The Farlex Financial Dictionary

Business and Investing Terms Explained

Explore more books by Farlex at
farlex.com/books

FARLEX INTERNATIONAL

FARLEX INTERNATIONAL LIMITED

a Farlex Group Company

• USA   • Ireland

farlex.com   farlex.ie

ISBN-10: 1539354237

ISBN-13: 978-1539354239

About the publisher

Farlex is the publishing team behind TheFreeDictionary.com, the trusted reference destination with 1 billion+ annual visits.

The most comprehensive reference resource online, The Free Dictionary is a massive, easily searchable collection of dictionaries and encyclopedias from the most trusted publishers, including McGraw-Hill, Houghton Mifflin, HarperCollins, and many more.

Since its founding in 2003, TheFreeDictionary.com has grown to include a vast and diverse amount of reference content, including multiple thesaurus sources and specialty dictionaries covering fields such as finance, law, science, medicine, idioms and slang, acronyms, computing, and more, as well as dictionaries in 14 other languages.

Farlex dictionary apps powered by The Free Dictionary have been downloaded tens of millions of times across multiple platforms, with top ratings after hundreds of thousands of user reviews.

With *The Farlex Financial Dictionary*, Farlex continues its reputation for the most comprehensive, trusted, and easy-to-use reference products in the world.

For more books from Farlex, visit **farlex.com/books**.

Preface

The world of finance is vast, complex, and rapidly changing—and filled with a vast amount of complex, rapidly changing language and jargon. If you're not well versed in the language of finance, you are most certainly missing opportunities. A piece of good financial advice may sound like a meaningless tangle of jargon. Worse still, a bad deal might sound golden. There's no use reading the fine print if you don't understand it.

Your understanding starts here. This dictionary was designed to present both basic and complex financial concepts in a way you can easily understand, remember, and—most importantly—put to use. Complicated topics are explained thoroughly and clearly, but they are not dumbed down. Rather, they are presented with historical context and examples that illustrate precisely what they mean and what they do not. By covering all aspects of the global market, from the subtle differences between similar investment strategies to the latest macroeconomic trends, this dictionary will give you the confidence and the know-how to thrive in today's financial world.

Any time you hear a financial term you don't recognize or understand, open this dictionary, and you will find it waiting to be understood. With each new term you learn, you will see ways it can be put to practical use. Then the vast world of finance will become smaller, and all your financial decisions will become clearer. Start defining your success.

1040 Form A document that individuals and some corporations must file with the IRS each year. The 1040 form calculates income, deductions, and credits, and ultimately arrives at how much, if any, tax the filer owes for the year. The form itself is short, but many taxpayers must use additional forms to calculate how things like dividend income and capital gains are taxed on the 1040. See also: 1040EZ.

1040A Form In the United States, a simplified version of the 1040 Form on which a taxpayer lists his/her income. In order to be eligible to use the 1040A, the taxpayer must not itemize deductions, own a business, or exceed a certain ceiling on income. It is more complex than the 1040EZ Form, but it appeals primarily to new taxpayers who do not have dependents and cannot claim other credits.

1040EZ Form In the United States, a simplified version of the 1040 Form on which a taxpayer lists his/her income. In order to be eligible to use the 1040EZ, the taxpayer must not itemize deductions, have any dependents, own a business, or exceed a certain ceiling on regular or interest income. The 1040EZ is the most straightforward tax return because its users have no need for most deductions or credits. See also: 1040 Form, 1040A Form.

1040PC Form A version of the 1040 Form that consisted of fewer pages. The 1040PC allowed taxpayers to prepare their tax return on a computer; it consisted of a bottom line number, a dollar amount, and an explanatory column called a legend page. It was introduced in 1993 and discontinued in 2000 as e-filing became more prominent.

1099 A form that payers of dividends send to payees and to the IRS declaring the dividends, interest, and similar payments made to the payees in a given tax year. Taxpayers report income listed on a 1099 on their 1040 forms when calculating their tax liabilities.

1099 B A form stating a taxpayer's capital gains and losses from security trades. A broker provides each client with a 1099 B form by January 31 each year; the client then uses this to report capital gains and losses from the sale of securities when filling out his/her 1040 to calculate his/her tax liability.

1099 DIV A form that every company is required to submit to all persons or companies earning taxable capital gains on the company. The form contains information on all dividends, interest, and other capital gains paid over the tax year. Publicly-traded companies, mutual funds, banks, and other companies paying dividends or interest must submit a 1099-DIV to each shareholder and bondholder, and report to the IRS how much it paid to each person or company.

1099 Income In the United States, income earned from independent contracting or other forms of self-employment. For example, a freelance writer receives 1099 income from his clients instead of from wages or salary from a single employer. Such income derives its name from the fact that it is reported on form 1099-MISC.

1099-INT A form one must file with the IRS declaring all the interest one receives in a year from taxable investment vehicles held at a financial institution. This includes interest on corporate bonds, savings accounts, certificates of deposit, and so forth.

1099-OID A form that an issuer sends to all investors listing all income from interest on discount issues. This includes income from zero-coupon bonds, Treasury bills, and other securities issued at a discount from par. Investors are to include this income when calculating their taxable income.

10-K A form the SEC requires publicly-traded companies and some private companies to file every year. It includes statements on equity and audited financials. While similar to the annual report to shareholders, it often contains more information, such as executive compensation and organizational structure. All publicly traded companies and any privately traded companies with more than 500 shareholders and $10 million in assets are required to file a 10-K. The SEC requires companies to provide the 10-K form to any shareholder who requests it and to state on the form whether or not the company's financials are available for free online. See also: Transparency.

10-Q A form the SEC requires publicly-traded companies and some private companies to file every quarter. It includes statements on equity and unaudited financial statements. While similar to a shareholder report, a 10-Q form often contains more information, such as executive compensation and organizational structure. All publicly-traded companies and any privately traded companies with more than 500 shareholders and $10 million in assets are required to file a 10-Q. Companies only file three 10-Q forms each year, as the final quarter's numbers are included in the 10-K. See also: Transparency.

10-Year Treasury Note A debt owed by the United States government for a period of 10 years. Each note has a stated interest rate, which is paid semi-annually. Because the United States is seen as a very low-risk borrower, many investors see 10-year Treasury Note interest rates as indicative of the wider bond market. Normally, the interest rate decreases with greater demand for the Notes and rises with lower demand. For example, in December 2008, 10-year interest rates were the lowest in history due to deteriorating economic conditions and the consequent desire of investors for low-risk investments. See also: yield, bond, treasury note, treasury bond, treasury bill.

11th District Cost of Funds Index An index of the interest rates paid on checking accounts and savings accounts in Arizona, California, and Nevada. This index measures the cost of funds for banks and some other financial institutions in the western United States; that is, the 11th District COFI measures what banks must pay to those who would offer them funding for their lending and other operations. The 11th District COFI is published on a monthly basis and is considered a lagging indicator of prevailing interest rates in the west.

12B-1 Fee A fee one must pay in a 12B-1 Plan. A 12B-1 plan is a mutual fund that, instead of a load (or sales fee), annually charges shareholders a small percentage of the fund's market value, which is called a 12B-1 fee. Instead of assessing a fee when buying or selling shares as most mutual funds do, 12B-1 fees are deductions from the fund's market value per shareholder. Usually a 12B-1 fee is less than 1% of the market value.

12B-1 Fund A mutual fund that charges shareholders a small percentage of the fund's market value, instead of a load (or sales fee). That is, a 12B-1 Plan does not require shareholders to pay a fee when buying or selling shares; rather, they simply deduct what is owed to the shareholder once per year. Usually a 12B-1 plan charges less than 1%.

1787 Brasher Dubloon A rare gold coin privately minted in the United States. One was once sold for $7.40 million. See also: Numismatics.

1794 Flowing Hair Dollar A silver dollar coin manufactured in the United States. Its obverse features Lady Liberty with her hair down. A 1794 Flowing Hair dollar was sold in 2010 for $7.85 million. See also: Numismatics.

1804 Class I Silver Dollar A silver dollar coin manufactured in the United States. One was sold in 1999 for $4.14 million. See also: Numismatics.

1907 Golden Eagle A gold $20 coin manufactured in the United States. One was sold in 2005 for $2.99 million. See also: Numismatics.

1913 Liberty Head Nickel A rare five-cent coin manufactured in the United States. One was sold in 2001 for $1.84 million. See also: Numismatics.

1927-D Golden Eagle A gold $20 coin manufactured at the Denver Mint in the United States. One was sold in 2005 for $1.89 million. See also: Numismatics.

1933 Saint-Gaudens Golden Eagle A gold $20 coin manufactured in the United States. Its reverse features a bald eagle in flight. One was sold in 2002 for $7.59 million. See also: Numismatics.

19c-3 Stock A stock listed on a given exchange that may be traded off the physical confines of the exchange. These stocks are eligible for over-the-counter trading. All stocks listed after April 26, 1979 are 19c-3 stocks. The name refers to SEC rule 19c-3, which permitted these transactions. The rule was adopted as part of a move toward an experimental National Market System.

20% Cushion Rule A rule of thumb for municipal bonds. Under the rule, the revenue a municipal bond raises should exceed the proposed budget of the project the bond intends to fund by at least 20%. This allows the bond to account for unforeseen expenses. Following a cushion rule is especially important because municipal bonds are ultimately financed by taxpayer money.

24-Hour Trading The trading of a security or contract on a constant basis. Some computer programs, notably Automated Screen Trading, allow 24-hour trading so buying and selling can continue even after exchanges close. Foreign exchange markets also permit trading 24 hours per day between Monday and Friday. See also: ECN.

30-Year Treasury A debt security owed by the United States government for a period of 30 years. Each 30-year Treasury has a stated interest rate, which is paid semi-annually. Because the United States is seen as a very low-risk borrower, many investors see 30-year Treasury interest rates as indicative of the state of the wider bond market. Normally, the interest rate decreases with greater demand for 30-year Treasury securities and rises with lower demand. As with other U.S. Treasury securities, 30-year Treasuries are negotiable and may be traded on an exchange or over-the-counter. See also: yield, bond, treasury note, treasury bond, treasury bill.

3C1 A section in the Investment Company Act of 1940 exempting certain investment companies from its provisions. Under the exemption, investment companies with fewer than one hundred investors and no intention of making a public offering are not required to register with the SEC. These companies are known as private investment companies, and include charitable organizations and pensions. Hedge funds often use this section to avoid SEC registration.

401(k) A retirement investment plan in which a contributor defers taxation on contributions until after withdrawal. Under a traditional 401(k), a worker places a portion of his/her pre-tax income into a 401(k) account and allows it to be invested. Taxation is deferred until withdrawal from the account, generally after retirement. Withdrawals prior to the age of 59 1/2 are subject to excise taxes, but the investor must begin disbursements before the age of 70 1/2, unless he/she is still employed with the company offering the 401(k). Most employees are allowed to place up to $16,500 (in 2009) into a 401(k), and some employers have matching contributions. In 2006, the U.S. Government instituted the Roth 401(k), which allows post-tax contributions in return for tax-free withdrawals after retirement. This gave retirement investors a wider range of choice based upon their specific needs. Most 401(k)s are employee benefits and workers must have a sponsoring employer to take advantage of one. However, a self-employed person may also set up a 401(k) for himself/herself.

403(b) A retirement investment plan for employees of certain non-profit organizations in which a contributor defers taxation on contributions until after withdrawal. Under a traditional 403(b), a worker places a portion of his/her pre-tax income into a 403(b) account and allows it to be invested. Taxation is deferred until withdrawal from the account, generally after retirement. 403(b)s are employee benefits, and workers must have a sponsoring employer such as a public school or a church in order to take advantage of one. They are the non-profit worker's equivalent of a 401(k).

457 A retirement investment plan for employees of state and municipal governments in which a contributor defers taxation on contributions until after withdrawal. A worker places a portion of his/her pre-tax income into a 457 account and allows it to be invested. Taxation is deferred until withdrawal from the account, generally after retirement. 457s are employee benefits, and workers must have a sponsoring employer, such as a public school or a church, in order to take advantage of one. It is equivalent to a 401(k) and a 403(b); the main structural difference is that 457s may allow for higher catch-up contributions.

48-Hour Rule A rule under the PSA Uniform Practices requiring that all information about the mortgages underlying a forward contract on a mortgage-backed security be communicated from a seller to a buyer by 3 p.m. two days before the delivery takes place. This contract is known as TBA.

501(c) A section of the Internal Revenue Code governing the status of several different kinds of non-profit organizations. In general, organizations registered under 501(c) are exempt from federal taxation and, in some cases, contributions and donations made to them are also tax exempt. In many instances, laws in individual states exempt 501(c) organizations from their own taxes. Examples of 501(c) organizations include churches, charities, lobbying groups, labor unions, social clubs, and even cemeteries.

501(c)(3) A subsection of the Internal Revenue Code governing the status of non-profit organizations devoted exclusively to religious, charitable, scientific, educational, and other, similar purposes. 501(c)3 organizations are exempt from federal taxation and, in most cases, contributions and donations made to them are also tax exempt. Nearly all major charities in the United States are 501(c)3 organizations; many philanthropic foundations do not provide grants to organizations not registered under 501(c)3. They are not allowed to lobby for political candidates.

501(c)3 Bond A tax-exempt municipal bond used by a local government entity to raise money for a 501(c)3 organization. That is, a 501(c)3 bond represents a sort of public-private partnership in which a municipality provides financing for a charity, educational foundation, or other organization organized under subsection 501(c)3 of the Internal Revenue Code. A 501(c)3 bond is not subject to the federal alternative minimum tax. It is a type of private activity bond.

501(c)4 A subsection of the Internal Revenue Code governing the status of non-profit organizations devoted to lobbying for political, civic, or other, similar causes. 501(c)4 organizations are exempt from federal taxation. However, contributions and donations made to them are not tax exempt. Examples of 501(c)4 organizations include political campaigns and groups that advocate for certain issues. In order to qualify for 501(c)4 status, all of the organization's earnings must be used for social welfare purposes.

501(c)5 A subsection of the Internal Revenue Code governing the status of non-profit organizations devoted to labor, agricultural, or horticultural purposes. That is, a 501(c)5 organization seeks to promote better conditions for persons or companies that belong to it. They may conduct lobbying for their causes, but not as their primary activity. 501(c)5 organizations are exempt from federal taxation.

501(c)6 A subsection of the Internal Revenue Code governing the status of non-profit organizations devoted to business purposes. That is, a 501(c)5 organization seeks to promote better business conditions for persons or companies that belong to it. Examples of organizations that may register under subsection 501(c)6 include chambers of commerce and real estate boards. They may conduct lobbying for their causes, but not as their primary activity. 501(c)6 organizations are exempt from federal taxation.

504 Corporation A nonprofit organization authorized under the Small Business Administration in the United States that provides loans and other assistance exclusively to small businesses. The 504 Corporation provides loans at below market interest rates, often with longer repayment schedules and lower collateral requirements. The 504 Corporation exists to create jobs and promote business. It is a certified development company based in Minnesota. See also: 504 Loan.

50-50 Plan A program by which lawyers contribute 50 hours per year pro bono and $50 per month to the local legal aid agency. A 50-50 plan seeks to ensure that all persons have adequate access to the justice system in the United States.

527 Organization A tax exempt organization in the United States dedicated to supporting or opposing candidates for political office or advocating or opposing certain issues. For example, a 527 organization may be formed to campaign for or against banking regulation. Unless a 527 promotes or denigrates a specific candidate, there are no limits on its contributions or spending. However, 527s must publish the names of their contributors as well as the donations they make.

529 College Savings Plan An account into which persons deposit funds to save for university-related expenses. The funds in a 529 college savings account are tax-deferred and, if used directly to pay for college, tax exempt at the federal level. They are sometimes exempt at the state level as well. The plan exists in an attempt to make post-secondary education more affordable. See also: IRA, 401(k).

52-Week High The highest price for a stock or other security over a trailing 52-week period. Investors often compare the current price for a stock to its 52-week high in order to determine its recent performance as well to help gauge whether it has become overvalued or undervalued.

52-Week Low The lowest price for a stock or other security over a trailing 52-week period. Investors often compare the current price for a stock to its 52-week low in order to determine its recent performance as well to help gauge whether it has become overvalued or undervalued.

5-Year Treasury Security A debt owed by the United States government for a period of five years. Each security has a stated interest rate, which is paid semi-annually. Unlike a 10-year Treasury note, it is not necessarily considered indicative of the state of the wider bondmarket. However, because the United States is seen as a very low-risk borrower, some investors seek out five-year Treasury securities (and other Treasury securities) when they are not confident in future stock performance. See also: yield, bond, treasury note, treasury bond, treasury bill.

800 Portability The ability of the owner of a toll free number to maintain the same number even upon changing long distance providers. For example, if a charity that operates an 800 number wishes to switch its long distance provider from Qwest to Verizon or vice versa, 800 portability allows the charity to keep the same number for donations or other purposes. The Federal Communications Commission has required long distance providers to offer 800 portability since 1993 in order to promote competition.

800-Number Promotion An advertisement, especially but not necessarily on television, in which a company encourages viewers to call a toll-free number (which usually starts with 800) to order the product. 800-number promotion is convenient for the customer as the product is nearly always shipped in the mail and payment can be made over the phone. It is especially popular for products on late-night television.

8-K A form that the SEC requires publicly-traded companies to file whenever a significant event happens. These events may affect the company's financial state and therefore the SEC believes that they should be known to the public. Examples of these events include an acquisition, merger, bankruptcy, or change in the composition of the board of directors. 8-K forms are required to be filed within four days of the event.

9/11 Terrorist Attacks An event on September 11, 2001, in which 19 al Qaeda terrorists flew two airplanes into the World Trade Center towers in New York and a third into the Pentagon in Washington, D.C. A fourth airplane failed to reach its target and crashed in Pennsylvania. Immediately after the attacks, which killed more than 2,000 people, U.S. President George W. Bush grounded all non-military airplanes and all stock exchanges in the United States were closed for several days. The attacks (and increased airport security that followed them) are thought to have hurt the airline industry. Additionally, stock prices fell significantly when markets re-opened; for example, the DJIA fell 685 points on September 17, 2001.

90-Day Letter A letter that the IRS sends to a taxpayer after an audit. The letter states that the audit has found inconsistencies or other errors in the tax returns and that the taxpayer will have to pay more unless he/she can show that the audit is in error. The letter derives its name from the fact that the taxpayer has 90 days to dispute the results of the audit before reassessment occurs.

A 1. A symbol appearing next to a stock listed on NASDAQ indicating that the stock is a class A share. All NASDAQ listings use a four-letter abbreviation; if an "A" follows the abbreviation, this indicates that the security being traded is class A. Publicly-traded companies sometimes issue common shares of different classes, which usually affects the shares' voting rights. Class A shares usually, but not always, carry more voting rights than class B shares. 2. Indicating a class of mutual fund with a front-end load. In this case, a certain amount of one's investment is deducted for the mutual fund's salesperson's commission. This lowers the size of the investment in the mutual fund. For example, if one invests $50,000 in a mutual fund, a certain amount, say $1,000, is deducted for the commission, resulting in an investment of only $49,000 in the fund.

A Classification of Residential Neighborhoods In marketing, a program that analyzes and attempts to understand the demographics of individual neighborhoods in the United Kingdom and their demand for goods and services. It utilizes nearly 300 lifestyle variables to break down all British postcodes into about 50 kinds of households.

A Priori Probability In statistics, the use of logic to estimate the probability of an event. For example, when considering a company's earnings, the company can make a profit, suffer a loss, or break even in a given year. All other things being equal, there is a 1/3 a priori probability of each scenario occurring.

A Random Walk Down Wall Street A 1973 book by Burton Malkiel arguing that security prices are completely unpredictable, especially in the short term. The book sets forth the idea that both fundamental analysis and technical analysis are wastes of time, as securities behave randomly. Thus, Malkiel holds that it is impossible to outperform the market by choosing the "correct" securities; it is only possible to outperform the market by taking on additional risk. Malkiel cites the fact that many actively managed mutual funds do not outperform the market over time, and in many cases revert to the mean. Critics of this idea contend that empirical evidence shows that security prices do indeed follow particular trends that can be predicted with a fair degree of accuracy. The title of the book gave birth to the term random walk theory. See also: Efficient markets theory.

A Rating The third-highest bond rating by S&P and Fitch. An A rating is subdivided (in decreasing order) into A+, A, and A-. Bonds with A ratings are investment-grade, meaning that banks are allowed to hold them. Bonds with A ratings are low-risk and low-return, though not as much as AA and AAA ratings. The rating is equivalent to the A1, A2, and A3 ratings by Moody's.

A Ton of Money A slang term for a great deal of profit or capital gains that can be made in a brief period of time. For example, a broker may give a client a tip to make a ton of money if he buys a certain stock at the right time.

A. Philip Randolph A 20th-century American socialist and union organizer. He was particularly known for his role in the civil rights movement, protesting against discrimination against Black Americans in military contracts and other areas. In 1925, he organized the Brotherhood of Sleeping Car Porters, the first major effort to unionize the Pullman Company, which was then a major employer of African Americans. He lived from 1889 to 1979.

A.G. Becker Paribas An investment bank that resulted from the acquisition of A.G. Becker by Banque Paribas in 1984. This acquisition was short-lived, as Banque Paribas sold A.G. Becker to Merrill Lynch later that same year. A.G. Becker was especially desirable to both companies for its knowledge and expertise in the commercial paper markets.

A.M. Best and Company A company known for its ratings of the credit quality of insurance companies. A rating issued by A.M. Best and Company measures an insurance company's ability to pay claims that might be made. The ratings can be between A and F, with A being the highest rating. Best's ratings have historically been issued for insurance companies exclusively, but, more recently, they have been applied to a few small banks.

A.P. Giannini An American banker who founded Bank of America. He established the Bank of Italy in San Francisco in 1904, which he merged with the Bank of America, Los Angeles, to form what became the Bank of America. He was one of the first bankers to offer services to the middle class; he was also an early pioneer of branch banking. He lived from 1870 to 1949.

A1 A subset of the third-highest bond rating by Moody's. The other subsets are A2 and A3, both of which are slightly lower. Bonds with an A1 rating are investment-grade, meaning that banks are allowed to hold them. Bonds with A1 ratings are low-risk and low-return, though not as much as Aa and Aaa ratings. The rating is equivalent to the A+ rating by S&P and Fitch.

AA The second-highest bond rating by S&P and Fitch. AA is subdivided (in decreasing order) into AA+, AA, and AA-. Bonds with AA ratings are investment-grade, meaning that banks are allowed to hold them. AA bonds are low-risk and low-return. The rating is equivalent to an Aa rating by Moody's.

AAA The highest bond rating by S&P and Fitch. A rating of AAA is considered to carry virtually no risk; U.S. Treasury securities, for example, always receive the AAA rating. A bond with an AA is investment-grade, meaning that banks are allowed to hold them. AA bonds are low risk and low return. The rating is equivalent of an Aaa rating by Moody's.

AAAA Spot Contract A standardized contract between an advertising agency and a television or radio station. The contract specifies the number of commercials the agency will air over what time, at what price, and under what conditions. The AAAA spot contract is published by the American Association of Advertising Agencies.

Aam An obsolete Dutch unit of volume roughly equivalent to 155 liters, with slight regional variations.

Aanaa A coin used occasionally in Nepal. One aanaa is worth 1/16 of a Nepalese rupee.

AATPO An international organization that promotes trade between countries in Africa. Specifically, it seeks to encourage member states to bring their trade laws into line with each other, and it provides training and research services. It was established in 1975 by the Organization for African Unity and the African Development Bank. Its headquarters are in Tangiers.

A-B Split A way to test the effectiveness of direct contact marketing. In an A-B split, the marketer will send, for example, different types of direct mail pieces to potential customers. For instance, it may send two sets of direct mail with different images, wording, or even colors. The marketer will determine which direct mail grouping receives the highest response rate and begin to concentrate its direct mail efforts on that grouping. An A-B split is used in a variety of different media, including banner ads, e-mails, and landing pages. It is also called A-B testing.

ABA Transit Number A nine-digit code at the bottom of a check indicating the bank that issued the check. The ABA transit number is issued and published by the American Bankers Association. It is also called the routing transit number or the association number.

Abacus An instrument allowing one to quickly add and subtract numbers. Generally, an abacus is composed of a rectangular frame in which horizontal rods are partially covered with beads. The beads may be moved one way or the other to make calculations. It was invented in China in the 2nd century CE and is considered the earliest calculator.

Abandon 1. To decide not to exercise an option. This occurs when an option is out-of-the-money on the exercise date. That is, one may abandon an option if it is currently unprofitable and thus highly unlikely to become profitable. **2.** To withdraw one's claim to an asset, especially an unprofitable one. Corporations must file appropriate paperwork with the government to abandon assets. Alternatively, an individual may abandon both real and personal property. For example, a homeowner may leave his/her house and never intend to return. A squatter may then come to possess the home through adverse possession. An important component of abandonment is the owner's intent never to return or otherwise possess the property again. **3.** To opt out of a forward contract according to the procedure specified therein. When one abandons a forward contract, one does not buy or sell the underlying asset and it is not delivered.

Abandon Rate The number of phone calls a telemarketer makes that the potential customer or contact hangs up on automatically without listening, expressed as a percentage of total phone calls made. A high abandon rate may indicate the telemarketer is not performing his/her job efficiently.

Abandoned Property Property that appears as if the owner deliberately left it with no apparent intention to return and claim it. For example, a car left on the side of the road for several days may be considered abandoned property. In general, abandoned property becomes the property of its finder, though, in some cases, it may become the property of the state. See also: Abandonment, Mislaid Property, Lost Property.

Abandonment 1. The act of fully and completely relinquishing ownership of some property or asset. One may abandon both tangible assets, such as tools or real estate, or intangible assets, such as patents or leases. For example, abandonment occurs when someone leaves his/her house empty, never intending to return or otherwise use the property. Legal abandonment sometimes requires filing declaration of intent to do so with the appropriate authorities. Sometimes, a person may obtain abandoned property for free, though this does not apply to real estate. See also: Adverse possession. **2.** See: Expiration.

Abandonment and Salvage A clause in a contract allowing one party to abandon (or forfeit ownership to) a property and thereby transfer ownership to another party, assuming the second party accepts. Abandonment and salvage clauses are most common in insurance covering goods being shipped overseas. That is, if the ship sinks and the owner does not wish to attempt to recover the goods, he may declare them abandoned, which would transfer ownership to his insurance company (though the insurance company may refuse to accept ownership). It is also present in some homeowner's insurance contracts. It should not be confused with an abandonment option.

Abandonment Option A clause in some contracts allowing one party or the other to terminate the contract before completion. The abandonment option adds value to a contract that can be traded because it allows both parties a great deal of flexibility in case the contract proves unprofitable. However, the clause is most common in contracts between financial advisers and their clients.

Abandonment Value The value of an asset if it were sold immediately and all debts associated with it were repaid. That is, the abandonment value is what would be left over after an asset is sold and all the bills were paid. It is also called the liquidation value. See also: Market Price.

Abasi A currency subdivision in Afghanistan between 1891 and 1925. An abasi was worth one-third of an Afghan rupee.

Abatement A decrease in the amount one owes in taxes. Abatement may come from a tax cut, a rebate, or a reduction in penalties or interest one owes on previous taxes.

Abatement Cost The expense a business incurs as a result of cleaning or removing an undesired byproduct of its goods and services. Abatement cost is often associated with large manufacturing plants that must abide by environmental standards or city noise ordinances. However, it may apply to a small business also. For example, a dental office must bear the cost of disposing of medically hazardous material.

Abbrochment The purchase of all goods in a market in order to control all retail sales of those goods in that market. Abbrochment is one way to create a monopoly.

ABC 1. See: Associated Builders and Contractors. **2.** See: American Business Center. **3.** See: Activity-Based Costing. **4.** See: ABC Agreement. **5.** See: Audit Bureau of Circulations.

ABC Agreement An agreement between a member of the New York Stock Exchange and the company for which the member works. The agreement contains three stipulations (referenced in the eponymous "A-B-C"). The first stipulation allows the member to transfer ownership of the seat to another employee of the company. The second allows the member to purchase a second seat on the trading floor on behalf of another employee of the company, while still maintaining ownership of the first seat. The third states that if the member sells the seat, he/she must give the gain to the company. An ABC agreement exists because members represent the companies that employ them (and the companies buy the seats for them), but they are recognized by the NYSE as independent. The agreement protects the company in case the employee ever leaves to go to another firm. The ABC agreement must be entered with the consent of the NYSE.

ABC Analyzed Issue In publishing, a semi-annual issue of a periodical that provides statistical information on itself. The Audit Bureau of Circulations uses the information in the ABC issues of different publications to form ABC Statements.

ABC Method A way to manage a company's inventory by categorizing the importance of the items in it. The items with the highest value are given the highest priority and therefore receive the most attention. This is a common method for managing inventory.

ABC News/Money Magazine Consumer Comfort Index A weekly survey on the perception of the national economy, the personal finance of the respondents, and the likelihood that respondents will continue to spend money. While the Index is published weekly, it contains responses gathered over a period of four weeks. The Index is not seasonally adjusted, but it breaks down responses by age, gender, income, education, employment, and region. Its value goes from -100 to +100; consistent declines may be a predictor for coming declines in consumer spending.

ABC Statement In publishing, a semi-annual statement detailing statistical information on a publication, especially its circulation. Companies file ABC Statements with either the Audit Bureau of Circulations or the Business Publications Audit of Circulations. ABC Statements help companies attract advertisers by providing succinct reports on their publications.

ABCD Counties A categorization of American counties by population. An "A County" is one of the top 25 counties by population in the United States. A "B County" is one with a population over 150,000 that is not already an A County. A "C County" has between 40,000 and 150,000 residents. Finally, a "D County" is any other county. ABCD counties are used when preparing media marketing strategies to maximize their effect.

Abend Informal; to end a project or process prematurely. This term is used especially in computer-related projects. It is a portmanteau of "abnormal end."

Abeyance 1. A situation in which a property's current or future owner is unknown, with the expectation of the true owner presenting himself/herself. For example, if one's will states that one's property shall go to one's youngest nephew at the time of one's death, the property is in abeyance because it is unknown whether the youngest nephew now will still be the youngest nephew when the will is executed. **2.** A situation in which a law ceases to be in effect, with the expectation that it will become effective again. For example, in the immediate aftermath of a coup, a country's constitution may be said to be in abeyance.

Abeyance Order 1. An order by a court declaring a property or claim in abeyance. That is, the court may issue an abeyance order declaring that the owner or holder of a claim in presently unknown. This is used in bankruptcy proceedings. **2.** An order by an advertiser to play a commercial during a time that is not available.

Ability to Pay A principle stating that persons or corporations who earn the same amount of money should be taxed in the same way, and that those who earn more should be taxed more. For example, the principle states that two individuals making $50,000 per year should be taxed the same amount, regardless of how they earned their income, while someone making $100,000 per year should be taxed more than either of the other persons. Ability to pay is the idea behind the progressive tax system in place in many countries. See also: Horizontal equity.

Abnormal Return The difference between the expected return and the actual return on an investment. Abnormal returns may be either positive or negative; indeed an abnormal return may be negative even if the actual return is positive. That is, suppose the expected return on an investment is 7% and the actual return is 5%. While the investor has 5% more than he/she had when he/she started, the abnormal return is still -2%. On the other hand, if the expected return is 5% and the actual return is 9%, then there is a positive abnormal return of 4%. One may use an abnormal return to gauge the accuracy of various asset pricing models.

Abnormal Spoilage Spoilage, or waste, of a product that occurs due to inefficiency in the process of making that product. Unlike normal spoilage, it is recorded on a balance sheet as a loss rather than a cost. While normal spoilage is seen as inevitable, companies seek to create processes to reduce or eliminate abnormal spoilage.

About Good In coin collecting, describing a well-worn coin that has only an outline (perhaps a faint outline) of its original features. These generally are not worth very much. See also: Numismatics.

Above Board In business, a slang term meaning honest. For example, an above board deal indicates a transaction with no illegal or unethical undertones.

Above Par Describing a bond or other fixed-income security that sells for a price above its face value. For example, a bond for $20 over its face value is selling above par. Generally speaking, securities sell above par when interest rates have declined and thus new issues of bonds will pay a lower coupon. A bond that sells above par will mature at a price less than what the bondholder paid, but he/she may still make a profit, if one takes coupons into account.

Above Poverty Line In India, a measure of persons who live above its nationally designated poverty threshold. India divides the poverty threshold into urban and rural areas. People in urban areas must meet higher monthly income minimums to be considered above the poverty line. The World Bank uses a more stringent poverty threshold than the Indian government.

Above the Line 1. Income and expenses a company incurs in its day-to-day operations. Above the line items increase or decrease the company's profit. These items are called above the line because they do not deal with how profits or losses are distributed. See also: Below the line. **2.** Advertising in which a company buys space or airtime as opposed to only paying commissions on the revenue earned from the advertising. For example, a commercial on television is above the line, while telemarketing is not. **3.** A tax deduction one takes on one's gross income instead of one's adjusted gross income.

Above the Market Describing an order to buy or sell a security at a price substantially lower (for a buy order) or higher (for a sell order) than the current market price. An above the market order is unlikely to be filled until the market price moves closer to the order's designated price. For example, one makes an above the market order when one makes a bid to buy a stock at $22 per share when the market price for a stock is $30 per share.

Above Water 1. Describing a company that is maintaining operations with little or no financial difficulty. It is a somewhat informal term that is used especially when a company is doing neither poorly nor terribly well. **2.** Describing a company's assets when their value exceeds their book value. The Generally Accepted Accounting Principles rarely allow the book value of an asset to change except in accordance with the rules of depreciation or appreciation. Thus, a book value may not state an asset's actual value. A company with above-water assets often attracts investors who have done a great deal of research into the value of its assets; these investors often stand to make a significant return on a comparatively small investment.

Above-the-Line Cost In advertising, the costs related to non-technical aspects of the production of a commercial to air on television or over the radio. Above the line costs include paying actors, script writers, and so forth. They do not include technical issues like special effects or equipment. See also: Below-the-line cost.

Absence Rate The full-time employees who do not work full-time in a given week, expressed a percentage of total employees in a given company or industry. The absence rate does not consider whether a given absence is legitimate; it only observes that the employee is not at work. In general, the absence rate is higher in companies with more generous employee benefits. Companies seek to keep their absence rates to the lowest level possible.

Absentee Owner An owner who is almost never physically present at a piece of real estate he/she owns. Absentee owners generally do not make repairs or improvements to their properties. If an absentee owner rents out a property, he/she does not interfere with what their tenants do (often even if what they do is illegal) and likewise often do not fulfill the legal requirements to maintain the property.

Absenteeism A situation in which a large number of workers consistently do not come to work, especially for illegitimate reasons. Absenteeism implies that the workers are not terminated for their actions. It can be a sign of poor management.

Absolute Advantage The ability for an economic actor to produce a good or service using fewer resources. For example, if an individual produces 100 bricks using 100 units of labor and a second individual produces 200 bricks using the same amount of labor, the second individual has an absolute advantage in the production of bricks. This concept is generally attributed to Adam Smith. See also: comparative advantage, replacement cycle.

Absolute Auction An auction in which the highest bidder receives the item for sale. That is, an absolute auction does not have a specified price below which the current owner will refuse to sell. See also: Reserve price.

Absolute Contraband In the laws of war, any goods that a belligerent may confiscate from a neutral party legally to prevent the possibility that they may be delivered to the enemy. Examples of absolute contraband include weapons, munitions, and machinery that can be used to manufacture weapons. Neutral parties have the right to trade with any or all belligerents in a war, and the confiscation of absolute contraband is not considered an act of war against the neutral party. See also: Conditional Contraband, Contraband.

Absolute Form of Purchasing Power Parity A theory stating that the same good or service costs the same amount regardless of the currency in which it is measured. For instance, if 1 pound is equivalent to 2 dollars, and a widget costs 1 pound in England, then the absolute form of purchasing power parity would state that the same widget would cost 2 dollars in the United States. This concept is also called the law of one price. In securities, any deviations from the absolute form of purchasing power parity create opportunities for arbitrage (profiting from inefficiencies in prices). See also: Purchasing power parity, Currency pair.

Absolute Liability In law, the legal liability the owner of a property has for all damages committed by other persons on his/her property. For example, if a lumberjack working on Farmer John's property chops down a tree and it falls on Rancher Frank's barn, Farmer John may have the absolute liability to pay for Rancher Frank's new barn.

Absolute Physical Life The period of time in which an asset can be used. Many assets, particularly those that become technologically obsolete, depreciate over time and eventually can no longer be used. The absolute physical life is often calculated to determine the risk involved in the purchase of assets.

Absolute Priority A rule stating that, in liquidation, certain creditors must be satisfied in full before any other creditors receive any payments. That is, in the liquidation of a company, the absolute priority rule states that holders of secured debt must be paid before holders of unsecured debt. Holders of unsecured debt have precedence over preferred shareholders, and, finally, preferred shareholders must be satisfied before common shareholders.

Absolute Rate In a plain vanilla swap, the fixed interest rate. In a plain vanilla swap, the two legs of the swap are a fixed interest rate, say 3.5%, and a floating interest rate, say LIBOR + 0.5%, each calculated over some notional value. Each party pays the other at set intervals over the life of the swap. In this case, the absolute rate is 3.5% over the notional value.

Absolute Return The return on an asset, fund, or other investment expressed in dollar or percentage terms. That is, the absolute return is the return relative to the investment itself. For example, if one buys shares in a stock for $1000 and sells them for $1500, one may say that one has an absolute return of $500 or 50%. There is little analysis of the absolute return beyond that. Most of the time, the absolute return is less helpful to investors than the relative return, which compares the return on an investment relative to other, similar investments or to the market as a whole. See also: Absolute Return Fund.

Absolute Return Fund A mutual fund or other investmentcompany that takes both long and short positions in order to produce a gain, or at least avoid a loss, regardless of overall market conditions. The idea behind an absolute return states that during a downturn, the gains on the short positions (which produce gains when security prices drop) offset the losses on the long positions. In other words, an absolute return fund seeks to combine the accessibility of a mutual fund with some of the strategies of a hedge fund. Critics contend that absolute return funds carry higher risks of loss than their proponents admit.

Absolute Terms Describing any measurement used without reference to other measurements. Considering measurements in absolute terms is often less useful than using relative terms.

Absolute Value The value of a variable without regard to whether it is positive or negative. For example, an absolute value of 6% applies whether a company's profits increase 6% or decrease by the same amount.

Absolute-Rate Swap An interest rate swap in which the fixed interest rate is given a numerical value. That is, the fixed interest rate is expressed by an absolute rate, say, 5%. Virtually all plain vanilla swaps are absolute rate swaps.

Absolutism The political theory that all power should belong to the state. According to absolutism, every corporation, religious organization, or other institution must give way to the state. Absolutism comes from the period in European history before and during the early development of capitalism during which monarchs attempted to centralize power. See also: Fascism.

Absolutist A person who believes all power should belong to the state. According to absolutism, every corporation, religious organization, or other institution must give way to the state. Absolutism comes from the period in European history before and during the early development of capitalism during which monarchs attempted to centralize. See also: Fascism.

Absorb 1. To trade a security without driving the market price in any direction. That is, a security is said to absorb transactions when they do not cause the price to go up or down. **2.** To refrain from passing on a cost to customers. For example, a business absorbs a cost when it must pay an additional $1 per unit in taxes but does not raise a unit's retail price by any amount.

Absorbed 1. In business, an expense that the company does not pass on to customers. For example, if a company's costs increase from $5 to $7 per unit, but it decides to maintain its price at $10 per unit, it is said to absorb the extra $2. **2.** Acquired. That is, an absorbed company is one that another company buys and then integrates into its current operations. **3.** In underwriting, fully subscribed.

Absorption 1. The total demand for all goods and services in an economy. One calculates the absorption by adding the value of all goods and services produced and consumed locally to that of all imports. **2.** A French term for acquisition.

Absorption Costing In accounting, the practice of recording as expenses all costs associated with producing a good. This includes both the costs of the raw materials and the fixed costs, such as employee wages, the cost of machinery, and so forth. External reporting must use absorption costing. It contrasts with variable costing, which does not consider fixed costs.

Absorption Rate The rate at which vacant business or residential space in an area is sold or rented over a given period of time. The absorption rate is expressed in square feet sold/leased as a percentage of the total available. Alternatively, one may express it as units (or homes) sold as a percentage of the total.

Abstract A brief summary at the beginning of an article, paper, or presentation. Abstracts are commonly associated with academia; for example, an economics professor may attach an abstract to a publication. However, it may also be used with a business presentation.

Abstract of Record In law, a brief summary of a trial that provides the major details for use by the appellate court.

Abstract of Title In real estate, a brief history of the ownership of a piece of property. That is, the abstract of title has a summary of all the previous owners and dates of sale. It also lists any potential, conflicting claims to the property. See also: Clear title.

ABTA A trade association for travel agents and tour companies in the United Kingdom. ABTA sets professional standards for members and conducts public relations for the British travel industry. It was established as the Association of British Travel Agents and changed its name to ABTA in 2007.

Abu Dhabi Fund for Arab Economic Development A financial institution owned by the government of Abu Dhabi that promotes investment in the developing world. It does this through concessionary loans, grants and equity investment provided to governments and private companies. It has funded projects in more than 50 countries since its foundation in 1971. See also: Abu Dhabi Investment Authority.

Abucco An obsolete unit of mass in Pegu, Burma, approximately equivalent to 196 grams. It was used to weigh gold and silver.

Abusive Tax Shelter An investment vehicle or other structure with no purpose other than to reduces one's tax liability. Often, an abusive tax shelter takes the form of a partnership or trust. Taxpayers caught using abusive tax shelters to avoid or evade taxation must pay the applicable taxes plus interest. To bypass accusation of arbitrary enforcement, the IRS publishes a list of investment vehicles that are considered abusive tax shelters, though one may face penalties for using a scheme that even resembles something on the list.

Abut To touch or to lie next to. The term is used in property to determine the obligations of a homeowner or the municipality.

ABW GOST 7.67 Latin three-letter geocode for Aruba. The code is used for transactions to and from Aruban bank accounts and for international shipping to Aruba. As with all GOST 7.67 codes, it is used primarily in Cyrillic alphabets.

Academic Year The period of time during which most classes are held at an educational institution. A student must accomplish a certain number of classes or credit hours each academic year in order to remain eligible for federal or other financial aid.

Academy of Accounting Historians An organization for historians who specialize in accounting. It publishes a newsletter and a semi-annual journal, in addition to sponsoring conferences. It was established in 1973; its headquarters are in Ohio.

Accelerated Cost Recovery System An accounting technique formerly used in the United States to tax a tangible asset based upon its estimated depreciation. The estimated depreciation bore only a rough relationship to an asset's actual life, and was designed to decrease the taxation in the early years of an asset's ownership. ACRS was instituted by the Economic Recovery Act of 1981 and amended in 1986 to create the Modified Accelerated Cost Recovery System. See also: Absolute Physical Life.

Accelerated Death Benefit A death benefit in some life insurance policies that may be paid before the policyholder's actual death. Generally speaking, one may use the accelerated death benefit only to defray medical expenses should the policyholder be diagnosed with a terminal illness. The idea of the accelerated death benefit originated in the 1980s to help pay for some of the medical expenses of AIDS patients.

Accelerated Depreciation Any of several systems of increasing the depreciation on an asset. Increasing the depreciation allows the asset's owner to write off more of the value of the asset, at least for some of the years of ownership. This can reduce the owner's tax liability. A common method of accelerated depreciation is the Modified Accelerated Cost Recovery System, which estimates depreciation in a way that bears only a rough relationship to an asset's actual life; it was designed to decrease the taxation in the early years of an asset's ownership.

Accelerated Option A clause in some insurance contracts allowing a policyholder to access some of the benefits of the policy before he/she otherwise would be able to do so. Very often, the accelerated option allows the holder of a whole life insurance policy to use the savings portion to pay off the remainder of the premiums in a single, lump sum.

Accelerated Reply Mail A service the U.S. Postal Service provides to businesses by which it delivers return mail more quickly than it would otherwise. This is especially useful when a company is mailing a check.

Accelerated Tariff Elimination A unilateral or mutual move to reduce or eliminate tariffs with another country, or between two countries, on a faster schedule than had been anticipated previously. Obviously, this allows the economic benefits (and problems) of free trade to take effect more quickly.

Acceleration Clause A clause in a contract, especially a loan or bond, allowing a creditor to call the debt if certain, stated events occur. For example, if a borrower defaults on two or more payments, an acceleration clause may allow a lender to force the borrower to repay the entire amount of the loan immediately. Failure to repay could absolve the lender of all obligations in the contract, including the requirement to refund any money the borrower had previously paid, and render it effectively null and void.

Acceleration Life Insurance A life insurance policy that allows the policyholder to access a portion of the death benefit (usually about 25%) in the event of a catastrophic illness. The policy states which illnesses are eligible for this benefit. Acceleration life insurance allows the policyholder to pay for treatment of what may be a final illness while still providing for his/her beneficiaries after death. See also: Accelerated Option.

Accelerative Endowment In insurance, a form of the accelerated option that allows a policyholder to have access to the savings portion of his/her whole life policy (or the equivalent in other policies). That is, the accelerative endowment transfers to the policyholder the portion of the premiums that were set aside for his/her future use. The accelerative endowment is paid as a lump sum and may be used for any purpose.

Accelerator Principle The idea that a small change in consumer behavior can have a large effect on a company's investment. For example, suppose $100 of investment in a bakery produces $100 worth of baked goods. If consumers usually buy $100 of baked goods each year but this increases to $110, the bakery must buy 10% more equipment, baking materials, and so forth, which can increase the amount it invests in its suppliers by more than 10%. The accelerator principle exacerbates advances and declines; it is used in various models of the business cycle. See also: Multiplier.

Accelerator-Multiplier Model A model for the business cycle at the macroeconomic level. The accelerator-multiplier model is cyclical and has three phases. First, the government increases its expenditures, which increases consumer income. The increase in income leads consumers to buy more goods and services, which increases economic output. The higher output leads to higher investment in the economy. As the name implies, it combines the Keynesian multiplier model with the accelerator model.

Accept 1. To honor. For example, a bank may accept a check by depositing it into the appropriate account. **2.** To take delivery for a commodity, security, or anything else one previously bought.

Acceptable Quality Level The maximum number of defects a product can have to be deemed acceptable to sell to wholesalers or retailers. The acceptable quality level is important in the quality control of a product, especially when it is mass-produced.

Acceptable Use Policy The principles guiding the appropriate use of a public computer network by a private individual. It may also apply to the use of a computer provided to an individual by a company or agency for work use. The acceptable use policy outlines the types of websites a user may or may not visit and/or the kinds of work that are prohibited. For example, an acceptable use policy at a company may ban the use of a social networking website like Facebook. More commonly, AUPs ban the viewing of pornography or websites likely to contain viruses.

Acceptance Credit A letter of credit in which the buyer authorizes the transfer of funds to the seller on or after a certain date assuming the conditions of the letter are met. Acceptance credit may be confirmed, meaning that a bank has promised to pay in the event of default, or unconfirmed, meaning the seller assumes the risk of the borrower's default. See also: Banker's Acceptance.

Acceptance Sampling A form of quality control for mass-produced products in which a certain number of the products are tested at random. Acceptance sampling is most useful when it is impossible to test all products. For example, if an armory tested all the bullets it produced, there would be none left. For that reason, acceptance sampling is used to determine whether the majority of the bullets are of sufficient quality to sell.

Acceptance Supra Protest A situation in which a third party (such as a bank) makes payment on a bill of exchange that a buyer did not pay, either because the buyer refused to accept delivery (usually for lack of quality) or simply because he/she refused to pay. It is also called acceptance for honor. See also: Dishonor by Nonpayment, Dishonor by Non-Acceptance.

Accepting Bank A bank in a country to which another bank sends a letter of credit on behalf of a client. The accepting bank honors the letter of credit and transfers requested funds to the client. This is similar to an advising bank, though the latter term refers exclusively to a bank in different country; an accepting bank may be (but is not necessarily) in the domestic country.

Accepting House Committee A term referring to a number of commercial banks operating under the aegis and regulation of the Bank of England.

Access The ability or authority to view restricted data or enter a restricted area.

Access Device A computer program that allows an authorized user to access information, either in a desired order or at random, depending on the type of access device.

Access Right The authority a user of a computer program or a network has to access that program or network. One using a program or network without access rights is a hacker.

Access Time In telecommunications, the delay between the time a request is made on a system and the time the system grants the request. As technology advances, access time is generally reduced.

Accession 1. In law, the process by which one acquires property from another property one already owns. Accession occurs when a produced property automatically belongs to the owner of the producing property. For example, a corn cob grown in a garden accedes to the owner of the corn stalk. Likewise, corn starch belongs to the owner of the original corn from which it was made. **2.** In international relations, the process by which a country joins the European Union. **3.** See: Acquisition.

Accession Country In international relations, a country that is a prospective member of the European Union. In order to qualify as an accession country, a state must have a democracy with a market economy, it must respect human rights, and it must accept the aims of the European Union. In order to actually join the EU, a treaty stating such must be ratified by both the accession country and the European Parliament.

Accessorial Charges Extra fees attached to transportation services for duties beyond simply shipping a good from point A to point B. Examples of services on which a company may attach accessorial charges include waiting time, storage, packing, extra fuel, and so forth. Accessorial charges are also called assessorial charges.

Accessorial Services Transportation services that a company performs beyond simply shipping a good from point A to point B. Examples of accessorial services include waiting time, storage, extra fuel, and so forth. A company may attach accessorial charges to compensate it for accessorial services.

Accident An unintended event that causes harm of any kind. An accident may be unavoidable; for example, one may hit a deer while driving a car, despite taking all appropriate precautions, simply because the deer ran in front of the car. Other accidents are the result of negligence; for example, a driver may unintentionally hit another car because he was speeding and under the influence of alcohol. The party responsible for paying damages in the event of an accident depends on a number of factors, notably which party, if any, was negligent. In some cases, one may be responsible for paying damages even if there was no negligence. Lawsuits attempting to determine responsibility are commonplace. See also: Indemnity.

Accident and Health Benefits An agreement by an employer to pay at least some of an employee's expenses in the event the employee suffers an accident (especially at work), becomes ill, or dies unexpectedly. In general, accident and health benefits involve the employer purchasing an insurance policy for the employee and paying for or at least subsidizing the premium. See also: Employee Benefits.

Accident and Health Insurance An insurance policy that provides coverage when the policyholder (or his/her dependent) becomes ill, is injured, or dies from an accident. For example, a health insurance policy may pay for most or all of the costs of a surgery. Accident and health insurance may cover doctor's visits, medical procedures, prescription drugs, and so forth. The policyholder pays a premium each month in exchange for the coverage; this premium may or may not be subsidized by one's employer. Additionally, the policyholder often must pay coinsurance and/or a copay for certain procedures. In the United States, many people procure accident and health insurance through their employers because it is often expensive to buy on one's own. Likewise, many people have group insurance to provide medical coverage.

Accident Frequency The number of times an accident occurs over a period of time. Accident frequency depends on the type of work an individual or company does, and the dangers inherent to certain actions. Accident frequency helps an insurance company determine the premium for accident insurance. Accident frequency in the workplace is likely to be higher if a company does not have or does not enforce safety standards.

Accident Insurance An insurance policy that provides coverage if the policyholder (or his/her dependent) is injured or dies as the result of an accident. For example, an accident insurance policy may pay for most or all of the costs of a surgery that occurs because of injuries sustained in a car accident. The policyholder pays a premium each month in exchange for the coverage; this premium may or may not be subsidized by one's employer.

Accident Prevention Measures an individual or company takes to attempt to reduce the number of accidents that occur. For example, a factory may require all workers to wear hard hats to reduce the risk of injury to their heads. Accident prevention measures may reduce insurance premiums.

Accident Severity The monetary value of the loss caused by an accident. Accident severity is useful in determining the premiums for accident insurance.

Accidental Death and Dismemberment Insurance An insurance policy that provides coverage if the policyholder (or his/her dependent) dies as the result of a non-work related accident. That is, accidental death insurance provides a death benefit over and above what the beneficiary would receive from a normal life insurance policy. Often, the insurance policy will also provide a benefit if the policyholder loses a limb or sustains some other, major injury.

Accidental Death Benefit The benefit paid on accidental death and dismemberment insurance. In general, the accidental death benefit is paid if the policyholder dies as the result of a non-work related accident. A policy may also pay an accidental death benefit if the policyholder loses a limb or sustains some other, major injury. This benefit is over and above what the beneficiary would receive from a normal life insurance policy.

Accidental Means A condition in most insurance policies requiring that an insured event be the result of an accident. For example, an accident insurance policy may provide coverage for a gunshot wound, but not if it was the result of a suicide attempt. The accidental means requirement helps insurance companies reduce fraud.

Accommodating Transactions Transfers of money, gold, or highly liquid assets that a central bank or other monetary authority makes to stabilize a country's balance of payments. That is, a central bank makes accommodating transactions when a country's balance of payments has become too positive or too negative and is therefore putting pressure on exchange rates. The accommodating transactions are not made for purposes of profit, but instead to help bring equilibrium to a country's currency.

Accommodation In the Uniform Commercial Code, a situation in which a seller makes delivery of goods of insufficient quality. The buyer may accept or reject the whole of the goods, but may not accept only a portion. See also: Partial Performance.

Accommodation Bill A bill of exchange that a third party guarantees without compensation. That is, the third party provides the guarantee as a favor. This reduces the risk to the bill of exchange. It is also called an accommodation note, accommodation paper, or a windbill.

Accommodation Endorsement A guarantee made on a bill of exchange without compensation for the guaranteeing party. That is, the third party provides an accommodation endorsement as a favor. The accommodation endorsement reduces the risk to the bill of exchange. See also: Accommodation Bill.

Accommodation Endorser A party that makes a guarantee on a bill of exchange without compensation. That is, the accommodation endorser provides the guarantee as a favor. The accommodation endorser reduces the risk to the bill of exchange. See also: Accommodation Bill.

Accommodation Line An insurance policy that is sold to a business that, under ordinary circumstances, would not qualify. The insurance company sells the accommodation line to the business either as a favor to the policyholder or to develop good relations with the community in which it operates so as to attract more profitable policyholders. See also: Loss leader.

Accord and Satisfaction In contract law, a situation in which a debtor buys debt forgiveness from the creditor. For example, suppose one owes $100,000 to a creditor and is paying monthly. The debtor may agree with the creditor to make accord and satisfaction for $75,000 immediately. This provides the creditor with immediate liquidity and relieves the debtor of the debt. In the event of a dispute, the burden of proof that accord and satisfaction have been made lie with the debtor.

Accordion Fold A way to fold paper in which one makes at least two parallel creases such that there are at least three equally sized folds. This is used in marketing literature, especially in direct mail, to compact as much information as possible into a small, easily deliverable space.

Accordion Insert A piece of marketing literature that has been folded using at least two parallel creases such that there are at least three equally sized folds. An accordion insert is designed to compact as much information as possible into a small, easily deliverable space. It is used commonly in direct mail.

Account An agreement between an institution and a person, or another institution, whereby the first institution agrees to hold money and/or other assets on behalf of the second. What the holder may do with those assets depends upon the nature of the account. In a checking account and a savings account, a bank holds money for the client and pays it (them or he/she) a certain percentage in interest. This payment gives the bank the right to lend the money to other clients or invest it within the confines of law and banking regulation. However, the client has the right to withdraw the total amount of money on demand. In a brokerage account, a brokerage holds money and securities for the client and makes transactions with them at the client's request. In exchange, the brokerage charges commissions for the transactions.

Account Activity Any event that results in a change to an account balance. For example, if one has an account at a bank, account activities include deposits, withdrawals, interest payments, and so forth. Unauthorized account activity may be a sign of identity theft. See also: Account statement.

Account Ad Valorem Duty A tax on an import that is expressed as a percentage of the value of the import. See also: Ad valorem.

Account Aggregation A practice or service in which information on a large number of accounts (such as credits, debts, and so forth) are available on a user friendly sheet or interface. Account aggregation makes management of multiple accounts easier, especially for a financial adviser or investment manager with a large number of clients. Account aggregation began to become common in the middle of the first decade of the 2000s.

Account Analysis 1. A summary of services a bank provides for a company. Examples of information in an account analysis include average daily float, accounts receivable turnover, and the account balance. Account analysis helps a company identify any potential weaknesses in its structure. **2.** A statement providing the account analysis for a company.

Account Balance The amount available in an account. Simply put, the account balance is the net of all credits less all debits. A positive account balance indicates the account holder has funds available to him/her, while a negative balance indicates the holder owes money. Account balances are important in banking because they determine whether or not an account holder has money for living expenses and in margin accounts because they show whether the holder can conduct more margin transactions.

Account Conflict A situation in which a single marketer has agreed to advertise for two competing companies or products. Account conflict usually occurs when two advertising agencies, each handling a company or product, merge or go through an acquisition. Advertisers seek to avoid account conflict because it could result in conflict of interest or at least result in accidental disclosure of confidential information. When an account conflict arises, the advertiser often drops one client or the other.

Account Current 1. A monthly statement an insurance company releases to a policyholder detailing premiums and claims paid. **2.** See: Checking account.

Account Executive A low ranking official at an advertising agency responsible for carrying out the wishes of higher officials in accordance with the client's needs. An account executive ranks above an account coordinator, which is the lowest, entry-level position at an advertising agency.

Account Fee An annual fee that a brokerage, bank, or any other organization assesses on all accounts for the ability to keep an account at that organization. An account fee compensates the organization for the cost of keeping the account open. See also: Inactivity fee, Maintenance fee.

Account Form A way to print a balance sheet whereby assets are listed on the left and liabilities (along with shareholder equity) are on the right. This contrasts with a report form.

Account Holder The owner of an account. That is, if an account has a positive balance, the account holder owns the money or securities contained in it. Likewise, if the account has a negative balance, the account holder owes money to the institution (often a bank or brokerage, but perhaps a private company) providing the account.

Account in Trust An account at a bank, brokerage, or insurance company that is held by one person but managed by another. That is, while one person owns the account in trust, another (often a parent or guardian) manages it. Often, the account is only held in trust until certain conditions are filled. For example, a child may take control of an account in trust upon reaching age 18.

Account Inquiry A request by an outside party to access the records of an account. For example, a credit agency may make an account inquiry to a credit card company to determine whether an account holder pays his/her bills on time and in full. Account inquiries are important in the risk analysis of individuals; however, too many account inquiries can lower one's FICO score.

Account Number A unique number of several (often eight or nine) digits used to identify the account at a bank or brokerage. Account numbers are meant to be complicated to eliminate the possibility that two persons will have the same number or that an identity thief will correctly guess a number.

Account Party An importer or other buyer that applies for a letter of credit from a bank. The account party, upon receiving the letter of credit, is able to guarantee the exporter (or other seller) that it will receive payment for the goods shipped even if the account party itself defaults.

Account Payee Only Words that one may write on a check indicating that no one other than the person or entity to which the check is addressed may cash or deposit

the check. This adds an extra layer of protection against fraud. One may also write "not negotiable" to have the same effect.

Account Reconcilement A service in which one balances all outlays and payments, finds out what outlays must still be made and what payments are still outstanding, and determines how much cash a company has on hand. Outside parties often conduct account reconcilement in order to provide a level of objectivity to their analysis. See also: Cash management, Outside audit.

Account Reconciliation The process of ensuring that one's personal records of transactions on a bank account matches the bank statement one receives each month or quarter. That is, each time one writes a check, uses a debit card, or otherwise makes a withdrawal from or deposit into a bank account, one keeps a record of the transaction. Account reconciliation involves making sure that these records match the bank's of the same transactions. Account reconciliation helps avoid, or at least remedy, such problems as identity theft and bank errors.

Account Representative The agent at a company who is responsible for a client. That is, the account representative meets with the client, determines its wishes, and devises plans of action that help the client accomplish its goals. Often, though not always, the account representative executes the plan himself/herself. Account representatives are common in many different kinds of business.

Account Statement 1. In banking, a statement detailing all credits and debits to an account over a given period of time. It is also called a bank statement. **2.** In investing, a statement detailing all long positions and short positions that an investor currently holds.

Accountability The responsibility of the person or organization responsible for a task to take credit for all positive outcomes and blame for all negative outcomes. Accountability is desirable in finance and economics because it promotes efficiency. See also: Transparency.

Accountable Plan A plan used by a business to reimburse its employees for expenses they incur for work purposes. For example, an employee on a business trip may be required to pay for a hotel room with his/her own money and later receive a reimbursement. Under an accountable plan, the reimbursement the employee receives is not included in his/her income. Because it is not part of one's income, the reimbursement is not a tax write-off, which is why the accountable plan was devised.

Accountant A professional who maintains financial records, notes expenses or revenue, and/or determines how much one owes or is owed. Accountants seek to assure that every individual or company pays, or is paid, the correct amount. There are several different types of accounting, each of which reports revenue and earnings differently from other methods. Two major methods accountants use are accrual accounting and cash accounting. Accrual accounting recognizes revenue and matches it with the expenses that generated that revenue. Cash accounting, on the other hand, recognizes revenue and expenses in the order in which they are received or spent. Accountants play an important role in personal finance as well. One may hire an accountant to maintain accurate records, to ensure that enough money remains to pay one's bills. Likewise, people use accountants to pay personal or corporate taxes in the correct amount. See also: CPA, LIFO, FIFO.

Accountant in Charge The person who supervises an audit. The accountant in charge has final responsibility for the accuracy of the results. He/she delegates tasks, reviews reports, and generally oversees other accountants.

Accountants for the Public Interest A society for accountants to volunteer their time to perform professional services for charities and other nonprofit organizations that cannot afford them. It also provides information on the accounting implications of public policy questions.

Accountants' Index A list of books and articles pertinent to accounting professionals, especially in the United States. The American Institute of Certified Public Accountants updates and publishes the Accountants' Index on a quarterly and an annual basis.

Accountants International Study Group A professional organization for accountants in Canada, the United Kingdom, and the United States. While the AISG does not provide professional certifications, it provides for the international exchange of ideas and issues for members. Members of the American Institute of Certified Public Accountants, the Canadian Institute of Chartered Accountants, and the Institute of Chartered Accountants in England and Wales all participate.

Accountant's Liability The legal responsibility an accountant has for fraud or gross negligence. That is, the accountant's liability is the potential exposure he/she has to a lawsuit. In general, an accountant who does not conform (whether deliberately or accidentally) to the Generally Accepted Accounting Principles or the Generally Accepted Auditing Standards is more likely to face legal action. See also: Accountants Liability Insurance.

Accountants Liability Insurance An insurance policy providing coverage in the event an accountant is involved in a lawsuit involving his/her professional conduct. That is, accountants liability insurance pays for the accountant's legal fees, and, if necessary, damages arising from a lawsuit. Many accountants purchase liability insurance to reduce their personal risk in case they make a mistake in their work.

Accountant's Magazine, The A monthly journal for accounting professionals. Articles in The Accountant's Magazine cover a variety of topics germane to accountancy. It was established in 1897 and is published in Scotland.

Accountant's Opinion An auditor's statement that he/she has reviewed the financial statements of a company and believes that they are accurate, complete, and in accordance with Generally Accepted Accounting Principles. Most of the time, a publicly-traded company's annual report contains an accountant's opinion; a report without one can be a matter of concern to investors. Instead of an accountant's opinion, the auditor may issue a qualified opinion, stating that the auditor is unable to render a full opinion about a company's finances, or a portion thereof, because the company's accounting does not meet the Generally Accepted Accounting Principles, or because the information was for some reason incomplete. An accountant's opinion is also called an auditor's report, a clean opinion, or simply an opinion.

Accounting The practice or profession of maintaining financial records, noting expenses or revenue, and determining how much one owes or is owed. Accounting seeks to assure that every individual or company pays or is paid the correct amount. There are several different types of accounting, each of which reports revenue and earnings differently from other methods. Two major accounting methods are accrual accounting and cash accounting. Accrual accounting recognizes revenue and matches it with the expenses that generated that revenue. Cash accounting, on the other hand, recognizes revenue and expenses in the order in which they are received or spent. Accounting is important in personal finance as well. One must maintain accurate records to ensure that enough money remains to pay one's bills. Likewise, accounting is necessary to pay personal or corporate taxes in the correct amount. See also: CPA, LIFO, FIFO.

Accounting Basis Any of several systems for recognizing revenue and expenses for accounting purposes. In the United States, the two main bases for accounting are cash accounting and accrual accounting. The cash accounting basis recognizes revenue and expenses in the order in which they are received or made. The accrual basis, on the other hand, matches revenue with the expenses that generated that revenue. Using a different accounting basis can have tax implications.

Accounting Change An adjustment to an accounting principle. For example, an accounting change may occur if new legislation allows companies to use a favorable depreciation method. Even without new legislation, the national governing body of accountants may make accounting changes. In all cases, accounting changes are announced publicly.

Accounting Control Quality control for a company's accounting practices. That is, accounting control is the series of processes a company undertakes to ensure accuracy in its financial reporting.

Accounting Convention An accounting procedure used informally. That is, an accounting convention has been neither endorsed nor prohibited by the SEC or another appropriate body. In general, when the SEC has neither endorsed nor prohibited an accounting convention, it is because it has not needed to rule on the matter, especially if the convention is new. A ruling may formalize or forbid a convention, or it may make the convention obsolete.

Accounting Currency The currency used in the internal accounting of an organization. For example, if a bank records all its transactions in British pounds, the pound is its accounting currency. Under some circumstances, a currency, notably Special Drawing Rights, may be used only as an accounting currency and for nothing else.

Accounting Cycle The events that occur between the beginning of a transaction and its recording in a company's records. For example, the accounting cycle for a sale may begin with the actual sale, continue with an accountant's analysis of the type of sale (mainly a cash or credit sale), and conclude with the posting of the sale in the company's ledger. The accounting cycle is often more complex than the above example, including steps such as quality control.

Accounting Department The staff members of a company or office who deal with accounting. In small companies, an accounting department may consist of one or two people who handle all accounting affairs. Larger companies, however, may have multiple accounting sub-departments; for example, one may deal with taxes, while another one deals with accounts receivable, and so forth.

Accounting Earnings A company's earnings as reported on its annual report or other statement. It may be calculated by any method approved in the Generally Accepted Accounting Principles.

Accounting Entity Any organization with assets and liabilities maintained on a completely separate balance sheet from other organizations. The accounting entity does not need to be a legal entity in order to have a separate balance sheet. Very often, an accounting entity is a subsidiary or department within a larger company. See also: Special Purpose Vehicle, Combined Financial Statement.

Accounting Equation A brief equation describing the relationship between the assets and the liabilities of a company. In other words, the accounting equation describes how a company's resources relate to the persons or entities with claims on those resources. It is stated as: Assets = Liabilities + Owners' Equity.

Accounting Error Any mistake on a financial statement or other accounting measurement. An accounting error is not the result of fraud or ill intent, but rather is simply an inaccuracy. An accounting error may (or may not) be the result of negligence and, for that reason, may expose the accountant to a lawsuit.

Accounting Event Anything that alters a company's financial statement. Accounting events may be external; for example, a sale is an accounting event because it reduces inventory and increases revenue. Likewise, they may be internal; for example, depreciation and amortization are accounting events because they show up on a balance sheet even though no cash changes hands.

Accounting Exposure The risk that a company may suffer a reduction in value because a change in exchange rates reduces the value of its accounts or assets denominated in foreign currencies. That is, if a particular currency in which a company has some assets denominated decreases in value, the value of those assets

also decreases with respect to the company's main currency. See also: Foreign exchange risk.

Accounting Firm A company that specializes in accounting services for clients. That is, an accounting firm may handle a client's payroll, accounts receivable and accounts payable, taxes, and/or any number of other services. Many accounting firms also offer auditing or advisory services. See also: Big 4.

Accounting Fraud Any act or attempt to falsify an accounting statement for financial gain. A clear example of accounting fraud is the act of deliberately overpricing a company's assets in order to drive up its share price. Another example is filing bankruptcy to avoid debt, rather than because of financial hardship. One of the biggest accounting frauds in history occurred during the Enron scandal in 2001.

Accounting Hall of Fame An award given by the American Accounting Association honoring individual accountants who have contributed to the advancement of the profession. As of 2009, 83 persons have been inducted into the Accounting Hall of Fame; it is considered an extremely prestigious award in the accounting industry. It is located at Ohio State University.

Accounting Historians Journal A journal for historians who specialize in accounting. Articles in the Accounting Historians Journal cover a variety of topics related to the history of accountancy. It is published twice a year by the Academy of Accounting Historians.

Accounting Information System An electronic system containing all documents that a company uses to prepare financial statements and that one may use to defend against an audit. Accounting records include receipts, ledgers, sales records, and so forth. An accounting information system has become a major means for a company to maintain accounting records. See also: Accounting software.

Accounting Insolvency A situation in which a firm or individual has a negative net worth. That is, accounting insolvency occurs when total liabilities exceed total assets on a firm's or individual's balance sheet. Accounting insolvency does not automatically equate to bankruptcy because the individual or organization may still be able to make monthly payments. This is what differentiates accounting insolvency from standard insolvency, which involves the inability to service debts. Nevertheless, creditors may force corporations with accounting insolvency to restructure payments or declare bankruptcy, depending on the specific situation.

Accounting Liquidity A measure of a company's ability to meet its short-term obligations using its most liquid assets. That is, accounting liquidity is the ease with which a company can pays its bills and liabilities over the next year, especially if it must convert its assets into cash in order to do so. Two common ways to measure accounting liquidity are the current ratio and the quick ratio.

Accounting Manual A book detailing the accounting methods used by a company. Because accountants have a certain amount of leeway in how to treat some (though not all) revenues and expenses, a company may standardize its own accounting procedures and publish them in an internal manual.

Accounting Measurement A unit of accounting. Very often, an accounting measurement is a unit of money. For example, if a company records its sales for a month as $25,000, its accounting measurement is U.S. dollars. However, an accounting measurement may also be a non-monetary unit, such as hours worked or jobs created.

Accounting Method Any system of accounting that uses a unique way for recognizing revenue and earnings. An accounting method reports revenue and earnings differently from other methods in order to assure that every company pays the appropriate amount in taxes. Two major accounting methods are accrual accounting and cash accounting. Accrual accounting recognizes revenue and matches it with the expenses that generated that revenue. Cash accounting, on the other hand, recognizes revenue and expenses in the order in which they are received or created. Regulations require different companies to use different accounting methods; for example, companies with inventories are required to use the accrual method.

Accounting Noise The act of making a firm's financial situation look better or worse than it really is by using or abusing the Generally Accepted Accounting Principles. Accounting noise is, to a certain extent, inevitable, as succinct statements very rarely give a full and complete picture of a firm's financial state. For this reason, potential and current investors are often advised to read the footnotes of financial statements to see a fuller picture. Accounting noise may make a firm look better by showing many one-time-only sales or worse by showing one-time-only expenses. Most of the time, accounting noise is incidental, but some firms abuse the GAAP to manipulate earnings in order to make themselves look healthy when they are not. See also: Aggressive accounting.

Accounting Period 1. The period of time reflected in financial statements. Usually, the accounting period is either the calendar year or a quarter. For example, publicly-traded companies must report their financial state for the accounting period since their previous report. 2. In the United Kingdom, the period for which corporate taxes are assessed.

Accounting Postulate An underlying assumption in accounting. An accounting postulate is not listed in any statement of accounting procedures because it is assumed that it is understood by everyone. For example, an accounting postulate in the United States may state that all transactions will be listed in U.S. dollars.

Accounting Principles Board A committee of the American Institute of Certified Public Accountants that advised on and set standards for financial record keeping. It was dissolved in 1973 and replaced by the Financial Accounting Standards Board.

Accounting Procedure The accounting methods used by a company. Because accountants have a certain amount of leeway in how to treat some (though not all) revenues and expenses, a company may standardize its own accounting procedures, often publishing them in an internal manual.

Accounting Profits The revenue a company derives from its operations, less all explicit costs. For example, if a company's revenue is $1 million and its total overhead is $750,000, its accounting profit is $250,000. Unlike economic profits, accounting profits do not consider an activity's opportunity cost.

Accounting Records All documents that one uses to prepare financial statements and that one may use to defend against an audit. Accounting records include receipts, ledgers, sales records, and so forth. In the United States, one generally must retain accounting records for seven years in order to verify any irregularities that may be discovered later.

Accounting Research Bulletins Recommendations by the American Institute of Certified Public Accountants on how accountants ought to treat certain facts or items. While Accounting Research Bulletins are not authoritative in themselves, the SEC often makes them so by adopting them.

Accounting Software A computer program that helps a company deal with its accounting needs. For example, accounting software may list accounts payable, account balances, and so forth. If information is entered accurately, it eliminates calculation errors. A company may buy accounting software, develop its own, or buy a program while making its own modifications.

Accounting Standards Executive Committee A committee of the American Institute of Certified Public Accountants that is permitted to make statements on the technical aspects of financial reporting without first clearing the statements with AICPA's board of directors. Its statements are not authoritative but have influence on the statements put out by other bodies, notably the FASB.

Accounting Trends and Techniques An annual report by the American Institute of Certified Public Accountants giving statistics and other information on how accountants treat various aspects of the financial statements for major corporations. It provides a number of examples drawn from real life.

Account-Only Check A check with an endorsement stating that it can only be deposited into an account and may not be paid in cash. This endorsement is irrevocable; that is, the depositor cannot cross out the endorsement to change it.

Accounts Payable 1. Money owed for a good or service purchased on credit. Accounts payable are a current liability for a company and are expected to be paid within a short amount of time, often 10, 30, or 90 days. **2.** A unit within a company's accounting department that deals with accounts payable, managing credit lines, purchase orders, and audit reports.

Accounts Payable Ledger A listing of all accounts payable by creditor. That is, the accounts payable ledger is a book listing accounts payable in which each credit has its own unique page. The accounts payable is useful as a quick reference detailing who is owed what.

Accounts Receivable 1. Money that a customer owes a company for a good or service purchased on credit. Accounts receivable are current assets for a company and are expected to be paid within a short amount of time, often 10, 30, or 90 days. See also: Collection period. **2.** A unit within a company's accounting department that deals with accounts receivable.

Accounts Receivable Discounted The sale of a company's accounts receivable in which the buyer has recourse and may demand payment from a third party in the event of default. See also: Factoring.

Accounts Receivable Financing The selling of a firm's accounts receivable to a third party, known as a factor. If a firm is not confident in its ability to collect on its credit sales, it may sell the right to receive payment to the factor at a discount. The factor then assumes the credit risk associated with the accounts receivable. This allows the firm access to working capital immediately, which is important especially if the firm might otherwise have a cash flow problem. The price of accounts receivable financing is determined by the creditworthiness of the firm's customer, not of the firm itself. See also: Debt assignment.

Accounts Receivable Insurance An insurance policy providing coverage in the event a company is unable to collect on its accounts receivable, especially under certain, specified circumstances. Accounts receivable insurance helps a company maintain regular cash flow. See also: Allowance for Bad Debts.

Accounts Receivable Turnover The average amount of time it takes for a business to collect on its accounts receivable. This is calculated by multiplying the amount in accounts receivable by the number of days in a given period and dividing into the total amount of credit sales. Accounts receivable turnover is a way to determine how a business' credit risk compares to that of its competitors.

Accredited Advisor in Insurance A professional designation awarded by the Insurance Institute of America. One receives an AAI certification upon the completion of the three-part exam. One part deals with insurance production, one deals with multi-line insurance production, and the last deals with operations and sales management. The Institute recommends people receive an AAI if they work in the business end of an insurance company.

Accredited Investor An investor with a net worth of more than $1 million or who has had an annual income of more than $200,000 ($300,000 with a spouse) in each of the past two years. Under Regulation D, accredited investors are exempt from the requirement that no more than 35 investors are allowed to participate in the private placement of a security, company, or hedge fund. As a result, many investment vehicles target high net-worth individuals.

Accreted Value The value of an original issue discount bond or other bond where the interest (or the equivalent) is not paid until maturity. The accreted value of such a bond often has only a rough relationship with its market value. See also: imputed interest.

Accreting Cap An interest rate ceiling on an obligation in which the principal increases over time. An interest rate ceiling is a floating interest rate with a stated, maximum rate above which it may not rise. Thus, while an interest rate with an accreting cap may only go to a certain level, the actual amount paid on it may increase without limit because the principal increases over time. See also: Accreting swap.

Accreting Swap A swap in which the notional amount increases over time. This is usually a fixed interest rate swap but also occasionally a currency swap. The legs of the swap are calculated at a fixed rate, but the principal over which they are calculated goes up over time. This is most commonly used in the construction industry and other projects in which costs rise over the life of the venture.

Accretion 1. The capital gains a bondholder receives when he/she buys a bond at a discount from par and expects it to mature at par. For example, if one buys a bond at 90% of par, the accretion is 10%. Unless the bond is tax exempt, accretion is taxable each year even though the bondholder does not actually receive any payments until maturity. See also: Imputed value. **2.** The addition of value as the result of an outside event. For example, an accretive acquisition occurs if an acquisition increases a company's earnings per share.

Accretion of Discount The increase in value of a security or other instrument as it approaches maturity. For example, suppose one buys a bond with a face value of $100 and pays $89. Because one is guaranteed to receive $100 when the bond matures, its value gradually increases between the purchase date and maturity. This increase is called the accretion of discount.

Accretive Acquisition An acquisition that increases a publicly-traded company's earnings per share. An accretive acquisition occurs when the price-earnings ratio of the acquiring firm is greater than that of the target firm. This means that the target firm's earnings are likely strong; this is often seen as a good investment. An accretive acquisition usually results in a higher share price for the acquiring company. See also: Dilutive Acquisition.

Accrual Accounting A system of accounting that recognizes revenue and matches it with the expenses that generated that revenue. Unlike other systems of accounting, which recognize revenue and expenses in the order in which they are received, the accrual accounting convention ignores the function of time and only considers what expenses generate what revenues, even if payments have not actually been made. Companies with inventories are required to use the accrual method for tax purposes.

Accrual of Obligation The maturity of an obligation or a portion of an obligation, which occurs on the date a payment must be made or some act must be performed.

Accrual Rate The interest rate that is charged on a loan or bond but is not paid until a later date. For example, if one pays the interest on one's mortgage every month, the accrual rate is the interest rate charged to the principal of the mortgage each day of a month until the payment is made.

Accruals On a balance sheet, an expense or asset that is recognized before it is paid. Accruals are recorded as liabilities or assets (depending on the type) and are recognized because of the extremely high likelihood of payment. Accruals are generally periodic payments; examples include salaries and accounts receivable from well-known customers. They are recorded as "accrued" on a balance sheet on the date the payment begins to be expected; they remain in this section of the balance sheet until they are actually paid.

Accrue To earn but not collect. For example, if a company makes $1 million in revenue but has not collected $250,000 before it must make its quarterly statement, it is said to have accrued $250,000 in revenue. By the same token, the interest a bond has earned between coupon payments is said to accrue. See also: Accruals.

Accrued Assets The revenue a company earns over a period of time but has not collected by the end of a reporting period. For example, if a company makes $1 million in revenue but has not collected $250,000 before it must make its quarterly statement, it lists that amount as its accrued assets. Accrued assets are also called accrued revenue.

Accrued Benefit Cost Method A way to calculate the future expense of an employee's retirement benefits. The accrued benefit cost method calculates the benefits an employee earns each year by participating in a retirement plan. One then calculates the present value of the benefits by considering the employee's life expectancy and assigns this value to the year the employee earns those benefits.

Accrued Benefits The pension, vacation, or other benefits that an employee earns in the course of a year. This is effectively income that the employee is not paid immediately. For example, an employee may accrue vacation benefits, but rather than receiving a check for the benefits, he continues to be paid his regular salary when he goes on holiday. If the employee is terminated or retires, he must be paid all previously unpaid accrued benefits.

Accrued Discount The interest paid on a savings bond at redemption or maturity. Some savings bonds do not have coupons; their accrued discounts are paid in a single sum at redemption or maturity. That is, when the bond matures or is redeemed, the bondholder receives payment all at once, but receives nothing during the life of the bond. Other savings bonds do have coupons paid in semi-annual tranches; for these bonds, the accrued discount includes the amount in all these tranches plus the money, whether par or below par, received at redemption or maturity. See also: Accrued bond, Income bond.

Accrued Dividend A dividend that a publicly-traded company has declared but on which payment is not yet due. For example, if a company declares a dividend on May 31 to be paid on June 30, it is considered an accrued dividend between those two dates. An accrued dividend is listed as a liability on the company's balance sheet. It should not be confused with an accumulated dividend.

Accrued Income The income a company earns over a period of time but has not collected by the end of a reporting period. For example, if a company earns $1 million but has not collected $250,000 before it must make its quarterly statement, it lists that amount as its accrued income.

Accrued Income Scheme In the United Kingdom, a way that interest on bonds is treated for tax purposes. Specifically, when a bondholder sells a bond, all interest that has accumulated since the last coupon payment but has not yet been paid is treated as if it had been paid to the bondholder. For example, suppose a bond pays coupons on June 30 and December 31. If one sells a bond on August 15, all interest accumulating between June 30 and August 15 is treated as income for the seller and is taxed as such, even though the interest is actually paid to the buyer.

Accrued Interest 1. The interest that accumulates on a bond between coupon payments. That is, the accrued interest begins to be calculated when a coupon is made. The total accrued interest for a given period becomes the next coupon payment. See also: Day count convention. **2.** See: Accrued expense.

Accrued Taxes The taxes assessed on a company, either on its earnings or on the value of its property, but which it has not yet paid. If the company does not pay the accrued taxes in full by the specified date, it may owe interest and penalties. Accrued taxes are listed as a liability on the company's balance sheet.

Acculturation The adaptation of a product, strategy, or anything else to fit another culture. Acculturation is often necessary when a product enters a new market in another country (or even another region or population in the same country). For example, Coca-Cola uses slightly different recipes in some countries because each recipe fits cultural tastes better in each area. Acculturation may also be practical: some American car manufacturers had a difficult time selling automobiles in Japan when they first entered that market because their side mirrors were too large to navigate in Japanese traffic.

Accumulated Amount The gain on any investment at a stated interest rate, plus the amount originally invested.

Accumulated Benefit Obligation The present value of the future liability of an employee's pension, assuming that the employee is fired or retires on the date the calculation is performed. For example, the accumulated benefit obligation is what the pension fund must pay the employee should the employer make no further contributions and the employee retires immediately. The accumulated benefit obligation therefore assumes that the employee will make no further contributions to the pension plan. See also: Projected Benefit Obligation.

Accumulated Depletion A total reduction to the value of an asset over time. Accumulated depletion comes about as a result of the physical reduction of the asset's features. For example, there is a limited amount of oil in an oil field. Accumulated depletion is the total reduction to the value of the oil field as the oil is drilled up over time. Accumulated depletion is recorded on a balance sheet most often in connection with natural resources. See also: Contra-Asset, Depreciation, Amortization.

Accumulated Depreciation The total depreciation on an asset, and not simply the depreciation that is added each year. One may calculate the accumulated depreciation by subtracting the original value of the asset from its current book value or by multiplying the yearly depreciation by the number of years the asset has been held.

Accumulated Earnings Tax In the United States, a tax on a corporation for retained earnings the IRS deems to be excessive. Retained earnings are profits that are not paid out in dividends. Companies with a low payout ratio generally experience higher price appreciation on their stock, which would subject shareholders to a higher capital gains tax when they sell, rather than a higher tax on dividends. However, the tax rate on capital gains is lower than the tax on dividends. Thus, the accumulated earnings tax exists to ensure that the government is able to receive roughly the same amount in revenue regardless of how much or how little the corporation distributes in dividends.

Accumulated Profits Tax A tax on the profits of a company. Owners of a company sometimes pay accumulated profits taxes as a way to reduce their personal income tax liabilities. See also: Corporation tax.

Accumulation 1. The gradual purchase of a single security over a long period of time as opposed to a single purchase all at once. This is done to avoid causing fluctuations in price. See also: Distribution, Accumulation Area. **2.** See: Market Outperform.

Accumulation Area A price range in which buyers buy large numbers of shares of a stock. One can identify an accumulation area if a stock only rarely falls below a certain price. On-balance Volume Method analysts use accumulation areas to recommend stock purchases because they believe such stocks will attract large numbers of buyers. See also: Distribution area.

Accumulation Benefits An addition to the death benefit of a life insurance policy. See also: Whole life insurance.

Accumulation Period 1. The period of time in which someone saves, especially for retirement. Generally speaking, the longer the accumulation period, the more one

saves. **2.** In annuities, the period of time in which one contributes to the annuity. Depending on the type of annuity, taxes may be deferred during the accumulation period. Generally speaking, the longer the accumulation period and the more one contributes to the annuity, the greater the resulting income stream.

Accumulation Plan 1. An investment strategy in which one gradually buys securities and takes positions in piecemeal fashion until one's portfolio reaches a desired size. **2.** See: Voluntary accumulation plan.

Accumulation Trust A trust into which the grantor places assets under the direction of a trustee. Unlike other trusts, the trustee is not allowed to give the assets themselves to the beneficiary. Rather, the trustee invests the assets and delivers the gains to the beneficiary.

Accumulation Unit 1. In a unit trust, a structure whereby a unit holder automatically reinvests profits from the trust, rather than accepts them as dividends. See also: DRIP. **2.** In a variable annuity, the shares that the annuity has purchased with the money the annuitant has invested in it.

Accumulation Unit Value The net asset value of an accumulation unit after all taxes and management fees have been deducted. An accumulation unit is the number of shares a variable annuity purchases with the money invested in it.

Accumulation/Distribution Line In technical analysis, a line plotting the number of stocks most investors are buying versus the number of stocks most investors are selling over a period of time. This shows whether investors are generally buying or selling. If the line slopes upward over time, it indicates an upward trend, and, if it slopes downward, the opposite is true.

Accuracy The state of being correct or true. Accuracy is important both in measuring present data and predicting future data. An accurate analyst or forecaster is rewarded with influence (and often bonuses), while a consistently inaccurate one rarely remains with a company.

Acetabulum An ancient Roman unit of volume approximately equivalent to 68 milliliters.

Acetate A derivative of acetic acid. Acetate is found in a number of chemical compounds with a wide variety of commercial uses. Notably, sodium acetate is used in textiles and processed foods, among other things. See also: Acetate Proof.

Acetate Proof In printing, a prototype of material printed on acetate paper. Advertisers use acetate proofs for greater opacity.

Achein Taya A Burmese unit of mass approximately equivalent to 16.33 kilograms.

Acid Rain Precipitation with low pH, usually resulting from excessive sulfur or nitrogen oxides in the atmosphere. Acid rain is detrimental to both plant and animal life. It has become less common since the 1970s, when governments began to take steps to reduce the sulfur released into the air.

Acid-Test Ratio A measure of a company's ability to meet its short-term obligations using its most liquid assets. It is calculated by subtracting inventories from current assets and dividing the quantity by its current liabilities. A higher acid-test ratio indicates greater short-term financial health. The acid-test ratio is more conservative than the current ratio, which measures much the same thing, because the current ratio excludes the value of inventory. This is because inventory can be less liquid than other current assets. The acid-test ratio thus measures a company's ability to meet obligations in a worst-case scenario. It is also called the quick ratio.

Acne A slang term for a break-out.

ACOnet Austrian Academic Computer Network. A network that gives members access to academic literature, databases, and other information. ACOnet was established to connect Austrian universities to one another. It traces its history to the early 1980s and is based at the University of Vienna.

Acquired Advantage The ability for an economic actor to produce a good or service with fewer resources using knowledge or skills that are acquired over time. For example, if Town A has more electrical engineers or a better engineering school than Town B, Town A may have an acquired advantage in the production of electrical circuits, even if all other resources are the same. See also: comparative advantage, absolute advantage, location-specific advantage.

Acquired Group Membership An affiliation with a club, church, professional organization, or any other group not determined by birth. Acquired group membership is a sign of recognition by a community and often reflects social status. It is important in business because it provides a starting place for networking and can be a medium for the exchange of information.

Acquiree A company that is the object of a takeover attempt. That is, another company is buying the acquiree's shares with the intent of obtaining a majority stake. This may occur with or without the authorization of the acquiree's board of directors. An acquiring company identifies potential acquirees based on a variety of factors, including share price and growth potential; in the event of a hostile takeover, the acquirer may buy up to 5% of the acquiree without publicly disclosing its intentions.

Acquirer A person or company that buys an asset or a company. An acquirer who purchases a publicly-traded company is almost always another company. That is, individual investors, even wealthy ones, rarely buy publicly-traded companies. See also: Mergers & Acquisitions.

Acquisition An investment in which a company or person buys a publicly-traded company, or, more commonly, most of the shares in that company. For example, if Corporation A buys 51% or more of Corporation B, then Corporation B becomes a subsidiary of Corporation A, and the activity is called an acquisition. A single investor may buy out a publicly-traded company; one calls this "going private."

Acquisitions occur in exchange for cash, stock, or both. Acquisitions may be friendly or hostile; a friendly acquisition occurs when the board of directors supports the acquisition and a hostile acquisition occurs when it does not. See also: Antitakeover measure.

Acquisition Cost 1. The total cost for a firm to buy an asset. The acquisition cost includes all legal fees, closing costs, or other increases. Likewise, it makes allowances for discounts. Importantly, however, the acquisition cost does not include any applicable sales tax. **2.** The total cost for a firm to gain a new client or customer. The acquisition cost includes marketing, discounts, networking, and other associated costs.

Acquisition Debt Any debt one uses to buy, make improvements on, or build a residence for oneself. See also: Mortgage.

Acquisition Fee Any and all fees one must pay in the process of buying a property. Examples of acquisition fees include closing costs, commission to the real estate broker, and any costs associated with construction. One may pay acquisition fees directly, or one may borrow them along with the mortgage. See also: All-in cost.

Acquisition Indigestion 1. A situation in which a company that has been bought out has difficulty integrating its corporate culture with that of the acquiring company. **2.** A situation in which an acquiring company has difficulty profiting from an acquisition.

Acquisition of Stock An acquisition by one company of another in which the acquiring company buys the target company's stock. That is, rather than paying with debt or some other means, an acquisition of stock occurs when the acquiring company buys a majority of the target company's shares outstanding. This may be associated with a hostile takeover, where the acquiring company buys shares directly from stockholders, but this is not always the case. See also: Leveraged buyout.

Acquisition Premium The difference between the estimated value of a target company and the price the acquiring company pays to buy it. The acquisition premium may be either above or below the original estimate and comes from revised estimates and changes in the acquisition agreement.

Acquittance The full satisfaction or discharge of a debt or other liability as witnessed by the issue of a receipt or other, similar document by the creditor.

Acre A measure of area, especially of land. The area of an acre is not standardized; an American acre is slightly larger than an international acre. It is roughly 4,840 square yards. Historically, an acre is said to be an approximation of the land a single ox could plough in a day. It is often used in real estate transactions.

Acre Breadth An obsolete unit of length equivalent to 22 yards.

Acreage Report An annual report listing the crops planted throughout the United States and the number of acres each one occupies. The U.S. Department of Agriculture publishes the Acreage Report and compiles it by taking a survey of American farmers.

Acrobat A computer program that converts any document into the form it would look like if it were printed. Sometimes these documents can be edited in Acrobat, but not always. It preserves all colors and formatting the document had in other programs.

Acronym An abbreviation made from the first parts (usually the first letters) of a multi-word term. Strictly speaking, acronyms form pronounceable words, such as STRIPS. Those that do not are called initialisms, such as SEC. However, the term has come to refer to all abbreviations. Acronyms are very common in business and finance, and often are used so commonly they nearly replace the original term. For example, price-earnings ratio is often shortened to P/E and a chief executive officer is usually called a CEO.

Across the Board Relating to or applying to a situation in which most or all members of a group behave the same way. This especially applies to a situation in which most securities on an exchange move in the same direction. For example, one might say, "Stocks are down across the board," meaning that the predominant market movement is downward. Across the board situations are normally responses to a market-wide event, such as a change in interest rate or a political situation.

Across the Board Tariff Reduction The unilateral decision by a country to reduce the tariffs it imposes on its imports. Tariffs are considered economically inefficient because they make imports less competitive than domestically produced goods, which can result in more expensive products for consumers. Across the board tariff reductions help prevent this; they also may be intended to encourage the country's trade partners to do the same and make the country's exports more competitive abroad. Opponents of across the board tariff reductions, however, argue that the increased competition can drive domestic companies out of business, eliminating jobs.

Across the Piece In business, a slang term describing any event or thing that will affect the entire organization. For example, a company conducting layoffs across the piece has layoffs in every department.

Across-the-Board Describing anything that applies to all affected parties equally. For example, if a company decides on an across-the-board pay reduction, all of its employees (including managers) have their pay reduced by the same percentage. Likewise, if an exchange is on an across-the-board upward trend, it means all or nearly all securities on that exchange are increasing in price.

Across-the-Board Movement A trend affecting all or nearly all securities in a market or sectors in an economy. For example, an across the board movement may describe a period of growth in which every industry sees increases in profitability. See also: Systematic risk.

Act 1. See: Activity. **2.** In insurance, any deed, especially one that foregoes the possibility of coverage. For example, life insurance policies rarely extend coverage if the policyholder commits suicide. In this case, the suicide is called an act.

Act of Bankruptcy An involuntary admission of bankruptcy by a debtor. In general, going into default and consistently missing payments may be considered acts of bankruptcy. Before 1978 in the United States, an act of bankruptcy involved the transfer of assets to another party with the intent to defraud creditors, but this is no longer the case. Upon committing an act of bankruptcy, creditors have the ability to petition to force the debtor into legal bankruptcy.

Act of God In law, any event outside of human control, especially one that causes damage. Examples of acts of God include tornados, hurricanes and earthquakes. Many contracts do not have to be completed in the event of an act of God; that is, one is usually immune from having to perform on a contract rendered impossible by an act of God. Many companies, notably agricultural and similar corporations, have insurance to compensate for losses resulting from an act of God. An act of God is also called vis major, which is Latin for "superior force." See also: Act of God bond.

Act of God Bond A high yield debt security backed by insurance premiums. Insurance companies issue act of God bonds in order to raise funds for hypothetical insurance payouts resulting from one or more stated events, such as floods or fires. The bondholder receives coupons from what the insurance company collects in premiums. However, if the insurance company suffers a loss from a payout of one of stated events, the obligation to repay the bond is either relaxed or forgiven. The main advantage to an act of God bond, despite the stated risk, is the fact that it offers a high yield without much regard for the performance of the broader economy because people as institutions will almost always set money aside for insurance premiums.

Act of State Doctrine A doctrine stating that each sovereign state has complete control over the laws within its own borders and that its acts cannot be questioned in the courts of another state. This is important to economics and trade because it means that investors in one country cannot sue to force a company or the government in another country to take an action favorable to them; they must go through the domestic courts for redress. While international agreements and conventions temper the act of state doctrine, it remains important.

Acting in Concert Describing two or more investors coordinating with each other to achieve the same investment goal. This especially applies to two institutional investors acting in concert; for example, they may act together to take over a smaller company and split the management duties between them. See also: Joint venture.

Action Device In marketing, a way to encourage a person to buy a product or otherwise spend money through the performance of a physical action. For example, a street canvasser looking for donations usually carries a binder and often has a much higher success rate if the canvasser can convince a potential donor to hold the binder.

Action Ex Contractu A legal action arising out of the accused violation of a contract.

Action Item Something that must be accomplished prior to the next meeting. For example, a board of directors may require the treasurer to find quotes for employee insurance before the next meeting. In this case, gathering quotes is an action item because they are to be presented (generally along with a recommendation) at the next board meeting.

Action Program A plan detailing the steps one must take to achieve a stated goal. For example, if one wishes to have a larger office in two years, one may make an action program detailing how to attain that goal. An action program must show the time horizon, the tasks one must complete, and the cost associated with each task. It is also called an action plan.

Actions Ex Delicto Legal actions arising out of some manner of wrong-doing. Actions ex delicto, for example, may refer to harm coming from trespass. The term is rare, as torts generally encompass actions ex delicto.

Activation Fee A one-time fee a company charges upon the creation of a new account. For example, a cellular phone company or an Internet service provider may assess an activation fee in addition to the first month's bill. The activation fee is intended to compensate the company for the expenses associated with setting up the account.

Active 1. Describing a security that is traded with relative frequency. Many investors look to active securities because they can be traded, even in rather large quantities, without affecting the price. Active securities usually have a low bid-ask spread. **2.** Describing a market or exchange with a high trading volume.

Active Account A brokerage account on which trades occur regularly. Active account holders generally do not have a buy and hold investment strategy; rather, they seek to profit from small changes in the prices of securities and high trading volume. Some brokerages charge a fee for managing active accounts, as doing so is more work for the broker(s) involved.

Active Bond Especially on the New York Stock Exchange, a bond or other debt security that trades with relative frequency. Many investors look to active bonds because they can be traded, even in rather large quantities, without affecting the price. Active bonds usually have a low bid-ask spread. See also: Active bond crowd.

Active Bond Crowd Traders on the New York Stock Exchange who deal with bonds that are traded frequently. Because they deal in active bonds, the active bond crowd is responsible for the lion's share of bond trading volume. Prices are usually higher for actively traded bonds because they are liquid investments. See also: Cabinet Crowd.

Active Box Collateral used to secure funds borrowed on a margin account. A margin account allows an investor to buy securities with money borrowed from a broker; the funds are payable on demand of the broker. They also must be secured by an active box, which usually consists of securities owned by the borrower. The "box" refers to a safe where the stock and bond certificates are kept until the margin account is paid off. It is also called an open box.

Active Buyer In marketing, a customer who has bought a product from a company recently. For example, an active buyer may be a customer who subscribed to a newspaper in the past year. An active buyer is more likely to be a continuing customer than other customers.

Active Corps of Executives A volunteer organization in which major executives donate time and expertise to help small businesses in the United States. It was established in 1969 and is affiliated with the Service Corps of Retired Executives.

Active Income The regular compensation that an individual receives in the form of salary, wages, tips, commissions, and/or any other source. For example, rents and dividends are not considered active income because an individual does not need to do anything in order to earn them. An individual earns active (and passive) income in order to pay for personal expenses, such as a mortgage, debt service, groceries, etc. Active income is necessary for an economy to function. See also: Passive income, Portfolio income.

Active Management The practice of a money manager or a team of money managers making investment decisions on what securities to include in a mutual fund or portfolio. Sometimes active management exists within certain parameters; for example, money managers may only buy blue-chip stocks for a certain fund and growth stocks for another. The basic premise of active management, however, states that the managers can maximize the return for investors by buying or selling securities on a fairly regular basis. See also: Passive management, Indexing.

Active Market A market for a security with a high trading volume. Many investors look to active markets because they can be traded, even in rather large quantities, without affecting the price. Securities with active markets usually have low bid-ask spreads.

Active Member A member of a securities exchange who makes trades on a regular basis. Active members represent most of the trade volume on the exchange and provide the most liquidity. See also: Market maker, Day trader, Active account.

Active Month In futures trading, the month immediately following the delivery month. Despite the name, trading on a contract is very inactive during the active month because the contract has already been performed, rendering it worthless.

Active Partner In a partnership, a partner who both owns a share in the company's equity and is responsible for the overall management of the company. An active partner sometimes (but not always) provides capital in order to fund the company's operations. An active partner often has unlimited liability in case the company fails. See also: General Partner.

Active Retention The practice of setting aside funds to pay for losses if and when they occur. Active retention especially refers to funds put away for small losses. It saves the company the expense of buying an insurance policy to cover routine losses. It is a concept similar to, but distinct from, a company's allowance for bad debts.

Active Return The actual return on an investment relative to some benchmark. The active return can be either positive or negative; for example, if the actual return is 5% and the benchmark is 6%, the active return is -1%. More broadly, the active return may be the difference between an investment or portfolio and some index against which it is measured. If a portfolio outperforms the market, it may be said to have a positive active return. See also: Required rate of return.

Active Risk The risk a portfolio or fund acquires when it is actively managed, especially when its money managers attempt to outperform some benchmark. That is, the more a fund or portfolio differs from the benchmark upon which it is based, the more likely it is to underperform or outperform that same benchmark. This extra risk is active risk.

Active Search In marketing, a process in which a consumer seeks information on a product he/she wants to buy. An active search often includes reading reviews, comparing prices, and generally attempting to find the best quality product for the lowest cost.

Active Subscriber A subscriber to a periodical who has bought or renewed a subscription within the last stated period of time. A large number of active subscribers makes the periodical attractive to advertisers and such a periodical may be able to command higher rates from them.

Active Underwriter An underwriter at Lloyd's.

Active Window On a computer, the window (or interface) one is currently using. Most computers only allow one active window at a time. For example, if one has a web browser and a word processor both open, one can only utilize one at a time even though both programs are open. The same applies for two windows of the same program.

Actively Managed Fund A pool of liquidity with a portfolio that an investment company trades actively in order to meet the fund's investment goals. For example, an actively managed fund may have a target return or a target level of risk. If the target is not being met, the investment company managing the fund makes appropriate trades in order to correct the situation. Mutual funds are actively managed funds. See also: Index fund.

Active-Participant Status The state of belonging to an employer-sponsored retirement plan. One may have active-participant status in an IRA, 401(k), 403(b), or other, similar investment vehicles. An employer generally indicates an employee's active-participant status on the employee's W-2 form so the employee may take advantage of the tax benefits of the plan.

Activist Investor A shareholder or group of shareholders in a publicly-traded company that tries to make changes in management and/or operations in a way that suits the shareholder(s)' interests. Activist investors deliberately acquire substantial stakes in certain companies and therefore wield enough influence that the company often must listen to them. Activist investors may choose to negotiate directly with the company or indirectly though methods like proxy wars or public shaming. Activist investors may be motivated by ethical concerns; they may want the company to pay its workers better, for example. More often, they wish to change the company in a way that will maximize their own return. Activist investors may be investment companies, institutional investors, shareholder groups, or even wealthy individual shareholders.

Activist Policy Any policy whereby a government seeks to direct or affect the economy in which it operates. For example, a government may offer a tax credit to homebuyers to stimulate homeownership. Likewise, it may cut taxes to encourage spending or it may increase its own spending to create demand for goods and services. All governments pursue activist policies inasmuch as they seek to encourage growth; however, the term connotes a policy in which the government plays a more direct role. See also: American Recovery and Reinvestment Act of 2009.

Activities of Daily Living Basic, mundane activities such as bathing, eating, taking medication, walking, dressing, and using the toilet. Long-term care insurance policies compile and maintain (slightly different) lists of activities of daily living that a policyholder generally should be able to do. If a policyholder is unable to perform two or more activities of daily living, he/she is usually able to receive benefits from the long-term care policy. They are also important in determining eligibility for benefits from Medicare, Medicaid, and other government assistance programs.

Activity 1. An act that requires use of resources or time. In Program Evaluation and Review Technique (PERT), an activity is represented by an arrow on a PERT chart. **2.** In investing, the amount of a security's relative trading volume; that is, the amount of money flowing into and out of a security in trading. A high amount of activity means that many shares of the security are being bought and sold at a high rate, while a low level of activity indicates the opposite.

Activity Account An account into which government funds are placed for a specific purpose or department. For example, in a city budget, police funds may be placed in a different activity account than public health funds. Activity accounts provide a useful way to segregate government appropriations.

Activity Accounting The analysis and reporting of financial and other information on activities, in which the analysis is conducted by the persons or departments responsible for those activities. Activity accounting allows those persons or departments to take credit or blame for the good and bad decisions made over the period of time indicated in the accounting statement. It is used especially in decentralized organizations. Activity accounting is also called responsibility accounting or profitability accounting. See also: Activity-Based Costing.

Activity Attributes Features inherent to an activity. Examples of activity attributes include time and cost. Analyzing activity attributes is an important part of activity analysis, which helps a business become more cost effective.

Activity Based Budgeting A way to budget that analyzes potential activities in which a company can engage. These activities are organized according to the company's goals, and the costs of each are organized to compile the budget. ABB contrasts with traditional budgeting, which usually simply increases the previous year's budget to account for inflation and the like; rather, ABB seeks out new opportunities and allocates resources in the budget based on them. Proponents say that ABB is a more accurate way to forecast budgeting.

Activity Based Management An area of management accounting that evaluates business activities so that management can make better-informed business decisions, especially by streamlining activity to reduce costs. ABM utilizes activity-based costing, which attempts to allocate overhead costs to specific goods and services and find ways to reduce them.

Activity Center The combined cost to a company of conducting two or more activities. See also: All-In Cost.

Activity Charge A fee a company or bank assesses for providing a service. For example, a bank may assess an activity charge if a person withdraws money from that bank's ATM. Likewise, an activity charge may also be assessed monthly on every checking account at a bank to keep them open. See also: Service Fee.

Activity Cost Assignment The process of matching a company's costs to the activities that produce those costs. This helps promote the company's cost effectiveness. See also: Activity Cost Assignment.

Activity Dictionary A list of activities in which a company can or does engage. The activity dictionary also includes a description of each activity. It provides a convenient reference for a company's current or possible activities.

Activity Driver Analysis The investigation and reporting of a company's activities with the highest cost. This helps promote the company's cost effectiveness. See also: Activity Cost Assignment.

Activity Level 1. See: Active Stocks. **2.** The level to which an activity incurs a cost for a company.

Activity-Based System Any computer system or other algorithm that provides quantitative information on a company's activities. This may be used in activity-based management.

Actual A physical, homogenous commodity underlying a contract. Actuals can be traded on the physical market and delivered immediately, or traded on the futures market and delivered at the completion of the contract. As such, actuals have an intrinsic value. Examples include oil, beef, and diamonds.

Actual Authority The legal authority a person has as the result of a law or contract. For example, the owner of a house has the actual authority to sell it because the law states that he is the owner. Likewise, the president of the United States has the actual authority to sign or veto legislation. Persons with actual authority are legally liable for their actions. Actual authority is distinct from apparent authority. It is also called express authority.

Actual Cash Value In insurance, the cost to the insurance company to replace a good covered by a policy. The actual cash value is the original cost of the good, less depreciation and obsolescence. In order to receive coverage for a good's actual market value, that good must be listed specifically in the insurance policy. The actual cash value is related to a good's market value.

Actual Cost The cost a company pays or is paid for a good or service. The actual cost may be more or less than the estimated cost. For example, a car shop may estimate that repairs will cost $700, but the actual cost may in fact be $800. One often is not informed of the actual cost until it is incurred.

Actual Damages In a lawsuit, the damages the judge or jury orders one party to pay the other to compensate for real losses the second party suffered resulting from the action or negligence of the first party. For example, if Joe sues Bob because Bob caused $5,000 in damage to Joe's property, the actual damages the jury awards will equal $5,000. Actual damages differ from both nominal damages and punitive damages.

Actual Market 1. A commodity market in which commodities are delivered immediately. For example, if one buys 100 barrels of oil on an actual market, the oil is delivered upon execution of the transaction. An actual market is the opposite of a futures market, where delivery is delayed until the futures contract expires. **2.** The price at which a trade occurs, as opposed to price at which a given economic theory states that it ought to occur.

Actual Return The return or yield on an investment or portfolio, as opposed to an estimation of the same. Before making an investment, one generally calculates the expected return, which is an important aspect of an investment's risk analysis. The actual return is what objectively happened to the investment. In addition to contributing to an investor's profit or loss on a given deal, the actual return may be measured against the expected return to determine the accuracy of risk analysis methodologies.

Actual Total Loss The total amount that an insurance company pays to a policyholder when an insured item is completely destroyed, damaged beyond use, or disappears without explanation. It is also called total loss.

Actuarial Adjustment In insurance and pensions, a change made to a company's premiums, reserves, or finances based on actual or expected changes to the benefits it must pay out. For example, if a disproportionate number of pensioners retire early, the company providing their pensions must adjust its reserves downward and/or its premiums upward to account for the benefits it must pay before it expected to do so. A company may also make actuarial adjustments to benefits themselves; for example, those persons retiring early may find their monthly pension payments are less than expected.

Actuarial Analysis An evaluation of the risk of loss to an investment done by an actuary. Actuaries use a variety of statistical models and other mathematical methods to conduct actuarial analysis. See also: Actuarial risk.

Actuarial Board for Counseling and Discipline An organization in the United States that establishes and enforces ethical guidelines for actuaries. It responds to actuaries' requests for advice on how to handle a given situation. It also responds to complaints on an actuary's conduct and, if necessary, takes disciplinary action. It was established by the American Academy of Actuaries and is based in Washington, D.C.

Actuarial Consultant A professional who assists an individual in making financial decisions, especially involving insurance or pensions. The actuarial consultant uses statistical models to assess the client's risk and gives advice based upon that information. Unlike actuaries who work for insurance companies, actuarial consultants have a fiduciary responsibility to work in the best interests of the person seeking to buy insurance or participate in a pension.

Actuarial Cost Assumptions The assumptions an actuary makes when calculating the cost of providing insurance or a pension. Actuarial cost assumptions include the expected benefit of the policy or pension, the age at which the pensioner is expected to retire, and the return on investment on the premiums the pensioner makes, among other things. As with all assumptions, actuarial cost assumptions may turn out to be wrong; this would result in an actuarial adjustment.

Actuarial Cost Method Any method used to determine how much money the premiums to a pension must be each month. In order to remain solvent, a pension's premiums plus the return of investment must equal or exceed the amount paid out to retirees. The company managing the pension uses an actuarial cost method to calculate premiums based on that assumption. It is also called an actuarial funding method.

Actuarial Equity An evaluation of the risk to an insurance company if it sells a policy to a particular person. Factors that may affect actuarial equity include family history, age body-mass index, occupation, and so forth. Actuaries use a variety of statistical models and other mathematical methods to calculate actuarial equity. See also: Actuarial Analysis.

Actuarial Equivalent A measurement in which the payment streams on two, different insurance policies or other plans have the same present value under a given set of actuarial assumptions. It is used to compare two plans with each other.

Actuarial Gains and Losses The actual amount a company pays on its pensions compared to previous estimates. An actuarial gain occurs if the company pays less than it thought it would, while an actuarial loss happens if it pays more than expected. Actuarial gains and losses may result in a change to a company's actuarial assumptions. See also: Actuarial adjustment.

Actuarial Rate An estimate of the future loss on a pension fund based on historical loss under similar circumstances. The actuarial rate may be right or wrong, and can result in an actuarial gain or an actuarial loss for the company. See also: Actuarial Assumptions.

Actuarial Risk The possibility that an actuary's assessment of a potential policyholder's risk may turn out to be incorrect. For example, if an actuary is using statistical models and determines a policyholder is likely to live for another 30 years, there is an actuarial risk that the policyholder will die tomorrow. This would result in a large loss for the insurance company. Actuaries work to improve their statistical models to minimize actuarial risk. See also: Actuarial analysis.

Actuarial Science The statistical study of risk as it relates to insurance. A practitioner of actuarial science computes various risk factors and determines the likelihood of whether (or when) an event will occur. For example, one may look at a person's medical information, such as height, weight, and pre-existing conditions, and mathematically determine how likely it is that the person will cost the insurance company more than he/she will pay in premiums. This helps the insurance company decide whether the person will receive coverage and, if so, what the monthly premium will be. Many universities offer degrees in actuarial science, though many insurance companies hire individuals with math degrees and teach them actuarial science directly.

Actuarial Surplus A measure of the amount by which the value of a company's pension fund exceeds the amount it must pay out in benefits. This should not be confused with an actuarial gain, which occurs when a company pays out less than expected. That is, a company can have an actuarial gain (and pay out less than it estimated) without having an actuarial surplus and vice versa.

Actuarial Value In health insurance, the estimated percentage of a typical policyholder's medical bills that an individual plan is expected to pay. A policyholder may receive less than the actuarial value in coverage if he/she has few medical expenses (because the bills may not exceed the deductible) and may receive more than the actuarial value if he/she has numerous expenses. The actuarial value is considered a good baseline for the coverage most policyholders will receive most of the time. The Affordable Care Act of 2010 in the United States requires health insurance providers to calculate and publicize the actuarial value of each plan.

Actuary A statistician who works for an insurance company or other organization that assesses risk. The actuary computes various risk factors and determines the likelihood of whether (or when) an event will occur. For example, an actuary will look at a person's medical information, such as height, weight, and pre-existing conditions, and mathematically determine how likely it is that the person will cost the insurance company more than he/she will pay in premiums. This helps the insurance company decide whether the person will receive coverage and, if so, what the monthly premium will be.

Actus An ancient Roman unit of length approximately equivalent to 35.5 meters.

Actus quadratus An ancient Roman unit of area approximately equivalent to 1,262 square meters. It was also called an acnua or a semis.

Actus simplex An ancient Roman unit of area approximately equivalent to 42.1 square meters.

AD 1. ISO 3166-1 alpha-2 code for the Principality of Andorra. This is the code used in international transactions to and from Andorran bank accounts. **2.** ISO 3166-2 geocode for Andorra. This is used as an international standard for shipping to Andorra. Each Andorran Parish has its own code with the prefix "AD." For example, the code for the Parish of Canillo is ISO 3166-2:AD-02. **3.** See: A-D.

A-D In technical analysis, a line plotting the advance-decline index over a period of time. The advance-decline index takes the total of stock issues increasing on a trading day and subtracts the number of stock issues declining on the same day. Technical analysts use the index as an indicator of market movements, and use the advance-decline line to confirm a movement. If the line slopes upward over time, it indicates an upward trend, and, if it slopes downward, the opposite is true.

Ad Beatissimi An encyclical letter written by Pope Benedict XV in 1914. Written during the early days of World War I, the letter condemns injustice between social classes, greed, and revolutionary activity against the state. As such, the letter represents an important part of Catholic teaching on social justice, which is critical of both communism and unrestrained capitalism.

Ad Hoc Describing anything constituted for a single purpose or to deal with a certain situation. It especially describes a reaction to a spontaneous situation. For example, the board of directors of a company may form an ad hoc committee to deal with a labor dispute. Once the dispute is resolved, the committee will cease to exist.

Ad Infinitum Describing anything that continues without limit. For example, if a government continually prints money, the money supply may increase ad infinitum.

Ad Valorem Equivalent In international commerce, a tax on an import that is expressed as a percentage of the value of the import. It is applied during a tariff adjustment. See also: Ad valorem tax.

Ad Valorem Tariff A tax on an import calculated as a percentage of the value of the import. This contrasts with tariffs on the weight, size, or quantity of the import. Like all tariffs, ad valorem tariffs are controversial, with opponents arguing that they are economically inefficient. See also: Ad Valorem Tax.

Ad Valorem Tax A tax calculated as a percentage of the value of an asset. Most property taxes are ad valorem taxes because the property owners owe a given percentage of the market value the property. Value-added taxes are another common example.

Ad-a-Card A coupon with perforated edges that one may detach from a newspaper or magazine. An ad-a-card is designed to attract attention and to generate a response from the reader.

Adam Smith A Scottish philosopher who is credited with developing most of the ideas of modern economics. Smith believed that economies work most efficiently when economic actors attempt to maximize their own self-interests, and that doing so tends to maximize the interests of society as a whole. He also coined the term Invisible Hand, which is a metaphor for the free market. He published a number of influential works, most notably the Theory of Moral Sentiments and the Wealth of Nations. He lived from 1723 to 1790.

Adaptive Expectations A theory stating that economic actors make decisions based upon past, recent performance, regardless of the actual state of the economy. Thus, it takes economic actors some time to realize that a recession has ended or is beginning and to adjust their behavior accordingly. Adaptive expectations can result in large losses. See also: Rational expectations, Irrational exuberance.

Adaptive Exponential Smoothing A form of exponential smoothing that uses a coefficient to account for seasonal variation. Adaptive exponential smoothing attempts to identify trends (e.g. in sales) while ignoring irrelevant information from normal fluctuations that occur throughout the year. See also: Seasonally adjusted.

Adashah An ancient Hebrew unit of area approximately equivalent to 35 square millimeters.

ADB 1. Adjusted Debit Balance. The amount of money an investor owes on a margin account. This is calculated as the amount the investor directly owes his/her broker less the paper profit the investor has made on short sales and similar transactions on a special miscellaneous account. The adjusted debit balance is important to determining the amount owed in case of a margin call. According to Regulation T, an investor can only make a cash or securities withdrawal if the adjusted debit balance is small. **2.** Asian Development Bank. A bank that promotes economic growth and international development in the Asia-Pacific region of the world. It finances its activities with bonds and works closely with the International Monetary Fund and the World Bank toward accomplishing its goals. Its two largest shareholders are the United States and Japan. It was established in 1966 and is headquartered in Manila.

Add to Cash Value Option In universal life insurance, the ability to place a portion of one's premium into a cash value account, which will invest that premium and may offer a higher return for the policyholder. This additional cash becomes available upon the death of the policyholder and adds to the guaranteed death benefit that is otherwise received. Because of the existence of the add to cash value option, premiums are higher for universal life policies than for other forms of life insurance.

Addendum A document used to amend or make further specifications to a contract. For example, an addendum may change a payment schedule or, if the contract itself did not do so, specify the amount of the payments. Lawyers often have standardized addendum forms in case parties to a contract wish to make changes.

Adding to a Loser Buying more shares in a publicly-traded company in which one already owns shares after the stock price has gone down, or short selling more shares after the price has gone up. Adding to a loser lowers (or raises, for a short sale) the average price at which one buys the stock, which, if the price goes back up (or down), will increase one's capital gains when one closes the position on the stock. However, adding to a loser carries the risk that the stock will continue to decline. As a result, some analysts recommend never adding to a loser. See also: Average Down, Average Up.

Additional Bonds Test A financial statement that a company must issue before making a new issue of a bond. The additional bonds test shows what assets the potential issuer has available to pay coupons on the bond. It helps ensure the issuer is able to service debt on the new issue. The additional bonds test increases the transparency of the market and helps one accurately gauge the risk of the new bond issue.

Additional Car Any car or other automobile owned or leased by an individual or his/her spouse other than the one under a car insurance policy. If the additional car is a passenger car and is not used for farming or business, it may be covered by the same insurance policy if and only if all of the cars owned by the individual or couple are under that policy.

Additional Collateral In a loan or bond, collateral that the lender requires over and above the original collateral. A lender may only require additional collateral if the loan contract permits it. Generally, lenders require additional collateral if there is

a sudden increase in the risk of the loan, or if shareholders demand the lender reduce its risk exposure on all loans. See also: After-Acquired Clause.

Additional Death Benefit In some life insurance policies, an extra benefit the beneficiaries of the policy receive upon the death of the policyholder, provided one's death occurs under certain, defined circumstances. For example, a policy may pay an additional death benefit if the policyholder dies before his/her retirement. The amount of the additional death benefit and the circumstances under which it is paid are defined in the policy.

Additional Deposit Privilege In some whole life insurance policies, the ability to make additional, unscheduled premiums at any time. These premiums are added to the cash value of the policy unless there is an outstanding loan against the cash value, in which case they are applied to the loan. The minimum additional deposit is usually around $1,000.

Additional First-Year Depreciation A provision in U.S. tax law that permits some assets purchased in a given year to be expensed, rather than depreciated, the first year of ownership. That is, one may write off the total value of the asset rather than the amount by which is depreciates. This reduces one's taxable income. There are limits on the value of property on which one may use additional first-year depreciation; this amount changes in different years.

Additional Hedge A way for a mortgage lender to protect itself from the risk that a potential borrower will reject a loan after the terms are set but before the deal is finalized. Such a rejection could result in a loss for the lender, particularly if it has already made arrangements to repackage and sell the mortgage to a third party. An additional hedge protects against this. See also: Fallout Risk.

Additional Insured A person or company listed on an insurance policy in addition to the primary policyholder. For example, the head of household may list her husband and children as additional insureds on her health insurance. This is often less expensive than buying separate policies. An additional insured is also called an additional interest.

Additional Living Expense Insurance An insurance policy (or a section of an insurance policy) that provides coverage for extra expenses that occur if the policyholder must temporarily leave his/her residence. For example, if one's home suffers from fire damage and one must temporarily live in a hotel, additional living expense insurance may pay for the cost of having to eat out three times a day. Additional living expense insurance may stand on its own or it may be part of a homeowner's insurance or similar plan.

Additional Mark-On An increase in the price of a retail product that occurs relatively soon after another increase. Additional mark-ons are most common during peak retail seasons, such as the weeks before Christmas.

Additional Paid-In Capital Capital that a company raises in a financing round in excess of the capital's par value. For example, additional paid-in capital may occur when a publicly-traded company makes a new issue of stock with a par value of $5 per share and places it with investors for $8 per share. Companies can only raise additional paid-in capital on the primary market because they do not receive any additional money from trades on the secondary market. It is important to note that it has become rare for stock to have a par value. See also: Paid-in Capital.

Additional Premium A premium on an insurance policy over and above the initial premium imposed at the beginning of the policy. An additional premium may be assessed if the insured's risk is found to have increased significantly.

Additional Voluntary Contribution Also called an AVC. In the United Kingdom, a contribution to a pension over and above what one is required to contribute. For example, one may have a pension structured such that one makes a 100-pound contribution each month automatically. If one makes a supplementary 50-pound contribution, this is called an AVC. This may increase the benefits the pension pays after retirement. Employers sometimes match additional voluntary contributions.

Add-On Certificate of Deposit Money deposited into a certificate of deposit after the initial deposit. Suppose one places $1,000 in a certificate of deposit and places a further $500 into the same account later. One refers to the $500 as an add-on. Only some financial institutions allow add-on certificates of deposit because they receive the same interest rate as the previous deposit, a fact that would be disadvantageous to the financial institution when interest rates are declining.

Add-On Financing Any issue of stock by a publicly-traded company other than the IPO. A company makes a public offering through underwriters, who have the responsibility to place the offering with individual and institutional investors. Companies make add-on financing issues in order to raise financing for expanded operations or because they have become cash poor and need to finance their current operations. The offerings themselves give investors a portion of ownership in the company issuing them. Add-on financing is also called a follow-on offering. See also: All Holders Rule, Anti-dilution provision.

Add-On Interest A method of determining interest in which the interest is calculated as a percentage of the original principal. For example, if one borrows $10,000 at an annual add-on interest rate of 10%, the interest one pays each year is $1,000 (10% of $10,000), regardless of how much principal remains at the beginning of each payment period. Using add-on interest will result in more interest paid and, as a result, higher monthly payments.

Add-On Plan In a subscription service, an additional service one may purchase for an extra amount of money. For example, if one has a cell phone plan that includes nationwide long distance for $50 per month, an add-on plan may permit international calling for $10 per month more. The term is most common in the telecommunications industry.

Add-On-Sale The sale to a buyer of a product associated with, but distinct from, the product the buyer originally wanted. For example, if person goes to a restaurant for dinner and the waiter convinces him to order dessert, the dessert is an add-on sale. Likewise, if a car dealer convinces a buyer to purchase the extended warranty for a vehicle, that is also an add-on sale

Address **1.** The physical place where a person or company resides or does business. Most places are on a road of some kind; each building on a road has an individual number so a person or company can receive mail at the address. **2.** The place where a person or company receives mail. For example, one's mailing address may be a box at the post office. One can retrieve mail there. **3.** A location in the World Wide Web where one can find a website. It is usually followed by a suffix such as .com, .org, or .net. For example, the address for TheFreeDictionary is www.TheFreeDictionary.com.

Address Change Service A computerized service offered by the U.S. Postal Service automatically correcting inaccurate addresses for companies that maintain electronic mailing lists. The ACS sends the new address electronically so as to reduce (indeed, almost eliminate) the time and expense of changing addresses on a list manually. The ACS charges a small fee for each correction.

Address Hygiene The accuracy of a list of addresses. If one has a list of addresses (such as subscribers to a newspaper or donors to a political campaign), one may generally sell the list to another party. Lists tend to have better address hygiene if they are newer and if the addresses came from individuals who signed up for the list voluntarily. Address hygiene is important in direct mail marketing.

Address Resolution Protocol A protocol whereby a computer can determine the address of a network host when certain information (namely the host's Internet layer or network layer) is known. It was designed in 1982.

Address Service Requested A request to a post office to forward a piece of mail to the forwarding address. The U.S. Postal Service generally does this free of charge for the first 18 months that a person or company resides at the new address. It may also inform the sender of a new address for an additional charge.

Address Validation Service A service whereby one can discover whether or not an address is valid. Address validation services are generally not available for commercial use.

Adequacy of Coverage The extent to which an asset or investment is protected from loss by insurance or hedging. For example, if one owns a house, there is the risk that it could burn down. Adequacy of coverage measures the extent to which the insurance benefit covers the value of the house.

Adequate Disclosure A convention in which accountants attempt to include all relevant or potentially relevant information in a financial statement, either in the statement itself or in a footnote.

Adequate Notice The clear disclosure of the major terms of a loan. Under the Truth in Lending Act, a lender is required to provide adequate notice before the loan is made. Information included under adequate notice includes the term of the loan, the APR, any applicable fees, and so forth.

Adequate Sample In statistics, a sample size considered to be sufficiently large to be predictive. This is important whether one is polling an election or the potential popularity of a new product. It is also important, especially in marketing, that the adequate sample include enough members of a product's target demographic.

ADF ISO 4217 code for the Andorran franc. In practice, the currency was identical to the French franc, which was replaced by the euro in 1999. The Andorran franc circulated alongside the Andorran peseta.

Adhesion Contract A standardized, take-it-or-leave-it contract that one party offers to another. That is, one party has no option to change any section of the contract through negotiation with the other party. Adhesion contracts are especially useful to companies that engage in a high volume of transactions because they give them greater predictability. However, it is not uncommon for one party to offer an adhesion contract that hides excessive penalties or other payments in the fine print; in such situations, courts often refuse to enforce the contract.

Adhesion Insurance Contract A standard insurance policy that a policyholder buys as a whole. That is, the policyholder has no option to change any section of the contract through negotiation with the insurer. All insurance policies are adhesion insurance contracts. This gives the insurer greater predictability in its possible liabilities. In the event of a lawsuit involving a misinterpretation of such a contract, however, courts have tended to rule in favor of the policyholder because there was no negotiation between the two parties.

Adhiya In Nepal, an agreement between an owner of land and a farmer whereby the farmer cultivates the land and splits the produce evenly with the owner.

Adhocracy A slang term for a business or other organization with few or no permanent structures. New situations are discussed and decided as they occur (that is, on an "ad hoc" basis). An adhocracy may encounter problems with efficiency.

Adjacent Describing a real estate property that is close to but not adjoining another. For example, a house is adjacent to the house across the street because they are in the same neighborhood.

Adjoining Describing a real estate property immediately next to another. For example, a house adjoins the house next door. See also: Adjacent.

Adjudication The settlement of a dispute by the declaration of a court. For example, a court adjudicates a lawsuit when it decides which party, if either, wins, and whether or how much money to award. What distinguishes adjudication is the fact that it involves a court. See also: Arbitration.

Adjustable Life Insurance A life insurance policy in which the policyholder has the ability to change the death benefit, premium, the term of the policy, or the frequency with which premiums are paid. It should not be confused with an adjustable premium.

Adjustable Premium A premium on an insurance policy that the insurer may alter. The premium may go either down or up, at least to a certain, stated limit. The premium may be adjusted depending on a change to the policyholder's life expectancy, the returns on the investments made with the premiums, and other factors.

Adjustable Rate An interest rate on a loan or convertible security that changes periodically. For example, an adjustable rate mortgage has a certain interest rate that changes with varying frequency. The frequency of the change is called the adjustment rate. Usually, the adjustable rate is set according to some outside benchmark; for example, a loan might set the interest rate at LIBOR + 1%. An advantage of adjustable rate loans is the fact that one's interest rate might fall over time; this is a particular advantage if prevailing interest rates are high at the time of the loan. A disadvantage to adjustable rates is the uncertainty associated with them: one's payments on the loan generally rise or fall.

Adjustable Rate Mortgage A mortgage with an interest rate that changes periodically. Generally speaking, an adjustable rate mortgage is linked to some major benchmark rate; for example, the interest rate may be stated as "LIBOR + 1%." The mortgage may or may not have a cap on how much the interest rate can rise or fall, or on how often the interest rate may change. Very often, the initial interest rate for an adjustable-rate mortgage is lower than that for a fixed-rate mortgage. This allows more people to qualify for an adjustable-rate mortgage; however, this kind of mortgage can be risky because the interest rate (and therefore the monthly payment) can rise unexpectedly. Indeed the prevalence of ARMs has been blamed for the housing bubble in the mid-2000s and the subsequent recession. See also: Credit Crunch, Teaser Rate.

Adjustable-Rate Preferred Stock A preferred stock paying a dividend that varies from time to time. Usually the dividend rate is the same as the interest rate on a Treasury security, which is adjusted quarterly. They may also be backed by mortgages or mortgage-backed securities. ARPS's tend to have stable prices because a drop in the common share's price is offset by a rise in bonds, and vice versa.

Adjusted Balance Method An accounting method that posts costs or recognizes revenue at the end of a time period after all activities over that time period have been processed. For example, a savings account usually uses an adjusted balance method because it calculates the interest at the end of each month or quarter, after all debits and credits over that month or quarter post to the account.

Adjusted Basis The cost of an asset after various deductions and additions such as depreciation, brokerage fees, or dividends. Tax on such an asset is calculated from the adjusted basis rather than the price that was actually paid.

Adjusted Capital Ratio A ratio of a bank's capital to its total assets. It is calculated by taking the bank's allowance for bad debt and gains on its securities, and subtracting its losses and probable bad debt. The adjusted capital ratio is one way to calculate the bank's capital adequacy.

Adjusted Cost Base In Canadian taxes, a calculation of the cost of an asset that includes expenditures indirectly related to the purchase price of the asset. For example, the adjusted cost base may include improvements made to real estate or commissions paid for a security. It is important to note that these expenses may be required expenses (one must pay commissions to brokers if one wishes to trade on the stock market), but they are not included in the purchase price, per se. The ACB may also include dividends that are reinvested. In Canada, one is liable for capital gains taxes on an asset sold for a price greater than the adjusted cost base.

Adjusted Debit Balance The amount of money an investor owes on a margin account. This is calculated as the amount the investor directly owes his/her broker less the paper profit the investor has made on short sales and similar transactions on a special miscellaneous account. The adjusted debit balance is important to determining the amount owed in case of a margin call. According to Regulation T, an investor can only make a cash or securities withdrawal if the adjusted debit balance is small.

Adjusted Exercise Price **1.** The strike price on an option after making allowances for stock splits. For example, suppose the exercise price for an option is $400 and the company doubles the number of shares. The adjusted exercise price would drop to $200. **2.** See: Nominal Exercise Price.

Adjusted Funds From Operations In real estate investment trusts (REITs), a measure of revenue from operations involving liquid transfers, like cash, rather than illiquid assets. In general, the FFO is determined by taking the REIT's earnings and adding back their depreciation and amortization of mortgages, then subtracting regular expenditures used to maintain the REIT's assets. It is widely considered a better measure of an REIT's earnings than its funds from operations.

Adjusted Gross Estate In estate tax, the sum total value of a decedent's assets plus certain additions, less the total value of all debts. Assets included in the adjusted gross estate include, but are not limited to: property (including community property and all savings), certain types of gifts made in the last three years of the decedent's life, property or income transferred before death but under which the decedent maintained use and/or enjoyment, revocable transfers, life insurance, and pensions and annuities with death benefits. The debts include mortgages, loans, liens, and other liabilities. If the value of the adjusted gross estate exceeds $1 million, it is subject to the estate tax. See also: Taxable estate.

Adjusted Gross Income In U.S. tax, an individual's taxable income after all specific deductions, but not standard or itemized deductions. Adjusted gross income is used to calculate one's tax liability, as well as eligibility for certain social programs. For example, contributions to health savings accounts are not taxable. Thus, one removes the amount contributed to such an account from his/her gross income before calculating his/her tax liability.

Adjusted Liabilities The statutory liabilities of an insurance company less its interest maintenance reserve and its asset valuation reserve. An insurance company's statutory liabilities are calculated according to the industry's accounting standards and sometimes overstate the company's liabilities because they do not account for the two reserves. Many financial ratios use adjusted liabilities because they are thought to be more accurate.

Adjusted Net Asset Value An expression of the underlying value of the company. It is calculated by taking the market value of assets and subtracting the value of all its liabilities, including those not reflected on a balance sheet. Critics maintain that the adjusted net asset value understates a company's real value because it does not properly account for intangible assets. It is also called the adjusted book value.

Adjusted Net Worth A way to measure the value of an insurance company. It is calculated by taking its net worth and adding its paper gains, capital surplus, and any other reserves the company may have set aside. The adjusted net worth represents a way for one to compare the financial health of an insurance company to that of other insurance companies.

Adjusted Premium Method A way to calculate the cash surrender value of a life insurance policy. The adjusted premium method involves calculating the expense allowance for the first year, then the adjusted premium, and finally the cash surrender value by substituting the net level premium for the adjusted premium.

Adjusted Present Value The net present value of any project financed exclusively by equity and the present value of debt. Using the adjusted present value can carry some tax benefits.

Adjusted Seasonal Installment Method In corporate taxation in the United States, a way to reduce underpayment penalties that result from the fact that most of a company's profit occurs during a portion of the year, and it has therefore underpaid during other portions of the year. In order to qualify for this method, an average of 70% of the company's profits must occur during the same six-month period for three years.

Adjusted Surplus The net assets of an insurance company less its adjusted liabilities, which are its statutory liabilities less its interest maintenance reserve and its asset valuation reserve. Many financial ratios use the adjusted surplus because the fact that it utilizes the adjusted liabilities is thought to be more accurate.

Adjusted Underwriting Profit The profit an insurance company realizes over a given period of time. It is calculated by taking the premiums it receives and the capital gains on the investments it makes with those premiums, and subtracting the company's overhead plus what it pays out in claims on its policies.

Adjuster A person who investigates a claim on an insurance policy. That is, an adjuster observes any damage, consults police reports and/or hospital records, and generally ensures that an event occurred the way it was said to have occurred. Adjusters may work for a policyholder (in which case they have an incentive to see a claim paid), an insurance company (in which case they have an incentive to see a claim denied), or some other interested party.

Adjusting Entry 1. An adjustment made to a company's financial records at the end of an accounting period to assign revenues and expenses to the days on which the events justifying them occurred or on which the revenue was received, depending on the situation. For example, if a company is paid in advance for the purchase of some good, an adjusting entry may recognize that revenue on the day the good was delivered. Likewise, if the company was paid after delivery, it may recognize the revenue on the day it was paid. See also: Accrued Expenses, Accrued Revenue, Prepaid Expenses, Unearned Revenue. **2.** Any correction to a previous entry in a company's financial records.

Adjustment 1. A tax deduction taken on a loss, especially on bad debt or accounts receivable that will likely not be collected. One is not liable for income that is not actually realized. **2.** In insurance, a payment on a claim. For example, if one has homeowner's insurance and his/her house floods, he/she is entitled to an adjustment, so long as the insurance covers flooding. Arriving at the amount of the adjustment is a complex process and insurance companies employ full-time adjusters to investigate claims and determine what amount, if any, the adjustment should be. **3.** In an adjustable-rate mortgage, a change in the interest rate paid on the mortgage. The adjustment may be upward or downward. See also: Adjustment frequency.

Adjustment Assistance Any program whereby a government helps to retrain workers whose jobs or careers have been rendered obsolete. Adjustment assistance may be provided when a technology makes a job redundant. More commonly, however, adjustment assistance refers to programs a government designs when it pursues policies antithetical to a particular line of work. For example, a country may pursue free trade policies that result in outsourcing to other nations, requiring adjustment assistance for laid off workers. Adjustment assistance is controversial, especially because it is unlikely that older workers will be rehired even after training.

Adjustment Bond A bond that a company issues to its current bondholders in exchange for its previously issued bonds. An adjustment bond usually offers less favorable terms to bondholders, such as lower coupon rates, and is usually issued when the company is in danger of bankruptcy and is unlikely to be able to make

payments on the previous bonds. An adjustment bond can be good for the company because it can help avoid bankruptcy; it can also be beneficial to bondholders in the long term because it may make more from the adjustment bond than it would if the company's assets were liquidated.

Adjustment Costs The costs associated with making any changes. For example, one must consider adjustment costs for hiring a new employee, or the costs of lost production in the event of layoffs. All companies have adjustment costs, especially when they seek to achieve greater efficiency.

Adjustment Credit A short-term loan by a Federal Reserve Bank to a member bank that the member bank takes in order to meet its reserve requirements. The adjustment credit is secured by the member bank's promissory note; it is a very common transaction.

Adjustment Date In an adjustable rate mortgage or other variable rate loan, the date on which the interest rate changes. The adjustment date occurs regularly, but how often it occurs depends upon the adjustment frequency.

Adjustment Frequency In adjustable-rate mortgages, the rate at which changes to a mortgage's interest rate occur. Usually, the interest rate changes once a year, but some mortgages change rates as often as once a month or as seldom as every five years. The higher the adjustment frequency, the higher the financial risk for the homeowner. For example, if the adjustment frequency is once a month, a homeowner could find his/her mortgage payment increasing every month for five months before it goes down again. This ties up more of the homeowner's income, and increases the likelihood of default.

Adjustment in Conversion Terms A change in the conversion price of a convertible security. The conversion price is the price the holder of a convertible security pays in order to exchange the convertible for a common share. Following a stock split, for example, the price per share drops. This results in an adjustment in conversion terms to reflect the change in the value of a share. Some convertible securities have adjustments in conversion terms built into the terms of the security, regardless of whether or not a stock split occurs. See also: Conversion ratio.

Adjustment Income In insurance, income paid to the survivors of a household's primary earner until they are able to make necessary lifestyle modifications. For example, suppose a husband works full time and makes $100,000 per year while a wife works part time and makes only $25,000 per year. If the husband dies, his life insurance policy may provide adjustment income over and above the death benefit until the wife can recover emotionally, find a full-time job, and make other changes.

Adjustment Index Any mathematical modification made to a data set to account and control for an exogenous situation that would otherwise distort the data. For example, temporary jobs are often created in November and December because of the Christmas season. A statistician likely will apply an adjustment index to the number of jobs created in those months so the unemployment rate is not artificially low.

Adjustment Interval In adjustable-rate mortgages and variable-rate mortgages, the time between two changes in the interest rate of the mortgage or loan. Often, the adjustment interval lasts one year, but some loans change rates as often as once a month or as seldom as every five years. The shorter the adjustment interval, the higher the financial risk is for the homeowner. For example, if the adjustment interval for a mortgage is one month, a homeowner's mortgage payment could increase every month for five months or longer before it decreases again. This ties up more of the homeowner's income, and increases the likelihood of default.

Adjustment on Conversion Money that must be paid to or by a bondholder when a convertible bond is changed into another type of security. The bondholder may have to pay the adjustment, for example, if there is a difference in the par value of the two securities favorable to the issuer. Alternately, the bondholder may receive all coupons previously due on the convertible bond.

Adjustment Programme A set of economic or monetary policies a government takes in conjunction with the International Monetary Fund to reduce a deficit in a country's balance of payments. An adjustment programme often includes measures designed to make the country more fiscally sound, but which are painful to the populace. For example, an adjustment programme may stipulate a reduction or elimination of food subsidies. See also: Structural Adjustment Loan Facility.

Adjustments in Appraisal A change in an estimate of real estate value based on a slight difference between two otherwise comparable properties. An adjustment appraisal may be expressed either as a percentage or a dollar amount.

Adjustments to Income In U.S. tax, deductions that reduce one's taxable income. When calculating a taxpayer's tax liability, one takes the amount of money he/she has made over the tax year and takes away deductions such as contributions to IRA accounts, business expenses, and so forth. One refers to these deductions as adjustments to income.

Administered Price A price dictated by any entity other than market forces. Most of the time, an administered price refers to a price set by a government, but it may also be set by a private company with sufficient control over the market that it can control prices. See also: Monopoly.

Administering Agency 1. A company that provides administration services for another company's employer-sponsored insurance policies, retirement plans, and/or other employee benefits. An administering agency is generally an insurance company. **2.** A company that administers its own employee benefits.

Administracion Nacional de Telecomunicationes A state-owned, telecommunications company in Uruguay. While other companies can provide mobile phone services, ANTEL has a monopoly on Uruguayan landlines. In 1992, the government attempted to privatize ANTEL (and other state-owned companies), but a popular referendum rejected the effort. It was established in 1974.

Administration 1. The implementation and management of a policy. A company's senior officers (such as the board of directors) set the policies and its managers (and sometimes the officers themselves) are responsible for administration. **2.** In an estate, the management of the assets of a decedent until they are discharged to his/her heirs.

Administration Bond A bond issued by the administrator of an estate. The administration bond provides security in case the administrator causes financial losses due to theft, fraud, or negligence. The administration bond is refunded to the administrator if he/she performs his/her duties in accordance with the law and the decedent's will.

Administration Order In bankruptcy or estates, an order by a court mandating that creditors appoint an administrator to handle, pay off, or discharge the debts. In the event of a bankruptcy, the administration order may also charge the administrator with winding down a business' operations.

Administrative Agency The government organization responsible for enforcing a body of laws. For example, the Internal Revenue Service is the administrative agency for U.S. tax law. It is also called a government agency.

Administrative Budget A formal and highly detailed budget that a company's management uses to control daily expenses and operations.

Administrative Charge A fee assessed on a purchase for the time and expense of processing the purchase. For example, if one buys baseball tickets online, one may have to pay an administrative charge in addition to the cost of the tickets themselves and applicable sales taxes. Administrative charges may compensate the seller, for example, for the cost of processing credit card information online.

Administrative Exception Note In international commerce, a document listing commodities that a country can export without first notifying the Coordinating Committee for Multilateral Export Controls (CoCom). Commodities listed on administrative exception notes can be exported at the discretion of the exporting country. Administrative exception notes became irrelevant when CoCom ceased to function in 1994.

Administrative Expense An expense that a company is required to spend but that is difficult to associate with a specific item. Examples of costs grouped under administrative expenses include utilities, office supplies, and postage costs.

Administrative Law A body of law created by government agencies. It consists of rules, regulations, and decisions made by an agency rather than a law passed by Congress or Parliament. That is, administrative law is not legislation, but it has the force of law. Administrative law became more common starting in the 20th century as government programs worldwide became both more common and more complex.

Administrative Law Judge A judge who presides and decides at the hearing of a dispute between a U.S. government agency and a plaintiff. An administrative law judge is appointed from a pool of persons who have passed an oral and a written examination. The hearing over which an administrative law judge presides is the original trial; either party has the right to appeal his/her decision.

Administrative Management Society An organization that promotes efficiency in management. It participates in research to lower costs, increase quality of products and improve relations between employers and employees. It is based in Washington, D.C.

Administrative Pricing Rules Rules the IRS formerly used to determine the income and therefore the taxation of foreign sales corporations. Administrative pricing rules were in Section 925 of the Internal Revenue Code and have since been repealed.

Administrative Protective Order An order issued by the U.S. Department of Commerce preventing the divulgence of any proprietary information it learns in the process of investigating a company. This is done to protect competition. APOs are most common when the Department is looking into the environmental impact of imports.

Administrative Receiver In corporate bankruptcy, a custodian appointed by a court or regulator who is charged with the administration of all assets and debts. The administrative receiver's duty is to pay off as many debts as possible as cheaply as possible without liquidating the company. In general, this means the receiver restructures the company to put it on a path toward solvency. See also: Receivership.

Administrative Services Only A plan a large employer buys from an insurance company whereby the employer assumes all risk for its employees' insurance. That is, the employer, rather than the insurance company, pays all benefits on the policy. The insurance company provides only assistance on matters such as preparation of manuals, communication with policyholders, and other, mundane services.

Administrative Skills The ability to perform organizational and basic, technical services. Administrative skills include (but are not limited to) the abilities to file papers appropriately, take dictation, set up meetings and help prepare presentations. Administrative skills are necessary for administrative assistants and personal assistants.

Administrator 1. Anyone authorized to act on behalf of a person, company, estate, trust, or any other entity. **2.** See: State Administrator.

Administrator's Deed A document transferring real estate from an intestate person to his/her heir. That is, if a person dies without a will, the administrator's deed conveys title to his/her property to the deceased person's next of kin.

Administrivia In business, a slang term for mundane matters (such as filling out forms) that managers do not want or simply refuse to do. Secretaries and lower-ranking managers may handle administrivia.

Admiralty Court Any court that has jurisdiction over maritime law. This jurisdiction covers criminal and civil law, torts, and many other things. In the United Kingdom, admiralty courts sit very rarely. In the United States, ordinary federal district courts are considered admiralty courts when the dispute involves maritime law.

Admiralty Liability The amount for which one is liable in certain events that occur on the high seas. For example, if a ship sinks, the ship's owner (under certain circumstances) may have to make restitution for the goods lost up to the total value of the ship. Admiralty liability varies according to circumstance and the specific event. See also: Jones Act.

Admiralty Proceeding Any hearing before an admiralty court. An admiralty proceeding is usually a lawsuit brought against another party over an event that occurred on the high seas. For example, if one is transporting a good overseas and the ship sinks, any lawsuit that results would be heard in an admiralty proceeding.

Admission Temporaire The import of a good into another country or territory for a limited period of time. For example, a good may receive admission temporaire to receive some improvement as one step in a supply chain and then sent to another country. Goods entering a country under admission temporaire are generally not subject to tariffs or similar fees, though they must leave the country within a certain period of time.

Admitted Assets In the United States, assets that a state permits an insurance company to include on its balance sheet. Admitted assets vary state to state, but they must be both liquid and able to be valued; they are important to determining an insurance company's solvency in the event an unusually large number of claims are made. Admitted assets usually include mortgages, stocks, bonds and accounts receivable that the company reasonably expects to be paid.

Admitted Company An insurance company licensed to operate in one state even though its main office is in another state. Insurance licensing in the United States is conducted on a state-by-state basis; admitted companies are, in effect, "foreign" corporations that have received permission to conduct business in-state. Both the companies themselves and the agents they use must be licensed in each state in which they work.

Admitted Insurance An insurance policy sold by an admitted company, which is an insurance company licensed to operate in one state even though its main office is in another state. Insurance licensing in the United States is conducted on a state-by-state basis; admitted insurance is, in effect, "foreign" insurance that one may buy. Both the insurance companies themselves and the agents they use must be licensed in each state in which they work.

Adnorm In marketing, the readers of a publication who remember a particular advertisement, expressed as a percentage of readers who ordinarily would remember advertisements of a given type. For example, an adnorm of 50 means 50% of readers remember a given advertisement. An advertisement's adnorm is determined through market research. Adnorm is important because it can influence the success or failure of a marketing campaign.

Adobe Systems, Inc. A publicly-traded company that designs and sells multimedia software for computers, especially for Internet use. It is particularly well-known for Adobe Acrobat (which is used for PDF documents), as well as Photoshop and video editing programs. It was established in 1982 and is based in San Jose, California. It is traded on NASDAQ.

Adopter Categories Categories of consumers based upon readiness to purchase a new product. Adopter categories include innovators (2.5% of the market), early adopters (13.5%), early majority (34%), late majority (34%) and laggards (16%). Targeting a product to the appropriate adopter category at the appropriate time can help it become a success with the group of consumers its makers are trying to reach. For example, a company may attempt to identify and sell to innovators before early adopters, early adopters before early majority, and so forth.

Adoption Credit In U.S. tax law, a direct dollar-for-dollar reduction in one's tax liability for each child under the age of 18 that a taxpayer adopts. The adoption credit is intended to reimburse the taxpayer for attorney's fees, court costs, and traveling expenses. The credit is non-refundable, but if the amount of the credit exceeds one's tax liability, it may be carried forward for up to five years. The maximum amount of the adoption credit is adjusted for inflation. See also: Carryforward.

Adowlie 1. An obsolete Indian unit of dry volume approximately equivalent to 2.509 liters. It was used for salt. **2.** An obsolete Indian unit of weight approximately equivalent to 1.982 kilograms.

ADP ISO 4217 code for the Andorran peseta. In practice, the currency was identical to the Spanish peseta, which was replaced by the euro in 1999. The Andorran peseta circulated alongside the Andorran franc.

ADR Index An index that tracks all American Depository Receipts. Different indices have different criteria for which ADRs they track. For example, the Bank of New York tracks all ADRs traded on the New York Stock Exchange, NASDAQ, and the American Stock Exchange. The Standard & Poor's ADR Index, on the other hand, tracks ADRs associated with companies tracked by the S&P 700. ADR indices are weighted for market capitalization.

Adult A person who has reached the age of majority. This age is usually 18, but may be 17 in criminal cases or 21 in other cases. An adult is legally permitted to enter a contract, do business,erm? by the or conduct any other activity without permission or countersignature by a parent or guardian

ADV Form A form that all investment advisers who manage more than $25 million in assets are required to file with the SEC. The form discloses the adviser's education, fees, investment strategies, disciplinary actions (if any), and other information.

Advance 1. To increase in price, especially for a security. If a stock's price is $10 per share at the start of the trading day and $15 at the end, the stock is said to have advanced. **2.** To make a payment before it is due to the payee. For example, an employer may advance an employee part of his/her paycheck the week before pay day so the employee may make a needed payment. If this happens, the amount of the employee's paycheck is reduced by the amount of the advance.

Advance Account Money given to an employee to spend for a specific purpose before the employee is expected to spend it. For example, a company may give an employee a corporate credit card in anticipation of that employee going on a business trip.

Advance Against Collection A short-term loan that a bank makes to an exporter, secured by what the exporter is owed by an importer. The bank may collect these funds from the importer directly. If the importer does not make payment, the bank retrieves the advanced against collection loan from the exporter.

Advance Canvass A practice in which marketers personally visit retailers in advance of the release of a new product. The purpose of the advance canvass is to inform the retailers about the product and, more importantly, to excite them about it so they are eager to sell the product to consumers when it becomes available. For example, the advance canvassers may encourage the retailer to offer the product in a prominent place.

Advance Commitment A promise to undertake some activity before it is done. For example, a futures contract is an advance commitment to buy or sell an asset for a certain price at some point in the future. Likewise, in short-selling, one sells a security one does not own, and thus makes an advance commitment to buy it at some point in the future to ensure a smooth transaction.

Advance Computerized Execution System On NASDAQ, an electronic system allowing the automatic execution of orders between clients and market makers. Only clients and market makers that already have a relationship with each other use the ACES.

Advance Corporation Tax In the United Kingdom, a former withholding tax made on dividends. That is, corporations were required to pay the advance corporation tax on dividends before they were paid to shareholders so that the shareholders themselves were not responsible for paying any taxes. Dividends paid to pensions or some other tax-exempt investment vehicles may have had the advance corporation tax refunded later. The tax was rescinded in 1999.

Advance Deposit Account An account a person or company may maintain with the U.S. Postal Service. The account holder deposits funds into the account periodically, and the Postal Service deducts from those funds when the account holder needs to mail something. This can expedite the shipping process.

Advance Directive A legal document expressing a person's medical wishes in the event of his/her mental or physical incapacity. An advance directive is made while the director is still competent, and comes into effect at incapacity. An advance directive may state whether or not the director wishes to be placed on life support or to receive a particular treatment. It may or may not assign another party, usually a family member, to make these decisions as they come up. It is important to note that in this situation, an advance directive is not a power of attorney and neither allows the other party access to the assignor's finances, nor obliges him/her to pay for any treatment. See also: Proxy directive.

Advance Estimate In calculating quarterly GDP, the first estimate published approximately one month after the end of a quarter. It includes all information then available, but because relevant information may not be available immediately or may be subject to revision, it is subject to scrutiny and is usually revised in the preliminary estimate and later in the final estimate. As a result, the advance estimate is considered important as a guideline to performance in a quarter, but it is not necessarily the most accurate measure.

Advance Funded Pension Plan A pension that has sufficient liquid assets to pay all of its liabilities, including (and especially) all future payments to beneficiaries, because the sponsoring employer periodically sets aside funds to ensure the pension's financial health. This presents the least risk to both the sponsoring employer and pensioners. See also: Unfunded pension plan.

Advance Funding Any payment on a future obligation. A very basic example of advance funding is a parent paying a child's allowance a week early. Sometimes advance funding is a loan; payday loans are common sources of advance funding. Often, however, advance funding is deducted against some future obligation that the payer otherwise owes the payee.

Advance Import Deposits A percentage of the value of an import that a country's customs authority requires the importer to deposit for a brief period of time. While the importer eventually receives the advance import deposit back, he/she does not earn any interest on it. Advance import deposits help countries control their currency values. Currency liberalization policies may involve the reduction or elimination of advance import deposits.

Advance Payment A payment on an obligation that is paid well in advance. For example, if one pays May's rent in April, the payment is an advance payment. Often, though not always, the advance payment results in a discount on the amount owed. It is also called a payment in advance.

Advance Premium The premium on an insurance policy that is paid well in advance. For example, if one pays May's premium in April, the payment is an advance premium. Often, though not always, the advance premium results in a discount on the amount owed.

Advance Premium Mutual A mutual company that sells insurance. That is, the policyholders of an advance premium mutual company own the company. The advance premium company does not sell insurance in order to make a profit; rather the premiums it charges are intended only to cover all claims and expenses.

Advance Rate The percentage of the value of collateral that a lender uses to determine the amount of a loan. For example, if one pledges a collateral worth $10,000, and the advance rate is 90%, the lender will only extend $9000 in credit. This may protect the lender from risks, such as depreciation on the collateral.

Advance Refunding The act or practice of a company issuing a second bond with a lower coupon rate in order to pay off a previously issued callable bond. In this circumstance, the callable bond is known as a prefunded bond. Companies engage in advance refunding when more favorable interest rates become available, which reduces the company's overall borrowing costs.

Advance Renewal A renewal of a subscription, especially to a periodical, made before the company has its normal promotion to encourage renewals. The advance renewal may be made at the customer's request, or perhaps because the company engages in an automatic renewal policy.

Advance Start A subscription, especially to a periodical, that begins with an issue after the one currently being sold. For example, if one buys a 12-month subscription to a newspaper beginning 1 April and it is currently 15 March, then one has purchased an advance start subscription. It is also called a preferred start or a delayed start.

Advance/Decline Spread In technical analysis, the total of stocks increasing on a trading day less the number of stocks declining on the same day. Technical analysts use the spread as an indicator of market breadth. A positive spread indicates that a trend is or will soon become bullish, while a negative spread shows a bearish trend.

Advanced Companies On the TSX Venture Exchange, publicly-traded companies that have higher stockholder distribution, market value, and other requirements relative to other companies on the Exchange. See also: Blue chip.

Advanced Corporation Tax In the United Kingdom, the tax on a dividend that a corporation pays before distributing the dividend to shareholders. That is, the corporation pre-pays the advanced corporation tax so the shareholder does not have to do so when it comes time to pay his/her other taxes. The tax reduces the corporate tax the company must pay on its profits. It was introduced in 1973.

Advanced Life Underwriting A complicated process by which an insurance company looks at a person's financial situation in order to determine his/her life insurance needs. Advanced life underwriting is usually done when the potential policyholder has a large number of assets and liabilities, and would owe the estate and other taxes upon death. Advanced life underwriting is usually done by an expert because ordinary insurance underwriters are often poorly equipped to handle the process.

Advanced Manufacturing Environment A situation in which manufacturers are in stiff competition with one another because of continuous improvement in technology, international trade and other factors. While this can make it difficult for a company to stay afloat (and harder still for a new company to come into the market), it often provides more and better choices for consumers.

Advanced Technology Product Electronic products such as computers, microchips, DVD players and so forth. Many countries (especially those that are resource poor) have devoted large swaths of their economies to the assemblage and export of advanced technology products from imported raw material. Israel is one of the world's most prominent examples of this phenomenon.

Advancement Any asset given to a person before the donor's death with the agreement that the asset will be considered part of the recipient's inheritance from the donor's estate when he/she dies. That is, if an elderly person has left his granddaughter 20% of his estate in his will, but gives her cash or assets equal in value to 5% of the estate as an advancement, then the granddaughter will only receive 15% of the estate when the elderly person dies.

Advancer An informal term for a stock or other security that has risen in price over a given period. For example, if a stock opens at $5 and closes at $5.25, it is said to be an advancer for that trading day. See also: Decliner.

Advancing Volume The trading volume of all advancing securities on an exchange or index on a given trading day. That is, advancing volume measures the cumulative volume of all securities on the exchange or index that had closing prices higher than their opening prices. Technical analysts use advancing volume and declining volume to determine buy and sell signals. Advancing volume should not be confused with up volume, which measures the same thing with respect to a single security.

Adventure Any activity that involves risk. Almost any investment, business opportunity, and even many jobs involve adventure of one kind or another. The willingness to undertake an adventure is a necessary component to the function of capitalism.

Adversary The other side in litigation. For example, in a lawsuit, the plaintiff and the defendant are adversaries with respect to each other.

Adverse Action The denial of an application for credit because of insufficient credit history or negative information on one's credit report. For example, one may be denied a loan to buy a house because of a recent bankruptcy. This denial is called an adverse action.

Adverse Balance The difference between the value of transactions in which money leaves a country and the value of transactions in which money enters it in which the former value is greater. An adverse balance means more money leaves a country than enters it. It is a strongly negative sign for that country's economy. See also: Balance of Payment.

Adverse Financial Selection 1. A situation in which a policyholder cancels an insurance policy because he/she believe he/she can earn a higher return by investing the policy's cash value in a different investment vehicle. **2.** A situation in which a policyholder cancels an insurance policy because a financial hardship has forced him/her to use the cash value to pay for other obligations.

Adverse Opinion A statement by an auditor that a company's financial statements are inaccurate, whether accidentally or deliberately. An adverse opinion usually follows a report from an internal audit or external audit. Auditors attach adverse opinions to reports if the company's financial statements diverge a great deal from the Generally Accepted Accounting Principles.

Adverse Possession In law, the process by which one lays claim and takes title to a piece of real estate without paying for it, by holding it for a specified period of time. For example, a person living on a property without its owner's knowledge or consent for a certain number of years may become the owner of that property through adverse possession. This concept effectively puts a limit on the number of years after an action in which one can undertake litigation claiming a property. There are a number of requirements before one can claim adverse possession on real estate. For example, one must openly possess the real estate and make no attempt to hide it. One shows this by living there in good faith, paying property taxes and/or making improvements on the land. See also: Abandonment, Clear Title.

Adverse Selection A sociological phenomenon in which those persons with the most dangerous lifestyles or careers are the most likely to buy life insurance policies. Adverse selection may also occur if those persons conceal or falsify relevant information when they apply for the insurance policy. This has the potential of economic hardship for life insurance companies because those most likely to receive a death benefit are the ones buying policies. This reduces profit potential. Life insurance companies attempt to counteract adverse selection by limiting coverage and/or raising premiums. Adverse selection is also called antiselection.

Adverse Supply Shock Any sudden event that dramatically but (usually) temporarily decreases supply for one or more goods or services. An adverse supply shock is often (but not always) a natural event. For example, a series of severe tornados on farms in western Oklahoma can cause adverse supply shock for wheat. This reduces the amount of wheat in the market, which raises the price, assuming demand remains constant. It is a type of supply shock.

Adversely Classified Assets Any loan that a bank doubts will be repaid. That is, adversely classified assets are loans with some impairment, usually due to the credit quality of the borrower. Adversely classified assets fall into three categories (from least severe to most severe): substandard, doubtful and loss. See also: Account Uncollectible.

Advertised Price The announced price at which a product is offered. When a gallon of milk has a price tag reading $3 or a house is offered at $100,000, both are examples of advertised price. The advertised price is often negotiable, depending on the situation.

Advertisement Any communication designed to raise awareness and produce a desired effect. An advertisement may occur through any medium, be that print, broadcast, imagery, or even word of mouth. Many advertisements are basic; for example, there may be a radio announcement to "buy X." Others are more complex, encouraging purchase by stating a product has a better price and/or better quality. Many advertisements are intended to entertain. They are an integral part of marketing. Informally, an advertisement is called an advert or an ad.

Advertiser The company that makes an advertisement to promote its product and/or itself. An advertiser usually does this by buying space in print media or time in broadcasting. Increasingly, advertisers are using the Internet to target their products to precise, desired demographics. See also: Marketing.

Advertisers Liability Insurance An insurance policy providing coverage for an advertiser or advertising agency in the event an advertisement makes a false statement or an omission that results in a lawsuit. For example, if an ad slanders a competing product and the competing company sues, advertising liability insurance protects both the company making the advertised product and the agency advertising it.

Advertising Age A weekly publication for and by the advertising industry. It covers the goings-on of the industry, including new trends, creative developments and so forth. It was established in Chicago in 1930.

Advertising Agency A company that produces advertisements to promote the products of its clients. An advertising agency writes ads, targets them to the appropriate demographics, and generally shepherds their production from beginning to end. Increasingly, advertisers are using the Internet to target their products to the precise, desired demographic. See also: Marketing.

Advertising Allowance Any funds or discounts a wholesaler provides to a retailer in exchange for advertising the wholesaler's products. The advertising allowance often reimburses the retailer for the cost of advertising the product and is intended to encourage more prominent displays of some products to increase the wholesaler's sales.

Advertising Appropriation The amount that an advertising agency collects in revenue over a given period of time. Theoretically, this is equal to what the agency charges its clients for services, though this is not always the case. Advertising appropriation is based on how much the company bills to its clients and the amount it actually collects.

Advertising Checking Bureau A company that gathers and disseminates the advertising costs, compliance levels and other information on the advertising activities of American retailers. It provides this information to advertisers for free so they can make more informed decisions on where to place their advertising. The Bureau is based in New York City.

Advertising Club of New York A voluntary, professional organization that helps to regulate the American advertising industry. It offers training and promotes good practices among members. Interestingly, it was the first supporter of the organization that ultimately became the Better Business Bureau. It was established in 1896 and was originally known as the Sphinx Club.

Advertising Contract 1. An agreement between a maker of a good or provider of a service and another party whereby the second party will provide space or time to promote the first party's good or service. Very often, though not always, the second party is a periodical or a broadcaster that allows the advertiser to prepare a specific ad. Increasingly, these contracts are being used for Internet advertising as well. An advertising contract specifies what is provided, for how long, and at what price. **2.** An agreement between a manufacturer or wholesaler and a retailer whereby the retailer undertakes some action to encourage customers to buy the wholesaler's product in exchange for a fee or some other consideration.

Advertising Costs An item on a balance sheet indicating what a company spends advertising its products. Very often, advertising costs are amortized over time and not listed as money is actually spent.

Advertising Council Inc. A non-profit organization in the United States established in order to promote the public good through advertisements. It disseminates ads encouraging civic duty, patriotism, hard work, lack of drug use and so forth. It was established in 1942 to encourage popular support for World War II efforts like war bonds.

Advertising Manager An official at an advertising agency responsible for developing and implementing advertising strategies in accordance with the client's needs. An advertising manager meets with the client and the organizations providing advertising in order to accomplish these goals. He/she may also have a hand in the actual production of an ad. An advertising manager may help the client decide how much advertising should be print-based, broadcasted, or online.

Advertising Research Foundation A non-profit organization in the United States that collects, analyzes and disseminates information on the American advertising industry. It conducts and publishes research in a number of ways; one of its most prominent tools is the Journal of Advertising Research, a peer-reviewed periodical it publishes. ARF was established in 1936 and is based in New York City.

Advertising Reserve An extra amount of money set aside to pay an advertising agency should an unforeseen event occur. For example, if a product proves more popular with younger consumers than older when a company expected the opposite, the company may use the advertising reserve to pay the agency to launch a new ad campaign aimed at youth.

Advertising Weight 1. The number of pages in a periodical consisting of advertising divided by the number of total pages. **2.** The actual or projected number of contacts an advertisement has. For example, if a stretch of highway has 1 million cars driving through it every day, a billboard on that highway has an advertising weight of 1 million per day.

Advertising Women of New York An organization dedicated to promoting women in the advertising industry. It was established in 1912 and is the oldest organization of its type. It hosts approximately 35 training and networking events per year.

Advertorial An advertisement in a newspaper or other periodical that appears at first glance to be an article.

Advice of Acceptance A statement issued by a bank notifying another bank of the positive result of a letter of credit or other demand for payment. That is, the advice of acceptance informs the second bank that the bill of lading was honored and paid as demanded. It is a type of advice of fate.

Advice of Fate A statement issued by a bank notifying another bank of the result of a letter of credit or other demand for payment. That is, the advice of fate informs the second bank whether or not the bill of lading was honored and paid as demanded. See also: Advice of Acceptance, Advice of Nonacceptance.

Advice of Nonacceptance A statement issued by a bank notifying another bank of the negative result of a letter of credit or other demand for payment. That is, the advice of nonacceptance informs the second bank that the bill of lading was not honored or paid as demanded. It is also called advice of nonpayment. It is a type of advice of fate.

Advise Fate A request by a bank to another bank for the result of a bill of lading or other demand for payment. That is, the advise fate request asks the second bank whether or not the bill of lading was honored and paid as demanded. See also: Advice of Fate.

Advised Credit An unconfirmed letter of credit of which an advising bank has informed the recipient of all terms and other conditions.

Advised Line of Credit A revolving line of credit of which the issuer has informed the recipient of all terms and other conditions. In the United States, the Truth in Lending Act requires credit card companies and banks to provide this advice to customers.

Advisers' Sentiment In technical analysis, a theory that the overall sentiment of investment advisers is usually wrong. That is, when most investment advisers believe that the market will be bullish, it maintains that it will in fact be bearish, and vice versa. Technical analysts who follow the advisers' sentiment theory attempt to measure overall belief and make investment decisions accordingly. See also: Sentiment index.

Advisory Account A brokerage account in which a broker can only make limited investment decisions without consulting the investor. Such decisions must be made in accordance with the customer's stated investment goals. This contrasts with a discretionary account, which gives the broker more independence.

Advisory Broker A broker or brokerage that, in addition to making trades on behalf of the client, provides investment advice. That is, the advisory broker recommends the client buys or sells certain securities, in accordance with his/her investment goals. The advisory broker receives a fee in addition to the commissions given for the actual trades.

Advisory Committee A board that provides expertise and other advice to the main governing body of an organization. For example, the board of directors of a publicly-traded company may consult with an advisory committee on important matters. The advisory committee does not decide the matter, but may represent a broader spectrum of interests than the governing body itself.

Advisory Committee for the Co-ordination of Information Systems A body under the United Nations intended to update and manage its information technology.

Advisory Committee on Export Policy An interagency body of the U.S. federal government that hears and resolves disputes between cabinet departments on matters of international trade policy. The agencies represented on ACEP include the Arms Control & Disarmament Agency and the Departments of State, Energy, and Defense. The Department of Commerce presides over ACEP.

Advisory Committee on Trade Policy and Negotiations A body that advises the United States Trade Representative on policy matters. The Committee consists of members from the private sector; for example, they may be drawn from consulting companies, banks, universities, lobbying groups, or almost any other organization. It consists of approximately 40 members.

Advisory Letter A newsletter offering financial advice to readers or subscribers. An advisory letter may be broad by discussing macroeconomic trends, or it may offer specific advice on particular sectors of certain markets. If an advisory letter offers advice on specific securities, the author(s) are normally registered investment advisors with the SEC, and investors should exercise caution if they are not.

Advisory, Conciliation and Arbitration Service A quasi-government body in the United Kingdom that mediates disputes between employers and workers (usually unions). It was established near the end of the 19th century. It was quite famous in the 1970s and 1980s, when labor disputes in Britain were very common.

Advocacy Advertisement An advertisement that promotes something other than a good or service. Specifically, advocacy advertising advances a political, social, religious or other, similar issue. A commercial asking viewers to vote for a certain candidate is an example of advocacy advertising. An advocacy advertisement may ask for donations for causes. Advocacy advertising is important in raising awareness.

Advocacy Center A division of the U.S. Department of Commerce that advocates for American businesses and companies internationally. That is, it lobbies for international contracts for U.S. companies in order to encourage exports and thereby create or save American jobs. It works with development banks (such as the World Bank) in accomplishing its goals.

Adweek A weekly publication for and by the advertising industry. It covers the goings-on of the industry, including new trends, creative developments, client-agency relationships and so forth. It was established in 1978; it is currently owned by Nielsen.

Adyndaky Etraplar In Turkmenistan, a political subdivision for an urban neighborhood.

AE 1. ISO 3166-1 alpha-2 code for the United Arab Emirates. This is the code used in international transactions to and from Emirati bank accounts. **2.** ISO 3166-2 geocode for the United Arab Emirates. This is used as an international standard for shipping to the United Arab Emirates. Each emirate has its own code with the prefix "AE." For example, the code for the Emirate of Dubai is ISO 3166-2:AE-DU.

AED ISO 4217 code for the Emirati dirham. It was introduced in 1971 upon the formation of the United Arab Emirates and their complete independence from Great Britain. Previously, both the Bahraini dinar and the Qatari riyal (then known as the Qatar-Dubai riyal) were used in what is now the UAE. While it was pegged to the IMF special drawing rights in 1978, the dirham has been pegged to the U.S. dollar unofficially for most of its history. The UAE officially pegged the dirham to the dollar in 1997.

Aeromexico An airline company in Mexico that, while not state-owned, is given preferential treatment by the Mexican government. It was established in 1934 and operates both domestic and international flights. See also: Flag Carrier.

Aesthetics Physical beauty. It is an important concept in marketing because consumers may be more inclined to buy a product they find aesthetically pleasing.

AF 1. ISO 3166-1 alpha-2 code for the Islamic Republic of Afghanistan. This is the code used in international transactions to and from Afghan bank accounts. **2.** ISO 3166-2 geocode for Afghanistan. This is used as an international standard for shipping to Afghanistan. Each province has its own code with the prefix "AF." For example, the code for the Province of Herat is ISO 3166-2:AF-HER.

AFA ISO 4217 representation for the Afghan afghani that was issued between 1925 and 2002. Formerly pegged to the Indian rupee and the U.S. dollar, it became a floating currency in 1992. During the political instability of the 1990s, the afghani experienced rampant inflation. After the U.S.-led invasion, the Afghan government began issuing a new afghani with the ISO 4217 symbol "AFN." The afghani was divided into 100 pul. See also: Currency pair.

Affarsvarlden General Index A prominent Swedish stock index. That is, the Affarvarlden General Index tracks the most important securities traded on Swedish exchanges.

Affective Behavior Any activity or other behavior intended to produce a desired effect. For example, a government may cut taxes to encourage people to spend more. Engaging in an affective behavior in no way guarantees the desired effect will actually occur.

Affiant A person who signs an affidavit. The affiant certifies under penalty of perjury that the statements contained in the affidavit are true to the best of his/her knowledge.

Affidavit A statement sworn to be true to the best of the maker's knowledge. An affidavit is notarized to prove its authenticity. A person who knowingly makes a false statement in an affidavit is guilty of perjury.

Affidavit of Domicile An affidavit issued by the executor of an estate stating the residence of the decedent at the time of his/her death. Before securities can be distributed to heirs, the executor must issue an affidavit of domicile to ensure there are not outstanding liens against the estate in the jurisdiction of the decedent's residence. An affidavit of domicile is notarized and is made under penalty of perjury. It is also called an affidavit of residence.

Affidavit of Loss A statement declaring the loss of a security. One files an affidavit of loss when the certificate of the security is stolen or destroyed in a flood or fire. The affidavit includes information such as the holder's name and the circumstances surrounding the loss. One must file an affidavit of loss in order to receive a bond of indemnity and replace the lost security.

Affidavit of Performance An affidavit submitted by a broadcaster to an advertiser stating that a commercial or other advertisement has been aired according to the specifications set by the advertiser. The affidavit of performance states the services rendered and the amount the advertiser owes. An affidavit of performance is notarized and is made under penalty of perjury.

Affiliate 1. A company that owns a minority interest in another company. This gives the first company a degree of control over the second, but not enough to make it a full-fledged subsidiary. **2.** One of two companies that have a structural relationship with each other. For example, both companies may be subsidiaries of the same parent company.

Affiliated Corporation A corporation of which another company owns a significant percentage, but not a majority, of its shares. This gives the company a great deal of influence, but not outright control, of the affiliated corporation. See also: Subsidiary, Parent company.

Affiliated Foreign Group A set of companies owned by the same person or parent company; the owner or parent company is located in a foreign country. See also: Foreign Corporation, Controlled Foreign Corporation.

Affiliated Group A set of companies owned by the same parent company. An affiliated group often files its tax returns as if it were a single company, but this is not always the case. See also: Affiliated Corporation.

Affiliated Retailer 1. A retailer owned by an affiliated wholesaler. An affiliated wholesaler owns either a majority or a significant minority stake in the affiliated retailer in order to control directly or indirectly how its products are marketed. That is, the affiliated retailer sells the affiliated wholesaler's products to consumers. **2.** A group of retailers that band together for marketing purposes.

Affiliated Wholesaler 1. A wholesaler who owns a majority or significant minority stake in one or more retailers. This allows the affiliated wholesaler either control or significant influence over how its products are marketed at a retail level. It also provides one or more guaranteed customers for the wholesaler's products. **2.** A group of wholesalers that band together for marketing purposes.

Affinities In the philosophy of Max Weber, the relationship between Protestant culture and capitalism. According to Weber, affinities exist between Protestantism and capitalism because the former provides a cultural framework for the latter to grow. This is why, in Weber's estimation, Protestant regions like Germany and Britain prospered more economically in the 19th century than Catholic areas like Ireland or Italy.

Affinity Card A credit card or debit card co-issued by a bank and another organization. The other organization's logo appears on the card. For example, one may have an affinity card with one's favorite hockey team's mascot on it. It may also have awards attached to it; for example, one may build up points toward box seats at a hockey game. The idea behind the affinity card is to encourage people to sign up for credit cards from banks offering certain affinities.

Affinity Fraud A type of fraud where a con artist targets members of a particular group. For example, a con artist may mail donation solicitations to political activists asking for money to pressure the government for a certain cause, when the donations, in fact, go to the con artist himself. Likewise, the con artist may convince members of a religious or ethnic group to donate to a made-up organization to protect the rights of the group. See also: Pyramid Scheme.

Affirmative Action A series of policies a government or organization pursues to help a given demographic group, especially a historical minority, in work and/or education. Affirmative action may be mild; for example, race may be one of a number of factors a university considers when deciding admission. On the other hand, it may impose stringent requirements; for example, a government may oblige companies to abide by gender quotas when hiring. Affirmative action as a policy is quite controversial. Proponents argue it helps engender equality among groups in society. Critics contend it does (or at least can) reward less qualified persons at the expense of more qualified persons. The term "affirmative action" is predominantly American. The concept is called positive discrimination in the United Kingdom, employment equity in Canada and reservation in India.

Affirmative Dumping Determination A statement by the U.S. Department of Commerce requiring an exporter to post funds as security on future goods that the exporter sends to the United States. The affirmative dumping determination is made if the Commerce Department finds that the exporter is in violation of American anti-dumping laws.

Affirmative Obligation Financial Industry Regulatory Authority requirements on NASDAQ market makers. Affirmative obligations include but are not limited to ensuring a two-sided market always exists, reporting price and trading volume within 90 seconds of each transaction, and participating in the Small Order Execution System. It should not be confused with an affirmative covenant.

Affirmative Relief In a lawsuit, relief or some other compensation the defendant demands over the incident. That is, when the defendant claims both that he/she is not responsible for any damage and that the plaintiff is responsible for damage to him/her because of the same series of events, the defendant asks for affirmative relief.

Affirmative Warranty A statement on an insurance policy made by the policyholder or an insured party indicating that a fact is currently true. The affirmative warranty must in fact be truthful in order for the policy to be effective.

Affluenza 1. A situation in which wealthy people find themselves unhappy. The term came to prominence in the mid-2000s, when the financial industry was doing extraordinarily well but people who worked on Wall Street or The City discovered that large bank accounts did not satisfy them at their deepest levels. **2.** A slang term for greed.

Afford To be able to buy something. Theoretically, one can afford anything so long as one has the money to purchase it. However, affordability is subjective to a certain extent, depending on one's other obligations, wants and needs. See also: Expensive, Cheap.

Affordability Index An index published monthly by the National Association of Realtors showing how easy or difficult it is for a family to buy a house. A rating of 100 indicates that a family making the national (or regional) median income can buy a house at the median price. A rating below 100 means that houses are less affordable, while one above 100 shows that they are more affordable. The National Association of Realtors publishes both national and regional affordability indices.

Affordable Method A way that a marketing company decides how much to spend on an advertising campaign. The affordable method is determined by how much the company believes the producer of the product can afford. Because this is a subjective measurement, it may or may not be effective.

Affreightment An agreement between the owner of a ship and another party whereby the owner agrees to transport the other party's goods on that ship from and to certain stated locations. Affreightment is the equivalent of a lease; that is, the ship's owner rents space on the ship for the other party's goods.

AFG GOST 7.67 Latin three-letter geocode for Afghanistan. The code is used for transactions to and from Afghan bank accounts and for international shipping to Afghanistan. As with all GOST 7.67 codes, it is used primarily in Cyrillic alphabets.

Afghan Afghani The currency of Afghanistan. Introduced in 1925, it was formerly pegged to the Indian rupee and the U.S. dollar. It briefly floated between 1978 and 1982, and it became a floating currency permanently in 1992. During the political instability of the 1990s, the afghani experienced rampant inflation, primarily because each warlord issued his own afghani. After the U.S.-led invasion in 2001, the Afghan government began issuing a new afghani, which has brought a certain amount of stability to the currency. See also: AFN, AFA.

Afghan Rupee The currency of Afghanistan prior to 1925. It was based on a coin of silver, and did not circulate universally throughout Afghanistan until 1891. It was replaced by the afghani.

Afianzadoras An organization in Mexico that promotes bond and security companies. Essentially, Afianzadoras promotes the investment sector of the Mexican economy. It became independent of the Bankers Association of Mexico in 1985.

Afloat 1. See: Going Concern. **2.** See: Float.

AFN ISO 4217 code for the new Afghan afghani. It was introduced in 2002, following the U.S.-led invasion of Afghanistan. It replaced the old afghani (code AFA), which was not a united currency, being issued separately by both the Taliban and the Northern Alliance. The new afghani has become a much more stable currency than its predecessor, even appreciating against the U.S. dollar starting in 2004.

AFN Korea A radio and television broadcast network for U.S. military personnel and their families who are stationed in South Korea. AFN Korea offers a variety of channels and stations. AFN Korea broadcasts are encrypted to avoid copyright violations. In lieu of commercials, AFN Korea sends out public service announcements.

Africa Enterprise Fund A division of the International Finance Corporation (which is itself a division of the World Bank) that promotes the creation and maintenance of small business and medium-sized business in sub-Saharan Africa.

Africa Project Development Facility An organization that seeks to promote business in Africa in order to encourage a self-perpetuating market without need for international aid. It provides advisory and other services for new businesses in Africa. It was established in 1986 by the United Nations under the aegis of the International Finance Corporation with the cooperation of the African Development Bank.

African Development Bank A bank in Africa that was established in order to reduce poverty and promote sustainable growth. Among other things, it makes loans and provides other forms of financial assistance for projects thought to contribute to African development. It also managed the African Development Fund and the Nigerian Trust Fund. It was established in 1963 and maintains its headquarters in Cote d'Ivoire.

African Development Foundation An independent agency of the U.S. government that provides grants to enterprises and community groups intended to promote development in Sub-Saharan Africa. That is, it promotes small businesses and non-profit organizations in its program area. It was established in 1980 and is considered one of the best-run U.S. government agencies.

African Export-Import Bank A bank established in order to promote African exports. Among its activities, the Bank provides credit to African exporters, finances the import of raw materials in order to make exportable products and generally attempts to encourage African countries to trade internationally. It was established in 1993 and maintains its headquarters in Cairo. Its name may be abbreviated to AFREXIMBANK.

African Groundnut Council An organization dedicated to the promotion of peanut (also known as groundnut) commerce in Gambia, Mali, Niger, Nigeria, Senegal and Sudan. It was established in 1964 and is based in Nigeria.

African Management Services Company An organization that seeks to promote business in Africa. It provides advisory and training services for new businesses and state-run companies in Africa. It was established by the United Nations under the aegis of the International Finance Corporation with the cooperation of the African Development Bank.

African Regional Organization for Standardization An organization that promotes trade by and within Africa by encouraging greater standardization. The standards ARSO seeks to harmonize include agriculture, food products, engineering and textiles, among other things. ARSO believes that greater standardization will lead to more trade because consumers will have an objective rule against which to measure products.

African Timber Organization An international organization dedicating to standardizing the forestry policies of member countries, with the goal of promoting sustainability in timber industries. The ATO follows international recommendations in conducting its activities. It has 13 members throughout sub-Saharan Africa.

African, Caribbean, and Pacific Countries A group of 79 independent states that have undertaken to reduce poverty, promote development and seek greater integration into the global economy. Nearly all the ACP countries are signatories to the Cotonou Agreement, giving members a special relationship with the European Union. Many ACP states are among the least developed in the world.

Aft A term describing anything toward the back or rear of a ship or aircraft. It is often used in sailing.

After Date In a bill of exchange, the date on which the bill comes due. The after date is a stated number of days after a dated indicated on the bill. See also: At Sight, After Sight.

After Hours Trading The practice of trading a security after an exchange has closed. After-hours trading occurs over-the-counter, but both listed and unlisted securities may be traded. After-hours trading is often less liquid than regular trading because participation by market makers is voluntary, whereas market makers are required to serve as a counterparty for a security during trading hours. The price of a security in after-hours trading may influence is price on the next trading day. The practice is less commonly called extended-hours trading.

After Sight In a bill of exchange, the date on which the bill comes due. It is a stated number of days after the bill is presented to the buyer. See also: At Sight, After Date.

After Tax Operating Income In accounting, a calculation of a business' operating income after all taxes are paid. The ATOI is not a recognized practice in the Generally Accepted Accounting Practices; thus, it is vital to note how each accountant and each firm arrive at the calculation. It is closely related to the net operating profit after tax calculation, which is also unrecognized in GAAP.

After the Bell Describing any period of time after a stock exchange has closed. It is often used in reference to after-hours trading.

After the Fact Accounting System A system of bookkeeping in which one uses the most recent transactions available online to record (or verify) revenues and expenses in the company's own books.

After-Acquired Clause In bond indentures and mortgages, a clause stating that assets acquired after the contract comes into effect may be regarded as additional collateral for the debt. For example, if a person buys a second house after taking out a mortgage on his/her primary house, the mortgage lender may regard the second house as extra security in the event of default. The after-acquired clause exists to provide additional protection to the lender to ensure that secured debts are paid.

After-Acquired Property **1.** Property that a person buys after an activity has taken place, usually after either a bankruptcy has been filed or a will has been made. For example, if one buys 10 acres after filing bankruptcy, those 10 acres are considered after-acquired property. How after-acquired properties affect an activity (such as whether they can be used to repay creditors in a bankruptcy or how they are distributed in a will) differs according to individual situations. **2.** In law, property one sells without owning but then subsequently buys. For example, suppose Joe sells Bob 10 acres, but those 10 acres in fact belong to Frank. If Joe takes Bob's money and buys Frank's 10 acres afterward, they are automatically transferred to Bob. See also: Fraud.

After-Hours Market Close The final price of a security being traded in the after-hours market. The after-hours market close is generally seen as an indication of the opening price at the beginning of the following trading day. It is often expressed as a percentage increase or decrease from the closing price during the trading day. That is, if the share price at market close is $20 and the after-hours market close is $30, it is expressed as a 50% increase.

Afternoon Drive In radio broadcasting, the period of time between 3 p.m. and 7 p.m. The afternoon drive occurs when people are going home from work and very often listening to the radio. Because of the higher volume of radio listeners during the afternoon drive, advertising rates are higher during this time period. The other peak time in radio listening is the morning drive.

After-Sales Service Any assistance a seller provides a buyer after a good or service is sold. For example, a car dealer may offer free or discounted service on a car for a year after purchase. Likewise, a computer manufacturer may offer free technical support to customers. After-sales services are important to building brand loyalty and generating repeat customers.

After-Tax Describing any financial data calculated after subtracting total tax liability. For example if one's income is $100,000 and one's tax liability is $33,000, then one's after-tax income is $67,000.

After-Tax Basis A comparison of net yield between taxable and tax-exempt bonds, especially corporate bonds and tax-free municipal bonds. A corporate bond yields less than its stated interest rate because of taxation, whereas a tax-exempt municipal bond does not. Thus, a municipal bond paying a lower interest rate will often net the bondholder more than a corporate bond with a slightly higher interest rate, depending upon one's tax bracket. See also: Municipals-over-bonds spread.

After-Tax Contribution A contribution made to a retirement plan with money one has left over after paying taxes. That is, when one makes after-tax contributions to a retirement plan, one has already paid taxes on the contribution. As a result, one does not pay taxes on the withdrawals on the plan made after retirement. After tax contributions are made on Roth IRAs and Roth 401(k)s. See also: Pre-Tax Contributions.

After-Tax Equity Yield The yield on an investment in real estate after subtracting taxes and other charges. One calculates the after-tax equity yield by taking the proceeds from the sale of real estate, subtracting expenses (such as paying off the remaining mortgage), and adding back in the cash flow that the real estate generated while one owned it. One then subtracts the total taxes owed on the profit from the sale and the cash flow and expresses the result as a percentage of the original investment.

After-Tax Proceeds from Resale When one sells an asset, the profit on that sale after any applicable taxes on it are paid. For example, if one sells a house for a $100,000 profit (after paying off the remaining mortgage and making realtor fees and so forth) but owes $25,000 in taxes from the sale, the after-tax proceeds from resale are only $75,000. The amount of the after-tax proceeds from re-sale may vary on the same investment depending on whether one owes income tax or capital gains tax.

After-Tax Profit Margin A measure of how well a company controls its costs after taxes. It is calculated by dividing the company's net income (profit after taxes) by its net sales. A high after-tax profit margin often means the company controls its costs well and provides a value for the shareholder's investment. However, a low after-tax profit margin is not necessarily a negative sign. Some companies and industries are expensive to run and have low margins by their nature, relying on sheer volume to generate profits. However, a high after-tax profit margin is generally seen as better if it is at all feasible.

After-Tax Real Rate of Return The rate of return on an investment after subtracting taxes and adjusting for inflation. It is calculated simply by taking the after-tax return and subtracting the inflation rate. For example, if the after-tax return is 7% and the inflation rate is 4%, the after-tax real rate of return is 3%.

After-Tax Return The return on an investment after any applicable taxes on it are paid. For example, if one sells a house for $100,000 but owes $25,000 in taxes from the sale, the after-tax return on the house is only $75,000. The amount of the after-tax return may vary on the same investment depending on whether one owes income tax or capital gains tax. It should not be confused with the after-tax value, which is similar but is not contingent on the sale of an asset or the closing of an investment.

After-Tax Value The value of an asset after any applicable taxes on it are paid. For example, if one sells a house for $100,000 but owes $25,000 in taxes from the sale, the after-tax value of the house is only $75,000. This remains the after-tax value whether or not one actually sells the house, which is what differentiates it from the after-tax return. See also: Net Salvage Value.

Aftertax Yield An investment's rate of return after subtracting all applicable taxes, expressed as a percentage. Most analysts prefer to look at afterax yield instead of pretax yield when weighting investment decisions. Mutual funds are required to disclose their aftertax yields to provide the most accurate picture possible. See also: Current yield.

Aftonomi Monastiki Politeia In Greece, a political subdivision for Mount Athos, which is an autonomous region consisting of monastic communities.

Ag **1.** ISO 3166-1 alpha-2 code for Antigua and Barbuda. This is the code used in international transactions to and from Antiguan and Barbudan bank accounts. **2.** ISO 3166-2 geocode for Antigua and Barbuda. This is used as an international standard for shipping to Antigua and Barbuda. Each parish and dependency has its own code with the prefix "AG." For example, the code for the Parish of Saint George is ISO 3166-2:AG-03.

Against **1.** See: Against the Grain. **2.** See: Against all Risk. **3.** See: Against the Box.

Against the Box Describing the action of short selling a security one owns. When one sells against the box, gains and losses are equalized by the long position on a security combined with the short position created by the short sale. One formerly sold against the box generally in order to be able to claim profits on the sale in the following tax year, but the Taxpayer Relief Act of 1997 largely removed this loophole.

Against the Grain The practice of folding paper or feeding it into a printer in a direction other than the one in which the fibers of the paper run. Going against the grain leads to bulkier material and as such is rarely recommended, especially in marketing.

Agate Line In newspapers and magazines, an area of space used to measure the size of classified ads and some other advertisements. An agate line is one column inch wide and one-fourteenth of an inch high.

Age & Life-Cycle Segmentation In marketing, a strategy that divides potential customers into various groups based upon their ages or their states in life and devises different campaigns for each. For example, given a product that appeals both to young people and to older people, an age and life-cycle segmentation strategy would use different tactics for the two age groups. It might produce commercials on daytime television for the older potential customers and viral Internet advertisements for the younger people.

Age Change In insurance, a person's birthday. The date on which a person's age changes may cause one's premiums to increase or decrease (depending on the type of insurance).

Age Discrimination The practice in which a company or other organization fires, refuses to hire, limits the benefits of or otherwise maltreats a worker of a certain age. For example, an employer may refuse to hire an otherwise qualified applicant for a position because he/she regards the applicant as too old to learn new skills. Likewise, the employer may refuse to hire a younger worker without regard for the worker's qualifications, because he/she believes young people cannot take directions. While legislation in the United States and elsewhere protects older workers from age discrimination, these laws do not necessarily protect younger employees. See also: Age Discrimination in Employment Act.

Age Discrimination in Employment Act Legislation in the United States, passed in 1967, that forbids discrimination against persons over the age of 40 in the hiring or firing of, and the distribution of benefits to, employees. The Act was deemed necessary because some employers were unlikely to hire otherwise qualified applicants because they were closer to retirement and therefore less likely to stay with the company. It provides for reinstatement and back pay for employees against whom companies have discriminated.

Age Limit The maximum age for which one is eligible for an insurance policy. For example, a life insurance company may refused to sell a policy to someone over the age of 90 because it is unlikely that the person will live long enough for the insurance company to recoup the death benefit in the person's premiums.

Age Relief A standard tax deduction in the United Kingdom for persons and married couples over the age of 65. That is, age relief is the income of older persons that is not considered income for tax purposes; only income over the age relief is taxable. The age relief amount increases at age 75.

Age Setback The number of years' difference between women and men at which they are paying the same amount in life insurance premiums. Because women tend to live longer than men, life insurance companies often charge them lower premiums because they expect women to pay premiums for a longer period of time. For example, a 66 year old woman may pay the same premium each month as a 62 year old man. In this case, the age setback is four years. Having age setback is sometimes considered discriminatory and is illegal in some jurisdictions.

Aged Fail A transaction that has not been settled more than 30 days after the trade date. An aged fail is subject to specific fines and other charges from the SEC. Aged fails occur most often between clearing houses and institutions; individual investors rarely commit an aged fail. See also: Fail, Settlement.

Age-Earnings Profile A chart showing the average or median income for workers over time. In general, earnings rise as workers become older, though this is not always the case. One may make age-earnings profiles for all workers, or one may customize them for workers in different industries or of different demographics.

Agence Canadienne de Developpement International A government agency in Canada that administers foreign aid and promotes international development. Among other things, it partners with other public and private organizations worldwide to alleviate poverty and encourage sustainable growth in developing countries. It was established in 1968. See also: DFID, USAID.

Agence de Cooperation Culterelle et Technique A former international organization for nations with a French-speaking majority or significant minority. It was established in 1970 and subsequently became the Organisation Internationale de la Francophonie.

Agencja Rozwoju Przemyslu S.A. A semi-public agency in Poland charged with developing industry in the country. It offers consulting services to Polish companies, provides financial assistance, and supports regional and international business cooperation. It is organized as a joint stock company; the State Treasury owns all stock and the Minister of the Treasury exercises all voting rights. While it traces its origins to 1987, it was established in its current form in 1990 to help the transition in Poland from communism to capitalism.

Agency Agreement An agreement between persons and/or organizations whereby one, called the agent, acts on behalf of the other, called the principal. The agency agreement states the functions the agent will perform for the principal, under what circumstances, and for what compensation. Agents have a fiduciary responsibility to act in the best interests of the principal. Common examples of agents include brokers and attorneys. An agency agreement is also called an agency contract. See also: Agency theory, Agency problem, Agency costs.

Agency Bank A separately incorporated branch of a foreign bank inside the United States. Agency banks cannot make loans or take deposits in their own name; rather, they do so on behalf of the parent bank in the foreign country. They also are the main issuers of American Depository Receipts.

Agency Basis A form of compensation to a broker through commissions that are established by bids submitted by different brokerages. Agency basis compensation is used for brokers who handle program trading.

Agency Bill 1. A bill of exchange that a client takes out from a local branch of a foreign bank. **2.** See: Agency security.

Agency Bond A debt obligation owed by an agency of the U.S. Government. While similar to a Treasury security, agency bonds are issued by a particular agency of the federal government, rather than the federal government itself. These agencies include Ginnie Mae, the Federal Farm Credit Bank, and the U.S. Postal Service. With the exceptions of the Postal Service and the Tennessee Valley Authority, all these obligations are guaranteed by the U.S. Government. They offer higher interest rates than Treasury securities. They are less formally called agencies.

Agency by Estoppel A situation in which a reasonable person may assume agency agreement exists when it does not. For example, if a person or company allows another person or company to use proprietary letterhead to send out correspondence, agency by estoppel may exist. Because the agency is assumed, the (presumed) principal may be legally bound by the agent's actions.

Agency by Necessity A situation in which one person acts as another person's agent outside the scope of a previous agreement in order to prevent harm to the principal. For example, two persons may have a principal-agent relationship in which one acts as the other's attorney. The attorney's responsibilities probably would not include making medical decisions in the event of the client's incapacity. However, if the client has some emergency and requires immediate surgery, and there is no one else to make the decision, the attorney may be the one to give consent for the surgery. In this case, the attorney is acting as an agent by necessity.

Agency by Ratification A situation in which a person or company inaccurately claims to be an agent for another person or company and conducts some act in that capacity, but which the principal (who is not actually a principal) later accepts and recognizes. Because the agent is not actually an agent, any act he/she conducts on behalf of the principal ordinarily would be invalid; however, agency by ratification exists because the "principal" confirmed the act.

Agency Commission 1. A fee that an advertising agency charges a client for the services it provides. This is usually a percentage of the costs the agency incurs in the process of providing the services. **2.** A discount that a broadcaster gives an advertising agency for bringing in advertisers. Because the agency acts as an intermediary and saves the broadcaster the time and expense of finding clients, the broadcaster usually gives the agency a 15% discount.

Agency Cost View A theory stating that agency costs, which are incremental costs occurring when an agent makes decisions on behalf of a client, are the lowest when the client finances some, but not all, of his/her transactions with debt.

Agency Costs Costs that arise from the inefficiency of a relationship between an agent and a principal. In a publicly-traded company, agency costs may arise because the company's executives (the agents) may act in their own interest in a way that is detrimental to shareholders (the principals). For example, they may raise their own salaries to an unrealistic level. Agency costs are best reduced by providing appropriate incentives to align the interests of both agents and principals.

Agency Cross A transaction on an exchange in which one person serves as broker to both the buyer and the seller. This occurs when a broker receives opposite orders for the exact same security in the exact same quantity. When this occurs the broker must still go on to the floor of the exchange and announce the trade and wait for a better offer before executing the orders. Agency crosses are regulated like this to ensure that the broker does not favor one customer over another.

Agency Disclosure A statement a real estate broker provides the potential buyer or seller of a property detailing the nature of the broker's prospective relationship with that buyer or seller. The agency disclosure outlines the rights and responsibilities the

broker has in a real estate transaction. In general, the agency disclosure states whether the broker will represent the buyer, the seller, or both.

Agency Fee A fee that an employee must pay if a company's workforce is represented by a union and the employee chooses not to join that union. The employee has that choice if the company is an agency plant. An agency fee is different from union dues, but is intended to cover the costs of collective bargaining, from which non-union employees benefit even if they do not join the union. See also: Right to work.

Agency Fund Any funds that a government or government unit holds on behalf of another. For example, if the State of Oklahoma holds money for the State of Texas, or the City of Tulsa for Tulsa Public Schools, these monies are called agency funds.

Agency Group A number of independent advertising agencies that agree not to compete and to help each other in markets with which other agencies in the group are not familiar. For example, Agency A may be based in New York and Agency B in New Orleans. If Agency B has a client who wants to expand into the New York market, it may call on Agency A for help. The first agency group was established in 1929. They are not as common as they once were, because advertising agencies are increasingly merging rather than working together. An agency group is also called an agency network.

Agency Loan A loan that an agency of the federal government may make available to a local government.

Agency Manager A person who manages a branch of an insurance company. Because the branch is located in a physical place, most of its clients will be local. The agency manager works for the company (unlike individual insurance agents, who are often self-employed). As a result, the manager receives a salary, rather than commissions, though he/she may receive a bonus periodically based on the number of policies sold.

Agency of Record In marketing, an advertising agency that a large corporation uses to coordinate all its advertising. That is, when a company uses several different advertising agencies, the agency of record deals directly with broadcasters and other media in order to make the advertising process more efficient. In general, the agency of record receives a fee from the other advertising agencies for this service.

Agency Pass-Throughs Mortgage-backed pass-through securities with principals and interest guaranteed by a U.S. Government agency. A pass-through security is backed by assets or debt; in an agency pass-through security, a government agency reduces the risk of default to the pass-through holder by guaranteeing payment. Ginnie Mae makes most of these guarantees, but Freddie Mac and Fannie Mae do as well.

Agency Plant A company whose employees are represented by a union the employees are not required to join. That is, employees do not have to join the union in order to receive the higher wages and other perks of collective bargaining. Employees do not have to pay union dues, but must pay an agency fee, which is intended to cover the costs of collective bargaining. See also: Right to work.

Agency Problem A situation in which agents of an organization (e.g. the management) use their authority for their own benefit rather than that of the principals (e.g. the shareholders). The agency problem also refers to simple disagreement between agents and principals. For example, a publicly-traded company's board of directors may disagree with shareholders on how to best invest the company's assets. It especially applies when the board wishes to invest in securities that would favor board members' outside interests.

Agency Recognition In marketing, the acknowledgement of an advertising agency by broadcasters and other media. While agency recognition does not demonstrate that the agency is entirely sound, it does indicate a minimum level of financial stability and trustworthiness. Some companies will not do business with an ad agency until it has received agency recognition.

Agency Risk The risk that the management of a company will use its authority to benefit itself rather than shareholder. For instance, managers may elect to pay themselves higher salaries, which increases overhead, rather than to pay out extra profits as dividends. In a more sinister example, managers may steal the business' money.

Agency Securities 1. Debt instruments issued by government sponsored entities, especially mortgage-backed securities from Ginnie Mae, Fannie Mae, and Freddie Mac, and the Federal Home Loan Banks. Because each of those organizations is sponsored by the U.S. government, agency securities are implicitly guaranteed, and, in the case of Ginnie Mae, are backed by the full faith and credit of the United States. As such, agency securities have historically had high credit ratings, though they were criticized for an alleged role in the 2007-08 credit crunch. **2.** An alternative term for government sponsored entities.

Agency Shop A company with a large number of employees represented by a union but in which workers are not required to join the union. That is, the agency shop has both union and non-union workers. The non-union workers are not required to pay union dues but must pay what is called an agency fee to cover the costs of collective bargaining. See also: Open shop, Closed shop, Right to work.

Agency Theory The study of the relationship between an agent (such as a broker) and a principal (such as a client). Agency theory seeks to explain the relationship in order to recommend the appropriate incentives for both parties to behave the same way, or more specifically, for the agent to have the incentive to follow the principal's direction. Agency theory also seeks to reduce costs in disagreements between the two.

Agency Trade A trade that a broker makes for a client in which the broker initiates the order. Only brokers managing discretionary accounts may make agency trades because, otherwise, they do not have the authority to execute orders without the client's explicit authorization.

Agency-Produced Program A show for radio or television produced entirely by an advertising agency. Often, though not always, the agency promotes the goods or services it is selling within the agency-produced program. The agency-produced program is sold or provided to a radio or television station with the proviso that the agency controls all ads broadcast within the show.

Agent A person who acts on behalf of an organization or another person. Agents have a fiduciary responsibility to act in the best interests of the principal. Common examples of agents include brokers and attorneys. See also: Agency theory, Agency problem, Agency costs.

Agent Bank 1. See: Lead manager. **2.** See: Agency bank. **3.** A bank that issues a credit card on behalf of the primary issuer. The agent bank does not finance the credit card transactions. Most credit card issuers are in fact agent banks.

Agent Commission A form of payment to an agent in which the agent receives a percentage of the value of each transaction that a client orders. Commissions are seen as advantageous to a client because if the client does not make orders, then he/she does not have to pay an agent commission. However, commissions create an incentive for agents to make as many transactions as possible. See also: Fee.

Agent Distributor Service A company that promotes and sells a product on behalf of its manufacturer, usually in another country. An agent distributor service is useful because it may know the local market much better than the manufacturer itself.

Agent for Exporter An agent who acts on behalf of an exporter. That is, the agent for exporter has the responsibility for opening up a new market for the exporter. He/she helps create or expand demand for the exporter's product. The agent generally also has information on local regulations and knows how to navigate them. He/she is paid a commission on the sales the exporter makes.

Agent License A license granting the holder the ability to sell insurance in the state issuing it. To qualify for an agent license, one usually must attain a certain educational level and/or pass a test. Because most insurance is regulated at the state level, each state has its own agent licensing requirements. See also: Agent's qualification laws.

Agent of Record An insurance agent who has sold a policy to a client. The agent of record receives a commission from the insurance company for the sale.

Agent Reinstate A situation in which a former subscriber to a periodical renews his/her subscription after some interruption. Usually, an agent reinstate occurs when the subscriber makes a late payment. For example, a person could forget to pay for a newspaper subscription, in which case newspaper delivery would stop. If the person then made the subscription payment, the next newspaper delivery would affect the agent reinstate. Agent reinstate is also called agency reinstatement or agent's reinstatement. It should not be confused with reinstatement, which is an insurance term.

Agent's Authority The ability of an agent to act on behalf of a client in a way that binds the client. There are four types of agent's authority. Actual express authority is authority the client states in a contract given to an agent. Apparent authority is given verbally by the client. Implied authority is considered by the agent to be necessary to perform duties given under actual express or apparent authority. Finally, inherent authority is that which occurs when the agent exceeds his/her actual express authority only slightly and performs similar actions.

Agent's Balance A commission that an insurance company owes to an insurance agent but has not paid. The agent's balance is created when the agent sells a policy to a client. It is a percentage of the amount the insurance company makes from the new policyholder.

Agent's Cancellation The cancellation of any order for a product sold by an agent. The agent may be a newspaper salesman, an insurance agent, a broker, or any other person who is paid on commission. The agent's cancellation means the agent is not paid (or must refund) his/her commission to the company.

Agent's Qualification Laws The laws in a U.S. state establishing the qualifications to become licensed as an insurance agent. Because most insurance is regulated at the state level, each state has its own agent's qualification laws.

Age-Weighted Profit-Sharing Plan A plan by which an employer distributes a set percentage of the company's profits to its employees' retirement accounts, with older employees receiving more. That is, a company sets up a series of accounts for employees and places a portion of its profits in them until employees retire. Under an age-weighted profit-sharing plan, accounts for older employees receive a larger amount each time the company makes a distribution. The company divides up the distributions in such a way that the older employees (who are closer to retirement) and the younger employees (whose account will benefit more from compound interest) will receive the same amount from the profit-sharing following retirement. The idea behind any profit-sharing plan is to give employees an incentive to work for the company's profitability.

Agglomeration Economies The net advantage of building one or more businesses in a city or other large population center. Agglomeration economies occur when the larger market, lower transportation costs, and other benefits outweigh the added expenses (such as higher rent or taxes) of living in a city. This concept is closely associated with economies of scale. See also: Diseconomies of agglomeration.

Aggregate Annual Deductible In insurance, the maximum amount that a policyholder must pay for a claim before the insurance company will make any payments at all. That is, if one or more insured events happen in a given year, the policyholder is responsible for covering damages up to a certain dollar amount, at which point the insurance company begins coverage. Because the deductible is calculated annually, if two insured events happen in a year, the deductible is only applied once. Generally, the higher one's deductible is, the less one pays in premiums on the policy.

Aggregate Demand The total demand of goods and services in an economy at a given overall price and time. Aggregate demand is tracked on an aggregate demand curve, which plots demand against price. When prices are rising, this indicates that the aggregate supply in the economy is inadequate to meet the aggregate demand; this leads businesses to expand their operations and produce more goods and services.

Aggregate Demand Curve A graph representing demand for goods and services in an economy at different prices. If prices are increasing while demand remains constant, this indicates the economy's aggregate supply is inadequate to meet demand. One calculates the aggregate demand curve by combining and properly weighting the demand curves for individual goods and services.

Aggregate Demand Schedule A graph representing the aggregate demand at each level of a country's GDP. On the aggregate demand schedule, the x-axis represents GDP and the y-axis represents aggregate demand. In general, aggregate demand (the overall demand in an economy for goods and services at a certain price) rises along with GDP.

Aggregate Dollar Limit 1. The maximum amount payable to an individual from a government program. For example, safety net programs like welfare or disability insurance may be subject to an aggregate dollar limit. **2.** See: Aggregate insurance limit.

Aggregate Excess Contract A form of stop loss insurance whereby an insurer agrees to pay 80% to 100% (depending on the specific policy) of all costs a person or company incurs over and above the aggregate limit on another insurance policy. The aggregate limit is the total amount an insurance company will pay on a policy; thus, an aggregate excess contract helps defray costs in the event of a catastrophic loss that another policy does not fully cover.

Aggregate Exercise Price The exercise price of an option that the holder actually pays or is paid (depending on the nature of the option). The aggregate exercise price is calculated by taking the exercise price per unit and multiplying by the number of units specified in the contract. For example, if an option holder has a call for 1,000 shares of a stock for a $35 exercise price, the aggregate exercise price will be $35,000.

Aggregate Income The total income earned by all persons and companies in a country or region. The aggregate income generally does not adjust for inflation, debt, taxes, or other things. There are a number of ways to measure aggregate income, but GDP is one of the best known and most widely used.

Aggregate Indemnity In the event a person or company has more than one insurance policy covering the same insured event, the total coverage both policies provide. See also: Aggregate limit.

Aggregate Limit The maximum amount that an insurance policy will provide over a given period of time or over the life of the policy. For example, if an insurance company has agreed to pay all of a person's medical bills up to $100,000 and the person incurs $135,000 in services, the policyholder must pay $35,000 out of pocket. Some supplemental insurance policies provide coverage over the aggregate limit. See also: Stop loss insurance.

Aggregate Mortality Table A table showing the number of deaths of policyholders relative to the total number of persons who have purchased life insurance. Unlike an ultimate mortality table, an aggregate mortality table does not account for the ages of policyholders or the number of years they owned their policies before dying. Therefore, it may not provide as accurate a picture as some other mortality tables; nevertheless, an actuary may use it to help price policies appropriately.

Aggregate Products Liability Limit The maximum coverage that a product liability insurance policy will provide to a policyholder over a given period of time, especially a year.

Aggregate Stop Loss Insurance A company insurance policy that provides coverage on all expenses when another insurance policy exceeds its projected costs. For example, if an employer provides insurance for its employees but the costs for the company exceed 115% of projected costs, an aggregate stop loss insurance policy would pay for all the company's costs over this amount. An aggregate stop loss insurance policy reduces the company's risk in providing employee benefits.

Aggregate Supply The total supply of goods and services in an economy at a given overall price and time. Aggregate supply is tracked on an aggregate supply curve, which plots supply against price. When prices are rising, this indicates that the aggregate supply is inadequate to meet aggregate demand; this leads businesses to expand their operations and produce more goods and services. In the short term, aggregate supply is responsive to price movements, but, in the long term, it only increases in response to increased productivity.

Aggregated Shipments The shipment of many units of a good on the same vessel, often as a container load.

Aggregation 1. A composite report of all futures positions held by a single trader. Aggregations are used to ensure that reports are accurate and regulations are followed. **2.** In corporate financial planning, the combination of several, small investments such that they are treated as one, large investment.

Aggressive Accounting The practice of incorrectly recognizing revenue in order to please investors. Aggressive accounting seeks to falsely inflate stock prices by improperly reporting income, failing to capitalize expenses, hiding losses in subsidiaries, or otherwise misrepresenting the company's financial state. In the early 2000s, aggressive accounting came into focus in the United States when it was revealed that Enron and several other companies were using the practice. See also: Sarbanes-Oxley Act of 2002.

Aggressive Growth Mutual Fund A mutual fund that invests primarily or exclusively in high-risk, high-return securities. They may invest in IPOs and quickly re-sell; they also commonly invest in options. Very little of the income from an aggressive growth mutual fund comes from dividends; rather, most of its earnings come from capital appreciation. They have a high degree of volatility, and tend to correlate highly with stock market performance; that is, they do well when stock markets do well and poorly otherwise. Some analysts believe that while aggressive growth mutual funds correlate in this way, they do so more strongly, meaning that their values increase and decrease more steeply than stock markets as a whole.

Aggressive Investment Strategy An investment strategy in which one takes higher risks in order to achieve higher returns. One using an aggressive investment strategy often seeks to invest in young industries with high growth potential, rather than low-risk, low-yield vehicles. For example, during a market bubble, aggressive investors are more likely to make speculative investment than to buy Treasury bonds.

Aggressive Market A market or exchange with a high trading volume. When a market becomes very aggressive, the prices of stocks can go up significantly, which in turn makes it more expensive for a trader to become involved in the market by buying stocks. As the market becomes more aggressive, some traders are unwilling to involve themselves, which can (but does not always) lead to prices leveling or reverting to the mean.

Aging The process of investigating a company's accounts receivable according to how long individual invoices have been outstanding. Analysts can use aging to identify bad debt and/or problems with the company's credit policy.

Aging Schedule A table arranging accounts receivable according to the days until due or days past due. For example, an aging schedule may list accounts receivable that are less than 30 days old, less than 45 days old, and/or more than 90 days old. An aging schedule helps a company determine which of its customers are paying on time and may also be useful in the estimation of cash flow.

Agio 1. See: Foreign exchange. **2.** A fee paid to a bank or other intermediary for exchanging two currencies.

Agiro An obsolete unit of mass in Pegu, Burma, approximately equivalent to 392 grams. It was used to weigh gold and silver.

AGO GOST 7.67 Latin three-letter geocode for Angola. The code is used for transactions to and from Angolan bank accounts and for international shipping to Angola. As with all GOST 7.67 codes, it is used primarily in Cyrillic alphabets.

Agora In Israel, a coin representing one-hundredth of a new shekel. It is the equivalent of the cent in the U.S. dollar or the pence in the British pound. Its plural is agorot.

Agreed Amount Clause A clause in a property insurance contract stating that if an insured event occurs, the insurance company will pay either the amount to repair or replace the property or a set maximum, which is called the agreed amount. In general, a policyholder pays a higher premium for a higher agreed amount.

Agreed Bid A bid by a company to buy a publicly traded company with the full knowledge and consent of the target company's board of directors. That is, an agreed bid is a bid for a friendly takeover. In an agreed bid, the acquiring company generally offers a premium to the current stock price for each share.

Agreed Upon Procedures The procedures an accountant uses when preparing a statement for a party when the party requires the accountant to use these procedures and takes responsibility for their adequacy and accuracy. The accountant does not express an opinion on the procedures, but must abide by them for purposes of preparing the requested statement.

Agreed Valuation The value of cargo being transported on a ship, as agreed by the owner and the shipper. The agreed valuation is important because it helps determine both what the shipper is paid to transport the cargo and the amount of liability for insurance purposes.

Agreed-Value Policy A property insurance policy stating that if an insured event occurs, the insurance company will pay either the amount to repair or replace the property or a set maximum, which is called the agreed amount. In general, a policyholder pays a higher premium for a higher agreed amount.

Agreement Among Underwriters A contract between members of an underwriting syndicate stating the responsibilities and rights of each member of the syndicate. Included in the agreement between underwriters is the amount of the new issue each underwriter is required to place, whether or not it is sold on a best efforts basis, and the structure as to how members of the syndicate are paid. An agreement among underwriters is vital because no syndicate is a permanent relationship; the contract helps avoid problems before they start. See also: Jointly and Severally, Severally but Not Jointly.

Agreement Corporation A corporation that has received a charter from a state to engage in international banking. Under the Agreement Corporation Act, agreement corporations are allowed to receive funds from national corporations and use them to engage in international banking. They are called "agreement" corporations because they agree to abide by the restrictions of the Agreement Corporation Act and the Edge Act, though many of those restrictions have since been relaxed.

Agreement Corporation Act Legislation in the United States, passed in 1916, that allows banks and some other corporations to engage in international banking. Under the Agreement Corporation Act, national banks may give some of their excess capital to state-chartered banks and other corporations, which then use them for international banking purposes. These state-chartered banks and other corporations are called agreement corporations because they agree to abide by the restrictions of the Act, though many of those restrictions have since been relaxed. See also: Edge Act.

Agreement of Antidumping Practices An international agreement prohibiting a signatory country from "dumping," which refers to exporting goods for lower than their market value. Specifically, the agreement states that a country cannot export any good to a country at a price that would negatively impact the local market for that good. Countries are allowed to charge a tariff or other duty to make up for the difference in price. This Agreement is overseen by the World Trade Organization.

Agreement of Customs Valuation An agreement to create a framework to unify the way countries value imports for customs purposes. This agreement was intended to make international trade more predictable and therefore carry less risk. The Agreement was negotiated in the 1970s by members of the General Agreement on Tariffs and Trade.

Agreement of Sale A contract by which two parties (a buyer and a seller) consent to the sale of some property. The agreement of sale usually contains a description of the property being sold, the price, the terms, and other relevant details. This term is used most commonly in real estate, but it may apply correctly to any sale involving a written document detailing a transaction.

Agreement on Government Procurement A treaty by members of the World Trade Organization mandating openness and transparency when signatory governments buy goods and services from foreign companies. It established a framework for signatories to follow in creating laws and regulations mandating this transparency. It came into effect in 1996.

Agreement on Import Licensing An agreement to create a framework to eliminate licensing requirements for imports. These licenses, while not actually tariffs, were considered an unnecessary barrier to international commerce because they added to exporters' expenses. The Agreement was negotiated in the 1970s by members of the General Agreement on Tariffs and Trade.

Agreement on Technical Barriers to Trade A 1979 agreement by members of the General Agreement on Tariffs and Trade that sought to ensure that administrative processes (such as certifications, testing, and other regulations) do not become a barrier to international commerce. It set up a series of voluntary standards to expedite and homogenize these administrative processes to reduce risk and cost for exporters. See also: ISO.

Agreement on Trade in Civil Aircraft An international agreement eliminating tariffs and other trade barriers on civilian aircraft, flight simulators, airplane engines, and related pieces of equipment. It is binding on all World Trade Organization members that have agreed to it. The Agreement came into effect in 1980.

Agreement Value 1. The current market value of a swap. One calculates the agreement value by determining how expensive it would be to establish the exact same swap position if one were to do so under present market conditions, rather than the conditions under which the swap was actually entered. **2.** See: Agreed valuation.

Agrement The approval and appointment by a government of an ambassador or other envoy by a foreign government. When one country sends an envoy to another, the second country's recognition of that envoy is an agrement.

Agribusiness A general term for all companies and business that engage in agriculture or food processing. Agribusiness includes farms, ranches, grocers, processing centers such as slaughterhouses, and so forth. While the term is used within agribusiness to describe itself, it often has a negative connotation describing corporate farms (as opposed to family farms). It is sometimes associated with practices deemed unethical by some, such as not giving animals sufficient space to move around before they are slaughtered. However, the term also correctly applies to food cooperatives and even family farms themselves.

AGRICOLA An online database of the National Agricultural Library, provided by the U.S. Department of Agriculture. AGRICOLA provides resources on livestock, food, history, rural development, and marketing, among other things. It allows one to request material from the National Agricultural Library without being physically present.

Agricultural Commodities Commodities that come from the raising of crops and/or animals. While some agricultural commodities, such as corn or beef, are direct products of the earth, others, like high fructose corn syrup, are derived from them. The trade of agricultural commodities gave rise to the first exchanges in the Middle Ages. Even now, agricultural products are among the most important commodities and futures contracts that are traded.

Agricultural Credit Any loan or other extension of credit that a bank provides for agricultural or other rural use. Most agricultural credit finances farmers or ranchers as they plant crops, buy equipment, harvest, or do other things necessary for operations but from which profits will not be realized for quite some time. The term of agricultural credit depends on how expensive the product or project it intends to finance is. See also: Federal Farm Credit Bank, Farmer Mac.

Agricultural Economy Any local or national economy heavily dependent on agriculture. Most jobs in an agricultural economy are rooted in farming and ranching, at least tangentially. For example, even if one does not farm, one may make a living selling tractors and other farm equipment. Agricultural economies are often in very rural areas. How well such an economy performs may depend heavily on exogenous factors like the weather.

Agricultural Equipment Insurance An insurance policy that provides coverage in the event of damage to property necessary for running an agricultural business. In general, agricultural equipment insurance covers equipment and machinery (including, for example, saddles for horses) against fire, lightning, mischief, theft, or vandalism. It does not cover exceptionally heavy equipment like aircraft or boats, or crops. As with all insurance, the policyholder pays a premium for this coverage.

Agricultural Futures Futures contracts in which the underlying assets come from the raising of crops and/or animals. That is, the underlying asset of an agricultural futures contract may be a direct product of the earth, such as corn or beef, or a derivative, such as high fructose corn syrup. Agricultural futures are among the most important futures contracts that are traded.

Agricultural Goods Goods that come from the raising of crops and/or animals. While some agricultural goods, such as corn or beef, are direct products of the earth, others, like high fructose corn syrup, are derived from them. The trade of agricultural goods gave rise to the first exchanges in the Middle Ages. Even now, agricultural goods are among the most important commodities and futures contracts that are traded.

Agricultural Marketing Services A division of the U.S. Department of Agriculture that tests and grades, as well as provides news for cotton, dairy, fruit and vegetable, livestock and seed, poultry, and tobacco products. It is responsible for the enforcement of some federal laws regulating agriculture. Among other things, it tests certain products to ensure they are not contaminated.

Agricultural Officer An employee of the Department of Agriculture, Food and Rural Development in the European Union who provides technical expertise for the Department's operations.

Agricultural Protection 1. Any policy that puts up tariffs or other trade barriers on agricultural products so as to prevent or discourage imports. The World Trade Organization seeks to discourage agricultural protection; it was a topic of discussion during the Doha Round. **2.** Any policy that seeks to promote agriculture in a given area. See also: Rural development.

Agricultural Real Estate Any piece of real estate designated for or permitted to undertake agricultural activity. For example, one may run a farm or raise certain kinds of animals only on agricultural real estate. Local zoning laws determine what properties in an area qualify as agricultural real estate.

Agricultural Trade Leads A business opportunity to buy or sell agricultural goods to a party in another country. This term is most common in import and export jargon. See also: Trade leads.

Agricultural Trade Office An office at a U.S. embassy that promotes American agriculture and seeks export opportunities for U.S. farmers and ranchers. Agricultural trade offices work with local companies, including importers, wholesalers, and retailers, to accomplish their goals.

Agriculture The production of food through the raising of crops and/or animals. The development of agriculture approximately 9,000 years ago is considered to be one of the most important revolutions in human thinking, one that made civilization possible. The trade of agricultural products, such as wheat or coffee, gave rise to the first exchanges. Even now, agricultural products are among the most important commodities that are traded. Very often, agriculture may only be performed in certain areas. Zoning laws regulate where farming and ranching may or may not take place. See also: Agribusiness.

Agriculture Information System A worldwide network of research organizations that share literature on agriculture with each other. Its goal is to disseminate agricultural information to a wide audience. It was established in 1974 under the auspices of the United Nations.

Agroterrorism The poisoning of the food supply in order to cause death and destruction, especially for a political end. While agroterrorism has not occurred on a large scale, it is speculated that its outbreak would cause panic in securities markets and in the wider economy, in addition to the obvious public health problems.

Ahead On an exchange, referring to a record of a trade that occurs at the same price as another trade, but is nonetheless listed before that other trade in a specialist's book. See also: Behind.

AHK ISO 4217 code for the Austo-Hungarian krone (which was called the korona in Hungary). It was issued in 1892 and was pegged to gold. Prices rose significantly during World War I and, following the breakup of the Austro-Hungarian Empire, its successor states gradually abandoned the krone.

Ahmed Abdul Rahman Al-Samawi A Yemeni banker and public official born in 1946. He served variously as minister of finance, executive director of the Arab Monetary Fund, and CEO of the Yemen Bank for Reconstruction and Development. From 1997 to 2010, he was governor of the Central Bank of Yemen.

Ahmed Mohammed Ali Al-Madani A Saudi banker born in 1934. Madani spent most of his early career in academia, including serving for a time as acting rector of King Abdulaziz University. He became president of the Islamic Development Bank upon its establishment in 1975.

AI 1. ISO 3166-1 alpha-2 code for French Afars and Issas before it changed its name to Djibouti. This was the code used in international transactions to and from bank accounts in the territory. **2.** ISO 3166-2 geocode for French Afars and Issas. This was used as an international standard for shipping to French Afars and Issas. In both cases, the code is obsolete.

AIA GOST 7.67 Latin three-letter geocode for Anguilla. The code is used for transactions to and from Anguillan bank accounts and for international shipping to Anguilla. As with all GOST 7.67 codes, it is used primarily in Cyrillic alphabets.

AIAF A professional certification indicating one has the ability to prepare financial statements for insurers in a way that complies with the standards of the National Association of Insurance Commissioners. In order to earn an AIAF certification, one must complete a course and pass a test administered by the Insurance Institute of America.

AIAFD Association des Institutions Africaines de Financement du Developpement (AIAFD). An organization that provides training and information services to members who specialize in international development in Africa. Membership is open to any bank or other financial institution. It was established by of the African Development Bank in 1975.

Aid to Families with Dependent Children A former social program in the United States that provided financial aid to low-income persons with children or other dependents. Aid to Families with Dependent Children is what most people in the U.S. called "welfare." Critics claimed the system was abused easily and created a culture of dependency. Proponents argued the program assisted the people who needed it most. It was replaced by Temporary Aid to Needy Families in 1996. See also: Personal Responsibility and Work Opportunity Act.

Aided Recall In marketing, a technique to determine how well viewers or listeners remember an advertisement. In aided recall, a test audience is shown an advertisement and is asked questions about it. The testers give verbal cues to help the test audience remember important points about the advertisement. This contrasts with unaided recall, where no such help is given.

Aide-Memoire An informal summary of a contract or other legal document. The aide-memoire helps the reader (or writer) remember the contract's important points.

AIDJ ISO 3166-3 code for French Afars and Issas, which changed its name to Djibouti in 1977. ISO 3166-3 codes are used to indicate names of countries and territories that are no longer used.

AIG A large insurance and financial services company. It was established in 1919 in Shanghai, where it was the first Western company to sell insurance in China. It went on to become one of the largest companies in the world, underwriting more commercial and industrial insurance in the United States than any other company. Its credit rating fell below AA in September 2008, which caused a liquidity crisis in the company. It subsequently required a bailout in the form of loans from the Federal Reserve to stay afloat. It also received money from TARP. At the time, it was the largest bailout of a private company in U.S. history.

Aimag In Mongolia, a political subdivision equivalent to a province.

AIOEC An organization established under the auspices of the United Nations for countries with iron ore as a major natural resource. The AIOEC was established to promote the export and other trade of iron ore. It is governed by a Conference of Ministers and a Board, both of which are appointed by member countries. The Conference and the Board give instructions to a Secretariat, which conducts research and is responsible for the AIOEC's daily operations. It was established in 1975.

Air Cargo Any goods being transported through the air, especially if they are to be sold later.

Air Cargo Insurance An insurance policy that protects the buyer of a good being transported through the air from the loss of that good. Most of the time, when a good is being shipped by air, either the buyer or the seller is required to purchase air cargo insurance (or at least to assume the risk of loss); their specific agreement determines which one is responsible. See also: Incoterm, Marine Cargo Insurance.

Air Check A recording of a broadcast given to an advertiser. The air check proves to the advertiser that a commercial or advertisement in fact aired. It also includes the announcer's introduction and/or a portion of his/her show. This is used by radio stations and advertisers to find new talent.

Air Date In advertising, the date on which a commercial is broadcast on the radio or television. The air date is important because the advertiser purchases the time on the air date from the broadcaster.

Air Freight The transportation of goods on an aircraft. Air freight is faster than shipping by land or sea, but it is subject to greater weight and other restrictions. See also: Air Parcel Post.

Air Freight Consolidator A company that ships goods by air on behalf of a client, but does not own or operate its own airplanes. An air freight consolidator receives the goods from the client and passes them on to a third party that operates aircraft. It issues house air waybills to indicate to customers that their goods have been received and have been passed on for freight by air. They often include tracking numbers so that the customer can check the status of the shipment.

Air Marshal An undercover law enforcement agent who boards a flight as a normal passenger to prevent a hijacking or other crime, should one occur. The air marshal is tasked with ensuring air travel, both for business and pleasure, occurs smoothly and safely. An air marshal is also called a sky marshal.

Air Parcel Post Any mail sent by air. See also: Air Freight.

Air Pocket Stock A stock that undergoes a sudden drop in price, normally as the result of bad news. For example, if a publicly-traded company announces that its earnings will be slightly less than expected, its stock price's drop may be described as an air pocket. Most of the time, an air pocket is temporary and does not indicate a deeper problem. The term comes from an airplane's sudden drop in altitude when it hits an air pocket.

Air Rights The right to build on, occupy, and/or profit from the air above a piece of real estate. Supposedly, air rights have existed as long as the concept of private property, but it became important in the 20th century as air travel became more common. In the United States, air rights only extend to the amount of air that one may reasonably occupy. As with other aspects of real estate, air rights may be sold, leased, or otherwise acted upon either in conjunction with or separate from the property to which they are attached. See also: Mineral Rights.

Airbag Swap An interest rate swap with a notional amount that fluctuates according to changes in prevailing interest rates. Most interest rate swaps have roughly the following structure: the counterparties agree to swap a fixed interest rate and a floating interest rate, both calculated over some notional amount. In an airbag swap, the notional amount may increase as interest rates increase and decrease as they decrease, or vice versa. An airbag swap is most useful when the counterparties wish to hedge investments that are highly sensitive to changes in prevailing interest rates, such as bonds.

Airbill Several copies of a form associated with a parcel sent by express mail. The airbill contains the addresses of the sender and recipient, along with other information. The sender fills out the airbill, keeps one copy, gives one to the mail service for its records, and sends one with the parcel to indicate the destination.

Air-Bubble Packing Plastic wrap with a series of air pockets. Air-bubble packing is used to wrap fragile goods for shipping. Air-bubble packing reduces the risk of shipping some goods over long distances.

Airbus Industries Group A major European aircraft manufacturer. It was established around 1970 as several European governments consolidated their manufacturing companies in order to compete with American companies, notably Boeing. Airbus produces both military and civilian aircraft, which are used by airlines worldwide. Its competitors, especially Boeing, have protested that the government aid Airbus receives gives it an unfair advantage.

Aircraft Hull Insurance An insurance policy providing coverage to the owners and operators of an aircraft in the event that it is damaged or destroyed. Aircraft hull insurance covers all losses to a plane not specifically excluded. For example, if a plane crashes or is filled with the wrong fuel, aircraft hull insurance pays for the repair or replacement of the plane.

Aircraft Liability Insurance An insurance policy providing coverage to the owners and operators of an airplane in the event that a person or property is damaged while on airplane. That is, if a person slips and falls in the bathroom, or if the plane crashes into another on the runway, aircraft liability insurance would protect the plane from any ensuing lawsuits.

Airport Liability Coverage An insurance policy providing coverage to the owners and operators of an airport in the event that a person or property is damaged while on the airport's premises. That is, if a person slips and falls in an airport bathroom, or if a plane crashes into another on the runway, airport liability coverage would protect the airport from any ensuing lawsuits.

Airport Mail Facility An office of the U.S. Postal Service that is located in or near an airport. An airport mail facility allows efficient sorting and delivery of mail received via aircraft. It is also called an airmail field.

Airport Revenue Bond A municipal bond used to construct or expand an airport. The bond is secured by the revenue the airport receives in the course of its operations, or by the revenue from lease payments made by a particular airline. In either case, the issuing municipality does not back the bond itself. Generally speaking, an airport revenue bond is riskier than other municipal bonds because airports have no power to tax, and thus a sudden fall in revenue may result in an inability to repay the bond.

Aiwas An ancient Persian unit of length approximately equivalent to 20 millimeters.

Aiyl Okmotus In Kyrgyzstan, a political subdivision equivalent to a rural municipality.

Ajustabonos An inflation-indexed bond issued by the Bank of Mexico. Ajustabonos have maturities of three to five years. They pay interest each quarter based on the inflation adjusted value of their 100-peso face value. That is, interest on ajustabonos is based on the worth of 100 pesos at the time the bond was issued. Ajustabonos guarantee a real return.

AKA An abbreviation for "also known as." It is used in business when a person or, less commonly, a company, has two names or a nickname that is often used.

Akaina An ancient Greek unit of area approximately equivalent to 9.5 square meters.

Akarere In Rwanda, a political subdivision roughly equivalent to a county.

Akio Morita A businessman who co-founded Sony. Trained in the family business of soy and sake, Morita established what became Sony in 1946 with Masaru Ibuka, whom he met during World War II. In 1950, Sony introduced the first tape recorder in Japan and went on to become a major electronics company. Morita remained chairman of Sony until 1994. He lived from 1921 until 1999.

Akmetal A theoretical global currency. Under the akmetal system, all central banks would subordinate their policies to a worldwide central bank. It was proposed in 2009 by Nursultan Nazarbayev, the president of Kazakhstan, but the idea attracted little support worldwide.

AKTB In Sweden, an abbreviation indicating a company is an "aktiebolag," which means "share company" or "stock company."

Aktiengesellschaft A German term for a publicly-traded company. The term is used in Germany, Austria, and Switzerland. Interestingly, Aktiengesellschaft companies in Germany have two boards of directors, a supervisory board that is roughly equivalent to an American or British board, and a management board, which is subordinate but is responsible for the company's day-to-day operations. It is abbreviated as A.G.

Aktieselskab A Danish term for a company whose ownership may be transferred by the trading of shares. The term is used both for publicly-traded companies and closely held companies. It is abbreviated A.S. or AKTS.

AL 1. ISO 3166-1 alpha-2 code for the Republic of Albania. This is the code used in international transactions to and from Albanian bank accounts. **2.** ISO 3166-2 geocode for Albania. This is used as an international standard for shipping to Albania. Each county and district has its own code with the prefix "AL." For example, the code for the district of Berat is ISO 3166-2:AL-BR.

Al Jazeera A major news organization. It began as an Arabic-language news network in 1996 and has since expanded to an English-language channel, a newspaper, multiple websites, and other mediums. Al Jazeera was established by a loan from the Emir of Qatar; because it has never relied on direct subsidies from the Qatari government, it is considered one of the most reliable news organizations in the Middle East.

Al Qaida A terrorist organization founded in the late 1980s. It was established in Pakistan to fight against the Soviets in Afghanistan. Its ideology is based on a certain interpretation of the writings of Sayid Qutb, who argued that "true" Islam had been lost over the years and has to be recovered. It is best known for the 9/11 terrorist attacks, which, among other things, destroyed the World Trade Center in the United States and served as the impetus for subsequent American wars in Afghanistan and Iraq. Since 2001, Al Qaida has become more decentralized, with various otherwise unrelated groups claiming the name as they conduct terrorist or other activities in different countries.

Alan Greenspan Chairman of the Federal Reserve from 1987 to 2006. He was chairman during both the 1987 stock market crash and the Asian financial crisis in the 1990s. In both circumstances, he saw to it that the Federal Reserve served as a source of liquidity in order to ensure the global economy continued to function. He kept interest rates low during the dot-com bubble of the 1990s. He was criticized during the late 2000s recession for supporting the unfettered free market policies that led to the housing bubble and unregulated derivatives. He became a friend and follower of Ayn Rand in the 1950s and remains controversial today.

ALAP As late as possible. A slang term in business indicating the submission of work very close to or on a deadline because one does not have to re-work any portion of the work. That is, an ALAP submission is done to avoid a redo, rather than because the work took until the deadline to complete.

Alaska Native Settlement Trust A trust set up under Alaska and federal law whose beneficiaries are the stockholders of an Inuit or other Native-owned corporation. For example, a trust may be set up to provide educational scholarships for qualified persons. Trustees must be individuals and may not be corporations or banks. Alaska Native Settlement Trusts are eligible for favorable tax treatment.

Alaska Trust Act A 1997 state law in Alaska that allows any American to place assets in an irrevocable trust that protects those assets from creditors and, in some circumstances, excludes them from the grantor's estate for tax purposes. In order for a trust to fall under the jurisdiction of the Act, at least one of the trustees must live or have a business in Alaska and the trust's records must be maintained in Alaska. Additionally, a certain percentage of the administration of the trust must take place in Alaska. The Act effectively made Alaska a tax shelter along the lines of the Cayman Islands, the Bahamas, and other offshore locations.

ALB GOST 7.67 Latin three-letter geocode for Albania. The code is used for transactions to and from Albanian bank accounts and for international shipping to Albania. As with all GOST 7.67 codes, it is used primarily in Cyrillic alphabets.

Albanian Franga The former currency of Albania. It was introduced in 1926. There were no franga banknotes and the currency consisted exclusively of gold coins. In 1939, the Albanian lek replaced the franga.

Albanian Lek The currency of Albania. It was introduced in 1926 and is a floating currency.

Alberta Securities Commission An organization in Canada that regulates the trade of securities in Alberta. Along with the British Columbia Securities Commission, it regulates the TSX Venture Exchange. Commission members are appointed by the Lieutenant Governor of Alberta with the advice and consent of the executive council.

Alcohol by Volume The number of milliliters of alcohol in a 100-milliliter beverage. This determines the strength of the drink and can affect the taxation on the drink.

Alcoholic Beverage Liability Insurance An insurance policy that protects a bar, restaurant, or other provider of alcohol from a lawsuit in the event that an intoxicated person causes damage to a third party. For example, a man may become intoxicated at Joe's Bar and then drive his car into a house. If the owner of that house sues Joe's and wins, alcoholic beverage liability insurance would pay the damages on behalf of the bar. As with all insurance policies, Joe's would pay a premium in order to receive coverage.

Alderney Pound The currency of Alderney. Because Alderney is part of Guernsey, and therefore a British crown dependency, the Alderney pound no longer circulates. The British pound circulates instead. However, commemorative coins are still produced.

Aleatory Contract A contract whose performance is dependent on the future occurrence of some event and/or in which the amount of money exchanged between the parties may be unequal. For example, an insurance policy is usually an aleatory contract because the insurance company does not have to do anything unless an insured event occurs.

Alen A Norwegian unit of length approximately equivalent to 627 millimeters.

Alevid In Estonia, a political subdivision approximately equivalent to a borough.

Alexander Graham Bell An inventor credited with the first marketable telephone. The telephone was an instant success and, along with the older invention of the telegraph, was responsible for the development of easier and more frequent communication worldwide. Bell was born in Scotland in 1847 and died in Canada in 1922.

Alfred P. Sloan Jr. An American businessman (1875-1966) who was president and chairman of the board for General Motors. He began his career as president of Hyatt Roller Bearing, which made ball bearings. In 1916, this company merged with United Motors Company, which became part of GM two years later. Sloan remained at GM for the rest of his career and became president in 1937. Sloan is believed to have been the first to change designs of car models from year to year. This concept became known as planned obsolescence. He was also a noted philanthropist; however, he was accused of assisting Nazis during World War II.

Algerian Dinar The currency of Algeria. It was introduced in 1964, replacing the Algerian new franc. The dinar underwent a period of high inflation in the 1990s during Algeria's transition to a capitalist economy, but this has since abated.

Algerian Franc The former currency of Algeria. It was introduced in 1848 upon France's occupation of Algeria. It was pegged to the French franc at a one-to-one ratio. The franc was replaced by the Algerian dinar in 1964, soon after Algeria's independence.

Algorithm Any organized set of steps used to help solve a problem. Algorithms are important in several fields, notably mathematics and computing.

Algorithmic Languages A set of early programming languages developed in the early 1950s. ALGOL languages were highly influential in the development of other programming languages over the next several decades.

Algorithmic Trading A computerized trading system that institutional investors use to make large transactions in securities while affecting their prices as little as possible. Algorithmic trading uses complicated mathematical formulas to identify the ideal times to buy and sell securities in large batches. Usually, algorithmic trading involves dividing trading a large number of securities as smaller groups so as not to cause panic buying or panic selling. Algorithmic trading contrasts with program trading, which is also a computerized system but does not attempt to minimize price changes. Algorithmic trading is also called black box trading.

Alias A pseudonym or fake name. An alias may be used when one is intending to commit identity theft or otherwise defraud another.

Alien A non-citizen. An alien is a citizen of a state other than the one in which he/she resides, works, and/or visits. Aliens usually have restrictions on working in other countries. Many countries also have restrictions on how much investment or ownership of property aliens are allowed to have. A few countries forbid foreign investment entirely, though many encourage investment by aliens as it brings capital into the countries.

Alien Corporation A corporation organized and registered according to the laws of another country but with operations in the domestic country. The alien corporation may or may not also have operations in the country in which it is registered. In order to attain tax advantages, some countries allow corporations to register and not maintain operations. See also: Multinational corporation, Tax haven.

Alien Insurer An insurance company that is organized according to the laws of another jurisdiction, especially another country or state. An alien insurer must alter its practices and perhaps separately incorporate if it wishes to enter a different jurisdiction.

Alienation In law, the ability to transfer a property to another party, either by sale or gift. Most property is alienable, but subject to certain restrictions. For example, a property may be temporarily inalienable because a third party has right of first refusal on it.

Alienation Clause A clause in a mortgage contract requiring that the owner of a property (that is, the debtor on the mortgage) pay the remaining balance of the mortgage should the property be sold. The alienation clause ensures the bank is repaid in full when the ownership of a property changes. Because of an alienation clause, a potential seller usually seeks to sell a property for at least as much as the remaining balance.

Aligned Export Documentation System In international commerce, a form on which as much information as possible is entered. An aligned export documentation system allows one to duplicate information easily (and possibly make minor changes) and thereby to avoid repetitive data entry.

Alimony Periodic payments made to a former spouse (or a current spouse from whom one is separated). Alimony is tax deductible for the paying person and is taxable income for the receiving person.

Alimony Payment A payment one makes periodically to a former spouse (or a current spouse from whom one is separated). Alimony payments are tax deductible for the paying person and are taxable income for the receiving person.

Alimony Substitution Trust An agreement between two divorced or divorcing spouses whereby the one paying alimony deposits assets into a trust and, rather than paying alimony directly, pays their spouse income that the assets generate. An alimony substitution trust is taxed slightly differently from regular alimony. Specifically, assets placed in the trust are not tax deductible.

ALL ISO 4217 code for the Albanian lek. It was introduced in 1926 and is a floating currency.

All Hands Meeting An internal meeting held before the initial public offering of a company. Accountants, lawyers, underwriters, and/or managers may be involved in the all hands meeting; the purpose of the meeting is to resolve all outstanding legal, financial or other issues before the IPO takes place. See also: Due Diligence Meeting.

All In Cost The total cost of a transaction after commissions, interest rates, and other expenses. For example, a student loan has a principal and interest rate, but the all in cost may include an origination fee, a federal default fee, and other expenses.

All Lines Insurance An insurance policy that combines most or all of the policyholder's needs. For example, if one needs car insurance, homeowner insurance, and health insurance, one may purchase an all lines insurance policy covering all of these. The policyholder pays a single premium for all his/her coverage because all lines insurance is a single policy.

All Ordinaries Index The oldest stock index in Australia. Established in 1980, it tracks the 500 largest publicly-traded companies traded on the Australian Securities Exchange. It is weighted for market capitalization. Its importance has declined since the introduction of a second stock index (the S&P/ASX), but it nevertheless remains a benchmark for the performance of Australian equities.

All Other Perils & Misfortune Any event that is similar to an insured event but not exactly the same. For example, a ship sinking from a fire may be an insured event, while sinking from a pirate attack may not be. However, it may fall under all other perils and misfortune. Some insurance policies specifically offer coverage for all other perils and misfortune.

All Risk Clause An insurance policy that covers all possible claims not specifically excluded. All risk insurance is found only in property insurance. Homeowners insurance in sometimes all risk insurance. If one's homeowners insurance is an all risk policy and his/her house burns down, the insurance policy covers it unless the agreement states categorically that it will not cover destruction by fire. All risk insurance is usually quite expensive.

All Risk Insurance An insurance policy that covers all possible claims not specifically excluded. All risk insurance is found only in property insurance. Homeowners insurance in sometimes all risk insurance. If one's homeowners insurance is an all risk policy and the house burns down, the insurance policy covers it unless the agreement states categorically that it will not cover destruction by fire. All risk insurance is usually quite expensive.

All Savers Certificate A type of certificate of deposit issued in the United States in 1981 and 1982. An all savers certificate required a minimum deposit of $500 and provided tax free interest for the depositor up to $1,000 (or $2,000 for a married couple filing jointly). All savers certificates were issued primarily by savings and loan associations seeking to build funds to provide mortgage loans. They were created by the Economic Recovery Tax Act of 1981 as a way to stimulate economic growth.

All the Boats Rise Slang; a term describing gains that most traders make when the stock market rises. For example, if the stock market is rising due to a real estate boom, even traders who have little exposure to real estate will tend to make gains as well.

All the Boats Sink Slang; a term describing losses that most traders make when the stock market falls. For example, if the stock market is falling due to a real estate decline, even traders who have little exposure to real estate will tend to suffer losses as well.

All the Traffic Will Bear A business practice in which a company charges an amount that seems excessive but is still within the range of what customers will pay. That is, the company pushes the price of its product to the limit without going over. See also: Expensive.

All Washed Up A business, company, or other venture that has failed and is no longer operating.

All Weather Fund A mutual fund that performs well regardless of the economic climate. There is no set definition of what qualifies as an all weather fund, but many diversified funds with a variety of different asset classes with consistent performance can be considered all weather funds. See also: Fair weather fund, Foul weather fund.

All-Cargo Aircraft An airplane that transports items such as goods or mail rather than paying passengers.

Allegation In law, a claim that a party to a proceeding makes and states that he/she is able to prove. For example, one may allege in a lawsuit that another party has committed fraud. If the second party is found liable for fraud, one is said to have proven one's allegation.

Allelse An alternate term for "miscellaneous" in business consulting. The term is most common in consulting for Christian churches and ministries.

Allfinanz 1. An Irish company that underwrites life insurance policies for its clients. **2.** See: Bancassurance.

All-Hands Meeting A meeting that every employee in a company or department is required to attend. An all-hands meeting may be used to make special announcements.

All-Holders Rule An SEC regulation requiring publicly-traded companies to offer all new issues of a security to all current shareholders of the same class. For example, if a company issues more Class A shares, it must allow all current Class A shareholders to participate in the offering. Likewise, if it wishes to buy back all class A shares, it must allow all shareholders to sell their shares back to the company.

Alliance An agreement between two or more companies to cooperate on a project or in business generally. For example, two companies may agree not to compete in certain areas or to honor each other's coupons or other marketing promotions. An alliance can provide a strategic advantage for both companies, though it is illegal if it is deemed to be collusion.

Alliance of American Insurers A lobbying organization for property and casualty insurance companies in the United States. It publishes material, presses for favorable legislation, conducts research, and generally seeks to promote its members. It is based in Chicago.

Allied Lines A housing insurance policy that covers most contingencies. Examples of events covered under allied lines include damage from falling timber, sprinkler systems, and vandalism. It does not cover fire damage and so is usually purchased with a standard fire policy.

Allied Member A shareholder or partner of a member firm of the New York Stock Exchange. Allied members may make trades on the exchange floor, but only after completing an exam on the NYSE's rules. One must own at least 5% equity in a member firm in order to be eligible to be an allied member.

Allied Military Currency Currency that was legal tender in some Allied-occupied areas during World War II. The Allied Military Currency was issued when soldiers could not be paid in the local currency and because paying them in U.S. dollars posed the risk of high inflation due to the fact that the dollar had a high value at the time relative to most European currencies. Military leaders declared Allied Military Currency legal tender and required local retailers and others to accept it as payment.

Alligator An option spread with unusually large commissions for the involved broker(s). In an alligator, the commissions are so large that the potential profit from the spread is not worth the expense. In such a situation, the investor holding the spread is said to be "eaten alive."

Alligator Spread Informal; a series of positions on different option contracts that is not and cannot be profitable, regardless of the direction of market movements.

All-Inclusive Facility Any place that can be used for a large number of purposes. For example, a room in a hotel may be an all-inclusive facility because it can be used for a conference, a wedding reception, or some other event.

All-In-Rate The rate that a bank charges a customer in exchange for honoring a banker's acceptance. The all-in-rate is the discount interest rate added to a commission.

Allocate On a balance sheet, to spread an expense over more than one accounting period. One of the most prominent examples of allocation is depreciation, which spreads the cost of an asset over a certain number of years.

Allocated Benefits Payments that one receives from a defined benefits plan. Allocated benefits are gradually paid for as an employee makes payments into the plan throughout his/her working life. As a result, the employee is guaranteed the benefits regardless of what happens to the company for which he/she works.

Allocated Promotion Goods that a manufacturer or supplier sells to a retailer at a lower price so the retailer can then offer them at a discount to consumers. The manufacturer or supplier makes the allocated promotion in order to generate sales without diminishing the retailer's profit. In general, there is a limit on the allocation promotion; that is, the retailer can only buy a certain number of goods. This prevents the retailer from buying more than he/she needs in order to sell them at a higher profit later.

Allocated Transfer Risk Reserve An allowance for bad debts that a bank keeps in order to protect against country risk. For example, a bank may keep an ATRR in case a country renders its currency inconvertible, which would prevent a foreign borrower in that country from making payments.

Allocation of Plan Assets on Termination When a company goes out of business or otherwise divests itself of a pension plan, the payment of all assets in the plan to all employees. The allocation may occur in one of two ways. Either the employees receive everything they have personally paid in premiums, plus interest, or they receive a portion of their benefits based upon what they would have been entitled to if the pension stayed active. In the latter option, employees paid more generally receive more than ones paid less.

Allocation under Lines of Credit A line of credit extended by an export development corporation to a foreign borrower (usually a bank) for a series of transactions that are not defined before the line of credit is extended.

Allocational Efficiency A condition in a market when all capital and other resources are assigned to projects with the highest profitability. Allocational efficiency is thought to benefit all economic actors to the greatest possible extent. In an environment of allocational efficiency, only the projects with the highest potential profitability receive funding and then only in the precise amount that is needed. Allocational efficiency assumes that the market is already informational and operationally efficient, that is, that all pertinent knowledge is public and non-income producing expenses (i.e. fees) are reasonably priced or non-existent. An allocatively efficient market has no imperfections and therefore does not exist in practice. However, markets can contain it to a greater or lesser extent. See also: Market failure.

Allocation-of-Income Rules Given two or more organizations controlled by the same persons or parties, rules allowing the IRS to treat some income, deductions, or credits claimed by one as claimed by another to reflect the true tax liability for the organizations. For example, if one company gives a loan to another and either charges no interest rate or does not charge an "arm's length" interest rate, the IRS may, in some circumstances, treat the companies as one entity for tax purposes. Allocation-of-income rules exist to prevent tax evasion by hiding some income in shell companies.

Allocative Efficiency A measure of the benefit one derives from distributing or investing his/her assets in one way as opposed to another. Allocative efficiency is difficult to measure, especially in advance. However, rational economic actors attempt to maximize their allocative efficiency. See also: Incremental internal rate of return.

Allodial System A system of ownership by which an owner has all rights associated with possessing a property, subject only to limitations such as police power or eminent domain. The allodial system in its most extreme form is expressed in late Roman law: a property owner has the right to "use and abuse" his/her property.

Allonge In countries operating under the Code Napoleon, an addendum to a contract or other transaction on which a party affixes his/her signature. The allonge often contains a summary of what the contract or transaction does, and a signature on the allonge indicates agreement to the contract. It was formerly often added to a bill of exchange, but this has become less common as bills of exchange have themselves become less common. It was never common in Anglo-American jurisdictions because, in common law, signing the contract itself is considered consent.

All-or-None Offering The offering of a security in which the entire issue must be sold or the offering is void. The lead underwriter has the ability to cancel the offering if the entire issue is not sold. Most best effort deals are all-or-none offerings.

All-or-None Order The order to a broker to buy or sell a security in which the entire order must be filled or it is void. See also: FOK.

Allotment In underwriting, the portion of an IPO that each underwriting firm in a syndicate receives or buys. Each firm has the responsibility to place its allotment with investors.

Allotted Shares In underwriting, the shares that each underwriting firm in a syndicate receives or buys. Each firm has the responsibility to place its allotted shares with investors.

Allowable Order Cost In marketing, the maximum amount a company can spend in attempting to attract a customer without reducing its profit by a significant amount. For example, a salesman can use the allowable order cost to determine whether he can afford to take a potential customer to a restaurant.

Allowance 1. See: Allowance method. **2.** See: Capital allowance. **3.** See: Allowance for depreciation. **4.** See: Allowance for doubtful accounts. **5.** See: Withholding allowance. **6.** See: Mileage allowance.

Allowance for Doubtful Accounts Extra funds from sales, or another source, set aside in order to pay off bad debt if and when it arises. The allowance helps a company ward off any potential cash flow problems should its credit sales not be repaid as expected. On financial statements, it is important to note that an allowance for bad debts exists for fiscal conservatism and not because one expects a large amount of bad debt to accumulate. An allowance for doubtful accounts is also called a cushion. Banks call these funds the loan loss reserve. See also: Savings account.

Allowance Method In accounting, a method by which one estimates the bad debt a company will acquire each accounting period. One calculates this estimate by assuming a certain percentage of sales will become accounts uncollectible. One automatically writes off this estimate each period. If the actual amount of bad debt differs from the estimate, an adjustment is made the following accounting period. See also: Direct write-off method.

Allowed Time The time during which an employee is paid while not working because of a situation beyond his/her control. Allowed time is granted more frequently to salaried employees than to wage earners,. Allowed time is usually finite; after its expiration, the employee often must begin to forgo payment. Examples of allowed time include sick time or grieving time. It is also called waiting time. It should not be confused with a waiting period.

All-Purpose Financial Statement A financial statement that contains information relevant to all interested parties. For example, an all-purpose financial statement may contain information for shareholders, bondholders, employees, managers, potential investors, and even independent analysts. Most annual reports and similar statements are intended to be all-purpose.

Alma-0 A programming language that primarily utilizes imperative commands but includes a few features that make it compatible with declarative programming languages.

Al-Maashiiyah In Islamic law, a privately owned animal. One includes the animals one owns when computing the zakat (mandatory charity) one owes.

Al-Marhalah In Islamic law, a measure of distance. One marhalah is roughly equivalent to 44 kilometers or 27.5 miles.

Al-Mata In Islamic law, permissible worldly possessions. Al-mata include necessities for living, investments, inventory, and property. The Arabic term, however, implies that this type of wealth has a fleeting nature.

Al-Mauziinat In Islamic law, an item sold in terms of quantity of weight. For example, gold is a mauziinat because one buys it by the ounce.

Al-Mil In Islamic law, a measure of distance. One mil is slightly longer than one mile and roughly equivalent to 1.8 kilometers.

Al-Milkal-al-'Aammah In Islamic law, publicly-owned infrastructure. A major example is a road. No one person may own al-milkal-al-'aammah, and likewise no one person may prevent another from using it.

Al-Mithlii In Islamic law, a term for fungibles.

Al-Mithqaal In Islamic law, a measure of weight used in the sale of commodities. One mithqaal is equivalent to four and a half grams.

Al-Mithqaal bi Dhahab In Islamic law, a measure of weight used in the sale of gold. One mithqaal bi dhahab is equivalent to four and a quarter grams.

Almost Uncirculated Describing a coin or banknote with only the slightest of abrasions or signs of wear. These coins may be worth a fair amount of money, though they are illiquid assets. See also: Numismatics.

Almsgiving The act or practice of giving money to the poor or to an organization dedicated to religious or social issues. Almsgiving is an important part of many religions, which generally encourage or commend taking care of the poor.

Al-Mu'aawamah In Islamic law, the sale of fruit from a tree before it has grown. The sale may occur up to three years before the growth of fruit. Because it is not certain whether the fruit will actually grow, this type of contract is considered gharar (excessive speculation) and is not permitted.

Al-Mubaadharah In Islamic law, a contract in which the owner of agricultural real estate hires another person to cultivate his land in exchange for a portion of the harvest. The specific portion varies between one-sixth and one-seventh.

Almude A Portuguese measure of liquid volume approximately equivalent to 16.8 liters. It became obsolete after Lusophone countries adopted the metric system in the 19th century.

Al-Mudharaba al-Muqayyadah In Islamic finance, a mudharaba contract that places some requirements or constraints on the entrepreneur. In a mudharaba, a provider of capital agrees to invest in an entrepreneur in exchange for a portion of the profit of the entrepreneur's venture. Al-mudaarabah al-muqayyadah specifies how and under what circumstances the entrepreneur may spend the capital.

Al-Mudharaba al-Mutlaqah In Islamic finance, a mudharaba contract that places no requirements or constraints on the entrepreneur. In a mudharaba, a provider of capital agrees to invest in an entrepreneur in exchange for a portion of the profit of the entrepreneur's venture. Al-mudharaba al-mutlaqah specifies which party receives what portion of the profit, but leaves all other things to the entrepreneur's discretion.

Al-Muhtakir In Islamic finance, a person who hoards commodities in hopes of raising the price in order to increase his own gains. For example, a grain farmer who controls a large portion of the market may refuse to sell his grain until the price goes up. This practice is considered unjust and is prohibited in Islam.

Al-Muqaassah In Islamic law, a term for the settlement of accounts.

Al-Musaaqah In Islamic law, an agreement whereby a landowner pays another party a portion of his harvest for the year in exchange for help irrigating his land so the plants can grow.

Al-Mustad'aafiin In Islamic law, the oppressed, poor persons in society who accept their fate of oppression. One of the goals of Islamic law is to promote equity (though not equality) between the rich and the poor.

Al-Mustakbiriin In Islamic law, the wealthy persons in society who exploit the poor. One of the goals of Islamic law is to promote equity (though not equality) between the rich and the poor.

Al-Mustarsil In Islamic law, a buyer or seller who, through ignorance, pays too much or receives too little for the goods he buys or sells. For example, a tourist may pay too much for a souvenir because he/she does not know how to reduce the price through negotiation.

Al-Muzaar'ah In Islamic law, an agreement whereby a landowner pays another party a portion of his harvest for the year in exchange for help tilling his land so the plants can grow.

Aln A Swedish unit of length approximately equivalent to 59.4 centimeters. Its plural is alnar.

Al-Naazirah In Islamic law, the agreement by a lender to postpone repayment if a borrower declares that he/she is unable to pay. In order to be sharia-compliant, the lender may not demand any compensation for granting al-naazirah.

Al-Najiz In Islamic law, a term for a cash sale.

Al-Naqdain An Arabic term referring to both gold and silver.

Al-Nashsh In Islamic law, a measure of weight. One nashsh is equivalent to approximately 59.5 grams.

Al-Nawaah In Islamic law, a measure of weight. One nawaah is approximately equivalent to 15 grams.

Alongside The side of a ship or other overseas vessel. A good that is about to be loaded onto a ship may be said to be alongside the ship if it is lying on the dock. See also: Free alongside ship.

Alpha 1. The measure of the performance of a portfolio after adjusting for risk. Alpha is calculated by comparing the volatility of the portfolio and comparing it to some benchmark. The alpha is the excess return of the portfolio over the benchmark. It is important to Markowitz portfolio theory and is used as a technical indicator. **2.** The excess return that a portfolio makes over and above what the capital asset pricing model estimates.

Alpha Coefficient In the capital asset pricing model, a measure of an investment's performance over and above the performance of investments of the same risk. It is graphically represented by the intersection of the security characteristic line and the x-axis. In a perfectly efficient market, the alpha coefficient ought to be zero (that is, all investments with the same risk should perform the same), but this rarely happens. It is also called Treynor's alpha. See also: Alpha.

Alpha Pup In business, a slang term for a young adult likely to set trends in consumer use. Alpha pups are most useful in focus groups and similar situations.

Alpha Risk When testing a hypothesis, the risk of rejecting a piece of data that should have been accepted. Many tests reject some data as unusable or irrelevant. Alpha risk is the probability that the wrong data will be eliminated from the sample. It is also called type I error or alpha error. See also: Beta risk.

Alpha Stocks The most commonly traded stocks on an exchange, especially those with the largest market capitalization. For example, an exchange with 2,000 companies trading on it may designate 150 alpha stocks.

Alpha-2 The most common code used by the International Organization for Standardization to identify countries and some territories. An alpha-2 code consists of two letters. For example, the code for the Kingdom of Bahrain is BH.

Alphabet Rounds The early attempts for a start-up to procure financing for itself through the issue of bonds or some other means. The term derives its name from the fact that the first attempt is called an A-round, the second attempt is called a B-round, and so forth.

Alphabet Stock A common stock with some feature distinguishing it from other common stock in the same company. Publicly-traded companies sometimes issue common shares of different classes, which usually affects the shares' voting rights. For example, class A shares usually carry more voting rights than class B shares. The name derives from the fact that these stocks usually are distinguished by different letters of the alphabet.

Alphanumeric Character A letter or number, as opposed to another character such as punctuation. Some programs can only read alphanumeric characters. For example, some e-mail programs may not recognize "!" or "+" as part of a password.

Al-Qasabah In Islamic law, a measure of area. One qasabah is approximately equivalent to 13.7 square meters.

Al-Qiimah In Islamic finance, a term for the prevailing market price of a good or service.

Al-Qiimii In Islamic law, a term for non-fungibles.

Al-Radkh In Islamic law, a small gift, especially one given to a non-combatant after a war.

Al-Ribaa al-Mu'taad In Islamic law, reasonable profit. It is forbidden for a business to exceed reasonable profit as this is considered exploitative and harmful to the poor. What qualifies as al-ribaa al-mu'taad is not defined.

Al-Riibah In Islamic law, income that bears resemblance to riba, which is a term for interest on debt. Because Islam prohibits riba, it is not always clear whether al-riibah is legal (and consequently if one may keep it).

Al-Safqah An Arabic term for a contract or a sale. The term literally denotes striking two hands together to finalize an agreement.

Alt Tab A computer command that changes the visible program. For example, one may press alt+tab to switch the visible program from Facebook to Microsoft Word. Alt tabbing may enable an employee to look busy when a manager passes by his/her desk.

Alteration of Share Capital A change in the number of authorized shares a company may issue. Authorized shares are the total shares a company is permitted to issue, as opposed to the number it actually has issued. To alter share capital, a company must amend its charter and/or bylaws and register the change with the appropriate regulatory authority.

Altered Check A check on which the name, amount, or other information has been changed in order to defraud someone. For example, one may change the name of the payee from John Smith to John Smythe, which will result in John Smythe receiving payment. The liability for funds lost on an altered check depends on which party involved displays negligence.

Alternate Director A temporary delegate for a member of a board of directors who stands in during his/her absence.. While laws vary, in most jurisdictions, the alternate director has the same rights and responsibilities as the member he/she represents.

Alternate Sponsorship An agreement in which two companies advertising different products buy the same broadcast time together, each paying for half, and alternate which product is advertised. For example, two companies may buy time from a station at 3:30 p.m. Monday through Thursday. Company A may broadcast its product Monday and Wednesday, while Company B does the same Tuesday and

Thursday. Alternate sponsorship reduces costs for advertisers and is most common when a timeslot has largely the same audience several days per week.

Alternate Weeks In broadcast advertising, an agreement whereby a radio or television station puts out a commercial for one week, then refrains for a week, then puts it out for one more week. The advertiser then pays for two weeks of advertising even though the commercial will be broadcast over the course of three weeks.

Alternate-Bundles Run In advertising, a method in which an advertiser requests that a periodical print different ads for the same product in different copies of the same issue. For example, an advertiser may purchase page 34 of a magazine, but request two different ads run in different copies. This allows the advertiser to test which ad is more effective and adjust its tactics accordingly.

Alternative Assets Highly valuable assets that are not usually found in a portfolio. Examples include rare coins and stamps, artwork, a Babe Ruth rookie card, and so forth. Alternative assets are usually less liquid than other assets because they are more difficult to sell and are often highly expensive. However, one may add alternative assets to a portfolio because they tend to maintain their values when the rest of the market is performing poorly. An alternative asset may aid in portfolio diversification. Some banks charge an additional fee to store alternative assets because of their sensitive nature. See also: Christie's.

Alternative Currency Option An option contract purchased in one currency with the payoff in another currency. For example, one may buy a call option with U.S. dollars, giving one the right to buy the underlying asset in Bahraini dinars. An alternative currency option can be used to hedge the foreign exchange risk of other investments.

Alternative Delivery Procedure Any provision in a futures contract that allows the buyer or the seller to make or receive delivery in a way that differs from the procedures set forth in the contract. A party often activates an alternative delivery procedure when it becomes advantageous for his/her investment strategy. See also: Cash settlement.

Alternative Depreciation Schedule In the Modified Accelerated Cost Recovery System, a system of depreciation in which the cost of purchasing an asset is recovered over a fairly long period of time. This shows the asset as having a higher value each year. Therefore, the owner has a higher net worth than he/she would using the General Depreciation Schedule.

Alternative Hypothesis A hypothesis the tester wishes to prove. When testing a hypothesis, a scientist often begins with an alternative hypothesis and a null hypothesis, which cannot be true. He/she then attempts to prove the alternative hypothesis, often by trying to prove the null hypothesis false.

Alternative Investment Any investment other than a stock, bond, or cash. Prominent examples include derivatives, hedge funds, real estate, and commodities. Most of the time, institutional investors and high net-worth individuals are the main holders of alternative investments. This is because they are subject to fewer regulations and are consequently riskier than most other investments. Alternative investments are rarely required to publish independently verifiable financial information. They also have particularly high minimum investments, which discourage casual investors. Alternative investments are controversial in many quarters. Because of the comparative lack of regulation and disclosure, they are subject to scrutiny from politicians and economic analysts. However, they often have high (sometimes very high) returns.

Alternative Investment Market Any investment other than a stock, bond, or cash. Prominent examples include derivatives, hedge funds, real estate, and commodities. Most of the time, institutional investors and high net-worth individuals are the main holders of alternative investments. This is because they are subject to fewer regulations and are consequently riskier than most other investments. Alternative investments are rarely required to publish independently verifiable financial information. They also have particularly high minimum investments, which discourage casual investors. Alternative investments are controversial in many quarters. Because of the comparative lack of regulation and disclosure, they are subject to scrutiny from politicians and economic analysts. However, they often have high returns.

Alternative Media Any non-mainstream media. For example, fringe right- and left-wing groups may operate their own radio stations or websites. More broadly, alternative media may include any small media outlet that is not controlled by a large corporation or a government. Advertising in alternative media may provide a cheap way to appeal to a niche audience.

Alternative Minimum Cost Method Either of two ways a company can choose to finance its pension plan. The company may use the actuarial cost method or the accrued benefit cost method, depending on which is cheaper.

Alternative Minimum Tax A tax in the United States intended to be levied on very wealthy persons who are eligible for so many deductions that they would otherwise have little or no tax liability. To arrive at the AMT, one adds certain deductions back into a person's adjusted gross income and then subtracts the AMT exemption, which results in the alternative minimum tax income. The taxpayer then pays a percentage of the alternative minimum tax income rather than his/her AGI. The AMT is controversial in the United States because it is not indexed to inflation, meaning that upper middle class families are gradually becoming subject to it, rather than only the very wealthy. See also: Tentative minimum tax, Bracket creep.

Alternative Minimum Tax Income In the United States, income subject to the alternative minimum tax. It is calculated by adding certain deductions back into a person's adjusted gross income and then subtracting the AMT exemption. The

taxpayer pays a percentage of the alternative minimum tax income rather than his/her AGI. See also: Tentative minimum tax, Bracket creep.

Alternative Mortgage Instrument Any mortgage loan other than a fixed rate, amortized, conventional mortgage. Examples include adjustable-rate mortgages and hybrid mortgages. They are most popular when interest rates are high and more people cannot afford a regular mortgage, or when a larger number of people are buying investment property. The proliferation of alternative mortgage instruments has been cited as a contributing factor in causing the 2008 economic crisis.

Alternative Risk Financing Facility An insurance company that provides a wide variety of products not otherwise available to its policyholders. While the products themselves are fairly standard, the policyholders of alternative risk financing facilities often cannot obtain them because policies are too expensive or because the individuals or companies involved cannot qualify as self-insurers. Most alternative risk financing facilities maintain their headquarters in Bermuda.

Alternative Tariff In international commerce, a tariff that charges two or more rates for the same goods going to and from the same places. A rational shipper seeks to pay the lowest alternative tariff possible.

Alternative Valuation Date Six months after the death of a person subject to the estate tax. If the executor of an estate believes that the value of an estate is declining or will decline, he/she may use the alternative valuation date for purposes of determining the value of the estate. This reduces the estate tax owed. Otherwise, the executor uses the date of the person's death.

Altman Z-Score A method for determining the likelihood of a company's bankruptcy in the coming two years. A company's Z-score is determined by the application of four or five ratios as variables, each weighted for importance according to a certain formula. The original ratios are working capital / total assets, retained earnings / total assets, EBIT / total assets, market value of equity / book value of liabilities, and sales / total assets. Different versions of the Altman Z-score may use slightly different variables and may weight them differently. A higher score is a positive sign, with a score over 2.99 meaning the company is "safe." The Z-score has predicted corporate bankruptcies with more than 70% accuracy.

Altyn A coin formerly minted in Russia. Thought to originally have been some denomination of gold, it became the nickname of a three kopek coin, though this has not been minted since 1991.

Aluminum The most abundant metal in the crust of the Earth. Because it is not very dense and is resistant to corrosion, it has a wide variety of commercial uses, notably in transportation, packaging, and construction. It is also used in home appliances. Aluminum is also spelled aluminium, especially in countries where British English predominates.

AM 1. ISO 3166-1 alpha-2 code for the Republic of Armenia. This is the code used in international transactions to and from Armenian bank accounts. **2.** ISO 3166-2 geocode for Armenia. This is used as an international standard for shipping to Armenia. Each Armenian region and the city of Yerevan have their own codes with the prefix "AM." For example, the code for the Province of Ararat is ISO 3166-2:AM-AR.

AM Station A station that broadcasts using radio waves. The technology is simpler than that used at an FM station. AM stations dominated radio until about 1980, when FM stations became more popular. Even still, AM stations broadcast a wide variety of programs, especially related sports and news.

Amah An ancient Hebrew unit of length approximately equivalent to 50 centimeters.

Amah al Amah An ancient Hebrew unit of area variously equivalent to values between 2,300 and 3,300 square centimeters.

Amakudari The practice in which a senior Japanese bureaucrat retires from the civil service and takes an executive position at a private company. The former bureaucrat's personal and professional ties to the former position are thought to help the company receive information or favors. Amakudari generally occurs between ages 50 and 60. The word is Japanese for "descent from heaven."

Amanah In Saudi Arabia, a political subdivision equivalent to a municipality.

Amani A former currency super-division in Afghanistan. One amani was worth 10 Afghan rupees.

Amaranthed A slang term for a hedge fund that takes on too much risk and spectacularly fails. An amaranthed may result from overexposure to a specific industry or sector.

Amass To gather or to collect. The term is used in business especially in relation to a person or company that has gathered something needed or desired. For example, a person may amass wealth or inventory.

Amateur Investor An investor who deals in securities but does not do so professionally. Amateur investors participate in the markets for any number of reasons. They may be unemployed and trade penny stocks to pay bills, or they may invest because they want to control their retirements directly. Some professional investors may look down on amateur investors out of a belief that they are motivated by emotion or they are ignorant of the best investment strategies. However, there is little evidence to support this idea. See also: Odd-lotter, Odd-lot theory.

Amazonian Cooperation Treaty A treaty, signed by eight South American nations in 1978, that protects approximately 3 million square miles in the Amazon. The treaty also protects the petroleum interests of indigenous peoples, among other things.

AMBAC Financial Group, Inc. A holding company whose subsidiaries provide guarantees and principal and interest payments on debt securities and some asset-backed securities. AMBAC's subsidiaries also provide other financial services, such as swaps and investment advice, mainly to state and local governments in the United States. It was founded in 1971 and is based in New York City.

Ambassador The highest ranking foreign diplomat representing a country to another government. For example, the highest ranking British representative in the United States is the ambassador from the United Kingdom. An ambassador speaks for the government he/she represents.

Ambiguity Unclear language in a contract. In the event of a dispute over ambiguous language, a court usually sides with the party, if it exists, that possesses less knowledge or experience in how contracts are constructed. The thinking behind this is that the more experienced party ought to know better than to put ambiguous language in a contract. See also: Ambiguous statement.

Ambiguous Statement In advertising, any statement that does not have a specific meaning. Ambiguous statements are particularly useful if a new product does not have a target audience or if the producer is unsure to whom it will appeal. For example, an advertiser may call a new product "fresh" in its advertising because, although it may mean different things to different people, it is usually interpreted positively.

AMD ISO 4217 code for the Armenian dram. It was introduced in 1993, replacing the Soviet ruble. It is a floating currency.

Amend To change by some formal process. For example, one may amend a charter to change how a company operates. Likewise, one may amend a tax return to make it more accurate.

Amended Return A tax return in the United States correcting one or more errors on a return from a previous year. One files an amended return if events have shown that a taxpayer likely has a greater or lesser tax liability than previously thought. The IRS uses File 1040X to file amended returns.

Amenities Anything that makes a property, good, or service more appealing. For example, a grocer may offer free home delivery for the elderly, or a condo may offer free access to a gym.

America Online An Internet company that was instrumental in bringing online services to the public. It provided an online community through its software that allowed customers to share information and communicate with each other. Eventually, AOL provided access to the Internet as a whole. At one time, 30 million people in the United States alone received their Internet connection through AOL.

American Academy of Actuaries A professional and lobbying organization for actuaries in the United States. In addition to promoting legislation on behalf of the actuarial industry, it creates and enforces professional standards for members, primarily through the Actuarial Standards Board.

American Accounting Association A professional organization for academics who specialize in the study of accounting. It publishes The Accounting Review, a journal with a variety of articles germane to the accounting profession. It also promotes accounting education through research and conferences. It was established in 1916 and its headquarters are in Florida.

American Advertising Federation A lobbying organization for advertisers and advertising agencies in the United States. It promotes legislation on behalf of the advertising industry and also conducts conferences and educates members on new and growing trends. Through its college chapters, it provides real-life case studies for university students interested in advertising. Its headquarters are in Washington, D.C.

American Agency System A way to sell insurance whereby a self-employed individual or an independent company offers policies through different, competing insurers. This person or company is responsible for finding potential policyholders and often explains the advantages and disadvantages of individual policies. If a client buys a policy, the person or company receives a commission from the insurer. The advantages to the American agency system are that it keeps costs down for insurance companies (because they do not have to pay for marketing themselves) and provides potential policyholders a wider array of options. It is also called the independent agency system.

American Annuity Table A table formerly used to calculate premiums for deferred annuities based upon the age (and therefore the expected mortality) of an annuitant. It was replaced in 1983.

American Arbitration Association A private company that provides support for arbitration. Arbitration is an extrajudicial means of resolving a dispute in which the parties agree to make their cases before an impartial person or panel. While the American Arbitration Association does not serve as this person or panel, it can provide assistance to the arbitrators. For example, it may provide the rules that the arbitrators must follow. It also may appoint an arbitrator if the disputing parties cannot agree on one. It is based in New York City.

American Association of Advertising Agencies A lobbying and trade organization for advertising agencies in the United States. In addition to promoting legislation on behalf of the advertising industry, it also provides resources for advertising agencies. For example, it publishes the AAAA spot contract, which is a standardized contract members may use to save the cost of creating special contracts for each client. Its headquarters are in New York City.

American Association of Exporters and Importers An organization that promotes the interests of companies that import into and export out of the United States. The AAEI lobbies before Congress, the U.S. Trade Representative, other government agencies and foreign powers. Members consist of manufacturers, distributors, and retailers, as well as banks, insurance companies, and others. It seeks the elimination of most trade barriers, promotes free trade, and monitors trade sanctions.

American Association of Individual Investors An organization that provides information by and for small investors. Its website provides much of its information; it also publishes a monthly journal. Local chapters provide information pertinent to individual members. Founded in 1979, the AAII has over 150,000 members and is based in Chicago.

American Automobile Association A non-profit organization that sells car insurance, provides assistance to members, and lobbies on behalf of motorists. It was established in 1902 in Chicago and is now based in Florida. It is often called AAA ("Triple A").

American Bankers Association A professional organization for banks and bankers in the United States. Among other things, it lobbies on behalf of the banking industry and conducts educational and professional development activities. It was established in 1875 and is based in Washington, D.C.

American Bar Association The most prestigious professional association for lawyers and law students in the United States. It provides law school accreditation, sets ethical standards for members, and offers continuing education. It was established in 1878 and is based in Chicago, with a large office in Washington, D.C.

American Buffalo A gold bullion coin minted in the United States. It is 99.99% pure gold and began to be minted in 2006. Its face value is $50 and it is largely uncirculated.

American Business Conference A lobbying organization for presidents, CEOs, and other executives in companies with at least $25 million in annual revenue. The American Business Conference states its goal is to help medium-sized businesses maximize their potential by promoting high growth government policies. It is based in Washington, D.C.

American Business Initiative An organization that promotes the export of American goods to countries in Eastern Europe. It especially promotes energy, telecommunications, agricultural, and housing products.

American Business Press, Inc. An organization for companies that specialize in business-to-business communication. Members include book publishers and software developers. It provides information on finance, government affairs, marketing, and other areas. It was established in 1907.

American College An educational institution that offers a variety of professional certifications in the financial field. Perhaps most prominently, it offers the ChFP and CFP certifications. Most of its students matriculate through distance learning programs, allowing the American College to reach more people. It is based in Bryn Mawr, Pennsylvania.

American Corporate Accrual Receipts Also called ACARS, a corporate bond whose coupons have been separated from the principal. ACARS therefore pay no interest. They are sold at a significant discount from par and mature at par. ACARS fluctuate in price, sometimes dramatically, because changes in interest rates make them more or less desirable. See also: zero-coupon bond, STRIPS.

American Council of Engineering Companies A lobbying group representing engineering companies in the United States. It represents approximately 5,500 private firms and advocates in their interest before the federal government. Its primary advocacy issues include tax, regulation, and the environment.

American Council of Life Insurance A lobbying organization for companies in the United States offering life insurance, retirement plans, long-term care insurance, and similar products. It presses for legislation favorable to the industry, conducts events, and provides networking activities for members. It is based in Washington, D.C.

American Customer Satisfaction Index An economic indicator in the United States. It measures satisfaction with various products in approximately 80,000 consumers a year. It uses econometric modeling to complement the surveys. The Index has been published since 1994 and is based at the University of Michigan.

American Depositary Receipt Fee A fee that an American bank assesses on the issuer of a foreign stock in exchange for re-issuing that stock as an American depository receipt.

American Depository Receipt A certificate issued by an American bank representing a share of a foreign stock that the bank holds in trust but that is traded on an American stock exchange. An American depository receipt is dollar-denominated and entitles the bearer to any dividends and other benefits associated with the stock underlying it. ADRs can be traded like any other security. ADRs shield investors from foreign exchange risk and any applicable tariffs they would have had to pay if they had bought the stock outright. They also exempt the investor from any other requirements the foreign exchange authority might have levied. See also: International Depository Receipt.

American Depository Receipt Ratio The number of foreign shares represented by a single American Depository Receipt (ADR). An ADR is a certificate issued by a bank representing a certain number of shares of a stock the bank holds in trust, but that are traded on a foreign stock exchange and denominated in U.S. dollars. The number of shares represented by a single ADR is at the discretion of the bank issuing the ADR. The ADR ratio can have an effect on the price of the ADR.

American Depository Share A certificate issued by an American bank representing a share of a foreign stock the bank holds in trust but that is traded on an

American stock exchange. An American depository share is dollar-denominated and entitles the bearer to any dividends and other benefits associated with the single share underlying it. In other words, an American depository share is a single share of an American depository receipt.

American Economic Association A professional organization for academics who specialize in the study of economics. It publishes several journals, in addition to sponsoring conferences, encouraging research, and hosting a job fair. It was established in 1885 in New York; its business office is in Tennessee.

American Experience Table An early table showing the number of deaths and the life expectancies of people who purchased life insurance at various ages. It was based on data collected between 1843 and 1858 and was published in 1868. It was used in the calculation of life insurance premiums until being replaced by the CSO table.

American Express A financial services company based in New York. It began in 1850 as an express mail service. In 1882, it began offering money orders and later developed traveler's cheques in 1891. Today, it offers charge cards and other forms of credit to individuals and companies. It is one of the 30 companies tracked by the Dow Jones Industrial Average.

American Federation of Labor and Congress of Industrial Organizations The largest umbrella organization for unions in the United States. It represents more than 11 million workers in the U.S. and Canada. While it has little direct control over member unions, it is a powerful political force for organized labor and carries a great deal of influence. It was established in 1955 as the result of a merger between the AFL and the CIO.

American Federation of Musicians of the United States and Canada A labor union for North American musicians. It lobbies and negotiates contracts for better pay and working conditions. It also attempts to protect copyrights for musicians' intellectual property. It was established in 1896 by members of the American Federation of Labor (now the AFL-CIO).

American Federation of Television and Radio Artists A labor union for American journalists, actors, and others who are broadcast on radio or television. It lobbies and negotiates contracts for better pay and working conditions; it also advocates for members in the event of a lawsuit. It was established in 1937 and is based in New York and Los Angeles. It is affiliated with the AFL-CIO.

American Gas Association A lobbying organization for natural gas producers in the United States. It also conducts research for the natural gas industry and generally promotes it to the public. More than 90% of natural gas customers in the United States buy from an AGA member. It was established in 1918 and is based in Alexandria, Virginia.

American Gold Eagle The official gold bullion coin minted in the United States. It is 91.67% pure gold and began to be minted in 1986. It is largely uncirculated.

American Guild of Musical Artists A labor union for American singers, dancers and other performers. Among other activities, it lobbies and negotiates contracts for better pay and working conditions. Unlike most other performers' unions, it does not forbid members from doing non-union work. It was established in 1936 and is affiliated with the AFL-CIO and the Associated Actors and Artistes of America.

American Institute for Property and Liability Underwriters An educational institute that offers the Chartered Property and Casualty Underwriter (CPCU) certification. In order to qualify for a CPCU, one must pass the Institute's coursework, which includes classes on accounting, finance, insurance, and so forth. It is located in Malvern, Pennsylvania.

American Institute in Taiwan A non-profit organization in the United States that effectively serves as its embassy to Taiwan. When American relations with the People's Republic of China were normalized in 1979, the United States had to revoke recognition of the Republic of China, which controls Taiwan. In response, the American Institute in Taiwan was established as a non-official organization by which the U.S. could communicate with the Taiwanese government. It is staffed by Department of State employees (though for a time they had to resign from the Department of State for the duration of their assignment at the Institute). While it maintains a small headquarters in Virginia, its largest office is in Taipei, Taiwan.

American Institute of Banking An educational organization that offers more than 100 courses on banking each year. It awards diplomas and certificates to those who complete its coursework, which is offered online. More than 150,000 people matriculate through the AIB each year. It was founded in 1907.

American Institute of Certified Public Accountants A professional organization for accountants. In addition to operating the Certified Public Accountant exam, it sets ethical standards and some professional standards, especially for accountants working as individuals and for privately held companies. Until the 1970s, they maintained the Generally Accepted Accounting Practices. It traces its history to the late 19th century and was formally established in 1916.

American Insurance Association A lobbying organization for property and casualty insurance companies in the United States. It represents companies that sell car insurance, catastrophe insurance, and malpractice insurance, among others. Among other lobbying activities, it presses for lower taxation and regulatory reform of the insurance industry. It traces its origins to the National Board of Fire Underwriters, established in 1866. It is based in Washington, D.C.

American Jobs Creation Act United States legislation, passed in 2004, that repealed a subsidy for American exporters and extended tax relief to them (and others) in order to compensate them. It cut taxes for farmers and manufacturers and increased penalties for tax shelters. Proponents argued it would provide an incentive to create American jobs, while opponents contended it only made the tax code more complex.

American Management Association A non-profit organization in the United States that provides continuing education and professional development to companies, governments, and individuals. It was founded in 1913 and is based in New York City.

American Marketing Association A professional organization in the United States for companies and individuals who practice or study marketing. Among other things, it manages educational and professional development activities, along with conducting research and providing networking opportunities. It is based in Chicago.

American National Standards Institute A non-profit organization that oversees development of voluntary standards of quality for products of governments and private companies. Members include government agencies, corporations, academics, and other individuals. While it was established by groups primarily interested in engineering standards, it works in other fields as well, notably health care. It was founded in 1918.

American Opportunity Credit A tax credit in the United States making a dollar-for-dollar reduction in the tax liability of a postsecondary student equivalent to 100% of tuition and education fees, up to $2,500. Up to 40% of the credit is a refundable tax credit. Certain income limits apply to a student's eligibility. It was instituted in 2009 and is scheduled to expire in 2012.

American Option An option contract that may be exercised at any time on or before the expiration date. For example, if one buys an American call giving him/her the right to buy shares in X expiring on the final Friday in March, the call may be exercised at any time on or before the final Friday in March. The differentiating feature of an American option is the fact that its value varies according to the value of the underlying asset over the life of the contract. This means that a holder may wait for an advantageous price and exercise the option. This contrasts with a European-style option, which may only be exercised on the expiration date.

American Plan A 1920s term for a non-union company. The term derives from a meeting of anti-union employers in Chicago in 1921. These employers agreed to refuse to negotiate with unions; they also required their employees to sign a pledge stating they would not join a union, deeming them "un-American." The American plan resulted in at least a 25% decrease in union membership in the United States between 1921 and 1923.

American Platinum Eagle The official platinum bullion coin minted in the United States. It is 99.95% pure platinum and began to be minted in 1997. It is largely uncirculated.

American Principles Project A nonprofit organization in the United States dedicated to promoting politically conservative causes. It is especially notable for its support of the return to the gold standard for the U.S. dollar. It is based in Washington, D.C.

American Risk and Insurance Association A professional organization for academics that specializes in the study of risk and insurance. It publishes two peer-reviewed journals, in addition to sponsoring conferences, conducting research, and providing grants. It was established in 1932 and its headquarters are in Malvern, Pennsylvania.

American Selling Price The way a tariff was calculated under the Fordney-McCumber Act of 1922. That is, the American selling price indicated that a tariff on an import into the United States would be calculated according to the price of a similar, American-made good rather than the manufacturer's price. For example, the tariff on a particular good might be 50% of a good's price. If a British company made that good for $20 and an American company for $50, the American selling price standard would put the tariff on the British-made good at $25 (50% of $50) rather than $10 (50% of $20). The American selling price standard, among other provisions of the Fordney-McCumber Act, is believed to have harmed the American economy.

American Silver Eagle The official silver bullion coin minted in the United States. It is 99.9% pure silver and began to be minted in 1986. It is largely uncirculated.

American Society for Quality A professional organization for quality control experts. It offers training and certification programs to members. It also advises nonprofits and government bodies at the federal, state, and local levels on how to implement quality control within their respective competencies. It was established in 1946 and is based in Milwaukee, Wisconsin. It used to be called the American Society for Quality Control (ASQC).

American Society of Appraisers A professional organization for persons who estimate the value of property. It represents persons who evaluate real estate, gems, machinery, and other forms of property. It offers a certification program to persons who have at least five years of experience, who have completed an examination, and who have had at least two appraisals reviewed. It was established in 1936 and is based in Herndon, Virginia.

American Society of Composers, Authors and Publishers An organization for American writers, musical composers, and others who have been published. It monitors public performances and distribution of members' works, collects fees, and distributes royalties. It was established in 1914 and is based in New York.

American Society of Women Accountants An organization dedicated to promoting women in the accounting field. It was established in 1938 in Indiana and has expanded nationwide. It hosts a large number of training and networking events per year. Members are encouraged to seek advice from one another on accounting and professional issues. It is based in Virginia.

American Statistical Association A professional organization for statisticians in the United States. It encourages the research and application of statistics in a variety of fields. The ASA also publishes a number of journals to further its work. Established in 1839, it is the second-oldest organization of its type still in existence. It is based in Virginia.

American Stock Exchange On October 1, 2008, it changed its name to NYSE Alternext U.S. Prior to its 2008 acquisition by NYSE Euronext, the American Stock Exchange was a mutually owned stock exchange located in Manhattan. Of the three main U.S. stock exchanges, it has the most liberal policies on company listing, having more small companies than either the NYSE or NASDAQ. As a result, it is smaller than either of those stock exchanges by trading volume, handling only about 10% of American securities.

American Television and Radio Commercials Festival A competition for the best broadcast commercial. It is held each year to honor excellence in the broadcast advertising field. Nominees are entered into a variety of categories, and winners receive an award called the Clio.

American Traders Index A list of all domestic clients of the U.S. and Foreign Commercial Service (US&FCS). It is used by US&FCS branches outside the United States to create mailing lists.

American Women's Society of Certified Public Accountants An organization dedicated to promoting women in the accounting field. In particular, it encourages continuing education for members and publishes a journal called The Woman CPA. It was established in 1933 and is based in Ohio.

Americans with Disabilities Act Legislation in the United States, passed in 1990, that extended civil rights laws to persons who are physically disabled. Among other provisions, it requires facilities to accommodate the disabled insofar as it is possible. Businesses must comply with the Act when they build or expand their buildings. For example, most new commercial buildings with steps are required to provide access for persons who use wheelchairs.

Americus Trust A trust containing common stock that issued two types of units representing that stock: primes and scores. Holders of primes received all dividends that were issued for the life of the trust plus, at maturity, the total value of the share up to a certain amount. Score holders received the excess of that certain amount. Americus trusts no longer exist as the result of a tax ruling in 1987 that eliminated most of their tax advantages. See also: PERC.

Amero A proposed currency for a hypothetical monetary union of Canada, Mexico, and the United States. Proponents of the amero argue that it would save billions in foreign exchange transactions and would increase trade. Critics cite both loss of independent monetary policies and national sovereignty as reasons for opposing the amero.

AMEX Composite Index An index, weighted for market value, of all stocks and other securities traded on the American Stock Exchange relative to their value on December 29, 1995.

AMEX Oil Index An index tracking approximately a dozen major petroleum companies, including ConocoPhillips and BP. It is considered an indicator of the performance of the oil industry. It is a price-weighted index.

Amicus Curiae Latin for "friend of the court." A person who is not a party to a case but offers expert or other relevant information on a point of law in order to help the judge or jury make a decision. An amicus curiae may offer testimony (provided it is unsolicited by either party in the case) or write a brief or legal treatise on the matter at hand. The court has full discretion whether or not to accept the statement of an amicus curiae.

Amidships At or near the middle of a ship. This term is used when transporting goods over water. See also: International commerce.

Amivest Liquidity Ratio A measure of the liquidity of a security. It is calculated by taking the dollar volume of a security for a given month and dividing by the percentage of change to the stock's price in that same month.

AM-Lira Currency that was legal tender in some Allied-occupied parts of Italy during World War II. The AM-lira was issued when soldiers could not be paid in the local currency and because paying them in U.S. dollars posed the risk of high inflation due to the fact that the dollar had a high value at the time relative to most European currencies. Military leaders declared Allied Military Currency legal tender and required local retailers and others to accept it as payment. Nevertheless, the AM-lira was subject to high inflation. It was issued between 1943 and 1945.

Amman Financial Market A securities exchange in Jordan. It was established in 1976 and traded in stocks, government and corporate bonds, and negotiable certificates of deposit, among other securities. It was the only exchange in Jordan and was replaced by the Amman Stock Exchange in 1999.

Amman Stock Exchange A securities exchange in Jordan. It was established in 1999; both stocks and bonds trade on its floor. It operates two indices, including, most notably, the ASE Market Capitalization Weighted Index.

Ammatu An ancient Akkadian unit of length approximately equivalent to 497 centimeters.

Amortization 1. A tax deduction for the gradual consumption of the value of an asset, especially an intangible asset. For example, if a company spends $1 million on a patent that expires in 10 years, it amortizes the expense by deducting $100,000 from its taxable income over the course of 10 years. It is often used interchangeably with

depreciation, which technically refers to the same thing for tangible assets. **2.** The act of repaying a loan in regular payments over a given period of time.

Amortization Term The period of time over which a mortgage or other loan is amortized. See also: Repayment period.

Amortized Loan A loan with the same payment each pay period. In an amortized loan, different amounts go to principal and interest each month. This allows the lender to receive the full amount of interest while also keeping periodic payments equal. See also: Self-Amortizing loan.

Amortized Value The value of a bond as determined by the process of amortization. The amortized value of a bond may be used as its asset value on a balance sheet.

Amortizing Cap An interest rate cap on a loan that gradually decreases as the principal on loan is repaid. This means that while the interest rate (and therefore one's payments) may change, the amount by which it may change lessens over time.

Amortizing Collar An interest rate collar on a loan that gradually changes as the principal on the loan is repaid. This means that while the interest rate (and therefore one's payments) may change, the maximum and minimum interest rates may also change over time.

Amortizing Interest Rate Swap An interest rate swap with no special features, except for the fact that the notional amount over which the interest is calculated declines over time. See also: Plain vanilla swap.

Amortizing Option An option in which the underlying asset is an interest rate or an interest rate swap. In both cases, the notional amount over which the interest rate is calculated gradually decreases (or is "amortized") over time. The amount by which it decreases is usually tied to repayment on a loan or other liability.

Amortizing Swaption An option in which the underlying asset is an interest rate swap with a notional amount (the theoretical amount over which the interest rate is calculated) gradually decreases (or is "amortized") over time. The amount by which it decreases is usually tied to repayment on a loan or other liability.

Amount Any number or value. For example, if one's net worth is $4 million, the amount of the net worth is $4 million.

Amount at Risk 1. The difference between the amount an insurer must pay if an insured event occurs and the reserves from which it makes payments. **2.** The different between the amount of a loan and the amount the borrower still owes the lender, including interest. **3.** The difference between the cash value of a life insurance policy and the amount the insurer must pay if the policyholder dies.

Amount Financed The amount a borrower receives from a lender. The amount financed is usually equal to the principal less any finance charges, such as an application fee or down payment.

Amount of Insurance to Value The ratio of the amount for which a property is insured to its value. For example, if a property is insured for $120,000 and its market value is only $60,000, the amount of insurance to value is 2:1.

Amount of One per Period The interest that a $1 deposit accumulates as it compounds over time. This is often used as an example to demonstrate the power of compounding.

Amount Outstanding and in Circulation The money in a country issued by a mint that is available in cash for transactions by any party.

Amount Realized The amount for which one sells an asset. The amount realized may be a realized gain (in which the sale price exceeds the original purchase price) or a realized loss (in which the sale price is less than the original purchase price). It may also break even. The amount realized likely will affect one's taxable income.

Amount Subject In insurance, the amount likely to be lost in a disaster, depending on the risk of disaster in the area of the insured property. Insurance underwriters must estimate the amount subject for each policy. See also: Probable maximum loss.

Amounts Differ A check a bank does not honor because the amount written in numbers differs from the amount written in words. Most checks include spaces where the writer puts down both in numbers and in words the amount he/she wishes to pay to the recipient of the check. If the two do not match, the bank is unlikely to pay it because it will not know which amount is correct. Banks usually assess charges for unpaid checks.

Amphoe In Thailand, a political subdivision equivalent to a district.

Amphora Quadrantal An ancient Roman unit of liquid volume approximately equivalent to 26.2 liters.

Amplitude of Oscillation The amount by which a measure diverges from the mean value as it moves through time. See also: Oscillator.

Amsterdam Exchange The oldest stock exchange in the world. It was established in 1602 by the Dutch East India Trading Company and operated for centuries as an open outcry exchange for the trade of stocks and bonds. In 1997, it merged with the European Option Exchange to create AEX, which traded derivatives along with stocks and bonds. In 2000, it became part of Euronext.

Amsterdam Exchange Index An index of stocks traded on Euronext Amsterdam. Begun in 1983, AEX consists of the 25 stocks that are most actively traded on the exchange. It is weighted for market capitalization.

Amsterdam Interprofessional Market Also called AIM. A system for block trading between banks on the Amsterdam Exchange. The AIM was introduced in 1986.

Amt In Denmark and Germany, a political subdivision equivalent to a county.

AMT Exemption The amount of a person or company's income or profit that is not subject to the alternative minimum tax. The AMT exemption gradually decreases as one's income or profit increases.

AMTEL An internal messaging system used by some stock exchanges.

Amter In Denmark, a political subdivision equivalent to a county that was abolished in 2007.

Amtrak A government-owned corporation in the United States providing rail service between cities. All preferred stock is owned by the federal government, and the President appoints members of the board of directors (subject to Senate confirmation). Amtrak has never been self-sufficient. Critics of government-owned companies often point to this as a sign that the private market is better at running companies. Amtrak's defenders, however, point out that the U.S. government also must subsidize air travel (which is privately run).

AN 1. ISO 3166-1 alpha-2 code for Netherlands Antilles prior to its separation into Bonaire, Sint Eustatius and Saba, Curacao, and Sint Maarten in 2011. This was the code used in international transactions to and from bank accounts in Netherlands Antilles. **2.** ISO 3166-2 geocode for Netherlands Antilles. This was used as an international standard for shipping to Netherlands Antilles. In both cases, the code is obsolete.

Analog Signal A continuous, electrical wave containing data. The magnitude of the signal corresponds to the amount of data contained in it. An analog signal is one of two ways to change raw data into an electrical wave. See also: Digital system.

Analysis The practice of examining information to determine what conclusions it indicates,. The information observed in analysis depends on the type of analysis being conducted. For example, technical analysis uses statistics to determine future price movements of securities, while fundamental analysis looks at indicators of a company's intrinsic value. Analysis may involve qualitative or quantitative information, or both. Most forms of analysis have both strengths and weaknesses.

Analysis of Property and Casualty Policy A process that determines what properties a property and casualty insurance policy covers, where the properties are covered, what risks and persons are covered, how much coinsurance the policyholder must pay, and other restrictions or features of the policy.

Analysis of Variance A process of determining similarities between like groups. Analysis of variance is used in marketing to determine how likely groups with similar demographic backgrounds are to respond to a particular campaign.

Analyst A person who examines information to determine what it indicates about a company, situation, or anything else. The information observed by an analyst depends on the type of analysis being conducted. For example, technical analysts use statistics to determine future price movements of securities, while fundamental analysts look at indicators of a company's intrinsic value. Analysts may use qualitative or quantitative information, or both.

Analyst Coverage The number of analysts who observe a particular stock or other security. Large and well-known companies often have greater analyst coverage of their stocks than other companies. Greater analyst coverage often results in higher demand and therefore lower prices. Some value investors recommend buying securities with low analyst coverage because they could be undervalued.

Analytical Marketing System Any system whereby marketers use computers or computer-generated data to make decisions on how to market a product. For example, marketers may create a database of potential customers and use an analytical marketing system with certain inputs to determine the best target audience.

Analytical Review Any process by which a person or company looks at an account or financial statement and attempts to identify any irregularities. This may involve comparing financial and non-financial information. An analytical review is less thorough than an audit. In general, an analytical review can lead to an audit if odd information is found. A CPA often leads an analytical review.

Anarchism The belief that no government is beneficial. Anarchism historically has been associated with violence, especially during the late 19th and early 20th centuries. Anarchism exists in many different forms. Some on the far right believe in total individualism and voluntarism, while others on the far left believe that complete collectivism can replace the state.

Anarchist A person who believes no government is beneficial. Anarchists historically have been associated with violence, especially during the late 19th and early 20th centuries. Anarchism exists in many different forms. Some on the far right believe in total individualism and voluntarism, while others on the far left believe that complete collectivism can replace the state.

Anchal In Nepal, a political subdivision approximately equivalent to a province.

Anchor Tenant A large store that rents space in a mall or other shopping center. An anchor tenant has the ability to attract more people to the mall than the other tenants, and because it rents more space, it will generate more of the mall's revenue. Anchor tenants are often large department stores. Agreements with anchor tenants must be in place before most banks will finance the construction of a mall or shopping center.

Anchoring The act of basing an investment decision on irrelevant information. For example, if one bases the value of a stock on its price a year ago, one is practicing anchoring. This can be a dangerous practice, but it is also easy to do. Anchoring is a concept in behavioral economics, which states that people often make decisions based on their perceptions and feelings in addition to (and sometimes instead of) facts.

Ancillary 1. See: Ancillary benefit. **2.** See: Ancillary charge. **3.** See: Ancillary revenue.

Ancillary Benefit Any extra profit or other benefit involved in a transaction but not directly related to it. For example, one may earn a salary through one's company and also keep the frequent flyer miles one earns on the company credit card. In this case, the frequent flyer miles are ancillary benefits.

Ancillary Charge Any cost or other expense involved in a transaction but not directly related to it. For example, one may see a concert ticket advertised for $13 (no sales tax) but actually spend $30 on the ticket because of convenience and processing fees. Those fees are collectively called ancillary charges

Ancillary Credit Business A business that is involved with credit but does not offer credit itself. Examples of ancillary credit businesses include debt collection agencies, which collect the credit extended by others, and credit brokerages, which are businesses that make introductions between customers and companies that give credit.

Ancillary Revenue Revenue that a company derives from anything other than its main business. To give a very basic example, a liquor store may receive ancillary revenue from the sale of cigarette lighters and magazines at the cash register. Most companies have ancillary revenue of one kind or another; at times it may become the main revenue source. For example, a pool hall may find itself making more from selling beer than from renting pool tables.

Ancillary Service Endorsement A service offered by the U.S. Postal Service in which it sends information to a mailer on the new address of a recipient if that address has changed. The Postal Service charges a fee for this service. See also: ACS.

And 1. And. Short for And Interest. **2.** AND. The GOST 7.67 Latin three-letter geocode for Andorra. The code is used for transactions to and from Andorran bank accounts and for international shipping to Andorra. As with all GOST 7.67 codes, it is used primarily in Cyrillic alphabets.

And Interest A promise that a bond buyer will receive the interest that has accrued since the last coupon payment if he/she buys the indicated bond. This ordinarily increases the price by the amount of that interest.

Andean Community An international trade organization consisting of Bolivia, Colombia, Ecuador, and Peru, along with some associate and observer countries also located in Latin America. It was established in 1969; in 1992, member nations signed a free trade agreement.

Andean Development Corporation A multilateral lending facility owned by governments throughout South America. The Andean Development Corporation extends credit to public and private organizations in member countries engaging in projects related to international development. It was established in 1970 in Caracas, Venezuela.

Andean Reserve Fund A lending facility associated with the Andean Group. The Andean Reserve Fund extends credit to public and private organizations in member countries to reduce balance of payment deficits.

Andean Trade Initiative The structure that implements the Andean Trade Preference Act (ATPA). The ATI eliminates tariffs and other preferential treatments on most imports coming from Bolivia, Colombia, Ecuador, and Peru. The ATI is meant to encourage production of goods other than narcotics, for which the Andean area is known. See also: Caribbean Basin Initiative.

Andean Trade Preference Act United States legislation, enacted in 1991 and expanded in 2002, that reduces or eliminates tariffs and provides other preferential treatment to most imports coming from Bolivia, Colombia, Ecuador, and Peru. The 2002 expansion likewise provides duty free treatment of some products. The Act is meant to encourage production of goods other than narcotics, for which the Andean area is known. The Act has encouraged Andean countries to reduce their own tariffs on American exports. The structure that implements the Act is called the Andean Trade Initiative (ATI). See also: Caribbean Basin Initiative.

Andorran Franc A former currency of Andorra. In practice, the currency was identical to the French franc, which was replaced by the euro in 1999. The Andorran franc circulated alongside the Andorran peseta.

Andorran Peseta A former currency of Andorra. In practice, the currency was identical to the Spanish peseta, which was replaced by the euro in 1999. The Andorran peseta circulated alongside the Andorran franc.

Andrew Carnegie An American early industrialist. He began working at a factory as a boy and ascended the corporate ladder until he founded Carnegie Steel Company, which later became U.S. Steel. Believed by many to be one of the richest men in history, he became a philanthropist in later life and gave away most of his money. Critics claim he was an opponent of organized labor who paid his employees poorly under harsh working conditions. His supporters contend he lived the American dream, rising from poverty to wealth through hard work and dedication. He lived from 1835 to 1919. See also: Robber Baron.

Andrew Fastow The chief financial officer at Enron from 1998 until 2001. That year, it was revealed that many of Enron's assets were either overpriced or completely fictional; losses were hidden in offshore subsidies, and most profits were fraudulent. Fastow shared responsibility for much of this; he traded his testimony against co-conspirators in exchange for a lighter prison sentence. He was born in 1961.

ANG ISO 4217 code for the Netherlands Antillean guilder. The currency traces its origins to the 18th century but took its current name in 1952. Throughout most of its history, it was pegged to the Dutch guilder; however, after the occupation of the Netherlands during the Second World War, it switched the peg to the U.S. dollar. It has maintained this peg at different values ever since. It is known colloquially as the florin.

Angel 1. Informal for angel investor, which is a high net worth individual who provides financing to a start-up, either in exchange for convertible debt or equity. Among start-ups, they are thought of as a bridge between loans from family and friends and venture capital, though angels are themselves often personally connected to the business. Angels take on a great deal of risk when they invest in these start-ups; they are also subject to dilution at the start-up's IPO. Therefore, they usually require a high rate of return in exchange for their financing. **2.** Informal for investment-grade, which describes a bond with a medium or high rating. Angel bonds are rated Baa3 by Moody's or BBB- by S&P or Fitch. Angel bonds are considered sufficiently low-risk that the law allows banks to invest in them. In addition to being low-risk, they provide a low return, greatly reducing the cost on the issuer. All Treasury and most municipal bonds are angel bonds.

Angel Bond Informal; an investment-grade bond, which is a bond with a medium or high rating. Angel bonds are rated Baa3 by Moody's or BBB- by S&P or Fitch, or higher. Angel bonds are considered sufficiently low-risk that the law allows banks to invest in them. In addition to being low-risk, they provide a low return, greatly reducing the cost on the issuer. All Treasury and most municipal bonds are angel bonds.

Angel Investor A high net worth individual who provides financing to a start-up, either in exchange for convertible debt or equity. Among start-ups, they are thought of as a bridge between loans from family and friends and venture capital, though angel investors are themselves often personally connected to the business. Angel investors take on a great deal of risk when they invest in these start ups; they are also subject to dilution at the start up's IPO. Therefore, they usually require a high rate of return in exchange for their financing. They are informally known as angels or informal investors.

Angelina Jolie Stock Index An index consisting of stocks in companies somehow related to Hollywood Actress Angelina Jolie. That is, the index consists of movie studios, film distributors, and similar companies. The philosophy behind the index states that because Angelina Jolie is a popular actress, people will see her movies, and companies connected to her will be profitable. The index was created by finance blogger Fred Fuld.

Anglo-Irish Bank Corporation Act 2009 Legislation in Ireland that nationalized the Anglo-Irish Bank, which was in the process of collapsing. The bank had admitted in late 2008 to having hidden more than 80 million euros in loans from its balance sheet. This caused its share price to crash 98%, which necessitated a bailout in order to keep the Irish economy afloat, as the Anglo-Irish Bank was the third largest bank in the country.

Anglophone A person, company, or country for which English is the primary language. Because of the importance of America and the UK in the global economy, English is one of the most common languages in international commerce.

Angolan Angolar The former currency of Angola. It was introduced in 1928 and was pegged to the Portuguese escudo at a one-to-one ratio. In 1958, the Angolan escudo replaced the angolar as part of a broader effort to unite the currencies used in Portuguese colonies.

Angolan Escudo The former currency of Angola. It was introduced in 1958, replacing the Angolan angular as part of a broader effort to unite the currencies used in Portuguese colonies. It was pegged to the Portuguese escudo at a one-to-one ratio. The Angolan kwacha replaced the escudo two years after Angola's independence in 1975.

Angolan First Kwanza The former currency of Angola. It was introduced in 1977, two years after Angola's independence from Portugal. It was subject to inflation for most of its existence. It was replaced by the novo kwanza at par in 1990.

Angolan Kwanza The currency of Angola. It was introduced in 1999. While it initially suffered from high inflation, it dropped to a reasonable rate. Due to inflation in Angola, the current kwanza is the fourth to be issued since 1977.

Angolan Kwanza Readjustado The former currency of Angola. It replaced the novo kwanza in 1995 to help reduce inflation. The kwanza readjustado did not result in lower inflation and was replaced by the (second) kwanza in 1999.

Angstrom A unit of length equivalent to one-one billionth of one meter.

Angula An ancient Indian unit of length variously equivalent to values between 16 and 21 millimeters.

ANHH ISO 3166-3 code for the Netherlands Antilles, which separated into Bonaire, Sint Eustatius and Saba, Curacao, and Sint Maarten in 2011. ISO 3166-3 codes are used to indicate names of countries and territories that are no longer used.

Animal Health Benefits A health insurance policy that covers one's pet(s). In general, animal health benefits are not available through one's employer and must be purchased separately. As with all insurance plans, one must pay a premium to receive the coverage.

Animal Spirits 1. An informal term for consumer confidence used by John Maynard Keynes. The term has made a comeback since the 2000s economic crisis renewed interest in Keynesianism. **2.** A slang term for the foolishness of taking a large risk in entrepreneurship by, for example, mortgaging one's house to finance an untried business venture.

Animatics In animation, a step within storyboarding in which the animators develop a simple process to determine how a scene will feel in relation to motion and time.

Animation The rapid showing of still pictures (especially drawings) such that they appear to be moving. In the United States, animation in television and movies has

historically been designed to appeal mainly to children, which may affect what commercials are broadcast in their timeslots.

Animation Camera A camera modified to film cartoons or other animation. See also: Animation Stand.

Animation Stand A system used to film cartoons or other animation on a flat surface. It is distinguished by the fact that it films while pointed downward. See also: Animation Camera.

Ankanam A customary unit of area approximately equivalent to 6.7 square kilometers. It is used in some parts of India in real estate transactions.

Ankare A Swedish unit of volume approximately equivalent to 39.26 liters.

Anker An obsolete Dutch unit of volume roughly equivalent to 39 liters.

Ankle Biter Informal for small-cap. Describing a publicly-traded company with a low amount of market capitalization. In general, a small-cap company has a market capitalization of less than $1 billion or $2 billion, but there is no specific definition. Some brokerages or exchanges have slightly different definitions of small-cap. Some indexes track ankle biter companies, as do some exchange traded funds.

Anna A customary unit of area approximately equivalent to 16.86 square meters. It is used in real estate transactions in some parts of Pakistan.

Annex 1. A section or amendment to an international agreement. This can be important in some treaties, such as the Kyoto Protocol, in which industrialized countries are called Annex I countries and others are known as non-Annex I countries. **2.** See: Annexation.

Annexation The process by which a city or township expands its borders. The city or township may annex an unincorporated area or another municipality. The process is governed by state law and may require a vote by the affected people.

Announcement A significant piece of news given to the public. For example, if a company hires a new CEO, the announcement occurs the day this news is given to the media to report to the public. As the announcement may affect the company's stock price, many analysts observe stock performance on the announcement date and consider it a gauge of how the market will treat the news.

Announcement Date 1. The date on which a significant piece of news is announced to the public. For example, if a company hires a new CEO, the announcement date is the day it is announced to the media. As the announcement may affect the company's stock price, many analysts observe its performance on the announcement date and consider it a gauge of how the market will treat the news. **2.** The date on which a dividend is announced. After the announcement date, the dividend becomes a legal liability and a company is obliged to pay it.

Announcement Effect A change in security prices or volatility as a result of some announcement. For example, if the Federal Reserve raises interest rates, stock prices are liable to fall. Likewise, if a company announces an acquisition, its stock may rise. The announcement effect may cause drastic price changes; as a result, companies and governments often selectively leak or hint at announcements before they occur to minimize surprises. The announcement effect is also called the signal effect. See also: Price out the News.

Announcer Voice-Over In marketing, the practice of an off-camera individual speaking in a commercial, especially to narrate. For example, a commercial for a fast food restaurant may show a person eating a hamburger, while an off-screen announcer describes how good it tastes. Announcer voice-overs are often easier to produce, and voice-over actors are usually less expensive to hire than on-screen talent.

Annual Describing a situation, event, or statement that occurs or is filed only once per year. See also: Annual Report.

Annual Addition In a defined-contribution plan, the maximum contribution an annuitant may make to a qualifying retirement account per year. The annual addition is usually the lesser amount of a percentage of income or a certain dollar amount, the latter of which is indexed to inflation.

Annual Basis The expression of a variable in yearly terms even though the variable does not directly apply to a year. That is, a variable expressed on an annual basis has been mathematically converted to yearly terms. For example, if the return rate on an investment is 2% after one month, one computes the return on an annual basis by multiplying by twelve, resulting in a 24% return rate. A variable on an annual basis is often theoretical; there is often no guarantee that the return rate in the example above will be 24% if it is calculated after a month or two. An annual basis usually does not take into account the effects of compounding. It is also called annualization.

Annual Budget A plan for an organization or company's expenditures for a fiscal year. Making an annual budget involves balancing an organization's revenue or income with its expenses. A budget is in balance if revenues equal expenditures, it is in deficit if the person or company must resort to borrowing to meet expenses, and it is in surplus if money is left over to be used for savings or expansion.

Annual Cap The maximum amount that an interest rate on an adjustable-ratemortgage may change in a single year. For example, an adjustable-rate mortgage may have an annual cap stating that the rate will not go up more than 1.5% each year. This concept is similar to an interest rate ceiling, but an annual cap does not specify a maximum interest rate. Instead, it limits the speed at which a rate increases.

Annual Clean Up A requirement for a borrower to completely repay a revolving line of credit at least once per year. For example, a lender may require an annual clean up for a company that uses a business line of credit to make payroll in its slow months. The annual clean up proves to the lender that the borrower is not overly dependent on the credit line and can generate its own revenue. It is also called a clean up requirement.

Annual Convention Blank A statement that an insurance company must file each year with the state regulator. The annual convention blank states an insurance company's revenues, expenditures, investments, and lists every employee who earns more than $40,000 per year. The annual convention blank ensures that an insurance company is able to pay benefits on all policies on which premiums have been paid. It is also called an annual statement.

Annual Debt Service The total amount of money required each year to make payments on the principal and interest on long-term loans, bond interest, and the principals of maturing bonds. One calculates the annual debt service by adding together all debt service an individual or company pays each year, or by adding debt service for a month and multiplying by 12. See also: Debt service coverage ratio.

Annual Depreciation Allowance The depreciation on an asset that a tax agency permits each year. This contrasts with accumulated depreciation, which is calculated by multiplying the annual depreciation allowance by the number of years the asset has been held.

Annual Earnings A company's total revenue for a calendar or fiscal year less its annual operating expenses, interest paid, depreciation, and taxes. For example, a widget manufacturer may earn $1,000,000 in total revenue in 2010. The widgets cost $200,000 to make, and the manufacturer's administrative and payroll expenses total $250,000. He also must subtract $50,000 in depreciation on his widget manufacturing equipment and pay $200,000 in taxes. His annual earnings are stated as: $1,000,000 - $200,000 - $250,000 - $50,000 - $200,000 = $300,000. See also: EBIT.

Annual Earnings Report An annual report a publicly-traded company publishes stating information over a given period of time. The report contains information on the company's financial state, most notably statements on revenue, expenses, and earnings. It is, in general, less detailed than a stockholder's report, but contains much of the same information. See also: Balance sheet.

Annual Exclusion The amount of a taxpayer's income that he/she may exclude from his/her taxable income. Examples of income that may go into the annual exclusion include business expenses and municipal bond coupons. The amount of the annual exclusion varies from taxpayer to taxpayer.

Annual Expected Dollar Loss A measure of risk that considers the average amount a person or business is likely to lose in a year if an investment performs poorly.

Annual Fee A fee that a company assesses on a customer simply for being a customer. Annual fees are most common in the financial industry. For example, a credit card company may charge a customer an annual fee of $60 in order to keep that customer's card active.

Annual Fund Operating Expenses The cost that a mutual fund or other investment company incurs for maintaining proper records, printing financial statements, and otherwise maintaining operations. Annual fund operating expenses sometimes include marketing costs as well. Most investment companies assess a fee to cover these expenses. This fee is separate and distinct from the load (or sales fee). See also: Management fee.

Annual General Meeting The main meeting of the shareholders of a publicly-traded company that takes place each year. At the annual general meeting, the company may present its financial reports. Shareholders may ask questions of the board of directors and they may vote on matters pertaining to the company that only shareholders may decide. Publicly-traded companies are required to have an AGM and must inform shareholders of where and when it will occur in a timely manner. See also: Extraordinary General Meeting.

Annual Gift Tax Exclusion The value of the gift(s) an individual or married couple may give in a year without being subject to the gift tax. The amount of the annual gift tax exclusion varies from year to year but is always over $10,000. In general, payments for medical, educational, and political purposes fall under the annual gift tax exclusion no matter how much they are, as do gifts to one's spouse.

Annual Income The money a person makes from labor, investment, or any other source in the course of a year. Receiving income is the goal of all commerce. Annual income is usually taxed by the government, though one's taxable income for a year may differ from his/her actual annual income. See also: Income tax.

Annual Insurance Policy An insurance policy in which the policyholder pays premiums and the insurer provides coverage for a full year. At the conclusion of that year, either party may choose to renew the policy. It is also called an annual policy.

Annual Mortgage Statement A statement that a mortgage lender sends to a borrower indicating the interest and points paid on a mortgage, the principal remaining, and the escrowed taxes and/or insurance that the lender paid on the borrower's behalf. This helps the borrower in taking the correct deductions on his/her tax return. It is also called Form 1098.

Annual Percentage Rate The cost of funds or interest rate for an entire year expressed as a single percentage. Significantly, the APR does not account for compounding. For example, if the APR is 36%, the percentage is 3% per month, but the interest rate or cost of funds for the entire year may be greater than 36% due to the effects of compounding. By law, a credit card company or other lender must inform the customer of the APR before any agreement is signed. The APR provides the customer with a convenient number against which to compare the cost of funds for other loans or investments. It is less commonly called the annual rate of return or the nominal annual rate.

Annual Percentage Yield The yield on an investment in one year, taking into account the effects of compounding. For example, if one has a fixed-income investment such as certificate of deposit that pays 3% in interest each month, the annual percentage yield is more than 3% because compounding the interest results in a (slightly) higher return each month. In this example, the annual effective yield is calculated thus: Annual percentage yield = $(1.03)^{12} - 1 = .43 = 43\%$, where 1.03 is 1 plus the monthly interest and 12 is the number of times in a year interest is compounded. It is also known as the annual effective yield.

Annual Premium Annuity An annuity one buys by making a series of equal payments over the course of one or several years. One pays an equal amount each year when purchasing an annual premium annuity.

Annual Renewable Term Insurance An insurance policy in which the insurer guarantees the policyholder will be insurable for a set number of years (often 10 to 30), but premiums are only guaranteed for a year at a time. That is, the insurer may raise premiums each year even though it may not cancel the policy for the stated number of years. Annual renewable term insurance is usually less beneficial for the policyholder than for the insurer.

Annual Renewal Agreement A contract that the parties agree to renew each year at a certain price and under set conditions.

Annual Report A report that a publicly-traded company is required to distribute to shareholders each year. The report contains information on the company's financial state, such as operational income and net profit. Sometimes, it also contains an accountant's opinion on the general health of the company. Generally, the front part of the annual report states the "bottom line," while the last part contains more detailed financial information. For example, the front part of the report may contain a brief essay stating, "Our company is healthy for reasons A, B, and C." At the conclusion of that essay, the stockholder may view its financial statements. See also: Stockholder's report.

Annual Return The revenue an investment generates over a year as a percentage of the amount of capital invested. The annual return shows the number of years it will take to recover one's investment. For example, if one invests $1,000 and receives $150 in the first year of the investment, the rate of return is 15%, and the investor will recover his/her initial $1,000 in six years and eight months. Investors vary their required rates of return for different levels of risk.

Annual Sales The revenue that a company derives from the sale of its products in a year. This is distinguished from sources of annual revenue like interest income and other investments. A company records its annual sales on its balance sheet. High sales are desirable, particularly when expenses are high.

Annual Statement 1. See: Annual Earnings Report. **2.** See: Annual Convention Blank.

Annual Wage The total amount paid in a year to an employee who is paid hourly instead of at a flat annual rate.

Annualize To express a variable in yearly terms even though the variable does not directly apply to a year. That is, an annualized variable has been mathematically converted to yearly terms. For example, if the return rate on an investment is 2% after one month, one computes the annualized return by multiplying by 12, resulting in a 24% return rate. An annualized variable is often theoretical; there is no guarantee that the return rate in the example above will be 12% if it is calculated after a month or two. Annualizing usually does not take into account the effects of compounding.

Annualized Gain A gain on an investment expressed in yearly terms, even though the variable does not directly apply to a year. That is, an annualized gain has been mathematically converted to yearly terms. For example, if the return rate on an investment is 2% after one month, one computes the annualized return by multiplying by 12, resulting in a 24% return rate. An annualized variable is often theoretical; there is no guarantee that the return rate in the example above will be 24% if it is calculated after only a month or two.

Annualized Income Installment Method In corporate taxation in the United States, a way to reduce underpayment penalties by assuming that a company's income is annualized for a certain period of time (for example, a quarter). For example, a company may pay estimated taxes based on its profit for one quarter and make the same payment for three more quarters regardless of the company's actual profit for each quarter.

Annuitant The beneficiary of an annuity. Depending on the type of annuity, the annuitant may be the person who paid into the annuity, or may be a relative or other designee of that person, such as a widow or widower.

Annuitization The reception of monthly payments from an annuity after an accumulation period. Depending on the type of annuity, one may annuitize payments for a period of time or for the remainder of one's life.

Annuitization Method A way to receive distributions from an annuity where the annuitant is guaranteed to receive a certain amount in income each month for the remainder of his/her life. This carries lower risk than a systematic withdrawal plan, where the annuitant receives income until his/her account runs out. However, should the annuitant using the annuitization method die prematurely, payments may stop and the annuitant may lose the remainder of his/her annuity.

Annuity A product offered by an insurance company or an employer to which one makes contribution(s) and immediately or later begins receiving payments, which usually last the remainder of the annuitant's life. An annuity usually refers to a retirement account into which the annuitant makes payments over his/her working life. The payments are then invested and the annuitant begins to receive the principal plus earnings after retirement. A qualifying retirement account is an annuity that allows for either contributions or withdrawals to be tax-exempt up to a certain amount. However, a wide variety of annuities exist. An annuitant may make a one-time contribution or monthly contributions over a period of time. Likewise, one may begin to receive payments immediately or defer them to a later date such as retirement. One may elect to make fixed or variable contributions as well as to receive fixed or variable payments. See also: 401(k), IRA.

Annuity Analysis All relevant facts on an annuity, such as the amount paid to the annuitant each year or any sales fees.

Annuity Consideration The purchase price of an annuity. Depending on the type of annuity, the annuity consideration may be a lump sum or spread out in payments over an agreed-upon length of time.

Annuity Contract The agreement outlining the terms of an annuity. Among other things, the contract spells out the contributions, employer matching contributions, benefit schedule, whether the annuity is fixed or variable, and what the early withdrawal penalties are. The annuitant and the insurance company agree on the annuity contract when the annuitant buys the annuity. Generally speaking, the insurance company maintains a standard set of annuity contracts to meet the needs of different annuitants.

Annuity Due A payment that must be made at the beginning, rather than at the end, of a period. For example, an annuity due may require payment at the beginning of the month instead of at the end. Many lease agreements have annuity due payments, while credit cards, for example, do not.

Annuity Factor The calculation of the present value of a cash flow or other income stream that produces $1 in income over so many periods of time.

Annuity Forms The various structures of annuity one may purchase from an insurer or other financial company. Some annuity forms include fixed annuity or variable annuity, period certain or life annuity, and qualifying annuity or non-qualifying annuity.

Annuity in Advance An annuity with payments that are made at the beginning, rather than the end, of a period. For example, an annuity in advance may require payments at the beginning of the month. Many rental agreements have annuity in advance payments, while most credit cards, for example, do not. See also: Ordinary Annuity.

Annuity in Arrears A payment that is made at the end of a period. For example, one usually makes a monthly mortgage payment at the end of the month, when a certain amount of interest has had a chance to accumulate. An annuity in arrears often, but not always, refers a loan payment. It should not be confused with "in arrears," which describes a payment that is late.

Annuity Income The income one derives from an annuity one previously purchased. Many pensions and other retirement plans are annuities. However, one may receive annuity income from other sources, such as a settlement from a lawsuit or from lottery winnings. Annuity income is generally taxed like ordinary income.

Annuity Method of Depreciation A way to calculate the depreciation of an asset. Under the annuity method, one begins by calculating the internal rate of return and multiplying that by the original book value of the asset. One then subtracts the product from the cash flow the asset generates each year. This difference is subtracted from the book value (or the previous year's depreciated value) to arrive at the depreciated value. The annuity method is not approved by the Generally Accepted Accounting Principles.

Annuity Payment Option Either of two ways that one may elect to receive payments from an annuity. One may receive a fixed dollar amount each month, guaranteeing payments but exposing the annuitant to inflation risk. On the other hand, one may decide to receive variable payments, tying payments to the performance of some underlying portfolio. One generally decides which annuity payment option one wishes to receive upon purchasing the annuity.

Annuity Principal The contributions one makes to an annuity. This may be a lump sum payment, but it is usually a series of contributions made on a monthly basis. The annuity principal is invested on behalf of the annuitant and forms the basis of the payments he/she begins to receive after the first withdrawal.

Annuity Rent A payment made to an annuitant from his/her annuity. For example, if one purchases an annuity and begins receiving payments after age 65, then those payments in retirement are called the annuity rent.

Annuity Starting Date The date on which an annuitant receives his/her first payment from an annuity. If it is an immediate annuity, the annuity starting date is soon after the annuitant purchases the plan; if it is a deferred annuity, the starting date may occur some years after purchase, especially following retirement.

Annuity Table, 1949 A mortality table of the likelihood a person of a certain age will die in the next year, taking into account the fact that people were living longer than they were when the Standard Annuity Table was published in 1937. It was used in determining one's eligibility for some insurance and annuity plans. It has since been replaced.

Annuity Unit Shares in an annuity. When one purchases an annuity, one purchases a fixed number of annuity units, which are set to represent the value of the portfolio in which the annuity invests. When one begins to receive payments from the annuity, this has the effect of selling annuity units so the annuitant may receive cash from them.

Anomaly An unusual or unrepeatable event. For example, a stock index inexplicably rising 20% in a week during a bear market may constitute an anomaly.

Anonymizing The process of removing identifying information from a transmission over the Internet. For example, one may anonymize an e-mail by removing information regarding the sender. It should not be confused with anonymous trading.

Anonymous Trading Trades that take place without the buyer and/or seller revealing his/her identity. Anonymous trading is most common among well-known or well-regarded investors who do not wish to set off speculation based on their trades. See also: Stalking horse.

Ansvarlig Selskap Also called ANS. In Norway, a corporate structure whereby all owners are fully responsible for all debts their company acquires. For example, if an ANS company has five owners who agree to split the debts five ways, but two owners refuse to pay, creditors can collect debts from the remaining three. An ANS does not require any investment capital to be registered with authorities, but owner(s) have unlimited liability for any losses. This structure is most common with small and medium-sized businesses. See also: Aksjeselskap.

Answer A formal rebuttal that the defendant in a lawsuit makes against the claims of the plaintiff. The answer asserts that the plaintiff's allegations are false, or, if they are true, that the defendant is not liable for them.

Answering Service A company that takes phone messages outside business hours. If an office hires an answering service, one who calls that office after hours is automatically forwarded to the answering service. The answering service can take a message, forward to caller to another number, or take whatever action the office/client has requested. This service gives the caller someone "real" on the other end and, ideally, helps ensure prompt attention once the office re-opens.

Antedate The practice of placing a date that has already passed on a contract or a check. On its own, this does not invalidate or negatively impact the contract or check, but it may affect how long it remains valid. For example, one may sign a 12-month contract on February 1 but antedate it to January 1. Because the contract then states that it expires 12 months from January 1, it has effectively become an 11-month contract. See also: Post-Date.

Antiboycott Law A law that forbids companies in a country from boycotting foreign nations unless the domestic government authorizes it. It may also prohibit agreements deemed discriminatory on racial, gender, or other grounds. American antiboycott laws effectively prohibit American companies from refusing to do business with Israeli companies. However, this is no longer as important as it once was, as many Arab League countries no longer enforce their boycott of Israel.

Anticipated Balance The expected balance of a savings account over a given period of time, assuming a compound interest rate and an unchanging principal(not including added interest).

Anticipated Growth Rate The return rate on a bond fund (a mutual fund in which most or all securities represented in it are bonds) based upon the weighted average maturity of the bonds represented in the fund. The anticipated growth rate assumes all dividends are reinvested and the underlying bonds are held to maturity. See also: Anticipated Value at Maturity.

Anticipated Holding Period In a long position, the period of time during which one expects to own a security or other asset. The anticipated holding period is important to calculating the position's expected return. One may also determine the anticipated holding period for tax purposes because long-term investments are not taxed as heavily as short-term ones. See also: HPR

Anticipated Interest The interest that an account or debt will accrue over a given period of time, assuming a compound interest rate and an unchanging principal (not including added interest).

Anticipated Value at Maturity The redemption value of one share in a bond fund (a mutual fund in which most or all securities represented in it are bonds) based upon the weighted average maturity of the bonds represented in the fund. The anticipated value at maturity has only a loose impact on the fund's share price. See also: Anticipated Growth Rate.

Anticipatory Breach In contracts, a declaration in which one party stops performing his/her obligations. The Uniform Commercial Code specifies how one may calculate damages in a lawsuit resulting from an anticipatory breach.

Anticipatory Hedge An investment or other transaction one makes in order to hedge against (or reduce the risk of) another investment or transaction one intends to make in the future.

Anticoercion Law A law or clause within a law forbidding coercion (the use of threats, intimidation, or deceit to force an action) in insurance and other businesses. Most U.S. states have adopted a version of the NAIC Unfair Trade Practices Act, which includes an anticoercion law.

Anti-Competitive A practice intended to subvert or eliminate competition. Many analysts believe competition is good for customers because it encourages companies to offer better quality products and/or lower prices. Anti-competitive measures, like price fixing or collusion, remove this incentive and thereby hamper innovation and growth. Many countries have laws banning or limiting anti-competitive activities, though opponents, notably Ayn Rand and her followers, argue that they encourage economic inefficiency and punish success.

Antidilution Clause 1. In common and preferred stock, the right of a shareholder to maintain the same percentage of ownership in a company, should the company issue more stock. This protects the investor from devaluation of his/her shares if the company decides to hold a round of financing. In preferred stock, the anti-dilution clause also indicates the right of a shareholder to purchase more shares in a new round of financing at the offering price up to his/her previous percentage of ownership. Most U.S. states only recognize the anti-dilution clause if it is made explicit in the corporation's charter. **2.** In convertible securities, the right of a holder to maintain the same conversion ratio in the event of a stock split. For example, if a convertible bond may be exchanged for 100 shares of common stock and there is a 2-for-1 stock split, the same convertible bond can be exchanged for 200 shares. This protects the investor from devaluation of the conversion option.

Antidilutive Effect The result of the retirement of shares, usually through a buyback. That is, a company may buy back some of its own shares from shareholders, which reduces the number of shares outstanding. This increases the company's earnings per share, which in turn usually increases the stock price.

Antidumping Any law, regulation, tariff, or other tactic used to prevent dumping, which is the act of exporting a good to a foreign country to capitalize on the price difference. Dumping can result in a handsome profit for the exporter, but it can also damage the importing country's local economy. Governments attempt to counteract the practice by implementing antidumping measures.

Antidumping Code A generic term given to the sections of GATT and WTO agreements governing dumping, antidumping duties, and related issues.

Antidumping Duty In international commerce, a tariff placed on an import that is unusually low-priced. Dumping is the act of exporting a good to a foreign country to capitalize on the price difference. Dumping can result in a handsome profit for the exporter, but it can also damage the importing country's local economy. Thus, many countries attempt to counteract the practice by implementing anti-dumping duties.

Antidumping Duty Order An order by a government agency imposing or expanding an antidumping duty on an import thought to be priced unfairly low.

Antidumping Investigation Notice A notice by a government agency announcing an investigation into potential dumping. Dumping is the act of exporting a good to a foreign country to capitalize on the price difference. This can cause harm to the domestic industry, especially in the short term. Once the government publishes an antidumping investigation notice, it must begin the investigation within 20 days.

Antidumping Petition A request by an American industry to the appropriate government agency requesting an investigation into potential dumping. Dumping is the act of exporting a good to a foreign country to capitalize on the price difference. This can cause harm to the domestic industry, especially in the short term. An antidumping petition starts an investigation that could result in the imposition of an antidumping duty to counterbalance the dumping.

Antidumping Suit A lawsuit in which a country accuses a trading partner of dumping, which is the practice of exporting a good to a foreign country to capitalize on the price difference. This can harm domestic industries. According to the World Trade Organization, in order to prove one's case in an antidumping suit, one must prove both that dumping took place and that it harmed a domestic industry in a tangible way.

Antidumping/Countervailing Duty System In international commerce, a system that places tariffs on imports that are unusually low-priced. Under an antidumping/countervailing duty system, the importing country places an antidumping duty on products sent from countries where the good is much less expensive than domestically produced goods of the same type. The system also imposes a countervailing duty on products subsidized by the government of the exporting country. This system is used in Australia.

Anti-Globalization A movement that opposes free trade, free movement of capital, and other policies intended to facilitate international business. Various types of people oppose globalization. Labor unions in developed countries may oppose it because it represents a threat to traditional, industrial jobs. Other factions on the left believe globalization favors the wealthy at the expense of the poor and working class.

Anti-Greenmail Provision A provision in a corporate charter forbidding the payment of a bon voyage bonus without the approval of a given majority of shareholders. Greenmailing is a practice in which a corporate raider buys a large amount of stock from another publicly-traded company and forces the latter to buy back the stock at a substantial premium in order to avoid a takeover. One refers to this buyback as the bon voyage bonus, as this enables the company to be left alone by the greenmailer. An anti-greenmail provision discourages corporate raiders from greenmailing in the first place as it makes the bon voyage bonus more difficult to receive, which may result in the greenmailer becoming stuck with ownership of shares he/she does not actually want.

Antihausse A French term for any action taken to combat inflation. For example, an increase in interest rates may be antihausse.

Anti-Inflationary Measure Any policy a central bank or other agency takes to reduce the inflation rate. In general, anti-inflationary measures involve raising key interest rates, sometimes dramatically, to cut down the money supply. Other anti-inflationary measures include things like instituting price controls, changing the peg of a currency, and outlawing inflation. Raising interest rates, however, is considered to be the best anti-inflationary measure for a floating, fiat currency. See also: Tight money.

Anti-Martingale System An investment strategy in which an investor increases the size of his/her investment with each gain. For example, if an investor buys stock at $10 per share and the price goes to $20 per share, he/she may sell the first stock and then buy another stock at $20 per share. In other words, with each profit the investor adds to the size of his/her portfolio, accepting additional risk only with additional earnings. This contrasts with the Martingale System, in which the investor

increases his/her risk more with losing investments. Both systems are used in gambling as well as investment.

Anti-Money Laundering Any law or regulation requiring an institution to perform due diligence on potential clients to ensure that it is not aiding in a money laundering scheme. If the institution does not conduct due diligence properly, it may be held legally liable for the money laundering activities. These regulations were an important part of the USA PATRIOT Act.

Anti-Monopoly Policy Any law or policy intended to oppose monopolies and other anti-competitive organizations or practices. Anti-monopoly policies are intended to regulate the market share an individual company can have in order to enforce competition. Proponents of anti-monopoly policies believe the added competition benefits the consumer, while opponents, notably Ayn Rand, argue that they encourage economic inefficiency and punish success. See also: Sherman Act, Clayton Act.

Antioffset Spray In printing, a spray used to keep ink on one sheet from leaking onto another sheet.

Anti-Pollution Measure Any law intended to reduce pollution and its effects. Examples include basic ordinances like littering prohibitions or controversial measures like a carbon tax or cap-and-trade. Some analysts believe anti-pollution measures will harm the global economy and increase poverty, while others hold that the environmental improvements will ultimately benefit business.

Antique A product or other item that is old but still desirable to a collector or an investor because of its rarity or quality. There is no set age that renders an item an antique. A car might be considered an antique after 50 years, but a coin after 100.

Antiquidate To render obsolete.

Antirebate Law A law banning the practice in which an insurance agent gives a certain percentage of his/her commission to a policyholder as an incentive to buy a policy from him/her. An antirebate law is intended to encourage fair business practices in the insurance industry. Most U.S. states have antirebate laws.

Anti-Reciprocal Rule A FINRA rule stating that two investment companies and/or brokerages may not collude to direct business to each other. For example, the anti-reciprocal rule prohibits a mutual fund from conducting their trades through a certain brokerage in exchange for that brokerage directing investors to that mutual fund.

Antitakeover Measure Periodic or continual measures a firm's management takes to discourage unwanted or hostile takeovers. One example of an antitakeover measure is the macaroni defense, in which the company issues a large number of bonds with the proviso that they must be redeemed at a high price if the company is taken over. See also: Shark Watcher.

Antitakeover Statute A law at the state level prohibiting hostile takeovers in certain circumstances. Different states have different antitakeover statutes, but most involve some way of limiting a potential acquirer's ability to take a bid directly to shareholders. Critics contend that these laws can work against shareholder interest, while proponents maintain that they promote stability in publicly-traded companies. Antitakeover statutes can only apply to companies registered in states having such laws.

Antitrust Opposing trusts, monopolies, and other organizations or practices deemed to be anti-competitive. Antitrust especially refers to opposition to price-fixing contracts, price discrimination, and tying. Proponents of antitrust laws believe they increase competitions, while opponents, notably Ayn Rand, argue that they encourage economic inefficiency and punish success. See also: Sherman Act, Clayton Act.

Antitrust Acts 1. See: Sherman Act. **2.** See: Clayton Act.

Antitrust Law Any law opposing trusts, monopolies, and other organizations or practices deemed to be anti-competitive. Antitrust laws especially refer to laws forbidding price-fixing contracts, price discrimination, and tying. Proponents of antitrust laws believe they increase competition, while opponents, notably Ayn Rand, argue that they encourage economic inefficiency and punish success. See also: Sherman Act, Clayton Act.

Antivirus Software A computer program designed to find, remove, and protect against malicious software such as viruses, worms, and Trojan horses. Antivirus software has become especially important for businesses as their activities have become increasingly reliant on the Internet.

Any Occupation for Which Reasonably Suited One of two ways an insurer determines a person's disability. Under this standard, a person is considered disabled if he/she is deemed unable to do any job suited to his/her educational background and work experience. This contrasts with the own occupation standard.

Any Quantity In shipping, a freight rate that does not depend on the amount or weight of the good being shipped.

Any Willing Provider Law In health care, a law requiring an insurer or a managed care organization to allow policyholders to receive treatment from any provider willing to accept the fee the insurer offers, even if he/she is not in the insurer's network of approved providers. About half of U.S. states have any willing provider statutes.

Any-and-All Bid A bid to buy all stock in a company available for sale at the specified price. Any-and-all bids are useful for acquiring companies during hostile takeovers. Rather than working through the board of directors, an acquirer can simply place an any-and-all bid for stock at, say, 10% over its current market price, and buy from any stockholder willing to sell.

Any-Interest-Date Call A provision in some municipal bonds giving the issuer the right to redeem a bond before maturity on any date that the issuer owes coupons to bondholders.

Any-Part-of Order An order to a broker in which the client instructs the a broker to execute only part of the order if necessary. This situation usually arises when the broker cannot find a corresponding order. For example, if an investor makes an order to a broker to sell 1000 shares at a certain price but there are only buyers for 600 shares, the broker partially executes the order and looks for buyers for the remaining 400. The leftovers from an any-part-of order are called leaves. This order contrasts with an all-or-none order.

ANZUS Pact A treaty between Australia, New Zealand, and the United States stating that signatories will coordinate and cooperate with one another on defense issues, especially those affecting the South Pacific. It came into effect in 1951. In the mid-1980s, the United States and New Zealand had a dispute over nuclear ships and now do not consider themselves bound by ANZUS with respect to each other. However, they both maintain treaty obligations with respect to Australia.

AO 1. ISO 3166-1 alpha-2 code for the Republic of Angola. This is the code used in international transactions to and from Angolan bank accounts. **2.** ISO 3166-2 geocode for Angola. This is used as an international standard for shipping to Angola. Each Angolan province has its own code with the prefix "AO." For example, the code for the Province of Bengo is ISO 3166-2:AO-BGO.

AOA ISO 4217 code for the Angolan kwanza. It was introduced in 1999. While it initially suffered from high inflation, it has dropped to a reasonable rate. Due to inflation in Angola, the current kwanza is the fourth to be issued since 1977.

AOK ISO 4217 code for the first Angolan kwanza. It was introduced in 1977, two years after Angola's independence from Portugal. It was subject to inflation for most of its existence. It was replaced by the novo kwanza at par in 1990.

AON ISO 4217 code for the Angolan new kwanza. It was introduced in 1990, replacing the first kwanza at a one-to-one ratio. However, Angolans were required to exchange 95% of their old kwanzas for government securities rather than cash. The new kwanza suffered from high inflation. It was replaced by the kwanza readjustado in 1995.

AOR ISO 4217 code for the Angolan kwanza readjustado. It replaced the novo kwanza in 1995 to help reduce inflation. The kwanza readjustado did not result in lower inflation and was replaced by the (second) kwanza in 1999.

Apartment A dwelling unit within a larger structure. An apartment has a kitchen, bathroom, and a place to sleep, and some have much more room and include many luxuries. While one may buy an apartment, they are generally rented out to tenants.

Apartment Building A structure with several apartments in it. The apartments share a hallway or exterior walkway, though they are not otherwise connected to each other. Investors may purchase an apartment building to collect the rental income from tenants.

APB Opinion An official opinion by the Accounting Principles Board on how to report a transaction. APB opinions set standards for the accounting industry and helped establish uniform practice insofar as it was possible. APB opinions have not been issued since 1973, when the APB was replaced by the Financial Accounting Standards Board. See also: FASB opinion.

API Weekly Report A report on the oil market issued each week by the American Petroleum Institute. It details the amount of oil imported into the United States (measured in thousands of barrels), the performance of petroleum stocks, and so forth.

APICS Business Outlook Index An index gauging sentiment in manufacturing. An index value above 50 indicates that the manufacturing industry is expanding while a measure below 50 indicates contraction. It is published monthly by the Association for Operations Management. See also: PMI.

Apothecaries' Ounce An obsolete unit of weight approximately equivalent to 31.1 grams.

Apparent Agency A situation in which a person or company inaccurately claims to be an agent for another person or company and conducts some act in that capacity, but which the principal (who is not actually a principal) later accepts and recognizes. Because the agent is not actually an agent, any act he/she conducts on behalf of the principal ordinarily would be invalid; however, agency by ratification exists because the "principal" confirms the act.

Appeal A request to a higher court to review a previously completed criminal or civil case. In general, only one of the parties involved in the original case may appeal it.

Appeal Bond In an appeal, a bond that guarantees payment of the original judgment. For example, if Joe sues Bob for $1 million and Joe wins, Bob may appeal to a higher court to reverse the ruling. However, the higher court may require Bob to post an appeal bond of $1 million plus the cost of the appeal just in case he loses the appeal as well. This assures Joe will be paid (assuming he also wins the appeal) and discourages frivolous appeals.

Appellant The party to a lawsuit or administrative hearing who previously lost a judgment and is trying to overturn it. For example, if Joe sues Bob for $1 million and Joe wins, Bob may appeal to a higher court to reverse the ruling. In this case, Bob is the appellant.

Appellate Court A court that reviews a previously completed, criminal or civil case upon request from one of the involved parties. For example, if Joe sues Bob for

$1 million and Joe wins, Bob may appeal to a higher court to reverse the ruling. The higher court in this case would be the appellate court.

Appellee The party to a lawsuit or administrative hearing who previously won a judgment that the other party (called the appellant) is trying to overturn. For example, if Joe sues Bob for $1 million and Joe wins, Bob may appeal to a higher court to reverse the ruling. In this case, Joe is the appellee.

Applause Mail In marketing, correspondence sent to a radio or television station praising something that station has done. A station may receive applause mail for a personality, a show, a commercial, or almost anything else. Applause mail helps that station determine the popularity of its programming and may help it make advertising decisions.

Apple Annie During the Great Depression, a slang term for a person who could not find a regular job and performed menial tasks, such as selling apples on a street corner, to earn a minimal living.

Applet In computing, an application program that has one and only one function. Very often, an applet is a small part of a larger application.

Appleton Rule A regulation in New York State requiring every insurance company doing business in New York to abide by New York's rules even regarding business it does in other states. The Appleton rule has had a large affect on insurance regulation because it applies to insurance companies that do any business in New York, even if that only forms a small part of their operations. It was instituted in the early 1900s.

Applicable Federal Rate The interest rate the IRS assumes when it calculates imputed interest. Imputed interest is interest that is assigned to an investment for tax purposes even when no interest has been paid. Thus, one pays taxes on the applicable federal rate. It is published by the U.S. Treasury.

Applicant A person who has made a formal request. For example, a person who has asked for a loan from the bank, but has not yet been approved, is said to be an applicant for that loan.

Application 1. A formal request. Generally, one must fill out an application form as part of the application process. **2.** See: Application Program.

Application Form A standardized form one completes in order to make a formal request. Items that may be on an application form include name, social security number, and the nature of the request. One may use an application form to apply for a job or a loan, among other things.

Application of Funds Any of six results of spending money. Spending money can result in a loss, an increase in current assets (other than cash), an increase in non-current assets, a decrease in current liabilities, a decrease in non-current liabilities, or a decrease in shareholders' equity.

Application Program A computer program that performs a specified function. Examples include browsers, word processors, spreadsheets, and databases.

Application Program Interface A portion of a software program that allows it to interact with other programs. An application program interface is necessary for many complex programs to function.

Application Service Provider A company that sells a computer application to a customer and delivers it over a network. The ASP owns both the application and the servers on which it is written.

Applications Programmer A computer programmer who writes programs to be used on a certain software system. An applications programmer is different from a systems programmer, who designs the software itself.

Applied Cost In cost accounting, the expense of an activity or product, allocated according to a predetermined formula. These costs may or may not be based on the costs that the activity or product actually incurs.

Applied Economics The study of observing how economic theory works in practice. Applied economics may be practiced at the macroeconomic or microeconomic levels. For example, one may conduct a study examining the performace of a government regulation in a national economy. This would involve gathering data from real businesses and/or individuals, as opposed to constructing a model on how such regulation should work. The term originated in the early 20th century.

Applied Overhead In cost accounting, the expense of each department in a company, allocated according to a predetermined formula. For example, a company may apply 60% of its overhead to R&D and 40% to its sales department. These percentages may or may not be based on the actual costs each department incurs.

Applied Research Research conducted for a specific, often commercial, purpose. That is, applied research is the opposite of research for its own sake. One may conduct applied research on how to make a more efficient light bulb; this would contrast with research on how electricity works in an ideal universe. See also: Research and Development.

Applied Tariff The tariff an exporter or importer owes on a particular transaction. This differs from the bound rate, which is the tariff writ large, or the tariff rates negotiated for all transactions between two countries.

Appointed Actuary An actuary employed by an insurance company to ensure compliance with all required reserve statutes. In the United States, insurance companies are required to have a certain percentage of their assets set aside to pay claims should the need arise. The NAIC requires insurance companies to employ appointed actuaries to make certain they are able to pay unexpected liabilities.

Appointment A designation in which a person or company allows an agent to act on their behalf. See also: Agency.

Appointment of Trustees for Terminated Plan A plan to protect beneficiaries in the event of the bankruptcy of a pension. The Pension Benefit Guaranty Corporation (PBGC) enacts this plan by appointing one or more trustees, who have the obligation to keep assets from being further reduced, to prevent new liabilities, and to generally advocate on behalf of pensioners as opposed to creditors or other interested parties. The U.S. District Court must approve the trustees the PBGC appoints.

Appointment Papers Documentation demonstrating that a person or company has allowed an agent to act on his, her, or its behalf. See also: Agency.

Apportionment A division. The term may be used in insurance to indicate which policy bears what percentage of a loss. Alternatively, it may be used in the sale of real estate to show the property tax or insurance the buyer and the seller each owe for a year. See also: Apportionment Clause.

Apportionment Clause When more than one property insurance policy covers the same event, a clause stating that each policy only provides coverage in proportion to the total coverage each policy provides. For example, one may have two policies covering one's home from fire damage. Policy A provides maximum coverage of $40,000 and Policy B provides $60,000, for a total of $100,000. If the home catches fire causing $50,000 in damage, the apportionment clause in each insurance policy requires that Policy A pay for $20,000 and Policy B pay for the remaining $30,000.

Appraisal The act of estimating the value of a property by a person licensed to do so. A person performing an appraisal must receive authorization from the appropriate body of the state in which he/she resides. An appraisal may take into account the quality of the property, values of surrounding properties, and market conditions in the area. It is important for determining the property taxes for which the owner is liable, as well as a potential sale price if the owner wishes to sell his/her property.

Appraisal Capital In accounting, an entry on a balance sheet for the amount by which an asset's appraised value exceeds its book value. When this occurs, the asset's book value is listed as its actual value and the difference is listed as appraisal capital, which is counted as equity. This practice is rare in the United States, but more common elsewhere.

Appraisal Clause In insurance, a clause in a policy giving both the insurance company and the policyholder the right to demand an appraisal to determine the value of an insured property. This protects both parties in the event of a dispute over the value of a loss.

Appraisal Costs The costs a company incurs in making sure its products conform to customer needs or desires. Examples include field testing and focus groups. Appraisal costs are a type of quality cost.

Appraisal Fee A fee that an appraiser assesses to perform his/her service. That is, when an appraiser estimates the value of a property, he/she usually charges an appraisal fee. This is usually a necessary cost to the buyer, seller, or lender in a real estate transaction. See also: Closing costs.

Appraisal Foundation An organization that sets standards for property appraisers in the United States. Based in Washington D.C., it seeks to ensure appraisers are qualified and certified and to standardize the criteria appraisers use to estimate the value of properties. It was established in 1989.

Appraisal Method of Depreciation A way to depreciate an asset in which one makes an appraisal of the asset at the beginning and end of each accounting period and records the difference as the depreciation amount, assuming that the asset decreases in value. If it does not, the depreciation is listed as zero. The appraisal method is not usually considered an acceptable way to record depreciation.

Appraisal Ratio A measure of a fund or portfolio's performance calculated by taking its alpha (a measure of the fund's return, assuming the market return is zero) and dividing by its unsystemic risk or standard deviation. Generally speaking, money managers use the appraisal ratio to measure the fund's performance relative to some benchmark. They may change the composition of funds and portfolios with suboptimal appraisal ratios.

Appraisal Report A report detailing the estimation of the value of a property by a person licensed to do so. An appraisal report may be self-contained, summary, or restricted. A self-contained report is 150 pages and highly detailed, discussing every element considered in the appraisal. A summary report is 20 pages and less detailed. A restricted report is 10 pages and is intended only for the owner's use.

Appraisal Right In mergers and acquisitions, the right of shareholders who object to being acquired to demand a fair price for their shares, as determined by a court. In theory, this guarantees that shareholders are adequately compensated for being overridden on the merger or acquisition. These shareholders may elect to have their shares purchased by the acquiring corporation at the price set by the court. In the United States, most states grant appraisal rights in their regulatory statutes.

Appraisal Value The value of a property as estimated by a person licensed to do so. The appraised value may take into account the quality of the property, values of surrounding properties, and market conditions in the area. It is important for determining the property taxes for which the owner is liable, as well as a potential sale price if the owner wishes to sell the property.

Appraiser A person licensed to estimate the value of a property. The appraiser may take into account the quality of the property, values of surrounding properties, and market conditions in the area. One becomes licensed or certified as an appraiser generally through education, testing and work experience, though the specific requirements vary by state.

Appreciated Property A property that has increased in value. Most property depreciates, and appreciated property is fairly rare. Real estate, however, is a major exception, and tends to appreciate over time.

Appreciated Value The increased value of a property or other asset. Most property depreciates, and it is fairly rare to discuss a property's appreciated value. Real estate and securities are major exceptions, since real estate tends to appreciate over time and securities may increase or decrease in value depending on market conditions. The appreciated value may be used to calculate capital gains or property taxes.

Appreciation An increase in value of a property or other asset. Most property depreciates, and it is fairly rare to discuss a property's appreciation. Real estate and securities are major exceptions, since real estate tends to appreciate over time and securities may increase or decrease in value depending on market conditions. Appreciation may be used to calculate capital gains or property taxes. See also: Capital appreciation.

Apprentice One who learns a trade or occupation by working directly under a skilled person. For example, an apprentice may study under a blacksmith to learn the trade. The apprentice may be paid a small amount or may simply receive room and board.

Apprenticeship A position in which one learns a trade or occupation by working directly under a skilled person. The student (called an apprentice) may be paid a small amount or may simply receive room and board.

Appropriated Expenditure The money that has been assigned to a department, project or something else. For example, a government may appropriate a certain amount of money to its defense department to fund the department's operations for a year. The monies given to the department form its appropriated expenditures.

Appropriated Retained Earnings The retained earnings a company does not make available as dividends. The appropriated retained earnings may be used for almost any purpose; for example, they may fund an expansion, an acquisition or debt reduction. See also: Plowback rate.

Appropriation An assignment of money to a department, project or something else. For example, a government may appropriate a certain amount of money to its defense department to fund the department's operations for a year.

Appropriation Account An account for a government unit that is credited with the amount the legislature appropriates to that unit. The unit debits its appropriation account every time it spends money.

Appropriation Bill Legislation that authorizes the government to spend money from the public treasury for a certain purpose. For example, an appropriation bill may enable the defense ministry to fund the military's activities for the year. If the amount authorized in all appropriation bills in a year exceeds the revenue the government collects, then the government goes into deficit. In many countries, appropriation bills must originate in the lower house of the legislature.

Appropriation Request A formal request to the proper authority for a significant amount of money, especially for a capital investment. A government department may make an appropriations request to the legislature to expand its services; likewise, a department within a company may make a request to senior management.

Approval An acceptance of an application. For example, an insurance company may give approval to an application for a policy, and a bank may do the same for a loan application.

Approval Conditional Premium Receipt An insurance policy that comes into effect when the insurance company approves an application. See also: Insurability conditional premium receipt.

Approved Charge In some health insurance plans, the amount that the insurer will pay for a medical procedure. Some insurers will only pay for medical procedures up to the approved charge. If the amount the physician or hospital bills exceeds the approved charge, the policyholder is responsible for paying it. See also: Coinsurance.

Approved Deferred Share Trust In the United Kingdom, a trust created by a publicly traded company consisting of shares in that same company. The company creates the ADST to benefit its employees. Shares in an ADST are not taxed until they are sold, and even then are taxed at a reduced rate. A company must receive approval from Inland Revenue before a trust is recognized as an ADST. See also: Employee stock option.

Approved Delivery Facility In futures contracts, the agreed-upon location authorized by an exchange where the seller or his/her representative must hand over the underlying good or commodity in order to fulfill the obligation to make delivery. Often, an approved delivery facility is a warehouse.

Approved List A list of companies and other investments in which certain organizations like state-chartered banks, insurance companies, and pensions are allowed to invest. The components of approved lists vary from state to state, but most approved lists contain low-risk, low-return investments designed to maintain the organizations' sustainability and protect the principal placed in them. An approved list is also called a legal list.

Approximate Describing a measure coming close to but not necessarily reaching the exact value. Approximate measures can be inaccurate but are often necessary when more precise information is unavailable.

Appurtenant In property law, an attachment to a deed or other document restricting an owner's rights. For example, an appurtenant may deprive an owner of land from the mineral rights attached to that land.

Appurtenant Structure Any building on a piece of real estate other than the main building. For example, a house may have a detached apartment on the same piece of property. Most insurance policies covering the main building on a piece of property also cover appurtenant structures.

Apreciacion de una accion A Spanish term for an increase in the price of a stock. See also: Appreciation.

Apsar The currency of Abkhazia, a state with limited recognition. Perhaps because of this limited recognition, apsars circulate much less frequently than the Russian ruble in Abkhazia. While apsar coins are made of silver and gold, the currency is pegged to the Russian ruble.

Apskritis In Lithuania, a political subdivision equivalent to a county.

Aptitude The natural ability to do something or to learn it quickly. Some aptitude is necessary to perform any job well. For example, one must have an aptitude for math in order to become a proficient technical analyst.

AQ ISO 3166-2 geocode for Antarctica. This is used as an international standard for shipping to Antarctica.

AR 1. See: Autoregressive Process. **2.** See: Accounts Receivable. **3.** ISO 3166-1 alpha-2 code for the Argentine Republic. This is the code used in international transactions to and from Argentinian bank accounts. **4.** ISO 3166-2 geocode for Argentina. This is used as an international standard for shipping to Argentina. Each Argentinian province has its own code with the prefix "AR." For example, the code for the Province of Buenos Aires is ISO 3166-2:AR-B.

ARA ISO 4217 code for the first Afghan afghani. It was introduced in 1925 and was initially pegged to silver. In 1949, the peg shifted to the U.S. dollar, which was maintained at various levels (except from 1979 to 1982) until 1992. Different factions within Afghanistan issued their own afghani notes. The first afghani was replaced by the second afghani (code AFN) after the American-led invasion of Afghanistan.

Arab Bank for Economic Development in Africa A bank established by the League of Arab States in 1974 to promote economic development in Africa. It provides grants to African governments for certain projects. In order to encourage regional integration, ABEDA provides funds for a single project that will be carried out in several countries. Its headquarters are in Khartoum, Sudan.

Arab Boycott of Israel An attempt by the Arab League to isolate the State of Israel by boycotting Israeli businesses, companies that buy from or sell to Israeli businesses and companies that ship their products through Israel. The Israeli Chamber of Commerce has stated that the boycott has hurt Israel's economy, though it nevertheless performs better than most Arab economies. The boycott became official in 1948 (following Israeli independence) and remains in effect. However, only Syria and Lebanon enforce it to any significant extent.

Arab Common Market A proposed market allowing the free movement of goods, services, labor, and capital between all Arab countries. The Arab Common Market began with a proposal to create a customs union in 2007; it is intended to be in place by 2020. See also: MEFTA.

Arab Cooperation Council An international organization that sought to emulate the economic integration of the Gulf Cooperation Council. It was established in 1989 and consisted of Egypt, Iraq, Jordan, and North Yemen. It became defunct following Iraq's invasion of Kuwait in 1990.

Arab Fund for Economic and Social Development A financial institution intended to benefit international development in Arab countries. AFESD was established in Kuwait in 1972 under the aegis of the League of Arab States. The AFESD has several billion dollars in assets. See also: Petrodollar.

Arab International Bank A bank in Egypt. It provides a full spectrum of retail banking services, primarily for export industries, notably natural gas, oil, pharmaceuticals, telecommunications, and tourism. It was established in 1974. See also: Arab-African International Bank.

Arab League An international organization intended to foster political and economic cooperation, and to deal with matters of regional concern. For example, it was able to prevent full-scale civil war in Lebanon in 1958 and has managed the Arab boycott of Israel since 1948. Since the early 2000s, it has been involved in the attempt to broker peace with Israel and the Palestinians. It was established in 1945 and is based in Cairo.

Arab Maghreb Union A regional organization consisting of the Arab countries in North Africa (with Egypt being a major exception). It aims for economic and political cooperation throughout the region. It was established in 1989.

Arab Monetary Fund An international organization that promotes trade and development of financial markets for and between Arab states. It also aims to correct deficits in members' balance of payments. All its activities were originally intended to pave way for a united, Arab currency, but this goal has largely faded. It was established in 1977 and is based in Abu Dhabi, United Arab Emirates.

Arab Money A slang term for tax free money, especially money procured illegally. The term is highly derogatory.

Arab Trade Financing Program A financial institution intended to foster trade between Arab countries and to make financing available for Arab exporters. It provides lines of credit to Arab exporters and importers through national agencies.

These national agencies are appointed by the monetary authorities in each country. The ATFP was established by the Arab Monetary Fund in 1989.

Arab-African International Bank A bank in Egypt. It promotes the increased use of retail banking among the Egyptian population and provides brokerage and investment services. It was established 1964 as a joint venture between the Central Bank of Egypt and the Kuwait Investment Authority.

Arabic Foot An obsolete Arabic unit of length approximately equivalent to 32 centimeters.

Aratni An ancient Indian unit of length variously equivalent to values between 375 and 500 millimeters.

Arbeidsmiljoloven Legislation in Norway intended to provide safe working environments for employees. It applies to all businesses operating in Norway other than shipping companies and fisheries. It includes regulations on working hours, maternity leave, and other things. It came into effect in 2006. The word "Arbeidsmiljoloven" translates to "Working Environment Act."

Arbiter An impartial third party asked to resolve a disagreement without forcing the disputants to go to court. The parties to the dispute agree to make their cases before one or more arbiters and to abide by whatever decision the arbiter or arbiters make, each party forgoing the right to an appeal. There are generally three arbiters, but there may be up to five. An arbiter is also called an arbitrator, or, less formally, an umpire.

Arbitrage An investment practice that attempts to profit from inefficiencies in price by making transactions that offset each other. For example, one may buy a security at a low price and, within a few seconds, re-sell it to a willing buyer at a higher price. Arbitrageurs can keep prices relatively stable as markets try to resist their attempts at price exploitation. Arbitrageurs often use computer programs because their transactions can be complex and occur in rapid succession.

Arbitrage Bond A municipal bond issued at a lower interest rate than another municipal bond. The funds from the second bond are invested in treasury securities until the call date of the first bond, when they are used to pay for the first bond's redemption. Depending on whether an arbitrage bond is also used for projects relating to municipal development, it may or may not be tax free.

Arbitrage Pricing Theory A pricing model that seeks to calculate the appropriate price of an asset while taking into account systemic risks common across a class of assets. The APT describes a relationship between a single asset and a portfolio that considers many different macroeconomic variables. Any security with a price different from the one predicted by the model is considered mispriced and is an arbitrage opportunity. An investor may use the arbitrage pricing theory to find undervalued securities and assets and take advantage of them. The APT is considered an alternative to the capital asset pricing model.

Arbitrage Trading Program A trading strategy taking a long or short position on a stock or commodity and taking the opposite position on a futures contract. This strategy often makes use of a computer program because the transactions involved can become complex and occur in rapid succession. A trader using an arbitrage trading program usually closes the positions toward the end of the futures contract when the prices of the contract and the underlying are approximately equal. This strategy is often used in trading whole baskets of stocks.

Arbitrage-Free Condition A situation in which all relevant assets are priced appropriately and there is no way for one's gains to outpace market gains without taking on more risk. Assuming an arbitrage-free condition is important in financial models, thought its existence is mainly theoretical.

Arbitrageur A trader who practices arbitrage. That is, an arbitrageur attempts to profit from inefficiencies in price by making transactions that offset each other. For example, one may buy a security at a low price, and, within a few seconds, re-sell it to a willing buyer at a higher price. Arbitrageurs can keep prices relatively stable as markets attempt to resist their attempts at price exploitation. They often use computer programs because their transactions can be complex and occur in rapid succession.

Arbitrary Value A value not linked to an asset or liability, but created solely for accounting purposes. Critics of capitalism contend that a disproportionate amount of the value the market creates is arbitrary, though others strongly dispute this. Arbitrary value is also called fictitious value.

Arbitration An extrajudicial means of resolving a dispute in which the parties agree to make their cases before an impartial person or panel. There are generally three arbitrators, but there may be up to five. Importantly, the parties in arbitration agree to allow the decision to be binding and to forego the right to an appeal.

Arbitration Clause A clause in a contract stating that, in the event of a dispute, parties shall follow an extrajudicial means of resolution in which they make their cases before an impartial person or panel. The clause may also indicate the specific process the parties shall follow in the event of arbitration. The clause is intended to save both parties the time and expense of a lawsuit.

Arbitration Panel A committee involved in an extrajudicial means of resolving a dispute. Parties to the dispute agree to make their cases before the arbitration panel and to abide by its decision, forgoing the right to an appeal. There are generally three members of an arbitration panel, but there may be up to five. Self-regulatory organizations such as FINRA sponsor arbitration panels for the equitable resolution of disputes.

Arbitron Company A company that provides clients with information about American radio markets; examples of such information include demographics, size and the products people in different markets are likely to buy. It provides similar information about online and other forms of broadcasting markets. It is based in New York.

Arbitron Information on Demand A computerized system available to subscribers providing information about American radio and some other markets; examples of such information include demographics, size and the products people in different markets are likely to buy. Arbitration Information on Demand provides a variety of reports. It is owned by the Arbitron Company.

Arc Elasticity A variable's elasticity (or relative stability of a variable with respect to another variable's change) when the two variables are between two given points. One calculates the arc elasticity by dividing the percentage change of one variable by the percentage change of the other. This is used to find a more accurate measure of the price elasticity of demand.

Archer In the United Kingdom, a slang term for 2,000 pounds. The term derives from a man named Jeffrey Archer, who was accused of bribing a prostitute with 2,000 pounds.

Archer Medical Savings Account An account into which one makes tax-deferred contributions that can be used for present and future medical expenses. An Archer MSA is used in conjunction with an insurance policy with a high deductible. An Archer MSA may be used in order to offset the high deductible on one's other insurance policy. One does not pay taxes on withdrawals from a health savings account, unless one withdraws funds for a non-medical reason, in which case they are taxed as ordinary income. If one is under 65, there may also be a penalty associated with a non-medical withdrawal.

Archipelago Exchange A former electronic communications network that facilitated over-the-counter trading by sending buy or sell orders to the appropriate specialist on the floor of a stock exchange, bypassing the floor broker. It merged with the New York Stock Exchange in 2006 to form NYSE Arca.

Archive Storage A physical place where one can store old documents with current or future value but that one does not immediately need. For example, one may place the deed to one's house or one's old tax returns in archive storage. Most archive storage units have some sort of security to prevent break-ins.

ARE GOST 7.67 Latin three-letter geocode for the United Arab Emirates. The code is used for transactions to and from Emirati bank accounts and for international shipping to the Emirates. As with all GOST 7.67 codes, it is used primarily in Cyrillic alphabets.

Are You Open? An inquiry as to whether an order to buy or sell a security has been filled. Some orders are only open for a certain amount of time, while some remain open until they are filled. The inquiry can help clarify the matter. See also: IOC, GTC.

Area The size of a two-dimensional space. One calculates the area by multiplying the area's length by its width.

Area Code A three-digit code affixed at the beginning of a telephone number in a geographic region. Sometimes, if a place has an exceptionally large number of phone numbers, a single region can have more than one area code. Area codes were introduced in 1951 to allow for direct long-distance dialing.

Area Distribution Center A U.S. Postal Service facility that receives a high volume of mail. The area distribution center accumulates mail and sends it out to individual post offices, which in turn deliver it to the appropriate addresses.

Area of Dominant Influence The geographic area that a television or radio station covers. For example, a radio station based in Tulsa usually can be heard through most of Northeastern Oklahoma. This is important in advertising, as more people can see or hear an ad broadcast over a larger ADI. The Arbitron Company publishes the ADI for American media markets.

Area Sample In statistics, all the possible values a random variable can take under a given set of circumstances in a geographic area, as well as the probability that it will take each value. That is, an area sample divides a large geographic area into subunits and calculates the probability that the variable will occur in each unit. An area sample is a form of probability distribution applied to geography. It is also called an area selection.

Area-by-Area Allocation A way to budget for advertising whereby a company allows its departments to spend a certain amount in each media market based on its size and relevance to the overall marketing strategy. For example, a company may allocate $10 million for advertising in Dallas, $7.5 million for Oklahoma City, and $5 million for Tulsa because each city is smaller than the one before it. Area-by-area allocation is also called market-by-market allocation.

ARG GOST 7.67 Latin three-letter geocode for Argentina. The code is used for transactions to and from Argentine bank accounts and for international shipping to Argentina. As with all GOST 7.67 codes, it is used primarily in Cyrillic alphabets.

Argentine Economic Crisis of 2001 A near collapse of the Argentine economy that began as a currency crisis. Argentina's currencies had historically seen high inflation; this inflation began to spiral out of control in the 1980s, and local vendors started to refuse local currency. In 1992, the government issued the convertible peso (ARS), which was pegged to the U.S. dollar, and the government maintained enough dollars at the central bank for people to exchange pesos for dollars on demand. This resulted in relative stability throughout the 1990s. However, the ease of convertibility led to capital flight as people would transfer their pesos to dollars and then send them out of the country. It also made imports cheap and led to unemployment, as companies preferred to import into Argentina rather than produce items domestically. Corruption was commonplace and the government's debt increased steadily. All of

this came to a head in 2001 when investors and ordinary people began a bank run, withdrawing their pesos to convert them to dollars and take them offshore. The government responded by effectively freezing all bank accounts, only allowing small amounts to be withdrawn. This led to riots. Eventually the government defaulted on its debt and ended convertibility to the dollar. It eventually ended the peg. At first, this caused inflation and unemployment, but the devalued peso encouraged exports while discouraging imports, which promoted growth in Argentina. Economic growth returned in 2003.

Argentine Peso The currency of Argentina. It was introduced in 1992, replacing the austral following a bout of hyperinflation. At introduction, it was pegged to the U.S. dollar at a one-to-one ratio, meaning that if one presented one peso to the Central Bank of the Republic of Argentina, it could be redeemed for one dollar. This peg was dropped during the Argentine economic crisis of 2001, but the Central Bank attempts to keep the value of the peso around three dollars to promote stability. It is also called the peso convertible.

Argument On a computer, information that the user enters in response to the requirements of a program. The program can only continue to function once the user has entered the argument. This is common in spreadsheet programs.

Ari Gold and His Friends A slang term for securities based on gold and similar metals, such as silver and platinum. The term derives from the television program Entourage.

Ariadne Network An organization of NGOs that intends to stop human trafficking from Eastern and Southeastern Europe. Members are located in countries of origin, transportation and destination for human traffickers and modern slaves. The Network attempts to raise awareness and improve communication so as to reduce and eventually eliminate the trade of persons.

Arithmetic Average Rate of Return The rate of return on an investment that is calculated by taking the total cash inflow over the life of the investment and dividing it by the number of years in the life of the investment. The average rate of return does not guarantee that the cash inflows are the same in a given year; it simply guarantees that the return averages out to the average rate.

Arithmetic Index An average in which no values count for more than others. That is, an arithmetic index simply adds the value of all data and divides by the number of data points. An arithmetic index is less common than a weighted average; that is, most indices weight for price or market capitalization. However, the Value Line composite index has an arithmetic version.

Arithmetic Mean Average An average calculated by adding the value of the points in a data set and dividing the sum by the number of data points. For example, suppose one wishes to calculate the average income of a country with exactly five people in it, and their incomes are $25,000, $26,000, $43,000, $70,000, and $72,000. It is calculated as: ($25,000 + $26,000 + $43,000 + $70,000 + $72,000) / 5 = $47,200. A limitation to the arithmetic mean average is that it can be overly affected by extremes in either direction. For example, if one of the five persons in the country earns $100 billion per year, the arithmetic mean average income would be in the billions and would not accurately count the other four citizens. For this reason, many analysts use the median in conjunction with the arithmetic mean average. The arithmetic mean average is also called simply the mean.

Arithmetic Progression A sequence of numbers in which the difference between any two succeeding numbers in the sequence is always the same. For example, given the sequence 0, 10, 20, 30, 40, and 50, the progression is arithmetic because the difference between each succeeding number is always 10.

Arizona Stock Exchange A former electronic exchange that allowed investors to trade NYSE, AMEX, and NASDAQ stocks after trading had ceased on other exchanges. It had low volume throughout its history and was exempt from SEC registration for that reason. It opened in 1990 and ultimately closed in 2001 due to lack of volume.

ARL ISO 4217 code for the Argentine peso ley. It was introduced in 1970, replacing the peso moneda nacional. It suffered from high inflation and was replaced by the peso argentino at a ratio of 10,000 to one in 1983.

ARM GOST 7.67 Latin three-letter geocode for Armenia. The code is used for transactions to and from Armenian bank accounts and for international shipping to Armenia. As with all GOST 7.67 codes, it is used primarily in Cyrillic alphabets.

Armed Islamic Group An Islamist group based in Algeria that has conducted terrorist activities since the early 1990s. In addition to civilian massacres within Algeria, it was responsible for the hijacking of an Air France flight in 1994.

Armenian Dram The currency of Armenia. It was introduced in 1993, replacing the Soviet ruble. It is a floating currency.

Armored Car and Messenger Insurance An insurance policy that covers shipments made by armored car. These shipments are usually large sums of money, precious metals, and similar assets. Armored car and messenger insurance is often tailored to the needs of the policyholder; it frequently covers all risks outside of war and fraud.

Arms Control and Disarmament Agency An agency of the U.S. government charged with conducting research and formulating policies and international agreements designed to prevent proliferation and to encourage disarmament of nuclear weapons and other weapons of mass destruction. It comes under the aegis of the Department of State.

Arm's Length Transaction A transaction in which the buyer and the seller have no significant, prior relationship. In an arm's length transaction, neither party has an incentive to act against his/her own interest. That is, the seller seeks to make the price as high as he/she can, and likewise the buyer seeks to make it as low as he/she can. The negotiations for an arm's length transaction result in the arm's length price, which is almost always close to the market value of the asset being sold. The term is often used in real estate transactions because family members often sell property to each other at something other than the arm's length price.

Arms Short-Term Trading Index Also called TRIN. In technical analysis, a measure of the strength of short-term market movements. It is calculated thusly: TRIN = (Advancing securities / Declining securities) / (Volume of advancing securities / Volume of declining securities) A TRIN measure below 1 indicates that there are more advancing securities on higher volume and is therefore a bullish indicator. A TRIN above 1 indicates the opposite and is thought to be bearish.

Armstrong Investigation An investigation into abuse and fraud that occurred in the New York State insurance industry in the early 20th century. The investigation was undertaken in 1905 and led to stricter regulation of the industry; for example, after the Armstrong investigation, insurance companies were required to put their policies' benefits in language a potential policyholder could understand.

Army Post Office A U.S. Army or Air Force office where American military personnel stationed overseas can send and receive correspondence. It operates just like a regular post office and must abide by all regulations set by the U.S. Postal Service. However, it is operated by the Department of Defense. See also: FPO.

Arnes Network Academic and Research Network of Slovenia. A publicly-owned foundation in Slovenia that provides Internet and other network services for universities, think tanks, cultural institutes, and similar organizations. It provides services for more than 200,000 people. Its board of directors is appointed by the Slovenian government.

Around In foreign exchange, a slang term for the premium or discount of a forward exchange rate relative to the current spot rate.

Aroura An ancient Greek unit of area approximately equivalent to 237.5 square meters.

ARP ISO 4217 code for the Argentine peso argentino. It was introduced in 1983, replacing the peso ley. It suffered from high inflation and was replaced by the austral at a ratio of 1,000 to one in 1985.

Arpanet The first digital network that utilized packet switching, which is the transmission of data, regardless of content, in manageable chunks called packets. This was a revolutionary technology and ultimately led to the creation of the modern Internet. It was developed in the 1960s by the Defense Advanced Research Projects Agency.

Arpent 1. An obsolete measure of length approximately equivalent to 58.47 meters. **2.** An obsolete measure of length approximately equivalent to 0.85 acres.

Arrangement 1. An agreement between a person or company and creditors whereby the person or company pays a fraction of what he/she/it owes to the creditors and, in exchange, the creditors forgive the remainder of the debt. This helps the creditors recover some of the debt and helps the person or company avoid bankruptcy. **2.** See: Treaty.

Arrangement on Guidelines for Officially Supported Export Credits An international agreement providing a framework for the provision of export credit guarantees. An export credit guarantee ensures that an exporter receives payment for goods shipped overseas in the event that the customer defaults, reducing the risk to the exporter's business and allowing it to keep its prices competitive. The guarantee is usually provided by a government or quasi-government agency. The Arrangement is intended to prevent a situation in which different countries use their export credit guarantees to attract business to the detriment of other countries. In other words, the Arrangement seeks to ensure that exports are sold on the basis of their quality rather than because an export credit guarantee offers unfairly favorable terms. The Arrangement is not binding in itself, but has been adopted by most OECD countries.

Arrangement Regarding Bovine Meat An international agreement to reduce tariffs and promote international cooperation in the trade of beef, veal and cattle. More than 20 countries have signed the Arrangement. It was negotiated at the Tokyo Round in the 1970s.

Arratel A Portuguese measure of weight approximately equivalent to 0.46 kilograms. It became obsolete after Lusophone countries adopted the metric system in the 19th century.

Array On a computer, a collection of data under a given name. Data points within an array are stored within a subset, usually with a name like x(1), x(2), etc.

Arrearage A previously due payment that has not been made. For example, because preferred stock has guaranteed dividends, a company is legally required to pay all dividends on preferred stock before it makes any dividend payments on common stock. If the company does not do so, usually because it has become cash poor, the preferred dividends are said to be in arrearage. This is also called being in arrears.

Arroba A Portuguese measure of weight approximately equivalent to 14.69 kilograms. It became obsolete after Lusophone countries adopted the metric system in the 19th century.

Arrondissement In French-speaking areas, a political subdivision equivalent to a borough. In the Netherlands, it is used to mean a district.

ARS ISO 4217 code for the Argentinian peso. It was introduced in 1992, replacing the austral following hyperinflation. At introduction, it was pegged to the U.S. dollar at a one-to-one ratio, meaning that if one presented one peso to the Central Bank of the Republic of Argentina, it could be redeemed for one dollar. This peg was dropped in the Argentine economic crisis of 2001, but the Central Bank attempts to keep the value of the peso around three dollars to promote stability. It is also called the peso convertible.

Arsani A Persian unit of length approximately equivalent to 55 or 60 centimeters.

Arshin A Russian unit of length equivalent to 2.33 feet. It was rendered obsolete when the Soviet Union began to use the metric system in 1924.

Arsin A Turkish measure of length approximately equivalent to 68 centimeters. It became obsolete when Turkey made the metric system mandatory in 1933.

Arson Deliberately setting fire with a destructive intent. Arson can be intended to incite terror; for example, a loan shark may set fire to a building owned by a debtor. Insurance for businesses and homes usually covers arson, though sometimes company owners set fire to their own buildings as a form of insurance fraud.

Art Any visual, creative material. Examples of art include drawings, videos and computer graphics. Art may be bought and sold as an asset (indeed, famous art such as the Mona Lisa is worth many millions of dollars), but it is also used in marketing to help a product appeal to buyers.

Art and Mechanical In marketing, describing the costs of producing and printing the artwork for an ad campaign.

Art Buyer A professional knowledgeable in art. An art buyer may scout talent for an advertising agency seeking to employ an art director. Alternatively, an art buyer may look for art for a collector or a company, among other reasons.

Art Director A professional who works at an advertising agency to provide artwork and similar products for ads, commercials and other marketing tools. For example, an art director may create a cartoon character to associate with a client's product. Art directors may be artists, graphic designers, or cinematographers, or have a number of other specialties.

Art Directors Club A professional organization for art directors, graphic designers and visual communication specialists. It hosts educational, networking and other events, and it provides scholarships for aspiring professionals. It was established in 1920 and is based in New York.

Art Service A company that provides artwork for commercials, ads and other marketing tools for an advertising agency. Many agencies have their own art departments, but an art service can supplement or, in some cases, even replace their work.

Arthur Andersen An accounting company once regarded as one of the finest in the world. It surrendered its license to operate as a certified public accountant in the wake of the Enron scandal in 2002. It has ceased most of its operations. See also: Big Five.

Arthur Levitt An American broker. He worked for a time as a broker for individual investors before becoming chairman of the American Stock Exchange. He was chairman of the Securities and Exchange Commission from 1993 to 2001.

Arthur Pigou A 20th-century English economist. He was noted for his contributions to welfare economics (the use of microeconomic data to measure the health of an economy) and externalities (the costs or benefits of a transaction to parties who do not directly participate in it). He lived from 1877 to 1959. See also: Pigouvian taxes.

Article 9 The section of the Uniform Commercial Code on collateral. It discusses what collateral can be used, who owns it in the event of default, and the circumstances under which a creditor can take possession of property.

Article XII Company A financial institution in New York that provides credit and other services for international commerce. Such institutions are usually owned by foreign companies and conduct activities like lending to borrowers outside the United States and exchanging foreign currencies. Article XII companies are not allowed to take deposits within New York and must receive permission from the banking board to take outside deposits. Its name is derived from Article XII of the New York State Banking Law.

Articles of Consolidation A document outlining the basic functions of a company formed by the merger of two or more companies. Among other things, it states the new company's corporate structure and how many authorized shares (if any) there will be. It also states how its corporate governance and operations will work. Some jurisdictions require companies to file articles of consolidation after a merger.

Articles of Dissolution A document filed with the appropriate jurisdiction to end the existence of a corporation or other legal entity. Articles of dissolution dispose of the corporation's assets in accordance with local law. For example, they may order payment of all debts and surrender of other assets to shareholders or other interested parties.

Articles of Incorporation A document outlining the basic functions of a company. Among other things, it states whether it will be an S Corporation or a C Corporation and how many authorized shares there will be. It also states how its corporate governance and operations will work. A company that seeks to incorporate must file articles of incorporation with the appropriate authority. In the United States, that authority is usually the states and sometimes the federal government. It is also called a corporate charter or simply a charter. See also: Charter Amendment Limitations.

Articles of Partnership A document outlining the basic functions of a company. Among other things, it states each partner's responsibilities, how profits are to be divided, and the type of business the partnership creates. Persons or companies that seek to form a partnership must file articles of partnership with the appropriate authority, which, in the United States, is usually the state in which the partnership is located. Articles of partnership are also called partnership agreements.

Articulate In accounting, describing the relationships, if any, between the different facts listed on a financial statement.

Artificial Currency A currency that does not circulate and is used for accounting purposes only. A prominent example is the special drawing right, which is based on a basket of different currencies and is used when accounting IMF transactions.

Artificial Intelligence Any computer program that seeks to imitate human thought. Artificial intelligence is useful in making some investment decisions because it eliminates emotional trading and is able to make most calculations more quickly and accurately. As a result it is often used in some more complex investment strategies, notably arbitrage.

Aruba Florin The currency of Aruba. This currency was introduced in 1986 upon Aruba's independence from Netherlands Antilles. The florin replaced the Netherlands Antilles guilder at a 1:1 ratio. Like the guilder, however, the florin is pegged to the U.S. dollar at a rate of 1.79 florins to 1 dollar; this peg is identical to the Netherlands Antilles guilder.

AS 1. ISO 3166-1 alpha-2 code for American Samoa. This is the code used in international transactions to and from American Samoan bank accounts. **2.** ISO 3166-2 geocode for American Samoa. This is used as an international standard for shipping to American Samoa. As a territory of the United States, American Samoa is also assigned the geocode ISO 3166-2:US-AS.

As Is Describing the sale of an asset in which the seller gives no guarantee on the quality of the asset and makes no repairs that may be necessary. An "as is" sale transfers all risk to the buyer. This may result in a lower price. Even so, it is often advantageous to the buyer only if he/she intended to make repairs or renovations anyway. The term is used frequently in real estate.

As per Advice A term on a bill of exchange indicating that the drawee has been informed that he/she is responsible for making payment on the bill.

ASA 1. See: American Society of Appraisers. **2.** See: American National Standards Institute. **3.** See: American Statistical Association.

Ascender An informal term for a stock or other security that has risen in price over a given period. For example, if a stock opens at $5.00 and closes at $5.25, it is said to be an ascender for that trading day. See also: Decliner.

Ascending Channel In technical analysis, a channel that trends upward. A price channel is the range between the support and resistance levels on a chart. In other words, an ascending channel is marked by higher highs and higher lows; this is a bullish signal that is likely to continue until the lows drop below the higher lows previously documented. See also: Descending Channel.

Ascending Sign In technical analysis, a series of high and low prices for a security that is generally trending upward. That is, both the highs and the lows are tending to rise over time. This is almost always a bullish signal. Examples of ascending signs include an ascending triangle and an ascending channel.

Ascending Tops In technical analysis, a series of peaks in price in which each peak is higher than the last. That is, a price may peak, then dip back down, then go to a higher peak, and so forth. Technical analysts often consider this a strong buy signal.

Ascending Triangle In technical analysis, a series of high and low prices for a security that, when plotted on a chart, looks vaguely like a triangle pointed to the right. One constructs an ascending triangle by first drawing a horizontal line on a chart representing a high price toward which a security is approaching and then drawing a diagonal line representing a security's upward price trend. An ascending triangle indicates that both the highs and the lows are rising. It is a bullish signal. See also: Descending triangle.

ASCII American Standard Code for Information Exchange. A code that represents as a binary number each of the 128 letters, numbers, punctuation marks and other characters used in English. This was developed in the 1960s for telegraphs and is used in computing.

Ascribed Group Membership The state of belonging to a social group from which one cannot cease to belong. Ascribed group membership may include race, gender, ethnicity, and, to lesser extents, religion and socio-economic class. Ascribed group membership can affect the economic or business choices one makes. It can hinder business development (for example, it can be more difficult to start a business if one comes from a less wealthy background). It can also help in some circumstances (for example, one may have a built-in customer base in members of one's ascribed group).

ASE Index The benchmark index of securities traded on the Athens Exchange. It lost more than a third of its value in the wake of the Greek financial crisis in 2009-2010.

ASE Market Capitalization Weighted Index The more important of the two indices of securities traded in Jordan. It was created in 1992 and, as the name implies, weights for market capitalization, meaning price changes to more highly capitalized companies affect the Index more. It tracks about 70 stocks listed on the Amman Stock Exchange; this list is reevaluated each year.

ASEAN Free-Trade Area An agreement between members of ASEAN that seeks the reduction and/or elimination of tariffs between members at the encouragement of foreign direct investment. Goods originating in an ASEAN member state and exported to another may not have a tariff higher than 5% of the value of the good. It was signed in 1992 and became operational in 2003. Since it was originally created, prospective members of ASEAN have been required to sign on to the Free-Trade Area.

ASEAN+3 An international forum for the members of the Association of Southeast Asian Nations along with China, Japan, and South Korea. Its first meeting occurred in 1997 but it was not established formally until 1999. It is noted for proposing the Asian currency unit, an accounting currency that would (if implemented) rationalize exchange rates among participating currencies to promote financial stability.

Aseguradora Mexicana An insurance company in Mexico.

Aseittha A Burmese unit of mass approximately equivalent to 408.23 grams.

Ashaan ad-Dukhaan An Arabic term for "something for cigarettes." In Egypt, it is a slang term for a small bribe.

Asia Ex-Japan All the countries in East Asia except for Japan. Asia Ex-Japan contains a number of high-growth, developing economies. Some indices and mutual funds track Asia Ex-Japan in order to observe or take advantage of the high return possible from investing in these countries. Japan is excluded because it is considered a developed country; investing in Japan carries lower risk and a lower return.

Asian and Pacific Coconut Community An international organization for countries that produce and export coconuts. It exists to promote the trade of coconuts and coconut products, and sets international standards for the quality of coconut oil. Most member nations are in the Indian Ocean or the South Pacific, though Jamaica is an associate member. It is based in Jakarta, Indonesia.

Asian Clearing Union An organization intended to provide a systematic way for transnational transactions in Asia to be settled. Eligible transactions are settled using an accounting currency equal to one U.S. dollar. A number of transactions are required to be settled through the Asian Currency Union, notably deferred-payment import/export transactions and direct transfers between residents of different member countries. It was established by the United Nations in 1974 and is based in Tehran, Iran.

Asian Currency Unit A proposed currency basket for the ASEAN + 3 currencies as a precursor to a currency union in East Asia. It is intended to model the European currency unit, which preceded the euro. The countries that would theoretically participate in this are Brunei, Burma, Cambodia, China, Indonesia, Japan, Laos, Malaysia, Philippines, Singapore, South Korea, Thailand, and Vietnam.

Asian Development Bank A bank that promotes economic growth and international development in the Asia-Pacific region of the world. It finances its activities with bonds and works closely with the International Monetary Fund and the World Bank toward accomplishing its goals. Its two largest shareholders are the United States and Japan. It was established in 1966 and is headquartered in Manila, Philippines.

Asian Development Fund An instrument of the Asian Development Bank that offers grants and low-interest loans to developing countries in Asia. The ADF seeks to reduce poverty and promote sustainable development in its program area. It was established in 1973 and is funded through its donor countries.

Asian Dollar Market The market in East Asia for loans or bank deposits denominated in U.S. dollars. Banks in Asia sometimes offer dollar market services.

Asian Dollars U.S. dollar deposits in banks in East Asia. Asian dollar futures contracts, which are based on Asian dollar deposits, are a highly liquid investment. Investing in Asian dollars may help an Asian company hedge its foreign exchange risk on investments in the United States. It is an example of a eurocurrency.

Asian Financial Crisis A situation in which a number of East Asian currencies collapsed in value, forcing the IMF to launch a $40 billion loan program to stabilize their economies. The crisis started in 1997, when the Thai baht began to float for the first time; this resulted in rapid devaluation of the currency and large price increases. Similar things began happening in Hong Kong, Laos, Malaysia, the Philippines, and especially Indonesia and South Korea. This occurred despite the fact that most of these governments had no national debt and were thought to have been pursuing rational monetary policies. The Asian financial crisis ended what was previously called the East Asian economic miracle. Analysts disagree about what caused the crisis. Some economists have argued that there was too much foreign capital investment in East Asia without a concomitant increase in domestic productivity. Others have cited supposed crony capitalism in many of these countries, while still others blame the IMF for exacerbating what they say was a minor situation.

Asian Futures A futures contract on a security issued by a company in East Asia. While some Asian economies are quite open for trade with foreigners, others are not.

Asian Option An option contract in which the payoff is related to the average price of the underlying instrument over a set period of time. There are two basic types of an Asian option. In an average strike option, the underlying instrument is bought or sold at its average price over the period of the contract. In an average rate option, the payoff is the difference between the average price of the underlying asset over the life of the contract and some stated strike.

Asian Productivity Organization An international organization dedicated to socioeconomic development and increased productivity in East Asia and the Pacific. It conducts research, advises member countries, and attempts to strengthen small- and medium-sized businesses, among other things. It was established in 1961 and consists of 20 countries in the region. It is headquartered in Tokyo.

Asia-Pacific The regions containing most countries and territories in East Asia, Southeast Asia, the South Pacific, and Oceania. Sometimes it also includes the North and South American nations on the eastern shore of the Pacific, as well as occasionally Russia and South Asia.

Asia-Pacific Economic Cooperation Pact An organization promoting trade and economic liberalization among countries with borders along the Pacific Ocean. It has 21 members including Australia, Canada, China, Chile, Japan, Russia, South Korea, and the United States. Heads of government of member nations meet annually to discuss trade and economic issues. It was established in 1989 and is headquartered in Singapore. See also: ASEAN, Free Trade Area of the Asia-Pacific.

Ask The lowest price for which a seller is willing to sell some asset. When one makes a buy order, one may order a broker to buy at the ask, which is simply the best price currently available. The difference between the ask and the bid is called the bid-ask spread, which is a key measure of liquidity.

Ask Rate The lowest exchange rate at which a seller is willing to sell a currency. See also: Ask.

Ask Size The number of shares in a stock that a potential seller is willing to sell in a given offer. For example, if the ask size is 1,000 shares, this means that the seller wishes to sell 1,000 shares at the stated price. See also: Bid Size.

Asked to Bid/Offer A situation in which a seller or buyer of a security has solicited a potential buyer or seller. When an investment bank is asked to bid/offer, the potential seller/buyer asks for money as a surety. See also: Bid-ask spread.

Askel A Finnish unit of length approximately equivalent to one meter. Its measure was never systemized and became obsolete when Finland adopted the metric system in 1880.

Aslu An ancient Akkadian unit of length approximately equivalent to 60 meters.

ASM GOST 7.67 Latin three-letter geocode for American Samoa. The code is used for transactions to and from American Samoan bank accounts and for international shipping to American Samoa. As with all GOST 7.67 codes, it is used primarily in Cyrillic alphabets.

Asociacion Latinoamericana de Institutiones Financieras de Desarrollo An organization dedicated to economic development and integration in Central and South America. It conducts research and attempts to improve the flow of information between countries in the region. It was established in 1968 and consists of 24 countries in the region, along with several North American and European nations. It is headquartered in Lima, Peru.

Asociacion Latinoamericana de Integracion An international organization dedicated to trade integration and the establishment of a common market in Latin America. Member states give each other preferential treatment in the form of tariff rebates as well as financial and other forms of cooperation. However, its scope is much less broad than the European Union, many of whose members hope for full political integration. ALADI was established in 1980.

Aspect Ratio The ratio of the longer dimension of a shape to its shorter dimension. For example, if the length of a rectangle is three inches and its width is two inches, its aspect ratio is 1.5. This is used in graphic design and in measuring the size of products like paper. As such it can be important to advertising.

Aspenize To turn an area, especially but not necessarily a municipality, into an expensive tourist attraction. Aspenization is accompanied by rising real estate prices, more restaurants, and sometimes by higher taxes. Aspenization tends to increase tax revenue, but is often controversial among residents. The term derives from Aspen, Colorado, a tourist city in the United States.

Asper A division of the muzuna, which was a subdivision of the Algerian budju. One muzuna was divided into two asper.

Aspirin Australian Stock Price Riskless Index Note. A debt security with no coupon with a return based on the return of a benchmark stock index. Unlike most zero-coupon bonds, an Aspirin is issued at near face value; however, like others, it is redeemed at face value at maturity, which is four years after issue. The return (or the equivalent of a coupon) on an Aspirin is the fact that the bondholder receives a percentage of the return on the Australian all-ordinaries stock index provided it is over a certain amount. For example, if the limit is 5% and the return is 9% over the four years of the Aspirin, the bondholder receives a return of 4%. However, if the return on the all-ordinaries index falls below the limit, the bondholder receives no return. Aspirins allow investors to participate in the stock market without assuming all of the risk involved.

Aspirin Count Theory A somewhat tongue-in-cheek theory stating that stock prices and aspirin sales are inversely related. That is, when stock prices are rising, aspirin sales are falling and vice versa. The idea behind this theory is that when stock prices are rising, fewer people are under stress, and, therefore, have less need for aspirin; likewise, when stock prices are falling, more people need aspirin and therefore buy it. The aspirin count theory has never been seriously tested.

Assailing Thieves In maritime insurance, an insured event providing coverage in the event that a ship's cargo is stolen.

Assault Unwanted and/or violent physical contact with another person. Assault is a crime and a tort in most jurisdictions, though specific definitions differ from place to place.

Assay To test precious metals for their purity. This is important to commodities and futures involving precious metals, in which the quality of the underlying metals must be specified in the contract.

Assba An obsolete Arabic unit of length approximately equivalent to 2.25 centimeters.

Assemblage The combination of two or more adjoining plots of real estate into a single plot. For example, a farmer may own 10 acres. If he buys the 25 acres next to him, he may combine the two plots so that they are from then on considered a single unit. Assemblage can increase the value of the real estate such that the new plot is worth more than the sum of its parts. This can have property tax implications.

Assembly Dailies In film, the best takes of two or more scenes shot on a day as put together by an editor. The editor may splice together several takes and scenes in order to create a relatively coherent assembly daily. Assembly dailies are the beginning of the editing process and are used in both television and cinema. They are also simply called dailies.

Assembly Language A computer language in which a command corresponds to only one statement in the language. For example, "A" in assembly language stands for "Add." This provides less flexibility than binary, but it is easier to learn and use.

Assembly Line A way to manufacture a product in which parts are added in sequence by different workers. For example, Joe may put the engine in a car and send it to Bob, who puts on the doors. Then it goes to Frank, who applies the wheels. Each worker has his/her post; the unfinished product comes to each worker in turn. This process allows workers to put together more products at a time; for instance, rather than putting together one car at a time, workers are able to use their expertise on multiple cars throughout the day. Assembly lines were developed by the Ford Motor Company in the early 20th century and were instrumental in beginning the mass production of automobiles.

Assembly Plant The place where a company manufactures its products. The term implies, but does not necessitate, the presence of assembly lines at the plant.

Assented Stock A stock owned by a shareholder who has agreed to a takeover of the company represented by the stock. The acquiring company in such a takeover usually offers a higher price for assented stock than for non-assented stock.

Assess 1. To estimate the value of a property, especially for property tax purposes. For example, a county may send an assessor to one's house to assess its value and base the property tax one owes on that assessment. **2.** To decide the cost of something. For example, an insurance company may assess the damage of a house fire at $120,000 and agree to pay that much toward repairs. Alternatively, the government may assess that one owes $50,000 in income tax based upon one's income the previous year.

Assessable Capital Stock 1. The capital stock of a bank that, in the event of insolvency, exposes shareholders to liabilities over and above what they originally invested. **2.** Capital stock that the holder has not paid in full and that is therefore subject to a call.

Assessable Insurance An insurance policy in which a premium is paid up front, but in which the insurer reserves the right to require another premium to be paid if losses resulting from claims exceed the amount the policyholder contributed in the initial premium. This is also called natural premium or stipulated premium insurance.

Assessable Mutual A mutual insurance company that charges a policyholder a premium in exchange for an insurance policy, but reserves the right to require another premium to be paid if losses resulting from claims exceed the amount the policyholder contributed in the initial premium.

Assessed Valuation The value of a property as determined by an appraisal conducted by a municipality. The assessed valuation usually occurs every year when a municipality asks for appraisal to determine the liability for property taxes. If a property owner wishes to dispute the value of an appraisal, he/she may request a reassessment. The assessed valuation may take into account the quality of the property, values of surrounding properties, and market conditions in the area.

Assessment Company An insurance company that charges a policyholder a premium in exchange for an insurance policy, but reserves the right to require another premium to be paid if losses resulting from claims exceed the amount the policyholder contributed in the initial premium. An assessment company is also called an assessment association or a stipulated premium company.

Assessment of Deficiency The amount that a taxpayer owes in back taxes as determined by the IRS and, if one was requested, an appeal. For example, if one owed $50,000 in taxes for 2009 but only paid $40,000, the IRS would make an assessment of deficiency for $10,000, plus interest and penalties.

Assessment Period In assessable insurance, the period of time during which the insurance company has the right to determine whether or not it should charge an additional premium. Assessable insurance is an insurance policy in which a premium is paid up front, but in which the insurer reserves the right to require another premium to be paid if losses resulting from claims exceed the amount the policyholder contributed in the initial premium. To protect the policyholder, this determination must be made during the assessment period.

Assessment Ratio A ratio of a property's assessed valuation to its market value. An assessed valuation is the value of a property as determined by an appraisal conducted by a municipality. The market value is the price for which one can sell a property on the open market. For example, if the assessed valuation of a piece of real estate is $180,000 and its market value is $200,000, its assessment ratio is 0.90, or 90%. The assessment ratio is used to determine one's property tax liability.

Assessment Roll A list of the assessed valuation of all properties in a given jurisdiction. Assessment rolls are usually maintained by a city or county for property tax purposes.

Assessor A person licensed by a municipality to conduct appraisals of local properties. An assessor may take into account the quality of a property, values of surrounding properties, and market conditions in the area. The purpose of an assessor's appraisals is to assess the value of properties so as to determine each owner's property tax liability.

Asset In accounting, anything of value that a person or firm buys. Assets can be physical, such as real estate or stocks, a claim on debts, such as accounts receivable or liens, or a right, such as a patent. Of crucial importance to assets is their relative liquidity, or the ease with which they can be converted to cash. Liquid assets are often thought to be more useful than illiquid assets. See also: Tangible asset, Intangible asset.

Asset Activity Ratios Any ratio that measures how well or how poorly a person or company is managing assets. For example, one may compare assets to debt to ensure that debt remains at a manageable level. Likewise one may compare assets to cash flow or any number of other metrics. See also: Asset Turnover Ratio.

Asset Adequacy Tested Reserve The liquid assets that a life insurance company must keep at all times. The asset adequacy tested reserve is set by law or regulation and equals the insurance company's total liabilities, assuming that it must pay all possible claims at once. This amount is tested under a number of different scenarios to ensure the company can pay claims regardless of prevailing interest rates. See also: Required reserve.

Asset Allocation An active management strategy for a portfolio or fund with a basic set of securities. The investor or money manager changes the securities represented in the portfolio or fund as one's investment goals change. It is important to note, however, that asset allocation implies diversification to the portfolio or fund. The investor or money manager may use fundamental, technical, and/or macroeconomic analysis in determining when and how to change the securities in the portfolio or fund.

Asset Allocation Fund A mutual fund with a portfolio mixing stocks, bonds, and cash equivalents in different types of securities. This is done to diversify the fund and avoid the volatility in any one market. There are three basic types of asset allocation funds. Balanced funds maintain a more-or-less fixed ratio of stocks and bonds. Life-cycle or target date funds start with higher-risk investments, but move toward lower-risk as the investor approaches some pre-determined date, usually retirement. Finally, life-style funds are actively managed according to an investor's or broker's specifications and market conditions.

Asset Backed 1. See: Asset-Backed Security. 2. See: Asset-Based Finance.

Asset Class Different types of investments that behave similarly and are subject to most of the same market forces. Many analysts believe that there are three main assets classes: equity securities or stocks, fixed-income securities or bonds, and cash equivalents. Some analysts would also include commodities, real estate, and derivatives. Including a variety of asset classes is important to constructing or maintaining a diverse portfolio.

Asset Coverage The extent to which a company can maintain operations at its level of debt. One of the most common ways to measure asset coverage is the asset coverage ratio, which divides the value of tangible assets less current liabilities by the company's total debt outstanding. These liabilities may include preferred dividends and rent. See also: Cash flow coverage ratio, Debt service coverage ratio.

Asset Coverage Ratio The ratio of the value of a company's assets less current liabilities to the company's total debt outstanding. These liabilities may include preferred dividends and rent. The asset coverage ratio measures how easily a company can maintain its operations with its level of debt. See also: Cash flow coverage ratio, Debt service coverage ratio.

Asset Depreciation Range System A system for determining the useful life of different kinds of assets that the IRS uses in determining depreciation. This is used in turn to determine the taxation for different assets. See also: Modified Accelerated Cost Recovery System.

Asset Depreciation Risk In insurance, the risk of loss to the company as the result of declining investments. An insurance company generally maintains a portfolio of securities. If a stock declines or a bond defaults, it may find itself with fewer assets and the same number of liabilities. In the United States, state governments determine the investments insurance companies are allowed to make to reduce asset depreciation risk. It is one of four types of risk to an insurance company; the others are interest rate risk, pricing inadequacy risk, and general business risk. Asset depreciation risk is also called asset quality risk. See also: Legal list.

Asset Financing The act of a company pledging a security interest in some asset in order to obtain cash. This term is most commonly used when a company is seeking short-term financing, such as working capital. Generally speaking, asset financing refers to a company's pledge of its accounts receivable or inventories in order to obtain a loan, but other assets may be used as well. See also: Factoring, Collateral.

Asset for Asset Swap A swap in which two creditors exchange one or more defaulting debts each. Creditors do this in order to reduce the amount of debt on their books while at the same time increasing the amount of interest they are owed.

Asset Impairment The state in which an asset has a market value less than its value listed on the company's records, especially when the value is unlikely to recover. The cash flow an impaired asset will generate is less than the difference between its market value and its book value. Impaired assets include bad debt, obsolete equipment and, most especially, goodwill. A company must write off its asset impairment each year.

Asset Ledger In accounting, a record of all assets. The asset ledger is normally divided into subaccounts covering different kinds of assets. To give a very simple example, an asset ledger may record long-term and short-term assets in different places. Larger companies nearly always have more complicated asset ledgers.

Asset Management The act or practice of an investment advisory firm making investment decisions on behalf of a client. Asset management often opens up more potential investment vehicles up to the client. Another advantage is that, theoretically, asset managers have more knowledge and experience in making appropriate investment decisions than their clients. Asset management is usually limited to institutional investors and high net-worth individuals, as it is usually expensive.

Asset Management Account An account at a bank or other financial institution that allows the account holder to place money for both banking and investment services. When money is placed into the account, it is automatically placed into a money market account, which carries a higher interest rate than normal checking or savings accounts. The account holder can then direct the money to various banking and investment services. Asset management accounts were allowed after the passage of the Gramm-Leach-Bliley Act, which allowed financial institutions to offer both banking and investment services for the first time since at least the Great Depression.

Asset Management Corporation 1. See: Investment advisory firm. 2. See: Sovereign wealth fund.

Asset Motive The demand for money over and above what one needs to live in order to make investments. That is, the asset motive describes the desire to have money in order to make more money. It may be divided into the portfolio motive and speculative motive. The portfolio motive is the desire for money to invest directly, while the speculative motive is the demand to place money aside (outside of one's portfolio) to make a better investment should the opportunity arise.

Asset Play A stock with a net asset value above its market capitalization. An asset play is undervalued and therefore is considered to be a good stock to buy. See also: Wallflower.

Asset Price The amount one pays for an asset when buying it. The price represents the amount of value the market has assigned, fairly or unfairly, to an asset. Normally, prices are expressed in terms of money, but this is not always the case; for example, one may trade four chickens for two sheep. Asset prices tend to be regulated by the law of supply and demand; that is, the price of an asset increases with smaller supply and/or greater demand. A corollary to this is the idea that commoditization drives prices down because it increases supply (sometimes vastly) while leaving demand the same. Prices likewise rise when the value of money declines. Governments can and have controlled the prices of certain assets by subsidy or decree. This is usually an anti-inflationary measure and tends to distort, rather than eliminate, the law of supply and demand. It is thus not generally sustainable as a mechanism for controlling price.

Asset Pricing Model Any of several models used to determine the appropriate price or return on an asset at a given level of risk. Prominent examples include the capital asset pricing model and the arbitrage pricing theory.

Asset Quality A measure of the likelihood of default of a loan or lease, combined with a measure of its marketability. That is, asset quality is a measure of the price at which a bank or other financial institution can sell a loan or lease to a third party, as determined by the borrower or lessee, especially by a bond issuer. Credit ratings agencies determine credit quality in order to provide bond ratings; they may change these from time to time. FICO scores are measures of the credit quality of individuals. See also: Investment-grade, Junk.

Asset Retirement Obligation In accounting, a requirement that a long-term liability that must be retired in the future be recorded at its estimated, fair market value at the time of retirement instead of its value at the time the liability was acquired. This is codified in FASB No. 143.

Asset Sale The sale of a loan by a bank to a third party. An asset sale ensures that the bank receives cash for a loan it has made and reduces its potential for bad debt. It removes the loan from the bank's portfolio, unless the bank has an agreement with the third party to take the loan back in the event of default.

Asset Share Value The equity that a policyholder has built up in an insurance company. The asset share value is calculated as the amount the policyholder has paid in premiums, less the cost of insurance and other expenses to the insurance company. The asset share value is computed using the amount the insurance company actually spends in expenses, and is not simply an estimate.

Asset Stripping A form of corporate raiding in which a company acquires a target company and then sells some of its assets, usually to repay its (the corporate raider's) debt. Often this debt is the debt incurred in the process of taking over the target company. The corporate raider conducts asset stripping because he believes that selling some of the assets will both repay the debt and leave the raider with enough extra assets to increase its net worth. In the process of deciding which companies to acquire, asset strippers look for companies worth more as individual assets than as companies.

Asset Substitution A company's exchange of lower-risk investments for higher-risk investments. Firms may use asset substitution as a form of financing, or as a move to please shareholders. It can be detrimental to the company's bondholders as it increases the possibility of default without any corresponding benefit because bonds have a fixed interest rate. On the other hand, asset substitution can benefit shareholders as it carries the possibility of higher returns.

Asset Sufficiency or Insufficiency A calculation of the surrender value, the required reserve and the asset share value. These calculations are compared with one another to ensure that an insurance company has enough liquid assets to maintain operations.

Asset Swap A swap in which the legs are two investments, one with a fixed return and one with a variable return. For example, two investors could agree to swap bonds, which have guaranteed coupons, and an index fund, which has a return linked to the performance of some index. The counterparties to an asset swap are usually seeking favorable cash flows to fulfill their investment goals. While it is not required, debt obligations are usually at least one of the assets that are swapped.

Asset Turnover A ratio of a company's net sales to total assets. It is a measure of how efficiently management is using the assets at its disposal to promote sales. A high ratio indicates that the company is using its assets efficiently to increase sales, while a low ratio indicates the opposite. It is also known as total asset turnover.

Asset Valuation The process of determining the fair market value of an asset. This is done periodically when determining the value of real estate, a portfolio, an investment, an item on a balance sheet, or any number of other assets. There are a number of tools used for asset valuation, including the historical value, values of similar assets, current supply and demand, fundamental analysis, and so forth.

Asset Valuation Reserve The assets that a company is required to maintain in order to pay unexpected liabilities should they arise. Banks, for example, are required to keep a reserve ratio of deposits to protect against a bank run. Likewise, insurance companies must keep an asset valuation reserve (which is set by the NAIC) to be able to pay an unusually large number of claims.

Asset Value In stocks, the market value of a company's assets per share. Asset value does not take into account the share price; one calculates the asset value by adding together the total value of the company's tangible and intangible assets and dividing by the shares outstanding. Fundamental analysts may use a company's asset value to determine whether it is undervalued or overvalued. A company with a share price below its asset value is considered undervalued and fundamental analysts may recommend buying shares in that company. On the other hand, a company with a share price above the asset value is overvalued and fundamental analysts may recommend selling it. See also: Net asset value.

Asset/Equity Ratio The total assets of a company divided by the value of its stockholder equity. This is one measure of a company's leverage.

Asset/Liability Management Any active management strategy that involves coordinating a company's or fund's assets and liabilities such that the two together form an adequate return. Generally speaking, one aims to invest such that assets exceed liabilities as much as possible.

Asset-Backed Alert A weekly newsletter that publishes information on mortgage-backed securities and other asset-backed securities. It disseminates statistics, as well as news on relevant regulation and investment strategies. The publication is based in New Jersey.

Asset-Backed Commercial Paper A short-term debt security issued by a corporation that is collateralized by some asset. In general, asset-backed commercial paper is secured by accounts receivables or something similar. It carries less risk than other commercial paper, which is unsecured. It is a highly liquid investment and forms part of the money market.

Asset-Backed Fund A mutual fund that invests in real estate, equipment, stocks and other tangible assets. The advantage to an asset-backed fund is the fact that the assets behind it have liquidation value (that is, if a company fails, one can sell the company's equipment or real estate to cover a portion of the investment). Funds that invest in bonds and other debt securities do not necessarily have this advantage.

Asset-Backed Security A debt security collateralized by some receivables on some credit sale. Common examples of this collateral include receivables on credit cards, automotive loans, and similar assets. Returns on these securities come from customers' payments on their credit cards and other loans that may be backing the securities. Banks and companies package and sell their receivables to investors in order to reduce the risk of loan defaults. See also: Mortgage-backed security.

Asset-Based Finance The practice of making a loan secured by an asset. While, in theory, many loans are asset-based mortgages, the term most commonly applies to loans secured by something unusual, such as accounts receivable or intellectual property. Businesses take out most asset-based loans and pledge something used in the conduct of their businesses as collateral, such as inventory. As with all secured loans, asset-based loans have lower interest rates than unsecured loans. The practice is also called asset-based lending.

Asset-Conversion Loan A loan secured by an asset. That is, an asset-conversion loan converts an asset into cash in order to finance a company's activities. This term is most commonly used when a company is seeking short-term financing, such as working capital. Generally speaking, an asset-conversion loan involves a company's pledge of its accounts receivable or inventories in order to obtain a loan, but other assets may be used as well. See also: Factoring, Collateral.

Asset-Coverage Test A test determining whether a company is allowed to issue bonds. It is calculated by subtracting a company's current liabilities from its net assets and dividing the quantity by its total debts and/or preferred stock obligations; it may be expressed as dollar amount or as a percentage. Generally, a higher asset-coverage test is desirable, as it indicates the level of debt is low compared to net assets. A significant limitation of the asset-coverage test is the fact that it does not account for liquidity when making the calculation.

Asset-Liability Committee Also called ALCO. A committee at a bank charged with ensuring the bank has enough assets to pay for its liabilities. It does this by monitoring the risk of the bank's investments as well as its capital structure. It reports to the board of directors and generally must also provide information to regulators.

Asset-Liability Gap A real or expected inability for a bank or other financial institution to pay its liabilities based upon the assets it currently holds. Because the asset-liability gap does not include assets expected to come in the near future, it is used in conjunction with other tools to determine a bank's solvency.

Assets and Valuation An estimation of the fair market value of the assets in a pension plan as conducted by an actuary.

Assets Requirement The minimum amount one must invest in order to participate in an activity. For example, a hedge fund may impose a minimum asset requirement of $1 million, meaning that one must place at least $1 million into the hedge fund in order to become an investor. Investment companies sometimes impose asset requirements in order to keep out small investors.

Assets Under Management The money or other assets for which an investment advisory firm makes investment decisions for a client. Assets under management may refer to the assets for a particular client, or to the total amount managed for all clients. For example, a company may say that it has more than $2 billion under management. Asset management often opens more potential investment vehicles to the client.

Assets-in-Place The securities, real estate, and other property that a company already owns, and therefore does not need to buy in order to execute a particular investment strategy.

Assign In futures and options, to select, usually at random, a client with a short position to make delivery on a contract. That is, a clearing house randomly assigns a brokerage with a short position on a futures contract or option to make delivery of the underlying asset to one of the clearing house's clients with a long position on the same contract. When a brokerage is assigned to make a delivery, it also randomly assigns a client with a short position to make the delivery to the brokerage.

Assignable Contract A futures contract that the holder may assign to another party. That is, the holder may give or sell the assignable contract to a third party, allowing this party to take on all rights and obligations associated with the contract. One may do this and still profit from the investment if the underlying asset has appreciated. This is a relatively unusual provision; most futures traded on exchanges are not assignable contracts.

Assigned Mailing Date The date on which the user of a mailing list is permitted to send direct mail to all persons thereon. The owner of the mailing list uses the assigned mailing date to regulate how often persons on the same list receive direct mail. The person or group who owns a list determines the assigned mailing date, though it is often not enforced.

Assigned Risk 1. A driver of an automobile who is uninsurable (usually because of a poor driving record), but is required, by law, to have automobile insurance. States assign their uninsurable drivers to insurance companies, which must provide coverage (known as automobile assigned risk insurance), though the companies charge higher premiums. **2.** In workers' compensation, a worker who performs labor considered so hazardous that an insurance company will not insure his place of employment. For example, a miner or an oil rig worker may be an assigned risk. As with automobiles, states assign their uninsurable workers to insurance companies, which must provide coverage, often at higher premiums.

Assigned Risk Plan 1. An insurance plan for drivers who otherwise would not be able to obtain automobile insurance. Each state in the U.S. requires insurers to offer automobile assigned risk insurance, at a higher premium than traditional insurance. States assign uninsurable drivers to insurance companies, which must provide coverage. This helps people who, by law, must obtain automobile insurance, but are unable to do so because of poor driving records or other reasons. Critics contend it drives up premiums for all policyholders. **2.** In workers' compensation, an insurance plan for workers who perform labor considered so hazardous that an insurance company ordinarily would not insure the worker's place of employment. As with automobiles, states assign uninsurable workers to insurance companies, which must provide coverage, often at higher premiums.

Assignee A person to whom a contract is given or sold. For example, if Bob sells a futures contract to Joe, or alternately allows Joe to take over the lease on Bob's apartment, Joe is the assignee. While assigning contracts is common, not all contracts are transferable. See also: Assignor.

Assignment A sale or gift, especially of a contract or an obligation. While assigning contracts is common, not all contracts are transferable. See also: Assignor.

Assignment Capsule Clearly stated parameters for a task; a detailed job description. One is not expected to do (and may be prohibited from doing) tasks outside the assignment capsule.

Assignment Form A standardized contract or other form effecting and providing evidence of an assignment, which is a sale or gift, especially of a contract or an obligation. Requirements for assignment forms vary state by state.

Assignment Method Any quantitative or qualitative methodology by which one determines how to assign capital, employees, and almost anything else as efficiently as possible. For example, an assignment method may help a company determine how many employees it puts on a task or how much a major project should cost.

Assignment of Accounts Receivable A loan collateralized by a company's accounts receivable. For example, if a company borrowed $1 million from a bank and then defaulted, the bank could collect the company's accounts receivable. In general assignment of accounts receivable, the lender may collect from all the company's receivables until it recoups the amount lent. In special assignment, the lender may only collect from certain accounts specified in the lending agreement. This concept is similar to, but distinct from, factoring.

Assignment of Income The splitting of a person or company's income to another person or company so that the first person or company pays less in taxes. The United States Supreme Court has disallowed assignment of income under most circumstances.

Assignment of Insurable Interest The transfer of insurable interest to another party. Insurable interest is the right to enter an insurance contract because one has a property or carries a risk that needs to be insured against. For example, one cannot buy life insurance providing coverage for one's friend's death. However, in assignment of insurable interest, one can purchase insurance on oneself and then sell or give it to another party. This allows the other party to collect the benefit should the insured event occur. Assignment of insurable interest is the only way by which one may collect insurance money when one does not have a direct interest in the insured event.

Assignment of Lease The transfer of a lease by the lessee to another party. For example, if one rents an apartment, one might sell or give one's friend the right to live there (and the obligation to make payments). The assignor (the original lessee) remains bound by the lease contract if the assignee fails to make his/her obligations, unless the lessor states otherwise. Because of the potential complications, some lessors do not allow lessees to engage in assignment of lease.

Assignment of Letter of Credit The transfer of the right to receive payment on a letter of credit to another party. That is, in the assignment of letter of credit, the beneficiary of the letter of credit may sell or give a person or company the right to be paid by the bank honoring the letter.

Assignment of Life Policies The transfer to another party of the right to receive the death benefit of a life insurance policy. While one cannot buy life insurance providing coverage in the event of another person's death, one can buy the right to receive the death benefit from a policyholder. See also: Assignment of Insurable Interest.

Assignor In the transfer of an asset, liability, or anything else, the party that makes the transfer. That is, the assignor originally holds the asset or liability and gives or sells it to the assignee.

Assimilation The sale of the totality of a new issue. That is, assimilation occurs when investors buy the issue from underwriters and begin trading it like any other security.

Assistant Art Director An employee at an advertising agency who works in conjunction with the art director to develop graphics and other art for marketing purposes. In general, the assistant art director works primarily or exclusively on one account at a time, while the art director works for multiple clients.

Assisted Area In the United Kingdom, an area designated as needing government assistance to promote economic development.

Assistive Technology A computer program or any other technology used to help physically impaired persons. One example of assistive technology is a computer program that reads newspapers aloud to blind persons.

Associate Bank A bank that belongs to a network of organizations that provides benefits for all members. For example, many banks are associate banks for Visa, which provides debit card and credit card services for these banks. Banks may pay to be associated with such ventures.

Associate Creative Director An employee at an advertising agency who works in conjunction with the creative director to develop concepts and general strategies for marketing purposes. In general, the assistant creative director works primarily or exclusively on one account at a time, while the creative director works for multiple clients.

Associate in Claims A professional certification indicating one has expertise in the processing of insurance claims. In general, one only pursues an AIC after several years in the insurance industry. In order to earn certification, one must complete four courses and pass a test in each. The certification is administered by the Insurance Institute of America.

Associate in Commercial Underwriting A certification in underwriting offered by the AICPCU. Courses include principles and property, liability and advanced techniques and commercial insurance. It is abbreviated AU.

Associate in Management A professional certification indicating one has expertise in management in insurance. In general, one only pursues an AIM if one already serves as a manager in an insurance company. In order to earn certification, one must complete four tests covering subjects like human relations and decision making. The certification is administered by the Insurance Institute of America.

Associate in Marine Insurance Management A certification for insurance workers who wish to deal in marine insurance. The AMIM requires coursework in the particular risks and structures of marine insurance. It is offered by the Institute of Internal Auditors.

Associate in Risk Management A certification offered by the American Institute of CPCU. To receive the certification, one must complete a series of courses on the science of risk management, skills used in reducing risk, risk assessment and risk financing, among other things.

Associated Business Publications An organization for companies that specialize in business-to-business communication. Two examples of industries that belong to Associated Business Publications include book publishers and software developers. Associated Business Publications provides information about finance, government affairs, marketing and other subjects to members. It was established in 1907 and is also called American Business Press, Inc.

Associated Financing Any additional money, whether it is grants or loans, that a government issues in conjunction with a package issued by the OECD for international development purposes.

Associated Gas Natural gas discovered with crude oil, either in the ground above the oil or dissolved within it.

Associated Person 1. On a futures exchange, any person affiliated with an investment advisory firm, brokerage or futures commission merchant. An associated person must be registered with the CFTC and must abide by the regulations of the exchange on which he/she works. **2.** A person affiliated with a company traded on NASDAQ.

Associated With Describing the duties of an auditor with respect to the footnotes of a financial statement. While the auditor does not audit the footnotes, he/she has a duty to ensure their basic reasonableness.

Association A word used to designate an organization, whether it is for-profit or non-profit. Some states list "association" as one of the acceptable names designating a corporation.

Association Captive An insurance company that caters only to members of an occupation, professional association, or other organization. For example, a labor union may own an association captive that provides insurance only to union members. Likewise, a lobbying group for banks may have an association captive for banks represented by that group.

Association des Banques Centrales Africaines An organization consisting of 32 central banks and two regional banks in Africa. It encourages regional cooperation between banks, policymakers, and other financial professionals. It was established in 1968; its headquarters are in Dakar, Senegal.

Association for Operations Management An organization that provides education, certification, and training on methods to improve efficiency in a company's operations, especially in manufacturing. It was established in 1957 and is based in Chicago. It is also called APICS.

Association Group An organization that purchases insurance for members in order to achieve a lower premium per member. In order to avoid adverse selection, associated groups are not formed exclusively to purchase insurance, but rather add it as a benefit of membership.

Association Group Insurance An insurance policy purchased through an organization that buys insurance for members in order to achieve a lower premium per member. In order to avoid adverse selection, associated groups are not formed exclusively to purchase insurance, but rather add it as a benefit of membership.

Association of African Development Finance Institutions An organization that provides training and information services to members who specialize in international development in Africa. Membership is open to any bank or other financial institution. It was established by of the African Development Bank in 1975.

Association of British Insurers A trade association for insurance companies in the United Kingdom. It lobbies and conducts public relations on behalf of the industry and sets standards of conduct for members. It was established in 1985 and is based in London.

Association of Central African Banks An organization consisting of 32 central banks and two regional banks in Africa. ACAB encourages regional cooperation between banks, policymakers, and other financial professionals. It was established in 1968; its headquarters are in Dakar, Senegal.

Association of Certified Fraud Examiners A professional organization for persons who investigate fraud. Among other activities, it provides the Certified Fraud Examiner designation to persons who fulfill requirements. It was established in 1988 and is based in Austin, Texas.

Association of Chartered Certified Accountants A professional organization for accountants. It traces its roots to the United Kingdom in the early 20th century but it offers certified chartered accountant and chartered accounting technician qualifications throughout the world. It remains headquartered in London and Glasgow but us maintains 80 offices globally.

Association of Coffee Producing Countries An international organization that attempted to influence global coffee prices much the way OPEC influences oil prices. It was unsuccessful in this mission and, as a result of financial problems, dissolved itself in 2002.

Association of Corporate Treasurers A professional organization for corporate treasurers in the United Kingdom. It sets standards for treasury management by requiring members and associate members to pass examinations before joining. It was established in 1979.

Association of Futures Brokers and Dealers Ltd. A self-regulatory organization in the United Kingdom that assists in the regulation of British futures exchanges. Primarily, the AFBD maintains a framework to which brokers and dealers on futures exchanges are expected to conform. It was established in 1984.

Association of Government Accountants A professional organization for accountants for federal, state and local government entities in the United States. Among other activities, it provides certification and sets ethical standards for members. It was established in 1955 and is based in Alexandria, Virginia.

Association of Governmental Risk Pools An organization of members that pool their risk together so as to pay lower premiums for their insurance. Membership is open to government agencies, local governments, public schools, and similar organizations in North America. It was established in 1998.

Association of Insurance and Risk Managers in Industry and Commerce An organization in the United Kingdom for insurers and risk management companies. It is intended to promote best practices in the risk management sector. It is based in London.

Association of Interactive Marketers A lobbying organization for online businesses. It provides networking opportunities for e-entrepreneurs, encourages people to buy online, and lobbies the government for favorable policies. It was established in 1993 and is affiliated with the Direct Marketing Association.

Association of International Bond Dealers A professional organization for financial institutions and other investors who trade bonds frequently. It lobbies for favorable regulation and legislation for the bond market in European countries. It also publishes bond yields and quotes. It was established in Zurich in 1969.

Association of Lloyd's Members An association of wealthy individuals who provide a great deal of capital that underwrites the activities of Lloyd's of London. For most of Lloyd's centuries-long history, these individuals (known as Names), had unlimited liability for any losses associated with being a Name. Lloyd's introduced Names with limited liability in 1994, and these have become increasingly important. The ALM provides a forum in which Names can voice ideas and lobby on behalf of Lloyd's.

Association of National Advertisers A trade association for marketing companies in the United States. Members include more than 400 companies that market products for their clients. It was established in Detroit in 1910. It maintains offices in New York and Washington, DC.

Association of Natural Rubber Producing Countries An international organization for countries that produce natural rubber. It exists to promote the trade of rubber in an economically and environmentally sustainable way. Most member nations are located in south or east Asia, or the South Pacific. It was established in 1970.

Association of Private Client Investment Managers and Stockbrokers A lobbying organization for investment managers and brokerages in the United Kingdom. It presses for regulation favorable to its members, provides information on the British business climate, and communicates with members on regulatory and other changes. It was established in 1990.

Association of Publicly Traded Companies An Israeli lobbying organization for publicly traded companies. It presses for favorable regulation and legislation for publicly traded companies. Members are listed primarily on NASDAQ and the Tel Aviv Stock Exchange. It is based in Tel Aviv.

Association of Southeast Asian Nations An economic and political alliance of sovereign states in southeastern Asia. It was established in 1967; its members are Brunei, Burma, Cambodia, Indonesia, Laos, Malaysia, the Philippines, Singapore, Thailand, and Vietnam. ASEAN promotes regional cooperation on cultural and political levels, and it provides a forum for the peaceful resolution of disputes. Perhaps most important is ASEAN's work in regional integration. For example, it operates the ASEAN Free Trade Area and encourages members to invest in each other with as few restrictions as possible. It has also concluded common free trade agreements with a number of non-member countries, including Japan and Australia.

Association sans but lucratif A French term for non-profit organization. It is a name for the legal corporate form of non-profits in Belgium and is abbreviated ASBL. See also: Vereniging zonder winstoogmerk.

Assumable Loan A mortgage that the borrower may transfer to another party. That is, upon the sale of real estate with an assumable loan, the seller (who is the borrower) lets the buyer take over the mortgage, which allows him/her to buy the real estate with the same terms as the original loan. Most VA and FHA loans are assumable.

Assumed Bond A bond issued by one organization but for which another organization has taken over responsibility to repay. This may change the risk associated with the bond. The term connotes a long-term bond.

Assumed Interest Rate In annuities, a component of how monthly payments to the annuitant are determined. It is the minimum interest rate that the annuity may accrue while the annuitant makes payments on it; the annuity may perform better than the assumed interest rate depending on how it is invested, but the assumed interest rate serves as a bottom for how much the annuitant will receive when he/she begins to draw payments.

Assumed Liability 1. See: Contractual Liability. **2.** See: Assumed Bond.

Assumed Loss Ratio In insurance, the money that a company supposes it is likely to pay for claims and other losses as a percentage of total premiums it collects.

Assumed Shelter Cost The money a company anticipates it will spend to pay for housing for an employee it will transfer to another country. Many times, when an employee is transferred overseas, the company will pay for housing for the employee and his/her family. The assumed housing cost helps the company estimate whether or not such a transfer is worth the expense.

Assumption The act of taking on the liabilities of another property. For example, if one is a co-signer on a loan and the borrower defaults, the co-signer assumes the responsibility to repay the loan.

Assumption Certificate A guarantee from a reinsurance company that it will pay for losses from an insured event if the original insurance company fails to do so. It provides the assumption certificate even though it does not bear a contractual relationship directly with policyholders. An assumption certificate is also called a cut-through endorsement.

Assumption Fee A fee that the buyer of a property with an assumable mortgage pays to the lender for the ability to take over the mortgage.

Assumption of Risk 1. In law, an agreement by which one party takes on the risk of another party, often for some compensation. **2.** In torts, a defense in a lawsuit in which the defendant argues that the plaintiff took a risky action after having been informed of risks in such a way that a reasonable person would understand such risks. This limits the defendant's liability in the lawsuit. However, some states limit the use of the assumption of risk defense.

Assumption Reinsurance A form of reinsurance in which an insurer simply takes the place of another insurer. That is, Insurance Company B assumes some or all of the policies previously serviced by Insurance Company A. Assumption reinsurance is rare compared to reinsurance in which the first insurance company remains liable for claims, and the reinsurer only pays in the event of default.

Assurance A chiefly British term for insurance.

Assurance Service Any service that improves the amount and/or quality of information available. A major example of an assurance service is an audit, which is intended to improve the accuracy of the information in a financial statement. Assurance services are supposed to reduce information risk.

Assured A chiefly British term for insured.

Assurer A chiefly British term for insurer.

Assuror 1. Informal; an individual or company that helps a small Christian church or ministry with its finances. An assuror may be paid or may be a volunteer. **2.** See: Assurer.

Astedader Akabibi In Ethiopia, a political subdivision equivalent to a chartered city not under the jurisdiction of a province.

Asterisk A character indicating the existence of a footnote or that some other information is available. This may be used, for example, on a financial statement. Its symbol is *.

Asylum Seeker A person fleeing from one place to another due to real or perceived persecution. This persecution may be political, religious, or economic. For example, a landowner may be forced to go to another country because the government nationalized all land and is imprisoning former owners. Asylum seekers may be eligible to stay in the country to which they flee longer than they otherwise would.

Asymmetric Information A situation in which one party to a transaction has information about the transaction to which the other party is not privy. Asymmetric information may result in a bad deal for one party (often but not always the buyer). To give an extreme example, the seller of real estate may know that his property is lined with land mines. This would ordinarily result in a (steep) drop in price, but if the buyer does not know this, it may not. Asymmetric information is not as prevalent as it once was because of increased transparency and legal requirements for disclosure, as well as better technology. Indeed, trading securities with asymmetric information is often illegal. See also: Insider trading, moral hazard, adverse selection.

Asymmetric Margining A situation in which the parties in a transaction have different margin requirements imposed by their respective brokerages. This could indicate one party to the transaction is considered lower risk than the other.

Asymmetric Payoff A situation in which the settlement valuation on a security changes in a way other than a linear increase or decrease. Options are common instruments with asymmetric payoff. Forwards, on the other hand, generally have symmetric payoff.

Asymmetric Risk Exposure A situation in which the potential gains and losses on an investment are uneven. For example, in an unhedged short sale, the potential gain is limited to the total potential loss of the underlying asset (because something cannot have less than no value), but potential losses are unlimited because the underlying asset could increase in value ad infinitum (resulting in a loss for the short seller). A collar option, on the other hand, may not have asymmetric risk exposure because the potential gains and losses are set at the beginning of the contract and are generally equal.

Asymmetric Taxes A situation in which two parties to a transaction pay different tax rates. This may affect what one party or the other desires about the timing, price, or other factors regarding the transaction.

Asymmetric Threat The possibility that a weak power will use surprise, deception, terrorism, new technologies, or some other unconventional method to defeat a strong power. Asymmetric threat poses a political risk to commerce.

Asymmetric Volatility A situation in which the volatility of a security is higher when the broader market is performing poorly than when it is performing well. Experts disagree on what causes asymmetric volatility, but factors such as leverage and panic are often cited. The fact that asymmetric volatility exists is important to hedging strategies and option pricing models.

Asymmetry A lack of equality between two things. For example, there may be asymmetry in how two types of income are taxed. Asymmetry may encourage certain business or investment decisions while discouraging others.

Asymptote In geometry, a line associated with a curve in such a way that the distance between the line and the curve approaches zero as both reach toward infinity. Asymptotes are used in calculus and are computed using limits.

Asynchronous 1. In computing, describing a process that occurs independently of other processes. **2.** In telecommunications, describing two signals within a network or between two networks that are sent at different times. **3.** More generally, describing two or more events that occur at a different time or something that occurs at the wrong time.

AT 1. ISO 3166-1 alpha-2 code for the Republic of Austria. This is the code used in international transactions to and from Austrian bank accounts. **2.** ISO 3166-2 geocode for Austria. This is used as an international standard for shipping to Austria. Each state has its own code with the prefix "AT." For example, the code for the State of Burgenland is ISO 3166-2:AT-1.

At Fault Describing a person or company that is legally liable for a situation. For example, if Joe trips Bob (deliberately or not) and Bob breaks his arm, Joe may be considered at fault and may be required to pay Bob's medical bills.

At Par 1. Describing the full price of a bond. This is usually, but not always, $1000 per bond. **2.** Describing any two equal values, especially of currencies. See also: Par.

At Par Forward Spread In foreign exchange, a situation in which the forward exchange rate is identical to the spot rate.

At Post Education Education one receives outside the United States because one or one's immediate family member is employed overseas by the U.S. Department of State. The State Department provides reimbursements for at post education up to a certain limit, depending on where the post is.

At Risk 1. See: Value at Risk. **2.** See: At Risk Rule. **3.** Describing any asset or investment one may lose for any reason whatsoever.

At Sign A character signifying the word "at." It is used in accounting to mean "at the rate of" and in e-mail addresses. Its symbol is @.

At the Bell 1. See: At the open. **2.** See: At the close.

At the Close Order 1. An order to buy or sell a security at the best price available when an exchange closes. **2.** An order to buy or sell a security at the security's price when an exchange closes. If this price is not available, the order is canceled.

At the Figure The nearest whole dollar price to a security's bid and ask. It is also called at the full.

At the Money An option contract with a strike price exactly equal to the price of the underlying asset. In this situation, the option contract has no intrinsic value. However, it can easily develop an intrinsic value if the option becomes in-the-money. At-the-money options are extremely volatile because they can become in-the-money or out-of-the-money quickly.

At the Opening Order 1. An order to buy or sell a security at the best price available when an exchange opens. **2.** An order to buy or sell a security at its opening price when an exchange opens. If this price is not available, the order is canceled.

AT&T One of the largest providers of landline telephones, mobile phone service, Internet, and cable in the United States. It traces its origins to the Bell Telephone Company, established by Alexander Graham Bell in 1875. By the second decade of the 20th century, it was approaching near monopoly status over the telephone industry. In 1913, it agreed to acquire no more competitors without the approval of the Interstate Commerce Commission. In 1982, it was ruled that AT&T was engaging in anti-competitive activities, and the company was forced to divest itself of many of its assets. In 2005, the company was acquired by one of its former subsidiaries, which took the name AT&T. It presently controls much of what it originally did before the monopoly settlement. See also: Baby Bell.

ATA GOST 7.67 Latin three-letter geocode for Antarctica. The code is used for international shipping to Antarctica. As with all GOST 7.67 codes, it is used primarily in Cyrillic alphabets.

ATA Carnet A Temporary Admission Carnet. A certificate allowing the import of a good into another country or territory for a period of one year. An ATA carnet allows a good to enter the country without tariffs or similar fees, provided it leaves the country within the year. See also: Admission Temporaire.

ATF GOST 7.67 Latin three-letter geocode for the French Southern Territories. The code is used for transactions to and from local bank accounts and for international shipping to the French Southern Territories. As with all GOST 7.67 codes, it is used primarily in Cyrillic alphabets.

ATG GOST 7.67 Latin three-letter geocode for Antigua and Barbuda. The code is used for transactions to and from Antiguan and Barbudan bank accounts and for international shipping to Antigua and Barbuda. As with all GOST 7.67 codes, it is used primarily in Cyrillic alphabets.

Athanni In India, a slang term for a 50-paisa coin, which is worth half of one Indian rupee.

Athens Exchange A major securities exchange in Greece. It was established as the Athens Stock Exchange in 1876. In 2002, it became the Athens Exchange in a merger with the Athens Derivatives Exchange. It trades stocks, bonds and derivatives. More than 300 publicly traded companies are listed on the Athens Exchange.

Athwartships In shipping, describing something lying sideways across a vessel.

Atlanta Fed Index An index of manufacturing in states under the jurisdiction of the Atlanta Federal Reserve. It is used along with other indices as a barometer of the state of manufacturing in the United States.

Atlanta Federal Reserve The Federal Reserve Bank that oversees banking in Alabama, Florida, Georgia, and parts of Louisiana, Mississippi and Tennessee. It has the authority to regulate member banks in its region, as well as to help regulate the money supply. Every member bank in the region is required to buy stock in the Atlanta Federal Reserve Bank in order to support its efforts.

Atni Tuqtawsiz Yuriyu A Tatar unit of length varying in distance from 15 to 25 kilometers. It was rendered obsolete when the Soviet Union began to use the metric system in 1924.

Atnin Konlek Yuli A Tatar unit of length varying in distance from 40 to 50 kilometers. It was rendered obsolete when the Soviet Union began to use the metric system in 1924.

Atomic Energy Commission A former agency of the United States government that oversaw development of atomic energy for peaceful civilian purposes. It existed from 1946 to 1974.

Atomistic Competition A situation in which perfect competition exists because of the existence of many small companies. Because there are so many companies, no one is able to dominate the market or set prices. This results in low profits but also low cost for clients or consumers. Many believe atomistic competition to be ideal, though it rarely exists in practice.

At-Risk Rule In tax law, a rule disallowing investors from deducting more investment money from their taxable income than they have actually invested. For example, if one places $10,000 in a stock and would otherwise derive $15,000 in tax deductions from the investment, the at-risk rule only allows the investor to deduct $10,000. The rule exists to prevent a person from investing in a way that avoids taxes excessively.

ATS ISO 4217 code for the Austrian schilling. It was introduced in 1945 following the Second World War, replacing the German Reichsmark. Under the Bretton Woods system, the schilling was pegged to a currency basket, and after 1976 was tied to the Deutsche Mark. It ceased circulation in 2002 with the introduction of the euro.

Att A subdivision of the Lao kip. One att is equal in value to 1/100 of one kip. It does not circulate in practice.

Attache A diplomat assigned to an embassy, often with a specific purpose.

Attached Mail Mail that is sent along with a periodical such as a newspaper or magazine and is charged a lower postage rate because of it. For example, a bill sent with a newspaper is attached mail and the sender pays less than he/she would otherwise. In order to qualify as attached mail, the mail must be secondary to the main periodical.

Attachment The seizure of property, especially (but not necessarily) real estate, from a defendant in a lawsuit in anticipation of its award to a plaintiff. Attachment occurs when a judge believes that the plaintiff will prevail in the suit and, therefore, permits the seizure. However, if the defendant does prevail in the end, the judge must compensate her with a bond to cover any potential damages the plaintiff causes.

Attachment Point The amount of money an insurer pays until the point at which supplemental insurance (which may come from another provider) begins to be paid. For example, if one purchases supplemental insurance with terms stating that coverage will begin after the policyholder's primary insurance exceeds $500,000 in claims, the attachment point is $500,000.

Attained Age 1. The age of a person holding an insurance policy. This may affect the premium that is paid. **2.** The age at which a beneficiary, policyholder, or pensioner begins to receive payments from a plan.

Attained Age Conversion When one switches between two life insurance policies, the change in premium due to the difference in ages when each policy starts. For example, if a person bought a life insurance policy at age 35 and changed to a different policy at age 55, attained age conversion would likely result in a higher premium.

Attention Economics A way to approach marketing that treats a person's attention as a scarce commodity that one must acquire in order to motivate that person to buy a good or perform some act. Attention economics is especially important in advertising; because of the sheer volume of advertisements people see and hear, advertisers must be aware of the need to grab and hold a person's attention.

Attention Line A line on a letter or in an address on an envelope stating the person within an organization to whom the correspondence is addressed. For example, one may address a letter to "Any Company" and write "Attention: John Smith" on the line immediately below. This second line is the attention line.

Attest 1. To certify or to state under oath. **2.** See: Testament.

Attest Function The acts an accountant performs when conducting an audit. That is, the attest function is the totality of the reviews, corrections, and reports an accountant makes when performing his/her duties.

Attestation The act of witnessing the signature or execution of a legal document. One proves attestation by signing the document along with other relevant parties; the attestation proves that the document is authentic and can be enforced. Attestation is especially important to a will.

Attestation Clause 1. A clause in an insurance policy contract stating that representatives of the insurer must sign it in order for it to be effective. **2.** A clause in a will stating the testator is legally able to execute the will and that he/she has abided by all laws and has signed the will in the presence of the appropriate number of witnesses.

Attitude A subjective measure of how one or more persons feel about an event, person, or object. Marketers attempt to measure attitudes of consumers to determine the products they may buy. Likewise, analysts measure investor attitudes to estimate future market movements. See also: Sentiment indicator, Behavioral economics.

Attitude Study A survey conducted to measure the success of an advertising campaign or a client's satisfaction with a company. See also: Marketing.

Attitudes, Interests and Opinions A survey of an individual's likes, desires and beliefs. Questions in this survey may include whether or not the respondent prefers staying indoors or going out, or whether he/she enjoys eating at restaurants. An individual's attitudes, interests and opinions are compared against his/her demographics to determine his/her likely preferences. This is used in marketing.

Attorney at Law A term for a lawyer in several countries, notably Japan and the United States. In order to practice, attorneys at law generally must have passed an examination measuring their knowledge of the law and also must have obtained a law degree.

Attorney in Fact A person to whom legal authority on behalf of another person has been given. An attorney in fact may sign legal documents and perform other duties for the designator in accordance with the parameters set by the designator. See also: Power of attorney.

Attorney's Fee A fee a lawyer charges for legal services. Lawyers may work by the hour, for a flat fee, or may even be paid a percentage of the amount one wins in a lawsuit.

Attorney's Letter In an audit, a letter an accountant sends to a lawyer verifying the client's lawsuits. In order to assess the financial state of a company, the accountant needs an accurate picture of the lawsuits it is facing and any actual or potential judgments against it. The attorney's letter requests this information.

Attorney's Professional Liability Insurance An insurance policy for a lawyer providing coverage in the event that his/her actions or omissions result in injury to a client or in the event that the client causes injury to another party. Attorney's professional liability insurance protects lawyers from negative events that may result from the performance of their duties.

Attornment The consent to the transfer of a right. Attornment may be expressed or implied. For example, if a renter continues to live in his/her apartment after the landlord sells the property to a new owner, the renter implies attornment and the new owner becomes the new landlord. The term derives from English feudalism.

Attractive Nuisance A feature, especially a dangerous one, on a property that outsiders may be encouraged to abuse, perhaps to their detriment. For example, a trespasser may be tempted to jump off a bridge into a pond. Property owners generally have the responsibility to take reasonable measure to prevent attractive nuisances from being mistreated.

Attribute Bias 1. A bias within the dividend discount model in which the model favors certain stocks. The dividend discount model is a method for valuing stock according to the present value of future dividends. Because of attribute bias, the model tends to rate more highly stocks with high dividend yields, and low P/E ratios. **2.** More broadly, a situation in which any model rates securities that share similar characteristics more highly. Some analysts caution against this bias because it eliminates some of the benefits of diversification, though others believe that attribute bias poses little problem as long as the securities have strong fundamentals.

Attribute Sampling The statistical analysis of a sample involving characteristics that units in the sample either have or do not have. For example, a loan is either in default or it is not. Attribute sampling is useful when attempting to determine the extent to which a characteristic exists in a sample.

Attributed Tip Income Program An IRS program in which employers who have tips added to at least 25% of their gross receipts use a predetermined formula to assume how much tipped employees likely are making from these tips. This amount is taxed by the IRS. ATIP does not require employees to self-report their tips. However, in order to participate, at least 75% of tipped employees, in addition to the employer, must agree to it.

Attribution The assignment of cause. For example, if one attributes a statement to a CEO, one says the CEO made the statement. Likewise, if one attributes a market bounce to GDP growth, one says the GDP growth caused the bounce.

Attribution Rules In Canada, a series of rules set by the Canada Revenue Agency governing transfers of assets between family members. For example, the attribution rules do not allow two spouses to divide income between themselves in such a way that it reduces their overall tax liability. Attribution rules were devised to prevent citizens from taking advantage of family relations to unfairly avoid taxes. See also: Tax evasion.

Attribution Theory The concept stating that people make decisions based on the factors they believe caused their present situations and seek to emulate or avoid those real or perceived causes. For example, if one believes investing in cotton caused one's bankruptcy, one may be unlikely to invest in cotton again, whether or not the supposition is true.

Attrition The slow, gradual reduction of members in a company or organization due to retirement, resignation or death. That is, members lost through attrition are not replaced in the same numbers. Attrition may be deliberate; that is, if a company is downsizing, it may prefer to lose employees through attrition rather than to conduct layoffs. Other times, however, attrition may be a sign of a weak company or organization unable to attract talent. Attrition is also called natural wastage.

AU 1. ISO 3166-1 alpha-2 code for the Commonwealth of Australia. This is the code used in international transactions to and from Australian bank accounts. **2.** ISO 3166-2 geocode for Australia. This is used as an international standard for shipping to Australia. Each Australian state and territory has its own code with the prefix "AU." For example, the code for the New South Wales is ISO 3166-2:AU-NSW.

Auction 1. A way to sell an item in which a moderator takes bids from a number of persons for a period of time and ultimately sells to the highest bidder. For example, the moderator (called an auctioneer) may set the opening bid at $5 and, once someone offers to pay $5, may incrementally increase the requested bids until they stop. Variations on an auction may involve any number of things; for example, a person

with more than one job offer may request higher salaries in turn and then finally take the highest paying position. See also: Bidding war. **2.** See: Auction market.

Auction Market A security exchange in which buyers make bids and sellers make offers in order to make transactions in a security. On an auction market, the current price for a share in a security is the highest price a buyer is willing to pay and the lowest price a seller is willing to accept. For example, if potential buyers for Security A enter bids of $50, $51, and $52, and potential sellers enter offers of $52, $53, and $54, the current share price is $52. Only the bid/offer for $52 is executed; others must make better bids and offers in order to conduct transactions. The New York Stock Exchange is a major auction market.

Auction Preferred Stock A preferred stock with an adjustable dividend that changes every seven weeks according to the results of a Dutch auction. Every preferred stock has a guaranteed dividend; an auction market preferred stock is distinguished by the fact that the amount of its dividends changes from time to time. An auction market preferred stock is beneficial for some investors because the auction reveals the current market yield every seven weeks, which helps in investment decisions on whether to buy, sell, or hold. It is also called an auction rate preferred stock or a Dutch auction preferred stock.

AUD ISO 4217 code for the Australian dollar. It was introduced in 1966, replacing the Australian pound. It was initially pegged to the British pound, but changed the peg to the U.S. dollar in 1967. It is now a floating currency and is the sixth-most widely traded currency in the world. It is especially important in the South Pacific region, where a number of small nations either use the dollar or peg their currencies to it at a 1:1 ratio.

Audan In Kazakhstan, a political subdivision approximately equivalent to a county.

Audience 1. The persons who watch, listen to, or read a medium such as a television show or a magazine, or who are likely to do so. **2.** The persons who are the targets of an advertising campaign, or the persons who have actually been exposed to it.

Audience Accumulation The total number of people exposed to an advertising campaign. Obviously, advertisers aim to have the highest audience accumulation possible in their target demographics. The higher the audience accumulation, the more likely it is for the campaign to be successful.

Audience Composition The age and gender demographics of the audience of a broadcast. The audience composition shows what percentages of an audience are male and female, and the age groups to which the audience belongs. An audience composition helps an advertiser target its ads better. It should not be confused with an audience profile, which measures socio-economic conditions.

Audience Duplication A measure of the percentage of viewers of an advertisement who previously saw the same advertisement. An advertiser may aim for high audience duplication if it is thought to result in higher response. On the other hand, if an advertiser wishes to reach as many people as possible, low audience duplication may be better.

Audience Flow A measure of how many viewers or listeners turn on or turn off a television or radio broadcast over a period of time.

Audience Fragmentation A situation in which viewers of a television program live in vastly different areas. For example, people in New York and Alaska can watch the same television channel and see the same show. Audience fragmentation has become more common since cable has become popular. It has made advertising more difficult because, for example, shoppers in New York and Alaska might not shop at the same grocery chain.

Audience Profile The social and economic demographics of the audience of a broadcast. The audience profile shows what percentages of an audience earn various levels of income, the amount of time spent on vacation, and similar information. An audience profile helps an advertiser target its ads better. It should not be confused with audience composition, which measures age and gender in an audience.

Audience Share A measure of the potential members of an audience for an advertisement who have the possibility of observing the advertisement and actually do observe it (even if they do not notice it). If an advertiser is targeting everyone in a city and takes out an ad in the newspaper, for example, the audience share is the percentage of the city's population who subscribe to or at least read the newspaper regularly. The audience share may be measured by a survey or with some other tool like Nielsen ratings.

Audience-Holding Index A measure of how long, on average, audience members listen to or watch a radio or television broadcast. The audience-holding index is measured on a minute-to-minute basis and can affect advertising rates, especially if the audience tunes in for only a small portion of the broadcast.

Audience-Participation Program A television or radio broadcast with a live audience, members of whom are involved in the program. For example, a game show may pick audience members at random to be contestants. An audience-participation program may appeal to certain demographics attractive to advertisers. This format also is used in infomercials.

Audimeter A devise attached to a television (or, originally, a radio) that records and transmits whether or not the television is turned on, and how long it broadcasts a particular channel. The audimeter was developed in 1936; the A.C. Nielsen Company has used it ever since to measure the popularity of different programs. The audiometer results affect advertising rates and even help determine whether programs continue to air.

Audio Sound transmitted electronically. Audio is integral to media like radio, television, and, increasingly, the Internet. For that reason, it is used in advertising on these media.

Audit 1. The process of reviewing activities to identify inefficiencies, reduce costs, and otherwise achieve organizational objectives. Audits may investigate potential theft or fraud and ensure compliance with applicable regulations and policies. They also help ensure the accuracy of reports. Audits are an essential part of a company's efficiency. **2.** In taxation, the process in which the tax collection agency reviewing the reports of an individual or company to see if all income, deductions, and/or credits reported accurately reflect reality. This is done to ensure that each individual or company pays his/her/its full tax liability. Audits are conducted on a random basis, or when something appears remiss on a tax return. See also: Tax avoidance, Tax evasion.

Audit Bureau of Circulations 1. A non-profit organization that monitors newspapers, magazines and other media that sell advertising space. It researches the audiences, readership and other information on non-traditional media in North America. Advertisers provide funding for the Bureau because they use this information in making business decisions. It was established in 1914. **2.** A non-profit organization that provides much the same service for British and Irish traditional media. It was established in 1931.

Audit Bureau of Verification Services A non-profit organization that monitors electronic media such as the Internet. It researches the audiences, popularity and other information on non-traditional media in North America. Advertisers provide funding for the Bureau because they use this information when making business decisions. It was incorporated in 1995 as the Audit Bureau of Marketing Services. It is associated with the Audit Bureau of Circulations.

Audit Committee A committee responsible for reviewing its own company's business activities to identify inefficiencies, reduce costs, and otherwise achieve organizational objectives. Audit committees may investigate potential theft or fraud and ensure compliance with applicable regulations and policies. They also assist in risk management. In a large company, especially a publicly traded one, the audit committee is independent from any management and is answerable only to the board of directors. See also: Internal audit.

Audit Cycle The period of time during which an audit is conducted. An audit cycle varies depending on the type of audit being made. For example, the audit cycle for a tax audit by its nature begins after tax returns are filed (or are supposed to have been filed).

Audit Department A department within a company responsible for conducting internal audits when deemed necessary. The audit department ensures accuracy of records and compliance with relevant regulation and company policies.

Audit Fee A fee a company pays an external auditor in exchange for performing an audit. Because the Sarbanes-Oxley Act made audits more complex, audit fees have increased significantly in the United States since 2001.

Audit Guide A pamphlet published by the American Institute of Certified Public Accountants providing information about how to conduct an audit under various circumstances. For example, an audit guide may cover a tax audit or an audit of personal finances. While they are not as detailed as the Generally Accepted Auditing Principles, statements in an audit guide are considered authoritative.

Audit Program The process by which an auditor reviews activities to identify inefficiencies, reduce costs, and otherwise achieve organizational objectives. The auditing process differs each time an audit occurs, depending on the client's size, complexity, and other factors. However, the auditing process always aims to ensure the accuracy of reports and compliance with regulations and policies. See also: Audit, Auditing procedure.

Audit Risk The risk to a company or investor that an audit will not discover some accidental or intentional irregularity, either through negligence or mal intent. This may result in significant losses to the company and its investors once the irregularity is finally discovered. It could also result in a lawsuit against the auditing firm that conducted the audit.

Audit Software In accounting, any computer program that assists in keeping records and therefore makes records easier to evaluate in an audit.

Audit Test In accounting, an experiment measuring a small sample of a larger population. The experimenter may extrapolate the results to apply them to a larger population. For example, if a company determines that it spent $5,000 to attract 500 customers, it may estimate that it spends an average of $100 to attract any one customer.

Audit Trail A record of the transactions in a trade from the beginning to the end. The SEC and the NYSE use the audit trail when investigating irregularities and potential trading violations.

Auditability The ability to obtain an accurate audit. Auditability depends on the transparency of the company being audited. That is, companies that keep more complete records and have managers who are honest with auditors have greater auditability.

Audited Statement A financial statement that an auditor has prepared according to the Generally Accepted Auditing Principles (GAAP). Audited statements are subject to more rigorous standards than unaudited statements and, as such, are less prone to errors. An audited statement should not be confused with an auditor's opinion.

Auditing Evidence In an audit, any substantiation proving or disproving the accuracy of a financial statement. See also: Auditing procedure, Auditing process.

Auditing Firm A company that reviews activities to identify inefficiencies, reduce costs, and otherwise achieve organizational objectives. Auditing firms may investigate potential theft or fraud and ensure compliance with applicable regulations and policies. They also help to ensure the accuracy of reports. Audits are an essential part of a company's efficiency. See also: Internal auditor, External auditor.

Auditing Procedure Any tactic used by an auditor to identify inefficiencies, reduce costs, and otherwise achieve organizational objectives. Examples of auditing procedures include reviewing documents, interviewing officials and checking irregularities. See also: Auditing process, Audit, Attest function.

Auditing Standards Guidelines for how audits should be conducted. The most commonly accepted auditing standards are the GAAS, which are set by the American Institute of Certified Public Accountants and provide a uniform set of standards for conducting audits in the United States.

Auditing Standards Board The branch of the American Institute of Certified Public Accountants that sets the Generally Accepted Auditing Standards. Its decisions about audit procedures are authoritative; auditors generally must abide by them. The Auditing Standards Board provides a uniform set of standards for conducting audits in the United States.

Audition The process by which a person or company decides to purchase advertisements for a radio or television program. An audition involves listening to or watching the program (or an early version of it) and weighing its target demographics and other variables against the product the company is trying to sell.

Auditor 1. A person who reviews activities to identify inefficiencies, reduce costs, and otherwise achieve organizational objectives. Auditors may investigate potential theft or fraud and ensure compliance with applicable regulations and policies. They also help ensure the accuracy of reports. Audits are an essential part of a company's efficiency. See also: Internal auditor, External auditor. **2.** In taxation, an employee of the tax collection agency who reviews the reports of an individual or company to see if all income, deductions, and/or credits reported accurately reflect reality. This is done to ensure that each individual or company pays his/her/its full tax liability. Audits are conducted on a random basis, or when something appears remiss on a tax return. See also: Tax avoidance, Tax evasion.

Aunt Millie 1. Derogatory; an uneducated investor who knows little or nothing about investment strategies. Investment advisors often recommend simple investments that carry little risk to Aunt Millies. **2.** Derogatory; a security thought to be a bad risk. The term derives from the idea that the security or strategy is so bad that only an "Aunt Millie" investor would buy it.

Aurar 1/100 of an Icelandic krone. Because the krone is a relatively weak currency, aurars do not circulate.

AUS GOST 7.67 Latin three-letter geocode for Australia. The code is used for transactions to and from Australian bank accounts and for international shipping to Australia. As with all GOST 7.67 codes, it is used primarily in Cyrillic alphabets.

Ausfuhrkredit-Gesellschaft A bank in Germany that extends credit to German and European exporters. It also provides guarantees of payment and insurance. It is intended to reduce the risk of European exports and thereby assist in the sale of European products abroad. This concept is controversial; critics allege that it negatively impacts international development, since developing countries cannot compete with such insured exports. Proponents, however, argue that Ausfuhrkredit-Gesellschaft's services enable developing countries to import products they otherwise would not be able to afford. It was established in 1952 and is owned by 20 German banks. See also: Export credit agency.

Aussie A slang term for the Australian dollar.

Austerity A program in which a government drastically reduces spending and/or increases taxes or other revenue sources. A government launches austerity programs when their deficit and/or national debt become unsustainable. The IMF and the World Bank often require austerity programs in exchange for restructuring or refinancing a country's debt. Austerity is usually politically unpopular because it may involve cutting programs like food subsidies or national health care.

Austerity Measure Any policy a government implements to reduce its deficit. Austerity measures are adopted when the deficit becomes unsustainable and the government is unable to borrow to finance further spending. Generally, austerity measures consist of some combination of tax increases and spending cuts, often in welfare and social service programs. They derive their name from the fact that they usually are politically unpopular.

Austian Netherlands Kronenthaler The currency of the Austrian Netherlands prior to its occupation by France in 1794. It was replaced by the French franc.

Austral The former currency of Argentina. It was introduced in 1985, replacing the peso argentine. It was subject to hyperinflation for its history and was replaced by the Argentine peso in 1991.

Australasia The area of southern Oceania consisting of Australia, Tasmania, New Zealand, and a few other small islands. It is distinguished from other areas of Oceania, namely Polynesia, Micronesia, and Melanesia.

Australia Group An informal international organization intended to identify exports needing to be controlled so as to prevent the spread of chemical and biological weapons. It was established in 1985 and held its first meeting in 1989. Its members include 40 countries and the European Commission.

Australian Dollar The currency of Australia. It was introduced in 1966, replacing the Australian pound. It was initially pegged to the British pound, but later pegged to the U.S. dollar in 1967. It is now a floating currency and is one of the most widely traded currencies in the world. It is especially important in the South Pacific region, where a number of small nations either use the Australian Dollar or peg their currencies to it at a 1:1 ratio.

Australian Dollar Area The area in which the Australian dollar circulates. The Australian dollar area includes Australia and seven Australian territories, as well as the nations of Kiribati, Nauru, and Tuvalu.

Australian Kangaroo A one-ounce gold bullion coin minted in Australia. The obverse is stamped with the Sovereign of Australia and the reverse with a picture of a kangaroo.

Australian Pound The former currency of Australia. It was introduced in 1910, nine years after the formation of the Australian federation. It was divided into 20 shillings, each containing 12 pence. It remained in circulation until 1966. See also: Australian dollar.

Australian Securities and Investments Commission An agency of the Australian government responsible for regulating corporations, investments, and insurance. Its goal is to protect consumers, creditors and investors from predatory or unfair business practices. Among other things, it co-regulates the Australian Securities Exchange. It was established in 1991 to consolidate several regulatory agencies that previously existed. It is based in Melbourne.

Australian Securities Exchange The largest securities exchange in Australia, established in 2006 as the result of a merger between the Australian Stock Exchange and the Sydney Futures Exchange. ASX is a publicly-traded company, which is traded on its own exchange. The exchange is fully electronic and trades both stocks and derivatives. It co-regulates itself with the Australian Securities and Investment Commission.

Austrian Krone The currency of Austria between 1919 and 1925. While intended to replace the Austro-Hungarian krone, it was prone to hyperinflation and was replaced by the Austrian schilling after only a few years.

Austrian Mint An organization in Austria that issues legal tender coins for general use. It traces its origins to 1194 and has been in its current building since 1837. It is located in Vienna.

Austrian Schilling The former currency of Austria. It was introduced in 1945 following World War II, replacing the German Reichsmark. Under the Bretton Woods system, the schilling was pegged to a currency basket, and after 1976 was tied to the Deutsche Mark. It ceased circulation in 2002 with the introduction of the euro.

Austrian School A school of economics that argues that human behavior is so complex it is extremely difficult or impossible to model. For that reason, it promotes deductive, as opposed to inductive, reasoning in its analysis. It is an extremely individualist school, advocating laissez faire policies and opposing all or nearly all government interventions in the economy. The Austrian School, and particularly its rejection of modeling, has faced criticism from both right- and left-leaning economists. It is so named because most of its founders were born in or around Austria. See also: Ludwig von Mises.

Austrian Shilling The former currency of Austria. It was introduced in 1945 following the Second World War, replacing the German Reichsmark. Under the Bretton Woods system, the schilling was pegged to a currency basket, and, after 1976, was tied to the Deutsche Mark. It ceased circulation in 2002 with the introduction of the euro.

Austrian Traded Index The primary index tracking the performance of stocks on the Wiener Borse. It consists of 20 stocks and is weighted for price. It is abbreviated ATX.

AUT GOST 7.67 Latin three-letter geocode for Austria. The code is used for transactions to and from Austrian bank accounts and for international shipping to Austria. As with all GOST 7.67 codes, it is used primarily in Cyrillic alphabets.

Autarky Economic self-sufficiency. That is, a country has autarky when it does not need to engage in any sort of international trade. Rather, it produces all of its goods and services within the country. Autarky is rare in the modern world, but some examples include Cambodia under the Khmer Rouge and India prior to 1991. Most analysts see autarky as economically inefficient, though some governments pursue the policy to encourage local industry or more rarely to keep their people from perceived threatening influences. See also: Import Substitution, Embargo, Economic Sanctions, Nonconvertible Currency.

Autex An electronic network allowing broker-dealers to communicate with each other easily when they receive orders to buy or sell a large block of securities. Autex allows broker-dealers to find a better, or at least a similar, counter-offer from another broker-dealer. This allows them to transact with other broker-dealers rather than automatically sending the block to the market maker, who is obliged to fill the order if need be. Autex is less commonly called the super message.

Authentication A legal certification that a document is genuine. In business, this is especially applied to bonds, showing that an issue was legitimate.

Authoritarian A person who believes in or is involved with a political or economic system characterized by submission to authority, whether it is a person, party, or class. In an authoritarian society, the individuals exist to serve the state or ruling power. The authority may rule arbitrarily; that is, it is not bound by its own laws. This concept is opposed to democracy, individualism, and the rule of law.

Democratic societies are thought to offer greater impetus for long-term economic growth, although authoritarian counterexamples exist.

Authoritarian Society A society characterized by political and/or economic submission to an authority, whether it is a person, party, or class. In an authoritarian society, the individuals exist to serve the state or ruling clique. The power having authority may rule arbitrarily; that is, it is not bound by its own laws. This concept is opposed to democracy, individualism, and the rule of law. Democratic societies are thought to possess more impetus for long term economic growth, although authoritarian counterexamples exist.

Authority A structure or organization established for a certain purpose with the legitimacy to carry out said purpose. In a business context, certain organizations have authority to police, and, if necessary, punish certain business activities. For example, the SEC has authority to regulate any and all business transactions occurring in the United States. These organizations derive their authority from the ruling government and international conventions.

Authority Bond A bond issued by an authority, especially a government, that is repaid to bondholders with expected revenues from the project that the authority bond intends to finance. For example, a city may issue an authority to finance improvements to the local museum. It expects to be able to pay back the bond with money raised on increased ticket sales at the museum after improvements are completed.

Authority to Pay In international commerce, notification given by an importer's bank to a seller stating that it (the bank) will accept a bill of exchange from the seller within a certain period of time to pay for a good. Authority to pay documents are used in East Asian countries, most notably in Japan. See also: Authority to purchase.

Authority to Purchase In international commerce, notification given to a seller stating that an importer (instead of the importer's bank) will accept a bill of exchange from the seller within a certain period of time to pay for a good. Authority to purchase documents are used in East Asian countries, most notably in Japan. See also: Authority to pay.

Authority to Terminate Plan The circumstances in which an employer can eliminate its pension plan without incurring adverse tax conditions. A company has authority to terminate plan if it is bankrupt, insolvent, or otherwise unable to continue making contributions. If it cancels a plan for any other reason, all previous contributions become taxable.

Authorization The granting of access to a document or the ability to conduct an activity. Authorization may be limited to a certain transaction or time period, or it may be unlimited. For example, a potential home buyer may grant a lender authorization to view his/her credit reports.

Authorization Code A code a financial institution submits electronically to a merchant stating that it approves of an attempted purchase with a debit card or credit card issued by that institution.

Authorized Auditor 1. A person in the United Kingdom given special permission by the Secretary of State to act as an auditor even if he/she would not qualify as one. This designation was stated in the Companies Act 1967, which has since been repealed. **2.** See: Auditor.

Authorized Control Level Risk-Based Capital The amount of capital an insurance company should have on hand, plus any surpluses.

Authorized Financial Adviser An investment adviser in the United Kingdom registered under and subject to the Financial Services Act 1986 and the Financial Services and Markets Act 2000.

Authorized Insurer A company that has received a license in a U.S. state to sell insurance in that state. Because each state has its own insurance regulations, each has the ability to set standards for authorized insurers. An insurance company operating in multiple states must be an authorized insurer in each state it does business.

Authorized Investment An investment made in accordance with a trust or a client's wishes or other instructions. It is illegal for a fiduciary agent or a trustee to make anything other than an authorized investment. This contrasts with a legal investment, which is an investment a regulated institution is allowed to make by the government.

Authorized Participant An institutional investor that takes part in the creation of an exchange-traded fund (ETF). An exchange-traded fund is an investment company that tracks all the stocks on a particular exchange. When an ETF is created, an authorized participant buys the shares that are to underlie it and gives them to the fund's sponsor in exchange for units (or shares) in the new ETF. The authorized participant then sells these units to investors. Authorized participants are handpicked by the sponsor of the ETF.

Authorized Settlement Agent A bank that may send checks and other demands for payment to a Federal Reserve bank to be honored. An authorized settlement agent submits these demands through the Automated Clearing House. The actions of authorized settlement agents help ensure smooth functioning of banks. An authorized settlement agent should not be confused with a settlement agent.

Authorized Shares The maximum number of shares a company is allowed to issue. Generally, the company's charter specifies the number of authorized shares, but shareholders can increase or decrease it according to procedures listed in the charter. Typically, the number of authorized shares is larger than the required amount in order to give a company the greatest amount of flexibility. Authorized shares are also called authorized capital stock or simply authorized stock.

Author's Alteration In publishing, a change made by an author after the book or article has gone to print for the first time. That is, an author's alteration occurs because the writer wishes to make a change and not because of some error in printing. Printers often charge for author's alterations. It is also called an author's correction.

Auto Sales The total amount of revenue from the sale of automotive vehicles in a given month. This revenue is seasonally adjusted and is published by the U.S. Department of Commerce. This is considered an important economic indicator because people tend to buy cars when the economy is doing well, and not to do so when the economy is performing poorly.

Autocracy A government system in which one person has complete and total power. While autocracy does not exist in practice, dictatorships often concentrate power in only a few persons.

Autocrat 1. A leader in a government who wields complete and total power. While autocrats do not exist in practice, dictatorships often concentrate power in only a few persons. **2.** A person who believes that autocracy is a desirable form of government.

Automated Bond System An electronic system on the New York Stock Exchange giving bid and ask quotes for inactive bonds. This allows investors, especially the cabinet crowd, to easily monitor the prices of bonds that are not frequently traded.

Automated Broker Interface A software system offered by U.S. Customs that allows importers to file information on the goods they bring into the United States. While using the ABI is voluntary, nearly all importers use it to file their paperwork.

Automated Business Mail Processing System Also called ABMPS. A way to sort U.S. mail using the five-digit zip code. While this zip code is still used in most correspondence, the ABMPS has been replaced by the Zip+4 code.

Automated Clearing House An electronic funds transfer system allowing for the instantaneous transfer of money between users for payroll deductions, tax refunds, direct deposits, and more transactions. It is run by the National Automated Clearing House Association.

Automated Commercial Environment A computerized system used in the United States to track all imports and related transactions coming over land. It is used at all points of entry from Mexico and most from Canada.

Automated Commercial System A computerized system used in the United States to track all imports and related transactions.

Automated Confirmation Transaction Service Also called an ACT Service. An automated system that reports information on the settling of transactions on NASDAQ. ACT is thought to increase transparency and quality of information in the NASDAQ market.

Automated Customer Account Transfer The transfer of securities from one account to another at a separate bank or brokerage. This may be done for any security or derivative: stocks, bonds, options, and futures may all be transferred via ACAT. However, each ACAT occurs over the Automated Customer Account Transfer System, which is only open to institutions eligible for membership in the National Securities Clearing Corporation and member banks of the Depository Trust Company.

Automated Customer Account Transfer Service A computerized system enabling the transfer of securities from one account to another at a separate bank or brokerage. This may be done for any security or derivative: stocks, bonds, options, and futures may all be transferred via the ACATS. However, each transfer may only occur between institutions on the ACATS system, which only includes institutions eligible for membership in the National Securities Clearing Corporation that are member banks of the Depository Trust Company. See also: ACAT.

Automated Export Reporting Program An electronic program the U.S. Census uses to collect data on exports from and imports to the United States.

Automated Export System In international commerce, the electronic filing of a shipper's export declaration with U.S. Customs. A shipper's export declaration is required with the shipment of certain controlled substances. The automated export system is designed to expedite the process.

Automated Information Exchange System Also called AIES. A computer system used in American customs that facilitates transfer of information between national import specialists and field import specialists. See also: International Commerce.

Automated Manifest Systems A computerized system that allows cargo-carrying vessels to declare their shipments electronically before they arrive in port. This is intended to expedite the importation system. It interacts with other computer systems in order to accomplish its goals.

Automated Order System A computerized order-entry system that sends buy or sell orders to the appropriate specialist on the floor of a stock exchange, bypassing the floor broker. It is used to automatically execute smaller orders, generally defined as fewer than 1000 shares.

Automated Pit Trading Electronic trading system introduced on the London International Financial Futures and Options Exchange in 1989 to replace outcry trading. See also: LIFFE CONNECT.

Automated Screen Trading The trading of a security or contract on a computer program that allows for trade 24 hours per day. GLOBEX (used for foreign exchange) is a famous example of an automated screen trading system.

Automated Search and Match A system provided by the New York Stock Exchange containing information on 500,000 executives and 75,000 companies. The

Automated Search and Match compares the information available to individual trades to find suspected insider trading.

Automated System for Customs Data Also called ASYCUDA. Software designed to administrate the customs process. It stores declarations, manifests, and other forms. It also assists workers in ensuring tariffs are paid and imports abide by law in the importing country. It was developed in Switzerland.

Automated Teller Machine Commonly called an ATM. A computer program located in a kiosk allowing the user to conduct certain banking transaction. Most often, an ATM allows the user to withdraw cash, but one may also check the balance of an account, make a deposit, make a payment, or conduct other transaction. The user may be assessed a fee to use an ATM, especially if the user's account is at a bank other than the one that owns the ATM.

Automated Trade Locator Assistance Network An organization in the United States sponsored by the Small Business Administration that provides automated market research for businesses.

Automated Underwriting A process in which a computer program reviews relevant information in a loan application and makes a decision based on the method built into it. For example, automated underwriting may make a decision automatically based on the applicant's credit history, income, and the amount asked. Difficult decisions may be referred to human underwriters. Automated underwriting is believed to be more efficient and less biased than human underwriting. It is used especially for mortgages.

Automated Valuation Model A computer model that estimates the value of a piece of real estate. While it is not as detailed as a full appraisal of the property, the automated valuation model is used as a substitute in some situations, such as the extension of a second mortgage or the assessment of property taxes. It is not used in considering a primary mortgage, which requires an appraisal.

Automatic Bill Payment A service in which a bank allows an account holder to pay personal bills by transferring funds out of an account with an order made over the telephone. Automatic bill payment originated with savings and loan associations, which allowed customers to make these transfers out of savings accounts at a time when they were not allowed to offer checking accounts. See also: Electronic Funds Transfer.

Automatic Checkoff A feature in some workplaces in which the employer deducts employees' union dues from their paychecks much as they would do for taxes or insurance. Often, automatic checkoff occurs because of an agreement between the employer and union representatives. It is also called compulsory checkoff.

Automatic Coverage A feature in some insurance policies that changes the amount of coverage in accordance with changes in the value of the property being insured. For example, if the value of a piece of real estate increases or decreases over time, a policy with automatic coverage would alter its coverage in proportion to the change.

Automatic Data Processing A publicly-traded company that provides computing and outsourcing services. Primarily, it processes clients' payrolls, but it also provides services related to insurance, retirement accounts, and other services. One in every six Americans has his/her paycheck processed by ADP.

Automatic Dialer A computer program that calls numbers and plays a pre-recorded message. This is used in marketing, often in political campaigns. For example, an automatic dialer may play a message from a celebrity endorser. Legislation limits the use of automatic dialers. See also: Dialing for dollars.

Automatic Dialing and Recorded Message Player In marketing, a program that calls a preset list of phone numbers and leaves a recorded message. Often (though not always), the message is recorded by a celebrity endorser of the product being marketed. Since the mid-2000s, it has become a fairly common feature of political campaigns.

Automatic Dividend Reinvestment A practice or agreement in which dividends on a security are used to buy more of the same security, rather than disbursed to the investor in cash. Automatic dividend reinvestment is relatively common in mutual funds; investors agree to use dividends and other capital gains to reinvest in more shares of the mutual fund. While this involves assuming more risk in the mutual fund, it carries the possibility of higher returns.

Automatic Enrollment An employer-sponsored retirement plan in which the employer is able to enroll an employee without that employee's express authorization. The employer determines what percentage of the employee's salary or wages is contributed to the plan. The employee is able to change this percentage and can even refuse enrollment in the plan, but he/she must do so in writing.

Automatic Error Correction A method to detect and correct errors (such as misspellings or faulty code) in a computer program or transmission.

Automatic Exercise The exercise of an in-the-money option without the holder's express authorization. That is, automatic exercise occurs at a certain point when the option is in-the-money even though the holder has not specifically requested the exercise. The Options Clearing Corporation practices automatic exercise when clearing option contracts, unless a holder requests otherwise.

Automatic Extension An extra amount of time some taxpayers are given to file their tax returns for a given year without needing to file an extension. For example, most U.S. citizens residing abroad are given an automatic extension for two months. See also: Form 4868.

Automatic Funds Transfer A transaction in which a person moves money from one of her accounts to another over the Internet, telephone, or other electronic service. Automatic funds transfers are a convenient way to move money easily and conduct different transactions. There may or may not be a fee assessed to conduct an automatic funds transfer. See also: Direct deposit.

Automatic Increase in Benefit Provision A clause in some disability income insurance policies allowing the policyholder to increase his/her monthly payments up to 6% at his/her discretion.

Automatic Increase in Insurance Endorsement An addendum to an insurance policy in which the amount of coverage for a property increases over time in accordance with changes to the construction cost index. This endorsement allows a policyholder to maintain coverage regardless of the inflation rate. It is also called the inflation endorsement.

Automatic Interaction Detector Analysis A statistical technique used to determine potential buyers of a product. It takes a universe of potential buyers and uses a series of steps to identify groups with certain buying habits. It expresses these persons with similar buying habits as clusters on a graph. It is used in multivariate analysis.

Automatic Merchandising The sale of goods through a vending machine. Automatic merchandising does not require a sales person and may occur at any time of day or night (assuming the machine is accessible). Both of these reduce the overhead to almost nothing. Soda and tobacco account for the large majority of automatic merchandising.

Automatic Non-Proportional Reinsurance A form of reinsurance in which the reinsurer pays the insurer for all losses exceeding a certain, stated amount.

Automatic Premium Loan Provision In some whole life insurance policies, a clause providing for a loan from the policy's cash value in the event the policyholder does not pay the premium. The automatic premium loan provision mandates the payment of the premium with this loan in order to prevent the lapse of the policy.

Automatic Proportional Reinsurance A form of reinsurance in which the insurer and the reinsurer share the risks on policies.

Automatic Rebalancing A strategy in which gaining investments in a portfolio are sold and the profits reinvested in an out-of-favor industry or stock. Because the out-of-favor stocks are not followed closely, they may be undervalued. Automatic rebalancing may therefore result in higher gains at the same level of risk.

Automatic Reinstatement Clause In some insurance policies, a clause restoring a limit after a claim is made and satisfied. For example, if a policy has a limit of $10,000 and a claim is made for $9,000, the next claim may be made for up to $10,000, regardless of the size of the previous claim.

Automatic Reinsurance An agreement between an insurer and a reinsurer in which the reinsurer takes over the risk for a certain class of policies from the insurer. See also: Reinsurance.

Automatic Renewal A way a business attempts to create residual income in which it sells a certain, stated order to a customer at regular intervals until the customer cancels. For example, an online dating site may renew a membership every 30 days until the client decides not to continue. The term especially applies to memberships and other intangible orders.

Automatic Reorder A way a business attempts to create residual income in which it sells a certain, stated order to a customer at regular intervals until the customer cancels. For example, a potato chip wholesaler may sell 1,000 bags of potato chips to a grocery store every week until the store decides to no longer buy them. This also helps the buyer control its inventory.

Automatic Rollover The transfer of a small amount of funds from one IRA to another owned by the same person without the owner's authorization. Rollovers happen most often when an employee changes jobs and therefore IRA accounts. Automatic rollovers occur when there is a small amount of money (usually $1,000 to $5,000) left in the first account; a plan administrator is responsible for transferring the funds between accounts. Since 2005, automatic rollovers into a traditional IRA have been required in this situation. See also: Involuntary cash-out.

Automatic Stabilizers Systems that involuntarily shore up GDP without any action by a government. For example, when a recession occurs, taxes usually decrease because persons and corporations make less. This gives them extra money to spend or invest, which helps GDP remain higher than it would otherwise. Most economists agree that automatic stabilizers work in the short term. They are also called automatic fiscal stabilizers and built-in stabilizers.

Automatic Stay In bankruptcy, an injunction against any ongoing collection process by any creditor. That is, all creditors must stop current attempts to collect debts during the bankruptcy proceedings. Chapter 13 bankruptcy also protects co-debtors who may not have filed bankruptcy. The automatic stay prevents creditors from filing lawsuits, making collection calls, or repossessing or foreclosing on property until the debts are discharged (or not) or the bankruptcy judge lifts the stay. American bankruptcy law limits the automatic stay for second-time filers to 30 days, and does not grant automatic stays for third and subsequent filings.

Automatic Transfer Service A service at a bank in which funds transfer from an account holder's savings account to his/her checking account when he/she makes a withdrawal that would otherwise result in an overdraft. For example, if there is $450 in one's checking account and one writes a check for $500, an automatic transfer service would transfer $50 to the checking from the savings account to cover the check.

Automatic Transfer Service Account A savings account at a bank that is structured in such a way that funds transfer into the same account holder's checking

account when the holder makes a withdrawal that would otherwise result in an overdraft. That is, if there is $450 in one's checking account and one writes a check for $500, an ATS account would transfer $50 to the checking from the savings account to cover the check.

Automatic Withdrawal A mutual fund that gives a certain, stated amount to each shareholder every month or quarter. For example, an automatic withdrawal fund could be structured to give shareholders one dollar per share per month. The money theoretically comes from dividends or coupons, but if there is not enough income to cover the withdrawal, the fund's managers must liquidate some securities to cover the obligation.

Automation The use of machinery, rather than persons, to complete a task. Automation has become increasingly common with leaps in technology that occurred in the 19th and 20th centuries. Automation is thought to have increased efficiency; for example, it made mass production of goods possible. Critics contend, however, that it renders jobs obsolete, undermining workers and reducing people's knowledge of how to "do" things. See also: Industrial Revolution.

Automation Rate In the U.S. Postal Service, the reduced rate offered on stamps for bulk mail if one fills out recipient information in a way compatible with automated machine processing. The automation rate incentivizes efficiency because machines can sort mail much faster than people.

Automobile Assigned Risk Insurance An insurance plan for drivers who otherwise would not be able to obtain automobile insurance. Each state in the U.S. requires insurers to offer automobile assigned risk insurance, at a premium higher than that of traditional insurance. States assign uninsurable drivers to insurance companies, which must provide coverage. This helps people who by law must obtain automobile insurance but are not able to do so because of poor driving records or other reasons. Critics contend it drives up premiums for all policyholders.

Automobile Comprehensive An insurance policy providing coverage for damage caused to one's car, the damage the car itself causes, and/or the car's theft. Automobile comprehensive insurance combines automobile liability insurance (which covers damage the car causes) and automobile collision (which covers damage to the car itself). All U.S. states require drivers to have liability insurance, but comprehensive coverage is not mandatory.

Automobile Fleet A large number of vehicles owned by the same entity, especially a corporation. An automobile fleet is covered under a single insurance policy.

Automobile Information Disclosure Act An American law, passed in 1958, requiring new automobiles to display a sticker stating the retail price suggested by the manufacturer, the vehicle's standard and optional equipment, information on the warranty, engine, and transmission, and gas mileage. This information is intended to protect the potential consumer.

Automobile Lease A way to structure the purchase of an automobile. Rather than buying a car outright, the buyer rents the vehicle from the seller for a certain period of time, after which the buyer either returns the car or purchases it for a price agreed upon in the lease. Payments are usually lower on a lease than on a car loan, and it is easier to qualify. The buyer also bears no risk for the car's depreciation because he/she can simply return the automobile at the end of the term. The seller, on the other hand, is allowed to effectively sell the car at least twice: once new and once used. However, automobile leases generally are not considered good investments if a person wishes to use a car for a long period of time. It often also comes with more stringent terms, such as a limit on the number of miles one may drive in a year. See also: Capital Lease.

Automobile Liability Insurance An insurance policy providing coverage for personal and property damage caused by one's car. This differs from other types of coverage because it does not cover damage to or theft of the car. See also: Car Insurance, Automobile Physical Damage Insurance.

Automobile Physical Damage Insurance An insurance policy providing coverage for personal and property damage caused to one's car. Events covered under automobile physical damage insurance may include vandalism, harm from weather, and car accidents. One may purchase this insurance on its own or as part of a more comprehensive policy. It is also called automobile collision insurance. See also: Car insurance, Automobile Liability Insurance.

Automobile Reinsurance Facility An insurance plan for drivers who otherwise would not be able to obtain automobile insurance. Each state in the U.S. requires insurers to offer an automobile reinsurance facility, at a higher premium. States assign their uninsurable driver to an insurance company, which must provide coverage. This helps people who, by law, must obtain automobile insurance, but are unable to do so because of a poor driving record or for some other reason. Critics contend that it drives up premiums for all policyholders. It is also called the automobile shared market or automatic assigned risk insurance.

Automobile Theft The act of stealing a motor vehicle from its proper owner or user. Many automobiles are stolen so the thieves can sell the parts. Other times, a car may be stolen for illicit purposes such as drug running. Car insurance often protects against automobile theft.

Automobile, Boat, and Aircraft Insurance An insurance policy providing coverage for damage caused to one's automobile, private boat, airplane or helicopter, as well as the damage the vehicle itself causes and/or its theft. One pays premiums to the insurance company in exchange for this coverage. The amount of the premium is determined by the relative danger that the car and driver pose.

Automotive Industry A division of manufacturing that produces, builds, and sells motor vehicles. As driving became more common in the early and mid-20th century, the automotive industry expanded significantly. In the early 21st century, it continued to expand in South America, China, India, and other newly developed countries, though it has stagnated in older markets like the United States and Japan. Most automobiles operate on an internal combustion engine, the use of which has become increasingly controversial because of concerns about emissions.

Automotive Products Trade Agreement A 1965 treaty between Canada and the United States eliminating tariffs on motor vehicles and auto parts. Almost immediately, the agreement resulted in significantly more automotive trade. Proponents of the treaty (and free trade in general) argue the agreement created thousands of jobs in Canada while eliminating its trade deficit with the United States. Critics, however, point out that Canada's own car companies were entirely replaced by American counterparts. The World Trade Organization declared the agreement illegal in 2001, though by that time it had been largely replaced by NAFTA. It was informally called the Auto Pact and APTA.

Autonomous Consumption An expenditure that does not vary with one's income. That is, autonomous consumption is what one must spend regardless of how much money one makes. Autonomous consumption is largely fixed during certain time periods. Examples of autonomous consumption include rent or mortgage payments and debt service. If one's income is zero, then autonomous consumption is financed by spending savings or by borrowing. See also: Induced Expenditure.

Autonomous Investment All investment in a country or region independent of GDP growth. Examples include government investment, inventory replacements, and other investments that must be made for the economy to continue to function, even in times of reduced or negative growth. Autonomous investment contrasts with induced investment, which is discretionary.

Autonomous System A set of different IP addresses on the Internet under the direct control of one or more networks. Before 2007, an autonomous system had to be under the control of only one network, but this is no longer the case. Each autonomous system has a unique number assigned by the Internet Assigned Numbers Authority.

Autonomy The state in which a company is not a subsidiary, department or other subdivision of another company. That is, an autonomous company is completely independent. Autonomy should not be confused with an autonomous expenditure or with autonomous consumption.

AUTOPER A computer system that facilitates trading on the American Stock Exchange for small orders. AUTOPER sends buy or sell orders to the appropriate specialist on the exchange floor, allowing him/her to execute and report trades at the same time. See also: ECN.

Autoregressive Anything that uses past data to predict future data. Technical analysis, for example, is by its nature autoregressive. See also: Forecasting.

Autoregressive Conditional Heteroskedasticity A statistical measure of the average error between a best fit line and actual data that uses past data to predict future performance. General Autoaggressive Conditional Heteroskedasticity is the most common way of doing this. See also: Fractal Distribution.

Autoregressive Process Any process or model that uses past data to predict future data. Technical analysis, for example, is an autoregressive process. See also: Forecasting.

Autorite du Bassin du Niger An international organization intended to advance international cooperation in the development and use of resources in the Niger River in West Africa. While many of its activities concentrate on hydroelectric development, the Autorite du Bassin du Niger promotes collaboration in other areas, such as agriculture and forestry. Member states include Benin, Burkina Faso, Cameroon, Chad, Cote d'Ivoire, Guinea, Mali, Niger and Nigeria. It is known in English as the Niger Basin Authority or the NBA, as well as by its French abbreviation, ABN.

Auxiliary Service Facility In the United States Postal Service, a satellite office for a bulk mail center, which assists the bulk mail center in processing large volumes of mail.

Availability The state of funds deposited into an account that a customer is able to withdraw. This especially applies to check deposits, because funds deposited by check often do not become available for a certain number of days while the bank ensures that the check is valid. Under the Expedited Funds Availability Act of 1987, banks in the United States must grant availability to funds within a certain number of days. See also: Check hold.

Availability Float A deposit into a bank account that has not yet cleared. For example, one may deposit a check for $1,000 from an out-of-state bank. The funds may be posted to the account immediately, but they will not become available to the account holder until the issuing bank honors the check and transfers the funds to the receiving bank. This process can take as long as five business days. See also: Check hold.

Availability Schedule The number of days it takes for a bank account deposit to clear. The availability schedule is set by the Expedited Funds Availability Act, which sets a different number of days for different circumstances (such as whether or not the deposit comes from an out of state account). The availability schedule can last as long as five business days. See also: Availability Float.

Available Asset 1. An asset that is not being used as collateral on a loan and may therefore be sold or donated. In other words, an available asset is any asset with no restrictions on its use. 2. See: Liquid asset.

Available Balance The balance in a bank account to which the account holder has access. The available balance usually is calculated by taking the account balance and subtracting credits and debits that have not yet cleared.

Available Cash Flow A measure of a company's ability to generate the cash flow necessary to maintain operations. It is calculated by taking the total cash inflow and subtracting total expenses before adding back the cash spent on debt service.

Available Credit 1. The credit one has on a credit card. For example, if one has a $650 limit on a credit and has made $200 in purchases with it, one's available credit is $450. 2. See: Available Balance.

Available Earnings The profit of a company that it may choose to pay out as dividends to common stockholders. One calculates the available earnings by taking the profit and subtracting depreciation, taxes, preferred dividends and other expenses. Available earnings are also used in calculating earnings per share. See also: Payout rate.

Available on the Way in Describing a stock that one may buy without much difficulty. The term is usually used in the context of inquiries about the stock. See also: Liquidity.

Available Reserve The difference between a bank's excess reserve (or its reserves over and above its reserve requirements) and the funds borrowed from a discount window at the Federal Reserve. That is, the available reserve is the bank's reserve that it is free to use as it pleases because it does not have to use it to repay any debt.

Available Seat Miles A measure of an airplane's ability to carry passengers. It is calculated by taking the number of seats available on the plane and multiplying by the number of miles the plane flies. Available seat miles are important because they are used to calculate the cost per available seat mile and the revenue per available seat mile, which are both used to help determine an airline's profitability.

Aval A third party guarantee, especially by a bank, that ensures payment on a note, bond, or other debt instrument in the event of default. This is practiced in Europe more often than in the United States, as American banks have tighter restrictions on bank guarantees.

Avalizor A third party guarantor, especially a bank, which ensures payment on a note, bond, or other debt instrument in the event of default. This is practiced in Europe more often than in the United States as American banks have tighter restrictions on bank guarantees. See also: aval.

Average A simple way to calculate the relative price of an index of stocks that involves adding the prices of all the stocks in the index and dividing by the total number of stocks. Market averages may be weighted, for example, for price or market capitalization. Movements in the market average of an index are considered a way to observe trends in the health of the companies represented in it. Some market averages are taken as an indicator of health in the broader economy; prominent examples of this include the Dow Jones Industrial Average and S&P 500 indices.

Average Accounting Return A measure of returns over the life of an investment. It is calculated by taking the average net profit (earnings minus taxes and depreciation) and dividing it by the average book value of the investment over its life. The average accounting return is used to help determine how efficiently assets are used to produce a profit.

Average Adjuster A person or company hired by an insurer to determine whether and how to pay a loss claimed on a maritime insurance policy. See also: General Average, Particular Average.

Average Age of Accounts Receivable The total amount of time a company's accounts receivable have been uncollected divided by the number of outstanding invoices. For example, suppose a company has three outstanding invoices, one for 30 days, one for 40 days, and one for 90 days. Their average age is accounted as follows: Average age of accounts receivable = (30 + 40 + 90) / 3 = 53.33 days

Average Age of Inventory The average amount of time it takes for a company to sell its inventory. One calculates the average age of inventory by dividing the value of average inventory by the cost of goods sold and multiplying the result by 365 days.

Average Agreement In marine insurance, a contract in which the shipper pays a premium in exchange for general average coverage. That is, in the event of a loss, the insurer agrees to pay a percentage of the value of the total value of the shipper's cargo.

Average Annual Growth Rate The average growth of an investment over a given number of years. It is calculated simply by adding together the growth rate in each year in question and dividing by the number of years. For example, if a portfolio grows 10% in year 1, -5% in year 2, and 6% in year 3, the average annual growth rate is calculated as (10 - 5 + 6) / 3 = 3.67%.

Average Annual Return The sum of the return rates of an investment over a given number of years divided by that number of years. For example, if one wishes to compute the average annual return over five years and the returns in each year were 2%, 5%, 7%, 9% and 4%, the AAR would be 5.4% per year (27% / 5 years). The average annual return is useful when gauging an investment's current annual return with respect to its historical return. In the above example, one may conclude that because the annual return in the most recent year (4%) is below the AAR, the investment may not be advisable.

Average Annual Yield The total yield on a multi-year investment or portfolio, often a certificate of deposit, divided by the total term of the investment. Calculating the average annual yield assumes that all interest accrued without any withdrawals over the length of the investment.

Average Audience Rating A measure of how long audience members listen to or watch a radio or television broadcast. The average audience rating is measured on a minute-to-minute basis; it is one way the A.C. Nielsen Company measures popularity of broadcasts.

Average Balance The balance still owed on a loan or line of credit over a period of time. One calculates the average balance by adding the balance at the beginning of an accounting period to the balance at the end and dividing by two. It is also called the average daily balance.

Average Collected Balance The balance in a bank account over a period of time. One calculates the average collecting balance by adding the balance at the beginning of an accounting period to the balance at the end and dividing by two.

Average Cost 1. A method of determining the value of securities in a tax year. One calculates the average cost by taking the total cost of buying shares in a security and dividing it by the number of shares one owns. The average-cost method is useful especially when the security has fluctuated significantly in price and when the investor has an automatic investment plan. **2.** In inventory, a method to determine the value of one unit. It is calculated by dividing the total cost of buying the inventory by the units available for sale. See also: Inventory Valuation.

Average Cost Flow Assumption A way to calculate the costs in which one weights the cost of inventory and the cost of goods sold against the value of inventory at the time a report is made. It is also called the average cost flow assumption.

Average Cost of Capital The total amount that a company must pay in dividends on preferred stock and in coupons on bonds, expressed as a percentage of the total amount raised through the issue of stock and bonds. This shows what a company must spend in order to raise the capital it needs to maintain or expand operations.

Average Daily Balance An accounting method in which cost and interest owed on a good or service are calculated at the end of each day rather than at the end of the month. Most credit cards calculate cost and interest on top of the balance at the previous pay period, but most department store cards use the average daily balance method. This, theoretically, reduces the amount one owes in interest on department store credit cards (though many charge higher rates of interest, canceling out the savings).

Average Daily Float The availability float over a period of time. One calculates the average daily float by adding the availability float at the beginning of an accounting period to the float at the end and dividing by two. It is also called items in collection.

Average Daily Rate The amount that a hotel or motel charges for a room each night on average over a period of time. The average daily rate is calculated by adding the amount charged each day over a period and dividing by the number of days in that period. See also: Revenue per Available Room.

Average Daily Volume The number of shares of a security traded each day averaged over some period of time. Generally speaking, the average daily volume is calculated over the course of the previous year. One may compare the current trading volume to the average daily volume to determine whether volume is particularly high or low. This can be useful in technical analysis.

Average Days' Inventory on Hand A measure of a company's sales strength. One calculates the average days' inventory on hand by dividing 365 days in a year by the cost of goods sold and dividing the result by average inventory. This indicates how often a company must replenish its inventory, which in turn shows how long it takes to sell its inventory.

Average Days Payable The average number of days it takes for a business to pay its bills. This is calculated by multiplying its payables turnover by 365. Companies aim to have a short average days payable because it indicates that necessary payments can be made relatively easily.

Average Down To buy more shares in a publicly-traded company in which one already owns shares after the stock price has gone down. Averaging down lowers the average price at which one buys the stock, which, if the price goes back up, will increase one's profit when one sells the stock. However, averaging down carries the risk that the stock will continue to decline.

Average Earnings Clause In disability insurance, a clause stating that if a person remains on disability for such a long time that the amount he/she is collecting in insurance exceeds the amount he/she earned while working, the person must refund a proportionate amount to the insurer and future payments are reduced.

Average Equity The average value that a client has invested in a brokerage account. That is, it is the cash value of the securities the client has bought with his/her own money, rather than what he/she has bought on margin. Brokerages calculate the average equity on a daily basis to ensure that clients are meeting margin requirements. See also: Mark-to-market.

Average Fixed Cost A measure of fixed costs per unit. One calculates the average fixed costs by adding up the total one spends over a period of time and dividing by the number of units. For example, if one pays $500 per month in rent and wishes to calculate the average fixed costs for a year, one divides the $6,000 one spends on rent by 12 months.

Average Frequency The average number of times the target of an advertising campaign encounters an advertisement. In general, advertisers seek high average frequency because the more times a person encounters an advertisement, the more

likely he/she is to respond to it and buy the advertised product. See also: Audience Duplication.

Average Hourly Earnings The average amount employees make per hour in the United States in a given month. It is calculated by the Bureau of Labor Statistics each month; the Federal Reserve uses average hourly earnings in deciding whether to raise or lower interest rates.

Average Indexed Monthly Earnings Also called the AIME. The inflation-adjusted, average income an individual earns each month over his/her working life, as calculated by the Social Security Administration. The AIME is calculated using the 35 highest-earning years (after the 21st birthday) of an individual's life. If one worked for fewer than 35 years, zeros are entered for years one did not work up to 35. AIME is used to determine one's Social Security benefits following retirement.

Average Inventory The value of a company's inventory over a period of time. One calculates the average inventory by adding the value of inventory at the beginning of an accounting period to the value at the end and dividing by two.

Average Irrespective of Percentage In marine insurance, an agreement whereby the insurer will pay the total value of a loss without regard to any percentage or other calculation.

Average Maturity In a mutual fund containing debt securities, the average amount of time until the debt securities mature. It is calculated by adding together the total amount of time until maturity and dividing by the number of debt securities in the mutual fund. The shorter the average maturity is, the less the fund's share price will fluctuate with changes in interest rates. See also: Weighted average maturity.

Average Monthly Earnings The average income an individual earns each month over his/her working life, as calculated by the Social Security Administration. The AIME is calculated using the 35 highest-earning years (after the 21st birthday) of an individual's life. If one worked for fewer than 35 years, zeros are entered for years one did not work up to 35. See also: Average Indexed Monthly Earnings.

Average Net Cost The cost of an insurance policy, taking into account the time value of money. There are several different ways to calculate the average net cost. It is also called the interest adjusted cost.

Average Net Paid Circulation The number of periodicals sold over a period of time divided by the number of issues published. For example, if a newsletter is published twice a month and it sells 4,000 letters in January, the average net paid circulation is 2,000. The Audit Bureau of Circulations uses the average net paid circulation to determine readership.

Average Outstanding Balance The balance still owed on a portfolio of credit cards divided by the number of credit card accounts represented in the portfolio. Investors considering buying a credit card portfolio may look at the average outstanding balance to measure the potential profitability of the investment.

Average Price 1. A measure of how much an investor pays for each share of stock calculated by taking the prices one pays and dividing by the number of prices. For example, suppose one buys five shares of the same stock, paying $10, $11, $12, $13, and $14, respectively. The average price in this case is $12. See also: Average up, Average down. **2.** A very rough measure of a bond's yield-to-maturity taken by adding the par value of the bond to the price the bondholder paid, and dividing by two. This is not always accurate, but it gives bondholders an approximate measure with little effort.

Average Price Call A call option giving the holder the right, but not the obligation, to buy the underlying asset, where the payoff is the average price by which the underlying asset exceeds the strike price over a given period of time. This gives both parties a certain level of predictability to the option contract. It is a type of exotic option.

Average Price per Share A measure of how much an investor pays for each share of stock calculated by taking the prices one pays and dividing by the number of prices. For example, suppose one buys five shares of the same stock, paying $10, $11, $12, $13 and $14, respectively. The average price in this case is $12. The average price per share affects the taxes owed when one sells the stock. See also: Average up, Average down.

Average Price Put A put option in which the payoff is the difference between the average price of the underlying instrument over the option's life and some stated strike price.

Average Pricing A way to set the price for a good or service in which one charges a premium over and above the average cost for that good or service. Average pricing should not be confused with average price.

Average Profit Margin A company or project's profit margin divided by the number of units it sells. For example, if a company sells 1,000 widgets in a year and makes a profit of $10,000, its average profit margin is $10 per widget.

Average Propensity to Consume The amount of money a person spends as a percentage of total income. For example, if one makes $50,000 and spends $40,000, the average propensity to consume is 80%. Countries with a high average propensity to consume generally have a lower unemployment rate because the demand to buy things creates jobs. However, it may be more susceptible to recession as people save very little. It should not be confused with the marginal propensity to consume.

Average Propensity to Import The amount of money a person spends on imports as a percentage of total income. For example, if one makes $50,000 and spends $10,000 on imported goods, the average propensity to import is 20%. It should not be confused with the marginal propensity to import.

Average Propensity to Save The amount of money a person saves as a percentage of total income. For example, if one makes $50,000 and spends $40,000, the average propensity to save is 20%. Countries with a low average propensity to save generally have a lower unemployment rates because the demand to buy things creates jobs. However, they may be more susceptible to recession as people save very little. It should not be confused with the marginal propensity to save.

Average Qualitative Opinion A number signifying how many analysts have recommended buying, holding, or selling, a security, respectively.

Average Rate of Return The rate of return on an investment that is calculated by taking the total cash inflow over the life of the investment and dividing it by the number of years in the life of the investment. The average rate of return does not guarantee that the cash inflows are the same in a given year; it simply guarantees that the return averages out to the average rate of return.

Average Revenue The total revenue a company or project collects from sales divided by the number of units sold over a period of time.

Average Revenue Per Unit A measure of the total amount of revenue a product generates, divided by the total number of users or units of that product. Companies use the ARPU to determine how profitable a certain product is, and, if necessary, make improvements, expand, or cancel the product. ARPU is commonly used in the telecommunications industry to determine the revenue generated per cell phone user on various plans and/or types of cell phone.

Average Semiprivate Rate The rate hospitals charge for a semiprivate room on average in a geographic area. Health insurers often reimburse for hospital stays at the average semiprivate room rate.

Average Shareholders' Equity The net asset value of a company at the beginning of an accounting period added to the value at the end of the period, divided by two. This is used as an alternate way to calculate a company's return on equity.

Average Shares Outstanding The number of shares an issuing entity, such as a publicly-traded company, has not repurchased at the beginning of an accounting period added to the number of shares at the end of the period, divided by two. See also: Shares Outstanding.

Average Stock The average value of a stock over an accounting period. One calculates the average stock by adding the stock price at the beginning of an accounting period to the price at the end and dividing by two.

Average Ticket The average amount one spends in a debit card transaction. One calculates the average ticket by taking the total amount spent over a period of time and dividing by the number of debit card transactions. This measures bank account activity.

Average Total Assets The value of assets a person or company has, on average, over a period of time. One calculates the average total assets by adding the value of assets at the beginning of an accounting period to the value at the end and dividing by two.

Average True Range In technical analysis, a measure of a security's volatility. It is calculated using one of three metrics: the current high less the current low, the current high less the previous close, and the current low less the previous close. The ATR is the highest of those metrics at any given time. A higher ATR indicates greater volatility. In order to have the most accurate measure possible, one generally uses a 14-day exponential moving average of the ATR.

Average Up To buy more shares in a publicly-traded company in which one already owns shares after the stock price has gone up. Averaging up increases the average price at which one buys the stock, which, if the price goes back down, will decrease one's profit when one sells the stock. However, averaging up carries the possibility of higher profits with more shares if the stock continues to increase.

Average Weekly Wage The average amount an employee makes in a week. This is used in calculating unemployment and workers compensation benefits.

Average Workweek The total number of hours employees work in a week divided by the number of employees. The Bureau of Labor Statistics compiles and publishes the average workweek for the United States. When the average workweek is decreasing, it indicates employers are cutting costs and may be a leading indicator of a recession. Likewise, an increase in the average workweek may portend a recovery.

Average-Cost Method 1. A method of determining the value of securities in a tax year. One calculates the average cost by taking the total cost of buying shares in a security and dividing by the number of shares one owns. The average-cost method is useful especially when the security has fluctuated significantly in price and when the investor has an automatic investment plan. **2.** In inventory, a method to determine the value of one unit. It is calculated by dividing the total cost of buying the inventory by the units available for sale. See also: Inventory valuation.

Aviation Accident Insurance An insurance policy protecting the policyholder (or his/her heirs) from injury or death in the event that the policyholder is a passenger involved in an airplane or helicopter crash. The policy generally requires the flight to be regularly scheduled.

Aviation Exclusion A clause in many life insurance policies stating that the death benefit will not be paid if the policyholder dies in a non-regularly scheduled flight. That is, the death benefit may be paid if the policyholder dies in the crash of a commercial flight, but not if he/she dies in a private plane crash.

Aviation Hazard The additional risk a person carries for being involved in air flights other than regular, commercial flights. An aviation hazard carries higher premiums on insurance policies.

Aviation Insurance An insurance policy protecting the owners and/or operators of an airplane from damage in the event of a crash. It also pays for medical bills and potential lawsuit damages from injured or killed passengers and other persons.

Aviation Trip Life Insurance A life insurance policy providing a death benefit in the event the policyholder is killed in the crash of a specific flight. Sometimes, the policy includes transportation to and from the airport. It only covers specific flights; that is, it is not an ongoing policy. Aviation trip life insurance is usually purchased at the airport.

Avo 1/100 of a Mecanese pataca.

Avoidable Cost A cost that a company does not have to pay if it does not take an intended action or cancels an ongoing action or activity. Avoidable costs are not necessary and generally are variable.

Avoidance of Contract A situation in which a contract is canceled because it has become impossible to fulfill without causing inequity between the parties. The parties are released from their obligations when it is canceled.

Avoiding Probate Steps one takes to prevent one's estate going through probate court after one's death. Probate court can be expensive and time-consuming for one's survivors and thus steps are often taken to avoid it. One may avoid probate in a variety of ways; examples include making gifts to relatives and sharing property ownership with a spouse.

Avoirdupois A system of measuring weight in which the basic unit is one pound, which is divided into 16 ounces. It is used in the United States, and to a lesser extent in the United Kingdom, Canada, and some former British colonies. Because it is not based on units of 10, it is not used in scientific settings.

Avtonomiuri Respublika In Georgia, a political subdivision equivalent to an autonomous region.

Avtonomna Respublika In Ukraine, a political subdivision for the Crimea, which is a province with a great deal of internal autonomy.

Avulsion In law, a situation in which the amount of land on a property increases or decreases due to a sudden (not a gradual) action of water. For example, a flood changing the course of a river may result in avulsion. Depending on the laws of the jurisdiction in which it occurs, an avulsion may or may not change property lines or even government borders.

Award To give a contract to a person or company, especially after competitive bidding from multiple persons or companies. That is, a company awards a contract when it decides to do business with somebody.

Award Letter The total reduction of a student's out-of-pocket expenses for attending a post-secondary educational institution for an academic year. The award letter outlines all grants, scholarships, work-study programs and some loans offered to the student. The award letter may determine whether or not the student can afford the institution. It is also called an award package.

Awareness The process by which, through advertising or word of mouth, a person comes to know of the existence of a product. Awareness is intended to arouse interest and ultimately lead to action.

Awareness, Interest, Desire, Action In marketing, a model of the four steps a person takes in deciding upon an action (especially a purchase). Awareness occurs when, through advertising or word of mouth, a person comes to know the existence of the product. Interest is a curiosity that causes the person to seek out more information. Desire is the state in which the person wants the product. Finally, action occurs when the customer buys the product or commits the desired act. This model is used in marketing both goods and intangibles, such as political campaigns. It is abbreviated AIDA.

Awareness, Trial, Repeat In marketing, a model of the three steps a person takes in becoming a buyer of a product. Awareness occurs when, through advertising or word of mouth, the customer comes to know of the existence of the product. Trial occurs when the customer purchases the product for the first time to see how he/she likes it. Finally, repeat occurs when the customer becomes a repeat buyer and perhaps develops loyalty to the product. It is abbreviated ATR.

Away from Home A category of travel where an individual is away from his/her general place of business or employment of a period of time substantially longer than an ordinary work day. The IRS allows individuals who are working away from home for any reason to deduct all meals, lodging, and other expenses from their taxable income.

Away from Post Education Boarding school education one receives when one's immediate family member is employed overseas by the U.S. Department of State. Away from post education occurs at a school located outside daily commuting distance from the family member's posting. The State Department provides reimbursements for away post education up to a certain limit.

Away from the Market Describing a quote that is either higher (for an ask) or lower (for a bid) than a security's current price. That is, an away from the market quote, if taken, would move the security's price in one direction or the other. If it is not taken it can lead to a wider bid-ask spread.

Away from Us Informal; describing a transaction conducted by another competing broker-dealer.

Awettha A Burmese unit of mass approximately equivalent to 204.12 grams.

AWG ISO 4217 code for the Aruban florin. This currency was introduced in 1986 upon Aruba's independence from Netherlands Antilles. The florin replaced the Netherlands Antilles guilder at a 1:1 ratio. Like the guilder, however, the florin is pegged to the United States dollar at a rate of 1.79 florins to 1 dollar; this peg is identical to the Netherlands Antilles guilder.

AX 1. ISO 3166-1 alpha-2 code for the Aland Islands. This is the code used in international transactions to and from Alandic bank accounts. **2.** ISO 3166-2 geocode for the Aland Islands. This is used as an international standard for shipping to the Aland Islands. Because the Aland Islands are part of Finland, they have their own ISO 3166-2 code under the FI entry.

Axe In bonds, an interest an investor has in buying or selling a given bond. A broker may match axes together to determine whether a trade can be executed. See also: Order.

Axe to Grind In equities, an interest an investor has in a stock. An investor has an axe to grind if he/she owns, has sold short, has ordered, or has inquired about taking a position in a stock.

Axis In Cartesian charting, a line that bisects a chart. The x-axis cuts a chart horizontally, while the y-axis cuts it vertically.

Axis of Evil Iran, Iraq, and North Korea, labeled as such by U.S. President George W. Bush, who accused them of sponsoring terrorism and of pursuing nuclear weapons and other weapons of mass destruction. The term evoked the Axis Powers, against which the United States and other Allies fought in World War II. The term was criticized for implying coordination between the three nations when none existed.

Ayak A Turkish measure of length approximately equivalent to 37.9 centimeters. It became obsolete when Turkey made the metric system mandatory in 1933.

Ayn Rand A philosopher and novelist closely associated with beliefs in limited government and in free market capitalism. Strongly individualist, Rand opposed most policies that directed any individual effort toward a collective goal. This led her to become an opponent of most social programs geared toward reducing poverty; she also opposed anti-trust laws, which she believed violated free market principles. She had a strong influence on future Federal Reserve chairman Alan Greenspan. She lived from 1905 to 1982.

Ayrton Senna In the United Kingdom, a slang term for 10 pounds. The term derives from the name of Ayrton Senna, a racecar driver in the 1980s and 1990s. In Cockney rhyming slang, Senna rhymes with a casual pronunciation of tenner. It is sometimes shortened to Ayrton.

AZ 1. ISO 3166-1 alpha-2 code for the Republic of Azerbaijan. This is the code used in international transactions to and from Azerbaijani bank accounts. **2.** ISO 3166-2 geocode for Azerbaijan. This is used as an international standard for shipping to Azerbaijan. Each subdivision has its own code with the prefix "AZ." For example, the code for the City of Baki is ISO 3166-2:AZ-BA.

AZE GOST 7.67 Latin three-letter geocode for Azerbaijan. The code is used for transactions to and from Azerbaijani bank accounts and for international shipping to Azerbaijan. As with all GOST 7.67 codes, it is used primarily in Cyrillic alphabets.

Azerbaijani Manat The currency of Azerbaijan. It was introduced in 1992, replacing the Soviet ruble at a ratio of 10 rubles to one manat. It is a floating currency. Its value has increased rather steadily since 2005 as a result of increased petrodollars in Azerbaijan. Interestingly, the Soviet ruble was called the manat in Azerbaijan even before the fall of the Soviet Union.

AZM ISO 4217 code for the Azerbaijani second manat. It was introduced in 1992, replacing the Soviet ruble at a ratio of 10 rubles to one manat. It is a floating currency; its value has increased rather steadily since 2005 as a result of increased petrodollars in the country. Interestingly, the Soviet ruble was called the manat in Azerbaijan even before the fall of the Soviet Union.

AZN ISO 4217 code for the Azerbaijani third manat. It was introduced in 2006, replacing the second manat at a ratio of 5,000 old manat to one new one.

Azorean Real The currency of the Azores prior to 1911. It was pegged to the Portuguese escudo at a ratio of 1,000 reis to one escudo. Because of this peg, the real continued to circulate for some 20 years after the escudo formally replaced it.

B 1. On the NASDAQ stock exchange, a symbol on the ticker board indicating that the issue being traded is class B stock. That is, B represents common stock designated by the publicly-traded company issuing it as having fewer rights than class A stock, especially fewer voting rights. **2.** A low bond rating used by the S&P and Fitch credit agencies. B-rated bonds are highly speculative and are thought to contain high risk and a relatively high chance of default. Banks are not permitted to invest in B-rated bonds. See also: Junk.

B1 Visa A visa granting the holder permission to enter the United States for business purposes. For example, a foreigner may procure a B1 visa in order to conduct a business deal with a client.

B2B E-Commerce A transaction conducted between two businesses over the Internet. For example, a publisher may sell books to a retailer, ship them to him/her, and receive payment online without meeting representatives from the retailer.

B2C Business to Customer. A sale between a business and the end user of the product that is sold. For example, a bookstore may sell a magazine to a customer who intends to read it (as opposed to re-sell it). See also: B2B.

B2C E-Commerce A transaction conducted over the Internet between a business and a consumer. For example, an online publisher may sell a book to a customer, ship it to him/her, and receive payment, all without ever meeting the customer. B2C e-commerce first became common in the 1990s with the popularization of the Internet. See also: dot-com bubble, B2B.

Ba A bond rating by Moody's. It is subdivided (in decreasing order) into Ba1, Ba2, and Ba3. A Ba rating is equivalent to a BB rating by S&P and Fitch. A Ba rating is the highest possible junk bond rating, meaning that a bond with this rating carries less risk than other junk bonds. Nevertheless, banks are prohibited from investing in them.

Baa A credit rating used by Moody's credit agency for long-term bonds and some other investments. It is subdivided (in descending order) into Baa1, Baa2, Baa3. A Baa rating is equivalent to the BBB rating range used by Fitch and S&P. A Baa rating represents a relatively low-risk bond or investment; banks are allowed to invest in Baa rated bonds. However, Baa is toward the bottom of investment-grade bond ratings, being only one grade above junk bond ratings. Risk-averse investors must therefore exercise caution in Baa investments, especially if the rating was recently downgraded.

Baa3 A credit rating used by Moody's credit agency for long-term bonds and some other investments. A Baa3 rating represents a relatively low-risk bond or investment; banks are allowed to invest in Baa3 rated bonds. However, Baa3 is at the bottom of investment-grade bond ratings, being only one grade above junk bond ratings. Risk-averse investors must therefore exercise caution in Baa3 investments, especially if the rating was recently downgraded. It is a subdivision of a Baa rating.

Baan In Laos, a political subdivision equivalent to a village or other municipality.

Baath Party A political party in the Middle East advocating secular, socialist policies intended to free Arab-majority countries from Western influence. It was established in 1940 in Syria. Its Syrian and Iraqi branches split in 1955 and became antagonistic toward each other. It became the ruling party of Syria in 1963 and was in charge of Iraq from 1968 until 2003.

Baby Bell Any of seven telecommunications companies that were formed from AT&T after its antitrust break-up in 1984. In that year, AT&T was determined to be so large that it violated antitrust law in the United States and it was forced to spin off seven subsidiaries, which became known as the baby bells. Few of the baby bells still exist as independent companies, as most have gone through a series of mergers and acquisitions in the years since.

Baby Bills A hypothetical, tongue-in-cheek name given to potential companies that would have been created if Microsoft had been broken up as a result of the antitrust suit brought against it in the late 1990s. The name derives from baby bells, which were the companies created after AT&T's break-up, and Bill Gates, the founder of Microsoft. As Microsoft was not broken up, the name became moot. See also: United States vs. Microsoft.

Baby Bond Informal; a bond with a face value of less than $1,000. Small companies issue baby bonds, especially when they wish to attract small investors and/or lack access to institutional investors.

Baby Bonus A payment a government makes to new parents, usually to reduce the pressure of the expense the baby brings. The baby bonus is given whether the child comes through adoption or natural birth. Only a few governments offer a baby bonus.

Baby Boomers A generation of children born in the years following World War II. While there is debate about the years in which baby boomers were born, the U.S. Census Bureau defines the generation as being born between 1946 and 1964. The baby boomer generation was one of the largest in U.S. history and had a significant cultural and economic impact. Their impact on American social programs like Social Security and Medicare is expected to increase significantly as they retire in larger numbers.

Babylonian Orgy In business, a slang term for a boring, mandatory conference in another town. The term is used sarcastically, indicating that there will be nothing fun at the conference for its participants.

Babysitter A slang term for a cosigner, which is a third party to a loan guaranteeing that the loan will be repaid.

Babysitting Slang; the act or practice of holding a losing investment for a relatively long period of time. One babysits an investment in hopes that the market will turn around and allow one eventually to break even.

Baccalaureate Bond A zero-coupon bond issued in some U.S. states to pay for college tuition expenses. That is, a student or his/her family purchases a baccalaureate bond, the proceeds of which help pay for tuition at its maturity. Baccalaureate bonds are usually issued in small denominations and have varying maturities that correspond to the due dates of tuition.

Baccone Italian for "little bite"; used as a euphemism for bribery.

Bachelor of Business Administration An undergraduate degree in business studies. Some BBA concentrations include accounting, entrepreneurship, finance, marketing, and supply chain management. See also: Masters of Business Administration.

Back Away To withdraw from a previously stated intent to conduct a certain transaction. For example, if a broker-dealer expresses an interest in buying shares of Stock X and then changes his/her mind, the broker-dealer is said to back away from the transaction.

Back Charge A fee that a company has charged but has not collected by the end of an accounting period. A company usually sends an invoice for back charges on its own or with the next bill. For example, if one's water bill is $20 per month and one did not pay in April, one will likely have a bill for $40 (plus late charges) in May.

Back Cover The outside of the last page of a magazine. Back covers very often have advertisements on them. As a result of its visibility, a back cover usually commands a higher price from an advertiser.

Back Door 1. In business, a slang term describing something unethical. It may also describe the action of circumventing a problem in an unusual (but still ethical) way. **2.** Any way to access a computer system other than logging in or using "normal" channels. Programmers often put back doors into their programs, or a hacker may create one. **3.** See: Back-Door Listing.

Back Door Listing Informal for reverse acquisition. An act in which a private company purchases a publicly-traded company and shifts its management into the latter. This allows private companies to become publicly traded while avoiding the regulatory and financial requirements associated with an IPO. In order for a reverse acquisition to happen smoothly, the publicly-traded company is usually a shell corporation, that is, one with only an organizational structure and little or no activity. The two businesses can then merge the private company's product(s) with the public company's structure. It also makes initial trading less dependent on market conditions, a key risk in IPOs. However, it is important to note that a reverse acquisition only provides the private company with more liquidity if there is a real market interest in it.

Back Fee In a compound option, the premium one pays on the second option contract. A compound option is an option on another option. For example, one may buy a call on a put, which is an option to buy an option to sell some underlying asset. An investor buying a compound option pays a premium on the first option, but does not pay a premium on the second option unless the first option is exercised. This second premium is the back fee.

Back Haul The return trip of a ship over its outbound route. It may or may not carry cargo on the back haul.

Back Issue Any periodical other than the most current issue. Libraries and other institutions often store back issues of periodicals for historical purposes.

Back Month Among several different futures contracts, the one with the longest maturity. For example, given three futures contracts, one expiring in March, one in June, and one in September, the back month is the one expiring in September.

Back of Book The section of a magazine that comes after most of the content. Advertisers argue that ads in the back of the book have the lowest response rate because so few people read magazines all the way to the end. Nevertheless, back of the book ads usually cost the same as ads elsewhere in the magazine.

Back of the Napkin Business Model A business model with few details. It provides a general idea of the products that a company intends to produce and of how it plans to monetize them. However, it may not include a detailed budget, a timeline, or other significant information.

Back Office The various administrative and support offices of a company, especially a financial services company. The back office departments handle internal accounting, compliance with government regulations, legal matters, settlements, and clearing services. While they do not generally deal with clients, they are necessary for the smooth function of the office. See also: Front office, Middle office.

Back on the Shelf Describing the permanent cancellation of an order to buy or sell a security. An order is placed back on the shelf when buying or selling the security would no longer be advantageous for the investor.

Back Order An order by a customer that cannot be filled because the seller does not have the good in stock. A retailer may have a back order at a wholesaler, which may cause a back order from a consumer to that retailer. A large number of back orders may indicate poor inventory management.

Back Pay Wages and salary a company is required to pay from a previous pay period but has not. Back pay may arise if a company is having cash flow problems, or if the company is insolvent. Non-payment of back pay can result in a lawsuit.

Back Stop In an issue of new stock, a guarantee made by an investor, usually an institution, to a publicly-traded company that it will buy the remainder of an issue if the company is unable to place it all with other investors. For example, an institution may announce that it will provide 100% back stop to a company's new issue up to $50 million. If the company only raises $35 million by placing the security with other investors, the institution will buy the remaining $15 million worth of stock.

Back Taxes Taxes that an individual or corporation did not pay in a given year. Back taxes incur interest and penalties that add up quickly. The IRS allows for plans to pay back taxes over time, though they continue to accumulate interest in the interim.

Back Test To use past data to predict future events. Researchers use back testing to find relationships between apparently unrelated events and determine if one causes the other. One may conduct back testing to inform one's investment decisions or strategy, though the practice is not always accurate because a great number of inputs cause economic events.

Back Translation The act of translating a previously translated text back into the original language. Back translation is used to confirm the reliability and accuracy of the translation. Back translation is used in market research in foreign countries, especially in high risk situations when one may not know very much about the local business culture.

Back Up 1. To sell a bond or other debt security with a longer maturity and buy another with a shorter maturity. One may do this when short-term interest rates are higher than long-term interest rates, for example. **2.** A change in a short-term trend. For example, if a bearish trend becomes bullish or vice versa, one may say the market has backed up.

Back Up the Truck Informal; to take or recommend an extremely bullish position, especially with a large investment. For example, if one believes that Stock A will soon rise in price, one may back up the truck on that stock by investing a particularly large amount of money in a long position. Backing up the truck implies a great deal of confidence in the proposed investment. The term derives from the image of a long-haul truck backing up to a warehouse to load up.

Back-and-Fill To change one's mind repeatedly. Backing and filling on an investment strategy can create a greater likelihood of loss. The term was originally nautical.

Backbone The largest channel of information on a network. The backbone processes and transmits the greatest amount of data. The size of a backbone is not based on an objective standard, but rather depends on the size of the network.

Backdating The act of dating a document before the date it was actually signed. For example, if one signs a contract on February 1, one may backdate it to January 31. Backdating is usually illegal; for example, one may use backdating to evade taxes. However, it can be permissible under certain circumstances. For instance, one may backdate an insurance claim if there was an unavoidable delay between the date the insured event occurred and the day the claim was made.

Backdoor Borrowing The act of a government borrowing without voter approval. This may or may not occur after the voters have refused to authorize a bond issue. The practice is controversial as it implies a lack of transparency in government actions and forces taxpayer money to be used to repay debt that voters did not want.

Backed In Informal; describing the circumstances that result in an expected jump or drop in a security's price. When a security is backed in, one may buy it at a discount or sell it at a premium; this often results in a quick profit.

Back-End Load Fund A mutual fund with a load that is paid when the shareholder sells his/her shares. That is, a back-end load fund carries a sales fee that a shareholder only pays when he/she sells shares in that mutual fund within a certain number of years. When an investor initially buys a share in a back-end load fund, he/she agrees to pay a third party (usually a financial institution or broker) a certain percentage of the share's value if he/she decides to sell it within five to 10 years, depending on the specific nature of the agreement. The amount of the load usually declines by the year until the maximum number of years is reached. See also: B-share.

Back-End Ratio In loans, the portion of a person's gross income that goes toward debt service. It is calculated by dividing all monthly debt payments by one's gross monthly income. Lenders use the back-end ratio when determining whether to extend credit to an individual. Some lenders use it in conjunction with the front-end ratio, while others consider the back-end ratio exclusively. The lower one's back-end ratio is, the more likely one is to receive a loan. Generally speaking, lenders do not make loans to a person with a back-end ratio of more than 0.36, but they make exceptions for good credit.

Back-End Value In a two-tier tender offer, the price paid to shareholders after the buyer already has control of the company. A two-tier tender offer is an offer to buy a company in which the buyer offers to buy enough shares to gain control of the company at a certain price, then offers to buy the remaining shares at a lower price. For example, a buyer may purchase 50% + 1 of a company at $20 per share and then offer to buy the rest of the company at $12 per share. In this case, the back-end value is the $12 per share offer. See also: Blended price.

Backer Card A small space available for an advertisement. A backer card is much like a small billboard. They are found in grocery stores and other places with a high level of foot traffic.

Backflush Costing A way to account for the cost of inventory in a just-in-time system. In backflush costing, no costs are accounted until a product is finished. After it is finished, costs are assigned over a period between the time product construction began and the time it finished. That is, costs are "flushed" back into the past. This is useful when a company has low inventory because it is simpler than tracking costs as they occur.

Background Anything used in an advertisement that is not the primary goal of that advertisement. Examples of background information include actors, music and colors. For example, the background in an ad for a vacation package may be an image of a family on the beach. Background is used in marketing to produce a desired response.

Background Investigation The process of verifying information a job applicant gives on his/her resume or in an interview. Examples of tasks completed during a background investigation include calling previous employers and co-workers, and checking for a criminal history. Background investigations are most common in jobs involving significant responsibility, such handling a great deal of money or working with children.

Background Music Music used in a situation in which music is not the primary goal. For example, background music may be played at a convention where people gather or in a commercial for a food product. Background music is used in marketing to produce a desired response. For example, it may be used to produce a calming mood at the convention or to make viewers of a commercial excited about buying the product.

Background Notes A publication by the U.S. Department of State detailing the land, economy, government, history and other information of independent countries and some other political units worldwide. It is available on the State Department's website.

Background Processing In computing, the performance of less important programs only when more important programs are idle or otherwise not in use. Background processing has become less common as more computers are able to multitask efficiently.

Backlighting A practice in which a person or object is lit from behind rather than from another angle. It can be used in video recordings or in other media like billboards. Backlighting is often used in advertising and marketing for dramatic effect.

Backlog The total value of orders for a product that have not been filled. The backlog can help a company estimate its future earnings or other performance more accurately. This metric is used most often in manufacturing.

Back-Office Crunch A situation in which the administrative office in a financial company has more tasks than it can physically do in a certain period of time. This creates a backlog in the company's operations.

Backspread An investment strategy in which an investor sells one or more option contracts and uses the proceeds to buy more option contracts than he/she sold. The options have the same underlying security or asset, and, ideally, the investor uses the premium(s) from the option(s) sold to finance the premiums for the options bought. If the underlying moves in the direction the trader wants, he/she can realize exceptional profits; however, even if the underlying moves away from the trader, he/she can make a small profit or at least break even because risk is limited to the premiums of the calls bought, which hopefully do not exceed the premium(s) of the option(s) sold. A backspread strategy may be used for calls or puts, but not both. See also: Put Ratio Backspread, Call Ratio Backspread.

Back-to-Back Commercials Advertisements aired on TV or radio immediately following each other. Radio stations and television networks do not allow competitors to air back-to-back commercials; rather, they often broadcast ads for unrelated or complementary products. Back-to-back commercials are less common on the Internet because ads often are shown one at a time.

Back-to-Back Commitment An agreement in which a bank makes a loan for a new construction and an investor promises to buy that loan from the bank at a specified future date. This commitment reduces the risk the bank takes on when it makes a loan. A back-to-back commitment is identical to a take-out commitment, but applies to loans on new constructions, rather than mortgages on existing properties.

Back-to-Back Credit An agreement by a bank to guarantee payment by a seller made at the same time another bank guarantees performance by a buyer. Back-to-back credit is intended to reduce the risk of a transaction to a minimum. Back-to-back credit is also called countervailing credit or reciprocal credit. See also: Back-to-Back Letter of Credit.

Back-to-Back Financing 1. In foreign exchange, two equivalent loans issued by two companies in two countries to offset each other's currency risk. For example, suppose an American company wishes to open a European office and a European company wants to open an American office. The American company may lend the European company $1 million for start-up costs. This loan is calculated in dollars. At the same time, the European company loans the American company the equivalent of $1 million in euros to help with their start-up costs. Because both loans are made in the local currencies, neither company needs to worry about whether the exchange rate will favor them as the loans are paid back. This practice has become less common as currency swaps have become more common. **2.** In international trade, see back-to-back letters of credit.

Back-to-Back Letter of Credit Two letters of credit issued by two banks, one guaranteeing payment by a seller and the other guaranteeing performance by a buyer. Back-to-back letters of credit are intended to minimize the risk of a transaction. See also: Back-to-Back Credit.

Back-to-Back Loan A situation in which two companies in different countries borrow an equivalent amount from each other in their respective currencies. That is, there is no net capital output because the companies are borrowing the same amount, only in different currencies. The companies repay these loans in an agreed-upon period of time. This used to be a common way to hedge against currency fluctuations, though currency swaps have largely replaced them.

Back-to-Back Swap A swap that reverses the terms of a previously agreed-upon swap. For example, the fixed rate payer in the first swap becomes the floating rate payer in the second swap. This eliminates the need for the two parties to pay each other, since each owes the other the same amount. It is sometimes used in lieu of simply canceling a swap.

Backup Line of Credit A bank's guarantee of an issuer's commercial paper. Commercial paper is a short-term, unsecured debt security usually issued by a company with a very high credit rating. As a result, commercial paper is very low-risk. The backup line provides additional security for the paper, but usually does not provide credit for the full value of the paper. The issuer pays a fee to the bank for the backup line.

Backup Space Memory space on a computer, external drive, or online available to save extra copies of computer data. That is, backup space is where one stores data in case the original data is lost. Having backup space is especially important if one keeps a great deal of information for work or taxes on a computer.

Backup Tape A hard drive with memory space available to save extra copies of computer data. That is, a backup tape is where one stores data in case the original data is lost. Having backup tape is especially important if one keeps a great deal of information for one's company on a computer. Businesses commonly use backup tape to keep their computer information in more than one place.

Back-Up Withholding The garnishment of both regular income and investments for tax purposes. In most developed countries, a certain percentage of wages and salaries are withheld from the employee and paid directly to the tax authority. The same applies with many investment profits, including, but not limited to, dividends,

commissions, and fees. It does not generally apply to real estate transactions. Governments instituted this regulation to avoid the possibility that a taxpayer may spend all his/her money before it is due to the tax authority, leaving it with the difficult process of collecting. In the United States, back-up withholding originated before the Civil War and was reinstituted in the 1940s.

Backup Withholding Rate The percentage of dividends, interest and other investment income one must pay if one fails to properly file one's tax identification number. The IRS informs companies and persons who are subject to backup withholding; this ensures the companies and persons pay the appropriate amount in taxes.

Backward Integration A business model whereby a company takes direct control of how its products are supplied. For example, a company may buy another company that previously supplied its raw material. That is, a butcher may own a ranch so that he does not have to buy slaughtered animals from an outside ranch. Alternatively, backward integration may involve the butcher buying the outside ranch. See also: Forward Integration.

Backwardation In Keynesian economics, a theory stating that the future spot price for a commodity will be higher than the forward price. This is because the producers of commodities expect to sell no matter what and are willing to sell at a loss, if necessary. In normal backwardation, no rational investor will buy on the future spot market if he/she can buy more cheaply on the forward market. The extent to which normal backwardation occurs in the market is debated.

Backwardation Swap A swap in which two parties exchange cash flows based on the current price and the future price of a commodity. That is, the two legs are the current price of a commodity and the expected price at some point in the future. This is used by commodity investors to hedge against future price fluctuations. For example, a farmer may use a backwardation swap to secure a certain price for his wheat before it is grown. See also: Futures Contract.

Backward-Bending Supply Curve The graphical representation of the theory that as income increases, work decreases. That is, people take more leisure time as they earn more.

Bacon Job In business, a slang term for a fun or interesting assignment or project for which people are willing to volunteer and work hard. A manager may have a relatively easy time in a bacon job.

Bad Bank A bank to which a bank holding company transfers non-performing assets from the banks it owns. This reduces the risk to which the transferring banks are exposed, which in turn increases their credit quality. A bad bank is also called a collection bank.

Bad Break Informal; an investment that turns out badly despite proper due diligence and other precautions.

Bad Debt Debt from a credit sale that the creditor is unable to collect. Debt becomes bad debt when the creditor has made all reasonable efforts to collect the debt but has been unable to do so. Often, this occurs when the debtor declares bankruptcy or when pursuing collection attempts further will cost more than the debt itself. A company writes off bad debt as an expense, which reduces its taxable income. However, it also deprives the company of cash flow that is ultimately necessary to keep it in business.

Bad Debt Expense An item on a balance sheet indicating debt from a credit sale that the creditor is unable to collect. Debt becomes a bad debt expense when the creditor has made all reasonable efforts to collect the debt but has been unable to do so. Many companies set aside an allowance for bad debts to pay for bad debt expenses. While this helps, bad debt expenses still deprive a company of cash flow that is ultimately necessary to keep it in business.

Bad Debt Recovery Partial or whole payment of a debt previously thought to be uncollectible. For example, if a credit card has been written off but then the credit card company receives a payment, this is considered bad debt recovery. This reduces a company's accounts receivable and generally increases income. Bad debt recovery may come from the receipt of a regular payment or from some other source, such as the sale of a loan's collateral.

Bad Delivery Describing a stock that cannot be transferred, especially because of improperly filed paperwork or another fairly innocuous reason. In other words, the delivery of such a stock is only stopped by legal and/or regulatory rules. See also: Good delivery, Dirty stock.

Bad Faith Abuse of the law by a party to a lawsuit. That is, one is acting in bad faith if one exploits the law for personal gain. Bad faith can result in the loss of a lawsuit and perhaps in punitive damages. See also: Insurance bad faith.

Bad Paper In business, a slang term for a bounced check (especially a paycheck), payment in a valueless currency, or some other unacceptable means of payment.

Bad Risk 1. A loan that is unlikely to be repaid because of bad credit history, insufficient income, or some other reason. A bad risk increases the risk to the lender and the likelihood of default on the part of the borrower. **2.** A person or company to whom lending would create bad risk.

Bad Title Title to a property that does not necessarily prove ownership. Bad titles are common when there are multiple claims to a single piece of real estate. See also: Quitclaim.

Baden-Wuerttemburg Mint An organization in Germany that issues legal tender coins for general use. It traces its origins to 1374 and is located in Stuttgart.

Badges of Trade In law, the circumstances under which a trade can take place. Badges of trade are important in accounting because non-trade transactions are taxed differently. Badges of trade originate in case law. Examples include the nature of the subject matter being exchanged, the length of ownership, and the reason for the transaction.

Bad-Pay List In marketing, a list of persons with a bad credit history. Persons on a bad-pay list may be removed from a universe of targets in a campaign because they will be unable to buy the good or service being advertised. For example, a cold caller may remove people on a bad-pay list from the file of persons he/she intends to call. A bad-pay list is also called a bad-risk list.

Baffle In film, a movable panel that absorbs light and sound in order to minimize unwanted reflections and echoes. A baffle is relevant to marketing because it improves film quality and therefore improves commercials.

Bag Man Informal; pejorative. **1.** A person who collects funds on behalf of a political candidate or organization. Campaign finance laws limit the amount of funds a bag man may collect from one person or interest group. **2.** A person who collects funds on behalf of a family or other unit of organized crime in exchange for protection. The bag man may also pay bribes to government officials. **3.** An IRS agent.

Bag Mark In numismatics, a scuff or other mark on a coin caused during the production or storage process. This may reduce a coin's value as a collector's item, even if the coin does not circulate.

Bag of Sand In the United Kingdom, a slang term for 1,000 pounds. The term derives from Cockney rhyming slang: sand rhymes with grand, another term for one thousand. It is sometimes shortened to bag.

Bag of Snakes A slang term for a business with difficult and often unforeseen problems. For example, an acquiring company may discover that a subsidiary it recently bought has low employee morale only after the purchase is completed. The company then may be said to have bought a bag of snakes.

Bag Stain In numismatics, a scuff or other mark on a coin caused due to contact with the cloth on a coin storage bag. This may reduce a coin's value as a collector's item, even if the coin does not circulate.

Bag Tag A label placed on a sack of bulk mail stating its contents and destination. A bag tag is also called a sack tag. See also: Bagging.

Bagel Land Describing a stock whose value is likely to drop toward zero. For example, if a company has declared bankruptcy and is about to be delisted, its stock may be said to be going to bagel land. The term is not applied to penny stocks.

Baggage Insurance A form of travel insurance that provides coverage in case one's checked or carry-on luggage is lost, stolen or damaged. Baggage insurance is purchased because the airline itself provides little or no coverage automatically. Baggage insurance generally only applies to airline travel, though theoretically one may purchase it for ocean or train transit.

Bagged Cargo Anything being transported in a bag or sack, especially if it is to be sold later.

Bagging The process of placing bulk mail into a large sack for delivery to the post office. Bagging has become less common as mailers increasingly use wooden planks capable of holding 2,000 pounds at a time.

Bags In Mongolia, a political subdivision approximately equivalent to a municipality. Most are sparsely populated due to the prevalence of nomads in Mongolia.

Bahaging lungsod In the Philippines, a political subdivision for a city.

Bahamas Dollar The currency of the Bahamas. Issued in 1966, it is pegged to the U.S. dollar at a 1:1 ratio. This allows the Bahamas to appeal to tourists economically; in fact, many businesses accept both American and Bahamian dollars.

Bahamian Pound The former currency of the Bahamas. It was pegged to the British pound at a one-to-one ratio; British coins circulated along with banknotes printed in the Bahamas. The Bahamian dollar replaced the pound in 1966.

Bahar 1. An obsolete Persian unit of length approximately equivalent to 3.25 centimeters. **2.** An obsolete Omani unit of weight approximately equivalent to 808 grams.

Bahidar In Nepal, a term for an accountant.

Bahraini Dinar The currency of Bahrain. It was introduced upon Bahrain's independence from the United Kingdom; it replaced the Gulf rupee. In 1980, the dinar was pegged to Special Drawing Rights, though in practice it was pegged to the U.S. dollar. The peg was officially changed to the dollar in 2001.

Bail Bond Money given by a third party to a court to ensure that the defendant appears at his/her court date. The third party (called a bail bond agent) charges a fee in exchange for placing the bail bond, which is returned to the agent if the defendant appears as ordered. Bail bonds are most common in the United States, where bails are higher than in other countries.

Bail Out To give money to a company so that it avoids bankruptcy and is able to continue operations. Generally speaking, the term often refers to a government bailing out a private corporation. A bailout may take the form of a direct transfer of capital, or it may occur indirectly through low or no interest loans and subsidies. For example, in September of 2008 the insurance conglomerate AIG found itself in dire straits. The Federal Reserve bailed it out by extending $85 billion (and eventually $182 billion) in credit to the company. Proponents of bailouts say that they keep an economy afloat when an industry thought too big to fail otherwise would collapse. Critics contend that bailouts are inefficient and that non-competitive companies ought to fail. See also: Cash for clunkers.

Baile An obsolete Irish unit of area equivalent to 1,440 acres.

Bailee In law, a person or company who temporarily takes possession of another's property. Unlike a lessee, a bailee is not allowed to use the property in question. Bailees do, however, have a fiduciary responsibility to return the property in the same condition. See also: Bailment.

Bailee's Customer Insurance An insurance policy providing coverage in cases in which a bailee does not return property to a bailor in appropriate condition. In a bailment, the bailor temporarily transfers possession of a property to the bailee, who has a fiduciary responsibility to return it in at least the same condition. If the bailee fails to do this through accident or negligence, the bailee's customer insurance pays for the damages.

Bailiwick The administrative term for the jurisdictions of Guernsey and Jersey, which are areas outside the United Kingdom belonging to the British Crown and in most ways subject to the United Kingdom. The term derives from a medieval jurisdiction presided over by a type of medieval sheriff's deputy. A bailiwick is headed by a bailiff.

Bailment In law, a situation in which one party (the bailee) temporarily takes possession of the property of another party (the bailor). Unlike a lease, a bailment does not transfer the ability to use the property, only its possession. The bailee does, however, have a fiduciary responsibility to return the property in the same condition. See also: Bailee's Customer Insurance.

Bailor In law, a person or company that temporarily gives possession of its property to another party. Unlike a lessor, a bailor does not allow the other party (called a bailee) to use the property in question. See also: Bailment.

Bailout Bond A bond issued by the Resolution Funding Corporation in order to raise funds for the Resolution Trust Corporation. That is, bailout bonds were issued in order to pay for the closure, reorganization, and the financing of savings and loans that went bankrupt during the S&L crisis. The principal on bailout bonds were guaranteed by zero-coupon Treasury bonds, meaning that they were backed by the full faith and credit of the United States government. See also: Financial Institutions Reform, Recovery and Enforcement Act of 1989.

Bailout Payback Method Payback Period A way to include the salvage value in the calculation of cash flow. That is, in the bailout payback method payback period, one adds the salvage value of an asset to the cash flow that asset generates to determine how long it will take for cash inflow to equal the cash outflow of purchasing the asset.

Bail-Out Provision In a variable annuity, a clause stating that the annuitant can make early withdrawals without penalty if the return on the annuity falls below a certain stated amount.

Bairro In Portuguese-speaking countries, a political subdivision equivalent to a neighborhood.

Bait and Switch Pricing A practice in which a retailer advertises exceptionally low prices for its products to attract customers and, later, when the customer asks, claims the products are out of stock or unavailable for some other reason. This forces the customer either to leave or to pay higher prices. Because this is considered an unfair business practice, bait and switch pricing is illegal. The advertisements promoting these artificially low prices are called bait ads.

Baiza A division of the Omani rial. One thousand baiza amount to one rial. See also: Fil, Penny.

Bake Off A final decision-making event in which two products are compared side-by-side in order to determine which is better. A company may conduct a bake-off, for example, to decide which product will receive the most funding for marketing purposes.

Baked In Describing a term that is included in a contract, business deal, or anything else. For example, an acquisition may include a provision requiring that the current managers of the acquired company remain on staff. This provision is said to be baked in to the acquisition.

Baked in the Cake Informal; a situation in which the market has already incorporated expected information into the price of a stock. That is, if a company's earnings are large for a particular quarter, it may leak the information so that investors bake it into the cake, reducing the pressure for an unsustainable jump in price when the earnings are actually announced. For this reason, the Federal Reserve issues statements indicating what policy changes it might make before it makes them, allowing the markets to adjust before the announcement. It is more formally called discounting the news.

Bake-Off A situation in which two or more investment banks compete to attract a client's business. For example, two banks may offer presentations to entice a client to use one (and not the other) as the broker in a merger or acquisition.

Baker Plan A plan formed by U.S. Treasury Secretary James Baker in 1985 to relieve debt in the developing world. The Baker Plan identified 15 countries with relatively healthy economies but also with a large amount of debt, and suggested the World Bank and private banks provide funding while these countries undertook liberalizing structural reform. Ultimately the plan was not implemented because no consensus could be reached on which 15 countries to include.

Baker's Dozen Thirteen, as opposed to a "normal" dozen, which is 12. The term may have originated as a practice among medieval bakers to avoid false charges of cheating their customers.

Bakhsh In Iran, a political subdivision equivalent to a municipality.

Baksheesh Arabic for "gratuity," which is used as a euphemism for bribery.

Baladiyah In Arabic-speaking areas, a political subdivision equivalent to a city or municipality.

Balance Concentration A practice in which several companies use the same bank account. Balance concentration is intended to reduce the likelihood of an accidental overdraft from their separate accounts.

Balance Due The total principal still owed on a loan or other debt. This does not include interest that has not yet accumulated. Thus, if one owes $1,000 on a credit card, one could pay more than $1,000 over time by making principal and interest payments, or one could simply pay the balance due (or the complete amount) at once.

Balance of Concessions An agreement in which one country reduces tariffs on its imports from another country in exchange for an equivalent, or at least similar, reduction from the second country. The balance of concessions is intended to stimulate international commerce between the two countries. It is also called reciprocity or simply a concession.

Balance of Indebtedness A summary of all the assets and liabilities held by a sovereign entity. That is, a balance of indebtedness states all the assets a country owns (examples include national art, taxes not yet spent, and stock in nationalized corporations) and all liabilities (including accounts payable to government workers, unpaid entitlement spending, and especially the national debt). One may consider the balance of indebtedness as the balance sheet for a country. See also: Investment Position.

Balance of Payments The difference between the value of transactions in which money leaves a country and the value of transactions in which money enters it. A positive balance of payments means more money enters a country than leaves it, while a negative BOP indicates the opposite. The balance of payments includes the trade balance, but also transactions such as foreign direct investment, transfers of currency, and payments for goods and services. Investors who deal in foreign investments use the BOP to help make investment decisions.

Balance of Retained Earnings A financial statement declaring a company's retained earnings at the beginning and end of an accounting period. It begins with the unadjusted retained earnings from the previous accounting period, then lists adjustments, adds net income, and subtracts dividends paid. The final entry lists the retained earnings at the end of the accounting period. The balance of retained earnings is published along with a balance sheet.

Balance of Risks Statement A statement the Federal Open Market Committee issues after each meeting indicating members' thoughts on potential, future policy decisions. The risks to which the name refers are the risk of inflation (combated with higher interest rates) versus the risk of recession (combated with lower interest rates). The balance of risks statement gives analysts some insight into what the FOMC is thinking. The FOMC began issuing balance of risks statements in 2000.

Balance of Trade The difference between the value of a country's exports and the value of its imports. If the value of exports exceeds that of imports, a country is said to have a trade surplus, while the opposite case is called a trade deficit. Analysts disagree on the impact, if any, of the balance of trade on the economy. Some economists believe that an overly large trade deficit causes unemployment and lowers GDP growth. Others believe that the balance of trade has little impact, because the more international trade occurs, the more likely it is that foreign companies will invest in the home country, negating any negative effects.

Balance Reporting Real time reports, usually to a corporation, of changes to the balance in its bank account. A bank issues balance reports so the corporation can manage its cash flows more effectively. Formerly, balance reporting was done daily, but companies are increasingly able to check their balances online at any time.

Balance Sheet A statement of a company's assets, liabilities, and stockholder equity at a given period of time, such as the end of a quarter or year. A balance sheet is a record of what a company has and how it has come to have it. A balance sheet is divided into two main sections, one that records assets and one that records liabilities and stockholder equity. The assets should generally equal the liabilities and stockholder equity because the latter two are how the company paid for its assets. Examples of items recorded as assets include accounts receivable and property, plants, and equipment. Examples of liabilities include accounts payable and long-term bonds.

Balance Sheet Account Any account owned by a company that is not closed out over the course of a year. Examples of balance sheet accounts include accounts payable and accounts receivable. A balance sheet account contrasts with an income account, which is closed out because it was paid in full. Balance sheet accounts are listed on a balance sheet.

Balance Sheet Normalization The practice of returning a balance sheet to its usual size. For example, if a company has taken on an unusual amount of debt to pay for a special circumstance, balance sheet normalization may involve repaying the debt in short order. For instance, it may not renew bonds when they mature.

Balance Sheet Reserves In insurance, an amount set aside and placed on a balance sheet as a liability. The balance sheet reserves exist in order to guarantee the insurance company is able to pay all claims that could be made. As such, balance sheet reserves are determined according to an actuarial formula.

Balanced Budget A budget in which revenues equal or exceed expenditures. A balanced budget is thought to be positive for a company, as it means that the company is not taking on any (additional) debt in order to conduct its operations; if revenues exceed expenditures, it results in a profit. Balanced budgets may be

recognized after a fiscal year is complete, or they may be projected for an upcoming year.

Balanced Budget Amendment A proposed amendment to the United States Constitution that would require the federal budget to be in balance or in surplus every fiscal year. Several different versions of the balanced budget amendment have been proposed, and most states have implemented a version of it. Proponents argue it would encourage fiscal responsibility, while critics contend investing with borrowed money can sometimes be beneficial.

Balanced Budget Multiplier A situation in which a government increases spending and taxes at a rate that keeps its budget in balance. It is thought that some of the money collected in increased taxes comes from what people otherwise would have saved. Because the government then spends the money, spending is increased in the aggregate, which drives economic growth.

Balanced Growth A situation in which capital intensity in an economy remains the same while other factors like GDP and productivity increase.

Balanced Investment Strategy An investment strategy that involves taking a certain amount of investment money and placing it equally or almost equally in high-risk and low-risk securities. This allows the investor to take some advantage of market upswings while not losing everything in a downturn. It requires less day-to-day management than an aggressive investment strategy, but more than a defensive one. For example, balanced investors are more likely to buy a certain speculative investment but also put an equal amount of money into Treasury notes.

Balanced Mutual Fund A mutual fund with a portfolio mixing stocks, bonds, and cash equivalents in different types of securities in a more-or-less fixed ratio. Balanced mutual funds are used for long-term investing. They also seek to diversify one's portfolio and avoid volatility in any one market. It is an example of an asset allocation fund.

Balanced Portfolio A portfolio with money invested equally or almost equally in high-risk and low-risk securities. This allows the investor to take some advantage of market upswings while not losing everything in a downturn. It requires less day-to-day management than an aggressive investment strategy, but more than a defensive one. For example, balanced investors are more likely to buy a certain speculative investment while putting an equal amount of money into Treasury notes.

Balanced Scorecard A type of internal audit. A balanced scorecard collects data and reports to management on four areas: learning and growth, business processes, customers, and finance. The balanced scorecard helps an organization monitor performance and, if necessary, make improvements.

Balance-of-Payments Crisis A situation in which a sovereign entity has developed an unsustainable balance of payments deficit. That is, a balance of payments crisis occurs when so much money is flowing outside a country that it has difficulty borrowing to make up the difference. A balance of payments crisis becomes acute in circumstances like an exceptionally large budget deficit that lasts for an extended period of time or a default on interest payments on publicly-held debt. See also: 1998 Russian Financial Crisis.

Balances with the Bank of England Accounts that banks hold with the Bank of England. British banks and building societies keep their required reserves and money owed to other banks as balances with the Bank of England.

Balancing Charge The amount by which the sale price of an asset exceeds its written-down value. The written-down value is considered the actual value of the asset for tax purposes. As a result, a balancing charge is considered profit and is taxable.

Balancing Item In accounting, an entry making an adjustment in cases in which two figures do not agree. For example, if two estimates of the value of an asset arrive at two different amounts, an accountant may enter a balancing item for the difference between the two to determine which calculation is correct.

Bale A standardized bundle of compressed material, tied together or placed in wrapping. Bales are standardized to weigh different amounts in different countries. They are used to measure shipments of commodities like paper and some agricultural products, such as hay.

Bale Cargo Cargo shipped, especially over sea or through the air, and grouped in bales.

Ball A slang term in Hong Kong for $1 million. The term is most common in Hong Kong securities exchanges and other trading platforms. See also: Hong Kong dollar.

Ballast Informal; anything that helps bring balance to an economy or company. For example, if strong auto sales lift an otherwise stagnant economy, it may be said to be a ballast preserving GDP growth. The term refers to the weight that helps balance a ship at sea.

Balle A slang term for the French franc. It is also used sometimes to refer to the euro. Literally, the word means "bullet."

Balloon Interest The interest on serial bonds, which are bonds that gradually mature at regular intervals until the whole issue matures. It is called balloon interest because it gradually rises over the life of the bond issue. See also: Balloon Maturity.

Balloon Loan A loan or bond in which the borrower makes only interest payments for a set period of time. At the end of the term, the borrower repays the entire principal at once. A balloon loan may be useful when the borrower expects interest rates to be low at the end of the term, allowing him/her simply to refinance the loan. However, there is a high risk of default because not all borrowers actually have the cash to repay an entire loan in one payment. See also: Balloon Mortgage.

Balloon Maturity A provision in some bond agreements in which a large number of bonds comes due at the same time, usually at maturity. Balloon maturity occurs only in bonds without a sinking fund provision; rather than retiring part of the principal at different times, balloon maturity returns most or all of the principal on a single date. Issuers of bonds with balloon maturities can have difficulty in repayment if they have not set aside a sufficient amount of money.

Balloon Mortgage A mortgage whereby the property owner makes only interest payments for a set period of time, usually five, seven or 10 years. At the end of the term, the owner repays the entire principal at once. A balloon mortgage is useful for an investment property where the owner does not expect to own for the full term of the mortgage. It may also be useful where the owner expects interest rates to be low at the end of the term and he/she can simply refinance the mortgage. However, there is a high risk of default because not all owners actually have the cash to repay the mortgage at one given time.

Balloon Option An option contract in which the strike price increases by a certain ratio after the price of the underlying asset reaches a stated threshold. For example, if the underlying asset goes above $50 per unit, the strike price may increase by $3 for every extra dollar that the underlying reaches. This type of option is most common when the underlying asset is a currency.

Ballot A document on which a shareholder records his/her preference for a decision, especially in elections for the board of directors. The ballot may represent one vote per shareholder, but more commonly, it represents one vote per share, giving persons and companies with more shares greater say. Ballots may be filled electronically, over the phone, or in person on paper. They are used at the annual meeting of shareholders and other meetings the company may call. See also: Proxy Ballot.

Ballpark Informal; an estimate. For example, when analysts are in the process of determining a company's earnings, they may release a "ballpark" as they continue their calculations.

Balop An image placed in front of a balopticon. A balopticon was a very early projector that looked much like a lantern. One placed the balop in front of the balopticon, which would project the image contained in the balop onto a wall or screen. The balopticon was important in the development of cinema and television, which are both important in advertising.

Balopticon A very early projector that looked much like a lantern. One could place an image (called a balop) in front of the balopticon, which would project the image onto a wall or screen. Often, the balopticon would project text so it could be copied. It was important in the development of cinema and television, which are both important in advertising.

Baltic Exchange A company that tracks information on goods being shipped internationally and the derivatives based upon them. That is, it tracks commodities, futures contracts, and options, provided they represent internationally shipped items. It also publishes a code of conduct for members, which include most of the world's shipping interests. The Baltic Exchange is based in London and was established in 1744.

Baltic Freight Index An index tracking futures contracts on goods being shipped internationally. It was used to settle contracts traded on the now defunct Baltic International Freight Futures Exchange.

Baltic International Freight Futures Exchange A former exchange in London on which futures contracts for dry goods being shipped internationally were traded. Futures on tanker freights were traded on the exchange briefly in 1986, but met with little interest. The Baltic International Freight Futures Exchange was established in 1985 and ceased operations in 2001 due to illiquidity.

BAM ISO 4217 code for the Bosnian and Herzegovinian convertible mark. It was introduced in 1995 and replaced three different currencies. It was pegged to the German mark on a 1:1 ratio. When the euro replaced the German mark, the convertible mark changed the peg to 1 euro : 1.95583 convertible marks. This was the same ratio that the German mark had with the euro before its replacement.

Bamboo 1. An obsolete Indian unit of length approximately equivalent to 12.8 meters. **2.** See: Dha.

Ban A subdivision of the Moldovan leu or Romanian leu. One ban is equal in value to 1/100 of one leu. Its plural is bani.

BANAMEX The second-largest bank in Mexico. It was the result of a merger in 1884 and, in 1926 became the first Latin American bank to establish a presence in New York. It has been a subsidiary of Citigroup since 2001. It should not be confused with the Bank of Mexico, which is the central bank.

Banana Republic A politically unstable country ruled by a wealthy and corrupt party or faction. Banana republics often are financed by one or a few cash crops, with little (or uneven) development beyond those. There is usually excessive collusion between the government and business interests.

Bancassurance Insurance provided by a bank. For example, a bank could offer life insurance in addition to its savings, loan, and investment services. Proponents argue that bancassurance can streamline internal and government regulations. For example, a bank offering a mortgage may require borrowers to buy homeowners insurance; if bancassurance is available, the borrower could purchase a policy directly from the bank without needing to shop around. However, bancassurance is somewhat controversial; critics contend that allowing banks to sell insurance gives them too much control over the financial services sector. As a result, some countries prohibit it. The United States has allowed it since the passage of the Gramm-Leach-Bliley Act.

Banco Interamericano de Desarollo An international organization established to promote international development and regional integration in Latin America. It works toward these goals by lending to governments and government-owned corporations in the area. Members eligible to borrow comprise all nations in Central and South America, while those who do not borrow include many European and OECD states. It was established in 1959 and is based in Washington, D.C.

Banco la Republica Oriental del Uruguay The largest bank in Uruguay. It has more than 120 branches throughout the country, as well as a few elsewhere. It was established in 1896.

Banco Latinoamericano de Exportaciones A bank that capitalizes other banks in Latin America in order to promote international trade in the area. It was established in 1979 and is based in Panama.

Banco Nacional de Comercio Exterior A government-owned bank in Mexico. It was established to provide financing for the promotion of Mexican exports. It especially attempts to assist small and medium-sized businesses. It is based in Mexico City with offices elsewhere in the country. See also: Export Credit Agency.

Bancor A proposed global accounting currency on which the currencies of the world would be based. The bancor would have been pegged to gold. John Maynard Keynes and E.F. Schumacher formulated the bancor in advance of the Bretton Woods Conference, but it was never adopted. See also: Special Drawing Rights.

Band Any range between two limits. For example, government regulation may establish a band of acceptable inflation rates and take steps to ensure they remain within that band.

Band of Investment An appraisal method for investment property that determines the amount one would pay for a piece of real estate such that it equals its operating income. One calculates the band of investment by multiplying the operating income by a capitalization rate. The appraiser must estimate the capitalization rate because it is not known for sure until the property is purchased. The band of investment can be used to analyze whether or not to buy an investment property.

Band-Aid Treatment Informal; a remedy for the appearance of a problem rather than a solution to the problem itself. For example, if a company is having cash flow problems, it may borrow, rather than take any concrete steps to increase collections or sales. While band-aid treatments may be inevitable in the short term, they generally do not resolve any problems and may ultimately make matters worse.

Bandwidth In investment banking, a slang term for extra time available to take on more work. For example, an employee has bandwidth if she can be assigned another project and still be able to complete all other assignments in the allotted time.

Bangalored In business, describing a position that was eliminated (resulting in the firing of the employee who filled it) because it was outsourced to India or elsewhere in South Asia. For example, many positions in American call centers were bangalored during the early 2000s.

Bangkok Stock Exchange The first stock exchange in Thailand. Established in 1963 as part of a program to improve Thai living standards, it lacked official government support. Moreover, potential investors did not have a great deal of education on the nature of stock markets. It was plagued by low trading volume throughout its history and closed in the early 1970s.

Bangladesh Bank The central bank of Bangladesh. It is responsible for issuing the Bengali taka and setting the country's monetary policy. In setting its policies, the Bank is required to attempt to maximize employment, productivity and real income. It was established in 1971.

Bangtail A small extension of an envelope with a detachable, perforated edge. A bangtail is used in direct mail marketing to solicit a response in a convenient fashion. For example, a political campaign may include a bangtail from a potential contributor that allows him/her to send money with minimal effort.

Bani A division of the Romanian leu equal in value to 1/100 of one leu.

Banica A subdivision of the Independent State of Croatia kuna, a currency that circulated between 1941 and 1945. One banica was equal in value to 1/100 of one kuna.

Bank An institution that provides a great variety of financial services. At their most basic, banks hold money on behalf of customers, which is payable to the customer on demand, either by appearing at the bank for a withdrawal or by writing a check to a third party. Banks use the money they hold to finance loans, which they make to businesses and individuals to pay for operations, mortgages, education expenses, and any number of other things. Many banks also perform other services for a fee; for instance they offer certified checks to customers guaranteeing payment to third parties. In some countries they may provide investment and insurance services. With the exception of Islamic banks, they pay interest on deposits and receive interest on their loans. Banks are regulated by the laws and central banks of their home countries; normally they must receive a charter to engage in business. Banks are usually organized as corporations.

Bank Account An agreement between a bank and a person or institution, whereby the bank agrees to hold money and/or other assets on behalf of the other party. What the holder may do with those assets depends upon the nature of the account. In a checking account or a savings account, the bank holds money and pays the client a certain percentage in interest. This payment gives the bank the right to lend the money to other clients or invest it within the confines of law and banking regulations. However, the client has the right to withdraw the total amount of money on demand.

Bank Administration Institute The oldest nonprofit organization in the United States that promotes best practices in the American banking sector. It sets industry standards, conducts research and holds educational programs for members. It was established in 1924 and is based in Chicago.

Bank Advisory Committee A board that provides expertise and other advice to a bank's board of directors. It may consist of former executives and other people deemed to have special knowledge of the bank or the banking sector. The board of directors may consult with an advisory committee on important matters. The advisory committee does not decide the matter, but may represent a broader spectrum of interests than the board of directors itself.

Bank Affiliate Export Trading Company A company, owned by a bank, that supervises the exportation process for clients. Often, there are legal requirements that must be fulfilled before a country allows its goods to be exported; export trading companies navigate these requirements and regulations. Because they are owned by banks, they may be able to assist with financing more easily than other companies. As with other export trading companies, they charge fees or commissions for their services.

Bank Anticipation Note A short-term note usually, but not always, issued by a municipality and used to finance some project. Bank anticipation notes are often issued with a maturity of one year or less; the proceeds are paid by the issue of a larger bond with a longer maturity. A construction loan note, in which a city finances private construction, is an example of a bank anticipation note. See also: IDC, RAN.

Bank Automated Credit System Also called BACS. An electronic system in the United Kingdom by which business-to-business transactions can be processed. That is, the BACS can transfer funds between banks in a more efficient fashion. Individual companies also use BACS to pay recurring bills. For example, they may use the system for large payments like dividends and wages/salaries for employees.

Bank Bill 1. See: Bank Note. **2.** See: Bank Draft.

Bank Branch A semi-independent office of a bank. For example, a bank may have five branches where account holders can make deposits and withdrawals and conduct other business at the place most convenient for them.

Bank Burglary and Robbery Insurance An insurance policy providing coverage to a bank in case of robbery or other malfeasance. For example, if a bank is vandalized or robbed, the insurance policy will pay for its losses. As with every policy, the bank pays a premium for burglary and robbery insurance.

Bank Call A quarterly report every bank must file with its primary regulator. The bank call includes information on the bank's income and its general state. Bank calls are published on the website of the FDIC in order to promote transparency in the banking sector.

Bank Capital Money that one has invested. Free flow of capital into investments is thought to be a major component of economic growth. Generally, businesses can only expand when they are able to raise capital from investors or borrow it from a bank or through a bond issue. See also: Capitalization, Capitalism.

Bank Card Association A network or organization owned by banks that processes transactions by bank cards. That is, a bank card association gives a bank the right to issue a card and authorizes debits and credits put on the card. It charges a fee (often assessed per transaction) for performing these services. Visa International and MasterCard International are the major bank card associations in the United States.

Bank Certificate Documentation confirming balances a bank owes or is owed on a certain date.

Bank Charge Any fee that a bank assesses on an account. An example of a bank charge is a monthly or annual fee for the privilege of maintaining an account. Other bank charges include overdraft fees (which are placed on a checking account when a holder withdraws more money than he/she has) and inactivity fees (which occur when a holder does not conduct a transaction for a certain period of time). Bank charges form a significant portion of banks' revenue.

Bank Clearing The process of settling transactions between banks. Because so many transactions take place between banks on a given day, bank clearing exists to process what each party owes or is owed in a central location so the least amount of money actually changes hands. For example, suppose Bank A owes $1 million to Bank B in cleared checks, but Bank B owes Bank A $1.5 million. Bank clearing is the process of determining that Bank B must only pay Bank A $500,000.

Bank Credit The total amount an individual may borrow from all banks. For example, suppose there are only three banks that will lend to a certain person. If that person can borrow $1,000 from the first, and $2,000 from each of the other two, her total bank credit is $5,000.

Bank Dealer 1. A department within a bank registered and therefore legally permitted to buy and sell municipal bonds on its own account, rather than only on the accounts of clients. **2.** A bank that is registered and therefore legally permitted to buy and sell government securities on its own account. Because the stability of the financial system depends on banks remaining solvent, bank dealers may only invest in securities deemed to be low risk, or "bank grade."

Bank Debit A reduction in the amount of one's bank account. While this technically could apply to any withdrawal, the term is used especially to refer automatic withdrawals made regularly with the account holder's permission. For example, one may allow for bank debits to pay one's car insurance bill each month. The account holder must explicitly authorize bank debits in order to prevent abuse.

Bank Delivery Order to an Airline An instruction from a bank to an airline to release some cargo to a stated party. Bank delivery orders are used when the bank is the consignee of the cargo.

Bank Deposit An amount of money held at a financial institution on behalf of an account holder for safekeeping. For example, one may keep a bank deposit in one's checking account to pay for daily expenses instead of hiding one's money "under the mattress." Most bank deposits are insured by organizations like the FDIC to reduce their risk.

Bank Endorsement A stamp or other authorization made by a bank on the back of a check (as proof that payment is owed) when it presents the check to the writer's bank for collection. Most checks require a bank endorsement if they go between two different banks. See also: Endorsement.

Bank Error A situation in which a bank incorrectly states the amount of money in an account. It may occur for a number of reasons, such as a payment that does not clear or a deposit that is placed in the wrong account. Persons benefiting from a bank error ordinarily are not entitled to keep the extra money because the bank (or the true owner) has a certain amount of time (usually years) to find and reclaim it.

Bank Examination A regular inspection performed by a regulator on a bank. An examination evaluates the number and quality of loans a bank makes, the quality of the bank's other assets and its compliance with regulation. An examination helps determine the stability and solvency of the bank in question. It often involves personal visits by examiners to the bank.

Bank Failure A situation in which a bank is unable to service its debts. This may occur when too many of a bank's loans default or, more rarely, when a bank has too few accounts providing it with cash flow. Bank failure used to cause great turmoil to the financial system, but since the Great Depression, the FDIC has insured bank accounts up to a certain amount to reduce the pressure for bank runs. When a bank fails, the FDIC takes it over and either sells it to another bank or operates the bank itself.

Bank for International Settlements An international organization composed of central banks that helps ensure the proper flow of money throughout the global economy. Based in Basel, Switzerland, the BIS seeks to increase transparency in monetary policy throughout the world, and to apply international standards where it is believed they are appropriate. The BIS regulates capital adequacy and encourages transparency in reserve requirement policies. Importantly, it does not provide financial aid to members. Critics allege that its standards are unenforceable. See also: International Monetary Fund.

Bank Giro A transfer of funds between banks without using a check. A giro transfer can be accomplished electronically or through the mail. It usually processes faster than a check. It originated in Europe, where in some countries it has largely replaced the use of checks, especially in international transactions.

Bank Guarantee A promise made by a bank to provide payment to another bank or lender on a bond, loan, or other liability in the event of default. Banks often make guarantees on behalf of certain clients to promise payment on loans. Bank guarantees reduce the risk to loans and liabilities and usually improve the credit agency ratings of bonds.

Bank Holding Company A company that is the majority shareholder in at least one bank. A bank holding company controls the operations of the banks it owns. Bank holding companies have access to liquidity from regulators through the loans made to the banks themselves. In the United States, bank holding companies must register with the Federal Reserve and are subject to its regulation, though they may also be responsible to other regulators as well. Re-registering as a bank holding company became a favored way for investment banks and other companies to increase their liquidity in the wake of the 2008 financial crisis.

Bank Holiday The term for a public holiday in the United Kingdom and the Republic of Ireland. As the term implies, banks are closed on bank holidays, as are many other businesses. Employees who work on bank holidays often are paid extra. Bank holidays may or may not coincide with cultural or religious festivals.

Bank Identification Number A former term for the unique number on a credit card or debit card. It has been replaced by the issuer identification number.

Bank Insurance A guarantee by a government or private company of all the deposits in a bank, at least up to a certain amount. Most bank insurance in the United States is provided by the Federal Deposit Insurance Corporation.

Bank Insurance Fund Also called the BIF. A pool of money created in 1989 by the FDIC to insure deposits made by banks that are members of the Federal Reserve System. The BIF was created to separate bank insurance money from thrift insurance money (which came from the Savings Association Insurance Fund). While this was likely beneficial for a time because of the savings and loan crisis, it created a perverse incentive for banks and thrifts to reclassify themselves as the other (ie. a bank to a thrift or a thrift to a bank), depending on which fund had lower fees at a given time. This led to the passage of the Federal Deposit Insurance Act of 2005, which abolished the Savings Association Insurance Fund and the BIF and created a single Deposit Insurance Fund.

Bank Investment Contract A bank-issued contract guaranteeing a specific portfolio a specific yield for a certain period of time. This contract usually has a maturity ranging from one to ten years. It is a low-risk, low-yield investment made mostly by corporations carrying 401(k) or profit-sharing plans. See also: Guaranteed Investment Contract.

Bank Letter of Credit Policy An insurance policy the Export-Import Bank offers to U.S. banks guaranteeing payment on letters of credit written by foreign banks. This reduces the political risk, and other risks, associated with honoring letters of credit from foreign countries. As such, the bank letter of credit policy facilitates international commerce.

Bank Loan The extension of money from a bank to another party with the agreement that the money will be repaid. Nearly all bank loans are made at interest, meaning borrowers pay a certain percentage of the principal amount to the lender as compensation for borrowing. Most loans also have a maturity date, by which time the borrower must have repaid the loan. A bank loan occasionally is called a bank advance. See also: Loan.

Bank Mandate 1. A document issued by a bank to another bank requesting that the second bank allow a customer to open an account, conduct transactions and generally receive privileges as if he/she were an existing account holder. **2.** A standardized, contractual agreement outlining the rights and responsibilities a bank and a customer have toward each other. The bank prepares the bank mandate and periodically updates it.

Bank Marketing Association An organization that publishes a number of newsletters and periodicals pertaining to the American banking sector. Among the subjects covered in BMA publications are regulation, bank marketing, and earnings growth advice. It is affiliated with the American Bankers Association.

Bank Merger A situation in which two banks pool their assets and liabilities to become one bank. Because this can have a significant impact on the financial industry, the Federal Reserve subjects mergers involving bank holding companies to more intensive regulation. See also: Too Big to Fail.

Bank Note A note issued by a bank and accepted as money. In a fiat money system (that is, in all modern monetary systems), a bank note is the same as cash. In general, bank notes are issued by the central bank (or by a bank authorized by the central bank to print money) and are legal tender. It is also called paper money.

Bank of America One of the largest banks in the United States. It traces its origins to the Bank of Italy in the early 20th century, which served immigrants in San Francisco. It grew to serve all of California and, through a number of acquisitions, spread throughout the United States. In the 1990s, while named BankAmerica, it lent a hedge fund more than $1 billion; when this hedge fund lost out in the Russian financial crisis, the bank was bought by NationsBank, which took the name Bank of America. It bought MBNA, at the time the world's largest credit card issuer, in 2005. In 2008, it acquired Merrill Lynch, which was near bankruptcy, after pressure from U.S. authorities. In 2008 and 2009 it received a federal bailout worth more than $150 billion in cash and guarantees.

Bank of Biafra The central bank of Biafra, a country that existed between 1967 and 1970 with limited recognition. In 1968, it began to issue the Biafran pound, which was not recognized as a currency in much of the rest of the world. Biafran notes have since become a collector's item.

Bank of Canada The central bank of Canada. It is structured as a Crown Corporation, which is theoretically owned by the Queen of Canada but is in practice by the Canadian federal government. The Bank of Canada sets the monetary policy for Canada, especially by key interest rates. Lowering and raising interest rates is how the Bank of Canada controls the amount of money in the economy. The Bank's goal in doing this is to keep inflation between 1% and 3% annually in order to promote sustainable growth. It is governed by the Board of Directors of the Bank of Canada and a Governor who is appointed by the Board.

Bank of Central African States The central bank of the Economic and Monetary Community of Central Africa. It issues the Central African CFA franc, which circulates in Cameroon, the Central African Republic, Chad, Equatorial Guinea, Gabon, and the Republic of the Congo.

Bank of Credit and Commerce International More commonly called BCCI. An international bank established in Pakistan, headquartered in London, and registered in Luxembourg. Its operations were structured to avoid regulation by any single authority. It was founded in 1972 with investments from the Emir of Abu Dhabi and Bank of America. It grew rapidly, making major loans and seeking deposits from high net-worth individuals. It became the seventh largest bank in the world. Because it was so poorly regulated, it was able to commit massive fraud, as well as deal with terrorist groups and questionable government operations. These crimes were ultimately exposed in 1991, and BCCI shut down, though lawsuits involving it continued for more than a decade.

Bank of Documentary Credit Insurance Also called BDCI. A bank that provides insurance to Canadian banks providing credit to exporters. That is, the BDCI reduces the risk to banks to make loans on Canadian exports. This is intended to increase exports and spur economic growth. See also: Export Credit Agency.

Bank of England The central bank of the United Kingdom. It is let by a Governor, which is at least nominally a civil service post. The Bank of England prints money for England and Wales (though not for Northern Ireland or Scotland) and acts as a lender of last resort for all banks in the UK. Through its semi-independent Monetary Policy Committee, the Bank of England sets monetary policy for the UK, particularly by attempting to ensure that inflation remains as close as possible to 2%. If the inflation rate is more than 1% in either direction of 2%, the Governor of the Bank of England must write the Chancellor of the Exchequer to explain how he/she will remedy the situation. It was established in 1694 and served as the model for the creation of most modern central banks. See also: Federal Reserve System, European Central Bank.

Bank of First Deposit A bank that takes deposits from individuals and/or businesses. See also: Retail Bank.

Bank of Japan The central bank of Japan. It is responsible for issuing the yen, setting monetary policy, issuing Japanese government securities, and providing settlement in order to preserve a strong financial industry. It works closely with the Japanese government. It was established in 1882.

Bank of New York The oldest bank in the United States. It was founded in 1784 by Alexander Hamilton, who later became the first Secretary of the Treasury. It merged with the Mellon Financial Corporation in 2007 to form the Bank of New York Mellon.

Bank of Scotland A major commercial bank in Scotland. It was established in 1695 and was the first bank in Europe to issue bank notes. In 1959, it became the first British bank to install a computer to process accounts. In 2009, it was acquired by Lloyds. It maintains the right to issue pound sterling notes, though it issues the Scottish version.

Bank Rate Monitor Index An index of 100 interest rates paid on savings account deposits in the United States. Bank Rate Monitor Inc. compiles and publishes the index each week; it is considered a benchmark for interest rates at different kinds of American banks.

Bank Rating A measure of a bank's likelihood of remaining solvent. Credit ratings agencies conduct analysis in order to determine bank ratings; the criteria and the ratings themselves may change from time to time. Bank ratings are important to investors as they make certain investment decisions, such as whether to buy stock in a bank or in another company heavily exposed to the banking system. A bank rating should not be confused with an investment grade rating, though the concepts are somewhat similar.

Bank Reconciliation The act or process of recording transactions that have occurred since one received one's bank statement in order to arrive at an accurate account balance. For example, if one spent $1,200 between bank statements, bank reconciliation involves recording those transactions so that they add up to $1,200.

Bank Reconciliation Statement A form on which one may compare a personal record of transactions on a bank account with the bank's record of the same. One uses a bank reconciliation statement to reconcile accounts and identify errors or omissions in records.

Bank Regulation The laws and bureaucratic rules governing banking. Banks have regulations at the federal, state, and sometimes local levels. Examples of bank regulations include capital requirements and limits on interest rates. Member banks of the Federal Reserve are subject to further regulations, such as the requirement to buy stock in the Federal Reserve System. Proponents of bank regulations state that they help maintain consumer confidence in banking, which in turn helps keep the economy running smoothly. Critics maintain that most bank regulations create market distortions and hamper economic growth. Perhaps predictably, these two groups disagree on whether too little or too much bank regulation caused the credit crunch of the mid and late 2000s and the subsequent recession.

Bank Release A statement given by a bank to a client giving the client permission to take delivery of some goods previously shipped. The bank gives the bank release after the client pays or is given a bill of exchange.

Bank Restriction Act of 1797 Legislation in the United Kingdom restricting the ability of the Bank of England from exchanging sterling notes for gold. At the time, the Bank of England was obligated to exchange the one pound sterling for one pound of gold on demand. However, the Napoleonic wars necessitated Parliament to order the printing of money to finance military operations. By 1814, 28.4 million pound notes were printed, but the Bank of England only held 2.2 million pounds in gold. This resulted in a 30% depreciation for the sterling. See also: Gold standard.

Bank Roi A colloquial term for 100 Thai baht.

Bank Run An event in which many account holders at a bank withdraw all of their funds at the same time because they do not believe the bank is solvent. Ironically, the pressure of a bank run itself can cause the bank to become insolvent. In the United States, bank runs were fairly common before the creation of the FDIC, which insures bank deposits up to a certain amount. See also: Panic.

Bank Secrecy Act United States legislation, enacted in 1970, that mandates greater disclosures by banks on transfers of money. Specifically, it requires banks to file reports on purchases of negotiable instruments (like commercial paper) for more than $10,000 if they are bought with cash. It also requires banks to inform the federal government of suspicious activities by account holders. The Bank Secrecy Act is intended to prevent money laundering. See also: Anti-Money Laundering Law.

Bank Swap 1. See: Swap Bank. **2.** See: Central Bank Liquidity Swap.

Bank Trust Custodial Account An individual retirement account from which contributions are placed either into an interest-bearing account at a bank or a brokerage account directed by the IRA holder. A bank trust custodial account gives the holder a great deal of flexibility as to how his/her retirement money is invested. This type of account was created in 1974.

Bank Trust Department A division of a bank that administers trusts, guardianships, and estates. It also may serve as a trustee for certain corporate bonds and pensions. Importantly, a bank trust department may manage the assets of customers who request it to do so. This is most often utilized by elderly persons with no next of kin, who allow the bank to handle their finances in case of illness and/or incapacity. Bank trust departments tend to be conservative and risk-averse in their investment decisions, making them attractive money managers to certain investors.

Bank Wire 1. An electronic communications system between banks. Employees at banks use the bank wire to inform other banks that an activity or transaction has taken place. Important: It is not used to actually transfer funds. **2.** See: Electronic funds transfer.

Bank-Based Corporate Governance System The design of a board of directors so that most or all members are either bankers or insiders. The term is used most often in publicly-traded companies, but it can theoretically be used for any organization.

Bankbook A ledger or book on which a depositor at a bank records all transactions in one's account, such as deposits, withdrawals and interest payments. It is also called a passbook.

Banker A person, especially an executive, who works for a bank. Bankers provide a wide variety of services, such as monitoring and safeguarding bank accounts, issuing loans, and accounting. Some bankers may also provide investment services such as underwriting or brokering. A banker's client may be an individual, company, or institutional investor, depending on the nature of the transaction and the type of bank.

Banker's Acceptance Short-term debt obligations that are secured by banks. That is, a bank promises to pay a creditor if a borrower defaults. It is also called a documented discount note.

Banker's Bank A bank that provides loans and other services to small banks in local communities. Because they provide capital to (and therefore spread risk over) a large number of local banks, banker's banks enable community banks to provide retail services for a lower expense than otherwise would be possible. Banker's banks originated in Minnesota in 1975.

Bankers Blanket Bond A bond or insurance policy covering a bank in the event it loses money as the result of employee theft or fraud. Blanket fidelity bonds generally only cover situations in which an employee commits fraud for personal gain; they do not cover situations in which the employee, without support or knowledge of management, falsifies transactions to make the bank appear healthier than it is. Some U.S. states require banks to have blanket bonds. It is a type of blanket fidelity bond.

Banker's Reference A letter a bank provides stating the creditworthiness of an account holder. It contains account history and similar information. Banker's references often are used in commerce when a bank is considering extending a loan and wishes to discover the likelihood of repayment.

Banking The network of institutions and laws that provide a great variety of financial services. At its most basic, banking involves an institution holding money on behalf of customers that is payable to the customer on demand, either by appearing at the bank for a withdrawal or by writing a check to a third party. The banking system also provides loans to businesses and individuals. Many banks also perform other services for a fee; for instance, they offer certified checks to customers guaranteeing payment to third parties. In some countries, they may provide investment and insurance services. With the exception of Islamic banks, banking almost always involves the payment of interest on deposits and reception of interest on loans. Banking is regulated by the laws and central banks of individual countries.

Banking (Special Provisions) Act 2008 Legislation in the United Kingdom authorizing the British government to nationalize failing banks under certain circumstances. The proximate cause of the act was the nationalization of Northern Rock, which collapsed in 2007. However, three other banks were taken over the same year under the act. See also: Late 2000s recession.

Banking Acts of 1979 and 1987 Two pieces of legislation in the United Kingdom. Under both Acts, the Bank of England has regulatory responsibility for British financial institutions.

Banking and Securities Industry Committee An organization established to write and promote a uniform set of rules for the settlement of securities trades. It was formed in 1970 as trading volume increased to the point that former systems could not keep pace. It was dissolved with the formation of the Deposit Trust Company.

Banking Books Textbooks and other educational materials published in order to teach the concepts, laws and practice of banking.

Banking Delay The time it takes a bank to collect the funds from a check deposit to the issuing bank. A banking delay may take only a day or two for a local check, and perhaps longer from an out-of-state or foreign check. It is important to note that a banking delay is different from a check hold, which is the maximum number of days a bank may refrain from crediting a depositor's account while it attempts to collect the funds. Unless the check bounces, the bank must credit the account at the end of the check holding period regardless of whether or not the banking delay has passed.

Banking Department A cabinet-level agency of a state government charged with regulating banking in that state. In some states, the banking department also has responsibility over other financial instruments, such as insurance companies.

Banking Directives Banking regulations instituted in Europe in the 1970s and 1980s in anticipation of the introduction of the euro. The first banking directive encourages cooperation between EU nations in the establishment and regulation of credit institutions. The consolidated supervision directive requires two institutions in different countries to be regulated on a supranational basis if one owns more than 25% of the other. Finally, the second directive created a single banking license throughout the EU.

Banking Ombudsman An institution that receives and deals with disputes related to banking and financial services. Examples of complaints an ombudsman might handle include non-payment of a check and refusal to honor a duly issued letter of credit. Banking ombudsman services exist in countries like the United Kingdom and India, though other nations have similar organizations.

Banking Power The ability of a bank to conduct activities. Banking power is given by the appropriate government agency. Activities permitted under banking powers are regulated; they may include retail banking or commercial banking, as well as permissible nonbank activities such as insurance, trading on the secondary market for

mortgages, or investment banking. See also: Glass-Steagall Act, Gramm-Bliley-Leach Act.

Bankline 1. A network connecting six banks and several hundred ATM machines in South Korea. **2.** See: Line of Credit.

Bankmail In acquisitions, an agreement between an acquiring company and a bank stipulating that the bank will not provide financing for any competing bid for the acquired company. For example, if Company A wishes to buy Company B, it may seek a guarantee from a bank that it will either finance Company A's bid or no bid at all. Companies use bankmail to reduce the risk that they will be outbid.

Bankroll To provide financing, whether as a loan, grant, or simply as part of a budget. For example, a company may bankroll its research and development by providing funding for it in the budget. Likewise, a credit union bankrolls a business when it allows a client to take out a second mortgage on a home.

Bankruptcy A legal declaration that one is unable to pay one's debts and thus needs to have debts forgiven or reorganized. That is, bankruptcy is a legal proceeding in which a person or corporation has become insolvent, and therefore cannot pay his/her/its obligations. Most of the time, the person or corporation files this declaration with a bankruptcy court, though in some cases the creditors may do so themselves. In bankruptcy proceedings, one's assets and debts are evaluated and debts are repaid according to the debtor's ability to pay, what the creditors will accept, and what the court and the law decide. In the United States, bankruptcy falls under federal jurisdiction. There are three main types of American bankruptcy. In Chapter 7, the person or company's assets are liquidated and creditors are repaid out of the proceeds from the liquidation. All remaining debts are then discharged. If a company files for Chapter 7 protection, it ceases operation. In Chapter 11 bankruptcy, a company files a reorganization plan with the court whereby it continues operation and creditors are repaid for part of what they are owed; all other debts are discharged. In Chapter 13, the person or company remains in debt, but payments are lowered, repayment periods are extended, and the company remains in business. See also: Absolute priority rule, Chapter 9, Chapter 12, Chapter 15.

Bankruptcy Abuse Prevention and Consumer Protection Act of 2005 United States legislation that made it more difficult to file Chapter 7 bankruptcy, instead encouraging Chapter 13. It requires persons with incomes over the median income in their state to calculate their incomes relative to what are considered reasonable expenses. Those with incomes over a certain amount are not allowed to file Chapter 7, which would forgive all debts not repaid. This and some other provisions in the bill were specifically designed to make it more difficult to file bankruptcy in the United States.

Bankruptcy and Insolvency Act Legislation in Canada laying out requirements for most bankruptcies. Individuals and most businesses (excepting banks, insurance companies, and some other financial companies) may file for bankruptcy under the Act. It forgives debts not repaid after all reasonable efforts have been made to preserve assets on behalf of creditors.

Bankruptcy Code A comprehensive law governing bankruptcy in a country or other jurisdiction. In the United States, the Bankruptcy Reform Act of 1978 forms the current bankruptcy code. It provides for three main types of bankruptcy. Chapter 7 provides for liquidation of a business and discharge of debts. Chapter 11 allows corporations to continue operations after reorganization. Chapter 13 restructures debt but does not forgive it.

Bankruptcy Cost View A theory stating that the costs of bankruptcy offset or exceed the benefits a company receives from a great deal of leverage. Followers of this view recommend companies maintain less than 100% leverage.

Bankruptcy Court A court constituted to hear bankruptcy cases exclusively. In the United States, bankruptcy courts are constituted under the federal government and are units of regional district courts.

Bankruptcy Financing Financing made available to a debtor in possession, which is a company that maintains its operations during a Chapter 11 bankruptcy. A debtor in possession is generally attempting to fulfill its reorganization plan, discharging certain debts and changing any structural weaknesses to put it on a path to profitability. A company often requires financing in order to restructure, and bankruptcy financing enables it to do so, though at a very high interest rate to compensate the lender for the risk of making money available to the debtor in possession.

Bankruptcy Fraud The deliberate attempt to discharge or restructure debts without needing to do so. One may accomplish bankruptcy fraud in a variety of ways, such as hiding assets or filing frequently. In the United States, bankruptcy fraud is punishable by five years in prison and/or a $250,000 fine.

Bankruptcy Petition 1. A formal request by an individual or a business to a bankruptcy court to declare bankruptcy and to discharge or restructure debts (after repayment is made insofar as possible). **2.** A formal request by an individual or a business' creditors to a bankruptcy court to declare bankruptcy and to require repayment or restructuring of debts. Some businesses and individuals (such as fishermen in Canada) are exempt from this type of forced bankruptcy.

Bankruptcy Reform Act of 1978 A major overhaul of previous bankruptcy law in the United States. The Act forms the basis for how bankruptcies have been conducted ever since. The Act provides for three main types of bankruptcy. Chapter 7 provides for liquidation of a business and discharge of debts. Chapter 11 allows corporations to continue operations after reorganization. Chapter 13 restructures debt but does not forgive it. See also: Bankruptcy Abuse Prevention and Consumer Protection Act, Bankruptcy and Insolvency Act.

Bankruptcy Risk The risk that an individual or especially a company may be unable to service its debts. Bankruptcy risk is greater when the individual or firm has little or no cash flow, or when it manages its assets poorly. Banks assess bankruptcy risk when considering whether to make a loan. It is also called insolvency risk.

Banks for Cooperatives Twelve privately-owned banks sponsored by the U.S. federal government that provide financing to American farmers. They make loans to farmers for marketing and supply purposes, as well as to rural utility companies. They pay for their operations through bonds and other debt securities issued by a federal farm credit bank. Banks for cooperatives were created in 1933.

Banner Ad An advertisement embedded in a webpage. A banner ad is commonly at the top or the bottom on a page, but may be placed anywhere. Advertisers may pay by the number of clicks or by the number of views. A banner ad is also called a web banner. See also: CPC, CPM.

Banner Advertising A type of advertising on the Internet in which the advertiser places an ad at the top of a website. This ad is 460 X 68 pixels almost always emphasizes graphics over text. Banner advertising is designed to attract the attention of the user of a website and usually to encourage him/her to click on the ad and go to the website of the advertiser. One may think of banner advertising as the online equivalent of a billboard. See also: CPM, CPC.

Banner Year Slang; an extremely profitable or otherwise successful year for a person or organization. For example, the CEO of a company has a banner year if she helps her company rebound from bankruptcy to near-record profit in only 10 months.

Bannerhead In advertising, a headline printed in large, bold type over a text. The bannerhead is intended to grab the attention of a viewer. It may entice him/her to read the remainder of the advertisement, or it simply may leave him/her with an impression about the product.

Banque Centrale des Etats de l'Afrique de l'Ouest The central bank of the West African Economic and Monetary Union. It issues the West African CFA franc, which circulates in Benin, Burkina Faso, Cote d'Ivoire, Guinea Bissau, Mali, Niger and Togo. It was established in 1961.

Banque d'Affaires A type of bank structure in France. A banque d'affaires provides financing and advisory services for companies and other organizations. Banques d'affaires usually sell their loans and other assets to investors only a short time after acquiring them.

Banque de Developpement des Etats de l'Afrique Centrale A bank that provides loans to support integration of member countries and to promote economic development. Members include Cameroon, Central African Republic, Chad, Republic of the Congo, Equatorial Guinea and Gabon. It was founded in 1975 and began operations in 1977. It is based in Brazzaville, Congo.

Banque de Developpement des Etats du Grand Lac A bank that provides loans and other services to promote economic development among member states. Members include Burundi, Rwanda, and the Democratic Republic of the Congo. It was founded in 1977. It is based in Goma, Democratic Republic of the Congo.

Banque de France The former central bank of France. It once issued and regulated the French franc. Since 1998, it has assisted the European Central Bank in regulating the euro in France.

Banque Francaise du Commerce Exterieur A former bank in France providing financing and bonds to French exporters. It was structured as a joint stock company; its major shareholders were state-owned banks, and its director was appointed by the Finance Minister. As part of a privatization program, BFCE was sold to Credit National in 1996.

Banque Ouest-Africaine de Developpement A bank that provides loans to promote economic development among member states. Members include Benin, Burkina Faso, Cote d'Ivoire, Mali, Niger, Senegal and Togo. It was founded in 1973 and began operations in 1976. It is based in Lome, Togo.

Banxquote Money Markets Index An index of money market rates in the United States. This information may be divided geographically or topically.

Baptism of Fire Informal; a difficult situation a company or manager is experiencing for the first time. Baptism of fire is generally thought to result in the company or manager's success or failure. Examples include the hiring of a new CEO at a time when a company is facing bankruptcy, or the entrance of a firm's first major competitor into the market.

Bar In technical analysis, a graphic indicating a security's open, high, low, and close prices over a given time period. This time period may be as long as a year or more or as short as a minute, and many technical analysts use bars on a daily basis. Bars are an important part of analyzing price trends and market movements. Bars are the equivalent of candlesticks on candlestick charts.

Bar Code A code placed on a product that a machine can read. Groceries and other products commonly have bar codes on them so a machine can display how much they cost. This ensures accurate prices are paid on retail goods. Bar codes were invented by a graduate student in Philadelphia, Pennsylvania, in 1948.

Bar Code Sorter A machine that reads bar codes corresponding to zip codes on envelopes and sends them to the proper destination.

Bar Graph A chart with rectangles (each representing a category) placed next to each other in which the length of each rectangle represents the amount of data in each category. For example, the rectangles could represent U.S. states and their sizes may correspond to their GDP.

Barangay In the Philippines, a political subdivision approximately equivalent to a neighborhood.

Barbados Dollar The currency of Barbados. It was issued in 1973, replacing the East Caribbean dollar at par. Since 1975, it has been pegged to the U.S. dollar at a ratio of two BBD to one USD.

Barbell Strategy An investment strategy whereby a portfolio consists predominantly or exclusively of bonds with very short and very long maturities. The investment strategy behind a barbell portfolio is to invest in high-yield bonds with long maturities to maximize return while also maintaining investment-grade bonds with short maturities to minimize risk and maximize liquidity.

Barber Dime A silver coin minted by the United States between 1892 and 1916. It was worth 1/10 of one dollar. It derives its name from Charles E. Barber, who designed it.

Barber Half Dollar A silver coin minted by the United States between 1892 and 1916. It was worth 1/2 of one dollar. It derives its name from Charles E. Barber, who designed it.

Barber Quarter A silver coin minted by the United States between 1892 and 1916. It was worth 1/4 of one dollar. It derives its name from Charles E. Barber, who designed it.

Barclays A global financial services company. It was established in London in 1690 and gradually increased its holdings over time. In 1966, it issued Britain's first credit card, and, in 1985, it issued the country's first debit card. It introduced the ATM machine and is one of the world's largest companies. In 2008, it purchased Lehman Brothers, which had filed bankruptcy as a result of the 2008 economic crisis.

Bare Option An option contract traded as its own security, as opposed to an embedded option, which is attached to a bond. Most options are bare options.

Bare Wall Insurance In a condominium property, an insurance policy that provides coverage only for its exterior features. It does not provide coverage for anything inside the unfinished wall of the property, such as countertops, sinks or toilets. A condo homeowners association may purchase a bare wall insurance policy, leaving the owners to buy insurance covering everything else. See also: Single entity insurance.

Bareboat Charter An agreement whereby one rents a boat without a crew. That is, the renter is responsible for providing a crew and, for that reason, is in complete control of the operations of the boat during the rental period. This differs from a voyage charter, whereby the renter can direct where the boat goes, but in which the owner provides the crew and maintains control over their activities.

Barefoot Pilgrim Informal; a small investor who takes excessive risk, makes dumb investments, and displays general financial ignorance. It especially applies when such an investor has lost most or all of his/her wealth. See also: Naive diversification.

Bargain 1. To negotiate. For example, if the asking price for a house is $300,000 and a potential buyer does not want to pay that much, he may bargain with the seller to lower the price to $280,000. **2.** A purchase with a price lower than fair market value, or at least lower than competitors' prices.

Bargain and Sale Deed A title used by a seller to transfer a piece of real estate to a buyer without guaranteeing the validity of the title. That is, a bargain and sale deed does not ensure that the seller has the right to sell the property. See also: Quitclaim deed.

Bargain Basement 1. A company that sells very cheap and often low quality items. **2.** An informal term describing the prices at a bargain basement.

Bargain Basement Price Informal; an extremely low price.

Bargain Hunter An investor who buys low-priced stocks either predominantly or exclusively. The investor may believe that the stock is undervalued and will soon rise, or that it will provide a steady return. See also: Bottom fisher.

Bargain Purchase A purchase with a price lower than fair market value, or at least lower than competitors' prices. It is also called simply a bargain.

Bargain Renewal Option The right but not the obligation for a lessee to renew a lease at the end of its term for a periodic payment significantly below market rates. For example, if an apartment ordinarily rents for $1,000 per month, but a lessee may renew his/her rental agreement for $600 per month, he/she has a bargain renewal option. This effectively gives the lessee some of the rights associated with property.

Bargain Sale The sale of an asset for less than fair market value with the intent of making a charitable contribution. For example, a grocery store may make a bargain sale if it sells food to a homeless shelter for $5,000 when it is worth $15,000. In this case, the grocery store may take a tax deduction for $10,000 (the difference between the sale price and the market value).

Bargaining Agent The union or other organization recognized by an employer as having the ability to conduct collective bargaining on behalf of all or a certain section of employees.

Bargaining Power The leverage available to a party in a negotiation that helps achieve the desired outcome. For example, in a negotiation between an employee and an employer, the employee has bargaining power because she has a skill the employer wants or needs and thus may have the ability to extract a higher salary. On the other hand, the employer has bargaining power because he has money to pay the employee, which the employee wants. See also: Collective Bargaining.

Bargaining Unit A group of employees represented by a union or other organization that is permitted to engage in collective bargaining with an employer.

Bargain-Purchase-Price Option A lease in which the lessee has the option to buy the underlying asset at less than its fair market value at the end of the lease. For example, one may enter into an agreement to rent a house for five years with the option to purchase the house at the end of five years; the price is determined at the beginning of the lease, but must be substantially less than the market value of the house. If the lease is non-cancelable, the Financial Account Standards Board requires that it be considered a capital lease. See also: Rent-to-own.

Barge A large boat with a flat bottom that does not propel itself. Barges must be attached to a tugboat or towboat to be transported. They are used on rivers and canals, primarily to convey cheap cargo in bulk. They were more common prior to the introduction of railroads during the Industrial Revolution.

Barid An obsolete Arabic unit of length approximately equivalent to 23.04 kilometers.

Ba-Ri-Ga An ancient Sumerian unit of volume approximately equivalent to 60 liters.

Barings Bank Collapse The disintegration of Barings Bank in 1995 due to unauthorized and fraudulent trading by Nick Leeson, a derivatives broker employed in Barings' Singapore office. Leeson was permitted to conduct arbitrage by buying futures on Nikkei and at the same time selling them on Simmex. Instead, he made unhedged futures transactions on Nikkei and reported his losses as gains. His trading was exposed following large losses on Nikkei after an earthquake. His losses totaled more than $1 billion, twice Barings' available capital. Barings quickly became insolvent and was sold to ING for 1 pound.

Barleycorn An obsolete measure of length equivalent to one-third of one inch.

Barmil A Maltese unit of volume approximately equivalent to 43.2 liters. It was originally used to measure alcohol. It is largely obsolete but is still used in some circumstances.

Barometer Stock A stock in a well-known or highly-regarded company in a given sector. The performance of a barometer stock is considered to be an indicator of the performance of its particular sector or industry. The term "barometer stock" is chiefly British; in the U.S., the primary term is bellwether stock.

Baronial Envelope An envelope with a flap that may be sealed. Baronial envelopes are large and are used in marketing for direct mail campaigns because they can hold standard letters and other literature.

BARRA's Performance Analysis A method used to determine how well or poorly a money manager invests the funds entrusted to him/her. Rather than comparing a money manager to others of the same class, BARRA's performance analysis compares money managers to the market and determines whether gains or losses are attributable to systematic factors. Institutional investors commonly use this method when evaluating their employees.

Barratry 1. In maritime commerce, an illegal act in which the captain or crew of a ship damages the transaction. Examples include stealing cargo or throwing it overboard. Barratry is a risk associated with the transaction; responsibility for the risk may rest with the buyer or the seller, depending on the terms of the shipping agreement. See also: Incoterm. **2.** The act or practice of filing repeated, usually frivolous lawsuits.

Barrel A container holding approximately 159 liters of liquid. Barrels are extremely important in international commerce, as they measure the volume of crude oil, one of the world's most important commodities.

Barrels per Day The most common measure of how much oil a well, company, or country produces. Barrels per day is especially important because oil is priced by the barrel in the commodities market.

Barren Money Money that is not earning interest or any other return. Essentially, barren money is all money that is not invested or is used in some other way. A simple example of barren money is cash that one places in a safe or under a mattress.

Barrier 1. See: Trade barrier. **2.** See: Barrier Option.

Barrier Option An option contract that may only be exercised when the underlying asset reaches some barrier price. A barrier option may either be a knock-in or a knock-out. A knock-in may only be exercised when the underlying asset rises above or falls below (depending on the particular terms) the barrier price. On the other hand, a knock-out automatically expires when the underlying asset rises above or falls below the barrier price. It is important to note that the barrier price is distinct from the exercise price, though, theoretically, they may be set at the same amount. See also: Exotic option.

Barrier Price The price at which a barrier option becomes active or inactive. A knock-in barrier option may not be exercised unless the price of the underlying asset reaches the barrier price, which is stated in the contract. For example, a contract may have a strike price of $35, but it may only be exercised if the spot price of the underlying asset falls below $40 at some point during the life of the option. On the other hand, a knock-out barrier option with a strike price of $35 may expire automatically if the price rises above $40. In both cases, the barrier price is $40.

Barrier to Entry A high cost or other difficulty that prevents or makes it difficult for new businesses to enter an industry. For instance, high regulation or customer loyalty may be barriers to entry for a new company. Barriers to entry provide a distinct advantage for companies already operating; these companies have high profit margins and few competitors. Examples of industries with barriers to entry are the telecommunications and energy industries, because of the high cost of infrastructure necessary to begin operations. See also: Barriers to exit.

Barriers to Exit Prohibitive costs associated with leaving a sector or market. For example, if a company operating in several sectors wishes to divest itself of its automotive interests, it may have a difficult time selling permanent assets or laying off workers because of high severance costs. Barriers to exit may discourage a company from divesting, or prevent it altogether. Barriers to exit are most common in sectors with high fixed costs.

Barrio In Spanish-speaking countries, a political subdivision equivalent to a neighborhood.

Barrister A lawyer who argues before a court and provides specialist advice. A barrister generally does not have direct contact with the client, and may only litigate before a court when instructed by a solicitor. A barrister is not an attorney and may not act on behalf of a client except in conjunction with the solicitor. Barristers and solicitors are most common in common law jurisdictions, especially those with legal roots in Great Britain. Many countries, including the United States, do not distinguish between barristers and solicitors.

Barron's A weekly periodical that provides information on American markets and securities. It is divided into four sections, covering technology companies, mutual funds, the past week's securities performance, and the financial outlook. Barron's is published by Dow Jones & Company.

Barron's Confidence Index A measure of how bullish or bearish a market is. To calculate the Index, one divides the average yield of high risk bonds by the average yield of medium risk bonds. A high Index figure indicates a bullish market because investors are willing to accept lower returns for higher levels of risk. A low figure indicates the opposite.

Barter To trade one item for another of roughly equal value. That is, bartering occurs without a medium of exchange like money. For example, one may trade 10 apples for 10 oranges. Bartering exists in all societies, though it is less common than monetary transactions. See also: Horizontal Security Exchange, Payment-in-Kind.

Bas Caribbean/Central America Business Advisory Service. An organization that provides guidance for entrepreneurs in the Caribbean and Central America. While the BAS does not invest or make loans itself, it also helps small businesses arrange financing. It was established in 1981 and is run by the International Finance Corporation.

Base In technical analysis, a situation in which the support level and the resistance level are roughly the same for a given (usually long) period of time. That is, a base occurs when a security trades only in a very narrow range. A base indicates that the supply and demand for a security are at an equilibrium. This means that the security is unlikely to be bullish or bearish in the near future.

Base Currency In foreign exchange, the first currency listed in a currency pair. Normally, it is either the domestic currency or the dominant forex currency. Firms dealing in multiple currencies calculate all profits and losses in the base currency. The base currency is assigned the value of 1 when calculating exchange rates. For example, if one is calculating the exchange rate of the U.S. dollar to the British pound and the pound is the base currency, it is expressed as GBPUSD and read as "dollars per one pound." See also: quote currency.

Base Date The date against which the performance of an index is measured. For example, suppose the base date is January 1, 2001, and the initial value of an index is 100. If the index is 150 on April 16, 2009, it means that the value of the index is 50% higher in 2009 than it was on New Year's Day in 2001. It is also called the reference date. See also: Base Value.

Base I A network that processes data transmitted by a card issued by a bank affiliated with Visa. Base I authorizes transactions made on a Visa card. It should not be confused with Basel I.

Base II A network that settles transactions made on Visa cards. Merchant banks and card issuing banks use Base II to ensure the least amount of money needs to change hands when settling Visa transactions. It should not be confused with Basel II.

Base Market Value 1. See: Market average. **2.** See: Base value.

Base Metal A metal other than a precious metal; iron is often excluded as well. Common examples include aluminum, tin and copper. Base metals may be traded as commodities and have a variety of uses. As currencies have increasingly gone to fiat money systems, coins are usually made out of a base metal such as zinc.

Base Pay The salary one earns to which one may add through good job performance. For example, a company may hire a sales representative with a low base pay plus a commission on each sale made. Base pay allows an employee to continue to make a living during slow times, but generally is low enough to incentivize performance.

Base Pay Rate The hourly wage an employee or contractor is paid. The base pay rate is used to calculate overtime, bonuses and some other fringe benefits.

Base Period The period of time against which an index is measured. For example, suppose the base period is 2001 and the initial value of an index is 100. If the index is 150 in 2009, it means that the value of the index is 50% higher in 2009 than it was in 2001. It is also called the reference period.

Base Premium The premium for an insurance policy that is used to calculate the premium for reinsurance. It is also called the subject premium or the underlying premium.

Base Record A form containing basic data about a customer. The base record includes information such as name, address and telephone number. Base records are used in places such as medical offices, marketing companies and consultancies.

Base Rent The minimum rent on a space with variable rent. For example, a company may rent retail space from a facility and pay $3,000 per month plus some percentage of its revenue. In this case, the base rent is $3,000 because it can never go below that amount.

Base Stock The minimum inventory a company needs in order to maintain operations without some interruption. Companies, especially retailers, strive to maintain at least their base stock at all times.

Base Stock Method A way to account for the value of a company's inventory. All base stock (the minimum needed to maintain operations) is calculated according to its purchase price, while the LIFO method is used for all additional inventory. The base stock method is not a generally accepted system. See also: Generally Accepted Accounting Principles.

Base Value An often arbitrary figure used as the initial value of an index. All future values of the index are comparisons against the base value. For example, suppose an index is formed in 2001 and its base value is 100. If the index is 150 in 2009, it means that its value is 50% higher in 2009 than it was in 2001. It is also called the index number. See also: Base Year.

Base Year The year against which the performance of an index is measured. For example, suppose the base year is 2001 and the initial value of an index is 100. If the index is 150 in 2009, it means that the value of the index is 50% higher in 2009 than it was in 2001. It is also called the reference year. See also: Base Value.

Base Year Analysis In accounting and statistics, the expression of financial information in a given year as a percentage of an amount in an initial year. A company may treat the first year of its operations or the first year it made a profit as the base year, expressing all financial information in those terms. Occasionally, governments or companies may change the base year to one that better represents "normal" performance.

Baseball Card A card containing the name, picture and statistics of a baseball player. Rare cards and first-year cards of players who later became famous (called "rookie cards") are often valuable as collectibles. A baseball card is an example of a valuable but illiquid asset because it can be difficult to sell to a non-collector.

Basel A town in Switzerland. It has been known for centuries as a meeting place where a number of international agreements have been formed. See also: Basel I, Basel II.

Basel Accord An agreement on international banking regulations dealing with how banks handle risk. The Basel Accord focuses mainly on credit risk; it divides banks' assets into five categories according to how risky they are. The five categories are assets with no risk, 10% risk, 20%, 50% and 100%. All banks conducting international transactions are required under the Basel Accord to hold assets with no more than 8% aggregated risk. The Accord was promulgated in 1988.Banks in most G-10 countries have implemented it since the early 1990s. It is now considered largely outdated and is in the process of being replaced by Basel II. It is also called Basel I.

Basel Committee on Banking Supervision An organization that seeks to provide a supranational framework for banking regulation. It prepares major overhauls to regulatory systems, such as the Basel II Accord. It does not have enforcement authority, but rather makes recommendations to member countries. It was established by the central banks of the G-10 in 1974. It is also called the BIS Committee. It takes both its names from the fact that it meets four times per year at the Bank for International Settlements (BIS) in Basel, Switzerland.

Basel Concordat A 1983 agreement by the Basel Committee stating banks opening subsidiaries in foreign countries must submit those subsidiaries to the full regulatory authority of the relevant countries. It also requires the parent banks to allow their own regulators to review the foreign subsidiaries. It accomplishes both of these by encouraging the regulatory authorities to share information with each other.

Basel Convention A treaty intended to reduce the transfer of hazardous waste across international lines, especially between developed countries and the developing world. Hazardous waste is defined in the treaty as anything considered hazardous waste in the country in which it originated. Interestingly, it does not deal with radioactive waste. It was signed in 1989 and went into effect in 1992.

Basel II An agreement on international banking regulations dealing with how banks handle risk. Basel II establishes risk management and risk capital requirements in an attempt to ensure banks remain solvent. Basel II consists of three pillars. The first deals with capital requirements and mandates that banks exposed to more risk (which is itself categorized and quantified) must maintain sufficient capital. The second pillar provides an outline that regulators can use to deal with non-quantifiable forms of risk. The third attempts to promote market discipline.

Basel Market Risk Amendment An amendment to the Basel Convergence Accord that allowed banks to use value-at-risk models in making internal calculations of risk. It was enacted in 1996 through the Bank for International Settlements.

Baseline Anything used for comparison. For example, a company that wishes to determine whether its profits are increasing or decreasing may compare them to a previous year's profits. In this case, the previous year's profits are considered the base line. A baseline is also called a base. See also: Benchmark, Base currency.

Baseload The minimum amount of power an electrical or other utility company must put out in a 24-hour time period to meet estimated demand from its customers. Many companies designate baseload power plants to put out only the baseload because it is less expensive and often safer. These companies also maintain other plants to provide for higher demand as it arises.

Basher A person who spreads (possibly false) negative information about a security in order to make its price fall. The goal of a basher is to drive the price artificially low so one can buy it and profit from the resulting price correction when the security rises back to its former price.

Bashki In Albania, a political subdivision equivalent to an urban municipality.

BASIC Beginners All-Purpose Symbolic Instruction Code. A programming language that allows a programmer to interact with a program while it is running. BASIC is very simple and was designed for instructional purposes. However, it underlies both the DOS and Windows operating systems.

Basic Balance The balance of payment for a country that calculates on the current account and the capital account. The balance of payment is the difference between the value of transactions in which money leaves a country and the value of transactions in which money enters it, while the current account and the capital account are only two of the measures used in calculating it most of the time. The basic balance is less affected by short-term changes in interest rates or exchange rates. It is often used in countries with pegged exchange rates.

Basic Banking Retail banking services offered for a low monthly fee for depositors. For example, basic banking services may include the ability to write a stated number of checks and visit a teller a given number of times. It usually also includes unlimited ATM visits. Basic banking originated in the 1980s with increased pressure to provide more affordable services.

Basic Business Strategies How a company intends to meet its financial needs or goals for the future. Corporate financial planning involves identifying these needs and goals; the company executes a business strategy to achieve them. Simply put, the main financial objective is to make money, and basic business strategies help the company make it. Despite the simplicity of the concept, this can be a complicated process.

Basic Health Insurance Policy A health insurance policy that provides only minimal coverage. For example, it may cover preventative visits to a physician and catastrophic events. Basic health insurance policies have high deductibles. As a result, they have low premiums. They tend to appeal to young adults and exceptionally healthy persons.

Basic Industry Multiplier A ratio of the total population of an area to those persons employed in industrial positions. Because industrial jobs tend to have high pay, their existence tends to create service-oriented jobs like waiters and shop clerks. As a result, each new industrial job is thought to increase the total population of the area by the basic industry multiplier.

Basic IRR Rule A rule of thumb stating that a person or company should conduct a project or make an investment if the internal rate of return exceeds the discount rate. That is, one should only do an activity if the discount value of the cash inflows exceeds cash outflows.

Basic Mortality Table In actuarial analysis, a table of the likelihood a person of a certain age will die in the next year. This is important in determining one's eligibility for some insurance and annuity plans.

Basic Network In marketing, a number of individual television stations belonging to a network (such as ABC, CBS, or NBC) on which an advertiser can purchase time for a commercial. Once an advertiser purchases time on the basic network, it is allowed to use the network's facilities. Each network determines its own basic network.

Basic Premium The portion of a life insurance premium that a policyholder pays, usually monthly, that compensates the insurer for administrative expenses, commission for the agent who sells the policy, and the likelihood that that policyholder will die in the coming year.

Basic Price 1. The price for a good or service, less any sales tax or VAT the buyer pays and plus any subsidy the seller receives. In other words, the basic price is what the seller collects for the sale, as opposed to what the buyer pays. **2.** The price for a periodical. Newspapers and magazines have separate basic prices for single issues and for subscriptions. It is also called the basic rate.

Basic Rate 1. See: Manual Rate. **2.** See: Rate of Return. **3.** See: Basic Rate of Income Tax. **4.** The price for a periodical. Newspapers and magazines have separate basic rates for single issues and for subscriptions. It is more commonly called the basic price.

Basic Rate of Income Tax The term for the second-lowest marginal tax rate in the United Kingdom. In 2008, one paid the basic rate on all personal income and savings (after personal allowances) below 37,400 pounds, unless one earned less than 2,440 pounds, in which case one paid the lower rate. The basic rate on dividend income in 2008 was 10%. Most Britons pay the basic rate on most of their income.

Basic Time Frame In life insurance, the time period in which a loss (that is, death) may occur.

Basing Point In accounting, the geographical location where a commodity has a certain price. The basing point is used to help determine the price for the same commodity in another location. In general, the price at the basing point is added to transportation costs to arrive at the price elsewhere.

Basing Rate In accounting, the freight rate from one location to another that is used to calculate the freight rate between two other locations. For example, one may add extra transportation costs to the basing rate to arrive at a new freight rate.

Basis 1. The cost of an asset less depreciation. This is used when calculating one's tax liability related to that asset. **2.** The all-in cost of a security when it is bought. That is, it is the price of the security plus any applicable fees. This is the price against which any capital gains or losses are calculated for tax purposes. For example, if the tax basis for a stock is $5 per share and the investor sells it for $7, then the capital gain for which one is liable is $2 per share. It is also called the cost basis.

Basis Book A table or book of tables showing the yields of bonds at different interest rates and maturities. For example, if one is considering the purchase of a bond, one can take the coupon rate and the maturity and compare them in the basis book to determine the yield. The basis book is good for approximating yields, but financial calculators tend to be more accurate, especially for more complex bonds.

Basis Grade The minimum acceptable quality of a commodity for delivery on a futures contract. The basis grade must be described in the contract, and can strongly affect the price. To use an extreme example (unlikely in real life), a futures contract for rotten corn would be worth less than one for high-quality corn. In both cases, however, the basis grade is described in the contract itself.

Basis Point A unit of percentage measure equal to 0.01%. Basis points are commonly used when discussing changes to interest rates, equity indices, and fixed-income securities. In the media, perhaps its most common use is in reporting a central bank's changes to prevailing interest rates. For example, a newspaper might report that the Federal Reserve cut interest rates 100 basis points when it means that prevailing rates have dropped from 1.5% to 0.5%.

Basis Price A quote for a bond expressed in terms of the bond's yield to maturity. For example, if the yield to maturity is 8%, the basis price is also 8%.

Basis Quote In futures contracts, a quote for a contract made with reference to another contract. For example, if a contract with expiry in June is $15 and another contract with expiry in September is $20, the basis quote for the September contract is June expiry + $5. Theoretically, basis quotes consolidate and make quoting futures contracts easier.

Basis Rate Swap An interest rate swap where both legs are variable interest rates calculated over the same notional value. For example, one interest rate may be LIBOR + 0.50%, and the other may be the yield on a 10-year Treasury note. A basis rate swap helps the counterparties hedge against their respective interest rate risks.

Basis Risk The risk that a change in prevailing interest rates will change the price of a company's or investor's interest-bearing liabilities disproportionate to the price of interest-bearing assets. This would increase liabilities and decrease assets, resulting in a loss.

Basis Swap An interest rate swap in which both legs (the interest rates that are swapped) are both floating rates. The floating rates are calculated over different bases; for example, one might be linked the LIBOR and the other to the fed funds rate. A basis swap is used to help a company hedge against its basis risk.

Basis Trading A form of arbitrage in which one buys an investment vehicle while selling or selling short a similar investment vehicle. For example, one may buy a stock while selling a futures contract on the same stock. Alternatively, one may buy a put while selling a put on the same underlying asset for a different strike price. Basis trading is advantageous when the trader believes there is priceinefficiency between the two investment vehicles such that the gain on one will offset the loss on the other. For instance, in the futures contract example, basis trading can be advantageous if the price of the stock plus the cost of carry is less than the price of the futures contract that the investor sells. It is also called relationship trading.

Basis Weight The weight of 500 sheets of standard-size paper. This weight varies by the type of paper because different papers have different standard sizes. The basis weight is used in shipping. It is also called the basic weight or the paper weight.

Basket 1. A group of securities often, but not always, derivatives, bought and sold as a single unit. Institutional investors often purchase baskets in order to pay only a single commission on an exceptionally large transaction. A basket is also useful in an index arbitrage transaction. **2.** See: Currency basket.

Basket Option An option contract in which the underlying asset consists of several different assets. For example, a basket call may give one the right, but not the obligation, to buy more than one currency at the strike price (which is denominated in a currency other than any in the underlying). A basket option provides a way for a corporation to hedge against several different risks at the same time and to do so more cheaply. However, a rainbow option is exposed to the risk that only some, rather than all, of the underlying assets will move in the direction benefiting the holder. A basket option is also called a rainbow option.

Basket Order An order to buy or sell a group of securities, often derivatives, as a single unit. Institutional investors often make basket orders in order to pay only a single commission on an exceptionally large transaction. Basket orders are also useful in index arbitrage transactions.

Basket Peg The policy of pegging a currency to a portfolio of several currencies with different weightings. For example, a basket peg may consist of 40% euros, 35% U.S. dollars and 25% British pounds; these percentages determine the basket's value. A country usually follows a basket peg to attach its currency to another without overexposing it to the fluctuations of a single currency. For example, Kuwait shifted to a basket peg in 2007 because the U.S. dollar, to which it was attached previously, was weak at the time, resulting in high inflation.

Basket Pegger A nation with a currency that is pegged to a portfolio of several currencies with different weightings. For example, a basket pegger may attach its currency to a portfolio consisting of 40% euros, 35% U.S. dollars and 25% British pounds; these percentages determine the basket's value. Basket peggers usually follow this policy to peg their currencies without overexposing them to the fluctuations of a single currency. For example, Kuwait shifted the peg of the Kuwaiti

dinar from the U.S. dollar to a currency basket in 2007 because the dollar was weak at the time and resulted in high inflation.

Basket Purchase The purchase of a large number of assets, as opposed to a single asset. For example, a company may buy 1,000 widgets instead of one widget at a time. Retailers commonly make basket purchases to manage their inventory. A basket purchase is also called a lump-sum purchase.

Basket Trade 1. A single order or trade in 15 or more securities, especially in large amounts. Basket trades can be open orders in which the computer is instructed to wait until a certain price prevails before buying or selling the large quantity of securities. This is a service offered exclusively to institutional investors and high net-worth individuals. **2.** See: Program Trading.

Batch A group of instruments, especially checks and other demands for payment, that a company keeps for processing later in the day. For example, if a retailer is paid with 30 checks in a given morning, these checks collectively are called a batch. Using batches is becoming less common among retailers as customers increasingly pay with debit and credit cards. A batch is also called a block.

Batch Balance The practice of double verifying a batch of checks or other demands for payment to ensure correct processing. For example, one may check the amounts written on the instruments against a deposit slip.

Batch Header A document entered into a computer stating the characteristics of a batch. For example, it may state that all checks in a batch were written on the same day, or perhaps they were used to pay for similar services. The batch header eliminates the tedium and wasted time of entering the same information for each individual check when it is recorded on a computer.

Batch Header Record 1. A 94-digit number identifying a bank. It is used in processing payments through the Automated Clearing House. **2.** See: Batch Header.

Batch Identification A unique number assigned to a batch of checks or other demands for payment. Batch identification is used to process these checks more efficiently.

Batch Processing The completion of a number of tasks by a computer without manual input by a person. A computer can be programmed to use batch processing in order to make it faster and more efficient. Batch processing traces its roots to the invention of the modern computer in the 1950s and 1960s.

Batch Trading On an exchange, a series of orders to buy or sell a security that are compiled together for a period of time and then executed as if they were one order. Batch trading is allowed only at the beginning of a trading day for un-executed orders that had accumulated after the previous day's close.

Batch-Level Activities The set of activities that need to be done each time a group of products is made or sold. Batch-level activities may include paying employees or recording sales. The specific tasks vary according to the type of product. The term is used most frequently in accounting

Batman A Turkish measure of weight approximately equivalent to 7.7 kilograms. It became obsolete when Turkey made the metric system mandatory in 1933.

Battery The use of excessive physical force against another person. If no injury results from battery, it is a tort; Otherwise, it is a crime.

Batting a Thousand A slang term in business meaning that no mistakes have been made. For example, a salesman is batting a thousand if the recipients of all of his cold calls for the day agree to purchase his products. The term is derived from the baseball statistic in which 1.000 indicates a perfect batting average.

Batting Average A slang term in business for one's success rate. For example, a salesman making cold calls has a solid batting average if half of his potential clients agree to purchase his products. The term is derived from baseball.

Battle Rhythm A slang term for a business plan, marketing plan, or any plan dealing with a complicated or adverse situation.

Baud A measure of signals per second that are transmitted over copper telephone wire. With increased speed, bauds largely have been replaced with bits per second. It is abbreviated Bd.

Bavarian State Mint An organization in Germany that issues legal tender coins for general use. It was established in 1158 and is owned by the government of Bavaria. It is located in Munich.

Bay al Salam In Islamic finance, a sale in which delivery is deferred until some stated date in the future. It is used for agricultural products and other fungibles. In order to comply with the sharia, a salam contract must specify the quality of the good to be delivered, and payment must be made at the time the contract is entered.

Bay Street A street in Toronto that forms the center of its financial district. Several major banks and law firms, among other things, are based on Bay Street, though, interestingly, the Toronto Stock Exchange is not. Because of its influence on the wider financial world, Bay Street is used often as a byword for the financial industry and its lobbyists in Canada. See also: Wall Street, The City.

Bayesian Approach to Decision Making A way to make decisions based on incomplete or imperfect information. When information is not available, the Bayesian approach makes mathematical assumptions about its likely content. As that information is gathered and disseminated, the Bayesian approach corrects or replaces the assumptions and alters its decision-making accordingly.

Bayesian Probability A revision of a previous probability based on new information. In Bayesian analysis, one makes mathematical assumptions about unavailable information. As that information is gathered and disseminated, the

Bayesian probability corrects or replaces the assumptions and alters its results accordingly.

Bayesian Statistics A statistical system using probabilities based on assumptions about unavailable information. As that information is gathered and disseminated, one corrects or replaces the assumptions and the statistical analysis alters its results accordingly.

Bazaar A market place, usually outdoors, where vendors sell goods such as fruits and vegetables, books, household items and so forth. A bazaar is usually held in a designated place, but vendors can pack up their wares at the end of the day and take them home. Bazaars are most common in the Mediterranean, the Middle East and South Asia.

BB **1.** A credit rating used by S&P and Fitch credit rating agencies for long-term bonds and some other investments. It is subdivided (in descending order) into BB+, BB, and BB-. A BB rating is equivalent to the Ba rating range used by Moody's. A BB rating represents a medium risk junk bond or investment; because it has junk status, banks are not allowed to invest in BB rated bonds. However, BB is at the top of the junk ratings, being only one grade below investment grade ratings. Risk averse investors must therefore exercise caution in BB investments but less caution than other junk bonds, especially if the rating was recently upgraded. **2.** ISO 3166-1 alpha-2 code for Barbados. This is the code used in international transactions to and from Barbadian bank accounts. **3.** ISO 3166-2 geocode for Barbados. This is used as an international standard for shipping to Barbados. Each Barbadian parish has its own code with the prefix "BB." For example, the code for Christ Church Parish is ISO 3166-2:BB-01.

BBB A credit rating used by the S&P and Fitch credit agencies for long-term bonds and some other investments. It is equivalent to the Baa2 rating used by Moody's. A BBB rating represents a relatively low-risk bond or investment; banks are allowed to invest in BBB rated bonds. However, it is toward the bottom of investment-grade bond ratings, being only two grades above junk bond ratings. Risk-averse investors must therefore exercise caution on BBB investments, especially if the rating was recently downgraded.

BBB- A credit rating used by the S&P and Fitch credit agencies for long-term bonds and some other investments. It is equivalent to the Baa3 rating used by Moody's. A BBB- rating represents a relatively low-risk bond or investment; banks are allowed to invest in BBB- rated bonds. However, it is the very bottom of investment-grade bond ratings, and is only one grade above a junk bond rating. Risk-averse investors must therefore exercise caution on BBB- investments, especially if the rating was recently downgraded.

BBD ISO 4217 code for the Barbados dollar. It was issued in 1973, replacing the East Caribbean dollar at par. Since 1975, it has been pegged to the U.S. dollar at a ratio of two BBD to one USD.

BCG Growth Share Matrix A chart with four quadrants that helps businesses analyze themselves by placing themselves (or their subsidiaries or products) into one of the four quadrants. The chart plots market share (on the x-axis) against growth rate (on the y-axis). A company with a low growth rate and a large market share is called a cash cow; it requires little capital to maintain operations and produces a solid profit. A company with a low growth rate and a small market share is a dog; it generally produces a small profit and is usually sold. A company with a high growth rate and a small market share is called a problem child or question market; it is expensive to operate and produces little or no profit, but has the potential to do so. Finally, a company with a high growth rate and a large market share is called a star; these are expensive to operate, but produce large profits. Analysts use the BCG Growth Share Matrix in order to analyze how well or poorly a company or corporation is using its resources for itself, its subsidiaries, and/or its products. It was developed in 1970 by the Boston Consulting Group.

BCICAC British Columbia International Commercial Arbitration Centre. An organization in Canada that resolves disputes between businesses outside the court system. It also handles domain name disputes and uninsured motorist cases. It is based on the model articulated by the UN Commission on International Trade Law. It was established in 1986 and is based in Vancouver.

BD **1.** ISO 3166-1 alpha-2 code for the People's Republic of Bangladesh. This is the code used in international transactions to and from Bangladeshi bank accounts. **2.** ISO 3166-2 geocode for Bangladesh. This is used as an international standard for shipping to Bangladesh. Each Bangladeshi division and district has its own code with the prefix "BD." For example, the code for the District of Bagerhat is ISO 3166-2:BD-05.

BD Form A form that broker-dealer firms must file with the SEC. It contains information on each firm's officers and finances. See also: Registration.

BDI GOST 7.67 Latin three-letter geocode for Burundi. The code is used for transactions to and from Burundian bank accounts and for international shipping to Burundi. As with all GOST 7.67 codes, it is used primarily in Cyrillic alphabets.

BDT ISO 4217 code for the Bangladeshi taka. It was introduced in 1972, replacing the Pakistani rupee at a 1:1 ratio. It has historically been a weak currency.

Bean Counter Slang; an accountant.

Beans In commodity trading, a slang term for soybean contracts. Beans refer only to soybeans, and not to any other beans traded on a commodity exchange or over-the-counter.

Bear An investor who believes, for any technical or fundamental reason, that a security or the broader market will decline significantly. A bear takes the appropriate steps to limit losses during the period that they believe that the security will decline. They may sell their long positions or short sell the security to profit from the decline in price. See also: Bull.

Bear Bond A bond that is likely to increase in price when stocks or the economy at large is performing poorly (that is, when interest rates are rising). Interest-only bonds and mortgage-backed securities that pay only interest are common examples of bear bonds because, in a bear market, people tend to pay only interest on large debts. See also: Flight to Safety.

Bear Call Spread In options, a strategy in which one buys call options on a security and then sells the same number of call options on the same security with the same expiration month at a lower strike price. A bear call spread limits both the potential profit and the potential risk, but is most profitable if the security drops moderately in price.

Bear CD A certificate of deposit with an interest rate that varies inversely to the performance of some benchmark index. When the index decreases, the CD's interest rate increases, and vice versa. One places money into a bear CD if one believes an index will decline. Alternatively, one invests in a bear CD to hedge against another position. For example, if one has a mutual fund tracking the same index, a bear CD will alleviate some of the risk that the index will decline.

Bear Closing The purchase of a security or derivative after having previously sold it. That is, a bear closing occurs when an investor believes that the security's or derivative's price has fallen to its bottom or has stabilized. A bear closing can cause a rally, or even out a bear market.

Bear Correction In technical analysis, a small gain after a series of increasing gains in a security. For example, if a security rises in price by $2 on Monday, $2.50 on Tuesday and $3 on Wednesday, but only rises by $2.25 on Thursday, a bear correction is said to occur on Thursday. It may predict a coming drop in price. The term is especially common in forex markets.

Bear Flag In technical analysis, a downtrend followed by roughly even trading on heavy volume. A bear flag is likely to be followed by a further drop and is a signal to sell, especially when the even trading begins to break downward. It derives its name from the fact that it looks roughly like an upside down flagpole when plotted on a graph.

Bear Flattener A situation in which the yield curve for bonds is flattening. That is, short-term interest rates on bonds rise more rapidly than long-term rates so that the two begin to converge, resulting in a flat (or flatter) yield curve when it is plotted on a graph. This is considered a bearish indicator because it means that investors believe that the higher interest rates on short-term bonds may produce a higher return than stocks will in the short-term. See also: Inverted yield curve, bullish flattener.

Bear Fund A mutual fund that invests predominately or exclusively in securities that tend to do well when most of the market is performing poorly and that do poorly when the market is performing well. Bear funds are intended to be a safe haven for investors in a down market. Examples of securities that may be found in a bear fund include stocks in budget retailers and fast food restaurants, since they tend to be stable and even experience some earnings growth during recessions.

Bear Hug An offer by a company to buy another company for a price per share far above the share price's fair market value. A company offers a bear hug when it believes the target company's management may decline the offer. Because the management has a fiduciary responsibility to act in the best interest of shareholders, the bear hug is essentially an offer the management cannot refuse, at least not without exposing itself to a lawsuit. It is a form of a hostile takeover and may be used as a form of risk arbitrage.

Bear Market A situation in which a large number of indices lose a significant percentage of their value over the medium or long term. While there is no hard-and-fast definition of a bear market, many analysts consider a 20% loss in the Dow Jones Industrial Average or the S&P 500 to be a good rule of thumb. It is difficult to make a positive return on stocks during a bear market, and some investors move into bonds. This leads to the sale of more stocks, and the bear market can become self-sustaining. Technical analysts attempt to find the bottom of bear markets and identify buy signals, but this is risky. A bear market is different from a recession, but one can lead to the other. See also: Bull market.

Bear Put Spread In options, a strategy in which one buys put options on a security and then sells the same number of put options on the same security with the same expiration month at a lower strike price. A bear put spread limits both the potential profit and the potential risk, but is most profitable if the security drops moderately in price.

Bear Raid The practice of short selling a stock and spreading unfavorable news (which may or may not be true) about the company. That is, a bear raid occurs when one borrows a security, sells it, and attempts to push the security's price downward. This would result in a significant profit on the short sale. While it was a popular speculative investment strategy in the early 1900s, it is not illegal.

Bear Rally A rapid increase in stock prices following a downturn. A bear rally occurs when investors begin buying stocks in large amounts, which represents an increase in demand and therefore raises the price. However, because fundamental information has not improved, the bear rally is short-lived and is unlikely to be sustained. A bear rally is thus a brief respite between two downturns.

Bear Slide A steady decrease in the price of a stock following a bear raid, which is the practice of short selling a stock and spreading unfavorable news about the company issuing it. The bear slide represents a successful attempt to push the security's price down so the bear raider can increase his/her gains on the short sale.

Bear Spread In options, the purchase and sale of a series of contracts designed to make a profit for an investor as the price of the underlying asset declines. One buys and writes these options at different strike prices; however it is important to note that all contracts have the same expiration date. The investor makes a profit if the price of the underlying declines. **2.** In futures, the sale of a contract expiring in a near month and the purchase of a contract in the same or a similar underlying asset expiring in a later month. In this situation, the investor makes a profit if the price of the underlying declines.

Bear Squeeze The intervention of a central bank to dissuade speculators from short selling its currency. In general, a bear squeeze occurs when a central bank buys its own currency to improve its exchange rate, which would result in a loss to speculators betting against that currency.

Bear Stearns A former investment bank and brokerage that provided services in capital markets, clearance and wealth management. It was noted for the issue of asset-backed securities, especially of mortgages. It was established in 1923 and became a subsidiary of JP Morgan Chase as the result of a fire sale in 2008.

Bear Stearns Bankruptcy The 2008 collapse of Bear Stearns, a major American investment bank. It occurred because Bear Stearns became overexposed to mortgage-backed securities based on subprime mortgages. As defaults on these mortgages (and therefore investor losses) became apparent in 2006 and 2007, Bear Stearns increased its exposure to this market, which compounded its losses. In March 2008, the Federal Reserve extended the company a loan to try to save it. This effort failed, and Bear Stearns was sold that same month to JP Morgan Chase for $10 per share (down from $133.20 per share less than a year before).

Bear Steepener A widening yield curve that happens when long-term interest rates increase at a faster pace than short-term interest rates. Bear steepeners occur when investors are pessimistic about stock prices over the short-term, and may not expect inflation over the long-term. See also: Bull steepener.

Bear Trap An indication that a security's increasing price has reversed itself, causing some investors to sell it. Unfortunately, the reversal is short-lived or non-existent, and the security continues to increase. Investors who have sold after a bear trap often have a difficult time buying back their securities because they cannot find sellers. See also: Bull trap, Bull market.

Bearer The owner of a security or other instrument. One may bear any type of security. While technically a bearer is identical to a holder, the term "bearer" implies one who holds a security with no ownership information, automatically making the bearer the presumed owner.

Bearer Bond A bond containing no ownership information and, therefore, the physical holder is presumed to be the owner. Coupons on bearer bonds are physically attached to the bonds and must be presented to the issuer to receive interest payments. Bearer bonds have not been issued in the United States since 1982, thus making them significantly less important. See also: Clip.

Bearer Form A security containing no ownership information and for which the physical bearer is presumed to be the owner. In the case of bonds, coupons are physically attached to the bond and must be presented to the issuer to receive interest payments. Bearer stocks may be bought and sold without endorsement. Bearer bonds have not been issued in the United States since 1982, and thus they have become a significantly less important activity. Bearer stocks are also quite rare.

Bearer Instrument A security that contains no ownership information and whose physical bearer is presumed to be the owner. Bearer instruments may be bought and sold without endorsement. Due to the increased digitization of the market, they are quite rare.

Bearer Stock A stock that contains no ownership information and whose physical bearer is presumed to be the owner. Bearer stocks may be bought and sold without endorsement. They are quite rare.

Bearish Describing a market for one or more securities in which there are few buyers and many sellers. A bearish market occurs due to declining prices, and it is sometimes associated with high trading volume. Investors may also describe having a bearish feeling about a market, meaning they believe (not necessarily with any analysis) that prices have been declining or soon will begin to do so.

Bearish Belt Hold In candlestick charting, a candlestick indicating a possible turnaround in a bull market. A bearish belt hold occurs after a series of gaining trading days, represented by white candles. The bearish belt hold is a losing trading day, represented by a black candle, in which the opening price is the highest price of the day and the closing price is only a little bit higher than the intraday low, both of which are much lower than the opening price. This is represented by a long candle with no wick (or shadow) at the top and only a short wick (or shadow) at the bottom. Some technical analysts consider this a reversal of the bullish trend, while others believe that it is an unreliable indicator.

Bearish Divergence In technical analysis, a situation in which two indicators move in opposite directions. For example, stock prices may decline while bond prices may increase. This can be either a bullish or a bearish indicator, depending on the nature of the divergence. Technical analysts use a number of related indicators to attempt to observe divergence and make investment decisions accordingly. See also: MACD.

Bearish Engulfing Pattern In candlestick charting, a pattern with a small, white candle (representing a trading day with a gain) followed by a larger, black candle (representing a trading day with a loss). The opening price and closing price in the black candle must both be higher than those in the white candle. A bearish engulfing pattern usually, but does not always, comes during a bullish trend; it may be a signal that the trend is peaking and is about to become bearish.

Bearish Harami A form of charting rendered using graphics of candlesticks indicating the reversal of a market uptrend. A bearish harami is conceptualized by a large white candlestick (representing one day) followed by much smaller black candlestick in which both the top and the bottom are no longer than the top or the bottom of the white candlestick (representing the next trading day). See also: Candlestick chart.

BEARS Bonds Enabling Annual Retirement Savings. A derivative security, the holders of which are entitled to receive the face value of bonds underlying call options represented in CUBS. That is, when the CUBS holders exercise their call options, BEARS receive the face value.

Beat the Averages To perform better than the market as a whole. Many money managers are rated on their ability to beat the averages (which refers to broad market indices such as the DJIA or the S&P 500) with the portfolios they manage. Beating the averages may also refer to individual securities. See also: Manager Universe (Benchmark), Market outperform.

Beat the Bushes To market a product in a rural or unusual area. Advertising a store in the newspaper of a town that is more than an hour away from the nearest location of that store is an example of beating the bushes.

Beat the Dow To perform better than the Dow Jones Industrial Average. Many money managers are rated on their ability to beat the Dow with the portfolios they manage. Beating the averages may also refer to the performance of individual securities. See also: Manager Universe (Benchmark), Market outperform.

Beat the Gun Slang; the act of buying (or selling) a security or asset at the perfect price. In such cases, immediately after the security or asset is bought (or sold), the price begins a significant increase (or decrease), resulting in a healthy gain for the buyer (or seller).

Beating the Gun Informal; in equities, describing the act of securing an advantageous position at the perfect time. Beating the gun may describe taking a short position immediately before the price begins to fall or a long position before it begins to rise. Investors account for different reasons for beating the gun. Some may ascribe it to luck, but most attribute it to appropriate technical or fundamental analysis.

Beatrice Webb A British economist who lived from 1858 to 1943. She was a supporter of social reform in Britain, writing in favor of trade unions and against the poor conditions of homes in certain parts of London. In 1909, Webb recommended that Britain adopt a welfare state. She was an early theorist regarding co-ops and is credited with creating the term collective bargaining. She also co-founded the London School of Economics. See also: Beveridge Report.

Beauty Contest In Keynesian economics, a concept describing how rational investors are expected to buy and sell securities. According to the theory, in a free market, rational investors tend to buy securities they believe everyone else thinks are valuable, rather than the ones they themselves believe are valuable. That is, because demand for securities drives prices up and down, rational investors attempt to estimate their demand rather than their intrinsic values. The term is based on a fictional newspaper contest in which contestants are asked to identify one woman among six that other people think to be the most beautiful, rather than the woman the contestant likes best himself.

Beauty Shot In television advertising, a close-up shot of the product. For example, in a commercial for shampoo, a beauty shot zooms in on a bottle of the shampoo being advertised.

Bed and Breakfast A small hotel, often a private home, that provides breakfast in addition to lodging. Bed and breakfasts are usually marketed to couples and families for romantic getaways or vacations. They often are found in rural areas, though this is not always the case.

Bedroom Community A primarily residential town where most residents commute to work in a larger city. For example, many industrial workers may live in a small town outside the city in which the factory is located; they must either drive or take public transportation to go to work each day. Bedroom communities generally have little economy of their own beyond retail shops for use by residents. They are often, but not always, suburbs.

Bee Sting Slang; a potential financial problem, especially if it comes from a decision made with insufficient information.

Beehive In the United Kingdom, a slang term for 5 pounds. The term derives from Cockney rhyming slang: beehive rhymes with five.

Beeks A slang term for economic information. The term derives from the film Trading Places.

Beemer Informal for a BMW, an expensive automobile and motorcycle brand. Beemers are seen culturally as a sign of sometimes conspicuous wealth, and companies often market luxury goods and services to people who own them.

Beep A slang term for basis point.

Beer Ticket In the U.S. Navy, a slang term for non-U.S. currency.

Beer Token In the United Kingdom, a slang term for one pound sterling. The term derives from the idea that young men spend a disproportionate amount of their money on beer.

Beer v. United States A U.S. case concerning judicial pay. The Constitution of the United States prohibits the reduction of a judge's pay during the course of his/her tenure. Representatives of judges contend that inflation effectively reduces their pay and have argued for the reinstatement of automatic cost of living adjustments that were previously in place.

Bees and Honey In the United Kingdom, a slang term for money. The term derives from Cockney rhyming slang: honey rhymes with money. It is sometimes shortened to bees.

Bee-Tee Informal; a bookkeeper or treasurer of the board of directors in a small Christian church or ministry. The bee-tee may work in his/her spare time, and might not be a professional bookkeeper. The term derives from "BT," which stands for "board treasurer."

BEF ISO 4217 code for the Belgian franc. It traces its origins to the conquest of the Low Countries during the Napoleonic Wars. It has been pegged to a number of different currencies throughout its history and was one of the currencies in the Latin Monetary Union for a time. It was replaced by the euro in 2002.

Before the Bell Describing any period of time before a stock exchange opens. It is often used to mean trading before the market opens.

Before-and-After Rule The practice of appraising a piece of real estate both before and after it is taken over by a government due to eminent domain. The before-and-after rule considers improvements (or injuries) the government makes to the property. For example, if the government tears down a condemned house to build a park, this likely will improve the property value, while the opposite is probably true if the government tears down a mansion for the same reason.

Before-Tax Basis Any calculation that does not account for either income taxes or capital gains taxes. The before-tax basis is not as useful as the after-tax basis for arriving at an accurate figure, particularly given the fact that some investments are tax-exempt. See also: Pretax contribution.

Before-Tax Cash Flow The cash flow a person or company realizes after subtracting debt service and other expenses but not tax liability. Before-tax cash flow represents cash available to pay off creditors in the event of liquidation. While it is an important measure, it is not as closely watched as earnings before interest and taxes.

Before-Tax Contributions Contributions made to a retirement plan with taxable withdrawals. That is, when one makes before-tax contributions to a retirement plan, one does not pay taxes on the contributions in the year they are made, but defers taxation until one begins to make withdrawals from the plan. One makes before-tax contributions to traditional IRAs and most 401(k)s. See also: After-tax contributions.

Beggar-Thy-Neighbor A protectionist policy involving the devaluation of one's currency and the construction of tariffs barriers on other countries. The goal of a beggar-thy-neighbor policy is to increase demand for a country's exports (by devaluing the currency and making a country's goods less expensive in other countries) while also reducing demand for the countries imports (by making them more expensive through the tariff barriers). A form of this policy, notably the tariff barrier, was implemented at the beginning of the Great Depression with almost no success. A beggar-thy-neighbor policy in the United States caused other countries to follow suit, resulting in a massive decrease in international trade. This made the Depression worse. See also: Smoot-Hawley Act.

Beginning Inventory Goods and materials available for sale at the beginning of an accounting period or fiscal year. Comparing the beginning inventory to the ending inventory may help a company determine whether it overestimated the materials it needs to operate, or customers' demand for its products. They may use these figures to estimate future sales and therefore future inventory. See also: Inventory turnover.

Behavior Segmentation In marketing, a strategy that divides potential customers into different groups based upon their lifestyles, spending habits, disposable income and other areas. Behavior segmentation is most useful when a product is likely to appeal to persons in a specific niche. It is a form of market segmentation.

Behavioral Accounting A form of accounting that attempts to value key personnel such as executives or technicians. That is, behavioral accounting places a number on what an important person in the company can contribute and includes this as an asset. As with other intangible assets, this can be extremely difficult, but it can result in a more accurate picture of a company's worth. It is also called human resource accounting.

Behavioral Economics A theory of economics that attempts to explain economic participants' decisions as those of rational actors looking out for their self-interest given the sometimes inefficient nature of the market. Tracing its origins to Adam Smith's The Theory of Moral Sentiments, one of behavioral economics' primary observations holds that investors and people in genera make decisions on imprecise impressions and beliefs rather than rational analysis. A second observation states that the way a question or problem is framed to an investor will influence the decision he/she ultimately makes. These two observations largely explain market inefficiencies; that is, behavioral economics holds that markets are sometimes inefficient because people are not mathematical equations. Behavioral economics stands in stark contrast to the efficient markets theory. See also: Naive diversification, Formula plan, Subjective probabilities.

Behavioral Economist A theorist who attempts to explain economic participants' decisions as those of rational actors looking out for their self-interest given the sometimes inefficient nature of the market. Tracing its origins to Adam Smith's The Theory of Moral Sentiments, one of behavioral economists' primary observations holds that investors and people in general make decisions on imprecise impressions and beliefs rather than rational analysis. A second observation states that the way a question or problem is framed to an investor will influence the decision he/she ultimately makes. These two observations largely explain market inefficiencies; that

is, behavioral economists hold that markets are sometimes inefficient because people are not mathematical equations. Behavioral economics stands in stark contrast to the efficient markets theory. See also: Naive diversification, Formula plan, Subjective probabilities.

Behavioral Finance A theory of finance that attempts to explain the decisions of investors by viewing them as rational actors looking out for their self-interest, given the sometimes inefficient nature of the market. Tracing its origins to Adam Smith's The Theory of Moral Sentiments, one of its primary observations holds that investors (and people in general) make decisions on imprecise impressions and beliefs rather than rational analysis. A second observation states that the way a question or problem is framed to an investor will influence the decision he/she ultimately makes. These two observations largely explain market inefficiencies; that is, behavior finance holds that markets are sometimes inefficient because people are not mathematical equations. Behavioral finance stands in stark contrast to the efficient markets theory. See also: Naive diversification, Formula plan, Subjective probabilities.

Behavioral Theory of the Firm A theory of how a firm or company makes decisions. The behavioral theory states that a company's decision makers may not make the best decisions all the time because of lack of information, how a question is framed or their own prejudices and fears. Because more than one person is usually involved in a company's decision-making process, firms often implement policies to reduce the incentive for the personal perceptions of multiple persons to result in inefficient decisions. See also: Theory of the Firm.

Behind On an exchange, referring to a record of a trade that occurs at the same price as another trade, but is nonetheless listed after that other trade in a specialist's book. See also: Ahead.

Beige Book A report issued by the Federal Reserve Board two weeks before each FOMC meeting. The report contains anecdotal information on the state of the market and the broader economy in each region of the United States. The Beige Book is compiled from interviews with key market players including Federal Reserve Branch presidents. The Beige Book is considered a window into what the upper managers of the Federal Reserve are thinking, and, as such, it fuels speculation on what the FOMC will decide to do when it meets. The Beige Book may be designed to reduce shock (and the potential for panic) in the market after the Federal Reserve actually announces its decisions.

Beirut Agreement An international treaty that promotes the exchange of ideas between countries. The Beirut Agreement provides for exemptions from tariffs for films and other works of education, science or culture. Because these works must be certified in their countries of origin as having educational or other value, critics contend the Beirut Agreement has had the opposite effect of its intent.

Beirut Stock Exchange The main stock exchange of Lebanon. It is a joint stock company created in 1920. Trading halted on the BSE between 1983 and 1996 as a result of the Lebanese Civil War and its aftermath. It began trading international depository receipts and derivatives in 1999.

Beit Kor An ancient Hebrew unit of area variously equivalent to values between 17.3 and 24.9 square kilometers.

Beit Rova An ancient Hebrew unit of area variously equivalent to values between 24 and 34 square meters.

Beit Seah An ancient Hebrew unit of area variously equivalent to values between 576 and 829 square meters.

BEL GOST 7.67 Latin three-letter geocode for Belgium. The code is used for transactions to and from Belgian bank accounts and for international shipping to Belgium. As with all GOST 7.67 codes, it is used primarily in Cyrillic alphabets.

Belarusian Ruble The currency of Belarus. It was issued in 1992, existing alongside the Soviet ruble for several months but eventually replacing it. It has been subject to high inflation. For most of its history, the currency has been variously tied to the U.S. dollar and the Russian ruble.

Belde In Turkey, a political subdivision equivalent to an urban municipality.

Belediye In Turkey, a political subdivision equivalent to a municipal government.

Belgian Franc The former currency of Belgium. It traces its origins to the conquest of the Low Countries during the Napoleonic Wars. It has been pegged to a number of different currencies throughout its history and was one of the currencies in the Latin Monetary Union for a time. It was replaced by the euro in 2002.

Belgian Option An option contract that provides a partial payoff to the holder if the spot price of the underlying asset moves toward the strike price. The holder receives a payoff for the remainder of the intrinsic value of the option if it is in-the-money at expiration. It is a type of exotic option.

Belgium Futures and Options Exchange A former exchange for options and futures contracts. It closed in 2003 following its acquisition by NYSE Euronext. It was more commonly called BELFOX.

Belgium-Luxembourg Economic Union Also called BLEU or UBEL. A treaty that fixed the values of the Belgian franc and the Luxembourg franc at a 1:1 parity. This established a single market between Belgium and Luxembourg. Signed in 1921, it was superseded by the Benelux Customs Union in 1948.

Belize Dollar The currency of Belize. This became the currency in 1973, when British Honduras changed its name to Belize. While it was initially pegged to the British pound, the peg switched to the U.S. dollar (to which the currency of British Honduras had previously been fixed) in 1978.

Bell A traditional bell that is rung to signify the beginning or the end of a trading day. The bell on the New York Stock Exchange is one of the more famous examples.

As an increasing number of securities exchanges do most or all of their trading online, a bell has become a symbol or informal term for the beginning or the end of a trading day, rather than a description of a real bell.

Bell Cow A retail item that sells well even though its price far exceeds the cost to the producer. For example, a cup of coffee at a cafe may sell for $3 even though it costs only 25 cents to make. If the cafe is nevertheless successful, the coffee may be considered a bell cow. See also: Cash cow.

Bell Curve A curve on a chart in which most data points cluster around the median and become less frequent the farther they fall to either side of the median. When plotted on a chart, a bell curve looks roughly like a bell.

Bellwether Issue A bond with a coupon that is close to market rates. Interest rates on bonds vary from time to time according to a number of factors, but are usually locked at issue. A bellwether issue is one with an interest rate very near to the prevailing rates, regardless of when it was issued. Bellwether issues are also called benchmark issues and perhaps, most commonly, current coupons bonds.

Bellwether Security A stock or other security that usually leads the direction of its industry or sector. For example, if a stock begins a bullish or bearish trend a little bit ahead of other stocks, it may be said to be a bellwether security. It should not be confused with a bellwether issue.

Belly On a ship or airplane, the place underneath the main deck where cargo can be stored. The belly is also called the pits or the holds.

Belly Cargo In shipping, cargo that is stored underneath the main deck of the ship or airplane.

Belly Up Informal; relating to a bankrupt or failed company or project. The term is also used with reference to financial institutions shut down by regulators due to insolvency. See also: Bankruptcy.

Below Market Rate An interest rate or return below prevailing rates. A below market interest rate may be given to a borrower if he/she has an exceptionally good credit history. On the other hand, a below market return rate usually happens if one takes too little risk relative to the market or too much risk relative to the potential return.

Below Par Describing a bond that is issued or sold at a price below its face value. For example, a bond with par of $10,000 might be issued to an investor for $7,000. All zero-coupon bonds are issued below par.

Below the Bar In investment banking, describing a client that is too small to be worth the effort to keep. For example, a bank may release a below the bar client if it has less than $100,000 to put under management.

Below the Line 1. In accounting, an extraordinary income or expense a company does not incur in its day-to-day operations. Because they are not repeated, below the line items are not considered to increase or decrease the company's profit. See also: Above the line. **2.** Advertising in which a company pays a commission based on the success of the campaign. Below the line advertising is most common in direct mail and similar campaigns that rely on a customer's reaction to the advertisement, rather than his/her previous research on the product. **3.** A tax deduction one takes on one's adjusted gross income instead of one's gross income.

Below the Line Item In accounting, an extraordinary income or expense a company does not incur in its day-to-day operations. Because they are not repeated, below the line items are not considered to increase or decrease the company's profit. See also: Above the line.

Below the Market An order to buy or sell a security for a price below the current market value. A below the market order may occur when an investor wishes to buy at a low price in order to sell later at a high price. It also may be a stop order to sell a security when its price goes below a certain level in order to limit losses.

Below-the-Line Cost In accounting, extraordinary expenses a company does not incur in its day-to-day operations. Because they are not repeated, below the line costs are not considered to decrease the company's profit. See also: Above the line.

Below-the-Line Deduction A tax deduction one takes on one's adjusted gross income instead of one's gross income.

Belt and Suspenders Informal; a lender who demands too much collateral relative to the risk of a loan and who files a lien at the slightest excuse.

Belts and Suspenders A slang term for an extremely cautious plan or behavior. It is an informal way to describe risk adversity.

Bema An ancient Greek unit of length approximately equivalent to 1.54 meters. It was also called a diploun bema.

BEN GOST 7.67 Latin three-letter geocode for Benin. The code is used for transactions to and from Beninese bank accounts and for international shipping to Benin. As with all GOST 7.67 codes, it is used primarily in Cyrillic alphabets.

Ben Bernanke An economist who became Chairman of the Federal Reserve in 2005. He presided over the 2000s economic crisis, supervising the bailouts and forced mergers of a number of American financial institutions. He was both lauded and criticized for favoring an expansive monetary policy, which proponents claimed kept the American economy from collapsing in the crisis, but which others argued would lead to inflation. He is considered an expert on the Great Depression.

Bench Error An error made in the production of a good resulting in a defect. A company's insurance policy usually covers losses from a bench error.

Benchmark A standard against which a security's performance is compared. A benchmark is usually an index of securities of the same or similar class. Stocks are usually compared against stocks; bonds against bonds, etc. Another type of

benchmark considers securities according to industry: a telecommunications stock may be compared to other telecommunications stocks. Likewise, mid-cap securities may be benchmarked against other mid-cap securities. Some indices, such as the Dow Jones Industrial Average and the S&P 500, are considered to be benchmarks for the wider economy.

Benchmark Bond The most recent issue of a bond with a given maturity. A benchmark bond's performance is used to compare the performances of other bonds with the same maturity and of similar issue sizes, coupons, and liquidity. See also: benchmark.

Benchmark Country A country against which the performances of other countries are compared, especially in economic analysis. A benchmark country may be chosen on basis of population, industrial base, and other similarities to other countries.

Benchmark Error The act of using the wrong benchmark when creating a market portfolio in the capital asset pricing model or a similar model. For example, when calculating a CAPM using European stocks, a benchmark error would involve using the Dow Jones Industrial Average (an American index) as the benchmark. A benchmark error can result in wildly incorrect calculations.

Benchmark Interest Rate An interest rate against which other interest rates are calculated. For example, LIBOR is considered a benchmark rate because floating-rate instruments are related to it (for example, one may be calculated as LIBOR + 1%). Central banks make loans to banks under their jurisdiction at certain interest rates, which are then used as benchmarks for the loans those banks make.

Benchmark Surplus The additional amount of capital an insurance company may make available to a policyholder for each premium the policyholder pays if an unforeseen disruption of cash flow occurs.

Benefactor A person or organization that provides financial or other support to an individual or company. An uncle who pays for his niece's college education is a benefactor, as is a company that donates some of its profits to a school. See also: Philanthropist.

Beneficial Interest The right of a person to enjoy or otherwise use a property or other asset even if he/she does not actually own it. For example, the beneficiary of a trust has beneficial interest because he receives the income derived from the assets in the trust, but he does not own the assets themselves. This concept is very similar to beneficial ownership.

Beneficial Owner A person who has effective ownership of a security or other property without actually holding title to it. This especially refers to holding voter proxy or investment power over a share or transaction, whether directly or indirectly. See also: Double-dip lease.

Beneficial Ownership The state of having effective ownership of a security without actually holding title to it. This especially refers to holding voter proxy or investment power over a share or transaction, whether directly or indirectly. See also: Double-dip lease.

Beneficiary 1. In insurance, the person or (more rarely) organization that receives money from the insurance company when the insured event occurs. For example, in life insurance, when the insured person dies, a beneficiary may be his/her spouse This means that the spouse receives the agreed-upon amount of money from the insurance company. **2.** In annuities, the annuitant. The annuitant is the person who receives the agreed-upon amount of money from the annuity starting at the agreed-upon time. Depending on the type of annuity, the annuitant may be the person who paid into the annuity, or may be a relative or other designee of that person, such as a widow or widower.

Beneficiary Clause A clause in a document creating a trust, annuity or insurance policy stating who the beneficiary is. The person or company creating the trust, annuity or insurance policy may or may not be able to change who the beneficiary is, depending on the nature of the clause. See also: Revocable beneficiary, Irrevocable beneficiary.

Beneficiary of Trust The person or company receiving the income from a trust. The beneficiary receives a certain amount of money (usually a percentage of the trust's investment income) starting at the agreed-upon time. Depending on the type of trust, the beneficiary may be the grantor, a trustee, or some third party.

Benefit In annuities, insurance and some government programs, the amount of money one receives under certain, stated circumstances. Benefits commonly refer to periodic payments one begins to receive following retirement, but they may also refer to welfare payments like rental assistance or food stamps. In general, benefits may be fixed at a certain amount (often determined by the amount one has contributed in premiums or taxes) or may vary according to inflation or an underlying investment portfolio.

Benefit Allocation Method A way to finance a retirement plan in which an employee pays a certain amount or percentage of salary each year that the company uses to fund benefits equal to the contribution. These contributions continue each year until retirement (or until the employee leaves the company). In other words, the benefits are based on an average of an employee's salary over time. The benefit allocation method gives more highly compensated employees more benefits in retirement because those employees paid more into the system.

Benefit Allowance The value of benefits one receives from an insurance policy, annuity or retirement plan based upon the premium one pays. If one or one's employer pays high premiums, one is more likely to have a high benefit allowance.

Benefit Approach to Pensions How benefits for a pension are calculated. The two primary benefit approaches are the accumulated benefits and the projected unit benefit. In the accumulated benefits approach, payouts are determined according to one's salary each year benefits were awarded; that is, benefits are an average of one's earnings over time. In the projected unit benefit, the payouts are based on one's salary on the date of retirement.

Benefit Corporation A corporation in which the members of board of directors have the statutory duty to provide some tangible benefit to the community and/or the environment. In other words, a benefit corporation is not prohibited from earning and distributing profits, but is expected to do these other things as well. A benefit corporation is informally called a b-corp.

Benefit Cost Ratio A ratio representing the benefits of a project or investment compared to its cost. The BCR may be a strictly financial ratio, comparing the expected return to the cost of investment, or it may account for approximations of qualitative measurements.

Benefit Differential In insurance, the difference between what an insurer pays a preferred provider for a service and what it pays a nonpreferred provider for the same service. Law or regulations aimed at protecting policyholders may limit how large the benefit differential can be.

Benefit Formula How benefits for an insurance policy, government program or annuity are calculated. The benefit formula varies according to the program or annuity; it may be based on one's most recent salary, an average of one's salary over a certain number of years and/or the performance of some stated portfolio of investments.

Benefit Offset A reduction of benefits that a retiree receives when he/she has not made sufficient contributions to a retirement plan. Many retirement plans and government programs allow benefit offsets when the beneficiary has overdue payments and/or has not contributed for a certain period of time. A benefit offset exists to protect the company or government from abuse by beneficiaries.

Benefit Period The time during which one receives payments from an insurance policy or government program. For example, the benefit period for a person receiving Medicare begins when he/she is admitted to inpatient care and ends 60 days following discharge. The benefit period may be used to help determine the amount and type of benefits one receives.

Benefit Principle A philosophy stating that those who benefit most from government programs have an obligation to pay more for those programs. For example, shareholders in companies subsidized by the government may pay more under a tax system using the benefit principle. This contrasts with the ability to pay principle.

Benefit Segmentation In marketing, a strategy that divides potential customers into different groups based on the benefits they seek to derive from products. For example, benefit segmentation may divide customers into those who look primarily for short-term fun in their purchases, and those who are after long-term advantage. Behavior segmentation is most useful when a product is likely to appeal to persons in a specific niche. It is a form of market segmentation.

Benefit Trigger Any event that causes a pension or annuity to start making payments to a beneficiary. Retirement and the attainment of a certain age are common benefit triggers.

Benefit-Based Pension Plan A pension plan in which the payer (usually a company) guarantees it will pay the agreed-upon benefits, regardless of any circumstances like reduced profits or even bankruptcy.

Benefits for International Service Any compensation or severance one receives if one serves or has served a company in a foreign country, especially in a dangerous, less developed or otherwise undesirable area. For example, an oil company may provide benefits for international service if one does work in the eastern deserts of Saudi Arabia.

Benefits in Kind Goods or services provided for free or for a very low price, especially as a donation for charitable purposes or as a fringe benefit for an employee or client.

Benefits System 1. See: Social Security. **2.** A predominately British term for welfare programs.

Benelux Customs Union A treaty that eliminated tariffs on goods traded between Belgium, the Netherlands and Luxembourg. It also established a common tariff for goods originating outside the three countries. In other words, the Customs Union allowed the members to be treated as a single country for purposes of international trade. The treaty was signed in 1944, came into effect in 1948 and was superseded by the Benelux Economic Union in 1960. See also: Belgium-Luxembourg Economic Union.

Benelux Economic Union An intergovernmental organization consisting of Belgium, the Netherlands, and Luxembourg. Created in 1958 and made effective in 1960, it allows the free movement of goods, services, capital and workers between the three countries. Decisions the governing bodies of the Benelux Economic Union make must be ratified by the parliaments of the three countries. While the Union remains in force, many of its responsibilities have been transferred to the European Union. It is the successor to the Benelux Customs Union.

Bengali Taka The currency of Bangladesh. It first was issued in 1972, replacing the Pakistani rupee at a 1:1 ratio. It has historically been a weak currency.

Benjamin A slang term for a $100 bill in the United States. The term is derived from Benjamin Franklin, who appears on the $100 bill.

Benjamin Graham An analyst who is considered the father of value investing. This is an investment strategy in which one seeks securities thought to be undervalued. His seminal works, Security Analysis and The Intelligent Investor, are both considered classics and are still studied. Among Graham's most important precepts is the idea that a share in a publicly-traded company confers ownership in a business, and one must treat investing as buying a business that one believes to be profitable. Graham's approach contrasts with investors who use methods such as arbitrage to make quick profits. He lived from 1894 to 1976.

Bequeath To give, especially in a will after death. For example, a grandfather may bequeath his house to his granddaughter in his will.

Bequest In wills and estates, the gift of part of the estate to a beneficiary. A bequest may be real estate or personal property. For example, if a decedent wishes her son to have her house and her daughter to have the family jewels, then each of these is specified in the decedent's will. In this case, the house and the family jewels are separate bequests. See also: Codicil.

Berid A Turkish measure of length approximately equivalent to 227 meters. It became obsolete when Turkey made the metric system mandatory in 1933. An equivalent term is menzil.

Berkeley Software Distribution A computer operating system that was used between 1977 and 1995. Berkeley Software Distribution was based on and was considered a subset of UNIX.

Berkovets A Russian unit of weight approximately equivalent to 163.8 kilograms. It was rendered obsolete when the Soviet Union began to use the metric system in 1924.

Berkshire Hathaway A company that holds a wide variety of investments for shareholders. It was founded in 1839 as a textile manufacturing company. In 1962, Warren Buffett began buying its shares and eventually took a controlling stake in the company. Buffett expanded Berkshire Hathaway into insurance and used the proceeds to finance other investments. Buffett used the value investing philosophy in picking Berkshire's investments, which in general have been highly profitable. For example, these investments returned 76% to shareholders between 2000 and 2010. It often is held up as a primary example of the success of value investing.

Berlin Mint An organization in Germany that issues legal tender coins for general use. It is a state-owned corporation.

Bermuda Swaption An option in which the buyer of the option has the right to enter into to an interest rate swap on certain dates throughout the option's life. The terms of the swaption specify whether the buyer will be the payer of the floating rate or the payer of the fixed rate. It is called a Bermudan swaption because, like a Bermudan option, the swaption may only be exercised on certain, specified dates over its life. See also: Call Swaption, Put Swaption, Plan Vanilla Swap.

Bermudian Dollar The currency of Bermuda. It was first issued in 1970, replacing the Bermudan pound. Since its introduction, the dollar has been pegged to the U.S. dollar at a 1:1 ratio.

Bermudian Pound The former currency of Bermuda. It was pegged to the British pound at a one-to-one ratio and was replaced by the Bermudian dollar in 1970.

Bernard J. Ebbers A Canadian businessman who served as CEO of WorldCom for much of its early history prior to 2002. He co-founded WorldCom (then called Long Distance Discount Services) in 1983. After becoming CEO in 2005, he oversaw a number of acquisitions of telecommunications companies, including some of the largest (at that time) takeovers in American history. In 2002, he resigned in an accounting scandal and was sentenced to 25 years in prison in 2005. See also: Enron scandal.

Bernard Madoff A broker and investment adviser whose firm was revealed in 2008 to be the largest Ponzi scheme in history. Before this revelation, Madoff was a well respected and supposedly successful investor and philanthropist. His penny stock company developed the computer technology that led to the foundation of NASDAQ. He served as chairman of NASDAQ and was on the board of the National Association of Securities Dealers. His victims included a large number of charitable organizations that had allowed Madoff's firm to invest their endowments. In 2009, he pleaded guilty to defrauding his victims of nearly $65 billion; he was sentenced to 150 years in prison.

Berne Convention A treaty governing international recognition of copyrights. The Convention requires members to apply the laws of their own country to works and inventions originally from other countries. For example, a book published in Australia is treated in Russia the same as if it had been published originally in Russia. This extension of copyright does not require additional registration. That is, the author in Australia does not have to re-register his/her book in Russia for it to be recognized as his/her intellectual property. Author Victor Hugo originated the idea for the Berne Convention, which was signed in 1886.

Berne Union The collective name for countries that are signatories to the Berne Convention, which governs international recognition of copyrights. The vast majority of the world's countries belong to the Berne Union.

Bernoulli Box An early computer disk onto which one could store several megabytes of memory. It was introduced in the 1980s and was made largely obsolete with the introduction of Zip drives in the mid-1990s. Bernoulli Boxes resembled floppy disks.

Bernoulli Trial A test in which there are precisely two random outcomes: success and failure. For example, if one is testing whether flipping a coin will result in heads, the two outcomes are yes (success) and no (failure). See also: Bernoulli's Law.

Berry Gordy Jr. An American businessman who founded Motown Records. Born into a fairly prominent Black family in Detroit, he started his first label in 1959 with an $800 loan from family members. He signed a large number of successful, primarily African American, artists. He was born in 1929.

Berth A place on a port or dock where a ship is tied when not in use. Large ports have different berths for different purposes. For example, a ship storing natural gas may dock at a berth away from other ships.

Bertrand Duopoly One of two major models of how duopolies operate. In the Bertrand model, two companies compete with each other for the lowest possible price, resulting in perfect competition. Bertrand duopoly is applicable in many circumstances but it does not express duopolistic behavior perfectly. See also: Cournot model.

Beru An ancient Akkadian unit of length approximately equivalent to 10.8 kilometers.

Bes 1. An ancient Roman unit of area approximately equivalent to 1,682 square meters. 2. See: Bessis.

Besloten Vennootschap A Dutch term for a limited liability company. This is the most common legal form businesses take in the Netherlands. It is often abbreviated BV.

Bessis An ancient Roman unit of weight approximately equivalent to 219.3 grams. It was also called a bes.

Best Efforts Test In Chapter 13 bankruptcy, one of two conditions that must be fulfilled in the debtor's repayment plan. According to the best efforts test, the debtor must pay unsecured creditors at least an amount equal to his/her monthly disposable income (as calculated when he/she files for bankruptcy) multiplied by either 36 or 60, depending on the whether the debtor makes below or above the median income in his/her state. It should not be confused with best efforts underwriting. See also: Best interest of creditors test.

Best Execution A rule requiring brokers to always execute orders for clients at the best possible price. The SEC requires brokers to follow the best execution rule in order to protect investors.

Best Fit A curve or line that comes most closely to following a set of data points plotted on a chart. Best fit curves and lines are used in technical analysis to find trends.

Best in Breed In marketing, a slang term describing the most popular or most excellent product among all similar types of products. For example, the best-selling peanut butter in a market may be called the best in breed.

Best in Class The security or company that is performing best in its sector or industry. It is also called the best of breed. See also: Benchmark.

Best Interest A duty or obligation to act in a manner one believes to be most beneficial to a person or organization. For example, a guardian must act in the best interest of a child, and a CEO must do the same for his/her company. See also: Fiduciary.

Best of Breed The company or investment in a sector that represents the lowest risk or the possibility of the greatest gain for the holder. The best of breed is a good quality investment, at least compared with those most similar to it.

Best Practices The most effective and/or most ethical actions a professional, company or industry can take. For example, a company may be engaging in best practices when it makes an extra effort to establish an ongoing relationship with customers to encourage repeat business. Many professional organizations exist to promote best practices in their respective industries.

Best Time Available In marketing, an instruction given to a radio or television station to air a commercial at the time when, in its estimation, the commercial is likely to be seen or heard by the widest audience.

Best-Efforts Basis An agreement between an underwriter and an issuer in which the underwriter agrees to place as much of an offering with investors as possible, but is not responsible for any portion of the offering it fails to sell. For example, suppose an issuer makes a new issue of 100,000 shares. The issuer may make a best effort basis agreement with an underwriting firm for the underwriter to sell those shares to investors. If the underwriting firm only sells 90,000, however, it is not required to buy the remaining 10,000 from the issuer. This reduces the risk to the underwriter; to reduce the risk to the issuer, most best efforts are all-or-none offerings.

Best-Interests-of-Creditors Test In Chapter 13 bankruptcy, a requirement that unsecured creditors receive at least as much as they would have in Chapter 7 bankruptcy. Chapter 7 bankruptcy is complete liquidation of assets while Chapter 13 bankruptcy allows the bankrupt person or business to continue operations so long as they submit a plan to repay debts over three to five years. It is usually used by persons or sole proprietorships with a heavy debt load but still significant income. The best-interest-of-creditors test exists to ensure that the person or business filing Chapter 13 is not simply trying evade liquidation or to escape repaying necessary debts. See also: Best Efforts Test.

Best-of-Two Option An option in which the payoff is equal to the payoff of the better performing of two different underlying assets. It is also called a better-of-two option. It is a type of exotic option.

Best-Price Rule An SEC rule stating that that a tender offer (an offer by a company to buy back some of its own shares) must be available to all holders of that class of share and that the highest price paid must be the price paid to all holders who take advantage of the tender offer. This rule exists to ensure fairness and prevent favoritism in tender offers.

Best's Rating A measure of the credit quality of an insurance company. That is, the rating measures an insurance company's ability to pay claims that might be made. Best's ratings can be between A and F, with A being the highest rating. Best's ratings have historically been issued for insurance companies exclusively, but, more recently, they have been applied to a few small banks. They are issued by the A.M. Best Company.

Beta A measure of a security's or portfolio's volatility. A beta of 1 means that the security or portfolio is neither more nor less volatile or risky than the wider market. A beta of more than 1 indicates greater volatility and a beta of less than 1 indicates less. Beta is an important component of the Capital Asset Pricing Model, which attempts to use volatility and risk to estimate expected returns.

Beta Alpha Psi An honorary society for American college students of accounting, finance and information systems. It promotes academic and professional development among members, and provides networking opportunities later in life. It was established in 1919.

Beta Equation A way to calculate beta, which is the measure of a security's volatility relative to that of the wider market. There are several different beta equations.

Beta Error When testing a hypothesis, the risk of a false negative in the results. It is also called a type II error or beta risk. See also: Alpha risk.

Beta Test A test of a product by outside users before the product goes into mass production. That is, a beta test occurs after an internal alpha test but before a product is produced in large quantities for consumers. The term is used most often in software development.

Betamaxed A slang term describing a situation in which a product using inferior technology is marketed so successfully that it drives a product using superior technology out of business.

Better Business Bureau An organization that promotes an environment in which buyers and sellers can trust each other. It encourages ethical business practices, provides information on fraudulent schemes against both businesses and their customers, and offers arbitration services in the event of disputes. It was established in 1912 and consists of local chapters throughout the United States and Canada.

Better Price Limit Order 1. A buy limit order in which the limit price is higher than the current ask. 2. A sell limit order in which the limit price is lower than the current bid. Better price limit orders indicate that the order makers are willing to pay more or accept less than the market price. This means they are filled immediately. As a result, they are only available at the opening.

Betterment 1. In real estate, an increase in the value of a property because of an improvement near the property that makes it more desirable for potential buyers. For example, if a municipality builds a highway or a park near a house, this may result in betterment for the homeowner. 2. In accounting, an increase in the value of an asset because of some improvement that increases its efficiency or profitability.

Betterment Insurance An insurance policy that the renter of a property procures on all improvements he/she makes to that property. This differs from insurance on the property itself. For example, if a dentist rents an office and adds three dental chairs and a laboratory, the property owner procures insurance for the office itself while the dentist buys betterment insurance for the chairs and the lab.

Beveridge Report A report to the British Cabinet recommending the creation of the modern Welfare State. The Beveridge Report cited five social evils in the United Kingdom: squalor, ignorance, want, idleness and disease. It recommended an expansion of the National Insurance program and the creation of what became the National Health Service. It was published in 1941 and most of its recommendations were adopted following the Labour Party victory in the 1945 election.

Bezier Drawing Tool A tool that allows one to draw curves on a computer. It takes its name from a Bezier curve, which is a smooth curve with at least three points. It is used in making graphics for marketing and other purposes.

Bezirk In Austria, a political subdivision equivalent to a district.

BF 1. ISO 3166-1 alpha-2 code for Burkina Faso. This is the code used in international transactions to and from bank accounts in Burkina Faso. 2. ISO 3166-2 geocode for Burkina Faso. This is used as an international standard for shipping to Burkina Faso. Each province has its own code with the prefix "BF." For example, the code for the Province of Bam is ISO 3166-2:BF-BAM.

BFA GOST 7.67 Latin three-letter geocode for Burkina Faso. The code is used for transactions to and from Burkinabe bank accounts and for international shipping to Burkina Faso. As with all GOST 7.67 codes, it is used primarily in Cyrillic alphabets.

BG 1. ISO 3166-1 alpha-2 code for the Republic of Bulgaria. This is the code used in international transactions to and from Bulgarian bank accounts. 2. ISO 3166-2 geocode for Bulgaria. This is used as an international standard for shipping to Bulgaria. Each Bulgarian subdivision has its own code with the prefix "BG." For example, the code for the Province of Montana is ISO 3166-2:BG-12.

BGD GOST 7.67 Latin three-letter geocode for Bangladesh. The code is used for transactions to and from Bangladeshi bank accounts and for international shipping to Bangladesh. As with all GOST 7.67 codes, it is used primarily in Cyrillic alphabets.

BGL ISO 4217 code for the third Bulgarian lev. It was introduced in 1962, replacing the second lev after a period of high inflation. It was likewise replaced by the fourth lev (code BGN) for the same reason in 1999.

BGN ISO 4217 code for the fourth Bulgarian lev. The fourth lev replaced the third lev in 1999 at a ratio of 1,000 third leva to one fourth lev. At its introduction, the lev was pegged to the Deutsche mark at a 1:1 ratio. When Germany changed over to the euro, Bulgaria unofficially switched its peg to the new currency at a ratio of 1.95583 leva to one euro.

BGR GOST 7.67 Latin three-letter geocode for Bulgaria. The code is used for transactions to and from Bulgarian bank accounts and for international shipping to Bulgaria. As with all GOST 7.67 codes, it is used primarily in Cyrillic alphabets.

BH 1. ISO 3166-1 alpha-2 code for the Kingdom of Bahrain. This is the code used in international transactions to and from Bahraini bank accounts. **2.** ISO 3166-2 geocode for Bahrain. This is used as an international standard for shipping to Bahrain. Each Bahraini governate has its own code with the prefix "BH." For example, the code for the Capital Governate is ISO 3166-2:BH-13.

BHD ISO 4217 code for the Bahraini dinar. It was introduced upon Bahrain's independence from the United Kingdom; it replaced the Gulf rupee. In 1980, the dinar was pegged to Special Drawing Rights, though in practice it was pegged to the U.S. dollar. The peg was officially changed to the dollar in 2001.

BHR GOST 7.67 Latin three-letter geocode for Bahrain. The code is used for transactions to and from Bahraini bank accounts and for international shipping to Bahrain. As with all GOST 7.67 codes, it is used primarily in Cyrillic alphabets.

BHS GOST 7.67 Latin three-letter geocode for the Bahamas. The code is used for transactions to and from Bahamian bank accounts and for international shipping to the Bahamas. As with all GOST 7.67 codes, it is used primarily in Cyrillic alphabets.

Bhutanese Rupee The former currency of Bhutan. It was pegged to the Indian rupee at a one-to-one ratio. It was replaced by the ngultrum in 1974

BI 1. ISO 3166-1 alpha-2 code for the Republic of Burundi. This is the code used in international transactions to and from Burundian bank accounts. **2.** ISO 3166-2 geocode for Burundi. This is used as an international standard for shipping to Burundi. Most provinces has their own codes with the prefix "BI." For example, the code for Bururi is ISO 3166-2:BI-BR.

Biafran Pound The currency of Biafra, a country with limited recognition that existed between 1967 and 1970. It was issued in 1968 but was not recognized as a currency in much of the rest of the world. However, Biafran notes have since become a collector's item.

Biannual Twice each year. It is used in business in a variety of circumstances. For example, a board of directors may meet or the company may distribute dividends biannually. Biennial means the same thing. See also: Quarter.

Bias 1. In statistics, a circumstance leading to inaccurate results because of conscious or unconscious manipulation of data. Bias is anything that reduces the randomness of the sample being tested. **2.** Anything that affects a decision other than facts. For example, a company may be disinclined to expand into an area of town because it is perceived as dangerous, whether or not it actually is. Bias is thought to reduce efficiency. See also: Behavioral economics.

Bibhag In Bangladesh, a political subdivision approximately equivalent to a province.

Bid 1. An offer by an investor to buy a security. **2.** The highest price a potential buyer is willing to pay for a security. See also: Ask, Bid-ask spread.

Bid and Ask Price 1. See: Bid. **2.** See: Ask.

Bid Away In over-the-counter trading, to make a bid higher than the previous price for which the security or derivative was sold. See also: Uptick.

Bid Bond A bond that a bidder to a construction project buys to guarantee that it has the means to complete the project should it be awarded the contract. The amount of a bid bond is a certain percentage of the price of the contract. It exists to reassure the company awarding the contract that the bidder has the cash flow needed for the project. The bidder is reimbursed for the bid bond if it does not receive the contract.

Bid Market A market in which the number of buyers exceeds the number of sellers. That is, demand to buy securities outstrips the supply for sale. This generally is temporary as the price tends to rise until sellers and buyers equalize. See also: Bull market.

Bid Rate The highest exchange rate at which a buyer is willing to buy a currency. See also: Bid.

Bid Size The number of shares in a stock that a potential buyer is willing to purchase in a given bid. For example, if the bid size is 1,000 shares, this means that the bidder wishes to buy 1,000 shares at the stated price.

Bid Tick The change in a bid. That is, a bid tick shows how much a bid for a stock has gone up or down, or if it has stayed the same. Bid ticks are important for day traders who may make many trades in a trading day. See also: Tick.

Bid Wanted An indication or announcement that an investor or broker-dealer wishes to sell a certain security at a certain price, especially when there are no current buyers. A bid wanted is analogous to a bid, which is essentially the same thing from the buyer's perspective. The price on a bid wanted is called the offer.

Bid-Ask Spread On an exchange, the difference between the highest price a buyer of a security or other asset is willing to pay and the lowest price a seller is willing to offer. Generally speaking, the more liquid an asset is, the lower the bid-ask spread is. As a result, currency, which is considered the most liquid asset, has an extremely low bid-ask spread.

Bidder A potential buyer. The term may apply regardless of what the bidder is seeking to buy. To give only a few examples, bidders seek to buy houses, stocks, bonds, and whole companies. A bidder may be an individual or a corporation. Generally speaking, a seller finds the bidder who offers the best deal and executes the sale with him or her.

Bidding Buyer An investor who wants to buy a security, but not necessarily immediately. That is, a bidding buyer is willing to wait until a seller offers him/her a sufficiently low price, as opposed to simply wanting to accumulate securities. A bidding buyer may believe that the security he/she wants to buy represents a solid company, but not one that is nearing an explosion of growth. See also: Bidding through the market.

Bidding Through the Market In general equities, referring to an investor who aggressively wants to buy securities. He/she is often willing to bid higher than the market value for a security. A buyer may bid through the market if he/she believes the price of a security is about to increase substantially. Alternatively, he/she may believe it is a good long-term investment, even if the security's market value does not yet reflect that.

Bidding up The act of an investor raising his/her buy limit price as a result of steadily rising prices for the security involved. When an investor makes a buy limit order, he/she sets a (relatively low) price at which the broker is to buy the security. If, however, the price increases significantly and shows no sign of approaching the buy limit price, then the investor risks not buying the security and missing out on further increases. One bids up in order to avoid this; while it means the investor must spend more to buy the security, it opens up the opportunity for a large return.

Bidding War A situation in which two persons or organization are so interested in a product, asset, or potential employee that they offer successively higher prices or salaries for it. For example, two potential employers for a recent graduate may be so interested that when the first offers $50,000, the other comes back with $55,000, which leads the first to increase to $60,000, and so forth. Bidding wars usually occur very rapidly.

Bid-to-Cover Ratio In the auction of U.S. Treasury securities, the ratio of the bids received in the auction to the number of bids actually accepted. The bid-to-cover ratio is an indicator (though not the only one) of relative demand for Treasury securities. A bid-to-cover ratio of over 2.0 indicates a successful auction with competitive bidding, while a lower ratio indicates the opposite.

BIF 1. Bank Insurance Fund. A pool of money created in 1989 by the FDIC to insure deposits made by banks who are members of the Federal Reserve System. The BIF was created to separate bank insurance money from thrift insurance money (which came from the Savings Association Insurance Fund). While this was likely beneficial for a time because of the savings and loan crisis, it created a perverse incentive for banks and thrifts to reclassify themselves as the other (i.e., a bank to a thrift or a thrift to a bank), depending on which fund had lower fees. This led to the passage of the Federal Deposit Insurance Act of 2005, which abolished the Savings Association Insurance Fund and the BIF and created a single Deposit Insurance Fund. **2.** ISO 4217 code for the Burundian franc. It was introduced in 1964, replacing the Rwanda and Burundi franc. There are currently plans to replace the franc with the East African shilling, a common currency structured along the lines of the euro, by the end of 2009.

Bifurcate A derogatory slang term meaning to divide one job into two jobs. For example, the director of communications position may be bifurcated into the director of internal communications and the director of external communications. The term is most common when the holder of the previous, unified position is asked to reapply for one or both of the new positions. See also: Breadcrumbing.

Big Bang An informal term referring to the deregulation of the London Stock Market on October 27, 1986. On that date, a number of changes occurred, including a shift from an open outcry system to an electronic exchange. Perhaps most important, however, was the abolition of fixed commissions, which completely changed the way brokers on the London Stock Market conducted their business. Big Bang significantly increased the volume on the London Stock Exchange and reversed its trend of falling behind other world stock markets. It was a major part of Prime Minister Margaret Thatcher's financial reform program. It is important to note that one does not refer to Big Bang as the Big Bang.

Big Bath The practice of making poor earnings of a company, especially of a publicly-traded company, appear worse than they really are. One may accomplish a big bath through write-offs, prepaid expenses, and so forth. The hidden earnings are revealed in a year, when earnings are better, to make them look even better than they really are. A new CEO sometimes takes a big bath to artificially inflate earnings in the second year of his tenure. This allows him to blame the previous bad year on the CEO who came before him. Not coincidentally, it also increases this CEO's chances of receiving a large bonus in the second year.

Big Bickies An Australian slang term for a great deal of money.

Big Blue Informal for IBM, a major computer and information technology company. IBM develops software and hardware, provides network hosting, and offers IT consulting services. It is one of the only IT companies to trace its origins back more than 100 years. It was established in New York in 1896. After Coca-Cola, IBM is considered the second-most valuable brand name in the world.

Big Board An informal name for the New York Stock Exchange. The name specifically refers to the famous NYSE electronic board announcing prices.

Big Bull A slang term for $500 in Hong Kong. See also: Hong Kong dollar.

Big Business A somewhat pejorative term for large corporations. The term especially connotes corporations that have a great deal of political power. The term originated in the middle and late 19th century, when a large number of mergers and acquisitions consolidated many large companies that previously existed. Opponents of big business on both ends of the political spectrum contend that large corporations have too much power in government and use their influence to extract favorable legislation.

Big Cracker A slang term for a one-dollar coin in Hong Kong. See also: Hong Kong dollar.

Big Dog 1. In business, a slang term for a large invoice. **2.** A slang term for an important person. For example, a major shareholder in a corporation may be said to be a big dog.

Big Enchilada A slang term for a boss, a CEO, or some other executive in an organization.

Big Figure The whole dollar amount of a quote. For example, if a security is trading at $26.45, its big figure is 26. Many traders do not include the big figure when providing quotes, especially for highly liquid assets like currencies, because they assume other traders already know them. The big figure is also called a handle, especially in the United States.

Big Four The four largest accounting firms in the United States: Deloitte Touche Tohmatsu, Pricewaterhouse Coopers, Ernst & Young, and KPMG. In addition to accounting, these firms all offer auditing and advisory services. The number of "big" accounting firms has decreased over time because of mergers and, most recently, the ruin of Arthur Andersen following the Enron scandal in 2002.

Big Mac PPP A measure of purchasing power parity that observes the price of a Big Mac in a given country relative to the price of a Big Mac in the United States, with a goal of determining the real value of a currency. Purchasing power parity is a theory stating that the same good or service costs the same amount regardless of the currency in which it is measured. For instance, if 1 pound is equivalent to 2 dollars, and a widget costs 1 pound in England, then purchasing power parity would state that the same widget would cost 2 dollars in the United States. Big Mac PPP attempts to see how well this holds by measuring the prices of Big Macs. It is calculated by taking the price of a Big Mac in a given country and dividing by the price of an American Big Mac. This gives a relative exchange rate of the two countries and helps one see if a currency is overvalued or undervalued. For example, if a Big Mac costs $1 in the United States and 0.75 pounds in the United Kingdom, the Big Mac PPP is 0.75 GBP:USD. If the official GBP:USD exchange rate is 0.50, then this indicates that the pound is overvalued. The Big Mac PPP is published by The Economist. See also: Currency pair.

Big Note Man In Australia, a slang term for a person who ostentatiously displays wealth. The term derives from Australian currency prior to decimalization, when larger denominations were printed on larger bills.

Big Picture 1. An informal term for long-term investing. **2.** A large trade that increases investor interest in a security.

Big Pix Informal; a one-page summary of a financial statement. The term is most common in business consulting for Christian churches and ministries.

Big Producer A well known and well regarded broker who generates a significant amount of business for his/her brokerage (and a great deal of money in commissions for himself/herself). See also: Rainmaker.

Big Push In international development, a model stating that companies decide whether or not to industrialize their operations based on what they believe other companies will do. Though industrialization is expensive, it can result in a tremendous competitive advantage over companies that do not do so. The big push posits that these facts significantly influence the judgments of companies mulling industrialization. See also: Game theory.

Big Steal Informal; a purchase for an exceptionally good (low) price. For example, if a wholesaler wishes to buy a retailer with which it has done business, it may wait until bad news about the retailer results in a steep (but temporary) decline in its share price. The wholesaler then buys the shares in a big steal.

Big Swinging Dick (Very) informal and somewhat derogatory; a trader who believes his methodology is perfect and will always result in sizable profits. However, it originally was a term of self-designation for major bond-traders. The term was popularized by the book Liar's Poker, which describes the author's experience as a bond trader on Wall Street in the 1980s.

Big Three The three largest automobile firms in the United States: General Motors, Chrysler, and Ford. Historically, their performance was considered an indicator of the performance of the wider American economy.

Big Uglies Informal; older, industrial companies involved in sectors considered "dirty" by some investors. Examples include companies in the coal mining or steel industries. Big uglies often are considered solid investments because they provide steady returns. However, the term implies that many investors ignore them because of ethical concerns or simply because they are not as trendy as newer companies.

Bigha A unit of area variously equivalent to values between 1,500 and 12,400 square meters. It is used in real estate transactions in Bangladesh, Nepal, and parts of India.

Big-Ticket Item An expensive retail good. A big ticket item may be regarded as a necessity for an individual or business. For example, a farm generally must purchase big ticket items like tractors. Big ticket items are ordinarily bought on credit, with the buyer making periodic payments.

BIH GOST 7.67 Latin three-letter geocode for Bosnia and Herzegovina. The code is used for transactions to and from Bosnian and Herzegovinian bank accounts and for international shipping to Bosnia and Herzegovina. As with all GOST 7.67 codes, it is used primarily in Cyrillic alphabets.

Bijzondere Gemeenten In Holland, a political subdivision equivalent to a province within the Caribbean Netherlands.

Bilateral Clearing Agreement An agreement in which two governments agree to allow trade between them up to a certain value for a given period of time. A bilateral clearing agreement limits the amount of trade that can take place under its terms; for that reason, it is considered inefficient by advocates of free trade.

Bilateral Contract A contract in which each party has obligations to the other. For example, in a contract of sale, one party provides a good or service and the other party provides remuneration in the form of payment. Bilateral contracts are extremely common. See also: Unilateral contract.

Bilateral Credit Limit The credit limit two banks extend to each other for securities trades that occur during a single day. That is, one bank may only borrow from the other up to the bilateral credit limit. Most of the time, the credit is netted at the end of the trading day, which allows one bank to borrow more than the credit limit in absolute terms, provided the other bank borrows an equivalent amount to bring it under the credit limit. For example, if the bilateral credit limit is $1 million, bank A may borrow $1.5 million from bank B provided bank B borrows at least $500,000 from bank A on the same trading day. See also: Bilateral netting.

Bilateral Grid A system in which the exchange rates for all currencies on the European Monetary System are listed in terms of the European currency unit.

Bilateral Investment Treaty An agreement between two countries establishing the rules under which individuals and companies in one country may provide foreign direct investment in the other. The rules work both ways unless the treaty states otherwise; that is, if the treaty sets a limit on foreign direct investment by a company, this applies to companies in both countries. Most bilateral investment treaties require arbitration (instead of lawsuits) for the resolution of disputes.

Bilateral Mistake A situation in which both parties to a contract misunderstand or misinterpret the terms of an item in the contract. A bilateral mistake voids a contract under most circumstances.

Bilateral Monopoly A situation in which there is a single buyer and a single seller of a product. Each party has an incentive to extract the most benefits it can; specifically, the buyer wants to pay the lowest possible price and the seller wants to extract the highest. The result of the ensuing negotiation is somewhere in between. Bilateral monopolies are seen in labor agreements in which one company provides nearly all the jobs in a town (and wants to pay the lowest possible wage) and nearly all citizens in the town work for the company (and want the highest wage).

Bilateral Netting Given two parties who carry a set of swaps between each other, an agreement to consolidate all the swaps into one net payment from one party to the other. That is, if, in a given period, the net swap favors one party, that party is paid the amount; however, if, during the next period, the net swap favors the counterparty, then the counterparty is paid. This tidies the accounting for both parties, and protects both in the event of bankruptcy. If one party declares bankruptcy, the counterparty only has to continue paying if the net swap favors the first party.

Bilateral Steel Agreement A treaty between two countries governing the trade of steel between them. In general, bilateral steel agreements reduce tariffs each country places on the other's steel and discourage subsidies they give to their own steel companies. See also: Free trade agreement.

Bilateral Trade The barter of goods between companies and/or governments in two countries, almost always without recourse to currency. Bilateral trades were more common during the Cold War; the Soviet Union conducted bilateral trades to allow for its government to serve as one party while a private company in another country served as the other. Bilateral trades have become rare since except for highly sensitive goods like nuclear material.

Bilateral Trade Agreement A trade pact between two parties. The parties are usually two countries, but one or both may be a supranational organization like the European Union. Bilateral trade agreements usually, but do not always, reduce tariffs and other trade barriers between the parties. They may extend privileges the parties do not give to other countries, or they may mirror similar treaties with other countries.

Bilateral Treaty A treaty between two parties. The parties are usually two countries, but one or both may be a supranational organization like the European Union.

Bilingual Person A person with the ability to speak two languages. In areas where two languages are common, bilingual persons are often paid more to do the same jobs as monolingual persons because they are able to service more customers with less difficulty.

Bilingualism The ability to speak two languages. In areas where two languages are common, bilingual individuals are often paid more to do the same jobs as monolingual persons because they are able to service more customers with less difficulty.

Bill 1. A statement given buy a seller to a buyer itemizing the sale and demanding payment. A bill may be for the sale of a good or a service. The bill usually states the names of the counterparties, the goods and/or services purchased, and adds any applicable sales tax or VAT. It may also include the terms of sale, especially if it is a credit sale. A bill is also called an invoice. See also: Receipt. **2.** Informal for Treasury bill.

Bill Gates A computer developer and entrepreneur and one of the richest people in the world. He became involved in computing in the middle and late 1970s and founded Microsoft. He was instrumental in developing DOS and the Windows operating systems. Gates helped make the personal computer accessible and affordable for most people, which revolutionized education, business, and many other fields. He also founded the Gates Foundation, a philanthropic organization.

Bill Group A collection of credit orders made over a certain period of time and later canceled for nonpayment.

Bill in a Set A bill that is grouped together with a number of other bills, such that it is considered a single bill for legal liability purposes.

Bill Insert Marketing material sent in the mail along with a regular bill. This allows a company to maximize its advertisements at the lowest possible price because it does not have to pay for extra postage. A bill insert is also called a bill stuffer.

Bill Key A code assigned to each credit sale over a given period of time. The bill key helps the seller track its accounts receivable.

Bill Me Informal; a credit sale in which one purchases a product and receives a demand for payment (often including interest) at a later date.

Bill Mountain Informal; a situation in which one has an unusually high number of bills to pay each month, or when the bills are exceptionally expensive. The term refers to a large stack of papers (representing individual bills) resembling a mountain.

Bill of Activities A catalog of all activities that must be completed to create a finished product. For example, the bill of activities for constructing a building may list mixing the concrete, putting up the steel beams, and so forth. See also: Bill of materials.

Bill of Credit 1. A bill issued by a government that may be traded as money and may be redeemed by the holder for actual money on a given day. **2.** A request for payment by a third party. For example, if one writes a check to a seller, the seller demands payment from the bank out of the funds it holds on behalf of the buyer. In this case, the check is a bill of credit.

Bill of Enclosure An act of the British Parliament that joined two or more strips of land into a single property. Since the Middle Ages, English landowners could, by mutual consent, join their properties into an enclosure, which consolidated use of land and was thus beneficial for farming. Many large landowners around villages enclosed their lands, leaving small landowners with patches surrounded by large tracts. The large landowners could petition Parliament to force the small landowners to cede their land to the enclosure. Parliament did this by passing a bill of enclosure. Bills of enclosure were passed most commonly in the late 18th and early 19th centuries. See also: Eminent domain.

Bill of Exchange A document requiring payment by one party to another for a good or service the party demanding payment provided. See also: Receipt.

Bill of Goods 1. A list of goods a salesman offers to sell. **2.** A communication a salesman makes to convince someone to buy something he/she otherwise would not.

Bill of Health A certificate stating a ship or other vessel embarked from a place not known to have any contagious diseases or other illnesses that might harm public health. Bills of health are especially common on ships coming from a part of the world thought, correctly or incorrectly, to contain an unusually high number of communicable diseases.

Bill of Lading A document in which a seller agrees to use a certain transportation to ship a good to a certain location. The bill of lading details the type, quality, and quantity of the good. It also serves as the receipt upon arrival at the destination.

Bill of Materials A catalog of all materials needed to create a marketable item. For example, the bill of materials for a chest of drawers may list the frame, the individual drawers, the handles, the screws, the packaging and so forth. A bill of materials is organized hierarchically; that is, the product is listed at the top and all materials are below. See also: Bill of activities.

Bill of Parcels A document stating the items contained in a package of goods being transported from the seller to the buyer. It also contains the price of each good. The bill of parcels helps resolve any disputes that may result from the transaction. It is also called a package list.

Bill of Rights A generic term referring to a (usually concise) list of rights that citizens of a state possess. For example, a bill of rights may include the freedom to practice religion and the freedom to vote for the candidate of one's choice. There are two types of bill of rights. An entrenched bill of rights may not be amended without a complicated process, such as a popular referendum. An unentrenched bill of rights, on the other hand, may be amended or changed by normal legislative procedure. See also: Constitution.

Bill of Sale A document a seller gives to a buyer stating that a sale occurred on a given date, at a given place, for a given amount of compensation. A bill of sale is a type of receipt and may be used as proof in court if there is a dispute. See also: Absolute bill of sale, Condition bill of sale.

Bill Pass A situation in which the U.S. Federal Reserve buys Treasury bills in order to finance the debt of the federal government.

Bill Payment The regular reception of compensation for a repeated service. For example, paying the rent is a form of bill payment because it is done each month.

Bill Presentment A message delivered to a debtor describing what he/she owes a creditor for a given month. Any person who pays his/her regular bills online is eligible for bill presentment. For example, a credit card company may present a bill each month to a card holder. See also: Electronic bill presentment.

Bill Rate 1. The amount that a company or professional charges per hour of work. For example, the bill rate for an attorney may be $300 per hour. **2.** The interest rate on a debt security with a maturity of one year or less.

Bill To/Ship To On an order to buy a good, an instruction to send the good itself and the invoice to different addresses.

Billboard A large structure found outside in a high traffic area on which a person or company can place an advertisement in exchange for a fee. A billboard is a common form of advertising for products likely to appeal to drivers or pedestrians, or to increase the visibility of companies in the immediate vicinity of the billboard. Less commonly, a billboard is called a bleed poster or a painted bulletin.

Billboard Advertising The practice of using a large structure found outside in a high traffic area to place an advertisement in exchange for a fee. Billboard advertising is common for products likely to appeal to drivers or pedestrians, or to increase the visibility of companies in the immediate vicinity of the billboard.

Billboard Allowance The money that a company allocates to advertise on billboards. The billboard allowance may be a subset of the wider marketing budget.

Billed Weight The weight of a good being shipped as recorded on the waybill. This is used in calculating the amount the shipper is paid for transportation services.

Billiard An alternate term for one quadrillion, or 10^15. The term was coined in Germany during the hyperinflation under the Weimar Republic in the early 1920s.

Billing 1. The process by which a seller sends demands for payment to one or more buyers. Billing may occur once if the buyer pays in full, or it may occur regularly (such as once a month) in an installment plan. **2.** A department in a company that deals with billing.

Billing Cycle In an installment plan, the time between the days on which a company sends two invoices to a customer. For example, if a company sends a bill on April 1 and another on May 1, the billing cycle runs from April 2 to April 30.

Billing Error Any mistake on a bill resulting from the seller's mistake. For example, a company may add what is owed incorrectly or accidentally omit a credit it should have included. The buyer does not have to pay billing errors, though the dispute may take some time to resolve.

Billing on a Long-Term Contract The amount that a company charges a customer for a project that takes a substantial period of time, often one year or longer.

Billing Series A way in which a company attempts to collect on a credit sale. A billing series takes the form of a series of progressively more stern letters. For example, the first letter may invite the customer to pay while thanking her for the purchase. The final letter often threatens legal action or to report the buyer to a credit agency. Employing a billing series is common for periodicals and similar companies.

Billion 1. One thousand million in the short scale numbering system. **2.** One million million in the long scale number system. This number is known, perhaps more commonly, as one trillion.

Billon An alloy of silver consisting of pure silver mixed with copper. It is used in the production of some coins.

Bill-Over-Bond Spread The difference in yield between a Treasury bill and some stated bond. The bill-over-bond spread measures the extra return one may receive from investing in one or the other, or it may measure the risk of the bond over the Treasury bill, which is considered riskless. See also: Municipals-over-bonds spread.

Bills Payable 1. Debt that a bank must pay to another bank, often but not always the central bank of the country in which it operates. **2.** More generally, any bill of exchange, trade acceptance or similar obligation a company must pay on or by a certain date. See also: Accounts payable.

Bills Receivable Any bill of exchange, trade acceptance, or similar obligation a company is owed and must be paid on or by a certain date. See also: Accounts receivable.

Bill-To Party The person or company listed on an invoice or some other demand for payment as the party responsible for paying for a good or service. The bill-to party is often, but not always, the buyer of the good or service.

Bimetal Plate In printing, a plate using two metals, copper and either stainless steel or aluminum. A bimetal plate is used to print several thousand copies because it more durable and less susceptible to corrosion than either of the metals on their own. Because of this, bimetal plates are more expensive than other printing plates.

Bimetallism A monetary system in which a currency is exchangeable for a certain amount of either gold or silver. Bimetallism establishes a fixed exchange rate between gold and silver. As with other hard money systems, bimetallism can be unstable, as currency may be hoarded when the supply and demand of either gold or silver exceeds the stated value of the currency. Proponents of bimetallism opposed the gold standard because they believed it to be excessively deflationary. This was a subject of intense debate in the late 19th century in the United States.

Bimodal Distribution A probability distribution with two outcomes more likely than all other outcomes and approximately equally probable with respect to each other. On a chart, a bimodal distribution looks roughly like two waves with the waves cresting at about the same point.

Binary Answer A slang term used when one asks for a yes or no answer. The term is most commonly used when the one asking a question believes a response is evasive or misleading.

Binary Numeral System A system in which all letters, numbers, and other characters are saved in a computer as some combination of the digits 0 and 1. This system is used in nearly all modern computing.

Binary Option An option contract in which the payoff is some set price or nothing. For example, suppose the strike price on a binary option is $100 and the payoff is $250. If the underlying asset is above $100 when the option is exercised, one receives $250. Otherwise, one does not receive anything. A binary option is also called an all-or-nothing option. See also: Exotic option.

Binational Dispute Settlement Panel A panel set up under a bilateral investment treaty or a free trade agreement to negotiate disputes between companies or governments of the signatory parties. Among other advantages, this enables parties to the treaty to avoid deciding which country's law applies in a particular case.

Binational Secretariat An office charged with the enforcement of a bilateral investment treaty or a free trade agreement. A binational secretariat may have an office in the capital cities of both parties to the treaty. A binational secretariat is charged specifically with helping to resolve disputes resulting from the treaty.

Binder Allowance A reduction in the purchase price of a bulk order of a periodical given to an airline, doctor's office, or other company to compensate them for the cost of the plastic binders to protect them from wear resulting from use by multiple readers.

Bind-In An advertisement in a periodical such as a magazine that includes a perforated card enabling the recipient to respond. That is, the bind-in makes it as easy as possible for a potential customer to buy the product being advertised.

Bind-In Order Card A perforated card attached to a bind-in allowing the recipient to respond. A bind-in is an advertisement in a periodical such as a magazine that includes the order card to make it as easy as possible for a potential customer to buy the product being advertised. The bind-in order card usually requires information like an address to which the product can be shipped, and some method of payment.

Binding 1. In printing, the process that collates and attaches pages to each other to create the finished book or periodical. Binding is also called the bindery line. **2.** See: Binding a Tariff. **3.** For insurance, see: Binding receipt.

Binding a Tariff A promise by a country not to raise its tariffs for the foreseeable future. Binding a tariff is considered favorable for international trade because it gives potential exporters and importers a level of certainty they otherwise would not have. The World Trade Organization encourages tariff binding.

Binding Authority A precedent decided by a higher court. Lower courts are required to follow binding authority when deciding similar cases. For example, precedents decided by the U.S. Supreme Court are binding authority on all American courts.

Binding Decision 1. A decision that binds the parties affected by it and that they may not appeal. A binding decision may be the result of arbitration, the appeal to the highest court possible or a decision by a regulatory agency. **2.** See: Binding authority.

Binding Receipt A temporary contract requiring an insurance company to provide stated coverage to a policyholder so long as that policyholder makes premium payments on time.

Binding Tariff Classification Ruling A decision by a regulator as to the tariff classification code used on a good. The binding ruling is effective for a certain number of years, and may affect the tariff paid on that good.

Binomial Distribution The distribution of successes and failures of a certain number of Bernoulli trials. A Bernoulli trial is a test in which there are precisely two random outcomes: success and failure. For example, if one is testing whether flipping a coin will result in heads, the two outcomes are yes (success) or no (failure). A binomial distribution, then, would be the number of heads compared to the number of tails in a given number of flips. It is also called a Bernoulli distribution.

Binomial Model A model for mathematically pricing options. The model divides the time between the writing of an option and its expiration into many small increments. It considers changes to the price of the underlying asset during each increment and how that would affect what the option price ought to be. Along with the Black-Scholes model, it is a very common option pricing model.

Binomial Process The division of a time period into several increments, during each of which one of two things may occur. During the next increment, one of two other things may happen. The binomial process is used in some decision making processes; it also provides the mathematical basis for the binomial model for pricing option contracts.

Biochemical Warfare The open use by a nation state of biological or chemical agents to kill, injure or incapacitate its enemy. There are numerous examples of biochemical warfare dating back thousands of years. See also: Biochemterrorism.

Biochemterrorism The use by a non-state group, or the secret use by a nation state, of biological or chemical agents to kill, injure or incapacitate one's political enemy. There are numerous examples of biochemterrorism dating back thousands of years. See also: Biochemical warfare.

Biochemterrorist A non-state person or group that uses biological or chemical agents to kill, injure, or incapacitate one's political enemy. A state that uses these agents may also be considered a biochemterrorist. There are numerous examples of biochemterrorism dating back thousands of years. See also: Biochemical warfare.

Biological Agent A living thing such as a fungus or virus that is used in biological ammunition. A biological agent is used in biowarfare and bioterrorism. Well known examples include anthrax and bubonic plague.

Biological Ammunition Ammunition in a weapon that primarily discharges biological agents. An example of a potential biological ammunition is anthrax.

Biological Weapons Convention An international treaty forbidding signatories from developing or possessing weapons that may be used in biowarfare. It requires signatories to dispose of or change the use of the biological weapons they possess at the time of signature and mandates assistance to countries suffering from violations of the treaty. Most of the world's countries are signatories to the Biological Weapons Convention. Twenty-two original nations signed the Convention in 1972, and it became effective in 1975.

Biometrics The process of recognizing a human being using one or more inherent physical traits. For example, one may identify a criminal using his/her fingerprints. Biometric products are used for a variety of government and commercial purposes, often for security.

Biotechnology The use of living things, such as one-cell organisms, in technological innovations. Biotechnology has particular applications in medicine, agriculture, engineering, and similar fields. Biotech organizations may make and market their own products, or they may be departments within another company, such as a pharmaceutical corporation.

Bioterrorism The use by a non-state group, or the secret use by a nation state, of germs and other living beings to kill, injure or incapacitate one's enemy. There are numerous examples of bioterrorism dating back thousands of years. See also: Biowarfare.

Bioterrorist A non-state person or group that uses germs and other living beings to kill, injure, or incapacitate an enemy. States that use biological weapons secretly may also be considered bioterrorists. There are numerous examples of bioterrorism dating back thousands of years. See also: Biowarfare.

Biowarfare The open use by a nation state of germs and other living beings to kill, injure or incapacitate its enemy. There are numerous examples of biowarfare dating back thousands of years. The Biological Weapons Convention was intended to stop biowarfare, but some analysts believe nation states have further developed their capacity to conduct war in this way. See also: Bioterrorism.

Bipartisan Describing any measure or policy that draws support from two political parties. For example, in the United States, a unanimously passed defense bill may be said to be bipartisan. The term is used in countries with de facto or de jure two-party systems.

Bird Dog In auto sales, a salesperson or other party who refers a potential customer to another salesperson in exchange for a portion of the commission.

Birdtable Slang; to discuss a matter before a formal meeting. Birdtabling may help participants prepare for a meeting. It may also involve assigning projects to the participants.

Birr The currency of Ethiopia. It was introduced in 1945, replacing the East African shilling, though an earlier birr had been the currency prior to the East African campaign and the Italian occupation of Ethiopia. It is noted for its high rate of inflation, estimated at over 11% in 2005 and 41% in 2008. Interestingly, the official translation of the birr was "dollar" until 1976, when "birr" became the appropriate word in both Amharic and English.

Birth Rate The number of babies born per 1,000 women of childbearing age in a population. This may be used to help calculate population growth. It is also called the fertility rate.

Biscuit In the United Kingdom, a slang term for 1,000 pounds. The term gained currency in the gambling industry as 1,000-pound chips are larger than others, looking like biscuits or cookies.

Bismerpund A Norwegian unit of weight approximately equivalent to six kilograms.

Bissi In India, a slang term for a 20-paisa coin, which is worth 1/5 of one Indian rupee.

Bit The smallest unit of information a computer can hold in its memory. A bit is always represented as a 0 or a 1 in binary code. The word is a contraction of "binary digit."

BITNET A network cooperative that predated wide use of the Internet. It allowed universities that joined and purchased modems to share information with each other. Formed between Yale and the City University of New York in 1981, it was used by many universities worldwide during the 1980s. By the mid-1990s, however, it had largely disintegrated.

Biweekly Describing anything that occurs every two weeks, such as a payment. Biweekly payments differ from other payments that occur once per month. See also: Biweekly loan, Biweekly mortgage.

Biweekly Loan A loan in which the property buyer makes payments every two weeks instead of once per month. Both payments could apply to principal and interest, or one of the payments could pay down the principal exclusively. Because of the extra payment, a biweekly loan is repaid faster, which saves the buyer additional interest payments. It is, however, more expensive in the short and medium terms; the bank may also charge extra fees for changing the payments to a biweekly structure.

Bi-Weekly Mortgage Loan A mortgage in which the property buyer makes payments every two weeks instead of once per month. Both payments could apply to principal and interest, or one of the payments could pay down the principal exclusively. Because of the extra payment, a bi-weekly mortgage is repaid faster, which saves the buyer additional interest payments. It is, however, more expensive in the short and medium terms; the bank may also charge extra fees for changing the payments to a bi-weekly structure.

Biza An obsolete unit of mass in Pegu, Burma, approximately equivalent to 1,568 grams. It was used to weigh gold and silver.

BJ **1.** ISO 3166-1 alpha-2 code for the Republic of Benin. This is the code used in international transactions to and from Beninese bank accounts. **2.** ISO 3166-2 geocode for Benin. This is used as an international standard for shipping to Benin. Each Beninese department has its own code with the prefix "BJ." For example, the code for Alibori Department is ISO 3166-2:BJ-AL.

Black Informal; describing a financial statement that ends with a positive assessment. For example, if a company produces a profit for a given period of time, it is said to be "in the black." The term comes from the color of ink used for such statements. See also: Red.

Black and White Describing an advertisement, especially one containing pictures, that lacks any color other than black and white. Because colors are more expensive than black ink on white paper, and because they are less likely to attract attention, black and white advertisements are comparatively inexpensive.

Black Book An optical disc that does not follow the standards for DVD, CD or Blu-ray players. Most video games for PlayStation, Xbox and similar consoles are stored and sold on black book discs.

Black Box **1.** Any complex investment strategy or model. In general, a black box involves a computer using complicated formulas to achieve returns in the desired way. Because an investor may not understand the model (and may not be able to do so), a black box can lead to unforeseen problems. See also: Black box syndrome. **2.** In Islamic finance, a strategy that allows one to invest funds in a Sharia-compliant way but still link the returns to non-compliant investments. Using a black box is very controversial and some Islamic finance scholars reject it as un-Islamic.

Black Box Model Any system into which one inputs information and receives output based on an algorithm the system uses. It is called a black box because one need not understand how a model works in order to use it.

Black Box Syndrome Unforeseen problems or difficulties arising from the use of a complex investment strategy, especially one involving complex mathematical formulas requiring a computer. The black box syndrome may result from lack of transparency in a model, or perhaps from an investor's misunderstanding of its ramifications.

Black Friday **1.** In the United States, the day after Thanksgiving. Black Friday is considered the first day of the Christmas shopping season each year. It is noted for discounts and special offers on retail goods. Some retailers open at midnight to create an air of importance for the day and thus maximize shopping hours. It is one of the busiest shopping days of the year. **2.** In the United Kingdom, the last Friday before Christmas. It is the most common day for office Christmas parties and, as such, is one of the busiest days of the year for restaurants, pubs and catering companies. **3.** September 24, 1869. On this day, the United States gold market fell precipitously following a price manipulation by James Fisk and Jay Gould. During the Civil War a few years before, American money was backed by the full faith and credit of the United States, but not by a commodity like gold or silver. Following the War, the federal government began buying back this currency with gold and then using the currency to redeem government bonds; this stabilized the currency but caused the price of gold to drop to its lowest level in years. Fisk and Gould took advantage of this and began buying gold, which caused the price to increase. In the process, they attempted to convince U.S. President Ulysses Grant to limit the release of gold, which drove the price even higher. The conspiracy came to a head on Black Friday when Treasury Secretary George Boutwell realized what was happening and released a large amount of government-owned gold. This caused the price to crash.

Black Hole Slang; a project that takes an inordinate amount of time to complete. For example, if a contractor spends so much time on one client that she cannot devote enough time to other clients to satisfy their needs, the first client is known as a black hole. The term is most common in accounting and auditing.

Black Knight A company that is offering or executing a hostile takeover. If a firm makes an offer to shareholders to acquire a publicly-traded company after the board of directors refuses, or if it bypasses the board completely, one refers to the acquiring firm as a black knight. This is a derogatory term, and so one might expect the board, management, or even employees to use it more than shareholders.

Black List A list of persons and/or organizations excluded from a privilege or service. For example, people who have written bad checks at a store may be put on a black list and not allowed to enter or buy from that store. The term has a pejorative connotation, and often refers to persons excluded for questionable reasons. For example, a business association may maintain a black list of union members or a union may do the same for current and former business lobbyists.

Black List State A U.S. state maintaining a list of insurance companies that are not allowed to provide surplus line insurance in that state. Surplus line insurance is provided in special circumstances by a company not otherwise authorized to provide insurance in a certain state. A black list state restricts these activities.

Black Market A market for products that are illegal, stolen, or otherwise need to be hidden from regulatory authorities. A black market encompasses the horrific (e.g. human trafficking) as well as the more mundane (e.g. participating in the market to evade taxes). Legal products on a black market are usually less expensive than on the regulated market because sellers do not pay taxes on their goods and services. That said, there is little or no recourse for the customer if and when a black market product fails. It is worth noting that black markets tend to be largest in jurisdictions where there are the most regulations and government monopolies. It is also known as an underground market.

Black Market Exchange Rate An exchange rate for a currency that differs from the official exchange rate set by a government. The black market exchange rate occurs when the official rate bears little or no relationship to the currency's actual value. Using the black market exchange rate can be a punishable offense in the country issuing the affected currency.

Black Mold A fungus associated with poor air quality indoors. Economically, it can be a concern when considering the purchase of a water damaged building. Its scientific name is Stachybotrys chartarum.

Black Monday October 28, 1929. The date of one of the large stock market crashes that presaged the Great Depression. While the Great Depression had already begun in some areas, Black Monday, which followed Black Thursday, showed that the crash of the previous week was not a one-time event and helped mark the end of the speculative bubble that had characterized most investing in the 1920s. Black Tuesday followed the next day. The Great Depression contributed to the formation of most regulation still in force today.

Black Money A scam in which the scammer attempts to convince a victim that black construction paper (or similar material) is in fact dyed money. Such scammers send e-mails stating that they have a large amount of money that has been dyed black to avoid customs. The scammer then asks the victim to pay for the chemicals to take off the dye in exchange for a percentage of the money. An alternate version of the scam involves actually showing the dyed "money" to a potential victim. It originated around 2000.

Black Plate A printing plate that only uses black ink. A print advertisement only using a black plate is less expensive that one using color.

Black Scholes Model A model for mathematically pricing options. The model takes into account the strike price, the time until the expiration date, the price of the underlying asset, and the standard deviation of the underlying asset's return. The model assumes that the option can only be exercised on the expiration date, that it will provide a risk-free return, and that the volatility of the underlying asset will remain constant throughout the life of the contract. The calculation is slightly different for calls and puts. See also: Option Adjusted Spread, Option Pricing Curve.

Black Thursday The date of the first large stock market crash that presaged the Great Depression. While the Great Depression had already begun in some areas, Black Thursday marked the end of the speculative bubble that had marked most investing in the 1920s. Black Thursday occurred on October 24, 1929, with Black Monday and Black Tuesday following the next week. The Great Depression contributed to the formation of most regulation still in force today.

Black Tuesday The date of the third large stock market crash that presaged the Great Depression. While the Great Depression had already begun in some areas, Black Tuesday confirmed fears felt by investors that the end of the speculative bubble that had marked most investing in the 1920s had arrived. Black Tuesday occurred on October 29, 1929; on this day, the Dow Jones Industrial Average lost nearly 12% of its value after having lost almost 13% the previous day on Black Monday. The Great Depression contributed to the formation of most regulation still in force today. See also: Black Thursday.

Black Wednesday September 16, 1992. The day that investor George Soros short sold more than $10 billion worth of British pounds, which forced the Bank of England to withdraw from the European Exchange Rate Mechanism and to devalue the pound. He is a noted critic of unfettered free enterprise and believes that reflexivity can change the fundamentals of an economy.

Blackberry A mobile phone with access to e-mail and the Internet as well as online faxing. Its modern model was introduced in 2002. It is commonly used in business and other professional communication because it allows portable access to e-mail.

Blackboard Trading The practice of trading on commodities or futures on an exchange floor with an actual blackboard. That is, trades are written on the blackboard and erased when they are no longer relevant. Blackboard trading has become rather unusual, but it is useful on small exchanges or for securities with light trading volume.

Black-Box Accounting A slightly pejorative term used to describe highly and deliberately complex accounting methods. Companies usually use black-box accounting when they wish to appear more financially stable than they are. In doing so, they may report their earnings using overly-sophisticated methods designed to hide losses or boost profits. In explaining the methodology, companies may use unnecessarily technical language and/or include extraneous information in order to confuse the casual reader. It is thought to take a skilled person to "decode" black-box accounting.

Black-Derman-Toy Model A popular model for predicting future interest rates. It assumes short-term interest rates determine future long-term rates. It also assumes these short-term rates revert to their mean and have a logarithmic distribution, meaning the logarithm of possible future rates has a normal distribution. The model was developed in the 1980s.

Blackmail A crime in which one threatens to reveal damaging information about another unless the former is paid some amount of money or is given something of value. For example, one may threaten to reveal information about an extramarital affair or evidence that the other person committed a crime unless one is paid $100,000. Legally, blackmail is a form of extortion.

Blackout **1.** A situation in which local television and radio stations do not broadcast a live sports match or similar event. A blackout is most common when a company wishes to increase ticket sales for the event. The blackout may be canceled if the event sells all tickets a certain number of days before. **2.** See: Blackout period.

Blackout Period The period of time during which an employee may not make any changes to his/her employer-sponsored retirement plan. This usually occurs when the plan is being restructured or when administrative changes are being made. For example, a company may institute a blackout period if it is moving management of its retirement plans to a different brokerage. A blackout period normally lasts approximately 60 days. It is also called the lockdown.

Black-Plate Change A change in a print-out that only involves altering text or something else printed with black ink. One may make a black-plate change to update an advertisement or to attach a special message to one segment of a campaign. A black-plate change is cheap compared to changes involving multiple colors.

Blair House Agreement An agreement between the United States and the European Union to reduce subsidies to exporters and domestic producers. These subsidies were given to make products cheaper at their final destinations; this type of arrangement is thought to reduce competition and to harm international trade. The Agreement was concluded in 1992 in order to bring the U.S. and the EU into compliance with the Uruguay Round.

Blamestorming The act, especially in a meeting setting, of seeking someone to blame (often but not always someone in the meeting) for a project or something else that has gone wrong. For example, if a marketing campaign fails, a company may have a blamestorming session to decide who has to take the fall for the whole company.

Blank Bill A bill of sale or bill of exchange on which the name of the payee (that is, the person or organization who receives compensation) is not listed. The payee is assumed to be the physical possessor of the blank bill. See also: Blank check.

Blank Check **1.** A check made payable to a certain person, organization, or to cash, and signed by the writer with the amount of the check left blank. That is, a blank check allows the payee (or anyone else) to determine the amount of the check. A blank check can be very dangerous, especially if one is made to a person the writer does not trust or if the payee does not know how much is in the writer's account. It easily can lead to (sometimes significant) overdrafts. **2.** Informal for a situation or transaction requiring a great deal of trust between the parties.

Blank Check Offering An initial public offering made by a company that has not yet defined its business operations. Black check offerings are usually penny stocks; the funds raised through a blank check offering must usually be placed in an escrow account until certain conditions have been met. Because a blank check company has not begun, or even defined, its operations, it effectively asks investors to trust it. Blank check offerings are therefore subject to extra regulation to protect these investors from the possibility that the company is a fraud. In any event, investing in a blank check offering is always speculative. See also: Rule 419.

Blank Check Preferred Stock An amendment to the charter of a publicly-traded company allowing the board of directors to issue new preferred stock without shareholder approval. Blank check preferred stock is usually an anti-takeover measure.

Blank Stock A stock that is issued to investors without any rights attached to it. That is, whether the stock comes with voting rights, guaranteed dividends, or anything else is determined by the board of directors after issue. See also: Blank Check Preferred Stock.

Blank Transfer The sale or other transfer of securities in which the name of the buyer or transferee is not recorded. Thus, the physical holder of the certificate is assumed to be the new owner of the securities. With the increase in electronic recording of security sales, blank transfers have become less frequent. It should not be confused with blank stock.

Blank-Check Company A company that has not yet defined its business operations. Blank check companies issue penny stocks; the funds raised through a blank check offering must usually be placed in an escrow account until certain conditions have been met. Because a blank check company has not begun or even defined its operations, it effectively asks investors to trust it. Blank check companies are therefore subject to extra regulation to protect these investors from the possibility that the company is a fraud. In any event, investing in a blank check company is always speculative.

Blanket **1.** See: Blanket insurance. **2.** See: Blanket mortgage. **3.** See: Blanket purchase order.

Blanket Appropriation In accounting, an appropriation to a department or project that does not specify the things on which that department or project can spend money. That is, the blanket appropriation gives the heads of departments the authority to spend the blanket appropriation as they see fit. Blanket appropriations are most common in government budgeting.

Blanket Bond A bond or insurance policy covering a company in the event it loses money as the result of employee theft or fraud. It is important to note that blanket bonds generally only cover situations in which an employee commits fraud for personal gain; it does not cover situations in which the employee (without support or knowledge of management) falsifies trading so that it makes the company appear healthier that it is. The Federal Bonding Program, which is run through the Department of Labor, insures or guarantees the insurance of ex-offenders whose employment adds significant risk of theft or fraud. See also: Bonding, Operational risk.

Blanket Certificate of Origin In international trade, a certificate of origin covering identical goods being sent to the same importer at intervals. For example, if an importer buys 100 barrels of refined oil every day for a year, the exporter may obtain a blanket certificate to cover all barrels for the entire year rather than procuring separate daily certificates of origin. A blanket certificate of origin may specify the period during which it is effective.

Blanket Contract A contract between an advertiser and a media company such as a television station or a newspaper that governs all products the advertiser attempts to sell through that media company. The blanket contract is directly between the advertiser and the media company; it excludes any relationship the advertiser may have with an advertising agency.

Blanket Crime Policy An insurance policy that provides coverage for all financial crimes that result in losses to a business. For example, a blanket crime policy covers employee theft, lost deposits, acceptance of counterfeit money and so forth. Blanket crime policies have become less common with the increase in popularity of specific policies provided in a commercial crime coverage form.

Blanket Fidelity Bond A bond or insurance policy covering a company in the event it loses money as the result of employee theft or fraud. It is important to note that blanket fidelity bonds generally only cover situations in which an employee commits fraud for personal gain; it does not cover situations in which the employee, without support or knowledge of management, falsifies trading so that it makes the company appear healthier than it is. The Federal Bonding Program, run by the Department of Labor, insures or guarantees the insurance of ex-offenders whose employment adds significant risk of theft or fraud. The SEC requires brokerages to be covered by a blanket fidelity bond. See also: Bonding, Operational Risk.

Blanket Honesty Bond A bond or insurance policy covering a company in the event it loses money as the result of employee or unidentified theft or fraud. A blanket honesty bond provides a limit of coverage without regard for the number of employees involved. That is, it pays for losses up to a certain amount whether one or several employees were guilty of a crime. This differentiates it from a blanket position bond. As with similar bonds and policies, it does not cover situations in which the employee (without support or knowledge of management) falsifies trading to make the company appear healthier than it is. See also: Bonding, Operational risk.

Blanket Insurance **1.** An insurance policy that covers two or more properties or the same property at two or more locations. For example, a blanket insurance policy may provide coverage for both a house and the furniture inside it. Alternatively, a policy may cover a person's furniture both at his/her house and in his/her storage unit in another town. **2.** See: Blanket bond.

Blanket Lien A lien on all or nearly all of a debtor's assets. In the event of default, the creditor has the right to take, and, at its discretion, sell off any or all of the assets covered under the blanket lien. Generally speaking, a blanket lien covers multiple assets that are specifically enumerated on the loan agreement, though, occasionally, a creditor can take other assets not listed as well. Some businesses use blanket liens to receive short-term financing.

Blanket Limit The maximum amount of money an insurance company will pay out in claims on all policies in a geographic area. That is, the limit on all policies that a company underwrites in a given area cannot exceed the blanket limit.

Blanket Medical Expense Insurance A health insurance policy that pays for all medical bills one incurs unless the policy specifically excludes them. For example, a blanket medical expense insurance policy may cover all illnesses and injuries provided they are not self-inflicted. Blanket medical expense coverage is considered the most comprehensive insurance policy one can have.

Blanket Mortgage A single mortgage used to buy more than one piece of property. The multiple properties serve as collateral for the blanket mortgage, but they may be sold individually. Real estate developers may use blanket mortgages to consolidate the borrowing necessary to buy properties for their businesses. In addition to paying for the properties underlying the mortgage, a real estate developer may use a blanket mortgage to cover the cost of developing the property.

Blanket Position Bond A bond or insurance policy covering a company in the event it loses money as the result of employee theft or fraud. Unlike a blanket fidelity bond, it provides a limit of coverage per employee rather than per event or per company. That is, it pays for losses up to a certain amount multiplied by the number of employees involved. As with similar bonds and policies, it does not cover situations in which the employee (without support or knowledge of management) falsifies trading to make the company appear healthier than it is. See also: Bonding, Operational risk.

Blanket Purchase Order An order to buy the same good or service regularly. For example, if a company buys 100 barrels of refined oil every day for a year, it may make a blanket order to cover all barrels for the entire year rather than making separate daily purchase orders. A blanket purchase order may specify the period during which it is effective.

Blanket Rate An interest rate or price that applies to all goods or services of the same type. That is, a blanket rate does not vary according to special circumstances.

Blanket Recommendation A recommendation to buy or sell a security that a broker or investment advisor makes to all her clients. Many analysts advise against following a blanket recommendation because doing so may not advance one's individual investment goals. In fact, following a blanket recommendation may seriously harm a client, depending on the client's risk tolerance, level of diversification and other matters.

Blauer A nickname for the 100-deutschmark banknote. It means "the blue one" since the 100 mark note was blue.

Bleed **1.** To lose money in a venture or investment over time. Bleeding may occur fast or slowly, but never improves. See also: Stop the bleeding. **2.** To extract an excessively high price in a transaction or venture under threat of force or some other harm. Bleeding in this sense is illegal.

Bleed Ad A full page advertisement in a newspaper or magazine that leaves no margin. That is, the ad extends all the way to the edge of the page on at least one side. Bleed ads are more expensive than other full page ads.

Bleed in the Gutter In marketing, an advertisement in a newspaper or magazine that extends on two pages down the middle column. See also: Bleed ad.

Bleeding a Project In real estate, overstating expenses in a new construction or neglecting to pay normal operating expenses in an existing structure in order to extract the highest possible profit. For example, a landlord may refuse to pay for a new air conditioner in a building it is renting to a restaurant. Bleeding a project is considered unsustainable because it is difficult to maintain quality tenants or customers and leads to a reduction in the value of the property.

Bleeding Edge The latest, flashiest graphic technology, especially on the Internet. The bleeding edge may be used in a pejorative sense to refer to advertisers that sacrifice quality for the perceived showiness of online ads.

Blemish Any scuff or other mark on the surface of a coin. This may reduce a coin's value as a collector's item, even if the coin does not circulate. See also: Numismatics.

Blend Fund A mutual fund that invests in some combination of value stocks and growth stocks. That is, a blend fund attempts to hedge its risk by investing in stocks that are considered to be generally stable while at the same time attempting a high return by investing in high risk, usually new, stocks. A blend fund may invest in small cap, medium cap, or large cap companies, or some combination of the three. A blend fund is also called a hybrid fund and became relatively common because of promotion by Morningstar, Inc. See also: Dual-Purpose Fund.

Blended Insurance Program Insurance that combines the profit-sharing and other advantages of finite insurance with the complete transfer of risk that comes with traditional insurance. It is also called an integrated insurance program.

Blended Price The average price of a share in a two-tier tender offer, weighted by tier. For example, if 70% of shares in Company A are bought for $10 and the remaining 30% are bought for $2, the blended price is expressed as ((.7)10 + (.3)2). Company A's blended price is $7.60.

Blended Rate 1. A weighted average interest rate on all of a person's or company's debt. The blended rate provides the aggregate interest rate for debt. For example, if one pays 5% on $50,000 in debt and 10% on $25,000 in other debt, the blended rate is calculated as: Blended Rate = (50,000 * 0.05 + 25,000 * 0.10) / 75,000 = 6.67%. **2.** When refinancing a loan, an interest rate higher than the previous rate, but lower than the rate the bank would charge on a new loan. A blended rate may be used after a bank has raised its prevailing rates.

Blended Value Describing a business model that combines profitability with social benefit. For example, a company that makes money writing grants for school districts has blended value because it carries the value of the company itself along with the added value of its social responsibility. Because ethics are difficult to quantify as value, the blended value is hard to calculate. However, retail products with blended value (such as free range eggs) are generally more expensive than comparable products without blended value.

Blending Describing a strategy, price or anything else that combines two or more factors. For example, a blended fund includes both value stocks and growth stocks. Likewise, a blended rate is often the average of two or more interest rates.

Blight Dilapidated or abandoned property. Blight causes low property values in the surrounding area, and is strongly associated with crime and capital flight. Many municipalities take steps to reduce blight; for example, a city may offer a tax incentive for a business to move into a blighted area or a grant to repair a building. Some blighted areas, however, are considered to be beyond repair.

Blighted Area A location where multiple buildings are dilapidated or abandoned. Blighted areas are marked by low property values, crime and capital flight. Many municipalities take steps to reduce blight; for example, a city may offer a tax incentive for a business to move into a blighted area or a grant to repair a building. Some blighted areas, however, are considered to be beyond repair.

Blind Bid A bid, usually by a portfolio manager, to buy a portfolio of stocks without knowing what stocks are included. Blind bids are useful when the portfolio manager wishes to buy stocks without affecting their market prices. Obviously, however, not knowing what stocks are included can be quite risky.

Blind Brokering A securities trade in which the buyer and the seller do not know each other's identities. Most transactions on an exchange occur on a blind broker basis; a major exception occurs when a brokerage is trading on its own account with its own client. Blind brokering ensures anonymity in trading unless conflict of interest requires disclosure.

Blind Copy A copy of a letter or e-mail sent to a person without the knowledge of the primary recipient. In e-mail, blind copy is represented on the "bcc" line.

Blind Embossing An impression made on paper without ink. For example, a seal may be blindly embossed on an official document, or it may prepare a paper for further modification. Blind embossing is also called blind stamping.

Blind Entry A debit or credit on an account that only includes the amount and a description of where the money came from or went. That is, a blind entry does not include an explanation of why the money was spent or collected.

Blind Headline In printing, a headline with no meaning or an unclear meaning. Blind headlines are sometimes used to attract eyes to an advertisement, but, in general, writers try to avoid them.

Blind Offer A textual advertisement that contains a request for reader response toward the end or in an otherwise inconspicuous place. The advertiser or advertising agency measures the number or responses a blind offer receives and uses this information to gauge how closely most viewers read the advertisement. A blind offer is also called a hidden offer or a buried offer.

Blind Perf A perforation that is only on one side of a page. A blind perf is usually used if a page has advertisements on each side and the publisher does not want the perforation of one to distract readers of the other.

Blind Pool A limited partnership without any stated investment goals. The blind pool gathers money from investors, who then trust the general partner(s) and managers of the pool to invest wisely. Blind pools have a shaky reputation as the result of some fraud scandals in the 1980s and 1990s. They are most common toward the end of a prolonged bull market, in which investors do not engage in the appropriate due diligence and risk analysis. Legitimate blind pools usually exist for reverse acquisition. In these cases, the general partner(s) choose not to reveal their purposes for fear of scaring away potential investors, especially if the reverse acquisition is high-risk. See also: Transparency.

Blind Trust A trust where the beneficiary is not given knowledge of the assets in it. The trustee has knowledge of the assets and is responsible for investing them on behalf of the beneficiary. A grantor usually sets ups a blind trust to avoid potential conflicts of interest.

Blister Agent A chemical that causes blisters or other severe irritation on human or animal skin. Occasionally, blister agents are used in medical treatments and may have a commercial value for this reason. However, blister agents are usually used in chemical weapons.

Blister Pack A form of packaging for small retail goods that forms fitted bubbles of plastic or aluminum around the individual products. For example, a blister pack forms a plastic cover over the individual pills in a box of medicine. Blister packs and similar packaging have been criticized for wastefulness, particularly because plastic is not biodegradable.

Blitzkrieg Tender Offer In a hostile takeover, an offer from the acquiring company to buy stock from the target company at a price so far above the current market value that investors sell quickly. Ideally, the blitzkrieg tender offer is successful before the target company can react in an organized fashion.

Bloatation Slang; a situation in which a company leaves essential jobs or positions open but instead hires non-essential personnel. Bloatation may be indicative of coming financial problems, perhaps including bankruptcy.

Block An exceptionally large amount or value of securities. While there is no specific definition of how many shares constitute a block, most people using the term refer to holding or trading more than 10,000 shares and/or shares worth more than $200,000. Almost invariably, trades of this magnitude involve institutional investors. See also: Block trade, Secondary issue.

Block Diagram A diagram in which principal ideas or concepts are represented in boxes with labels. The boxes are connected by lines so that ideas related or leading to one another have lines joining them. Block diagrams are commonly used in computer engineering.

Block Grant A large amount of money that a national government gives to a regional government with only general parameters on how it should be spent. For example, the national government may fund a province's medical program, but leave the specifics to the province's own government.

Block Group A location used by the U.S. Census Bureau where approximately 800 to 1,000 people live. As the name indicates, a block group is usually a collection of city blocks. It is a subdivision of a census tract and is the smallest geographical unit for which the Census reports data.

Block Group Selector A computer program that identifies block groups reported by the U.S. Census Bureau most likely to respond to a particular marketing campaign. It may also be used to test which block groups respond.

Block Limit The maximum amount of money an insurance company will pay out in claims on all policies on a city block. That is, the limit on all policies that a company underwrites on a certain block cannot exceed the block limit. It is a type of blanket limit.

Block Move In word processing, the act of copying text (or less commonly, images) from one section of a document and pasting it to another place in that same document. Block moves make editing faster and more efficient.

Block of Policies The insurance policies a company underwrites with the exact same terms and conditions. For example, a particular block of policies may include all life insurance policies with coverage of $100,000 and a monthly premium of $50.

Block Order Exposure System Also called BLOX. A computerized system on the SEAQ allowing institutional investors and London Stock Exchange members' clients to trade large blocks of securities. BLOX reduces the time and expense of working through a broker-dealer. See also: SOES, Small order automatic execution facility.

Block Out 1. In broadcasting, time that ordinarily would be available for sale to advertisers but is not because of a public service announcement, government speech or other reason. **2.** In photography, a portion of a picture that one covers over and re-photographs. This may be used in advertising.

Block Policy An insurance policy that provides coverage for goods while they are in transit between two locations, while they are being delivered to another party, and while they are present on another's property (such as a warehouse). A block policy is a type of all risks policy; that is, it provides coverage for all losses that may occur while the policy is in effect.

Block Positioner A dealer who buys large numbers of securities from an investor in hopes of profiting from future, positive price movements. Block positioners usually use short sales and other hedging strategies to reduce the risk associated with their long positions. They must register with the SEC.

Block Programming In radio and television broadcasting, the practice of airing similar shows for a two to four hour span of time. Block programming is intended to appeal to the same demographic so the audience remains relatively constant for the block programming period. This gives advertisers a long space of time in which to target their products to their most likely customers. It is also called a broadcast block.

Block Trade A trade involving the sale of a large block of securities, usually more than 10,000 shares or $200,000 in value at a time.

Block Trader A dealer who buys and sells large blocks of securities, usually more than 10,000 shares or $200,000 in value at a time.

Block Voting A voting system where a large number of shareholders band together and vote the same way with all of their shares. This gives the block more leverage over shareholder votes. Block voting should not be confused with a block trade, which is a different concept altogether.

Blockade The act of preventing food, medicine, materials and/or other supplies from entering or leaving a country. A blockade occurs when one country sends its military and sets up a perimeter, disallowing the blockaded supplies from being exported or imported. A blockade is an act of war and is obviously disruptive to international trade.

Blockage Discount A discount that an institutional investor applies to a block trade with another institutional investor. That is, if an institutional investor wishes to divest itself of all or most of its holding in a security, it may apply a blockage discount to sell it more quickly. This has the added advantage of not causing a crash in the price of the security because of increased trading volume because the blockage discount causes a trade below the market price.

Blockbuster A real estate agent or company that convinces a homeowner to sell his/her property at a loss because racial and/or ethnic minorities are moving into the area. For example, a blockbuster may hire a Latino woman to walk around a neighborhood and act as though she lives there. Blockbusters seek both to profit from the resale of the house and to encourage people to buy homes in new developments. Blockbusting became common after desegregation, and became very controversial after its public exposure in the 1960s. By the 1980s, the practice had largely disappeared.

Blockbusting An unethical business practice in which a real estate agent convinces a homeowner to sell his/her property at a loss because racial and/or ethnic minorities are moving into the area. For example, a company may hire a Latino woman to walk around a neighborhood and act as though she lives there. Blockbusting was done both to profit from the resale of the house and to encourage people to buy homes in new developments. Blockbusting became common after desegregation, and became very controversial after its public exposure in the 1960s. By the 1980s, the practice had largely disappeared.

Blocked Account A margin account in which the amount of equity is below SEC or brokerage requirements. Such an account is not allowed to buy any more stocks until the level of equity is raised; a portion each sale of stock must be used to pay down the account's debt. Regulation T sets the minimum equity standards, but individual brokerages may set higher standards. In general, however, an account becomes blocked when the market value of the stocks purchased on margin falls below the amount owed on the stocks. A blocked account is sometimes referred to as a restricted account.

Blocked Funds Money generated by a company's foreign operations that cannot be moved from one country to another because of one or more regulations in the country in which the money was generated. For example, a government may place a limit on the maximum amount that may be moved out of a country over a given period of time. Having an excessive amount in blocked funds may harm a company's cash flow. See also: Political risk.

Blockface The side of a city block between two intersections. That is, if a block is a square, a blockface is one side of that square. The U.S. Census Bureau uses this designation.

Blockholder A shareholder with an exceptionally large amount or value of stock. While there is no specific definition of how many shares constitute a block, most people using the term refer to holding or trading more than 10,000 shares and/or shares worth more than $200,000. Almost invariably, blockholders are institutional investors. See also: Block trade, Secondary issue.

Blocking Law A law that restricts an individual's access to a website. A blocking law serves a number of functions. It may prevent the viewing of websites posting copyrighted material without authorization, or it may try to block pornography. Some countries, notably China, block websites thought to be subversive to the government.

Blog A website to which a person or persons may regularly post journal entries or commentaries. A blog may be a personal diary, a collaboration concentrating on a theme or nearly anything in between. Most blogs allow readers to comment on each entry. Some blogs attract large followings and are monetized through advertisements and in other ways. As of 2007, there were more than 100 million blogs worldwide.

Blogger A person who maintains or posts to a blog, which is a website featuring journal entries or commentaries. A blogger may post a personal diary or may be one

of many collaborators concentrating on a theme such as politics or entertainment. Some blogs attract large followings and are monetized through advertisements and in other ways. As of 2007, there were more than 100 million blogs worldwide.

Blood Agent A chemical that causes sickness or death in humans or animals as it is absorbed in the blood. Many blood agents are based on arsenic or cyanide. Blood agents are usually used in poisons or chemical weapons.

Blood Diamond A diamond used to finance a war or rebellion. Blood diamonds are most common in Africa, where diamonds are plentiful and where there a great deal of conflict has taken place in the late 20th and early 21st centuries. Trade in blood diamonds is illegal. In 2003, the United Nations put in place the Kimberley Process to certify diamonds as legitimate. Blood diamonds are also called conflict diamonds.

Bloodletting An intense bear market. Bloodletting occurs when a security or market declines significantly in price very quickly. See also: Panic sell.

Bloomberg A news company that offers real time and historic prices, trends, and analysis of securities, as well as information and reporting on the economy as a whole. Bloomberg covers news in a variety of media, notably using television, radio, the Internet, and its own Bloomberg Terminal, a software program that offers a great deal of information in real time. To a lesser extent, it also offers general news and other coverage. Bloomberg was established by Michael Bloomberg in 1981.

Bloomberg Terminal A software program that offers a great deal of information in real time. It provides prices, trends, and analysis of securities. It is available as a subscription service for a fee. It is owned by Bloomberg LP.

Bloombergsmanship Slang; the ability to read and understand the Bloomberg news service such that one is able to cover the fact that one lacks experience in finance or investing. Bloombergsmanship can be dangerous as it can give the appearance of knowing more than one actually does.

Blotter A book or computer program (more commonly the latter) where a brokerage records all trades on a trading day to which it is a party. The blotter records all relevant details of each trade, such as whether the brokerage bought or sold shares, how many, what price, what time, and so forth. The blotter also indicates whether or not the trade settled as appropriate.

Blow up a Customer Slang; to convince a client to take a position on an investment vehicle that causes the client to lose a great deal of money and close the position (possibly withdrawing from the market) at a large loss. The term was popularized by the book Liar's Poker, which describes the author's experience as a bond trader on Wall Street in the 1980s.

Blowing a Budget Slang; the act of spending too much time or money on a single project. Blowing a budget is inefficient and may cause problems in either the short or the long term. The term is most common in accounting and auditing.

Blow-Off Top A sudden, rapid increase in a security's price followed by an equally sudden, rapid decrease. A blow-off top can result in large short-term gains, provided one sells the security at exactly the right moment. Just as likely, however, is the possibility that one will incur a loss by buying at the top price. A blow-off top can result from either sudden news or a rumor. See also: Reversion to the mean.

Blowout A new issue of a security that is placed with investors almost immediately and with no difficulty because of high demand on the part of investors. A blowout may be a sign of a well-regarded company; it could also occur during a speculative bubble. See also: Hot Issue.

BLR GOST 7.67 Latin three-letter geocode for Belarus. The code is used for transactions to and from Belarusian bank accounts and for international shipping to Belarus. As with all GOST 7.67 codes, it is used primarily in Cyrillic alphabets.

Blue Book A publication estimating the value of automobiles. It is especially known for used vehicles, but is also provides values for new cars, motor homes and other vehicles. It was first published in 1926, and is formally known as the Kelley Blue Book.

Blue Book Value The market value of an automobile as determined by the Kelley Blue Book. The blue book value is used as a guideline for car dealers and others who buy and sell used cars.

Blue Chip Index An index that predominately or exclusively tracks stocks in well-known and highly respected publicly-traded companies. Blue chip indices track companies that are usually financially sound and are thought to be relatively low-risk investments. These indices tend to be less volatile and are used sometimes as indicators of wider economic performance. A prominent example of a blue chip index is the Dow Jones Industrial Average.

Blue Chip Stock Stock in a well-known and highly respected publicly-traded company. Blue chip companies are usually financially sound and are thought to be relatively low-risk investments. They tend to be less volatile than other companies and to provide solid growth to portfolios. Examples in the United States include General Electric and Coca-Cola. Indices such as the Dow Jones Industrial Average tracks blue chip stocks.

Blue Collar Describing an employee or occupation marked by skilled labor, especially manual labor earning an hourly wage. Examples of industries requiring blue collar workers include manufacturing, mining, and truck driving, among many others. The term is often used to describe a culture influenced by or an area populated largely with blue collar workers. Developed countries have seen a decline in blue collar occupations to developing countries, where labor is less expensive.

Blue Cross and Blue Shield A group of 39 insurance companies in the United States. It provides health insurance to about one-third of the American population.

Each affiliated company is separately incorporated to offer insurance in a single state or within a region. Primarily, it offers PPOs and HMOs, but it is also an administrator of Medicare. It is based in Chicago and traces its origins to 1929.

Blue Dog Coalition A caucus of Democrats in the United States House of Representatives who are moderate to conservative on fiscal issues. The Blue Dog Coalition does not have a cohesive ideology but tends to stand between Republicans and more liberal Democrats on matters like federal spending, entitlement programs and national security. Many members of the Blue Dog Coalition are also socially conservative..

Blue Law A law intended to enforce religious morality. In general, blue laws refer to public observance of holy days through the restriction of commerce. While most blue laws in the United States have been repealed, many states restrict the sale of alcohol on Sunday, the Christian Sabbath. Other countries have similar restrictions on Jewish, Islamic and other holidays.

Blue List A daily publication of new issues of bonds, along with commentary, analysis, and other information. It contains information that may be useful for bond investors. It was first published in 1935 by Standard & Poor. It is called the Blue List because it was historically printed on blue paper, though it is now available online. See also: Advisory letter.

Blue Money Slang; money that a person or business spends with poor management or accountability.

Blue Month The month during which trade on an option or futures contract is most active.

Blue Ocean A slang term for untapped market share. For example, persons who have never bought a cell phone represent blue ocean for cellular providers. See also: Blue ocean opportunity.

Blue Ocean Opportunity A slang term for a business opportunity in a new area that competitors may not have explored or considered. Blue ocean opportunities are risky but can be highly lucrative, depending on interest and timing. See also: Blue ocean.

Blue Pan In film, a camera movement that blurs the images the camera captures because it is moved so quickly. It is used to transition between scenes in commercials and other media. It is also called a whip shot or a whizz pan.

Blue Room A room on the trading floor of the New York Stock Exchange.

Blue Screen In photography and video making, a physical blue screen against which a shot is taken. The screen enables a second shot (usually a background) to be combined with the first image. Blue screens are used in filming to make an actor look as if he/she is somewhere else. This can be less expensive than shooting on location, though blue screens are also used to superimpose very expensive CGI images into the film. A blue screen may also be a green screen.

Blue Sky Laws Laws requiring research and transparency to ensure that a new issue of a security complies with applicable laws in the state in which they are issued. It especially refers to laws protecting investors from securities fraud. The term became popular when U.S. Supreme Court Justice Joseph McKenna wrote in Hall vs. Geiger-Jones Company (1917) that he wished to protect investors from securities with "no more basis than so many feet of 'blue sky.'" See also: Due Diligence.

Blue Skying Referring to research done to ensure that a new issue of a security complies with applicable laws in the state in which it is issued. It especially refers to laws protecting investors from securities fraud. The term became popular when U.S. Supreme Court Justice Joseph McKenna wrote in Hall vs. Geiger-Jones Company (1917) that he wished to protect investors from securities with "no more basis than so many feet of 'blue sky.'" See also: Due Diligence.

Blue Tongue A slang term for a $10 note in Australia. The term is derived from the blue tongue skink, an Australian lizard, as well as the fact that $10 notes are mostly blue.

Blueprint 1. A construction plan. It is called a blueprint because it historically has been printed on blue paper with white lines. **2.** In photography, a copy of a periodical printed before final editing in which images are shown on blue paper. **3.** Informal, a plan.

Blurb Informal for an advertisement, especially a brief one.

BLZ GOST 7.67 Latin three-letter geocode for Belize. The code is used for transactions to and from Belizean bank accounts and for international shipping to Belize. As with all GOST 7.67 codes, it is used primarily in Cyrillic alphabets.

BM 1. ISO 3166-1 alpha-2 code for Bermuda. This is the code used in international transactions to and from Bermudan bank accounts. **2.** ISO 3166-2 geocode for Bermuda. This is used as an international standard for shipping to Bermuda.

BMD ISO 4217 code for the Bermudan dollar. It was first issued in 1970, replacing the Bermudan pound. Since its introduction, the dollar has been pegged to the U.S. dollar at a 1:1 ratio.

BMU GOST 7.67 Latin three-letter geocode for Bermuda. The code is used for transactions to and from Bermudan bank accounts and for international shipping to Bermuda. As with all GOST 7.67 codes, it is used primarily in Cyrillic alphabets.

BN An abbreviation for brown. The abbreviation is used most frequently by coin collectors and investors to indicate copper coins. An equivalent abbreviation is BR.

BND ISO 4217 code for the Brunei dollar. In Malay, the dollar is called the Brunei ringgit. Established in 1967, it is pegged to the Singaporean dollar at a 1:1 ratio. This means that the Brunei dollar effectively floats, but is monitored against an undisclosed currency basket maintained by the Monetary Authority of Singapore.

BO 1. ISO 3166-1 alpha-2 code for the Plurinational State of Bolivia. This is the code used in international transactions to and from Bolivian bank accounts. **2.** ISO 3166-2 geocode for Bolivia. This is used as an international standard for shipping to Bolivia. Each Bolivian department has its own code with the prefix "BO." For example, the code for the Department of La Paz is ISO 3166-2:BO-L.

Bo Derek Stock Informal; a stock that is thought to be very likely to appreciate or that is otherwise of high quality. The term comes from the film 10, in which actress Bo Derek plays the "perfect" woman.

Board Broker 1. A member or candidate for a membership on a commodity exchange who is asked to help ensure the smooth flow of trades. Specifically, the board broker matches and executes orders, provides quotes, and sees that all trading accounts are accurate and up-to-date. Generally speaking, a board broker is assigned a single commodity for which to provide this service. See also: Specialist, Market Maker. **2.** An employee of the Chicago Board Options Exchange who maintains orders that are unable to be executed immediately because the prices requested are far away from current market prices. See also: Away from the market.

Board Broker System A system for making markets on commodity exchanges where a particular member or nominee for membership is assigned a commodity and charged with maintaining liquidity for that commodity. That is, the member matches and executes orders for its assigned commodities, maintains records, and prepares to buy or sell on its own account to prevent the market from becoming illiquid. Each commodity is given one board broker, though one board broker may be assigned several commodities. This system helps keep trading regular and orderly, and is similar to the market maker system on stock exchanges.

Board Foot A unit of volume used to measure quantities of wood in Canada and the United States. One board foot is equivalent to 2.360 cubic meters.

Board Independence The state in which all or a majority of the members of a board of directors do not have a relationship with the company except as directors. For example, they may not be relatives of the company's founders, key players or major employees. In the United States, the SEC and individual exchanges require board independence.

Board Insurer An insurance company that provides coverage to boards of directors of publicly traded companies, nonprofits and other organizations. See also: D&O Insurance.

Board Lot A lot as defined by the security exchange on which it is traded. Most trading takes place in multiples of board lots. On the TSX Venture Exchange, for example, board lots are composed of 100 shares if the share price is $1 or more, 500 shares if the price is between $0.11 and $0.99, and 1,000 shares if the price is $0.10 or less.

Board of Arbitration A panel of impartial persons appointed to resolve a dispute in an extrajudicial process. There are generally three arbitrators, but there may be up to five. Parties in arbitration agree to allow the decision of the board of arbitration to be binding and to forego the right to an appeal.

Board of Customs and Excise A former agency of the British government responsible for the collection of tariffs and customs. It was merged with Inland Revenue to form HM Revenue and Customs.

Board of Directors A body elected to govern a corporation on behalf of shareholders. Generally chosen to represent both management and shareholder interests, it establishes general policies for the organization, including dividend policies, and hires/fires major executives. It is answerable to shareholders for its decisions. A publicly traded company must have a board of directors.

Board of Directors of the Bank of Canada The governing body of the Bank of Canada, which is Canada's central bank. It appoints the Governor of the Bank of Canada and is responsible for general oversight of the institution. It sets the budget, monitors employees and performs other tasks of a board of directors. Because the Bank is independent of the government, it is one of the only government-owned organizations in Canada that sets its own policies.

Board of Equalization A generic term for a government agency responsible for tax collection. In the United States, different states use their boards of equalization to collect different taxes. However, they tend to deal with property tax and, less commonly, sales tax.

Board of Governors of the Federal Reserve System A committee of the Federal Reserve charged with implementing monetary policy of the United States. It consists of seven members appointed by the President of the United States and confirmed by the Senate. The chairman of the Board also serves as Chairman of the Federal Reserve. Members serve for staggered, 14-year terms. The length of service is designed to give the Board as much independence from Congress, and therefore immediate political expediency, as possible. The Board makes an annual report on its operation to the Speaker of the House of Representatives and its members serve ex officio on the Federal Open Market Committee.

Board of Investments A generic term for a government agency responsible for managing a government's assets, attempting to attract investment to the country or region and/or regulating investment.

Board of Realtors A generic term for an association of realtors, especially a local organization. Boards of realtors may provide support to realtors, and they generally provide potential property buyers with information on the area.

Board of Trade 1. In Canada, an alternate term for a chamber of commerce. **2.** In the United Stets, an alternate term for an exchange, especially for commodities and/or derivatives.

Board of Trade of City of Chicago vs. Olsen A 1923 decision by the U.S. Supreme Court holding that Congress has the authority under the Constitution to require all futures contracts on grain to be traded on an exchange. This allowed the Grain Futures Act of 1922 to remain in effect. This decision has formed the basis of subsequent regulation of futures trading of commodities.

Board of Trustees A body elected or appointed to govern a nonprofit organization. It establishes general policies for the organization, manages its finances and hires/fires major executives. A board of trustees is usually a self-perpetuating body.

Board Room 1. The room where the board of directors for any organization meets. **2.** A room in a brokerage where clients and brokers can watch an electronic ticker where security prices are updated on a constant basis. See also: The Big Board.

Board-Out Clause In a publicly-traded company's charter or bylaws, a provision allowing the board of directors to invoke the supermajority provision. If a board exercises the board-out clause, the consent of more than a simple majority of shareholders is needed for certain actions, especially a merger or acquisition. The board-out clause is almost always used as an anti-takeover measure. For example, the board may invoke the board-out clause to require that two thirds of shareholders approve of a merger or acquisition the board does not favor. The board-out clause exists to make hostile takeovers more difficult, while allowing leeway for friendly takeovers.

Boat Owners Package Policy An insurance policy purchased by the owner of a boat. It includes coverage for physical damage to the boat in the event of an accident, as well as medical bills for injured persons and liability from lawsuits. It may also include over coverage. It is intended to be as comprehensive as possible so the boat owner only has one policy (and one payment).

Bob ISO 4217 code for the second Bolivian boliviano. It was introduced in 1987, replacing the peso boliviano at a ratio of 1 million pesos to one boliviano. It is a floating currency.

Bobtail Liability Insurance An insurance policy that guards the policyholder from legal expenses from a lawsuit over a truck after it has delivered its load. That is, bobtail liability insurance provides coverage if an 18-wheeler carrying cargo delivers its load and then, on its way home, causes an accident resulting in a lawsuit. The policy pays for actual and punitive damages as well attorneys' fees.

Bochka A Russian unit of liquid volume approximately equivalent to 492 liters. It was rendered obsolete when the Soviet Union began to use the metric system in 1924.

Bodily Injury Damage to a person's physical being. Examples include bruises, burns, lacerations, poisonings and so forth. Bodily injury may result from an accident, negligence or a deliberate effort. Causing bodily injury on purpose is a crime, while accidental and negligent harm may result in a lawsuit. See also: Bodily injury liability insurance.

Bodily Injury Coverage An insurance policy purchased in conjunction with car insurance that provides coverage in the event of serious injury as the result of an automobile crash. Bodily injury coverage pays for medical bills of all persons injured up to a certain limit. Usually each person has an individual limit (e.g. $25,000) and the event causing the injuries has a total limit (e.g. $50,000).

Bodily Injury Liability Insurance An insurance policy that guards the policyholder from legal expenses resulting from a lawsuit over a bodily injury. For example, if Joe is negligent and causes bodily harm to Frank, Joe's bodily injury liability policy would pay for Frank's attorneys' fees as well as the actual and punitive damages Joe otherwise would have paid.

Body The main part of a document or advertisement. The body provides the most detailed information compared to other parts of a document. Especially in marketing, it is intended to elicit the desired response from the reader.

Body Language Non-verbal communication. Examples include smiles, gestures and sitting or standing positions. Body language is important in face-to-face marketing. For example, salespersons are encouraged (or required) to smile when talking to a customer.

Body Text 1. In word processing, the default font for typing in the body of a document. The body type is usually a basic font like Arial or Times New Roman. **2.** See: Body type.

Body Type The primary text of a print advertisement. Body type gives information about the product in the ad. It is generally large and easy to read so as many people as possible see it. It is also called body copy or body text.

Bogey Informal; a benchmark.

Boiler and Machinery Insurance An insurance policy that covers industrial equipment. It provides compensation in the event of damage to the machine. It may pay for new equipment, medical bills and other expenses resulting from the damage to the equipment, as well as other costs like lost income.

Boiler Room Informal; a place where workers make unsolicited telephone calls to completely unknown persons in an attempt to convince them to invest in a particular venture. Boiler rooms are controversial and some jurisdictions have put in place laws limiting their legitimate use. In any event, the term has a negative connotation; one often hears of boiler rooms in the context of shady and perhaps illegal investments.

Boilerplate Informal; standard language in a legal document. For example, a contract with few or no special conditions may use largely boilerplate language. In investing, the term often refers to a prospectus or a registration document.

Boilerplate Copy Any standard writing used in a variety of documents. For example, boilerplate copy may be a paragraph about the history of a nonprofit that the nonprofit publishes on its website, grant applications, promotional literature and anywhere else that is relevant. Boilerplate copy is also used in contracts, so that the parties can make changes to standardized language rather than write new contracts from scratch.

Boiling the Ocean In business, the act or practice of attempting a project that is impossible because it is too broad or poorly defined. For example, a grant proposal to build a youth center could be described as boiling the ocean if it does not specify what programs would be offered there. The term is used most commonly by persons trying to avoid projects of this nature.

BOL GOST 7.67 Latin three-letter geocode for Bolivia. The code is used for transactions to and from Bolivian bank accounts and for international shipping to Bolivia. As with all GOST 7.67 codes, it is used primarily in Cyrillic alphabets.

Boldface In printing, a typeface that is thicker than other typefaces of the same font. It is often used for emphasis.

Bolivar The currency of Venezuela. It came into circulation in 1879. While it was originally pegged to the French franc, it has been pegged to the U.S. dollar for much of its history. Since the 1970s, it has suffered from a high rate of inflation. It is named for Simon Bolivar, the controversial revolutionary who liberated much of South America from Spain.

Bolivian Peso Boliviano The former currency of Bolivia. It was introduced in 1963 and was pegged to the U.S. dollar. It suffered from high inflation, resulting in several devaluations and finally abandonment of the peg in favor of a managed float. Devaluation continued until the peso boliviano became a floating currency, resulting in a near total loss of its value. In 1987, the second boliviano replaced the peso boliviano at a rate of 1 million peso bolivianos to one boliviano.

Boliviano The currency of Bolivia. It was introduced in 1987, replacing the peso boliviano at a ratio of 1 million pesos to one boliviano. It is a floating currency.

Boll An obsolete Scottish unit of dry volume. For beans, grass seed, peas, rye, salt, and wheat, one boll was approximately equivalent to 145.145 liters. For barley, malt, and oats, however, it was approximately equivalent to 211.664 liters.

Bollinger Bands In technical analysis, charts or tables that compare a security's volatility to its price over time. Bollinger Bands? consist of a simple moving average of the security's price over a given number of days (usually 20 or 21), plus one upper limit and one lower limit. The limits are calculated as the amount of the moving average plus or minus two standard deviations. The purpose of Bollinger Bands is to provide a working definition of a security's upper and lower price limit, to indicate if volatility is increasing, decreasing, or staying the same. Bollinger Bands are one of the most popular technical analysis tools. Bollinger Bands are the registered trademark of John Bollinger, who developed them.

Bolsa The Spanish term for "stock exchange." Many stock exchanges in Spanish-speaking countries are known by both their Spanish and English names.

Bolsa de Barcelona A regional exchange in Spain. Like other Spanish exchanges, it is owned by Bolsas y Mercadoes Espanoles.

Bolsa de Commercio de Santiago The main stock exchange in Chile. Founded in 1893, it deals in stocks, bonds, options, futures, and some commodities and currencies, notably the U.S. dollar. It publishes three indices: the General Stock Price Index, which is weighted by capitalization and revised annually, and the Selective Stock Price Index and the Inter-10 Index, which are both weighted for volume and revised quarterly.

Bolsa de Mercadorias & Futuros A former commodities and futures exchange in Brazil. It merged with BOVESPA in 2008 to form the BM&F BOVESPA.

Bolsa de Valores de Sao Paulo Also called BOVESPA. A former stock exchange in Brazil. It was founded in 1890 and owned by the government until the 1960s. It merged with the Brazilian Mercantile and Futures Exchange in 2008 to form the BM&F BOVESPA.

Bolsa de Valores do Rio de Janeiro The second-largest stock exchange in Brazil. Many types of securities trade on its floor. It is an important player in Brazil's carbon trading market.

Bolsas y Mercados Espanoles A company that owns the stock exchanges in Spain. In addition to managing the operations of the securities exchanges, it also offers settlement services and deals with warrants. Additionally, it sells technology consulting services. It was founded in 2002.

Bolt A computerized order-entry system that sends buy or sell orders for block, over-the-counter trades. It is used to automatically execute orders, and allow users to monitor their positions. It operates much like the continuous on-line trading system, but only for block trades.

Bombay Stock Exchange One of the oldest stock exchanges in India, responsible for approximately one third of the country's trading volume. Tracing its origins to the 1830s, it is notable for the Sensex, an index of the 30 most actively traded stocks on its floor that is considered one of the most important benchmark indices in India. It is also known as Stock Exchange, Mumbai or BSE.

Bon Voyage Bonus The payment to a greenmailer. Greenmailing is a practice in which a corporate raider buys a large amount of stock from another publicly-traded company and forces the latter to buy back the stock at a substantial premium in order to avoid a takeover. One refers to this buyback as the bon voyage bonus, as this enables the company to be left alone by the greenmailer.

Bona Fide In law, belief that a statement or act is made or done honestly and with no ill intent, even if ill effect results. Liability for ill effect may be lessened or eliminated if the statement or act causing it was bona fide. The term is Latin for "in good faith," and the concept is sometimes referred to in this way.

Bona Fide Error A mistake made without negligence or ill intent. Bond fide errors are common simply because of human nature. If a bona fide error is corrected upon discovery, it is unlikely that the party who made it will have legal liability for any losses resulting from it.

Bona Fide Purchaser The purchaser of a property who does not know the seller lacks the right to sell it. The bona fide purchaser, because he is unaware of competing claims to the property, is usually considered the proper owner. However, most of the time the owner with the true claim to the property may sue the seller. In any case, the bona fide purchaser is held harmless in the transaction.

Bona-Fide Foreign Resident A person from the U.S. who resides in a foreign country for an entire tax year and who generally intends to remain outside the United States for an extended period of time. For example, a person who lives abroad during a one-year graduate program generally does not qualify as a bona fide foreign resident even if she is outside the U.S. for the full tax year. A bona fide foreign resident is not required to pay American income tax on income earned outside the U.S., subject to a certain limit.

Bond A security representing the debt of the company or government issuing it. When a company or government issues a bond, it borrows money from the bondholders; it then uses the money to invest in its operations. In exchange, the bondholder receives the principal amount back on a maturity date stated in the indenture, which is the agreement governing a bond's terms. In addition, the bondholder usually has the right to receive coupons or payments on the bond's interest. Generally speaking, a bond is tradable though some, such as savings bonds, are not. The interest rates on Treasury securities are considered a benchmark for interest rates on other debt in the United States. The higher the interest rate on a bond is, the more risky it is likely to be. There are several different kinds of bonds. The most basic division is the one between corporate bonds, which are issued by private companies, and government bonds such as Treasuries or municipal bonds. Other common types include callable bonds, which allow the issuer to repay the principal prior to maturity, depriving the bondholder of future coupons, and floating rate notes, which carry an interest rate that changes from time to time according to some benchmark. Along with cash and stocks, bonds are one of the basic types of assets.

Bond Act of 1917 1. See: First Liberty Bond Act of 1917. **2.** See: Second Liberty Bond Act of 1917.

Bond Anticipation Note A short-term note, usually but not always issued by a municipality, used to finance some project. BANs are often issued with a maturity of one year or less; the proceeds are paid by the issue of a larger bond with a longer maturity. A construction loan note, in which a city finances private construction, is an example of a bond anticipation note. See also: IDC, RAN.

Bond Attorney A lawyer hired by a bond issuer to represent the interests of potential bondholders. Before a new issue of a bond, a bond attorney must generally present a legal opinion stating that everything that the issuer says about the bond is true, and that the issuer has adhered to all applicable laws. Issuers hire bond attorneys to reduce the risk to bondholders and therefore to attract more investors.

Bond Bank A government agency that buys whole issues of municipal bonds from local governments. Bond banks buy these bonds using funds they accumulate from the issue of their own bonds.

Bond Basis Book Table or book of tables showing the yields of bonds at different interest rates and maturities. For example, if one is considering the purchase of a bond, one can take the coupon rate and the maturity and compare them in the bond basis book to determine the yield. The bond basis book is good for approximating yields, but financial calculators tend to be more accurate, especially for more complex bonds.

Bond Broker A broker on an exchange whose business consists predominately or exclusively of bond trading. That is, a bond broker buys and sells bonds on behalf of clients in exchange for commissions.

Bond Buyer A daily newsletter providing information on the bond market in the United States. It is published in hardcopy and online, and gives some of the most detailed information available. It is especially renowned for its knowledge of the municipal bond market. The publication is based in New York and was established in 1891.

Bond Buyer's Municipal Bond Index An index of yields on highly-rated municipal bonds. The Bond Buyer's Index is published daily in the Bond Buyer, a daily advisory letter on debt securities. Investment advisers use the Bond Buyer's municipal bond index to evaluate and track changes in new issues of municipal bonds.

Bond Calendar A list of bonds nearing issue over a certain period of time. That is, the bond calendar lists new issues that have not been made but are about to be. A large number of new issues on a bond calendar may be a leading indicator of rising interest rates as issuers must raise interest rates to attract bond investors.

Bond Certificate A physical document that gives the person or company listed the right to collect on a debt. Bond certificates often contain a great deal of information, such as the holder's name and any right attached to the ownership, among other things. One may use bond certificates in court to prove a fact alleged. However, many issuers use electronic documents rather than physical bond certificates.

Bond Circular A legal document detailing the structure of a bond. The bond circular states the coupon rate, the maturity, and whether or not it may be redeemed early, among other relevant information.

Bond Conversion The exchange of a convertible bond for common shares, nearly always in the company issuing the convertible bond. See also: conversion option.

Bond Counsel An attorney who writes an official opinion stating that a local government is legally permitted to issue a municipal bond. A new issue of a municipal bond is required to have this statement from a bond counsel.

Bond Covenant An agreement between the issuer and holder of a bond, requiring or forbidding certain actions of the issuer. Positive covenants require actions while negative covenants forbid them. The exact terms of a bond covenant must be written in the bond indenture.

Bond Crowd Members of an exchange to trade bonds primarily or exclusively. See also: Active bond crowd, Cabinet crowd.

Bond Dedication The practice of selling a bond with a low yield to maturity and buying a bond with a high yield to maturity. Insurance companies and pensions practice bond dedication to ensure sustainable payouts on future liabilities like claims and payments to pensioners.

Bond Discount A situation in which a bond's market value is lower than its face value. Short-term bonds are often issued at a bond discount, especially if they are zero-coupon bonds. However, bonds on the secondary market may trade at a bond discount, which occurs when supply exceeds demand. A bond discount is likely when the issuer has poor or recently downgraded credit, or when current interest rates are higher than the bond's. See also: Unamortized bond discount.

Bond Equivalent Yield The non-annual yield of a bond expressed in annual terms. The bond equivalent yield helps an investor compare the return of a bond that pays a coupon on an annual basis with a bond with semi-annual, quarterly, or any other coupons. It is calculated thusly: Bond equivalent yield = ((face value - purchase price) / purchase price) * (365 / days until maturity). See also: Annual Percentage Rate.

Bond Futures An agreement to buy or sell a bond at a certain date at a certain price. That is, Investor A may make a contract with Investor B in which A agrees to buy a certain number of B's bonds at 90% of their par value on January 15. This contract must be honored whether the price of the bonds goes to 80% or 125% of par. As with all futures contracts, bond futures contracts can help reduce volatility in certain markets, but they contain the risks inherent to all speculative investing. These contracts may be sold on the secondary market, but the person holding the contract at its end must take delivery of the underlying asset.

Bond Insurance Company A company that sells insurance on bonds. That is, a bond insurance company guarantees that the principal and coupon on a bond will be paid at the appropriate times. The bond insurance company does this in exchange for a premium. Insured bonds carry a higher credit rating.

Bond Investor A person or company who invests significantly in municipal or corporate bonds. The bonds represent debt that the bond issuer owes to the bond investors. Thus, a bond investor usually has the right to receive principal and interest on this debt, though some derivatives separate the two. Investors buy bonds because they usually have less risk than other securities, and, in the event of the bankruptcy of the issuer, bonds have priority over stock in the liquidation of assets.

Bond Issue A set of bonds that a company or government offers for sale. That is, when one sells bonds to the public (or offers them for private placement) the collection of those bonds is said to be an issue. If the company or government is selling a set for the first time, it is said to be making a new issue. Typically, bond issues may be bought and sold on the open market, although there are many non-tradable bonds.

Bond Issue Costs The expenses a company or government incurs in the process of issuing a bond. Bond issue costs may include registration with regulators, marketing the issue to investors, procuring insurance and so forth. An issuer must consider bond issue costs when weighing whether issuing a bond is worth the risk.

Bond Issuer An organization that registers, distributes and sells a bond on the primary market. A bond issuer can be a private company or a government. For example, if a company registers a stock with the SEC, makes arrangements to underwrite it, and keeps the proceeds from its sale, it is said to be the issuer of that stock.

Bond Market The supply and demand for the buying and selling of bonds. The bond market involves both government and corporate bonds in both the primary market (the first sale at issue) and the secondary market (all subsequent sales). Most transactions involving bonds occur over-the-counter. Bond prices both affect and are affected by the current state of the stock market.

Bond Market Unit A currency that does not circulate but is used only on the international bond market.

Bond Mutual Fund A mutual fund that invests exclusively in bonds. It pays dividends based on coupon payments and maturities of the bonds. A bond mutual fund tends to yield more than a money market or certificate of deposit, and it pays dividends more often than an individual bond. Bond mutual funds may be composed of convertible, corporate, treasury, mortgage, or municipal bonds, or some combination of the five. They may also be classified by average yield, or by length of time before maturity.

Bond Option An option to buy or sell (depending on whether it is a call or a put) a bond at a certain price on or before the expiry date. One buys a call bond option if one believes that interest rates will fall, causing an increase in bond prices. Likewise, one buys a put bond option if one believes that the opposite will be the case. See also: Stock option.

Bond Outstanding Method In accounting, a way to amortize the discount or premium of a bond's par value by spreading it out over the course of its life. The way it is spread is determined by the ratio of the bonds outstanding at a given moment to the total amount outstanding over the life of the issue.

Bond Paper Very high quality paper originally used to print bond certificates. Increasingly, it is also used for stationary and graphic design, among other uses. Its weight is more than 50 grams per square meter.

Bond Points A percentage of a bond's face value that is used to indicate its purchase price. For example, if a bond is trading at 95 bond points, this means that it is trading at 95% of its face value. Generally speaking, a bond's face value is $1,000, so 95 bond points indicates a purchase price of $950.

Bond Portfolio A portfolio that invests predominately or exclusively in bonds. It collects coupons that are based on the aggregated risk and maturities of the bonds represented in the portfolio. Bond portfolios may be composed of convertible, corporate, treasury, mortgage or municipal bonds, or some combination of the five. They may also be classified by average yield, or by length of time before maturity.

Bond Power A form used to transfer a bond from a seller to a buyer without endorsing the bond certificate. See also: Stock power.

Bond Prices The amount one pays to buy a bond. A bond price is usually represented as a percentage of par value. For example, if a bond has a par of $1,000 and is sold for $900, the price is published as 90%.

Bond Quote The price of a bond on an exchange. A bond quote is usually expressed as a percentage of the bond's face value. Occasionally, however, it is quoted as a dollar amount.

Bond Rating A measure of the likelihood of a bond's default. Credit ratings agencies conduct credit analysis in order to provide bond ratings; the criteria and the ratings themselves may change these from time to time. Bond ratings are important to bond investors as they make investment decisions. For example, if a bond has a low rating and an investor is risk averse, he/she will be unlikely to invest in that bond, as it will lead to an increased possibility that the investor will lose the amount invested. See also: Investment-grade, Junk.

Bond Ratio One of many measures of a company's leverage. A bond ratio is calculated by taking the value of a company's bonds and dividing by the quantity of its long-term debt and its stockholder equity. A lower bond ratio indicates that a company has less debt and is therefore less risky to investors. An exceptionally high bond ratio may indicate that the company has too much debt.

Bond Ration The supply of bonds a company has to sell.

Bond Risk The risk associated with investing in bonds. Major examples of bond risk include interest rate risk, which is the possibility one may not be able to reinvest at the same interest rate upon maturity; credit risk, which is the risk of default by the issuer; and inflation risk, which is the possibility that the inflation rate may outpace the return on the investment.

Bond Room A specially designated place on the New York Stock Exchange for the trading of bonds. The active bond crowd gathers in one area of the floor while the cabinet crowd gathers in another. It is not on the main NYSE trading floor.

Bond Sinking Fund A fund or account into which an issuer deposits money on a regular basis in order to repay a bond that will come due in the future. For example, if a company issues a bond with a balloon maturity of seven years, one may put money into a bond sinking fund for seven years in order to be ready to pay off the principal when it comes due. Some bonds have sinking fund provisions, requiring the issuer to put money aside to repay bondholders at maturity. See also: Sinking fund call.

Bond Spread The difference in yield between one bond and another with a lower credit rating. In general, the bond with a lower rating has the higher yield because of the added risk involved. As such, bond spreads are used to compare risk.

Bond Strategy Basic standards and beliefs guiding one's bond positions. Factors influencing one's bond strategy include risk tolerance, investment goals and personal beliefs about what guides the bond market. Bond strategies may vary greatly from each other. For example, a risk averse investor may buy government bonds, while a risk lover may prefer junk bonds from start-ups.

Bond Swap A situation in which one sells a bond while buying another bond at the exact same time. One may conduct a bond swap for any number of reasons, such as to receive a better coupon, to increase or decrease risk, or to attain a tax advantage from the sold bond and maintain a diversified portfoliowith the bought bond. See also: Swap.

Bond Trading The buying and selling of bonds. Bond trading involves both government and corporate bonds in both the primary market (the first sale at issue) and the secondary market (all subsequent sales). Most transactions involving bonds occur over-the-counter. Bond prices both affect and are affected by the current state of the stock market.

Bond Transaction Table A table in a newspaper giving information on bonds, such as price, yield and special features.

Bond Trustee An organization, almost always a financial institution, hired by a bond issuer to ensure the terms of the indenture and all applicable laws are being followed. The trustee has a fiduciary responsibility to act on behalf of the issuer, rather than in its own interests.

Bond Valuation Analysis The process of determining the intrinsic value of bonds. Factors considered in bond valuation analysis may include the presence of a sinking fund, insurance, the financial stability of the issuer and so forth. Bond valuation analysts buy or recommend buying bonds with the best value.

Bond Washing The act or practice of selling a bond before a coupon is paid and buying it back immediately after the payment. After a coupon is paid, the price of the bond usually decreases by the amount of the coupon. Bond washing, then, is a way to produce a capital gain without having to pay tax on it.

Bond Yield The income one receives from a bond investment, rather than its capital appreciation. The yield is calculated as the coupons the investor receives in a year expressed as a percentage of the cost of the investment. In general, riskier bonds have higher yields. Measuring the direction of bond yields over time is one way to try to predict future economic movements. See also: Yield curve.

Bonded Describing any debt or liability on which payment is guaranteed by a bond.

Bonded Debt The total debt that a company has issued as bonds, as opposed to loans or other forms of financing.

Bonded Exchange Anything that would impede a transaction. The term is especially applied to problems in foreign exchange transactions.

Bonded Goods Imports stored in a bonded warehouse, which is a location where the goods can be stored without payment of tariffs or other duties for a certain period of time. The warehouse provides not only space but also facilities to clean, repackage or even complete the manufacture of the bonded goods. Importers have a given period of time (such as five years) to pay the tariffs and remove the bonded goods from the warehouse. They are called bonded goods because the importer must post a bond to compensate the government if the goods are released without tariff payment. See also: Bonded warehouse.

Bonded Storage Exemptions The ability to be stored without payment of tariffs or other duties for a certain period of time. Bonded storage exemptions occur when goods are in a bonded warehouse.

Bonded Warehouse A warehouse in which imports may be stored without payment of tariffs or other duties for a certain period of time. A bonded warehouse provides not only space but also facilities to clean, repackage or even complete the manufacture of the imports. Importers have a given period of time (such as five years) to pay the tariffs and remove the goods from the bonded warehouse. It is called a bonded warehouse because the importer must post a bond to compensate the government if the goods are released without tariff payment. It is also called bonded storage or a bonded terminal. See also: Bonded goods.

Bondholder A person or company that owns a municipal or corporate bond. The bond represents a debt that the bond issuer owes to the bondholder. Thus, a bondholder usually has the right to receive principal and interest on this debt, though some derivatives separate the two. In the event of the bankruptcy of the issuer, bondholders have priority over shareholders in the liquidation of assets.

Bonding A background check on a potential employee, followed by the procurement of insurance against any theft from the company that the employee may commit. Some financial service or other companies whose employees handle large amounts of cash conduct this process. The United States Department of Labor runs the Federal Bonding Program, which issues bonds insuring or guaranteeing the insurance of ex-offenders whose employment adds significant risk of theft or fraud.

Bond-Over-Bill Spread The difference in yield between two bonds or other debt securities with different credit quality. For example, an investment grade bond and a junk bond have different yields to appropriately compensate the bondholder for the level of risk. The difference between these is called the yield spread.

Bond-Over-Stock Warrant An option in which the payout is the yield on a stated bond index less the return on a stated stock index.

Bonus Compensation in money and/or stocks over and above one's salary. Bonuses are given after a company realizes exceptionally high profits and for extremely good work employees perform. Bonuses often are given near the end of the year or major holidays.

Bonus Circulation An extra publication of a periodical above what the publication has promised to advertisers. The bonus circulation includes advertisements, but because it was not part of the original contract, the publication does not charge advertisers. In other words, the bonus circulation provides free exposure for advertisers.

Bonus Issue The free distribution of new shares to existing shareholders. A bonus issue is most common when the issuer does not wish to increase its dividend when it is expected to do so, especially when it may be cash poor. Instead of the increased dividend, shareholders receive the additional shares. Shareholders receive the bonus issue in proportion to the number of shares they already own. A bonus issue is also called a scrip issue. See also: Antidilution Provision.

Bonus Method In accounting, a method to calculate the capital that each partner in a partnership contributes. According to the bonus method, partners who contribute intangible assets (such as sweat equity or expertise) are providing more capital to the company than they actually did in cash.

Bonus Pack In marketing, two products sold in one package. Generally, one of the products is smaller or less valuable and is included to entice potential customers to purchase the product. For example, a bonus pack may include a booklet of recipes along with a set of kitchenware. See also: Sweetener.

Bonus Plan The policies a company follows in paying out bonuses. The bonus plan includes details on eligibility, the circumstances under which bonuses are paid and how amounts are determined. For example, a bonus plan may state that employees are eligible for a bonus after a certain number of months with the company when the company collects more than a certain percentage of its accounts receivable.

Bonus Rate An interest rate that is added to the interest rate of an annuity in the first year of its existence. For example, an insurance company may sell a fixed annuity with a 5% rate but apply a bonus rate of 2% in the first year so that the principal increases by a total of 7%. In the second and subsequent years, the bonus rate reverts to 5%. The bonus rate is a sweetener to attract customers.

Book 1. An informal term for an accounting record such as an income statement. See also: Cook the books. **2.** A general term for a record of any sort. **3.** See: Subscribe.

Book Balance The total amount of money a bank has on deposit before adjusting for uncleared checks or deposits, as well as reserve requirements. That is, the book balance is a measure of what the bank has on hand prior to adding or subtracting regulatory obligations and items that will soon appear on its books. The book balance is also called the gross balance.

Book Building The process of canvassing potential investors for interest in a new issue of a security, especially before the SEC has approved the issue. Building a book allows a syndicate to have a rough idea of the demand for the new issue, which may affect its price when it is actually issued. See also: Overbooked, Underbooked, Fully booked.

Book Closure The date on which a publicly-traded company announces that a shareholder is entitled to a dividend. Theoretically, only those who own a stock on the announcement date should be entitled to a dividend; however, because shares change hands so often, actually calculating this can become quite complex. To make the process easier, the company may simply announce a book closure date at some point in the near future, which means that whoever owns a share on that day may claim a declared dividend.

Book Depreciation A depreciation method based on the accounting method a company uses. That is, book depreciation is used for a company's internal and external accounting reports. It contrasts with tax depreciation, the method used to conform to the rules of the relevant tax agency.

Book Inventory The record a company has of the stock in its portfolio. This may differ from its actual stock portfolio because it is sometimes difficult to maintain entirely accurate records due to the sheer amount of stock a large company often has.

Book of Business Informal; a financial adviser's or salesman's list of clients and the amount of money each one generates. This term is used most frequently in brokerages or investment advisory firms.

Book of Original Entry A book or other record on which transactions are recorded when or immediately after they occur.

Book Paper Paper of a quality high enough to use for printing books. Book paper comes in a variety of types and styles, including thick, thin, plain, and glossy, among many others.

Book Profit A gain on an investment that has not yet been realized. That is, book profit occurs when the current price of a security is higher than the price the holder paid for it, but the holder still owns the security. As a result, there is the possibility that the book profit might be erased if the price goes back down. A book profit represents an increase in one's net worth, but it may or may not affect one's lifestyle. Under most circumstances, one is not taxed for book profit; the government waits until gains and losses are realized. See also: Paper loss.

Book Rate The amount one pays to mail books, films, sound recordings and some other publications. The book rate varies by weight.

Book the Goods In business and investing, a slang term meaning to place an order.

Book to Bill A ratio of orders taken to invoices sent over a set period of time. In other words, a book-to-bill ratio compares current customers (orders taken) to previous customers (invoices sent). This is a tool used to calculate whether demand for a good or service is rising or falling. A book-to-bill ratio of less than one indicates falling demand, while a ratio of greater than one shows growth, after accounting for seasonal or other fluctuation. The semi-conductor industry makes particular use of this ratio.

Book Transfer A change in ownership, especially of a security, that does not result in a change of location. For example, a stock may be sold between two clients of the same brokerage. In such a case, the stock certificate is unlikely to move at all.

Bookends In advertising on television or radio, the practice of airing the same commercial twice, once at the beginning and once at the end of the commercial break. The idea behind using bookends is that doing so will help viewers recall the commercial and will therefore increase the likelihood that those viewers will buy the product.

Book-Entry 1. A certificate of ownership in a security that is maintained electronically. Rather than printing paper certificates, issuers of securities sometimes rely upon book-entries to reduce the risk of theft or destruction of the certificate. **2.** Describing a security that has book-entries rather than paper certificates.

Book-Entry Callable Corpus Also called BECC. A zero-coupon bond that formerly had a physical certificate but has since has been changed to a book-entry security (meaning ownership records are kept electronically). This term is used most commonly in literature for bond funds.

Book-Entry Security A security where the certificate is not actually given to the holder. Instead, the holder is given a receipt and the information is held electronically. Book-entry securities have become more common as computers

become more sophisticated and exchanges increasingly decide to close their trading floors. Book-entry securities are settled by the DTCC.

Booking the Basis In some forward contracts, an agreement between a buyer and a seller allowing one or the other to determine the price of the underlying asset described in the forward at some future date. Booking the basis occurs according to some formula agreed at the outset so the party does not simply make up a price. Once the future date occurs, the price of the underlying asset is set and remains that way until the forward contract matures. Booking the basis should not be confused with a basis book.

Bookkeeper A person who records financial transactions. That is, bookkeepers maintain financial records, noting expenses or revenue, and determining how much one owes or is owed. Bookkeeping is related to, but distinct from, accounting. While accountants create reports based on financial information, bookkeepers record the information itself.

Bookkeeping The practice or profession of recording transactions. That is, bookkeeping involves maintaining financial records, noting expenses or revenue, and determining how much one owes or is owed. It is related to, but distinct from, accounting. While accountants create reports based on financial information, bookkeepers record the information itself.

Booklet A short book, usually less than 20 pages. Booklets have a wide variety of both business and non-business uses. For example, they may be used in marketing.

Bookout To close a position on an over-the-counter derivative, especially a swap. One may bookout by selling a long position, buying a short position, or simply paying the market value of the derivative to the other party of the transaction.

Book-to-Market Ratio A ratio of a publicly-traded company's book value to its market value. That is, the BTM is a comparison of a company's net asset value per share to its share price. This is a useful tool to help determine how the market prices a company relative to its actual worth. A ratio greater than one indicates an undervalued company, while a ratio less than one means a company is overvalued. Value managers seek out companies with high BTMs for their portfolios.

Boom A period of rapid, strong economic and/or stock growth. For example, some developing countries post GDP growth of 10-12% per year, especially after they have liberalized their economic policies. Likewise, some stocks may become suddenly very popular, resulting in a boom. The dot-com bubble is one of the most famous examples of a stock boom. The problem with booms is that the growth is rarely sustainable, as investors become more and more speculative and take needless risks. Thus, most booms ultimately result in busts. Many economists believe the boom-and-bust cycle is an inevitable part of doing business, while others believe that government regulation can limit both booms and busts.

Boomerang Effect In marketing, a way to calculate how well an investment performs. The boomerang effect consists of three parts: the initial investment, the work done to create an advertising campaign, and the return. One investigates the investment and the execution of the campaign to determine if the return is sufficient relative to the marketing work involved.

Boomernomics An investment strategy in which one invests in companies likely to be patronized by baby boomers. Baby boomers are persons, especially in the United States, born immediately after World War II (usually defined as between 1946 and 1964). When they were born, boomers were the largest generation in history. Boomernomics assumes that as this generation ages, demand will increase for geriatric medical products as well as for luxury products like vacation homes. Boomernomics is a long-term investment strategy because it assumes that demand (and therefore profits) for these products will increase only gradually over time.

Boon Any event or condition thought to benefit investors. It is not a technical term, and indeed is seen more often in newspaper headlines than heard in common parlance. Events as different as the central bank's lowering of interest rates and an individual company's better-than-expected earnings report may both be described as boons.

Boondoggle A large, expensive project of no particular use. It especially refers to squandering government or corporate money. The term refers to perceived wasteful recreational activities provided to the unemployed during the New Deal in the United States.

Booster Shot The first report by an underwriter recommending that investors buy a new issue of a security. A booster shot intends to make the new issue more attractive to investors.

Boot Money or an asset added to a trade in order to make it reflect the fair market value of the assets being traded. A common example of a boot is a trade between a new car and an old car. The person trading the old car will usually add money or another asset to the deal in order to make it "even." The boot is often taxable even in an otherwise tax-free transaction.

Boot Disk Any storage disk one can use to load and run an operating system or a program on a computer. Historically, the most common boot disks have been floppy disks and CD-ROMs. Increasingly, however, flash drives are being used instead.

Booth Informal; a cubicle on the New York Stock Exchange. Member firms use booths to take orders for trade, which are then executed on the trading floor. Members then use the booths to communicate the trade back to a client. With the advent of Blackberries and other personal digital devices, some members have begun using these instead of the booths. See also: Telephone booth.

Bootstrap 1. To start a company with personal finances rather than through loans or venture capital. This is obviously a large risk to the entrepreneur as he/she has no recourse should the business fail. On the other hand, it allows the entrepreneur to maintain control of the business and has the potential to be very successful. It is famously said that Ross Perot established Electronic Data Systems with $1,000 in personal savings; he maintained complete control of the company until its IPO six years later. This is an example of bootstrapping. See also: Seed money. **2.** To calculate the yield curve on a zero-coupon Treasury bill. Because the U.S. Treasury does not issue new T-bills constantly, bootstrapping is used to create a yield curve by filling in the missing yields on the T-bills.

Bootstrap Acquisition A way to finance the acquisition of a publicly-traded company. In a bootstrap acquisition, one buys some shares and then uses them as collateral to borrow cash to buy more shares. These shares are used to borrow more money, and so forth until one owns a majority stake in the company. If one defaults on any of the loans, however, the shares go to the lender. A bootstrap acquisition is a type of leveraged buy-out.

Bootstrap Business A company started with little or no capital. The term may be especially applicable if the company goes on to become successful. For example, one might call Electronic Data Systems a bootstrap business because Ross Perot started it with only $1,000 in personal savings.

BOP ISO 4217 code for the Bolivian peso boliviano. The currency was introduced in 1963 and was pegged to the U.S. dollar. It suffered from high inflation, resulting in several devaluations and finally abandonment of the peg in favor of a managed float. Devaluation continued until the peso boliviano became a floating currency, resulting in a near total loss of its value. In 1987, the second boliviano replaced the peso boliviano at a rate of 1 million peso bolivianos to one boliviano.

Boracic In Cockney rhyming slang, a term for poor or otherwise out of money.

Borax Sodium borate, a compound used in detergents and makeup as well as in insecticides and metallurgy. As such, it has both industrial and consumer product uses.

Border A set line denoting the extremities of a country, government, legal jurisdiction or property. Borders for governments or jurisdictions are agreed between parties or set by a higher authority. Borders between properties are set by a government or the original owner. An owner of property sometimes may subdivide and sell pieces, thereby creating new borders within his old property.

Border Cargo Selectivity Also called the BCS. A computerized system used in the United States to distinguish between risky and non-risky imports and related transactions coming over land through high-volume ports of entry. Other than distinguishing between high-volume and other ports of entry, it is identical to the Cargo Selectivity used by the Automated Commercial System.

Border Environment Cooperation Commission Also called BECC. An international organization intended to promote economic development along the U.S.-Mexico border. It seeks to develop infrastructure on both sides of the border to improve water, waste management, wastewater and air quality, as well as to promote clean energy. It works in cooperation with the North American Development Bank to achieve these goals. BECC was established in 1994 as a side agreement with NAFTA.

Border Tax Adjustment A tax to which domestically produced goods and imports are subject but from which exports are exempt. Border tax adjustments are intended to encourage exports while not making imports excessively competitive against domestic goods. This may be seen as a barrier to trade.

Bordereau A report made by an insurance company stating the risks to which it is exposed, but which it has reinsured. That is, the bordereau lists the risks for which the company has itself purchased insurance policies.

Borderline Risk An applicant for an insurance policy whose risks either have not been fully assessed or which the insurer may not be able to cover.

Boris A slang term for a security trading in Russia.

Borrow To receive money from another party with the agreement that the money will be repaid. Most borrowers borrow at interest, meaning they pay a certain percentage of the principal amount to the lender as compensation for borrowing. Most loans also have a maturity date by which time the borrower must have repaid the loan. Borrowing occurs informally from family and friends, at the retail level through a bank, and also on a large scale involving governments and institutional investors.

Borrowed Funds Money one has received from another party with the agreement that it will be repaid. Most borrowed funds are repaid with interest, meaning the borrower pays a certain percentage of the principal amount to the lender as compensation for borrowing. Most borrowed funds also have a maturity date by which time the borrower must have repaid the loan. Borrowing and lending occur informally between family and friends, at the retail level through banks and on a large scale through governments and institutional investors.

Borrowed Reserves Money that a member bank of the Federal Reserve System borrows from its Federal Reserve bank in order to maintain its required reserves. The interest rate on borrowed reserves is an important benchmark interest rate.

Borrower A person or company that has received money from another party with the agreement that the money will be repaid. Most borrowers borrow at interest, meaning they pay a certain percentage of the principal amount to the lender as compensation for borrowing. Most loans also have a maturity date by which time the borrower must have repaid the loan. Borrowing and lending occur informally between family and friends, at the retail level through banks and on a large scale through governments and institutional investors.

Borrowing Authority of Pension Benefit Guaranty Corporation The statutory ability of the Pension Benefit Guaranty Corporation (PBGC) to borrow from the U.S. Treasury. The Secretary of the Treasury must approve all loans and all interest rates.

Borrowing Base The amount of money that a lender may advance for each dollar (or other currency unit) the borrower pledges as collateral. More liquid collateral results in a higher borrowing base. See also: Margining.

Borrowing Costs The amount of money paid in interest on a loan or other debt. In other words, it is what one must spend in order to receive money. Borrowing costs are expenses for both personal and business loans.

Borrowing Power 1. The ability to borrow more funds. A person or company with a great deal in assets and little in debt is likely to have greater borrowing power than a person or company in the opposite position. **2.** The amount an investor may buy on margin. This varies from investor to investor, generally according to credit risk and the amount of collateral his/her brokerage keeps. The brokerage sends each investor a statement each month informing him/her of the amount of borrowing power the investor has.

Borrowing Power of Securities The amount that a person or company may borrow to purchase securities on margin. The borrowing power of securities is determined by the market value of the securities one has placed as collateral on the margin account. In general, the market value of the collateral must be at least 25% of the amount one borrows.

Borsa Italiana The main stock exchange in Italy. Founded in 1808 and publicly owned until 1998, the London Stock Exchange acquired it in 2007. It is the primary market for derivatives traded in Italy, as well as for Italian government bonds and eurobonds. It also trades in other fixed income investments. All trading take place electronically.

Bosnia and Herzegovina Convertible Mark The currency of Bosnia and Herzegovina. It was introduced in 1995 and replaced three different currencies. It was pegged to the German mark on a 1:1 ratio. When the euro replaced the German mark, the convertible mark changed the peg to 1 euro : 1.95583 convertible marks. This was the same ratio that the German mark had with the euro before its replacement.

Boston Consulting Group A major management consulting firm. It is responsible for developing the BCG Growth Share Matrix, which describes the level of capital a company requires and the growth of which it is capable. It has likewise developed similar systems to help companies conceptualize their business.

Boston Equity Exchange A defunct stock exchange. It closed in 2007.

Boston Exchange Automated Communication Order-Routing Network A computerized system allowing for the automatic execution of orders on any exchange in the United States at the consolidated market price.

Boston Options Exchange An electronic exchange that deals primarily in stocks and equity options. It was established in 2002 by Bourse de Montreal, the Boston Stock Exchange, and a brokerage called Interactive Brokers. It began its operations in 2008.

Boston Stock Exchange A small, regional stock exchange in the United States. It was established in 1834 and is currently owned by NASDAQ.

BOT 1. Build own transfer. To transfer responsibility for a project from one party to another. **2.** Balance of trade. The difference between the value of a country's exports and the value of its imports. If the value of exports exceeds that of imports, a country is said to have a trade surplus, while the opposite case is called a trade deficit. Analysts disagree on the impact, if any, of the balance of trade on the economy. Some economists believe that an overly large trade deficit causes unemployment and lowers GDP growth. Others believe that the balance of trade has little impact, because the more international trade occurs, the more likely it is that foreign companies will invest in the home country, negating any adverse effects.

Botao In Portugal, a nickname for the one eurocent coin. The name means "button," and refers to its low value. An alternate nickname is feijao, which means "bean."

Both to Blame Clause In marine insurance, a clause stating that in the event two or more ships are determined to be responsible for a collision at sea, the owners and transporters are jointly responsible for all damages in proportion to the value of the property each was originally transporting.

Bottle A British slang term for either 2 pounds or 200 pounds. The term derives from "bottle of glue," which rhymes with two. It is an example of Cockney rhyming slang.

Bottle Hanger A piece of cardboard or heavy paper with an advertisement printed on it. It is cut in such a way so as to hang from the neck of a bottle. Bottle hangers are used in marketing in grocery stores, especially to announce a lower price or a free product with the purchase of a bottle of soda or other drink.

Bottleneck In project management and other fields, a situation in which output is limited by the lowest capacity system in the project. For example, the output of book publishing is limited by how quickly writers write, regardless of how quickly books can be edited and printed. Bottlenecks have a wide variety of applications in business, technology and elsewhere.

Bottlenecking In an audit, a situation in which most of the work is scheduled to be done close to the deadline, rather than consistently throughout the project. This results in a great deal of work being done in a short amount of time, which can be stressful and lead to mistakes.

Bottom Fishing An investment strategy in which one buys high-risk stocks in companies that have recently dropped dramatically in price. The investor buys the stock in the belief that the drop is due to panic selling, rather than a serious fault in the company, and that the company will recover. The number of bottom fishers may increase in a prolonged bear market. See also: Distressed securities.

Bottom Line An informal term for net income. That is, the bottom line is a company's total revenue less its operating expenses, interest paid, depreciation and taxes. For example, suppose a widget manufacturer earns $1,000,000 in total revenue. The widgets cost $200,000 to make and administrative and payroll expenses total $250,000. The manufacturer also must subtract $50,000 in depreciation on widget manufacturing equipment and pay $200,000 in taxes. The manufacturer's bottom line is stated as: $1,000,000 - $200,000 - $250,000 - $50,000 - $200,000 = $300,000.

Bottom Line It A slang term meaning to summarize. For example, a manager may state that she does not wish to hear a whole presentation. She may instead request that the presenters "bottom line it" by stating the main point.

Bottomry A loan the owner of a ship takes with the ship as collateral. Bottomry finances the ship's ability to transport cargo for one or more clients. Upon the ship's return, the ship's owner must repay the lender with interest (the payment comes from what the owner collects from clients); if the owner fails to do so, he/she loses the ship. Bottomry is also called bottomage.

Bottom-Up Investing An investment philosophy that primarily considers factors affecting individual companies. That is, when making investment decisions, a bottom-up investor considers the financial health, products, supply and demand, and other aspects of a company's performance over a given period of time. Proponents of bottom-up investing argue that it lets the investor know the details of each, specific stock in which he/she invests while also allowing him/her to do well in a market downturn. Critics maintain that the ability to perform well in a bad market if overstated. See also: Top-Down Investing, Value Investing.

Bought Deal A new issue that a single underwriter purchases in order to place with investors. Most of the time, new issues are made through a syndicate of several underwriters. Likewise, most underwriters are reluctant to buy part of a new issue if they are unsure of how much demand there will be. Thus, an underwriter only agrees to a bought deal if it believes there will be a good deal of demand so that it can quickly re-sell the entire issue.

Bought Ledger 1. A book or electronic document that a company uses to record its expenditures for purchases. 2. Recently, the term has come to mean the department or system a company uses to keep control of the credit it extends.

Boulewarism An offer that a company makes directly to its employees, bypassing a labor union. The employees may either accept the offer or go on strike. However, they may not amend it. Because there is no possibility of negotiating with the union for a better deal, boulewarisms are illegal under the National Labor Relations Act of 1935.

Bounce 1. To not pay a check because there are insufficient funds in the payer's account. For example, suppose Joe writes a check to Bob for $500, but there is only $400 in Joe's checking account. When Bob deposits the check, his bank will refuse to credit the $500 to his account, because Joe's bank will advise that Joe does not have enough money to honor the check. In such a situation, the check is said to bounce. 2. An increase in a security's price following a period of flat or downward performance. A bounce can occur when the company or an analyst announces favorable news.

Bounce Back A catalog or order form included with shipment to a customer that encourages him/her to buy the same or similar products from the seller. The bounce back is a very cheap form of marketing because it does not require the seller to spend any more on postage than it otherwise would have (indeed, much of the time the buyer pays for postage anyway).

Bounce Message A message from a server to an e-mail sender that the e-mail did not reach the recipient. There may be a variety of reasons for a bounce message, ranging from an invalid e-mail address to a full mailbox to a busy server.

Bouncebackability A slang term for the ability to turn an adverse situation into a success.

Bounced Check A check from which funds are not transferred because there are insufficient funds in the payer's account. For example, suppose Joe writes a check to Bob for $500, but there is only $400 in Joe's checking account. When Bob deposits the check, his bank will refuse to credit the $500 to his account, because Joe's bank will advise that Joe does not have enough money to honor the check. In this case, the check is called a bounced check. In the United Kingdom, the common term is an unpaid cheque.

Bound Describing a party to a contract who is legally obligated to follow that contract. A bound party who violates the contract may be sued for damages.

Bound Rate A tariff, expressed as a percentage of the value of an import, that a country has agreed to levy on goods from another country. The tariff may not rise above the bound rate as long as the relevant treaty remains in force. It is also called a bound tariff or tariff binding. See also: World Trade Organization.

Boundary Conditions The limitations to which a mathematical equation is subject under certain circumstances. Boundary conditions are important in solving problems dealing with real world issues.

Bounded Rationality The theory that humans attempt to make rational decisions, but their ability to do so is limited by knowledge, ability to know, inadequate time to consider and other factors. Bounded rationality may explain situations like panic buying, in which investors continue to buy a security long after it ceases to be rational

to do so. Investors may believe the price for the security may continue to rise and may not believe they have enough time to find out for certain. Bounded rationality claims people aim for rationality but cannot be reasonable all the time. See also: Behavioral economics.

Bounty A payment a local government or a bail bondsman gives to an individual who finds, arrests and takes a fugitive to jail. A bounty helps ensure that the government or bail bondsman recovers at least part of the bail owed if a person fails to come to a court date.

Bourse 1. A term for a stock exchange in Europe. 2. Informal for the Paris Bourse.

Boutique A small brokerage and investment advisory firm that offers highly personalized services to a select group of individuals. Boutiques have only a few clients.

Boutique Agency A company that creates advertisements for both advertisers and advertising agencies. That is, a boutique agency deals exclusively with the creative aspects of advertising. It develops concepts and employs writers and artists almost exclusively.

BOV ISO 4217 code for the Bolivian MVDOL. It is a unit of account in Bolivia that does not circulate. It is adjusted for inflation relative to the U.S. dollar so that its value does not change with inflation. Because of this stability, financial instruments in Bolivia are quoted in BOV terms. MVDOL is a Spanish abbreviation for "boliviano maintaining value with respect to the dollar."

Bow Wave A slang term for the initial shock of a change decreed by upper management. The term has a slightly negative connotation, but the situation is usually considered to be temporary.

Bowie Bonds An issue of bonds with a 10 year maturity collateralized by the royalties on all 25 albums David Bowie released before 1990. David Bowie issued the Bowie bonds in 1997 in order to raise the capital to buy the rights to a number of his songs owned by his former manager. In exchange, Bowie gave up the royalties to the songs he did own for a period of 10 years. Since 2007, Bowie has owned the royalties to all of his songs. Bowie bonds were one of the first bond issued collateralized by intellectual property, though several such bonds have been issued since.

Bow-Tie Loan A short-term loan with a variable interest rate; if the interest rate rises above a predetermined level, the payment collected toward the higher interest is instead applied to the principal of the loan. This effectively sets a maximum monthly payment the borrower pays, but may extend the term of the loan as the principal may increase over time.

Box The physical location where a brokerage keeps securities being held as collateral on loans. Boxes are used for collateral on margin accounts and other transactions. A box is also called an open box. See also: Free box.

Box Size In point & figure charts, the amount of change in price needed to move the chart. Point & figure charts do not account for time and are a series of X and O columns, each representing a price. Thus, the box size may be thought of as the amount of price movement needed to create a new X or O column on the chart. There is no rule governing how large or small the box size needs to be; this is left up to the individual analyst. See also: Reversal amount.

Box Spread An option strategy in which one holds both a bull spread and a bear spread. A bull spread is a series of options (either calls or puts, but not both) structured so that one makes a profit if the price of the underlying asset increases, while a bear spread is a similar series designed to do well if the price declines. A box spread therefore reduces or eliminates the risk associated with both a bull spread and a bear spread. Most of the time, it also reduces or eliminates the opportunity for profit, but pricing inefficiencies between the two spreads can lead to profit from arbitrage. A box spread is considered a very complex investment strategy.

Box-Jenkins Model A methodology that makes forecasts of future economic behavior by applying a best fit model to past behavior. In using the model, one applies an autoregressive moving average to past data. In order to do this accurately, one must identify the data being measured and ensure it is independent of other variables, define the parameters of investigation, and check the model. The model is used in econometrics.

Boxtop Offer The offer of a free or reduced price item from a manufacturer if the buyer presents the top of a box (usually a cereal box) upon purchase. A boxtop offer is made to encourage people who buy cereal (or some other common item) to also purchase the stated product. Some manufacturers have standing relationships with cereal companies for boxtop offers.

Boycott The conscious refusal to buy products from a certain company or country. Boycotts are often organized on a large scale in an attempt to influence the behavior of companies or countries. Very often, boycotts are ethical or political.

BP Curve A line on a chart indicating the series of interest rates at which a country's balance of payments (that is, the amount of money entering a country less the money leaving it) is at equilibrium. It generally trends upward. It affects the exchange rates of currencies.

BPA Statement A statement giving information on the number of persons an advertisement reaches. It is issued by BPA Worldwide, a nonprofit that independently verifies market penetration for ads. A BPA statement may cover media in any of 25 countries.

BQ 1. ISO 3166-1 alpha-2 code for British Antarctic Territory. 2. ISO 3166-2 geocode for British Antarctic Territory. This was used as an international standard for shipping to the territory. In both cases, the code is obsolete.

BQAQ ISO 3166-3 code for the British Antarctic Territory, which was re-designated as part of Antarctica in 1979. ISO 3166-3 codes are used to indicate names of countries that are no longer used.

BR 1. ISO 3166-1 alpha-2 code for the Federative Republic of Brazil. This is the code used in international transactions to and from Brazilian bank accounts. **2.** ISO 3166-2 geocode for Brazil. This is used as an international standard for shipping to Brazil. Each Brazilian state has its own code with the prefix "BR." For example, the code for the State of Acre is ISO 3166-2:BR:AC.

BRA GOST 7.67 Latin three-letter geocode for Brazil. The code is used for transactions to and from Brazilian bank accounts and for international shipping to Brazil. As with all GOST 7.67 codes, it is used primarily in Cyrillic alphabets.

Braca A Portuguese measure of length approximately equivalent to 2.2 meters. It became obsolete after Lusophone countries adopted the metric system in the 19th century.

Bracero An agreement between the United States and Mexico whereby agricultural, industrial and other laborers from Mexico were permitted to enter the United States in order to work. The program came from an agreement between U.S. President Franklin Roosevelt and Mexican President Manuel Avila Camacho to help with the American labor shortage resulting from the war effort. It began in 1942 and ended in 1964.

Bracket A group of underwriters responsible for placing a certain amount of a new issue with investors. Brackets are arranged in a hierarchy, which indicates how much of an issue each bracket is placing with respect to the others. The brackets are called, from largest to smallest: bulge bracket, major bracket, minor bracket, underwriter, selling group. The second largest bracket is sometimes called the mezzanine bracket. Brackets are listed in order of size on an advertisement detailing each new issue, known as the tombstone.

Bracket Creep A situation in which inflation pushes people into higher tax brackets, resulting in a higher tax liability, even though the purchasing power of their income has not increased. When inflation is high, the dollar amounts of people's incomes goes up, but because prices for products also go up this does not correlate to an increase in purchasing power. However, because tax brackets are listed by dollar amounts, it may mean that the government is entitled to a greater share of one's disposable income. To avoid bracket creep, a legislature may link a tax bracket to inflation or change tax brackets every few years.

Bracket Indexation The practice of increasing or decreasing the income falling under various tax brackets to adjust for inflation. This is done to prevent (or at least reduce) bracket creep, which occurs when inflation pushes people into higher tax brackets, resulting in a higher tax liability, even though the purchasing power of their income has not increased. Bracket indexation reduces government revenue, but lessens arbitrary tax increases that could be harmful to the economy.

Bracketed Buy Order An order to a broker consisting of three parts. The primary part is the order to buy a security at a certain price; this is attached to a limit order to sell the security at a price above the buy price and a stop order to sell it at a price below the buy price. For example, suppose one makes a bracketed buy order to buy at $200 per share. It may also include a limit order to sell at or above $225 and a stop order to sell at $175. A bracketed buy order tells the broker exactly what the client expects. It also allows the buyer to lock in profits and limit losses without the need to monitor the security and make follow-up orders.

Bracketing The process of arranging groups of underwriters responsible for placing a new issue with investors into a hierarchy. This hierarchy indicates how much of an issue each group of underwriters is placing with respect to the others. The brackets are called, from largest to smallest: bulge bracket, major bracket, minor bracket, underwriter, selling group. The second largest bracket is sometimes called the mezzanine bracket. Brackets are listed in order of size on an advertisement detailing each new issue, known as the tombstone.

Brady Bond A bond issued by the International Bank for Reconstruction and Development to Latin American countries starting in 1989 and continuing into the 1990s. It effectively refinanced the bonds issued by Latin American countries after many defaulted on their national debt in the 1980s. Many bonds issued in the region prior to this were illiquid; Brady bonds were tradable and, for that reason, were more attractive to investors. Because many of them were guaranteed by U.S. Treasury bonds, they also carried less risk. In 1999, Ecuador defaulted on its Brady bonds. However, in 2003, Mexico retired its Brady bond debt completely.

Brady Commission A group assembled by U.S. President Ronald Reagan in 1988 to investigate the causes behind the 1987 stock market crash and to make recommendations to prevent it from happening again. It recommended that limits be put on how much a security can rise or fall in price during periods of volatility (which was adopted) and that the Federal Reserve take a stronger regulatory role in securities (which was not).

Brain Drain A situation in which the smartest, best educated people in a society or country leave for elsewhere. For example, brain drain may occur if the best doctors in a country leave to work abroad. Brain drain can occur for any number of reasons. Common examples, however, include political instability, better career opportunities or simply higher salaries. Brain drain is a problem in many developing countries.

Brainstorming A usually informal meeting in which participants try to think of ideas to solve a problem or accomplish a goal. The idea behind brainstorming is to come up with as many suggestions as possible, in hopes that one of them will stand up to scrutiny and become the solution. Criticism is discouraged during brainstorming, and participants are encouraged to discuss unusual proposals and to

build upon what others say. This is a common and useful way to solve problems both in business and in other situations.

Branch 1. An office or subsidiary of a company that exists and conducts operations in a country other than the one in which the company is headquartered. See also: MNC. **2.** A semi-independent office of a bank. For example, a bank may have five branches in a city where account holders can make deposits and withdrawals and conduct other business at the place most convenient for them.

Branch Accounting The practice of keeping separate bank accounts for each branch of a company even though the branches together with the home office form a single, legal entity. Because branches are responsible for earning money for the company as a whole, the home office may take funds from the branch accounts and put them in its own account. Likewise, it may credit funds to a branch if the branch is having cash flow problems.

Branch Bank A semi-independent office of a bank. For example, a bank may have five branches in a city where account holders can make deposits and withdrawals and conduct other business at the place most convenient for them. Many banks maintain branches in other states. This was permitted for the first time since the 1920s by the Riegle-Neal Act of 1994. See also: McFadden Act.

Branch Office Manager 1. The person who is responsible for the smooth function of an office or subsidiary that exists and conducts operations in a place other than where the company is headquartered. The branch office manager is usually responsible to one or more managers at the home office. See also: MNC. **2.** The person who is responsible for the smooth function of a semi-independent office of a bank. For example, a bank may have five branches in a city where account holders can make deposits and withdrawals and conduct other business. Each has its own branch office manager.

Branch Post Office A post office outside the city limits. A branch post office provides basic services like mailing certain letters and packages. For special services, however, one must travel to the main post office to which the branch is linked.

Branch Store A retail store that exists and conducts operations in a place other than the main store location. The branch store usually has fewer items for sale and may sell only the most common goods so customers do not have to go all the way to the main store to purchase certain things. See also: Branch.

Brand Anything that distinguishes a company's product from other, similar products. Examples of brands include logos, catchphrases, or symbols. Brands make a product more recognizable and therefore are likely to attract customers and customer loyalty. There is often a sense among consumers that brand products are somehow better than off-brand or generic products; as a result, brand products are usually more expensive.

Brand Association The extent to which a brand name is used to refer to a group of products. For example, in the American South, carbonated soda pop is usually called Coke (referring to Coca-Cola), regardless of brand or flavor. It is considered an extremely good sign when a single brand name becomes a byword for a whole class of products.

Brand Attitude The consensus attitude of potential consumers toward a product. Brand association refers to what the consumers believe the product does, how well it does it, and how likely they are to find it useful. Knowledge of a product's brand association is developed through market research such as asking focus groups. It is used in preparing advertising campaigns for products.

Brand Awareness The ability for a potential consumer to differentiate a brand name from other, similar products. For example, in the American South, carbonated soda pop is usually called Coke (referring to Coca-Cola), regardless of brand or flavor. This is an example of brand awareness because it shows the extent to which many Southerners automatically think of Coca-Cola when they think of soda pop. Building brand awareness is an important component of marketing, especially when products have very few aspects to distinguish themselves in terms of quality.

Brand Category A group of products that compete against each other to satisfy the same need among potential consumers. For example, Coke and Pepsi are in the same brand category because they are very similar products.

Brand Development The number of persons per thousand who buy a product. This is used to measure sales or the success of a marketing campaign.

Brand Development Index The percentage of persons in a certain area in the U.S. who buy a product compared to the percentage of total Americans who buy the same product. For example, if 10% of people in Oklahoma buy a certain product and 30% of Americans as a whole buy it, the BDI is 33.3 (BDI = 10% / 30%). This may be used to measure relative market penetration in certain areas.

Brand Equity The value of brand recognition. Brand equity increases the value of an otherwise indistinguishable product. For example, consider two soft drinks that taste exactly the same. If one has a great deal of brand recognition, and the other does not, consumers will be more likely to buy the one they recognize. This increases the value of the drink with brand recognition in the minds of consumers. Brand equity is difficult to measure (as are all intangible assets), but is important in determining the value of a good or the company that produces that good.

Brand Extension The act or practice of adding a new product under the same brand name. This allows a company to introduce a new product without having to build up a whole new customer base for it. For example, when Jimmy Dean introduces a new flavor of sausage, it may put the Jimmy Dean name and logo on the wrapping. This is intended to encourage people who like other Jimmy Dean sausages to view the new flavor favorably and be more inclined to buy it.

Brand Franchise An agreement between a wholesaler or retailer and the holder of a brand for the distributor to use that brand exclusively in an area. That is, the wholesaler or retailer is the only company permitted to sell that brand product within certain boundaries. This helps the wholesaler or retailer boost its sales, because it can tap into customers' brand loyalty.

Brand Leader The products in a certain sector of the economy that sell the most relative to competing products. For example, Pepsi and Coca-Cola are considered brand leaders among soft drink products because nearly all such products in the United States are produced by one or the other. Brand leaders generally have developed a great deal of brand loyalty from their customers.

Brand Loyalty The propensity for a consumer to buy a product again. Brand loyalty begins when a customer has a positive experience with a product; however, such purchasing may end up as simply a habit (albeit a revenue-producing habit). It is important for companies to build their brand awareness (or knowledge that their products are available) and to produce quality goods in the first place in order to build brand loyalty.

Brand Management The steps a company takes in order to build brand awareness and eventually brand equity for its products. Brand management is a marketing strategy designed to differentiate products through logos, catchphrases, symbols or even the name of the company itself, rather than through differences in quality or price. Brand management can increase the revenue potential for a product, and can ultimately increase the value of the company itself.

Brand Manager A marketer who takes steps to build brand awareness and eventually brand equity for its products. Brand managers market strategies to differentiate products through logos, catchphrases, symbols or even the name of the company itself, rather than through differences in quality or price. Brand management can increase the revenue potential for a product, and can ultimately increase the value of the company itself.

Brand Name Anything that distinguishes a company's product from other, similar products. Examples of brands include logos, catchphrases, symbols or even the name of the company itself. Brand names make a product more recognizable and therefore are likely to attract customers and customer loyalty. There is often a sense among consumers that brand name products are somehow better than off-brand or generic products; as a result, brand name products are usually more expensive.

Brand Potential Index Also called the BPI. A measure of potential, future sales based on the customers a product may be able to attract. It is taken by comparing a product's market development index (itself a comparison of actual versus potential customers in an area to those in the U.S. as a whole) to its brand development index (the percentage of persons in a certain area in the U.S. who buy a product compared to the percentage of total Americans who buy the same product). One calculates the BPI for a limited geographic area.

Brand Preference The extent to which a consumer makes purchasing decisions based on a brand name rather than the quality of a product or the price. Brand names include logos, catchphrases, symbols or even the name of the company itself. Most marketing campaigns are designed to convince consumers that a brand's product is superior, whether or not it actually is. For this reason, brand name products are often more expensive.

Brand Switching A customer's act of buying a product different than one of the same kind that he/she previously purchased. For example, a customer may buy Coke on Wednesday and Pepsi on Friday. Any number of factors may cause brand switching, including but not limited to a lower price, a negative experience with the first product, or simply better placement on a shelf at the store. However, it is most common when a consumer does not believe that one product is qualitatively different from another; that is, it happens when there is little brand awareness.

Brand Terrorist A slang term for an employee who intentionally or unintentionally causes harm to his/her company and damages its reputation. For example, a trader who illegally trades on an investment bank's account and causes a scandal is a brand terrorist for that investment bank.

Brandatories A slang term for all the steps that must be taken before a marketing campaign can begin. The term is a portmanteau of branding and inventories.

Branding The process of creating differentiation between a product and other products of the same kind. Branding is a marketing strategy to create the impression that one product is better than the other, whether or not that is true. Branding makes a product more recognizable and therefore is likely to attract customers and customer loyalty. There is often a sense among consumers that brand products are somehow better than off-brand or generic products; as a result, brand products are usually more expensive. Examples of brands include logos, catchphrases, symbols, or even the name of the company itself.

Brandt Report A 1980 report recommending more transfer of resources between developed and developing countries. It criticized developed countries' export of finished goods while developing nations export primarily intermediate goods and raw material. The report claimed that this perpetuated the division between the two parts of the world. The report divided the world into the developed global north (which included the Northern Hemisphere plus Australia and New Zealand), and an impoverished global south (including most of the Southern Hemisphere).

Brass An alloy of copper and zinc. It has low friction and so is used in manufactured products such as gears and valves. It is also used in musical instruments.. It may be traded as a commodity on exchanges such as the London Metal Exchange.

Brazilian Federal Board of Accountancy An organization that helps set the accounting standards for Brazil. It also helps coordinate efforts to bring Brazil's accounting standards in line with the International Financial Reporting Standards. It was created by the federal government.

Brazilian Identity Card A card containing the name, photograph and birth date of an individual, along with his/her parents' names, his/her signature and his/her thumbprint. While this card is not legally required, one must present it to buy real estate, obtain a drivers license and apply for a job, among other things. The cards are issued by state governments, but they are accepted in every Brazilian state.

Brazilian Institute of Accountants Also called IBRACON. An organization that helps set the accounting standards for Brazil. It also lobbies on behalf of accountants and auditors.

Brazilian Real The currency of Brazil. It was introduced in 1994 following the Latin American economic crisis. It is currently a floating currency, though it was semi-pegged to the U.S. dollar for most of the 1990s. It suffered two different currency crises in 1999 and 2002, but has since become one of the stronger currencies in the region.

BRB GOST 7.67 Latin three-letter geocode for Barbados. The code is used for transactions to and from Barbadian bank accounts and for international shipping to Barbados. As with all GOST 7.67 codes, it is used primarily in Cyrillic alphabets.

BRC ISO 4217 code for the first Brazilian cruzado. It was introduced in 1986 and circulated through 1989. During this time, Brazil's currencies were subject to high inflation.

BRE ISO 4217 code for the third Brazilian cruzeiro. It was introduced in 1990 and circulated through 1993. During this time, Brazil's currencies were subject to high inflation.

Breach A violation. For trade and legal contexts, see breach of concession agreement and breach of contract.

Breach of Concession Agreement The deliberate raising of a tariff in violation of a concession. A concession is an agreement in which one country reduces tariffs on its imports from another country in exchange for an equivalent, or at least a similar, reduction from the second country. Concessions are intended to stimulate international commerce between the two countries. A breach of concession occurs when one country unilaterally raises its tariffs higher than the level stipulated by the agreement. It may result in a complaint to the World Bank, a reciprocal hike in tariffs against the offending country, or, in the worst case scenario, a trade war.

Breach of Contract The nonperformance of a contract by one of its parties, or the interference by the party in the other party's performance. For example, if a company has a contract to build a house and does not build it, or does not build it to proper specifications, the company may be in breach of contract. Breach of contract entitles the offended party to sue and to collect damages resulting from loss of value he/she has suffered. Depending on the nature of the breach, the contract may be irreparably harmed and the offended party may be exempted from performance on his/her part.

Breach of Specified Governmental Obligations 1. The violation of a treaty by a government. Because there is no supranational authority regulating international law, there is no specific remedy for this type of breach. However, it harms the country's reputation and may result in diplomatic action up to and including war. **2.** A breach of contract by a government. This is governed by the law of the country in question.

Breach of Warranty The manufacture of a dangerous or defective product such that it opens the manufacturer and/or seller to a lawsuit. The consumer protections put in place during the 20th and 21st centuries have increased the number of lawsuits for breach of warranty. This is controversial, as consumer advocates tend to applaud this development, while manufacturers contend that the protections do not protect consumers but do add to costs, which raises prices.

Breadcrumbing The act or practice of combining multiple jobs or positions into a single job or position. For example, the director of internal communications and the director of external communications may be breadcrumbed into a director of communications position. It is the opposite of bifurcating.

Breadth Indicator Any indicator that measures the relative strength of a price movement either upward or downward. One may think of a breadth indicator as a measure of the likelihood of the persistence of an upswing or a downturn in a security's price. Technical analysts use various breadth indicators to make their recommendations or investments.

Breadth of the Market The relative strength of a price movement either upward or downward. One may think of breadth of the market as the likelihood of the persistence of an upswing or a downturn in a security's price. Technical analysts use various measure of market breadth to make their recommendations or investments.

Breadwinner The person who provides most or all of the income for his/her household. Stereotypically, the husband/father of a family is the breadwinner in the United States and other Western countries. However, the feminist movement in the mid-20th century and increases in the cost of living have resulted in many homes having two breadwinners. Other households have a single breadwinner of either sex out of choice or necessity.

Break 1. A sudden, unexpected change in a security's price or in a market's value. While a break could indicate either upward or downward change, the connotation is negative. Especially on the futures market, a break means a steep decline in price, usually the result of a natural disaster affecting the underlying. **2.** Less frequently, break refers to a discrepancy in a brokerage's accounting books.

Break Bulk Cargo Cargo on a ship stored without a container, or in only a small container like a barrel or a small box. Historically, nearly all cargo transported from one place to another has been break bulk cargo. However, since the 1960s, large containers built according to ISO specifications have become more common.

Break Even 1. To make the sales or revenues necessary to cover costs and prevent a firm from operating at a loss. The breakeven may be relatively stable or it may fluctuate, depending on the company or industry. Companies with high breakevens tend to have large fluctuations in earnings from year to year. **2.** To sell a security at a price that causes the seller to neither make a profit nor lose money on the sale.

Break Fee 1. In a contract between two parties, an amount of money one party may pay the other in order to agree to dissolve the contract. In many cases, the amount of the break fee is contained in the contract itself. It may diminish over time, depending on the nature of the contract. Break fees are common in leases. **2.** In mergers and acquisitions, a fee the target pays to the acquirer in case a deal fails before completion. Theoretically, this is done to reimburse the acquirer for due diligence expenses, but, in practice, it is often used to attempt to restore good relations between the two companies.

Break Forward A derivative of a forward contract in which the buyer agrees to sell the underlying forward at a discount to its current value. However, the buyer may cancel this agreement if the value of the underlying rises above a stated level. A break forward contract imitates an option contract and is used primarily on forwards in foreign exchange. See also: Deferred payment option.

Break in Service A situation in which an employee temporarily ceases to be an employee. For example, an employee may find another job but then come back to the original workplace. Alternatively, he/she may be fired and then re-hired. In general, this does not negatively impact the employee's pension or other benefits provided the break in service was not longer than an agreed-upon period of time.

Break Issue A new issue of a security that drops below its first offer price very quickly. For example, a company may make an IPO and ask $15 per share. If its price drops to $12 per share that trading day, it is said to be a broken issue (in this particular case, a broken IPO). Broken issues are commonly the result of lack of trust in the company's management, or bad news regarding the company that occurred during or just before the issue was made. Speculators buy broken issues with the hope that the crashed price is too low and that a correction will result in gains.

Break Price To increase a bid or decrease an offer to a price where a trade is more likely to take place. Breaking price can narrow the bid-ask spread and makes a market more liquid.

Breakage 1. In accounting, an amount of money set aside to cover the cost of goods that break during transport. Because these goods cannot be sold, the company loses the revenue they would produce. A company may prevent this revenue loss from adversely affecting its finances by setting aside a breakage allowance. This exists due to fiscal conservatism and not because a company expects an unusual number of goods to break. **2.** In retail, a gift card that is purchased but not used. The revenue a retailer generates from breakage is all profit, except for the minimal costs necessary to produce the cards.

Breakeven Analysis An analysis of a product or company's sales required to neither lose money nor make a profit, but simply to cover costs. A company needs to at least break even in order to make the expense of producing a product worth the effort. As a result, breakeven analysis is an important feature in evaluating the risk of an activity. Breakeven analysis calculates the relationship between the fixed costs, variable costs, and profit of the product.

Break-Even Chart A chart onto which two lines are plotted, one representing a company's costs and the other representing its revenue. The point where the two lines intersect is the company's breakeven point.

Break-Even Equation An equation representing the sales a company requires to simply to cover costs, without losing money or making a profit. A company needs to at least break even in order to make the expense of producing a product worth the effort. As a result, a breakeven equation is an important feature in evaluating the risk of an activity. Breakeven equations calculate the relationship between the fixed costs, variable costs and revenue of the product.

Break-Even Point 1. The sales or revenues necessary to cover costs and prevent a firm from operating at a loss. The breakeven may be relatively stable or it may fluctuate, depending on the company or industry. Companies with high breakevens tend to have large fluctuations in earnings from year to year. **2.** The price of a security that, if one sells at it, will cause the investor to neither make a profit nor lose money on the sale. **3.** In options, the price of the underlying asset that will ensure that the option holder will neither make a profit nor lose money on exercising the option. In calls, the break-even point is the strike price added to the premium, while in puts, it is the strike price minus the premium.

Break-Even Sales The revenue from sales necessary to cover costs and prevent a firm from operating at a loss. The breakeven sales may be relatively stable or may fluctuate, depending on the company or industry. Companies with high breakeven sales points tend to have large fluctuations in earnings from year to year.

Break-Even Tax Rate The tax rate at which it would neither be advantageous or disadvantageous for a company to conduct a certain transaction. This allows the investor or business to consider the potential transaction on its own merits, rather than basing the decision on whether it increases or decreases one's tax liability. See also: Going Galt.

Breakeven Time The length of time for the discounted value of future cash flow from an investment to equal the cost of making the investment. That is, if one spends $1,000 buying a stock, the breakeven time is the time it takes for the investor to make

at least $1,000 from that stock. A longer breakeven time equates to higher risk for the investment.

Break-Even Yield The yield necessary to cover costs and prevent a firm from operating at a loss. The breakeven yield may be relatively stable or it may fluctuate, depending on the company or industry. Companies with high breakeven yields tend to have large fluctuations in earnings from year to year. Calculating the breakeven yield is an important part of risk analysis.

Breaking a Buck A situation in which the net asset value of a money market fund drops below $1. Generally, the NAV of a money market fund remains at $1, but it may drop below if the returns on the fund's investments do not cover operating expenses. Breaking a buck occurs when interest rates drop to an unsustainably low level or when the fund has used leverage to make investments. Because money market funds are ordinarily risk-free investments, breaking a buck is relatively uncommon; the first occurrence did not happen until 1994.

Breaking the Syndicate The act of the members of a syndicate parting ways at the end of the relationship. A syndicate is a group of underwriters who work together to place an issue with investors. Once the issue is placed (or once it becomes clear that no more of the issue can be placed), the syndicate is said to break. Every syndicate is a temporary arrangement.

Breakout 1. In technical analysis, a situation in which the price of a security rises above a resistance level. The resistance level is a price above which a security only rarely climbs. This is a highly bullish signal because it indicates the price likely will continue to rise until it finds another resistance level. **2.** In technical analysis, a situation in which the price of a security falls below a support level. The support level is a price below which a security only rarely drops. This is a highly bearish signal because it indicates the price likely will continue to fall until it finds another support level.

Breakout Trader A trader that makes investment decisions based on technical indicators in order to make a large return. The breakout trader may use a variety of indicators, but often relies on support and resistance levels. When a security rises above its resistance level, the breakout trader buys it because it is highly likely that the security will continue to rise. Thus, the trader relies on "break out" prices to amass an abnormal return.

Breakpoint In loaded mutual funds, a dollar amount an investor must buy into the fund in order to be eligible for a reduced load or sales fee. For example, if the breakpoint for a certain mutual fund is $50,000, and investments beyond that amount will halve the load, it becomes advantageous for an investor to invest $50,000 instead of, say, $45,000, because this will entitle him/her to half the load for the entire investment, and not just for the amount invested past $50,000. Mutual funds that allow investors to buy at just below the breakpoint may run afoul of Financial Industry Regulatory Authority regulations. An investment need not come all at once to pass the breakpoint; an investor putting two tranches of $25,000 into the above mutual fund will usually find his excess load refunded. See also: Right of accumulation.

Breakpoint Sale In loaded mutual funds, the sale of shares to an investor that qualifies the investor for a reduced load or sales fee. For example, if the breakpoint for a certain mutual fund is $50,000 and investments beyond that amount will halve the load, it becomes advantageous for an investor to invest $50,000, instead of, say, $45,000, because this will entitle him/her to half the load for the entire investment, and not just for the amount invested past $50,000. Mutual funds that allow investors to buy at just below the breakpoint may violate Financial Industry Regulatory Authority regulations. An investment need not come all at once to pass the breakpoint; an investor putting two tranches of $25,000 into the above mutual fund will usually find his excess load refunded. See also: Right of accumulation.

Breakup A situation in which two or more divisions of a company split into two or more independent companies. A breakup can occur as the result of anti-trust action by a government or if the company simply believes the divisions will be more profitable separately. A breakup should not be confused with a break. See also: Spin-off.

Breakup Fee In some agreements, a fee that a seller must pay a buyer if the seller decides not to close the deal. The seller usually does this if it receives a better bid from another buyer after it has already entered negotiations. The breakup fee exists to compensate the first buyer, who has no control over the change in situation. It is usually 1-3% of the sale price. See also: Topper fee.

Breakup Value The value of a division in a company if that division were its own independent company. Companies considering taking over another use the breakup value, among other metrics, to determine whether a takeover is worth the time and expense. It is also called the private market value.

BREC An informal term for bank reconciliation.

Breeder's Insurance Policy An insurance policy providing coverage in the event of the theft, death, injury or illness of a breeding animal, which is an animal used for mating to produce animals of a high quality. Breeder's insurance policies are most common in professions like dog and livestock breeding. It is important to replace lost income in ranching and similar sectors.

Brent Blend A blend of light, sweet crude oil drilled in the North Sea. Brent blend futures are traded on the International Petroleum Exchange and are considered an important benchmark for oil prices: much of the oil coming the Middle East, Africa, and Europe is priced relative to Brent blend.

Brent Crude Futures A futures contract on crude oil drilled in the North Sea. Prices for Brent crude futures are used as benchmarks for future oil prices in Africa,

Europe and the Middle East. As such, Brent crude futures are important indicators of oil and other energy markets.

Bretton Woods Agreement An international agreement on monetary and currency policy for the period following World War II. Initially crafted in 1944 while the war was ongoing, it came into effect the following year. Among other things, the Bretton Woods Agreement created the International Monetary Fund and the International Bank for Reconstruction and Development. The latter organization was created to finance post-war reconstruction, while the IMF was intended to stabilize exchanges rates between currencies and to serve as a country's lender of last resort. A key component of the Bretton Woods Agreement was the requirement that all countries peg their currencies to a certain amount of gold. In practice, most currencies were pegged to the U.S. dollar, which was itself pegged to gold. This helped the IMF accomplish its stated goals to stabilize currencies that had experienced a large amount of wartime inflation. The Agreement worked relatively well until the United States unilaterally depegged from gold in 1971. See also: Keynesian economics, Nixon shock.

Bre-X Minerals Ltd. A former Canadian mining company that has been accused of perpetrating the largest stock fraud in the history of mining and one of the largest in the history of Canada. In 1993, Bre-X bought a piece of land near the Busang River in Indonesia that was initially estimated to contain 2 million ounces of gold. Estimates consistently rose throughout the early and mid-1990s, culminating in a stated 200 million ounces by 1997. In the process, Bre-X went from being a penny stock to one of the most valuable stocks in Canada. When an independent company found little or no gold in the area, Bre-X collapsed and became the subject of investigation by the Royal Canadian Mounted Police. It finally went bankrupt in 2002.

Brezhnev Stagnation Slower than normal economic growth that occurred in the Soviet Union in the 1960s and especially the 1970s, roughly corresponding with the time Leonid Brezhnev was General Secretary of the Communist Party. Brezhnev put an end to many of the reforms begun under Nikita Khrushchev, which resulted in severe shortages of many goods. The Soviet Union had difficulty balancing supply with demand in the economy, and many goods were unavailable in stores for long periods of time. Stagnation continued even after Brezhnev's death in 1982 and may have been a contributing factor in the USSR's collapse.

Bribe To give money or some other compensation to another party so that party will violate rules. For example, a restaurant owner may offer a bribe to a health inspector so he/she will overlook a restaurant's violation of the city's health code. Bribery is a crime and a form of corruption. It is possible (and in many places common) in both the government and the private sector.

Briber A person who offers a bribe, which is money or some other compensation given to another party so that party will violate rules. For example, a restaurant owner may offer a bribe to a health inspector so he/she will overlook a restaurant's violation of the city's health code. In such a case, the restaurant owner is a briber. Bribery is a crime and a form of corruption.

BRIC An acronym for Brazil, Russia, India and China. The BRIC countries are considered four of the most important developing countries to have graduated to developed nations. They are noted for growing liquidity, stability, infrastructure and other positive features, and have been projected by some to be the four largest economies in the world by 2050.

Brick and Mortar A company with a physical presence in the real world. Example of brick and mortar companies are grocery stores, auto shops, and so forth. While they have higher overhead and less flexibility than online companies, they can often provide more personalized services to customers. See also: Click and mortar.

Bricks In auto sales, a house or other residence put up as collateral on a loan for an automobile.

Bricks-and-Clicks A company with a physical presence in the real world as well as online. Example of brick and click companies are retail book sellers with a physical store and a website from which one may order books. A brick and click company attempts to combine the flexibility of a purely online company with the personal service available from a brick and mortar company.

Bridge 1. In broadcasting, a fade-out between two scenes indicating a transition. 2. An advertisement in a magazine or other periodical that goes across two pages.

Bridge Bank In the United States, a bank the FDIC has declared insolvent and has taken over. A bridge bank is separately incorporated from the original bank, which ceases its function altogether. The FDIC administers deposits and loans for the bridge bank for up to three years, until a buyer is found or the bank's operations wind down. A bridge bank must be registered as a national bank.

Bridge Financing Financing or credit that an investment bank or venture capital firm extends until long-term financing can be arranged or an obligation is removed. If bridge financing is a loan, interest rates are relatively high, often 12-15%. Some institutions, however, accept payment in the form of equity in the company receiving the financing, often in order to sell to investors later. Bridge financing is used to satisfy working capital needs; for example, if a company is arranging for an IPO or a bond issue in the coming months, but needs capital before then, it may arrange bridge financing. See also: Angel investor.

Bridge Insurance An insurance policy that provides coverage for fire, accidents or other damage against a bridge. A municipality or other government may purchase bridge insurance to avoid paying for damages that may result from mischief or natural disaster on a bridge it owns. It generally does not cover damage resulting from acts of war or defects in the design.

Bridge Insurance for Bridges under Construction An insurance policy that provides coverage for fire, accidents or other damage against a bridge while it is being constructed. A contractor may purchase bridge insurance to avoid paying for damages that may result from mischief or natural disaster on a bridge it is building.

Bridge Loan A loan for a short-term period, usually two weeks to three years, until long-term financing can be arranged or an obligation is removed. Interest rates are relatively high, often 12-15%. Bridge loans are used to satisfy working capital needs; for example, if a company is arranging for an IPO or a bond issue in the coming months, but needs capital before then, it may take out a bridge loan. In doing so, it will plan to pay back the bridge loan with the money raised in the longer-term financing.

Brilliant Uncirculated In numismatics, describing a coin with no scuffs or other marks that has never been circulated (which would expose it to blemishes). These coins may be valuable as collector's items, though they are illiquid assets.

Bring-Down Comfort Letter Before or during a new issue, a statement by an auditor that a comfort letter previously published is still valid. A comfort letter is a statement indicating that, while a full audit has not been done, a review of the issue's prospectus has revealed nothing inaccurate or misleading. The bring-down comfort letter indicates the previous comfort letter is still valid.

Brique A slang term for 10,000 French francs. Literally, the word means "brick."

Britannia Coins Gold and silver bullion coins made by the Royal Mint in the United Kingdom. A Britannia coin is one troy ounce (or some fraction thereof). One ounce gold coins have a face value of 100 pounds, while a silver coin is two pounds.

British Bankers Association A professional association of banks and financial service firms. With over 200 members in dozens of countries, the BBA is one of the leading organizations in its field. It is responsible for working with European government organizations on improvements for banking regulations, in addition to setting a banking code and small business code. Importantly, the BBA is responsible for setting the LIBOR every day.

British Caribbean Currency Board The central bank of British Guiana and various British possessions in the Caribbean before 1955. It issued the British West Indies dollar and, starting in 1949, maintained a peg to the British pound.

British Clearer Informal for a large, commercial bank in the United Kingdom that deals predominantly or exclusively in the domestic market.

British Columbia Dollar The currency of British Columbia between 1865 and 1871. It replaced the British pound and was equal in value to the Canadian dollar. It was replaced by the Canadian dollar when British Columbia joined the Canadian Confederation.

British Columbia Securities Commission An organization in Canada that regulates the trade of securities in British Columbia. Along with the Alberta Securities Commission, it regulates the TSX Venture Exchange. It was established in 1996 and is based in Vancouver.

British East India Company One of the world's oldest joint stock companies, founded in 1600. A British company, it traded cotton, silk, opium and other products with India, China and Southeast Asia. It received a number of legal privileges from the British government, and eventually came to rule large parts of India until the mid-19th century.

British High Commission A British embassy in a Commonwealth country. The high commissioner ranks as ambassador to that country. The term dates to the title used for the administrators who indirectly ruled by the British Empire.

British Know How Fund A program of the British government that assisted former Soviet-bloc nations in the transition to free market democracies. While this assistance is still provided to some countries, the Know How Fund as such no longer exists.

British Overseas Trade Board A board that advises the British government on trade and export issues. Among other activities, it conducts road shows promoting British exports and provides consulting services to new companies. It was established in 1972.

British Pound The currency of the United Kingdom. It is the third largest reserve currency in the world. It traces its origins to Anglo-Saxon times and is the oldest currency still in use. It is issued by the Bank of England and the Bank of Scotland. Like most currencies, it was pegged to the U.S. dollar under the Bretton Woods System, but is now a floating currency. The pound did not use a decimal system for its subdivisions until 1971. See also: Decimalisation, Quid.

British Thermal Unit The energy needed to raise the temperature of one pound of water one degree Fahrenheit. It is used in the United Kingdom, the United States, and a few other countries to measure the energy used by appliances like heaters and air conditioners. In the metric system, the equivalent of the British thermal unit is the joule. It is abbreviated BTU.

British West African Pound The currency used in the former British territories in West Africa. It was pegged to the British pound but was not legal tender in the United Kingdom. It began to be minted in 1912 and became gradually obsolete as the territories became independent. It was fully defunct by 1968.

British West Indian Dollar The former currency of British Guiana and some small states in the Eastern Caribbean. It was first issued in 1935 and was pegged to the British pound. Starting in the 1950s, states began withdrawing from the currency union and the British West Indian Dollar was replaced by the East Caribbean dollar in 1965.

BRL ISO 4217 code for the Brazilian real. It was introduced in 1994 following the Latin American economic crisis. It is currently a floating currency, though it was semi-pegged to the U.S. dollar for most of the 1990s. It suffered two different currency crises in 1999 and 2002, but has since become one of the stronger currencies in the region.

BRN GOST 7.67 Latin three-letter geocode for Brunei. The code is used for transactions to and from Bruneian bank accounts and for international shipping to Brunei. As with all GOST 7.67 codes, it is used primarily in Cyrillic alphabets.

Broad Evidence Rule A rule allowing the admission of any evidence regarding a property's value in the process of determining the property's actual cash value. The broad evidence rule is used to determine how much an insurance company or other party should compensate for a property in the event of its loss, theft or damage.

Broad Form Personal Theft Insurance An insurance policy that provides coverage for theft, damage or other loss to personal property named within it. The policy includes most personal property that could be in the insured area, as well as damage to the interior of the area itself. This insurance is usually a part of a homeowner's insurance policy.

Broad Market An index that consists of many stocks or stocks in many different industries. Broad market indices are not terribly useful in gauging the performance of individual industries they help give an indication of movements in the broader economy. An example of a broad market is the Wilshire 5000. See also: Narrow market.

Broad Money The widest possible definition of money supply. There is no universal agreement as to what constitutes broad money. In general, it includes highly liquid instruments like all physical currency and deposits in checking accounts, but also less liquid deposits like those in savings accounts, certificates of deposit, institutional money market accounts, repurchase agreements and other assets that do not circulate very often. It may also include debt securities with maturities of less than two years, repurchase agreements and other assets.

Broad Named Perils A homeowner's insurance policy that only provides coverage for events named in the policy. For example, a broad named perils policy may cover tornadoes and fires, burglaries, civil disturbances and so forth, but not floods. These policies are less expensive than comprehensive policies; broad form named perils insurance is designed to cover only the most likely events.

Broad Tape A service provided by Dow Jones & Company to brokerages that gives information on securities trades. It derives its name from the large amount of information it provides (relative to ticker tape) and the fact that it is printed on wider paper than ticker tape.

Broadband A method of transmission that allows multiple media to be transferred over a single wire or line, at the same time, and very rapidly, at least several megabits per second. Colloquially, the term is often applied to any Internet connection other than a dial-up connection. Broadband (and Internet connections generally) have allowed global businesses to operate much more closely to real time.

Broadbanding In human resources, the practice of a company to have only a few pay grades but a great deal of latitude within each grade. For example, a company may have only three pay grades: one ranging from $35,000 to $55,000, one from $60,000 to $80,000, and one from $85,000 to $105,000. Broadbanding gives a company the leeway to reward good performance with increased salary without necessitating promotion to a higher position. This helps keep the company from becoming top heavy.

Broad-Based Index An index that consists of many stocks or stocks in many different industries. Broad-based indices are not terribly useful in gauging the performance of individual industries, but help give an indication on movements in the broader economy. An example of a broad-based index is the Wilshire 5000. See also: Narrow-based.

Broad-Based Weighted Average An anti-dilution provision in which a company makes a new issue and gives or sells all stockholders new shares so that they maintain the same percentage of ownership in the company. Importantly, preferred stockholders are allowed to take advantage of the new issue. This differs from other anti-dilution provisions that consider common stockholders, but not preferred stockholders. However, this average is not as commonly used as some other anti-dilution provisions.

Broadcast Adjacency A television or radio show that starts immediately before or after another show. A popular program will likely have a large number of viewers who watch at least the beginning or the end of the adjacent program. This allows the broadcaster to charge advertisers more for adjacent time.

Broadcast Advertisers Reports An organization that examines the products and services advertised in broadcast media. It publishes reports on such topics and includes information on where ads for certain products generally fall in a commercial break. It provides these reports to paid subscribers.

Broadcast Advertising Adjacency The time within a television, radio, or (increasingly) online broadcast set aside for commercials. For example, if a television show takes a commercial break half way through, the break is said to be adjacent to that show. Because viewers want to watch (or listen to) the remainder of the show, it is likely that they will watch (or listen to) the adjacent advertising break.

Broadcast Media 1. The electronic transmission of data to televisions, radios or the Internet. Broadcast media is used to transmit shows or movies for entertainment. It is monetized through the sale of advertising space during or between shows. 2. A broadcast media company.

Broadcast Music, Inc. A nonprofit organization that collects royalties on the broadcast of music and distributes them to their composers and songwriters. The broadcast may occur on radio or television, in a nightclub, or elsewhere. It also issues licenses to organizations to broadcast this music in the first place. It was established in 1939 and has offices in seven locations across the United States.

Broadcaster 1. An announcer on radio or television. 2. An advertiser on radio or television. 3. The owner of a radio or television station.

Broadside A large piece of paper on which only one side has print. A broadside is used to make an announcement. It formerly was used as a common way to publish newspapers, though this is rare now. It is also called a broadsheet.

Brochure A pamphlet giving information. A brochure may display information on a tourist destination, a new company or nearly anything else. Brochures are generally graphic intensive and are used frequently in advertising and marketing.

Brochureware A website that rarely updates the information contained on it. For example, it may contain basic information on a company and include contact details. Small businesses may use brochureware if they want to have a web presence but do not offer products online.

Broken Date 1. In foreign exchange, a term for a futures contract or other derivative with an unusual delivery date. For example, a forward contract to buy U.S. dollars 54 days in the future is said to have a broken date. 2. An unusual value date. A value date is the delivery date in a eurocurrency or foreign exchange transaction and is usually a standard period such as one week or one month. A broken date, then, may be a value date 13 days after the trade date.

Broken Up 1. Referring to a trade on a securities exchange that is not executed due to a priority bid. For example, even if an offer of $15 per share for a security is accepted, the trade may be broken up if another offer is made for $20 per share before the initial trade takes place. 2. Referring to a company that splits into several parties, as a result of antitrust action or to preserve a company's financial health. For example, a company may spin off an unprofitable division.

Broker A person or firm that conducts transactions on behalf of a client. Some brokers only conduct transactions while others also offer different types of investment advisory services. Brokers derive their profit from commissions on orders given. That is, they usually collect a percentage of the value of each transaction, though some charge flat fees. Clients may give orders in a variety of ways. One may meet with a broker, call on the telephone, or give orders over the Internet. Brokers handle two main types of brokerage accounts: advisory accounts and discretionary accounts. Brokers are only allowed to conduct transactions on advisory accounts on the specific orders of the account holder, or under very specific instructions. On the other hand, they have much more leeway over discretionary accounts, conducting transactions not prohibited by the account holder in accordance with the holder's investment goals and the prudent man rule. In practice, most brokerage firms are in fact broker-dealer firms. Most brokers must register with the SEC.

Broker Association A voluntary organization of members of an exchange in which members share responsibility for filling client orders, making trades, and so forth. That is, a broker association is a group of individual brokerages that acts as one brokerage. A broker association is useful especially for small brokerages that can "team up" with each other to make better deals for clients.

Broker Call Loan A loan that must be paid on demand. Broker call loans are often used to fund margin accounts; the interest rate on such a loan is calculated with reference to the broker call, which is published in the Investor's Business Daily and the Wall Street Journal each day. Broker call loans require securities as collateral.

Broker Comparison Statements two brokers give to each other to confirm the details about a trade of a security to which they agreed. Details include the price and size of the transaction. The comparisons the brokers give one another must agree before the trade can be settled. A broker comparison is informally called a comp. See also: Don't Know.

Broker ITS An estimate of opening prices for securities traded on the New York Stock Exchange. The broker ITS is sent to floor brokers before the opening of each trading day.

Broker Loan Rate The interest rate at which banks make loans to brokers in order to finance margin loans for their clients. Because the broker wishes to make a profit on his/her own margin loans, he/she offers margin loans at a premium to the broker loan rate. It is also called the call money rate.

Broker of Record An insurance agent who manages a policy for a client. The agent of record gives all quotes to and receives questions from the client. He/she receives a commission or other compensation for these services.

Broker Price Opinion An estimation of the value of a property by a real estate broker. A broker price opinion may take into account the quality of the property, values of surrounding properties and market conditions in the area. However, the estimation is not as detailed or as definitive as a full appraisal. A BPO may be done at the request of a bank when the owner of the property is attempting to refinance a loan or when it is attempting to find an alternative to foreclosure. It also may be done to help a seller determine the best asking price for his/her property.

Broker Recommendations A broker's estimate about the future performance of a stock or security. A broker may use any number of technical, fundamental and/or macroeconomic factors when analyzing a security. The broker then recommends that clients buy, sell or hold the security based on the estimate or rating. Some brokers are particularly well-regarded on certain securities and, for that reason, their advice is often followed and may affect the security's price.

Brokerage Account Money given to a broker or brokerage for investment purposes. One manages one's brokerage account differently according to the type of brokerage; that is, one may meet with a broker, call on the telephone, or give orders over the Internet. Brokerage accounts are divided into two main categories: advisory accounts and discretionary accounts. Brokers are only allowed to conduct transactions on advisory accounts on the specific orders of the account holder, or under very specific instructions. On the other hand, brokers have a great deal more leeway over discretionary accounts, conducting transactions not prohibited by the account holder in accordance with the holder's investment goals and the prudent man rule.

Brokerage Department A department of an insurance company that sells policies to customers. The brokers within the department often work purely for commissions and do not collect salaries or wages. Some, though not all, brokerage departments have their own underwriters to facilitate the quick sale of policies.

Brokerage Firm A firm that conducts transactions on behalf of a client. Some brokerage firms only conduct transactions, while others also offer different types of investment advisory services. Brokerage firms derive their profit from commissions on orders given. That is, they usually collect a percentage of the value of each transaction, though some charge flat fees. Clients may give orders in a variety of ways. One may meet with a broker, call on the telephone, or give orders over the Internet. Brokerage firms handle two main types of brokerage accounts: advisory accounts and discretionary accounts. Brokers are only allowed to conduct transactions on advisory accounts on the specific orders of the account holder, or under very specific instructions. Brokerages have much more leeway over discretionary accounts, conducting transactions not prohibited by the account holder in accordance with the holder's investment goals and the prudent man rule. In practice, most brokerage firms are in fact broker-dealer firms. Most brokerage firms must register with the SEC.

Brokerage General Agent In insurance, a person who finds and trains insurance brokers. The brokerage general agent sells insurance policies to the brokers, who then sell them to individuals and/or companies.

Brokerage Supervisor A person who finds and trains brokers. The brokerage supervisor ensures that the other brokers follow all applicable laws and regulations and may be legally liable if one of the brokers under his/her direction commits securities fraud. The brokerage supervisor also sells securities to the brokers, who then sell them to clients.

Brokerage Window The ability for an account holder to have control over at least some of the investments made on his/her IRA or 401(k). That is, either the account holder or a designated representative has the ability to make investments with the contributions made to the account. This increases the potential return on a retirement account, but also increases the risk associated with it. See also: Self-directed IRA.

Broker-Dealer A person or, more often, a firm that acts as a broker for some transactions and a dealer for others. That is, as a broker, he/she conducts transactions on behalf of clients, and, as a dealer, he/she trades on his/her own account. In practice, most brokerages are in fact broker-dealer firms. Most broker-dealers must register with the SEC.

Brokered CD A certificate of deposit (CD) that one buys through a brokerage. A bank originates the CD, which a brokerage then buys and sells to its clients, usually in smaller pieces. A brokered CD pays a higher interest rate than most CDs to which a small investor has access, and may be traded. As with all CDs, they are insured by the FDIC.

Brokered Deposit A large sum of money composed of many smaller sums offered to a broker by investors. The small sums are compiled into a brokered deposit to qualify for a higher interest rate when the broker deposits it into an investment vehicle.

Brokered Market The buying and selling of anything where a broker represents one or both counterparties. The broker is thought to be able to extract the best price on behalf of those whom he/she represents. Most securities and real estate transactions occur in brokered markets.

Broker's Call The interest rate at which banks make loans to brokers in order to finance margin loans for their clients. Because the broker wishes to make a profit on his/her own margin loans, he/she offers margin loans at a premium to the broker's call rate. Margin loan rates are quoted with respect to the broker's call rate, which is published daily in different periodicals.

Broker's Loan A loan to a broker or brokerage by a bank. Brokers take out broker's loans usually to fund margin accounts for their clients, but also to fund underwriting purchases. Occasionally, brokerages borrow these loans to buy securities for themselves as well. Broker's loans are payable on 24 hours notice, and carry interest rates that are about one point higher than short-term rates. See also: Broker call loan.

Bronzing The process of applying chemicals or metal powder to a material to make it appear bronze. Bronzing may increase the value of a good, or at least improve its appearance. It is most common with baby shoes and other memorabilia.

Brookings Institution A think tank in Washington, D.C. It performs research on the American and international economies, as well as on foreign policy and other issues. It was established in 1916.

Brought Over the Wall Describing a situation where a research analyst at an investment bank works temporarily in the underwriting department on a particular client about whom the analyst is knowledgeable. The "wall" refers to the imposed lack of communication between the investment banking and brokerage services of a financial institution. The wall exists in order to prevent brokers and investment bankers working for the same company from deliberately or accidentally sharing inside information that could lead to illegal insider trading. Bringing someone over the wall, albeit temporarily, allows for the communication of inside information when doing so is both legal and necessary. The term is also called "brought over the Chinese wall." See also: Chinese Wall.

Brown Bag A lunch meeting. That is, a brown bag is a luncheon in which business or other pertinent matters are discussed. If a brown bag is catered, the company generally pays for it.

Brown Goods Relatively small electronic goods like televisions, radios, and so forth. Brown goods are fairly inexpensive compared to white goods (such as air conditioners and refrigerators). Brown goods are also replaced more frequently than white goods.

Brownfield **1.** Unused land previously utilized for industrial or other commercial purposes, especially land that is polluted or otherwise contaminated. Municipalities and private businesses sometimes attempt to clean up brownfields and/or find new uses for them. **2.** More generally, land no longer in use. The term in this sense is most common the United Kingdom and Australia.

Brownfield Investment The purchase of a previously constructed factory or other facility in order to use it for a new activity. For example, a company that makes hammers may buy a factory that previously made screwdrivers in order to expand their hammer-making operations. Brown field investment is relatively common in foreign direct investment.

Browser A computer program used to find files or to surf the Internet. Web browsers are necessary to engage in e-commerce. That is, one cannot buy a book online without a browser to access a website from which to order books.

BRR ISO 4217 code for the Brazilian cruzeiro real. It was introduced in 1993 and circulated through 1994. During this time, Brazil's currencies were subject to high inflation.

Brunei Dollar The currency of Brunei. In Malay, the dollar is called the Brunei ringgit. Established in 1967, it is pegged to the Singaporean dollar at a 1:1 ratio. This means that the Brunei dollar effectively floats, but is monitored against an undisclosed currency basket maintained by the Monetary Authority of Singapore.

Bruneian Pitis The former currency of Brunei. A coin, it was introduced in the 16th century and was minted periodically until 1868. It was withdrawn from circulation and replaced with the Straits dollar in the early 20th century.

Brussels Principles of Valuation Principles used to standardize the value of an import for tariff purposes. The Brussels principles state that a good is worth the price to which uninterested buyers and sellers would agree at the time the valuation is made. The principles were devised for the General Agreement on Tariffs and Trade.

Brussels Stock Exchange A former stock exchange in Belgium. Established by Napoleon in 1801, it merged with several other European exchanges in 2000 to form Euronext. Trading continued on the exchange under its new name, Euronext Brussels.

BRZ ISO 4217 code for the firstcruzeiro, which was the currency of Brazil between 1942 and 1967. It replaced the reis at a rate of 1,000 reis to one cruzeiro. The cruzeiro began to experience high inflation and as a result was replaced by the second cruzeiro.

BS **1.** ISO 3166-1 alpha-2 code for the Commonwealth of the Bahamas. This is the code used in international transactions to and from Bahamian bank accounts. **2.** ISO 3166-2 geocode for the Bahamas. This is used as an international standard for shipping to the Bahamas. Each Bahamian district has its own code with the prefix "BS." For example, the code for the District of High Rock is ISO 3166-2:BS-HR.

BSD ISO 4217 code for the Bahamian dollar. Issued in 1966, it is pegged to the U.S. dollar at a 1:1 ratio. This allows the Bahamas to appeal to tourists economically; indeed, many businesses accept both American and Bahamian dollars.

BSE **1.** See: Boston Stock Exchange. **2.** See: Bombay Stock Exchange.

B-Share A share in a mutual fund to which a fee is charged when the share is sold within a certain number of years. That is, when an investor initially buys a B-share, he/she agrees to pay a third party (usually a financial institution or broker) a certain percentage of the share's value if he/she decides to sell it within five to 10 years, depending on the specific nature of the agreement. The fee usually declines by the year until the maximum number of years is reached. A B-share is one type of load fund. See also: A-share, C-share, No-load fund.

BTG A British pharmaceutical company. It develops drugs for cancer, neurological disorders and other diseases and sells them to hospitals and others. It traces its origins to the 1940s and was founded in its current form in 1991 as the British Technology Group. It is publicly traded and is included on the FTSE 250.

BTN GOST 7.67 Latin three-letter geocode for Bhutan. The code is used for transactions to and from Bhutanese bank accounts and for international shipping to Bhutan. As with all GOST 7.67 codes, it is used primarily in Cyrillic alphabets.

Bu **1.** ISO 3166-1 alpha-2 code for Burma before it changed its name to Myanmar. This was the code used in international transactions to and from Burmese bank accounts. **2.** ISO 3166-2 geocode for Burma. This was used as an international standard for shipping to Burma. In both cases, the code is obsolete.

Bubble A situation in which prices for securities, especially stocks, rise far above their actual value. This trend continues until investors realize just how far prices have risen, usually, but not always, resulting in a sharp decline. Bubbles usually occur when investors, for any number of reasons, believe that demand for the stocks will continue to rise or that the stocks will become profitable in short order. Both of these scenarios result in increased prices. A famous example of a bubble is the dot-com bubble of the 1990s. Dot-com companies were hugely popular investments at the time, with IPOs of hundreds of dollars per share, even if a company had never produced a profit, and, in some cases, had never earned any revenue. This came from the theory that Internet companies needed to expand their customer bases as much as possible and thus corner the largest possible market share, even if this meant massive losses. NASDAQ, on which many dot-coms traded, rose to record highs. This continued until 2000, when the bubble burst and NASDAQ quickly lost more than half of its value.

Bubble Economy An economy market in which prices for goods and services rise far above actual values. This trend continues until investors realize just how far prices have risen, usually but not always resulting in a sharp decline. Bubbles usually occur when investors, for any number of reasons, believe that demand in the economy will continue to rise far beyond what is sustainable. This results in the increased prices. See also: Bubble.

Bubble Theory A theory of investing stating that prices for securities, especially stocks, occasionally rise far above their actual value. This trend continues until investors realize just how far prices have risen, usually, but not always, resulting in a sharp decline. A famous example of a bubble is the dot-com bubble of the 1990s. Dot-com companies were hugely popular investments at the time, with IPOs of hundreds of dollars per share, even if a company had never produced a profit, and, in some cases, had never earned any revenue. This came from the theory that Internet companies needed to expand their customer bases as much as possible and thus corner the largest possible market share, even if this meant massive losses. NASDAQ, on which many dot-coms traded, rose to record highs. This continued until 2000, when the bubble burst and NASDAQ quickly lost more than half of its value.

Buck 1. Among traders, informal for $1 million. **2.** More generally, informal for one dollar or one euro. See also: Breaking the buck. **3.** In bond trading, 1/10 of one dollar of a bond price. Because bonds often are quoted in terms of 1,000 points (and not in terms of dollars), a buck is equivalent to one point.

Buck the Trend To perform well when the market as a whole is doing poorly, or, rarely to perform badly when the market as a whole is doing well. Bucking the trend may apply to individual securities or to whole industries. In technical analysis, bucking the trend is often seen as a bullish signal, as it indicates that investors are still interested in the security or industry involved despite the downtrend in the rest of the market.

Bucket Shop 1. A brokerage that aggressively and often illegally sells its own securities to is clients because it wishes to divest itself and not because selling them is in the interests of the clients. The federal government limits bucket shop activities by limiting the over-the-counter transactions that brokerages are allowed to make. **2.** A brokerage that agrees to buy or sell securities on behalf of clients at a given price, but instead buys at a lower price or sells at a higher price in order to keep the difference as profit.

Bucketing The practice in which a brokerage that agrees to buy or sell securities on behalf of clients at a given price instead buys at a lower price or sells at a higher price in order to keep the difference as profit. Bucketing is illegal in the United States because it is a violation of the brokerage's fiduciary responsibility to act in the best interest of the client (in this case, to find the best available price). Brokerages that routinely engage in bucketing are known as bucket shops. The practice is occasionally called bucketeering. See also: Profiteering, Bucketeer.

Buckeye A small retail seller of cigars.

Buckslip In fundraising, a small rectangular piece of paper in a direct mail package. It may contain information on planned giving or simply summarize the contents of the rest of the package. It nearly always includes information about how the recipient can respond and send money to the direct mailer.

Buda'ah In Islamic law, goods that one party gives to another without compensation. For example, an owner of a company may leave another entrepreneur in charge when he (the owner) goes on vacation.

Buddam An obsolete Indian unit of weight approximately equivalent to 622.4 grams.

Budget A plan for a person or company's expenditures. Making a budget involves looking at one's revenue or income and matching that to expenses such that the person or company pays for all necessary expenses. A budget is in balance if revenues equal expenditures, in deficit if the person or company must resort to borrowing to meet expenses, and in surplus if money is left over to be used for savings or expansion.

Budget Account An individual bank account into which one deposits funds sufficient only to cover one's recurring expenses. For example, at the beginning of the year, one may deposit funds to cover annual rent, health insurance, cell phone bills and so forth. These expenses are automatically debited each month as they come due.

Budget Authority Ability conferred by law upon government organizations to receive and spend the state's money. In the United States, Congress may confer budget authority on federal agencies according to various classifications. They may classify budget authority by the amount available (definite or indefinite), the timing of congressional action (current or permanent), or duration (one-year, multiyear, or no year).

Budget Committee A committee in a legislature that provides oversight in the preparation of the government budget. Depending on the particular committee, it may directly write the budget, receive expenditure estimates from government agencies and/or draft legislation implementing the budget.

Budget Constraint The goods and services an individual is able to purchase over a given period of time at his/her current income. A budget constraint may be represented on a chart according to the following equation: $P_xx + P_yy = m$ P_x is how much a good costs; x is the quantity of that good one purchases; Py is the price of all other goods and services; y is the quantity of all other goods; and m is the amount of money one has allocated for consumption.

Budget Cut A reduction in the amount a department within a company or government may spend over a given period of time. Budget cuts often result from reduced revenue, or sometimes from prioritization of other resources. For example, if the state of Oklahoma receives 10% less tax revenue in a year than it received the previous year, it may institute 10% budget cuts on all state agencies so the state remains in balance.

Budget Dust A minor line item in a budget. For example, if a family has a mortgage of $2,000 and monthly credit card debt service of a further $1,800, the $40 it spends on parking each month may be considered budget dust.

Budget Line An item in a budget. For example, the amount of money a company expects to spend in manager salaries may be listed as a budget line.

Budget Manual A series of instructions on how departments in a company should prepare their budgets for the following year. The manual helps standardize how the company prepares its aggregated budget.

Budget Mortgage A mortgage that consolidates insurance and tax payments into the principal and interest. This allows the property owner to write one check each month for all housing expenses. Most mortgages on residential properties are budget mortgages. See also: PITI.

Budget Planning Calendar The schedule by which a company prepares its budget for the following year. The budget planning calendar allows time for research and discussion. It generally consists of several proximate goals on the way toward compiling the actual budget. The budget planning calendar is often several months long.

Budget Report A report detailing a company's planned expenditures and allowing comparison to what they actually were. The budget report contains two columns, one for budgeted outlays and one for actual. The budget report helps a company determine how closely its budgets mirror reality and how well it manages its costs. The difference between the budgeted and actual amount is called the budget variance.

Budget Retailer A store or other company that sells inexpensive goods or services to consumers. For example, a budget retail clothing store sells cheap clothes. Critics contend budget retailers sell poor quality goods, though supporters maintain that poor and lower middle class people would have few options without them.

Budget Surplus The amount by which revenue exceeds expenditures. A budget surplus means that the budget is likely healthy, at least in the short-term, and that the government, company or individual it regards does not have to resort to borrowing. A company must have a budget surplus in order to make a profit. See also: Deficit.

Budget Variance In accounting, the difference between the estimated and actual cost of a project or other operation. See also: Budget report.

Budgetary Accountability The act or requirement to record the reasoning behind all recommendations or decisions when preparing a budget. This includes both estimates of revenue and desired expenditures. This is used to help ensure the budget is prepared in the most responsible way possible. How well a company or government does this may be published in the budget report.

Budgetary Control Any process a company or government puts in place to help ensure accuracy and honesty in its budget. Budgetary control may set goals for expected revenues or planned expenditures. It almost always includes a system to monitor compliance over time.

Budgetary Slack The deliberate overestimation of expenses or underestimation of revenue for a project. Budgetary slack may be built into a project so that if expenses are less and/or revenues are more than expected, the project and its managers are viewed favorably by investors and/or executives.

Budgeted Balance Sheet A balance sheet listing estimated assets, liabilities and shareholder equity for the coming year. The budgeted balance sheet is used to check the accuracy of other budgets the company prepares, as well as to show financial strengths or weaknesses at the beginning of each year.

Budgeted Income Statement A balance sheet listing the estimated revenues and expenses for the coming year. It also states the company's expected profit. The budgeted income statement is used to show financial strengths or weaknesses at the beginning of each year.

Budgeting Fund A government budget listing estimated revenues and expenditures for the coming year. Each government department creates a budgeting fund to show financial strengths or weaknesses at the beginning of each year, as well as to systematically manage how it allocates its money.

Budgeting Model Any quantitative system used to help prepare a budget. A budgeting model helps a company ready itself in case revenues and/or expenditures are different from estimations. That is, it assists in determining what a company ought to do if it performs particularly well or poorly in a given year. Most budgeting models involve calculations done on a computer.

Budju The currency of Algeria prior to its occupation by France in 1848. It was not a decimalized currency, being divided into 24 muzuna.

Buenos Aires Stock Exchange The main stock exchange in Argentina, established in 1854. Importantly it operates MERVAL, a price-weighted index of the most important publicly-traded companies in Argentina. See also: Burcap.

Buffalo Nickel A copper coin minted by the United States between 1913 and 1938. It was worth 1/20 of one dollar.

Buffalo Plan A computer program that tracks sales and profits of magazines. It was developed in Buffalo, New York.

Buffer In computer science, a temporary storage for data before it can be processed. For example, a word processor may put data in a buffer before sending it to a printer, because a computer operates faster than a printer.

Buffer Stock Scheme A practice in which a large investor, especially a government, buys large quantities of commodities during periods of high supply and stores them so they do not trade or circulate. The investor then sells them when supply is low. This is done to stabilize the price by roughly equalizing supply regardless of other factors. This practice was first used in China more than 2,600 years ago. It is most common with agricultural products. The usefulness of the scheme is controversial.

Buffer Zone In political science, an area between two antagonists that is put in place so they do not attack each other. A famous example of a buffer zone is the demilitarized zone separating North and South Korea. Occasionally, the buffer zone is a third country.

Buffett Rule A proposed tax policy in the United States. The rule would impose a special tax on those earning more than $1 million per year. The rule is intended to circumvent the fact that many wealthy persons pay less in taxes than they otherwise would because much of their income comes from capital gains and so is subject to (lower) capital gains tax rates. The Buffett Rule was proposed in 2011. It is named for Warren Buffett.

Bug A problem with a computer or similar device that causes it to function incorrectly. A bug can cause significant slowdown or even failure of a project. As a result, many companies spend a great deal of time "de-bugging," or fixing as many bugs as they can find, before releasing software or other programs.

Build Own Transfer To transfer responsibility for a project from one party to another.

Build to Suit An agreement whereby the owner of real estate pays to construct a building to the specifications of a potential tenant. In exchange, the tenant agrees to rent both the land and the building from the owner.

Builders' All Risk An insurance policy for the construction industry. Contractors and home builders purchase builders' all risk policies to protect themselves from liability and/or loss in case the project fails.

Builders Risk Hull Insurance An insurance policy for the ship-building industry. Contractors and ship builders purchase builders risk hull policies to protect themselves from liability and/or loss in case the building cannot be completed, or in case a faulty job results in an accident or wreck.

Building and Personal Property Coverage Insurance that a business owner purchases providing coverage for most damage to its office or any of the property contained in it. This insurance covers all damages named in the policy, such as damage from fire, vandalism or theft. A building and personal property policy reduces some of the risks of doing business.

Building Code Municipal or sometimes national ordinances governing the safe construction and renovation of buildings. A building code helps ensure that a building is not a hazard to people entering and leaving it, or to the broader public. For example, a building code may prohibit hazardous substances like asbestos from being used in construction. In general, building codes do not apply to existing buildings unless an addition or reconstruction is being done.

Building Line The closest a building (such as a house) may be to the demarcation dividing two real estate properties. A building line may ensure that houses abide by the fire code or may simply ensure that residents and businesses have some degree of privacy. Building lines are set by either the local government or, less commonly, a neighborhood association.

Building Loan Agreement An agreement by a bank or other financing entity to extend capital to build a new construction. For example, a building loan agreement may be signed so a developer can build a new house or neighborhood. The money is disbursed at intervals, rather than all at once, once the builder reaches certain, defined stages of construction.

Building Permit Permission by a local government to build a new construction or renovate an existing one. A building permit helps ensure that the construction will be safe and that it will comply with inspections (and therefore with the building code). It also helps raise revenue for the municipality, since building permits usually require a fee.

Building Societies Act 1986 Legislation in the United Kingdom that expanded the services building societies are allowed to offer. Under the Act, building societies became able to conduct banking services other than receiving deposits and making loans. The Act resulted in a process by which most building societies demutualized and became regular banks.

Building Societies Ombudsman In the United Kingdom, an administrator who investigates complaints individuals make against building societies. See also: Regulation.

Building Society A bank owned by its depositors and borrowers, who are called members. Building societies primarily make mortgage loans to their members. The first building societies were started in England in the late 18th century; most of them were voluntarily dissolved when all their members owned houses. Building societies became able to conduct banking services other than deposits and loans in the mid-1980s. Since then, most of them have demutualized and have become regular banks. In 2010, there were approximately 50 building societies left in the United Kingdom.

Bulgarian Lev The currency of Bulgaria. The fourth lev replaced the third lev in 1999 at a ratio of 1,000 third leva to one fourth lev. At its introduction, the lev was pegged to the Deutsche mark at a 1:1 ratio. When Germany adopted the euro, Bulgaria unofficially switched its peg to the new currency at a ratio of 1.95583 leva to one euro.

Bulgarian Mint An organization in Bulgaria that issues legal tender coins for general use. It was established in 1952 and is owned by the Bulgarian National Bank. It is located in Sofia.

Bulge Especially in commodities, a rapid and sometimes short-lived increase in a security's price. It is an informal term, often synonymous with bubble.

Bulge-Bracket Firm In bracketing, an underwriting firm responsible for placing a certain amount of a new issue with investors. If a bulge bracket firm is the single largest underwriter, it may be responsible for assigning parts of the issuer to other underwriters. Brackets are listed in order of size on an advertisement detailing each new issue, known as the tombstone.

Bulk Buying The act or practice of buying a large quantity of a good at once. This may occur at either the retail or the wholesale level. For example, a coffee shop purchases coffee in bulk because it needs to sell to its customers. An individual may buy the same amount simply because he/she does not want to go shopping for it very often. Bulk buying is often less expensive per unit because marginal costs tend to decrease the more a company produces or sells.

Bulk Cargo A large amount of a commodity on a ship stored without a container, or in only a small container like a barrel or a small box. Bulk cargo may be wet, like oil, or dry, like coal. See also: Break bulk cargo.

Bulk Carrier A ship designed to transport bulk cargo, which is a large amount of a commodity on a ship stored without a container, or in only a small container like a barrel or a small box. Bulk carriers sometimes have only one deck to maximize room for transportation. Many, though not all, are very large. Almost half of the world's merchant fleets are bulk carriers.

Bulk Circulation A way to circulate a periodical such as a magazine or a newspaper. A periodical is in bulk circulation if its publisher places a large number of issues in a central location. For example, a magazine may be distributed exclusively at coffee shops, or a daily newspaper may place several issues at the student union at a university.

Bulk Discount A discount on the purchase of a product if one buys more than a certain number or amount. For example, one may receive a $1 per unit discount on TV dinners if one purchases 10 at the same time. However, the term usually applies to large purchases, such as those used in wholesaling and international commerce.

Bulk Filing A way checks are processed whereby they are sorted by the account statement cycles (for example, by month) rather than by account number. This means that canceled checks are not filed with or returned to their individual account holders unless requested. Bulk filing is less time consuming than other check filing systems.

Bulk Freight The fee a shipper collects for the overseas transportation of bulk cargo, which is a large amount of a commodity on a ship stored without a container, or in only a small container like a barrel or a small box.

Bulk Mail The dissemination of mail to a large number of people. For example, a supermarket may send bulk mail containing coupons and other discounts. Bulk mail may be solicited or unsolicited, and its use is a common tactic in marketing. Bulk mail is entitled to reduced postage from the U.S. Postal Service.

Bulk Mail Center One of 21 centers in the United States where mail is processed and distributed to the appropriate destinations. Bulk mail centers are highly automated.

Bulk Mail System A system the U.S. Postal Services uses in which letters and other mail are sent to a processing center for routing to their final destinations. There are roughly 300 regional centers for this purpose and a smaller number of national centers for inter-regional correspondence.

Bulk Order An order to buy a large quantity of a good at once. This may occur at either the retail or the wholesale levels. For example, a coffee shop may make a bulk order for coffee because it needs to sell to its customers. An individual may order the same amount simply because he/she does not want to go shopping for it very often. Buying in bulk is often less expensive per unit than buying otherwise, because marginal costs tend to decrease the more a company produces or sells.

Bulk Sale The sale of a large number of real estate properties at the same time as if they were one unit. The properties are not connected and usually have nothing in common except that they are sold in the same transaction. Bulk sales developed as a way to divest oneself of a real estate investment.

Bulk Sales Escrow An escrow agreement in which unsecured creditors force a business to give proceeds from sales of large a amount of inventory and certain other assets to a third party, known as the escrow agent. The escrow agent holds the proceeds until the sales are final and then gives them to the creditors. If a business has acquired too much debt in its activities, a bulk sales escrow is introduced to ensure that the business does not spend the money it receives on still more bad ventures. This protects creditors who do not have liens on specific assets. As with all escrow agreements, the escrow agent receives a fee for his/her services, which are usually split between the business and its creditors.

Bulk Segregation The practice in which a brokerage places a client's securities in street name and keeps them separate from the securities the brokerage itself owns. Securities in street name are owned by a client, but the brokerage holds title to reduce the client's risk and to facilitate trade at the client's request. Bulk segregation occurs to keep these two very different types of securities separate from each other.

Bulk Shipping The overseas transportation of bulk cargo, which is a large amount of a commodity on a ship stored without a container, or in only a small container like a barrel or a small box. Bulk shippers charge fees (called bulk freight) for the service of transportation. Almost half of the world's merchant fleets are bulk carriers, which perform this service.

Bulk Solids A large amount of a dry commodity stored without a container or anything else indicating its quantity. See also: Bulk cargo.

Bulking A brokerage's practice of combining a large number of orders to buy or sell a security and executing them as one. Bulking may occur for odd lot orders, or for orders below the minimum the counterparty wishes to sell or buy.

Bull **1.** An investor who believes that the market or a security will rise and makes investment decisions accordingly. See also: Bear. **2.** Informal for bull market.

Bull Bond A bond that is likely to increase in price when stocks or the economy at large is performing well (that is, when interest rates are falling). This contrasts with most other bonds, which tend to increase in price when interest rates are rising. Principal-only bonds are common examples of bull bonds because, in a bull market, people tend to pay down the principal on their large debts.

Bull CD A certificate of deposit in which the interest rate is tied to the value of a stock market over the course its life. There is, however, a minimum interest rate so that the CD is exposed to market upswings, but not downturns. A bull CD is often used by investors who want to have involvement with the stock market but with a low risk.

Bull Correction In technical analysis, a small drop after a series of increasingly large drops in a security. For example, if a security falls in price by $2 on Monday, $2.50 on Tuesday, $3 on Wednesday, but only by $2.25 on Thursday, a bull correction is said to occur on Thursday. It may predict a coming rise in price. The term is especially common in forex markets.

Bull Flag In technical analysis, an uptrend followed by roughly even trading on heavy volume. A bull flag is likely to be followed by a further rise and is a signal to buy, especially when the even trading begins to break upward. It derives its name from the fact that it looks roughly like a flagpole when plotted on a graph. See also: Bear flag.

Bull Market A market for a security, commodity, currency, or anything else where prices are consistently increasing. For example, if an index increases 10-20% over a relatively brief period of time, it is said to be in a bull market. There is a great deal of money that can be made in a bull market, but the danger exists that a bull market can undergo a price correction or become a speculative bubble. See also: Bear market.

Bull Power One of two indicators used in the Elder-Ray Index, which is a technical measure of the upward or downward pressure on a security's price. The bull power is the daily high minus the exponential moving average of the security's price for a certain period of time. The bull power is used along with the bear power to find buy and sell signals.

Bull Spread A high-risk option strategy in which one buys and sells option contracts in such a way that one benefits the most if the price of the underlying asset rises. For example, one can buy a call with a low strike price and sell another call with a high strike price. If the underlying asset rises, the investor stands to make a great deal of money very quickly. However, if the price does not rise, one can lose the investment.

Bull Steepener A widening yield curve that happens when short-term interest rates decrease at a faster pace than long-term interest rates. Bull steepeners occur when investors are optimistic about stock prices over the short term. See also: Bear steepener.

Bull Trap An indication that a security's declining price has reversed itself, causing some investors to buy it. Unfortunately, the reversal is short-lived or non-existent and the security continues to decline. Investors who have bought after a bull trap indication often have a difficult time unloading their securities because they cannot find buyers. See also: Bear trap, Bear market.

Bull/Bear Ratio A ratio measuring market sentiment. It is calculated by polling investment advisers on whether they feel bullish or bearish about the market trend. One then divides the number of bullish investment advisers by the number of bearish ones. It is published weekly by Investor's Intelligence.

Bulldog Bond A foreign bond denominated in British pounds and traded in the United Kingdom. In order to raise capital from British investors, a non-British company may choose to sell a bond in the U.K. See also: Yankee Bond, Samurai Bond.

Bulldog Market Informal; a stock market in the United Kingdom. The term is most often used by those outside the U.K.

Bulldog Security Informal; a security in the United Kingdom. The term is most often used by those outside the UK.

Bullet The final, large payment a loan whereby the property owner makes only small payments for a set period of time (often five, seven or 10 years). At the end of the term, the owner repays the bullet, which is the entire principal and interest at once. For example, during the 2000s real estate bubble, balloon mortgages were common; homeowners made only interest payments followed by a bullet for the entire principal of the mortgage's maturity. Loans with bullets may be useful if the owner expects interest rates to be low at the end of the term and he/she can simply refinance the loans. However, there is a high risk of default because not all owners have the cash to repay the loan at one given time.

Bullet Bond A bond with no special features that cannot be redeemed prematurely. That is, the bullet bond repays the entire principal at maturity and at no other time. It is also called a virgin bond. See also: Bullet.

Bullet GIC A guaranteed investment contract with a single premium and a single payout at the maturity of the contract. Like all GICs, a bullet GIC provides the investor with a guaranteed principal repayment plus interest; it is usually offered by insurance companies. It is a fairly low-risk investment.

Bullet Repayment **1.** A way to structure the repayment of a loan in which the borrower does not pay the principal over the life of the loan, but rather makes a lump sum payment at maturity. This is relatively common in mortgage loans; the borrower pays the interest each month and refinances the house in order to make the bullet repayment at the end of the mortgage term. **2.** The lump sum payment in a bullet repayment structure.

Bullet Strategy In bonds, an investment strategy in which one takes a long position (that is, buys) medium-term bonds while taking no position in short-term notes or long-term bonds. A bullet strategy can be useful if prevailing interest rates for medium-term bonds are higher than either short-term or long-term. A bullet strategy is the exact opposite of a bullet strategy.

Bullet Trade The act of buying a put option in which the underlying asset is in the money; that is, the market value of the underlying instrument is lower than the strike price. This allows the buyer of the option to capitalize in a bear market without waiting for the market to recover.

Bulletin A brief report of news. For example, a company may issue a bulletin on hiring a new CEO. See also: Press release.

Bulletin Board On NASDAQ, electronic listing of over-the-counter securities. The Bulletin Board lists several thousand securities, including stocks, bonds, ADRs, and others. Since 1999, the SEC has required all companies listed on the Bulletin Board to report their financial information.

Bulletin Board Exchange Also called BBX. A proposed electronic exchange that was intended to replace the OTCBB. Securities to be listed on the BBX would have no financial requirements, but would have to abide by the corporate governance standards of NASDAQ securities. It was intended to come into existence in 2003.

Bullion Precious metal that may be bought and sold for investment. Most types of bullion are at least 99.9% pure. Bullion is a commodity that investors may use as a hedge against recession and inflation. Thus, while it is volatile like most commodities, it always maintains a relatively high value.

Bullion Coins Coins struck from a precious metal that may be bought and sold for investment. Most bullion coins are at least 99.9% pure. Bullion coins are commodities that investors often use as a hedge against recession and inflation. Thus, while it is volatile like most commodities, it always maintains a relatively high value. Bullion coins trade for higher prices than the metals from which they are made, accounting for costs associated with their manufacture.

Bullish Describing an indicator that prices are likely to rise. A simple example of a bullish indicator is a large number of margin transactions, which means investors are buying and generally leads to higher prices. See also: Bearish.

Bullish Belt Hold In candlestick charting, a candlestick indicating a possible turnaround in a bear market. A bullish bear hold occurs after a series of losing trading days, represented by black candles. The bullish bear hold is a gaining trading day, represented by a white candle, in which the opening price is the bottom price and the closing price is only slightly lower than the intraday high, both of which are much higher than the opening price. This is represented by a long candle with no wick (or shadow) at the bottom and only a short wick (or shadow) at the top.

Bullish Divergence In technical analysis, a situation in which the price of a security goes to a new low while another indicator shows the trend is likely to reverse. That is, bullish divergence occurs when a bullish indicator shows a bearish sign (the new low) is unlikely to be true. This is a bullish sign. Technical analysts use a number of factors to attempt to observe divergence and make investment decisions accordingly. See also: MACD.

Bullish Engulfing Pattern In candlestick charting, a pattern with a small, black candle (representing a trading day with a loss) followed by a larger, white candle (representing a trading day with a gain). The closing price and high price in the white candle must both be higher than those in the black candle. A bullish engulfing pattern usually, but not always, comes during a bearish trend; it may be a signal that the trend is approaching its bottom and is about to become bullish.

Bullish Flattener A situation in which the yield curve for bonds is flattening. A bullish flattener occurs when long-term interest rates on bonds fall more rapidly than short-term rates so that the two begin to converge, resulting in a flat (or flatter) yield curve when it is plotted on a graph. This is considered a bullish indicator: it means investors believe stocks will rise in the short term, which causes the comparatively higher short-term rates. See also: Inverted yield curve, bearish flattener.

Bullish Harami In candlestick charting, a bullish sign in which candlesticks show the reversal of a market downtrend. A bullish harami is conceptualized by a large black candlestick (representing one trading day with a large loss) followed by a much smaller white candlestick in which both the top and the bottom are no longer than the top or the bottom of the black candlestick (representing the next trading day with a smaller gain). Technical analysts often recommend buying a security undergoing a bullish harami.

Bullpen Informal; a term for the center of a brokerage office where younger brokers keep their desks and do their work. This contrasts with the offices reserved for senior brokers.

Bultu An ancient Akkadian unit of weight approximately equivalent to 30 kilograms.

Bum A person unable or unwilling to work, and who therefore must beg for money. The term has a derogatory connotation, implying laziness. A large number of bums in an area may indicate economic dilapidation.

Bumbershoot Policy An insurance policy that covers shipyards for various marine and some non-marine risks. The policy covers all claims that the yard's other insurance policies do not. For example, it protects the shipyard from liability, indemnity, collisions and so forth. It is a type of umbrella policy.

Bumblebee Slang; a needlessly cumbersome financial statement, especially one that obscures the true financial statement. The term is most common in the context of small Christian churches and ministries.

BUMM ISO 3166-3 code for Burma, which changed its name to Myanmar. ISO 3166-3 codes are used to indicate names of countries that are no longer used.

Bumper Sticker In marketing, a small poster with adhesive on one side. Bumper stickers are usually affixed to a vehicle. They are commonly used to display political messages, though they may be used for business, humor, or any other purpose.

Bump-Up CD A certificate of deposit in which the holder has the right to increase the interest rate paid on it if prevailing interest rates increase at some point over the term of the CD. The holder may only do this once; if interest rates decline, the new, higher rate on the CD remains the same. A bump-up CD protects the investor from some of the interest rate risk inherent to normal CDs.

Bun A unit of weight in Taiwan approximately equivalent to 37.5 milligrams. It is used primarily in the sale of bulk foodstuffs.

Bunch To combine orders for a security for execution at the same time. A broker may bunch either odd-lot or round-lot orders, but only if all affected clients agree to it. Bunching may be particularly advantageous for odd-lotters (investors with orders for fewer than 100 securities) as it helps them to avoid extra fees they are otherwise charged.

Bund A bond issued by the federal government of Germany. Because it is guaranteed by the federal government, it is considered the safest asset in Germany. See also: U.S. Treasury security.

Bunder A Dutch unit of area equivalent to one hectare. It was adopted in 1817, soon after the establishment of the Kingdom of the Netherlands.

Bundesanleihen A bond issued by the German federal government with a maturity of 10 to 30 years. It has a coupon fixed upon issue. Because it is issued by a prominent government, it is considered very low risk. A Bundesanleihen is also called a bund.

Bundesbank The central bank of Germany. Established in 1957, it issued the Deutsche mark until 2002 when it was replaced by the euro. However, the Bundesbank remains the most influential member of the European System of Central Banks. Both the Bundesbank and the European Central Bank (ECB) are headquartered in Frankfurt. Among other duties, it is responsible for issuing euros and regulating banks under its jurisdiction. However, it is not a lender of last resort, as the ECB fulfills this duty.

Bundesbond A bond issued by the German federal government. It has a coupon fixed upon issue. Because it is issued by a prominent government, it is considered very low risk. On the primary market, Bundesbond issues are sold to investors at auction.

Bundesland In Austria and Germany, a political subdivision equivalent to a state or province.

Bundesministerium fur Wirtschaft und Technologie Federal Ministry of Economics and Technology. A cabinet department in Germany. It is responsible for setting policies for small business, industry, energy and other areas in accordance with applicable law. It traces its origins to 1917 and was established in its curren form in 2005.

Bundle A slang term for a large amount of money.

Bundle of Goods Multiple products that are sold as if they were a single product. For example, all seven books in the Harry Potter series may be sold as a box set.

Bundled Software Multiple software products that are sold as if they were a single product. For example, Microsoft Office contains a word processor, a spreadsheet, a slideshow program and an e-mail program.

Bundle-of-Rights Theory The total rights that come with the sale of real estate. The bundle of rights includes the ability to live on the property, to make improvements, to sell or rent it and otherwise to do anything to the property that does not violate the law.

Bundling 1. The practice of selling multiple products as if they were one. For example, all seven books in the Harry Potter series may be bundled and sold as a box set. **2.** The practice of compiling a number of financial products and selling them as securities. Mortgages are frequently bundled as mortgage-backed securities.

Bungalow A small, single-family home, usually with only one story. A bungalow is a term used by real estate agents for affordable housing available for working class and lower middle class persons to buy. Bungalows originated in India.

Bungee A slang term for an oversold security. The term derives from the fact that an oversold security has declined significantly in price but generally hits a bottom and begins to rise.

Bunker A large container on a ship used to hold fuel. See also: Bunker adjustment factor.

Bunker Adjustment Factor An increase in a shipping rate as the result of increased oil prices. Because higher oil prices add to expenses, a shipper may set a bunker adjustment factor so as not to reduce profits. Each shipping company sets its own bunker adjustment factor; regulators monitor BAFs so collusion does not take place.

Bunker Fuel Refined oil on a ship and used as fuel. See also: Bunker adjustment factor.

Bunny Bond A bond with a provision that bondholders may, at their discretion, reinvest coupon payments in other bonds with the same interest rate and maturity. This protects bondholders from the risk that interest rates will fall by the time coupon payments are made, resulting in lower returns. It is also called a multiplier bond or a guaranteed coupon reinvestment bond. See also: Reinvestment risk, PIK.

Buoyant Describing a market where prices are trending upward, especially when they are doing so gradually.

Bur An ancient Sumerian unit of area approximately equivalent to 64.8 square kilometers.

Burden of Proof The obligations one party must meet to prove a fact in court. The party holding the burden of proof in a case must back each of his/her assertions with evidence for them to be legally acceptable. In a criminal case, the burden of proof rests with the prosecutor; in a civil case, it resides with the plaintiff. See also: Beyond a reasonable doubt, Preponderance of evidence.

Bureau An agency or department, especially of a government. The U.S. Census Bureau is a prominent example.

Bureau Insurer An insurance company that belongs to a cooperative organization that helps the company set its premium rates. A bureau insurer may join such an organization if it is new to a state or to a market and lacks the experience to set rates on its own.

Bureau of Advertising An organization that promotes the American newspaper industry to advertisers. It attempts to encourage advertisers to buy space in newspapers and thereby keep the industry profitable. It provides potential advertisers and advertising agencies with information on local markets, paper circulation and other data. It is a non-profit organization and is a division of the American Newspaper Publishers Association.

Bureau of Economic Analysis An organization within the U.S. Department of Commerce that conducts research and statistics on the American economy. Perhaps most importantly, the BEA produces information on the American gross domestic product and balance of trade. It also researches foreign economies. Government policy and private investment decisions often are based on research from the Bureau of Economic Analysis. It should not be confused with the National Bureau of Economic Research.

Bureau of Federal Credit Unions A former agency of the U.S. federal government that chartered and regulated federal credit unions. It was a subset of several different divisions of the government throughout its history. It belonged at various times to the Farm Credit Agency, the FDIC, the Social Security Administration and the now-defunct Department of Health, Education, and Welfare. As the number of credit unions increased, the Bureau was replaced by the National Credit Union Administration. It existed from 1934 to 1970.

Bureau of Industry and Security An agency of the U.S. Department of Commerce charged with regulating exports to ensure that they are sent abroad in a safe and efficient manner. It also monitors exporters to help enforce applicable law, particularly arms control agreements and trade sanctions. It works with private companies as needed to perform its duties.

Bureau of International Expositions The governing body for World Expos. It organizes these expositions every five years as well as periodic, specialized expositions. These expositions are attended by tens of millions of people each time they are held. It was established in Paris in 1928.

Bureau of Labor Statistics A bureau of the U.S. Department of Labor responsible for the collection and publication of statistics on the state of the American economy. It publishes various statistics on employment and unemployment and is responsible for compiling the Consumer Price Index, which measures inflation. To avoid the appearance of partiality toward the policies of one political party or the other, it schedules the publications of its statistics more than a year in advance.

Bureau Rate A premium per unit of insurance established by a cooperative organization for insurance companies in individual states.

Bureaucracy The set of government employees who write, implement, and enforce regulations set under their purview by appropriate legislation. Examples of bureaucratic organizations in the United States include the IRS, the Department of Justice, and the Consumer Financial Protection Bureau. Max Weber argued that bureaucrats have no interests of their own, and that their incentives are identical to those of the state. Karl Marx, on the other hand, believed that bureaucrats protect themselves and their own positions ahead of the state. The term can have a negative connotation depending on its use.

Bureaucrat An administrator, especially of a government or large corporation. A bureaucrat is charged with enforcing the rules and ensuring that proper procedures are followed. The word has a negative connotation because bureaucrats are often thought to slow down progress or innovation. However, because bureaucrats help create a level playing field, Max Weber argued that they are necessary for the rule of law to function.

Burglary The act of entering a building unlawfully with the intention of committing a crime, usually but not always theft. Burglary is illegal in nearly every jurisdiction.

Burglary Insurance An insurance policy covering losses resulting from a burglary, which is the act of entering a building unlawfully with the intention of committing a crime, usually but not always theft. Burglary insurance for businesses is usually part of a larger policy. It ordinarily requires relatively high coinsurance, in the range of 40% to 80%.

Burial Insurance An insurance policy that pays for the policyholder's funeral upon his/her death. Burial insurance pays for expenses such as preparation of the body, the casket, the flowers, and so forth. The benefits from burial insurance are paid upon death, provided the policyholder does not live past 100. As with all insurance, one pays a premium to receive the benefits. Burial insurance is also called funeral insurance.

Burke Test A survey measuring the effectiveness of a television advertisement. The day following the broadcast of an ad, the Burke test is conducted on a portion of the target audience. The people selected are called on the telephone and asked questions about what the ad was trying to sell, how well they remembered it and so forth. This is used to gauge the success of both the advertising campaign itself and the effect it has on the advertiser's brand recognition.

Burmese Rupee The former currency of Burma. For much of its history, the Burmese rupee was identical to the Indian rupee as both countries were British colonies. Before 1937, the only differences were the languages printed on the currencies. The rupee did not circulate during World War II, since Japan, which conquered Burma, issued its own colonial currency. In 1948, Burma became independent and issued its own rupee, but this was replaced by the Burmese kyat in 1952.

Burn 1. In printing, the time at which an image is put on a plate. **2.** In film, a ghost of an image that remains after the image has disappeared.

Burn and Churn To make more trades on a discretionary account in order to inflate commissions, rather than client profits. That is, burning and churning occurs when a broker makes unnecessary trades on an account for his/her own profit, rather than the client's. Burning and churning is illegal.

Burn Rate The amount of money that a company spends each month from the amount it has raised from venture capital. For example, if a company is spending $100,000 per month, it is said to have a burn rate of 100,000. The burn rate is measured until the company begins to have a positive cash flow. If the burn rate exceeds expectations or cash flow remains negative for too long, the company may have a difficult time becoming profitable.

Burning Cost Ratio In insurance, the ratio of losses for which a reinsurer pays to the insurer's premium income. It is also called pure less cost.

Burnout In a mortgage-backed security, the percentage of mortgages underlying the security that were not re-financed following a drop in interest rates. Historically, a mortgage that is not re-financed is less likely to re-finance at the next drop in interest rates. As a result, potential investors in mortgage-backed securities often look for a high burnout rate because it reduces prepayment risk, or the risk that investors will be deprived of future interest payments because too many mortgages are prepaid.

Bursa Malaysia A holding company that operates a number of exchanges in Malaysia. It was established in 1964.

Burst In marketing, an ad on a product that looks vaguely like an explosion. For example, a burst may be placed on a cereal box touting the number of vitamins and minerals it contains. A burst is meant to call attention to itself in order to entice buyers. It is used both in consumer goods and in direct mail.

Burst Advertising Visual advertising with bright colors. Burst advertising is intended to attract attention in hopes that viewers will notice the ad. It is also called saturation.

Buru An ancient Akkadian unit of area approximately equivalent to 64.8 square kilometers.

Burundian Franc The currency of Burundi. It was introduced in 1964, replacing the Rwanda and Burundi franc. Plans have been proposed to replace the franc with the East African shilling, a common currency structured along the lines of the euro.

Bush Doctrine A neoconservative foreign policy idea in the United States. It is most commonly associated with efforts to prevent future terrorist attacks on the United States through the invasion of foreign countries thought to be safe havens for terrorist groups. It is also used to express regime change, or the attempt to replace a dictatorship with a fledgling democracy. More generally, the term describes American unilateralism.

Business 1. A company or other organization engaged in commerce. A business sells goods and/or services to clients. For example, a widget maker selling widgets to wholesalers or retailers is a widget business. A business may be for-profit or non-profit. **2.** Informal; an industry. For example, one may refer to the automotive

industry as the "car business." **3.** Informal; commerce. One who buys or sells with a company is said to "do business" with that company.

Business Activity Code A six digit code used in business to classify the principal activity a company performs. The business activity code is used by the IRS to categorize companies for tax purposes.

Business and Personal Property Coverage Form Also called a BPPCF. An insurance policy providing coverage for a building one owns, the additions and fixtures in it, the personal property contained in it, and/or the fixtures installed in a building one has leased. For example, a BPPCF covers a dance studio; the dance floor installed after purchasing the studio; all the tables, chairs, and other supplies; and/or the dance floor installed in another building the studio has leased.

Business Auto Coverage Form An insurance policy providing coverage for damage caused to an automobile owned by a business, the damage the automobile itself causes, and/or theft of the automobile. One pays premiums to the insurance company in exchange for this coverage. All U.S. states require drivers to have some form of car insurance.

Business Bad Debt A bad debt an individual incurs in an activity related to his/her primary line of work. For example, a mechanic might repair a car and allow the owner to pay on credit. If the mechanic does not collect payment, he incurs a business bad debt. In American tax, business bad debt is completely deductible, even if the debt has some remaining value. This contrasts with non-business bad debt, which is only deductible when entirely worthless.

Business Code A line on a Schedule C on which a self-employed person lists the principal activity he/she does for a living.

Business Combination Laws Laws in most U.S. states limiting the transactions between publicly-traded companies and their most prominent minority shareholders. Generally speaking, a company may not merge or conduct other major transactions with a company owned by a minority shareholder for a certain number of years after the minority shareholder takes on a certain, defined percentage of the company's equity.

Business Conditions The general state of an economy as it affects individual businesses. Examples of business condition indicators include profits, revenues and productivity.

Business Council for International Understanding Also called the BCIU. An organization that encourages dialogue between business and political leaders in different countries. It holds events, briefings and programs for networking and education. Members consist of more than 150 companies; government officials are usually invited to meetings as well. It was established in 1955 with the support of U.S. President Dwight Eisenhower.

Business Credit 1. Any loan or line of credit to a company or an individual for business purposes as opposed to personal use. **2.** A loan or line of credit that a company extends to another in order for the second company to buy goods and services, especially those necessary to conduct its operations. It is more commonly called trade credit.

Business Crime Insurance An insurance policy that provides coverage for losses resulting from theft or other crime committed against a business. For example, if a business is the victim of arson or burglary, business crime insurance will pay for damages.

Business Cycle The continuous expansion and contraction of economic growth in fairly regular intervals. That is, a business cycle involves GDP growth and the creation of wealth for a period of time, followed by overheating and a recession. When the recession reaches its bottom the business cycle starts again. Some economists believe that the length and strength of business cycles are easily predictable, while others dispute this. A business cycle is seen as an inevitable part of the capitalist system. It is informally called a boom-and-bust cycle. See also: Industry Life Cycle, Kondratiev Wave.

Business Cycle Indicators An index of a variety of indicators thought to predict the tops and bottoms of a business cycle. The BCI includes leading, lagging, and coincident indicators in order to provide the most accurate view possible. Nonetheless, many argue that because business cycles are always unpredictable to some degree, the BCI must taken with a grain of salt. It is published by The Conference Board. See also: CCI, CEO Confidence Index, Help Wanted Advertising Index.

Business Date The date on which a document or other information is processed. It should not be confused with the business day.

Business Day A time during which securities markets and most retailers and other shops are open. In much of the world, every day is a business day except for Saturday and Sunday. However, this is not a hard and fast rule. For example, in Bahrain, Sunday is a business day while Friday is not.

Business Development Bank of Canada A government-owned corporation in Canada that provides financing, advisory, and venture capital services for small businesses and start-ups. The BDC helps promote economic growth, particularly for exporters and technology companies. Bonds issued by the BDC are guaranteed by the Canadian government. It was established as the Industrial Development Bank in 1944.

Business Enterprise A company or other organization engaged in commerce. A business enterprise sells goods and/or services to clients. For example, a widget maker selling widgets to wholesalers or retailers is a widget business enterprise. A business enterprise may be for-profit or non-profit.

Business Environment Risk Index Also called the BERI. An index that measures risk to business in a specific country. The BERI is intended to help companies weigh the risk versus the potential return of expanding their operations abroad.

Business Etiquette Good manners that facilitate business by allowing one to be taken seriously and to prevent unintended offense. For example, it is customary in many areas for a man to wear a suit to business meetings; a person who does not follow this etiquette is often thought to be less likely to land a contract with a client. Business etiquette varies from country to country and even region to region. For this reason, it is helpful to investigate the etiquette of various areas before traveling to those areas.

Business Executive Enforcement Team A forum that allows for executives of exporting companies to communicate with the Bureau of Export Administration to discuss how to enforce American trade policies.

Business Expansion Scheme Also called the BES. A structure in the United Kingdom that assisted new and small businesses in raising capital. Individuals and companies received tax incentives to invest in new companies and other high-risk ventures. It resulted in a large increase in investment in new companies. The BES was introduced in 1983 and was replaced by the Enterprise Investment Scheme in 1994.

Business Expense Costs that result from having and maintaining a business. Rent and employee salaries are primary (and expensive) examples of business expenses, as are office supplies and raw materials from which to make products. Under most circumstances, business expenses are tax deductible.

Business Expense Deduction A reduction in a business's taxable income by costs that result from having and maintaining the business. Rent and employee salaries are primary (and expensive) examples of business expenses that are qualified for the deduction. For example, if a business has $1 million in revenue and $400,000 in overhead eligible for the business expense deduction, its taxable income is only $600,000.

Business Facilitation Office A booth at an international trade fair promoting American goods, services and companies.

Business Failure A situation in which a company or other business ceases operations because it is unable to generate sufficient revenue to cover its expenses. For example, if a company is unable to service debt it may file for bankruptcy and stop operating. Business failure is relatively common in the first year or so of operations because the owner is unable to compete for any number of reasons.

Business Fundamentals The facts that affect a company's underlying value. Examples of business fundamentals include debt, cash flow, supply of and demand for the company's products, and so forth. For instance, if a company does not have a sufficient supply of products, it will fail. Likewise, demand for the product must remain at a certain level in order for it to be successful. Strong business fundamentals are considered essential for long-term success and stability. See also: Value Investing, Fundamental Analysis.

Business Gift A gift given to another on behalf of a company. Gifts up to $25 per recipient per year are tax deductible, as are gifts of small items, such as pens and calendars, costing $4 or less each.

Business Income The money a person or company receives from doing business, especially in the course of a year. For example, if a mechanic repairs a car and is paid, he/she receives business income. It is taxable, but one may remove expenses from business income when calculating the portion that is taxed.

Business Incubator A program to help a start-up stay in business. A business incubator may offer management consulting or other services to provide a new company with needed resources to overcome common problems. Very commonly, business incubators also offer more concrete aid, such as free or discounted rent on an office for the first six months of operations. Companies that pass through a business incubator stage have a much higher success rate than those that do not.

Business Information Office 1. The department at a company responsible for information technology and often other technological aspects of the company's operations. Some companies may combine the information office with the security office. See also: Chief information officer, Chief information security officer. 2. See: Business facilitation office.

Business Information Service for the Newly Independent States A program of the American government to assist former Soviet-bloc nations in the transition to the free market. BISNIS promotes American exports to and investment in these countries, as well as encourages collaboration between U.S. and Eastern Europe and Central Asia.

Business Intelligence The use of data to discover what is happening with a company. An example of business intelligence is the use of a computer program to look at financial statements to detect irregularities or other patterns. A company may do this to improve its own efficiency, an outside observer may do it to make recommendations or to invest, and a competitor may do it to find potential advantages.

Business Interruption An event that causes a business to relocate or temporarily close. For example, an office may flood and becomes unusable, or a natural disaster may make commerce unfeasible in an entire area. A company may purchase business interruption insurance to guard against losses resulting from this.

Business Interruption Insurance An insurance policy that provides coverage in case some event causes a business to relocate or temporarily close. For example, if an office floods and becomes unusable, business interruption insurance will replace the profits the company would have made during the time it is closed and also will cover its operating expenses. It is also called business income coverage.

Business Judgment Rule In American business law, the concept granting members of the board of directors of a corporation the presumption that they intend to work for the company's profitability, provided they act in good faith. That is, courts assume boards of directors think they are doing the right thing even if an act harms the company in retrospect. This protects members from shareholder lawsuits in the event their actions do not go as planned. On the other hand, if a board of directors is found to have squandered the company's resources by, for example, grossly overpaying when buying or receiving far too little when selling assets, it may still be found legally liable.

Business Liability Insurance An insurance policy protecting the owners of a business both from paying for damage resulting from a fire, vandalism, and other misfortunes and from legal liability in case the business's actions or negligence result in an injury. The premium of a business property and liability insurance package may be lower than the sum of two separate policies.

Business List 1. A mailing list of companies. This may be used in b2b communications. 2. A list of companies in a particular sector or geographical area. This may be published in a phone book, online, by a chamber of commerce, or in some other form.

Business Model A plan a company or other business uses in order to make a profit from its operations. Some business models are complex, while others are simple. For example, a hedge fund's business model may involve encouraging high net worth individuals to make a large investment that will be used in a series of complicated (and sometimes obscure) transactions. On the other hand, a freelance editor's business model is simply to write and edit for clients in order to receive payment.

Business Office An office from which a company conducts some or all of its back office activities. A business office may provide offices for managers, accountants, human resources personnel and other employees necessary for the smooth function of a company. These employees may not be directly involved with the creation or distribution of products. A business office contrasts with properties, such as factories, where operational activities take place.

Business Overhead Expense Insurance An insurance policy that provides coverage in case the owner of a business is disabled and temporarily, but completely, unable to work. For example, if a business owner contracts cancer and is unable to work during treatment, business overhead expense insurance will pay his/her operating expenses during the period of disability so the business can continue to function. Examples of included expenses are property taxes, insurance premiums, interest on debt, employee salaries, and so forth. The expenses must be incurred during the period of disability (for instance, the company cannot close its main office and expect compensation for rent it is not paying). The maximum period during which coverage is paid is usually one or two years. See also: Business income coverage.

Business Plan A formal statement of what a business wants to accomplish and how it intends to accomplish it. A business plan includes a vision statement, which is a brief summary of the company's goals (usually some variation of "to make money by creating a superior product"). It also includes details of the products the company makes or intends to make, how it will sell them, and how much they will cost. A business plan nearly always includes a budget. Such plans are important to investors, who want to know how their money is supposed to be used, and to management to help keep a company on track.

Business Practice Any tactic or activity a business conducts to reach its objectives. Ultimately, a business's objective is to make money. Business practices are the ways it attempts to do so in the most cost effective way. A company may have rules for business practices to ensure that its employees are efficient in their work and abide by applicable laws. See also: Business ethics.

Business Process The series of activities undertaken to create a product or deliver a service. Companies often lay down specific rules for business process to ensure activities are completed in an organized and efficient manner. Business process may involve division of labor between multiple persons and/or technologies. For example, in a publishing company, one person may write material, a second may edit it, a third may add graphics, and a fourth may print it. Business process is also called business function.

Business Process Management The process by which a company seeks to align all its departments and activities toward the same goal. In general, this goal is to deliver the best product to customers or clients. Business process management aims for high efficiency, particularly by openness to new ideas in both information technology and human resources. BPM activities are divided into design, modeling, execution, monitoring and optimization. See also: Six Sigma.

Business Process Reengineering The use of computers and information technology to improve a company's efficiency. For example, an automobile factory may automate and use more machines, rather than workers, to make cars. Because such companies need fewer workers, they often need fewer managers, who usually command higher salaries. Business process reengineering can increase the speed with which products are made (because machines can work 24 hours a day) and can reduce overhead (because the company needs to pay fewer employees). This is considered beneficial for consumers because it results in less expensive products. However, it is controversial, since some perceive BPR as a cause of unemployment.

Business Property Property (other than capital assets) that a person or company holds for business purposes. Examples include real estate, inventory, receivables and depreciating personal property.

Business Property and Liability Insurance Package An insurance policy protecting the owners of a business both from paying for damage resulting from fire, vandalism and other misfortunes and from legal liability in case the business's actions or negligence result in injury. The premium for a business property and liability insurance package may be lower than the sum of the premiums of two separate policies.

Business Property Relief In the United Kingdom, the reduction or elimination of inheritance tax on the transfer of some types of property used for business purposes. For example, shares in unquoted companies in which the transferor had majority control are not subject to an inheritance tax because of business property relief. Likewise, land and machinery used primarily for a business before the transfer are taxed at half the ordinary rate.

Business Publication Audit of Circulation A non-profit organization that monitors business-to-business magazines, periodicals, and other media that sell advertising space. It researches audiences, readership and other information about business-to-business publications. Advertisers provide funding for the BPA because they use this information in making business decisions. It was established in 1931. See also: BPA statement.

Business Purpose A transaction with any purpose other than to reduce taxes. An act with a business purpose may have the side effect of reducing taxes (which may be the primary reason a business conducted it), but it must also advance the goals or objectives of the business. Having a legitimate business purpose is a key standard the IRS uses in determining whether an act is tax avoidance or tax evasion.

Business Rate A property tax on a business or other non-residential property. Business rates are used to fund local government services and projects such as road construction and improvement. Business rates are used in England and Wales; they trace their origins to at least the 16th century.

Business Reply Card In marketing, a small, preaddressed card included in a piece of mail allowing the receiver to reply to the sender without charge. This is used for mail sent to a large number of people and/or organizations. A card may be inside a periodical, for example, and it may allow the receiver to submit his/her subscription renewal without a stamp. A mailer pays the U.S. Postal Service a flat, annual fee to be able to use business reply cards.

Business Reply Envelope In marketing, a preaddressed envelope included in a piece of mail allowing the receiver to reply to the sender without charge. This is used for mail sent to a large number of people and/or organizations. For example, an envelope may be sent along with a letter promoting a political candidate, and it may allow the receiver to submit a contribution without a stamp. A mailer pays the U.S. Postal Service a flat, annual fee to be able to use business reply envelopes.

Business Reply Mail In marketing, a preaddressed card or letter included in a piece of mail allowing the receiver to reply to the sender without charge. This is used for mail sent to a large number of people and/or organizations. Business reply mail may be inside a periodical, for example, and it may allow the receiver to submit his/her subscription renewal without a stamp. A mailer pays the U.S. Postal Service a flat, annual fee to be able to use business reply mail.

Business Risk The risk that a company will go bankrupt. Every company carries the business risk that it will produce insufficient cash flow in order to maintain operations. Business risk can come from a variety of sources, some systemic and others unsystemic. That is, every company has the business risk that the broader economy will perform poorly and therefore that sales will be poor, and also the risk that the market simply will not like its products.

Business Risk Exclusion A clause in a business's insurance policy stating that it does not provide coverage for products that do not meet the company's quality specifications. For example, if a company produces widgets guaranteed to last 15 years and they only last four, the company's insurance may not cover refunds or other losses because of the business risk exclusion.

Business Roundtable A lobbying organization for major corporations in the United States. Members consist of the CEOs of large companies. It is known for opposing legislation favored by labor unions and for supporting free trade. It was established in 1972 and is based in Washington, D.C.

Business Sales and Inventories An estimate of the total value of all sales and inventories in the manufacturing, retail and wholesale industries. This is an indicator of consumer spending; that is, when the figure is high, it shows that consumers are spending more on goods. Thus, changes to business sales and inventories can be a signal of economic growth or decline. It is published monthly.

Business School A college that offers undergraduate and/or postgraduate degrees representing study of business. These schools offer theoretical, and perhaps also practical, coursework in how to manage a company, construct a business model and generally run a business. In business school, one may concentrate in fields like accounting, entrepreneurship, finance, marketing and supply chain management, among others. See also: Masters of business administration, Bachelor of business administration.

Business Segment A division or subset of a business' operations, especially in large corporations. For a division to be considered a segment, it must directly earn revenue for the company. For example, a heavily diversified corporation may have one segment dedicated to telecommunications, another to manufacturing, and a third

to energy. It is also known simply as a segment. Internally, each segment's expenses and revenues are accounted for separately.

Business Starts Index The number of businesses started in the United States each week. These businesses may or may not be incorporated. Data is categorized by state for the sake of comparison. The index is an indicator of economic growth or decline. It is published by Dun & Bradstreet.

Business Strategy The principles guiding how a business uses its resources to achieve its goals. A strategy states a business's focus and indicates the basic steps the business will use to achieve it. The ultimate aim of any strategy is to make money, but each company takes a different (sometimes very different) approach to achieve this goal. Business strategies are widely studied and discussed in management consulting.

Business Structure The way a business is organized. The business structure states who owns the company, how profits are distributed and which managers perform what jobs. It is also important for tax and liability purposes, as companies are often taxed differently from each other and managers may have differing levels of responsibility in the event of wrongdoing or a lawsuit. In the United States, the three business structures recognized by the IRS are sole proprietorship, partnership and corporation. Other structures that are legally important (but not for tax purposes) include limited liability company, S-Corporation, and C-Corporation.

Business Studies The academic study of how businesses operate. It may be pursued at the undergraduate and postgraduate levels, and occasionally even in secondary education. Generally, business studies involve theoretical, and perhaps also practical, coursework in how to manage a company, construct a business model and generally run a business. They may also involve the study of accounting, entrepreneurship, finance, marketing and/or supply chain management. See also: Masters of business administration.

Business Transacted with Producer Controlled Property Act Also called the Business Transacted with Producer Controlled Property/Casualty Insurer Act. Model legislation to regulate insurance brokers in U.S. states. The act allows state insurance commissioners (or their equivalent) to hold brokers liable for civil penalties if their conduct results in the bankruptcy of an insurance company regulated by that state. The commissioners may also require the broker to pay into the guarantee fund. It was written by the National Association of Insurance Commissioners so states would have roughly the same guidelines.

Business Valuation The process of determining how much a business is worth. Business valuation is highly subjective because it involves estimating the value of intangible assets like trade secrets and brand recognition. It also involves valuation of tangible assets like machinery and stockholder equity. A business valuation may be performed for a potential investor or buyer.

Business Value How much a business is worth. Business value is a highly subjective measure because it involves estimating the value of intangible assets like trade secrets and brand recognition. It adds to this the value of tangible assets like machinery and stockholder equity. Business value is especially important for potential investors or buyers.

Businessowners Policy An insurance policy that provides coverage in case some event causes a business to relocate or temporarily close. It also provides coverage for damage to the property owned by the business. For example, if an office floods and becomes unusable, a businessowners policy will replace the profits the company would have made during the time the company was closed and also will pay to repair the damage from the flood.

Businessowners Policy-Section I: Property Coverage The portion of businessowners policy that provides coverage for damage to the property owned by the business. For example, if an office floods and becomes unusable, the property damage portion of a businessowners policy will pay to repair the damage from the flood.

Businessowners Policy-Section II: Liability Coverage An insurance policy that provides coverage in case an accident or injury results in the business being found legally liable. For example, if a person trips in a company's office because of an uneven floor and the company is found liable, liability coverage would pay the damages on its behalf.

Business-to-Business A transaction conducted between a business and another business. For example, a publisher may sell books to a retailer, ship it to him/her, and receive payment without the books ever going to their end users (i.e. readers). The term is often associated with e-commerce, that is, with business-to-business transactions over the Internet.

BusinessWorks A computer program for small businesses with fewer than 50 employees. It allows companies to record transactions, expenses and revenue, and to perform other activities related to accounting.

Bust 1. The cancellation of an order to a broker after it has been executed. Busts usually occur if some error has been made. **2.** A period of rapid decline for a security or market. A bust is associated with a bear market. See also: Boom-bust cycle.

Bustarella Italian for "little envelope." It is a euphemism for a bribe.

Busted Bond 1. A bond that has defaulted and on which further payments are extremely unlikely or impossible. Busted bond certificates have become collectors' items. A busted bond is also called an old bond. **2.** See: Busted convertible.

Busted Convertible Security A convertible security in which the underlying stock is trading 50% or more below the value of the convertible option. This renders the convertible option nearly worthless, and the security acts like common debt. This is considered a low risk investment with the possibility of high return because a busted convertible usually has a fixed return, and there is a small chance that the stock will recover allowing the investor to exercise the convertible option.

Busted Takeover An acquisition of one company by another in which the acquiring company finances the purchase with debt and then sells various assets of the target company in order to repay the debt. A busted takeover is most advantageous when the acquiring company is cash poor and the target company has a surplus of undervalued assets.

Busy In marketing, an informal term for an advertisement with so many graphics, sound effects or other such features that it detracts from the overall message, thus leaving no impression about the product being marketed.

Butt An obsolete measure of volume equivalent to 126 gallons.

Butterfly 1. See: Butterfly shift. **2.** See: Butterfly spread.

Butterfly Shift A change in the yield curve for bonds in which yields on short-term bonds and long-term bonds change the same amount but the yield on medium-term bonds does not. For example, if yields on short- and long-term bonds move up 1.5% but the yield on medium-term bonds moves up only 0.5%, this is considered a butterfly shift. A butterfly shift may be positive, as in the example described, or negative, in which short- and long-term yields move down at a rate greater than medium-term yields. The term comes from the shape of the yield curve in these situations; it looks like a butterfly flapping its wings.

Butterfly Spread An option strategy wherein one sells two options with the same strike price and buys two other options, one with a low strike and one with a high strike. The butterfly spread limits both the risk and the profit potential; it is profitable only if the price of the underlying asset remains in a relatively narrow range. One may use a butterfly spread on both calls and puts, but not on both mixed together. See also: bull spread, bear spread.

Button A link to a file on a computer represented by a place the user can click with a mouse. A button may open a program, a directory or almost anything else contained in the computer. It may or may not be positioned on the desktop.

Butut A division of the Gambian dalasi equal in value to 1/100 of one dalasi.

Butylka Vinnaya A Russian unit of liquid volume approximately equivalent to 768.7 milliliters. It was rendered obsolete when the Soviet Union began to use the metric system in 1924. It was based on the size of a bottle of wine.

Butylka Vodochnaya A Russian unit of liquid volume approximately equivalent to 615 milliliters. It was rendered obsolete when the Soviet Union began to use the metric system in 1924. It was based on the size of a bottle of vodka.

Buxbox 1. A way of budgeting for small organizations in which each department or task is allocated a certain amount of money and in which spending is permitted for that department or task only if there is money left for that line department or task. For example, an organization may set aside a certain amount of money each month for client entertainment. If it has already spent the money for client entertainment for the month, the buxbox method will not permit the organization to borrow from other line items to take a client to lunch. The buxbox method is used most commonly for small Christian churches and ministries. **2.** In the buxbox method, the allocation of money made for each department or task.

Buy To take ownership of some asset in exchange for some monetary remuneration. Buying may take any of several forms. In a cash purchase, the buyer gives cash or a cash equivalent immediately in exchange for the asset. In a credit sale, the buyer takes ownership immediately in exchange for future payment, often with interest. An example of buying is a simple transaction involving widgets. If the buyer is willing to pay $2 per widget and the seller wishes to sell 100 widgets, then the seller gives to the buyer 100 widgets and, in their place, receives $200. See also: Sale.

Buy a Spread An options position in which an investor buys an option at a given premium and writes another option with a lower premium and a different strike price. It is important to note that both options expire on the same day. An investor buys a spread to create a position in which he/she will make a profit whether or not the options are exercised. If the investor exercises the option he/she bought, it is because he/she expects to profit on the resale of the underlying asset. If the option with the lower premium is exercised, the investor profits on the sale of the underlying. See also: Exotic option, Spread.

Buy American Restrictions A section of the American Recovery and Reinvestment Act prohibiting the use of most foreign iron, steel or manufactured items in projects sponsored by the Act. Proponents argued the restrictions were intended to stimulate American manufacturing and thereby to create American jobs. Critics contended they were inefficient and had the potential to incite retaliatory measures from other countries, which could have a net negative impact on the U.S. economy. See also: Trade War.

Buy and Hold An investment strategy in which one does not do any trading on a portfolio between the initial selection of the securities and the end of a certain time period (which is usually a long time). A buy-and-hold strategy ignores short and medium-term trends and concentrates exclusively on the long-term. A buy-and-hold strategy attempts to eliminate any emotional trading that may be done foolishly during a particular bear market. In general, a buy-and-hold strategy yields a solid return as the market trends upward with time. However, it can be exceptionally risky during a prolonged and severe bear market or recession. For example, if an investor had used a buy-and-hold strategy starting in 1929 and had held it throughout the Great Depression, he/she would have had to wait most of his/her life to see a profit on the portfolio. See also: Active investing, Value investing.

Buy Break A situation in which the price of a security rises above its resistance level (the price above which the security rarely rises). In technical analysis, a buy break is a highly bullish signal as it indicates the security will probably continue to rise.

Buy In To buy the same security a second time because the seller did not deliver in a timely manner the first time. In a buy in, the buyer informs the exchange of the delivery failure; if the second transaction is more expensive, the original seller must pay the difference.

Buy Limit Order An order to a broker to buy a security if and only if the best available price is equal to or less than some set price. See also: limit order.

Buy Low, Sell High The practice of buying a security when its price is (or is perceived to be) low and selling it when its price is high. The ability to buy low and sell high requires one to be able to determine roughly when the low and high prices for a security occur. There are a number of technical indicators analysts use to find these, but critics of the practice contend it is impossible or at least excessively risky.

Buy Minus Order An order to buy a security with very specific price requirements. The price at which the order is executed may not be higher than the security's last price if the last price was a downtick or a zero-minus tick. If the previous trade was an uptick or a zero-plus tick, the price may not be higher than the difference between the last price and its change (which is itself the difference between the current price and the close on the previous trading day).

Buy on Close An order to buy a security at the end of the trading day at the best available price. See also: at-the-close order.

Buy on Margin To buy a security with money borrowed from a brokerage. Doing so opens up investment opportunities for an investor that he/she might not otherwise have been able to afford. More importantly, however, a margin security increases the possibility of a higher return and the risk of more losses. The practice of buying on margin is governed by Regulation T. See also: Margin call, Maintenance, Margin account.

Buy On Opening An order to buy a security when an exchange opens at the best price available in the opening range.

Buy on the Bad News Informal; to buy a stock after its price has recently declined because of a negative rumor or report. One buys on the bad news when one assumes that the recent price decline has resulted in an undervalued stock. That is, one buys with the hope that the price will recover. However, it carries the risk that the stock will continue to decline.

Buy on the Dips Informal; to buy a stock after its price has recently declined. One buys on the dips when one assumes that the recent price decline has resulted in an undervalued stock. That is, one buys with the hope that the price will recover. However, it carries the risk that the stock will continue to decline.

Buy Order An instruction from an investor to a broker to buy a certain amount of a security. Buy orders may take various forms. For example, an investor may instruct the broker to buy immediately at the best available price, or to wait until a certain price is reached. See also: Sell order.

Buy Side The institutional investors that buy most securities available for sale on Wall Street. See also: Sell side.

Buy Signal In charting and technical analysis, any condition thought to be favorable to buying. Examples include a double bottom and achieving a new high price in heavy trading volume. See also: Sell Signal.

Buy Stop Order A stop order that becomes a market order to buy a security if it rises above its current price. That is, a buy stop order is not executed so long as the security is at or below the price when the order was made, but is executed at the best available price when it rises above that order. An investor who makes a buy stop order operates on the premise that if a security rises, it will likely continue to rise. In other words, the maker of a buy stop order hopes to profit from a security's upward momentum.

Buy the Book An order to a broker to buy all shares of a security available at the current offer price, whether from one specialist or from everyone willing to sell. Large institutional investors usually make this order. The term comes from record books specialists kept before they began to use computers.

Buy the Rumor, Sell the Fact A catchphrase meaning that positive rumors about a company often cause stock prices to rise (because of increased buying on the part of investors), but then the prices fall (because of increased selling) after actual reports do not bear out the rumors.

Buy to Close Informal for closing a position, especially in options. See also: Buy to cover, Buy to open.

Buy To Cover To buy a security one has previously sold short in order to close a position. In order to make a profit on a short cover, one must buy the security at a price lower than the price at which one short sold it. Likewise, one may buy to cover to avoid or pay a margin call, if it appears that one will lose in a short sale and the brokerage demands the return of cash or securities. See also: Maintenance margin.

Buy to Open Informal for opening a position, especially in options. See also: Buy to cover, Buy to close.

Buy-and-Write Strategy An investment strategy in which an investor writes an option while holding an equal and opposite position on the underlying asset. A buy write call option occurs when the investor owns the underlying asset and writes a call so that the underlying is on hand to sell to the option holder if the option is exercised. A buy write put option occurs when the investor writes a put has enough cash to cover the strike if the put is exercised. It is thought that utilizing buy-and-write strategy is a beneficial tactic as the investor may profit from the option premium. See also: Covered option.

Buyback The act of a publicly-traded company buying its own stock, sometimes at a price well above fair market value. Buyback is not intended to stop trade on its stock. Rather, it is an attempt either to reduce the supply of shares in the market (with the hope of driving up the share price) or to prevent a real or suspected hostile takeover. If a company becomes its own majority or plurality shareholder, it either makes a hostile takeover impossible or more expensive for the acquiring company. A buyback may occur all at once or gradually over time. See also: Antitakeover measure, Self-tender offer.

Buydown A prepayment on a loan, especially a mortgage, that reduces monthly payments thereafter. A buydown may temporarily reduce payments, for example, by reducing the loan's interest rate for a certain period. On the other hand, a permanent buydown reduces the interest rate by a lesser amount for the life of the loan. A buydown is often made by a third party, but this is not always the case.

Buyer The person or company that takes ownership of some asset in exchange for some monetary remuneration. Buying may take any of several forms. In a cash purchase, the buyer gives cash or a cash equivalent immediately in exchange for the asset. In a credit sale, the buyer takes ownership immediately in exchange for future payment, often with interest.

Buyer Behavior The motivations behind a buyer's purchases. For example, a consumer's buyer behavior may tend toward personal consumption, and he/she therefore may buy in small quantities relative to a wholesaler.

Buyer Credit A credit given to an importer's account by the recipient of a letter of credit (that is, a bank) in exchange for on-time payment. The originator of the letter of credit (the importer's own bank) may negotiate with the recipient for buyer credits.

Buyer Credit Protocol A guarantee of payment made by the Canadian Export Development Corporation to foreign buyers. The buyer credit protocol is intended to promote Canadian exports.

Buyer Readiness Stages The six psychological stages through which a person passes when deciding to purchase a product. The six stages are awareness of the product, knowledge of what it does, interest in the product, preference over competing products, conviction of the product's suitability, and purchase. Marketing campaigns exist in large part to move the target audience through the buyer readiness stages.

Buyer's Agent A person or company that represents the potential buyer in a real estate transaction. The buyer's agent, in exchange for a commission or fee, attempts to negotiate the seller to a more favorable price and/or better terms. A buyer's agent contrasts with a real estate agent, who represents the seller.

Buyer's Broker In a real estate transaction, the agent who represents the potential buyer of a property. The buyer's broker is responsible for representing the buyer's interest and trying to achieve the best price and terms on the deal. The buyer's broker receives a commission on the value of the sale of property.

Buyer's Call A contract between a buyer and seller whereby the parties agree to trade a commodity on the spot market (which the seller has) in exchange for a futures contract on the same commodity (which the buyer purchases). Alternatively, the buyer may simply agree to buy the commodity on the spot market at some point in the future. Buyer's calls are useful when a buyer needs something that the seller will not need until later.

Buyer's Fee In an auction, a fee paid by the purchaser to the person or organization holding the auction on top of the top bid. For example, if one bids $1,000 for an antique bed, one may have to pay a 10% buyer's fee (or $100) if one wins the auction. A buyer's fee is one way an auctioneer makes money from the auction.

Buyer's Market A market situation in which lower prices prevail due to excess supply and a shortage of demand. A buyer's market may occur in one particular sector or across the wider economy. For example, if there are 10 houses in a neighborhood and eight of them are up for sale, it is likely that their prices will race toward the bottom. This means that a prospective homebuyer looking in that area will almost certainly find a good deal on a house. See also: Seller's market.

Buyer's Remorse Regret a buyer may feel, especially after making a major purchase. The buyer may feel like he/she was pressured, spent too much, and/or purchased an inferior product. Some laws or policies may allow a buyer to return a product within a certain number of days and to receive a refund, but usually there is very little one can do about buyer's remorse.

Buyers Strike A situation in which a large number of buyers stop purchasing one or more commodities over an extended period of time in order to reduce the price. For example, everyone in a city may choose to bike to work instead of drive as part of an effort to reduce gas prices. A buyers strike is similar to but distinct from a boycott, which may be undertaken for moral reasons.

Buy-In Management Buy-Out Also called a BIMBO. A situation in which both the current managers of a company and one or more outside investors collectively purchase a controlling interest in the company. A BIMBO is thought to give the new owners both the experience of the current management and new ideas from the outside investors.

Buying Climax A situation in which a security's price has risen very quickly and very high on heavy trading volume. A buying climax is often followed by steep price correction. See also: Selling climax.

Buying Habits An individual's or group's normal purchases. Buying habits may shift over time with an individual's or society's changing needs. Marketing is an attempt to influence buying habits.

Buying Panic The rapid buying of a security by a large number of investors. This decreases the supply of the security available for sale and therefore drives up the price. Buying panics occur for a number of reasons. For example, a stock may rise suddenly in price if its company issues an unexpectedly positive earnings report. The panic comes from investors' desire to buy into the stock immediately before the price rises even more. See also: Panic sale, Sell-off.

Buying Power Money in a margin account that an investor has available to purchase securities. An investor with a margin account has buying power if the market value of securities placed as collateral in the margin account does not drop below a predetermined level. For example, if one has $10,000 in collateral in a margin account and the account has a maintenance level of 25%, one's buying power is $40,000. See also: Margin call.

Buying Rate The highest price a potential buyer is willing to pay for a security. A buying rate is also called a bid.

Buying the Index The act of buying all stocks tracked in the S&P 500 in proportion to their representation in that index. One buys the index when one wants to achieve the same return as the S&P 500 itself. The S&P 500 is the index used for this because it is considered an indicator of the state of the broader economy.

Buy-or-Die Message In direct mail marketing, a message to an inactive recipient in which the recipient is told he/she will be removed from the list unless some response is made. A response to a buy-or-die message often results in more loyalty from the recipient; no response saves the mailer the expense of keeping the recipient on the list.

Buyout 1. An investment in which an entire company, or, more commonly, the controlling interest in the company, is sold. For example, if Jack and Frank each own a 50% stake in a mechanic shop, Frank may conduct a buyout by purchasing Jack's half of the company. In publicly-traded companies, buyouts are usually acquisitions by another company. However, a single investor may buy out a publicly-traded company; one calls this "going private." Other types of buyouts include venture capital buyouts or management buyouts. See also: Friendly takeover, Hostile takeover. **2.** In a contract, the act of one party paying a fee to the other party to end the contract before its completion. The term especially applies to employer-employee contracts. See also: Break fee.

Buyout Program A program in which an employer asks employees to quit voluntarily in exchange for a lump sum payment, or a series of payments over a brief period of time. A buyout program generally is created when the employer is facing long-term financial difficulties. It releases the employer from the liability of continuing to pay salary, insurance, pension payments, and so forth. If a sufficient number of employees participate in a buyout program, the financial situation of the employer may improve sufficiently to avoid involuntary layoffs.

Buy-Side Analyst An analyst who researches and evaluates the institutional investors that buy most securities available for sale on Wall Street. See also: Sell side.

Buyuk Donum A Turkish measure of area approximately equivalent to 2.72 square kilometers. It became obsolete when Turkey made the metric system mandatory in 1933.

BV 1. ISO 3166-1 alpha-2 code for Bouvet Island. This would be the code used in international transactions to and from Bouvet Island bank accounts, though as the island is uninhabited, this is unlikely to be used. **2.** ISO 3166-2 geocode for Bouvet Island. This is used as an international standard for shipping to Benin.

BVT GOST 7.67 Latin three-letter geocode for Bouvet Island. The code is used for international shipping to Bouvet Island. As with all GOST 7.67 codes, it is used primarily in Cyrillic alphabets.

BW 1. ISO 3166-1 alpha-2 code for the Republic of Botswana. This is the code used in international transactions to and from Botswanan bank accounts. **2.** ISO 3166-2 geocode for Botswana. This is used as an international standard for shipping to Botswana. Each district has its own code with the prefix "BW." For example, the code for the Central District is ISO 3166-2:BW-CE.

BWA GOST 7.67 Latin three-letter geocode for Botswana. The code is used for transactions to and from Botswana bank accounts and for international shipping to Botswana. As with all GOST 7.67 codes, it is used primarily in Cyrillic alphabets.

BWP ISO 4217 code for the Botswanan pula. It was introduced in 1976, replacing the South African rand. It has historically been one of the strongest currencies in Africa, and is used in Zimbabwe (along with other currencies) because the Zimbabwean dollar is effectively worthless.

Bwrdeistref In Wales, a political subdivision equivalent to a county.

BY 1. ISO 3166-1 alpha-2 code for the Republic of Belarus. This is the code used in international transactions to and from Belarusian bank accounts. **2.** ISO 3166-2 geocode for Belarus. This is used as an international standard for shipping to Belarus. Each Belarusian province has its own code with the prefix "BY." For example, the code for the Province of Brest is ISO 3166-2:BY-BR.

BYAA ISO 3166-3 code for Byelorussian Soviet Socialist Republic, which changed its name to Belarus in 1991. ISO 3166-3 codes are used to indicate names of countries that are no longer used.

BYB ISO 4217 code for the first Belarusian ruble. It was issued in 1992, existing alongside the Soviet ruble for several months but eventually replacing it. It was subject to high inflation and was replaced by the second ruble (code BYR) in 2000.

Bylaw Amendment Limitation A restriction on the process of amending the bylaws of a publicly-traded company. Examples of bylaw amendment limitations include requirements for a supermajority of shareholders to agree, or a provision rendering certain bylaws unamendable. Bylaw amendment limitations can be part of an anti-takeover measure and are governed by state law. See also: Charter amendment limitations.

Bylaws Rules established by a company or other organization setting forth details on how it is to be organized. Bylaws do not set forth the basic structure of the company; this is done in the organization's charter. For example, a charter may indicate that the company or organization must have a board of directors, while its bylaws state how many directors there are to be and how often they are elected. Bylaws are approved by shareholders (or the equivalent in other organizations) and may be amended by them.

Byline In journalism, the text usually immediately below the headline giving the name, company and/or position of an article's writer.

Bypass Trust An irrevocable trust into which the trustor deposits funds and other assets to provide for a surviving spouse. In a bypass trust, the trustor names his/her surviving spouse as beneficiary and provides that the income and/or principal from the trust shall pass to that spouse upon the trustor's death. A bypass trust is common when a person wishes to avoid estate taxes on assets passing to the spouse. See also: Q-TIP.

BYR ISO 4217 code for the Belarusian ruble. It was issued in 2000 after an earlier ruble suffered from inflation. While there are periodic discussions of a currency union with Russia, the Belarusian ruble has been pegged to the U.S. dollar since 2008.

Byte A unit of digitally stored information. A byte is the number of bits (or the 0 or 1 characters in binary code) needed to print a single letter or other character of text.

BZ 1. ISO 3166-1 alpha-2 code for Belize. This is the code used in international transactions to and from Belizean bank accounts. **2.** ISO 3166-2 geocode for Belize. This is used as an international standard for shipping to Belize. Each district has its own code with the prefix "BZ." For example, the code for the District of Toledo is ISO 3166-2:BZ-TOL.

BZD ISO 4217 code for the Belize dollar. This became the code in 1973, when British Honduras changed its name to Belize. While it was initially pegged to the British pound, the peg switched to the U.S. dollar (to which the currency of British Honduras had previously been fixed) in 1978.

C 1. A symbol appearing next to a stock listed on NASDAQ indicating that the stock is temporarily exempt from listing requirement. All NASDAQ listings use a four-letter abbreviation; if a "C" follows the abbreviation, it indicates that the security being traded is currently exempt. **2.** In money market mutual funds, a symbol indicating that the fund is exempt from federal income taxes. **3.** In dividends, a symbol, which appears mainly in newspapers, that the dividend is liquidating.

C Corporation A business that is legally completely separate from its owners. Most publicly-traded companies (and all major ones) fall under this classification. For United States tax purposes, C corporations are required to pay income taxes on their profits. The advantage to a C corporate structure is the fact that, unlike S corporations, there is no limit to the number of shareholders. A disadvantage is the fact that, because a C corporation is taxed itself and its individual shareholders are taxed on dividends, it is subject to double taxation.

CA 1. ISO 3166-1 alpha-2 code for Canada. This is the code used in international transactions to and from Canadian bank accounts. **2.** ISO 3166-2 geocode for Canada. This is used as an international standard for shipping to Canada. Each province and territory has its own code with the prefix "CA." For example, the code for the Territory of Nunavut is ISO 3166-2:CA-NU.

Cabda An obsolete Arabic unit of length approximately equivalent to nine centimeters.

Cabinet Office A department of the British government that provides ancillary and support staff to the government and has some oversight on the civil service. The office traces its origins to 1916.

Cabinet Security An inactive or infrequently traded bond or stock. They are usually traded in small batches, around five shares at a time. Cabinet securities are kept in cabinets on the trading floor until they are needed.

Cable 1. Informal; the exchange rate between the British pound and the U.S. dollar. This term is used by currency traders, and it originates from the transatlantic cables used to wire the exchange rate between the two currencies in the 19th century. **2.** Informal for the GBP.

CAD ISO 4217 code for the Canadian dollar. The dollar traces its antecedents to the dollar of the Province of Canada, which was issued in 1858 and gradually adopted by the territories of British North America as they formed modern Canada over the course of the next century. The Canadian dollar was pegged to the United States dollar at various values, often at par, until 1950. The currency began to float that year, though it briefly reverted to the U.S. dollar peg between 1962 and 1970.

CAF GOST 7.67 Latin three-letter geocode for the Central African Republic. The code is used for transactions to and from Central African bank accounts and for international shipping to the Central African Republic. As with all GOST 7.67 codes, it is used primarily in Cyrillic alphabets.

Cafeteria Plan 1. An employee benefit in which an employee may contribute so much of his/her pretax income into a special account that may be used for a broad range of purposes. One may use the funds in a cafeteria plan for matters such as medical expenses, life insurance premiums, or other things. This allows the employee to structure his/her employee benefits in a way that best suits their needs for a given period of time. For example, a young, healthy employee may have the ability to choose a less expensive, less comprehensive insurance plan than he/she might otherwise receive from an employer. It is formally called a Section 125 plan. See also: Flexible Spending Account. **2.** An employee benefit plan in which employees may choose from multiple options. For example, an employee may choose among a health insurance plan with no deductible, one with a $500 deductible, or one with a $1,000 deductible.

Cage A department at a brokerage responsible for receiving and distributing funds, as well as maintaining records. The cage enables the rest of the brokerage to function, especially by keeping records of dividends and other payouts and receiving payments from clients. It is more formally called the cashier's department.

Caida A Spanish term for fall. It is used in reference to a market downturn.

Caja A term for a savings and loan in Spain. Cajas began as a way for the economically disadvantaged to save their money; however they have gradually become more like traditional retail and commercial banks.

Calculation Agent A person who calculates the value of a derivative and/or determines who owes what to whom in a swap. The calculation agent is usually a market maker. Sometimes both parties use a single calculation agent for a transaction, but sometimes each party uses a different agent. In this case, the two calculation agents jointly share responsibilities and must work together on the transaction. See also: Clearing Corporation.

Calendar A list of bonds nearing issue over a certain period of time. That is, the calendar lists new issues that have not been made, but are about to be. A large number of new issues on a calendar may be a leading indicator of rising interest rates, as issuers must raise interest rates to attract bond investors.

Calendar Effect The extent to which holding a stock at a particular time helps or harms returns. That is, some analysts believe that stocks perform better or worse on given days, months, or even years. Analysts disagree on which, if any, calendar effects are "real," but they can have an impact on the psychological outlook of investors, which can help or harm returns. For example, some investors believe that October is a bad month to buy because many of the great stock market crashes took place in October. Whether or not there is any evidence for this, it may discourage enough investors from buying that it actually will harm stock prices. Major examples of calendar effects include the January effect and the presidential election cycle theory.

Calendar Year The 12-month period between 1 January and 31 December. In the United States and many other places, the tax year, or the period of time during which annual taxes are calculated, is identical to the calendar year. An unusual number of trades often occur toward the end of the calendar year as investors seek to achieve the lowest, legal, tax liability. A company's fiscal year, or the period of time for which it creates its annual budget, may run for a different 12-month period.

Call an Option In a call option, to buy the underlying asset. The option holder has no obligation to call the option and only does so if he/she believes it benefits him/her. Depending upon the nature of the option, this may be done at any point during the life of the contract, or it may only be done on the contract's expiry date. The strike price of the sale is agreed upon in the option contract (that is, before the option is exercised).

Call Date The first date on which a callable bond may be called by the issuer. Most callable bonds contain a provision preventing a bond from being called for a certain period of time. Interest payments are guaranteed during this period, but not afterward. The bond may be prematurely redeemed at any point after the call date. See also: Call protection.

Call Feature A provision in an indenture that makes a bond callable. A callable bond allows the issuer to redeem the bond before maturity. When the bond is called, the bondholder receives the par value (or sometimes more) and does not receive any more coupons. Callable bonds are issued to allow the issuers to hedge against interest rate risk. That is, if interest rates fall significantly, the issuers can call the bond and issue a new bond at a lower interest rate, reducing their liabilities. However, to protect the bondholder, most callable bonds also include call protection, which prevents the bonds from being called for a certain period of time, and thereby guarantees the current interest rate for that time.

Call Loan Rate The interest rate at which brokers make loans to clients in order to finance margin accounts. The call loan rate may be changed on a daily basis, and the call loans themselves may be canceled on 24 hours' notice. See also: Broker loan rate.

Call Market An exchange or place on an exchange where trading occurs only at particular times, rather than throughout a trading day. On a call market, brokers take orders to buy and sell securities, record them, and execute orders at the appropriate time along with other brokers. Call markets are most common where there is little trading volume.

Call Option An option contract in which the holder has the right (but not the obligation) to buy the underlying asset at an agreed-upon price on or before the expiration date of the contract, regardless of the prevailing market price of the underlying asset. One buys a call option if one believes the price for the underlying asset will rise by the end of the contract. If the price does rise, the holder may buy and resell the underlying asset for a profit. If the price does not rise, the option expires and the holder's loss is limited to the price of buying the contract. Call options may be used on their own or in conjunction with put options to create an option spread in order to hedge risk.

Call Price **1.** The price at which a bond may be redeemed by the issuer before maturity. The price is set at the time of the issue. Call prices are set to reduce the issuer's risk of default; that is, the issuer may have a concern that it will not be able to make all coupon payments and redemptions at maturity and may cut its losses by redeeming at the call price. **2.** The price at which a company may buy out its own preferred stock. The price is set at the time the preferred stock is issued. Reasons for exercising a stock call price include a desire to reduce dividends paid to preferred stockholders and a desire to increase earnings on common stock.

Call Protection A provision in callable bonds that prevents the bond from being called for a certain period of time. Interest payments are guaranteed during the call protection period but not afterward. The bond may be prematurely redeemed at any point after the call date. Call protection exists to protect bondholders from the risk that interest rates will fall before the call date. The period of time during which the bond cannot be called is often called the cushion.

Call Provision A provision in an indenture that makes a bond callable. A callable bond allows the issuer to redeem the bond before maturity. When the bond is called, the bondholder receives the par value (or sometimes more) and does not receive any more coupons. Callable bonds are issued to allow the issuers to hedge against interest rate risk. That is, if interest rates fall significantly, the issuers can call the bond and issue a new bond at a lower interest rate, reducing their liabilities. However, to protect the bondholder, most callable bonds also include call protection, which prevents the bonds from being called for a certain period of time and thereby guarantees the current interest rate for that time.

Call Ratio Backspread A bullish investment strategy in which an investor sells a call option at a low strike price and then uses the proceeds from that sale to buy two call options at a higher strike price. The calls have the same underlying security or asset, and ideally have the same premiums; importantly, they must have the same expiration date. If the underlying moves modestly in the direction the trader wants, he/she can realize exceptional profits; however, even if the underlying moves away from the trader, he/she can make a small profit or at least break even. This is a hedging strategy in which the investor is likely to attain neither significant profit nor loss, but may return a modest profit. Risk is limited to the premiums of the calls bought, and profits are theoretically (though rarely actually) unlimited. This is a favored investment strategy of many risk-averse option traders. See also: Put Ratio Backspread.

Call Report **1.** A record of all calls and visits a salesperson makes. The call report includes the result of each call or visit so one can measure the salesperson's success rate. The salesperson files his/her call reports with his/her supervisor. **2.** See: Bank Call.

Call Risk A risk that a callable bond will be repaid early and that the money earned may not be able to be reinvested in a security with a comparable return. Suppose one invests in a callable bond with coupon payments of 4%. However, interest rates fall and the issuer calls the bond and pays the par value. The investor may make a profit, but now he/she may only purchase a bond with a coupon of 2.5%. Most callable bonds include call periods in the indenture, protecting the bondholder from this risk for a certain period of time. Call risk is one of the most common kinds of reinvestment risk.

Call Rule A rule on an exchange stating that the opening price for a cash commodity is set at the end of the previous trading day. This price is always close to the closing price for that trading day. The call rule helps reduce the volatility that can occur in overnight trading. See also: After-hours trading.

Call Spread An option spread in which one has a long position in a call while having a short position on another call on the same underlying asset with a different strike price and/or expiration date. One uses a call spread to profit from price movements in the underlying asset. See also: Put spread.

Call Swaption An option in which the buyer of the option has the right to enter into to an interest rate swap as the fixed-rate payer. That is, the seller becomes the floating rate payer if the buyer decides to exercise the option. It is called a swaption because it is an option on a swap. A swaption is useful if an interest rate swap may be useful for the buyer's investment strategy, but there is still some uncertainty as to whether that will be the case. See also: Put swaption, Plain vanilla swap.

Call Warrant A call option contained within a warrant. That is, a call warrant is a certificate issued with a security giving the holder the option of buying an underlying asset (in this case, usually more securities) at a certain strike price. Unlike options, call warrants are issued by companies during a round of financing, rather than by an individual investor or brokerage.

Callability A provision in an indenture that allows a bond to be redeemed before maturity. Callability allows the bond to be called at the discretion of the issuer, within certain limits. When the bond is called, the bondholder receives the par value (or sometimes slightly more) and does not receive any more coupons. Callable bonds are issued to allow the issuers to hedge against interest rate risk. That is, if interest rates fall significantly, they can call the bond and issue a new bond at a lower interest rate, reducing their liabilities. However, to protect the bondholder, most callable bonds also include call protection, which prevents the bonds from being called for a certain period of time and thereby guarantees the current interest rate for that time.

Callable Bond A bond that may be redeemed before maturity. Callability allows the bond to be called at the discretion of the issuer within certain limits. When the bond is called, the bondholder receives the par value (or sometimes a bit more) and does not receive any more coupons. Callable bonds are issued to allow the issuers to hedge against interest rate risk. That is, if interest rates fall significantly, the issuer can call the bond and issue a new bond at a lower interest rate, reducing its liabilities. However, to protect the bondholder, most callable bonds also include call protection which prevents the bonds from being called for a certain period of time and thereby guarantees the current interest rate for that time.

Callable Common Stock Common stock in a publicly-traded company that the issuing company may buy back from shareholders. This price schedule under which the issuer may buy back the stock is determined when the stock is issued and the price itself gradually increases over time. Callable common stock allows the company the flexibility to buy back shares at a price for which it can budget. See also: Self-tender offer, Puttable common stock.

Callable Preferred Stock A preferred stock that the issuing company may redeem under certain, stated circumstances. That is, the company may require the callable preferred stock to be exchanged for a given amount of cash. A company may issue callable preferred stock to protect itself from the possibility that its obligations to pay guaranteed dividends may become too expensive in the future.

Called Away Describing a situation in which a contract must be completed, depriving an investor of potential gains. For example, if an option is exercised, the person who owns the underlying must buy or sell it at the agreed upon price, which is usually different from its fair market value, to the disadvantage of the owner. "Called away" is a term most often used with options that are exercised, short sales that must be delivered, or a bond redeemed before maturity.

Cambist A trader or other expert in foreign exchange. Cambists are usually successful in trading currencies in their own right, and companies engaged in international trade may employ them to help reduce currency risk. Cambists must be able to read market factors that may affect a currency's value, but must also consider political factors as well. For example, in 1992 George Soros short sold $10 billion worth of British pounds on the United Kingdom's reluctance to either let its currency float or raise interest rates. Soros earned over $1 billion by considering both the economic and political situations surrounding the sterling.

Cambodian Franc The former currency of Cambodia. Issued in 1875 to replace the tical, it was pegged to the French franc at a one-to-one ratio. It was replaced by the French Indochinese piastre, which circulated alongside the franc.

Cambodian Tical The former currency of Cambodia (and Siam, now Thailand). The tical was a silver coin weighing about 15 grams. In 1875, after the French invasion of Southeast Asia, the tical was replaced by the Cambodian franc.

Cambrist **1.** A foreign exchange trader. **2.** Any person regarded as an expert on currencies and foreign exchange. See also: Numismatist.

CAMELS Rating System A mnemonic device for the factors by which regulators determine banks' riskiness. The rating system goes on a scale from one to five, with one showing the least risk and five the most risk. The factors break down as follows: C - Capital Adequacy A - Quality of Assets M - Quality of Management E - Earnings L - Liquidity S - Sensitivity of the Bank to Market Risk

Camouflage Compensation A part of a major executive's pay package other than salary, especially if it is not required to be disclosed to shareholders. An example may be a stock option. Camouflage compensation may result in employee compensation well above what is listed on company filings.

Campaign Finance Law Any law governing who may contribute or how much may be contributed to a political campaign. For example, a campaign finance law may prohibit corporations from donating more than $1,000 to a campaign. Campaign finance laws are fairly controversial in the United States.

Campbell Harvey Duke University professor who authored the first major glossary of financial terms for publication on the Internet.

Camptown In Lesotho, the capital of a district, which is the equivalent of a province.

CAN GOST 7.67 Latin three-letter geocode for Canada. The code is used for transactions to and from Canadian bank accounts and for international shipping to Canada. As with all GOST 7.67 codes, it is used primarily in Cyrillic alphabets.

Canada A Portuguese measure of liquid volume approximately equivalent to 1.4 liters. It became obsolete after Lusophone countries adopted the metric system in the 19th century.

Canada Education Savings Grant A grant from the Canadian Government to individual Registered Education Savings Plans (RESPs). The grant matches between 20% and 40% of the first $500 of a family's contribution to an RESP, depending on the family's income. It then matches 20% of the family's contributions after $500, regardless of income, up to a maximum benefit of $2,500.

Canada Premium Bond A savings bond, issued by the Canadian government, with a fixed interest rate and a provision limiting redemption. That is, unlike Canada Savings Bonds, Canada Premium Bonds may only be redeemed at par once per year, within 30 days of the anniversary of issue. This protects the government from the risk that too many bondholders will redeem their bonds whenever interest rates rise. To compensate bondholders, however, Premium Bonds pay a higher interest rate than Savings Bonds from the outset.

Canada Revenue Agency The tax collection agency for the Canadian government. It is responsible for collecting all federal taxes derived from sources other than tariffs and associated fees. It also collects income taxes on behalf of all provinces except Quebec and provincial corporate taxes except for Alberta and Quebec. The CRA is also responsible for collecting the goods and services tax, which is the Canadian VAT. See also: IRS, Notice of seizure.

Canada Savings Bond A savings bond offered by the Government of Canada and guaranteed by the Bank of Canada. Originally offered in 1946 as a Victory War

Bond, a CSB pays a low, but safe, interest rate. The interest rate at which a CSB is offered is guaranteed for one year, and then fluctuates according to prevailing interest rates. A CSB is redeemable for cash at any time, but usually has a maturity of 10 years. See also: Canada Premium Bond.

Canadian Agency A Canadian agency bank in the United States. An agency bank is a separately incorporated branch of a foreign bank inside the United States. As with other agency banks, Canadian agencies cannot make loans or take deposits in their own name; rather they do so on behalf of the parent bank in Canada.

Canadian Dealing Network An organized system for over-the-counter trading in Canada. It is a subsidiary of the Toronto Stock Exchange.

Canadian Derivatives Clearing Corporation An organization in Canada that settles futures and options transactions on the Bourse de Montreal. It is charged with matching orders together, ensuring that delivery is made to the correct party, and collecting margin money. Its previous name was Trans Canada Options.

Canadian Dollar The currency of Canada. The dollar traces its antecedents to the dollar of the Province of Canada, which was issued in 1858, and gradually adopted by the territories of British North America as they formed modern Canada over the course of the next century. The Canadian dollar was pegged to the United States dollar at various values, often at par, until 1950. The currency began to float that year, though it briefly reverted to the U.S. dollar peg between 1962 and 1970.

Canadian Gold Maple Leaf A coin minted in Canada containing some fraction of one troy ounce of gold. It is legal tender in Canada, but does not circulate.

Canadian Investor Protection Fund A not-for-profit organization mandated under Canadian law to insure investors against the potential bankruptcy of a broker-dealer. If a broker or dealer goes bankrupt after a client has entrusted it with cash or securities, the CIPF will compensate the client up to $1 million. Over 200 brokers, dealers, and others are members of the CIPF, and fund its activities. It is important to note that the CIPF does not insure against losses by investors, only against the possibility that a broker-dealer may be unable to conduct a transaction because of bankruptcy.

Canadian Originated Preferred Securities A security that combines aspects of preferred stock and long-term debt issues. It is structured as a bond and pays interest instead of dividends, but provides higher yields than Canadian bonds. COPrS are subordinated to other debt but are ahead of preferred stock. The interest may be stopped for up to five years, but only if dividends for common stock have been stopped first. They are taxable investments.

Canadian Palladium Maple Leaf A coin minted in Canada containing some fraction of one troy ounce of palladium. It is legal tender in Canada but does not circulate. It was minted between 2005 and 2007, and again in 2009.

Canadian Platinum Maple Leaf A coin minted in Canada containing some fraction of one troy ounce of platinum. It is legal tender in Canada but does not circulate. It was minted between 1988 and 1999, and again in 2002 and 2009.

Canadian Pound The currency of the Province of Canada prior to 1858. Initially, the pound was based on the Spanish dollar, making it worth somewhat less than the British pound. In 1853, Canada adopted the gold standard as part of a larger policy to encourage trade with the United States without alienating the United Kingdom. Like the British pound at the time, the Canadian pound was divided into 20 shillings or 240 pence.

Canadian Securities Course A course one must complete in order to become a securities dealer or agent in Canada. It also fulfills one requirement to become licensed to sellCanadian mutual funds. To pass the course, one must pass two 100-question, multiple-choice exams.

Canadian Securities Institute An educational institute for securities professionals in Canada. It offers classes and certifications in real estate, derivatives, investment advice, and estate planning, among others, and its members agree to abide by a code of ethical conduct. It was founded in 1970.

Canadian Silver Maple Leaf A coin minted in Canada containing one troy ounce of silver. Its face value is five dollars but it generally trades for some amount higher than that.

Cancel Order An instruction from an investor to a broker to cancel a previously made order that has not yet been filled. Cancel orders are made when an investor changes his/her mind about making a transaction and decides to make a different one or none at all. It is important to issue a cancel order, especially when the replacement transaction involves the same security. Otherwise, the broker may fill both orders, perhaps resulting in a loss.

Cancellation A notice by a broker to a client that the broker has made a mistake and has taken steps to rectify it. For example, if a client makes an order to buy 1,000 shares and the broker mistakenly buys 2,000, he/she must sell the extra 1,000 shares and bear any losses himself/herself. Afterwards, the broker must inform the client of what has transpired and provide full documentation. This ensures that the broker simply made a mistake and was not trading maliciously or improperly.

Cancellation Markings and Date In scripophily, any hole punched into or other marking on a certificate indicating that it has been canceled. It may also state the date on which the certificate was canceled.

Candareen A measure of weight in East Asia roughly equivalent to 378 milligrams. In Imperial China, it was used as a currency denomination equivalent to 1/100 of one renminbi, but this is no longer the case. See also: Troy candareen.

Candlestick Chart A chart of a stock's performance over a given period of time where each trading day is represented by a drawing of what looks like a candle. The candle has wicks (called shadows) coming out of each end representing the high and low prices for each trading day. The candles are colored white a days where the price increases and black on days it decreases. For white candles, the bottom of the candle represents the opening price and the top is the closing price. It is the opposite for black candles. Candlestick charts are very important in technical analysis.

Candy An obsolete South Asian unit of weight approximately equivalent to 227 kilograms.

Candy Store A slang term for an automotive dealership with an exceptionally large inventory.

CANSLIM A mnemonic device for deciding which stocks to buy. It was developed by William O'Neil of Investor Business Daily. It breaks down as follows: C: Current quarterly earnings per share. O'Neil advises buying stocks with recent, large increases in quarterly EPS. A: Annual earnings. Companies with increases in annual earnings each year for five years are thought to be good stocks to buy. N: New products, management, or events. Each of these is usually thought to be positive. S: Supply and demand. Stocks with small supply and large demand usually increase significantly in price in a short period of time. L: Leader or laggard. O'Neil argues that stocks that lead an industry are better than those that lag behind in price. I: Institutional investors. A large number of institutional investors or a few institutional investors that own much of the stock are thought to be negative influences. M: Market direction. It is thought to be a good sign when the major stock indices are increasing.

Can't Find In marketing, a computer file that a computer cannot locate because it no longer exists or is misfiled.

Caoga Pingin A coin that circulated in the Republic of Ireland between 1970 and 2002. It was equal in value to 1/2 of one Irish pound.

Cap **1.** Informal for market capitalization. **2.** In a floating-rate note or an adjustable-rate mortgage (ARM), the highest possible interest rate. For example, if one has an adjustable-rate mortgage on a house, the interest rate fluctuates periodically. However, if the homeowner has a cap on the interest rate, there is a guarantee that it will never rise above a certain percent, no matter what the ARM formula would otherwise dictate. A cap is designed to protect the person or company making the interest payments. See also: Floor, Collar.

Capacity The theoretical maximum number of products a company can produce at a given time. For example, an oil pump may have a capacity of X barrels per day, meaning that it cannot produce more than X. Companies rarely operate at full capacity, both to allow themselves leeway in the event of increased demand and because capacity may not be possible at a given time because of worker illness, machinery maintenance, or other reasons.

Capacity Utilization Rate The extent to which a company uses its facilities at capacity, expressed as a percentage. That is, the capacity utilization rate states how much a company produces as a percentage of what it can produce. For example, if a factory produces 1,000 widgets per day but could produce 2,000 for the same cost, it has a capacity utilization rate of 50%. The capacity utilization rate is most useful for companies producing goods rather than services because goods are simply easier to quantify.

Capital Money that one has invested. For example, one uses capital when building a factory to make a new product. Likewise, one uses capital when one buys a single share of a stock. Free flow of capital into investments is thought to be a major component of economic growth. Generally speaking, businesses can only expand when they are able to raise capital from investors or borrow it from a bank or through a bond issue. See also: Capitalization, Capitalism.

Capital Account A calculation of the amount of money coming into and going out of a country. The capital account is calculated by netting the public and private investments within the country with those the government and domestic companies are making outside the country. For example, one must net the foreign direct investment in the country with the FDI the government and businesses are making in other countries to come up with part of the calculation of the capital account. Other inputs into the capital account include (but are not limited to) bank accounts and changes in the amount of domestic and foreign holders of stocks, bonds, and currencies.

Capital Adequacy Ratio A measure of a bank's ability to meet its obligations relative to its exposure to risk. The capital adequacy ratio exists to ensure that a bank is able to handle losses and fulfill its obligations to account holders without ceasing operations. It is calculated as: CAR = (Tier 1 Capital + Tier 2 Capital) / Risk-weighted assets.

Capital Allocation Decision A company's or manager's decision on where to place recourses such that they produce the maximum possible return for shareholders. Capital allocation decisions represent attempts to produce profit in the most efficient way possible. They can be quite difficult to make, as the options for capital allocation are virtually limitless. Capital allocation decisions may involve making more of the same product, investing in research to invent new products, paying out more in dividends, or making any number of different decisions.

Capital Allocation Line In Markowitz Portfolio Theory, a line plotting the return at a given level of risk of all portfolios that can be formed using a risky asset and a riskless asset. The line is designed to show investors the return they are likely to make at different levels of risk. See also: Markowitz efficient set of portfolios.

Capital Allowances A reduction in a company's corporate tax in order to encourage it to make capital investments. In general, when a company buys capital assets or makes some other long term investment, its corporate taxes are reduced by some amount over and above what the depreciation on the asset would have been. This amount is called the capital allowance.

Capital Asset An asset that the owner intends to hold and derive benefits from for a period of more than one year. Capital assets include long-term investments such as land and major equipment. It is difficult to liquidate capital assets, and companies usually do so when they are extremely cash poor. They are intended to help produce a business' profits and are therefore usually necessary investments. For tax purposes, one represents the value of capital assets with the "property, plant, and equipment" figure.

Capital Asset Pricing Model A model that attempts to describe the relationship between the risk and the expected return on an investment that is used to determine an investment's appropriate price. The assumption behind the CAPM is that money has two values: a time value and a risk value. Thus, any risky asset or investment must compensate the investor for both the time his/her money is tied up in the investment and the investment's relative riskiness. This compensation must be in addition to the risk-free rate of return. There are a number of variations on the CAPM, notably the multifactor CAPM and the two-factor model. The CAPM is calculated according to the following formula: ra = rf + Betaa(rm - rf) where: ra is the asset price, rf is the risk-free rate of return, Betaa is the risk premium, and rm is the market rate of return.

Capital Assistance Program In the United States, a program dedicated to the purchase of convertible preferred stock of banks in the United States. The stock pays a 9% dividend and converts to common stock after seven years unless the bank repurchases it. The program is intended to spur lending in the wake of the 2008 financial crisis by shoring up at-risk banks. It was established in February 2009.

Capital Budget A plan for a company's capital expenditures. Capital expenditures are payments made over a period of more than one year. They are used to acquire assets or improve the useful life of existing assets; an example of a capital expenditure is the funding to construct a factory. Making a capital budget must account for the potential profitability of the plans involved. Calculating the net present value or the internal rate of return are two methods for determining a capital budget.

Capital Builder Account A brokerage account in which the client may use the loan value (or maximum amount a brokerage may lend for margin purchases) of securities in a margin account to finance the purchase and sale of different securities. Generally speaking, the extra funds from the loan value are placed in a money market account that the investor may use at will. Capital builder accounts are offered exclusively through Merrill Lynch.

Capital Construction Fund An investment vehicle fishermen may use to defer taxation on income invested in it, provided it is used later to build, purchase or repair fishing vessels. The CCF is co-managed by the IRS and the National Marine Fisheries Service.

Capital Dividend A dividend that comes from what an investor has paid into a publicly-traded company, rather than from its earnings. That is, a capital dividend occurs when a company gives back what the investor has invested. It may occur when a company must pay a required dividend but earnings make it unable to do so from its profits. Capital dividends may be a sign that a company is not financially healthy. In any case, they reduce the amount of capital that the company has to invest in its operations. They are also called return of capital.

Capital Expenditure Payments made in cash or cash equivalents over a period of more than one year. Capital expenditures are used to acquire assets or improve the useful life of existing assets. An example of a capital expenditure is the funding to construct a factory. In accounting, capital expenditures must be capitalized; that is, the expenditure is recognized on a balance sheet gradually over the course of an asset's useful life. Capital expenditures are recorded as liabilities on a balance sheet. They are also called capital outlays. See also: Capital asset.

Capital Flight A situation in which foreign investors remove their investments from a particular country because of some increase in country risk. Capital flight may occur because of government instability, the sudden appearance of high inflation, or because another country's government offers a better deal. Governments almost always try to prevent capital flight from occurring, but this is not always possible. See also: Foreign direct investment.

Capital Formation The transfer of capital from individuals, organizations, or government for business use. For example, a widget company experiences capital formation when people buy widgets. The company can then use the profit to encourage investment or to expand its operations, among other options. Capital formation is crucial to economic growth.

Capital Gain In real estate and investments, the difference between the purchase price and the sale price when the sale price is more. That is, when an investor buys a security or real estate and sells it for a higher price, he/she incurs a capital gain. Capital gains in the United States are taxed at a lower rate than other income if the asset is held for longer than one year. One may use capital losses to offset capital gains to minimize one's liability for capital gains taxes; indeed, some investors do so deliberately. See also: Paper gain.

Capital Gains Distribution An amount of money paid to shareholders of a mutual fund from its capital gains over the course of a year. That is, a mutual fund takes its capital gains over a year and divides them among shareholders, who are then responsible for capital gains taxes. Capital gains distributions are usually made at the end of each calendar year and they reduce the fund's net asset value. Because of the existence of capital gains distributions, some analysts advise against purchasing

mutual funds at the end of a calendar year because a shareholder will become instantly liable for capital gains taxes.

Capital Gains Tax The tax paid on profits realized by selling a position held for longer than one year. For example, if someone buys a stock or bond and sells it five years later for more than what he/she paid, that person is assessed the capital gains tax. In the United States, capital gains taxes are lower than regular income taxes. This is because the government wishes to encourage long-term investment. It is important to note that the capital gains tax is only assessed on long-term capital gains, not on short-term capital gains. See also: Long-term capital loss.

Capital Gains Treatment How a government taxes capital gains, which are gains from investing in securities and other investment vehicles. In the United States, capital gains treatment is divided into short term and long term categories. The IRS taxes long term capital gains at a much lower rate (a maximum of 15% as of 2009) than short term gains (a maximum of 35%, which is identical to the highest income tax bracket). This is done in order to encourage long-term investing while discouraging (or at least not encouraging) short-term or speculative investing. In practice, accountants and investors have developed a variety of ways to attain long term capital gains treatment.

Capital Gains Yield The price appreciation on an investment relative to the amount one initially invested. For example, if one buys a stock for $10 and the share price goes to $15, the capital gains yield is 50%. It is calculated as follows: Capital gains yield = (market price of a security - original purchase price) / original purchase price.

Capital Goods Goods that are used to create other goods that can be sold to customers. Examples include fixed assets like factories and current assets like raw material to make a product. Capital goods are an important concept in Marxist economics where it refers to any means of production. See also: Consumer Goods.

Capital Goods Price Index A measure of inflation in New Zealand that considers what companies spend on capital assets, which are assets used to produce other assets. It is calculated by considering changes to prices in a basket of capital assets each quarter. Assets included in the index are: buildings (both residential and non-residential), land improvement costs, plant construction and machinery, and transportation equipment.

Capital Growth Strategy An investment philosophy that aims to maximize the return on a portfolio over the long-term. Investors utilizing the capital growth strategy often have approximately two thirds of their portfolios in equities, with the rest in fixed-income investments and cash. This third of the portfolio is designed to provide a minimum hedge against the risk of investing in equities. However, some practitioners of the capital growth strategy invest exclusively in equities.

Capital Guarantee Fund Any investment vehicle where the investor is guaranteed not to lose the capital he/she places into the vehicle. That is, the company offering the investment must bear any losses suffered itself. Because this completely eliminates the investor's risk, capital guarantee funds offer a very low rate of return. See also: Principal Protected Note, Risk-Free Rate of Return.

Capital Infusion 1. Within a firm, the provision of funds to a relatively unsuccessful division from the profits of another division. Management may infuse a division with capital if it believes that it will eventually become profitable. **2.** Funds received from a venture capital firm. Capital infusion may help a start-up survive the first few months or years before it becomes profitable, or it may help a failing business maintain its operations as it restructures or reforms.

Capital Intensive Describing a company or industry requiring a great deal of capital to maintain operations. For example, the automobile industry is capital-intensive because, in order to make cars, it requires a lot of workers and expensive equipment that must be properly maintained. Another, smaller scale example is a dentist office, which requires expensive equipment and materials. In order to stay afloat, capital intensive companies need either consistently large profits or inexpensive credit.

Capital Lease A long-term lease in which the lessee must record the leased item as an asset on his/her balance sheet and record the present value of the lease payments as debt. Additionally, the lessor must record the lease as a sale on his/her own balance sheet. A capital lease may last for several years and is not callable. It is treated as a sale for tax purposes. It is also called a financial lease.

Capital Loss In real estate and investments, the difference between the purchase price and the sale price when the sale price is less. That is, when an investor buys a security or real estate and sells it for a lower price, he/she incurs a capital loss. One may use capital losses to offset capital gains to minimize one's liability for capital gains taxes; indeed, some investors do so deliberately. See also: Paper loss.

Capital Market Any market in which securities are traded. Capital markets include the stock and bond markets. Companies and governments use capital markets to raise funds for their operations; for example, a company may issue an IPO while a government may issue a bond in order to conduct new or expand ongoing activities. Investors purchase securities in the capital markets in order to extract a return and earn profit on the securities. Capital markets include primary markets, such as IPOs that are placed with investors through underwriters, and secondary markets, in which all subsequent trading takes place. Government agencies in different countries regulate local capital markets, though some, especially exchanges, play some role in regulating themselves.

Capital Market Line In the capital asset pricing model, a line that plots the extra return an investor expects for each change in the level of risk. Rational investors expect higher returns for riskier assets and the capital market line shows this graphically. A portfolio that accurately reflects the capital market line is considered a Markowitz efficient portfolio. The slope of the capital market line is a calculation of theequilibrium market price of risk. See also: Beta.

Capital Note A short-term, corporate bond. A company issues a capital note in order to pay its short-term liabilities. Capital notes are unsecured and, in the event of liquidation, receive the lowest priority of all bonds (thought they still rank higher than preferred or common stock).

Capital Outflow A situation in which money leaves an economy at an extremely high rate. That is, capital outflow occurs when economic actors liquidate their investments and deposit their capital in another economy. Capital outflow is generally indicative of a larger problem, such as a weakening currency. It is most common in developing countries and is considered a highly negative event.

Capital Purchase Program In the United States, a portion of the Troubled Asset Relief Program dedicated to the purchase of preferred stock and warrants of banks in the United States. The program was created to spur lending in the wake of the 2008 financial crisis by shoring up at-risk banks. The program lasted from 2008 until February 2009 when it was replaced by the Capital Assistance Program.

Capital Rationing The act or practice of limiting a company's investment. That is, capital rationing occurs when a company's management places a maximum amount on new investments it can make over a given period of time. The two methods of capital rationing are forbidding investments over a certain amount or increasing the cost of capital for such investments. Capital rationing is most common when a company's previous investments have not performed well.

Capital Requirements In banking regulation, the amount of money a bank must have available to cover withdrawals, closed accounts, and other account-related expenses. While each jurisdiction computes capital requirements differently, Basel II provides a framework many countries follow; it describes capital requirements as a percentage of a bank's risk-weighted assets. Capital requirements are important for bank solvency, and, in difficult times, reduce the pressure for bank runs.

Capital Risk The risk that a company will lose the amount of an investment. An investor takes on capital risk each time he/she invests in anything other than a risk-free security. Capital risk is limited to the amount one has invested. For example, if one buys a $1,000 bond, he/she will not lose more than $1,000.

Capital Share In a dual purpose fund, a share that is entitled to appreciation on the firm's investments. Dual purpose funds issue two types of shares: capital shares and income shares, which are entitled to the firm's ordinary income. A dual purpose fund has the advantage of allowing shareholders to choose which shares in which to invest (according to their investment goals) without the difficulty of changing investment vehicles.

Capital Structure How a company finances its operations. The three most basic ways to finance are through debt, equity (or the issue of stock), and, for a small business, personal savings. Capital structure usually refers to how much of each type of financing a company holds as a percentage of all its financing. Generally speaking, a company with a high level of debt compared to equity is thought to carry higher risk, though some analysts do not believe that capital structure matters to risk or profitability.

Capital Surplus Capital a company raises in a financing round in excess of the capital's par value. For example, capital surplus may occur when a publicly-traded company makes a new issue of stock with a par value of $5 per share and places it with investors for $8 per share. Companies can only raise capital surplus on the primary market because they do not receive any additional money from trades on the secondary market. It is important to note that it has become rare for stock to have a par value. See also: Paid-in capital.

Capital Trust An American real estate investment trust that specializes in commercial real estate. It also underwrites and manages high-yield debt for clients. It was established in 1997 and is based in New York.

Capital Turnover A ratio of how effectively a publicly-traded company manages the capital invested in it to produce revenues. It is calculated by taking the total of the company's annual sales and dividing it by the average stockholder equity, which is the average amount of money invested in the company. A high ratio indicates that the company is using its capital well, while a low ratio indicates the opposite. It is also called equity turnover.

Capitalism The economic system in which the means of production is privately held. In capitalism, the most important means of production is money rather than land (as in feudalism) or labor (as in socialism). That is, the ability to raise and use money for the production of goods and services is more important than owning the land from which goods come, or the ability to work in order to create a good or service. As a result, government policies generally target the regulation (or not) of money and its uses rather than those of property and/or labor. While capitalism is often associated with laissez-faire policies, governments often involve themselves in capitalist countries. The appropriate amount of government intervention in a capitalist system remains hotly debated.

Capitalist A person who believes in or is involved with an economic system in which the means of production are privately held. In capitalism, the most important of the means of production is money, rather than land (as in feudalism) or labor (as in socialism). That is, the ability to raise and use money for the production of goods and services is more important than owning the land from which goods come, or the ability to work in order to create a good or service. As a result, government policies generally target the regulation (or not) of money and its uses rather than those of property and/or labor. While capitalism is often associated with laissez-faire policies,

governments in capitalist countries often involve themselves. The appropriate amount of government intervention in a capitalist system remains hotly debated.

Capitalization Change An increase or decrease in the number of shares outstanding. A capitalization change may occur due to a new issue, a share buyback, or any similar activity.

Capitalization Effective Date The date on which an increase or decrease in the number of shares outstanding takes effect. A capitalization change may occur due to a new issue, a share buyback, or any similar activity.

Capitalization Method A method of building a portfolio in which one enters a long position on the securities in some benchmark index in proportion to each security's market capitalization. For example, if the benchmark index has three stocks in it (one representing 50% of the capitalization of the index and the other two each representing 25%) 50% of a portfolio using the capitalization method would be composed of the first stock, while the rest would be equally divided between the other stocks.

Capitalization Rate The net income an asset produces in a given year divided by its purchase price. The capitalization rate is used to help determine the rate of return, or how fast an asset pays for itself and begins to make a profit. For example, if an asset cost $1,000,000 and it produces $100,000 in a given year, the capitalization rate is 10% and it will take 10 years to pay for the asset with the money it produces. However, it is important to note that the capitalization rate may change from year to year. For example, the same asset could produce $100,000 in year one but $250,000 in year two. It is informally known as the cap rate.

Capitalization Table A table detailing all the securities a firm has issued. The securities are organized according to type, dates of issue, and the amount the firm has raised in issuing them.

Capitalization-Weighted Index An index in which the price is determined by the price of individual stocks, weighted for total market value. For example, if the price of a component stock of the index changes, its effect on the index as a whole is proportionate to share's price multiplied by the number of shares the company has outstanding. This means that changes in price will affect the index more if the component company has greater value. Most non-American market value-weighted indices give further weighting (called float-weighted indexing) to properly account for partial government ownership of many large corporations. This method of index weighting contrasts with a price-weighted index, in which all price changes are weighted differently, and a market share-weighted index, which weights only by the number of shares outstanding and not by their value. Major examples of a market value-weighted index include the NASDAQ Composite Index and the Standard & Poor's 500. The latter uses float-weighted indexing to match its calculations more closely with foreign counterparts.

Capitalize In accounting, to recognize expenses on long-term liabilities over a long period of time. This allows a company to spread out its expenses so they do not appear to reduce profits at any particular time. For example, a company may have a $1 million profit and a $1 million loan to acquire machinery for its factory. If it does not capitalize the loan, its balance sheet will show no profit for that year. Capitalizing the loan allows the company to recognize the liability over a certain period, usually the usable life of the machinery.

Capitalized Interest Funds that an issuer places into a separate account in order to pay for future coupons on a bond. Capitalized interest is considered an asset and may be deducted from the issuer's taxes over time. There is disagreement about the benefits of this deduction; some issuers prefer to receive the deduction at once, rather than over time.

Capitulation A situation in which a market gives back many or all of its previous gains. That is, prices drop significantly during a capitulation. Some investors believe that capitulation is an opportunity to buy because some securities tend to drop too much and will eventually recover nicely. However, capitulation can result in significant losses to those who already own the securities involved.

Capoluogo In Italy and San Marino, a political subdivision equivalent to the main city in a county.

Capped Floating Rate Note A variable-rate note with a maximum interest rate that the variable rate cannot exceed. For example, a variable-rate note may have a cap stating that the rate will not exceed 9% even if the formula used to calculate the interest rate would have it do so. A capped rate reduces the risk to the issuer of the note.

Capped Option An option contract that establishes a maximum profit for the holder. Capped options contain a provision stating that the option is automatically exercised if the underlying security closes on a trading day above (for a call) or below (for a put) some established price. This means that if the underlying security moves in a direction disadvantageous for the writer, there is a maximum amount the writer can lose. A capped option is also called a capped-style option.

Capping A practice in which the writer of a call option who holds a long position in the underlying asset sells large quantities of the underlying asset. A call option gives the holder the right but not the obligation to buy the underlying asset from the writer at an agreed-upon price regardless of what the spot price is when the option is exercised. If the underlying asset rises in price, this is advantageous to the holder but not to the writer. Therefore, the writer may practice capping to increase supply in the market and to keep the price of the underlying asset from rising. If successful, the holder of the call does not exercise the option and the writer is able to profit from the premium (or price the holder paid to buy the option).

CAPS A preferred stock that pays a dividend tied to U.S. Treasury securities. CAPS are convertible to common stock at par value at any time, especially after profits are announced, but before dividends are paid. CAPS have the advantage of protecting the investor's principal while also allowing him/her to take advantage of upswings in the company's value.

Captive Finance Company A subsidiary financial institution whose primary or sole operation is the provision of credit for customers of the parent company. For example, a captive finance company owned by a dental corporation may make loans for the expensive dental services. Captive finance companies have historically been prominent in the automotive industry, easing the purchase of cars from whichever company owns them. Captive finance companies are typically wholly owned subsidiaries.

Caput A call option contract on a put option. A caput has two expiration dates and two strikes; there are also two premiums: one paid up front and another paid if the underlying option is exercised. A caput gives the holder the right, but not the obligation, to buy a put option, which he/she does if the price on the asset underlying the put option declines. Like other compound options, it is often used in markets where there are doubts about the risk for the underlying option, such as currency or fixed income markets. Significantly, caputs trade only over-the-counter, not on an exchange.

Caqrim A Tatar unit of length approximately equivalent to one kilometer. It was rendered obsolete when the Soviet Union began to use the metric system in 1924.

Car **1.** Informal; a loose term for the number of commodities underlying a single contract. The amount varies by commodity. **2.** See: CARS.

Car Insurance An insurance policy providing coverage for damage caused to one's car, the damage the car itself causes, and/or its theft. One pays premiums to the car insurance company in exchange for this coverage. The amount of the premium is determined by the relative danger that the car and driver pose. For example, a sports car will likely command a higher premium than a sedan, and a young driver almost always pay more than an older driver. All U.S. states require drivers to have some form of car insurance.

Caracas Stock Exchange The only securities exchange in Venezuela. Completely electronic since 1992, it trades in both equity and debt instruments. The Caracas Stock Exchange has experienced significant declines since the 1990s, at one time only functioning by trading in Venezuelan government debt. Much trade that would otherwise happen on the Caracas Stock Exchange occurs through American Depository Receipt transactions, which occur on American exchanges, rather than the Caracas Stock Exchange. It is abbreviated BVC after its Spanish name, Bolsa de Valores de Caracas.

Carbon Trade A market proposed by the Kyoto Protocol in which each country participating receives a limit on the carbon emissions it and companies operating in it are allowed to produce. Countries (and/or companies) may buy and sell the emissions limits assigned to them. Carbon trade is intended to be an attempt to reduce overall carbon emissions while still allowing companies that may have difficulty doing so to have an outlet for transition. It is also called emissions trading.

Cardboard Box Index A measure of the production of cardboard boxes. The cardboard box index is used to gauge the production of consumer goods. Because the vast majority of non-durable goods are shipped in cardboard boxes, higher demand for them usually equates to higher production of these goods. As such, the cardboard box index is considered a fairly reliable indicator of industrial production.

Career The job or sequence of jobs a person has in his/her chosen field. A career may or may not involve multiple jobs, but it generally remains in the same field of expertise. Traditionally, one receives the necessary education or training to start a career, takes an entry-level job, and gradually receives increasingly greater responsibility (and higher pay). However, many people do not follow the traditional career path, notably entrepreneurs who take responsibility on to themselves. Additionally, some people have two or more careers throughout their life as they move, by will or necessity, into different fields.

Career Limiting Move Any action that will limit an employee's ability to be promoted within a company. For example, making a major mistake in a presentation in front of the CEO may be a career limiting move. It is analogous to, but less severe than, career suicide.

Career Suicide Any action that will limit or eliminate an employee's ability to find jobs in his/her own field. For example, a graphic designer who performs unusable work and persistently sues employers when he is laid off may find it nearly impossible to find a graphic design job.

Career-Specific Scholarship A scholarship available to persons wishing to use their education to pursue a certain line of work. For example, an engineering firm with a need for electrical engineers may make a scholarship available to undergraduate students majoring in that field.

Cargo Anything being transported, especially if it is to be sold later.

Cargo Insurance An insurance policy that protects the buyer of a good from the loss of that good while it is being transported. Most of the time, when a good is being shipped, either the buyer or the seller is required to purchase cargo insurance (or at least to assume the risk of transit); their specific agreement determines which one is responsible. See also: Incoterm.

Carib A Tatar unit of area approximately equivalent to 1,821 square meters. It was rendered obsolete when the Soviet Union began to use the metric system in 1924.

Carload A railroad car that can hold up to 40,000 pounds or 25,000 bushels of a commodity. Carloads can be important to commodity trading because some commodities are sold in such large quantities that one needs carloads to transport them to the approved delivery facility.

Carpool Tunnel Syndrome A slang term for a sleepy or tired state when one first arrives at work. Carpool tunnel syndrome comes from carpooling with co-workers; because one is not driving, one does not have to pay attention and thus may take more time to fully wake up.

Carriage and Insurance Paid To In international commerce, an agreement between a buyer and a seller stating that the seller is responsible for paying for shipping and providing a minimum amount of insurance coverage until some named destination, while the buyer is responsible for the transportation risk beyond the minimum coverage as soon as the good or product is delivered to the carrier. It is also called a CIP. See also: Incoterm, CFR.

Carried Interest In a limited partnership, the percentage of the profit that goes to the general partner. For example, if a fund is structured as a limited partnership, the limited partners receive a certain return on their investments and the general partner, who is the fund manager, receives the carried interest. Carried interest exists despite the fact that the general partner does not contribute capital to the partnership; it encourages him/her to make profitable investment decisions for the partnership.

Carrot Equity The right of a shareholder to purchase more shares in a publicly-traded company if the company's performance reaches a certain benchmark. If the company's performance outpaces expectations or reaches a stated level (for example, if its net income or operating income reaches a certain amount) the holders of carrot equity may purchase more shares. Carrot equity operates much like a call option, but it is given automatically and the shareholder need not buy it. Carrot equity is designed to give shareholders a vested interest in the company's medium or long-term performance.

Carry **1.** See: Cost of carry. **2.** A slang term for net financing cost.

Carryback In accounting, a way for a company to reduce its tax liability by applying a net operating loss to previous years in which it made a profit. If a company deducts more than its net income in a given tax year, it may take the difference between the deduction and the net income (a negative number) and apply it as a deduction on taxable income for the previous five years. For example, if a company makes $1,000,000 in one year, and loses $500,000 the following year, it may only be liable for a $500,000 profit on the year it makes a profit. That is, it may receive a tax refund on part of what it paid for the profitable year. See also: Future Income Tax.

Carryforward In accounting, a way for a company to reduce its tax liability by applying losses to future tax years in which the company makes a profit. That is, carryforward allows companies to apply losses to profits that have not yet occurred and thereby reduce the taxes they pay on those profits. Carryforward is limited to seven years. For example, suppose a company loses $500,000 in year one, then nets $1,000,000 in year five. The company may carry forward the losses and only be liable for taxes on $500,000 of its profit in year five. Independent contractors who file Schedule C with the IRS are required to use carryforwards, which is useful since most independent contractors lose money in their first few years of business. Some publicly-traded companies opt not to use it, as appearing to reduce profits may scare off potential investors who do not realize that the profits upon which taxes are paid do not equal the company's actual profits.

Carrying Broker **1.** A member of a commodity exchange who provides clearing services for other members or brokers. A carrying broker does this in addition to his/her other duties as a member of the exchange in return for a fee. **2.** A broker who, in exchange for a fee, performs the duties of other brokers who may be overworked or are otherwise unable to fill an order.

Carrying Charge **1.** The cost of storing a commodity over a period of time. It includes incidental costs, insurance coverage, and the physical cost of storage. It does not include depreciation, if any. The carrying charge is incorporated to the price of a commodity on the futures market. **2.** In interest rate futures, the difference between the cost of purchasing an instrument and its yield. See also: Profit, Loss. **3.** Fees a firm charges for making a loan. The largest single carrying charge is the interest, but it also includes charges such as an origination fee or an application fee. See also: All-in cost.

Carrying Charge Market When considering two futures contracts on the same commodity with two different delivery months, a market in which the price for the contract with the later delivery when it equals the price of the contract with earlier delivery plus the cost of storing the underlying commodity for the remaining period of time. For example, suppose the price of a July expiry futures contract on gold is $995 per ounce, and the cost of storing it for a month is $5 per ounce. In a carrying charge market, the price of an August expiry futures contract on gold would be $1,000 per ounce. A carrying charge market is also called a full carry market.

Carrying Cost of Inventory The cost to a business of storing its inventory over a period of time. It includes taxes, insurance, the physical cost of storage, and opportunity cost. It does not include depreciation, if any. For example, if a business sells perishable goods and some of them spoil before they are sold, the carrying cost of inventory includes the costs associated with insuring and/or replacing the spoiled goods.

Cartel A small group of companies or governments that regulate the price of a good or service by having total or near total control of a market. Suppose four airline companies control 98% of the market share for passenger flight. If these four companies formed a cartel they could agree to set prices together, which would guarantee profits for all companies because it is extremely unlikely that a fifth company would be able to successfully undercut them. A prominent example of a cartel of governments is OPEC, which effectively can set the price of a barrel of oil by mandating quotas for each company to follow and thereby controlling supply. See also: Price collusion.

Carter Quarter A tongue-in-cheek term for the Susan B. Anthony dollar, which was minted while Jimmy Carter was president and was often confused with the 25-cent coin.

Cartwheel A nickname of a silver U.S. dollar coin. The term is most common in numismatics. It derives its name from the reflection of an unblemished coin for collectors, which is said to look like the spokes of a wagon wheel.

Cash Physical currency printed on banknotes and coins. Cash may be exchanged for goods or services because it is legal tender in the country or region recognizing it. See also: Cash and cash equivalents.

Cash a Check To deposit a check at a bank other institution and to receive cash in exchange. For example, suppose Joe writes Bob a check for $10. Rather than place the check in the bank, Bob may go to his bank, present the check, and receive $10 in cash. The bank then directs the check to Joe's bank and receives $10 from Joe's account to compensate itself for the cash it gave to Bob.

Cash Accounting A system of accounting that recognizes revenue and expenses in the order in which they are received or made. For example, if a company receives $200 in revenue on Tuesday, it must record $200 in revenue on Tuesday. Cash accounting contrasts with accrual accounting, which matches expenses with the revenue it generates, regardless of when each one occurs. Cash accounting can result in a different tax liability from accrual accounting. For this reason, regulations require different companies to use different accounting methods; for example, companies carrying inventory are not allowed to use the cash accounting method.

Cash Advance Cash one receives from one's credit card account, especially from an ATM. A cash advance usually carries a high interest rate, in part because credit cards have high interest rates anyway, and in part because the interest on a cash advance often begins to accrue immediately.

Cash and Carry Trade A transaction in which one takes a short position on a futures contract and a long position on the underlying asset where the spot price, or current price, of the underlying commodity is below the price in the futures contract. Making a profit from a cash and carry trade is considered a form of arbitrage. That is, one uses a cash and carry trade to make money from uncertainty or inefficiency in the market, in this case, with regard to the future price of the underlying asset. This is also called buying the basis.

Cash and Cash Equivalents Balance sheet items that represent either physical currency printed on notes or assets that can easily be changed into that. Examples of cash equivalents include savings accounts, bonds (especially near their maturities), and money markets. Cash and cash equivalents represent a company's or individual's liquidity, which can be important for investors and banks. See also: M1, M2.

Cash Asset Ratio A ratio of a company's cash and liquid assets to its total liabilities. A cash asset ratio measures a company's liquidity and how easily it can service debt and cover short-term liabilities if the need arises. As a result, potential creditors use this ratio in determining whether or not to make short-term loans. It is also called the liquidity ratio and the current ratio.

Cash Available for Debt Service A ratio of a company's cash on hand to its debt service. A ratio of less than 1 indicates that the company is unable to service its debt while a ratio of 1 means that it can service its debt, but that doing so will result in no remaining cash on hand. Thus, shareholders and potential lenders prefer to have the cash available for debt service to be as high as possible.

Cash Balance Plan A pension plan that combines features of a defined-benefit plan and a defined-contribution plan. Like a defined-benefit plan, a cash balance plan guarantees the pensioner a certain benefit upon retirement. That is, the amount one receives from a cash balance plan does not vary according to the performance of some portfolio. Like a defined-contribution plan, the employer agrees to place a certain percentage of one's salary into the plan each year, and accounts are created on an individual basis. A cash balance plan can be rolled over into another account if the employee changes jobs. As a result, it is relatively popular with younger workers.

Cash Basis Accounting A system of accounting that recognizes revenue in the order in which it is received, and expenses on the same basis. Cash basis accounting does not deal with accounts receivable or accounts payable and only recognizes transactions actually paid for. This accounting system is easiest and perhaps best for organizations with few or no credit sales. See also: Accrual Accounting Convention.

Cash Budget An estimate of the expected cash inflows and cash outflows for a company or individual for a given period of time. A cash budget is vitally important because it measures the liquidity of a company (or individual) and therefore how much one can spend before beginning to have financial difficulties. See also: Budget.

Cash Charge A one-off expense that a company pays, especially when it is attempting to improve its efficiency. For example, if a company wishes to find less expensive employees, it may offer retirement plans to its current employees and take the expense as a cash charge. Cash charges are almost never repeated. A cash charge is reported on a balance sheet as an extraordinary item.

Cash Contract A trade of a security or a derivative where settlement occurs on the same trading day. This is fairly unusual; most contracts are settled between one and three days later. Generally speaking, cash contracts are most common in the last week of the calendar year when many trades must be settled sooner to guarantee tax advantages for one or both parties. It is also called a cash trade.

Cash Conversion Cycle The time between an expenditure of money to make a product and the collection of accounts receivable from the sale of that product. Obviously, a shorter cash conversion cycle is preferable. A longer cash conversion cycle may indicate a current or potential problem with cash flow.

Cash Cow In growth share matrices, the quadrant representing companies, especially subsidies, that produce large profits with little need for cash injection because they have large market shares in slow-growing markets. A cash cow is not necessarily experiencing growth; if it is growing, it is almost always very slow. Corporations want to own cash cows, as they require little oversight compared to the profits they produce. See also: Marketing, Portfolio analysis.

Cash Deficiency Agreement In project finance, especially construction, an agreement in which one party provides the other up to a certain amount so that the second party may temporarily alleviate its cash flow problems until it becomes profitable. This especially applies to a situation in which one or more of the second party's products are not selling as well as expected. This agreement allows the borrower to service its debt without risking default.

Cash Dividend A share in the profit of a publicly-traded company or another investment vehicle that is distributed to each shareholder in cash in proportion to the percentage of ownership in the company each shareholder has. Cash dividends contrasts with automatic dividend reinvestment, whereby companies and investment vehicles enter into agreements with shareholders to automatically buy more shares with dividends. They also differ from dividends that are paid in the form of stocks or bonds. Companies tend to pay more in cash dividends when they do not wish to reinvest profits into expanded operations. See also: Plowback ratio.

Cash Earnings per Share A measure of a publicly-traded company's cash on hand, calculated by dividing the company's cash flow by the number of shares outstanding. Cash earnings per share helps determine a company's ability to service debt, pay dividends and perform other transactions. A high cash earnings per share, coupled with a low share price, indicates that the company likely has strong earnings and that the share price will soon rise. It is also called cash flow per share.

Cash Equivalent An asset that can easily be changed into cash. Examples of cash equivalents include savings account, bonds (especially near their maturities), and money markets. Cash and cash equivalents represent a company's or individual's liquidity, which can be important for investors and banks. See also: M1, M2.

Cash Flow 1. Cash that comes into or goes out of a person's or company's account. Cash flow can come from any number of sources and is crucial for a business' continued operation and a person's continued survival. Cash inflow may come from wages, salary, sales, loans, revenue from operations, or even personal gifts. Cash outflow usually comes from expenses and investments. It is crucially important to maintain a positive net cash flow insofar as possible. **2.** In accounting, an item on a financial statement indicating cash flow.

Cash Flow After Interest and Taxes In accounting, a measure of a company's cash flow after all taxes and interest expenses are paid. It is calculated by taking the company's net income and adding back in the value of all non-cash expenses, notably amortization and depreciation. Publicly-traded companies with a high cash flow after interest and taxes are in a better position to distribute cash dividends than those with a low cash flow after taxes. In addition, it is also used as a measure of general performance and financial health.

Cash Flow After Taxes In accounting, a measure of a company's cash flow after all taxes are paid. It is calculated by taking the net income and adding back in the value of all non-cash expenses, notably amortization and depreciation. Publicly-traded companies with a high cash flow after taxes are in a better position to distribute cash dividends than those with a low cash flow after taxes. In addition to this, it is also used as a measure of general performance and financial health.

Cash Flow Break-Even Point The cash flow necessary to cover costs and prevent a firm from operating at a loss. The break-even point may be relatively stable or it may fluctuate, depending on the company or industry. Companies with high break-even points tend to have large fluctuations in earnings from year to year.

Cash Flow Coverage Ratio The ratio of a company's annual earnings before interest and taxes to its annual debt service and other liabilities. These liabilities may include preferred dividends and rent. Banks use the cash flow coverage ratio to help determine whether to make or refinance loans. A cash flow coverage ratio equal to or greater than one indicates that the debtor is able to service the debt on its profit. See also: Debt-service coverage ratio.

Cash Flow from Financing Activities Cash flow that a company acquires from a financing round instead of from operations. That is, cash flow from financing activities is the net amount that a company receives from issuing stock and bonds. Generally speaking, shareholders prefer to see positive cash flow from financing activities, but a negative amount could mean that a company is buying back its own stock, which drives up the share price. It is calculated thus: Cash flow from financing activities = Cash from stock and bonds - debt service on bonds - dividends paid to stockholders - Stock buybacks - called debt.

Cash Flow from Investing Activities On a cash flow statement, an item summarizing the change to a company's cash flow from its investments in securities. Cash flow from investing activities includes capital gains and losses. It is important to the cash flow statement because investments in securities may result in negative cash flow even when the company is otherwise profitable. Depending on the liquidity of the company's portfolio, the negative cash flow may actually be positive.

Cash Flow From Operations A ratio of a company's cash flow to either its net income or operating income. The latter ratio provides a more accurate description of a company's cash flow, while the former takes into account the effects of non-operation transactions on income. Cash flow from operations shows the difference, if any, between a company's reported income and actual cash on hand.

Cash Flow Matching The practice of matching returns on a portfolio to future capital outlays. That is, cash flow matching involves investing in certain securities with a certain expected return so that the investor will be able to pay for future liabilities. Pension funds and annuities perform the most cash flow matching, as they have future liabilities that are both large and relatively easy to estimate. Portfolios that perform cash flow matching usually invest in low-risk, investment-grade securities. The practice is also called portfolio dedication, matching, or the structured portfolio strategy.

Cash Flow per Common Share The net cash flow a company makes in a given period of time, less dividends on preferred stock, divided by the common shares outstanding.

Cash Flow Return on Investment A model of determining the value of a company that assumes that the market sets prices based on cash flow instead of earnings. It is calculated thusly: CFROI = Cash flow / Total investment.

Cash Flow Statement A statement every publicly-traded company must file with the SEC each quarter indicating all cash inflows and cash outflows from all sources, whether they are business activities or the company's investments. This is considered one indication among many of a company's financial health. A business activity may be reported as income if a company has agreed to a contract, even if no money has actually changed hands; a cash flow statement seeks to avoid this by showing how much cash the company has on hand. It is also called an application of funds statement.

Cash Flow Time Line A line or chart showing a company's cash inflows and cash outflows and the business activities that caused them over a given period of time.

Cash in Advance Commonly abbreviated CIA. A transaction in which the good or service is paid in full before the good is delivered or the service is rendered. It is also called cash before delivery (CBD) and cash with order.

Cash Investment A short-term investment into which one deposits cash and receives the return in 90 days or less. Its name derives from the fact that it can quickly be converted to cash if necessary. Examples include money market funds and Treasury bills. They are also called cash reserves or money market investments.

Cash Management 1. The ability or strategy a company uses to ensure that it collects all cash owed to it. For example, cash management may involve contracting a debt collection service to retrieve what is owed by a customer, or, more simply, it may involve depositing cash into a lock box to ensure that it is not stolen. **2.** See: Asset management.

Cash Management Bill A U.S. Treasury security with a minimum purchase of $1 million and a maturity of 10 to 20 days. The U.S. Treasury sells cash management bills to institutional investors when it needs to raise cash quickly for a very short period of time.

Cash Matching Strategy The practice of matching returns on a bond portfolio to future capital outlays. That is, a cash matching strategy involves investing in certain securities with a certain expected return so that the investor will be able to pay for future liabilities. The practice is essentially the same as cash flow matching, except it applies exclusively to bond portfolios. See also: Duration matching strategy.

Cash Offer In mergers and acquisitions, an offer to buy a publicly-traded company in exchange for cash. A cash offer may be either friendly or hostile. It differs from other types of takeover offers that may buy the company in exchange for stock and/or debt.

Cash Position The cash and cash equivalents that a company, fund, or bank has available to pay short-term obligations. The cash position is a measure of the institution's liquidity. See also: Quick ratio, Accounting liquidity.

Cash Price On an exchange, the price of a security or commodity at the present moment. If one buys or sells a security or commodity, one pays the cash price. The cash price contrasts with the futures price. It is also called the current price and the spot price. See also: Spot rate.

Cash Ratio 1. A ratio of a company's cash and liquid assets to its total liabilities. A cash ratio is a measure of company's liquidity and how easily it can service debt and cover short-term liabilities if the need arises. As a result, potential creditors use this ratio in determining whether or not to make short-term loans. It is also called the liquidity ratio and the cash asset ratio. **2.** In banking, a ratio of a bank's cash and cash equivalents to its demand deposits. See also: Reserve requirement.

Cash Refund Annuity An annuity with a provision stating that if the annuitant does not receive payments at least equal to the amount he/she paid as contributions, then some beneficiary (such as a relative of the annuitant) receives the difference in a lump sum. This reduces the risk to the annuitant that the annuity will prove to be a bad investment. However, it does not protect the insurance company providing the annuity. A cash refund annuity is also called a lump sum refund annuity. See also: Installment Refund Annuity.

Cash Settlement Contracts Futures or option contracts in which the counterparties agree that instead of delivering the underlying assets at the execution of the contract, one delivers their cash equivalent. For example, suppose someone bought a call contract taking on the obligation to buy a certain number of barrels of oil, should the option be exercised. If/when the option is exercised, the call holder

pays the strike price. In exchange, the counterparty delivers the cash value of the agreed upon number of barrels of oil. Such a transaction is usually netted between the parties so that cash only changes hands once.

Cash Transaction Any transaction that does not occur on the futures or forward market. That is, the participants in a cash transaction agree to buy and sell, respectively, at the present market value and to settle the transaction a few (usually three or fewer) days later. Technically, there is no difference between a cash transaction and a spot transaction, but the latter term is more common on the foreign exchange market.

Cash Value The amount of cash that becomes available to an insured person upon the cancellation of his/her insurance policy. Most often, this applies to the savings portion of a canceled whole life policy. This value is considered an asset and can be borrowed against or used as collateral. It may also be called a cash surrender value or a surrender value.

Cash Value Account An account into which cash is deposited that becomes available to an insured person upon the cancellation of his/her insurance policy. Most often, this applies to the savings portion of a canceled whole life policy. This value is considered an asset and can be borrowed against or used as collateral. It may also be called a cash-surrender value or a surrender value.

Cash Value Added The cash flow a company is able to generate relative to the cash flow it must generate to remain in business. The CVA is calculated by taking a company's operating cash flow and subtracting its operating cash flow demand. A high CVA is considered desirable; a CVA under 1 indicates the company cannot meet its cash flow needs. See also: Economic value added.

Cashbook A record of a company's cash deposits and withdrawals. The cashbook is part of a company's ledger and is periodically checked against its bank statements to ensure that the accounting it accurate.

Cashed Up A slang term in Britain describing one who has a great deal of money to spend, especially temporarily. For example, one may say he is cashed up right after pay day.

Cashier's Department A department at a brokerage responsible for receiving and distributing funds, as well as maintaining records. The cashier's department enables the rest of the brokerage to function, especially by keeping records of dividends and other payouts and receiving payments from clients. It is informally called the cage.

Cashish A slang term for cash on hand.

Cashless Exercise A method of exercising employee stock options in which the employee borrows enough money from a broker to buy the underlying stocks and immediately resells enough shares to pay the loan, in addition to taxes and commissions. This is a form of buying on margin; ordinarily, most brokers would not allow the employee to buy on margin, but, in cashless exercises, they receive repayment almost at once. This results in a profit for both the broker and usually for the employee as well.

Cash-on-Cash Return A way to calculate the rate of return on an investment, especially in real estate. One calculates the cash-on-cash return by dividing the cash inflow on the investment in a given year by the cash outflow originally made. For example, if one buys a property for $100,000, this amount is the denominator when calculating the cash-on-cash return each year.

Cash-or-Nothing Call In European options, a call option in which the payoff is some fixed amount of money if the market value of the underlying asset is above the strike price, but no payoff if it is below the strike price. In American options, the payoff occurs if the underlying's value ever "touches" the strike price, and is nothing if it never does by the expiry date of the contract. Because they are considered exotic or obscure, cash-or-nothing calls have historically been fairly illiquid investments. The SEC did not allow these options to be listed on exchanges until 2008; because of this, they formerly traded exclusively over-the-counter. Analysts use the prices of cash-or-nothing options to determine the market's best guess as to the likelihood of an event occurring.

Cash-or-Nothing Put A put option that results in either a predetermined payoff, if the underlying asset trades below the strike price at the close of the expiration date, or no payoff, if it trades above the strike price. For example, suppose one holds a cash-or-nothing put to sell a certain amount of shares of Google at $400 per share. If Google is trading below $400 on the expiration date, the holder automatically receives the set payoff. If it is trading above $400, the payoff is zero. See also: Cash-or-nothing call.

Cashout A situation in which a person or company is cash poor and cannot meet expenses and is also unable to sell its assets easily to raise cash. A cashout often means that the person or company must resort to borrowing. See also: Cash Out Refinancing.

Cash-Secured Put A put option in which the writer deposits an amount equal to the strike price of the put into an account in case the option is exercised. For example, if one writes a put for 100 shares with a strike price of $10, the writer agrees to place $1,000 into an account and does not use that money for anything. In a put option, the writer agrees to buy the underlying asset from the holder at the agreed-upon strike price should the holder exercise the option. Securing the put with cash reduces the risk to the holder that the writer will be unable to meet the obligations of the contract.

Casino Finance A slightly derogatory term for highly risky, speculative investing. The term especially refers to buying and selling stocks, which can easily result in a large gain or an enormous loss.

Castello In San Marino, a political subdivision equivalent to a county.

Castles in the Sky Slang; a term describing an extremely overvalued security or market. The price rises because investors believe it will keep rising indefinitely. This continues right up to the moment that the price crashes. The term describes a market bubble.

Casualty Insurance A category of insurance that covers unforeseen events on a stated asset or assets. Car insurance, workers compensation insurance, and elevator insurance all fall under this general category. Often, casualty insurance only covers a particular event or asset. That is, car insurance covers one's car (and perhaps the persons within it) only. Casualty insurance provides coverage to the policyholder in the event the insured event occurs; the coverage is contingent upon the timely payment of premiums.

Casualty Loss A loss that occurs as a result of an unforeseen, catastrophic event. Casualty losses can occur, for example, when one drives a car through the garage or when a tornado destroys a business. Financial losses from gradual, environmental degradation would not qualify as casualty losses. One may deduct a casualty loss from one's taxable income, subject to certain conditions. Specifically, the first $100 of a casualty loss is not deductible and one must reduce the amount of the deduction by 10% of one's adjusted gross income. For example, if one suffers a casualty loss of $25,000 and has an adjusted gross income of $100,000, the casualty loss deduction is calculated thusly: Casualty loss = 25,000 - 100 - (0.10 * 100,000) = $14,900.

Casuistry 1. In law, the act of applying a rule or principle to a theoretical situation in order to see how it holds up. **2.** In law, the act of generalizing an unusual situation in order to form a rule or principle based on it. **3.** Derogatory, faulty reasoning.

Catalyst An event that directly or indirectly causes another event. For example, a positive earnings report may be a catalyst for a stock to rise in price. Likewise, conservative financial management may be a catalyst for long-term sustainability.

Catastrophe Bond A high-yield debt security backed by insurance premiums. Insurance companies issue catastrophe bonds in order to raise funds for hypothetical insurance payouts resulting from one or more stated events such as floods or fires. The bondholder receives coupons from what the insurance company collects in premiums. However, if the insurance company suffers a loss from a payout of one of stated events, the obligation to repay the bond is either relaxed or forgiven. The main advantage to a catastrophe bond, despite the stated risk, is the fact that it offers a high yield without much regard for the performance of the broader economy because people and institutions will almost always set money aside for insurance premiums.

Catastrophe Call The call of a bond that occurs when an asset secured by that bond is destroyed. For example, suppose a company issues a bond to build a factory, with the coupon and principal payments secured by the revenue that factory produces. If that factory burns down, there is nothing securing the future coupon payments, and the issuer may make a catastrophe call to save itself from a liability it may not be able to pay.

Catastrophic Illness Insurance An insurance policy covering extraordinarily expensive medical bills. Catastrophic illness insurance usually is released as a lump sum when the insured event occurs. Often, catastrophic illness insurance is triggered when a policyholder has a major medical problem and still needs treatment after surviving more than a stated number of days. For example, catastrophic illness insurance may cover the extended hospitalization necessary after a major surgery.

Catch-Up Contribution Contributions to an IRA or a 401(k) over and above the maximum allowed otherwise. Account holders are allowed to make catch-up contributions if they are over 50 years of age. They were first allowed under the Economic Growth And Tax Relief Reconciliation Act of 2001 and are designed to let persons save more for retirement as they near retirement without being taxed.

Category Killer An exceptionally large retailer that sells a wide range of products and, in doing so, drives smaller, specialized companies out of business. For example, when Wal-Mart became popular, it drove into bankruptcy a wide range of individual and small chain clothiers, hardware stores, and eventually groceries. Category killers are able to do this by providing essentially the same product at a much lower price, which they achieve by tightly controlling costs and the supply chain. See also: JIT.

Cats and Dogs A slang term for highly speculative stocks with little history or documentation indicating likelihood of success.

Catty A unit of weight in Taiwan approximately equivalent to 600 grams. It is used primarily in the sale of bulk foodstuffs.

Caucus A meeting of members of a political party, a faction within a party, or other likeminded individuals. For example, in a legislative chamber, the represented political parties form their own caucuses to present a unified front in public.

Caveat Emptor Latin for "let the buyer beware." It is used in many transactions to indicate that all sales are final and all due diligence is the sole responsibility of the buyer. The phrase is especially common in real estate.

Cawnie An obsolete Indian unit of area approximately equivalent to 5.349 square kilometers. It was used in Chennai for real estate transactions.

CAX ISO 4217 code for the Canadian cent. It is worth 1% of a Canadian dollar.

Cayawlenen Ayliq Yuli A Tatar unit of length approximately equivalent to 1,120 kilometers. It was rendered obsolete when the Soviet Union began to use the metric system in 1924.

Cayawlenen Konlek Yuli A Tatar unit of length approximately equivalent to 37.34 kilometers. It was rendered obsolete when the Soviet Union began to use the metric system in 1924.

CBO 1. Collateralized Bond Obligation. An asset-backed security backed by the receivables on junk bonds. Issuers of CBOs package and sell their receivables on

bonds they hold to investors in order to reduce the risk coming from defaults. Returns on CBOs are lower risk than the individual bonds backing them. This is because it is unlikely that all or even most of the junk bonds will default. This makes the collateralized bond obligations investment grade and therefore banks are allowed to invest in them. See also: Collateralized Loan Obligation, Collateralized Mortgage Obligation. **2.** Congressional Budget Office. An agency of the United States Congress that provides the Congress with economic data. Among other duties, it calculates the national debt and the impact that individual bills and the budget generally have on the federal deficit. It was created in 1974; its director is appointed jointly by the Speaker of the House and the President pro tempore of the Senate.

CBOE NASDAQ Volatility Index A mathematical measure of the implied volatility of options trading on NASDAQ 100. The VXN attempts to measure the likelihood of option prices to vary unpredictably in the context of the Black-Scholes model. A higher number on the index represents greater volatility, while a lower number represents lower volatility. While critics maintain that its usefulness is overstated, the index is considered an indicator of option volatility in the wider market. See also: VIX.

CBOE S&P 500 BuyWrite Index An index showing the performance of a buy-write strategy involving the stocks on the S&P 500. That is, the BuyWrite Index shows an investor what would happen if she/he purchased the stocks on the S&P 500 and wrote call options in which the S&P 500 index were the underlying asset. See also: Covered call.

CBOE S&P 500 PutWrite Index An index showing the performance of a covered strategy involving the stocks on the S&P 500. That is, the PutWrite Index shows an investor what would happen if she/he purchased put options on the S&P 500 index and had sufficient cash on hand to buy the stocks in case the options were exercised. See also: Covered put.

CBOE Volatility Index A mathematical measure of the implied volatility of options trading on the S&P 500 index. That is, the CBOE Volatility Index attempts to measure the likelihood of option prices to vary unpredictably in the context of a particular pricing model in this case, the Black-Scholes model. A higher number on the index represents greater volatility, while a lower number represents lower volatility. While critics maintain that its usefulness is overstated, the index is considered a leading indicator of option volatility in the wider market. The CBOE Index is operated by the Chicago Board of Options Exchange, and is also known as the VIX.

CBV Midcap Index An index tracking 30 mid-cap companies in Vietnam. The companies on the index each have a market capitalization between 150 billion and 500 billion Vietnamese dong. The index is used as an indicator of the performance of midcap companies on the Vietnamese market.

CBV Smallcap Index An index tracking 30 small-cap companies in Vietnam. The companies on the index each have a market capitalization between 50 billion and 150 billion Vietnamese dong. The index is used as an indicator of the performance of small companies on Vietnamese market.

CBV Total An index tracking 110 publicly-traded companies in Vietnam. It includes all companies tracked on the CBV Largecap, CBV Midcap, and CBV Smallcap indices. The index is used as an indicator of the performance of the Vietnamese market.

CC 1. ISO 3166-1 alpha-2 code for the Territory of the Cocos Islands, also known as the Keeling Islands. This is the code used in international transactions to and from Cocossian bank accounts. **2.** ISO 3166-2 geocode for the Cocos Islands. This is used as an international standard for shipping to the Cocos Islands.

CCC 1. A credit rating used by the S&P and Fitch credit agencies for long-term bonds and some other investments. It is equivalent to the CAA rating used by Moody's. A CCC rating represents an extremely high risk bond or investment; banks are not allowed to invest in CCC rated bonds. CCC bonds are junk bonds. **2.** Cash conversion cycle. The time between an expenditure of money to make a product and the collection of accounts receivable from the sale of that product. Obviously, a shorter cash conversion cycle is preferable. A longer cash conversion cycle may indicate a current or potential problem with cash flow.

CCK GOST 7.67 Latin three-letter geocode for the Cocos Islands. The code is used for transactions to and from Cocossian bank accounts and for international shipping to the Cocos Islands. As with all GOST 7.67 codes, it is used primarily in Cyrillic alphabets.

CD Annuity An instrument that combines features of an annuity and a certificate of deposit. Like a fixed annuity, it gives the annuitant a series of payments each month for the duration of the annuity. Like a CD (and unlike many fixed annuities), the return is guaranteed for the entire life of the instrument. In other words, a CD annuity gives a return similar to a CD, though it is structured like an annuity.

CDF ISO 4217 code for the Congolese franc. It was issued in 1997 when Zaire became the Democratic Republic of the Congo (not to be confused with the Republic of the Congo). The franc replaced the new zaire.

CDO Squared Slang; a collateralized debt obligation collateralized by other collateralized debt obligations rather than directly by debt. A CDO squared may have less risk than a regular CDO, as it has more underlying debts.

Cease-and-Desist Order An order from a government regulator to halt an action. Cease-and-desist orders are used to enforce licensing regulation, halt the sale of unregistered securities, or stop transactions believed to be fraudulent. The order states a period of time in which the recipient can contest it in court. If the recipient does not contest the order, or if the contest fails, the order becomes enforceable in a court of law.

Ceiling The maximum interest rate that may be charged on a contract or agreement. For example, an adjustable-rate mortgage may have an interest rate ceiling stating that the rate will not go over 9% even if the formula used to calculate the interest rate would have it do so. An interest rate ceiling reduces the risk of the party paying the interest. It is also called an interest rate cap. See also: Interest Rate Floor.

Ceim An obsolete Irish unit of length approximately equivalent to 62.5 centimeters.

Ceki A Turkish measure of weight approximately equivalent to 226 kilograms. It became obsolete when Turkey made the metric system mandatory in 1933.

Celler-Kefauver Antimerger Act An American antitrust law passed in 1950 that closed a major loophole in the Clayton Act. While the Clayton Act prohibited mergers that reduced competition, it allowed companies to buy individual assets of competitors. Some companies did this to such an extent that it reduced competition, which had the potential to effectively sideline the Clayton Act. The Celler-Kefauver Act closed this loophole, giving the government the power to stop vertical mergers and asset acquisitions regarded as reducing competition. It is often simply called the Antimerger Act.

Census Bureau A division under the Department of Commerce that collects data on the population, demographics, and economics in the United States. The Census Bureau is required to conduct an exhaustive survey of the U.S. population at least once every 10 years; this determines the apportionment of seats in the U.S. House of Representatives. However, it also provides a great deal of useful information on the state of the American economy. For example, it publishes figures on the trade balance. See also: The Conference Board.

Cent A division of several currencies in English-speaking countries equal in value to 1/100 of one unit of each currency.

Centas A division of the Lithuanian litas equal in value to 1/100 of one litas. Its plural is centai.

Centavo A division of several currencies in Spanish- and Portuguese-speaking countries equal in value to 1/100 of one unit of each currency. An equivalent term is centimo.

Centesimo A division of several currencies in Italian-speaking (and some Spanish-speaking) countries equal in value to 1/100 of one unit of each currency.

Centime A division of several currencies in French-speaking countries equal in value to 1/100 of one unit of each currency.

Centner An obsolete measure of weight equivalent to 110 pounds.

Central African CFA Franc The currency of five former French colonies and one former Spanish colony in Africa: Cameroon, Central African Republic, Chad, Congo (Republic of), Equatorial Guinea, and Gabon. It was introduced in 1945. For most of its history, it was pegged to the French franc, but, in 1999, the peg switched to the euro. While it is of equal value to the Central African CFA franc, the two currencies are not interchangeable.

Central Bank A bank that is constituted by a government or international organization to issue and regulate currency, regulate banks under its jurisdiction, act as a lender of last resort, and generally ensure a sustainable monetary policy. Oftentimes, central banks are charged with one or more specific duties such as attempting full employment or a certain exchange rate for the currency. Most commonly, however, central banks are charged with finding the balance between maintaining low inflation and high economic growth. They do this primarily by setting interest rates at which they lend to banks under its jurisdiction which, in turn, highly influences interest rates throughout the country or region. Prominent central banks include the Federal Reserve, the Bank of England, the European Central Bank, the Bank of Japan, and the People's Bank of China.

Central Bank Intervention The practice in which a central bank buys and sells one or more currencies in order to affect the exchange rate of its own currency. To give a very simple example, if a central bank believes its own currency is overvalued it may sell that currency on the open market to increase supply. The extra supply will likely drive down the exchange rate to a lower level.

Central Bank of Brazil The organization charged with issuing currency and regulating monetary policy. It is responsible for printing the Brazilian rial and for setting the overnight loan rate known as the SELIC. The Central Bank is informally called the Bacen. It was established in 1964.

Central Bank of Iceland The supreme monetary authority in Iceland. It is responsible for issuing the Icelandic kronur and for setting target inflation rates. While it is expected to follow the government's lead in many areas, it remains an independent agency. It was established in 1961.

Central Bank of Liberia The supreme monetary authority in Liberia. It replaced the National Bank of Liberia in 2000, following the end of a civil war. See also: Liberian dollar.

Central Bank of Nigeria The supreme monetary authority in Nigeria. It issues the Nigerian naira, maintains foreign currency reserves and is charged with maintaining monetary stability. It is also the lender of last resort for Nigerian banks. It was established by law in 1958.

Central Bank of Russia The central bank of Russia. The Russian constitution charges the Central Bank with maintaining the stability of the Russian ruble. It sets interest rates for interbank loans in Russia and also regulates the banking industry. It was established in 1990, but traces its origins to the central bank of the Russian Empire in the mid-1800s.

Central Bank of Swaziland The supreme monetary authority in Swaziland. Among other things, it manages the country's foreign exchange and issues government securities to Swazi banks. It was established in 1974.

Central Bank of Syria The supreme monetary authority in Syria. It is responsible for issuing the Syrian pound and for implementing monetary policy.

Central Bank of the Philippines The supreme monetary authority of the Philippines. It issues the Philippine peso, maintains foreign currency reserves and is charged with maintaining monetary stability. It is also the lender of last resort for Philippine banks. It was established in 1949 and re-chartered in 1993.

Central Bank of the Republic of Argentina The supreme monetary authority of Argentina. It issues the Argentine peso, maintains foreign currency reserves and is charged with maintaining monetary stability. It is also the lender of last resort for Argentine banks. It was established in 1935.

Central Clearing Time In England and Wales, the amount of time it takes for a cheque to be cleared. That is, the central clearing time is how long it takes for money to be transferred by cheque. Central clearing time is typically three business days, though it may take longer if a cheque is deposited after 4:30 pm.

Central Limit Order Book A proposed database for all limit orders received by specialists and market makers throughout the United States. Such a system would allow limit orders to be fulfilled immediately or later, depending on the nature of the order, on any American exchange. The SEC proposed the establishment of CLOB, but it never occurred because most exchanges believe that such as a database would cause them to lose trading volume.

Central Limit Theorem In statistics, a theory stating that as the sample size of identically distributed, random numbers approaches infinity, it is more likely that the distribution of the numbers will approximate normal distribution. That is, the mean of all samples within that universe of numbers will be roughly the mean of the whole sample.

Central Mint of China An organization in Taiwan that issues legal tender coins for general use. It was established in mainland China in 1920 and moved to Taiwan in 1949. It is owned by the Central Bank of China (Taiwan) and is located in Taoyuan County.

Central Processing System A computer system on which FAFSA data is processed. The CPS uses algorithms to determine post-secondary students' eligibility for federal financial aid.

Central Rate In the European Monetary System, an exchange rate for a currency relative to the European currency unit. Each currency is permitted to move within a narrow range of the central rate, making each currency in the European Monetary System a semi-pegged currency.

Central Treaty Organization A former international organization consisting of Iran, Iraq, Pakistan, Turkey and the United Kingdom. The United States was also involved peripherally. It was modeled after NATO and was intended to resist Soviet expansion into the Middle East and South Asia. It was largely unsuccessful in this mission; for example, Iraq left the organization after it opened diplomatic relations with the Soviet Union in 1958. It was also known as CENTO and the Baghdad Pact. It existed from 1955 to 1979.

Centralized Cash Flow Management The practice of a large corporation, especially a multinational, making all cash management decisions from headquarters. That is, individual units have little autonomy under centralized cash flow management. This has the advantage of being a uniform policy throughout the company, but management may be time consuming and possibly not as efficient.

Centro poblado In Peru, a political subdivision approximately equivalent to a municipality.

Cents per Share The dividend that a mutual fund or publicly-traded company gives to shareholders for each share owned.

Centuria An ancient Roman unit of area approximately equivalent to 50.5 hectares.

CEO Confidence Survey A survey of 100 CEOs in the United States on their perceptions of the state of their business and the economy in general. Topics covered in the survey include long-term and short-term outlooks, prospects for hiring or laying off workers, and concerns unique to particular industries. The CEO Confidence Survey attempts to quantify these feelings on a scale of 0 to 100, with a higher score indicating bullish feelings. The survey is taken monthly and published by The Conference Board.

Cercle In Mali, a political subdivision approximately equivalent to a county.

Ceres Principles Ten rules guiding the investment practices of the Ceres, a nonprofit whose members include both investors and environmental organizations. The Ceres Principles require one to make investment decisions that minimize risk to the environment and promote sustainable use of natural resources. They were originally called the Valdez Principles because they were written in 1989 following the Exxon Valdez disaster.

Certainty Equivalent A small, zero-risk return an investor may trade for a larger potential return with an associated risk. Companies offer certainty equivalent returns on certain investments and use their demand to determine the level of risk an investor will accept for a given return from the company.

Certificate A physical document that declares a fact and that may be used to prove said fact. One of the most common types of certificates is a stock certificate, which gives the person or company listed a portion of ownership in a publicly-traded company. Certificates often contain a great deal of information, such as what the certificate entails, whether that be ownership, a right attached to the ownership (such as a warrant), or something else entirely. Certificates of ownership also state the name of the owner; for example, a deed to a house contains the name of the owner(s). Certificates are vitally important, as one may use them in court to prove a fact alleged.

Certificate of Accrual on Treasury Securities A formerly-issued Treasury security whose coupons had been stripped by an intermediary. CATS therefore paid no interest. They were sold at a significant discount from par and matured at par. CATS fluctuated in price, sometimes dramatically, because changes in interest rates made them more or less desirable. CATS could be invested IRAs and other pension accounts; they were also exempt from state and local taxes. They were issued between 1982 and 1986, becoming obsolete when the U.S. Treasury began issuing its own stripped bonds. See also: Zero-Coupon Bonds.

Certificate of Automobile Receivables A derivative whose value is derived from the receivables on a car loan. This entitles the owner to a claim on the principal and interest payments on the particular car loans underpinning the security. The equivalent of the coupon on CARS is a percentage of the interest and principal paid on car loans. An obvious risk associated with CARS is the possibility that a substantial number of loans will default. See also: Credit risk, Mortgage-backed security.

Certificate of Deposit A deposit at a bank or other financial institution that has a fixed return (usually via an interest rate) and a set maturity. The depositor does not have access to the funds in a certificate of deposit until maturity; in exchange, he/she is usually entitled to a higher interest rate. CDs are insured by the FDIC up to a certain amount and as such are a way to increase return for no extra risk. See also: Demand deposit, Real estate certificate of deposit, Negotiable certificate of deposit.

Certificate of Government Receipts Treasury securities that have been stripped of their coupons. This means that COUGRs are bonds that pay no interest and simply mature at face value. The financial firm A.G. Becker Paribas offers COUGRs as synthetic debt securities, selling them at a discount to their face value, which guarantees a profit for buyers. Because they are U.S. Treasury securities, COUGRs are risk-free. See also: CATS, TIGRs.

Certificate of Origin A document stating the country in which a product was manufactured. Many countries require certificates of origin as part of the paperwork necessary for importing goods. This is because most nations give certain other nations preferential or detrimental treatment with regard to trade. That is, it may charge no or very low tariffs on some countries while charging very high tariffs on others. A certificate of origin lets customs agents know what fees are applicable to a given shipment of goods.

Certificated Stock Inventory of a commodity that has been inspected by a designated official and determined to be of the appropriate quality. Certificated stock may be used in delivery on a futures contract or option. Certificated stock is also called certified stock. It should not be confused with a stock certificate, which indicates ownership of a stock.

Certificateless Municipal A municipal bond with no physical bond certificate. Instead, the holder is given a receipt and the information is held electronically. Certificateless municipals have become more common as computers have become more sophisticated and exchanges have increasingly closed their trading floors. Certificateless municipals are settled by the DTCC.

Certificates for Amortizing Revolving Debts Pass-through securities backed by the receivables on credit cards. That is, they are debt securities in which the holders are entitled to the principal and interest on the credit card payments underlying them. CARDs are structured in a similar way to mortgage-backed securities.

Certified Check A check whose payment is guaranteed by a bank. In exchange for a fee, a bank issues a certified check to a person, who is very often both the payer and the payee. That is, a person gives the bank the amount for which the certified check is written, either in cash or by deducting the appropriate amount from the payer's account; the bank then makes the check payable to that person. The person may cash the check at any bank, or deposit it at a different bank without being subject to a check hold. A certified check is also known as a registered check or banker's draft. See also: Traveler's cheque, Commercial draft.

Certified Financial Planner A professional certificate offered through the Certified Financial Planner Board of Standards. The certification qualifies one to consult on financial matters. In order to qualify for a CFP, one must complete a series of tests measuring knowledge of retirement issues, estate planning, tax, and financial planning. One must also remain current on continuing education requirements. CFPs often advice clients on how best to manage their money. See also: ChFC.

Certified in Financial Management A professional designation for financial managers awarded by the Institute of Management Accountants. These professionals specialize in the study of how managers use accounting and/or financial information in current or future business decisions. Holders of the CFM designation must pass a four-part exam and follow established common practices and ethical standards set by the Institute. See also: Certified Management Accountant.

Certified Investment Management Consultant A professionally certified investment manager. To become a CIMC, one must complete required coursework and complete a four-part examination covering asset allocation, modern portfolio management, measurement of portfolio performance, and ethics. The exam is administered by FINRA. See also: CFA, ChFC.

Certified Investment Management Specialist An associate investment manager. To become a CIMS, one must complete an examination and work in investment management for a certain period of time. The designation is administered by the Institute for Investment Management Consultants. The designation ranks below a CIMC. See also: CFA, ChFC.

Certified Management Accountant An accountant who specializes in the study of how managers use accounting and/or financial information in current or future business decisions. Management accountants use both qualitative and quantitative information in their work. Unlike other accountants, they primarily report to the internal management of a company, rather than to an external body like shareholders or tax collection agencies. In order to become a certified management accountant, one must pass a series of tests sponsored by the Institute of Management Accountants. These tests examine one's knowledge in four subjects: business analysis, management accounting and reporting, strategic management, and business applications.

Certified Public Accountant A professionally licensed accountant. In the United States, CPA eligibility conditions vary by state, but all require the successful completion of a four-part CPA exam. CPAs can legally give public attestation to advice on financial statements; for example, only a CPA can sign an in-house audit. See also: Accountancy.

Ceteris Paribus Literally, a Latin phrase meaning "with other things the same." In economic and financial models, ceteris paribus is a shorthand indicating that the model holds true if other market forces do not intervene. One often finds "ceteris paribus" in simple models and in simplifications of complex models. For example, one might say: "If supply decreases, price increases, ceteris paribus." The statement is true assuming constant (and substantial) demand regardless of supply, among other factors. Ceteris paribus acknowledges other facts without letting them overwhelm the point of the model.

C-EZ A short form for the Schedule C. It is used by business owners who report a profit, but have expenses under $5,000, no inventory, no business property to depreciate, no expenses for the business use of home, no carryovers from passive activity losses, and no employees. Additionally, it cannot be used to report a business loss. Schedule C-EZ is aimed at microbusiness owners, or those who have businesses to supplement their primary incomes.

Cf 1. On a bond transaction table, an abbreviation indicating that a bond has matured, but is still trading. **2.** ISO 3166-1 alpha-2 code for the Central African Republic. This is the code used in international transactions to and from Central African bank accounts. **3.** ISO 3166-2 geocode for the Central African Republic. This is used as an international standard for shipping to the Central African Republic. The capital and each prefecture have their own codes with the prefix "CF." For example, the code for the Prefecture of Ouaka is ISO 3166-2:CF-UK.

CFA Franc Zone A collective term for the countries that use either the Central African CFA franc or the West African CFA franc, which are both guaranteed by the French government. The CFA franc zone consists of Cameroon, the Central African Republic, Chad, the Republic of the Congo, Equatorial Guinea, and Gabon (for the Central African franc), and Benin, Burkina Faso, Cote d'Ivoire, Guinea-Bissau, Mali, Niger, Senegal and Togo (for the West African franc).

CFA Institute A professional organization of financial analysts. In addition to operating the Chartered Financial Analyst (CFA) and Certified Investment Performance Measurement (CIPM) exams, its members agree to abide by a code of ethical conduct in financial reporting known as the Global Investment Performance Standards (GIPS). Founded in 1925 in Chicago, the CFA Institute has 135 member societies in 56 countries.

CFR A CPT involving ocean freight. In a CFR, the seller is responsible for paying for shipping, while the buyer is responsible for transportation risk as soon as the good or product is loaded onto the ship. Legally, risk transfers when the good or product crosses the outer rail of the ship.

CG 1. ISO 3166-1 alpha-2 code for the Republic of the Congo (not to be confused with the Democratic Republic of the Congo). This is the code used in international transactions to and from Congolese bank accounts. **2.** ISO 3166-2 geocode for the Congo. This is used as an international standard for shipping to the Congo. Each region and the capital have their own codes with the prefix "CG." For example, the code for the Region of Pool is ISO 3166-2:CG-12.

CH 1. ISO 3166-1 alpha-2 code for the Swiss Confederation. This is the code used in international transactions to and from Swiss bank accounts. **2.** ISO 3166-2 geocode for Switzerland. This is used as an international standard for shipping to Switzerland. Each Swiss canton has its own code with the prefix "CH." For example, the code for the Canton of Geneva is ISO 3166-2:CH-GE.

Chaikin Oscillator In technical analysis, a measure of market movements created by subtracting a 10-day exponential moving average (EMA) from a 3-day exponential moving average of the accumulation/distribution line, which is a measure of whether investors are generally buying or selling. Exponential moving averages are weighted to emphasize more recent market movements; the Chaikin oscillator does this while also accounting for older trends, such as the 10-day EMA.

Chain Cent A one-cent piece minted by the United States in 1793. It was the first U.S.-made coin to circulate. It was worth 1/100 of one dollar.

Chainsaw Consultant An outside person or company brought in to conduct lay-offs. A chainsaw consultant is hired if a company's managers are unable or unwilling to lay off employees themselves.

Chair of the Board In a publicly-traded company, the highest ranking member of the board of directors. The chair is elected by the board, presides over meetings, and acts as a liaison between management and shareholders. The chair has the responsibility to ensure that the company's policies are being properly enforced to benefit shareholders. As such, he/she guides the board in establishing general policies for the organization, including dividend policies, and hiring or firing major executives. He/she is answerable to shareholders for his/her decisions, but is, in general, the most powerful officer in the company.

Chairman of the Council of Economic Advisers The head of the Council of Economic Advisers, which advises the president on economic matters. The chairman is permitted to attend cabinet meetings. Among his/her duties are helping the president formulate policy, interpreting data, and generally serving as one of the White House's resident experts on the economy. The chairman is appointed by the president upon approval of the Senate.

Chalder An obsolete Scottish unit of dry volume. For beans, grass seed, peas, rye, salt, and wheat, one chalder was approximately equivalent to 2,324.9 liters. For barley, malt, and oats, however, it was approximately equivalent to 3,362.5 liters.

Chaldron An obsolete unit of dry volume variously equivalent to values between 32 and 72 bushels.

Chalkoi A small coin of little value in ancient Greece. One oblus was subdivided into eight chalkoi. One drachma was subdivided into six obloi.

Chameleon Option An option whose features can change. For example, a call option that can become a put option is a chameleon.

Champagne Stock Slang; stock that has very quickly risen in price. It especially refers to stocks with prices that have recently doubled or tripled.

Chancellor of the Duchy of Lancaster An officer of the British government responsible for the administration of expenses and rents (and other income) of the Duchy of Lancaster, a large tract of land belonging to the Crown that provides much of the monarch's income. In practice, the chancellor serves as a minister without portfolio in the British cabinet and leaves administration of the duchy to a subordinate. The chancellor is appointed by the monarch on the advice of the prime minister.

Chancellor of the Exchequer The head of HM Treasury in the United Kingdom. He/she is responsible for advising on and executing economic and fiscal policy in the United Kingdom. Through Inland Revenue and Customs, he/she oversees tax collection.

Chande Momentum Oscillator In technical analysis, an indication of whether a security is overbought or oversold. It is calculated by adding together all gains over a given period (a positive number) and all losses over the same period (a negative number) and dividing the sum by the total price movement over the period. The result will be between -100 and +100. A security is thought to be overbought when the oscillator is greater than +50 and oversold when it is less than -50. Some analysts add a moving average to the oscillator to help clarify buy and sell signals.

Change The difference between the closing price on a trading day and the closing price on the previous trading day. The change may be positive or negative. For example, if a stock closes at $11 on Tuesday and $12 on Wednesday, it has a change of +$1. On the other hand, if the stock falls to $10 on Friday, it has a change of -$2. Change is also called net change. See also: Technical Analysis.

Change Agent An employee or outside consultant who believes that he/she is making positive changes to a company. The term is used most commonly when certain employees encourage the use of new technologies. These changes may or may not be popular among other employees.

Change in Stock List Any alteration to the set of stocks traded on an exchange. Examples of changes in stock list include new listings, delistings, and changes to company names.

Changer A clearing house, especially on the Merc, that takes the opposite position of an exchange's member firm's futures position. In other words, the changer bears the risk of a futures contract on behalf of this member firm. Changers charge a fee for this service.

Changes in Financial Position Activities from operations that alter the cash a company has on hand. Changes in financial position include cash outflows, such as capital expenditures, and cash inflows, such as revenue. It may also include certain non-cash changes, such as depreciation.

Changwat In Thailand, a political subdivision equivalent to a province.

Channel Check A way of analyzing a stock, where one uses information supplied by parties other than the company being analyzed. A channel check is useful because the information is independently verified and, because it is not provided by the company being analyzed, there is no incentive to make the company appear healthier than it is.

Channel Stuffing An illegal practice in which a company willfully sells more of its product to distributors than the distributors can sell to customers. The company makes these sales on credit, which temporarily boosts its accounts receivable and by extension its current assets. This makes the company look healthier than it really is which can raise its stock price. Eventually, when the distributors are unable to sell the product they return it to the company instead of paying, which reduces the accounts receivable and brings the company's balance sheet in line with reality.

Chaos Theory A theory stating that seemingly unrelated events affect each other in a predictable, mathematical way. In investing, chaos theory is used to predict future stock prices using information that does not seem to affect prices directly, such as

trading volume and trader sentiment. Computing these factors using chaos theory is as complex as it is controversial.

Chapter 10 A chapter of the U.S. bankruptcy code stating the terms under which a small company may file for bankruptcy protection while it prepares a reorganization plan. In order to be eligible for Chapter 10 protection, the company cannot have more than $2.5 million in debt and the reorganization plan must include provisions where the debt will be repaid within three years. See also: Chapter 7, Chapter 11, Chapter 13.

Chapter 11 The process of the reorganization of a bankrupt company under the supervision of a court or the appropriate regulator. Chapter 11 proceedings require a reorganization plan, which is filed with the bankruptcy court or regulator and describes how an insolvent company will change structurally to help it pay its debts and stay in business. This plan is subject to court or regulator oversight to ensure enforcement. Depending upon the specific plan, a company's original owner or managers may maintain control. Other times, the company's creditors become the new owners of the business; this especially happens when one or more creditors have had their debt completely discharged. Changes also must occur structurally (perhaps in risk management or marketing or perhaps in something more fundamental) to ensure that the bankruptcy does not repeat itself.

Chapter 13 A form of bankruptcy in which a person or company reorganizes his/her/its debts so they are repaid over a period of three to five years. This form of bankruptcy is most commonly used if one continues to have significant income even though one's debts have become too burdensome. A disadvantage to Chapter 13 is the fact that one's debts are not discharged. However, Chapter 13 may allow one to maintain ownership of assets that would otherwise be liquidated. It is also called a wage earner plan. See also: Chapter 7, Chapter 11, Best interests of creditors test.

Chapter 7 In the United States, a type of bankruptcy where a person's or company's assets are required to be liquidated. The court appoints a trustee, who may or may not be a part of the company, to oversee the liquidation process. If a company files for chapter 7, it ceases operations. The company's creditors receive the proceeds from liquidation according to the system of absolute priority; that is, secured creditors are paid first, then if anything is left unsecured creditors are paid, then preferred stockholders, and finally common stockholders. A company files for chapter 7 proceedings when its management believes that reorganizing according to a court-mandated plan would not result in the company becoming profitable.

Chaqian A Chinese term for tea money. It is a slang term for a small bribe.

Charge 1. To sell at a certain price. For example, if a grocery store sells coffee beans for $7 per pound, it is said to charge $7 per pound for coffee. **2.** Informal; to buy something on credit, especially with a credit card or charge card. That is, one who uses a credit card for transactions is said to charge those transactions.

Charge Card A revolving line of credit with no interest rate that requires the holder to repay the entire balance each month. That is, a charge card allows one to borrow without limit or interest so long as it is repaid in full by the due date. The charge card company makes a profit through annual fees and large late fees on card holders who do not repay their balances. In essence, however, a charge card operates much like a credit card. American Express and Diner's Club are two prominent charge card companies.

Charge d'Affaires An official at an embassy who is the head of mission in the absence of the ambassador. That is, a charge d'affaires may act as ambassador if the ambassador is temporarily out of the country, or if an ambassador is yet to be appointed.

Chargeback A refund made by a credit card company to a credit card holder. Chargebacks occur when a card holder disputes an item on one's credit card statement, usually because he/she claims that he/she never authorized the charge. For example, if a person is a victim of identity theft because someone stole and used his/her credit card, that person may receive a chargeback on all unauthorized transactions. Other reasons for receiving a chargeback include receiving goods late or damaged, or not receiving them at all.

Charitable Contribution Deduction A reduction in one's taxable income as a result of donations to a charity or other non-profit. A charitable contribution deduction reduces the income on which one pays taxes up to 50% of one's adjusted gross income. Donations to most non-profits qualify for the charitable contribution deduction with the notable exception of political organizations such as labor unions or lobbyists.

Charitable Lead Trust An irrevocable trust into which the grantor deposits assets, with the income from the investment of these assets going to a designated charity for a certain period of time. After that time expires, the remainder of the assets and income are given to the trust's beneficiaries. A charitable lead trust allows the grantor to provide for his/her survivors after death while reducing to a minimum the estate tax because some of the assets were given to charity. See also: Charitable remainder trust.

Charitable Remainder Trust An irrevocable trust in which the grantor deposits assets with the income from the investment of these assets given to beneficiaries for a certain period of time. After the time expires, the remainder of the assets and income are donated to charity. A charitable remainder trust allows the grantor to provide for his/her survivors after death while reducing to a minimum the estate tax because the assets are ultimately directed to charity.

Charitable Trust An irrevocable trust into which the grantor deposits assets, with at least some of the proceeds going to a charity. There are two types of charitable trusts. In a charitable lead trust, the income from the investment of the assets in the trust goes to a designated charity for a certain period of time. After that time expires, the remainder of the assets and income are given to the trust's beneficiaries. In a charitable remainder trust, the income from the assets goes to the beneficiaries for a certain period of time, after which the assets themselves are donated to charity. In the United States, both types of charitable trust receive favorable treatment for estate tax purposes.

Charka A Russian unit of liquid volume approximately equivalent to 123 milliliters. It was rendered obsolete when the Soviet Union began to use the metric system in 1924.

Charles M. Schwab An American industrialist and steel manufacturer (1862-1939). He began to work as a stake driver for the Carnegie Steel Company and quickly rose to become its president. He secretly negotiated Carnegie's sale to J.P. Morgan and other investors in 1901. He continued as president of U.S. Steel, Carnegie's successor company, until 1903, when a conflict with another executive caused him to form Bethlehem Steel Company. It became the largest steel producing company in the world. He became very wealthy, but lost most of his money in the 1929 stock market crash. He was not related to Charles R. Schwab.

Charles Merrill An American stockbroker. In 1915, he co-founded the company that created Merrill Lynch and was able to avoid much of the Great Crash of 1929 by diversifying his investments. Merrill was noted for investing in retail chains, notably Safeway and the company that became K-Mart. He lived from 1885 to 1956.

Charm School A derogatory term for a corporate training program for mangers or employees, especially a program to which one is sent for disciplinary purposes. For example, an employee may be sent to charm school to learn why racism is unacceptable if he/she is punished for making racially insensitive remarks.

Chart Formation The graphical representation on a chart of a trend in security prices. Technical analysts identify chart formations for a security and predict future price movements in part by matching current patterns with previous patterns.

Chart Service A company that sells charts of security prices. A chart service compiles information and composes a chart, usually on a monthly basis, in order to send to a client. It saves the client the time of creating a chart himself/herself and, as such, may expedite investment decisions, especially those made with technical analysis. However, chart service charts are often delayed by a few days, meaning that the chart does not display a security's most recently available information.

Charter Amendment Limitation A restriction on the process of amending the charter of a publicly-traded company. Examples of charter amendment limitations include requirements for a supermajority of shareholders to agree or a provision rendering certain parts of the charter unamendable. Charter amendment limitations can be part of an anti-takeover measure and are governed by state law. See also: Bylaw amendment limitations.

Chartered Accountant A professionally licensed accountant in the United Kingdom and several current and former Commonwealth countries. In England and Wales, in order to qualify as a chartered accountant, one must pass 15 exams and have 450 days of work experience in the field. Furthermore, a chartered accountant must abide by ethical guidelines set by the relevant body and take continuing education classes. See also: Accountancy, Certified Public Accountant, Institute of Chartered Accountants in England and Wales, Institute of Chartered Accountants of Scotland, Institute of Chartered Accountants in Ireland.

Chartered Bank A bank that has received the appropriate regulatory approval to operate and/or to receive certain government guarantees. Banks are regulated by the laws and central banks of their home countries; normally, they must receive a charter to engage in business. A charter indicates that the bank complies and must continue to comply with appropriate regulations, such as maintaining a certain minimum capital. See also: Participating bank.

Chartered Financial Analyst A professional certificate offered through the CFA Institute. The certification qualifies one to be a financial analyst. In order to qualify for a CFA, one must have worked a certain number of years in the financial industry and complete three tiers of exams on accounting, money management, economics, security analysis, and ethics.

Chartered Financial Consultant A professional certificate offered through the American College in Pennsylvania. The certification qualifies one to consult on financial matters, especially for individuals and small businesses. In order to qualify for a ChFC, one must have worked a certain number of years in the financial industry and complete eight to nine courses in income tax, insurance, employee benefits, investment, and estate planning, among others. The certification itself is awarded after an exam. See also: Certified financial planner.

Chartered Insurance Professional A professionally licensed insurance agent in property and casualty. In Canada, the CIP certification requires passage of 10 exams given by the Insurance Institute of Canada. The CIP is designed to set and promote professional standards among insurance agents in Canada. Chartered insurance professionals are required to pay an annual fee in order to retain their certifications.

Chartered Investment Counselor A professional designation for CFAs who work as investment advisers. In order to qualify as a CIC, one must first become a chartered financial analyst, have at least five years of work experience as an investment adviser or a similar field, and work at a member firm of the Investment Counsel Association of America. A CIC designation is considered a sign of vast experience in investment advisory services and/or asset management.

Chartered Market Technician A professional designation for a technical analyst. Technical analysts use statistics to determine trends in security prices, and make or recommend investment decisions based on those trends. In order to be certified as a CMT, one must be a member of the Market Technicians Association (MTA) and pass a series of examinations measuring one's knowledge of the theory and practice of technical analysis. Furthermore, one must agree to abide by the MTA's standards of ethical practice.

Chase a Stock To place limit orders for a stock that is increasing in price. One places the limit orders at successively higher prices in order to take advantage of the stock's capital appreciation when it is rising while not exposing oneself to the possibility that it will not rise to a higher price. For example, one may place limit orders at $5.50, $5.70, and $5.90. This means that if the stock goes to $5.60 and then falls to $5, the stock chaser will only be lose the amount invested in the first tier of purchases. On the other hand, if the stock rises to $8, one receives the capital appreciation on all three tiers of purchases. See also: Average Up.

Chasing Down Smokestacks Slang; the act or practice of making sales calls at industrial or manufacturing companies.

Chasing Nickels Around Dollar Bills The act or practice in which a company or government cuts small costs but leaves larger issues unaddressed and acts as if its actions represent fiscal responsibility. For example, if a government cuts highway funding, which represents 2% of spending, but leaves an unfunded liability in an entitlement program representing 65% of spending, the government may be said to be chasing nickels around dollar bills.

Chasing Returns Slang; the act or practice of taking on more (or excessive) risk in hopes of generating larger gains. For example, an investor who overexposes his portfolio to a security that happens to be bullish is said to be chasing returns. This may or may not turn out well for the investor.

Chasing the Market The act of making investment decisions based on market trends after those trends have been in place for quite some time. Chasing the market applies to both buying and selling securities. For example, one may buy a stock after it has already gone up in price considerably, and may already have become overvalued. Alternatively, one may sell the same stock after its downward trend has become well established and it may have already become undervalued. Chasing the market is closely related to both panic buying and panic selling and is usually considered an irrational investment strategy.

Chast A Russian unit of dry volume approximately equivalent to 109.33 cubic centimeters. It was rendered obsolete when the Soviet Union began to use the metric system in 1924.

Chastity Bond A corporate bond that matures automatically in the event the issuer is acquired by another company. Some companies issue chastity bonds as an antitakeover measure; this gives potential acquiring companies have an incentive not to attempt a hostile takeover if it will immediately have to repay bonds.

Chavanni In India, a slang term for a 25-paisa coin, which is worth one quarter of one Indian rupee.

CHE GOST 7.67 Latin three-letter geocode for Switzerland. The code is used for transactions to and from Swiss bank accounts and for international shipping to Switzerland. As with all GOST 7.67 codes, it is used primarily in Cyrillic alphabets.

Cheap Of or related to the low cost of a good, service, or security. Cheapness is determined by comparing the cost to similar goods, services, and securities. Cheapness is also related to one's ability to buy: what seems cheap to one person may seem expensive to another. Cheapness may, but does not always, indicate a low quality in the good, service, or security.

Cheap Money A monetary policy in which a central bank sets low interest rates so that credit is easily attainable. This makes borrowing easy for business, which stimulates investment and expansion of operations. The immediate result of cheap money is a boost in stock prices; in the medium term, cheap money promotes economic growth. However, if cheap money remains in the economy for too long, it can lead to a situation in which there is a glut of currency or too many dollars chasing too few goods and services leading to inflation. For this reason, most central banks alternate between policies of cheap money and tight money in varying degrees to encourage growth while keeping inflation under control.

Cheap Stock The practice of issuing stock in a company at too low a price immediately before an IPO. Generally, the cheap stock is offered at only a small fraction of the company's expected share price after the IPO. An underwriter may offer cheap stock in order to attract investors who might make a quick profit from the company or to potential managers in the company. Offering cheap stock is illegal.

Cheapest to Deliver The individual units of an underlying asset that would be least expensive for the seller of a futures contract to deliver to the buyer. Some derivatives specify the quality of product that the seller must deliver. If there is no specification, the seller has the right to deliver any quality and still fulfill the requirements of the contract. In such a case, the rational seller will always deliver the CTD. This may be a product of lower quality, and the price of such a futures contract will reflect this.

Cheapjack A primarily British term for cheapskate.

Cheapskate A slang term for a person or organization that spends less than it needs to. For example, a dentist who consistently orders an insufficient supply of cotton balls for patients' mouths may be considered a cheapskate. Being a cheapskate may cause more problems than it solves.

Chebel 1. An ancient Persian unit of length approximately equivalent to 24 meters. 2. A Persian unit of length approximately equivalent to 20 or 25 meters.

Chechen Naxar A proposed currency for Chechnya during its failed war of secession. Naxar notes were printed in 1994 but were never introduced into circulation as they were largely destroyed by the Russian military.

Check A document in which the writer orders his/her bank to pay to the receiver of the check a stated amount of money. For example, Joe may write Andrew a check for $10. In doing so, Joe is signing a document stating that he wishes to give Andrew $10, that it is available in Joe's bank, and Andrew can receive it from there. Andrew can either go to Joe's bank, present the check, and collect $10, or he may go to his own bank to deposit the check into his own account. In that case, Andrew's bank contacts Joe's bank and collects the $10 that way. Checks can be for any amount. See also: Check hold.

Check Clearing The process in which a bank collects the funds on a check deposit from the issuing institution. Check clearing involves the bank in which the check was deposited mailing the check to the issuing bank. The issuing bank then credits the deposit bank the funds on the check, assuming the check writer had the funds in his/her account. The deposit bank in turn credits the individual account into which the check was deposited. In the United States, the Federal Reserve operates a national check clearing system to expedite the process. See also: Check hold.

Check Hold In the United States, the number of days a bank is legally allowed to hold uncollected funds from a check deposit before crediting the funds to the depositor's account. According to the Expedited Funds Availability Act of 1987, the length of a check hold is two days for a local check and five days for a non-local check, with the first $100 being available the next business day. The length of the check hold is designed to approximate the number of days it takes for a bank to collect funds from the check writer.

Check Representment A process in which a check is deposited as many times as is necessary in order for it to clear. That is, if a check does not have sufficient funds in the account to be deposited, the bank continues to deposit it until funds become available and the check finally clears. This allows the recipient of the check to (eventually) receive funds on a check that would otherwise bounce and saves the writer of the check from having to pay an NSF fee.

Check Writer The person or company on whose account a check is drawn. That is, the check writer indicates how much money should be withdrawn and to whom it is directed, and gives the check to the recipient, who may cash or deposit it.

Checked Eskimo A slang term for a situation in which an unqualified applicant is given a job or a promotion. The term jokingly refers to the idea that the applicant claimed to be an Eskimo so he/she would benefit from the company's affirmative action policies.

Checking Account An account at a bank in which a customer deposits money for immediate use. For example, one may utilize a checking account for one's monthly expenses, such as a mortgage payment or groceries. Because most customers keep money in a checking account for a shorter period than in a savings account, a current account pays a slightly lower interest rate. Typically, one can write a check or use a debt card on a checking account, and banks expect customers to do so. The term "checking account" is more common in the United States. In the United Kingdom, the common term is "current account."

Checking the Market The act of reviewing the current quotes for a security in order to find the best price. If one seeks to sell, checking the market involves reviewing the bids. On the other hand, if one seeks to buy, it means reviewing the asks. See also: Bid-ask spread.

Checkwriting The act or process of writing a check. When one writes a check, one makes an order to one's bank to transfer funds to another account, perhaps at a different bank. To write a check, one must indicate who the payee is by writing his/her/its name. One must also date the check and sign it. Generally, one also writes the amount of the payment (in both numbers and words) unless one is writing a blank check. Under most circumstances, one gives the check to the payee, who then deposits it into his/her bank account. At this point the check clearing process begins.

Chef-Lieu In French-speaking countries, a political subdivision equivalent to the capital city of a district or province.

Chenica A Persian unit of volume approximately equivalent to 1.32 liters.

Cheques Act 1992 Legislation in the United Kingdom that made cheques non-transferrable. That is, the Act forbade the recipient of a cheque (for whom the money is intended) from giving to another the right to receive the money represented on a cheque. The Cheques Act was intended to reduce cheque fraud.

Cherry A British slang for one pound. It is an example of Cockney rhyming slang.

Cherry Picker In numismatics, a collector or dealer who looks through collections and buys only the rare or otherwise valuable coins. These coins may be valuable, but they are illiquid assets.

Cherry Picking 1. In bankruptcy, a decision by a court to uphold contracts with favorable terms toward the company declaring bankruptcy and to nullify contracts with unfavorable terms. Laws restrict the use of cherry picking. **2.** An investment strategy in which one picks securities that have been performing well with the expectation that they will continue to perform well. This carries the risk of loss due to an unexpectedly changing trend.

Chetrum A subdivision of the Bhutanese ngultrum. One chetrum is equal in value to 1/100 of one ngultrum. Its plural is chhertum. See also: Cent.

Chetverik A Russian unit of dry volume approximately equivalent to 26.24 liters. It was rendered obsolete when the Soviet Union began to use the metric system in 1924.

Chetvert 1. A Russian unit of dry volume approximately equivalent to 210 liters. **2.** A Russian unit of liquid volume approximately equivalent to 1.5 liters. **3.** A Russian unit of length equivalent to seven inches. An equivalent term was piad. All versions of the term were rendered obsolete when the Soviet Union began to use the metric system in 1924.

Chewog In Bhutan, an electoral subdivision of a municipality. See also: Gewog.

CHF ISO 4217 code for the Swiss franc. Although the first Swiss franc was used briefly at the end of the 18th century, the modern franc was introduced in 1850, replacing almost two dozen local currencies. Switzerland was a member of the Latin Monetary Union until its demise in 1927 and later belonged to the Bretton Woods System. Until 2000, at least 40% of the franc was required to be backed by gold. The Swiss franc is known for having almost no inflation and as such is considered a very safe currency for investment.

Chhioh A unit of length in Taiwan approximately equivalent to 30 centimeters.

Chhun A unit of length in Taiwan approximately equivalent to three centimeters.

Chi A unit of length in China approximately equivalent to 33.33 centimeters. It is sometimes called a Chinese foot.

Chiarella vs. U.S. A U.S. Supreme Court case holding that an employee of a company handling takeover bids who infers the names of the target companies using nonpublic information and buys or sells stock in them has not violated insider trading law. However, the employee may not reveal to anyone the names of the target companies. The case was decided in 1980.

Chicago Board of Trade Established in 1848, it was the oldest options and futures exchange in the world when it ceased operations in 2007 after being acquired by and merged into the Chicago Mercantile Exchange.

Chicago Board Options Exchange The largest options exchange in the United States by trading volume. Established in 1973, option contracts on more than 2000 companies and indices trade on the CBOE. Its trading floor uses a hybrid system; that is, investors may choose whether to use the open outcry format or to conduct trades electronically. It was the first exchange to offer exchange-traded options.

Chicago Mercantile Exchange The largest options and futures exchange in the world. Founded as a non-profit at the end of the nineteenth century, it demutualized in 2000 and went public in 2002. Approximately 70% of its business takes place electronically on CME Globex, the oldest electronic futures exchange in the world with well over one billion transactions since its introduction in 1992. In October 2008, in light of the credit crunch, the CME allied with the Citadel Investment Group LLC to create a transparent electronic trading platform for default credit swaps.

Chicago Stock Exchange A stock exchange in the United States. Established in 1882, it merged with a number of other exchanges during the 20th century and was known as the Midwest Stock Exchange until 1993. In the 1980s, it became one of the first stock exchanges to automate its order executions. A publicly-traded company does not need to be listed on the Exchange in order to tradeon it. It provides the CHX Matching System, which allows some of its securities to trade on other exchanges, and vice versa.

Chicken Shop A company that does not meet deadlines and does not perform adequate work. An example of a chicken shop is a company hired to design a website that goes over budget and over time to produce a website that looks like it was copied directly from a free online template. The term implies that such companies do little repeat business.

Chicken Stuff A slang term in Hong Kong that can mean either $10,000 or $1. See also: Hong Kong dollar.

Chief Credit Officer The officer at a credit ratings agency responsible for setting the criteria against which the risk of debt is judged. The chief credit officer manages the standardization and enforcement of these criteria, as well as ensuring that they accurately quantify the risk of rated instruments.

Chief Executive Officer In a corporation, the highest ranking officer in the company. In smaller companies, the chief executive officer may be combined with the president (the second-highest officer). The CEO has the responsibility of setting the overarching goals of the company and ensuring that they are met. He/she often serves as a point person between the company's management and the board of directors. The CEO is usually a member of the board of directors himself/herself. Generally speaking, the smaller a firm is, the more day-to-day management responsibilities the CEO has.

Chief Finagle Officer A slang term for a chief financial officer, especially one who works hard to make a company's finances appear sound. See also: Aggressive accounting.

Chief Financial Officer In a corporation, the official charged with overseeing all financial matters. The CFO is the equivalent of a treasurer: he/she is responsible for ensuring the long-term financial health of the corporation. This includes mundane matters like signing checks and record keeping, but the CFO is also head of financial forecasting, budgeting, and managing the company's financial risk. The CFO is often a member of the board of directors, and reports to the CEO. In the United States, it is common for CFOs to have an MBA degree, but not necessarily a professional designation like CPA or CFA.

Chief Information Officer The officer at a company that is responsible for information technology and often other technological aspects of the company's operations. The CIO reports to the CEO; the position often has a negative connotation because of the (relatively) high turnover rate of chief information officers. Because of the graying line between information and security, some companies combine the CIO and the chief security officer into the role of chief information security officer.

Chief Operating Officer The manager of a company (often but not always a publicly-traded company) who is responsible for the overall day-to-day operations. That is, the COO ensures smoothness in the process of producing and distributing the company's goods or of providing its services. A COO is responsible to the CEO and the board of directors.

Chief Secretary to the Treasury A major position in HM Treasury, ranking after the prime minister and the chancellor of the exchequer. The chief secretary is responsible for coordinating with other departments in formulating the national budget, negotiating on pay for public sector workers, procuring materials and contractors from the private sector, and managing other similar issues.

Chief Security Officer The officer in a corporation responsible for the safety and security the company's employees, assets (including cash), and products. The chief security officer is especially important to technology companies because of the specific dangers posed by hackers and others who would disrupt operations electronically. Because of the graying line between information and security, some companies combine the CSO and the chief information officer into the role of chief information security officer.

Chiefdom In Sierra Leone, a political subdivision equivalent to a municipality.

Chikhalsi 1. In North Korea, a political subdivision equivalent to a city outside the jurisdiction of any province. **2.** In South Korea, a city governed directly by the central government.

Child Labor The employment of persons under a certain age. Child labor generally is restricted. For example, a jurisdiction may prohibit children under 16 from working during school hours, and children under 18 from working in hazardous conditions. Employment of young children is sometimes associated with sweat shops.

Child Tax Credit In U.S. tax law, a direct dollar-for-dollar reduction in one's tax liability per eligible child in the household. Depending on the modified AGI of the person(s) filing, the child tax credit is generally $1,000 per child. See also: Tax credit.

Chilean Escudo The former currency of Chile. It was introduced in 1960, replacing the old peso in a bid to control inflation. However, it was subject to high inflation as well and was replaced by the Chilean peso in 1975.

Chilean Peso The currency of Chile. It was introduced in 1975, replacing the Chilean escudo. It has historically been subject to high inflation. See also: Unidad de Fomento.

Chill Any restriction on the purchase or sale of a security imposed by the Depository Trust Company. The DTC may put a chill on a stock, for example, if it is at risk of overheating.

China Banknote Printing and Minting An organization in China that issues legal tender coins and banknotes for general use. It is a state-owned corporation of the government of China. It is located in Beijing.

China Concepts Stock A stock in a company operating in the People's Republic of China that trades on the Hong Kong Stock Exchange, or sometimes on another stock exchange. Generally speaking, only Chinese citizens are allowed to invest in Chinese stock exchanges. Therefore, China concepts stocks are separately incorporated in another country in order to allow foreign investment in Chinese companies. Their existence is part of the slow liberalization process in China.

Chinese Fire Drill A slang term for a chaotic, frenetic meeting or project.

Chinese Hedge In arbitrage, the practice of taking a short position on a convertible security and taking a long position on the underlying asset of that convertible security. The investor makes a Chinese hedge in hopes that the price of the underlying asset will fall, allowing him/her to profit from the decrease in the price of the convertible security. On the other hand, if the underlying asset rises in price, the investor profits from the increase as well. A Chinese hedge is also called a reverse hedge because it is the opposite of a set-up hedge.

Chinese Metric Ounce A unit of weight equivalent to 50 grams.

Chinese Wall Informal; the imposed lack of communication between the investment banking and brokerage services of a financial institution. The Chinese wall exists in order to prevent brokers and investment bankers working for the same company from deliberately or accidentally sharing inside information that could lead to illegal insider trading. The Chinese wall protects both the financial institution at large and the individual investment bankers and brokers.

Chinese Yuan The currency of the People's Republic of China. It was introduced in Communist areas of China in 1948 during the Chinese Civil War, replacing multiple currencies previously in use. For much of its history, it was pegged to the U.S. dollar, which became especially important during the 1980s when China began opening itself to international trade. In 2005, the peg was changed to a currency basket, though the dollar remains important. In 2009, the Chinese government started to signal further dissociation from the dollar, though analysts disagree on how serious such moves are given the amount of dollar debt held by China.

CHIPS Clearing House Interbank Payments System. A wire transfer system allowing participating banks to exchange large amounts of money between themselves as needed. See also: Fedwire.

CHL GOST 7.67 Latin three-letter geocode for Chile. The code is used for transactions to and from Chilean bank accounts and for international shipping to Chile. As with all GOST 7.67 codes, it is used primarily in Cyrillic alphabets.

CHN GOST 7.67 Latin three-letter geocode for China. The code is used for transactions to and from Chinese bank accounts and for international shipping to China. As with all GOST 7.67 codes, it is used primarily in Cyrillic alphabets.

Cho A unit of length in Japan equivalent to approximately 119 yards.

Choinix An ancient Greek unit of dry volume approximately equivalent to 1.09 liters.

Choke Price The price at which demand for an asset drops to zero. That is, when a company charges the choke price or higher for a good or service, all potential customers believe that the price is too high and, as a result, do not buy. Most often, the choke price is associated with natural resources. For example, economists may discuss the price per barrel of oil at which consumers simply no longer buy oil. Colloquially, a choke may refer to a price at which demand drops, but it is important to note that the choke price refers to no demand at all.

Chon A subdivision of the North Korean won. One chon is equal in value to 1/100 of one won.

Chooser Option An option contract in which the option holder may choose at some point during the life whether the option is a call or a put. This allows the option holder the greatest possible leeway depending on price movements in the underlying asset. A chooser option sets the expiration date and the strike at the time it is entered. See also: Exotic option.

Chop Mark A mark imprinted on a coin, usually to prove authenticity. They have become rather unusual since the advent of fiat money, but they were more common when coins were made out of precious metals.

Chopin An obsolete Scottish unit of liquid volume approximately equivalent to 0.848 liters.

Choppy Market A situation in which prices in a market or index fluctuate, sometimes wildly, but end at a rough equilibrium. A choppy market may be a short-term trend. For example, NASDAQ may begin a week or month at 1,500 and fluctuate as low as 1,100 or as high as 1,900, but end the period at roughly 1,500.

Chous An ancient Greek unit of liquid volume approximately equivalent to 3.27 liters.

Chow An obsolete Indian unit of weight approximately equivalent to 0.389 grams.

Christ the King In Catholic theology, the idea that Jesus Christ is the ultimate source of law and that therefore human law should attempt to conform to divine law. This does not extend only to religious matters, but also to social and economic ones. For example, the notion of Christ the King has been used to defend the right to private property, the right of workers to unionize, and the obligation to follow secular law. For that reason, it has been used to criticize both capitalism and communism in the context of Catholic teaching on social justice.

Christmas Tree An investment strategy in which an investor buys a call option at a low strike price and then uses the proceeds from that sale to sell two call options at two different (but higher) strike prices. When one draws this strategy graphically, it vaguely resembles a Christmas tree. The calls have the same underlying security or asset; importantly, they must have the same expiration date. If the underlying moves modestly in the direction the trader wants, he/she can realize exceptional profits; however, if the underlying moves away from the trader, he/she has the possibility to lose a great deal. The staggered strikes for the two call options the investor sells are intended to hedge against loss in this situation.

Christopher Pissarides A Cypriot economist who was born in 1948. He is noted for his work in labor markets and for helping to develop the matching function, which represents the relationship between the number of unemployed persons and the number of jobs available over time. Pissarides won the Nobel Prize for economics in 2010.

Chubu Economic Federation An organization that promotes economic development in central Japan. It consists of several hundred companies and nonprofit organizations. Its activities include conducting research for legal reforms and promoting improvement to infrastructure. It was established in 1951.

Chungah An obsolete Indian unit of volume approximately equivalent to 0.758 liters.

Chunnel A slang term for the euro-British pound exchange rate. The term derives from the name of the underground tunnel connecting Britain with continental Europe.

Churn To make both buy and sell orders through different brokers, usually in large quantities, to create the impression of increased interest in a security and thereby raise its price. An investor churns if he/she has a long position on the security and wishes to sell it at an artificially high price. Churning is a form of manipulation, and is illegal under the Securities Exchange Act of 1934. See also: Fix.

Churn Rate The rate at which customers terminate their relationships with a company over a given period of time. For example, if five customers in 50 discontinue their cable every month, the churn rate is 5%. The church rate contrasts with the growth rate, which, in this case, is defined as the number of new clients or customers. If a company is to grow, the growth rate must consistently exceed the churn rate. The churn rate is important in the telecommunications industry, where several companies operate in a geographical area and compete for customers.

CHW ISO 4217 code for the WIR euro, which is an accounting currency used by medium-sized and small businesses in Switzerland. The WIR euro is used by members of the WIR Bank, which encourages member businesses to trade with each other and facilitates transactions between them. Although the WIR euro does not circulate, it helps maintain the stability of the Swiss economy.

CI 1. ISO 3166-1 alpha-2 code for the Republic of Cote d'Ivoire. This is the code used in international transactions to and from Ivoirian bank accounts. **2.** ISO 3166-2 geocode for Cote d'Ivoire. This is used as an international standard for shipping to Cote d'Ivoire. Each Ivoirian region has its own code with the prefix "CI." For example, the code for the Region of Bafing is ISO 3166-2:CI-17.

CIDP Crop Insurance and Disaster Payments. Any payments one receives from an insurance policy covering agricultural real estate. One lists CIDP on Form 4835 or Schedule F.

Cilak A Tatar unit of volume approximately equivalent to 12,299 liters. It was rendered obsolete when the Soviet Union began to use the metric system in 1924.

Cinnebar A slang term for coins in Hong Kong. Literally, the term refers to mercury ore. An alternate slang term with the same meaning is ground.

Circle Informal; to attempt to find investors for underwriting purposes. Before a new issue, underwriters circle potential investors, who may or may not book an order to buy a portion. Potential investors are provided with a preliminary prospectus if they are circled and indicate interest. It is important to note that circling is non-binding because it is illegal to sell a security that has not been issued. See also: Overbooked, Underbooked, Fully Subscribed, Indication of Interest.

Circle Back Slang; to discuss an issue after it was previously discussed, especially if nothing was decided. For example, if a board of directors tables an agenda item and then discusses it at the next meeting, it could be said to be circling back to the issue.

Circuit Breaker On an exchange, a measure designed to prevent panic selling by stopping trading after a security or an index has fallen by a certain amount. For example, if the Dow Jones Industrial Average falls 10% in a trading day, the New York Stock Exchange suspends trade for at least one hour. A circuit breaker is intended to allow investors to determine whether a situation is really as bad as it looks. It is sometimes called a collar. See also: Suspended trading.

Circuit Court A generic name for a court in several jurisdictions. Circuit courts have a variety of duties. For example, in the U.S. State of Louisiana, circuit courts are appellate courts, while in the state of Alabama they are courts with original jurisdiction.

Circular 1. See: Bond circular. **2.** See: Information circular.

Circular Trading A scheme in which a broker enters a sell order with the knowledge that an exactly offsetting buy order is being entered or will be entered at roughly the same time. Circular trading does not allow for competition and does not result in a change of beneficial ownership. For that reason, it is illegal.

Cirek 1. A Tatar unit of length equivalent to 177.8 millimeters. It was rendered obsolete when the Soviet Union began to use the metric system in 1924. **2.** A Tatar unit of area approximately equivalent to 5,463 square meters. It was rendered obsolete when the Soviet Union began to use the metric system in 1924. **3.** A Tatar unit of volume approximately equivalent to 210 liters. It was rendered obsolete when the Soviet Union began to use the metric system in 1924.

Cirektan Sigez A Tatar unit of volume approximately equivalent to 26.24 liters. It was rendered obsolete when the Soviet Union began to use the metric system in 1924.

Citizen Bond A certificateless municipal bond that may be registered and traded on an exchange. A certificateless municipal bond does not issue individual certificates in order to facilitate trade. A citizen bond provides an extra layer of ease by trading on an exchange. Unlike other municipal bonds, many citizen bonds have their prices listed in daily publications.

City Hall 1. A building that serves as a headquarters for most or all municipal services, such as parks and public works departments. City hall is usually home to city council meetings and the office of the mayor or other executive. **2.** A euphemism for municipal or local government.

City Mail Mail directed to the same city. In the United States, most residents and businesses in the same city have the same first three digits in their zip codes. City mail is directed to places with the same first three digits. City mail is sorted into a city sack.

City Sack A bag of city mail, which is sorted mail that is directed to the same city. In the United States, most residents and businesses in the same city have the same first three digits in their zip codes. The city sack is directed to places with the same first three digits and is distributed to specific post offices from there.

Ciudad autonoma In Spain, a political subdivision for an autonomous city controlled by Spain but surrounded by Morocco. That is, a ciudad autonoma is a Spanish enclave in Morocco. There are two such territories.

CIV GOST 7.67 Latin three-letter geocode for Cote d'Ivoire. The code is used for transactions to and from Ivorian bank accounts and for international shipping to Cote d'Ivoire. As with all GOST 7.67 codes, it is used primarily in Cyrillic alphabets.

Civil Money Penalty A fine assessed by a court on a person or entity that has profited from violations of securities law and regulation. For example, if a broker makes illegal insider trades from information gleaned from a client, he/she may have to pay a civil money penalty. Ordinarily, the civil money penalty is equal to the profit that the violator made from his/her activities.

Civil Rehabilitation Law A bankruptcy law in Japan allowing a company to force a lender to change the terms of the loan in order to alleviate the company's bad debt. The law was enacted in 2000 in the wake of the Asian financial crisis.

Civil Rights Act of 1964 Legislation in the United States that prohibited racial discrimination in government, education and employment. It prohibited businesses from refusing to serve persons on the basis of race and it required judges to apply voter registration requests equally to all races. It invalidated state laws establishing racial segregation, and had the effect in some states of requiring school districts to bus students to other districts to conform to racial quotas. The Act is considered a landmark of the American civil rights movement.

Civil Society A collection of persons who associate together to explore or promote their interests or goals. While civil society is not necessarily political or economic, it provides a sphere outside of the state or private sector in which people are motivated by their own goals, apart from profit or the good of the state. For that reason, civil society can exercise significant political influence. The growth of civil society is considered a mark of successful economic development of a country or region.

CK 1. ISO 3166-1 alpha-2 code for the Cook Islands. This is the code used in international transactions to and from Cook Island bank accounts. **2.** ISO 3166-2 geocode for the Cook Islands. This is used as an international standard for shipping to Cook Islands.

CL 1. ISO 3166-1 alpha-2 code for the Republic of Chile. This is the code used in international transactions to and from Chilean bank accounts. **2.** ISO 3166-2 geocode for Chile. This is used as an international standard for shipping to Chile. Each Chilean region has its own code with the prefix "CL." For example, the code for the State of Los Lagos is ISO 3166-2:CL-LL.

CL1 A service that provides quotes, index, and other corporate information for junior stocks listed on the TSX Venture Exchange.

CL2 A service that provides committed orders and trades for stocks listed on the TSX Venture Exchange.

Clad Coin A coin made of two different metals, one at the center of the coin and one that is plating.

Claim Dilution A situation in which it becomes less likely that a party to a loan, security, or other contract will be paid in full as agreed. It can occur in mortgage-backed securities, for example, if more securities are issued without a proportionate number of new mortgages being bought and incorporated into the security. See also: Anti-dilution provision.

Clarence Birdseye An American inventor and entrepreneur who developed the modern method of freezing food. Previous freezing methods occurred more slowly, which resulted in larger ice crystals and reduced food quality. Birdseye overcame this by freezing at lower temperatures. This development led directly to the retail sale of frozen food. He lived from 1886 to 1956.

Class 1. See: Asset Classes. **2.** See: Stock Class. **3.** An option contract of one type or another. For example, calls and puts are different classes of option, as are American style and European style options.

Class A Shares Shares in a mutual fund with a front-end load. For class A shares, a certain amount of one's investment is deducted for the commission of mutual fund's salesperson. This lowers the size of the investment in the mutual fund. For example, if one invests $50,000 in a mutual fund, a certain amount, say $1,000, is deducted for the commission, resulting in only $49,000 actually being invested in the fund.

Class Action Lawsuit A lawsuit that occurs when multiple people, who claim to have been wronged by the defendant in the same or a similar way, seek restitution, even if the alleged wrongs occurred at different times. For example, multiple shareholders may file a class action suit against a company if they suffered losses from similar fraudulent actions. Proponents of class actions lawsuits contend that they allow "the little guy," however defined, to seek justice. Opponents argue that they enrich attorneys and do not necessarily help the actual plaintiffs. See also: Tort reform, Class Action Fairness Act of 2005.

Class B Shares Shares in a mutual fund with a back-end load. For class B shares, a certain amount of one's investment is deducted for the commission of mutual fund's salesperson when one sells the shares. That is, one gives the salesperson a certain percentage of the share's value if one decides to sell it within five to 10 years, depending on the specific nature of the agreement. The size of the fee usually declines by the year until the maximum number of years is reached.

Class Lives The useful life of a type of property as defined by the Alternative Depreciation System or the General Depreciation System.

Class of Options All option contracts of the same type and style on the same underlying security. For example, when one speaks of a class of options, one may refer to all the American-style calls on Google. This includes all expiration dates and strike prices, but not contracts of different types, such as puts or European-style options.

Class Warfare In political science, the idea that social classes are perpetually in conflict for more economic and political power. For example, a corporation's management has the incentive to make the most money possible for shareholders, while unionized employees have the incentive to make the most money possible for themselves. Thus, a collective bargaining negotiation will be treated like a zero-sum game, in which one side wins and the other loses. The idea that class warfare is inevitable is not universally accepted, but it is a foundational element of communism and some forms of capitalism.

Classic Head Cent A one-cent piece minted by the United States between 1808 and 1814. It was worth 1/100 of one dollar.

Classical Economics A set of related economic theories that trace their origins to the Enlightenment. Adam Smith is commonly thought to be the father of classical economics. He and those who followed him believed that economies work most efficiently when economic actors attempt to maximize their own self-interests, and that doing so tends to maximize the interests of society as a whole. For example, a man may open a mechanic shop to make a profit for himself, but, in the process, he may hire otherwise unemployed mechanics and service otherwise broken cars, which then facilitates business for the rest of the community. See also: Invisible hand, Neo-classical economics, Socialism.

Classical Economist A person associated with a set of related economic theories tracing their origins to the Enlightenment. Adam Smith is commonly thought to be the father of classical economics. He and those who followed him believed that economies work most efficiently when economic actors attempt to maximize their own self-interests, and that doing so tends to maximize the interests of society as a whole. For example, a man may open a mechanic shop to make a profit for himself, but, in the process, he may hire otherwise unemployed mechanics and service otherwise broken cars, which then facilitates business for the rest of the community. See also: Invisible hand, Neo-classical economics, Socialism.

Classical Unemployment Unemployment that occurs because the wages for an employee rise above what a company is willing to pay. For example, if a company is willing to pay $30,000 per year for a job but potential employees will not accept less than $40,000, the job will go unfilled. Some economists claim government interventions such as minimum wage laws and unemployment benefits cause unemployment because they raise the cost of hiring an employee, making companies less likely to create jobs. Other economists dispute this idea.

Classified Board A board of directors where members start their terms at different times and only a certain number are elected in a given year. For example, a board of directors may have 10 members serving five-year, staggered terms where two new members are elected each year. In addition to giving the board consistency in its membership, a classified board makes hostile takeovers more difficult because the potential acquirer can replace only so many directors at a time.

Classified Stock **1.** A type of stock in a publicly-traded company that issues more than one type of stock. Each type of classified stock has distinct rights attached to it. Two common classified stocks are preferred stock, which carries the right to guaranteed dividends, and common stock, which carries the right to vote in the annual meeting. **2.** In mutual funds, a stock with a particular load. The load, which is the sales fee for buying into the mutual fund, is charged at different times depending on the stock class. For example, a class A stock has a load that is paid up front, while a class B stock has a load that is paid when one sells the shares in the mutual fund.

Claused Bill of Lading A bill of lading indicating some damage to, or loss of, a good during transport. A bill of lading is a document in which the parties agree to ship a good to a certain location, and also serves as the receipt upon arrival at the destination. Most banks or other institutions financing the shipment refuse to accept or honor claused bills of lading, which means that sellers often have difficulty receiving payment on them. It is also called a dirty bill of lading. See also: Clean bill of lading.

Clawback **1.** A drop in a security's price after a previous rise. **2.** Money that must be refunded or given back for some reason or other. The term especially applies to tax advantages extended to a taxpayer subject to certain conditions that the taxpayer did not fulfill.

Clayton Act A 1914 American antitrust law that expanded and clarified the Sherman Act of 1890. The act prohibited price discrimination, mergers that substantially decrease competition, and other practices that the Sherman Act left for court interpretation. Significantly, the Clayton Act exempted unions and labor organizations from its provisions because the Sherman Act had been used to restrict the ability to strike.

CLE ISO 4217 code for the Chilean escudo. It was introduced in 1960, replacing the old peso in a bid to control inflation. However, it was subject to high inflation as well and was replaced by the Chilean peso in 1975.

Clean **1.** Describing a block trade in which the buyer agrees to buy all of the seller's securities or inventory he/she is offering. It often happens that a buyer is only interested in, say, half or three quarters of the securities a seller is offering. This leaves the seller with extra securities he/she does not want, and exposes him/her to the risk that they will be sold either at a low price or not at all. A clean transaction spares the seller from this risk, as the buyer takes all the securities offered off of the seller's hands. **2.** Describing a company or individual with little or no debt. See: Clean balance sheet.

Clean Balance Sheet Somewhat informal; a company with little or no debt. Clean balance sheets are seen as desirable for many investors as they represent little risk. However, maintaining a clean balance sheet is not always possible, particularly if a company's revenues are highly seasonal.

Clean Bill of Lading A bill of lading indicating that there is no damage to or loss of the goods during transport. A bill of lading is a document in which the parties agree to ship a good to a certain location and also serves as the receipt upon arrival at the destination. Most banks or other institutions financing the shipment will only accept clean bills of lading. See also: Foul Bill of Lading.

Clean Price The price of a coupon bond that does not include any interest that accrues. That is, a clean price is the price of a bond discounting future cash flows. Because the dirty price does include interest between coupon payments, the dirty price and the clean price will equal each other only immediately following a coupon payment. Most American exchanges use the clean price when quoting bond prices.

Clean Report of Findings In international commerce, a report issued by an inspector stating that no damage to or loss of goods occurred before shipment. A clean report of findings also states that both parties have agreed to the same price and that the goods are in the condition that a buyer specified. See also: Clean bill of lading, Incoterm.

Clean Sheeting A crime in which an insurance agent and a potential policyholder purchase a life insurance policy without discussing a preexisting condition. Clean sheeting allows the policyholder to buy the policy at a low price and quickly re-sell it at a higher price.

Clean Trade A trade in which a brokerage is able to match clients' buy and sell orders precisely. This is beneficial for the brokerage as it means that it does not have to find more securities or sell from its own inventory in order to fill the orders. It is also called a clean cross.

Clean Up To sell what remains of a position of a security such that it closes the position. For example, if one owned 1,000 shares in a stock and sold 750 of them, one cleans up the position by selling the remaining 250 shares.

Cleanup Call Also called a cleanup buyback, an option in securitization transactions in which the issuer may reduce its own administrative expenses by buying back the remaining issue when the principal has been reduced to an insignificant amount, usually to less than 10% of the original issue. This option is often exercised for mortgage-backed securities.

Clear To settle a transaction by the payment of the price and often the delivery of the goods. Because so many transactions occur at a given time, and because they may directly or indirectly involve a number of third parties, such as brokers, dealers, or specialists, clearing firms settle most transactions in exchange for a fee.

Clear Title The title to a property where there are no competing claims, liens, or anything else that would hinder its transfer. That is, if a property has undisputed ownership, its owner is said to have clear title. An owner with clear title may sell the property without any legal difficulties. Generally speaking, a real estate broker researches a property to ensure that there are no competing claims. See also: Quitclaim deed, Title search.

Clearance The process of settling transactions. Most exchanges have one or more clearing houses, which are charged with matching orders together, ensuring that deliveries are made to the correct parties, and collecting margin money. Because so many trades take place on an exchange in a given day, clearing houses exist to process what each party owes or is owed in a central location so the fewest securities actually change hands. For example, suppose that a broker-dealer buys 1000 shares of a security and then, in a completely separate transaction, sells 700 of the same shares. At the end of the trading day, the clearing house would determine that the broker-dealer must only buy 300 shares as the other 700 belong to another party. Clearing houses receive a clearing fee in exchange for clearance services.

Clearing Corporation An agency or corporation on an exchange that settles transactions for a fee. Most exchanges have one or more clearing corporations that are charged with matching orders together, ensuring that delivery is made to the correct party, and collecting margin money. Because so many trades take place on an exchange in a given day, clearing corporations exist to process what each party owes or is owed in a central location so that the fewest securities and the least amount of money actually change hands. For example, suppose that a broker-dealer buys 1,000 shares of a security and then, in a completely separate transaction, sells 700 of the same shares. At the end of the trading day, the clearing house would determine that the broker-dealer must only buy 300 shares as the other 700 belong to another party. Clearing corporations receive a clearing fee in exchange for these services.

Clearing Fee A fee a clearing house charges for its services of handling unsettled transactions.

Clearing House Automated Payment System A company that operates a computer system to perform clearing services for funds and some other investment vehicles denominated in the British pound. It is allied with other clearing houses in the Association for Payment Clearing Services. It began operations in 1984.

Clearing House Electronic Subregister System An electronic system that settles transactions made on the Australian Securities Exchange. Under Australian corporate law, all equity securities must be held and settled through CHESS. It is operated by the ASX Settlement and Transfer Corporation Pty Limited.

Clearing House Funds Money that passes between Federal Reserve banks that is not available because the check by which the money is deposited has not cleared. It may take up to three days for the funds to clear and become available in the depositor's account.

Clearing Member A member firm on an exchange that is also a member of a clearing house. Clearing members have access to the clearing house for the settlement of transactions. Non-member firms on an exchange must work with and through a member firm in order to settle their own transactions. See also: Clearing fee.

Clearing Member Trade Agreement An agreement whereby an investor uses different brokers to conduct trades. However, at the end of the trading day, the investor is allowed to use a single broker to present his/her trades to a clearing house for clearing purposes. A clearing member trade agreement is used exclusively for options, futures, and other derivatives. Under the agreement, the investor is given the option of choosing among several brokers who participate in the agreement.

Clearing Number The identifying number assigned to any company that uses a clearing corporation.

Clearing-House Statement A document that a participating firm submits to a clearing house on an exchange. The statement contains information on the positions the firm holds and the amount that must be paid to each client of the firm. The clearing house nets all information submitted on clearing house statements and ensures that the least amount of money has to change hands.

Clearstream International A clearing house that is one of the largest security depository and post-trade financial services companies in the world. Formed in 2000 as the result of a merger between Cedel International and Deutsche Borse Clearing, Clearstream serves as the principle clearing house for transactions in the Euromarket. Now fully owned by Deutsche Borse, it provides clearing services for companies in more than 80 countries. Its main competitors are Euroclear and the Depository Trust and Clearing Corporation.

CLF ISO 4217 code for the Chilean unidad de fomento. It is a unit of account in Chile that does not circulate. It is adjusted for inflation relative to the Chilean peso (and earlier the Chilean escudo) so that its value remains constant. It was created in 1967 and was originally used to help the Chilean government pay its loans for international development.

Clickie A slang term for a tech stock in an Internet company. Examples of clickies include Google and Facebook.

Click-Through Rate The number of visitors to a website that click on the advertisements present on that website as a percentage of total visitors. Click-through rates are vitally important to e-commerce businesses that derive their revenue predominantly or exclusively from ads. Because click through rates have declined over time, some websites rely on sheer volume of visitors to compensate for low click-through rates. CPM, PPC, Impression.

Clientele Effect A theory stating that a company's stock price increases or decreases according to changes in the company's policies. For example, if a company raises its dividend, investors are more likely to buy that company's stock, which would increase the price. Likewise, if a company has an excessive amount of debt, investors are unlikely to want to buy the stock and the price will decrease. The clientele effect stands in contrast with the capital structure irrelevance principle. See also: Material News.

Cliff Effect In economics, the disproportionately positive or negative results of an action. For example, suppose a company takes on too much debt and a credit ratings agency downgrades its bond rating. This may increase the company's borrowing costs significantly, which in turn gives it less cash on hand to make coupon payments. This can lead to a further downgrade and the cycle continues. The cliff effect implies that relatively little separates a company from being seen as quite healthy to being seen as a poor investment.

Clifford Trust An irrevocable, but temporary, living trust into which one deposits assets on behalf of a beneficiary. In a Clifford trust, assets are invested and all income from these investments are given to the beneficiary, who is usually a minor child. Once the trust expires, however, the assets revert to the donor. A Clifford trust must exist for at least 10 years unless the donor dies in the meantime. Formerly, income on the assets in Clifford trusts were taxed at the minor child's tax rate (which was usually very low) after the child turned 14. As a result, Clifford trusts could be used as a tax loophole. However, the loophole was closed in 1986.

Clima An ancient Roman unit of area approximately equivalent to 315 square meters.

Climax A situation in which a security's price has risen (or fallen) very quickly and very high (or low) on heavy trading volume. A climax is often followed by steep price correction. See also: Buying climax, Selling climax, Reversion to the mean.

Climber Slang; an extremely successful salesperson. A climber is able to sell his/her product to even the most difficult customer.

Clinton Bond A bond with no coupon and no principal. That is, a Clinton bond is a bond that is literally worth nothing. The term originally referred to low-bond interest rates when Bill Clinton was president of the United States, which caused bond traders to lose money. The term is more of a buzzword; that is, it may be used to complain about fiscal policy than refer to real bonds. A Clinton bond is also called a Quayle bond, after former U.S. Vice President Dan Quayle.

Clip To separate a coupon from a bearer bond. A bearer bond contains no ownership information and the physical bearer is presumed to be the owner. The bond contains physical coupons that must be clipped in order to receive the interest payments. Bearer bonds have not been issued in the United States since 1982, and thus clipping has become a less common activity, applying only to long maturity bonds issued before then.

Cliquet A series of forward start options in which the first option is active (and its strike price is set) immediately. The second option becomes active on the expiration date of the first option, with the strike set as the market value of the underlying on that day. The process continues for as many options as exist in the cliquet. Importantly, the entire premium is paid at once. Cliquets are useful for an investor who wants to lock in an option for a significant period of time, with the strike price adjusting to reflect market realities. It is also known as a reset option or a ratchet option.

Clock Tower Attrition A slang term for a situation in which a new manager fires a large number of his/her subordinates in a short period of time. Clock tower attrition may occur because the previous employees were incompetent, or simply because the new manager wants to bring in his/her own allies. The term may refer to the clock tower massacre at the University of Texas in 1966.

Clocksucker A highly derogatory slang term for an unproductive employee. An equivalent term is pigeon.

Clone Fund A mutual fund that is actively-managed in theory, but, in practice, tracks another mutual fund. Clone funds were formerly common in Canada because of limits on foreign investments that existed on Registered Retirement Savings Plans. That is, if one wanted to invest in a non-Canadian mutual fund but doing so put one over the limit, one could invest instead in a clone fund that was registered in Canada but tracked the foreign fund. They have become less common since 2005 when legal changes lifted limits. See also: Closet index fund.

Close 1. The end of a trading day on an exchange. **2.** The final price of a security at the end of a trading day. It is also called the closing price.

Close a Position To end an investment; to change from a long position to a short position or vice versa. A long position is ownership of a security or option, while a short position is debt. Thus, to close a long position is to sell a security or option and to close a short position is to buy out the debt.

Close Market A market for a security with a very low bid-ask spread. That is, there is a very small difference between the highest price a buyer is willing to pay and the lowest price that a seller is willing to take. A close market occurs when trading is very active and there are a larger number of market makers working on the same security.

Close of Business The end of a business day, usually between 4 p.m. and 5 p.m. Communication generally must be received by the close of business in order to be acted on before the next business day, though the advent of the Internet and smart phones has changed this somewhat.

Close of Play A slang term for the deadline for a bid, project, contract, or anything else. For example, a company soliciting bids for a major project may state that the close of play is the last Friday of the month. The term refers to cricket and thus is most frequently used in areas where cricket is popular.

Close Period The time between the preparation of a company's balance sheet and its announcement to the public. The close period usually lasts about two months. During this time SEC rules prohibit insiders from buying or selling the company's shares in any way.

Closed Corporation A company in which a small group of shareholders controls the majority of the shares. These majority shareholders tend to hold on to the company's stock, and, for that reason, only minority shares are traded, leading to light trade volume. Closed corporations are, by their nature, resistant to hostile takeovers and proxy wars. They tend to be more stable than other companies because their share prices are not determined by (sometimes irrational) investment decisions, but by the value of the company itself. However, closed corporations do not have access to as much working capital as corporations with more shareholders. They are also called closely held companies.

Closed Fund A mutual fund that is closed to new investors, whether permanently or temporarily. A mutual fund's management may decide to close the fund because it may believe that there are too many investors and/or assets in the fund to generate a return appropriate to its investment strategy. Sometimes such a fund prevents even current investors from buying more shares of the fund, although this is less common. A closed fund should not be confused with a closed-end fund, which is a different concept altogether.

Closed Out Concerning the liquidation of a position because of a failure to cover a short sale or margin call. More broadly, it refers to the sale of any position for any reason.

Closed-End Fund A mutual fund that issues a fixed number of shares at its establishment, and, afterwards, neither increases nor decreases the number of shares. Like other mutual funds, a closed-end fund is actively managed, meaning that the securities underlying the fund change from time to time in accordance with the fund's investment goals. A shareholder in a closed-end fund redeems shares with the issuer as with open-end funds, but may trade shares as if they were stocks. The value of shares in a closed-end fund is determined by supply, demand, and the fund's net asset value. See also: Exchange-traded fund.

Closed-End Indenture A provision in an indenture stating that the collateral securing a bond may not secure any other bond issues. A closed-end indenture means that the issuer may only use the stated collateral on a single bond issue; this ensures that only bondholders of that issue have a claim to that collateral in the event of default. As a result, a secured bond with a closed-end indenture carries less risk than a secured bond with an open-end indenture, which allows collateral to secure multiple bonds.

Closed-End Mortgage 1. In banking, a bond secured by a mortgage in which the mortgage may not be paid off before maturity, and the property in question may not be used as collateral on any other transaction without the bondholder's permission. **2.** In real estate, a mortgage in which the principal amount may not be increased. Further borrowing is not permitted using the same mortgage as collateral.

Closed-Market Transaction A situation in which an insider buys or sells restricted shares in a company from or to the same company. Because the person involved is an insider, he/she must file appropriate documentation with the SEC in order for the transaction to be legal. However, closed-market transactions are not considered insider trading because the counterparty is the company itself rather than another investor without inside information.

Close-End Credit A loan agreement in which the lender expects the entirety of the loan, including principal, interest, and other charges, to be paid in full by a stated due date. For example, in an automotive loan, the lender might extend credit for five years; the borrower must completely satisfy the terms of the loan in that period of time.

Closely Held Shares Shares in a publicly-traded company in which a small group of shareholders control the majority of the shares. These majority shareholders tend to hold on to the company's stock, and, as such, only minority shares are traded, leading to light trade volume. Closely held companies are, by their nature, resistant to hostile takeovers and proxy wars. They tend to be more stable than other companies because their share prices are not determined by (sometimes irrational) investment decisions, but by the value of the company itself. However, closely held companies do not have access to as much working capital as corporations with more shareholders.

Closet Index Fund A mutual fund that is actively managed in theory, but more or less tracks a benchmark stock index. Closet index funds generally exist because their managers believe it is safer to generally track indices rather than take on the greater risks incumbent with more active management. Closet index funds do not advertise themselves as such, but one may determine whether a mutual fund is one by comparing its R square to a given index. Some advisors counsel staying away from closet index funds as they carry fees and commissions associated with mutual funds, and one can directly invest in an index for less expense, while achieving the same result.

Closing The time trading ends on an exchange. This is important to matters like a security's closing price or closing bid. See also: Open.

Closing Balance The balance of a bank account at the end of a period, such as a month or year. If the closing balance is listed on a bank statement, it indicates the closing balance on the date the statement was printed.

Closing Bell A traditional bell that is rung to signify the end of a trading day. The closing bell on the New York Stock Exchange is one of the more famous examples. As an increasing number of securities exchanges do most or all their trading online, a closing bell has become a symbol or informal term for the end of a trading day, rather than a description of a real bell.

Closing Costs Costs associated with the completion of a sale of real estate. Closing costs are not usually included in the sale price of the property. Some examples of closing costs are appraisal fees, deed-recording fees, and applicable taxes. Mortgage loans often include money for closing costs. They are also called settlement costs.

Closing Dinner A dinner or brief vacation an investment bank buys for its employees who have worked and completed a major deal. A closing dinner is used to congratulate employees on their success and to boost morale. Closing dinners are especially useful if employees have been working significant overtime to finish the deal.

Closing Price The final bid and ask price of a security at the end of a trading session. It is also called the closing quote or the market close.

Closing Purchase 1. Any transaction that closes a position, especially a short position. **2.** An option seller's purchase of another option that cancels out the provisions of the previous option by having the same provisions.

Closing Purchase Transaction An option seller's purchase of another option that cancels out the provisions of the previous option by having the same provisions.

Closing Range The highest bid and the lowest offer made on an exchange during the period immediately preceding the close. The closing range is closely related to the closing price.

Closing Rate The exchange rate for two currencies at the end of a period of time, such as a trading day or month.

Closing Sale 1. Any transaction that closes a position, especially a long position. **2.** An option buyer's sale of a second option that cancels out the provisions of the previous option by having the same provisions.

Closing Tick The number of stocks on an exchange where the closing price is higher than the trade immediately before the closing trade minus the number of stocks, where the closing price was lower than the next-to-last trade. A positive closing tick is seen as bullish, while a negative closing tick is seen as negative. This is a technical indicator.

Cloud on Title Any claim to the title on a property that puts another claim into question. That is, one may own a property that another person claims with some (though by no means clear) legal justification. Clouds on title normally arise in the sale of a property when a buyer or real estate broker is conducting due diligence.

Clove An obsolete unit of weight variously equivalent to values between seven and 10 pounds. It was used in the sale of cheese and wool.

CLP ISO 4217 code for the Chilean peso. It was introduced in 1975, replacing the Chilean escudo. It has historically been subject to high inflation. See also: Unidad de Fomento.

Club Deal A situation in which a group of private equity firms acquires a publicly-traded company. A club deal can be beneficial to the private equity firms because it reduces the capital each must use in order to buy the company. However, because a club deal reduces the number of competing bids, shareholders may receive a smaller price for their shares. See also: Hostile takeover.

Clydesdale Bank A commercial bank in the United Kingdom. Established in Scotland in 1838, it expanded throughout Scotland and grew to have some presence in London and North England as well. It is one of three banks permitted to issue banknotes in Scotland.

CM 1. ISO 3166-1 alpha-2 code for the Republic of Cameroon. This is the code used in international transactions to and from Cameroonian bank accounts. **2.** ISO 3166-2 geocode for Cameroon. This is used as an international standard for shipping to Cameroon. Each region has its own code with the prefix "CM." For example, the code for the Central Region is ISO 3166-2:CM-CE.

CMO REIT A real estate investment trust that invests in collateralized mortgage obligations. The CMO REIT derives its return from the difference in the interest and principal paid on the mortgages underlying the CMOs and the coupons paid to the CMO holders. A CMO REIT is considered a very risky investment vehicle.

CMR GOST 7.67 Latin three-letter geocode for Cameroon. The code is used for transactions to and from Cameroonian bank accounts and for international shipping to Cameroon. As with all GOST 7.67 codes, it is used primarily in Cyrillic alphabets.

CN An abbreviation for cupro-nickel. The abbreviation is used most frequently by coin collectors and investors to indicate coins made out of 88% copper and 12% nickel.

CNN Effect A theory stating that the market suffers during intense news coverage of a major event because persons stay home and watch the coverage, rather than go out and buy goods and services. This is a controversial theory and little evidence documents it. However, its effect, if any, would likely impact services more negatively than goods. For example, watching a natural disaster on television may prevent one from going to the cinema and watching a film about a natural disaster. It will not, however, prevent one from buying groceries. More generally, the CNN effect refers to the idea that 24-hour cable news has given the public the impression, but not necessarily a correct one, that it is more engaged with current events.

CNY ISO 4217 code for the Chinese renmimbi. It was introduced in Communist areas of China in 1948 during the Chinese Civil War, replacing multiple currencies previously in use. For much of its history, it was pegged to the U.S. dollar, which became especially important during the 1980s when China began opening itself to international trade. In 2005, the peg was changed to a currency basket, though the dollar remains important. In 2009, the Chinese government started to signal further dissociation from the dollar, though analysts disagree on how serious such moves are given the amount of dollar debt held by China.

CO 1. ISO 3166-1 alpha-2 code for the Republic of Colombia. This is the code used in international transactions to and from Colombian bank accounts. **2.** ISO 3166-2 geocode for Colombia. This is used as an international standard for shipping to Colombia. Each Colombian department and the capital district have their own codes with the prefix "CO." For example, the code for the Department of Bolivar is ISO 3166-2:CO-BOL.

Coattail Investing An investment strategy in which one buys most or all of the same securities as a historically successful and usually well-known investor. One buys these securities as soon as the famous investor's decision is made public. It is a risky strategy as it ignores portfolio implications and risk analysis. For example, one may buy a stock after it has already gone up in price considerably, and may already have become overvalued. Alternatively, one may sell the same stock after its downward trend has become well established and it may have already become undervalued. However, it can be a profitable strategy if the coattail investor adopts a buy-and-hold mentality because, in the long term, the famous investor is often correct. See also: Chasing the market.

Cockroach Theory A non-scientific market theory that bad news comes in large bunches, rather than a little at a time. In other words, the cockroach theory states that if one company in a sector or industry is revealed to have problems, it is likely that other companies in the same sector or industry have problems as well. For example, when it was revealed that Enron's accounting had been deliberately falsified, it was soon known that other companies, notably WorldCom, also had massive accounting problems. See also: Enron scandal.

Code of Procedure Rules used by the National Association for Securities Dealers to settle disputes between members. See also: Arbitration, FINRA.

Codicil An amendment or modification to a will that is not intended to displace or abolish the will. Codicils are subject to the same legal requirements as a will, such as the signatures of a certain number of witnesses. Courts sometimes have difficulty in determining whether a document is a codicil or an entirely new will, but, in general, documents dealing with only a portion of an estate are presumed to be codicils unless they specifically abolish previous wills.

Coefficient of Variation In statistics, the ratio of the standard deviation of a series of data points to the expected return. In investing, the coefficient of variation is used to measure the volatility (represented by the standard deviation) to the expected return on an investment. A lower coefficient of variation indicates a higher expected return with less risk. See also: Beta.

Coface A corporation in France that extends credit to French exporters. It was established by the French government and has subsequently been privatized. Coface also provides guarantees and insurance accounts receivable for exports, and it is known for providing information on country risk and other political risk matters. Like other export credit agencies (ECAs), Coface is controversial; critics allege that ECAs negatively impact international development, as developing countries cannot compete with such insured exports. Proponents of ECAs argue that they enable developing countries to import products they otherwise would not be able to afford.

Coffee, Sugar, and Cocoa Exchange An exchange, tracing its roots to 1882, on which futures contracts and options on coffee, sugar, cocoa, and the S&P Commodity Index are traded. It is based in New York City and is a subsidiary of the Intercontinental Exchange.

Co-Financing The act or practice in which two different lenders agree to finance a single project for a borrower. For example, two lenders may agree to extend loans to start a business. The co-financiers use the same information and documentation when executing this arrangement, but the loans may have different terms. See also: Cofinancing agreement.

Cofinancing Agreement An agreement between the World Bank and another bank or financial institution to extend credit to a government or private organization in the developing world. Cofinancing agreements exist to assist in international development while also spreading the risk between the lenders.

COG GOST 7.67 Latin three-letter geocode for the Republic of the Congo. The code is used for transactions to and from Congolese bank accounts and for international shipping to the Congo. As with all GOST 7.67 codes, it is used primarily in Cyrillic alphabets.

Coherent Market Hypothesis A model on how markets work that purports to improve upon the efficient markets theory. It states that market movements may be predicted within certain broad limits, depending on a combination of investor sentiment and fundamental bias. The coherent market hypothesis claims that markets go through four phases: random walk, unstable transition, chaos, and coherence. The coherent markets hypothesis attempts to curb the perceived overstatements of random walk theory and the efficient markets theory. See also: Capital Market Theory.

Coiled Market A market that has been going down (or up) for a while and thus has a strong possibility of making a rapid movement up (or down). This may occur if prices have been kept artificially low (or high) for too long and the market is ready to make a correction.

Coin It In A slang term meaning to make a good profit or to earn a large salary or wage.

Coincident Indicator An economic indicator that provides information on the current state of the economy. That is, a coincident indicator does not show which way the economy is heading, but where it is at present. For example, coincident indicators move up when GDP is growing and down when GDP is shrinking. A common example is personal income. It is also called a concurrent indicator. See also: Leading indicator, Lagging indicator.

Coinsurance In insurance, a structure in which the policyholder and the insurer split the responsibility for paying for covered items. Coinsurance is most common with health and real estate insurance. For example, if a policyholder has surgery that is covered under the plan, coinsurance might require the policyholder to pay 20% and the insurer to pay the remaining 80%. This helps the insurer control costs by avoiding flippant claims, but also provides most of the coverage needed for the policyholder.

Coinsurance Effect A theory stating that a merger of any two companies renders bankruptcy less likely for the merged company than for the two previously constituted companies. The idea behind the coinsurance effect is that spreading assets and liabilities more widely makes default less likely. Theoretically, the coinsurance effect makes bond issues for the merged company lower-risk than those of the previous companies, driving down bond yields.

COK GOST 7.67 Latin three-letter geocode for the Cook Islands. The code is used for transactions to and from Cook Islander bank accounts and for international shipping to the Cook Islands. As with all GOST 7.67 codes, it is used primarily in Cyrillic alphabets.

COL GOST 7.67 Latin three-letter geocode for Colombia. The code is used for transactions to and from Colombian bank accounts and for international shipping to Colombia. As with all GOST 7.67 codes, it is used primarily in Cyrillic alphabets.

Cold Calling Informal; the practice of a broker making an unsolicited telephone call to a completely unknown person in an attempt to convince the person to become a client of that broker or brokerage. This practice is controversial and some jurisdictions have enacted laws limiting its legitimate use. It is also called dialing and smiling. See also: order period.

Cold Towel A slang term meaning to wait or put off a decision. For example, an employee may cold towel a decision on a project until he returns from vacation.

Collaborative Commerce The sharing and distribution of information online to encourage the integration of businesses.

Collar 1. A way to hedge against the potential of loss by buying an out-of-the-money put while writing an out-of-the-money call. A collar is most beneficial when an investor holds a stock that has recently experienced significant gains. If the stock falls, the investor can exercise the put, ensuring a profit. If it continues to rise, the call places a cap on the profit. **2.** On an exchange, a measure designed to prevent panic selling by stopping trading after a security or an index has fallen by a certain amount. For example, if the Dow Jones Industrial Average falls 10% in a trading day, the New York Stock Exchange suspends trade for at least one hour. A collar is intended to allow investors to determine whether a situation is really as bad as it looks. It is sometimes called a circuit breaker. See also: Suspended trading.

Collateral Trust Bond A bond usually issued by a holding company that is collateralized with securities rather than physical assets. Holding companies are the primary issuers of these bonds because their primary operation is to hold stock in other companies; their main assets are these securities.

Collateralize To offer an asset as a surety that a debt will be repaid. The asset may be kept by the lender until the debt is repaid, or the borrower may maintain possession with the proviso that the lender may take possession of the borrower defaults. For example, one collateralizes a mortgage loan with the real estate one purchases with the loan. If the loan is not repaid, the lender has the right to seize the real estate in question. See also: Lien.

Collateralized Bond Obligation An asset-backed security backed by the receivables on junk bonds. Issuers of CBOs package and sell their receivables on

bonds they hold to investors in order to reduce the risk coming from defaults. Returns on CBOs are lower risk than the individual bonds backing them. This is because it is unlikely that all or even most of the junk bonds will default. This makes the collateralized bond obligation investment grade and therefore banks are allowed to invest in them. See also: Collateralized Loan Obligation, Collateralized Mortgage Obligation.

Collateralized Debt Obligation An asset-backed security backed by the receivables on loans, bonds, or other debt. Banks package and sell their receivables on debt to investors in order to reduce the risk of loss due to default. Returns on CDOs are paid in tranches; that is, the individual loans backing each CDO have different levels of risk, and investors are paid out according to the level of risk they have acquired. Banks offer higher interest rates to investors willing to buy CDOs backed by higher-risk loans. From a bank's perspective, in addition to reducing risk, CDOs also reduce their capital requirements because they can raise funds through the issue of CDOs. While, theoretically, CDOs can be backed by mortgages, one usually refers to these as collateralized mortgage obligations.

Collateralized Loan Obligation An asset-backed security backed by the receivables on loans. Banks package and sell their receivables on loans to investors in order to reduce the risk coming from loan defaults. Returns on CLOs are paid in tranches; that is, the individual loans backing a CLO have different maturities, and investors are paid out as each matures. Banks offer higher interest rates to investors willing to buy CLOs backed by higher-risk loans. From a bank's perspective, in addition to reducing risk, CLOs also reduce their capital requirements by raising funds through the issue of CLOs. See also: Collateralized mortgage obligation.

Collateralized Mortgage Obligation An asset-backed security backed by mortgages. Banks package and sell their receivables on mortgages to investors in order to reduce the risk coming from defaults. Returns on CMOs are paid in tranches; that is, an individual mortgages backing CMOs have different maturities and investors are paid out according to their level of investment. Banks offer higher interest rates to investors willing to buy CMOs backed by higher-risk mortgages, such as subprime mortgages. See also: Collateralized loan obligation.

Collectible An asset of limited quantity and the perception of high value. Many collectibles are antiques. For example, a Babe Ruth baseball card is a collectible. Perhaps the main market for collectibles exists among persons who simply like collectibles; that is, a person who enjoys baseball is more likely to be a buyer of collectible baseball cards. However, because collectibles tend to maintain their value, investors may buy collectibles in addition to securities as a hedge against inflation. The problem with collectibles as an investment is the potential lack of liquidity: an investor may not be able to find an avid baseball card collector to whom to sell his/her collectibles.

Collection The act of receiving payment for goods or services. Collection occurs on the spot in a cash sale, while it may occur some weeks or even months later in a credit sale. See also: Accounts receivable, Collection policy.

Collection Float 1. Synonymous with shares outstanding. A collection float refers to the number of shares an issuing entity has not repurchased and that are available for trade by the general public. Sometimes it is simply known as a float. **2.** A deposit into a bank account that has not yet cleared. For example, one may deposit a check for $1,000 from an out-of-state bank. The funds may be posted to the account immediately, but they will not become available to the account holder until the issuing bank honors the check and transfers the funds to the receiving bank. This process can take as long as five business days. See also: Check hold.

Collection Fraction The percentage of accounts receivable for a month collected in a given month. For example, a small business may have $20,000 in sales for the month of July. If it collects $10,000 in July, $5,000 in August, and $2,500 each in September and October, the collection fractions for July's sales are 50% in July, 25% in August, and 12.5% in September and October.

Collection Policy The steps that a company follows in ensuring timely payment of its accounts receivable. Collection policies vary by company. An example of the steps a company can takes involves a friendly phone call to make sure payment is made on time, followed by a firm phone call when a payment is late, followed by a threatening letter, and finally turning the client over to a collection agency. Companies may deviate from their collection policy for long-standing or otherwise trusted customer.

Collective Bargaining A process by which an employer negotiates with employees toward an agreement that applies to all employees. That is, collective bargaining is not a negotiation involving individual employees but rather all employees at a company, or at least all who choose to be represented by a trade union. In the United States, companies are not allowed to discipline employees for attempting collective bargaining. See also: Bargaining Unit.

Collective Fund 1. A fund that has a set number of shares, which are then traded. Due to the finite number of shares, the fund's value rises and falls according to supply and demand. See also: open-ended fund. **2.** A fund that has special permission from the IRS to include tax-exempt or tax-deferred investments such as IRAs or pensions in its portfolio in order to diversify.

Collectivism Any political or economic system that centralizes the means of production at the expense of individual ownership. Collectivism is associated with socialism, which advocates state ownership of resources. However, collectivism may exist in capitalist systems if corporations own most or all of the means of production.

Collectivist One who believes in or advocates the centralization of the means of production at the expense of individual ownership. Collectivism is associated with socialism, which advocates state ownership of resources. However, collectivism may exist in capitalist systems if corporations own most or all of the means of production.

Cologne Terms A form of debt relief for heavily indebted poor countries in which the present value of payments is reduced by up to 90%. The Cologne terms were introduced by the HIPC Initiative in 1999. This form of debt relief is a type of concessional restructuring.

Colombian Peso The currency of Colombia. Instituted in 1837, it was pegged to the U.S. dollar for a time. Since 1955, however, the peso has floated. It has gradually deteriorated in value since.

Colombo Stock Exchange Sri Lanka's main stock exchange. The Colombo Stock Exchange has two indices and lists 234 companies representing approximately one-quarter of Sri Lanka's GDP. It is well known for the high degree of trading automation and its technological sophistication.

Colonia Any rural population center in Arizona, California, New Mexico or Texas within 150 miles of the U.S. border with Mexico. Colonias very often are unincorporated and are set up without government approval. As a result, colonias frequently have substandard or nonexistent municipal infrastructure.

Color Break In printing, the point or line at which one color gives way to another color. For example, in a piece of paper that is half red and half yellow, the color break is a line half-way down the page. It is also called the break for color.

Colorful Crab A slang term for $10 in Hong Kong. This term began to be used when the color of the $10 banknotes was changed from green to red and blue. An equivalent term is colorful paper. See also: Hong Kong dollar, Green crab.

Column Shaking The act or practice of changing a company's corporate culture in a fundamental way. Column shaking is generally conceived as a way to change a company's bad habits in order to make employees and others more productive, happier, and ultimately more profitable.

COM GOST 7.67 Latin three-letter geocode for Comoros. The code is used for transactions to and from Comorian bank accounts and for international shipping to Comoros. As with all GOST 7.67 codes, it is used primarily in Cyrillic alphabets.

Co-Manager In a syndicate placing a eurobond, the underwriter ranking just below the lead manager, which in turn ranks below the arranger, which is the senior-most underwriter.

Comarca 1. In Spanish-speaking countries, a political subdivision equivalent to a county. **2.** In Portuguese-speaking countries, a judicial district.

Comarca indigena In Panama, a political subdivision with a large Indian population. Some are equivalent to a province while others are considered municipalities.

Combat Zone A place where a war is taking place. If the U.S. Department of Defense designates an area is a combat zone, troops deployed there are not required to pay income taxes on earnings made while there. Likewise, any income earned while treating an injury sustained in a combat zone is tax-free.

Combination Bond A municipal bond with the coupon and principal guaranteed both by the general revenue of the municipality issuing the bond and by the revenue of the project the bond finances. If the revenue from the project is less than expected and is not enough to make payments, the municipality will make them instead. A combination bond is intended to reduce the risk to the bondholder to the least possible amount; therefore, interest rates on them are fairly low. It is also called a double-barrel municipal bond.

Combination Option A series of option contracts consisting of at least one call and one put with the same underlying asset. The combination option is written as a single unit but each of the component contracts may be resold on the secondary market separately. Each of the contracts has different strike prices and/or different expiration dates. Combination options exist in order to hedge one's investments. An investor may exercise either the call or the put, depending on the underlying price trends over the life of the contract, and still make a profit on the transaction. See also: Cliquet, Straddle, Strangle.

Combination Security Any complex security that includes features of two or more basic securities. One of the most common combination securities is a convertible bond, which is a bond that may be exchanged for common stock. In other words, a convertible bond combines features of bonds (with a fixed return and repayment at maturity) with features of stocks (with equity in the issuing company and the possibility of a high return).

Combination Strategy An option strategy in which one buys or sells two options on the same underlying asset with the same expiration date but with different strike prices. A combination strategy allows one to profit from the difference in strike prices on or before the expiration date. See also: Spread, Straddle.

Combined Financial Statement 1. A financial statement giving information on the assets, liabilities, profits, and losses of a corporation containing multiple companies. Each company's financial statement is given individually (that is, statements are not reconciled) and released together. This gives investors and shareholders an idea of the relative standing of each affiliated company and subsidiary, and thus the prospects for the corporation as a whole. It is important to note that a combined financial statement is different from a consolidated financial statement, which reconciles the numbers. **2.** A service a bank provides to customers giving each a statement containing information on all accounts with the bank, not only one at a time.

Come In Informal; a price decline.

Come Out of the Trade Idiom in general equities; it describes the impressions and expectations of each party to a trade immediately after the trade takes place. It also describes the condition of a trader's account in relation to the security being traded (i.e. long or short) immediately after the trade takes place. See also: Going into the trade.

Come to Jesus Meeting A slang term for a meeting at which serious topics will be discussed, perhaps with major implications. For example, a manager may have a come to Jesus meeting with an employee to tell her that her work has been unacceptable and, that if it does not improve, she will soon be fired. The term comes from American evangelical Christianity.

Comfort Letter Before or during a new issue, a statement by an auditor stating that, while a full audit has not been done, a review of the issue's prospectus has revealed nothing inaccurate or misleading. The comfort letter also states that the auditor is confident that a full audit would not uncover anything unusual that would negatively affect the issue.

Commerce The practice of buying and selling goods and services, whether for use or investment. Commerce usually refers to buying and selling on a large scale; that is, the sale of one widget is a transaction, while the sale of all the widgets in a country is the commerce of widgets. See also: E-commerce.

Commercial 1. Describing a company or other organization that produces, transports, or sells a commodity. **2.** An advertisement, especially one broadcast on television. See also: Marketing.

Commercial Bank A bank offering checking accounts, savings accounts, certificates of deposit, personal and business loans, and other, similar services. Commercial banks charge fees and/or interest for many of their services, though they may pay interest on other services. A retail bank is often an individual branch of a commercial bank where one may procure these services. A commercial bank contrasts with an investment bank, though their services have become more intertwined since the late 1990s.

Commercial Draft A request or demand for payment made by a bank on behalf of a third party. While the recipient of the commercial draft is not bound to honor it, refusal to do so may hurt his/her credit at the bank issuing the demand. For example, if Fred owes Joe money, Joe may ask a bank to issue a commercial draft, which Joe or a courier presents to Fred. Fred is not legally obliged to pay Joe, but if he does not, he may find difficulty securing a loan from the bank and other banks associated with it.

Commercial Grain Stock Any place where grain is stored. This especially refers to grain elevators and shipping vessels. Commercial grain stocks are important to investing because grain is traded as a commodity.

Commercial Hedgers Companies that take positions (often long positions) on the futures market for their operations. That is, commercial hedgers buy futures contracts in order to secure the price for the commodities they will need for their business purposes at a later date. Commercial hedgers seek to reduce the risk of the rising costs of materials later by guaranteeing their prices now.

Commercial Loan A loan made to a business to finance capital expenditures. "Commercial loan" is a fairly broad term, covering revolving lines of credit, as well as long and short-term debt. In any case, a commercial loan is made by a bank and is used to pay for expenses that the business, especially a small business, might not otherwise be able to afford.

Commercial Mortgage Alert A weekly newsletter that publishes information on the commercial mortgage backed security and real estate investment trust markets. It disseminates statistics and news on relevant investment strategies. The publication is based in New Jersey.

Commercial Mortgage-Backed Security A mortgage-backed security in which the mortgages on commercial building, offices, factories, apartments, and other buildings other than single-family homes collateralize the security. Unlike most other mortgage-backed securities, the structure of a CMBS is not standardized and as a result, it is difficult to assess its risk. It is also called a collateralized mortgage-backed security.

Commercial Paper An unsecured, short-term debt security issued by a corporation. Commercial paper is usually issued at a discount from par, and is a popular investment with mutual funds. It usually is issued in large denominations (over $250,000) and has a maturity of less than 270 days, with most maturing within one or two months of issue. It is a highly liquid investment and forms part of the money market. It is often simply called paper.

Commercial Paper Funding Facility A program implemented by the Federal Reserve System in response to the 2008 financial crisis. The New York Federal Reserve Bank (through a special purpose vehicle) purchased commercial paper from U.S.-based issuers in order to promote liquidity and the availability of credit in the wake of collapse of Lehman Brothers and other investment banks. The Commercial Paper Funding Facility expired in 2010.

Commercial Property Real estate and improvements thereon that the local government has specifically designated for business use. Commercial property may be set aside for farming, industrial use, or professional offices. Municipalities usually group commercial property together to maintain orderliness in the city, and to prevent new developments from interfering with existing homes and businesses. For example, a city may set aside an area for commercial development so a business does not build a large factory next to personal homes. Commercial property usually has to comply with certain standards set by the municipality; for example, a building may be required to have a certain aesthetic. Commercial property may be taxed differently from other property. See also: Zoning.

Commercial Trader A trader who uses the futures market to hedge against current business activities. For example, if a trader invests in a commodity believing the price will increase, he/she may lock in futures contracts at a certain price in case he/she is wrong. The term is a designation used by the Commodity Futures Trading Commission.

Commingled Fund 1. A mutual fund in which money from several customers is pooled together to reduce risk and cost. Any fund investing a large amount of money is subject to a lower percentage of brokerage fees, and large accounts usually have smaller administrative costs than individual accounts. They also benefit from economies of scale, mitigating risk. However, capital gains in a commingled fund are distributed equally among investors, usually resulting in a smaller return. **2.** A normally illegal practice in which a broker mingles his own funds with those of his/her client, making it difficult to distinguish to whom to give returns.

Commingled Securities Securities owned by a customer and held by a brokerage that are kept together with securities owned by the brokerage itself. This especially refers to margin securities kept as collateral. Commingled securities are legal with the permission of the customer. See also: Hypothecation.

Commission A form of payment to a brokerage in which the brokerage receives a percentage of the value of each transaction that a client orders. Commissions are seen as advantageous to a client because if the client does not make orders, then he/she does not have to pay a broker. However, commissions create an incentive for brokers to make as many transactions as possible; this has resulted in the regulation of commissions by the SEC. The percentage of a commission varies by brokerage, with those charging higher commissions offering a wider variety of investment advisory services. Low-commission brokerages usually offer no investment advice and simply fill orders. See also: Fee.

Commission Broker A person on the floor of an exchange who trades securities on behalf of a brokerage or investor. He/she may only make trades as directed by the client, or may have some leeway in the trades he/she makes. For his/her services, this person is paid a commission, which is a percentage of value of each transaction the broker makes. In order to guard against abuse, commission brokers working with discretionary accounts are required to follow suitability rules, which mandate that the broker only make trades in good faith, that is, only makes trades a "reasonable person" would make.

Commission-Only Compensation A form of payment to a brokerage in which the brokerage receives a percentage of the value of each transaction that a client orders. Commissions are seen as advantageous to a client because he/she does not have to pay a broker if he/she does not make orders. However, commissions create an incentive for brokers to make as many transactions as possible; this has resulted in the regulation of commissions by the SEC. The percentage of a commission varies by brokerage, with those charging higher commissions offering a wider variety of investment advisory services. Low-commission brokerages usually offer no investment advice and simply fill orders.

Commitment 1. The legal obligation to undertake an activity in a given way at a given time in the future. Usually, commitment refers to the requirement for parties to a futures contract to make or receive delivery of the underlying commodities on the expiration date of the contract. **2.** A liability. A commitment is the obligation to make good on an agreement at some point. For example, a borrower makes a commitment to pay back a loan by a certain time.

Commitment Fee A fee that a lender assesses on a borrower to keep a credit line open regardless of use. For example, a credit card company may charge a card holder $60 per year to allow him/her to continue to use the credit card. This should not be confused with interest, which is only calculated if a loan is made or a credit line is used.

Commitment of Traders Report A report that institutional investors and some speculators must file weekly with the Commodity Futures Trading Commission to declare their futures and option positions on certain commodities. The reports are designed to improve the information available to the market and thus make futures and option trading more efficient.

Commitments of Traders Report A report published each week by the Commodity Futures Trading Commission detailing major changes in traders' positions over the previous week. Specifically, it records and publishes changes to open positions on derivatives with more than 20 traders. The COT provides a quick reference for investors to understand the complex procedures and trades that occur on the CFTC. This in turn helps them make investment decisions.

Committed Facility Credit that is available to the borrower if and only if the borrower meets the requirements imposed by the lender. These requirements are often very strict. See also: Facility.

Committee of European Banking Supervisors A former group that advised the European Union on banking regulation. The committee was established to improve communication, to prepare draft policy changes, and to help implement regulatory decisions. It consisted of representatives of EU central banks and banking regulatory agencies. It was established in 2004 and dissolved in 2011. It was replaced by the European Banking Authority.

Committee on Foreign Investment in the United States Also called CFIUS. An interagency group in the United States responsible for advising the president on how foreign investment affects the U.S. It consists of the heads of 16 departments and agencies and is chaired by the Secretary of the Treasury. Among

other things, it is responsible for ensuring that foreign direct investment does not negatively impact U.S. national security. It was established by executive order in 1975. See also: Exon-Florio Amendment.

Committee on Uniform Securities Identification Procedures A board that assigns a nine-digit number to every stock and registered bond that trades in the United States. CUSIP is owned by the American Bankers Association and is operated by S&P. A CUSIP number facilitates trade and settlement by making each security unique from every other of the same class. CUSIP numbers are recorded in each trade.

Commodities Exchange Center A building in New York that once provided the offices and trading floors for Coffee, Sugar & Cocoa Exchange, Commodity Exchange, Inc, New York Cotton Exchange, New York Futures Exchange, and New York Mercantile Exchange. It was built in 1977 and used until the 9/11 terrorist attacks, when the Center was badly damaged. After this, the five exchanges found different offices.

Commoditization Movement toward perfect competition; the process by which a good or service thought to be unique or superior becomes like other, similar goods and services in the eyes of the market. Commoditization is the movement toward undifferentiated competition between two or more companies offering the same good or service. This leads to lower prices.

Commodity Block Currency A currency with foreign exchange price movements that strongly correlate to the movements of a single commodity. This happens when the economy of the country issuing such a currency is largely tied to one commodity, or a few similar commodities. For example, Canada has more oil in its ground than any other country except Saudi Arabia. As a result, the Canadian dollar appreciates when oil prices are high and depreciates when they are low.

Commodity Channel Index In technical analysis, an equation using a moving average to determine whether a commodity is overbought or oversold. It is calculated as follows: $CCI = (P - MA) / 0.015D$ where: P = the commodity's current price. MA = a moving average of the price over a given period of time. D = normal deviations from the moving average. This has become a popular tool among technical analysts, who use it to find highs and lows in a commodity's price to make their investment decisions. Some even use it for equities and currencies, in addition to commodities.

Commodity Currency A currency with an exchange rate highly correlated to the price of a commodity that is important to the economy of the currency issuer. For example, the Canadian dollar tends to be strong when oil and soybean prices are high because these are two major commodities produced in Canada. Other commodity currencies include the Australian dollar and the New Zealand dollar.

Commodity Exchange Act Legislation in the United States, passed in 1936, that imposed regulations upon the trading of commodities as well as some futures and options. Among other things, the Act provides that any option on a commodity and all futures must occur on an exchange and not over-the-counter. This Act replaced the Grain Futures Act of 1922. See also: CFTC, New Deal, Onion Futures Act.

Commodity Futures Contract An agreement to buy and sell a commodity at a certain date at a certain price. For example, Investor A may make a contract with Farmer B in which A agrees to buy a certain number of bushels of B's corn at $15 per bushel. This contract must be honored whether the price of corn goes to $1 or $100 per bushel. Commodity futures contracts can help reduce volatility in the normally volatile commodity markets, but contain the risks inherent to all speculative investing. These contracts may be sold on the secondary market, but the person holding the contract at its end must take delivery of the underlying. See also: Carrying charge, Options contract.

Commodity Futures Trading Commission A commission of the United States Government created in 1974 to regulate the market for futures contracts. It consists of five commissioners appointed by the President and confirmed by the Senate. Among other duties, the CFTC regulates the settlement of derivatives, oversees derivative exchanges, and sets and enforces rules on trading derivatives. It also works with the SEC to regulate futures contracts on single stocks. Futures traders and investment advisers must register with the CFTC as commodity trading advisers.

Commodity Indices Indices that track the price of different types of commodities. A commodity index may track commodities directly, or indirectly by tracking futures contracts for certain commodities. For example, commodity indices may track energy products or currencies, or may tracks futures contracts in either of those. Commodity indices operate much like exchange-traded funds or mutual funds in day-to-day trading: investors may buy, sell, or short sell shares in commodity indices as if they were stocks. An advantage to trading commodity indices is that it gives investors access to commodity markets without needing to buy or accept delivery on the underlying commodities.

Commodity Mudharaba In Islamic finance, a mudharaba contract in which the provider of capital gives the entrepreneur the initial investment in kind. For example, the provider of capital may give initial inventory and supply computers. In any mudharaba, a provider of capital agrees to invest in an entrepreneur in exchange for a portion of the profit of the entrepreneur's venture. Most Islamic law scholars reject the use of commodity mudharabas because they do not utilize cash.

Commodity Option An option contract giving the holder the right but not the obligation to buy (for a call) or sell (for a put) a futures contract on a certain stated commodity at a given strike price on or before the expiration date.

Commodity Paper A loan or cash advance secured by commodities, bills of lading, or warehouse receipts.

Commodity Pool A pool of liquidity that an investment company places in futures and options with the goal of producing a certain return. Because a commodity pool contains more liquidity than investors could afford on their own, it distributes risk between investors and allows them to forego margin requirements. Commodity pools are actively managed by the company to maintain the investment goals. Commodity pools are designed for investors who wish to take advantage of a highly diversified futures and options portfolio without a large amount of capital. See also: Commodity pool operator.

Commodity Pool Operator An individual or a limited partnership that operates a commodity pool. That is, a commodity pool is a fund in which investors contribute capital for participation in the futures and option markets. The commodity pool operator is either the management of the commodity pool or, more commonly, is hired by management to make investment decisions on behalf of the pool. Generally speaking, a person or company hired to serve as a commodity pool operator is a licensed commodity trading adviser.

Commodity Product Spread A spread involving different but related commodities. In it, one buys (or sells) futures in a raw commodity at the same time one sells (or buys) futures in a product of that commodity. For example, one may buy futures for crude oil while selling futures in refined oil. Commodity product spreads are useful because they can take advantage of price spread between the underlying commodities and the products that can be derived from soybeans. See also: Crush, Crack.

Commodity Research Bureau An organization that produces an index that tracks the price movements of 17 commodities. The CRB index does not follow any one commodity sector, but rather the general direction of commodities overall. The CRB index is watched by both commodity and bond investors because the prices of commodities and bonds tend to move in opposite directions due to inflation.

Commodity Research Bureau Index An index that tracks the price movements of commodities. The CRB does not follow any one commodity sector but rather the overall direction of commodities generally. The CRB is watched by both commodity and bond investors because the prices of commodities and bonds tend to move in opposite directions due to inflation.

Commodity Selection Index In technical analysis, a measure of how strong a trend on a commodity is. A high value on the CSI indicates that the current trend on a security, whether upward or downward, is strong. Investors use the CSI for short-term commodity trades. That is, if a CSI shows a strong upward trend, it is likely that rises will continue for the immediate future. However, using the CSI alone can be risky, as it cannot show when a reversal will take place.

Commodity Swap A swap involving the market price of a commodity. In a commodity swap, a financial institution is usually one of the counterparties. A user of the commodity may agree to pay the financial institution a fixed price for the commodity in exchange for the institution paying the user the spot price for the same commodity. On the other hand, a producer of a commodity may agree to pay the financial institution the market price in exchange for receiving a fixed price. A commodity swap usually involves oil and is used to protect against price fluctuations.

Commodity Trading Advisor An individual, or, more commonly, a firm that provides investment advice on the options or futures market. All individuals and companies doing this as their business must register with the CFTC unless they advise fewer than 15 people per year. Registration takes place through the National Futures Association.

Commodity-Backed Bond A bond with a coupon or principal tied to the price of some, stated commodity such as gold. A commodity backed bond may carry a low coupon rate but it allows the bondholder to hedge against inflation because the price of commodities usually rises over time. That said, some commodities are highly volatile, and the bondholder assumes the risk of a loss due to a fall in the commodity's price. Commodity backed bonds are relatively rare and are usually issued by companies that have some stake in the underlying commodities. It is also called a gold bond.

Common Equity The amount that all common shareholders have invested in a company. Most importantly, this includes the value of the common shares themselves. However, it also includes retained earnings and additional paid-in capital.

Common Good That which is seen as best for a whole community and not simply for any individual or small group within that community. This may be seen in purely utilitarian ways, but it may be founded upon natural law theory. The ideas behind law and democracy assume that the common good is something that can be achieved, or at least should be pursued. Proponents of both regulation and deregulation (or almost any other policy) believe their views best suit the common good.

Common Market 1. A market with the free movement of goods, services, labor, and capital between two or more places. For example, even though Texas and Oklahoma are different places with different governments and regulations, the two have a common market because workers do not need permission to move between them, and one may transfer money between them without incurring any tariffs or fees. See also: Free trade. **2.** An informal term for the European Economic Community.

Common Size Balance Sheet A balance sheet in which the items are expressed as percentages of total assets or total liabilities instead of as dollar amounts. For example, a common-size statement may express all cash as 10% of total assets, fixed assets as 25%, and so forth. A common-size statement is most useful when one attempts to compare a company to similar companies of different size or when one is comparing year-to-year variations in capital structure in the same company.

Common Stock Stock in a publicly-traded company that entitles holders to vote in the annual meeting, to elect the board of directors, and to generally exercise control of the company. While common stockholders are important in terms of their level of control, they have the least precedence in the event of liquidation. That is, if the company goes bankrupt, common stockholders do not receive any money until all bondholders, other debt holders, and preferred shareholders are paid in full. Likewise, common stock is not entitled to a guaranteed dividend. Common stock is also called ordinary stock.

Common Stock Equivalent A convertible security that is traded as if it was a common stock. The common stock equivalent is traded like common stock because it can be exchanged for actual common stock on demand from the holder.

Common Stock Fund A mutual fund consisting only of common stocks. A common stock fund may be high-risk if it invests primarily in start-ups and recent IPOs, or it may be low-risk if it invests in established companies with stable returns.

Common Stock Market 1. A stock market on which only common shares are traded. **2.** The supply and demand for common shares, whether of a single company, sector, or a whole economy.

Common Stock Ratio The ratio of the value of a company's common stock to its total capitalization, expressed as a percentage. A common stock ratio is an expression of how much a company is financed by equity. A high ratio indicates that the company finances a great deal of its operations through equity and, perhaps, is averse to debt. This signifies a conservative financial plan, though some analysts question whether or not this is beneficial.

Common-Base-Year Analysis In accounting and statistics, the expression of financial information in a given year as a percentage of an amount in an initial year. A company may treat the first year of its operations or the first year it made a profit as the base year, and express all financial information in those terms. For example, it may issue statements saying that profits in year five were 125% of year one's profits. Occasionally, governments or companies may change the base year to one that is more representative of "normal" performance.

Commons Real estate, especially open space, that belongs to a community as a whole. Regulations governing how commons may be used (for example, how they may be used for commerce) vary by jurisdiction.

Common-Size Statement Any financial statement in which the items are expressed as percentages of some figure instead of as dollar amounts. For example, a common-size statement may express all cash inflows as a percentage of total revenue. A common-size statement is most useful when one attempts to compare a company to similar companies of different size. It is also called a one hundred percent statement.

Commonwealth Development Corporation An international aid organization established by the British government after the Second World War to aid in post-war development. It has since been partially privatized and assists in international development in various parts of the world. See also: DFID.

Community Bank An independent, locally-owned commercial bank. It operates exclusively in and derives its funds from the community in which it is based. It is sometimes easier to obtain a loan from a community bank because it may have better knowledge of the local market. It is also known as an independent bank.

Community Council In Lesotho, the equivalent of a municipality.

Community Interest Company A for-profit company in the United Kingdom that has statutory duties other than making a profit for owners. It may be formed for many purposes, such as to improve a community or to protect the environment. It is treated as a for-profit company for legal and tax purposes. It is not prohibited from making a profit, but it is subject to fewer regulatory requirements than a non-profit in the United Kingdom.

Community Property A property owned by a married couple. Community properties have rights of survivorship. In other words, when one spouse dies, the property does not become part of the decedent's estate; rather, the other spouse continues to own the property. A couple may jointly own their home, for example. Generally speaking, a spouse is considered to be the primary beneficiary of the other's assets, such as retirement accounts, unless both spouses state otherwise.

Community Reinvestment Act A 1977 U.S. law encouraging banks and other lending agencies to extend credit to low and moderate income persons wishing to buy a home. The original contained no penalties, but prohibited lending institutions from discriminating against a potential homeowner based on where he/she lives. Regulatory changes in 1995 and legislative amendment in 1999 are often blamed for encouraging banks to make excessively risky loans in exchange for the ability to offer investment and insurance services. Because of this, some believe the CRA is responsible for the housing bubble that contributed to the recession that began in 2008. See also: Credit Crunch, Gramm-Leach-Bliley Act

Comorian Franc The currency of Comoros. It began with the Madagascar-Comoros CFA franc, which ended with Madagascar's withdrawal in 1973. It was pegged to the French franc and since 1999 has been pegged to the euro.

Comp Informal for comparison or comparison ticket; statements two brokers give to each other to confirm the details about a trade of a security to which they agreed. Details include the price and size of the transaction. The comps the brokers give one another must agree before the trade can be settled. See also: Don't Know.

Company Any organization that engages in business. There are many different structures a company can have, depending primarily on tax considerations and the type of business it does. Among some of the more prominent examples are a sole proprietorship, where an individual works on his/her own and all income is reported as personal income; a partnership, where two or more people create an organization partially distinct from each and where each partner has his/her own role; and a corporation, which is separate and distinct from its owners and is often a legally recognized person. See also: Limited liability company, Publicly-traded company.

Company Doctor An executive who is well-regarded for managing a distressed business back to financial health. A company may hire a company doctor from outside as a CEO or as some other officer if it is in danger of bankruptcy.

Company Risk Risk that might cause a loss to one company but not to other, similar companies. An example of company risk is the possibility of a strike by a company's employees. One may mitigate company risk by buying securities of multiple companies in the same industry. For example, a particular oil company has the company risk that it may drill little or no oil in a given year. An investor may mitigate this risk by investing in several different oil companies. Company risk is a type of nonsystematic risk.

Company-Specific Risk An unsystemic risk specific to a certain company's operations and reputation. For example, if a widget wholesaler has only one supplier and the supplier goes bankrupt, this could greatly impact the wholesaler's sales, profits, and other operations. Also, a company may have a bad reputation, making their operations difficult in a certain area. For example, a company that refuses to hire union workers might prove unprofitable if it opens a branch in a strongly pro-union town. Company-specific risks are difficult to quantify and thus qualitative analysis is needed to determine their natures and likelihoods. They may be reduced by appropriate diversification.

Comparables Characteristics of an asset that are similar to those of another asset. Comparables are especially important in real estate when appraising the value of a property. For example, if an appraiser is attempting to determine the value of a house, he may use the comparables of other houses in the neighborhood, such as the number of bedrooms or the square footage, when making the determination.

Comparative Advantage The ability of an individual, company, or economy to conduct an activity better than another for some fixed, almost unchangeable reason. Comparative advantage is important in making decisions such as what products one should make or sell; if a company is unable to make a product as well as another and that is unlikely to change, the company might be well advised to make a different product. For example, a lumber company in Oregon has a comparative advantage to a lumber company in Arizona because there are simply more trees in Oregon. This makes it unlikely that the company in Arizona will be able to fill orders as well or as quickly as the company in Oregon. For this reason, the Arizona company's management might consider investing in mining instead of lumber.

Comparative Credit Analysis The act or practice of comparing the bond rating or other credit rating of different, but similar, firms. Comparative credit analysis helps one determine what investments best fit one's investment goals relative to one's risk tolerance.

Comparative Financial Statements Financial statements from different quarters or years that are set side-by-side to gauge how a company has performed over time. This is useful when determining whether a company's earnings, revenue, or other items are considered "good." It also helps in predicting future performance.

Comparison Ticket One of the statements that two brokers give to each other to confirm the details about a trade of a security to which they agreed. Details include the price and size of the transaction. The comparison tickets that the brokers give one another must agree before the trade can be settled. See also: Don't Know.

Comparison Universe A group of comparable peer money managers against whose performance a single money manager is assessed. This is done periodically to maintain competitiveness and to judge a particular manager's performance. The practice has become controversial as some believe that comparison universes are too broadly defined to demonstrate the skill of a particular manager accurately and that they suffer from survivor bias because bad managers drop out or are fired. See also: Evaluation Period.

Compensating Balance Money from a loan that a borrower keeps in an account with a lender providing some surety that the lender will be repaid. A compensating balance is especially common with corporate loans. It increases the cost of capital to the borrower because he/she is paying interest on more money than he/she is permitted to use.

Compensation Payment for services rendered. One is due compensation when one has performed a service for an employer or client. Examples of compensation include wages, salaries, tips, fees, and commissions. Compensation is usually the primary component of an individual's tax liability. It is also called remuneration.

Compert A local person who knows how to use computers and is willing to help a small organization with its information technology needs. The compert may be paid or may be a volunteer. The term is an abbreviation of "computer expert" and is most commonly used in the context of small Christian churches and ministries.

Competence The ability to complete a project, make a product, or otherwise do what is required. Both individuals and companies have competence. For example, an engineer would not likely find a job as a nurse because it is outside his competence, that is, his ability to do the required work. Likewise, a dental office is unlikely to be hired to design a skyscraper.

Competition The attempt by two or more companies or other organizations to secure the business of a customer. Competition occurs when different companies offer better quality products and/or lower prices in order to encourage economic actors to become and remain customers. For example, two grocery stores may advertise that they offer better quality meat or lower prices for peanut butter so

shoppers patronize one grocery store and not the other. Nearly all economists believe that competition is necessary for innovation and growth, though few agree on how best to foster competition.

Competitive Bid A sealed bid, given to an issuer by an underwriter, containing a prospective price and terms for a contract. At the close date of bidding, the issuer picks the best offer. U.S. Government agencies are usually required to use this process and award the contract to the least expensive option. This is also used for various other ventures, from IPOs to project finance.

Competitive Bidders Institutions that make sealed bids to a bond issuer containing a prospective price and terms for an issue. On the close date of bidding, the issuer picks the best price and terms from among the competitive bidders. Competitive bidding is one of two processes by which the U.S. Government issues Treasury securities. This is also used for various other ventures, from IPOs to project finance.

Competitive Tender A way to distribute a bond to investors. In a competitive tender, the issuer receives bids from large companies or other investors to buy the bond issue; the highest bid receives the issue. The winner, at its discretion, may or may not distribute portions of the issue on the secondary market. The Bank of Canada uses competitive tenders to sell its bonds.

Complementary Financing A loan made by more than one lender that is secured by the same stock or other security. All lenders have a lien on a given security until the loan is paid off. In complementary financing, two or more lenders make two or more loans to a single borrower and secure those loans by a certain security. The amount of the lien on the security is in proportion to the amount of the loan each lender makes. For example, if Lender A loans $60,000 and Lender B loans $40,000 to Borrower C and they both secure their loans with a certain number of shares of Stock D, then, in the event of default, Lender A has the right to 60% of the shares, while Lender B has the right to 40%.

Complete 1. See: Fill. **2.** To finish a project. For example, one completes a construction project when all buildings are finished and there is no further work to do. See also: Physical completion.

Complete Audit An audit of both financial statements and the documents underlying them. That is, a complete audit does not only look at financial statements to make sure they make sense, it also makes sure that statements compare well with the documents used to create them. Complete audits are less likely than other audits to contain errors.

Complete Fill A communication from a broker to a client stating that the broker was able to buy or sell all the shares the client requested. See also: Fill or kill.

Complete Portfolio An investor's entire portfolio, and not simply his/her risky or risk-free securities.

Completed-Contract Method In construction and project finance, a method for calculating profits and losses in which revenue is recognized only after the physical completion of the contract. This differs from the completed-contract method, which recognizes revenue as it is received, provided that it is prorated according to the percentage of the project that is complete. Each method may have its own tax advantages.

Completion In project finance, the time at which a project has been finished, functions, and is generating enough revenue such that its cash flows become the primary way the project is repaying debt. Completion applies especially to construction and other infrastructure projects. For example, an oil company may build a series of oil pumps and finance the construction though bonds. Completion occurs when the oil pumps are completed and are working, and the cash flows generated by the oil are repaying the bonds. See also: Sales Completion, Physical Completion.

Completion Bonding A loan guarantee that a project will be paid for even if it is abandoned. Producers or publishers will make this guarantee to a bank in order to secure loans to finance their projects. Completion bonding benefits the bank as it guarantees that its loan will be paid. It also benefits the producer or publisher as the loan generally does not become payable until the project is completed, improving his/her accounting position. Finally, it benefits the person who actually develops a given project as the producer or publisher is discouraged from suddenly terminating that project. This form of financing is common to the video game and film industries.

Completion Risk The risk that a project may not be completed and/or produce revenue, either because the financing was cut off before completion or because the project's construction was done poorly. See also: Completion Test.

Completion Undertaking An agreement between two companies in which one undertakes a project and the other provides financing. The first company agrees either to complete the project according to certain specifications or to repay the second company for all debt it incurred in financing the project. This reduces the risk to the financing company that the other company will be unable to complete the project and thereby leave it unable to service debt.

Complex Capital Structure A company's capital structure that consists of anything other than (or in addition to) stock and bonds. Capital structure consists of, in brief, the vehicles by which a company raises capital in order to maintain or expand operations. A complex capital structure may consist of convertible stock, warrants, rights, or convertible bonds, among other vehicles. A company may also have a complex capital structure if it divides its common stock into more than one class.

Complexity Theory A theory stating that seemingly independent variables and/or data can organize into a system. Complexity theory argues that an economy is an adaptive field. That is, economic and non-economic factors interact continually and no equilibrium is ever reached. In other words, complexity theory states that chaos is inevitable in economics.

Compliance Department A department in a brokerage with the duty of ensuring that all trades comply with applicable laws and SEC regulations. A compliance department oversees employees and principals of the brokerage and monitors their activities. It must also investigate suspicious activity and, if necessary, report it to the appropriate authority.

Compliment Sandwich A management technique in which one pays an employee a compliment on his/her work, delivers a criticism, and then compliments him/her again. A compliment sandwich is a way to make an employee aware of his/her problems while attempting to preserve his/her morale.

Composite Index An alternate term for an index.

Composite Index of Lagging Indicators An index tracking a number of economic indicators considered to be lagging. A lagging indicator is one that occurs after an economy has started moving in a particular direction. For example, a drop in the unemployment rate is considered a lagging indicator of recovery following a recession. Among the indicators used by the Composite Index of Lagging Indicators are the change in the inflation rate and the average length of time each person has held his/her current job. It is used to confirm whether a particular economic movement is sustainable.

Composite Index of Leading Indicators An index tracking a number of economic indicators considered to be leading. A leading indicator is one that occurs before an economy has started moving in a particular direction. For example, a reduction in the average number of hours worked by manufacturing employees is considered a leading indicator because it usually precedes an economic slowdown or a recession. Among the indicators used by the Composite Index of Leading Indicators are the change in the money supply and the number of new building permits issued for residences. It is used to help predict the direction of the economy so investors and businesses can make decisions accordingly.

Composite Tape A record of the transactions occurring on an exchange on a given trading day, updated in real time or with only a slight delay. Before electronic tickers became common, most records of trading were printed out on strips of paper known as the composite tape. It is more common now to refer to an exchange's live record as a ticker. When tape was common, trading volume sometimes became so heavy for a security that the tape publicly announcing quotes was delayed by a significant amount of time, usually a minute or two. This was called a tape is late situation.

Composite Trading A report at the end of each trading day of the changes in price, trading volume, and closing prices for securities that trade on a given exchange or in a given country. Because some securities trade on multiple exchanges in different time zones, the composite trading report may not be completely accurate, but it provides a quick look at how different securities did over the trading day.

Composition The securities in a portfolio or fund, organized according to type. For example, the composition of a portfolio may be 60% stocks and 40% bonds.

Composition with Creditors A contract in which two or more creditors agree to accept a lump sum partial payment of a debt and write off the remainder of the debt. The creditors then split the sum in proportion to how much each one is owed. For example, suppose a debtor owes Creditor A $60,000 and Creditor B $40,000. If the debtor cannot make repayment, he/she may enter a composition with creditors for $10,000. Creditor A receives $6,000 and Creditor B $4,000; they then consider the debt paid in full.

Compound Annual Return The average year-on-year growth rate of an investment over a number of years. While investments usually do not grow at a constant rate, the compound annual return smoothes out returns by assuming constant growth. This makes accounting for the investment tidier. It is calculated as: Compound annual return = (Ending Value / Beginning Value)^((1 / n) - 1) where n is the length of time of the investment in years. It is also called the compound annual growth rate. See also: Average Annual Growth Rate.

Compound Interest The interest on a loan or other fixed-income instrument where interest previously paid is included in the calculation of future interest. For example, if one has a certificate of deposit for $1,000 that pays 3% in interest each month, The interest paid in the first month is $30 (3% of $1,000), in the second month it is $30.90 (3% of $1,030), and so forth. The more frequently interest is compounded, the higher the yield will be on the instrument. See also: Amortization.

Compound Interest Rate The interest rate on a loan or other fixed-income instrument in which interest previously paid is included in the calculation of future interest. For example, if one has a certificate of deposit for $1,000 with a 3% compound interest rate (compounded monthly), the interest paid is $30 (3% of $1,000) in the first month, $30.90 (3% of $1,030) in the second month, and so forth. The more frequently interest is compounded, the higher the yield will be on the instrument.

Compound Option An option contract on an option contract. There are four basic types: a call on a call; a put on a call; a call on a put; and a put on a put. A compound option has two expiration dates and two strikes. There are also two premiums: one paid up front and the other paid if the underlying option is exercised. It is often used in markets where there are doubts on the risk for the underlying option, such as currency or fixed income markets. It is also called a split-fee option.

Compounding The process of earning interest on a loan or other fixed-income instrument where the interest can itself earn interest. That is, interest previously calculated is included in the calculation of future interest. For example, suppose

someone had the same certificate of deposit for $1000 that pays 3%, compounding each month. The interest paid is $30 in the first month (3% of $1,000), $30.90 in the second month (3% of $1,030), and so forth. In this situation, the more frequently interest is compounded, the higher the yield will be on the instrument. See also: Amortization, Time value of money, Simple interest.

Compounding Frequency How often the interest is added to the principal of a loan each year. The greater the compounding frequency is, the more money the lender will make from the loan. See also: Continuously compounded interest.

Compounding Period The period of time between the compounding of interest. For example, if one has a bank account in which the interest is compounded monthly, then the compounding period is one month. Continuously compounded interest has no compounding period.

Comprehensive Due Diligence Investigation During a company's security offering, an investigation to determine whether the company has adequately disclosed its financial status in the offering's prospectus. An investor interested in buying the security may conduct a comprehensive due diligence investigation. Alternatively, investment advisers may do so in order to truthfully advise their clients on whether to invest in it. See also: Due diligence meeting.

Comprehensive Income The income of a company from any transaction that does not involve an owner's investment or distribution to an owner. For example, if a company exchanges two currencies for practical, rather than investment, purposes, any profit from the transaction may be considered comprehensive income. Comprehensive income contrasts with net income.

Comptroller of the Currency The head of the Office of the Comptroller of the Currency, which is an agency of the U.S. Government that regulates and supervises all banks (but not thrifts) in the United States. The Comptroller of the Currency is charged with enforcing banking regulation, prosecuting crimes committed by bank officials in the performance (or non-performance) of their duties, and helping to ensure equal access to banks by all American citizens. He or she is appointed by the President and confirmed by the Senate.

Compustat A database that provides extensive information on publicly-traded companies worldwide. Information available on Compustat includes earnings reports, Standard & Poor's ratings of its bonds, insider and institutional holders of its stock, and so forth. Its information is available to customers by subscription. Compustat is owned by Standard & Poor's.

Computer-Assisted Execution System A computerized order-entry system that sends buy or sell orders to market makers for over-the-counter trades.

Computerized Investing A computerized order-entry system that sends buy or sell orders for automatic execution, bypassing the floor broker or specialist. Computerized investing has historically been limited to institutional investors and traders, but small investors are beginning to use it more commonly. See also: ABS, ACAT, SOES, Ameritrade.

Computerized Market Timing System Any computerized system that makes buy and sell recommendations to users based upon information gleaned from large numbers of trades. The advantage to such a system is its ability to compute the combined significance of a large amount of data in a short period of time.

Comuna In Romania, a political subdivision equivalent to a rural village.

Comunidad In Spain, a political subdivision equivalent to a province or autonomous region.

Comunidad autonoma In Spain, a political subdivision equivalent to an autonomous province. These provinces belong to nationalities or ethnic groups within Spain and have a great deal of internal independence.

Comunidade intermunicipal In Portugal, a political subdivision in which municipal governments band together to provide certain services collectively.

Comunidade urbana In Portugal, a political subdivision equivalent to an urban community.

Concave Describing a curve segment whose ends fall below an arbitrarily set straight line. Concave properties are important to charting; for example, when tracking a stock market's performance, a dip in the chart with respect to the previous day's close followed by a rally going up to but not necessarily meeting that close may be described as a concave curve.

Concelho In Portugal and Cape Verde, a political subdivision equivalent to a municipal government.

Concentration Account A large account kept by a bank or other financial institution for its own internal purposes. Financial institutions use the funds in their concentration accounts to settle numerous transactions that occur on a particular day. For example, if a customer closes his/her bank account, the money given to him/her likely comes from the concentration account. Often, the money in a concentration account comes from regional branches of a bank, which transfer funds to a central location. This is the origin of the name. It was formerly relatively common for customers to transfer their own money through the concentration account of their banks, for both legitimate and illegitimate purposes. However, the USA PATRIOT Act forbade this practice.

Concentration Banks A small group of large banks that a firm periodically asks to collect its deposits from a larger group of smaller banks.

Concentration Service A service that a bank provides in which it processes payments for a company. The company directs its customers to send payments to a lockbox at the bank, which then collects the payments and deposits them directly into the company's account. A concentration service reduces time between the receipt and

Concept Company A company that has not yet made a profit but has developed a product thought likely to be profitable in the future. For example, a company in the process of developing a revolutionary computer technology may attract investors because they believe the company possibly might become the next Microsoft or Google. On the other hand, value investors tend to stay away from concept companies because they lack the fundamentals to make themselves attractive.

Concession Agreement An agreement in which a government, especially a local government, gives preferential treatment to a private-sector company. Generally speaking, a concession agreement involves special tax considerations, and is designed to encourage a company to come to or stay in an area. Governments make concession agreements to promote job growth or stability.

Concessional Restructuring A form of debt relief in which the present value of payments is reduced. That is, the borrower is able to pay less each month (or other period of time).

Concordat A treaty between the Holy See (or the Vatican) and a secular state. Historically, these treaties were used to secure the privileges of the Roman Catholic Church within a state, but frequently also gave the state a role in Church matters, as in the nomination or deposition of bishops. Since the Second Vatican Council (which ended in 1965), however, concordats generally have been concerned with matters like the promotion of Catholic education, especially through the use of state funding.

Conditional Call A provision in a convertible security agreement outlining the circumstances under which the issuer of the convertible security may call it without allowing the holder to exercise the convertible option. Most of the time, the conditional call states that the issuer may call the convertible security if the price of the underlying stock is trading outside a certain range, such that exercising the convertible option will put an undue strain on the issuer.

Conditional Call Option A term in some callable bonds requiring the issuer to replace it with a non-callable bond with the same maturity and similar terms if the bond is called prematurely. This protects the bondholders in the event that the bond is called. This provision is exclusive to junk bonds.

Conditional Listing Application The application that a company must file in order to be publicly traded on the Toronto Stock Exchange. A company must include its prospectus with the conditional listing application.

Conditional Order An order to buy or sell a security, but only under certain conditions. For example, an investor may make a stop-limit order to buy or sell a security at a certain price, but only after another price has already been reached. Conditional orders allow investors greater flexibility in trading to meet their particular investment goals.

Conditional Sales Contracts A sale of an asset in which the buyer assumes possession and may have use of the asset, but the seller retains title until the buyer pays its full price and may repossess the asset if the buyer does not. In exchange for the right to use the asset, the buyer makes payments over an agreed-upon period of time, whether months or years. This arrangement is most common with heavy equipment, machinery, and real estate. See also: Beneficial ownership, Lease.

Condominium In the United States and most of Canada, a piece of housing property attached to other properties, each individually owned, but with co-ownership of all common areas. This is usually associated with an apartment building in which residents own their apartments, but collectively (acting through a homeowners' association) own things like elevators, electric wiring, the outside of the buildings or the courtyards. In the event of an accident, liability is often apportioned according to where the accident occurred. For example, if a pipe bursts in a condominium and ruins the floors, its owner is responsible. However, if a pipe bursts in a condominium and ruins a neighboring unit's floors, liability rests with the homeowner's association. It is informally called a condo.

Condor In options, a strategy in which four contracts are bought or sold at four different strike prices. In a call condor, the investor buys the calls with the highest and lowest strike prices and sells the calls with the middle strike prices. In a put condor, the investor sells the contracts with the highest and lowest strikes and buys the middle ones. An investor engages in a condor strategy if he/she expects a great deal of volatility on the underlying asset; it allows him/her to make a profit regardless of the price of the underlying as long as it remains in a certain (broad) range. See also: Butterfly spread.

Conduit Financing A type of financing in which a government or private company issues debt on behalf of a non-profit organization. The debt is guaranteed by the revenue the project that the debt finances generates. Conduit financing is used for the non-profit's capital expenditures.

Conference Call A telephone call in which there are more than two participants. In investing, a publicly-traded company schedules conference calls where any analyst following that company may hear about its recent happenings. That is, a company executive speaks on a conference call and attempts to present information, such as quarterly earnings or a merger, in the best possible light for analysts. The SEC requires companies to schedule conference calls in advance and to allow as many analysts as possible to listen in on them.

Confidence Indicator A measure of the willingness of investors to attempt higher returns by assuming more risk. A confidence indicator may be calculated in a number of different ways. It may be calculated by compiling an index of stocks categorized according to risk, where a higher measure indicates higher confidence. A confidence indicator also may be determined subjectively; for example, a person may take a survey of industry insiders to see how they feel about taking more risk.

Confidence Level In polling and statistics, the degree of certainty in the confidence interval. The confidence level is how likely a pollster or statistician believes the results of a poll are repeatable and non-random. This is expressed as a percentage. For example, if a poll finds that 48% of those polled intend to vote for Candidate A with a 3% confidence interval and a 95% confidence level, this means that the pollster is 95% certain that between 45% and 51% of the population at large will vote for Candidate A.

Confirmation 1. A written statement a broker issues after a trade spelling out what exactly transpired, including the price, commissions, applicable fees, and the terms of trade. Confirmations are sometimes sent out immediately, but often within a week of the transaction. **2.** A market indication corroborating a previous indication. This shows that a predicted market trend will in fact take place, reducing uncertainty in the market.

Confirmed Letter of Credit A letter of credit guaranteed by two banks. That is, a bank agrees to honor the letter of credit and make the required payment in case both the letter's holder and the original, issuing bank both fail to make payment. This reduces the risk of the letter of credit to an absolute minimum.

Confirming Bank A bank that makes assurances to the relevant party that a letter of credit from another bank is genuine.

Conforming Loan A mortgage loan that Freddie Mac and Fannie Mae are allowed to buy. These organizations buy mortgages from the original lenders so as to reduce risk to the lenders and, thereby, maintain a smooth flow of mortgage credit. Conforming loans must meet certain guidelines. Included among these guidelines are requirements, such as a maximum debt-to-income ratio for the property owner, but the most important rule states that neither organization may buy a loan worth more than a certain amount. This amount changes every year according to changes in the median home price. See also: Jumbo loan, Mortgage-backed security.

Congestion A situation where a demand for a security exceeds supply or vice versa. In both cases, a large change in price is likely because investors will have a difficult time entering or leaving a position at its current price. Congestion can lead to a security trading either below its support level (if supply exceeds demand) or above its resistance level (if demand exceeds supply).

Congestion Area In technical analysis, a series of very similar prices at which a security trades for an extended period of time. For example, if a stock trades between $12.50 and $13.25 for several trading days, this price range is said to be that stock's congestion area. A congestion area indicates that supply and demand for a security are relatively equal; as a result, most technical analysts do not recommend buying or selling such a security until it breaks the congestion area in one direction or another.

Congius An ancient Roman unit of liquid volume approximately equivalent to 3.27 liters.

Conglomerate A corporation that runs and manages many, unrelated businesses. The businesses are in different industries and generally have nothing at all to do with each other in terms of what products are produced. The theory behind a conglomerate states that the individual businesses can be managed at lower cost because they are able to pool resources while also reducing risks inherent to any particular industry. Conglomerates are not as popular in the United States as they once were because some became so complex, they were impossible to operate. See also: Keiretsu, Chaebol.

Conglomerate Merger A merger in which the merging firms are in completely different industries. Two companies may complete a conglomerate merger for any number of reasons. Among the most prominent are the desire to expand into new markets and thereby reduce unsystematic risk and a need to eliminate redundant activities by consolidating certain departments (a process known as synergy). Pure conglomerate mergers occur when the parties have absolutely nothing in common, while mixed conglomerate mergers come from the desire of the parties to extend their markets or products. A potential drawback to a conglomerate merger is the fact that a firm may become too big and difficult to operate, resulting in inefficiency.

Congolese Franc The currency of the Democratic Republic of the Congo (not to be confused with the Republic of the Congo). It was introduced in 1997, replacing the new zaire when the country changed its name from Zaire. The currency in circulation consists exclusively of paper notes. No coins ever circulated, even though a few were designed and sold to collectors.

Consensus Estimate The average of different analysts' estimates about a stock's or security's performance. One may make a consensus estimate for any number of measures, such as earnings, sales, or revenue. A consensus rating or estimate may be published and, assuming the estimate is well-regarded, announcements of actual measures that differ from the consensus may affect the security's price significantly.

Consensus Forecast The average or median forecast made by well-respected analysts on the future performance of a security or derivative. Forecasting is the process of using certain data to predict future market movements. Various methods exist for forecasting; experts differ on which ones, if any, work. See also: Technical analysis, Fundamental analysis, Random walk theory.

Consensus Recommendation The mean or median recommendation that analysts make on a stock. The consensus recommendation is calculated simply by compiling recommendations and taking the average or median. Importantly, the consensus recommendation does not consider past accuracy or respect of the different analysts.

Consent Dividend A dividend that is not actually paid to a shareholder but is kept as part of a company's retained earnings. A shareholder may agree to have a dividend added to his/her gross income even if it not paid. This may increase the shareholder's personal tax liability but may decrease the company's corporate tax liability, which may in turn help the share price.

Consent Solicitation An offer by the issuer of a security to change the terms of the security agreement. For example, a bond issuer may ask bondholders if the terms of the indenture may be changed. Consent solicitations are made because security agreements require mutual consent in order to be altered.

Conservatism The philosophy that what has been done should continue to be done as long as there is not a positive reason to change it. Conservatives may favor class distinctions as natural, or at least not harmful. In modern times, conservatism has become associated with the political right, or the belief that capitalism and the free market tend to best determine how an economy ought to be organized.

Conservative A person who believes that what has been done should continue to be done as long as there is not a positive reason to change it. Conservatives may favor class distinctions as natural, or at least not harmful. In modern times, conservatism has become associated with the political right, or the belief that capitalism and the free market tend to best determine how an economy ought to be organized.

Consideration Money or other payment provided in exchange for an act or service that helps a business. Consideration may be cash in which case, it is more like a sale or payment-in-kind. For example, a person may receive a certain amount of equity in a business in exchange for giving or allowing the business to use the person's intellectual property.

Consignee In a bill of lading, the party entitled to receive the goods upon their arrival.

Consignment The act or practice of the owner of a good transferring the good to a second party, usually to be sold. The parties split the proceeds from the sale according to some agreed-upon arrangement. At all times before the sale, the original owner of the good retains ownership and may end the consignment by requesting the good's return. Generally speaking, a consignment lasts for a certain period of time, after which the good is returned to the owner, unless it first is sold.

Consolidated Bond A bond that pays off two or more outstanding bonds. A consolidated bond can come with a lower combined coupon rate that helps the issuer reduce its liabilities. See also: Consolidation loan, Refinancing.

Consolidated Financial Statement A financial statement that combines the assets and liabilities of a parent company and its subsidiaries. A consolidated financial statement presents an aggregated picture of the whole corporation, rather than its individual parts.

Consolidated Income Statement An income statement that combines the revenue, expenses, and income of a parent company and its subsidiaries. A consolidated income statement presents an aggregated picture of the whole corporation rather than its individual parts. Any money owed between the companies included in the statement is not considered.

Consolidated Mortgage A mortgage that one takes out in order to pay off two or more mortgages. The mortgages may or may not be for the same piece of property. A mortgage holder may take out a consolidated mortgage to lower monthly payments or for some other reason. See also: Blanket mortgage, Debt consolidation, Consolidated mortgage bond.

Consolidated Mortgage Bond A bond guaranteed by more than one mortgage on more than one property. Sometimes, the bonds are backed by refinanced mortgages. Payments are dependent on payments on the underlying mortgages. See also: Mortgage-backed security, Collateralized mortgage obligation.

Consolidated Quotation System An electronic service, regulated by the SEC, containing quotation information for securities listed on the New York Stock Exchange, the American Stock Exchange, and other, regional exchanges, as well as member firms in the National Association of Securities Dealers. NASDAQ also processes the data and provides it to subscribers under the name Composite Quotation Service.

Consolidated Short Position Report A report that lists all shares on the Toronto Stock Exchange and the TSX Venture Exchange that have been sold short. The report also states the change from the previous report.

Consolidated Tape A ticker tape that reports all trades on a security, regardless of where the trades take place. For example, a consolidated tape quote for IBM would show its prices on all exchanges on which IBM is traded, and not simply one or two. See also: Network A, Network B.

Consolidated Tax Return A tax return providing information on the assets, liabilities, profits, and losses of a group of affiliated companies. Each company's tax return is reconciled so that the return is treated as if it were for a single company. A parent company may file a consolidated tax return if it owns at least 80% of its subsidiaries.

Consolidation A type of merger in which two or more companies create an entirely new corporate entity and transfer all their assets and liabilities to the new entity. The former companies may continue to exist on paper, but they have no assets or liabilities. For example, the lawyers for the consolidating companies may go the secretary of state and form a new limited liability company (usually by paying a fee of $50 or so). After this is done, all assets and liabilities are given to the new LLC.

Consolidation Loan A loan that pays off two or more loans. A consolidation loan often comes with a lower monthly payment and/or interest rate than the previous

loans, as well as a longer repayment period. The process is usually called debt consolidation, and is often used for student loans.

Consolidation Service A service in which a company combines several different shipments on a single vessel or airplane in order to extract bulk rates and other favorable treatment from the transportation service. A consolidation service is also called an assembly service, cargo consolidation, and freight consolidation.

Consortium A group of independent companies participating in a joint venture for mutual benefit. Companies in a consortium cooperate with one another, often sharing technology as needed. A consortium allows the companies to conduct operations that they would not be able to do individually. It is important to note, however, that a consortium is not a merger and the companies remain independent.

Consortium Bank A subsidiary bank owned by several different banks. Each owner bank has an equal share so that no bank is the majority shareholder. The owner banks are often in different countries. A consortium bank is created to finance a specific project; once the project is complete, the consortium bank dissolves itself. While they are not as common as they once were, they are useful when a project involves multiple currencies.

Conspicuous Consumption The purchase of items one does not need simply to show that one is able to afford them. For example, a person who buys an exotic automobile may be engaging in conspicuous consumption.

Constant Currencies A calculation of international sales that eliminates fluctuations in currency values. This calculation exists to make financial statements "cleaner." For example, suppose a Japanese company does most of its business in U.S. dollars. If its sales increase or decrease in dollar terms, this may or may not be reflected in yen because of changes to the exchange rate. Assuming a constant exchange rate for the financial statement helps the company accurately report information.

Constant Dollar A measure of a dollar's value with respect to some year. One may use a constant dollar analysis to account for inflation. For example, suppose one wishes to measure changes in the U.S. national debt. It would be most useful to use a constant dollar format, for example, by measuring the national debt for all years in the dollar's value in the year 2000. This eliminates inflation as a consideration when analyzing the national debt.

Constant Maturity Describing all bonds with a maturity on a certain date. This is used to help compare the yields on Treasury, corporate, and other bonds. Mortgage banks also use constant maturity yields to help them determine interest rates on mortgages. Most often, the Federal Reserve provides constant maturity quotes to investors.

Constant Maturity Swap An interest rate swap where the buyer is permitted to pick the maturities of the interest rates swapped. For example, the buyer may choose to receive the six month interest rate (calculated over some notional amount) while paying a one-year rate. One buys a CMS when one believes he/she knows the direction of future rates.

Constant Ratio Plan An investment strategy in which the market value of stocks and bonds are kept at a predetermined ratio. That is, when compiling a portfolio, an investor may decide that 60% of its value will consist of bonds and 40% will be stocks. When prices rise or fall on the securities in the portfolio, the investor will buy and sell accordingly in order to maintain the ratio. A constant ratio plan is a form of active management and is done in order to reduce the risk in the portfolio.

Constant Yield Method A way to calculate the yield on a discount bond or zero-coupon bond for tax purposes. The constant yield method usually results in a lower tax liability but is often more difficult to calculate. One may choose to use the constant yield method or the ratable accrual method when one buys the bond. Afterward, however, one must continue to use the same method until the bond matures or becomes sold.

Constitution The basic law of a polity. The constitution states how the polity governs itself and usually enshrines the rights that its citizens have. For example, a constitution may state how often legislative elections occur and indicate the limits of legislative purview. It also may guarantee rights such as freedom of religion and the right to vote for the candidate of one's choosing. See also: Bill of rights.

Construction Loan A short-term loan used to finance the building of some real estate project. The builders take out a construction loan in order to begin the project while they obtain long-term funding. Because there is no guarantee that the builders will be able to obtain long-term funding and a construction loan is not intended to fund an entire project, construction loans are fairly risky, and, as a result, have high interest rates.

Constructive Dividend In American taxation, any payment to a shareholder that is not classified as a dividend by the company. The IRS treats these payments as dividends and taxes them as such. Constructive dividends are most common in closely-held corporations in which shareholders are often also employees or landlords of the company. For example, if a company rents its offices from a shareholder and pays in excess of the offices' fair market value, then the IRS considers the company's rent (or a portion of it) as a constructive dividend. Unlike business expenses, which are tax-deductible, constructive dividends are taxable. Thus, the company from the example will not be able to write off its rent like most other companies do.

Constructive Insider A person who is not considered an insider of a publicly-traded company but may still have access to nonpublic information that is expected to remain nonpublic. For example, a lawyer working for a firm retained by a publicly-traded company may be a constructive insider. Constructive insiders are expected to abide by the same rules as actual corporate insiders; that is, they may not reveal or profit from nonpublic information. The term was first used in the U.S. Supreme Court case Dirks vs. SEC.

Constructive Sale Rule A section of the Internal Revenue Code clarifying the transactions that are subject to capital gains taxation. Basically, any transaction that essentially offsets a previously held position is subject to the tax, even if it is not a straight sale of a security. An example of a transaction that falls under the Constructive Sale Rule is a short sale against the box. It is formally called Section 1259.

Consular Invoice In international commerce, an invoice signed and sealed by a consul of the importing country who is posted in the exporting country. A consular invoice builds trust between the buyer and seller and helps reduce the possibility that the seller (exporter) will overcharge the buyer (importer).

Consulenza An Italian term for advice. It may be used in the context of investment advice.

Consumed-Income Tax A tax only on income that one spends on goods and services. A common example of a consumed-income tax is a sales tax. Most countries have consumed-income taxes at some level and proposals exist in the United States to shift from a mainly progressive tax system to a system that utilizes consumed income taxes predominantly or exclusively. Proponents of a consumed-income tax argue that it encourages saving and makes the economy more efficient, while opponents maintain that it adversely affects the poor, who must by necessity spend more of their income.

Consumer Advisory Council An organization that advises the Federal Reserve on issues affecting consumers, especially the availability of credit. The Council consists of 30 representatives and meets in Washington, D.C. It is one of three Federal Reserve advisory committees; the others are the Thrift Institutions Advisory Council and the Federal Advisory Council.

Consumer Class The class of persons able to buy goods and services other than those that satisfy their basic needs. For example, members of the consumer class may buy cellular phones and multiple automobiles. The consumer class may broadly correspond to the middle class, but if a country is sufficiently wealthy, even its lower classes may belong to the consumer class in some way.

Consumer Confidence Index An index published by The Conference Board measuring public opinion about the economy. The Consumer Confidence Index surveys consumers' buying habits, level of optimism, and expectations for the future. The index has a base value of 100; The Conference Board declares a recession whenever two consecutive quarters have values below 100. Information contained in the index is based on monthly surveys of 5,000 American households.

Consumer Credit Any loan or line of credit that a borrower uses to purchase goods and services at the retail level. Typically, consumer credit finances any asset that depreciates quickly and is not used for investment purposes. Credit cards are a common example of consumer credit because one pays for ordinary expenses such as groceries or gasoline with a credit card; one ordinarily would not purchase stock with a credit card. Loans for education and cars are also examples of consumer credit. However, consumer credit expressly excludes loans for real estate.

Consumer Credit Protection Act of 1968 Legislation in the United States requiring lenders to disclose to potential borrowers all terms of loans, including, but not limited to, the interest rates, applicable fees, and the length of loans. The Act also allows consumers to cancel some credit transactions that require a lien to be placed on the consumer's primary residence. For the most part, the Act does not place limits on the fees lenders may charge, but instead requires transparency. It is also called the Truth in Lending Act.

Consumer Debenture A debenture or other debt security that a financial institution sells directly to the public. That is, the financial institution does not use any intermediaries, such as underwriters, when selling a consumer debenture.

Consumer Debt The debt individuals use to purchase consumer goods. In macroeconomics, consumer debt is used for individual purchase rather than investment. A common example of consumer debt is the balance on a credit card.

Consumer Finance Company A non-bank lender. A consumer finance company does not receive deposits, but does make loans to customers for business or personal use. It derives its profits from the interest on these loans. It is also called simply a finance company.

Consumer Goods Goods intended to be used by themselves, rather than as part of the production of another good. The most common consumer goods are food and clothing. Most of the time, consumer goods are sold byretailers, as opposed to wholesalers.

Consumer Interest The interest one owes on a loan used to buy a consumer good. For example, if one uses a credit card to buy groceries, the interest one pays on this loan, if any, is called consumer interest.

Consumer Internet Barometer A quarterly report publishing the results of a survey on Internet usage of 10,000 American households. It reports how often respondents are online, how satisfied they are with their providers, information on online purchases, and perceptions on the security of online purchases. The Consumer Internet Barometer has become more important as more commerce has come to be conducted over the Internet. It is published by The Conference Board.

Consumer Price Index A measure of inflation in the United States that considers what people spend on staple goods and services. It is calculated by taking the average of changes in price to a basket of goods and services compiled by the U.S. Department of Labor. The goods and services in the basket are weighted according to their perceived importance. The CPI is considered a primary tool in determining how people are experiencing inflation.

Consumer Product Personal property designed for personal, family or other non-business use, whether on a temporary or permanent basis. Examples of consumer products include toys and furniture.

Consumer Product Safety Commission Also called the CPSC. An agency of the U.S. federal government charged with enforcing safety of consumer products such as toys or furniture. The Act authorized the Commission to work with industries to develop voluntary standards, to implement mandatory standards, to recall products and even to ban dangerous products.

Consumer Products Safety Act of 1972 Legislation in the United States that created the Consumer Product Safety Commission. The Commission was charged with improving safety of consumer products such as toys or furniture. The Act authorized the Commission to work with industries to develop voluntary standards, to implement and enforce mandatory standards, to recall products and even to ban dangerous products.

Consumer Products Safety Commission An agency of the U.S. federal government that seeks to protect consumers from injury resulting from the use of goods. For example, the CPSC is responsible for ensuring that cribs manufactured and sold in the United States are safe for babies. It is headed by three commissioners appointed by the president and confirmed by the Senate. It was established in 1972 and is based in Bethesda, Maryland.

Consumer Protection Telemarketing Act Legislation in the United States prohibiting telephone salespersons from using certain practices. Among other provisions, the Act disallows telemarketers from lying to potential buyers and requires orders made over the telephone to be delivered within a certain period of time. It was passed in 1993.

Consumer Reporting Agency A company measures of an individual's creditworthiness and sells information regarding it. Consumer reporting agencies quantify a variety of factors in an individual's background, including a history of default, the current amount of debt, and the length of time that the individual has made purchases on credit. Banks and other financial institutions may purchase information from a consumer reporting agency to determine whether or not an individual is likely to default on a loan, mortgage, or other debt. See also: Fair Isaac Corporation, Credit bureau.

Consumer Staples Companies, industries, and products that are used for personal and household purposes. Consumer staples include food, alcohol, tobacco, medicine, clothing, and so forth. Companies that sell consumer staples have a reputation of resistance to economic downturn, but this is not always the case. In any event, they are often sold long-term investments.

Consumption Tax A tax only on income that one spends on goods and services. A common example of a consumption tax is a sales tax. Most countries have consumption taxes at some level and proposals exist in the United States to shift from a mainly progressive tax system to a system that utilizes consumption taxes predominantly or exclusively. Proponents of a consumption tax argue that it encourages saving and makes the economy more efficient, while opponents maintain that it adversely affects the poor, who must, by necessity, spend more of their income.

Contagion A recession or economic crisis that begins in one country and extends to others. For example, the late 2000s recession began with a large number of defaults on subprime mortgages in the United States. However, because investors worldwide invested in mortgage-backed securities backed by those mortgages, it affected portfolios and funds internationally and became a global meltdown. See also: Great Recession.

Contango A situation in which the futures price for an asset is higher than the expected future spot price. The futures price in contango declines to the future spot price as the futures contract approaches maturity. See also: Backwardation, Keynesian economics.

Contingency A negative situation that may occur and for which one ought to prepare. For example, a company may maintain extra cash reserves to cover unexpected liabilities. See also: Cushion.

Contingency Graph A graph showing the profit or loss a currency speculator will realize on his/her positions under various exchange rates. That is, the contingency graph shows how much the speculator will gain or lose if the currency on which he/she is speculating moves to anywhere within the range of the graph. This can be useful in the risk analysis of speculative currency position.

Contingent Annuity An annuity that does not begin making payments to the annuitant or the beneficiary until a certain stated event occurs. Annuities that do not begin payments until an individual's retirement or death are common examples.

Contingent Asset An asset that a company may have or receive but only if a certain future event occurs. Usually, a contingent asset refers to the outcome of a lawsuit: that is, the company may be awarded a significant amount of money if it wins the lawsuit. Contingent assets are not ordinarily recorded on a balance sheet because of the uncertainty surrounding them. Their existence may or may not affect the company's share price. See also: Contingent Liability.

Contingent Beneficiary In wills and insurance, a beneficiary who receives the benefit in case the primary beneficiary dies or is otherwise unable to receive the benefit. In cases where the primary beneficiary is mentally incapacitated, a contingent beneficiary is often named to ensure that assets are used to help the primary beneficiary. Attorneys commonly recommend that wills include at least one contingent beneficiary, and sometimes a list of successive contingent beneficiaries so as to remove any ambiguity.

Contingent Conversion Trigger In contingent convertible bonds, the price that the underlying stock must reach before conversion is allowed. All convertible bonds have a conversion price, which is the price one pays in order to exchange the bonds for stocks. Contingent convertible bonds, however, have a second, higher price that the underlying stock must meet before a bondholder is allowed to convert. This is called the contingent conversion trigger. For example, the conversion price for a contingent convertible bond may be $10 per share, but if the stock price is above $20 per share, the investor may not convert the bond. In this case, the contingent conversion trigger is $20. See also: Provisional Call Trigger Price, Trigger Price.

Contingent Convertible A convertible bond in which the price of the underlying stock must reach a certain level before conversion is allowed. All convertible bonds have a conversion price, that is, the price one pays in order to exchange the bonds for stocks. Contingent convertible bonds, however, have a second, higher price that the underlying stock must meet before a bondholder is allowed to convert. For example, the conversion price for a convertible bond may be $10 per share, but if the stock price is below $20 per share, the investor may not convert the bond.

Contingent Deferred Sales Charge The formal name for the load in a back-end load fund. A CDSC is the fee paid when a shareholder sells shares in a mutual fund within a certain number of years. That is, when an investor initially buys a share in a back-end load fund, he/she agrees to pay a third party, usually a financial institution or broker, a certain percentage of the share's value if he/she decides to sell it within five to 10 years, depending on the specific nature of the agreement. The CDSC usually declines by the year until the maximum number of years is reached. See also: B-share.

Contingent Guarantee A guarantee made by a third party to the buyer of a good or service stating that the seller will receive payment on time and in the correct amount. If the buyer fails to make the payment, the third party will make payment on his/her behalf. Contingent guarantees, known as letters of credit, have become very common in international commerce, as distance and other factors make it difficult for sellers to establish the credit worthiness of every buyer. See also: Co-signer.

Contingent Immunization An investment strategy in which an asset manager or investor makes investments of varying risk until something goes wrong. When an investment suffers a loss and brings the portfolio down to some pre-defined return, the asset manager or investor begins making low- or no-risk investments that guarantee that same, pre-defined return. A contingent immunization strategy opens an investor up to large returns while minimizing losses as much as possible.

Contingent Issue An issue of a security that occurs automatically, but only when certain conditions are met. A contingent issue may be an anti-takeover measure. For example, a publicly-traded company may plan for a contingent issue in the event of a hostile takeover to make the takeover more expensive for the acquiring company. See also: Poison pill.

Contingent Liability A liability that a company may have to pay, but only if a certain future event occurs. Usually, a contingent liability refers to the outcome of a lawsuit: that is, the company may have to pay a significant amount of money if it loses the lawsuit. Contingent liabilities are recorded under accounts payable; their existence may also affect the share price.

Contingent Order An order to a broker to conduct a transaction on the assumption that a related transaction is conducted. The related transaction may occur before, after, or at the same time as the contingent order. That is, an investor may give an order to his/her broker to buy Stock A contingent upon the sale of Stock B. A common example of a contingent order is a buy-write, in which an investor orders his/her broker to buy a security and at the same time write an option with that security as the underlying asset.

Contingent Rent Rent that varies depending on a certain condition. For example, the owner of a property may index its rent to the tenant's monthly income. A contingent rent system may be more beneficial for the lessee than the lessor.

Contingent Value Right A right attached to a stock entitling the holder to the difference between the share price and some stated amount of money should the share price not exceed that amount in a given period of time. CVRs are most often attached to stocks after a merger or acquisition to encourage shareholders not to sell, and to give the new situation a chance to become profitable.

Contingent Voting Rights Voting rights that go to a shareholder or other stakeholder who does not ordinarily have them. For example, a shareholder may receive contingent voting rights in the event that the company does not fulfill obligations that it promised the shareholder it would fulfill. Contingent voting rights are agreed between the company and the shareholder or stakeholder.

Continuation Pattern In technical analysis, a temporary deviation from a previous trend that signals that it will soon begin to follow that trend again. Continuation patterns are most accurate in the medium term (one to three months). Common continuation patterns include widgets, triangles, and flags.

Continuous Compounding Describing interest that accumulates on a constant basis. That is, if a loan has continuous compounding interest, the interest accumulates all the time, which means that the interest added to the loan balance also begins earning interest on itself. In the short and medium term, this has almost the same yield as daily compounding interest but over the long term, the continuous compounding interest can earn much more. Albert Einstein was once reported as saying that there is no more powerful force in the universe than continuous compounding interest. See also: Compounding.

Continuous Disclosure The legal requirement of a company to inform the public about positive and negative situations affecting the company. For example, the company has an obligation to report losses resulting from a failed merger even if the disclosure reflects poorly on the CEO and board of directors.

Continuous Net Settlement A clearing practice in which all buy and sell orders are settled within a brokerage firm. That is, all buy and sell orders are offset against each other on a particular trading day, such that only orders that are "left over" remain to be settled. This results in fewer securities needing to be moved into or out of a particular brokerage.

Continuous Online Trading System A computerized order-entry system that sends buy or sell orders for over-the-counter trades. It is used to automatically execute orders, and allow users to monitor their positions.

Continuous Random Variable A random variable that may take any value within a given range. That is, unlike a discrete variable, a continuous random variable is not necessarily an integer.

Continuous Trading Orders for trade that are executed immediately. On some exchanges, brokers wait to accumulate a number of orders before filling them. Continuous trading, on the other hand, demands that the broker carry out the order at once, or as soon as the appropriate price becomes available. Limit orders are an example of continuous trading: when they are made, the price may not be available, but the broker must execute the order as soon as it is to avoid missing out on the proper price. In the United States, all trading is continuous except at the open.

Conto A slang term for one Brazilian real. An equivalent term is pila.

Contra Account An account whose value offsets the value of an equivalent account. This applies whether the account is debited or credited. For example, two firms may have contra accounts in which each owes the other money. They might agree to offset the mutual debt and make a single payment to whichever is owed more. Perhaps the most common example of a contra account is an asset's depreciation, which is subtracted from its original price to calculate its book value. In this case, the depreciation and the original price are contra accounts with respect to each other.

Contra Broker In a transaction, the broker for the counterparty. For example, the contra broker for a seller is the buyer's broker.

Contract 1. A legal agreement between two parties in which each agrees to do, make, buy, or sell a good or service, or in which one party grants a right or undertakes an obligation, often in exchange for a fee. A contract is less commonly called a binding agreement. See also: Option contract, Futures contract. 2. Informal for a unit of trade in options and futures.

Contract For Differences A futures contract that is settled in cash. That is, the underlying does not trade hands, and neither party needs to own it. Two parties simply designate each other as seller and buyer, and at the close of the contract one party pays the other the difference in value between the underlying's opening and closing prices, multiplied by the number of shares specified in the contract. If the difference is positive, the seller pays the buyer; if the difference is negative, the buyer pays the seller. An advantage to CFDs is the fact that they are exempt from taxes like stamp duties, because the underlying asset does not actually exist. However, they tend to work better as short-term investments because they are subject to daily financing charges.

Contract for Purchase or Sale A contract for the sale of real estate. Realtor organizations set standard contracts for purchase or sale, but these forms may be changed depending on the specific nature of each transaction.

Contract Holder The owner of a security, derivative, or anything else to which an obligation is owed.

Contract Market A futures or options exchange. Examples include the Chicago Board Options Exchange and Euronext LIFFE. A contract market is also called a designated exchange.

Contract Price In common law, the amount of money one receives in exchange for providing a good or service outlined in a contract. The contract price must be stated in the contract. For example, if two parties make a contract to sell a house for $100,000, the contract price is $100,000.

Contract Unit A standardized size represented in a single option or futures contract. For example, a contract unit may be so many bushels or so many kilograms. The contract unit differs according to the commodity that underlies the contract.

Contraction In a business cycle, the time between the peak and the bottom. That is, a contraction occurs between the end of economic growth and the end of the subsequent recession. Contractions are characterized by layoffs, a decline in GDP, and other negative factors. However, historically, contractions have tended not to last as long as expansions.

Contraction Risk The risk that the duration of a debt security will decline because of prepayment. Duration is the length of time it takes to receive the present value of future principal and interest payments on a debt security; prepayment will deprive the holder of a bond of future coupons, resulting in less interest and therefore a shorter duration. Contraction risk is most prominent in mortgage-backed securities. See also: Prepayment risk.

Contractual Claim An amount to which one party of a contract is entitled. For example, if two parties agree to transfer a security in exchange for a fee, that fee is the contractual claim.

Contractual Intermediary A financial institution that stands between counterparties in a transaction. For example, in the sale of a house, a bank usually serves as a contractual intermediary by providing a mortgage to the homebuyer. In some non-traditional transactions, a bank may buy a product (e.g. corn) and immediately re-sell it for a profit to a third party. Most transactions requiring a loan to one of the parties, including intermediaries. See also: Murabaha.

Contramarket Stock Stocks that tend to do well when most of the market is performing poorly and that do poorly when the market is performing well. A key to finding contramarket stocks, in addition to regular due diligence like surveying past performance, is finding companies that might profit when people either do not have money or think that they do not. For example, budget retailers and fast food restaurants tend to be stable and even experience some earnings growth. Likewise they may not do as well during economic expansion because more consumers seek luxury products.

Contrarian An investor who buys securities that others are selling and sells those that others are buying. A contrarian operates on the premise that most other investors are wrong most of the time since they tend to overreact to both good news and bad news. As a result, a contrarian assumes that either prices will revert to the mean and he/she will make a small profit, or that investors are entirely wrong and the market is moving in another direction, in which case the contrarian will realize a larger profit. See also: Crowd.

Contribution Money placed into an annuity or retirement account. Most of the time, contributions are small and are made on a regular basis, especially monthly. Occasionally, however, one may make a large, one-time contribution to purchase the annuity or retirement account. Contributions are combined and invested and, along with any earnings, are eventually repaid to the annuitant or account holder in monthly installments.

Contribution Margin The profit a company makes on a product calculated by subtracting its variable revenues from its variable costs. Because variable revenues and costs are largely dependent on the business cycle, a company with a high contribution margin is likely to have an even higher margin during economic expansion.

Contributory Pension Plan A pension where the pensioner (or employee) must make contributions. The employer often makes matching contributions to increase the value of the pension plan. Most pensions are contributory pension plans. See also: Noncontributory Pension Plan.

Contributory Value In real estate, a portion of the land or the improvements on it that increases its value. For example, the contributory value of the mother-in-law suite in a back yard may increase the value of a home by $25,000.

Control Half plus one of ownership of a company. Control gives the person or group having it the ability to make all decisions on how the company operates. In a publicly-traded company, control comes from buying more than half of the common stock.

Control Person An important person in a corporation. Control persons include senior managers, members of the board of directors, and officers such as the CEO and CFO. Control persons are able to use both their authority and their influence to make decisions on the corporation's activities. A control person is also called an affiliated person.

Control Value The number of shares outstanding in a company that is sufficient to be able to control the company. In a publicly-traded company, the control value may be 50% + 1 for ordinary decisions, or a supermajority of shares for more important decisions. If one person or company owns a control value, such shares command a higher price than other shares because each share represents a level of oversight in the company that non-control shares do not possess.

Controlled Commodities Commodities regulated by the Commodity Exchange Act of 1936. This Act provided that all futures and options on commodities be traded on an exchange. Controlled commodities are thus all exchange-traded.

Controlled Foreign Corporation A company registered in and regulated by a foreign country that has at least 50% American ownership. Setting up a corporation in a foreign country may have tax advantages; for example, a country may encourage companies to register in it by having no corporate tax. The IRS works within the context of foreign treaties to determine how earnings from controlled foreign corporations are taxed in the United States.

Controller The chief accountant in a company or government. The controller is the head of the accounting department and is responsible for financial and managerial accounting. He/she helps management interpret and appropriately respond to accounting data. A controller is also called a comptroller.

Controlling Interest Fifty percent plus one ownership of the stock in a publicly-traded company. This gives the person or company with the controlling interest outright control of the company's operations, especially the election of its board of directors. Some investors with controlling interest are not involved in the daily operations of the company, but most are. Indeed, an individual person with controlling interest is often the company's founder. The person or company with controlling interest is called the majority shareholder. See also: Parent company.

Convenience Yield The extra gain that an investor receives for holding a commodity rather than an option or futures contract on that commodity. Because of the uncertainty of future events, the convenience yield can be (though is not always) quite high. For example, if one holds so many barrels of oil and there is a sudden disruption in a major pipeline, the value of the physical barrel will increase while the value of a futures contract on oil likely will decrease.

Convention A method under the Modified Accelerated Cost Recovery System one uses to calculate the depreciation of an asset in the year it is purchased (or first used) and the year of the end of its useful life.

Convention Expenses Expenses incurred when a person attends a business-related convention. For example, if a dentist travels to another location to attend an American Dental Association meeting, lodging, meals, and transportation costs usually count as convention expenses. One may deduct convention expenses from one's taxable income, provided they are, in fact, directly related to business. For this reason, convention expenses are somewhat controversial; some companies, for example, book a business meeting at a major resort and then deduct the entire cost. Whether or not this is an actual convention expense is a source of debate.

Convention Statement A statement a life insurance company must file with a state government each year. Requirements for convention statements vary by state, but all states mandate that the company report its assets, liabilities, and current surplus. A single life insurance company must file a convention statement in each state where it does business.

Conventional Option An American option or European option that is not traded on an exchange. That is, a conventional option has no special features that would exclude it from an exchange but, nonetheless, is privately negotiated and agreed between the parties. A conventional option is illiquid because there is little secondary market for it. It has become a rare investment vehicle, as trading options on exchanges have become more common.

Conventional Project A project that currently has negative cash flow but is expected one day to have positive cash flow. The length of time it takes for a conventional project to go from negative to positive cash flow largely determines its success.

Convergence The fact that the futures price and the spot price for a given asset approach one another as a futures contract on that asset approaches maturity. At maturity, the two prices should be equal. The existence of convergence is the basis for the theory that forward rates equal future spot rates, though this idea is more controversial.

Conversion The act of exchanging a convertible security for the underlying common stock. For example, if one holds a convertible bond in company A, conversion occurs when the holder gives the convertible bond back to company A and, in return, either receives for free or buys at a stated price, common shares in the same company.

Conversion Feature The ability to change from one investment vehicle to another. For example, one may be able to switch between mutual funds in a fund family without incurring a penalty. Likewise, one may exchange a convertible bond to common stock in the issuing company. Sometimes, one even may be able to change an adjustable-rate mortgage into a fixed-rate mortgage. All of these examples describe a conversion feature on the investment vehicles.

Conversion Period The period of time during which a convertible security may be exchanged for common stock. The length of the conversion period depends upon the particular security; sometimes it lasts until maturity and sometimes it expires. If a conversion period has an expiration date, the issuing company may extend it at its discretion. See also: Conversion ratio.

Conversion Premium The amount by which a convertible security is trading above the common stock into which it may be converted. Most convertible securities trade at a conversion premium, though it usually lessens as the common stock increases in price.

Conversion Price In a convertible security, the price at which the owner is allowed to buy an equal number of common shares in exchange for trading in the convertible security. This price is set at the sale of the convertible security. For example, a company may buy an issue of convertible bonds (a low-risk investment) from another company with the agreement that if the company's stock increases greatly in value, the first company may trade its bonds for the right to a certain number of the company's stocks at a set, low price. This price is the conversion price.

Conversion Privilege 1. In insurance, a policy in which both the premiums and the coverage are guaranteed for a certain number of years, regardless of the health of the insured person. This privilege is operative as long as premiums are paid on time. The insurer may only increase the premium if premiums are increased to the whole class of policyholders. **2.** The right of a policyholder to convert a group policy to an individual policy without a health examination. This right is usually exercised after the termination of employment, and the premium is determined by the policyholder's attained age.

Conversion Ratio The number of common shares obtainable for each convertible security should the investor exercise the convertible option. A higher ratio means that more common shares are available per convertible security. It is calculated using the following formula: Conversion Ratio = Face Value of Convertible Security / Conversion Price.

Convert To change a convertible security into the underlying security. For example, if one converts a convertible bond for Johnson & Johnson, one exchanges the bond for the agreed-upon number of common shares in Johnson & Johnson. See also: Conversion option, Conversion price.

Converted Put The purchase of a call option and the short sale of the underlying asset. This is effectively the same as buying a put option because one makes a profit if the underlying asset decreases in price. For this reason, a converted put is also called a synthetic put.

Convertibility The state of or the ease with which a currency may be exchanged for a foreign currency. Currency convertibility is vitally important in the foreign exchange market; higher convertibility means that a currency is more liquid and, therefore, less difficult to trade. Factors affecting convertibility include the availability of foreign currency reserves in a given country and domestic regulations seeking to protect local investors from bad investment decisions in, say, a currency undergoing a period of hyperinflation. A few socialist governments even issue inconvertible currencies, such as the Cuban peso, in order to protect their citizens from perceived capitalist infiltration. See also: Inconvertibility.

Convertible A bond or preferred stock that may be exchanged for common stock in the company issuing the convertible at a certain ratio and/or a certain price. A convertible security gives the holder a great deal of flexibility. It reduces risk by guaranteeing a coupon payment or dividend while also allowing the holder to take advantage of a potential, larger return through the ability to convert the security. See also: Convertible option.

Convertible Adjustable Preferred Stock A preferred stock that pays a dividend tied to U.S. Treasury securities. CAPS are convertible to common stock at par value at any time, especially after profits are announced but before dividends are paid. CAPS have the advantage of protecting the investor's principal while also allowing him/her to take advantage of upswings in the company's value.

Convertible Arbitrage An investment strategy in which one buys a convertible bond and short sells the underlying common stock. The idea behind convertible arbitrage is to profit from inefficiency in the pricing of the convertible bond. However, convertible arbitrage is risky and requires monitoring because the pricing inefficiencies may only be temporary. It is a strategy associated with hedge funds. See also: Chinese hedge.

Convertible Bond A bond that a bondholder may exchange, at a certain price, for common stock in the company issuing the bond. The number of shares one receives for each bond and the price one pays for those shares are determined when the convertible bond is issued. A convertible bond is a low-risk investment, but it affords the investor a great amount of leeway because he/she can exchange it for another security with higher risk and a higher return. Certain convertible bonds may only be exchanged at certain points in their lives. The extent to which bondholders exchange convertible bonds is sometimes seen as an indication of whether the share price is overvalued or undervalued. See also: Busted convertible, Overhanging bond, Convertible preferred stock.

Convertible Currency A currency that may be exchanged for a foreign currency. Currency convertibility is vitally important in the foreign exchange market; higher convertibility means that a currency is more liquid and, therefore, less difficult to trade. Factors affecting convertibility include the availability of foreign currency reserves in a given country and domestic regulations seeking to protect local investors from bad investment decisions in, for example, a currency undergoing a period of hyperinflation. A few socialist governments even issue inconvertible currencies, such as the Cuban peso, in order to protect their citizens from perceived capitalist infiltration. See also: Inconvertibility.

Convertible Debenture An unsecured, convertible bond. That is, a convertible debenture is a bond with no collateral that may, at the bondholder's discretion, be exchanged for common stock in the company issuing the bond. See also: Compulsory convertible debenture.

Convertible Dinar A currency used in the former Yugoslavia. It was introduced in 1990, replacing the hard dinar. Most of the constituent countries of Yugoslavia became independent, and it was replaced by the reformed dinar in 1992.

Convertible Eurobond A bond denominated in a currency, other than that of the issuing country, that may be exchanged for common shares or other assets. Generally speaking, one exercises the conversion option of a Eurobond indirectly through warrants attached to it.

Convertible Exchangeable Preferred Stock Preferred stock in a publicly-traded company that, at the discretion of the stockholder, may be exchanged for either common stock or convertible bonds. If the stockholder elects to trade for convertible bonds, he/she retains the ability to exchange the bond for common stock on the exact same terms.

Convertible Floating-Rate Note A debt security with a floating interest rate that may be exchanged for another debt security with a higher, fixed interest rate. Most floating-rate notes expose holders to the risk that declining interest rates will reduce their returns. A convertible floating-rate note protects holders by giving them the option to lock-in their return, should interest rates fall significantly.

Convertible Hedge A position in which one owns a convertible bond in a publicly-traded company while also selling short the common stock in the same company. The idea behind a convertible hedge is to profit regardless of whether the common stock increases or decreases in price. If the stock goes up, the investor loses on the short sale, but can profit by exercising the conversion option on the bond and selling the underlying stock. If the stock goes down, the investor profits from the short sale and does not exercise the conversion option, keeping the coupon payments from the bond.

Convertible Preferred Stock A preferred stock that a stockholder may exchange, at any time after a waiting period, for common stock in the company issuing the bond. The number of shares one receives for each preferred share is determined when the convertible preferred stock is issued. A convertible preferred stock is a relatively low-risk investment because of the guaranteed dividends, but it affords the investor a great amount of leeway because he/she can exchange it for

common shares, which have higher risk and higher returns. See also: Conversion ratio, Convertible bond.

Convertible Security A bond or preferred stock that may be exchanged for common stock in the company issuing the exchangeable security at a certain ratio and/or a certain price. A convertible security gives the holder a great deal of flexibility. It reduces risk by guaranteeing a coupon payment or dividend while also allowing the holder to take advantage of a potentially larger return through the ability to convert the security to common stock. It is less commonly called an exchangeable security. See also: Convertible Option.

Convertible Subordinate Note A short-term, convertible bond that, in the event of the issuer's liquidation, has lower priority with respect to other debt. That is, a convertible subordinate note is a bond that may be changed into common stock at the discretion of the bondholder. If the issuer goes bankrupt and liquidates, one or more other debt securities must be repaid before the convertible subordinate note may be repaid. However, as with all debt securities, it has priority over all stock.

Convertible Term A term life insurance policy that the policyholder may convert into a whole life insurance policy without a health exam. A whole life insurance policy carries more risk for the insurance company, especially if there is no health exam to help determine the premium. As a result, convertible term policies have higher premiums at the outset than other term life policies.

Convex Describing a curve. Generally speaking, analysts use convex to describe the price-yield relationship of coupon bonds.

Convexity Describing a curve segment whose ends fall above an arbitrarily set straight line. Convex properties are important to charting; for example, when tracking a stock market's performance, a rise in the chart with respect to the previous day's close followed by a correction going down to but not necessarily meeting that close may be described as a convex curve. See also: Concave.

Conveyance A written document transferring property from one owner to the next. Most often, conveyance is applied to real estate; that is, when one sells his/her house, he/she conveys the deed to the next owner. Conveyance may also apply, however, to the transfer of bulk commodities. Depending on local law and practice, all parties involved in a conveyance (or their attorneys) must be present and literally trade documents to effect the change in ownership.

Conveyance Tax A tax that a government (usually a local government) imposes on the transfer of real estate. See also: Stamp duty.

Cook Islands Dollar The currency of the Cook Islands. It was introduced in 1972, replacing the New Zealand dollar, to which it is still pegged at a one-to-one ratio.

Cook the Books Informal; to falsify an accounting statement deliberately. Cooking the books usually involves overstating revenue and/or understating expenses. A person can use aggressive accounting to cook the books by using creative ways to make a company look healthier than it is. More directly, a person can simply lie on a financial statement. Cooking the books is illegal.

Cookie Jar Accounting An accounting method in which a company understates how healthy it is when its finances are doing well and likewise, overstates its health when it is performing poorly. The company generally does this by applying excess revenues from good years to bad years. While this is common and expected to an extent, it can be detrimental to the company and its investors if taken too far. See also: Carryforward, Carryback, Aggressive Accounting.

Cooler An investor who has lost money in stocks and attempts to liquidate some or all of his/her positions.

Cooling Degree Day A day on which the temperature in a certain area is above 65 degrees Fahrenheit, necessitating the use of air conditioners. Cooling degree days are used in some weather futures, which are contracts in which the buyer is required to pay the seller some multiple of $20 for each cooling degree day in a month, depending on how much warmer it is. Weather futures allow businesses to hedge against potential losses resulting from unexpected changes in weather. Energy companies are the most common sellers of weather futures. They have become relatively popular investments. See also: Heating degree day.

Cooling-Off Period An SEC rule mandating that several days transpire between the filing of a new issue's prospectus and the actual offering of the issue. This allows potential buyers and the seller to have a final chance to investigate the new issue and attempt to determine if there will be any previously unforeseen problems. The cooling off period is usually 20 days, but the SEC may change that for individual offerings at its discretion. It is also called the waiting period.

Cooling-Off Rule 1. A rule of the SEC mandating that several days transpire between the filing of a new issue's prospectus and the actual offering of the issue. This allows potential buyers and the seller to have a final chance to investigate the new issue and attempt to determine if there are any previously unforeseen problems. The cooling-off period is usually 20 days, but the SEC may change that for individual offerings at its discretion. 2. A clause in many contracts allowing the buyer of a good to return it to the seller in exchange for the amount paid for it for up to three days, without committing breach of contract. The cooling-off rule allows a buyer to restore the status quo before the contract was entered for any reason for a limited period of time. It is also known as buyer's remorse.

Cooperative Any organization owned by its members. A cooperative may be a business owned by its employees and/or customers, a residential complex owned by the people who live in it, or even a bank owned by its depositors. Certain legal requirements are incumbent upon cooperatives; for example, there is often a cap on how much of their profits may be distributed. See also: Cooperative economics.

Cooperative Competition A term referring to the benefits two or more companies experience while competing with each other for customers or markets. The term may be used ironically since it is, at first glance, an oxymoron.

Cooperative Education A program in which an educational institution combines theoretical study with practical experience. Traditionally, cooperative education alternates semesters between classroom study and full-time, paid employment in a position related to one's field. It is also called work study.

Coopetition Competition within an organization to the organization's detriment. For example, the attempt by departments in the company to maximize their own budgets may result in an inefficient allocation of resources such that the company cannot be profitable.

COP 1. ISO 4217 code for the Colombian peso. Instituted in 1837, it was pegged to the U.S. dollar for a time. Since 1955, however, the peso has floated. It has gradually deteriorated in value since. 2. Certificate of Participation. An investment in which the investor purchases the right to a share of a municipality's or government entity's lease revenues instead of a bond secured by those revenues. Government entities issue COPs to avoid limitations on debt legally placed upon them. This is roughly a government entity's equivalent to accounts receivable financing. In the United States, the organizations issuing or guaranteeing COPs are Ginnie Mae, Fannie Mae, Freddie Mac, and Sallie Mae. They are also called participation certificates or PCs. See also: Lease revenue bond.

Copayment In insurance, a fee that a policyholder must pay for certain covered items for which the insurance company otherwise pays. For example, a check-up with a doctor may cost the policyholder a copayment of $25, with the insurance company paying for the remainder of the cost due. A copayment is also called a co-pay and should not be confused with a deductible. It exists to discourage policyholders from abusing the insurance policy.

Copenhagen Stock Exchange An electronic stock exchange in Denmark. It is owned by the NASDAQ OMX Group and is itself the parent company of FUTOP, the derivatives exchange in Denmark. See also: OMX Copenhagen 20.

Coppock Curve In technical analysis, a system for determining stock market rallies. The system uses a ten-month weighted moving average of the sum of eleven- and fourteen-month rates of change. Buy signals are determined when the curve turns upward after being below zero; analysts disagree as to whether the curve shows sell signals. The curve is thought to be a good way to determine rallies for stock markets, but not for more volatile commodity markets.

Copyright The right to distribute, copy, or change an original work for a limited period of time. A state grants copyright to the creator of the work, but the creator may assign or sell the right. During the time the copyright persists, one must (with some exceptions) receive permission from the owner to publish or distribute the copyrighted material. After a certain period of time, any person may distribute the work without permission. See also: Public domain.

Cord A unit of volume used to measure quantities of firewood in Canada and the United States. The cord is equivalent to 3.62 cubic meters.

Core Bank A commercial bank that is a major presence globally or in a certain area. For example Goldman Sachs is a core bank worldwide. Core banks have highly diversified assets but carry a great deal of systemic risk. Some may be considered too big to fail.

Core Capital The capital that a thrift is required to maintain. According to FHLB rules, a thrift must have enough core capital to cover 2% of its assets.

Core Competence The primary field in which a business operates or is believed to be a leader. Core competence is the expertise in which a company is thought to excel and provide the greatest benefit to customers. This is important both in marketing and in the creation of business models. For example, a company will likely be able to charge higher fees for goods or services in its core competence.

Core Holding A stock in a portfolio that one holds for the long-term. For example, if one buys a blue-chip stock and never sells it, this is considered a core holding in one's portfolio. Stocks that investors include in their core holdings are usually relatively low-risk and have a history of a solid (if not very large) return.

Core Holdings Assets or other holdings an investment company or other organization keeps over the long-term. Core holdings generally are low-risk securities with a history of solid performance. Poor performance for core holdings can be disastrous for the holder.

Core Inflation A measure of inflation that attempts to predict future inflation by excluding price volatility. It is thought to be a better measure of underlying inflation as it does not account for temporary price shocks. Some economists who measure core inflation exclude certain markets that tend to be volatile, such as energy and food, while others include all markets but exclude the markets that have had the greatest volatility over the last given period.

Core Plus An investment strategy in portfolios and mutual funds in which the majority (sometimes up to 75%) of the portfolio consists of low-risk and risk-free securities, such as Treasury and investment-grade bonds, that are held for the long-term, while the remainder consists of securities carrying higher risk. One adopts a core plus strategy in order to attempt to capitalize on certain securities while also limiting risk. It is one of the more common investment strategies.

Corner a Market 1. To own a significant enough amount of a stock to be able to manipulate its price. More specifically, an investor corners a market when he/she owns so many shares in a company that he/she can trigger a sell off if he/she dumps the stock. For this reason, persons and institutions owning or buying more than a

certain percentage of shares in a company must register with the SEC and are subject to certain restrictions. 2. To have the greatest market share in a particular industry without having a monopoly. Companies that have cornered their markets usually have greater leeway in their decisions; for example, they may charge higher prices for their products without fear of losing too much business. Large companies, such as Wal-Mart or Microsoft, are considered to have cornered their markets. See also: Gorilla.

Cornish Acre A Cornish unit of area equivalent to either 64 or 120 acres.

Cornish Apple Gallon A Cornish unit of weight equivalent to seven pounds.

Cornish Burn A Cornish unit of measure equivalent to 21 fish.

Cornish Bushel A Cornish unit of volume equivalent to 18 gallons. It is used for barley, potatoes and wheat.

Cornish Cran A Cornish unit of measure equivalent to 800 fish.

Cornish Fathom A Cornish unit of length equivalent to five feet.

Cornish Ferling A Cornish unit of area equivalent to either 16 or 30 acres.

Cornish Gallon A Cornish unit of weight equivalent to 10 pounds.

Cornish Hundred A Cornish unit of measure equivalent to 132 fish.

Cornish Knight's Fee A Cornish unit of area equivalent to either 256 or 480 acres.

Cornish Lace A Cornish unit of area equivalent to 18 square feet.

Cornish Land Rod A Cornish unit of area equivalent to nine square feet. It is also called a Cornish lorgh.

Cornish Last A Cornish unit of measure equivalent to 132,000 fish.

Cornish Lease A Cornish unit of area equivalent to 12 square yards.

Cornish Long Hundred A Cornish unit of measure equivalent to 965 fish.

Cornish Mease A Cornish unit of measure equivalent to 505 herring.

Cornish Metric Gallon A Cornish unit of weight equivalent to five kilograms.

Cornish Mile A Cornish unit of length equivalent to one and a half miles.

Cornish Ounce A Cornish unit of measure equivalent to a 1/16 of a piece of real estate or a set of fish.

Cornish Pound A Cornish unit of weight equivalent to 18 ounces. It is used for butter.

Cornish Rod A Cornish unit of area equivalent to 2,880 square feet.

Cornish Stick A Cornish unit of area equivalent to three square yards.

Cornish Ton A Cornish unit of weight equivalent to 2,100 pounds.

Cornish Warp A Cornish unit of measure equivalent to four fish.

Coronet Large Cent A one-cent piece minted by the United States between 1816 and 1839. It was worth 1/100 of one dollar. It was sometimes called the Matron Head cent.

Corporate Action Any action a publicly-traded company takes that affects its shareholders and/or bondholders, whether positively or negatively. Common examples of corporate action include stock splits, where the company doubles the number of its shares, and calling bonds, where a company deprives bondholders of coupons to which they would otherwise have been entitled. Corporate actions must be approved by the board of directors and in many circumstances shareholders may vote on the measures as well.

Corporate and Criminal Fraud Accountability Act of 2002 The portion of the Sarbanes-Oxley Act (which strengthened accounting disclosure requirements) that states the criminal penalties for falsification or destruction of records and interference with an investigation. It also protects whistleblowers.

Corporate Anorexia A situation in which a company does not have a sufficient number of employees to remain profitable. Corporate anorexia sometimes occurs after large layoffs. It is a difficult position for a company: it cannot make money with the employees it has, but cannot afford any more employees. An anorexic company can have difficulty remaining in business.

Corporate Bankruptcy The legal process by which a company or other business declares that it is unable to pay its debts and requires relief. In the United States, there are two kinds of corporate bankruptcy. Chapter 7 provides for liquidation of a business and the discharge of debts. Chapter 11 allows corporations to continue operations after reorganization and forgives debts that companies cannot repay.

Corporate Bond Debt securities issued by a for-profit company instead of a government. Corporate bonds are a major way companies raise funds for their operations or for a specific project. The risk of a corporate bond for a bondholder depends on the creditworthiness of the issuing company. As with all bonds, corporate bonds have a maturity, at which time the principal is repaid to bondholders. They also usually have a stated coupon rate. Corporate bonds are taxable.

Corporate Bond Fund A mutual fund consisting only of corporate bonds. A common stock fund may be high-risk if it invests primarily in junk bonds, or it may be low-risk if it invests in established investment-grade bonds.

Corporate Bond Short-Term Fund A mutual fund that invests predominantly or exclusively in corporate bonds (that is, bonds issued by private sector companies) with maturities of less than a year or so. These funds are considered beneficial when interest rates are falling (and therefore when bond prices are rising) because the funds sell bonds, creating gains from the higher prices. Corporate bond short-term funds generally carry lower risks than mutual funds investing primarily in stocks, but the levels of risk vary according to the credit ratings of the companies whose bonds are represented in the fund.

Corporate Cannibalism An act or strategy in which a company introduces a new product into a market where the same company's products are already well established. A company engaging in corporate cannibalism is effectively competing against itself. There are two main reasons companies do this. First, the company wants to increase its market share and is taking a gamble that introducing the new product will harm other competitors more than the company itself. Secondly, the company may believe that the new product will sell better than the first, or will sell to a different sort of buyer. For example, a company may manufacture cars, and later begin manufacturing trucks. While both products appeal to the same general market (drivers) one may fit an individual's needs better than the other. However, corporate cannibalism often has negative effects: the car manufactures customer base may begin buying trucks instead of cars, resulting in good truck sales, but not increasing the company's market share. There may even be a decrease. It is also called market cannibalization.

Corporate Citizenship A company's responsibility to its community and to the world as a whole. A company's corporate citizenship includes passive acts such as avoiding pollution or positive acts such as building a park near its factory. A company may engage in corporate citizenship for charitable or philanthropic reasons, but may also do so to protect its profits. That is, a company known for poor corporate citizenship is more likely to invite boycotts or to drive away potential customers. See also: Ethical investing.

Corporate Equivalent A comparison of yield between taxable bonds selling at par and tax-exempt bonds selling at a discount. A corporate bond yields less than its stated interest rate because of taxation, whereas a tax-exempt municipal bond does not. Thus, a municipal bond paying a lower interest rate will often net the bondholder more than a corporate bond with a slightly higher interest rate, depending upon one's tax bracket. The corporate equivalent yield measures how much this difference is. See also: Municipals-over-bonds spread.

Corporate Financial Management The act or practice of developing strategies and plans and making investment decisions that positively affect the operations of a corporation. Corporate financial management involves setting goals, planning how to achieve them, and, perhaps most importantly, deciding the best way to pay for them.

Corporate Financial Planning The process of determining a company's financial needs or goals for the future and how to achieve them. Corporate financial planning involves deciding what investments and activities would be most appropriate under both the company's individual and broader economic circumstances. All things being equal, short-term financial planning involves less uncertainty than long-term financial planning because, generally speaking, market trends are more easily predictable in the short term. Likewise, short-term financial plans are more easily amendable in case something goes wrong.

Corporate Financing Committee A body of FINRA that reviews SEC filing materials prior to a new issue of a security. Its most important duty is to ensure that mark-ups that underwriters charge for shares of the new issue are fair. It also existed when FINRA was the National Association of Securities Dealers.

Corporate Governance The manner in which the stakeholders in a corporation relate to one another. Corporate governance has a positive connotation and a company with "good" corporate governance is said to be a company in which all stakeholders relate to each other in a positive way. Good corporate governance is considered an important quality of sustainable growth for a company; that is, if the shareholders, management, and employees all fulfill their fiduciary responsibilities to one another, the corporation is thought to have a greater likelihood of success. Corporate governance is laid out in the corporation's charter and other applicable documents.

Corporate Income Fund A unit investment trust with highly-rated securities in a fixed portfolio. Corporate income funds usually pay out applicable interest monthly, and they can be traded on the secondary market.

Corporate Inflation-Linked Securities A bond or other debt security issued by a private (that is, non-government) company with an interest rate that varies according to inflation. A corporate inflation-linked security, for example, may pay a fixed coupon plus an additional coupon with the amount adjusted every so often according to some inflation indicator, such as the Consumer Price Index. If these securities are held to maturity, then the investor guarantees that the return will exceed the rate of inflation. Corporate inflation-linked securities exist to provide a low-risk investment vehicle in which the return is guaranteed not to fall below the rate of inflation. See also: I Bond.

Corporate Inversion The act of a parent company based in the United States switching its registration address with that of one of its offshore subsidies in order to take advantage of lower corporation taxes. Corporate inversion has gradually become more popular, though the U.S. government is attempting to limit its use.

Corporate Kleptocracy A slang term for greed among executives that harms shareholders or the general public. An example was Enron's use of aggressive accounting techniques to artificially inflate stock prices, which ultimately destroyed employees' retirement plans and the value for shareholders. The term is highly derogatory.

Corporate Processing Float The time required to process a customer's payments. A company may receive a payment, but due to its bank's regulations, or a holiday, or some other reason, it may not be able to process the payment and take the money out of the customer's account for several hours to several days. See also: Check hold.

Corporate Raider A person or company that is offering or executing a hostile takeover by buying shares directly from shareholders. If a firm makes an offer to shareholders to acquire a publicly-traded company after the board of directors refuses, or if it bypasses the board completely, one refers to the acquiring firm as a corporate raider. Often, the corporate raider does not actually intend to take over the target company, but is simply trying to force the board of directors to repurchase shares at a premium to their market value. A corporate raider that accumulates more than 5% of a company's outstanding shares must register with the SEC. It is also known simply as a raider. See also: Greenmail, Premium raid.

Corporate Tax A tax levied on corporations' profits. Because corporations are legal entities separate from their owners, they may be taxed as if they were persons. A corporate tax, then, is the equivalent of the income tax for natural persons. Corporate taxes vary from country to country; in the United States, they are levied at both the federal and state levels. Proponents of the corporate tax argue it guards against excessive profits that may result from unethical or illegal corporate practices, while opponents say that corporations simply pass on the tax to their customers.

Corporate Tax View An argument stating that double taxation makes the issuing of stocks more expensive than debt financing. That is, those who hold the corporate tax view argue that since the owners of a corporation must pay both corporate taxes and individual taxes, rather than forming a corporation and issuing stock, owners of the corporation ought to consider borrowing, as it is a cheaper way to pay for expanded operations in the long run.

Corporate Taxable Equivalent The yield to maturity on a bond issued at par that would equal the after-tax yield to maturity on a similar bond that is issued at a premium or discount to par. See also: Taxable equivalent yield.

Corporate Trust A trust that a corporation creates to secure a bond or other debt security. That is, a corporate trust is effectively money set aside to ensure that bondholders are covered in the event of default on the issue.

Corporate Veil The legal separation of a corporation from its shareholders. That is, because of the corporate veil, shareholders are not responsible for paying the debts of the corporation (beyond the level of their own investment) and generally are not legally liable for any crimes the corporation might commit. While the corporate veil protects shareholders, it may be disregarded under certain circumstances, notably if a shareholder assisted the corporation in the commission of a crime. See also: Piercing the corporate veil.

Corporate Welfare Bum Highly derogatory; an executive or company taking money from the public treasury through subsidies, large contracts or other means. The term connotes an individual or company that enriches itself without contributing to the development of an economy or creating jobs to any significant extent.

Corporation A business that is legally completely separate from its owners. Most publicly-traded companies (and all major ones) fall under this classification. For United States tax purposes, corporations, legally known as C corporations, are required to pay income taxes on their profits. The advantage to a corporate structure is the fact that, unlike other structures, there is no limit to the number of shareholders. A disadvantage is the fact that, because a corporation is taxed by itself and its individual shareholders are taxed on dividends, it is subject to double taxation. It is important to note that the term corporation almost never refers to an S corporation, which is not entirely separate from its owners.

CORR In ticker tapes, shorthand used to indicate that a previous statement was inaccurate and needs to be corrected. "CORR" is stated at the beginning of the statement to show that it is a correction.

Corrective Advertising Advertising, usually required by a regulatory agency, that corrects a perceived inaccuracy in previous advertising. For example, a commercial for dog food may give the impression, without scientific evidence, that it improves tooth health in canines. A watchdog group may require the manufacturer to run corrective advertising to clarify the matter.

Corregimiento In Panama, a political subdivision roughly equivalent to a municipal government.

Correlation Coefficient A measure of whether and by how much two variables are related. A correlation coefficient may be between -1 and +1. Suppose there are two variables, A and B, with -A and -B indicating their opposites. A correlation coefficient of -1 indicates that A and -B are correlated and vice versa. On the other hand, a correlation coefficient of +1 means that A and B are correlated.

Correspondent Bank A bank that has limited access to certain financial markets and therefore must use the services of another bank to conduct certain transactions. Correspondent banks are usually small. Agreements with other banks allow it to provide necessary services for account holders without incurring the expense of setting up a branch in another city or country.

Cosigner A third party to a loan who provides a guarantee that a loan will be repaid. The guarantee by the cosigner reduces the risk that the lender will lose the money he/she has distributed to the borrower. The cosigner signs an agreement with the lender stating that if the borrower fails to repay the loan, the cosigner will assume legal liability for it. A cosigner may be an institution, but is often a relative or friend of the borrower, especially for personal loans. Persons with little or poor credit history sometimes cannot receive a loan without a cosigner. See also: Surety.

Cost The amount of money or property paid for a good or service. Cost is an expense for both personal and business assets. If a cost is for a business expense, it may be tax deductible. A cost may be paid immediately in the form of cash or over time in a credit sale or similar transaction. Cost is the opposite of revenue: It may be thought of as money spent instead of made.

Cost Accounting A branch of accounting that observes and calculates the actual costs of a company's operations. Internal managers, rather than auditors, use cost accounting most of the time to identify aspects of their company where costs can be cut. For example, a manager may enlist a cost accountant to determine the most expensive aspects of his/her business that is, where the money goes. The accountant may make a detailed report so that the manager may make decisions based upon it. Because cost accounting is primarily internal, it need not conform to the Generally Accepted Accounting Principles. It is also called managerial or management accounting. See also: Assurance, Activity-based costing.

Cost and Freight A CPT involving ocean freight. In a CFR, the seller is responsible for paying for shipping, while the buyer is responsible for transportation risk as soon as the good or product is loaded onto the ship. Legally, risk transfers when the good or product crosses the outer rail of the ship. See also: Incoterm.

Cost Basis 1. The price of an asset for tax purposes. That is, one uses the cost basis of an asset to determine the capital gain or loss on an investment. For example, if an investor buys 1,000 shares of a stock for $10 per share and, at the end of the tax year, the stock is worth $15 per share, the cost basis is $10 per share. The investor uses this to determine that his/her capital gain on that stock for the tax year was $5 per share. It is important to note, however, that the cost basis is rarely the simple purchase price; it also includes applicable fees or commissions paid to the broker. This would increase the cost basis in the above example and thereby reduce the investor's capital gain. **2.** The difference between the present price of a commodity and the futures price. See also: Spread.

Cost Center A department or other section of a company where managers are directly responsible for costs. For example, consider a company that has a manufacturing department, a research and development department, and a payroll department. Each department could be a cost center, and the directors of each department would be responsible to keep costs to as low a level as possible. The company thus accounts for each cost center separately, which allows managers to take immediate responsibility for cost growth and credit for cost cutting.

Cost Company Arrangement An agreement between the producers of a product or project and its financiers whereby the financiers are entitled to receive the product for free, provided they pay all the costs associated with producing it.

Cost Containment Any act or strategy that attempts to reduce a company's spending. Limiting use of the corporate credit card by managers or disallowing personal long distance phone calls are both examples of cost containment.

Cost Equivalent In inventories, an estimation of the cost for older items in inventory calculated when the actual records are unavailable.

Cost Hierarchy A listing of all a company's or department's activities according to how expensive they are. While more expensive activities are not automatically reduced or eliminated, a cost hierarchy may make prioritization of activities easier, which may in turn influence budgeting decisions.

Cost of Attendance The amount of money one must spend to study at a post-secondary educational institution for a year while maintaining himself/herself. The cost of attendance includes tuition, room and board, and books. The cost of attendance may be paid directly or it may be borrowed and repaid over time.

Cost of Capital The difference in return between an investment one makes and another that one chose not to make. This may occur in securities trading or in other decisions. For example, if a person has $10,000 to invest and must choose between Stock A and Stock B, the cost of capital is the difference in their returns. If that person invests $10,000 in Stock A and receives a 5% return, while Stock B makes a 7% return, the cost of capital is 2%. One way of conceptualizing the cost of capital is as the amount of money one could have made by making a different investment decision. Many companies calculate the cost of capital when deciding whether to issue stock or a bond, to determine which would be cheaper.

Cost of Carry The cost of storing a commodity over a period of time. It includes incidental costs, insurance coverage, and the physical cost of storage. It does not include depreciation, if any. The carrying charge is incorporated in the price of a commodity on the futures market. See also: Carrying costs.

Cost of Equity The required rate of return that a stockholder demands from a publicly-traded company in exchange for buying a share and assuming the risk associated with it. It is calculated thusly: Cost of Equity = (Dividends per share / Price per share) + Dividend growth rate.

Cost of Funds The amount of money paid in interest on a loan. The cost of funds is an expense for both personal and business loans. It also refers to the interest rate in addition to the absolute amount in interest.

Cost of Goods Sold The cost to a business of making the products it sells over a given period of time. The cost of goods sold includes parts and labor expenses, but does not include shipping, advertising, or other indirect costs. COGS is included on a company's balance sheet and may be subtracted from revenue when calculating the company's gross margin.

Cost of Lease Financing The discounted future cash flow necessary for a lease financing project to be worth the expense of doing. See also: Internal Rate of Return.

Cost of Living The amount one must pay to maintain one's standard of living. That is, the cost of living measures how much one must spend to finance one's lifestyle. Cost of living varies by area; it may be lower in a small city, for example, than in a large city. Changes to the cost of living are related to, but are distinct from, underlying inflation. For example, gasoline prices may rise faster than inflation, which may increase the cost of living more than inflation itself does.

Cost of Tender The cost of delivery of the underlying asset of a futures contract on a commodity. For example, if one holds a long position (i.e., owns) a futures contract on corn, the seller must deliver the corn to the holder when the contract expires. The holder must compensate the seller for any transportation, carrying costs, and any other expenses that accrue in the process of delivering the corn. The costs are collectively called cost of tender.

Cost per Click In online advertising, the measurement of cost paid by an advertiser per click on its advertisement. Most search engines and many blogs advertise by cost per click, the three largest of which are Google, Yahoo!, and MSN. See also: Pay Per Click.

Cost per Thousand In online advertising, the measurement of cost paid by an advertiser per 1,000 impressions of its advertisement. One impression is one view of the advertisement by a website viewer. Many websites, especially those with high traffic, charge advertisers on a per 1,000 impression basis. It differs from a cost per click scheme, in that the viewer does not have to click on the ad in order for the advertiser to be charged.

Cost Records An investor's personal records of the prices at which he/she bought and sold securities. The investor keeps cost records in order to calculate capital gains.

Cost Recovery Period The amount of time that it takes for an asset to depreciate from its purchase price to its salvage value. In other words, the cost recovery period is an amount of time equal to the useful life of the asset. Very often, the IRS assigns a cost recovery period for different assets to head off disputes before they begin. See also: Modified Accelerated Cost Recovery System.

Cost Synergy The financial benefit two companies may derive from a merger or acquisition. For example, two companies that merge may be able to produce more revenue than either one could independently by combining the most efficient processes each brings to the merger. Cost synergy may also refer to the cost reduction a merger brings about by eliminating or streamlining redundant processes. Cost synergy usually has a positive connotation; as a result, press releases and media reports often use the term to refer to layoffs following a merger that are intended to make the newly merged company more efficient.

Cost, Insurance and Freight A CPT involving ocean freight. In a CIF, the seller is responsible for paying for shipping and providing a minimum amount of insurance coverage up to the named port of destination, while the buyer is responsible for the transportation risk beyond the minimum coverage as soon as the good or product is loaded onto the ship. Legally, risk transfers when the good or product crosses the outer rail of the ship. A CIF is similar to a CFR, but also requires the seller to provide minimal insurance. See also: Incoterm.

Costa Rican Colon The currency of Costa Rica. It began circulating in 1896, replacing the Costa Rican peso. It was on a crawling peg with respect to the U.S. dollar until 2006. In October of that year, it was allowed to float within a range with a set floor and a changing ceiling. In many places in Costa Rica, the dollar circulates alongside the colon.

Cost-Benefit Analysis The formal or informal process of comparing the expected costs of a project against its expected revenue. When a company conducts a cost-benefit analysis, it assigns dollar amounts to costs and benefits in order to determine whether a particular project is likely to be profitable. Cost-benefit analysis is important when making investment decisions.

Cost-Benefit Ratio A ratio of whether or not and how much profit will result from an investment. It is calculated by taking the net present value of expected future cash flows from the investment and dividing by the investment's original cost. A ratio above one indicates that the investment will be profitable while a ratio below one means that it will not. A cost-benefit ratio is also called a profitability index.

Cost-of-Living Adjustment An increase to a wage, salary, or pension designed so that the real value remains the same. That is, a cost-of-living adjustment increases the underlying wage, salary, or pension so that it keeps pace with (but does not run ahead of) inflation. Federal pensions and Social Security include cost-of-living adjustments, though few other pensions do.

Cost-Plus Contract An agreement between a buyer and seller in which the seller agrees to make or produce a good for the buyer. The selling price is the cost to the seller of making or producing the good in addition to some fixed fee or percentage of the cost. See also: Cost-plus pricing.

Cost-Push Inflation Inflation caused by rising costs of production. For example, if the price of a barrel of oil rises significantly, this could cause fuel prices to increase which, in turn, increases costs for transportation of food, tools, and other goods, which can cause some level of inflation across an economy. Cost-push inflation contrasts with demand-pull inflation, which is caused by a rise in demand on the part of consumers.

Cotation Assistee en Continu 40 Index An index tracking the 40 largest and most liquid companies traded on the Paris Bourse stock exchange. Established in 1987, it is the premier index tracking the general direction of the French market and economy; it is roughly the French equivalent of the Dow Jones Industrial Average. The CAC 40 is weighted for market capitalization.

Coto A Spanish measure of length approximately equivalent to 4.1 inches. It is largely obsolete.

COU ISO 4217 code for the Colombian unidad de valor real. It is a unit of account in Colombia that does not circulate. It is adjusted for inflation relative to the

Colombian peso so that its value remains stable. Because of this stability, major purchases (notably mortgages) in Colombia may be quoted in COU terms.

Council for Economic and Fiscal Policy A Japanese council formed to improve communication between cabinet ministries and to discuss the country's policies. Its recommendations are presented to the cabinet and, in general, are incorporated into government strategy. The council was established in 2001.

Council of Economic Advisers A committee of three members charged with advising the President of the United States on economic matters. Among its duties are helping the President formulate policy, interpreting data, and generally serving as the White House's resident experts on the economy. Each year, the Council prepares a report, which gives information on the state of the economy of the previous year and contains predictions for the coming year. The Council consists of a chairperson and two members, who are appointed by the President upon approval of the Senate. It is the subject of criticism at times because political considerations have been known to color its reports.

Council of Institutional Investors A non-profit organization that promotes the interests of institutional investors in the United States. The Council of Institutional Investors provides members with lobbying, educational, networking, and other similar services. There are more than 140 members, mainly pension funds, of the Council of Institutional Investors; members control a combined $3 trillion in assets. The Council was established in 1985 and maintains its headquarters in Washington, D.C.

Council of Petroleum Accountants Societies A professional organization consisting of accountants working in the oil and gas industry. It provides members with networking opportunities, education on how to use the accounting profession in a way most relevant to the oil and gas industry, and publishes articles and accounting guidelines. It is based in Denver, Colorado.

Count On a point & figure chart, an estimation of future price movements. Point & figure charts seek to identify support and resistance levels. Counts are estimates on the likelihood that a security will break through one or the other and result in a large profit or loss.

Counterfeit Describing anything fake. In the context of finance, the term is usually used to describe money minted or printed by any person or institution not duly authorized to do so. While counterfeit money is not legal tender, its proliferation may debase the value of money if it is not readily identifiable as fake.

Counteroffer A second or subsequent offer to purchase an asset. For example, if the asking price on a house is $150,000, a potential buyer may make an initial offer of $125,000. In such a case, the seller may make a counteroffer for $140,000. Counteroffers are only made if the price is subject to negotiation.

Counterparties The persons or institutions engaging in a transaction. That is, the buyer and the seller of a good are the counterparties to the sale of that good. While it could apply to any transaction, the term is most common when referring to the counterparties of a swap.

Counterparty Risk 1. In options, the risk that the option holder will not exercise the option. This may be good if the price moves in the option writer's favor, but counterparty risk is small in that situation. **2.** More generally, the risk that one party in a contract will default or otherwise not fulfill his/her obligations. Counterparty risk can be diminished when one party mandates a co-signer or highly-rated guarantor. See also: Intermediated market.

Counterposing A slang term for the practice of an employee avoiding work by using jargon or vague statements to confuse and outsmart management.

Counterpurchase An agreement between two persons or companies to buy goods or services from each other, usually at different times. For example, Company A may buy goods from Company B in March, and then sell different goods to Company B in April. Counterpurchases are made for the mutual benefit of both companies.

Countersignature A second signature by a second person on a document. Countersignatures exist for authentication. For example, the prime minister may be required to countersign a law the president approves in order to guarantee approval. Likewise, a witness may countersign a will to show that it really represents the testator's wishes.

Countersignature Law In the United States, a law requiring an insurance policy to be signed by an insurance agent who is licensed to practice in the state where the policy is issued. Countersignature laws are not federal, but rather exist at the level of individual states.

Countertrade The exchange of goods and services for other goods and services. Countertrade is relatively common in trade with or between cash-poor countries. Most economists estimate that countertrade accounts for between 20% and 25% of global trade volume. See also: Buyback, Switch trading, and Counter purchase.

Countertrend Strategy An investment strategy in which an investor buys when other investors are selling with the intention of selling when others are buying. A countertrend strategy follows the investment philosophy of "buy low, sell high." Those who utilize countertrend strategy often use technical analysis in making decisions about when it is appropriate to buy and sell.

Country Basket An unmanaged portfolio that tracks the stock markets for a particular country. For example, a country basket may contain all stocks traded on every major stock market in Italy. The company managing the country basket issues shares in this portfolio; these shares may be traded as if they were stocks. Most country baskets are traded on the New York Stock Exchange. See also: iShare, Closed-end investment company, Index fund.

Country Diversification Investment of one's portfolio in securities that are traded in various countries. This is done to reduce risk, often political risk. For example, if one country's government announces a larger than normal budget deficit, or the central bank raises interest rates, this may affect security prices in one country but not necessarily in other countries that did not take equivalent steps. Likewise, if a whole industry fails in one country but thrives in another, investing in the same industry in both countries hedges one's risk. Some analysts argue that country diversification is less effective in an era of globalization, but other analysts dispute that.

Country Economic Risk The likelihood that economic developments in one country may negatively impact international transactions. Suppose Country A and Country B enjoy a free trade agreement, which greatly increased trade between the two nations. A protectionist party may be elected to office in Country B and immediately revoke the FTA. Not only will this affect business, perhaps both positively and negatively, within Country B, but exporters from Country A will suddenly find that their investments have evaporated. See also: Country political risk.

Country Financial Risk The risk that a government will default or miss a payment on its national debt. Country financial risk is important in determining the value of a currency.

Country Risk The risk that a foreign government will significantly alter its policies or other regulations so that it negatively impacts the business climate in that country or the returns on a particular industry, company, or project. Macro-country risk deals with policy changes that harm, say, exporters or foreign-owned businesses in general, while micro-country risk implies that a government will deliberately target a particular company or way of making a living. For example, the political climate of a country in which defense contractors operate may turn against one particular company because of its perceived excesses or against defense contractors in general. This may cause the government revoke contracts for one or more defense contractors See also: Reputational risk, political risk, sovereign risk, geographic risk.

Country Screening When making international investment decisions, the process of organizing potential investments by country. Country screening can be useful as it may help one recognize risks associated with each specific country. See also: Country risk.

Country Similarity Theory The idea that countries with similar qualities are most likely to trade with each other. These qualities may include level of development, savings rates, and natural resources, among others. The country similarity theory is based on the idea that economic actors with similar qualities are going to want many of the same things.

Country Size Theory The idea that countries with a larger physical territory are more self-sufficient than smaller countries. This may be because greater territory increases the potential access to natural resources and other foundations for economic growth. This may affect decisions for foreign direct investment.

County A subdivision of government in most American states. Most of the time, a county is a municipal level below the state government but above a city or township. Counties serve different purposes, depending on the state. In some states, they have courts and a sheriff's office. The chief prosecutor (district attorney) for an area is often employed at the county level. In Oklahoma and many other states, counties have jurisdiction over all land in their boundaries not otherwise incorporated into a city or other municipality. In some states like Maryland, counties have quite broad responsibilities, including the provision of public health services and education. On the other hand, counties have no authority in Rhode Island. In Louisiana, counties are called parishes. In Alaska, they are called boroughs. See also: ABCD Counties.

Coupon The interest paid on a bond. That is, the coupon is the amount that the issuer must pay to the holder of each bond in exchange for investing in that bond. Coupons usually are paid every six months. They are called coupons because formerly they were represented by physical coupons on the bond certificate that had to be clipped and returned to the issuer to receive the interest payment. With the advent of computers, this has become much less common.

Coupon Bond A bond containing no ownership information and for which the physical bearer is presumed to be the owner. Coupons are physically attached to the bond and must be presented to the issuer to receive interest payments. Coupon bonds have not been issued in the United States since 1982, and thus they have become a significantly less important activity; most references to bearer bonds apply to very old bonds that have not yet matured. See also: Clipping.

Coupon Clipping The practice of finding discounts on consumer goods such as groceries. One presents pieces of paper representing these discounts (called coupons) to receive the discount. The coupons are cut out of ("clipped" from) a periodical such as a newspaper or magazine. These coupons should not be confused with the coupons on bonds.

Coupon Date One of the dates on which bondholders are sent coupon payments. That is, the coupon dates are the dates on which bondholders receive the interest that they are guaranteed. Coupon dates are fixed for bonds, and usually occur twice a year. See also: Dividend payment date.

Coupon Equivalent Rate An alternative method of calculating the yield on a bond. It is used for zero-coupon bonds, as these are issued at discounts to their face value; that is, the CER states what the coupon rate would be if it carried a coupon and had been sold at face value. As such, it gives a more accurate picture of the yield of a zero-coupon bond. It is calculated as: CER = ((Market Price - Face Value) / Market Price) * (365 / Days until Maturity).

Coupon Payments Annual interest paid on a bond, usually in semi-annual tranches. Coupon payments are expressed as a percentage of the face value (par) of a bond. For example, if one holds a bond worth $100,000 at 5% interest, the bondholder will receive $5,000 in coupon payments per year (or, more strictly, $2,500 every six months) until the bond matures or he/she sells the bond.

Coupon Rate The interest rate that a bond pays to a bondholder, usually semi-annually. The coupon rate is stated on the bond. This is also called the nominal yield or the yield rate.

Coupure A French term that is used in English to refer to paper money. The French term literally refers to a plaster structure that covers a hole in a wall. The term is meant to convey the ease with which paper money can change hands.

Cout, Assurance, Fret A French term for cost, insurance and freight. It may be abbreviated CAF.

Covado A Portuguese measure of length approximately equivalent to 0.66 meters. It became obsolete after Lusophone countries adopted the metric system in the 19th century.

Covariance The degree to which two variables are correlated. That is, covariance is the measure of how much two variables are related to one another. It is important in security analysis to determine how much or how little price movements in two companies or industries are connected.

Covenant A provision in an indenture. An indenture sets the terms of a bond; its terms include the coupon rate, the period until maturity, and whether the bond comes with any special features like convertibility or whether it is callable. A covenant within an indenture states what actions the issuer and the bondholder may or may not take in certain situations. Covenants (and indentures generally) exist to reduce the risk to all parties to a bond.

Cover Bid In an auction or other competitive sale, the second-highest bid. The term carries a slight connotation that the bidder was a plant who was simply trying to drive the price higher. This may or may not imply collusion.

Coverage 1. The specific insured events for which an insurance company will pay a benefit. For example, a life insurance policy provides coverage in the event of death. Likewise, a health insurance policy provides money in the event of illness. Generally speaking, an insurance policy outlines what it covers and the benefits it provides under different circumstances. **2.** A measure of a company's ability to pay its fixed liabilities. It is calculated by determining by subtracting its fixed payments from its operating income. High coverage indicates that the company can easily make its payments and indeed is able to set funds aside to do so in the event its income declines. Low coverage means that the company can make its payments but that it has less flexibility in doing so. A negative number indicates that the company cannot pay its fixed liabilities. The payments included in this calculation are lease payments, dividends on preferred stock, and debt service. It is also called fixed-charge coverage.

Coverage Initiated The date on which a brokerage or research firm begins giving buy or sell ratings to a particular publicly-traded company. The term is most commonly used in the media when a first rating is reported.

Coverage Ratio Any ratio measuring one's ability to pay a certain expense. There are various kinds of coverage ratio. For example, one may take a ratio of a company's monthly cash flow to its monthly debt service. Generally speaking, a coverage ratio at or above 1 indicates that a company can pay the stated expense, while a ratio below 1 indicates the opposite.

Coverdell Education Savings Account An account into which one may deposit funds on a tax-deferred basis, on the assumption that they will be used to pay for the education of the account holder. The funds are invested in a portfolio, much like an IRA or another retirement account. If the funds are in fact used for education, withdrawals from a Coverdell account are tax-exempt up to the total cost of education. Importantly, any tax liability on a Coverdell account is assessed at the account holder's bracket, rather than the contributor's. This protects the account holder from an excessive tax liability in the event a wealthy parent made most or all of the contributions. It was formerly called an education IRA.

Covered Call A position in which an investor short sells or writes an option contract, giving the buyer the ability to buy the underlying asset on demand while also owning the underlying asset. For example, an investor has a covered call position when he writes a call for 100 shares of AT&T and owns at least 100 shares of AT&T. This means that if the holder of the call exercises the option, the investor will be able to sell the shares without a problem. Investors often use a covered call strategy when they do not expect the option to be exercised and simply want to collect the premiums without exposing themselves to the risk of loss if the option is actually exercised.

Covered Call Writing Strategy In options, a strategy in which one writes a call option with the intention to avoid a margin account. Because a call writer is obligated to sell the underlying should the option buyer exercise the option, the writer must either already own the underlying or be able to borrow. Using a covered call strategy means the writer already owns the underlying and does not borrow it from a broker. If the writer sells the call at the same time he/she buys the underlying, this is called a "buy-write." If the writer already owned the underlying it is referred to as an "overwrite." In both these situations, the option is immune to margin calls.

Covered Foreign Currency Loan A loan made in a currency other than the one in which the borrower usually operates. For example, a borrower in the U.S. may take out a loan in pounds sterling to finance new operations in the U.K. The loan is "covered" because the parties use a foreign currency forward contract, an agreement in which the parties agree to trade certain currencies in the future at a given exchange rate to hedge against foreign exchange risk.

Covered Interest Arbitrage A strategy in which one enters a long position in an investment in a foreign currency and simultaneously enters a short position in a

forward contract on that same currency. The amount one receives in the sale of the forward contract should equal what one spends on the long investment in the base currency. One enters the short position in order to hedge the exchange risk.

Covered Interest Rate Parity The principle stating that yields from two equivalent investments in the domestic market and the foreign market, respectively, are equal after accounting for fluctuations in the exchange rate. See also: Purchasing power parity, Covered interest rate arbitrage.

Covered Option A situation in which an investor writes an option while holding an equal and opposite position on the underlying asset. A covered call option occurs when the investor owns the underlying asset and writes a call so that the underlying is on hand to sell to the option holder if the option is exercised. A covered put option occurs when the investor writes a put and has enough cash to cover the strike if the put is exercised. It is thought that utilizing covered options is a beneficial tactic, as the investor may profit from the option premium.

Covered Put Option A situation in which an investor writes an option while holding an equal and opposite position on the underlying asset. A covered call option occurs when the investor owns the underlying asset and writes a call so that the underlying is on hand to sell to the option holder if the option is exercised. A covered put option occurs when the investor writes a put and has enough cash to cover the strike if the put is exercised. It is thought that utilizing covered options is a beneficial tactic as the investor may profit from the option premium.

Covered Security A security that has special exemption from state and local regulations. Thus, a covered security is only subject to federal regulations. This type of security was created in 1996 by the National Securities Markets Improvement Act, which was intended to standardize regulations for securities trading throughout the United States. As a result, most stocks traded in America are covered securities.

Covered Straddle An options strategy in which an investor takes a position on a call and a put with the same strike price and expiration date on an underlying security that the investor already owns. One may have a covered straddle when he/she believes that the market for the underlying asset will be volatile and will undergo dramatic price changes, but is unsure of which direction the changes will go. Like all straddles, a covered straddle allows the investor to profit regardless of which direction the underlying moves, provided there is a significant movement. A small price change in either direction will result in a loss. It is important to note that a covered straddle differs from a covered option.

Covered Straddle Write An option strategy in which an investor writes (sells) a call and a put with the same strike price and expiration date on an underlying security that the investor already owns. A person may have a covered straddle when he/she believes that the market for the underlying asset will be volatile and will undergo dramatic price changes but is unsure of which direction the changes will go. Like all straddles, a covered straddle allows the investor to profit regardless of which direction the underlying asset moves (provided there is a significant movement). A small price change in either direction will result in a loss. It is important to note that a covered straddle differs from a covered option.

Covered Writer The writer (or seller) of an option contract who either owns the underlying asset (for a call) or has sufficient cash to buy the underlying asset if need be (for a put). That is, a call option gives the holder (or buyer) the right but not the obligation to buy the underlying asset for the stated strike price. When the call is exercised, it poses little risk for the covered writer because he/she already owns the underlying asset and can simply sell it to the holder rather than needing to buy the asset at the current market price, which is usually higher than the strike price. Likewise, a put gives the holder the right but not the obligation to sell the underlying asset to the writer at the strike price. A covered writer is able to buy the underlying asset with no problem because he/she has the cash on hand. This eliminates the risk that he/she will have to sell other securities, perhaps at a loss, to raise the cash. See also: Covered Option, Uncovered Writer.

Covering 1. Informal for buying back. **2.** The act of completing a transaction. For example, covering a long position may mean making payment for securities one has bought. **2.** Informal; to close a position.

Cowboy A slang term for an employee who is hard to manage either because he/she does not work well with others, has a difficult personality, or for some other reason.

Cowboy Marketer A marketer who was supposed to promote a stock to persons who opt in to an e-mail campaign but rather spams anyone with an e-mail address. The term implies that the company that hired the marketer does not know what is going on. The practice is considered unethical because it may increase the marketer's compensation without actually producing results.

Cowboy Marketing The practice in which a marketer who was supposed to promote a stock to persons who opt in to an e-mail campaign in fact spams anyone with an e-mail address. The term implies that the company that hired the marketer does not know what is going on. The practice is considered unethical because it may increase the marketer's compensation without actually producing results.

CPB A slang term for a situation in which an employee is taking care of personal matters while at work. For example, an employee who sits at his desk and works on his novel instead of dealing with customers is CPB. The term is an abbreviation for "conducting personal business."

CPF Franc A currency used in former French colonies in the South Pacific, namely French Polynesia, New Caledonia and Wallis and Futuna. It was introduced in 1945 to spare French colonies from the severe devaluation necessary to the French franc following World War II. Between 1949 and 1999, it was pegged to the French franc; since then, it has been pegged to the euro. See also: CFA franc.

CPT Carrier Paid To. In international commerce, an agreement between a seller and a buyer indicating that the seller is responsible for the costs of shipping a good while the buyer assumes the risk of damage to the good once it is transferred to a carrier. This means that the buyer is responsible for any insurance he/she may wish to purchase. A carrier is any person who transports the good to an agreed upon destination; in cases where the transportation involves multiple carriers, risk is transferred when the good is delivered to the fist carrier. See also: United Nations Convention on Contracts for the International Sale of Goods, Incoterm.

CPV GOST 7.67 Latin three-letter geocode for Cape Verde. The code is used for transactions to and from Cape Verdean bank accounts and for international shipping to Cape Verde. As with all GOST 7.67 codes, it is used primarily in Cyrillic alphabets.

CR 1. ISO 3166-1 alpha-2 code for the Republic of Costa Rica. This is the code used in international transactions to and from Costa Rican bank accounts. **2.** ISO 3166-2 geocode for Costa Rica. This is used as an international standard for shipping to Costa Rica. Each Costa Rican province has its own code with the prefix "CR." For example, the code for the Province of Limon is ISO 3166-2:CR-L.

Crack Spread A spread involving oil futures. In a crack spread, an investor takes a long position in crude oil futures and a short position in refined oil futures. This allows the investor to create an artificial position on the price of refining oil. Refineries are the most likely investors to enter into a crack spread. See also: Crush spread.

Cracker A slang term in Hong Kong for $10,000. See also: Hong Kong dollar, Big cracker.

Cram Down To force an investor to accept a deal he/she considers unfair. For example, in a hostile takeover, some shareholders may be forced to accept junk bonds instead of cash in exchange for their stock. Likewise, in an uncovered option, the writer may be forced to purchase the underlying asset at a price that is far away from the prevailing market price. Usually, cramming down occurs when an investor is legally obliged to accept a deal, or when not taking the deal would result in an even greater loss.

Cramdown In bankruptcy, the ability of a court to formulate and implement a Chapter 11 reorganization plan over and above the objections of creditors. Generally speaking, unsecured creditors object to a debtor's bankruptcy because they have no recourse for retrieving the debt. The rationale behind a cramdown is the fact that unsecured creditors will usually receive part of the debt back under a Chapter 11 reorganization, but would receive nothing in a Chapter 7 liquidation. Cramdown is therefore thought to be the least negative option for both the debtor and the creditors. Courts are required, however, to formulate a cramdown that is as equitable as possible for all parties.

Cram-Down 1. See: Cram Down. **2.** See: Cramdown.

Crash A sudden, dramatic, and usually sustained drop in securities market prices. It may be followed by a steep economic downturn, like the 1929 Crash that precipitated the Great Depression. In order to prevent crashes from hurting investors too much at once, most exchanges mandate a cutoff point below which trading stops. For example, the by-laws of a stock market may say that if it loses 10% of its value in intraday trading, the exchange officials automatically stop trading. See also: Panic selling.

Crawling Peg A situation in which one currency links its value to that of another currency, but allows it to fluctuate within certain limits. This differs from a straight peg, which has one currency permanently valued at a certain amount in relation to another currency; it also differs from a floating currency, which changes in value according to market factors. A crawling peg may be valuable if a currency would otherwise be exceptionally volatile; it allows the currency to fluctuate to an acceptable level.

CRC ISO 4217 code for the Costa Rican colon. It began circulating in 1896, replacing the Costa Rican peso. It was on a crawling peg with respect to the U.S. dollar until 2006. In October of that year, it was allowed to float within a range with a set floor and a changing ceiling. In many places in Costa Rica, the dollar circulates alongside the colon.

CRD A central database with information on individual brokers, investment advisors, and so forth. The CRD provides information on their backgrounds, education, licensing, and perhaps, most importantly, whether or not clients have complained about them or if they have ever been disciplined by an exchange, the SEC, or a professional organization.

Createalytics A slang term for the manipulation of data to support one's favored conclusion. Createalytics may be used in finance, marketing, or in many other areas. For example, a focus group manager may use createalytics to show management that participants liked a product more than they actually did.

Creation Unit The set of securities underlying an exchange-traded fund. A creation unit is a basket of securities traded on a particular exchange that are assembled and repackaged as a single share of the exchange-traded fund.

Creative Accounting The practice of recognizing revenue in a way that makes a company look better than it is while still conforming to the GAAP. Creative accounting seeks to inflate stock prices, for example, by selling assets at the end of a year to create a profit that offsets a loss. One could argue that creative accounting hides a company's true financial state, but, unlike aggressive accounting, creative accounting is generally legal. See also: Sarbanes-Oxley Act of 2002.

Creative Destruction A concept in capitalist theory stating that innovation causes failure, but that failure, in turn, creates more innovation. For example, suppose someone invents a better widget. If he/she markets this widget effectively, he/she will eventually drive all previous widget manufacturers out of business. However, this forces older widget manufacturers to create their own innovations that will either keep themselves in business or improve their financial situations in other ways. This is considered one of the most important concepts in capitalism.

Credit 1. An agreement between a buyer and a seller in which the buyer receives the good or service in advance and makes payment later, often over time and usually with interest. For example, a buyer may purchase a computer on credit for $600 and pay $100 per month over several months with interest. One of the most common ways of buying on credit is to use a credit card, but many companies have their own credit schemes. A steady flow of credit in an economy is considered important for financial health. See also: Accounts receivable, Accounts payable. **2.** The amount in a bank account or some other account. For example, if one has $800 in his/her bank, he/she is said to have an $800 credit. Likewise, if he/she receives a check for another $200, he/she receives a further $200 credit.

Credit Analysis The process of determining the likelihood of default, especially by a bond issuer. Credit rating agencies conduct credit analysis in order to provide bond ratings; they may change these from time to time. Bond investors likewise conduct credit analysis. For example, if an investor's credit analysis indicates that a bond rating is about to decrease, he/she will be unlikely to invest in that bond, as it will lead to locking in a lower interest rate at a higher level of risk. On the other hand, if credit analysis shows that a bond rating is about to increase, an investor will be more inclined to buy that bond, as it provides a lower level of risk while also giving him/her a higher coupon. See also: Investment-grade, Junk.

Credit Balance The profit from a short sale that is deposited into a margin account. The credit balance consists of any maintenance margin the account holder must keep in the account as well as additional funds that may be withdrawn or used to buy more securities. This latter is called the free credit balance.

Credit Card A card entitling the owner to use funds from the issuing company up to a certain limit. The holder of a credit card may use it to buy a good or service. When one does this, the issuing company effectively gives the card holder a loan for the amount of the good or service, which the holder is expected to repay. Most credit cards have variable and relatively high interest rates on these loans. Credit cards also have a limit, which may be raised or lowered depending on the creditworthiness of the card holder. Most analysts recommend treating a credit card as a short-term loan, as allowing the interest to compound for too long may result in dire financial straits.

Credit Cliff Informal; a situation where a decline in credit availability can make a bad situation for a company even worse. For example, suppose a company has a large amount of debt. It may default on one loan or bond, causing its credit rating to be reduced. This will cause banks and investors to require higher interest rates for further extensions of credit. This increases the company's liabilities and can cause further defaults on loans and bonds. In short, a credit cliff is a compounding of a bad situation caused by credit problems.

Credit Default Swap A swap in which the buyer makes a series of payments and, in exchange, receives a guarantee against default from the seller on a designated debt security. That is, the buyer transfers the risk that a debt security, such as a bond, will default to the seller, and the seller receives a series of fees for assuming this risk. In some ways, a credit default swap is like insurance, but there are significant differences. Prominently, the buyer of the credit default swap need not own the underlying debt security. Thus, the buyer may be speculating on the potential for default on the designated security. Likewise, the seller is not required to have the cash available to pay the buyer in case the designated security does default. This lack of regulation has raised concern, especially during the late 2000s credit crunch.

Credit Derivative Any derivative that allows an investor to hedge its credit risk. For example, if a brokerage is concerned that a client may be unable to pay a margin call, it may transfer this risk to another investor in exchange for paying a fee. Regular derivatives, like forward contracts and options, may be used as credit derivatives, depending on the credit risk of an investor's other positions.

Credit Flow The availability of credit. High credit flow indicates low interest rates, loose credit requirements, and ease of borrowing money. Low credit flow indicates the opposite.

Credit History A record of one's payment history on current and previous debt. If one makes payments on time and does not acquire an excessive amount of debt, one's credit history is likely to be good. This makes an individual a good risk if he/she wishes to borrow more money. On the other hand, if one has a history of late payments and/or default, the individual is likely to be a bad risk and may be denied credit. One's FICO score is a measure of one's credit history.

Credit Insurance An insurance policy protecting a company in the event that it does not collect an unusually large amount of its accounts receivable. A company's accounts receivable represent what it is owed on its credit sales. Every company that makes credit sales takes the risk that its customers will not or cannot pay what they owe. Credit insurance is one way to reduce this risk. See also: Factoring.

Credit Limit The maximum amount of money one is allowed to borrow. A bank or another financial services company may extend a credit line to a client, which is essentially approval for a loan or series of loans to be given on demand from the borrower. The borrower is under no obligation to actually take out a loan at any particular time. The maximum amount for which a particular borrower is approved is known as the credit limit. Banks and financial services company do not extend loans past the credit limit. For example, one may have a credit card with a credit limit of

$2,000; if one attempts to put $2,100 on the card, the bank will decline payment. A good credit report and a regular history of loan payments may result in the credit limit being raised. See also: Facility.

Credit Period The period of time during which a firm grants credit to a customer. At the end of the credit period, the customer is expected to have paid for all goods or services he/she has purchased.

Credit Policy Delay The time between the sale of a good or service on credit and the receipt of payment. The length of the credit policy delay depends on a number of factors, such as the buyer's creditworthiness and the seller's policy on credit sales. See also: Accounts receivable.

Credit Quality A measure of the likelihood of default, especially by a bond issuer. Credit ratings agencies determine credit quality in order to provide bond ratings; they may change these from time to time. FICO scores are measures of the credit quality of individuals. See also: Investment-grade, Junk.

Credit Rating 1. See: Bond rating. **2.** See: FICO score.

Credit Rating Agency A company that provides investors with assessments of an investment's risk. The issuers of investments, especially debt securities, pay credit rating agencies to provide them with ratings. A high rating indicates low risk and may therefore encourage investors to buy a security. Additionally, banks may only invest in securities with a high rating from two or more credit rating agencies. The SEC recognizes 10 firms as credit rating agencies; Fitch, S&P, and Moody's are the three most prominent. However, the methods of credit ratings agencies have been subject to criticism. For example, most agencies gave high-risk mortgage-backed securities top ratings until they defaulted at the collapse of the housing bubble.

Credit Score A measure of an individual's creditworthiness. Credit scoring involves the quantification of a variety of factors in an individual's background, including a history of default, the current amount of debt, and the length of time that the individual has made purchases on credit. Banks and other financial institutions may use a credit score to determine whether or not an individual is likely to default on a loan, mortgage, or other debt. The FICO score is the most common credit score in the United States.

Credit Squeeze A situation in which it is difficult to finance through borrowing. A credit squeeze often occurs when economic growth is declining and/or when interest rates rise. The Federal Reserve is often blamed for credit squeezes when they raise target interest rates, but it may occur through private sector actions as well, such as a systemic rise in bad debt. See also: Credit crunch.

Credit Standards The set of standards that a company or bank uses to determine whether to extend a loan or line of credit to an applicant. Credit standards may include having a certain FICO score, recent good credit history, and a certain income.

Credit Union A non-profit cooperative organization that offers many of the same services as a bank. Specifically, credit unions offer checking accounts, savings accounts, and some loans. Most of the time, credit unions were founded by and/or cater to a particular profession, church, or community. Many credit unions serve rural or poor areas. Because they are non-profits, they often offer better interest rates than retail banks; however, they usually have fewer services.

Credit Watch Notice from a credit rating agency to a bond issuer that a negative factor has arisen in the agency's review of the issuer's credit rating. If the issuer does not take steps to explain or alleviate the factor, the credit watch may be the first step toward a reduction in the issuer's rating. For example, a credit rating agency may discover a dramatic drop in an issuer's liquidity ratio, which increases the likelihood of default on a debt. It would then send a credit watch to the issuer.

Credit-Balance Theory In technical analysis, a theory stating that large cash balances on investors' brokerage accounts are an indicator of market uptrends. The theory contends that investors with cash balances in their accounts are extremely likely to eventually use that cash to buy securities. This increases demand for securities, which in turn drives up prices. Credit balance theory contrasts with debit-balance theory, which contends the exact opposite.

Credito fondiario An Italian term for land credit. The term corresponds to a medium-term or long-term mortgage loan.

Creditor A person or company to whom one owes money. A creditor may be a bank or another company. In the case of bonds and personal debt, the creditor is often an individual. A creditor may be secured, meaning that the debt has a collateral, or unsecured, meaning that the debt has no specific collateral.

Creditor's Committee In bankruptcy, an ad hoc committee of creditors who have an interest in seeing as much debt as possible recovered from the person or company filing for bankruptcy.

Creditworthiness The ability to borrow money. The better one's creditworthiness, the more likely it is that a bank or other financial institution will extend credit. One establishes creditworthiness by repaying loans and other bills on time, spending prudently, and generally showing that one can behave in a financially responsible way. Individual creditworthiness is measured by the FICO score while a company's or other organization's creditworthiness usually is measured by its credit rating.

Credo A short statement of principles and/or goals to guide a company in the conduct of its business. See also: Mission statement.

Creeping Expropriation The continual restriction of private property rights gradually over time by a government. Creeping expropriation involves legislation, regulation, and taxation, which together over time make it difficult for a person or business to own property. Creeping expropriation, where it exists, makes it increasingly difficult to conduct commerce.

Creeping Inflation Low, persistent inflation over time. Creeping inflation generally is not noticed at first, but nevertheless reduces the value of a currency significantly. For example, if the inflation rate is 3%, prices will double in only 33 years.

CREST The central securities depository for many British and Irish securities. In particular, it is used to settle gilts in the United Kingdom. Using CREST carries tax advantages for U.K. investors. It allows shares to be traded between investors without the physical certificates needing to change hands. Euroclear has owned it since 2002.

CRI GOST 7.67 Latin three-letter geocode for Costa Rica. The code is used for transactions to and from Costa Rican bank accounts and for international shipping to Costa Rica. As with all GOST 7.67 codes, it is used primarily in Cyrillic alphabets.

Crisp Set A term for a mathematical model that does not use fuzzy logic. Fuzzy logic is a mathematical or computer program that attempts to approximate the ambiguity inherent to human reasoning. Thus, a crisp set is any program that organizes data into neat categories where each data point can belong to one, and only one, category.

Critical Level 1. A variable that has reached a sufficiently high or low value as to change the nature of what is discussed. For example, if the revenue of a small business reaches a certain level, it may need to hire additional employees, which could subject the business to more regulation, and this may result in the small business becoming a medium-sized business or even a large corporation. In this case, the revenue necessary to make this happen is called the critical level of revenue. **2.** The time when a company's operations have become sufficiently profitable that it can sustain itself without further capital infusions or other sources of outside funding. Critical level is the goal of all start-ups, many of which may remain in the development stage for years or never leave it. In both cases, the critical level is also called critical mass.

Critical Mass 1. A situation that can no longer be ignored. For example, if an employee who makes co-workers of the opposite sex uncomfortable makes unwanted sexual advances toward the chief financial officer, the situation is said to have reached critical mass, and the employee must immediately be disciplined or fired. **2.** The point at which a product or company has become sufficiently popular to take off and become commonly used. For example, a company that has posted a profit for three years in a row and has respectable financials may reach critical mass and become extremely attractive to investors.

Criticality A slightly incorrect term for extreme importance. For example, a supervisor may emphasize to an employee the criticality of performing well at an upcoming presentation to investors.

Croatian Dinar The former currency of Croatia. It replaced the Yugoslav convertible dinar at a one-to-one ratio in 1991. The Croatian dinar was a transition currency between the Yugoslav dinar and the Croatian kuna, which replaced it in 1994. The dinar was subject to high inflation.

Croatian Kuna The currency of Croatia. First issued in 1939 while Croatia was part of Yugoslavia, it was originally pegged at a dual exchange rate to the German reichsmark. Pulled from circulation in 1945, the kuna was reintroduced in 1994, replacing the Yugoslav dinar. The new kruna was introduced at an exchange rate of 1 kruna per 1,000 dinars; it is a floating currency.

Crop Year 1. In agricultural commodities, the period of time between two harvests. For many crops, this approximates a calendar year but some may have two crop years each calendar year. Due to weather and other conditions, the quality of the commodity may vary by crop year and thus affect pricing. Examples of commodities with crop years include corn, rice, and wheat. **2.** In crop insurance, the fiscal year in which claims are processed. This is used in bookkeeping simply to keep as many claims and payments as possible in the same fiscal year. This is particularly important because crop insurance claims tend to be made around the same time, that is, following a bad harvest.

Cross To match and execute two orders made to the same broker. Suppose a broker receives one order to buy 1,000 shares at $45 and another to sell 1,000 shares at $45. If he matches these two together, he is said to cross the orders. Crossing is subject to some regulation to prevent conflict of interest on the part of the broker.

Cross Currency In foreign exchange, two currencies that are exchanged without first converting one or the other into United States dollars. At the end of World War II, most currencies were pegged to the dollar as the United States was the only major country to come out of the war with little damage. This meant that confidence in the dollar was strong, especially since it was also pegged to gold. Since then, currencies have begun to be traded without reference to the dollar; these are known as cross currencies. See also: Bretton Woods.

Cross Default A provision in some bonds stating that the issuer shall be considered in default if the issuer defaults on any other of its obligations or liabilities. This provides extra protection for bondholders.

Cross Foot In accounting, a slang term for adding numbers horizontally across a page.

Cross Funds Referring to internal purchases and other transactions that improve or reduce the standing of an organization's accounting books but do not necessarily result in revenues or expenditures.

Cross Hedge An investment strategy that involves taking a position on a commodity followed by an equal but opposite futures position on a different commodity with similar price movements. Because the price movements of the two commodities should be closely correlated, a negative movement on the present commodity should be offset by a positive movement on the opposite futures position, and vice versa. Cross hedging is often used in markets where there is no viable futures market for the presently-owned commodity. See also: Commercial trader.

Cross Holding The situation in which one publicly-traded company owns stock in another publicly-traded company. This situation can lead to double-counting of securities, especially when the two corporations are listed on the same index. Thus, one needs to account for cross holdings when aggregating the capitalizations of firms. If two firms cross hold each other, it is difficult to displace the management in one without the consent of the other corporation.

Cross Margining The practice of a brokerage using the excess margin on one client's margin account to cover another margin account that has fallen below the margin requirement. An account that has fallen below the margin requirement is subject to a margin call, but some financial institutions practice cross margining to reduce the risk that a client will be unable to pay a margin call, which would create problems for all parties involved. Cross margining is also called a spread margin.

Cross Option Two option contracts giving two companies the right, but not the obligation, to buy a significant amount of stock in each other for a certain strike price. Cross options are most common when the companies are in the process of merging anyway. The companies enter the cross option in order to reduce the risk that a third party will come and disrupt the merger by buying one of the companies.

Cross Rate In foreign exchange, the exchange rate of currencies being traded in a country that does not utilize either of those currencies. For example, a trader in Britain dealing in Mexican pesos and euros will trade them at the cross rate. Less frequently, the cross rate refers to any exchange rate that does not involve the U.S. dollar. See also: Cross currency.

Cross Trade A trade in which a broker offsets buy and sell orders without recording the orders on the exchange where the trade is taking place. Suppose a broker receives one order to buy 1,000 shares at $45 and another to sell 1,000 shares at $45. If he simply matches these two orders without publicizing them on an exchange to see if better prices are available, he conducts a cross trade. This could prevent investors from taking advantage of a better price. A cross trade may be considered a form of price manipulation and, as such, is prohibited.

Crossborder Bond A bond issued in a country or currency other than that of the investor or broker. They include eurobonds, which are issued in a foreign currency, foreign bonds, which are issued by a foreign government or corporation in the domestic market, and global bonds, which are issued in both domestic and international markets. Unlike domestic bonds, crossborder bonds are usually subject to currency risk. Caution is required when investing in crossborder bonds because they may be subject to different regulatory and taxation requirements than the ones with which the investor or broker is familiar.

Cross-Border Factoring Concluding an international transaction by using a more than factor; that is, an institution that buys others institutions' accounts receivable. In this situation, an exporter sells its accounts receivable to a factor, which then contacts other factoring institutions in order to collect what was owed to the exporter. This helps the exporting business because it may divest itself of credit risk (and perhaps currency risk as well).

Cross-Collateral 1. In project finance, a pool of assets owned by several different persons and/or organizations that is collectively used as collateral on a loan. 2. Collateral on one loan that is also used as collateral on another loan. In the event of default, both creditors have a claim on the collateral.

Cross-Default A provision in a loan agreement or other debt obligation stating that the borrower defaults if he/she goes into default on any other obligation. For example, a cross-default provision may state that a person defaults on his car lease if he defaults on his mortgage. This provision exists to protect the lender.

Crossed Market A situation in which the bid for a security exceeds the ask. That is, a crossed market occurs when the highest price that a buyer is willing to pay is higher than the lowest price a seller is willing to take. This is fairly unusual and characterizes a highly volatile security. A crossed market is most common on NASDAQ when orders are entered before the opening.

Crossed Trade A trade in which a broker offsets buy and sell orders without recording the orders on the exchange where the trade is taking place. This prevents traders from taking advantage of a better price. A crossed trade may be considered a form of price manipulation and, as such, is prohibited.

Crossing Session The time during which the buyers and sellers of securities match orders so the least amount of cash or number of securities actually needs to change hands. This occurs after a trading session on an exchange. See also: Clearing house.

Crossover In technical analysis, a situation in which a price crosses a threshold thought to be bullish or bearish. For example, if a stock price goes above its resistance level, the resistance level is said to be a crossover because it indicates that the stock will likely continue to rise and the overall trend has changed.

Crossover Credit A situation in which a bond is speculative grade but very close to investment grade or vice versa. It often refers to a split rating in which one credit rating agency gives the bond an investment grade rating and another gives it a junk rating. Generally speaking, regulators require bonds to receive investment grade ratings from two different agencies. Thus, crossover credit is often not strong enough to allow banks to invest in them.

Crossover Fund A mutual fund that invests in both publicly-traded companies and private equity. A crossover fund usually has higher risk than most mutual funds, depending on the types of companies in which it invests, but it normally has both

high yield and growth. Crossover funds are considered better as long-term investments, rather than short-term.

Crossover Investor An investor who buys an interest in a company at numerous stages in its life cycle. This especially refers to one who buys stock in a company before, during, and after its IPO. The crossover investor's strategy is to buy at different stages of the life cycle to maximize returns. See also: Buy and hold.

Crossover Rate When comparing two different but similar projects, the specific returns required for the projects to have the same net present value. Because two similar securities may have different volatility, calculating the crossover rate helps to determine which will be more profitable in the short and long terms. For example, one dotcom company may achieve a steady rate of growth, but only slowly over time, while a second dotcom may achieve the same returns in a shorter timeframe, but with greater vulnerability to market downturns. Calculating the rate at which each will achieve a desired net present value, assuming no massive changes in circumstances, may help an investor make decisions regarding which to buy and which to sell.

Crossover Refunding Bond A bond that is issued to redeem another bond before maturity. It differs from other refunding bonds in that proceeds from a crossover refunding bond are held in escrow until the date at which the first bond is actually redeemed.

Cross-Sectional Ratio Analysis The analysis of a financial ratio of a company with the same ratio of different companies in the same industry. For example, one may conduct a cross-sectional ratio analysis of the debt ratios of multiple companies in the telecommunications industry. Quite simply, one does this by taking the debt ratios of each company and comparing them to one another. An analyst does this in order to find the company with healthiest financial status. This is helpful in making informed investment decisions.

Cross-State Air Pollution Rule A rule mandated by the U.S. Environmental Protection Agency requiring states to reduce the air pollution emitted by companies in their state. The rule applies if the EPA declares that the state permits too much air pollution. The rule was adopted in 2011.

Cross-Training The act or practice of training employees to perform multiple jobs if necessary. For example, a salesperson may train the office manager to make sales calls and the office manager may show the salesperson how to pay vendors. This way, if the salesperson goes on maternity leave or the office manager is fired, the company is able to function while a replacement is found.

Crowd 1. Members of an exchange who congregate in a certain area on a trading floor to make transactions. Crowds especially trade in certain securities. For example, the active bond crowd may gather in one area of the floor while the cabinet crowd may gather in another. 2. Informal for most investors. People with different investment philosophies alternately advise to either follow or avoid following the crowd.

Crowding Out A situation in which a government, especially the U.S. Government, borrows so much money that it discourages lending to private businesses. Crowding out generally occurs because lenders prefer the government as a borrower because it is much less risky and the government is able to pay any interest rate. Thus, when the government is borrowing heavily and lenders have only a finite amount they can lend, it may crowd out private borrowers.

Crown A former coin in the United Kingdom equal in value to five shillings, or 1/4 of one British pound. The last crown was minted in 1965. Following decimalization in 1971, a 25-pence coin was minted to replace the crown. Informally, crowns were called dollars, recalling the time when one pound was worth four U.S. dollars.

Crown Corporation A corporation owned by the government of Canada or one of its provincial governments. The federal or provincial government has a large say in setting the budget of crown corporations and appoints the board of directors, but in general they operate as private companies on a day-to-day basis. However, crown corporations are sometimes thought to be less efficient than other companies and several, such as Air Canada, have been privatized. A famous example of a current crown corporation is the Canadian Broadcasting Corporation.

Crown Jewel 1. A particularly valuable or important asset that a company owns. For example, a car manufacturer's three best producing factories may be considered its crown jewels. 2. Describing an antitakeover measure in which a company sells many or all of its crown jewel assets. A crown jewel policy is designed to make the company less attractive to potential acquirers. The obvious disadvantage to a crown jewel policy is the possibility that, even if the company remains independent, the lack of its crown jewels may render it unable to maintain its operations easily. It is a type of scorched earth policy. See also: Poison pill, Suicide pill.

Crown Jewel Lockup Agreement An offer to sell the stock or assets of a company to an investor most desirable to management. A company makes a crown jewel lockup agreement when it is the target of a hostile takeover. A crown jewel lockup agreement is beneficial to management because the friendly investor will likely let managers keep their jobs, but it may violate management's fiduciary responsibility to act in the best interest of shareholders.

Crown Law The legal system in the United Kingdom. Crown law also serves as the basis for law in many Commonwealth countries, such as Canada, Australia, and Singapore. Importantly, Crown Law serves as the basis for financial law in some organizations within countries that do not belong to the Commonwealth. The Dubai International Financial Centre, for example, operates under British common law.

CRSP Tapes Records of stock prices compiled on magnetic tapes and released in monthly and daily batches by the Center for Research in Security Prices.

Crunching Slang; a situation in which the price of an investment rapidly drops below its support level.

Crush Spread A commodity spread involving soybean products. In it, one buys soybean futures at the same time one sells futures in soybean meal and soybean oil. Crushes are useful because they can take advantage of price spread between the underlying soybeans and products that can be derived from soybeans. See also: Reverse crush.

Cruzado The currency of Brazil between 1986 and 1989. It replaced the second Brazilian cruzeiro at a rate of one cruzado for 1,000 cruzeiro. The cruzado was issued in an attempt to control Brazilian inflation; this attempt failed and the cruzado was replaced by the cruzado novo in 1989.

Cruzado Novo The currency of Brazil between 1989 and 1990. It replaced the first cruzado at a rate of one new cruzado to 1,000 old cruzado. The cruzado novo was issued in an attempt to control Brazilian inflation; this attempt failed and the cruzado novo was replaced by the third cruzeiro in 1990.

Cruzeiro Real The currency of Brazil from 1993 to 1994. It replaced the third cruzeiro at a rate of 1,000 cruzeiro to one cruzeiro real. Like its predecessor currency, it experienced high inflation. It was quickly replaced by the Brazilian real.

Crystallization The act of selling an asset and immediately buying the same asset back. One does this for tax purposes; that is, one sells the asset in order to realize a capital loss, but buys it back because one believes it still represents a solid investment. Most tax agencies have rules forbidding or limiting crystallization.

CS 1. ISO 3166-1 alpha-2 code for Serbia and Montenegro before it separated into two independent countries. This was the code used in international transactions to and from bank accounts in Serbia and Montenegro. **2.** ISO 3166-2 geocode for Serbia and Montenegro. This was used as an international standard for shipping to Serbia and Montenegro. In both cases, the code is obsolete.

CSD ISO 4217 code for the Serbian dinar prior to 2006. It was introduced in 2003 when Yugoslavia formally separated into Serbia and Montenegro. It replaced the Yugoslav dinar at par. The code changed to RSD when Serbia became fully independent.

C-Share A class of mutual fund with a constant load. The load is a fee that the investor pays in order to maintain his/her investment in a mutual fund; it is designed to cover the fund's costs. A constant load, unlike a front-end or back-end load, is paid on an ongoing basis, usually annually. See also: 12b-1 fee.

CSHH ISO 3166-3 code for Czechoslovakia, which separated into the Czech Republic and Slovakia in 1993. ISO 3166-3 codes are used to indicate names of countries that are no longer used.

CSK ISO 4217 code for the Czechoslovak koruna. The koruna was introduced in 1945, after the end of World War II. As Czechoslovakia was under Communist rule for much of the latter half of the 20th century, the koruna was under tight government control. The currency was replaced by the Czech koruna and the Slovak koruna in 1993, when Czechoslovakia split into two countries.

CSXX ISO 3166-3 code for Serbia and Montenegro, which ceased to exist in 2006 when Serbia and Montenegro separated into two completely separate countries. ISO 3166-3 codes are used to indicate names of countries that are no longer used.

CT 1. ISO 3166-1 alpha-2 code for the Canton and Enderbury Islands prior to their transfer to Kiribati. This was the code used in international transactions to and from bank accounts on the islands. **2.** ISO 3166-2 geocode for the Canton and Enderbury Islands. This was used as an international standard for shipping to the Canton and Enderbury Islands. In both cases, the code is obsolete.

CTKI ISO 3166-3 code for the Canton and Enderbury Islands, which acceded to Kiribati in 1979. ISO 3166-3 codes are used to indicate names of countries and territories that are no longer used.

CU 1. ISO 3166-1 alpha-2 code for the Republic of Cuba. This is the code used in international transactions to and from Cuban bank accounts. **2.** ISO 3166-2 geocode for Cuba. This is used as an international standard for shipping to Cuba. Each province and special municipality has its own code with the prefix "CU." For example, the code for the Province of Granma is ISO 3166-2:CU-12.

Cuata A nickname for the 25-cent coin in Panama, which is worth 1/4 of one Panamanian balboa. The word is derived from the quarter coin of the U.S. dollar, which circulates alongside the cuata.

CUB GOST 7.67 Latin three-letter geocode for Cuba. The code is used for transactions to and from Cuban bank accounts and for international shipping to Cuba. As with all GOST 7.67 codes, it is used primarily in Cyrillic alphabets.

Cuban Convertible Peso One of two currencies in Cuba. It is pegged to the U.S. dollar at a one-to-one ratio, meaning that one could present one convertible peso to the Central Bank of Cuba and redeem it for one dollar. Because the other currency in Cuba, the Cuban peso, is an inconvertible currency, the convertible peso is Cuba's only point of access to international foreign exchange markets.

Cuban Peso One of two official currencies in Cuba. The other is the convertible peso. The Cuban peso has no official value outside of Cuba. To convert pesos, one must first convert them to convertible pesos, which are then exchangeable for other currencies. Most workers receive portions of their salaries in both currencies. They buy basic items like food with Cuban pesos, and use convertible pesos for luxury goods.

Cubicle Vulture An employee who takes office supplies or other things from the desk of a co-worker who has been fired or laid off. It may also refer to one who jockeys to take over a desk or cubicle thought to be more desirable than his/her own.

Cubitus An ancient Roman unit of length approximately equivalent to 444 millimeters.

CUC ISO 4217 code for the Cuban convertible peso. The peso is one of two official currencies in Cuba, the other being the "ordinary" Cuban peso. One may exchange convertible pesos for other currencies. That is, in order to convert pesos, one must first convert them to convertible pesos, which are then exchangeable for other currencies. Most workers receive portions of their salaries in both currencies; they buy basic items like food with pesos and use CUC for luxury goods.

Cuig Phingin A coin that circulated in the Republic of Ireland between 1969 and 2002. It was equal in value to 1/20 of one Irish pound.

Culeus An ancient Roman unit of liquid volume approximately equivalent to 254 liters.

Cullingey An obsolete Indian unit of weight approximately equivalent to 5.265 grams.

Cullishigay An obsolete Indian unit of dry volume approximately equivalent to 44 liters.

Cum Dividend Describing a share being traded where the buyer is entitled to the next dividend. That is, the seller sells the right to the next dividend along with the actual share. Shares are traded cum dividend before the ex-dividend date.

Cum Warrant A situation in which a security has a warrant attached to it. That is, the buyer of the security is eligible for a warrant that was declared prior to the purchase of the security, but had not been distributed.

Cumulative A preferred stock where the publicly-traded company must pay all dividends. If a company misses a dividend payment for any reason, it still owes it to cumulative preferred stockholders. That is, all dividends that were "skipped" must be paid to cumulative preferred stockholders before any dividends are paid to common stock holders. This contrasts with non-cumulative preferred stock, where stockholders must forgo dividend payments that are missed. Most preferred stock is cumulative.

Cumulative Abnormal Return In stocks, the sum of all the differences between the expected returns and the actual returns up to a given point in time. Since the expected return is computed by an asset pricing model, the cumulative abnormal return may be used to determine how accurate the model is. More often, it is used to investigate the affect extraneous events have on stock prices.

Cumulative Audience The total number of persons a radio or television broadcast reaches. Productions with higher cumulative audiences receive higher revenue from advertisers because there are more people watching or listening to the broadcast. The cumulative audience is also called the unduplicated audience or the reach.

Cumulative Dividend Feature A characteristic of preferred stock in which all dividends on preferred stock must be paid before any dividends are paid on common stock. That is, if a publicly-traded company stops paying dividends on preferred stock, it must stop paying dividends on all stock. If the company wishes to begin paying dividends on common stock again, it must pay what are called dividend arrears; that is, it must pay all back preferred stock dividends before any common stock dividends.

Cumulative Preferred Stock Preferred stock for which the publicly-traded company must pay all dividends. If a company misses a dividend payment for any reason, it still owes it to cumulative preferred stockholders. That is, all dividends that were "skipped" must be paid to cumulative preferred stockholders before any dividends are paid to common stock holders. This contrasts with non-cumulative preferred stock, for which stockholders must forgo dividend payments that are missed. Most preferred stock is cumulative preferred stock.

Cumulative Total Return The return or yield on an investment or portfolio over a given period of time, expressed in non-annualized terms. Before making an investment, one generally calculates the expected return, which is an important aspect of an investment's risk analysis. The cumulative total return is what objectively happened to the investment. It is vitally important to note that the cumulative total return is not expressed in annualized terms.

Cumulative Translation Adjustment Account On a balance sheet, an account where a company reports fluctuations in exchange rates that have occurred since it acquired an asset in a foreign currency. CTA accounts exist because FASB No. 52 requires companies to report assets held in foreign currencies to be reported at their current exchange rates.

Cumulative Volume Index In technical analysis, an index tracking possible future price movements for the broader market. It is calculated by subtracting the volume of declining stocks from the volume of advancing stocks and adding the difference to a running count. A declining CVI is thought to be bearish while an advancing CVI is thought bullish. See also: OBV.

Cumulative Voting In electing members of a board of directors, a system where common shareholders have one vote per share multiplied by the number of directors to be elected. Cumulative voting allows shareholders to apply all votes to one person or to divide them up between candidates. For example, if a person owns a single share and there are five empty seats on the board, that person has five votes.

Cun A unit of length in China approximately equivalent to 3.33 centimeters. It is sometimes called a Chinese inch.

Cuna A Spanish term for wedge. It is used to refer to a triangle pattern.

Cunji In China, a political subdivision equivalent to a village.

CUP ISO 4217 code for the Cuban peso. The peso is one of two official currencies in Cuba, the other being the convertible peso. The CUP has no official value outside of Cuba; to convert CUP, one must first convert it to convertible pesos, which are then exchangeable for other currencies. Most workers receive portions of their salaries in both currencies; they buy basic items like food with CUP and use convertible pesos for luxury goods.

Cup and Handle In technical analysis, a price trend that resembles a cup and a handle on a chart. It occurs when the price of a security reaches a high and then takes a U-shaped downtrend and uptrend. This is the cup. When the price approaches its previous high, investors who bought at or near the previous high tend to sell their shares, which causes the price to drop slightly. This is the handle. After the handle "completes," the price of the security tends to increase significantly. Technical analysts view cups and handles as buy signals under the correct circumstances.

Curb Exchange Informal for the American Stock Exchange.

Curb Market The market for securities trading outside normal exchange hours. The curb market may affect the price of a security once the exchange re-opens. See also: Over-the-counter.

Curb Trading The act or practice of trading outside an exchange's regulation. Generally speaking, curb trading occurs online or over a telephone. It is a form of over-the-counter trading. It should not be confused with a trading curb.

Cure 1. To correct an error. **2.** To make a payment, either in full or in part, on a liability that is in default.

Currency Money generally accepted in circulation in a certain jurisdiction. That is, currency is any form of money that businesses in a certain jurisdiction will accept in exchange for goods and services. Usually, the domestic government sets its own currency and provides penalties to persons and businesses in its jurisdiction that do not accept it. However, some countries (especially those experiencing hyperinflation) accept other countries' currencies informally. Alternatively, a country may use the currency of another (as some countries have done with the U.S. dollar) or pool resources to make an international currency accepted in several countries (the euro being the most prominent example). See also: Foreign exchange.

Currency Appreciation An increase in the value of one currency with respect to another. This means that one unit of the appreciating currency buys more units of the other currency than it did previously. While this can be a good sign, as it may indicate a low rate of inflation, it also makes exports from the country with the appreciating currency more expensive, while making imports less expensive.

Currency Arbitrage An investment strategy in which one buys a currency on one market and instantly sells it on another market. Currency arbitrage takes advantage of temporary discrepancies in price between the two markets. Because currency markets are so liquid, opportunities for currency arbitrage are few and generally last only for a few seconds. Conducting it requires sophisticated computer software.

Currency Basket A portfolio of several currencies with different weightings. For example, one may construct a currency basket with 40% euros, 35% U.S. dollars, and 25% British pounds; the percentages determine the basket's value. Using a currency basket is a common way to peg a currency without overexposing it to the fluctuations of a single currency. For example, Kuwait shifted the peg of the Kuwaiti dinar to a currency basket from the U.S. dollar in 2007 because the dollar was weak at the time, resulting in high inflation.

Currency Board An agency of a government that determines the value of the domestic currency. Specifically, the currency board decides whether to peg the currency to another or to allow it to float. Theoretically, it may also peg the currency to the value of some commodity, such as gold, but that is exceedingly rare. In most developed countries, central banks perform the duties of currency boards. As separate entities, they are found mainly in developing countries.

Currency Call Option A call option in which the underlying asset is a foreign currency. The option gives the holder the right but not the obligation to buy a set amount of the currency at a certain exchange rate on or before the expiration date. As with other currency options, these are largely used when international corporations wish to hedge against the possibility of adverse movements in foreign exchange rates.

Currency Carry Trade A position in which a trader borrows money in one currency at a low interest rate and lends the same money in another currency at a higher interest rate. A currency carry trade derives its profit from the exchange rate between the two currencies and the difference in interest rates. The major risk associated with a currency carry trade is that the exchange rate will move in an adverse direction, eliminating the profit from the interest rate difference.

Currency Centre An organization in Ireland that issues legal tender coins and banknotes for general use. It was established in 1978 and is based in Dublin. It is also called the Irish Mint.

Currency Depreciation A decrease in the value of a currency with respect to other currencies. This means that the depreciated currency is worth fewer units of some other currency. While depreciation means a reduction in value, it can be advantageous as it makes exports in the depreciated currency less expensive. For example, suppose one unit of Currency A is worth one unit of Currency B. If Currency A depreciates such that it becomes worth half of one unite of Currency B, then exports denominated in Currency A are only half as expensive when trading in a Currency B market. See also: Floating currency.

Currency Diversification Any investment strategy that involves investing in securities denominated in several currencies. For example, one may buy stocks that trade in U.S. dollars, British pounds, Japanese yen, and euros. One conducts a currency diversification strategy to reduce the foreign exchange risk involved in trading with only one or two currencies.

Currency Fluctuation A change in an exchange rate. If the British pound is worth $2 on Monday, and $1.80 on Tuesday, a (somewhat dramatic) currency fluctuation has occurred. Currency fluctuations happen constantly and occur for all floating currencies.

Currency Forward An agreement between two parties to exchange a certain amount in currencies at a certain rate at a certain time. When a forward contract of any sort is made, terms are negotiated directly between the parties, unlike a futures contract, which trades on an exchange. Partly because there is little secondary market for forward contract, determining the forward price is a zero-sum game: one party will gain on the contract and one will lose. Thus, in a currency forward, each party believes that the prevailing exchange rate will move in a direction favorable to him/her by the expiry of the contract.

Currency Futures A futures contract in which the underlying asset is a currency. Two parties agree to buy and sell a certain currency at a given exchange rate with respect to another currency at some point in the future. The market for currency futures contracts is important in estimating the future value of different currencies.

Currency Futures Option An option contract where the underlying asset is a currency futures contract. That is, a currency futures option gives the holder the right, but not the obligation, to buy (for a call) or sell (for a put) a currency futures contract;, which is a contract to exchange two currencies at an agreed-upon exchange rate at a certain point in the future, regardless of what the exchange rate is at that future time. This helps the holder manage his/her foreign exchange risk.

Currency Hedge In equities, the act of holding a position in a stock denominated in a foreign currency while holding an equal but opposite position in the currency itself. This protects the investor from fluctuations in the value of a currency adversely affecting the stock holdings.

Currency in Circulation The cash, coins, and demand deposits that constitute the money in an economy that may be easily exchanged for goods and services. The currency in circulation is one of the most liquid measurements of the money supply. See also: M0, M1.

Currency Option An option contract in which the underlying asset is a foreign currency. The option gives the holder the right but not the obligation to buy (for a call) or sell (for a put) a set amount of the currency at a certain exchange rate on or before the expiration date. They are largely used when international corporations wish to hedge against the possibility of adverse movements in foreign exchange rates.

Currency Overlay The practice of using a firm specializing in currency hedging. This firm is called the overlay manager. The overlay manager takes a number of positions in various foreign currencies in order to reduce the client's foreign exchange risk.

Currency Overvaluation A situation in which the exchange rate of a currency exceeds what the open market is willing to pay. For example, currency overvaluation may occur when central banks buy more of a currency that they ordinarily do when other trading is flat. Currency overvaluation makes a country's exports more expensive and may thus be detrimental to international trade.

Currency Pair In foreign exchange, two currencies whose values are compared. The first currency is called the base currency and is given a value of 1, while the second is called the quote currency and is expressed as "quote currencies per one base currency." For example, if one compares the British pound to the U.S. dollar and the pound is the base currency, it is written as GBPUSD and expressed as "dollars per one pound."

Currency Put Option Option contract allowing the holder to sell a currency at a given foreign exchange price within or at a certain period of time.

Currency Revaluation The active decision of a government to increase or decrease the value of its own currency in relation to other currencies. Revaluation occurs exclusively in fixed currencies, when the currency in question is pegged to another currency. A government generally revalues its own currency when it wishes to make adjustments to its peg to another currency. If the revaluation is a devaluation, it makes the country's exports less expensive in foreign markets.

Currency Risk In currency exchange, the possibility that one currency will devalue to the exchanger's detriment. For example, someone may move to the United Kingdom from the United States and change all of his/her money from dollars to pounds. If he/she moves back to the United States with the same amount of pounds, there is the possibility that the pound will have devalued, resulting in fewer dollars than he/she brought to the U.K. In 1996, economist Conway Lackman suggested an extension of the Capital Asset Pricing Model to help calculate exchange risk in international trade.

Currency Risk Sharing An agreement between two parties where they share the foreign exchange risk associated with a transaction. For example, a buyer in Britain and a seller in the United States may agree to split the difference between any gains or losses that may result from the sale of the good or service. Currency risk sharing reduces foreign exchange risk for both parties.

Currency Selection An active management strategy for a portfolio or fund with a basic set of securities denominated in different currencies. The investor or money manager changes the securities represented in the portfolio or fund as changes to one's investment goals change. A currency selection strategy exposes the portfolio or fund to foreign exchange risk, but the money manager can also take advantage of changes to foreign currency values.

Currenex An online exchange for the trading of currencies. Currenex is used most often by governments and institutional investors. It was established in New York in 1999.

Current Account Balance The balance of trade within a country, less the value of financial transfers. That is, the current account balance is the difference between the value of goods and services a country exports and the value of the goods and services it imports.

Current Assets Cash and other assets expected to be converted to cash within a year. Examples include accounts receivable, prepaid expenses, and many negotiable securities. Current assets are calculated on a balance sheet and are one way to measure a company's liquidity. Current assets tend not to add much to the company's assets, but help keep it running on a day-to-day basis. See also: Fixed asset, Gross working capital.

Current Cost of Supplies Referring to the net income of a company after accounting for changes in expenses, especially those that affect the company's products. Calculating net income that accounts for the current cost of supplies is most common for companies that produce and sell commodities. For example, because oil and natural gas prices are quite volatile, the current cost of supplies can greatly impact an energy company's net income.

Current Delivery Among several different futures contracts, the one with the shortest maturity. For example, given three futures contracts, one expiring in March, one in June, and one in September, the current deliver is the one expiring in March. It is also called the nearby deliver. See also: Most distant futures contract.

Current Dollar The value of a dollar at the time at which it is measured. This varies from year to year, and, in times of high inflation, it may vary more often. For example, the current dollar value of $10 in 1950 is different from the current dollar value of $10 in 2009. Comparing current dollars may help in determining the rate of inflation.

Current Income Describing a portfolio containing primarily fixed-income securities and blue chip stocks that pay high dividends. A current income portfolio provides a steady income to the portfolio holder. As such, a portfolio does not hold high-growth or start up stocks; it follows a relatively conservative investment strategy. Most commonly, current income portfolios are held by retirees and others who seek a modest (but still substantial) return at little risk.

Current Issue In Treasury securities, the most recent issue. Current issues trade much more actively than older issues of Treasury securities. At any given time, there is a current issue for each type of Treasury security: notes, bills, and bonds and all their subcategories with different maturities. For example, a 20-year Treasury bond and a 30-year Treasury bond have two different current issues, but, in both cases, it is the most recently auctioned one. The current issue is also the on-the-run issue. See also: Off-the-run issue.

Current Liabilities On a balance sheet, any liability expected to be paid off in one year or less. Common examples of current liabilities are short-term bills and accounts payable.

Current Market Value The value of a portfolio. This is calculated by aggregating the market values of the securities represented in the portfolio. One may have a paper gain or a paper loss on one's portfolio when measuring the current market value. However, it is important to note that these gains or losses are not locked in until one closes the positions in the portfolio.

Current Maturity The time between today's date and the maturity date for a particular bond. For example, if a company issued a 20 years bond five years ago, its current maturity is 15 years. The current maturity is important for a bond's valuation. See also: Yield to maturity, Duration.

Current Order The payment on a loan or other liability that is due next. For example, if a student loan is due on the third of each month, and it is currently December 8th, the current order is the loan payment due on January 3rd of the following year.

Current Portion of Long-Term Debt On a balance sheet, the part of a company's long-term debt that must be paid within a year. The current portion of long-term debt is a liability and is recorded on the balance sheet separately from current liabilities and long-term liabilities. Investors may add the current portion of long-term debt to the current liabilities and compare them to current cash flow to determine if the company is at risk of default. A high amount of current portion of long-term debt compared to poor cash flow is considered a sign of poor financial health.

Current Production Rate The highest interest rate payable on mortgage-backed securities guaranteed by the Government National Mortgage Association (Ginnie Mae). The current production rate is usually half a point less than what the homeowners are paying in interest on their mortgage. For example, if homeowners whose mortgages back the securities are paying 6% on their mortgages, the maximum interest payable is almost always 5.5%. See also: Ginnie Mae Pass-Through.

Current Rate Method On a balance sheet, a way to recognize all expenses and revenues made in a foreign currency by translating them according to their spot exchange rate. The current rate method, while technically correct, makes financial statements more difficult to compile and evaluate because of the fluctuations in exchange rates that inevitably occur. See also: Constant currencies, Foreign currency translation.

Current Yield The income from dividends (for stocks) or coupons (for bonds) divided by the market price of the security, expressed as a percentage. This is sometimes used in making the decision of whether or not to buy a security, but it does not accurately reflect its return, as the market price changes constantly. It is also called the current return or the running yield.

Current/Noncurrent Method In accounting, a convention where all current assets and liabilities in a foreign currency are translated to the domestic currency at the current exchange rate while all long-term assets and liabilities are translated at the exchange rate in effect when each asset or liability was acquired. See also: Temporal Method.

Curtailment The act or process of reducing a company's operations in order to bring stability to the company. Curtailment usually occurs when the company has been experiencing unsustainable growth that it is unable to manage effectively. Tactics of curtailment include spinning off subsidiaries, laying off staff, and generally focusing the company's operations on the best products that it is able to create effectively. Curtailment is intended to improve efficiency and increase profits.

Cushion 1. Period of time during which a bond cannot be called. Interest payments are guaranteed during the cushion, but not after, as the bond may be prematurely redeemed at any point after the call date. **2.** A reserve account, or the function a reserve account serves, usually to pay off bad debt. **3.** An advantageous debt-to-equity ratio, usually less than 40%.

Cushion Bond A callable bond with coupons that are above prevailing interest rates. A cushion bond is more expensive than other bonds. If interest rates rise, the value of a cushion bond depreciates less than other bonds because its interest rate was already high compared to others. However, if interest rates fall, the issuer may call the bond, resulting in less appreciation and a greater prepayment risk.

Cushion Theory In investing, a theory stating that a stock on which there are a large number of short positions will eventually rise in price as investors move to cover the short positions. That is, a stock that many investors have sold over a period of time eventually has upward pressure build as buyers move to buy the shares being sold, creating demand. See also: Short selling.

CUSIP Number A nine-digit number assigned to every stock and registered bond that trades in the United States. The number is assigned by CUSIP, which is owned by the American Bankers Association and is operated by S&P. A CUSIP number facilitates trade and settlement by making each security unique to every other of the same class. CUSIP numbers are recorded in each trade.

Custo Brasil A term used to describe the high cost of business in Brazil. Custo Brasil comes at least in part from corruption, regulation, and lack of infrastructure. The term itself is Portuguese for "Brazil cost."

Custodial Account An account at a bank, brokerage, or insurance company held by an adult guardian on behalf of a minor child. That is, the minor child owns the custodial account, but the parent or guardian manages it and makes all decisions related to it. The child takes control of the account at a certain age: 18, 21, or 25, depending on the jurisdiction. Importantly, the account is taxed at the guardian's marginal tax rate until the child turns 18, at which point it is taxed at the child's rate.

Custodial Care Non-medical care given to individuals who are unable to perform activities of daily living. Examples of custodial care include helping a person dress herself, cook or feed herself, and use the bathroom. Custodial care at home is available through some private insurance plans. That is, the insurance may pay for a nurse to come to a disabled person's house and help with the activities of daily living. Medicare may also pay for custodial care but generally only within a nursing home. See also: Long-Term Care Insurance.

Custodial Fee A fee a brokerage or other financial institution charges for safekeeping services. Safekeeping or custody is a service in which the brokerage or financial institution holds securities on behalf of the client, which reduces the risk of the client losing his/her assets or having them stolen. They are also available to the brokerage to sell at the client's demand. Like a bank, custody provides an investor a place to store assets with little risk. Unlike a bank, custodians are not allowed to use the items in safekeeping for their own ends. Assets in custody are not fungible for the brokerage because they remain in the client's name.

Custodian A brokerage or other financial institution that holds and manages a client's securities or other assets on his/her behalf. This reduces the risk of the client losing his/her assets or having them stolen. They are also available to the brokerage to sell at the client's demand. Like a bank, a custodian provides an investor a place to store assets with little risk. Brokerages normally require a fee for custodial services. See also: Safekeeping.

Custodian Bank A bank that holds and manages a client's securities or other assets on his/her behalf. For example, the bank may hold stock certificates for the client. This reduces the risk of the client losing his/her assets or having them stolen. A custodian bank provides an investor a place to store assets with little risk. Custodian banks normally require a fee for this service. See also: Safekeeping.

Custody A service in which a brokerage or other financial institution holds securities on behalf of the client. This reduces the risk of the client losing his/her assets or having them stolen. They are also available to the brokerage to sell at the client's demand. Like a bank, custody provides an investor a place to store assets with little risk. Unlike a bank, custodians are not allowed to use the items in safekeeping for their own ends. Assets in custody are not fungible for the brokerage because they remain on the client's name. For this reason, these institutions normally charge custodial fees for safekeeping services.

Custody-Only Trading A system in which shares of a stock may only be traded if the holder's name appears on the stock certificate. That is, the shares may be traded only if the certificate physically changes hands. Not all companies use a custody-only trading system; those that do adopt the system use it to protect the share price against naked short sellers.

Customary Law A practice in a group or society that has never been codified but has been so common for so long that it is considered legally enforceable. English common law is largely derived from customary law. Likewise, most international law is customary.

Customer An individual or organization that buys (or has the potential of buying) a good or service from a seller. A customer can be new or long standing and can tend toward large or small purchases, depending both on the customer and the type of business being patronized. Marketing and customer service are used to attract and retain customers.

Customer Activated Terminal A kiosk at which a customer can insert a card and retrieve information or receive other services. The most common type of customer activated terminal is an ATM.

Customer Base The group of customers to whom a company primarily sells its products. A customer base may be rooted in a geographic area, or its constituents may have some common need regardless of where they are located. A customer base may expand or contract over time.

Customer Information File A file a bank keeps on each of its account holders and other clients. It contains information on account balances, outstanding loans, assets and so forth. It is updated frequently to ensure correct information.

Customer Initiated Entry An electronic transaction with a bank that occurs at the order of a customer. Examples of customer initiated entries include transactions on an ATM or over the telephone.

Customer List A list of previous buyers from a company. The company maintains a customer list in order to continue the business relationship. That is, companies use customer lists to keep up with buyers and to promote customer loyalty.

Customer Loyalty The likelihood that a customer will continue to patronize the same businesses. A number of factors may influence customer loyalty, including length of the business relationship, quality of customer service, and prices.

Customer Profile A dossier detailing the demographic background, buying habits, credit history and other information of a customer. Customer profiles may help a company market its products to individual customers more effectively. See also: Customer information file.

Customer Type Indicator Code A numbered code used on futures exchanges to indicate different types of transactions. CTIs are filed (along with other paper work) with the exchange's clearing house. The codes are numbered one, two, three, and four. A code of one means that an exchange member was trading on his/her own account. Two indicates transactions by clearing members on their proprietary accounts. Three is a transaction conducted by a member for another member. Finally, four is a transaction by a member for a client.

Customer's Loan An agreement that a client may make with a brokerage allowing the brokerage to borrow the client's margin securities to cover short sales and fail to delivers made by other clients. Margin securities are securities that the client uses as collateral in order to borrow from the brokerage and buy other securities. Even though the brokerage possesses the margin securities, they still belong to the client. As a result the brokerage must have a customer's loan agreement on file to use the securities for other purposes. A customer's loan agreement should not be confused with a margin agreement. See also: Margin account.

Customer's Man Informal for broker.

Customers' Net Debit Balance The amount of money an investor owes on a margin loan. This is calculated as the amount the investor directly owes his/her broker. It does not account for the paper profit the investor has made on various transactions. When determining the amount owed in the case of a margin call, one generally uses the adjusted debit balance, which starts with the debit balance and subtracts the amount of applicable paper profit. The customers' net debit balance is usually called simply the debt balance, but the former term is used most often on the NYSE.

Customized Benchmark Any benchmark designed by a broker, investment advisor, or a similar party that is tailored to meet the investment goals of a particular client.

Customs A general term for an agency in a country responsible for controlling the flow of goods into the country. Customs agencies attempt to prevent dangerous, hazardous or illegal materials from entering the country, and also collect tariffs and other taxes. They may also enforce import quotas.

Customs Bond A bond or insurance policy covering a company in the event that it loses money as the result of failing to comply with customs regulations. A customs bond is posted with the government of the importing country to guarantee payment of fines and other fees.

Customs Broker An individual or firm licensed to represent an importer or exporter in front of customs authorities. A customs broker must ordinarily be authorized to act as such by the local government. The broker files the appropriate paperwork and helps ensure that the goods being imported comply with all applicable regulations. A customs broker is also called a customshouse broker, especially in the United States.

Customs Clearing Agent A person who is responsible for a client's customs procedures. A customs clearing agent ensures compliance with relevant laws in order to expedite the import or export process.

Customs Cooperation Council Also called the CCC. An early name for the World Customs Organization.

Customs Cooperation Council Nomenclature A system for categorizing imports to determine the appropriate tariff or regulation to apply. It was established as the Brussels Tariff Nomenclature and changed to its later name in 1976. In 1989, it was replaced by the Harmonized Commodity Description and Coding System.

Customs Court A federal court in the United States with jurisdiction over disputes relating to customs law. For example, if an importer disagrees with the government over the proper tariff to be paid, it may take the matter to the Customs Court. It was established in 1926.

Customs Gold Unit A currency used in the Republic of China before its evacuation to Taiwan. It was issued in 1930, originally only to settle international trade transactions. It was pegged to the U.S. dollar and was backed by silver. In 1942, it began to circulate throughout Republic of China-controlled areas. In 1948, the year before the ROC retreated to Taiwan, the customs gold unit ceased to circulate.

Customs Modernization Act Legislation in the United States, passed in 1993, that sought to improve enforcement of customs and audits. At the time, it was one of the most sweeping changes to U.S. Customs in more than 200 years. The Act, which is commonly called the Mod Act, was part of larger legislation to bring the U.S. into compliance with the North American Free Trade Agreement.

Customs Union A market with the free movement of goods, services, labor, and capital between two or more jurisdictions. For example, even though Texas and Oklahoma are different places with different governments and regulations, the two have a customs union because workers do not need permission to move between them and one may transfer money between them without incurring any tariffs or fees. Most often, however, a customs union refers to a union between two or more countries, not regions within the same country. For example, the European Union is a customs union. See also: Free trade.

Customs Union of Belarus, Kazakhstan and Russia An international organization with the goal of eliminating all tariffs and trade barriers between member states. It is speculated that the union eventually might become a European Union-type organization for the former Soviet Union. It was established in 2010 and is sometimes called simply the Russian Customs Union.

Cut Off Date 1. In property law, the date at which an unclaimed security or other property is turned over to the state in which the last known owner was last known to reside. See also: Escheat. **2.** The date a discount, sale, or other especially lowered price on a product or products expires. **3.** The last day of a month in which a bank calculates the activity on its accounts. For example, if the cut off date is the fifteenth of the month, the bank calculates its accounts' activities from the fifteenth of one month to the fifteenth of the next. Statements are based on activities between cut off dates.

Cut Out To refuse to clear a transaction. See also: Clearing house, Settlement, Fail.

Cut, Cap and Balance Act Proposed legislation in the United States that would have made a debt limit increase contingent on significant spending cuts, a reduction in the size of the federal government to no greater than 18% of GDP, passage of a Balanced Budget Amendment to the U.S. Constitution by the House and Senate, and the rejection of all future tax increases without a two-thirds vote in both houses. The Cut, Cap and Balance Act passed the House of Representatives in 2011, but did not pass the Senate.

Cutoff Point The required rate of return needed to make an investment worth the expense. The cutoff point is subject and varies from investor to investor. However, in general, cutoff points vary by risk. That is, the cutoff point is almost higher for a riskier investment, meaning that the investor will not invest in a risky venture that is unlikely to have a high rate of return. Some investors adopt cutoff points as their personal investment policies, while others decide based on the situation.

Cut-Throat Competition Competition between two or more companies so fierce that they are unable to recoup the costs of making their products. This may happen especially if there are frequent or seasonal drops in demand. Over the long term, cut-throat competition is unsustainable for all companies involved. It is also called ruinous or destructive competition.

Cutting a Melon Informal; the act or practice of a publicly-traded company declaring an extra dividend. After a period of particularly high earnings, a company may cut a melon in order to share the additional profits with stockholders. Cutting a melon may involve a cash dividend, extra stock, or property.

CV 1. ISO 3166-1 alpha-2 code for the Republic of Cape Verde. This is the code used in international transactions to and from Cape Verdean bank accounts. **2.** ISO 3166-2 geocode for Cape Verde. This is used as an international standard for shipping to Cape Verde. However, it is not locally used; the nation uses its own National Geographic Code of Cape Verde.

CVE ISO 4217 code for the Cape Verdean escudo. It was introduced in 1914 and was pegged to the Portuguese escudo until the Cape Verde Islands became independent in 1975. Depreciation of the CVE led the Cape Verde Islands to re-establish the peg in 1998. It is currently pegged to the euro.

CX 1. ISO 3166-1 alpha-2 code for the Territory of Christmas Island. This is the code used in international transactions to and from Christmas Islander bank accounts.

2. ISO 3166-2 geocode for Christmas Island. This is used as an international standard for shipping to Christmas Island.

CXL On a ticker tape, an abbreviation indicating that a previously reported transaction has been canceled.

CXR GOST 7.67 Latin three-letter geocode for Christmas Island. The code is used for transactions to and from Christmas Islander bank accounts and for international shipping to Christmas Island. As with all GOST 7.67 codes, it is used primarily in Cyrillic alphabets.

CY 1. ISO 3166-1 alpha-2 code for the Republic of Cyprus. This is the code used in international transactions to and from Cypriot bank accounts. **2.** ISO 3166-2 geocode for Cyprus. This is used as an international standard for shipping to Cyprus. Each Cypriot district has its own code with the prefix "CY." For example, the code for the District of Pafos is ISO 3166-2:CY-05.

Cyathus An ancient Roman unit of volume approximately equivalent to 45 milliliters.

Cyberslacking In business, the act or practice of avoiding work by doing other things on one's computer. For example, one may chat on Facebook instead of doing work. Sometimes cyberslacking can, at first glance, appear to be work.

Cycle 1. See: Business cycle. **2.** See: Product cycle. **3:** See: Industry life cycle.

Cycle Billing The practice in which a company bills different customers at different times. For example, the company may send invoices to half its customers on the first of the month and the other half on the 15th. Cycle billing may help customers manage their cash flows. It may also help a company easily determine who has been billed and who has not.

Cyclical Industry An industry that tends to do poorly when most of the economy as a whole is performing poorly, and well when the economy is doing well. Cyclical industries may represent publicly-traded companies that are perceived to sell luxuries or products. For example, car companies sell expensive products (cars) that many people perceive to be necessities. However, because cars are expensive, consumers in bad economic times may decide to wait to buy cars until the economy improves. On the other hand, car companies tend to do rather well when the economy is doing well.

Cyclical Stock Stocks that tend to do poorly when most of the economy as a whole is performing poorly and vice versa. Cyclical stocks may represent publicly-traded companies that are perceived to be luxuries or that sell expensive products. For example, car companies sell expensive products (cars) that many people perceive to be necessities. However, because they are expensive, consumers in bad economic times may decide to wait to buy cars until the economy improves. On the other hand, car companies tend to do rather well when the economy is doing well.

Cyclical Unemployment Unemployment that increases when economic growth decreases and vice versa. Cyclical unemployment increases when demand for products is insufficient for businesses to justify the expense of keeping so many employees on staff. Likewise, the unemployment decreases when demand rises.

Cylinder A series of two transactions involving derivatives in which there is no initial cost to the investor. A common example of a cylinder is the sale of one derivative and the use of the proceeds to buy another. It is similar to a positive carry, but does not necessarily involve offsetting positions.

CYM GOST 7.67 Latin three-letter geocode for the Cayman Islands. The code is used for transactions to and from Cayman bank accounts and for international shipping to the Cayman Islands. As with all GOST 7.67 codes, it is used primarily in Cyrillic alphabets.

CYP GOST 7.67 Latin three-letter geocode for Cyprus. The code is used for transactions to and from Cypriot bank accounts and for international shipping to Cyprus. As with all GOST 7.67 codes, it is used primarily in Cyrillic alphabets.

Cypriot Pound The former currency of Cyprus. It was introduced by the British in 1879 and was pegged to the British pound at par until 1972. The pound was taken out of circulation and replaced by the euro in January 2008.

Cyrus Eaton A Canadian-American industrialist and investor. He made his fortune in oil, electricity and later worked in automotives and railroads. Despite an early association with John D. Rockefeller, Eaton opposed "eastern financiers" whom he thought had too much influence in American capitalism. He lived from 1883 to 1979.

CZ 1. ISO 3166-1 alpha-2 code for the Czech Republic. This is the code used in international transactions to and from Czech bank accounts. **2.** ISO 3166-2 geocode for the Czech Republic. This is used as an international standard for shipping to the Czech Republic. Each region and district has its own code with the prefix "CZ." For example, the code for Vysocina Region is ISO 3166-2:CZ-VY.

CZE GOST 7.67 Latin three-letter geocode for the Czech Republic. The code is used for transactions to and from Czech bank accounts and for international shipping to the Czech Republic. As with all GOST 7.67 codes, it is used primarily in Cyrillic alphabets.

Czech Koruna The currency of the Czech Republic. It was introduced in 1993, replacing the Czechoslovakian koruna when the Czech Republic separated from Slovakia. It is a floating currency. There has been much discussion of replacing the koruna with the euro, but, historically, there has been a great deal of opposition to this move within the Czech Republic.

Czechoslovak Koruna The currency of the former Czechoslovakia. It was introduced in 1919 and remained until 1993 (with a six-year exception during World War II). After the breakup of Czechoslovakia it was replaced by the Czech koruna and the Slovak koruna.

CZK ISO 4217 code for the Czech koruna. It was introduced in 1993, replacing the Czechoslovakian koruna when the Czech Republic separated from Slovakia. It is a floating currency. There has been much discussion of replacing the koruna with the euro, but, historically, there has been a great deal of opposition to this move within the Czech Republic.

D 1. A symbol appearing next to a stock listed on NASDAQ indicating that the stock is a new issue, especially the result of a reverse stock split. All NASDAQ listings use a four-letter abbreviation; if a "D" follows the abbreviation, this indicates that the security being traded is a new issue. **2.** A symbol appearing on a stock transaction table meaning that the share price is a new 52-week low. It is especially used in newspapers.

Daca Trayas An ancient Persian unit of length approximately equivalent to three meters.

Daerah In Brunei, a political subdivision approximately equivalent to a county.

Daerah Tingkat I In Indonesia, a political subdivision equivalent to a province.

Daerah Tingkat II In Indonesia, a political subdivision equivalent to a municipal government.

Daiei A Japanese company that manages one of the largest grocery store chains as well as clothing shops and department stores. It was established in 1957 and was, for a time, Japan's largest retailer. It is a publicly-traded company.

Daily Driver Technology one uses each day at work. Examples of daily drivers include personal computers and smart phones. A daily driver implies reliability and steadiness in the face of new technologies that are flashy but may take time to accept.

Daily Trading Limit The maximum amount of gain or loss that can occur on a particular security or, more commonly, derivative on a trading day. Derivatives, currencies, and commodities can be extremely volatile investments. In order to prevent this volatility from spiraling out of control, options and futures exchanges enact daily trading limits stating that a security cannot rise or fall more than a certain percent in a given trading day. If a security reaches the daily trading limit, trading on that security is suspended for the remainder of the day. This is called a locked market. See also: Limit up, Limit down.

Dain An obsolete Burmese unit of length approximately equivalent to 3.912 kilometers.

Daira In Algeria, a political subdivision equivalent to a county.

Daisy Chain A series of manipulative transactions on a security intended to create an impression of a high trading volume, suggesting interest in assets or securities that may not actually be there. This tends to increase the share price, which in turn encourages other investors to buy the security. When other investors become interested, the manipulating traders dump the security at an artificially high price. See also: Churning, Round-Trip Trading.

Daktylos An ancient Greek unit of length approximately equivalent to 19.3 millimeters.

Dalal Street An informal term for the Bombay Stock Exchange or for the investing community in India. See also: Wall Street.

Dam A subdivision of the mohar, the currency of Nepal prior to 1932. A dam was equivalent to 1/128 of a mohar.

Damages Money a jury gives to a party in a lawsuit to compensate for some injury. Damages may be divided into actual damages, which compensate for a real loss (such as the cost of repairing a car), and punitive damages, which penalize the other party. For example, a jury may require a defendant to pay $30,000 in actual damages to pay for the plaintiff's medical bills, and a further $100,000 to show how displeased the jury is with the defendant's actions.

Daman al-Mal In Islamic law, the legal liability to pay the debts of a partnership. Daman al-mal may be divided among the partners in various ways, depending on the nature of the partnership. See also: Musharika, Mudharaba.

Daman al-Talaf In Islamic law, the legal liability to pay for or replace damaged property under a partnership's care. For example, if a partnership receives a car to perform repairs, daman al-talaf stipulates which party is responsible if the car is accidentally destroyed.

Dan A unit of mass in China approximately equivalent to 50 kilograms.

Da-Na An ancient Sumerian unit of length approximately equivalent to 10.8 kilometers.

Danda An ancient Indian unit of length variously equivalent to values between 1.5 and two meters.

Dandy Roll A metal stamp coated with water and imprinted on a piece of paper during manufacture in order to create a watermark.

Daniel Starch and Associates A market research company that surveys advertisements in a wide variety of media and investigates their effectiveness. It disseminates its findings to clients in order to improve their advertising strategies.

Danish Krone The currency of Denmark. It was introduced in 1873, replacing the Danish rigsdaler. It was part of the Scandinavian Monetary Union until the beginning of World War I. During this time, the krone was pegged to gold. It was variously pegged to the German Reichsmark and the British pound in the middle 20th century. Denmark later joined the Bretton Woods Agreement, which tied the krone to the U.S. dollar (and, by extension, to gold). It is currently pegged to the ERM II, which ties the krone to the euro but allows it to remain somewhat independent.

Dao In ancient China, a political subdivision roughly equivalent to a province.

Dark Cloud Cover In candlestick charting, a bearish indicator in which a large black candle (representing a loss on the trading day) follows a large white candle (representing a gain on the previous trading day). The close of the current trading day must be about halfway between the opening and closing prices of the previous trading day. This is represented on the chart by drawing the bottom of the black candle next to the middle of the white candle. A dark cloud cover may represent the reversal of a previous bullish trend, and technical analysts look for confirmation in the following day's trading.

Dark Liquidity Pool A private securities exchange or trading platform. Dark liquidity pools do not publish the prices of their transactions, which allows investors to make larger transactions at lower cost than they might otherwise. Most traders in dark liquidity pools are institutional investors, such as mutual funds or hedge funds, that wish to protect the anonymity of their investments and/or investors. They also may not wish to cause price movements by the disclosure of their transactions. No dark liquidity pool is completely secretive: they must register with the SEC as either a securities exchange or a broker-dealer; they are governed by Regulation ATS, which stipulates certain transactions and prices that they must disclose under various circumstances. See also: Transparency.

Dassi In India, a slang term for a 10-paisa coin, which is worth 1/10 of one Indian rupee.

Data Mining The practice of looking for a pattern in a large amount of seemingly random data. Data mining is usually done with a computer program and helps in marketing. That is, a company can look at the (publicly available) purchase patterns of a person or group of persons and determine what products to direct at them.

Data Release Number A unique four-digit number attached to a student aid report, which outlines the federal financial aid available to students at a post-secondary educational institution.

Data Universal Numerical System More commonly called the DUNS system. A system developed by Dun & Bradford in which a business entity is assigned a unique, nine-digit number. The DUNS system is used by the United States government, the European Commission and the United Nations. It was introduced in 1963 to help organize Dun & Bradford's credit investigations.

Date Certain The date on which a contract expires or by which it must be completed. For example, every option contract has a date on which or by which the option must be exercised if it is to be exercised at all. This is the date certain on an option contract. The date certain is considered legally binding. See also: Quadruple witching day.

Dated Date The date on which interest begins to accrue on a bond or other fixed-income security. The dated date is usually the date on which coupon payments are made, or, in the case of the first dated date, the issue date. If one buys a fixed-income security between dated dates, one must compensate the seller for all interest that has accrued in addition to the purchase price. See also: Dirty price.

Dates Convention In accounting, the practice of recognizing cash flows on the date they actually occur. This applies to both incoming and outgoing cash flows. The dates convention affects the calculation and discounting of future cash flows. It is the opposite of the end-of-year convention, which treats cash flows as if they occurred on the last day of the fiscal year.

Dating The extension of credit by a bank to a customer for a longer-than-normal period of time.

Daugh An obsolete Scottish unit of area approximately equivalent to 640 acres.

David Packard An American businessman who co-founded Hewlett-Packard. He established the company in his garage with William Hewlett in 1939. Packard handled the management while Hewlett was responsible for the technical innovations. Packard served as president, CEO and chairman of the board for most of HP's history prior to 1993. He also served in the Nixon administration. Packard lived from 1912 to 1996.

Dawn Raid In a hostile takeover, the act of an acquiring firm or, more rarely, an individual investor buying a substantial amount of a target firm's stock at the beginning of the trading day. One perpetrates a dawn raid to take the target firm by surprise; by not making a formal offer to buy the company before the dawn raid, the acquiring firm does not give the target firm the chance to enact an antitakeover measure that would increase the cost of the takeover. Regulations allow an acquiring firm to buy only 15% of the target firm in a dawn raid; many acquiring firms thus make formal offers after they have a significant stake in the target firm.

Day Around Order A day order that cancels another day order. A day around order is usually the same type of order (that is, it orders the broker to buy or sell the same security), but it changes the terms of the previous day order, such as the price or the quantity.

Day Loan A loan that a bank extends to a broker in order to buy securities. The loan is due at the end of the same day it is extended. A day loan exists to provide a broker with funding until an ordinary broker call loan can be made. It is also called a morning loan.

Day of Deposit to Day of Withdrawal Account A bank account on which interest is paid for the period during which money is in the account. Nearly all bank accounts are day of deposit to day of withdrawal accounts.

Day Order An order to a broker to buy or sell a security that expires at the end of the trading day if not filled. For example, one may make a day order to sell a stock at $35 or better. If the stock never rises above $30, the order is not filled and expires worthless at the end of the day. If the shareholder still wishes to sell the stock the next day, he/she must make a new order.

Day Trade An investment practice in which one buys (or sells short) a security and then sells (or buys) the same security in the same trading day. That is, a day trade involves the opening and the closing of a position on the same trading day, in order to profit from short-term changes in price. For example, a day trader may buy Stock A at $15 per share because he/she believes it will be $17 a few minutes or hours later. The activities in which day traders engage are high risk because there is no guarantee that the price will move in the desired direction. However, day traders provide a great deal of liquidity to the market.

Day Trader An investor who makes many trades throughout a trading day, buying and selling securities in order to profit from short-term changes in price. For example, a day trader may buy Stock A at $15 per share because he/she believes it will be $25 a few minutes or hours later. The activities in which day traders engage are high risk because there is no guarantee that the price will move in the desired direction. However, day traders provide a great deal of liquidity to the market.

Day-Count Convention An assumption used to calculate the frequency of coupon payments for a bond. This is used to calculate accrued interest and may therefore be important to the valuation of a bond, especially just before or just after the coupon date. There are two main day-count conventions. The 30/360 convention assumes that there are 30 days each month and 360 days in a year. On the other hand, the actual/actual convention uses the real number of days each month and year.

Days Payable Outstanding The average amount of time it takes a company to pay its accounts payable. A company's accounts payable are short-term liabilities resulting from purchases the company has made on credit. Days payable outstanding is calculated thusly: DPO = (accounts payable / cost of sales) * number of days.

Days' Sales in Inventory Ratio A measure of how quickly a company turns its inventory into sales. It is calculated by dividing the value of inventory by the value of sales and multiplying by 365. A shorter DSI is considered preferable, as it means there is a shorter period between the acquisition of inventory and its sale, but different industries have different standards with regard to the length of the DSI. It is used with days sales outstanding and days payable outstanding to help determine the financial health of a company.

Days' Sales Outstanding In accounting, a company's average collection period. Usually calculated monthly, it indexes the relationship between outstanding accounts receivable and total sales over a given period and is a common tool in measuring liquidity. Tracking trends in days' sales outstanding can also indicate the level of credit risk a company is willing to extend at different points of time. It is also called the collection ratio.

Dc On a bond transaction table, an abbreviation indicating that a bond was issued at a deep discount.

DD 1. ISO 3166-1 alpha-2 code for East Germany prior to its reunification with West Germany. This was the code used in international transactions to and from bank accounts in East Germany. **2.** ISO 3166-2 geocode for East Germany. This was used as an international standard for shipping to East Germany. In both cases, the code is obsolete.

DDDE ISO 3166-3 code for East Germany, which merged with West Germany in 1990. ISO 3166-3 codes are used to indicate names of countries that are no longer used.

DDM 1. Discounted dividend model. A formula for determining the projected return on a stock by estimating the present value of future dividends. One compares the discounted dividend return to the current stock price, and, if the former is higher, it indicates that the stock is undervalued. More than one DDM is used to calculate the dividend discount return, but it is important to note that they all assume that the stock will in fact pay dividends, which may not always be the case. **2.** ISO 4217 code for the East German mark. It was in use between 1948 and 1990, when it was theoretically pegged to the (West German) deutschemark at par, but it was largely inconvertible. After German reunification in 1990, the deutschemark replaced the East German mark.

DE 1. ISO 3166-1 alpha-2 code for the Federal Republic of Germany. This is the code used in international transactions to and from German bank accounts. **2.** ISO 3166-2 geocode for Germany. This is used as an international standard for shipping to Germany. Each German state has its own code with the prefix "DE." For example, the code for the State of Hamburg is ISO 3166-2:DE-HH.

De Facto Existing in fact, but not by legal standard. In business, one occasionally makes reference to "de facto" monopolies in situations where alternatives to a certain brand may exist, but the brand has such a large market share that the alternatives may as well not exist. Likewise, some analysts of the 2008 recession have discussed the "de facto" nationalization of the banking industry, in which some governments, notably the British, bought some banks outright and implicitly guaranteed the existence of all other banks.

Dead Account In banking, an account with no activity whatsoever over a lengthy period of time. That is, the account holder makes no deposits to or withdrawals from a dead account. See also: Inactive account.

Dead Assets Assets with no value that are listed on a balance sheet.

Dead Cat Bounce Slang; a small rally after a significant decline. The term implies that the decline will continue and will be sustained. For example, if a stock price drops from $150 to $125, then rises to $130, then drops to $110, the rise is said to be a dead cat bounce.

Dead Hand Poison Pill A provision in some antitakeover measures stipulating that only persons who were members of the board of directors at the time the antitakeover measure was put into place have the power to rescind the antitakeover measure. More specifically, it may refer to the right of the board of directors to dilute the stock holdings of the person or institution taking over by issuing more stocks and giving them to themselves. The intent is to make the hostile takeover prohibitively expensive for the party taking over. Dead hand poison pills are controversial and have been challenged in some jurisdictions.

Dead Money Slang; an investment that results in no profit or in only mediocre profit.

Dead Presidents In the United States, a slang term for money. The term derives from the fact that the faces of past U.S. presidents appear on some bills.

Dead Stick A slang term for a project with no forward progress that is in danger of failure. The phrase derives from an aviation term for a plane that is about to completely lose control.

Dead Wood A slang term for a formerly productive employee who no longer contributes in any significant way.

Deadbeat A person or company who intentionally and repeatedly does not pay his/her bills. For example, a deadbeat may refrain from paying his/her rent. While there is recourse for those dealing with deadbeats (for example, a landlord can evict a person who does not pay rent), this can be expensive and time-consuming. In nearly all cases, a deadbeat has a poor credit history. A deadbeat is also called a bad pay, but should not be confused with a freeloader.

Dead-End Job A job with little or no hope of advancement or increased pay. One may be in a dead-end job because one lacks the skills to advance or simply because there are no better jobs available. One may be able to exit a dead-end job through education or training.

Deadhead An employee of a transportation company who travels for free in order to return home or arrive at his next assignment.

Deadline The time at which a project or other assignment is due. For example, a supervisor may give an employee a Thursday deadline to prepare a presentation for the supervisor to deliver on Friday. In business, keeping deadlines may indicate efficiency.

Deadweight Loss The loss of economic activity due to excessive taxation. For example, suppose a person on welfare is offered a job that pays more than he/she receives in welfare benefits. If taxes are too high, however, the person may find that his/her aftertax income is in fact lower than what he/she was receiving on welfare. The person might then rationally decide to stay on welfare. The deadweight loss is both the cost of keeping that person on welfare and the loss incurred from the economy at large from losing that person's production. It is also called the excess burden of taxation.

Deadwood Anything that significantly reduces efficiency in an economy, company, or other organization. For example, if a company hires more employees than it needs so that there is not enough work for them all to do, then the extra employees are deadwood because they cost without adding value. Some social projects may encourage deadwood: for example, a government may deliberately hire too many postal workers to keep down unemployment figures even though the extra personnel may actually reduce the efficiency of the post office. See also: Dead weight loss, Featherbedding.

Deal Flow The rate at which new proposals are made to a funding firm. Deal flow is also used to indicate the general feeling of how often a firm receives new offers. The term is used almost exclusively in venture capital, and not in banking. Some venture capitalists, notably Bill Burnham, have criticized the concept, believing that venture capital firms should seek out potential deals rather than allow the proposals to come to them. See also: Venture capital.

Deal Stock Stock in a publicly-traded company that may be acquired by or merged into another company. The term especially applies when the merger or acquisition is rumored but has not been announced.

Deal Ticket Slang; the contract containing the terms and conditions for a trade. It is also called a trading ticket.

Dealer A person or company that trades securities on its own behalf. That is, a dealer is a principal in a transaction; it neither does business on behalf of a client nor facilitates transactions between parties. In the United States, dealers are regulated by the SEC, and must be trading securities as a business. If an individual trades securities privately, that person is said to be a trader and is subject to different regulations. See also: Agent, Broker, Broker-dealer.

Dealer Bank A commercial bank that buys and sells U.S. Treasury securities, municipal bonds, and/or agency securities. Dealer banks are registered with the Municipal Securities Rulemaking Board. Investing in dealer banks is very low risk because the securities they hold are virtually risk-free and often are exempt from taxation.

Dealer Loan A loan to a dealer by a bank. Dealers take out dealer loans in order to finance inventory for their trades. Dealer loans are payable in 24 hours of receipt, and must carry collateral.

Dealer Market The market for traders who are trading on their own accounts, as opposed to traders to conduct transactions on behalf of clients. Dealer markets exist to create the greatest liquidity possible for other transactions. One of the most prominent dealer markets is NASDAQ. See also: Dealer, Broker-dealer.

Dealer Option An over-the-counter, option contract in which the underlying asset is a physical commodity. Most of the time, clearing houses write dealer options when they hold the underlying asset (for a call) or sufficient cash to buy the underlying asset (for a put).

Dealer Paper Commercial paper issued by a company to a dealer, who in turn sells the paper to investors. Commercial paper is a short-term debt security. Dealer paper describes one way a company may issue it. This method generally excludes small investors because there is a large minimum investment, often $250,000 or more. See also: Direct paper.

Dealer's Spread The amount a dealer earns by buying a security and then selling it to an investor. The dealer's spread is the difference between the dealer's purchase price and his/her sale price. The dealer's spread is how dealers (other than broker-dealers) make most of their profits.

Dear Money A market or security with high trading volume and a small bid-ask spread. However, an investor can profit in a dear money market, especially if he/she trades large numbers of securities. When the bid-ask spread is narrow, an investor may have difficulty making more than a small return for each trade, but sheer numbers can make returns add to a substantial amount. The term is mainly used in the United Kingdom and corresponds to the American term tight market.

Death Benefit In life insurance and annuities, the amount of money that is paid to the policyholder's survivor(s) upon the policyholder's death. That is, the amount may be a lump sum determined at the outset of the policy or annuity that is paid when the policyholder dies, or it may be a monthly payment that begins to be paid when the policyholder passes away and remains payable until the survivor's death. The former death benefit is more common in life insurance and the latter is more common in annuities.

Death Cross In charting and technical analysis, a crossover in which a security's long-term moving average falls below its support level or short-term moving average. That is, a death cross is the point on a chart where the long-term moving average price of a security crosses a bearish indicator on the chart. The death cross must be reinforced by high trading volume. The death cross indicates that the security has become bearish and some technical analysts see this is as a time to sell. The death cross becomes the security's resistance level in a rising market.

Death Put A provision in some indentures giving the survivors of a bondholder the right, but not the obligation, to sell a bond back to its issuer at the bondholder's death or legal incapacitation. The bond is sold at is face value and the proceeds are deposited into the estate of the bondholder. If interest rates are declining, the survivors may be able to make a great deal of profit.

Death Spiral A loan that investors give to a publicly-traded company in exchange for convertible bonds. The convertible bonds give the investor a right to buy shares in the company at a low, agreed-upon price. However, issuing these bonds creates more shares outstanding when they are converted, which results in a drop in the share price. The low share price encourages more bondholders to convert their bonds to equity, which causes a further drop in price and the process continues. Because of this disadvantage, companies only engage in death spirals if they badly need cash.

Death Tax An informal, pejorative term for the estate tax and the inheritance tax. The term is most commonly used by politicians and pundits who favor the abolition of one or both taxes.

Death Valley Curve An informal term for the period of time between a company's receipt of venture capital financing and its establishment of a secure cash flow. During the death valley curve, the company is unlikely to receive more financing. The term refers to the extremely high probability that the company will fail during the death valley curve.

Death-Backed Bonds Bonds secured by a pool of life insurance policies. Coupons on death-backed bonds come from the profit the insurance company derives from each life insurance policy. Death-backed bonds carry little risk because every life insurance policyholder eventually dies.

Debasement The act of lowering the value of something, especially a coin. In the past, a government would melt coins down and mix them with a metal of lower value in order to create more coins of the same denomination. This inevitably caused inflation, though it is unclear how well these governments understood that. Because few currencies are now based on a precious metal, debasement it rare.

Deben An ancient Egyptian unit of weight approximately equivalent to 13.6 grams during the Old and Middle Kingdoms or 91 grams during the New Kingdom.

Debenture A debt security, issued by a government or large company, that is not secured by an asset or lien, but rather by the all issuer's assets not otherwise secured. That is, a debenture carries no collateral and is considered unsecured; in case of bankruptcy, the debenture holder is considered a general creditor. A debenture can be traded, and the term is often interchangeable with a bond. Debentures issued by governments are considered risk-free. See also: Treasury security.

Debenture Stock A stock entitling the bearer to a certain fixed dividend at set periods of time. Like debenture debt, debenture stock offers fixed payments with no collateral beyond the company's performance. Unlike debenture debt, however, debenture stock is a form of equity, which puts it in a position behind all debts in the event of liquidation. Debenture stock operates almost identically to preferred stock.

Debit Balance The amount of money an investor owes on a margin loan. This is calculated as the amount the investor directly owes his/her broker. It does not account the paper profit the investor has made on various transactions. When determining the amount owed in the case of margin call, one generally uses the adjusted debit balance, which starts with the debit balance and subtracts the amount of applicable paper profit.

Debit Card A card entitling the owner to make automatic withdrawals from a bank account to make purchases or to receive cash. That is, when one uses a debit card, the issuing bank transfers funds from the holder's account to the seller electronically. The holder of a debit card may therefore use it to buy a good or service. Debit cards operate much like credit cards but, while credit cards are essentially short term loans, debit cards are more like electronic checks. They are also called check cards, bank cards or, less commonly, asset cards.

Debit Spread An option strategy in which one buys an option for a higher premium and sells another option on the same underlying asset at a lower premium. One profits from a debit spread when there is a large change in the price of the underlying asset that will increase the value of the option with the higher premium; the option with the lower premium hedges the investor's risk.

Debit-Balance Theory In technical analysis, a theory dealing with the measure of debts owed to a brokerage on margin accounts. A high debit balance indicates that large or important investors are buying on margin in greater amounts, which is thought to be a bullish indicator. Likewise, a low debit balance indicates that many investors are not buying on margin; this is thought to be bearish. Debit-balance theory assumes that investors thought to be "sophisticated" usually make wise investment decisions; not all analysts agree with this assumption. See also: Crowd theory, Credit-balance theory.

Debt Any money owed to an individual, company, or other organization. One acquires debt when one borrows money. Generally speaking, one acquires debt for a specific purpose, such as funding a college education or purchasing a house. In business and government, debt is often issued in the form of bonds, which are tradeable securities entitling the bearer to repayment at the appropriate time(s). Occasionally, especially for personal loans, debt is issued without interest or other compensation; one simply pays back what was lent. This is exceedingly rare in business and a debtor almost always compensates a creditor with a certain amount of interest, representing the time value of money. However, some areas of finance, especially Islamic banking, do not allow debt with interest.

Debt Assignment The transfer of debt, and the right of receiving repayment, from a creditor to a third party, usually, but not always, a subsidiary of the original creditor. A company may assign debt to a subsidiary to protect investors who do not wish to invest in a new, risky deal, or it may simply wish to hide losses from shareholders. The debtor is unaffected unless the third party draws up new terms. See also: Enron scandal, Aggressive accounting.

Debt Bomb A situation in which a major institutional investor, especially a bank, defaults on a debt. A debt bomb can cause massive confusion and panic throughout the national and global economies, particularly in an economy heavily dependent on debt and easy credit availability. A debt bomb can trigger government intervention such as a bailout. See also: Lehman Brothers bankruptcy, Bear Stearns bankruptcy, Credit crunch, Too-big-to-fail.

Debt Capacity 1. See: Debt ceiling. 2. The amount of debt that a person or company can repay in a reasonable amount of time using current resources and assuming income neither increases nor decreases. See also: Creditworthiness.

Debt Ceiling The maximum amount that a government can borrow. The term especially applies to municipalities; rising above the debt ceiling may trigger a reduction it a municipality's credit rating. Cities and other local governments that are near the debt limit may issue participation certificates--a right to the receivables for a certain project--instead of direct debt. The United States also has a national debt ceiling, but Congress simply raises it every time the national debt approaches the ceiling.

Debt Consolidation The process of taking out a loan that pays off two or more loans. Debt consolidation often comes with a lower monthly payment and/or interest rate than the previous loans, as well as a longer repayment period. The loan by which debt consolidation take place is called a consolidation loan; the process is often used for student loans.

Debt Displacement The reduction in a company's ability to borrow because it leases its assets. While debt displacement occurs when a company receives income from its leases, it prevents the company from using those assets as collateral for a loan. Debt displacement can be detrimental, depending on the nature of the business and how much income the leases bring.

Debt Financing The act of a business raising operating capital or other capital by borrowing. Most often, this refers to the issuance of a bond, debenture, or other debt security. In exchange for lending the money, bond holders and others become creditors of the business and are entitled to the payment of interest and to have their loan redeemed at the end of a given period. Debt financing can be long-term or short-term. Long-term debt financing usually involves a business' need to buy the basic necessities for its business, such as facilities and major assets, while short-term debt financing includes debt securities with shorter redemption periods and is used to provide day-to-day necessities such as inventory and/or payroll. See also: Equity financing.

Debt Limitation A negative covenant in a bond indenture limiting the issuer's ability to acquire more debt before the bond matures. Debt limitation may take a variety of forms. For example, the indenture may restrict the debt service coverage ratio, meaning that the company can acquire theoretically unlimited debt provided it increases it income to such a level that it can service the debt. On the other hand, debt limitation may set a maximum dollar amount of debt that the issuer may acquire

during the life of the bond, or even may prevent the issuer from becoming any more indebted at all. These latter debt limitations are more likely when the issuer is not on sound financial footing and possibly is issuing junk bonds. A debt limitation should not be confused with a debt limit, which is similar but is a legal requirement on a government.

Debt Management Any strategy that helps a debtor to repay or otherwise handle their debt better. Debt management may involve working with creditors to restructure debt or helping the debtor manage payments more effectively. A debtor may appeal to a debt management company if he/she does not know how to manage the debt himself/herself or if there is so much debt that outside management becomes necessary.

Debt Management Ratio A ratio of a company's debt to its total financing. The debt management ratio measures how much of a company's operations comes from debt instead of other forms of financing, such as stock or personal savings. The debt management ratio is one measure among many of a company's risk and likelihood of default. See also: Debt ratio, Debt-to-equity ratio.

Debt Price In debt securities, the price paid per $100 of face value. For example, if one purchases $1,000 worth of bonds for $989, the debt price is $98.90.

Debt Ratio A measure of a company's total debt to its total assets. A ratio less than one means that a company has more assets than debt, while a ratio of more than one means the opposite. A debt ratio is a measure of how risky it would be for a bank to extend a loan to a company, with a higher ratio indicating great risk.

Debt Restructuring The process of a person or business negotiating and agreeing with its creditors to reduce its debt or to revise a repayment plan. Debt restructuring often occurs when a person or company has taken on too much debt and is in danger of bankruptcy. Debt restructuring is beneficial to the person or company requesting it because it often results in a significant discount and/or a more flexible repayment schedule. It is usually less expensive than a bankruptcy would be. Likewise, it is beneficial to the creditors because a bankruptcy will likely result in some debt being discharged; creditors generally prefer debt restructuring because they would rather be paid less than not paid at all. See also: debt-to-equity swap, restructuring, capital structure.

Debt Retirement The act of paying off a debt completely. If one borrows a certain amount, one must eventually repay it to the lender and retire the debt.

Debt Securities Any debt issued by a government or corporation that may be traded. That is, the original buyer of the debt security effectively lends the issuer money in exchange for the security, which gives the holder the right to receive interest payments and, at maturity, the principal. The holder may, at his/her/its discretion, sell the security to someone else, who then gains the right to receive interest and principal from the issuer. In general, debt securities are less risky than stocks; their riskiness relative to each other is determined by the creditworthiness of the issuer.

Debt Service The amount of money required to make payments on the principal and interest on outstanding loans, the interest on bonds, or the principal of maturing bonds. An individual or company unable to make such payments is said to be "unable to service one's debt." An example of debt service is a monthly student loan payment. See also: Debt service coverage ratio.

Debt Warrant A warrant, usually attached to a bond or other debt security, giving the holder the right to purchase more bonds or debt securities from the same issuer at a stated price. A debt warrant is a sweetener designed to encourage potential investors to buy the bond to which the warrant is attached.

Debt/Equity Ratio In risk analysis, a way to determine a company's leverage. The ratio is calculated by taking the company's long-term debt and dividing it by the value of its common stock. Put graphically: Debt/equity ratio = Long-term debt / Common stock The greater a company's leverage, the higher the ratio. Generally, companies with higher ratios are thought to be more risky because they have more liabilities and less equity. See also: Long-Term Debt/Capitalization Ratio.

Debt/Equity Swap A situation in which a debtor (which is a company) replaces the debt held by one or more creditors with a percentage of ownership in the company. A debt-equity swap often occurs if the company would otherwise be unable to repay the creditor(s) anything without going bankrupt. However, the swap may be a result of change from a debt-based to an equity-based capital structure. In either case, these swaps are often considered part of a company's attempt to restructure itself. Some debt agreements restrict the debtor's ability to force a debt-for-equity swap.

Debt-Based Asset A debt where one is entitled to principal and (usually) interest payments from the borrower. One may hold a debt-based asset by directly lending to the borrower, or one may hold it by purchasing the right to receive repayment from the actual lender. Debt-based assets are recorded as assets on a balance sheet, though there is risk of default. Some debt-based assets, notably (but not exclusively) bonds, may be traded on or off an exchange, while others are non-negotiable.

Debtor A person, company, or other organization that owes money to another individual, company, or organization. Generally speaking, a debtor acquires debt for a specific purpose, such as to fund a college education or to purchase a house. In business and government, debt is often issued in the form of bonds, which are tradeable securities entitling the bearer to repayment at the appropriate time(s), making the issuing government or business the debtor. A debtor almost always compensates a creditor with a certain amount of interest, representing the time value of money. However, some areas of finance, especially Islamic banking, do not allow debt with interest.

Debtor in Possession A company that maintains its operations during a Chapter 11 bankruptcy. A debtor in possession is generally attempting to fulfill its reorganization plan, discharging certain debts and changing any structural weaknesses to put it on a path to profitability. As such, a debtor in possession is drastically different from a company in liquidation, which ceases operations and sells all its assets.

Debtor-in-Possession Financing Financing made available to a debtor in possession, which is a company that maintains its operations during a Chapter 11 bankruptcy. A debtor in possession is generally attempting to fulfill its reorganization plan, discharging certain debts and changing any structural weaknesses to put it on a path to profitability. A company often requires financing in order to restructure, and DIP financing enables it to do so.

Debt-Service Coverage Ratio 1. In investment real estate, the ratio of annual net operating income on a piece of investment property to its annual debt service. Banks use the DSCR to help determine whether to make or refinance loans for investment property. A DSCR equal to or greater than 1 indicates that the debtor is able to service the debt on the income from the investment property. In personal finance, banks usually require a DSCR of at least 1 to make such a loan, while they generally expect a ratio of 1.2 for commercial projects. **2.** In government finance, the ratio of annual export earnings to its annual debt service on external debt.

Debt-to-GDP Ratio A ratio of a country's national debt to its GDP. The debt-to-GDP ratio is one way to estimate whether or not a country will be able to repay its debt. The higher the ratio is, the more likely a country is to default because its government has borrowed too much relative to the ability of the country as a whole to repay. This may affect the country's sovereign credit rating. However, this ratio is not the only metric used. For example, the United States and the United Kingdom maintain national debts that approach 100% of GDP, but both have AAA credit ratings because the political risk in both countries is very low.

Debt-to-Income Ratio The amount of an individual or company's gross income that it spends on debt service as a percentage of its total gross income. The higher the DTI is, the less likely is it that the individual or company will be able to repay debt. As a result, financial institutions use the DTI in informing decisions on whether or not to make loans. Often, the "debt" in the term refers to all liability payments (such as employee wages, taxes, and utility bills) and not simply to debt.

Deceased Alert A statement attached to an individual's credit report stating that the individual is dead. A deceased alert is necessary to prevent identity theft. For example, an identity thief could steal a deceased person's information and apply for a loan without any intention of repayment. Without a deceased alert, the bank may be otherwise inclined to extend credit to the identity thief. In such a case, the estate of the deceased could be held legally liable for repaying the loan. The family of the deceased must inform credit agencies of the death before the deceased alert is placed on the credit report.

December Effect The tendency of stocks to perform better in December than in any other month of the year. This may be because of increased sales and earnings due to the Christmas season, or because of expectations for new products at the start of the next year. In any case, December has usually, historically, been the best month for stock performance. It is also noteworthy that, in general, fewer bankruptcies are filed in December. See also: Monday effect.

Decempeda An ancient Roman unit of length approximately equivalent to 2.96 meters. It was also called a pertica.

Deceptionist A slang term for an administrative assistant among whose primary responsibilities is to limit access to his/her boss. A deceptionist may be hired if the boss is extremely busy, or if he/she simply does not want unnecessary issues to bother him/her. Deceptionists enable their bosses to avoid people without creating enemies.

Decile Rank In funds and securities, measure of performance on a scale of 1 to 10. A rank of 1 indicates that the fund or security performed in the top 10% of similar funds or securities, while a rank of 10 indicates performance in the bottom 10%. See also: Decile.

Decimal Pricing The listing of a security's price in decimals instead of fractions. For example, decimal pricing means that a security would be listed as, say, $25.25, instead of $25 1/4. Decimal pricing makes prices and the market more understandable for investors and laypeople.

Decimal Trading Trading in which the price of a security is quoted using decimals rather than fractions to represent divisions of a dollar. That is, a quote in decimal trading would be $10.25 instead of $10 1/4. Decimal trading as become more common with digitalization. See also: Drill Bits.

Decimalization 1. The process of changing listings of security prices from fractions to decimals. Decimalization makes prices and the market easier for investors and laypeople to understand. **2.** In the United Kingdom, the process of changing the calculation of the pound sterling to a decimal system. Prior to 1971, the UK had a very complex way of calculating subdivisions of the pound. Since then, the currency has been decimalized into 100 pence.

Decimel A customary unit of area approximately equivalent to 40.46 square meters. It is used in some parts of India and Bangladesh in real estate transactions.

Decision Tree In risk analysis, a diagram of decisions and their potential consequences. It is used to help determine the most straightforward (and cheapest) way to arrive at a stated goal. It is represented by potential decisions (drawn as squares), branching off into different proximate consequences (drawn as circles), and potential end results (drawn as triangles).

Deck In futures and options, an informal term for open orders. Brokers have a deck they attempt to fill at the desired prices. A deck is the equivalent of a book on the equity market.

Deck Corn In futures trading, a slang term for a futures contract on corn that expires in December.

Declaration 1. An announcement by the board of directors of a publicly-traded company that it will issue a dividend. See also: Declaration date, Ex-dividend date. **2.** More generally, any formal announcement that a person or activity intends to undertake a certain activity. Sometimes regulators require companies to make declarations of actions like a hostile takeover attempt. This is intended to increase transparency in the market.

Declaration Date 1. See: Announcement date. **2.** See: Expiration date.

Declaration of the Rights of Man and Citizen A document written by French revolutionaries in 1789. It is based on the concept that humans (or at least men) have natural rights that the state must respect. Ideas contained within the declaration include the concept that all men are equal and that law must reflect popular will. It is one of the foundational documents of modern liberalism.

Declaratory Judgment A ruling by a court (or, less commonly, a regulator) that resolves a dispute but does not order an action. That is, a declaratory judgment states a fact. For example, a declaratory judgment may state who owns a patent or a piece of property.

Declare To authorize or announce a dividend. A publicly-traded company that declares a dividend binds itself with an obligation to later pay that same dividend to shareholders. See also: Declaration date, Ex-dividend date.

Declared Dividend A dividend that a company has been announced but not yet paid. See also: Ex-dividend.

Decline A situation in which a stock or other security that has dropped in price over a given period. For example, if a stock opens at $5 and closes at $4.45, it is said to have declined for that trading day.

Decliner Informal for a stock or other security that has dropped in price over a given period. For example, if a stock opens at $5 and closes at $4.45, it is said to be a decliner for that trading day.

Declining Balance Method A way of calculating the depreciation of an asset whereby one subtracts a certain percentage of its current value each year. For example, suppose an asset costing $100,000 depreciates 10% each year. After the first year, it depreciates to $90,000. In the second year, one deducts 10% from the $90,000, rather than the original $100,000. Thus, the depreciated value after the second year is $81,000. This is a common means of calculating depreciation.

Declining Industry An industry producing one or more products that are declining in demand, profitability, or both. A declining industry may be suffering losses, or it may still be making a profit that has been shrinking consistently. An industry may go into decline for a number of reasons. The economy may decline and the industry's products may suddenly be considered luxuries. Alternatively, a new technology may be developed that renders an industry obsolete. For example, the video cassette recording (VCR) industry was performing well for approximately 20 years. However, the introduction of DVDs, which are more efficient and of higher quality, turned the VCR industry into a declining industry. See also: Industry Life Cycle.

Decoupling A situation in which returns on two assets or asset classes that normally move together move separately. For example, oil and natural gas prices usually move together: when one goes up, so does the other, and vice versa. Likewise, stocks and corporate bonds usually behave the same way. Decoupling in both cases occurs when oil moves in one direction while natural gas moves in the opposite, or when stocks' and corporate bonds' returns diverge.

Decreasing Term Insurance A term life insurance policy in which the policyholder pays a constant premium but the benefit decreases over time, either on a monthly, quarterly, or yearly basis. For example, one may purchase a decreasing term life insurance policy for a period of 20 years at a premium of $150 per month. At first, the benefit may be as high as, say, $200,000, but it may gradually shrink each year to, say, $50,000. A decreasing term policy is primarily beneficial to young people who have a considerable amount on liabilities but do not expect to have them in the future.

Decriminalization The act of making a previously illegal act legal. For example, a state may decriminalize usury by allowing banks to charge higher interest rates.

Decruit A slang term meaning to fire or lay off, especially if those affected are senior managers.

Dedicated Capital The face value of an entire issue. It is calculated by determining the face value of individual shares or bonds and multiplying by the whole number issued. It is also called the dedicated value.

Dedicated Short Bias In hedge funds, an investment strategy where the funds take more short positions than long positions. The hedge fund uses this strategy in the belief that more securities will decline in price than rise. This can be a risky investment strategy, especially in a prolonged bull market.

Deductible 1. Able to be taken off of one's tax liability. See: Deduction. **2.** In insurance, the amount that a policyholder must pay for a claim before the insurance company will make any payments at all. That is, if an insured event happens, the policyholder is responsible for covering damages up to a certain dollar amount, at which point the insurance company begins coverage. Some insurance policies have an annual deductible; that is, if two insured events happen in a given year, the deductible is only applied once. Other policies have a per event deductible; that is, the deductible applies each time a claim is made. Generally, the higher one's deductible is, the less one pays in premiums on the policy.

Deductible Contribution A contribution that one may place into an IRA, 401(k), or other retirement plan each year that can reduce one's taxable income by the same amount. That is, the deductible contribution is the portion of one's retirement contribution that is tax deductible. The IRS generally sets the limits on deductible contributions. For example, the limit on deductible contributions for 401(k) plans was $16,500 in 2009.

Deduction An amount of money that one may subtract from one's gross annual income when calculating one's income tax liability. A common misconception about tax deductions is that they represent a dollar-for-dollar reduction of one's tax liability. Rather, a deduction removes a certain dollar amount from the income the IRS uses to calculate the percentage of one's income that is owed in taxes. Common deductions are charitable contributions, business expenses, and interest on mortgages. See also: Tax credit.

Deelgemeente In the Netherlands, a political subdivision roughly equivalent to a neighborhood or sub-municipal district. The term is also used in Belgium, but it has little political significance.

Deep Background Describing an interview that may not be used as an official source, but improves the interviewer's perception. Information from a deep background interview generally must be confirmed before it is published. The term is used largely in American journalism.

Deep Discount Bond A bond or other debt instrument that is issued at a price far below its face value. For example, a bond with par of $10,000 might be issued to an investor for $5,000. Junk bonds are often deep-discount bonds.

Deep Discount Brokerage Firm A brokerage that offers clients no commissions and usually a flat fee for trades. Unlike most brokerages, a deep discount brokerage provides only trading services; it does not, for example, provide custody services. The idea behind a deep discount brokerage firm is that it will still make a good deal of money from the sheer volume of transactions it facilitates. See also: Discount brokerage firm.

Deep in the Money 1. A call option with a strike price less than half the value of the underlying asset. 2. A put option with a strike price more than double the value of the underlying asset. In both these situations, the option contract has intrinsic value. It is unlikely that the option will be out of the money by the time the option is exercised.

Deep Market A market with high trading volume and a small bid-ask spread. However, an investor can profit in a deep market, especially if he/she trades large numbers of securities. When the bid-ask spread is narrow, an investor may have difficulty making more than a small return for each trade, but sheer numbers can make returns add to a substantial amount. In any case, a deep market is almost always highly liquid.

Deep Out of the Money 1. A put option with a strike price less than half the value of the underlying asset. 2. A call option with a strike price more than double the value of the underlying asset. In both these situations, the option contract has no intrinsic value. It is unlikely that the option will be in the money by the time the option is exercised.

Deep Pockets A slang term for wealth or an exceptionally wealthy investor. See also: Angel investor.

Deep See Diver In Cockney rhyming slang, a term for five British pounds.

Default The failure to make payments on a debt. One may default on any debt, such as a mortgage or a bond. Default is a very serious matter and may entitle the lender or bondholder to take possession of one's assets in order to recover the amount lost in principal and interest payments on the debt. Default also has a negative impact on one's creditworthiness in the future.

Default Interest The higher interest that a borrower must pay after default. If a borrower defaults on a loan, he/she must pay default interest in order to compensate a lender for the added risk of extending credit to him/her.

Default Premium The return over and above the risk-free rate of return that an investor demands in exchange for accepting the risk inherent to an investment. The default premium becomes larger with greater amounts of risk. For example, an investment grade bond has a lower default premium than a junk bond, which carries more risk, but a higher premium than a Treasury security, which is riskless.

Default Risk The risk that a debtor will be unable to pay back its loans. Default risk goes up if a debtor has large number of liabilities and poor cash flow. Generally speaking, companies and persons with high default risk stand a greater chance of a loan being denied and pay a higher interest rate on the loans they do receive. See also: Bankruptcy.

Defeasance 1. A provision in a loan or bond removing it as a liability on a balance sheet if cash or a portfolio is set aside for debt service. Usually defeasance occurs when a borrower owns a portfolio of Treasury securities, the coupons of which are used to service a debt. When the borrower has set aside sufficient assets to cover the debt, the debt does not need to be recorded on a balance sheet. 2. More broadly, a provision in an agreement voiding the agreement under certain defined circumstances.

Defense Advanced Research Projects Agency An agency of the U.S. Department of Defense responsible for developing new military technologies. It is perhaps best known for its development of Arpanet, which is the direct precursor of the modern Internet. It was established in 1958 and is based in Arlington, Virginia.

Defensive Acquisition An acquisition that a company makes in order to keep from being taken over. For example, if Company A may acquire a much smaller Company B, which will make Company A so large that any takeover will result in the acquirer running afoul of antitrust laws. A defensive acquisition most commonly applies to acquiring a company, but it may also involve acquiring a particular product that will make the company more difficult to take over. It is an example of an antitakeover measure.

Defensive Buy An investment decision to buy stock in a publicly-traded company that is resistant to market downturn. Examples of these companies include those in the pharmaceutical and budget retail industries. Defensive buys are relatively low risk, low return stocks, and investors often enter long positions in them if they anticipate a market downturn.

Defensive Investment Strategy An investment strategy in which a money manager seeks to protect the client's investment. A defensive investor seeks low risk, low return securities such as bonds, certificates of deposit, and some blue chip stocks.

Defensive Securities Low-risk securities, especially stocks in companies relatively unaffected by business cycles. In times of market downturn, investors tend to seek defensive securities to provide a steady rate of return, or at least to lose less money than the market as a whole. Examples include stocks in utility companies and the health care industry.

Deferred Account An annuity or other investment vehicle in which one does not pay taxes on the contributions until after withdrawal. Common examples of deferred accounts are a 401(k) and a traditional IRA. Generally speaking, one places a portion of his/her pre-tax income into a deferred account and allows it to be invested. Taxation is deferred until withdrawal from the account, generally after retirement.

Deferred Acquisition Costs In insurance, an expense to a customer that an insurance company initially pays, but recoups the funds from the customer gradually over the life of the insurance policy or other contract.

Deferred Annuity An annuity in which the annuitant does not begin to receive payments until some future date. A deferred annuity has two phases: a savings phase and an income phase. During the savings phase, the annuitant places money into the annuity, which invests it on behalf of the annuitant. In the income phase, the annuitant receives payments. It is important to note that a deferred annuity is not taxed until the income phase begins. It also pays a death benefit to the survivor(s) of the annuitant. Nearly all retirement plans are deferred annuities. See also: IRA, 401(k).

Deferred Charge An asset on a balance sheet that comes about from a business making payment for a good or service it has not yet received, but will in the near future. Prepaid expenses are expensed over time as the goods or services are received. A common example of a prepaid expense is an insurance policy. Another example is a lump sum payment for rent; if a company pays for a year's worth of rent in advance, it is recorded as a deferred charge. A deferred charge is also called a prepaid expense.

Deferred Compensation Money or other compensation that has been earned but not yet received by the earner. Deferred compensation is not taxed until it is actually received, and is usually taxed at a lower rate when it is received (depending on one's income later in life). The most common form of deferred compensation is a retirement plan such as an IRA or 401(k), but stock options and other pensions also qualify.

Deferred Dividend A type of whole life insurance in which the policyholder does not receive any dividends the policy earns until a certain time (called the dividend period) has passed. If a policyholder dies during the dividend period, any dividends he/she would have earned are deposited in a fund that pays the dividends of policyholders who survive the period. As with all insurance, one must pay premiums receive any benefits at all.

Deferred Equity A convertible bond. One often refers to a convertible bond as a deferred equity because it is likely that the bondholder will exercise the convertible option and turn the bond into stock.

Deferred Income Tax On a balance sheet, a tax that a company will owe on its income, but that has not yet been assessed. Because of differences between tax regulations and the Generally Accepted Accounting Principles, income may be recognized on a balance sheet for accounting purposes, but not for tax purposes. However, that income will eventually be recognized for tax purposes and income tax will then be assessed. This tax is called deferred income tax, and is recorded as a liability on the balance sheet.

Deferred Interest Bond A bond that pays no coupons until a certain point in the future. An example is a zero-coupon bond, which pays no interest at all, but the par value one receives at maturity provides the equivalent.

Deferred Liability 1. Money that a company receives from a customer as prepayment for some good or service. A deferred liability is listed on a balance sheet as a liability until the good or service is delivered. This is because the company would have to return the money if it does not keep its end of the bargain as promised. A deferred liability is also called a deferred credit or deferred revenue. 2. See: Past-Due Payment.

Deferred Nominal Life Annuity An annuity that one may purchase where one receives a fixed dollar amount each month for the remainder of one's life, following retirement. It is deferred because the annuitant does not begin to receive payments immediately and nominal because the fixed dollar amount is not adjusted for inflation.

Deferred Payment Option An option contract (whether a call or a put) in which the premium is not paid until the expiration date. A deferred payment option is a form of an American option; that is, the option may be exercised at any point until the expiration date. Generally speaking, a deferred payment option is a long-term investment; the expiration date (and hence the premium payment) is usually at least a year after the date the contract is first entered. It is also called a deferred premium option or a Boston option.

Deferred Profit Sharing Plan A pension plan in which an employer distributes a set percentage of the company's profits into accounts for the employees participating in the plan. The DPSP operates like most other pensions and retirement plans, but instead of placing a set dollar amount into the accounts, it places profits. The idea behind a DPSP is to encourage employees to work for the company's profitability. Employees do not pay taxes on their DPSPs until they begin to make withdrawals after retirement. DPSPs are available in Canada and must be registered with the Canada Revenue Agency.

Deferred Success A euphemism for failure with the (perhaps slim) possibility of success later. For example, if a marketing campaign failed to achieve better sales numbers, but the company wishes to portray the hope that the sales numbers will improve later, it may call the campaign a deferred success.

Deferred Tax Expense Money that an individual or company owes for taxes but has not yet paid. Deferred tax expenses are placed aside and kept until the company or individual pays taxes, either once per quarter or once per year. Deferred tax expenses are most common for corporations and independent contractors who do not have their taxes deducted from their cash inflows.

Deferred-Interest Bond A bond that does not pay a coupon for a certain period of time. After this period, which is usually three to 10 years, coupon payments begin normally. These bonds sell at a discount to par during the time they are not paying coupons.

Deficiency 1. The amount by which cash flow falls short of debt service. For example, if a company has $300,000 in current liabilities and only $250,000 in cash flow for a given year, its deficiency is $50,000. **2.** In taxation, the amount by which one's tax liability exceeds what the individual person or organization reported. For example, if the IRS disallows certain deductions that the taxpayer applied, he/she will owe more in taxes than he/she reported on the return. Deficiency is the amount this taxpayer still owes to the IRS.

Deficiency Dividend A dividend a personal holding company, real estate investment trust, or regulated investment company pays after the IRS has determined that certain taxes are owed, but before these taxes are paid. A company pays deficiency dividends in order to reduce its tax liability.

Deficiency Letter A letter from the SEC stating that there is a problem with a particular filing, especially a prospectus. A deficiency letter is submitted to the filer if the SEC determines that there is a major omission or error in the filing. The company making the filing is expected to deal with the deficiency immediately and make an amended filing. Generally speaking, the submission of a deficiency letter delays a new issue and may be accompanied by a stop order, forbidding a new issue until the matter is resolved.

Deficit A situation in which outflow of money exceeds inflow. That is, a deficit occurs when a government, company, or individual spends more than he/she/it receives in a given period of time, usually a year. One's deficit adds to one's debt, and, therefore, many analysts believe that deficits are unsustainable over the long-term. See also: Surplus.

Deficit Net Worth A situation in which a person or company has more liabilities than assets. This may happen to a person if, for example, he/she owes more on his/her mortgage than the home is worth. A company may have a deficit net worth after consistently posting operating losses over an extended period of time. It is important to note that a deficit net worth does not necessarily mean that bankruptcy is inevitable, but it may prevent the debtor from receiving new credit necessary to maintain operations. It is also called negative net worth.

Deficit Reduction Act of 1984 Legislation in the United States that closed some loopholes and eliminated some taxes, but for the most part increased American tax levels. Among other provisions, the Act did this by increasing the number of years over which some assets are depreciated, ending the net interest exclusion up to $900, and established stricter rules for income averaging. Its name in the House of Representatives was the Tax Reform Act of 1984.

Deficit Spending A situation in which a company, or especially a government, spends more money than it collects for a given period of time, usually a quarter or a year. Companies and government finance deficit spending with borrowing; for example, the U.S. government could issue Treasury securities. Some economic theories, notably Reaganomics and Keynesian economics, minimize the importance of government deficit spending, especially during recessions. However, deficit spending adds debt, which can be detrimental in the long term. See also: national debt.

Defined Asset Fund A unit investment trust that exists only for a limited period of time, after which it is liquidated. A unit investment trust consists of an unmanaged portfolio of securities, the rights to which are sold to investors as shares or units. The dividends and/or coupons from these securities are passed on to unit holders, just as in a mutual fund. A defined asset fund works like this, with the addition that, at a certain maturity, the assets in the fund are liquidated and distributed to unit holders.

Defined Contribution Plan A retirement plan in which the employee and/or employer contribute a set dollar amount each month. The benefits of a defined contribution plan are not set, and depend upon how well the contributions are invested before the pensioner starts to make withdrawals. The disadvantage of a defined contribution plan is the possibility that the investments will not perform as well as expected, giving the pensioner a less secure retirement. The advantage is that the pensioner, while still making contributions, has the ability to determine how the contributions are invested, at least to a certain extent. See also: 401(k).

Defined-Benefit Plan A retirement plan in which the retiree receives a set amount in benefits each month once he/she begins receiving benefits. That is, the benefits the retiree receives are not dependent on the performance of the portfolio in which the contributions are invested; the company sponsoring the plan assumes the entire liability. The amount of the benefit is determined according to some formula that usually accounts for the amount of contributions and the length of time the retiree worked for the company. The disadvantage to a defined-benefit plan, from the company's perspective, is the possibility that the investment portfolio will not perform as expected, forcing the company to make payments from its earnings, or, worse, to borrow money. See also: Defined-contribution plan.

Deflation A situation in which a currency gains value, often resulting from a decrease in prices. Many economists believe that deflation is the result a fall in demand for goods and services, which causes producers to reduce prices. This reduces their profits and causes a reduction in investment, which contributes to a further drop in demand. Because of this deflationary spiral, deflation is often associated with recessions and depressions and has been known to cause unemployment. It is also called negative inflation. See also: Lost Decade, Inflation.

Deflator A mathematical tool used to adjust for inflation when comparing two prices from two different periods of time. One uses a deflator when one seeks to determine whether or not prices are rising in real terms.

Defrayment An expense that is later reimbursed. In accounting, a defrayment should not be listed as income since it is used simply to offset expenses that have already been incurred.

Degearing The process of a company repaying debt and issuing equity in order to alter its capital structure. A capital structure is how a company finances itself. Some (though not all) analysts believe that minimizing debt and maximizing equity can reduce the company's risk because, most of the time, paying coupons on debt is required while paying dividends on equity is not. Degearing is therefore a strategy to decrease risk while also maintaining the same level of financing. See also: Deleverage.

De-Horse In auto sales, to allow a potential customer to drive a new automobile instead of his/her own before he/she has officially bought it. A seller de-horses a customer from his/her current vehicle to discourage him/her from going to other dealerships. De-horsing may encourage a customer to finalize the purchase of the automobile he/she is driving.

Deich Pingin A coin that circulated in the Republic of Ireland between 1969 and 2002. It was equal in value to 1/10 of one Irish pound.

Deich Scilling A coin that circulated in the Republic of Ireland between 1966 and 2002. It was equal in value to 1/2 of one Irish pound.

Deindustrialization A situation in which an economy begins producing more services than goods. An analyst may say that deindustrialization is occurring when decreases in manufacturing are accompanied by increases in consulting companies. This can be beneficial to some sectors; indeed, some investors look for evidence of deindustrialization to know what industries are likely to be profitable. However, deindustrialization can be detrimental to some workers and regions. For example, as the United States has deindustrialized, the city of Detroit, which is home to many automakers, has lost approximately half of its population, and consistently maintains a high unemployment rate relative to the rest of the country.

Deisceim An obsolete Irish unit of length approximately equivalent to 1.5 meters.

Delagatorship A slang term for a business or company run by a poor decision maker. That is, the owner or manager of a delegatorship allows subordinates to decide nearly all major and minor issues.

Delayed Convertible A convertible security where the conversion option may not be exercised until some specified date after the security is issued. See also: Period of call protection.

Delayed Opening A situation in which security does not open for trade by an exchange's management or by regulators. The opening on a security is delayed usually in order to discourage volatility. It happens especially when there is an exceptionally large number of buy or sell orders relative to their opposite. This may happen immediately following an announcement of good or bad news. Opening remains delayed until the imbalance is corrected. See also: Suspended Trading.

Delayed Settlement A situation in which a buyer or, more commonly, his/her broker, does not receive delivery of the securities he/she bought by the settlement date. A delayed settlement may or may not be by mutual consent of the counterparties to the transaction. A seller may deliberately arrange a delayed settlement so the securities remain on his/her records until a certain event, such as the ex-dividend date, has passed. See also Fail to deliver, Aged fail.

Deleverage To repay a company's debts in order to make it more attractive to investors. Companies acquire leverage (or debt) to expand operations in the most efficient way possible. However, acquiring too much debt may increase the company's risk so that it may be in danger of default or bankruptcy. Deleveraging reduces these risks.

Deliberation Council A working group consisting of government officials, business leaders and sometimes consumer and labor advocates. The deliberation council discusses and helps design economic policy. Deliberation councils were common in the high performance Asian economies during their periods of economic development.

Delinquency The state of being late for a payment on a loan or other liability. If a payment is due on the third of each month and one does not pay until the ninth, the account is said to be in delinquency until the payment is made. Some liabilities have grace periods to allow for late periods up to a certain point without causing delinquency. A late fee may or may not be assessed on a delinquent payment. Serious and prolonged delinquency can lead to default.

Delinquent Tax Tax one did not pay by the due date. Ordinarily, one owes interest and/or penalties on delinquent tax, which increase over time.

Delisting The removal of a stock from trading on an exchange. Delisting occurs when a publicly-traded company violates the exchange's rules, or, more commonly, when the company ceases to meet listing requirements. For example, when a company's market capitalization falls below a certain level, it is in danger of delisting.

Deliverable Instrument The underlying asset in a forward contract. A deliverable instrument is a commodity or security that is given to the buyer of a forward contract at the expiration date in exchange for a certain price. See also: Delivery.

Delivered at Frontier In international trade, an agreement between a buyer (importer) and a seller (exporter) in which the seller assumes all expense and risk of delivering a good up to the borders of the buyer's country. At that point, the buyer assumes all expense and risk. This term is most common when the good is delivered over land. It is less common in maritime or air transportation. See also: Incoterm.

Delivered Duty Paid In international commerce, an agreement between a buyer and a seller stating that the seller is responsible for paying for shipping and all transportation risk up to some agreed-upon delivery point. Of all incoterms, DDP gives the most responsibility to the seller and the least risk to the buyer. It is also called free domicile.

Delivered Duty Unpaid In international commerce, an agreement between a buyer and a seller stating that the seller must pay for all transportation and insurance up to a named destination in the importing country. Once the goods arrive in the importing country, the buyer is responsible for all transportation and risk and must also pay any tariffs or duties. The seller is not responsible for unloading the goods from the ship or other vessel unless both parties explicitly agree. See also: Incoterm.

Delivered Ex Quay In international commerce, an agreement between a buyer and a seller where the seller must bear all cost and risk of transporting a good until it has arrived and been unloaded at a port. That is, the seller has total responsibility while the good is loaded, being shipped overseas, and unloaded. The seller must pay the shipping company and purchase insurance for the good. The buyer may or may not be responsible for paying duties and customs, depending on the specific nature of the agreement. See also: Incoterm.

Delivered Ex Ship In international commerce, an agreement between a buyer and a seller in which the seller must bear all costs and risks of transporting a good until it has arrived at a port and has been made available for the buyer or his/her agent to retrieve it. That is, the seller has total responsibility while the good is being shipped overseas. The seller must pay the shipping company and purchase insurance for the good. See also: Incoterm.

Delivering Short The practice of borrowing shares and using them to deliver on an option contract. For example, suppose one holds a call option on 100 shares of Johnson & Johnson. If the option writer does not own 100 shares of Johnson & Johnson if the option is exercised, he must borrow them from another investor in order to fill the terms of the option. The writer must later buy the shares on the open market in order to return the borrowed shares. This can result in large losses if the price of Johnson & Johnson increases in the meantime. See also: Short Sale.

Delivery The transfer of a security or an underlying asset to a buyer. The term is often used in options, forward, and futures contracts, in which payment and delivery are separated by a relatively long period of time. Most of the time, however, delivery does not occur, as most traders offset their positions with opposite contracts.

Delivery Date The date on which the underlying asset of a futures contract or forward contract is delivered to the contract holder. A contract holder may offset the contract by taking an opposite position before it matures, but any investor holding such a contract on the expiration date must take delivery on the delivery date. See also: Notice day.

Delivery Instructions An order by a client to a broker as to where the broker should place securities or other assets once they are received from a seller. They could be given directly to the customer, placed in a brokerage account, or put somewhere else entirely.

Delivery Instrument A receipt or other document that the holder of a futures contract may exchange for the actual, underlying asset at expiration. The delivery instrument is easier to physically transfer than the underlying asset, but gives the holder the ability to receive the underlying at the end of the contract. They are especially useful because many futures contracts are ultimately settled in cash rather than with the actual underlying.

Delivery Month The month in which an option or futures contract expires and delivery must be made. The seller generally must inform the buyer of delivery during the delivery month.

Delivery Notice In futures trading, the written notice by the seller of a commodity of the intent to deliver to the buyer or other appropriate person/institution. The delivery notice may take place at any time during the notice period, which is specified in the futures contract. The delivery notice must specify the exact commodities to be delivered.

Delivery Option In some futures contract, the right of the seller to determine where and how the underlying asset will be delivered when the contract expires. It also gives the seller some leeway in the quality of the underlying asset to be delivered. The seller informs the buyer of these details.

Delivery Point In international commerce and futures contracts, the agreed-upon location where the seller or his/her representative must hand over the underlying good or commodity in order to have fulfilled the obligation to make delivery. Often, a delivery point is a warehouse.

Delivery Price The price at which a futures contract is settled. Clearing houses set delivery prices to reduce confusion when the futures contract expires and the seller must make delivery.

Delivery versus Payment A settlement procedure in which the buyer and the seller of a security agree that the seller will pay the buyer upon the security's delivery to the seller. This agreement is designed to reduce risk to both parties: if the delivery and payment do not occur at the same time there is a risk, however small, of theft by one party or the other. It is more commonly known as cash on delivery.

Delors Report A report outlining a three-phase plan to integrate the markets and currencies of Europe. It laid the foundation for the establishment of the European Union in 1993 and led to the introduction of the euro in 1999. The report was presented in 1989 by the European Commission, at the time presided over by Jacque Delors.

Delphi Technique A system of forecasting in which different experts give their professional opinions without knowing what the other experts' opinions are. That is, the experts share their opinions anonymously and discuss them in a series of rounds. These rounds continue until they reach some consensus. The Delphi technique exists to ensure that a famous or well-regarded expert's opinion does not drown out those of lesser known analysts.

Delta Cross-Hedge An investment strategy that involves taking a position on a call and a put on the same underlying asset. Because the price movements of the two options are closely correlated, a negative movement on the call should be offset by a positive movement on the put and vice versa. A delta cross-hedge should create a delta neutral position.

Delta Hedging An options strategy that involves offsetting a long position on an option contract with a short position on the underlying asset, or vice versa. An investor uses a delta hedging strategy when a change in the price of the underlying asset results in a change to the premium of the option. The relationship between the change in premium and the change in the price of the underlying is known at the hedge ratio; delta hedging profits from changes in the hedge ratio.

Delta Neutral Describing a portfolio containing option contracts where changes in the price of the underlying assets do not change the value of the portfolio. One can construct a delta neutral portfolio, for example, by buying calls and puts on the same underlying asset where each has an equal but opposite delta with respect to the other. So when the price of the underlying asset changes, the two options change prices in opposite directions so that there is no net effect on the value of the portfolio.

Delta Spread A situation in which the difference in price of two or more related options is zero. An investor holding these options will find that a small change in the price of the underlying asset will not affect the price of his/her options, but a large movement in any direction will result in a large profit. A delta spread is a hedging strategy designed to minimize risk while maximizing return. The most common type of delta spread is a calendar spread. See also: Call ratio backspread.

DEM ISO 4217 code for the deutschemark. It was introduced in 1948, replacing the Reichsmark. It became one of the most important currencies in the world. For example, it was one of the currencies included in the basket that determined the value of Special Drawing Rights. After 1990, the deutschemark became the currency of the unified Germany. It was replaced by the euro in 1999 and ceased circulation in 2002.

Demand The need or desire for a good, service, or asset among consumers at a given price. The amount of demand at a given price is determined by supply and the availability of similar or replacements goods and services, among other factors. While demand for some staple products is relatively constant regardless of price, most of the time the price has a large influence on the level of demand. Demand for a good or service tends to increase as its price decreases. See also: Law of supply and demand, Demand curve.

Demand Deposit Funds in a bank account that may be withdrawn on demand of the customer. Most demand deposits are in checking accounts and savings accounts, because funds in these accounts are available to the customer at any time (unless they are under a check hold). Under the Expedited Funds Availability Act of 1987, banks in the United States must grant availability to demand deposits within a certain number of days.

Demand Loan A loan that must be paid on demand from the lender. Demand loans are often used to fund margin accounts; alternatively, they are common for personal loans with no set maturity. Demand loans often require collateral and are also called call loans. See also: Margin call.

Demand Price The price for a good or service as determined by how much potential buyers want the good or service at a given level of supply. As demand for

163

the product rises (assuming a constant supply), so does the demand price. Likewise, the demand price falls as demand drops. One uses the demand curve to calculate the demand price.

Demand Shock Any sudden event that dramatically but (usually) temporarily increases or decreases demand for one or more goods or services. The event may result from government intervention, such as a change in money supply, or may be a random occurrence in the market. For example, a company announcing that it is discontinuing a certain product may see an increase in demand for that product because people want to buy it while they can. This results in an increase in price for that product. However, if that company decides not to discontinue the brand, demand will likely taper off, resulting in a return to equilibrium.

Demand-Pull Inflation In Keynesian economics, a significant increase in prices that occurs when there is an increase in demand for goods and services such that the increase outpaces supply. The equivalent of demand-pull inflation can occur for any one product, but the term refers to situations where this happens throughout the economy. Demand may increase for a number of reasons; one example is an increase in the money supply. If persons have more money, they are more likely to buy goods and services which, in turn, drives up prices. One way to think of demand-pull inflation is to conceptualize it as too many dollars chasing too few products.

Dematerialization The process by which stocks and other securities cease to be represented by a physical certificate and become electronically recorded. Dematerialization has gradually become more common as computers have become more sophisticated and exchanges increasingly decide to close their trading floors.

De-Merger A situation in which a company sells one or more of its subsidiaries. Shareholders in the original company are usually given the same proportion of shares in the newly independent company. See also: Spin-off, Divestiture.

Demo A public or semi-public display of a product. A company may put out a demo to a limited audience as part of its market research to see how well the product works, what needs to be changed, and so forth. Alternately, it may put on a demo during marketing to show potential buyers how good it already is. The term is short for demonstration and is sometimes also used as a verb.

Democracy Self-rule in a polity. In a democracy, the citizens vote on issues of governance. Often, the term also refers to a republic, in which citizens elect representatives who vote on issues of governance, but the two terms are not identical.

Democrat A person or scholar who believes in self-rule in a polity. In a democracy, the citizens vote on issues of governance. Often, the term also refers to a republican, who believes that citizens should elect representatives who vote on issues of governance, but the two terms are not identical.

Democratic Party of Japan A center-left political party in Japan. The Democratic Party favors restructuring the civil service (believing it to be too large) and in general favors free market and social justice principles. It was founded in 1998.

Demos In Greece, a political subdivision equivalent to a municipality.

Demutualization The process by which a mutual company becomes a publicly-traded company. A mutual company is a company owned by its members or users for the benefit of those members or users. In demutualization, the members give up their rights and receive shares in the company in return, which the (now former) members may then sell. Demutualization happens most often when a stock exchange owned by its members goes public. As an aside, a mutual company should not be confused with a mutual fund.

Deng Xiaoping A 20th-century Chinese statesman. Active in the Communist Party of China throughout his entire career, he served as China's de facto leader from 1978 until 1992. He was the major force behind China's pro-market reforms, including the establishment of a private sector and the acceptance of international trade. His reforms are credited with turning China into a global economic player. Deng lived from 1904 to 1997.

Denga A former coin in Russia. It was minted sporadically from the 14th century until 1916. It was worth half a kopek.

Deni A division of the Macedonian denar equal in value to 1/100 of one denar.

Dennis Kozlowski An American former executive on Wall Street. He became CEO of Tyco International in 1992 and expanded its operations dramatically throughout the 1990s. However, he was later convicted of taking more than $80 million in unauthorized bonuses. He was born in 1946.

Denomination The face value of money or a bond. The denomination for a bond is most often $1000, which the par paid at maturity. Denominations on money indicate how much cash one has. For example, if one has a bill with a $10 denomination, this indicates that one has $10.

Deny An ancient Egyptian unit of volume approximately equivalent to 50 cubic centimeters.

Departament In the Duchy of Warsaw, a political subdivision equivalent to a province. These existed between 1807 and 1815.

Departamento In Spanish-speaking areas of Latin America, a political subdivision roughly equivalent to a province.

Departement In France, a political subdivision equivalent to a province.

Department for Business, Enterprise and Regulatory Reform A former department of the British government responsible for business regulation, enforcement of employment law, promotion of business growth and entrepreneurship,

and economic growth in sub-national regions. It was established in 2007 and in 2009 became part of the Department of Business, Innovation and Skills.

Department for Business, Innovation and Skills A department of the British government responsible for advising the government and implementing law related to corporate governance, business regulation, intellectual property, international trade, and other business issues. For example, it is the department that issues export licenses. The department was created in 2009 but traces its origins to the 17th century.

Department for Culture, Media and Sport A department of the British government responsible for internet and media regulation in the United Kingdom and for the promotion of the arts, sports, and creative economic sectors in England alone. It was established in 1992 as the Department of National Heritage and took its current name in 1997.

Department for Environment, Food and Rural Affairs Also called DEFRA. A department of the British government responsible for regulation of agriculture and fishing, enforcement of safety standards in food, and protection of the environment. It was established in 2001 as part of a merger of previously existing departments and offices.

Department for Innovation, Universities and Skills A former department of the British government responsible for the administration of universities, adult learning programs, and other public bodies (such as the Medical Research Council) intended to promote education. It was established in 2007 and in 2009 became part of the Department of Business, Innovation and Skills.

Department for International Development Commonly called DFID. A department of the British government responsible for the administration of foreign aid. It donates money and sponsors programs all over the world to assist in international development. It traces its origins to the 1970s.

Department for Transport A department of the British government responsible for highway maintenance, motor vehicle registration, the coastguard, and other similar issues. It was created in 2002, but traces its origins to the early 20th century.

Department for Work and Pensions A department of the British government responsible for administration of welfare policy, British Social Security, state pensions, and similar matters. Because it handles most government payments to citizens, it oversees the largest budget of any department in the U.K. It was established in 2001, but traces its origins to the beginnings of the welfare state in the early 20th century.

Department of Communities and Local Government A department of the British government responsible for administration of municipalities in England (but not elsewhere in the United Kingdom). It is responsible for a wide variety of matters, including issues such as fire services, building regulations, and urban planning. It was established in 2006.

Department of Energy and Climate Change A department of the British government responsible for managing and advising government energy policy. For example, it oversees efforts to gradually decrease the United Kingdom's reliance on fossil fuels. It was created in 2009, but existed in various forms at various times during the 20th century.

Department of Justice A cabinet-level body of the U.S. federal government responsible for the prosecution of federal crimes. It also provides counsel for the government and supervises law enforcement agencies such as the FBI and the Bureau of Alcohol, Tobacco, Firearms and Explosives. The department was created in 1870.

Department of Labor A department of the United States government that is responsible for enforcement of laws regulating workplace conditions, minimum wages, and other federal labor laws. It is also administers unemployment insurance and collects some economic statistics, particularly regarding unemployment.

Department of Veterans Affairs A department of the U.S. federal government devoted to serving the interests of American military veterans. Among other things, the Department guarantees mortgages borrowed by veterans to increase veteran homeownership.

Depeg To remove a previously instituted peg on a currency. For example, if Currency A is pegged to Currency B at a 1:1 ratio, but the central bank for Currency A decides to let it float, it is said to be depegged from Currency B. Depegging may occur if the peg is causing inflation or if the central bank is unable to sustain the peg for other reasons.

Dependency Ratio The ratio of the rough number of persons who are financially dependent on another person to the rough number of persons of working age, expressed as a percentage. The dependency ratio shows how easy or difficult it is for the persons of working age to take care of those who are not of working age. It is calculated thus: Dependency ratio = (Number of persons under 15 + Number of persons over 65) / (Number of persons between 15 and 65) *100

Dependent An individual for whom another individual is financially responsible. For example, if a working mother has a child, the child is her dependent. Likewise, if a man is taking care of his father in his old age, the father is a dependent. One may normally receive a tax credit for dependents. See also: Child Tax Credit.

Dependent Student A post-secondary student in the United States who does not earn income sufficient to be an independent student. A dependent student must report parental income on his/her FAFSA when attempting to qualify for federal financial aid. In other words, because there is no way a dependent student has enough income to pay for his/her education, the government considers the possibility that his/her parents may be able to do so.

Dependent Variable In technical analysis, a variable whose value is determined by the value of other variable(s), but plays no part in determining the value of those other variable(s). For example, if a product's price is determined by some equation involving the product's supply and its demand, the price is the dependent variable because the price does not affect the supply or demand.

Depletion A reduction of the value of an asset on a balance sheet that comes about as a result of the physical reduction of the asset's features. For example, there is only so much oil in an oil field. Depletion reduces the value of the oil field in a way related to the amount of oil drilled up over a given period of time. Depletion is used most often with natural resources. See also: Depreciation, Amortization.

Deposit 1. An amount of money held at a financial institution on behalf of an account holder for safekeeping. For example, one may keep a deposit in one's checking account to pay for daily expenses instead of hiding one's money "under the mattress." Many deposits are insured by organizations like the FDIC to reduce their risk. 2. See: Earnest Money.

Deposit Insurance A guarantee by some organization that funds in a bank deposit will be available to the account holder. That is, if the bank becomes insolvent, insured deposits are safe and depositors will be able to access them. Deposit insurance is made by a government-sponsored organization such as the FDIC. Deposit insurance exists in order to reduce pressures that might result in bank runs.

Deposit Insurance Corporation of Japan A semi-governmental organization in Japan that insures deposits in banks. That is, if a bank fails, the DICJ will reimburse all lost funds of depositors up to 10 million yen. Unlike some other deposit insurers, the DICJ does not cover foreign currency deposits. The DICJ was established in 1971.

Deposit Insurance Law Legislation in Japan that established the Deposit Insurance Corporation of Japan. The law requires the DICJ to reimburse all lost funds of depositors up to a certain amount in the event of a bank failure. The Deposit Insurance Law was designed to stabilize the Japanese banking sector and to reduce the pressure for bank runs. It was passed in the early 1970s and has been amended several times since.

Deposit Note A certificate of deposit that the bank may redeem and return to the holder before it matures. Deposit notes usually have a long maturity and may be traded on the secondary market. See also: Negotiable CD, Jumbo CD.

Deposit Rate Control A government mandate of a maximum interest rate it may pay on deposits in banks. Deposit rate controls are implemented to encourage liquidity in an economy. They have played a role in the economic development of some countries.

Deposit/Withdrawal at Custodian A computerized system on the DTCC for automatic transfers of cash and securities. This allows the DTCC to settle transactions more quickly and efficiently.

Depositary 1. A person entrusted with something of value, especially an agent in an exchange offer. The depositary in this sense acts as a go-between for the persons or firms making a transaction, ensuring that all securities and/or cash are given to the appropriate recipients. 2. A person or firm who keeps assets or securities on behalf of a client; for example, a bank. See also: Depository.

Depositary Bank A bank that keeps assets or securities on behalf of a client. All retail banks are depositary banks, because they hold money for account holders.

Depositors Forgery Insurance An insurance policy a company purchases providing coverage in the event of a loss due to a forged check or other financial instrument. It is also called a forgery bond.

Depository Institution An organization, which may be either for-profit or non-profit, that takes money from clients and places it in any of a variety of investment vehicles for the benefit of both the client and the organization. Common examples of depository institutions are retail banks and savings and loan associations, both of which take deposits into safekeeping and use them to make loans to other customers.

Depository Institutions Deregulation and Monetary Control Act Legislation in the United States that deregulated banks while giving the Federal Reserve more authority over non-member banks. Particularly, it required non-member banks to abide by Federal Reserve decisions but allowed greater leeway in bank mergers and in individual banks setting their own interest rates. The Act also raised deposit insurance to $100,000 per account. It is informally known as the Monetary Control Act.

Depository Transfer Check A check made by a bank to a company. A depository transfer check is useful when a company collects revenue at multiple locations in a given day. For example, if a company has several branches in the same city, the company's bank may collect funds from all locations, amass them in a single location, and then issue the depository transfer check to the company. The company may then deposit the check at that bank or at another one. A depository transfer check physically appears like an ordinary check, with the only difference being that it states "depository transfer check" on it.

Depository Trust & Clearing Corporation A clearing house that is the largest security depository and post-trade financial services company in the world. Based in New York, the DTCC settles the large majority of securities transactions in the United States, totaling $1.86 quadrillion in value in 2007. Along with its subsidiaries, the corporation provides services on mutual funds, insurance, corporate and municipal bonds, equities, mortgage- and government-backed securities, and various other derivatives. Its main competitors are Euroclear and Clearstream.

Depreciation The gradual reduction of an asset's value. It is an expense, but because it is non-cash, it is often effectively a tax write-off; that is, a person or company usually may reduce his/her/its taxable income by the amount of the depreciation on the asset. Because there are many different ways to account depreciation, it often bears only a rough resemblance to the asset's useful life. This may further benefit the company as they may continue to use the asset tax-free after its value has technically depreciated to nothing. See also: Amortization.

Depreciation Recapture A procedure the IRS uses to maximize tax revenue from depreciating assets by requiring the profit on the sale of a depreciating asset to be reported as ordinary income rather than capital gain. Because capital gains are taxed at a lower rate than most ordinary income, the IRS uses depreciating recapture to make up for some of the tax revenue lost in the depreciating asset. Depreciation recapture is assessed if the assets are sold for a price higher than their depreciated value.

Depreciation Tax Shield A tax deduction that comes from the depreciation of an asset. For example, if one spends $1,000 on an asset and its book value is reduced to $800 the following year, the depreciation tax shield is $200.

Depressed Price A price for a stock that is lower than other stocks in the same or similar markets. Bargain hunters and bottom fishers often buy securities with depressed prices on the assumption that they are undervalued, which will cause higher prices. A depressed price occurs especially in a buyer's market.

Depression A particularly long and/or deep recession. While there is no technical definition of a depression, conventionally it is defined as a period featuring severe declines in productivity and investment and particularly high unemployment. During the Great Depression, for example, GDP in the United States dropped 12% between 1929 and 1930 and a further 16% the following year. Likewise, unemployment rose to more than 25% nationwide and higher in some places.

Depth The ability of a security to withstand greater or smaller demand without affecting the price. Deep securities tend to be highly liquid and can be bought or sold in large quantities without their prices greatly moving in either direction. Among the factors affecting depth is the minimum price increment at which trades can be made (the tick size), market transparency, and restrictions on trade due to a futures or option contract on the security.

Deputizer A person who raises money for a non-profit organization, especially on a small scale. The term is most common in small Christian churches or ministries.

Deputizing Slang; the act or practice of raising money for a non-profit organization, especially on a small scale. The term is most common in small Christian churches or ministries.

Deregulate To reduce the amount of regulation over a market or economy. It may include reduced or eliminated requirements for reporting or filing statements with regulators. Deregulating may allow an organization to conduct more activities than it could before; for example, it may allow a bank to make more high risk investments. Deregulation is intended to increase efficiency in the market by letting the Invisible Hand guide the economy apart from government intervention. Opponents, however, argue that deregulation increases the likelihood of fraud and unfair practices such as insider trading. Many analysts agree that deregulation helps firms on solid financial footing and hurts those that are not.

Derekh Yom A Talmudic unit of length approximately equivalent to 40 or 45 kilometers.

Derivative Market The market for the sale of futures, forwards, options, and other securities except for regular stocks and bonds. Derivatives may be traded on an exchange or over-the-counter. Derivatives are often traded as speculative investments or to reduce the risk of one's other positions. Prominent derivative exchange includes the Chicago Mercantile Exchange and Euronext LIFFE.

Derivative Security Futures, forwards, options, and other securities except for regular stocks and bonds. The value of nearly all derivatives are based on an underlying asset, whether that is a stock, bond, currency, index, or something else entirely. Derivative securities may be traded on an exchange or over-the-counter. Derivatives are often traded as speculative investments or to reduce the risk of one's other positions. Prominent derivative exchanges include the Chicago Mercantile Exchange and Euronext LIFFE.

Desa In Indonesia, a political subdivision equivalent to a rural village.

Descending Tops In technical analysis, a chart pattern marked by a security price climbing, peaking, and dipping down repeatedly where each peak is lower than the last. For example, a stock price may climb to $35, drop to $25, climb back $32, and so forth. Descending tops is considered a bearish indicator.

Descending Triangle In technical analysis, a series of high and low prices for a security that, when plotted on a chart, looks vaguely like a triangle pointed to the right. A descending triangle indicates that both the highs and the low are lowering. It is a bearish signal. See also: Triangle, Ascending Triangle.

Descope To reduce the number of deliverables to be completed. For example, if a project has three deliverables but has only finished two of them by the deadline, the project may be descoped to make it appear successful.

Design Risk The risk associated with potential flaws in the design of a good or its production and their effect on the project's cash flow. It is also known as engineering risk.

Designated Order Turnaround A computerized order-entry system on the New York Stock Exchange that bypasses brokers and automatically executes orders at the best available price through a specialist on the trading floor. It is used predominantly for small and odd-lot orders. See also: SOES.

Desk Any trading desk or department at which transactions are carried out. One example is the home loan department at a bank. However, it especially applies to the Securities Department at the New York Federal Reserve, which carries out all of the Federal Reserve's orders to increase or decrease the dollar supply when it changes interest rates.

Desk Jockey A slang term for an office worker. Examples of desk jockeys include insurance adjusters and tax preparers.

Desk Trader An employee at a brokerage who takes orders from clients and trades on their behalf. A desk trader does not trade on the brokerage's own account. See also: Dealer.

Despot A person or group that rules a country without recourse to democratic elements like free elections. Despots believe that they should rule because they know best how people ought to live. Most governments now are democracies (at least officially), but despots continue to thrive in many areas.

Despotism 1. A theory that the best form of government is rule by one person (or group) who knows best how people ought to live. Most governments now are democracies (at least officially) and so despotism has been more or less discredited as a theory. **2.** A despotic state or government.

Destination Control Statement A form placed with American exports stating the authorized destinations of the goods. It is also called an antidiversion clause.

Detailed Audit The process of reviewing activities to identify inefficiencies, to reduce costs, and otherwise to achieve organizational objectives in a more complete way than other audits. Detailed audits may investigate potential theft or fraud and ensure compliance with applicable regulations and policies. They also help ensure the accuracy and legality of reports, as well as whether they conform to the Generally Accepted Accounting Principles .

Determinism In economics, the theory that occurrences are caused directly by other occurrences, and that economic agency by individuals plays little or no role. For example, a company's success occurs because social and economic pressures cause its products to be demanded, and not because of any marketing strategy its management devises. Determinism is associated with Karl Marx, who believed in the importance of historical analysis in explaining economic phenomena. However, some Marxist analysts have rejected that Marx taught economic determinism.

Determinist A person subscribing to the theory that economic occurrences are caused directly by other occurrences, and that economic agency by individuals plays little or no role. For example, determinism holds that a company's success occurs because social and economic pressures cause its products to be demanded, and not because of any marketing strategy its management devises. Determinism is associated with Karl Marx, who believed in the importance of historical analysis in explaining economic phenomena. However, some Marxist analysts deny that Marx taught economic determinism.

Detrend The removal of a trend from the consideration of several variables. A detrend may be necessary to discover a company's true financial health. For example, one may detrend increased sales around Christmas time to see a more accurate account of a company's sales in a given year.

DEU GOST 7.67 Latin three-letter geocode for Germany. The code is used for transactions to and from German bank accounts and for international shipping to Germany. As with all GOST 7.67 codes, it is used primarily in Cyrillic alphabets.

Deuce A slang term for $200. The term is most common in auto sales.

Deunx 1. An ancient Roman unit of area approximately equivalent to 2,313 square meters. **2.** An ancient Roman unit of weight approximately equivalent to 301.5 grams.

Deutsche Borse AG A firm that operates a number of high-profile securities and derivative exchanges, among other financial companies. Formed in 1993, it owns the Frankfurt Stock Exchange and Eurex. Just as prominently, Deutsche Borse AG also owns the Clearstream clearing house.

Deutsche Terminborse Formerly a German exchange for options and futures contracts. It was the first fully computerized exchange in Germany and the first to trade futures. In 1998, Deutsche Terminborse merged with the Swiss Options and Financial Futures Exchange to form Eurex.

Deutschemark The former currency of Germany. It was introduced in 1948, replacing the Reichsmark. It became one of the most important currencies in the world. For example, it was one of the currencies included in the basket that determined the value of Special Drawing Rights. After 1990, the deutschemark became the currency of the unified Germany. It was replaced by the euro in 1999 and ceased circulation in 2002.

Deutscher Aktienindex A blue chip index in Germany. It tracks the performance (dividends added in) of the 30 most actively traded stocks on the Frankfurt Stock Exchange. Prices are taken from the Xetra electronic trading system and are updated every minute.

Devaluation The active decision of a government to reduce the value of its own currency vis a vis other currencies. Devaluation occurs exclusively in fixed currencies, when the currency in question is pegged to another currency. Governments devalue their own currencies to make their exports less expensive in foreign markets. If a company exports its products for the same price in the local (devalued) currency, it is cheaper for consumers to buy those products in their own currency. See also: Depreciation.

Development Economics The subset of economics concerned with improving the economic growth of low-income countries. Development economics may focus on how to implement infrastructure or develop the business environment for growth to take place. It also studies what government policies (if any) would promote growth. Development economics became a major field within economics in the latter part of the 20th century, as more former European colonies became independent.

Development Stage The period that a company undergoes while it is in the process of discovering what goods and services best suit the company's needs and developing those products in order to sell them. Some companies have divisions for this kind of research, while other companies are devoted exclusively to it. Biotech companies, for example, often go through a relatively long development stage before they make and sell their products. Companies in the development stage often produce little or no revenue.

Developmental Oil and Gas Partnership A lower-risk oil and gas limited partnership. The general partner uses the investment money from the limited partners to drill in a proven oil or gas field, and not in an unproven field. This gives the limited partners a good chance at a steady return, but little hope for sudden profit. The typical partnership unit for a limited partner costs $5,000, and the limited partner risks no more than this investment.

Developmental State View A view of economic development holding that capital markets cannot provide the necessary liquidity and growth for development without significant government intervention. The developmental state view advocates that, at minimum, a government in a developing country should coordinate resource allocation with the private sector. Others contend that the government should conduct resource allocation itself. Economists disagree on how well the developmental state view works.

Devisenkommisar In Weimar Germany, an official appointed to help control the rapid depreciation of the German mark. The devisenkommisar office was created in September 1923 to help tame the hyperinflation experienced in Germany at this time. The office soon take on the right to seize gold, other precious metals, and hard currencies. These attempts to curb inflation failed.

Dexia A Belgian-French bank that provides insurance, wealth management, public finance, and commercial and retail banking services. It traces its origins to 1860. It came under financial pressure during the late 2000s recession. In 2011, its Belgian division was nationalized, with Luxembourg and France providing guarantees of its debt.

Dextans 1. An ancient Roman unit of area approximately equivalent to 2,103 square meters. **2.** An ancient Roman unit of weight approximately equivalent to 274.1 grams.

Dha An obsolete Burmese unit of length approximately equivalent to 3.912 meters.

Dha Phingin A coin that circulated in the Republic of Ireland between 1971 and 2002. It was equal in value to 1/50 of one Irish pound.

Dhaka Stock Exchange Bangladesh's main stock exchange. The Dhaka Stock Exchange began in 1954 when Bangladesh was still known as East Pakistan, and came into existence in its current form in 1976, five years after independence from Pakistan. The DSE operates two indices with more than 300 companies listed. It is a public limited company.

Dhanu An ancient Indian unit of length variously equivalent to values between three and four meters.

Dhanu Graha An ancient Indian unit of length variously equivalent to values between 62 and 83 millimeters.

Dhanu Musti An ancient Indian unit of length variously equivalent to values between 125 and 167 millimeters.

Diagonal Spread An option strategy in which one enters into a long position on a call (or a put) while taking a short position on another call (or put) with the same underlying asset, but with different strike prices and expiration dates. One gains (or loses) on the change in the spot price of the underlying asset over the life of the spread. It derives its name from the fact that it shares features with a vertical spread (where the calls or puts have different strike prices) and a horizontal spread (where they have different expiration dates).

Dialing for Dollars Informal; the practice of making an unsolicited telephone call to a completely unknown person in an attempt to convince the person to become an investor of a particular venture. This practice is controversial and some jurisdictions have put in place laws limiting its legitimate use. In theory, dialing for dollars is the same practice as cold calling, but the former term has a negative connotation. One often hears of dialing for dollars in the context of a suspicious and perhaps illegal investment.

Dialogue Marketing A marketing strategy or tactic in which one tries to make sales by developing a friendly business relationship with a potential customer. Assuming the product itself is good, dialogue marketing may result in repeat business.

Diamond Top Formation In technical analysis, the end of an uptrend and the beginning of a downtrend. In a diamond top formation, the price peaks and then begins to decline. It derives its name from the fact that it vaguely resembles the top of a diamond when the prices are plotted on a chart.

Diamonds 1. A unit investment trust in which the underlying asset is the Dow Jones Industrial Average. That is, diamonds are shares in a closed-end index fund tracking the DJIA. It is traded on the American Stock Exchange. It operates much like an exchange-traded fund, but, like all unit investment trusts, it has an expiration date, while ETFs do not. Its ticker symbol is DIA. **2.** A valuable commodity consisting of very hard gem stones used in jewelry and tools. Diamonds may be traded on any of a number of exchanges. See also: Blood diamonds.

Diarize A slang term meaning to record, especially the findings of a study or the minutes of a meeting.

Diary Forward Slang; to record an event on a calendar at regular intervals until further notice. For example, one may diary forward meetings for the board of directors if it is announced that they are to be held on the first Monday of each month for the foreseeable future.

Diaspora The persons of a community living outside their area or ancestral homeland, especially but not necessarily as a community. A diaspora can create and sustain trade and other economic ties between two areas. For example, a businessman from one ethnic group may communicate with a relative in the homeland in order to set up an import-export company.

Diaulos An ancient Greek unit of length approximately equivalent to 369.9 meters.

Die A metal stamp that forms the design of a coin. It does not refer to the coin color, but instead to the imprints, such as the portrait, value, or other engraving on the coin. See also: Numismatics.

Die Clash In numismatics, a situation in which the die (the metal stamp engraving each coin) stamping the top of a coin collides with the die stamping the bottom, damaging the coin. This may affect the value of the coin for collectors.

Die Defect In numismatics, any damage that affects the die, which is the metal stamp engraving a coin. This may damage the coin, which could affect its value for collectors.

Diff A futures contract traded on the Chicago Mercantile Exchange where the underlying asset is the interest rate spread between the U.S. dollar and either the British pound or the Japanese yen. The German mark has been used as well. A diff can be used to hedge foreign exchange risk. See also: Interest rate parity.

Difference Check A check that one counterparty in a swap gives to another at the end of the swap agreement. For example, in an interest rate swap, the counterparties swap two different interest rates calculated over the same nominal value. In order to make things easier, the counterparty who owes more writes a check for the difference between the two interest rates, instead of both counterparties writing checks for the whole amount owed to the other.

Difference from S&P A measure of how a security or fund performs relative to the market as a whole. It is calculated by taking the percentage change to the S&P 500 and subtracting the percentage change to the security or fund. The S&P is used because it is a very broad, benchmark index. The difference from the S&P can help one determine if a security or fund is cyclical or counter-cyclical.

Differential 1. The degree of change in quality of the underlying asset on a futures contract that is allowed. Every futures contract specifies the quality of the commodity underlying it that must be delivered in order for the seller to fulfill the contract. The differential allows the seller to deliver a good of a different quality, at least within certain limits. Not all futures contracts allow for differentials. **2.** A change in the location of delivery that some futures contracts allow the seller to make at his/her discretion.

Differential Disclosure The practice of a publicly-traded company placing contradictory earnings information on two different reports, especially so as not to have the discrepancy discovered.

Differential Swap A plain vanilla swap in which one of the legs is paid in a currency other than the one in which it is calculated. For example, the notional amount over which the interest rates are calculated may be in U.S. dollars, but one of the payments may be made in yen. A differential swap may be entered in order to take advantage of a favorable exchange rate. See also: Exchange rate risk, Currency swap.

Digit An obsolete unit of length equivalent to 0.75 inches.

Digits Deleted On a ticker tape, an indication that only a partial quote is given. Specifically, only the final digits are listed in order to save room on the ticker tape. For example, if a quote is 54.75, it may read on the tape as 4.75 on the assumption that investors know to add $50 to the quote. Digits are deleted when the tape is late due to heavy trading volume.

Digitus An ancient Roman unit of length approximately equivalent to 18.5 millimeters.

Dijishi In China, a political subdivision roughly equivalent to a metropolitan area. A dijishi ranks below a province but above a county.

Diluted Earnings per Share The earnings per share of a publicly-traded company calculated on the assumption that all convertible securities were exercised. That is, instead of considering only common stock currently in existence, the diluted EPS assumes that all securities such as stock options, convertible bonds, and anything else that can be changed into common stock is actually changed. The diluted EPS is useful for common shareholders because it represents the earnings one would receive in the worst possible situation. Many companies report both the basic EPS and the diluted EPS. The actual EPS usually falls between the two. See also: Dual Presentation.

Diluted Founders In venture capital, founders of companies who have sold most of their ownership. This occurs when the founders approach venture capitalists for funding and in exchange give a portion of the company's ownership to the venture capital firm. Over time, through successive financing rounds, the founders' stake in the company becomes increasingly diluted.

Dilutive Acquisition An acquisition that reduces a publicly-traded company's earnings per share. A dilutive acquisition occurs when the price-earnings ratio of the acquiring firm is less than that of the target firm. A dilutive acquisition usually results in a lower share price for the target company. See also: Accretive acquisition.

Dilutive Effect The result of an increase in the number of shares, usually through a new issue. That is, a company may issue more shares to shareholders and other investors, which raises the number of shares outstanding. This decreases the company's earnings per share, which, in turn, can decrease the stock price. See also: Anti-dilution provision.

Dim Sum Market The market for bonds denominated in Chinese yuan and issued internationally in Hong Kong. The dim sum market exists as part of the Chinese government's attempt to establish itself as a global, stable financial market.

Dimidium scrupulum An ancient Roman unit of area approximately equivalent to 4.38 square meters.

Dinosaur 1. An employee with a great deal of experience. The term is somewhat of a backhanded compliment as it connotes a curmudgeonly demeanor and resistance to change. **2.** A slang term for obsolete technology.

Diorama A three-dimensional model, especially of a real or historical event. For example, a miniature or full scale model of Appomattox Courthouse on the day that General Robert E. Lee surrendered to General Ulysses S. Grant may be called a diorama.

Dip A small decrease in a security's price after a significant uptrend. Some investment advisers and technical analysts recommend buying after a dip if there are signals that the uptrend will continue afterwards. However, it is sometimes difficult to determine whether a dip is temporary or if it is the beginning of a trend reversal.

Diqu In China, a political subdivision below a province but above a county.

Diram A subdivision of the Tajikistani somoni. One diram is equal in value to 1/100 of one somoni.

Direct Informal for a debt security issued by the United States government, as opposed to one of its agencies. Perhaps the most prominent example of a direct security is a U.S. Treasury security. Direct securities are considered risk-free because they are guaranteed by the full faith and credit of the United States government.

Direct Access Trading A system on NASDAQ allowing the user to make trades without going through a broker. Direct access trading allows investors to make trades very quickly, which is important for day traders, who seek to make a profit from price movements that take place in a single trading day. Most investors do not use direct access trading because their investments do not depend on the speed of buying or selling a given security.

Direct Costs of Financial Distress Any fees or penalties that result from a bankruptcy or liquidation. An obvious example is the fee one must pay to a bankruptcy attorney. However, other fees, perhaps broker fees resulting from the liquidation of stock, may also be attached.

Direct Deposit An electronic service in which a payment, especially but not limited to a paycheck, pension, or tax refund, is transferred immediately into the recipient's bank account. The direct deposit replaces a check for which the recipient would otherwise have to wait to arrive in the mail. A direct deposit service also allows the recipient to have access to his/her funds immediately without waiting on the holding period, which is required for many check deposits.

Direct Estimate Method A budget forecast based on detailed, category-by-category estimates of cash inflows and outflows. See also: Cash budgeting.

Direct Investment The act or practice of buying stock in a publicly-traded company without using a broker as an intermediary. Perhaps the most common means of direct investment is dividend reinvestment, which is the act of using one's dividends to buy more shares in the same company. Some companies also offer plans called direct purchase plans, which allow investors to bypass their broker. However, direct purchase plans are rather illiquid (it is difficult to sell one's shares without a broker), and are therefore bought for long-term investing.

Direct Loan Program A division of the ExIm Bank that makes loans to foreign companies with the requirement that they use the proceeds to buy American exports. Direct loans are made for the foreign company's capital outlays; they carry a fixed interest rate. See also: Federal Direct Student Loan Program.

Direct Marketing Block The use of a block group in a direct mail or other marketing campaign. A block group is a location used by the U.S. Census Bureau where approximately 800 to 1,000 people live. As the name indicates, a block group is usually a collection of city blocks. A marketer uses block groups and the demographic information contained in them to identify the persons most likely to respond to a particular marketing campaign. It may also be used in a marketing campaign to test which block groups respond.

Direct Overhead Costs of business that result directly from having and maintaining a business. Rent is a primary (and expensive) example of direct overhead, as are office supplies and raw material from which to make products.

Direct Paper Commercial paper issued by a company to an investor without the use of a dealer to intermediate the transaction. Commercial paper is a short-term debt security. Direct paper describes one way a company may issue it. See also: Dealer paper.

Direct Participation Program A business venture, especially, but not necessarily, a limited partnership or an S corporation, that allows the investors to participate in the profits and tax avoidance of some underlying investment. Generally speaking, direct participation programs invest in real estate or energy products. The idea behind a direct participation program is to allow investors to participate in certain tax benefits usually available only to corporations, such as depreciation deductions. However, the United States government has limited many of the tax benefits available to direct participation programs.

Direct Play A stock in a non-diversified, publicly-traded company. For example, a company with business predominantly or exclusively in automobile manufacturing issues direct play stocks. Investors buy direct plays when they believe that a certain industry is about to perform exceptionally well. This brings with it the possibility of a high return for the investor, but direct plays are also much riskier than shares in diversified companies.

Direct Public Offering An offering of stock in a company to its employees, customers, suppliers, and other stakeholders. A direct public offering differs from a normal issue of stock, in which underwriters sell the issue to whomever will buy it. A DPO is usually less expensive to the company making the offering (as it does not have to pay underwriters), but it raises less capital.

Direct Registration System An electronic system allowing a person or corporation to own shares without being issued stock certificates. In a direct registration system, the shareholder's information is maintained on a computer system. Transfer of shares maintained on a direct registration system may take place either through a transfer agent or the shareholder's ordinary broker.

Direct Repurchase The act of a publicly-traded company buying back its own shares from shareholders. This is done to reduce the number of shares outstanding and is a common practice when the company's management believes that its shares are undervalued.

Direct Rollover The transfer of funds from an IRA to another qualified retirement account owned by the same person or vice versa. Rollovers happen most often when an employee changes jobs and therefore IRA accounts. A direct rollover goes directly from one account to the other; it is not distributed to the account holder at any point. A direct rollover may only be done once per year for each account. One must report a direct rollover to the IRS, but it is not taxable.

Direct Search Market A situation in which buyers and sellers, especially of securities but also of other goods and services, seek each other out and conduct trades without brokers or other financial institutions mediating. This is the opposite of an intermediated market.

Direct Stock-Purchase Program A plan in which a publicly-traded company allows an investor to buy stock directly from the company rather than through a broker-dealer. Some companies offer direct stock purchase plans to raise financing at less expense to the investor (mainly through not charging commissions or fees). Some advisers recommend that first-time investors use direct stock purchase plans because of the reduced cost. It should not be confused with an employee stock option plan because direct stock purchase plans are open to anyone.

Direct Tax A tax that cannot be shifted to another person or entity. For example, taxes on income or assets are direct taxes, as the person or organization on whom they are levied must pay them directly. Direct taxes differ from indirect taxes, such as sales tax, which is levied on a seller but is paid by buyers. There is disagreement as to whether a corporate tax is a direct tax or indirect tax.

Direct Terms In foreign exchange, the expression of a currency in terms of one unit of a different currency. For example, to say there are two U.S. dollars per one British pound is to express the dollar in direct terms to the pound. See also: Indirect terms, Currency pair.

Directed Order An order from a client to a broker that includes instructions on what exchange to use. For example, if the client is only interested in buying the stated security on the American Stock Exchange, a directed order will include this information.

Directed Sale In underwriting, the sale of a large block of a security to a single investor. The lead underwriter handles a directed sale and withholds shares in the block from other members of the underwriting syndicate.

Directional Movement Index A moving average indicating whether and how strongly a security's price is changing. The DMI is based on the assumption that if a price is trending in one direction or the other, the highest (or lowest) price on a given trading day is always higher (or lower) than the highest (or lowest) price on the previous trading day. For example, if the intraday high for security X is $10 on Monday and $12 on Tuesday, the DMI reckons that security X is trending upward. It is calculated on a scale of 0 to 100, depending on the strength of the trend, and may be positive (indicating upward movement in price) or negative (indicating downward movement). It helps analysts determine whether to buy or sell securities.

Directional Trading A fairly straightforward investment strategy that involves buying securities one believes will rise in price and selling those one believes will decline in price. The success of the strategy involves the ability to accurately predict market movements, and the largest risk is the possibility that the investor may make a mistake. Many long-term investors use a directional trading strategy. See also: Market timer, Market neutral trading strategy.

Director of the Office of Management and Budget The head of the U.S. federal government office charged with preparing the budget and measuring the effectiveness of government programs. He or she is appointed by the president of the United States and confirmed by the Senate.

Directorate General for Economic and Financial Affairs An administrative office of the European Union. It monitors the economic performance of the EU, the organization's budget, economic aspects of other countries and international organizations, and financing of EU activities. It operates under the auspices of the European Commission.

Directors' and Officers' Liability Insurance Insurance a publicly-traded company purchases to reimburse senior management, or the company itself, for damages and legal expenses incurred as the result of a lawsuit for negligence. For example, if the board of directors' actions led to a massive loss for the company resulting in a lawsuit, directors' and officers' liability insurance will cover the cost of the lawsuit for the company as a whole and the individual directors. It is important to note that directors' and officers' liability insurance does not cover intentionally wrong actions, only negligence. It is often called D&O insurance for short.

Directorship A seat on the board of directors of a company or other organization. A directorship allows one to have a direct say in a company's policies, particularly regarding dividend payments, the hiring and firing of major executives, and so forth. One receives a directorship as the result of a shareholder vote. Generally speaking, directors are nominated on the basis of whom they intend to represent, whether that be management, a particular block of shareholders, or even the company's employees.

Dirhem A Turkish measure of weight approximately equivalent to 3.21 grams. It became obsolete when Turkey made the metric system mandatory in 1933.

Dirigisme In political science, the theory that the state ought to drive economic growth. Dirigisme argues that the state may do this by controlling the means of production (as in communism) or simply through careful economic planning. Proponents believe that dirigisme is an effective tool of development, while critics contend that it is inefficient and not respectful of individual rights. See also: State capitalism.

Dirks vs. SEC A U.S. Supreme Court case holding that one who receives inside information may be in violation of insider trading laws if he/she believes the person who revealed the information had a duty to keep it a secret. The case was decided in 1984. See also: Constructive insider.

Dirty Pool An informal term. **1.** Unethical behavior. **2.** The act or practice of aggressively negotiating to achieve the best possible result.

Dirty Price The price of a coupon bond that includes the present value of all future cash flows. That is, a dirty price is the price of a bond plus the interest that accrues between coupon payments. Therefore, the dirty price of a bond gradually increases between coupon payments, then retreats immediately after a coupon payment. Many European exchanges use the dirty price when quoting bond prices.

Dirty Stock A stock that cannot be transferred, especially because of improperly filed paperwork or another fairly innocuous reason. In other words, the delivery of a dirty stock is only stopped by legal and/or regulatory rules. See also: Good delivery.

Disability **1.** Any brokerage account with a restriction, or the restrictions themselves. Disabilities exist generally to prevent conflicts of interest in investment. For example, an employee of the brokerage may be unable to make certain transactions on his account with the brokerage. **2.** See: Disability insurance.

Disability Income Insurance In the United States, a program, run by the Social Security Administration, that provides for the lost income of individuals who become disabled for an extended period of time. Persons who have paid enough of the FICA tax for a long enough period of time are eligible for Social Security Disability Income Insurance. Payments begin at the start of the sixth month of a person's disability. The amount of the benefit varies according to a number of factors.

Disabled Person A person with less mental or physical ability than the average person. For example, a disabled person may use a wheelchair or may be blind or deaf. Mentally disabled persons often (but do not always) have lower earning potential than the average person, but this is not by any means the case for the physically disabled. Laws exist in many jurisdictions to protect the rights of disabled persons. See also: Americans with Disabilities Act, Handicapped Person.

Disatina A Tatar unit of area approximately equivalent to 1.1 hectares. It was rendered obsolete when the Soviet Union began to use the metric system in 1924.

Disbursement A payment. The term is used especially in the context of loans. When the borrower receives all or a portion of the loan funds, he/she is said to receive a disbursement.

Disbursement Float Money that a person or company has spent but that has not yet been taken out of one's bank account. A disbursement float occurs when a person or company writes a check; when the check is deposited, it usually takes a few days for the payment to clear. The disbursement float may be thought of as the difference between what is in one's bank account and what the bank shows to be in the account as the result of an uncleared check. See also: Net float, Collection float, Check hold.

Discharge in Bankruptcy The act of a bankruptcy court forgiving the debt of the person or company that has filed for bankruptcy. A discharge in bankruptcy means that the creditors have received as much as they are going to receive and that they no longer have the right to attempt to collect on debts.

Discharge of Lien The act of terminating a lien on a property after the claim on the lean has been satisfied to the claimant's or some other expectations.

Disclosure The voluntary or required release of information relevant to a security, company, fund, or anything else. In order to be listed on an exchange, a company must provide disclosure on itself by registering with the SEC and abiding by regulations that govern what information about itself that the company releases. Disclosure exists to prevent price manipulation and anything else that would disrupt the efficiency of trade. See also: Transparency.

Disclosure Statement **1.** A document given to a potential borrower by a lender stating all the terms of the loan. This includes the interest rate, the length of the loan, and any applicable fees. Lenders are required to provide disclosure statements. See also: Truth in Lending Act. **2.** A document given to a potential IRA account holder stating all the terms of the IRA. This includes the rules, penalties, and applicable fees associated with the IRA. IRA providers are required to provide disclosure statements and give the account holder seven days to opt out of the account with no penalties.

Discontinued Operations Divisions within a business that have either stopped operations due to lack of profitability or have been sold. A business may discontinue operations of a division if it loses money for the business or if it wishes to expand in other directions, among other reasons. The Financial Accounting Standards Board requires publicly-traded companies to report earnings per share of all divisions in its business, including discontinued operations. See also: Cost accounting.

Discount Arbitrage 1. An option strategy in which a person buys a call at a discount from its usual price and at the same time sells or short sells the underlying asset. **2.** An option strategy in which a person buys a put at a discount from its usual price and at the same time buys the underlying asset. In both cases, the person engages in a covered option strategy.

Discount Bond A bond or other debt instrument that is issued at a price below its face value. For example, a bond with par of $10,000 might be issued to an investor for $7000. All zero-coupon bonds are discount bonds.

Discount Brokerage Firm A brokerage firm that provides transaction services predominantly or exclusively. That is, a discount broker provides clients with little or no research or investment advice; rather, it specializes in completing the transactions for which clients ask. Discount brokers usually rely on computer programs to find matching offers or bids. They charge lower commissions than other brokers and rely on a high volume of orders for a profit. See also: Deep Discount Brokerage Firm.

Discount Interest 1. A situation where all the interest on a loan is paid at once. That is, the interest is deducted from the amount the borrower receives at the beginning of the loan. For example, if a bank makes a loan of $20,000 at a simple interest rate (that is, a non-compounding rate) of 5%, the bank simply does not give the borrower $1,000 (or 5% of $20,000). The borrower effectively borrows $19,000 and repays it with no interest. Discount interest is very rare in retail banking. **2.** See: Discount rate.

Discount Margin The average, expected return over a given reference rate for a floating-rate security. Because a floating-rate security by definition changes its return over time, the discount margin estimates the return over the reference rate by assuming that the floating rate will follow a certain pattern between issue and maturity.

Discount Note A debt security with a maturity of one year or less issued at a discount to its face value. For example, if a discount note has a face value of $1,000, it may be issued to the holder at $900. When it matures, the holder receives the full $1,000. A discount note does not pay a coupon; rather, the difference between the discount and the face value takes the place of the coupon. See also: coupon-equivalent yield.

Discount Payment The amount one pays for a security when that amount is less than the security's face value. See also: Discount bond.

Discount Period The period of time between the date a bill of exchange is drawn and the date on which payment is due.

Discount Point One percentage point of the principal of a mortgage loan that some lenders require borrowers to pay immediately as a condition of making the loan. That is, if the lender makes a mortgage loan, it may require the borrower to pay a certain amount of discount points up front. The amount paid is deducted from the interest the borrower would otherwise owe on the loan. Discount points are tax deductible for the borrower because they qualify as prepaid interest.

Discount Rate The interest rate at which the Federal Reserve makes short-term loans to member banks. The discount rate is an indicator of the direction in which the Federal Reserve is trying to push the broader economy. In general, a low interest rate indicates that it is trying to promote growth by making liquidity easily available, and a high interest rate shows that the Fed is concerned about inflationary pressures on the economy and trying to reduce the amount of money in the economy. Along with the sale of Treasury securities and the determining of the fed funds rate, setting the discount rate is one of the primary ways the Federal Reserve sets the monetary policy of the United States.

Discount Window An agency from which member banks of the Federal Reserve can borrow funds. Banks borrow short-term funds at the discount rate from the discount window, and must provide collateral for the transaction. The idea behind the discount window is to provide liquidity to banks when they need it without making them too reliant upon it. The Federal Reserve accomplishes this by raising or lowering the discount rate: a low interest rate indicates that it is trying to promote growth by making liquidity easily available, and a high interest rate shows that the Fed is concerned about inflationary pressures on the economy and trying to reduce the amount of money in the economy. While the discount window provides services electronically now, the term comes from an actual bank where representatives of member banks used to go to borrow money from the Federal Reserve.

Discount Yield A way to quote the price for bonds. It is calculated as the annualized yield assuming a 360 day year. One calculates the discount yield thusly: Discount yield = (Discount from par value / par value) * (360 / Days until maturity) The discount yield is also called the discount basis or the bank-discount basis.

Discounted Basis The sale of an investment vehicle, especially a bond, at a price below its value at maturity. This sale price must be the difference between the maturity value and the remaining interest or carrying cost on the investment vehicle.

Discounted Bill A debt security issued at a discount to its face value. For example, if a discounted bill has a face value of $1,000, it may be issued to the holder at $900. When it matures, the holder receives the full $1,000. A discounted bill, especially a short-term issue, often does not pay a coupon; rather, the difference between the discount and the face value takes the place of the coupon. See also: Coupon-equivalent yield.

Discounted Cash Flows Future, expected cash flows from a project or venture that have been adjusted to arrive at their present value. One uses the calculation of discounted cash flows to determine whether a particular investment is likely to be profitable.

Discounted Payback Period Rule In investment decisions, the number of years it takes for an investment to recover its initial cost after accounting for inflation, interest, and other matters affected by the time value of money, in order to be worthwhile to the investor. It differs slightly from the payback period rule, which only accounts for cash flows resulting from an investment and does not take into account the time value of money. Each investor determines his/her own discounted payback period rule and, as such, it is a highly subjective rule. In general, however, short-term investors use a short number of years, or even months, for their discounted payback period rules, while long-term investors measure their rules in years or even decades.

Discounting The act of determining the present value of future cash flows. Because money is subject to inflation and has the ability to earn interest, one dollar today is worth more than one dollar tomorrow. Discounting, then, is the act of determining how much less tomorrow's dollar is worth. For example, a bank may loan a sum of money and schedule repayments at $100 per month for 10 years. The bank may then discount the value of payments and determine exactly how much (in today's dollars) it will have received once the loan is paid off.

Discounting the News Describing a situation in which the market has already incorporated expected information into the price of a stock. That is, if a company's earnings are large for a particular quarter, it may leak the information so that investors discount the news, reducing the pressure for an unsustainable jump in price when the earnings are actually announced. For this reason, the Federal Reserve issues statements indicating what policy changes it might make before it makes them, allowing the markets to adjust before the announcement.

Discouraged Worker A person in the labor force who is not actively looking for work or who has been unable to find a job for an extended period of time. Discouraged workers are considered "marginally attached" to the labor force. Somewhat controversially, discouraged workers are generally not included in official estimations of unemployment.

Discrepancy 1. A letter of credit where the holder does not comply with the terms set forth in it. A discrepancy voids the letter of credit. **2.** More generally, any deviation from an agreement or contract.

Discrete Random Variable A variable that can take only one of several definite values. For example, one's FICO score is a discrete random variable because it can only be a positive integer between 300 and 850.

Discretion The ability to make decisions on one's own without the need to consult others. For example, a discretionary account gives a broker the right to make significant investment decisions without permission from or even consultation with the account's owner. Likewise, certain investments give an investor more discretion than others. An option contract allows but does not require the holder to buy (or sell) the underlying, while a futures contract requires the exchange to take place.

Discretionary Account A brokerage account in which a broker is able to make decisions without the need to consult others. For example, a discretionary account gives a broker the right to make significant investment decisions without permission from or even consultation with the account's owner. However, decisions made on a discretionary account must be made in accordance with the client's stated investment goals and according to the prudent man principle.

Discretionary Cash Flow The cash flow available to a company after its capital expenditures have been financed to their net present value and after all liabilities, such as employee wages and others, have been paid. The discretionary cash flow may be used to pay dividends to shareholders, to provide bonuses to executives, or for any number of other purposes.

Discretionary Order An order to buy or sell a security where the broker has the ability to decide when is the best time and price at which to execute the order, in accordance with the client's investment goals and the prudent person rule.

Discretionary Proposition The ability of a broker, holding a stock on behalf of a client, to vote for that client at the annual meeting of shareholders in the event that the broker mailed the proxy card to the client but has not heard any direction from the client. The discretionary proposition allows the broker to vote in favor of the company's management only. See also: Beneficial Owner, 10-Day Rule.

Discretionary Trust A trust in which a trustee is able to make decisions without the need to consult others. For example, a discretionary trust gives the trustee the right to make significant investment decisions without permission from or even consultation with the trustor or the beneficiary. However, the trustee has a fiduciary responsibility to manage the assets as well as possible; decisions made in a discretionary trust must be made in accordance with the prudent man principle.

Diseconomies of Scale The decrease of efficiency in the making of a product by producing more of it. That is, diseconomies of scale occur when a company increases its output for a product such that it increases the cost per unit of the product. For example, assume that labor costs at a factory are constant as long as the factory produces between 100,000 and 500,000 units per month. If the factory produces more than 500,000 units per month, it may have to hire more workers, which would increase the cost per unit. It is easier for smaller companies to fall into diseconomies of scale because they have less control over their costs; indeed this can cause many smaller companies to be at a significant competitive disadvantage. See also: Economies of Scale.

Disgorgement Stolen money that must be repaid to victims of theft, fraud, or some other financial crime. That is, when a person or business has made profits through illegal or unethical means, it must pay disgorgement plus interest to all victims in so far as it is possible. This is done to attempt to restore the status quo before the illegal or unethical actions were committed. The perpetrator must pay disgorgement over and above any punitive damages that have been assessed.

Dishonor To refuse payment on a check, receipt, or some other document demanding payment. One usually dishonors a document if there is something irregular about it, such as a check drawn with insufficient funds. See also: Honor.

Disinflation A situation in which the inflation rate decreases, but does not reverse. For example, disinflation occurs when the inflation rate goes from 5% to 2%. Importantly, it is not deflation when the inflation rate becomes negative. Disinflation is considered a normal and healthy part of a business cycle.

Disinflation Stock Stocks that do well when inflation is decreasing. Disinflation stocks tend to be in industries that must borrow heavily. Disinflation stocks tend to perform poorly when inflation is high because high inflation leads to higher interest rates, which increases the cost of capital for the companies issuing disinflation stocks. Most utility stocks are disinflation stocks, for example.

Disintermediation The act of making a withdrawal from a bank or other financial institution in order to use the funds for investment purposes. For example, one may withdraw $10,000 from his savings account in order to buy a stock without the bank's intermediation. This has become less common with deregulation of banking because more banks can offer investment services, reducing the incentive to withdraw.

Disinvestment The sale or elimination of a department, subsidiary, or any other major investment. Disinvestment is most common when a company must raise capital quickly to finance new operations or pay a certain liability, or when it determines that the investment is unlikely to become or remain profitable in the future.

Disloyalty Fee A small fee that a bank customer pays for using an ATM belonging to another bank. In the United States, the disloyalty fee ranges from $2 to $5.

Dismissal for Cause The termination of employment because of an employee's misconduct. For example, an employee may be dismissed for sexual harassment or absenteeism. Dismissal for cause may render the former employee ineligible to collect unemployment insurance.

Dismissal of Petition A court's decision not to hear a case any further. Generally, this occurs because of some defect in the petition. For example, one party may not have standing to sue, or a prosecutor may not have met the burden of proof. In the United States, dismissal without prejudice leaves the petition open to be re-filed once the defect is rectified. However, dismissal with prejudice means the matter is closed.

Disorderly Market A situation in which trading on a security is exceptionally volatile, especially when there is no apparent reason for it. A disorderly market may arise when short sellers are attempting to cover their positions, or when there is an order imbalance, among other reasons. Exchanges sometimes stop trade in a disorderly market to encourage smooth trading as much as possible.

Disparity Index In technical analysis, an indicator that measures a security's current price to its most recent closing price and expresses the difference as a percentage. A positive disparity index measure indicates that pressure to buy the security is increasing while a negative measure shows the opposite. Extreme values in either direction may indicate that a price correction is about to occur. Technical analysts use the disparity index to measure momentum.

Dispersion In statistics, the placement of data points along a chart relative to an average or mean line. Dispersion is important to finance as the data points of say, a stock, determine the mean, which in turn helps determines the stock's trend. Dispersion is also used to determine volatility: data points all over the chart indicate that a stock has wild fluctuation in price.

Displaced Moving Average A moving average that has been moved forward or backward in time according to a certain formula. The displaced moving average allows traders to make an educated guess about continued market movements, while removing some of the noise in simple moving averages. Some believe that displaced moving averages are more accurate for this reason.

Disposable Income A person's income after he/she has paid taxes. Disposable income determines what sort of lodging one can afford, how often one can go out to eat, how much one can save, etc. A negative disposable income indicates that an individual is borrowing in order to cover his/her expenses. A country's average disposable income is an important indicator of economic health.

Disposition The sale of a security. See also: Close a position.

Dispute Resolution Any method of resolving a conflict without resorting to a lawsuit. Dispute resolution involves the disputing parties agreeing that a neutral arbiter will hear the arguments of both sides and render a binding decision. In investing, arbiters in dispute resolution may be FINRA, the New York Stock Exchange, or the SEC, depending on the type of disagreement. Dispute resolution is nearly always less expensive than a lawsuit because there are no appeals (and fewer lawyers).

Disqualifying Disposition A sale or other transaction in stock that one acquired to an employee stock option plan within two years of enrollment in the plan or one year of purchase. The profit on a disqualifying disposition is not considered capital gains and is taxed like ordinary income, which is usually at a higher rate.

Dissident Director A member of the board of directors who speaks out against the company or organization's policies and tries to change them, but lacks to votes to do so.

Distansminut A Swedish unit of nautical distance equivalent to 185.2 meters.

Distress Sale A rapid, urgent sale of assets, often at a loss. Distressed sales often occur when cash is needed to cover immediate needs or debts. They are also associated with margin calls. A common example of a distressed sale is the rapid sale of real estate when the owner can no longer make the mortgage payments; he/she must sell the property immediately to pay off the mortgage, even if it involves losing money on the property. See also: Distressed securities.

Distressed Debt A debt security in an unprofitable company that is likely to go bankrupt. This is considered to be a high-risk security with the potential for high return because financial distress often precedes corporate restructuring, which could keep the company from bankruptcy, or at least liquidation, enabling the security to be repaid in full. On the other hand, the potential for default is very high. Distressed debt usually sells for a very small percentage of its par value.

Distressed Security A security in an unprofitable company, or in a company believed to be unprofitable. This is considered to be a high-risk security with the potential for high return because financial distress often precedes corporate restructuring. This may make the company profitable very rapidly. On the other hand, the potential for default is very high.

Distribution 1. A situation in which a security's or market's trading volume is higher on a given trading day than the previous trading day without any price appreciation. This is taken as an indicator that the security or market has hit its highest price and will soon decline. 2. The payment of the assets in an IRA or other retirement account to the account holder or his/her beneficiary. Distributions usually begin after retirement, but may begin before with the payment of applicable penalties. 3. A dividend paid to a company's or mutual fund's shareholders. 4. An institution's consistent sale of a single security over a long period of time as opposed to all at once. This is done to avoid causing fluctuations in price. See also: Accumulation.

Distribution by Coupon A listing of all the fixed-income securities in a portfolio according to their coupon rates.

Distribution by Credit Quality A listing of all the securities in a portfolio according to their credit ratings.

Distribution by Issuer A listing of all the securities in a portfolio according to their issuers.

Distribution by Maturity A listing of all the securities, especially debt securities, in a portfolio according to their issuers. Distribution by maturity is a way of calculating the interest rate risk of a portfolio. The fewer long-term securities that are in a portfolio, the less likely its current market value is to change according to changes in prevailing interest rates.

Distribution Cost Advantage A comparative advantage that one company has over another because of its ability to deliver goods or services more quickly and less expensively. For example, a flower delivery service in the town where the order was placed has a distribution cost advantage over an identical service out of state, as it can deliver flowers more quickly and cheaply.

Distribution Period The time between the declaration date and the record date. The declaration date is the day on which the board of directors announces the amount of a dividend that will be distributed to common stockholders, while the record date is the day by which one much own stock in that company to be entitled to the dividend. Depending on the size of the dividend and the desirability of the stock, there may or may not be a rush to buy a stock during the distribution period.

Distribution Schedule The frequency with which a mutual fund pays dividends from its portfolio to shareholders. It also may refer to the frequency with which the fund collects fees from shareholders to defray its own costs. See also: Load.

Distribution Stock A small number of shares within a larger number of shares of a single security that are sold consistently over a long period of time as opposed to all at once. This is done to avoid causing fluctuations in price. See also: Distribution area.

Districten In Suriname, a political subdivision equivalent to a province or district.

Distritu In East Timor, a political subdivision equivalent to a municipality.

Diuturnum Illud An encyclical letter written by Pope Leo XIII in 1881 in response to increased civil unrest in Europe by anarchists and communists. It states that Christians owe obedience to the state and recommends that they work within the state for positive social change. It also criticizes social contract theory.

Diuym A Russian unit of length equivalent to one inch. It was rendered obsolete when the Soviet Union began to use the metric system in 1924.

Divergence In technical analysis, a situation in which two indicators move in opposite directions. For example, stock prices may decline while bond prices may increase. This can be either a bullish or a bearish indicator, depending on the nature of the divergence. Technical analysts use any number of related indicators to attempt to observe divergence and make investment decisions accordingly. See also: MACD.

Diversification In risk management, the act or strategy of adding more investments to one's portfolio to hedge against the investments already in it. Ideally, this reduces the risk inherent in any one investment, and increases the possibility of making a profit, or at least avoiding a loss. This may also reduce the expected return on a portfolio, but it depends on level and type of diversification. There are two main types of diversification. Horizontal diversification involves investing in similar investments. Examples include investing in several technology companies or in different types of bonds. Vertical diversification involves investing in very different securities; for example, one may choose to invest in securities traded in different countries, or in both winter clothing and swimsuit companies. Both types of diversification may be as broad or as narrow as the investor chooses. In general, broader diversification equates to less risk and less return. See also: Markowitz Portfolio Theory.

Diversified Common Stock Fund A mutual fund that invests in the common stock of a wide variety of publicly-traded companies. A diversified common stock fund often holds shares in companies with different market capitalization and in different industries. This reduces the risk to a particular industry or stock while also allowing investors to take advantage of dividends from common stock.

Diversified Company A company that operates and/or invests in several different business sectors. A diversified company exists to reduce unsystematic risk; that is, when one industry is doing poorly, a diversified company may still do well if its other industries are performing well. As a result, stock in a diversified company is generally more stable than the average stock. See also: Conglomerate merger.

Diversified Fund A fund that has invested in many different types of securities in order to hedge against the securities already in the fund. Ideally, this reduces the risk inherent in any one investment, and increases the possibility of making a profit, or at least avoiding a loss. This may also reduce the expected return on the fund, but it depends on the level and type of diversification. There are two main types of diversification that a fund may utilize. Horizontal diversification involves investing in similar investments. Examples include investing in several technology companies or in different types of bonds. Vertical diversification involves investing in very different securities; for example, one may choose to invest in securities traded in different countries, or in both winter clothing and swimsuit companies. Both types of diversification may be as broad or as narrow as the fund's manager chooses. In general, broader diversification equates to less risk and less return.

Diversity Score A measure of the diversification (by industry) of a collateralized debt obligation. Moody's was the creator and the original user of the diversity score.

Diversity Segmentation The use of a cost driver (which is a factor that directly contributes to a company's expenses) to account for changing demand.

Divestiture The removal of assets from a person or firm's balance sheet through sale, exchange, closure, bankruptcy, or some other means. Divestiture may occur when a person or company has acquired more than he/she/it can properly administer. This sort of divestiture may occur slowly; for example, a corporation may slowly sell subsidiaries to concentrate exclusively on its core competence. On the other hand, divestiture may occur because a person or company has become cash poor and needs to build liquidity very quickly.

Divided Account In underwriting, a portion of a new issue that a member of a syndicate is responsible for placing with investors. Each underwriting firm in a syndicate is responsible only for its own divided account. If a member of the syndicate fails to place its portion with investors, other underwriters are under no obligation to assist that member. This contrasts with an undivided account, in which underwriters are each assigned a portion of a new issue, but each underwriter is responsible for placing the whole issue.

Dividend A portion of a publicly-traded company or fund's earnings that is distributed to shareholders. The amount of earnings distributed as dividends is usually determined by the board of directors and divided by the number of shares, but preferred stock often has guaranteed dividends. Dividends exist in order to encourage investment in the company and to allow shareholders (who are really co-owners) to participate in the profits. A rapidly expanding company often pays little or nothing in dividends, as most of its earnings are reinvested in the company. On the other hand, a well-established company with solid profits likely pays relatively high dividends.

Dividend Adjustment A dividend given to a convertible preferred stock holder when he/she exercises the conversion option and exchanges the preferred shares for common shares. A dividend adjustment is designed to compensate a preferred stockholder for any dividends he/she otherwise would have received as a common stockholder. It is a fairly unusual practice.

Dividend Capture The practice of buying a stock before the ex-dividend date and selling immediately thereafter. The ex-dividend date is the date after which a dividend belongs by right to the seller, rather than the buyer, of a stock. Thus, dividend capture allows the investor to keep the dividend after selling the stock. An investor practicing dividend capture is only interested in a stock for the dividend it produces and therefore sells the stock as soon as he/she can retain the dividend.

Dividend Clawback An agreement whereby stockholders use previous dividends to finance the future operations of the company. That is, the stockholders agree to use dividends to buy more stock in case the company becomes cash poor and needs liquidity for its operations.

Dividend Clientele Shareholders who pressure a publicly-traded company to follow a certain dividend policy, usually in order to minimize their own tax liability. Often, the dividend clientele asks the company to change the schedule of dividend payments to that which is most favorable to them. However, these policies are not always in the best long-term interests of the company.

Dividend Coverage The amount by which a company's earnings exceed its dividends. The higher a company's earnings are relative to its dividends, the better its dividend coverage and the more flexibility the company has. A company with good dividend coverage has the option to raise the dividend if it wishes and likewise may still pay the same dividend with little difficulty if earnings decline. Maintaining adequate dividend coverage is especially important if the company has issued a lot of preferred stock, which carries guaranteed dividends.

Dividend Disbursing Agent A financial institution that, for a fee, distributes dividends to shareholders in a publicly-traded company, investment company, or a similar company. A dividend disbursing agent is particularly important because so many investment companies have a large number of investors who each have a small amount of equity. See also: Transfer Agent.

Dividend Discount Model An estimate of what the price per share of a stock or other security should be, based on the present value of future dividends. This estimate allows investors to determine whether the stock is undervalued or overvalued. If the model says the stock should cost more than it does, investors often buy it. Likewise, if the real cost is higher than the estimate, the investor is likely to sell or refrain from buying.

Dividend Discount Return The projected return on a stock that is calculated by estimating the present value of future dividends. One compares the dividend discount return to the current stock price, and if the former is higher, this indicates that the stock is undervalued. There are various ways to calculate the dividend discount return, but it is important to note that they all assume that the stock will in fact pay dividends, which may not always be the case.

Dividend Enhanced Convertible Stock Preferred stock entitling the holder to guaranteed dividends and to which are attached a put option and a call option. That is, if the stock declines in price the holder of DECS may sell it for the stated strike price. Likewise if the stock increases in price, he holder may exercise the call and buy more stock for a discount. DECS also have a convertible option allowing the holder to exchange the DECS for common stock.

Dividend Equivalent Right In some employee stock options, the right of a shareholder to take more shares in the company for which he/she works in lieu of dividends on the shares he/she already holds.

Dividend Exclusion The percentage of received dividends that a corporation may exclude from its taxable income. That is, a company may deduct a certain amount of dividends received from its investments. When a corporation owns less than one-fifth of another company's shares outstanding, it may deduct 70% of dividends. When it owns less than 80% of the company, it may deduct 75%. When it owns more than 80% of the other company, it may deduct all dividends. Dividend exclusion helps avoid double taxation, but is not available to any individual investor.

Dividend Imputation In Australia, a statement attached to a dividend indicating that the company issuing the dividend has already paid taxes on its profits. This exempts the dividend receiver from taxation on the dividend. Dividend imputations exist to avoid double taxation, which occurs when a company pays corporate tax on its profits and then a shareholder pays income or capital gains taxes on a dividend coming out of those same profits.

Dividend Income Dividends paid to shareholders in a publicly-traded company or mutual fund. Various factors, notably how long one has held the shares and whether one reinvests the dividend, determine whether dividend income is taxed as ordinary income or capital gains, or not taxed until one sells the shares. Dividend income is also called dividend distribution. See also: Dividend reinvestment plan.

Dividend Limitation A provision in some bond indentures placing a maximum amount on what a company can pay out in dividends. A dividend limitation reduces the risk that the issuer will default on a bond because it foolishly decides to pay out too much in dividends to common shareholders. This provision is designed to protect bondholders but has the possibility to scare away potential stockholders.

Dividend Order A written instruction from a bondholder or shareholder to a corporation to forward interest payments and/or dividends to a person or institution other than the holder, usually a broker or bank.

Dividend Payable A dividend that a company has declared but not yet paid. See also: Ex-Dividend, Dividend Payment Date.

Dividend Paying Agent A person or, more commonly, a corporation that a publicly-traded company hires to pay dividends to shareholders. The dividend paying agent receives a fee for this service. See also: Transfer agent.

Dividend Payment Date The dates on which stockholders are sent dividend payments. That is, the dividend payment dates are the dates where stockholders receive dividends that they are either guaranteed (for preferred stock) or that was previously declared by the company (for common stock). Dividend payment dates are fixed for preferred stock because the dividends are contractually guaranteed; however, they may change for common stock, particularly when the company changes its plowback rate. See also: Interest Dates.

Dividend Payout Ratio In fundamental analysis, the opposite of the plowback ratio. That is, the dividend payout ratio is a company's dividends paid to shareholders expressed as a percentage of total earnings. A higher ratio indicates that a company pays more in dividends and thus reinvests less of its earnings into the company. Whether or not this is desirable depends on the rate of growth; investors tend to prefer a higher payout ratio in a slow-growing company and a lower one in a fast-growing company.

Dividend per Share The portion of a publicly-traded company's earnings distributed to shareholders divided by the total number of shares outstanding. The dividends per share formula determines how much each investor receives each time a dividend payment is made. For example, if a company declares a $0.35 dividend per share and one owns 1,000 shares, one receives $350 in dividends.

Dividend Period A period of time during which a policyholder of a deferred dividend policy may not receive any dividends that the policy earns. If a policyholder dies during the dividend period, any dividends he/she would have earned are deposited in a fund that pays the dividends of policyholders who survive the period.

Dividend Policy The amount of a dividend that a publicly-traded company decides to pay out to shareholders. The dividend policy may change from time to time. Factors affecting a dividend policy include the company's earnings for the relevant period and its expected performance in the near future. Many companies, especially startups, have a rather stingy dividend policy because they plow back much of their earnings into further development. Established companies, such as blue chips, tend to have relatively liberal dividend policies. However, some research, notably Miller and Modigliani's irrelevance proposition, suggests that a company's dividend policy does not impact its performance in any way. See also: Dividend clientele, Signaling approach (on dividend policy).

Dividend Record A publication by S&P showing the dividend policies and payment histories of various publicly-traded companies.

Dividend Reinvestment Plan A practice or agreement in which dividends on a security are used to buy more of the same security rather than be disbursed to the investor in cash. A dividend reinvestment plan is relatively common in mutual funds; investors agree to use dividends and other capital gains to reinvest in more shares of the mutual fund. While this involves assuming more risk in the mutual fund, it carries the possibility of higher returns.

Dividend Requirement The earnings of a publicly-traded company that the company has contractually obliged itself to pay out as dividends for preferred stockholders. Most of the time, when a company issues preferred stock, it guarantees buyers a certain dividend. This can be beneficial as it may attract buyers, but at the same time the dividend requirement can put a financial strain on the company. See also: Payout Rate, Plowback Rate.

Dividend Right The right of a shareholder to receive the same dividend that other shareholders of the same class receive. That is, if one holds common stock with no special features and the company declares that each shareholder is entitled to a 9 cents per share dividend, the company cannot arbitrarily decide to pay one shareholder any more or less than 9 cents per share.

Dividend Rollover Plan An investment strategy in which one buys a stock immediately before the ex-dividend date and sells it immediately after. This allows the investor to keep the dividend without accepting (much) of the risk associated with owning the stock. The main risk to a dividend rollover plan is the possibility that the sale of the stock will result in a loss exceeding the dividend.

Dividend Tax Credit In Canada, a tax credit that reduces one's tax liability if one receives dividends from a company. The credit is 13.33% of the value of a dividend for Canadian federal taxes, with additional credits at the provincial levels. The dividend tax credit treats a dividend as 125% of its actual value. For example, suppose one receives $1000 in dividends and would otherwise owe 22% (or $220) in taxes. The federal dividend tax credit would take 125% of the $1000 (or $1250) and reduces one's tax liability of 13.33% of that amount. 13.33% of $1250 is $166.63, which means that one would only owe $56.37 ($250 - $166.63) in taxes on the dividend at the federal level. One may owe less if the province applies its own dividend tax credit. This credit exists in order to avoid double taxation of dividends.

Dividend Test A provision in some lending agreements where the borrower is a company that forbids or restricts the borrower's ability to make dividends payments to shareholders. That is, the dividend test may place a limit on the company's earnings that may be distributed as dividends. Obviously, the dividend test works to the detriment of shareholders, but it improves the lender's likelihood of being repaid because it increases the resources the borrower had to service debt.

Dividend Trade Roll/Play An investment practice in which an investor buys and sells shares near the ex-dividend date, the date after which the next dividend belongs to the seller of the share, rather than the buyer. An advantage of dividend trade roll/play is the fact that dividends are 80% tax exempt with the remaining 20% offset by capital losses. The practice is only profitable if the investor is entitled to the normal 80% exemption on dividends.

Dividend Yield The dividend per share that a company pays divided by the share price. This is reported on the financial statements of a publicly-traded company. It is a measure of the return an investor makes for every dollar invested in the company. If there are no capital gains, the dividend yield is the entire return on the stock. It is also called the price-dividend ratio.

Dividends in Arrears Dividends on preferred stock that are past due. Because preferred stock has guaranteed dividends, a company is legally required to pay the dividends before it makes any dividend payments at all on common stock. Dividends in arrears go to the current owners of preferred stock when they are paid; the person who owned it when the dividends originally should have been paid receives nothing. They are also called accumulated dividends.

Dividends Payable The amount that a publicly-traded company is legally obligated to pay for a given period. Some dividends payable, notably for preferred stock, are guaranteed and must always be paid, while others are not and may change from time to time depending upon the company's earnings or cash flow.

Dividends per Share The total amount a publicly-traded company pays in ordinary dividends over a given period of time divided by the average number of shares outstanding. Dividends per share gives a potential investor an idea of how much he/she will receive in dividends if he/she buys a given stock. Typically, blue chip or other well-established companies pay high dividends per share, while start-ups pay small dividends per share.

Dividends-Received Deduction A reduction in the taxable income of a company when it receives dividends from stock it owns in another company. A company is eligible for a 70% dividends-received deduction if it owns less than 20% of the second company, 80% if it owns between 20% and 80% of the company, and 100% if it owns more than that. A dividends-received deduction exists in order to reduce the effects of triple taxation on publicly-traded companies; that is, the company must pay corporate taxes and its shareholders must pay capital gains taxes. The dividends-received deduction allows companies to mostly avoid a third tax on the same earnings.

Divini Redemptoris An encyclical letter written by Pope Pius XI in 1937. The letter is primarily a condemnation of communism, which Pius XI believed to be antithetical to the common good. It forms part of modern Catholic social justice theory.

Divisional Secretariat In Sri Lanka, a political subdivision roughly equivalent to a municipality.

Divisor In division, the number by which another number if divided. For example, in the equation 8 / 4 = 2, the divisor is 4. This is used in indexes to account for stock splits and dividends. See also: Dow divisor.

Diwan al-Mal In the early Middle Ages, the name of provincial tax and revenue agencies of the Abbasid Empire. They were also called mustawfii.

Diworsification Diversification of a portfolio without regard, or with incorrect regard, for the necessary mathematical formulation such that it makes the portfolio riskier without any chance of a higher return.. Diworsification especially refers to investing in several mutual funds with the same or similar investment strategies. This exposes the investor to the unsystemic risks associated with the individual funds without hedging the systemic risk associated with all of them. See also: Naive diversification, Markowitz portfolio theory.

DJ 1. ISO 3166-1 alpha-2 code for the Republic of Djibouti. This is the code used in international transactions to and from Djiboutian bank accounts. **2.** ISO 3166-2 geocode for Djibouti. This is used as an international standard for shipping to Djibouti. Each major Djiboutian subdivision has its own code with the prefix "DJ." For example, the code for the Region of Dikhil is ISO 3166-2:DJ-DI.

Dja An ancient Egyptian unit of volume approximately equivalent to 300 milliliters.

Djeser An ancient Egyptian unit of length approximately equivalent to 30 centimeters.

DJF ISO 4217 for the Djiboutian franc. It was introduced in 1908 when Djibouti was a French colony, and pegged to the French franc. It became an independence currency in 1949 and was pegged to the U.S. dollar under the Bretton Woods System). Even after the Bretton Woods System collapsed, the franc has maintained the peg to the dollar.

DJI GOST 7.67 Latin three-letter geocode for Djibouti. The code is used for transactions to and from Djiboutian bank accounts and for international shipping to Djibouti. As with all GOST 7.67 codes, it is used primarily in Cyrillic alphabets.

Djiboutian Franc The currency of Djibouti. It was introduced in 1908 when Djibouti was a French colony, and pegged to the French franc. It became an independent currency in 1949 and was pegged to the U.S. dollar under the Bretton Woods System. Even after the Bretton Woods System collapsed, the franc has maintained the peg to the dollar.

DK 1. ISO 3166-1 alpha-2 code for Denmark. This is the code used in international transactions to and from Danish bank accounts. **2.** ISO 3166-2 geocode for Denmark. This is used as an international standard for shipping to Denmark. Each Danish region has its own code with the prefix "DK." For example, the code for the Region of Sjaelland and is ISO 3166-2:DK-85. **3.** Don't know. A trade that cannot be settled by a clearing house because the counterparties have contradictory or otherwise inconsistent information on the trade. The clearing house may become aware of the discrepancy by reviewing the comps the brokers give one another, or by some other method. In this trade, it is said that one or both of the counterparties "does not know the trade."

DKK ISO 4217 code for the Danish krone. It was introduced in 1873, replacing the Danish rigsdaler. It was part of the Scandanavian Monetary Union until the beginning of the First World War. During this time, the krone was pegged to gold. It was variously pegged to the German Reichsmark and the British pound in the middle 20th century. Denmark joined the Bretton Woods Agreement, which tied the krone to the U.S. dollar (and, by extension, to gold). It is currently pegged to the ERM II, which ties the krone to the euro, but allows it to remain somewhat independent.

DM 1. ISO 3166-1 alpha-2 code for the Commonwealth of Dominica. This is the code used in international transactions to and from Dominican bank accounts. **2.** ISO 3166-2 geocode for Dominica. This is used as an international standard for shipping to Dominica. Each parish has its own code with the prefix "DM." For example, the code for the Parish of St. Joseph is ISO 3166-2:DM-06.

DMA GOST 7.67 Latin three-letter geocode for Dominica. The code is used for transactions to and from Dominican bank accounts and for international shipping to Dominica. As with all GOST 7.67 codes, it is used primarily in Cyrillic alphabets.

DNK GOST 7.67 Latin three-letter geocode for Denmark. The code is used for transactions to and from Danish bank accounts and for international shipping to Denmark. As with all GOST 7.67 codes, it is used primarily in Cyrillic alphabets.

Do 1. ISO 3166-1 alpha-2 code for the Dominican Republic. This is the code used in international transactions to and from DR bank accounts. **2.** ISO 3166-2 geocode for the Dominican Republic. This is used as an international standard for shipping to the DR. Each DR province has its own code with the prefix "DO." For example, the code for the Province of Hato Mayor is ISO 3166-2:DO-30.

Do Not Increase In a good til canceled order, an instruction to a broker not to increase the number of shares ordered in the event of a stock split. A stock split increases the number of shares outstanding by some stated ratio, and many brokers increase the number of shares asked or bid to compensate for this. A DNI instructs the broker not to do so.

Do Not Reduce Order In a limit order following the ex-dividend date, an instruction not to reduce the limit price by the amount of the dividend. Most of the time, following the ex-dividend date, the price of the limit order is reduced because the coming dividend will belong to the current owner, rather than the buyer. One issues a do not reduce order if one believes that demand for the stock justifies the higher price.

Do the Needful In India, a slang term for bribery.

Dobra The currency of Sao Tome and Principe. It was introduced in 1977, replacing the Sao Tome and Principe escudo. In the mid-2000s, the dobra's inflation rate accelerated significantly. In 2009, it was pegged to the euro.

Docra An obsolete Indian unit of weight approximately equivalent to 38.9 grams.

Doctrine of Sovereign Immunity A legal principle that a nation may not be tried in another nation's courts without its own consent. This is important when a foreign corporation has a legal claim against another nation's government. It must go to that nation's courts in order to seek redress.

Documentary Collections International transactions in which banks act on behalf of the importer and exporter to collect payment for a good. The exporter presents the appropriate documents to a bank in his/her country, which forwards them to a bank in the importer's country. This bank presents the documents to the importer and accepts payment, which it then forwards back to the first bank. The banks have no responsibility in a documentary collection except to fulfill instructions of the importer and exporter; that is, they make no guarantees of payment. See also: Documents against payment, Documents against acceptance.

Documents Against Payment A terms of payment arrangement in which an exporter entrusts the ownership documents of an assetto his/her bank, which then presents them to an importer only after the bank has received payment for the asset. Essentially, the bank holds hostage the ownership documents, which the importer needs to take possession of the merchandise, until the bank, and, by extension, the exporter, are paid. A risk for the exporter is the possibility that the importer will refuse to pay, and, while he/she will not be able to take possession of the merchandise, the exporter has little legal recourse. The terms of this agreement are set between the importer and exporter at the time of the sale.

Dodrans 1. An ancient Roman unit of area approximately equivalent to 1,893 square meters. **2.** An ancient Roman unit of weight approximately equivalent to 246.7 grams.

Doesn't Justify Investing Anything A derogatory nickname for the DJIA, or the Dow Jones Industrial Average. The name is used sarcastically when the DJIA is bearish. Another nickname with the same connotation is the Dow Jones Insufferable.

Dog In the BCG growth share matrix, the quadrant representing companies, especially subsidies, that require minimal cash injections but have low market shares, and therefore usually operate with little or no profit. These companies usually exist in mature industries with well established but not very profitable markets, products, or brands. Some analysts recommend selling dogs, as they have little potential for growth; however, because they require little capital to operate, they may be useful and may perhaps produce an earnings surprise. See also: Marketing, Portfolio analysis.

Dog Eat Dog Informal; describing brutal competition. For example, dog eat dog competition occurs when two companies repeatedly attempt to undercut each other's prices. Dog eat dog competition is designed to increase the market share of one company at the expense of all others', even if it reduces the company's profit margin in the short and medium term. Dog eat dog competition can make it difficult for a start-up to break in to the same industry. See also: Duopoly.

Dog in this Fight Informal for market share or other interest in a market or event. For example, a software company has to keep abreast of developments in technology as its competitors may use them to their own advantage. Thus, the software company is said to a dog in the fight.

Dogs of the Dow 1. The 10 stocks (of 30) on the Dow Jones Industrial Average with the lowest prices and consequently the highest yields. **2.** An investment strategy in which one buys the dogs of the Dow on the first of the calendar year and sell them exactly one year later. Theoretically, the extra risk involved in this strategy gives an investor a higher return than buying all 30 stocks on the DJIA.

Doing the Reverse Desk Informal; the act of a hedge fund misleading other hedge funds that seek to imitate its strategy and/or tactics. Doing the reverse desk involves making small transactions with a great deal of publicity while quietly making large transactions that fit with the hedge fund's true investment goals. If hedge funds are imitating each other, this means that they are making the same or similar transactions, which increases prices and makes it more expensive for a hedge fund to do its business. Doing the reverse desk is intended to reduce this risk. It is comparatively easy for a hedge fund to do the reverse desk because hedge funds are not required to be as transparent as other investment vehicles.

Doji In candlestick charting, a candlestick indicating that the open price and close price for a security are almost equal. It is formed by candlestick that is very short and only slightly thicker than a line. As a result, dojis often look like plus signs.

Dokdo A subdivision of the kori, the currency of Kutch while it was part of British India. A dokdo was worth 1/24 of one kori. Its plural was dokda.

Dolia A Russian unit of weight approximately equivalent to 44.4 milligrams. It was rendered obsolete when the Soviet Union began to use the metric system in 1924.

Dolichos An ancient Greek unit of length approximately equivalent to 2,219 meters.

Dollar Accountability Group A person or small group of persons who are responsible for a certain amount of money. The term is most common in the context of small Christian churches and ministries. For example, a church's food pantry may have an administrative team responsible for managing all expenses associated with the pantry. This team is called the dollar accountability group. One may also refer to it as a department accountability group.

Dollar Bears Traders who buy foreign currencies with U.S. dollars because they believe that the dollar is falling or will soon fall. Any number of indicators may influence this decision for dollar bears.

Dollar Bond 1. A bond issued in U.S. dollars, especially one issued by a non-American government or company. **2.** A bond quoted by price rather than yield. Generally speaking, municipal revenue bonds are the only bonds that use a dollar bond convention.

Dollar Overhang The amount by which U.S. dollars outside the United States (called eurodollars) exceed American gold reserves. While the dollar is no longer pegged to gold, under the Bretton Woods System, dollar overhang could make it more difficult to convert dollars to gold.

Dollar Price The price of a bond, expressed as a percentage of the face value. For example, if a bond has a face value of $1,000 (which most bonds do) and it is trading at $990, one quotes the price as 99% in dollar terms. The dollar price is one of two ways bonds are quoted on different exchanges. The other way is a percentage of the bond's yield.

Dollar Price of a Bond The price of a bond, expressed as a percentage of the face value. For example, if a bond has a face value of $1000 (which most bonds do), and it is trading at $990, the price is quoted as 99% in dollar terms. The dollar price is one of two ways bonds are quoted on different exchanges. The other way is a percentage of the bond's yield.

Dollar Return The dollar amount of the rate of return over a given period of time. For example, suppose one invests $100,000 and these investments return 6% in its first year. The dollar return on this portfolio for this year is $6,000 (6% of $100,000 over a year).

Dollar Safety Margin In a contingent immunization strategy, the dollar amount of the return at which the contingent immunization takes place. In a contingent immunization strategy, an asset manager or investor makes investments at varying risks until something goes wrong. When an investment suffers a loss and brings the portfolio down to some pre-defined return, the asset manager or investor begins making low- or no-risk investments that guarantee that same pre-defined return. The dollar amount of that return is the dollar safety margin.

Dollar-Cost Averaging An investment strategy in which one makes investments in the same dollar amount at regular times. For example, one may buy $1,000 in Stock A every month, regardless of Stock A's current price. Because this means one buys fewer shares when the price is high and more when the price is low, dollar-cost averaging aims to reduce the average cost of the shares one buys. This increases the profit per share when one sells the stock. Dollar cost averaging is most common with shares of a mutual fund or a retirement plan. It is also called a constant dollar plan.

DOM GOST 7.67 Latin three-letter geocode for the Dominican Republic. The code is used for transactions to and from DR bank accounts and for international shipping to the DR. As with all GOST 7.67 codes, it is used primarily in Cyrillic alphabets.

DOMA A category of customer loyalty in which customers do not switch to a competitor unless they, as the abbreviation states, die or move away.

Dome In technical analysis, a price trend indicated on a chart by a gradual rise to a high, followed by a gradual decline. Traders seek to sell at the top point of the dome. Generally speaking, the sell signal is reached when trading is characterized by low volume and flat prices. This is seen as a shift from bull market to a bear market, albeit a slow one. It is also called an inverted saucer. See also: Saucer.

Domestic Bonds Bonds issued in the country and currency in which they are traded. Unlike international bonds, domestic bonds are not subject to currency risk. They usually carry less risk, as the regulatory and taxation requirements are usually known to investors in domestic bonds, or at least to their brokers and accountants.

Domestic Corporation A corporation that operates in the country in which it was organized and is based. Like all corporations, it must abide by domestic regulations and business practices. Many corporations operate in multiple countries, and are considered domestic corporations only in the home country. See also: Foreign corporation, International corporation.

Domestic Life Work or recreation done with or for one's family, however defined. Family has been defined differently at different points in history, as have how social relations within families ought to work. However, many political and economic theories hold that family is the basic building block upon which society is founded and therefore that domestic life is something that ought to be protected by the state. For example, Roman Catholic teaching on social justice assumes that domestic life is a foundational right. Likewise, the right to start and raise a family is guaranteed by the Universal Declaration of Human Rights.

Domestic Market The supply and demand for a good, service, or security in a particular country. Many companies cater to the domestic market because they know applicable laws and regulations the best. There also may be a unique demand for a certain product in the domestic market. For example, an American flag supplier will likely sell more flags in the United States than in Canada. The size of the domestic market is calculated in the gross domestic product.

Domicile A place where one maintains one's primary residence for tax purposes. One proves a domicile by registering to vote, maintaining a driver's license, and/or actually living in the place. It is important to note that one usually but does not always live in the domicile. Indeed, domiciles are somewhat controversial, especially in Britain. This is because many foreign workers claim other places as their domicile in order to avoid taxes on worldwide income. For example, a resident of Britain with a house in Oklahoma may register to vote in Oklahoma and claim this as their domicile. Thus, the resident only pays taxes on income earned in the United Kingdom. Lawmakers have made various suggestions on how to close to loophole but one may still take advantage of it.

Domini Social Index 400 An index tracking 400 publicly-traded companies in the United States known for socially responsible investing. The index excludes companies that produce alcohol, tobacco, weapons, nuclear power, and other controversial products. The Domini 400 includes around 250 companies on the S&P 500 and other companies known for sustainable business practices. It was launched in 1990 and is weighted for market capitalization. See also: Ethical investing, Green fund, Islamic finance.

Dominican Peso The currency of the Dominican Republic. It was issued in 1937. It has periodically been subject to high inflation. The U.S. dollar is also accepted in the Dominican Republic.

Donald J. Johnston A Canadian lawyer and politician. He served in various Liberal Party capacities in the 1980s and 1990s and became Secretary-General of the OECD in 1996. During his tenure, which lasted until 2006, the OECD promoted social responsibility for multinational corporations. He was born in 1936.

Donamail A master database of names and addresses maintained by a non-profit organization. The donamail database is used to solicit donations, to distribute news, and for all other direct mail purposes.

Donchian Channels In technical analysis, a moving average stating the highest high and the lowest low for a security over the desired time period. The highest high and the lowest low are each replaced as the previous ones move out of the current time period. According to this device, a buy signal occurs if the price of a security closes above the current highest high and a sell signal occurs if it closes below the lowest low.

Dong In South Korea, a political subdivision for a neighborhood within a city.

Donor A person or institution who gives assets to another person or institution, either directly or through a trust. Under most circumstances, donors can deduct the value (or depreciated value) of the assets given from their taxable income. While many donors give out of the goodness of their hearts, many do so in order to avoid taxes, especially when donating through a trust.

Donor Advised Fund A way to structure a charity in which a third party manages the funds donated and gives them to the organization at the request of the donor. That is, a philanthropist (or a family or a foundation) may set up a donor advised fund and direct money to any of a number of organizations. A donor advised fund is a relatively inexpensive way to set up charitable donations while allowing the maximum amount of flexibility for the donor.

Don't Fight the Tape A maxim stating that one should not trade against the general trend. Essentially, the phrase advises investors to follow the crowd; that is, one should only buy when prices are rising (and when everyone else is buying) and sell when prices are falling (and everyone else is selling). See also: Behavioral economics.

Don't Know Describing a trade that cannot be settled by a clearing house because the counterparties have contradictory or otherwise inconsistent information on the trade. The clearing house may become aware of the discrepancy by reviewing the comps the brokers gave one another, or by some other method. In this trade, it is said that one or both of the counterparties "does not know the trade."

Doomsday Call A provision in a bond or other fixed income security allowing the issuer to redeem the security before maturity. When a doomsday call is exercised, bondholders are paid a fixed amount, either the par value or a certain percentage depending on the nature of the provision. Bond issuers include doomsday calls in some agreements to hedge against interest rate risk. That is, if interest rates lower significantly, they can exercise the doomsday call and issue a new bond at a lower interest rate. Informally, they are known as Canada calls, as they are relatively common on Canadian corporate bonds. See also: Callable bond.

DOP ISO 4217 code for the Dominican peso. It was issued in 1937. It has periodically been subject to high inflation. The U.S. dollar is also accepted in the Dominican Republic.

Dorn An obsolete Irish unit of length approximately equivalent to either 10.4 or 12.5 centimeters.

Dosh A chiefly British slang term for money or cash.

Dot-Com A business, especially a publicly-traded company, that conducts most or all of its business over the Internet. Dot-coms may conduct business in one or more of the following areas: Content, Commerce, and Connection. Content companies provide information, either for free or for a charge, and earn most of their operating income from advertising. Commerce companies sell new and/or used goods directly over the Internet. Connection companies provide Internet services directly to customers. Dot-coms were hugely popular investments in the 1990s, with IPOs of hundreds of dollars per share, even if a company had never produced a profit and, in some cases, had never earned any revenue. This came from the theory that Internet companies needed to expand their customer bases as much as possible and thus corner the largest possible market share, even if this meant massive losses. While this worked for some dot-coms, notably Google, which did not produce a profit for its first several years of operation, the theory was unsustainable because, in a given industry, only one or two companies could corner large market shares, meaning most dot-coms were doomed to failure. This dot-com bubble burst in 2000.

Double The purchase of a call and a put on the same underlying asset with the same strike price and the same expiration date. A double enables one to profit from whatever price movement the underlying takes. That is, if the price goes up, the holder exercises the call, and if it goes down, he/she exercises the put. If one of the options is in the money, the other must be out of the money.

Double Barrier Option An option contract that may only be exercised if the price for the underlying asset remains within or breaks into a certain range. For example, a double barrier option may specify that the price of the underlying asset must remain between $10 and $15 per share in order for the option to be exercised. This contrasts with a regular barrier option, which specifies only one price. See also: Knock-In, Knock-Out.

Double Bottom In technical analysis, a situation in which the price of a security hits a low, rises 10-20%, and then hits roughly the same low before rising again. A double bottom in a relatively short period of time indicates that the low is a price support for the security. A situation where trading volume rises as the security increases from the second bottom is thought to be a bullish indicator. See also: W-shaped recovery.

Double Bottom Base In technical analysis, a sharp fall in the price of security, followed by a sharp rise, followed by another sharp fall, followed by another sharp rise. While the fall in price indeed can be deep, it may be a bullish sign as the price tends to rise significantly after the second drop. Some analysts recommend buying when the price during the second rise matches the peak during the first rise. See also: W-shaped recovery.

Double Die In numismatics, a situation in which the engraving on a coin appears to have been stamped twice. This may affect the value of the coin for collectors.

Double Dime A coin minted in the United States in the 1800s worth 1/20 of one dollar, or 20 cents. The double dime circulated but proved unpopular and was eventually discontinued.

Double Dip 1. See: Double dipping. **2.** See: Double dip recession.

Double Dip Recession A long-term macroeconomic trend characterized by a recession, a recovery, then another recession. For example, the United States economy entered a recession in 1929, which continued until 1933. Recovery continued until 1937, at which point a second recession began. Double-dip recessions often have weak recoveries in between the recessions (though the example above included some years of very strong growth); analysts therefore tend to worry about a double-dip recession when a recovery is weak.

Double Dipping The practice of receiving two incomes from the same source. It especially, but not exclusively, refers to a broker placing commission-based securities into a fee-based account. This means that the broker receives both commissions and fees from transactions on that account. While this is not illegal in itself, double dipping must conform to the prudent person rule.

Double Eagle A gold coin minted in the United States between 1849 and 1933. It was worth $20.

Double Florin A former coin in the United Kingdom equal in value to four shillings, or 1/5 of one British pound. Double florins were minted briefly in the late 1800s as part of a failed attempt to decimalize the pound (which did not occur until 1971).

Double Gearing The act or practice of two or more companies pooling their risk in which each places capital in the other company. In one of the most common examples of double gearing, an insurance company buys shares in a bank, and, in exchange, the bank extends credit to the insurance company.

Double Heqat An ancient Egyptian unit of volume approximately equivalent to 9.6 liters.

Double Nugget A British slang term for a two-pound coin.

Double Option A call and a put rolled into a single option contract. A double option gives the holder the right (but not the obligation) either to buy or to sell the underlying asset at the strike price. That is, there are three choices for a double option: buy, sell, or do nothing and allow the option to expire. Double options are traded in Europe.

Double Sawbuck In the United States, a slang term for $20. It is rarely used.

Double Taxation A situation in which the same earnings are taxed twice. One of the most common examples of double taxation occurs when a publicly-traded company pays corporate taxes on its earnings. It then passes on some of those earnings to shareholders as dividends, on which they must pay individual income tax or capital gains tax. Various means exist to reduce double taxation. See also: Tax avoidance.

Double Time Payment of twice one's ordinary hourly wage. For example, a company may pay its waged employees double time if they have to work on Christmas or New Year's day. See also: Time and a half.

Double Top A situation in which a security's price peaks, drops back down, then peaks again at the same price as before. For example, a stock may rise to $30 per share, drop to $27, then rise back to $30. A double top is useful in identifying a resistance level, which is a price above which a security has difficulty rising. This, in turn, can be helpful in finding buy signals and sell signals.

Double Up To buy more of a security in which one already has a long position after the price declines. For example, one may buy 500 shares in Company A at $50 per share, and then 500 more when the price declines to $35 per share. One doubles up on a security when one is exceedingly confident in its long term prospects. Doubling up carries relatively high risks.

Double-Declining-Balance Depreciation Method A way of calculating the depreciation of an asset that assumes the asset loses value at double the rate of the straight-line method. One calculates the DDB by depreciating double the straight-line value for the first year, and then depreciating the same percentage for each remaining year of the asset's usable life. DDB is a form of accelerated depreciation.

Double-Dip Lease A cross-border lease that, due to tax regulations in two different countries, allow both parties to be considered the owner for tax purposes. In most European countries, the holder of a legal title is considered the owner of an asset for tax purposes, while in the United States, legal title is only one of several factors considered. One example of a double-dip lease is the sale of an asset to a foreign agent, who then leases it back to the original owner for mutual tax advantage. This was a common tax avoidance scheme until the JOBS ACT in the United States made most double-dip leases unprofitable in 2004. See also: Lease buyback, sukuk al-ijara.

Double-Entry Bookkeeping A system of accounting where every transaction is recorded as a debit to one account and a credit to another. That is, one who uses a double-entry bookkeeping system records each transaction twice, such that each credit (representing revenue) is recorded as a credit to one's capital account and as a debit on one's bank account. For example, if a company sells a product for $100, it adds $100 to its capital account and subtracts $100 to its bank account. One way of conceptualizing the bank account is from the bank's perspective: the debits are debits because any asset in a bank account represents a liability for the bank; this is why they are subtracted instead of added. However, the data are recorded twice to prevent errors in bookkeeping: the total debits and credits recorded should add to zero.

Doublespeak A political term referring to the practice of issuing contradictory statements. For example, doublespeak may involve a government publicly blaming the previous administration when things go poorly and taking credit when things go well. The term is strongly associated with government propaganda. See also: Doublethink.

Double-Tax Agreement An agreement between the governments of two countries stating that the taxes one pays on dividends in one country may be deducted from one's income from foreign dividends in the other country. This is especially important for multinational corporations and individuals who have overseas interests when one or both countries tax worldwide income. See also: Foreign Tax Credit, Double Taxation.

Doublethink A political term referring to the act of willingly believing two contradictory statements. For example, doublethink may involve trusting the government when one's preferred party is in power and never trusting it when the preferred party is not in power. The term is strongly associated with government propaganda. See also: Doublespeak.

Doubling Option A provision in some bond indentures allowing the issuer to repurchase up to twice the number of bonds specified in the indenture's sinking fund provision. That is, the doubling option allows the issuer to redeem a large number of bonds prematurely. The redemption occurs at face value, or close to it. The issuer usually exercises the doubling option when interest rates are low and it can re-issue the same bonds at less expense to itself. The doubling option reduces the return for investors.

Douglas T. Breeden An American economist. Breeden developed a version the capital asset pricing model by arguing that the appropriate price for an asset relative to its risk depends on overall consumption in the economy, and not simply its risk relative to the risk of the market as a whole. Breeden called this concept the consumption beta.

Dovish Describing a statement from the Federal Reserve indicating that it may lower interest rates. The statement is called dovish because it indicates that the Fed does not believe that the inflation rate is high enough to warrant concern. See also: Hawkish.

Dow Divisor A mathematical tool the Dow Jones Industrial Average uses to account for stock splits. Stock splits change the share price of a company without changing its underlying value, because it simply issues more shares. The DJIA, as a price-weighted index, calculates the average by adding the share prices together and dividing by the number of stocks that it indexes. If it did not have a tool like the Dow divisor, the average would become distorted every time a stock split occurs.

Dow Jones & Company, Inc. A financial publishing company based in New York. It publishes a large number of products, both in print and online. It is particularly well known for publishing The Wall Street Journal and Barron's

Magazine. Additionally, it publishes thousands of indices on securities; the three best known are the Dow Jones Industrial Average, the Dow Jones Utility Average, and the Down Jones Transportation Average. It was established in 1882 and is a subsidiary of News Corporation.

Dow Jones AIG Commodity Index A futures commodity index listing 19 different commodities in the United States. It is designed to be a diversified and liquid index tracking the performance of physical commodities in the United States. It weights the commodities listed according to liquidity and dollar-adjusted production data. However, unlike other commodity indices, the DJ-AIGCI sets limits on its weighting so as to maintain its own diversification. It is a rolling index, which means that futures near their delivery dates must be sold so as to avoid delivery of the underlying.

Dow Jones Averages Measures of changes in the market value of blue chip stocks traded on the New York Stock Exchange (and occasionally NASDAQ), weighted by price. Price-weighting means that stocks with higher prices per share affect the averages more. There are four Dow Jones Averages: the Dow Jones Industrial Average (DJIA), the Dow Jones Transportation Average (DJTA), the Dow Jones Utility Average (DJUA), and the Dow Jones Composity Average (DJCA). The DJIA tracks 30 major companies in different industries, such as General Electric and Bank of America. The DJTA tracks 20 transportation companies, including railroads and airlines. The DJUA tracks 15 utility companies, most of which are defensive securities. The DJCA tracks all 65 companies in the other averages. See also: Publicly-traded company.

Dow Jones CDX Indexes A series of indices that track credit derivatives in various countries around the world. Credit derivatives include options, swaps, and similar securities. The Dow Jones CDX Indices provide benchmarks for individual investors and mutual funds that primarily invest in credit derivatives to know which derivative markets are bullish or bearish at a given time.

Dow Jones Industrial Average A stock market index founded in 1896 by Charles Dow tracking 30 companies in various industries thought to be representative of the American economy. It is a price-weighted index, meaning that stocks with higher prices per share affect the average more. It also scales its averages to account for stock splits and other changes in the companies tracked. All stocks tracked in the DJIA are traded on either the New York Stock Exchange or NASDAQ. It is considered the premier securities index in the United States.

Dow Jones Transportation Average A stock market index founded in 1884 by Charles Dow tracking (usually) 20 companies in the transportation industry. It is a price-weighted index, meaning that stocks with higher prices per share affect the average more. It also scales its averages to account for stock splits and other changes in the companies tracked. It includes stocks in shipping, airlines, trucking, railroads, and similar industries. It is the oldest actively used stock index in the world.

Dow Jones Utility Average A stock index tracking fifteen large, American utility companies. Utility companies borrow more than most companies and thus benefit from low interest rates. Because of this, a downturn on the DJUA is considered a predictor signaling an expected rise in interest rates. See also: Dow Jones Industrial Average, Dow Jones Transportation Average.

Dow Theory In technical analysis, a theory stating that when the Dow Jones Industrial Average and the Dow Jones Transportation Average both hit a new high or a new low for a period of time, it can confirm a previous, bullish or bearish signal. It is important that both the averages must reach a new high (or a new low) in order to confirm the trend.

Dower In wills and estates, a percentage of a husband's assets to which a widow is entitled, regardless of how much she is given in her husband's will. Thus, a husband may will her more than the dower, but not less. The amount of the dower varies, and few jurisdictions still have laws requiring one.

Down Payment An initial payment one makes on an asset financed with debt or otherwise paid in installments. For example, when buying a house, one usually makes a down payment of between 5% and 25% (depending largely on the buyer's FICO score and the availability of credit), and pays for the remainder of the house with a mortgage. Often, a large down payment qualifies one for a lower interest rate on the loan financing the remainder of the purchase.

Down Round In venture capital, a round of financing in which a company issues more stock with less valuation than previous financing rounds. This devalues all other stock in the company and results in less equity per share. A down round is usually a response to a major or minor cash flow problem, and ideally result in immediate cash on hand to cover operating costs. When the dotcom bubble burst, many tech companies held down rounds as an emergency measure to stay in business. See also: Antidilution provision.

Down Volume The trading volume of a security on a trading day during which the security closed down for the day. That is, when the closing price is lower than the opening price, all volume on that security for that day is considered down volume. Technical analysts use down volume and up volume to determine buy and sell signals.

Downgrade A change in the rating of a bond or other security in a downward direction. For example, a bond that had previously been rated AAA may be downgraded to AA. Downgrades are considered detrimental because they mean the ratings agency believes that the issuer of the security is less likely to be able to fulfill its obligations, such as coupon payments. A downgrade increases the cost of funds for the issuer because investors expect a higher return in exchange for the increased risk on the security. See also: Upgrade.

Downside In technical analysis and fundamental analysis, an estimate of the potential percentage or dollar amount by which a security may fall in the near-term. There are various methodologies used to determine an upside. For example, an analyst may look at recent trends on a bank stock and believe that it has the potential to fall in value by 15% in the next few weeks. This might be an indication for investors to sell the stock. Downside is also known as downside risk. See also: Upside Potential.

Downside Protection A position on a security that hedges risk such that it protects the holder from loss under most circumstances. One of the more common forms of downside protection is a covered option, in which one takes a long position on an option on a security that the investor already owns. This limits the loss that the investor could sustain on the security.

Downsize To reduce the size of a company. A company downsizes when its operations are perceived to become inefficient and it wishes to concentrate on certain competencies in order to improve profitability and reduce expenses. Downsizing often reduces the number of jobs at the company. Because downsizing reduces expenses, it often increases the company's value and/or dividends for shareholders.

Downstream In energy companies, relating to operations after production up to the point of sale. For example, an oil company's operations related to refining oil and selling gasoline to certain distributors are considered downstream. Some companies provide downstream operations exclusively, but most are integrated, providing both upstream and downstream operations.

Downstream Merger A merger in which a partially-owned subsidiary takes over its parent company. Contrary to the belief of some, the accounting of a downstream merger is different from a pooling of interests.

Downtick Volume In technical analysis, the trading volume of a security that is trading lower than its previous price. This is used to calculate the net volume, which is the uptick volume minus the downtick volume. Some analysts use this to indicate buy signals and sell signals.

Downtime In investment banking, a slang term for a situation in which a bank employee does not have much to do, especially if he/she is waiting for superiors to give further directions. An employee may spend downtime working on personal matters, or he/she may simply avoid work altogether.

Downtrend A situation in which a security price is moving mostly downward. Though there may or may not be a few upticks in between, this does not stop the overall bearish trend. For example, a security may be priced at $100 per share on January 1, $90 on January 10, and $85 on January 31. This indicates a downtrend, even if the security closed higher on certain days in January.

Downturn A decline in a security or market, especially after a long bullish period. A downturn is considered an inevitable part of the business cycle. See also: Bear market.

Downwardly Mobile A person who leaves a high-paying, prestigious job to take another position that pays less and is in a less lucrative field. One may be downwardly mobile by necessity (for example, if the previous company conducts lay-offs), or by choice (for example, if one was not satisfied in the previous position and wishes to do something more personally rewarding).

Draft A document in which a payer agrees to make a payment in a certain amount to a payee from an account held with a third party, usually a bank. A common example is a check. There are two main types of draft: a sight draft must be paid by the third party on demand of the payee, while a time draft may only be paid at a stated time.

Draft Check Slang; a post-dated check. That is, a check with a date after the current one written on it. In most circumstances, a draft check may not be deposited until the date written on it is reached. This gives the writer time to collect money so as not to write a bad check. Post-dating checks is strongly discouraged.

Drag-Along Rights The right of majority shareholders to force minority shareholders to sell their shares to a third party or to liquidate the company. Majority shareholders may exercise drag-along rights if a potential buyer will only agree to purchase 100% of a company.

Dragon Bond A eurodollar bond issued in Asia but denominated in U.S. dollars. The dollar is thought to be a lower risk currency than most East Asian currencies (the yen perhaps being the major exception). Some Asian companies therefore issue dragon bonds to encourage investors to buy their debt. Dragon bonds are usually long-term bonds.

Draining Reserves The practice of a central bank reducing the money supply. Examples of draining reserves include selling Treasury securities (or the equivalent in different countries), raising interest rates at which banks borrow from the central bank or from each other, and increasing banks' reserve requirements. All these measures are designed to reduce the amount of money in circulation in order to combat inflation.

Drama Price A price for real estate that has been reduced in order to entice more potential buyers. The term implies that there were no interested buyers at the previous, higher price.

Draped Bust Dollar A $1 coin minted in the United States between 1795 and 1804. It featured a picture of Lady Liberty with her bust rather prominently displayed. It was 90% silver.

Draw a Call To conduct any action that provokes a reaction from a client. For example, one may make trades that increase the trading volume on a security that one's client holds, causing the client to buy or sell that security.

Drawdown 1. In construction, a situation in which a company receives part of the funding necessary to complete a project. The company may receive the funding gradually over the course of the project. See also: IDC. 2. The gradual decline in the price of a security or other investment between its high and low over a given period. See also: Bear market.

Drawee 1. The party, often a bank, directed to pay the stated amount to the payee on a draft or check. 2. The party to whom a bill of exchange is addressed. A drawee, in this sense, is also called an acceptor.

Drawer One who makes a draft. For example, with a check, the drawer is the party writing the check who demands that his/her bank pay to some third party the indicated amount of money. See also: Drawee.

Drayage In international commerce, a fee trucking companies charge to carry an import from the ship on which it came into the country to its buyer. Drayage is important to incoterms as some agreements mandate that the seller pay for drayage, while others have the buyer pay this fee.

Dread Disease Rider A provision in some life insurance policies in which the insurance company must pay the policyholder a portion of the death benefit if the beneficiary develops a serious illness, or a "dread disease." Common illnesses covered under the dread disease rider are heart disease and some kinds of cancer. This rider exists in order to help the policyholder pay the medical cost of the illness.

Drill-Bit Stock A stock with a share price of less than one dollar. The imagery of a drill-bit comes from the days before decimalization, when stocks were quoted in fractions of a dollar; likewise, drill-bits are sized in fractions of an inch. In the present day, a drill-bit stock may be a new company or it may be an old company. A drill-bit stock may be in danger of delisting, depending on the rules of the exchange on which it trades.

Drip Feed 1. In venture capital, the practice of making small investments in a start-up as the need for capital arises. That is, a venture capital firm may sponsor a start-up, but a drip feed protects the firm from the risk that a start-up will collapse, resulting in the loss of the whole investment. A drip feed can be useful because it allows the start-up to maintain and expand operations while not forcing too much risk on its sponsor. 2. See: Dollar-cost averaging.

Drive-by VC A situation in which a venture capital (VC) firm invests in a start-up but takes little or no role in managing it. This is because the venture capital firm seeks to sell its investment in the shortest possible timeframe. Drive-by VC is often advantageous to both the start-up and the venture capital firm, though critics maintain it can lead to unsustainable growth, as the VC firm can pressure the start-up can go public before it is fully prepared.

Drop To remove a security from a list of securities for which a dealer serves as a counterpart in the over-the-counter market.

Drop-Dead Day Informal; a firm deadline that one cannot miss. A drop-dead day is often the last day of the quarter or year by which financial figures must be reported.

Drop-Dead Fee A fee that a borrowing company pays a lender if the borrower intends to use the funds from the loan to finance the acquisition of another company. The drop-dead fee is only paid if acquisition does not take place. That is, suppose Company A borrows from a bank to buy Company B. If Company B's shareholders refuse the offer and Company A has already borrowed the money, Company A must return what it has borrowed to the bank and pay the drop-dead fee to compensate the bank for lost interest. The term is most common in the United Kingdom.

Droplock Bond A floating rate bond that changes into a fixed rate bond if the interest rate on which the floating rate is based falls below a certain level. If this conversion occurs, the bond remains at the fixed rate until maturity. This is designed to protect the bondholder by providing a guaranteed minimum coupon, but it also protects the issuer because it locks in a fixed rate under certain circumstances, no matter how high interest rates go after those circumstances. See also: Floor, Convertible bond.

Drought Sale In farming and ranching, the sale of more livestock than is usual because of some unexpected incident out of the control of the farmer or rancher. That is, if there is a drought or disease that requires one to sell more livestock than one otherwise would, this is called a drought sale. Taxes on the profits from drought sales may be deferred to another year so that the tax code does not punish farmers and ranchers in difficult times.

Dry Powder Informal; a term for cash reserves, especially to cover unforeseen, future obligations. In personal finance, dry powder can also refer to low-risk liquid assets that can be converted to cash with minimal effort. The term is associated often with venture capital, when it refers to keeping ventures funded in a downturn, and with home building, when it refers to a reserve used to buy real estate when the market is favorable. The term derives from the need for dry gunpowder in the heat of battle in early modern warfare.

Dual Banking In the United States, the regulatory situation in which a bank may receive a charter from either the Federal Reserve or the state in which it operates. This is a function of federalism in the United States, and is different from banking regulation in many other countries. See also: Member bank, Non-member bank.

Dual Class Recapitalization The new issue of common stock that a company distributes to current stockholders in exchange for previously-issued common stock. The new common stock usually has fewer voting rights. Dual class recapitalization increases the board of directors' control over the management of the company.

Dual Class Stock A stock in a publicly-traded company that issues two types of stock. Each stock class has distinct rights attached to it. Generally speaking, dual-class stocks include preferred stock, which carries the right to guaranteed dividends, and common stock, which carries the right to vote in the annual meeting.

Dual Currency Deposit A deposit made at a financial institution in one currency in which withdrawals could be made either in the first currency or another one, selected by the depositor and the institution. It is important to note that a dual currency deposit creates a foreign exchange risk for the depositor. See also: Currency swap.

Dual Currency Issue A bond in which coupons are paid in one currency while the principal is paid in another. Dual currency issues set an exchange rate that usually allows payments in the stronger currency to appreciate more. There are number of ways to calculate the exchange rate; the three most common are to use the exchange rate at the time of issue, the spot rate at the time payments are made, and to use a third currency to determine the value of the other two. Dual currency issues are most commonly used by (and are most valuable to) multinational corporations and traders on the eurobond market.

Dual Exchange Rate A situation in which a currency has two official exchange rates, one pegged to another currency and the other floating. Each is used for different things. The exchange rate for money used for sectors seen as essential, such as food, is fixed, while "non-essential" sectors are allowed to float. A dual exchange rate allows a country to devalue its currency to reflect market realities without the pain of high inflation that usually accompanies severe devaluation. Critics allege that a dual exchange rate is less efficient than a straightforward devaluation and acts as a tariff on industries the government sees as luxuries.

Dual Income with No Kids Also called DINKS. In marketing, a term for households with two adults, either a married couple or life partners, with no children. Usually both partners are employed but occasionally one partner brings home two incomes. They are important to marketers trying to sell luxury items such as vacations or expensive household items. Because DINKS tend to have large disposable incomes, marketers often target new technologies at them. Many DINKS ultimately have children and become, in marketing terms, DEWKS.

Dual Listing The practice of listing the same security on two or more stock exchanges. Dual listing is thought to increase liquidity and improve the bid-ask spread for stocks by providing more competition. It can also allow a stock to continue trade after one exchange has closed for the day, but another remains open. However, dual listing is not very common. It should not be confused with multiple listing, which is a term in real estate.

Dual Presentation A report of a company's earnings per share on both a basic and diluted basis. This is used for companies with complex capital structures in which neither presentation accurately reflects the company's earnings on its own.

Dual Purpose Fund A closed-end fund that offers two types of shares: income shares and capital shares. Income shares offer holders a portion of the fixed return on the fund's portfolio, and attract low-risk investors. Capital shares do not offer a portion on the fixed return, but instead offer holders a portion of the returns on stocks or similar investments, attracting medium- or high-risk investors. An advantage to the dual purpose fund is that it offers shareholders a choice as to which type of investment they would like to make.

Dual Syndicate Equity Offering A new issue of a stock made through two syndicates. When making a dual syndicate equity offering, the issuer hires two separate groups of underwriters. The first group offers the stock to investors in the issuer's own country while the second offers it internationally. Using two syndicates allows each underwriter the ability to respond to the different needs and concerns of domestic and global investors.

Dually Employed with Kids In marketing, a term for households with two adults and an unknown (but usually small) number of children. Usually both adults are employed, but occasionally one adult brings home two incomes. They are important to marketers trying to sell children's items such as toys and videos games. The idea behind this is that DEWKS tend to spoil their children. See also: DINKS.

Dubbeltje A slang term for a 10-eurocent coin in the Netherlands. The term was used for the equivalent Dutch guilder coin.

Duck Shove Slang; the act or practice of giving work to a co-worker or subordinate if one does not want to do it oneself. A duck shove may reduce morale, but can help one to avoid work.

Duck Shuffler Slang; a person who makes a change to a report or project after it is done or sufficiently planned. The term refers to the phrase "ducks in a row," implying that the duck shuffler moves one's ducks.

Due Describing a debt or its maturity. For example, one may say that a $250,000 mortgage is due in 30 years, which means that the mortgage must be completely paid off 30 years from the time of that statement.

Due Date The date by which a debt or other payment must be paid in order not to be late. Due dates occur for all kinds of liabilities; for example, the due date for one's rent may be 15th of each month. See also: Delinquency, Default.

Due Diligence The investigation of an asset, investment, or anything else to ensure that everything is as it seems. Due diligence helps a buyer or investor make sure that there are no unexpected problems with the asset or investment and that he/she does not overpay. Due diligence can be a complex and formalized process in the acquisition of a company. Even when buying a house, for example, due diligence involves time consuming and at times expensive endeavors, like a home inspection. However, due diligence is seen as a necessary part of doing business or buying an asset. See also: 10-K, Due diligence meeting.

Due Diligence Meeting An internal meeting held after the registration of a new security with the SEC but before the registration's effective date. Under the Securities Act of 1933, all accountants, counsel, underwriters, and managers can be held civilly liable for knowingly making false or misleading statements in the registration documents. In order to shield themselves from liability, representatives of the registrant conduct a meeting before the registration becomes effective to discuss and if necessary remedy any issues that may have arisen. This is considered a necessary part of due diligence prior to the issuance of a new security.

Due-on-Sale Clause In mortgages, a clause stating that the borrower must repay the entirety of the principal on the mortgage if he/she sells the property before the mortgage matures. This protects the lender from the risk that the borrower will sell the property, pocket the proceeds (or, worse, lose them in other investments), and then default on the mortgage. It further protects the lender from the risk that the borrower will transfer the mortgage to the new owner of the property when prevailing interest rates are higher than what the new owner would pay.

Duim An obsolete Dutch unit of length roughly equivalent to two and a half centimeters, with slight regional variations.

Duit A coin that circulated in the Netherlands prior to the Dutch guilder's decimalization in the 19th century. It was worth 1/160th of one guilder.

Dumbbell A portfolio consisting predominantly or exclusively of bonds with very short and very long maturities. The investment strategy behind a dumbbell portfolio is the invest in high-yield bonds with long maturities to maximize return while also maintaining investment-grade bonds with short maturities to minimize risk and maximize liquidity.

Dummy A buyer of real estate who has no interest in owning what he/she buys. That is, if a developer wishes to buy up a large amount of land without attracting attention, he/she may hire dummies to purchase (with the developer's capital) on his/her behalf. The dummies in turn re-sell (or simply give) the properties to the developer.

Dummy Activity In accounting, a fabricated activity put into a record to show precedence among two or more activities taking place at the same time.

Dummy Director A member of the board of directors that acts and votes in the interests or on behalf of a non-member. Dummy directors are most common in start-ups that have just become publicly-traded companies, because managers need to fill up a certain number of directors in order to meet legal requirements and therefore appoint or elect a number of dummy directors to serve temporarily until permanent directors can be found. In the interim, they tend to act on behalf of the management.

Dummy Shareholder A person or company that owns shares in a publicly-traded company on behalf of another person or company. That is, while the shares are in the dummy shareholder's name, another party makes all decisions related to their use. See also: Beneficial ownership.

Dumping 1. The act of exporting a good to a country where the exported good is much less expensive in the importing country than domestically produced goods of the same type. This can result in a handsome profit for the exporter. Importing countries attempt to counteract dumping by setting up tariff barriers. Some countries peg their currencies artificially low so as to enable dumping. See also: Outsourcing. **2.** The act of selling at a loss. This may apply to selling a stock, especially in a panic sale, to minimize losses. Alternatively, it may apply to a company selling low on purpose to gain market share or force competitors into a costly price war.

Dun & Bradstreet A company specializing in the investigation of credit worthiness, financial standing, and/or reputation of other businesses. It provides this information to third parties for a fee. Some mercantile agencies compile information into large databases, which they then distribute to subscribers. The first mercantile agency was founded in 1841 in New York under the name of "Mercantile Agency," and it is now known as Dun & Bradstreet. See also: Business intelligence, Due diligence.

Dunning The process of attempting to collect on accounts receivable. Dunning occurs when customers do not pay promptly and/or in full. See also: Collections agency.

Duo scrupula An ancient Roman unit of area approximately equivalent to 17.5 square meters.

Duopoly A situation in which two companies split all or nearly all the market share of a good or service. There are two models for duopoly: the Cournot model and the Bertrand model. In the Cournot model, the two companies assume the output of the other, resulting in greater output than in a monopoly, but less than in a state of perfect competition. This pushes prices lower, but not as low as they would be in perfect competition. In the Bertrand model, the duopolistic companies compete for the lowest possible price, resulting in perfect competition. Both models are applicable in different situations and times and neither expresses duopolistic behavior perfectly. Major examples of duopolies include Pepsi and Coca-Cola in the soft drink market and Microsoft and Apple in the computer operating system market.

Duplicate Proxy A vote in a shareholder meeting that undoes a previous vote. That is, a shareholder who has, for example, voted for a merger may submit a duplicate proxy to vote against the same merger. When counting votes, the company counts the most recently dated duplicate proxy. This system allows an investor time for a sober second thought; however, he/she must make sure to submit the vote in time to be counted.

DuPont Analysis An alternative calculation of the return on equity of an investment. DuPont analysis utilizes the investment's gross book value instead of its net book value. It is calculated as: (Profits / Sales) * (Sales / Assets) * (Assets / Equity) = DuPont Analysis return on equity The theory behind DuPont analysis states that forms of return on equity using net book value discourage investment in new, potentially risky ventures because they underestimate the return for the first few years of the investment. The DuPont calculation attempts to remedy this situation.

Durable Goods Orders Orders that companies make for consumer products designed and intended to last longer than three years. Some examples of durable goods, such as cars, are expensive, while others, such as forks and knives, are not. If durable goods orders increase, it is a sign of a healthy economy because it shows that consumers are willing to make major purchases. As such, durable goods orders are a major economic indicator.

Durable Merchandise Consumer products designed and intended to last longer than three years. Some examples of durable merchandise, such as cars, are expensive, while others, such as forks and knives, are not. Companies that produce durable merchandise can be volatile, as their profits fluctuate according to how often their customers need more of their products. Durable merchandise is also called consumer durables or durable goods.

Durable Power of Attorney The legal transfer of the authority to act on behalf of another person. That is, durable power of attorney gives the designee (called an agent) the ability to sign legal documents and manage the finances of the principal in the event of the principal's incapacitation. For example, one may designate durable power of attorney to a relative in case one develops Alzheimer's disease and is unable to manage one's own affairs. See also: Advanced directive.

Duration The amount by which a bond's price increases or decreases as the result of a 1% change in interest rates. When interest rates rise above a bond's own interest rate, its price usually declines because an investor can earn a higher yield with another bond. Likewise, when interest rates fall, the bond's price usually rises. Duration measures how much the price changes and, for that reason, is a measure of a bond's volatility.

Duration Matching Strategy An immunization strategy in which one matches the duration of assets in a portfolio to the duration of the liabilities. Duration is the number of years until the investor receive the present value of all income from a bond (including interest and principal), and is used to gauge a bond's sensitivity to interest rate changes. A duration matching strategy is intended to reduce the portfolio's sensitivity to interest rates in order to reduce the risk of loss to the holder.

Duress Force, coercion or threat of either. A contract signed under duress is usually invalid and unenforceable. To give a very simple example, one may not hold a gun to the head of another party and expect him/her to sign a valid contract. Likewise, one may not be guilty of a crime if one commits it under duress.

Dusin A Danish unit of 12.

Dutch Auction An auction of a new issue of securities where the highest price offered to buy a portion of the issue becomes the price at which the entire issue is sold. Dutch auctions are particularly important because they are the means used to sell new issues of U.S. Treasury securities. A Dutch auction begins with the securities offered at a high price and the price is gradually lowered until there is a bid. This contrasts with a commercial option that begins at a low price that is gradually raised.

Dutch Disease The phenomenon in which the manufacturing sector of a country declines when it begins to make significant profits from the exploitation of a natural resource. For example, if a country suddenly discovers oil and sells it on the international market, it may see a decline in the competitiveness of its manufacturing companies. It is thought that the Dutch disease comes from the fact that the sale of the natural resource leads to a stronger currency, which makes the country's exports more expensive and causes scaling down in manufacturing.

Dutch East India Trading Company The first modern corporation in the world. Established in 1602 by the Dutch government as a legal monopoly, it controlled much of the trade of spices and other goods between Europe and East Asia for the next 200 years. The Dutch East India Trading Company also exercised government control over much of the East Indies; it exercised law and order powers and ran a military to fight against European (mostly British) and other competitors. It was the first company to issue stocks and helped spur the existence of modern exchanges. It dissolved in 1800.

Dutch Metric Ounce A unit of weight equivalent to 100 grams.

Duty A tax that a country imposes on its imports and, occasionally, exports. A duty exists to make an import more expensive and to thereby encourage people to buy goods produced in their own country. Proponents of their use argue that duties discourage outsourcing of jobs to other countries and make the country more self-sufficient, but most economists agree that they are economically inefficient and some contend that they may ultimately harm the people they are intended to help. A duty is also called a tariff. See also: WTO, International trade, Globalization.

Duureg In Mongolia, a political subdivision for a district in Ulan Bator, the capital. One duureg is divided into several khorroo.

Duym A Tatar unit of length equivalent to 25.44 millimeters. It was rendered obsolete when the Soviet Union began to use the metric system in 1924.

Dva An ancient Persian unit of length approximately equivalent to 100 millimeters.

Dwarf A mortgage-backed security pool, issued by Fannie Mae, with a maturity of 15 years.

Dwelling Loan A mortgage on the primary residence of an individual or family. This contrasts with a mortgage on an investment property or business property.

Dwelling loans may be eligible for benefits from social programs for troubled homeowners, while other mortgages generally are not.

DY 1. ISO 3166-1 alpha-2 code for Dahomey before it changed its name to Benin. This was the code used in international transactions to and from Dahomean bank accounts. **2.** ISO 3166-2 geocode for Dahomey. This was used as an international standard for shipping to Dahomey. In both cases, the code is obsolete.

DYBJ ISO 3166-3 code for Dahomey, which changed its name to Benin in 1975. ISO 3166-3 codes are used to indicate names of countries that are no longer used.

Dynamic Describing any situation that may change. It is especially important in options strategies.

Dynamic Asset Allocation An active management strategy for a portfolio or fund with a basic set of securities. The money manager changes the securities represented in the portfolio or fund as needed in order to take advantage of short-term profits. However, once the portfolio or fund has attains those profits, the money manager returns to the basic set of securities originally in it. The money manager may use fundamental, technical, and/or macroeconomic analysis in determining when and how to change the securities in the portfolio or fund.

Dynamic Hedging An investment strategy in which one reduces risk by taking various positions in put options according to changing market conditions. For example, one may buy a put to hedge risk to one security in a portfolio thought to be particularly risky at one time, and then sell that put and buy another when matters change.

Dynamic Momentum Index A technical measure indicating whether a security is overbought or oversold. It is calculated thusly: DMI = 100 - (100 / (1 + RS)) where RS is the average measure of the security's price on days it closes up divided by the average price on days it closes down. A DMI over 70 means that a security is overbought while a measure under 30 means that the security is oversold. The measure is similar to a relative strength index, with the main difference being the length of time accounted in the RS measure. The DMI uses shorter time periods when volatility is high and longer periods when it is low.

Dynamic Risk The risk of loss resulting from changes in culture, taste or policy. For example, if one sells only black socks in the United States, one takes the dynamic risk that no one will buy black socks after Labor Day. Likewise, if one sells for-profit insurance, one takes the dynamic risk that the government will ban this type of insurance. It is related to political risk, but primarily connotes cultural changes.

Dynamical Systems A series of equations in which the output of one becomes the input of another. One equation may determine a company's earnings for a particular period. The earnings, then, may be put into another equation to determine the earnings per share. This is a simple example of dynamical systems. It may (and often does) include a long string of equations.

DZ 1. ISO 3166-1 alpha-2 code for the People's Democratic Republic of Algeria. This is the code used in international transactions to and from Algerian bank accounts. **2.** ISO 3166-2 geocode for Algeria. This is used as an international standard for shipping to Algeria. Each Algerian province has its own code with the prefix "DZ." For example, the code for the Province of Medea is ISO 3166-2:DZ-26.

DZA GOST 7.67 Latin three-letter geocode for Algeria. The code is used for transactions to and from Algerian bank accounts and for international shipping to Algeria. As with all GOST 7.67 codes, it is used primarily in Cyrillic alphabets.

DZD ISO 4217 code for the Algerian dinar. It was introduced in 1964, replacing the Algerian new franc. The dinar underwent a period of high inflation in the 1990s during Algeria's transition to a capitalist economy, but this has since abated.

Dzielnica In Poland, a political subdivision equivalent to a district within a city.

Dzongkhag In Bhutan, a political subdivision equivalent to a province.

E A symbol appearing next to a stock listed on NASDAQ indicating that the share being traded represents a company that has not filed a necessary report with the SEC by the deadline. All NASDAQ listings use a four letter abbreviation; if an E follows the abbreviation, this indicates that the share comes from a company that did not file on time.

E&OE An abbreviation for "errors and omissions excepted," a disclaimer stating that information in a document is not necessarily accurate. E&OE, statements are most common when information changes quickly. It is intended to reduce the legal liability of the party making the statement. The term is most common in the United Kingdom and current and former Commonwealth countries.

E. George Schaefer An investor who was a major proponent of Dow theory, which states that when the Dow Jones Industrial Average and the Dow Jones Transportation Average both hit a new high or a new low for a period of time, it can confirm a previous bullish or bearish signal. Unlike Dow theorists who came before him, he also strongly believed in value investing. He died in 1974.

E.A.O.N. An abbreviation for "except as otherwise noted." For example, a financial statement may indicate that all figures are provided in U.S. dollars E.A.O.N.

E.F. Schumacher A 20th-century German economist. For much of his career, he served as an adviser to the National Coal Board in the United Kingdom, in which capacity he promoted the use of coal instead of oil, fearing oil eventually would become prohibitively expensive due to its depletion. In his later career, he worked in economic development, advocating that the most sustainable means of development was to use local resources for local needs. He lived from 1911 to 1977.

Each Way Describing a commission that a broker receives when he/she is involved in both the purchase and the sale of an asset or security. That is, the broker receives two commissions, one from the buyer and one from the seller.

Eager Beaver Informal; a person who performs one's duties diligently and enthusiastically and who may request more duties as a result. An eager beaver may be ambitious or may simply have an exceptional work ethic. An eager beaver may become a good employee or a successful business owner.

Eagle A gold coin minted in the United States between 1795 and 1933. It was worth $10.

Earl A slang term sometimes used in finance and trading for oil. The term derives from the way the word "oil" is said to be pronounced in an American Southern accent.

Earliest Finish Time In industry and manufacturing, the earliest possible time an activity can end. The earliest finish time determines the earliest start time for succeeding activities. See also: Supply chain.

Earliest Start Time In industry and manufacturing, the earliest possible time an activity can begin. The earliest start time is determined by the earliest finish time of preceding activities. See also: Supply chain.

Early Amortization Early repayment of an asset-backed security, usually occurring when something goes wrong. Most commonly, if there are more than a certain number of defaults on the assets (such as mortgages) underlying the security, early amortization occurs. It is intended to reduce the risk to the investor and therefore to entice buyers.

Early Bargain A discount only available to the first several people who take advantage of it, or only until a certain, stated time. For example, a retail store may offer a 25% discount to everyone who makes a purchase before 11 a.m. Early bargains are associated with holiday sales such as Black Friday.

Early Exercise A situation in which an option contract is exercised before its expiration date. American-style options allow early exercise, while European-style options do not.

Early Extinguishment of Debt The payment of a debt in full before it is due. Early extinguishment of debt is good for the borrower because it relieves him/her of the debt, but it deprives the lender of interest he/she would have received otherwise. As a result, some lenders attach prepayment penalties to loans to disincentivize early extinguishment. Early extinguishment of debt is also called prepayment, which has other meanings as well. See also: Prepayment risk.

Early Fringe In television broadcasting, the late afternoon and early evening. The early fringe has fewer viewers than prime time, but the audience consists of similar demographics. As a result, some advertisers who wish to appeal to prime time audiences (that is, families) may air commercials during the early fringe because it is less expensive.

Early Harvest A situation in which the weather causes the harvest of a crop to come earlier than it usually does. An early harvest can result in a drop in the price for that crop because the excess supply was unanticipated. Various derivatives for agricultural products (and even for the weather) exist to hedge against the risk of early harvest and other acts of God.

Early Intervention Program A program in the United States providing nutrition, nursing, physical therapy and similar services to infants and toddlers with developmental disabilities. It is designed to help these children to be able to reach their intellectual and other potential when they start school. It was created by Congress in the 1980s and is administered by each state.

Early Retirement Retirement before the normal age, which is generally between 55 and 65. Early retirement may occur because a person attains financial security for the remainder of his/her life before most of his/her peers. Unfortunately, it may also occur due to injury or inability to work in one's field. People in early retirement may qualify for pension or government benefits, but generally they are less than those who retire at full age.

Early Settlement The practice of settling a trade before the usual settlement date. This is fairly unusual; most contracts are settled between one and three days later. Generally speaking, early settlement is common in the last week of the calendar year when many trades must be settled sooner to guarantee tax advantages for one or both parties. Likewise, one may desire early settlement for other reasons, such as to receive a dividend on a certain date. See also: Cash contract.

Early Withdrawal The withdrawal of funds from a fixed-income investment before the prescribed time. Early withdrawal may come from a certificate of deposit before its maturity. More often, however, it refers to a withdrawal from a retirement account before the appropriate age (usually 65 or the date of retirement, whichever is later). Early withdrawals are usually assessed a fee to discourage frequent or abusive use. As a result, early withdrawals usually occur when the account holder is in great financial need. An early withdrawal is also called an early distribution or a premature distribution.

Early Withdrawal Penalty A fee assessed on the withdrawal of funds from a fixed-income investment before the prescribed time. Early withdrawal may come from a certificate of deposit before its maturity. More often, however, early withdrawals refer to withdrawals from a retirement account before the appropriate age (usually 65 or date of retirement, whichever is greater). Early withdrawal penalties exist to discourage the frequent or abusive use of early withdrawals. As a result, early withdrawals usually occur when the account holder is in great financial need.

Early-Retirement Benefits The benefits from a pension or government program one receives after early retirement. Most pensions and government programs pay benefits based on how much an individual contributes to the system during his/her working life. That is, people who work longer (and/or earn more) contribute more than those who do not. As a result, early-retirement benefits are usually less than benefits for those who retire at full age.

Earmark 1. To set aside money to use only for a certain, stated purpose. Earmarking is common in both personal savings and in corporate finance, as well as in government. For example, an individual may earmark reserves for his/her honeymoon and a company may do the same to pay off bonds when they mature. Likewise, a politician may earmark government funds for a project in his/her district. When politicians earmark funds, the word takes on a slightly negative connotation. See also: Pork barrel spending. **2.** Money that has been earmarked.

Earmarked Reserves Money in savings that one intends to use only for a certain, stated purpose. Earmarked reserves are common in both personal savings and in corporate finance. For example, an individual may earmark reserves for his/her honeymoon and a company may do the same to pay off bonds when they mature.

Earn a Living To make money in order to provide for personal and family expenses. In general, one earns a living with a job, which is an occupation for which one is compensated. Some earn their livings through investments or through owning a business.

Earned Income Income from salaries, wages, commissions, tips, bonuses, and any other source related to the work one does. Earned income specifically excludes income from investments. Earned income is taxed at one's regular income tax rate. See also: Marginal tax rate.

Earned Income Tax Credit Also called the EITC. A dollar-for-dollar reduction in the tax liability for lower and middle income persons in the United States. The credit is applied against taxes owed on wages, salaries, tips and other forms of earned income. Investment income is excluded and one may not have more than a certain amount of investment income to be eligible for the credit. Households with children may receive larger credits. The EITC is refundable, meaning if the credit causes one's tax liability to go below zero, one receives the difference from the IRS.

Earned Premium In insurance accounting, the prepaid premium that an insurance company may count as profit because of the length of its exposure to risk. For example, suppose a policyholder pays three years' worth of premiums up front. After a year has gone by, the insurer may count one third of that premium as earned premium and therefore profit. Earning the premium only works if no claims exceeding the amount of the premium are filed; it there are claims, the insurer may take a loss.

Earned Rate A reduced amount of money per advertisement that an advertiser pays in exchange for high volume. For example, if an advertiser agrees to purchase 30 seconds of time every commercial break for an extended period, that advertiser may be eligible for an earned rate.

Earned Revenue Revenue a company derives from its operations. For example, if a company sells its inventory and receives money, it is earning revenue. This contrasts with revenue from other sources, such as the company's investments, and from profit, which is revenue less expenses.

Earned Right In Social Security in the United States, the right an individual has to receive benefits following retirement according to how much he/she paid into the system during his/her working life. That is, people who work longer (and/or earn more) contribute more than those who do not, and, as a result, they collect higher Social Security benefits.

Earnest Money A small amount of money that a seller requires a potential buyer to deposit before a transaction is completed. Earnest money ensures that the potential buyer is serious about the transaction and will be likely to complete it when the time comes. If the buyer subsequently withdraws from the deal, he/she usually forfeits the earnest money. It is common in real estate and securities (where it is usually called a good faith deposit). Earnest money reduces the risk to the seller. It is also called a binder.

Earning Asset An asset that produces money for a company without any work needing to be done. Earning assets include such things as stocks, bonds, certificates of deposit, and generally anything that earns interest or dividends.

Earning Power 1. See: Earnings per share. **2.** The ability of a company to make a profit on its operations. There is no single way to estimate a company's earning power, and indeed it varies from company to company. For example, a well-established company's earning power may be best estimated by its dividend yield. On the other hand, one may determine a start-up's earning power through other metrics, like return on assets.

Earning the Points Somewhat informal; in foreign exchange, the act of selling a futures contract on a currency at a high exchange rate and buying a currency on the spot market at a lower exchange rate. When one must deliver the underlying currency on the futures contract, earning the points guarantees a gain because one sells the currency at a higher rate than the one at which one bought it. See also: Losing the points.

Earnings A company's total revenue less its operating expenses, interest paid, depreciation, and taxes. For example, suppose a widget manufacturer makes $1,000,000 in total revenue. The widgets cost $200,000 to make and his administrative and payroll expenses total $250,000. He also must subtract $50,000 in depreciation on his widget manufacturing equipment and pay $200,000 in taxes. His earnings are stated as: $1,000,000 - $200,000 - $250,000 - $50,000 - $200,000 = $300,000.

Earnings Announcement The public announcement of a company's earnings. Earnings announcements mean investors will know how a company is performing and may make comparisons to past performance and to other companies. As an earnings announcement may affect the company's stock price, many analysts observe stock performance on the announcement date and consider it a gauge of how the market will treat the news.

Earnings Before Interest After Taxes A measure of a company's ability to produce income on its operations in a given year. It is calculated as the company's revenue less its expenses (such as overhead) and tax liability, but not subtracting its interest paid on debt. The EBIAT does not account for one-off or otherwise unusual revenues and expenses, only recurring ones. EBIAT represents cash available to pay off creditors in the event of liquidation and, as such, it is closely watched, especially when the company incurs little depreciation or amortization. It is a less common measure than earnings before interest and taxes.

Earnings Before Interest and Tax A measure of a company's ability to produce income on its operations in a given year. It is calculated as the company's revenue less its expenses (such as overhead) but not subtracting its tax liability or interest paid on debt. It is important to note that EBIT does not account for one-off or otherwise unusual revenues and expenses, only recurring ones. EBIT represents cash available to pay off creditors in the event of liquidation and, as such, it is closely watched, especially when the company incurs little depreciation or amortization. It is also called operating profit.

Earnings Before Interest, Taxes, and Depreciation A measure of a company's ability to produce income on its operations in a given year. It is calculated as the company's revenue less its expenses (such as overhead), but including its tax liability, interest paid on debt, and depreciation. It is important to note that EBITD does not account for one-off or otherwise unusual revenues and expenses, only recurring ones. Depreciation is excluded because it is a deduction from profit that does not have to be paid in cash and is thus not useful for determining cash on hand. EBITD represents cash available to pay off creditors in the event of liquidation, and, as such, it is closely watched, especially when the company has little amortization. See also: EBIT.

Earnings Before Interest, Taxes, Depreciation and Amortization A measure of a company's ability to produce income on its operations in a given year. It is calculated as the company's revenue less most of its expenses (such as overhead) but not subtracting its tax liability, interest paid on debt, amortization or depreciation. It is important to note that EBITDA does not account for one-off or otherwise unusual revenues and expenses, only recurring ones. It is a less common measure than EBITD or EBIT.

Earnings Before Interest, Taxes, Depreciation, Amortization, and Rent A measure of a company's ability to produce income on its operations in a given year. It is calculated as the company's revenue less most of its expenses (such as overhead) but not subtracting its tax liability, interest paid on debt, amortization, depreciation, or rent on its facilities. It is important to note that EBITDAR does not account for one-off or otherwise unusual revenues and expenses, only recurring ones. It is a less common measure than either EBITD or EBIT.

Earnings Before Taxes A measure of a company's ability to produce income on its operations in a given year. It is calculated as the company's revenue less its expenses (such as overhead), but not subtracting its tax liability. EBIT represents cash available to pay off creditors in the event of liquidation, and, as such, it is closely watched, especially when comparing companies in jurisdictions with different tax laws. However, it is not as common a measure as earnings before interest and taxes.

Earnings Calendar The schedule according to which various publicly-traded companies announce their earnings for a certain period such as a quarter or a year. The earnings calendar organizes these announcements by date and company. For example, it may provide an alphabetical listing of all companies making earnings announcements on a certain date in October, also indicating the time and manner of the announcement. Earnings calendars exist for investor convenience.

Earnings Credit Rate Also called an ECR. The interest rate a bank pays on customer deposits. Rather than being applied to the deposit directly, ECRs are used to reduce the fees the customers pay for other banking services. For example, if a bank is paying a 0.05% ECR on a $10,000 deposit, the depositor earns a $5 reduction in his/her other fees. An ECR is usually connected to a Treasury bill rate.

Earnings Enhancement Benefit An additional, optional death benefit on an annuity. One may elect to include an earnings enhancement benefit in exchange for a fee or a percentage of the total value of the annuity.

Earnings Estimate An analyst's best guess as to what a company's earnings will be for a given quarter or year. Analysts use a variety of methods, mostly involving past information and current news, to arrive at earnings estimates. They are circulated prior to a company's announcement of its earnings statement. If earnings are lower than most estimates, this can cause a decline in its share price. Likewise, unexpectedly high earnings can cause a price jump.

Earnings Expectations The consensus estimate of analysts and other experts as to a company's earnings for a given period of time. If earnings expectations are high, the price of a company's stock may increase as investors seek to take advantage of the added value or dividend. Companies may hint about their earnings before the earnings announcement so as to prevent their stocks from unsustainably rising or falling in price.

Earnings Forecast The act or process of using certain data to predict future earnings of a publicly-traded company. Earnings forecasts can cause significant changes in share price for companies, since forecasts may influence earnings

expectations. Various methods exist for forecasting; experts differ on which ones, if any, work.

Earnings Growth The actual or expected increase in profits over two comparable periods of time. For example, if a company had a $1 million profit in 2009 and a $1.2 million profit in 2010, it is said to have experienced 20% earnings growth.

Earnings Momentum Year-on-year growth in earnings per share, usually sustained over a number of years. There does not need to be a particular pattern to the rate of growth in different years; all that is needed is for growth to be sustained. High earnings momentum often leads to increases in share price as investors tend to believe companies with earnings momentum have achieved relatively sustainable growth. Negative earnings momentum is also possible, with steady, year-on-year decreases in growth.

Earnings Multiplier The price of a security per share at a given time divided by its annual earnings per share, adjusted for current interest rates. Often the earnings used are trailing 12-month earnings, but some analysts use other forms. The earnings multiplier is a way to help determine a security's stock valuation, that is, the fair value of a stock in a perfect market. It is also a measure of expected, but not realized, growth. It is a variation on the price-earnings ratio.

Earnings per Share In a given fiscal year, a publicly-traded company's profit divided by the number of shares outstanding. This is considered the single most important aspect in determining a share's price and value, because the calculation of earnings per share shows the amount of money to which a shareholder would be entitled in the event of the company's liquidation. In general, earnings per share applies only to common shares. It is calculated thusly: Earnings per share = (Net income - Preferred dividends) / Average shares outstanding.

Earnings Potential The amount a person or company might be able to earn. There is no time frame implied in the definition. For example, one may discuss the earnings potential of a company next year or of a person over his/her lifetime. A number of factors, notably experience, expertise, connections and competence may affect earnings potential.

Earnings Quality A condition describing how earnings are recognized. Earnings of high quality are attributable to conservative accounting standards and/or strong cash flows. Low quality earnings come from artificial sources, such as inflation or aggressive accounting. For example, a publicly-traded company may claim strong earnings and consequently have a high stock price. However, the company may have low cash flow from operations and the strong earnings may come mainly from the accounting structures it uses. Therefore, its stock is overvalued. Quality of earnings ratings is subjective, but it does take into account matters such as corporate governance, inventory to sales ratios, and other factors.

Earnings Report An annual report and other quarterly reports a publicly-traded company publishes giving information over a given period of time. The report contains information on the company's financial state, most notably statements on revenue, expenses, and earnings (which is the difference between the two). It is, in general, less detailed than a stockholder's report, but contains much of the same information. See also: Balance sheet.

Earnings Response Coefficient The relationship between a change in a company's stock price and any unusual statements in a company's earnings announcement. Unexpectedly high earnings can create a buying panic and while low earnings can create a selling panic. This can drive the stock price up or down. Arbitrageurs use the earnings response coefficient to estimate how much the price may change and make decisions on how to exploit the pricing inefficiency. See also: Capital Asset Pricing Model, Arbitrage.

Earnings Retention Ratio The percentage of a publicly-traded company's post-tax earnings that are not paid in dividends. Most earnings retained are re-invested into the company's operations. Tracking year-on-year earnings retention ratios is important to fundamental analysis to investigate whether a company is increasing or decreasing its rate of re-investment. The earnings retentions ratio is calculated thusly: Earnings retention ratio = (Net income - dividends) / Net income For example, a company with a net income of $10 million that pays out $3.5 million in dividends has an earnings retention ratio of (10 million - 3.5 million) / 10 million = 65%. It is also called simply the retention ratio.

Earnings Season The first month of each quarter when earnings statements from the previous quarters are released. That is, earnings seasons are January, April, July, and October.

Earnings Surprise A situation in which a publicly-traded company's earnings report indicates higher or lower profit than analysts expected. This can lead to a sharp (and often unsustainable) increase or decrease in the share price. Many companies seek to avoid earnings surprises by pricing out, or slowly leaking information before the earnings report is published.

Earnings Test In Social Security in the United States, a test to determine whether a person under normal retirement age (between 62 and 67) is eligible for reduced benefits. The test sets two levels of income (which vary year to year); if one's own income is above the lower level but below the upper level, one may receive benefits at a $1 reduction for every $2 in wages. One receives full benefits in later years after one has passed proper retirement age.

Earnings Variability 1. Differences in a publicly traded company's year-on-year earnings or earnings per share in both positive and negative directions. Earnings variability is sometimes considered a negative sign as investors do not know whether the company's earnings in one year can be sustained in the next. This can lead to a low P/E ratio as high earnings in a given year do not equate to an increase in share price. It is the opposite of earnings momentum. **2.** The amount a worker's wages or salary change from year to year. Earnings variability can occur due to a job change, among other reasons. Between 2003 and 2007, approximately one in five workers saw their earnings increase by 25% or more and one in five saw them decrease by the same amount.

Earnings Warning An announcement by a publicly-traded company, often over a conference call, that its earnings will not be as high as previously expected. Earnings warnings give investors and analysts a basis from which to make their investment decisions and recommendations. It also helps the company price out the bad news so its share price is not subject to wild drops when the earnings are actually announced.

Earnings-Age Profile A graph showing the average income of persons in a group at various ages. The earnings-age profile may be specific; for example, it may show the average earnings for college graduates or for women. It may also be general, including everyone in a given economy.

Earnings-Price Ratio The annual earnings of a security per share divided by its price per share at a given time. It is the inverse of the more common price-earnings ratio. Often, the earnings one uses are trailing 12-month earnings, but some analysts use other forms. The earnings-price ratio is a way to help determine a security's stock valuation, that is, the fair value of a stock in a perfect market. It is also a measure of expected, but not realized, growth. It may be used in place of the price-earnings ratio if, say, there are no earnings (as one cannot divide by zero). It is also called the earnings yield or the earnings capitalization ratio.

Earn-Out In an acquisition, an additional payment made to the acquired company's former owner(s) in the event that certain earnings are met. For example, a company may acquire another for $75 million, with an additional $10 million in cash and/or stock if the acquired company's earnings outperform expectations by a certain percentage. Earn-outs are based on the acquired company's potential future earnings.

Earn-Out Agreement An agreement in which one pays a lump sum to buy a company and states that he/she will pay a further sum if certain, stated conditions are met. An earn-out agreement is a type of contingent contract.

Earthquake Insurance An insurance policy protecting the policyholder in the event an earthquake damages or destroys his/her home or other property. In general, the insurance pays to repair or rebuild the property. Deductibles on earthquake insurance tend to be quite high compared to other types of insurance.

EASDAQ A defunct European electronic securities exchange headquartered in Brussels. Founded originally as a European equivalent to NASDAQ, it was purchased by the American exchange in 2001 and became NASDAQ Europe. In 2003, it shut down operations as a result of the burst of the dot-com bubble.

Ease of Movement In technical analysis, a measure of the price of a security relative to its volume. A positive number indicates an upward movement in price, while a negative number indicates the opposite. However, a high number, whether positive or negative, indicates low volume. Thus, a high positive number shows price accumulation on low volume, while a low positive number indicates the same on high volume. Ease of movement is designed to show how much volume is needed to move the price of a security.

East African Community An international organization that seeks economic and political integration for member states. Originally established in 1967, it fell apart some years later and was re-established in 2000. It became a free trade zone for members. In 2010, it founded a common market for all goods and services across the borders of member states. It is in the process of establishing a single currency as well. Its members are Burundi, Kenya, Rwanda, Tanzania and Uganda.

East African Development Bank A bank that was established in order to promote growth in East Africa. Among other things, it provides loans and other forms of financial assistance for projects thought to contribute to African development. It was established in 1967 by the East African Community and re-chartered in 1980 as an independent entity. It maintains its headquarters in Uganda.

East African Shilling 1. A currency used between 1921 and 1969 in the parts of East Africa controlled by the British. It was pegged to the British pound. **2.** A proposed currency for the East African Community, which consists of Burundi, Kenya, Rwanda, Tanzania and Uganda. Circulation is expected to begin between 2012 and 2015.

East Asian Economic Grouping A proposed free trade zone for East and Southeast Asian nations. Originally suggested in 1990, it never came to fruition in part because it specifically excluded non-Asian nations, and Japan did not want to alienate the United States, one of its major trade partners. It was also called the East Asian Economic Caucus.

East Caribbean Dollar The currency for all members and associate members of the Organisation of Eastern Caribbean States except for the British Virgin Islands. It traces its origins to the Spanish dollar, the world's leading currency in the 18th century, but it was first issued in 1965, replacing the British West Indian dollar at par.

East German Mark The currency of the former East Germany. It was in use between 1948 and 1990, when it was theoretically pegged to the (West German) deutschemark at par, but it was largely inconvertible. After German reunification in 1990, the deutschmark replaced the East German mark.

East/West Labels In marketing, a list of addresses that may be affixed to envelopes that are arranged geographically. This may be useful in a direct mail campaign in which one seeks to target people in a certain area.

Eastern Account An offering of a new issue in which underwriters are jointly and severally responsible for placing the total offering. Each underwriting firm is liable for placing unsold portions of the issue from other underwriters. For instance, suppose an underwriting firm is responsible for placing 15% of an issue and does so. If the entire issue is not placed, the firm must assist in placing the remainder, even if it is greater than the original 15%. This contrasts with a Western account, in which underwriters are liable for placing only their assigned percentage of the offering.

Eastern Caribbean Central Bank The central bank of the Organisation of Eastern Caribbean states, which consists of Anguilla, Antigua and Barbuda, Dominica, Grenada, Montserrat, Saint Kitts and Nevis, Saint Lucia, and Saint Vincent and the Grenadines. It is responsible for issuing and stabilizing the East Caribbean dollar.

Eastern Europe Business Information Center Also called the EEBIC. An organization that provides American companies with investment opportunities, new ventures, applicable laws and other information in former Soviet bloc nations. The EEBIC was established in 1990 to assist Eastern European nations in the transition to capitalism. It is based in Washington, D.C.

Easy Fiscal Policy A policy in which a government cuts taxes and increases spending. Governments pursue easy fiscal policies most commonly during recessions or when the economy is in need of stimulus. While this can help in the short term, it can also lead to debt problems once the economy recovers.

Easy-to-Borrow List A list of securities that are easily attainable for short sellers. The easy-to-borrow list contains securities with a high degree of liquidity or a lot of outstanding shares. This guarantees delivery for shorts sellers who wish to borrow the securities and sell them immediately. It is published on a daily basis and helps short sellers and hedge funds make investment decisions more quickly.

Eat Well, Sleep Well Informal; a phrase used to describe the difference between a high risk portfolio and a low risk portfolio. One with a high risk portfolio eats well because there is a possibility of a high return, granting the investor a more luxurious lifestyle. On the other hand, one with a low risk portfolio sleeps well because he/she does not need to worry about the possibility of losing one's investment in the way one taking more risks does. See also: Markowitz portfolio theory.

Eat Your Own Dog Food Slang; to use one's company's own products. For example, an employee at Pepsi eats his own dog food when he refuses to buy or drink Coca Cola for any reason whatsoever and only drinks Pepsi products. Most of the time, however, the term refers to companies that use their own products in their operations. For instance, an internet service provider may use its own network to connect its own computers to the internet. This term became popular in the 1990s.

Eating Someone's Lunch Informal; a situation in which a company uses aggressive marketing or other techniques to increase its own market share by decreasing the market share of one or more competitors. Eating someone's lunch is obviously beneficial for the aggressive company and detrimental for the competitor. Examples of eating someone's lunch include cutting prices and issuing flashier advertising. See also: Loss leader.

Eating Stock The act of buying stock one is legally required to buy, especially when doing so is disadvantageous. For example, an underwriter may eat stock when it is required to buy stock it was unable to place with investors. Likewise, an investor with a short position on a put may be forced to buy stock at a price over its market value.

EBITDA Margin A measure of revenue relative to cash expenses from operations. One calculates the EBITDA margin as follows: EBITDA Margin = Earnings before interest, taxes, depreciation and amortization / Revenue

EBITDAX Earnings before interest, taxes, depreciation, amortization and exploration. A measure of an oil, gas, or mineral company's ability to produce income on its operations in a given year. It is calculated as the company's revenue less its expenses (such as overhead), but including its tax liability, interest paid on debt, depreciation, amortization, and what it spends in exploring for new oil, gas, or mineral deposits. It is important to note that EBITDAX does not account for one-off or otherwise unusual revenues and expenses, only recurring ones. It is used when determining whether an energy or similar company can repay a loan; often a loan used to acquire another company.

Ebone A large system of data routes and networks that became Europe's leading broadband provider during the 1990s. It operated between 1992 and 2002 when its owner company declared bankruptcy following the burst of the dot-com bubble.

EBS 1. Swiss Electronic Bourse. A computerized system linking the trading floors of the Basel, Zurich, and Geneva stock exchanges. This allows a bid or an offer made on one exchange to be executed on any of the three. **2.** Electronic Blue Sheet. A filing system the SEC requires companies and self-regulatory organizations to use when reporting some trade records. It derives its name from the fact that it was filed with physical blue sheets before the change to an electronic system.

EC 1. ISO 3166-1 alpha-2 code for the Republic of Ecuador. This is the code used in international transactions to and from Ecuadorian bank accounts. **2.** ISO 3166-2 geocode for Ecuador. This is used as an international standard for shipping to Ecuador. Each province has its own code with the prefix "EC." For example, the code for the Province of Cotopaxi is ISO 3166-2:EC-X.

Echo Award A major award in the direct marketing field. Echo awards are given in 11 categories during annual ceremonies.

Echo Bubble A small bubble that forms after another bubble bursts. That is, an echo bubble forms when the economy or, more commonly, the stock market begins to recover from a burst bubble prematurely. Analysts and investors form echo bubbles, in part, because they begin to feel more confident than the situation warrants. As with all bubbles, echo bubbles eventually burst.

Echo Chamber The tendency of members of a group to reinforce each other's views and not to contradict each other because there is little or no information presented from outside the group. An echo chamber is dangerous in business as one member may not see a flaw in another's thinking or may be afraid to point it out. However, the term is most commonly used in media to describe a self-reinforcing story. See also: Groupism.

Eclectic Paradigm An approach to analyzing whether it is beneficial for a company to make a foreign direct investment. The eclectic paradigm considers three factors. The first factor is whether a comparative advantage exists for the product the company wishes to develop in the foreign country. The second factor considers whether there is an advantage to developing that product in one country instead of another. Finally, the third factor considers whether it would be better for the company to develop the product in that foreign country itself rather than outsource development to a local company already in that country.

Eco A proposed common currency for the West African Monetary Union. Potential adoptees are Gambia, Ghana, Guinea, Liberia, Nigeria, and Sierra Leone.

Eco-Dumping The act of exporting a good from a country with new or poorly enforced environmental protection laws. These laws generally add to the cost of producing a good, so the export likely is much less expensive in an importing country than domestically produced goods of the same type. This can result in a large profit for the exporter. In addition to the costs to the environment (and the accompanying ethical questions), this can be detrimental to domestic business in the importing country. Many jurisdictions attempt to counteract dumping by setting up tariff barriers. See also: Dumping.

Eco-Label A label attached to a consumer good indicating that it is energy efficient, was produced sustainably, or is otherwise environmentally friendly. Different jurisdictions have different rules governing what products may qualify for eco-labels. Some countries and industries have voluntary schemes with standards set by professional bodies, while others use mandatory, government-issued labels.

Ecology The study of how living things interact with their surroundings. For example, an ecologist may study how a plant operates in different types of soil or whether or not bacteria thrive in various environs. Ecology is important in sustainable development to ensure that an action does not irreparably harm an environment.

E-Commerce Commerce conducted over the Internet. For example, an online publisher may sell a book to a customer, ship it to him/her, receive payment, and conduct the entire matter without ever meeting the customer. E-commerce became common in the 1990s with the popularization of the Internet. See also: dot-com bubble.

Econometrics The use of mathematics to assess economic data. There are two broad subdivisions in econometrics. Theoretical econometrics uses statistics to find strengths or weaknesses of an economic model considered on its own terms. Applied econometrics, on the other hand, considers how well a model conforms to real life data. For example, one may look at average wages for those with different levels of education to determine whether or not higher education is cost effective.

Economic Activity An act that requires use of resources or time. Examples include buying a stock or making a product to sell. The level of economic activity throughout an economy can be measured in a number of ways, with perhaps the most common being GDP.

Economic Actor A person or unit able to use land, labor or capital. An economic actor uses these resources to shape an economy, usually (though not always) for his own benefit. An economic actor may be an individual, a company, a government or even a society as a whole. In general, economic actors are assumed to be rational (that is, they make decisions that would maximize their self interest), though some analysts would contend that many actors are too short sighted to be fully rational. See also: Homo economicus.

Economic Agency A person or unit's ability to use land, labor or capital. Economic agency renders one able to help shape an economy. For example, a person with $5 in his pocket has the economic agency to decide whether to buy a beer from Arnie's or McNellie's. Likewise, a farmer with a piece of land has the ability to decide whether to grow corn or beans. Most analysts believe the agency of numerous economic actors decides how successful (or unsuccessful) an economy is. Followers of determinism, on the other hand, dispute this.

Economic Analysis The application of data to a theory of how people produce, trade, and use goods and services. One may use both qualitative and quantitative tools in economic analysis. For example, given a theory of what causes unemployment, an economic analyst may take the data in an attempt to find its true causes and compare them to the original theory. However, economic analysis may be colored by the analyst's preconceived notions, to the point in which some data is over- or underemphasized to prove one's point. On the other hand, economic analysis is vital to find the truth (or its closest approximations) about what makes an economy work.

Economic and Monetary Union A group of independent countries with a common market, no trade barriers between members, and a single currency. That is, in addition to the single currency, there are no tariffs on goods and services and citizens of participating countries may live and work in other countries with no restrictions. An economic and monetary union may be considered, for many (but not all) economic purposes, a single country. Political union and some autonomy in each country with respect to economic policy are the only aspects that keep an economic and monetary union from complete economic integration.

Economic and Social Commission for Asia and the Pacific A commission established by the United Nations to foster economic and other cooperation among states in Asia, Oceania and the South Pacific. The United States and several European countries also participate. It was founded in 1947.

Economic and Social Commission for Western Asia A commission established by the United Nations to foster economic and other cooperation among Arab states in the Middle East, along with Egypt and Sudan. It was founded in 1973 and is based in Beirut, Lebanon.

Economic and Social Council Also called ECOSOC. An organization under the United Nations charged with encouraging social and economic development worldwide. ECOSOC conducts a four-week meeting in New York each July. Its work is supplemented by the five United Nations Regional Economic Commissions. ECOSOC was established in 1945.

Economic and Social Research Council A quasi-governmental organization in the United Kingdom that conducts research in social science, especially as it relates to public policy and economic development. It was established in 1965 and is based in Swindon.

Economic Bulletin Board An Internet database containing thousands of files and documents issued by various agencies of the U.S. government. Agencies include the Department of Commerce, the Treasury Department, the Federal Reserve and others.

Economic Commission for Europe A commission established by the United Nations in 1947 to foster economic and other cooperation among European states. It discusses land administration, urban development and environmental issues.

Economic Community of Central African States Also called ECCAS. An organization founded to promote economic development and raise living standards among member nations in Central Africa. It was established in 1985 but was largely inactive until the late 1990s due to conflict in the region and non-payment of membership dues. See also: CEMAC.

Economic Community of the Great Lakes Countries An organization founded to promote economic development and commerce in Burundi, the Democratic Republic of the Congo, and Rwanda. It was established in 1976 and controls a development bank and a number of groups dealing with electricity, mining and energy. See also: CEMAC.

Economic Community of West African States Also called ECOWAS. An organization founded to promote economic integration among 15 countries in West Africa. Institutionally, it is modeled on the European Union, with a Commission, Parliament, and Court of Justice. ECOWAS controls a development bank and works to reduce barriers between member nations. It was founded in 1975.

Economic Cooperation Organization An international organization consisting of 10 non-Arab, Muslim-majority countries in central and western Asia. Its goal is to create a common market modeled along the lines of the European Union. It was established in 1985 and is based in Tehran, Iran.

Economic Cycle The period of time during which an economy evolves from a state of health to fragility to recession to recovery and back to health. Every capitalist economy has cycles to a greater or lesser extent. However, regulations may be designed to curtail them (or, more accurately, to attempt to maximize the good times while preventing the bad times); this is rarely successful. Factors affecting economic cycles include the level of inflation, the availability of capital, natural disasters, and political events. Some industries are considered countercyclical, meaning that demand for their products remains relatively constant regardless of economic circumstances; some even do better in recessions. Other industries, mainly those considered luxuries, are greatly dependent on economic cycles. An economic cycle is often colloquially called a boom-and-bust cycle.

Economic Dependence A situation in which the success of one thing depends on the success of another. This may occur within a company; for example, a project may not have funding unless another project is successful. Likewise it may occur within an economy; for example, an agricultural economy may be excessively dependent on the value of corn such that if the price of corn drops it can have serious repercussions on that economy. Many companies and economies seek to diversify to avoid economic dependence.

Economic Earnings The cash flow a company expects to realize in perpetuity, assuming no change in its capacity to produce goods or services.

Economic Exposure The risk of loss that a company experiences when investing or operating abroad. That is, when a company has interests in more than one country, economic exposure is the risk that a change in the economy in one of the countries will negatively impact its investments or operations. Examples of economic exposure include the possibilities that exchange rates could fluctuate or that a government could defaults on its debt, which would affect the foreign currency. See also: Foreign-exchange risk.

Economic Growth and Tax Relief Reconciliation Act of 2001 Legislation in the United States that reduced marginal tax rates for most American taxpayers. For example, it reduced the lowest bracket from 15% to 10% and the highest from 39.6% to 35%. It also simplified tax consequences of gifts and retirement plans. Proponents of EGTRRA claim that such policies spur economic growth. Critics point to lost government revenues and claim that the tax cuts primarily benefited the wealthy.

Economic Growth Rate The change in a nation's GDP from one period of time (usually a year) to the next. The economic growth rate shows by how much GDP has grown or shrunk in raw dollar amounts. It is considered one of the most important measures of how well or poorly an economy is performing. It is calculated thusly: Economic growth rate = (GDPyear 2 - GDPyear 1) / GDPyear 1 * 100 The economic growth rate does not adjust for inflation; therefore, the real economic growth rate is sometimes considered more accurate. One may use GNP instead of GDP in calculating the economic growth rate, but this is rare.

Economic Imperialism The deliberate or implied policy in which one country makes another dependent upon the first country's resources. This effectively gives one country control over another. See also: Imperialism.

Economic Imperialist A person or group that believes in or promotes a policy in which one country makes another dependent upon the first country's resources. This effectively gives one country control over another. See also: Imperialism.

Economic Income Income over and above what covers a person's or company's bare essentials. For example, if, after covering one's rent, food, and other basic expenses, one has a certain amount of money left over, this is one's economic income. One can spend his/her economic income and not endanger one's financial position.

Economic Moat Informal; a competitive advantage over other companies in the same industry. This comparative advantage may be cost-related; that is, one company may be able to produce a good or service more cheaply and can therefore sell it for less. However, the economic moat may also be intangible; one company's name recognition may encourage more consumers to buy its products. A "wide" or "deep" economic moat indicates a company with an economic moat difficult to overcome. See also: Comparative Advantage, Absolute Advantage.

Economic Officer An employee of the U.S. Department of State responsible for economic analysis in the country to which he/she is assigned. An economic officer studies the local economy and assesses its implications for the United States. He/she may also work in trade negotiations.

Economic Order Quantity The number of orders a brokerage receives and must fill that minimizes its obligation to keep inventory. The economic order quantity reduces the brokerage's costs to the least possible level.

Economic Output The quantity of a product that a company, sector, or economy can produce over a limited period of time. For example, if a widget factory produces 30,000 widgets in April and is open seven days a week, its output may be measured as 1,000 widgets per day. Economic output may be expressed as a monetary value and may be compared against the costs to produce the output (sometimes called the input).

Economic Planning Agency A former independent agency in Japan that helped advise the government on economic issues. In 2001, it was merged into the Ministry of Economy, Trade and Industry.

Economic Recovery Tax Act United States legislation, passed in 1981 and signed by President Ronald Reagan that cut marginal tax rates significantly. For example, it cut the top tax rate from 70% to 50% over three years and the bottom rate from 14% to 11%. The Act was intended to stimulate economic growth by putting more money in people's pockets; this concept is a key component of what became known as Reaganomics. Government revenue declined by nearly 3% of GDP as a result of the Act. It is also called the Kemp-Roth tax cut after its two principal sponsors in Congress.

Economic Rents 1. Profits in excess of what the market would otherwise command. A company can receive economic rents if it is a monopoly, or if it is part of a cartel. See also: Rent-seeking behavior. **2.** The amount of money the owner of a property can reasonably demand in order to rent that property.

Economic Risk The possibility that an economic downturn will negatively impact an investment. For example, launching a luxury product immediately before or during a recession carries a great deal of economic risk. Economic risk is closely related to political risk as government decisions impacting the economy may also affect an investment. For example, a central bank may raise interest rates or the legislature may raise taxes, and this may result in economic conditions impacting an investment.

Economic Shock An event that can cause a sudden, drastic change in an economy. For example, if it were suddenly discovered that there is no more oil in the world, this would cause economic shock, causing prices to skyrocket. Likewise, if the technology was developed to make oil obsolete and was announced with no notice, it would cause an economic shock in the other direction. An economic shock can be either positive or negative; likewise, it can be temporary or permanent. See also: Price in.

Economic Slowdown A situation in which GDP growth slows but does not decline. For example, if GDP goes from 5% growth to 3% growth, an economy is experiencing a slowdown. Most analysts do not consider a slowdown to be a recession, but unemployment may rise and productivity may decline. See also: Depression.

Economic Stimulus Act of 2008 Legislation in the United States that paid tax rebates to certain households, provided tax incentives to small businesses to encourage hiring and investment, and allowed Fannie Mae and Freddie Mac to purchase mortgages above previous limits. The act was intended to avert a recession, but it did not, and the U.S. entered a serious financial crisis later the same year.

Economic Surplus The value of a company or other organization's total assets less its total liabilities.

Economic Union A common market across more than one sovereign state with a united currency and the free exchange of capital and labor. This involves the transfer of a portion of sovereignty, especially control over monetary policy, to a central organization. Neo-Liberal economists, notably Ludwig von Mises and Friedrich von Hayek, consider an economic and monetary union the fifth stage of economic integration. The largest and most famous example of an economic union is the eurozone.

Economic Value Added A company's after-tax earnings less its opportunity cost. The economic value-added measure is a metric of how well it has performed over a given period of time compared to how it could have performed.

Economic Variable Any data accounted for in an economic model. An economic variable is any measurement that helps to determine how an economy functions. Examples include population, poverty rate, inflation, and available resources. See also: Indicator.

Economics The study of how people produce, trade, and use goods and services. Economists look at how different actors, such as individuals, companies, and governments, interact with one another to maximize the fulfillment of their needs through the use of scarce resources. Economics also includes the study of supply, demand, and the relationship between the two. There are a number of schools of thought within economics. Some major schools are classical economics, which considers the sources of production as well as the role of the Invisible Hand of the market, and Marxism, which considers the exploitation of labor by holders of capital. Other, modern schools of thought include Keynesianism, which emphasizes the role of demand as opposed to supply, and monetarism, which promotes the use of the free market and the considers the role of money supply in economic growth. See also: Macroeconomics, Microeconomics.

Economies of Scale The increase of efficiency in the making of a product by producing more of it. Economies of scale control costs carefully and extracts as much value out of every dollar spent as possible. For example, assume that labor costs at a factory are constant as long as the factory produces between 100,000 and 500,000 units per month. All other things being equal, economies of scale demand that the factory produce 500,000 units each month. Economies of scale are easier for larger companies that have greater control over their costs; indeed, it can give many larger companies a significant competitive advantage. See also: Diseconomies of scale.

Economist A person, especially but not necessarily an academic, who studies how people produce, trade, and use goods and services. Economists look at how different actors, such as individuals, companies, and governments, interact with one another to maximize the fulfillment of their needs through the use of scarce resources. Economists also study supply, demand, and the relationship between the two. There are a number of schools of thought among economists. Some major schools are classical economics, which considers the sources of production as well as the role of the Invisible Hand of the market, and Marxism, which considers the exploitation of labor by holders of capital. Other, modern schools of thought include Keynesianism, which emphasizes the role of demand as opposed to supply, and monetarism, which promotes the use of the free market and considers the role of money supply in economic growth. See also: Macroeconomics, Microeconomics.

Economy The production, trade, and use of goods and services. The economy is the interaction between different actors, such as individuals, companies, and governments, in order to maximize the fulfillment of their needs through the use of scarce resources. The relationship between supply and demand is vitally important to how an economy operates, though economists disagree on exactly how. There are a number of schools of thought within the study of the economy. Some major schools are classical economics, which considers the sources of production as well as the role of the Invisible Hand of the market, and Marxism, which considers the exploitation of labor by holders of capital. Other, modern schools of thought include Keynesianism, which emphasizes the role of demand as opposed to supply, and monetarism, which promotes the use of the free market and considers the role of money supply in economic growth. See also: Macroeconomics, Microeconomics.

Ecoterrorism Acts of terrorism committed by those who want to protect the environment. The possibility of ecoterrorism is a type of political risk for construction companies, developers and others.

Ecoterrorist A person or group that plans or commits acts of terrorism in order to protect the environment. The possibility of ecoterrorism is a type of political risk for construction companies, developers, and others.

Ecotourism Tourism structured in a way that causes the least damage or has the least impact on the area visited. It may also involve visiting places of ecological interest. Ecotourism is considered sustainable and can be beneficial for the local economy.

Ecotourist A person or group that takes trips structured in a way that causes the least damage or has the least impact on the area visited. Ecotourists may also visit places of ecological interest. Ecotourism is considered sustainable and can be beneficial for the local economy.

ECS ISO 4217 code for the Ecuadorian sucre, which was the currency of Ecuador between 1884 and 2000. Originally based on gold, it was placed on a crawling peg to the U.S. dollar in 1983. In 1999, it lost two-thirds of its value, and fell 17% in the first week of 2000. This prompted President Jamil Mahuad to replace the sucre with the dollar as the national currency. Sucres ceased to be legal tender in September 2000 and became unexchangeable in March 2001.

ECU GOST 7.67 Latin three-letter geocode for Ecuador. The code is used for transactions to and from Ecuadorian bank accounts and for international shipping to Ecuador. As with all GOST 7.67 codes, it is used primarily in Cyrillic alphabets.

Ecuadorian Sucre The national currency of Ecuador between 1884 and 2000. Its ISO 4217 code is ECS. Originally based on gold, it was placed on a crawling peg to the U.S. dollar in 1983. In 1999, it lost two-thirds of its value, and fell 17% in the first week of 2000. This prompted President Jamil Mahuad to replace the sucre with the dollar as the national currency. Sucres ceased to be legal tender in September 2000 and became unexchangeable in March 2001.

ECV ISO 4217 code for the Ecuadorean Unidad de Valor Constante, which was an accounting currency introduced in 1993 to control inflation of the Ecuadorean sucre. Its initial value was set at 10,000 sucres to one UVC. This value was readjusted to account for inflation of the sucre. The UVC was abandoned in 2000 when Ecuador adopted the U.S. dollar.

EDGAR Electronic Data Gathering, Analysis and Retrieval. An electronic system that the SEC uses to allow publicly-traded companies to make necessary filings more quickly and efficiently. Every publicly-traded company in the United States with an asset value greater than $10 million and more than 500 shareholders, as well as other companies listed on a major stock exchange, must use EDGAR to file its quarterly and annual reports and any other information it must submit to the SEC. Since its institution in 1996, filing efficiency has improved considerably.

Edge Act Legislation in the United States, passed in 1919, that allowed the Federal Reserve to charter banks that could conduct international transactions without needing to abide by the banking laws of an individual state. Because banking is more international today, there are fewer distinctions between Edge Act corporations and ordinary banks.

Edge Act Corporation A bank chartered by the Federal Reserve to conduct international banking transactions without needing to abide by the banking laws of an individual state. Edge Act corporations were established by the Edge Act in 1919 and have since undergone several legal revisions. Because banking is more international today there are fewer distinctions between Edge Act corporations and ordinary banks.

Edgy In auto sales, a slang term describing a customer with a short or questionable credit history. An edgy customer may have difficulty obtaining financing for his/her purchase.

Edict An announcement of a new law or regulation. This word is now rarely used in an economic context. However, a famous French edict in the 1600s mandated the sale of better quality cloth. Repeat violators were tied to a post with their cloth attached to their bodies.

Edward George The Governor of the Bank of England between 1993 and 2003. During his tenure, the Bank of England was given the ability to set interest rates independently from the government. He was known to keep a higher profile in the media than most of his predecessors. He lived from 1938 to 2009.

EE 1. ISO 3166-1 alpha-2 code for the Republic of Estonia. This is the code used in international transactions to and from Estonian bank accounts. **2.** ISO 3166-2 geocode for Estonia. This is used as an international standard for shipping to Estonia. Each Estonian county has its own code with the prefix "EE." For example, the code for the County of Harjumaa is ISO 3166-2:EE-37.

EEK ISO 4217 code for the Estonian kroon. It was issued in 1992, replacing the Soviet ruble. It was pegged to the deutschemark and then to the euro. In January 2011, the euro replaced the kroon.

Effective Debt The total debt of a company plus the value of its lease payments. Effective debt helps potential investors and lenders determine the ongoing expenses of a company due to debt service and similar costs. If the effective debt rises above a certain level, the company is unlikely to be profitable because of a low net cash flow.

Effective Interest Rate The interest rate on a debt or debt security that takes into account the effects of compounding. For example, if one has a fixed-income investment such as certificate of deposit that pays 3% in interest each month, the effective interest rate is more than 3% because compounding the interest results in a (slightly) greater principal each month on which the interest rate is calculated. In this example, the effective interest rate rate is calculated thus: Effective interest rate = (1 + .03/12)^12 - 1 = .0304 = 3.04%, where .03 is the simple interest rate and 12 is the number of times in a year interest is compounded. It is also known as the annual effective rate or the annual equivalent rate. See also: Stated annual interest rate, annual percentage yield.

Effective Margin The profit margin produced from an asset if one assumes financing at a certain interest rate. That is, one calculates potential profits as if income remains constant but cost of funds varies. See also: Effective yield.

Effective Net Worth The net worth of an individual or company plus what he/she/it owes in junior debt. Because, in the event of liquidation, junior debt is paid only after all senior debt is paid, the individual or company has a great deal more flexibility in repayment. This flexibility has the effect of adding to the individual or company's net worth.

Effective Sale The sale of a round lot (100 shares) of a security that determines the price of an odd lot trade. Thus, the effective sale is the first trade that takes place after a specialist receives an odd lot order.

Effective Tax Rate The tax rate one pays assuming that one pays a flat rate rather than under a progressive system. Under progressive tax systems, one pays different rates for different amounts in income. For example, one may pay 10% for the first $10,000 of income and 25% for all additional income. In practice this means that one would pay somewhere between 10% and 25%. One calculates the effective tax rate simply by taking the total tax liability, dividing by one's taxable income and multiplying by 100. Suppose one makes $20,000 in a year and is taxed under the above system. This person pays $1000 (10%) of the first $10,000 and 2500 (25%) of the second $10,000. The total tax liability is $3500, which when divided by the $20,000 of income and multiplied 100, is found to have an effective tax rate of 17.5%.

Efficiency Ratio In banking, a ratio of expenses to revenue. For example, if a bank spends $10 million and makes $15 million in a given month, its efficiency ratio is .67.

Banks desire a lower efficiency ratio because this means that the bank is making considerably more than it is spending and is therefore on sound fiscal footing. One way to conceptualize the efficiency ratio is to say it is the measure of what a bank must spend in order to make one dollar. In the above example, the bank must spend 67 cents.

Efficient Capital Market Any market in which securities are traded where new information is incorporated into prices very quickly. How efficient capital markets really are is the subject of intense debate. See also: Efficient Markets Hypothesis.

Efficient Market Theory A controversial model on how markets work. It states that the market efficiently deals with all information on a given security and reflects it in the price immediately. The model holds that technical analysis, fundamental analysis, and any speculative investing based on them are useless. The model has three forms: weak efficiency, which holds that technical analysis is ineffective, semi-strong efficiency, which holds that fundamental analysis is ineffective, and strong efficiency, which states that even insider information is immediately reflected in the security prices. Investors and academics disagree on how well the model works.

E-Filing The act or practice of filing necessary paperwork online or otherwise electronically. E-filing has become increasingly common with the advent of the Internet. Individuals may e-file their tax returns, for example. Likewise, corporations often e-file their SEC statements through EDGAR.

EG 1. ISO 3166-1 alpha-2 code for the Arab Republic of Egypt. This is the code used in international transactions to and from Egyptian bank accounts. **2.** ISO 3166-2 geocode for Egypt. This is used as an international standard for shipping to Egypt. Each Egyptian governorate has its own code with the prefix "EG." For example, the code for the Governorate of Minya is ISO 3166-2:EG-MN.

Ege A Finnish slang term for the euro.

Eggshell An obsolete Irish unit of volume approximately equivalent to 55 milliliters.

E-Government Act Legislation in the United States, passed in 2002, that created a federal Chief Information Officer who is responsible for improving citizen access to government information by publishing and otherwise promoting it over the Internet.

EGP ISO 4217 code for the Egyptian pound. It was introduced in 1834, replacing the piastre, which continued to circulate at a value of 1% of a pound. Between 1885 and 1914, the pound was effectively pegged to gold. Afterward, it was formally pegged to the British pound until 1962, when the peg switched to the U.S. dollar at various rates. The pound became a floating currency in 1989.

Egress The right to leave an area. Denial of egress may lead to conviction for false imprisonment or a similar crime.

EGY GOST 7.67 Latin three-letter geocode for Egypt. The code is used for transactions to and from Egyptian bank accounts and for international shipping to Egypt. As with all GOST 7.67 codes, it is used primarily in Cyrillic alphabets.

Egyptian Finger An ancient Egyptian unit of length approximately equivalent to 1.88 centimeters.

Egyptian Fist An ancient Egyptian unit of length approximately equivalent to 10.75 centimeters.

Egyptian Hand An ancient Egyptian unit of length approximately equivalent to 9.38 centimeters.

Egyptian Palm An ancient Egyptian unit of length approximately equivalent to 7.5 centimeters.

Egyptian Pound The currency of Egypt. It was introduced in 1834, replacing the piastre, which continued to circulate at a value of 1% of a pound. From 1885 to 1914, the pound was unofficially pegged to gold. Afterward, it was officially pegged to the British pound until 1962, when the peg switched to the U.S. dollar at various rates. The Egyptian pound became a floating currency in 1989.

Egyptian Shoulder An ancient Egyptian unit of area approximately equivalent to 13.7 square meters.

EH 1. ISO 3166-1 alpha-2 code for the Western Sahara. This is the code used in international transactions to and from Western Saharan bank accounts. **2.** ISO 3166-2 geocode for the Western Sahara. As Western Sahara is a disputed territory, there are no Western Saharan subdivisions that use the prefix "EH." However, the part of the area under Moroccan control uses the Moroccan geocode, with provinces corresponding to the prefix "MA." For example, the code for the Province of Es-Smara is ISO 3166-2:MA-ESM.

Eier A slang term for money in some German-speaking countries. Literally, the word means "eggs."

Eighth One eighth of a point or dollar. Prior to the decimalization of quotes, one might find a quote for so many eighths of a dollar. See also: Drill bit.

Eisenhower Dollar A $1 coin minted in the United States between 1971 and 1978, featuring former President Dwight D. Eisenhower.

Either/Or Facility A loan agreement whereby a bank allows a customer to borrow a certain amount of money, either in the domestic currency from one of its domestic branches or in a eurocurrency from one of its foreign branches.

Either-Way Market In eurocurrency deposit transactions between banks, a situation in which there is no difference between the bid and the ask. An either-way market is highly liquid.

Ejectment In common law, a legal action to recover title to land one owns by right. Ejectment originated in the Middle Ages but is rarely employed today. See also: Eviction.

Ekwele The currency of Equatorial Guinea between 1975 and 1985. It was replaced by the Central African CFA franc. Its plural was bipkwele.

El An obsolete Dutch unit of length roughly equivalent to 70 centimeters, with slight regional variations.

El Coloso del Norte Spanish for "the Giant of the North." This is a slang term in Latin America for the United States, and especially refers to its economic strength.

El Macho Maximo A slang term for the President of Mexico.

E-Lancer An independent contractor who performs his/her duties predominantly or exclusively online. For example, an e-lancer may edit books or design websites at home, communicating with clients and colleagues via phone and e-mail. E-lancers have fewer expenses than other independent contractors; for example, an e-lancer generally does not have to pay for an office.

Elasticity of an Option The change in a price of an option given a 1% change in the price of the underlying asset. This price is likely to change more if the option is near-the-money than if it is deep-in-the-money or deep-out-of-the-money. See also: Volatility.

Elasticity of Demand The relative stability of a security's or product's price in the face of increased or decreased demand. Elastic securities or products have prices that move as independently as possible from changes in demand. In securities, elasticity is strongly influenced by the number of shares outstanding; if a company has many shares outstanding, a large order to buy or sell them is less likely to affect the price as strongly as a similar order for a company with comparatively few shares outstanding. In other products, elasticity largely comes from whether a given product is considered a necessity or a luxury. A "necessary" product is likely to be more elastic. See also: Income Elasticity of Demand.

Elasticity of Demand and Supply 1. See: Elasticity of demand. 2. See: Elasticity of supply.

Elasticity of Supply The relative stability of a security's or product's supply in the face of increased or decreased price. Typically, an increased price results in greater supply because fewer people are buying the product; these products are considered inelastic. For example, Rolex watches are considered inelastic because a higher price results in fewer people purchasing the watches, which, in turn, results in an increased supply. On the other hand, staple products like food and clothing are considered elastic because an increased price does not necessarily lead to more supply. This is because people continue to buy food and (some) clothing. See also: Elasticity of demand.

Elder-Ray Index In technical analysis, a measure of the upward or downward pressure on a security's price. The Elder-Ray index uses two indicators: a bull power, measured as the daily high minus the exponential moving average for a certain period of time, and a bear power, measured as the daily low minus that same exponential moving average. A buy signal occurs when the bear power is negative but moving upward and the bull power has recently increased. Likewise, a sell signal occurs when the bull power is positive but moving downward and the bear power has recently fallen. One may also plot the Elder-Ray index on a chart and measure the slope of the line to confirm trends.

Elect To order a broker to change a stop limit order or a stop order to a limit order or a market order.

Electing Sale The sale that triggers a stop order. For example, suppose one makes a stop order to buy at the best available price after the price reaches $8 per share. The electing sale is a transaction on that security made for $8 a share. This sale activates the stop order. See also: Stop price.

Election Period In extendable bonds and retractable bonds, a period of time during which a bondholder must inform the issuer whether or not he/she intends to exercise the option to extend or retract. Both types of bonds allow a bondholder to change the maturity date and either move it forward or push it back, depending upon the bondholder's interests and investment goals. However, if he/she is to take advantage of this feature, he/she must inform the issuer during the election period.

Elective-Deferral Contribution A contribution to an IRA or 401(k) made from an employee's pretax income. That is, an elective-deferral contribution is tax-deferred, meaning that the retirement account holder does not pay taxes on what goes into the account until he/she begins making withdrawals.

Electrical Exemption Clause A clause in some insurance policies stating that damages caused to electrical appliances by an improper or artificial electrical current are only covered if the current causes a fire. Even then, the clause states that the policy will only provide coverage for fire damages and not for repairs to the electrical appliances or anything else. An electrical exemption clause is also called a dynamo clause.

Electronic Benefits Transfer A system in which a government grants a citizen a card with features like a debit card to dispense public service benefits. For example, most U.S. states use electronic benefits transfer for food stamps. The recipient of food stamps receives a debit card with a certain amount of money pre-programmed into it and the recipient can use it to buy food. Not all establishments accept electronic benefits transfers for payment (just as not all stores accepted actual food stamps), but many do. Electronic benefits transfers are also sometimes used for other welfare programs.

Electronic Bill Presentment A message delivered via e-mail or access to a secure website describing what a debtor owes a creditor for a given month. Any person who pays his/her bills online is eligible for electronic bill presentment, and many companies offer it.

Electronic Blue Sheet A form that clearing firms submit to the SEC to record transactions. The term derives its name from the fact that forms were actual blue sheets before electronic submission became common.

Electronic Check Conversion A form of payment in which the payer writes the payee a check, but in which the actual funds are debited/credited electronically. The U.S. Treasury has used electronic check conversion to make large payments online.

Electronic Communication Network A computer system that facilitates over-the-counter trading as well as exchange trading. The electronic communication network sends buy or sell orders to the appropriate specialiston the floor of a stock exchange, bypassing the floor broker. A company running an ECN charges a fee for its services.

Electronic Communications Privacy Act Legislation in the United States, passed in 1986, that protects most communication sent over a computer network from search or seizure without a warrant. The Act requires law enforcement officials to abide by the same requirements for computer communications as they do for telephone communications. Exemptions established by the Act, such as access to records kept by service providers, have proven controversial.

Electronic Data Interchange A strictly structured form of business-to-business communication. Electronic data interchange involves the transfer of formal documents, such as orders, invoices, and even checks. Companies provide EDI services to more than 80,000 clients, but the system receives significant competition from various services offered over the Internet.

Electronic Exchange A securities exchange in which traders do not physically meet to buy and sell securities. Instead, all trading takes place over a computer system, which may be operated from almost anywhere. Electronic exchanges may or may not have specified trading hours. Electronic exchanges differ from physical location exchanges, which have a central location to meet.

Electronic Fund Transfer Act Legislations in the United States, passed in 1978, that establishes rights and responsibilities for persons and institutions that use electronic funds transfers. Persons who discover errors on their statements have 60 days to report the error or they are responsible for the loss. Legal liability for lost or stolen EFT cards is limited provided that the financial institution is informed of the loss or theft.

Electronic Funds Transfer System Any computerized system that facilitates a transaction in which money, securities, or some other good changes hands. Examples of electronic funds transfer include receiving cash out of an ATM and placing an order to buy a stock over the telephone.

Electronic Quotation Service An online service provided for brokers and dealers in the over-the-counter markets. The service allows participants to see the current price for OTC securities and make investment decisions accordingly. It is operated by Pink Sheets LLC.

Electronic Wallet Software that allows an online shopper to pay for his/her purchases easily and conveniently. See also: Paypal.

Elephant Informal; a very large institutional investor. Elephants can have huge impacts on the market for both good and bad. See also: Too-Big-to-Fail.

Eleven Bond Index An index of the average yield of 11 municipal bonds tracked by Bond Buyer's. These bonds have 20-year maturities and an average rating of AA. The eleven bond index is considered an important benchmark index for the bond market.

Eli Lilly and Company A major pharmaceutical company in the United States. It manufactures drugs for diabetes, cancer and other diseases. It was established in 1876 and is based in Indianapolis.

Eligible Margin Collateral that may be used for a margin account. When one borrows funds from a broker in order to buy on margin, one must generally put up collateral in order to guaranteerepayment. Very often the collateral is the security (or securities) bought on the margin account; however, certain low-priced stocks are sometimes not accepted as collateral and the investor must use some other collateral. The collateral a broker accepts is known as the eligible margin. See also: Restricted account.

Eligible Rollover Distribution The amount of money in an IRA or other qualified retirement plan that may be rolled over into another plan. Rollovers occur most often when a person changes employers; they may occur without penalty once per year.

Elimination Period In disability income insurance or loss of income insurance, the period of time that must transpire before the insurer begins to make payments covering the claim. That is, if one suffers an injury or a long term illness that results in substantial loss of income, the insurance policy sets an elimination period, at least in part to ensure that the disability or sickness is in fact long-term. The elimination period is often thought of as the deductible for disability and loss of income insurance as the policyholder is responsible for expenses incurred during it. For the disability income insurance run by the Social Security Administration, the elimination period is five months. Private plans often include 90-day periods, or shorter periods in exchange for higher premiums.

Eliot Spitzer An American politician. As attorney general of New York, he was known for prosecuting white collar crime, particularly securities fraud and other crimes related to the financial sector. He served as governor of New York in 2007 and 2008. Spitzer was born in 1959.

Elizabeth Phillips An American socialist and game designer, also known as Lizzie Magie. She is best known for her invention of The Landlord's Game, a board game that was the precursor to Monopoly. She created it around 1903 to demonstrate what she thought of as the abuses created by the capitalist system. Phillips lived from 1866 to 1848.

Elizur Wright An American mathematician. He developed the first modern mortality tables to determine premiums, which helped ensure that life insurance remained a viable business model. He was also a noted abolitionist. Wright lived from 1804 to 1885.

Ell An obsolete unit of length equivalent to 45 inches.

Elle A German unit of length. Its measure varied in different German-speaking areas, but generally was between 400 and 800 millimeters. It became obsolete with the adoption of the metric system in the 1870s.

Elliott Wave Theory A theory of price movements stating that all stocks move in waves roughly analogous to waves found in nature. The Elliott Wave Theory holds that stock prices move up a total of five times and down a total three times in succession; once the cycle is completed, it starts again. Unlike other, similar theories, the Elliott Wave Theory does not apply any particular time frame to its waves.

Elves The analysts who appeared on the television show Wall Street Week, which aired between 1970 and 2005. The elves used technical analysis to predict future price movements in the stock market. They operated two indices using technical indicators; the Wall Street Week Index was used between 1970 and 1989 and was well regarded for its usefulness. The Elves Index, used between 1989 and 2001, was noted more for its uses as a contrarian index; at least one analyst suggested one should do the opposite of what the Elves Index advised. The term "elf" itself was a playful reference to the Gnomes of Zurich.

Elves Index An index featured on the television program Wall Street Week, which aired between 1970 and 2005. The index consisted of 10 indicators of analysts' personal views on the direction of the market over the coming three months. The Elves Index was noted more for its use as a contrarian index; at least one analyst suggested one should do the opposite of what the Elves Index advised. The index was used between 1989 and 2001. See also: Gnomes of Zurich, Elves.

Em A unit of length used in printing. An em is one-sixth of an inch. It is also called a pica.

Embargo The legal prohibition of the sale of goods to or purchase of goods from a country. An embargo may be partial. For instance, a country may boycott all bananas from a certain country. An embargo usually occurs for political or security reasons. For example, in 1962 the United States imposed an embargo on nearly all trade with Cuba in response to the nationalization of American business interests in Cuba.

Embassy 1. A group of diplomats charged with representing the interests of a country to a foreign government. For example, the embassy of the United States in London represents the U.S. in the United Kingdom. The head of an embassy is usually called an ambassador. **2.** More commonly, the building in which an embassy keeps its office. This office is extraterritorial, which means it is the sovereign territory of the embassy's government, not of the host country.

Embedded Option An option or other special provision attached to a bond. For example, an embedded option in a convertible bond is the ability of the bondholder to exchange the bond for shares in the underlying common stock. Likewise, an embedded option may enable the issuer to call a callable bond before maturity. It differs from a bare option, which is the trading of a standalone security separately from any bond.

Embedded Value The value of a company that is calculated by adding together its adjusted net asset value and the present value of potential future profits. That is, the embedded value considers what the owners of the company have received in the past and what they are likely to receive in the future. Embedded value is an inherently conservative valuation method, excluding intangible assets and assuming that earnings will not increase in the future. The measure is most common outside North America, especially in the insurance industry.

Embezzle To steal funds placed under one's responsibility. For example, a trustee has a fiduciary responsibility to use the funds in a trust for the beneficiary and for no other purpose. If he pockets some of the funds instead, he commits embezzlement. This crime can result in significant jail time, depending on the amount stolen. See also: White collar crime.

Emblements An agricultural crop, such as corn or wheat, that the renter of a piece of real estate grows each year. The renter has the right to maintain the emblements as personal property, even if the lease to the land expires before the crop matures.

Emergency Banking Act of 1933 Legislation in the United States that was used to respond to the banking crisis of the Great Depression quickly until more long-lasting legislation could be passed. It established regulations for the orderly liquidation of banks that could not be saved and the reorganization of those that could. It also gave the President power to declare a national banking emergency, which would give the President complete control over the nation's finances and render it illegal for banks to operate without presidential approval. It was largely replaced later in 1933 by the Glass-Steagal Act.

Emergency Economic Stabilization Act of 2008 Legislation in the United States that authorized $700 billion for the government to purchase high risk assets (particularly mortgage-backed securities) from banks and other financial institutions to keep these institutions from collapsing due to defaults. It also allowed this money to be used to provide capital directly to banks. The Act was passed because it was thought that the U.S. (and indeed the global) financial industry was on the verge of collapse because of excessive risk taking. It is widely considered a bailout of American (and some foreign) banks. See also: Late 2000s recession.

Emergency Fund An account where an individual deposits funds to use in an emergency. That is, if one finds himself laid off and unable to work due to a medical emergency (or, otherwise, in a financially difficult position) the emergency fund helps prevent destitution while one finds another job or recuperates. Many analysts recommend keeping three to six months of living expenses in an emergency fund, while others recommend setting aside a year's worth of expenses. See also: Rainy day fund, Equalization Reserve.

Emergency Home Finance Act of 1970 Legislation in the United States that created Freddie Mac, a federally chartered company that guarantees mortgages granted to low- or middle-income households. The Act came about as a result of pressure to provide competition to Fannie Mae, which is another federally chartered company that does much the same thing. There was concern in the investment community that without this competition, government guaranteed mortgages would crowd out the market, which would be detrimental to non-guaranteed mortgages. Both Freddie Mac and Fannie Mae were put in federal receivership in 2008.

Emerging Company Marketplace On the American Stock Exchange, a service once offered to help new and small-cap publicly-traded companies meet listing requirements. The emerging company marketplace no longer exists.

Emerging Industry An industry producing one or more products without an established market or customer base. Companies in emerging industries often spend a great deal on research and development and nearly always have little to no revenue in their early years. As a result, stocks in emerging industries carry very high risk; however, if a company becomes successful, it can result in large returns. For example, most dot-com companies had little or no revenue in their early years, and, indeed, most went bankrupt. However, a few, such as Google and Amazon, became prominent and profitable for their shareholders. See also: Industry Life Cycle.

Emerging Issues Task Force A standing committee formed by the Financial Accounting Standards Board with a directive to investigate and make recommendations on issues in accounting as they arise. It seeks to establish uniform practices on new issues before divergent practices become widely accepted for different regions and/or firms. To this end, the EITF holds public meetings from time to time to discuss new issues and to receive input on the recommendations it ought to make. It consists of accountants from the larger accounting firms and the chief accountant at the SEC.

Emerging Market An economy in a country noted for growing liquidity, stability, infrastructure and other positive features, though not to the same extent as exists in the developed world. That is, emerging markets are economies that have increasingly important roles in the international stage and may one day become principal players, but they have not yet arrived at that level. Political factors may help or encumber emerging markets as they attempt to gain wealth and prominence. Major examples of emerging markets are Brazil, Russia, India, and China. Smaller economies, such as Bahrain, Egypt, Colombia, and others are also considered emerging markets. Emerging markets exist in less developed countries relative to the United States and Europe; these countries nonetheless have vibrant, active economies. See also: International development, BRIC.

Emerging Market Clearing Corporation A clearing corporation that performs clearing services for bonds and other debt securities issued in developing countries. Established in 1998 with expanded clearing services becoming operational in 2002, it is associated with the Depository Trust & Clearing Corporation.

Emerging Market Equity Fund A mutual fund that invests exclusively in stocks issued by companies in a developing country. Emerging market equity funds may concentrate in a region, such as the Middle East, or in a given industry, such as telecommunications stocks in emerging markets. Emerging market equity funds tend to be volatile, as they are heavily exposed to political risk. However, they offer the possibility of a high return. At least some emerging markets, notably Eastern Europe, experienced high growth in the 1990s. See also: BRIC.

Emerging Market Fund A mutual fund that invests predominantly or exclusively in the securities of a developing country or a group of developing countries. Emerging market funds may concentrate in a region, such as the Middle East, or in a given industry, such as oil in emerging markets. Emerging market funds tend to be volatile as they are heavily exposed to political risk. However, they offer the possibility of a high return because at least some emerging markets, notably Eastern Europe, experienced high growth in the 1990s. See also: BRIC.

Emerging Markets Free Index An index published by Morgan Stanley Capital International (MSCI) that tracks stocks in developing countries with a great deal of foreign direct investment. Example countries with stocks tracked by the index include Argentina, Jordan, and Mexico. As with all MSCI indices, it is weighted for market capitalization.

Emilio Botin A Spanish banker born in 1934. In 1986, he became president of Banco de Santander, a role he inherited from his father. As the result of mergers and acquisitions, this bank became the largest in Spain in 1999 and the second largest in Europe in 2004.

Eminent Domain The right of a government to force the sale of real estate by a private individual or corporation in certain cases. For example, if a municipality is building a road, it may exercise eminent domain to purchase the land along which the road is going to run. While the private owners are paid for these purchases, they may not refuse to sell. The term is most common in the United States. The concept is called compulsory purchase in the United Kingdom and compulsory acquisition in Australia.

E-Mini A futures contract in which the underlying asset is a small portion of an index future, which is a futures contract where the underlying asset is a stock index. For example, an e-mini may represent a fraction of an index future on the NASDAQ 100. E-minis are more affordable and easier to sell than standard index futures. However, they are still speculative investments and subject to the same risks as other futures. As with other index futures, they are settled in cash. They are traded on the Chicago Mercantile Exchange.

Emirati Dirham The currency of the United Arab Emirates. It was introduced in 1971 upon the formation of the United Arab Emirates and their complete independence from Great Britain. Previously, both the Bahraini dinar and the Qatari riyal (then known as the Qatar-Dubai riyal) were used in what is now the UAE. While it was pegged to the IMF special drawing rights in 1978, the dirham has been pegged to the U.S. dollar unofficially for most of its history. The UAE officially pegged the dirham to the dollar in 1997.

Empire-Building The act or practice of a manager or employee attempting to increase his/her influence over the company for which he/she works without regard for what is best for the company. A variety of factors may influence empire-building, such as the possibility for a higher salary or simply the prestige that comes from being an important person. Empire-building is frowned upon in most sectors, as it does not benefit shareholders and can in fact harm them if an empire-builder is neglecting the actual business at hand.

Employable Describing a person who is likely to find gainful employment. A person may be employable because he/she has a skill set matching the available jobs in the area. A long gap in employment may reduce a person's employability as his/her skills may become obsolete. Education or training, on the other hand, may increase a person's employability.

Employee A person who works for another on a full-time or part-time basis. An employer directs where the employee perform work, what he/she does, and so forth. In general, an employee is paid a wage or salary by the employer in exchange for his/her time and/or production.

Employee Benefits Security Administration An agency under the U.S. Department of Labor responsible for enforcing the Employee Retirement Income Security Act. Specifically, EBSA enforces a number of regulations designed to ensure that employers and other involved parties do not misuse the funds entrusted to them in retirement accounts. Among other provisions, EBSA requires retirement account managers to provide information to account holders on a regular basis. It also enforces standards for managers' use of discretionary authority. Until 2003, EBSA was known as the Pension and Welfare Benefits Administration, and before 1986 it was the Pension and Welfare Benefits Program.

Employee Contribution Plan An employer-sponsored retirement plan in which the employee makes contributions through payroll deductions. That is, rather than receiving the full amount in salary or wages, the employer automatically places a portion into the retirement plan on behalf of the employee. These contributions may or may not be tax deductible, depending on the type of plan. Sometimes, though not always, employers provide matching contributions for employee contribution plans. See also: IRA, 401(k).

Employee Retirement Income Security Act of 1974 Legislation in the United States, passed in 1974, that established a number of regulations to ensure that employers and other involved parties do not misuse the funds entrusted to them in retirement accounts. Among other provisions, the Act requires retirement account managers to provide information to account holders on a regular basis. It also sets standards for managers' use of discretionary authority and allows account holders to sue their pensions for unpaid benefits.

Employee Share Ownership Trust An employee benefit in which employees are sold shares in the publicly-traded company for which they work through a trust. ESOTs are designed to help give employees equity in the company to boost morale and thereby improve productivity. It also provides the company with a source of revenue. Buying shares through an ESOT gives employees various tax benefits, and may give employees a greater say in the election of the board of directors. It is similar to, but different from, an employee stock ownership plan.

Employee Stock Ownership Plan An employee benefit in which employees are issued or sold shares in the publicly-traded company for which they work after a certain number of days of employment. ESOPs are designed to give employees equity in the company to boost morale and thereby improve productivity. ESOPs receive various tax benefits, and may give employees a greater say in the election of the board of directors.

Employee Stock Purchase Plan An employee benefit that some firms offer allowing employees to use payroll deductions to buy shares in the firm at a discount from their fair market value. The firm offers this to employees at certain times; those who participate in the program allow the payroll deductions to accumulate for a certain number of pay periods. At the end of the period the firm uses the funds to purchase the number of shares worth that amount. The percentage discount varies from firm to firm, but can be as much as 15%.

Employer A person or company that hires one or more persons to perform work on a full-time or part-time basis. The employer directs where the employee performs work, what he/she does, and so forth. In general, an employer is responsible for paying a wage or salary to the employee in exchange for his/her time and/or production. An employer may be required to pay a portion of employees' taxes.

Employer Matching Contribution Money an employer offers to an employee's IRA or other retirement fund. Normally employers will offer an equal amount that the employee contributes up to a certain dollar amount or percentage of income. This is considered an employee benefit and allows a worker to save more (and accrue applicable interest) without enduring financial hardship.

Employer Sponsored Retirement Plan A retirement plan in which both an employer and an employee make contributions into an account each month. The contributions are invested on behalf of an employee, who may begin to make withdrawals after retirement. Typically, employer sponsored retirement plans are tax-deferred, meaning that the employee does not pay taxes on the funds in the pension until he/she begins making withdrawals. However, some plans are not tax-deferred, and, instead, employees make tax-free withdrawals. Employers are not legally required to offer retirement plans, though most major companies do. Plans may have defined contributions, defined benefits, or both. See also: 401(k), IRA.

Employer's Liability Insurance Insurance that protects an employer from damages from a lawsuit resulting from an injury due to the employer's negligence. It does not cover lawsuits resulting from discrimination, wrongful dismissal and so forth. Employer's liability insurance is required in some jurisdictions and may be rolled in with a worker's compensation policy.

Employment at Will A form of employment in which either the employee or the employer may terminate employment with or without cause and with or without notice. For example, an employee may quit as soon as he/she finds a better job. Likewise, the employer may fire an employee even if he/she comes to work on time and performs diligently. Employment at will is not allowed in all jurisdictions and it is restricted even where it exists. For example, an employer ordinarily may not fire a worker on racial or religious grounds.

Employment Cost Index An index compiled by the Bureau for Labor Statistics estimating the cost of hiring and paying the American workforce. Analysts closely monitor the employment cost index: an unexpectedly large increase may result in downward pressure in the market. This is because a rise in the cost of paying employees reduces profits, which in turn reduces stock prices. It may also reduce bond prices because rises in the ECI are seen as a harbinger of inflation.

Employment Rate The number of persons who have jobs, expressed as a percentage of the total workforce. The employment rate is not used as commonly as the unemployment rate but it is still an important indicator of the state of the wider economy. It is a lagging indicator; that is, following a recession, the employment rate tends not to grow to any significant extent until the remainder of the economy has recovered. This is because of the high risk and expense of creating jobs.

Empty Head and Pure Heart Test An SEC rule stating that under most circumstances, the only investor allowed to trade with insider information is one who is making a tender offer, which is an offer to buy shares in a company directly from shareholders at a price well in excess of its market value. The empty head and pure heart test is governed by Rule 14e-3b.

EMTA A professional association for traders and investors in emerging markets. It provides a forum for these market participants to discuss current issues in emerging market investing and, when possible, to devise solutions to problems by consensus. It was established in 1990 in the wake of the debt rescheduling in Mexico and Venezuela. See also: Brady plan.

E-Nail A slang term for an e-mail in which a person or concept is soundly criticized. In general, senior persons in a company or organization are copied on an e-nail so that it is circulated as widely as possible.

Encashment The act of paying a loan or other liability in cash, as opposed to some other means such as check or credit card.

Encryption The coding of sensitive information for transfer online or otherwise electronically. One may encrypt data to prevent anyone other than the intended recipient from accessing it. For example, if one buys a product online and enters credit card information into an electronic form, that information is usually encrypted so hackers and potential identity thieves cannot use it for illicit purposes.

Encumbered Describing securities or assets that are subject to one or more liens. That is, encumbered securities belong to one person or entity but are subject to a claim by another. Encumbered securities or assets may not be sold until the lien or debt on them is satisfied. One of the most common encumbered assets is a house with a mortgage. A homeowner may not sell the house until the mortgage is paid off (though, in practice, the proceeds from the sale of the house pay off the mortgage).

Encumbrance 1. In accounting, an amount of money that one is required to spend on a stated thing in the future. For example, a portion of the proceeds of a sale may be encumbered to pay for the cost of goods sold. **2.** In real estate, any claim of ownership that may cloud the legitimacy of a sale. See also: Bad title.

Endaze A Turkish measure of length approximately equivalent to 65 centimeters. It became obsolete when Turkey made the metric system mandatory in 1933.

Ending Inventory Goods and materials available for sale at the end of an accounting period or fiscal year. Comparing the ending inventory to the beginning inventory may help a company determine whether it overestimated the materials it needs to operate, or customers' demand for their products.

End-of-Year Convention In accounting, treating cash flows as if they occurred only on the last day of the fiscal year. This applies to both incoming and outgoing cash flows. The end-of-year convention affects the calculation and discounting of future cash flows. It is the opposite of the dates convention, which recognizes cash flows on the date they are received or paid.

Endogenous Uncertainty Uncertainty regarding a firm's state, or a financial situation that could be resolved if the firm would simply announce it. For example, speculative investing may increase prior to the release of an earnings statement, driving the stock price up or down because of the endogenous uncertainty stemming from the fact that the company has not yet released the statement. In other words, endogenous uncertainty is under the control of the company it regards. See also: Exogenous uncertainty.

Endogenous Variable A variable with a value determined by the equation in which it exists. See also: Dependent Variable.

Endorsement 1. The payee's signature on the back of a check indicating that the payee has received the check. Banks require that payees endorse checks before they may be cashed or deposited. **2.** An amendment to a document, especially an insurance policy. Informally, they are called riders.

Endorsement in Blank The signature of the owner of a security transferring ownership to another without any other party being named as the recipient. Whoever holds an endorsement in blank is assumed to be the owner. This is risky because there is no guarantee that the intended recipient will actually receive it. This has become less common over time as ownership records increasingly are kept electronically.

Endorser The payee on a check whose signature appears on the back of the check. The signature (called an endorsement) indicates that the payee has received the check. Banks require payees to endorse checks before they can be cashed or deposited.

Endowment 1. Money or property that one or more donors leaves to an institution, especially a non-profit, with the expectation that it will be invested. That is, the institution invests its endowment and helps finance its activities with the profit from the investments. Examples of institutions that commonly have endowments are charities, scholarship funds, and universities. **2.** A provision in some life insurance agreements whereby the insurance company pays the death benefit when the policyholder reaches a certain age. For example, rather than waiting for death to actually occur, the company may pay the death benefit when the policyholder turns 100 years old.

Endowment Funds Portfolios for some non-profits, especially universities, hospitals, and foundations. Endowment funds are usually set aside for capital expenditures, and are only used on an as-needed basis. Having a great deal of money in an endowment fund indicates that the organization is likely on sound financial footing.

Endowment Life Insurance A term life insurance policy whereby the insurance company agrees to pay the death benefit when the policyholder reaches a certain age. For example, rather than waiting for death to actually occur, the company may pay the death benefit when the policyholder turns 100 years old. Because the insurance company will pay the death benefit whether or not the policyholder dies in the designated period of time, premiums on endowment life insurance are high.

Enduring Purpose A statement of principles, beliefs, and/or goals to guide a company in the conduct of its business. See also: Mission Statement.

Energy Mutual Fund A mutual fund that invests predominantly or exclusively in energy stocks. As with other sector funds, energy mutual funds are exposed to systematic risk inherent to energy companies. For example, an energy mutual fund will likely perform less well if oil prices drop because many energy companies are largely dependent on profits from oil and related commodities.

Energy Stock A stock in a company whose predominant business is the production or sale of energy. Energy stock may include shares in both upstream companies, such as oil exploration firms, and downstream companies, such as oil refineries. Energy stocks have historically been dominated by oil and natural gas, but alternative energy companies are sometimes publicly-traded as well. Energy stock prices are largely determined by the supply and demand for energy and as such tend to be seasonal; they are also quite sensitive to political events. See also: Political risk.

Energy Tax Incentives Act of 2005 Legislation in the United States that provided $14.5 billion in tax deductions and tax credits for businesses and individuals who invest in energy conservation, renewable energy, domestically-produced fossil fuels and/or energy infrastructure.

Enforcement Standards How an organization chooses to enforce its rules or to adjudicate disputes. For example, suppose a government criminalizes tax fraud but not tax avoidance. In lieu of more specific rulings from the government, the tax collection agency may set its own rules as to the difference between the two. These rules are the agency's enforcement standards.

Enhanced Indexing A portfolio management strategy that mainly tracks a certain index but is designed to perform slightly better than that index. Typically, enhanced indexing involves holding roughly the same securities as the index in roughly the same proportion; however, the portfolio manager often overweights certain stocks or industries if he/she believes them to be undervalued. This process is called tilting. See also: Enhanced index fund.

Enhanced Structural Adjustment Facility Loans formerly made by the IMF to developing countries to finance projects, such as infrastructure, that will promote economic growth in the long term. Loans were made at 0.5% interest and repayment was deferred for five and a half years. They came due in 10 years. These loans were issued from 1987 to 1999.

Enhancement Any change that leads to an increase in the value of any good, service, or product. Two obvious examples of enhancement are a decrease in supply and an increase in demand.

Enrico Braggiotti A Turkish-Monegasque banker born in 1923. He joined Banca Commerciale Italiana in 1950, becoming its president in 1988. He was noted for his role in the privatization of a number of Italian banks in the 1980s. He began working for an investment bank in Monaco in 1990, retiring in 2006.

Enrolled Agent A person authorized to represent a taxpayer to the IRS administrative courts for audit and other purposes. In order to become an enrolled agent, one must pass an exam and file Form 23 with the IRS. It should be noted that certified public accountants and attorneys may serve as enrolled agents without special licensing.

Enrolled Retirement Plan Agent A person authorized to represent an employer to the IRS administrative courts for tax purposes related to their annuities, pensions, and other retirement plans. In order to become an enrolled retirement plan agent, one must pass an exam and file Form 23-EP with the IRS.

Enron An energy company that perpetrated one of the largest accounting frauds in history. Established in its latest form in 1985 in Omaha, it moved its headquarters to Houston and provided oil, natural gas, electric, water, and bandwidth products. Its share price eventually climbed to $85 because it used what it termed "innovative" techniques, including weather futures, to build its profit. In 2001, however, it was revealed that many of its assets were either overpriced or completely fictional; losses were hidden in offshore subsidies; and most profits were fraudulent. Its share price collapsed to $0.30 and Enron filed for bankruptcy in December 2001. See also: Arthur Andersen, WorldCom, Tyco International.

Enronitis Informal; the attribution of a share price decline to bad accounting. The word derives from the Enron scandal of 2001.

Enroute Expenses The expenses an employee incurs whilst traveling internationally for an employer. Enroute expenses include airfare, lodging and food, among other things. An employer either must pay the enroute expenses directly or reimburse the employee.

Enterprise A company or any other business.

Enterprise for the Americas Initiative A program of the U.S. government allowing countries in Latin America and the Caribbean to redirect a portion of the debt owed to the United States to a fund aimed at helping local children and the environment. In order to be eligible for the EAI, a government first must have moved toward opening itself for foreign direct investment. It was established by President George H.W. Bush in 1991.

Enterprise Fund A government-owned fund that sells goods and services to the general public. Enterprise funds are common at the local level. They must abide by the same generally accepted accounting principles that private companies do.

Enterprise Multiple A way to determine the value of a company, especially if a person is considering buying shares or the company as a whole. It is calculated by taking its enterprise value and dividing by its EBITDA. The enterprise multiple is useful because, unlike other ratios like the P/E, it takes the company's debt into account (because the enterprise value considers debt). A low enterprise multiple indicates that the company is undervalued while a high multiple indicates that it is overvalued.

Enterprise Value The market value of a company if it were (hypothetically) to be taken over. It is calculated by adding its market capitalization to its debt, minority interest, and preferred equity at market value, then subtracting its cash or cash equivalents. This is an important aspect of business valuation and accounting.

Enterprise Zone An area that has special incentives available for those who start companies or other organizations. For example, an enterprise zone may offer tax cuts to small businesses that open inside its jurisdiction. Enterprise zones are a popular way to rejuvenate dilapidated areas or otherwise to promote economic development.

Enterprise-Value-to-Sales A ratio of a company's enterprise value to its sales. The enterprise value is the theoretical price of a takeover and includes a wide variety of assets and liabilities, while sales is the value of the products the company sells in a given year. Generally speaking, a low ratio is considered better because it indicates that a company has high sales relative to its value. However, a high ratio may indicate that investors believe that its sales will soon rise.

Entertainment Expense Deduction A reduction in one's income for purposes of calculating one's income tax. The entertainment expense deduction is equal to up to 50% of what a business spends in the course of buying meals for or otherwise entertaining a client, customer, or employee. In order to be eligible for the deduction, one must be able to prove that one conducted business with the person being entertained.

Entrepot 1. A port where goods can be imported from a ship, stored, and then re-exported or transported to their final destination. **2.** More generally, a warehouse.

Entrepreneur The possessor or owner of a for-profit organization. The term is usually applied to small business owners, who bear the majority of the risk and reap the most benefit from a company. It can also relate to (individual) majority shareholders who are involved in the operation of his/her business. Entrepreneurs are generally accepted as integral to the success of a capitalist system.

Entropy Disorder in any system. It is the opposite of efficiency.

Entry Level Job A job available to a person with academic or some other qualification but little practical experience in the area. For example, a recent graduate engineer may take an entry level job at a firm where he/she assists a senior engineer in his/her own projects. An entry level job may give one the opportunity to develop experience and may lead to advancement of one's career. However, some entry level jobs do not pay well.

Envelope In technical analysis, two moving averages of a security's price indicating its upper and lower limits. That is, a price tends not to move above the higher moving average or below the lower moving average. Analysts use envelopes to help them determine buy and sell signals. When a price reaches the higher moving average, analysts may declare a sell signal, while they may declare a buy signal when a price reaches the lower moving average.

Environmental Risk The risk that a certain business venture or activity will cause destruction to the surrounding natural environment. For example, if oil reserves were discovered in a national park, there would be the environmental risk that exploiting the reserves might harm or destroy some of the park's wildlife. While environmental risk implies some moral or at least reputational risk, it also carries economic consequences. A company with environmental risk often has to pay fees for exemptions from certain policies, and it is usually responsible for cleaning up the environment in case it causes a slow or sudden disaster. See also: Cap-and-trade.

EOMMEX Hellenic Organization for Small and Medium Sized Enterprises & Handicraft. A quasi-governmental organization in Greece that works with small and medium sized businesses to maximize their competitiveness. It also advises the government on policies that would best benefit these businesses. It was established in 1977 and is based in Athens.

EOY An abbreviation for end of year. A company must have its records in order by the end of the year, especially to pay its taxes and compute profits and losses.

Eparchy In Cyprus, an administrative subdivision approximately equivalent to a county or province.

Equal Credit Opportunity Act Legislation in the United States passed in 1974, outlawing discrimination against race, sex, national origin, age, welfare status, and other identifiers in the extension of credit. That is, the Act forbids banks and other financial institutions from using these factors when it decides whether or not to make a loan or open a line of credit for a client. Under the Act, the creditor can only consider the individual's creditworthiness. It also requires potential creditors to approve or deny applications for credits within 30 days and to explain why upon request. It is enforced by the Federal Trade Commission.

Equal Dollar Swap The sale of common stock in a publicly-traded company and the use of the proceeds to buy as many convertible securities in the same or a similar company as the proceeds will buy. For example, one may sell 1000 shares of AT&T at $25 per share and use the money to buy as many convertible bonds in AT&T as can be had for $25,000. An equal dollar swap gives the investor greater flexibility for the same investment than simply owning the common stock. See also: Equal Shares Swap.

Equal Percentage Contribution Rule The requirement that certain pension plans sponsored by employers receive equal contributions from both employers and employees.

Equal Shares Swap The sale of common stock in a publicly-traded company and the use of the proceeds to buy just as many convertible securities such that one may use the conversion option to have the same amount of common stock as before. For example, one may sell 1000 shares of AT&T and use the money to buy as many convertible bonds in AT&T as needed to be able to convert to 1000 shares. An equal shares swap gives the investor greater flexibility than simply owning the common stock while at the same time allowing the investor the ability to have the same amount of common stock if needed or desired.

Equalization Reserve An account where an insurance company deposits funds to use in an emergency. That is, if an insurer finds itself in a position where it needs to pay more claims than it had anticipated, it may use funds from the equalization reserve to ensure that it fulfills its contractual obligations. An equalization reserve helps prevent any potential cash flow problems for the insurance company. It is especially useful in the event of an act of God, such as a flood or fire, where many policyholders live in the affected area. See also: Rainy day fund, Emergency fund.

Equalizing Dividend A one-time, special dividend a publicly-traded company may declare and pay when it changes its dividend schedule. When a company changes its dividend schedule, it often deprives shareholders of income they would have received otherwise. The equalizing dividend is intended to compensate shareholders for this loss.

Equatorial Guinean Ekwele The former currency of Equatorial Guinea. It was introduced in 1975, seven years after the country's independence. Until 1979, it was spelled ekuele. After the "ekwele" spelling was adopted, its plural became bipkwele. In 1985, it was replaced by the CFA franc at a rate of four bipkwele to one franc.

Equilibrium A state of stable prices brought about by the rough equality of supply and demand. This applies for consumer goods, securities, and most other goods and services.

Equilibrium Exchange Rate The exchange rate at which the demand for a currency and supply of the same currency are equal. The equilibrium exchange rate indicates that the price of exchanging two currencies will remain stable. See also: Equilibrium rate of interest.

Equilibrium Market Price of Risk In the capital asset pricing model, the extra return on an investment that an investor expects in exchange for accepting a greater degree of risk. The riskier an investment is, the greater return an investor expects. The equilibrium market price of risk is shown graphically as the slope of the capital

market line, which plots the extra return expected for each change in level of risk. See also: Beta.

Equilibrium Price The price brought about by the rough equality of supply and demand. This applies for consumer goods, securities, and most other goods and services.

Equilibrium Rate of Interest In money markets, an interest rate at which the demand for money and supply of money are equal. When a central bank sets interest rates higher than the equilibrium rate, there is an excess supply of money, resulting in investors holding less money and putting more into bonds. This causes the price of bonds to rise, driving down the interest rate toward the equilibrium rate. The opposite occurs when interest rates are lower than the equilibrium rate: there is excess demand for money, causing investors to sell bonds to raise cash. This decreases the price of bonds, causing the interest rate to rise to the equilibrium point. Central banks can use the equilibrium rate of interest as a tool in determining the appropriate money supply.

Equipment Tangible assets that are peripheral to a company's operations but are nonetheless necessary. Equipment is generally moveable and may be more or less expensive than other equipment. Trucks to transport materials and toilet paper for customer bathrooms are both examples of equipment.

Equipment Bond A bond that a railroad issues in order to purchase trains and anything else that moves on the railway. The bond is secured by the assets purchased; that is, if coupon or other payments are not made, bondholders may confiscate and sell the equipment financed by the bond.

Equipment Leasing Limited Partnership A limited partnership in which the limited partners contribute funds that are used to buy expensive equipment, which is then leased to businesses. For example, an equipment leasing limited partnership may purchase a set of tractors and lease them to agricultural corporations. The partnership receives lease payments for the equipment, which are then distributed among the partners. An advantage to an equipment leasing limited partnership is the fact that much of the income from the lease payments is not subject to taxation because of deductions for interest and depreciation.

Equipment Trust Certificate A certificate entitling the holder to the revenue from the lease of an asset. In an equipment trust, the trust owns the asset and leases the asset to a company (which usually set up the trust). Certificate holders receive lease payments until the certificates mature, at which point ownership of the asset is transferred to the company leasing it. Rail and airline companies use equipment trust certificates in order to finance the purchase of trains and planes.

Equities in Dallas Slang; an unwanted and lackluster job at a Wall Street trading firm. The term connotes a job with no future given to a person unlikely to do well at the company, perhaps because he or she has fallen into disfavor with an executive. The term was popularized by the book Liar's Poker, which describes the author's experience as a bond trader on Wall Street in the 1980s.

Equity Ownership. Equity is what a person, company, or account has to its name if all debts were liquidated. Because of this, it is an alternate term for a stock. Equity is important to accounting, trading, among others.

Equity Accounting A method of accounting where a company lists undistributed profits from an affiliated company (or a company in which it holds a substantial, but not controlling, interest) on its balance sheet. This may improve the appearance of the company's financial health, whether or not the undistributed profits are eventually distributed to the company.

Equity Cap 1. The maximum amount of equity in a company an investor or class of investors is allowed to hold. A government may place an equity cap on the amount of equity a foreign national or company may possess in domestic companies, or in certain industries thought to be important. **2.** Informal for equity capital. Equity capital is money raised by owners of a company. A common example of equity capital is the funding raised by issuing stock.

Equity Capital Markets Department The department of an investment bank that deals with traders who work on exchange floors. Equity capital markets departments exist to prevent traders from dealing with the ordinary investment banking divisions, which may accidentally breach confidential information. This helps promote stability in the market, protects the bank's deals with clients and prevents it from running afoul of insider trading laws.

Equity Carve Out The act or process of a company making an IPO on one of its subsidies without fully spinning off. During an equity carve-out, the parent company becomes majority shareholder and only offers a minority share to the market. This gives the subsidiary a degree of autonomy (such as its own board of directors) while still retaining access to resources at the parent company. Most of the time, an equity carve-out ultimately results in the parent company fully spinning off the subsidy. It is also called a partial spin off.

Equity Claim The right of a shareholder or some other party to the profit of a company after all prior obligations have been paid. Equity claims are perhaps most important in the event of the company's liquidation. Equity claims are also called residual claims.

Equity Contribution Agreement An agreement in which the parties provide capital for a project in exchange for equity either in the company conducting the project, or in the project itself.

Equity Fund A mutual fund consisting predominantly or exclusively of stocks. An equity stock fund may be high-risk if it invests primarily in start-ups and recent IPOs, or it may be low-risk if it invests in established companies with stable returns. Equity funds are often classified according to the types of companies in which they invest, such as a green fund that invests in environmentally friendly companies. They may also classify themselves according to some other metric, such as equity funds that invest in large-cap or small-cap stocks. An equity fund is also called a stock fund.

Equity Funding 1. An insurance policy paid for by a mutual fund. That is, the value of the shares of the mutual fund pays the premiums of the insurance policy. Equity funding can be useful because it provides the risk reduction of an insurance policy while allowing the policyholder to keep any returns from the mutual fund over and above what is owed for the premium. It is most common with life insurance. However, the practice is controversial, as it has been associated with the Equity Funding Corporation of America, which offered this investment vehicle. This company perpetrated massive accounting fraud in the 1960s and 1970s. Perhaps because of this, equity funding is not very popular with investors. **2.** See: Equity financing.

Equity Income 1. Dividends that a shareholder in a stock earns over the time he/she owns the stock. **2.** A mutual fund that invests predominantly or exclusively in stocks known for paying moderate dividends and modest-to-strong capital appreciation. An equity income fund is a relatively low-risk mutual fund.

Equity Kicker An option to purchase stock attached to a bond. A bond issuer may attach an equity kicker as a sweetener to encourage investment in the bond.

Equity Linked Foreign Exchange Option A position involving a combination of an option contract on a currency and a forward contract on a stock. If the currency's value moves in a direction favorable to the investor, the investor receives a payoff depending on the performance of the stock underlying the forward contract. If not, the investor does not receive a payoff. An ELF-X helps an investor hedge against foreign-exchange risk. It is also called a portfolio currency protection option.

Equity Market Capitalization The aggregate value of an equity market. It is calculated by adding together market capitalization of each stock on the equity market. It may be used to compare the stock market to other investment vehicles.

Equity Market Neutral In hedge funds, an investment strategy that involves taking a long position in some equities and a short position on equities in the same industry. For example, a hedge fund may buy an oil company's stock while selling short the stock of another oil company. Theoretically, this reduces risk to the portfolio because stocks in a single industry tend to move in generally the same direction. Thus, a gain on one stock would offset a loss on another.

Equity Note A medium-term debt security that automatically turns into common stock at maturity. That is, rather than receiving back the principal, the holder exchanges the equity note for common stock. Before maturity, the equity note pays coupons like an ordinary debt security and has a higher priority than common stock in the event of the issuer's liquidation. An equity note combines the guaranteed return of a bond or other debt security with the potential for a higher return that comes with holding common stock.

Equity Option An option contract on a stock. The holder of an equity option has the ability to buy (in a call) or sell (in a put) some number of stocks in a certain company at a given strike price on or before the expiration date. See also: NEO.

Equity Participation Loan A loan where the lender takes some portion of ownership in the project or has the right to do so. See also: Mudaraba.

Equity REIT A real estate investment trust (REIT) that buys and owns property outright, rather than investing in mortgages. The revenue for equity REITs comes mainly from rents on the properties owned. Like all REITs, they may be traded as if they were stocks. Owning an equity REIT is more liquid than directly owning the real estate underlying it.

Equity Risk Premium The return that an investor expects over and above the risk-free rate of return in exchange for investing in common stock instead of U.S. Treasury bonds. The equity risk premium may be calculated as the return such a stock actually earns over a given period. For example, if the interest rate on a Treasury bond is 4% and the stock returns 9%, the equity risk premium is 5%. Whether or not this is worth the investment depends on the cost of the stock, the risk relative to other stocks with similar returns, and the investor's own risk aversion. The equity risk premium is also called simply the equity premium.

Equity Swap A swap in which the at least one of the two legs is the cash flow from some equity instrument like a stock. For example, the counterparties to an equity swap may agree to exchange the dividends from two stocks of roughly the same value. Alternatively, they may exchange the capital gains from a stock index for an interest rate calculated over a nominal value. Equity swaps may take a variety of forms, but all exist in order to diversify the cash flows of the parties without requiring them to buy anything new. An equity swap may also help one or both parties legally avoid taxation.

Equity Unit Investment Trust An investment company that contains an unmanaged portfolio of stocks for approximately one year. Investors may buy shares (called units) in the trust and hold them for the year or redeem them from the trust at any time. The units operate much like shares in a mutual fund; the holder is entitled to any capital gains and is responsible for any losses on the portfolio. The main differences are that the portfolio is unmanaged and there is a time limit on the life of the trust. At the end of the year, the trust is either liquidated or rolled over into a new equity unit investment trust. See also: UIT.

Equity Warrant A warrant in which the underlying security is a stock. That is, an equity warrant is a certificate issued with a security giving the holder the option of buying a stock at a certain strike price for a certain period of time. Equity warrants are the most common warrants. Unlike options, warrants are issued by companies during a round of financing as an added incentive to buy a security; they are not

issued by individual investors or brokerages. Warrants also usually have a longer maturity.

Equity Withdrawal 1. The act or practice of borrowing against the value of one's home. One may withdraw equity only if the value of the home exceeds the remaining mortgage (otherwise, the borrower has negative equity). One may make an equity withdrawal to fund home improvements, a new home, an education, or almost anything else. See also: Home equity loan. **2.** The amount by which the sale price of real estate exceeds the amount the seller paid for it.

Equity-Indexed Annuity An annuity with an interest rate linked to the performance of an equity index. Most annuities pay the interest rate stated in the contract, but an equity-indexed annuity pays a minimum interest rate, with the possibility of a higher rate depending on the performance of the relevant stock or equity index. Each plan uses a different methodology in determining how the higher interest rate is calculated. Common features in its calculation include a participation rate, which determines how much of the annuity is linked to the index, and the rate cap, which sets a maximum interest rate on some plans. Many equity-index annuities use the Standard & Poor's 500 Composite Stock Price Index (S&P 500) as their benchmark.

Equity-Linked Eurobond A bond denominated in a currency other than the one used in the country where it is issued that offers a return based on the performance of some stock or stock index. That is, the equity-linked Eurobond generally offers a small, guaranteed return with the possibility of a larger return dependent on the underlying stock or index. Equity-linked Eurobonds combine some of the advantages of both stocks and bonds, and also can help an investor hedge against foreign exchange risk.

Equity-Linked Policy A whole life insurance policy in which some or all of the premium is allocated to a separate account, which is invested in common stock. If the common stock portfolio does well, the death benefit increases accordingly; if it performs poorly, it decreases. However, all equity-linked policies have a benefit floor. A significant advantage to an equity-linked policy is the fact the policyholder does not have to pay taxes on earnings from the portfolio until it is cashed in, usually through death. In the United States, equity-linked policies are considered securities contracts and, as such, they are regulated by federal law. An equity-linked policy is a type of variable life insurance policy.

Equivalent Annual Annuity The amount one would receive annually, over a certain number of years, from an annuity that has a present value equal to some stated amount.

Equivalent Annual Cash Flow The cash flow required for the annual return on an annuity to equal the return on another investment vehicle. The equivalent annual cash flow is important in analyzing the risk and opportunity cost of an annuity.

Equivalent Annual Cost The cost of an asset over the time it is held, expressed in annualized terms. It is calculated as: EAC = (Price + Discount Rate) / (1 - (1 + Discount Rate)-Years Held) The EAC may be compared to the revenue that the asset produces in a year to determine whether acquiring the asset is cost effective.

Equivalent Bond Yield An alternative method of calculating the yield on a bond. It is used for zero-coupon bonds, as these are issued at discounts to their face value, that is, the equivalent bond yield states what the yield would be if it carried a coupon and had been sold at face value. As such, it provides a more accurate picture of the yield of a zero-coupon bond. See also: Coupon-equivalent rate.

Equivolume A chart that plots price and volume as one data point. Graphically, equivolume looks like a candlestick chart, but the length of the candlestick represents price and the width represents volume. Technical analysts consider a price increase with high volume more significant than a price increase with low volume, and thus equivolume charts assist in their investment decisions.

ER 1. ISO 3166-1 alpha-2 code for the State of Eritrea. This is the code used in international transactions to and from Eritrean bank accounts. **2.** ISO 3166-2 geocode for Eritrea. This is used as an international standard for shipping to Eritrea. Each Eritrean province has its own code with the prefix "ER." For example, the code for the Province of Debub is ISO 3166-2:ER-DU.

Erasure Guarantee A guarantee made by a representative of a financial institution or stock exchange that a change to a security's terms is accurate. It is similar to a notary public's guarantee, but it must be made by an accredited person from the financial institution or exchange. See also: Medallion STAMP Program.

ERI GOST 7.67 Latin three-letter geocode for Eritrea. The code is used for transactions to and from Eritrean bank accounts and for international shipping to Eritrea. As with all GOST 7.67 codes, it is used primarily in Cyrillic alphabets.

Eritrean Nakfa The currency of Eritrea. It was introduced in 1997, replacing the Ethiopian birr. It is issued by the Bank of Eritrea and is pegged to the U.S. dollar.

Eritrean Tallero The former currency of Eritrea. It was introduced in 1890 and was divided into five lire. Each lira was equivalent to the Italian lira, effectively pegging the tallero to the lira at a ratio of five lire to one taller. It was replaced by the Italian lira in 1921.

ERN ISO 4217 code for the Eritrean nakfa. It was introduced in 1997, replacing the Ethiopian birr. It is issued by the Bank of Eritrea and is pegged to the U.S. dollar.

Ernst Welteke A German politician who served as president of the Bundesbank from 1999 to 2004. Welteke served as president during the transition from the deutschemark to the euro. He was born in 1942.

Erosion 1. The gradual loss of an asset's value. See also: Depreciation. 2. The wearing away of real estate caused by natural events. For example, a rising sea level may erode a beach front property. Erosion can reduce the property's value.

ERR On a ticker tape, an indication that the previous quote was an error. This advises the person reading the tape to ignore that quote.

Error Coin A coin minted with some blemish. In general, attempts are made not to release error coins into circulation, so they are sufficiently rare that some error coins may be valuable for collectors. However, they are illiquid assets.

Errors and Omissions Insurance An insurance policy providing coverage for a professional in the event he/she does not perform his/her duties well and it results in harm to a client. That is, errors and omissions insurance covers negligence. It is offered to attorneys, physicians, architects, etc. It is known by its abbreviation, E&O.

ES 1. ISO 3166-1 alpha-2 code for the Kingdom of Spain. This is the code used in international transactions to and from Spanish bank accounts. 2. ISO 3166-2 geocode for Spain. This is used as an international standard for shipping to Spain. Each province and autonomous community has its own code, with provinces having the prefix "ES." For example, the code for the Province of Avila is ISO 3166-2:ES-AV.

Escalation Clause A clause in a contract stating that the price of a good or service will increase if a cost increases correspondingly. For example, a supermarket may enter a contract with an apple distributor to buy apples at a certain price. However, an escalation clause may cause that price to increase if the cost of transporting the apples to the store goes up by a certain amount.

Escalator Clause A clause in a contract stating that a certain payment increase will grow each year according to some formula stated in the contract. For example, an employment contract may have an escalator clause allowing for small increases in salary each year. An escalator clause usually exists to protect one party to the contract from inflation.

Escheat The acquisition of property by a state or government from the estate of a deceased person. An escheat occurs when the deceased person has no will, no relatives, and no survivors to whom the property would otherwise go. Because it is rare for a person to have no relatives at all, escheats are fairly unusual. The concept has its origins in feudalism, when the immediately superior feudal lord would inherit property that would otherwise be left without an owner. Different states have different laws governing escheats.

Escheat Period The amount of time required by law for an unoccupied property to be considered abandoned. In the United States, the escheat period varies state by state. See also: Lost, Mislaid, or Abandoned Property, Escheat.

Escropula A Portuguese measure of weight approximately equivalent to two grams. It became obsolete after Lusophone countries adopted the metric system in the 19th century.

Escrow A certificate stating that an asset is being held by a third party on behalf of two parties to a transaction until certain conditions are filled. An escrow agreement is issued by the bank or other institution holding the asset in escrow and is useful to prove to one party or the other that the escrow has in fact taken place. See also: Escrow agent.

Escrow Agent A third party who agrees to hold funds or assets in escrow. The escrow agent provides this service to two parties in a transaction until certain conditions are filled. The escrow agent holds the assets until the transaction is finalized and then gives them to the appropriate party. See also: Bulk sales escrow.

Escrow Receipt A statement by a bank to the holder of a call option stating that the writer (or seller) of the option has deposited the underlying asset with the bank. This guarantees that delivery will be made in proper course should the holder exercise the option.

Escrowed Shares Shares in a publicly-traded company held by a third party on behalf of two parties to a transaction until certain conditions are filled. For example, a third party may hold escrowed shares that a potential acquiring company placed as the equivalent of earnest money for the target company. See also: Escrow Agent.

Escrowed to Maturity Describing a bond that has had its proceeds placed in an escrow account until another bond matures. That is, the issuer places the funds from the ETM bond into an account to set them aside in order to pay off a second bond at its maturity.

Escudo The name of several current and former currencies. The word derives from the Portuguese word for shield. The Portuguese escudo was the currency of Portugal until the introduction of the euro in 1999. Most other escudos circulated in former Portuguese colonies. The only current currency with the name is the Cape Verdean escudo.

Ese An ancient Sumerian unit of length approximately equivalent to 60 meters.

ESH GOST 7.67 Latin three-letter geocode for the Western Sahara. The code is used for transactions to and from Western Saharan bank accounts and for international shipping to the Western Sahara. As with all GOST 7.67 codes, it is used primarily in Cyrillic alphabets.

Eski Donum A Turkish measure of area approximately equivalent to 919 square meters. It became obsolete when Turkey made the metric system mandatory in 1933.

Eski Mil A Turkish measure of length approximately equivalent to 1.89 kilometers. It became obsolete when Turkey made the metric system mandatory in 1933.

ESP GOST 7.67 Latin three-letter geocode for Spain. The code is used for transactions to and from Spanish bank accounts and for international shipping to Spain. As with all GOST 7.67 codes, it is used primarily in Cyrillic alphabets.

Esquisse In art, a rough sketch that gives the general overview of what the final product will look like. Esquisse is an important step in marketing because it allows for suggestions or corrections before too much work has been done. Esquisse is the equivalent of loose rendering, which is used in graphic design.

Essential Purpose Bond A municipal bond that intends to fund the normal functions of a local government. Examples of institutions and activities that an essential purpose bond finances are municipal buildings, police cars, firefighter salaries, and so forth. Essential purpose bonds differ from private activity bonds, which are municipal bonds intended to help private business in the community. It is also called a traditional government purpose bond. See also: General obligation bond.

EST GOST 7.67 Latin three-letter geocode for Estonia. The code is used for transactions to and from Estonian bank accounts and for international shipping to Estonia. As with all GOST 7.67 codes, it is used primarily in Cyrillic alphabets.

Estacode Money set aside for travel expenses for a corporate officer, politician, or even an athlete.

Estado In Brazil, Mexico, and Venezuela, a political subdivision equivalent to a province.

Estate The assets that a person owns when he/she dies. The estate includes all personal property, real estate, securities and other assets. The estate is used to repay all of the person's outstanding debt. After debts are repaid, the estate may be taxed, depending on the value of the remaining assets. After all debts and taxes are repaid, the estate is distributed according to the provisions of the decedent's will and/or state law.

Estate Planning The process of preparing one's assets for one's death. Estate planning involves matters such as writing a will in order to designate beneficiaries, or who will receive one's assets following death. It may also involve setting up trusts in such a way as to reduce estate tax liability. Estate planning is especially important if one is wealthy and has a large number of assets of which to dispose or if one has minor children who will need tending in the event of the parent's untimely death. Estate planning is an ongoing process. See also: ChFC, CFP, Life Insurance.

Estate Planning Distribution The distribution between bequests made before death and those made after death. For example, one may distribute 40% of his/her property before death by putting it in a trust and keep the remaining 60% until he/she dies. This may have positive estate tax implications by reducing one's personal net worth.

Estate Tax A tax on the assets a deceased person leaves behind. These assets include all personal property, real estate, securities and other things. In the United States, the estate tax is applied to the value of an estate that remains after all the debts of the deceased are paid, if the value of the estate exceeds a certain amount, which is always over $1 million. The estate tax should not be confused with an inheritance tax, which is a tax on the income one receives from an estate.

Estate Tax Liability The amount an estate owes to the government before it can be distributed to heirs. The estate tax liability is calculated as a certain percentage of the value of an estate after all the debts of the deceased are repaid and certain deductions are taken. However, there is no estate tax liability calculated on the first $1 million (sometimes more) of an estate's value.

Estatutos A Portuguese term for the articles of incorporation of a non-governmental organization.

Estimated Financial Aid A tentative financial aid package offered by the U.S. federal government through the FAFSA system. Estimated financial aid requires further action on the part of a student, such as verifying income.

Estimated Tax Taxes paid to the IRS on a quarterly basis on all income not subject to withholding. Estimated taxes most prominently affect self-employed persons, but they must also be paid on alimony, rents, and capital gains. Persons who file estimated taxes must also file 1040 forms and, if necessary, pay any taxes they may have underpaid on their estimated taxes.

Estonian Kroon The former currency of Estonia. It was issued in 1992, replacing the Soviet ruble. It was pegged to the deutschemark and then to the euro. In January 2011, the euro replaced the kroon.

Estoppel Clause A clause in a contract stating that certain facts are true as of the date the contract is signed. For example, the estoppel clause may state the collateral or amount of a loan. It is put in a contract to eliminate any ambiguity.

Estovers In English law, the amount of wood the renter of a piece of land was permitted to take each year for home repair, firewood, animal husbandry and other, necessary purposes.

ET 1. ISO 3166-1 alpha-2 code for the Federal Democratic Republic of Ethiopia. This is the code used in international transactions to and from Ethiopian bank accounts. 2. ISO 3166-2 geocode for Ethiopia. This is an international standard for shipping to Ethiopia. Each administration and state has its own code with the prefix "ET." For example, the code for the State of Afar is ISO 3166-2:ET-AF.

Et Al. A Latin abbreviation meaning "and others." It is used in many contexts to state that there are other parties involved. For example, one may refer to the authors of a book written by Marinelli, Moreno and Sookiasian as "Marinelli et al." Likewise, legal documents would use the same shorthand if all three decided to sue their publisher.

Et Non A Latin phrase meaning "and not." It is used in legal documents and proceedings to strongly deny an assertion. For example, one may plead innocent to a crime et non.

Et Uxor A Latin phrase meaning "and the wife." It is used in legal documents to identify a man's wife as party to a proceeding even though she is otherwise unmentioned. This is most common in property and marital cases. It is often abbreviated "et ux." The equivalent when a woman's husband is mentioned but not named is "et vir."

ETB ISO 4217 code for the Ethiopian birr. It was introduced in 1945, replacing the East African shilling, though an earlier birr had been the currency prior to the East African campaign and the Italian occupation of Ethiopia. It is noted for its high rate of inflation, estimated at over 11% in 2005 and 41% in 2008. Interestingly, the official translation of the birr was "dollar" until 1976, when "birr" became the appropriate word in both Amharic and English.

ETH GOST 7.67 three-letter geocode for Ethiopia. The code is used for transactions to and from Ethiopian bank accounts and for international shipping to Ethiopia. As with all GOST 7.67 codes, it is used primarily in Cyrillic alphabets.

Ethical Dilemma A difficulty in which one is presented with two equally good (or equally bad) options and the correct decision is not immediately apparent. For example, the manager of a company may be put in a position in which she must choose between the interests of her employees and her investors.

Ethical Fund A mutual fund in which the asset managers make investment decisions based upon some ethical code. An ethical fund is marketed to investors who may have moral objections to certain investment vehicles or companies. For example, an individual may have a moral objection to smoking and may therefore buy shares in a mutual fund that refrains from investing in tobacco companies. Ethical funds may have positive or negative guidelines; that is, a fund's ethics may inform where it makes investments (e.g. in environmentally friendly companies) and where it does not (e.g. in arms manufacturers). See also: Green fund, Islamic finance.

Ethical Investing Any investment philosophy that recommends investment decisions based upon a decision's ethical implications for individuals and companies. For example, an individual may have a moral objection to smoking, and therefore refrain from investing in tobacco companies. Ethical investing may be both positive and negative; that is, it may inform where an individual makes investments (e.g. in environmentally friendly companies) and where he/she does not make investments (e.g. in arms manufacturers). Some mutual funds, and even whole subdivisions of companies, are dedicated to promoting ethical investing. See also: Green fund, Islamic finance.

Ethics The study and practice of appropriate behavior, regardless of the behavior's legality. Certain industries have professional organizations setting and promoting certain ethical standards. For example, an accountant may be required to refrain from engaging in aggressive accounting, even when a particular type of aggressive accounting is not illegal. Professional organizations may censure or revoke the licenses of those professionals who are found to have violated the ethical standards of their fields. In investing, ethics helps inform the investment decisions of some individuals and companies. For example, an individual may have a moral objection to smoking and therefore refrain from investing in tobacco companies. Ethics may be both positive and negative in investing; that is, it may inform where an individual makes investments (e.g. in environmentally friendly companies) and where he/she does not (e.g. in arms manufacturers). Some mutual funds and even whole subdivisions are dedicated to promoting ethical investing. See also: Green fund, Islamic finance.

Ethics Audit An investigation into how well (or poorly) a company conforms to the ethical standards of its industry or society generally. An ethics audit may consider the company's own practices, how it redresses grievances, how it discloses its finances, whether it punishes whistleblowers, and even the general cultural surrounding its business dealings. Some companies may formally adopt a code of ethics and conduct periodic ethics audits to see how closely they follow their own rules.

E-Trade The trade of a security over the Internet. Brokerages offering e-trade services automatically forward these orders to the appropriate person on the exchange floor to make the trade.

Etrap In Turkmenistan, a political subdivision approximately equivalent to a county.

Etzba An ancient Hebrew unit of length approximately equivalent to two or two and a half centimeters.

Euclidean Geometry A system of geometry that deals with objects on a plane. Its theory is based on five postulates, from which a number of theoretical proofs are derived.

Eup In South Korea, a political subdivision equivalent to a town with at least 20,000 residents.

EUR ISO 4217 code for the euro. It was introduced in 1999 in hopes of integrating the economies of the European Union. At introduction, it was an accounting currency; banknotes entered circulation in 2002. After the U.S. dollar, the euro is the most traded currency in the world, and it is the second-largest reserve currency. It circulates in the eurozone, which includes a majority of the states in the European Union. It was intended to remove the exchange rate risk of businesses participating in the EU's common market and free trade association. Proponents of the euro state that it is more valuable than the former currencies, while opponents say that it has made goods and services in their home countries more expensive. A number of countries outside the eurozone have formally or informally adopted the euro as well. See also: ECU, EMU, European Central Bank.

Eurace A Slovak slang term for a euro coin. Literally, the term means "letter E."

EUREX An exchange for options, futures, and other derivatives, formed in 1998 by the merger of Deutsche Terminborse and SOFFEX. Trading on Eurex takes place electronically. It is, along with NYSE Euronext and the Merc, one of the three most prominent derivatives exchanges in the world.

Euro The currency of participating member nations of the European Union. The euro was introduced in 1999 and became the official currency of participating nations in 2002. It was intended to remove the exchange rate risk of businesses participating in the EU's common market and free trade association. It has become one of the world's most important currencies. Proponents of the euro state that it is more valuable than the former currencies, while opponents say that it has made goods and services in their home countries more expensive. The euro's ISO 4217 code is EUR. See also: European Central Bank, EURIBOR, Eurozone.

Euro Area Reference Note A bond issued by the European Investment Bank. Originally issued in 1999, the notes were among the first ever denominated in euros and were intended to help create a market for euro securities.

Euro Interbank Offer Rate The average interest rate participating banks offer each other for unsecured loans. The loans are denominated in the euro even though not all participating banks operate in the European Union. Because these banks operate the largest share of the European money market, the EURIBOR is a benchmark for short term interest rates. It is also a benchmark for euro-denominated forward rate agreements and interest rate swaps. Likewise, EURIBOR is used in some floating rate bonds, with the interest rate spread being expressed as: "EURIBOR + X base points." See also: LIBOR, panel bank.

Euro LIBOR The LIBOR calculated in euros. It is a rare occurrence to calculate the euro LIBOR and is mainly used as a convenience for contracts that predate the euro.

Euro Line A line of credit granted by a bank or other financial institution in a foreign currency. For example, a British bank may give a British client a line of credit denominated in U.S. dollars. A euro line may be useful if one has significant business dealings in another country and wishes to hedge one's foreign exchange risk.

Euro Overnight Index Average The weighted average EURIBOR, which is the interest rate European banks charge one another on overnight loans. The European Central Bank calculates the EONIA each day.

Euro Straight A eurobond with a fixed coupon. Eurobonds are bonds issued or traded in a country using a currency other than the one in which the bond is denominated. This means that the bond uses a certain currency, but operates outside the jurisdiction of the central bank that issues that currency. Eurobonds are issued by multinational corporations; for example, a British company may issue a eurobond in Germany, denominating it in U.S. dollars. Euro straight bonds provide a degree of certainty unavailable to variable coupon bonds, but expose an investor to interest rate risk. It is important to note that the term has nothing to do with the euro, and the prefix "euro-" is used more generally to refer to deposits outside the jurisdiction of the domestic central bank.

Euro.NM A network of European exchanges dedicated to promoting growth companies. It accomplishes this goal by linking member exchanges, allowing financial intermediaries to operate on all exchanges, and by having similar rules on settlement of transactions. Member exchanges include Borsa Italiana, Deutsche Bank AG, Euronext Amsterdam, Euronext Brussels, and Euronext Paris.

Eurobank 1. A bank that regularly or primarily accepts deposits in currencies other than the one used in the country where the bank is located. Eurobanks also make loans primarily in different currencies. See also: Eurocurrency. **2.** See: EuroBancshares, Inc.

Eurobond Bonds issued or traded in a country using a currency other than the one in which the bond is denominated. This means that the bond uses a certain currency, but operates outside the jurisdiction of the central bank that issues that currency. Eurobonds are issued by multinational corporations; for example, a British company may issue a eurobond in Germany, denominating it in U.S. dollars. It is important to note that the term has nothing to do with the euro, and the prefix "euro-" is used more generally to refer to deposits outside the jurisdiction of the domestic central bank.

Eurocent A division of the euro equal in value to 1/100 of one euro.

Eurocheck A traveler's check issued by a European bank. A Eurocheck may be exchanged for cash at over 200,000 institutions worldwide. Each Eurocheck has identification so that if it is lost or stolen, the holder may still retrieve the money he/she has placed in it.

Euroclear A clearing house that serves as one of the largest security depository and post-trade financial services companies in the world. Based in Brussels, Euroclear settles transactions on behalf of clients, many of whom trade on European exchanges. It was established in 1968 and is owned by its users. Its main competitors are the DTCC and Clearstream.

Eurocommercial Paper A short-term, unsecured loan issued by a corporation in a currency other than the one in which the corporation operates. Corporations issue eurocommerical papers in order to tap into the international money markets for their financing. Like other commercial papers, eurocommercial papers are rarely for a term longer than a few months and they are usually issued at a discount. An example of a eurocommercial paper is a British firm issuing debt in U.S. dollars to encourage investment from dollar-investors in international money markets. See also: Eurodollar.

Eurocredit Credit extended in a currency outside the jurisdiction of the central bank of the bank extending the credit. For example, an American bank may make a loan denominated in Japanese yen. The term has nothing to do with the euro; and the prefix "euro-" is used more generally to refer to deposits outside the jurisdiction of the local central bank, e.g. "euroruble." Eurocredit loans are usually large and long-term. Banks participating in the eurocredit market generally also participate in the eurocurrency market.

Eurocredit Market Banks who make and receive loans in currencies outside the jurisdiction of the issuing central bank. The term has nothing to do with the euro; and the prefix "euro-" is used more generally to refer to deposits outside the jurisdiction of the local central bank, e.g. "euroruble." Eurocredit loans are usually large and long-term. Banks participating in the eurocredit market generally also participate in the eurocurrency market.

Eurocurrency Deposits in banks that are denominated in currencies other than the one in which that bank operates. For example, a eurodollar is a U.S. dollar deposit outside the jurisdiction of the Federal Reserve, that is, outside the United States. Eurodollar investments may be traded in any country other than the United States, but are usually traded in London. Likewise, a euroyen is a yen deposit outside Japan, thought it usually refers to a euroyen CD. It is important to note that term has nothing to do with the euro, and the prefix "euro-" is used more generally to refer to deposits outside the jurisdiction of the local central bank, e.g. "euroruble."

Eurocurrency Deposit A short-term certificate of deposit with a fixed interest rate made in a currency outside the jurisdiction of the issuing central bank. For example, one may purchase a CD in U.S. dollars and deposit it in a bank in Great Britain. Eurocurrency deposits help persons and businesses hedge against short-term fluctuations in exchange rates.

Eurocurrency Market The market for investments denominated in currencies other than the one in which the investment is traded. For example, a eurodollar is a U.S. dollar deposit outside the jurisdiction of the Federal Reserve (that is, outside the United States). Eurodollar investments may be traded in any country other than the United States but are usually traded in London. Likewise, a euroyen is a yen deposit outside Japan, thought it usually refers to a euroyen CD. The eurocurrency market may also refer to the trading of eurocurrency bonds. It is important to note that term has nothing to do with the euro, and the prefix "euro-" is used more generally to refer to deposits outside the jurisdiction of the local central bank (e.g. "euroruble").

Eurodollar U.S. dollar deposits in banks outside the jurisdiction of the Federal Reserve; that is, outside the United States. Eurodollar futures contracts, which are based on eurodollar desposits, are a highly liquid investment traded on the Chicago Mercantile Exchange. Prices are determined by forecasting the three month USD LIBOR interest rate. Likewise, eurodollar sweeps are a popular short-term investment for large businesses. The term has nothing to do with the euro, and the prefix "euro-" is used more generally to refer to deposits outside the jurisdiction of the local central bank, e.g. "euroruble."

Eurodollar Bond A bond denominated in U.S. dollars issued by a non-American company outside of the United States and the issuer's home country. It is important to note that these are traded worldwide, not just in Europe. Like other Eurocurrency securities, Eurodollar bonds are subject to fewer regulatory restrictions because the central bank that issued the currency (in this case, the U.S. Federal Reserve System) does not have any jurisdiction over the dollars because the bonds are issued and traded outside the U.S. For example, a Japanese company may issue a Eurodollar bond to attract foreign investors for its financing needs. Eurodollar bonds are one of the more common eurocurrency bonds because of the international importance of the dollar. See also: Eurobond, Eurodollar.

Eurodollar CD A certificate of deposit denominated in U.S. dollars, but issued and held outside the United States. Almost all Eurodollar certificates of deposit are issued by banks in London.

Eurodollar Deposit A short-term certificate of deposit with a fixed interest rate issued in U.S. dollars outside the jurisdiction of the Federal Reserve. For example, one may purchase a CD in U.S. dollars and deposit it in a bank in the UK. Eurodollar deposits help persons and businesses hedge against short-term fluctuations in U.S. dollar exchange rates.

Eurodollar Obligations Bonds or, more commonly, certificates of deposit issued in U.S. dollars but outside the jurisdiction of the Federal Reserve. Most of the time, a eurodollar obligation is held by a non-American bank or a foreign branch of an American bank. However, a dollar-denominated obligation is considered a eurodollar obligation if it is held anywhere outside the United States. See also: eurodollar.

Euroequity Issue An IPO that occurs on two exchanges in two different countries at the same time. Euroequity IPOs allow as many investors as possible to take advantage of the IPO; this increases the possibility that the newly public company will raise more capital in a round of financing. Euroequity is nearly always placed by an international underwriting syndicate.

Euroeuro A euro deposit in a bank outside the jurisdiction of European Central Bank; that is, outside the eurozone. It should be noted that the prefix "euro-" is used generally to refer to deposits outside the jurisdiction of the local central bank, such as in "euroruble."

Eurofranc A French franc deposit in a bank outside the jurisdiction of the Bank of France; that is, outside France. Since the introduction of the euro, the eurofranc has become obsolete. The term has nothing to do with the euro, and the prefix "euro-" is used generally to refer to deposits outside the jurisdiction of the local central bank, such as in "euroruble."

Eurogroup An informal, periodic meeting of the finance ministers of the eurozone. The Eurogroup meets to influence the monetary policy of the eurozone, though the

European Central Bank actually sets this policy. It held its first meeting in 1998 and received formal mandate in 2009.

Eurolira An Italian lira deposit in a bank outside the jurisdiction of Banca d'Italia; that is, outside Italy. Since the introduction of the euro, the eurolira has become obsolete. The term has nothing to do with the euro, and the prefix "euro-" is used generally to refer to deposits outside the jurisdiction of the local central bank, such as in "euroruble."

Euromark A German mark deposit in a bank outside the jurisdiction of Deutsche Bundesbank; that is, outside Germany. Since the introduction of the euro, the euromark has become obsolete. The term has nothing to do with the euro, and the prefix "euro-" is used generally to refer to deposits outside the jurisdiction of the local central bank, such as in "euroruble."

Euronext 100 Index The index for largest and most liquid blue chip stocks traded on Euronext exchanges. Companies listed the Euronext 100 must trade at least 20% of their issues annually (calculated on a rolling basis). It is considered a major benchmark index for European stocks.

Euronext Brussels A stock exchange in Belgium. It was founded as the Brussels Stock Exchange in 1801 at the order of Napoleon. It took its current name in 2000 when it merged with the Amsterdam Exchange and the Paris Bourse to form Euronext.

Euronext NV A company that owns and operates a number of stock exchanges in Europe. It was formed in 2000 with the merger of the Amsterdam, Brussels and Paris Bourses. The following year, it acquired LIFFE and in 2002 merged with the exchange that became Euronext Lisbon. In 2007, it merged with the New York Stock Exchange to form NYSE Euronext. Euronext provides common trading and clearing for all securities traded on any exchange it operates. It is known for publishing the Euronext 100, a major stock index.

Euronext Paris A major stock exchange in France. Established in the early 19th century as the Paris Bourse, it was run for many years by an elected council of brokers. It became fully automated in 1989 and took its current name in 2000.

Euro-Note A debt security with a maturity of less than a few years traded in the Eurocurrency market. This means that the Euro note is denominated in a currency other than the one of the country in which it is traded.

Europe 1992 An agreement between European states to eliminate tariffs and other trade barriers on agricultural products in order to promote intra-European trade. It was established in 1992. See also: Common Agricultural Policy.

Europe, Australia, Far East The regions containing most major markets outside North America. The MSCI EAFE Index tracks securities in Europe, Australia, and the Far East and is considered a major indicator of the direction of global markets.

Europe, Middle East and Africa The branch of a multinational corporation that operates in Europe, the Middle East, and Africa. EMEA companies have their own officers and operating structures independent of, say, the American or Japanese branches. For example, Multinational Corporation A has one board of directors and set of shareholders, but its EMEA branch has its own CEO, CFO, and so forth.

European Academic and Research Network A former computer network connecting European and American servers. It was especially useful in the period before the Internet became prominent. It was established in 1984 and merged with RARE to create TERENA in 1995.

European Agricultural Guidance and Guarantee Fund A fund that financed rural development in the European Union as part of the Common Agricultural Policy. It was established in 1962 and was replaced by the European Agricultural Guarantee Fund and the European Agricultural Fund for Rural Development.

European Bank for Reconstruction and Development A bank created after the end of the Cold War to help Central and Eastern European nations in the transition to capitalism. Among other things, it provides loans to companies and governments for new and expanded operations, assists in privatization of former state-owned businesses, and helps with bank stabilization. In 2006, it began changing its focus from helping former Soviet bloc nations in Europe to former members of the Soviet Union in Central Asia, including Russia itself. It is financed by member nations across the world, including most Western European countries and the United States.

European Banking Authority An agency responsible for banking regulation in the European Union. Among other responsibilities, it conducts stress tests of troubled banks and sets standards for bank reporting in the EU. It also has the power to veto decisions made by national regulators of member states. It was established in 2011 and is based in London.

European Central Bank The central bank for the eurozone. It was established in 1998 prior to the introduction of the euro in 1999. It issues the euro and sets monetary policy, especially by setting key interest rates. Raising interest rates is how the ECB reduces the amount of money in the economy, which slows unsustainable growth and curbs inflation. Lowering interest rates increases the amount of money in the economy and is used to spur growth. The ECB is independent of all other government bodies of the European Union and its member states. It is governed by an Executive Board and Governing Council. The Governing Council is the highest body; it consists of members of the Executive Board and heads of the central banks of the states participating in the eurozone.

European Commission The executive department of the European Union. It is responsible for enforcing treaties, implementing laws and proposing legislation to the

European Parliament. It consists of a president nominated by the European Council and confirmed by Parliament and one commissioner nominated by each state of the EU (except the president's home country) in consultation with the president and confirmed by Parliament. The Commission traces its origins to the High Authority of the European Coal and Steal Community; it took its current form in 1967.

European Court of Justice The supreme court of the European Union. It was established in 1952, predating the foundation of the EU by several decades. It has jurisdiction over EU law, but not over the national laws of member states. It consists of one judge per member state, though the full court meets rarely and decisions are made generally by a panel of judges.

European Currency Unit Prior to the adoption of the euro, the ECU was set up as currency basket to provide a methodology for reconciling differing exchange rates between currencies who wished to participate in the single European currency. Established in the 1979, it was known as a "semi-pegged" system in which currencies were variable with respect to each other only within a certain range. After the introduction of the euro in 1999, the exchange rate mechanism was replaced by ERM II, which reconciles exchange rates for countries wishing to join the eurozone. See also: Exchange rate mechanism.

European Financial Stability Mechanism A lending facility established by the European Union to bail out member states in danger of default and other fiscal stress. The EFSM is permitted to borrow up to 60 billion euros to finance its objectives. Its debt is collateralized by the EU budget. It began operations in 2011 with a bond issue to assist the Irish government.

European Financial Stabilization Mechanism A lending facility established by the European Union to bail out member states in danger of default and other fiscal stress. The EFSM is permitted to borrow in order to finance its objectives. Its debt is collateralized by the EU budget. It began operations in 2011 with a bond issue to assist the Irish government.

European Investment Bank A bank owned by the members of the European Union. It was established to finance EU policies, especially in infrastructure, energy, medium-sized and small businesses, and similar projects. It was established in 1958 and is based in Luxembourg.

European Monetary System A system established in 1979 whereby most member states of the European Economic Community linked their currencies to each other in anticipation of monetary integration. The first stage of the EMS was the European currency unit, then the ERM I, and, finally, the introduction of the euro and the ERM II. The European Monetary System also called for greater extension of credit between European countries. Among the methods the EMS used included the relative synchronization of national interest rates.

European Option An option contract that may only be exercised on the expiration date. For example, if one buy a European call giving him/her the right to buy shares in X expiring on the final Friday in March, the call may only be exercised on the final Friday in March. The implication of a European option is the fact that its value is entirely dependent on the value of the underlying asset at the end of the contract. A holder may not wait for an advantageous price and exercise the option. This contrasts with an American option, which may be exercised at any time prior to expiry.

European Terms In the United States currency market, an exchange rate stated in U.S. dollars per unit of a foreign currency. That is, the act of stating an exchange rate in European terms means stating the dollars needed to buy one unit of that currency. European terms contrasts with direct terms, which state the units of the foreign currency needed to buy one dollar.

European Union A supranational economic and political organization consisting of the majority of the countries in Europe. While it lacks the authority of a federal union, it provides a common market and free trade between members. Importantly, it created and operates the euro, which is one of the most important global currencies. See also: European Central Bank.

European, Australia, and Far East Index An index consisting of a wide selection of stocks traded in most major markets outside North America. It is considered a major indicator of the direction of global markets. It is weighted for market capitalization and is managed by MSCI.

Euroruble A Russian ruble deposit in a bank outside the jurisdiction of the Bank of Russia; that is, outside Russia. The term has nothing to do with the euro, and the prefix "euro-" is used generally to refer to deposits outside the jurisdiction of the local central bank, such as in "eurodollar."

Eurosecurity A security issued or traded in a country using a currency other than the one in which the security is denominated. This means that the security uses a certain currency, but operates outside the jurisdiction of the central bank that issues that currency. Eurosecurities are issued by multinational corporations; for example, a British company may issue a bond in Germany, denominating it in U.S. dollars. The term has nothing to do with the euro; the prefix "euro-" is used more generally to refer to deposits outside the jurisdiction of the domestic central bank.

Eurostat Statistical Office of European Communities. An arm of the European Union government that collects and disseminates statistics related to EU member countries, as well as candidate countries and certain trading partners. Eurostat publishes information on economic growth, the labor force, the state of regions and cities, interest rates, and other matters. It was founded in 1953.

Eurosterling A British pound deposit in a bank outside the jurisdiction of the Bank of England; that is, outside the United Kingdom. The eurosterling is also called the europound. The term has nothing to do with the euro, and the prefix "euro-" is used

generally to refer to deposits outside the jurisdiction of the local central bank, such as in "euroruble."

Eurosterling Bond A bond denominated in British pounds issued by a non-British company outside the United Kingdom. It is important to note that these are traded worldwide, not just in Europe. Like other Eurocurrency securities, Eurosterling bonds are subject to fewer regulatory restrictions because the central bank that issued the currency (in this case, the Bank of England) does not have any jurisdiction over the pounds because the bonds are issued and traded outside Britain. For example, an American company may issue a Eurosterling bond to attract non-British sterling investors for its financing needs. See also: Eurobond, Eurodollar.

Euroterrorism A term pertaining to any of a number of terrorist organizations that operated throughout Europe, and occasionally worked together, in the 1970s and 1980s. Euroterrorist groups had different goals: for example, the Irish Republican Army opposed British presence in Northern Ireland, while the Cellules Communistes Combattantes in Belgium fought against capitalism. Some groups were nationalist, while others focused on promoting a left wing ideology.

Euroterrorist Any of a number of terrorist organizations that operated throughout Europe, and occasionally worked together, in the 1970s and 1980s. Euroterrorist groups had different goals: for example, the Irish Republican Army opposed British presence in Northern Ireland, while the Cellules Communistes Combattantes in Belgium opposed capitalism. Some groups were nationalist, while others focused on promoting a left wing ideology.

Eurotrack 100 Index An index tracking 100 publicly-traded companies listed on exchanges in continental Europe. It is managed by the FTSE. Like many other FTSE indices, it is calculated in real time, with prices updated every few seconds. It is weighted for market capitalization and is considered an indicator of health in the European market.

Eurotrack 200 Index An index tracking 100 publicly-traded companies listed on exchanges in continental Europe and the 100 British companies listed on the FTSE 100. It is managed by the FTSE. Like many other FTSE indices, it is calculated in real time, with prices updated every minute. It is weighted for market capitalization and is considered an indicator of health in the wider market.

Eurowarrant A system in the European Union whereby member states extradite prisoners to other member states upon demand. The Eurowarrant replaced extradition requests, which could be granted or denied. Barring abuse of the system, extradition under a Eurowarrant is automatic. The system was adopted in 2002.

Euroyen Yen deposits in banks outside the jurisdiction of the Central Bank of Japan, that is, outside of Japan. Euroyen bonds are a highly desired investment because they are highly liquid and subject to fewer regulatory restrictions than other bonds. It is important to note that the term has nothing to do with the euro, and the prefix "euro-" is used more generally to refer to deposits outside the jurisdiction of the local central bank, e.g. "euroruble."

Euroyen Bond A bond denominated in Japanese yen issued by a non-Japanese company outside of Japan. It is important to note that these are traded worldwide, not just in Europe. Euroyen bonds became more common after 1984, when Japan began opening its financial markets to foreigners. Like other Eurocurrency securities, Euroyen bonds are subject to fewer regulatory restrictions because the central bank that issued the currency (in this case, the Bank of Japan) does not have any jurisdiction over the yen because the bonds are issued and traded outside Japan. For example, an American company may issue a Euroyen bond to attract non-Japanese yen-investors for its financing needs. See also: Eurobond, Eurodollar.

EUTELSAT A company in France that provides satellite coverage in Europe, the Middle East, Africa, India and the Americas. It broadcasts radio, television and Internet signals to homes and offices all over the world; it also provides Internet access on airlines and elsewhere. It was established as an inter-governmental organization 1977 and was privatized in 2001.

Evaluation of Internal Control In accounting, the study of the procedures that a company uses to check its own work for accuracy. In an audit in the United States, an auditor is required to evaluate internal controls to ensure that they are sufficient and to report on real or potential problems with them. See also: Internal audit.

Evaluation Period The time period in which a money manager's performance is measured against some subjective or objective standard. This is done periodically to assess the effectiveness of a money manager's work for his/her firm. The evaluation period is especially important at the beginning of employment, but remains so throughout one's career. See also: Manager Universe (Benchmark).

Evaluator In investing, an outside party who estimates the value of an illiquid asset, such as an antique or an inactive bond. Evaluators sometimes perform their services after a death to appraise rare or one-of-a-kind items. See also: Appraisal.

Even Up To offset a position by buying or selling an amount equal to the opposite position. For example, if one owns 1,000 shares in stock A, one evens up by selling those 1,000 shares.

Even-Par Swap The sale of a bond with a given face value (usually $1,000) and the purchase of another bond with the same face value. That is, an even-par swap does not consider the present market value of the bonds.

Event Information that can cause a security price to rise or fall. Examples of events include earnings reports, new regulations or even wider occurrences like elections. Events are particularly important in the efficient markets hypothesis.

Event Anomalies Occurrences that present the opportunity for an abnormal return. For example, a company may announce the hiring of a well-regarded executive as

CEO. This could cause the company's stock price to jump temporarily; a shareholder could sell some shares at the artificially high price, generating a higher return than the shareholder expected when he/she bought the stock. See also: Excess return.

Event Driven In hedge funds, an investment strategy of using many different investment strategies in reaction to various events. For example, if a merger is announced, a hedge fund may conduct transactions according to one strategy and, if the merger falls through, the fund may make transactions using a completely different strategy. The idea behind an event driven strategy is to use the best investment strategy befitting a particular moment in time.

Event Risk The risk that an unpredictable, non-repeating event will cause a loss. A strike at a factory or an accident that renders a mine inoperable are examples of event risk. Insurance is intended to lessen many event risks.

Event Study A study to determine what effect the release of information or its timing has on a security's price. Most analysts believe that information should be released in portions so that the market can price out good or bad information and reduce volatility. However, followers of the efficient markets hypothesis argue that doing that is unnecessary because information is reflected in the security's price immediately. Event studies help shed light on which school, if either, is correct; as with anything, there is the potential for bias within the study itself.

Events Marketing A form of marketing in which one holds one or more events to promote a product or company. For example, one may have an open house to entice people to come to a new dental office. Likewise, one may hold a seminar demonstrating a new product at a hotel. Events marketing can be expensive and one generally does not immediately reach people who do not come to an event.

Events of Default In a loan, an event allowing the lender to call the full amount of the loan from the borrower. Events of default are specifically laid out in the loan contract, and often include chronically late payments or other breaches of contract.

Evergreen Describing a long-term contract that is renewed automatically after a short-term period unless it is terminated. For example, an evergreen contract may last five years with an option to terminate at the end of one year. Unless one party or the other terminates the contract by the end of the first year, it is renewed for an additional five years after the end of the first five years.

Evergreen Credit A revolving line-of-credit without a maturity date. As with other revolving lines-of-credit, the borrower may take and repay funds as needed up to a certain limit. See also: Evergreen loan.

Evergreen Funding A situation in which a start-up receives funding in small amounts over a long period of time. This differs from an IPO or some venture capital investments, which tend to be large, one-time-only capital infusions. This tends to be a lower risk arrangement for those providing capital to the start-up, because if it fails in the meantime, no further capital infusions will be required.

Evergreen Option 1. An employee stock option with no expiration date where the employee is granted a certain percentage of the company's shares outstanding automatically each year. The evergreen option requires no approval and the employee does not need to do anything extra to acquire the new shares. This allows the employee to gradually increase his/her holding in the company for which he/she works every year. **2.** An option contract that is renewed automatically after a short-term period unless it is terminated. For example, an evergreen contract may last five years with an option to terminate at the end of one year. Unless one party or the other terminates the contract by the end of the first year, it is renewed for an additional five years after the end of the first five years.

Evergreen Stock Option Plan An employee stock option with no expiration date in which the employee is granted a certain percentage of the company's shares outstanding automatically each year. The evergreen option requires no approval and the employee does not need to do anything extra to acquire the new shares. This allows the employee to gradually increase his/her holding in the company for which he/she works every year.

Everyday Low Pricing A pricing strategy in which a retail store consistently carries low prices and rarely holds sales promotions in which it lowers prices temporarily. Everyday low pricing is intended to promote customer loyalty so buyers persistently shop at a store because they know prices will always be low. Everyday low pricing also means a retailer spends less in advertising. Everyday low pricing stores may have higher sales than hi-low pricing stores, but may also experience lower profits.

Everything but Arms An agreement between the European Union and the world's 49 least developed countries. Under the agreement, all exports except weapons from these countries may enter the EU without paying any tariffs or going through any other trade barriers. The Everything but Arms agreement came into effect in 2001, but a few commodities (bananas, sugar and rice) were still subject to tariffs until the mid- and late-2000s.

Eviction The casting out of a tenant from a tenancy. For example, a landlord may evict a resident of an apartment for non-payment of rent. Eviction may occur for a tenant's violations of the lease agreement. In general, however, the landlord must give notice a certain number of days before an eviction may take place.

Evidence of Insurability Documentation that an applicant for life or health insurance is sufficiently healthy to be sold a policy. Many policies do not require evidence of insurability, but others mandate a health exam prior to the policy's issue.

Evidence of Origin Reasonable attestation that an import comes from the country that the importer or exporter claims. Usually, a certificate of origin is sufficient to provide evidence of origin. A good's origin may affect the tariff paid on it.

Evidence of Right to Make Entry Documentation that the party attempting to bring an import into the United States is a licensed agent of either the importer or the exporter. Evidence of right to make entry is required by U.S. customs.

Evidence of Title A document proving ownership. An example is a deed to a car.

Evolutionary Theory of the Firm A theory that no one business model or strategy ensures a company's survival over the long term. According to the evolutionary theory, success or failure is determined by how well the business model fits the needs of the present moment. Sheer chance also plays a large role.

Ex Shorthand indicating that a security is being traded without something attached to it. The term is most common when that "something" is an extra that would usually be attached to the security but is not. See also: Ex-dividend, Ex-right, Ex-warrant.

Ex Div. 1. See: Ex-dividend. **2.** See: Ex-dividend date.

Ex Dock An agreement between a buyer and a seller in which the seller delivers a good, at his own expense and risk, to a certain dock from which the good may be loaded onto a ship. Once it arrives at the dock, expense and risk transfer to the buyer, who is responsible for transporting the good from there. It is not a recognized incoterm.

Ex Gratia Payment A payment one makes when he/she has no obligation to do so. For example, an employer may give an unannounced bonus to employees at the end of a particularly good year. An ex gratia payment generally is non-recurring, but, in any case, is not the result of a legal obligation.

Ex Mine An agreement between a buyer and a seller relating to the price one owes to the other with respect to the development of a mineral.

Ex Officio Describing a member of an organization who serves in his/her position because he/she already has another post. For example, the Lieutenant Governor of Oklahoma serves ex officio as a member of the Oklahoma Native American Cultural and Education Authority. Serving ex officio does not mean one has more or fewer powers than other members (this depends upon the organization's bylaws). Rather, it simply means that the holder of the stated post has the right to sit in that organization.

Ex Post Describing the data from an event that has already happened. For example, an investor may analyze a company's earnings ex post, and then compare them with her predictions to gauge her accuracy. See also: Ex ante.

Ex Post Facto Describing anything, especially a law, that is applied retroactively. For example, a law criminalizing a certain action, which was passed on November 20, 2010, but gives the state the power to prosecute offenders retroactively to January 1, 2010, is an ex post facto law. Many jurisdictions do not permit their governments to enact ex post facto laws, at least in criminal cases.

Ex Warehouse An agreement between a buyer and a seller in which the seller delivers a good, at his own expense and risk, to a certain warehouse. Once it arrives at the warehouse, expense and risk transfer to the buyer, who is responsible for transporting the good from there.

Ex Works In international commerce, an agreement between a seller and a buyer indicating that the seller has fulfilled his/her obligation to deliver a good when he/she has made it available at his/her premises for the buyer to pick up. The seller is therefore not responsible for transporting the good and risk is transferred to the buyer as soon as the good is available. The buyer is responsible for all costs related to the transport of the good, as well as charges associated with exporting and importing. The place where the good is to be made available is specified in the agreement and is usually a warehouse or other facility owned by the seller. Of all international commerce agreements, an Ex Works agreement carries the least responsibility for the seller. See also: United Nations Convention on Contracts for the International Sale of Goods, Incoterm.

Exact Interest Interest that is calculated and therefore repaid on the basis of a 365-day year (that is, an actual year), as opposed to a 360-day year, which is used in some calculations. While this is only a small difference in calculation, the difference in amount can be large, especially with large debt transactions. See also: Ordinary interest.

Ex-All The sale of a security without any of the "extras" that otherwise would have belonged to it. Examples include dividends, warrants, and other rights. When a stock, for example, is sold ex-all, all of the rights associated with it remain with the seller. Selling ex-all almost invariably reduces the price for which the security is sold. See also: Ex-dividend date.

Examination of Title In real estate, research done to investigate the legitimacy of a title. An examination of title is done before the sale of property to ensure that there are no competing claims for the same property. An examination of title looks into only recent history and does not trace the property back to its source. For that reason, its findings may not be as accurate as a full title search, which tracks the property back to its beginnings or a statutory date.

Examined Business A life or health insurance policy on which the potential policyholder has not paid the first premium. However, the policyholder has passed a relevant medical examination to confirm eligibility for the policy.

Examiner 1. See: Auditor. **2.** A doctor who performs a physical on a life or health insurance applicant to determine whether or not the applicant is eligible for a policy.

Ex-Ante Describing any predicted future event. For example, an analyst may predict a company's earnings ex-ante and then compare its actual earnings to gauge the accuracy of her prediction. See also: Ex-Post.

Exante Average Rate of Return An estimated, as opposed to actual, average rate of return over the life of an investment. In cases in which there was uncertainty as to the average rate of return before the investment was made, one calculates the exante average rate of return to gauge how much one may expect to make from it. This may inform one's investment decisions. One may compare the exante average to the expost average rate of return after the investment is complete to determine how accurate the estimates were.

Ex-Bonus Describing the sale of a stock in which a bonus issue that has been announced but not distributed remains with the seller. That is, the buyer does not receive the bonus when it is distributed even though she owns the stock. A bonus in this context is a free issue of shares given by the issuing company to current stockholders. This is also called ex-capitalization or ex-scrip.

Except for Opinion An auditor's statement that he/she is unable to render an opinion about a company's finances, or a portion thereof, because regulatory or managerial encumbrances prevented a full investigation.

Exception 1. In a publicly-traded company, a proxy that does not authorize the proxy committee to act on his/her behalf. Such a proxy makes his/her own arrangements. **2.** In an audit of a financial statement, a note stating that the auditor agrees with a majority of the statement, but not with certain parts. That is, exceptions are written when the auditor believes that the majority of the financial statement is accurate, but that there are a few inaccuracies scattered throughout. Exceptions are noted in the auditor's report.

Exceptional Item An unusual charge that a company accrues in the ordinary course of its business. For example, the wages a company pays may be exceptionally large in a given year because of the amount of overtime that employees work. This differs from an extraordinary item which is also unusual but does not accrue in the ordinary course of business. Under the Generally Accepted Accounting Principles, exceptional items must be reported on a balance sheet while extraordinary items need not be reported.

Excess Contribution Contributions made to an IRA over and above the maximum allowable contribution. One must withdraw excess contributions from the IRA in the current tax year or be subject to a 6% excise tax. Excess contributions are banned in order to remove the incentive for excessive tax avoidance.

Excess Deferral Contributions to an IRA, 401(k), or other tax-deferred account over and above the limits on what may be deferred. Most plans place limits on how much can be contributed to the account each year and written off of one's taxable income. If one contributes too much, one runs the risk of paying taxes on the excess deferral in the year it is contributed as well as the year it is distributed after retirement. One may avoid this if one requests a refund of the excess deferral in the same tax year. If one does this, one only owes taxes for the current year.

Excess Demand Demand for a good or service well over supply. Excess demand leads to high prices for the good or service.

Excess Interest In whole life insurance, the return on the policy over and above the death benefit that the policy guarantees. The amount of the excess interest (if any) depends on the performance of the portion of the premium that is put in a cash value account and is invested.

Excess Kurtosis A measure of the fatness of the tails of kurtosis where there is higher likelihood of large gains or large losses on an investment. That is, excess kurtosis indicates that the volatility of the investment is itself highly volatile.

Excess Loan A loan a bank makes to an individual over and above statutory limits. A national bank in the United States may not lend more than 15% of its capital to one person. For a state bank, the limit is 10%. An excess loan is any loan over these percentages.

Excess Margin Cash or securities that one has deposited in a margin account over and above the minimum maintenance requirement. The excess margin is available to be used as collateral for margin loans, or it may be withdrawn and used for any other purpose.

Excess Profits Tax A tax imposed on a company's profits over a certain amount. Excess profit taxes are imposed in order to generate more revenue for the government, especially during national emergencies. In the United States, excess profit taxes have been implemented during wartime. There are also periodic debates on whether to impose an excess profit tax on private industries thought to be necessary for consumers in order to discourage profiteering or price gouging. Particularly, oil and gas companies have been targeted for this form of the excess profit tax. See also: Windfall Tax.

Excess Reserves Money a bank keeps in addition to the legally required reserves. Historically, most banks have kept little or nothing in excess reserves because they earn no interest on excess reserves. Government policies such as FDIC deposit insurance encouraged keeping less in reserves because banks were not required to cover all withdrawals in the event of a run. However, in the United States, the Emergency Economic Stabilization Act of 2008 allowed the Federal Reserve to pay interest on excess reserves, which is began doing in October 2008. In the ensuing months, the amount of excess reserves in American banks increased substantially. This is thought to have reduced insolvency risk for banks by encouraging them to keep more money on hand, but critics contend that this discourages banks from lending.

Excess Return A return that is larger than some benchmark, especially the risk-free return. A portfolio, for example, may have an excess return above the index on which it is based. This occurs when the portfolio manager makes certain investment decisions that pay off for the investor. It is important to note that receiving an excess return almost always requires one to take on more risk.

Excess Return on the Market Portfolio The difference between the return on the market portfolio, a hypothetical portfolio of all securities, and the riskless rate of return, which is usually defined as the return on a 90-day Treasury bill. This may be taken as an indicator of how well (or poorly) the stock market is performing.

Excess Supply Supply of a good or service well over demand. Excess supply leads to low prices for the good or service.

Excess-Accumulation Penalty A 50% tax that one must pay if one neglects to take the required minimum distribution from one's IRA. The required minimum distribution is the portion of an IRA that must begin to be distributed to an annuitant by the age of 70.5 or the date of retirement, whichever comes later. The amount of the minimum required distribution is determined by the value of the IRA, the length of time the annuitant has contributed, and the amount of contributions. In any case, the excess accumulation penalty exists in order to prevent an IRA from becoming unfairly valuable during the annuitant's retirement. See also: Excise tax.

Excess-Currency Country A country in which the U.S. government representation has more of the local currency than it needs. Officials stationed in excess-currency countries are encouraged to minimize purchases made in U.S. dollars and to use the local currency instead.

Excessive Insurance Insurance over and above the policyholder's needs. For example, if one's homeowners insurance has a $500,000 benefit but it would only take $150,000 to rebuild one's house and replace one's possessions, one has excessive insurance. A person or company with excessive insurance likely is paying too much in premiums.

Excessive Purchases A higher than normal number of purchases made on a credit card. Excessive purchases may be a sign of fraud or may even indicate that a card has been stolen. Ordinarily, the fraud protection unit of the credit card company contacts the card holder to discuss excessive purchases.

Exchange Acquisition A trade in which a number of small sell orders are placed together and executed in order to fill a single, very large buy order. An exchange acquisition may create the appearance of a single trade (indeed, it is reported as such), but in fact it is the result of a streamlining process whereby a broker makes what would have been smaller trades at once. The broker receives a special commission for making an exchange acquisition. See also: Block.

Exchange Against Actual A transaction where an investor trades a cash position on a commodity for a futures contract on the same commodity. An exchange against actuals is useful when two investors have offsetting, hedged positions they wish to close. An exchange against actuals is also called an exchange against physicals or an exchange versus cash.

Exchange Controls Laws or regulations that a government may institute limiting foreign exchange of its currency. A government may enact exchange controls on one currency (that is, a government may say that its currency is not convertible into Zimbabwean dollars, for example), or it may enact exchange controls over all currencies. Some countries have exchange controls to prevent citizens from making bad investment decisions in, say, a country experiencing hyperinflation, while a few communist countries enact exchange controls to prevent capitalist influences. See also: Inconvertibility.

Exchange Distribution A trade in which a number of small buy orders are placed together and executed in order to fill a single, very large sell order. An exchange distribution may create the appearance of a single trade (and indeed it is reported as such), but, in fact, it is the result of a streamlining process whereby a broker makes what would have been smaller trades at once. The broker receives a special commission for making an exchange distribution. See also: Block.

Exchange Fund An investment vehicle allowing investors with large holdings in a single stock to exchange them for a diversified portfolio. This allows the investors to diversify their holdings without selling any stocks, thereby avoiding taxes on their capital gains until the shares are actually sold. Exchange funds are controversial as investors could avoid taxes completely by never selling the portfolio and simply borrowing against it. They were originally introduced in 1999. An exchange fund is also called a swap fund.

Exchange Member A person, normally a broker, who has membership on a stock exchange. This means that he/she is allowed to make trades on the floor of that exchange. Most exchanges do not allow firms to be members, so the membership for a member firm formally belongs to one or more of its employees. Memberships are bought and sold at market price because most exchanges have a finite number. See also: Seat.

Exchange of Assets An acquisition in which the acquirer buys the target company indirectly by buying its assets. The assets may be bought in exchange for cash and/or stock.

Exchange of Futures for Cash An agreement between two parties in which a buyer of a commodity exchanges futures contracts for the commodity. Either the buyer gives the seller a certain amount in long position futures or he/she receives from the seller an equivalent amount of short position futures. If there is a difference between the futures and the price of the commodity, it is settled in cash. This transaction is also known as an exchange for physicals.

Exchange of Stock A way of accomplishing an acquisition in which the acquiring company buys all of the target company's stock and gives to shareholders either cash or stock in the acquiring company.

Exchange Offer An offer by a company to trade stocks or bonds for other stocks or bonds. For example, a firm may redeem bonds with other bonds of equivalent value. This often occurs when the firm has poor cash flow. Likewise, a company may redeem stocks in itself for other stocks, either in the same or another firm. An exchange offer of stocks is common following a merger or acquisition.

Exchange Privilege The right of a shareholder in a mutual fund to sell his/her shares and buy shares in another mutual fund within the same fund family, generally with no additional load (or sales fee). Different mutual funds within a fund family have different investment goals and/or strategies. However, because the same company manages the whole group, individual investors may generally exercise the exchange privilege to move money from one fund to another without extra commissions or fees, or with only a nominal charge. The exchange privilege allows investors to be flexible in their own investment goals according to their particular needs at a given time.

Exchange Rate The value of two currencies relative to each other. For example, on a given day, one may trade one U.S. dollar for a certain number of British pounds. A currency's exchange rates may be floating (that is, they may change from day to day) or they may be pegged to another currency. A floating exchange rate is dependent on the supply and demand of the involved currencies, as well as the amount of the currency held in foreign reserves. On the other hand, a government may peg its currency to a certain amount in another currency or currency basket. For example, the Qatari riyal has been worth 0.274725 dollars since 1980. An advantage to a floating exchange rate is the fact that it tends to be more economically efficient. However, floating exchange rates tend to be more volatile, depending on the particular currency. Pegged exchange rates are generally more stable, but, since they are set by government fiat, they may take political rather than economic conditions into account. For example, some countries peg their exchange rates artificially low with respect to a major trading partner to make their exports to that partner artificially cheap. See also: Currency pair, Eurodollar.

Exchange Rate Bands The range of exchange rates a central bank allows its currency to take. Exchange rate bands are used when one currency links its value to that of another currency but allows it to fluctuate within certain limits. Proponents maintain that exchange rate bands give a currency a certain level of flexibility so that it can respond to market factors while leaving control with the central bank. Critics contend that this system is inefficient and leads to unfair practices in international trade. The Chinese renmimbi is a prominent example of a currency that traditionally has existed within exchange rate bands. See also: Crawling peg.

Exchange Rate Mechanism Used prior to the adoption of the euro, a method for reconciling differing exchange rates between currencies, allowing participation in the single European currency. Established in 1979, it was known as a "semi-pegged" system in which currencies were variable with respect to each other only within a certain range. After the introduction of the euro in 1999, the exchange rate mechanism was replaced by ERM II, which reconciles exchange rates for countries wishing to join the eurozone.

Exchange Ratio In mergers and acquisitions, the number of shares an acquiring firm distributes for each validly rendered share of the acquired company. Each exchange ratio is calculated in accordance to the merger or acquisition agreement. Factors considered in determining the ratio are the relative value of each company prior to the closing of the merger or acquisition, any potential tax advantages for both parties, and applicable regulations.

Exchange Traded Note A debt security issued by a financial institution with no coupon and no principal protection. That is, unlike other bonds, the issuer of an exchange traded note is not required to repay the principal at maturity. Rather, the return on an exchange traded note is determined by the performance of some stated market index. Exchange traded notes are negotiable securities traded on an exchange. They often have maturities as long as 30 years.

Exchange Value The theoretical value of a commodity if it were to be traded. In Marxist economics, this is similar to but distinct from the concept of price, which is a money value of a commodity in a transaction. It differs from use value in that use value measures quality while exchange value measures quantity.

Exchangeable Debt A debt security that the holder may exchange, at a certain price, for common stock in the company other than the one that issued the debt security. The number of shares one receives for each security and the price one pays for those shares are determined when the exchangeable debt is issued. Most of the time, the common stock is in a subsidiary of the company that issued the exchangeable debt. Exchangeable debt is a low-risk investment, but it affords the investor a great amount of leeway because he/she can exchange it for another security with higher risk and a higher return. Exchangeable debt operates like a convertible bond; the main difference is the fact that in a convertible bond the common stock that one may buy is the stock of the company issuing the bond rather than that of a subsidiary.

Exchange-Traded Fund A security that represents all the stocks on a given exchange. For example, an exchange-traded fund may track the Standard and Poor's 500. The organization issuing the exchange-trade fund owns each of the stocks traded on the S&P 500 in approximate ratio to their market capitalization. ETF shares can be bought, sold, short-sold, traded on margin, and generally function as if they were stocks. Investors use exchange-traded funds as a way to easily diversify their portfolios at relatively low cost. See also: SPDR.

Exchange-Traded Option An option contract that is traded on an exchange. An exchange-traded option is subject to all of the exchange's applicable regulations; this reduces uncertainly for the investor because exchange-traded options are standardized contracts. They contrast with over-the-counter options, the provisions of which may be customized.

Exchequer **1.** See: HM Treasury. **2.** A general term, especially in the United Kingdom, for a fund or account.

Excise Tax A tax on the manufacture or sale of a good or service over and above all other taxes paid on it. For example, a person may owe sales tax on the purchase of tobacco, but the state may also levy an excise tax on top of it. Likewise, one may owe both income taxes and excise taxes on a premature distribution of an IRA. See also: Sin tax.

Exclusion **1.** Injuries, illnesses, or other conditions for which a health insurance policy does not provide coverage. Exclusions exist because they are thought to be too risky for the health insurance provider. For example, many insurance providers exclude treatment for some types of cancer because they are so expensive to treat. See also: Pre-existing condition. **2.** Income that is not considered gross income for tax purposes. Exclusions include gifts, inheritance, and some others. It is important to note that just because a type of income is an exclusion, it does not mean that it is not taxed; it simply may be taxed differently. Exclusions are stated in the U.S. Tax Code.

Exclusion Ratio The percentage of an investor's return that is not subject to taxes. The exclusion ratio is a percentage with a dollar amount equal to the payback on one's initial investment. Any return above the exclusion ratio is subject to taxes. Most of the time, the exclusion ratio applies to non-qualified annuities.

Exclusionary Self-Tender A self-tender offer in which a company offers to buy its own shares from shareholders while excluding a particular class of shareholders. See also: Go Private.

Exclusions from Medical Benefits Injuries, illnesses, or other conditions for which a health insurance policy does not provide coverage. Exclusions exist because they are thought to be too risky for the health insurance provider. For example, insurance providers may exclude treatment for some types of cancer because they are expensive to treat. See also: Pre-existing condition.

Exclusions of Policy Anything for which an insurance policy does not provide coverage. Exclusions exist because they are thought to be too risky for the insurance provider or because they constitute an abuse of the policy. For example, life insurance providers may exclude coverage for suicide. See also: Pre-existing condition.

Exclusive Describes a broker-dealer who has a client's order or indication of interest without competing with other broker-dealers. That is, an exclusive broker-dealer is not competing for a better commission or anything else with other broker-dealers.

Ex-Coupon The sale of a bond after a stated date before a coupon is distributed. When a bond is sold ex-coupon, the right to receive the coupon remains with the seller. Selling ex-coupon almost invariably reduces the selling price of the bond. See also: Ex-dividend, Ex-bonus.

Ex-Date **1.** See: Ex-dividend date. **2.** The date on which the new price of a stock is listed following a stock split. A stock split reduces the price per share, and tickers on exchanges reflect this on and after the ex-date.

EXDEC Shipper's Export Declaration. A form that an exporter or a shipping company must file with the U.S. Department of Commerce if the value of the commodity one is exporting exceeds a certain value. In 2000, this value was $2,500. The form is administered by the U.S. Census Bureau. See also: International trade.

Ex-Dividend The sale of a security after a dividend has been announced but before it has been distributed. When a security is sold ex-dividend, the dividend remains with the seller. Selling ex-dividend almost invariably reduces the price for which the security is sold by the amount of the dividend. See also: Cum dividend, Ex-dividend date.

Ex-Dividend Date The date on which any dividend on a stock that has been declared but not distributed belongs legally to the seller, rather than the buyer. That is, when one sells a stock on or after the ex-dividend date, it will go to the seller when the next dividend comes. On the other hand, if it is sold before the ex-dividend date, the dividend will go to the buyer.

Ex-Dividend Share A share in a stock sold after a dividend has been announced but before it has been distributed. When a security is sold ex-dividend, the dividend remains with the seller. Selling ex-dividend almost invariably reduces the price for which the security is sold by the amount of the dividend. See also: Cum dividend, Ex-dividend date.

Execution The act of filling an order to buy or sell a security. That is, when a broker executes an order, he/she actually makes a trade on behalf of the client. The date of execution is known as the trade date.

Execution Costs The difference between the market price of a security and what that price would have been had a certain transaction affecting the price not taken place. See also: Market impact cost, market timing cost.

Executive Order 6102 A 1933 executive order by U.S. President Franklin D. Roosevelt forbidding persons and corporations in the United States from owning more than a token amount of gold. All gold over the legal limit was required to be sold to the federal government at a price of $20.67 per ounce. The order was made moot a year later with the passage of the Gold Reserve Act of 1934.

Executor/Executrix A person who administers the estate of a deceased person. The executor (if male) or executrix (if female) is responsible for gathering all of the decedent's assets and giving them to the appropriate beneficiaries. He/she is often a family member or lawyer who is either appointed in the decedent's will or by a court. The executor/executrix has a fiduciary responsibility to act on behalf of the decedent and to fulfill, as closely as possible, the wishes set forth in the will. Persons under 18 and convicted felons cannot serve as executors.

Exempt Income Any income that is not subject to taxation. Examples of exempt income in the United States include income from municipal bonds, some retirement contributions, interest paid on mortgages, and the personal exemption, among other things. See also: Earned Income Tax Credit.

Exempt Securities Securities that do not need to be registered with the SEC under the Security Act of 1933 or the Securities Exchange Act of 1934. Examples of exempt securities include small issues, agency securities, most other debt instruments issued by the federal or a local government, and issues made only in a single state. Private placements are also usually exempt from registration.

Exempt Status The state of not being subject to taxation. Examples of organizations with exempt statues (in some jurisdictions) include religious groups and charities. Additionally, certain income an individual or corporation derives may be tax exempt. For example, coupons from a municipal bond are tax exempt at the federal level. See also: Tax credit, Tax deduction, 501(c)3.

Exemption Trust A trust set up by a married couple into which both spouses agree to deposit all assets of the first spouse to die, even if they would otherwise go to the second spouse. When the second spouse dies, the trust is dissolved and assets from both spouses are distributed to survivors. An exemption trust exists because the assets deposited into it are not subject to the estate tax when the second spouse passes away because they are not technically part of the estate.

Exercise In option contracts, to buy (in the case of a call) or sell (in the case of a put) the underlying asset. The option holder has no obligation to exercise the option, and only does so if he/she believes it benefits him/her. Depending upon the nature of the option, this may be done at any point during the life of the contract, or it may only be done on the contract's expiry date. The strike price of the sale is agreed-upon in the option contract, that is, before the option is exercised.

Exercise Limit A rule on many derivative exchanges preventing the exercise of too many option contracts by one investor over a given period of time. The exercise limit usually lasts five days; that is, no person or company may exercise more than the stated number of options on the same underlying asset over any five business days. Exercise limits exist in order to promote market stability by preventing a single investor from taking over too much of a market too quickly.

Exercise Loan A loan that an employer gives to an employee to enable the employee to exercise his/her stock options. An exercise loan may be forgiven under certain, defined circumstances.

Exercise Notice The written notice of the holder of an option contract of his/her intent to exercise the option. Exercise notice may occur on or before the expiration date, depending on the type of option contract. The exercise notice is sent to the Options Clearing Corporation, which is responsible for settling the transaction by finding an investor with an opposite position on the same contract.

Exercise Settlement Amount The amount that the writer (for a call) or the holder (for a put) of an index option is paid if the option is exercised. Because one cannot actually transfer an index, these options are subject to cash settlement for the exercise settlement amount. It is calculated as the difference between the strike price and the aggregate price of the index on the day the option is exercised with the quantity multiplied by the index multiplier.

Exercise Value The profit that an option holder would receive by exercising an in-the-money option. That is, the exercise value of an option is how much the strike price is below the underlying asset (for a call) or above the underlying asset (for a put). These options have value because they always result in a profit. As a result, they may be sold for much higher price than the investor paid for the option. See also: Intrinsic Value.

Ex-Food and Energy A measure of inflation in the United States that considers what people spend on staple goods and services other than food and energy. It is calculated by taking the average of price changes to a basket of goods and services compiled by the U.S. Department of Labor. The ex-food and energy index is identical to the Consumer Price Index except that it leaves out food and energy. Some consider the ex-food and energy index a more reliable measure of inflation, as food and energy prices are quite volatile. Critics, however, contend that leaving these prices out does not adequately measure short-term changes in the real value of money.

Ex-Gracing The practice of sending new issues of a periodical to a former subscriber after his/her subscription has expired, perhaps to encourage him/her to re-subscribe.

Exhaustion A situation in which demand has overwhelmed supply or vice versa. The term is especially used in investing when too many traders have taken a short position or a long position relative to the number of traders on the other side. This can be an indication that the price for a security has peaked (if there are too many buyers) or bottomed (if there are too many sellers). See also: Price correction.

Exhaustion Gap In technical analysis, a gap on a chart representing a large difference in price between two succeeding trades after prices have been rising significantly. The second price is higher than the first. The exhaustion gap indicates that buying pressure is ending and the security in question will soon begin to decline in price.

Existing Home Sales A measure of the number and price of sales of single-family homes other than new constructions. It is considered an economic indicator of the availability and affordability of mortgages and real estate in the United States. It is also considered a lagging indicator as it tends to react after changes in mortgage interest rates. Existing home sales tend to rise after a decline in mortgage rates and fall when the opposite happens. The U.S. National Association of Realtors publishes existing home sales monthly.

Exit Strategy **1.** In entrepreneurship and venture capital, a plan to end one's involvement with a business or investment while making the greatest possible profit (or smallest possible loss). An exit strategy is designed to turn an illiquid asset into liquid cash for the investor. The most straightforward exit strategy is simply selling one's business. If this is impossible, difficult, or unprofitable, another example is discounting one's products to sell as much as possible in as short a time as possible, as in a going-out-of-business sale. **2.** In trade, a plan to close a position at a certain point. For instance, a trader may make a stop-loss order in order to close an unprofitable position.

Ex-Legal A municipal bond that does not have the written endorsement of a bond law firm. An ex-legal bond has not been checked to ensure that it has followed all applicable laws in the course of issue (or, worse, it has been checked and a firm refused to endorse it). As a result, ex-legals are more highly exposed to legal risk than other bonds.

Ex-New The sale of a stock in which the buyer does not receive the right to take advantage of a coming bonus issue or the right to receive a warrant that has been announced but not distributed. These rights remain with the seller. In other words, an ex-new sale is both ex-scrip and ex-warrant.

Exogenous **1.** Describing anything outside a company's control. For example, a company may fail because of a recession even if it does everything right. In this case, the recession is an exogenous factor. **2.** See: Independent Variable.

Exogenous Uncertainty Anything outside a company's control. For example, a company may fail because of a recession even if it does everything right. In this case, the possibility of recession is an exogenous uncertainty.

Exogenous Variable In a model, any independent variable whose value is not determined by the model. An exogenous variable is not affected by the model, but still may determine the value of one or more dependent variables. See also: Endogenous variable.

Exonumia The hobby or practice of collecting commemorative coins and medals. These coins can be valuable to the study of economic history and often have value as collectibles.

Exonumist A person who studies or collects commemorative coins and medals. These coins can be valuable to the study of economic history and often have value as collectibles.

Exordium Clause A clause at the beginning of a will. The exordium clause identifies the testor (or person making the will), states his/her residence and the fact that he/she is of sound mind. It also revokes all previous will. See also: Last Will & Testament.

Exotic Option Any option contract that is not an American or European option. That is, an exotic option contains some provision that makes it different from a straightforward option contract with a strike price, underlying asset, and expiration date. For example, a chooser option allows the holder to decide whether the contract is a call or a put at some point over the contract's life. Also, an Asian option has no set strike price and is calculated as the average of some price listed in the contract and the market value of the underlying asset at the time of exercise. Most exotic options trade over-the-counter because their provisions make them too complex for the regulations of exchanges.

Expansion In a business cycle, a period of growth during which an economy moves from its trough to its peak. For example, if an economy dips to growth of -2.5% and then recovers to 3% growth, this period is called expansion. It is considered a normal and inevitable part of a business cycle following a recession or other contraction. Expansion is also called recovery.

Expatriate An employee at a company who is a citizen of another country. Some governments require companies hiring expatriates to show cause that the job could not be performed by a local citizen. Expatriates are generally subject to taxation only in the country where they are working, though citizens of the United States often must pay American taxes as well as local taxes, depending on their levels of income. See also: Foreign Tax Credit.

Expectations Index A survey of 5,000 households in which respondents are asked their impressions and sentiments regarding economic conditions in the coming six months. Specifically, they are asked their impressions on employment prospects, business opportunities, and, perhaps most importantly, their expected spending habits. The Expectations Index is the most important component of the Consumer Confidence Index, which businesses use to help make investment decisions. For example, if the Expectation Index shows that consumers are unlikely to spend more on luxury items in the next six months, the leisure industry will probably not build new hotels in that time period. See also: Friedman unit.

Expected Dividend Yield The yield an investor expects to receive over one year when he/she purchases a stock or other security that pays dividends. The dividend yield is the amount an investor receives in dividends in one year divided by the purchase price of the security. The expected dividend yield is what the investor expects to receive at purchase, rather than what he/she actually receives. While calculating the expected dividend yield has a role in making investment decisions, it is important to note that the expected dividend yield may not match up with the actual dividend yield. See also: Expected return, Actual return.

Expected Family Contribution The amount that a student and his/her family are calculated to be able to pay for an academic year at a post-secondary educational institution. The expected family contribution is used in the FAFSA system. It is calculated by taking the tuition and subtracting the federal financial aid for which the student is eligible.

Expected Future Cash Flows The cash flow an investor or company expects to realize from a project before that project begins. The actual cash flows received may be greater or less than the expected future cash flows. They are often measured according to their present value. See also: Expected return.

Expected Rate of Inflation Investor and public expectations of current or future inflation. These expectations may or may not be rational, but they may affect how the market reacts to changes in target interest rates. For example, the market usually responds well to a cut in interest rates, but if investors expect inflation to go higher in the near future and the Federal Reserve cuts rates, the market may not react positively.

Expected Return The return on an investment as estimated by an asset pricing model. It is calculated by taking the average of the probability distribution of all possible returns. For example, a model might state that an investment has a 10% chance of a 100% return and a 90% chance of a 50% return. The expected return is calculated as: Expected Return = 0.1(1) + 0.9(0.5) = 0.55 = 55%. It is important to note that there is no guarantee that the expected rate of return and the actual return will be the same. See also: Abnormal return.

Expected Return-Beta Relationship In the Capital Asset Pricing Model, a statement that the expected rate of return on an investment is directly proportional to its risk premium, as signified by its beta.

Expected Value of Perfect Information An estimate of the price an investor would pay for perfect information on an investment. See also: Efficiency.

Expedited Funds Availability Act Legislation in the United States, passed in 1987, that requires banks to make checks and other deposits available within a certain number of days. Depending on circumstances such as the size of the deposit and how long the account has been open, the bank must make the deposit available on the first, second, seventh or ninth day. See also: Check hold.

Expense Account An account a company keeps with a budgeted amount of money in it to allow an employee to pay expenses on a business trip. For example, a company may authorize an employee to use a company credit card to pay for hotel, food and similar expenses while she attends a marketing event. Less commonly, an expense account refers to a situation in which an employee spends his/her own money and receives a reimbursement from the employer.

Expensed Charged to an expense account, reducing the profit for a given project or assignment. The term is associated with charges connected to networking and other events used to attract clients or investors. Expensed items are written off on taxes as they reduce profit.

Expenses Costs of living or doing business. Examples of personal expenses include the mortgage payment, groceries, and gas for the car. Examples of business expenses include the cost of materials, employee salaries, and other overhead. Expenses also include unusual costs like medical bills or employee bonuses. Businesses attempt to keep costs to the lowest possible amount without sacrificing revenue. This maximizes profit. Likewise, households generally attempt (and in many cases must) keep expenses lower than household income. While business expenses are generally tax deductible, most personal expenses are not.

Expensive Of or related to the high cost of a good, service, or security. Expensiveness is determined by comparing the cost to similar goods, services, and securities. Expensiveness is also related to one's ability to buy: what seems expensive to one person may not seem so to another. Expensiveness may be justified depending on the quality of the good, service, or security.

Experience Rating In insurance, a calculation of a policy's premium based on the likelihood of a claim on that policy. This calculation takes into account the policyholder's history of past claims with the aim of discouraging dangerous activities that would lead to a claim. For instance, a policyholder with a history of claims due to work-related injuries will likely pay higher premiums because of his/her experience rating than a policyholder with no such history. Indeed, an experience rating showing few or no claims can lead to discounts on premiums.

Expiration Cycle The period of time during which an option contract is valid. Most options that trade on an exchange belong to one of three expiration cycles. The January cycle expires in the first month of each quarter, the February cycle expires in the second month, and the March cycle expires in the third month. It is also called the option cycle.

Expiration Date The date by which an option contract is abandoned and becomes worthless unless it is exercised. In an option contract, the holder has the right, but not the obligation, to buy or sell (depending on the type of option) the underlying asset within a certain period of time. The expiration date is the time at which the holder will lose the right to exercise the option. A European option can only be exercised on the expiration date, while an American option can be exercised at any point prior to the expiration date.

Expiration Effect The rapid trading of a futures or option contract immediately before expiration. The expiration effect can cause large and rapid changes in the price of the contract, and usually is the result of traders seeking to close their positions to fulfill their various investment strategies before expiration.

Expiration Friday The expiration date for three types of standardized contracts: stock options, stock index futures, and index options. Expiration Friday occurs four times a year, on the third Friday in the last month of each quarter. Investors often unwind their positions on these contracts on or immediately before expiration Fridays, which leads to increased trading volume and price volatility on those days.

Expiration Series All options or futures that expire in a given month. See also: Expiration cycle.

Expiration Time The specific time of day on the expiration date by which an option must be exercised or it will expire. On exchanges in the United States, the expiration time is either 11:59 a.m. or 5:30 p.m., eastern time.

Ex-Pit Transaction A futures transaction that does not occur on the trading floor. These transactions are called ex-pit because the futures trading floor is informally called the pit.

Explicit Bankruptcy Costs Expenses that an individual or company incurs directly in the process of a bankruptcy. Explicit bankruptcy costs include attorney's fees, court costs, and so forth.

Explicit Cost A direct expense that a business incurs in conducting an activity. Examples of explicit costs include salaries, wages, materials, etc. An explicit cost can be recurring, or it can be a one-off expense. Likewise, it can be predictable, like the rent, or it can vary from time to time, like the electric bill. Less commonly, an explicit cost is called an outlay cost. See also: Implicit cost.

Explicit Tax A tax levied and collected by a government. Examples include income tax, value added tax, sales tax, estate tax, and so forth. This compares to hidden regulatory fees, which add to the cost of doing business without necessarily adding to government revenue. For example, some argue for a carbon tax that would, theoretically, increase government revenue by taxing the emission of carbon dioxide. This compares to a proposed cap-and-trade system, which requires carbon emitters to buy permission to emit without changing how they are actually taxed.

Exploding Offer An offer (to buy or sell a good or service) with an expiration date. For example, one may make an exploding offer to buy an automobile on Friday and expect an answer by the following Monday. Exploding offers put pressure on the counterparty to make a decision.

Exploding Term Sheet In venture capital, a term sheet for a business agreement that may not be finalized. A term sheet is a preliminary agreement between a venture capital firm and a business it intends to finance; it outlines the terms of what each party expects from the other, usually in a bullet point fashion. It is not usually binding. A term sheet may "explode" if either party backs out of the deal and the term sheet does not culminate in a final contract between the venture capital firm and the business.

Exploration Cost The cost an oil or gas company incurs while searching for oil or gas to drill. Exploration costs include the cost of researching appropriate places to drill and the cost of actually drilling. There is no guarantee that there will be a return on the investment of exploration costs because there is no guarantee that the company will find oil or natural gas. Exploration costs can also be quite expensive. See also: Exploration oil & gas limited partnership, Upstream.

Exploratory Oil and Gas Partnership A higher-risk oil and gas limited partnership. The general partner uses the investment money from the limited partners to drill in an unproven oil or gas field, and not in a proven field. This gives the limited partners the possibility of high profit if a large amount of oil or gas is discovered, but there is a chance that nothing will be found and the limited partners will lose their investments. The typical partnership unit for a limited partner costs $5000, and the limited partner risks no more than this investment.

Exponential Moving Average The average price of a security calculated by adding closing prices from the most recent trading days (for example, the last 10 days) and dividing by the number of trading days considered (in this case, 10), with more recent trading days being weighted so that they affect the average more. An exponential moving average is more difficult to calculate than a simple moving average, but it provides a quick look at a security's trend. See also: Moving Average Convergence Divergence, Envelope.

Export A good produced in one country and sold to a customer in another country. Exports bring money into the producing country; for that reason, many economists believe that a nation's proper balance of trade means more exports are sold than imports bought. Exports may be difficult to sell in some countries, as the importers may put up various protectionist measures such as import quotas and tariffs. Most governments seek to promote exports, while they have differing positions on imports. See also: Free trade, NAFTA.

Export Administration Act of 1979 Legislation in the United States that gave the president the authority to control exports to other countries when national security and/or short supply demand it. The Act expired in 1994 but its regulations have been renewed by executive order every year since. Since 1990, the Act has not applied to agricultural products under some circumstances.

Export Administration Review Board An organization that hears and resolves disputes on American trade licensing. That is, if two or more cabinet departments disagree on whether or not to grant a company an export license, the EARB has the final decision. The Departments of Commerce, Defense, Energy, State and the Arms Control and Disarmament Agency are all voting members, while the Joint Chiefs of Staff and the CIA are nonvoting members. It was established in 1970.

Export America A former monthly publication by the International Trade Administration of the U.S. Department of Commerce. It folded in July 2004.

Export and Import Permits Act Legislation in Canada that authorizes the Minister for International Trade to restrict goods that may be imported or exported. The Act sets out the criteria the Minister uses in making these determinations; steel, textiles and weapons may all be controlled under the Act. The Minister issues permits to regulate the import and export of restricted goods.

Export Assistance Center One of dozens of offices run by the U.S. Department of Commerce providing advice and expertise to small businesses on how to export one's products. There are export assistance centers in about 100 American cities and in 80 other countries.

Export Contact List Service Also called the ECLS. A service giving American companies lists of potential customers and partners in other countries. The lists include manufacturers, distributors and others. It is provided by the International Trade Administration to promote American exports.

Export Control Any restriction a country places on its exports. For example, a country may impose export controls on weapons or nuclear materials in the interest of national security. Alternatively, it may place a control on wheat during a famine to help prevent food shortages.

Export Control Automated Support System Also called ECASS. A database of license information compiled and maintained by the Bureau of Industry and Security in the U.S. Department of Commerce. ECASS assists the BIS in its enforcement duties.

Export Control Classification Number Also called an ECCN. An alphanumeric code used to identify the level of control required for an export. An ECCN is used for technological goods and helps ensure applicable laws are being followed.

Export Control List A list of dangerous substances that a country subjects to more stringent regulations. Poisons, weapons and goods relating to national security are examples of items that might be included on an export control list.

Export Credit Agency A private or semi-governmental body that extends credit to local exporters. ECAs also provide guarantees and insurance for exports, and occasionally for imports as well. Sometimes governments use ECAs to subsidize exporters and related businesses, but this is generally frowned upon in international circles. ECAs are controversial; critics allege that their existence negatively impacts international development as developing countries cannot compete with such insured exports. Proponents of ECAs argue that they enable developing countries to import products they otherwise would not be able to afford.

Export Credit Guarantee A guarantee of payment made by an export credit agency (ECA). ECAs are government or semi-government agencies that provide guarantees and insurance for exports, and occasionally for imports as well. An export credit guarantee ensures that an exporter receives payment for goods shipped overseas in the event the customer defaults, reducing the risk to the exporter's business and allowing it to keep its prices competitive. The use of export credit guarantees is controversial; critics allege that their existence negatively impacts international development, as developing countries cannot compete with such insured exports. Proponents argue that they enable developing countries to import products they otherwise would not be able to afford.

Export Development Corp. A government owned corporation in Canada that extends credit to Canadian exporters. Export Development Canada also provides guarantees and insurance for exports. Like other export credit agencies (ECA), Export Development Canada is controversial; critics allege that ECAs negatively impact international development, as developing countries cannot compete with such insured exports. Proponents of ECAs argue that they enable developing countries to import products they otherwise would not be able to afford.

Export Enhancement Act of 1992 Legislation in the United States that created the Trade Promotion Coordinating Committee (TPCC), which advises the president on how best to promote American exports. The Act gives the president the authority to appoint members of the TPCC and to define its specific duties.

Export Finance Insurance Corp. A government owned corporation in Australia that extends credit to Australian exporters. The EFIC also provides guarantees and insurance for exports, and encourages private banks to do the same. Like other export credit agencies (ECAs), the EFIC is controversial; critics allege that ECAs negatively impact international development, as developing countries cannot compete with such insured exports. Proponents of ECAs argue that they enable developing countries to import products they otherwise would not be able to afford.

Export Financing Interest Income coming from interest on a credit line an exporter extended to a buyer on goods the exporter manufactured in the United States. That is, if a seller in the United States lends a foreign buyer an amount to buy one of the seller's products, the interest on that loan is export financing interest. The IRS categorizes export financing interest as passive income as long as less than half the value of the final product comes from imports into the United States.

Export House A company in India that has received a permit to sell exports.

Export Jobber A buyer of a good from a foreign country; an importer.

Export Levy A tax that a country imposes on its exports, which makes them more expensive. Export levies may encourage domestic consumption of domestically produced goods. They are less rare than import tariffs. See also: Import substitution industrialization.

Export License A license that a government issues to an exporter granting permission to sell certain goods to a given country. Because countries have different trade agreements with other governments, and sometimes do not allow any trade with some nations, export licenses ensure that exporters are adhering to all applicable laws.

Export Management Consultant A professional who supervises the exportation process for clients. Often there are legal requirements that must be filled before a country allows its goods to be exported; export management consultants

navigate these requirements and regulations. They operate like an export division for a company that does not have an export division. They may be local or foreign; sometimes they even operate in the country that imports the goods. Export management consultants may operate as freelancers, but they usually work for export management companies. They charge either a fee or a commission for their services.

Export Push Strategy In development economics, the approach in which a government makes a concerted effort to promote exports in order to encourage economic growth. A government may do this by keeping its currency weak, by subsidizing favored industries, or by adopting trade agreements with other countries. In an export push strategy, a country seeks to maintain a favorable balance of trade.

Export Quota A limit a country sets on the number of units of a good that may be exported over a period of time. Export quotas are usually instituted in order to maximize the domestic supply, which helps keep prices low within the country. While this may be good for consumers, it is not necessarily beneficial for producers. See also: Export control.

Export Rate The amount by which the value of an economy's exports grows (or declines) over a period of time. Because net exports are one component in GDP, the export rate contributes to overall growth or decline in an economy.

Export Trading Company A company that supervises the exportation process for clients. Often, there are legal requirements that must be filled before a country allows its goods to be exported; export trading companies navigate these requirements and regulations. They operate like an export division for a company that does not have an export division. They may be local or foreign; sometimes they even operate in the country that imports the goods. They charge either a fee or a commission for their services. They are also called export management companies.

Export Trading Company Act of 1982 Legislation in the United States that eased the ability for persons to form trade associations and other groups for exporters. The Act was intended to increase American exports.

Exporter Counseling Division A division of the Bureau of Industry and Security of the U.S. Department of Commerce responsible for educating exporters on regulations and how to abide by them. To this end, it responds to inquiries and participates in educational events.

Export-Import Bank The United States government's export credit agency, which extends credit to American exporters. The ExIm Bank also provides guarantees and insurance for exports. Unlike some other export credit agencies, it is not allowed to compete with private banks; it simply extends credit for transactions that would not otherwise receive it. Like other export credit agencies, however, the ExIm Bank is controversial; critics allege that ECAs negatively impact international development as developing countries cannot compete with such insured exports. Proponents of ECAs argue that they enable developing countries to import products they otherwise would not be able to afford.

Export-Import Bank of Japan A former bank that was responsible for providing financing to encourage Japanese international trade. It ceased to exist in 1999 when it merged with the Overseas Economic Cooperation Fund to form the Japanese Bank for International Cooperation.

Ex-Post Actual returns or other historical data. Analysts use ex-post data on price movements, earnings, and other metrics to try to predict expected returns on an investment. See also: Ex-ante.

Expost Average Rate of Return A calculation of the actual, as opposed to estimated, average rate of return over the life of an investment. In cases where there was uncertainty as to the average rate of return before the investment was made, one calculates the expost average rate of return after the investment is complete to determine how closely the investment matched estimates. The calculation of the expost average rate of return is fairly straightforward: one takes the total return on an investment and divides by the number of years in the life of the investment. It is important to note that these are the actual figures rather than estimates. See also: Exante average rate of return.

Exposure Draft A version of a document released internally and opened for discussion before the final document is published.

Expropriation The act of a government or, rarely, a private organization taking property away from its owner(s). Generally speaking, expropriation implies that the owner will be compensated for the loss, though not always at fair market value. Compensation does not always occur when citizens have little legal protection against government takeovers.

Expunge On AUTEX, to cancel an order such that it leaves no record either on the electronic board or in the historical archives of the board. A straight cancellation leaves a record in the archives of AUTEX, which may not be desirable for some traders who do not wish other traders to know that they were once interested in a certain transaction. Expunging the order removes this risk. See also: Cancel.

Ex-Rights Date The date on which any right on a stock that has been declared, but not distributed, belongs legally to its seller rather than the buyer. That is, when one sells a stock on or after the ex-rights date, the right will remain with the seller when it is distributed. On the other hand, if it is sold before the ex-rights date, the right will go to the buyer. See also: Ex-dividend date.

Extendable Note A bond in which the date of maturity may be extended. Whether the issuer, bondholder, or both have the authority to extend the maturity depends upon the specific terms of the bond agreement. If a maturity is extended, the issuer continues to pay coupons. Thus, extendable notes usually sell at a higher price than other bonds because there is the possibility for a higher return. They are also called extendable bonds.

Extended Blue Room A room added to the Blue Room of the New York Stock Exchange to provide extra space for traders in order to meet added volume. The Extended Blue Room was opened in 1988 and closed in 2007.

Extended Coverage Endorsement An optional addition to a Standard Fire Policy that provides coverage for additional and more uncommon risks. Covered events include riots, explosions, airplane damage and so forth. One pays an additional premium for the extended coverage endorsement.

Extended IRA An IRA from which a second generation beneficiary receives funds after both the account holder and the first generation beneficiary have died. The second generation beneficiary is the heir of the first generation beneficiary, who was the heir of the account holder. An IRA may be extended when the second generation beneficiary does not need or want to receive all the funds at once. This may be beneficial, as the second generation beneficiary retains all the tax benefits associated with the IRA.

Extension 1. In options, the expiration date. Occasionally the parties to an option contract will agree to extend the expiration to a certain date in the future. **2.** In taxes, the day that one must file one's return if one asked the tax agency for more time to do it. For example, in the United States the deadline to file tax returns is 15 April. If a taxpayer is unable to make this deadline, he/she may ask the IRS for an extension until 15 October. In this case, 15 October is the extension date. **3.** In an offer for bids on a contract, the date to which a deadline is lengthened. If there is either a lack of interest or no good bids on a contract, the company or government offering it may extend the deadline to allow other companies to decide whether to make a bid. This second deadline is the extension date.

Extension Date 1. In options, the expiration date. Occasionally, the parties to an option contract will agree to extend the expiration to a certain date in the future. **2.** In taxes, the day that one must file one's return if one asked the tax agency for more time to do it. For example, in the United States, the deadline to file tax returns is April 15. If a taxpayer is unable to make this deadline, he/she may ask the IRS for an extension until October 15. In this case, October 15 is the extension date. **3.** In an offer for bids on a contract, the date to which a deadline is lengthened. If there is either a lack of interest or no good bids on a contract, the company or government offering it may extend the deadline to allow other companies to decide whether to make a bid. This second deadline is the extension date.

Extension of Time for Filing In taxes, the process by which one receives permission to file one's return at a later date. For example, in the United States, the deadline to file tax returns is April 15. If a taxpayer is unable to make this deadline, he/she may ask the IRS for an extension until October 15. In this case, October 15 is called the extension date.

Extension Risk The risk of a loss to an investor in a mortgage-backed security that comes from a lower prepayment rate. The mortgages underlying a mortgage-backed security may be prepaid, which will return the principal amount to the investor sooner. However, this is unlikely to occur when interest rates are rising because mortgage payers have no incentive to refinance to lock in a lower interest rate. This extends the amount of time that the investor has his/her funds in the mortgage-backed security; this could deprive him/her of investing in another security with a higher interest rate. See also: Opportunity cost, interest rate risk.

Extension Swap A swap in which one investor exchanges a bond for another bond with the same or almost the same terms, but with a longer maturity. An investor may do this directly by swapping one bond for another, or indirectly by selling the bond with the shorter maturity and buying the bond with the longer maturity.

External Affairs and International Trade Canada An organization of the Canadian government that promotes Canadian exports and international trade. In the 1980s, it was also responsible for immigration policy. Its name was changed to Department of Foreign Affairs and International Trade Canada in 1995.

External Audit A measurement and report on the state of a person's or business' finances, made by an external agency. A common (and feared) example of an external audit is an audit by the IRS, which is done to ensure that the person or business being audited has paid the appropriate amount in taxes. Often, companies hire audit firms to look at their financial states and to receive an objective assessment. It is also called an outside audit. See also: Internal audit, Audit.

External Auditor An outside person who measures and reports on the state of a person's or business' finances. A common example of an external audit is an audit by the IRS, which is done to ensure that the person or business being audited has paid the appropriate amount in taxes. Often, companies hire external auditors to look at their financial states and to receive an objective assessment. See also: Internal audit, Audit.

External Balance A situation in which the money a country brings in from exports is roughly equal to the money it spends on imports. That is, external balance occurs when the current account is neither excessively positive nor excessively negative. An external balance implies capital movement. That is, a country needs to have both imports and exports to maintain an external balance; it is not sufficient simple to note no balance by not buying and selling goods. An external balance is considered sustainable. See also: Internal balance.

External Benefit The benefit of a transaction to parties who do not directly participate in it. Externality can be either positive or negative. For example, a merger can lead to higher share prices and bonuses for employees, benefiting shareholders and employees at the two companies merging. This can create wealth and positively impact a community. A transaction may have both external benefits and external costs: a transaction may result in a factory opening in one city and one closing in another. An external benefit is also called positive externality. See also: Externality.

External Cost The cost of a transaction to parties who do not directly participate in it. For example, a merger can drive a competitor out of business, which results in layoffs and reduced wealth, which can hurt a community. A transaction may result in a factory opening in one city and one closing in another. An external cost is also called negative externality. See also: Externality.

External Finance Financing for a company that comes from a new issue of stocks or bonds. That is, external finance occurs when a company looks outside itself to raise capital; rather than using its retained earnings or depreciation, it issues securities. See also: Internal Finance.

External Fund 1. A mutual fund that invests predominantly or exclusively in securities issued in foreign countries. An external fund does not necessarily concentrate on any single country, but it does not invest in securities from the country in which it operates. An external fund should not be confused with a global fund, which invests in both domestic and foreign securities. An external fund is also called an international fund. **2.** Funding that a company raises from any source other than itself. Two common types of external funds are bond and stock issues. A company seeks external funds when it wishes to expand its operations or other activities, but lacks the cash flow to do it independently. Providers of external funds almost always expect to receive something in return; for example, bondholders expect interest and principle repayment, while stockholders expect to receive a portion of the ownership of the company.

External Funding Funding that a company raises from any source other than itself. Two common types of external funding are bond and stock issues. A company seeks out external funds when it wishes to expand its operations or other activities, but lacks the cash flow to do it independently. Providers of external funds almost always expect to receive something in return; for example, bondholders expect interest and principle repayment, while stockholders expect to receive a portion of the ownership of the company.

External Market The market or trade of any securities that are offered to investors in multiple countries and are outside the jurisdiction of any particular country. For example, a British company may issue a bond on an external market if it issues it in Germany and France and denominates it in U.S. dollars. External markets are also called euromarkets. It is important to note, however, that the term has nothing to do with the euro, and the prefix "euro-" is used more generally to refer to deposits outside the jurisdiction of the domestic central bank.

External Trade Act of 1987 Legislation in South Korea that significantly liberalized its international trade policies. For most of the postwar period, South Korea severely restricted imports of finished products so it could develop its own industry. As a result of the Act, South Korea began to permit more imports and to promote policies closer to free trade. Agriculture, however, has remained largely restricted.

External Value The value of a currency expressed in terms of another currency. For example, if an analyst says one pound is worth two dollars at a given time, he/she is expressing an external value of the pound. This contrasts with expressing a currency in terms of itself (which is especially relevant because of inflation). See also: Purchasing power parity.

Externality The cost or benefits of a transaction to parties who do not directly participate in it. Externality can be either positive or negative. For example, a merger can lead to higher share prices and bonuses for employees, benefiting shareholders and employees at the two companies merging, This can create wealth and positively impact a community. On the other hand, the merger can drive a competitor out of business, which results in layoffs and reduced wealth, which can hurt a community. Externality is also called spillover or the neighborhood effect. See also: External benefit, External cost.

Extinction Pricing A pricing strategy in which a company attempts to drive its competition out of business by setting its prices significantly lower. This can even involve selling products at a loss for a period of time. A company can engage in extinction pricing if it already has large market share and wishes to expand it or if it can make up the losses in some other way (for example, by increasing prices for other products). See also: Loss leader, Monopoly.

Extinguish To cause a security to cease to exist. This especially applies to debt securities; for example, when a bond matures, it is said to be extinguished. See also: Repay.

Extortion An illegal act in which one coerces another into providing money or something else of value. For example, one may extort money from a business by threat of force. Extortion historically has been common in organized crime.

Extortion Insurance An insurance policy providing coverage in the event that the insured party is threatened with violence toward him/her or his/her property unless a payment is made. As with all insurance, one must pay a premium in exchange for coverage. See also: Political risk, Blackmail.

Extra Fine In numismatics, describing a coin with a little bit of wear on some of the higher points. The coin is still easily readable and there are no or few obvious blemishes. These coins may be valuable as collector's items, though they are illiquid assets.

Extraordinary Gain Non-recurring, non-operating profit in a given fiscal year. Publicly-traded companies must include extraordinary gains (and extraordinary losses) on their annual and quarterly reports; they are usually explained separately so as not to detract from the companies' usual gains and losses. One of the most common extraordinary gains a company may report is the sale of a subsidiary or stake in another company for an amount greater than the asset value carried on the company's balance sheet.

Extraordinary General Meeting Any shareholders meeting other than the annual general meeting. Extraordinary general meetings are usually called to deal with an urgent matter, such as the replacement of an executive or perhaps some legal trouble with the company. Any decision that shareholders must make but cannot wait until the next annual general meeting is made at an EGM.

Extraordinary Item A large gain or loss in a company's earnings due to a non-recurring event that is out of the company's control. For example, a water distribution company may have unusually high earnings from sales because a natural disaster required relief organizations to purchase large quantities of clean water. On the other hand, it may have low earnings from sales because all the relief organizations had previously stocked up on water and did not need to buy any more. Extraordinary items are reported separately from the company's other financial statements so as to give a clearer picture of how the company is actually performing. Publicly-traded companies must report extraordinary items to shareholders in quarterly and annual reports and explain why they do not constitute a substantial increase or decrease in the company's health.

Extraordinary Loss A loss that occurs because of an unforeseen and generally unforeseeable event that affects the company. For example, a company may suffer a loss if it sells one of its factories for less than its market value. Extraordinary losses are generally not repeatable. Balance sheets usually record extraordinary losses separately from other losses to account for this. See also: Extraordinary Gain.

Extraordinary Positive Value A positive net present value. A net present value is a measure of discounted cash inflow to present cash outflow to determine whether a prospective investment will be profitable. For example, if a dentist wishes to purchase a new dental practice, he may calculate the net present value over a number of years to see if he will recover his investment in a reasonable period of time. If the ask price for the dental practice is $500,000, this is the present cash outflow used in the calculation. If the discounted cash inflow over two years is greater than $500,000, then the investment has an extraordinary positive value and will likely be profitable.

Extraordinary Redemption A situation in which a bond issuer redeems a bond before its maturity because the revenue source paying the coupons disappears. For example, suppose a callable bond is issued to build a factory, and the revenue from the factory pays the interest on the bond. If the factory burns down, the company may redeem the bond at par so it no longer has to make interest payments. While the above example is catastrophic, most extraordinary redemptions occur for more mundane reasons; for instance, a mortgage-backed security may be extraordinarily redeemed if too many mortgages are refinanced. An extraordinary redemption is also called a special call.

Extrapolative Statistical Model Any model that attempts to use past trends in data in order to predict future trends. This may be used in any number of business or non-business situations. However, technical analysts commonly use extrapolative statistical models in order to predict future prices of securities. This can be quite important in the futures and option markets.

Extraterritoriality The state of being exempt from a country or region's law. This may occur in an embassy, for example, which legally is not part of the territory in which it resides. Historically, extraterritoriality referred to the colonial right to be tried only by one's own justice system, even if one was in a foreign country.

Extraview Slang; a second interview that a company is required by policy or for some other reason to hold, even though it has decided which candidate will be offered a position. An extraview may be scheduled, for example, if a department has to prove to corporate that is has conducted due diligence before hiring an employee.

Extreme Value Theory In statistics, any way to estimate or measure the likelihood of an extremely unlikely event. That is, extreme value theory measures the probability that a data point that deviates significantly from the mean will occur. It is useful in insurance to measure the risk of catastrophic events, such as tornados and wildfires.

Extrinsic Value The value of an asset that occurs by mutual agreement. Fiat money, for example, has value because everyone in an economy agrees that it has value, even though the paper on which it is printed does not have any more value than other paper. The line between extrinsic and intrinsic value is sometimes blurry.

Ex-Warrant Describing the sale of a security after a warrant has been announced but before it has been distributed. When a security is sold ex-warrant, the warrant remains with the seller. Selling ex-warrant almost invariably reduces the price for which the security is sold. See also: Cum warrant.

Eye Camera A specialized camera that focuses on the human eye and measures eye movements. An eye camera is used in eye movement analysis, which measures how one's eyes respond to a visual advertisement. For that reason, eye cameras are important to marketing.

Eye Movement Analysis In marketing, the practice of measuring how one's eyes respond to a visual advertisement. In general, one's eyes rest longer on a pleasing image than on a displeasing one. As a result, marketers use eye movement analysis to find the images most likely to attract and maintain attention in an effort to maximize an ad's visibility.

Eyebrow In print marketing, a small bit of text placed over the main headline of an advertisement. For example, an eyebrow may read "Local Opera Presents" over the larger headline, "FIGARO."

Eyrir A subdivision of the Icelandic krona. It takes 100 aurar (the plural of eyrir) to make one krona. The eyrir is not used in practice.

F A symbol appearing next to a stock listed on NASDAQ indicating that the stock belongs to a foreign company. All NASDAQ listings use a four-letter abbreviation; if an F follows the abbreviation, this indicates that the security being traded represents a foreign company.

F.O.B. Airport In international commerce, an agreement between a seller and a buyer indicating that the seller has fulfilled his/her obligation to deliver a good when he/she has transferred it to the airport from which it will be transported. All cost and risk transfers to the buyer when the good comes to the airport. The buyer designates the specific airport to which the seller must deliver the good.

F.O.B. Freight Allowed An agreement between a seller and a buyer indicating that the seller has fulfilled his/her obligation to deliver a good when he/she has transferred it to the point from which it is to be transported to the buyer. The seller pays for transportation indirectly. That is, the seller quotes the buyer a cost for transportation, which the buyer pays. The seller then deducts this amount from the invoice.

F.O.B. Freight Prepaid An agreement between a seller and a buyer indicating that the seller has fulfilled his/her obligation to deliver a good when he/she has transferred it to the point from which it is to be transported to the buyer. While risk transfers to the buyer when the good is delivered to this point, the seller is responsible for transportation costs.

F.O.B. Named Inland Carrier In domestic commerce, an agreement between a seller and a buyer indicating that the seller has fulfilled his/her obligation to deliver a good when he/she has transferred it to a stated place from which it will be transported. All cost and risk transfers to the buyer when the good comes to that place. The buyer designates the specific place to which the seller must deliver the good.

F.O.B. Named Port of Exportation In maritime international commerce, an agreement between a seller and a buyer indicating that the seller has fulfilled his/her obligation to deliver a good when he/she has transferred it to a port from which it will be transported. All cost and risk transfers to the buyer when the good arrives at the port. The buyer designates the port to which the seller must deliver the good.

F.W. Woolworth An American businessman who founded one of the first five-and-dime stores, in which all items were sold for five and ten cents. This company, Woolworth's, began in 1879 on a $300 loan and made Woolworth into a multi-millionaire. In order to pay for the discounts he offered customers, he purchased goods directly from manufacturers. He also fixed prices for consumers, which was uncommon at the time. Woolworth lived from 1852 to 1919. See also: Sam Walton.

F/C An abbreviation for the date the first coupon is paid on a bond. The F/C sometimes occurs at an irregular time; that is, if the bond pays coupons every six months, the F/C may be longer or shorter than six months. See also: Long coupon, Short coupon, Grace period.

Fabless Company In the semiconductor industry, a company that specializes in the development and sale of semiconductor chips. Fabless companies do not make the chips themselves; rather, they outsource manufacture to foundry companies, which make the chips according to fabless companies' specifications. A fabless company is thus able to keep it capital expenditures to a minimum as it does not have to invest in the construction of foundries to make the semiconductor chips. Most of the time, fabless companies concentrate predominantly in research and development.

Face Interest Rate The interest rate listed on a loan agreement. The face interest rate may bear little relation to the interest actually paid because the face rate does not indicate how often interest compounds. The annual effective rate is a better measure of interest. However, for the sake of simplicity, some lenders may list the annual effective rate as the face interest rate. It should not be confused with the nominal interest rate.

Face of Policy The face value of a life insurance policy. For example, if the death benefit is $100,000 upon the death of the policyholder, the face of policy is $100,000.

Face Time In investment banking, a slang term for staying at work late but not to do any extra work. An employee puts in face time because a supervisor has not noticed that she does not have enough work to do, but the employee does not want to be caught and assigned another project.

Face Value The amount of money stated on a bond or (rarely) a stock certificate. For example, if a bond certificate says $1,000, the face value is $1000. Bonds pay the face value at maturity, and calculate coupons as a percentage of the face value. Many bonds are issued at their face value, though discount bonds are not. The face value is also called the par value or simply par.

Face-Amount Certificate A debt security with a face value printed on its certificate. A face-amount certificate obligates the issuer to pay the face value to the holder of the security at its maturity. Face-amount certificates ordinarily have face values of $1,000, though this may be higher or lower depending upon the issue.

Faced Mail Envelopes arranged in such a way that all addresses face the same direction. Some mail-sorting machines require faced mail to operate.

Facilitating Intermediary In international commerce, a party that helps a transaction occur, but is not directly involved in the transaction and does not take possession of the goods. Major examples of facilitating intermediaries include banks and insurance companies.

Facilitation The act of providing or preserving the liquidity of a market. For example, market makers facilitate markets when they trade on their own accounts to try to preserve an equilibrium of supply and demand.

Facility A loan extended by a bank to a business in need of operating capital. This may take several forms, from a short-term loan to a line of credit. Different banks have different facility plans for their clients who own or run businesses. See also: Debt financing.

Facility Fee A fee that a borrower pays to a lender in exchange for a loan. See also: Closing Costs.

Facility License A license required to open certain types of businesses. For example, a municipality may require the procurement of a facility license before opening a childcare center.

Facility of Payment Clause A provision in some life insurance policies allowing the insurer to pick a beneficiary if the policy's designated beneficiary is a minor or is deceased. For example, the insurer may pay the next closest relative of the decedent or may simply pay the funeral home.

Facing Slip A label on a U.S. Postal Service package indicating the destination and the consolidation level, which measures the extent to which the package has been sorted.

Facsimile Draft A scanned or faxed copy of a sales draft. Facsimile drafts are especially important in the event of a dispute over a sale or payment.

Factor A third party that buys a firm's accounts receivable. If a firm is not confident in its ability to collect on its credit sales, it may sell the right to receive payment to the factor at a discount. The factor then assumes the credit risk associated with the accounts receivable. This provides the firm immediate access to working capital, which is important, especially if the firm has a cash flow problem. The price of factoring is determined by the creditworthiness of the firm's customer, not of the firm itself. It is also known as accounts receivable financing.

Factor Analysis The analysis of seemingly unrelated phenomena and their disparate and combined effect on an investment. Factor analysis takes a large number of dependent variables and seeks to isolate the independent variables determining them. Isolating the independent variables (called factors in this context) helps reduce the number of variables that the analyst must study in order to make accurate statements and predictions about the direction of an investment.

Factor Cost The market value of a good or service at the retail level. The factor cost is equal to the price the customer pays, less any taxes (such as a VAT or a sales tax), and plus any subsidies the customer receives from the government.

Factor Endowment The means of production (namely land, labor, capital and sometimes entrepreneurship) contained in an area. In general, greater factor endowment portends greater economic success. However, some resource-poor countries and regions become successful simply by efficient use of the little factor endowment they have.

Factor Income The income one derives from the sale of the means of production, namely land, labor and capital. Rent is the factor income from land; wages and salaries are the incomes from the sale of labor. Finally, dividends represent factor income from capital.

Factor Incomes from Abroad The income a person or company derives from its operations in other countries. Factor incomes from abroad include foreign profits and remittances that workers send back to their home countries. See also: Factor Income.

Factor Market The market for the means of production. That is, the factor market is the buying and selling of land, labor and capital, as well as raw materials and entrepreneurship. The most important component of the factor market is labor. See also: Factor Income.

Factor Mobility The ease with which the means of production (that is, land, labor, capital and sometimes entrepreneurship) can be moved to another location or put to a different use. For example, capital has factor mobility if one may easily sell one security and purchase another, or move money to another bank or town. A country or region with greater factor mobility may experience greater economic success.

Factor Model A mathematical calculation of the extent to which macroeconomic factors affect the securities in a portfolio. Factor models attempt to account for contingencies like changes in interest rates or inflation. Factor models fall into three main categories. A statistical factor model attempts to explain risks particular to an investment. A fundamental factor model looks at risks to an industry or market that may affect a portfolio. Finally, a macroeconomic factor model considers relevant risks to the wider economy. See also: Risk analysis.

Factor Price The price at which the means of production (that is, land, labor, capital and sometimes entrepreneurship) are sold. Economists disagree about what determines factor prices. Marxists and classical economists argue that factor prices represent the intrinsic value of the means of production. Other economists, however, believe that factor prices come from demand for the means of production.

Factor Price Equalization The theory that the prices of two identical means of production in different areas will eventually equal each other. For example, if wages in one region exceed wages in another, they will gradually fall in the first region and rise in the second until they are the same. Factor price equalization works best when factor mobility exists. See also: Factor Price.

Factor Return The return a factor receives on its investment. A factor is a company that buys the accounts receivable from another company in exchange for a smaller fee, which is paid up front. If and when the factor eventually receives the total amount accounts receivable, it makes a profit.

Factory Orders Orders that companies make for both durable goods and non-durable goods that they wish to sell to customers. Examples of durable goods include cars and flatware (because they are intended to last longer than three years), while examples of non-durable goods include food and clothing. If factory orders increase, it is a sign of a healthy economy because it shows that consumers are willing to make purchases. As such, factory orders are a major economic indicator.

Fade Informal; in over-the-counter trading, to fill an order.

FAFSA A form that a post-secondary student files with the federal government to determine eligibility for federal financial aid for school. The FAFSA outlines the student's (or his/her family's) assets and income and determines the amount he/she is expected to pay for education.

FAFSA on the Web An online form used to file the FAFSA, which a post-secondary student files with the federal government to determine eligibility for federal financial aid for school.

Fai In Islamic law, the spoils of war that a Muslim army may take if the territory is taken without bloodshed.

Fail 1. See: Business failure. **2.** See: Fail to deliver.

Fail to Deliver A situation in which a buyer, or, more commonly, his/her broker does not receive delivery of the securities he/she bought by the settlement date. A fail to deliver occurs because of the negligence or deliberate withholding on the part of the seller. If a buyer does not receive the securities, he/she is not obligated to make payment until delivery is made. See also: Aged fail.

Failure of Issue In law, the death of a person without children. Because such a person has no immediate heirs, peripheral relatives inherit his/her property. If no relatives or other inheritors can be found, the state may take over the property. See also: Escheat.

Fair In numismatics, describing a well-worn coin on which the date may be visible only with some difficulty. These coins generally are less valuable for collectors.

Fair and Accurate Credit Transaction Act of 2003 Legislation in the United States requiring the three major credit reporting agencies to disclose an individual's credit reports to that individual once per year for free. One may request a free report through a website or telephone number managed by the three agencies, Experian, Equifax, and TransUnion, in cooperation with the Federal Trade Commission. The Act contains provisions making identity theft more difficult. See also: Fair Credit Reporting Act.

Fair Credit Billing Act Also called the FCBA. Legislation in the United States, passed in 1974, that allowed credit card customers to dispute (in writing sent by mail) a charge made on their cards. For example, if an unauthorized person makes a charge on a card or if the credit card company bills an incorrect amount, the FCBA allows the customer to ask the charge to be removed or changed. The card holder is usually not liable for erroneous or fraudulent charges. The FCBA was an amendment to the Truth in Lending Act.

Fair Disclosure An SEC regulation requiring that all publicly-traded companies in the United States disclose relevant, or "material," information to all shareholders at the same time. Adopted in 2000, this was a response to a common practice in the 1990s, in which large companies disclosed financial information on conference calls to certain analysts while excluding the public and even all shareholders. The regulation mandates that intentional disclosures be made publicly and that unintentional disclosures be made public within twenty-four hours. Controversial when introduced, it has increased access to information on larger firms, but some analysts suggest that it has decreased the information available and therefore increased stock volatility for smaller firms.

Fair Funds for Investors A provision of the Sarbanes-Oxley Act that allows courts to extract funds from companies that have used aggressive accounting techniques to defraud investors in order to repay those investors. That is, if one suffers a loss because a company was conducting an illegal activity, the Fair Funds for Investors provision allows them to recover their losses from the company. This provision was enacted following the Enron scandal to maintain confidence in the stock market and to reduce risk for investors.

Fair Game 1. An investment without a risk premium. That is, fair game describes an investment without a higher return for more risk accepted. Thus, an investor may take on higher risk without the possibility of higher return. Risk-averse investors tend to avoid these investments. **2.** See: Zero-sum game.

Fair Housing Act Legislation in the United States, passed in 1968, that prohibited discrimination in the sale or rental of a private home based on the buyer's or renter's race, religion, or national origin. The Act was later amended to include gender, ability, and families with children under its protected classes. Critics allege that it provides few enforcement mechanisms and discrimination still occurs. It is also called the Civil Rights Act of 1968. See also: Community Reinvestment Act.

Fair Labor Standards Act Also called the FLSA. Legislation in the United States, passed in 1938, that required employers engaged in interstate commerce to provide a minimum level of employee benefits. For example, the FLSA prohibits child labor and established the first federal minimum wage. For purposes of this Act, "interstate commerce" is interpreted so broadly as to include basically all employers not specifically exempted. It was part of the New Deal.

Fair Market Price What a willing buyer pays a willing seller for a given asset. In a perfectly efficient market, fair market prices are determined by the law of supply and demand and no other factors. In securities, the fair market price is the price of the most recent transaction of that security. Open markets and capitalism, in general, can only exist if prices are set by the market, at least most of the time. See also: Fair Market Value, Invisible Hand.

Fair Market Value A subjective estimate of what a willing buyer would pay a willing seller for a given asset, assuming both have a reasonable knowledge of the asset's worth. Fair market value is important in both law and accounting. In the former, it is often used in assessing damages as the result of a lawsuit. In the latter, determining the fair market value of an asset (e.g. after depreciation) is important to determining the amount of tax owed on it.

Fair Packaging & Labeling Act Legislation in the United States requiring the label on a consumer product to state clearly the name of the product, its maker or manufacturer, and its quantity. The Act was passed so consumers are able to know what they are buying. It came into effect in 1967.

Fair Plan A program in several American states by which the state government provides or subsidizes insurance on properties that otherwise would be uninsurable because they are in high risk areas. For example, a fair plan may insure a coastal property in a hurricane area. As with all insurance, the policyholder must pay a premium to receive the coverage.

Fair Presentation In International Accounting Standards, the requirement for companies not to obfuscate their financial statements so as to mislead shareholders or the wider market.

Fair Price Provision A provision in the bylaws of some publicly-traded companies stating that a company seeking to acquire it must pay a fair price to targeted shareholders. The formula for determining a fair price may be indicated in the bylaws; it is often a calculation based on historic prices. Additionally, the fair price provision mandates that the acquiring company must pay all shareholders the same amount per share in multi-tiered shares. The fair price provision exists both to protect shareholders and to discourage hostile acquisitions by making them more expensive. See also: Antitakeover measure.

Fair Rate of Return The profit that a government allows an industry to make if it deems that industry to be necessary for public function. A state may impose a fair rate of return on industries, such as utilities, to keep services affordable for consumers. Critics of this practice contend that this is economically inefficient and ultimately harms consumers, though this is a matter of considerable dispute.

Fair Trade Acts State laws in the United States allowing manufacturers or distributors of goods to require retailers to charge a minimum price. Fair trade acts were designed to protect manufacturers from retailer price-cutting, which otherwise would reduce manufacturers' profits. Fair trade acts are currently rare to nonexistent.

Fair Trading Act of 1986 Legislation in the United States intended to protect consumers from misleading advertisements for products. Under the Act, companies are required to reveal potentially hazardous materials in or uses for certain baby and toddler products, among other things. The country of origin must be revealed on most articles of clothing. Finally, advertisers are prohibited from lying in their ads.

Fair Weather Fund Mutual funds that tend to do poorly when most of the economy as a whole is performing poorly and perform well when the economy is performing well. Fair weather funds may contain publicly-traded companies that are perceived to be luxuries or that sell expensive products. For example, car companies sell expensive products (cars) that many people perceive to be necessities. However, because they are expensive, consumers in bad economic times may decide to wait to buy cars until the economy improves. On the other hand, car companies tend to do rather well when the economy is doing well. As a result, a fair weather fund may contain a number of automotive stocks.

Fairway Bond A bond with a coupon that is linked to some short-term benchmark interest rate. That is, a fairway bond carries a variable interest rate that changes according to a specified short-term interest rate. For example, a fairway bond may have a coupon of LIBOR + 0.5%. When investors believe interest rates will soon rise, they have an incentive to stay out of the bond market because their return would be locked at the lower interest rate. Fairway bonds reduce this incentive by allowing investors to take advantage of higher interest rates as they occur. A fairway bond is also called a floater. See also: Inverse floater.

Fairy Dust A slang term for the final, minor changes before a project, presentation, or anything else is completed. For example, cute images added at the last minute to a PowerPoint presentation are fairy dust.

Fakelaki A Greek term for "little envelope." It is a slang term for a small bribe.

Fakeout In technical analysis, an informal term for a situation in which an analyst takes or recommends taking a position because technical indicators show that some market movement will take place, but it never does. Technical analysts base their recommendations and investments on the idea that past market movements predict future movements; a fakeout occurs when they apply this methodology and the opposite of what was expected occurs. To reduce the possibility of fakeouts, most technical analysts look at multiple indicators before making any recommendations. See also: Noise.

Faker's Dozen A situation in which an employee takes 12 dubious sick days in a period of time. A person who does a faker's dozen may have difficulty keeping his/her job.

Falce A largely obsolete Romanian measure of area approximately equivalent to 14.3 square meters.

Falkland Islands Pound The currency of the Falkland Islands. It was introduced in 1833 and is pegged to the British pound at par. British pounds are usually accepted on the Falkland Islands as if they were Falkland Islands pounds.

Fall An obsolete Scottish unit of length equivalent to 222 inches.

Fall Down Informal; to be or become unable to deliver a good, service, or return as promised due to lack of cooperation by partners in a deal and/or changing conditions in the market. For example, if a consultant does not deliver a finished product to his client because his research contractors did not perform their duties, that consultant is said to have fallen down.

Fall Money Money a person guilty of a criminal offense uses to pay for attorney's fees and associated costs.

Fall Out of Bed Describing a situation in which a stock drops significantly in price, especially after a rumored or proposed merger, acquisition, or other major deal does not occur.

Fallen Angel 1. A junk bond that was once investment-grade. **2.** A stock that has fallen steeply in price from its previous high. In both cases, fallen angels may be undervalued, value investments or bad investments nearing bankruptcy. This makes investing in a fallen angel very risky but it has the possibility of a high return.

Fallout Risk In mortgages, the risk that a potential borrower (that is, a property buyer) will withdraw from the deal before it is finalized. Banking regulation requires that banks offering a given interest rate hold that rate for 60 days, during which the potential borrower is under no obligation to actually take out the mortgage loan. During that time, the bank usually makes preparations to sell the mortgage as a mortgage-backed security or as some other investment vehicle. If the potential borrower withdraws during those 60 days, the bank is exposed to the risk that it will lose out on the return it could have made from the MBS or other investment vehicle. Fallout risk is also called borrower fallout.

Fama and French Three Factor Model An expansion of the capital asset pricing model that considers the facts that small cap stocks outperform large cap stocks and that value stocks do the same with respect to growth stocks. The model accounts for these facts when determining the appropriate price for these stocks.

Family Business A company in which one person or a group of related persons is the controlling shareholder. The term connotes a small business, but some family businesses are large, publicly-traded corporations. In the latter case, family members often serve on the board of directors and may appoint some of their number to major executive positions.

Family Contribution The amount a student and his/her family pay for an academic year at a post-secondary educational institution. The amount by which the cost of education exceeds the family contribution must be borrowed or awarded in some other form of financial aid.

Family Trust A trust into which the trustor places assets to be distributed to children following his/her death. Specifically, a family trust does not name the trustor's spouse as a beneficiary. See also: Q-TIP.

Famn A Swedish unit of length approximately equivalent to 178 centimeters.

Fannie Mae Federal National Mortgage Association (FNMA). A publicly-traded company chartered by the U.S. Congress to guarantee mortgages granted to low- or middle-income households. In order to do this, it buys mortgages and repackages them, selling them as mortgage-backed securities. It also maintains its own portfolio of mortgage-backed securities. With the collapse of the housing bubble, Fannie Mae was placed in federal receivership in 2008 as a result of overexposure to this market. See also: Freddie Mac, Community Reinvestment Act, Credit crunch.

Far Month Among several different futures contracts or options, describing the one with the longest maturity. For example, given three futures contracts, one expiring in March, one in June, and one in September, the far month futures contract is the one expiring in September.

Faritany mizakatena In Madagascar, a political subdivision equivalent to a province.

Faritra In Madagascar, a political subdivision equivalent to a county. These were dissolved in 2009.

Farmer Mac Informal for Federal Agricultural Mortgage Corporation. A publicly-traded company chartered by the U.S. Congress to provide a secondary market for mortgages granted for agricultural real estate and rural housing. In order to do this, it buys mortgages and repackages them, selling them as mortgage-backed securities. Farmer Mac was established to make real estate easier to purchase for farmers, ranchers, and rural citizens. It was established in 1988. See also: Farm Credit System, Fannie Mae, Freddie Mac.

Farmowners and Ranchowners Insurance An insurance policy that provides coverage for damage to barns, fences, stables, or other physical structures on a farm or ranch. It also protects the policyholder from legal liability in the event that an accident or negligence in a covered property causes injury to a person. As with all insurance, one must pay a premium to receive the coverage.

Faroese Krona The currency of the Faroe Islands. It is the same currency as the Danish krone in that both are issued by the same central bank and are identical on international exchange markets. Additionally, banks exchange them without charge on a one-to-one ratio. However, Danish krone are not legal tender in the Faroe Islands (though generally they are accepted), and Faroese kronur generally are not accepted in Denmark.

Farsang 1. An obsolete Persian unit of length equivalent to 6.23 meters. **2.** A Persian unit of length equivalent to 10 meters.

Farsax A Tatar unit of length varying in distance from 6.4 to 7.4 kilometers. It was rendered obsolete when the Soviet Union began to use the metric system in 1924.

Farthing A former coin in the United Kingdom equal in value to one quarter of one penny. Farthings were used in the United Kingdom prior to the decimalization of the British pound. They ceased to be legal tender in 1960.

FASB No. 113 A rule of the Financial Accounting Standards Board requiring insurance companies to report their total positions on reinsurance, not just the net positions that affect their regular insurance policies.

FASB No. 115 A rule of the Financial Accounting Standards Board requiring insurance companies to report their securities with fixed maturities according to their current market value. This rule applies to most negotiable and nonnegotiable bonds.

FASB No. 52 An FASB guideline that requires American companies to record foreign exchange items on a balance sheet according to prevailing exchange rates. Adjustments for changes to market rates are only made when they affect the company's cash flow. It replaced the Statement of Financial Accounting Standards No. 8.

FASB No. 8 An FASB rule requiring transactions in foreign currencies be reported according to their historical cost assuming the current, market exchange rate. This rule was quite controversial and FASB No. 8 was replaced by FASB No. 52 in 1981.

FASB Statement An official opinion by the Financial Accounting Standards Board on how to report a transaction. FASB statements set standards for the accounting industry and help establish uniform practice insofar as it is possible.

Fascism A political system characterized by extreme nationalism. When it emerged in the early 20th century, it rejected both left-wing and right-wing thought and advocated a system in which the citizens of a nation work together for a common goal (usually under the command of a strong leader). Fascism is noted for corporatist economic policies, in which interests of the state, businesses and workers cooperate to set policies. It is strongly associated with racism and/or expansionism.

Fascist A person or group that believes in or promotes a political system characterized by extreme nationalism. When fascism emerged in the early 20th century, it rejected both left-wing and right-wing thought and advocated a system in which the citizens of a nation work together for a common goal (usually under the command of a strong leader). Fascists are noted for corporatist economic policies, in which interests of the state, businesses, and workers cooperate to set policies. They are strongly associated with racism and/or expansionism.

Fast Market An exchange or financial market undergoing an extreme amount of volatility with high trading volume. A fast market may occur as the result of both positive and negative events: an IPO may attract greater interest than expected or a publicly-traded company may release unexpectedly pessimistic earnings forecasts. Trades occur so rapidly that market orders may be executed at a very different price from the price at the time the order was placed. Fast markets are often thought to be unsustainable and some analysts advise investors to exercise caution when buying or selling securities in them.

Fast Market Rule In the United Kingdom, the right of an exchange to declare that trading has become too volatile to maintain current quotes and therefore allow trades to occur outside quoted ranges. The fast market rule exists as an alternative to a circuit breaker, which would allow exchanges to slow down or halt trading in such circumstances. See also: Fast market.

Fast Money Slang; in the bond market, price movements caused by speculators without regard for fundamentals. For example, if speculators buy bonds and the prices rise (and yields fall) without a corresponding shift in risk, the price movement was caused by fast money.

Fast Tape In futures trading, a situation where trading on a contract is so active that an accurate quote cannot be given on its price. That is, a fast tape occurs when the price is changing very rapidly because of the large number of trades. When this happens, a ticker gives the range of prices within which the contract is trading and notes "fast" after it. This indicates that the situation is changing quickly. See also: ticker tape.

Fat Cat Informal; a wealthy person. The term is derogatory and connotes a person who flaunts his/her wealth ostentatiously and/or does not work to earn it.

Fatah A secular, left-wing political party that forms the largest component of the Palestinian Liberation Organization. It is a nationalist party that advocates a Palestinian state in the whole region of Palestine, including the parts claimed by Israel, though some factions within Fatah have backed away from this latter platform. Unlike its main rival, Hamas, it is not regarded as a terrorist group. It was established in 1958.

Father Tape In computing, a backup tape, disc or drive one generation older than the most recent one. For example, if data is backed up each week, the father tape is the backup record from last week. See also: Grandfather tape.

Fatwa An opinion on Islamic law made by a scholar regarded as having authority. For example, a fatwa may state that a new financial vehicle complies with the sharia and that Muslims may invest in it. A fatwa may not be universally accepted, and scholars have deep disagreements as to what Islamic finance products are indeed Islamic.

Faultytasking A slang term in business for multitasking inefficiently. That is, faultytasking involves working on so many projects that one does not do any of them well.

Faux Pas A social mistake. An example is belching loudly at a cocktail hour. An excessively embarrassing or insulting faux pas can make business difficult or impossible to conduct.

Favn A Norwegian unit of length approximately equivalent to 1.9 meters.

Fear Appeal In marketing, the use of fear to generate the desired response. For example, a company may launch an advertising campaign implying that persons who do not purchase flood insurance are in imminent danger of a flood. Fear appeal is most common in marketing related to health care.

Fear Premium An increase in prices because of investor nervousness about a future event. For example, the price of contracts on oranges may increase if a hurricane is expected to hit Florida (where oranges are grown). The price may return to normal if the event does not take place (or is not as bad as predicted).

Feasible Target Payout Ratio The payout ratio (or what a company pays in dividends as a percentage of its earnings) that it can afford based on its free cash flow. Maintaining feasible target payout ratios helps ensure that a company does not pay more than it can afford in dividends.

Feather One's Nest Informal; to take advantage of one's authority to make money for oneself, especially using unethical or illegal means. For example, a bureaucrat may feather his nest by taking bribes from companies that he regulates.

Featherbedding 1. Pejorative; a term for the hiring or maintaining the employment of more workers than a company needs, or of instituting unnecessary work procedures so that workers may have something to do without increasing the company's production. Historically, this has applied to union contracts in which a union insists the employer hire more union members than he/she needs. However, the term is also used to describe unnecessary or nepotistic management level positions. **2.** Under the Taft-Hartley Act, an illegal agreement providing for payment for services that are unperformed and not to be performed. This was passed as an anti-union measure limiting the ability to create "make-work" programs, but the U.S. Supreme Court ruled such programs to be legal in American Newspaper Publishers Association vs. National Labor Relations Board (1953). This decision defined featherbedding exclusively as paying a worker not to work.

Feature Creep A situation in which a new aspects or features are added to a product as it goes through development. Feature creep may improve the final product, but it also may delay development and complicate problems.

Fed Bias An announcement by the Federal Open Market Committee on the state of inflation of the U.S. dollar. If the Fed believes inflation is high or will begin to increase, the Fed bias indicates that interest rates may soon rise. Belief in future, low inflation indicates the opposite.

Fed Model A theory used by some analysts to determine whether to buy stocks or bonds. The theory postulates that there ought to be relative equality between the yield on the S&P 500 and that of 10-year Treasury notes. If the S&P 500 yield is higher, this indicates that the S&P 500 (and by extension stocks in general) are undervalued; it is seen as a buy signal for stocks. If 10-year note returns are higher, this is seen as a buy signal for bonds. Contrary to the name, the Federal Reserve does not endorse the model.

FED Pass An action of the Federal Reserve System by which it adds to the reserves of banks, making credit more easily attainable. A FED pass is meant to spur economic growth during slowdowns. However, it can also increase the amount of money in circulation, which raises the possibility of inflation.

Fed Speak Informal term for the statements made by former Federal Reserve Chairman Alan Greenspan. Greenspan was known to make long, vague statements on future changes in Federal Reserve policy; it was speculated he did so on purpose to prevent overreactions to his statements in the stock market. Analysts spent a great deal of time and energy trying to decipher Fed Speak. Some even analyzed (only half-jokingly) what Greenspan would say in his reports to Congress by judging the size of his briefcase.

Fed Wire An electronic system allowing the quick transfer of funds and securities between banks. The fed wire exists to settle large transactions between banks so that they can continue to extend credit to each other and to customers. It is operated by the Federal Reserve and is more formally known as the Federal Reserve Wire Network. See also: Real-time gross settlement system (RTGSS).

Federal Advisory Council A committee consisting of representatives from each of the 12 Federal Reserve Banks, along with a President and a Vice President. The FAC conducts research on behalf of the Federal Reserve and advises the Board of Governors on potential policy changes.

Federal Agency Security A debt obligation owed by an agency of the U.S. government. While similar to a Treasury security, federal agency securities are issued by a particular agency of the federal government, rather than the federal government itself. Agencies that offer these securities include Ginnie Mae, the Federal Farm Credit Bank, and the U.S. Postal Service. With the exceptions of the Postal Service and the Tennessee Valley Authority, all federal agency securities are guaranteed by the U.S. government. They also offer higher interest rates than Treasury securities.

Federal Bonding Program A program of the U.S. Department of Labor issuing bonds to insure or guarantee the insurance of ex-offenders. Bonding is the process of acquiring insurance against employee theft or malfeasance, and is required in some jobs in which the employee handles a large amount of money. The Federal Bonding Program assists in the rehabilitation of ex-offenders by providing this insurance if a potential employee has too high a risk to be commercially insured. It was established in 1966.

Federal Cartel Office An agency in Germany that enforces antitrust law. It ensures that companies compete fairly with one another and that illegal monopolies are not created. It was established in 1958 and is based in Bonn.

Federal Charter A document placing a bank under federal regulation. A federal charter is required in order to operate in more than one state.

Federal Cigarette Labeling & Advertising Act Legislation in the United States, passed in 1967, that required packs of cigarettes to carry warnings advising of their harmful effects.

Federal Covered Advisor In the United States, an investment manager who manages more than $25 million of other people's money. They are required to register with the SEC annually and to abide by any applicable state laws.

Federal Crime Insurance An insurance policy in the United States providing coverage to a homeowner or business owner against theft or burglary when such coverage is not available or is not affordable. That is, federal crime insurance provides insurance for persons and businesses in high-crime areas. The Federal Insurance Administration manages the program.

Federal Deficit The amount by which the expenditures of the United States Federal Government exceed its revenue from taxes, tariffs, and other sources. In order to finance the deficit, the Government must borrow money, especially by the issue of Treasury securities. Some economists believe that the federal deficit has only minor importance, while others believe it could cause inflation if left unchecked, because the Government would eventually have to print money repay the deficit. It should not be confused with the national debt.

Federal Deposit Insurance Act of 2005 Legislation in the United States that created the Deposit Insurance Fund, which insures American banks and thrifts. Before the passage of the Act, banks and thrifts were separated into two insurance pools. While this was likely beneficial for a time because of the savings and loan crisis, it created a perverse incentive for banks and thrifts to reclassify themselves as the other (i.e., a bank to a thrift or a thrift to a bank), depending on which fund had lower fees. The Federal Deposit Insurance Act abolished these two funds to simplify banking regulation.

Federal Deposit Insurance Corporation A corporation owned by the United States government that insures bank deposits up to a certain level, so as to reduce pressure for bank panics. Created by the Glass-Steagal Act of 1933, the FDIC backs all bank deposits and some retirement accounts with the full faith and credit of the United States up to either $100,000 or $250,000, depending on the type of account. This amount may be changed by statute. A bank must purchase bank insurance from the FDIC in order to be eligible for this coverage. The FDIC helps maintain consumer confidence in banks and, by extension, the financial system.

Federal Deposit Insurance Corporation Improvement Act Commonly abbreviated FIDCIA. Legislation in the United States, passed in 1991, that allowed the FDIC to borrow from the United States Treasury in order to save or to liquidate savings and loan associations that were deemed to be in danger of insolvency. It required the FDIC to handle these S&Ls in the least expensive way possible. See also: Bailout Bond.

Federal Employer Liability Act Legislation in the United States that requires railroad companies to compensate employees in the event that they are injured on the job due to employer negligence. While the employee has the obligation to prove negligence, benefits under the Act are quite generous, including rewards of pain and suffering, which partly distinguishes these benefits from workers comp. The Act was passed in 1908.

Federal Energy Regulatory Commission An agency of the U.S. federal government with regulatory authority over liquefied natural gas, oil pipelines, interstate and wholesale electricity sales and hydroelectricity. Its duties include making and enforcing electric reliability standards, licensing projects and investigating energy markets. It has some authority over pricing. It was established in 1977.

Federal Estate Tax A tax in the United States applied to the value of the estate of a deceased person after all debts of the deceased are paid. The federal estate tax has a large exemption; the amount varies, but is always more than $1 million. The federal estate tax derives fairly little income for the federal government, but it is used to prevent (or at least reduce) the proliferation of dynastic wealth. See also: Death Tax.

Federal Farm Credit Bank A bank that provides loans for agricultural or other rural use. Most loans from federal farm credit banks are for commercial agriculture, but they also finance personal and recreational projects. They also issue short-term securities to finance their activities. Federal farm credit banks form part of the Farm Credit System. See also: Farm Credit Act, Farmer Mac, Agency bond.

Federal Funds Money that a commercial bank in the United States has in excess of its reserve requirement. Banks deposit their federal funds at the Federal Reserve Bank of their district. Federal funds are available for lending to other banks on an overnight basis. The amount of federal funds is seen as a signal of the state of American credit markets, with more money available signaling loose credit and a less indicating the opposite. See also: Federal Funds Rate.

Federal Funds Market The market for loans that the Federal Reserve makes to member banks. The fed funds market is an indicator of the direction in which the Federal Reserve is trying to push the broader economy. In general, if the Federal Reserve has a low interest rate range in the fed funds market, this indicates that it is trying to promote growth by making liquidity easily available; a high interest rate shows that the Fed is concerned about inflationary pressures on the economy and is trying to reduce the amount of money in the economy. Along with the sale of Treasury securities and determining the discount rate, influencing the federal funds market is one of the primary ways the Federal Reserve sets the monetary policy of the United States. See also: LIBOR.

Federal Funds Rate The interest rate at which fed funds are lent to a bank. Fed funds refer to the amount of money that a commercial bank in the United States has in excess of its reserve requirement that is deposited at the Federal Reserve Bank of their district. Federal funds are available for lending to other banks on an overnight basis. The FOMC sets a target for the federal funds rate, but the actual interest rates at which banks lend to one another are set by market forces. Generally speaking, however, when one speaks of the Fed raising or lowering "interest rates," this refers to the federal funds rate.

Federal Guarantee Insurance Corporation A private company providing financial guarantee insurance for different types of transactions. For example, an insurance policy may cover a lender from liability resulting from the failure of the borrower to repay the loan. The FGIC originally provided this insurance exclusively for municipal bonds, but expanded into different transactions, such as IPOs. Clients pay the FGIC the appropriate premium in exchange for a guarantee of repayment in case of default; this increases the bond's credit rating and, usually, decreases its interest rate. The services that the FGIC provides are similar to sureties or co-signed loans.

Federal Home Loan Bank System A system of 12 American banks whose purpose is to provide low-cost loans for mortgages, businesses, and urban and rural economic development. The FHLB is not publicly traded, but rather is owned by several thousand banks and other financial institutions. These institutions buy stock in the system in order to become eligible for subsidized loans, which they then make to high-risk customers. Established in 1932 during the Great Depression, the FHLB largely succeeded in its original purposes of putting people in affordable homes. However, in the late 2000s, the FHLB began to have cash flow problems due in part to overexposure to the housing bubble and became the largest borrower from the United States government.

Federal Housing Administration An agency of the United States federal government responsible for encouraging homeownership. It does this primarily by providing insurance to private mortgage lenders. It finances its activities by buying mortgages from the lender, repackaging them as mortgage-backed securities, and re-selling them. It also makes mortgage loans directly. It was established in 1934.

Federal Housing Administration Mortgage A mortgage provided by the Federal Housing Administration. The FHA offers several different types of mortgage, including (but not limited to) fixed-rate mortgages, adjustable-rate mortgages, energy efficient mortgages, and so forth. There are various requirements to be eligible for an FHA mortgage, including steady or increasing income for at least two years and at least two years since a bankruptcy.

Federal Housing Finance Board An organization of the U.S. federal government that regulates the Federal Home Loan Banks. It was created in response to the savings and loan crisis and replaced the Federal Home Loan Bank Board. It consists of five members; four are appointed by the President of the United States and the fifth is the Secretary of Housing and Urban Development or his/her representative.

Federal Insurance Administration An agency of the U.S. federal government that provides flood insurance in areas where flooding would not be covered under an ordinary homeowners policy. That is, the FIA provides flood insurance in high risk areas. It operates under FEMA.

Federal Insurance Contributions Act Legislation in the United States that requires employees to contribute a certain percentage of their wages or salaries via payroll deductions to finance Medicare and Social Security. Employees are required to contribute 6.2% of each paycheck toward Social Security, up to a certain income limit. They are also required to pay 1.45% to pay for Medicare, with no income limit. Employers are required to make matching contributions for each employee. Under the Federal Insurance Contributions Act, employees do not actually receive this percentage of their wages or salaries. Proponents of the Act argue that that this allows employees to budget their taxes better while critics state that the tax is regressive. See also: FICA Tax.

Federal Intermediate Credit Bank One of 12 government-sponsored banks that provide loans to farms, ranches, and other agricultural companies. These loans are short-term; farmers, ranchers and their companies own the stock in Federal Intermediate Credit Banks, much like member banks own stock in the Federal Reserve. The FICB derives most of its capital from short-term debt securities.

Federal Land Bank A bank that provides loans for agricultural or other rural use. Most loans from federal land banks are for commercial agriculture, but they also finance personal and recreational projects. Federal land banks form part of the Farm Credit System. See also: Farm Credit Act.

Federal Maritime Commission An agency of the U.S. Government responsible for the ocean-borne international commerce of the United States. Among other things, the FMC regulates shipping lines (which is calls ocean common carriers) and other ocean freighters that bring goods into the United States. It also enforces laws requiring the cruise ships maintain enough insurance to cover loss or damages. It issues licenses for commerce involving U.S. goods. It was established in 1961. See also: ICE, United States Merchant Marine.

Federal Officials Bond A bond or insurance policy covering losses resulting from malfeasance by a federal employee. For example, if a bureaucrat steals a government-owned bank account, the federal officials bond will compensate the government. See also: Public Employees Blanket Bond, Public Official Bond.

Federal Open Market Committee An arm of the Federal Reserve System charged with setting standards for open market operations. That is, the FOMC sets the monetary policy for the United States by buying and selling securities and setting key interest rates, especially the rate at which banks lend each other money for overnight loans. Selling government securities and raising interest rates are how the Federal Reserve reduces the amount of money in the economy; these tools are used to slow unsustainable growth and to curb inflation. Buying securities and lowering interest rates increase the amount of money in the economy and are used to spur growth. The Committee meets eight times per year and consists of the seven members of the Federal Reserve Board of Governors and five of the 12 Reserve Bank presidents. Four of the five presidents alternate for one-year terms, while the President of the New York Federal Reserve serves ex officio. It operates independently, although the Chairman of the Federal Reserve is required to appear before Congress at intervals. Somewhat controversially, its meetings are conducted in secret.

Federal Open Market Committee Minutes A record of a meeting of the Federal Open Market Committee. The FOMC is responsible for changes in interest rates; these changes are announced after the meeting with no context. The minutes are released some six weeks after each meeting. They reveal the specific matters discussed at the meeting and any dissenting votes on interest rate changes.

Federal Poverty Level The minimum yearly income that a person or family needs in order to provide for its basic needs. The Department of Health and Human Services calculates the Federal Povery Level and publishes it each February. The actual dollar amount varies according to family size. Different agencies of the U.S. Government use the FPL in determining eligibility for certain programs, notably TANF and Medicaid.

Federal Power Commission A former agency of the U.S. federal government that licensed hydroelectric projects on federally owned land and regulated natural gas and interstate electric sales. It was established in 1930 and was replaced by the Federal Energy Regulatory Commission in 1977.

Federal Register A daily publication of the U.S. federal government that disseminates new rules, changes to rules, public announcements and other information pertinent to federal employees and other interested parties. It was first published in 1936.

Federal Reserve Act of 1913 Legislation in the United States that created the Federal Reserve System. Prior to the Act's adoption, the United States had been without a central bank since the charter of the Second Bank of the United States expired in 1836. This led to a number of panics, including several in the first decade of the 20th century, which led many to believe that a central bank ought to control American monetary policy. The Act mandated the creation of between eight and 12 Federal Reserve banks 12 ultimately were founded to operate under the guidance of a Federal Reserve Board, whose seven members were appointed by the President. The Act gave the Federal Reserve System the authority to print money, a controversial measure at the time. It further required that all federally-chartered banks belong to the System and purchase a certain amount of stock in the Federal Reserve bank in charge of their particular regions. The Federal Reserve System was ordered to set the monetary policy of the United States, which it does by printing money, selling Treasury securities, and adjusting the discount rate and the fed funds rate. While the Federal Reserve Act has been amended more than 200 times since 1913, it remains the most significant law governing American finances.

Federal Reserve Bank One of 12 banks that make up the Federal Reserve System. Each Federal Reserve Bank has the authority to regulate member banks in its region, as well as regulate the money supply. Every member bank is required to buy stock in its district's Federal Reserve Bank in order to support its efforts. There are Federal Reserve Banks in Atlanta, Boston, Chicago, Cleveland, Dallas, Kansas City, Minneapolis, New York, Philadelphia, Richmond, San Francisco, and St. Louis. Of these, the New York Federal Reserve is the most important and has the most responsibilities.

Federal Reserve District The region over which a Federal Reserve Bank has jurisdiction. Each Federal Reserve Bank has the authority to regulate member banks in its district, as well as to help regulate the money supply. Every member bank is required to buy stock in its district's Federal Reserve Bank in order to support its efforts. Each district consists of multiple states and parts of states. For example, the Kansas City Federal Reserve District includes Colorado, Kansas, Nebraska, Oklahoma, and parts of Missouri and New Mexico.

Federal Reserve System The central bank system of the United States. The Federal Reserve regulates the monetary policy of the United States, especially by setting the discount rate and the fed funds rate and by buying and selling U.S. Treasury securities. It consists of 12 regional banks that operate under the guidance of a Federal Reserve Board, whose seven members are appointed by the President of the United States. The Federal Reserve System has the authority to print money, a controversial measure both now and at the time it was founded. All federally-chartered banks must belong to the Federal Reserve System and purchase a certain amount of stock in the Federal Reserve bank in charge of their particular regions. The Federal Reserve System was established in 1913.

Federal Savings and Loan Association A federally chartered bank that specializes in taking deposits for checking and savings accounts, as well as making home mortgages. Savings and loan associations tend to be smaller than other banks and are more focused on the local communities in which they operate. It is sometimes (but not always) easier to obtain a loan from a savings and loan association because it may have better knowledge of the local market. They derive most of their funds from customer savings accounts, but they also generally have easy access to loans from the Federal Home Mortgage Banks. They are also known as thrifts. They are regulated by the Office of Thrift Supervision.

Federal Stafford Subsidized Loan A low-interest loan available to post-secondary students with demonstrated financial need. Payments are deferred until six months after a student has ceased to be enrolled at least half-time in a degree or certificate-seeking program. The U.S. federal government makes interest payments for the student during this time. One must file the FAFSA to determine eligibility for a federal Stafford subsidized loan.

Federal Stafford Unsubsidized Loan A low-interest loan available to post-secondary students regardless of demonstrated financial need. Payments are deferred until six months after a student has ceased to be enrolled at least half-time in a degree or certificate-seeking program. The U.S. federal government defers interest payments for the student during this time; the interest is added to the principal at the end of the period. One must file the FAFSA to determine eligibility for a federal Stafford unsubsidized loan.

Federal Trade Commission A government organization with the responsibility of protecting consumers from predatory or unfair business practices. As such, it is responsible for the enforcement of antitrust laws, protecting against anti-competitive mergers and acquisitions. Citizens may complain to the Federal Trade Commission for perceived wrongdoings in the business practices of a company. While adjudicating these complaints takes time, the FTC provides a recourse against exploitation of the consumer.

Federal Trade Commission Act of 1914 Legislation in the United States that established the Federal Trade Commission (FTC). The Act gave the FTC the responsibility for protecting consumers from predatory or unfair business practices. The Act also provided a forum for citizens to complain about perceived wrongdoings in the business practices of a company. Additionally, the Act gave the FTC the ability to issue cease and desist orders to companies engaging in these practices. Its ability to enforce antitrust laws did not come until the 1930s.

Federal Unemployment Tax Act Commonly called FUTA. Legislation in the United States authorizing the federal government to levy an unemployment compensation tax, which pays for the unemployment insurance of the unemployed labor force. The taxes permitted under FUTA pay for the federal government's half of unemployment insurance; the other half is provided by states. However, FUTA sets up a fund from which states can borrow to pay for their half.

Federalism A political system in which the central government has certain, enumerated powers, and other government responsibilities are delegated to lower levels of government. For example, a federalist system may designate the central government to handle monetary policy and foreign affairs, but delegate most other matters to the provinces or states. Examples of federalist countries include the United States and Canada.

Federalist One who believes in or advocates a political system in which the central government has certain, enumerated powers, and other government responsibilities are delegated to lower levels of government. For example, a federalist system may designate the central government to handle monetary policy and foreign affairs, but delegate most other matters to the provinces or states.

Federally Sponsored Corporate Security A debt obligation owed by a private company chartered by the U.S. government. While similar to an agency security, federally sponsored corporate securities are issued by a private company with an implicit guarantee from the federal government. Agencies that offer these securities include Fannie Mae and Freddie Mac. While these securities are not directly guaranteed by the U.S. government, they are considered fairly safe investments.

Fee An agreed-upon, stated amount one pays for a service or privilege. For example, one may be required to pay a fee to attend college, to open an account with a brokerage, or to do any number of other things. Fees are stated and are usually standardized for the person or organization receiving them.

Fee Table A table in the prospectus of a mutual fund stating what fees are and how one incurs them. It tells whether the sales charge is front-end, back-end, or an even loan. A fee table increases transparency in the market.

Fee-Based Compensation A way to pay a broker, investment adviser or money manager in which the client gives a set hourly wage and/or a percentage of the assets under management in exchange for financial services. The contrasts with commission-based compensation, though some managers receive a combination of both.

Fee-Based Investment A fund or portfolio where the money manager is paid a percentage of the fund or portfolio's market value rather than commissions based on the number of transactions conducted. Fee-based investment is thought to better align the incentives of investors and money managers; specifically, money managers have a reason to provide increased value for the investment. Fee-based investment also reduces the temptation to overtrade simply to extract higher commissions.

Feed Ratio A ratio of the total cost of food for an animal over the course of its life to the animal's sale price. Futures and commodity traders use the feed ratio to determine whether investing in animal commodities is worth the overhead costs. A ratio of less than one indicates that one can make a net profit from selling the animal while a ratio greater than one indicates the opposite. See also: Corn-Hog Ratio.

Feed the Gorilla A slang term meaning to spend the minimum amount of time required on core competencies in order to devote more time to other projects. Feeding the gorilla is high risk as one may ignore the most sustainable parts of a business.

Feeder Cattle Cattle separated from a herd's breeding stock. They are kept in a different area and fed food intended to fatten them for slaughter. See also: Beef.

Feeder Fund A mutual fund or other fund that invests exclusively in another fund. Shares of the feeder fund represent shares in the second fund (called a master fund), which, in turn, represent shares in the underlying securities. Feeder funds are relatively common when the master fund contains tax disadvantages for shareholders that the feeder fund remedies. See also: Fund of funds.

Feeder Lines In infrastructure, rail or air lines that take passengers to a primary hub, where they can take different lines to their final destinations.

Feeding Frenzy 1. A slang term for intense buying. This may occur at a retail level or it may refer to a bullish market for securities. **2.** During the 1980s, the custom among certain bond traders on Wall Street to order far more takeout food than they could eat. The point of the feeding frenzies was to see which trader could display the most conspicuous consumption. Feeding frenzies were exposed in the book Liar's Poker, which describes the author's experience as a bond trader on Wall Street in the 1980s. . k-Doorer secrets to Israel, Wolf Hopper: ecisie

Fee-for-Service A form of health insurance where the policyholder pays for medical expenses out-of-pocket and receives a reimbursement from the insurer. That is, a fee-for-service plan reduces the insurer's risk that the plan might be abused by requiring the policyholder to pay for expenses first, and only reimburses him/her afterward. Generally speaking, a fee-for-service policy includes some co-insurance. Some medical practices require fee-for-service payment to reduce the risk that it cannot perform a procedure if the insurer denies coverage. That is, the practice expects the patient to pay when the service is given and to file with the insurer for reimbursement afterward.

Felines Formerly-issued Treasury securities whose coupons had been stripped by an intermediary. Felines therefore paid no interest. They were sold at a significant discount from par and matured at par. Felines fluctuated in price, sometimes dramatically, because changes in interest rates made them more or less desirable. There were a variety of different felines during the early 1980s, all with "feline" acronyms, such as CATS, COUGRS, and TIGRS. They became largely obsolete after 1986, when the U.S. Treasury began issuing its own stripped bonds. See also: zero-coupon bonds, STRIPS.

Fellow Servant Rule A former defense used in lawsuits whereby an employer claimed he/she was not responsible for an employee's work-related injury because another employee caused it. Workers compensation laws have replaced the fellow servant rule.

Fen A unit of length in China approximately equivalent to 3.33 millimeters.

Fence A position in which an investor is long (or short) on an out-of-the-money put, long (or short) on an opposite out-of-the-money call in addition to being long (or short) on the underlying asset. Both options have the same expiration date. A fence position sets a floor and ceiling for the underlying asset and limits potential losses for the investor. It is often used by traders in farm commodities.

Fencing The act of buying stolen property with the intention of re-selling it to unsuspecting persons. For example, a person may steal jewelry to sell to a middleman (called a fence), who then re-sells it a buyer who may or may not realize that the jewelry is stolen. Fences profit from paying low prices for the stolen property and re-selling it at retail prices (prices comparable to those on the legitimate market). Fencing is illegal in most jurisdictions, but it may be difficult to prove in court.

Fening A subdivision of the convertible mark in Bosnia and Herzegovina. One fening is equal in value to 1/100 of one mark. Its plural is feninga.

Fennig A subdivision of the Bosnia and Herzegovina convertible mark. One fennig is worth 1/100 of one convertible mark.

Feorirling A coin that circulated in the Republic of Ireland between 1928 and 1962. It was equal in value to 1/960 of one Irish pound. See also: Farthing.

Feredela A largely obsolete Romanian measure of area approximately equivalent to 1.25 square meters.

Fermi A unit of length equivalent to one-one quadrillionth of one meter.

Fersah A Turkish measure of length approximately equivalent to 5.7 kilometers. It became obsolete when Turkey made the metric system mandatory in 1933.

Fertach An obsolete Irish unit of length approximately equivalent to three meters.

Feu An inexact unit of capacity equal to the size of a cargo container 40 feet (or sometimes 45 feet) in length. See also: TEU.

FFELP Federal Family Education Loan Program. A former program of the U.S. federal government in which the government subsidized or guaranteed private, low interest rate loans to students enrolled in degree-seeking post-secondary education programs. The program offered Stafford loans (both subsidized and unsubsidized) and PLUS loans. The program was eliminated in 2010 when the federal government directly took over the lending programs.

FH In numismatics, an abbreviation meaning "full head." It is used to describe Standing Liberty quarters on which the head of Lady Liberty it visible in full detail. This is unusual even among some uncirculated Standing Liberty quarters and may positively affect the value.

FI 1. ISO 3166-1 alpha-2 code for the Republic of Finland. This is the code used in international transactions to and from Finnish bank accounts. **2.** ISO 3166-2 geocode for Finland. This is used as an international standard for shipping to Finland. Each Finnish province has its own code with the prefix "FI." For example, the code for the Province of Lapin laani is ISO 3166-2:FI-LL.

Fiat Money Money that is not backed by anything other than a government trust. Fiat money has no intrinsic value; it only has value at all because all participants in an economy agree to trust the government issuing the currency. All modern money is fiat money. While deflation is possible for fiat money, it is much more susceptible to inflation.

Fiber A slang term for the euro-U.S. dollar exchange rate.

Fibonacci Fan In technical analysis, a way of determining the support and resistance levels for a security's price. One calculates a Fibonacci fan by finding the high and low prices for a given period of time and dividing the difference between those two by three Fibonacci ratios: 38.2%, 50%, and 61.8%. One then draws lines on a chart based on these calculations.

Fibonacci Numbers A sequence of numbers in which each number is the sum of the two previous numbers (1, 1, 2 and so on). Some technical analysts use Fibonacci numbers to determine which securities are bullish or bearish. Some of the ways they use Fibonacci numbers are Fibonacci time zones, Fibonacci retracement, Fibonacci fans, and Fibonacci arcs.

Fiche Pingin A coin that circulated in the Republic of Ireland between 1986 and 2002. It was equal in value to 1/5 of one Irish pound.

FICO Score A way of measuring an individual's creditworthiness. A FICO score is a quantification of a variety of factors in an individual's background, including a history of default, the current amount of debt, and the length of time that the individual has made purchases on credit. A FICO score ranges between 350 and 850. In general, a score of 650 is considered a "fair" credit score, while 750 or higher is considered "excellent." A FICO score is a convenient way to summarize an individual's credit history and is included in a credit report. The term comes from the Fair Isaac Corporation, which created the system.

Fictitious Credit The credit available on a margin account. This refers to the proceeds from a short sale that are deposited in the account, resulting in extra credit available to the account holder. However, because this credit comes from securities being used as collateral, the fictitious credit is not locked in and, more importantly, the account holder cannot withdraw it directly.

Fiduciary 1. A person appointed to handle another person's finances. A fiduciary holds the assets of another person and is required to act in the best interests of that person; he/she is not allowed to invest for personal profit. See also: Prudent person rule. **2.** Describing a duty or obligation to act in the best interest of another person or institution. For example, an elected government might state that it has a fiduciary duty to wisely use the taxes it collects. **3.** An unsecured loan.

Fiduciary Bond A bond that the executor of an estate posts to ensure he/she performs his/her duties properly. Among these duties is preparing an inventory and disposing it according to the terms of the will of the deceased. The executor forfeits the bond if a probate court determines he/she has failed to live up to his/her duties. It is also called a probate bond.

Fiduciary Out A provision in some merger agreements allowing the board of directors of one of the companies to terminate the deal before it is finalized if it receives a better offer from another company. A fiduciary out provision exists because boards of directors have a responsibility to always act in the best interests of shareholders. A better offer for shareholders is almost always thought to be in their best interests.

Fiduciary Risk The risk that an agent handling funds on behalf of a principal will not live up to his/her full fiduciary responsibility. That is, fiduciary risk is the possibility that an agent will not act in the client's best interest. This does not necessarily include foul play or fraud. It could simply mean that the agent is not handling the client's funds in the best possible way.

Field Bet The act or practice of buying stocks in several companies in the same, declining industry. The idea behind a field bet is to accept the losses for a time, hoping that several companies will go bankrupt and that the remaining companies will reform themselves, resulting in solid gains. Field betting is a highly risky strategy.

Field Warehouse A warehouse owned by a company other than the one using it. The company using the warehouse pays rent to the owner. It should not be confused with field warehousing, which is a financing arrangement.

Fifteen-Year Mortgage A mortgage with a maturity of 15 years. A 15-year mortgage usually has a higher payment than a 30-year mortgage because one pays a higher portion of the principal each month.

Fifth A unit of liquid volume equivalent to one-fifth of one gallon. It is used in the sale of liquor.

Fifty Percent Principle In technical analysis, a general rule stating that a security on an upward trend will lose between 50% and 75% of its recent gains before the upward trend continues. The 50% principle exists because some investors, seeing an upward trend, become concerned that a security is overvalued and sell their shares even though the upward trend has not ceased. Once investors realize this, they begin to buy the security and the upward trend continues.

Fight the Tape To buy when most traders are selling and vice versa. Generally speaking, investors are advised not to fight the tape; most analysts consider it irrational behavior.

Fiji Dollar The currency of Fiji. It was introduced in 1969, replacing the Fijian pound. The Fijian dollar is a floating currency. Interestingly, all dollars currently in circulation feature a portrait of Queen Elizabeth of the United Kingdom even though she is no longer Fiji's head of state.

Fijian Pound The former currency of Fiji. It was pegged to the British pound along with the Australian and New Zealand pounds. In 1969, it was replaced by the Fijian dollar in order to maintain rough parity with the newly issued Australian and New Zealand dollars (and thereby encourage Fijian exports to those countries).

File an Extension To request extra time to complete one's tax return for a year. It is common to file an extension if one does not gather all relevant information or complete all forms by the deadline. For example, one may file an extension on one's federal taxes from April 15 to October 15.

Filing Status A group into which one classifies oneself when filing a tax return. In the United States, there are five filing statuses: single individual, married filing separately, married filing jointly, head of household, and qualifying widow(er) with dependent child. One's filing status is important to determining one's tax bracket and the credits and deductions to which one is entitled.

Fill To conduct a trade such that it satisfies a client's order. That is, a broker fills an order when he/she makes the requested trade. The price at which an order is filled is called a fill price.

Fill or Kill An order to a broker to buy or sell a security or derivative, usually in large quantities, in which investors have a short period of time to partially or completely fulfill the order before it is cancelled. An FOK may be considered the opposite of a good 'til cancelled (GTC) order; it differs from an immediate or cancel (IOC) order because an IOC may only be partially filled, while an FOK must be entirely filled or the whole offer is void. An FOK is considered a type of day order, but has a much shorter time frame. See also: All-or-None Offering.

Fill Price The price at which an order for a security is executed. The fill price, in other words, is the market price of a security in practice, as opposed to the price in theory. The fill price may or may not be an investor's requested price, depending on the type of order.

Filler A subdivision of the Hungarian forint. One filler is equal in value to 1/100 of one forint. It does not circulate in practice.

Fils A division of the currency in several Arabic speaking countries. Many currencies, such as the Emirati dirham and the Bahraini dinar, are divided into 100 or 1,000 fils.

Filter Rule In technical analysis, an arbitrarily set percentage of increase or decline in a stock's price that the analyst sees as an indicator to buy or sell the stock. For example, the analyst may set his/her own filter rule at 15%. If the stock rises 15%, the analyst recommends buying; if it falls 15%, he/she recommends selling. While the particular percentage is subjective, one arrives at it by observing the stock's historical trends. The filter rule exists to help the investor avoid buying or selling at insignificant or anomalous changes in price. However, many analysts do not believe that the filter rule consistently produces profits for the investor.

FIM ISO 4217 code for the Finnish markka. It was introduced in 1860, replacing the Russian ruble. Like most currencies, it was pegged to the U.S. dollar during the Bretton Woods period, and later to various currency baskets. It was replaced by the euro in 1999 and ceased circulating in 2002.

FIN GOST 7.67 Latin three-letter geocode for Finland. The code is used for transactions to and from Finnish bank accounts and for international shipping to Finland. As with all GOST 7.67 codes, it is used primarily in Cyrillic alphabets.

Final Dividend The last dividend declared in a given fiscal year. The final dividend is determined after all financial reports have been made and the company has the clearest pictures of its performance that year. As a result, the final dividend is often the largest, as the company does not have to worry about being conservative if expected revenues do not match actual revenues. The term is most common in the United Kingdom.

Final Prospectus **1.** The last prospectus distributed prior to a new issue of a security. The final prospectus contains similar information to a preliminary prospectus, but is updated, and, importantly, contains the security's price. **2.** The most recent prospectus distributed by a mutual fund. Mutual funds update their prospecti from time to time as the types of securities represented in the fund, or perhaps its investment philosophy, change. The final prospectus is issued annually.

Final Take Informal; the profit or revenue that a participant in a project receives from the project's proceeds.

Finance The study of money and how it is used. Finance considers the relationship of money to time and risk. One of the main subsets of finance is the study of credit and banking, as this involves money, time, and risk all together. Finance may deal with personal or corporate issues, such as how will an individual or company acquires the money needed to perform a certain act.

Finance Act Annual legislation in the United Kingdom making changes to the tax structure. The Finance Act may raise or lower taxes or provide tax incentives for various reasons, depending on the government's financial needs. The Finance Act is passed as part of the budget process each year.

Finance Charge The cost of obtaining financing, especially through debt. Often it refers to the interest one must pay, expressed as the annual percentage rate. See also: Cost of capital.

Financial Accounting A branch of accounting involving the preparation and publication of financial statements, earnings reports, and other forms for disclosure to shareholders, regulators, and any other stakeholders. Financial accounting is necessary for publicly-traded companies and some other corporations. It must be accomplished in accordance with the Generally Accepted Accounting Principles or the equivalent in different countries. The primary difference between financial accounting and managerial accounting is the fact that financial accounting involves explanation to outside parties, while managerial accounting is primarily internal.

Financial Accounting Standards Board In the United States, a non-governmental body the SEC has charged with establishing and maintaining generally accepted standards for professional accountants. Founded in 1973, the FASB has published a variety of rules and clarifications on how accounting ought to be done in the United States. It is important to note that the FASB does not govern accounting ethics; rather, its purpose to govern the fundamentals of how accounting is conducted. For example, it has published guidelines on how to report a company's cash flows. The Financial Accounting Foundation oversees the FASB.

Financial Accounting Standards Foundation A private sector body in Japan charged with establishing and maintaining standards for professional accountants. Founded in 2001, the FASF has published a variety of rules and clarifications on how accounting ought to be done in Japan.

Financial Aid Loans, grants, and scholarships available to help students pay for education expenses, especially by an educational institution or a government. For example, a university may offer grants and academic scholarships while the government may subsidize low-interest loans so a student can attend the school. Financial aid is designed to make education more affordable, though schools also may use it to attract competitive students.

Financial Analysis Research into data relating to the stability and profitability of businesses, especially to guide one's investing practices. At its most basic, financial analysis involves looking at financial statements to determine if a company is healthy. Balance sheets are important to financial analysis as they provide a ready-made means of investigating performance. However, it is important to note that quantitative financial analysis has limits: the accounting methods a particular business employs, for example, may make it look more or less healthy than it really is. See also: Fundamental analysis.

Financial Analyst A person who researches and reports on the state of securities. An analyst uses technical or fundamental signals to determine which securities are likely to be profitable, and which are not. Financial analysts help persons and organizations in making investment decisions. See also: CFA.

Financial and Operational Combined Uniform Single Report A report the SEC requires members of the New York Stock Exchange to file with the exchange on a monthly and quarterly basis. The report includes information on each member's capital position; that is, how much each member owns in cash, securities, and other liquid assets. The report is filed on Form X-17A-5.

Financial Asset A non-physical asset. Examples of financial assets include bank accounts and shares in a publicly-traded company. Financial assets are distinguished from physical assets like real estate and personal property. In general, when one speaks of "investing" and the "market," one is referring to financial assets, though both those terms may include non-financial assets like corn or wheat.

Financial Center **1.** A term for a large bank or bank branch. **2.** A term for a city or country with a large financial sector.

Financial Close The period of time after an agreement has been entered when all conditions have been fulfilled (or waived) and all documents have been properly filed and executed. After the financial close, drawdowns are allowed.

Financial Community of Africa A collective term for countries that use the West African CFA franc. The Financial Community of Africa includes Benin, Burkina Faso, Cote d'Ivoire, Guinea-Bissau, Mali, Niger, Senegal, and Togo.

Financial Contagion A negative occurrence in one market, industry, or country that impacts other markets, industries, or countries. For example, problems in the U.S. financial markets starting in 2007 spread to other industries quickly and by 2008 had become a global financial crisis. Likewise, Japan's financial crisis in the 1990s had repercussions all over East Asia and elsewhere. See also: Globalization.

Financial Control Any measure of how well a company or department controls its costs, sometimes expressed as how far under or over budget it is.

Financial Crimes Enforcement Network A network of agencies under the direction of the U.S. Department of the Treasury that monitors transactions and helps enforce financial laws, especially those against money laundering. FinCEN examines required filings by companies, and tracks and investigates irregularities. FinCEN operates both inside and outside the United States, and relies upon information from law enforcement, financial institutions, and regulators.

Financial Distress A stage before bankruptcy where a company's creditors are not being paid or are paid with significant difficulty. While a company can avoid moving from financial distress to bankruptcy, it can be very difficult. Often, financial distress can come with its own costs, such as fees paid to lawyers or the costs of extra interest for late payments. See also: Costs of financial distress.

Financial Distress Cost The cost of liquidation. Financial distress costs include fees for lawyers and money needed to file paperwork. They also include the losses incurred from slowing or ceasing operations.

Financial Engineering The process of creating a new investment vehicle. For example, one may create a new derivative by taking existing structures and altering them to mitigate risk and/or increase the return. One may also theoretically invent a completely new financial product from nothing. Financial engineering is often mathematically intensive, as a number of risks and other factors must be considered before the new product is marketable.

Financial Future A futures contract on a financial product. Examples of financial futures include trading on currencies, stock indices, and Treasury securities. In a financial future, the counterparties agree to trade the underlying financial product at a certain time for a certain price. Some financial futures are settled in cash, especially if the underlying assets are indices. Financial futures may be traded like other futures.

Financial Guarantee Insurance An insurance policy covering a lender from liability resulting from the failure of the borrower to repay the loan. It may also cover losses from a decrease in interest rates to the detriment of the lender. Financial guarantee insurance may cover different types of loans, but, in most U.S. states, usually does not include mortgages or certain credit lines. It is similar to a surety or a co-signed loan.

Financial Guaranty Insurance Corporation A private company providing financial guarantee insurance for different types of transactions. For example, an insurance policy may cover a lender from liability resulting from the failure of the borrower to repay the loan. FGIC originally provided this insurance exclusively for municipal bonds, but expanded into different transactions such as IPOs. Clients pay FGIC the appropriate premium in exchange for a guarantee of repayment in case of default; this increases the bond's credit rating and usually decreases its interest rate. The services FGIC provides are similar to sureties or co-signed loans.

Financial Highlights In a financial report, especially a publicly-traded company's report to shareholders, an overview or summary of the major occurrences in the company since the last report. The financial highlights may include major statistics and figures, such as net cash flow from operations, or it may include qualitative information on an acquisition or a new product. Government departments may also include financial highlights in their reports.

Financial Holding Company In the United States, a financial company that engages in nonbanking activities. For example, a financial holding company may be a bank, but it also may offer insurance and investment products. A financial holding company must have at least 85% of its assets in financial services and must divest all nonfinancial services within 10 years of its registration as an FHC. Financial holding companies are regulated by the Federal Reserve.

Financial Incentive An incentive to do something because it is less expensive than not doing so. For example, a company may have a financial incentive to open a factory in Town A instead of Town B because Town A's property taxes are lower.

Financial Industry Regulatory Authority A self-regulatory organization that assists the SEC in regulating financial markets, notably exchanges and companies that deal with securities. Among other duties, FINRA enforces rules, arbitrates disputes, and provides training and licensing services. Contrary to the belief of some, it is not a government agency. It was created in 2007 with the merger of the National Association of Securities Dealers and the NYSE regulatory board.

Financial Innovation The creation of a new investment vehicle. For example, one may structure a derivative in a way that has never been done before. Financial innovation can increase efficiency and profits for certain parties. However, it often takes time for regulation to catch up to financial innovation, which can make it risky.

Financial Institution An organization, which may be either for-profit or non-profit, that takes money from clients and places it in any of a variety of investment vehicles for the benefit of both the client and the organization. Common examples of financial institutions are retail banks, which take deposits into safekeeping and use them to make loans to other customers, and insurance companies, which do not take deposits, but provide guarantees of payment if a certain situation occurs in exchange for a premium. See also: Depository institution, Non-depository institution.

Financial Institutions Reform, Recovery and Enforcement Act of 1989 Legislation in the United States passed in response to the savings and loan crisis. The FIRREA created the Resolution Trust Corporation, which was charged with closing thrifts declared to be insolvent. It also created new funds within the FDIC to administer the depositor's insurance to account holders at insolvent institutions. Importantly, it created the Office of Thrift Supervision, a bureau of the U.S. Department of the Treasury to regulate federal savings associations, savings and loan associations (thrifts), and some holding companies. The OTS both provides charters and creates regulations for thrifts and other institutions that fall under its supervision. Additionally, it audits the practices of financial institutions that specialize in personal savings and mortgage loans to ensure that they comply with applicable regulations.

Financial Instrument Any document with monetary value. Examples include cash and cash equivalents, but also securities such as bonds and stocks which have value and may be traded in exchange for money.

Financial Intermediary A financial institution that stands between counterparties in a transaction. For example, in the sale of a house, a bank usually serves as a financial intermediary by providing a mortgage to the homebuyer. In some non-traditional transactions, a bank may buy a product, such as corn, and immediately re-sell it for a profit to a third party. Most transactions requiring a loan to one of the parties include financial intermediaries. See also: Murabaha.

Financial Investment and Loan Program A government-owned trust fund in Japan managing the assets comprising the life insurance for postal workers, the savings of the postal service, national pensions, and welfare programs.

Financial Leverage 1. To use debt to finance an activity. For example, one usually borrows money in the form of a mortgage to buy a house. One commonly refers to this as leveraging the house. Likewise, one leverages when one uses a margin in order to purchase securities. **2.** The amount of debt that has been used to finance activities. A company with much more debt than equity is generally called "highly leveraged." Too much leverage is often thought to be unhealthy, but many firms use leverage in order to expand operations.

Financial Leverage Clientele Investors, especially clients at a single brokerage, who prefer to invest predominantly or exclusively in companies with a given amount of leverage. That is, the financial leverage clientele prefers to invest in companies with a certain level of borrowing. Some financial leverage clientele may prefer companies with less borrowing, while others may prefer more. What unites them is the importance leverage has in determining their investment choices.

Financial Market Any place where trading occurs, regardless of whether it is on an exchange or over-the-counter.

Financial Need The difference between the cost of an educational program and what the student can afford to pay. One's financial need may qualify one for grants, scholarships, or low-interest loans. Otherwise, the student must borrow or save. See also: Expected family contribution.

Financial Objectives A company's financial needs or goals for the future. Corporate financial planning involves identifying these financial objectives and determining how to achieve them. Simply put, the main financial objective is to make money, but financial objectives often also determine the amount that is needed or desired, the timeframe in which it must be made, and how the money will be spent. This can be a complicated process.

Financial Obligation Ratio In personal finance, the ratio of mortgage payments, consumer debt payments, car payments and other debt to total disposable income. The financial obligation ratio shows how easily a person can make his/her debt service each month. This shows how likely a person is to default, which may affect his/her ability to take on more debt.

Financial Performance Any of many different mathematical measures to evaluate how well a company is using its resources to make a profit. Common examples of financial performance include operating income, earnings before interest and taxes, and net asset value. It is important to note that no one measure of financial performance should be taken on its own. Rather, a thorough assessment of a company's performance should take into account many different measures.

Financial Plan A summary of a company's financial needs or goals for the future and how to achieve them. Corporate financial planning involves deciding what investments and activities would be most appropriate under both the company's individual and broader economic circumstances. All things being equal, short-term financial planning involves less uncertainty than long-term financial planning because, generally speaking, market trends are more predictable in the short term. Likewise, short-term financial plans are more easily amended in case something goes wrong.

Financial Planner A professional who consults with clients on financial matters. A financial planner may help a client prepare income taxes, insurance, investments, and estate planning, among others. Generally speaking, a financial planner must have a certification such as a ChFC or a CFP.

Financial Planning The process of determining a person's or firm's financial needs or goals for the future and the means to achieve them. Financial planning involves deciding what investments and activities would be most appropriate under both personal and broader economic circumstances. All things being equal, short-term financial planning involves less uncertainty than long-term financial planning because, generally speaking, market trends are more easily predictable in the short term. Likewise, short-term financial plans are more easily amendable in case something goes wrong as a result of the short time frame.

Financial Porn An excessive amount of information, especially from the 24 hour news cycle, that purports to help investors but may not. For example, analysts on the news may spend a significant amount of time discussing one stock, which may cause investors to buy it without doing sufficient research. In addition to the potential for loss, there is the opportunity cost of not investing in a better stock that was not discussed on the news. Financial porn is effectively investment advice for those unwilling to perform due diligence themselves.

Financial Portal A website that provides the user with a wide variety of investing information. This information can include news, quotes, recommendations, and a number of other things. Some financial portals offer all information for free, but many have some free material and other, "exclusive" material available for a fee. Examples of financial portals include Bloomberg and The Motley Fool.

Financial Position The total assets, liabilities, and/or equity a person or company holds. This term especially applies to investment positions. See also: Long Position, Short Position.

Financial Press Newspapers, magazines, or other media specializing in financial news. Prominent examples include Bloomberg and the Financial Times. The financial press is important to the overall financial sector as some companies often publish information, such as bond yields, in certain periodicals to disseminate it to the widest possible audience.

Financial Price Risk The risk that the price of something will change significantly such that it results in a loss. For example, if one has an investment in a foreign currency and that currency changes in value, it may adversely affect the investment's value. Likewise, if one holds a long position in a commodity and the price crashes for any reason, one may take a loss. Financial price risk can be mitigated by any number of hedging strategies, but these almost always limit returns.

Financial Public Relations A department of a company that attempts to portray the company's investments and financial state in the best possible light, or a public relations firm hired for this purpose. A financial public relations department interprets applicable laws and regulations, and it generally employs lawyers in order to defend the interpretations to the regulator if need be. Financial public relations also deal with disclosure forms and press releases made available to journalists and the public; these seek to promote and, if necessary, defend the company.

Financial Pyramid An investment strategy that structures portfolios according to the risk associated with each investment. The majority of investments are low-risk and non-speculative; these form the "base" of the pyramid. A smaller number are medium-risk, forming the "middle" of the pyramid. A few are high-risk, high-return investments that may be highly speculative. The idea behind a financial pyramid is to allow for the possibility of high return for the investors without acquiring too much risk in the portfolio.

Financial Rand An accounting currency used in South Africa between 1985 and 1995. Under this system, the South African rand continued to circulate but investments made by non-South Africans could be sold only for the financial rand, which had strict conditions placed on its convertibility. The financial rand was introduced in order to prevent massive outflows of capital that began in response to South Africa's apartheid policy. It was abolished after apartheid was ended.

Financial Ratio The division of one piece of financial information by another. Financial ratios are very common in fundamental analysis, which investigates the financial health of companies. An example of a financial ratio is the price-earnings ratio, which divides a publicly-traded company's share price by its earnings per share. This helps analysts determine whether a company's share price properly reflects its performance.

Financial Reconstruction Commission A former agency of the Japanese government that oversaw financial policy. It managed and disposed of assets nationalized in the wake of the Asian financial crisis. It was established in 1998 as part of the response to the crisis. It was merged into the Financial Services Agency in 2001.

Financial Revitalization Law Legislation in Japan that overhauled financial regulation in that country. Among other things, it established the Financial Reconstruction Commission to manage and dispose of nationalized assets. It also provided companies and banks with tools to remain in business. Some have argued that the law marked a shift from relation-based to rule-based regulation in Japan. The law was passed in 1998.

Financial Risk Any risk that comes from giving money to another person or entity. For example, if one lends money, one carries the financial risk that the borrower will not repay it. A venture capital firm carries the financial risk that its investments will never become profitable. Likewise, an investor who purchases an asset carries the financial risk that he/she will be unable to re-sell it.

Financial Service Income Income from services such as banking and brokering. Much financial service income comes from fees and commissions. In the case of leases, it comes from lease payments.

Financial Services Act 1986 Legislation in the United Kingdom that largely deregulated financial services. Specifically, it removed from courts the ability they previously held to regulate derivative contracts. Most of the Act (though not the aforementioned example) was repealed by the Financial Services and Markets Act 2000.

Financial Services and Markets Act 2000 Legislation in the United Kingdom that established the Financial Services Authority. The Act gave the FSA the power to regulate financial services. It also established a requirement for companies to reveal information that the FSA requests.

Financial Services Authority The primary regulatory body for the British financial industry. It is a non-government agency, though its board of directors is appointed by HM Treasury. It is charged with maintaining efficiency and competition in banking, insurance and the securities trade. It also is responsible for protecting consumers insofar as possible. It was established in 2001.

Financial Services Modernization Act of 1999 Legislation in the United States that deregulated much of the American financial industry. It permitted banks, insurance companies and investment banks to offer each others' products for the first time since the Great Depression. That is, the same companies could offer insurance, brokerage services and/or regular banking services. The legislation resulted in a great deal of consolidation in the financial sector. Critics maintain that it caused banks to take on unnecessary risks that led to the late 2000s recession. It is more commonly called the Gramm-Leach-Bliley Act after its principal authors.

Financial Slack Extra money that a company has available in case of a downturn in sales, revenue, or profit. Financial slack may help a company make it through a difficult period. It is the equivalent of a company's savings.

Financial Stabilization Law Legislation in Japan authorizing the injection of 30 trillion yen into the banking sector to protect depositors and shore up banks themselves. The law was passed in 1998 due to the Asian financial crisis. It is considered to have been a failure.

Financial Statement Any list of the assets and liabilities of a company designed to show its financial health, profits or losses, and/or other variables. The two most common financial statements are the balance sheet and the income statement. Publicly-traded companies and some others are legally required to publish certain financial statements.

Financial Supermarket A financial institution that offers a wide variety of services to clients. For example, a financial supermarket may serve as a broker, insurance company, and real estate agent. Some financial supermarkets may even offer services approximating banking services. This is both convenient for the client and profitable for the supermarket. Financial supermarkets are made possible largely through deregulation.

Financial Supervisory Agency An agency in Japan responsible for regulating securities exchanges, banks, and insurance. It has been independent of any ministry since its creation in 1998.

Financial System Planning Bureau A division of the Japanese Ministry of Finance partially responsible for regulating securities and banks. It was created in 1998 by merging the banking and securities bureaus of the ministry.

Financial Times All-Share Index An index tracking approximately 600 publicly-traded companies listed on the London Stock Exchange and representing approximately 98% of the LSE's market capitalization. Like many other FTSE indices, it is calculated in real time, with prices updated every 15 seconds. Each quarter, the FTSE reevaluates the companies tracked on the index and makes necessary adjustments to ensure that it represents the correct companies. It includes all companies tracked by the FTSE 100, the FTSE 250, and the FTSE Small Cap. It is weighted for market capitalization.

Financing The process or means of acquiring capital necessary to conduct a business activity. Two of the most common forms of financing are debt financing and equity financing. In debt financing, one borrows money, usually from an institution, with the promise to return the money with interest at some point in the future. This provides capital to the borrower and a profit to the lender. In equity financing, a company sells portions of ownership to those who are interested. Unlike debt financing, equity financing usually raises capital without incurring liabilities, but the risk exists that the company will not raise enough. An alternative to both debt financing and equity financing, especially for start-ups, is using money from personal savings to pay for activities.

Financing Agreements A statement outlining the terms of credit between a lender and a borrower. While this may apply to any loan agreement, the term is most commonly used in project finance.

Financing Corporation A bond-issuing entity established by the U.S. Congress in 1987 to recapitalize the Federal Savings and Loan Insurance Corporation. The bonds it issued were to be repaid with FSLIC insurance premiums and funds made available by the Federal Home Loan Bank System. The funds it raised were insufficient to prevent insolvency and the FSLIC was abolished in 1989.

Financing Cost Savings The act of gaining a competitive advantage in business because of access to low-cost capital. For example, if two competing firms both borrow $1 million for operating expenses, but Firm A secured a 4.5% interest rate while Firm B had to settle for 8%, then Firm A has financed cost savings with respect to Firm B.

Financing Round Any organized attempt by a company to raise capital for its operations. A financing round may involve the sale of stock or bonds, or a company may seek an angel investor. A financing round is often necessary for a company to begin or to expand operations. See also: Down round.

Finder An intermediary who seeks and discovers a potential deal that can be made. For example, a finder may know that a person or company is seeking to sell a certain asset and may find a potential buyer. A finder is paid for this service, but only if the deal is finalized. See also: Finder's fee.

Finder of Fact In law, person or group assigned to determine whether and how an event occurred. For example, a finder of fact may be asked whether an accused person in fact robbed a bank. The finder of fact is generally a judge or jury. The finder of fact is also called the trier of fact.

Finder's Fee A fee that a person or company is paid in exchange for facilitating a transaction or other deal. For example, one may be paid a finder's fee if one knows both a potential buyer and a potential seller of a company, introduces the two, and the deal is finalized. The finder often has no role except to make parties aware of each other's existence and the finder's fee is usually a percentage of the value of the deal.

Fine A monetary penalty for an act. For example, one may have to pay $100 if one is caught driving over the speed limit. Fines are imposed instead of or (especially for financial crimes) in addition to prison sentences.

Fine Print Informal; all of the terms of a contract, rather than simply its main provisions. The fine print of a contract, as its name suggests, often appears in a smaller font, and can be cumbersome to read completely. For this reason, restrictions or terms disadvantageous to one party might be hidden in the fine print. This fact is the origin of the phrase, "Always read the fine print."

Fineness A measure of the purity of a precious metal as a unit of 1,000. That is, a fineness measure of 1 means that 0.1% of a substance is a given precious metal, while a measure of 1,000 means that 100% is the metal. Fineness is important to commodities and futures involving precious metals, in which the quality of the underlying metals must be specified in the contract.

Fingerprint In technical analysis, a particular security's unique or unusual price movements. For example, a stock may have a tendency to move slightly upward when similar stocks are moving slightly downward. Any number of factors may cause this, but the factors are often unique to the company issuing the security. A fingerprint often has a pattern that technical analysts may detect and track in order to take advantage of fluctuations.

Finish To fill an order. That is, once a broker finishes an order, he executes it according the conditions set forth by the client.

Finite Reinsurance Reinsurance that only covers a limited amount of risk. That is, an insurance company purchases finite reinsurance from a reinsurer to cover certain, very large payouts. The insurance company takes steps to reduce the remainder of its risk in other ways, such as by selling the risk to other parties. Finite reinsurance is available to insurance companies for lower premiums than other forms of reinsurance.

Finite-Life Real Estate Investment Trust A real estate investment trust (REIT) designed to sell all of its assets within a certain period of time in order to profit from capital gains. Before the assets are sold, the revenue for REITs comes mainly from rents on the properties it owns. Like all REITs, a finite-life REIT may be traded as if it were a stock. Owning a REIT is more liquid than directly owning the real estate underlying it.

Fire Somewhat informal; to terminate the employment of an employee. An employee may be fired for cause, such as for sexual harassment or absenteeism, or, in many cases, without cause. A fired employee is often eligible to collect unemployment insurance for a certain period of time.

Fire Drill In investment banking, a slang term for the pressing need to finish a presentation or other project as soon as possible.

Fire Sale A situation in which security prices are exceptionally low. This may be a buy signal, especially if the securities are fundamentally sound.

Fire Starter A slang term for an employee or executive who intentionally or unintentionally causes trouble wherever he/she goes. See also: Career-limiting move.

Firefighter A slang term for a person who solves problems as they arise. The term connotes the idea that the firefighter is distracted from dealing with larger issues because minor problems prevent him/her from doing so.

Firefighting A slang term for solving problems as they arise. The term connotes the idea that the firefighter is distracted from dealing with larger issues because minor problems prevent him/her from doing so.

Firkin An obsolete unit of volume equivalent to one-quarter of one barrel.

Firlot An obsolete Scottish unit of dry volume. For beans, grass seed, peas, rye, salt, and wheat, one firlot was approximately equivalent to 36.286 liters. For barley, malt, and oats, however, it was approximately equivalent to 52.916 liters.

Firm 1. A company or any other for-profit business. 2. Describing an order to buy or sell a security that may be executed fwithout confirming the order with the person or company making it. Most firm orders have a time limit.

Firm Anomalies A trading strategy that involves investing in a certain firm believing that characteristics specific to that firm will cause it to outperform its industry or the market as a whole. Firm anomalies may include a particularly good or well-regarded management team, for example. Firm anomaly is a characteristic of behavioral economics, which takes into account non-quantifiable matters such as human capital.

Firm Offer An offer to buy a security, company, property or anything else in which the price is not subject to negotiation. For example, one may make a firm offer to purchase a $400,000 house for $500,000 provided the seller makes all requested repairs. In this situation, the seller may either accept or decline the offer, but he/she cannot change it.

Firm Order 1. An order to a broker to buy or sell a security, where the order is not dependent on later confirmation by the client. Rather, the client makes the order and the broker fills it. 2. An order made by a broker-dealer itself rather than an individual investor or other client of the broker-dealer.

Firm Quote A bid or ask made by a dealer or market maker that is not up for negotiation. For example, if a dealer offers to sell 5,000 shares of a stock at $10 per share and the quote is firm, then potential buyers need not come back with a counteroffer of $8 per share. They can either take the offer or not. See also: Nominal quote.

Firm's Net Value of Debt A firm's market value less its total debt. See also: Net asset value.

Firm-Specific News News regarding a single company as opposed to an industry or the wider market. Examples include an earnings announcement, the hiring or firing of an executive, and so forth. Firm-specific news may affect the company's own stock price, but is unlikely to have ramifications on other companies unless the news becomes part of a trend. See also: Pricing out the News.

First Call Date The first date on which a callable bond or other fixed income security may be called. A callable bond allows the issuer to redeem the bond before maturity. When the bond is called, the bondholder receives the par value and does not receive any more coupons. Callable bonds are issued to allow the issuers to hedge against interest rate risk. That is, if interest rates lower significantly, they can call the bond and issue a new bond at a lower interest rate, reducing their liabilities. However, to protect the bondholder, most callable bonds also include a first call date, which guarantees the current interest rate for a certain period of time. The first call date is included in the bond agreement. See also: Doomsday call, Yield to first.

First Coupon The date on which a bond makes its first interest payment to bondholders. The first coupon date sometimes occurs at an irregular time; that is, if the bond pays coupons every six months, the first coupon may be longer or shorter than six months. See also: Long coupon, Short coupon, Grace period.

First Cruzeiro The currency of Brazil between 1942 and 1967. It replaced the reis at a rate of 1,000 reis to one cruzeiro. The cruzeiro began to experience high inflation and as a result was replaced by the second cruzeiro.

First Dollar Coverage An insurance policy where the insurer pays for all expenses once an insured event occurs. There is usually a (high) maximum amount limiting first dollar coverage, but the policy does not include a deductible, coinsurance, or anything else; the insurer is responsible for all expenses up to that

maximum amount. Because these plans carry more risk for the insurer, first dollar coverage comes with higher monthly premiums. First dollar coverage is available for many types of insurance, whether it is homeowner's insurance, car insurance, health insurance, or something else.

First East African Shilling A subdivision of the British pound that circulated in parts of Africa while they were under British control. It was equal in value to the British shilling, which was 1/20 of one pound.

First Fundamental Welfare Theorem The theory that a market equilibrium (that is, when the number of buyers equals the number of sellers) is always Pareto efficient. That is, in market equilibrium, no other allocation of resources can improve the lot of one economic actor without hurting the lot of another economic actor. The first fundamental welfare theorem states that the free market tends to assign resources in the most efficient way possible.

First Home A private residence purchased by a person who has never previously purchased a residence. Buying a first home is considered a major accomplishment as it gives one a stake in society and in the prosperity of the area where one lives. A first home may also be subject to favorable tax treatment.

First Icelandic Krona A former currency of Iceland. It was introduced as the Danish krona in 1874. Notes and coins began to be issued within Iceland in 1885. It became an independent currency following the demise of the Scandinavian Monetary Union after World War I. It was replaced by the second Icelandic krona in 1981.

First In, First Out In accounting, a technique for valuing inventory by treating inventory acquired first as if it were sold first. The sale of inventory is recorded against the purchase price of the oldest inventory, even if the physical goods are not the same. In times of high inflation, the first-in, first out technique increases a business' inflation risk. For this reason, most American firms have used the last-in, first-out technique in their accounting since the 1970s.

First Mortgage A mortgage on a property in which the lender has the right to full payment before any other lenders or liens on the same property are paid. That is, if the borrower defaults on the mortgage, the lender of the first mortgage has first right to the property and other lenders using the same property as collateral may only use it after the first lender has been fully satisfied. Generally speaking, first mortgages carry lower risk for lenders than other mortgages.

First Mover The first company that enters a new market. For example, the first mover may be the first soft drink company to come to a recently liberalized country. This helps the first mover dominate the market early so as to maintain a competitive advantage over the long term as other companies come to the market. The term may refer to Aristotle's concept of God as the first mover of the universe. See also: Barriers to entry.

First Notice Day The first day on which a clearing house may inform an investor that it intends to make delivery of a commodity that the investor previously bought in a futures contract. The date is governed by the rules of different exchanges and clearing houses, but may also be stated in the futures contract itself. It also occurs in the delivery month in which the contract expires.

First Section Stocks in the largest companies traded on the Tokyo Stock Exchange. See also: Second Section, Mothers (Tokyo Stock Exchange).

First Sudanese Pound The former currency of Sudan. It was issued in 1956, replacing the Egyptian pound and another Sudanese currency linked with the Egyptian pound. It was pegged to the British pound from 1969 to 1971. In 1992, it was replaced by the Sudanese dinar (which was itself replaced by the second Sudanese pound in 2007).

First Turkmenistani Manat The former currency of Turkmenistan. It was introduced in 1993, replacing the Soviet ruble. It suffered from high inflation in the 1990s and 2000s, and was replaced by the new Turkmenistani manat in January 2009 at a ratio of 5,000 old manat to one new manat.

First Ugandan Shilling The former currency of Uganda. It was introduced in 1966, replacing the East African shilling. It was marked by high inflation and in 1987 was replaced by the new Ugandan shilling.

First World A term for the most highly developed nations. It may be applied to any member of the OECD, though its usage is somewhat archaic. Originally, the term referred to the allies of the United States during the Cold War. The term still is still sometimes associated with the Cold War and has some negative connotations. As a result, so-called First World nations frequently are called developed nations. See also: OECD.

First Zimbabwean Dollar The former currency of Zimbabwe. It replaced the Rhodesian dollar following (official) independence from Britain in 1980 and was used until hyperinflation forced the government to issue the second Zimbabwean dollar in 2006.

First-Time Homebuyer A person or couple who buys a primary residence for the first time. Buying a home usually requires a large down payment; for this reason, first-time home buyers are permitted to make a withdrawal from an IRA without penalty provided it is used to help purchase the home. Additionally, first-time home buyers are eligible for a substantial tax credit.

Fiscal Agency Services Services that Federal Reserve Banks perform for the United States government. The most important of these services include maintaining the Treasury Department's bank accounts and issuing and redeeming Treasury securities.

Fiscal Agent A bank or similar institution that, in exchange for a fee, takes over fiscal responsibilities of another party. For example, a publicly-traded company may hire a fiscal agent to distribute dividends or coupons on its behalf. A fiscal agent allows the client to streamline its operations such that it can concentrate on its actual business, rather than worrying about who receives the proper dividends. See also: Outsourcing.

Fiscal Drag Reduced activity in an economy as a result of a progressive tax system set up in such a way as to penalize extra earnings. For example, suppose a gross income more than $50,000 per year increases one's tax liability such that a person effectively earns less than he/she would have at $45,000 gross. A rational economic actor would therefore endeavor to lower his/her gross income. This in turn lowers spending and reduces the supply of money in an economy available to purchase goods and services. The diminished activity is called fiscal drag.

Fiscal Neutrality A situation in which a government does not use tax incentives to encourage or discourage behavior. Fiscal neutrality especially refers to a balanced budget because it requires neither the government borrowing of a budget deficit nor the investment of a budget surplus.

Fiscal Period The period of time reflected in financial statements. Usually, the fiscal period is either the calendar year or a quarter. For example, publicly-traded companies must report their financial state for the fiscal period since their previous report. A fiscal period is also called an accounting period.

Fiscal Policy Government policies related to taxes, spending, and interest rates. Fiscal policy is intended positively influence macroeconomic conditions. The primary debate within this field is how active a government should be. Proponents of a tight fiscal policy argue that government acts best when it acts least; they promote low taxes and spending and ideally limit government involvement to the setting of prevailing interest rates. Proponents of a loose government policy believe that government has a larger role in promoting economic well-being. See also: Reaganomics, Keynesian economics.

Fiscal Quarter One fourth of the calendar that businesses use to calculate revenue and expenses. This may or may not correspond to a calendar quarter. For example, the first calendar quarter includes January, February and March because they are the first three months of the calendar year. However, if a business' fiscal year runs from October to September, the first fiscal quarter includes October, November and December.

Fiscal Reconstruction Law Legislation in Japan, passed in 1997, requiring a balanced budget. In effect, this coupled bailouts of Japanese companies with tax increases. See also: Asian financial crisis.

Fiscal Year 1. A calendar businesses use to calculate revenue and expenses. Most businesses also use their fiscal year as the period their annual budgets operate. Most jurisdictions require businesses to issue financial statements each year but often do not specify when they must do so. Thus, fiscal years vary by business and jurisdiction. They tend to begin in the middle of the calendar year, particularly in retail, as the end of the calendar year is an exceptionally busy time. The U.S. Government's fiscal year starts on October 1. In nomenclature, if a fiscal year covers more than one calendar year it is designated by the calendar year in which it ends; for example, the U.S. government's fiscal year from October 1, 2008 to September 30, 2009 is called "FY 09." **2.** In the United Kingdom, the tax year.

Fiscal Year End Describing anything that occurs toward the end of a fiscal year. For example, if a company's fiscal year runs from July 1 to June 30, the fiscal year end report may be issued in June.

Fiscal Year-End The end of the 12-month period constituting a company's fiscal year. The company is responsible for preparing various financial statements such as profit-loss statements, inventory reports, and other things.

Fischer Black An American economist known for his development of mathematical models for pricing investments. In particular, he helped create the Black-Scholes model, which is used to determine the appropriate price for option contracts. In the 1970s, he argued against both Keynesians, who believed central banks ought to have discretion to raise or lower the money supply, and monetarists, who thought the money supply should grow at a constant rate. Black lived from 1938 to 1995.

FISH An abbreviation for "first in, still here." The term is a tongue-in-cheek reference to the first in, first out accounting method. It refers to a company that keeps its inventory for a long time, often because of poor sales. Ultimately, this may render inventory obsolete. A company dealing with FISH may be in or near financial trouble.

Fisher Effect A theory stating that real interest rates are independent of monetary considerations. According to the Fisher effect, a currency's real interest rate is equal to its nominal interest rate less the inflation rate. Thus, if the inflation rate rises, the real interest rate eventually rises as well; likewise, if inflation falls, the real interest rate will fall. See also: International Fisher Effect.

Fisher's Separation Theorem An economic theory stating that the investment decisions of a firm are independent from the wishes of the firm's owners. Fisher's Separation Theorem states that the productive value of a firm's management neither affects nor is affected by the owner's business decisions. As a result, the performance of a firm's investments has no relation to how they are financed, whether stock, debt, or cash. The theorem was devised by economist Irving Fisher. See also: Irrelevance result.

Fishyback Describing the transportation of a truck or other vehicle on a ship or other water-going vehicle. See also: Piggyback freight.

Fisk-Gould Scandal September 24, 1869. On this day, the United States gold market declined precipitously following a price manipulation by James Fisk and Jay Gould. During the Civil War a few years before, American money was backed by the full faith and credit of the United States, but not by a commodity like gold or silver. Following the War, the federal government began buying back this currency with gold and then using the currency to redeem government bonds; this stabilized the currency, but caused the price of gold to drop to its lowest level in years. Fisk and Gould took advantage of this and began buying gold, which cause the price to increase. In the process, they attempted to convince U.S. President Ulysses Grant to limit the amount of gold released, which drove the price still higher. This conspiracy came to a head on Black Friday when Treasury Secretary George Boutwell realized what was happening and released a large amount of government-owned gold. This caused the price to crash.

Fit To meet the needs of an investor or portfolio. That is, a security fits a portfolio if it has the acceptable amount of risk, return, meets the investor's ethical preferences, and so forth.

Fit Investment An investment that meets a person's or institution's goals. Fit investments vary from investor to investor and can even change for the same investor over time. For example, a person may have the goal to extract a high return from her investments when she is young in order to finance a certain lifestyle; fit investments for this person are likely to include high risk securities and ventures. Over time, however, this person may be concerned about protecting savings for retirement. As a result, fit investments may shift to primarily bonds and blue-chip stocks.

Fitch Investors Service A financial services company that primarily offers credit ratings for different kinds of bonds. That is, it serves as a credit ratings agency (CRA) and a research firm. It is one of only ten firms the SEC recognizes as a credit rating agency, though, like other CRAs, its methods have been subject to criticism. For example, it gave the nation of Iceland a near top rating until the nation's bankruptcy in 2008. It is based in New York and was established in 1909.

Fitch Ratings A credit rating by Fitch. As with other credit ratings, a Fitch rating measures the level of risk associated with a particular issuer of debt securities. Credit ratings are extremely important to some issuers, as banks are only allowed to invest in low-risk debt securities. Fitch is one of only 10 firms the SEC recognizes as a credit rating agency, and, along with S&P and Moody's, it is one of the three most prominent. However, the methods of credit ratings agencies have been subject to criticism. For example, most agencies gave high-risk mortgage-backed securities top ratings until they defaulted.

Fitch Sheet In equities, a data sheet showing the history of a security. The information on a Fitch sheet includes trading volume, price, and exact times of trades. Fitch sheets are used to analyze past performance and/or confirm that a security was in fact traded. Regulators also use Fitch sheets in their investigations of suspicious activity. They are obtained from financial databanks, notably Quotron.

Fitel A Maltese unit of length approximately equivalent to 13.1 centimeters. It is largely obsolete but is still used in some circumstances.

Fitel Kubu A Maltese unit of cubic volume approximately equivalent to 2.25 liters. It is largely obsolete but is still used in some circumstances.

Fitel Kwadru A Maltese unit of area approximately equivalent to 171.5 square centimeters. It is largely obsolete but is still used in some circumstances.

Five Against Bond Spread A spread in which an investor has offsetting positions on five-year Treasury notes and long-term Treasury bonds with maturities from 15 to 20 years. That is, an investor takes a short position on five-year notes and a long position on the long-term notes or vice versa. In doing so, the investor hopes to take advantage of the difference in the interest rates between the two instruments.

Five Against Note Spread A spread in which an investor has offsetting positions on five-year and 10-year Treasury notes. That is, an investor takes a short position on five-year notes and a long position on 10-year notes, or vice versa. In doing so, the investor hopes to take advantage of the difference in interest rates between the two notes.

Five Cs of Credit Five factors a lender considers when evaluating whether or not to extend credit to a potential borrower. Importantly, the five Cs of credit include both quantitative and qualitative measures. They are: character (or the borrowers' reputation), capacity (a measure of the borrower's ability to repay by comparing his/her debt service to income), capital available, collateral pledged against the loan, and the conditions of the loan (such as the interest rate, monthly payment, and so forth).

Five Hundred Dollar Rule An SEC rule prohibiting broker-dealers from liquidating a client's investment to cover a margin call if the deficiency in the margin account is less than $500. In a margin account, one borrows from a broker-dealer to buy securities. One must offer other securities as collateral, such that the value of the securities is a certain percentage of the value of the amount one borrows. If the value of those securities drops below that percentage, the broker-dealer may require the client to offer more securities or, failing that, may liquidate the client's positions to cover the deficiency. The five hundred dollar rule prevents the broker-dealer from treating the client unfairly by liquidating positions to cover minor deficiencies.

Five Percent Rule 1. An ethical guideline for FINRA members. While the rule does not impose any particular restrictions, it discourages dealers from having an excessive dealer's spread and brokerages from charging excessively high commissions. **2.** An SEC rule stating that a person or organization must report buying or acquiring more than 5% beneficial ownership in any one equity stock.

Five-Year Plan A multiyear plan for economic development prepared by a government. For example, a five-year plan may state the methods and the amount of development that should be experienced by the industrial sector by the end of the plan. Five-year plans were introduced in the Soviet Union and were adopted by most other 20th-century communist states. For that reason, the term is associated with command economies.

Five-Year Rule An option for the heir of an IRA account holder who dies before the required beginning date. Under the five-year rule, the appropriate heir must receive all assets from the IRA by December 31 of the fifth year following the account holder's death. The heir may opt out of the five-year rule and receive the assets over his/her life expectancy, effectively treating the heir as if he/she were the account holder. It is important to note that the five-year rule only applies to account holders who die before the required beginning date.

Fivondronana In Madagascar, a political subdivision approximately equivalent to a municipality.

Fix To set the price of a good or service, especially by the collusion of two or more companies. For example, two railroad companies may agree to set an artificially high price for train tickets. If these companies control a sufficient market share of railroads, then customers have no choice but to pay the high prices. In general, price fixing is illegal, but some governments, especially in developing economies, both allow and encourage the practice. Neo-liberal economists consider price fixing an inefficient practice, and in the United States it is a criminal offense under the Sherman Act. See also: Antitrust.

Fixed Annuity An annuity that allows the annuitant a fixed return for the life of the annuity. Like any annuity, the annuitant buys into a policy, either with a lump sum or premiums over a period of time. When the annuitant reaches a certain age, or retirement (whichever is greater), he/she begins to receive payments. Typically, the insurance company issuing a fixed annuity invests the premiums in low-risk investment vehicles such as bonds. This results in a smaller likelihood that the insurance company will be unable to make the payments, but also exposes the annuitant to inflation risk. See also: Variable annuity.

Fixed Asset An asset with a long-term useful life that a company uses to make its products or provide its services. Strictly speaking, a fixed asset is any asset that the company does not expect to sell for at least a year, but the term often refers to assets a company expects to have indefinitely. Common examples of fixed assets are real estate and factories, which a company holds for long periods of time.

Fixed Asset Turnover Ratio A measure of how efficiently a business generates sales from its investments. That is, it is the ratio of the amount a company earns in sales to the average value of its fixed assets. Fixed assets are investments that cannot easily be converted into cash, e.g. a factory or computer system, and can be quite expensive. Thus, if a company has a high ratio, this means that its sales have kept pace with or exceeded the amount it has invested in fixed assets, which is a positive sign for the company.

Fixed Benefits In annuities and insurance, benefits that guarantee the annuitant a fixed return for the life of the annuity. Like any annuity, the annuitant buys into a policy, either with a lump sum or premiums, over a period of time. When the annuitant reaches a certain age or retirement (whichever is greater), he/she begins to receive the fixed benefits. Generally speaking, the insurance company issuing an annuity with fixed benefits invests the premiums in low-risk investment vehicles, such as bonds. This results in a smaller likelihood that the insurance company will be unable to make the payments, but also exposes the annuitant to inflation risk. See also: Variable benefits.

Fixed Capital Formation The process by which a company acquires its fixed assets. Fixed assets are productive assets a company holds for longer than one year. Thus, fixed capital formation occurs, for example, when a company builds a factory or installs a pipeline. Fixed capital formation is often expensive, but is necessary for growth in manufacturing and similar industries.

Fixed Cost An expense that does not change from time period to time period. For example, a company may rent a piece of property for $4,000 per month. A company often prefers to have fixed costs because they reduce uncertainty, but this is not always possible.

Fixed Coupon An interest rate on a bond that does not change over the life of the bond. If one purchases a bond with a fixed coupon of 10%, then 10% is calculated over the principal balance each time the interest compounds. A fixed coupon differs from a variable coupon, which may change from time to time, at least within certain parameters.

Fixed Currency A currency to which the government has linked the value of another currency or, rarely, some valuable commodity like gold. For example, under the Bretton Woods System, most world currencies fixed themselves to the U.S. dollar, which in turn fixed itself to gold. A government may fix its currency by holding reserves of the other currency (or the asset to which it is fixed) in the central bank. For example, if a country fixes its currency to the British pound, it must hold enough pounds in reserve to account for all of its currency in circulation.

Fixed Exchange Rate An exchange rate for a currency where the government has decided to link the value to another currency or to some valuable commodity like gold. For example, under the Bretton Woods System, most world currencies fixed themselves to the U.S. dollar, which in turn fixed itself to gold. A government may fix its currency by holding reserves of the peg (or the asset to which it is fixed) in the central bank. For example, if a country fixes its currency to the British pound, it must hold enough pounds in reserve to account for all of its currency in circulation. Importantly, fixed exchange rates do not change according to market conditions. It is also called a pegged exchange rate.

Fixed Income 1. An income that does not increase over time, except perhaps for inflation. For example, a retired person lives on a fixed income as he/she only receives payments from his/her pension, Social Security, or something similar. A person on a fixed income may have little leeway if prices rise significantly. **2.** See: Fixed-income security.

Fixed Income Clearing Corporation A company that matches, nets, and settles trades on fixed-income securities in the United States. Specifically, it provides clearance and settlement services on U.S. Treasury securities (as well as other government securities) and mortgage-backed securities. It was formed in 2003 with the merger of the Government Securities Clearing Corporation and the Mortgage-Backed Securities Clearing Corporation.

Fixed Income Market The market for the trading of securities paying a guaranteed yield. Examples of fixed-income securities include bonds and preferred stock. The fixed-income market is lower risk and lower return than the variable income market.

Fixed Interest Rate An interest rate that does not change over the life of a loan or other form of credit. If one borrows money at a fixed interest rate of 10%, then 10% is calculated over the principal balance each time the interest compounds. A fixed interest rate differs from a variable interest rate, which may change, at least within certain parameters. Most home mortgages in the United States have fixed interest rates. It is also called simply a fixed rate.

Fixed Premium A payment for an insurance policy or annuity that does not change over the life of the policy or annuity. Fixed premiums have fewer risks for the policyholder or annuitant, and are very common. See also: Variable premium.

Fixed Price 1. See: Offering price. **2.** A price that is not subject to negotiation. The fixed price may be set by a government, or may indicate that the seller has no interest to lower the price for any reason. One must either pay the fixed price or not buy the product. Many products must specify whether or not they have fixed prices because price negotiation is common in many parts of the world. For example, if Wal-Mart sells milk for $3 per gallon, milk is offered on a fixed price basis because the customer cannot make a counter-offer for $2.50. One either buys the milk at $3 or does not.

Fixed Rate Loan A loan with an interest rate that does not change over the life of the loan. For example, if one borrows money at a fixed interest rate of 10%, then 10% is amortized over the maturity of the loan and thus payments never change. A fixed interest rate differs from a variable interest rate, which may change, at least within certain parameters. Most home mortgages in the United States are fixed rate loans.

Fixed Term Lease A lease binding the parties to each other for a specified period of time, such as a month or a year. That is, the fixed-term lease requires the lessee to make periodic payments and requires the lessor to surrender use of his/her property. A fixed term lease is also called (somewhat misleadingly) a tenancy for years.

Fixed-Charge Coverage Ratio A measure of a company's ability to pay its fixed expenses, such as rent and interest, on debt without resorting to more debt. A ratio over 1 indicates that the company is able to pay its fixed charges, while a ratio below one indicates the opposite. The fixed charge coverage ratio is calculated thus: Fixed-charge coverage ratio = (EBIT + fixed charges before tax) / (fixed charged before tax + interest)

Fixed-Dollar Security 1. See: Savings bond. **2.** See: Fixed-income security.

Fixed-Income Arbitrage An arbitrage strategy in which one seeks to profit from small differences in interest rates between two bonds or other fixed-income securities that are otherwise essentially the same. One conducts this by taking opposite positions in the two securities. Fixed-income arbitrage rarely results in a large profit and can be quite risky. As a result, many analysts advise against using it.

Fixed-Income Security A security with a guaranteed return. Common examples include bonds, which pay periodic coupons representing a certain interest rate, and preferred stocks, which are legally required to receive a specified dividend at certain times. Typically, fixed-income securities offer lower risk and lower returns than common stock and similar investment vehicles.

Fixed-Rate Capital Security A security that combines features of bonds and preferred stock. Fixed-rate capital securities provide the holder with a fixed coupon with payments on a regular basis, and like bonds, these coupons are tax deductible for the issuer. Likewise, most have a maturity date and are fairly liquid. However, like preferred stock, the issuer may suspend payments on fixed-rate capital securities when it is having cash flow problems, though only if it also stops all dividend payments on stock. Because of these features, fixed-rate capital securities are fairly low risk investments.

Fixed-Rate Mortgage A mortgage on real estate with an interest rate that does not change over the life of the loan. As a result, payments on a fixed-rate mortgage do not change. This carries the least risk for the borrower, but it can make it more difficult to qualify for a mortgage in the first place. See also: Adjustable-rate mortgage.

Fixed-Rate Payer In a plain vanilla swap, the investor who pays the fixed interest rate and receives the floating interest rate. The two legs of a plain vanilla swap are a fixed interest rate, say 3.5%, and a floating interest rate, say LIBOR + 0.5%. In such a swap, the only things traded are the two interest rates, which are calculated over a notional value. The fixed rate payer gives 3.5% of the notional value to the floating rate payer and, in return, receives LIBOR + 0.5% of the same notional value. Each party pays the other at set intervals over the life of the swap.

FJ 1. ISO 3166-1 alpha-2 code for the Republic of the Fiji Islands. This is the code used in international transactions to and from Fijian bank accounts. **2.** ISO 3166-2 geocode for Fiji. This is used as an international standard for shipping to Fiji. Each division and dependency has its own code with the prefix "FJ." For example, the code for the Central Division is ISO 3166-2:FJ-C.

Fjardingsvag A Swedish unit of length approximately equivalent to two and a half kilometers.

FJD ISO 4217 code for the Fijian dollar. It was introduced in 1969, replacing the Fijian pound. The Fijian dollar is a floating currency. Interestingly, all dollars currently in circulation feature a portrait of Queen Elizabeth of the United Kingdom even though she is no longer Fiji's head of state.

Fjerdingsvei A Norwegian unit of length approximately equivalent to 2.82 kilometers.

FJI GOST 7.67 Latin three-letter geocode for Fiji. The code is used for transactions to and from Fijian bank accounts and for international shipping to Fiji. As with all GOST 7.67 codes, it is used primarily in Cyrillic alphabets.

FK 1. ISO 3166-1 alpha-2 code for the Falkland Islands. This is the code used in international transactions to and from Falkland bank accounts. **2.** ISO 3166-2 geocode for the Falkland Islands. This is used as an international standard for shipping to the Falkland Islands.

FKP ISO 4217 code for the Falkland Islands pound. It was introduced in 1833 and is pegged to the British pound at par. Indeed, British pounds are usually accepted on the Falkland Islands as if they were Falkland Islands pounds.

Flag In technical analysis, a situation on a chart in which a security's price undergoes a steep rise or fall, then trades within a narrow price range. When a steep rise proceeds the narrow trading, it looks somewhat like a flag raised on a pole. Many analysts believe that when a flag occurs, the narrow trading is only temporary and will soon be followed by another steep rise or fall. That is, a rise will follow a rise and a fall will follow a fall.

Flagable Slang; describing something that may pose a problem or is otherwise worthy of attention and immediate action. The term is most common in the context of the financial management of small Christian churches and ministries.

Flake Slang; in auto sales, a term for a non-creditworthy customer with a small or no down payment. Flake customers are very high risk for the seller, and likely will not obtain financing.

Flan In numismatics, a coin on which no stamp has been made. These coins are not considered money, though their base metals may still be valuable. See also: Die.

Flash When the tape is late by more than five minutes, the current price of a security that periodically displays, or "flashes," on the ticker. This interrupts the delayed prices and keeps investors abreast of where the current price is even if they do not know how it arrived there. The flash price displays every five or 10 minutes.

Flash Price On a ticker tape, the current price of a security that interrupts a long-delayed price. That is, in a situation in which trading volume is so heavy that the ticker publicly announcing quotes is delayed by a significant amount of time, usually more than five minutes, the ticker might interrupt the series of delayed prices with a flash price to keep investors as up to date as possible. This was fairly common before electronic tickers were used, but has become largely a non-issue since then because electronic tickers announce prices in real time.

Flat 1. Describing a stock or other security that is neither rising nor falling in price. **2.** In foreign exchange, having no position. That is, an investor is flat if he/she has neither bought nor short sold a given currency. **3.** Describing a bond that trades without interest that has accumulated since the last coupon payment. It is fairly unusual for bonds to trade flat, as the buyer is normally expected to compensate the seller for the next coupon that the seller will no longer receive from the issuer. However, bonds in default trade flat.

Flat Loan A loan without interest. Investors who borrow securities for short sales often provide flat loans to lenders as collateral for borrowed securities. Personal loans are also commonly flat loans. In Islamic finance, flat loans are the only loans directly allowed.

Flat Market A market in neither an uptrend nor a downtrend. That is, the securities in a flat market are relatively constant in price, at least for a certain period of time. A market may be flat while investors wait to hear some relevant information, such as an earnings report. A flat market is sometimes associated with low trading volume. It is also called a sideways market or a deer market.

Flat on a Failure The act or practice of selling a stock if it reaches a certain (higher) price level but fails to break through to still higher levels. Flat on a failure is analogous to cutting one's losses, but there are no losses. Rather, there simply isn't as much profit as the investor hoped. See also: Ceiling.

Flat Price Risk The risk to an investment one takes without taking an offsetting position. For example, if one buys Johnson & Johnson stock at $60 per share without hedging at all, the flat price risk is the possibility that J&J will drop below $60. See also: Spread, Straddle.

Flat Tax A way to structure an income tax where everyone (or nearly everyone) pays the same marginal rate. For example, a flat tax may be set at 15%, and everyone will pay that rate regardless of how much they earn. This contrasts with progressive taxation, where the marginal tax rate increases with increased income. Proponents of a flat tax argue that it provides an incentive for people to earn more (because they keep more of what they earn than under a progressive tax system), which in turn spurs economic growth. Opponents contend that a flat tax deprives the government of

revenue and progressive taxation does not disincentivize earning more because, even at higher rates, people keep more after taxes than they would have done if they earned less.

Flat Trades 1. Securities that do not trade with accrued interest included in the price. For example, most American exchanges trade bonds without including interest. See also: Clean price. **2.** Securities, especially bonds, that normally trade with accrued interest but are not because of a significant problem. Normally, a bond flat trades when it is in default.

Flattening of the Yield Curve A change in the yield curve for bonds in which the yield spread on short-term and long-term Treasury bonds decreases. That is, a flattening of the yield curve occurs when either the yield increases for short-term bonds and decreases for long-term bonds, or vice versa. It is important to note that the yield curve is a graphic representation, plotting yield against maturity.

Fleet Post Office A U.S. Coast Guard, Marine Corps or Navy office where American military personnel stationed overseas can send and receive correspondence. It operates just like a regular post office and must abide by all regulations set by the U.S. Postal Service. However, it is operated by the Department of Defense. See also: APO.

FLEX Option An option that does not have standardized features. The writer and the buyer of a FLEX option negotiate the specific terms, such as the strike price and the expiration date. It is important to note the FLEX options do not trade in the continuous market. Generally speaking, clearing houses are the main writers of FLEX options.

Flexible Budget A budget that considers different levels of production or sales. A flexible budget makes different amounts available to departments depending on what production or sales are realized. For example, a flexible budget may make 6% more money available to its research and development department if its revenue increases 6%.

Flexible Expenses Unnecessary expenses that may be foregone if necessary. Personal flexible expenses might include luxury goods and services such as those associated with a vacation. Business flexible expenses might include personal accounts used to take potential clients out to dinner. In certain circumstances, even necessary expenses can be considered flexible if one may cut back on them. For example, one may spend less on groceries in a given week.

Flexible Income Fund A bond fund that invests in many different types of bonds. For example, a flexible income fund may include U.S. Treasury securities, investment-grade corporate bonds, and junk bonds in its portfolio. The goal of a flexible income fund is to create a diversified portfolio with higher yields than the risk-free yield.

Flexible Purpose Corporation A corporation in which the members of the board of directors have statutory duties other than making a profit for shareholders. A flexible purpose corporation may be formed for many purposes, such as to provide steady jobs to employees or to protect the environment. In other words, a flexible purpose corporation is not prohibited from earning and distributing profits, but is expected to do other things as well.

Flexible Spending Account An employee benefit in which an employee may contribute so much of his/her pretax income into a special account that may be used for a broad range of purposes. One may use the funds in a flexible spending account for matters such as uncovered medical expenses, life insurance premiums, or other things. Some flexible spending accounts expect the account holder to pay for these things out-of-pocket and then receive reimbursement. Others have a debit card attached to the account that the account holder may use. Flexible spending accounts are not taxed.

Flight Risk An employee thought to be considering leaving the company. A flight risk may harm the company if he/she quits, particularly if he/she is an important employee. A company may take measures to protect itself against flight risks. See also: Key man insurance.

Flight to Cash A situation in which traders and other investors close their positions and take refuge in highly liquid assets such as cash or U.S. Treasury securities. A flight to cash occurs during a precipitous, and apparently sustained, drop in security prices. When markets are highly volatile and seem likely to decline in value, investors may fly to cash because it is an asset likely to retain its value in the short term.

Flip Side The opposite position in an equities transaction. For example, if an investor wishes to enter a long position, the flip side is a short position. See also: Flip.

Flip-Flop Note A debt security backed by two different debts, one with a variable interest rate and one with a fixed interest rate. The holder of a flip-flop note may choose which interest rate to receive at any time, depending on which one is higher for a given period.

Flip-Over Pill A provision in some antitakeover measures stipulating that shareholders on the receiving end of a hostile takeover may buy shares in their own company at a price below fair market value. Once the acquisition is complete, the provision allows these same shareholders to buy more shares in the new company for below market value. This forces shareholders in the acquiring company to suffer a devaluation and dilution of their own shares. This is done to discourage hostile takeovers among the shareholders of the acquiring companies. See also: Dead-hand poison pill.

Flipper 1. A trader who buys stock and quickly sells it for a profit. A flipper may be a day trader, buying and selling on a constant basis, or a (slightly) more long-term trader, holding for a day or two. Flipping is a high risk venture because a slight decline in share prices in the short term can severely hurt the flippers positions. On the other hand, a slight uptick can result in enormous profit. **2.** An investor who buys real estate, usually a house, makes a few improvements, and sells it at a higher price. Colloquially, flippers are thought to buy the house, "slap a coat of paint on it," and re-sell for a large profit. Flippers were common even among casual investors during the housing bubble of the early and mid-2000s.

Flipping 1. The act or practice of buying IPOs only to resell them at a substantial profit very quickly. Flipping is a short-term investment strategy that operates on the assumption or existence of liquid markets. Institutional investors engage in flipping at a greater rate than individual investors as they have the most shares available to them at the offer price. Flipping, when done over and over by a large number of investors, can lead to a speculative bubble. See also: Stock jobbing. **2.** The act or practice of buying real estate at a low or moderate price with the intent to resell it for a profit in a short amount of time. Flipping takes two main forms. One may buy several properties, intending to sell them in only a few months hoping that that price goes up. This is most common in areas expected to become big developments. On the other hand, one may buy a single property often with improvements already on it and renovate it with the intention to sell it for a much higher price.

FLK GOST 7.67 Latin three-letter geocode for the Falkland Islands. The code is used for transactions to and from Falkland Islander bank accounts and for international shipping to the Falkland Islands. As with all GOST 7.67 codes, it is used primarily in Cyrillic alphabets.

Float 1. The number of shares of a publicly-traded company available to trade. It is important to note that this may be different from the shares outstanding: some shareholders may buy and hold, reducing the size of the float. The size of a float greatly affects a stock's volatility. If a float is small, any number of activities could affect greatly its price, especially a single large order to buy or sell it. This would greatly alter the number of shares available to trade, creating too little or too much supply and therefore drive the price up or down. A large float tends to have less volatility because large orders do not affect the supply as much. It is also called a floating supply. See also: Technical condition of a market. **2.** In foreign exchange, a currency that is not pegged to another currency's value.

Floater Insurance An insurance policy, or an addition to another insurance policy, that covers personal property deemed to be easily movable. That is, floater insurance reimburses the owner if easily movable property is lost, damaged, or destroyed. Examples of easily movable property include electronics, jewelry, and perhaps furniture. Floater insurance usually covers only the specific property named in the policy; for example one must purchase separate floater insurance policies for the couch, the love seat, and the dining room table.

Floating Currency A currency whose value is determined by the free market. That is, the value of a floating currency changes constantly depending on the supply and demand for that currency, as well as the amount of the currency held in foreign reserves. An advantage to a floating currency is that it tends to be more economically efficient. However, floating exchange rates tend to be more volatile depending on the particular currency. A floating currency may undergo currency appreciation or currency depreciation, depending on market fluctuations. Most major currencies are floating currencies See also: Fixed exchange rate, Crawling peg, Managed float.

Floating Debt Short-term debt that a company refinances continuously. A company may utilize floating debt instead of long-term debt because short-term loans have lower interest rates. Also, if interest rates fall, the company will be able to refinance at a lower rate to reduce its expenses. The risk of floating debt is the possibility that interest rates will rise, increasing the company's expenses.

Floating Exchange Rate The exchange rate in which the value of the currency is determined by the free market. That is, a currency has a floating exchange rate when its value changes constantly depending on the supply and demand for that currency, as well as the amount of the currency held in foreign reserves. An advantage to a floating exchange rate is that it tends to be more economically efficient. However, floating exchange rates tend to be more volatile depending on the particular currency. A currency with a floating exchange rate may undergo currency appreciation or currency depreciation, depending on market fluctuations. A floating exchange rate is also called a flexible exchange rate. See also: Fixed exchange rate, Crawling peg, Managed float.

Floating Exchange Rate System The practice in which a central bank buys and sells one or more foreign currencies in order to affect the exchange rate of its own currency. To give a very simple example, if a central bank believes its own currency is overvalued, it may buy other currencies on the open market to increase demand and therefore the price of these currencies. The extra demand will likely drive down the exchange rate of its own currency to a lower level.

Floating Rate 1. Floating exchange rate. **2.** Floating interest rate.

Floating Security 1. See: Floater. **2.** A security that a broker buys in his/her own name on behalf of a client. The floating security is held in the broker's name to make it easier to sell quickly if need be. See also: Beneficial ownership, Safekeep.

Floating Supply The number of shares of a publicly-traded company available to trade. It is important to note that this may be different from the shares outstanding: some shareholders may buy and hold, reducing the size of the float. The size of a floating supply greatly affects a stock's volatility. If it is small, any number of activities could affect greatly its price, especially a single large order to buy or sell it. This would greatly alter the number of shares available to trade, creating too little or too much supply and, therefore, drive the price up or down. A large floating supply tends to have less volatility because large orders do not affect the supply as much. It is also called a float. See also: Technical condition of a market.

Floating-Rate Contract A pension plan purchased through a bank or an insurance company for a lump sum where the principal is guaranteed by the issuer and where the payoff varies according to a variable interest rate. One may receive payments from a floating-rate contract either in installments or as a lump sum after retirement. A floating-rate contract provides the pensioner with a small interest rate that may change and is not guaranteed, but the fact that the principal is guaranteed makes it a relatively low-risk investment. A floating-rate contract is a type of guaranteed investment contract.

Floating-Rate Note A bond with a variable interest rate. These bonds typically have coupons renewable every three months and pay according to a set calculation. For example, a note may have an interest rate of "EURIBOR + 1%" and pay whatever the EURIBOR rate happens to be at the time plus 1%. Some FRNs have maximum and minimum interest rates, known as capped FRNs and floored FRNs, respectively. An FRN with both a maximum and a minimum interest rate is called a collared FRN. In the United States, government sponsored enterprises issue most FRNs while banks do the same in Europe. See also: Adjustable-rate mortgage.

Floating-Rate Payer In a plain vanilla swap, the investor who pays the floating interest rate and receives the fixed interest rate. The two legs of a plain vanilla swap are a fixed interest rate, say 3.5%, and a floating interest rate, say LIBOR + 0.5%. In such a swap, the only things traded are the two interest rates, which are calculated over a notional value. The floating rate payer gives LIBOR + 0.5% of the notional value to the fixed rate payer and, in return, receives 3.5% of the same notional value. Each party pays the other at set intervals over the life of the swap.

Floating-Rate Preferred Stock A preferred stock paying a dividend that varies from time to time. Usually, the dividend rate is the same as the interest rate on a Treasury security. They may also be backed by mortgages or mortgage-backed securities. Floating-rate preferred stocks tend to have stable prices because a drop in the common share's price is offset by a rise in bonds, and vice versa.

Floirin A coin that circulated in the Republic of Ireland between 1928 and 1994. It was equal in value to 1/10 of one Irish pound. See also: Florin.

Floor 1. See: Exchange floor. **2.** The lowest price or some other limit that can occur. For example, in an adjustable-rate mortgage, the lender will often specify a floor for the interest rate, which means that even though the interest rate on the mortgage changes from time to time, it will never drop below the specified floor. These exist to protect one or both parties to a contract or investment. See also: Ceiling, Collar.

Floor Broker A broker who is employed by a member firm of an exchange who executes trades on behalf of the member firm's clients. These clients make their orders to the member firm, which is also a brokerage, and these orders are relayed to floor brokers, who conduct the desired trades. Importantly, unlike floor traders, floor brokers do not trade on their own accounts.

Floor Give-Up The announcement of the investors represented by floor members in a transaction. When two floor members conduct a transaction on behalf of clients, they must tell each other whom they represent before the trade is settled.

Floor Official An employee of an exchange that judges between disputes on the trading floor. For example, if two traders disagree on the terms of a trade to which they previously agreed, they may call upon a floor official to settle the dispute. It is important to note that floor officials do not decide points of trading law; they merely arbitrate disputes.

Floor Picture Details on the crowd for a security. A floor picture includes the major traders, the size of most orders, and perhaps the average bid-ask spread.

Floor Trader On an exchange floor, a member who trades predominantly or exclusively on his/her own account. That is, the member does not represent a particular firm or client. A floor trader tends to profit from short-term price changes; they provide approximately 75% of liquidity in the market on a trading day. They contrast with floor brokers, who fill orders on behalf of clients. A floor trader is also called a registered trader or a registered competitive trader.

Florin 1. A gold coin struck in Florence in 1253. Used as a currency, it was so successful that other countries in medieval Europe adopted their own gold coins and called them florins. **2.** See: Aruban florin.

Flotation Cost The costs that a company incurs when it makes a new issue of either stocks or bonds. Flotation costs include the costs of printing the certificates, paying the underwriters, government fees, and other associated costs. As new issues are intended to raise capital for the company, it is important for it to ensure that it will at least make back what it spends.

Flotsam In maritime law, property seen floating on the water after having been ejected from a ship involuntarily. Flotsam is usually the result of a shipwreck. Under maritime law, flotsam remains the property of its original owners, while jetsam, which is deliberately thrown overboard in an emergency, is the property of its finder.

Flow of Funds Statement 1. In municipal bonds, a statement listing the priorities of how the bond's revenue will be used. Usually, the priorities are listed in the following order: the project for which a bond was issued, the debt service, and saving to repay the principal. **2.** In mutual funds, a statement of money moving into and out of the funds.

Flow Trader Slang; traders who buy and sell securities on behalf of their company's clients, rather than for the company itself. Because flow traders generally are paid commission for each trade, they have no incentive to work against clients' interests (and in fact are legally prohibited from doing so).

Flowing Hair Dollar A $1 coin minted in the United States between 1794 and 1795. It was the first dollar coin authorized by the U.S. government. Based on the

Spanish dollar, it derived its name from the hair on the picture of Lady Liberty featured on the obverse.

Fluctuation A change to a price or interest rates. Prices may fluctuate according to supply and demand. Interest rates may do the same, but their fluctuations are usually more regulated.

Fluctuation Limit On a futures exchange, the maximum amount that a contract can rise or fall in price before the exchange's management institutes suspended trading. Trading on a security is suspended usually in order to discourage volatility. This is especially important for futures contracts and options, which are almost always volatile.

Flurry A large, and usually temporary, increase in a security's trading volume.

Flying Eagle Cent A one-cent piece minted by the United States between 1856 and 1858. It was worth 1/100 of one dollar. Unlike previous one cent pieces, it featured an eagle in flight on the obverse instead of a portrait of Lady Liberty.

FM 1. ISO 3166-1 alpha-2 code for the Federated States of Micronesia. This is the code used in international transactions to and from Micronesian bank accounts. **2.** ISO 3166-2 geocode for Micronesia. This is used as an international standard for shipping to Micronesia. Each Micronesian state has its own code with the prefix "FM." For example, the code for the State of Pohnpei is ISO 3166-2:FM:PNI.

FMAN Abbreviation for February, May, August, and November. This is used in option cycles to determine the expiration date of an option contract.

FO 1. ISO 3166-1 alpha-2 code for the Faroe Islands. This is the code used in international transactions to and from Faroese bank accounts. **2.** ISO 3166-2 geocode for the Faroe Islands. This is used as an international standard for shipping to the Faroe Islands.

Focus List A list of securities that an investment bank or investment advisory recommends buying or selling. Each bank's or advisory's research department compiles the focus list and updates it periodically. The research department uses a number of criteria in writing the focus list, including growth potential, riskiness, and business practices. Sometimes, a watchdog group may compile its own focus list of companies to patronize or boycott based on their corporate ethics or lack thereof.

FOCUS Report A report that all members of the New York Stock Exchange are required to submit at monthly and quarterly intervals. The report contains information on each member firm's capital gains.

Focused Fund A mutual fund that invests in only a few stocks. That is, a focused fund may only hold positions in 10 to 30 stocks, as opposed to the several hundred that most mutual funds have. A focused fund intends to invest only in the stocks of the highest quality, and often engages in rigorous research prior to entering a position on a stock. Ideally, this will guarantee a solid return; however, critics contend that focused funds are deliberately undiversified, and are therefore exposed to a large amount of risk.

Fod An obsolete Danish unit of length approximately equivalent to 313.85 millimeters.

Fokontany In Madagascar, a political subdivision equivalent to a village or group of villages.

Folding A slang term for a large amount of money, especially cash.

Folio A portfolio of stocks and other securities that an investor may buy or sell as a single unit, much like a mutual fund. Unlike a mutual fund, however, the investor may add or subtract securities from the portfolio at his/her discretion for a flat monthly or annual fee to the brokerage providing the folio. This gives the investor substantial control over the portfolio, especially in its tax consequences, while still providing the main advantage of a mutual fund, namely disbursing risk over a wide variety of securities.

Follow the Smart Money An investment practice in which one buys and sells the same securities as institutional investors and/or market insiders. Supposedly, these investments perform better than others because institutional investors and market insiders are thought to to be better informed than most investors. Many analysts, however, dispute the idea that smart money is any "smarter" than that of the average investor.

Food for Progress A United States federal program giving or lending food and other commodities to developing countries while they grow the capacity to function as free market economies. Food for Progress was created in 1985.

Food Sovereignty The concept that a group of persons have the right to determine what livestock and crops they will raise and grow, and therefore what they will eat. Food sovereignty is favored by some small farmers and others who prefer trade barriers and other measures to protect their traditional way of life. Critics contend that this is inefficient and more expensive than allowing the free market to regulate food production.

Food, Drug and Cosmetics Act Legislation in the United States, passed in 1938, that gave the Food and Drug Administration the authority to certify the safety of food, food additives, medicines, and so forth. It also gives the FDA the ability to classify goods as cosmetics, though it does not regulate cosmetics. The Act gave consumers grounds to sue companies for selling unsafe products; the government may pursue criminal penalties for repeated or fraudulent violations.

Fool's Gold Iron pyrite, or a metal that superficially looks like gold. It is used to produce sulfur dioxide, which is important in making paper. Fool's gold was often mistaken for real gold during gold rushes and at other times, but is vastly less valuable.

Foot In accounting, a slang term for adding numbers vertically on a page.

Footnote An explanation of an item in a financial statement or of the financial statement generally. A footnote may expand upon the company's accounting methods, or it may show why a negative item is unlikely to be repeated. Footnotes are usually found at the end of financial statements; they are considered useful because they give more information than the financial statement itself does.

For Valuation Only Describing a quote for the price of a security in which the price is subject to change. That is, an FVO quote may be a bid or an offer where a potential counterpart may try to extract a better price. Market makers occasionally make FVO quotes for information purposes.

For/At Describing the desired price for a transaction. For example, one may bid for $10 per share or make an offer at $15 per share. The terms are used on orders to buy or sell a security.

Forbearance The temporary suspension of loan repayments due to demonstrated financial hardship on the part of the borrower. Interest continues to accrue during forbearance and thus may extend the repayment period or cause payments to increase once they re-commence. A borrower must apply to the lender to be considered for forbearance.

For-Benefit Describing a sector of the economy that is not opposed to making a profit but primarily exists for another purpose. A for-benefit company uses profit to promote efficiency but has statutory responsibilities beyond maximizing value for stockholders or owners.

Forbes 500 A list formerly compiled and published annually by Forbes magazine of the 500 largest publicly-traded companies in the United States. The Forbes 500 consisted of four separate lists, detailing the largest companies by sales, profits, assets, and market value; companies could appear on more than one list. To be listed on the Forbes 500 was considered very prestigious. The Forbes 500 was replaced by the Forbes Global 2000 in 2003.

Forbes Global 2000 A list compiled and published annually by Forbes magazine of the 2000 largest publicly-traded companies in the world. The Forbes Global 2000 uses four criteria to arrive at its list: sales, profits, assets and market value. To be listed on the Forbes Global 2000 is considered very prestigious. The Forbes Global 2000 replaced the Forbes 500 in 2003.

Force Majeure Risk The risk of loss to a company from an act of God. For example, force majeure risk is the risk that company will lose production from a factory if a tornado comes and destroys the factory. See also: Act of God bond.

Forced Conversion In a callable convertible security, a situation in which the issuer calls the security, which requires the holder to exercise the conversion option and exchange the security for common stock. An issuer may authorize a forced conversion when interest rates decline and it can issue the same amount of debt at a lower cost of capital. However, a forced conversion may not be advantageous to the security holder because common stock is riskier and the combination of dividends and capital appreciation may not equal the coupon rate the holder was receiving prior to conversion.

Forced Liquidation A situation in which an outside party can force the sale of an asset belonging to another. For example, a bank may force a borrower to sell his/her collateral in order to repay the debt. Likewise, a brokerage can force a client to sell securities if the client is unable to meet a margin call and preferred stockholders can (sometimes) force the liquidation of a publicly-traded company if it does not make preferred dividend payments.

Forecasting The act or process of using certain data to predict future market movements. Various methods exist for forecasting; experts differ on which ones, if any, work. See also: Technical analysis, Fundamental analysis, Random walk theory.

Foreclosure A situation in which a mortgage lender takes possession of the property because the borrower has not made payments on interest or principal for a certain period of time. Once the lender takes over the property, it usually sells at a discounted price so as to recover the amount lost on the mortgage loan. Foreclosure results in a loss for the lender and is obviously quite detrimental to the borrower; as a result, it is the last resort. Most of the time, lenders attempt to work with the borrower to come up with a better solution, such as extending the repayment period in order to lower payments. See also: Forbearance.

Foreign and Commonwealth Office The department of the British government responsible for advising on and executing foreign policy and matters related to the Commonwealth of Nations (which primarily consists of former territories of the British Empire). It also has an administration role in British overseas territories. It was created in its current form in 1968 but traces its origins to 1782. The chancellor of the exchequer is appointed by the monarch on the advice of the prime minister.

Foreign Assistance Act of 1961 Legislation in the United States that consolidated a number of civilian foreign aid programs under a new organization, the U.S. Agency for International Development. It also split military from non-military foreign aid.

Foreign Bank Supervision Enhancement Act Legislation in the United States, passed in 1991, that gave the Federal Reserve the power to authorize (or not) foreign banks to operate in the U.S. This applied both to future foreign banks and those already in operation when the Act was passed.

Foreign Banking Market The loans that a bank makes to foreign nationals for use outside the country. Typically, these loans are made in the domestic currency.

Foreign Base Company Income Sales that a company earns or passive income that a holding company receives from a foreign source. Foreign base company income must be reported to the IRS and it is taxable in the United States. It is reported on Subpart F.

Foreign Bond A bond traded in a given country that was issued by a foreign government or company. The foreign bond market trades in the domestic currency and is regulated by domestic regulators.

Foreign Bond Market Bonds traded in a given country that were issued by a foreign government or company. The foreign bond market trades in the domestic currency and is regulated by domestic regulators.

Foreign Branch A branch of a foreign company that operates in the United States, or a branch of an American company operating outside the U.S. In both cases, the branch is legally part of the company and is not its own entity. Each type of foreign branch is subject to special tax considerations.

Foreign Corporation A corporation that operates in one country but was organized and is based in a different country. Foreign corporations must abide by domestic regulations and business practices, but may (or may not, depending on the specific organization) submit their profits to shareholders in the home country. Many corporations operate in multiple countries, and are considered foreign corporations in each country except the home country. See also: Domestic corporation, International corporation.

Foreign Corrupt Practices Act Legislation in the United States, passed in 1977, that banned U.S. corporations and others from bribing foreign officials in order to secure better business conditions. Prior to the passage of this Act, many American companies made unethical payments to high government officials in other countries to secure a contract or perhaps a legal change that would make it easier for an American company to conduct business in the foreign country. The Act also increased transparency requirements for some security issuers. It was amended by the International Anti-Bribery Act of 1998.

Foreign Credit Insurance Association A group of insurance companies that, along with the Export-Import Bank, serve as export credit agencies (ECAs), which extend credit to American exporters. They also provide guarantees and insurance for exports. In general, the FCIA provides insurance for lower risk clients, with the ExIm Bank taking those the FCIA cannot insure. Like call ECAs, the FCIA is controversial. Critics allege that they negatively impact international development, as developing countries cannot compete with such insured exports. Proponents of ECAs argue that they enable developing countries to import products they otherwise would not be able to afford.

Foreign Crowd Members of the New York Stock Exchange who deal primarily or exclusively in foreign bonds. See also: Crowd.

Foreign Currency A currency printed in a different country. Generally speaking, a foreign currency may not be used to buy goods and services in any country other that the one in which it is printed, unless the government of that country agrees to use it. For example, the Federated States of Micronesia uses the U.S. dollar, but if the Micronesian government had not agreed to this one would not be able to use dollars in Micronesia. However, exceptions to this rule exist, particularly when the domestic currency has a low value. For example, many merchants in Zimbabwe accept the U.S. dollar in addition to (or even instead of) the Zimbabwean dollar. See also: Foreign Exchange.

Foreign Currency Contract 1. See: Foreign currency option. 2. See: Foreign currency future.

Foreign Currency Convertible Bond A convertible bond that is issued in a currency other than the issuer's own. A company may issue an FCCB if it intends to make a large investment in a country using that foreign currency. For example, when an American company issues a convertible bond in euros because it intends to build a factory in Germany, this is a foreign currency convertible bond. Like all convertible bonds, an FSSB is a bond that a bondholder may exchange, at a certain price, for common stock in the company issuing the bond. The number of shares one receives for each bond and the price one pays for those shares are determined when the convertible bond is issued. This allows bondholders to take advantage of both the low risk of a bond and the potential price appreciation of the underlying stock. The FCCB also reduces the foreign exchange risk for the issuer.

Foreign Currency Effect The gain or loss on an investment denominated in a foreign currency due to changes in the exchange rate. For example, a rising domestic currency will result in a loss in a foreign investment because each foreign currency unit converted will result in fewer domestic currency units. The opposite is true for a falling domestic currency or a rising foreign currency. Foreign currency effects theoretically do not occur with pegged currencies if the foreign currency is pegged to the domestic one or vice versa. See also: Foreign exchange risk, Sovereign risk.

Foreign Currency Future A futures contract in which the underlying asset is a currency. Two parties agree to buy and sell a certain currency at a given exchange rate with respect to another currency at some point in the future. The market for currency futures contracts is important in estimating the future value of different currencies.

Foreign Currency Option An option contract giving the holder the right, but not the obligation, to buy (for a call) or sell (for a put) a futures contract on a certain currency with a given exchange rate on or before the expiration date (depending on the type of option). A foreign currency option effectively gives one the option to lock in an exchange rate on the currency in question if it moves in a favorable direction, while letting the option expire, worthless, if the currency does not move in the desired direction. This helps hedge an investor's foreign exchange risk.

Foreign Currency Translation When a parent-subsidiary relationship exists between two companies in different countries using different currencies, the act or practice of changing the financial statements of the subsidiary to conform to the accounting standards of the parent's country, as well as re-denominating the subsidiary's currency into the parent's currency. According to the Generally Accepted Accounting Principles in the United States, the translation of a foreign currency to U.S. dollars must be accurate as of the date on the financial statement. If there have been substantial changes to the exchange rate since that date, the consolidated financial statement must note this.

Foreign Debt The debt one government owes to a foreign government or corporation. Foreign debt may occur when one buys the debts securities issued by another government. While foreign debt can be advantageous because it may allow a country to finance its development or other government functions, a government owing too much foreign debt (or too much debt generally) may find itself beholden to another country. It is also called external debt or international debt. See also: Debt crisis.

Foreign Direct Investment A major investment by a foreign corporation. A common example of foreign direct investment is a situation in which a foreign company comes into a country to build or buy a factory. Many economists believe that foreign direct investment is good for an economy, as it provides jobs and increases domestic capital. Critics point out that profits from foreign direct investment usually leave the country and go to the foreign company. Encouraging foreign direct investment is a major part of some IMF restructuring programs.

Foreign Equity Market The trading of stocks issued in a certain country by a foreign publicly-traded company. See also: International depository receipt.

Foreign Exchange Broker A broker who operates predominantly or exclusively in currency markets. That is, a foreign exchange broker fills orders to buy and sell currencies in exchange for a commission.

Foreign Exchange Control Act Legislation in South Korea, passed in 1961, that liberalized currency conversion of the South Korean won. That is, the Act permitted international trade of the won. The Act required the Minister of Finance to maintain a record of exchange rates and allowed him to suspend convertibility in the event of an emergency. See also: Exchange controls.

Foreign Exchange Controls Restrictions on foreign currencies in a country. These controls may range from the basic, such as banning the use of a foreign currency in domestic stores and shops, to the dramatic, such as banning currency conversion. Every country has some foreign exchange controls to protect their currencies, but nations with weak currencies are more likely to impose more controls. See also: Pegged Currency, Crawling Peg.

Foreign Exchange Dealer A trader who buys and sells currencies. For example, a foreign exchange dealer may buy dollars from one party and sell them to another at a different exchange rate. The dealer profits from the difference in exchange rates between currencies.

Foreign Exchange Market A market for the trading of currencies. For example, one may buy dollars or sell pounds on a forex market. Foreign exchange is one the largest and most liquid markets in the world. Trading occurs over-the-counter, and most of the major players are governments, banks, and speculators. Forex markets are often used in hedging strategies.

Foreign Exchange Risk The risk that the return on an investment may be reduced or eliminated because of a change in the exchange rate of two currencies. For example, if an American has a CD in the United Kingdom worth 1 million British pounds and the exchange rate is 2 USD: 1 GBP, then the American effectively has $2 million in the CD. However, if the exchange rate changes significantly to, say, 1 USD: 1 GBP, then the American only has $1 million in the CD, even though he/she still has 1 million pounds. Foreign exchange risk is also called exchange rate risk.

Foreign Exchange Swap An agreement between two parties to exchange two currencies at a certain exchange rate at a certain time in the future. For example, if a company knows that it will need British pounds in the future and another company knows that it will need U.S. dollars, they agree to swap the two at the agreed-upon exchange rate. This eliminates the risk that the exchange rate will change in a way that is disadvantageous to one party or the other. They are also called currency swaps. See also: Swap.

Foreign Investment Risk Matrix Also called a FIRM. A methodology that organizes different countries according to the political risk and economic risk investing in each country poses. For example, a FIRM would likely list the United States in a different place from Zimbabwe, where investments carry significantly more political and economic risk.

Foreign Market The market in one country for the trading of securities registered and based in another country. Trading in a foreign market may involve trading on a foreign exchange electronically, or it may involve trading those foreign securities on a domestic exchange. Foreign markets often, but do not always, expose the investor to foreign exchange risk.

Foreign Market Beta In the Capital Asset Pricing Model, a measure of the risk to an investment in a foreign market. See also: Beta.

Foreign Official Institutions The national government of another state, including all its departments, regulatory authorities, and diplomatic and consular missions. Knowledge of foreign official institutions is important to international businesses because they set their laws of commerce independently from the local government, and the laws may be quite different from each other.

Foreign Plan A retirement plan created by a person in Canada intended to benefit someone who does not live in Canada. The creator of the retirement plan may also be the beneficiary if he/she intends to retire outside Canada, or the beneficiary may be someone different. Foreign plans are known for the complexities they create on Canadian tax returns.

Foreign Restricted List A list of securities offered by foreign corporations in violation of SEC registration requirements. The list exists to caution investors from taking a position on securities that might land one in legal trouble.

Foreign Sales Corporation An exporting corporation in the United States. Exporters may register as foreign sales corporations in order to receive certain tax advantages. Foreign sales corporations must have an office in a country with an exchange of information agreement with the United States and have at least one member of the board of directors residing in that country. This structure was created by the Tax Reform Act of 1984, and was formerly called a Domestic International Sales Corporation.

Foreign Tax Credit A direct, dollar-for-dollar reduction in one's U.S. tax liability because of taxes levied by a foreign government. The United States is one of the only countries that taxes income that citizens earn abroad. However, the foreign tax credit exempts income paid as taxes to foreign governments, eliminating the possibility of double taxation.

Foreigner Any person, company, bank, or other organization outside the United States. This includes foreign subsidies or branches of American companies. Generally speaking, foreigners are not subject to U.S. law unless they are doing business with a U.S. citizen, company, or government.

Foreign-Source Income Personal income earned outside the United States. Unlike many other countries, foreign-source income is taxable in the United States.

Foreign-Targeted Issue Treasury securities issued between October 1984 and April 1986 to entities in countries outside the United States. Targeted entities included foreign branches of American banks, foreign central banks, and some international organizations. They were convertible to regular Treasury notes.

Forensic Accountant An accountant who uses investigative skills to determine the accuracy of a company's financial statements in a legal dispute. The word forensic means "suitable for a court of law." Thus, forensic accountants are used in fraud investigations, breach of contract disputes, and other disagreements that require court action. Forensic accountants are often retained by one or both parties in such disputes to bolster their cases.

Forensic Accounting A branch of accounting that uses investigative skills to determine the accuracy of a company's financial statements in a legal dispute. The word forensic means "suitable for a court of law." Thus, forensic accountants are used in fraud investigations, breach of contract disputes, and other disagreements that require court action. Forensic accountants are often retained by one or both parties in such dispute to bolster their cases.

Forfaiting In international trade, the selling of an exporter's receivables for a particular transaction. It is similar to factoring except in scope. While a company sells all of its accounts receivable in factoring, an exporter only sells one receivable for one, perhaps high risk, transaction. In forfaiting, the buyer is known as a forfaiter, and assumes all the risks associated with collecting the receivables. Generally, the exporter forfaits the receivable at a discount. This improves cash flow but reduces income.

Forfeiture The loss of a right or property. Forfeiture usually occurs when one has neglected to fulfill one's obligations necessary to keep the right or property. For example, one may forfeit one's house if the mortgage defaults.

Forfinjaan Ahwa An Arabic term for a cup of coffee. In Syria, it is a slang term for a small bribe.

Forint The currency of Hungary. It was issued in 1946, not long before Hungary became a communist country. It was an inconvertible currency until the fall of the Iron Curtain, when Hungary transitioned to capitalism. It dealt with high inflation in the 1990s but stabilized afterwards.

Form 1000 A worksheet published by the IRS that a taxpayer uses to claim ownership of a tax exempt bond issued before 1934. The information is reported and filed with the IRS on Form 1042.

Form 1023 A form that an organization files with the IRS to apply for tax exempt status under Section 501(c)3 of the Internal Revenue Code. Form 1023 generally is not necessary if the organization is a place of worship or if it has gross receipts for the tax year under $5,000.

Form 1024 A form that an organization files with the IRS to apply for tax exempt status under various sections of the Internal Revenue Code. For example, social clubs may use Form 1024 to achieve tax exempt status.

Form 1028 A form published by the IRS that a farmers' cooperative uses to file for tax exempt status.

Form 1040 (PR) A document that individuals and some corporations in Puerto Rico must file with the IRS each year. The 1040 (PR) form calculates income, deductions, and credits, and ultimately determines how much tax the filer owes for the year. The form itself is short, but many taxpayers must use additional forms to calculate how things like dividend income and capital gains are taxed on the 1040.

Form 1040 (PR) (Anejo H-PR) A form that a taxpayer in Puerto Rico files with the IRS to report wages and salaries paid to domestic employees such as maids and butlers. The form is also used to calculate the taxes the employer owes on the wages and salaries.

Form 1040 (Schedule C) A form that one attaches to Form 1040 to report the profit or loss from one's business. An individual files Schedule C if he/she is self-employed in a sole proprietorship or is the only member of a limited liability company. The filer lists all revenues and business expenses on Schedule C. He/she may only be taxed on the profit.

Form 1040 (Schedule D-1) A form published by the IRS allowing one to continue to report gains and losses from securities and other assets that may be subject to the capital gains tax. One files Schedule D-1 if there is not enough room on Schedule D to list all relevant gains and losses.

Form 1040 (Schedule E) A form that one attaches to Form 1040 to report profit or loss from royalties, partnerships, rental real estate, trusts, estates, S-corporations, or real estate mortgage investment conduits.

Form 1040 (Schedule EIC) A form that one files with the IRS to claim the earned income tax credit.

Form 1040 (Schedule F) A form that one files with the IRS along with Form 1040 to claim profits or losses from farming or other agricultural activities.

Form 1040 (Schedule H) A form that a taxpayer files with the IRS to report wages and salaries paid to domestic employees such as maids and butlers. The form is also used to calculate the taxes the employer owes on the wages and salaries.

Form 1040 (Schedule J) A form that a farmer or a fisherman files with the IRS along with Form 1040 to average his/her income over the previous three years. This can reduce one's tax liability over those three years. It is especially useful in farming and fishing, two occupations for which incomes can be quite volatile. A farmer or fisherman may file Schedule J even if he/she was not engaged in farming or fishing during the three years under consideration.

Form 1040 (Schedule L) A form published by the IRS allowing certain taxpayers to calculate the standard deduction for which they are eligible. One uses Schedule L if one suffered a loss from a federally-declared disaster between 2007 and 2009, or if one paid excise taxes or other taxes to a state on the purchase of a new vehicle between February 2009 and the beginning of 2010.

Form 1040 (Schedule M) A form that one attaches to Form 1040 to claim the Making Work Pay credit, a $400 to $800 credit that was available in 2009 and 2010 for employed persons in the United States as part of the American Recovery and Reinvestment Act.

Form 1040 (Schedule R) A form that one attaches to Form 1040 or Form 1040A to claim a tax credit available to the elderly and disabled. One qualifies for the credit if one is at least 65 years old, or if one is under 65 and receives disability income.

Form 1040 (Schedule SE) A form that self-employed persons and certain employees of religious organizations file with the IRS to calculate the self-employment tax they owe. One owes self-employment tax if one is in business for oneself (and therefore has no employer to pay half of one's FICA taxes) or if one works for a religious organization exempt from collecting FICA taxes. Half of the self-employment tax is tax deductible.

Form 1040-C A form that non-resident aliens of the United States must file with the IRS upon departure. Form 1040-C calculates income, deductions, and credits, and ultimately determines how much tax the filer owes for the year.

Form 1040-ES A form that an individual files with the IRS to calculate and pay taxes based what he/she believes his/her ultimate tax liability will be. In other words, one uses Form 1040-ES to estimate taxes and pay them, usually on a quarterly basis. One must file Form 1040-ES if one has income that is not subject to withholding. If the estimation is wrong, the filer may receive a refund (or pay more to the IRS) when he/she files the actual tax return.

Form 1040-ES (NR) A form that a non-resident alien files with the IRS to calculate and pay taxes based what he/she believes his/her ultimate tax liability will be. In other words, one uses Form 1040-ES (NR) to estimate taxes and pay them. One must file Form 1040-ES (NR) if one has income that is not subject to withholding. If the estimation is wrong, the filer may receive a refund (or pay more to the IRS) when he/she files the actual tax return.

Form 1040-ES (PR) A form that an individual in Puerto Rico files with the IRS to calculate and pay taxes based what he/she believes his/her ultimate tax liability will be. In other words, one uses Form 1040-ES (PR) to estimate taxes and pay them. One must file Form 1040-ES (PR) if one has income that is not subject to withholding. If the estimation is wrong, the filer may receive a refund (or pay more to the IRS) when he/she files the actual tax return.

Form 1040-NR A document that non-resident aliens of the United States must file with the IRS each year. Form 1040-NR calculates income, deductions, and credits, and ultimately determines how much income tax the filer owes for the year.

Form 1040-NR-EZ A simplified tax return that may be used by some non-resident aliens of the United States. One may use Form 1040-NR-EZ if one claims no dependents, cannot be claimed as a dependent, has no interest or investment income, does not exceed income limits, and claims no credits and no deductions other than the deduction for state and local tax refunds. Form 1040-NR-EZ is more straightforward and easier to file than the normal Form 1040-NR.

Form 1040-SS A tax return in the United States that self-employed persons and certain employees of religious organizations file with the IRS to pay the self-employment tax they owe. It is also used to claim an additional child tax credit available to residents of Puerto Rico. See also: Form 1040 (Schedule SE).

Form 1040-V A payment voucher that one sends to the IRS with an estimated tax payment. Form 1040-V is filed along with Form 1040-ES, which calculates what the payment should be.

Form 1040-X A form that one uses to amend a previously filed Form 1040, which is used to report one's income and pay the income tax.

Form 1041 A form that one files with the IRS to report the assets and liabilities of an estate or a trust. The assets considered include all personal property, real estate, and securities. Form 1041 is used to calculate what estate tax, if any, is owed after all the debts of the deceased are paid and all deductions and credits are applied.

Form 1041 (Schedule D) A form that one files with the IRS along with Form 1041 to report the sale of capital assets associated with an estate. For example, if one sells a business or a home of a decedent, the gain or loss from this sale is reported on Schedule D. See also: Estate tax.

Form 1041 (Schedule D-1) A form published by the IRS to report the sale of capital assets along with Form 1041 (Schedule D). Schedule D-1 is used if there is not enough room on Schedule D to report all capital assets sold.

Form 1041 (Schedule I) A form that one files with the IRS to calculate the alternative minimum tax that an estate may owe. See also: Estate tax.

Form 1041 (Schedule J) A form that one files with the IRS to report distributions from a complex trust above the proper distributions usually made, provided that the distributions exceed the trust's income for the year. Schedule J is filed along with Form 1041, and is used in calculating estate tax liability.

Form 1041 (Schedule K-1) A form that one files with the IRS to report the income, credits, or deductions of an estate in which a beneficiary has a share. Schedule K-1 is filed along with Form 1041 and is used in calculating estate tax liability.

Form 1041-A A form that one files with the IRS if a trust is claiming deductions for charitable contributions. These contributions must be itemized by the specific charitable purpose of each contribution.

Form 1041-ES A form that one files with the IRS to report and pay the estimated tax of an estate or trust. One must file Form 1041-ES if the estate or trust is expected to owe at least $1,000 for the tax year.

Form 1041-N A form that one files with the IRS to choose special tax treatment options available to an Alaska Native Settlement Trust. Trusts that file Form 1041-N are taxed at a 10% rate.

Form 1041-QFT A tax return calculating the income, credits, deductions, and ultimately the tax liability of a qualified funeral trust, which is a trust set up specifically to pay for the funeral expenses of beneficiaries.

Form 1041-T A form that a trust or estate files with the IRS to elect estimated tax payments that the trust or estate makes to be considered as having been made by a beneficiary. For example, if a trust makes an estimated tax payment of $10,000, it may use Form 1041-T to ask the IRS to consider that $10,000 as having been paid by one of the trust's beneficiaries.

Form 1042 A form that one files with the IRS to report withholding of taxes from the U.S. income earned by a foreign person. It is also used to report the 2% excise tax on certain payments of foreign procurements. The form is filed annually. See also Form 1042-S.

Form 1042-S A form that one files with the IRS to report certain U.S. income of a foreign person that is subject to withholding. It is especially used for income derived from a nominee or a publicly-traded partnership. Many common types of income, notably income reported on W-2 or 1099 forms, is not reported on Form 1042-S.

Form 1042-T A form that one files with the IRS to summarize Form 1042-S and to transmit the information contained on it to the IRS.

Form 1045 A form that one files with the IRS to request a tentative tax refund. One may do this for a carryback from a net operating loss, the carryback of an unused tax credit, the carryback of certain contract losses, or certain tax overpayments.

Form 1065 A form that one files with the IRS stating the profits, losses, credits and/or deductions of a partnership. Form 1065 is filed whether the partnership is foreign or domestic, or if it is a general or limited partnership. While a partnership is not taxed directly, the profits and losses are passed to the partners, who pay taxes on the partnership's behalf.

Form 1065 (Schedule B-1) A form that one files with the IRS to report information on the persons or entities that own more than 50% of a partnership. Information reported on Schedule B-1 includes the name, the type of entity (if it is an organization), and the country in which the person or entity is based.

Form 1065 (Schedule C) A form that one files with the IRS to answer certain questions about a partnership pertaining to Form 1065 (Schedule M-3). Questions include whether the partnership transferred any assets to a partner and whether or not it changed its accounting method during the tax year.

Form 1065 (Schedule D) A form that a partnership files with the IRS to report the sale of capital assets, distributions of capital gains, and bad debts unrelated to the business of the partnership.

Form 1065 (Schedule D-1) A form that one files with the IRS to continue Form 1065 (Schedule D), which is used to report a partnership's sale of capital assets, distributions of capital gains, and bad debts unrelated to the business of the partnership. Schedule D-1 is used if there is not enough room on Schedule D to state all sales, distributions, and bad debts.

Form 1065 (Schedule K-1) A form that a partner in a partnership uses to state his/her own share of profits, losses, deductions, and credits ascribed to him/her. Because a partnership does not pay taxes directly and the tax liability is passed through to each partner, Schedule K-1 is not filed with the IRS. The partner keeps it for his/her own records.

Form 1065 (Schedule M-3) A form that a partnership files with the IRS to reconcile its profit and loss statements. A partnership must file Schedule M-3 if its assets or adjusted assets exceed $10 million in value, if its total receipts exceed $35 million, or if a second partnership meeting those criteria owns 50% or more of the partnership.

Form 1065-B A form that a large partnership files with the IRS stating its profits, losses, deductions, and credits, as well as its partners' shares of the same. While Form 1065-B may be used to pay some minor taxes, most partnerships do not pay taxes directly and the tax liability is passed through to each partner. Companies that may be required to file Form 1065-B include general partnerships, limited partnerships, and limited liability companies.

Form 1065-B (Schedule K-1) A form published by the IRS on which a partnership declares the share of profits, losses, deductions, and credits ascribed to each partner. Because a partnership does not pay taxes directly and the tax liability is passed through to each partner, Schedule K-1 is not filed with the IRS. It is sent to the partner, who is responsible for reporting the information on his/her own tax return.

Form 1066 A form that one files with the IRS to state the income, losses, deductions, and credits applicable to a real estate mortgage investment conduit. The form is also used for the REMIC to pay taxes on prohibited transactions, additional contributions of capital, and income from foreclosures. Other taxes are passed through to the REMIC holders.

Form 1066 (Schedule Q) A form that a real estate mortgage investment conduit sends to a holder each quarter stating the holder's portion of the REMIC's taxable income. The holder is liable for this taxation and must report this income on his/her own tax return.

Form 1096 A form published by the IRS that one submits in order to file paper copies of Form 1098, Form 1099, Form 3921, Form 3922, Form 5498, and/or Form W-2G. Form 1096 is not necessary if these forms are submitted electronically.

Form 1097-BTC A form that the issuer of a bond files with the IRS to report tax credits available to bondholders. Use of this form is available to regulated investment companies that decide to distribute their bond tax credits to shareholders. This distribution was first permitted in the American Recovery and Reinvestment Act of 2009.

Form 1098 A form published by the IRS that a lender uses to report the interest that a borrower pays on a mortgage in a year in excess of $600. The form is reported to the IRS and sent to the borrower. Because the interest on one's home mortgage is tax deductible, receiving Form 1098 and reporting the interest paid to the IRS may significantly impact one's tax liability.

Form 1098-C A form published by the IRS that a non-profit organization uses to report the value of the donation of a boat or motor vehicle. The form is reported to the IRS and sent to the donor. Because charity donations are tax deductible, receiving Form 1098-C and reporting the value of the donation to the IRS may significantly impact one's tax liability.

Form 1098-E A form published by the IRS that one uses to report tax deductible tuition paid to a qualified educational institution in a year. The form is reported to the IRS and sent to the party paying the tuition. Because tuition may be tax deductible, receiving Form 1098-E and reporting the tuition to the IRS may significantly impact one's tax liability.

Form 1098-MA A form that state housing finance agencies file with the IRS to report loans and other payments made to homeowners in disaster zones and certain disadvantaged areas.

Form 1098-T A form published by the IRS that a lender uses to report the interest that a borrower pays on a student loan in a year in excess of $600. The form is reported to the IRS and sent to the borrower. Because student loan interest is tax deductible up to a certain limit, receiving Form 1098-C and reporting the interest paid to the IRS may significantly impact one's tax liability.

Form 1099-A A form that a lender files with the IRS if it receives ownership in any collateral instead of partial or total repayment. Lenders are required to file 1099-A even if they do not lend as part of their business.

Form 1099-C A form that a lender files with the IRS if it cancels a debt in excess of $600. Lenders are required to file 1099-C whether the borrower is a natural person or legal person.

Form 1099-CAP A form that a corporation files with the IRS to report payments to a shareholder if control of the corporation changes hands or if it changes its capital structure. The form is filed if the shareholder receives cash, stock, or some other form on in-kind payment.

Form 1099-G A form that a government agency files with IRS to report any payments made to an individual. For example, if a local government gives a citizen a tax refund, it reports this payment to the IRS on Form 1099-G. This is done because many of these payments are taxable for the individual.

Form 1099-H A form that an insurer files with the IRS to report advance payments of the health care tax credit made by a government entity.

Form 1099-K A form that one files with the IRS to report the settlement of a debt on a gift card, credit card, or similar instrument by a third party.

Form 1099-LTC A form that an insurer files with the IRS to report accelerated death benefits or long-term care benefits paid to a policyholder on behalf of the insured. The policyholder receives a copy of Form 1099-LTC, which may affect his/her taxable income.

Form 1099-MISC A form one files with the IRS on which one reports royalties, lotteries, commissions, golden parachute payments, income earned by an independent contractor, and similar payments. The person earning this income receives a copy of the 1099-MISC, which he/she uses to determine income for filing his/her own taxes.

Form 1099-PATR A form one files with the IRS on which one reports income from dividends received from a cooperative organization. The form must be filed if the amount of the dividend is $10 or greater. The form may also be used to report any tax withheld according to the back-up withholding rules.

Form 1099-Q A form that one files with the IRS to report payments made by qualified educational plans. For example, the fiduciary of a Coverdell savings account files Form 1099-Q to report disbursements from the account.

Form 1099-R An IRS form reporting income from distributions from an IRA, 401(k), pension plan, profit-sharing plan, insurance plan, or another, similar instrument. The form indicates how much was withheld for taxes, if any, and the total amount of income one derived from a plan. This helps the plan holder calculate his/her tax liability from these plans.

Form 1099-S A form one files with the IRS to report the sale of real estate. Any profit on the sale of real estate is taxable.

Form 1099-SA A form that one files with the IRS to report payments made by a qualified medical savings plan. For example, the fiduciary of a health savings account files Form 1099-SA to report disbursements from the account.

Form 1116 A form that one files with the IRS in order to claim the foreign tax credit, which is a direct, dollar-for-dollar reduction in one's U.S. tax liability due to taxes levied by a foreign government. Form 1116 is used whether the filer is an individual, a trust, or an estate.

Form 1118 A form that a corporation files with the IRS in order to claim the foreign tax credit, which is a direct, dollar-for-dollar reduction in the corporation's U.S. tax liability due to taxes levied by a foreign government.

Form 1118 (Schedule I) A form that a corporation files with the IRS to claim the foreign tax credit for taxes paid on oil and gas income derived outside the United States.

Form 1118 (Schedule J) A form that a corporation files with the IRS to make certain adjustments to income or losses when claiming the foreign tax credit.

Form 1118 (Schedule K) A form that a corporation files with the IRS to reconcile the loss carryover from the current year with the loss carryover from the previous year in claiming the foreign tax credit.

Form 1120 A corporate tax return in the United States. A corporation files Form 1120 to report its revenue, expenses, and profits or losses. It also uses Form 1120 to claim deductions and credits, which is especially important in the United States because corporate tax rates historically have been high compared to other countries. Form 1120 generally is filed three months after the end of the corporation's tax year.

Form 1120 (Schedule B) A form filed with the IRS to report information on the reconciliation of income or loss of corporations with total assets greater than $10 million. It is a supplemental form for Form 1120 (Schedule M-3).

Form 1120 (Schedule D) A form that a corporation files with the IRS to report the sale and dispositions of capital assets, including like-kind exchanges. The gains or losses from these exchanges may affect the corporation's tax liability.

Form 1120 (Schedule G) A form that a corporation files with the IRS to report information on corporations, partnerships, and other legal persons that own at least 20% or control at least 50% of voting shares.

Form 1120 (Schedule H) A form that a personal service corporation must file with the IRS in order to have a tax year other than the calendar year. In order to qualify as a personal service corporation for tax purposes, a company must have been engaged in the principal business of a personal service on the last day of the previous tax year or the last day of the calendar year of the company's tax year. Thus, Schedule H may affect the company's tax treatment.

Form 1120 (Schedule M-3) A form filed with the IRS to reconcile the income or loss of a corporation with total assets greater than $10 million.

Form 1120 (Schedule N) A form that a corporation files with the IRS reporting information on any activities it conducts outside the United States. Schedule N is required for multinational companies operating in the United States.

Form 1120 (Schedule O) A form that a controlled group of corporations files with the IRS to report how profits, losses, and other things are apportioned out among the members of the group. For example, a parent company with three subsidiaries would file Schedule O to declare which companies are assigned which profits and losses.

Form 1120 (Schedule PH) A form that a corporation files with the IRS to calculate the personal holding company tax, which is a tax levied on a corporation if five or fewer persons control at least half of the company's stock and if at least 60% of the company's income is passive income from companies it owns.

Form 1120 (Schedule UTP) A form that a corporation files with the IRS if it has uncertain tax positions that may affect its tax liability. A corporation may file Schedule UTP if it has audited financial statements and has assets greater than $100 million.

Form 1120-C A tax return for a cooperative association in the United States. A coop files Form 1120-C to report its revenue, expenses, and profits or losses. It also uses Form 1120 to claim deductions and credits, which are used to determine its tax liability.

Form 1120-F A tax return for the U.S.-sourced income of a foreign corporation. A foreign corporation files Form 1120-F to report its U.S. revenue, expenses and profits or losses. It also uses Form 1120-F to claim deductions and credits, which is especially important in the United States because corporate tax rates historically have been high compared to other countries.

Form 1120-F (Schedule H) A form that a foreign corporation files with the IRS to claim deductions for its business expenses. Foreign corporations may only claim these deductions if the expenses relate to their activities in the United States.

Form 1120-F (Schedule I) A form that a foreign corporation files with the IRS to report interest expenses connected to certain income. These interest expenses are tax deductible.

Form 1120-F (Schedule M-3) A form filed with the IRS to reconcile the income or loss of a foreign corporation with total assets greater than $10 million.

Form 1120-F (Schedule P) A form that a foreign corporation files with the IRS to report its partnership interests. That is, it reports all companies in which it is a partner. If these partnerships are connected to income (or losses) in the United States, these interests may be taxable (or deductible).

Form 1120-F (Schedule S) A form that a foreign corporation files with the IRS to claim the exclusion of certain income from sea or air transportation from its taxable income. Foreign companies are eligible for this exclusion if the countries in which they are based provide the equivalent courtesy to companies based in the United States.

Form 1120-F (Schedule V) A form that a foreign corporation files with the IRS to report certain assets used in transportation (such as ships and airplanes) that are subject to a 4% tax on all U.S.-sourced income derived from those assets.

Form 1120-F (Schedules M-1, M-2) A form that a foreign corporation files with the IRS to report its retained earnings and the reconciliation of its income or loss statements.

Form 1120-FSC A tax return for the income of a foreign sales corporation. A foreign sales corporation files Form 1120-FSC to report its revenue, expenses, and profits or losses. It also uses Form 1120-FSC to claim deductions and credits, which is especially important in the United States because corporate tax rates historically have been high compared to other countries.

Form 1120-FSC (Schedule P) A form that a foreign sales corporation files with the IRS to report gross receipts from the resale of an export to a company controlled by the same owners as the foreign sales corporation. It is also used if the foreign sales corporation has receipts from serving as an intermediary to accomplish the same goal.

Form 1120-H A tax return that a homeowners' association may file with the IRS to claim certain tax benefits available to it.

Form 1120-IC-DISC A tax return for the income of an IC-DISC, which is a company in the United States that exports to non-U.S.-based clients. An IC-DISC files Form 1120-IC-DISC to report its revenue, expenses, and profits or losses. It also uses Form 1120-IC-DISC to claim deductions and credits, which is especially important in the United States because corporate tax rates historically have been high compared to other countries.

Form 1120-IC-DISC (Schedule K) A form that an IC-DISC sends to a shareholder reporting actual or deemed distributions to that shareholder. The shareholder uses this form to report capital gains on his/her tax return.

Form 1120-IC-DISC (Schedule P) A form that an IC-DISC files with the IRS to report gross receipts from serving as an intermediary for inter-company transfers.

Form 1120-IC-DISC (Schedule Q) A form that a company files with the IRS to claim a loan from an IC-DISC as a producer's loan.

Form 1120-L A tax return for the income of a life insurance company. A life insurance company files Form 1120-L to report its revenue, expenses, and profits or losses. It also uses Form 1120-L to claim deductions and credits, which is especially important in the United States because corporate tax rates historically have been high compared to other countries.

Form 1120-L (Schedule M-3) A form filed with the IRS to reconcile the income or loss of a life insurance company with total assets greater than $10 million.

Form 1120-ND A tax return for the income for a nuclear decommissioning fund. A nuclear decommissioning fund files Form 1120-L to report its revenue, expenses, and profits or losses. It also uses Form 1120-ND to claim deductions and credits.

Form 1120-PC A tax return for the income of a casualty and property insurance company. An insurance company files Form 1120-PC to report its revenue, expenses, and profits or losses. It also uses Form 1120-PC to claim deductions and credits, which is especially important in the United States because corporate tax rates historically have been high compared to other countries.

Form 1120-PC (Schedule M-3) A form filed with the IRS to reconcile the income or loss of a casualty and property insurance company with total assets greater than $10 million.

Form 1120-POL A tax return for the income of a political action committee or other politically-oriented tax exempt organization. While these organizations are not taxed directly, they may use Form 1120-POL to receive credits for federal taxes paid, for example, on gasoline.

Form 1120-REIT A tax return for the income of a real estate investment trust. An REIT files Form 1120-REIT to report its revenue, expenses, and profits or losses. It also uses Form 1120-REIT to claim deductions and credits, which is especially important in the United States because corporate tax rates historically have been high compared to other countries.

Form 1120-RIC A tax return for the income of a casualty and property insurance company. An insurance company files Form 1120-PC to report its revenue, expenses, and profits or losses. It also uses Form 1120-PC to claim deductions and credits, which is especially important in the United States because corporate tax rates historically have been high compared to other countries.

Form 1120-S A tax return for the income of an S-corporation. A corporation files Form 1120-S to report its revenue, expenses, and profits or losses. It also uses Form 1120-S to claim deductions and credits, which is especially important in the United States because corporate tax rates historically have been high compared to other countries.

Form 1120-S (Schedule D) A form that an S-corporation files with the IRS to report the sale of capital assets, distributions of capital gains, and bad debts unrelated to the business of the corporation.

Form 1120-S (Schedule K-1) A form that a shareholder in an S-corporation uses to state his/her own share of profits, losses, deductions, and credits ascribed to him/her. The company files Schedule K-1 with the IRS; the shareholder receives a copy for his/her own records and uses it in filing his/her tax return.

Form 1120-S (Schedule M-3) A form filed with the IRS to reconcile the income or loss of an S-corporation with total assets greater than $10 million.

Form 1120-SF A tax return for the income of a qualified settlement fund. A fund files Form 1120-SF to report its revenue, expenses, and profits or losses. It also uses Form 1120-SF to claim deductions and credits, which is especially important in the United States because corporate tax rates historically have been high compared to other countries.

Form 1120-W A form that a corporation files with the IRS to report and pay its estimated tax. A corporation must file Form 1120-W if it is expected to owe at least $500 for the tax year.

Form 1120-X A form that one files with the IRS to amend a previously filed Form 1120, which is a corporate tax return.

Form 1122 A form that one files with the IRS to include a subsidiary on its parent company's tax return. See also: Consolidated tax return.

Form 1127 A form one files with the IRS to request an extension of the time to file taxes due to an economic or other hardship. Form 1127 is used only if the extension of time is used to pay the full amount owed. It is not used to request a monthly installment plan.

Form 1128 A form that a company files with the IRS to adopt a tax year other than the calendar year. For example, if a company desires a tax year that runs from July 1 to June 30, it files Form 1128 to inform IRS of this choice. Form 1128 is also used to change the tax year.

Form 1138 A form that a corporation files with the IRS to request an extension of the time necessary for filing a tax return. The corporation may file Form 1138 only if it expects loss carryback for the tax year.

Form 1139 A form that a corporation files with the IRS to request a speedy tax refund due to a tax loss carryback or overpayment of taxes due to certain income adjustments.

Form 11-C A form the owner of a gambling establishment must file if he/she hires agents who take bets on behalf of the establishment. On Form 11-C, the owner must list the names, addresses, and employer identification numbers of these agents. For example, if Tom is a bookie and has six employees who take bets for his business, he must list all six on Form 11-C. However, he does not have to list his other employees who do not take bets. The purpose of the form is to ensure that all bet takers pay the appropriate occupational tax.

Form 1310 A form that one files with the IRS to claim a tax refund that is due to a deceased person. The spouse or executor of the decedent's estate has the right to file Form 1310.

Form 1363 A form that an exporter files with the IRS to claim an exemption from an excise tax on the air transportation of goods that take off and land in the United States. An exporter may file this form if the goods are transported directly outside the country or to a U.S. overseas possession.

Form 13-F A form that institutional investors managing more than $100 million in Section 13(f) securities must file with the SEC each quarter. Among other things, form 13-F discloses the names of investment managers, the types and numbers of securities owned (along with their CUSIP numbers), and the value of each security. Form 13-F helps the SEC promote transparency in the market.

Form 144 A form that an executive of a publicly-traded company must file with the SEC to demonstrate compliance with Rule 144. That is an SEC rule allowing executives who owns restricted stock in their own company to sell some shares without registering them with the SEC. An executive may do this once every six months if he/she has held the shares for at least two years. Filing Form 144 ensures that the executive has complied with the terms of the rule.

Form 2032 A form that a U.S. company files with the IRS to receive the ability to continue to pay Social Security taxes on U.S. citizens and resident aliens working outside the United States for a foreign affiliate of the company. Form 2032 exists so as not to penalize U.S. persons who relocate outside the United States.

Form 2063 A tax return that a non-U.S. citizen files with the IRS upon departure from the United States. Form 2063 certifies the non-citizen has satisfied all taxation requirements placed upon him/her.

Form 2106 A form an employee files with the IRS to report any expenses incurred in the course of employment for the year. Form 2106 is filed only when the expenses were not reimbursed; these expenses are tax deductible.

Form 2106-EZ A form that an employee files with the IRS to claim a tax deduction for unreimbursed expenses that the employee has incurred in the ordinary course of his/her employment. Form 2106-EZ is also used for deductions related to the business use of the employee's vehicle, provided the employee uses the standard mileage rate.

Form 211 A form one files with the IRS to report unpaid taxes by another party. For example, an employee may file Form 211 if she has information indicating that her company is skimping on its corporate taxes. If the IRS collects additional taxes (and penalties) based on the information provided in Form 211, the filer may be eligible to receive a reward of up to 30% of the collection. In order to file this form, the accused tax cheat must make at least $2 million per year (if a corporation) or $200,000 (if an individual).

Form 211A A form that a state or local law enforcement agency files with the IRS to claim reimbursement for expenses incurred during a tax investigation. That is, if the IRS asks a state or local agency to assist in an investigation, the agency files Form 211A so that it will be compensated for the staff time and other expenses utilized in helping the IRS.

Form 2120 A form that an individual files with the IRS declaring the names of a person who paid more than 10% of the expenses of an individual that the filer claims as a dependent. Form 2120 also declares that the filer has received a signed statement from this person that he/she will not claim the individual as a dependent. Form 2120 is filed when no single taxpayer provided more than half of the individual's support but when at least two taxpayers provided more than 10%.

Form 2159 A form one files with the IRS allowing it to withhold more than usual from an employee, generally to pay back taxes as part of an offer in compromise. Form 2159 exists because such withholding requires the employer's consent before it may begin.

Form 2210 A form that an individual, estate, or trust files with the IRS to calculate whether and how much the filer owes as a penalty for underpayment of estimated taxes. In general, one must file Form 2210 only if one is requesting a waiver or otherwise attempting to reduce the amount of the penalty.

Form 2210-F A form that an individual, estate, or trust files with the IRS to calculate whether and how much the filer owes as a penalty for underpayment of estimated taxes on income related to fishing or farming. In general, one must file Form 2210-F if at least two-thirds of the filer's gross income comes from fishing or farming and his/her estimated taxes were less than two-thirds of the actual taxes owed. One can also file Form 2210-F to request a waiver from the penalty.

Form 2220 A form that a corporation files with the IRS to calculate whether and how much the filer owes as a penalty for underpayment of estimated taxes. A corporation must file Form 2220 if the underpayment is $500 or more and if it is a large corporation estimating its first installment or if it uses the adjusted seasonal installment method or the annualized income installment method to pay estimated taxes.

Form 2290 A form one files with the IRS to report any taxes due on a highway-traveling vehicle weighing more than 55,000 pounds. A logging vehicle is an example of a vehicle for which Form 2290 might be filed.

Form 23 A form one files to apply to become a representative before the IRS.

Form 2333-X A form that one files with the IRS to order more information from the Stakeholder Partnerships, Education and Communication program. This program aims to build relationships with local communities to ensure that community members pay their taxes.

Form 2350 A form that one files with the IRS to request an extension of the time to file Form 2555, which is used to claim a foreign earned income exclusion from U.S. taxation of income earned in a foreign country. One may file Form 2350 if one needs more time to pass residency tests necessary to claim the exclusion.

Form 23-EP A form one files to apply to become a representative before the IRS on matters pertaining to the tax treatment of retirement plans.

Form 2438 A form that a real estate investment trust or regulated investment company files with the IRS to declare its undistributed capital gains and pay taxes on them. A trust's shareholders can claim a credit for the taxes the trust pays.

Form 2439 A form a mutual fund or other investment company files with the IRS to report any capital gains that were not distributed to shareholders over the course of the year. Shareholders also receive copies of Form 2439.

Form 2441 A form that one files with the IRS to claim a tax credit for expenses incurred for child care. A parent may file Form 2441, for example, if the parent paid a daycare service or a nanny to babysit while the parent was at work.

Form 2553 A form that a small business files with the IRS to be treated as an S-corporation for tax purposes.

Form 2555 A form that one files with the IRS to claim a foreign earned income exclusion from U.S. taxation of income earned in a foreign country. One may file

Form 2555 regardless of the amount one earns abroad, but the maximum exclusion is $92,900 (as of 2011).

Form 2555-EZ A simplified form that one files with the IRS to claim a foreign earned income exclusion from U.S. taxation of income earned in a foreign country. One may file Form 2555-EZ (instead of Form 2555) if one's foreign income is less than $92,901 (the maximum amount as of 2011), if one is not self-employed, and if one does not claim deductions for moving expenses or housing.

Form 2587 An application that one files with the IRS to register for the Special Enrollment Examination. Passing the exam enables one to become an enrolled agent. One must have a preparer tax identification number to be eligible to file Form 2587.

Form 2678 A form that a person or company files with the IRS to empower another party to make deposits or payments to the IRS on the filer's behalf. One may also use it to revoke the appointment. The IRS must approve the filing before it may take effect.

Form 2848 A form that a person files with the IRS to give another party the power to represent that person before the IRS. For example, one may file Form 2848 to ask a volunteer at a Low Income Taxpayer Clinic to act as a liaison between that individual and the IRS.

Form 3 A form that an individual or company must file with the SEC after buying 10% or more of shares outstanding in a publicly-traded company or when an insider (one in possession of nonpublic knowledge) becomes affiliated with a company's operations. Form 3 exists to help prevent insider trading and monopolization.

Form 3115 A form that a company files with the IRS to apply for a change in accounting method. For example, one files Form 3115 it one finds it more advantageous to begin to use the accrual method than to continue with the cash method.

Form 3468 A form that one files with the IRS to claim a tax credit for making a qualifying investment in renewable or clean energy technology. Examples of potentially qualifying investments include clean coal and solar energy.

Form 3491 A form that a cooperative files with the IRS to apply for exemption from filing Form 1099-PATR, which is used to report income received from a cooperative. In order to receive the exemption, at least 85% of its income must come from qualified retail sales.

Form 3520 A form that a U.S. person files with the IRS to report some transactions with a foreign trust, ownership of a foreign trust, or certain gifts from a foreign person or corporation. One must file a separate Form 3520 for each foreign trust with which one interacts.

Form 3520-A A form one files with the IRS providing information on a foreign trust owned by a U.S. person. Each U.S. owner of a single foreign trust must file a separate Form 3520-A. This is an information return, but some of the income or assets reported may be taxable.

Form 3800 A form that a company files with the IRS to claim any general business credit. Examples of general business credits include the Indian employment credit and the welfare-to-work credit.

Form 3903 A form that one files with the IRS to calculate moving expenses. This is used in order to find the maximum allowable tax deduction for moving expenses. It should be noted that in order to deduct moving expenses at all, one's new workplace must be at least 50 miles farther from one's previous home than the old work place, and one must work at the new location for at least 39 weeks during the 12 months immediately following the move.

Form 3911 A form that one files with the IRS to update contact information in order to receive a tax refund. The IRS sends Form 3911 to a taxpayer if a previous attempt to send the refund failed or if the check was not deposited within a year of its issue.

Form 3921 A form that a corporation files with the IRS upon an employee's exercise of a stock option. Form 3921 is used when the employee eventually sells the stock in order to calculate the capital gain or loss.

Form 3922 A form a corporation files with the IRS upon an employee's exercise of a stock option at a price less than 100% of the stock's market price. Form 3922 is used when the employee eventually sells the stock in order to calculate the capital gain or loss.

Form 3949-A A form that a law enforcement official may file with the IRS to receive information on someone alleged to have violated tax laws. The form includes information such as the taxpayer's name and contact details, the nature of the offense, and whether or not law enforcement considers the taxpayer dangerous.

Form 4 A form that an insider must file with the SEC within two days of conducting a trade on a company with which the insider is involved. Directors, senior management, and large shareholders must file Form 4. This is done to promote transparency in the market and to discourage insider trading. See also: Form 3, Form 5.

Form 4029 A form that one files with the IRS to apply for a religious exemption from payment of FICA taxes and to opt out of the Social Security and Medicare programs. One only files Form 4029 if one is a layperson objecting on religious grounds. Clergy file Form 4361.

Form 4136 A form that one files with the IRS to claim a tax credit for certain federal excise taxes paid on automotive fuel. It is also used to claim a tax credit for the use of alternative fuels.

Form 4137 A form one files with the IRS to declare income from tips that were not reported to one's employer, and to calculate FICA taxes owed on that income. Form 4137 is attached to Form 1040 or another tax return that the tipped employee files.

Form 4255 A form that one files with the IRS to calculate an increase in taxes due to the recapture of an investment or a therapeutic grant tax credit. For example, one may have to file Form 4255 if one claimed an investment credit in a previous year, but sold the investment within the first five years.

Form 433-A A form one files with the IRS when an individual makes an offer in compromise. The form provides financial information to the IRS to help determine how much to withhold each month in paying the individual's back taxes.

Form 433-B A form one files with the IRS when a business makes an offer in compromise. The form provides financial information to the IRS to help determine how much to withhold each month in paying the business's back taxes.

Form 433-D A form one files with the IRS when one agrees to pay back taxes in installments. That is, in Form 433-D, one agrees to pay a certain amount each month until the total tax liability is paid. One must include direct debit payment information on the form.

Form 433-F A form one files with the IRS in which one documents income and expenses each month. One files this form as part of working out an installment plan with the IRS in order to pay back taxes.

Form 4361 A form a priest, minister or other clergy member (or the equivalent) files with the IRS claiming exemption from self-employment tax due to his/her status as a clergy member. In order to be eligible to file Form 4361, the clergyperson may not be under a vow of poverty.

Form 4419 A form that one files with the IRS to request permission to file certain forms electronically. The forms covered under Form 4419 are Form 1042-S, Form 1097, Form 1098, Form 1099, Form 3921, Form 3922, Form 5498, Form 8027, Form 8955-SSA, and Form W-2G.

Form 4421 A form that one files with the IRS to declare the commission paid to the executor of an estate and any associated attorney's fees. These fees are deducted from the value of the estate for the purpose of calculating the estate tax owed.

Form 4422 A form that one files with the IRS to apply for a discharge of an estate tax lien on real estate. In addition to the form, the IRS requires a description of the property (including its value), a copy of a will mentioning the property, and similar documentation.

Form 4461 A form filed with the IRS to request approval for master and prototype or volume submitter defined contribution plans. That is, when multiple companies adopt the same or nearly the same defined contribution plan, they file Form 4461-B to receive approval to have these plans treated in the same way for tax purposes.

Form 4461-A A form filed with the IRS to request approval for master and prototype or volume submitter defined benefit plans. That is, when multiple companies adopt the same or nearly the same defined benefit plan, they file Form 4461-B to receive approval to have these plans treated in the same way for tax purposes.

Form 4461-B A form filed with the IRS to request approval for master and prototype or volume submitter pension plans. That is, when multiple companies adopt the same or nearly the same pension plan, they file Form 4461-B to receive approval to have these plans treated in the same way for tax purposes.

Form 4466 A form that a corporation files with the IRS to apply for an early refund of overpaid estimated taxes. In order to be eligible to file Form 4466, a corporation must have overpaid at least $500 or 10% of its tax liability for the year.

Form 4506 A form one files with the IRS to request a copy of a tax return filed for a previous year. One may request the copy be sent to him/her, or one may direct that it be sent to some other party.

Form 4506-A A form one files with the IRS to request a copy of a tax return filed by a tax exempt political organization. Because these returns are matters of public record, almost anyone can request copies. Form 4506-A is not necessary for all political organization returns, however. Form 8871, for example, is available for inspection online.

Form 4506-EZ A form that one files with the IRS to request some of the information contained on a tax return filed in the previous three years. The information is called the transcript of the tax return, and does not include information such as penalties assessed, payments made, or adjustments made by the IRS. One may request the copy be sent to him/her, or one may direct that it be sent to some other party.

Form 4506-T A form that one files with the IRS to request the information contained on a previously filed tax return without requesting the return itself. The information is called the transcript of the tax return. One may request the copy be sent to him/her, or one may direct that it be sent to some other party.

Form 4562 A form that one files with the IRS to claim a tax deduction for the depreciation or amortization of property one owns or to declare that property should be considered business property under Section 179 of the tax code. It also is used to explain the rules governing the tax treatment of the business or investment use of certain types of personal property.

Form 4563 A form that one files with the IRS to declare income earned in American Samoa that may be excluded from one's gross income for tax purposes. One is eligible to file this form if one lives in American Samoa and has earned the relevant income there. The form is used to calculate the amount of income that may be excluded.

Form 4626 A form that a corporation files with the IRS to compute the alternative minimum tax that the corporation owes. A company must file Form 4626 if it is not a small company (since small companies are exempt from alternative minimum taxes), if its profit before the net operating loss deduction exceeds $40,000 (or some other stated amount), and/or if it claimed certain, stated tax credits.

Form 4669 A form that one files with the IRS to declare any payment received on which income taxes, FICA taxes, or other taxes were not withheld. The form includes spaces to list the amount of the payment, as well as the names of the payer and payee. The form declares that all taxes were paid on the payment.

Form 4670 A form that a payer files with the IRS to apply for relief from paying withholding taxes on a payment made to a payee. In order to file Form 4670, the payer must certify that the payee has paid all appropriate taxes.

Form 4684 A form that one files with the IRS to report losses from theft or casualty. With a few exceptions, these losses are tax deductible, provided that they do not come simply from misplaced property and that proper insurance claims are filed.

Form 4685 A form one files with the IRS to report losses (or gains) from theft or destruction of property. These losses may be tax deductible.

Form 4720 A form that a tax-exempt charitable organization files with the IRS to calculate and pay taxes on certain activities and investments that fall outside the organization's charitable purpose and that may result in loss of 501(c)3 status. For example, it is used to pay taxes on excess or unauthorized lobbying activities.

Form 4768 A form that one files with the IRS in order to ask for a six-month extension of time to file Form 706, which is the estate tax return, and other forms in the 706 series. The first extension is granted automatically. The form may also be used to apply for additional extensions, though these are granted on a discretionary basis.

Form 4797 A form one files with the IRS to report the profits (or losses) from the sale or exchange of an asset. For example, if a company sells the equipment from one of its factories, it reports the results of the sale on Form 4797.

Form 4810 A form that one files with the IRS to request quick assessment of taxes. On the form, one lists the other forms filed for which the quick assessment is requested. Form 4810 may not be filed before one has filed these other forms.

Form 4835 A form that the owner of agricultural real estate files with the IRS to report income from rent of the land based upon crops grown or livestock tended. This income is taxable but is not subject to the self-employment tax. The owner of the real estate files Form 4835 only if he/she owns (or leases) the land but leased it to a tenant and did not participate in actual farming or ranching.

Form 4852 A form that one files with the IRS to report income if one did not receive (or incorrectly received) Form W-2, Form W-2c, or Form 1099-R. Before filing this form, one must make a serious effort to obtain the relevant forms.

Form 4868 A form that one files with the IRS to apply for a six-month extension to file Form 1040 or any other form in the 1040 family. The extension is granted automatically the first time it is requested. The extension lasts for four months if the citizen or resident lives outside the United States.

Form 4876-A A form that a corporation files with the IRS to be treated as an interest charge domestic international sales corporation (a type of exporter) for tax purposes. These corporations are entitled to substantial tax savings.

Form 4913 A flyer published by the IRS outlining various ways that one can retrieve tax information relevant to victims of the 2010 Gulf of Mexico oil spill. One can retrieve this information online, over the phone, through the mail, or at designated locations.

Form 4952 A form one files with the IRS to calculate the interest one spends on investments each year. One may deduct this interest from his/her income for tax purposes, provided that it does not exceed his/her net investment income.

Form 4970 A form that one files with the IRS to calculate and pay the tax owed on accumulation distributions from certain trusts based in the United States.

Form 4972 A form that one files with the IRS to calculate and pay the tax owed on lump-sum distributions from qualified retirement plans. Filing this form may result in paying lower taxes on the distribution than one would if it were taxed as ordinary income.

Form 4977 A form that one files with the IRS to report weekly withholding tax liability (which is calculated on Form 1042) and quarterly taxes on unemployment benefits (which are calculated on Form 940).

Form 4996 A form that one files with the IRS to accompany electronic or magnetic transfers of tax returns on wages or withholding. For example, if one transmits several Forms 940 to the IRS electronically, Form 4996 is used to accompany the transmission.

Form 5 A form that an executive or other insider must file with the SEC reporting and disclosing all previously undisclosed, legal insider trading that he/she conducted over the previous fiscal year. Form 5 is especially used for small insider trading transactions that are not required to be disclosed under Form 4. Form 5 exists to promote transparency in the market.

Form 5074 A form that one files with the IRS to report income earned in Guam or the Northern Mariana Islands. The IRS uses this form to calculate taxes owed to Guam and the Northern Mariana Islands, respectively. Residents of Guam and the Northern Mariana Islands are not required to file this form. Rather, it is for non-residents who earn income in either of the two places.

Form 5129 A form that one files with the IRS in which the filer answers questions about his/her marital status, number of dependents, and exemptions. This information is used to determine a taxpayer's filing status.

Form 5213 A form that an individual, trust, partnership, or corporation files with the IRS to ask the IRS to postpone determination of whether the filer engages in an activity to earn a profit. Most activities are assumed to be for profit if a profit results. However, if there is no profit, the IRS may, under some circumstances, determine that the activity is not for profit, which would limit the tax deductions for which the filer is eligible.

Form 5227 An information return that a split-interest trust files with the IRS to report its activities. It reports contributions and distributions that may affect the deductions or tax liabilities of those making the contributions or receiving the distributions. It is also used to determine if the split-interest trust is subject to any excise taxes.

Form 5300 An application filed with the IRS requesting a determination of whether an employee benefit plan qualifies as a defined benefit or defined contribution plan for tax purposes. It is also used to request the determination of the tax status of any trust related to an employee benefit plan.

Form 5300 (Schedule Q) A form filed with the IRS along with Form 5300 to ask the IRS to consider coverage, minimum participation, and non-discrimination in an employee benefit plan as it determines whether the plan is a defined benefit or defined contribution plan for tax purposes.

Form 5304-SIMPLE A model form published by the IRS that is used to set up the terms of a SIMPLE IRA plan. An employer uses a separate Form 5304-SIMPLE for each employee. It is kept for the employer's own records. It is not filed with the IRS.

Form 5305 A model form published by the IRS that is used to set up the terms of a traditional IRA trust plan. An employer files Form 5305 with the bank or other financial institution that serves as trustee for the IRA. It is not filed with the IRS.

Form 5305-A A model form published by the IRS that is used to set up the terms of a traditional IRA custodial plan. An employer files Form 5305-A with the bank or other financial institution that serves as custodian for the IRA. It is not filed with the IRS.

Form 5305-A-SEP A model form published by the IRS that is used to set up the terms of a salary reduction SEP plan, which is an SEP plan in which an employer withholds a portion of the employee's salary and deposits it into the plan. An employer uses a separate Form 5304-A-SEP for each employee. It is kept for the employer's own records. It is not filed with the IRS.

Form 5305-B A model form published by the IRS that is used to set up the terms of a health savings account trust. The form is filed with the bank, insurance company, or other trustee for the HSA. It is not filed with the IRS.

Form 5305-C A model form published by the IRS that is used to set up the terms of a health savings custodial account. The form is filed with the bank, insurance company, or other custodian of the HSA. It is not filed with the IRS.

Form 5305-E A model form published by the IRS that is used to set up the terms of a Coverdell education savings account trust. The form is filed with the bank, savings and loan, or other trustee for the Coverdell ESA. It is not filed with the IRS.

Form 5305-EA A model form published by the IRS that is used to set up the terms of a Coverdell education savings custodial account. The form is filed with the bank, savings and loan, or other custodian for the Coverdell ESA. It is not filed with the IRS.

Form 5305-R A model form published by the IRS that is used to set up the terms of a Roth IRA trust. The form is filed with the bank, savings and loan, or other trustee for the Roth IRA. It is not filed with the IRS.

Form 5305-RA A model form published by the IRS that is used to set up the terms of a Roth individual retirement custodial account. The form is filed with the bank, savings and loan, or other custodian for the Roth IRA. It is not filed with the IRS.

Form 5305-RB A model form published by the IRS that is used to set up the terms of a Roth IRA annuity. The form is a contract between the issuer of the annuity and the annuitant. It is not filed with the IRS.

Form 5305-S A model form published by the IRS that is used to set up the terms of a SIMPLE IRA trust. The form is filed with the bank, savings and loan, or other trustee for the SIMPLE IRA. It is not filed with the IRS.

Form 5305-SA A model form published by the IRS that is used to set up the terms of a SIMPLE individual retirement custodial account. The form is filed with the bank, savings and loan, or other custodian for the SIMPLE IRA. It is not filed with the IRS.

Form 5305-SEP A model form published by the IRS that is used to set up the terms of an SEP plan. An employer uses a separate Form 5305-SEP for each employee. It is kept for the employer's own records. It is not filed with the IRS.

Form 5305-SIMPLE A model form published by the IRS that is used to set up the terms of a SIMPLE plan. An employer uses a separate Form 5305-SIMPLE for each employee. It is kept for the employer's own records. It is not filed with the IRS.

Form 5306 A form an employer files with the IRS requesting determination that an individual retirement account meets the qualifications for deductibility of contributions (or distributions) and other special tax benefits.

Form 5306-A A form an employer files with the IRS requesting determination that an SEP or SIMPLE IRA meets the qualifications for deductibility of contributions (or distributions) and other special tax benefits.

Form 5307 An application filed with the IRS requesting a determination of whether a master and prototype or volume submitter plan qualifies as a defined benefit or defined contribution plan for tax purposes. It is also used to request the determination of the tax status of any trust related to an M&S or VS plan.

Form 5309 A form that a company files with the IRS requesting a determination letter stating the tax status of an employee stock ownership plan. It is filed along with Form 5300.

Form 5310 A form that a company files with the IRS requesting a determination letter stating the tax status of a pension, profit-sharing, or deferred compensation plan upon the cancelation of the plan.

Form 5310-A A form that a company files with the IRS to declare the merger, consolidation, transfer of assets or spin-off of a pension, profit-sharing or deferred compensation plan. It is also used if the plan is to be treated as a qualified separate line of business.

Form 5316 A form that a retirement plan or other trust files with the IRS to request a treatment pooled trust, which is a trust managed by a non-profit organization in which each beneficiary maintains a separate account.

Form 5329 A form that one files with the IRS to report excise taxes related to early or otherwise taxable distributions from an IRA, education savings account, health savings account, or similar structures.

Form 5330 A form that one files with the IRS to report excise taxes assessed for various types of inaccurate filings related to employee benefit plans. For example, a company may have to file Form 5330 if it deducted non-deductible contributions or used an impermissible vehicle as a tax shelter.

Form 5405 A form that one filed with the IRS to claim a tax credit for purchasing one's first home (or one's first home in a number of years) during 2011. For first-time buyers, the credit was worth 10% of the value of the home or $8,000, whichever was less.

Form 5434 A form that one files with the IRS in order to enroll as an IRS-recognized actuary. A filer must declare information like experience in the field and other qualifications.

Form 5434-A A form that one files with the IRS in order to renew enrollment as an IRS-recognized actuary. A filer must declare information like details about his/her continuing education and whether or not he/she has been accused of professional misconduct.

Form 5452 A form that a corporation files with the IRS to report distributions other than dividends to shareholders. An example of a non-dividend distribution is a return of capital. These distributions are sometimes not taxable.

Form 5471 A form that an individual files with the IRS if he/she is a director, officer, or major shareholder in a foreign corporation. The form reports information on the filer as well as potentially taxable transactions between the filer and the company.

Form 5471 (Schedule J) A form that one files with the IRS along with Form 5471 to report the accumulated earnings of a controlled foreign corporation. This is used if the filer is a director, officer, or major shareholder in a foreign corporation.

Form 5471 (Schedule M) A form that one files with the IRS along with Form 5471 to report transactions between a controlled foreign corporation and the filer or a company in which the filer has a substantial interest. This is used if the filer is a director, officer, or major shareholder in the foreign corporation.

Form 5471 (Schedule O) A form that one files with the IRS along with Form 5471 to report the organization or reorganization of a foreign corporation, or the purchase/sale of its stock. This is used if the filer is a director, officer, or major shareholder in the foreign corporation.

Form 5472 A form that an American corporation files with the IRS if it is at least 25% owned by non-U.S. interests. The form reports information on the non-U.S. shareholders as well as potentially taxable transactions between these shareholders and the company.

Form 5495 A form that one files with IRS to request an exemption from the income tax, gift tax, and/or estate tax otherwise owed by a deceased person or his/her estate. The executor of the decedent's estate may file Form 5495.

Form 5498 A form that one files with the IRS to report contribution and other information on an individual retirement account. A company managing IRAs must report contributions, rollovers, traditional to Roth IRA conversions, account closures, and required minimum distributions on each IRA under management. However, they are not required to report the individual investments that each IRA makes.

Form 5498-ESA A form that an education savings account files with the IRS for each plan participant declaring information like the amount contributed and the amount rolled over in a year. This information is used to help plan participants file their tax returns.

Form 5498-SA A form that one files with the IRS to report contributions made to and other information about a qualified medical savings plan. For example, the fiduciary of a health savings account files Form 5498-SA to report contributions to the account.

Form 5500 A form a plan administrator files with the IRS to report information on the retirement plans offered to employees. This form is filed in order to ensure compliance with the Employee Retirement Income Security Act.

Form 5500-EZ A form that a pension fund or other retirement plan files with the IRS for annual reporting purposes. In order to be eligible to file Form 5500-EZ, the pension or plan must have one and only one participant (including a spouse) or be a foreign plan required to report to the IRS.

Form 5500-SF A form that a small pension fund or similar small retirement plan files with the IRS for annual reporting purposes. In order to be eligible to file Form 5500-SF, a pension or plan must have fewer than 100 participants, be held by one employer, hold no securities in that employer's company, and have independently audited books. This form is filed electronically.

Form 5558 A form that one files with the IRS to request an extension of time for filing various forms related to employee retirement plans. The forms covered by Form 5558 are Form 5500, Form 5500-SF, Form 5500-EZ, Form 8955-SSA, and Form 5330.

Form 5578 A form that a private school files with the IRS to declare that it does not discriminate in hiring or student selection on basis of race. A private school must file this form annually if it is exempt from federal taxation.

Form 56 A form one files with the IRS to declare that a fiduciary relationship exists between the filer and an estate or trust. The form is relatively simple, requiring the name, address, and other pertinent information of the fiduciary agent. One also files Form 56 to announce the termination of the relationship. See also: Form 56-F.

Form 5695 A form that one files with the IRS to claim tax credits for energy efficient products used in a residence, especially one's home.

Form 56-F A form that a financial institution files with the IRS to declare that a fiduciary relationship exists between the filer and an estate or trust. The form is relatively simple, requiring the name, address, and other pertinent information of the fiduciary agent. The financial institution also files Form 56-F to announce the termination of the relationship. See also: Form 56.

Form 5713 A form that a corporation or individual files with the IRS to report operations in a country boycotting Israel. For example, a company may be required to file Form 5713 if it exports to Saudi Arabia. These operations do not automatically mean that a company loses tax benefits, but the operations must be declared anyway.

Form 5713 (Schedule A) A form that a corporation or individual files with the IRS to report purchases, sales, and payroll during what is called a "boycott operation," which in general is any operation inside a country conducting an international boycott. For example, an American oil company in Saudi Arabia must report its operations because Saudi Arabia boycotts Israel.

Form 5713 (Schedule B) A form that a corporation or individual files with the IRS to report taxes paid or tax benefits derived from what is called a "boycott operation," which in general is any operation inside a country conducting an international boycott. For example, an American oil company in Saudi Arabia must report its tax benefits because Saudi Arabia boycotts Israel.

Form 5713 (Schedule C) A form that a corporation or individual files with the IRS to calculate the loss of tax benefits during what is called a "boycott operation," which in general is any operation inside a country conducting an international boycott. For example, an American oil company in Saudi Arabia must report its loss of tax benefits because Saudi Arabia boycotts Israel.

Form 5735 A form that a corporation files with the IRS in order to claim a tax credit for contributing to the economic development of American Samoa. In order to qualify for the credit, the company must have had ongoing operations and derive most of its profits from trade in American Samoa.

Form 5754 A form filed with the IRS to claim gambling winnings, which are taxable.

Form 5768 A form that a 501(c)3 organization files with the IRS to claim (or revoke a claim to use) its right under the tax code to influence legislation. Ordinarily, 501(c)3 organizations are not permitted to try to influence legislation. However, if they file Form 5768 they will be permitted to do so without losing tax exempt status if they follow appropriate guidelines. An organization files this form to declare that it will start or stop trying to influence legislation.

Form 5884 A form that a company files with the IRS to claim a tax credit for the wages paid in the first two years of employment to a person belonging to a qualified group, such as an ex-felon, veteran, or SNAP recipient.

Form 5884-B A form that a company files with the IRS to claim a tax credit for previously unemployed employees who were hired between February and December 2010 and remained employed for the same company for 52 consecutive weeks. The credit was designed to find jobs for unemployed workers.

Form 5884-C A form that a tax-exempt organization files with the IRS to claim a tax credit for the wages paid to a veteran in the first two years of employment. Because these organizations ordinarily do not pay taxes, the credit is applied to the employer portion of Social Security taxes.

Form 6069 A form that a coal mining company files with the IRS to calculate the tax deduction permitted for its contributions to a black lung benefit trust. It is also used to calculate the excise tax owed on contributions over and above the allowed level.

Form 6088 A form that the trustee of a retirement plan files with the IRS upon termination of the plan to request a determination letter indicating that the plan qualified for favorable tax treatment upon its termination.

Form 6118 A form that a tax preparer or promoter files with the IRS to request a refund of penalties that he/she believes were incorrectly imposed. For example, if a preparer was required to pay a penalty for reckless conduct but disputes whether this conduct occurred, he/she uses Form 6118 to request a refund.

Form 6197 A form that a manufacturer or importer of automobiles files with the IRS to pay an excise tax on automobiles that do not meet specified standards for fuel efficiency. This tax is imposed on the sale, lease, or use of these automobiles.

Form 6198 A form one files with the IRS to claim profit or loss in the current year for capital put at risk in a previous year. A loss listed on Form 6198 may be tax deductible up to the amount of the capital put at risk originally.

Form 6251 A form that an individual files with the IRS to calculate how much alternative minimum tax he/she owes.

Form 6252 A form one files with the IRS to report income in the current year from an installment sale made in a previous year. For example, if one sells a truck in October for $1,000 and accepts $200 installments, one reports the installments received in January and thereafter on Form 6252.

Form 6317 (PR) A feedback form published by the IRS inviting trainees using Publication 678 (PR) to state how satisfied or unsatisfied they are with the course.

Form 637 A form one files with the IRS to register as a payer or beneficiary of an excise tax. Persons or companies who sell products on which excise taxes are filed may be required to file Form 637. For example, importers of alcohol and most biodiesel are two types of sellers who may have to file the form.

Form 6466 A form that one files with the IRS to declare that Form W-4 has been filed electronically. One may use Form 6466 for up to five employers. If one wishes to file for more employers, one uses Form 6467.

Form 6467 A form that one files with the IRS to declare that Form W-4 has been filed electronically. One may use Form 6467 as a continuation of Form 6466 if one has to declare more than five employers.

Form 6478 A form that a gas station or similar company files with the IRS in order to claim a tax credit for the use of ethanol and similar substances in gasoline. This reduces the amount the gas station (and therefore the consumer) must pay in excise taxes on gasoline.

Form 6497 An information return that a company files with the IRS to report tax exempt energy grants, as well as subsidized financing made for energy purposes. Any organization (generally a federal, state, or local government entity or an Indian tribe) that administers an energy grant or energy financing program must file this form.

Form 6559 A form that one files with the IRS to identify the sender of magnetic media files, especially for the transmission of Form W-2 data.

Form 656 A form one files with the IRS to request an offer in compromise, which is a program whereby a person or company owing delinquent taxes asks to settle the debt for less than the full amount owed. In order to file Form 656, the taxpayer must state that he/she will never be able to pay his/her taxes in full or show that there are other circumstances, such as age or disability, that will hinder payment. See also: Form 433.

Form 656-A A form one files with the IRS along with a Form 656 declaring that one has paid the appropriate application fee for an offer in compromise, which is a program whereby a person or company owing delinquent taxes asks to settle the debt for less than the full amount owed. If one claims not to owe an application fee (due to low income or other factors) and the IRS determines otherwise, the application for offer in compromise is denied automatically.

Form 656-B A form published by the IRS explaining how to file for an offer in compromise. It also contains Form 433-A and Form 433-B, which are used to actually file.

Form 656-L A form one files with the IRS declaring that the filer believes he/she does not owe the delinquent taxes, interest, and/or penalties that he/she is accused of owing. On the form, the filer explains the circumstances of his/her case and offers to pay a certain amount (the amount the filer believes he/she owes). A Form 656-L is used in an offer in compromise.

Form 656-PPV A form one files with the IRS to make a payment on an offer in compromise, which is a program whereby a person or company owing delinquent taxes asks the IRS to settle the debt for less than the full amount owed. One files a Form 656-PPV periodically if one has not opted for automatic withdrawals through a Form 433-D or some other means.

Form 6627 A form that some refineries, importers, and exporters file with the IRS to calculate the tax owed on the manufacture or use of petroleum or other ozone-depleting chemicals. This tax is levied in order to incentivize the development of environmentally-friendly energy.

Form 6729 A quality control sheet published by the IRS that is used to ensure that volunteer sites for VITA, TCE, and similar programs are operating according to IRS standards.

Form 6729-B A quality control sheet published by the IRS that is used to ensure that tax returns prepared under the SPEC program are filled out correctly.

Form 6729-C A quality control sheet published by the IRS that is used to ensure that tax returns prepared under the VITA, TCE, and similar programs are filled out correctly.

Form 673 A form one files with the IRS to claim that one is not subject to withholding tax under the foreign earned income exclusion. In general, an American employer must withhold from U.S. citizens working outside the United States, but the employee may claim an exemption to this if he/she does not believe his/her income earned overseas will exceed the threshold for U.S. taxation, as one generally does not pay taxes on foreign income below a certain level. Form 673 is one way to make this declaration, though there are other forms with which to do so.

Form 6744 A test administered by the IRS that a volunteer must pass before qualifying to prepare tax returns as part of the Volunteer Income Tax Assistance or Tax Counseling for the Elderly programs. The test presents various hypothetical scenarios; the volunteer must correctly assess the tax impact of these scenarios.

Form 6765 A form that a company files with the IRS to claim a tax credit for increasing its research and development operations. In general, commercial research conducted in the United States before commercial production begins qualifies for this credit.

Form 6781 In U.S. tax, a form used for reporting income relevant to calculating one's capital gains tax liability. The form deals with the taxation of open positions under Section 1256 of the U.S. Tax Code, namely, any regulated futures contract, any foreign currency contract, any non-equity option, any dealer equity option, and any dealer securities futures contract. Form 6781 directs the taxpayer to report any gains or losses from these contracts on the assumption that they were closed at market value on the last day of the tax year.

Form 7004 A form that one files with the IRS to request a five- or six-month extension to file tax returns for business income taxes and certain related taxes. While one must estimate and pay the tax owed, Form 7004 allows one extra time to calculate the actual tax.

Form 706 A tax return one files with the IRS to claim one's estate tax liability. On a Form 706, one lists the assets, liabilities, and exemptions of a deceased person. The executor of the decedent's estate has the capacity to file a Form 706. The value of an estate necessary for an estate tax to be imposed varies from year to year, but is always higher than $1 million.

Form 706-A A tax return that the heir of an estate files with the IRS if specially valued property that he/she inherited is sold or is no longer used in a permissible fashion. In such cases, the form indicates how much estate tax (if any) the heir owes on the sold property. The form must be filed even if no tax is owed.

Form 706-CD A form that a U.S. citizen or resident alien files with the IRS to declare an estate tax that was paid to a foreign government. One may receive a tax credit for foreign estate taxes, but must file this form in order to claim the credit.

Form 706-D A form that one files with the IRS to declare certain taxable events related to the business interests of the heir of an estate. When one files a Form 706 to declare an estate tax liability, one may be able to deduct for the portions of one's business owned by heirs. If the heir sells this interest, or some other taxable event occurs, one must file Form 706-D to declare any additional tax liability brought about by the loss of this deduction.

Form 706-GS(D) A form one files with the IRS to assess the tax liability due on a distribution from a generation-skipping trust. One is required to file this form if one receives any distribution from such a trust.

Form 706-GS(D-1) A form a trustee in a generation-skipping trust files with the IRS and delivers to a beneficiary declaring a distribution from that trust. This form may be used in filing a Form 706-GS(D), which declares the tax liability due on such a distribution.

Form 706-GS(T) A form one files with the IRS to assess the tax liability due on the termination of a generation-skipping trust. The trustee is required to file the form if the trust terminates under certain circumstances.

Form 706-NA A form one files with the IRS to compute the estate tax liability for non-resident persons who are not U.S. citizens. One must file a Form 706-NA if the gross value of the decedent's estate in the United States exceeds $60,000.

Form 706-QDT A form one files with the IRS to declare the estate tax liability for distributions from a qualified domestic trust or for the remaining value of the trust after the death of a second spouse.

Form 709 A form one files with the IRS to declare the gift tax liability on transfers exceeding a certain value, as well as that on some transfers involving a generation-skipping trust.

Form 712 A form one files with the IRS to state the value of a life insurance policy at the time of death of the policyholder or when it is transferred (as a gift) to another party. Form 712 is submitted along with forms used to calculate an estate tax or gift tax.

Form 720 A form a company files with the IRS on a quarterly basis to report its liability for federal excise taxes, especially those on gasoline and air travel. The return is due by the last day of April, July, October and January.

Form 720-CS A form that ship, barge, and pipeline owners must file with the IRS to report the liquid material (such as gasoline) that they transport from place to place. Form 720-CS helps the IRS keep track of the liquid materials subject to federal excise taxes. The form must be filed each month. See also: Form 720.

Form 720-TO A form that the owner of a terminal where certain liquid material (such as gasoline) is stored must file with the IRS to report the liquid material that has come into and gone out of the terminal. Form 720-TO helps the IRS to keep track of liquid materials subject to federal excise taxes. The form must be filed each month. See also: Form 720.

Form 720-X A form that a company files with the IRS to amend a previously filed Form 720. That is, Form 720-X corrects a mistake on a previous declaration of the liability for federal excise taxes.

Form 730 A tax return that one files with the IRS to declare the tax liability on bets and wagers. Companies that takes wagers and organizations that conduct lotteries are required to file Form 730 on a monthly basis.

Form 8023 A form that a corporation files with the IRS if it is purchased by another corporation and elects to have the purchase treated as a stock (as opposed to a cash or debt) transaction. This affects the tax treatment of the purchase.

Form 8027 A form that a restaurant or bar files with the IRS to report all tips reported by employees. All employees who receive $20 or more in tips per month must report tips to their employer, who in turn reports this information to the IRS.

Form 8027-T A form filed with the IRS to confirm the transmission by an employer of an employee's tip income. This form is used because tips are taxable but difficult to verify.

Form 8038 An information return that the issuer of a tax-exempt private activity bond files with the IRS. The information required on the return includes what the bond is used for (airport, dock, sewage facility, etc.) and the proceeds of the issue.

Form 8038-B A form that the issuer of certain taxable state or local bonds files with the IRS to receive tax credits or direct payments for issue. Under the American Recovery and Reinvestment Act, qualified bonds may be used to provide construction and similar jobs to Americans. These bond issuers receive credit or direct payment.

Form 8038-CP A form that the issuer of certain bonds files with the IRS to receive reimbursements for coupon payments. Under the American Recovery and Reinvestment Act and similar legislation, qualified bonds may be used to pay for certain environmentally sustainable projects, certain school construction projects, and other projects intended to provide construction and similar jobs to Americans. These bond issuers receive credit up to a certain level of coupon payments.

Form 8038-G An information return that the issuer of a government tax-exempt bond worth more than $100,000 files with the IRS. The information required on the return includes the issue price, what the bond is used for, and the maturity date.

Form 8038-GC An information return that the issuer of a government tax-exempt bond, installment sale, or lease worth less than $100,000 files with the IRS. The information required on the return includes the issue price and the function of the lease.

Form 8038-R A form that the issuer of a tax-exempt bond files with the IRS to request the refund of an overpayment of arbitrage profits from the investment of bond proceeds that the issuer had agreed to rebate to the U.S. Treasury. These rebates to the Treasury are necessary in order for state and local bonds to be tax-exempt. See also: Form 8038-T.

Form 8038-T A form that the issuer of a tax-exempt bond files with the IRS to rebate to the U.S. Treasury arbitrage profits from the investment of bond proceeds, and to make similar payments. Coupons on state and local bonds are not tax-exempt unless the issuer files this form.

Form 8038-TC A form that the issuer of a qualified bond files with the IRS in order to claim a tax credit for the coupons. For example, an issuer of a bond used to build a new school may be eligible to file this form.

Form 8050 A form that a corporation files to inform the IRS of the bank account and routing number to be used for the direct deposit of its corporate tax refund.

Form 8082 A form that one files with the IRS to declare that one wishes to treat an asset or income differently from how it was reported on Schedule K-1. One files this form if one is a partner in a partnership, a stockholder in an S-corporation, an owner of a foreign trust, or a residual interest holder in a REMIC.

Form 8160-T A form published by the IRS informing tax exempt organizations of the forms they may be able to file in lieu of Form 990. It states, for example, that some organizations may file the much simpler Form 990-N.

Form 8233 A form that a non-resident alien files with the IRS to claim exemption from withholding for certain personal services. For example, a foreign politician who makes a paid speaking engagement at a college in the United States may have to file Form 8233 to exempt himself from withholding.

Form 8274 A form that a church or other religious organization files with the IRS in order to exempt itself from payment of Social Security or Medicare taxes. A religious organization may file this form only if it has a theological or other religious objection to social safety net programs.

Form 8275 A form one files with the IRS in order to report inaccuracies previously declared on a tax return, except those made in violation of U.S. Treasury regulation. One uses this form in order to avoid penalties otherwise assessed on inaccurate returns. It is used by individuals and corporations.

Form 8275-R A form that one files with the IRS in order to report declarations made on a tax return in violation of U.S. Treasury regulation. One uses this form in order to avoid penalties otherwise assessed on inaccurate returns. It is used by individuals and corporations.

Form 8281 An information return that the issuer of an original issue discount bond files with the IRS. The form reports information like the issue date, the maturity date, and the interest rate.

Form 8282 A form that one files with the IRS providing information on the recipient of an item or other asset donated to charity. This information may affect whether the value of the item or asset is tax deductible. The form has spaces for the original recipient as well as any successor recipients.

Form 8283 A form that one files with the IRS to report non-cash contributions to charitable organizations, such a clothes or vehicles, if the combined value of these contributions exceeds $500. It is not used to determine the tax deduction for these contributions, though they are tax deductible.

Form 8283-V A form that one files with the IRS if one intends to claim a tax deduction for charitable contributions in excess of $10,000. One must pay a $500 filing fee to file Form 8283-V.

Form 8288 A tax return that one files with the IRS on matters related to the withholding of taxation from the proceeds of the sale of real estate in the United States in which the seller is a non-resident alien or other non-U.S. person. This ensures that taxes are paid on the sale.

Form 8288-A A form that one files with the IRS providing the information related to the withholding of taxation from the proceeds of the sale of real estate in the United States in which the seller is a non-resident alien or other non-U.S. person. The form requires information like the name of the seller and the name of the withholding agent.

Form 8288-B An application that one files with the IRS for a withholding certificate, which would reduce the withholding of taxation from the proceeds of the sale of real estate in the United States in which the seller is a non-resident alien or other non-U.S. person.

Form 8300 A form one files with the IRS to report cash payments in excess of $10,000 that one receives in the conduct of business. These payments are documented in order to discourage potential money laundering. Publication 1544 explains how to file Form 8300.

Form 8302 A form that one files to inform the IRS of the bank account and routing number to be used for the direct deposit of a tax refund in excess of $1 million.

Form 8308 A form that one files with the IRS to report the sale (or other transfer) of one's ownership interest in a partnership. The form requires one to state the names and other information of the seller (transferor) and the buyer (transferee). The form may affect the tax treatment of both the seller and the buyer.

Form 8316 A form that a non-resident alien of the United States files with the IRS to request the refund of Social Security tax withheld incorrectly.

Form 8328 A form that the issuer of a tax-exempt private activity bond files with the IRS to carry forward the excess volume cap it has at the end of a period of time. Once the decision to carry forward is made, it cannot be undone.

Form 8329 An information return that a lender files with the IRS each year to report mortgage credit certificates. A mortgage credit certificate is a security issued by a state or local government allowing holders to claim a tax credit on a portion of the interest they pay on their mortgages. This form keeps track of the total number and value of certificates that a lender applies to the mortgages it makes.

Form 8330 An information return that the issuer of a mortgage credit certificate files with the IRS each quarter. A mortgage credit certificate is a security issued by a state or local government allowing holders to claim a tax credit on a portion of the interest they pay on their mortgages. This form keeps track of the total number and value of certificates that an issuer has in circulation.

Form 8332 A form that a custodial parent files with the IRS in which the parent agrees not to claim the child tax credit for a child. This allows the non-custodial parent to take the credit. This form is also filed to revoke the previous agreement.

Form 8379 A form one files with the IRS to claim an overpayment of a back tax liability owed by his/her spouse. If the filer is judged to be an injured spouse, he or she may be entitled to a refund for his or her part of the overpayment.

Form 8396 A form that one files with the IRS to report a tax credit for holding a qualified mortgage credit certificate issued by a municipal agency or government.

Form 8404 A form that a stockholder in an interest charge domestic international sales corporation files with the IRS to report interest owed on his/her tax liability, which, per the structure of an IC-DISC, is deferred.

Form 843 A form one files with the IRS to request a refund for certain overpaid taxes. For example, if one pays more in taxes on an employee than one withheld from the employee's paycheck or if one overpays FICA taxes, one may use Form 843 to receive back the owed money.

Form 8453 A form that an individual files with the IRS to declare that his/her tax return was e-filed.

Form 8453-B A form that an electing large partnership files with the IRS to declare that it e-filed its tax return.

Form 8453-C A form that a U.S. corporation files with the IRS to declare that it e-filed its tax return.

Form 8453-EO A form that a tax-exempt organization files with the IRS to declare that it e-filed its information return.

Form 8453-EX A form that a payer of an excise tax files with the IRS to declare that its tax return was e-filed.

Form 8453-F A form that an estate or trust files with the IRS to declare that it e-filed its tax return.

Form 8453-I A form that a foreign corporation files with the IRS to declare that it e-filed its tax return.

Form 8453-PE A form that a partnership files with the IRS to declare that it e-filed its tax return.

Form 8453-S A form that an S-corporation files with the IRS to declare that it e-filed its tax return.

Form 8453-X A form that a political organization files with the IRS to declare that it e-filed its declaration of Section 527 status.

Form 8498 An application a person or organization files with the IRS to request permission to be a registered provider of continuing education on tax matters. The form also includes a request for a continuing education provider identification number.

Form 8508 A form that one files with the IRS to request a waiver from the requirement to file certain forms electronically. Forms covered by this filing are Form W-2, Form W-2G, Form 1042-S, Form 1097-BTC, Form 1098 series, Form 1099 series, Form 3921, Form 3922, Form 5498 series, and Form 8027.

Form 8546 A form that one files with the IRS to request the reimbursement for bank fees incurred due to a lost tax refund check, an incorrect tax levy, or similar reasons.

Form 8554 A form that one files with the IRS to renew his/her enrollment for the right to practice before the IRS. This form must be filed every three years, along with an application fee.

Form 8554-EP A form that an enrolled retirement plan agent files with the IRS to renew his/her enrollment. This form must be filed every three years, along with an application fee.

Form 8569 A form declaring one's geographic availability for a training program in various cities around the country. It is used by applicants for the Senior Executive Service Candidate Development Program, as well as by applicants for other executive training programs.

Form 8582 A form one files with the IRS to report passive activity losses. One may deduct passive activity losses from passive income for tax purposes, but not from other income.

Form 8824 A form one files with the IRS to report like-kind exchanges, which are exchanges of two assets of the same type, even if of different quality, that are used for a business for investment purposes. See also: Section 1031.

Form 8829 A form one uses to calculate allowable expenses for the business use of one's home. Form 8829 is used by persons who are self-employed at least part-time.

Form 886-H-AOC A form one files with the IRS to provide supporting documentation proving eligibility for the American Opportunity Credit, which is a tax credit offered to postsecondary students. One must provide canceled checks or other documentation in order to receive the credit.

Form 886-H-FTHBC A form filed with the IRS to provide supporting documentation proving eligibility for the first-time home buyer credit, which was a tax credit of up to $8,000 offered to persons who purchased homes before April 2010. One needed to provide both proof of purchase and proof of residency on the Form 886-H-FTHBC to receive the credit.

Form 8941 A form that a small business files with the IRS to claim the health care tax credit. This credit is a direct, dollar-for-dollar reduction of the company's tax liability up to a certain percentage of the premium it pays for employees' health insurance.

Form 907 A form one files with the IRS to extend the statute of limitations for filing a request for a refund of an overpaid tax. In general, one must file for a refund within three years of filing a tax return or within two years of the overpayment, whichever occurs later. If one needs more time to make this request, one must file a Form 907.

Form 911 A form one files to request help from the Taxpayer Advocate Service. The Taxpayer Advocate Service is a branch of the IRS that provides free assistance to individual and corporate taxpayers who are experiencing trouble with the IRS. If one is facing immediate IRS action, Form 911 enables one to start the process of receiving this assistance. The Taxpayer Advocate Service may be able to stop asset seizures and similar measures while a case is being processed.

Form 921 A form one files with the IRS to request an extension of the time necessary to file an income tax return due to the fact that real estate owned by the taxpayer is under contract to be sold but has not been sold yet. As the price of the sale may affect one's tax liability, Form 921 allows the taxpayer to wait for a certain period of time before filing taxes.

Form 921-A A form a corporation or partnership files with the IRS to request an extension of the time necessary to file an income tax return due to the fact that real estate owned by the corporation or partnership is under contract to be sold but has not been sold yet. As the price of the sale may affect one's tax liability, Form 921-A allows the taxpayer to wait for a certain period of time before filing taxes.

Form 921-I A form an investor in a corporation files with the IRS to request an extension of the time necessary to file an income tax return due to the fact that real estate owned by the corporation is under contract to be sold but has not been sold yet. As the price of the sale may affect the investor's tax liability, Form 921-I allows the taxpayer to wait for a certain period of time before filing taxes.

Form 921-P A form a limited liability company or partnership files with the IRS to request an extension of the time necessary to file an income tax return due to the fact that real estate owned by the company or partnership is under contract to be sold but

has not been sold yet. As the price of the sale may affect one's tax liability, Form 921-P allows the taxpayer to wait for a certain period of time before filing taxes.

Form 926 A form one files with the IRS to report the sale or other transfer of tangible or intangible property to a non-U.S. person, that is, a foreign person or corporation.

Form 940 A form a company files with the IRS to pay unemployment insurance taxes on its employees. Many employers file this form annually, though some are required to do so more frequently. See also: Federal Unemployment Tax Act.

Form 940 (Schedule A) A form a company files with the IRS if it paid unemployment insurance taxes on employees in more than one state. This form may reduce tax credits for employers.

Form 941 A form a company files with the IRS each quarter to declare income and FICA taxes on its employees. The form lists federal income tax, Social Security and Medicare withholdings paid by both the employees and the employer.

Form 941 (PR) A form a company in Puerto Rico files with the IRS each quarter to declare income and FICA taxes on its employees. The form lists federal income tax, Social Security and Medicare withholdings paid by both the employees and the employer.

Form 941 (Schedule B) A form a company files with the IRS to list the payroll tax liability for each day of a quarter. A company is required to file Form 941 if it is a semi-weekly depositor with more than $50,000 in payroll taxes during the lookback period or more than $100,000 on any day in the present or most recent calendar year.

Form 941 (Schedule D) A form a company files with the IRS if the payroll tax liabilities it files for its employees on Form 941 differ from what is reported on each employee's W-2 due to a merger or acquisition.

Form 941 (Schedule R) A form an accountant files with the IRS reporting all aggregate information for each Form 941 the accountant filed on behalf of a client. That is, each client is listed separately on Schedule R, and the accountant lists the total amount each client reports to the IRS.

Form 941-SS A form a company in American Samoa, Guam, Mariana Islands or the U.S. Virgin Islands files with the IRS each quarter to declare income and FICA taxes on their employees. The form lists federal income tax, Social Security and Medicare withholdings paid by both the employees and the employer.

Form 941-X A form a company files with the IRS to amend a previously filed Form 941, which is used to declare income and FICA taxes for employees.

Form 941-X (PR) A form a company in Puerto Rico files with the IRS to amend a previously filed Form 941 (PR), which is used to declare income and FICA taxes for employees.

Form 943 A form an agricultural employer files with the IRS each year to report income and FICA taxes it withholds from its employees. The form lists federal income tax, Social Security and Medicare withholdings paid during the course of the year.

Form 943 (PR) A form an agricultural employer in Puerto Rico files with the IRS each year to report income and FICA taxes it withholds from its employees. The form lists federal income tax, Social Security and Medicare withholdings paid during the course of the year.

Form 943-A A form some agricultural employers must file with the IRS to declare their payroll tax liabilities. The form is filed annually, but the tax liabilities are delineated by month. Agricultural employers must file if they deposit tax liabilities semiweekly or if their liability for any one month is greater than $100,000.

Form 943-A (PR) A form some agricultural employers in Puerto Rico must file with the IRS declaring their payroll tax liabilities. The form is filed annually, but the tax liabilities are delineated by month. Agricultural employers must file if they deposit tax liabilities semiweekly or if their liability for any one month is greater than $100,000.

Form 943-V A payment voucher an agricultural employer sends to the IRS along with income and FICA tax payments it withholds from its employees. See also: Form 943.

Form 943-X A form an agricultural employer files with the IRS to amend a previously filed Form 943, which is used to report income and FICA taxes the employer withholds from its employees.

Form 943-X (PR) A form an agricultural employer in Puerto Rico files with the IRS to amend a previously filed Form 943 (PR), which is used to report income and FICA taxes the employer withholds from its employees.

Form 944 A form a company files with the IRS each year to declare income and FICA taxes on its employees. The form lists federal income tax, Social Security and Medicare withholdings paid by both the employees and the employer. Form 944 is designed for small businesses that have low tax liabilities. As a result, it is filed once a year instead of once a quarter as some large businesses are required to do. See also: Form 941.

Form 944 (PR) A form a company in Puerto Rico files with the IRS each year to declare income and FICA taxes on its employees. The form lists federal income tax, Social Security and Medicare withholdings paid by both the employees and the employer. Form 944 (PR) is designed for small businesses that have low tax liabilities. As a result, it is filed once a year instead of once a quarter as some large businesses are required to do. See also: Form 941 (PR).

Form 944-SS A form companies in American Samoa, Guam, Northern Mariana Islands or the U.S. Virgin Islands file with the IRS each year to declare income and

FICA taxes on their employees. The form lists federal income tax, Social Security and Medicare withholdings paid by both the employees and the employer. Form 944-SS is designed for small businesses that have low tax liabilities. As a result, it is filed once a year instead of once a quarter as some large businesses are required to do.

Form 944-X A form a small company files with the IRS to amend a previously filed Form 944, which a small company uses to declare income and FICA taxes on its employees each year.

Form 944-X (PR) A form a small company in Puerto Rico files with the IRS to amend a previously filed Form 944 (PR), which small companies use to declare income and FICA taxes on their employees each year.

Form 945 A form a company files with the IRS to declare the taxes withheld on non-payroll payments made to an employee. For example, a company may file Form 945 to declare withholdings from an employee's pension distributions.

Form 945-A A form an employer must file with the IRS to declare tax liabilities on all non-payroll payments made to employees. The form is filed annually, but the tax liabilities are delineated by month. Employers must file if they deposit tax liabilities semiweekly or if their liability for any one month is greater than $100,000.

Form 945-V A voucher an employer sends to the IRS along with withholding tax payments from non-wage and non-salary payments it makes to employees. See also: Form 945.

Form 945-X A form a company files with the IRS to amend a previously filed Form 945, which is used to declare the taxes withheld on non-payroll payments made to an employee.

Form 952 A form a corporation files with the IRS to extend the deadline for assessing taxes on all proceeds of the liquidation of a subsidiary. The form may be filed only if the liquidation is completed within three years of the first receipt of proceeds.

Form 966 A form a corporation (or agricultural coop) must file with the IRS to declare its dissolution and/or liquidation of stock. Form 966 must be filed because liquidation may create a taxable event.

Form 970 A form a company files with the IRS to declare that the company is using the last in, first out accounting method for its inventory.

Form 972 A form a stockholder in a corporation files with the IRS to consent to have a dividend considered as part of the stockholder's own income for tax purposes, even though no dividend was paid. If the stockholder consents to such a dividend, the company may deduct the amount of the dividend from its own taxable income.

Form 973 A form a corporation files with the IRS to claim a tax deduction on a dividend it does not actually pay. That is, if a stockholder consents to have a dividend considered as part of the stockholder's own income for tax purposes, the corporation may claim a deduction for this dividend even though it is not paid.

Form 976 A form published by the IRS for a company to claim a deduction for the payment of a deficiency dividend. A deficiency dividend is a dividend a personal holding company, real estate investment trust, or regulated investment company pays after the IRS has determined that certain taxes are owed, but before these taxes are paid. These dividends may be tax deductible.

Form 982 A form one files with the IRS to reduce certain discharged debts from inclusion in one's gross income (and therefore potentially in one's taxable income). In general, a discharge of debt is included in gross income and therefore may be taxable. Form 982 is an application to reduce some of this inclusion.

Form 990 The tax return for a tax exempt organization in the United States. Charities, for example, must file Form 990 every year to maintain their legal nonprofit status.

Form 990 (Schedule D) A form that a non-profit organization files with the IRS to report financial information regarding its donor-advised funds, endowments, and similar structures. For example, a university may file the gains or losses from its endowment fund on Form 990 (Schedule D).

Form 990 (Schedule F) A form that a non-profit organization files with the IRS to report all activities it conducts outside the United States. The organization files Schedule F for any activity, whether or not it is related to its core purposes. For example, a charitable foundation may file Schedule F to report any grants it makes to overseas development groups.

Form 990 (Schedule H) A form that a non-profit organization files with the IRS to report financial activities regarding any hospitals the organization operates.

Form 990 (Schedule I) A form that a non-profit organization files with the IRS to disclose the grants the organization made over the course of the tax year. In addition to ensuring that the organization makes tax-free grants in accordance with the law, Schedule I is helpful to grant seekers as it indicates what organizations are most likely to be sympathetic.

Form 990 (Schedule I-1) A form that one attaches to Form 990 (Schedule I), which is used to disclose grants that the filer makes over the course of the tax year. Schedule I-1 is used if there is not enough room on Schedule I to state all grants made.

Form 990 (Schedule J) A form that a non-profit organization files with the IRS to report compensation that the organization pays to members of the board of directors, certain corporate officers, the persons with the highest salaries, and key employees.

Form 990 (Schedule J-1) A form that one attaches to Form 990 (Schedule J), which is used to report compensation that a non-profit organization pays to certain

employees. Schedule J-1 is used if there is not enough room on Schedule J to list employees for whom compensation must be disclosed.

Form 990 (Schedule J-2) A form that one attaches to the portion of Form 990 on which one must list board members, corporate officers, and key employees. One uses Schedule J-2 if there is not enough room on Form 990 to list all key employees.

Form 990 (Schedule K) A form that a non-profit organization files with the IRS to report outstanding liabilities from tax exempt bonds that the organization issues. Organizations with bond receipts under $100,000 and those that issued bonds before 2002 do not have to file Schedule K.

Form 990 (Schedule M) A form that a non-profit organization files with the IRS to report non-cash contributions it received in the tax year. For example, the organization uses Schedule M to report any securities or works of art that a donor bequeathed to it in his/her estate.

Form 990 (Schedule O) A form that a non-profit organization attaches to Form 990 or Form 990-EZ to answer questions that the filer did not have room to answer on the form. Alternately, Schedule O is used to provide any information that the filer believes to be relevant.

Form 990 (Schedule R) A form that a non-profit attaches to Form 990 to provide information on transactions with disregarded organizations and other organizations related to it.

Form 990 (Schedule R-1) A form that one attaches to Form 990 (Schedule R) to provide additional information if one does not have sufficient room to do so on Schedule R.

Form 990 or 990-EZ (Schedule A) A form that a non-profit organization attaches to Form 990 or Form 990-EZ stating the reason why the organization is a non-profit and the source of its revenue.

Form 990 or 990-EZ (Schedule C) A form that a 501(c)3 or 527 organization files with the IRS to report any money it spends on political activities.

Form 990 or 990-EZ (Schedule E) A form that a private school files with the IRS to report information on its racial non-discrimination policies.

Form 990 or 990-EZ (Schedule G) A form that a non-profit organization files with the IRS to report information on its fundraising activities, including those involving gaming. For example, if a school conducts a fundraising raffle, it reports this information on Schedule G.

Form 990 or 990-EZ (Schedule L) A form that a non-profit organization files with the IRS to report excess benefit transactions with disqualified persons.

Form 990 or 990-EZ (Schedule N) A form that a non-profit organization files with the IRS to report its dissolution or the sale or other disposition of more than 25% of its assets.

Form 990 or 990-EZ (Schedule N-1) A form that a non-profit organization attaches to Form 990 or 990-EZ (Schedule N) to report the sale or other disposition of more than 25% of its assets. Schedule N-1 is filed if there is not sufficient room on Schedule N to report all sales or dispositions.

Form 990, 990-EZ, 990-PF (Schedule B) A form that a non-profit organization files with the IRS to report the names and information of its primary contributors, whether these contributor make cash or non-cash donations.

Form 990-BL A form that a non-profit organization specializing in black lung benefits files with the IRS to report its income, expenses, and other financial information.

Form 990-EZ A form that some non-profit organizations file with the IRS to report their income, expenses, and other financial information. A non-profit is eligible to file Form 990-EZ in lieu of Form 990 if it takes in less than $200,000 in gross receipts and has less than $500,000 in total assets.

Form 990-PF A form that some private foundations file with the IRS to report the tax owed on their investment income, as well as to report grants and other charitable distributions made during the tax year.

Form 990-T A form that a tax exempt organization files with the IRS to report its unrelated business income and to figure the tax owed on that income.

Form 990-W A worksheet published by the IRS allowing a tax exempt organization to estimate the tax owed on unrelated business income.

Form F-6 A form that one must register with the SEC to offer an American Depository Receipt. An America Depository Receipt is security representing a foreign stock held by a financial institution that is traded in U.S. dollars. Form F-6 includes information such as the issuer of the receipt and what foreign stock it represents.

Form FR-1 A form that foreign dealers are required to file with FINRA when they are involved with new issues in which demand exceeds supply. Form FR-1 ensures that the foreign dealers do not attempt to sell shares of the new issue above the offering price or to certain prohibited organizations with which there may be a conflict of interest. Foreign dealers only fill out Form FR-1 with they buy new issues for resale. Less formally, it is called a blanket certification form.

Form N-1A A form used to register mutual funds and other investment companies with the SEC. The form gives information about the investment company, such as its investment strategy, organization, and potential risks associated with it. An investment company is required to fill out Form N-1A unless it is an insurance company associated with a mutual fund or if it is already registered under the Small Business Administration. This form exists to promote transparency in the market. See also: Prospectus.

Form N-2 A form that a closed-end investment company must file with the SEC in order to offer shares in itself to investors. The form details information that may be relevant to investors when deciding whether or not to buy shares of the investment company. It is also used in ensuring that it complies with the SEC's other regulations.

Form N-SAR A form that an investment company must file with the SEC twice per year detailing information on its fees, portfolio turnover rate, loads, and so forth.

Form PD 4632 A registration form one must file to be eligible to purchase U.S. Treasury bills (which have maturities under one year) at auction. In filling out the form, one must specify the specific maturity one wishes to buy. Forms may be filed at any Federal Reserve Bank or any of its branches.

Form PD 4633-1 A form that an investor must file with the Federal Reserve in order to roll over the investor's Treasury securities that are maturing into newly issued Treasury securities. Form PD 4633-1 must be filed at least 20 days before the currently held securities mature.

Form S-1 A document filed with the SEC explaining an initial public offering of securities. Form S-1 must contain a complete description of the security and the terms of the sale. It must also include applicable information about the issuer's financial situation and applicable risk factors. This is done to protect investors from fraud.

Form S-11 A registration form that real estate investment trusts and some other investment companies must file with the SEC before offering securities. Any company that owns real estate for investment purposes and intends to offer securities must file form S-11. The form contains information on the company and is intended to give potential investors as much information as possible before buying the securities.

Form S-18 A form the SEC formerly used to register issues of securities with less value, that is, with a value of $7.5 million or less. This form required less information than other security registration forms, but after complaints from some start-ups that it was still too complex, the SEC abolished Form S-18 and replaced it with Form SB-2.

Form S-2 A form the SEC formerly used to register issues of securities with less value, that is, with a value of $7.5 million or less. This form required less information than other security registration forms, but, after complaints from some start-ups that it was still too complex, the SEC abolished it and replaced it with Form SB-2.

Form S-6 The form that a unit investment trust must file with the SEC to register its securities.

Form S-8 A form that a company must file with the SEC when it issues stock or stock options to its own employees. The form details the terms of the issues; the S-8 is short compared to other mandatory filings.

Form T A form that one must fill out and file with FINRA for making a trade over-the-counter or on NASDAQ outside normal business hours. Form T helps maintain transparency and appropriate regulation in the market.

Form X17-A5 A form filed with the SEC by brokers and dealers regarding their financial position over a given year.

Formal Tax Legislation The process by which tax legislation becomes law in the United States. As with all federal laws, formal tax legislation requires the consent of both houses of Congress and the approval of the President (or a congressional override of a presidential veto by a two-thirds vote in both houses). However, unlike other laws, tax bills must be introduced in the House of Representatives. This is because the House is supposed to represent individual citizens, rather than whole states, as with the Senate. Formal tax legislation must work its way through the House Ways and Means Committee before its approval by the House; after this, the bill goes to the Senate Finance Committee and, if approved, moves to the whole Senate.

Formation A pattern on a chart indicating price movement in a security. See also: Technical analysis.

Formula Basis A way to make a new issue of common stock in which the SEC approves the determination of the initial price according to a certain, stated formula.

Formula Plan An investment strategy that calls for the buying and selling of securities according to a set formula. Both long-term and short-term formula plans exist, as well as high- and low-risk plans, but most rely heavily on previous market indicators. For this reason it is difficult to include a new issue of stock in a formula plan. Formula plans aim to eliminate personal opinions, emotions, and judgments from investing by never deviating from the formula.

Forrach An obsolete Irish unit of length approximately equivalent to 36 meters.

Fortune 500 A list compiled and published annually by Fortune magazine of the 500 largest publicly-traded and closely held companies in the United States. The Fortune 500 measures "largeness" by revenue minus excise taxes; that is, a company with larger revenue is listed higher on the Fortune 500, regardless of other measures such as profit margin. To be listed on the Fortune 500 is considered very prestigious.

Fortune 500 Company A company on the Fortune 500, a list compiled and published annually of the 500 largest publicly-traded and closely held companies in the United States. The Fortune 500 measures "largeness" by revenue minus excise taxes; that is, a company with larger revenue is listed higher on the Fortune 500, regardless of other measures such as profit margin. To be listed on the Fortune 500 is considered very prestigious.

Forward Averaging A former practice allowing certain pensioners in the United States to treat lump sum retirement plan withdrawals as if they occurred over a period of five or 10 years. This allowed qualifying retirees to pay only one-fifth or one-tenth of the taxes that they would otherwise have had to pay in a given year. Forward averaging was discontinued in 2000.

Forward Contract An agreement to buy or sell an asset at a certain date at a certain price. That is, Investor A may make a contract with Farmer B in which A agrees to buy a certain number of bushels of B's corn at $15 per bushel. This contract must be honored whether the price of corn goes to $1 or $100 per bushel. Forward contracts can help reduce volatility in certain markets, but they contain the risks inherent to all speculative investing. These contracts may be sold on the secondary market, but the person holding the contract at its end must take delivery of the underlying asset. Forward contracts are identical to futures contracts except that their provisions are not standardized. That is, forwards may be written with any provisions the parties desire. While this allows for greater flexibility, this makes the contracts less liquid on the secondary market and prevents them from being traded on an exchange.

Forward Cover A purchase of an asset, especially a commodity, in order to be able to deliver a short position on a forward contract. For example, if one sells a forward contract stating that one must deliver 100 barrels of oil and one only owns 90 barrels, one must make a forward cover of 10 barrels of oil to fulfill the contract.

Forward Currency Contract An agreement between two parties to exchange two currencies at a given exchange rate at some point in the future, usually 30, 60, or 90 days hence. A forward currency contract mitigates foreign exchange risk for the parties and is most useful when both parties have operations or some other interest in a country using a given currency. Forward currency contracts are over-the-counter contracts.

Forward Delivery The delivery of the underlying asset in a forward contract. In a forward delivery, the seller gives the buyer the asset and the buyer makes payment according to the terms of the contract.

Forward Differential The percentage difference between the spot price and the forward price of an asset. The forward differential is expressed in annualized terms, and may help the investor determine the general price trend of an asset.

Forward Discount In currency trading, a situation in which the forward price for the currency is less than the spot price. A forward discount occurs when the market expects the currency to depreciate over time. It is important to note, however, that this does not always actually happen.

Forward Earnings An estimation of a company's future earnings, usually for the coming quarter or year. Forward earnings are essentially what an analyst or a company thinks its profits will be, rather than what they actually are. Forward earnings are often used in conjunction with trailing earnings in making investment decisions. Trailing earnings are known, but are less relevant because they are in the past. On the other hand, forward earnings are relevant, but it is unknown how accurate their estimation will prove to be. See also: Expected return.

Forward Federal Funds The funds that the Federal Reserve will allow member banks to borrow to cover a deficiency in reserve requirements at some future date.

Forward Foreign Exchange Rate The agreed-upon exchange rate for a forward contract on a currency. When a forward contract is made, the parties agree to buy/sell the underlying currency at a certain point in the future at a certain exchange rate. The rate is negotiated directly between the parties, unlike a futures contract, which trades on an exchange. Partly because there is little secondary market for forward contracts, determining the forward foreign exchange rate is a zero-sum game: one party will gain on the contract and one will lose, depending on the movements of the relevant currencies between the formation of the contract and its maturity.

Forward Forward Contract An over-the-counter forward contract on a eurocurrency. In this contract, one party agrees to deliver to the other a certain amount of a eurocurrency at a certain price at some future date.

Forward Integration A business model whereby a company takes direct control of how its products are distributed. For example, a company may market its products directly to consumers rather than selling them to a retailer. Alternatively, forward integration may involve the company simply acquiring the retailer. See also: Backward integration.

Forward Interest Rate An interest rate to which a borrower and lender agree for a loan to be made in the future. According to the unbiased expectations hypothesis, forward interest rates predict spot interest rates at the time the loan is actually made, but many analysts dispute whether this is true.

Forward Market The trading of forward contracts between investors. Because forward contracts are not standardized and are traded over-the-counter, the forward market is relatively informal compared to the futures market.

Forward Outright A forward foreign exchange contract with an expiration date any time after the delivery date for the spot rate contract.

Forward Parity In currency trading, a theory stating that the forward exchange rate for a currency is an unbiased predictor of the future spot rate. That is, all other things being equal, forward parity states that exchange rate trades for some future dates will accurately predict what the exchange rate will be on that date in the future. See also: Forward discount.

Forward Price The agreed upon price of the underlying asset in a forward contract. When a forward contract is made, the parties agree to buy/sell the underlying at a certain point in the future at a certain price. The price is negotiated directly between the parties, unlike a futures contract, which trades on an exchange. Partly because there is little secondary market for forward contracts, determining the forward price is a zero-sum game: one party will gain on the contract and one will lose.

Forward Price to Earnings The price of a security per share at a given time divided by its projected earnings per share over the coming year. A forward P/E ratio is a way to help determine a security's stock valuation (that is, the fair value of a stock in a perfect market). It is also a measure of expected, but not realized, growth. See also: P/E, PEG.

Forward Pricing A practice in which a mutual fund determines the price of its shares based on the next net asset value following an order to buy or sell shares. The SEC requires mutual funds to use forward pricing to arrive at their share prices.

Forward Rate The interest rate or exchange rate on a forward contract with a certain expiration. Some analysts believe that forward rates accurately predict future spot rates, though others dispute this.

Forward Rate Agreement An agreement between two parties to exchange two currencies or interest rates at a given rate at some point in the future. A forward rate agreement mitigates foreign exchange risk or interest rate risk for the parties. It is most useful when both parties have operations or some other interest in a country using a given currency or investment vehicle with a floating interest rate. Forward rate agreements are over-the-counter contracts and are also called future rate agreements.

Forward Sale 1. The sale of a future loan in which the lender (seller) guarantees an investor a certain payment flow and interest rate. This is usually done to hedge against the investor's future foreign exchange risk and interest rate risk. **2.** In Islamic banking, the purchase of and payment for a specified good or service at a price usually lower than market value, with delivery deferred until a set future date. A bank buys a commodity before it is grown or manufactured, then may re-sell it to a third party in order to turn a profit on the transaction. This is used as a form of financing for farms and businesses, and is governed by a salam contract.

Forward Spread A price on a forward contract used to change the price on a spot contract, which in turn is used to calculate the price on a forward contract. The number of days until delivery, the spot exchange rate, and the interest rate differential are used to calculate the forward spread.

Forward Swap An agreement between two investors to swap assets, interest rates, or almost anything else on a set date in the future. A forward swap exists in order to provide investors with flexibility in accomplishing their investment goals; for example, the counterparties may wish to use a swap to hedge their risk, but are willing to accept the risk for the first year of an investment. A forward swap can consist of more than one swap: for example, the counterparties can agree to swap interest rates beginning in six months and then to swap different interest rates a year after that.

Forward Trade A transaction involving a forward contract.

Forward Triangular Merger A merger where an independent company combines with the subsidiary of another country. For example, a forward triangular merger may occur when Company A merges with Subsidiary B of Company C. In this forward triangular merger, Company A (or at least its resources and assets) becomes a subsidiary of Company C.

Forwarder A company that arranges transportation services for importers and exporters. A forwarder prepares the appropriate documents, contacts and arranges services from the companies that actually transport goods, and handles insurance matters. In other words, a forwarder handles the large number of details associated with international transportation so the importer and/or exporter do not have to do so themselves. It is also called a freight forwarder. See also: NVOCC.

Forward-Looking Statement A projection of a company's financial health for a certain period of time, such as a year. A forward-looking statement makes certain assumptions; for example, management may assume that sales will increase or decrease by a certain amount based on current trends. As a result, forward-looking statements are subject to revision, as reality may not match the assumptions. A forward-looking statement is nonetheless useful for making certain decisions about a company's future, such as whether or not to expand operations.

Fot A Norwegian unit of length approximately equivalent to 314 millimeters.

Foul Weather Fund A mutual fund designed to perform as well or better than the overall market when the overall market is performing poorly. For example, a foul weather fund may invest predominantly in securities with low volatility or in countercyclical stocks. Foul weather funds exist to reduce the risk to the investor during a downturn.

Found Money 1. Money that an individual or company possesses unawares. A mundane example of found money is $5 that one finds in the pocket of the jacket one had last worn several months ago. Banks maintain accounts with found money; for instance, an individual may have opened an account and forgotten it, or one may have inherited such an account from a relative. Likewise, governments keep tax refund checks that they are unable to deliver. **2.** An informal term for money one does not earn. It may apply to an inheritance, for example.

Four C's Informal for carat, cut, clarity, and color. The four Cs determine a diamond's value, with more carats, better cuts, greater clarity, and less color equating to a more expensive diamond.

Fourth Market The over-the-counter market for the sale of listed securities between institutional investors. For example, if a mutual fund sells stock in Google to a hedge fund without going through an exchange, the transaction is said to occur on the fourth market. These transactions occur in large blocks without the use of brokers, which save counterparties from significant fees.

Fourth Zimbabwean Dollar The former currency of Zimbabwe. The fourth dollar was introduced in February 2009, when the government of Zimbabwe dropped 12 zeros from the third dollar in response to hyperinflation. However, inflation continued, and, in April, the government permitted Zimbabweans to use any currency for transactions (which most people were doing anyway). This effectively ended the Zimbabwean dollar.

Foxing In scripophily, a situation in which brown spots appear on a stock or bond certificate due to too much bleach being used during the manufacturing process.

Fox-Trot Economy An economy characterized by two periods of rapid growth followed by two periods of slow growth. The term derives its name from the fox trot dance, which has two fast steps followed by two slow steps. See also: Business Cycle.

FQ 1. ISO 3166-1 alpha-2 code for French Southern and Antarctic Territory. **2.** ISO 3166-2 geocode for French Southern and Antarctic Territory. This was used as an international standard for shipping to the territory. In both cases, the code is obsolete.

FQHH ISO 3166-3 code for the French Southern and Antarctic Territories, which were re-designated separately as Antarctica and the French Southern Territories in 1979. ISO 3166-3 codes are used to indicate names of countries and territories that are no longer used.

FRA GOST 7.67 Latin three-letter geocode for France. The code is used for transactions to and from French bank accounts and for international shipping to France. As with all GOST 7.67 codes, it is used primarily in Cyrillic alphabets.

Fractal 1. In technical analysis, an indicator of the reversal of the previous trend. It is shown on a candlestick chart as a series of five candles, representing five trading days. A bullish fractal occurs when the lowest low of any trading day is represented by the middle candle, with two successively less low trading days on each side. This is seen as a buy signal. A bearish fractal occurs when the highest high of the five days is represented by the middle candle, with two successively less high trading days on each side. This is seen as a sell signal. **2.** Any whole made up of parts that are self-similar.

Fractal Dimension A description of how a discontinuous object fills the space it occupies. For example, a basketball is not smooth; rather it has lines and grooves all over it. Because it is not a perfect sphere, it requires fractal dimensions to explain how it exists.

Fractional Brownian Motion A random walk with some bias. That is, fractional Brownian motion means that a security's price moves seemingly randomly, but with some external event sending it in one direction or the other.

Fractional Coins Coins minted by a government that are denominated as fractions of the basic currency unit. For example, the U.S. dollar is divided into 100 cents. Fractional coins are any coins that represent less than one dollar. Thus, 50-cent pieces, quarters, dimes, nickels, and cents are all fractional coins.

Fractional Discretion Order An order to a broker to buy or sell a security at a certain price that allows the broker to accept a lower price if the desired price is unavailable. An example of a fractional discretion order is an order to buy 100 shares of Wal-Mart at $47 per share, with a 50-cent discretion. This means that if $47 is not available, the broker may buy Wal-Mart at the best available price up to $47.50.

Fractional Share Less than one share of a stock or a mutual fund. One almost always purchases fractional shares as part of a dividend reinvestment program. That is, when one automatically uses dividends to buy more shares, there may be extra cash left over but not enough to buy a full share. The company or fund sponsoring the dividend reinvestment program then allows the shareholder to buy a fractional share.

Fragmentation 1. A means of production in which different parts of the supply chain are located in different countries. Fragmentation occurs to reduce costs of production. For example, the least expensive materials may be in India and the cheapest factory workers in China, while the target retail customer is in the United States or Canada. Fragmentation can occur most easily when there is free trade, or at least low tariffs between all the countries on the supply chain. See also: Globalization. **2.** A situation in a decentralized market. This often renders investors unaware of the best price available for their trades, resulting in inefficiency in the market. Fragmentation has become less of a problem with the advent of electronic exchanges and other, similar products.

Framework Agreement A term for the first draft of the Baker Plan, which was proposed in order to provide for the self-determination of people living in Western Sahara, which is claimed by Morocco. The Framework Agreement was informally discussed in 2000, but it was never presented to the United Nations Security Council.

Franc The name for several current and former currencies. The original franc was issued by King John the Good of France in 1360. Various countries around France and most French colonies call their currencies the franc, though France itself discontinued the franc, replacing it with the euro in 1999.

Franchise An agreement in which an entrepreneur buys a license to use another business' products, brand, proprietary knowledge, and trade secrets. This allows the entrepreneur to start a business without building up his/her own brand or products. This is a common way to start a business, especially in highly competitive industries. An industry that utilizes franchises on a regular basis is fast food; because of stiff competition, it is generally more profitable for one who wishes to start a fast food restaurant to buy a franchise.

Franchise Tax In the United States, a state-level tax on a businesses and partnerships registered or chartered in that state. The franchise tax is paid annually and gives a business or partnership the right to continue to operate in that state. Franchise taxes are calculated differently in each state.

Franchisee One who owns a franchise. A franchisee usually pays a start-up fee and an annual licensing fee for the privilege to maintain the franchise.

Franchisor A company that sells the right to use its products to an individual or company. McDonald's is a prominent example of a franchisor. If one wishes to open a McDonald's franchise, everything from the food to the uniforms has already been determined by the corporation. McDonald's sells the right to use these to the franchisee. See also: Turnkey business.

Francis Mer A French businessman who served as Minister of Economy, Finance, and Industry from 2002 to 2004. He has also been involved in a number of industrial companies.

Francophone A person, company, or country for which French is the primary language. Because of the historical importance of French as an international language and of France as a world power, French is one of the most common languages in international commerce.

Frank P. Quattrone An investment banker who specializes in high tech companies. During the 1990s, he facilitated the initial public offerings for a number of dot-coms, including Amazon and Cisco. He was convicted of obstruction of justice in the early 2000s for asking for the deletion of e-mails possibly related to IPO spinning, but this was later overturned and Quattrone returned to investment banking. He was born in Philadelphia in 1955.

Franked Dividend In Australia, a dividend issued with a tax credit attached to it. Franked dividends exist in order to avoid double taxation of dividends. The amount of the tax credit depends upon the issuer's tax rate and the amount of the dividend. See also: Franked Income.

Franked Income In the United Kingdom, a dividend issued with a tax credit attached to it. Franked income exists in order to avoid double taxation of dividends. The amount of the tax credit depends upon the issuer's tax rate and the amount of the dividend. See also: Franked Dividend.

Frankfurt Stock Exchange One of the oldest and most prominent stock exchanges in the world. Tracing its origins to the ninth century, the Frankfurt Stock Exchange was one of the first exchanges to trade in currencies as early as the late 16th century. Today, a sizable percentage of European trading and upwards of 90% of German trading occurs on the Frankfurt Stock Exchange. It is owned and operated by Deutsche Borse.

Franklin Half Dollar A silver coin minted by the United States between 1948 and 1963. It was worth 1/2 of one dollar. It featured a portrait of Benjamin Franklin on the obverse.

Fraud Any attempt to deceive another for financial gain. A clear example of fraud is selling a new issue that does not really exist. That is, the company can collect money from investors and, rather than use it to finance operations, pocket the money and do nothing. There are a number of types of fraud. Common types include forgery of documents, false claims in insurance, and filing bankruptcy to avoid debt rather than because of financial hardship.

Fraud Enforcement and Recovery Act of 2009 Legislation in the United States that allocated more money to various inspection divisions of the federal government with the intention of improving fraud investigations. It also included mortgage lenders for the first time in the definition of financial institution, enabling the government to investigate them for fraud as well. The act was adopted in response to the sub-prime mortgage crisis, which had led to the global financial crisis that began in 2008.

Fraudulent Conveyance The transfer of property to another party in order to defraud a creditor. For example, if a person owes the bank for a loan for $15,000, the person may give or sell $15,000 worth of property to a relative, often while still maintaining use of the property, in order to prevent the bank from being repaid. Legally, fraudulent conveyance requires the intention to defraud a creditor.

Frazione In Italy and San Marino, a political subdivision approximately equivalent to a village or small town.

Freddie Mac Federal Home Loan Mortgage Corporation (FHLMC). A publicly-traded company chartered by the U.S. Congress to guarantee mortgages granted to low- or middle-income households. In order to do this, it buys mortgages and repackages them, selling them as mortgage-backed securities. It also maintains its own portfolio of mortgage-backed securities. It was established in 1970 to provide competition for Fannie Mae, which provides the same services and also had an implicit guarantee of federal backing. With the collapse of the housing bubble, Freddie Mac was placed in federal receivership in 2008 as a result of overexposure to this market. See also: Community Reinvestment Act, Credit Crunch.

Frederick W. Smith An American businessman. In 1971, he founded Federal Express, the first overnight delivery service in the world. He started the company with several million dollars in inheritance and much more money in venture capital. He served as CEO for the first 40 years of FedEx's history. Smith was born in 1944.

Free Without cost. Free goods and services usually come with some strings attached. For example, one may receive a free item with an order to buy another item. Some dispute whether such bonuses are really free. See also: Sweetener.

Free Alongside Ship In maritime, international commerce, an agreement between a buyer (importer) and a seller (exporter) in which the seller is responsible for the transportation and risk of the good until it is within reach of the ship's crane, at which point the buyer assumes responsibility for both. That is, the seller does not bear the expense or risk of actually loading the good onto the ship. The buyer is responsible for clearing the good through customs in both the home country and the country of delivery.

Free and Clear Describing property, especially real estate, that one owns with no liens, mortgages, or other encumbrances upon it. Free and clear property has no competing claims on it.

Free Asset Ratio A measure of an insurance company's ability to expand its services. It is calculated as the total value of its assets over and above the value of its assets that are used to collateralize individual policies.

Free Box An area in a brokerage where security certificates are stored, especially when the securities are completely owned by clients and are not being used as collateral on a margin account. See also: Safety Deposit Box.

Free Carrier In international commerce, an agreement between a seller and a buyer indicating that the seller has fulfilled his/her obligation to deliver a good when he/she has transferred it to the port, airport, or other place from which it will be transported. All cost and risk transfers to the buyer when the good is delivered to this agreed-upon place. The buyer designates the place to which the seller must deliver the good. See also: United Nations Convention on Contracts for the International Sale of Goods, Incoterm.

Free Cash Flow A measure of a company's ability to generate the cash flow necessary to maintain operations. There is more than one way to calculate free cash flow, but perhaps the simplest is to subtract a company's capital expenditures from its cash flow from operations. Some analysts believe that free cash flow is more important than other measures of financial health because it measures how much cash a company has and can make. This differs from other measures, which are sometimes accused of using both legitimate and illegitimate forms of accounting to make a company look healthier than it really is.

Free Cash Flow for the Firm A measure of a firm's cash on hand. It is calculated by taking the firm's operating cash flow and subtracting expenses, taxes, and changes to net working capital and investments. It is a way of calculating profit, among many others, to determine a company's financial health. A positive FCFF indicates that the company has raised more than enough revenue to cover its costs, while a negative FCFF indicates the opposite.

Free Cash Flow per Share A measure of a publicly-traded company's cash on hand, calculated by dividing the company's free cash flow by the number of shares outstanding. Free cash flow per share helps one determine a company's ability to service debt, pay dividends, and perform other transactions. A high free cash flow per share, coupled with a low share price, indicates that the company likely has strong earnings and that the share price will soon rise.

Free Cash Flow to Equity The cash that a company has on hand after all debt service and expenses have been paid and reinvestment has been made. The free cash flow to equity is calculated thusly: FCFE = Net income + newly borrowed debt - capital expenditures - change in net working capital - debt service. FCFE is a measure of a company's value and is considered an alternative to the dividend discount model.

Free Cell A slang term for the empty cubicle formerly used by an employee who has been fired.

Free Credit Balance The cash in a brokerage account to which the account holder may receive at any time or use to buy more securities. The free credit balance usually comes from dividends or coupon payments. The account holder may elect to receive the free credit balance each month or may direct the brokerage to make certain investments with it.

Free Delivery An agreement between a buyer and a seller of a security in which the seller makes delivery on the security even if full payment has not been made. This obviously exposes the seller to the risk that the buyer will not pay.

Free Entry A situation in which there are no barriers to entry. That is, any seller wishing to bring a product to market may do so with little or no trouble. While free entry is rare in practice, a market is more efficient if there are few barriers to entry because it leaves open the possibility that new competition with lower prices or better products may arrive at any time.

Free Float 1. See: Floating currency. 2. See: Floating shares.

Free Good 1. In economics, a good that is not scarce. That is, a free good is available to as many people as could ever want it in whatever quantity they want it. A major example is air. A free good is not subject to the law of supply and demand. 2. A good not subject to a tariff.

Free In and Out In shipping, an agreement between the charterer (the party that hires a vessel) and the vessel's operator in which the charterer is responsible for the expense of both loading and unloading cargo from the vessel. That is, under the agreement, loading and unloading cargo is free from the purview of the vessel's operator.

Free Indices A series of indices developed by Morgan Stanley tracking securities that trade in various countries; the indices are weighted for market capitalization and the ability for foreigners to invest in them. For example, a free index may have a market capitalization of $1 billion, but if the laws of the countries in which the securities trade only allow up to 25% foreign ownership, the free index lists a market capitalization of $250 million. A prominent free index is the emerging markets free index. See also: BRIC.

Free into Wagon In transportation, an agreement between the charterer (the party that hires a vessel) and a train's operator in which the charterer is responsible for the expense of loading and unloading cargo from the vessel. That is, under the agreement, loading cargo is free from the purview of the train's operator.

Free Market A system of economics that minimizes government intervention and maximizes the role of the market. According to the theory of the free market, rational economic actors acting in their own self interest deal with information and price goods and services the most efficiently. Government regulations, trade barriers, and labor laws are generally thought to distort the market. Proponents of the free market argue that it provides the most opportunities for both consumers and producers by creating more jobs and allowing competition to decide what businesses are successful. Critics maintain that an unfettered free market concentrates wealth in the hands of a few, which is unsustainable in the long term. In practice, no country or jurisdiction has a completely free market. See also: Deregulation, Classical economics, Keynesian economics, Marxism, Monetarism, Chicago School, Austrian School.

Free Marketeer A person who believes in the system of economics that minimizes government intervention and maximizes the role of the market. A free marketeer believes that rational economic actors acting in their own self interest deal with information and price goods and services more efficiently than individuals acting under any other system. Free marketers generally believe that government regulations, trade barriers and labor laws distort the market. They argue that the market provides the most opportunities for both consumers and producers by creating more jobs and allowing competition to determine which businesses are successful.

Free of Particular Average A provision in maritime transport insurance stating that the insurer is not responsible for losses up to a certain percentage of the value of the covered products. The specific percentage varies according to the insurance agreement. Free of particular average provisions normally occur if the covered products are likely to sustain minor losses in transport. This allows the insurer to only be liable for catastrophic losses resulting from transport; for example, the insurer will be liable if the ship sinks or all the products catch fire. It will not be liable if some of the products break in transit, up to a certain percentage of the total value.

Free On Board In maritime international commerce, an agreement between a seller and a buyer indicating that the seller has fulfilled his/her obligation to deliver a good when he/she has transferred it to the ship on which it will be transported. All cost and risk transfers to the buyer when the good crosses the ship's rail. The buyer designates the ship onto which the seller must deliver the good. See also: United Nations Convention on Contracts for the International Sale of Goods, Incoterm.

Free Port A port where ships can dock and unload goods without paying tariffs or other fees on those goods. The goods can be held duty-free at the free port for a certain period of time, though generally they must be re-exported at the end of the period. Free ports may be used to make final improvements on unfinished goods.

Free Reserves Bank reserves over and above a bank's reserve requirements, less the amount it has borrowed from the Federal Reserve. That is, free reserves are extra cash a bank keeps in liquid assets (that is, what it does not loan out) beyond its legal requirement, minus what it must repay.

Free Rider An investor whose investment decisions mimic those of another larger investor or firm. A free rider effectively places his/her hope in the larger investor to make profitable decisions. This is, of course, risky for the free rider because he/she does little to no research on his/her own, but this saves the expense of doing so. See also: Free Rider Problem.

Free Right of Exchange The right of an owner of a security to give it away or trade it for another security without any charges or fees. The free right of exchange differs from a sale in that money does not change hands. As a result, the transaction is exempt from fees on a security exchange.

Free Shit A highly derogatory term for social welfare policies. The term is used almost exclusively by the opponents of these policies. Examples of so-called free shit include food stamps, national health services, and housing subsidies.

Free Stock A stock a person may sell, short sell, use as collateral on a loan, or otherwise use without restriction. Free stock either was not bought with borrowed funds or has been paid in full.

Free Supply The amount of a commodity or other asset available for trade on an exchange. The free supply may have a significant effect on the liquidity of an investment. For example, a large free supply indicates a very liquid commodity or asset that may be easily traded, while a small free supply indicates the opposite.

Free to Trade In equities, describing a trader on an exchange who is not subject to any restrictions on his/her actions. A trader who is free to trade may make and solicit offers at will.

Free Trade The state in which there are few or no tariffs or other trade barriers discouraging international trade. For example, a country with a free trade policy does not subsidize favored industries in order to make them less expensive compared to international competitors. Proponents of free trade argue that it is more economically efficient and helps consumers by promoting competition to keep prices low. Critics contend that free trade is detrimental to local jobs, especially in the developed world.

Free Trade Agreement An agreement between two or more countries that reduces or eliminates most trade restrictions between the participants. For example, a free trade agreement may abolish subsidies to favored industries in order to make them less expensive compared to international competitors. Proponents of free trade argue that it is more economically efficient and helps consumers by promoting competition to keep prices low. Critics contend that free trade is detrimental to local jobs, especially in the developed world. NAFTA is a major (and controversial) example of a free trade agreement. In particular, NAFTA allowed for the more or less free importation and exportation of agricultural products and textiles.

Free Trade Zone An area, especially consisting of two or more countries, in which there are few or no tariffs or other trade barriers discouraging international trade. For example, the countries in a free trade zone do not subsidize favored industries in order to make them less expensive compared to international competitors. Proponents of free trade argue that it is more economically efficient and helps consumers by promoting competition to keep prices low. Critics contend that free trade is detrimental to local jobs, especially in the developed world. For example, Canada, Mexico and the United States form a free trade zone because they are all members of NAFTA.

Free-Crowd System A system of trading on a commodity exchange that allows floor traders to enter orders and execute them simultaneously.

Freed Up **1.** Describing a situation in which underwriters in a new issue are released from their previous obligation to place the issue at a certain price. That is, upon being freed up, the underwriters may sell the new issue to investors for whatever price the investors are willing to pay. This is especially common when there is an unusually large demand for the new issue, which drives the market price upwards. The issuer frees up underwriters to raise more capital. **2.** Describing money available to an investor after he/she liquidates a position. That is, freed up capital is the extra cash the investor now has on hand.

Freedom Support Act Legislation the United States, passed in 1992, intended to help former Soviet nations in the transition to capitalism. Among other provisions, it established American Business Centers in several countries to provide resources to encourage American businesses to expand into the Eastern bloc.

Free-Riding **1.** The practice of buying a security and then selling it without having enough cash or cash-equivalent to pay for the original purchase. In the United States, transactions do not settle for three days; that is, a buyer does not pay for a security until three days after he/she buys it. If the buyer does not have the cash to pay for the purchase, he/she may theoretically sell the security on the same day and use that money to pay for the purchase. Free-riding is illegal under SEC rules and is prohibited by the Financial Industry Regulatory Authority. **2.** An illegal practice in which an underwriter does not place a new issue of a security and then later sells it for a higher price.

Freeze Out **1.** In an acquisition, a provision in a charter allowing the acquiring company to buy out all minority shareholders in the target company for a fair price for a limited period of time. The freeze out provision usually lasts from two to five years following the acquisition. **2.** A situation in which the majority shareholder(s) of a company pressure minority shareholders to sell their holdings. For instance, majority shareholders may conduct a freeze out by completely shutting minority shareholders out of the decision making process or by withholding pertinent (but not legally required) information.

Freeze Out Provision In an acquisition, a provision in a charter allowing the acquiring company to buy out all minority shareholders in the target company for a fair price for a limited period of time. The freeze out provision usually lasts from two to five years following the acquisition.

Freguesia In Portugal, a political and judicial subdivision equivalent to a neighborhood. It is used in judicial districts.

Freight **1.** Goods to be transported. The term is especially used in international commerce. **2.** The cost of goods being transported, including the actual cost and the insurance. There are a number of ways for the buyer and seller of goods to divide responsibility for freight. See also: Incoterm.

Freight All Kinds A group of companies providing trucking and other transportation services in the United States. It was established in 1983 and is based in Denver.

French Cameroonian Franc The former currency of Cameroon. It was introduced in 1922, replacing the German mark and French franc. In 1958, it was replaced by the Central African CFA franc.

French Fold A way to fold paper printed on one side so that only the printed side shows. In marketing, French folding is part of some direct mail campaigns.

French Franc The former currency of France. It traces its origins to the currency issued by King John the Good in 1360. The franc became the national currency following the French Revolution. It was initially pegged to silver, but wars of the 18th century led to the issue of paper currency, which caused inflation. In 1803, it was repegged to gold and silver. The franc was abandoned when France was part of the Latin Monetary Union but was readopted during World War I. Following World War II, the franc joined the Bretton Woods System and floated after that system's collapse. It was replaced by the euro in 1999 and was withdrawn from circulation in 2002.

French Indian Rupee The currency of the portions of India under French control. It was equal in value to the Indian rupee and the two currencies circulated alongside each other. The currency became obsolete when France ceded its remaining possessions in the area to the Republic of India in 1954.

Frequency of Compounding The number of times that interest is calculated on a loan or other fixed-return investment in a given year. For example, if the frequency of compounding is three, interest is calculated three times per year. The higher the frequency of compounding, the greater return one will make (or one will spend) on the loan or other investment at the same interest rate. See also: Continuously Compounded Interest.

Fresh Picture A new price of a stock or market after a certain amount of trading has occurred following new information that has recently come to light. For example, a broker, who knew a stock's price earlier in the day, may ask for a fresh picture to receive updated information in making investment decisions.

Fresh Signal In fundamental analysis and technical analysis, an indicator. A fresh signal is a sign that a security will behave in a certain way, and the term especially applies if it indicates that the security's trend is about to change from positive to negative or vice versa. Before a fresh signal is taken too seriously, it needs confirmation, or a separate indicator showing that the fresh signal is part of a trend, rather than an anomaly. See also: Buy signal, Sell signal.

FRF ISO 4217 code for the French franc. The original franc was issued by King John the Good of France in 1360. It was taken out of circulation in 1641 and was reintroduced in 1795. Before World War I, it was variously pegged to gold, silver and the value of property confiscated from the church. It was part of the Bretton Woods System after World War II and became a floating currency after its collapse. It was replaced by the euro in 2002.

Friction Costs The total cost, both direct and indirect, of a transaction after commissions, interest rates, taxes, research, time, and other expenses. For example, a student loan has a principal and interest rate, but the friction cost may include an origination fee, a federal default fee, and other expenses.

Frictional Cost The difference between the return on an index fund and the index it tracks. For example, if the return on the S&P 500 for a period of time is 5% and the return on an index fund tracking the S&P 500 is 3%, the frictional cost is 2%. The return on the index fund is nearly always lower than the return on the index itself because of fees, expenses, and other costs associated with managing the fund. A high frictional cost, however, may indicate that the investment company is either charging excessive fees or the fund does not track the index as closely as is claimed.

Frictional Unemployment Unemployment that results from incomplete information. Examples of frictional unemployment include first-time job seekers who do not have jobs because they do not have the resources to look for jobs successfully. Frictional unemployment may also occur when a company does not know where to look for qualified individuals. It is thought to be impossible to completely eliminate frictional unemployment.

Frictions The processes involved in making a transaction. For example, if one wishes to buy a stock, one must first determine the price, conduct research, comply with regulations, and spend time doing each of those things. Frictions include both monetary and non-monetary costs. They are associated with the relative difficulty of conducting a transaction. See also: Friction costs, Frictional unemployment.

Friendly Fire A fire that is set with no foul intentions and that does not go out of control. For example, a fire in a fireplace and a bonfire on a farm are both friendly fires. Insurance policies generally do not cover losses from friendly fire, such as damage to a chimney. Rather, the insurance only provides coverage if the fire leaves the fireplace and burns down the house or if the fire accidentally destroys a crop.

Friendly Hands A slang term for an investor who buys an IPO with the intention of holding the stock for an extended period of time. Friendly hands reduce volatility in an IPO (which can be quite volatile). Thus, they help maintain price stability as the market tries to decide how much an IPO is worth.

Friendly Takeover The acquisition of one company by another with the full knowledge and consent of the target company's board of directors. Generally speaking, a friendly takeover requires the approval of shareholders in addition to the board of directors, but, in this case, shareholders tend to follow the board's lead. This is because, in a friendly takeover, the acquiring company offers a premium to the current stock price for each share. See also: Hostile takeover.

Friend-of-a-Friend A person one does not know well. A friend of a friend is useful in word of mouth marketing: a person may recommend a product in the general company of many people, even if he only directs the comment to his friend. The social reach of individuals has become more important in marketing with the advent of social networking.

Friends and Family Share Stock that is sold to executives in a company or their friends and relatives before an IPO. This helps the company raise financing before its IPO. However, the issue of friends and family stock can lead to conflict of interest and, as such it must abide by applicable laws.

FRO GOST 7.67 Latin three-letter geocode for the Faroe Islands. The code is used for transactions to and from Faroese bank accounts and for international shipping to the Faroe Islands. As with all GOST 7.67 codes, it is used primarily in Cyrillic alphabets.

Front Burner A slang term for an important issue that should be handled promptly.

Front Fee In a compound option, the premium one pays on the first option contract. A compound option is an option on another option. For example, one may buy a call on a put, which is an option to buy an option to sell some underlying asset. An investor buying a compound option pays a premium on the first option but does not pay a premium on the second option unless the first option is exercised (if it is exercised). This first premium is the front fee. See also: Back Fee.

Front of Book In magazine publishing, the pages toward the beginning of a magazine. The front of book is usually reserved for shorter articles and normally comes before the features.

Front Office The sales and corporate finance offices of a financial services company. The front office departments deal with customers, provide services, and are generally responsible for the production of revenue for the company. See also: Back office, Middle office.

Front Running The act of entering a trade, either with a long or short position, knowing that other investors are about to take a position that will positively influence one's own. For example, one may buy Security A knowing full well that other investors are also about to buy Security A in large blocks, causing its price to increase. This will allow the investor to sell Security A at a much higher price. Front running is forbidden by the SEC as a form of insider trading. It is also known as stepping in front or pennying.

Front-End Load A sales fee in a mutual fund that one pays when one buys shares in the fund. That is, when an investor buys a share in a mutual fund with a front-end loan, he/she agrees to pay a third party, usually a financial institution or broker, a certain percentage of the share's value. Unlike back-end load, the shareholder does not pay the fee upon sale, but rather upon purchase. A share in a mutual fund with a front-end load is called an A-share. See also: B-Share, C-Share, No-Load Fund, CDSC.

Front-End Ratio A ratio of an individual's monthly mortgage expenses to his/her monthly income. The expenses used in this calculation are usually the principal, interest, taxes, and insurance that an individual owes on a monthly basis. Mortgage lenders often use front-end ratios to determine whether an individual has sufficient income in order to qualify for a mortgage. Generally speaking, lenders look for a front-end ratio of less than 0.30 - 0.33. Persons with ratios in excess of that have more difficulty securing mortgages. See also: Back-end ratio.

Frontier Markets Developing countries or stocks listed in those countries with less infrastructure, capitalization, and/or liquidity than other developing countries. A frontier market is considered a type of emerging market, but is considered less prominent or important than markets like India or Brazil. Examples of frontier markets include Bahrain and Nigeria.

Front-Load Fund A mutual fund with a sales fee one pays when one buys shares. When an investor buys a share in a front-load fund, he/she agrees to pay a third party, usually a financial institution or broker, a certain percentage of the share's value. Unlike a back-end load fund, the shareholder does not pay the fee upon sale, but rather upon purchase. A share in a front-load fund is called an A-share. See also: Back-load fund, No-load fund.

Frozen Account A bank account that the customer may not use because of a debt that has not been paid. This means that money can neither go into nor come out of an account. A creditor is allowed to freeze an account for up to twice the amount owed if the debtor is consistently delinquent. The account remains frozen until the debt is settled or the creditor is otherwise satisfied. Generally speaking, an account holder is notified in writing that his/her account has been frozen, but this is not always the case.

Frozen Asset An asset that the owner may not sell or use because of a debt that has not been paid. A frozen asset is often, but not always, the pledged collateral on the debt. The asset remains frozen until the debt is settled or the creditor is otherwise satisfied. Generally speaking, the asset's owner is notified in writing that his/her asset has been frozen, but this is not always the case.

Frozen Collateral Collateral on a loan that the lender may not seize. The possibility of frozen collateral is a risk the lender takes when he/she accepts any collateral for a loan. Most of the time, collateral becomes frozen when there is a dispute as to whether the borrower owns it, or when two lenders disagree as to who has prior claim to it.

Fry a Bigger Fish In equities, to conduct a trade larger than the trade one just completed.

FS In numismatics, an abbreviation meaning "full steps." It is used to describe five-cent coins on which the complete Jefferson Memorial is clearly visible on the reverse. This is somewhat unusual due to wear and tear and may positively affect the value.

FSB In numismatics, an abbreviation meaning "full split bands." It is used to describe Mercury Head dimes on which the band holding the arrows on the reverse together is clear and fully visible. This is somewhat unusual and may positively affect the value.

Fshatra In Albania, a political subdivision equivalent to a village.

FSM GOST 7.67 Latin three-letter geocode for Micronesia. The code is used for transactions to and from Micronesian bank accounts and for international shipping to Micronesia. As with all GOST 7.67 codes, it is used primarily in Cyrillic alphabets.

FTSE 1. A company that researches and publishes thousands of indices tracking securities and other investment vehicles. Created in 1962 as a joint venture between the London Stock Exchange and the Financial Times, the FTSE is particularly famous for maintaining the FTSE 100 Index. It charges fees to companies that make use of its indices, and maintains offices in around 10 cities in financial centers all over the world. 2. Informal for FTSE 100 Index.

FTSE 100 Index An index tracking the 100 publicly-traded companies listed on the London Stock Exchange with the most market capitalization. Like many other FTSE indices, it is calculated in real time, with prices updated every 15 seconds. Each quarter, the FTSE reevaluates the companies tracked on the index and makes necessary adjustments to ensure that it represents the most highly capitalized companies. The FTSE 100 Index is considered a prime indicator of health in the wider market.

Fuang A subdivision of the Cambodian tical, the currency of Cambodia before 1875. One fuang was worth one-eighth of a tical.

Fuchs A slang term for a 50-deutschemark banknote that circulated in Germany prior to the adoption of the euro.

FUD Factor In sales, hesitancy that a potential customer feels due to fear, uncertainty, and/or doubt. A capable salesperson convinces the customer to overcome the FUD factor and buy the product anyway.

Fuel Subsidy A program in which a government or other organization pays for a portion of gasoline, heating oil, or some other fuel. Fuel subsidies tend to be politically popular, especially when the market price of fuel climbs. However, they have caused unsustainable financial problems in some countries in which they have been implemented.

Fuenfer A nickname for the 5-pfennig coin, which was worth 1/20 of one deutschmark.

Fuffziger A nickname for the 50-pfennig coin, which was worth 1/2 of one deutschmark.

Fulcrum Fee A fee than an investment adviser may charge a client if the return on a portfolio exceeds some agreed-upon benchmark. A fulcrum fee is one the few performance-based fees than an investment adviser may assess; one cannot charge it to small investors, only to institutional investors and high net-worth individuals.

Fulcrum Point In technical analysis, a chart's representation of the top or bottom price for a security or index. For example, if Stock A has been on a bearish trend for a long time and later begins to climb again, the fulcrum point is the lowest point on the chart. Likewise, if Stock B has been bullish and begins to decline, the fulcrum point is the highest point on the chart.

Full Bore Slang; to sell an automobile at full price. In auto sales, prices are almost always subject to negotiation and it is unusual to pay full price. To sell full bore is a rare treat for the salesperson.

Full Carry When considering two futures contracts on the same commodity with two different delivery months, a market in which the price for the contract with the later delivery equals the price of the contract with earlier delivery plus the cost of storing the underlying commodity for the remaining period of time. For example, suppose the price of a July expiry futures contract on gold is $995 per ounce and the cost of storing it for a month is $5 per ounce. In a full carry market, the price of an August expiry futures contract on gold would be $1,000 per ounce. A full carry market is also called a full carrying charge market.

Full Coupon Bond A bond with a coupon near or equal to the current interest rates. A full coupon bond sells at face value. If prevailing interest rates rise or fall, the bond is no longer considered full coupon and its price changes accordingly.

Full Disclosure The act of revealing all relevant information to the public, especially to avoid the appearance of bias or fraud. The SEC requires publicly-traded companies to render full disclosure of their financial state as much as possible. See also: Transparency.

Full Duplex In telecommunications, a system that allows transmission between two endpoints simultaneously. For example, if two people are talking on the telephone, sound will be transmitted at the same time in both directions. This contrasts with a half duplex, in which information may only be transmitted one way at a time.

Full Employment A situation in which there is no cyclical unemployment. Full employment does not mean there is no unemployment, since there may be frictional unemployment as persons move from old positions into new ones. Some economists hold that full employment occurs when unemployment falls to the rate below which inflation accelerates, though other economists dispute this idea. See also: NAIRU.

Full Employment and Balanced Growth Act of 1978 Legislation in the United States, enacted in 1978, that sought to curtail the stagflation that marked most of the 1970s. The Act set up four goals for the federal government: full employment, economic growth, balanced budget, and elimination of inflation. It stated that the government preferred private investment to accomplish these goals, but, if it was not forthcoming, then the government could make investments to spur demand and, if necessary, create make-work jobs along the lines of the New Deal. It set goals to be reached by certain dates; for example, it stated that inflation should be 4% by 1983 and 0% by 1988. Critics of the Act maintained that the four goals are different and that it is often impossible to fulfill them all.

Full Faith and Credit A situation in which a government agrees to repay a debt no matter what. For example, if a bond is backed by the full faith and credit of the United States, the U.S. government must find some way to repay the bond. U.S. Treasury securities, Ginnie Mae bonds, and some other debt securities are call full-faith-and-credit bonds because they have this backing. Municipalities may also attach full faith and credit to their bonds, but this means less than the credit of the United States.

Full Faith-and-Credit Obligation A bond secured by an unconditional promise to pay by another entity. The term usually refers to a debt security backed by the United States government. For example, a U.S. Treasury security and a Ginnie Mae pass-through are both full faith-and-credit obligations. These securities carry very low risk.

Full Handle In energy and grain trading, a point in price change. For example, if oil drops from $99 to $98, it is said to drop a full handle.

Full Ratchet The option for existing shareholders in some publicly-traded companies to exchange their shares for more shares in a new issue of stock where the newly issued stock is made at a lower price. For example, if one purchases shares for $60 per share and the company later makes a new issue at $20 per share, the shareholder may exchange the shares purchased at $60 for an equivalent amount in

$20 shares. This will triple his/her number of shares. This is an anti-dilution provision.

Full Recourse Describing a loan for which there is a co-signer. That is, if the borrower defaults on the loan, the co-signer becomes legally liable for repayment. Thus, in addition to any collateral that may secure the loan, the lender is further protected from default by the existence of the co-signer. See also: Non-recourse loan.

Full Retirement Age The age at which one becomes eligible for a full government or private pension. Full retirement age varies according to the rules of the particular pension. It may be a stated age or it may depend on how many years one has worked. Normally, however, full retirement age is between 55 and 65.

Full Showing When advertising on a train, taxi cab or other mode of transportation, the placing of the ad in all cars. This gives the ad the maximum level of exposure. See also: Quarter showing.

Full Stock Stock with a face value of $100. Full stock (and indeed any stock with a face value) is rare and one only may buy them directly from the issuer.

Full Trading Authorization An authorization by a client for the broker to make any trades on a discretionary account without conferring with the client. In other words, full trading authorization means that the client makes no demands on the broker's actions and the broker is bound only by the prudent person rule.

Full Vesting Describing a stock option or qualified retirement plan to which a person is entitled to the benefits of ownership, even if he/she no longer works at the company providing it. Vesting occurs after an employee has worked at the company for a certain number of years; once a benefit is fully vested, the benefits of the stock option or plan cannot be revoked.

Full-Service Broker A brokerage that provides transaction services in addition to research and investment advice. That is, a full-service broker works with clients to determine and execute clients' investment goals; brokers may conduct the transactions the clients direct or they may independently manage portfolios for clients. Full-service brokerage firms provide individual services, and, as a result, charge much higher commissions than discount brokerage firms. However, they are not as exclusive as boutiques.

Full-Time Student A person who takes more than 12 credit hours, or the equivalent, at a post-secondary institution in a school term. A full-time student is eligible for certain tax advantages, as is a parent, if he/she financially supports the student.

Fully Depreciated An asset that has, over time, depreciated to no book value. A company may no longer write off part of the value of a fully depreciated asset because, legally speaking, there is no value. However, the fully depreciated asset may still be used because depreciation often bears only a rough relationship to an asset's actual usable life.

Fully Distributed Describing a new issue of a security that underwriters or dealers have sold in total to the general public. All trading on a security after it has been fully distributed occurs on the secondary market. See also: Primary market.

Fully Invested Describing a fund or company that has committed all or nearly all of its capital to securities. For example, a fully invested mutual fund keeps little or none of its capital in money market accounts, but rather places it in bonds or stock. A fully invested company is bullish on the future performance of the market.

Fully Modified Pass-Throughs Pass-through securities with principals and interest guaranteed by a U.S. Government agency. A pass-through security is backed by assets or debt; in a fully modified pass-through security, a government agency reduces the risk of default to the pass-through holder by guaranteeing payment. Ginnie Mae makes most of these guarantees, but Freddie Mac and Fannie Mae do as well.

Fully Subscribed Describing a situation in which an underwriting syndicate places a new issue in the exact amount it is issued. Before a new issue, underwriters canvass potential investors, who may or may not book an order to buy a portion the new issue. If investors agree to buy the exact amount that is issued, the security is said to be fully subscribed. A fully subscribed issue indicates that the issuer priced it perfectly, creating an equilibrium of supply and demand. This can be quite difficult to do. See also: Overbooked, Undersubscribed.

Fun A unit of weight in Japan equivalent to 375 milligrams.

Fun Money Money used for non-business purposes. For example, one may set aside money for a vacation or to finance an expensive hobby. More rarely, it may also refer to start-up capital for a business based on one's hobby.

Functional Expenses The expenses a non-profit organization incurs in executing its programs, in addition to fundraising and management. Functional expenses are reported on the organization's Form 990 and are useful in ensuring that its income is reinvested in the organization and is not in fact profit.

Fund Balance On a financial statement, the reporting of an organization's net assets (that is, the extent to which assets exceed liabilities).

Fund Family A set of mutual funds managed by a single company. The funds within a fund family have different investment goals and/or strategies. However, because the same company manages the whole family, individual investors may generally move money from one fund to another without extra commissions or fees. This allows investors to be flexible in their own investment goals according to their particular needs at a given time. A fund family is also called a group of funds.

Fund Flows 1. In municipal bonds, a statement indicating a list of priorities for which the municipality will use the funds raised by the bond. Generally speaking, the flow of funds priorities begin with maintenance of city functions, followed by operations, debt service, expansion of the city's facilities, and reserving cash prepay debt. **2.** In mutual funds, the balance of money going into and coming out a mutual fund.

Fund Manager A bank, business, or, less often, a person that makes investment decisions for a mutual fund. Fund managers make these decisions in accordance with the parameters set by the fund's prospectus. The goal is to make the most profit for the fund as possible. Unlike brokers, fund managers are not paid on commission but by a percentage of the total amount of money under the fund's management. This gives the fund manager an incentive to work for shareholders' profit because the more money the manager accumulates, the more he/she/it makes. See also: Markowitz Portfolio Theory.

Fund of Funds A mutual fund that invests exclusively in other mutual funds. Theoretically, funds of funds allow the investor to diversify risk even more than in a regular mutual fund without reducing return significantly. One disadvantage is the fact that most funds of funds have higher fees because shareholders have to pay fees for the funds of funds themselves and must also pay fees for the underlying funds. Funds of funds were especially popular in the 1960s.

Fund Overlap A situation in which two or more investment vehicles in a portfolio hold largely the same securities. For example, one may hold an index fund tracking the S&P 500 and a mutual fund that is actively managed in theory but, in reality, largely tracks the S&P 500. Fund overlap may result in a portfolio that appears diversified but is, in fact, not. This can add to the portfolio's risk; as a result, risk averse investors need to exercise the most caution over fund overlap. See also: Closet index fund.

Fund Supermarket A brokerage that provides investors access to many mutual funds from various fund families. This permits greater variety in their portfolios while allowing the investors to receive all their statements from a single source. Fund supermarkets also have the potential for deep customer bases because of the sheer variety of funds offered.

Fund Switching The practice of selling shares in a mutual fund and using the proceeds to buy shares in another mutual fund. An investor does this when economic conditions or his/her investment goals have changed. Because of the fees (known as loads) associated with buying and selling mutual funds, fund switching can be expensive unless one is switching within a fund family or between no-load funds.

Fundamental Analysis In making investment decisions, the analysis of the facts that affect a company's underlying value. Examples of factors considered in fundamental analysis include debt, cash flow, supply and demand for the company's products, and so forth. For instance, if a company does not have a sufficient supply of products, it will fail. Likewise, demand for the product must remain at a certain level in order for it to be successful. Fundamental analysts recommend buying stocks in companies with strong fundamentals because they are essential for long-term success and stability. Fundamental analysis contrasts with technical analysis, which considers primarily short-term indicators. See also: Value Investing.

Fundamental Analyst In making investment decisions, a person who analyzes the facts affecting a company's underlying value. Examples of factors considered by fundamental analysts include debt, cash flow, supply and demand for the company's products, and so forth. For instance, if a company does not have a sufficient supply of products, it will fail. Likewise, demand for the product must remain at a certain level in order for it to be successful. Fundamental analysts recommend buying stocks in companies with strong fundamentals because they are essential for long-term success and stability. Fundamental analysis contrasts with technical analysis, which considers primarily short-term indicators. See also: Value investing.

Fundamental Forecasting The practice of using fundamental analysis to predict future exchange rates. This involves looking at all quantitative and qualitative aspects that might affect exchange rates, including macroeconomic data and political factors. Critics contend that fundamental forecasting is limited as some of the data it includes is difficult to quantify and it may miss some data that have an immediate effect of exchange rates.

Fundamental Information The facts that affect a company's underlying value. Examples of fundamental information include debt, cash flow, supply of and demand for the company's products, and so forth. For instance, if a company does not have a sufficient supply of products, it will fail. Likewise, demand for the product must remain at a certain level in order for it to be successful. Strong fundamental information is considered essential for long-term success and stability. See also: Value investing, Fundamental analysis.

Funded Pension Plan A pension that has sufficient liquid assets to pay all of its liabilities, including (and especially) all future payments to beneficiaries.

Fundies A slang term for fundamental information.

Funding 1. See: Refinancing. **2.** The act of raising capital to conduct an activity. For example, if a company issues a bond to finance the construction of a factory, it is said to be funding the factory.

Funding Agreement A low-risk, fixed-income investment that an institutional investor may purchase. In a funding agreement, one provides a lump sum to the seller, and, in exchange, one receives a fixed return, often based on LIBOR. Mutual funds and pensions often purchase funding agreements because of the certainty associated with them. It is structured much like a guaranteed investment contract.

Funding Ratio A ratio of a pension or annuity's assets to its liabilities. A funding ratio above 1 indicates that the pension or annuity is able to cover all payments it is obligated to make. A ratio below 1 indicates that it is either unable to make payments or is in danger of not being able to do so.

Funds from Operations In real estate investment trusts, a measure of revenue from operations involving liquid transfers like cash, rather than illiquid assets. In general, the FFO is determined by taking the REIT's earnings and adding back their depreciation and amortization of mortgages.

Funds Management The practice of ensuring that the assets of a financial institution are timed such that they can pay liabilities. For example, a funds manager times a loan such that, upon repayment, a bank can use the funds to pay a time deposit when it comes due. Funds management should not be confused with investment management.

Fungibility The state of being interchangeable. For example, money has fungibility because there is no difference between one dollar and another dollar. Likewise, stocks of the same type in the same company and commodities of the same quality are generally fungible. On the other hand, assets like land or baseball cards are not fungible because each unit has unique qualities that add or subtract value.

Fungible Issue A newly issued bond with the same terms as a previous one. That is, a fungible issue and the previous bond will have the same coupon rate, maturity and so forth.

Fungibles Assets in which one unit is completely interchangeable with another. For example, there is no difference between one ounce of gold of a given quality and one ounce of gold of exactly the same quality. Money is another example of a fungible asset: $10 in cash is $10 in cash whether the bills are crisp and new or old and tattered. Some investment vehicles are fungible, while others are not. Standardized contracts such as options and futures are largely fungible, while forward contracts are not. Fungible assets are more liquid than non-fungible assets.

Funt A Russian unit of weight approximately equivalent to 409.5 grams. It was rendered obsolete when the Soviet Union began to use the metric system in 1924.

Fur and Jewelry Floater An option addition to a property insurance policy that provides coverage for damage to fur or leather clothing or jewelry. Fur insurance does not cover damage due to insects or normal wear and tear. As with all insurance, one must pay a premium for fur insurance.

Fur Insurance An insurance policy that provides coverage for damage to fur or leather clothing or other items. Fur insurance does not cover damage due to insects or normal wear and tear. As with all insurance, one must pay a premium for fur insurance.

Furlong A measure of length equal to 220 yards or one-eighth of a mile. It is derived from the approximate length of one plowed furrow on an acre of land. Except in horseracing, it is rarely used today.

Furthest Month Among several different futures contracts or options, describing the one with the longest maturity. For example, given three futures contracts, one expiring in March, one in June, and one in September, the furthest month futures contract is the one expiring in September.

Fuss A German unit of length. Its measure varied in different German-speaking areas, but generally was between 250 and 400 millimeters. It became obsolete with the adoption of the metric system in the 1870s.

Fut A Russian unit of length equivalent to one foot. It was rendered obsolete when the Soviet Union began to use the metric system in 1924.

Futes A slang term for futures contracts. The term is most commonly used in the plural.

Future Deadline In investment banking, a slang term for any project due more than 24 hours after the present moment.

Future Income Tax In accounting, a way for a company to avoid taxes following years in which it had a net operating loss. If a company deducts more than its net income in a given tax year, it may take the difference between the deduction and the net income (a negative number) and apply it as a deduction on taxable income for up to 7-10 years. For example, if a company loses $500,000 in one year, and makes $1,000,000 the following year, it may only be liable for a $500,000 profit.

Future Interest In real estate, ownership of a property without the right to use it at present. For example, the owner of an apartment has a future interest if she rents it to a tenant. She may own the apartment, but the tenant has the right to live there. Generally, the owner may enter without permission or at least prior notice.

Future Investment Opportunities An opportunity to profit from an investment that will take place in the future, but that results from an opportunity in the present.

Future Proof Slang; describing anything unlikely to become obsolete. For example, paper could be considered future proof because it will be a needed office supply regardless of what new technology develops. This concept is the opposite of planned obsolescence.

Future Value The value of an asset or investment at a certain point in the future when its return is a known factor. That is, the future value of an investment is useful only when the security being measured has a fixed rate of return. Stocks are highly unlikely to be measured for future value because their returns are too volatile. The future value is used for bonds, interest-bearing accounts, certificates of deposit, and other, similar assets.

Futures Bundle A futures contract enabling one to make or receive delivery of the same commodity at the same price every month or quarter for three, four, or five years. This is particularly useful for producers of commodities as it allows them to stabilize their prices for a long period of time. For example, a wheat farmer may sell a futures bundle so he knows how much he will make from a certain amount of wheat for a period of several years.

Futures Commission Merchant A broker or brokerage on a futures exchange. A futures commission merchant receives and executes orders on behalf of clients and extends credit for margin transactions. It is also called a commodity broker.

Futures Contract An agreement to buy or sell an asset at a certain date at a certain price. That is, Investor A may make a contract with Farmer B in which A agrees to buy a certain number of bushels of B's corn at $15 per bushel. This contract must be honored whether the price of corn goes to $1 or $100 per bushel. Futures contracts can help reduce volatility in certain markets, but they contain the risks inherent to all speculative investing. These contracts may be sold on the secondary market, but the person holding the contract at its end must take delivery of the underlying asset. Futures contract are standard instruments; that is, unlike forward contracts, their provisions are standardized. As such, they may be traded on an exchange.

Futures Equivalent The number of futures contracts needed to have the same risk as a given options strategy.

Futures Exchange An exchange on which futures contracts are traded. A futures contract is traded on a futures exchange; this allows them to be standardized contracts, which reduces uncertainty for investors. Futures exchanges are useful because it allows investors to make either speculative investments or hedges based on the expected future price for a commodity or other underlying asset. Many futures exchanges are also options exchanges.

Futures Market The supply and demand for the trading of futures contracts. A futures contract is an agreement to buy and sell an asset at a certain date at a certain price. That is, Investor A may make a contract with Farmer B in which A agrees to buy so many bushels of B's corn at $15 per bushel. This contract must be honored whether the price of corn goes to $1 or $100 per bushel. Futures contracts can help reduce volatility in certain markets, but they contain the risks inherent to all speculative investing. These contracts may be traded on the secondary market, creating the futures market. The investor holding the contract at its end must take delivery of the underlying asset. Trading on the futures market often occurs on a futures exchange, such as the Merc.

Futures Option A contract giving the holder the right (but not the obligation) to buy (if a call) or sell (if a put) a futures contract. In other words, the underlying asset of a futures option is a futures contract (which itself has a separate underlying asset). A futures option may be useful if it is not readily apparent whether taking a certain futures position would be beneficial to one's investment strategy.

Futures Pack A group of futures contracts enabling one to buy a certain number of contracts for delivery in each month for four, consecutive months. For example, one may buy a futures pack in January for delivery in June, July, August, and September.

Futures Position The state of owning or owing a futures contract, which is an agreement to buy or sell an asset at a certain date at a certain price. One has a long futures position when one owns a contract, while one has a short position when the contract is sold, especially sold short.

Futures Price The price on a futures contract. For example, if an investor enters a futures contract to sell a certain number of barrels of oil in six months for $90 per barrel, the futures price is $90.

Futures Spread In arbitrage, the purchase of a future contract and the simultaneous sale of another contract on the same commodity when the price differs. For example, an arbitrageur may take advantage of a situation in which the purchase price and the sale price of a futures contract are different. In practice, a futures spread is relatively rare, as futures contracts are a liquid market, which holds down any price discrepancy.

Futures Trader An investor who trades in futures contracts on an exchange. If Investor A and Investor B on the Chicago Mercantile Exchange make a contract in which A agrees to buy a certain number of bushels of B's corn at $15 per bushel six months in the future, both investors are futures traders.

Futures Trading Act of 1921 Legislation in the United States that imposed a 20 cent per bushel tax on all grain futures that were not registered and regulated by the U.S. Department of Agriculture. The Act was intended to impose regulation on futures contracts and exchanges. It was declared unconstitutional in 1921.

Fuzzy Logic A form of logic programmed into some computers to allow them to use probability. That is, fuzzy logic allows computers to deal with uncertainty and to make decisions based on the information available. Unlike pure logic, which requires certainty, fuzzy logic helps computers make decisions the way humans do, only faster. This can be important in some investment strategies, such as arbitrage, that require decisions to be made very quickly.

FX 1. ISO 3166-1 alpha-2 code for Metropolitan France, which includes all of France except for its overseas departments, collectivities, and territories, as well as New Caledonia. This was the code used in international transactions to and from French bank accounts. **2.** ISO 3166-2 geocode for Metropolitan France. This was used as an international standard for shipping to Metropolitan France. In both cases, the code is obsolete.

FXFR ISO 3166-3 code for Metropolitan France, which consists of all of France except for overseas departments, collectivities, and territories, as well as New Caledonia. All of France was re-designated with the code FR in 1997. ISO 3166-3 codes are used to indicate names of countries and territories that are no longer used.

FXX GOST 7.67 Latin three-letter geocode for Metropolitan France, which is the part of France located in Europe. The code is used for transactions to and from Metropolitan French bank accounts and for international shipping to Metropolitan France. As with all GOST 7.67 codes, it is used primarily in Cyrillic alphabets.

FYI A quote for the price of a security in which the price is subject to change. Market makers occasionally make FYI quotes for valuation purposes only. It may also refer to a quote that is not an offer, but simply supplied for informational purposes.

G.I. Insurance 1. See: SGLI. **2.** See: VGLI.

G-8 Finance Ministers The heads of the financial and economic regulatory departments in each G-8 country. G-8 finance ministers are known by different names. For example, the finance minister in the U.S. is the Secretary of the Treasury, while in the U.K., the finance minister is called the Chancellor of the Exchequer. G-8 finance ministers meet four times a year to discuss mutual concerns, problems and other issues.

GA 1. ISO 3166-1 alpha-2 code for Gabon. This is the code used in international transactions to and from Gabonese bank accounts. **2.** ISO 3166-2 geocode for Gabon. This is used as an international standard for shipping to Gabon. Each Gabonese province has its own code with the prefix "GA." For example, the code for the Province of Nyanga is ISO 3166-2:GA-5.

GAB GOST 7.67 Latin three-letter geocode for Gabon. The code is used for transactions to and from Gabonese bank accounts and for international shipping to Gabon. As with all GOST 7.67 codes, it is used primarily in Cyrillic alphabets.

Gadfly A slightly derogatory term for a shareholder who attends annual meetings of shareholders and asks the executives difficult questions. That is, the gadfly may question executive pay, ask why a dividend was not larger when it could have been, and may also generally point out issues about which other shareholders may not be aware. Obviously, many executives do not like the presence of gadflies, though shareholders may find them useful.

Gaffer In film, the person in charge of lighting effects. Because different lights draw out different emotions, a gaffer may be used in marketing to find the lighting (for example, for a commercial) most likely to elicit a positive response from a targeted consumer.

Gaffoon In television, the person in charge of sound effects. Because different sounds draw out different emotions, a gaffoon may be used in marketing to find sound effects (for example, for a commercial) most likely to elicit a positive response from a targeted consumer.

Gag Writer A comedy writer, especially for television. A gag writer may be hired to compose a humorous commercial intended to increase sales of a product.

Gai Atsu A Japanese term for external pressure. It refers to postwar demands, especially by the United States and others, intended to influence Japanese economic and financial policies.

Gaijin The Japanese word for foreigner. The term is often used to describe non-Japanese persons and organizations who invest in Japanese securities.

Gain An increase in price or value. For example, if a stock opens at $10 and closes at $12, it is said to gain $2. Likewise, if one buys a house for $200,000, and its value is later assessed $325,000, the house has gained $125,000. See also: Capital gains, Paper gain, Uptick.

Gain Contingency A possible future event that will increase revenue or profits. A common example of a gain contingency is a lawsuit that might be successful. For the sake of fiscal conservatism, gain contingencies are not reported as assets or revenue until the suspected events actually occur.

Gain Sharing A bonus given to an employee who finds and implements creative ways to increase revenue or reduce costs. In general, gain sharing involves giving the employee a portion of the extra revenue or the cost savings. The idea behind gain sharing is to encourage employees to work for the good of the company by making it in their best interests to do so.

Gainer A security that increase in price during a trading day. That is, a gainer has a higher price at the close than it did at the open. See also: Loser.

Gainful Employment A job that allows self-sufficiency. There is no hard-and-fast definition of what constitutes gainful employment. For example, pizza delivery may pay the bills for one person but only serve as a cash generator for another. Gainful employment usually (but not always) implies work in a white collar or skilled blue collar position. Debt level, family commitments and other monthly bills affect the extent to which one is gainfully employed.

GAINSr A convertible, municipal bond with aspects of both zero-coupon and interest-bearing bonds.

Gakubatsu In Japan, a group of alumni from the same school or university. Historically, members of gakubatsu have maintained ties with each other, which has impacted Japanese government and business.

Galley Proof In publishing, a preliminary text that has not been subdivided into pages. Galley proofs are produced before a text goes to print for proofreading and other editing purposes.

Gallic leuga An ancient Roman unit of length approximately equivalent to 2.22 kilometers.

Galloping Inflation An informal term for double digit inflation or hyperinflation. The term conjures the image of a horse running at top speed.

Gallup and Robinson, Inc. A market research company in the United States that specializes in advertising. Gallup and Robinson assists clients in honing their advertisements so they have maximum effect. For example, the company researches the extent to which people recall various ads the next day. Gallup and Robinson was established in 1948 and is based in New Jersey.

Galvanic Skin Response A physical response in the skin due to some stimulus. For example, turning red when one is nervous is a galvanic skin response. Some marketers measure galvanic skin responses on test subjects of advertisements. Proponents believe this is an objective way to determine a test subject's response to an advertisement, though critics contend that this practice does not sufficiently account for outside stimuli that may affect measurements.

Gambia River Basin Development Organization An international organization established to promote economic development along the Gambia River. It provides financing for projects assigned by member nations. It was established in 1978 and consists of the Gambia, Guinea, Guinea-Bissau and Senegal.

Gambian Dalasi The currency of Gambia. It was adopted in 1971, replacing the Gambian pound. It is a floating currency.

Gambian Pound The currency of Gambia before 1971. Until 1964, the Gambian pound was simply the British pound issued in Gambia. It was replaced by the Gambian dalasi.

Gambling The act of wagering on an event or a game of chance in which the outcome is uncertain. This includes card games such as poker or bets on sporting events. In U.S. tax, all gambling income, regardless of where or how it was obtained, is taxable income and must be reported to the IRS. Professional gamblers may deduct all gambling losses against gambling income, but casual gamblers may only do so up to the amount of their gambling income.

Gambling Income Winnings from wagers on events or games of chance in which the outcome is uncertain. This includes all cash won and the market value of non-cash winnings such as vacations. In U.S. tax, all gambling income, regardless of where or how it was obtained, is taxable income and must be reported to the IRS. Professional gamblers may deduct all gambling losses against gambling income, but casual gamblers may only do so up to the amount of gambling income.

Gambling Insurance An insurance policy that provides coverage for gambling losses. Gambling insurance is quite unusual in practice because it may encourage a policyholder to place bets recklessly, compounding losses. As with all insurance, one must pay a premium to receive the coverage.

Gambling Loss Losses from wagers on events or games of chance in which the outcome is uncertain. This includes all cash lost and the market value of non-cash losses such as vacations. Professional gamblers may deduct all gambling losses against gambling income, but casual gamblers may only do so up to the amount of gambling income.

Game Theory A model of how decisions are made that includes not only the thought processes of the individual, but also interaction between individuals. Game theory attempts to explain how one seeks to maximize one's own benefit given the information one has received from other persons. It attempts to mathematically weigh the odds of a person making a decision under certain circumstances with limited information. See also: Prisoner's dilemma.

Gaming Contract A contract in which participants agree to play a game of chance. For example, if two friends make a bet on who will win the World Series, they have entered a gaming contract and the loser is obliged to pay the winner the agreed-upon amount. However, a gaming contract may not be enforceable in a jurisdiction where gambling is illegal.

Gamma A measure of how fast the delta changes. That is, gamma is a mathematical measurement of how fast the price of an option contract changes for each unit of change in the price of the underlying asset. The larger the gamma, the more volatile the option contract is. If an option is at the money or near the money, gamma is large, but if it is deep in or deep out of the money, gamma can become quite small. This is because when an option is near the money, a small change in the underlying asset's value can greatly change the level of demand for the contract. This is not the case for deep in and deep out of the money options.

Gamma Neutral Describing a portfolio with a delta of zero. Delta is a measure of how much the price of a derivative increases (a positive delta) or decreases (a negative delta) for each increase in the price of the underlying asset. One constructs a gamma neutral portfolio by purchasing derivatives with equal, but opposite, deltas. See also: Hedging strategy.

Gang An organized group (often rather small) of persons with a common identity. The term is usually used to describe organized crime groups, especially those run by racial and ethnic minorities. As with most organized crime groups, gangs have symbols, rituals and are generally involved in drug trafficking and other illegal activities. Gangs and other organized crime groups pose a significant and persistent problem for law enforcement. See also: RICO.

Gang Run A method in which several projects are printed using the same printer. Gang runs are intended to reduce printing costs.

Gangway The opening on a ship through which cargo can be carried on or off.

Gann Angles In technical analysis, a series of angles plotted over a chart representing price and time. There are nine angles, each representing a different price movement; for example, when the angle is 45 degrees, it shows that price and time are moving identically with one another. A change in angle represents a possible change in price movement, which can either be confirmed or not by the following change in angle. Gann angles were first introduced in 1935, and their effectiveness of remains controversial.

Gap 1. In technical analysis, a break on a chart representing a sudden and large price movement accompanied by high trading volume. Generally speaking, charts do not show gaps because price movements, even when large, occur smoothly enough to not require a break in the chart. Gaps may occur, for example, when the price of a security suddenly doubles or halves. As with many charting terms, it may be bullish or bearish; a sudden movement upward is a bullish gap, while a sudden movement downward is bearish. It is also called a breakaway gap. **2.** Financing that is needed but unavailable. A common solution to filling a gap is borrowing.

Gap Down In technical analysis, a break on a chart representing a sudden and large price movement downward on high trading volume. That is, a security gaps down when its price drops by a significant amount with little or no warning. It is represented on a chart by a break with no line representing the price. This is considered a bearish signal.

Gap Loan Financing that is needed but unavailable. A common solution to filling a gap is borrowing. See also: Bridge loan.

Gap Opening An opening price for a security on an exchange that is significantly higher or lower than the closing price on the previous trading day. A gap opening almost always occurs if there was positive or negative news (or a rumor) overnight or during the weekend.

Gap Ratio The ratio of a company's rate sensitive assets to its rate sensitive liabilities. Rate sensitive assets and liabilities are those likely to increase or decrease substantially in value due to changes in interest rates. A gap ratio over 1 indicates that there are more rate sensitive assets than liabilities, meaning revenue or profits will likely increase as interest rates rise. A ratio below 1 indicates the opposite. The gap ratio is most commonly used in banking.

Gap Risk The risk that a stock will fall dramatically in price from one trade to the next. For example, gap risk is the possibility that one will lose on an investment if a stock falls from, say, $120 to $95 per share in a single trade. This only occurs when there is a significant and sudden drop in demand for the stock.

Gap Up In technical analysis, a break on a chart representing a sudden and large price movement upward on high trading volume. That is, a security gaps up when its price rises a significant amount with little or no warning. It is represented on a chart by a break with no line representing the price. This is considered a bullish signal.

Garage A trading floor on the New York Stock Exchange that is an annex to the main floor. It is located on the north side of the main floor.

Garage Insurance An insurance policy protecting a garage owner from damages caused by vehicles while on the garage's property. This type of insurance is most popular with auto dealerships and similar businesses because it protects owners from accidents that other drivers cause. As with all insurance, one must pay a premium to receive garage coverage.

Garbatrage An increase in the price of a security when another company in the same or a similar sector is acquired by a third company. For example, if Holding Company A buys Mining Corporation B, garbatrage occurs when the share price for Mining Corporation C goes up. Garbatrage occurs when speculation surrounds the initial acquisition and rumors abound that more takeovers are likely. It is also called rumortrage and is an example of behavioral economics. See also: Arbitrage.

Garce 1. An obsolete Indian unit of weight approximately equivalent to 4,199 kilograms. **2.** An obsolete Indian unit of dry volume approximately equivalent to 5,244 liters. **3.** An obsolete Indian unit of dry volume approximately equivalent to 5,085 liters.

Garden Apartment An apartment complex with a large courtyard. Garden apartments usually have only one or two stories so the courtyard looks close to all tenants. These apartments may give the impression of being in the country, regardless of where one actually lives. Depending on how well kept garden apartments are, they may be more expensive than other rental units.

Garnets A Tatar unit of volume approximately equivalent to 3.3 liters. It was rendered obsolete when the Soviet Union began to use the metric system in 1924.

Garnishee A person from whom a portion of his/her full salary or wages is withheld, especially in order to pay a creditor or the tax agency. For example, suppose one's regular paycheck is $1,500. A garnishee may receive a check for only $1,050 because the government is withholding $450 for taxes. Garnishment may also occur for other reasons, such as to pay child support, back taxes, or some debts.

Garnishment The withholding of a person's full salary or wages, especially in order to pay a creditor or the tax agency. For example, suppose one's regular paycheck would be $1500. Garnishment occurs when the person receives a check for only $1050 because the government is withholding $450 for taxes. Garnishment may also occur for other reasons, such as to pay child support, back taxes, or some debts.

Garn-St. Germain Depository Institutions Act Legislation in the United States allowing federal savings and loan associations to offer adjustable-rate mortgages.. The Act was passed to encourage homeownership by making loans available to more persons. However, it is considered to have contributed to the savings and loan crisis, whereby a large number of S&Ls failed in the late 1980s. The Act was passed in 1982.

Garra A Maltese unit of volume approximately equivalent to 10.8 liters. It was originally used to measure alcohol. It is largely obsolete but is still used in some circumstances.

Gas Guzzler Tax A tax levied on manufacturers and importers producing or importing cars with gas mileage of less than 22.5 miles per gallon. Instituted in 1978 as part of a wider effort to reduce reliance on oil, the gas guzzler tax largely halted the production and sale of extremely large family cars seen previously. It does not apply to trucks or sport utility vehicles. See also: Green Fund.

Gaseoso A Portuguese term for a soda or soft drink. It is a slang term for a small bribe.

Gastarbeiter A migrant worker in Germany. A gastarbeiter temporarily lives in Germany and is usually employed in manual labor. The word has become common in other European countries as well.

Gatekeeper In insurance, requirements that a policyholder must fulfill before becoming eligible for a benefit. This especially applies to eligibility for long-term care in health insurance.

Gather in the Stops An investment strategy in which traders sell a security in large quantities such that it lowers the price in order to trigger stop orders. When the stop orders are triggered, more shares are sold, which triggers more stop orders, and the cycle continues. One may do this in order to drive the price down so that one may buy the security back at an artificially low price. However, if gathering in the stops runs out of control, an exchange may suspend stop orders for that security.

Gaucho A proposed regional accounting currency for South America. Argentina and Brazil attempted to implement the gaucho in 1987 to make international payments in the region, but it was never actually issued.

Ga-Wout A Burmese unit of length approximately equivalent to 5.12 kilometers.

Gazelle Company A slang term for a company that has increased its revenues by at least 20% each year for four years running. This may result in a much higher share price. The term implies that a company is growing, like a gazelle, by leaps and bounds.

Gazump In the sale of real estate, the unexpected raising of the price immediately before the deal closes. That is, after the parties have agreed to the price but before they have signed the appropriate papers, the seller may decide to raise the price. This surprise move is called a gazump. See also: Gazunder.

Gazumping 1. Informal; the act of withdrawing a promise in business, especially a promise to sell. For example, if a company agrees in principle to sell a factory to a second company, but receives a better offer from a third company, which it accepts instead, it is said to "gazump" the second company. **2.** See: Gazump.

Gazunder A situation in which a potential buyer of real estate revises his/her bid for less money before the transaction is finalized. For example, if one originally offers $200,000 and the seller accepts this, a gazunder occurs when one reduces the bid to $175,000. A gazunder is risky because the seller is under no obligation to accept the gazunder. Generally speaking, a gazunder occurs when the buyer is confident that the seller will accept the new price, especially when there are no other potential buyers and real estate prices are crashing.

GB 1. ISO 3166-1 alpha-2 code for the United Kingdom of Great Britain and Northern Ireland. This is the code used in international transactions to and from British bank accounts. **2.** ISO 3166-2 geocode for the United Kingdom. This is used as an international standard for shipping to the United Kingdom. Most British subdivisions have their own codes with the prefix "GB." For example, the code for the Unitary Authority of Brighton and Hove is ISO 3166-2:GB-BNH.

GBP ISO 4217 code for the British pound sterling. It is the third largest reserve currency in the world. It traces its origins to Anglo-Saxon times and is the oldest currency still in use. It is issued by the Bank of England and the Bank of Scotland. Like most currencies, it was pegged to the U.S. dollar under the Bretton Woods System, but is now a floating currency. The pound is interesting in part because it did not use a decimal system for its subdivisions until 1971. See also: Decimalisation, Quid.

GBR GOST 7.67 Latin three-letter geocode for the United Kingdom. The code is used for transactions to and from British bank accounts and for international shipping to the United Kingdom. As with all GOST 7.67 codes, it is used primarily in Cyrillic alphabets.

GBX In stocks, a notation used to indicate that a price is quoted in terms of pence instead of British pounds. See also: GBP.

GD 1. ISO 3166-1 alpha-2 code for Grenada. This is the code used in international transactions to and from bank accounts in Grenada. **2.** ISO 3166-2 geocode for Grenada. This is used as an international standard for shipping to Grenada. Each parish in Grenada has its own code with the prefix "GD." For example, the code for the Parish of St. Andrew is ISO 3166-2:GD-01.

GDP Gap The economic growth that an economy would experience if all persons willing to work had jobs. The GDP gap represents growth that can never happen because the economy has not allocated jobs to all willing workers. This can occur for a number of reasons, including excessive government regulation and corporate fear for future earnings. See also: Unemployment rate, Full employment.

GDP Price Deflator A ratio of nominal GDP to real GDP expressed as a percentage. The GDP price deflator is used as a measure of the inflation rate; it does not account for price changes in commodity baskets like the Consumer Price Index. Rather, it shows changes in GDP compared with a base year.

GE 1. ISO 3166-1 alpha-2 code for the Gilbert and Ellice Islands prior to their re-designation as Kiribati and Tuvalu. This was the code used in international transactions to and from bank accounts in the islands. **2.** ISO 3166-2 geocode for the Gilbert and Ellice Islands. This was used as an international standard for shipping to the Gilbert and Ellice Islands. In both cases, the code is obsolete. **3.** See: You ting.

Geary-Khamis Dollar A hypothetical currency equal in value to the U.S. dollar at a stated point of time. It is used in economics textbooks to demonstrate topics such as purchasing power parity. For example, the Geary-Khamis dollar might be set as equal to the value of the U.S. dollar in 2000.

Geek Informal and somewhat derogatory; a new hire at a Wall Street trading firm. The term was popularized by the book Liar's Poker, which describes the author's experience as a bond trader on Wall Street in the 1980s.

GEHH ISO 3166-3 code for the Gilbert and Ellice Islands, which became Kiribati and Tuvalu in 1976. ISO 3166-3 codes are used to indicate names of countries that are no longer used.

GEL ISO 4217 code for the Georgian lari. It was introduced in 1995, replacing the kupon lari, which had replaced the Soviet ruble and was suffering from hyperinflation. The lari is a floating currency.

Gem In numismatics, a high quality coin. These coins may be valuable as collector's items, though they are illiquid assets. It may also refer to the beauty of the coin regardless of quality.

Gemeente In the Netherlands and Flemish-speaking parts of Belgium, a political subdivision equivalent to a municipal government.

Gemeenten In the Netherlands, a political subdivision equivalent to a municipality.

Gemeinde In German-speaking countries, a political subdivision approximately equivalent to a municipality.

Gemeinschaft A German word translated roughly as community. It is used sometimes to describe an economy or society marked by strong personal relationships and moderate division of labor. For example, all members of a family may work together on a farm. While each family member may have his/her specialty, everyone can perform everyone else's job if need be. Feudal and idealistic socialist societies are examples of Gemeinschaft economies.

General Acceptance The agreement by a bank to pay a bill of exchange in full. This differs from a qualified acceptance, in which the bank honors only a portion of the bill or changes the terms under which payment is made.

General Account 1. In the parlance of the Federal Reserve, a margin account. **2.** In insurance, the account into which all premiums are deposited, unless the policyholder has designated a different account (especially in a whole life policy). Funds in a general account are invested and the proceeds are used to pay claims.

General Agent An agent authorized to perform a limited number of transactions on behalf of a client over a specified period of time. The general agent's authority and responsibilities are terminated at the conclusion of this period of time.

General Agreement on Tariffs and Trade An international treaty, originally written in 1947, intending to establish a framework for international trade, with the goal of the reduction and elimination of tariffs. Its provisions were amended a number of times since its promulgation, but its goals remained the same until 1995, when it was replaced by the World Trade Organization. See also: Doha round.

General Arrangements to Borrow Also called the GAB. A collective agreement between the nations of the G-10 and the International Monetary Fund in which the G-10 members lend a certain amount of capital. The IMF utilizes the funds of the GAB when its normal funds fall short of its borrowers' needs. See also: New Arrangements to Borrow.

General Average In maritime law, a form of insurance with the condition that if one company's cargo must be thrown overboard in order to save the ship from sinking, all other companies with cargo on the ship pay restitution. The form of the general average is agreed upon in advance; normally, the companies pay in proportion to the amount of cargo they each had on the ship. This is done to reduce risk to all companies using a ship to transport their goods.

General Average Contribution The amount a company pays the shipping company or the losing company in a general average. A general average is a form of insurance in maritime law stating that if one company's cargo must be thrown overboard in order to save the ship from sinking, all other companies with cargo on the ship must pay restitution. Normally, each company's general average contribution is in proportion to the amount of cargo each had on the ship. This is done to reduce risk to all companies using a ship to transport their goods.

General Collateral Financing Trades Repurchase agreements of fixed-income investment vehicles, usually by institutional investors. The trades occur on a blind broker basis and allow for transactions to take place more quickly.

General Creditor One who is owed an uncollateralized debt. A general creditor has no lien or collateral on the debt except perhaps a claim on unpaid-for goods, depending on the nature of the goods. In the event of bankruptcy in the United States, a general creditor has no automatic right to any part of the debtor's property, and must file a proof of claim in bankruptcy court. In a no-asset Chapter 7 bankruptcy, most debts are discharged to the detriment of the general creditor. In an asset Chapter 7 case, unsecured property is liquidated and distributed to general and other creditors according to the bankruptcy court's ruling. See also: Secured creditor.

General Depreciation System In depreciation, the most common method used in the Modified Accelerated Cost Recovery System. Under the General Depreciation System, one uses either the declining balance method or straight-line depreciation, depending on which will result in a greater amount depreciated for the time period in question.

General Ledger A record of all of a company's financial statements. It contains two columns: one for credits and one for debits. See also: Balance sheet.

General Lien In a loan or liability, a lien against all personal property, and not simply on the property that the loan was used to buy. A general lien applies only to personal property; that is, real estate cannot be seized. Tax liens imposed by the IRS are general liens.

General Mortgage A mortgage secured by all properties the borrower owns that are not specifically excluded. For example, a real estate owner may have a general mortgage to cover all of his/her properties.

General Obligation Bond In the United States, a municipal bond in which the issuing locality pledges to use all revenues at its disposal to pay bondholders, including the raising of property taxes. Should a sufficient number of residents not pay their property taxes that it impacts revenue for bondholders, the terms of the bond legally require the municipality to raise property taxes to make up the shortfall. There are two basic types of general obligation bonds. A limited GO allows for the raising of property taxes up to a certain percentage, while an unlimited GO theoretically allows the municipality to levy taxes of up to 100% of a property's value. Because an unlimited GO provides a great incentive to pay property tax on time, and because many states only allow such a bond to be issued following a vote on the matter, credit ratings agencies usually rate them higher. However, both types of GO are generally rated highly.

General Order A situation in which imports do not clear customs within 15 days of arriving to the country. Generally, goods are placed under a general order if they are missing needed documentation or if the owner does not claim them. The owner still carries the risk of damage to the goods, and it is the owner's responsibility to rectify the situation. If goods remain under general order for more than six months, the government either confiscates or auctions them.

General Partner In a company, one who shares with at least one other person, jointly and severally, the business' management authority, the ability to hire and fire employees, the right to share revenue, and the financial risk for the company's debts. General partners exist in general partnership and limited partnerships. There is no immediate difference between the rights and responsibilities for general partners in each type of business, except that general partners in a limited partnership must share a certain amount of profit and financial liability with limited partners according to an arrangement between them.

General Partnership A business structure in which two or more persons share in the ownership and profits and losses of the business. In a general partnership, two or more partners, jointly and severally, share all profits, losses, management authority, and risk for the business. Importantly, all partners have unlimited liability, which means that they may lose more than they originally invested. In most jurisdictions, partnerships are preferable to corporations because partnerships' profits are not taxed prior to distribution to the partners. In other words, there is no equivalent to a corporate tax on partnerships. On the other hand, partners have more legal and financial liability in case of liquidation than would shareholders and most management in a corporation. See also: Limited partnership, Limited liability partnership.

General Revenue Revenue that a state or local government raises through taxation and that may be used for any purpose. That is, general revenue is not earmarked automatically for functions such as road maintenance or payroll for state workers. Rather, the government may use general revenue for discretionary functions.

General Sales Tax A sales tax applied to all goods and services sold in a jurisdiction that are not specifically exempted. For example, a general sales tax may be implemented at the local level on all goods and services except groceries in order to finance municipal government. See also: VAT.

General Strike 1. A strike in which all or most workers in a city or region stop working. A general strike is not limited to one company and generally extends beyond a single industry. It is intended to show solidarity between all workers and may be a statement against capitalism as a system. General strikes were most common in the 19th and early 20th centuries. **2.** More generally, any large strike, even if confined to a single company.

General Tariff A tariff a country imposes on imports from all countries other than most favored nations and nations with which it has a free trade agreement. The general tariff is higher than other tariffs and may harm trade with countries to which it is applied.

General Utilities Doctrine A former provision in U.S. tax law allowing a corporation to liquidate its assets at a profit and pass on the profit to its shareholders without paying a corporate tax. Shareholders, however, remained responsible for taxes on what amounted to a special dividend. The general utilities doctrine allowed shareholders to avoid double taxation in the liquidation of assets. It was abolished by the Tax Reform Act of 1986.

Generally Accepted Accounting Principles Rules to which accountants adhere when preparing financial statements. The Generally Accepted Accounting Principles exist to ensure that American accountants are using the same or almost the same standards so that comparison of financial statements between or within a company is easy and accurate. They also promote transparency in accounting. The GAAP are set by the FASB. See also: International Financial Reporting Standards.

Generally Accepted Auditing Standards Guidelines for how audits ought to be conducted. The Generally Accepted Auditing Standards are set by the American Institute of Certified Public Accountants and provide a uniform set of standards for how to conduct audits in the United States.

Generational Accounting A way to conduct accounting that primarily considers how current income and spending will impact long-term financial sustainability. The term is used most frequently in government accounting. For example, generational accounting may consider whether or not the state pension can pay all liabilities for at least 60 years.

Generation-Skipping Transfer or Trust A trust into which assets are deposited and invested, but for different beneficiaries. That is, the assets of the trust are held on behalf of the grantor's grandchildren; they are divided among them when the grantor's children all die. On the other hand, income from the investment of those assets is distributed among the grantor's children. Generation-skipping trusts allow the grantor's assets to bypass estate taxes that the children would have to pay if the assets were directly transferred.

Generic Describing a product without a famous brand name. Generic products are basically the same as brand products but are generally less expensive.

Generic Bond 1. A bond with no distinguishing features. **2.** An alternate term for a public official bond.

Generic Credit Spread The difference in yield between two debt securities with the same features except riskiness. That is, the generic credit spread is the difference between a yield on a debt security with a given credit rating and the yield on another with the same coupon rate and maturity but a different credit rating. In all cases, the riskier debt security will have a higher yield. It is also simply called a credit spread. See also: Risk premium.

Generic Market The market for goods and services needed by most consumers. For example, groceries and clothing may be considered part of the generic market.

Generic Security A security that has not been traded long enough to establish a positive reputation for liquidity and trade volume. Generic securities have usually been traded for less than a year. Because of the relatively high risk, generic securities have lower prices than older, seasoned securities.

Gentlemen Prefer Bonds A term used during a bear market to indicate that investors prefer bonds. In a bear market, stocks decline in price while bonds (whose prices usually move inversely relative to stocks) tend to rise. As a result, investors will prefer to buy bonds while the bear market lasts. The term derives from the 1953 Marilyn Monroe film, Gentlemen Prefer Blondes.

GEO GOST 7.67 Latin three-letter geocode for the Republic of Georgia. The code is used for transactions to and from Georgian bank accounts and for international shipping to Georgia. As with all GOST 7.67 codes, it is used primarily in Cyrillic alphabets.

Geographic Risk The risk to an investment in a specific geographic area. Specifically, it refers to the possibility that a natural disaster to which an area is prone will negatively impact an investment. For example, a company pumping oil in the Gulf of Mexico carries a geographic risk that a hurricane will destroy its infrastructure. See also: Country risk.

George Akerlof An American economist and academic born in 1940. He is most noted for his work on information asymmetry, which summarizes how economic actors use and share information in order to gain advantages in the market. Akerlof argues, contrary to neo-classical economics, that markets usually are inefficient because information is not spread evenly. He shared the Nobel Prize for Economics in 2001 for this work. Akerlof has also been noted for his work on the social effects of economic choices, particularly with regard to the availability of contraceptives and legal abortion.

George Eastman An inventor and entrepreneur who created roll film. His invention made photography accessible to more people and led to the invention of motion pictures. Eastman founded Kodak to market the modern camera, which he invented. In later life, he became a major philanthropist. He lived from 1854 to 1932.

George Soros A famous investor and hedge fund speculator. Born in Hungary in an Esperanto-speaking home, he fled to England and later the United States to escape Nazism. In 1970, he founded Soros Fund Management, which returned an average of 42.5% per year for the next 10 years. In 1992, he short sold more than $10 billion worth of British pounds, which forced the Bank of England to withdraw from the European Exchange Rate Mechanism and to devalue the pound. He is a noted critic of unfettered free enterprise and believes that reflexivity can change the fundamentals of an economy. See also: Black Wednesday.

Georgian Lari The currency of the Republic of Georgia. It was introduced in 1995, replacing the kupon lari, which had replaced the Soviet ruble and was suffering from hyperinflation. The lari is a floating currency.

Geppy A slang term for the British pound-Japanese yen exchange rate.

Geris An ancient Hebrew unit of area approximately equivalent to 314 square millimeters.

Germanophone A person, company, or country for which German is the primary language. Because of the historical importance of German as an international language and of German-speaking countries as a world power, German is an important language in international commerce. German has official status in about 11 countries.

Gestation Repo A repurchase agreement between a mortgage provider and a security dealer. In a gestation repo, the mortgage company sells agency securities to the dealer and agrees to buy them back at a stated price at a certain point in the future. This provides a profit for the security dealer and short-term funding for the mortgage provider. See also: Double sale.

Get Down to Brass Tacks Informal; to discuss the essentials of the matter at hand. For example, shareholders discussing declining dividends may get down to brass tacks when they discuss why sales are lagging, rather than whether the CEO is being paid too much.

Get Hit Informal; to decline in price or to lose on an investment. Stocks can get hit for any number of reasons, whether technical or fundamental.

Getting Paid In investment banking, a slang term for the commissions or other forms of payment made for trading on a client's behalf.

Gewog In Bhutan, a political subdivision equivalent to a municipality.

GF 1. ISO 3166-1 alpha-2 code for French Guiana. This is the code used in international transactions to and from French Guianan bank accounts. **2.** ISO 3166-2 geocode for French Guiana. This is used as an international standard for shipping to French Guiana.

GG 1. ISO 3166-1 alpha-2 code for the Bailiwick of Guernsey. This is the code used in international transactions to and from Guernesiais bank accounts. **2.** ISO 3166-2 geocode for Guernsey. This is used as an international standard for shipping to Guernsey. Because Guernsey is a British Crown Dependency, it has its own ISO 3166-2 code under the UK entry.

GGK ISO 4217 code for the German goldmark, which was the currency of Germany between its unification in 1873 and the end of World War I. It was based on gold, but it replaced the Vereinsthaler, which was based on silver. While it circulated, it was called simply the mark; the name goldmark was invented later to distinguish it from later German currencies.

GGP A currency code for the Guernsey pound. Because Guernsey is a British Crown dependency, it is in a monetary union with the United Kingdom. As a result, a Guernsey pound is equivalent to a British pound. This code is not recognized by the ISO.

GH 1. ISO 3166-1 alpha-2 code for the Republic of Ghana. This is the code used in international transactions to and from Ghanaian bank accounts. **2.** ISO 3166-2 geocode for Ghana. This is used as an international standard for shipping to Ghana. Each region of Ghana has its own code with the prefix "GH." For example, the code for Volta is ISO 3166-2:GH-TV.

GHA GOST 7.67 Latin three-letter geocode for Ghana. The code is used for transactions to and from Ghanaian bank accounts and for international shipping to Ghana. As with all GOST 7.67 codes, it is used primarily in Cyrillic alphabets.

Ghabara A Maltese unit of dry volume approximately equivalent to 303.1 milliliters. It is largely obsolete but is still used in some circumstances.

Ghalva An obsolete Arabic unit of length approximately equivalent to 230.4 meters.

Ghanaian Cedi The currency of Ghana. The first cedi was issued in 1965 and was pegged to the British pound. Two years later, the second cedi was issued with a different peg. It briefly floated in the late 1970s but was subject to high inflation. To counteract the inflation, the third cedi was issued in 2007, after which inflation eased significantly.

Ghanaian Pound The currency of Ghana between 1958 and 1965. It replaced the British West African pound shortly after Ghana's independence. In 1965, it was changed to the first Ghanaian cedi.

GHC ISO 4217 code for the second Ghanaian cedi. It was introduced in 1967, replacing the first cedi, which in turn had replaced the Ghanaian pound. It was initially pegged to the British pound at various values. It became a floating currency briefly in 1978 but too-rapid depreciation led Ghana to re-peg the cedi to the U.S. dollar very quickly. It floated again in 1990; consistently high inflation led to its replacement by the third cedi (code GHS) in 2007.

Ghost Payroll 1. Persons on a list of employees who either do not exist or are not required to show up for work. Money paid to the ghost payroll is remitted to an organized crime syndicate. Ghost payrolls are used to make extortion schemes appear legitimate. **2.** The money paid to the ghost payroll.

Ghost Stock A stock that is sold short when the short seller has not actually borrowed it. As a result, the ghost stock cannot be delivered to the buyer. It should not be confused with ghosting.

Ghost Work Projects or other work that laid off or fired employees did not complete. It remains for other employees to finish ghost work.

Ghosting An illegal practice in which two or more market makers collude in order to artificially inflate or deflate the price of a stock, hoping to profit on the uptick or downturn. One firm will buy or sell large amounts of a certain stock and the second firm does the same, causing a buy or sell frenzy. The supposed competitors then have the opportunity to profit as the market is unaware of their collusion. See also: Insider trading, antitrust.

GHS ISO 4217 code for the third Ghanaian cedi. It was issued in 2007 due to the second cedi's consistently high inflation.

Gi 1. ISO 3166-1 alpha-2 code for Gibraltar. This is the code used in international transactions to and from Gibraltar bank accounts. **2.** ISO 3166-2 geocode for Gibraltar. This is used as an international standard for shipping to Gibraltar. For example, a package being shipped to the area from abroad would bear the designation "ISO 3166-2:GI."

GIB GOST 7.67 Latin three-letter geocode for Gibraltar. The code is used for transactions to and from Gibraltarian bank accounts and for international shipping to Gibraltar. As with all GOST 7.67 codes, it is used primarily in Cyrillic alphabets.

Gibraltar Pound The currency of Gibraltar. It was introduced in 1927, replacing the British pound. It is pegged to the British pound at par.

Gibson's Paradox An observation that interest rates are correlated with wholesale prices rather than the inflation rate. Gibson's Paradox was first discussed by John Maynard Keynes in 1930; at the time, the idea was controversial, as most economists believed that interest rates correlated with changes to prices rather than the prices themselves. It is important to note that Gibson's paradox only applied when money was on the gold standard. See also: Keynesian economics.

Gift An asset of any kind that an individual transfers to another individual while neither receiving nor expecting anything in return. A gift one receives is taxable in the United States, but only if its value exceeds $13,000 (in 2009) and is not specifically excluded. For example, gifts between spouses are not taxable under any circumstances. See also: Estate, Gift Tax.

Gift Aid Scholarships or grants used to pay for one's education. Unlike loans, gift aid is not repaid, and unlike work-study programs, there are no requirements beyond academic performance to keep gift aid.

Gift Causa Mortis A gift made upon the giver's death. A gift causa mortis contrasts with a gift inter vivos, which the giver bequeaths while still living. A large gift causa mortis may be subject to the gift tax.

Gift Inter Vivos A gift one gives to another while one is still living. A gift inter vivos contrasts with a gift causa mortis, where the giver bequeaths the gift pending his/her own death. A large gift inter vivos may be subject to the gift tax.

Gift Splitting The act of a married couple giving gifts to a single beneficiary separately in order to avoid the gift tax. Givers of gifts in excess of $10,000 are required to pay the gift tax. In order to avoid this through gift splitting, spouses may separately give up to $10,000, meaning that the beneficiary receives up to $20,000 without subjecting the giver to the tax.

Gift Tax A tax that the federal government levies on givers of gifts in excess of a certain value. If the value of a gift is over a certain amount, which varies from year to year but is always over $10,000, the government assesses the gift tax. The tax applies even if the recipient pays for the gift, so long as he/she does not pay for the full value. Generally speaking, payments for medical, educational, and political purposes are exempt from the gift tax, as are gifts to one's spouse.

Gifting Phase A period of one's life during which one's investment goals shift from making money to giving to charitable or philanthropic causes. The term is most commonly associated with highly successful investors who wish to give back some or all of their earnings to the community at large. An investment adviser may make different decisions during the gifting phase.

Gifts in Kind Any donation other than cash to a non-profit organization. For example, gifts in kind may consist of stocks, bonds, or inventory. In general, gifts in kind are tax deductible at their fair market value.

Gilded Age The period of American history from approximately the end of the Civil War to the early 20th century. The Gilded Age was marked by rapid industrialization, development of infrastructure (such as railroads), and virtually no government regulation of the economy. Important industrialists, such as Andrew Carnegie, John W. Rockefeller, Cornelius Vanderbilt, and others, led a period of development that created what became the modern American economy. This age saw the early development of organized labor, which the industrialists often violently opposed. Apologists for the Gilded Age point out that this era laid the foundations for American philanthropy and employed many people who might have gone without jobs otherwise. Critics denounce the era's alleged conspicuous consumption on the part of the wealthy and economic instability that they claim came from lack of regulation. See also: Panic of 1873, Panic of 1893, Panic of 1907, Cross of Gold, Robber baron.

Gill An obsolete Scottish unit of liquid volume approximately equivalent to 0.053 liters.

Gilt Edged Bond A private-issued, investment grade bond. Only blue chip companies issue gilt edged bonds and, for that reason, they have high ratings. Gilt edged bonds are considered sufficiently low-risk that the law allows banks to invest in them. In addition to being low-risk, investment-grade bonds are low-return, greatly reducing the cost on the issuer. They are considered the next safest bond to a Treasury security.

Gilt Fund A mutual fund composed primarily or exclusively of gilts. Gilts are a debt security issued by the British government, and thus are the equivalent of U.S. Treasury securities. As such, a gilt fund provides a steady (if small) return at little to no risk.

Gin GOST 7.67 Latin three-letter geocode for Guinea. The code is used for transactions to and from Guinean bank accounts and for international shipping to Guinea. As with all GOST 7.67 codes, it is used primarily in Cyrillic alphabets.

Ginnie Mae Mutual Fund A mutual fund that invests exclusively in mortgage-backed securities issued by Ginnie Mae. The returns on Ginnie Mae mutual funds vary according to the interest rates currently being paid on the mortgages underlying the MBSs. Ginnie Mae mutual funds are relatively low-risk, as Ginnie Mae mortgages are guaranteed or insured by various branches of the U.S. government. Additionally, each mutual fund contains many Ginnie Mae mortgages, reducing the investor's exposure to prepayment risk. Some buy shares in Ginnie Mae mutual funds simply because they are available in smaller denominations than the individual MBSs underlying them.

Ginnie Mae Pass-Through Mortgage-backed pass-through securities with principals and interest guaranteed by Ginnie Mae. A pass-through security is backed by assets or debt; in a Ginnie Mae pass-through security, Ginnie Mae reduces the risk of default to the pass-through holder by guaranteeing payment. It is the most common agency pass-through security.

Ginnie Mae Trust A unit investment trust that invests exclusively in Ginnie Mae certificates. It operates much like a Ginnie Mae mutual fund, but returns for a Ginnie

Mae trust are given to the investor rather than reinvested. Thus, if one purchases a Ginnie Mae trust, one receives progressively smaller coupon payments as the mortgages underlying the trust are paid off.

GIP ISO 4217 code for the Gibraltar pound. It was introduced in 1927, replacing the British pound. It is pegged to the British pound at par.

Girah An obsolete Indian and Pakistani unit of length approximately equivalent to 5.715 centimeters.

Giri An ancient Sumerian unit of length approximately equivalent to one meter.

Giscard Bond A bond once issued by the French government in which the payoff was indexed to the price of gold. Giscard bonds were issued in the early 1970s, immediately before the price of gold rose significantly. As a result, the bonds were very expensive for the French government to repay.

Giulio Tremonti A professor and politician who has served several times as the Italian Minister of Economy and Finance, including in the 1990s and 2000s. Tremonti is noted for spearheading significant tax cuts and abolitions in Italy, though tax rates remained high compared to neighboring countries. He was born in 1947.

Give Up For a broker to execute an order on behalf of another broker. Giving up occurs as a professional courtesy when a broker receives an order from a client that he/she is too busy to execute. It is important to note that the broker who receives the order, rather than the broker who conducts the transaction, is the one who earns the applicable commissions and fees. The term originates from the fact that the broker who executes the transaction must "give up" the commission to other broker.

Giveback The surrender of benefits or wages by the employees of a company. That is, a giveback occurs when the management persuades the workers to agree to a reduction in wages and/or benefits. Givebacks reduce a company's overhead and, for that reason, tend to please shareholders. However, critics maintain that they are bad for the company's long-term sustainability. See also: Labor relations.

GL 1. ISO 3166-1 alpha-2 code for Greenland. This is the code used in international transactions to and from Greenlander bank accounts. **2.** ISO 3166-2 geocode for Greenland. This is used as an international standard for shipping to Greenland.

Glamour Stock A popular stock that is held by a large number of investors, especially institutional investors. A glamour stock usually has a high price and almost always has a high P/E ratio because of the larger than normal demand for it.

Glanders A bacterial disease characterized by fever, coughing, nasal discharge and sometimes the development of nodules underneath the skin. It can cause death in days or months. Glanders is most common in horses and similar animals but can be contracted by humans. It was used in biological warfare during both world wars.

Glasnost A policy to increase the transparency of the government of the Soviet Union. Glasnost was instituted in the late 1980s, relaxing censorship of the media and permitting greater freedom of speech. It made public many of the atrocities committed under Joseph Stalin and the dilapidation of many aspects of Soviet life. Some historians view this loosening of state policy as one of the causes of the fall of the Soviet Union. See also: Perestroika.

Glass Ceiling A situation in which a person cannot advance in an organization because of real or perceived sexism, racism or some other form of discrimination. For example, very few CEOs in the United States are women; this fact forms a glass ceiling for women in business. Glass ceilings are usually illegal but are difficult to prosecute because choosing one candidate over another is often unquantifiable.

Glass Insurance An insurance policy that provides coverage for damage to an expensive piece of glass. This type of insurance is useful for replacing, for example, the windows in one's home if they are vandalized. Glass insurance is often offered as a rider to another policy. As with all insurance, one must pay a premium to receive the coverage.

Glass-Steagal Act Legislation in the United States, enacted in 1933, intended to restore confidence in the banking system. Among its most important provisions was the creation the FDIC, which provided insurance on bank deposits up to a certain amount. The act also prohibited bank holding companies from owning brokerages or certain securities. This provision was designed to prevent banks from engaging in most investment activities and thereby to reduce the risk they carried. Most of the Glass-Steagal Act was repealed by the Gramm-Leach-Bliley Act in 1999. It is formally called the Banking Act of 1933.

Gliding Clause A clause in a contract allowing the seller of a good to charge the market value of the good upon delivery, rather than when the contract is signed. For example, if the market value of a car is $15,000 when the car is sold but $17,000 when the buyer picks it up, the buyer must pay $17,000. A gliding clause may be used as a hedge against inflation.

Global Bond A bond that may be traded in any domestic or euro market. A global bond may be issued in the domestic currency, but the same issue may be offered in several countries at the same time. Thus, global bonds may be traded either in domestic or foreign markets.

Global Crossing A telecommunications company that filed for bankruptcy during the Enron scandal of the early 2000s. It had previously inflated its profits by recording as revenue its conduit swaps, a transaction in which telecommunications companies exchange carriers with each other without trading money. In 2005, it was found to have violated several accounting laws and was forced to settle with the SEC. See also: Sarbanes-Oxley Act.

Global Fund A mutual fund or other investment company that invests in securities that are traded in various countries. This is done to reduce risk, often political risk. For example, if one country's government announces a larger than normal budget

deficit, or the central bank raises interest rates, this may affect security prices in one country, but not necessarily in other countries that did not take equivalent steps. Likewise, if a whole industry fails in one country, but thrives in another, investing in the same industry in both countries hedges one's risk. Some analysts argue that country diversification is less effective in an era of globalization, but other analysts dispute that. A global fund is also called a world fund. See also: Country diversification.

Global Investment Performance Standards A code of ethical conduct in financial reporting. The CFA Institute puts out the GIPS and all members agree to abide by them. The GIPS seek to promote transparency and honesty in financial analysis. An important component of the GIPS is the concept that the money manager must report all discretionary accounts he/she controls, not simply those that perform well.

Global Macro Strategy A hedge fund strategy in which the money manager makes investment decisions based on the macroeconomic or political conditions in a country. For example, if a government is contemplating major health care legislation and one hedge fund manager believes this will help insurance companies, the manager will likely invest in those insurance companies. However, if another manager believes that the legislation will harm insurance companies, he/she will likely short sell those same insurance stocks.

Global Registered Share Shares that trade on multiple exchanges with different currencies. For example, if a publicly-traded company issues shares in dollars on the New York Stock Exchange and in pounds on the London Stock Exchange, it is issuing global registered shares. These are fairly uncommon, and are certainly less common than International Depository Receipts, whereby a company issues its shares in one currency but allows banks effectively to trade them in another. Global registered shares are also called simply global shares.

Globalization The integration of global markets by the reduction trade barriers, improved communication, foreign direct investment, and other means. Globalization allows a multinational corporation to make a product in one country and sell it in another. This provides jobs in one country and less expensive goods in the other. Globalization also allows for the free flow of capital between countries, which many believe spurs economic growth. Proponents of globalization argue that it allows developing countries to continue and hasten their levels of development, and that it protects consumers in developed countries. Opponents believe that globalization serves the interests of multinational corporations at the expense of small businesses, which sends jobs to other countries needlessly.

Globex A trading platform that allows investors to trade futures, commodities, and other derivatives without regard for time zone. Trading takes place electronically. It was established by Reuters in 1992. It has become less popular as exchanges, notably the CBOT, have adopted similar platforms. See also: National Market System.

Glossy Bright or shiny, especially on paper or in print. Glossy items are used in marketing in order to attract attention.

GLP GOST 7.67 Latin three-letter geocode for Guadeloupe. The code is used for transactions to and from Guadeloupean bank accounts and for international shipping to Guadeloupe. As with all GOST 7.67 codes, it is used primarily in Cyrillic alphabets.

Glut Oversupply; too many units of a product in an area or economy relative to demand. A glut almost always causes the price of the product to drop.

GM 1. ISO 3166-1 alpha-2 code for the Republic of the Gambia. This is the code used in international transactions to and from Gambian bank accounts. **2.** ISO 3166-2 geocode for Gambia. This is used as an international standard for shipping to Gambia. Each Gambian division has its own code with the prefix "GM." For example, the code for the Lower River Division is ISO 3166-2:GM-L.

GMB GOST 7.67 Latin three-letter geocode for the Gambia. The code is used for transactions to and from Gambian bank accounts and for international shipping to the Gambia. As with all GOST 7.67 codes, it is used primarily in Cyrillic alphabets.

GMD ISO 4217 code for the Gambian dalasi. It was issued in 1971, replacing the Gambian pound.

Gmina In Poland, a political subdivision equivalent to a municipality.

GNB GOST 7.67 Latin three-letter geocode for Guinea-Bissau. The code is used for transactions to and from Bissau-Guinean bank accounts and for international shipping to Guinea-Bissau. As with all GOST 7.67 codes, it is used primarily in Cyrillic alphabets.

GNE ISO 4217 code for the syli, which was the currency of Guinea between 1971 and 1985. It replaced the first Guinean franc and itself was replaced by the second franc. The second franc's initial value matched the syli's at a 1:1 ratio. See also: GNF.

GNF ISO 4217 code for the second Guinean franc. It was introduced in 1985, replacing the syli. Throughout the 2000s decade, the franc has experienced high inflation.

GNMA Midget Informal for mortgage-backed securities with principals and interest guaranteed by Ginnie Mae and having certain features. In particular, the mortgages underlying GNMA midgets have fixed-rates and 15-year maturities. As with other agency pass-through securities, a government agency (in this case Ginnie Mae) reduces the risk of default to the pass-through holder by guaranteeing payment.

GNMA-I A straightforward mortgage-backed, pass-through security issued by Ginnie Mae. All mortgages backing each GNMA-I were made by the same issuer and all have the same interest rate. All mortgages were issued within the three months immediately preceding the issue of the GNMA-I. Because these securities have no special features, they have more risk than other mortgage-backed securities such as collateralized mortgage obligations. GNMA-I is pronounced "Ginnie Mae One."

GNMA-II A certain type of mortgage-backed, pass-through security issued by Ginnie Mae. Mortgages backing each GNMA-II may be made by different issuers and/or have different interest rates. The mortgages may be more geographically diverse or have other special features that reduce their risk. GNMA-II is pronounced "Ginnie Mae Two."

Gnomes Pass-through, mortgage-backed securities offered through Freddie Mac where the mortgages underlying the security have a maturity of 15 years.

Gnomes of Zurich A pejorative term for bankers in Switzerland. They acquired this nickname because of their reputation for discrete and indeed secretive policies. Harold Wilson coined the term in 1956 when he was the British shadow chancellor of the exchequer and believed that Swiss bank speculators were artificially weakening the pound.

GNQ GOST 7.67 Latin three-letter geocode for Equatorial Guinea. The code is used for transactions to and from Equatorial Guinean bank accounts and for international shipping to Equatorial Guinea. As with all GOST 7.67 codes, it is used primarily in Cyrillic alphabets.

Go Along To buy or sell a security at the price currently being offered or bid. That is, one goes along with a transaction when one takes an offer or bid rather than makes one.

Go Galt Informal; to cease working in response to punitive taxes. That is, when taxes become sufficiently high as to disincentivize work, one goes Galt as a form of protest. For example, if taxes are 100% on all income over $90,000, no one has an incentive to earn more than $90,000 and one may therefore work less. Going Galt under a marginal tax system is generally irrational because one's post-tax income is almost always higher than it would have been had one stopped working and gone Galt. The term derives from a major character in Ayn Rand's novel, Atlas Shrugged.

Go Home A slang term meaning to close a position.

Go Long To take a long position. That is, one goes long when one buys a security or derivative.

Go Short To take a short position. That is, one goes short when one conducts a short sale, writes an option, sells a futures contract, or sells any other security where further action may be necessary. See also: Go long.

Go to Black In film, to fade the screen until no image appears and the screen is simply black. Going to black may be used between scenes or to create dramatic effect. It may therefore be used in commercials and some other forms of marketing.

Go Unable To become impossible to fill (an order) on an exchange floor. For example, if an investor orders a broker to buy at $15 but the price suddenly jumps to $25 and appears headed upward, the order is said to have gone unable.

Goal What a person or institution seeks to gain from an investment. Goals vary from investor to investor and can even change for the same investor over time. For example, a person may have the goal to extract a high return from her investments when she is young in order to finance a certain lifestyle; this person is likely to invest in high risk securities and ventures. Over time, however, this person may be concerned about protecting savings for retirement. As a result, the goals may shift and the person may invest primarily in bonds and blue-chip stocks instead. Goals influence one's investment philosophy and strategy. See also: Portfolio Restructuring.

Goat Rodeo A slang term for a bad meeting. For example, if shareholders spend most of the annual meeting criticizing management and attempting to remove the board of directors, the meeting may be described as a goat rodeo.

Gobolka In Somalia, a political subdivision equivalent to a province.

Gobrecht Dollar A $1 coin minted in the United States between 1836 and 1839. It featured Lady Liberty on the obverse and is named for Christian Gobrecht, who engraved it. It was about 90% silver.

Godfather Offer An offer by an acquiring company to buy a target company for far more than the target's market value. Often, the board of directors may be inclined to refuse a godfather offer (primarily because it could cause them to lose their jobs), but the price is so high that actually refusing would expose the board to lawsuits by shareholders. A godfather offer is usually made when the target company's stock has been stable or declining for an extended period. The term gets its name from the film The Godfather, because it is an offer the board cannot refuse.

Godo Gaisha A Japanese term for a limited liability company. Godo geisha were introduced in Japan in 2006, replacing yugen-kaisha.

God's Work A slang term for investment banking. It was coined in 2009 by a Goldman Sachs executive attempting to defend investment banking against populist, anti-banking sentiment. However, it is more commonly used ironically by those who oppose perceived excesses in the financial sector.

Godzilla In numismatics, a slang term for an extremely high quality coin, such as a gem. These coins may be valuable as collector's items, though they are illiquid assets.

Goes To trade, especially at a given price. For example, one may say that a stock "goes" at $10, meaning that one may trade at its current share price of $10.

Gofer An employee responsible for making coffee, picking up dry cleaning and other menial tasks. While gofers have low status and usually are poorly paid, they may have access to important persons in the company or industry. This may in turn help gofers advance their careers. This is especially the case in the entertainment sector.

Go-Go Fund Informal; a mutual fund that invests predominantly or exclusively in high growth companies. Because many of these companies will eventually go bankrupt, a go-go fund carries high risk. However, it has the possibility of a high return if some of the companies establish themselves and become highly profitable.

Going Ahead The act or practice of a broker making a trade on his/her own account before filling a similar order on behalf of a client. Going ahead is considered a form of insider trading and as such is illegal.

Going Away 1. Buying a bond with the intention to immediately resell it. Dealers practice going away; this only rarely affects the bond's price. **2.** Buying a large amount of a serial bond with a given maturity. Institutional investors practice this form of going away most often.

Going Concern A term describing a company with enough cash flow and/or other resources to maintain operations for the foreseeable future. A company that is no longer a going concern has gone bankrupt.

Going into the Trade Idiom in general equities; describing the impressions and expectations of each party to a trade immediately before the trade takes place. It also describes the condition of a trader's account vis a vis the security being traded (i.e. long or short) immediately before the trade takes place.

Going Out In equities, referring to the advertising the sale of a security over NASDAQ, Autex, or SSI.

Going Private A process in which the senior management of a publicly-traded company or a small group of investors buys all of the company's shares outstanding. Going private gives the management or investor group complete control of the company and allows it to operate without recourse to shareholders. Going private is often highly leveraged. When the management purchases the company, one usually refers to the act as a management buyout.

Going Public The act or process of a company selling stock in itself when it moves from private ownership to public trade. More generally, it refers to the actual first sale of stock to the public. Small companies looking for a new source of financing often go public, but large companies who wish to be publicly traded can do so as well. Investing in a company that is going public is generally risky because one does not know how much demand will exist for the stock after its initial offering. This risk comes from the uncertainty of the stock's resale value. See also: Publicly-traded company.

Going Rate Informal; the current or prevailing price, especially of a major asset like real estate. See also: Spot price.

Going South Informal; the process of a stock or market declining in price gradually over time.

Going Suit Slang; a situation in which a technical worker becomes a manager (and has to wear a suit to work). The term is somewhat derogatory, connoting a person who has forgotten his/her roots. It may also indicate a person who becomes less technically proficient the longer he/she remains in management.

Going-Concern Value The value of a company as long as it remains in business. One calculates the going-concern value by adding the value of its goodwill and income to its net asset value. This is an important calculation when determining the appropriate purchase price in a merger or acquisition. Mortgage lenders also use it to determine the value of an income-producing property.

Gold A particularly valuable precious metal. Gold is an element with the atomic number 79. It is used for jewelry, electronics and for other purposes. Historically, gold was used in many cultures as the basis for currency, but this is no longer the case. Investments in gold are often used as a hedge against inflation because it tends to maintain its value over time.

Gold Ball Slang; in auto sales, a term for a highly creditworthy customer with a large down payment. Gold ball customers are very low risk for the seller.

Gold Bars Bars of gold bullion that may be bought and sold for investment. Most gold bullion is at least 99.9% pure. Gold bars, like all gold bullion, are commodities that investors often use as a hedge against recession and inflation; Thus, while it is volatile like most commodities, it always maintains a relatively high value. Gold bars are measured by mass and purity rather than face value.

Gold Bug An investor or investment adviser who keeps a portfolio consisting largely or exclusively of gold and gold-related products, especially when most other investors are not doing so. A gold bug may believe that the economy is about to undergo a period of high inflation or that a speculative bubble is about to burst. He/she invests in gold because it tends to maintain its value, even in bad economic times, and because it is usually protected from inflation. Other investors often believe that gold bugs are alarmists. In the late 2000s recession, some gold bugs were associated with the Austrian School of economics, but this is not always the case. See also: Peter Schiff.

Gold Bullion Pure gold that may be bought and sold for investment. Most gold bullion is at least 99.9% pure. It is usually smelted into either gold bars or gold coins. Gold bullion is a commodity that investors often use as a hedge against recession and inflation; Thus, while it is volatile like most commodities, it always maintains a relatively high value. Gold bullion is measured by mass and purity rather than face value.

Gold Certificate A document entitling one to ownership of a certain, stated amount of gold. Most of the time, gold investors hold gold certificates rather than the physical gold itself in order to avoid the expense, security issues, and other difficulties associated with owning gold. However, the holder of the gold certificate can take possession of the gold he/she owns upon demand.

Gold Clause A clause in a contract allowing payment to be made in gold instead of currency. A gold clause is placed in a contract if it is suspected that payment in currency may be rendered impossible due to inflation, war or some other reason. Gold clauses were common at the first part of the 20th century, but were illegal in the United States between 1934 and 1977.

Gold Clause Cases Several U.S. Supreme Court cases arising out of the Gold Reserve Act of 1934. According to this act, private citizens were no longer allowed to own more than a token amount of gold. However, many contracts enacted before the act contained gold clauses, which allowed one party to demand payment in gold (in order to protect against inflation of the U.S. dollar). The Supreme Court ruled that these clauses became invalid upon the passage of the act and that no party could demand such payment. The argument behind this ruling states that Congress has the authority to invalidate valid contracts if these contracts go against any monetary policy Congress may adopt. These cases were decided jointly in 1935.

Gold Coin 1. A coin of gold bullion that may be bought and sold for investment. Most gold bullion is at least 99.9% pure. Gold coins, like all gold bullion, are commodities that investors often use as a hedge against recession and inflation. Thus, while they are volatile like most commodities, they always maintain a relatively high value. Gold coins are measured by mass and purity rather than face value. **2.** A coin of a currency that is minted from gold and intended for circulation. See also: Kruggerand.

Gold Dollar A $1 coin minted in the United States between 1849 and 1889. It was 90% pure gold.

Gold Fixing The determination of the price of gold. Gold fixing is done twice per day by the London gold pool, which consists of five members who investigate the supply and demand for gold on the world market. The price that gold fixing determines serves as a benchmark for gold trading worldwide.

Gold Franc An accounting currency used by the Bank for International Settlements between 1930 and 2003. The gold franc was equal in value to 0.290 grams of fine gold, which was also the peg used by the Swiss franc for a time. The BIS replaced the gold franc with Special Drawing Rights.

Gold Futures An agreement to buy and sell a certain amount of gold at a certain date at a certain price. For example, Investor A may make a contract with Farmer B in which A agrees to buy a certain number of bars of B's gold at $800 per ounce. This contract must be honored whether the price of corn goes to $100 or $2,000 per ounce. Gold futures contracts can help reduce volatility in the normally volatile commodity markets, but contain the risks inherent to all speculative investing. These contracts may be sold on the secondary market, but the person holding the contract at its end must take delivery of the underlying.

Gold Market The supply and demand for the buying and selling of gold, a major precious metal. Because gold is considered a hedge against inflation (that is, it retains its value during bouts of inflation), one may buy gold if one thinks the inflation rate might accelerate. Conversely, one may sell gold if one is concerned about disinflation.

Gold Mutual Fund A mutual fund or other investment company that invests predominantly or exclusively in securities related to gold. For example, it may invest in futures contracts or options in gold itself or in stock in gold mining companies. See also: Precious Metals Fund.

Gold Option A contract giving the holder the right (but not the obligation) to buy (in a call) or to sell (in a put) a certain quantity of gold at a stated price on or before the expiration date of the contract. Because gold is considered a hedge against inflation (that is, it retains its value during bouts of inflation), one may purchase a gold call if one thinks the inflation rate might accelerate. Conversely, one may purchase a gold put if one is concerned about disinflation.

Gold Reserve Act of 1934 Legislation in the United States that required citizens to sell their privately owned gold to the federal government. After the passage of this act, it was illegal for U.S. citizens to own more than small amounts of gold until the end of 1974. The Gold Reserve Act was intended to stabilize the U.S. dollar during the Great Depression. Scholars differ on how well it accomplished this goal.

Gold Standard A system whereby a currency is linked to the value of gold. That is, one would be able to exchange one unit of the currency for so many ounces of gold on demand. The gold standard makes monetary policy independent from policymaker decisions. Many currencies have been linked to gold over the years, most recently under the Bretton Woods System. The gold standard reduces the likelihood of inflation, but tends to cause higher interest rates and renders a country less able to pursue full employment. The gold standard contrasts with fiat money. See also: Cross of Gold, Silver Standard.

Gold Stock Reserves of gold kept by the U.S. Treasury. They consist of both gold bullion and certificates of gold that the Treasury issues to Federal Reserve Banks.

Gold Tranche Before 1978, 25% of an IMF member state's membership fees. Any IMF member had access to its reserve tranche without preconditions, and was not obligated to repay what it withdrew. It derived its name from the fact that it was paid in gold. Reserve tranches replaced gold tranches. Special Drawing Rights were formerly based on gold.

Goldbrick Shares Shares in a stock that appear to have value, but are in fact worthless. While this may describe simply a bad investment, the term connotes shares in a fraudulent company.

Goldbricker A person who appears to be working, but in fact is surfing the Internet, making personal phone calls, or generally not working. A goldbricker tries to look busy but in fact is not very productive at all.

Goldbricking The appearance of working, when in fact one is surfing the Internet, making personal phone calls, or generally not working. A goldbricker tries to look busy but in fact is not very productive at all.

Golden Boot A lucrative severance package used to encourage an aging worker to voluntarily resign. The package may include cash and stock options, as well as equity in the company. Golden boots are most common when a company wishes to hire younger workers that may have skills that the older worker does not possess. It would cost the company money to retrain the older worker, and he/she may not learn the new skill as well. On the other hand, age discrimination laws may prevent the company from firing the older worker. The golden boot attempts to serve everyone's interest to the best of its ability. See also: Golden handshake.

Golden Bull A slang term for $1,000 in Hong Kong. The term refers to the color of $1,000 banknotes. See also: Hong Kong dollar.

Golden Cross 1. In technical analysis, a situation in which a short-term moving average of a stock's price exceeds its long-term moving average. The long-term moving average is seen as the stock's resistance level, or price over which the stock rarely rises. Thus, when a golden cross occurs, this is seen as a bullish indicator, at least in the short-term. **2.** In foreign exchange, a technical indicator in which short-term and long-term moving averages for a currency are moving in the same direction, meaning that the currency will continue this trend in the short-term.

Golden Handcuffs An incentive that makes it very unlikely that an employee will leave a company. For example, an employer may offer an exceptionally good health insurance policy at a reduced cost to an employee. The term has a slightly negative connotation because some believe these incentives reduce innovation in an economy.

Golden Handshake A clause in a high-ranking executive's hiring contract describing a lucrative severance package once the executive leaves the company. The package often includes cash and stock options worth millions of dollars, as well equity in the company. The executive is normally eligible for a golden handshake regardless of the circumstances under which he/she left the company, whether retirement, redundancy brought about from a merger or acquisition, or termination for mismanagement. Controversy surrounding the practice tends to increase in times of increased mergers, as well as in economic downturns.

Golden Hello A large signing bonus that a securities company such as a brokerage or a hedge fund pays to an employee that it "steals" from a competitor. The golden hello exists to entice the employee to change jobs. The company pays a golden hello when it believes that the employee will be a valuable resource for the company and, perhaps more importantly, his loss to the other company will create a competitive disadvantage.

Golden Life Jacket In an acquisition, an offer by an acquiring company to the executives of the target company of lucrative compensation packages in exchange for remaining with the company. The packages often include large bonuses and in-the-money options, as well equity in the company. A golden life jacket helps the acquiring company retain executives who have run the target company, thus reducing the risk that the acquiring company will make some large mistake in management. It also reduces the inconvenience of hiring numerous executive as once. The practice is controversial, as golden life jackets may encourage executives to make decisions that are not in the best interest of shareholders.

Golden Share A share in a publicly-traded company that gives the shareholder power to veto changes to the charter. Golden shares were originated when the British government began privatizing previously nationalized companies in the 1980s and wished to retain a great deal of control over these companies. Other European countries later took similar measures, though many forms of golden share have since been ruled illegal in the European Union.

Goldilocks Economy An economy that is performing well enough to avoid a recession and even provide a solid return for investors, but not so well that it causes inflation. The term references the story of Goldilocks and the Three Bears because the economy is neither too cold nor too hot.

Goldilocks Market A market that is performing well enough to avoid losses and even provide a solid return for investors, but not so well that it creates a bubble. The term references the story of Goldilocks and the Three Bears: the economy is neither too hot nor too cold, it is "just right."

Goldman Sachs Commodity Index An index of 24 futures contracts on various commodities. It is an important benchmark index of the commodities market.

Goldmark The currency of Germany between its unification in 1873 and the beginning of World War I. It was based on gold, but it replaced the Vereinsthaler, which was based on silver. While it circulated, it was called simply the mark; the name goldmark was invented later to distinguish it from the papiermark, which technically was the same currency but was not pegged to gold.

Goloid An alloy metal consisting of copper, gold, and silver. In 1877, it was proposed that goloid coins consisting primarily of silver, about 10% copper, and 3% to 4% gold be used in the United States. Some proofs were made but they were never released into circulation due to the ease with which one could make counterfeit goloid coins without gold.

Good Delivery and Settlement Procedures Standardized practices for how and when trades are settled and underlying goods delivered. Among other things, good delivery and settlement practices indicate when a seller may notify a buyer of intent to deliver and at what point payment must be made. The PSA Uniform Practices set out good delivery and settlement procedures.

Good Faith Deposit 1. In municipal bonds, a small amount of money, usually less than 5% of an issue, that underwriters give to the issuer in exchange for the right to place part of the issue. A good faith deposit is a sign that an underwriter has a vested interest in placing the issue and will therefore act vigorously on behalf of the issuer. **2.** In securities, a small amount of money from an order that a brokerage requires a new client to deposit in exchange for filling the order. The good faith deposit ensures that the new client is serious about the order and will be likely to settle or make delivery when the time comes. This is done to reduce the risk to the brokerage when it takes a new client. It is also called earnest money. **3.** See: Initial margin amount.

Good Faith Estimate In mortgages, a detailed list of all the all-in costs of a loan, which the prospective lender must provide to the prospective borrower within three days of applying for the mortgage. Commonly included in a good faith estimate are origination fees, government fees, the cost of the credit report, etc. Each fee is preceded by a number on the good faith estimate; the number comes from the HUD-1 Real Estate Settlement Statement, which assigns a number to each type of fee.

Good Faith Money 1. See: Good faith deposit. **2.** See: Earnest money.

Good Money 1. Federal funds that are transferred over the fed wire and are received by the recipient bank on the same day. Good money contrasts with clearinghouse funds, which are not received for three days. **2.** See: Sound money.

Good Risk 1. An investment that one believes is likely to be profitable. The term most often refers to a loan made to a creditworthy person or company. Good risks are considered exceptionally likely to be repaid. **2.** A person or company on which a good risk is taken.

Good Through/Until Date Order An order to a broker to buy or sell a security at a certain price whenever that price becomes available at any time before a certain date. Such an order stands indefinitely until either the security is bought or sold at the specified price or the expiration date is met, or the investor cancels the order. The order may be partially filled; that is, if the expiration date passes, any part of the order filled remains filled while the rest is cancelled. Most good-'til-cancelled orders are in fact good-through-date orders because they generally expire 30 to 60 days after they are made, if they have not been filled, unless the investor reiterates them. See also: FOK, IOC, open order.

Good 'Til Cancelled Order An order to a broker to buy or sell a security at a certain price whenever that price becomes available. Theoretically, such an order is standing indefinitely until either the security is bought or sold at the specified price or the investor cancels the order. In practice, GTCs generally expire 30-60 days after they are made if they have not been filled, unless the investor reiterates them. A GTC is also known as an open order.

Goods and Services 1. See: Good. **2.** See: Service.

Goods and Services Tax A term for a VAT in Australia, Canada, Hong Kong, India, New Zealand and Singapore.

Good-This-Month Order An order to a broker to buy or sell a security at a certain price, with the order expiring at the end of the calendar month if that price does not become available. If the price does become available during that month, the order is executed. A GTM is similar to a day order, but it remains open for the remainder of the month, instead of the remainder of a day. See also: GTC.

Goodwill Intangible assets relating to a company's business practices. Goodwill includes assets with value that are exceptionally difficult to quantify. Examples include brand recognition, customer loyalty, and employee happiness. Goodwill helps a company remain competitive in the long term, even if the company does not produce the best product. For example, a customer will be more likely to buy peanut butter from one company and pay more for it, if he/she thinks the company produces better-tasting peanut butter, regardless of whether or not this is the case. When a company buys another company, it will often pay above the target company's book value to account for goodwill.

Google A publicly-traded company primarily offering a web portal. Originally a search engine in the 1990s and early 2000s, Google expanded to online messaging, e-mail services, web video, mobile phones and so forth. Google monetizes its operations primarily through advertisements. It was founded in 1998. See also: Yahoo.

Gopik A subdivision of the Azerbaijani manat. One gopik is equal in value to 1/100 of a manat. See also: Cent.

Gordon Brown A British politician who served as Prime Minister of the United Kingdom from 2007 to 2010. A historian and political scientist by training, he was elected to Parliament in 1983. In 1997, he became Chancellor of the Exchequer. As Chancellor, he gave the Bank of England control of monetary policy independent of government influence and adjusted tax rates according to inflation rather than earnings. As Prime Minister, he bailed out British banks during the late 2000s recession. The recession resulted in a significant increase in Britain's national debt.

Gordon Growth Model A simple model to estimate the value of a stock. The model assumes one knows the dividend per share in the stock one year hence and, more importantly, that the dividends will grow at a constant rate indefinitely. Because of the latter assumption, the model is useful primarily for blue chip companies and other mature companies where dividend growth is unlikely to change. It is calculated thusly: Stock Value = Dividend per share in one year / (Required rate of return - dividend growth rate)

Gorilla A company that has the greatest market share in a particular industry without having a monopoly. A gorilla usually has greater leeway in its decisions; for example, it may charge a higher price for its products without fear of losing too much business. Large companies, such as Wal-Mart or Microsoft, are considered gorillas.

Gorod In Serbia, a political subdivision equivalent to a city.

Gosbank The central bank of the Soviet Union. Founded in 1921, it was the only bank in the USSR between the Great Depression and 1987. It helped prepare the state budget and financed both government operations and private projects that furthered Soviet economic goals. It also issued the Soviet ruble. See also: Five year plan, Perestroika.

Gosplan A committee that designed the economic plans for the Soviet Union. Initially planning for five years in advance, it later tried to plan for 10 to 15 years ahead. While Gosplan successfully industrialized the Soviet Union in only a few years, its plans were generally quite inefficient. It was created in 1921 and lasted until the end of the Soviet Union.

Gouge In numismatics, a significant scratch or other blemish on a coin, usually more than normal wear and tear. This may affect the coin's value for collectors.

Government Accounting Office Also called the GAO. The highest auditing organization within the U.S. federal government. It is responsible for investigating appropriations of funds to ensure they are spent as they ought to be. It also recommends policies that may result in the more efficient use of government money. It was established in 1921 as the General Accounting Office. It is headed by the Comptroller General of the United States.

Government Accounting Standards Board In the United States, a non-governmental body charged with establishing and maintaining generally accepted standards for professional accountants who work in state and local governments. Founded in 1984, the GASB has published a variety of rules and clarifications on how government accounting ought to be done in the United States. Its primary purpose is to govern the fundamentals of how accounting is conducted. For example, it has published guidelines on how to report a municipality's cash flows.

Government Bond Any bond issued by an agency of the United States government. Government bonds are backed by the full faith and credit of the government and are considered risk-free. Most are negotiable, with prominent examples being Treasury securities or Ginnie Mae bonds. U.S. savings bonds, however, are not negotiable.

Government Broker A broker authorized to buy and sell UK government securities. The government broker conducts these transactions on the instructions of the Bank of England. Since 1986, market makers for gilt-edged securities have largely replaced government brokers.

Government Debt 1. See: National debt. **2.** See: Government security. **3.** See: Municipal bond.

Government Depository In the United States, one of many libraries at which copies of federal documents are kept and are available for public use. Government depositories may be useful for one researching laws and regulations dealing with finance, investment and other issues.

Government Equalities Office An office of the British government responsible for encouraging equality for all persons in the United Kingdom regardless of gender, race, disability, ethnicity, or sexual orientation. It manages anti-discrimination legislation for the U.K. It was created in 2007.

Government Failure A situation in which government intervention leads to the inefficient allocation of resources. This is not the same as a government intervention leading to an unpopular result. A government failure may prove popular, for example, if it subsidizes local jobs at the expense of more efficient companies elsewhere. Examples of government failure include crowding out and pork-barrel spending.

Government Grant Money given by a government to fund a project. One may receive a government grant for academic or scientific research, to further one's education, or to engage in charity work. The United States government makes many grants, often of an educational or scientific nature.

Government Money Mutual Fund A mutual fund investing primarily or exclusively in short-term securities issued by a government agency. Returns on government money mutual funds are low because short-term government securities tend to be low risk. However, they may offer higher returns than, say, savings accounts, and may offer tax advantages.

Government National Mortgage Association Also called GNMA or Ginne Mae. A United States government-owned enterprise that buys mortgages from banks and pools them, selling the pools as mortgage-backed securities. Ginnie Mae securities are backed by the full faith and credit of the United States and as such are consider risk-free investments. Ginnie Mae's activities are designed to help facilitate the provision of credit for home purchases among middle and low-income Americans.

Government Puddee An obsolete Indian unit of dry volume approximately equivalent to 1.64 liters.

Government Purchases The money that a government spends procuring goods or services from the private sector. Examples include a local government hiring a company to repair a road or the national government buying artillery for the military. In Keynesian economics, government purchases are important for stimulating demand in times of economic downturn. That is, when no one will buy goods or services, Keynesian economics states that the government ought to do so in order to keep commerce going.

Government Securities Clearing Corporation A subsidiary of the National Securities Clearing Corporation that provides clearing services for U.S. government securities. For example, the GSCC specializes in transactions such as those involving Treasury bonds.

Government Security 1. See: U.S. Treasury Security. **2.** See: Agency security. **3.** See: Municipal bond.

Government Spending The payment of money by a government for some service it offers. A major example of government spending is payment of salaries for military personnel. Because government spending is financed by some combination of taxes and public debt, the level and recipients of government spending are usually matters of some controversy.

Government Sponsored Enterprise A privately held or publicly traded company created by the U.S. Government for some purpose thought to benefit the American economy. For example, Freddie Mac was originally a GSE created to encourage homeownership among middle class and working class Americans. Because it is "sponsored" but not owned by the government, GSE stocks carry higher risk than, say, Treasury securities, which are backed by the full faith and credit of the United States. However, GSEs have an implicit guarantee that the government will not allow them to fail. Indeed, when Fannie Mae and Freddie Mac collapsed in 2008 they almost instantly received federal assistance.

Government-Sponsored Retirement Arrangement A retirement plan for persons who are employed by a private agency that derives its revenue from the Canadian federal government. Contributions to a GSRA are not tax deductible and regulations limit the amount that one can contribute to an RRSP if one also has a GSRA.

Governor 1. The head of a bank, especially but not necessarily a central bank. For example, the highest post in the Bank of England is called the Governor. **2.** More generally, a term for some chief executives, especially heads of political subdivisions. For example, the head of an American state is called a governor.

Gower Report Proposed regulations of the British financial sector. The Gower Report came out of the perceived need for greater regulation in the light of various scandals in the 1960s and 1970s. The report recommended the creation of the Securities and Investment Board and several self-regulatory organizations to protect investors and consumers. The recommendations were adopted and eventually resulted in the formation of the Financial Services Authority.

Goznak A state-owned corporation in Russia that issues legal tender coins and banknotes for general use. It also produces credit cards, passports, phone cards, and similar products. It was established in 1919 and is based in Moscow.

GP 1. ISO 3166-1 alpha-2 code for the French Department of Guadeloupe. This is the code used in international transactions to and from Guadeloupean bank accounts. **2.** ISO 3166-2 geocode for Guadeloupe. This is used as an international standard for shipping to Guadeloupe.

GPM ISO 4217 code for the German papiermark. It was introduced in 1914, when the mark's peg to gold was abandoned. The papiermark is strongly associated with hyperinflation as prices rose exponentially following World War I. In 1924, it was replaced by the Rentenmark at a ratio of 1 trillion to one.

GQ 1. ISO 3166-1 alpha-2 code for the Republic of Equatorial Guinea. This is the code used in international transactions to and from Equatorial Guinean bank accounts. **2.** ISO 3166-2 geocode for Equatorial Guinea. This is used as an international standard for shipping to Equatorial Guinea. Each province has its own code with the prefix "GQ." For example, the code for the Province of Bioko Sur is ISO 3166-2:GQ-BS.

GQE ISO 4217 code for the Equatorial Guinean ekwele. It was introduced in 1975, seven years after the country's independence. Until 1979, it was spelled ekuele. After the "ekwele" spelling was adopted, its plural became bipkwele. In 1985, it was replaced by the CFA franc at a rate of four bipkwele to one franc.

GR 1. ISO 3166-1 alpha-2 code for the Hellenic Republic (Greece). This is the code used in international transactions to and from Greek bank accounts. **2.** ISO 3166-2 geocode for Greece. This is used as an international standard for shipping to Greece. Each subdivision has its own code with the prefix "GR." For example, the code for the Department of Arkadia is ISO 3166-2:GR-12.

Grace Period 1. The time after the due date for a loan payment during which one may make the payment without any late fees or penalties. The length of the grace period depends on the loan terms, but is usually around 15 days. **2.** The time after rent is due, during which one may pay rent without a late fee. The grace period for rent is usually five days. **3.** In bonds, the time between the issue of the bond and the first coupon payment. This grace period usually applies to long-term bonds, where interest payments do not begin to occur for a few years after issue.

Grad In Croatia, a political subdivision equivalent to a city.

Grada In Serbia, a political subdivision equivalent to an urban municipality.

Grading Certificate A document that states the quality of a commodity. For example, given a bushel of corn, a grading certificate would indicate whether or not the corn is of a certain caliber. Grading certificates are prepared by professional inspectors and are important to options and futures, which often state the quality that an underlying commodity must have in order to fulfill the contract's terms.

Gradske Opstine In Serbia, a political subdivision equivalent to a neighborhood within a city.

Gradualist Monetarism The policy in which the growth of the money supply is slowly reduced until it equals the economy's growth rate. Proponents of gradual monetarism argue that this policy controls inflation without unnecessarily slowing down GDP growth. Critics question the policy's ability to control inflation.

Gradualist Monetarist A scholar or other person who promotes the policy in which growth of the money supply is slowly reduced until it equals the economy's growth rate. Gradualist monetarists argue that this policy controls inflation without unnecessarily slowing down GDP growth. Critics question the policy's ability to control inflation.

Graduated Call Writing The investment strategy of writing covered calls, which are calls where the writer owns the underlying asset, and gradually increasing the strike price as the price of the underlying asset rises. For example, if one writes a covered call with a strike price of $20 which expires unexercised, but the price of the call has still risen, the writer may issue another call on the same asset with a strike price of $25. This process continues until an option is exercised. Graduated call writing allows the writer to collect the premiums and eventually sell the underlying asset for a higher price.

Graduated Flat Tax A progressive income tax with only a few, usually low tax brackets. For example, a graduated flat tax would tax all income up to $20,000 at 5% and income above that at 15%. A graduated flat tax seeks a compromise between those who say that a flat tax is regressive and those who say that a progressive tax is extortionary.

Graduated Lease A long-term lease on a property where the rent is changed periodically to reflect the market value of the property. This is used in real estate. For example, suppose one signs a 99 year, graduated lease on an office building. The rent may increase (or, less likely, decrease) every 10 years as the value of the office building increases (or decreases) over time. Graduated leases are designed to protect the owner/lessor of the property.

Graduated Mortality Table In actuarial analysis, a table of the likelihood that a person of a certain age will die in the next year, taking into account potential errors and biases in the data collection underlying the table. For example, a graduated mortality table may make adjustments to adjust for small sample size. Mortality tables are important in determining one's eligibility for some insurance and annuity plans.

Graduated Payment A system of making payments on a loan in which the payments increase gradually over the life of the loan. That is, the payments start low and increase by a certain percentage, usually 7% to 12% each year, until the full payment level is reached. When a bank determines whether to make a graduated payment loan, it only considers whether the borrower can make the low, initial payments. This allows a person who would not otherwise qualify for a loan to borrow, usually in order to buy property. The risk is the possibility that needed income will not materialize in the future, making the borrower unable to repay the loan. Graduated payment loans usually have fixed interest rates and involve negative amortization.

Graduated Payment Mortgage A method of amortizing a mortgage such that payments are initially lower than they would be for a comparable mortgage with flat payments, and gradually increase over three, five, or seven years. When payments reach their full amount, they are usually higher than they would have been had the mortgage holder made flat payments over the life of the mortgage. This is because the difference between the initial payments and what the initial payments would have been in a flat payment scheme is added to the principal. A mortgage holder may opt for a GPM if he/she does not have the cash flow for the full mortgage when he/she buys the property, but expects to have it in the future. This entails risk for both the borrower and the lender as those cash flows may or may not be there when the time comes. See also: ARM.

Graduated Security A stock that was once traded on one stock exchange that moves to another, more prestigious exchange. For example, a company may move its listing from the Pacific Stock Exchange to the New York Stock Exchange. A graduated security makes this move to increase interest in the company and thereby increase its trading volume.

Graduated Wage The scheduled increase (or decrease) of wages for an employee. Factors affecting graduated wages for an employee may include performance, length of service, changes in job description and so forth.

Gradus An ancient Roman unit of length approximately equivalent to 740 millimeters. It was also called a pes sestertius.

Graft An informal term for bribery.

Graham and Dodd See: Benjamin Graham, David Dodd.

Grain A unit of weight equivalent to one 7,000th of one pound.

Grain and Feed Trade Association Also called GAFTA. An international organization intended to promote international trade between members. It conducts research and analysis of corn and other agricultural goods and works with other organizations to influence trade policy. It was established in 1878 as the London Corn Trade Association.

Grain Futures Act of 1922 Legislation in the United States that required all futures contracts on grain to be traded on a futures exchange. It also required these exchanges to publish more information and prevent price manipulation. It created the Grain Futures Commission, which was the predecessor organization of the Commodity Futures Trading Commission. It replaced the Futures Trading Act of 1921, which was declared unconstitutional. See also: Board of Trade of City of Chicago vs. Olsen.

Grain Futures Commission A former organization that regulated the futures trade of some agricultural products in the United States. The Commission was the first of its kind to be found to be constitutional by the U.S. Supreme Court. It was a predecessor of the Commodity Futures Trading Commission.

Grain Stocks Report A quarterly report released by the U.S. Department of Agriculture detailing inventories of soybeans, corn, wheat and other grains in the United States. Because it effectively reveals the supply of American grains, the report's release can greatly impact commodity prices, especially if the report does not match expectations.

Grameen Bank A bank in Bangladesh that pioneered modern microfinance. Grameen Bank makes very small loans to extremely impoverished persons to help them achieve self-employment so they are able to lift themselves out of poverty. Borrowers belong to five member groups; members encourage each other to repay the loan. Borrowers must agree to abide by 16 rules for social betterment. While critics contend that too many of Grameen's loans extract high interest rates, some are interest-free. Historically, Grameen has had very low default rates, though many borrowers pay late. It was founded in 1983 by Muhammad Yunus.

Grammage The grams of weight per square meter of area. This is used to weigh bulk paper.

Gramm-Bliley-Leach Act Legislation in the United States, passed in 1999, that deregulated the banking industry. Specifically, it repealed the portion of the Glass-Steagal Act that prohibited commercial banks, investment banks and insurance companies from working in each other's sectors. Critics claim that this deregulation led directly to the late 2000s recession by allowing banks to take excessive risks, essentially putting their customers' deposits at risk. Many others claim that this assessment is inaccurate, and contend that the Act prevented the crisis from being even worse than it was.

Gramm-Rudman-Hollings Act Legislation in the United States, passed in 1985, that mandated automatic cuts in federal discretionary spending if the government deficit rose above stated target levels. The severity of the cuts was considered draconian and the Act was found largely unconstitutional in 1987. It was replaced by the Budget Enforcement Act of 1990.

Grana An obsolete unit of weight in the early metric system approximately equivalent to 50 grams.

Grand In the United States, a slang term for multiples of $1,000. The term "big ones" is also used. For example, "10 grand" and "10 big ones" both mean $10,000.

Grandfather Clause A clause in a new law, regulation, or anything else that exempts certain persons or businesses from abiding by it. For example, suppose a country passes a law stating that it is illegal to own a cat. A grandfather clause would allow persons who already own cats to continue to keep them, but would prevent people who do not own cats from buying them. Grandfather clauses are controversial, but they are also relatively common.

Grandfather Tape In computing, a backup tape, disc or drive two generations older than the most recent one. For example, if data is backed up each week, the grandfather tape is the backup record from two weeks ago. See also: Father tape.

Grandfathered Activities Activities that are permitted when they otherwise would not be permitted because of a grandfather clause. A grandfather clause is a portion of a new law, regulation, or anything else that exempts certain persons or businesses from abiding by it. For example, suppose a country passes a law stating that it is illegal to own a cat. A grandfather clause may allow persons who already own cats to continue to keep them, but would prevent people who do not own cats from buying them. In this case, owning a cat is a grandfathered activity. Grandfathered activities are controversial, but they are also relatively common.

Granny Bond A savings bond with an interest rate linked to an index such that the return stays ahead of inflation. This is useful for people on fixed incomes who otherwise might suffer from an inflation tax; that is, they may otherwise see their savings decrease in real value. It is available in the United Kingdom to people over retirement age.

Grant An amount of money given, usually by a government or nonprofit organization, to fund certain projects. One may receive a grant for academic or scientific research, or to further one's education, or to engage in charity work. The United States government makes many grants, often of an educational or scientific nature. Grants are also a key part of many philanthropic foundations' activities.

Grant Anticipation Note A bond issued by a state government or state highway bank that is secured by future, expected federal highway funding. States issue grant anticipation notes to provide cash for immediate or time sensitive needs related to highway construction or maintenance. There is no guarantee the state will receive anticipated funding; however, once it is received, it is used to repay the bond. A grant anticipation note is also called a grant anticipation revenue vehicle or a GARVEE.

Grant Date The date on which an employee is given a stock option. The grant date is usually later than the date on which it is announced that stock options will be distributed.

Grant in Aid Funding that a government gives to a private entity for a specific purpose. For example, a government may give a grant in aid to a charity that assists persons in buying their own homes or to a business that invests in a favored industry such as green energy. Grantees must abide by government regulations upon receiving a grant in aid (for example, they may be required to account for government funds separately), but they have general autonomy over how to specifically spend the money.

Grant of Administration In England and Wales, authorization by a court for an appointed person to begin to administrate the assets of a decedent. A grant of administration is given when the decedent dies intestate, that is, when he/she dies without a will. This contrasts with a grant of probate, which is a similar authorization given to the executor of a will.

Grant of Probate In England and Wales, authorization by a court for the executor of an estate to begin to administrate the assets of a decedent. This contrasts with a grant of administration, which is a similar authorization given to a person if the decedent dies without a will.

Grantee 1. The recipient of a gift. **2.** The beneficiary of a trust. A grantor places assets in the trust on behalf of the grantee and allows a trustee to administer them for a certain period of time.

Grantor 1. The writer of an option contract. **2.** The person who creates a trust. The grantor places assets in the trust on behalf of a beneficiary and allows the trustee to administer them for a certain period of time.

Grantor Retained Income Trust A trust in which the grantor places some assets for the beneficiary, but retains the right to receive income from those assets up to a certain point, at which time the beneficiary begins to receive the income. This allows the beneficiary to receive income from the trust without being subject to the estate tax. A disadvantage is the possibility that the grantor will die before the expiration of the trust, which results in the assets transferring to the grantor's estate. In that case, the beneficiary does not receive anything. It is also called a grantor retained annuity trust.

Grantor Trust A trust where the grantor retains usufruct of the assets in the trust. That is, the grantor may continue to use the assets she has placed into the trust even after ceding technical ownership. A grantor trust is usually considered part of the grantor's estate when the grantor dies and, as such, can be subject to the estate tax.

Grantor Underwritten Note A mechanism in which a group of banks collectively purchase fixed-rate debt securities and then sell them at auction. A grantor underwritten note is similar to a euronote.

Grao A Portuguese measure of weight approximately equivalent to 0.05 grams. It became obsolete after Lusophone countries adopted the metric system in the 19th century.

Grape Slang; in auto sales, a customer who believes whatever the salesperson tells him/her and who is generally agreeable. The term connotes a customer who will pay top price for an automobile.

Graph A representation of numbers signifying different data sets. Graphs are vitally important in tracking past performance of economic data with the aim of predicting its future behavior. For example, a government agency may create a graph of unemployment claims over time. If claims have trended downward, the agency may predict that unemployment may remain low. Graphs are also crucial for technical analysts, who use them to track securities' performance to help make investment decisions. Graphs are also known as charts.

Grass A slang term for $10 in Hong Kong. Bowl and stripe are equivalent terms. See also: Hong Kong dollar.

Gratis Free or without cost.

Graveyard Market A bear market in which few investors wish to enter or close a position. That is, potential sellers do not wish to sell their positions, as doing so would lock in their losses, and they wish to wait until the market recovers at least somewhat. On the other hand, potential buyers do not wish to enter a long position because they believe the market will continue its decline. Graveyard markets tend to occur near the end of a bear market, but they are usually slow to improve.

Graveyard Shift The overnight shift at a 24-hour establishment. The graveyard shift may last from 12 a.m. to 8 a.m., 11 p.m. to 7 a.m., or a similar period of time. Because of the inconvenience (and occasionally danger) of working the graveyard shift, these employees are occasionally paid slightly more. Other companies rotate their employees in and out of the graveyard shift.

Gravure Printing A way to print paper in which the image is carved into the printing plate. That is, the image consists of indentations on the plate. This contrasts with relief printing, in which the image is raised from the plate's surface.

Gray Knight A company that outbids a white knight in a friendly acquisition. A gray knight is not after a hostile takeover, but does serve its own interests, as opposed to those of the target company. Often, a gray knight makes an unsolicited bid for the target company after the initial, friendly bid. The management of the target company prefers a gray knight to a black knight, but, of course, would most prefer to be acquired by a white knight.

Gray List A list of stocks in which the risk arbitrage division of an investment bank is not allowed to invest. However, the block trading division is allowed to invest in companies on the gray list. The gray list consists of companies working closely with the investment bank on any number of projects, but especially mergers and acquisitions. Because of this, the gray list is unpublished and may not be known outside this risk arbitrage division.

Gray Market Trade using unofficial and unregulated, but still legal, means. In securities, a gray market typically refers to trade in bonds or stocks not yet issued. These sales are contingent upon the issuance actually taking place, and are sometimes considered benchmarks for how successful the issuance will be. Another example of a gray market is the pharmaceuticals industry, in which buyers in different countries sometimes pay very different amounts. Buyers in the more expensive country may travel to the other country to buy their medicines, creating a gray market.

Gray Money Money one derives from tax evasion. For example, gray money includes illicit deductions or funds hidden in an offshore bank. Gray money is similar to, but distinct from, black money, which is the revenue from a criminal enterprise, such as drug dealing.

Gray Sourcing A slang term for finding an older IT worker because he/she is the only one who knows how to work the company's older computer system.

Graymail 1. To force a government to alter its policy by threatening to reveal state secrets. Graymail especially refers to situations in which one forces the government to drop criminal or civil proceedings. In other words, graymail is blackmail of a government. **2.** To request the use of state secrets in a criminal or civil proceeding in order to bolster one's case.

GRC GOST 7.67 Latin three-letter geocode for Greece. The code is used for transactions to and from Greek bank accounts and for international shipping to Greece. As with all GOST 7.67 codes, it is used primarily in Cyrillic alphabets.

GRD ISO 4217 code for the Greek drachma. It was introduced in 1832, two years after Greece's legal independence from the Ottoman Empire. During the Nazi occupation in the early 1940s, the drachma suffered from hyperinflation. Inflation slowed after the end of World War II, but remained high until Greece joined the Bretton Woods System in 1953, when the drachma was pegged to the U.S. dollar. After the end of the Bretton Woods System, the value of the drachma gradually declined until it was replaced by the euro in 2001.

Grease A slang term for bribery.

Great Call In general equities, a potential customer. A broker or firm may look at an investor's past buying and selling history and, believing that he/she may be interested in a particular trade, approach a great call. Alternately, a great call may make himself/herself known to the broker by inquiring about his/her desired type of trade.

Great Crash 1. Three trading days where the New York Stock Exchange lost a significant amount of value very quickly. The Great Crash presaged the Great Depression, though it had already started in some areas. See also: Black Thursday, Black Monday, Black Tuesday. **2.** An alternative (and slightly inaccurate) term for the Great Depression.

Great Society A series of programs launched by U.S. President Lyndon B. Johnson in the 1960s to improve quality of life for Americans. The Great Society saw a number of innovative programs. Some were more successful than others. Medicare and Medicaid, which greatly reduce medical expenses for the elderly and the poor, proved popular though expensive. Food stamps were intended to improve food security, though critics maintain that they encourage recipients to eat unhealthily. The Great Society also increased federal funding for universities and created the National Endowment for the Arts.

Greater Fool Theory The idea that there is always a buyer for a security who will pay a better price than the seller paid. That is, the greater fool theory states that if an investor buys a security at a high price, he/she will be able to find a buyer who will pay an even higher price. The origin of the theory's name comes from the idea that if an investor makes a foolish decision to buy an expensive security, he/she can find a greater fool to take it off his/her hands. The greater fool theory is important to the formation and continuation of speculative bubbles, and only works until the bubble bursts.

Greed The intense, perhaps inordinate, desire for wealth. There is no consensus as to how much desire qualifies as greed. Some believe greed to be positive as it motivates business, which spurs economic growth. Many others, however, believe greed can go too far and create unsustainable growth or growth at the expense of social justice. The morality of greed is a concern in the field of business ethics.

Greeddobo In numismatics, a slang term for an unscrupulous coin dealer who does inappropriate or simply dumb things in order to make a quick profit. The term originated in the Southern United States.

Greek Drachma The former currency of Greece. It was introduced in 1832, two years after Greece's legal independence from the Ottoman Empire. During the Nazi occupation in the early 1940s, the drachma suffered from hyperinflation. Inflation slowed after the end of World War II, but remained high until Greece joined the Bretton Woods System in 1953, when the drachma was pegged to the U.S. dollar. After the end of the Bretton Woods System, the value of the drachma gradually declined until it was replaced by the euro in 2001.

Greeks Mathematical measures of risk. See also: delta, gamma, rho, theta, and vega.

Green Book A 1975 book by Muammar al-Qaddafi advocating a "third way" between capitalism and communism. The Green Book rejects republicanism in favor of direct democracy and promotes a form of socialism based on Islam and Arab nationalism. The Green Book reflected the governing philosophy of Libya, though critics contend that the country in fact was a dictatorship under Qaddafi.

Green Box A cardboard box made completely from recycled material. See also: Green energy.

Green Clause A clause in a letter of credit allowing one to take out an advance loan before a shipment is sent if one puts up some collateral, often demonstrated by warehouse receipts. For example, a farmer may utilize a green clause to receive financing for operations, using his crops in a warehouse as collateral. A green clause is most common in contracts relating to agricultural commodities.

Green Coffee Association A trade association for investors, exporters and importers, insurers and others involved in the uncooked coffee bean business. It recommends best practices for the industry, conducts arbitration and provides other professional services for members. It was established in 1923 and is based in New York City.

Green Coffee Warehouse Stocks A report issued on a monthly basis by the Green Coffee Association stating the supply of uncooked coffee beans held in 11 major warehouses in the United States. Low stock may raise prices for coffee contracts, while a large inventory may result in the opposite. As such, traders in coffee contracts greatly anticipate the Green Coffee Warehouse Stocks. See also: Coffee, Sugar, and Cocoa Exchange.

Green Crab A formerly used slang term for $10 in Hong Kong, which referred to the green color of banknotes. These banknotes are no longer used. See also: Hong Kong dollar, Colorful crab.

Green Field 1. A slang term for a potential client or customer who has never purchased or used a product before. It is important to make a positive first impression on a green field in order to promote repeat business. **2.** An untapped market.

Green Fund A mutual fund that invests exclusively in securities in environmentally-friendly companies. Different green funds have different methodologies for determining what constitutes an environmentally-friendly company. Some may avoid certain industries (notably oil and gas) entirely, while others may look at the environmental records of particular companies. Each green fund describes its methodology in its prospectus. It is also called an environmental fund.

Green Investing Any investment practice that involves buying securities exclusively in environmentally-friendly companies. Different green investing practices have different methodologies for determining what constitutes an environmentally-friendly company. Some may avoid certain industries such as oil and gas, entirely, while others may look at the environmental records of particular companies. Many investment companies offer green funds. Green investing is a form of socially conscious investing.

Green Investment Any investment that involves taking a position in securities exclusively in environmentally-friendly companies. Different green investments involve different methodologies for determining what constitutes an environmentally-friendly company. Some may avoid certain industries, such as oil and gas, entirely, while others may look at the environmental records of particular companies. Many investment companies offer green funds. Green investing is a form of socially conscious investing.

Green Pea In auto sales, a slang term for an inexperienced salesperson.

Green Pound The European currency unit used to establish uniform agricultural prices throughout the European Union.

Green Tax A tax levied on actions that are deemed to be detrimental to the environment. For example, a government may put a green tax on non-recyclable plastic grocery bags. The idea behind a green tax is to reduce the incentive to harm the environment by using other, less expensive products. It is a type of Pigouvian tax.

Greenback Informal for the U.S. dollar. The term derives from the fact that dollar bills are green; it dates back to the American Civil War. See also: Loonie.

Greenmail A practice in which a corporate raider buys a large amount of stock from another publicly-traded company and forces the latter to buy back the stock at a substantial premium in order to avoid a takeover. The corporate raider has no intention of actually buying the target company; it merely seeks to profit from the buyback. One refers to this buyback as a bon voyage bonus, as this enables the company to be left alone by the greenmailer. Some companies formulate anti-greenmail provisions in their charters or bylaws to prevent the situation from occurring in the first place.

Greenmailer A corporate raider who buys a large amount of stock from a publicly-traded company and forces it to buy back the stock at a substantial premium in order to avoid a takeover. The corporate raider has no intention of actually buying the target company; it merely seeks to profit from the buyback. One refers to this buyback as a bon voyage bonus, as this enables the company to be left alone by the greenmailer. T. Boone Pickens was a prominent greenmailer in the 1980s.

Greensheet An informational booklet that an underwriting firm prepares to assist its employees in placing a new issue with investors. A greensheet contains information on a new issue; generally, it is a summary of the prospectus along with brief commentary on its advantages and disadvantages. The greensheet is designed to help sales staff when canvassing potential investors; it is not distributed to the investors themselves.

Greenshoe Option A provision in some underwriting contracts allowing the underwriter to sell more shares to investors than were originally agreed. In an underwriting agreement, the underwriter agrees with the issuer of a security to place a certain amount with investors. If demand for the security exceeds the underwriter's supply, the greenshoe option allows the underwriter to avoid a sudden jump in price by increasing supply. Normally, the greenshoe option allows the underwriter to increase supply up to 15%. It is important to note that not all underwriting contracts have greenshoe options, especially in situations in which the issue is for a limited project for which the issuer only needs a certain amount of capital. It is also called an overallotment option.

Greenspan Put A term coined in the late 1990s describing Federal Reserve chairman Alan Greenspan's loose monetary policy. Throughout this period, Greenspan and the Fed kept interest rates rather low to encourage growth in the stock markets. Investors assumed from this policy that stocks would continue to rise and, thus, they could enter long positions and sell them at a higher price on or before a certain date, creating a put option in practice, if not in contract. While this was likely not the intent of the Federal Reserve at this time, investors used this investment strategy anyway. See also: Irrational exuberance.

Greenwashing A slang term for a situation in which a company takes token steps to be more environmentally conscious, but advertises its steps in such a way as to make them appear more significant than they are. For example, if a company places recycling bins next to its trash cans but does nothing to curb its corporate jet use, it may greenwash its decisions by playing up the recycling bins.

Greenwich Mean Time The time of day as calculated by the Royal Observatory in London. This clock is used to determine time zones worldwide. It is used in business.

Gresham's Law The theory that given two types of money with the same nominal value but different real values, the "bad" money will be spent while the "good" money will be hoarded. Strictly, the law only applies if the exchange rate between the two monies is decreed by the state, but it is sometimes invoked more broadly. While it does not always hold true, one example was the hoarding of U.S. coins in the 20th century as they gradually came to be minted with less valuable metals.

Gridlock A situation in which a business does not function, or functions ineffectively, due to conflicting orders from management and/or insufficient operating procedures. Gridlock may occur when two or more parties are attempting to control a business, or when project goals are incompletely defined because of incompetent management. Gridlock can be very costly to a business' operations, especially when it is prolonged.

Grinder Informal; an investor or investment adviser who specializes in small trades and investments. The term connotes hard work to extract the maximum value out of each investment; in any case, grinders do not rely upon large profits from only a few, large transactions. Rather, they profit from the sheer volume of small transactions they conduct.

GRL GOST 7.67 Latin three-letter geocode for Greenland. The code is used for transactions to and from Greenlander bank accounts and for international shipping to Greenland. As with all GOST 7.67 codes, it is used primarily in Cyrillic alphabets.

Groat In England and Scotland (and later the United Kingdom), a coin equal in value to four pence. Groats were first issued in the Middle Ages and ceased to be minted in 1856. However, they continued to circulate in British Guiana until 1955.

Groatland An obsolete Scottish unit of area. A groatland was the amount of land on which rent of four pennies (or one groat) could be charged. This system was used in western Scotland.

Gromada In Poland, an archaic political division for a village. Gromadas were largely obsolete by the 19th century, and were briefly revived between the 1950s and 1970s.

Gros A Danish unit of 144.

Groschen A subdivision of the Austrian schilling, which is the former currency of Austria. One groschen was equal in value to 1/100 of schilling. See also: Cent.

Gross The amount before any subtractions are made. For example, the amount that a person earns from an employer represents his gross income. He then subtracts his tax liability and other deductions to arrive at his net income.

Gross Domestic Product A measure of the value of the total production in a country, usually in a given year. Gross domestic product is calculated by adding together total consumer spending, total government spending, total business spending, and the value of net exports. GDP is considered one of the leader indicators of the health of a nation's economy. GDP growth is considered desirable and represents the fact that businesses are producing and that consumers and the government are buying. It is often used as a way to measure a country's standard of living. See also: GNP.

Gross Estate In estate tax, the sum total value of a decedent's assets plus certain additions before any applicable tax credits or deductions. Gross estate includes, but is not limited to: property (including community property and all savings), certain types of gifts made in the last three years of the decedent's life, property or income transferred before death but under which the decedent maintained use and/or enjoyment, revocable transfers, life insurance, and pensions and annuities with death benefits. See also: Taxable estate.

Gross Income An individual or company's income before taxes and deductions. For individual income, it is calculated as the individual's wages or salary, investment and asset appreciation, and the amount made from any other source of income. In a company, it is calculated as revenues minus expenses. An individual's gross income is important to determining eligibility for certain social programs, while a company's gross income is one measure among many of how well it uses its resources to produce a profit. See also: Adjusted gross income.

Gross Interest Interest one receives before accounting for taxes. For example, a bondholder receives interest payments on the bond periodically. The gross interest is the amount the bondholder receives from the issuer, and not what he/she keeps after paying taxes.

Gross Lease A lease in which the lessee pays the lessor (the property owner) a flat fee at agreed upon intervals (usually once per month), and, in exchange, the lessor is responsible for all maintenance and other expenses associated with the property. Most rental agreements on residences are gross leases. See also: Net lease.

Gross National Product A measure of the value of what a country's citizens produce in a given year, whether or not the production occurred in that country. To calculate GNP, one takes the GDP and adds to it all earnings made by domestic citizens in a different country. One then subtracts from this quantity all earnings made

in the home country by non-citizens. GNP is less commonly used now because it has become a less accurate tool for calculating what a domestic economy produces, as more countries have citizens working abroad.

Gross Per Broker The commissions a broker earns over a given period. Every time a broker executes a trade on behalf of a client, that broker earns a commission, which may be a flat fee, but is usually a percentage of the value of the transaction. Many brokerages calculate their revenue in terms of gross per broker, and most expect their brokers to earn a certain gross as quota. Typically, individual brokers receive approximately one third of their gross as salary.

Gross Processing Margin The gain or loss one realizes by taking a long position in a commodity and a short position on a finished product made from that commodity. This allows the investor to create an artificial position on the price of making the finished product. The gross processing margin measures how successfully one does this. See also: Crack spread, Crush spread.

Gross Production Tax In the United States, a tax levied by some individual states on mining and drilling companies on the value of what is mined or drilled. For example, the State of Oklahoma levies a gross production tax on oil companies equal to 7% of the value of oil drilled from the ground. Gross production taxes are generally deductible from federal taxes.

Gross Profit A company's revenue from sales in a given period of time less its cost of goods sold. Gross profit is easy to calculate and may provide a rough idea of a company's performance. However, it does not account for a number of very important expenses, such as marketing or employee salaries. For that reason, it is not as accurate of a measurement as net profit or EBIT.

Gross Profit Margin A measure of how well a company controls its costs. It is calculated by dividing a company's profit by its revenues and expressing the result as a percentage. The higher the gross profit margin is, the better the company is thought to control costs. Investors use the gross profit margin to compare companies in the same industry and well as in different industries to determine what are the most profitable. It is also called the profit margin or simply the margin.

Gross Revenue Pledge A provision in the indentures of some municipal bonds stating that the first priority of the revenue from the bond shall service debt or be set aside to pay the coupons to bondholders. The project a bond intends to finance is relegated to second place, and may be funded from other sources in addition to the bond. This places a difficulty on the issuer, but reduces the risk of default to bondholders. It also allows the bond to be issued at a lower interest rate, which is good for the issuer.

Gross Sales The revenue a company derives from sales before making any deductions for discounts, transportation, and some other expenses. Gross sales contrast with net sales, which account for some of these basis expenses. They also contrast with cash flow because gross sales include credit sales that the company may not have collected.

Gross Settlement In foreign exchange, a way to settle a transaction in which the buyer directly pays the seller. This contrasts with the normal way to settle securities transactions, which involves using a clearing house. See also: Clearance.

Gross Spread In a public offering, the difference between the price an underwriter pays an issuer and the price at which it sells the offering to the public. That is, an underwriter pays the issuer an agreed-upon price to purchase an issue, which it then attempts to place with investors. When it places the issue, it charges the investor a certain price like any other trade. The difference is known as the gross spread; it forms the bulk of an underwriting firm's profits. See also: Fully subscribed, Overbooked, Underbooked.

Gross Weight The weight of a good that is being shipped, including the good itself, its container, and all packing materials. Knowing the gross weight helps companies price their services. See also: Tare weight.

Gross Working Capital Cash and short-term assets expected to be converted to cash within a year. Businesses use the calculation of gross working capital to measure cash flow. Gross working capital does not account for current liabilities, but is simply the measure of total cash and cash equivalent on hand. Gross working capital tends not to add much to the business' assets, but helps keep it running on a day-to-day basis. See also: Fixed asset, Net working capital.

Grosz A division of the Polish zloty equal in value to 1/100 of one zloty. The plural of grosz is groszy.

Grote palm An obsolete Dutch unit of length roughly equivalent to 10 centimeters.

Ground A customary unit of area approximately equivalent to 203 square meters. It is used in real estate transactions in some parts of India.

Ground Lease A lease of real estate. A ground lease differs from other types of leases, such as those where one rents an apartment or a factory. Generally speaking, one may use a ground lease to occupy a piece of land and make improvements to it. For example, one may build an office on the land. Ground leases are important to some investment vehicles in Islamic finance, notably sukuk al-ijara.

Group Annuity An annuity purchased by a number of people who negotiate collectively. A group annuity operates like other annuities, except that contributions are paid by (and payments are made to) more than one person under a single plan. See also: Group insurance.

Group Exemption A determination by the IRS that several organizations have tax exempt status due to connection to a single, parent non-profit organization. It should be noted that this tax exempt status may be given even before the parent organization has received 501(c)3 status.

Group Insurance Insurance provided to a whole number of people who negotiate collectively. Group insurance is thought to provide better insurance at a lower rate to members of the group because the insurer is able to spread its risk over a larger number of people that it otherwise would be able to do. Unions and other trade groups often procure group insurance policies.

Group of 15 An informal organization of developing nations. It was established to promote cooperation in trade, technology, and other matters, as well as to present a united face in negotiations with other groups such as the World Trade Organization. It was established in 1989. Despite the name, there are in fact 18 members, which are Algeria, Argentina, Brazil, Chile, Egypt, India, Indonesia, Iran, Jamaica, Kenya, Malaysia, Mexico, Niger, Peru, Senegal, Sri Lanka, Venezuela, and Zimbabwe.

Group of Eight An informal group composed of United States, Japan, Germany, the United Kingdom, France, Italy, Canada, and Russia (listed by nominal GDP). The European Union participates also but does not host or chair events. The G-8 members are the world's leading industrial democracies. Their leaders meet annually to discuss economic cooperation and other matters. The G-8 does not have a permanent secretariat, but rather gives an informal forum for leaders to meet and discuss ideas.

Group of Eleven Also called the G-11. An informal group of developing nations seeking to reduce their collective debt burden so they can use their resources to pursue economic growth. The G-11 works with the G-8 (which consists primarily of the wealthiest countries) to achieve this goal. It was established in 2006. Members include Croatia, Ecuador, El Salvador, Georgia, Honduras, Indonesia, Jordan, Morocco, Pakistan, Paraguay and Sri Lanka.

Group of Five 1. The United States, Japan, Germany, the United Kingdom, and France (listed by nominal GDP). The G5 are the world's leading industrial powers. Their leaders meet periodically to discuss economic cooperation, and the five nations have generally friendly trade relations. Representatives of the central banks of these nations also meet periodically to discuss monetary matters. **2.** Group of Five is also occasionally used to describe representatives of the five Wall Street investment firms who jointly designed subprime mortgage securities: Deutsche Bank, Goldman Sachs, Bear Stearns, JP Morgan Chase, and Citigroup.

Group of Seven Also called G-7. An informal group composed of the United States, Japan, Germany, the United Kingdom, France, Italy, and Canada (listed by nominal GDP). The G-7 represents the world's leading industrial democracies. Their finance ministers/secretaries meet annually to discuss economic cooperation and other matters. The G-7 does not have a permanent secretariat, but rather gives an informal forum for leaders to meet and discuss ideas.

Group of Ten An informal group composed of United States, Japan, Germany, the United Kingdom, France, Italy, Canada, the Netherlands, Belgium, and Sweden (listed by nominal GDP). Switzerland also plays a small role in the Group. Members of the G-10 are some of the world's leading industrial democracies. Representatives of the G-10 meet every other month at the Bank for International Settlements.

Group of Thirty An informal group composed of 30 of the world's central bankers, thinkers, practitioners, academics and others. The G-30 meets twice annually to discuss economics, foreign exchange, capital markets and other matters. It was established in 1978 and is based in Washington, D.C.

Group of Three 1. Germany, Japan and the United States, collectively referred to this way because of their large GDPs relative to the rest of the world. The Group of Three once comprised the largest industrialized nations in the world. **2.** A free trade agreement between Colombia, Mexico and Venezuela. The Group of Three reduced tariffs between the countries and pledged cooperation on investment, intellectual property and other matters. It came into effect in 1995. Although it remains in effect, Venezuela withdrew in 2006.

Group of Twenty Four An informal group composed of 24 developing countries all over the world. The G-24 exists to ensure developing countries are represented at international discussions of monetary issues. It was established in 1971 and maintains its headquarters at the IMF, even though the two are not formally affiliated.

Group Rotation 1. The tendency for some industries and sectors to perform better than others at different times. Group rotation is a result of economic cycles. **2.** An active management strategy in which a money manager changes the industries or sectors represented in a portfolio or fund in order to always hold securities in the strongest sectors. The goal of group rotation is to outperform the market by actively managing the portfolio or fund. This form of group rotation is also called sector rotation.

Group Rotation Manager A money manager who allocates capital under management according to the economic cycle or business cycle. For example, a group rotation manager may invest in a large number of IPOs (high risk investments) during periods of economic expansion and then switch most of the capital over to U.S. Treasury securities (low risk investments) when the economy is near or in recession. A group rotation manager primarily considers macroeconomic conditions when allocating capital. That is, a group rotation manager uses top-down investment strategies.

Group Sales The sale of a new issue in large quantities to institutional investors.

Group Universal Life Policy A universal life insurance policy that one purchases as a member of a collective group. A universal life insurance policy operates much like a whole life policy, with the main difference being that the interest earned on the savings portion of the policy can be used to pay premiums. If a large number of people pool their resources to buy a universal life policy that covers them individually, they are said to buy a group universal life policy.

Groupement d'Interet Economique A structure in France in which a group of businesses join together for mutual interest in order to form a competitive advantage. For example, businesses in a single town may band together to compete more efficiently against other towns both inside and outside France.

Group-Home Care Medical care provided to a number of people in a group setting. The persons involved live together in a facility and receive care from physicians and nurses who work at the facility. Some insurance policies provide coverage for group-home care, as do Medicare and Medicaid under some circumstances.

Groupism The tendency of members of a group to agree with each other and not to contradict each other out of a desire for status, recognition or acceptance. Groupism is dangerous in business as one member may be afraid to point out a flaw in another's thinking or the group as a whole may be disinclined toward innovation.

Growing Equity Mortgage A mortgage with a fixed interest rate and monthly payments that increase over time, at least up to a certain amount. The increased payments go toward paying down the principal on the mortgage. A growing equity mortgage allows the mortgage holder to shorten the period of the mortgage with the increased payments. A GEM makes the most sense if the home owner expects to increase his/her income over the life of the mortgage.

Growth The change in a company's or nation's earnings, revenue, GDP or some other measure from one period of time (usually a year) to the next. Growth shows by how much the measure has grown or shrunk in raw dollar amounts, but may be expressed as a percentage as well. It may or may not be adjusted for inflation.

Growth Accounting The study and analysis of factors affecting economic growth. For example, growth accounting may measure things like productivity and growth of capital in order to account for changes to the gross domestic product of a country or region.

Growth and Income Fund A mutual fund that invests in both high growth companies and companies known for paying dividends. Growth and income funds combine aspects of growth funds and income funds. As a result, they have more risk and higher returns than income funds and lower risk and lower returns than growth funds.

Growth at a Reasonable Price An equity investment strategy, popularized by Peter Lynch, that seeks to find a balance between the growth strategy and the valuation strategy. The strategy aims at investing in stocks with sustainable growth in a relatively low (compared to growth investing) price range. GARP investors tend to favor older companies with solid growth rates, such as General Electric.

Growth Company A company performing better, or expected to perform better, than its industry or the market as a whole. Companies generating a return on equity of greater than 15% are generally classified as growth companies, but not all growth companies are classified as such. These companies usually pay little to nothing in dividends as the companies reinvest most of their earnings. Some believe that many or most growth companies are overvalued, citing, for example, the large number of growth companies during the dotcom bubble. See also: Industry life cycle.

Growth Fund A portfolio or mutual fund in which the primary goal is capital appreciation of the securities represented therein. That is, the investor or shareholder does not expect dividends and most returns on investments come in higher share prices. This involves investing in companies with higher risk than other portfolios. For example, a growth fund will likely invest in a promising start-up with a great outlook instead of a blue-chip company with a reliable, but not exciting, outlook. In addition to risk, a growth fund requires a relatively long time horizon, as start-ups and similar companies often take time to appreciate. See also: Plow back, Buy low, sell high, Income fund, Growth and income fund.

Growth Industry An industry in an early phase of existence marked by an end to technological innovation and the beginning of an attempt by different companies in the industry to gain larger market shares. That is, even if two competing companies make exactly the same product, they will use marketing, pricing, and other methods to become a leader in that product's market. These companies experience high earnings and/or revenue, though they often reinvest their profits into further growth of the company and as a result tend to pay out low dividends. See also: Industry Life Cycle, Three-Phase DDM.

Growth Investing An investment strategy in which one purchases securities deemed likely to rise in price, especially in the short or medium term. In growth investing, one prioritizes the theoretical future price of a company's shares over its current price or actual value. One may use a variety of technical or fundamental means to find growth securities. Growth investing can result in large gains in a relatively short period of time; however, it can fuel speculative bubbles. After the burst of the dot-com bubble, the growth at a reasonable price strategy became more popular than straight growth investing.

Growth Opportunity An investment or project that has the potential to grow significantly, leading to a profit for the investor. New investments are often presented to potential investors as growth opportunities.

Growth Phase In an industry life cycle, an early phase marked by an end to technological innovation and the attempt by different companies in the industry to gain larger market shares. That is, even if two competing companies make exactly the same product, they will use marketing, pricing, and other methods to become a leader in that product's market.

Growth Rate The amount by which a variable increases over a given period of time as a percentage of its previous value. For example, a 3% growth rate in GDP for a year means that the value of an economy is 103% of the value of the previous year.

Growth Recession An economy in which GDP growth is occurring but unemployment is high. A growth recession can be politically complicated, as politicians either must convince the majority of people that things are going well or a minority that things are going poorly. See also: Jobless recovery.

Growth Stock Share in a company performing better, or expected to perform better, than its industry or the market as a whole. Shares generating a return on equity of greater than 15% are generally classified as growth stocks, but not all growth stocks are classified as such. Such stocks usually pay little to nothing dividends as the companies reinvest most of their earnings. Some believe that many or most growth stocks are overvalued, citing for example the large number of growth stocks during the dotcom bubble.

Grzywna A measure of weight for gold and silver in medieval eastern Europe. While the specific weight varied, a grzywna was usually around 200 grams. The Ukrainian hryvnia derives its name from it.

GS 1. ISO 3166-1 alpha-2 code for South Georgia and the South Sandwich Islands. This would be the code used in international transactions to and from local bank accounts. **2.** ISO 3166-2 geocode for South Georgia and the South Sandwich Islands. This is used as an international standard for shipping to the area.

GT 1. ISO 3166-1 alpha-2 code for the Republic of Guatemala. This is the code used in international transactions to and from Guatemalan bank accounts. **2.** ISO 3166-2 geocode for Guatemala. This is used as an international standard for shipping to Guatemala. Each Guatemalan department has its own code with the prefix "GT." For example, the code for the Department of Alta Verapaz is ISO 3166-2:GT-AV.

GTM GOST 7.67 Latin three-letter geocode for Guatemala. The code is used for transactions to and from Guatemalan bank accounts and for international shipping to Guatemala. As with all GOST 7.67 codes, it is used primarily in Cyrillic alphabets.

GTQ ISO 4217 code for the Guatemalan quetzal. It was introduced in 1925 and was pegged to the U.S. dollar and the French franc, as well as gold, at different points in its history. Since 1987, it has been a floating currency. Interestingly, it is named after the quetzal, a local bird whose feathers were used as a currency during the Mayan period.

G-Type Reorganization A form of corporate reorganization in which a bankrupt company sells some or all of its assets to repay as much of its debt as possible. See also: Liquidation.

Guanxi A Chinese word indicating the personal networks and relationships over which a person has influence. That is, guanxi indicates a relationship in which the persons involved may persuade each other to perform favors. The term's meaning also incorporates the advantages that such relationship can have. As such, guanxi is important in business relationships.

Guap A large amount of money. The term is thought to derive from guacamole.

Guarani The currency of Paraguay. It was introduced in 1944, replacing the Paraguayan peso. It was pegged to the U.S. dollar between 1960 and 1985. It is now the least valuable currency in North and South America.

Guarantee A promise made by a third party to provide payment on a bond, loan, or other liability in the event of default. While many guarantees apply to debt instruments, they may also be used in day-to-day life. For example, a parent may sign a guarantee with a rental agency promising to pay rent on behalf of an adult child if he/she does not do it. Banks often make guarantees on behalf of certain clients, but, just as often, private parties make guarantees to banks to promise payment on private loans. Guarantees reduce the risk to loans and liabilities, and usually improve the credit agency ratings of bonds.

Guarantee Fee A fee charged to holders of a mortgage-backed security by the issuer. The guarantee fee helps cover the issuer's expenses but its most important use is to lessen the issuer's risk of loss or default in case too many of the mortgages underlying the security themselves default.

Guarantee Letter In put options, a guarantee of delivery of securities made by a bank to a brokerage on behalf of the bank's client. When an investor is writing a put option and does not have the cash available to buy the underlying asset if the option is exercised, the brokerage may require a guarantee letter in order to eliminate the risk that the investor will not be able to buy the underlying asset. See also: Cosigner, Letter of guarantee.

Guarantee of Signature A statement issued by a bank or other financial institution stating that the signature on an associated legal document is authentic. The guarantee of signature is attached to the main document, and is used to provide protection against risk of fraud. Some documents, notably statements of transfer of stocks or bonds, require a guarantee of signature to be valid.

Guaranteed Account 1. A margin account at a brokerage where the maintenance requirement is secured by the assets or the excess margin on another account. This reduces the risk to both the brokerage and the account holder. **2.** See: Insured Account.

Guaranteed Annual Wage A pledge by a company to provide sufficient work for an employee to make an agreed-upon amount each year. The work may be irregular; that is, an employee may not be required to work one week but work overtime another.

Guaranteed Bond A bond on which payment is guaranteed by a third party such as a government or a bond insurance company. A guaranteed bond is doubly protected because it is payment can come either from the issuer or from the third party in case the issuer defaults. As such, a guaranteed bond is low risk and therefore usually carries a lower coupon rate than an uninsured bond or other bond without a guarantee. A bond guaranteed by the U.S. government is generally thought to be riskless.

Guaranteed Cost Premium A premium on an insurance policy in which coverage does not change based on the severity of an insured event.

Guaranteed Dividend A dividend that a company is required to pay on its preferred stock. Guaranteed dividends are generally cumulative, meaning that if a company skips a payment, it can make no dividend payments on common stock until preferred stockholders are satisfied in full. Under some circumstances, preferred stockholders can force the liquidation of a company that does not pay its guaranteed dividends.

Guaranteed Insurability A provision in some life and health insurance contracts stating that the insurance contract will be renewed at the end of its term at a certain, stated premium without regard for the policyholder's health when the contract expires. One generally must pay extra for guaranteed insurability. It should not be confused with a guaranteed insurance contract. See also: Pre-Existing Condition.

Guaranteed Introducing Broker A brokerage that does not actually handle transactions and for which a futures commodity merchant agrees to be responsible for all liabilities. In general, introducing brokers make recommendations while delegating the task of executing trades to a person or firm operating on a trading floor. Most of the time, an introducing broker must raise its own capital to do this, but a guaranteed introducing broker may pass off these expenses to the futures commodity merchant.

Guaranteed Investment Contract A pension plan purchased through a bank or an insurance company for a lump sum in which the principal is guaranteed by the issuer. One may receive payments from a GIC either in installments or as a lump sum after retirement. A GIC provides the pensioner with a small interest rate that is not guaranteed, but the fact that the principal is guaranteed makes it a relatively low-risk investment.

Guaranteed Issue The legal requirement for an insurance company to issue a policy to an applicant regardless of his/her level of risk. This especially applies to health insurance. For example, an insurance company may be compelled to issue a policy to a person with a pre-existing condition. In general, higher risk policyholders still must pay a higher premium for their insurance. In the United States, Obamacare mandates guaranteed issue of health insurance.

Guaranteed Loan A loan on which payment is guaranteed by a third party such as a government, an insurance company or a co-signer. A guaranteed loan is doubly protected because repayment can come either from the issuer or from the third party in case the issuer defaults. As such, a guaranteed loan is low risk and therefore usually carries a lower interest rate than another loan without a guarantee.

Guaranteed Mortgage Certificate A mortgage-backed security issued by Freddie Mac. As with all mortgage-backed securities, the coupons on guaranteed mortgage certificates are paid out of the principal and interest on a pool of mortgages underlying the securities. However, GMCs have a guaranteed average life, meaning that Freddie Mac protects the investor from prepayment risk buy guaranteeing principal and interest payments in the event that too many mortgage holders pay back their loans early, depriving the pool of interest it otherwise would have received. See also: collateralized mortgage obligation.

Guaranteed Renewable Policy Insurance A health insurance policy that the insurer is required to renew provided the policyholder pays premiums in a timely manner. Additionally, guaranteed renewable policies may only raise their premiums if premiums are raised on a whole class of policyholders; that is, insurers may not raise premiums on individual policyholders arbitrarily.

Guaranteed Replacement Cost Coverage Insurance An insurance policy in which the insurer will pay the entire cost of replacing the insured asset if it is damaged or destroyed. That is, there is not maximum benefit on the policy; the insurer simply pays the replacement cost regardless of what it is. Importantly, a guaranteed replacement cost coverage plan does not take depreciation into account.

Guaranteed Return A return that a company is required to pay. Bonds and coupons have guaranteed returns because the issuing company agrees to pay coupons and guaranteed dividends. This contrasts with non-guaranteed returns, such as the dividends on common stock, which a company may decide not to pay. A guaranteed return does not necessarily mean that the company will pay (the company may, for example, default or go bankrupt). However, under some circumstances, the holders of securities with guaranteed returns may force the liquidation of the company.

Guaranteed Return Structure A way to structure a security in which the amount invested is protected. For example, a bond has a guaranteed return structure because, in the event of liquidation, bondholders have prior claim to their initial investment over other investors. Likewise, a co-signed loan has a guaranteed return structure because a third party agrees to take on the liability in the event of default. Many guaranteed return structures are based on debt.

Guaranteed Share A share of stock in a company for which another company or bank promises to pay dividends in case the issuing company defaults. Because guaranteed shares carry lower risk, they are usually more expensive than non-guaranteed stocks.

Guaranteed Stock A stock in a company for which another company or bank promises to pay dividends in case the issuing company defaults. Because guaranteed stocks carry lower risk, they are usually more expensive than non-guaranteed stocks.

Guaranteed Student Loan A student loan on which repayment is guaranteed by a third party, especially the U.S. federal government. A student loan is financing used to pay for one's education, especially at the postsecondary or technical level. Because these loans do not purchase any asset to offer as collateral, they are high risk. However, a guaranteed student loan reduces the risk by promising that the third party will repay if the student defaults. Examples of federally guaranteed student loans in the United States include the Stafford loan and the PLUS loan.

Guaranteeing Bank A bank that ensures payment on a note, bond, or other debt instrument in the event of default. It is important to note that the avalising bank is not a party to the transaction in any other way. Avalising banks are more common in Europe than in the United States, as American banks have tighter restrictions on bank guarantees. See also: aval.

Guarantor A third party who promises to provide payment on a bond, loan, or other liability in the event of default. While many guarantees apply to debt instruments, they may also be used for day-to-day expenses. For example, a parent may be a guarantor for an adult child and promise to pay rent to a rental agency if the adult child does not do it. Banks often serve as guarantors on behalf of certain clients, but, just as often, private parties serve as guarantors and promise payment on private loans. Guarantors reduce the risk to loans and liabilities, and usually improve the credit agency ratings of bonds.

Guaranty 1. See: Guarantee. **2.** See: Collateral.

Guardian A non-parent who is legally responsible for a minor child or mentally incompetent person. A guardian may be designated by a parent, perhaps in a will, or one may be appointed by a court. More than one guardian may be designated for a single person, each with his/her own areas of responsibility. For example, a child may live with one guardian while another is responsible for administering assets left to the child in his/her parent's estate.

Guardian Deed Title to real estate given to the guardian of a minor child or a mentally incompetent person. The guardian deed allows the guardian to sell the real estate because its owner is not capable of doing so himself/herself. Guardian deeds are issued by a court.

Guardian IRA An IRA created and administered on behalf of a minor or mentally incompetent adult by a legal guardian. The IRA is registered in the name of the minor, but the guardian is responsible for all paperwork. When the minor reaches adulthood (either 18 or 21 years of age, depending on the state), he/she must complete necessary paperwork recognizing him/her as the administrator of the IRA.

Guardianship Legal responsibility by a non-parent for a minor child or mentally incompetent person. Guardianship may be designated by a parent, perhaps in a will, or a guardian may be appointed by a court. More than one guardian may be designated for a single person, each with his/her own areas of responsibility. For example, a child may live with one guardian while another is responsible for administering assets left to the child in his/her parent's estate.

Guardianship Expenses The amount one spends as part of one's legal responsibility to care for a mentally incompetent person or a child other than one's own. In the United States, guardianship expenses are tax deductible at the federal level. See also: Guardian.

Guatemalan Quetzal The currency of Guatemala. It was introduced in 1925 and was pegged to the U.S. dollar and the French franc, as well as gold, at different points in its history. Since 1987, it has been a floating currency. It is named after the quetzal, a local bird whose feathers were used as a currency during the Mayan period.

Guberniya In Russia prior to 1917, a political subdivision equivalent to a province.

Guerilla Warfare A type of warfare in which small groups of soldiers and/or armed civilians strike suddenly against an exposed target and then withdraw quickly. Guerilla warfare is used when one military cannot meet another successfully in the open field, or when the regular army already has been defeated. Guerilla warfare can be very bloody, but has been successful in the past. It is a kind of political risk in some areas.

Guernsey Pound The currency of Guernsey. Because Guernsey is a British Crown dependency, it is in a monetary union with the United Kingdom. As a result, a Guernsey pound is equivalent to a British pound.

Guertin Laws Laws in each U.S. state requiring an insurer to pay a cash surrender value to a term life policyholder under certain circumstances. If the policyholder has had the policy for three years or longer and lapses due to non-payment of a premium, the Guertin laws apply and the cash surrender value must be paid. These laws are designed to protect long-term policyholders even though term life policies usually do not have cash surrender values.

Guest Law A law allowing the passenger in an automobile to bring a lawsuit against the driver in the event of an accident. In order to be liable for injuries and/or damages, the driver must be negligent. That is, the driver must be found to be in some way at fault for the accident.

Guest Worker The holder of an H1-B visa, which gives one permission to live and work the United States for three years, renewable once. Guest workers must possess sufficient skills to perform the work for which they are hired (though there has been controversy as to what level of skill is required) and, if they quit or are fired, they must return home, find another job or apply for a change in status. While the H1-B visa is not an immigrant visa, guest workers may apply for green cards.

GUF GOST 7.67 Latin three-letter geocode for French Guiana. The code is used for transactions to and from French Guianese bank accounts and for international shipping to French Guiana. As with all GOST 7.67 codes, it is used primarily in Cyrillic alphabets.

Guidance An announcement, often over a conference call, by a publicly-traded company of its projected earnings for a quarter or year. Guidance gives investors and

analysts a basis from which to make their investment decisions and recommendations. Guidance also helps the company price out any potential good or bad news so its share price is not subject to wild fluctuations when the earnings are actually announced. Guidance is also called earnings guidance.

Guild An association of persons with a particular skill or trade. For example, the electricians in an area may form a guild for mutual support, to route business to each other, or for other reasons. A guild contrasts with a union primarily because it includes both employers and employees; it is based on trade, rather than class. Guilds were most common in medieval Europe, but still exist and have a great deal of sway in some industries, notably filmmaking. Bar associations of lawyers and realtor groups may also be considered guilds.

Guilder 1. See: Dutch guilder. **2.** See: Netherlands Antillean guilder.

Guilder Share A share in any of a number of Dutch companies that are not allowed to trade outside Holland. A guilder share would not be remarkable except that Dutch regulations do not even allow it to simply be bought and incorporated into an international depository receipt or IDR. As a result, when an IDR buys shares in these companies, the shares are canceled and guilder shares are issued in their stead.

Guilt-Edged Investment Informal for any unethical or illegal investment. The term comes from the guilt the investor supposedly feels for making money unethically.

Guinea A gold coin issued in the United Kingdom between 1663 and 1816. From 1717 on, its value was fixed by law at 21 shillings, or just over one British pound. After it was withdrawn from circulation, "guinea" remained a slang term for 21 shillings. After decimalization, the term was still used in horse racing and the sale of rams to mean 1.05 pounds.

Guinea-Bissau Peso The former currency of Guinea-Bissau. It was introduced in 1975 and was replaced by the West African CFA franc in 1997.

Guinean Franc The currency of Guinea. It was introduced in 1985, replacing the Guinean syli (which itself replaced the first franc) at par. It is a floating currency and has been subject to high inflation.

Gulden An alternate term for the Dutch guilder.

Gulf Cooperation Council An international organization fostering greater political and economic unity for Arab countries in the Arabian Gulf. Among other things, it exists to promote similar regulatory regimes, to unify military presence and to advance the private sector. Most members had pledged to create a common currency by 2010, but this has been postponed indefinitely. See also: Khaleeji.

Gulf Rupee A currency that circulated in several parts of the Persian Gulf between 1959 and 1970. It was issued by the Indian government and pegged to the Indian rupee at par; by extension, this meant it was also pegged to the British pound. It was replaced by a number of currencies once Kuwait, Bahrain and others gradually became fully independent of Britain.

GUM GOST 7.67 Latin three-letter geocode for Guam. The code is used for transactions to and from Guamanian bank accounts and for international shipping to Guam. As with all GOST 7.67 codes, it is used primarily in Cyrillic alphabets.

Gum Arabic A gum made from sap of the acacia tree. In the 19th century, it was a major export in parts of east Africa and Sudan. Gum arabic is used in painting and in textiles, as well as in some foodstuff and as a desert in its own.

Gun An ancient Sumerian unit of weight approximately equivalent to 30 kilograms.

Gun Jumping The act or practice of soliciting orders for a new issue of a security before it has been registered with the SEC, or before its registration has been approved. Gun jumping amounts to soliciting orders outside the SEC's regulation and is, as such, illegal. Engaging in gun jumping can delay the actual issue of the security.

Guns and Butter Curve A curve on a chart demonstrating a theoretical construction of opportunity cost. Given an economy of only two products, guns and butter, and limited resources, economic actors must decide how much of each to produce. The more guns it produces, the less butter it can produce and vice versa. The guns and butter curve demonstrates this graphically.

Gunslinger A money manager who is willing to take big risks to increase the potential return on investments. A gunslinger, for example, would be more likely to invest in the IPO of a company with a new and exciting product about which little is known, than to invest in the secured bond issued by a company everyone knows and trusts. The term especially refers to money managers who buy the risky securities on margin. See also: Risk lover.

Guntha A customary unit of area approximately equivalent to 101.17 square meters. It is used in real estate transactions in some parts of India and Pakistan.

Gur An ancient Sumerian unit of volume approximately equivalent to 300 liters.

GUST Restatement Adjustments annuities and retirement plans were required to make because of changes in American legislation. The term comes from four laws and international agreements: the General Agreement on Tariffs and Trade, Uniformed Services Employment and Reemployment Rights Act of 1996, Small Business Job Protection Act of 1996, and Taxpayer Relief Act of 1997. However, GUST restatement must also comply with the IRS Restructuring and Reform Act of 1998 and Community Renewal Tax Relief Act of 1997. GUST restatements may require a number of revisions to the foundational agreements of annuities and retirement plans. For example, the Community Renewal Act changed the definition of compensation to include some transportation benefits. This could affect a plan's maximum allowable contribution. Plans were required to make the necessary changes and inform plan participants that they had done so.

Gutter 1. In newspapers and journalism, the space between columns. **2.** In books and magazines, any crease in a page, especially the center margin.

GUY GOST 7.67 Latin three-letter geocode for Guyana. The code is used for transactions to and from Guyanese bank accounts and for international shipping to Guyana. As with all GOST 7.67 codes, it is used primarily in Cyrillic alphabets.

Guyanese Dollar The currency of Guyana. Introduced in 1839, it was originally related to the Spanish dollar (which widely circulated in Caribbean colonies) and was intended to facilitate the transition from a currency based on the Dutch guilder to one based on the British pound. It was pegged to the pound until 1975.

Guz An obsolete Nepalese unit of length approximately equivalent to 0.9144 meters or one yard.

GW 1. ISO 3166-1 alpha-2 code for the Republic of Guinea-Bissau. This is the code used in international transactions to and from Guinea-Bissauan bank accounts. **2.** ISO 3166-2 geocode for Guinea-Bissau. This is used as an international standard for shipping to Guinea-Bissau. Each region has its own code with the prefix "GW." For example, the code for the Region of Bafata is ISO 3166-2:GW-BA.

Gwangyeoksi In South Korea, a political subdivision equivalent to a city outside the jurisdiction of any province.

Gwangyeok-Si In South Korea, a political subdivision equivalent to a metropolitan area.

GWP ISO 4217 code for the Guinea-Bissau peso. It was introduced in 1975 and was replaced by the West African CFA franc in 1997.

GY 1. ISO 3166-1 alpha-2 code for the Co-operative Republic of Guyana. This is the code used in international transactions to and from Guyanese bank accounts. **2.** ISO 3166-2 geocode for Guyana. This is used as an international standard for shipping to Guyana. Each region has its own code with the prefix "GY." For example, the code for the Region of Barima-Waini is ISO 3166-2:GY-BA.

GYD ISO 4217 code for the Guyanese dollar. It was introduced in 1966, replacing the East Caribbean dollar at par.

Gypsy Swap A swap in which the legs are common stock and restricted stock. A gypsy swap generally occurs when an investor wishes to liquidate a position in a publicly-traded company. That is, because a restricted stock may only be sold under certain circumstances, an investor holding one may exchange it for a more liquid investment.

Gyugh In Armenia, a political subdivision equivalent to a village.

H.W. Heinrich An early researcher of workplace safety. He encouraged employers to adopt standards for safer offices and factories, but also pointed out that failure to act safely caused most accidents. His work flourished in the 1930s.

H-1B Visa A visa granting the holder permission to live and work the United States for three years, with the opportunity to renew once. H-1B visa holders must possess sufficient skills to perform the work for which they are hired (though there has been controversy about the level of skill required) and, if they quit or are fired, they must return home, find another job, or apply for a change in status. While the H1-B visa is not an immigrant visa, its holders may apply for green cards.

Habatsu Political factions within the Liberal Democratic Party (LDP) of Japan. Except for 11 months in 1993 and 1994, the Liberal Democratic Party was the ruling party of Japan constantly between 1955 and 2009, when it lost reelection to the Democratic Party. Because the LDP was effectively the only party in Japan for so long, habatsu functioned much like parties themselves; that is, they vied with each other for dominance within the LDP. However, habatsu largely centered on personality, rather than policy or ideology. Their influence has declined since the 1990s.

Habeas Corpus A writ one may file requiring the custodian of a prisoner to justify in court that the imprisonment is legal. For example, if one is arrested without proper warrant, one may file habeas corpus for one's release. It should be noted that the right to file habeas corpus may be suspended in national emergencies or for other reasons. The concept comes from English common law.

Habendum In a lease or similar contract, a clause stating the extent to which the lessor is giving the lessee control of a property. For example, a habendum may state how long the lessee may use the property and what he may or may not do to it.

Habit A normal custom of an individual or group. Habits greatly influence economic behavior at both the micro- and macro- levels. For example, one may develop the habit of only shopping at certain stores, whether or not they have the best products or prices. Likewise, the majority of farmers in a country may only grow certain crops, whether or not those are the best for the land or the market. Habits may be positive or negative, and are often both, depending on one's perspective.

HABITAT Formally called the United Nations Human Settlements Programme. An organization within the United Nations that aims to provide housing. HABITAT seeks to encourage sustainable cities and towns because of increasing urbanization worldwide. It was established in 1978 and is based in Nairobi.

Hacker A person who infiltrates a computer system, usually in order to gather information. A hacker finds a way past the system's protocols. Some hackers do this simply for the thrill, though many others hack for nefarious purposes. For example, a hacker may be hired by a company or government to conduct espionage on a competitor or enemy. Other hackers freelance in order to find things like credit card numbers to facilitate identity theft and other crimes. However, the word is not always used in a negative context.

Hague System Formally called the Hague Agreement Concerning the International Deposit of Industrial Designs. An international agreement allowing one to register an industrial design as one's own intellectual property in all participating countries using a single application form and paying only one set of fees. This is especially important in international business because the agreement makes it easier to protect one's idea when marketing it in several countries at once. More than 50 countries belong to the Hague System.

Hail Insurance An insurance policy that provides coverage for damage to agricultural crops due to hail. Hail insurance helps reduce the weather-related uncertainty that farmers experience. In the event of an insured loss, damaged crops are compensated for in proportion of the total crop. As with all insurance, one pays a premium for hail insurance coverage.

Hair Shirt An informal term for an austerity measure. The term derives from shirts made of animal hair that religious figures have worn as a sign of penance. Austerity measures are adopted to make up for (or even to do penance for) excessive government debt.

Haircut 1. The reduction of value to securities used as collateral in a margin loan. That is, when one places securities as collateral, the brokerage making the loan treats them as being worth less than they actually are, so as to give itself a cushion in case its market price decreases. **2.** The bid-ask spread at which a market maker buys and sells securities. It is called a haircut because it is a thin spread.

Haitian Dollar In Haiti, a term for five gourdes. Between 1912 and 1989, the Haitian gourde was pegged at a rate of five gourdes to one U.S. dollar. Even though the gourde is now a floating currency, the peg is maintained in colloquial speech. Prices in shops are sometimes given in Haitian dollars.

Haitian Gourde The currency of Haiti. It was introduced in 1872, replacing another currency that was also called the gourde. It was initially pegged to the French franc, but this was switched to the U.S. dollar in 1912 at a rate of five gourdes to one dollar. Since 1989, the gourde has been a floating currency. Interestingly, the peg is maintained in colloquial speech, in which people refer to five gourdes as a Haitian dollar. Often, prices are even given in Haitian dollars.

Hajr In Islamic law, the act of imposing a restriction on what a person may do with a property. For example, an insane person may have hajr imposed preventing him from selling his house.

Halal Describing anything that is permissible in sharia, or Islamic law. The word most often refers to moral decisions or food items. However, it may also refer to investments acceptable to Islamic finance.

Halala A subdivision of a Saudi riyal. One halala is equal in value to 1/100 of a riyal. See also: Cent.

Halation 1. In photography, blurred lines due to light. When done deliberately, halation may call attention to a certain part of an image. This may be used in advertisements or other forms of marketing. **2.** See: Blooming.

Haler A division of the Czech koruna equal in value to 1/100 of one koruna.

Half a Ton In the United Kingdom, a slang term for 50 pounds.

Half Cent A coin minted in the United States between 1793 and 1857 worth 1/200 of one dollar.

Half Crown A former coin in the United Kingdom equal in value to 1/8 of one British pound. Half crowns were demonetized in 1970, the year before the pound was decimalized.

Half Dime A coin minted in the United States between 1792 and 1873 worth 1/20 of one dollar.

Half Duplex In telecommunications, a system that allows transmission between two endpoints, but not simultaneously. For example, if two people have walkie talkies, each may speak to the other, but the signal will not transmit if both try to speak at the same time. This contrasts with a full duplex, in which information may be transmitted both ways at the same time.

Half Eagle The first gold coin the United States authorized. It was minted between 1795 and 1929 and was worth $5.

Half Farthing A coin produced in the United Kingdom between 1828 and 1856. It was equal in value to 1/8 of one penny, or 1/1920 of one British pound. Half farthings were demonetized in 1869.

Half Life In a pool of mortgages underlying a mortgage-backed security, the length of time it takes for half the aggregate principal to be repaid. A half life is normally about 12 years, but this may vary depending on how often homeowners refinance their mortgages (which pays off all principal at once). Half lives are calculated for mortgage-backed securities issued or guaranteed by Freddie Mac, Fannie Mae, and Ginnie Mae.

Half Union A non-circulating, commemorative coin minted in the United States in 1877 and again in 1915. It had a face value of $50.

Half-Commission Man In investing, a person who introduces a potential client to a broker and, in exchange, receives half the commission the broker generates from that client. Half commission men help brokers find more and better clients such that volume compensates for the reduced commission. See also: Introducing broker.

Half-Inch In Cockney rhyming slang, a term meaning to steal.

Half-Page Double Spread An advertisement in a magazine that spreads across the top or bottom half of two consecutive pages.

Half-Sovereign A former coin in the United Kingdom equal in value to 10 shillings, or half of one British pound. Half-sovereigns were minted from gold and thus have not circulated since the end of the gold standard.

Half-Stock Informal; common stock or preferred stock with a face value of $50. Most stocks, when they have a face value at all, are issued with a face value of $100; thus, stock issued at $50 is called "half stock." It is important to note that stocks rarely have face value anymore.

Halftone An engraving used to print an illustration, such as in a book or magazine. This word is most common in publishing.

Half-Year Convention In accounting, the assumption that an asset is purchased at its value exactly half-way through the calendar year in which it is purchased. For example, if one buys an asset for $1,000 on January 1st and it is worth $1,200 at the end of the second quarter, the half-year convention would assume that it was bought for $1,200. This can affect taxes owed on the asset and the depreciation allowed each year. Obviously the half-year convention can have both positive and negative impacts, depending on the price movement of the asset.

Halier A division of the Slovak koruna equal in value to 1/100 of one koruna.

Hall vs. Geiger-Jones Company A 1917 United States Supreme Court decision that confirmed the right of states to pass laws regulating the securities trade. The decision is perhaps best known today for its application of the term "blue skying," coined when Justice Joseph McKenna asserted that states may and should protect investors from securities with "no more basis than so many feet of 'blue sky.'" See also: Due Diligence.

Hallmark In marketing, a distinguishing feature of a product that makes it recognizable to potential buyers. A hallmark may be a significant intangible asset for a product.

Halloween Strategy In investing, the strategy of buying securities after October 31 and selling them in May. The strategy is based on the idea that securities perform the best between October and May. It is an example of a calendar strategy.

Halo Effect In psychology, the concept that persons with one positive quality are perceived as having multiple positive qualities. For example, an attractive person may be thought to be more intelligent than he/she really is. In business, the halo effect is seen when one popular product from a company improves sales for other products.

Hamas A political party and paramilitary organization in Palestine. Established in 1987, it originated in the older Muslim Brotherhood but combined Islamism with Palestinian nationalism. It was responsible for numerous suicide bombings in the 1990s and early 2000s, but ended this policy in 2005. In 2006, it won parliamentary elections in Palestine and the following year expelled rival Fatah from Gaza. Hamas (or at least its paramilitary wing) is regarded as a terrorist organization by much of the world.

Hamaynk In Armenia, a political subdivision equivalent to a municipal government.

Hamburg Mint An organization in Germany that issues legal tender coins for general use. It traces its origins to the 9th century and is a state-owned corporation.

Hamburg Rules Rules established by the United Nations governing the rights and obligations that carriers, shippers and consignees have with respect to each other when transporting goods by sea. The Rules were intended to mitigate the negative impacts previous rules had on developing countries. The Hamburg Rules are formally called the United Nations Convention on the Carriage of Goods by Sea. They were adopted in 1978 and came into effect in 1992. See also: UNCITRAL.

Hameau In France, a political subdivision equivalent to a rural village.

Hamlet In Oregon, a political subdivision equivalent to a rural village. While hamlets are organized, they do not have the ability to tax and do not provide utilities.

Hamma An ancient Greek unit of length approximately equivalent to 18.5 meters.

Hammer In candlestick charts, the representation of a trading day where a security trades significantly below its opening price for most of the day, but closes either above or close to the opening price. It is called a hammer because the candlestick representing the trading day looks somewhat like a hammer. It is not necessarily a bullish indicator, but a hammer may mean that the market is nearing a bottom.

Hammering the Market Informal; in a stock market, selling in heavy volume. Hammering the market usually occurs upon unexpected bad news, such as a terrorist attack. Most companies try to price out bad news by leaking it gradually, so as to avoid this situation, but, obviously, this is not always possible.

Hammersmith and Fulham Swaps A series of interest rate swaps on which the Borough of Hammersmith and Fulham (in London) took positions in the 1980s. The Borough was the floating rate payer, which, when interest rates rose, gave it liabilities well in excess of its statutory debt ceiling. These swaps were declared to be illegal in 1988 in part because they were too risky for local governments.

Hand A unit of length equivalent to four inches. It is used in the sale and use of horses.

Hand Tool A tool used by a person rather than by a machine. Examples include hammers, screwdrivers, welders and so forth. Hand tools are used in various blue collar positions, though a number have been rendered obsolete over time by automation.

Handbill A pamphlet one hands out to another, especially a stranger. Handbills are used in direct marketing, especially involving street canvassers. Handbills are known for their low response rates.

Hand-Held Addressing A tool one uses to apply address labels to envelopes. These tools are used by hand and usually require application of water for the label to "stick." As a result, hand-held addressing tools are almost obsolete and have been largely replaced with automated addressing tools.

Handicap A disability. The term is sometimes considered derogatory. In the United States, the Rehabilitation Act of 1973 used the word "handicap" to refer to a disability, while the Americans with Disabilities Act of 1990 used the word "disability" on the assumption that it had the same definition as "handicap." Courts interpreted this differently and applied a higher standard to the definition of "disability." Congress changed this with the passage of the ADA Amendments Act of 2008, which declared the two words to have the same meaning.

Handicapped Person A disabled person. The term is sometimes considered derogatory. In the United States, the Rehabilitation Act of 1973 used the word "handicap" to refer to a disability, while the Americans with Disabilities Act of 1990 used the word "disability" on the assumption it had the same definition as "handicap." Courts interpreted this differently and applied a higher standard to the definition of "disability." Congress changed this with the passage of the ADA Amendments Act of 2008, which declared the two words to have the same meaning.

Handle 1. On an exchange, a point in price change. For example, if stock goes from $11 to $10, it is said to drop a handle. **2.** On the S&P, 100 points in price change. **3.** See: Big figure.

Handling Allowance A discount offered by a manufacturer to a retailer for a product that requires special care or inconvenience. The handling allowance gives an incentive to the retailer to purchase a product in which it may not otherwise be interested.

Handling Charge The cost to package and ship a good. The seller often (but not always) passes on handling charges to the buyer. A handling charge may be called "shipping and handling."

Handsetting The act or process of setting type manually. That is, type on a printer is put in place by hand. Handsetting is rare because it is expensive, but it has a distinguished look, which is useful in some contexts.

Handshake Agreement An informal agreement in which major points are decided, but details may still need to be discussed. A handshake agreement is not finalized but indicates that the deal in question is likely to take place. A handshake agreement is often, but is not always, oral, rather than in writing.

Hands-Off Investor A shareholder or other investor who has enough equity to affect the company's management, but elects not to do so. A hand-off investor usually has an exceptionally large stake in the company, but chooses to accept his/her profits and ignore how the company is being run. A hands-off investor can be a show of confidence in the current management; in any case it allows the management a great deal of autonomy. The disadvantage, from the management's perspective, is the possibility that a hands-off investor will become dissatisfied and demand a greater role in the company. See also: Silent partner.

Hands-On Investor A shareholder or other investor who has enough equity to affect the company's management and elects to do so. A hand-on investor usually has an exceptionally large stake in the company and chooses to take an active role in how the company is being run. A hands-on investor may have little confidence in the current management; in any case, the situation results in the investor either appointing the management or allowing the existing management little autonomy. See also: Hands-off investor.

Handyman Special Slang; in real estate, a house in need of significant repairs. A handyman special is usually inexpensive and may be a good deal for buyers who are able to make repairs themselves at a relatively low cost.

Hang Seng Index An index tracking several dozen publicly-traded companies listed on the Hong Kong Stock Exchange, weighted for market capitalization. Started in 1969, Hang Seng includes approximately 70% of the capitalization of the Hong Kong Stock Exchange. It is considered to be an indicator of health in the wider market.

Hang the Bell on the Cat Slang; to take risks. The term has a positive connotation and implies leadership.

Hangarkeepers Legal Liability Insurance 1. An insurance policy that provides coverage to the owner of an airplane hangar in the event that a plane docked at that hangar but owned by someone else causes injury to a person or property. The policy covers the legal fees and damages that may result from the insured event. **2.** An insurance policy that provides coverage to the owner of an airplane in the event the plane causes injury to a person or property while another party is operating it. The policy covers legal fees and damages that may result from the insured event. In both cases, as with all insurance, the policyholder must pay a premium to receive the coverage.

Hangout A place frequented by one or more persons. Hangouts for groups such as young people are likely to attract advertisements (like billboards) different from hangouts for other groups.

Hans Eichel The German finance minister from 1999 to 2005. During his tenure, he tried unsuccessfully to reduce the German federal deficit. He was born in 1941.

Hanua In Papua New Guinea, a political subdivision equivalent to a village.

Hao A unit of length in China approximately equivalent to 33.33 micrometers.

Haploun Bema An ancient Greek unit of length approximately equivalent to 770 millimeters.

Hara-Kiri Swap A swap offering no profit for the offering party. That is, a hara-kiri swap involves an interest rate or exchange rate so low that it is impossible for the originator to make a profit. In general, hara-kiri swaps are advantageous only if they build a client base or if they allow one to enter a profiting position that one could not have entered previously. Nevertheless, it derives its name from hara-kiri, Japanese ritual suicide, because it is seen as a slow death for a company.

Haram In Islam, anything forbidden. For example, eating pork is considered haram. This is important in finance and economics because many investments, notably futures contracts and anything involving interest, are haram. See also: Islamic finance.

Harami Cross In candlestick charting, a large candle followed by a small candle (or doji) located completely within the previous candlestick's body. In candlestick charting, a candlestick represents a single trading day, with a larger candlestick indicating that the opening price is significantly different from the closing price. A doji following a large candlestick indicates that the previous trend is about to change. A bearish harami cross follows a day in which the price rose and a bullish harami cross follows a day on which it fell.

Harbor Fee A fee assessed on a boat or other vessel for the privilege to dock at a particular harbor. These fees are often small compared to a voyage's total costs.

Harbormaster A person who directs ships into or out of a harbor. Harbormasters are important to international trade because it is their duty to keep cargo safe.

Hard Budget Constraint A spending limit that cannot be exceeded without drastic consequences. For example, a country cannot exceed its debt ceiling without incurring panic in its bond markets. More commonly, however, this term refers to the requirement that a money manager or investment company at least break even and preferably meet some target profit for clients or shareholders. Companies that fail to meet hard budget constraints may see shake-ups in their management, perhaps with major executives losing their jobs.

Hard Call Protection A provision in callable bonds that prevents the bond from being prematurely redeemed for a certain period of time. Interest payments are guaranteed during the hard call protection period, but not afterward. The bond may be redeemed at any point after the call date, which means that the issuer would return the principal to bondholders and interest payments would cease. Hard call protection exists to protect bondholders from the risk that interest rates will fall before the call date. The period of time is often called the cushion. See also: Soft call protection.

Hard Capital Rationing A capital budget to which a company must adhere. A company may engage in hard capital rationing if it has limited resources and has allocated them in such a way as to allow little or no room for error. A project that goes over budget under hard capital rationing may land the company in trouble. See also: Capital rationing.

Hard Commodity A commodity that is mined or obtained from some other non-agricultural source. Hard commodities include gold, oil and diamonds. See also: Soft commodity.

Hard Copy A physical document containing information. For example, a printed paper of a spreadsheet is a hard copy, while the same spreadsheet saved to a flash drive is not.

Hard Currency A currency that is issued by a politically and economically stable country and is therefore well-respected in FX trade. Large, international transactions are often settled in one hard currency or other. The market to buy and sell hard currencies is especially liquid, even by the standards of foreign exchange trading. The price of a hard currency often remains stable in the short-term. Examples of hard currencies include the U.S. dollar, the British pound, the euro, and the Japanese yen.

Hard Dinar A currency used in the former Yugoslavia. It was introduced in 1966 and suffered from high inflation throughout its history, especially toward the end of its circulation. The convertible dinar replaced the hard dinar in 1990.

Hard Dollars Fees paid in cash to a brokerage for services. For example, an investor may pay hard dollars for research or investment advice from the brokerage. Hard dollar payments are made in cash rather than deducted from the value of a security transaction. See also: Soft dollars.

Hard Dot A portion of a halftone image with a sharp edge. A halftone image is used to print an illustration, and a hard dot produces better quality print. Often, new halftones have hard dots, but they degenerate over time to soft dots, which have less defined edges. A hard dot should not be confused with a hard edge.

Hard Ecu A pan-European currency proposed in 1990 by John Major, then Chancellor of the Exchequer in the United Kingdom. The hard ecu would have been managed by a fund, rather than a central bank. It was proposed as an alternative to what became the euro in 1999.

Hard Edge A sharp, clearly defined edge in printed material. Sometimes, hard edges are used in marketing to draw attention to a particular part of an image. However, a hard edge may be a flaw in printing. It should not be confused with a hard dot.

Hard Hat A helmet some workers are required to wear when employed in a hazardous position. For example, construction workers or oil drillers may have to wear hard hats as a condition of employment. Hard hats are closely associated with blue collar work.

Hard Insurance Market A period of time during which insurance companies are able to assess high premiums and therefore achieve high profits. A hard insurance market may occur after a disaster, which enables insurers to tighten their underwriting standards and therefore write fewer policies on lower risk clients. This contributes to their profitability. However, it may be difficult to obtain insurance during a hard insurance market. It is considered a normal part of the business cycle of insurance. See also: Soft insurance market.

Hard Landing A situation in which a central bank raises interest rates significantly to curb inflation and, in doing so, drives the economy into recession. For example, in 1981, the Federal Reserve raised the fed funds rate to 20%, which caused inflation to drop from 13.5% in 1981 to 3.2% in 1983. However, high interest rates led directly to a deep recession in the early 1980s. A hard landing is effective at reducing inflation, but is nonetheless undesirable. As a result, central banks only attempt it when there are no other viable options. See also: Soft Landing.

Hard Loan A loan made in a foreign currency that is stronger than the domestic currency. For example, a Turkish company may loan money to a Syrian company in euros because the euro is a stronger currency than either the Turkish lira or the Syrian pound. A hard loan carries foreign-exchange risk, but this is considered an acceptable risk compared to making the loan in a weak currency. See also: Hard currency.

Hard Manufacturing An asset used, usually in a factory or similar setting, to make products in large quantities. A hard manufacturing asset often may not be adapted easily and may only be able to make a defined set of products. A hard manufacturing asset is a major business expense but is necessary in some sectors to make what a company sells. It is one of the most important types of fixed assets.

Hard Money A currency backed by a tangible commodity such as gold, silver, or platinum. Hard money has an intrinsic value, but is more susceptible to deflation than fiat money. Many countries used hard money throughout most of their histories; indeed, in the United States there was a significant debate in the late 19th century about whether the dollar should be based on gold or silver. However, most countries today use fiat money and have since the United States left the Bretton Woods System in the 1970s.

Hard Offer In marketing, an offer to purchase a product with advance payment. For example, a hard offer may ask a potential customer to send $15 in exchange for a magazine subscription. A hard offer contrasts with a soft offer, in which the product is presented first. Companies making hard offers have lower response rates than those making soft offers, but they generally carry less bad debt.

Hard Proof Page In publishing, a hard copy of a proof. A proof is effectively a final draft of a publication before it goes to print; it is used to correct errors. A hard copy is a physical document, as opposed to something on a computer screen. Using a hard proof page to correct errors is the traditional way in which publishing has operated, but the advent of computers has slowly changed this.

Hard Red Winter Wheat A variety of wheat that is used in bread and some unbleached flour. It is traded as a commodity, primarily on the Kansas City Board of Trade.

Hard Sell An advertisement that aggressively commands attention and strongly encourages the target to purchase the product. For example, a hard sell commercial may simply state repeatedly, "Buy Smith's soap." A hard sell contrasts with a soft sell, which is less demanding.

Hard Side An informal term for the financial and operational issues a company faces in trying to remain in business. It contrasts with the soft side, which refers to customer care and relationship management.

Hard Stop A definite time at which a meeting must end. A hard stop is usually announced beforehand. For example, if the CEO has to catch a plane at 6 p.m., the board meeting may have a hard stop at 4 p.m.

Hard-Core Unemployed Persons without jobs for extended periods of time. Hard-core unemployed persons often lack necessary skills for employment, either from lack of education or because their skills have become obsolete. Hard-core unemployed may not be eligible for unemployment benefits. See also: U6.

Harden 1. To secure a computer system to make it more likely to withstand an attack from a hacker. **2.** See: Hard asset.

Hardening 1. The process by which a sudden change to the price of a commodity or futures contract slow and gradually corrects itself, bringing the price into alignment with fundamentals. See also: Reversion to the Mean. **2.** A slow but steady rise in price for a futures market or contract.

Hardship A financial or personal need that must be addressed. For example, one may make a hardship withdrawal from a retirement account in order to pay for unexpected medical bills one may not be able to afford otherwise. Likewise, one may be able to cancel an employment contract early if a spouse dies and one must take care of one's children.

Hardship Allowance Additional pay that an expatriate employee may receive for living and working in a potentially dangerous area. For example, if an oil company sends an employee to work a rig in a warzone, he/she likely will receive a hardship allowance in the form of a higher salary. In addition to the hardship allowance, the employee may receive additional vacation time and other benefits.

Hardship Withdrawal A withdrawal from a retirement account such as a 401(k) or an IRA made before the age of 59 1/2 because of financial need. In order to make a hardship withdrawal, one must demonstrate the financial need, such as the need to pay medical bills or tuition for college. Even so, a hardship withdrawal is usually subject to a penalty tax.

Hard-to-Borrow List A list of securities deemed to have an insufficient supply that therefore would be difficult to sell short. Brokerages use the list as part of their due diligence in determining which securities would be the most profitable to sell short. According the SEC, any security found on the hard-to-borrow list is considered in short supply and/or demand. Therefore, an investor may have a hard time finding buyers.

Harmless Warrant A provision in some bonds requiring a bondholder to surrender a bond if he/she buys another bond from the same company. Harmless warrants allow issuers to protect themselves from suddenly finding themselves with too much debt. Hypothetically, all bondholders could decide to buy more debt from an issuer, resulting in an excessive amount of debt. Requiring a bondholder to exchange one bond to buy another prevents this. Harmless warrants only apply if the bonds are similar in every way except maturity.

Harmonic Average In mathematics, an average used primarily for calculating an average rate, such as an average interest rate. It is calculated as the reciprocal of an arithmetic mean with inverse values. It is also known as the harmonic mean.

Harmonized Index of Consumer Prices A measure of inflation used by the European Central Bank that considers what people spend on important goods and services. It is calculated by taking the average of changes in price to a basket of goods and services compiled by EU member states. The goods and services in the basket are weighted according to their perceived importance. The HICP is considered a primary tool in determining how people are experiencing inflation. The European Central Bank attempts to keep inflation as measured by the HICP a little bit below 2% in the medium term.

Harmonized Sales Tax In Canada, the combination of the federal VAT and provincial sales taxes into a single tax collected by the Canada Revenue Agency. Each province sets sales taxes separate from the federal government to pay for provincial expenses. However, five provinces streamline the collection of their sales taxes by allowing the Canada Revenue Agency to collect them along with the VAT and to distribute proceeds to the provinces accordingly.

Harmonized System A nomenclature system for goods and services that countries import and export. The Harmonized System assigns numeric codes to goods and services. Participating countries are required to use this code when describing their tariff schedules. Nearly all international trade occurs under the Harmonized System. It was developed by the World Customs Organization.

Harmonized System Committee A committee of the World Customs Organization that periodically reviews and updates the Harmonized System, which is a global nomenclature system for goods and services that countries import and export.

Harmonized Tariff Schedule The classification of tariffs for goods and services imported by the United States. For example, in 2010, the schedule stated that live chickens weighing less than 186 grams were subject to a 0.9 cent duty upon entry. The numeric codes for goods and services upon which the Schedule is based come from the Harmonized Code, which is a global nomenclature system for goods and services that countries import and export. The Harmonized Tariff Schedule went into effect in 1989.

Harrod-Domar Growth Model A model for what creates economic growth. According to Harrod-Domar, growth equals a country's savings rate multiplied by the marginal product of capital less depreciation. Essentially, high savings generates growth because savings are eventually invested. The Harrod-Domar model has been used to explain lack of development in some parts of the world: because there is little capital to be saved, there is less capital to invest. Critics, however, contend that the model confuses growth and development (which are distinct) and that it can encourage reckless borrowing to spur development.

Harrod-Neutral Technical Progress Improvements in technology that increase the efficiency of labor. That is, harrod-neutral technical progress allows producers to make more with less. This generally results in lower expenses and, on a large scale, it can spur economic growth. However, it can also cause unemployment by making employees with certain skills unnecessary.

Harry Dexter White An American economist who served in a senior capacity at the Treasury Department. Following World War II, he was instrumental in the creation of the Bretton Woods System and the International Monetary Fund. He was a noted Keynesian who favored U.S. President Franklin Roosevelt's New Deal. He was later revealed to be a spy for the Soviet Union.

Harry Markowitz One of the first economists to apply mathematics to the operations of the stock market. A student of the Chicago School, he theorized that every rational investor, at a given level of risk, will accept only the largest expected return. This led him to develop Modern, or Markowitz, Portfolio Theory, which attempted to account for risk and expected return mathematically to help the investor find a portfolio with the maximum return for the minimum about of risk. A Markowitz efficient porfolio represented just that: the most expected return at a given amount of risk (excluding zero risk, though later economists explored zero-risk investments in the context of Markowitz's work). He first explored this theory in an article published in 1952 and received the Nobel prize for economics for his work in 1990. See also: Homogenous expectations assumption, Markowitz efficient set of portfolios.

Harter Act Legislation in the United States that removes the legal liability of the owner of a shipping vessel for losses resulting from errors in navigation if the owner has exercised due diligence. However, the Act specifically makes the owner liable for losses resulting from negligence in the loading, unloading or storage of goods being transported. The Harter Act has been replaced partially by the Carriage of Goods by Sea Act of 1936.

Hart-Scott-Rodino Act Legislation in the United States requiring any investor or company that buys 15% of equity or more than $15 million in stock in a publicly-

traded company to register with the Justice Department and the Federal Trade Commission. It requires the same registration from some mergers and acquisitions. Once this registration occurs, those organizations have 30 days to determine whether the transaction violates any antitrust laws or regulations. During this time, the transaction is not allowed to close.

Harvesting Strategy In marketing, the plan to discontinue a product after sales drop below a certain, defined point. Under a harvesting strategy, a company frontloads its marketing expenditures in order to maximize market share early. The company then gradually eliminates these expenditures. The product continues to be sold on the power of its market share and goodwill until sales decline to the stated point; it is then withdrawn. A harvesting strategy is intended to reduce costs while extracting as much revenue as possible from a product.

Hash Total The sum of unrelated numbers. The hash total does not provide useful data, but is used as a check to ensure inputs were entered correctly.

Hasit A Talmudic unit of length approximately equivalent to 15 or 20 centimeters.

Hat A Turkish measure of length approximately equivalent to 2.63 millimeters. It became obsolete when Turkey made the metric system mandatory in 1933.

Hatch A gateway or cover for a divide between decks of a ship. See also: International trade.

Hatchet Man A person who is charged with the task of destroying the reputation of an enemy. Hatchet men are most common in politics (the term was popularized due to the Watergate scandal), but they may be used in business as well.

Hat'h An obsolete unit of length once used in Bombay and some other parts of India approximately equivalent to 18 inches.

Hau A super-division of the Tongan pa'anga. One hau is equal in value to 100 pa'anga; hau are issued as commemorative coins and generally do not circulate.

Haul A slang term for a profit, especially the profit from a single project as opposed to that for the whole company.

Haulage 1. The sector of an economy that transports goods by land. For example, companies that carry goods by truck or train are said to be haulage companies. **2.** Goods being transported by land.

Haurlan Index In technical analysis, a measure of market breadth, which is an indicator of the number of advancing stocks relative to the number of declining stocks. The Haurlan Index consists of three parts: a three-day, 20-day and 200-day exponential moving averages of advancing stocks minus declining stocks on the New York Stock Exchange. Each of these is used to look at short-term, medium-term, and long-term trends in market breadth, respectively.

Have Hair Slang; in investing, to carry a great deal of risk. It may also mean to be more complicated than previously thought.

Havenstein Ruble A derogatory term for the German mark during the hyperinflation period in the early 1920s. The term derives from Rudolf Havenstein, who was in charge of the Reichsbank (the central bank of Germany) during this period.

Hawaiian Dollar The currency of Hawaii prior to its annexation by the United States in 1898. It was pegged to the U.S. dollar (which replaced it) at a one-to-one ratio.

Hawk An adviser or policymaker who is consistently concerned with inflation. That is, hawks favor maintaining low inflation over promoting high economic growth. As a result, hawks tend to prefer central banks to set relatively high interest rates. The term "hawk" may apply to persons who are concerned with another economic policy (e.g. deficit hawk), but the term, by itself, usually refers to an inflation hawk.

Hawkish Describing a statement from the Federal Reserve indicating that it may raise interest rates. The statement is called hawkish because it indicates that the Fed believes that the inflation rate is high enough to warrant concern. See also: Dovish.

Hawthorne Effect The phenomenon in which subjects of study alter their behavior simply because they are being studied. The Hawthorne effect is important in marketing. For example, test audience members may unintentionally skew their responses one way or another simply because they know they are part of a test audience. The concept originated in 1950 when analysis of a study from the 1920s and 1930s saw that productivity in a factory improved during a study of employees and declined after the study's conclusion.

Hazard 1. See: Physical hazard. **2.** See: Moral hazard.

Hazard Increase Resulting in Suspension or Exclusion of Coverage A clause in an insurance contract that gives the insurer the right to terminate a policy if the risk to a policyholder increases significantly. The clause is used especially in fire insurance.

Hazard Insurance A property insurance policy that provides coverage for catastrophic events named in the policy. For example, hazard may cover hurricanes and fires, but not tornadoes. Hazard insurance may not cover even the most common events, especially in high-risk areas. For this reason, some property owners buy named perils policies to supplement hazard insurance.

Hazardous Material Material that may cause damage because of its inherent nature. Examples include toxic or radioactive items. Most countries have regulations restricting the transportation of hazardous material. For example, the transporter may be required to take certain precautions or may not be permitted to transport in bulk.

Hazardous Waste Waste material that may cause damage because of its corrosiveness, toxicity, reactivity or flammability. Examples include byproducts from an oil refinery or used gauzes from a dental clinic. In the United States, one generally must dispose of hazardous waste according to EPA regulations.

H-Bond A former savings bond in the United States that paid interest on its principal semi-annually. Unlike Series E bonds, which paid interest only at redemption, H-bonds provided bondholders with current income on their investments. H-bonds were issued at face value, were exempt from state and local taxes, and had a fixed interest rate. They were issued between 1952 and 1979 and were replaced by the Series HH bond in 1980.

Head and Shoulders In technical analysis, an indicator in which the price of a security rises to a peak, falls, rises to a higher peak and then falls again, and, finally, rises to a third peak roughly equal to the first and falls again. While, in general, a head and shoulders pattern is considered a bearish indicator, it contains various bullish points, namely immediately before the price rises. These bullish points are called the neckline. When technical analysts see a security falling toward the neckline, they view this as a buy signal because historical patterns have shown that the security's price will rise soon thereafter. On the other hand, the third peak is considered a sell signal.

Head Count 1. The number of persons in a given group. **2.** The act of counting said persons.

Head Margin In publishing, the top of a page where nothing is printed. See also: Header.

Head of Household A taxpayer who pays more than half of the expenses of a household and is therefore taking care of a dependent. Heads of household are usually entitled to preferential tax treatment. A head of household must be unmarried unless his/her spouse files an individual tax return and has not lived with the head of household for more than six of the last 12 months.

Head Shunting The practice in which a manager encourages a headhunter to hire away an employee who is unproductive or simply difficult. Head shunting avoids embarrassment as the manager does not have to fire the employee.

Head Teller A bank teller who supervises other bank tellers. While specific duties vary, most of the time, a head teller assists other tellers if they cannot balance debits and credits at their drawers and prepares an end-of-the day report for the bank.

Head-and-Shoulder Bottom In a head-and-shoulders pattern, one of two price bottoms. A head-and-shoulders pattern is an indicator in which the price of a security rises to a peak, falls, rises to a higher peak and then falls again, and, finally, rises to a third peak roughly equal to the first and falls again. While, in general, a head and shoulders pattern is considered a bearish indicator, the bottoms are bullish points because they occur immediately before the price rises. These bullish points are sometimes called the neckline.

Header In publishing, an area toward the top of a page where one may print a headline, a date or other relevant information. Often, though not always, the text in a header is in larger print and may be repeated on each page of a document.

Headhunter A person or company that recruits potential employees for clients. The term is most often applied to recruiters who seek executives and other professionals such as doctors and lawyers.

Headline A brief statement at the beginning of an article, usually in larger type than the rest of the article, that describes what the article will state. Headlines are often abbreviated and may be deliberately sensational, especially in tabloids. A famous example of a headline occurred during the Great Crash in 1929, when Variety magazine reported, "WALL ST. LAYS AN EGG."

Headline Inflation The total inflation present in an economy. That is, headline inflation indicates the percentage by which prices rise over a period of time without making any major adjustments. While headline inflation is a good indicator of the inflation that consumers feel, it may not accurately show the amount by which the value of a currency is reduced. This is because headline inflation includes changes in prices to things like food and energy, which are quite volatile and may move up or down independently of underlying inflation. For this reason, some analysts prefer to use the core inflation metric (which excludes volatile commodities) when calculating inflation. See also: CPI.

Headline Risk The risk that a company may decline in share price because of negative news coverage. For example, rumors that a company's earnings are declining may cause shareholders to sell their stock. Even if the news itself is not true, headline risk can cause significant volatility for the stock in the short-term. For this reason, companies often price out the news by slowly leaking information before it is announced to minimize surprises and reduce the power of false rumors. See also: CNN effect.

Headquarters The administrative headquarters of an organization. The headquarters maintains all paperwork and other documents for the organization's operations. It is also where the organization conducts many of its major meetings.

Heads of Agreement An informal agreement between two parties seeking to form a partnership outlining the rights and responsibilities each would have in the partnership. Heads of agreement are intentionally vague and are usually the first step toward a full contract. Negotiations continue after the MOU is signed. Heads of agreement are similar to a memorandum of understanding for partnerships, but heads of agreement are not enforceable in a court of law, unlike an MOU. See also: Handshake Agreement.

Health and Beauty Aids Cosmetics and items used for personal grooming. Examples include make-up, toothpaste and deodorant. At the retail level, health and beauty aids are often placed in a separate section for easy access.

Health and Safety at Work Act Legislation in the United Kingdom, passed in 1974, that established duties for employers, employees and others to create a safe work environment. The Act contains a number of provisions and obligations. For example, employers are required to provide information and instruction to promote safety, and employees are required to cooperate with employers on these matters.

Health Care Marketing The process of advertising hospitals, medical offices, pharmaceuticals and so forth. Health care marketing has been controversial in the past (especially with regard to pharmaceuticals), but it can help the health care industry remain profitable. It uses many of the same strategies and tactics that other types of marketing use.

Health Care Power of Attorney The legal transfer of the authority to make medical decisions on behalf of another person. That is, health care power of attorney gives the designee (called an agent) the ability to determine what medical procedures may be done on the principal in the event of the principal's incapacitation. For example, one may designate health care power of attorney to a relative in case one develops Alzheimer's disease and is unable to make these decisions oneself. See also: Advanced directive.

Health Care Tax Credit A tax credit available to some small businesses that provide health insurance for their employees. The health care tax credit is a direct, dollar-for-dollar reduction in a business' tax liability up to a certain percentage of the premium it pays for employee health insurance. The credit phases out for average employee incomes between $25,000 and $50,000 and for business with between 10 and 25 full-time employees. This credit became available in 2010.

Health Certificate A form a physician fills out describing a person's medical condition. A health certificate contains information such as height, weight, blood pressure, communicable diseases and so forth. A health certificate may be required before a visa is issued. Alternatively, a health certificate may inform an insurer about a potential insured. It should be noted that, in some circumstances, animals must receive their own health certificates from a veterinarian before they may be transported.

Health Insurance An insurance policy that provides coverage when the policyholder (or his/her dependent) becomes ill. For example, a health insurance policy may pay for most or all of the costs of a surgery. Health insurance may cover doctor's visits, medical procedures, prescription drugs, and so forth. The policyholder pays a premium each month in exchange for the coverage; additionally, the policyholder often must pay coinsurance and/or a copay for certain procedures. In the United States, many people procure health insurance through their employers because it is often expensive to buy on one's own. Likewise, many people have group insurance to provide medical coverage. A significant amount of debate exists as to the appropriate role of the U.S. government in regulating health insurance providers and whether the government should assume this role directly.

Health Insurance Association of America Also called the HIAA. An organization for insurance companies that deal in health insurance. The plans offered by members of the HIAA provide coverage for about two-thirds of the American population. The HIAA hosts conferences, provides education and lobbies for favorable legislation. It is based in Washington, D.C.

Health Insurance Benefits The specific coverage offered by a health insurance policy. For example, health insurance benefits may pay for most or all of the costs of a surgery. They also may cover doctor's visits, medical procedures, prescription drugs, and so forth. How generous these benefits are depends largely on the premium the policyholder (and/or his employer) pays each month in exchange for the coverage. Additionally, the policyholder often must pay coinsurance and/or a copay for certain procedures.

Health Insurance Credit In the United States, a direct, dollar-for-dollar reduction in one's tax liability due to the health insurance premiums one pays for oneself or one's dependents. Health insurance credits are available to low-income persons as part of the earned income tax credit.

Health Insurance Futures A one-year futures contract structured to help insurance companies and other relevant parties to hedge losses on health insurance. Under a health insurance futures contract, if actual payments on health insurance claims exceed a certain level, the payoff of the contract increases by the amount of the excess. Health insurance futures are traded on the Chicago Board of Trade.

Health Insurance Renewability The ability of a policyholder to reactivate a health insurance policy after its term expires. Depending on the nature of the renewability, an insurer may be able to raise (or, less frequently, lower) premiums, provided all members of a risk class are treated in the same way.

Health Maintenance Organization Commonly called an HMO. A nonprofit organization that offers health insurance to a group of persons and charges members of the group the same monthly premium. Most HMOs require policyholders to have a primary physician who provides referrals for specialists and other medical services. Without these referrals, medical care generally will not be covered. This fact has made HMOs somewhat controversial. However, they generally operate at a lower out-of-pocket cost to consumers. They trace their origins to the early 20th century, but became more popular after the Health Maintenance Organization Act of 1973.

Health Maintenance Organization Act of 1973 Legislation in the United States that offered grants and other incentives to start or expand a health maintenance organization (HMO), which is a nonprofit organization offering health insurance to a group of people at the same monthly premium. It also required companies with more than 25 employees to offer employees the option to buy into an HMO if these companies also offered standard health insurance. (This latter provision expired in

1995.) The Act made HMOs a popular health insurance choice for many companies and individuals.

Health Plan Flexible Spending Account A structure in which an employee makes tax-free contributions to a special account that can be used for medical expenses not reimbursed by his/her ordinary health insurance. One may use funds in the account to make premium payments or to pay for unexpected expenses. A flexible spending account helps reduce one's risk of being underinsured. However, if one does not spend everything in the account by the end of a calendar or fiscal year, the remainder reverts to one's employer. See also: Health savings account.

Health Reimbursement Account A structure in which an employer makes contributions to a special account that can be used to pay for participating employees' medical expenses not reimbursed by his/her ordinary health insurance. The employee may use funds in the account to make premium payments or to pay for unexpected expenses. The employee does not pay taxes on these benefits. A health reimbursement account helps reduce one's risk of being underinsured. See also: Health savings account.

Health Savings Account A form of health insurance in which a policyholder makes tax-free contributions to a special account that can be used for present and future medical expenses. Health savings accounts may be purchased individually or through an employer, but, in order to qualify for one, a policyholder must have an insurance policy with a high deductible. A health savings account may be used in order to offset the high deductible on one's other insurance policy. One does not pay taxes on withdrawals from a health savings account, unless one withdraws funds for a non-medical reason, in which case there may also be a penalty, depending on the age of the policyholder.

Hearing A court proceeding that determines a stated issue. For example, a hearing may be held to determine whether or not certain evidence is admissible in a lawsuit.

Hearsay Evidence gathered from a second-hand or even further removed source. That is, the person giving hearsay evidence did not witness or experience the evidence himself/herself. In many jurisdictions, hearsay evidence is not admissible in court, especially in criminal proceedings. There are, however, a number of exceptions to this rule, notably if the original witness is unavailable or dead.

Heart Bond A bond where the issuer is a church, school, or other non-profit. The term may also refer to a bond that the underwriter attempts to sell by appealing to the investor's better angels, rather than his/her desire for profit.

Heat-Activated Label A label requiring the application of heat to become adhesive. That is, a head activated label will not stick to a surface unless one applies heat. These labels are generally no longer in use.

Heath-Jarrow-Morton Model A model that uses forward interest rates to determine prices for securities that are affected by changes in interest rates. The model is quite complex and used mainly by arbitrageurs. It may also be used in asset liability management.

Heating Degree Day A day on which the temperature in a certain area is below 65 degrees Fahrenheit, necessitating the use of heaters. Heating degree days are used in some weather futures, which are contracts in which the buyer is required to pay the seller some multiple of $20 for each heating degree day in a month, depending on how much cooler it is. Weather futures allow businesses to hedge against potential losses resulting from unexpected changes in weather. Energy companies are the most common sellers of weather futures; they have become relatively popular investments. See also: Cooling degree day.

Heating Oil A petroleum product used to heat private homes, offices and so forth. Approximately 25% of the world's crude oil is developed into heating oil. It is traded as a commodity on the Intercontinental Exchange and the New York Mercantile Exchange.

Heat-Transfer Label A label with an image on the back; the image can be transferred to another surface up to three times by applying heat to the label. Heat-transfer labels are generally no longer in use.

Heavily Indebted Poor Countries The 40 least developed countries with a large amount of foreign debt. The IMF and the World Bank help heavily indebted poor countries restructure their debt by offering low interest loans and some forms of debt relief. The two organizations have offered this service since 1996.

Heavy Adowlie An obsolete Indian unit of weight approximately equivalent to 2.031 kilograms.

Heavy Crude Unrefined oil that does not flow very well, as opposed to light crude, which does. Compared to light crude, heavy crude is expensive to refine. As a result, it is a lower-priced commodity.

Heavy Gold Electroplate A band of gold attached to the outside of a coin using an electric field. The term is most common in numismatics.

Heavy Industry A generic term for sectors producing or using heavy machinery or items. For example, heavy industry may refer to an automobile factory or the construction of a building. It may also be a designation in zoning law for places where such facilities may be built. See also: Light industry.

Heavy Lift The transportation of cargo or individual items that weigh more than one ton or that are larger than 100 meters. Heavy lifts often require heavy machinery such as cranes. Examples of equipment requiring heavy lifts include generators, turbines and oil rigs.

Heavy Lift Charge In maritime transport, a charge assessed to load or unload exceptionally heavy material. Heavy lifts are more difficult than loading or unloading lighter material and they often require specialized equipment such as cranes and may

require a particular type of ship (called a heavy lift vessel). The heavy lift charge helps compensate for this.

Heavy Lift Vessel A maritime vessel with specialized equipment such as cranes. A heavy lift vessel is equipped for a heavy lift, which is the transportation of cargo or individual items that weigh more than one ton or are larger than 100 meters. See also: Heavy lift charge.

Heavy Market A market for a security characterized by more sell orders than buy orders. Trading in such a market usually involves declining prices because of the downward pressure created by the glut of sell orders.

Heavy Share A stock on the London Stock Exchange with a share price over 10 pounds. Small investors are unlikely to buy heavy shares (especially in large quantities) because of the high price.

Heavy Share Price A share price on the London Stock Exchange over 10 pounds. Small investors are unlikely to buy heavy shares (especially in large quantities) because of the high price.

Heavy Users The segment of consumers that consumes the most. For example, if 10% of all widget users buy 90% of all widgets, these are considered the heavy users for widgets. In general, about one-third of consumers of a product are the heavy users. Marketers may target heavy users to maximize their use of the product.

Heavy-Up In marketing, the purchase of a great deal of advertising concentrated in a brief period of time. For example, a fireworks store in the United States may purchase radio and print advertising for the four weeks leading up to Independence Day, but not advertise at all the rest of the year.

Hectare A measure of area of land. A hectare is equal to 10,000 square meters. It traces its origins to the French revolutionary government. It is often used in real estate transactions. See also: Acre.

Hecteus An ancient Greek unit of dry volume approximately equivalent to 8.73 liters.

Hedge To reduce the risk of an investment by making an offsetting investment. There are a large number of hedging strategies that one can use. To give an example, one may take a long position on a security and then sell short the same or a similar security. This means that one will profit (or at least avoid a loss) no matter which direction the security's price takes. Hedging may reduce risk, but it is important to note that it also reduces profit potential.

Hedge Against Inflation To take steps to limit the reduction of the value of an investment due to inflation. Inflation decreases the value of money such that an investment's return is not worth as much as it might have been when the investment was made originally. Hedging against inflation helps reduce this pressure. Examples of hedging against inflation include buying commodities such as gold or purchasing an inflation-protected security, in which the return is linked to the inflation rate. See also: Real Rate of Return.

Hedge Clause A clause in a published document stating that the writer(s) believe the information contained therein to be accurate, but that accuracy is not guaranteed. For example, the author of an advisory newsletter may say that he/she retrieved all information in the newsletter from reliable sources and has taken reasonable measures to ensure accuracy, but that these measures do not guarantee that the information is correct. Hedge clauses exist to protect authors from legal liability in case the information they disseminate turns out to be wrong and investors make bad trades as a result.

Hedge Fund A pool of liquidity that is allowed to use aggressive techniques prohibited in mutual funds and other funds. That is, hedge funds often engage in short selling, arbitrage, and leverage trading, among others. Hedge funds are exempt from many regulatory requirements; for example, they are often exempt from registration with the SEC. Generally speaking, hedge funds are set up as partnerships into which an investor may buy for a minimum investment, usually anywhere from $250,000 to over $1,000,000. As a result, most hedge fund investors are institutional investors and high net-worth individuals. In order to avoid as many regulations as possible, most hedge funds are limited to 100 investors or less. Like mutual funds, they charge management fees, but, unlike other funds, they often take a percentage of the profits from investors. Hedge funds tend to be illiquid as they often require investors to maintain their investment for at least one year.

Hedge Fund Alert A weekly newsletter that publishes information on the hedge fund market. It disseminates news on relevant regulation and investment strategies. The publication is based in New Jersey.

Hedge Ratio 1. A ratio of the value of the proportion of a position that is hedged to the value of the entire position. A hedge ratio shows how exposed an investment is to risk. For example, if a hedge ratio is -.65, then 65% of the investment is protected from risk, while 35% remains exposed. **2.** A ratio of the value of a futures contract to the value of the underlying asset. This is used to identify and minimize risk in the contract.

Hedge Wrapper An option strategy in which an investor who owns the underlying asset buys an out of the money call and sells an out of the money put. The hedge wrapper sets a limit on the loss and gain one can realized from the price movements of the underlying asset; if it moves too far in one direction or the other one of the options will be exercised.

Hedged Position An investment in which risk is reduced by making an offsetting investment. There are a large number of hedging strategies that one can use. For example, one may take a long position on a security and then sell short the same security or a similar security. This means that one will profit (or at least avoid a loss) no matter which direction the security's price takes. A hedged position may reduce risk, but it is important to note that it also reduces profit potential.

Hedged Tender During a tender offer, the act of selling short shares one already owns. A tender offer is an offer by an outside party to buy some or all of a shareholder's shares in a company, usually for more than their market value. If a shareholder receives a tender offer, he/she may make a hedged tender in order to protect himself/herself from the risk that the tender offer will be canceled. The hedged tender is made at the same price as the tender offer, which locks in the shareholder's profit regardless of what happens to the tender offer.

Hedger An investor who takes steps to reduce the risk of an investment by making an offsetting investment. There are a large number of hedging strategies that a hedger can use. Hedgers may reduce risk, but in doing so they also reduce their profit potential.

Hedgie Informal for hedge fund.

Hedging Demand Demand or orders for securities that are used to diversify or otherwise reduce risk beyond normal mean-variance diversification. Hedging demands represent a desire for a risk-averse portfolio. See also: Risk analysis, Modern Portfolio Theory.

Hedging Effectiveness The extent to which hedging an investment actually reduces risk. There are a large number of hedging strategies one can use. For example, one may take a long position on a security and then sell short the same security. However, some strategies may be forms of naive diversification, which reduce hedging effectiveness. In an extreme example, if one buys a stock and then short sells a bond in a completely different industry, one is more likely to increase risk rather than decrease it.

Hedonic Damages Compensation for the loss of value of life in an injury case. For example, if Fred's negligence causes Bob to break his neck and become paralyzed, a jury in the resulting lawsuit may award Bob hedonic damages to repay him for the fact he can no longer enjoy his life in the same way as he once did. Hedonic damages are distinct from damages award for loss of income, earning potential and so forth. Most jurisdictions in the United States permit the award of hedonic damages.

Hehto A Finnish unit of volume approximately equivalent to 100 liters. It was used to measure the volume of potatoes and became obsolete when Finland adopted the metric system in 1880.

Heiermann A slang term for a five-deutschemark coin that circulated in Germany prior to the adoption of the euro.

Heir A person entitled to receive property (and, in some jurisdictions, title) from a deceased person. An heir may be designated by custom or statute, or may be selected in the decedent's will.

Heirloom An asset passed down within a family for several generations. Heirlooms refer to personal property, such jewelry or furniture, and not to major assets like real estate. Heirlooms often have intrinsic value, but because they may appeal to a limited demographic (family members and collectors), they may be illiquid.

Heirs and Assigns A term for the persons to whom property is bequeathed in a will (the heirs) and the persons to whom they may in turn give, sell or bequeath the same property (the assigns). The term may be used in a will to indicate that an heir is given unconditional ownership and is free to assign it as he/she wishes.

Hejaz Riyal The currency of the Hejaz from 1916 to 1925. It was introduced following the Hejaz' proclamation of independence from the Ottoman Empire. It was replaced at par by the Saudi riyal following Hussein bin Ali al-Hashemi's defeat by Ibn Saud.

Hektos An ancient Greek unit of area approximately equivalent to 158.3 square meters.

Held 1. Describing a situation in which a security is temporarily unavailable for trade. A security may be held for a variety of reasons, including an inability to give or receive a quote. See also: Suspend trading. **2.** Describing a security or other asset on which one has a long position. That is, one holds a security when one owns it.

Held at the Opening Describing a stock that is not allowed to trade when an exchange opens. A stock held at the opening is thought to be temporarily and excessively volatile because of news, or for some other reason that could cause unsustainable rises and falls in price. See also: Suspended trading.

Held-to-Maturity Securities Securities, especially debt securities, which an investor owns until they mature and therefore cease to exist. This entitles the holder to all coupon and other payments, as well as reimbursement for the principal amount. Because these securities are held until maturity, investors generally do not need to care about fluctuations in their prices that occur in the meantime.

Hell or High Water Contract A contract including a clause stating that payments must be made regardless of what happens. Specifically, a hell or high water contract requires one party to continue to receive payments even if an act of God prevents the contract from being completed. For example, suppose two parties sign a contract renting an apartment. The contract may contain a hell or high water clause saying that the renter must pay rent every month even if the apartment floods or burns down. It is also called a promise to pay contract.

Hellenic Export Promotion Organization Also called HEPO. An organization that works with Greek companies seeking to expand into foreign markets. HEPO helps companies abide by Greek export policies and with foreign governments to promote Greek products. It especially works in the agricultural, industrial, service-oriented and technological sectors. It is based in Athens with offices in Thessaloniki and Ioannina.

Heller 1. A subdivision of various German and Austrian currencies in use at different times throughout history. **2.** See: Czech heller. **3.** See: Slovakian heller.

Helms-Burton Act Legislation in the United States, passed in 1996, that strengthened the existing trade embargo on Cuba. The U.S. had prohibited most trade with Cuba since 1960. The Act extended this prohibition to companies doing business with Cuba and to companies that use property Cuba had nationalized from American companies. The Act was quite controversial internationally.

Help Wanted Advertising An advertisement in a newspaper for a job. The help wanted section of a newspaper is divided according to type of job. For example, an ad for receptionist at a dental practice may be placed in administrative jobs, while an ad for a dental assistant may be in health care. The amount of help wanted advertising is a leading indicator of the future job market. A large number of ads in the help wanted section indicates that jobs are being created, while a small number indicates the opposite.

Help-Wanted Index An index of the number of job advertisements in major American newspapers. This is used as an indicator of job openings and the general strength of the labor market. When the HWI is low, this means that few firms are hiring, which may result in increased unemployment. On the other hand, when the HWI is high, this means that many firms are hiring and potential employees have a great deal of choice regarding for whom they work. This may cause the firms to raise wages and salaries, which can (but does not always) have a negative impact on equities and bonds.

Helsinki Accords A 1975 international agreement that dramatically reduced tensions between the United States and allies and Soviet bloc nations. The Accords effectively recognized Soviet hegemony in Eastern Europe in exchange for assurances that the Soviet Union would improve its human rights record. Canada, the United States and all European countries except Andorra and Albania signed the Helsinki Accords. It was seen as a first step toward improved Soviet-Western relations.

Helsinki Stock Exchange The primary exchange in Finland. It trades in both equities and derivatives. It was established in 1912. In 1990, it adopted an electronic system that allowed trades to occur both on and off the floor.

Hemiekton An ancient Greek unit of dry volume approximately equivalent to 4.36 liters.

Hemiektos An ancient Greek unit of area approximately equivalent to 79.2 square meters.

Hemina 1. An ancient Roman unit of volume approximately equivalent to 273 milliliters. It was also called a cotyla. **2.** See: Kotyle.

Hemipodion An ancient Greek unit of length approximately equivalent to 154.1 millimeters. It was also called a dichas.

Hemline Theory A theory of investing stating that market trends follow the length of women's skirts. That is, when women wear short skirts, there is or will be a bull market; when they wear long skirts, there is or will be a bear market.

Hemorrhagic Fever Any virus that causes both fever and excessive bleeding due to the reduced ability of blood to coagulate. Hemorrhagic fevers are spread from person to person through respiration. As such, there is concern that hemorrhagic fevers have potential in bioweapons.

Henri Fayol A French mining company manager who devised one of the first systematic management systems. Fayol asserted that management had six goals: forecasting, planning, organizing, commanding, coordinating and controlling. He argued that employees must be expected to follow rules, but managers must compensate them appropriately and treat them fairly. According to Fayol, both employees and employers must subordinate their individual goals to those of the whole company. He lived from 1841 to 1925.

Henry George A 19th-century American politician and economist. He believed that individuals should own what they create, but he promoted common ownership of nature and especially land. He was a proponent of property taxes as a way to promote equality. George lived from 1839 to 1897. See also: Henry George theorem.

Henry George Theorem The idea that, under ideal conditions, government spending equals aggregate rent on land in a country. While this does not happen in real life, spending and aggregate rent do in many cases approximate each other. It has been discussed as a guide for the ideal population for a country or country subdivision. The theorem derives its name from Henry George, the 19th-century economist who first articulated it.

Henry Kravis An American private equity investor. He began his career at Bear Stearns, where he engineered a number of leveraged buyouts. In the 1970s, started his own firm. He was born in 1944 in Tulsa, Oklahoma.

Henry Luce An American publisher and businessman (1898-1967). Among other things, he founded TIME and Fortune magazines. He was also active in the anti-communist movement in the mid-20th century.

Hepburn v. Griswold A U.S. Supreme Court case holding that fiat currency issued during the U.S. Civil war was not legal tender and violated the Constitution of the United States. Specifically, the court held that the power Congress has to coin money requires that currency be backed by gold, silver or something similar. For that reason, one may refuse payment made in a currency not so backed. The case was decided in 1870 but was overturned the following year in Knox v. Lee and Parker v. Davis.

Heqat An ancient Egyptian unit of volume approximately equivalent to 4.8 liters.

Herd Instinct A sociological phenomenon in which everyone does what everyone else seems to be doing. In investing, the herd instinct is seen most commonly in panic sells and rallies that occur without regard for broader indicators. That is, regardless of the sustainability of a rally or the overreaction of the sell-off, the concept of a herd instinct suggests that traders will continue to follow the trend until contrary evidence becomes overwhelming (or simply until they calm down). See also: Behavioral economics, Crowd.

Heredium An ancient Roman unit of area approximately equivalent to 5,047 square meters.

Herfindahl-Hirschman Index An index of market concentration the U.S. Department of Justice uses to determine whether a monopoly is forming. The scale goes from zero to 10,000, with 10,000 indicating that a single company controls 100% of the market share in a given industry. An HHI of less than 1000 indicates a market with little concentration, which the Justice Department prefers. Any merger or acquisition leading to an increase of more than 100 when the HHI was previously greater than 1,800 may lead to antitrust action against the company involved.

Hermes An export credit guarantee issued by the German state. Hermes covers guarantee payment on certain exports in case the importer defaults. They are used to cover between 2% and 3% of German exports. This allows the exporters to charge lower prices for their products because of the reduced risk. As with all export credit, Hermes is controversial; critics allege that it negatively impacts international development, as developing countries cannot compete with such insured exports. Proponents argue that they enable developing countries to import products they otherwise would not be able to afford.

Herstatt Risk The risk that a foreign exchange trade will not settle. For example, a buyer may not receive delivery of the currency he/she bought by the settlement date, or the seller may not receive payment. This may occur because of the negligence or deliberate withholding by one party or the other. If a party does not receive the securities or payment, he/she is not obligated fulfill his/her end of the bargain until delivery or payment is made, but this can render him/her unable to conduct other activities that would advance his/her investment goals. Herstatt risk takes its name from the Herstatt bank, which notoriously failed to settle currency transactions and went into bankruptcy in 1974.

Hertogenbossche voet An obsolete Dutch unit of area roughly equivalent to eight square centimeters, with slight regional variations.

Herud In Iceland, a political subdivision approximately equivalent to a region. It is used for statistics and for district courts.

Heseb An ancient Egyptian unit of area approximately equivalent to 6.8 square meters.

Heterarchy 1. In politics, rule by a foreign power, even if masked by a puppet government. For example, Nazi Germany imposed heterarchy on France during World War II despite the presence of the Vichy government. **2.** In human relations, governance in which no single participant has direct power over others, but in which any participant may come to possess such power. Heterarchy is very complicated and is marked by multiple, overlapping or even contradictory power structures. It may be contrasted with a hierarchy, but one may exist within the other.

Heteroskedastic A sequence of variables in which each variable has a different variance. Heteroskedastics may be used to measure the margin of the error between predicted and actual data. See also: ARCH.

Heuristic A device one uses to learn or find. Heuristics are easy to remember, but are understood to not apply exactly to every situation. They are useful in all types of problem solving, including in business. Examples of heuristics include educated guesses, past experience and common sense.

Hexapodes An ancient Greek unit of area approximately equivalent to 3.42 square meters.

Hezbollah A Shi'a Muslim political party and paramilitary organization in Lebanon. Hezbollah was established in the 1980s in response to the Israeli invasion of Lebanon in 1982. It operates a number of social services, though some countries regard it as a terrorist organization. It was responsible for the capture and killing of two Israeli soldiers in a cross-border raid, an incident that led to the 2006 Israel-Lebanon War. This war, and Hezbollah's response to it, increased the organization's popularity in Lebanon among Sunni Muslims, Christians and others.

Hiccup 1. A brief decline in a price during a general uptrend. **2.** A brief rise in a price during a general downtrend. In both cases, any number of factors may cause a hiccup, but the trend soon resumes.

Hickenlooper Amendment Legislation in the United States, passed in 1962, that cut off foreign aid to countries inimical to American business interests. Specifically, it prohibited recipients of foreign aid from passing discriminatory taxes, seizing assets or doing anything else that targeted American operations in their territories. The Amendment was passed in response to Cuban seizure of U.S.-owned sugar farms.

Hickey An imperfection in printing, usually resulting from dirt or dust on the printer.

Hidden Agenda An ulterior motive for accomplishing a task. For example, a politician may appear to favor a piece of legislation because of the public good, but actually does so because it will benefit a company he owns. A hidden agenda does not have to be illegal or even unethical, but generally it does advance the interests of the person or persons pursuing it.

Hidden Asset Value that a person or company possesses that does not appear on its balance sheet. One may have a hidden asset due to an accounting convention. For example, a company may be required to depreciate an asset faster than its actual value declines. This results in a higher net worth for the company than would be reflected in its books. A hidden asset is also called a hidden reserve or a hidden value.

Hidden Camera Commercial A television commercial that shows (possibly edited and cherry-picked) examples of real users of a product describing their feelings. These feelings are unrehearsed and usually describe what the person actually believes about the product. Hidden camera commercials are produced to portray public support for a product.

Hidden Camera Technique The practice of filming real users of a product describing their feelings. These feelings are unrehearsed and usually describe what the person actually believes about the product. This footage may be edited together to form a hidden camera commercial, which attempts to portray public support for a product.

Hidden Damage Damage to an asset that is not immediately apparent. For example, a roof with hidden damage may appear unharmed until it leaks during a rain storm. Insurance policies provide coverage for both hidden and obvious damage.

Hidden Inflation A reduction in the purchasing power of money that one does not immediately notice because a company maintains the same prices for retail products, but begins to make those products with lower quality materials.

Hidden Load A loan or sales charge for purchasing shares in a mutual fund that is not obviously stated in the fund's prospectus. Colloquially, it may also refer to a 12b-1 fee.

Hidden Tax A tax that is built in to the price of a good or service that the buyer does not see. That is, rather than being added at the end of a transaction, like a sales tax, hidden taxes are included in the price. Examples of hidden taxes include corporate taxes, which can cause companies to raise their prices so as not to reduce profit, and VAT, in which taxes are added at every stage of production. See also: Inflation tax.

Hidden Unemployment A term used to describe persons who are unemployed or underemployed but who are not counted in official unemployment statistics. For example, the hidden unemployed include persons who no longer actively look for work because they have returned to school for retraining, or persons who have decided to stay at home with their children but would in theory be open to go back to work. These persons are not considered part of the labor force and thus are not included in statistics. Some analysts believe that the existence of hidden unemployment means that unemployment statistics are inherently skewed, but this is not a universal opinion.

Hide An obsolete unit of land area equivalent to 120 acres.

Hierarchy In human relations, governance in which who is in power over whom is clearly defined. For example, a hierarchy may exist with a company owner and three employees in that the owner is in charge of the employees. Hierarchy is easy to understand; power structures are marked and followed. It may be contrasted with a heterarchy, but one may exist within the other.

Hi-Fi A reproduction of a sound or image of such high quality that it imitates the real thing. The term is short for "high fidelity."

Hi-Fi Insert In print advertising, a high quality reproduction of an image of wallpaper that resembles real wallpaper. A hi-fi insert is pre-printed but can be given to a publication so it can print its own material on the other side of the sheet.

High Ball In auto sales, to give a potential customer an artificially large trade-in value for his/her vehicle in order to encourage him/her to purchase another automobile.

High Beta Index An index of highly volatile stocks. A stock's beta is a measure of its volatility compared to the wider market; as a result, a high beta index consists only of volatile stocks. An investment that tracks a high beta index is considered risky.

High Close A tactic in which traders buy a stock in relatively small amounts the final minutes of a trading day so that its closing price is higher than it otherwise would be. A high close exists because closing prices are widely quoted in the media and in other reports; this practice makes the stock appear robust.

High Credit The total amount in loans and other debt that a person or company owes to a bank. This may affect the person or company's ability to borrow any more money.

High Deductible Health Plan A form of health insurance in which the policyholder is responsible for all medical expenses up to a relatively high point. For example, a high deductible health plan may require the insured to pay all bills up to $5,000. The trade-off for these plans is a lower premium. High deductible health plans are popular among young people, healthy people and those who only want to have health insurance for emergencies.

High Finance The universe of extremely large, expensive and/or complex financial instruments. Most of the time, only institutional investors are interested in high finance; the barriers to entry are very high for other investors.

High Flyer A highly volatile, highly priced stock. Generally speaking, a high flyer has a high price-earnings ratio and moves significantly up and down in price in a short period of time. High flyers are attractive to high-risk investors because of the possibility for high capital gains in a very short period of time. The increases in price come about as investors expect a positive announcement, such as high earnings. If this announcement does not occur, or is not as optimistic as expected, the price collapses.

High Growth Company A company performing better, or expected to perform better, than its industry or the market as a whole. Companies generating a return on equity of greater than 15% are generally classified as high growth companies. Stocks in these companies usually pay little to nothing in dividends as they reinvest most of their earnings. Some believe that many or most growth companies are overvalued, citing for example the large number of growth companies during the dotcom bubble.

High Loan-to-Value Mortgage A mortgage in which the ratio of the amount of the loan is relatively high compared to the value of the property securing it. For example, if the value of a house is $100,000 and the value of the mortgage is $98,000, the loan-to-value ratio is 98%, which is considered high. A high loan-to-value mortgage indicates high risk to the lender because, if it forecloses, it may not be able to sell the house for enough money to compensate itself for the principal plus interest of the original mortgage.

High LTV Equity Loan A home equity loan in which the amount of the loan approaches (or possibly exceeds) the owner equity in the home that acts as collateral. Like other home equity loans, a high LTV equity loan is borrowed against the value of one's home. Because a high LTV equity loan represents a comparatively high risk for the lender, it may come with a high interest rate compared to other home equity loans. See also: Loan-to-value.

High Net Worth Individual An individual whose assets exceed his/her liabilities in value by a large figure. There is no hard-and-fast definition of a high net worth individual, though a net worth in excess of $1 million usually qualifies. The SEC, however, defines a high net worth individual as someone who has at least $750,000 under management or whom an investment adviser believes to have a net worth of $1.5 million or more. Many investment vehicles target high net worth individuals because they have more money to invest. Likewise, high net worth individuals are sometimes the only individuals (as opposed to organizations) who are permitted to invest in some vehicles.

High Penny In auto sales, to increase a customer's monthly payment by less than one dollar (or the equivalent). For example, to raise the payment from $237.45 to $237.95 is to high penny a customer. High pennying may increase revenue significantly if done at high volume.

High Price The highest price of a security over the past 52 weeks. The high price includes intraday price, not merely opening and closing prices.

High Ratio Loan A loan in which the ratio of the amount of the loan is relatively high compared to the value of the asset securing it. For example, if the value of a bulldozer is $100,000 and the value of the loan a company uses to buy it is $98,000, the loan-to-value ratio is 98%, which is considered high. A high ratio loan indicates high risk to the lender because, if it forecloses or repossesses, it may not be able to sell the asset for enough money to compensate itself for the principal plus interest of the original loan.

High Return A higher-than-normal amount of revenue an investment generates over a given period of time as a percentage of the amount of capital invested. There is no hard-and-fast definition of high return; it is compared to other return rates. In general, an investment that generates a high return usually has a high level of risk.

High Rise A tall building for residential and/or office space. High rises are most common in urban and densely populated areas. Buying or renting space in a high rise may be more expensive than buying or renting space in an outlying area.

High Risk Pools for the Medically Uninsurable A government-sponsored pool of liquidity for persons who, because of a severe illness or a pre-existing condition, cannot purchase health insurance. In the pool, one pays a premium (which is comparatively high due to the level of risk); the pool pays for medical expenses for policyholders up to a certain point and in most respects operates as a regular insurer. The main difference is the lack of need for profit, which enables the government to provide the insurance in the first place.

High Street Bank A large bank in the United Kingdom with branches spread out in many towns all over the country. It takes its name from "high street," which is a term for a main thoroughfare.

High Watermark The highest value of a benchmark over a certain period of time. High watermarks are mainly used to calculate bonuses for fund managers. That is, a manager may receive a bonus only if his investment decisions earn more than a certain percentage over the high watermark for a previous period.

High Wire Act A slang term for a highly risky venture, project, or investment. See also: Risk lover.

High Yielder A security with a high return. For example, a bond paying 15% per annum and a preferred stock paying 12.5% per quarter are both considered high yielders. High yielders usually carry higher than average risk, which is why they attempt to entice investors with the promise of a large yield.

High-Context Culture A culture in which a great deal of emphasis is placed upon the context, tone or circumstance of words used in addition to the meaning of the words themselves. For example, suppose one says, "I am fine," in response to the question, "How are you?" In a high-context culture, it should not necessarily be assumed that one is doing fine and that no further query needs to be made. Confusing cultural signals between a high-context and a low-context culture can create significant misunderstandings in both business and politics.

High-Coupon Bond Refunding A bond that retires another bond before the earlier bond matures in order to take advantage of a lower coupon rate. A company issues a high-coupon refunding bond after a decline in interest rates, which reduces the cost of funding. Refunding the bond deprives bondholders of the first bond from future coupon payments to which they would otherwise of have been entitled. See also: Interest Rate Risk.

High-End 1. Describing a luxury item. **2.** More generally, describing anything expensive.

Higher Education Act of 1965 Legislation in the United States that increased federal funding for colleges and universities. It also created the Pell grant, Stafford loan, PLUS loan, and similar programs to make post-secondary education more affordable for students. It has been reauthorized and amended several times since its original passage. It was part of the larger Great Society movement in the United States.

Higher Rate of Income Tax In progressive taxation, a tax rate above another rate. In most cases, the higher rate of income tax only applies to income over a defined level. For example, if one is taxed 10% on all income under $15,000 and 20% on all income over $15,000, 20% is the higher rate of income tax.

Highest and Best Use In real estate appraisals, the use of a property that leads to its highest possible value. The highest and best use may not be the current use of a property; in such cases, one may be able to buy the property for less than its ideal value. The highest and best use must be legal, physically possible, financially feasible and maximally productive.

High-Growth Describing a company, stock, economy or anything else performing better, or expected to perform better, than its industry, the wider market, or other economies. High-growth stocks may generate significant wealth in a short period of time, but are at risk of over-heating and undergoing a price correction. See also: Growth stock, Growth fund.

Highjacking Informal for a takeover. The term is most common in Japan.

Highlight Halftone In printing, a halftone negative in which all dots have been etched out or otherwise removed.

High-Low Index In technical analysis, an index of the number of stocks reaching a new high minus the number of stocks reaching a new low. This is used to determine whether a market movement is sustainable. A positive high-low index when the market has gone up means that that market is likely to continue to rise. However, mixed signals (i.e. a negative high-low index when the market has risen or vice versa) indicates that the current market movement is unlikely to continue.

Highly Compensated Employee An employee who owns 5% or more of the company for which he/she works or who makes more income than a certain amount set by the IRS. For tax purposes, highly compensated employees contribute less in tax deductible earnings to a qualifying retirement plan. This is because IRAs and other retirement plans do not qualify for tax advantages if their structures seem to favor highly compensated employees more than other employees.

Highly Confident Letter A letter issued by an investment bank stating that is believed it can arrange the necessary financing for an acquisition. A highly confident letter is made at the behest of the potential acquirer. While they have no legal status, highly confident letters can assuage nervous investors and persuade them that a deal can be completed, even though not all financing mechanisms have been arranged. Highly confident letters originated in the 1980s and were primarily used by corporate raiders.

Highly Leveraged Company A company or other institution with a high level of debt. A highly leveraged company carries a great deal of risk and may increase the likelihood of default or bankruptcy. A highly leveraged company may have to pay high interest rates on its debt.

Highly Leveraged Transaction A loan to a company or other institution that already has a high amount of debt. A highly leveraged transaction carries a great deal of risk and may increase the likelihood of bankruptcy. A highly leveraged transaction tends to command a large interest rate from the borrower.

Highly Protected Risk A risk that is highly unlikely to happen and, if it does, is unlikely to cause a great deal of damage. Insurance policies covering highly protected risks carry low premiums

High-Premium Convertible Debenture A convertible bond with a market price that exceeds par by a high percentage. Additionally, high-premium convertible debentures pay a relatively high coupon, and are long-term bonds. They are marketed to investors who generally invest in bonds, but wish to protect against inflation risk.

Highs Stocks, especially on a single index, that arrive at their new highest prices for the trailing 52-week period. They are also called new highs.

High-Technology Stock A stock in a company that sells products involving sophisticated technology. Commonly, high-technology companies deal in electronics, computers, and scientific research. Investing in high-technology stocks is high risk because the market is stiffly competitive, but it may yield a high return, particularly if a technology becomes very popular. This was the case in the 1990s when the Internet became a part of daily life. Many high-technology stocks trade on NASDAQ. See also: Dot-com bubble.

High-Valuation Stock An expensive stock compared to others, especially others in the same sector. Generally, a high-valuation stock has a comparatively high price-earnings ratio. Analysts may recommend a high-valuation stock if the price is expected to continue to rise.

Highway Contract Route A service in which a private, independent contractor carries mail on behalf of the U.S. Postal Service from one location to another along a highway. The USPS offers highway contract routes occasionally when it is deemed more efficient to do so.

High-Yield Bond A bond with a low rating. Bonds rated less than Baa3 by Moody's or BBB- by S&P or Fitch are considered high-yield bonds. They have higher yields because they have a higher risk of default on the part of the issuer. High-yield bonds are considered sufficiently high-risk that the law does not allow banks to invest in them. They are also called low-grade bonds, and, informally, junk bonds.

High-Yield Bond Fund A mutual fund that invests predominantly or exclusively in junk bonds. Because junk bonds have low credit ratings, they offer a comparatively high return. High-yield bond funds generally have portfolios containing at least two-thirds junk bonds. They provide a way for investors to take advantage of the return offered by a junk bond while also avoiding the risk of investing in a single bond at a high risk of default. See also: Investment grade.

High-Yield Financing The act of financing an activity or broader operation through the issue of junk bonds. These bonds have low credit ratings and have comparatively high risk. As a result, the issuer must pay higher interest rates. High-yield financing is used in some takeover situations where the acquiring company is cash poor.

Hijrah Calendar The Islamic religious calendar. It starts from the date in 622 when Mohammad fled from Mecca to Yathrib, which became Medina. It is not used commonly in Islamic finance, but appears sometimes in marketing literature.

Hinu An ancient Egyptian unit of volume approximately equivalent to 480 milliliters.

HIPC Initiative A joint program of the World Bank and the International Monetary Fund providing debt forgiveness and low-interest loans to the least developed countries with the greatest levels of debt. The HIPC Initiative began in 1996 in order to assist in international development. See also: Heavily Indebted Poor Countries.

Hippikon An ancient Greek unit of length approximately equivalent to 739.7 meters.

Hippo A slang term for the deciding opinion in a meeting, when it is delivered by the senior-most person. The term is an acronym for highest paid person's opinion.

Hire To initiate employment for a person. That is, one hires an employee when one asks him/her to accept a job and he/she agrees. The employer agrees to pay wages and/or salary to the employee, who agrees to perform certain services for the employer. See also: Fire.

Hire Purchase A British and Commonwealth term for closed-end leasing. See also: Rent-to-own.

Hiring Contract A contract giving a person employment at a company. A hiring contract generally gives a job description, the compensation, and the terms under which employment may end. A hiring contract may last for a certain number of years or it may state that it may end at any time with an agreed-upon notice.

Historic Rehabilitation Tax Credit A direct, dollar-for-dollar reduction in one's tax liability by a portion of the amount one spends renovating, restoring or rebuilding a historic building. The credit is intended to incentivize historic preservation and therefore does not apply to expansions or new constructions on historic buildings. The tax credit is equal to 20% of expenditures on certified historic buildings and 10% of expenditures on any structure built before 1936.

Historical Cost In the Generally Accepted Accounting Principles, the original cost of an asset on a balance sheet. Many assets, particularly illiquid assets, are recorded on a balance sheet according to their historical cost. A notable exception to this rule is the recording of marketable securities, which are recorded according to their market value. The historical cost usually bears little or no relationship to the market value after an asset has been held for several years.

Historical Cost Accounting Convention In accounting, the practice of recording the historical cost of an asset as its cost on a balance sheet. Under the Generally Accepted Accounting Principles, the historical cost is the original cost of an asset that the buyer paid. Many assets, particularly illiquid assets, are recorded on a balance sheet according to the historical cost accounting convention. A notable exception to this rule is the recording of marketable securities, which are recorded according to their market value. It is important to note that the historical cost usually bears little or no relationship to the market value after an asset has been held for several years.

Historical Trading Range The range of prices between the highest and lowest prices at which a security has traded since its IPO.

Historical Volatility A measure of a security's stability over a given period of time. While there are various ways to calculate it, the most common way is to compute the average deviation from the average price over the period of time one wishes to measure. The historical volatility is often compared to the implied volatility to determine if a security is overvalued or undervalued. Generally, securities with a higher historical volatility carry more risk. It is also called realized volatility or the standard deviation. See also: Volatility.

Historical Yield A mutual fund's yield over a given period of time. The historical yield may be measured over one, two or even five years. It provides a reference for the mutual fund's current performance. For example, if the yield in year five is 4%, one might compare it to the historical yield in years one through four to see whether or not 4% is a good return on that particular mutual fund.

Hit A unit measuring a person or IP address visiting a website. In general, the more hits a website generates, the higher revenue it earns from advertising and other sources.

Hit List In banking, a group of persons convinced or required to attend a presentation or listen to a request for money.

Hit the Bid To agree to sell a security at a previously quoted bid. This term is often used when one dealer sells to another. It is the opposite of the term, "take the offer."

Hit the Bricks Informal; to go on strike.

Hit the Ribbon Informal; to execute a trade such that it appears on a ticker. The term comes from the days when ticker tape was used; the tape was colloquially called "ribbon." It is also called to print.

Hitchhike To rely upon a foreign company or industry for one's own development. For example, a company may hitchhike if it does not produce any of its own products but instead sells those made in other countries. Hitchhiking is a model used in the context of international development.

Hitchment On a sea-going vessel, the combination of two or more shipments under a single bill of lading.

HK 1. ISO 3166-1 alpha-2 code for Hong Kong. This is the code used in international transactions to and from bank accounts in Hong Kong. **2.** ISO 3166-2 geocode for Hong Kong. This is used as an international standard for shipping to Hong Kong.

HKD ISO 4217 code for the Hong Kong dollar. It was first issued in the 1860s and for a number of years circulated in Hong Kong along with several other currencies. From 1963 to 1935, it was pegged to silver. It then adopted a crawling peg to the British pound, which continued until the yen was introduced during Japanese occupation in World War II. The dollar and the peg to the pound were reintroduced after the war, though the peg was eventually changed to the U.S. dollar. It floated in 1974, but readopted the U.S. dollar peg in 1983. It is an important currency because of Hong Kong's position as an international trade center.

HKG GOST 7.67 Latin three-letter geocode for Afghanistan. The code is used for transactions to and from Afghan bank accounts and for international shipping to Afghanistan. As with all GOST 7.67 codes, it is used primarily in Cyrillic alphabets.

Hkwe A Burmese unit of volume approximately equivalent to 2.04 liters.

Hkwet A Burmese unit of volume approximately equivalent to 127.86 milliliters.

HM Department for Education A department of the British government responsible for schools and other services for children up to the age of 19. It also advises the government on education policy. It was created in 2010, but traces its origins to the 19th century.

HM Department of Health A department of the British government responsible for advising on and managing government health policy. Most importantly, it administrates the National Health Service, the comprehensive, government medical program, in England (though not elsewhere in the United Kingdom). The Department of Health was created in 1988, but traces its origins to the 19th century.

HM Ministry of Justice A department of the British government responsible for administering the British (and in some cases only the English and Welsh) justice system. It prosecutes criminal cases, hears appeals of immigration decisions, handles civil liberty issues, advises the government on sentencing and penalty laws, and has other similar responsibilities. It also advises the government on matters relating to the British constitution. The Ministry of Justice was created in 2007.

HM Revenue and Customs The office of the British government responsible for tax collection. It also pays certain state benefits, notably refundable tax credits and other payments related to taxation. It is governed by a board of directors and is responsible to the chancellor of the exchequer. It was created in 2005 by the merger of Inland Revenue and HM Customs.

HM Treasury The department of the British government responsible for advising on and executing economic and fiscal policy in the United Kingdom. Through Inland Revenue and Customs, it has oversight of tax collection. The Treasury traces its origins to the 12th century.

HMD GOST 7.67 Latin three-letter geocode for Heard Island and McDonald Islands. The code is used for international shipping to HIMI. As with all GOST 7.67 codes, it is used primarily in Cyrillic alphabets.

HN 1. ISO 3166-1 alpha-2 code for the Republic of Honduras. This is the code used in international transactions to and from Honduran bank accounts. **2.** ISO 3166-2 geocode for Honduras. This is used as an international standard for shipping to Honduras. Each Honduran department has its own code with the prefix "HN." For example, the code for the Department of Colon is ISO 3166-2:HN-CL.

Hnan A Burmese unit of length equivalent to 0.79375 millimeters.

HND GOST 7.67 Latin three-letter geocode for Honduras. The code is used for transactions to and from Honduran bank accounts and for international shipping to Honduras. As with all GOST 7.67 codes, it is used primarily in Cyrillic alphabets.

HNL ISO 4217 code for the Honduran lempira. It is named after Lempira, a 16th century chieftain who led a resistance against the Spanish. It was introduced in 1931, replacing the Honduran peso. In the 1990s and early 2000s, the lempira underwent a great deal of inflation, but it has since stabilized. However, tourist centers and some other areas of the Honduras accept the U.S. dollar in addition to the lempira.

Hoarding A British term for a billboard.

Hobbet A unit of dry volume equivalent to two and a half bushels.

Hobby Loss A loss a taxpayer may not deduct from his/her taxable income because it occurred in the pursuit of personal pleasure. Suppose one sells lemonade for fun on Saturdays and takes a loss in doing so. This will likely be considered a hobby loss because one is not likely to be actively pursuing profit. The IRS applies what is called the "hobby loss rule" to determine whether it considers a loss to be hobby or business related; this rule states that an activity profitable three years out of every five can be considered a business. So the lemonade stand, which may never be profitable, will probably be considered a hobby loss.

Hobby Loss Rule A rule that the IRS applies to determine whether it considers a loss to be hobby or business related. This rule states that an activity profitable three years out of every five can be considered a business. If a loss is considered hobby related, it is not tax deductible. The hobby loss rule is also called the loss denial rule.

Hockey Stick A period of rapid growth followed by little or no growth. A hockey stick may represent a start up that is enormously successful at first and remains stable afterward, but does not continue to grow. It derives its name from the fact that, when plotted on a chart, it looks slightly like an upside down hockey stick.

Hockey Stick Bidding A situation in which a trader offers an exceptionally high price for a small unit of a good or service. This is considered anti-competitive and can be illegal.

Hodrick-Prescott Filter A mathematical technique used to smooth the non-linear data points in a time series. The HP filter helps analysts better determine trends. It is used most often to smooth out indices of macroeconomic data, such as the Help Wanted Index.

Hogshead An obsolete unit of volume equivalent to 63 gallons.

Hold **1.** To not sell. That is, to continue to own a security. See also: Buy-and-hold strategy. **2.** A recommendation by an analyst to neither buy nor sell a security. An analyst makes a hold recommendation when technical and/or fundamental indicators show middling performance by a security. It is also called a neutral or market perform recommendation.

Holdback Pay Money withheld from an employee's paycheck regularly until certain conditions are met. For example, an employer may be required to hold back pay until an employer pays back taxes or back child support.

Holder The owner of a given security. One may hold any type of security, and the term is often part of a compound word indicating which type is held. For example, the owner of share is called a shareholder, while the owner of a bond is called a bondholder. On its own, the term often applies to owners of derivatives, as in an option holder.

Holding **1.** The act of not selling. That is, when holding, one continues to own a security. See also: Buy-and-hold strategy. **2.** A security or other asset one currently owns.

Holding Company A company that owns enough stock in another company to control its operations. That is, the holding company can appoint the board of directors, set policies, and generally operate as the sole owner of another company, even if it does not actually own 100% of the stock. Some holding companies do not have operations of their own; that is, they exist simply to own and control other companies. In the United States, if a holding company owns at least 80% of the stock in another company, dividends paid to that holding company are not taxed. See also: Double Taxation.

Holding Company Depository Receipt Shares in several publicly-traded companies packaged together and traded as if they were one stock. HOLDRs are printed on one stock certificate. HOLDRs are put together in situations where some stocks pay higher dividends, while others have the higher potential for appreciation. They were created and are administered by Merrill Lynch, and trade on the American Stock Exchange. HOLDRs exist in many different industries.

Holding Fee An additional fee paid to an actor in a commercial allowing the advertiser to continue to use that actor's image after the commercial's initial run without seeking further permission.

Holding Gain An increase in the value of an asset or a decrease in the value of a liability that occurs without any action on the part of the holder. For example, if the value of one's house increases from $100,000 to $150,000 over three years, one has a holding gain of $50,000 over that period. Holding gains improve one's net worth.

Holding Loss A decrease in the value of an asset or an increase in the value of a liability that occurs without any action on the part of the holder. For example, if the value of one's house decreases from $150,000 to $100,000 over three years, one has a holding loss of $50,000 over that period. Holding losses reduce one's net worth.

Holding Period **1.** In a long position, the period of time during which one owns a security. The holding period is important to calculating an investment's returns and performance. The holding period also applies to taxation on capital gains, as long-term investments are not taxed as heavily as short-term ones. **2.** In a short sale, the period of time between the borrowing of securities and the return to their owner. That is, the holding period is the entire time elapsed for all the transactions of a short sale.

Holding Period Return The return on an investment during the time one holds the investment. The HPR is calculated by taking the income and other gains on the investment and dividing it by the historical cost. It is a useful way to compare the expected return to the actual return. The HPR may be calculated for any type of investment. It is also called the holding period yield (HPY).

Holding the Market A normally illegal practice in which a broker places or maintains buy orders for a security whose price is rapidly falling in order to artificially inflate demand and create a price floor. The main exception to its illegality is a situation in which the SEC gives an underwriter permission to attempt to hold the market for a new issue. Even in situations where it is legal, holding the market is a high-risk practice as the broker must normally buy large numbers of shares in order to curb falling demand, and, if he/she fails to create a price floor, he/she stands to lose a great deal of money. See also: Depth.

Holdout A homeowner (often the only one) who refuses to sell to make way for a new development. For example, if a company attempts to buy all the houses in a neighborhood to make way for a shopping center, a holdout is the one who does not sell. Holdouts can force the buyer to abandon or redesign the project.

Holdover **1.** A check received too late in the day to be processed. Holdovers are local or in-state, but a hold is placed on them until the next business day. See also: Check hold. **2.** See: Holdover tenant.

Holdover Tenant A tenant who remains in possession of a rented residence or office after the expiration of the lease. The holdover tenant may be evicted, but is often permitted to remain on a month-to-month basis. However, some leases avoid the situation entirely by automatically renewing unless one party or the other elects in advance not to do so.

Holiday Effect The tendency for a stock market to gain on the final trading day before an exchange-mandated long weekend or holiday such as Labor Day or Christmas. The holiday effect can be beneficial for traders, who may buy a security in the days leading up to the last trading day and then sell for a higher price on the final day. See also: Calendar effects.

Holiday Float A delay in a deposit or withdrawal because a bank is closed on a national or other holiday. See also: Float, Mail Float, Bank Holiday.

Holographic Will A handwritten will. A holographic will is often not on file with a lawyer or court and may have been written in haste. Holographic wills are valid, but in most jurisdictions must be witnessed to prove their validity. Some jurisdictions allow handwriting to be used to prove the identity of a testator.

Home Affordable Refinance Program A federal program in the United States allowing persons who are underwater on their home mortgages to refinance. Eligibility for HARP includes homeowners whose mortgages are owned by Freddie Mac or Fannie Mae and who are current on their payments. Additionally, the value of the mortgage cannot exceed 125% of the value of the home.

Home Asset Bias The fact that an investor is more likely to invest in assets that are in his/her own country than in similarly or better priced assets in another country. A variety of factors may explain the home asset bias, including government interventions such as tariffs. However, it is most likely that an investor simply has the most and the best information on assets in his/her own country.

Home Business Insurance An insurance policy that provides coverage for losses to a business run from home. For example, home business insurance may pay to replace computers, inventory and other items lost in a home accident such as a fire. Home business insurance is important because homeowners insurance does not cover most home business losses (and, in Canada, a home business can invalidate one's homeowners insurance). As with all insurance, one must pay a premium for the coverage. See also: Home office deduction.

Home Country The country in which one was born, regardless of where one currently lives. One's home country may have tax and other consequences. For example, one born in the United States is a citizen of the United States and so may be taxed on worldwide income, whether or not one lives there.

Home Equity Debt Debt collateralized by the value of one's home. The amount of this debt is generally the difference between the homeowner's equity in his/her house and the market value of the house. If home equity debt is not paid off, the lender may take possession of and sell the house in order to pay for the loan. This can occur even if the homeowner continues to make payments on his/her mortgage. This debt generally has a variable interest rate, which is nonetheless still lower than most other lines of credit.

Home Equity Line of Credit A line of credit in which one borrows against the value of one's home. That is, the collateral on a home equity line of credit is one's house. The amount of these loans is usually the difference between the homeowner's equity in the house and the market value of the house. A home equity line of credit operates like a credit card with a credit limit in that one may borrow, through a debit card or a check, at one's discretion, up to the maximum amount of the line of credit. The homeowner may use this credit line to finance other purchases or ventures. However, if a home equity line of credit is not repaid, the lender may take possession of the house and sell it in order to pay for the credit line; this can occur even if the homeowner continues to make payments on his/her mortgage. These loans generally have variable interest rates, which are nonetheless still lower than most other lines of credit.

Home Equity Loan A loan in which the one borrows against the value of one's home. That is, the collateral of a home-equity loan is one's house. The amount in these loans is generally the difference between the homeowner's equity in the house and the market value of the house. The homeowner receives the amount of the loan in a lump sum, and may use it to finance other purchases or ventures. If a home-equity loan is not paid off, the lender may take possession of and sell the house in order to pay for the loan; this can occur even if the homeowner continues to make payments on his/her mortgage. These loans generally have variable interest rates, which are nonetheless still lower than most other lines of credit. Home-equity loans are sometimes called second mortgages or equity loans. See also: Reverse mortgage.

Home Improvement Loan A loan used to remodel or repair a private residence. Home improvement loans are usually short-term. They may or may not be secured by the homes whose work they finance, but those that are secured generally carry lower interest rates.

Home Leave Extra vacation time earned by employees of the federal government who serve outside the United States. Home leave allows one to return home, visit family, and so forth. The longer one serves abroad, the more home leave one earns.

Home Modification Changes to the physical structure of a house made to make it more easily livable for a senior citizen or a physically disabled person. For example, one may add lower cabinets so a person in a wheelchair can reach them. Likewise, one may add handlebars to a shower to reduce the risk of slipping. While many home modifications are inexpensive, one can usually find reduced rates or financing options for more expensive modifications. See also: Activities of Daily Living.

Home Mortgage A loan used to buy real estate where one resides. A home mortgage is secured by the property it is used to purchase. One must make monthly payments on a home mortgage, and there is a set term before full payment is due, often 15, 20 or 30 years. Some mortgages have fixed interest rates, while others have variable interest rates. If one defaults on a home mortgage, the bank making it may take possession of the real estate and sell it to recover its investment. Some banks, notably savings and loans, specialize in making mortgage loans. In the United States, home mortgages have more favorable tax implications than mortgages on other properties. See also: Mortgage-backed security.

Home Mortgage Disclosure Act Legislation in the United States, passed in 1975, that requires financial institutions to keep records on mortgages, refinancing loans and other loans made on single and multi-family homes. The Act is designed to help HUD police banks make sure they do not discriminate against geographic regions or other protected criteria in making loans.

Home Mortgage Interest The interest paid on a loan securing one's primary residence. This excludes interest paid on investment properties and most vacation homes. In the United States, one may reduce one's taxable income by the amount one pays in interest on all eligible mortgages. There are some limits to the mortgage interest deduction. For example, one may only deduct interest on the first $1,000,000 worth of mortgages, aggregated with other home debt. However, most homeowners can deduct all of their mortgage interest.

Home Office 1. A place in one's residence in which one primarily performs tasks associated with self-employment or with one's job for an employer. For example, one may use the second bedroom in one's house as a home office, keeping one's desk, computer, files and so forth there. A home office may be eligible for a home office deduction if the space is used exclusively for business purposes. **2.** A department of the British government responsible for immigration, police, and other matters related to law enforcement. At various times throughout its history, it has overseen other issues, such as adoption, fire services, and worker's compensation. It was established in 1782.

Home Office Deduction A reduction in one's taxable income for the expenses of maintaining a home office. For example, a self-employed person may deduct the costs of office supplies, depreciation on one's computer and similar expenses. Likewise, one may deduct a portion of one's rent or mortgage for an office space used exclusively for business purposes. However, the amount deducted must be proportionate to the office's size relative to the home. Employees who work from home are eligible for the same deduction under the same restrictions.

Home Office Expense An expense one incurs by maintaining an office at home where one performs at least half of one's work. A home office expense includes a portion of the rent, property taxes, or perhaps the Internet bill. One may deduct home office expenses from one's taxable income up to the total amount one earns from the work performed at the home office. See also: Work from home, Independent contractor.

Home Ownership The state of owning one's primary residence. Homeownership gives the owner a stake in his/her neighborhood or town's long-term stability, and is a significant investment. The U.S. federal government thus attempts to encourage homeownership by allowing owners to deduct the interest on their mortgages from their taxable income.

Home Run An investment that results in an especially large capital gain in a very short period of time. For example, one may buy a stock that jumps from $5 per share to $55 per share in only six months. A home run results in huge capital gains for the stockholder or other investor. This term can be used for any investment vehicle, especially an IPO. See also: Hot issue.

Homemade Dividend When one owns a stock, the sale of some of the shares to imitate a dividend. One creates a homemade dividend especially when the company represented in the stock does not declare a dividend for a particular period of time. Importantly, a homemade dividend is subject to, at worst, capital gains tax; if the shares are sold at a loss, there may be not taxation at all. This contrasts with a "normal" dividend, which is usually taxed at a higher rate that capital gains.

Homemade Leverage Leverage resulting from borrowing or lending to oneself, particularly to enter into a riskless investment. An example of homemade leverage is borrowing from a personal account in order to buy U.S. Treasury securities. This concept is important to the Capital Asset Pricing Model and the Modigliani-Miller Theorem.

Homeowner A person who owns his/her primary residence. Homeownership gives the owner a stake in his/her neighborhood or town's long-term stability, as we as a significant investment. The U.S. federal government thus attempts to encourage homeownership by allowing owners to deduct the interest on their mortgages from their taxable income.

Homeowners Affordability and Stability Plan A program in the United States to help distressed homeowners in the wake of the late 2000s recession. It offers incentives for lenders to reduce the PITI of certain mortgages to 38% of the homeowner's net income. In turn, the government shares the cost so the homeowner only pays 31% of his/her net income on the mortgage. The plan was established in February 2009.

Homeowner's Insurance Insurance that the buyer of a private residence purchases providing coverage for most damage to the residence. Typically, homeowner's insurance covers damage from fire, deliberate or accidental destruction of the home by a person, and other, similar matters. Nearly all homeowner's insurance policies exclude acts of God like earthquakes and floods from coverage, though one may buy supplementary policies to cover these eventualities.

Homer A volunteer or employee of a non-profit organization who works primarily from home. The term is primarily used in the context of small Christian churches or ministries. See also: Telecommuting.

Homies A slang term for stocks in home building companies. The term is most commonly used in the plural.

Homo Economicus A person that desires to maximize his/her needs or desires. Homo economicus is used most of the time to refer to the rational economic actor, who desires wealth, does not desire to work if it can be avoided, and is able to find ways achieve those ends. This assumption is accepted by many economists, especially those who follow rational choice theory, but it remains controversial. The concept of homo economicus was developed by utilitarian thinkers, and contrasts with the constructs of behavioral economics.

Homogeneity The state of being alike or similar. In investing, a portfolio may be homogeneous if its securities are largely in the same industry or type. For example, a portfolio consisting exclusively of stocks is said to be homogeneous.

Homogeneous Expectations Assumption In Markowitz Portfolio Theory, the assumption that, under a given set of circumstances, all investors will want the same thing. Specifically, when presented with plans having different returns at a given risk, an investor will choose the plan with the highest return. Likewise, when presented plans with different risks at a given return, the investor will pick the plan with the lowest risk. While few researchers believe the assumption holds entirely true, many defend it as holding "approximately" in a given situation. Developed in the 1950s and 1960s, the homogenous expectations assumption is important to capital asset pricing models.

Homoskedastic Describing a sequence of variables where each variable has the same or a very similar variance. Homoskedasticity is often assumed in statistics but is not always true. See also: Heteroskedastic.

Honcho 1. Informal for a CEO. **2.** Informal for any senior officer or person in charge of an organization or department.

Honduran Lempira The currency of Honduras. It is named after Lempira, a 16th century chieftain who led a resistance against the Spanish. It was introduced in 1931, replacing the Honduran peso. In the 1990s and early 2000s, the lempira underwent a great deal of inflation, but it has since stabilized. However, tourist centers and some other areas of the Honduras accept the U.S. dollar in addition to the lempira.

Hong One of several major companies in Hong Kong or another special administrative region of China. The term began in the early 19th century and referred to companies that provided financing for Hong Kong business; it has since expanded to include large conglomerates based in Hong Kong. Prior to the 1997 handover to the Chinese, hongs were owned by British companies.

Hong Kong Commodities Exchange Ltd. An exchange in Hong Kong on which contracts for commodities, notably sugar futures, are traded. It was established in 1977.

Hong Kong Dollar The currency of Hong Kong, a special administrative region of China. It was first issued in the 1860s and, for a number of years, circulated in Hong Kong along with several other currencies. From 1963 to 1935, it was pegged to silver. It then adopted a crawling peg to the British pound, which continued until the yen was introduced during Japanese occupation in World War II. The dollar and the peg to the pound were reintroduced after the war, but the peg was eventually changed to the U.S. dollar. It began to float in 1974, but readopted the U.S. dollar peg in 1983. It is an important currency because of Hong Kong's position as an international trade center.

Hong Kong Exchanges and Clearing Limited The primary exchange in Hong Kong. It was established in 2000 with the merger of the Stock Exchange of Hong Kong, the Hong Kong Futures Exchange and the Hong Kong Securities Clearing Company. It provides a floor for traders to buy and sell securities and derivatives. It also provides clearing services. It is one of the largest exchanges (by market capitalization) in the world.

Hong Kong Futures Exchange A former futures exchange in Hong Kong. Established in 1976, it went bankrupt in 1987 because of speculative investing, notably as a result of illegal trades conducted by Robert Ng. It was finally absorbed into the Stock Exchange of Hong Kong in 2000.

Hong Kong Interbank Offer Rate The interest rate that banks in Hong Kong charge one another for interbank loans with terms of up to one year. It is considered a key benchmark interest rate in the wider Asian economy. Interest rate swaps in Asia, for example, often use HIBOR as the reference rate for the floating payer. See also: LIBOR, EURBOR.

Honne A Japanese word for a person's true feelings. Because it may conflict with social necessities and expectations, honne is often kept secret from all except one's closest confidantes. Honne contrasts with tatemae, which corresponds to the feelings one displays in public.

Honorarium An extra fee paid to a person or company who provides a service exceptionally well. An honorarium goes to a person who goes above and beyond the call of duty; it confers respect and honor on the person.

Hont An obsolete Dutch unit of area roughly equivalent to 1,400 square meters, with slight regional variations.

Hook 1. In marketing, a tool that arouses interest in an advertisement or in a product. **2.** Informal; to steal or defraud.

Hope Now Alliance An organization created to respond to distressed homeowners in the United States. The Hope Now Alliance consists of investors in mortgage-backed securities, mortgage lenders, agencies of the U.S. government, and other organizations. It created an 800-number to provide free financial counseling to callers. Counselors advise on the options available to callers, including modified payment plans and loss mitigation. The Hope Now Alliance was established in 2007.

Hope Scholarship A scholarship for degree-seeking, postsecondary students in Georgia who attend a public or private university in the state. The scholarship pays full tuition at a public university (or an equivalent amount for a private university), along with most mandatory students fees and an allowance to buy textbooks. The scholarship was created in 1993 and is funded by the Georgia lottery.

Hope Scholarship Credit A direct, dollar-for-dollar reduction in a taxpayer's tax liability for expenses paid for post-secondary education. One may apply the Hope scholarship credit for oneself, one's spouse, or a dependent child. To be eligible for the credit, one must have no more than the modified adjusted gross income designated each year, and one may not take it if one also deducts education expenses from one's income.

Hope Tax Credit A reduction of one's tax liability for one's education expenses for the first two years of college. That is, in order to be eligible for the credit, one must be enrolled at least half time in a degree or certificate granting program and must not have completed the first two years. (Additionally, one must be free of a felony drug conviction.) The credit may be applied to tuition, but generally not to room and board or similar expenses.

Horatio Alger An American writer who authored popular books in which the main characters (often historical figures) rise from poverty to relative wealth. In other words, Alger wrote about people who achieved the American dream. Critics maintain he gave his readers (and their intellectual descendants) false hope of success.

Horizon The length of time an investment is intended to last, usually expressed in years. Having a horizon helps an investor set his/her short-term and long-term investment plans. See also: Horizon analysis, Horizon return.

Horizon Analysis Analysis of the discounted return on an investment over one or more time frames (called horizons) that differ from the investment's actual maturity. For example, one might calculate the yield on a 10-year Treasury bond over its first year or first five years. Horizon analysis is done to see if an investment can or will perform well enough to meet one's investment goals over a given time. See also: Horizon analysis.

Horizon Return A discounted, total return on an investment or portfolio over a given time frame, called a horizon. For example, one might calculate the return on an investment over its first year or first five years, etc. See also: Horizon analysis.

Horizontal 1. See: Horizontal acquisition. **2.** See: Horizontal agreement. **3.** See: Horizontal contiguity. **4.** See: Horizontal contract.

Horizontal Acquisition The acquisition of one company by another in the same or a similar industry. This is often a part of the market consolidation process, when too many companies exist for the market to support. They then acquire each other in order to create fewer companies that are more competitive. In venture capital, horizontal acquisitions and horizontal mergers may be part of a roll up process.

Horizontal Agreement An agreement between two companies at the same level on the supply chain to work together. At its worst, a horizontal agreement can indicate collusion. However, this is ordinarily not the case; for example, companies may agree to pool their marketing resources for mutual benefit.

Horizontal Analysis In fundamental analysis, the comparison of a financial ratio or some other benchmark to the same ratio or benchmark for a different period of time. For example, horizontal analysis may investigate whether a company's earnings have gone up or down over a given quarter or year. Horizontal analysis may be used in making investment decisions to determine a company's financial health. In general, a horizontal analyst chooses a timeframe to match the timeframe of a possible investment.

Horizontal Audit An audit that investigates the same activity across multiple departments. For example, a horizontal audit may measure the effectiveness of one aspect of management common to several departments in a company. This contrasts with a vertical audit, which investigates all activities in the same department.

Horizontal Combination The acquisition by one company of several companies in the same or a similar industry. This is often a part of the market consolidation process, when too many companies exist for the market to support. Companies then acquire each other in order to create fewer companies that are more competitive. See also: Horizontal Acquisition.

Horizontal Conflict In marketing, stiff competition between two large companies or products. Horizontal conflict results in oversaturation of the market because competitors are targeting the same demographics. It is nearly impossible for a small competitor to enter the market during horizontal conflict. See also: Vertical Conflict.

Horizontal Contiguity The purchase of several advertisements on television or radio for broadcast at the same time of day for several days in a row. Buying horizontal contiguity may lead to a horizontal discount.

Horizontal Contract In social contract theory, an actual or implied contract binding a person to a community. A horizontal contract establishes the rules of social engagement that the community and its members expect from each other. See also: Vertical Contract.

Horizontal Count On a point-and-figure chart, the physical width of a congestion area. This is used to estimate the future price of a stock after it leaves the congestion area.

Horizontal Cume The total number of persons a radio or television program reaches from day to day. A rising horizontal cume represents a growing audience, which may generate greater revenue from advertisers. A declining horizontal cume indicates the opposite. The horizontal cume essentially measure the unduplicated audience over time.

Horizontal Discount A reduced price to broadcast an advertisement on television or radio at the same time of day over a period of at least several days. See also: Vertical Discount.

Horizontal Diversification In risk management, the act or strategy of adding more investments of like kind to one's portfolio to hedge against the investments already in it. Ideally, this reduces the risk inherent in any one investment, and increases the possibility of making a profit, or at least avoiding a loss. That is, horizontal diversification involves investing in similar instruments. Examples include investing in several technology companies or in different types of bonds. Horizontal diversification may be as broad or as narrow as the investor chooses. In general, broader diversification equates to less risk and lower return. See also: Markowitz Portfolio Theory, Vertical diversification.

Horizontal Equity A theory that persons or corporations who earn the same or a similar amount of money should be taxed in the same or a similar way. For example, horizontal equity states that two individuals making $50,000 per year should be taxed the same amount, regardless of how they earned their income. Horizontal equity is the idea behind the progressive tax system in place in many countries, though few countries implement it entirely.

Horizontal Expansion Growth of a company in which it purchases new facilities, tools and/or other assets to increase the volume of the product it makes. That is, horizontal expansion allows a company to make more of a product, but does not diversify its product line or the company's place in the supply chain.

Horizontal Export Trading Company An export company that buys goods from multiple manufacturers and sells them abroad, even if the manufacturers compete with each other domestically.

Horizontal Half Page An advertisement in a periodical that is printed on half of a page, divided laterally.

Horizontal Integration 1. A business strategy in which a company expands its operations to provide similar goods and services at the same point on the supply chain. For example, a widget retailer may begin selling whatsits in addition to widgets. More concretely, an oil exploration company may also begin exploring for natural gas. It is important to note that horizontal integration always occurs at the same point on the supply chain: a retailer does not move into wholesale and vice versa. See also: Vertical integration. **2.** See: Horizontal acquisition.

Horizontal Keiretsu In Japan, a number of independent but related companies centered on and financed by a single bank and/or a joint stock company. A horizontal keiretsu is essentially a diversified conglomerate; that is, it may have companies in several completely unrelated industries so as to reduce the risk of loss if one industry or other has a bad year. A horizontal keiretsu is thought to promote sustainability over quick profits; however, critics of this system contend that it is inefficient.

Horizontal Market 1. The market for a product that is used in a wide number of industries. For example, the market for utilities may be considered horizontal because nearly every person and every industry needs electricity and water. Horizontal markets may be considered more stable than vertical markets. **2.** The market for a product that complements or substitutes the market for another product. For example, cake and ice cream have horizontal markets because they appeal to the same people, who often buy them together.

Horizontal Marketing System An agreement between two or more companies at the same level in the supply chain to work together on marketing for the good of all parties. For example, two retailers in different areas (which therefore are not competing directly) may pool their marketing resources so as to help each other in their respective locations. See also: Synergy.

Horizontal Promotion A promotion to a position of greater responsibility (and therefore more compensation), but without greater managerial authority. For example, an analyst may receive a horizontal promotion to senior analyst. See also: Vertical Promotion.

Horizontal Publication A periodical intended for multiple companies, industries or trades. For example, a company may publish a magazine on small business financial management. This would have broad appeal for small business owners, regardless of the industry in which they work.

Horizontal Security Exchange A transaction in which one barters one security for a similar one. For example, one may trade a stock or a stock or a bond for a bond. Ideally, the securities involved should have roughly the same value, but, if not, the investor who receives the more valuable security does not owe taxes on the capital gain. However, if either investor sells his/her security, capital gains taxes will be levied.

Horizontal Specialization A management style in which several persons with equal authority are given oversight over specific departments or tasks. For example, one manager may be assigned to human relations, a second to operations and a third to accounting. However, no manager has authority over another. See also: Vertical Specialization.

Horizontal Third Page An advertisement in a periodical that is printed on one third of a page, divided laterally.

Horizontal Union A labor union representing all workers with a given skill set in a geographic area, regardless of the company for which they work. For example, a horizontal union may represent all the plumbers in town.

Horn of Africa A peninsula in northeastern Africa including Somalia, Ethiopia, Eritrea and Djibouti. The Horn of Africa is a major coffee exporter. However, because of political instability in Somalia, the waters around the Horn suffer from piracy.

Horsemen A slang term for large cap tech stocks. The term is most commonly used in the plural.

Horst Koehler A German economist, banker and politician. He served in the Finance Ministry and as president of the European Bank for Reconstruction and Development. From 2000 to 2004, he was chief at the International Monetary Fund and from 2004 to 2010 he was President of Germany. He was born in 1943.

Hospice Medical care provided for the terminally ill when death is thought to be imminent. One's health insurance policy may cover hospice care but this is not always the case.

Hospital Expense and Surgery Insurance An insurance policy that provides coverage for room and board and the medical procedures that one undergoes while in the hospital. Hospital expense and surgery insurance may supplement one's ordinary health insurance, especially if it does not provide sufficient benefits for hospital stays or surgeries. As with all insurance, one must pay a premium to receive the coverage.

Hospital Expense Insurance An insurance policy that provides coverage for the room and board and other basic expenses associated with a stay in a hospital. Hospital expense insurance may supplement one's ordinary health insurance, especially if it does not provide sufficient benefits for hospital stays. As with all insurance, one must pay a premium to receive the coverage.

Hospital Liability Insurance An insurance policy protecting a hospital associated with the cost of a medical malpractice or other lawsuit. For example, if a doctor makes an error resulting in the death of a patient during surgery, hospital liability insurance would protect the hospital from the ensuing suit. As with all insurance, the hospital must pay a premium to receive coverage.

Hospital Revenue Bond A municipal bond used to construct or expand a hospital. The bond is secured by the revenue the hospital receives in the course of its operations; that is, the issuing municipality does not back the bond itself. Generally speaking, a hospital revenue bond is riskier than other municipal bonds because hospitals have no power to tax and many carry an unusual amount of bad debt as a result of patients being unable to pay for services.

Hospitalization Insurance 1. See: Hospital expense insurance. **2.** See: Hospital indemnity insurance.

Host Bond A bond with a warrant or other sweetener attached. For example, a convertible bond is a host bond because it includes the option to change the bond to stock. A host bond is also called a package or a back bond.

Host Country A foreign country in which an ambassador and diplomatic staff reside while on assignment. The ambassador and staff represent the interests and policies of their own nation while in the host country.

Host Government The government of a foreign country in which an ambassador and diplomatic staff reside while on assignment. The ambassador and staff represent the interests and policies of their own nation while they are guests of the host government.

Host Liability The legal liability of a person or company that serves alcohol to a guest for any negative consequences of the consumption of alcohol. For example, in some jurisdictions, if a restaurant serves too many drinks to a patron and that patron kills a motorist in a car accident on the drive home, the restaurant may be held legally responsible. In some other jurisdictions, host liability only applies to persons or companies serving alcohol to underage persons.

Host Security A security with a warrant attached to it. A warrant is a certificate issued with a security giving the holder the option of buying a stock at a certain strike price for a certain period of time. They are issued by companies during a round of financing as an added incentive to buy a security. Most of the time, the host security is also a stock, but this is not always the case. See also: Equity warrant.

Hostile Fire A fire anywhere other than where it is controlled. Fires that spread from the fireplace to the carpet or from a bonfire to the pasture are both examples of hostile fire. Insurance covers damage caused by hostile fire. Hostile fire is also called unfriendly fire.

Hostile Leveraged Buyout The acquisition of a publicly-traded company by a person or group not favored by current management, where the acquisition is financed with debt. Often, the acquirer in a hostile leveraged buyout issues junk bonds in order to raise the capital necessary for the acquisition. Alternatively, the buyout may be underwritten by one or more investment banks. Hostile leveraged buyouts are fairly unusual because most organizations that finance leveraged buyouts prefer that current management remain at the helm to reduce risk.

Hostile Takeover The acquisition of one company by another without the consent of the target company's board of directors. Generally speaking, a hostile takeover involves the acquiring company buying stock directly from shareholders, sometimes by offering a particularly high price. The acquiring company may buy up to 5% of the target company without registering the move with the SEC. See also: Friendly takeover, Corporate raider.

Hostile Tender Offer In a hostile takeover, an offer to buy the target company's stock from shareholders. A hostile tender offer occurs when the target company's board of directors has recommended that shareholders not sell, and it will usually try to make a better offer than the hostile tender offer to buy out shareholders and avoid being taken over. The success of a hostile tender offer depends on how high it is compared to what the board of directors is willing to offer. See also: Antitakeover measure.

Hot Informal; describing an active security. That is, a hot security is one that is traded frequently.

Hot Card A debit or credit card that may not be used because it has been reported lost or stolen. If a thief (or anyone else) attempts to use a hot card, the transaction will be declined. See also: Identity theft.

Hot Desking The practice in which employees in an office are assigned to an area with several desks, but no one desk belongs to any one person. That is, employees can choose the desk they use each day within the designated area. Hot desking is an alternative to assigning each employee a cubicle.

Hot IPO An IPO that is extremely popular, leading to a dramatic rise in price immediately after the IPO. Hot IPOs are usually overbooked. They were especially popular in the 1990s during the dot-com bubble when it was common for IPOs to occur at, say, $10 per share, and almost instantly spike to $50 or $60 per share. An IPO is a risky investment in general; a hot IPO may be even riskier, especially when the company's earnings are small or non-existent, as was the case in the dot-com bubble. See also: Publicly-traded company.

Hot Issue A new issue that trades at a large premium to its original offer price. For example, suppose a company issues its IPO at $25 per share. If early trading on the secondary market is $50 per share, it is said to be a hot issue. These are relatively common during economic expansion or bubbles. They were especially associated with the dot-com bubbles in the late 1990s.

Hot List A weekly publication of all credit cards that are past due, or that have been canceled or stolen. It is published jointly by MasterCard and Visa. It is also called the Warning Bulletin.

Hot Money Funds that an investor moves from one investment vehicle to another in response to higher interest rates. For example, an investor may move hot money from an investment-grade bond to a certificate of deposit at another institution where the certificate of deposit has a higher return. Likewise, one may move funds from one country to another when interest rates in the second country are higher. Hot money may be moved when a country or institution lowers its interest rates.

Hot Stock 1. See: Hot Issue. **2.** A stock that rises significantly in a short period of time. This occurs when buyers greatly outnumber sellers.

Houdini A computer chip compatible with both IBM and Apple computers. A Houdini helps facilitate business between companies (or persons within a company) using different types of computers.

Hounding Analysts The act of a hedge fund manager calling an analyst, especially repeatedly, to persuade him/her to upgrade the hedge fund's rating. An upgrade in rating usually results in the fund's price increasing. When managers hound analysts, they are attempting to create a favorable situation for their investors (and perhaps increase their own commissions). However, it can result in the hedge fund having an inaccurate rating. It is important to note that hounding analysts is not always successful.

Hours of Work The period of time during which one engages in paid work. Labor law in many countries establishes maximum or minimum hours of work to protect employees. In other places, overtime hours (usually more than 40 hours of work) require extra pay. Hours of work are one way to measure the labor a person performs.

House A broker-dealer or underwriting person or firm. Houses are usually large institutions, but may also be an individual. They provide investment advising services, place and execute orders on behalf of clients, and place new issues with investors.

House Account 1. An investment account a brokerage firm uses for its own investments, rather than those on behalf of a client. **2.** An investment account in a brokerage that is large or otherwise important enough to be managed from the brokerage's main office, often with a major executive as the broker.

House Agency An advertising agency owned by an advertiser. That is, a house agency handles all advertising for all products that a company (the advertiser) makes. House agencies were once common because they gave large companies control over their own advertising. However, they lacked an outside perspective necessary to find potential flaws or areas of improvement in the advertiser's marketing strategy and are less common today. See also: In-house agency.

House Air Waybill A receipt issued by an air freight consolidator. A house air waybill indicates to the customer that his/her goods have been received by the company and have been passed on for freight by air. They often include tracking numbers so that the customer can check the status of the shipment.

House Appropriations Committee A committee of the U.S. House of Representatives responsible for drafting legislation to spend federal money. According to the U.S. Constitution, any federal spending must be authorized by legislation. The Appropriations Committee spearheads that effort in the House. It consists of approximately 60 members, most of whom belong to the House majority party. It was established in 1865. See also: House Ways and Means Committee.

House Excess In a margin account, the amount of cash or securities in excess of the minimum margin. The minimum margin is the collateral used for the brokerage to allow a client to buy securities with borrowed money. When a client has more than the minimum margin deposited with the brokerage at the end of a trading day, the brokerage informs him/her that he/she has a house excess. The client may use this to borrow more for margin transactions or may use it as a cushion to avoid a margin call in case the value of the client's portfolio declines.

House Maintenance Requirement The money or securities an investor must keep in a margin account at a brokerage over and above what FINRA requires in order to be able to borrow for short sales or other purposes. The maintenance is kept as collateral until the brokerage calls the margin and the client pays back what is owed. FINRA requires that the maintenance kept must be at least 25% of the amount borrowed; some brokerages have house maintenance requirements of up to 50%. See also: Restricted account.

House Poor Describing an individual with significant income, but with such a large mortgage on his/her house that he/she has little discretionary income. Historically, this term referred to farmers and ranchers, most of whose cash went to debt service on their land, but it has expanded to include anyone who spends so much on his/her mortgage that he/she cannot spend on other goods and services he/she wants or needs. Being house poor is also known as being land poor. See also: Upside down mortgage, McMansion, Foreclosure.

House Rules Rules followed only at a certain location. For example, each stock exchange has its own rules in addition to regulations set down by a government authority.

House Stock A stock that a brokerage keeps in its inventory. A brokerage may keep house stocks for clients or may trade them it its capacity as a market maker.

House to House Transportation between the office or residence of the sender and the office or residence of the receiver.

Housewife A woman who stays home while her husband works to earn a living. Housewives generally are responsible for cooking, cleaning and child-rearing. For that reason, they form a strong demographic for products related to these activities. Housewives are less common today as women have gradually entered the workforce and more households have two breadwinners. See also: Housewife time.

Housewife Time The late morning through the mid-afternoon on weekdays. The largest demographic of television viewers during this time are housewives, or at least are women over 16. Because housewives generally are responsible for cooking, cleaning and child-rearing, commercials during housewife time may often be geared toward these activities.

Housing and Economic Recovery Act of 2008 Legislation in the United States that guarantees sub-prime mortgages up to $300 billion, provided the lenders write down the value of the mortgage up to 90% of the actual value of the real estate. The Federal Housing Administration was charged with implementing the guarantees. The act was passed in July 2008 and enabled the government to put Freddie Mac and Fannie Mae into federal receivership in September.

Housing Market Index An index of more than 300 home building companies measuring demand for the construction of new homes. The housing market index goes from 0 to 100, with a measure over 50 meaning that demand for new homes is rising. This is considered an indicator of the state of the real estate and construction markets.

Housing Starts The number of new homes that construction companies have begun building in a given area over a certain period of time. The U.S. Census Bureau measures and publishes housing starts in the United States as a way of gauging the state of the housing market. See also: Housing Market Index.

Housing Unit A place where a person or persons live separate and apart from other persons. A housing unit may be a house, apartment, or even a self-contained room. See also: Zoning, Census.

HR 1. ISO 3166-1 alpha-2 code for the Republic of Croatia. This is the code used in international transactions to and from Croatian bank accounts. **2.** ISO 3166-2 geocode for Croatia. This is used as an international standard for shipping to Croatia. Each county (along with the City of Zagreb) has its own code with the prefix "HR." For example, the code for the County of Zadar ISO 3166-2:HR-13. **3.** See: Human resources.

HRD ISO 4217 code for Croatian dinar. It replaced the Yugoslav convertible dinar at a one-to-one ratio in 1991. The Croatian dinar was a transition currency between the Yugoslav dinar and the Croatian kuna, which replaced it in 1994. The dinar was subject to high inflation.

HRK ISO 4217 code for the Croatian kuna. First issued in 1939 while Croatia was part of Yugoslavia, it was originally pegged at a dual exchange rate to the German reichsmark. Pulled from circulation in 1945, the kuna was reintroduced in 1994, replacing the Yugoslav dinar. The new kruna was introduced at an exchange rate of 1 kruna per 1000 dinars; it is a floating currency.

HRV GOST 7.67 Latin three-letter geocode for Croatia. The code is used for transactions to and from Croatian bank accounts and for international shipping to Croatia. As with all GOST 7.67 codes, it is used primarily in Cyrillic alphabets.

H-Shares Shares in Chinese companies that trade on the Hong Kong Stock Exchange. H-shares are denominated in Hong Kong dollars and allow companies incorporated in the People's Republic of China to have access to capital from Hong Kong. H-Shares are subject to Chinese regulations and are included on the Hang Seng index.

HT 1. ISO 3166-1 alpha-2 code for the Republic of Haiti. This is the code used in international transactions to and from Haitian bank accounts. **2.** ISO 3166-2 geocode for Haiti. This is used as an international standard for shipping to Haiti. Each Haitian department has its own code with the prefix "HT." For example, the code for Nord Department is ISO 3166-2:HT-ND

HTG ISO 4217 code for the Haitian gourde. It was introduced in 1872, replacing another currency that was also called the gourde. It was initially pegged to the French franc, but this was switched to the U.S. dollar in 1912 at a rate of five gourdes to one dollar. Since 1989, the gourde has been a floating currency. Interestingly, the peg is maintained in colloquial speech, in which people refer to five gourdes as a Haitian dollar. Often prices are even given in Haitian dollars.

HTI GOST 7.67 Latin three-letter geocode for Haiti. The code is used for transactions to and from Haitian bank accounts and for international shipping to Haiti. As with all GOST 7.67 codes, it is used primarily in Cyrillic alphabets.

Htwa A Burmese unit of length equivalent to 228.6 millimeters.

Hu 1. ISO 3166-1 alpha-2 code for the Republic of Hungary. This is the code used in international transactions to and from Hungarian bank accounts. **2.** ISO 3166-2 geocode for Hungary. This is used as an international standard for shipping to Hungary. Each subdivision has its own code with the prefix "HU." For example, the code for the City of Budapest is ISO 3166-2:HU-BU.

Huckster 1. Informal; a seller, especially an unscrupulous one. **2.** A copywriter for radio or television.

HUD-1 Form In the sale of real estate, a form itemizing the closing costs that the buyer and the seller are each responsible for paying. The costs for the buyer ought to be close to the good faith estimate.

HUF ISO 4217 code for the Hungarian forint. It was issued in 1946, not long before Hungary became a communist country. It was an inconvertible currency until the fall of the Iron Curtain, when Hungary transitioned to capitalism. It dealt with high inflation in the 1990s, but stabilized afterwards.

Huge A slang term for the Finnish markka issued after 1963. It is derived from a Swedish term for "hundred," due to the fact that a 1963 revaluation increased the value of the markka 100-fold. The term was most common in Helsinki.

Hukm In Islamic law, a judicial ruling or decision made by one with authority. The term's plural form, ahkam, refers more specifically to rules derived from fiqh, or Islamic jurisprudence.

Hulbert Financial Digest An advisory letter specializing in other advisory letters. The Hulbert Financial Digest ranks different advisory letters based on their accuracy and insight. It provides different rankings for different sorts of advisory letters (e.g. long-term investment advice vs. short-term). It is published monthly by MarketWatch.

Hulbert Rating A rating by Hulbert Financial Digest for an advisory letter. Hulbert Financial Digest is an advisory letter specializing in other advisory letters. It provides ratings to different advisory letters based on their accuracy and insight. It provides different ratings for different sorts of advisory letters (e.g. long-term investment advice vs. short-term).

Hull Marine Insurance An insurance policy that provides coverage for the physical integrity of a ship. That is, hull marine insurance covers the ship's hull, life boats, railings and so forth. This contrasts with cargo marine insurance, which covers goods moved onto or off of a ship. As with all insurance, one must pay a premium to receive the coverage.

Human Capital The measure of the output an employee with a certain skill set is able to make. The concept of human capital was developed in the 1960s and is founded on the idea that hard work, education, and skill development all lead to more output. As a result, companies are encouraged to invest in human capital through various means such as education and bonuses for exceptionally good work, among others.

Human Resources 1. The department of a company that deals with hiring and retaining employees, firing those who do not perform, and managing disputes between employees or between an employee and a manager. Human resources departments often manage pensions, insurance, and other benefits as well. They are most common in medium- and large-sized companies. **2.** See: Human Capital.

Human Shield A military and political tactic in which civilians go to (or are placed in) a military target to dissuade an enemy attack. Human shields can protect military targets and have propaganda value if the enemy attacks anyway (which obviously could kill the civilians).

Humanitarian A person who helps others or believes people ought to be helped, regardless of their race, class, religion, sex, or other aspects of their identity. Humanitarians send money, food or other necessities to those in need. The term is often associated with charitable organizations. Critics claim that humanitarians have limited impact, while supporters argue that everyone should give what they can to make a larger, aggregate impact.

Humanitarianism The idea that persons ought to be helped, regardless of their race, class, religion, sex, or other aspects of their identity. Humanitarians send money, food, or other necessities to those in need. The term is often associated with charitable organizations. Critics claim that humanitarians have limited impact, while supporters argue that everyone should give what they can to make a larger, aggregate impact.

Human-Life Approach A way to calculate the benefit of a life insurance policy. One takes the human-life approach when one considers the financial loss to a family if the policyholder died immediately. This includes after-tax wages, benefits, insurance, and so forth. The human-life approach seeks to compensate the dependents of the policyholder for these losses. The human-life approach is used almost exclusively in situations where the policyholder is working.

Hump Informal; a period of rising security prices followed by a period of declining security prices. The period may be long term, short term or any period between the two. On a chart, this looks somewhat like a camel's hump. See also: Inverted Saucer.

Hun GOST 7.67 Latin three-letter geocode for Hong Kong. The code is used for transactions to and from Hong Kong bank accounts and for international shipping to Hong Kong. As with all GOST 7.67 codes, it is used primarily in Cyrillic alphabets.

Hund A nickname of the 100 Danish krone banknote. The name means "dog" in Danish, but is also a contraction of the Danish word for hundred.

Hundi-Stick A slang term for a $100 note in Australia.

Hundred Weight 100 pounds. Cwt is used in some futures contracts and other derivatives in which the weight of the underlying asset is required. For example, a contract may state that the seller will deliver 3 Cwt, meaning 300 pounds. This convention has been in use in the United States since the 19th century.

Hundredweight Pricing A system to determine the price of cargo being shipped. Under hundredweight pricing, cargo that weighs less than 100 pounds is priced by package, while cargo over 100 pounds is priced by total weight. See also: Cwt.

Hung Up Describing a situation in which an investor owns securities that are worth significantly less than they were when the investor purchased them. For example, an investor may have bought a stock at $10 per share, which may later fall to $2 per share. When an investor is hung up, he/she has the option of either holding the securities in hopes that they will rise, while still risking further losses, or selling them and locking in the current losses.

Hunkering Down Informal; the act of selling a large position in stock. That is, an investor hunkers down when he/she closes a position suddenly, especially when the position was particularly large. See also: Panic sell.

Hunting Elephants The act or practice in which an investment banker convinces a client to buy a security beneficial to the investment bank's portfolio, whether or not it is beneficial to the client. The term does not imply illegality; that is, one generally can make the argument that the security benefits the client. However, the investment banker encourages his/her client to buy it primarily because of how it benefits the bank.

Hurdle Rate In capital budgeting, the required return for a project. That is, when a company is planning its outlays in the medium and long-term, it requires a certain rate of return on projects, because they can be quite expensive and the outlays tie up capital that can be used elsewhere. This required return is called the hurdle rate.

Hush Money A bribe given in exchange for silence. That is, hush money is given to prevent a party from reporting a criminal. Hush money is common in organized crime, financial crime and other illegal acts.

Hustle A slang term meaning to cheat or otherwise earn money unethically or illegally.

Huyen In Vietnam, a political subdivision roughly equivalent to a county. It is also used to indicate a rural district.

HV 1. ISO 3166-1 alpha-2 code for Upper Volta before it changed its name to Burkina Faso. This was the code used in international transactions to and from bank accounts in Upper Volta. **2.** ISO 3166-2 geocode for Upper Volta. This was used as an international standard for shipping to Upper Volta. In both cases, the code is obsolete.

Hvalp A nickname for the 50-Danish krone banknote. The term means "puppy" in Danish, and derives from the word hund, which means "dog" and is a nickname for the 100 krone note.

HVBF ISO 3166-3 code for Upper Volta, which changed its name to Burkina Faso in 1984. ISO 3166-3 codes are used to indicate names of countries that are no longer used.

Hwan The currency of South Korea between 1953 and 1962. It suffered from high inflation throughout its use and was replaced by the South Korean won.

Hyakume A unit of weight in Japan equivalent to 375 grams.

Hybrid Annuity An annuity that allows the annuitant to make contributions to both a fixed annuity and a variable annuity at once. For example, if an annuitant contributes $1000 per month to the hybrid annuity, $800 may be allocated to the fixed annuity and $200 to the variable annuity. This provides the holder of the hybrid annuity the stability of a fixed annuity with the potential for a higher return that a variable annuity brings. A hybrid annuity is most useful for retirees who expect to live for a long time and wish to participate in the stock market.

Hybrid Debt A general term for a type of debt with some features of equity. Two of the most common examples are a convertible bond, which is a bond that the holder may exchange for stocks, and a preferred share, which is stock with a guaranteed

dividend. Both of these examples combine the guaranteed payments of a bond with a stock's potential for equity.

Hybrid Market An exchange with both a trading floor and electronic trading. That is, a hybrid market allows traders to decide whether to use the open outcry system, in which securities are traded between people who see each other, or to use a computer system to make transactions. A major example is the New York Stock Exchange.

Hybrid Mortgage An adjustable-rate mortgage in which the interest rate is locked for a rather long period of time. That is, the interest rate is locked for a certain period, often seven years, at which point it may move either upward or downward. Many hybrid mortgages have interest rate caps to offer further protection to the mortgage holder. The initial interest rate on a hybrid mortgage is often lower than market rates, but it carries the risk that after a certain number of years the interest rate will rise to a point resulting in payments that the mortgage holder will not be able to afford.

Hybrid Security A security that combines features of two or more different investment vehicles. The most common example is a convertible bond, which is a bond that the holder may exchange for stocks. This combines the guaranteed payments of a bond with a stock's potential for equity.

Hybrid Vehicle A motor vehicle that uses both gasoline and electricity to power the engine. In general, the internal combustion engine is used to charge the electric motor or when the electric motor is idle. Hybrid vehicles have become more popular with increased concern for the environment and alternative energy.

Hydrophilic Describing any substance that absorbs or attracts water. This is important in the petroleum industry.

Hydrophobic Describing any substance that repels water. This is important in the petroleum industry.

Hyperinflation A very high rate of inflation, especially sustained over a long period of time. While there is no set numeric definition, it is associated with inflation percentages in the millions and billions. Hyperinflation is almost always caused by poor monetary policy on the part of the government. For example, a government that rapidly increases the money supply without a corresponding growth in GDP often undergoes hyperinflation. This situation often leads to (though it may also be caused by) wider economic instability, and may lead to a lack of confidence in the government. As a result, hyperinflation that persists for a long time may lead to the government issuing a new currency entirely.

Hypothecate To pledge an asset as collateral on a loan without the lender taking possession of the collateral. It especially applies to mortgages: the borrower hypothecates when he/she pledges the house as collateral for payment of the mortgage, or he/she may hypothecate the mortgage in order to borrow against the value of the house. In both situations the borrower retains the house, but the lender has the right to take possession if the borrower does not service the debt. Hypothecation also occurs in trading: a broker will allow an investor to borrow money to purchase securities with those securities as collateral. The investor owns the securities but the broker may take them if the debt is not serviced, or if the value of the securities falls below a certain level. See also: Foreclosure, Margin account.

Hypothecation Agreement An agreement between a borrower and a lender where by the borrower pledges asset as collateral on a loan without the lender taking possession of the collateral. It especially applies to mortgages; the borrower hypothecates when he/she pledges the house as collateral for payment of the mortgage, or he/she may hypothecate the mortgage in order to borrow against the value of the house. In both situations, the borrower retains possession of the house, but the lender has the right to take possession if the borrower does not service the debt. Hypothecation agreements also occur in trading; a broker will allow an investor to borrow money in order to purchase securities with those securities as collateral. The investor owns the securities, but the broker may take them if the debt is not serviced or if the value of the securities falls below a certain level. See also: Foreclosure, Margin account.

Hysteresis In economics, a situation or indicator that persists despite evidence that it should not. For example, the unemployment rate tends to remain high even after GDP growth has resumed, in part because business owners are afraid that growth will turn negative again even if they have no rational reason for believing so. One may think of hysteresis as an economy's collective memory. See also: Lagging indicator.

I 1. On a stock transaction table, a symbol indicating that a dividend was paid after a stock split. **2.** A symbol appearing next to a bond listed on NASDAQ indicating that the bond is a company's third preferred bond. All NASDAQ listings use a four-letter abbreviation; if the letter "I" follows the abbreviation, this indicates that the security being traded is a third preferred bond.

I-9 A form that an employer must file with the U.S. federal government to verify that an employee is eligible to work in the United States. The employee fills out a portion of the form and the employer completes and files it. The form states that the employee has shown appropriate identification and documentation proving his/her legal ability to work. Employers have been required to file the I-9 form since 1986.

I'arah In Islamic law, the lending of a non-fungible item. For example, a person may lend use of a horse to his neighbor. I'arah may last for an indefinite period of time. See also: Ariyah.

Ibahah In Islamic law, the principle that anything is permitted as long it is not specifically prohibited. Ibahah especially applies in economic and commercial matters. That is, one may conduct any business one pleases so long as it does not contradict some definite injunction of the sharia.

Ibbotson & Associates A former research company for financial information. It was established by Professor Roger Ibbotson and was purchased by Morningstar in 2006.

IBD 50 An index of 50 growth stocks as determined by the Investor's Business Daily. Stocks in the index are chosen based on their fundamentals and price growth compared to that of the broader market. An updated index is published each Monday.

IBEX 35 The primary stock index for securities traded on the Madrid Stock Exchange. It tracks large-cap stocks and is weighted for market capitalization. It was established in 1992.

IBM Originally called International Business Machines. A major computer and information technology company. IBM develops software and hardware, provides network hosting, and offers IT consulting services. It is one of the only IT companies to trace its origins back more than 100 years. It was established in New York in 1896. After Coca-Cola, IBM is considered the second-most valuable brand name in the world.

Icarus Economy Informal; an economy that grows at an unsustainably fast pace, ultimately crashing. For example, an economy may grow at a healthy rate due to a bubble in one sector. When that bubble bursts, the economy as a whole suffers. The terms comes from the Greek story of Icarus, who made wings for himself but flew too close to the sun, which caused him to fall.

IC-DISC Interest Charge Domestic International Sales Corporation. An S-corporation, closely-held C-corporation or limited liability company in the United States that exports to non-U.S.-based clients. IC-DISCs are eligible for favorable tax treatment.

Ice Clause A clause in a shipping contract stating what action the ship is required to take in case ice prevents it from reaching its original destination. The ice clause can affect maritime trade.

Iceberg Order An order to buy or sell a large amount of a security in smaller quantities. Iceberg orders are often executed using a computer program that executes each tranche in succession at certain time. Institutional investors may use iceberg orders so observers do not see the sudden increase in interest in a security, which would likely cause a fluctuation in price. The term comes from the observation of a tip of an iceberg above the water, which only reveals a small part of the full iceberg.

Iceland Stock Exchange A stock exchange in Iceland. It was established in 1986 exclusively to trade government bonds. However, it began trading stocks in 1990. Only 11 stocks are listed on the Iceland Stock Exchange; they are relatively illiquid due to the small size of Iceland's economy.

Icelandic Krona The currency of Iceland. It came into existence in 1981 after a revaluation of the first Icelandic krona. It is not a widely traded currency, and, while it is a floating currency, the Central Bank of Iceland manages it closely.

ICMS A value-added tax in Brazil. The abbreviation stands for Imposto sobre circulacao de mercadorias e servicos.

ID A paper verifying a person's identity. Examples of IDs include birth certificates, passports, driver's licenses and government-issued cards. Some IDs may be issued by an organization other than a government, such as a school or workplace, but these IDs ordinarily are not accepted as authoritative.

Ideal Capacity The most output a company can produce with perfect efficiency and no waste (even inevitable waste). Ideal capacity is impossible to attain; assuming ideal capacity in budgeting may result in a company or project going over budget. It is also called maximum capacity.

Ideal Point Model A theory of how a consumer makes purchase decisions. According to the ideal point model, a consumer buys a product based on how closely it fits with the consumer's attitude of how the product "should" be. For example, given two brands of peanut butter with similar labels, prices and so forth, a consumer will buy the brand that conforms (or is thought to conform) most to what the consumer thinks peanut butter should taste like.

Identical Goods Two goods that are alike in all major respects. Identical goods have the same quantity and quality and are produced in the same country. Identical goods have the same value. They may have slight differences in appearance, however, but this does not affect their value. For example, two bricks of 14-carat gold fashioned in Belgium are considered identical goods.

Identical Reciprocity A situation in which foreign companies are allowed to operate in a country, but are subject to the same restrictions as in their home countries. For example, suppose Country A does not allow widget companies to make whatsits, but Country B does. Under identical reciprocity, a widget company based in Country A can open a factory in Country B, but still would not be permitted to make whatsits.

Identical Treatment In law, the concept that all persons deserve equal treatment regardless of circumstances. Identical treatment is almost never applied in practice; for example, minors generally cannot marry without parental consent. It should not be confused with equal treatment.

Identification Problem In econometrics, the difficulty in regressing an equation when too many variables change. For example, if a good's supply changes but demand does not, one can devise an estimation of the demand at a particular price. However, this is difficult if both supply and demand change.

Identified Renewal A renewal of a subscription to a publication in which the renewal card contains a code identifying the subscriber. An identified renewal may be entered more accurately into the publication's system and takes less time than manually entering the subscriber's information all over again.

Identified Transaction Payment sent to a company with an invoice, computer matchcode or other clearly identifying information. Identified transactions help a company keep its records straight: that is, they reduce the chance that the company will think that payment was not made when it in fact was.

Identify Shares To match shares sold with those bought. An investor may buy shares in a stock slowly over a number of years at many different prices. When he/she sells some of those shares, he/she identifies which shares he/she intends to sell. This is done to minimize his/her capital gains tax liability. For example, suppose an investor buys 5,000 shares at $10 per share and 5,000 shares at $20. If this investor later decides to sell 3,000 of her 10,000 shares at $25, she will likely identify the shares as the ones bought at $20. This means that her profit is only $5 per share instead of $15. That means her capital gains taxes will be less than it otherwise would have been.

Identity Theft A crime in which a person pretends to be another person for the purpose of using his/her financial information for personal gain. Identity theft can be fairly basic; for example, one may steal and use a credit card. Often, however, identity theft involves using computer programs to find a person's financial information and conduct large transactions with that person's money. Identity theft is a serious crime, as it can ruin the victim's credit, making it difficult to obtain a loan when one is needed. Many banks and credit card companies provide identity theft protection to reduce a client's liability for identity theft and to minimize its occurrence.

Identity Theft and Assumption Deterrence Act of 1998 Commonly abbreviated ITADA. Legislation in the United States that made it a federal offense to use another person's identifying information to commit a federal, state or local crime. It also authorized the Federal Trade Commission to register complaints of identity theft and all federal law enforcement agencies to investigate and prosecute them. The passage of ITADA marked the first time that identity theft became a crime in itself in the United States.

Identity Thief A person who pretends to be another person for the purpose of using the latter's financial information for personal gain. Identity theft can be fairly basic; for example, one may steal and use a credit card. Often, however, identity thieves use computer programs to find a person's financial information and conduct large transactions with that person's money. Identity theft is a serious crime, as it can ruin the victim's credit, making it difficult to obtain a loan when one is needed. Many banks and credit card companies provide identity theft protection to reduce a client's liability for identity theft and to minimize its occurrence.

IDIN International Development Information Network. A network that maintains information on international development projects related to research and training. It also tracks experts in various fields within international development so relevant organizations can be made aware of them. IDIN is maintained by the Development Research Institute in the Netherlands.

Idiot Card In broadcasting, an informal term for a cue card. This helps actors and/or announcers remember what they are supposed to say in order to ensure a smooth (and enjoyable) broadcast, which pleases viewers and, by extension, advertisers.

Idle Describing a project or asset that is not being used and therefore is not generating revenue. An idle asset usually has a maintenance cost associated with it. Companies therefore attempt not to have idle assets unless demand drops below a certain level.

Idle Capacity The capacity of a company not currently being used. One calculates idle capacity thusly: Idle capacity = Capacity / Utilization * 100% Because idle capacity usually has costs associated with it, companies attempt not to have idle capacity unless the cost of waste (such as unsold products) exceeds the cost of idle capacity.

Idle Funds Money that is not being invested. Idle funds do not make a return and are usually used for spending. Common examples of idle funds include cash and money in checking accounts.

Idle Time Time during which an employee, computer, or other aspect of the company is non-productive due to extenuating circumstances. This results in a loss for the company, because the employee or machine still needs to be paid or paid for. However, idle time is not the fault of anyone within the company. For example, if a patient at a dental office does not keep an appointment, the dental assistant accumulates idle time because she is not cleaning the patient's teeth. On the other hand, if the dental assistant spends an excessive amount of time making personal phone calls from the office, this is not idle time because she could theoretically be working.

IDN GOST 7.67 Latin three-letter geocode for Indonesia. The code is used for transactions to and from Indonesian bank accounts and for international shipping to Indonesia. As with all GOST 7.67 codes, it is used primarily in Cyrillic alphabets.

IDR ISO 4217 code for the Indonesian rupiah. It was first issued in the 1940s during and immediately after World War II. It circulated alongside a specially minted Dutch currency until Indonesia's independence was recognized in 1949. It is a weak currency.

IE 1. ISO 3166-1 alpha-2 code for the Republic of Ireland. This is the code used in international transactions to and from Irish bank accounts. 2. ISO 3166-2 geocode for Ireland. This is used as an international standard for shipping to Ireland. Each subdivision has its own code with the prefix "IE." For example, the code for County Galway is ISO 3166-2:IE-G.

IEA Petroleum Reserves The required oil reserves members of the International Energy Agency (IEA) must maintain as a condition of membership. The IEA is established to prevent or at least reduce energy crises caused by disruptions in the oil market. For that reason, it requires member states to maintain oil reserves containing at least 90 days' worth of the previous year's net import of oil.

IEP ISO 4217 code for the Irish pound. It was introduced in 1928, replacing the British pound sterling, though it was pegged to the sterling at a one-to-one ratio for quite some time. The peg was abandoned in the 1970s when Ireland joined the European Monetary System. The Irish pound was taken out of circulation in 2002 and replaced with the euro.

IFO Business Climate Index A monthly survey of business conditions in Germany. Surveys are sent to 7,000 business leaders each month and respondents are asked about their current positions and their expected outlook over the next six months. It is considered a significant leading indicator for the German economy.

IHS Global Insight A major economic research company. Global Insight provides consulting and advisory services to clients, using macroeconomic models and statistics, along with knowledge of specific industries, to guide its recommendations. It was established in 2001 and is based in Massachusetts.

I-I Page In over-the-counter trading, a computerized display of a customer's buy/sell orders received after the customer has made a block call.

Ijara Wa Iktina A type of capital goods financing compatible with Islamic law. Under the structure, a financial institution purchases capital goods and rents them to a client. The client makes rental payments to a special account; these payments are invested and the client receives the profits. At the end of an agreed-upon period, the client purchases the goods using the rental payments in the special account. This is also used for sharia-compliant mortgages.

Ijarah A type of lease compatible with Islamic law. Under the structure, the owner of a property gives the renter the ability to use the property in exchange for a periodic payment. The owner remains responsible for maintenance. Under an ijarah, the terms of the agreement must be clear and known to both parties.

Iku An ancient Sumerian or Akkadian unit of area approximately equivalent to 3,600 square meters.

IL IL **1.** ISO 3166-1 alpha-2 code for the State of Israel. This is the code used in international transactions to and from Israeli bank accounts. **2.** ISO 3166-2 geocode for Israel. This is used as an international standard for shipping to Israel. Each Israeli district has its own code with the prefix "IL." For example, the code for Jerusalem District is ISO 3166-2:IL-JM. Il **3.** In Turkey, a political subdivision equivalent to a province.

Ilce In Turkey, a political subdivision equivalent to a district or county.

ILEC A local telephone company that was in existence at the time AT&T was broken up into the baby bells.

Illegal Act An act in violation of a law in the jurisdiction in which it is committed. Examples of illegal acts include theft, or the unauthorized taking of property, perjury, or lying under oath, and murder. The criminality of some illegal acts (notably fraud, theft and others) helps to ensure smooth operation of businesses.

Illegal Alien A foreigner not permitted to reside or work in a country. One may be an illegal alien if one overstays a visa, works in violation of one's visa or enters a country illegally in the first place. Illegal aliens may face jail time and/or deportation. Companies that hire illegal aliens also are subject to sanctions. The term is sometimes considered derogatory; some prefer "undocumented worker."

Illegal Contract A contract that violates the law. Most of the time, an illegal contract is not enforceable. In a dispute over an illegal contract, a court generally cannot intervene.

Illegal Dividend A dividend that is calculated in such a way that it violates either the charter of the corporation or applicable laws. Illegal dividends are sometimes declared, but they may not be distributed.

Illegal Income Income from an illegal act. Examples of illegal income include income from theft and drug dealing. Illegal income is taxed in the United States as if it were ordinary income. Interestingly, expenses one incurs in the conduct of an illegal activity (other than drug trafficking) may be tax deductible. For example, the IRS may allow deductions for bribes paid to foreign governments.

Illegal Partnership 1. A partnership formed for the purpose of committing illegal acts. For example, two organized crime groups may form an illegal partnership. **2.** A partnership that does not conform to applicable regulations governing partnerships. For example, a partnership with more than 20 partners is, under most circumstances, illegal.

Illegal Strike A strike in violation of the law. Examples of illegal strikes include those that contravene court orders, do not have authorization from union membership, or are undertaken by certain groups of workers, notably police offers, not permitted to go on strike. Participants in an illegal strike may face legal sanctions.

Illiquid Describing an asset that is difficult to sell because of its expense, lack of interested buyers, or some other reason. Examples of illiquid assets include real estate, stocks with low trading volume, or collectibles. Illiquid assets still have value and, in many cases, very high value but are simply difficult to sell. See also: Liquid.

Illiquid Asset An asset that is difficult to sell because of its expense, lack of interested buyers, or some other reason. Examples of illiquid assets include real estate, stocks with low trading volume, or collectibles. Illiquid assets still have value and, in many cases, very high value, but are simply difficult to sell. See also: Liquid.

Illiquid Market A market in which that is difficult to sell assets because of their expense, lack of interested buyers, or some other reason. Examples of illiquid markets include real estate, some stocks with low trading volume, or collectibles. Assets in illiquid markets still have value and, in many cases, very high value, but are simply difficult to sell. See also: Liquid.

Illustration A graphic design or image. An illustration may be in a book, magazine, advertisement or in any number of other media. An illustration is usually distinguished from a photograph. They frequently are used in marketing, as images may affect purchasing decisions.

Illustrator A person who makes graphic designs or images. An illustrator's creation may be in a book, magazine, advertisement or in any number of other media. An illustrator is usually distinguished from a photographer. They are important in marketing, as images may affect purchasing habits.

ILP ISO 4217 code for the Irish pound. The pound was introduced in 1928, replacing the British pound sterling. However, it was pegged to the sterling at a one-to-one ratio until the peg was abandoned in the 1970s when Ireland joined the European Monetary System. The Irish pound was taken out of circulation in 2002 and replaced with the euro.

ILR ISO 4217 code for the old Israeli sheqel. It was introduced in 1980, replacing the Israeli lira, which was criticized for having a non-Hebrew name. It suffered high inflation throughout its history and was replaced by the new sheqel in 1985.

ILS ISO 4217 representation for the Israeli new sheqel. The ILS replaced the old sheqel in 1985 due to the former currency's high rate of inflation. The new sheqel is a floating currency, and because it is traded on the Merc, it is one of the few currencies for which futures and other derivative contracts are widely available. The new sheqel is a hard currency, indicating consumer confidence on the foreign exchange markets. See also: Currency pair.

IM 1. ISO 3166-1 alpha-2 code for the Isle of Man. This is the code used in international transactions to and from Manx bank accounts. **2.** ISO 3166-2 geocode for the Isle of Man. This is used as an international standard for shipping to the Isle of Man. It should be noted that because the Isle of Man is a British Crown Dependency, it has its own ISO 3166-2 code under the UK entry.

Imarah In the United Arab Emirates, a political subdivision equivalent to an emirate or province.

Imbalance 1. See: Order imbalance. **2.** See: Trade deficit.

Imbalance of Orders The excess of buy orders or sell orders for a given security. That is, an imbalance of orders occurs when more brokers or investors have made more orders of one type such that they cannot be matched to orders of the opposite type. Order imbalance in either direction reduces the liquidity of a security and thus specialists and market makers attempt to keep imbalance at the lowest possible level. Extreme order imbalance may result in the temporary suspension of trade.

ImClone A former publicly-traded company specializing in biotechnology, particularly the development of drugs treating cancer. It is known for the insider trading scandal involving its CEO, Sam Waksal, and television personality Martha Stewart. Both served time in federal prison for attempting (Waksal) or conducting (Stewart) insider trading. Since November 2008, ImClone has been a wholly-owned subsidiary of Eli Lilly and Company. Prior to its acquisition, ImClone was traded on NASDAQ.

Imiphakatsi In Swaziland, a political subdivision roughly equivalent to a municipality.

Immaterial Describing any circumstance or outcome of little to no importance. For example, a price movement in a stock of a single penny one way or another is almost always immaterial to the company's continued operations.

Immediate Annuity An annuity that the annuitant purchases with a lump sum payment and from which he/she begins to receive payments immediately. An annuitant often buys an immediate annuity after he/she has reached retirement age and wishes to receive his/her savings or other money in an organized manner. An immediate annuity may either be fixed or variable; that is, payments may remain constant throughout the life of the annuity (or the annuitant's natural life) or they may change according to the performance of the investments made by the lump sum payment. See also: Deferred annuity.

Immediate Family Close blood relatives, in-laws, and every person one supports financially. FINRA prohibits providing broker-dealer services to members of one's immediate family. In life insurance, the beneficiary of the death benefit is almost always a member of one's immediate family.

Immediate Settlement A situation in which the settlement of a trade occurs in the shortest possible amount of time. Immediate settlement usually describes a settlement date of five days following the trade date, but it may occur sooner. See also: Next day, Regular-Way trade.

Immediate Vesting Describing a stock option or qualified retirement plan to which a person is entitled to the benefits of ownership immediately upon receiving the option or plan, even if he/she no longer works at the company providing it. Vesting usually occurs after an employee has worked at the company for a certain number of years, but in immediate vesting, as the name implies, the person has full benefits immediately. Once a benefit is vested, the benefits of the stock option or plan cannot be revoked.

Immediate-or-Cancel Order An order from a broker to buy or sell a security or derivative, usually in large quantities, in which investors have a short period of time to partially or completely fulfill the order before it is cancelled. An IOC may be considered the opposite of a good 'til cancelled (GTC) order; it differs from a fill-or-kill (FOK) order because an IOC may only be partially filled, while an FOK must be entirely filled or the whole offer is void. An IOC is considered a type of day order, but has a much shorter time frame. See also: All-or-none offering.

Immigration and Customs Enforcement Also called ICE. An agency of the U.S. Federal Government that carries out immigration and customs law. Among other duties, it deports persons in the country illegally and investigates cyber crimes, human trafficking and intellectual property violations. It was established in 2003 with the merger of the U.S. Customs Service and Immigration and Naturalization Services.

Immortale Dei An encyclical letter written by Pope Leo XIII in 1885. It was written in response to controversy in France about whether a Catholic could obey a state not founded on Catholic principles. Leo held that a Catholic does have the obligation to obey such a state and to work within it to promote the common good, regardless of the state's origins. It is one of the foundational documents of modern Catholic teaching on social justice.

iMoneyNet's Money Fund Report A spreadsheet, published weekly, showing data on major, triple-A-rated institutional mutual funds. The report tracks seven- and 30-day yields, changes in assets in six different categories, monthly and annual returns, and other categories. The information is compiled by iMoneyNet, an American brand owned by London-based Informa plc.

IMP A currency code for the Isle of Man pound. It is pegged to the British pound at a one-to-one ratio; the two currencies circulate alongside each other. This code is not recognized by the ISO.

Impact Day The day on which a company makes a new issue or secondary offering of securities available for public trade. More shares outstanding become available on the impact day, which usually decreases the share price.

Impaired Asset An asset with a market value less than its value listed on the company's records, especially when the value is unlikely to recover. The cash flow an impaired asset will generate is less than the difference between its market value and its book value. A company must write down the value of impaired assets once per year. Common impaired assets include accounts receivable, long-term assets, and, especially, good will.

Impaired Capital A situation in which the total value of the capital in a publicly-traded company is less than the par value of its capital stock. Companies with impaired capital have usually taken out too many loans or have made a series of poor investments. Impaired capital may force a company to issue more stocks (for example, in a down round) or to liquidate.

Impaired Credit A credit rating or FICO score that has recently been reduced. A company or individual may have impaired credit if its financial situation changes in such a way that there is a greater likelihood of defaulting on a bond or business or personal loan. Impaired credit makes it more difficult for a company or person to borrow more funds.

Impairment A reduction in a company's working capital as a result of a loss on an investment or a distribution (such as a coupon or dividend) to investors.

Impeachment The act of attempting to remove a public official from office. An impeachment does not necessarily result in removal, since another step is required before the official is forced to leave office. For example, in the United States, the House of Representatives may impeach the president by a majority vote. The case is then passed on for trial to the Senate, which may remove the president with a two-thirds vote.

Imperfect Market 1. See: Market inefficiency. **2.** A market where costs are too high, encouraging producers either to stop producing or to find ways to lower costs. For example, if labor costs are too high in an imperfect market, producers have an incentive to lower salaries, lay off employees, or cease operations altogether.

Implicit Bankruptcy Costs Costs of bankruptcy other than attorney's fees, payments to creditors, and other direct costs. Implicit bankruptcy costs include the revenue one could have made from concentrating the company's energy on sales rather than the bankruptcy, or the increased interest rates the company will have to pay on loans. Implicit bankruptcy costs are difficult to measure and are an example of opportunity cost.

Implicit Cost The opportunity cost of an activity. Implicit costs are what a company or individual could have earned had a different decision been made. For example, suppose an independent consultant has two clients and she spends some time working on the first client's project. The implicit costs are what the consultant would have made had she worked on the second client's project instead. Implicit costs contrast with explicit costs, which are what someone actually spends on an activity. It is also called an indirect cost.

Implicit Tax The cost of an activity that is not collected by the government but may be the result of government policy. For example, if the government is encouraging economic growth and accepting a high inflation rate, one may consider this an implicit tax on personal savings because inflation renders them worth less over time. An implicit tax should not be confused with an indirect tax, which is a different concept altogether. See also: Explict tax.

Implied Call The right of a mortgage borrower to pay off his/her mortgage loan at any time. Unless there are penalties attached in the loan contract, this causes the lender to lose any interest that would have accumulated had the mortgage continued to exist. This right is usually implied in the contract, and is assumed to exist unless the contract states otherwise. Theoretically, it could be exercised if a homeowner accumulated enough cash to pay off the mortgage outright; most often it is exercised when the homeowner re-finances his/her loan.

Implied Rate The interest rate as calculated from the difference between a forward exchange rate and a spot exchange rate.

Implied Repo Rate The rate of return on the short sale of a futures or forward contract on a bond. That is, one may sell a future or forward in which a bond is the underlying asset without owning that bond. One may then buy that bond, collect coupons in the meantime, and deliver the bond when the futures or forward matures. The implied repo rate is the return rate on such a transaction.

Implied Volatility An estimation of the volatility of a stock as calculated by the price of an option on that stock. The factors used in determining a stock's implied volatility are the maturity date, exercise price, and riskless rate of return. One of the most common models used in estimating implied volatility is the Black-Scholes Option Pricing Model.

Implied Volatility Skews The extent to which the implied volatility of an option contract on a given underlying asset with a given expiration date changes with different strike prices.

Import A good produced in a country other than the one in which it is sold. Imports bring money into the producing country and can remove money from the country in which the good is sold. For that reason, many economists believe that a nation's proper balance of trade means more exports are sold than imports bought. Some countries set up various trade barriers against imports, notably import quotas and tariffs. Most governments seek to promote exports, while they have differing positions on imports. See also: Free trade, NAFTA.

Import Absorption In macroeconomics, the aggregate demand for imports in an economy by all economic actors. It is calculated as part of the total absorption.

Import Certificate A proposed system to lower the U.S. trade deficit. Under the system, exporters would be issued import certificates allowing them to import up to the total value they export. Exporters may then sell these certificates to importers, who need them to conduct their business. The concept would maximize the value of imports, allowing it to be no greater than the value of exports. While this is not technically a tariff, it has much the same effect. Import certificates were proposed by Warren Buffett in 2003.

Import Credit A loan a bank makes to a buyer of a good from another country. An import credit is generally a revolving line of credit.

Import Duties Act 1932 Legislation in the United Kingdom that levied a flat, 10% tariff on nearly all imports. It also gave a commission the ability to alter the tariffs; rates therefore soon rose to 15% and 33% on various products. Some imperial dominions were, for a time, exempt from the bill.

Import for Export An import into a country that is refined or otherwise further developed for export to another country. In the United States, imports for export are not necessarily bound by FDA regulations on food, drugs and other items that may enter the country.

Import Quota A protectionist regulation setting a maximum number of imports for a certain good over a given period of time, usually a year. For example, if a country wants to encourage domestic production of automobiles, it might set a limit on how many foreign cars may be brought into the country each year. While import quotas were once a relatively common form of protectionism, the 1995 renegotiation of the General Agreement on Tariffs and Trade put tougher international restrictions on them. Critics allege that import quotas, in addition to depriving the state of tariff revenue, lead to corruption (in the form of bribing customs agents) and smuggling. Many economists therefore believe that import quotas are less efficient than tariffs.

Import Substitution Development Strategy A development strategy whereby a government restricts or forbids the import of industrial material and subsidizes local material. For example, a country may not allow the import of refined oil and instead encourage development of local oil refineries. The ides behind this strategy is to make a less developed country less dependent on international assistance and foreign direct investment until such time as it is can absorb investment more easily and also trade its own products. This development strategy was followed in Latin America and some other regions for most of the mid and late 20th century. It has its theoretical foundations in Keynesian economics, though some analysts have claimed that each nation industrializing after the United Kingdom has followed some form of import substitution.

Imported Inflation A rise in price due to currency appreciation. For example, suppose the United States buys oil from Canada and then the Canadian dollar appreciates relative to the U.S. dollar. This will make Canadian oil more expensive to buy in the United States, which gives the appearance of inflation even though the U.S. dollar has not actually lost any value.

Importer A person or company that receives a good produced in another country. An importer may be the end user of the good or may wish to re-sell it. Sometimes importers buy a good and refine it in order to export to the original (or to a third) country.

Impost 1. See: Tax. **2.** See: Tariff.

Impression A user's view of an online advertisement. Each time a website viewer sees an online ad, this is one impression. The more impressions an ad receives, the more likely it is that a user will click on it. Most online ads are sold by cost per thousand of impressions. See also: CPC.

Imprest Accounting slang; a small amount of money appropriated for a particular purpose. The imprest is periodically replenished. See also: Petty cash.

Improvement The act of adding something to a property such that it increases the property's value. For example, if one builds a house on a piece of land, the land usually becomes more valuable. Thus, the house is considered an improvement.

Impulse Wave Pattern In Elliot Wave Theory, a sudden increase or decrease in a stock's price that coincides with the underlying trend. That is, if the trend is upward, the impulse wave is a sudden spike in price; if the trend is downward, the opposite is the case. Unlike other, similar theories, the Elliott Wave Theory does not apply any particular time frame to its waves.

Imputed Act An illegal act a court considers to have been done with full knowledge of its illegal status, whether or not a person actually knows it is against the law. This concept underlies the idea that ignorance of the law is not a valid excuse.

Imputed Interest Rate The minimum interest rate that the government assumes is paid on a loan, even if the actual interest rate is lower. The U.S. government places an imputed interest rate on some loans to reduce tax avoidance by some organizations that make loans well below market interest rates. The IRS also applies imputed interest on some bonds so that tax is paid every year on the interest, even if the bondholder does not receive coupon payments until maturity.

Imputed Value The value of a company including its opportunity cost and intangible assets.

IN 1. ISO 3166-1 alpha-2 code for the Republic of India. This is the code used in international transactions to and from Indian bank accounts. **2.** ISO 3166-2 geocode for India. This is used as an international standard for shipping to India. All states and Union territories have their own codes with the prefix "IN." For example, the code for the State of West Bengal ISO 3166-2:IN-WB.

In and Out 1. Describing a situation in which one opens and closes a position on a security very quickly. **2.** A clean trade on the over-the-counter market.

In Between In equities, describing a price higher than the bid price but lower than the offer price. More generally, the term may describe a moderately priced good or service.

In Competition Describing a situation where an investor has indicated interest to many different brokers in buying or selling a security. An investor in competition will do business through the broker able to find the best price for the desired trade.

In Kind 1. See: In-kind distribution. **2.** See: In-kind income. **3.** See: Payment in kind bond.

In Pari Delicto In law, describing a situation in which a court rules that two parties to a dispute are equally at fault for the dispute. If a court rules in pari delicto, it refuses to involve itself in the dispute or to award damages or other money to one party or the other. This ruling amounts to a dismissal of a case. See also: Dirty hands.

In Play Describing a company believed to be a target company in a hostile takeover. A company that is in play may receive offers from gray knights or white knights, or simply from investors seeking to profit from speculation on the takeover attempt.

In Rem Describing a lawsuit or other action directed at a property rather than a person. That is, one files a lawsuit in rem if there is a dispute over ownership of property and one wishes the court to determine the real owner. In rem actions are most common in disputes involving land.

In Street Name Describing securities where a brokerage holds legal ownership on behalf of a client. Even though the client is the actual owner, the brokerage holds title to the security because this makes the legalities of transferring the security easier if, and when, it is sold. The brokerage must turn the security over to the client if requested. See also: Beneficial ownership, Safekeeping.

In the Box Informal; describing a statement between two traders stating the delivery has been made.

In the Hole 1. Informal; at a discount. For example, if an investor is trying to sell a stock very quickly, he/she may sell "in the hole," meaning at a deep discount from its market value. One may do this if one needs to raise cash immediately. The term is most common in equities. **2.** Informal; a loss. A company that fails to generate enough revenue to meet its expenses is said to be "in the hole."

In the Middle In equities, describing a price exactly between the current bid and offer.

In the Penalty Box A slang term describing a stock that has dropped in price and is expected to remain low for some time.

In the Pink A slang term describing a financially stable and healthy company or economy.

In the Tank Informal; Describing a security or market in which price(s) are dropping rapidly. The term may refer to drops in a single trading day or over several trading days. When a market goes in the tank, it may trigger a panic sale.

In Touch With Soliciting for a bid. That is, one in touch with an investment is seeking to sell. It is important to note that "in touch with" an investment does not equate to asking but is rather an indication of interest. See also: Looking For.

Inactive Account A brokerage account on which the client makes few or no transactions for a lengthy period of time. As brokers make their profits from fees on transactions, some brokerages levy a special fee on inactive accounts to encourage trading.

Inactive Asset An asset that is rarely used. Examples include back-up power generators and a spare warehouse. Inactive assets can be expensive, but they help ensure the smooth operation of a business or other organization.

Inactive Bond Crowd Traders on the New York Stock Exchange who deal with infrequently traded bonds. Because they deal in inactive bonds, the inactive bond crowd is responsible for only a small portion of the bond trading volume. Prices are usually lower than actively traded bonds because inactive bonds have a wider bid-ask spread. The inactive bond crowed is commonly called the cabinet crowd because they normally issue limit orders that are kept on steel racks called cabinets until the orders are needed. See also: Active Bond Crowd.

Inactive Post A place on the New York Stock Exchange where infrequently traded securities are traded. These securities are usually traded in batches of five or 10, rather than batches of 100. See also: Cabinet crowd, Inactive security.

Inactive Security An infrequently traded bond or stock. Inactive securities are usually traded in small batches, approximately five shares at a time. Inactive securities are fairly illiquid and may be difficult to sell in a downturn. Their prices are also volatile because a small change in demand can greatly affect the price. Inactive securities are sometimes called cabinet securities because they are kept in cabinets on the trading floor until they are needed. See also: Cabinet crowd, Inactive post.

Inactivity Fee A fee a brokerage levies on an account on which the client has made few or no transactions for a lengthy period of time. Because brokers make their profits from fees on transactions, some brokerages levy an inactivity fee to encourage trading.

Inc. A designation indicating that a company or other organization has been incorporated, or has received legal status apart from its owners or members, in the state in which it is based.

Incentive Fee A fee paid to an asset manager or other investment adviser whose investment decisions perform particularly well. When an asset manager makes money for clients, he/she also makes money for the company for which he/she works. These companies offer incentive fees in order to encourage wise (and profitable) investments. Incentive fees usually come out of the portfolios that do well, rather than out of the company's general funds. They are also called performance fees. See also: Bonus, Manager Universe (Benchmark.)

Incestuous Share Dealing The act or practice of two companies buying and selling securities between themselves in order to gain mutually beneficial tax advantages.

Incidental Expenses Minor expenses that an employee incurs in the execution of his/her work. For example, an employee may a pen and a notebook on the way to a work conference. Incidental expenses may be reimbursed; otherwise, they are tax deductible.

Incipient Default An account that is in danger of default. An incipient default may occur when a company's sales are not as strong as expected or when it has an inordinately large amount in illiquid assets. Some loan and bond agreements require a borrower or issuer to inform the lender or bondholder if one is in incipient default. Some banks, especially mortgage providers, likewise encourage persons to inform the bank of an incipient default. Many financial institutions are willing to renegotiate the terms of payment to prevent a default from occurring.

Income The money a person makes from labor, investment, or any other source, especially in the course of a year. Receiving income is the goal of all commerce. It is usually taxed by the government. See also: Income tax.

Income Annuity A fixed or variable annuity that pays a certain monthly or (rarely) annual sum for the term of the annuity. The payments begin as soon as the annuitant buys the annuity. Usually, the annuity's term is the remainder of the annuitant's life, and sometimes the life of his/her surviving spouse, depending on the nature of the particular contract. An income annuity is usually purchased for a lump sum, and is designed to provide a stable income for the annuitant, generally in retirement. See also: Lifetime annuity, Pension.

Income Averaging A former method of spreading out one's tax liability by averaging one's income over 10 years. Income averaging was particularly beneficial to farmers and ranchers, as well as members of other professions with significant variations in annual income. Income averaging was eliminated in President Reagan's Tax Reform Act of 1986.

Income Baskets Several categories of income used for tax purposes. Unless the U.S. Tax Code states otherwise, a loss in one income basket can be used to offset a profit in another income basket. Thus, one only owes taxes on the net income after all, relevant baskets have been offset.

Income Bond A bond in which the issuer is only responsible for making coupon payments when it has sufficient income to do so. Income bonds are most common in reorganization plans in which the issuer is attempting to maintain operations in bankruptcy. An income bond is useful for the issuer because it provides capital quickly. However, it can be disadvantageous for the bondholder because there is little or no guarantee of repayment. As a result, income bonds are relatively rare securities.

Income Deposit Security A security that combines common stock and bonds. That is, when one purchases an IDS, one has effectively purchased a common share and part of a bond issue. This combines the stability of coupon payments with the potential for high returns of common stock. After a certain period of time, the investor may split an IDS into its component parts and sell them separately. An income deposit security is also called an income participating security and an enhanced income security.

Income Dividend In mutual funds, a dividend distributed to shareholders that comes from the dividends or interest on the stocks or bonds represented in the mutual fund. It does not include income from the capital appreciation of the mutual funds.

Income dividends are taxed as ordinary income at each shareholder's marginal tax bracket; they are not taxed as capital gains. See also: Capital gains distribution.

Income Elasticity of Demand A measure of whether a good is considered a necessity or a luxury. It is measured as a ratio of the change in demand for a good to the change in consumer income. Demand for a necessity tends to change slowly with changes in income; that is, as consumers become wealthier, they do not necessarily buy more of a necessity because they already have all they need. On the other hand, demand for luxury increases quickly with increases in income, as consumers buy more of a luxury when they become wealthier.

Income Exclusion Rule An IRS rule stating that certain income is always tax-exempt. Examples of income falling under the income exclusion rule are welfare payments, child support, and coupons from municipal bonds.

Income Fund A portfolio or mutual fund in which the primary goal is the provision of income to shareholders from the securities represented in the fund. That is, the investor or shareholder makes money from the dividends and coupons from the securities in fund, not from higher bond or share prices. This involves investing in securities with lower risk than other portfolios. For example, an income fund will more likely invest in a blue chip with a reliable, but not exciting, outlook instead of a promising start-up. An income fund is most popular with those nearing or in retirement who prefer steady investment income rather than the possibility of becoming rich. See also: Growth fund, Growth and income fund.

Income Immunization Strategies Any of several strategies a company may take in order to guarantee future cash flow. See also: Hedge.

Income Limited Partnership A limited partnership that is intended to produce income for the general partner(s) and limited partner(s), each of which would not be able to produce on his/her own. For example, the general partner may have knowledge of the business but no capital, while the limited partner has capital but no knowledge of the business. A common example of an income limited partnership is an oil & gas limited partnership.

Income Not If-come A catchphrase meaning that a business needs to make money immediately, and should not waste resources on projects with uncertain outcome.

Income Property Property intended to produce income for its owners, especially from rent. Examples of income properties include apartments and office buildings. See also: Passive income.

Income Risk The risk that the yield of a fund investing in short-term debt securities will decrease because of a decline in interest rates. For example, suppose a mutual fund invests in money market securities with maturities of less than a year. If interest rates decline, then the yield on the money market fund will also decline because when the money market securities mature, the returns are reinvested at lower interest rates. Income risk is the same concept as interest rate risk, but the former applies to funds, while the latter pertains to individual debt securities.

Income Share In a dual purpose fund, a share that is entitled to a portion of a firm's ordinary income. Dual purpose funds issue two types of shares: income shares and capital shares, which are entitled to appreciation on the firm's investments. A dual purpose fund has the advantage of allowing shareholders to choose which shares in which to invest (according to their investment goals) without the difficulty of changing investment vehicles. An income share carries lower risk than a capital share.

Income Stock A stock that pays a high dividend compared to other stocks. Income stocks are typically issued by blue chip or other well-established companies that have stable earnings and a solid financial outlook. They are able to pay the high dividends because there is little reason to reinvest earnings in a new product. The price of an income stock is largely dependent on interest rates; when interest rates increase, income stocks decrease, and vice versa.

Income Stream The money a company generates on a regular basis. For example, a company may have a steady income stream from its primary client, and periodic revenue from other, smaller clients. An income stream connotes steady pay. See also: Cash flow.

Income Tax A tax on a person's individual income from wages and salary, gambling winnings, and some other sources. Importantly, capital gains are usually excluded from income taxes and are subject to their own system of taxation. An income tax may be a flat tax, which means that all citizens pay the same percentage of their incomes to the government. Most of the time, however, an income tax refers to a progressive income tax, in which citizens with higher incomes pay higher percentages. For example, one who makes $100,000 per year pays a higher percentage, called a marginal tax rate, than one who makes $25,000. However, it is important to note that the marginal tax rate does not increase for one's entire income, merely each dollar over a certain threshold. Suppose one pays 10% of one's income up to $25,000, and 20% thereafter. The taxpayer making $25,001 does not suddenly have to pay 20% of his/her entire income merely on the one dollar over $25,000. That is, he/she owes 10% of $25,000 (or $2,500) and 20% of the $1 over that (or $0.20). All things being equal, this taxpayer owes $2,500.20 in taxes. See also: Adjusted gross income.

Income Velocity of Money In economics, the number of times one unit of currency is spent over a given period of time. It is indicative of how much economic activity occurs or is possible at a certain level of money supply. The income velocity of money tends to rise and fall concurrently with interest rates. It is calculated thus: Income velocity of money = GDP / money supply (however defined).

Income-Equity Fund A portfolio or mutual fund in which the primary goal is the receipt of dividends on the securities represented therein. That is, the investor or shareholder expects dividends and is less concerned with capital appreciation. This involves investing in companies with lower risk than other portfolios. For example, an income-equity fund will likely invest in a blue-chip company with a reliable, but not exciting, outlook, and will be less interested in a promising start-up with a great outlook. See also: Income fund, Growth and income fund.

Incontestability Clause A provision in some life insurance policies preventing the insurance company from canceling a policy after a certain period of time, usually one or two years. An incontestability clause protects the policyholder from being dropped if he/she develops an illness or health problem that is likely to shorten his/her life, which would be detrimental to the insurance company.

Inconvertibility The state in which a currency may not be exchanged for a foreign currency. A few socialist governments issue inconvertible currencies such as the Cuban peso in order to protect their citizens from perceived capitalist infiltration. Most of the time, however, domestic regulators may deem a foreign currency inconvertible in order to protect local investors from bad investment decisions. For example, regulators may deem a currency going through a period of hyperinflation as inconvertible; that way, investors do not make investments in that currency as they are likely to soon be worthless. See also: Foreign exchange.

Inconvertibility Coverage Insurance that covers losses resulting from the inability to change one currency for another. Inconvertibility is the state in which a currency may not be exchanged for a foreign currency. Inconvertibility coverage reduces the risk associated with this possibility. For example, if one makes a capital gain on an investment denominated in Currency A, but cannot exchange it for Currency B, inconvertibility coverage will provide compensation.

Incorporated Administrative Agency A legal structure for some agencies of the Japanese government. Unlike ministries and similar organizations, incorporated administrative agencies are responsible for the operations, rather than the planning, of government. The Japanese government does not guarantee debt issued by these agencies. Examples of incorporated independent agencies include the Japan Mint and the National Printing Bureau.

Incorporated Joint Venture A joint venture in which the companies involved create a separate corporation and divide its shares between themselves as an equitable way to distribute income from the joint venture.

Incorporation The process by which a business becomes a legal entity separate from its owner(s). Incorporation presents a number of advantages: becoming a separate legal entity means that the business itself makes or loses money, which protects owners from liability for its debts. Likewise, a corporation is taxed on its earningsseparately from its owners, and, in many countries, the corporate tax rates are lower than personal tax rates. The process of incorporation involves writing articles of incorporation and registering them with the appropriate government entity in order to receive a corporate charter, which confers corporate legal status.

Incoterms A series of standardized contracts for international commerce. Incoterms specify the rights and obligations of the buyer and the seller and what each must contribute to ensure that the good is delivered in good order. The most important aspects of incoterms are at what point risk transfers from the seller to the buyer and which is responsible to pay for transportation. Incoterms are agreed upon between the buyer and the seller. They are often expressed as an abbreviation. Common examples include EXW and FOB. See also: International Chamber of Commerce.

Incremental Cash Flows The difference between a company's cash flow and its potential cash flow, should it undertake a certain project. That is, a company nets the potential cash flow from a project it is considering and subtracts its current cash flow in order to calculate the incremental cash flow. This is important in the risk analysis of a potential project; a negative incremental cash flow indicates that the project is likely not worth the risk. A positive incremental cash flow shows that, all other things being equal, the project may be beneficial for the company.

Incremental Cost of Capital The average cost to a company to issue one more unit of debt or equity. The incremental cost of capital varies according to how many more or fewer units a company wishes to issue. See also: Incremental cost.

Incremental Internal Rate of Return When analyzing two investments, one more expensive than the other, the internal rate of return on the difference (increment) in their prices; that is, a measurement of the extra potential return of the more expensive investment. An internal rate of return is an estimate for the potential yield on an investment; calculating the incremental internal rate of return is a tool to help an investor decide whether the added risk of increased expenditure is worth the potential reward. Generally, if the incremental internal rate of return is higher than the minimum acceptable rate of return, the more expensive investment is considered the better one.

Incubator A non-profit or for-profit company that ensures that clients, which are all start-ups, have sufficient resources, technical knowledge, and other tools needed to succeed on their own. Incubator firms may charge a fee for these services, take equity in the company, or in some cases, even provide advice for free. A venture capital firm may or may not provide incubator services.

Incumbency Certificate An official document, issued by a corporation's secretary, listing the names and positions of the corporation's officers. Offices listed on the incumbency certificate usually include the chief executive officer and the chief financial officer. Incumbency certificates are usually available to the public upon request. Some jurisdictions prepare standard incumbency certificate forms that corporate secretaries may fill out.

Incumbent Any officer in a company, especially a large corporation. Incumbents include the CEO, managing director, and members of the board of directors.

Corporations usually must provide an incumbency certificate, which lists the names and positions of the corporation's officers, on demand of any member of the public.

Incurred but not Reported Losses A claim that an insurer has not yet paid. Incurred but not reported losses do not show up in the insurer's expenditures because of the non-payment. However, they do form part of the insurer's liabilities.

Incused In numismatics, describing an image on a coin that is pressed into the background and does not rise above it.

IND GOST 7.67 Latin three-letter geocode for India. The code is used for transactions to and from Indian bank accounts and for international shipping to India. As with all GOST 7.67 codes, it is used primarily in Cyrillic alphabets.

Indemnification The collection of money for damages. For example, indemnification occurs in insurance when the policyholder receives money to compensate for an insured event. Likewise, a company may receive indemnification from an employee, especially a major executive, if the company suffers damages in a lawsuit as a result of the employee's illegal or unethical actions.

Indemnity In law, compensation that one party is required to make to another for some loss, even if the compensating party did not directly cause the loss. For example, if Joe and Bob have a contract whereby Joe will pay for Bob's medical expenses should they arise and Bob is injured, then Joe must pay indemnity even if Joe did not cause the injury. If there is no contract specifying otherwise, however, the obligation to pay indemnity usually falls to the party that caused the loss.

Indemnity Insurance An insurance policy that pays the policyholder a certain amount per day after the insured event occurs. For example, if a policyholder is hospitalized, he/she may make a claim on his/her indemnity insurance policy and receive $150 per day. Thus, indemnity insurance does not cover specific expenses, but rather provides a flat fee. It is useful as a supplement to primary insurance because indemnity insurance may not provide enough to cover the policyholder by itself.

Indenture A contract for a bond. An indenture sets the terms of the bond; for example, it includes the coupon rate, the period until maturity, and whether the bond comes with any special features like convertibility or whether it is callable. All bonds must have an indenture. Indentures are usually summarized in a bond's prospectus.

Independent Agent An insurance agent who sells policies on behalf of several different companies. That is, an independent agent is self-employed and keeps commissions from whatever company for which he/she sells policies. Theoretically, an independent agent can offer objective advice, though if one company offers higher commissions than the others this can create a perverse incentive.

Independent Auditor A CPA who reviews a company's business activities to identify and resolve discrepancies. Independent auditors may investigate potential theft or fraud and ensure compliance with applicable regulations and policies. Importantly, an independent auditor is not employed by the company he/she is investigating. An independent auditor must review a company and provide it with an accountant's letter when it releases financial statements to shareholders. The accountant's letter certifies that the financial statements have been reviewed and are accurate. See also: Internal auditor.

Independent European Program Group Also called the IEPG. An international organization that seeks to maintain and improve the defense industry in Europe. It fosters cooperation between members and with the United States and allies on the other side of the Atlantic. Members include European members of NATO. The IEPG was established in 1976.

Independent Investments Investments an individual or firm makes that are not related to each other. That is, independent investments are intended to achieve different investment goals. One may buy independent investments individually or in groups.

Independent Project A project that is not part of or dependent on any other project. Thus, the funding of an independent project does not depend on another project receiving funding first.

Independent State of Croatia Kuna The currency of Croatia between 1941 and 1945. It replaced the Yugoslav dinar and was pegged to the German reichsmark. After the end of World War II, Croatia moved back to the Yugoslave dinar.

Independent Student A post-secondary student in the United States who is considered to have income sufficient to pay for his/her education without recourse to his/her family. An independent student is not required report parental income on his/her FAFSA when attempting to qualify for federal financial aid.

Independent Variable In technical analysis, a variable whose value is not determined by the value of other variable(s), but rather determines the value of those other variable(s). For example, if a product's price is determined by some equation involving the product's supply and its demand, supply and demand are independent variables because together they determine the product's price. See also: Dependent variable.

Index A statistical measure of the value of a certain portfolio of securities. The portfolio may be for a certain class of security, a certain industry, or may include the most important securities in a given market, among other options. The value of an index increases when the aggregate value of the underlying securities increases, and decreases when the aggregate value decreases. An index may track stocks, bonds, mutual funds, and any other security or investment vehicle, including other indices. An index's value may be weighted; for example, securities with higher prices or greater market capitalization may affect the index's value more than others. One of

the most prominent examples of an index is the Dow Jones Industrial Average, which is weighted for price and tracks 30 stocks important in American markets.

Index Amortizing Note A debt security that is structured to increase its maturity when prevailing interest rates are rising, and shorten it when they are falling. Thus, IANs are structured to protect holders from interest rate risk. See also: Collateralized mortgage obligation.

Index Amortizing Swap An interest rate swap in which the notional principal changes according to the movement of an underlying interest rate. Index amortizing swaps are often associated with collateralized mortgage obligation. The swap is designed to protect the fixed rate receiver from prepayment risk on a CMO, but the protection is not always effective. A common underlying interest rate used in index amortizing swaps is LIBOR.

Index and Option Market A division of the Merc that trades stock index futures and most options. It was established in 1982. See also: IMM.

Index Arbitrage A form of arbitrage in which an investor takes advantage of discrepancies in price between a stock index and a futures contract on that index. Index arbitrage occurs when an arbitrageur takes one position on a stock index (or on the individual stocks underlying the index) while taking an equal but opposite position on a futures contract on the index. He/she is then able to profit from the difference in the price between the two.

Index Fund A mutual fund that is not actively-managed and simply tracks a benchmark index. That is, the investment company managing the mutual fund places the liquidity in securities represented in a certain index. Thus, when that index increases in price, so does the mutual fund, and vice versa. An exchange-traded fund is a prime example of an index fund. Many popular tracker funds track the S&P 500 and other S&P indices. An index fund is less commonly called an index fund. See also: Closet index fund, SPDR.

Index Future A futures contract in which the holder agrees to buy an index (such as the Dow Jones Industrial Average) at a certain price on a stated date in the future. One makes a profit from an index future if the price of the index is above the price of the index future on the date the contract matures. One loses if the price of the index is below the price of the future. Because one cannot physically buy an index, index futures are settled in cash.

Index of Industrial Production An index of the total output from manufacturing, mining, and utility companies. The Federal Reserve Board compiles the industrial production index and publishes it monthly. It is seen as an indicator of macroeconomic trends. A high industrial production index indicates that economic growth and is seen as good for stockholders, especially in industrial sectors. A low industrial production index indicates that industry is falling, which is bad for stockholders, but good for bondholders, as the Fed may use the index as a reason to cut interest rates. Low industrial production also means that there are fewer inflationary pressures on the economy.

Index of Leading Economic Indicators An index of indicators that have, in the past, predicted market downturns. It is published monthly by The Conference Board and is considered an important index of future movements. When the index rises, analysts expect the markets to continue to rise, and when it falls, they anticipate a fall in the markets. The components of the index change from time to time, but they generally include interest rates, price movements on the S&P 500, and the change in money supply. It is important to note that the index is not entirely accurate: it has, in the past, indicated downturns that never actually happened.

Index Option A call or put option contract in which the underlying asset is an index of any sort. For example, in a call, an investor may buy the right to an index on or before the expiration date at a certain strike price. Obviously, one cannot buy or sell a physical index, so the underlying asset is said to be the dollar value of an index at a certain date and time multiplied by $100. Because physical delivery is not possible, when a stock index option is exercised, the delivery is the cash value of the strike price. See also: Exchange-traded fund, Index fund.

Index Swap Any swap where one of the legs is an index of any kind. For example, one may swap an index for a portfolio of bonds, or for anything else. Because it is impossible to actually own an index fund, these swaps are settled in cash. See also: Cash Settlement.

Index Warrant An option on a stock index or other security index. Those who buy and sell index warrants are often hedging against the overall movement of the index that the option tracks. For example, one may take a long position on an index fund, where the investor benefits if the index rises, and simultaneously purchase put index warrants locking in a certain price to sell the index fund if the long position does not rise.

Indexation The practice of connecting a return on an investment to some index. For example, if the return on a pension is linked to the consumer price index, it is said to be indexed to inflation.

Index-Based Offer An offer to buy or sell a security at a floating price based on an index. That is, the price is determined by the value of some index at the time the sale takes place; it is not a set amount.

Indexed Annuity An annuity with an interest rate linked to the performance of some index. Most annuities pay the interest rate stated in the contract, but an indexed annuity pays a minimum interest rate (which may be 0%, but never lower), with the possibility of a higher rate depending on the performance of the relevant index. Each plan uses a different methodology in determining how the higher interest rate is calculated. Common features in its calculation include a participation rate, which determines how much of the annuity is linked to the index, and the rate cap, which sets a maximum interest rate on some plans. Many index annuities use the S&P 500 as their benchmark.

Indexed Currency Option Note Also called an ICON. A debt security in which the borrower's repayment is determined by the exchange rate of two currencies. This allows one to hedge on one's currency speculations.

Indexed Loan A loan with a payment that changes periodically. For example, the payment may increase if the Consumer Price Index rises to a certain level. Likewise, it may fall if the CPI drops. An indexed loan protects against risks such as inflation risk that would reduce the yield for the lender. Indexed loans are most commonly long-term loans as the changing payment reduces the uncertainty attached to any long term investment. See also: Variable-rate loan.

Indexed Stock Option A stock option that may only be exercised if the company outperforms some stated index such as the S&P 500. This provides extra incentive for the employee (who is usually a senior executive) to see to it that the company performs well. Indexed stock options are favored by some ethical investment groups, as well as by some unions, because they reward performance for the company's work rather than the executive's ability to detect an advantageous moment in the market.

India Government Mint An organization in India that issues legal tender coins for general use. It operates four branches throughout the country located in Mumbai, Calcutta, Hyderabad, and Noida. It is controlled by the government of India. .

Indian Head Cent A one-cent piece minted by the United States between 1859 and 1909. It was worth 1/100 of one dollar. It featured Lady Liberty wearing a Native American headdress on the obverse.

Indian Rupee The currency of India. Prior to the independence of India, there were various Indian rupees and other currencies in circulation, many issued by different colonial powers. The modern rupee is descended from the rupee issued by the British. It was pegged to gold for much of its history, finally floating after the end of the Bretton Woods System in 1971.

Indicate To give some sign of a security's or the broader economy's health. An indication may cause a company's stock to rise or fall in price. Signals can indicate both technical and fundamental information. There are three basic types of indicators. A leading indicator occurs before an event or trend takes place and is thought to be predictive. A coincident indicator happens at the same time as the general trend. Finally, a lagging indicator occurs after the trend is well established, and is thought to confirm it.

Indicated Dividend The total dividend a company will pay on its stock in the next 12 month period, assuming each payment is the same as the most recent dividend. Indicated dividends are reported on many stock tables. See also: E.

Indication 1. Before the start of a trading day, a rough quote given so investors and traders know the range in which a stock will begin trading. The indication may be given by officers of the stock exchange or by someone else. **2.** See: Indicator.

Indication of Interest 1. A situation in which a potential buyer tells an underwriter that he/she might wish to buy a portion of a new issue. Before a new issue, underwriters canvass potential investors, who may or may not book an order to buy a portion. Investors are required to be provided with a preliminary prospectus if he/she indicates interest. It is important to note that indications of interest are non-binding because it is illegal to sell a security that has not been issued. See also: Overbooked, Underbooked, Fully Subscribed. **2.** More broadly, any situation in which a potential buyer makes an inquiry of a seller about a security. This shows that the buyer may wish to buy the security.

Indication Pricing Schedule In a currency swap or interest rate swap, the statement of the exchange rate or interest rates at which the counterparties swap. For example, in an interest rate swap, the fixed rate receiver may agree to pay LIBOR + 1% while the floating rate receiver may agree to pay 3.5%, both calculated over some notional amount. These interest rates are recorded in the swap agreement and are often referred to as the indication pricing schedule.

Indicative Quote An FYI quote on a security offered by a market maker. While the quote is not firm and is subject to change, it presents the general range in which the real price is likely to lie.

Indicator A signal of a security's or the broader economy's health. An indicator may cause a company's stock to rise or fall in price. Indicators can be technical or fundamental in nature. There are three basic types of indicator. A leading indicator occurs before an event or trend takes place, and is thought to be predictive. A coincident indicator happens at the same time as the general trend. Finally, a lagging indicator occurs after the trend is well established, and is thought to confirm it. See also: Signal.

Indifference Curve A curve on a graph where the x-axis represents a quantity of one good and the y-axis represents a quantity of a second good where the curve represents the universe of quantities with the same utility for a rational investor. The indifference curve is convex, or roughly U-shaped.

Indirect Convertible A convertible security that may be exchanged for another convertible security. For example, a bond may be exchanged for convertible preferred stock, which then may be exchanged for common stock. An indirect convertible is priced according to the price of the second underlying security. That is, the price of the bond from the example fluctuates according to the price of the common stock, rather than the price of the preferred stock.

Indirect Cost A cost to a business that is not directly related to making a product. For example, market research is an indirect cost because, while it may assist in making decisions about production, it does not affect the production of any one unit.

Another common indirect cost is the purchase of office supplies. Indirect costs are necessary to running a business. See also: Direct cost, Overhead.

Indirect Costs of Financial Distress Revenue or profit that a company could have made, had it not gone bankrupt. Indirect costs of financial distress are lost business that occurs because potential customers do not wish to take the risk of using a company that may not be able to deliver its goods or services. As with other indirect costs, the indirect costs of financial distress are difficult to calculate with certainty.

Indirect Method A measure of a company's cash flow. It is calculated by taking the company's net income and making a series of adjustments based on accounting conventions. The indirect method may be easier to calculate than netting cash inflows and cash outflows since companies required to report their accounting to an independent agency should have all the tools needed to use the indirect method.

Indirect Tax A tax that is shifted to another person or entity. For example, sales taxes are levied on a seller but are paid by buyers; that is, the government expects sellers to pay the sales tax, but they pass the cost on to their customers. An indirect tax differs from a direct tax like a tax on income or assets, which the person or organization on whom they are levied must pay directly. There is disagreement as to whether a corporate tax is a direct tax or indirect tax.

Individual Account An account at a brokerage, bank, company or anywhere that a single person is responsible for debits and credits thereto. An individual account contrasts with a joint account and a partnership account, both of which may have more than one account holder.

Individual Development Account A savings account for persons with lower income. The funds put into an IDA are matched by a public or private organization. One may use the funds in an IDA for educational purposes, starting a business, or buying a first house. IDAs are accompanied by programs for credit improvement and other classes to help account holders move up from poverty and into the middle classes.

Individual Fidelity Bond A bond or insurance policy covering a company in the event that it loses money as the result of theft or fraud by a particular employee. Individual fidelity bonds generally only cover situations in which an employee commits fraud for personal gain; they do not cover situations in which the employee, without support or knowledge of management, falsifies trading so that it makes the company appear healthier than it is. See also: Bonding, Operational Risk, Federal Bonding Program.

Individual Retirement Account An account into which a worker makes contributions up to a certain limit throughout his/her working life, and from which he/she begins to take distributions following retirement. There are two types of IRA. A traditional IRA allows for tax deductible contributions and taxable distributions, while a Roth IRA has non-deductible contributions and tax-free distributions. The limit to annual contributions to an IRA varies each year and is indexed to inflation. IRAs are invested in securities and usually own common stock and certificates of deposit. See also: 401(k).

Individual Retirement Account Rollover The transfer of funds from a retirement account to an IRA. This usually occurs when an account holder takes a new job or otherwise wishes to take advantage of the tax benefits an IRA offers over, say, a 401(k). Most IRA programs only allow one rollover per year; with a Roth IRA, there is an income limit beyond which a rollover is not allowed. An IRA rollover may be accomplished through a direct transfer or by check; however, a check transfer brings a 20% withholding charge, so account holders are advised to make direct transfers. See also: Automatic Rollover.

Individual Retirement Annuity A structure similar to an individual retirement account, with the key difference being that the contributions invested are not actively managed. Individual retirement annuities have the same contribution limits and tax advantages as individual retirement accounts. The annuities are purchased from an insurance company and are invested according to some defined scheme.

Indonesian Rupiah The currency of Indonesia. It was first issued in the 1940s during and immediately after World War II. It circulated alongside a specially minted Dutch currency until Indonesia's independence was recognized in 1949. It is a weak currency.

Inductive Reasoning A way of forming reasonable conclusions by gathering evidence and then forming principles based upon them. For example, if one wishes to find out how a stock will perform, one gathers as much evidence on that stock as possible and makes a conclusion based on that, regardless of one's feelings or suppositions beforehand. The advantage of inductive reasoning is that its evidence offers applicability to "real world" scenarios; however, a disadvantage is that one's evidence may be inaccurate or anecdotal. It is sometimes difficult to know how much evidence is needed to justify coming to a general conclusion. See also: Deductive reasoning, Analogy.

Industrial Describing a company or economy that engages largely or exclusively in the manufacture of products. An industrial company, for example, makes a good, which it then sells either to retailers or directly to consumers. An industrial economy is characterized by having a disproportionate amount of its GDP growth in industrial companies and government agencies. See also: Industrial Revolution.

Industrial Bond A long-term bond issued by a private company intending to construct or make improvements to a factory, plant, or something else industrial.

Industrial Development Board A nonprofit, usually government-owned organization intended to promote the business community in a local area. A municipal or county government may form an industrial development board to design and implement strategies to bring new businesses to that municipality or county. For example, an industrial development board may issue a bond to pay for the construction of an industrial park, which is then marketed to potential businesses locally and nationally.

Industrial Development Revenue Bond A municipal bond in which a local government entity is seeking to raise money for a private company. A municipality issues an IDRB when it wishes to attract a business and the jobs in brings to the area, especially when the business may be otherwise unable to obtain financing for the project.

Industrial Revenue Bond A tax-exempt municipal bond in which a local government entity is seeking to raise money for a private company. It may be used, for example, to build a factory or some other facility on behalf of a private company. A municipality issues an industrial revenue bond when it wishes to attract a business and the jobs in brings to the area, especially when the business may be otherwise unable to obtain financing for the project. The municipality issuing the bond must be able to prove that a public benefit will be derived from the industrial revenue bond in order to qualify for tax-exempt status.

Industrial Revitalization Corporation An agency in Japan that buys loans from distressed small and medium-sized banks and manages their liquidation or restructuring. The IRC may work with a large bank in carrying out its operations. It was established in 2003 as part of a program to fight deflation in Japan.

Industrial Vacation A business trip in an ideal location for vacation. One may stay longer than strictly necessary on an industrial vacation under the guise of tying up loose ends. The advantage of an industrial vacation is that it enables one to enjoy oneself while not having to use any vacation time.

Industrialization Fund for Developing Countries A fund that promotes sustainable, economic growth investing in developing countries in conjunction with Danish companies. It operates under the auspices of the Danish Ministry of Development Cooperation. It was established in 1967.

Industry Allocation The act or practice of including securities in different industries in one's portfolio. This is done to reduce systemic risk. For example, if one includes both Industry A and Industry B stocks in one's portfolio, and most Industry A companies go bankrupt, this will not necessarily affect Industry B stocks. Industry allocation thus increases the possibility of making a profit, or at least avoiding a loss. This may also reduce the expected return on a portfolio, but it depends on the level and type of diversification. In general, the broader the industry allocation, the less risk and the less return. See also: Horizontal diversification, Vertical diversification.

Industry Bet The act of an investor buying or selling stock in an entire industry rather than in only one company in that industry. Investors make industry bets instead of "company bets" because it is thought to be easier to predict an uptrend or downtrend for a set of related stocks rather than any individual stock. See also: Industry diversification.

Industry Consultation Program A body that advises the United States Trade Representative and the Secretary of Commerce on trade policy, particularly in the negotiation of trade agreements with other countries. The Program consists of approximately 500 members, which are industry executives from the private sector. It is also called the Industry Sector Advisory Committee.

Industry Life Cycle The period of time from the introduction of an industry to its decline and stagnation. Different analyses posit different stages of an industry life cycle (usually four to five), but all emphasize that an industry has a beginning, with technological innovation; a period of rapid growth; maturity and consolidation; and finally decline and possibly death. For example, in the video cassette recording (VCR) industry, the mid-1970s were a period of decentralized technological innovation, with VHS and Betamax formats vying for dominance. Later, video cassettes very quickly became a common household item. In the maturity phase, different companies selling VCRs attempted to corner a greater market share for their own (identical) versions of the product. Finally, the industry declined and was eventually supplanted by DVD players. An industry life cycle can be prolonged by several factors, including opening new markets to the product, finding new uses for the same product, or even attaining government subsidies. The concept of an industry life cycles applies most readily to the sale of goods and it is difficult to gauge how it works in a service economy.

Inefficient Market A market where prices do not always reflect available information as accurately as possible. Inefficient markets may result from a lag in information transferring to one place to another, deliberate withholding of information by an insider, or other reasons. Inefficient markets give rise to arbitrage opportunities. Most analysts believe that no market is perfectly efficient and that some inefficiency is inevitable. See also: Efficient Markets Hypothesis.

Inefficient Portfolio A portfolio that provides too low a return for the risk. That is, an inefficient portfolio has taken on so much risk that the return is not worth the effort. In Markowitz portfolio theory, an inefficient portfolio is graphically represented as any portfolio that does not follow the efficient frontier, or the set of portfolios that provide the highest return at each different level of risk.

Infant Industry Argument A policy position stating that new industries developing in a country need government protection. That is, the infant industry argument states that a government must subsidize these industries and/or protect them through tariffs. Proponents of this argument note that several East Asian tigers used this policy following World War II with a great deal of success. Critics maintain that these policies are capital intensive and not all states can afford them. It could also lead to retaliatory moves in countries to which a country seeks to export. See also: Import-substitution industrialization.

Inflation The reduction in the purchasing power of a currency. Inflation has historically occurred when a country prints too much of its currency in too short a period of time. Central banks attempt to control inflation by raising interest rates when necessary, which decreases the amount of money in circulation. Inflation is inevitable whenever wealth is created, but central banks attempt to keep it between 2% and 3% whenever possible. See also: Deflation, Disinflation, Inflation tax.

Inflation Accounting A method of accounting that includes inflation. In inflation accounting, one records price changes that affect the purchasing power of current assets and the value of the company's long-term assets and liabilities. This can provide a more accurate picture of a company's value. It is used to supplement a company's ordinary financial statements. It is less commonly called general price level accounting.

Inflation Premium The higher return that investors demand in exchange for investing in a long-term security where inflation has a greater potential to reduce the real return. The inflation premium is the reason that most yield curves trend upward. Thus, a bond with a maturity of 30 years almost always has a higher coupon rate than one with a maturity of 30 days. Investors expect to make a larger nominal return in part to compensate them for the lower real return that is almost inevitable because of the nature of inflation. See also: inflation risk.

Inflation Rate A measure of how fast a currency loses its value. That is, the inflation rate measures how fast prices for goods and services rise over time, or how much less one unit of currency buys now compared to one unit of currency at a given time in the past. The inflation rate may increase due to massive printing of money, which increases supply in the economy and thus reduces demand. Equally, it may occur because certain important commodities become rarer and thus more expensive. Central banks attempt to control the inflation rate by increasing and decreasing the money supply. The inflation rate is important to fixed-income securities, as the returns on these securities may not keep up with inflation, and thus result in a net loss for the investor. See also: CPI, Deflation.

Inflation Risk The risk that the rate of inflation will exceeds the rate of return on an investment. For example, if the rate of inflation is 5% over a year and the rate of return is 3%, then the investor has effectively taken a loss even though he/she has made a profit in absolute terms. Inflation risk applies especially to fixed-return securities as there is no possibility that the rate of return will increase to surpass inflation. For this reason, some fixed-return securities are inflation-indexed, which means that their nominal returns change, while their real returns stay the same. See also: Treasury Inflation Protected Securities.

Inflation Tax A term used to describe the negative impacts of inflation. That is, holders of cash and other highly liquid investments tend to see their holdings decline in value over time due to the effects of inflation. As a result, persons who keep their money in a savings account may not save as much (in real terms) as those who keep the same amounts of money in IRAs.

Inflation Uncertainty The concept that the future inflation rate is unknowable. Inflation uncertainty is the reason that the yield curve on a bond (usually) trends upward. That is, investors expect extra compensation for accepting the possibility that inflation may outpace the yield on the bond.

Inflationary Gap A situation in which the real GDP (GDP adjusted for inflation) exceeds the potential for what the economy can actually produce. This occurs when demand for products exceeds the labor or other resources required to produce them. Ultimately, this leads to demand-pull inflation.

Inflationary Psychology How increased inflation influences the behavior of economic actors. It is commonly believed that people borrow more during high inflation because they wish to have more cash to buy goods and services in case prices continue to rise. Prices then rise anyway because of the increased cash in circulation and higher demand for goods and services. In other words, inflationary psychology predicts that inflation can become self-perpetuating. See also: Behavior Economics.

Inflation-Indexed Securities A bond or other fixed-rate security with an interest rate that varies according to inflation. An inflation-indexed bond, for example, may pay a fixed coupon plus an additional coupon with the amount adjusted every so often according to some inflation indicator, such as the Consumer Price Index. If these securities are held to maturity, then the investor guarantees that the return will exceed the rate of inflation. Inflation-indexed securities exist to provide a low-risk investment vehicle in which the return is guaranteed not to fall below the rate of inflation. See also: I Bond.

Inflation-Linked Certificates of Deposit A certificate of deposit issued by the U.S. government that protects the holder from inflation. Most CDs, like most fixed dollar obligations, pay a fixed interest rate periodically and mature at par. While this carries low risk, it exposes investors to the possibility that the inflation rate will outpace the interest rate. In order to protect against this, an inflation-index certificate of deposit states its rate of return as the "inflation rate plus" whatever rate of return it would otherwise give. This means that the rate of return will give the real rather than nominal rate. See also: Real Return Bond, TIPS, Inflation-protected annuity.

Inflation-Linked Savings Bond In the United States, a savings bond with an inflation-indexed interest rate. This bond pays a fixed coupon plus an amount adjusted every six months according to the Consumer Price Index. These bonds are sold at face value and pay par upon maturity, which is 30 years after purchase. Series I bonds not held for at least five years are subject to a redemption penalty. Federal taxes on interest are deferred until redemption or maturity. Savings bonds are non-transferrable and must either be held or redeemed.

Inflation-Protected Annuity An annuity that protects the annuitant from inflation. Many annuities pay a fixed rate of return periodically for a fixed period or the life of an annuitant. While this carries low risk, it exposes annuitants to the possibility that the inflation rate will outpace the rate of return. In order to protect against this, an inflation-protected annuity states its rate of return as the "inflation rate plus" whatever rate of return it would otherwise give. This means that the rate of return will give the real rather than nominal rate. Because inflation-protected annuities are safer, they tend to offer lower rates of return than other annuities. See also: Real Return Bond, TIPS, Inflation-linked certificates of deposit.

Inflation-Protected Security A bond that protects the bondholder from inflation. Most bonds pay a fixed coupon rate periodically and mature at par. While this carries low risk, it exposes investors to the possibility that the inflation rate will outpace the interest rate represented on the coupon. In order to protect against this, an inflation-protected security automatically increases its principal according to the inflation rate. Thus, while the coupon rate does not increase, the dollar amount paid does. Because an IPS is so safe, it offers a very low rate of return. See also: Real Return Bond, TIPS.

Inflator A politician or other person who favors policies promoting inflation. For example, a business organization may be an inflator if it believes that easy credit afforded by inflationary policies outweighs the problems of higher prices.

Inflection Point In technical analysis, a high or a low on a chart that comes immediately before a market movement in the opposite direction.

In-Flight Survey A survey of foreigners traveling to and from the United States regarding their perceptions of Americans and the United States. The In-Flight Survey is given while respondents are in transit on an airplane, which leads to very high response rates. It is collected by the International Trade Administration but dissemination is fairly limited. The In-Flight Survey is formally called the Survey of International Air Travelers or the SIAT.

Information Agent An individual or company that is charged with explaining the various transactions of another party to anyone who needs to know.

Information Circular The agenda for a shareholder meeting. The board of directors or other, appropriate body sends the information circular to shareholders in anticipation of the meeting. Possible items on the information circular include board of directors elections, charter amendments, possible mergers, and so forth.

Information Coefficient A measure of the correlation between expected and actual returns. The IC is used internally within a firm to judge the performance of individual financial forecasters. The IC is measured on a scale between 0 to 1, with 1 indicating no difference between expected and actual returns. An analyst with a consistently high IC on his/her predictions will likely receive promotions and bonuses, while one with low information coefficients will likely lose his/her job.

Information Content Effect An increase or decrease in a security's price resulting from some relevant information. For example, a stock my rise in price following a positive earnings report or fall in price if the company's CEO is arrested. To reduce the information content effect, many companies seek to price out the information by hinting or building expectations before the official announcement.

Information Costs Costs that come from due diligence. That is, information costs include everything an individual or company spends when investigating whether a particular investment or activity is prudent and/or likely to be profitable.

Information Disclosure Law Legislation in Japan, passed in 2001, requiring government agencies to disclose information about the money they spend. It also requires agencies to publish their communications to the industries that they regulate in order to promote transparency and discourage inappropriately close relations between the government and the private sector.

Information Ratio In statistics, a measure of expected return to risk as a standard deviation. The information ratio is used in active management to gauge a manager's performance against some benchmark. See also: Manager Universe.

Information Services A company that provides individuals and other companies with research and advisory services. Many information service companies sell advisory letters. Some companies research and discuss broad macroeconomic trends, while others offer specific advice, providing in-depth coverage of one or two stocks. Still other companies provide both kinds of services. Many information service companies also create benchmark indices. Some information service companies are also registered investment advisors.

Information Signaling Hints as to a company's financial state and/or goals given through its actions. For example, a new issue of bonds may be an indication of plans for future expansion of operations and may affect the stock price.

Informationless Trades Trades made without regard to information available on the securities being traded. Informationless trades occur primarily when an investor wishes to change his/her investment goals or simply implement them differently. A common example of an informationless trade is the sale of a stock because the investor may wish to use the proceeds from the sale for other investments, rather than out of any concern about the stock itself.

Information-Motivated Trades Trades that an investor makes when he/she believes that he/she has information showing that the trade will ultimately result in a profit, whether or not the price is immediately advantageous. An investor may use technical analysis, fundamental analysis, or some other form of analysis when making information-motivated trades. However, one may also make trades based on inside information, which is illegal in most circumstances.

Infrastructure The basic system that allows a country or economy to function. Examples of infrastructure include roads, train tracks, telephone lines, and so forth. Infrastructure is often, but not always, provided by the government. Infrastructure must meet a certain minimum standard to allow commerce to occur. For example, one is unlikely to drive to the store if the roads are so muddy that they are impassable. Likewise, the more advanced infrastructure is, the more efficiently an economy functions. For example, the existence of a telephone allows an investor to make orders quickly while also performing other tasks.

Infrastructure Risk The risk of loss due to the possibility that the infrastructure in an area may be insufficient to complete a project or transport a good. For example, there may be no highways or major roads in an area, which will make it difficult or impossible to transport goods to the area in a timely manner. This may result in a loss to the seller. Infrastructure risk is higher in developing countries or in remote areas of developed countries. It is also called transportation risk.

Infrequent Exporter A company that makes between one and 50 export shipments per year. The U.S. Department of Commerce works with infrequent exporters in the United States to sustain and expand their markets internationally.

Ingot A bar of gold. The Federal Reserve, most banks, and some brokerages store gold in ingot form.

Ingress An entrance or, in the context of real estate, the right to enter a property.

Inheritance Any form of property that one receives when a person dies. One may receive an inheritance because the deceased person had so specified in a will, or, if there is no will, one may receive an inheritance simply by being a close relative of the deceased. In most countries, inheritances are taxed if they are valued over a certain amount. See also: Estate.

Inheritance Tax A tax on the money or assets that one inherits from an estate, as opposed to a tax on the estate itself. In the United States, inheritance taxes are levied at the state level and apply to the inheritors rather than the estate of the deceased. Generally speaking, inheritance taxes vary according to the inheritor's relationship with the deceased. For example, a spouse rarely, if ever, is responsible for an inheritance tax. It should not be confused with an estate tax, which is a tax on the estate before it is distributed.

Inheritance Tax Return A tax return that an executor must file on behalf of a decedent's estate to determine the tax liability owed to a state government as an inheritance tax. It should not be confused with the federal estate tax return, which does the same thing for the federal tax liability

Inherited IRA An IRA in which distributions continue after the primary beneficiary's death. For an IRA to be inherited, the primary beneficiary must have already been receiving the required minimum distribution; the distributions either continue or are re-calculated based upon the secondary beneficiary's life expectancy. If the secondary beneficiary is the widow(er) of the primary beneficiary, she/he may roll over the inherited IRA into her/his own IRA without penalty.

In-House 1. The business practice of implementing a certain project, sometimes outside a company's specific expertise, using the company's own staff and resources. **2.** In hiring practices, referring to the promotion of a company worker to a higher position rather than finding someone outside the company to fill the vacancy. See also: Outsourcing.

In-House Processing Float A deposit into a bank account that has not yet cleared. For example, one may deposit a check for $1,000 from an out-of-state bank. The funds may be posted to the account immediately, but they will not become available to the account holder until the issuing bank honors the check and transfers the funds to the receiving bank. This process can take as long as five business days. See also: Check Hold.

In-House Trade A trade that occurs within a brokerage. In an in-house trade, a broker who receives an order from a customer to buy a security does not find an outside seller, but rather fills the order from within the brokerage's own inventory of the security. This may or may not result in the best price for the client, but is almost always profitable for the brokerage.

Initial Delivery In a new issue, the date the security is transferred from the issuer to the first holder. It is also called original delivery. See also: Issue date.

Initial Filing 1. The act of a company registering with the SEC, such as before its initial public offering. **2.** The forms that must be filed in order to conduct a legal inside transaction.

Initial Margin The money or securities an investor keeps in a margin account in order to be able to borrow from a brokerage for short sales or other purposes. The initial margin requirement is kept as collateral until the brokerage calls the margin and the client pays back what is owed. FINRA requires that the initial margin requirement kept must be at least 25% of the amount borrowed, while some brokerages have initial margin requirements of up to 50%.

Initial Public Offering The first price for which a company offers to sell stock in itself when it moves from private ownership to public trade. More generally, it refers to the actual first sale of stock to the public. Small companies looking for a new source of financing offer most IPOs, but large companies who wish to be publicly traded can offer them as well. An IPO is generally a risky investment, because one does not know how much demand will exist for the stock after its initial offering; the risk comes from the uncertainty about the stock's resale value. See also: Publicly-traded company.

Initiate Coverage In technical analysis, to begin tracking the performance of a stock. Initiating coverage involves looking at a stock's past performance in the hope of observing indicators for future performance. When a brokerage or other organization initiates coverage, it usually announces that it is doing so, along with its first assessment. For example, a brokerage may announce that it has initiated coverage of Stock ABC with the recommendation of strong sell.

Injections to the Circular Flow of Incomes Any structure that adds money to the circular flow of incomes, which is a simple model for the flow of money. Under the model, consumers buy goods and services from producers, which causes the producers to make money. The producers then use that money to pay consumers to make their products (for example, in factories). The consumers use that money to buy more goods and services and the cycle continues. Withdrawals from the circular flow include exports (in which money is brought into the economy), investments (in which previously unspent money is spent) and government spending.

In-Kind Distribution 1. The act of giving away property or portions of property rather than selling it and then giving away the proceeds. For example, one may give one's house to an adult child in one's will. **2.** See: Payment-in-Kind.

Inland Bill of Lading A bill of lading (a document in which the parties agree to ship a good to a certain location) that is used for transport by truck, railroad, or basically any form of transport other than a ship or airline. A bill of lading also serves as the receipt upon arrival at the destination.

Inland Revenue A former agency of the British government responsible for the collection of income taxes, VAT and other taxes on goods and services originating in the United Kingdom. It was merged with the Board of Customs and Excise to form HM Revenue and Customs.

In-Line A situation or announcement that meets or nears the expectations of most analysts. For example, a company's earnings are said to be in-line when there are no surprises in the earnings report.

Input Tax In the United Kingdom, the value added tax that a business pays on the products it buys. This contrasts with the output tax, which is the VAT that the business charges customers on what it sells. If the output tax exceeds the input tax, the business must pay the difference to the government. On the other hand, if the input tax exceeds the output, the government refunds the difference to the business.

Inquiry 1. A request in which one investor asks another to make a bid or offer on a security. **2.** An indication of interest by a potential customer or client. Generally speaking, an inquiry follows an advertisement or word-of-mouth information about the company. The number of inquiries can help a company determine the effectiveness of its marketing. Likewise, the number of inquiries relative to the number of actual customers or clients can help the company determine the quality of its products and/or staff.

Inquiry Run A process by which a computer finds and utilizes the information on a file without changing the file itself. This may be used in a direct mail campaign; a computer may do an inquiry run on a mailing list to find and use every fifth name.

INR ISO 4217 code for the Indian rupee. Prior to the independence of India, there were various Indian rupees and other currencies in circulation, many issued by different colonial powers. The modern rupee is descended from the rupee issued by the British. It was pegged to gold for much of its history, finally floating after the end of the Bretton Woods System in 1971.

Insa-Dong A district in Seoul, South Korea. Following World War II, it became known for antique shops, and later as an arts district. It historically has been a popular area for tourists to visit.

Inscribed Stock A stock in which ownership information is recorded. The owner's name may be placed on a certificate, but, increasingly, stocks are recorded electronically to expedite trade. Only the owner of an inscribed stock is entitled to ownership rights. An inscribed stock contrasts with a bearer security.

Inscrutabili An encyclical letter written by Pope Leo XIII in 1878. Among other things, it condemns revolutionary activity and materialism. While the letter blames these and other ills on the abandonment of God, Leo saw social injustice in industrial capitalism and danger in the socialist response to it. As such, this letter forms the basis of much of modern Catholic teaching on social justice.

Insect Exclusion In transportation insurance, the denial of coverage for damage to goods due to insects.

In-Service Withdrawal A withdrawal from a retirement plan made before a certain event occurs, such as an age threshold or departure from a job. Typically, an in-service withdrawal results in a penalty for the account holder. For example, if one makes a withdrawal from a 401(k) before the age of 59 1/2, one must pay an excise tax on the withdrawal. These penalties exist to discourage in-service withdrawals.

Inside Director A member of the board of directors who is either employed by the company or is a major shareholder. Inside directors exist to represent the interests of stakeholders in the company. See also: Outside director.

Inside Market Buying and selling between dealers and/or institutional investors. The inside market provides liquidity to the market and thus has a lower bid-ask spread than other markets. Inside markets may also refer to over-the-counter trading.

Inside Quote The highest price a potential buyer is willing to pay for a security and the lowest price a potential seller is willing to receive. The inside quote is similar to the bid-ask spread, but refers to the prices themselves, rather than the difference between them.

Insider A person who has knowledge of or access to restricted or otherwise nonpublic information about a publicly-traded company. Examples include senior management and shareholders with more than a 10% stake in the company. Under most circumstances, it is a crime for an insider to make trades on the special information he/she possesses. See also: Inside information, Insider trading.

Insider Information Relevant information on a company that has not been released to the public. For example, a person may have access to a company's financial state prior to its official announcement. It is a serious crime to make a trade based on insider information or even to divulge such information to another person without authorization.

Insider Loan A loan in which the borrower is a corporation and the lender is one of its corporate officers, stockholders, or members of the board of directors. With sufficient documentation, an insider loan may be tax deductible; otherwise, it may be classified as paid-in capital and repayment subject to taxation.

Insider Trading A trade one makes because one has relevant information on a company that has not been released to the public. For example, a person may have access to a company's financial state prior to its official announcement, and then buy or sell that company's stock accordingly. Generally speaking, those who engage in insider trading are a company's board of directors, executives, major shareholders, and other investors who have access to non-public information. Insider trading is a serious crime when it is done without proper authorization.

Insider Trading and Securities Fraud Enforcement Act of 1988 In the United States, a 1988 law that significantly increased the penalties associated with insider trading and securities fraud. For example, for insider trading, the Act provided for fines of up to three times the profit an offender made as a result of the inside information. It also provided for cash payments to "whistle-blowers" and civil penalties for managers who, knowing that persons working under them are likely to engage in insider trading, fail to act.

Insider Trading Sanctions Act of 1984 Legislation in the United States that increased criminal and civil penalties for insider trading.

Insolvency Describing a situation in which an individual or firm is unable to service its debts. This occurs when the individual or firm has a little or no cash flow, and may occur due to poor cash management. An insolvent individual or firm often declares bankruptcy, or it may arrive at an understanding with creditors in which it restructures payments.

Inspectorial Power The ability for a regulator to conduct an investigation, especially of possible violations of the Uniform Securities Act. Inspectorial powers include the ability to take statements, issue subpoenas, request warrants from the relevant authorities, and so forth. Inspectorial powers are critical in the enforcement of market and economic laws.

Inspectors of Election In a publicly-traded company, a person or persons appointed to count ballots. They tabulate votes from shareholders who came to the annual meeting or other special meetings, as well as proxies, to determine that ballots were properly cast, and announce the results. Inspectors of election must not have a vested interest in the outcome, and they may not be overruled. See also: Inspector's or Judge's Certificate.

Inspector's or Judge's Certificate A certificate completed after a vote at a stockholders' meeting stating the results. For example, if shareholders are voting for a new member of the board of directors, a judge's certificate states who won and tallies how many votes each candidate received. The certificate is completed by the inspector of election.

Inst 1023 A form published by the IRS stating the instructions for filing Form 1023, which is used to apply for 501(c)3 status.

Inst 1024 A form published by the IRS stating the instructions for filing Form 1024, which various types of non-profits use to apply for tax exempt status.

Inst 1028 A form published by the IRS stating the instructions for filing Form 1028, which farmers' cooperatives use to file for tax exempt status.

Inst 1040 A form published by the IRS stating the instructions for filing Form 1040, which individuals and some corporations use to calculate their tax liability for the year. Inst 1040 also contains instructions for filing various schedules often attached to 1040.

Inst 1040 (General Inst) A form published by the IRS stating the instructions for filing Form 1040, which individuals and some corporations use to calculate their tax liability for the year. Unlike Inst 1040, Inst 1040 (General Inst) does not contain instructions for filing various schedules often attached to 1040.

Inst 1040 (PR) A form published by the IRS stating the instructions for filing Form 1040 (PR), which individuals and some corporations in Puerto Rico use to calculate their tax liability for the year.

Inst 1040 (PR) (Anejo H-PR) A form published by the IRS stating the instructions for filing Form 1040 (PR) (Anejo H-PR), which is used in Puerto Rico to report wages and salaries paid to domestic employees such as maids and butlers.

Inst 1040 (Schedule A) A form published by the IRS stating the instructions for filing Schedule A, which is used to report itemized deductions.

Inst 1040 (Schedule B) A form published by the IRS stating the instructions for filing Schedule B, which is used to report dividend and interest income greater than $400 per year.

Inst 1040 (Schedule C) A form published by the IRS stating the instructions for filing Form 1040 (Schedule C), which is used to report profit or loss from a sole proprietorship or a limited liability company with a single member.

Inst 1040 (Schedule D) A form published by the IRS stating the instructions for filing Schedule D of Form 1040, which is used to report gains and losses from securities and other assets that may be subject to the capital gains tax.

Inst 1040 (Schedule E) A form published by the IRS stating the instructions for filing Form 1040 (Schedule E), which is used to report profits or losses from various types of passive investments.

Inst 1040 (Schedule F) A form published by the IRS stating the instructions for filing Form 1040 (Schedule F), which is used to claim profits or losses from farming or other agricultural activities.

Inst 1040 (Schedule H) A form published by the IRS stating the instructions for filing Form 1040 (Schedule H), which is used to report wages and salaries paid to domestic employees such as maids and butlers.

Inst 1040 (Schedule J) A form published by the IRS stating the instructions for filing Form 1040 (Schedule J), which farmers and fishermen use to average their incomes over the previous three years.

Inst 1040 (Schedule M) A form published by the IRS stating the instructions for filing Form 1040 (Schedule M), which is used to claim the Making Work Pay credit.

Inst 1040 (Schedule R) A form published by the IRS stating the instructions for filing Form 1040 (Schedule R), which is used to claim a tax credit available to the elderly and disabled.

Inst 1040 (Schedule SE) A form published by the IRS explaining how to file Form 1040 (Schedule SE), which is used to calculate the self-employment taxes one owes.

Inst 1040 (Tax Tables) A form published by the IRS stating the tax liability for various incomes and filing statuses. The tables break down incomes in $10, $25, and $50 increments between no taxable income and taxable income of $98,000. It also states the differing liabilities for persons with the same income who file as single, married filing jointly, married filing separately, or head of household.

Inst 1040-A A form published by the IRS stating the instructions for filing Form 1040A, which is a simplified version of the 1040 Form on which a taxpayer lists his/her income. In order to be eligible to use the 1040A, the taxpayer must not itemize deductions, own a business, or exceed a certain amount of income.

Inst 1040-C A form published by the IRS stating the instructions for filing Form 1040-C, which non-resident aliens use to report and pay their tax liabilities upon departure from the United States.

Inst 1040-EZ A form published by the IRS stating the instructions for using Form 1040EZ, which is a simplified version of the 1040 Form on which a taxpayer lists his/her income. In order to be eligible to use the 1040EZ, the taxpayer must not itemize deductions, have any dependents, own a business, or exceed a certain ceiling on regular or interest income. The 1040EZ is the most straightforward tax return because its users have no need for most deductions or credits.

Inst 1040-NR A form published by the IRS stating the instructions for filing Form 1040-NR, which non-resident aliens of the United States file to calculate their income tax liabilities.

Inst 1040-NR-EZ A form published by the IRS stating the instructions for filing Form 1040-NR-EZ, which is a simplified tax return that may be used by some non-resident aliens of the United States.

Inst 1040-SS A form published by the IRS stating the instructions for filing Form 1040-SS, which is a tax return used to pay self-employment tax.

Inst 1040-X A form published by the IRS stating the instructions for filing Form 1040-X, which is used to amend a previously filed Form 1040.

Inst 1041 A form published by the IRS stating the instructions for filing Form 1041, which is used to calculate the tax liability of an estate. Inst 1041 also contains instructions for filing various schedules often attached to 1041.

Inst 1041 (Schedule D) A form published by the IRS stating the instructions for filing Form 1041 (Schedule D), which is used to report the sale of capital assets associated with an estate.

Inst 1041 (Schedule I) A form published by the IRS stating the instructions for filing Form 1041 (Schedule I), which is used to calculate the alternative minimum tax that an estate may owe.

Inst 1041-N A form published by the IRS stating the instructions for filing Form 1041-N, which is used to elect special tax treatment available to an Alaska Native Settlement Trust.

Inst 1042 A form published by the IRS stating the instructions for filing Form 1042, which is used to report withholding of taxes from the U.S. income earned by a foreign person.

Inst 1042-S A form published by the IRS stating the instructions for filing Form 1042-S, which is used to report certain U.S. income of a foreign person that is subject to withholding.

Inst 1045 A form published by the IRS stating the instructions for filing Form 1045, which is used to request a tentative tax refund.

Inst 1065 A form published by the IRS stating the instructions for filing Form 1065, which is used to report the profits, losses, credits and/or deductions of a partnership.

Inst 1065 (Schedule C) A form published by the IRS stating the instructions for filing Form 1065 (Schedule C), which is used to answer certain questions about a partnership pertaining to Form 1065 (Schedule M-3).

Inst 1065 (Schedule D) A form published by the IRS stating the instructions for filing Form 1065 (Schedule D), which a partnership files to report the sale of capital assets, distributions of capital gains, and bad debts unrelated to the business of the partnership.

Inst 1065 (Schedule K-1) A form published by the IRS stating the instructions for filling out Form 1065 (Schedule K-1), which a partner in a partnership uses to state his/her own share of profits, losses, deductions, and credits ascribed to him/her.

Inst 1065 (Schedule M-3) A form published by the IRS stating the instructions for filing Form 1065 (Schedule M-3), which some partnerships use to reconcile their profit and loss statements.

Inst 1065-B A form published by the IRS stating the instructions for filing Form 1065-B, which a large partnership uses to report its profits, losses, deductions, and credits, as well as its partners' shares of the same.

Inst 1065-B (Schedule K-1) A form published by the IRS stating the instructions for filling out Form 1065-B (Schedule K-1), which a partnership uses to declare the share of profits, losses, deductions, and credits ascribed to each partner.

Inst 1066 A form published by the IRS stating the instructions for filing Form 1066, which is used to state the income, losses, deductions and credits applicable to a real estate mortgage investment conduit.

Inst 1097-BTC A form published by the IRS stating the instructions for filing Form 1097-BTC, which bond issuers use to report tax credits available to bondholders

Inst 1098 A form published by the IRS stating the instructions for filing Form 1098, which is used to report interest paid on a mortgage in excess of $600.

Inst 1098-C A form published by the IRS stating the instructions for filling out Form 1098-C, which is used to report the value of the donation of a boat or motor vehicle to charity.

Inst 1098-E and 1098-T A form published by the IRS stating the instructions for filing Form 1098-E and Form 1098-T, which are used to report tax deductible student loan interest and tuition, respectively.

Inst 1099 General Instructions A form published by the IRS stating the instructions for a wide variety of forms, including Form 1098 and Form 5498.

Inst 1099-A and 1099-C A form published by the IRS stating the instructions for filing Form 1099-A and Form 1099-C, which are used to report the acquisition of collateral in lieu of repayment and the cancellation of a debt, respectively.

Inst 1099-B A form published by the IRS stating the instructions for filing Form 1099-B, which is used to state a taxpayer's capital gains and losses from security trades.

Inst 1099-CAP A form published by the IRS stating the instructions for filing Form 1099-CAP, which a corporation uses to report payments to a shareholder if control of the corporation changes hands or if it changes its capital structure.

Inst 1099-DIV A form published by the IRS stating the instructions for filling out Form 1099-DIV, which is used to declare all dividends, interest, and other capital gains paid to a security holder over the tax year.

Inst 1099-G A form published by the IRS stating the instructions for filing Form 1099-G, which government agencies use to report any payments made to an individual.

Inst 1099-H A form published by the IRS stating the instructions for filing Form 1099-H, which an insurer uses to report advance payments of the health care tax credit made by a government entity.

Inst 1099-INT and 1099-OID A form published by the IRS stating the instructions for Form 1099-INT and Form 1099-OID, which are used to report interest received from taxable investment vehicles held at financial institutions and interest paid on discount issues, respectively.

Inst 1099-K A form published by the IRS stating the instructions for filing Form 1099-K, which is used to report the settlement of a debt on a gift card, credit card or similar instrument by a third party.

Inst 1099-LTC A form published by the IRS stating the instructions for filing Form 1099-LTC, which an insurer uses to report accelerated death benefits or long-term care benefits paid to a policyholder on behalf of the insured.

Inst 1099-MISC A form published by the IRS containing the instructions for filing 1099-MISC, which is used to report royalties, lotteries, commissions, golden parachute payments, income earned by an independent contractor, and similar payments.

Inst 1099-PATR A form published by the IRS containing the instructions for filing Form 1099-PATR, which is used to report income from dividends received from a cooperative organization.

Inst 1099-Q A form published by the IRS stating the instructions for filing Form 1099-Q, which is used to report payments made by qualified educational plans.

Inst 1099-R and 5498 A form published by the IRS stating the instructions for filing Form 1099-R and Form 5498, which are used to report payments made by annuities, IRAs, pensions, or similar retirement plans, and contribution information on an individual retirement account, respectively.

Inst 1099-S A form published by the IRS containing the instructions for filing Form 1099-S, which is used to report the revenue from the sale of real estate.

Inst 1099-SA and 5498-SA A form published by the IRS stating the instructions for filing Form 1099-SA and Form 5498-SA, which are used to report payments made by a qualified medical savings plan and contributions made to these plans, respectively.

Inst 1116 A form published by the IRS stating the instructions for filing Form 1116, which is used to claim the foreign tax credit for individuals, trusts, and estates.

Inst 1118 A form published by the IRS stating the instructions for filing Form 1118, which is used to claim the foreign tax credit for corporations.

Inst 1118 (Schedule J) A form published by the IRS stating the instructions for filing Form 1118 (Schedule J), which is used to make certain adjustments to income or losses when claiming the foreign tax credit for a corporation.

Inst 1118 (Schedule K) A form published by the IRS stating the instructions for filing Form 1118 (Schedule K), which is used to reconcile the loss carryover from the current year with the loss carryover from the previous year in claiming the foreign tax credit.

Inst 1120 A form published by the IRS stating the instructions for filing Form 1120, which is the basic corporate tax return in the United States.

Inst 1120 (Schedule D) A form published by the IRS stating the instructions for filing Form 1120 (Schedule D), which a corporation uses to report the sale and dispositions of capital assets, including like-kind exchanges.

Inst 1120 (Schedule M-3) A form published by the IRS stating the instructions for filing Form 1120 (M-3), which is used to reconcile the income or loss of a corporation with total assets greater than $10 million.

Inst 1120 (Schedule O) A form published by the IRS stating the instructions for filing Form 1120 (Schedule O), which a controlled group of corporations uses to report how profits, losses, other things are apportioned out among the members of the group.

Inst 1120 (Schedule PH) A form published by the IRS stating the instructions for filing Form 1120 (Schedule PH), which is used to calculate a corporation's personal holding company tax.

Inst 1120 (Schedule UTP) A form published by the IRS stating the instructions for filing Form 1120 (Schedule UTP), which a corporation uses if it has uncertain tax positions that may affect its tax liability.

Inst 1120-C A form published by the IRS stating the instructions for filing Form 1120-C, which is the tax return for a cooperative association in the United States.

Inst 1120-F A form published by the IRS stating the instructions for filing Form 1120-F, which is the tax return for the U.S.-sourced income of a foreign corporation.

Inst 1120-F (Schedule H) A form published by the IRS stating the instructions for filing Form 1120-F (Schedule H), which foreign corporations use to claim deductions for business expenses.

Inst 1120-F (Schedule I) A form published by the IRS stating the instructions for filing Form 1120-F (Schedule I), which foreign corporations use to report interest expenses on certain income.

Inst 1120-F (Schedule M-3) A form published by the IRS stating the instructions for filing Form 1120 (M-3), which is used to reconcile the income or loss of a foreign corporation with total assets greater than $10 million.

Inst 1120-F (Schedule P) A form published by the IRS stating the instructions for filing Form 1120-F (Schedule P), which a foreign corporation uses to report its partnership interests.

Inst 1120-F (Schedule S) A form published by the IRS stating the instructions for filing Form 1120-F (Schedule S), which foreign corporations use to claim the exclusion of certain income from sea or air transportation from their taxable income.

Inst 1120-F (Schedule V) A form published by the IRS stating the instructions for filing Form 1120-F (Schedule V), which a foreign corporation uses to report certain assets used in transportation (such as ships and airplanes) that are subject to a 4% tax on all U.S.-sourced income derived from those assets.

Inst 1120-FSC A form published by the IRS stating the instructions for filing Form 1120-FSC, which is the tax return used for foreign sales corporations.

Inst 1120-H A form published by the IRS stating the instructions for filing Form 1120-H, which a homeowners' association may file with the IRS to claim certain tax benefits available to it.

Inst 1120-IC-DISC A form published by the IRS stating the instructions for filing Form 1120-IC-DISC, which is a tax return for companies in the United States that export to non-U.S.-based clients.

Inst 1120-L A form published by the IRS stating the instructions for filing Form 1120, which is a tax return for a life insurance company.

Inst 1120-L (Schedule M-3) A form published by the IRS stating the instructions for filing Form 1120-L (Schedule M-3), which is used to reconcile the income or loss of a life insurance company with total assets greater than $10 million.

Inst 1120-ND A form published by the IRS stating the instructions for filing Form 1120-ND, which is the tax return for a nuclear decommissioning fund.

Inst 1120-PC A form published by the IRS stating the instructions for filing Form 1120-PC, which is the tax return for casualty and property insurance companies in the United States.

Inst 1120-PC (Schedule M-3) A form published by the IRS stating the instructions for filing Form 1120-PC (Schedule M-3), which is used to reconcile the income or loss of a casualty and property insurance company with total assets greater than $10 million.

Inst 1120-REIT A form published by the IRS stating the instructions for filing Form 1120-REIT, which is the tax return for a real estate investment trust.

Inst 1120-RIC A form published by the IRS stating the instructions for filing Form 1120-RIC, which is the tax return for a regulated investment company.

Inst 1120-S A form published by the IRS stating the instructions for filing Form 1120-S, which is the tax return for an S-corporation.

Inst 1120-S (Schedule D) A form published by the IRS stating the instructions for filing Form 1120 (Schedule D), which an S-corporation uses to report the sale of capital assets, distributions of capital gains, and bad debts unrelated to the business of the corporation.

Inst 1120-S (Schedule K-1) A form published by the IRS stating the instructions for filing Form 1120 (Schedule K-1), which a shareholder in an S-corporation uses to state his/her own share of profits, losses, deductions, and credits ascribed to him/her.

Inst 1120-S (Schedule M-3) A form published by the IRS stating the instructions for filing Form 1120-S (Schedule M-3), which is used to reconcile the income or loss of an S-corporation with total assets greater than $10 million.

Inst 1120-SF A form published by the IRS stating the instructions for filing Form 1120-SF, which is the tax return for a qualified settlement fund.

Inst 1120-W A form published by the IRS stating the instructions for filing Form 1120-W, which corporations use to pay their estimated taxes.

Inst 1128 A form published by the IRS stating the instructions for filing Form 1128, which a company uses to adopt a tax year other than the calendar year.

Inst 1139 A form published by the IRS stating the instructions for filing Form 1139, which a corporation uses to request a speedy tax refund due to a tax loss carryback or overpayment of taxes due to certain income adjustments.

Inst 2106 A form published by the IRS stating the instructions for filing Form 2106, which is used to claim a tax deduction for expenses that an employee has incurred in the ordinary course of his/her employment, or to claim deductions for business use of the employee's vehicle.

Inst 2210 A form published by the IRS stating the instructions for filing Form 2210, which is used to calculate whether and how much the filer owes as a penalty for underpayment of estimated taxes.

Inst 2210-F A form published by the IRS stating the instructions for filing Form 2210-F, which is used to calculate whether and how much the filer owes as a penalty for underpayment of estimated taxes on income related to fishing or farming.

Inst 2220 A form published by the IRS stating the instructions for filing Form 2220, which is used to calculate whether and how much the filer (always a corporation) owes as a penalty for underpayment of estimated taxes.

Inst 2290 A form published by the IRS stating the instructions for filing Form 2290, which is used to declare and pay taxes owed on vehicles weighing 55,000 pounds or more.

Inst 2441 A form published by the IRS stating the instructions for filing Form 2441, which is used to claim a tax credit for expenses incurred for child care.

Inst 2553 A form published by the IRS stating the instructions for filing Form 2553, which small businesses use in order to be treated as S-corporations for tax purposes.

Inst 2555 A form published by the IRS stating the instructions for filing Form 2555, which is used to claim a foreign earned income exclusion from U.S. taxation of income earned in a foreign country.

Inst 2555-EZ A form published by the IRS stating the instructions for filing Form 2555-EZ, which is used under limited circumstances to claim a foreign earned income exclusion from U.S. taxation of income earned in a foreign country.

Inst 2848 A form published by the IRS stating the instructions for filing Form 2848, which a person uses to give another party the power to represent that person before the IRS.

Inst 3115 A form published by the IRS stating the instructions for filing Form 3115, which is used to apply for a change of accounting method.

Inst 3468 A form published by the IRS stating the instructions for filing Form 3468, which is used to claim a tax credit for making a qualifying investment in renewable or clean energy technology.

Inst 3520 A form published by the IRS stating the instructions for filing Form 3520, which is used to report some transactions with a foreign trust, ownership of a foreign trust, or certain gifts from a foreign person or corporation.

Inst 3520-A A form published by the IRS stating the instructions for filing Form 3520-A, which is an information return on a foreign trust owned by a U.S. person.

Inst 3800 A form published by the IRS stating the instructions for filing Form 3800, which is used to claim any general business credit.

Inst 3921 & 3922 A form published by the IRS stating the instructions for filing Form 3921 (which is used to report the exercise of a stock option) and Form 3922 (which is used to report the exercise of a stock option at a price less than 100% of the stock's market price).

Inst 4136 A form published by the IRS stating the instructions for filing Form 4136, which is used to claim a tax credit for excise taxes paid on automotive fuel.

Inst 4506-A A form published by the IRS stating the instructions for filing Form 4506-A, which is used to request a copy of a tax return filed by a tax exempt political organization.

Inst 4562 A form published by the IRS stating the instructions for filing Form 4562, which is used to claim a tax deduction for the depreciation or amortization of property one owns or to declare that such property should be considered business property under Section 179 of the tax code.

Inst 4626 A form published by the IRS stating the instructions for filing Form 4626, which is used to compute the alternative minimum tax that a corporation owes.

Inst 4684 A form published by the IRS providing the instructions for filing Form 4684, which is used to report losses from theft or casualty. These losses generally are tax deductible.

Inst 4720 A form published by the IRS stating the instructions for filing Form 4720, which tax-exempt charitable organizations file with the IRS to calculate and pay taxes on certain activities and investments that fall outside the organization's charitable purpose and that may result in loss of 501(c)3 status.

Inst 4768 A form published by the IRS stating the instructions for filing Form 4768, which is used to ask for a six-month extension of time to file Form 706, which is the estate tax return, and other forms in the 706 series.

Inst 4797 A form published by the IRS containing the instructions for filing Form 4797, which is used to report the profits (or losses) from the sale or exchange of an asset.

Inst 4952 A form formerly published by the IRS containing the instructions for filing Form 4952, which is used to calculate the interest one spends on investments each year.

Inst 5227 A form published by the IRS stating the instructions for filing Form 5227, which is an information return that a split-interest trust files with the IRS to report its activities.

Inst 5300 A form published by the IRS stating the instructions for filing Form 5300, which is an application filed with the IRS requesting a determination of whether an employee benefit plan qualifies as a defined benefit or defined contribution plan for tax purposes.

Inst 5300 (Schedule Q) A form published by the IRS stating the instructions for filing Form 5227 (Schedule Q), which is filed along with Form 5300 to ask the IRS to consider coverage, minimum participation, and non-discrimination in an employee benefit plan as it determines whether the plan is a defined benefit or defined contribution plan for tax purposes.

Inst 5307 A form published by the IRS stating the instructions for filing Form 5307, which is used to request a determination of whether a master and prototype or volume submitter plan qualifies as a defined benefit or defined contribution plan for tax purposes.

Inst 5310 A form published by the IRS stating the instructions for filing Form 5310, which is used to request a determination letter stating the tax status of a pension, profit-sharing, or deferred compensation plan upon the cancelation of the plan.

Inst 5310-A A form published by the IRS stating the instructions for filing Form 5310-A, which is used to declare the merger, consolidation, transfer of assets, or spin-off of a pension, profit-sharing, or deferred compensation plan.

Inst 5329 A form published by the IRS stating the instructions for filing Form 5329, which is used to report excise taxes related to early or otherwise taxable distributions from an IRA, education savings account, health savings account, or similar structures.

Inst 5330 A form published by the IRS stating the instructions for filing Form 5330, which is used to report and pay taxes assessed for various types of inaccurate filings related to employee benefit plans.

Inst 5405 A form published by the IRS stating the instructions for filing Form 5405, which is used to claim a tax credit for purchasing one's first home (or one's first home in a number of years).

Inst 5471 A form published by the IRS stating the instructions for filing Form 5471, which an individual uses to report certain transactions if he/she is a director, officer, or major shareholder in a foreign corporation.

Inst 5498-ESA A form published by the IRS stating the instructions for filing Form 5498-ESA, which an education savings account files to declare information like the amount each plan participant contributes or rolls over in a year.

Inst 5500 A form published by the IRS stating the instructions for filing Form 5500, which pension funds and other retirement plans file for annual reporting purposes.

Inst 5500-EZ A form published by the IRS stating the instructions for filing Form 5500-EZ, which a pension fund or other retirement plan with only one participant files for annual reporting purposes.

Inst 5500-SF A form published by the IRS stating the instructions for filing Form 5500-SF, which a small pension fund or similar small retirement plan uses for annual reporting purposes.

Inst 5713 A form published by the IRS stating the instructions for filing Form 5713, which companies use to report operations in a country boycotting Israel.

Inst 5735 A form published by the IRS stating the instructions for filing Form 5735, which some corporations may use to claim a tax credit for contributing to the economic development of American Samoa.

Inst 6198 A form published by the IRS stating the instructions for filing Form 6198, which is used to calculate the profit or loss one receives from putting money at risk during the tax year.

Inst 6251 A form published by the IRS stating the instructions for filing Form 6251, which is used to calculate how much alternative minimum tax an individual owes.

Inst 6252 A form published by the IRS containing the instructions for filing Form 6252, which is used to report income in the current year from an installment sale made in a previous year.

Inst 7004 A form published by the IRS stating the instructions for filing Form 7004, which is used to request a five- or six-month extension to file tax returns for business income taxes and certain related taxes.

Inst 706 A form the IRS publishes containing the instructions for a Form 706, which is a tax return one files to claim one's estate tax liability. On a Form 706, one lists the assets, liabilities and exemptions on the estate of a deceased person. The executor of the decedent's estate has the capacity to file a Form 706. The value of an estate necessary for an estate tax to be imposed varies from year to year, but is always higher than $1 million.

Inst 706-A A form published by the IRS containing the instructions for a Form 706-A, which is a tax return that the heir of an estate files if specially valued property that he/she inherited is sold or is no longer used in a permissible fashion. In such cases, the form indicates how much estate tax (if any) the heir owes on the sold property. The form must be filed even if no tax is owed.

Inst 706-D A form the IRS publishes giving the instructions for Form 706-D, which one files to declare certain taxable events related to the business interests of the heir of an estate. When one files a Form 706 to declare an estate tax liability, one may be able to deduct for the portions of one's business owned by heirs. If the heir sells this interest, or some other taxable event occurs, one must file Form 706-D to declare any additional tax liability brought about by the loss of this deduction.

Inst 706-GS(D) A form published by the IRS stating the instructions for a Form 706-GS(D), which one files to assess the tax liability due on a distribution from a generation-skipping trust.

Inst 706-GS(D-1) A form published by the IRS stating the instructions for a Form 706-GS(D-1), which declares a distribution from a generation-skipping trust to the IRS and the beneficiary.

Inst 706-GS(T) A form published by the IRS stating the instructions for a Form 706-GS(T), which one files to assess the tax liability due on the termination of a generation-skipping trust.

Inst 706-NA A form published by the IRS stating the instructions for filing a Form 706-NA, which computes the estate tax liability for non-resident persons who are not U.S. citizens. One must file a Form 706-NA if the gross value of the decedent's estate in the United States exceeds $60,000.

Inst 706-QDT A form published by the IRS stating the instructions for filing a Form 706-QDT, which declares the estate tax liability for distributions from a qualified domestic trust or for the remaining value of the trust after the death of a second spouse.

Inst 709 A form published by the IRS stating the instructions for filing a Form 709, which is used to declare the gift tax liability on transfers exceeding a certain value, as well as on some transfers involving a generation-skipping trust.

Inst 720 A form published by the IRS stating the instructions for filing a Form 720, which is used to report the liability for federal excise taxes, especially those on gasoline and air travel, each quarter.

Inst 720-CS A form published by the IRS stating the instructions for filing a Form 720-CS, which ship, barge, and pipeline owners must file with the IRS to report the liquid material (such as gasoline) that they transport from place to place.

Inst 720-TO A form published by the IRS stating the instructions for filing a Form 720-TO, on which the owner of a terminal where certain liquid material is stored must report the liquid material that has come into and gone out of the terminal.

Inst 8023 A form stating the instructions for filing Form 8023, which a corporation files with the IRS if it is purchased by another corporation and elects to have the purchase treated as a stock (as opposed to a cash or debt) transaction.

Inst 8027 A form published by the IRS stating the instructions for filing Form 8027, which a restaurant or bar files with the IRS to report all tips reported by employees.

Inst 8038 A form published by the IRS stating the instructions for filing Form 8038, which the issuer of a tax-exempt private activity bond files to report information about the issue.

Inst 8038-B A form published by the IRS stating the instructions for filing Form 8038-B, which the issuer of certain taxable state or local bonds files with the IRS in accordance with the American Recovery and Reinvestment Act to receive tax credits or direct payments for issue.

Inst 8038-CP A form published by the IRS stating the instructions for filing Form 8038-CP, which is used to receive reimbursements for coupon payments qualified under the American Recovery and Reinvestment Act and similar legislation.

Inst 8038-G A form published by the IRS stating the instructions for filing Form 8038-G, which is an information return that the issuer of a government tax-exempt bond worth more than $100,000 files with the IRS.

Inst 8038-T A form published by the IRS stating the instructions for filing Form 8038-T, which the issuer of a tax-exempt bond uses to rebate to the U.S. Treasury arbitrage profits from the investment of bond proceeds, and to make similar payments.

Inst 8038-TC A form published by the IRS stating the instructions for filing Form 8038-TC, which the issuer of a qualified bond uses to claim a tax credit for the coupons.

Inst 8082 A form published by the IRS stating the instructions for filing Form 8082, which is used to declare that one wishes to treat an asset or income differently from how it was reported on Schedule K-1.

Inst 8233 A form published by the IRS stating the instructions for filing Form 8233, which a non-resident alien uses to claim exemption from withholding for certain personal services.

Inst 8275 A form published by the IRS stating the instructions for filing Form 8275, which is used to report inaccuracies previously declared on a tax return, except those made in violation of U.S. Treasury regulation.

Inst 8275-R A form published by the IRS stating the instructions for filing Form 8275-R, which is used to report declarations on a tax return made in violation of U.S. Treasury regulation.

Inst 8283 A form published by the IRS stating the instructions for filing Form 8283, which is used to report non-cash contributions to charitable organizations, such as clothes or vehicles, if the combined value of these contributions exceeds $500.

Inst 8288 A form published by the IRS stating the instructions for filing Form 8288, which is used on matters related to the withholding of taxation from the proceeds of the sale of real estate in the United States in which the seller is a non-resident alien or other non-U.S. person.

Inst 8379 A form published by the IRS stating the instructions for filing Form 8379, which one files with the IRS to claim an overpayment of a back tax liability owed by his/her spouse.

Inst 843 A form a parent company files with the IRS to report all affiliated companies that are bound to it. Form 851 also states the tax credits and estimated tax payments that the affiliated companies made over the course of the year.

Inst 8582 A form published by the IRS containing the instructions for filing Form 8582, which is used to report passive activity losses.

Inst 8824 A form published by the IRS containing the instructions for filing Form 8824, which is used to report like-kind exchanges.

Inst 8829 A form published by the IRS containing the instructions for filing Form 8829, which is used to calculate allowable expenses for the business use of one's home.

Inst 8941 A form published by the IRS stating the instructions for filing Form 8941, which a small business uses to claim the health care tax credit.

Inst 926 A form published by the IRS stating the instructions for Form 926, which one uses to report the sale or other transfer of tangible or intangible property to a non-U.S. person, that is, a foreign person or corporation.

Inst 940 A form published by the IRS stating the instructions for a Form 940, which companies file to pay unemployment insurance taxes on their employees.

Inst 941 A form published by the IRS stating the instructions for filing Form 941, which a company uses to declare the income and FICA taxes it withholds from its employees each quarter.

Inst 941 (PR) A form published by the IRS stating the instructions for filing Form 941, which a company uses to declare income and FICA taxes it withholds from its employees each quarter.

Inst 941 (Schedule B) A form published by the IRS stating the instructions for Form 941 (Schedule B), which a company files to list its payroll tax liability for each day of a quarter. A company is required to file Form 941 if it is a semi-weekly depositor with more than $50,000 in payroll taxes during the lookback period or more than $100,000 on any day in the present or most recent calendar year.

Inst 941 (Schedule D) A form published by the IRS stating the instructions for filing a Form 941 (Schedule D), which a company uses if the payroll tax liabilities it files for its employees on Form 941 differ from what is reported on each employee's W-2 due to a merger or acquisition.

Inst 941-SS A form published by the IRS explaining how to file Form 941-SS, which companies use in American Samoa, Guam, Mariana Islands and the U.S. Virgin Islands to declare each quarter the income and FICA taxes they pay for their employees.

Inst 941-X A form published by the IRS explaining how to file Form 941-X, which a company uses to amend a previously filed Form 941.

Inst 943 A form published by the IRS stating the instructions for filing Form 943, which an agricultural employer files with the IRS each year to report income and FICA taxes it withholds from its employees.

Inst 943 (PR) A form published by the IRS stating the instructions for filing Form 943 (PR), which an agricultural employer in Puerto Rico files with the IRS each year to report income and FICA taxes it withholds from its employees.

Inst 943-X A form published by the IRS stating the instructions for filing Form 943-X, which an agricultural employer uses to amend a previously filed Form 943.

Inst 943-X (PR) A form published by the IRS stating the instructions for filing Form 943-X (PR), which an agricultural employer in Puerto Rico uses to amend a previously filed Form 943 (PR).

Inst 944 (PR) A form published by the IRS stating the instructions for filing Form 944 (PR), which small companies in Puerto Rico use to declare income and FICA taxes on their employees each year.

Inst 944-SS A form published by the IRS stating the instructions for filing Form 944-SS, which small companies in Samoa, Guam, Northern Mariana Islands or the U.S. Virgin Islands use to declare income and FICA taxes on their employees each year.

Inst 944-X A form published by the IRS stating the instructions for filing Form 944-X, which is used to amend a previously filed Form 944.

Inst 944-X (PR) A form published by the IRS stating the instructions for filing Form 944-X (PR), which is used to amend a previously filed Form 944 (PR).

Inst 945 A form published by the IRS stating the instructions for filing Form 945, which a company uses to declare the taxes withheld on payments made to an employee other than wages and salary.

Inst 945-X A form published by the IRS containing the instructions for filing Form 945-X, which is used to amend a previously filed Form 945.

Inst 990 A form published by the IRS stating instructions for filing Form 990, which tax exempt organizations use to report income and losses.

Inst 990 (Schedule D) A form published by the IRS stating instructions for filing Form 990 (Schedule D), on which tax exempt organizations report information on endowment funds, donor advised funds and similar structures.

Inst 990 (Schedule F) A form published by the IRS stating instructions for filing Form 990 (Schedule F), on which tax exempt organizations report all financial information on activities outside the United States

Inst 990 (Schedule H) A form published by the IRS stating the instructions required for filing Form 990 (Schedule H), which is used to report financial activities regarding any hospitals the filer operates.

Inst 990 (Schedule J) A form published by the IRS stating how to file Form 990 (Schedule J), which is used to report compensation that a non-profit organization pays to members of the board of directors, certain corporate officers, the persons with the highest salaries, and key employees.

Inst 990 (Schedule K) A form published by the IRS stating how to file Form 990 (Schedule K), which is used to report outstanding liabilities from tax exempt bonds that the organization issues.

Inst 990 (Schedule R) A form published by the IRS stating the instructions for filing Form 990 (Schedule R), which is used to provide information on a non-profit's transactions with disregarded organizations and other organizations related to it.

Inst 990 or 990-EZ (Schedule A) A form published by the IRS stating the instructions for filing Form 990 or 990-EZ (Schedule A), which states the reason why the filer is a non-profit organization and the source of its revenue.

Inst 990 or 990-EZ (Schedule C) A form published by the IRS stating the instructions for filing Form 990 or 990-EZ (Schedule C), which certain non-profit organizations use to report any money they spend on political activities.

Inst 990 or 990-EZ (Schedule G) A form published by the IRS stating the instructions for filing Form 990 or 990-EZ (Schedule G), which a non-profit organization uses to report information on its fundraising activities, including those involving gaming.

Inst 990 or 990-EZ (Schedule L) A form published by the IRS stating the instructions for filing Form 990 or 990-EZ (Schedule L), which is used to report excess benefit transactions with disqualified persons.

Inst 990-BL A form published by the IRS containing the instructions for filing Form 990-BL, which black lung benefit organizations use to report their income, expenses, and other financial information.

Inst 990-EZ A form published by the IRS stating the instructions for filing Form 990-EZ, which some non-profits use in lieu of Form 990 to report their income, expenses, and other financial information.

Inst 990-PF A form published by the IRS stating the instructions for filing Form 990-PF, which private foundations use to report the tax owed on their investment income, as well as to report grants and other charitable distributions made during the tax year.

Inst 990-T A form published by the IRS stating the instructions for filing Form 990-T, which tax exempt organizations use to report their unrelated business income and to calculate the tax owed on that income.

Installment A payment made as part of a series of payments on the same good, service, or obligation. For example, if one buys expensive consumer goods (such as furniture), one may agree with the seller to pay in installments until the furniture is paid in full. Likewise, one also makes installment payments on loans. Installments may or may not require interest to be paid.

Installment Debt A debt one repays with a series of payments made regularly over time. For example, if one buys an expensive consumer good, such as furniture, one may agree with the seller to pay a certain amount each month for one year when the furniture will be paid in full. Installment debt usually carries interest.

Installment Loan A loan that is repaid in a certain number of payments in the same amount. Interest is computed in advance and is rolled into the payments. For example, a mortgage amortized over 30 years is an installment loan because the payments are equal to each other and the loan is repaid after the 30 years have expired.

Installment Method In accounting, a way to recognize revenue from the sale of an asset in which one records revenue as installment payments are made. For example, when one sells an expensive asset, such as land, he/she may record the profit (or loss) on that sale as installment payments are received, rather than all at once. This spreads out the recognition of revenue over a longer period of time, possibly several years. This can reduce one's capital gains tax liability.

Installment Payments A series of payments that a buyer makes instead of a lump sum to compensate the seller. Installment payments often, but do not always, include interest to pay the seller for accepting the credit risk that the buyer will not make payments in a timely manner. Installment payments can have tax advantages for the seller. Most importantly, they make expensive goods and services available to buyers who would not otherwise be able to afford them. See also: Credit sale.

Installment Refund Annuity An annuity with a provision stating that if the annuitant does not receive payments at least equal to the amount he/she paid as contributions, then some beneficiary (such as a relative of the annuitant) receives the difference in monthly installments over a period of time. This reduces the risk to the annuitant that the annuity will prove to be a bad investment. However, it does not protect the insurance company providing the annuity. See also: Cash Refund Annuity.

Installment Sale A sale in which the buyer makes a series of payments instead of a lump sum in order to compensate the seller. The payments in an installment sale often, but do not always, include interest to pay the seller for accepting the credit risk that the buyer will not make payments in a timely manner. An installment sale can have tax advantages for the seller. See also: Credit sale.

Institute for Fiscal and Monetary Policy A research institution that operates under the Japanese Ministry of Finance. It advises the ministry on matters of policy.

Institute for Supply Management An organization in the United States that conducts research and educational activities regarding supply management and the professionals involved with it. It publishes a monthly magazine and is well known for collecting and distributing the Purchasing Managers Index each month. It was established in 1915.

Institute of Chartered Accountants in England and Wales A professional organization for accountants. In order to become a member, one must pass a series of exams and work in the accounting field for at least 450 days. The Institute sets ethical standards and some professional standards. It was established in 1880.

Institute of Chartered Accountants in Scotland A professional organization for accountants. In order to become a member, one must possess a university degree and complete a three-year training program through a sponsoring employer The Institute sets ethical standards and some professional standards. It was established in 1854.

Institute of Chartered Financial Analysts A professional organization of financial analysts in India. It trains students and executives in financial analysis. It was established in 1984.

Institute of Chartered Secretaries and Administrators Also called ICSA. An organization for company secretaries, or management professionals responsible for ensuring that corporate decisions are carried out. It sponsors certification programs for students and promotes good corporate governance for both for-profit companies and non-profits. It is based in London and has representation in a number of Commonwealth countries. The ICSA was established in 1891.

Institute of Electrical and Electronics Engineers Also called the IEEE. An international, professional organization for individuals involved in electrical technology. IEEE publishes more than 100 peer-reviewed periodicals, provides continuing education for members and sets scientific standards. It was established in 1963 through the merger of the Institute of Radio Engineers and the American Institute of Electrical Engineers.

Institute of Internal Auditors An international trade association for internal auditors. In addition to offering the Certified Internal Auditor certificate, it conducts research, sets professional ethical standards and provides educational and networking opportunities for members. It was established in 1941 and is based in Florida.

Institute of London Underwriters A group of insurance companies in the United Kingdom that pool risk for marine and air insurance. It draws up standardized contracts for members and settles claims. While the Institute is not part of Lloyd's, the two organizations work together for common goals. It was established in the late 19th century.

Institute of Management Accountants A professional organization in the United States for management accountants and financial managers. These professionals specialize in the study of how managers use accounting and/or financial information in current or future business decisions. Unlike other accountants, they primarily report to the internal management of a company, rather than to an external body like shareholders or tax collection agencies. The Institute establishes common practices and ethical standards for these professionals, and awards the Certified Management Accountant designation upon the successful completion of an examination testing one's knowledge in four subjects: business analysis, management accounting and reporting, strategic management, and business applications.

Institute of Social Research A think tank that investigates the effect of the economy on individual consumers. Aspects of research include poverty, political and sexual behavior and even cognition. It was established in the 1940s and is based at the University of Michigan.

Institutional Account A brokerage account of a registered investment company, insurance company, pension fund or any similar organization. Some regulators, such as the MSRB, apply the term more generally to include banks and individuals investing an unusually large amount of money. Institutional accounts often receive preferential treatment from their brokers, such as lower commissions.

Institutional Broker A broker whose clients are predominantly or exclusively large, institutional investors. Examples of an institutional broker's clients include hedge funds and banks. Given the sheer size of the trades in which institutional investors engage, an institutional broker may specialize in these types of investors because the commissions, while small, add up to a significant amount.. See also: Block trade.

Institutional Brokers' Estimate System A database established by the Lynch, Jones, and Ryan brokerage that compiles different analysts' at different brokerages forecasts on future earnings for many different publicly-traded companies. The IBES allows users to look at the high, low, and average predictions as well as see individual analysts' predictions. It is designed to assist in making investment decisions, especially to provide second opinions on one's own investment advisor's recommendations.

Institutional Fund A mutual fund that offers low fees and an exceptionally high minimum investment. An institutional fund markets itself to institutional investors such as pension funds and hedge funds, as well as high net-worth individuals.

Institutional Investor A business devoted to holding and managing assets, either for clients or for itself. Examples include mutual funds, banks, holding companies, and brokerages. Institutional investors are important to placing new issues of stocks and bonds, as they can afford to buy more of an issue than individual investors.

Institutional Ownership A situation in which a company's majority shareholder or sole owner is an institutional investor such as a mutual fund, insurance company, closed-end investment company, or something else. For example, Acme Brick is under the institutional ownership of Berkshire Hathaway which is an insurance and investment company. See also: Wholly Owned Subsidiary.

Institutional Shareholder A business, such as a mutual fund, bank or insurance company, that holds shares in a publicly-traded company. Institutional shareholders are important to placing new issues of stocks and bonds, as they can afford to buy more of an issue than individual investors. If an institutional shareholder owns a majority of the shares in a company, the company is said to be under institutional ownership.

Institutional Shareholder Services A company that institutional investors use as their proxy in the annual meetings of publicly-traded companies in which institutional investors have shares. It advises institutional investors how to vote in these meetings and casts votes on their behalf. It provides these services in exchange for a fee. See also: Proxy firm.

Institutionalization A situation in which institutional investors come to provide the vast majority of liquidity in the market, to the point that it is difficult for individual investors to participate.

Instrument 1. See: Security. **2.** Any tool that a government may use to influence the economy. Common instruments include setting prevailing interest rates, raising or lowering taxes, and awarding contracts to the private sector to stimulate demand for goods and services. **3.** See: Contract.

Instrumentality 1. An agency that issues debt obligations guaranteed by the full-faith-and-credit of the U.S. government even though the agency is not part of the government itself. See also: Indirect government obligation. **2.** The tools or means by which an organization or subset of that organization accomplishes its projects and goals.

Instruments of International Traffic Transportation vehicles and other tools used to bring goods into the United States. Instruments of international traffic include cargo vans, pallets, shipping tanks and textile fabric cores. Instruments of international traffic may be released into the U.S. without paying a tariff, subject to the posting of a customs bond.

In-Substance Debt Defeasance A provision in a loan removing it from a balance sheet if cash or a portfolio is set aside for debt service. Usually, defeasance occurs when a borrower owns a portfolio of Treasury securities whose coupons are used to service a debt. When the borrower has set aside sufficient assets to cover the debt, the debt does not need to be recorded on a balance sheet.

Insufficient Funds A situation in which one does not have enough deposited in a bank account to cover all checks and/or electronic withdrawals. For example, if Bob writes Joe a check for $200, but there is only $175 in Bob's account, Bob has insufficient funds in his bank account and the bank likely will refuse to transfer the funds to Joe's account. However, some banks make requested transfers with insufficient funds but assess an overdraft fee on the account holder. This is especially true with electronic transactions. See also: Bounce.

Insurable Interest The ability to derive profit or another benefit from an object, business or something else. For example, dentists have an insurable interest in their dental equipment because without it they would be unable to make a living. As the name implies, one may purchase an insurance policy to provide coverage for the loss of an insurable interest.

Insurance A contract between a client and a provider whereby the client makes monthly payments, called premiums, in exchange for the promise that the provider will pay for certain expenses. For example, if one purchases health insurance, the provider will pay for (some of) the client's medical bills, if any. Likewise in life insurance, the provider will give the client's family a certain amount of money when the client dies. The insurance company spreads the risk of any one expense by pooling the premiums from many clients. See also: Takaful.

Insurance Advertising Any advertisement intended to encourage persons or companies to buy insurance. It may accomplish this by directly marketing insurance products (for example over the television), by encouraging a potential customer to become more willing to receive sales calls (through direct mail, for example) or any number of other methods.

Insurance Agent A person licensed by a state and generally employed by an insurance company to sell insurance policies on the company's behalf. The agent generally receives a commission for this service. He/she attempts to extract the maximum value for the insurance company in all his/her dealings. An insurance agent should not be confused with an insurance broker or an insurance underwriter.

Insurance Broker A person who sells insurance policies. An insurance broker does not work for an insurance company, but rather represents the buyer of the policy to ensure that he/she receives a fair deal.

Insurance Claim A document or request filed by a policyholder stating that an insured event has occurred and that the insurance company should provide coverage. For example, if a person has health insurance and breaks his leg, he must file an insurance claim in order for the insurance company to pay for some or all of the medical expenses. Depending on the policy, a third party may or may not be able to file an insurance claim on behalf of a policyholder.

Insurance Company A company, which may be for-profit, non-profit or government-owned, that sells the promise to pay for certain expenses in exchange for a regular fee, called a premium. For example, if one purchases health insurance, the insurance company will pay for (some of) the client's medical bills, if any. Likewise, in life insurance, the company will give the client's beneficiary a certain amount of money when the client dies. The insurance company covers its expenses and/or makes a profit by spreading the risk of any one client over the pool of premiums from many clients.

Insurance Coverage The specific insured events for which an insurance company will pay a benefit. For example, a life insurance policy provides coverage in the event of death. Likewise, a health insurance policy provides money in the event of illness. In general, an insurance policy outlines what it covers and the benefits it provides under different circumstances.

Insurance Dividend An annual fee an insurance company pays to whole life policyholders. The amount of the dividend is determined by the company's board of directors and is not guaranteed. This allows whole life policyholders access to at least part of their benefit before death. The insurance dividend can be taken in cash, but is almost always applied as a discount against future premium payments. This is a distinct advantage of whole life policies, though some analysts believe that insurance dividends do not make up for the expense of whole life insurance compared to term insurance.

Insurance Fraud Prevention Act Legislation in the United States criminalizing insurance fraud at the federal level. The Act prohibits persons and companies from embezzling or stealing premiums or other funds due to an insurance company. Many states also have their own insurance fraud protection acts.

Insurance Guaranty Act Legislation in several American states establishing a fund to protect policyholders and pensioners from the default of an insurance company. That is, if an insurance company is licensed to operate in a given state, policyholders within that state are protected because, if the company defaults on its payments, the fund created by the insurance guaranty act will pay the policyholder instead. See also: State guaranty fund.

Insurance Policy The contents of an insurance contract. The policy describes the specific types of coverage (life, health, etc.), the restrictions that apply, and the applicable deductibles and premiums. Only the insurer makes legally enforceable promises in an insurance policy: the insurance company cannot legally compel the insured person to pay his/her premiums, but the insured person can sue to compel the insurer to provide coverage if it does not do so. All insurance policies, however, include a provision allowing the insurer to refuse coverage if the insured person does not pay the premiums.

Insurance Premium A payment that a policyholder makes, usually monthly, in order to be covered by an insurance policy.

Insurance Premium Tax A tax paid by insurers and insurance brokers in the United Kingdom. Insurers and brokers must pay the tax on all policies other than long-term insurance, such as life insurance, reinsurance and export finance.

Insurance Risk The likelihood that an insured event will occur, requiring the insurer to pay a claim. For example, in life insurance, the insurance risk is the possibility that the insured party will die before his/her premiums equal or exceed the death benefit. Insurance companies compensate for this risk by adjusting premiums according to how great the risk is.

Insurance Score A way of measuring the risk a potential policyholder poses to an insurance company. The insurance score is a numerical value and measures factors such as the number of claims the potential policyholder has made in the past. A higher score indicates that the potential policyholder poses little risk, is unlikely to make many claims, and is unlikely to make frivolous ones. As a result, one with a high insurance score pays a lower premium than one with a low insurance score.

Insurance Settlement A payment on an insurance claim. That is, when a valid insurance claim is made, the insurer makes a payment to the policyholder. This is called the insurance settlement.

Insurance Trust An irrevocable trust set up by a policyholder in which he/she places his/her life insurance policy. This removes the policy from the policyholder's estate, shielding it from estate taxes. Importantly, the insurance trust must be set up at least three years prior to the death of the policyholder in order to exclude it from the estate. One might set up an insurance trust in order to set aside cash to pay estate

taxes otherwise owed, or to provide for the policy's beneficiaries without concern for the tax. Normally, one sets up an insurance trust when one expects to have an estate worth more than the maximum exclusion figure. It is also called an irrevocable life insurance trust.

Insured Describing a person or organization with an insurance policy of any kind.

Insured Account A bank account on which some organization has placed a guarantee that funds will be available to the account holder. That is, if the bank becomes insolvent, insured accounts are safe and depositors will be able to access/retrieve their money, at least up to a certain amount. These accounts are almost always insured by government-sponsored organizations, such as the FDIC. Insured accounts exist in order to reduce pressures that might result in bank runs.

Insured Asset An asset with an insurance policy of any kind. That is, an insured asset is one for which an insurance company must compensate the owner if the asset is damaged or destroyed. Most companies have insurance policies on their assets, or at least their tangible assets, to transfer the risk associated with owning them. Likewise, most individuals have insurance policies on their major assets, such as their houses and cars.

Insured Bond A municipal bond on which payment is guaranteed by a bond insurance company, especially one with a high credit rating. An insured bond is doubly protected because it is guaranteed by both the revenues from the issuing municipality itself and by the bond insurer in case the issuer defaults. As such, an insured bond is very low risk, and therefore usually carries a lower coupon rate than an uninsured bond.

Insured Event Any event that would cause an insurer to pay a claim. For example, in car insurance, an insured event may be a car accident because it would cause the insurance company to compensate the policyholder for property damage and/or medical bills. Insurance companies base their premiums on the likelihood that an insured event may happen. For example, a younger driver may pay a higher premium than an adult because younger drivers may be statistically more likely to cause an accident.

Insured Loan A loan on which payment is guaranteed by an insurance company, especially one with a high credit rating. An insured loan is protected against default because, if default does occur, the insurance company will pay the lender what is owed. Insured loans carry lower interest rates than uninsured loans because there is less risk involved.

Intangibility The state in which an asset cannot be seen or touched. Intangible assets include things like patents and brand recognition, which add value to a company, but are difficult to price. Intangibility explicitly does not include actual things, such as widgets, a widget factory, or the land upon which the widget factory is built. Because of the difficulty in pricing, intangible assets are sometimes not included in a company's valuation. However, not including them may not express the company's true value. See also: Tangible assets.

Intangible Asset In accounting, any asset that cannot be seen or touched. Intangible assets include things like patents and brand recognition, which add value to a company, but are difficult to price. Intangible assets explicitly do not include actual things, such as widgets, a widget factory, or the land upon which the widget factory is built. Because of the difficulty in pricing, intangible assets are sometimes not included in a company's valuation. However, not including them may not express the company's true value. See also: Tangible assets.

Intangible Drilling Costs Expenses a company has when it drills for oil or natural gas. Intangible drilling costs are sometimes convenient for a company's tax purposes because it can deduct intangible drilling costs in one year when the company perhaps found little or no oil from profits made in a different year when the company does find oil.

Intangible Tax A tax imposed on an intangible asset. For example, an intangible tax may be levied on a brand or a stock. Intangible taxes can be difficult to assess because of the difficulties inherent in valuing intangible assets. In the United States, intangible taxes are imposed at the state and local levels.

Intangible Value In accounting, the value of an asset that cannot be seen or touched. Intangible assets include things like patents and brand recognition, which add value to a company. It is very difficult to determine intangible value because its liquidity and intrinsic value are often unknowable. Intangible values are sometimes not included in a company's valuation. However, not including them may not express the company's true value.

Intara In Rwanda, a political subdivision equivalent to a province.

Integer Programming In mathematics, a process or technique for finding the maximum or minimum value of a linear function subject where the solution must be an integer. It is a form of linear programming, which is important to securities analysis as it helps determine the maximum or minimum rate of return on a particular investment. While the maximum rate of return is not necessarily the expected rate of return, integer programming may help an investor decide if a security is worth a certain level of risk.

Integrated Financial Market Any market where capital may flow freely. For example, a country with uniform tax laws and regulation usually has an integrated financial market because there are no circumstances where one's return will be reduced because of tax restrictions or different regulation. In other words, in an integrated financial market, investments of the same risk always have exactly the same expected return. See also: National market system.

Integrated Pension Plan An employer-based pension in which the employer counts the employee's social security benefits as part of the pension, and therefore reduces the pension's benefits by some or all of the employee's social security check. Since 1988, however, employers have been required to pay at least 50% of the pension's defined benefit.

Intel A major manufacturer of semiconductor computer chips. It makes motherboards, integrated circuits, embedded processors, and similar products. Founded in 1968, it originally developed and manufactured SRAM and DRAM memory chips. Intel is publicly-traded on exchanges all over the world and is a component on the DJIA, NASDAQ 100, and S&P 500 indices.

Intellectual Property Rights The right of a person or company to exclusively use its own ideas, plans, and other intangible assets without competition, at least for a certain period of time. Examples of intellectual property include copyrights, trademarks, patents, and trade secrets. Intellectual property rights may be enforced by court through a lawsuit. The idea behind the protection of intellectual property is to encourage innovation without fear that a competitor may steal the idea and/or take credit for it.

Inter-African Coffee Organization An international organization consisting of more than two dozen coffee producing countries in Africa. It establishes policies for members to help ensure the highest level of production at the most favorable price. It was established in 1960.

Interagency Group on Countertrade A committee in the United States that negotiates with other countries on countertrade, which is the exchange of goods and services for other goods and services. This is especially important in trade with cash-poor countries. The Group was established in 1988 by executive order; it consists of the Secretaries of Agriculture, Defense, Energy, Labor, State and Treasury, as well as the U.S. Trade Representative and the Directors of FEMA, OMB and USAID. It is chaired by the Secretary of Commerce.

Inter-American Commercial Arbitration Commission Also called the IACAC. An international organization that provides out-of-court dispute resolution services for issues affecting trade in the Western Hemisphere. The IACAC consists of representatives from most countries in North and South America; it makes arrangements for arbitration or conciliation when two companies request it. It charges a fee for its services. It was originally established in 1934.

Inter-American Development Bank Also called the IADB. A bank that provides funds to assist international development in Latin America and the Caribbean. It primarily loans money to governments and state-owned corporations. It is owned by 48 country-shareholders, which are divided into borrower countries and creditor countries. Interestingly, borrower countries own a slight majority of shares in the IADB. It was established in 1959 and is headquartered in Washington, D.C.

Inter-American Investment Corporation An organization that provides loans to small and medium sized businesses in Latin America and the Caribbean. It aims for job creation and environmentally sustainable economic development in the region. It was established in 1985 and is based in Washington, D.C.

Inter-Arab Investment and Export Guarantee Corporation Also called the IAIGC or DHAMAN. The IAIGC provides guarantees for foreign direct investment in the Arab world against non-commercial risks, which makes it safer to invest in Arab countries. It also provides export credit to Arab countries exporting to other countries. Members include most Arab countries and several Arab banks. It was established in 1974.

Interbank Describing any loan, deposit, transaction or other relationship between two banks. Interbank transactions provide a great deal of liquidity to the market. Interbank interest rates are often used as benchmarks for other rates. See also: Interbank loan, Interbank rate, Interbank deposit.

Interbank Bid Rate The interest rate at which participating banks are willing to borrow deposits from other banks. Unlike an interbank offer rate, which is the rate at which banks lend money, an interbank bid rate is the rate at which banks ask to borrow. See also: London Interbank Bid Rate.

Interbank Loan A loan that one bank makes to another. Interbank loans may be made to ensure that banks meet their capital requirements at the end of each day. Interbank loans involving a central bank may be a way to control the money supply. Interbank loans must be repaid with interest in a stated period of time, often within a day. In such cases, interbank loans are called overnight loans.

Interbank Market The market for the trade of currencies, loans, and other financial instruments between banks. See also: Fed Funds.

Interbank Offer Rate The interest rate that banks in a jurisdiction charge one another for short-term, interbank loans. Major interbank offer rates, notably LIBOR and HIBOR, are considered key benchmark interest rates in the wider economies. Interest rate swaps, for example, often use an interbank offer rate as the reference rate for the floating payer.

Interbank Rate 1. See: Interbank offer rate. **2.** See: Interbank bid rate.

Interchangeable Bond A bond that was issued as a bearer bond but later changed to a registered bond, or vice versa. These were most common during the 1880s and 1890s.

Intercommodity Spread A spread in which an investor creates an artificial position on a commodity in a certain state. One has an intercommodity spread when one buys a futures contract for a given delivery month and sells a futures contract for a different delivery month on the same commodity but in a different state. For example, an investor can take a long position in crude oil futures for one month and a short position in refined oil futures for another month. This allows the investor to create an artificial position on the price of refining oil. This particular intercommodity spread is called a crack. See also: Crush spread.

Intercompany Loan A loan in which both the lender and the borrower are divisions of the same corporation. Such a loan may have tax consequences, depending on the jurisdiction.

Intercompany Transaction A transaction that occurs between two companies. For example, if a supplier sells to a retailer, this is said to be an intercompany transaction. It should not be confused with an intracompany transaction.

Inter-Dealer Broker 1. A brokerage that intermediates trades between dealers in the bond market and some over-the-counter markets. **2.** A member firm on the London Stock Exchange that only deals with market makers. That is, this inter-dealer broker does not trade securities with members of the public. In both cases, inter-dealer brokers work with huge transactions with very small spreads. This means that the percentage of profit on an individual is likely small, but the sheer size of transactions makes up for this.

Interdealer Quotation System An electronic exchange system giving member access to NASDAQ, NASDAQ small-cap market, and the OTCBB. This gives participating dealers and investors access to thousands of stocks with one of the widest possible ranges of market capitalization.

Interdelivery Spread An investment strategy in which one buys an option or futures contract while selling another option or futures contract on the same underlying asset with identical characteristics except that the second contract has a later expiration date. In an interdelivery spread, one expects that the prices on the contracts will move in such a way that the investor makes a profit.

Interest Money that is paid in exchange for borrowing or using another person's or organization's money. Interest is calculated as a percentage of the money borrowed. There are two kinds of interest, simple interest and compound interest. In simple interest, the interest is calculated only over the original principal amount. For example, if one borrows $1,000 at 3% interest, the interest is $30 (3% of $1,000) each time it is calculated. In compound interest, interest previously paid is included in the calculation of future interest. For example, with the above loan, interest paid in the first month is $30 (3% of $1,000), in the second month it is $30.90 (3% of $1,030), and so forth. Compound interest is more common because it yields more for the lender.

Interest Adjustment In an adjustable-rate mortgage or other debt, a change in the interest rate that the borrower must pay on the mortgage or debt. The adjustment may be upward or downward, and is usually calculated as some percentage above or below a stated benchmark rate. See also: Adjustment frequency, Interest rate risk.

Interest and Dividend Tax Compliance Act A rule in the United States whereby the Internal Revenue Service levies a 20% tax on a company paying dividends if that company does not provide the IRS with valid tax identification numbers for dividend recipients.

Interest Arbitrage The practice of buying a currency on the spot market, selling it on the forward market, and investing the difference in exchange rate. Interest arbitrage is done in order to profit from a (usually temporary) inefficiency in an exchange rate. One can conduct interest arbitrage with a foreign currency, or one can use one's own currency (provided one can buy it using a foreign currency).

Interest Bearing 1. See: Interest bearing deposit. **2.** See: Interest bearing debt.

Interest Coverage Ratio A ratio of a company's EBIT to its total expenses from interest payments. The interest coverage ratio measures the company's ability to make interest payments, such as in its debt service. A ratio above one indicates that the company is able to pay its interest, while a ratio below one means that its interest payments exceed its earnings.

Interest Coverage Test A rule that some companies have forbidding them from issuing more long-term debt securities if doing so would drive their interest coverage ratio below some, defined ratio. See also: Debt limitation.

Interest Dates The dates on which bondholders receive coupon payments. That is, the interest dates are the dates on which bondholders receive interest on the debt they hold. Almost without exception, interest dates occur twice per year on either the first or the fifteenth of the month. Whenever they occur, the interest dates are stated in the bond agreement and do not change. See also: Payment date.

Interest Deduction A reduction in one's taxable income that comes from expense from certain interest payments. For example, the interest one pays on one's mortgage is tax deductible so as to encourage home ownership. Likewise, interest paid on a margin account is often deductible. The United States government uses interest deductions, among other statutory tax advantages, to encourage behavior it supports without mandating it.

Interest During Construction In project finance, the interest that accumulates on a loan that finances the construction of a building or development. The IDC is a cost for the project, though it is not always calculated as such. The IDC is calculated until the project begins to generate revenue, when the company financing the project begins to service its debts.

Interest Equalization Tax A 15% tax on interest received from bonds originating outside the United States. Levied in 1963, its original intent was to stimulate dollar investment in American securities. The effect, however, was to stimulate the growth of euromarkets, that is, the growth of investment in dollars outside the jurisdiction of the United States. The interest equalization tax was removed in 1974.

Interest Expense The amount that an individual or company pays in interest on the debt it borrows. For example, if one borrows $1,000 for one year at an annualized interest rate of 10%, one will ultimately repay $1,100. In this case, the interest expense is $100. In the United Kingdom, the interest expense is called the interest payable.

Interest in Arrears 1. Interest on a loan that has not been paid, especially after payment has become late. **2.** Interest on a loan that is not paid over the life of the loan, but rather in full upon maturity.

Interest Only Strip A derivative security whose cash flow derives exclusively from interest payments on various debt securities. That is, the underlying asset of an interest-only strip is interest paid on debt securities, rather than the debt securities themselves. Many interest only strips are backed by mortgage interest, but some are also backed by Treasury securities and other debt securities. Interest-only strips are derived from bonds whose coupons are legally separated, or "stripped", from the bonds themselves.

Interest Parity A situation in which the interest rates in two currencies are equal because of differences in their exchange rates. For example, if the U.S. dollar has a 4% interest rate and the British pound has a 5% interest rate, but the exchange rate difference is 1%, the dollar and the pound are said to have interest parity.

Interest Payable The interest that a company owes for the present accounting period but has not yet paid. Interest payable is listed as a liability on a balance sheet.

Interest Payment The amount of interest that a borrower pays to a lender on a loan each month. Depending on how a loan is amortized, the interest payment may vary each month, even if the total payment is the same.

Interest Rate The percentage of the value of a balance or debt that one pays or is paid each time period. For example, if one holds a bond with a face value of $1,000 and a 3% interest rate payable each quarter, one receives $30 each quarter. The percentage of the interest rate remains constant (usually), but the amount one pays or is paid changes according to the amount of the balance or debt. For example, if one pays off part of the principal on a loan each month, the amount one pays in interest decreases even though the rate remains the same. See also: Time Value of Money.

Interest Rate Agreement A transaction between two investors in which one (Investor A) agrees to compensate another (Investor B) if a certain variable interest rate, known as the reference rate, rises above some agreed-upon strike rate. Investor A makes this compensation at certain periods of time over the life of the agreement each time the reference rate exceeds the strike. In exchange, Investor B gives Investor A a premium or purchase price for the agreement. See also: Interest rate swap.

Interest Rate Anchor An interest rate on a bond lower than its risk ordinarily would allow. An interest rate anchor may occur if there are no safer bonds available. That is, even though the risk of a bond may justify a higher interest rate in a vacuum, the bond is still safer than similar options, which keeps the rate low.

Interest Rate Floor The minimum interest rate that may be charged on a contract or agreement. For example, an adjustable-rate mortgage may have an interest rate floor stating that the rate will not go below 3.5% even if the formula used to calculate the interest rate would have it do so. An interest rate floor reduces the risk to the bank or other party receiving the interest. See also: Interest Rate Ceiling.

Interest Rate Futures Contract An agreement to buy and sell a debt obligation at a certain date at a certain price. For example, Investor A may make a contract with Creditor B in which A agrees to buy a certain number of B's bonds at a certain date for a certain amount. The value of an interest rate futures contract varies according to changes in the interest rates. For example, if interest rates rise, the value of the futures contract falls because a potential buyer will be able to buy another interest rate futures contract with a better interest rate. See also: Plain vanilla swap.

Interest Rate on Debt The cost of capital on a loan or other debt obligation. See also: Interest.

Interest Rate Option An option contract giving the holder to buy (for a call) or sell (for a put) a security with a certain interest rate at a given strike price on or before the expiration date. An interest-rate option is useful to hedge the interest rate risk inherent to portfolios consisting mainly of bonds.

Interest Rate Parity A theory stating that the difference between interest rates in two countries is the difference between the foreign exchange rate and the spot rate of their two currencies. According to this theory, when one makes two fixed investments in two different currencies, the return on both investments are the same even though interest rates may be different in absolute terms. See also: Purchasing power parity.

Interest Rate Risk The risk of loss due to a change in interest rates. Interest rate risk is important to transactions like interest rate swaps. In such a transaction, the party receiving the floating rate will receive a smaller amount should the floating rate decrease. Interest rate risk is also important to bonds; if interest rates rise, the prices of bonds fall. This affects the secondary market for bonds; for example, if one purchases a bond with a 3% interest rate and the prevailing rate rises to 5%, it becomes difficult or impossible to resell the bond at a profit. Finally, interest rate risk is important to project finance. If interest rates rise, funding may not be available for a new loan for a project that has already started.

Interest Rate Swap The exchange of interest rates for the mutual benefit of the exchangers. The exchangers take advantage of interest rates that are only available, for whatever reason, to the other exchanger by swapping them. The two legs of the swap are a fixed interest rate, say 3.5%, and a floating interest rate, say LIBOR + 0.5%. In such a swap, the only things traded are the two interest rates, which are calculated over a notional value. Each party pays the other at set intervals over the life of the swap. For example, one party may agree to pay the other a 3.5% interest rate calculated over a notional value of $1 million, while the second party may agree to pay LIBOR + 0.5% over the same notional value. It is important to note that the notional amount is arbitrary and is not actually traded. This is also called a plain vanilla swap.

Interest Receivable In a loan, the interest that is owed to the lender, especially over a period of time such as a month.

Interest Sensitive Stock A stock whose value is likely to increase or decrease substantially due to changes in interest rates. Most interest sensitive stocks represent publicly-traded companies with high rates of long-term debt. These companies' stocks decrease in value when interest rates rise because the higher cost of borrowing may result in lower profits and dividends. Conversely, their stocks rise on lower interest rates. For this reason, utility companies tend to have interest sensitive stocks.

Interest Subsidy The value of the tax deductions of an individual's or company's earnings resulting from interest payments on its debt over the course of a year. Some interest may be deducted from one's taxable income, depending on the type of loan or how it was borrowed. Common examples of interest subsidies include the deduction on home mortgage interest and student loan interest. Under most circumstances, interest on one's business is fully tax deductible.

Interest Tax Shield A reduction in tax liability coming from the ability to deduct interest payments from one's taxable income. For example, a mortgage provides an interest tax shield for a property buyer because interest on mortgages is generally deductible. An interest tax shield may encourage a company to finance a project through debt because dividends paid on stock issues are never deductible.

Interest-Bearing Eligible Liabilities Deposits at a bank in the United Kingdom on which the bank must pay interest. Certificates of deposit and saving accounts are example of interest-bearing eligible liabilities. The Bank of England may limit the growth of these liabilities; it did so in the 1970s.

Interested Shareholder A shareholder or group of shareholders with enough common stock that they can influence the company's decisions and policies. The concept of an interested shareholder assumes that there is no majority shareholder. The exact amount of stock one must own in order to be considered an interested shareholder varies according to jurisdiction, but it is normally around 20%.

Interest-Free Describing a loan, mortgage or other debt on which interest does not accumulate. Rather, the borrower must only repay the principal. For example, one may borrow $5,000 and pay the lender $5,000 over a period of two years, at which point the debt is considered repaid.

Interest-Only 1. Describing a derivative in which the underlying asset is future interest payments on a pool of mortgages or other debt obligations. Interest-only derivatives are highly exposed to prepayment risk as homeowners who pay off their mortgages or loans early do not generate any more interest payments. **2.** Describing a non-amortized loan. During the payment period of interest-only loans, one only pays on the interest that accumulates but not on the principal. At the end of the loan's term, the entire principal is due. An example is an interest-only mortgage, in which one makes interest payments for the term of the mortgage and then refinances in order to pay the principal at maturity.

Interest-Only Loan A non-amortized loan. During the payment period of interest-only loans, one only pays on the interest that accumulates but not on the principal. At the end of the loan's term, the entire principal is due. An example is an interest-only mortgage, in which one makes interest payments for the term of the mortgage and then refinances in order to pay the principal at maturity.

Interest-Only Mortgage A non-amortized mortgage. During the repayment period of an interest-only mortgage, one only pays on the interest that accumulates but not on the principal. At the end of the mortgage's term, the entire principal is due. Unless one saves sufficient cash during the term of the mortgage (a relatively rare event) one must refinance in order to repay the principal at maturity.

Intergovernmental Authority on Drought and Development Also called IGADD. A former organization of countries in East Africa. IGADD received and managed international support for various natural disasters (notably drought) that plagued the area in the 1970s and 1980s. IGADD was established in 1986 and dissolved in 1996. It was succeeded by the Intergovernmental Authority on Development.

Intergovernmental Conference Also called an IGC. An ad hoc committee formed periodically to amend the foundational treaties of the European Union. It consists of representatives of EU members, along with the European Commission. The European Parliament also participates. An intergovernmental conference is convoked at the behest of the European Council, which also meets at the conclusion of an IGC to work out any political problems. After the IGC, a treaty text is prepared and presented to member states for signature and ratification.

Intergovernmental Council of Copper Exporting Countries Also called the ICCEC. A former international organization of countries representing more than half of the world's proven copper reserves. The ICCEC was formed in 1967 in an attempt to form a cartel that would control the price of copper. It failed in this endeavor, and was disbanded in 1988.

Interim Dividend In the United Kingdom, a dividend declared and paid before the company has compiled or released its final financial statements for a given year. In the U.K., dividends are commonly declared twice per year; the dividend given before a company's annual meeting (at which financial statements are announced) is called the interim dividend. It is often, but not always, smaller than the final dividend.

Interim Financing A short-term loan intended to maintain a company's operations while it makes arrangements for longer-term financing. For example, a start-up may take out a loan for a few months while it prepares its initial public offering.

Interim Rate of Return The rate of return between two stated dates where the second date is not the final date of the investment. See also: Average rate of return.

Interim Receipt A record issued to a shareholder or bondholder while physical certificates are being printed or manufactured. The interim receipt may be exchanged for the certificate when it is ready.

Interim Report Any report that a publicly-traded company distributes to shareholders on a monthly, quarterly, and semi-annual basis. The report contains information on the company's financial state, such as operational income and net profit, for the period covered in the report. Unlike annual reports, interim reports are not usually audited. See also: Quarterly report.

Interlocking Directorates A situation or state in which one person is a member of the board of directors in more than one publicly-traded company. This creates the possibility of a conflict of interest; indeed, interlocking directorates are illegal when two companies are competitors.

Intermarket Sector Spread The difference in expected yield between two bonds in different sectors with the same maturity. The intermarket sector spread is important in determining which bond in which to invest, especially if one is more expensive than the other. See also: Incremental internal rate of return, Municipals-over-bonds spread.

Intermarket Spread The purchase of a futures contract and the simultaneous sale of the same contract on a different exchange. An investor enters an intermarket spread when the price for the contract is higher on the second exchange than on the first. One must watch prices on both exchanges in order to enter the spread responsibly; computer programs can assist in this. See also: Arbitrage.

Intermarket Spread Swap The sale of one bond and the purchase of another with completely different terms, such as a different coupon rate or maturity. Alternatively, one may directly swap one bond for the other. Intermarket spread swaps occur when the market and/or one's investment goals have changed, rendering it necessary to adopt a different bond strategy.

Intermarket Surveillance Information System A database, compiled by the New York Stock Exchange, containing option and equity information on eight major security exchanges. Published online, its purposes are to increase transparency and reduce violations in trade. Information on price, clearance, and the names of the brokers and institutions involved are all available on the database.

Intermarket Trading Trading a single security on two different exchanges. For example, one may buy a stock on the American Stock Exchange and sell it on the NYSE. Intermarket trading is a fairly common arbitrage strategy, whereby one takes advantage of the difference in price on the same security on two different exchanges in order to make a profit.

Intermarket Trading System A computerized trading system allowing investors and brokers access to more than one stock exchange. That is, the ITS effectively lists securities of participating exchanges on each other's boards. This allows investors to find the best price available for securities. The Cincinnati Stock Exchange was the first major exchange to adopt the ITS. See also: NMS.

Intermediate Bond A debt security with a maturity in the medium-term. While there is no set definition of what constitutes the medium-term, it is generally accepted that intermediate bonds are those that mature somewhere between one and 15 years. One of the most common intermediate bonds, the U.S. Treasury Note, usually has a maturity of 10 years. Intermediate bonds have become increasingly popular for what were formerly called long-term investors. This is especially true among Treasury securities; Treasury Notes have increasingly replaced Treasury Bonds as benchmarks of the bond market.

Intermediate Target Anything under indirect as opposed to direct control of a central bank. An example is money supply; a central bank usually cannot shred dollars when it wishes to reduce the money supply. Rather it raises interest rates, which provides an incentive for people to reduce the amount of money they pump into the economy.

Intermediate Trend In technical analysis, a security's likely performance over a certain period of time, usually a few weeks to six months. Analysts look for cyclical behavior in a security to account for an intermediate trend; that is, if a long-term bull market is observed, but with a fairly consistent series of reactions and rallies every few weeks, an analyst might view the intermediate trend as moderately bearish without detracting from the long-term bullish trend.

Intermediated Market A situation in which one or more financial institutions stand between counterparties in a transaction. For example, in the sale of a house, a bank usually intermediates the market by providing a mortgage to the homebuyer. In some non-traditional transactions, a bank may buy a product (e.g. corn) and immediately re-sell the corn for a profit to a third party. Most transactions requiring a loan to one of the parties are de facto intermediated markets. See also: Murabaha.

Intermediate-Term Describing a plan, strategy, security, or anything else with a term longer than the short term but shorter than the long term. The exact length varies according to the usage; it could be a few weeks or a few years. For example, an intermediate term financial plan outlines investment and other financial goals for any time between roughly six months and one year, while an intermediate term bond has a maturity of five to 10 years.

Intermediation A situation in which a financial institution stands between counterparties in a transaction. For example, in the sale of a house, a bank usually serves as a financial intermediary by providing a mortgage to the buyer and pay the seller. In some non-traditional transactions, a bank may buy a product (e.g. corn) and immediately re-sell it for a profit to a third party. Most transactions requiring a loan to one of the parties include intermediation. See also: Murabaha.

Intermodal Container Transfer Facility The place where cargo is transferred between two types of transportation. For example, cargo may be unloaded from a ship and onto a truck at an intermodal container transfer facility.

Internal Audit The process of reviewing business activities in-house to identify inefficiencies, reduce costs, and otherwise achieve organizational objectives. Internal audits may investigate potential theft or fraud and ensure compliance with applicable regulations and policies. They also assist in risk management. In a large company, especially a publicly traded one, internal auditing is conducted by a board independent from any management and answerable only to an audit committee, a subcommittee on the board of directors. The growth of internal audits accelerated following the 2002 passage of the Sarbanes-Oxley Act, which increased the accounting regulations for public companies.

Internal Audit and Risk Compliance Service A service offered by KPMG, a major consulting company that assists clients in managing risk and compliance with government regulation.

Internal Auditor A person or persons employed by a company who review their own company's business activities to identify inefficiencies, reduce costs, and otherwise achieve organizational objectives. Internal auditors may investigate potential theft or fraud and ensure compliance with applicable regulations and policies. They also assist in risk management. In a large company, especially a publicly traded one, internal auditing is conducted by a board independent from any management and answerable only to an audit committee, a subcommittee on the board of directors. The growth of internal audits accelerated following the 2002 passage of the Sarbanes-Oxley Act, which increased the accounting regulations for public companies.

Internal Balance A situation in which the consumption in an economy roughly equals production. That is, external balance occurs when what is spent and what is produced in the economy are never too far from being even. Internal balance may be characterized by both full employment and low inflation, though not all economists believe this is possible. Maintaining internal balance is considered sustainable. See also: External balance.

Internal Expansion Growth on an investment or asset as the result of internally-generated cash flow or appreciation on the assets. An example of internal expansion occurs when a company owns land and the value of the land increases.

Internal Financing Finance that does not come from issuing stocks or bonds but rather from the company's retained earnings and/or depreciation. One may think of internal finance as a company's savings account that it may use to buy assets when it needs.

Internal Funds Money that a person or company raises from within to begin or expand operations. Internal funds often form a company's seed money; that is, one may start a company with one's own funding rather than with a loan or an IPO. There is a famous story that Ross Perot established Electronic Data Systems with $1,000 in personal savings; in this case, Perot's savings account contained internal funds. See also: Bootstrap, External funds.

Internal Growth Rate The maximum amount of growth a company can sustain without needing to borrow money, make a new issue of stocks, or otherwise obtain a new source of financing. One calculates the internal growth rate by taking the company's retained earnings and dividing by its total assets.

Internal Market The market for, or trade of, any securities for investors in a single country inside the jurisdiction of that country. For example, a British company may issue a bond on the internal market if it issues it within the U.K. and denominates it in the pound sterling. The bond is thereby subject to all normal British securities and trading law. Internal markets contrast with external markets, which are more commonly called euromarkets.

Internal Measure A measure of the cash a company has on hand. The internal measure shows how long the company can maintain operations without additional revenue or financing.

Internal Rate of Return The discount rate at which the cash inflow on an investment equals its cash outflow. That is, the internal rate of return is the return necessary for the present value of an investment to equal what one spends in making the investment. Importantly, the internal rate of return accounts for inflation. See also: Yield to maturity.

Internal Revenue Code The unified law of taxation in the United States. It outlines how individuals and corporations are taxed as well as which deductions and credits are allowed, and how they are to be applied. The Code also covers estate taxes, gift taxes, and payroll taxes. The current version of the Internal Revenue Code was introduced in 1986, though it has been amended since. Critics of the code contend that it is needlessly complicated.

Internal Revenue Service The tax collection agency for the United States government. It is responsible for collecting all federal taxes derived from sources other than tariffs and associated fees. Nearly half of its revenues comes from taxes on personal incomes, with much of the rest coming from corporate taxes and employment taxes. The IRS has the ability to place and enforce liens on property and other assets for nonpayment of taxes. The activities of the IRS fund (many of) the functions of the American government. It is not responsible for collection of state and local taxes. See also: Notice of seizure.

Internal Revenue Service Restructuring and Reform Act of 1998 Legislation in the United States that amended the Internal Revenue Code of 1986 in a variety of ways. Among its major provisions were the institution of tax deductions for interest on some student loans and the exclusion of individuals who do not provide their tax identification numbers from the earned income tax credit. It also provided a five year term for the Commissioner of Internal Revenue.

Internalization A trade between an investor and his/her brokerage. That is, the client makes an order to the brokerage to buy or sell a security and the brokerage fills the order from its own inventory of the security. This can be advantageous to the brokerage because it is less expensive than going out and finding another buyer or seller. Some exchanges prohibit these trades, and brokerages are required to report internalization on exchanges that permit it.

International Accounting Standards A former system for standardizing accounting practices across the world. International Accounting Standards were issued by the International Accounting Standards Committee. Though it had no authority to enforce its rulings, a number of countries followed its guidelines anyway. In 2001, the IAS were replaced by the International Financial Reporting Standards.

International Accounting Standards Committee Also called the IASC. An organization established to standardize accounting practices across the world. Although the IASC had no authority to enforce its rulings, a number of countries followed its guidelines anyway. In 2001, the IASC was replaced by the International Accounting Standards Board.

International Accounting Unit Also called the IAU. The accounting currency for NATO. It does not circulate and is only used to calculate the cost of NATO's operations. Its value is determined every six months and is based on the exchange rates of NATO member nations.

International Accreditation Forum Also called the IAF. An organization consisting of numerous accrediting bodies. The IAF sets accreditation for compliance assessments, which are programs that certify whether products, goods, and services meet with industry standards. IAF members mutually recognize each other's accreditations.

International Air Transport Association Also called the IATA. A trade association for airlines all over the world. It promotes flight safety, encourages technical developments, and, perhaps most importantly, lobbies for favorable legislation from governments. It was established in 1945 in Havana and is based in Montreal.

International Anti-Bribery Act of 1998 Legislation in the United States, passed in 1998, that forbade U.S. citizens from bribing or attempting to unduly influence any government official. The Act was intended to bring the U.S. into compliance with the OECD.

International Anticounterfeiting Coalition Also called the IACC. A nonprofit organization in the United States that promotes intellectual property. The IACC conducts a number of activities toward this goal. It participates in global conferences to improve enforcement standards, trains police and other law enforcement officials, and lobbies the U.S. and foreign governments for favorable legislation. It was established in 1979 and is based in Washington, D.C.

International Arbitrage The practice of buying and selling a security registered in a foreign country and an International Depositary Receipt based on that same security. This allows the arbitrageur to profit from inefficiencies in price resulting from the exchange rate, the difference in price on different exchanges, and other factors. See also: Arbitrage.

International Asset Pricing Model A version of the Capital Asset Pricing Model applied to international investments. Like the CAPM, it attempts to describe the relationship between the risk and the expected return on an investment, which is used to determine an investment's appropriate price. The assumption behind the CAPM is that money has two values: a time value and a risk value. Thus, any risky asset or investment must compensate the investor for both the time spent with his/her money tied up in the investment and the investment's relative riskiness. This compensation must be in addition to the risk-free rate of return. It is important to note that in addition to these factors (which the CAPM and the IAPM hold in common), the IAPM assumes that purchasing power parity holds true in the countries it is investigating.

International Association of Financial Engineers A professional organization for persons who engage in financial engineering, which is broadly defined as the study of financial theory and mathematical and computer applications of the same. The IAFE was established in 1992 and consists of academics and market practitioners worldwide. Among other activities, it holds educational events, provides a venue for the discussion of research, and holds networking opportunities for members. It also presents the Financial Engineer of the Year Award.

International Atomic Energy Agency Also called the IAEA. It was established in 1957 to promote nuclear energy while discouraging the spread of nuclear weapons. The IAEA reports to the United Nations General Assembly, but is an autonomous entity.

International Atomic Energy List Also called the IAEL. A list of materials that could be used in the manufacture of nuclear weapons. IAEL materials cannot be exported to non-nuclear states except under certain circumstances. The list ceased to be updated in 1994 to avoid duplication with the Trigger List.

International Bank for Economic Cooperation Also called the IBEC. A bank established to promote international development and cooperation between member states. The IBEC was founded in 1963 with the Soviet Union and several Eastern European nations as members. Other communist countries joined as well. It finances trade imbalances, takes deposits in gold and convertible currencies, and provides investment services for governments. It reformed following the fall of the Soviet Union.

International Bank for Reconstruction and Development A division of the World Bank that provides loans to governments and public organizations in developing countries in order to alleviate poverty. Founded in 1946, it was established to rebuild Europe and Asia after World War II. It loans money for infrastructural, business, and environmental development worldwide. It charges developing countries low interest rates, raising its funds from bonds issued to governments and institutions. See also: International Monetary Fund.

International Banking Act Legislation in the United States, passed in 1978, that requires American branches of foreign banks to abide by the same regulations as U.S. banks. While this increases regulation by mandating capital adequacy requirements and so forth, it provides FDIC insurance to foreign banks.

International Banking Facility A bank or other financial institution that makes loans and accepts deposits for foreign clients. IBFs are not subject to the same reserve requirements or interest rate restrictions as banks providing services for domestic clients. This allows them to be competitive with banks in foreign countries. See also: Eurodollar.

International Bond A bond issued in a country or currency other than that of the investor or broker. They include Eurobonds, which are issued in a foreign currency, foreign bonds, which are issued by a foreign government or corporation in the domestic market, and global bonds, which are issued in both domestic and international markets. Unlike domestic bonds, international bonds are usually subject to currency risk. Caution is required when investing international bonds because they may be subject to different regulatory and taxation requirements than the ones with which the investor or broker is familiar.

International Business Opportunities Service Support services offered by Scottish Development International to Scottish companies doing business abroad. The services are intended to help participating companies find new prospects and learn how to take advantage of them.

International Business Reply Service A service offered by the U.S. Postal Service allowing mail with a reply card or envelope to be sent internationally. The reply card or envelope may be returned to the United States without postage, which is collected from the initial mailer upon delivery. It may be used in international direct mail marketing or in other business correspondence.

International Cargo Handling Coordination Association Also called the ICHCA. An organization that promotes safety standards for international shipping. It was established in 1952 and is based in the United Kingdom.

International Center for Theoretical Physics Also called the ICTP. A research organization in Italy. Its members study mathematics and physics, especially in order to encourage progress in developing countries. The ICTP conducts research into applied physics, condensed matter and statistical physics, high energy, cosmology and astroparticle physics, and mathematics. It was established in 1964 and is based in Trieste, Italy.

International Centre for Science and High Technology Also called ICS-UNIDO. An agency that promotes environmentally sustainable industrial development in developing countries. It operates under UNIDO but is funded by the Italian Ministry of Foreign Affairs. ICS-UNIDO was established in 1996 and is based in Trieste, Italy.

International Centre for Settlement of Investment Disputes Also called ICSID. An organization under the World Bank Group that serves as an arbitration board for disputes involving investment treaties. That is, when member countries disagree on the interpretation of an investment treaty applying to both of them, they may refer the matter to ICSID. More than 150 countries belong to ICSID. It was established in 1966 and is based in Washington, D.C.

International Chamber of Commerce The largest business organization in the world. It provides arbitration services for disputes between member companies in different countries. The ICC also examines potential policies and other measures that can be taken to promote international commerce. It was established in 1919 and maintains its secretariat in Paris.

International Civil Aviation Organization Also called the ICAO. An agency of the United Nations that develops standards for safe international flight. It recommends principles for inspections, infrastructure, accidents procedures, and so forth. Nearly every member of the UN is also a member of the ICAO. It was established in 1947 and is based in Montreal.

International Cocoa Organization An international organization for both cocoa importing and exporting countries. It promotes sustainability and advises on all facets of the cocoa sector. It was established in 1973 and is based in London.

International Commodities Clearing House An agency in London that settles futures contracts for exchanges worldwide. The ICCH matches orders together, ensures that delivery is made to the correct party and collects margin money. It is owned six British banks. Because so many trades take place on an exchange in a given day, the ICCH determines what each party owes or is owed in a central location (in London) so that the fewest securities and the least amount of money actually change hands. Primarily, it works for exchanges in the United Kingdom in Europe.

International Commodity Agreement A general term for a treaty regulating the trade of one or more commodities between countries. Usually, an international commodity agreement eases commodity trade, with allowances keeping up certain subsidies or other trade barriers for particularly important sectors such as agriculture.

International Competitive Bidding A system the World Bank uses to reduce the risk of the loans it makes. It requires borrowers to advertise the project a loan is funding in an international language and to accept the lowest (reasonable) bid from subcontractors. Agreeing to abide by international competitive bidding is a condition of borrowing from the World Bank.

International Confederation of Free Trade Unions A former association of trade unions in the Americas, Asia, Europe and Africa. It formed in 1949 as a number of unions (including the AFL-CIO in the United States) objected to the increasingly communist leanings of the World Federation of Trade Unions. Its membership increased to over 100 million following the end of the Cold War. In 2006, it merged with the World Confederation of Labor to form the International Trade Union Confederation.

International Congress of Accountants A meeting of accountants worldwide to discuss issues of concern and to facilitate the removal of differences in accounting standards. The meeting occurs every five years.

International Congress Office An agency of the U.S. Federal Government that encourages organizations to hold their meetings and conventions in the United States. It is based in the U.S. embassy in France.

International Cotton Association A nonprofit trade association for cotton investors. The ICA sets standards for members and arbitrates disputes. It also serves as the governing body for the Liverpool Cotton Exchange. It was established as the Liverpool Cotton Association in 1841 and took its present name in 2004.

International Court of Justice Also called the ICJ. The supreme judicial body of the United Nations. It decides disputes between states and rules on questions submitted to it by various international organizations, notably the UN General Assembly. It claims global jurisdiction but this is not universally accepted. It began in 1946 and is based in the Hague. It should not be confused with the International Criminal Court.

International Data Base An office under the U.S. Census Bureau that compiles and maintains information on the global population. It has information on the population for the world's largest countries from 1950 to the present. It also researches trends such as birth rates and death rates.

International Depository Receipt A certificate issued by a bank representing shares of a stock the bank holds in trust but that are traded on a foreign stock exchange. The IDR is denominated in the local currency, and entitles the bearer to any dividends and other benefits associated with the shares. IDRs can be traded like any other security. Using IDRs shields the investor from foreign exchange risk and any applicable tariffs he/she would have had to pay if he/she had bought the stock outright. It also exempts the investor from any requirements the foreign exchange might have levied. It is also known as a global depository receipt (GDR). See also: American Depository Receipt.

International Development Association A division of the World Bank that provides long-term, interest-free loans to the world's 80 poorest countries. The IDA is responsible for poverty reduction and other aspects of international development in the Third World. Nearly half of the countries it assists are in Africa. The IDA was established in 1960; its loans assist in public health, business development, education, and infrastructure development.

International Development Research Center Also called the IDRC. A crown corporation in Canada that conducts research into international development. Specifically, it works with developing countries to find scientific solutions to economic, environmental and other problems faced in the developing world. It was established in 1970.

International Diversification Investment of one's portfolio in securities that are traded in various countries. This is done to reduce risk, often political risk. For example, if one country's government announces a larger than normal budget deficit, or the central bank raises interest rates, this may affect security prices in one country, but not necessarily in other countries that did not take equivalent steps. Likewise, if a whole industry fails in one country but thrives in another, investing in the same industry in both countries hedges one's risk. Some analysts argue that international diversification is less effective in an era of globalization, but other analysts dispute that.

International Electrotechnical Commission Also called the IEC. An organization established to standardize the use of electricity. Members consist of national boards. The IEC attempts to incorporate the interests of governments and the private sector. It was founded in 1906 and is based in Geneva.

International Emergency Economic Powers Act Legislation in the United States, passed in 1977, that allows the president to declare a national emergency in the event of a foreign threat to the U.S. After such a declaration, the president may embargo the country from which the threat originates, and may also freeze assets or conduct other activities to deal with the situation. The emergency declaration must be renewed every year to remain in effect, and Congress has the ability to rescind it.

International Energy Agency Also called the IEA. An international organization under the OECD that promotes energy security, economic development and environmental protection among member states. It was established to prevent or

at least reduce energy crises caused by disruptions in the oil market. As such, it requires member states to maintain oil reserves containing at least 90 days' worth of the previous year's net import of oil. The IEA also provides energy advisory services to both members and non-members. It was established in 1974 and is based in Paris.

International Executive Service Corps Also called the IESC. A nonprofit organization in the United States that implements international development projects designed to strengthen private business in developing countries. Specifically, it offers assistance in the tourism, information technology, trade and financial services sectors. It was established in 1964 by David Rockefeller and is based in Washington, D.C.

International Finance Corporation A division of the World Bank that provides loans for private companies and projects in developing countries. Founded in 1956, it seeks to promote private-sector investment in the developing world. It charges market interest rates, and its loans do not have government guarantees. See also: International Monetary Fund.

International Finance Subsidiary A subsidiary of an international company that is incorporated in the United States and that issues bonds in order to invest the proceeds in foreign operations. The way an international finance subsidiary is structured, the yields on the bonds are not subject corporate withholding taxes. Since the U.S. has eliminated the corporate withholding tax, this structure has become less common.

International Financial Reporting Standards A system for standardizing accounting practices across the world. International Financial Reporting Standards are issued and interpreted by the International Accounting Standards Board. Though it has no authority to enforce its rulings, a number of jurisdictions, including the European Union, Singapore, and the Gulf Cooperation Council follow its guidelines anyway. The IFRS replaced the International Accounting Standards in 2001.

International Fisher Effect In international finance, a theory stating that an expected change in the exchange rate between two currencies is roughly equivalent to the difference between their nominal interest rates. This is based on the Fisher hypothesis, which states that real interest rates are independent of monetary considerations. If this is true, then a state with a low nominal interest rate has a low inflation rate; likewise, a country with a high nominal interest rate has a higher inflation rate. The real value of the high interest rate country will depreciate over time, leading to a circumstance in which its exchange rate, in relation to the low interest rate country, will change approximately according to the difference between their interest rates. This theory is controversial because, in practice, currencies with higher nominal interest rates tend to have lower inflation than currencies with lower interest rates.

International Fund A mutual fund that invests predominantly or exclusively in securities issued in foreign countries. An international fund does not necessarily concentrate on any single country, but it does not invest in securities from the country in which it operates. An international fund should not be confused with a global fund, which invests in both domestic and foreign securities.

International Fund for Agricultural Development An agency of the United Nations that provides loans and grants to developing countries for agricultural purposes. It aims to improve food security and thereby to eliminate rural poverty in the developing world. It was established in 1977 and is based in Rome.

International Intellectual Property Alliance Also called the IIPA. An organization in the United States that seeks to protect members' copyrights internationally. The IIPA consists of seven trade associations representing print, film, television, software and similar sectors. It was established in 1984 and is based in Washington, D.C.

International Investment Bank 1. A former bank established in 1971 to provide capital investment funding for Soviet bloc states. It was disestablished in 1991. **2.** An investment bank whose practices comply with Islamic law. It was established in 2003 and is based in Bahrain.

International Labour Organization Also called the ILO. An agency of the United Nations that seeks to promote and standardize labor practices. It makes recommendations to member states and calls for the elimination of child labor, slavery, and discrimination. It also promotes the right to unionize. It was established in 1919 and is based in Switzerland.

International Law The area of law dealing with relations between countries. International law consists of many aspects, both written and unwritten, but often refers to matters of war and peace, respect for human rights, international trade and commerce, and similar things. Institutions like the United Nations and the International Criminal Court purport to enforce international law, though their effectiveness is limited by the cooperation given by member states. In general, international law is governed by treaties between sovereign states.

International Market Index An index of 50 stocks in foreign companies who have American depository receipts that are traded on the New York Stock Exchange, American Stock Exchange, and NASDAQ. It is weighted for market capitalization.

International Monetary Fund An international organization that seeks to maintain stability in the global economy. It does this primarily by monitoring the balance of payments for different countries and implementing restructuring agreements with countries in need of help. It was established by Bretton Woods in 1944. See also: Special Drawing Rights, World Bank System.

International Monetary Market A division of the Merc that trades currencies, interest-rate options, and interest rate futures. Established in its current form in 1972 when its predecessor merged with the Merc, it also trades in eurodollar and LIBOR-based securities. It is the second largest futures exchange in the world and the largest in the United States.

International Monetary System In foreign exchange, the complete network of governments and institutions that affect currencies. The system has a set of agreed-upon rules that allows for international trade of goods and services. It is important to note that one government's decisions may affect the international monetary system. For example, many countries peg their currencies to the U.S. dollar; when the Federal Reserve makes changes to American monetary policy, it affects those currencies as well. Likewise, import and export laws and decisions on the convertibility of currencies have sometimes significant effects on the international monetary system. See also: Bretton Woods.

International Organization for Standardization A non-governmental organization that sets standard codes for countries and currencies. ISO sets the ISO 3166 codes for countries and provinces, which are used in international banking transactions and shipping. Likewise, it sets the ISO 4217 codes for individual currencies. ISO has its headquarters in Geneva, Switzerland, and, because its standards are usually adopted into the law of member states, it is more powerful than most other NGOs.

International Organization of Securities Commissions An international organization consisting of most security regulators in the world. For example, the SEC is a member of IOSCO. Other regulators, such as the CFTC, and self-regulatory organizations, such as the NYSE, may also participate in IOSCO, but not as full members. IOSCO seeks to provide an open forum for members and to establish a general framework for worldwide securities regulation, while also respecting the right of each country to regulate its own markets.

International Petroleum Exchange Futures and options exchange for energy commodities. Based in London and founded in 1980, the exchange deals with contracts on electricity, oil, natural gas, coal, and carbon emissions allowances. Notably, Brent Crude futures, one of the world's leading oil price indicators, trades on the IPE.

International Pow Wow An annual trade show for the travel industry designed to showcase and promote travel to the United States.

International Securities Exchange An exchange for options based in New York. Established in 2000, the International Securities Exchange lists options on a number of different investment vehicles, including stocks, indices, and ETFs. It also provides investors with tutorials on option strategies. In late 2008, the International Securities Exchange established a separate exchange for trading stocks.

International Securities Identification Number A number that is assigned to almost every stock and registered bond that trades throughout the world. An ISIN facilitates trade and settlement by making each security unique to every other security of the same class. Most countries have independent agencies that assign ISIN numbers to securities traded in their countries. ISIN numbers are recorded in each trade.

International Swaps and Derivatives Association A professional organization for traders in swaps and other derivatives. It serves as a lobbying group for the profession with the United States government, and sets uniform practices for members. Importantly, it writes and periodically updates the ISDA Master Agreement, which is a standardized contract for OTC derivatives. It maintains its headquarters in New York City.

International Trade Administration A branch of the U.S. Department of Commerce that promotes exports of non-agricultural goods. The ITA provides information to exporters and assures that they have access to international markets. It was established in 1980.

Internationalization Index Also called the II. The number of foreign affiliated companies in a country divided by the number of total companies. The United Nations uses the II to estimate the extent to which a country is integrated into the global economy.

Internet Service Provider A company that provides access to the internet for customers. Typically, an ISP provides this service in exchange for a monthly fee. It may also provide website hosting services.

Internet Tax Freedom Act Legislation in the United States, originally passed in 1998 and renewed several times since, that prohibits state and local governments from taxing the use of the Internet. For example, states and municipalities may not tax e-mails or bandwidth use. The Act was intended to increase Internet use in the United States.

Interpolation An estimate of an unknown variable using known variables that are somehow related to the unknown variable.

Interpositioning The act or practice of adding another broker-dealer to a transaction when there is no reason to do so and the extra broker-dealer does not provide a necessary service. Generally speaking, interpositioning occurs when two broker-dealers agree to insert the one into the dealings of another. This allows both to extract commissions without doing any work; obviously this is detrimental to the client because it forces him/her to pay money he/she does not need to pay. Interpositioning is illegal under the Investment Company Act of 1940, but it still occurs. Indeed, it was relatively common during the first few years of the 2000s.

Interstate Commerce Commission A former organization of the U.S. federal government established to regulate railroads. Among other things, it ensured fair prices for consumers and attempted to prevent racial discrimination on rail. Its jurisdiction was later expanded to include trucking. It was established in 1887 and was abolished in 1995.

Interstate Land Sales Full Disclosure Act Legislation in the United States, passed in 1968, that requires some sellers of land across state lines to register with the Department of Housing and Urban Development and provide potential buyers with reports on the state of the property. A seller is subject to the Act if he/she wishes to sell more than 100 lots in a subdivision. The Act is intended to protect buyers from dishonest practices in situations when the normal regulator (an individual state) does not have jurisdiction.

Interval Fund A mutual fund with shares that may be sold or redeemed on certain, stated dates. That is, an interval fund combines features of an open end mutual fund with a closed end mutual fund.

Inter-Vivos Trust A trust into which the grantor deposits certain assets for the management by another party while the grantor is still living. That is, the inter-vivos trust is created and maintained before the grantor dies. Generally speaking, an inter-vivos trust exists to help avoid estate taxes after death and other taxes while still living. One may also set up an inter-vivos trust to facilitate long-term property management. It is also called a living trust.

Intestacy A situation in which one dies without a will. The assets of such a person are distributed according to the statutes of the jurisdiction where he/she resided, but the estate generally is administered by probate court.

Intestate Describing a person who dies without a will. When an intestate person passes away, his/her assets are distributed to the next of kin and/or the state according to the law where the intestate person lived. It is important to note that courts do not take into account the intestate person's wishes in this circumstance.

In-the-Money 1. A call option with a strike price less than the value of the underlying asset. **2.** A put option with a strike price more than the value of the underlying asset. In both these situations, the option contract has intrinsic value. If an option is deep in the money, it is unlikely that the option will be out-of-the money by the time the option is exercised.

Intifaq In Islamic law, the gift or sale of the ability to use one's property for a certain purpose. For example, one may grant intifaq to allow a neighbor to graze his livestock on one's property.

Intracommodity Spread In futures contracts, the spread in which a trader buys a commodity future expiring in one month for a certain price, then sells a future for the same underlying commodity expiring a different month at the same time on the same exchange. Profit is determined by the price difference between the two contracts. The advantage of an intracommodity spread is that the trader does not need to rely on market movements in order to make a profit, but only needs his/her short position to have a higher price than the long position.

Intracompany Trade A transaction that occurs between two subsidiaries of the same parent company. For example, if a supplier sells to a retailer, and both are owned by the same conglomerate, this is said to be an intracompany transaction. It should not be confused with an intercompany transaction.

Intraday Referring to trade within a single day. As the price of a security fluctuates during a trading day, intraday prices are especially important to short-term investors. The term is also used to describe a security's high or low price during a trading day. For example: "Shares of Company X opened at $5 per share and closed at $6, with an intraday high of $7.50."

Intraday High The highest price at which a security trades on a given trading day. It is usually higher than the closing price and is also called the daily high.

Intraday Intensity Index A measure of the volume on a security over a given trading day, especially when block traders are heavily involved with it. It is calculated thusly: Intraday Intensity Index = (2 * close - high - low) / (high - low) * volume

Intraday Limit The largest position (either long or short) that a dealer working for an investment bank is permitted to take on a trading day. This limit is set by the bank for which each dealer works.

Intramarket Sector Spread The yield spread between two corporate bonds with the same maturity when the issuers are both in the same sector. A common example of an intramarket sector spread is the difference in yields between two 10-year bonds issued by an oil company and a natural gas company, respectively.

Intrapreneur A person who develops an idea and sees it to fruition within a large organization. For example, an intrapreneur may be an employee at a corporation who sees a problem with the way inventories are stored, and develops and implements a new way to store inventory. Intrepreneurs, in other words, are innovators within their organizations, but they usually do not start new organizations.

Intrapreneurship The development of an idea within a large organization. For example, intrapreneurship may involve the development and implementation of a new way to store inventory so as to improve a company's efficiency. In other words, intrapreneurship is innovation within an organization, but not the creation of a new one.

Intrastate Offering A new issue of a security in a single state. An intrastate offering is not subject to SEC regulations, but is required to follow the applicable laws of the state in which it is registered. Some companies make intrastate offerings because doing so is less expensive than registering with the SEC. In order to qualify for an intrastate offering (and thereby escape SEC regulation), the offering may only be to residents of a single state, in which the company must have a significant presence.

Intrinsic Value 1. The actual value of an asset. That is, the intrinsic value is what an asset is actually worth, rather than its current market value, which is overly influenced by market conditions such as a recession or a speculative bubble. One may think of the intrinsic value of an asset as its value "in a perfect world," because one may not always be able to receive the intrinsic value. For example, the intrinsic value of a baseball card may be $10,000, but if prevailing market conditions render investors uninterested in buying baseball cards, one may only be able to sell the card for $5,000. That said, the line between intrinsic and extrinsic value is sometimes blurry. **2.** The gain that an option holder would receive by exercising an in-the-money option. That is, the intrinsic value of an option is how much the strike price is below the underlying asset (for a call) or above the underlying asset (for a put). These options have intrinsic value because they always result in a profit. As a result, these options may be sold for a much higher price than the investor paid for the option.

Intrinsic Value of an Option The profit that an option holder would receive by exercising an in-the-money option. That is, the intrinsic value of an option is how much the strike price is below the underlying asset (for a call) or above the underlying asset (for a put). These options have intrinsic value because they always result in a profit. As a result, they may be sold for a much higher price than the investor paid for the option.

Introducing Broker A person or business that provides investing advice or counsel to an investor, but does not actually handle transactions. Generally speaking, introducing brokers make recommendations while delegating the task of executing trades to someone at the same or a different firm who operates on a trading floor. The introducing broker and the person(s) who execute a transaction split the fees and commissions according to some agreed upon arrangement. The term most often applies to brokers in the futures market.

Inure To cause or to result in. The word is most commonly used in legal documents, such as wills.

Inv 1. See: Inventory. **2.** See: Investor. **3.** See: Invoice.

Invasion Powers The ability of the trustee of a trust to give part of the principal (or original assets deposited in the trust) to the beneficiary if the investment income from the trust is insufficient for the beneficiary's needs. Using invasion powers can reduce the life of the trust and certainly threaten its sustainability. Because of this, the trustee may only exercise these powers under certain circumstances following procedures set forth in the trust agreement.

Inventory The raw materials and the products made from them that a company possesses and intends to sell in short order. It also includes raw materials that are in the process of being made into a final product. Inventory is considered an asset on a balance sheet, but because it comes with costs (such as storage and spoilage), most companies seek to find a balance between having too much inventory, which comes with these costs, and too little, which could result in the company not filling orders for the product. Inventory may be accounted on a last-in-first-out or a first-in-first-out basis, which each has advantages and disadvantages. See also: Just-in-Time, Just-in-Case.

Inventory Accounting A branch of accounting that values the inventory of companies. Inventory accounting may (or may not, depending on the tool being used) increase an inventory's value if its market price increases or if its carrying costs are low. On the other hand, it may (or many not) decrease the value if its depreciation is high or if the inventory is becoming obsolete.

Inventory Financing A loan or line of credit available to a business secured by its own inventory. That is, a business places its inventory as collateral in exchange for an operating loan. Inventory financing is advantageous for businesses with a large amount of physical inventory ready to ship. Inventory financing is used as a stop-gap against temporary cash flow problems resulting from inventory ready to sell but not sold. It is not recommended as a long-term financing tool.

Inventory Profit In accounting, the increase in value of an asset during the time it is held. Inventory profit may occur through appreciation, but it is most often the result of inflation. That is, the increase in the asset's value is usually the result of the reduction in the value of the currency. Inventory profit is typically only a minor piece of a company's total profit. See also: LIFO, FIFO.

Inventory Turnover A measure of how long it takes, on average, for a company to sell and replace its inventory. Inventory turnover can help a company or potential investor determine how well the company manages its inventory. Higher inventory turnover is considered to be desirable. The turnover is calculated as follows: Inventory turnover = Cost of goods sold / ((Beginning inventory + ending inventory) / 2)

Inventory Valuation In accounting, any way to estimate and report how much a company's inventory is worth. There are two primary ways to calculate inventory valuation. The first in, first out technique treats inventory acquired first as if it were sold first. That is, the sale of inventory is recorded against the purchase price of the oldest inventory, even if the physical goods are not the same. The last in, first out technique does the opposite: it records sales against the purchase price of the most recently acquired inventory. Both of these techniques are designed to estimate the value of inventory in a way that will decrease the company's tax liability while not reducing the book value of its assets.

Inverse Floating-Rate Note A bond or other debt security with a variable coupon rate that changes in inverse proportion to some benchmark rate. For example, an inverse floating-rate note may be linked to LIBOR; as the LIBOR decreases, the coupon rate increases and vice versa. An inverse floating-rate note allows a bondholder to benefit from declining interest rates. It is also called an inverse floater.

Inverse Order In an annuity or other vehicle with periodic payments, a way of reviewing payments beginning with the last and continuing on to the first.

Inverted Formation In technical analysis, a pattern that looks like the opposite of another pattern. For example, a saucer formation looks like a teacup on a chart, while an inverted saucer looks like a teacup that has been turned upside down. Obviously, an inverted formation gives the opposite signal from the "normal" formation. For example, a saucer is a bullish indicator, while an inverted saucer is a bearish indicator.

Inverted Market In options and futures, a situation where prices on contracts with short expirations or maturities are higher than those with longer expirations or maturities. This is rather unusual, as most investors demand a premium for longer term investments. An inverted market usually occurs when the underlying securities have low supply in the short term.

Inverted Yield Curve A yield curve in which the long-term yields on bonds are lower than short-term yields. A normal yield curve trends upward because bondholders expect a larger interest rate for a longer investment; however, if a yield curve turns negative, it indicates that the market believes that demand for long-term debt securities is increasing or will increase, which will drive yields downward. Higher demand for bonds usually occurs when investors believe that stock prices will fall. As a result, an inverted yield curve is a highly bearish indicator and indeed is seen as a predictor of a coming recession. An inverted yield curve is the rarest yield curve. It is also called a negative yield curve.

Invest in Canada An organization that promotes foreign investment in Canada. Among other things, it takes inquiries from potential investors, conducts market research and assists in the process of setting up companies in Canada. It was established in 1974 as the Foreign Investment Review Agency.

Invest, Then Investigate A risky and highly speculative investment strategy in which one performs no due diligence at all prior to buying a security. Rather, one does this afterward when deciding whether or not to sell the security. One may do this when one has a "feeling" that the security will rise in price or value, which, obviously, does not always happen. See also: Behavioral economics.

Invested Capital The capital that a company has invested or can invest in itself. It is calculated by adding the company's long-term debt, stock, and retained earnings. It may also apply to an individual by adding his/her net worth and long-term debt.

Investing Sage An individual investor who is well known and exceptionally well regarded. Investing sages have reputations for producing double digit returns for themselves and/or their clients. Some investors seek to imitate the strategies or methods of sages in hope of higher gains. Prominent investing sages include Warren Buffet and George Soros.

Investment The act of placing capital into a project or business with the intent of making a profit on the initial placing of capital. An investment may involve the extension of a loan or line of credit, which entitles one to repayment with interest, or it may involve buying an ownership stake in a business, with the hope that the business will become profitable. Investing may also involve buying a particular asset with the intent to resell it later for a higher price. Many types of investing exist, and each is subject to greater or lesser regulation in the jurisdiction in which it takes place. Legally, investing requires the existence and protection of individual property rights. Investing wisely requires a combination of astuteness, knowledge of the market, and timing.

Investment Advice Counsel given to an investor as to which securities to buy or strategies to pursue, usually in exchange for a fee. Investment advice may involve interacting directly with a client (e.g. by managing assets), or simply giving passive, general advice about which securities or industries are bullish or bearish. Investment advisors managing a certain amount of money must register with the SEC; the actions of all investment advisory services are governed by the Investment Advisors Act of 1940. Importantly, it is a criminal offense for investment advisory services to provide false or misleading information, and to sell or buy their own securities to or from a client.

Investment Adviser A person or business that provides investing advice or counsel to an investor in exchange for a fee. Investment advisers may interact directly with a client (e.g. by managing assets), or may provide passive, general advice on which securities or industries are bullish or bearish. Investment advisers managing more than a certain amount of money must register with the SEC; the actions of all investment advisers are governed by the Investment Advisers Act of 1940. Importantly, it is a criminal offense for investment advisers to provide false or misleading information, and to sell or buy their own securities to or from a client.

Investment Adviser Representative Any person who is employed by an investment adviser and assists him/her in making recommendations and other decisions for clients. An investment adviser representative must ordinarily possess a Series 65 license.

Investment Advisers Act Legislation in the United States defining an investment adviser as a person who provides professional advice on how to manage investments or makes investments on behalf of a client. Under amendments to the Advisers Act, investment advisers with more than $25 million under management are required to register with the SEC. The act defines the liability of investment advisers and provides guidelines on the fees and commissions they may collect. Additionally, the Act provides certain anti-fraud provisions protecting investors from predatory advisers, even those not registered with the SEC.

Investment Advisory Service A business that provides investing advice or counsel to an investor in exchange for a fee. Investment advisory services may interact directly with a client (e.g. by managing assets), or may provide passive, general advice on which securities or industries are bullish or bearish. Investment advisory services managing a certain amount of money must register with the SEC; the actions of all investment advisory services are governed by the Investment Advisors Act of 1940. Importantly, it is a criminal offense for investment advisory services to provide false or misleading information, and to sell or buy their own securities to or from a client. See also: Investment adviser.

Investment Agreement A contract stating the rights and responsibilities of two parties to an investment. Parties could be two partners, a client and an investment adviser, or a company and a government, among others. The investment agreements sets forth the parameters of the investment; for example, it includes what money, if any, one party must pay to the other and the goods or services each must provide or produce.

Investment Analysis Research into data relating to the stability and profitability of businesses, especially to guide one's investing practices. At its most basic, investment analysis involves looking at financial statements to determine if a company is healthy. Balance sheets are important to investment analysis as they provide a ready-made means of investigating performance. However, the accounting methods a particular business employs may make it look more or less healthy than it really is. Investment analysts attempt to assess a business' actual health. See also: Fundamental analysis, Financial analysis, Investment adviser.

Investment Analysts Persons who conduct research into data relating to the stability and profitability of businesses, especially to guide one's investing practices. At their most basic, investment analysts look at financial statements to determine if a company is healthy. Balance sheets are important to investment analysis as they provide a ready-made means of investigating performance. However, it is important to note that quantitative financial analysis has limits: the accounting methods a particular business employs, for example, may make it look more or less healthy than it really is. Investment analysts attempt to see through this and assess a business' actual health. See also: Fundamental analysis, Financial analysis, Investment adviser.

Investment Bank A financial institution that provides a variety of services for clients. Among the services of an investment bank are underwriting, facilitating transactions, assisting in mergers and acquisitions, and brokering. In general, an investment bank's clients are institutional investors, but high net-worth individuals also use them. The name can be misleading since investment banks rarely provide retail banking services.

Investment Banker A person who works for an investment bank, which is a financial institution that provides a variety of services for clients. Included among the services an investment banker may provide are underwriting, facilitating in transactions, assisting in mergers and acquisitions, and brokering. Typically, an investment banker's clients are institutional investors, but high net-worth individuals also hire them. The name can be misleading because investment bankers rarely provide retail banking services.

Investment Climate The situation in which an investment is made. Factors affecting the investment climate include macroeconomic considerations, the political situation, and consumer confidence. The investment climate is a significant contributing factor in the performance of an investment. A strong investment climate can help spur investments toward growth, while a weak climate can do the opposite. It should be noted that an investment climate may be beneficial for some investments and detrimental to others.

Investment Club A group of individual investors who pool their money and make investment decisions together. The advantage of an investment club is that it allows small investors to take advantage of a diversified portfolio when they otherwise may not be able to afford it. An investment club may be informal or it may be legally constituted. See also: Investment company.

Investment Company A company that provides investment advisory services and/or operates mutual funds. An investment company that operates mutual funds allows its clients to carry greater or lesser risk, depending on their particular investment goals. The investment company may or may not actively manage mutual funds. Investment companies managing more than a certain amount of money must register with the SEC. See also: Asset management, Brokerage.

Investment Company Act of 1940 Legislation in the United States regulating investment companies such as mutual funds. The act placed restrictions on the activities in which investment companies are allowed to engage. For example, it forbade short selling in many circumstances. It required investment companies to file financial disclosure and set limits on the fees they are allowed to charge; it also required that investment companies with more than a certain number of investors register with the SEC. The Investment Company Act is enforced by the SEC. See also: Investment Advisers Act of 1940.

Investment Company Amendments Act of 1970 Legislation in the United States revising and expanding the Investment Company Act of 1940. Specifically, it set controls on mutual fund sales fees. The Act set a maximum load fee that a mutual fund may charge, and regulated withdrawal penalties on annuities. It limited the formation of fund holding companies and disallowed foreign holding companies from buying shares of investment companies.

Investment Company Institute An association for mutual funds in the United States. Membership is limited to open-end investment companies, closed-end investment companies, unit investment trusts, exchange-traded funds, and individuals associated with them. Its goals are to establish and enforce ethical practices among members, to lobby policymakers on behalf of the industry, and to educate the public about mutual funds and other investment companies. It was established in 1940.

Investment Consultant A person or business that provides long-term investment advice to a client in exchange for a fee. Generally speaking, investment consultants interact directly with a client e.g. by managing assets and/or making specific recommendations in accordance with the client's long-term investment goals. Investment consultants are a type of investment adviser, and as such, if they manage more than a certain amount of money, they must register with the SEC. See also: Investment Advisers Act of 1940.

Investment Counsel Association of America Now known as the Investment Adviser Association; a non-profit professional association of investment advisers. Founded in 1937, the IAA has over 500 institutional members representing a variety of individuals and organizations. The IAA provides professional information to members in the form of events, publications, and newsletters. It is also a lobbying organization representing the investment advising profession to the U.S. government. Significantly, it was instrumental in the passage of Investment Advisers Act of 1940. See also: Investing.

Investment Decision Determination of where, when, how, and how much capital to spend and/or debt to acquire in the pursuit of making a profit. An investment decision is often reached between an investor and his/her investment advisors. Depending on the type of brokerage account an investor has, investment managers may or may not have tremendous leeway in making decisions without consulting the investor himself/herself. Factors contributing to an investment decision include, but are not limited to: capital on hand, projects or opportunities available, general market conditions, and a specific investment strategy.

Investment Farm A farm one owns as an investment. That is, the personal or corporate owner of an investment farm has the right to all profits and typically must pay for its operations, but the owner does not live on the farm and generally does not conduct operations himself/herself. For example, one may buy a farm and hire workers to grow crops. The actual farmers in this case are paid employees rather than the owners of the land. With the decline of family farming, investment farms have become more common. See also: Agribusiness.

Investment Grade Describing a bond with a medium or high rating. Bonds rated Baa3 by Moody's or BBB- by S&P or Fitch. Investment-grade bonds are considered sufficiently low-risk that the law allows banks to invest in them. In addition to being low-risk, investment-grade bonds are low-return, greatly reducing the cost on the issuer. Most American Treasury and municipal bonds are investment-grade. See also: Junk, High-Rating.

Investment History The transactions that a member firm or investor has conducted in the past, especially with a given broker-dealer. Investment history must be considered in making some decisions.

Investment Income The income one derives from capital gains, dividends, and other activities related to the purchase and sale of securities. This differs from wages and salary primarily in that one does not need to work for investment income. One can manage one's investments oneself, or one can hire a money manager to do it. Both individuals and companies can have investment income; indeed, a publicly-traded company must list its investment income on its balance sheet. Investment income is often taxed differently from other income. See also: Capital gains tax.

Investment Letter A document that the buyer of a restricted security must file with the SEC. The investment letter states that the security is exempt from registration with SEC because the buyer does not intend to sell the security for at least two years. The investment letter helps ensure that all private placement offerings comply with applicable law, especially those concerning insider trading. If the buyer does not offer an investment letter, then he/she must register the restricted security. See also: Private placement.

Investment Manager A person or, more often, a bank or business who controls an investment portfolio on behalf of a client. Investment managers make investment decisions on behalf of the client in accordance to the parameters set by the client. The goal is to make the most profit for the client as possible. Some investment managers have more autonomy than others, depending upon the client's needs and desires. Institutional investment managers normally hire a team to work on the different accounts it has under management. Unlike brokers, investment managers are not paid on commission, but rather by a percentage of the total amount of money under management. This gives the investment manager an incentive to work for the client's profit, as the more money the manager accumulates, the more he/she/it makes. An investment manager is also known as a money manager or portfolio manager. See also: Advisory account, Discretionary account, Markowitz Portfolio Theory.

Investment Opportunity Set All of the investments that a person or company is able to make at a given point in time. What determines an individual investment opportunity set is largely what the investor is able to afford, whether through equity financing, debt financing, venture capital, or even personal savings.

Investment Philosophy Basic standards and beliefs guiding one's investing practices. Factors influencing one's investment philosophy include risk tolerance, investment goals, and personal beliefs about what guides markets. Investment philosophies may vary widely from each other. For example, when investing in securities, one investor may use technical analysis, which utilizes statistical information exclusively, while another may use fundamental analysis, which uses both quantitative and qualitative information. It is also called an investment strategy. See also: Naive diversification, Markowitz Portfolio Theory.

Investment Policy A form outlining the investment philosophy of an investment company, investment advisor, or some other institution that invests on behalf of clients.

Investment Policy Statement In a discretionary account, an agreement between a portfolio manager and a client stating the client's needs and desires with regard to the portfolio. That is, the IPS states how the client expects the portfolio to perform and what the portfolio manager may and may not do in order to achieve this goal. The IPS prevents misunderstandings, such as when the manager takes on too much or too little risk for the clients investment goals. See also: Asset management.

Investment Pyramid An investment strategy in which an investor diversifies the risk of his/her portfolio while also leaving the possibility for a large return. One does this by putting most of the investor's money in low risk investment vehicles; this forms the "base" of the pyramid. One then puts a moderate amount of money in medium risk investments, and finally forms the "top" of the pyramid by placing a small amount of money in high risk, speculative investments. See also: GARP.

Investment Real Estate Real estate, usually residential real estate, that one purchases with the intent of earning from it. That is, investment real estate is real estate purchased with the intent of renting it, selling at a higher price, or using for almost any purpose other than using it as a residence. Common examples include apartment buildings and second houses. Investment real estate is often taxed differently from other real property. For example, one may not be able to deduct the interest paid on an investment real estate mortgage.

Investment Risk The risk that an investment will result in a loss. Nearly all investments have some investment risk: a stock may decline; a bond may default, and the underlying asset of a derivative may not behave in a certain way. See also: Return.

Investment Sector Loan Program A program that evaluates the need for reform in the industrial sectors in Latin America and negotiates with governments for the terms of development loans. The ISLP seeks the input of U.S. government agencies in making its evaluations. It is part of the Enterprise for the Americas Initiative.

Investment Software Software that helps identify securities that are most likely to meet an investor's stated investment goals. It also helps investors make their financial plans; some programs also offer technical and fundamental analysis.

Investment Strategy Committee A group in a brokerage that researches and reports to both the firm and the firm's clients on market trends and how they affect the firm's investment philosophy. The investment strategy committee advises clients on how much capital to invest in different types of securities; it may also identify industries that the committee believes are particularly bullish or bearish. The firm's chief economist and research director are usually members of the investment strategy committee.

Investment Tax Credit 1. A tax credit on capital expenditures that was abolished in 1986. **2.** A tax credit a business may receive for making adjustments to its building and other facilities to make them more energy efficient.

Investment Turnover The number of shares traded in a portfolio over a given period of time, expressed as a percentage of the number of shares in the portfolio. A low turnover means that the portfolio is not being very actively managed; it also means that one's broker is making less in commissions, as he/she is paid per trade. See also: Churning.

Investment Valuation Model A mathematical calculation of the value of an investment. An IVM computes this value as the present value of all returns the investment is likely to generate. This can help in making investment decisions. For example, if a company's share price is $5 and an IVM computes that the present value of returns will be $7 per share, the investment is likely to be profitable. See also: option pricing model.

Investment Vehicle A security or derivative. An investment vehicle may be rigidly structured, as in an asset-backed security, or it may be quite basic, like a stock or bond. One uses an investment vehicle in order to make a profit on the capital one has invested in it. An investment vehicle may involve the purchase of a debt obligation, which entitles one to repayment with interest, or it may involve buying an ownership stake in a business, with the hope that the business will become profitable. Many different investment vehicles exist, and each is subject to greater or lesser regulation in the jurisdiction in which it takes place. Each one has its own risks and rewards; choosing the correct investment vehicles for a portfolio requires a combination of astuteness, knowledge of the market, timing, and good luck.

Investor One who places capital into a project or business with the intent of making a profit from the initial placing of capital. An investor may be one who extends a loan or line of credit, which entitles one to repayment with interest, or he may buy an ownership stake in a business with the hope that the business will become profitable. Investing may also involve buying a particular asset with the intent to resell it later for a higher price. Many types of investing exist and each is subject to greater or lesser regulation in the jurisdiction in which it takes place. Legally, investors can only exist in places where individual property rights exist and are protected. Good investors require a combination of astuteness, knowledge of the market, and timing.

Investor and Capital Markets Fee Relief Act Legislation in the United States that reduced fees related to the securities trade. For example, it lowered mandatory fees for securities traded on exchanges from a percentage to a set dollar amount. It also abolished some application fees and the like. It was passed in 2002.

Investor Relations The department of a publicly-traded company that deals directly with shareholders and potential shareholders. The investor relations department answers questions, provides information, and generally serves as a direct link between shareholders and the company they partially own.

Investor's Equity The balance of money or securities an investor keeps in a margin account in order to be able to borrow from a brokerage for short sales or other purposes. Investor's equity is kept as collateral until the brokerage calls the margin and the client pays back what is owed. FINRA requires that investor's equity must be at least 25% of the amount borrowed at all times, while some brokerages require equity of up to 50%. See also: Maintenance.

Invisible Balance The aggregate value of a country's exports and imports of services but not goods. The invisible balance is a subset of the balance of trade, which is the same thing but includes goods.

Invisible Hand A metaphor for the free market. Adam Smith coined the phrase, which refers to the idea that in the pursuit of maximizing one's self-interest, one tends to maximize the interests of society as a whole, as if an invisible hand were guiding both. For example, a man may open a mechanic shop to make money for himself, but in the process he may hire otherwise unemployed mechanics and service otherwise broken cars, which then facilitates business for the rest of the community. Proponents of deregulation have used the metaphor to illustrate their points, though others, notably Noam Chomsky, have argued that Smith did not intend to phrase to imply a lack of government intervention.

Invisible Item In accounting, intangible assets that are counted as part of a country's balance of payments. Examples of invisible items include international travel and consulting services offered in a different country. They are considered in the balance of payments because they involve transfers of money across international borders.

Invisible Supply Commodities underlying a futures contract that are available for delivery but whose quantity is unknown. The quantity of the invisible supply is difficult or impossible to determine because it is held by more than one person or company. Despite the uncertainty of the invisible supply, it may still be traded.

Invisible Trade The sale of a service or an intangible asset (such as a copyright) as opposed to a good. See also: Visible trade.

Invisible Transaction An exchange in which a service is traded across international borders and money changes hands, but in which no tangible assets are traded. An example of an invisible transaction is a consulting service offered to a client in a different country. Invisible transactions are included as invisible items when calculating a country's balance of payments.

Invoice A statement given by a seller to a buyer itemizing the sale and demanding payment. An invoice may be for the sale of a good or a service. The invoice usually states the names of the counterparties and the goods and/or services purchased, and adds any applicable sales tax or VAT. It may also include the terms of sale, especially if it is a credit sale. An invoice is also called a bill or a due bill. See also: Receipt.

Invoice Billing A system of billing a client according to goods and services provided. That is, the company provides a bill to the client for each time he/she buys goods and services. This contrasts with other ways to bill a client, such as providing a bill each month regardless of how many goods and services are purchased.

Invoice Date The date on which an invoice for a good is issued, which is usually the same day the good is sent to the buyer. Payment is due a certain number of days after the invoice date.

Invoice Price 1. In Treasury futures contracts, the amount the buyer must pay the seller when the Treasury note is delivered. This is calculated as the settlement price of the future, plus interest that has accrued. **2.** In international trade, the price against which an ad valorem tariff is levied. The tariff is calculated as a percentage of the price listed on an invoice. **3.** In the automotive industry, the price a manufacturer charges a dealer before any applicable discounts or rebates.

Involuntary Bankruptcy A situation in which a creditor may force a debtor into bankruptcy. A creditor may file for involuntary bankruptcy if the debtor has become severely and consistently delinquent or if a custodian has been appointed for the debtor in the previous six months. After the petition is filed, the debtor usually has 20 days in which to contest it. If the debtor objects to involuntary bankruptcy, he/she must show either that payments are not as delinquent as claimed or that he/she is taking steps to restore solvency. If the debtor does not show this, the bankruptcy court can force liquidation to repay the creditor(s).

Involuntary Lien A non-consensual claim to the property of another as collateral to ensure the repayment of a debt. An involuntary lien may be imposed by a court, often for non-payment of taxes. The involuntary lien gives the tax authority (or other body) the right to confiscate one's property if the debt is not settled. An involuntary lien contrasts with a voluntary lien, to which the debtor consents.

Involuntary Reduction in Force Lay-offs that a company conducts after offering buy-outs or other incentives for employees to quit. A company has an involuntary reduction in force if not enough employees decided to leave on their own.

Involuntary Unemployment In Keynesian economics, unemployment that results from low levels of investment and high levels of savings. That is, because entrepreneurs and others are saving more than they are investing, they may not have enough money remaining to keep employees on staff. See also: Cyclical unemployment.

IO 1. ISO 3166-1 alpha-2 code for the British Indian Ocean Territory. This is the code used in international transactions to and from BIOT bank accounts. **2.** ISO 3166-2 geocode for the BIOT. This is used as an international standard for shipping to the BIOT. **3.** Interest only. A derivative security whose cash flow derives exclusively from interest payments on various debt securities. The underlying asset of an interest-only strip is interest paid on debt securities, rather than the debt securities themselves. Many interest only strips are backed by mortgage interest, but some are also backed by Treasury securities and other debt securities. Interest-only strips are derived from bonds whose coupons' ownership is legally separated (or "stripped") from the debt securities themselves.

IOT GOST 7.67 Latin three-letter geocode for British Indian Ocean Territory. The code is used for transactions to and from BIOT bank accounts and for international shipping to the BIOT. As with all GOST 7.67 codes, it is used primarily in Cyrillic alphabets.

IPO Lock-Up A practice in a publicly-traded company that forbids management and large stockholders from selling their shares for a period of time following an initial public offering. Depending on the company, the IPO lock-up usually lasts 90 to 180 days. It exists to ensure that the market is not flooded with shares in the company at any given time, which would increase supply and cause a drop in price. Large shareholders selling their shares may also be seen as equating to a lack of confidence in the company, triggering a panic sell.

IQ 1. ISO 3166-1 alpha-2 code for the Republic of Iraq. This is the code used in international transactions to and from Iraqi bank accounts. **2.** ISO 3166-2 geocode for Iraq. This is used as an international standard for shipping to Iraq. Each Iraqi province has its own code with the prefix "IQ." For example, the code for the Province of al-Anbar is ISO 3166-2:IQ-AN.

IQD ISO 4217 code for the Iraqi dinar. It was introduced in 1923, replacing the Indian rupee. It was pegged to the British pound until 1959, when the peg was switched to the U.S. dollar. The peg was maintained at various levels until the First Persian Gulf War in 1991, though the black market rate did not always reflect the official exchange rate. After the Gulf War, the Iraqi government was no longer able to use the Swiss printer it had previously used to print the dinar. It began using inferior technology to print its money. However, the older notes remained in circulation and became known as Swiss dinars. Both old and new notes were replaced following the U.S. invasion in 2003.

IR 1. ISO 3166-1 alpha-2 code for the Islamic Republic of Iran. This is the code used in international transactions to and from Iranian bank accounts. **2.** ISO 3166-2 geocode for Iran. This is used as an international standard for shipping to Iran. Each province has its own code with the prefix "IR." For example, the code for the Province of Fars is ISO 3166-2:IR-14.

IRA Adoption Agreement and Plan Document The final agreement between the holder of an IRA and the financial institution providing it. The Adoption Agreement and Plan Document states the terms of the IRA, such as the contribution limit, age at which withdrawals may begin, and so forth. One must sign the document before the IRA can go into effect.

IRA Transfer The exchange of assets in an IRA between two money managers or trustees. That is, an IRA transfer occurs when an account holder wishes to change trustees. In an IRA transfer, the account holder never has direct possession of the assets. It is important not to confuse an IRA transfer with an IRA rollover.

Iraimbilanja A division of the Malagasy ariary equal in value to 1/5 of one ariary.

Iranian Rial The currency of Iran. Issued to replace the qiran in 1932, it was pegged to the British pound at various rates until 1945. After this, it was pegged to the U.S. dollar until 1975. Since the Islamic Revolution in 1979, the rial has been marked by high inflation and low value.

Iraqi Dinar The currency of Iraq. It was introduced in 1923, replacing the Indian rupee. It was pegged to the British pound until 1959, when the peg was switched to the U.S. dollar. The peg was maintained at various levels until the Persian Gulf War in 1991, though the black market rate did not always reflect the official exchange rate. After the Gulf War, the Iraqi government was no longer able to use the Swiss printer it had previously used to print the dinar. It began using inferior technology to print its money. However, the older notes remained in circulation and became known as Swiss dinars. Both the old and the new notes were replaced following the U.S.-led invasion in 2003.

Iridium A precious metal that is extremely resistant to corrosion. It is used mainly for scientific and industrial purposes for which resistance to corrosion at high temperatures is needed. With only three metric tons of iridium produced and used each year, it is traded as a commodity on various security exchanges. Like many precious metals, iridium is volatile, but generally maintains relatively high prices.

Irish Budget 2010 An Irish government budget noted for its tax increases and spending cuts. This budget cut some 4 billion euros from Ireland's deficit, in part by controversially cutting welfare programs. These policies, considered to be austerity measures, were enacted in response to Ireland's sovereign debt problems resulting from the financial crisis that began in 2008. See also: Late 2000s recession.

Irish Pound The former currency of the Republic of Ireland. It was introduced in 1928, replacing the British pound sterling. However, it was pegged to the sterling at a one-to-one ratio until the peg was abandoned in the 1970s when Ireland joined the European Monetary System. The Irish pound was taken out of circulation in 2002 and replaced with the euro.

Irish Stock Exchange Also called the ISE. The only stock exchange in Ireland. Both stocks and bonds are traded on the ISE, which has been entirely electronic since 2000. It also has a special section for growth stocks. It was established in 1793, merged to form the London Stock Exchange in 1973, and became independent again in 1995.

IRL GOST 7.67 Latin three-letter geocode for Ireland. The code is used for transactions to and from Irish bank accounts and for international shipping to Ireland. As with all GOST 7.67 codes, it is used primarily in Cyrillic alphabets.

IRN GOST 7.67 Latin three-letter geocode for Iran. The code is used for transactions to and from Iranian bank accounts and for international shipping to Iran. As with all GOST 7.67 codes, it is used primarily in Cyrillic alphabets.

Iron Butterfly An option strategy in which one takes a position on four options with three different strike prices. One buys an out-of-the-money put with a low strike price, sells a call and a put with the same at-the-money strike price, and, finally, buys an out-of-the-money call with the highest strike price. One profits from the price movement of the underlying asset over the life of the options. It is most beneficial when the underlying asset is expected to have low volatility.

Iron Condor In options, a strategy in which four contracts are bought or sold at four different strike prices. In a call iron condor, the investor buys the calls with the highest and lowest strike prices and sells the calls with the middle strike prices. In a put iron condor, the investor sells the contracts with the highest and lowest strikes and buys the middle ones. An investor engages in an iron condor strategy if he/she expects a great deal of volatility on the underlying asset; it allows him/her to make a profit regardless of the price of the underlying so long as it remains in a certain (broad) range. See also: Butterfly spread.

Iron Dollar A slang term for the silver U.S. dollar. The term originated in the Northeastern United States. It was used primarily when the coin was in circulation as a way to complain about is heavy weight.

IRQ GOST 7.67 Latin three-letter geocode for Iraq. The code is used for transactions to and from Iraqi bank accounts and for international shipping to Iraq. As with all GOST 7.67 codes, it is used primarily in Cyrillic alphabets.

IRR ISO 4217 code for the Iranian rial. Issued to replace the qiran in 1932, it was pegged to the British pound at various rates until 1945. After this, it was pegged to the U.S. dollar until 1975. Since the Islamic Revolution in 1979, the rial has been marked by high inflation and low value.

Irrational Exuberance A term used by Alan Greenspan in 1996 to describe the dot-com bubble and, more broadly, the fact that the markets were overvalued. He was criticized at the time for talking down the market and stocks fell worldwide after he said it. However, his opinion was vindicated when the dot-com bubble burst, and irrational exuberance is still used as a catch phrase for overvalued markets.

Irredeemable 1. See: Irredeemable bond. **2.** See: Irredeemable security.

Irredeemable Bond 1. Any bond that is not a callable bond. The issuer of an irredeemable bond may not call, refinance, or otherwise prevent the bond from reaching its maturity. **2.** See: Perpetual bond.

Irregularity In law, a departure from standard procedure. Irregularities are not illegal, but may be (depending on the circumstances) sufficiently grave to render a lawsuit invalid.

Irrelevance Result An economic theory stating that the performance of a firm's investments has no relation to how they are financed, whether stock, debt, or cash. The irrelevance result postulates that the quality of the investment, rather than the financing behind it, is the relevant question for a firm. It is part of the Modigliani-Miller theorem. See also: Fisher's Separation Theorem.

Irrelevant Costs In managerial accounting, costs over which executives have no control and therefore which cannot be cut to reduce expenses. Examples of irrelevant costs include rent and insurance. Some costs may be irrelevant under some circumstances but relevant under others.

Irrevocable Beneficiary The beneficiary of an insurance policy or a segregated fund who may not be deprived of his/her right to receive the benefit without his/her own consent. This differs from other types of beneficiaries whose benefit may be changed or eliminated at the discretion of the policyholder or other appropriate party.

Irrevocable Corporate Purchase Order The final draft of a purchase order. It is sent to the seller on a company letterhead.

Irrevocable Letter of Credit A letter of credit that neither the bank granting it nor the letter holder (who is the buyer of some good) may cancel under any circumstances. This provides the seller with extra assurance that he/she will be paid on time and in the correct amount. Irrevocable letters of credit are most common in international commerce.

Irrevocable Trust A trust into which a grantor deposits assets for use by a beneficiary where the terms of the trust cannot be modified or abrogated without permission of the beneficiary. That is, when a grantor sets up an irrevocable trust, he/she completely relinquishes ownership of the assets placed in the trust. As a result, an irrevocable trust is not usually considered part of the grantor's estate for estate tax purposes.

IRS Restructuring and Reform Act of 1998 Legislation in the United States that made a number of changes to the Internal Revenue Code. Among other provisions, it lowered the length of time to hold an investment for capital gains treatment from 18 to 12 months. It also mandated a five-year term for the Commissioner of the IRS.

Irtihan In Islamic law, the act of mortgaging. For example, one practices irtihan by placing one's home as collateral for a loan.

Irving Fisher A major 20th-century American economist. He was one of the first to suggest that the burst of an asset bubble caused by excessive debt results in deflation. He also advocated the idea that changes in the money supply directly cause price changes. He laid much of the intellectual foundation for what became monetarism. He lived from 1867 to 1947.

IS **1.** ISO 3166-1 alpha-2 code for the Republic of Iceland. This is the code used in international transactions to and from Icelandic bank accounts. **2.** ISO 3166-2 geocode for Iceland. This is used as an international standard for shipping to Iceland. Each region has its own code with the prefix "IS." For example, the code for the Region of Reykjavik is ISO 3166-2:IS-0.

iShares A family of exchange-traded funds that tracks various stock or bond markets. iShares can be traded like stocks or other securities and operate much like mutual funds but without any net asset value. The largest issuer of exchange-traded funds, iShare funds are traded on several stock exchanges globally.

Ishtirak An Arabic term for partnership. The term is used in the context of Islamic finance.

ISJ ISO 4217 code for the old Icelandic krona. It was introduced in 1874 and was identical to the Danish krone until around 1918. It was revalued in 1981, at which point the code changed to ISK.

ISK ISO 4217 code for the second Icelandic krona, which came into existence in 1981 after a revaluation of the first Icelandic krona. It is not a widely traded currency and, while it is a floating currency, the Central Bank of Iceland manages it closely.

ISL GOST 7.67 Latin three-letter geocode for Iceland. The code is used for transactions to and from Icelandic bank accounts and for international shipping to Iceland. As with all GOST 7.67 codes, it is used primarily in Cyrillic alphabets.

Islamic American Relief Agency A defunct organization in Missouri that provided health clinics, orphan sponsorship and other charitable services in various parts of the world. It was founded in 1985 and was shut down in 2004 because of alleged ties to terrorist organizations. In 2007, its leaders were charged with sending more than $1 million to Iraq during the sanctions in place before 2003.

Islamic Bank A bank that only offers products that conform to the sharia, or Islamic law. For example, deposits in Islamic banks do not accrue interest. They either lie dormant until withdrawal or are invested. Because this involves higher risk than conventional banking services, various highly technical products have been developed to mitigate risk and generally imitate "regular" banks as much as possible while still complying with Islamic law. Considerable debate exists as to whether these products are in fact sharia-compliant.

Islamic Banking A system of banking that only offers products that conform to the sharia, or Islamic law. For example, in Islamic banking, checking and savings deposits do not accrue interest. They either lie dormant until withdrawal or are invested. Because this involves higher risk than conventional banking services, various highly technical products have been developed to mitigate risk and generally imitate "regular" banks as much as possible while still complying with Islamic law. Considerable debate exists as to whether these Islamic banking products are in fact sharia-compliant.

Islamic Development Bank Also called the IDB. A bank that provides development financing for countries and businesses in accordance with sharia law. Specifically, it does not charge interest on its loans but rather structures them so that profits from projects may be shared with the IDB. It also provides strictly interest-free loans for infrastructure and similar projects. Its shareholders include 54 Muslim-majority nations. It began operations in 1975.

Islamic Finance The range of financial transactions that conform to the sharia, or Islamic law. Islamic finance forbids investment in industries considered sinful, notably alcohol, pornography and armaments. Islamic law also forbids the payment or receipt of interest. This forces credit to be either interest-free, or, more commonly, to take the form of a partnership or joint venture. For example, a bank could buy an asset for cash and then re-sell it to the "borrower" for a profit such that the profit is the same as the bank would have made had it extended a regular loan. Islamic finance also forbids speculation. Thus, futures contracts and options are not permissible. These restrictions have made Islamic finance rather risk averse; it has a tendency to invest in fixed assets with an intrinsic value apart from the transaction. Critics within Islam claim that Islamic finance imitates conventional finance and therefore is not truly "Islamic." However, it became a major growth sector within finance in the early 2000s. See also: Sukuk, Murabaha, Mudharaba, Musharika.

Islamic Loan Any form of financing made according to Islamic law, which forbids the payment or receipt of interest. An Islamic loan may be an interest-free loan, but often it is a more complex transaction. For example, a bank could buy an asset for cash and then re-sell it to the "borrower" for a profit such that the profit is the same as the bank would have made had it extended a regular loan. Other types may involve the bank becoming a partner with the "borrower" so that both co-own the asset or business that the loan finances, and the borrower gradually buys the bank's share of ownership with a series of payments. Strictly speaking, most Islamic loans are partnerships or joint ventures, but they are called loans because they accomplish much the same thing as conventional loans. See also: Islamic finance, Murabaha, Mudharaba, Musharika.

Islamic Mortgage A mortgage made according to the sharia, or Islamic law, which forbids the payment or receipt of interest. An Islamic mortgage may be an interest-free loan, but often it is a more complex transaction. For example, a bank could buy a house for cash and then re-sell it to the "borrower" for a profit through amortized payments such that the profit is the same as the bank would have made had it extended a regular loan. Other types involve the bank becoming a partner with the "borrower" so that both co-own the house or business, a scenario in which the borrower gradually buys the bank's share of ownership with a series of payments.

Island An electronic network used to execute limit orders on the NYSE, NASDAQ, and American Stock Exchange, among others. The Island matches limit orders for execution; if a matching order is not available, an order is displayed on the Island until one is found.

Island Council In Kiribati, a political subdivision approximately equivalent to a municipality. This is the only national subdivision in Kiribati.

Island Display In retail, the prominent display of products away from other products to increase their visibility. An island display may be at the end of an aisle, by itself in the middle of a store, or in any other highly noticeable place.

Island Group In Tuvalu, a political subdivision equivalent to a province or district.

Island Position The position occupied by an advertisement on television, radio or in print that has been placed between two stories or programs. This contrasts with other ads placed between other ads.

Island Reversal In technical analysis, a pattern in which a security's price does one of two things. It may suddenly gap up (i.e. it suddenly begins trading well above its previous high) and then gap down again to its previous level. This is considered a bearish signal. On the other hand, island reversal may involve a gap down to a new low, and then a gap back up to the previous level. This is thought to be bullish. In any case, island reversal is a short-term indicator.

Isle of Man Pound The currency of the Isle of Man. It is pegged to the British pound at a one-to-one ratio; the two currencies circulate alongside each other.

ISO 3166-1 Numeric Code A code used for international trade of goods and for international transactions involving securities or banking. These codes are used primarily in languages not based on the Latin alphabet.

004	Afghanistan
010	Antarctica
016	American Samoa
020	Andorra
024	Angola
028	Antigua and Barbuda
031	Azerbaijan
040	Austria
056	Belgium
070	Bosnia and Herzegovina
074	Bouvet Island
076	Brazil
086	British Indian Ocean Territory
092	British Virgin Islands
100	Bulgaria
112	Belarus
120	Cameroon
140	Central African Republic
148	Chad
158	Taiwan
162	Christmas Island
166	Cocos Islands
175	Mayotte
178	Republic of the Congo
180	Democratic Republic of the Congo
184	Cook Islands
188	Costa Rica
196	Cyprus
204	Benin
212	Dominica
218	Ecuador
222	El Salvador
226	Equatorial Guinea
231	Ethiopia
233	Estonia
234	Faroe Islands

239	South Georgia and the South Sandwich Islands
246	Finland
248	Aland Islands
250	France
254	French Guinea
258	French Polynesia
260	French Southern and Antarctic Territories
266	Gabon
268	Republic of Georgia
275	Palestinian Territories
276	Germany
288	Ghana
296	Kiribati
300	Greece
304	Greenland
308	Grenada
312	Guadeloupe
316	Guam
334	Heard Island and the McDonald Islands
336	Vatican City
372	Ireland
380	Italy
384	Cote d'Ivoire
438	Liechtenstein
442	Luxembourg
450	Madagascar
466	Mali
470	Malta
474	Martinique
492	Monaco
499	Montenegro
500	Montserrat
508	Mozambique
520	Nauru
528	Netherlands
531	Curacao
534	Sint Maarten
535	Bonaire
540	New Caledonia
562	Niger
570	Niue
574	Norfolk Island
580	Northern Mariana Islands
581	U.S. Minor Outlying Islands
584	Marshall Islands
585	Palau
591	Panama
612	Pitcairn
616	Poland
620	Portugal
624	Guinea-Bissau

626	Timor-Leste
630	Puerto Rico
638	Reunion
642	Romania
652	Saint Barthelemy
659	Saint Kitts and Nevis
660	Anguilla
662	Saint Lucia
663	Saint Martin
666	Saint Pierre and Miquelon
670	Saint Vincent and the Grenadines
674	San Marino
686	Senegal
688	Serbia
703	Slovakia
705	Slovenia
716	Zimbabwe
724	Spain
729	Sudan
732	Western Sahara
740	Suriname
744	Svarbald and Jan Mayen
756	Switzerland
762	Tajikistan
768	Togo
772	Tokelau
792	Turkey
795	Turkmenistan
796	Turks and Caicos Islands
798	Tuvalu
804	Ukraine
831	Guernsey
832	Jersey
833	Isle of Man
850	U.S. Virgin Islands
854	Burkina Faso
862	Venezuela
876	Wallis and Futuna
887	Yemen

ISO 4217 Numeric Code A code used especially when financial transactions are made using non-Latin alphabets or scripts.

008	Albanian lek
012	Algerian dinar
032	Argentine peso
036	Australian dollar
044	Bahamian dollar
048	Bahraini dinar
050	Bangladeshi taka
051	Armenian dram
052	Barbados dollar
060	Bermudian dollar

064	Bhutanese ngultrum	418	Lao kip
068	Bolivian boliviano	422	Lebanese pound
072	Botswana pula	426	Lesotho loti
084	Belize dollar	428	Latvian lats
090	Solomon Islands dollar	430	Liberian dollar
096	Brunei dollar	434	Libyan dinar
104	Myanma kyat	440	Lithuanian litas
108	Burundian franc	446	Macanese pataca
116	Cambodian riel	454	Malawian kwacha
124	Canadian dollar	458	Malaysian ringgit
132	Cape Verdean escudo	462	Maldivian rufiyaa
136	Cayman Islands dollar	478	Mauritanian ouguiya
144	Lankan rupee	480	Mauritian rupee
152	Chilean peso	484	Mexican peso
156	Chinese renminbi	496	Mongolian tugrik
170	Colombian peso	498	Moldovan leu
174	Comorian franc	504	Moroccan dirham
191	Croatian kuna	512	Omani rial
192	Cuban peso	516	Namibian dollar
203	Czech koruna	524	Nepalese rupee
208	Danish krone	533	Aruban florin
214	Dominican peso	548	Vanuatu vatu
230	Ethiopian birr	554	New Zealand dollar
232	Eritrean nakfa	558	Nicaraguan cordoba
238	Falkland Islands pound	566	Nigerian naira
242	Fijian dollar	578	Norwegian krone
262	Djiboutian franc	586	Pakistani rupee
270	Gambian dalasi	590	Panamanian balboa
292	Gibraltar pound	598	Papua New Guinean kina
320	Guatemalan quetzal	600	Paraguayan guarani
324	Guinean franc	604	Peruvian new sol
328	Guyanese dollar	608	Philippine peso
332	Haitian gourde	634	Qatari rial
340	Honduran lempira	643	Russian ruble
344	Hong Kong dollar	646	Rwandan franc
348	Hungarian forint	654	Saint Helena pound
352	Icelandic krona	678	Sao Tome and Principe dobra
356	Indian rupee	682	Saudi riyal
360	Indonesian rupiah	690	Seychellois rupee
364	Iranian rial	694	Sierra Leonean leone
368	Iraqi dinar	702	Singaporean dollar
376	Israeli new sheqel	704	Vietnamese dong
388	Jamaican dollar	706	Somali shilling
392	Japanese yen	710	South African rand
398	Kazakhstani tenge	728	South Sudanese pound
400	Jordanian dinar	748	Swazi lilangeni
404	Kenyan shilling	752	Swedish krona
408	North Korean won	760	Syrian pound
410	South Korean won	764	Thai baht
414	Kuwaiti dinar	776	Tongan pa'anga
417	Kyrgyzstani som	780	Trinidad and Tobago dollar

784	UAE dirham
788	Tunisian dinar
800	Ugandan shilling
807	Macedonian denar
818	Egyptian pound
826	British pound
834	Tanzanian shilling
840	U.S. dollar
858	Uruguayan peso
860	Uzbekistani som
882	Western Samoan tala
886	Yemeni rial
894	Zambian kwacha
901	Taiwanese dollar
931	Cuban convertible peso
932	Zimbabwean dollar
934	Turkmenistani manat
936	Ghanaian cedi
937	Venezuelan bolivar
938	Sudanese pound
941	Serbian dinar
943	Mozambican metical
944	Azerbaijani manat
946	Romanian new leu
948	WIR Euro
949	Turkish dollar
950	Central African CFA franc
951	East Caribbean dollar
952	West African CFA franc
953	CFP franc
959	Gold
960	Special Drawing Rights
961	Silver
962	Platinum
964	Palladium
968	Surinamese dollar
969	Malagasy ariary
971	Afghan afghani
972	Tajikistani somoni
973	Angolan kwanza
974	Belarusian ruble
975	Bulgarian lev
976	Congolese franc
977	Bosnia and Herzegovina convertible mark
978	Euro
979	Mexican Unidad de Inversion
980	Ukrainian hryvnia
981	Georgian lari
985	Polish zloty
986	Brazilian real
990	Chilean Unidad de Fomento

Isoquant On a chart, a line or curve representing identical outputs when one changes one of two inputs.

I-SPY Act Proposed legislation in the United States that would ban all forms of data collection on the Internet except for cookies. The I-SPY Act would increase penalties for persons who create spyware. It passed the House of Representatives in 2005.

Isqat In Islamic law, the expiration of the right to conduct an action.

ISR GOST 7.67 Latin three-letter geocode for Israel. The code is used for transactions to and from Israeli bank accounts and for international shipping to Israel. As with all GOST 7.67 codes, it is used primarily in Cyrillic alphabets.

Israeli Lira The former currency of Israel. It was introduced upon Israeli independence in 1948. The fact that it had a non-Hebrew name proved controversial. As a result, it was replaced by the old Israeli sheqel in 1980.

Israeli New Sheqel The currency of Israel. It replaced the old sheqel in 1985 due to the former currency's high rate of inflation. The new sheqel is a floating currency, and because it is traded on the Merc, it is one of the few currencies for which futures and other derivative contracts are widely available. The new sheqel is a hard currency, indicating consumer confidence on the foreign exchange markets. See also: Currency pair.

Israeli Old Shekel The former currency of Israel. It was introduced in 1980, replacing the Israeli lira, which was criticized for having a non-Hebrew name. It suffered high inflation throughout its history and was replaced by the new sheqel in 1985.

Issar An ancient Hebrew unit of weight approximately equivalent to 0.177 grams.

Issue A set of securities that a company or government offers for sale. That is, when a company sells stocks or bonds to the public (or offers them for private placement) the collection of stocks or bonds is said to be an issue. If the company or government is selling a set for the first time, it is said to be making a new issue. Typically, issues of securities may be bought and sold on the open market.

Issue Date 1. The date on which a company or government makes a new issue of securities to the public. For example, if a company makes its IPO on January 1, this is said to be the issue date for its IPO. It is also called the offering date. **2.** The date on which interest begins to accrue on a bond or other fixed-income security. If one buys a fixed-income security between issue dates, one must compensate the seller for all interest that has accrued in addition to the purchase price. The issue date for a security is also called the dated date. See also: Dirty price.

Issue Price The initial price of a new issue on the primary market. That is, the issue price is what the issuer requests from the market in exchange for a share, bond, or other security.

Issuer An organization that registers, distributes, and sells a security on the primary market. An issuer can be a private company or a government. For example, if a company registers a stock with the SEC, makes arrangements to underwrite it, and keeps the proceeds from its sale, it is said to be the issuer of that stock.

Issuing Bank A bank that writes a letter of credit, especially on behalf of an exporter. The issuing bank operates in the country of the importer, and facilitates trade between the importer and exporter by providing credit for the transaction. It is also called an opening bank.

Issuing House A bank or other financial institution that registers, distributes, and sells a security on the primary market on behalf of another company. For example, if a company wishes to make an initial public offering, it may hire an issuing house to register the IPO with the SEC and make arrangements to underwrite it. See also: Underwriter.

Istanbul Stock Exchange The only securities exchange in Turkey. Stocks, bonds, derivatives, and other securities are traded on the Istanbul Stock Exchange. More than 300 companies are listed on the Exchange. It was established in 1986 but traces its origins to the late 19th century.

Istihqaq al-Ribh In Islamic law, the right to profit from a business or asset. In order to have this right under Islamic law, one must take a risk. That is, there is no profit without risk. This excludes the ability to profit from arbitrage or similar structures.

Istisna In Islamic law, a contract in which a buyer purchases an item for deferred delivery. The item must be described in detail and construction must fit the specifications. There is no set delivery date for the item. Usually, an istisna contract is made for specially made items. For example, one may make a contract to build a custom table for a client. Payment may be made in a lump sum or in installments.

IT 1. ISO 3166-1 alpha-2 code for the Italian Republic. This is the code used in international transactions to and from Italian bank accounts. **2.** ISO 3166-2 geocode for Italy. This is used as an international standard for shipping to Italy. Each Italian region and province has its own code with the prefix "IT." For example, the code for the Province of Perugia is ISO 3166-2:IT-PG.

ITA GOST 7.67 Latin three-letter geocode for Italy. The code is used for transactions to and from Italian bank accounts and for international shipping to Italy. As with all GOST 7.67 codes, it is used primarily in Cyrillic alphabets.

Itaewon District A tourist district in Seoul, South Korea. It is noted for its many restaurants, shops and brothels. Most visitors to the district are foreigners visiting or living in South Korea, including American military personnel.

Italian Derivatives Market One of two markets for derivatives managed by the Italian Stock Market. Options and futures both trade on IDEM.

Itemize To list a specific expense the taxpayer has had over the course of the tax year in order to reduce one's taxable income. One may itemize most medical expenses, for example, and deduct them from one's taxable income. The same is the case for interest on mortgages and business expenses. The IRS allows itemized deductions as an alternative to the standard deduction, which takes a flat amount out of one's taxable income. Itemized deductions are subject to certain restrictions; for example, some expenses must exceed a certain percentage of the adjusted gross income to be deductible.

Itemized Deduction A deduction from one's taxable income as the result of a specific expense the taxpayer has had over the course of the tax year. Most medical expenses, for example, may be deducted from one's taxable income. The same is the case for interest on mortgages and business expenses. The IRS allows itemized deductions as an alternative to the standard deduction, which takes a flat amount out of one's taxable income. Itemized deductions are subject to certain restrictions; for example, some expenses must exceed a certain percentage of the adjusted gross income to be deductible.

Itemized Statement An invoice or other statement listing entries individually. For example, a grant writer who worked on three grants for a client may issue an itemized statement that lists each grant and the number of hours spent on it on a separate line. Itemized statements are considered more detailed and thus are usually preferred.

Itinerant Worker A person who moves from place to place to find a job. An itinerant worker is not confined to a single place and often does not own property. Itinerant workers are most common in sectors with a large number of temporary jobs or a high degree of seasonality. For example, an itinerant worker may be an agricultural worker who moves between two regions with slightly different growing seasons. The number of itinerant workers may increase during recessions or other times with low levels of job security.

ITL ISO 4217 code for the Italian lira. It was introduced at the foundation of the modern Italian state in 1861. Between 1865 and the First World War, Italy belonged to the Latin Monetary Union. The lira intermittently suffered from high inflation until it was taken out of circulation and replaced with the euro in 2002. See also: Quota 90.

Itsehallinnollinen maakunta In Finland, a political subdivision for the Aland Islands, which are an autonomous region.

Ittifaq Dhimni In Islamic finance, the sale of an asset with an agreement to repurchase at a stated price.

Itumalo In Samoa, a political subdivision equivalent to a county or province.

Iugar A largely obsolete Romanian measure of area approximately equivalent to 5,700 square meters.

Ivan F. Boesky An American investor known for insider trading in the mid-1980s. An arbitrageur, he received tips from colleagues and made major stock purchases in publicly traded companies a few days before mergers or acquisitions were announced. He accumulated $200 million, but paid much of it in fines after he was caught. He later served time in jail.

J A symbol appearing next to a stock listed on NASDAQ indicating that the stock is a voting share. All NASDAQ listings use a four letter abbreviation; if a J follows the abbreviation, this indicates that the security being traded is voting stock.

J Curve 1. In charting, the theoretical trend of a country's trade balance after the devaluation of its currency. After a devaluation in currency, there is often a slight increase in the trade deficit, but the long-term effect is a trade surplus due to the fact that a good sold in a devalued currency makes a good less expensive for international buyers. This is represented graphically as a curve that briefly dips below the x-axis, representing time, before turning upwards, resembling the letter J. On this graph, the y-axis represents the trade balance. **2.** In equity funds, the theoretical trend of the internal rate of return over several years. Most funds operate at a loss at their beginning, due in part to their start-up costs. Later, if the fund is successful, the internal rate of return rises significantly. This is represented graphically as a curve that briefly dips below the x-axis, representing time, before turning upwards, resembling the letter J. On this graph, the y-axis represents the internal rate of return.

J-1 Visa A visa allowing one to stay in the United States for cultural or business exchange. Many times, a J-1 visa is issued for work purposes or for training, such as an internship or schooling. In order to be eligible for a J-1 visa, one must receive sponsorship from a government or private entity. One must leave the United States within 30 days of the visa's expiration.

Jack Grubman A formerly well regarded Wall Street analyst who specialized in the telecommunications industry. In 2002, he was accused of purposely giving bad advice to buy WorldCom and other stocks immediately before their companies went into bankruptcy. He was subsequently barred from the securities sector for life.

Jackson A slang term for a $20 bill in the United States. The term is derived from Andrew Jackson, who appears on the $20 bill.

JAJO Abbreviation for January, April, June, and October. This is used to option cycles to determine the expiration date of an option contract.

Jakarta Stock Exchange A former stock exchange in Indonesia. Originally opened in 1912, it closed and re-opened a number of times until 1977, when it was re-organized and experienced several years of steadily increasing trade. It was privatized in 1992 and introduced an automated trading floor in 1995. In 2007, it merged with the Surabaya Stock Exchange to form the Indonesia Stock Exchange.

Jalka A Finnish unit of length approximately equivalent to 297 millimeters. It became obsolete when Finland adopted the metric system in 1880.

JAM GOST 7.67 Latin three-letter geocode for Jamaica. The code is used for transactions to and from Jamaican bank accounts and for international shipping to Jamaica. As with all GOST 7.67 codes, it is used primarily in Cyrillic alphabets.

Jamaica Accord An international agreement that ratified the end of the Bretton Woods System by allowing the managed float of the price of gold with respect to the U.S. dollar. The agreement was concluded in 1976. A 1978 amendment to the Jamaica Accord allowed for the creation of Special Drawing Rights.

Jamaican Dollar The currency of Jamaica. It was introduced in 1968, replacing the Jamaican pound. It has historically been a very weak currency. It is a floating currency.

Jamaican Pound The former currency of Jamaica. It was issued in 1840 and pegged to the British pound. It was replaced by the Jamaican dollar in 1969.

James Goodfellow A Scottish inventor who patented personal identification number technology and was also instrumental in developing the automated teller machine. He was born in 1937.

James Tobin A 20th-century American economist. A Keynesian, he promoted government intervention in economies to prevent or end recessions. He also suggested that a fairly priced company ought to have a price equal to its total asset value, which formed the basis of the Q ratio, which is used to value companies. Tobin served on the Federal Reserve Board of Governors and Council of Economic Advisors. He received the Nobel Prize for Economics in 1981. He lived from 1918 to 2002.

James Wolfensohn President of the World Bank between 1995 and 2005. He spent part of his tenure discussing corruption in providing financing to the developing world. Born in Australia, he became a U.S. citizen in 1980. He was born in 1933.

Jamoat In Tajikistan, a political subdivision equivalent to a municipality.

Janitor Life Insurance A life insurance policy owned by a corporation on a large number of its employees. Janitor life insurance is an abuse of key person insurance, which compensates a company for the loss generated by the death of a significant employee. In the 1990s, it became common for companies to purchase key person insurance on many employees and even keep them after these employees left the company. Companies deducted the premiums and collected the death benefit when employees finally died. Janitor life insurance is legally limited, but still occurs. The term is slightly derogatory, as is its alternative, dead peasants life insurance.

January Barometer A theory stating that the performance of the S&P 500 in January predicts its performance for the remainder of the year. That is, if the S&P ends January higher than it began, there will be a rising stock market and vice versa. Investors using the January barometer make investment decisions based on this performance; they buy S&P 500 stocks when performance is strong in January and sell when it is not. The January barometer has had mixed results over the years.

January Dinar A currency used in the former Yugoslavia. It was introduced in January 1994 but suffered from hyperinflation so extreme that it was withdrawn only a month later. It was replaced by the new Yugoslav dinar, which was pegged to the deutschemark.

Japan Bank for International Cooperation A state-owned bank in Japan responsible for promoting trade relations internationally. It encourages Japanese exports and provides resources for foreign direct investment. It was established in 1999 with the merger of the Export-Import Bank of Japan and the Overseas Economic Cooperation Fund.

Japan Business Federation A trade association for Japanese businesses. It lobbies the government for favorable legislation and is considered one of the most politically conservative of Japanese business groups. It was established in its current form in 2002.

Japan Corporate Program A five-year program aimed to improve American exports to Japan. The U.S. Department of Commerce, which sponsored the program, selected 20 companies and helped them market their products in Japan. For example, it printed marketing literature in Japanese and held road shows in Japan. The program ran from 1991 to 1996.

Japan Defense Agency The former name of the Japanese Ministry of Defense. It changed its name in 2006.

Japan Development Bank A bank owned by the Japanese government that provided loans to foreign companies interested in foreign direct investment in Japan. It was established in 1951 to help reconstruct the Japanese economy. It was dissolved and replaced by the Development Bank of Japan in 2008.

Japan Export Information Center Also called the JEIC. An organization that provides market research and other information on doing business in Japan. It is run by the U.S. Department of Commerce and is based in Washington, D.C.

Japan External Trade Organization Also called JETRO. A government agency in Japan that promotes Japanese exports. It maintains offices in dozens of countries for this purpose. It also provides market research and other information for foreign companies considering investing in Japan. It was established in 1951.

Japan Federation of Economic Organizations A former trade association for Japanese businesses. It lobbied the government (particularly the Liberal Democratic Party) for favorable legislation. It merged into the Japan Business Federation in 2002.

Japan Inc. Informal for the close relationship between the Japanese government and the private sector. The Japanese government guided private sector development following the Second World War, often using personal relationships between bureaucrats and executives rather than actual regulation. This term came to prominence in the 1980s and was used by Western businessmen. While some credit Japan Inc. with playing a major role in the Japanese miracle, others believe it led to corruption and contributed to the Asian financial crisis.

Japan International Cooperation Agency Also called JICA. A government agency in Japan that coordinates foreign aid to other countries. It was established in its current form in 2003 but traces its origins to 1974, when it was a department in the Foreign Ministry.

Japan Local Government Bond Association An organization in Japan that assists municipalities in financial management so as to improve their ability to issue bonds and receive credit. It conducts research and provides training and educational programs. Members consist of local and provincial governments in Japan, while banks and other organizations may become associate members. It was established in 1979.

Japan Mint An organization in Japan that issues legal tender coins for general use. It was established in 1871 and is owned by the government of Japan as an incorporated administrative agency. It is headquartered in Osaka with branches in Hiroshima and Tokyo.

Japan Special Fund Also called the JSF. A fund established in 1988 by the Asian Development Bank and the government of Japan to assist in international development projects in Asia. The JSF offers grants and loans to recipient countries of the Asian Development Bank to help restructure their economies and promote growth.

Japanese Association of Securities Dealers Automated Quotation System An electronic securities exchange headquartered in Tokyo. Founded in 1963 as an over-the-counter exchange, it reorganized as a securities exchange in 2004. At reorganization, it became the first new securities exchange in Japan in nearly a half century. While its operations are similar to NASDAQ in the United States, the two are unrelated.

Japanese Auction A way to run an auction in which all participants must bid each new price in order to remain in competition for the item. For example, if the opening bid for a good is $500, all participants must bid $500. If the next bid is $600, anyone who does not bid $600 is eliminated. This continues until only one bidder remains. Each bidder is able to observe how many other bidders remain after each round.

Japanese Bankers Association An organization in Japan that represents banks and bank holding companies. It promotes compliance, helps set standards, and lobbies for favorable legislation. It traces its origins to 1945.

Japanese Civil Service Exam An examination one must pass in order to receive most jobs in the Japanese bureaucracy. The exam routinely has passage rates under 10%. Those who pass the exam and go on to be hired into the bureaucracy enjoy a great deal of social prestige.

Japanese Government Bond Any bond issued by the government of Japan. Japanese government bonds are backed by the full faith and credit of the government and are considered relatively low risk.

Japanese Institute of Certified Public Accountants A professional organization for accountants in Japan. It sets accounting and professional standards. Membership is required for anyone acting as a CPA in Japan. It was established in 1949.

Japanese Ministry of Defense A cabinet-level agency in Japan responsible for national defense. Though it traces its origins at least to the 19th century, it acquired its current name in 2006. Under the 1947 constitution, the Japanese government is not permitted to wage war. Nevertheless, the Ministry of Defense operates the Japan Self-Defense Forces, which effectively act as a military.

Japanese Miracle A term for the remarkable economic growth Japan experienced after its devastation in World War II. The growth is credited to a combination of American investment immediately after the war and government regulation of the economy. The Japanese government restricted imports and promoted exports. Meanwhile, the Bank of Japan lent vast amounts to companies to stimulate private investment. This combined with a close relationship between corporate executives and bureaucrats allowed the government to pick winners successfully. The Miracle lasted until the Japanese financial crisis, which started in 1991.

Japanese Yen The currency of Japan. It was introduced by the Meiji government in 1871. The yen decimalized the previously used Tokugawa currency. It was originally pegged to gold (smaller units were pegged to silver). Following World War II, the yen switched its peg to the U.S. dollar through the Bretton Woods System. In 1971, the yen began to float because it had become undervalued and because the United States left the Bretton Woods System. The currency suffered from exceptionally low value in the wake of the Asian financial crisis, but stabilized by the mid- and late-2000s. It is a common reserve currency, and is one of the most commonly traded currencies in the world.

Jareeb A customary unit of area approximately equivalent to 405 square meters. It is used in real estate transactions in some parts of Pakistan.

Jarrow Turnbull Model A model for pricing credit investment vehicles. The Jarrow Turnbull model considers interest rates and how they relate to the probability of default.

Java A programming language. It is especially useful because it allows for software distribution to a wide audience. It was developed by Sun Microsystems.

Jay Gould A successful American banker and one of the so-called "robber barons." After starting in his father's hardware store, he moved into the lumber business and banking. He became very wealthy and was, along with James Fisk, responsible for the gold buying spree that led to a price crash after the Civil War (it is called the Gould-Fisk scandal). He came to control 15% of American railroad tracks, though a failed attempt to kidnap an investor ensured that he never acquired the Erie Railroad. He was known for opposing unionization among his employees, sometimes violently. Gould lived from 1836 to 1892.

Jean-Claude Trichet A French banker. In the 1980s, he was part of the Group of 30, an organization specializing in economic issues. In 1993, he became the governor of Banque de France. Ten years later, he was made the second president of the European Central Bank. Trichet was born in 1942.

Jefferson Nickel A coin minted by the United States starting in 1938. It is worth 1/20 of one dollar. It features a portrait of Thomas Jefferson on the obverse.

Jeffrey K. Skilling A businessman who served as President of Enron. He worked for Enron periodically starting in 1987. Skilling adopted the strategy in which Enron itself did not possess any assets; he also adopted mark to market accounting. In 2006, he was convicted of insider trading, securities fraud, and other crimes. See also: Enron scandal, Kenneth Lay.

Jekyll and Hyde 1. Informal for strong and weak points in a company's financial statement. **2.** A volatile asset or investment whose value increases and decreases significantly in short periods of time. **3.** Informal for a situation where two major executives in a company have conflicting and incompatible views about the direction the company should take.

Jemaah Islamiah An Islamic militant organization active in Indonesia and other places in Southeast Asia. It was formed in 1993 in opposition to the Suharto regime. In 2002, the United Nations designated it as a terrorist organization.

Jennifer Lopez Informal for a security's rounded bottom, which occurs when its price reaches a bottom and gradually begins to increase. Technical analysts see this as a positive sign, as it indicates that the security is gradually transitioning from low prices to high prices, meaning that increases are likely to be sustained.

Jensen's Index A measure of the return on a portfolio over what the capital asset pricing model predicts, given the beta and market return on that portfolio. The index also adjusts for risk. It is also called Jensen's alpha or Jensen's measure. It is calculated as: Jensen's Index = ((Portfolio's return - Risk-free return) + (Market return - Risk-free return)) * Beta

Jeon A division of the South Korean won. One won is divided into 100 jeon; however, the jeon is not circulated in practice.

JEP A currency code for the Jersey pound. It is pegged to the British pound at a one-to-one ratio; the two currencies circulate alongside each other. This code is not recognized by the ISO.

Jersey Pound The currency of Jersey. It is pegged to the British pound at a one-to-one ratio; the two currencies circulate alongside each other.

Jet Lag The state of being unadjusted to a new time zone. One generally experiences jet lag after traveling rapidly over a brief period of time. For example, if one flies from Oklahoma to Bahrain, one is likely to experience jet lag because of the eight-hour time difference. Jet lag is a common result of travel for international business.

Jetsam Property seen floating on the water after having been thrown overboard from a ship in an emergency. Under maritime law, jetsam becomes the property of its finder, while flotsam, which usually results from a shipwreck, remains the property of its original owners.

Jettison To throw property overboard from a ship, especially in an emergency. Under maritime law, property that has been jettisoned (called jetsam) becomes the property of whoever finds it.

Jeweler's Block Insurance Policy An insurance policy providing coverage to a jewelry seller while his/her jewelry is being transported. This policy is particularly useful when the jeweler has ordered new inventory or has custody of jewels owned by his/her client. Jeweler's block insurance is an all-risks policy, meaning it covers all or nearly all contingencies resulting in loss.

Jewelry Gems, gold, silver and other precious items worn as personal accessories. Jewelry is often worn on a daily basis, and is also kept as a family heirloom (and worn rarely). Because jewelry is both small and expensive, it is a target for thieves and may easily be lost. Some jewelry owners purchase jewelry insurance, which protects against these possibilities.

Jewelry Floater An addition to a homeowner's insurance or renter insurance policy providing coverage in the event of loss, theft or damage to one's jewelry. Some jewelry floaters give cash for a claim, while others simply pay to replace the jewelry. A jewelry floater is important because many homeowner's insurance and renter insurance policies do not cover damage or loss of jewelry, and pay a low amount for theft. As with all insurance, one must pay a periodic premium in exchange for coverage.

Jewelry Insurance An insurance policy providing coverage in the event of loss, theft or damage to one's jewelry. Some jewelry insurance gives cash for a claim, while others simply pay to replace the jewelry. This type of insurance is important because many homeowner's insurance and renter insurance policies do not cover damage or loss of jewelry, and pay a low amount for theft. As with all insurance, one must pay a periodic premium in exchange for coverage.

Jiao A currency unit in China and Taiwan. It is equal to 1/10 of one renminbi or one Taiwanese dollar. The jiao is more commonly used in China.

JIBOR Jakarta Interbank Offer Rate. The interest rate participating banks offer to other banks for loans to each other. JIBOR may be used as a benchmark for short-term interest rates in Asia. It may also be used in other transactions, such as swaps. For example, an interest rate swap may give the floating rate as "JIBOR +/- X base points." See also: LIBOR, EURIBOR.

Jieban In China, a political subdivision equivalent to a township, usually within an urban area.

Jig A slang term for positive momentum.

Jigged Out Slang; describing a situation in which one opens a position, followed by a brief turnaround in the market prompting one to close the position at a loss, and finally a return to normalcy. In other words, one is jigged out when one is scared of a loss when one would have in fact made a gain.

Jihad A religious obligation for Muslims. The word is Arabic for "struggle," though its technical meaning has been disputed. Historically, many scholars have argued that jihad primarily entails a struggle against one's base instincts. However, it was used both in the Quran and by rulers of some Muslim-majority countries to justify war, whether to end persecution of Muslims or to provide religious grounds for conquest. The meaning of the term remains controversial, though some groups, notably al-Qaida, emphasize its militant element.

Jilla In Nepal, a political subdivision approximately equivalent to a county.

Jin A unit of mass in China approximately equivalent to 500 grams.

Jingle In marketing, a short song with lyrics intended to become "stuck in one's head." The jingle emphasizes the quality, price, and/or desirability of a product. Jingles evolved gradually, but originated with the invention of the radio in the 20th century.

Jinmyaku A Japanese term for a personal network. Using one's jinmyaku is important for finding a job or increasing one's customer base. See also: Networking.

Jinx A slang term for Japanese securities markets.

Jitney 1. An illegal act in which two or more investors buy and sell the same security at pre-arranged, agreed-upon prices. This directly results in neither profit nor loss for the investor, but creates the impression that the security is undergoing heavy trading, which could drive up the price or generate unwarranted interest. **2.** A situation in which a broker who is a floor member conducts a transaction on behalf of a broker who is not.

Jizya A tax historically imposed on non-Muslims living in under Islamic law. The jizya was levied on a per capita basis and formed a major source of state revenue in some Muslim societies. In exchange for paying the jizya, non-Muslims were not required to pay zakat.

JM 1. ISO 3166-1 alpha-2 code for Jamaica. This is the code used in international transactions to and from Jamaican bank accounts. **2.** ISO 3166-2 geocode for Jamaica. This is used as an international standard for shipping to Jamaica. Each Jamaican parish has its own code with the prefix "JM." For example, the code for the Parish of Hanover is ISO 3166-2:JM-09.

JMD ISO 4217 code for the Jamaican dollar. It was introduced in 1968, replacing the Jamaican pound. It has historically been a very weak currency. It is a floating currency.

JO JO 1. ISO 3166-1 alpha-2 code for the Kingdom of Jordan. This is the code used in international transactions to and from Jordanian bank accounts. **2.** ISO 3166-2 geocode for Jordan. This is used as an international standard for shipping to Jordan. Each governorate has its own code with the prefix "JO." For example, the code for the Governorate of Aqaba is ISO 3166-2:JO-AQ. Jo **3.** A unit of length in Japan equivalent to approximately 10 feet.

Joachimsthal A 16th-century name for Jachymov, a town in what is now the Czech Republic that was known for its silver deposits. Coins minted from silver found in Joachimsthal became common throughout the Holy Roman Empire and elsewhere. This coin was called the Joachimsthaler, which was shortened to thaler. This in turn became the origin for the word "dollar."

Job Gainful employment. Strictly speaking, a job refers to employment by another person or company, but the word is often used to describe self-employment as well. Because individuals are compensated for their work at their jobs, these are considered necessary for a society to function. According to Keynesian economics, the money one earns from a job can create more jobs because the money creates demand for goods and services that must be provided. Supply-side economics, on the other hand, maintains that lower taxes are best for job creation.

Job Acceptance Schedule The job conditions to which a potential employee is willing to agree. The conditions involved in a job acceptance schedule are pay, working environment, advancement prospects, type of work, and location. In general, an unemployed person is more likely to have a lower job acceptance schedule than an employed person who is looking for a career move. For example, an unemployed actor is more likely to take a job waiting tables than an employed actor.

Job Analysis In human resources, determination of the duties of a job, the nature of performance evaluation, the costs associated with hiring someone and so forth. Job analysis helps establish whether or not hiring someone is cost effective.

Job Analyst A person who determines the duties of a job, the nature of performance evaluation, the costs associated with hiring someone and so forth. Job analysts help establish whether or not hiring someone is cost effective. A job analyst may work in human resources.

Job Bank A database, especially but not necessarily online, where job openings are listed. A job bank may show positions for a single company, in a certain industry or even in a geographic area. A job bank consolidates the job hunting process and in theory makes finding suitable positions easier.

Job Center A public or private agency that seeks to connect the unemployed with potential employers. It may do this in a variety of ways, especially by setting up interviews, finding temporary work and/or providing resources for retraining.

Job Classification The arrangement of positions in a company or industry according to responsibility and/or compensation. For example, one's job classification may start as analyst, and then change to senior analyst, junior manager, senior manager and finally partner.

Job Cost Sheet An itemized list of the estimated or actual costs of materials and labor to complete a project or make a product.

Job Costing The process by which a construction company determines the expenses associated with a particular work order. For example, if a company is asked for a quote to build a parking lot, it first must conduct job costing for labor, materials and so forth to ensure that it is able to produce a profit. It is a type of managerial accounting. See also: Process costing.

Job Creation The process by which the number of jobs in an economy increases. Job creation often refers to government policies intended to reduce unemployment. Job creation programs may take a variety of forms. For example, a government may lower taxes and reduce regulation to make hiring less expensive. On the other hand, a government may hire workers itself, for example, to build a road. See also: New Deal, Reaganomics.

Job Creation and Worker Assistance Act of 2002 Legislation in the United States that reduced taxes on businesses without changing tax brackets. It accomplished this by temporarily increasing deductions, exemptions, and the number of years for which one may use a tax loss carryback. The idea behind the Act was to encourage job creation by allowing businesses to keep more of their earnings. The effects of this type of policy are disputed.

Job Depth The ability to control one's work environment. In general, the more self-direction one has, the greater one's job depth. That is, a person with job depth may be able to set his/her own hours, decide which tasks to accomplish every day, and so forth. A manager may have job depth, but circumstances incumbent on management (such as dealing with employee misconduct or an irate client) may reduce the level of depth.

Job Description A list of the duties associated with a job. It may also include compensation information and minimum education or experience requirements. A job description is used when a company or organization attempts to hire someone. It helps the company find qualified candidates. Likewise, it helps job seekers to find positions they are both willing and able to do.

Job Enrichment The practice of allowing employees to use the full range of their skills within their positions. Job enrichment consists of three parts: giving multiple tasks with varying levels of difficulty, ensuring each unit of work completed is meaningful, and offering encouragement and motivation to employees. Job enrichment is intended to improve employee morale.

Job Evaluation The process of determining how valuable a position is to a company. It helps a company decide the extent to which a job produces revenue, improves efficiency or adds value in some other way. A job evaluation does not judge the person in a position, but the position itself. It helps a company make wage, salary and/or benefit decisions for the jobs it creates.

Job Hunting Expenses Money that one spends in the course of attempting to find a new job. In the United States, one may deduct job hunting expenses from one's taxable income, regardless of whether one actually finds a new job. This deduction is subject to certain restrictions. Specifically, the job for which one is looking must be in the same field as one's previous job, and expenses are not deductible if it is one's first job after finishing education.

Job Jumper A person who changes jobs repeatedly in a relatively brief period of time. Companies frequently shy away from hiring job jumpers because job jumping may indicate that the applicant has an inability to commit to a single career, has difficulties with co-workers, or has some other impediment to being a good employee. A job jumper is also called a job hopper.

Job Lock A situation in which an employee wants to quit his/her job, but is unable to because he/she is afraid of losing health insurance or other employee benefits. A job lock may hold back one's career or, just as seriously, one's personal satisfaction at work.

Job Loss Mortgage Payment Insurance An insurance policy that pays all or a portion of a mortgage payment for a homeowner for a certain period of time in the event that the homeowner loses his/her job. For example, a policy may provide up to $1,200 per month in payments for up to nine months following a job loss. Job loss mortgage payment insurance encourages people to buy homes if the only consideration holding them back is fear of a job loss. While one generally must pay a premium for coverage, some organizations offer free policies to first-time home buyers.

Job Lot In commodities, a small number of units. For example, one may refer to 10 or 20 barrels of oil as a job lot. These are used primarily in futures contracts in which both parties are interested in trading in small numbers.

Job Market The supply and demand for jobs. That is, the job market is the amount of job openings available compared to the workforce capable of taking them. A large number of job openings may indicate lack of demand for jobs (that is, there are not enough skilled workers to fill available positions), while the opposite may indicate few jobs relative to the labor force.

Job Openings and Labor Turnover Survey A survey published by the Bureau of Labor Statistics each month on the state of the American job market. It collects and disseminates data on job openings, recruitment activity, hires and layoffs, and other criteria in several different sectors. JOLTS are used along with the Help Wanted Index to show whether the number of jobs is growing or shrinking at a given time.

Job Placement The process by which a worker finds a job or, alternately, a company finds an employee to fill a position.

Job Printer In publishing, a specialized printer for cards, circulars and similar items.

Job Project-Performance Cost Variance In accounting, the difference between the budgeted and the actual costs a construction company incurs on a project. The variance may be divided into costs due to prices (that is, if materials are unexpectedly more or less expensive) and due to efficiency (for instance, if there is a work stoppage because of inclement weather or extra time needed to receive zoning permits).

Job Rotation The practice in which a person changes positions in an organization frequently for a certain period of time. For example, a new hire may work in operations for a few months, then accounting and finally in human resources. Job rotation is intended to give a person well-rounded insight into how an organization functions. It may be done especially for management trainees.

Job Satisfaction A measure of how much a person likes his/her work. Job satisfaction encompasses a variety of tangible and intangible aspects, including pay, contentment with co-workers, and how much one likes the work itself. Some companies take various steps to improve job satisfaction in the belief that happy employees make good employees.

Job Security An objective or subjective measure of the likelihood a person will keep his job. Outsourcing, efficiency, company revenue, the expense of employment and an employee's own attitude all affect his/her job security. See also: Job Security Index.

Job Security Index A quantitative measure of job security in different locations in the United States. A variety of factors affect the Job Security Index, including international trade, outsourcing, job migration, and demographics, among others. The index uses the Job Security Scores of thousands of persons to arrive at its figures. It was established in 2004 and is published monthly by Scorelogix.

Job Security Score A calculation of an individual's job security, which measures the likelihood that the individual will keep his/her job. Personal demographics, one's skill set, levels of outsourcing and job migration all affect one's Job Security Score. One may think of it as analogous to a credit score.

Job Sharing The practice in which two or more persons work part-time in the same position that ordinarily one full-time person would fill. Job sharing may reduce employer costs as a company may not provide benefits to part-time employees. Likewise, it can be beneficial for employees with unusual scheduling needs. For example, parents of young children or persons active in religious communities may share jobs. However, it can be difficult, as lack of communication between the job sharers can cause problems for the company and reduce efficiency.

Job Shop 1. A small-to-medium manufacturing company that primarily provides custom and semi-custom work for businesses. A job shop contrasts with a manufacturing firm that makes large volumes of the same product on a constant basis. **2.** See: Job center.

Jobber In the United Kingdom, informal for a market maker.

Jobs And Growth Tax Relief Reconciliation Act of 2003 Legislation in the United States that lowered most marginal tax brackets and reduced taxes in other ways. For example, the Act reclassified many dividends as long-term capital gains, which caused them to be taxed at a much lower rate. Proponents of the Act argued that it would spur economic growth and job creation following the 2001-2002 recession, while critics contended that it would increase the deficit unnecessarily and shift the tax burden from the wealthy to the middle class.

Jobs Growth The number of jobs created in the United States in a given month. While this can affect the unemployment rate, the two figures are separate. For example, there can be positive jobs growth and unemployment can still rise. This is because population growth adds new members to the workforce at all times. Jobs growth must at least keep pace with this in order to prevent unemployment from rising. Jobs growth is included in the Employment Situation Summary published by the Bureau of Labor Statistics each month.

Jobseeker's Allowance A welfare benefit in the United Kingdom for unemployed persons who are looking for a job. It is available to all unemployed persons of working age (the exact age depends on the minimum age for the state pension). In order to be eligible, one must present oneself to a job center every two weeks to prove one is looking for work. The Jobseeker's Allowance traces its origins to 1911.

JOD ISO 4217 code for the Jordanian dinar. It was introduced in 1949, replacing the Palestinian pound. It has been pegged to Special Drawing Rights since 1995, but in practice it is more or less pegged to the U.S. dollar. In addition to circulating in Jordan, the dinar is used in the West Bank along with the Israeli new sheqel.

Joe Granville Wednesday January 7, 1981. The day before the Dow Jones Industrial Average reached 1,000 points for the first time since early 1973. As a

result, analyst Joe Granville wrote an advisory letter stating, "Sell everything!" The market dipped for several weeks and did not break 1,000 points again for more than a year and a half.

Johannesburg Securities Exchange The only stock exchange in South Africa and the largest in Africa. Established in 1887 as a means to trade gold, it has become one of the largest commodities exchanges in the world.

John D. Rockefeller A famous American industrialist. He started his career in foodstuffs, but constructed an oil refinery with a partner in 1859. He co-founded Standard Oil in 1870, and by 1880 had virtually monopolized oil refining in the United States. He was known for his heavy-handed business tactics, including corporate espionage and buying out competitors. Rockefeller's supporters contend that he improved efficiency and made oil accessible to the general public in the age of industrialization. His critics claim that he hurt small businesses and was guilty of unethical business dealings. In later life, he became a noted philanthropist. He lived from 1839 to 1937, and is regarded as perhaps the richest person who ever lived.

John L. Lewis A 20th-century American union organizer. He served as president of the United Mine Workers of America and was instrumental in founding the Congress of Industrial Organizations. He fought for higher wages for coal workers and other industrial employees in the United States. He lived from 1880 to 1969.

John Manley A Canadian politician who served as the first Minister of Industry in the mid- and late-1990s. He also served as Minister of Finance in 2002 and 2003. As minister of industry, he was responsible for economic development in Canada, with the goal of preventing brain drain. He was born in 1950.

John Maynard Keynes A major British economist. He provided much of the intellectual foundation for the theory that government intervention is necessary to ensure an active and vibrant economy. According to this theory, government should stimulate demand for goods and services in order to encourage economic growth. It thus recommends tax cuts and increased government spending during recessions to reinvigorate growth; likewise, it recommends tax increases and spending cuts during economic expansion in order to combat inflation. His thought was extremely popular for much of the 20th century prior to the 1970s, when stagflation (which under Keynesian theory should not be possible) was prevalent in the UK and the US. However, Keynesianism resurged at the end of the first decade of the 2000s. Keynes lived from 1883 to 1946.

John Rigas An American businessman who co-founded Adelphia Communications. He built it into a large cable provider with customers in 30 states. In 2004, he was convicted of wire fraud and other fraud charges. He was sentenced to 15 years in prison. He was born in 1924.

John Rusnak A former currency trader who attempted to hide nearly $700 million in losses that he incurred. In 2003, he was sentenced to seven and a half years in prison for bank fraud. He served six years combined in prison and house arrest.

John W. Rockefeller An American engineer. He invented the bombsight used on Allied planes during World War II and was active in developing new printers and paper for the publishing industry. He was only distantly related to John D. Rockefeller and was not considered part of the "Rockefeller family." He died in 1987.

John W. Snow An American politician and businessman who served as Secretary of the Treasury from 2003 to 2006. He began his career at the Department of Transportation. When he left, he became an executive at various railway and other transportation companies, rising to CEO of the CSX Corporation upon his appointment as Treasury Secretary. After leaving Treasury, Snow became Chairman of Cerberus Capital Management, which began management of Chrysler following its 2009 government bailout. Snow was born in 1939.

Joint Describing anything in which two or more persons hold equal rights and responsibilities. For example, every account holder may use the funds in a joint account (though not always independently from the other holders), and each owner is equally liable for a jointly-held property.

Joint Account An account at a bank or a brokerage where there are two or more account holders. The holders of a joint account share all rights and responsibilities regarding the account. That is, one may deposit or withdraw money from a joint account without the consent of the other and both may be held liable for an overdraft or loss. Joint accounts are most common for married couples.

Joint Account Agreement An agreement between the holders of a joint account detailing how the account will operate. Specifically, the joint account agreement states whether the account holders will each be able to withdraw and deposit funds into the account, or whether all account holders must agree before this can be done. Joint account agreements are required for both bank accounts and brokerage accounts held in the names of two or more persons.

Joint Agent A person who is authorized to facilitate business between two principals. For example, a joint agent may assist both the buyer and the seller of an asset.

Joint and Survivor Option In life insurance, the ability of a potential policyholder to choose a joint and survivor annuity among other options.

Joint Clearing Member A clearing house that operates on more than one exchange. An example is the DTCC, which operates on several American stock exchanges.

Joint Committee for Investment and Trade Also called a JCIT. A standing committee formed by two or more governments to discuss matters of international trade between the countries represented. A JCIT may be formed in anticipation of a free trade agreement. The United States formed JCITs with Israel before the U.S.-Israel Free Trade Agreement and with Mexico before NAFTA.

Joint Endorsement A requirement by a bank that both holders of a joint account endorse a check before it can be cashed. Not all checks on joint accounts require joint endorsements, and different banks have different regulations. Joint endorsements exist to keep one party to an account from conducting certain transactions without the knowledge or consent of the other.

Joint Float An agreement between the central banks of two or more different countries where their currencies remain at the same exchange rate relative to each other, but are otherwise floating currencies. The two central banks make the relevant purchases and sales of each other's currencies in order to maintain the joint float. See also: Peg.

Joint Life Annuity An annuity that two persons, almost always a married couple, open in order to provide for both in retirement. A joint life annuity makes payments to the designated party as long as one of the spouses remains alive. Depending on the nature of the agreement, the amount in the payments may decrease when the first spouse passes away. It is also called a joint and survivor annuity.

Joint Life with Last Survivor Annuity An annuity that makes payments to both the annuitant until death and then to a designated second party until the death of a designated third party (who is usually, but not always, the same person). A joint life with last survivor annuity allows the annuitant to provide for his/her spouse on a continuing basis, rather than giving a lump sum at death. The annuitant may also designate another party, such as a charity to receive payments until the death of the spouse. If there are funds remaining at the death of both spouses, the annuity pays a death benefit to the designated party or his/her survivors.

Joint Loan A loan in which two or more borrowers assume responsibility for repayment. That is, if one borrower stops paying, the others must pay on that borrower's behalf. A joint loan reduces the risk for the lender, which may reduce the interest rate. A joint loan also may be eligible for certain tax benefits.

Joint Note A promise by two or more parties to pay a debt. If the debt is not paid, the creditor may not single out any one debtor. That is, the creditor must sue all debtors or none.

Joint Ownership A situation in which two or more persons co-own a property. In other words, if two or more persons jointly own a property and one of them dies, the property does not become part of a decedent's estate; rather, the other owner(s) continue to own the property. A married couple may jointly own their house, for example. Likewise, two business partners may jointly own a business property. If two persons own an apartment complex and one of them dies, the whole of the complex belongs to the co-owner, and not the decedent's heirs. However, the decedent's liabilities may remain attached to this property and may be used to pay off creditors, even if the creditor had nothing to do with the property in question.

Joint Product Cost In accounting, the cost of two or more products derived from the same source. For example, natural gas and oil from the same well share joint product costs. Because it is impossible to distinguish which product caused a particular cost, joint product costs are distributed according to the expected sale price of each product.

Joint Products Two or more products derived from the same source using the same tools. For example, natural gas and oil from the same well are joint products. See also: Joint Product Cost.

Joint Rate A single price paid on a shipment transported by two or more carriers between its origin and destination.

Joint Stock Company A company that issues stock and requires shareholders to be held liable for the company's debt. In other words, a joint stock company combines features of a general partnership, in which owners of a company split profits and liabilities, and a publicly-traded company, which issues stock that shareholders are able to buy and sell on an exchange. See also: Publicly-traded partnership.

Joint Tax Return A tax return filed by a married couple. Joint tax returns are advantageous, as husbands and wives usually have a lower tax liability filing together than they would filing separately.

Joint Tenancy 1. See: Joint tenants with right of survivorship. **2.** See: Joint tenants in common.

Joint Tenancy with Right of Survivorship The ownership of property for which the co-owners have right of survivorship. In other words, if two or more persons jointly own a property with right of survivorship and one of them dies, the property does not become part of a decedent's estate; rather, the other owner(s) continue to own the property. A married couple may be joint tenants with right of survivorship on their house, for example. Less commonly, two business partners may be joint tenants with right of survivorship on a business property: if two persons own an apartment complex and one of them dies, the whole of the complex belongs to the co-owner, and not the decedent's heirs. It is important to note, however, that the decedent's liabilities may remain attached to the property and the property may be used to pay off creditors, even if the creditor had nothing to do with the property in question.

Joint Tenants in Common A way for two or more persons to own property together. Joint tenants in common may own equal or unequal shares of the property (but shares are usually equal), and there are no rights of survivorship. That is, when one of the co-owners dies, his/her share of the property becomes part of his/her estate and passes on to heirs. This is an arrangement common in joint business ventures: if two persons own an apartment complex and one of them dies, the decedent's share of the complex passes to his/her beneficiaries and does not pass to the other co-owner.

Joint Venture A project or other business activity in which two persons or companies partner together to conduct the project. In a joint venture, each of the persons or companies in the joint venture is responsible for profits, losses, and operations. A joint venture operates like a partnership and is usually taxed like one. A key difference between a joint venture and a partnership is the fact that a joint venture, when it involves companies, does not necessitate the merging of all the companies' operations and interests; rather, they cooperate for purposes of the joint venture only.

Jointly and Severally Relating to an agreement between the issuer of a new security and its underwriting syndicates mandating that the underwriters are responsible for any unsold portion of the issue in proportion to their participation in the issue, even if they sold their initially agreed upon participations. For instance, suppose an underwriting firm is responsible for placing 15% of an issue and does so. If the entire issue is not placed, the firm is still responsible for placing 15% of the unsold portion of the issue. This process continues until the entire issues is sold or the remainder cancelled.

Joint-Stock Bank A bank that issues stock and requires shareholders to be held liable for the company's debt. In other words, a joint stock bank combines features of a general partnership, in which owners of a company split profits and liabilities, and a publicly-traded company, which issues stock that shareholders are able to buy and sell on an exchange. A joint-stock bank is not owned by a government.

Jones Act Legislation in the United States, passed in 1920, that requires ships transporting cargo between U.S. ports to fly a U.S. flag, to be owned by American citizens, and to be crewed by U.S. citizens and residents. The Act was designed to protect merchant marine jobs. The Jones Act remains controversial. Critics maintain it is protectionist and results in higher prices for consumers, while supporters contend that it helps preserve American jobs and ensures trained seamen are available in times of national emergency. It is formally called the Merchant Marine Act; its colloquial name comes from Senator Wesley Jones, who sponsored it.

Jonestown Defense Any antitakeover measure so extreme that it may drive the target company into bankruptcy. For example, a Jonestown defense may stipulate that shareholders in the target company may buy shares in their own company at a price below fair market value in the event of a hostile acquisition. Once the acquisition is complete, the defense may allow these same shareholders to buy more shares in the new company at below market value. This forces shareholders to suffer a devaluation and dilution of their own shares. This is done to discourage hostile takeovers. In essence, a Jonestown defense is identical to a poison pill, except for degree; the term indicates that the target company may intentionally go bankrupt, rather than simply weaken itself. The term takes its name from the Jonestown massacre.

JOR GOST 7.67 Latin three-letter geocode for Jordan. The code is used for transactions to and from Jordanian bank accounts and for international shipping to Jordan. As with all GOST 7.67 codes, it is used primarily in Cyrillic alphabets.

Jordanian Dinar The currency of Jordan. It was introduced in 1949, replacing the Palestinian pound. It has been pegged to Special Drawing Rights since 1995, but in practice it is more or less pegged to the U.S. dollar. In addition to circulating in Jordan, the dinar is used in the West Bank along with the Israeli new sheqel.

Joseph Effect The concept that any movement in a given time series is more likely to be part of a trend than it is to be random. The extent to which a phenomenon is a Joseph effect is quantified on the Hurst component, which is measured between 0 and 1. A Hurst reading of more than 0.5 indicates that a movement is less random and therefore more likely to be a Joseph effect. The term comes from the Old Testament story in which Joseph predicted seven years of plenty followed by seven years of famine.

Joseph P. Kennedy A 20th-century American businessman and politician. After making a fortune in investing, Kennedy was appointed the first chairman of the Securities and Exchange Commission in 1934, serving until the following year. He later became the U.S. ambassador to the United Kingdom. He was the father of a number of prominent American politicians, notably President John F. Kennedy. He lived from 1888 to 1969.

Joseph Stiglitz An American economist and academic born in 1943. He is most noted for his work on information asymmetry, which summarizes how economic actors use and share information in order to gain advantages in the market. Stiglitz argues, contrary to neo-classical economics, that markets usually are inefficient because information is not spread evenly. He shared the Nobel Prize for Economics in 2001 for this work.

Joseph Wilson A U.S. diplomat and businessman who has served as the ambassador to several African countries. His private consulting work has dealt with political risk issues in Africa. Wilson was born in 1949.

Journal of Government Financial Management A quarterly journal for accountants, auditors, professors and others interested in federal, state and local government accounting in the United States. It was established in 1950 as the Government Accountants Journal. It is published by the Association of Government Accountants.

Jow An obsolete Indian unit of length approximately equivalent to 0.63 centimeters.

JP 1. ISO 3166-1 alpha-2 code for Japan. This is the code used in international transactions to and from Japanese bank accounts. **2.** ISO 3166-2 geocode for Japan. This is used as an international standard for shipping to Japan. Each Japanese prefecture has its own code with the prefix "JP." For example, the code for the Prefecture of Akita is ISO 3166-2:JP-05.

JPN GOST 7.67 Latin three-letter geocode for Japan. The code is used for transactions to and from Japanese bank accounts and for international shipping to Japan. As with all GOST 7.67 codes, it is used primarily in Cyrillic alphabets.

JPY ISO 4217 code for the Japanese yen. It was introduced by the Meiji government in 1871. The yen decimalized the previously used Tokugawa currency. It was originally pegged to gold (smaller units were pegged to silver). Following World War II, the yen switched its peg to the U.S. dollar through the Bretton Woods System. In 1971 the yen began to float because it had become undervalued and because the United States left the Bretton Woods System. The currency suffered from exceptionally low value in the wake of the Asian financial crisis but had stabilized by the mid- and late-2000s. Along with being a common reserve currency, it is one of the most commonly traded currencies in the world.

JT 1. ISO 3166-1 alpha-2 code for Johnston Island prior to its re-designation as one of the U.S. Minor Outlying Islands. This was the code used in international transactions to and from bank accounts on Johnston Island. **2.** ISO 3166-2 geocode for Johnston Island. This was used as an international standard for shipping to Johnston Island. In both cases, the code is obsolete.

JTUM ISO 3166-3 code for the Johnston Atoll islands, which were re-designated as part of the U.S. Minor Outlying Islands. ISO 3166-3 codes are used to indicate names of countries and territories that are no longer used.

Judet In Romania, a political subdivision equivalent to a county.

Judgment An order from a judge or jury to pay a certain amount of money. Judgments usually come after a lawsuit or a criminal conviction. For example, if a company is sued and found liable, it may receive a judgment for, say, $1 million, which it must pay to the plaintiff. Also, if one is convicted of theft, one may be ordered to repay what one has stolen. See also: Out-of-Court Settlement.

Judgmental Forecast A forecast made on subjective information. A judgmental forecast is made by a person thought to be knowledgeable about the company or market about which the forecast is being made. It may consider quantitative information, but it relies on a great deal of subjective feeling.

Jugerum An ancient Roman unit of area approximately equivalent to 2,523 square meters.

Juice In futures trading, the maintenance margin a trader must keep in an account in order to be able to keep a position open.

Julliard v. Greenman A U.S. Supreme Court decision holding that fiat currency issued during the U.S. Civil War was legal tender and had to be accepted as payment. That is, the court held that a contract requiring a certain number of dollars in payment was satisfied by the payment of that number of dollars, even if the value of the dollar declined in the meantime. The case was decided in 1885.

Jumbo Certificate of Deposit A certificate of deposit of large value, usually more than $1 million, that can be bought and sold, but not redeemed before maturity. See also: Negotiable CD.

Jumbo Loan 1. A mortgage loan so large it exceeds the limits for securitization by U.S. government mortgage banks. As such, a jumbo loan cannot be guaranteed or securitized by Freddie Mac or Fannie Mae. Because of this, jumbo loans carry higher credit risk and have historically been traded at a premium to conventional mortgages. **2.** A loan of $1 billion or more.

Jumbo Mortgage A mortgage loan so large that it exceeds the limits for securitization by U.S. government mortgage banks. A jumbo mortgage cannot be guaranteed or securitized by Freddie Mac or Fannie Mae. Because of this, jumbo mortgages carry higher credit risk and have historically been traded at a premium to conventional mortgages.

Juminqu In China, a political subdivision equivalent to an urban neighborhood.

Jumpru A Finnish unit of volume approximately equivalent to 8.18 milliliters. It became obsolete when Finland adopted the metric system in 1880.

Junior Capital Pool A capital structure where a company can issue shares, and even make an IPO before it has begun operations. It requires a minimum investment of $100,000, but can give a company access to the market to raise capital to begin operations. This is unusual and is only available in Canada. Obviously, investing in a company with a junior capital pool is very high risk.

Junior Debt A class of debt that, in the event of insolvency, is prioritized lower than other classes of debt. The most common kind of junior debt is an unsecured loan, which has no collateral. Another kind of junior debt is a secured loan in which another loan has priority on the collateral; a second mortgage is an example of a secured junior debt. This class of debt carries higher risk but also pays higher interest than other classes.

Junior Issue A security that has a lower priority compared to another in the event of liquidation. That is, if a company goes bankrupt and is liquidated, holders of secured debt must be paid before the holders of unsecured debt. Holders of unsecured debt must be paid before preferred shareholders, and finally, preferred shareholders must be satisfied before common shareholders. In the forgoing, each security is a junior issue compared to the previous one. See also: Absolute Priority Rule.

Junior Mortgage A mortgage secured by a lien on a property that is subordinate to another mortgage on the same property. One may take out a junior mortgage to pay for home repairs or for any number of other reasons. A junior mortgage carries a higher interest rate than a primary mortgage because the lien is less secure. A second mortgage is a junior mortgage, as are third and fourth mortgages. See also: Piggyback mortgage.

Junior Refunding The refinancing of a government's debt by issuing new debt securities, such as Treasuries, with a maturity in the short or medium term.

Junior Stock A stock that has a lower priority compared to another in the event of liquidation. That is, if a company goes bankrupt and is liquidated, holders of junior stock are only paid after all holders of senior stock are fully satisfied. For example, preferred shareholders must be paid before common shareholders; thus, common shares are junior stock with respect to preferred shares. See also: Absolute Priority Rule.

Junk Financing The act of financing an activity or broader operations through the issue of junk bonds. These bonds have low credit ratings and are comparatively high risk. As a result, the issuer must pay higher interest rates. Junk financing is used in some takeover situations where the acquiring company is cash poor.

Junk Muni-Bond Fund A mutual fund or other investment company that invests predominately or exclusively in municipal bonds with junk ratings. That is, these funds invest in bonds with so much risk that banks cannot invest in them and that were issued by government entities other than the federal government. The advantages to a junk muni-bond fund are the facts that the extra risk results in higher returns and that municipal bonds are exempt from federal taxes.

Junk Silver A slang term for silver coins that were released into circulation. Many of the silvers were alloys; that is, they were mixed with one or more different metals. In the United States, dimes, quarters, and half dollars released in 1964 or earlier are examples of junk silver.

Jurat 1. In law, the portion of an affidavit stating who makes the sworn statement, when it was made, and in front of whom it was made. **2.** In the Channel Islands and historically in some areas of France, a municipal official, roughly equivalent to a town councilor.

Jurgen Stark A German economist who served as interim president of the Bundesbank in 2004. In 2006, he became part of the Executive Board of the European Central Bank.

Jurisdiction Risk 1. The added risk of making a loan to a borrower in a foreign country. Such risks include exchange risk, political risk, and legal risk. **2.** The risk of placing funds under the jurisdiction of a foreign central bank. These risks include exchange risk and political risk. For example, jurisdiction risk includes the possibility that the foreign government will confiscate all foreign currency in the country.

Jurisdictional Arbitrage The practice of moving an office, factory or something else in order to come under the jurisdiction of a different regulatory agency with more lenient rules. For example, a corporation unwilling to pay corporate taxes to the state of California may move its head office to Arizona, outside the jurisdiction (in most circumstances) of the California tax authorities. Jurisdictional arbitrage is a type of regulatory arbitrage.

Juristic Act Any legally binding act. A common example of a juristic act is signing a contract.

Jury of Executive Opinion A way to forecast future trends in which one gathers the opinions of a number of known experts on a security or other matter at hand. The members of the jury perform their initial assessments on their own, then review each other's work, revising their own estimates as needed. The jury of executive opinion is useful because it provides a sort of peer review to point out errors in a non-adversarial way. See also: Consensus opinion.

Jurydyka In Poland, an archaic political subdivision equivalent to a rural village. All jurydykas are currently neighborhoods in Warsaw.

Jusen Non-bank financial institutions in Japan that made mortgage loans. Jusen were created in the 1970s as subsidiaries of banks. Excessive lending by jusen in the 1980s contributed to Japan's real estate bubble. Several received bailouts in the 1990s but they nevertheless ceased operations in 1995.

Just In Case A business strategy in which a company maintains high inventory at all times to compensate for sudden increases in demand. A JIC strategy incurs higher carry costs for inventory, but protects the company from the possibility of losing revenue if it runs out of inventory. It is common for companies and industries that have a hard time estimating demand for their products. It contrasts with a just in time (JIT) strategy. See also: Supply chain.

Just In Time A supply chain management system designed to reduce carrying costs to a minimum. A firm only orders what it expects for its immediate needs; therefore, it keeps a low inventory. For example, if a retailer believes it will sell 1,000 widgets in a week, it orders precisely 1,000 widgets from its manufacturer. JIT systems require that the retailer at the end of the supply chain can accurately predict demand for its products. They also require that each stage of the supply chain knows exactly how much time it takes to fill an order when it is made. The automotive industry and budget retailers commonly use JIT systems. See also: Lead time, Just in case.

Justice The virtue by which each person is given what he or she deserves. For example, justice requires that an employee be paid for work done, or that a scofflaw be punished for his or her crimes. Justice is perhaps the most important concept in law. Many people seeking social change do so because they believe current systems are unjust in some way. For example, a socialist may believe it is unjust that a worker does not have the legal right to profit from the value he/she adds, while a capitalist may argue that it is unjust to deprive the owners of capital or other assets of their property.

K 1. Shorthand for 1,000. **2.** A symbol appearing next to a stock listed on NASDAQ indicating that the share being traded has no voting rights. All NASDAQ listings use a four letter abbreviation; if a K follows the abbreviation, this indicates that the share comes without voting rights attached to it.

Kaapelinmitta A Finnish unit of nautical distance approximately equivalent to 185.2 meters. It became obsolete when Finland adopted the metric system in 1880.

Kabellangd A Swedish unit of nautical distance approximately equivalent to 178 meters.

Kabuki Dance A well-presented falsehood. A kabuki dance is a report, project, or anything else presented in a flashy way with little (or sometimes misleading) substance. While the term was originally used in politics, it has come to refer to corporate reports and projects as well.

Kabupaten In Indonesia, a political subdivision equivalent to a municipal government. It is also called a regency.

Kafalah bi al-Thaman In Islamic law, money a guarantor places as collateral in case the responsible person does not pay. For example, a parent may place kafalah bi al-thaman on an apartment to promise payment in case his son does not make rent.

Kaffekok An archaic Norwegian unit of length approximately equivalent to nine kilometers. The term was most common among the Sami, an indigenous people in northern Norway.

Kaffirs Informal for shares in a South African publicly-traded company, especially a gold mining company. Kaffirs trade on both the London Stock Exchange and the Johannesburg Stock Exchange, as well as in the United States as American Depository Receipts.

Kaghak In Armenia, a political subdivision equivalent to a township.

Kagi Chart In technical analysis, a chart representing changes in the supply and demand for a security. On a Kagi chart, a thick line indicates increased demand represented by a rising price, while a thin line shows increased supply represented by a falling price. The direction of the chart changes when the price rises or falls by a certain percentage, usually 4%. For example, when a security price declines by 4% or more, an upwards moving chart begins to move downward and vice versa. Kagi charting has the advantage of being mostly independent of time, which helps reduce the noise found in other charting.

Kalamos An ancient Greek unit of length approximately equivalent to 3.08 meters. It was also called an akaina or a dekapous.

Kall In Iceland, an informal term for the Icelandic krona.

Kalo-Kalo Slang; the financial services industry in Nigeria. The term derives from the name for slot machines used in Nigeria.

Kamikaze Pricing The practice in which a bank offers loans and other financial products at exceptionally low interest rates and prices. Very often, kamikaze pricing involves selling at a loss, and, for that reason, it is not sustainable in the long term. However, it can increase market share, and give the bank the opportunity to raise its prices later. See also: Loss leader.

Kampung In Malaysia, a political subdivision equivalent to a municipality.

Kan A unit of weight in Japan equivalent to 3.75 kilograms. An equivalent term is kanme.

Kanban A scheduling system indicating how many goods one must produce in a given period of time, how one must produce them, and by when they must be completed. It developed in Japan as a means to achieve just-in-time inventory control.

Kanee A customary unit of area approximately equivalent to 1,619 square meters. It is used in real estate transactions in some parts of Pakistan.

Kangaroo Informal; a stock in Australia. It especially refers to a stock on the All Ordinaries Index, which is the most prominent index of Australian stocks. The term is most often used by foreigners outside of Australia.

Kannaland A Swedish unit of area approximately equivalent to 88.15 square meters.

Kannu A Finnish unit of volume approximately equivalent to 2.62 liters. It became obsolete when Finland adopted the metric system in 1880.

Kannunala A Finnish unit of area approximately equivalent to 88.15 square meters. It became obsolete when Finland adopted the metric system in 1880.

Kansas City Board of Trade A derivatives exchange based in Kansas City on which commodities, futures, and options are traded. Primarily, the exchange trades derivatives related to hard red winter wheat, which is a primary ingredient in bread and an important agricultural product in the area. Additionally, in 1982, the KCBT became the first exchange to offer an index futures on a stock exchange when it introduced Value Line futures. It was established in 1856 and is regulated by the CFTC.

Kantar A Turkish measure of weight approximately equivalent to 56.44 kilograms. It became obsolete when Turkey made the metric system mandatory in 1933.

Kapanala A Finnish unit of area approximately equivalent to 154 square meters. It became obsolete when Finland adopted the metric system in 1880.

Kapeik 1/100 of one Georgian maneti, which was the currency of the Republic of Georgia between 1919 and 1923.

Kappa A Finnish unit of volume approximately equivalent to 5.5 liters. It became obsolete when Finland adopted the metric system in 1880.

Kappland A Swedish unit of area approximately equivalent to 154.3 square meters.

Kapyeyka A subdivision of the Belarusian ruble. One kapyeyka is equal in value to 1/100 of one ruble. It does not circulate in practice.

Karachi Inter Bank Offered Rate Commonly called KIBOR. The average interest rate that prime banks in Pakistan offer for term deposits.

Karachi Stock Exchange The oldest and largest stock exchange in Pakistan. It was established in 1947, and has historically been known for strong performance and high liquidity. However, the 2008 economic crisis and political instability in Pakistan caused the Karachi Stock Exchange to drop by more than a third between April and June 2008. See also: KSE 100 Index.

Karaniwang bayan In the Philippines, a political subdivision roughly equivalent to a township.

Karat 1. A way of measuring the mass of a gem. One karat is 200 milligrams. **2.** A way of measuring the purity of gold or platinum. One karat is 1/24 purity; that is, 24 karat gold is pure gold. In both cases, karat can also be spelled carat.

Karl Marx A 19th-century economic philosopher. He espoused common ownership (not state ownership) of the means of production. He taught that the capitalist class of persons (who control the money) exploits the proletariat (who provide most of the labor) to the detriment of the latter. According to Marx, as the direct result of industrialization, the proletariat inevitably will overthrow the capitalist class and, after a brief period in which the state controls the means of production, the state will fade away to create a communist society. His philosophy, Marxism, significantly influenced communist thinking for the next century. He lived from 1818 to 1883.

Kartocc 1. A Maltese unit of volume approximately equivalent to 1.14 liters. It was originally used to measure alcohol. It is largely obsolete but is still used in some circumstances. **2.** A Maltese unit of volume approximately equivalent to 1.23 liters. It was originally used to measure milk and oil. It is largely obsolete but is still used in some circumstances.

Kaspar Villger A Swiss politician. He was elected to the Federal Council (the seven member executive branch) in 1989 and served until 2003. He served as President of the Confederation twice. In 2009, he became chairman of the board of directors of UBS bank. He was born in 1941.

Kasselrij In the Netherlands, a political subdivision equivalent to a county.

Kassenobligation A German word for a medium-term debt security issued by a government. The maximum term for a Kassenobliation in Germany is four years. In Austria, it is five years, and in Switzerland, eight years.

Katastralgemeinde In Austria and some other central European countries, a subdivision of a country with no political authority that is used to organize the country for purposes of recording real estate ownership.

Katastralne uzemia In Slovakia, a subdivision with no political authority that is used to organize the country for purposes of recording real estate ownership.

Katha A customary unit of area approximately equivalent to 67 square meters. It is used in real estate transactions in some parts of India and Bangladesh, but its exact measure varies.

Kaupstadir In Iceland, a political subdivision equivalent to a township. It is used primarily for police precincts and bankruptcy courts.

Kawtha A Burmese unit of length equivalent to 1,280.16 meters.

KAZ GOST 7.67 Latin three-letter geocode for Kazakhstan. The code is used for transactions to and from Kazakhstani bank accounts and for international shipping to Kazakhstan. As with all GOST 7.67 codes, it is used primarily in Cyrillic alphabets.

Kazakhistani Tenge The currency of Kazakhstan. It was issued in 1993, replacing the Soviet ruble. Kazakhstan was one of the last former Soviet republics to issue a new, national currency.

KDD Corp A former Japanese telecommunications company. It was founded in 1953 and in 2000 merged with several other companies to form KDDI.

Kebeles In Ethiopia, a political subdivision approximately equivalent to a neighborhood within a city.

Kecamatan In Indonesia, a political subdivision equivalent to a section of a city or kabupaten.

Keepwell Agreement An agreement between a parent company and a subsidiary in which the parent company provides a guarantee on the subsidiary's debt for the duration of the agreement. The keepwell agreement reduces the risk to the subsidiary's debt securities and may be beneficial for its stockholders.

Keidanren A former organization in Japan that represented the interests of large corporations. It was established in 1946 and, in 2002, it merged with other groups to form the Japanese Business Federation.

Keiretsu In Japan, a number of independent but related companies centered on and financed by a single bank and/or a joint stock company. That is, the institution (and no other) provides financing for companies in the keiretsu. There are two main types of keiretsu. A horizontal keiretsu is essentially a diversified conglomerate; that is, it may have companies in several, completely unrelated industries so as to reduce the risk of loss if one industry or other has a bad year. A vertical keiretsu, on the other hand, is more centrally controlled such that companies in the same keiretsu provide all steps on the supply chain. For example, a mining company may sell a metal to a refinery in the same keiretsu, who then sells it to an auto company, who then sells cars to consumers. In Japan, these consumers are often employees of the very same keiretsu. Critics of this system contend that they are inefficient; proponents, however, argue that they are sustainable and have helped Japan recover from the post-war period. See also: Japanese miracle, Zaibatsu, Chaebol.

Keizai Doyukai Also called the Japanese Association of Corporate Executives. A nonprofit organization that promotes the economic and political interests of major business leaders in Japan. It conducts research, hosts events and lobbies the government for favorable legislation. Keizai Doyukai has more than 1,000 members representing nearly as many companies. It was founded in 1946 and is based in Tokyo.

Kejla A Maltese unit of volume approximately equivalent to 128 milliliters. It was originally used to measure milk and oil. It is largely obsolete but is still used in some circumstances.

Kelja A Maltese unit of land area approximately equivalent to 18.74 square meters. It is largely obsolete but is still used in some circumstances.

Keltner Channel In technical analysis, an indicator that tracks a stock's price along with two moving averages, calculated such that one is intended to be above the current price and one is below it. A Keltner channel shows an overpriced stock when the current price rises above the upper moving average and shows an underpriced stock when it falls below the lower moving average.

Kelurahan In Indonesia, a political subdivision equivalent to a village. It is a subdivision of a kecamatan.

Ken GOST 7.67 Latin three-letter geocode for Kenya. The code is used for transactions to and from Kenyan bank accounts and for international shipping to Kenya. As with all GOST 7.67 codes, it is used primarily in Cyrillic alphabets.

Ken Lay Chairman of the board and CEO of Enron from 1985 to 2002. During his tenure, Enron committed one of the largest accounting frauds in history. As CEO, Lay presided over a company in which many of its assets were either overpriced or completely fictional; losses were hidden in offshore subsidies; and most profits were fraudulent. He was charged with and convicted of securities fraud and other crimes, but he died before he was sentenced. He lived from 1942 to 2006.

Kengen A publicly-traded company that provides the vast majority of electricity in Kenya. It was established in 1997 and went public in 2006. It is more formally called the Kenya Electricity Generating Company.

Kentter In Kazakhstan, a political subdivision approximately equivalent to a municipality.

Kenyan Shilling The currency of Kenya. It was introduced in 1966, replacing the first East African shilling.

Keogh Plan An account into which a self-employed person makes contributions up to a certain limit throughout his/her working life, and from which he/she begins to take distributions following retirement. Under a Keogh plan, contributions are tax deductible and withdrawals are taxed. The limit on annual contributions to a Keogh plan varies each year and is indexed to inflation, but in any case, it is higher than the limit for an IRA or a 401(k). Contributions to Keogh plans are invested in securities and usually own common stock and certificates of deposit.

Keramion An ancient Greek unit of liquid volume approximately equivalent to 26.2 liters.

Kerberos A network protocol allowing machines connected to an unsecured network (called nodes) to identify each other securely. It was developed at MIT in the 1980s.

Kerpo A Finnish unit meaning 31 lampreys.

Kerrab A Turkish measure of length approximately equivalent to 4.25 centimeters. It became obsolete when Turkey made the metric system mandatory in 1933.

KES ISO 4217 code for the Kenyan shilling. It was introduced in 1966, replacing the first East African shilling.

Key Currency A currency pegged to a currency basket. Small, export-oriented countries may adopt key currencies because they may provide stable exchange rates for their currencies, which may reduce risk in international trade.

Key Date In numismatics, describing a coin that is expensive or difficult to find because comparatively few were made in the desired year. Key date coins may prevent the completion of a coin collection.

Key Employee A very important employee. A key employee may have contacts highly beneficial to the company, may work hard and generate more revenue than any other employee, or may have some other skill that would be difficult or impossible to replicate in another employee. Often, but not always, a key employee is a manager. A company may purchase key person insurance to protect itself against the possibility that an employee may unexpectedly die or become unable to work, which would deprive the company of his/her skills.

Key Industry An industry that is pivotal to the growth (or sometimes the survival) of an economy. Companies in a key industry are often major employers in an area and have a great deal of political power. For example, for much of its history until the 1980s, the economy of Oklahoma was very dependent on the oil and gas industry; it remained important even in the 2000s. For this reason, oil and gas may be considered a key industry in Oklahoma.

Key Man Insurance A life insurance policy that a company purchases on one or more of its most important employees. The company pays the premiums and is the beneficiary. If the employee dies unexpectedly the company receives the benefit to offset the financial loss from the employee's demise. Partnerships often have key man insurance on each of the partners, while publicly-traded companies carry policies for major executives and managers. Companies use key man benefits to buy back stock in the company from the decedent's estate. It is also common to use the benefit to offset lost production or to pay a headhunter to find a replacement employee.

Key Performance Indicators Quantitative and qualitative measurements showing how successfully an organization is achieving its investment goals. Key performance indicators vary from firm to firm, depending on one's particular needs and goals. Firms determine internally both the key performance indicators and the process of measuring them. They are used in marketing, manufacturing, and supply chain management.

Key Rate An interest rate that a bank uses to determine the interest rates it charges borrowers and pays depositors. Common key rates include the fed funds rate, the fed discount rate, and the LIBOR.

Keynesian A scholar or other person who believes that government intervention is necessary to ensure an active and vibrant economy. According to this theory, government should stimulate demand for goods and services in order to encourage economic growth. It thus recommends tax cuts and increased government spending during recessions to reinvigorate growth; likewise, Keynesians recommend tax increases and spending cuts during economic expansion in order to combat inflation. Many economists believe that Keynesian economic theory is more efficient than supply-side economics, though critics point to the theory's inability to explain stagflation in the United States during the 1970s.

Keynesian Economics A theory stating that government intervention is necessary to ensure an active and vibrant economy. According to this theory, government should stimulate demand for goods and services in order to encourage economic growth. It thus recommends tax cuts and increased government spending during recessions to reinvigorate growth; likewise, it recommends tax increases and spending cuts during economic expansion in order to combat inflation. Many economists believe that Keynesian economic theory is more efficient than supply-side economics, though critics point to the theory's inability to explain stagflation in the United States during the 1970s.

KG 1. ISO 3166-1 alpha-2 code for the Kyrgyz Republic. This is the code used in international transactions to and from Kyrgyzstani bank accounts. 2. ISO 3166-2 geocode for Kyrgyzstan. This is used as an international standard for shipping to Kyrgyzstan. Each Kyrgyzstani province has its own code with the prefix "KG." For example, the code for the Chuy Province is ISO 3166-2:KG-C.

KGS ISO 4217 code for the Kyrgyz som. It was introduced to replace the Soviet ruble; indeed, the som was the local name for the ruble while Kyrgyzstan was under Soviet rule.

KGZ GOST 7.67 Latin three-letter geocode for Kyrgyzstan. The code is used for transactions to and from Kyrgyzstani bank accounts and for international shipping to Kyrgyzstan. As with all GOST 7.67 codes, it is used primarily in Cyrillic alphabets.

KH 1. ISO 3166-1 alpha-2 code for the Kingdom of Cambodia. This is the code used in international transactions to and from Cambodian bank accounts. 2. ISO 3166-2 geocode for Cambodia. This is used as an international standard for shipping to Cambodia. Each Cambodian municipality and province has its own code with the prefix "KH." For example, the code for the Province of Pursat is ISO 3166-2:KH-15.

Kha An ancient Egyptian unit of area approximately equivalent to 275.65 square meters.

Kha Yaing In Myanmar (Burma), a political subdivision approximately equivalent to a county. It is also called khayai.

Khaleeji A proposed currency for the countries of the Gulf Cooperation Council, except for Oman and the United Arab Emirates, which have opted out of the program.

Khan In Cambodia, one of eight subdivisions of the capital, Phnom Penh. A khan is roughly equivalent to a district or neighborhood.

Khar An ancient Egyptian unit of volume approximately equivalent to 96.5 liters during the Middle Kingdom or 76.8 liters during the New Kingdom.

Kharub A division of the muzuna, which was a subdivision of the Algerian budju. One muzuna was divided into two kharub.

Kha-Ta An ancient Egyptian unit of area approximately equivalent to 27,565 square meters.

Khet An ancient Egyptian unit of length approximately equivalent to 52.5 meters.

Khett In Cambodia, a political subdivision equivalent to a prefecture or province.

KHM GOST 7.67 Latin three-letter geocode for Cambodia. The code is used for transactions to and from Cambodian bank accounts and for international shipping to Cambodia. As with all GOST 7.67 codes, it is used primarily in Cyrillic alphabets.

Khokha A slang term for 10 million Indian rupees. See also: Crore.

Khoroo In Mongolia, a political subdivision for a neighborhood inside Ulan Bator, the capital.

Khoroolol In Mongolia, a political subdivision for a neighborhood or other densely populated area. It was more common in Soviet times. See also: Khoroo.

Khot In Mongolia, a political subdivision equivalent to a city outside the jurisdiction of any province. The only khot in Mongolia is Ulan Bator.

Khoueng In Laos, a political subdivision equivalent to a province.

Khoum A subdivision of the Mauritanian ouguiya. The ouguiya is one of only two currencies not based on factors of 10, as each ouguiya is divided into five khoums. However, the khoum is not used in practice because of the ouguiya's low value.

KHR ISO 4217 code for the Cambodian riel. It was issued in 1980, ending five years where Cambodia had no monetary system. The U.S. dollar also circulates in Cambodia, particularly in urban areas. Additionally, merchants along the border often accept the Thai baht.

Khum In Cambodia, a political subdivision of a district. A khum is divided into more than one phum, or village.

Khun One of several words for "you" in Thai. It is also a title used in front of persons' names. It is a polite word and is used to speak with strangers or to speak in a business context.

KI 1. ISO 3166-1 alpha-2 code for the Republic of Botswana. This is the code used in international transactions to and from Kiribati's bank accounts. **2.** ISO 3166-2 geocode for Kiribati. This is used as an international standard for shipping to Kiribati. Each island group has its own code with the prefix "KI." For example, the code for the Gilbert Islands is ISO 3166-2:KI-G.

KIBOR 1. See: Kuwait Inter Bank Offered Rate. **2.** See: Karachi Inter Bank Offered Rate.

Kickback A payment or discount that one may receive in exchange for performing certain services. A kickback may be both legal and proper, or it may be a bribe. This depends on the specific nature of the kickback and the rules surrounding different transactions.

Kicking Goals Achieving success, especially by making high sales. The term comes from Australian rules football.

Kicking the Tires Informal; initial research done on a potential investment. Kicking the tires may involve a cursory look at the investment's fundamentals and possibly a request for more information from a reliable source. Kicking the tires implies that there is no commitment on the part of the investor. See also: Indication of interest.

Kiddie Tax A tax on the earnings of a minor child under the age of 18 who earns more than a certain amount in a given year when he/she are not working a paid job. The earnings over and above this amount (which is determined annually) are taxed at the child's parent's or guardian's tax rate. The kiddie tax was created in 1986 to remove the incentive for people to avoid taxes by "giving" stock to their children in a way to make it exempt from taxes. The kiddie tax was introduced in 1986.

Kidnap-Ransom Insurance An insurance policy providing coverage in the event that one is kidnapped and a ransom is demanded. For example, if a high level executive is kidnapped while visiting a branch office in a high risk area, a company that carries kidnap-ransom insurance on that executive will be reimbursed for the amount it spends providing ransom for him/her to the kidnappers. As with all insurance, one must pay a premium to receive the coverage.

Kihayr Izin In Islamic law, a contract that either party may cancel with no advance notice.

Kiihtelys A Finnish unit meaning 40 squirrel pelts.

Kikor An ancient Hebrew unit of weight approximately equivalent to 0.354 grams.

Kilderkin An obsolete unit of volume equivalent to 18 gallons.

Kile A Turkish measure of volume approximately equivalent to 0.037 cubic meters, or slightly less than 10 gallons. It became obsolete when Turkey made the metric system mandatory in 1933.

Kilil In Ethiopia, a political subdivision equivalent to a province.

Kill To cancel an order that has not yet been filled. See also: Fill-or-kill, Immediate-or-cancel.

Killer Application An informal term for a computer program so much better than its competitors that it drives them all out of business.

Killer Bee An investment banker who helps publicly-traded companies take periodic or continual measures to discourage unwanted or hostile takeovers. One example of an antitakeover measure in which a killer bee might assist is the macaroni defense, in which the company issues a large number of bonds with the proviso that they must be redeemed at a high price if the company is taken over.

Killing Informal; an extremely large profit.

Kimberley Process A structure set up to ensure that diamonds sold internationally do not finance wars or other conflicts. Countries subscribing to the Kimberley Process must put in place regulations requiring diamond dealers to buy diamonds only from known sources. Diamonds shipped across international borders must be certified as conflict-free or they may not be sold. The Kimberley Process was established in 2003.

Kin A unit of weight in Japan equivalent to 600 grams.

Kinderkrankdeiten A German term for teething troubles, as of an infant. The term was used in the early 1920s to describe the utter failure of the German office founded to control foreign exchange and stop the devaluation of the German mark.

King Sigismund A king of Poland who lived from 1467 to 1548. Sigismund is notable for being among the first to recognize that inflation occurs when there is too much money in circulation.

Kink In auto sales, a problem with a sales contract that prevents a deal from closing. A kink results from misrepresentation by one side or the other, or simply from a mistake in drawing up the contract.

Kip A unit of weight equivalent to 1,000 pounds.

Kippunta A Finnish unit of weight approximately equivalent to 170 grams. It became obsolete when Finland adopted the metric system in 1880.

KIR GOST 7.67 Latin three-letter geocode for Kiribati. The code is used for transactions to and from I-Kiribati bank accounts and for international shipping to Kiribati. As with all GOST 7.67 codes, it is used primarily in Cyrillic alphabets.

Kirat A Turkish measure of weight approximately equivalent to 0.2004 grams. It became obsolete when Turkey made the metric system mandatory in 1933.

Kiribati Dollar The currency of Kiribati. Kiribati dollars only circulate as coins because Kiribati uses Australian dollar banknotes; Australian coins are used as well. The two dollars are pegged at a one-to-one ratio. The Kirbati dollar was issued in 1979.

Kisterseg In Hungary, a political subdivision smaller than a county but larger than a municipality.

Kite An ancient Egyptian unit of weight approximately equivalent to 1.36 grams during the Old and Middle Kingdoms or 9.1 grams during the New Kingdom.

Kiting 1. The illegal practice of deliberately misrepresenting the value of a security or transaction in order to extract more funds from a counterparty. **2.** The illegal practice of writing a bad check on an account at one bank, depositing it at a second bank, and withdrawing cash. Check holds have made kiting more difficult than it once was. **3.** The illegal practice of defacing a check by increasing the amount of money written on it. One may take advantage of bad handwriting, for example, by changing "ten" to "twenty" on the check.

Kivenheitto A Finnish unit of length approximately equivalent to 50 meters. It became obsolete when Finland adopted the metric system in 1880, but is still used to mean "nearby."

Kiwi A nickname of the New Zealand dollar.

Kjordaemi In Iceland, a political subdivision approximately equivalent to a province.

Klafter 1. A German unit of length equivalent to 10 feet. **2.** A German unit of volume approximately equivalent to 2.9 cubic millimeters.

KLCE Kuala Lumpur Commodity Exchange. See: Malaysia Derivatives Exchange.

Kleine palm An obsolete Dutch unit of length roughly equivalent to three centimeters.

Klinger Oscillator In technical analysis, a measure of market movements created by comparing a 13-day moving average of a security's volume to a 13-day moving average of its price. A Klinger oscillator is designed to detect long-term trends while also showing short-term reversals. Theoretically, if one follows a Klinger oscillator, one may profit from a long-term uptrend while avoiding temporary losses from short-term downtrends. This allows the investor to maximize his/her return.

KMF ISO 4217 code for the Comorian franc. It began with the Madagascar-Comoros CFA franc, which ended with Madagascar's withdrawal in 1973. It was pegged to the French franc and since 1999 has been pegged to the euro.

KN 1. ISO 3166-1 alpha-2 code for the Federation of Saint Kitts and Nevis. This is the code used in international transactions to and from bank accounts in Saint Kitts and Nevis. **2.** ISO 3166-2 geocode for Saint Kitts and Nevis. This is used as an international standard for shipping to Saint Kitts and Nevis. Each parish has its own code with the prefix "KN." For example, the code for the Parish of Christ Church Nichola Town is ISO 3166-2:KN-01.

KNA GOST 7.67 Latin three-letter geocode for Saint Kitts and Nevis. The code is used for transactions to and from local bank accounts and for international shipping to Saint Kitts and Nevis. As with all GOST 7.67 codes, it is used primarily in Cyrillic alphabets.

Kneecapping Informal; the act of stopping a trend. The term is highly derogatory. For example, an analyst may accuse a government of kneecapping GDP growth by adopting a certain policy.

Knights of Labor A labor union founded in 1869. It reached its heyday in the 1880s when its size overreached its capacity. It finally dissolved in 1949. The Knights pushed for an eight-hour work day and the abolition of child labor. Some of their affiliates were early adopters of desegregation. The Knights opposed socialism.

Knock-In Option An option contract that becomes active only when a certain price is reached. For example, one may purchase a knock-in option with a "knock-in price" of $35 and a strike price of $45. If the price of the underlying asset never reaches $35 at any point over the course of the option's life, the option is treated as if it never existed in the first place. If it does, however, it becomes a plain vanilla option (that is, a regular option) with a strike price of $45. See also: Up-and-In Option, Down-and-In Option, Knock-Out Option.

Knock-Out Option An option contract that automatically expires, even before the expiration date, if the underlying asset reaches a certain price that would be disadvantageous to the option writer. If this price (called the knock-out) is reached, the option becomes worthless. Most of the time, the knock-out results in the holder losing the premium, though some knock-out options, known as rebate barrier options, refund part of it. See also: Barrier option.

Know Your Client A form containing detailed information on the risk tolerance and investment goals of the client of a brokerage. The KYC form helps ensure that an investment adviser or broker does not make decisions that do not conform to the client's intentions. Filling out a KYC form does not mean that the investment adviser always makes correct decisions; it merely requires him/her to make decisions that will be generally accepted as sound for someone who seeks to do what is in the client's best interests. See also: Prudent-Person rule.

Knox v. Lee A U.S. Supreme Court case holding that fiat currency issued during the U.S. Civil War was legal tender and had to be accepted as payment. The court held that one could not demand payment in gold or another commodity instead of legal tender currency. The case was decided in 1871, overturning the precedent set the year before in Hepburn v. Griswold.

KOBACO Korea Broadcasting Advertising Corporation. A government agency in South Korea that sets advertising rates for all television and radio stations in the country. It was established in 1981.

Kobo A subdivision of the Nigerian naira. One kobo is equal in value to 1/100 of a naira. See also: Cent.

Kochliarion An ancient Greek unit of volume approximately equivalent to 4.5 milliliters.

Kofi Annan Secretary-General of the United Nations from 1997 to 2006. He worked on a variety of international development projects during his tenure, including the Iraq Oil-for-Food program. He was a recipient of the 2001 Nobel Peace Prize.

Kokumin kai hoken A state-sponsored slogan in Japan meaning, "All people should have insurance." It was introduced in the postwar period to promote the nascent Japanese welfare state.

Kokumin kai nenkin A state-sponsored slogan in Japan meaning, "All people should have pensions." It was introduced in the postwar period to promote the nascent Japanese welfare state.

Kommanditgesellschaft Abbreviated KG. A German word for a limited partnership. It is a type of corporate structure in Austria, Germany and elsewhere.

Kommanditgesellschaft auf Aktien Abbreviated KgAA. A corporate structure in Germany equivalent to a master limited partnership.

Kommun In Finland and Sweden, a political subdivision equivalent to a municipality.

Kommune In Denmark, a political subdivision equivalent to a municipality.

Komuna In Kosovo, a political subdivision equivalent to a municipality.

Komune In Albania, a political subdivision equivalent to a rural municipality.

Konche An ancient Greek unit of liquid volume approximately equivalent to 22.7 milliliters.

Kondratiev Wave A theory stating that capitalist economies go through phases much longer than ordinary business cycles. That is, capitalist economies have cycles of 45-60 years, where they perform alternately well and then poorly. The cycle then starts over. For example, the Second Industrial Revolution lasted from approximately 1850 to 1900; the global economy performed well in the first half of the cycle and was characterized by depression in the second half. Kondratiev wave theory was proposed by a Soviet economist and is more popular in Marxist circles than outside of them. See also: Kremlinomics.

Kondylos An ancient Greek unit of length approximately equivalent to 38.5 millimeters.

Kone A major engineering company in Finland. It is one of the world's largest manufacturers of elevators and escalators. It was established in 1910 and its stock is one of the components of the OMX Helsinki 25.

Kop A Dutch unit of volume equivalent to one liter. It was adopted in 1817, soon after the establishment of the Kingdom of the Netherlands.

Kopanka An obsolete Polish unit of area approximately equivalent to 0.001995 hectares.

Kopeck The term for 1/100 of a Russian ruble, a Ukrainian hryvnia, and formerly a number of other currencies in Eastern Europe. See also: Cent.

Kopejek A subdivision of the Tuvan aksa. One kopejek was worth 1/100 of one aksa.

Koper In Flemish-speaking areas, a nickname for the one, two and five eurocent coins. The name means "copper," and refers to their color. Alternate Flemish nicknames are ros and rostjes, which mean "redhead" and "little redhead," respectively.

Kopiyka A subdivision of the Ukrainian hryvnia. One kopiyka is equal in value to 1/100 of one hyrvnia.

KOR GOST 7.67 Latin three-letter geocode for South Korea. The code is used for transactions to and from South Korean bank accounts and for international shipping to South Korea. As with all GOST 7.67 codes, it is used primarily in Cyrillic alphabets.

Korea Exchange A stock exchange in South Korea. It was created through the merger of the Korea Stock Exchange, the Korea Futures Exchange and KOSDAQ. Stocks, bonds, ETFs, REITs, futures and options are all traded on the Korea Exchange.

Korean Composite Stock Price Indexes 1. Any of several indices tracking the Korean Stock Exchange. They are weighted for market capitalization and are used to gauge the performance of South Korean securities and its wider economy. The most important KOSPI index is the KOSPI 200, which tracks the 200 largest stocks (by market capitalization) in South Korea. 2. An index of all stocks traded on the Korean Stock Exchange. See also: East Asian Tiger, NIC, Asian Financial Crisis.

Korean Yen The currency of Korea between 1910 and 1945. It was pegged at par to the Japanese yen and monetary policy was controlled by Japan. It was replaced by the North and South Korean wons following the end of World War II.

Korntonde An obsolete Danish unit of volume approximately equivalent to 1,391 liters. It was used to measure barrels of corn.

Korrel A Dutch unit of weight equivalent to 1/10 of one gram. It was adopted in 1817, soon after the establishment of the Kingdom of the Netherlands.

Kortteli A Finnish unit of volume approximately equivalent to 327.15 milliliters. It became obsolete when Finland adopted the metric system in 1880.

Koruna 1. See: CZK. 2. See: SKK.

KOSPI 200 An index tracking 200 large companies that trade on the Korea Exchange. Companies are weighted for market capitalization and the index is used to gauge the performance of South Korean securities and the country's wider economy. Derivatives based on the KOSPI 200 are among the most widely traded in the world.

Kotyle An ancient Greek unit of volume approximately equivalent to 272.8 milliliters. It was also called a hemina or, when measuring liquid volume, a trublion.

Kozhuun In Russia, a political subdivision equivalent to a rural municipality.

KP 1. ISO 3166-1 alpha-2 code for the People's Democratic Republic of Korea (North Korea). This is the code used in international transactions to and from North Korean bank accounts. 2. ISO 3166-2 geocode for North Korea. This is used as an international standard for shipping to North Korea. Each province and special city has its own code with the prefix "KP." For example, the code for Pyongyang is ISO 3166-2:KP-PYO.

KPW ISO 4217 code for the North Korean won. It was introduced in 1947, replacing the Korean yen. For some period of time before 2001, it was pegged to the U.S. dollar at rate of 2.16 won to one dollar, but this has been re-adjusted as the won's black market value was nowhere near the peg. The won is an inconvertible currency. Visitors must use foreign exchange certificates in North Korea officially, but many vendors simply accept foreign currencies.

KR 1. ISO 3166-1 alpha-2 code for the Republic of Korea (South Korea). This is the code used in international transactions to and from South Korean bank accounts. 2. ISO 3166-2 geocode for South Korea. This is used as an international standard for shipping to South Korea. Each province and metropolitan has its own code with the prefix "KR." For example, the code for the City of Seoul is ISO 3166-2:KR-11.

Krai In Russia, a political subdivision equivalent to a province. The term is largely customary; administratively, a krai is identical to an oblast.

Kraj In the Czech Republic and Slovakia, a political subdivision equivalent to a province.

Krajina Dinar The currency of Serbian Krajina, an unrecognized state that existed between 1991 and 1995. The dinar was introduced in 1992 and was subject to hyperinflation for its entire history. It was revalued twice, once in 1993 at a ratio of 1 million to one and once in 1994 at a ratio of 1 billion to one. It was replaced by the Croatian kuna.

Kran A currency subdivision in Afghanistan between 1891 and 1925. A kran was worth half of an Afghan rupee.

Kreis In Germany, a political subdivision equivalent to a district, which is larger than a county but smaller than a state.

KRI A currency code for the Kiribati dollar. Kiribati dollars only circulate as coins because Kiribati uses Australian dollar banknotes; Australian coins are used as well. The two dollars are pegged at a one-to-one ratio. The Kirbati dollar was issued in 1979. The code is not recognized by the ISO.

Krom In Cambodia, a subdivision of a village.

Krona 1. See: Swedish krona. 2. See: Icelandic krona.

Krone 1. See: Danish krone. 2. See: Norwegian krone.

Krong In Cambodia, a political subdivision equivalent to a municipality.

Krosha An ancient Indian unit of length variously equivalent to values between three and four kilometers. It was also called a gorata.

Krossi A Finnish unit meaning 144 pencils.

Krugerrand A coin minted in South Africa containing one troy ounce of gold. It is legal tender in South Africa but is not used. It is the first gold coin minted to be legal tender at the market value of one troy ounce of gold rather than for an amount indicated by the face value of the coin. It is one of the more frequently traded coins in the world. See also: Silver Krugerrand.

Kruzhka A Russian unit of dry volume approximately equivalent to 1.3 liters. It was rendered obsolete when the Soviet Union began to use the metric system in 1924.

Kruzhkha A Russian unit of liquid volume approximately equivalent to 12.3 liters. It was rendered obsolete when the Soviet Union began to use the metric system in 1924.

KRW ISO 4217 code for the South Korean won. It became the currency of South Korea in 1962, replacing the hwan. It was pegged to the U.S. dollar at various rates until 1997, when it became a floating currency. See also: Asian financial crisis.

Krysha A Russian word meaning roof. It became a common term for protection money in Russia following the collapse of the Soviet Union.

Kswacsh Dva An ancient Persian unit of length approximately equivalent to 600 millimeters.

KT Knowledge Transfer. A slang term for training a new employee, especially when an outgoing employee trains the new employee to replace him/her.

Kuai 1. A Chinese term for accounting. 2. A Chinese term for broker. An alternate Chinese term is jing ji ren. 3. A slang term for Chinese renminbi. It is roughly equivalent to buck or quid in English.

Kubikkfavn A Swedish unit of volume approximately equivalent to 5,850 liters.

Kudos Informal; praise for exemplary work. For example, a supervisor may offer kudos to an employee who gives an excellent presentation.

Kula A customary Moroccan unit of weight approximately equivalent to 11.165 kilograms.

Kulac A Turkish measure of length approximately equivalent to 1.83 meters. It became obsolete when Turkey made the metric system mandatory in 1933.

Kulad In Estonia, a political subdivision equivalent to a village.

Kun In North Korea, a political subdivision equivalent to a county.

Kunsilli lokali In Malta, a political subdivision equivalent to a municipality.

Kunta In Finland, a political subdivision of a municipal government.

Kupang A slang term for 10 cents in certain parts of Malaysia. For example, 80 cents is called eight kupang. The term is most common in Kedah, Penang, and Perlis. See also: Malaysian ringgit.

Kuroi Kiri A Japanese term for bribery or for corruption generally. Literally, the term means "black mist."

Kurru An ancient Akkadian unit of volume approximately equivalent to 300 liters.

Kurus A subdivision of currency in Turkey. A kurus is equal to 1/100 of a Turkish lira. See also: Cent.

Kus An ancient Sumerian unit of length approximately equivalent to 497 centimeters.

Kutch Kori The currency of Kutch, a portion of British-ruled India. Upon Indian independence in 1947, it was replaced by the Indian rupee. See also: Dokto, Trambiyo.

Kuwait Fund for Arab Economic Development An agency of the government of Kuwait intended to encourage international development. It was the first organization established by a developing country to assist developing countries. It was founded in 1961 with profits from Kuwait's oil reserves. See also: Petrodollar, AFESD.

Kuwait Inter Bank Offered Rate Commonly called KIBOR. The interest rate at which prime banks in Kuwait lend money to other banks.

Kuwaiti Dinar The currency of Kuwait. It was issued in 1961, replacing the Gulf rupee. It was initially pegged to the British pound. Between 1975 and 2003, it was pegged to a currency basket. In 2003, it shifted the peg to the U.S. dollar. However, Kuwait shifted the peg back to a currency basket in 2007 because the dollar was weak at the time, resulting in high inflation for the dinar.

Kvadratmil A Swedish unit of area approximately equivalent to 10.7 square kilometers.

Kvarter A Swedish unit of length approximately equivalent to 14.8 centimeters.

Kvartmil A Swedish unit of nautical distance equivalent to 1,852 meters.

KW 1. ISO 3166-1 alpha-2 code for the State of Kuwait. This is the code used in international transactions to and from Kuwaiti bank accounts. 2. ISO 3166-2 geocode for Kuwait. This is used as an international standard for shipping to Kuwait. Each Kuwaiti governate has its own code with the prefix "KW." For example, the code for the Prefecture of Jahrah is ISO 3166-2:KW-JA.

Kwacha 1. See: Malawian kwacha. 2. See: Zambian kwacha.

Kwaeng In Thailand, a political subdivision for a neighborhood or district within Bangkok.

Kwart A Maltese unit of weight approximately equivalent to 6.6 grams. It is largely obsolete but is still used in some circumstances.

Kwarta 1. A Maltese unit of volume approximately equivalent to 5.4 liters. It was originally used to measure alcohol. It is largely obsolete but is still used in some circumstances. 2. A Maltese unit of volume approximately equivalent to 5.1 liters. It was originally used to measure milk and oil. It is largely obsolete but is still used in some circumstances.

Kwartin A Maltese unit of volume approximately equivalent to 32 milliliters. It was originally used to measure milk and oil. It is largely obsolete but is still used in some circumstances.

Kwartje A slang term for a coin worth 0.25 Dutch guilders. The term has fallen out of use since the introduction of the euro.

KWD ISO 4217 code for the Kuwaiti dinar. It was issued in 1961, replacing the Gulf rupee. It was initially pegged to the British pound. Between 1975 and 2003, it was pegged to a currency basket. In 2003, it shifted the peg to the U.S. dollar. However, Kuwait shifted the peg back to a currency basket in 2007 because the dollar was weak at the time, resulting in high inflation for the dinar.

KWT GOST 7.67 Latin three-letter geocode for Kuwait. The code is used for transactions to and from Kuwaiti bank accounts and for international shipping to Kuwait. As with all GOST 7.67 codes, it is used primarily in Cyrillic alphabets.

KY 1. ISO 3166-1 alpha-2 code for the Cayman Islands. This is the code used in international transactions to and from Cayman bank accounts. 2. ISO 3166-2 geocode for Cayman. This is used as an international standard for shipping to the Cayman Islands, and is expressed as ISO 3166-2:KY.

Kyat The currency of Burma (or Myanmar). It was introduced in 1953, replacing the Burmese rupee. The Burmese government has been known to follow unusual policies with regard to printing money. For example, it introduced 45 and 90 kyat banknotes in 1987 because they both incorporated a leading general's favorite number (nine). Also in 1987, the government demonetized the 25, 35 and 75 kyat banknotes without warning. This led to a general uprising because those notes composed three-fourths of the currency in circulation.

Kyathos An ancient Greek unit of volume approximately equivalent to 45.5 milliliters.

Kyattha A Burmese unit of mass approximately equivalent to 16.33 grams.

Kyay Ywa In Myanmar (Burma), a political subdivision equivalent to a village, which is contained inside a kyay ywa ok su (group of villages).

Kyay Ywa Ok Su In Myanmar (Burma), a political subdivision equivalent to a group of villages, which are contained within a township (myo ne).

KYD ISO 4217 code for the Cayman Islands dollar. First introduced in 1972, replacing the Jamaican dollar, it has been pegged to the United States dollar since 1974. As of 2009, the peg was US$1.20 per C$1, making the Cayman Islands dollar one of the highest valued currencies in the world.

Kyndemil A Swedish unit of length approximately equivalent to 16 kilometers.

Kyoto Protocol An international treaty intended to combat global warming that limits the amount of greenhouse gases that nations may emit. Every major country in the world has ratified the Kyoto Protocol except the United States (which never ratified it) and Canada (which withdrew in 2011). The treaty was signed in 1997 and came into effect in 2005.

Kyrgyz Som The currency of Kyrgyzstan. It was introduced to replace the Soviet ruble; the som was the local name for the ruble while Kyrgyzstan was under Soviet rule.

Kyynara A Finnish unit of length approximately equivalent to 593.76 millimeters. It became obsolete when Finland adopted the metric system in 1880.

KZ 1. ISO 3166-1 alpha-2 code for the Republic of Kazakhstan. This is the code used in international transactions to and from Kazakh bank accounts. 2. ISO 3166-2 geocode for Kazakhstan. This is used as an international standard for shipping to Kazakhstan. Each Kazakh province and free city has its own code with the prefix "KZ." For example, the code for the Province of Akmola is ISO 3166-2:FM-AKM.

KZT ISO 4217 code for the Kazakhstani tenge. It was issued in 1993, replacing the Soviet ruble. Kazakhstan was once of the last former Soviet republics to issue a new national currency.

L On a stock transaction table, a symbol indicating that a security's price is its lowest price in a rolling 52-week period. See also: New low.

L.A. 1. See: LA. **2.** See: Local agent.

L.C. 1. See: Letter of credit. **2.** See: Limited company.

LA 1. ISO 3166-1 alpha-2 code for the Lao People's Democratic Republic. This is the code used in international transactions to and from Laotian bank accounts. 2. ISO 3166-2 geocode for Laos. This is used as an international standard for shipping to Laos. Each Laotian subdivision has its own code with the prefix "LA." For example, the code for the Province of Attapu is ISO 3166-2:LA-AT.

La Me A Burmese unit of volume approximately equivalent to 31.96 milliliters.

La Myet A Burmese unit of volume approximately equivalent to 15.98 milliliters.

La Myu A Burmese unit of volume approximately equivalent to 7.99 milliliters.

Laani In Finland, a political subdivision equivalent to a province.

Laari A currency subdivision in the Maldives. It is equal to value to 1/100 of a Maldivian rufiyaa. See also: Cent.

Labor Force The portion of a population available for work. For example, if there are 10,000 people in a town including 2,000 children and 3,000 retirees and chronically ill persons, the labor force is the remaining 5,000. The labor force may or may not include unemployed persons who do not wish to work. The unemployment rate is determined by calculating the unemployed persons in the labor force, not the general population.

Labor Hoarding The practice in which a company does not lay off employees when it otherwise would (as during a recession). Labor hoarding is high risk as it reduces a company's profitability during a difficult time, but it guarantees employee talent will be available to that company (and, just as importantly, not to its competitors) when growth resumes.

Labor Intensive Describing an industry or sector in which it is difficult to produce a good or service without a large amount of labor. Labor intensive industries require either a large number of employees or a large number of hours worked by employees, or both, in order to be successful. Labor intensity may be quantified by taking a ratio of the cost of labor (i.e. wages and salaries) as a proportion of the total capital cost of producing the good or service. The higher the ratio, the higher the labor intensity. Labor intensive industries may control costs in bad economies by laying off workers. Examples of labor intensive industries include agriculture, mining, and hospitality.

Labor Piracy The practice in which a company attempts to "steal" highly skilled or talented employees from competitors or other industries by offering better pay and benefits. For example, an accounting firm may hire a government auditor. Labor piracy is more common when labor is in high demand. See also: Headhunting.

Labor Pirate A person or company that attempts to "steal" highly skilled or talented employees from competitors or other industries by offering better pay and benefits. For example, an accounting firm may hire a government auditor. Labor piracy is more common when labor is in high demand. See also: Headhunting.

Labor Relations The study or practice of how a company relates to its employees, especially if those employees are unionized. Labor relations may be governed by law or a regulatory agency.

Laches In law, a doctrine stating that one cannot knowingly let one's rights lie dormant and then suddenly assert them. For example, if one builds a home on another's property without the objection of the property owner, the property owner cannot sue for ownership of the house 10 years later. There is no time limit on laches.

Lachter A German unit of length. Its measure varied in different German-speaking areas, but generally was about two meters. It became obsolete with the adoption of the metric system in the 1870s.

Ladder Strategy An investment strategy in which one invests in several securities with different maturities. When the first one matures, the yield may or may not be used to buy another security. It is used most often with bonds and certificates of deposit. Laddering protects the investor from interest rate risk by locking in interest rates at once. Suppose one does not use laddering: one may invest $30,000 in a five-year bond with a 4% coupon. When the bond matures, prevailing interest rates may have dropped to 2%, making it impossible to achieve the same profit reinvesting in the same type of bond. Had this investor used laddering, he/she would have put, say, $10,000 into three bonds: a five-year bond at 4%, a seven-year bond at 5.5%, and a 10-year bond at 6%. That way, if prevailing interest rates drop to 2% in five years, this only affects the reinvestment of one third of the initial $30,000 investment. This practice is also called staggering maturities or liquidity diversification.

Laddering a Stock An investment practice in which an investor buys a significant amount of stock when it is rising in price in order to push the price even higher. The investor then sells when the price is at its peak. Laddering a stock is a form of price manipulation.

Lady Godiva Accounting Principles A theoretical system of accounting that would disclose information not required to be disclosed under the generally accepted accounting principles (GAAP). LGAP include all off-balance sheet items, among other things. They were devised in the wake of the Enron scandal, and while the Sarbanes-Oxley Act of 2002 improved accounting transparency in the United States, the LGAP remain largely theoretical.

Lady Macbeth Strategy In a hostile takeover, a strategy in which a company poses as an ally of the takeover target, but ultimately joins the bidders. The erstwhile ally may use a Lady Macbeth strategy in order to gain information about the takeover target.

Lady of the House A woman who manages a household while her husband or partner earns the family income. In marketing, household products may be targeted to ladies of the house.

Laffer Curve An upside down parabola on a chart referring to a theoretical optimal tax rate that will maximize government revenues. The theory behind the Laffer curve states that there is a certain point, known as T*, at which a government collects the greatest possible amount in taxes. If taxes are lower than T*, the government collects less because taxpayers are not required to pay. If it is higher than T*, people have an incentive to work less because more of their money goes to the government and, as a result, the government collects less. Economists disagree about whether the Laffer curve is true, but even supporters agree that T* is only an approximation.

Lag 1. A late payment. 2. In a quantitative model, the length of time considered in the past that is used to predict a future variable.

Lag Response of Prepayments The time between the point at which interest rates falls to the point at which it become advantageous for mortgage borrowers to refinance their mortgages and the point at which prepayments actually increase. The lag response of prepayments is usually about three months and can be used to determine changes to the prepayment rate of mortgage-backed securities.

Laggard Industry An industry that may be growing but not as quickly as the economy at large. A laggard industry may be outdated or it may be simply out-of-favor.

Lagging 1. See: Late payment. 2. See: Lagging indicator.

Lagging Indicator Statistics of economic performance that follow other indicators. Lagging indicators are used to confirm a previous economic trend. For example, an increase in job creation and a fall in the unemployment rate are considered lagging indicators of economic recovery. That is, they occur after other indicators of recovery, such as GDP growth. As such, job creation and lower unemployment show that the GDP growth has been, and will likely continue to be, sustained. See also: Leading indicator, Coincident indicator.

Lagting The name of the parliaments of Aland (an autonomous territory of Finland) and the Faroe Islands (an autonomous territory of Denmark). The word means roughly "law thing" or "law assembly."

Laid Away In auto sales, a slang term describing a customer who adds all frills, extras, and insurance available to him/her when purchasing an automobile. In other words, a laid away customer pays the maximum possible price to the seller.

Laissez Passer A one-way travel document often issued as an emergency passport. A laissez passer may be issued by a national government or sometimes an international organization. Most frequently, one is issued to a stateless person, to a person fleeing a humanitarian crisis, or to a citizen of an unrecognized government.

Laissez-Faire A term describing an economic theory that promotes government non-intervention. Laissez-faire theory states that most government interventions make an economy less efficient and hamper growth. According to this, government ought to restrict itself to safeguarding the right to private property. In its extreme form, it is opposed to any law limiting economic activities short of theft or extortion. Laissez-faire economists are philosophically opposed to minimum wages, protectionism, antitrust laws, and most laws intended to benefit workers at the expense of employers. Proponents of laissez-faire economics argue that it benefits employers and workers alike. For example, a man may open a mechanic shop to make money for himself, but, in the process of doing so, he may hire otherwise unemployed mechanics and service otherwise broken cars, which then facilitates business for the rest of the community. If there were environmental or wage restrictions on his business, however, he might not hire as many employees and may not start the mechanic shop at all. Critics of the theory contend that its benefits are overstated and that a laissez-faire structure without regulation lends itself to the creation of bubbles, which harms both businesses and their employees. See also: Reaganomics, Invisible Hand, Keynesian economics, Marxism, Regulation.

Laissez-Faire Leadership A management style in which the manager provides little or no oversight to employees. The manager may be available to answer questions, but, in general, lets the employees perform their work. Laissez-faire leadership works best with employees who are highly competent and/or experienced.

LAJ ISO 4217 code for the Pathet Lao kip. It was issued in 1976, though it was in circulation in some parts of the country before then. It replaced the royal kip after the Laotian Civil War. It was re-valued and replaced by the new kip in 1979.

LAK ISO 4217 code for the Laotian new kip. It was issued throughout the whole of Laos in 1976, but it had been in circulation in parts of the country before then. It has suffered from bouts of steep inflation, and is one of the least valued currencies in the world.

Lake Chad Basin Commission An international organization established to protect the environment of Lake Chad. It aims to preserve the basin around Lake Chad, as well as the upper Chari-Logone and Komadugu-Yobe basins. It was established in 1964 and consists of Cameroon, the Central African Republic, Chad, Niger and Nigeria.

Lalawigan In the Philippines, a political subdivision equivalent to a province.

Lame Duck An ineffective trader who is in or near bankruptcy due to a series of bad trades, often over a long period of time. A lame duck has suffered heavy losses, not from a bear market or something similar, but simply due to his/her ineptitude. This is a slightly pejorative term that is most common in Europe.

Lan A Burmese unit of length equivalent to 1.8288 meters.

Lana In Mexico, a slang term for money. Equivalent terms are baro and feria.

Land Real estate or property. It is the primary (and indeed one of the only) assets whose values do not depreciate over time. Depending on the particular title, ownership of land may include mineral rights to any geophysical aspects occurring thereon. Ownership of land does not automatically include the right to develop it, depending on local regulations. While supply of land does not vary, demand may change greatly depending on its particular features, number of people in the area, and cultural differences regarding land ownership. It is an attractive form of collateral because it cannot be stolen or destroyed. See also: Plot, zoning law.

Land Banking The practice of buying real estate with the intent to re-sell it at a higher price. Land banking is common when the buyer expects the value to go up in a relatively short period of time. For example, if a university is in the process of expanding, one may buy empty land half a mile away in expectation that the university will one day want it as part of the campus.

Land Contract A contract in which a buyer agrees to purchase real property from the seller for a certain price and on a certain payment schedule, but in which the seller retains title to the land until all payments have been made. A land contract may or may not amortize payment evenly, so that it may require a large balloon payment at some point in order to transfer title. Land contracts are most common either for buyers who would not qualify for a normal mortgage or for purchases made for investment purposes. In the United States, different states have different regulations and restrictions on land contracts. See also: Lease with an option to buy, Rent-to-own.

Land Improvement The addition of buildings or beauty to a piece of real estate. A land improvement can be as simple as a new coat of paint or a better maintained lawn, or it may involve something more complicated like tearing down an existing house and building a mansion. In any case, a land improvement increases the value of the property. It is sometimes simply called an improvement.

Land Reform Any direct action by a government to change who owns land in a country. For example, a government may confiscate property held by large, foreign corporations and distribute it among poor and small farmers. Land reform is highly controversial whenever it is practiced.

Land Trust 1. A trust in which a grantor deposits one or more pieces of real estate. A trustee is given the right to manage the real estate. All profits or other gains are given to a beneficiary chosen by the grantor. 2. A government or private nonprofit organization responsible for managing and conserving real estate, especially undeveloped or unspoiled land. Such trusts exist to prevent environmental degradation of the land.

Land Value How much land and the improvements on it are worth, especially in its sale. One calculates capital gains (or losses) on the sale of land by subtracting the land value at purchase from the land value at sale. Generally speaking, land value increases over time, but this is by no means a universal rule.

Landbridge A railroad that connects two stations on opposite sides of a continent. A landbridge may be used to transport persons or cargo.

Landed Value The value of cargo when it is removed from a ship following a voyage. The landed value may be less than the value of the cargo when it was shipped originally, especially in the case of perishable goods.

Landesbank One of several regionally organized banks owned by the German government. Landesbanken are wholesale banks; that is, they offer services to institutional investors, businesses (especially large businesses), other banks, and investment vehicles such as mutual funds or pensions.

Landlocked A region or country with no coastline or with only an inland sea. In commerce, infrastructure such as roads, railroads or airports is required to transport cargo to a landlocked area.

Landlord A person who owns real estate and rents it to someone, allowing the renter to live and/or use the real estate in exchange for a fee. The fee is also called rent and is usually paid once per month. In exchange for the rent, the landlord is responsible for the basic upkeep of the property. For example, if the roof collapses, the landlord, rather than the renter, must pay for it. Landlords usually may not deduct the interest they pay on the mortgages of their properties from their taxable incomes, but the rent can provide a steady income with little or no actual work. A female landlord is called a landlady. See also: Passive income.

Landrum-Griffin Act Legislation in the United States, passed in 1959, that required labor unions to conduct secret elections of officers on a regular basis. It also required unions to disclose their financial states to the Department of Labor. It allowed union members to seek recourse from the Labor Department or through the courts in case the Act's provisions were not followed. The Act came about as a response to substantiated allegations that organized crime had infiltrated some American unions.

Landskap In Sweden, an archaic political subdivision equivalent to a province that was abolished in the 17th century.

Lanham Act Legislation in the United States, passed in 1947, that forbids trademark infringement and false advertising. It sets the criminal and civil penalties to which one may be liable for violations of the Lanham Act.

LAO GOST 7.67 Latin three-letter geocode for Laos. The code is used for transactions to and from Laotian bank accounts and for international shipping to Laos. As with all GOST 7.67 codes, it is used primarily in Cyrillic alphabets.

Laotian Kip The currency of Laos. It was issued throughout the whole of Laos in 1976, but it had been in circulation in parts of the country before then. It has suffered from bouts of steep inflation, and is one of the least valuable currencies in the world.

Lapse The termination of a right or privilege due to inaction. In insurance, lapses occur on a policy if the policyholder fails to pay premiums. In this case, the right to receive the benefit lapses. In options, the contract lapses if the option is not exercised on or by the expiration date. In this case, the right to buy or sell the underlying asset lapses.

Lapsed Option An option that the holder does not exercise by the expiration date. A lapsed option has no value. Generally speaking, an option lapses if it is out of the money at the end of the expiration date or if exercising it would be otherwise detrimental to the holder's position.

Lapsed Policy The termination of an insurance policy due to inaction on the part of the policyholder. In general, lapses occur if the policyholder fails to pay premiums. In this case, the right to receive the benefit if an insured event occurs ceases to exist.

Lapsed Rights Rights attached to a security that have expired. For example, a stock may have rights attached to it contingent upon future payment of some amount. If the amount is not paid, the rights lapse.

Large Bundle A superdivision of a tin ingot, which was a currency used in Malacca in the 15th century. Forty tin ingots were equivalent to one large bundle.

Large Span An ancient Egyptian unit of length approximately equivalent to 25 centimeters.

Large Trader A trader on a futures exchange that buys, holds, and sells sufficiently large positions to require the trader to report activities to the Commodity Futures Trading Commission. The amount of a commodity one must hold to qualify as a "large" trader varies by commodity.

Large Value Transfer System An electronic system allowing Canadian banks to transfer large amounts of funds instantaneously. The banks may use the LVTS on behalf of clients, but perhaps the most common usage is the transfer of funds for short-term loans between banks, including the Central Bank of Canada. Importantly, LVTS transfers are irreversible so as to reduce the possibility of fraud and other risks.

Large-Capitalization Describing a publicly-traded company with large amount of market capitalization. Though there is no fixed measurement, a large-capitalization company typically has a market capitalization over $5 billion or $10 billion. Some brokerages or exchanges have slightly different definitions of large-capitalization. Some indexes track large-capitalization companies, as do some exchange traded funds. See also: Mid-Cap, Low-Cap.

Last Fiscal Year The fiscal year that ended most recently. For example, if the fiscal year runs from January through December and it is currently April 2010, the last fiscal year is the calendar year 2009. The last fiscal year may be referenced in financial statements.

Last In, First Out In accounting, a technique for valuing inventory by treating inventory acquired most recently as if it were sold first. The sale of inventory is recorded against the purchase price of the most recently acquired inventory, even if the physical goods are not the same. In times of high inflation, the last-in, first out technique reduces a business' inflation risk. It also may reduce one's tax liability. For these reasons, most American firms have used this technique in their accounting since the 1970s.

Last Notice Day The last day on which a clearing house may inform an investor that it intends to make delivery of a commodity that the investor previously bought in a futures contract. The date is governed by the rules of different exchanges and clearing houses, but may also be stated in the futures contract itself. It occurs in the delivery month in which the contract expires.

Last Sale The most recent trade on a security, especially an exchange. The price of the last sale is considered the security's market price.

Last Sale Rule A rule stating that an investor has the right to inquire about all relevant information regarding the last sale of a security. Specifically, the investor may inquire on the sale price, among other things. The last sale rule gives the investor access to more information than simply the current bid-ask spread.

Last Split The extra shares one receives in exchange for former shares following a stock split. A stock split is a situation where a company increases the number of shares outstanding by declaring that each share is now worth a given number of new shares. For example, a stock split may divide each share in three. The last split is the number of new shares a stockholder receives.

Last Survivor Annuity An annuity between two or more persons in which benefits increase for surviving members as the annuitants die. For example, if there are two persons in a last survivor annuity, each receiving $500 per month, and one of them dies, the remaining annuitant receives $1,000 per month. Payments stop after the last annuitant finally passes away. A last survivor annuity is also called a tontine annuity.

Last Trade 1. The most recent transaction of a security, especially on an exchange. **2.** The price of the most recent transaction of a security, especially on an exchange. This is the security's current price.

Last Trading Day 1. In options, the expiration date. **2.** In futures, the last day on which a contract may be traded. After the last trading day, whoever holds the contract must either take delivery of the underlying assets or agree to settle in cash.

Lasti 1. A Finnish unit of dry volume approximately equivalent to 2,110 liters. **2.** A Finnish unit of liquid volume approximately equivalent to 1,507 liters. Both versions of the term became obsolete when Finland adopted the metric system in 1880.

Last-Sale Reporting A practice of NASDAQ in which every transaction over a lot in size is reported to the ticker within 90 seconds of taking place. Last-sale reporting must include the price and number of shares.

Late Charge A fee that a creditor assesses on a debtor when the borrower makes a late payment. For example, suppose a student loan carries a monthly payment of $150 and is due on the last day of each month. If the borrower does not pay the full $150 on the due date (or within a certain grace period), the lender may assess a $15 late charge. Late charges may occur with loans or other liabilities, such as a rent payment.

Late Fee An extra charge assessed on a person or organization if a payment is made after a stated date. For example, if the electric bill is due on the 12th and one pays it on the 15th, a late fee may be added. A late fee may be a flat amount or a percentage of what is owed.

Late Filer A person or company that files a tax return after the appropriate deadline. The term does not apply if the filer receives an extension on the deadline; the term late filer is only given to scofflaws.

Late Payment A debt service payment made after the end of a grace period. That is, a late payment may be made more than 30 days after the original due date. There may be late fees attached to late payments.

Late Retirement A situation in which one delays one's retirement until after the usual time. For example, if the general retirement age is 65, one takes late retirement if one works until one is 70. In the United States, late retirement can increase one's Social Security benefits because one continues to pay into the system.

Late Tape A situation in which trading volume for a security is so heavy that the ticker publicly announcing quotes is delayed by a significant amount of time, usually one or two minutes. This was fairly common before electronic tickers were used, but has largely become a non-issue since electronic tickers announce prices in real time.

Late-Day Trading A practice in which a hedge fund buys or sells shares in a mutual fund after the end of a trading day, but asks the fund to record the transactions at the end of the trading day. Because the net asset value (NAV) of a mutual fund is determined at the end of each trading day, transactions that occur after the end of the trading day may distort the fund's true NAV. This allows a hedge fund to close their positions the next trading day at a profit. Late-day trading is considered unethical, but it is not illegal.

Latent Default A liability that is near or in default, but has not been identified as such by the company carrying it.

Lateral A transfer to another department or division without a promotion or increase in responsibility. A lateral may not come with a raise or bonus, and the term implies that it may not be desirable.

Latest Finish Time The time by which a portion of a project must end. If that portion does not begin by the latest start time, the finish time for the whole project will be delayed. It is used in the Program Evaluation and Review Technique.

Latest Start Time The time by which a portion of a project must begin. If that portion does not begin by the latest start time, the finish time of the project will be delayed. It is used in the Program Evaluation and Review Technique.

Latino A person in the United States with roots, however defined, in a predominately Spanish-speaking country, especially but not necessarily in Latin

America. Latino is an ethnicity rather than a race for U.S. Census Bureau purposes. Latinos form one of the largest American minorities.

Latvian Lats The currency of Latvia. It was introduced in 1993, replacing the Latvian rublis, which replaced the Soviet ruble. Since 2005, the lats has been pegged to the euro in a band set by the European Exchange Rate Mechanism; this is in preparation for replacement of the lats with the euro at some point during or after 2012.

Latvian Rublis A transitional currency in Latvia between 1992 and 1993. It was introduced because the inflation of the Russian ruble, which previously circulated, was negatively impacting the Latvian economy. It was equal in value to the ruble. The Latvian rublis was replaced by the lats.

Laup A Norwegian unit of weight approximately equivalent to 18 kilograms. It is used most commonly to measure the weight of butter.

Lavish or Extravagant Expense A business expense that is significantly higher than what is considered reasonable. For example, if a company pays triple the market rate for office supplies, that amount may be a lavish or extravagant expense. These expenses are not tax deductible and so may increase a company's tax liability.

Law Concerning Personnel Exchange Law Concerning Personnel Exchange between National Government and Private Enterprise. Legislation in Japan, adopted in 1999, regulating civil servants who take high positions in private companies and vice versa. Under the law, the civil servants (or executives) may only take positions in each other's fields on contracts under three years, and the National Personnel Authority must publish the names of those who do so. The law was intended to limit the effect of amakudari.

Law of Blood A citizenship law stating that all or nearly all persons born to citizens of a given state are themselves citizen of that state, regardless of where they were born. For example, one with a parent who has been a U.S. citizen for one year is a citizen of the U.S., regardless of where one was born. Some countries (including the United States) also follow the law of the soil in addition to the law of blood.

Law of Demand In microeconomics, the idea that demand falls as prices rise and vice versa. For example, if prices for widgets rise, fewer people will buy widgets. See also: Supply and demand.

Law of Diminishing Marginal Returns In economics, the theory stating that each additional employee of a business is slightly less productive than the previously hired one. If all other factors remain constant, there is only so much production a business can provide. If it keeps hiring more employees, each employee will have less to do; in an extreme case, this can lead to payment for virtually no work. This may also apply to other factors of production; for example, if a factory increases the number of widget making machines but does not increase the number of employees to run them, eventually the widget machines simply take up space and tie up capital. The law of diminishing marginal returns is important to determining how much supply of a product a business can handle without diminishing productivity. See also: Austrian school, Law of Diminishing Marginal Utility.

Law of Diminishing Marginal Utility In economics, the theory that for each additional unit of a product an individual consumes, the less utility or satisfaction the person derives from it. This is important to determining how much supply of a product the market can handle without diminishing demand. Historically, it has been thought that one can quantify the marginal utility of each unit, but some economists disagree with this. See also: Austrian school.

Law of Large Numbers A mathematical theory that states that the statistical likelihood of a sample having a certain value approaches the statistical likelihood of the whole universe of samples as the sample becomes larger. For example, this is the reason political polls tend to be more accurate the larger they are. This is also called Bernoulli's Law.

Law of the Sea An international treaty under the auspices of the United Nations that defined nautical borders as being 12 nautical miles from the shore of a country. Under the treaty, each country has fishing and mining rights within those 12 miles. It was signed in 1982.

Law of the Soil A citizenship law stating that all or nearly all persons born in the physical jurisdiction of a state are citizens of that state. That is, under the law of the soil, the citizenship of one's parents is irrelevant. What matters is where one is born. The United States is a major example of a country abiding by law of the soil. Some countries also follow the law of blood in addition to the law of the soil.

Lay Off To terminate employees because the company is not making sufficient profits to pay them or to sustainably keep them on staff. While a lay off could affect one employee, the term usually refers to a group of employees that are let go because of budget cuts, restructuring, or other, similar situations. If and when the company returns to its previous profitability, it may hire back those employees who were laid off. Often, the company offers a severance or other final compensation to laid off employees.

Lay Underwriter An insurance underwriter who uses probability and statistics rather than personal interaction with a potential policyholder to determine whether or not to grant a policy. A lay underwriter works out of the company's home office.

Layout Person A graphic artist who is responsible for developing the graphics and drawings for an advertising campaign. A layout person is important in marketing because campaigns often succeed or fail based on how effective the graphics are.

Layup Informal; an order to a broker that can be executed easily. Layups are made on highly liquid securities at a reasonable price. A layup is also called a lead pipe.

LB **1.** ISO 3166-1 alpha-2 code for the Republic of Lebanon. This is the code used in international transactions to and from Lebanese bank accounts. **2.** ISO 3166-2 geocode for Lebanon. This is used as an international standard for shipping to Lebanon. Each governate has its own code with the prefix "LB." For example, the code for Beirut is ISO 3166-2:LB-BA.

LBN GOST 7.67 Latin three-letter geocode for Lebanon. The code is used for transactions to and from Lebanese bank accounts and for international shipping to Lebanon. As with all GOST 7.67 codes, it is used primarily in Cyrillic alphabets.

LBP ISO 4217 code for the Lebanese pound. It was introduced in 1939, replacing the Syrian pound, though both were pegged to the French franc at the same rate and were therefore worth exactly the same. It was pegged to the British pound briefly during the Second World War, and suffered a great deal of inflation during the Lebanese Civil War. It is also called the Lebanese lira because its Arabic name derives from the Ottoman lira.

LBR GOST 7.67 Latin three-letter geocode for Liberia. The code is used for transactions to and from Liberian bank accounts and for international shipping to Liberia. As with all GOST 7.67 codes, it is used primarily in Cyrillic alphabets.

LBY GOST 7.67 Latin three-letter geocode for Libya. The code is used for transactions to and from Libyan bank accounts and for international shipping to Libya. As with all GOST 7.67 codes, it is used primarily in Cyrillic alphabets.

LC **1.** ISO 3166-1 alpha-2 code for the Republic of Saint Lucia. This is the code used in international transactions to and from Saint Lucian bank accounts. **2.** ISO 3166-2 geocode for Saint Lucia. This is used as an international standard for shipping to Saint Lucia. Each Saint Lucian quarter has its own code with the prefix "LC." For example, the code for the Quarter of Praslin is ISO 3166-2:LC-09.

LCA GOST 7.67 Latin three-letter geocode for Saint Lucia. The code is used for transactions to and from local bank accounts and for international shipping to Saint Lucia. As with all GOST 7.67 codes, it is used primarily in Cyrillic alphabets.

L-Curve A graphical representation of the distribution of income in which the income of high earners vastly outweighs the income of all others. On an L-curve, the x-axis represents population and the y-axis represents income. The more income one earns in a year, the higher one's place on the L-curve. The curve increases gradually until it reaches the very wealthy, at which point it increases exponentially.

Lead Arranger In investment banking, an underwriting firm that leads a syndicate. A syndicate is a group of underwriters responsible for placing a new issue of a security with investors. Every syndicate is a temporary arrangement. The lead arranger assigns parts of the new issue to other underwriters for placement and usually takes the largest part itself. It is also called a managing underwriter or a syndicate manager or, less formally, a book runner.

Lead Bank An investment bank responsible for underwriting an issue of securities. The term is especially applied to an investment bank managing several investment banks in underwriting a project. The lead bank usually charges a larger fee for its services than other banks.

Lead Manager In a syndicate, an underwriting firm immediately subordinate to the managing underwriter. A syndicate is a group of underwriters responsible for placing a new issue of a security with investors. Every syndicate is a temporary arrangement. The lead manager is assigned the second-largest part of the new issue for placement. A lead manager is also called an arranger.

Lead Month Among several different futures contracts or options, the soonest month in which a contract expires. For example, given three futures contracts, one expiring in March, one in June, and one in September, the lead month is March.

Lead Regulator A self-regulatory organization that assists government regulators in enforcing some aspects of trading law. Prominent examples include the New York Stock Exchange and NASDAQ.

Lead Sheets Balance sheets in which all accounts are listed by category, notably cash, fixed assets, accounts receivable, accounts payable, and so forth. Lead sheets are intended to provide a comprehensive picture of a company at a glance.

Lead Time In supply chain management, the amount of time between a supplier receiving an order and its delivery to the distributor or customer. This is important for both custom-made products and mass production, and suppliers are expected to know the lead times for their different products. It is particularly important for just-in-time supply chains, in which each step in the supply chain is expected to know precise lead time. It is also called turnaround time.

Leadership The stocks with the highest trading volume over a given period of time. Leadership may give an indication of future market movements. That is, a large amount of interest in certain stocks may mean that the market will continue to be interested in them. Leadership may be either good or bad for the market. For example, poor leadership may result from too much speculation, while solid leadership comes from sustainable investing practices. It is also called market leadership.

Leading Economic Indicator An indicator that occurs before an economy has started moving in a particular direction and is therefore used to predict the economy's movement. For example, a reduction in the average number of hours worked by manufacturing employees is considered a leading indicator because it usually precedes an economic slowdown or a recession. Among the indicators used by the Composite Index of Leading Indicators are the change in the money supply and the number of new building permits issued for residences. Leading economic indicators are used to help predict the direction of the economy; investors and businesses can use them to make their decisions accordingly.

Leading Lipstick Indicator An indicator of future economic performance in which lipstick sales increase when consumers are not confident about the future. It is thought that people buy more lipstick when they are uncertain about the future because it is a relatively cheap luxury; that is, it is less expensive than a full makeover. The leading lipstick indicator has accurately predicted many market downturns in the past.

Leading the Market Describing a group of securities that move in the same direction as the market as a whole, but begin the movement before the market. For example, a group of stocks may increase when most stocks are increasing, but start going up when the rest of the market tends to be either flat or is declining. See also: Leading indicator.

League A unit of length equivalent to three miles.

League Table A list of investment banks by revenue (in underwriting) and size of transaction (in mergers and acquisitions). League tables list market leaders in different sectors; for example, a table might list leaders in equity underwriting while another may list the banks extending the most money in loans. Thomson Reuters and Euromoney publish several prestigious league tables.

Leak Slang. 1. In stocks or other securities, to lose value slowly. 2. In bonds, to slowly increase in yield over the risk-free rate of return, which indicates gradually increasing risk.

Leakage 1. In Keynesian economics, the process of removing money from the economy. Savings, imports, and taxes are leaked out of the economy, though they may come back in through the spending of one's savings, exports, and government injections. Keynes' circular flow model subtracted the value of leakages from national output to identify aggregate output. Thus, it is necessary to know the value leakages in order to calculate the aggregate national output. 2. In credit, money borrowed from a bank that is not redeposited into that bank, which primarily occurs through default. In this sense, leakage reduces the ability of a bank to extend credit.

Lease An agreement between two parties whereby one party allows the other to use his/her property for a certain period of time in exchange for a periodic fee. The property covered in a lease is usually real estate or equipment such as an automobile or machinery. There are two main kinds of leases. A capital lease is long-term and ownership of the asset transfers to the lessee at the end of the lease. An operating lease, on the other hand, is short-term and the lessor retains all rights of ownership at all times.

Lease Acquisition Cost The cost to either party when entering a lease agreement. It often refers to legal fees, but it can be any cost related to the lease.

Lease Fund A mutual fund that invests predominantly or exclusively on the receivables from lease agreements. Because there is little or no secondary market for leases, the fund must directly purchase the leases in the fund. A lease fund operates much like a bond fund, but with shorter maturities for the underlying assets.

Lease Rate In a leasing agreement, the interest rate. For example, when one leases a car, the bank or leasing company buys the car from the dealer, and lends its use to the driver until he/she pays back the purchase price plus some extra money. The extra money is the interest or lease rate. It is presented as a very small number, say .00220. One arrives at this number by dividing the APR by 2400. In this case, .00220 is the equivalent of a 5.28% interest rate. It is also called the money factor or simply the factor.

Lease Term The interval between the time a lease goes into effect and its expiration. This applies to both open-end leases and close-end leases. For example, one may rent an apartment (usually open-end) with a 12 month lease term, or one may lease a car (generally close-end) with a five year lease term. The lease term may or may not be renewed, depending on the type of lease and the agreement between the parties.

Leasehold The accounting status of assets under operating leases. An operating lease gives the lessee fewer rights to use the assets than a capital lease would; expenses on leaseholds are considered rental expenses. See also: Freehold.

Lease-Purchase Agreement An agreement between an owner and a renter to rent a property, often but not always real estate, for a certain period of time during which the renter can apply his/her rental payments toward the purchase of property, if he/she desires. For example, suppose one rents a house for $600 per month. In a lease-purchase agreement, the $600 may be held in escrow and may be applied to a down payment on the house at the end of the lease, if the renter so chooses. If the renter does not choose to buy the house, the money in escrow goes to the owner of the property as if it had been rent all along. It is also called a rent-to-own agreement.

Lease-Rental Bond A long-term municipal or other government bond that is used to finance public works, especially public buildings. Most of the time, the bond is repaid with rents or lease payments from these buildings. Occasionally, however, a lease-rental bond is also a general obligation bond.

Least-Developed Countries The countries with the lowest GDP relative to the remainder of the world. The least developed countries are characterized by little or no industry and/or a high dependence on foreign aid. Some of the least developed countries are dependent on worker remittances from relatives working in other countries. See also: International development.

Leath Choroin A coin that circulated in the Republic of Ireland between 1928 and 1970. It was equal in value to 1/8 of one Irish pound. See also: Half Crown.

Leath Phingin 1. A coin that circulated in the Republic of Ireland between 1928 and 1969. It was equal in value to 1/480 of one Irish pound. See also: Half penny. **2.**

A coin that circulated in the Republic of Ireland between 1971 and 1985. It was equal in value to 1/200 of one Irish pound. See also: Penny.

Leath Reul A coin that circulated in the Republic of Ireland between 1928 and 1972. It was equal in value to 1/80 of one Irish pound. See also: Threepence.

Leaves What remains of an order after a partial execution. For example, if an investor makes an order to a broker to sell 1,000 shares at a certain price and the broker is able to immediately sell 600 shares, the remaining 400 are said to be leaves.

Lebanese Loop A device that prevents a debit card or credit card that has been inserted into an ATM from being released back to its owner. A Lebanese loop is used to steal the card.

Lebanese Pound The currency of Lebanon. It was introduced in 1939, replacing the Syrian pound, though both were pegged to the French franc at the same rate and were therefore worth exactly the same. It was pegged to the British pound briefly during World War II, and suffered a great deal of inflation during the Lebanese Civil War. The Lebanese pound is also called the Lebanese lira because its Arabic name derives from the Ottoman lira.

Ledger Cash The amount in cash and cash equivalents a company has on hand. A publicly-traded company reports its ledger cash in its annual statements. Ledger cash is also called book cash.

Lee Iacocca An American automobile executive. He spent his early career at Ford, where he devised marketing strategies. He was made CEO of Chrysler in 1978, when it was on the verge of bankruptcy. He successfully negotiated loan guarantees from the U.S. Congress and introduced better-selling models, saving Chrysler. He retired in 1992.

Left-Hand Side In foreign exchange, a slang term for selling a currency.

Leg In a swap, the individual future cash flows that are swapped. The legs are calculated over a notional principal amount, which is not exchanged between the counterparties. Thus, in a swap, the only things traded are the two legs, which each party pays the other at set intervals over the life of the contract. For example, in an interest rate swap, one party may agree to pay the other a fixed interest rate over a notional value while the second party may agree to pay a variable interest rate over the same notional value. In this case, the fixed interest rate and the variable interest rate are the swap's two legs.

Leg Lifting The act or practice of selling one option contract in a combination option while maintaining one or more different ones. This will likely destroy the option strategy of the combination option. Therefore, one only does it when the premium makes the entire combination profitable. See also: Cliquet, Straddle, Strangle.

Leg On To buy or write the option contracts in a combination option separately from each other.

Legacy Cost Ongoing costs to a company that come from funding activities that, by definition, do not increase revenue. Perhaps the most prominent example of legacy costs is the funding of pension plans. Legacy costs often accrue when a company takes on too many responsibilities in times of strong performance or when it takes on an appropriate level of responsibility and then its priorities change. Critics of legacy costs contend that they make industry uncompetitive, while proponents, notably labor unions, argue they are part of an employer's moral obligation to its employees.

Legal Bankruptcy A bankruptcy that has resulted in legal proceedings. See also: Chapter 7, Chapter 11, Chapter 13.

Legal Capital The par value of all of a company's shares outstanding. Legal capital may not be distributed as dividends, or as anything else. It is also called stated capital.

Legal Defeasance 1. A provision in a loan or bond removing it as a liability on a balance sheet if cash or a portfolio is set aside for debt service. Usually defeasance occurs when a borrower owns a portfolio of Treasury securities, the coupons of which are used to service a debt. When the borrower has set aside sufficient assets to cover the debt, the debt does not need to be recorded on a balance sheet. **2.** More broadly, a provision in an agreement voiding the agreement under certain, defined circumstances.

Legal Entity A person who can enter a contract and therefore may be sued. A legal entity can be held liable for damages. It is important to note that a legal entity need not be an individual person. A corporation or other duly constituted organization is recognized as a person and, as such, is considered a legal entity.

Legal Investment An investment allowed for institutional investors under the legal and regulatory rules of the country in which it is made. Institutional investors, notably banks, handle funds on behalf of clients, who may or may not be interested in investing themselves. As a result, many institutional investors are restricted from making certain high-risk investments. In the case of bonds, legal investments are called investment-grade.

Legal List State A state in the United States that allows insurance companies and pensions only to invest from among a list of approved funds and other investment vehicles. The funds are low risk and have low volatility and are designed to protect policyholders and pensioners.

Legal Monopoly A monopoly constituted as such by the state. Legal monopolies are often heavily regulated and may have their rates and charges set by the government, at least within certain limits. The government may run the monopoly directly or contract it out to private companies; it also usually prohibits competition. A government may set up a legal monopoly if it deems it necessary for the citizenry to have a service that the monopoly provides at a reasonable rate. For example, the postal service may be considered a legal monopoly because, even though it has competition for some of its services, it remains the only organization that can legally deliver regular mail. This is because it is considered vital for the mail to run in a timely manner at affordable prices.

Legal Opinion An opinion by a lawyer or other qualified professional stating that a proposed municipal bond complies with all legal requirements and regulations. It also states whether or not the issue as structured will be exempt from federal taxes. Most municipal bonds are required to have legal opinions before issue.

Legal Risk The potential loss that may occur to an investment as a result of insufficient, improperly applied, or simply unfavorable legal proceedings in the country in which the investment is made. For example, a country may have inadequate bankruptcy protection or, in an extreme circumstance, the government may be able to seize property without provocation. On the other hand, legal risk exists even in countries that operate under the rule of law: a court, for instance, may find against a company in a given lawsuit, creating a precedent for other companies with similar operations.

Legal Scrub A slang term for a lawyer's review of a document for the purpose of removing potentially actionable language.

Legal Tender Anything that a jurisdiction has declared to be money. Historically, legal tender currency has been based on something like gold or silver; however, most money is now fiat money. That is, fiat money is that which has been declared to be legal tender by a government and would not be regarded as such without government backing. Legal tender may be used to pay a debt. In general, a merchant who does not accept legal tender currency has the debt canceled; that is, one is required to accept the legal tender or nothing at all.

Legal Transfer The transfer of a security that requires extra documentation. For example, the sale of a security by the estate of a dead person may require the executor of the estate or someone else to submit a death certificate in addition to the security's own certificate. In this case, legal transfer ensures that the executor has not stolen the security from the deceased.

Legend 1. A statement, often on a stock certificate, indicating the restrictions of ownership on the share. Many stocks do not have legends, but those that do usually place them directly on the certificate. Others include the legend on a separate document that is traded along with the stock. **2.** On a chart, an explanation of the symbols used. For example, given a candlestick chart, a legend may say that white candles represent trading days with gains and black candles represent trading days with losses.

Legging Out In a hedged investment, the act of closing one position while keeping the other open. For example, suppose one owns a stock and also holds a put option to sell that stock at a certain price in case the stock price drops significantly. In this case, legging out would involve selling the put option while continuing to own the stock.

Legislative Bureau A division of the Japanese government consisting of career bureaucrats who assist members of the Diet in writing legislation.

Legislative Overkill A pejorative term referring to a law that intends to close or prevent the abuse of a loophole but instead imposes new restrictions. Some believe that most regulation comes from legislative overkill, though others dispute this. For example, libertarian critics of the Sarbanes-Oxley Act argue that the law in fact did more harm than good by imposing excessive requirements that hurt profits and by extension the economy.

Legislative Risk The risk of loss due to a change in law in a particular jurisdiction. In general, legislative risk is the same is political risk, though the latter encompasses situations like coups and terrorism while legislative risk refers to changes in law according to due process. An (extreme) example of legislative risk is the possibility that the holder of a real estate investment trust will suffer a loss if the government passes a law that nationalizes all land in the country. More commonly, legislative risk deals with changes such as requirements to provide more benefits to employees or free trade agreements that make an industry less competitive against its foreign counterpart.

Legitimate Describing a security or trade in which a prospective buyer intends to buy without any illegal intentions, such as price manipulation.

Legua A Spanish measure of length approximately equivalent to 4.18 kilometers. It is largely obsolete.

Lehman Brothers Adjustable-Rate Mortgage Index An index that tracks most investment-grade mortgage-backed securities guaranteed by an agency. It is a subset of the Lehman Brothers Aggregate Bond Index. Following Lehman Brothers' bankruptcy, it began to be managed by Barclays.

Lehman Brothers California Municipal Bond Index An index that tracks most investment-grade municipal bonds in California. Specifically, it tracks bonds with maturities of more than two years and with issues greater than $50 million. It is a subset of the Lehman Brothers Aggregate Bond Index. Following Lehman Brothers' bankruptcy, it began to be managed by Barclays.

Lehman Brothers Commercial Mortgage-Backed Securities Index An index that tracks mortgage-backed securities in which the underlying mortgages are commercial properties rather than residential homes. It is a subset of the Lehman Brothers Aggregate Bond Index. Following Lehman Brothers' bankruptcy, it began to be managed by Barclays.

Lehman Brothers Corporate Bond Index An index that tracks most investment-grade corporate bonds in the United States. It is a subset of the Lehman Brothers Aggregate Bond Index. Following Lehman Brothers' bankruptcy, it began to be managed by Barclays.

Lehman Brothers Government Bond Index An index that tracks most Treasury and agency bonds in the United States. It is a subset of the Lehman Brothers Aggregate Bond Index. Following Lehman Brothers' bankruptcy, it began to be managed by Barclays.

Lehman Brothers Government/Corporate Bond Index An index that tracks most investment-grade corporate bonds and government bonds. Specifically, it tracks bonds with maturities of more than one year and with issues greater than $100 million. It is a subset of the Lehman Brothers Aggregate Bond Index. Following Lehman Brothers' bankruptcy, it began to be managed by Barclays.

Lehman Brothers Mortgage-Backed Securities Index An index that tracks mortgage-backed securities. Specifically, it tracks securities backed by Ginnie Mae, Freddie Mac, and Fannie Mae with 15-year and 30-year maturities. It is a subset of the Lehman Brothers Aggregate Bond Index. Following Lehman Brothers' bankruptcy, it began to be managed by Barclays.

Lehman Brothers Municipal Bond Index An index that tracks most investment-grade municipal bonds. Specifically, it tracks bonds with maturities of more than two years and with issues greater than $50 million. It is a subset of the Lehman Brothers Aggregate Bond Index. Following Lehman Brothers' bankruptcy, it began to be managed by Barclays.

Lehman Brothers New York Municipal Bond Index An index that tracks most investment-grade municipal bonds in New York. Specifically, it tracks bonds with maturities of more than two years and with issues greater than $50 million. It is a subset of the Lehman Brothers Aggregate Bond Index. Following Lehman Brothers' bankruptcy, it began to be managed by Barclays.

Lehman Formula A formula for determining a broker's commission for exceptionally large transactions. While there are variations on the formula and the numbers involved have changed over the years, the basic concept behind the Lehman formula remains that a broker charges a smaller percentage for each certain dollar amount that the transaction is worth. For example, in its original form, the Lehman formula charged a 5% commission for the first million dollars, 4% for the second million, 3% for the third million, 2% for the fourth million, and, finally, a 1% commission for everything above $4 million. It was developed by Lehman Brothers in the 1970s.

Leistungfaehigkeit A German term for efficiency. This term was invoked by Rudolf Havenstein, the head of the Reichsbank (the central bank of Germany) during the hyperinflation period in the early 1920s, to describe the success of his monetary policy of printing more money. Havenstein famously did not see the connection between this policy and the hyperinflation.

Leiviska A Finnish unit of weight approximately equivalent to 8.5 kilograms. It became obsolete when Finland adopted the metric system in 1880.

Leku Zogut A slang term for the Albanian franga, which was formerly the currency of Albania. The term refers to Ahmed Zogu (later called King Zog), who ruled Albania while the franga was in circulation.

Lemming An investor who follows the crowd without doing sufficient (or any) research on his/her investments. This almost inevitably leads to significant losses. The term has a negative connotation because a lemming (the animal) has a reputation for following his pack off of a cliff.

Lemon 1. Informal; an investment that performs exceptionally poorly, especially when the poor performance was completely unforeseen. **2.** Informal; a product that does not perform as promised. For example, if one buys a car and it stops running on the way home from the dealership, that car is said to be a lemon.

Lemons Problem The problem of asymmetric information in investing. In most investments, the buyer takes a risk that the seller is trying to sell because he/she knows that the investment is a lemon, that is, a nearly guaranteed loss. To compensate for the lemons problem, many buyers offer prices lower than they otherwise would in a perfectly symmetrical market.

Lendable Funds Money that a bank has available to lend to borrowers. That is, lendable funds are those funds a bank has over and above its operating expenses, reserve requirement, and other liabilities.

Lender A person or organization that makes a loan. That is, a lender gives money to a borrower with the expectation of repayment in a timely manner, almost always with interest.

Lender Liability Lawsuit A lawsuit between a lender and a borrower alleging that the lender failed to fulfill the loan contract. For example, a customer may sue his/her bank for not providing a mortgage after the mortgage contract was signed. However, most lender liability lawsuits involve a person or firm suing a creditor for pursuing the debt so aggressively that it drove the person or firm into bankruptcy. Most suits derive from a claim that the creditor did not act in good faith, rather than a claim of specific violation of the lending agreement. During the 2008 credit crunch, it became increasingly common for construction companies to sue banks under lender liability for not providing promised funding.

Lender of Last Resort An agency, usually a central bank, guaranteeing loans and extending credit when an institution is no longer creditworthy. The term especially applies to a country's central bank lending to other banks when they have become or are becoming insolvent. This is done to prevent bank runs and stabilize the wider economy. At the international level, the International Monetary Fund acts as a lender of last resort to sovereign states that are facing insolvency. In the Free Banking Era, private banks or even very wealthy individuals operated as lenders of last resort. The term can also apply to private institutions that specialize in extending credit to very high-risk customers. These institutions charge a high rate of interest and only appeal to persons and organizations that are not otherwise creditworthy. See also: Federal Reserve System.

Lending Agreement A contract specifying the terms of a loan. Included in a lending agreement are the amount to be borrowed, the interest rate, and the maturity, or time until the loan comes due. A lending agreement is legally binding, giving each party certain obligations toward the other, namely the lender's obligation to provide funds and the borrower's obligation to repay them..

Lending at a Premium A loan of a security between two brokers where the lending broker charges a fee to the other. Lending at a premium occurs to cover the cost of the short sale of the security by a client. It is not common to lend at a premium (most brokers lend securities to each other for free as a courtesy); it primarily occurs for illiquid securities.

Lending at a Rate The interest a brokerage pays to a client whose funds it is holding in escrow. When a client borrows securities from a brokerage and sells them, the brokerage usually collects the sale price and holds it until the client repays the borrowed securities. If the brokerage lends at a rate, it pays the client interest for holding securities.

Lending Securities In short selling, the act or practice of placing one's own securities into the trust of another person or institution with the expectation that identical securities will be returned within a certain number of days (often three). The practice of lending securities is crucial to the borrower's hedging of risk: if the borrower were unable to obtain such a security, he/she would be unable to make a profit on a decline in the security's value. Securities are often lent by a broker and placed in a margin account. See also: Hedge fund.

Leone The currency of Sierra Leone. It was introduced in 1964, replacing the British West African pound. It has been marked by high inflation for much of its history.

Leontief Paradox The concept that countries with a great deal of capital available import capital intensive commodities and export labor intensive commodities. This contradicts what one would expect: before the paradox was uncovered, economic theory held that countries would export according to their competitive advantages (that is, capital intensive countries would import labor intensive products and export capital intensive products). The Leontief paradox led to rejection or revision of the Heckscher-Ohlin theorem.

Leprechaun Leader Informal; an executive who illegally places money in an offshore account for personal use. Leprechaun leaders may acquire this money by stealing it from their firms or by some other means. The term comes from the legend of leprechauns, who are said to possess hidden treasure.

Leptokurtosis A state in which the volatility of a security is itself not volatile. That is, lepkurtosis is a state in which the volatility of a security changes at a relatively low rate. This is shown on a chart by a distribution line with data points resembling fat tails and a higher mean, with an even distribution. See also: Kurtosis, Platykurtosis.

Lepton A division of the Greek drachma. One lepton was worth 1/100 of a drachma. Its plural is lepta. While the drachma no longer circulates, lepton remains the slang term for euro cents in Greece.

Leru In Spain, a slang term for one euro.

Lesotho Loti The currency of Lesotho. It was issued in 1966 and began to circulate in 1980. It is pegged to the South African rand such that one is equal in value to the other. Both the rand and the loti are accepted in shops in Lesotho. Its plural is maloti.

Less Developed Country A country with lower GDP relative to other countries. Less developed countries are characterized by little industry and sometimes a comparatively high dependence on foreign aid. Less developed countries often undertake programs of development, with greater or lesser interventions on the part of the national governments. They are major borrowers from organizations such as the World Bank. While no strict definition of which countries are less developed exists, most countries that do not belong to the OECD are considered less developed. See also: International development.

Less Than Container Load In shipping, a term describing cargo of insufficient weight to qualify for a freight rate. That is, when one ships an LCL good, one must usually pay a higher fee.

Less Than Fair Value The deliberate sale of an export so that the export is significantly less expensive than a domestically produced good. A less than fair value sale is not simply less expensive, it is determined to be anti-competitive. Importing countries attempt to counteract less than fair value sales by setting up tariff barriers or countervailing duties. See also: Dumping.

Lessee A tenant; one who has obtained the right to use land, a house, and/or property from its owner. Sometimes, this includes the right to develop land belonging to another, but normally it is the right to live on an already developed property. The contract governing a lessee's rights is a lease; it generally includes the lessee's right to use the property under certain conditions without undue interference from the lessor for the period of time described in the lease. In exchange, the lessee pays rent.

Lessor The owner of land, a house, or other property who sells the right to use the property for a set period of time. Sometimes, this includes the right to develop land belonging to another, but normally it is the right to live on or use an already developed property. The contract governing a lessor's rights is a lease; it generally includes the lessee's right to use the property under certain conditions without undue interference from the lessor for the period of time described in the lease. In exchange, the lessee pays rent.

Let Thit A Burmese unit of length equivalent to 19.05 millimeters.

Let Your Profits Run An informal saying reminding investors not to panic when investments are performing well and not to maintain false hope when they are performing poorly. It is said when an investor wishes to sell a profitable position early out of fear that the investment will fall, giving back the profits. It is also applicable when the investor wishes to hold a losing investment in a probably vain hope that it will recover. In other words, one says "let your profits run" in order to keep investors from selling good investments or keeping bad ones.

Letter Bond A bond not registered with the SEC or other regulatory agency and privately placed with an investor. Because letter bonds are not registered, they are not allowed to be traded publicly. For this reason, when a letter bond is issued, the bondholder must send a letter to the SEC stating that he/she does not intend to resell the bond, and he/she has it only for long-term investment purposes. See also: Letter security.

Letter of Comfort 1. Before or during a new issue, a statement by an auditor stating that, while a full audit has not been done, a review of the issue's prospectus has revealed nothing inaccurate or misleading. The letter of comfort also states that the auditor is confident that a full audit would not uncover anything unusual that would negatively affect the issue. **2.** A letter that a parent company submits to a bank on behalf of a subsidiary. When the subsidiary is applying to borrow funds from the bank, the letter of comfort states that the parent company approves of and supports the application.

Letter of Comment A letter from the SEC to a company that is in the process of registering a new issue, especially for the first time. The letter suggests changes to the company's registration statement to ensure that it is as accurate and transparent as possible. The letter of comment is not a cause for concern; that is, it is not an indication that the SEC believes that the company has done something illegal. Rather, it is a way to ensure that the new issue occurs as smoothly as possible for all involved.

Letter of Credit A statement issued by a bank to the buyer of a good stating that the seller will receive payment on time and in the correct amount. If the buyer fails to make payment, the bank will do so on his/her behalf. The buyer presents a letter of credit to the seller, which eliminates the risk that the seller will not be paid. Letters of credit have become very common in international commerce, as distance and other factors make it difficult for sellers to establish the creditworthiness of every buyer.

Letter of Guarantee In call options, a guarantee of delivery of securities made by a bank to a brokerage on behalf of the bank's client. When an investor is writing a call option and does not have the underlying asset in his/her brokerage account, the brokerage may require a letter of guarantee in order to eliminate the risk that the investor will not deliver the securities should the call be exercised.

Letter of Indemnity A clause in a contract stating that payments must be made regardless of what happens. Specifically, a letter of indemnity mandates that if one party is unable to complete the contract, that party will pay reparation to the other. See also: Indemnity insurance, Hell or high water contract.

Letter of Intent 1. A document detailing a parent's wishes with regard to his/her minor children in the event of his/her death. For example, a letter of intent may state with whom the parent wants the children to live. While it is not a legal document, judges often use letters of intent along with other documents when determining the best interests of the children with regard to their future. **2.** A document indicating a corporation's intent to undertake a merger or acquisition. A letter of intent outlines the details of the merger or acquisition, including the purchase price and whether it will be paid in cash, stock, and/or debt. It is important to note that a letter of intent it not legally binding and may not be enforced. However, an LOI shows that the company is serious in its intention and there may be reputational risk in not following it.

Letter of Testamentary A statement from a probate court stating what person or organization shall serve as the executor of a deceased person's estate.

Lettered Edge An inscription on the edge of a coin. The lettered edge may be raised or imprinted into the coin. It makes the coin more difficult to counterfeit.

Leu A term for the currencies of Moldova and Romania. See also: MDL, New leu.

Level 1 A list of quotes for over-the-counter securities on NASDAQ. The quotes are made in real time. See also: OTCBB.

Level 2 An electronic service showing real-time quotes for each market maker on NASDAQ and the OTCBB. Level 2 allows the investors to find the market maker with the lowest bid-ask spread as trades are being executed.

Level Debt Service A provision in many city and other local government charters stating that debt payments must be relatively equal from year to year. This allows the municipality to make revenue projections more easily, but may impose constraints on municipal bond issues. See also: Debt ceiling.

Level Load A load for a mutual fund that is paid on an ongoing basis. A load is a fee that the investor pays in order to maintain his/her investment in a mutual fund; it is designed to cover the fund's costs; one may think of it as a sales fee. A level load contrasts with a front-end or a back-end load, in that it is paid in (usually annual) increments over the period of time during which one owns shares in the fund. See also: C-Share.

Level Premium A premium on a term life insurance policy that remains the same throughout the term. A level premium is higher than other policies with similar coverage, but the coverage increases over the term of the policy. This means that by the end of the term, the premium is lower than other policies with similar coverage. See also: Level premium insurance.

Level Term Insurance A term life insurance policy in which premiums remain the same throughout the term. Most level term policies have lives of 10 or 20 years, but this is not always the case. The distinguishing feature is that both the death benefit and the premium are fixed for the life of the policy. This means that premiums may be more expensive at first, but they will not increase as the policyholder becomes older or if he/she suddenly becomes ill.

Level Yield Curve A yield curve in which the long- and short-term yields on bonds are largely the same. A normal yield curve trends upward because bondholders expect a larger interest rate for a longer investment. If the yield curve levels, it indicates that bondholders are willing to except a lower long-term interest rate because they are uncertain about the future direction of the economy and would prefer to guarantee their interest rates in the present. A level yield curve may become an inverted yield curve, indicating an expected economic downturn.

Level-Coupon Bond A bond with coupon payments that are constant throughout the life of the bond. That is, a level-coupon bond is not indexed to inflation or anything else; it entitles the bearer to receive a percentage of the bond's principal at certain intervals until maturity. Unlike zero-coupon bonds, level-coupon bonds are sold at or close to par value because the coupons carry a stream of income that zero-coupon bonds lack. Level-coupon bonds are the most basic form of bond.

Level-Load Fund A mutual fund where the load is paid on an ongoing basis. A load is a fee that the investor pays in order to maintain his/her investment in a mutual fund; it is designed to cover the fund's costs; one may think of it as a sales fee. A level load contrasts with a front-end load or a back-end load, in that it is paid in (usually annual) increments over the period of time during which one owns shares in the fund. See also: C-Share.

Level-Premium Insurance A term life insurance policy in which the premium remains the same throughout the term. The premium one pays for level-premium insurance is higher than other policies with similar coverage, but the coverage increases over the term of the policy. This means that by the end of the term, the premium is lower than other policies with similar coverage.

Leverage 1. To use debt to finance an activity. For example, one usually borrows money in the form of a mortgage to buy a house. One commonly speaks of this as leveraging the house. Likewise, one leverages when one uses a margin in order to purchase securities. **2.** The amount of debt that has been used to finance activities. A company with much more debt than equity is generally called "highly leveraged." Too much leverage is thought to be unhealthy, but many firms use leverage in order to expand operations.

Leverage Clientele Investors who wish to buy shares in companies with a given amount of leverage. Generally speaking, leverage clientele are interested in companies that maintain the same amount of debt as the investors themselves.

Leverage Ratio In risk analysis, any ratio that measures a company's leverage. One example of a gearing ratio is the long-term debt/capitalization ratio, which is calculated by taking the company's long-term debt and dividing it by its long-term debt added to its preferred and common stock. Another example is a simple debt-to-equity ratio, which is calculated by dividing total debt by total equity. Generally, companies with higher leverage as determined by a leverage ratio are thought to be more risky because they have more liabilities and less equity. A leverage ratio is also called a gearing ratio or an equity multiplier.

Leverage Up To increase a firm's amount of debt. In general, a firm leverages up by issuing a bond, often in order to finance an expansion of operations. A publicly-traded company may leverage up to repurchase its own stock, which usually increases the share price; this was a relatively common way to discourage hostile takeovers in the 1980s.

Leveraged Describing the amount of debt that has been used to finance activities. A company with much more debt than equity is generally called "highly leveraged." Many analysts consider too much leverage to be unhealthy, but many firms use leverage in order to expand operations.

Leveraged Beta The volatility of a company relative to the market as a whole after adjusting for the amount of leverage. The leveraged beta is often lower than the unlevered beta (that is, the leveraged beta indicates less volatility) because debt can result in tax advantages that reduce volatility. See also: Beta.

Leveraged Buyout The acquisition of a publicly-traded company, often by a group of private investors, that is financed with debt. Often, the acquirer in a LBO issues junk bonds in order to raise the capital necessary for the acquisition. A leveraged buyout allows a company to be taken over with little capital, but it can be a high risk endeavor.

Leveraged Company A company that uses any debt to help finance its operations. Most companies are leveraged to some degree, but others take on so much debt they have difficulty servicing it and may file for bankruptcy. Highly leveraged companies often have more volatile profits than other companies. Some analysts, however, dispute the idea that leverage (or the lack of it) affects a company's performance in any way. See also: Capital Structure, Capital Structure Irrelevance Principle.

Leveraged Equity Stock in a publicly-traded company with a significant amount of debt. Leveraged equity carries the same risk as debt; that is, the company must service the debt to remain out of bankruptcy. On the other hand, leveraged equity can increase returns for shareholders when the cost of capital of debt is low.

Leveraged ESOP An employee stock ownership plan in which the sponsoring company borrows funds in order to purchase shares from itself, which it then distributes or sells to employees as part of their compensation. It repays the loan with annual contributions.

Leveraged Lease A lease in which a bank or other financial institution provides the lessor (the party granting the lease and retaining title to the lease good) with credit, which the lessor then uses to finance the lease. For example, suppose a car dealer (lessor) extends a lease to someone buying a car (lessee). The lessor may take a loan from a bank in order to receive capital from the lease of the car while the lessee drives away with the car. The lessee then makes payments on the lease, which the lessor then uses to repay the loan to the bank. Importantly, the lessor may take the leased asset away from the lessee if the lessee defaults, and the bank may do the same if the lessor defaults.

Leveraged Management Buyout A tactic in which the senior management of a publicly-traded company borrows heavily to buy all of the company's shares outstanding. A leveraged management buyout gives the management complete control of the company and allows it to operate without recourse to shareholders. Most management buyouts are leveraged. It is a form of going private.

Leveraged Portfolio A portfolio that includes at least some securities that were bought with borrowed money. A leveraged portfolio is risky because the securities may result in a loss, which would leave the investor liable to repay the borrowed capital. However, if the securities result in a gain, the investor has essentially made a profit without using his/her own money.

Leveraged Recapitalization The act of a publicly-traded company borrowing a significant amount of capital and using it either to pay an extraordinary dividend or to buy back a portion of its own stock. Leveraged recapitalization increases the company's liabilities (because of the extra debt) while reducing its equity. This can make it less attractive to potential acquirers. As a result, leveraged recapitalization is used most often as an anti-takeover measure. See also: Shark repellent.

Leveraged Required Return The required return on an investment that one makes in part or in full with debt.

Leveraged Stock A stock bought on credit, especially on a margin account. Generally, one purchases a leveraged stock with one's broker's money, with the stock and cash as collateral. This increases the stock owner's profit when the net value goes up and increases his/her debt to the broker when it goes down.

Levy 1. To impose an obligation to pay. For example, a government may levy a tax. **2.** To collect what is owed. For example, a creditor may levy a debt, meaning that it may collect it from the debtor.

LexisNexis A company that provides online research services for legal professionals in the United States and other countries. It provides users with thousands of American court decisions from the 18th century forward, statutes from several countries, as well as articles and other documents. LexisNexis was established in 1977.

Li 1. ISO 3166-1 alpha-2 code for the Principality of Liechtenstein. This is the code used in international transactions to and from Liechtensteiner bank accounts. **2.** ISO 3166-2 geocode for Liechtenstein. This is used as an international standard for shipping to Liechtenstein. Each commune has its own code with the prefix "LI." For example, the code for the Commune of Balzers is ISO 3166-2:LI-01.

Liability Funding Strategy Any investment strategy in which one seeks to match cash flows from investments to one's debt and other obligations. That is, when selecting securities in a portfolio, an investor following a liability funding strategy seeks to find those most likely to have a return that will allow the investor to make payments on his/her mortgage, student loans, and/or other liabilities. An individual or a business may follow a liability funding strategy.

Liability Insurance An insurance policy that guards the policyholder from legal expenses resulting from a lawsuit. This includes both attorneys' fees and damages that the policyholder must pay. Liability insurance is common in professions in which lawsuits are common, such as the medical field. A physician may buy liability insurance to protect himself/herself from the possibility that a patient will sue her for malpractice, negligence, or for any other reason. Premiums on liability insurance are sometimes considered prohibitively expensive, depending on the profession.

Liang A unit of mass in China approximately equivalent to 50 grams.

Liard A subdivision of the Austrian Netherlands kronenthaler, which circulated prior to 1794. There were 216 liards in a kronenthaler.

Liar's Loan A loan made to a person who has not been truthful about some aspect of the loan application. For example, if the borrower overstates his/her income, he/she is said to take out a liar's loan. In most jurisdictions, it is a crime to make false statements on a loan application.

Liberal A person who believes that one ought to be able to do what one would like provided it does not hurt another person. Liberalism was conceived in the 19th century primarily as an economic and social philosophy espousing religious liberty, the free market, and capitalism. In the 20th century, it became associated with the left, especially in the United States, due to a concern for social justice. As a result, a liberal tends to favor regulation of private enterprise. However, adherents to what is sometimes called "19th-century liberalism" or "European liberalism" are presumably more amenable to the free market.

Liberal Democratic Party of Japan A center-right political party in Japan. Except for 11 months in 1993 and 1994, the LDP ruled Japan between 1955 and 2009. Because it was so dominant, it has lacked a coherent ideology. It favors the free market but has also fostered a bureaucratic system that held significant influence over the private sector for most of the postwar period.

Liberal Trade Policy The policy in which a country reduces its tariffs and other trade barriers, often in conjunction with other countries. Liberal trade policies are intended to encourage international trade, which fuels economic growth. However, some economists and others believe liberal trade policies can be harmful because they are detrimental to domestic industries unable to compete with their foreign counterparts.

Liberalism The philosophy that one ought to be able to do what one would like provided it does not hurt another person. It was conceived in the 19th century primarily as an economic and social philosophy espousing religious liberty, the free market, and capitalism. In the 20th century, it became associated with the left, especially in the United States, due to a concern for social justice. As a result, a liberal tends to favor regulation of private enterprise. However, adherents to what is sometimes called "19th-century liberalism" or "European liberalism" are presumably more amenable to the free market.

Liberian Dollar The currency of Liberia. The dollar was introduced in 1943. After a coup d'etat in 1980, many businessmen took currency out of the country, creating a shortage. During the civil war (1990-2004), Liberian dollars were looted from the Central Bank of Liberia; in response, it created a new design for some currency notes. This created effectively two currencies: a legal one authorized by the Central Bank, and an illegal one based on the looted dollars. The Liberian economy still relies on a large amount of foreign aid.

Libertarian A person who believes government policies should be limited to preventing harm, rather than promoting goodness. Libertarians holds that people have the right to do whatever they wish provided that they do not prevent others from doing whatever they want. For example, a libertarian would oppose slavery (because it violates the rights of the slave) but would also oppose minimum wages (because they violate the employer's right to pay whatever the employee will take).

Libertarianism A political philosophy characterized by minimalist governance. Libertarians favor little or no government intervention in the economy beyond basic protection of property rights. They also strongly oppose perceived infringements of civil liberties. For example, a libertarian would likely oppose the indefinite detention of a suspected subversive without charges.

Liberty Cap Cent A one-cent piece minted by the United States between 1793 and 1796. It was worth 1/100 of one dollar.

Liberty Head A U.S. coin on which Lady Liberty appears on the obverse. The appearance of Lady Liberty contrasts with, say, a U.S. president or a Native American bust. Prior to the 20th century, most U.S. coins were liberty heads. See also: Numismatics.

Liberty Head Nickel A copper coin minted by the United States between 1883 and 1912. It was worth 1/20 of one dollar.

Libra 1. An obsolete unit of weight in the early metric system approximately equivalent to 500 grams. 2. An ancient Roman unit of weight approximately equivalent to 328.9 grams. It was also called an as.

Libyan Dinar The currency of Libya. It was issued in 1971, replacing the Libyan pound. It is colloquially called a jni in Western Libya or a jneh in Eastern Libya. The official name is rarely used in daily transactions.

Licence Raj A term used to describe the regulation of the private sector in India between 1947 and the early 1990s. In India at that time, one needed the approval of numerous agencies in order to set up a business legally. Manufacturing in particular was heavily regulated. The Licence Raj was the result of a mixed economy that used a government planning commission established after India's independence. The Licence Raj was largely successful in the 1950s and after, but eventually led to low rates of growth and investment. India began to liberalize its economy in the 1980s, ending the Licence Raj.

License Agreement A contract between the inventor or patent holder of a product and another party which grants that party the legal right to market, sell, or otherwise profit from that product. The license agreement may or may not give the other party exclusive right to sell the product, and it may be permanent or temporary. In return, the inventor or patent holder receives a royalty or some other compensation.

License Fee An amount of money one must pay in order to acquire a license. For example, one may be required to pay $25 for a driver's license, even after one passes the driver's test. See also: Import license, Export license.

Lichas An ancient Greek unit of length approximately equivalent to 192.6 millimeters.

Lick and a Promise A slang term for poor preparation, especially for something important. For example, if an entrepreneur goes to a meeting with a potential investor without writing down the business plan, he may be said to be going to the meeting with nothing but lick and a promise.

LIE GOST 7.67 Latin three-letter geocode for Liechtenstein. The code is used for transactions to and from Liechtensteiner bank accounts and for international shipping to Liechtenstein. As with all GOST 7.67 codes, it is used primarily in Cyrillic alphabets.

Lien The ability of a lender to sell the collateral if the borrower defaults on a loan. For example, if a loan is secured by one house, the bank or other lender has a lien on the house. It may foreclose and sell the house if the borrower does not make payments in a timely manner. A lien makes a loan less risky for the lender and may entitle the borrower to a lower interest rate or even a higher line of credit. See also: Secured Bond, Mortgage.

Lienholder The lender on a loan with collateral. When one has placed collateral on a loan, the lienholder has the right to take possession of the collateral in the event of default. One cannot sell the collateral until the loan is repaid.

Life Annuity A fixed or variable annuity that pays a certain monthly or (rarely) annual sum for life of the annuitant. Generally speaking, an annuitant buys a life annuity and makes installment payments for it throughout his/her working life. Following retirement, the annuitant begins to receive the benefit, the amount of which may or may not be fixed in the annuity contract. A life annuity is designed to provide a stable income for the annuitant in retirement. See also: Income annuity, Pension, IRA, 401(k).

Life Beneficiary A person designated in will to receive a certain asset or instrument for the remainder of his/her life. For example, in a will, a farmer may grant ownership of his farm to his children, but they may not take possession of it while their mother is alive. In this situation, the mother is the life beneficiary and has the right to live in the farm house for the rest of her life.

Life Care Community A place where retired persons can live semi-independently while maintaining easy access to health care and community activities. Life care communities may include a small apartment or living area and community recreation areas. Life care communities may be more cost effective for some retired persons than living completely on their own.

Life Estate Real estate owned only for the duration of one's life, at which time it reverts to the original owner. The owner of a life estate, called a life tenant, has all rights associated with ownership of property except the right to sell the property. Upon the death of the life tenant, the life estate reverts back to the owner, or to a third party designated by the owner. For example, in a will, a farmer may grant ownership of his farm to his children, subject to the life estate of their mother. In this situation, the mother holds the life estate and has the right to live in the farm house for the rest of her life. A life estate may be included in one's gross estate.

Life Expectancy The length of time the average person is anticipated to continue living. An insurance company may use the "official" life expectancy of a person at a certain age in determining the risk of a life insurance policy or annuity. Likewise, the IRS uses the average life expectancy to determine the required minimum distribution from IRAs. Often, the official life expectancy has only a rough relationship with an individual person's actual life expectancy.

Life Expectancy Term Insurance Term life insurance in which the death benefit gradually increases to a predetermined amount, after which it gradually decreases to zero.

Life Income 1. See: Life income fund. 2. See: Life income policy.

Life Income Fund In Canada, a pool of liquidity into which one may deposit pension contributions. The government sets minimum and maximum withdrawals that retirees may make from their life income funds each year. Life income funds are not mandatory.

Life Income Policy An annuity in which a designated beneficiary receives payments for a certain number of years upon the death of the insured. For example, a husband may purchase a life income policy in order to provide for his wife (the beneficiary) upon his death. The payments begin upon the death of the insured and terminate a stated number of years later. If the beneficiary does not survive the full number of years, a contingent beneficiary receives payments instead. As with all annuities, the insured must purchase it before payments are made, either by a lump sum or periodic payments made through one's working life.

Life Income with Period Certain An annuity in which the annuitant receives payments for the remainder of his/her life. If the annuitant dies before a stated period of time has elapsed, payments continue to be made to a designated beneficiary until the completion of that period. As with all annuities, the annuitant must purchase it before payments are made, either by a lump sum or periodic payments made through one's working life.

Life Insurance An insurance policy where, in exchange for a premium, the insurance company pays a certain benefit to the survivors of the policyholder upon his/her death. Life insurance can help defray costs of the funeral, pay off the estate's debts, and may provide for the survivors' (notably a widow or widower) future. There are two main types of life insurance. Term life insurance lasts only for a certain period of time and pays the death benefit only if the policyholder dies during that time. Whole life insurance lasts as long as the policyholder remains alive and provides a savings component against which the policyholder can borrow under most circumstances.

Life Insurance Assignment Clause A clause in a life insurance contract allowing the policyholder to give or sell the right to receive the death benefit or other benefits to another party. A common example of life insurance assignment occurs when a bank accepts a life insurance policy as collateral for a loan. In this circumstance, if the policyholder dies before the loan is repaid, the bank becomes the beneficiary.

Life Insurance Cost The amount one spends on premiums for life insurance. One considers life insurance costs, for example, when comparing term life to whole life insurance. Term life is more advantageous if one expects to die before the term expires. Otherwise, one simply loses the entire life insurance cost without receiving the death benefit.

Life Insurance in Force The total value of life insurance policies that a company has issued. One may think of the life insurance in force roughly as the total amount that the insurance company would have to pay if all its life insurance policyholders died tomorrow as well as the dividends it must pay to whole life policyholders.

Life Insurance Settlement A payment on a life insurance claim. That is, when the policyholder dies, the insurer makes a payment to the beneficiaries. This payment is called the life insurance settlement.

Life Insured Describing a person on whom a death benefit is paid. That is, when a life insured person dies, someone receives a death benefit. In general, the life insured person is the policyholder. However, some companies take out life insurance policies on employees and receive the death benefit when that person dies.

Life of Contract The time between the issue of a futures contract or option and its maturity or expiration. A contract may be traded at any point during its life, subject to the rules of the exchange on which it trades.

Life Office An insurance agency that sells life insurance predominately or exclusively.

Life Option A fixed annuity that pays a certain monthly sum for life of the annuitant. Generally speaking, an annuitant buys a life option and makes installment payments for it throughout his/her working life. Following retirement, the annuitant begins to receive the benefit. A life option is designed to provide a stable income for the annuitant in retirement. Risk is split between the annuitant and the company providing the life option: the annuitant benefits financially if he/she lives for a long time after retirement while the company benefits if he/she dies sooner. See also: Income Annuity, Pension, IRA, 401(k).

Life Paid Up at Sixty Five A life insurance policy in which the policyholder must pay premiums until he/she turns 65. That is, after the policyholder turns 65, he/she owes no more premiums, even though the policy remains in effect. This reduces the policyholder's costs, especially as he/she ages.

Life Risk Factor Information about a potential policyholder that affects life underwriting. Life risk factors include age, gender, height, weight, and tobacco use. Life risk factors demonstrate the likelihood that a policyholder will die before a certain period of time has passed. This informs an insurer as to whether to offer a policy and, if so, what premium to charge.

Life Tenant One who holds a life estate. A life tenant has all rights associated with ownership of real property, except the right to sell the property, until his/her (or someone else's) death. Upon the death of the life tenant, the property reverts back to the owner, or to a third party designated by the owner. For example, in a will, a farmer may grant ownership of his farm to his children, subject to the life estate of their mother. In this situation, the mother is the life tenant and has the right to live in the farm house for the rest of her life. A life tenancy may be included in one's gross estate.

Life Underwriter 1. See: Life insurance agent. 2. See: Insurance underwriter.

Life Underwriter Political Action Committee Also called LUPAC. A lobbying organization for insurance agents in the United States. It makes contributions to political candidates and causes. It is part of the National Association of Life Underwriters.

Life Underwriting Training Council Also called LUTC. An organization that supplies materials and classes to train life insurance agents.

Life with Guaranteed Term A type of annuity where the annuitant receives income payments from the annuity for the rest of his life and receives income for a certain number of years even if he dies before that time expires. For example, a person may purchase a life with guaranteed term annuity where he receives $2,000 per month for the remainder of one's life with a guarantee that payments will continue to his survivors for 20 years, regardless of when he dies. That is, the annuitant (or his survivors) will receive $2,000 per month for 20 years or the remainder of the annuitant's life, whichever is longer. This protects the annuitant's survivors from financial hardship in the event of an early death, but these annuities often come with smaller monthly payments.

Life-Cycle Budget An estimate of all expenses and revenues a company incurs and derives from a product. The life cycle budget includes all expenses from research and development, marketing, customer services and so forth. It also includes revenues from sales, royalties and other sources. It is calculated from the beginning of a product's research to its estimated date of withdrawal from the market. Life cycle budgets help a company determine whether or not a product is going to be profitable.

Life-Cycle Costing An estimate of all expenses a company incurs and derives from a product. Life cycle costing includes all expenses from research and development, marketing, customer services and so forth. It is calculated from the beginning of a product's research to its estimated date of withdrawal from the market. Life cycle costing helps a company determine whether or not a product is going to be profitable.

Lifecycle Fund Any mutual fund in a fund family that offers funds with varying levels of risk that are targeted at potential shareholders in different age groups. For example, a fund family may offer three lifecycle funds, one aimed at investors in their 20s and 30s, one at persons in their 40s and 50s, and one for those nearing or in retirement. In this situation, the first fund will carry the most risk because younger investors often seek to make a large return while the third will carry the least risk as investors wish mainly to protect their savings and pensions.

Lifeline Account A checking account with no minimum balance and no monthly fees. A lifeline account may have certain limitations; for example one may only be able to write a certain number of checks each month. Lifeline accounts exist to ensure that even low income persons have access to banks. As such, some U.S. states require banks to offer them.

Lifestyle Fund A portfolio strategy that targets persons according to age group. That is, a lifestyle fund may invest in low risk, low return securities if the prospective investor is approaching retirement and simply wants a steady income. On the other hand, a lifestyle fund may invest in precisely the opposite securities if the potential holder is young and looking to make a good deal very quickly. A lifestyle fund has the advantage of a great deal of flexibility depending on the investment goals of most persons in each age group.

Lifetime Cap The maximum interest rate on an adjustable rate loan that may be charged over the total repayment period. For example, a loan may be made at 5% with a 7% lifetime cap, meaning the interest rate cannot rise above 7%.

Lifetime Employment A situation in which an employee is practically guaranteed to keep his/her job. A person with lifetime employment may only be fired for gross violations such as sexual harassment or chronic absenteeism. Work performance has little or no bearing. Lifetime employment is rare except in the government sector and some nonprofits, though law firm partners may be said to have lifetime employment.

Lifetime Learning Credit A direct, dollar-for-dollar reduction of one's tax liability for money spent on higher education. In order to be eligible for the lifetime learning credit, one must have modified adjusted gross income within the limits set by Congress and have a family member enrolled in at least one class at a college, university, technical school, or vocational training. The credit is worth up to $2,000 per year and is non-refundable. Generally speaking, one may not claim a lifetime learning credit if one paid for the class through a 529 plan or if it is deducted as a business expense. Notably, one does not need to pursue a degree in order to be eligible for the credit.

LIFO Liquidation A situation in which a company using LIFO accounting sells its oldest inventory. Under LIFO accounting, inventory purchased last is treated as if it is sold first. Thus, LIFO liquidation occurs when a company appears to sell the inventory it purchased first. This may not be the actual inventory it purchased first but is treated as such for accounting purposes. LIFO liquidation happens when the company's sales outpace its purchases for inventory.

Lift 1. An increase in price. 2. An increase in the measure of some economic indicator. 3. See: Uptick.

Lifted Having risen; often refers to a rise on a stock market index. For example, one may hear that stocks in industry A have "lifted" the market. This word is often used in journalism.

Lighten Up To sell part of a security while still keeping it in one's portfolio. One may lighten up on a security because one believes that it will fall (but not necessarily by much) or because it is overrepresented in the portfolio.

Ligula An ancient Roman unit of volume approximately equivalent to 11.4 milliliters.

Like-for-Like Sales The comparison of a company's sales over a given period of time to the sales from a different period of time that resulted from the same or similar activities. For example, if a company has $3 million in sales in 2009 from its flagship store, this is compared to its sales from the same flagship store in 2008 and not to any of its satellite stores. Comparing like-for-like sales ignores the effects of expansion or other changes in activities that could distort comparisons from year to year.

Like-Kind Property Properties of the same type that are not necessarily the same property. Under U.S. tax law, two parties may exchange like-kind property without being subject to capital gains taxes. For example, if a person trades a rusty 1993 Chevrolet Cavalier for a mint-condition 1968 Chevrolet Corvette, he will not be liable for capital gains taxes on the extra value of the Corvette because both properties are automobiles. However, if he then trades the Corvette for 100 acres of farm land, he is liable for capital gains taxes because cars and real estate are not like-kind properties.

Likuta A division of the Zairean zaire. One likuta was worth 1/100 of a zaire. Its plural is makuta.

Lima Stock Exchange The only stock exchange in Peru. Established in 1971, it is one of the more important Latin American exchanges. Lima has historically been a major economic and financial center, making the Lima Stock Exchange one of the most watched in the region.

Limbo Informal; a proposed business deal or anything else in which the outcome is uncertain. For example, if two companies are discussing a merger and are in general agreement, but there are disagreements over the terms, the merger may be said to be in limbo.

Limit 1. The maximum amount of price change a futures contract is allowed to undergo on a given trading day. Limits are mandated by the exchanges on which futures contracts trade, and exist in order to reduce volatility in the market. It is also called a trading limit. 2. The maximum number of transactions in commodities that an individual may make on an exchange on a given trading day. Limits are mandated either by the Commodity Futures Trading Commission or by the exchanges on which commodity contracts trade. It is also called a trading limit. 3. See: Limit order.

Limit Down On a futures exchange, the maximum amount by which a futures contract may decline in price on a trading day. This may be a dollar amount or some percentage of its opening price. Exchanges set limits down in order to reduce volatility in the market and to reduce pressure for panic selling.

Limit if Touched An order to a broker to buy or sell a security at a certain stated price once a different stated price is reached. For example, suppose the second price is $50. A limit if touched order remains inactive until that security begins trading at $50, at which point the broker may fill the order at the investor's preferred price. A limit if touched order is identical to a stop limit order, except for the fact that a limit if touched sell order is made when the security is trading below the stop price, while a stop loss sell order is made when the security is trading above the stop price.

Limit Move The maximum price change a security or derivative is allowed to undergo on a given trading day. Limit moves are mandated by many exchanges in order to reduce volatility in the market.

Limit on Close Order An order to a broker to buy or sell a security at the end of the trading day at the best available price, provided it is equal to or better than some set price. See also: at-the-close order, limit order.

Limit Order An order to a broker to buy or sell a security at a certain price. That is, a limit order is not an immediate order; rather, it orders the broker to hold the security until the desired price is reached. For example, if stock A is trading at $50 per share, an investor may give his/her broker an order to buy stock A at $35 per share. The limit order may have a time limit on it, or it may remain open until filled. It is also called simply a limit.

Limit Order Book A list of all limit orders for a certain security that were placed by members of the public. The limit order book contains orders that have not yet been filled. The orders, however, are not public; only the book keeper has access to the details of most orders. Market makers and specialists have access only to the highest and lowest orders in order to facilitate trade.

Limit Order Display Rule A rule stating that market makers must include limit orders with better prices than those the market makers are bidding or asking to be included in market maker quotes. The limit order display rule helps improve investors' access to the best available prices.

Limit Order Information System An electronic system containing quotes for securities listed on different exchanges. Specialists and market makers may use the Limit Order Information System in order to find the best price for an order of a security of a certain size.

Limit Price 1. The price above or below which one is willing or not willing to buy or sell a security. For example, one may wish to buy a stock if the price drops to $20 per share, hold if the price goes above $40, or sell at $30. Both cases represent limit prices. An investor tells his/her broker any applicable limit prices, by which the broker is required to abide. **2.** A price of a product, especially a mass-produced product, sufficiently low so as to discourage new entry into that product's market. Monopolists set a limit price by increasing production to more than they otherwise need, which requires potential competitors to spend a greater amount in production in order to match the price. This renders competition unprofitable and maintains the monopolist's control of the market. The practice is illegal in most countries. See also: Antitrust.

Limit Up The maximum amount of price increase a futures contract or commodity is allowed to undergo on a given trading day. Limits up are mandated by the exchanges on which derivatives trade and exist in order to reduce volatility in the market. See also: Limit down, Trading limit.

Limitation on Asset Dispositions A provision in some bond indentures limiting the issuer's ability to sell certain stated assets. A limitation on asset dispositions reduces the risk to bondholders that the issuer will sell its assets and then default on the bond, which would mean that the bondholders would be completely unable to recover their investments. See also: Secured bond.

Limitation on Conversion In convertible securities, a delay or restriction on the ability to exercise the conversion option. For example, the holder of a convertible bond may have a limitation on conversion preventing him/her from changing that bond into the underlying stock on certain dates around the time of dividend payments.

Limitation on Liens An aspect of some bonds in which the issuer is only allowed to grant liens on its assets in certain circumstances. A bond with a limitation on liens generally carries lower risk because, in the event of default, the issuer's assets have fewer liens from secured creditors. This means that the bondholders have a higher priority on the proceeds of liquidation.

Limitation on Merger, Consolidation, or Sale A negative covenant in some bond indentures restricting or prohibiting mergers and/or acquisitions while the bond remains outstanding. This clause is designed to protect bondholders from unexpected occurrences changing the credit rating or other aspects about the issuer. However, it limits the issuer's options should it find itself in a difficult situation.

Limitation On Sale-and-Leaseback A provision in some bond indentures prohibiting or curtailing the issuer's ability to enter sale-and-leaseback agreements. A sale-and-leaseback agreement is an arrangement whereby a company sells a fixed asset to a bank or other institution and then rents it back and maintains usufruct of the asset. This increases the debt-to-asset ratio, which is usually seen as negative. It may be used when a company cannot otherwise obtain financing; in either case it can increase the risk to the bond, and so some bond indentures limit the use of sale and leasebacks.

Limited Audit An audit with a narrow scope. There are three types of limited audit. Some may only involve the investigation of certain departments, accounts or other units. Others may be short-term; that is, they may cover only the previous year. Finally, some may be limited to a specific subject, such as taxes or potential fraud.

Limited Company In the United Kingdom, a company with limited liability amongst its owners; that is, shareholders who are not liable for more than their investment in case of insolvency. In other words, an owner of a limited company would lose the value of his/her investment if the company declares bankruptcy, but would not be held liable for other outstanding debts. A limited company is the most common corporation structure in the United Kingdom and is designated by "Ltd"

after its name. There are two types of limited companies. A limited company by guarantee has no shareholders but instead contains members who contribute a small amount to cover outstanding debts following a potential liquidation. This structure is common among British charities, and is used by the Financial Services Authority. A public limited company usually (but not always) trades publicly, and shareholders are only liable for the value of their individual investments. These companies are designated by "p.l.c." See also: Limited liability company, U.S. Corporation.

Limited Convertibility The situation in which the residents of a country may not buy foreign currencies, but in which non-residents are permitted to by the domestic currency. A country may adopt limited convertibility to encourage foreign direct investment (in the domestic currency) while discouraging capital flight (by the residents). See also: Inconvertibility, Foreign exchange.

Limited Discretion Permission from an investor giving his/her broker the ability to make some investment decisions on a brokerage account without consulting the investor. Such decisions must be made in accordance with the customer's stated investment goals. This contrasts with a discretionary account, which gives the broker much more independence. Limited discretion is also called limited trading authorization.

Limited Liability A situation in which a partner is not liable for more than his/her/its investment in case of insolvency. That is, limited liability means that the relevant partner would lose the value of his/her investment if the company declares bankruptcy, but would not be held liable for other outstanding debts. A limited liability company, where all partners and owners have limited liability, is one of the most common corporate structures in the United States. It is designated by the letters "LLC" after its name.

Limited Liability Company In the United States, a company with limited liability amongst its owners, that is, one in which a partner is not liable for more than his/her/its investment in case of insolvency. In other words, a co-owner of a limited company would lose the value of his/her investment if the company declares bankruptcy, but would not be held liable for other outstanding debts. A limited liability company is one of the most common corporate structures in the United States. It is designated by the letters "LLC" after its name. A limited liability company is taxed as if it were a partnership, but has the ability to raise capital by acquiring new partners as if it were a corporation. However, because a limited liability company is not publicly-traded, it may have more difficulty raising capital than corporations. A limited liability company is designed to give at least some employees a share in the company's equity, while protecting them from potential losses. See also: Limited company.

Limited Partner In a company, one who shares with at least one other partner, jointly and severally, a business' ownership. Limited partners exist in limited partnerships and limited liability partnerships, but in both situations they are only liable for the capital they have invested in case of bankruptcy. In limited partnerships, the limited partners have no management authority and confine their participation to their capital investment. In limited liability partnerships, all partners are limited and therefore at least some have management authority. Profits are divided among limited partners according to an arrangement formed at the creation of the partnership.

Limited Partnership A business model in which at least one general partner and at least one limited partner share a business' ownership. In a limited partnership, the general partner does not usually make invest any capital, but has management authority and unlimited liability. That is, the general partner runs the business and, in the event of bankruptcy, is responsible for all debts not paid or discharged. The limited partners have no management authority and confine their participation to their capital investment. That is, limited partners invest a certain amount of money and have nothing else to do with the business. However, their liability is limited to the amount of the investment. In the worst case scenario for a limited partner, he/she loses what he/she invested. Profits are divided between general and limited partners according to an arrangement formed at the creation of the partnership.

Limited Payment Policy A life insurance policy where the death benefit remains constant but the policyholder may stop making premium payments after a certain period of time. For example, a limited payment policy may require payments to run for 20 years and then cease. Premiums on limited payment policies are likely to be higher than those on other life insurance policies.

Limited Price Order In general equities, an order to a broker to buy or sell shares in which the broker is constrained by the investor's limit price.

Limited Recourse Describing a loan that is secured up to a certain amount. For example, a loan on which one-third of the principal is secured or collateralized is a limited recourse loan. These loans may be used in project finance; a company may issue a bond with limited recourse for the first five years of its life, after which it becomes fully secured. Limited recourse loans carry lower interest rates than without recourse loans. In the event of liquidation, limited recourse debt is paid after secured debt and before unsecured debt.

Limited Risk The risk on an investment in which the risk has a ceiling. That is, when an investor enters a position with limited risk, he/she is aware of the maximum amount he/she could possibly lose. Limited partners have limited risks on their investments as they cannot lose more than they originally invested. Likewise, buying a stock carries limited risk as the investor cannot lose more than the buy price of the stock. See also: Unlimited risk.

Limited Safety Net A social safety net that assists a narrower range of persons than other social safety nets. For example, a limited safety net may only provide nutritional assistance to children and not to impoverished adults. Proponents of limited safety nets argue that safety nets drag on an economy and that restricting eligibility spurs job creation and innovation. Critics maintain that limiting the safety net harms the most vulnerable members of society.

Limited Warranty An agreement between a seller and a buyer in which the seller agrees to pay for damage to a good under certain conditions. For example, the limited warranty may only cover certain types of damage and/or damages up to a certain amount. For example, if one buys a computer with a limited warranty, the seller may refuse to pay for damages from water or deliberate abuse. See also: Unlimited warranty.

Limited-Liability Instrument An investment vehicle in which the maximum amount one may lose is the initial amount of the investment. An example is a long position on an option contract. If one does not exercise the option, the most one may lose is the premium. Likewise, a limited partner in any partnership is only liable for the amount of his/her investment in the event of liquidation.

Limited-Tax General Obligation Bond A municipal bond with two distinguishing features. First, as a general obligation bond, it is secured by all revenues the issuing municipality generates that are not otherwise secured. That is, unless a municipality's revenue specifically secures another bond, the municipality must theoretically use all of its other revenue to pay the bond. Secondly, because it is a limited-tax bond, its provisions place a maximum possible tax increase that the municipality can levy if its other revenues come up short. The first provision reduces the bond's risk, while the second provision increases it.

Limited-Voting Stock Common stock designated by the publicly-traded company issuing it as having fewer voting rights than other common stocks. This gives a shareholder of limited-voting stock less control over the company than he/she would otherwise have. For example, a company can designate its limited-voting stock as having half a vote and its regular common stock as having one vote. Limited-voting stock is beneficial for the board of directors and the company's management, as it allows the company to raise financing from limited-voting stockholders while giving them less control over the company. See also: Supervoting stock, Golden share.

Limit-On-Open Order An order to a broker to buy or sell a security at the beginning of the trading day if the best available price is equal to or better than some set price. See also: at-the-opening order, limit order.

Lincoln Cent A one-cent piece minted by the United States starting in 1909. It is worth 1/100 of one dollar. It features a portrait of Abraham Lincoln on the obverse.

Line 1. In technical analysis, a situation in which the supply and demand for a security are largely the same. A line means that the security is unlikely to see any rapid fluctuation in price. It is called a line because, when plotted on a graph, it looks like a roughly horizontal line. Technical analysts look for signals that a line is ready to break one way or another before recommending that investors take a position on a security. 2. Informal; workers in a large, industrial company. They are called the line because, historically, they assembled the parts of a product while literally standing next to each other in a long line, also called an assembly line.

Line Chart In technical analysis, a chart that shows a security's price over a period of time, such as a day, a month, or a year. A line chart is constructed by placing points representing the price at different points in time, and then connecting the points with lines. It is useful in showing a security's trend over time. However, it does nothing to indicate the security's high, low, open, or close.

Line of Credit An agreement between a bank and a company or an individual to provide a certain amount in loans on demand from the borrower. The borrower is under no obligation to actually take out a loan at any particular time, but may take part of the funds at any time over a period of several years. This agreement is fairly common in situations in which a business must make payroll but does not always have the operating income to do so, especially when its operating income is seasonal or otherwise varies from month to month. It is also called open-end credit or a revolving line of credit. See also: Credit Card.

Line Wrap In word processing, a feature that formats or re-formats the margins of a text so that it is viewable on a computer or other screen without scrolling horizontally.

Linea A Spanish measure of length approximately equivalent to 1.94 milliliters. It is largely obsolete.

Linear Programming In mathematics, a process or technique for finding the maximum or minimum value of a linear function subject to certain restraints. Linear programming is important to securities analysis as it helps determine the maximum or minimum rate of return on a particular investment. While the maximum rate of return is not necessarily the expected rate of return, it may help an investor decide if a security is worth a certain level of risk.

Linear Regression A statistical technique in which one takes a set of data points and plots them on a line. Linear regression is used to determine trends in economic data. For example, one may take different figures of GDP growth over time and plot them on a line in order to determine whether the general trend is upward or downward.

Line-of-Business Reporting A convention some companies use in their financial statements in which they report information by sector. For example, a single publicly-traded company that engages in agriculture, mining, and manufacturing may report revenue, sales, and profits/losses for each field individually. This allows a company to show its investors what parts of the company are performing better relative to the others. It also prevents one sector that is overperforming or underperforming from unduly influencing a financial statement.

Lingua Franca A language used when two or more speakers do not share a native language. A lingua franca is useful in international business, because participants

may have different backgrounds. English and French are both examples of a lingua franca commonly used in business.

Linha A Portuguese measure of length approximately equivalent to 2.29 millimeters. It became obsolete after Lusophone countries adopted the metric system in the 19th century.

Linie An obsolete Danish unit of length approximately equivalent to 2.18 millimeters.

Liniya A Russian unit of length equivalent to 1/10 of one inch. It was rendered obsolete when the Soviet Union began to use the metric system in 1924.

Linja A Finnish unit of length approximately equivalent to 2.1 millimeters. It became obsolete when Finland adopted the metric system in 1880.

Linje A Norwegian unit of length approximately equivalent to 2.18 millimeters.

Link A unit of length equivalent to 7.92 inches. It is used in the surveying of land.

Linkage The ability to buy and sell the same security on different exchanges. Because the prices may differ on different exchanges, linkage may create opportunity for arbitrage. Linkage has become easier with the advent of electronic exchanges and trading platforms.

Linn In Estonia, a political subdivision equivalent to an urban municipality.

Linnad In Estonia, a political subdivision approximately equivalent to a township.

Lino A high-quality, high-resolution print out of art, especially for an advertisement.

Lintner's Model A model theorizing how a publicly-traded company sets its dividend policy. The model states that dividends are paid according to two factors. The first is the net present value of earnings, with higher values indicating higher dividends. The second is the sustainability of earnings; that is, a company may increase its earnings without increasing its dividend payouts until managers are convinced that it will continue to maintain such earnings.

Lipa A subdivision of the Croatian kuna. A lipa is equal in value to 1/100 of a kuna. See also: Cent.

Lipper Mutual Fund Industry Average A series of indices that establish benchmarks for mutual fund performance. That is, the Lipper mutual fund industry averages allow investors to compare the performance of their mutual funds against other, similar mutual funds. Each index consists of the 30 largest mutual funds for each category. For example, a Lipper index of mid-cap funds consists of the 30 largest mid-cap funds, against which owners of shares in mid-cap funds can compare the performance of their investments.

Lipper, Inc. A research firm specializing in mutual funds. It provides clients with information on multiple kinds of mutual fund as well as individual funds themselves. Lipper's indices are regarded as benchmarks for the performance of mutual funds generally.

Lippie An obsolete Scottish unit of dry volume. For beans, grass seed, peas, rye, salt, and wheat, one lippie was approximately equivalent to 2.268 liters. For barley, malt, and oats, however, it was approximately equivalent to 3.037 liters. A lippie was also called a forpet.

Liquid Yield Option Note A convertible, callable, and putable zero-coupon bond. A LYON is a bond that is convertible to common stock and may be bought or sold as an option, but which does not pay interest. Because it pays no interest, it is issued at a considerable discount from par value of the bond. This guarantees a positive return to the investor, at least until such time as it becomes profitable for the investor to put the bond back to the issuing company for an amount over the issue price. Generally, the total return on a LYON is less than that of the company's common stock, assuming the company does well.

Liquidated Damages In some contracts, a set fee that one party must pay the other in cases of breach of contract. The amount of the liquidated damages is stated in the contract and is designed to compensate the grieved party when valuation of the breach would be difficult to ascertain.

Liquidated Debt 1. Debt that has been forgiven, either by the creditor or by a bankruptcy court. 2. In bankruptcy, debt that neither the creditor nor the debtor disputes is a real debt that ordinarily would be owed to the creditor.

Liquidating Dividend A dividend paid to shareholders out of a company's capital or assets, rather than its earned income. That is, a liquidating dividend occurs when a company pays more than its total profit in dividends. This usually happens when shareholders believe that the company is no longer sustainable or profitable. Therefore, liquidating dividends are considered a return of shareholders' investments, rather than profit on them. All of the firm's debts must be paid before it can pay liquidating dividends. See also: Final dividend.

Liquidation The conversion to cash. Liquidating a position may simply mean selling stock or bonds; the seller in this case receives the cash. Liquidation also refers to a situation in which a company ceases operations and sells as many assets as it can; the company uses the cash to repay debt and, if possible, shareholders. Liquidation often has a negative connotation for this reason. See also: Panic selling.

Liquidation by Assignment The sale of a company's assets when it becomes apparent that the individual assets are worth more than the company itself. A company and its creditors agree when and how liquidation by assignment occurs. See also: Chapter 7 Bankruptcy.

Liquidation Right The right of certain stakeholders in a firm to receive the proceeds of the firm's liquidation. Liquidation rights vary according to a hierarchy; that is, interested parties higher in the hierarchy have the right to receive all their proceeds before those lower in the hierarchy. Generally speaking, secured creditors have the highest liquidation rights, followed by general creditors, preferred stockholders, and, finally, common stockholders. See also: Bankruptcy.

Liquidator In bankruptcy, a person placed in charge of a company sometimes by creditors or shareholders, but often by court order who must oversee the winding down of operations and sell all assets. As the liquidator sells off assets, he/she uses the proceeds to pay creditors, starting with secured creditors, by giving them proceeds from sold collateral, followed by unsecured creditors. If there is any money remaining, the liquidator distributes this to the shareholders, if any, or the owner. The liquidator is paid a fee for these services. See also: Receivership.

Liquidity Easy convertibility into cash. A liquid asset or security can be easily bought or sold with little or no impact on price. Most methods of counting money supply include some highly liquid investments such as certificates of deposit. Liquid assets and investments are highly desirable as they may be sold to allow an investor to enter other investments as they arise. On exchanges, liquid investments usually have low bid-ask spreads. See also: Illiquid, Liquidity preference hypothesis.

Liquidity Path The plan by which the owner or founder of a company increases his/her liquidity. One may take out a line of credit against the value of the company, but the most common liquidity paths are either to sell the company in a merger or acquisition, or to make an IPO. The liquidity path may be the way the founder cashes out and relinquishes ownership of the company, or it may be the way by which he/she reinvests to expand the company. Without a liquidity path, the owner or founder may have a difficult time tapping into the value of the company he/she has built. See also: Sweat equity.

Liquidity Preference Hypothesis A theory stating that, all other things being equal, investors prefer liquid investments to illiquid ones. This is because investors prefer cash and, barring that, prefer investments to be as close to cash as possible. As a result, investors demand a premium for tying up their cash in an illiquid investment; this premium becomes larger as illiquid investments have longer maturities. This theory is more formally stated as: forward rates are greater than future spot rates. John Maynard Keynes was the first to propose the liquidity preference hypothesis. See also: Keynesian economics.

Liquidity Premium The rate of return that an investor expects above other rates or return in order to make an illiquid investment. All other things being equal, an investor generally expects a higher return for investing in something that may be difficult to convert to cash. For example, an inactive bond may pay a higher coupon rate than an active bond with a similar credit rating.

Liquidity Risk The risk that an individual or firm will have difficulty selling an asset without incurring a loss. That is, there may be a lack of interest in the market for a particular asset, forcing the owner to sell it for less than its actual value. Liquidity risk may be quantified as the difference between an asset's value and the price at which it can likely be sold. It is highest for lightly traded securities and small issues, as well as during a bear market.

Liquidity Theory of the Term Structure A theory stating that forward rates do not accurately predict future spot rates because forward rates are more liquid and therefore include a liquidity premium. The theory attempts to explain with the unbiased expectations theory is not borne out in real life.

Liquidity Trap A recession during which banks are unwilling to lend and nominal interest rates are already at or near zero. Because interest rates are so low, the central bank can do nothing further to expand the money supply. At the same time investors are unwilling to invest to help the economy grow because banks are unwilling to lend because their returns are so low. This extends the recession and indeed makes it worse. Many economists believe that the best way to end a liquidity trap is a money gift, where the government directly transfers money to consumers in hopes that they will spend it to spur investment.

Lira A term for a currency. It derives its name from "libra," which is the Latin word for a Troy pound of refined silver. It formerly was the name of the currencies in a number of states on the Italian peninsula, including Italy, San Marino and the Vatican. It continues to be the name for currencies in Jordan, Lebanon, Syria and Turkey.

Lis Pendens 1. Describing property or another asset subject to a pending lawsuit. Because the new owner of such a property or asset is subject to the same lawsuit, it can be difficult or impossible to sell a lis pedens property. **2.** Public announcement of a pending lawsuit. The term is Latin for "suit pending."

Lisbon Stock Exchange Also known as Euronext Lisbon; the largest stock exchange in Portugal. More than 70 companies are traded on its floor. It trades in bonds, stocks, exchange traded funds, and a wide variety of derivatives. Formed as the result of a merger in 2002, the Lisbon Stock Exchange has a market capitalization of nearly 300 billion euros. It is owned by NYSE Euronext.

Lisente The plural of a subdivision of a Lesotho loti. A loti is divided into 100 lisente. The singular form is sente.

Lispund A Swedish unit of weight approximately equivalent to 8.5 kilograms.

List Buyer In direct marketing, a person who purchases the one-time use of a list of names, numbers, addresses or other information. A list buyer is also called a list user.

List Cleaning The process of removing names and addresses from a mailing list. Bad addresses, persons who have opted out of the list and persons who have not responded recently all may be eliminated in a list cleaning. Periodic list cleaning improves the information available on a mailing list.

List Maintenance The process of adding and removing names and addresses from a mailing list. Bad addresses, persons who have opted out of the list and persons who

have not responded recently all may be eliminated during list maintenance. Likewise, new contacts may be inserted. Periodic or constant list maintenance improves the information available on a mailing list.

List Manager The person or organization that markets a set of names, numbers, addresses or other information to potential renters or buyers. A list manager attempts to entice organizations, especially direct marketers, to purchase mailing lists. The manager receives a fee from the list owner for this service.

List Owner The person or organization that owns a set of names, numbers, addresses or other information. A list owner may rent or sell this information to other parties, especially for direct marketing purposes.

List Price The advertised price for a good or service. It is common for a seller to reduce the list price or at least to permit negotiation, especially for large items such as houses and automobiles.

List Rental In direct marketing, the purchase of the one-time use of a list of names, numbers, addresses or other information.

List Royalty In direct marketing, a payment a list user must make to a list owner each time he/she uses the names, addresses, numbers or other information the list owner has provided.

List Segment In direct marketing, a section of a mailing list meeting certain criteria set by the user. For example, a list segment may be all the women in a mailing list or all persons of any gender living in a certain postal code.

Listed Describing a security or derivative that is traded on an exchange. It contrasts with the term "over-the-counter."

Listed Option An option that is traded on an exchange. Listed options must conform to exchange rules; for example, they must conform to one of two types: American style and European style. Over-the-counter options are not subject to these restrictions, but they are less liquid than listed options.

Listed Property A property for sale that a real estate agent includes in its inventory for potential buyers. Listed properties may be published in a variety of media, notably in pamphlets and on the Internet.

Listed Security Stock in a publicly-traded company that is traded on a particular stock exchange. For example, companies that trade on the NYSE are said to be listed securities for that exchange. Listed securities must conform to each exchange's listing requirements, which usually mandate having a certain market capitalization, number of shareholders, and/or revenue. Listing requirements exist to enforce stability on an exchange as much as possible. A listed security may be delisted if it fails to meet the listing requirements for too long. However, some listed securities may be temporarily exempt from listing requirements if they show some sign of a potential recovery. It is important to distinguish firms with listed securities from member firms, which are companies that conduct trades on an exchange. See also: C.

Listing Broker In equities, the broker who puts a security up for trade on an exchange, also called listing the security. The broker must be a registered member of the exchange in question, and the security must meet the exchange's listing requirements.

Listing Department The department of a stock exchange responsible for ensuring compliance with listing requirements. These listing requirements mandate that every stock on the exchange have a certain market capitalization, number of shareholders, and/or revenue. Listing requirements exist to enforce stability on the exchange as much as possible. As such, the listing department decides which companies may be listed, which must be delisted, and even which are temporarily exempt from the listing requirements. The listing department is also called the stock list. See also: Listed company, C.

Listing Requirement Rules to which a publicly-traded company must adhere in order to qualify for trading on a stock exchange. Each exchange has its own rules, but they usually pertain to having a certain market capitalization, number of shareholders, and/or revenue. Listing requirements exist to enforce as much stability on an exchange as possible. A previously listed company may be delisted if it falls below the listing requirements for too long, especially if it shows no sign of recovery.

Lithuanian Litas The currency of Lithuania. It was introduced in 1993, replacing the talonas, which was itself a temporary currency to replace the Soviet ruble. Between 1994 and 2002, the litas was pegged to the U.S. dollar. Since then, it has been pegged to the euro in preparation for Lithuania joining the eurozone. While the Lithuanian government hoped to replace the litas with the euro in 2010, high inflation has pushed the date back to 2013.

Lithuanian Mint An organization in Lithuania that issues legal tender coins for general use. It was established in 1990 and is owned by the government of Lithuania. It is located in Vilnius.

Litra In Romania, a term used to indicate one quarter of one liter.

Little Board An informal term for the American Stock Exchange.

Little Dragons An informal term for the economies of Hong Kong, Singapore, South Korea and Taiwan. Prior to the Asian financial crisis, the little dragons were considered threats to Japan because lower costs had the potential to draw business away from Japan. See also: Outsourcing.

Lituanian Talonas The temporary currency of Lithuania between 1991 and 1993. It replaced the Soviet ruble, though both continued to circulate for some time. The talonas was criticized because it required persons to pay effectively double for goods, which hindered growth while not controlling inflation. It was replaced by the litas.

Live Animal Insurance 1. See: Livestock mortality insurance. **2.** See: Livestock floater. **3.** See: Livestock insurance.

Livestock Floater An addition to a property insurance policy providing coverage for losses due to the death or injury of one's livestock. Livestock floaters generally cover accidents, acts of God, thefts and so forth. They usually exclude illegal acts, confiscation, and quarantines. As with all insurance, one must pay a premium to receive the coverage.

Livestock Insurance An insurance policy providing coverage for losses due to the death or injury of one's livestock. Livestock insurance generally covers accidents, acts of God, thefts and so forth. It usually excludes illegal acts, confiscation, and quarantines. As with all insurance, one must pay a premium to receive the coverage.

Livestock Mortality Insurance An insurance policy providing coverage due to the death of one's livestock. That is, livestock mortality insurance provides a death benefit as if the animal were a person. Livestock mortality insurance may allow the owner to purchase new livestock or to be compensated for loss of income due to the death. As with all insurance, one must pay a premium to receive the coverage.

Livestock Transit Insurance An insurance policy providing coverage due to the death or injury of one's livestock while they are being transported. Livestock transit insurance may allow the owner to pay for the animals' medical bills or to be compensated for loss of income due to the death or injury. As with all insurance, one must pay a premium to receive the coverage.

Liv-Ex Fine Wine Investables Index An index tracking sales of red wine from 24 chateaus in Bordeaux, weighted for scarcity. Though fine wine is an illiquid investment, it may be used as a hedge against inflation as it tends to maintain its value over time.

Living Benefits In life insurance, all or a portion of the death benefit that the policyholder may receive prior to death. The policyholder usually elects to receive living benefits during a terminal or catastrophic illness, especially one where health insurance does not cover all the bills. They are also called accelerated benefits. See also: Viatical settlement.

Living Wage The lowest wage necessary for a person to be able to provide himself/herself with food, clothing and shelter. A living wage varies from place to place depending on an area's cost of living. A living wage may also bear only a rough resemblance to the minimum wage, which is the lowest wage a company may offer legally. Some jurisdictions, however, have mandated a living wage as the local minimum wage.

Livre The name of several obsolete currencies. Livre currencies were used in parts of France, the Channel Islands, and a number of former French colonies.

LK 1. ISO 3166-1 alpha-2 code for the Democratic Socialist Republic of Sri Lanka. This is the code used in international transactions to and from Sri Lankan bank accounts. **2.** ISO 3166-2 geocode for Sri Lanka. This is used as an international standard for shipping to Sri Lanka. Each Sri Lankan province and district has its own code with the prefix "LK." For example, the code for the Province of Uva Palata is ISO 3166-2:LK-8.

LKA GOST 7.67 Latin three-letter geocode for Sri Lanka. The code is used for transactions to and from Sri Lankan bank accounts and for international shipping to Sri Lanka. As with all GOST 7.67 codes, it is used primarily in Cyrillic alphabets.

LKR ISO 4217 code for the Sri Lankan rupee. The rupee was instituted as the sole currency in 1869; it separated from the Indian rupee following Sri Lanka's independence from the United Kingdom.

Lloyd's of London An insurance and reinsurance market in London. Active since the 1600s, it is not a company, but instead a society of individual and corporate members, who come together to spread and pool risk between themselves. Thus, Lloyd's insurance policies are backed by the financial stakes of its members. Lloyd's does not underwrite policies itself (it leaves that to members), but instead acts an a de facto regulator for the conditions under which its members offer policies. Lloyd's has a three-tiered corporate structure: members, managers, and syndicates. Members provide capital and employ one or more underwriting syndicates. Managers provide the business infrastructure to syndicates for insurance and reinsurance policies. Syndicates underwrite risks and handle claims on particular policies. Complex and/or expensive policies often involve multiple syndicates. Lloyd's also employs brokers and service companies to facilitate transactions between clients and Lloyd's.

LMS Last Man Standing. A slang term for the senior manager or executive remaining after lay-offs. The term is derogatory and connotes the idea that the LMS is unqualified for his/her new responsibilities.

Load A sales charge or commission one pays for purchasing a mutual fund. The charge is paid to the person(s) who sold the investor shares in the fund. There are three types of load. A front-end load occurs when the shareholder pays the fee when buying into the fund. A back-end load means that the investor pays when selling his/her shares. Finally, an investor with a level-load fund pays. periodically throughout his/her time as a shareholder. Studies have shown that load funds perform neither better nor worse than no-load funds.

Load Fund A mutual fund that charges shareholders a sales charge or commission. The charge, or load, pays the person(s) who sold the investor shares in the fund. There are three types of load fund. A front-end load means that the shareholder pays the fee when buying into the fund, while a back-end load means that he/she pays when selling his/her shares. Finally, an investor with a level-load fund pays periodically throughout his/her time as a shareholder. Studies have shown that load funds perform neither better nor worse than no-load funds.

Load-to-Load A payment arrangement in which a customer pays a seller for a shipment of goods when the next shipment is received. A load-to-load arrangement is beneficial especially for companies that are inventory intensive.

Loan The extension of money from one party to another with the agreement that the money will be repaid. Nearly all loans (except for some informal ones) are made at interest, meaning borrowers pay a certain percentage of the principal amount to the lender as compensation for borrowing. Most loans also have a maturity date, by which time the borrower must have repaid the loan. A loan may be guaranteed by collateral, meaning that the lender either keeps an asset belonging to the borrower until the loan is repaid or has the right to seize such an asset in the event of default. Often, loans are obtained to purchase a major asset, such as a house. These loans are generally guaranteed by the asset they are used to buy. Lending is a foundational component of capitalism.

Loan Agreement A contract governing the extension of money from one party to another with the agreement that the money will be repaid. A loan agreement states the interest rate, the repayment period, the collateral (if any) and any special terms.

Loan Amortization Schedule The schedule according to which one repays a loan. The loan amortization schedule shows the amount of each installment and how much principal and/or interest is repaid each month. See also: Amortization.

Loan Cap The policy of a higher education institution forbidding students from taking out student loans in excess of a certain amount. A school may enforce a loan cap by covering a portion of the debt with grants, by giving scholarships, or by other means.

Loan Capital Long-term capital employed from sources other than common stock or savings. That is, loan capital is what a company has borrowed or issued in preferred stock. Loan capital is distinguished by the fact that a company is required to pay coupons or dividends periodically. That is, unlike common stock, loan capital carries a fixed liability for a company. Likewise, it is usually collateralized by one or more of the company's assets.

Loan Commitment The amount in loans that a bank will make or may be required to make in the near future, but has not yet made. Loan commitments may be open-ended or closed-ended. Suppose a bank approves two loans in a year; one is a revolving line of credit for $50,000 and the other is a business loan for $100,000. One would say that this bank has an open-ended loan commitment of $50,000 (because the principal amount in the loan, when repaid, may be borrowed again) and a closed-ended loan commitment of $100,000 (because once its principal is repaid, it no longer must be committed to that borrower). Banks must disclose their loan commitments.

Loan Consent Agreement The agreement between a brokerage and a client governing a margin account. The SEC requires the parties to sign a loan consent agreement before the brokerage can lend securities to the client.

Loan Constant The cash flow required to pay the principal and interest on a loan as a percentage of the original principal. This is expressed by dividing the monthly loan payment by the amount of original principal. While less useful now, before financial calculators came to prominence loan constant tables were developed in real estate finance to amortize home loans more easily. Multiplying by a percentage (set in the table) was seen as an easier way to determine a monthly payment.

Loan Covenant A provision in a loan agreement binding the borrower or lender. A loan covenant states what actions the borrower and the lender may or may not take in certain situations. Covenants exist to reduce the risk to all parties to a loan.

Loan Crowd Members of the New York Stock Exchange that lend and borrow securities to cover their clients' short sales. See also: Margin account.

Loan Fee A fee assessed when credit is extended. A loan fee may be an annual fee on a credit card or a loan origination fee for a mortgage. It is separate from the interest.

Loan Loss Provision A non-cash expense for banks to account for future losses on loan defaults. Banks assume that a certain percentage of loans will default or become slow-paying. Banks enter a percentage as an expense when calculating their pre-tax incomes. This guarantees a bank's solvency and capitalization if and when the defaults occur. The loan loss provision allocated each year increases with the riskiness of the loans a given bank makes. A bank making a small number of risky loans will have a low loan loss provision compared to a bank taking higher risks.

Loan Note A contract stating the terms of a loan, such as the principal, the interest rate, and the payment schedule. A loan note states the rights and obligations of both the lender and the borrower. If one party does not fulfill his/her obligations, the other may sue for redress.

Loan Portfolio The loans that a lender (or a buyer of loans) is owed. The loan portfolio is listed as an asset on the lender's or investor's balance sheet. The value of a loan portfolio depends on both the principal and interest owed and the average creditworthiness of the loans.

Loan Preference Principle In foreign exchange, a theory that if a covered loan is less expensive than another loan in one currency, it will be less expensive in all other currencies. See also: Purchasing Power Parity.

Loan Servicer A person assigned to collect debt service payments on behalf of a bank or other financial institution.

Loan Shark A person who makes illegal loans, usually by charging an extraordinarily high interest rate. For example, a loan shark may lend $1,000 at a 2,000% annualized interest rate, which is illegal in most states. Loan sharks are not financial institutions; they often "collateralize" their loans with threats of violence. Loan sharking often is associated with organized crime. See also: Usury.

Loan Sharking The practice of making illegal loans, usually by charging an extraordinarily high interest rate. For example, a loan shark may lend $1000 at a 2000% annualized interest rate, which is against the law in most states. Loan sharks are not financial institutions; indeed they often "collateralize" their loans with threats of violence. Loan sharking often is associated with organized crime. See also: Usury.

Loan Syndication A practice in which several banks each lend an amount of money to a borrower at the same time and for the same purpose. The banks participating in the loan syndication cooperate with each other for the duration of the project, even if they are otherwise competitors. Bank syndicates usually only lend large amounts of money that the individual banks could not afford easily. Loan syndication is a temporary arrangement between the banks. See also: Syndicate.

Loan to Value Ratio 1. In mortgages, the ratio of the amount of a potential mortgage to the value of the property it is intended to finance, expressed as a percentage. It is used as a way to assess the risk of making a particular mortgage loan. A lower loan-to-value ratio is seen as a lower risk to the lender. Most mortgage lenders require a maximum loan-to-value ratio of 75%. That is, a borrower is usually expected to pay for 25% of the value of a property out-of-pocket. **2.** More broadly, a ratio of the amount of a potential loan to the asset it is intended to finance. In addition to gauging the risk involved in making the loan, it tells the borrower whether or not the loan can be repaid if he/she sells the asset. This can be important if the borrower becomes unable make payments.

Loan Value The maximum amount an individual or company may borrow to buy securities on margin on a certain amount of collateral. The amount of a loan value is governed by Regulation T and by individual companies. See also: Maintenance Requirement.

Loanback The ability to borrow money using one's life insurance or retirement fund as collateral. Loanbacks are available for whole life insurance but not term life insurance. Loanbacks are useful in that they allow one to access the equity of borrowers' savings.

Lobbying The business, act, or practice of attempting to influence legislation or policy. For example, a lobbyist may call a legislator and urge him/her to vote for a bill that, if passed, would favor the industry or interests of lobbyist's client. Lobbying can be a lucrative business. However, a variety of rules exist in many jurisdictions to guard against the possibility that it can degenerate into bribery.

Lobbyist A person who attempts to influence legislation or policy, especially if he/she does so professionally. For example, a lobbyist may call a legislator and urge him/her to vote for a bill that, if passed, would favor the industry or interests of lobbyist's client. Lobbying can be a lucrative business. However, a variety of rules exist in many jurisdictions to guard against the possibility that it can degenerate into bribery.

Lobster A slang term for a $20 note in Australia. The term is derived from the fact that $20 notes are mostly red.

Lobster Trap An antitakeover strategy in which a publicly-traded company prohibits some convertible security holders from voting in the event that they exercise the conversion option. Specifically, if a single shareholder has more than 10% of the company's equity in convertible securities of any kind, that shareholder will be disallowed from converting their securities into voting stock. The conversion option may still allow the holder to own and have all other rights associated with common stock, but voting is not permitted. A lobster trap must be incorporated into the company's charter.

Local A member on a futures exchange that conducts trades predominantly or exclusively for one's own account. That is, a local is not a broker for other parties.

Local Authority Bill A debt security issued by a local government. Local authority bills are usually used to raise capital for improvements in infrastructure or other aspects of the municipality. For example, a city or school district may issue a bill to build a new school or a new playground. Risk varies with the municipality and the particular type of municipal bond. The term is most common outside of the United States. See also: Municipal bond.

Local Authority Stock A chiefly British term for a municipal bond.

Local Expectations Hypothesis A theory that bonds identical in every way except the length of maturity will have the same rate of return over a holding period. That is, if an investor buys the same amount of two bonds, each paying 5% interest payable twice per year but with one having a maturity of 10 years and the other 15, the investor will receive the same return from each bond if he/she holds both for the same amount of time. This is because the coupon payments are identical for both bonds, and coupons form the bulk of a bond's return.

Local Government Area In Nigeria, a political subdivision approximately equivalent to a municipality.

Local Hire A new employee who lives in the same area as the job. A company does not have as many start-up costs for a new hire because it does not cover any relocation expenses. Local hires may also be paid less than others, especially in the developing world and some other areas.

Local Level Government In Papua New Guinea, a political subdivision roughly equivalent to a municipality.

Local Listing A security that trades on a regional exchange and on no other exchange.

Local Rate A tax rate assessed by a local government, as opposed to the national or regional government. There may be limits on how high the local rate is permitted to be. Local taxes are used to pay for municipal functions such as schools, police and roads.

Local Tax A tax levied and collected by a state/province and or municipality. Local taxes are collected in order to fund local government services, but they often are also used to pay coupons and principals on municipal bonds. Local taxes sometimes come in the form of income or sales taxes, but the largest example of a local tax is property tax.

Localidad In Mozambique, a political subdivision approximately equivalent to a municipality.

Location A physical place. The location of a business is vitally important. For example, an oil company needs to station itself near oil. Likewise, a retail grocery store needs to be accessible from major roads.

Location Card A card or other record showing the amount of insurance coverage allowed for various locations. See also: In-Network, Out-of-Network.

Location, Location, Location A phrase indicating the supreme importance of location in business. Selecting a high-traffic or otherwise favorable location is paramount for building, for example, a successful restaurant business. The phrase is less relevant than it once was because of the increased use of the Internet in business. However, it remains very important.

Locational Arbitrage An arbitrage strategy in which one seeks to profit from differences in exchange rates for the same currency at different banks.

Location-Specific Advantage The ability of an individual, company, or economy to conduct an activity better than another for reasons related to location. Location-specific advantages are important in making decisions such as the products one should make or sell; if a company is unable to make a product as well as another because resources are unavailable or difficult to acquire in a certain location, the company might be well advised to make a different product. For example, a lumber company in Oregon has a location-specific advantage to a lumber company in Arizona because there are simply more trees in Oregon. This makes it unlikely that the company in Arizona will be able to fill orders as well or as quickly as the company in Oregon. For this reason, the Arizona company's management might consider investing in mining instead of lumberjacking.

Lock In To close a position such that the profit or loss from an investment is realized. For example, if an investor buys a stock at $5 per share and the price goes to $10, the investor has a paper profit of $5 per share. However, if the investor waits to sell the stock until the price drops to $8, the locked in profit is only $3 per share. Investors often wait before locking in substantial profits or losses, as locking in a profit may result in higher taxation, while locking in a loss removes the possibility that the investment can be recovered.

Lock Limit A price that a futures contract may not exceed or drop below on a given trading day. For example, if the lock limit is $25 for a given contract and it had previously been trading at $22, the exchange will not allow the contract to trade above $25. Likewise, if it were previously trading at $28, it would not be permitted to trade below $25. Futures exchanges set lock limits in order to protect investors from the excessive volatility often involved in futures trading.

Lock, Stock, and Barrel Informal for complete or full. For example, upon completing a business project, one may describe the project as "lock, stock and barrel."

Lockbox A service that a bank provides in which is processes payments for a company. The company directs its customers to send payments to a lockbox at the bank, whose employees then collect the payments and deposit them directly into the company's account. A lockbox reduces time between the receipt and processing of payments, which can be beneficial for the company using the service. On the other hand, it opens the possibility of fraud by bank employees, who could theoretically steal the payments by taking the funds from the payments and not depositing them.

Locked Limit Down A price that a futures contract may not drop below on a given trading day. For example, if the locked limit down is $25 for a given contract and it previously had been trading at $28, the exchange will not allow the contract to trade below $25. A futures exchange sets a lock limit in order to protect investors from the excessive volatility often involved in futures trading.

Locked Limit Up A price that a futures contract may not exceed on a given trading day. For example, if the locked limit up is $25 for a given contract and it previously had been trading at $22, the exchange will not allow the contract to trade above $25. A futures exchange sets a lock limit in order to protect investors from the excessive volatility often involved in futures trading.

Locked Market A situation in which a security has no bid-ask spread. That is, the bid and the ask in a locked market are identical. A locked market is both a temporary phenomenon and relatively uncommon. When it occurs, it usually happens with NASDAQ securities in trading before the open.

Locked-In Interest Rate A proposed interest rate on a mortgage loan that a bank agrees not to change unless the loan has not been finalized after a certain period of time. This period of time usually lasts for 60 days.

Lock-In Amendment An amendment to a corporate charter making it more difficult to repeal amendments that have previously passed. A lock-in amendment is usually used as an anti-takeover measure. For example, a company may pass a lock-in amendment stating that a previous anti-takeover amendment to the charter requires a 75% majority of shareholders to be repealed.

Lock-Out The act of an employer not permitting its employees to work. That is, an employer may close down its place of business (such as a factory) so that employees cannot work and thereby earn a living. Lock-outs are useful in situations such as when a union only represents a portion of a company's workforce. If the employer believes the union is making unreasonable demands, it can declare a lock-out to encourage non-union workers to put pressure on the union workers to give up on those demands. Because this has the effect of punishing all workers, lock-outs are usually illegal.

Lockup Agreement 1. See: Crown jewel lockup agreement. **2.** During an IPO, a contract prohibiting executives, underwriters, and/or venture capitalists from selling their shares in the company for a certain period of time. The period of time is usually about six months, but may be longer or shorter. A lockup agreement exists to reduce the pressure for volatility as the company goes through its first few months of public trade.

Lock-Up CD A certificate of deposit that the depositor agrees not to trade for the duration of the CD. Because this is not legally binding, a bank issuing a lock-up CD may require the depositor to keep the certificate of deposit at the bank to physically prevent the depositor from trading it. It should not be confused with a lock-up agreement, which is a different concept altogether.

Lockup Option An antitakeover measure in which a target company offers stock options to a white knight to purchase a great deal of equity in the company at a price that would be disadvantageous to a potential acquiring company. This is designed to encourage the potential acquiring company to abandon a hostile takeover attempt. It is also called a lock-up defense.

Lockup Period A time during which a publicly-traded company forbids management and large stockholders to sell their shares, usually following an initial public offering. Depending on the company, the lockup period may be 90 to 180 days. It exists to ensure that the market is not flooded with shares in the company at any given time, which would increase supply and cause a drop in price. Large shareholders selling their shares may also be seen as an indication of a lack of confidence in the company, triggering a panic sell. After the lockup period ends, however, shareholders may sell without restriction.

Logarithmic Scale A scale where the same percentage of change between two data points (with respect to two other data points) may represent different, raw amounts of change. For example, a logarithmic scale of a stock may show a graph where a change from $4 per share to $8 per share is the same distance as a change from $40 per share to $80.

Log-Linear Least-Squares Method In statistical analysis, a method of determining the relationship between dependent variables and independent variables calculated by taking the logarithm of all variables. One takes the logarithm because the calculation gives the same percentage changes to all variables equal weight. One then applies least-squares regression to the variables and plots them on a line.

Lognormal Distribution A way to calculate long-term returns on an investment where the natural log of some variable has a normal distribution.

Logo A graphic or seal that is uniquely identifiable with a company or other organization. A logo may be of a certain color and contain certain text and images. A logo helps build brand recognition and eventually customer loyalty. See also: Marketing.

Loi Royer Legislation in France, passed in 1973, limiting the physical size of some businesses. Among other provisions, it required a special permit for businesses larger than 1,000 square meters in towns with fewer than 40,000 residents and 1,500 square meters in larger towns. The intent of the law was to protect small grocers from supermarkets, which were thought to be encroaching at the time.

Lokiec An obsolete Polish unit of length. Its measure varied but generally was between 55 and 65 centimeters.

Lokiec Wiedenski An obsolete Polish unit of area approximately equivalent to 0.9 square meters.

Lombard 1. A banker or lender. The term is used especially when referring to a person rather than an institution. **2.** Slang; a wealthy person who is greedy, stingy or otherwise morally obnoxious.

Lombard Credit Credit extended in exchange for some collateral that remains with the lender. For example, a lender may extend Lombard credit if the borrower pledges jewelry in exchange. The borrower receives the collateral back upon repayment of the loan. Lombard credit may involve retail pawnbrokers, but the Federal Reserve System makes loans to member banks on a similar basis.

Lombard Loan A loan advanced by a pawnbroker to a customer. The term derives from the prosperous pawn shops in Italy in the early modern period.

Lombard Rate The interest rate the Deutsche Bundesbank charges other banks for collateralized loan obligations. Previously, the Lombard rate could be raised or lowered in keeping with Germany's monetary policy. However, since the euro came into being, Germany no longer controls its own monetary policy.

Lombard Street One of the first books to attempt to explain the intricacies of finance and banking regulation to the lay person. It takes its name from the fact that it was written following the infamous collapse of a bank on Lombard Street in London. It was written by Walter Bagehot and was published in 1866.

Lome Convention A former agreement between the European Community and 71 developing countries allowing for the duty-free export of most goods to Europe, provided they did not compete with European goods. It also increased foreign aid to the developing countries. Most developing participants were former British, Belgian, Dutch or French colonies. The Lome Convention came into effect in 1976 and was

renegotiated a number of times before the World Trade Organization ruled it anti-competitive in 1995. In 2000, it was replaced by the Cotonou Agreement.

London and New Zealand Futures Association An exchange in the United Kingdom on which contracts based on New Zealand wool are traded. It was founded in 1953 and is based in Bradford.

London Bullion Market An over-the-counter market for the trade of gold and silver. One must be a member of the London Bullion Market Association in order to trade on this market. While the Bank of England may regulate the market, the LBMA operates primarily as a self-regulatory organization.

London Club An informal group of major creditors. The London Club meets periodically to discuss matters of mutual interest. It was formed in 1976. See also: Paris Club.

London Cocoa Terminal Market A former exchange in London on which options and futures for cocoa were traded. It was established in 1928.

London Commodity Exchange A former exchange in London on which agricultural contracts were traded. It merged with LIFFE in 1996.

London Futures and Options Exchange A former exchange in London on which options and futures for grain, sugar, cocoa and other soft commodities were traded. It merged into LIFFE.

London Gold Pool The deposit of gold reserves made by eight central banks in 1961 in order to preserve the price of $35 per ounce of gold. The London Gold Pool sold gold on the London bullion market periodically whenever the market price of gold began to rise above $35. The sales were intended to help preserve the Bretton Woods System, whereby most currencies were pegged to gold. The London Gold Pool gradually dissolved with the failure of the Bretton Woods System in the late 1960s and early 1970s.

London Interbank Bid Rate The interest rate at which participating London banks are willing to borrow eurocurrency deposits from other banks. Unlike LIBOR, which is the rate at which banks lend money, LIBID is the rate at which banks ask to borrow. It is not set by any body or organization, but is calculated as the average of the interest rates at which London banks bid for borrowed eurocurrency funds from other banks. It is also the interest rate London banks pay for deposits from other banks. It is an important benchmark in euromarkets.

London Interbank Offer Rate The interest rate participating banks offer to other banks for loans on the London market. LIBOR is the most widely used benchmark for short term interest rates in the world, primarily because most of the world's largest borrowers borrow money on the London market. Because it is so prominent, it is often used in other transactions, such as swaps. For example, an interest rate swaps may give the floating rate as "LIBOR +/- X base points." It is set each day by the British Bankers Association, which calculates it by averaging short term, inter-bank, deposit interest rates among the most creditworthy banks. See also: EURIBOR.

London International Financial Futures and Options Exchange An electronic exchange on which a variety of derivatives are traded. Popular investments on LIFFE include futures and options on agricultural goods and financial instruments such as interest rates. It was established in 1982 and in 2000 it became completely electronic by closing its trading floor. In 2002, it became part of Euronext.

London Metal Exchange The world's largest futures and options exchange for metals. It was established in 1877, though it traces its roots back to 1571. The LME trades derivative products based on copper, lead, zinc, aluminum and aluminum alloy, nickel, steel, and tin. Since 2005, plastic has traded on the LME.

London Rules A set of non-binding principles developed by the Bank of England to handle bankruptcy. The London rules attempt to avoid liquidation of assets except in emergencies. The London rules are also called the London approach.

London Securities and Derivatives Exchange An exchange on which options and futures based on stocks from Sweden and Norway are traded. It is part of NASDAQ OMX.

London Stock Exchange A stock exchange in the United Kingdom. It is one of the largest exchanges in the world and its movements are indicative of the state of the larger market. More than 3200 stocks, bonds, and derivatives are traded on the London Stock Exchange. Many indices, notably the FTSE 100 track securities on the London Stock Exchange. It was established in 1801 but traces its origins to the British East India Company at the end of the 17th century.

London Terms A form of debt relief for heavily indebted poor countries in which the present value of payments is reduced by up to one-half. The London terms were introduced by the Paris Club in 1991. This form of debt relief is a type of concessional restructuring.

London Traded Options Market A former exchange in London on which options and futures for stocks were traded. It merged into LIFFE in 1993.

London Underwriting Centre A building in London where insurance underwriters and brokers who are not members of Lloyd's may meet and discuss business. It is located on Mincing Lane. See also: City of London.

Long Bonds A bond with a long time until maturity, often defined as more than two years. This is also called a long coupon.

Long Hedge The purchase of a futures contract with the intention of accepting delivery of the underlying asset. One conducts a long hedge in order to lock in a price for an asset one must purchase in the future. This protects the holder of the futures contract from volatility in the underlying asset's price. If the spot price of the underlying asset moves in a direction more beneficial for the holder, he/she can sell the futures contract and buy the asset at the spot price. An example of a long hedge is a situation in which a company needs to buy oil by June. The spot price of oil may be $70 per barrel, but the futures price for June delivery may be only $60. The company would choose to buy the futures contract at $60 per barrel. A long hedge is also called a buy hedge.

Long Jelly Roll An options strategy that involves buying and selling four different option contracts. Initially, one buys a put and sells a call that have the same strike price and the same expiration date. Then, one buys a call and sells a put with a later expiration date and the same strike price with respect to each other, but a different price than the first two contracts. This creates a short-term short position and a long-term long position. All contracts have the same underlying assets. The idea behind a long jelly roll is to profit from the spread in futures prices over the lives of the contracts. See also: Christmas tree.

Long Leg In an option spread, the portion that is a long position. For example, if a spread consists of a long position on one option and a short position on a similar option, the long position is called the long leg. It should not be confused with a leg in a swap.

Long Market Value The market value of a security or group of securities as of the close of the most recent trading day or business day.

Long Position The ownership of a security or derivative, or the state of having bought one or the other. A long position brings with it the right to coupon payments or dividends attached to the security or derivative. Informally, one who owns 100 shares of a stock is said to be "long 100 of the stock." Likewise, an investor who has bought (or holds) an option is said to be "long the option" because he/she has the right to exercise the option at a later date. See also: Short position, Close a position.

Long Position in an Option The state of holding an option or the state of having bought one. A long position in an option brings with it the right to exercise the option at the investor's discretion, subject to the terms of the contract. Colloquially, an investor who has a long position in an option is said to be "long the option." See also: Long position.

Long Rate 1. See: Long-term interest rate. 2. A long position on an instrument involving interest rates.

Long Run Informal for long term. The term is notable for John Maynard Keynes' quote, "In the long run, we are all dead."

Long Run Incremental Cost A foreseen, future change in the incremental cost to a company, which is the cost of a company producing one more unit of a product. Long run incremental costs are likely changes to the inputs of making a product, such as the cost of raw materials. For example, if making a product requires a significant amount of oil, and oil prices are thought to be likely to decline, the long run incremental cost is also likely to decline. While there is no guarantee that the long run incremental cost will change in the exact amount expected, attempting to calculate it helps a company make future investment decisions.

Long Shot Informal; an action involving high risk. A long shot may result in a significant gain but has a high likelihood of failing.

Long Straddle The act or state of having a long position in both a put option and a call option with the same underlying asset, strike price, and expiration date. An investor may take a long straddle when he/she believes that the market for the underlying asset will be volatile and will undergo dramatic price changes, but is unsure of which direction the changes will go. The long straddle allows the investor to profit regardless of which direction the underlying moves. It is also called a bullish straddle. See also: Straddle.

Long Term Describing a plan, strategy, security, or anything else with a term of longer than one year. The exact number of years varies according to the usage. For example, a long term financial plan outlines investment and other financial goals for any time more than one fiscal year, while a long term bond has a maturity of 10 or more years. Anything long term involves more uncertainty than anything short term because, generally speaking, market trends are more easily predictable in the short term. Thus, while planning for the long term is necessary, one's plan must be flexible to account for its inherent uncertainty.

Longevity Insurance An insurance policy that pays a benefit if the policyholder lives to a certain age. For example, in exchange for the premium, longevity insurance provides a lump sum to the policyholder, for example, if he/she lives to 90. Longevity insurance is comparable to life insurance; the chief difference is that the policyholder collects the benefit merely if he/she lives long enough. Longevity insurance protects against longevity risk.

Longevity Pay The higher pay one earns for remaining at the same company for a certain period of time. For example, one may receive a raise after six months, one year, two years and so forth. Proponents of longevity pay believe it encourages stability and lowers the employee turnover rate. Critics contend longevity pay discourages innovation by rewarding those who take few risks and are merely "good enough" to stay.

Longevity Risk The risk that an individual will outlive his/her retirement savings. For example, if one's retirement consists of personal savings and a fixed-term annuity, the possibility exists that the money will run out before one dies. The risk is especially large if one has health problems in one's old age. One may mitigate longevity risk in a number of ways. For example, one may purchase investment vehicles such as a lifetime annuity, which guarantees payments for the remainder of one's life, or longevity insurance, which provides a lump sum benefit if one lives to a certain age.

Long-Range Budget A budget with a term usually longer than one year. A long-range budget involves more uncertainty than a short-term budget because, typically, market movements and the business cycle are more easily predictable in the short term. On the other hand, planning for the long-term is necessary in order to ensure sustainable profitability. Thus, while planning for the long term is necessary, one's plan must be flexible to account for the uncertainty inherent to it.

Longshoreman A person who loads and unloads cargo from ships. Because these jobs are often both temporary and dangerous, longshoremen in the United States are entitled to coverage under the Longshore Act. A longshoreman is also called a docker or a stevedore.

Longshoreman and Harbor Workers Act Liability Government coverage under the Longshore Act to longshoremen injured while working. A longshoreman loads and unloads cargo from a ship. If he is injured on the job, he is entitled to approximately 2/3 of his average wage each week while he receives medical treatment. He also may receive 2/3 of his lost earnings potential or a specific amount for each injured body part. The liability applies to any longshoreman who works on boats of a certain capacity in the waters of the United States.

Longshoreman and Harbor Workers Endorsement An addition to a workers comp insurance policy that provides coverage to employees who must perform some of their tasks on board a ship. See also: Longshoreman and Harbor Workers Act liability.

Long-Term Bond A debt security with a maturity in the long-term. While there is no set definition of what constitutes the long-term, it is generally accepted that long-term bonds are those that mature several years in the future, often more than 15 or 20. One of the most low-risk long-term bonds, the U.S. Treasury Bond, usually has a maturity of 30 years.

Long-Term Capital Gain The profit one realizes by selling a position one has held for longer than one year. For example, if one buys a stock or bond and sells it five years later for more than what one paid, this is considered a long-term capital gain. The government wishes to encourage long-term investment, and as such, long-term capital gains are usually entitled to preferential treatment for tax purposes; that is, they are taxed at a lower rate than most other income. See also: Long-term capital loss.

Long-Term Capital Management A defunct hedge fund, established in 1993, that, at its height, held positions worth more than $1 trillion. Its investment strategy was to take advantage of arbitrage opportunities in bonds and other fixed-income securities; profits on individual transactions were small, so LTCM was required to borrow massive amounts of money in order to operate. It was at first enormously successful, with a 40% annualized return after fees. However, when Russia defaulted on its government bonds in 1998, there was a steep drop in bond prices, endangering LTCM's positions because of its high leverage. Because LTCM controlled upwards of 5% of the bond market at the time, defaulting on its loans would have caused global financial panic. It was eventually bailed out by a consortium of organizations under the supervision of the Federal Reserve.

Long-Term Care Long-term medical care for a debilitating but non-life threatening condition. For example, one may require long-term care if one is involved in a car accident or has a non-terminal disease that does not allow him/her to live independently. Long-term care often involves the inability to perform at least some of the activities of daily living. One may purchase long-term care insurance to pay for some of the expenses associated with long-term care.

Long-Term Care Insurance Insurance that is purchased against the possibility that the beneficiary will require long-term medical care for a debilitating but non-life threatening condition. For example, one may require long-term care if one is involved in a car accident or has a non-terminal disease that does not allow the sufferer to live independently. Long-term care insurance is designed to pay for at least some of the medical expenses associated with this. These policies provide a per diem or monthly allowance for expenses, as well as an elimination period, a period of time after the illness is diagnosed or the accident occurs, but before the insurer begins coverage. Policies with a higher per diem and shorter elimination period come with higher premiums.

Long-Term Contract 1. A contract to perform work over a significant period of time. For example, a construction company may have a contract to build a skyscraper, which may take several years. 2. A futures contract or similar instrument that does not expire for several months or longer. 3. See: Long-term lease.

Long-Term Debt Bonds, loans, and any other debt with a maturity of longer than one year. Long-term debt is used for capital outlays, which usually involves a business' need to buy the basic necessities for its operations, such as facilities and major assets. It is also called funded debt.

Long-Term Debt/Capitalization Ratio In risk analysis, a way to determine a company's leverage. The ratio is calculated by taking the company's long-term debt and dividing it by the sum of its long-term debt and its preferred and common stock. Put graphically: Ratio = Long-term debt / (Long-term debt + Preferred stock + Common stock) The greater a company's leverage, the higher the ratio. Generally, companies with higher ratios are thought to be more risky because they have more liabilities and less equity.

Long-Term Debt-to-Equity Ratio In risk analysis, a way to determine a company's leverage. The ratio is calculated by taking the company's long-term debt and dividing it by the total value of its preferred and common stock. Put graphically: Ratio = Long-term debt / (Preferred stock + Common stock) The greater a company's

325

leverage, the higher the ratio. Generally, companies with higher ratios are thought to be more risky because they have more liabilities and less equity.

Long-Term Equity Anticipation Securities Stock options with expiration of two to three years following issue. Most stock options expire nine months after issue; an advantage to LEAPS is the fact that there is a longer period of time for a desired price movement to take place, maximizing the possibility of profit. However, LEAPS are more expensive than other stock options.

Long-Term Financial Plan An investment plan or strategy with a term of usually longer than one year. A long-term financial plan involves more uncertainty than anything short-term because, typically, market trends are more easily predictable in the short term. On the other hand, planning for the long-term is necessary in order to enjoy financial security in retirement. Thus, while planning for the long term is necessary, one's plan must be flexible to account for the uncertainty inherent to it.

Long-Term Financing Capital extended for a term of greater than a year. In both investing and personal finance, long-term financing often takes the form of a loan with a payback period of longer than one year. Examples of long-term financing include a 30 year mortgage or a 10-year Treasury note. Equity is another form of long-term financing, such as when a company issues stock to raise capital for a new project.

Long-Term Forward Contract A non-standardized, over-the-counter agreement in which one party agrees to buy a certain asset from the other at a certain price, at a certain time more than one year in the future. Because there is little secondary market for any forward contract, long-term forward contracts are zero-sum games; one party will win and the other will lose.

Long-Term Goals Any and all objectives, especially financial ones, that a company intends to accomplish over the next five to 10 years.

Long-Term Greed In investment banking, a term describing the placing of one's client's interests above those of the bank because doing so will inspire client loyalty and, ultimately, make more money for the bank. Long-term greed is considered important for the sustainability of an investment bank. If an investment bank consistently makes bad decisions for clients, they are unlikely to stay with the bank, which will reduce the bank's capital and make it less likely to succeed.

Long-Term Interest Rate An interest rate on a financial instrument with a maturity of longer than one year. A long-term interest rate is usually (but not always) higher than a short-term rate because of the added risk of committing capital to a person or project for such a long period of time.

Long-Term Investing The practice of buying and holding a security, portfolio or investment strategy for a term of longer than one year. The exact number of years varies according to the usage. For example, a long-term stock investor may outline investment goals for any time longer than one year, while a long-term bond investor may hold a bond until it matures 10 or more years later. Long-term investing involves more uncertainty than short-term investing because, in general, market trends are more easily predictable in the short term. Thus, while planning for the long term is necessary, one's plan must be flexible to account for the uncertainty inherent in it. See also: Value investor.

Long-Term Investor An investor who intends to hold a security, portfolio, or investment strategy for a term of longer than one year. The exact number of years varies according to the usage. For example, a long-term stock investor may outline investment goals for any time longer than one year, while a long-term bond investor may hold a bond until it matures 10 or more years later. Long-term investing involves more uncertainty than anything short-term because, generally speaking, market trends are more easily predictable in the short term. Thus, while planning for the long term is necessary, one's plan must be flexible to account for the uncertainty inherent in it. See also: Value investor.

Long-Term Lease A lease for longer than one, five or 10 years, depending on the specific asset being leased. For example, commercial property usually has long-term leases for five or more years, while residential property often carries long-term leases for more than one year. A long-term lease locks in the price one pays for the asset, which is usually advantageous because prices often trend upward. However, long-term leases offer little flexibility. For example, one may have to pay significant penalties if one cancels a long-term lease. One humorous example of a long-term lease is the Guinness brewery in Ireland, which Arthur Guinness rented for 9,000 years for 45 pounds per year.

Long-Term Liability Any liability with a term of greater than a year. In both investing and personal finance, a long-term liability often is a loan with a long payback period. Examples include a 30-year mortgage or a 10-year Treasury note. See also: Long-term financing.

Long-Term Loss A loss on a security one holds for longer than one year, or a loss from the sale of a capital asset. In both cases, a long-term loss may be used to offset a long-term gain in order to reduce one's tax liability for that year. Additionally, one may carry forward the first $3,000 of a long-term loss to a different tax year, giving one an even lower tax liability.

Long-Term Moving Average The average price of a security over several weeks or months, calculated continuously. For instance, one may calculate a long-term moving average by adding the closing prices from each day for the past 52 weeks and dividing by the number of trading days considered. As with all moving averages, long-term moving averages may or may not be weighted. Moving averages help smooth out noise that may be present in a security's price on a given trading day. See also: Simple Moving Average, Exponential Moving Average.

Long-Term Prime Rate The interest rate charged by certain Japanese banks on loans made to highly creditworthy institutions for longer than one year. The long-term prime rate is used as a benchmark for determining other interest rates in Japan.

Long-Term Rate Risk The risk of loss due to a change in interest rates on a long-term bond. If interest rates rise, the prices of bonds fall. This affects the secondary market for bonds; for example, if one purchases a bond with a 3% interest rate and the prevailing rate rises to 5%, it becomes difficult or impossible to resell the bond at a profit. Because long-term bonds have a maturity of several years, there is a greater possibility that interest rates will move in an adverse direction. Long-term rate risk is part of the reason that rates on long-term bonds are (usually) higher than those on short-term bonds. See also: Yield curve.

Long-Term Trend Any price movement that occurs over a significant period of time, often over one year or several years. Long-term trends are difficult to predict and they are often interrupted by brief movements against the trend. For example, the dot-com bubble of the 1990s resulted in consistently high growth on the NASDAQ average, but this did not mean that NASDAQ rose every single day or even every week. See also: Secular market.

Long-Term Unemployed Persons who have been unemployed for an extended period of time. Measurements of long-term unemployment vary, but generally it is thought to be experienced by those who are without work for six months to a year or longer. Long-term unemployed persons may experience added difficulty in finding new jobs due to the length of the gap in their resumes, or, in some industries, because their skills quickly become obsolete. In some jurisdictions, the long-term unemployed may not be eligible for unemployment benefits.

Long-Term Unemployment The lack of work for an extended period of time, often defined as six months or longer. Long-term unemployment can be extremely harmful to the unemployed person because he/she may lose eligibility for certain government benefits if he/she has been out of work for too long. Likewise, significant long-term unemployment can create a vicious cycle for the economy at large: the skill set of the long-term unemployed workers may languish or even become obsolete in some industries, which makes it more difficult for them to find work when employers begin to hire again.

Lood A Dutch unit of weight equivalent to 10 grams. It was adopted in 1817, soon after the establishment of the Kingdom of the Netherlands.

Look **1.** In equities, the price at which a dealer or broker is willing to buy or sell a security. See also: Bid-ask spread. **2.** See: Quote.

Look Thru In accounting, a method of calculating tax liability of a controlled foreign corporation. It applies to U.S. taxpayers who own at least 10% of the voting stock of a foreign subsidiary of a foreign corporation.

Lookback Call Option A call option giving the holder the right (but not the obligation) to buy the underlying asset on or by the expiration date at its lowest price that occurred between the start of the option and the time it is exercised. Because there is no set strike price and the lookback gives the option holder the highest possible flexibility, it carries a high premium (or sale price). See also: Lookback Put Option.

Lookback Option An option contract where the holder is permitted to choose the strike price. That is, the buyer of a lookback call may choose a low strike price and the buyer of a lookback put may choose a high one. A lookback option is always in the money.

Lookback Put Option A put option giving the holder the right (but not the obligation) to sell the underlying asset on or by the expiration date at the highest price that occurs between the start of the option and the time it is exercised. Because there is no set strike price and the lookback gives the option holder the highest possible flexibility, it carries a high premium (or sale price). See also: Lookback Call Option.

Looking For Soliciting for an offer. That is, one looking for an investment is seeking to buy. It is important to note that "looking for" an investment does not equate to bidding, but is rather an indication of interest. See also: In touch with.

Looking Over Your Shoulder Slang; accounting and/or business consulting services provided to a non-profit organization, especially a small Christian church or ministry. It may be abbreviated LOYS.

Lookup To search for a previously saved record, especially but not necessarily on a computer. Looking up is necessary to guarantee information that is as accurate as possible.

Loonie Informal for the Canadian dollar. The term comes from the picture of the common loon, a Canadian bird, on the reverse of the one-dollar coin. The nickname originated in 1987 with the introduction of this coin. See also: Greenback.

Loophole A deliberate or accidental provision in a law that allows an individual or corporation to which it would otherwise apply to be exempt from it. Most loopholes are deliberate and are placed there to ensure that the law is not draconian, to please a lobbyist, or for some other reason. For example, a country may pass a law requiring most companies to register with the government. However, it may contain a loophole allowing the exemption of companies that find registration too difficult or expensive. Occasionally, the government may close a loophole, which means that it takes away the exemption.

Loose Rein A management style in which employees are given a great deal of autonomy and in which individual contributions are encouraged. An advantage to loose reins is the potential to foster creativity; that is, proponents believe that the relaxed atmosphere encourages innovation and productivity. Critics maintain that loose reins lead to laziness and, at worst, insubordination.

Loose Rendering In graphic design, a rough sketch that gives the general overview of what the final product will look like. Loose rendering is an important step in marketing because it allows for suggestions or corrections before too much work has been done.

Lorenz Curve A graph showing what percentage of a population possesses a certain percentage of a thing. For example, a Lorenz curve may show that the top five percent of the people in a country control 40% of the wealth. While it may be used in ecology as well as some other fields, it is frequently used in economics to represent social inequality. It was developed in 1905.

Loser A security that has fallen in price over a given period, often a trading day. Each day, the number of losers are compared to the number of gainers as one method, among many, of determining the market's overall mood. Often, media reports take the stocks that have lost the largest percentage or dollar amount on a given day and report them as the biggest losers, especially when the losers' industries are thought to be in a general slump.

Losing the Points Somewhat informal; in foreign exchange, the act of selling a futures contract on a currency at a low exchange rate and buying a currency on the spot market at a higher exchange rate. When one must deliver the underlying currency on the futures contract, losing the points guarantees a loss because one sells the currency at a rate lower than the one at which one bought it. Obviously, losing the points is inadvisable. See also: Gaining the points.

Losing Your Shirt Informal; a situation in which one makes such a bad investment decision that he/she loses everything he/she owns. For example, if a business venture goes bankrupt, an investor may be said to lose their shirt if they also must sell their house to repay the business' debt. Losing your shirt has a strongly negative connotation because it implies that one must sell one's shirt to pay liabilities. See also: Rio trade.

Loss Extracting less money from a transaction than one put into it. For example, a business' expenses may be $1 million for a year but it may only take in $800,000 in revenue. In such a case, the business has suffered a $200,000 loss. This is not always bad; most businesses lose money in the first few years of operation and this can reduce their tax liability when they do make a profit. However, losses over an extended period of time ultimately result in failure. See also: Gain, Paper Loss, Loss Carryforward, Loss Carryback.

Loss Adjuster A predominately British and Commonwealth term for a claims adjuster.

Loss Avoidance The strategy in which one does not take a position in order to guarantee that a loss does not occur. For example, one may decide not to purchase a house in order to guarantee that one never has to pay to repair the roof. Loss avoidance, however, guarantees no profit. As a result, investors seek to hedge risk rather than avoid it altogether.

Loss Exposure The amount that one risks. For example, if one spends $100,000 buying stock, one has a loss exposure of $100,000 because there exists the theoretical possibility that the value of that stock could go to zero.

Loss Leader Strategy A business strategy whereby a company sells a product at a loss in order to sell the customer associated products for a profit. This is common when a company is new and wishes to build brand loyalty and other goodwill. For example, a grocery store may sell its bread for a loss and advertise its low price for bread in order to attract customers, who will likely then buy that same store's milk, eggs, and cheese. A loss leader strategy can be very profitable if executed properly. See also: Pricing strategy.

Loss Payee The person or company to whom an insurance company makes a payment should the insured event occur. For example, in a health insurance policy, the loss payee will likely be the policyholder if he/she becomes ill. In a life insurance policy, the loss payee is likely the policyholder's survivors.

Loss Ratio In insurance, the ratio of what an insurance company pays in benefits and associated expenses (such as adjustments) to what is collected in premiums, expressed as a percentage. It is calculated thusly: Loss ratio = (Benefits paid out + Adjustment expenses) / Premiums collected For example, if a company pays out $8,000,000 in benefits and adjustment and collects $10,000,000 in premiums, its loss ratio is 80%. Traditionally, the loss ratio has been used as a gauge for both an insurance company's financial health and whether it was overcharging policy holders. For example, a high loss ratio indicated that the company was not making a reasonable profit, while a low ratio showed that it was either charging too much or covering too little. However, this view has been criticized, at least in relation to health insurance, on the grounds that the integration of insurers and providers makes it difficult or impossible to calculate the ratio properly.

Loss Reduction Policies that a company adopts to eliminate or alleviate losses. For example, management may hire new sales staff to try to increase revenue. Likewise, it may reduce staff hours or even conduct layoffs. Loss reduction tactics may also include public relations directed at current and potential shareholders.

Loss Run Business losses (as opposed to profits) that extend over two or more periods. For example, losses over two consecutive quarters may be considered a loss run.

Loss-Control Activities In insurance, actions taken by a policyholder at the behest of the insurance company to ensure that reasonable steps are taken to avoid a situation on which a claim might be made. For example, if a loss-of-income insurance policy covers a situation in which an employee's long-term injury results in a loss of production, the insurance company may require the policyholder to put in place appropriate safety measures to minimize claims. One does not conduct loss-control activities for policies that cover loss of income due to acts of God, such as tornados or hurricanes, but rather for policies covering primarily or exclusively foreseeable incidents.

Losses Outstanding In insurance, legitimate claims that an insurer has not paid to a policyholder.

Losses Paid In insurance, legitimate claims that an insurer has paid to a policyholder.

Loss-of-Income Insurance Insurance that covers the interruption of a policyholder's business activities, whether in whole or in part. A policy may cover loss of income from the cessation of business activities due to an act of God, such as a tornado or a hurricane, or a foreseeable incident. Likewise, it may cover partial interruption of activites, such as a situation in which an employee's long-term injury results in a loss of production. Loss-of-income insurance may also refer to personal insurance providing income for a person's disability or long-term illness.

Lost Card A credit card or debit card that the cardholder has reported missing. A lost card may also be one that the cardholder never received because it never came in the mail. Lost cards are canceled and replaced.

Lost in the Sauce A slang term for confusion about one's role or job description. The term may be used if one is overwhelmed by a new job or significant changes to his/her responsibilities.

Lot A Russian unit of weight approximately equivalent to 12.8 grams. It was rendered obsolete when the Soviet Union began to use the metric system in 1924.

Lot Line A line on a geographic survey denoting the boundary of a property. This is important in determining property ownership.

Lots 1. Pieces of land that are bought or sold as units. **2.** Groups of securities or derivatives traded as units, often in groups of 100. Some derivatives, especially exchange-traded funds, set a minimum lot that may be traded; for example, one may only trade a certain ETF in lots of 100. Exchanges and regulators set standard lots, which are used in contracts of trade. This practice means that an investor knows how many securities or derivatives he/she is buying or selling in a given transaction.

Lottery Bond 1. A bond guaranteed by the proceeds from a lottery. That is, an agency (usually a government agency) collects revenue from a lottery and uses this revenue to secure the bond. This reduces the risk to the bondholder that the bond will default. **2.** A bond with a provision stating that the issuer will redeem a certain number of bonds at a premium to their face value. For example, an issuer may sell 10,000 bonds with a face value of $1,000 each, and then announce that it will redeem 2,000 of them for $1,300 at maturity. A lottery bond exists to attract investors because it otherwise has no special features and usually carries a rather low coupon rate. Lottery bonds are issued by a number of European governments, notably France and Belgium.

Loukhai An ancient Indian unit of area approximately equivalent to one-eighth of a hectare.

Lourak An ancient Indian unit of area approximately equivalent to half a hectare.

Loushal An ancient Indian unit of area approximately equivalent to 1/16 hectare.

Love Money Money from family or friends used for the initial market research and/or operations for a company. Love money is vitally important when a start-up cannot otherwise qualify for financing because without it, a company can hardly come into being, let alone become successful. Love money may be given in exchange for equity, but it is usually a loan, sometimes with no fixed repayment date.

Low The smallest price of a stock over a given period of time, especially when the price has first been reached. That is, when a stock's prices have dipped below the previous record for a given period of time, analysts and reporters say that prices have reached "a new low." This is generally considered a bearish sign, especially when other indicators are also bearish.

Low Balance Method A way to calculate interest on a loan or account where one considers the lowest amount that is owed over a given period. This results in less interest paid to the lender or other entity to which the account is owed.

Low Decision Latitude The lack of authority to make important decisions. In a company, the lowest-ranking persons in management are said to have low decision latitude.

Low Hanging Fruit In investment banking, a potential client who is very likely to agree to put assets under the bank's management. For example, if an internationally known bank opens its first office in the capital of a small country, that country's biggest companies are likely to be low hanging fruit because they would want to associate themselves with a famous, successful bank.

Low Income Describing persons who earn less than, or at least not significantly more than, the poverty level. Low income persons have less disposable income than others and may sometimes struggle to pay their bills. Low income persons often have low job security and are strongly correlated with low education levels. Some low income persons may qualify for government assistance programs, though many do not because they earn too much, but not enough to live comfortably.

Low Price The lowest price at which a security trades on a given trading day. It is usually lower than the closing price and is also called the daily low. See also: Daily High.

Low Price-Earnings Ratio Effect A phenomenon whereby stocks with low price-earnings ratios tend to perform better than stocks with high price-earnings ratios. The low price-earnings ratio effect occurs because stocks with low price-earnings ratios are often undervalued, and their prices eventually rise.

Low Profit Limited Liability Company A limited liability company in some U.S. states that has statutory duties other than making a profit for owners. It may be formed for many purposes, such as to provide steady jobs to employees or to protect the environment. It is treated as a limited liability company for legal and tax purposes. It is not prohibited from making a profit, but it is subject to fewer regulatory requirements than a non-profit in the United States.

Lowball 1. Of or related to the low cost of a good, service, or security. A lowball cost is determined by comparing the cost to similar goods, services, and securities. Lowball costs may indicate a low quality in the good, service, or security. **2.** Informal; to make an offer to buy something for an exceptionally low price. For example, if the asking price on a house is $200,000, a potential buyer may lowball the seller by offering $125,000.

Low-Ball Offer An offer to buy something for an exceptionally low price. For example, if the asking price on a house is $200,000, a potential buyer may make a low-ball offer of $125,000.

Low-Content Culture A culture in which a great deal of emphasis is placed upon the words one uses, rather than their context, tone or circumstance. For example, suppose one says, "I am fine," in response to the question, "How are you?" In a low-context culture, it is assumed that one is doing fine and that no further query needs to be made. Confusing cultural signals between a low-context and a high-content culture can create significant misunderstandings in both business and politics.

Low-Coupon Bond Refunding The act of an issuer redeeming a bond with a low coupon and replacing it with a bond with a higher coupon. For example, one may wish to give a company back a bond, receive the principal amount, and buy a bond with a higher interest rate in order to receive a greater return. It is important to note that not all bond indentures allow such premature redemption.

Lower Deck Containers Containers designed to fit inside an aircraft. Cargo may be transported in lower deck containers. If the aircraft carries passengers as well, lower deck containers are placed below the cabin.

Lower Middle Class 1. The economic demographic including persons who earn more than the working class but less than the upper middle class. Members of the lower middle class may have some degree of job security and commonly have at least some college education. Teachers, accountants and many small business owners fall into the lower middle class. **2.** An alternate term for the working class, in which case middle class refers to the lower middle class described above.

Lower of Cost and Market Method A provision of the Generally Accepted Accounting Principles stating that an inventory must be valued on a balance sheet as either its historical cost (or what the company paid for it) or its current market value, whichever is lower. This method provides a conservative valuation for a company's inventory.

Lower of Cost or Market At the end of an accounting period, a convention used to mark the current value of remaining inventory. Under this convention, the inventory is recorded as either the historical cost (what the company originally paid) or the fair market value (what the inventory is now worth), whichever is lower. A company does this in order to minimize its tax liability.

Lower Rate of Income Tax The preferential tax treatment given to certain types of income. Lower rates of income tax are given to promote certain types of behavior. For example, capital gains are given a lower rate of income tax in order to encourage investment.

Low-Income Housing Limited Partnership A limited partnership in which partners buy or construct housing for persons with low or moderate income such that their rent cannot exceed a certain amount. Because rent is controlled, cash flow from the investment is minimal; however, the United States provides tax credits on these partnerships for up to 150% of the amount invested. One thus invests in a low-income housing limited partnership for the cash flow from the tax credits, rather than from the investment itself. One may not sell one's interest in this type of partnership for 15 years.

Low-Income Housing Tax Credit A dollar-for-dollar reduction in one's tax liability due to an investment in a housing complex for low and moderate income persons. The rent on this type of housing is controlled, so return on investment is minimal. The low-income housing tax credit provides some cash flow on these investments; as a result, it accounts for the vast majority of low-income housing investments in the United States. See also: Low-income housing limited partnership.

Low-Key Lighting In film, lighting that provides contrast between the light and dark areas of a scene, creating the impression of shadow. It is used to create the mood of suspense or mystery and may be used in marketing campaigns.

Low-Load Fund A mutual fund in which the load or sales fee that one must pay to the fund is low compared to other funds. Generally speaking, a low-load fund has a load between 1% and 4% of the value of the shares purchased or sold. Low-load funds became popular in the 1980s.

Low-Price Strategy In marketing, a strategy in which a newcomer to a market establishes a low price for products, especially when there is already significant competition. This can be advantageous when the seller must rely on high volume for profit; that is, even though profit margins would be low, the net income would still be high because of the large number of sales. A low-price strategy also helps create market share.

Low-Tech 1. Describing any technology in use prior to the Industrial Revolution. **2.** Describing any technology that is no longer the latest available. For example, fax machines may be considered low-tech compared to e-mail. However, low-tech tools and technologies may still be usable and profitable. To continue the example, fax machines are still sold because they are still useful.

Loyalty Program A program that encourages customers to shop consistently at the same place. Generally, a loyalty program issues a card (much like a credit card) to a customer, who swipes the card before she pays for her goods. The card identifies the customer and makes the purchase eligible for a discount or some other benefit. Loyalty programs are most common at the retail level.

LR 1. ISO 3166-1 alpha-2 code for the Republic of Liberia. This is the code used in international transactions to and from Liberian bank accounts. **2.** ISO 3166-2 geocode for Liberia. This is used as an international standard for shipping to Liberia. Most Liberian counties have their own codes with the prefix "LR." For example, the code for the County of Bong is ISO 3166-2:LR-BG

LRD ISO 4217 code for the Liberian dollar. The LRD was introduced in 1943. After a coup d'etat in 1980, many businessmen took currency out of the country, creating a shortage. During the civil war (1990-2004), Liberian dollars were looted from the Central Bank of Liberia; in response, it created a new design for some currency notes. This created effectively two currencies: a legal one authorized by the Central Bank, and an illegal one based on the looted dollars. The Liberian economy still relies on a large amount of foreign aid.

LS 1. ISO 3166-1 alpha-2 code for the Kingdom of Lesotho. This is the code used in international transactions to and from bank accounts in Lesotho. **2.** ISO 3166-2 geocode for Lesotho. This is used as an international standard for shipping to Lesotho. Each district has its own code with the prefix "LS." For example, the code for Berea District is ISO 3166-2:LS-D.

LSL ISO 4217 code for the Lesotho loti. It was issued in 1966 and began to circulate in 1980. It is pegged to the South African rand such that one is equal in value to the other. Both the rand and the loti are accepted in shops in Lesotho. Its plural is maloti.

LSO GOST 7.67 Latin three-letter geocode for Lesotho. The code is used for transactions to and from local bank accounts and for international shipping to Lesotho. As with all GOST 7.67 codes, it is used primarily in Cyrillic alphabets.

LT 1. ISO 3166-1 alpha-2 code for the Republic of Lithuania. This is the code used in international transactions to and from Lithuanian bank accounts. **2.** ISO 3166-2 geocode for Lithuania. This is used as an international standard for shipping to Lithuania. Each Lithuanian county has its own code with the prefix "LT." For example, the code for the County of Vilniaus is ISO 3166-2:LT-VL.

LTL ISO 4217 code for the Lithuanian litas. It was introduced in 1993, replacing the talonas, which was itself a temporary currency to replace the Soviet ruble. Between 1994 and 2002 the litas was pegged to the U.S. dollar. Since then, it has been pegged to the euro in preparation for Lithuania joining the eurozone. While the Lithuanian government hoped to replace the litas with the euro in 2010, high inflation has pushed the date back to 2013.

LTU GOST 7.67 Latin three-letter geocode for Lithuania. The code is used for transactions to and from Lithuanian bank accounts and for international shipping to Lithuania. As with all GOST 7.67 codes, it is used primarily in Cyrillic alphabets.

LU 1. ISO 3166-1 alpha-2 code for the Grand Duchy of Luxembourg. This is the code used in international transactions to and from Luxembourger bank accounts. **2.** ISO 3166-2 geocode for Luxembourg. This is used as an international standard for shipping to Luxembourg. Each district has its own code with the prefix "LU." For example, the code for the District of Diekirch is ISO 3166-2:LU-D.

Luca Pacioli A Franciscan friar who is widely regarded as the father of modern accounting. While he did not invent double-entry bookkeeping, he was the first to write a treatise on it. He was also the first to describe balance sheets and income statements. He famously said, "A person should not go to sleep at night until the debits equal the credits." He died in 1517.

Lucas Critique The concept that one cannot draw accurate conclusions about present macroeconomic phenomena based purely on past data. The Lucas critique states that every policy change affects the circumstances under which different situations occur. Thus, a policy that worked under one set of circumstances may not apply under a different set. The name comes from a 1976 paper by Robert Lucas.

Lucite A somewhat tongue-in-cheek trophy presented to an investment banker at a dinner celebrating the close of a major deal. A lucite usually is designed to remind the banker of the experience. For example, if a deal involves a merger in the meat-packing industry, the lucite may be shaped like freeze-dried chicken.

Luddite A term for workers in the early 19th century in Britain who opposed the Industrial Revolution because increased mechanization was changing the economy and leaving them without jobs. The term has come to mean any person who opposes technological changes, especially those that impact the economy.

Ludwig von Mises A major economist and philosopher. He promoted individualism as the basis for social science. Based on this belief, he advocated laissez faire policies and opposed nearly all government interventions in the economy. He was a proponent of the gold standard in monetary policy. He had significant influence of the Austrian School. He lived from 1881 to 1973.

LUF ISO 4217 code for the Luxembourgish franc. It was introduced in 1854 and remained in circulation until 2002, except for the period of German occupation during World War II. It was pegged to the Belgian franc at par for much of its history. It was replaced by the euro. See also: Belgium-Luxembourg Economic Union.

Luma A currency subdivision of the Armenian dram. A luma is equal in value to 1/100 of a dram. See also: Cent.

Lumber Wood cut in such a way as to be used for building. Lumber may be traded as a commodity and is especially important in the construction industry. Sustainable woodcutting has become a significant issue in the lumber industry.

Lumin A Maltese unit of dry volume approximately equivalent to 30.31 milliliters. It is largely obsolete but is still used in some circumstances.

Lump of Labor The idea that the amount of work that can be done in an economy is fixed. According to this idea, competition for a job is a zero-sum game because there can only be so many possible jobs. Most economists reject the lump of labor hypothesis.

Lump of Water A slang term for $100 in Hong Kong. Equivalent terms are red back and red snapper. See also: Hong Kong dollar.

Lump Sum A large amount of money one spends at once, especially to make a large purchase. For example, if a house costs $175,000, and the buyer pays the total amount up front, the buyer is said to make a lump sum payment.

Lump-Sum Distribution A one-time payment of the entire amount owed to another party. Examples of lump sum distributions include life insurance pay outs, or death benefits from a pension. It is important to note that, by definition, lump-sum distributions do not occur in annuities, as annuities pay out a certain amount over time.

Lump-Sum Tax A tax in which the taxpayer is assessed the same amount regardless of circumstance. An example of a lump-sum tax is a $55 fee on all employees who work in a township. Another example is tag fees on vehicles, which are the same regardless of the income of vehicle owners. Lump-sum taxes are regressive, meaning persons with lower income pay more as a percentage of their income.

Lunch and Learn A seminar offered during a free lunch. For example, a company may invite potential clients to a lunch and learn in which it describes its products while the potential clients eat the food provided.

Lungsod In the Philippines, a political subdivision equivalent to a city.

Luoti A Finnish unit of weight approximately equivalent to 14 grams. It became obsolete when Finland adopted the metric system in 1880.

Lusophone A person, company or country for which Portuguese is the primary language. While it is not as important in international commerce as English or French, it is the fifth most spoken language in the world and has official status in nine countries.

Luster In numismatics, the shininess of a coin. Coins in mint condition have the greatest luster. As a result, coins with a great deal of luster may have the most value.

Lutine Bell A bell formerly used to inform brokers and underwriters at Lloyd's of the fate of late ships. If a ship was tardy in coming to port in London, its cargo obviously would not arrive on the market and it could trigger an insured event. The Lutine Bell was struck once if a ship was reported sunk or otherwise lost, and twice if it returned. Lloyd's used a bell so all interested parties were made aware of the news at the same time. The Lutine Bell was recovered from the shipwrecked HMS Lutine in 1858.

LUX GOST 7.67 Latin three-letter geocode for Luxembourg. The code is used for transactions to and from Luxembourgish bank accounts and for international shipping to Luxembourg. As with all GOST 7.67 codes, it is used primarily in Cyrillic alphabets.

Luxembourg Franc The former currency of Luxeumbourg. It was introduced in 1854 and remained in circulation until 2002, except for the period of German occupation during World War II. It was pegged to the Belgian franc at par for much of its history. It was replaced by the euro. See also: Belgium-Luxembourg Economic Union.

Luxembourg Stock Exchange An exchange in Luxembourg established in 1928. Both stocks and bonds are traded on its floor, though it is especially known for the bond trade. It was the first exchange on which eurobonds were traded. See also: LuXx index.

Luxembourgish Franc The former currency of Luxembourg. It was introduced in 1854 and remained in circulation until 2002, except for the period of German occupation during World War II. It was pegged to the Belgian franc at par for much of its history. It was replaced by the euro. See also: Belgium-Luxembourg Economic Union.

Luxury A good or service not considered essential. Examples of luxuries include massages, gold watches and sail boats. Luxuries are often, but not always, fairly expensive. Luxury industries tend to be fairly prone to hard downturns during a recession. For example, if one is concerned for one's own job security, one is less likely to splurge on a massage. However, some luxury products, such as custom yachts, are considered recession-proof because they only appeal to the ultra-wealthy, who remain wealthy even in hard times.

Luxury Automobile An automobile with extra features for comfort and/or status of the driver. Luxury automobiles are more expensive than comparable automobiles. Because they tend to attract buyers who have money regardless of economic circumstances, the luxury automobile industry tends to hold up well during recessions. Two notable exceptions, however, have been the Great Depression and the late 2000s recession.

Luxury Tax A tax on a good or service that is not considered essential. Luxury taxes may be levied, for example, on sail boats or gold watches. Luxury taxes primarily impact wealthy persons, but are otherwise structured like a sales tax or a VAT. That is, a luxury tax is a percentage of the value (or the added value) of the good or service being sold.

LV 1. ISO 3166-1 alpha-2 code for the Republic of Latvia. This is the code used in international transactions to and from Latvian bank accounts. **2.** ISO 3166-2 geocode for Latvia. This is used as an international standard for shipping to Latvia. Each subdivision has its own code with the prefix "LV." For example, the code for the District of Ventspils Aprinkis is ISO 3166-2:LV-VE.

LVA GOST 7.67 Latin three-letter geocode for Latvia. The code is used for transactions to and from Latvian bank accounts and for international shipping to Latvia. As with all GOST 7.67 codes, it is used primarily in Cyrillic alphabets.

LVL ISO 4217 code for the Latvian lats. It was introduced in 1993, replacing the Latvian rublis, which in turn replaced the Soviet ruble. Since 2005, the lats has been pegged to the euro in a band set by the European Exchange Rate Mechanism; this is in preparation for replacement of the lats with the euro at some point during or after 2012.

Lwei A subdivision of the first Angolan kwanza. One lwei was equal in value to 1/100 of a kwanza. The equivalent for the current kwanza is the centimo. See also: Cent.

LY 1. ISO 3166-1 alpha-2 code for the Libyan Arab Jamahirya (Libya). This is the code used in international transactions to and from Libyan bank accounts. **2.** ISO 3166-2 geocode for Libya. This is used as an international standard for shipping to Libya. Each district has its own code with the prefix "LY." For example, the code for al-Marj district is ISO 3166-2:LY-MJ.

LYD ISO 4217 code for the Libyan dinar. It was issued in 1971, replacing the Libyan pound. It is colloquially called a jni in Western Libya or a jneh in Eastern Libya. The official name is rarely used in daily transactions.

Lyon Terms A form of debt relief for heavily indebted poor countries in which the present value of payments is reduced by up to 80%. The Lyon terms were introduced by the HIPC Initiative in 1996. This form of debt relief is a type of concessional restructuring.

M 1. A symbol (M) indicating that a bond has matured. It is used most often on transaction tables in a newspaper. **2.** A symbol (M) indicating that the dividend on a stock has been reduced by a certain amount. It is used most often on transaction tables in a newspaper. **3.** A symbol (m) indicating that the closing price of a security is lower than the closing price of the previous trading day. **4.** A symbol (m) indicating the percentage by which the net asset value per share of a closed-end investment company exceeds its share price. **5.** A symbol for 1,000.

M&IE Meals and Incidental Expenses. The allowable reimbursement the federal government gives to employees who travel on business. The M&IE one receives is determined by a table, which details permitted expenses based on where one is traveling and other factors.

M1 A measure of money supply used by various central banks that includes only currency in circulation and very near money instruments. In the Federal Reserve System, M1 includes all physical currency and deposits in checking accounts as well as Negotiable Orders Withdrawal accounts. It does not include savings accounts, certificates of deposit, or money market accounts. The European Central Bank defines M1 as the aggregation currency in circulation and overnight deposits. While different central banks have slightly different definitions of M1, all include money currently in circulation and the money most likely to come into circulation in the shortest possible amount of time. Therefore, it is the most liquid calculation of the money supply. See also: M0, M2, M3, M4.

M2 A measure of money supply used by the various central banks. In the Federal Reserve System, M2 includes all physical currency and deposits in checking accounts, and adds to this the amount of money in savings accounts, certificates of deposit up to $100,000 (or their equivalents), and money market accounts. The European Central Bank defines M2 as the aggregation currency in circulation, overnight deposits, deposits with maturities of up to two years, and deposits redeemable with notice of up to three months. The Japanese, Indian, and New Zealand central banks have definitions similar to (but not exactly the same as) the Federal Reserve's. While different central banks have slightly different definitions of M2, all include money currently in circulation and the money most likely to come into circulation. Therefore, it is the most common measure used in forecasting inflation. See also: M0, M1, M3, M4

M3 A measure of money supply used by the various central banks. In the Federal Reserve System, M3 includes all physical currency and deposits in checking accounts, deposits in savings accounts, certificates of deposit, institutional money market accounts, repurchase agreements, and other large liquid assets that do not circulate very often. The European Central Bank defines M3 as the aggregation of currency in circulation, overnight deposits, all money market accounts, debt securities with maturities of up to two years, and repurchase agreements. M3 includes money that circulates very little or not at all and, therefore, the Federal Reserve no longer calculates M3 when determining the money supply. However, it is useful to some economists seeking to determine the entire amount of money in a given economy. See also: M0, M1, M2, M4

MA 1. ISO 3166-1 alpha-2 code for the Kingdom of Morocco. This is the code used in international transactions to and from Moroccan bank accounts. **2.** ISO 3166-2 geocode for Morocco. This is used as an international standard for shipping to Morocco. Each province has its own code with the prefix "MA." For example, the code for the Province of Ait Baha is ISO 3166-2:MA-BAH.

Ma Bell A colloquial term for AT&T prior to the 1980s. It was used to refer to the fact that AT&T had total or near total monopoly over the provision of telephone service in most areas of the United States. After 1984, Ma Bell was forcibly broken up into several "baby Bells."

Ma'ah An ancient Hebrew unit of weight approximately equivalent to 0.7 grams.

Maakond In Estonia, a political subdivision equivalent to a county.

Maakuntaa In Finland, a political subdivision approximately equivalent to a province.

Maatje A Dutch unit of volume equivalent to 100 milliliters. It was adopted in 1817, soon after the establishment of the Kingdom of the Netherlands.

MAC GOST 7.67 Latin three-letter geocode for Macau. The code is used for transactions to and from Macanese bank accounts and for international shipping to Macau. As with all GOST 7.67 codes, it is used primarily in Cyrillic alphabets.

Macanese Pataca The currency of Macau. It was introduced in 1894. Macau is a special administrative region of China. Perhaps because of this the pataca is pegged to the Hong Kong dollar using a currency board system. That is, the Monetary Authority of Macau it legally obligated to redeem pataca for the equivalent amount of Hong Kong dollars on demand.

Macaroni Defense An antitakeover measure in which a company issues a large number of bonds with the provison that they must be redeemed at a high price if the company is taken over. The macaroni defense expands the cost of a hostile takeover (just like macaroni expands when it cooks). However, it can make a friendly takeover more difficult.

Mace A unit of weight in Taiwan approximately equivalent to 3.75 grams. It is used primarily in the sale of bulk foodstuffs.

Macedonian Denar The currency of Macedonia. It was introduced in 1992 following the fall of the former Yugoslavia, replacing the Yugoslav dinar at face value. The following year, it was devalued such that the new denar was equivalent to 100 of the old denar.

Macro In hedge funds, describing a medium or long term investment strategy. For example, a hedge fund manager may purchase futures contracts or options that do not expire for six or nine months, believing that the fund can profit from trends in the meantime or that the market will move in the desired direction during that timeframe.

Macro Country Risk The risk that a foreign government will significantly alter its policies or other regulations so that it significantly affects all investment in that country. More broadly, it can apply to the risk that a nation will refuse to comply with an agreement to which it is a party, or that political violence will hurt an investment or business. For example, if one exports goods to a foreign nation, and that nation elects a new government that enacts protectionist tariffs, this will negatively impact all exports, rather than simply one export business.

Macroeconomics The study of an economy in its largest sense. That is, macroeconomics studies gross domestic product, unemployment, inflation, and similar matters. It does not look at the function of individual companies and only tangentially studies individual industries. It is useful in helping determine the aggregate effect of certain policies on an economy as a whole. See also: Microeconomics.

Macromanager A manager who tries to exert authority outside his/her department. That is, a macromanager is a micromanager who believes his/her authority extends further than it actually does.

MAD ISO 4217 code for the Moroccan dirham. It was introduced in 1960, replacing the Moroccan franc. It is illegal to export locally circulating dirhams.

Mad Hatter A CEO or other major executive who is not trusted and whose ability to lead is being questioned. A mad hatter may soon be fired. See also: Golden handshake.

Made-to-Measure Tariff A tariff that brings the price of an import to the same level as the price of a comparable domestic good. A made-to-measure tariff is intended to make imports competitive without negatively impacting domestic producers.

Madison Avenue A street in Manhattan. It is known as the headquarters for a number of advertising agencies, as well as for its upscale shopping.

Madrid Stock Exchange The largest stock exchange in Spain, founded in 1831. It attracts considerably more foreign investment than the other three exchanges. It trades in equity shares and convertible bonds, as well as sovereign and corporate bonds and other fixed income securities. More than 1,000 domestic and foreign companies trade their shares on the Madrid Stock Exchange. Ninety percent of all transactions, including all fixed-income trading, occurs electronically.

Maekawa Report A report to the Japanese government recommending promotion of domestic demand and a lower emphasis on exports. It recommended deregulation of legal barricades between banking and securities sectors to accomplish this goal. The report was published in 1986, when Japan's balance of payments surplus was considered to be unsustainably high.

MAF ISO 4217 code for the Moroccan franc. It was introduced in French Morocco in 1921, and became the currency of the independent Morocco in 1957. The Moroccan dirham was introduced in 1960, but the franc remained as a subdivision of the dirham until the santim replaced it in 1974.

Mag In the United Kingdom, a slang term for a farthing. The term fell out of general use after the farthing was withdrawn from circulation in the years immediately before the decimalization of the British pound.

Mag Track A magnetic tape on which one can record both images and sound. It is used in film.

Maghreb Permanent Consultative Committee An international organization dedicated to economic development in the Arab Maghreb of North Africa. It was established in 1966 and is based in Tunis.

Maghreb States Algeria, Libya, Mauritania, Morocco, Tunisia and perhaps the Western Sahara. The Maghreb states are most of north Africa apart from Egypt; they belong to the Arab Maghreb Union, which promotes economic cooperation.

Magnuson-Moss Warranty Act Legislation in the United States, passed in 1975, that gave the Federal Trade Commission the authority to enforce warranties on consumer goods. The Act does not require goods to carry warranties, but rather states that companies must honor the warranties that they issue.

Mahayojan An ancient Indian unit of length variously equivalent to values between 13,000 and 16,000 kilometers.

Mahjoor In Islamic law, a person who is not permitted to do business. For example, an insane person or a minor may be a mahjoor.

Mahoz In Israel, a political subdivision equivalent to a district.

Maik A Burmese unit of length equivalent to 152.4 millimeters.

Mail Delay A delay in payment resulting from the mailing, rather than the handing over, of a check. It especially applies if the check is delayed or lost in the mail. See also: Check hold.

Mail Float A delay in payment resulting from the mailing, rather than the handing over, of a check. It especially applies if the check is delayed or lost in the mail. See also: Check hold.

Mailer's Technical Advisory Committee A committee responsible for advising the U.S. Postal Service on matters of direct mail policy. The Committee consists of catalogue companies, publishers, printers and other interested parties.

Mailing Date The date on which dividends, reports, and other relevant material are mailed the stockholders and/or bondholders.

Mailroom A place in an office where incoming mail is directed to the proper recipient and outgoing mail is passed on to the post office. A mail room should not be confused with a post office because a mailroom is privately owned and controlled internally.

Main Home The place where one lives most of the time. The main home is important to persons who own multiple properties because vacation homes and investment properties are taxed differently than the main home. In particular, one is not required to pay capital gains tax on the sale of a main home, provided one then buys another main home of equal or greater value. A main home is also called a principal residence.

Maintenance and Replacement Call In a secured bond, a provision in the indenture that allows the issuer to call the bond (or redeem it before maturity) if it sells or otherwise divests itself of the asset securing the bond. For example, if the collateral on a bond is a factory the issuer owns, a maintenance and replacement call would allow the issuer to call the bond if it sells the factory, or faces foreclosure, or enters into other stated circumstances. It should not be confused with a maintenance call, which has to do with margin accounts.

Maintenance Bond A bond that one company issues to another guaranteeing repayment in case some project fails to work properly after a certain period of time. For example, if a company hires a firm to build industrial equipment for a factory, the firm may issue a maintenance bond to the company. If the equipment is not constructed according to specifications and therefore does not function correctly, the company will not incur any losses because the firm must repay the bond. This reduces the risk to the bondholder that another party to a contract will not fulfill its obligations.

Maintenance Call An order by a brokerage for an account holder to deposit more cash or securities into a margin account when the value of the cash and securities currently in it falls below some defined percentage. Every margin account has a maintenance margin requirement, which is money or securities an investor must keep in his/her margin account in order to be able to borrow from the brokerage. FINRA requires that the maintenance margin must be at least 25% of the amount borrowed, while some brokerages require maintenances of up to 50%. If the maintenance margin falls below this, the account may be subject to a maintenance call. If the account holder is not able to make the necessary deposit, he/she must close out enough positions in order to make the deposit, or risk the account becoming blocked. A maintenance call is a form of a margin call.

Maintenance Fee 1. An annual fee that a brokerage assesses on all accounts for the ability to keep an account at that brokerage. The maintenance fee may be larger if an account has few transactions on it for a given year. See also: Inactivity fee. **2.** See: Homeowners' association fee.

Maintenance Margin The money or securities an investor keeps in a margin account in order to be able to borrow from a brokerage for short sales or other purposes. The maintenance is kept as collateral until the brokerage calls the margin and the client pays back what is owed. FINRA requires that the maintenance kept must be at least 25% of the amount borrowed, while some brokerages require maintenances of up to 50%. See also: Restricted account.

Major Bracket In bracketing, the second largest underwriting group responsible for placing a certain amount of a new issue with investors. The major bracket is the second largest, and is sometimes used interchangeably with "mezzanine bracket."

Brackets are listed in order of size on an advertisement detailing each new issue, known as the tombstone.

Major Currency One of the most commonly traded currencies in the world. Exchange rates are often quoted against one or more major currencies. These currencies are the U.S. dollar, the British pound, the Japanese yen, the Swiss franc and the euro.

Major Market Index An index of 20 stocks in different industries. Its composition is very similar to the Dow Jones Industrial Average. The Major Market Index is considered an important benchmark, though it is not as widely known as the DJIA. Its ticker symbol is XMI and it is managed by the American Stock Exchange.

Major Turn A change in a security's medium or long term prospects. A major turn may occur when a bull market is about to become a bear market or vice versa.

Majority Shareholder A person or company that owns 50% plus one of the stock in a publicly-traded company. This allows the majority shareholder outright control of the company's operations, especially the election of its board of directors. Some majority shareholders are not involved in the daily operations of the company, but most are. Indeed, the majority shareholder is often the company's founder. See also: Parent company.

Majority Stake The ownership of 50% plus one of the stock in a publicly-traded company. This gives the person or company holding majority stake outright control of the company's operations, especially the election of its board of directors. Some majority stake holders are not involved in the daily operations of the company, but most are. Indeed, the majority shareholder is often the company's founder. See also: Parent company.

Make a Market To be ready to trade at any time at the quoted price. The job of a dealer is to be able to make a market to promote liquidity for a security. When a broker-dealer makes a market, it allows the brokerage to trade from its own inventory, which is easier and less expensive than looking for other brokerages willing to trade. See also: Market maker.

Make It Rain Informal; to make a large amount of money, especially for someone else. For example, a broker who earns exceptional gains may be said to make it rain for his/her clients.

Make Whole Call Provision A provision in some bond agreements allowing the issuer to redeem the bond before maturity if it gives bondholders a lump-sum payment equal to the net present value of coupons they would have received, had the bond not been called. A make-whole call provision allows the issuer to reduce the amount of debt on its balance sheet, if need be, while also limiting bondholders' risk.

Makegood A free advertisement that a periodical runs as a courtesy to a client. A periodical runs a makegood ad after it previously published an ad for that client incorrectly.

Make-Up The amount by which that a cash flow or some other capital must increase in order to break even. For example, if a margin account is in deficiency by $500, it may be said to have a $500 make-up.

Making a Line In technical analysis, a situation in which the price of a security moves up and down slightly but generally maintains equilibrium. This makes a chart of the security's price look roughly like a straight line. If the price breaks away from the line and goes downward, this is a bearish indicator. On the other hand, if the price breaks upward, this is a bullish indicator.

Malagasy Ariary The currency of Madagascar. Issued in 1961, it existed alongside the Malagasy franc until 2005, during which time one ariary was equal to five francs. It is divided into five iraimbilanja, making it one of two currencies in the world not divided into 100 subunits.

Malagasy Franc The currency of Madagascar from the early 1970s until 2005. From 1963 until the early 1970s, Madagascar belonged to the Financial Community of Africa, but subsequently issued the franc, pegging it to the French franc. An inconvertible currency, it underwent a series of devaluations and floated in the last period of time prior to its abolition. It existed alongside the Malagasy ariary, which is the current currency in Madagascar.

Malawian Kwacha The currency of Malawi. It replaced the Malawian pound in 1971 at a ratio of two kwachas to one pound. It is a floating currency.

Malawian Pound The former currency of Malawi. It was introduced in 1964 when Malawi became an independent nation. It was replaced by the Malawian kwacha in 1971.

Malayong bayan In the Philippines, a political subdivision for Paternos, the only municipality in the Philippines contained inside metropolitan Manila.

Malayong lungsod In the Philippines, a political subdivision equivalent to a city outside the jurisdiction of any province.

Maldivian Rufiyaa The currency of the Maldives. It was issued in 1947 and was pegged to the Ceylonese rupee. It is currently pegged to the U.S. dollar.

Male Chauvinism The belief that men are superior to women. Most societies deal (or have dealt) with male chauvinism in some form or other. In business, male chauvinism may express itself in bias toward hiring or promoting men. Laws exist in many jurisdictions to limit or eliminate male chauvinism in business.

Male Chauvinist A person who believes men are superior to women. Most societies deal (or have dealt) with male chauvinism in some form or other. In business, male chauvinism may express as a bias in favor of hiring or promoting men. Laws exist in many jurisdictions to limit or eliminate male chauvinism in business.

Malian Franc The former currency of Mali. It was issued in 1962, replacing the West African CFA franc at a one-to-on ratio. The Malian franc was a weak currency. In 1984, Mali adopted the CFA franc again at a ratio of two Malian francs to one West African CFA franc.

Malicious Obedience 1. A tactic in which an employee follows a manager's instructions literally, doing exactly what was asked even if he/she knows that is not what is meant. Malicious obedience is a way for an employee to make his/her manager look bad because it is done in hopes that the manager's project will fail. **2.** A situation in which an employee hides his/her manager's mistakes so a more senior manager (or a client) will discover them later. This is also done in hopes that the manager's project will fail.

Maloney Act United States legislation passed in 1938 that allowed self-regulatory organizations to assist the SEC in some financial regulation. That is, the Maloney Act encouraged what was essentially a public-private partnership between the federal government and the financial industry. Currently, only FINRA is registered as such an organization under the Maloney Act.

Maltese Lira The currency of Malta from 1972 until 2007. Prior to 1972, Malta used the British pound; when the pound decimalized, Malta decided to issue its own lira, which it pegged to the pound on a 1:1 basis. It later was pegged to a currency basket and became the second highest valued currency in the world. It was replaced by the euro on January 1, 2008.

Maltese Scudo The currency of the Sovereign Military Order of Malta. While this circulated in Malta until 1798, the Order is currently extraterritorial and issues scudi only for souvenir purposes. It does not have an ISO 4217 code.

Mammon A derogatory term for money or greed. Mammon is used to refer to an excessive desire for wealth or security, especially at the expense of others. It is derived from the New Testament.

Ma-Na An ancient Sumerian unit of weight approximately equivalent to 497.7 grams.

Managed Account A brokerage account or any other account where the monies therein are invested by another party. For example, a person may have a discretionary account at his/her brokerage. This allows the brokerage to invest the funds in the account as it sees fit, in accordance with the account holder's investment goals and the prudent person rule. Other examples of managed accounts include annuities and IRAs. What distinguishes a managed account from other accounts is the fact that the account holder does not manage it himself/herself. See also: Separately managed account, Managed money.

Managed Currency A currency with an exchange rate set or influenced by a government. Often, the local government makes this intervention, but this is not always the case. For example, in 1994, the American government bought large quantities of Mexican pesos to stop the rapid loss of the peso's value. Strictly speaking, even a central bank's intervention to raise or lower interest rates creates a managed currency. However, because most floating currencies manage their regimes with occasional central bank involvement, the term applies mainly to frequent or dramatic interventions. See also: 1994 Mexican economic crisis, Floating currency, Fixed exchange rate.

Managed Earnings The practice of the managers of a company performing any action that misrepresents the company's financial health. The practice of managed earnings may include falsely inflating stock prices by improperly reporting income, failing to capitalize expenses, hiding losses in subsidiaries, or prematurely recognizing revenue. See also: Sarbanes-Oxley Act of 2002, Aggressive accounting.

Managed Float A floating exchange rate in which a government intervenes at some frequency to change the direction of the float by buying or selling currencies. Often, the local government makes this intervention, but this is not always the case. For example, in 1994, the American government bought large quantities of Mexican pesos to stop the rapid loss of the peso's value. Strictly speaking, even a central bank's intervention to raise or lower interest rates could be considered a managed float. However, because most floating currencies manage their regimes with occasional central bank involvement, the term applies mainly to frequent or dramatic interventions. A managed float is also known as a dirty float. See also: 1994 Mexican economic crisis, Floating currency, Fixed exchange rate.

Managed Futures Account An investment company that invests in government securities, futures contracts, and options on futures contracts. Managed futures accounts operate much like a mutual fund, specifically because they are both actively managed. Managed futures accounts tend to be less volatile than other investment vehicles. Managed futures accounts use technical analysis in most of their management practices. In the United States, they are regulated by the Commodity Futures Trading Commission and the National Futures Association.

Managed Money Any investment vehicle where the investor directly controls the funds placed therein. For example, an investor may place funds in a mutual fund or other investment company. The investment manager of the investment company then handles the money and makes investment decisions related to it. Managed money may also apply to an individual brokerage account where the broker has the discretion to make investment decisions without the specific approval of the account holder. See also: Managed account.

Management 1. The persons or institutions that administer a company. That is, management has the responsibility to direct employees, set and enforce policies, and generally ensure that the company fulfills its goals (which management itself often sets). Management is responsible to the board of directors (of a publicly-traded company) and ultimately to the company's owners. In small companies, owners and managers are often the same people. **2.** See: Asset management.

Management Audit A measurement and report of the effectiveness and results of certain business procedures. Management audits are usually performed internally, and check to see that procedures have their intended effect. Unlike a compliance audit, which simply ensures that procedures are being followed, management audits challenge the assumptions and goals of procedures, with an eye toward improving efficiency. A management audit may recommend changes in procedures resulting from observed inefficiencies in existing procedures. See also: Audit, Assurance.

Management Buy-In The act or practice of an outside investor buying a controlling interest in a publicly-traded company and leaving the current management intact. That is, unlike most acquisitions, the outside investor does not fire the top or middle level managers and bring in his own managers. Instead, the outside investor usually only places representatives on the board of directors.

Management Buyout The act of the senior management of a publicly-traded company buying all of the company's shares outstanding. A management buyout gives the management complete control of the company and allows it to operate without recourse to shareholders. A management buyout is usually heavily leveraged and is a form of going private.

Management by Objectives A goal-oriented management tool in which managers and employees come together to agree upon a set of objectives to achieve for the company's short-, medium-, or long-term future. Management by objectives is a multi-step process in which previous goals are periodically evaluated and changed with employee input, then put into practice with occasional performance evaluation and rewards to high achievers. Goals are expected to be explicitly defined by the SMART Principle. That is, goals must be Specific, Measurable, Achievable, Relevant, and Time-Specific. Critics of management by objectives argue that the tool only works when goals are defined more specifically than is usually possible. Proponents argue that this arrangement helps employees avoid a workaday mentality in which activities are performed without any reference to greater objectives. The term 'management by objectives' was coined and first explained by Peter Drucker in his 1954 book, The Practice of Management.

Management Contract A contract allowing another party to manage a firm or fund. Management contracts are common among mutual funds, which often hire outside companies to provide management services. See also: Asset management.

Management Fee A fee that an investment advisory firm charges for making investment decisions on behalf of a client. Asset management often opens up more potential investment vehicles to the client, and, theoretically, asset managers have more knowledge and experience in making appropriate investment decisions than the client. Managers charge fees for these services. Usually, the fee is a small percentage of the assets under management, but because asset management is often open only to institutional investors and high net-worth individuals, the management fee is usually a large dollar amount. It is also called an advisory fee.

Management Porn A derogatory term for a presentation with more graphs and charts than necessary. Management porn may not be terribly informative, but it is said to make managers happy either to see the charts and graphs or to present them.

Management Risk The risk of a loss due to incompetent management. That is, if a money manager consistently makes bad investment decisions for a fund or portfolio, there is a substantial risk that investors will lose money. Alternatively, the managers of an individual publicly-traded company may choose to suspend its most profitable operation and invest in unprofitable ones. This may result in a loss to shareholders. Various incentives and benchmarks exist in companies to reduce management risk; all have their proponents and critics. See also: Manager Universe (Benchmark).

Management's Discussion and Analysis In a stockholder's report, a summary at the beginning stating what the management believes about the company's previous year or quarter. Generally speaking, management's discussion and analysis state the "bottom line" while the remainder of the report contains more detailed financial information. For example, the discussion and analysis may contain a brief essay stating, "Our company is healthy for reasons A, B, and C ." At the conclusion of that essay, the stockholder may view the financial statement.

Manager Universe A comparison of one money manager's performance to a group of comparable peer money managers, or another term for the manager peer group. This is done periodically to maintain competitiveness and to judge a particular manager's performance. The practice has become controversial, as some believe that manager universes are too broadly defined to accurately demonstrate the skill of a particular manager and that they suffer from survivor bias because bad managers drop out or are fired. See also: Evaluation period.

Managerial Decision Any decision regarding the operations of a firm. These decisions include setting target growth rates, hiring or firing employees, and deciding what products to sell.

Managerial Flexibility The ability of the management of a company or fund to make investment decisions and other decisions based on current or projected market conditions, as opposed to any preconceived notions.

Managing Director 1. The person responsible for the management of a business unit, as opposed to the company as a whole. For example, an oil company may have one managing director for its upstream operations and another managing director for its downstream operations, both of whom are responsible to the chief executive officer. **2.** A member of a company's board of directors who also has management responsibility within the company. **3.** A primarily British and Commonwealth term for chief executive officer.

Manat A name for a currency in Central Asia. The currencies of both Azerbaijan and Turkmenistan are called the manat. In Azerbaijan, the Soviet ruble was called the manat locally.

Manatiq In Saudi Arabia, a political subdivision equivalent to a province.

Mancomunidad In Spain, a political subdivision consisting of municipalities that band together to perform certain functions. For example, mancomunidads may offer common utilities. They may be temporary or permanent arrangements.

Mandate 1. See: Order. **2.** The appointment of a person to make arrangements for the financing of a project.

Mandated Sick Leave Sick leave that a company is legally required to provide to employees. Governments may mandate sick leave in order to protect workers from termination when they are ill. Proponents of mandated sick leave argue that this helps workers keep their jobs when they can least afford to lose them. Critics maintain that mandated sick leave represents an unsustainable cost for businesses.

Mandatory Convertible A bond that must be converted into common stock in the company issuing it on or before a certain date. An advantage of a mandatory convertible to the investor is the fact that it guarantees a certain return up to the conversion date, after which there is no guaranteed return but the possibility of a much higher return. A publicly-traded company issues mandatory convertibles when it needs to raise the capital provided by issuing stock, but when doing so would put a strain on the price of existing shares.

Mandatory Redemption Schedule The schedule according to which the issuer of a bond with a sinking fund provision must set aside funds to repay the bond at maturity. Bonds with sinking fund provisions require the issuer to put money aside to repay bondholders at maturity. This reduces the risk of default. The schedule according to which these funds are put aside is the mandatory redemption schedule.

Manila Stock Exchange A former stock exchange in the Philippines. It was established in 1927 and in 1992 it merged with the Makati Stock Exchange to form the Philippine Stock Exchange.

Manipulation The attempt or act to artificially change the price of a security or a market movement with the intent to make a profit. One example is wash selling, in which an investor both sells then quickly re-buys the same security, hoping to create the impression of increased trading volume, and therefore raise the price. Another is churning, in which an investor makes both buy and sell orders through different brokers to create the impression of increased interest in the security and raise the price. Manipulation can be used to both increase and decrease prices, depending on the investor's perceived needs. Manipulation is illegal under the Securities Exchange Act of 1934. See also: Antitrust, Fix.

Mano River Union An international organization to encourage economic cooperation in parts of West Africa. It was established in 1973 but was dormant for much of its history because of political instability in the region. In 2004, however, it became active again. As of 2008, the Mano River Union consisted of Cote d'Ivoire, Guinea, Liberia and Sierra Leone.

Manu An ancient Akkadian unit of weight approximately equivalent to 497.7 grams.

Manufactured Payment The requirement that the borrower of a stock must pay dividends to the lender. The manufactured payment occurs because the lender of stock, because he/she remains the owner, normally retains the right to receive dividends. Manufactured payments have tax implications.

Mao In China, a slang term for jiao, a subdivision of currency equivalent to 1/10 of a yuan.

Maple Leaf A type of gold bullion coin in Canada. Maple leafs usually trade at a price slightly higher than the bullion's value. Like gold bullion, a maple leaf is a commodity that investors often use as a hedge against recession and inflation; thus, while it is volatile like most commodities, it always maintains a relatively high value.

Maquiladora A factory in Mexico established by a U.S. company to make finished products and ship them to the United States. Maquiladoras are close to the U.S. border with Mexico. They are controversial in the United States because they are thought to take away jobs from Americans who otherwise would have manufactured the products. They are also controversial in Mexico because they are thought to exploit Mexican workers. NAFTA made maquiladoras more cost effective. In the mid-2000s, maquiladoras accounted for more than half of U.S.-Mexican trade. A maquiladora is also called a maquila.

MAR GOST 7.67 Latin three-letter geocode for Morocco. The code is used for transactions to and from Moroccan bank accounts and for international shipping to Morocco. As with all GOST 7.67 codes, it is used primarily in Cyrillic alphabets.

Marabba A customary Indian unit of area approximately equivalent to 10.117 hectares.

Marche des Options Negociables de Paris A section of Euronext Paris on which stock and index futures and options are traded. All trades occur electronically.

Margin 1. Money that an investor has borrowed from a broker in order to buy securities. An investor who buys on margin can realize huge gains if the price of the security moves in a favorable direction; however, he/she also takes on a great deal of risk because it may not move in such a direction. See also: minimum maintenance, margin call. **2.** A measure of how well a company controls its costs. It is calculated by dividing a company's profit by its revenues and expressing the result as a percentage. The higher the margin is, the better the company is thought to control costs. Investors use the margin to compare companies in the same industry as well as between industries to determine which are the most profitable. It is also called the profit margin.

Margin Account A brokerage account in which the brokerage lends money to the account holder, which the account holder then uses to buy securities. That is, a margin account is one in which an investor makes investments with borrowed money. This opens up investment opportunities that an investor might not otherwise be able to afford. More importantly, however, a margin account increases both gains and losses for the investor.Regulation T and other regulations require margin accounts to have money or securities kept as collateral. See also: Margin call, Maintenance.

Margin Agreement An agreement between a brokerage and a client governing a margin account. The margin agreement enables the client to borrow from the brokerage in order to buy securities. The agreement details what collateral must be placed on the account and the other duties each party must fulfill. The client must sign the margin agreement before the margin account is created.

Margin Call An order by a brokerage for an account holder to deposit more cash or securities into a margin account when the value of the cash and securities currently in it falls below some defined percentage. Every margin account has a maintenance margin requirement, which is money or securities an investor must keep in his/her margin account in order to be able to borrow from the brokerage. FINRA requires that the maintenance margin must be at least 25% of the amount borrowed, while some brokerages require a maintenance margin of up to 50%. If the maintenance margin falls below this, the account may be subject to a margin call. If the account holder is unable to make the necessary deposit, he/she must close out enough positions in order to make the deposit, or risk the account becoming blocked.

Margin Department The department in a brokerage firm that deals with margin accounts. It monitors margin accounts opened by clients and ensures that they meet the minimum maintenance required by law and the brokerage itself. Additionally, the department makes margin calls and generally ensures smooth management of the margin accounts by the brokerage. It is also called the credit department.

Margin Loan Money that an investor has borrowed from a broker in order to buy securities. An investor who buys on margin can realize huge gains if the price of the security moves in a favorable direction; however, he/she also takes on a great deal of risk because it may not move in such a direction. See also: Minimum maintenance, Margin call.

Margin of Safety In business, the amount by which sales or other revenue can fall before it reaches the breakeven point. That is, the margin of safety is how much worse a company can do before it ceases to be profitable. For example, if a company's breakeven point is $200,000 per year, and it is currently producing $300,000, its margin of safety is $100,000. This is also called the safety margin.

Margin Requirement Options The initial margin or maintenance margin that an investor must deposit with a brokerage as collateral in order to purchase options with borrowed money. The margin requirement for options is set by Regulation T, but some brokerages have higher requirements.

Margin Security A security that one has purchased or sold on a margin account. A margin account is a brokerage account in which the brokerage lends the account holder money, which the account holder then uses to buy securities. Thus, a margin security is one that an investor buys with borrowed money. The fact that an investor is able to do this opens up investment opportunities that he/she might not otherwise be able to afford. More importantly, however, a margin security increases the possibility of a higher return and the risk of more losses. Margin securities are governed by Regulation T. See also: Margin call, Maintenance.

Margin Trading Trading securities that an investor has bought with money borrowed from a broker for that purpose. An investor who trades on margin can realize huge gains if the price of the security moves in a favorable direction; however, he/she also takes on a great deal of risk because it may not move in such a direction. See also: minimum maintenance, margin call.

Marginal Describing the effect, if any, of adding one additional unit to a calculation.

Marginal Cost The total cost to a company to produce one more unit of a product. The marginal cost varies according to how many more or fewer units a company wishes to produce. Increasing production may increase or decrease the marginal cost, because the marginal cost includes all costs such as labor, materials, and the cost of infrastructure. For example, if a widget manufacturer increases the number of widgets it produces, it may need to buy more material, but the costs of labor and factory maintenance remain the same, and are spread out over a greater number of widgets. This may reduce the marginal cost. On the other hand, if the manufacturer hires more workers and builds another factory, it will likely increase the marginal cost. It is also known as the incremental cost.

Marginal Efficiency of Capital The extra yield that an investor earns for each additional dollar of capital invested in the venture or security. The marginal efficiency of capital helps measure how much investment capital is worth the risk at a given return. It is also called marginal productivity of capital.

Marginal Propensity to Consume In Keynesian economics, the amount of a person's increase in income spent on goods and services as opposed to saved. It is measured as a ratio of a change in consumption to a change in income. For example, if one receives a $5,000 raise in salary and spends $3,000, the MPC is 0.6. Factors affecting the MPC include interest rates and the relative expense of goods and services. See also: Marginal propensity to save.

Marginal Revenue The revenue that a company generates over what it previously generated for each additional unit of output. For example, suppose a company generates $1000 in revenue from 100 units of a product (in other words $10 per unit).

In order to sell 101 units it may have to reduce its price to $9.99 per unit. In this case, its revenue becomes $1008.99. Thus, the marginal revenue is $8.99.

Marginal Risk The risk that the holder of a forward contract will declare bankruptcy before the contract matures. In such a case, the holder may not have sufficient funds to actually take possession of the underlying asset.

Marginal Tax Rate A percentage of one's income that one must pay in taxes. Marginal tax rates vary according to income levels. One who makes $100,000 per year has a higher marginal tax rate than one who makes $25,000. However, the marginal tax rate does not increase for one's entire income, merely each dollar over a certain threshold. Suppose one pays 10% of one's income up to $25,000, and 20% thereafter. The taxpayer making $25,001 does not suddenly have to pay 20% of his/her entire income, only on the one dollar over $25,000. That is, he/she owes 10% of $25,000 ($2,500) and 20% of the $1 over that (or $0.20). All things being equal, this taxpayer owes $2,500.20 in taxes.

Marginal Utility In economics, the level of satisfaction a person derives from a good or service. Marginal utility is inherently subjective and thus difficult to measure, but it is important to determining how much supply of a product the market can handle without diminishing demand. Historically, it has been thought that one can quantify the marginal utility of each unit, but some economists disagree with this. See also: Austrian school, Law of Diminishing Marginal Utility.

Marhala An obsolete Arabic unit of length approximately equivalent to 46.08 kilometers.

Maria Theresa Ounce A unit of weight approximately equivalent to 28.07 grams. It is used in Ethiopia and previously was used in Eritrea.

Marigold In British financial circles, a slang term for 1 million pounds. See also: The City.

Marine Cargo Insurance An insurance policy that protects the buyer of a good being transported over water from the loss of that good. Most of the time either the buyer or the seller is required to purchase marine cargo insurance (or at least to assume the risk of transit); their specific agreement determines which one is responsible. See also: Incoterm.

Marine Mammal Protection Act Legislation in the United States, passed in 1972, that prohibited the hunting or killing of marine mammals such as dolphins and whales. It also imposed a moratorium on the sale, import and export of marine mammals. Later legislation provided for exceptions for marine mammals captured in the process of fishing, but this remained controversial. The Act was intended to prevent species depletion. See also: Endangered Species Act.

Marital Deduction A deduction one may take when one transfers assets to one's spouse. All gifts and other transfers to a spouse are tax free; one may take advantage of this to reduce one's taxable income (within certain limits). Most marital deductions occur when one is planning one's estate.

Marital Status The state of being married or unmarried. Some definitions divide groups into single, married and divorced (or separated). Marital status qualifies one for various tax advantages; for example, married persons generally may exempt more of their income from taxes.

Marital Trust A trust into which one spouse deposits assets that transfer to the other spouse at some point in the future or upon the first spouse's death. A marital trust exists in order to avoid paying the estate tax. See also: Unlimited marital deduction.

Maritime Administration Also called MARAD. A branch of the U.S. Department of Transportation that provides and maintains ships for use during times of national emergency. MARAD also supports military operations when requested and determines sea routes best suited for American maritime commerce.

Mark 1. See: Mark to market. **2.** See: Deutschemark.

Mark Adelson An American credit analyst. A lawyer by training, Adelson worked for various investment banks and credit ratings agencies prior to becoming chief credit officer at Standard & Poor's in 2008. He was educated at Princeton University and the University of Michigan.

Mark gleich Mark A German phrase meaning "a mark is a mark." It was a catchphrase during and after World War I indicating public confidence in the German mark. It also referred to a German cultural preference for cash, under the belief that the Reichsbank would always redeem it. Following the hyperinflation of the early Weimar Republic, the phrase ceased to be believed.

Mark to Market To record a change in the value of an asset or fund to reflect its current fair market value. Marking to market occurs on a daily basis and is used for a number of purposes. Notably, investors mark to market a portfolio or security to ensure that a margin account is meeting its minimum maintenance.

Markaz In Egypt and Saudi Arabia, a political subdivision approximately equivalent to a county.

Markdown 1. The amount by which a seller reduces a price for a product or asset in order to make it desirable for buyers. See also: Markup. **2.** The difference between the price a broker-dealer charges for a retailer to buy a security and the price at which the broker-dealer sells the same security to a market maker. This may or may not be considered a commission.

Marker A slang term for documentation indicating that a debt is owed.

Market 1. Informal for an exchange or over-the-counter medium for the trading of securities. **2.** The economic actors with the need or desire for a certain product. For example, if telephone users desire more efficient service, this is a market for a new company to offer a better product. **3.** To take steps to encourage customers to buy a product or patronize a business. See also: Marketing.

Market Amount The usual and normal amount that investment banks trade with each other on a trading day. The level of the market amount may affect trading volume in the broader market.

Market Analysis Research into data relating to the stability and profitability of businesses, especially to guide one's investing practices. Market analysis involves looking at financial statements to determine if a company is healthy or technical indicators to see if it is profitable in the short-term. Balance sheets are important to balance analysis as they provide a ready-made means of investigating performance. However, it is important to note that quantitative financial analysis has limits. For example, the accounting methods that a particular business employs may make it look healthier or less healthy than it really is. Market analysts attempt to see through this and arrive at a business' actual ability to make a profit for investors. See also: Fundamental Analysis, Technical Analysis, Investment Adviser.

Market Arbitrage An investment strategy that attempts to profit from inefficiencies in price by making transactions that offset each other. For example, one may buy a security at a low price and, within a few seconds, re-sell it to a willing buyer at a higher price. Arbitrageurs can keep prices relatively stable as markets attempt to resist their attempts at price exploitation. They often use computer programs because their transactions can be complex and occur in rapid succession.

Market Bottom The lowest level of support in price for a security, index, or market over a given time frame. The security, index, or market is highly unlikely to go below the bottom; if it does so, it may cause panic selling. During a prolonged bear market, when a market is dropping more or less continuously for a long time, investors often question when the market will find bottom, which means that they wish to know when the market will begin to rise again, or at least stabilize.

Market Break A sudden, unexpected change in a security's price or in a market's value. While a market break could indicate either upward or downward change, the connotation is negative. Especially on the futures market, a market break means a steep decline in price, usually the result of a natural disaster affecting the underlying assets.

Market Capitalization The total value of all outstanding shares of a publicly-traded company. The market capitalization is calculated by multiplying the shares outstanding by the price per share. Market capitalization is one of the basic measures of a publicly-traded company; it is a way of determining the rough value of a company. Generally speaking, a higher market capitalization indicates a more valuable company. Many exchanges and indices are weighted for market capitalization. It is informally known as market cap. See also: Large cap, Mid cap, Small cap.

Market Clearing A situation in which the demand for loans equals the supply of loans. That is, borrowers want to borrow the same amount of money that lenders are willing to lend. During a market clearing, the equilibrium rate of interest prevails, which ideally means that the cost of borrowing is neither excessively high nor low.

Market Conversion Price The price one effectively pays for common stock when one exercises the conversion option of a convertible security. One calculates the market conversion price by dividing the price one paid for the convertible security by the conversion ratio, which is the number of shares of common stock one receives by exercising the conversion option. In order for the exercise of the option to be worthwhile, the market conversion price must be lower than the market price of common stock. It is also called the conversion parity price and the conversion value.

Market Correction A drop in the price of a security when that security has been overbought and therefore overpriced. Market corrections are usually short-term and are necessary for the stability of the security.

Market Cycle The period of time during which the stock market evolves from a bull market to a bear market, then back to a bull market. That is, a market cycle is the time during which stock prices rise, then fall, then rise again. Every stock market has market cycles, to a greater or lesser extent. However, regulations may be designed to curtail them (or, more accurately, to attempt to maximize the good times while preventing the bad times), though this is rarely successful. Some industries are considered countercyclical, meaning that demand for their products remains relatively constant regardless of broader market circumstances; some industries even do better when the market, as a whole, is performing poorly. Other industries, mainly those considered luxuries, are greatly dependent on market cycles.

Market Economy A social and economic system in which prices are fixed by the law of supply and demand rather than by a government or other body. In its pure form, a market economy is an economy absent of government subsidies, incentives, or regulations. A market economy contrasts with both a planned economy and a mixed economy. No economy is a complete market economy: most countries claiming to have market economies in fact have a market economy combined with greater or lesser government regulation, sometimes called a social market. Proponents of a market economy argue that it is more efficient than any alternatives, promotes fair competition between its participants, and rewards skill and hard work. Critics allege that a market economy perpetuates class differences and rewards ruthlessness over actual labor. Milton Friedman, Friedrich Hayek, and Ludwig von Mises were three major 20th-century proponents of the market economy. See also: Capitalism, socialism, John Maynard Keynes.

Market Efficiency The extent to which the price of an asset reflects all information available. Economists disagree on how efficient markets are. Followers of the efficient markets theory hold that the market efficiently deals with all information on a given security and reflects it in the price immediately, and that technical analysis, fundamental analysis, and/or any speculative investing based on those methods are useless. On the other hand, the primary observation of behavioral economics holds that investors (and people in general) make decisions on imprecise impressions and beliefs, rather than rational analysis, rendering markets somewhat inefficient to the extent that they are affected by people.

Market Enhancing View A view of economic development holding that capital markets provide much of the liquidity necessary for development, but that government invention is necessary to provide markets with incentives to promote sustainability and long-term growth. The market enhancing view advocates limited government in some matters, but strategic government involvement in others. Economists disagree on how well the market enhancing view works.

Market Exposure **1.** The amount of money one risks in an investment. For example, if one invests $10,000 in a stock, one accepts a market exposure of $10,000. One also may speak of being exposed to particular type of risk. For example, if one invests in a bond, one is exposed to the risk that inflation will outpace the yield on the bond. **2.** The proportion of a portfolio or fund invested in a single company or industry. For example, if 50% of one's portfolio consists of financial stocks, one has a 50% market exposure. Most investors seek diversification so as to avoid "over-exposure" in any one industry. See also: Markowitz Portfolio Theory.

Market Eye The information service that provides general investment advice, technical analysis, and other statistics. It is sponsored by the International Stock Exchange of the UK and Ireland.

Market Failure A situation in which the market does not allocate resources efficiently. Market failure can occur for one of three reasons. It may occur when one party has power that can prevent efficient transactions from occurring. An example is a monopoly. A second reason is the possibility that an efficient transaction can have externalities (side effects) that reduce efficiency elsewhere in the market or the broader economy. Finally, market failure can occur because of the nature of certain goods or services. Some analysts believe that market failure is usually the result of insufficient government protection of property rights. Market failure has been cited as a reason for government intervention in the economy. See also: Government failure.

Market Friendly View A view of economic development holding that capital markets provide the necessary liquidity and growth for development with little or no government intervention. The market friendly view advocates limited government that provides a legal framework but that has no role in resource allocation. Economists disagree on how well the market friendly view works.

Market Fund A mutual fund that is not actively-managed and simply tracks a benchmark index. That is, the investment company managing the mutual fund places the liquidity in securities represented in a certain index. Thus, when that index increases in price, so does the mutual fund, and vice versa. An exchange-traded fund is a prime example of an index fund. Many popular index funds track the S&P 500 and other S&P indices. See also: Closet index fund, SPDR.

Market If Touched An order to a broker to buy or sell a security at a certain price when that price becomes available. MITs are common in futures markets, and often come from technical analysis. An MIT may be a day order or a GTC order, but not an immediate or cancel order. For example, if shares are trading at $10 and an MIT is made to buy at $11, the broker buys no securities until the price is actually $11 per share.

Market Interest Rate The interest rate offered most commonly on deposits in banks, other interest-bearing accounts, as well as on loans. The market interest rate is different for different investment vehicles, though all are determined by the supply and demand for credit.

Market Internalization Advantages Situations in which a multinational corporation is able to deliver goods and services in places where other companies cannot. A market internalization advantage allows the multinational corporation to use a market failure to its advantage to make a profit. Multinational corporations are thought to have the greatest market internalization advantages.

Market Is Off Informal; a phrase indicating that a market index is trading below the previous day's closing price. Depending on the particular type of investment one has made, this may be a good or bad situation. Short-selling or trading in bonds are only two of many ways to profit on days when the market is off. However, an off-day for a market usually indicates a loss of money for someone who owns stocks, exchange-traded funds, or many other securities.

Market Jitters General agitation among traders because of real or expected bad news. Market jitters tend to push down equity prices and may push down bond prices as well.

Market Letter A newsletter offering financial advice to readers or subscribers. A market letter may discuss broad macroeconomic trends, or it may offer specific advice on particular sectors of certain markets. If a market letter offers advice on specific securities, the author(s) are normally registered investment advisors with the SEC, and investors should exercise caution if they are not.

Market Maker A dealer available to trade a stated security on its own account at any time at the quoted price. The job of a dealer is to be a market maker in order to promote liquidity for a security. When a broker-dealer makes a market, it trades from its own inventory, which is easier and less expensive for an investor than looking for other brokerages willing to trade. Many exchanges designate a market maker for each of its listed securities to promote ease of trade.

Market Maker Spread A bid-ask spread involving a market maker. A market maker is limited in the size of spreads he/she is allowed to have because the spread represents the market maker's profit on a given transaction.

Market Maven Informal; a well-connected or knowledgeable investor or analyst who is known as a leader in giving accurate and timely opinions on the performance of one or more securities. Some investors may watch the moves of market mavens and allow them to influence their own investment decisions.

Market Mechanism The use of the purchase and sale by some medium of exchange (money) to distribute goods and services throughout an economy. The market mechanism contrasts with other ways of distributing goods and services, including redistribution of wealth and bartering. While the market mechanism is associated with the free market, the two are separate concepts. For example, one can have a heavily regulated economy that still uses the market mechanism.

Market Microstructure The way a market or exchange functions under a given set of rules. The study of market microstructure deals with how well or poorly an exchange's rules encourage efficient trading. For example, one who studies market microstructure might conduct research into the similarities and differences in exchanges that have open outcry trading and those that are exclusively electronic.

Market Model The relationship between a security's performance and the performance of a portfolio containing it. The market model states that the security's performance is related its portfolio's performance according to its beta; that is, if a security has a beta of 2, and the portfolio rises 10%, then that particular security generally rises 20%. See also: Markowitz Portfolio Theory.

Market Not Held Order An order to a broker to buy or sell a security at a certain price or better. This gives the broker the discretion to execute it at any time. As a result, he/she is not held responsible for missing the desired price and executing at a worse price. A market not held order is not executed immediately, but rather when the broker believes it is the best time to do so.

Market Order An order to buy or sell a security at the best price available when the order is made. Brokers who execute these orders must make a good faith effort to find the best possible price. It is also called an at-the-market order.

Market Out Clause A clause in some underwriting agreements abolishing the agreement under certain, defined circumstances. For example, if the economy suddenly enters a severe recession or the stock market falls 25%, it is unlikely that investors will be interested in a risky IPO. The market-out clause could then absolve the underwriting syndicate of its responsibility without penalty.

Market Outperform A broker's or brokerage firm's rating of a security. Such a security is expected to do marginally better than the market as a whole for the period of time it holds the "market outperform" rating. Some firms call the rating "accumulate," "moderate buy," or simply "outperform." Different firms have different rating systems, but "market outperform" is usually one rating above "market perform" or "neutral," and one rating below "buy." For example, if the market is expected to go down slightly, but a certain company's fundamentals are thought to be sound, a brokerage firm might change that company's rating from market perform to market outperform.

Market Overhang Shares in a security or commodity contracts that are likely to be sold in certain circumstances, creating downward pressure on the price. That is, the market overhang supply is a block that investors are holding but will likely attempt to sell. For example, if a security hits its resistance level, more investors are likely to sell their shares which increases the number of shares available on the market and, assuming demand does not increase, will lead to a decline in the price. Market overhang is also called the overhanging supply or simply the overhang.

Market Penetration/Share The percentage of an industry or sector that a single company controls. For example, if Retail Company A conducts 10% of all retail sales in the United States, it is said to have a 10% market share or penetration. It is important that a company, especially a large company, maintains a substantial market share in order to remain competitive. However, companies that achieve too high a market share through mergers, acquisitions, or other methods may become regarded as monopolies and violate local antitrust laws. Some companies have a large market share compared to their competitors, but not enough to be considered a monopoly: these are called gorillas. See also: Herfindahl-Hirschman Index.

Market Perform A recommendation by an analyst to neither buy nor sell a security. An analyst makes a market perform recommendation when technical and/or fundamental indicators show middling performance by a security. The term indicates that the security is likely to perform neither better nor worse than the market as a whole. It is also called a neutral or hold recommendation.

Market Performance Committee A committee on the New York Stock Exchange that monitors and evaluates market makers. That is, the MPC is charged with ensuring that market makers do their job to maintain the orderly and liquid exchange of securities.

Market Portfolio In Markowitz portfolio theory, a theoretical portfolio of all assets in the world, weighted for value.

Market Power The ability of a company to be able to heavily influence the price charged for its product because no other companies have the same product or a similar product of the same quality. That is, a company with a great deal of market power is essentially able to charge whatever it wants so long as it does not run afoul of antitrust laws. See also: Monopoly, Price maker.

Market Price What a willing buyer pays a willing seller for a given asset. In an efficient market, market prices are determined by the law of supply and demand and no other factors. In securities, a market price is the price of the most recent transaction of that security. Open markets, and capitalism in general, can only exist if prices are set by the market, at least most of the time. See also: Fair market value, Invisible Hand.

Market Reform Act of 1990 Legislation in the United States that for the first time permitted the SEC to restrict certain kinds of trading, notably program trading, during "periods of extraordinary volatility." The Act also provided for more efficient reporting measures for securities trading and authorized the SEC to create a national system for the settlement of transactions. It was passed in response to the S&L crisis of the late 1980s.

Market Research Research into consumer or client needs or desires so a company can make or customize products to fit them. For example, market research may involve conducting surveys of target clients (say, a particular demographic) to identify what they most would like to see in the industry in which the company is involved. Market research is important for most companies but especially for companies with a high client turnover.

Market Researcher A professional who researches consumer or client needs or desires so a company can make or customize products to fit them. For example, a market researcher may conduct surveys of target clients to identify what they most would like to see in the industry in which the company is involved. Market research is important for most companies but especially for companies with a high client turnover.

Market Return In Markowitz Portfolio Theory, the return on a theoretical portfolio of all assets in the world where the portfolio is weighted for value.

Market RRR Schedule In charting, a graphic representation of a portfolio's minimum acceptable rate of return at given levels of risk. On this chart, one axis represents a level of risk and the other axis represents the minimum acceptable rate of return. Under the homogenous expectations assumption, the market RRR schedule will always have a positive slope. The market RRR schedule is important in calculating whether an investment fits one's investment philosophy. See also: Markets efficient set of portfolios.

Market Sector 1. See: Sector. 2. A system for the classification of bonds whereby bonds are organized according to their sector as well as the type of bond each is. For example, bonds may be organized according to whether they are government or corporate.

Market Segmentation In marketing, a strategy that divides potential customers into different groups that are likely to respond to a certain marketing tactic. For example, given a product that would appeal to both young people and older people, a market segmentation strategy would divide tactics between the two age groups. That is, it might produce commercials on daytime television for the older people and viral internet advertisements for the younger people.

Market Sentiment A subjective measure of how investors are feeling about a security or market. Generally speaking, market sentiments are positive when stock prices are going up and negative when they are going down. Because feelings sometimes change more slowly than a market's underlying fundamentals, market sentiment helps explain why securities have a tendency to become either overvalued or undervalued. Some investors plan to make investment decisions in a way that disregards market sentiment, while others attempt to profit from it. See also: Crowd theory, Subjective probabilities, The Theory of Moral Sentiments.

Market Share-Weighted Index An index in which the price is determined by the price of individual stocks, weighted for the number of shares outstanding. For example, if the price of a component stock of the index changes, its effect on the index as a whole is proportionate to the number of shares the company has outstanding. This means that changes in price will affect the index more if the component company has more outstanding shares.

Market Surveillance On NASDAQ, a department that investigates and reports any suspected illegal behavior. Market Surveillance is an important department in maintaining a free, fair, and transparent market. Because NASDAQ is an electronic exchange, Market Surveillance conducts most of its investigations on computers.

Market Sweep An offer of a stock allowing institutional investors and (occasionally) high net-worth individuals to buy a large percentage of a company's equity, usually at a price higher than the previous offer of stock. Market sweeps are fairly common in takeovers; they may also be used as antitakeover measures.

Market Technicians Association A professional organization for technical analysts. Technical analysts use statistics to determine trends in security prices, and make or recommend investment decisions based on those trends. They do not attempt to determine the intrinsic value of securities, but instead focus on matters such as trade volume, demand, and volatility. The MTA establishes standards of ethical practice among technical analysts, provides a forum for discussing issues in the field, and operates the Chartered Market Technician program.

Market Timer A money manager who seeks a profit for clients from his/her own ability to predict when the market will climb and fall. That is, a market timer buys securities when he/she believes that they are about to increase in price and sells when he/she believes their prices will fall. A market timer may use technical analysis to discern future price movements.

Market Timing Costs Costs coming from a change in a security's price during a transaction from some source other than the transaction itself.

Market Tone The state of the market. A market tone may be either good or bad. A high trading volume with strong or at least decent prices is seen as a positive market tone, while any sort of instability or downturn is seen as a negative market tone.

Market Top The highest price for a security or index over a given period of time. For example, if Stock A has been on a bullish trend for a long time and later begins to decline, the market top is the highest price during its bull market. See also: Fulcrum point, Market bottom.

Market Value A subjective estimate of what a willing buyer would pay a willing seller for a given asset, assuming both have a reasonable knowledge of the asset's worth. Market value is important in both law and accounting. In the former, it is often used in assessing damages as the result of a lawsuit. In the latter, determining the market value of an asset (e.g. after depreciation) is important to determining the amount of tax owed on it. Value investors look for companies with market values below their book values, believing these companies to be undervalued.

Market Value Added The difference between the market value of an asset or company and the capital that shareholder or other investors have invested into it. A positive MVA means that the asset or company has increased in value while a negative MVA indicates the opposite. Obviously, an investor wants the highest MVA possible for his/her investments.

Market Value Ratios Any ratio that compares a security's current market price (or average market price over a period of time) to any item on its financial statement. One of the most common market value ratios is the price-earnings ratio, which measure the market price against the company's earnings for a given period of time. Fundamental analysts use market value ratios to help determine whether a security is overvalued or undervalued.

Market Versus Quote The difference between the last price at which a security was traded and the current bid or ask price. The MVQ is often low because the bid or ask is usually close to the last trade price. Illiquid securities, however, can have a higher MVQ. See also: Bid-Ask Spread.

Marketable Good A good that can be easily bought or sold with little or no impact on price. Examples of marketable goods include stocks in blue chip companies and U.S. Treasury securities. On exchanges, marketable goods usually have low bid-ask spreads.

Marketable Title Title to real estate where ownership is not disputed and documented so clearly that it is not disputable. Most of the time, property may only be sold if it has a marketable title.

Market-Based Corporate Governance System A form of corporate governance where representatives of shareholders, managers, employees, and others all sit on the board of directors. As with most forms of modern corporate governance, there is a heavy bias toward shareholders in a market-based corporate governance system because they provide most or all of the company's capital for operations. This system is both praised as efficient and derided for not taking broader interests into account.

Market-Based Forecasting The process of predicting the future spot rate by analyzing the current spot rate and/or the forward rate.

Marketecture A slang term for advertising that uses an unusual number of technical terms. Marketecture may be directed to experts, or it simply may be poorly executed marketing to the general public.

Marketer A person or company that conducts activities in order to acquire and retain customers or clients. This may include basic courtesies like returning phone calls and taking meetings. Very often, however, a marketer conducts large, expensive campaigns to encourage as many people as possible to buy a certain product. Marketing techniques in the latter instance include buying advertisements in the media, receiving endorsements from well-known experts and/or personalities, and generally aggressively pushing the product onto the target audience.

Market-Facing Describing a position or department that deals with customers. Market-facing departments include sales and customer service. They are responsible for the production of most of a company's revenue.

Market-Indexed CD A certificate of deposit with a variable interest rate that changes according to the performance of some stated market index. For example, the interest rate could be tied to the value of the Dow Jones Industrial Average. As with most CDs, however, the principal of a market-indexed CD is guaranteed.

Marketing All activities a company conducts in order to acquire and retain customers or clients. This may include basic courtesies like returning phone calls and taking meetings. It may also refer to a large, expensive campaign to encourage as many people as possible to buy a certain product. Marketing techniques in the latter instance include buying advertisements in the media, receiving endorsements from well-known experts and/or personalities, and generally aggressively pushing the product onto the target audience.

Market-Neutral Investing An investment strategy in which one seeks to make the same return regardless of the performance of the broader market. There is no single way of executing a market neutral strategy, but it usually involves taking a combination of long positions and short positions. For example, one may take a long position on one index while also taking a short position on a similar but not identical index. Market neutral investing may also involve some form of arbitrage.

Market-on-Close Order An order to buy or sell a security at the best price available as close as possible to the closing of an exchange.

Market-Out Clause A clause in some underwriting agreements abolishing the agreement under certain, defined circumstances. For example, if the economy suddenly enters a severe recession, or the stock market falls 25%, it is unlikely that investors will be interested in a risky IPO. The market-out clause could then absolve the underwriting syndicate of its responsibility without penalty.

Market-with-Protection Order A market order that is canceled and changed to a limit order if the market price for the security changes suddenly. For example, one may issue a market-with-protection order to buy a stock for $10 per share. If the price of that stock jumps to $18 per share before the order is entirely filled, the order is canceled and a limit order of a lesser amount (say, $12) is made. If the stock falls back to $12, the remainder of the order is filled. A market-with-protection order exists to protect investors from paying more than they wanted (or receiving less than they wished) for securities.

Markka The former currency of Finland. It was introduced in 1860, replacing the Russian ruble. Like most currencies, it was pegged to the U.S. dollar during the Bretton Woods period, and later to various currency baskets. It was replaced by the euro in 1999 and ceased circulating in 2002.

Markland An obsolete Scottish unit of area. A markland was the amount of land on which rent of eight (sometimes 12) ounces of silver could be charged. This system was used in western Scotland.

Markovian Dependence A situation where the observation of one data point in a time series is dependent on other observations in the same time series. See also: Markov property.

Markowitz Diversification Diversification of a portfolio with appropriate regard for the mathematical formulas in Markowitz portfolio theory. That is, Markowitz diversification occurs when one uses mathematical models to find the securities to place in a portfolio such that the portfolio has the highest possible return for its level of risk. One may engage in Markowitz diversification when one wishes to increase or decrease one's portfolio's risk, or when the portfolio was previously not diversified. See also: Markowitz portfolio theory.

Markowitz Efficient Frontier A graphical representation of the set of portfolios giving the highest level of expected return at different levels of risk. Harry Markowitz theorized that each level of risk contains one combination of assets giving the highest expected return. An efficient set of portfolios is represented as a line on a graph with risk as the x-axis and expected return as the y-axis; this representation is the Markowitz efficient frontier. See also: Markowitz Efficient Portfolio, Homogeneous Expectations Assumption.

Markowitz Efficient Portfolio In Markowitz Portfolio Theory, a portfolio with the highest level of return at a given level of risk. One who carries such a portfolio cannot further diversify to increase the expected rate of return without accepting a greater amount of risk. Likewise one cannot decrease his/her exposure to risk without proportionately decreasing the expected return. A Markowitz efficient portfolio is determined mathematically and plotted on a chart with risk as the x-axis and expected return as the y-axis. See also: Markowitz efficient set of portfolios, Homogeneous expectations assumption.

Marks and Numbers Symbols used to identify individual pieces of cargo on a ship. This is important in shipping to help ensure that all goods are delivered to the correct parties. See also: CUSIP number.

Markup 1. The additional price one pays when one buys a security from a broker-dealer. That is, when one buys a security, one pays the broker-dealer an extra percentage or a flat fee as commission. This markup forms the bulk of the broker-dealer's income. **2.** See: Spread. **3.** The extra amount a retailer charges a customer for a good over and above what it paid the wholesaler. For example, if one pays Wal-Mart $20 for a toaster, and Wal-Mart bought it from the manufacturer for $15, the markup is $5.

Marlboro Friday April 2, 1993. On this day, Philip Morris, the cigarette maker, told the market it would cut its prices to compete with generic brands. This marked part of a larger movement in the market away from consumer loyalty to brand name cigarettes. Philip Morris lost about a quarter of its share price and $10 billion in market capitalization on this day.

Marquee Asset A particularly valuable or important asset that a company owns. For example, a car manufacturer's three best producing factories may be considered its marquee assets. A marquee asset is also called a trophy asset. See also: Crown jewel.

Marriage Penalty The higher tax rate that some married couples pay when they file jointly for their income taxes. Married couples filing jointly have different tax brackets than single persons; this can work to the advantage of couples with highly disparate income and single income households; however, it can work to the disadvantage of couples with roughly the same income. One refers to this as the marriage penalty. Some married couples file as single person to avoid the marriage penalty.

Married Filing Jointly A situation in which a married couple files a single tax return. Married persons usually file jointly if only one spouse makes the majority of the income; if both spouses make a significant income, filing jointly may be more complicated than it is worth. When a married couple files jointly, each spouse is completely responsible for the tax liability.

Married Filing Separately A filing status in which a married couple files individual tax returns instead of a single return. When two spouses file separately, each is taxed like a single individual. This usually results in a higher combined tax liability, but it may be advantageous if one spouse has significantly higher expenses or deductions.

Married Put A strategy to reduce or eliminate the risk of price depreciation on a stock by buying a put option on that stock. When an investor owns a stock and is concerned about price depreciation, he/she may buy a put option, giving him/her the right but not the obligation to sell the stock at a relatively high strike price on or before the expiration date. If the price does depreciate, the investor exercises the option and sells the stock to cover losses and perhaps make a profit. If the price appreciates instead, the investor simply lets the option expire and may keep the stock or sell it at the higher price. A married put may be thought of as insurance against price depreciation.

Married Put and Stock A situation in which an investor buys a put while holding an equal position on the underlying asset. That is, an investor has a married put and stock when he/she buys a put and either buys or already owns the underlying asset. If the underlying asset increases in price, the investor allows the put to expire worthless. If it goes down in price, the investor can exercise the put and sell the underlying asset at the (higher) strike price. A married put and stock limits the investor's risk.

Married Taxpayer A person who is legally married on the final day of a tax year (which is usually the calendar year). In the United States, a married taxpayer has the option of being married filing separately or married filing jointly, depending on which option offers the most tax advantages.

Marry To match orders such that the net position is zero. That is, a dealer marries two clients when he/she finds a buyer and a seller for the same security in the same quantity.

Marry a Stock To buy and hold a stock regardless of its market movements. One who marries a stock has no intention to sell it for any foreseeable reason, irrespective of other opportunities, or of the stock's positive or negative performance. Most investment advisers recommend against marrying a stock, even for long-term investors.

Marshall-Lerner Condition In international trade, a theory stating that if the sum of price elasticity of a country's exports and the price elasticity of its imports is greater than one, a devaluation of that country's currency will improve its balance of trade. Devaluation does not improve the balance of trade if the sum is any lower.

Martin Act Legislation in New York State that, as amended, gives the New York Attorney General wide power and discretion in investigating financial fraud. The Martin Act allows the Attorney General to question brokers and other interested parties without first specifying whether he/she intends to pursue criminal charges or file a civil suit. The Attorney General does not need to show whether the person(s) being charged under the Act intended to commit misconduct.

Martin S. Feldstein An American economist. He was a prominent economic adviser to President Ronald Reagan, though the two disagreed on the increasing deficit. He served as president of the National Bureau of Economic Research from 1978 to 2008. Feldstein was born in 1939.

Martingale System An investment strategy in which an investor increases the size of his/her investment with each loss. For example, if an investor buys stock at $10 per share and the price goes to $5 per share, he/she may buy more stock at the new, lower price. In other words, with each loss the investor adds to the size of his/her portfolio, accepting additional risk. The idea behind ther Martingale system may be summarized as: "What goes down must come up." That is, eventually the security will begin to rise in price, resulting in must larger profits. This contrasts with the Anti-Martingale system, in which the investor increases his/her risk more with gains. Both systems are used in gambling as well as investment.

Marubozo In candlestick charting, the representation of a trading day where a security does not trade outside the range of its opening price and closing price. This is represented by a candle without upper or lower shadows which are the "wicks" on the candle. When a marubozo occurs on a gaining day, the opening price is the daily low and the closing price is the daily high; this is a bullish signal. When it occurs on a losing day, the opening price is the daily high and the closing price is the daily low; this is a bearish signal.

Marxian Unemployment Unemployment due to the nature of the capitalist system. Karl Marx argued that the capitalist class has an incentive to keep some workers unemployed because doing so keeps wages low. For example, if there are two workers for every available job, the employed workers are not in a position to demand a wage increase because the employers can simply hire the other workers. Marxism therefore views unemployment as an example of the failure of capitalism.

Marxism The economic and social philosophy espousing free access to goods and services, the lack of distinction between classes, the lack of state or government, and common ownership (not state ownership) of the means of production. Marxism asserts that the proletariat (those with no access to capital but who provide most of the labor) will inevitably overthrow the capitalist class and that the state, after a brief period in which it controls the means of production, will fade away to create an ideal society. Marxism is a type of communism. It is named for 19th-century economic philosopher Karl Marx.

Marxist A person who espouses free access to goods and services, the lack of distinction between classes, the lack of state or government, and common ownership (not state ownership) of the means of production. Marxists believe that the proletariat (those with no access to capital but who provide most of the labor) will inevitably overthrow the capitalist class and that the state, after a brief period in which it controls the means of production, will fade away to create an ideal society. Marxism is a type of communism.

Marz In Armenia, a political subdivision equivalent to a province.

Masajuro Shiokawa A Japanese economist and politician. Elected to the House of Representatives in 1967, he served (except for a period from 1996 to 2000) until 2003. He was Minister of Finance from 2001 to 2003. He was born in 1921.

Masaru Hayami A Japanese businessman who served as governor of the Bank of Japan from 1997 to 2003. He was known for following a tight monetary policy, which was very controversial because the yen was subject to deflationary pressures at the time. He justified this by claiming that the yen could not be loosened until Japan's economy deregulated and ended the power of monopolies. He lived from 1925 to 2009.

Masha A customary Indian unit of dry volume approximately equivalent to 0.97 grams.

Mass Customization A strategy in which a company attempts to market a product to a customer's individual wants and needs while still producing the products at high level. That is, mass customization combines features of custom service, where a company makes a product upon demand from the customer, and mass production, where a company makes a large number of products exactly the same and sells them to a large number of customers. A company engaging in mass customization may offer a basic package for a product and then allow a customer to add or subtract different features at his/her discretion.

Massachusetts Trust A trust whereby the trustee or trustees run a business on behalf of beneficiaries. That is, the trustees act as the managers and the beneficiaries act as shareholders. Beneficiaries may sell their position as beneficiaries. The trustees own all property associated with the business. Income from a Massachusetts trust may be taxed more favorably than other income. The term derives from the first such trust, which was formed in Massachusetts in the late 19th century to avoid local real estate regulation. It is also called a business trust or an unincorporated business organization.

Master Air Waybill A document describing goods to be transported by multiple airlines, usually internationally. The first airline issues a waybill to prove that the goods have been received and are ready for transport.

Master Fund A mutual fund or other fund that allows a shareholder to have access to other investment vehicles. For example, a master fund may be a fund of funds, which is a mutual fund that invests in other mutual funds. Likewise, it may be a mutual fund in which a feeder fund invests. In the latter case, shares of the feeder fund represent shares in the master fund, which, in turn, represents shares in the underlying securities. Master funds and similar structures are relatively common when the one fund or the other contains tax disadvantages for shareholders that the other fund remedies.

Master Limited Partnership A limited partnership with ownership units that may be traded on an exchange. A limited partnership consists of a general partner, who manages the venture, and limited partners, who simply provide capital. A master limited partnership allows limited partners to buy and sell units of the venture as if they were shares in a publicly-traded company. Limited partners often receive cash distributions, which are similar to dividends, on a regular basis. This business form combines the tax advantages of a partnership, which does not pay tax on its profit, with the liquidity of a publicly-traded company. It is also called a publicly traded partnership.

Master Notes Short-term debt securities issued by the Federal Farm Credit Bank with a face value of $25 million. They mature one year after issue and pay a coupon linked to LIBOR or another benchmark rate. The holder of a master note may change the principal amount by up to 25% or use it as the underlying asset in a put or a call. These features give master notes a great deal of flexibility.

Master of Business Administration A graduate degree that represents advanced study of business. An MBA shows that the recipient has completed theoretical, and perhaps also practical, coursework in how to manage a company, construct a business model, and generally run a business. A person holding an MBA ordinarily commands a much higher starting salary than one who does not, at least in finance, consulting, and a few other sectors.

Master Pension Plan A retirement plan designed by a bank or other financial institution. When creating or updating employee benefits for a company, an employer may look at a master pension plan and adapt it to the company's individual needs. It is also called a prototype plan.

Master Trust A trust into which a large number of investors deposit money. The investors then allow the trustee to invest the money on their behalf and keep the profits. A master trust is useful because the larger number of securities in the investors' combined funds can entitle them to discounts or other preferential treatment. An example of a master trust is a unit investment trust, which is an unmanaged portfolio the investor may buy.

Mat A general term for Russian profanity. The use of mat is illegal in Russia, though this is only enforced sporadically. However, inadvertently using mat can make it more difficult (or at least awkward) to conduct business in Russian.

Matador Bond A bond issued in Spain on a Spanish exchange by a non-Spanish company. Before the introduction of the euro, matador bonds were denominated in pesetas. All matador bonds were corporate bonds, but they could be any other type of bond. See also: Domestic bond, Foreign bond.

Matador Market Informal; a stock market in Spain. The term is most often used by foreigners outside of Spain.

Matched and Lost A broker's report to a client that an order was not executed because another order with equal priority was executed instead. When an order is made, a broker seeks to match and execute it with an equal but opposite order. If two orders are made at the same time with the same price and are competing to be executed, they have equal priority. Brokers then flip a coin to determine which order is executed. The losing broker makes the matched and lost report to the client.

Matched Book A situation in which the funds a bank or brokerage has borrowed equal the funds it has lent to customers, where both borrowed and lent funds have the same maturity. A matched book is one way a financial institution can reduce its risk because a matched book does not add to its liabilities.

Matched Maturities A situation in which a bank or other financial institution has arranged it such that loans it has made and debts it has incurred mature at the same time. When a bank matches maturities, it ensures that it can pay its obligations with the proceeds from its assets, as long as no one defaults.

Matched Orders 1. Two equal but opposite orders to buy and sell a security. A clearing house matches orders so that all orders can be filled in due order. **2.** The practice of two investors buying and selling a security to each other in order to create the impression of higher trading volume. This is an illegal practice intended to artificially inflate the security's price.

Matched Sale Purchase Transactions A practice in which the Federal Reserve sells government securities with the proviso that it will buy back these same securities from the same party at the same price, usually within a week or two. This is a way for the Federal Reserve to tighten the money supply temporarily. It is a type of reverse repurchase agreement.

Matching Contribution Money an employer offers to an employee's IRA or other retirement plan. Normally employers will offer an equal amount that the employee contributes up to a certain dollar amount or percentage of income. This is considered an employee benefit and allows a worker to save more (and accrue applicable interest) without enduring financial hardship.

Matching Function The mathematical relationship between the number of unemployed persons who find jobs and the number of jobs available over time. It is used in the study of frictional unemployment, which is unemployment experienced by those who have lost their positions and are actively looking for another. See also: Christopher Pissarides.

Matching Grant A grant made in the same amount as another grant. For example, a company may match the money its customers donate for breast cancer research up to $10,000. Matching grants are commonly made by corporations, charitable organizations, and governments.

Matching Strategy An immunization strategy in which one matches the duration of assets in a portfolio to the duration of the liabilities. Duration is the number of years until the investor receives the present value of all income from a bond (including interest and principal), and is used to gauge a bond's sensitivity to interest rate changes. A matching strategy is intended to reduce the portfolio's sensitivity to interest rates in order to reduce the risk of loss to the holder.

Material 1. Describing information that is or may be relevant for a firm's operations. For example, if a VCR company is experiencing a dearth of demand because most of its potential customers are buying DVD players, this is material information that will likely need to be disclosed to shareholders. See also: Immaterial. **2.** Raw substances that a company uses to make its product. For example, an oil refinery's material is crude oil, which it makes into refined oil.

Material Adverse Change or Effect A clause in some merger and acquisition contracts allowing the acquiring to cancel a deal before it is finalized if material information is revealed that negatively impacts the target company's stock price. See also: Due diligence.

Material Goods A somewhat derogatory term for goods and services, especially those considered unnecessary luxuries. The term is used most frequently by critics of capitalism and/or conspicuous consumption.

Material Man A person or company that provides raw material to a construction site, where it is assembled or put in place. A material man is paid for this service.

Material Naturalism In Roman Catholic social justice teaching, an all-encompassing term for the belief of political and economic systems not based upon reverence for God. Examples of material naturalist systems include both capitalism and communism. Catholic social justice teaching holds that material naturalism inevitably tends toward injustice of one sort or another.

Material News Information likely to affect a stock's price. Examples include mergers and acquisitions, information on earnings over the most recent quarter or year, or announcements of regulatory changes. If material news is particularly good or bad, it can cause large fluctuations in the stock's price, increasing its volatility. For this reason, publicly-traded companies usually hint about what material news will say before they actually announce it. This allows the market to absorb the information gradually so as to reduce pressure for volatility. Material news is also called material information. See also: Priced out.

Material Participation The regular involvement in the running of a business. Material participation separates passive income (that is, the income of an investor) and active income (that is, wages, salary, and profit from one's business). For that reason, material participation affects the tax treatment of income.

Materiality The relevance of information that may cause a security's price to increase or decrease. Companies must report material information to the SEC and, by extension, to the public, in order to promote transparency and efficiency in the market.

Materials Requirement Planning An early computer system for managing inventory. The materials requirement planning created forecasts of future sales that helped businesses determine the materials they needed to have ready for sale at a given time. As other programs became more common, the materials requirement planning program was integrated into more sophisticated systems.

Mathematical Programming The use of a computer or other program that seeks to maximize return on an investment or find the most efficient use of limited resources by simulating real life situations with mathematical models. Mathematical programming seeks to predict future events by using probabilities and other mathematical devices. There are a number of types of mathematical programming; among the most important are linear programming, decision theory, and queuing theory.

Matilda Bond A foreign bond denominated in Australian dollars and traded in Australia. In order to raise capital from Australian investors, a foreign company may choose to sell a bond in Australia. A Matilda bond is also known as a kangaroo bond. See also: Bulldog bond, Samurai bond, Yankee bond.

Matrix Trading An investment strategy involving profiting from unusual yield curves on different-rated bonds. For example, when a junk bond and an investment-grade bond have, by some anomaly, similar yields temporarily, an investor owning a junk bond may initiate a bond swap and purchase the investment-grade bond with the proceeds. When the yield curves return to normal, the investor swaps them back. This allows the investor to have the greatest possible yield at the lowest possible risk. See also: Fixed income market.

Matte In numismatics, a finish on the surface of a coin that is deliberately grainy to the touch. Matte finishes have become rare for modern coins.

Matte Proof In numismatics, a proof coin that is deliberately grainy to the touch. Matte finishes have become rare for modern coins, but were made occasionally in the early 20th century.

Mattha A Burmese unit of mass approximately equivalent to 4.08 grams.

Mature Company A company at the stage in its life cycle when it grows at the rate of the economy at large. This is marked by earnings growth (or shrinkage) in line with most of the rest of the economy. Mature companies often pay higher dividends than those in a growth industry or a transition industry. See also: Three-phase DDM.

Mature Economy A stable economy with low growth and generally low inflation. It especially refers to an economy with a stable population; that is, there are fewer pressures to create jobs for a larger workforce, but at the same time, there is enough growth for the economy to financially support retirees as they age and need more care. See also: Mature company.

Mature Industry An industry at the stage in its life cycle where it grows at the rate of the economy at large. This is marked by earnings growth (or shrinkage) in line with most of the rest of the economy. Companies in mature industries often pay higher dividends than those in a growth industry or a transition industry. See also: Three-Phase DDM.

Matured Noninterest-Bearing Debt Bonds and other debt that have matured and no longer earn interest, but which the holder has not redeemed. For example, if one purchases a savings bond with a 20 year maturity and forgets about it until 25 years later, the savings bond is matured noninterest-bearing debt during the five years after its maturity. The term is most often used with respect to government bonds, such as war bonds, that are no longer issued and in which all previous issues have matured.

Matured RRSP In Canada, an RRSP (which is the equivalent of an IRA) into which the annuitant is no longer making payment. Instead, the annuitant receives payments. RRSPs generally mature after the annuitant's retirement.

Maturing Liability A debt one must repay in full in a short period of time. It especially refers to a medium- or long-term debt.

Maturity The time when the issuer of a bond or other debt security must repay the principal or when a borrower must repay a loan in full. For example, if a company issues $1 million in bonds with a maturity of 10 years, the company must repay $1 million to bondholders 10 years after the issue. The amount owed at maturity is usually the same as the debt or loan's face value. After maturity, the loan or debt ceases to exist, assuming all parties have fulfilled their obligations. See also: Expiration.

Maturity by Maturity Bidding A form of underwriting for bonds in which underwriters make bids to the issuer on part of the new issue by maturity. That is, the issuer places parts of the issue on auction according to the length until maturity. This allows underwriters to make bids on part, rather than all, of the issue, which allows more small underwriters to participate. See also: Auction, AON.

Maturity Date The date on which the issuer of a debt instrument must repay the principal in total. For example, a bond with a period of 10 years has a maturity date 10 years after its issue. The maturity date also indicates the period of time during which the lender or bondholder will receive interest payments. It is important to note that, despite the existence of a maturity date, many debt securities are callable and the issuer may redeem them before the maturity date under some circumstances.

Maturity Guarantee The benefit of an insurance policy or annuity to which the policyholder or annuitant is entitled after a certain number of years. The amount of the benefit as well as the number of years (which is usually 10) is stated in the contract.

Maturity Phase In an industry life cycle, the period of time after an industry has grown rapidly but before it begins to decline. Different analyses posit different stages of an industry life cycle (usually four to five), but all emphasize that an industry's maturity phase reduces redundant products and processes, and is usually marked by companies in the industry acquiring one another. For example, in the video cassette recording (VCR) industry, after a period of rapid growth and technological innovation, a maturity phase occurred. The VHS technology overran the Betamax technology, and different companies selling VCRs attempted to corner a greater market share for their own (identical) versions of the product. It is also called the consolidation phase.

Maturity Spread The difference in return between two bonds, one with a longer maturity than the other. Most of the time, the bond with the longer maturity has the higher return, though this is not always the case. See also: Yield Curve.

Maun In Islamic law, a small item one may lend to another person. For example, one may lend a book to a friend. Ariyah is the practice of lending a maun.

Maund An obsolete Indian unit of weight variously equivalent to values between 15 and 50 kilograms.

Mauritanian Ouguiya The currency of Mauritania. It was introduced in 1973, when Mauritania left the CFA franc currency zone. It is one of only two currencies not based on factors of 10; each ouguiya is divided into five khoums.

Mauritian Dollar The currency of Mauritius between 1820 and 1877. It was pegged at first to the Indian rupee and later to the British pound. It was replaced by the Mauritian rupee.

Mauritian Rupee The currency of Mauritius. It was introduced in 1874, replacing the Mauritian dollar and the Indian rupee. It was pegged at par to the Indian rupee until 1934, when it changed its peg to the British pound (the currency to which the Indian rupee was itself pegged). Mauritius maintained the peg to the pound until 1979.

Max Pain The expiration date of an unexercised option. The term is short for "maximum pain," which implies that a trader who does not exercise an option will lose money most of the time. See also: Maximum pain theory.

Maximizer A software program used by brokers and investment advisers. Maximizer allows users to track a client's investments and changes to the client's investment goals. It also allows users to network with other users to communicate information on market movements to each other and to clients. Maximizer also serves as a computerized central location for all of one's business files.

Maximum Price Fluctuation On an exchange, the maximum amount by which a contract or security may decline in price during a trading session. This may be a dollar amount, but is usually some percentage of its opening price. Exchanges set maximum price fluctuations in order to reduce volatility in the market and to reduce pressure for panic selling or panic buying.

Maximum Return Criterion The principle of seeking the highest possible return. More specifically, the MRC states that an investor, when presented with plans having different returns at a given risk, will choose the plan with the highest return. While not all researchers believe that all investors use the MRC even unconsciously, many defend it as holding "approximately" in a given situation. See also: Homogenous expectations assumption.

May Day 1. Informal; the first date on which brokerages were allowed to charge commissions below the previous minimum commissions. On May Day, brokers were permitted to negotiate commissions directly with clients for the first time. May Day occurred on 1 May 1975. **2.** A holiday for workers that occurs on the first of May. May Day is a significant day for leftist groups and other proponents for the working class. It is more commonly celebrated in Europe than in the Americas. See also: Labor Day.

May Expand In investing, an indication by a broker to another that he/she may increase the size of an order to buy or sell a security.

Mayaw A Burmese unit of length equivalent to 4.7625 millimeters.

MBIA, Inc. A private corporation that guarantees principal and interest payments on debt securities and some asset-backed securities. Founded in 1974 upon the merger of several casualty insurance companies, MBIA originally specialized in guaranteeing municipal bonds. It has since expanded to other investment vehicles such as corporate bonds and mortgage-backed securities. Clients are issuers who pay a fee to MBIA in exchange for the insurance. MBIA insurance typically guarantees the highest possible credit rating and lowers the overall cost of the issue.

MBS Clearing Corporation A clearing corporation for transactions involving mortgage-backed securities. That is, it settles MBS transactions and ensures that the appropriate securities change hands and that all of the correct parties are paid the correct amount. It was established in 1979.

MC 1. ISO 3166-1 alpha-2 code for the Principality of Monaco. This is the code used in international transactions to and from Monegasque bank accounts. **2.** ISO 3166-2 geocode for Monaco. This is used as an international standard for shipping to Monaco.

McCain-Feingold Act Legislation in the United States, passed in 2002, that changed the way that campaigns for federal political offices are financed. It banned soft money contributions, which were unregulated, usually large, contributions to the national party committees, instead of individual candidates. It also required political advertisements to state what person or group paid for them.

McCarran-Ferguson Act Legislation in the United States, passed in 1945, that exempts insurance companies from anti-trust law, except in cases of boycott, intimidation or coercion. It also states that federal law does not preempt state regulation of insurance (that is, state regulations trump federal law) unless federal legislation explicitly states otherwise. The act remains controversial.

McClellan Oscillator An indicator of future market movements related to the number of advancing or declining securities on the NYSE, as opposed to the average price change. The McClellan Oscillator is calculated by taking a 19-day exponential moving average (EMA) of the net number of securities that are advancing and subtracting a 39-day EMA of the same thing. That is, the McClellan Oscillator is

expressed as: Oscillator = (19-day EMA of securities advancing - securities declining) - (39-day EMA of securities advancing - securities declining). The importance of the McClellan Oscillator comes from the fact that price averages may be driven by only a few securities. That is, a few securities may be making large gains while the rest of the securities on the NYSE are posting losses, or vice versa. A price average, then, may not reflect the true conditions of the market. The McClellan Oscillator attempts to control for this.

McClellan Summation Index A version of the McClellan Oscillator adapted for long-term trends. It is an indicator of future market movements related to the number of advancing or declining securities on the NYSE as opposed to the average price change. The McClellan Summation Index is calculated by taking a 19-day exponential moving average (EMA) of the net number of securities that are advancing and subtracting a 39-day EMA of the same thing (which is the calculation of the McClellan Oscillator) and adding that to the previous trading day's Summation Index. That is, the McClellan Summation Index is expressed as: Oscillator = (19-day EMA of securities advancing - securities declining) - (39-day EMA of securities advancing - securities declining) + Previous day's McClellan Summation Index. The importance of the McClellan Summation Index comes from the fact that price averages may be driven by only a few securities. That is, a few securities may be making large gains while the rest of the securities on the NYSE are posting losses, or vice versa. A price average, then, may not reflect the true conditions of the market. The McClellan Summation Index attempts to control for this.

McCulloch v. Maryland An 1819 United States Supreme Court case holding that the federal government has the ability to pass laws for which the Constitution does not expressly provide, so long as they are used to further the powers that the Constitution gives to the federal government. Specifically, the Court ruled that Congress had the authority to charter the Second Bank of the United States even though the Constitution did not specify a power to charter banks. McCulloch v. Maryland was one of the most important early cases establishing federal supremacy over the states in matters even tangentially related to the powers that the Constitution gives Congress.

MCF ISO 4217 code for the Monegasque franc. It was introduced in 1837. From 1960 until its replacement by the euro in 1999, all coins in circulation corresponded with those of the French franc. The Monegasque franc was pegged to the French at a one-to-one ratio and the two currencies circulated alongside each other in Monaco.

McFadden Act Legislation in the United States, passed in 1927, that prohibited federally-chartered banks from operating in multiple states except to the extent permitted by state law. The McFadden Act was largely repealed by the Riegle-Neal Act.

McJob Slang; a job with low pay and few or no benefits that requires few skills and offers few opportunities for advancement. McJobs have low prestige and may be temporary. In any case, they have high turnover. Generally they are in the retail or service sectors. The term is derived from McDonald's, a fast-food restaurant chain.

MCO GOST 7.67 Latin three-letter geocode for Monaco. The code is used for transactions to and from Monegasque bank accounts and for international shipping to Monaco. As with all GOST 7.67 codes, it is used primarily in Cyrillic alphabets.

MD 1. ISO 3166-1 alpha-2 code for the Republic of Moldova. This is the code used in international transactions to and from Moldovan bank accounts. **2.** ISO 3166-2 geocode for Moldova. This is used as an international standard for shipping to Moldova. Each Moldovan subdivision has its own code with the prefix "MD." For example, the code for the City of Cahul is ISO 3166-2:MD-CA.

MDA GOST 7.67 Latin three-letter geocode for Moldova. The code is used for transactions to and from Moldovan bank accounts and for international shipping to Moldova. As with all GOST 7.67 codes, it is used primarily in Cyrillic alphabets.

MDG GOST 7.67 Latin three-letter geocode for Madagascar. The code is used for transactions to and from Malagasy bank accounts and for international shipping to Madagascar. As with all GOST 7.67 codes, it is used primarily in Cyrillic alphabets.

MDL ISO 4217 code for the Moldovan leu. It was introduced in 1993, replacing the cupon, which was itself a temporary currency to replace the Soviet ruble.

MDV GOST 7.67 Latin three-letter geocode for Maldives. The code is used for transactions to and from Maldivian bank accounts and for international shipping to Maldives. As with all GOST 7.67 codes, it is used primarily in Cyrillic alphabets.

Meals and Entertainment Expense Money that a business spends in the course of buying meals for or otherwise entertaining a client, customer, or employee. In the United States, one may deduct meals and entertainment expenses from one's taxable income, subject to certain restrictions. In general, one may only deduct up to 50% of meals and entertainment and must be able to prove that one conducted business with the person that one was entertaining.

Mean Return 1. See: Expected return. **2.** See: Average return.

Meandrathal A slang term for a person who cannot speak in public very well. The term is especially applied when such a person botches a presentation.

Mean-Variance Analysis The process of portfolio selection that assumes that every rational investor, at a given level of risk, will accept only the largest expected return. More specifically, mean-variance analysis attempts to account for risk and expected return mathematically to help the investor find a portfolio with the maximum return for the minimum about of risk. A Markowitz efficient porfolio represents just that: the most expected return at a given amount of risk (sometimes excluding zero risk). Harry Markowitz first began developing this form of analysis in an article published in 1952 and received the Nobel prize for economics for his work in 1990. See also: Homogenous expectations assumption, Markowitz efficient set of portfolios.

Measurement Error The difference between the value of some quantity and the value obtained by measuring it. It is nearly impossible to attain accurate measurements all the time, especially when one uses a single means of calculation. For this reason, when measuring the value of a company or asset, many analysts will check and double-check their work, and perhaps calculate the value using a different method, in order to ensure accuracy. See also: Audit, Due diligence.

Mecate A Mexican unit of area approximately equivalent to 1/10th of one acre.

Mechanical Investing Any investment strategy that uses a computerized system to make trades according to a certain algorithm. That is, one may program a mechanical investing system to buy or sell different security under specified circumstances. Mechanical investing often uses complicated mathematical formulas to identify the ideal times to buy and sell securities in large batches. Its use is intended to minimize the role human emotion plays in investing. See also: Computerized investing, Algorithmic Trading, Program Trading, Behavioral finance.

Medaky A Slovak slang term for a eurocent. Literally, the term means "copper."

Medallion Signature Guarantee In securities transactions, a guarantee by members of the Medallion Program that the signature(s) of the seller of a security is in fact the signature of the person(s) authorized to sell that security. The guarantee is backed up by an insurance policy and protects the buyer from any financial loss as the result of securities fraud. It reduces risk to buyers and allows securities transactions to be processed immediately. The guarantor is a bank or other member firm of the Securities Transfer Association.

Median In a data set, the value that half the data points fall below and half the data points fall above. It is used along with the mean; it is not as influenced by extreme values as the mean.

Median Market Cap A market capitalization figure where half of the securities in a portfolio have a higher market capitalization and half have a lower one.

Median Voter The theoretical person who is precisely in the middle of the political spectrum of his/her community. That is, the median voter's political views are equidistant from both the most right-wing and the most left-wing person in his community. In electoral politics, it is thought that the median voter (or group of median voters) tips the election to one candidate or the other. As a result, many politicians seek to appear to be moderate prior to an election.

Mediation An extrajudicial means of resolving a dispute between a broker and a client in which the parties agree to make their cases before an impartial person or panel. Very often, mediation is conducted through FINRA. Mediation is less expensive than arbitration and is certainly cheaper than a lawsuit.

Medicaid In the United States, a government program providing certain kinds of medical care to those who do not have or cannot afford health insurance. Medicaid is funded by the federal government, but administered by individual states. As a result, coverage varies state-by-state and is sometimes very limited. See also: Medicare.

Medicare A United States government program providing certain kinds of medical care to persons over 65 years of age. Medicare is funded by the federal government and divided into several parts. Medicare Part A is free (or rather paid with taxes) and pays for visits to the hospital, as well as some other costs. Medicare Part B covers doctor visits if the elderly person pays an extra premium, and Medicare Part D pays for prescription drugs in exchange for a premium. Participation in Parts B and D is voluntary, but participation in Part A is automatic. See also: Medicaid, Social Security, Obamacare.

Medicare Tax A certain percentage of wages or salaries used to finance Medicare. Employees are required to contribute 1.45% of their income to pay for Medicare, with no income limit. Employers are required to make matching contributions for each employee.

Medicare Wage Any wage or salary that is subject to the Medicare tax. As the name implies, the Medicare tax is a tax on top of one's income tax and Social Security tax that goes to fund Medicare. Generally speaking, only ordinary wages and salaries are Medicare wages. Tips and bonuses usually are exempt from the tax.

Medimnos An ancient Greek unit of dry volume approximately equivalent to 52.4 liters.

Medium of Exchange Anything used as money. A medium of exchange is most commonly a currency, but it may be a commodity agreed-upon in a certain area as having a value. Examples include gold, silver, or even seashells.

Medium Term Note An unconventional bond note with a maturity period usually between five and 10 years continually offered through various brokers, rather than issued all at once like other bonds. Unlike most bonds, which are bought and sold on exchanges, MTNs are normally purchased through an MTN brokerage, which operates on a best effort basis and is under no obligation to sell a certain amount on behalf of the issuer. Unlike corporate bonds, MTNs are almost always marketed to institutions and high net-worth individuals and have few or no small and medium investors. Beyond that, they functions much like corporate bonds: unsecured, non-callable, with fixed coupons and investment grade ratings. MTNs have become a favorite form of fundraising for large corporations, government agencies, and sovereign states. This demand has led to more complex MTNs, with floating interest rates and maturity periods from nine months to 30 years or longer. See also: Euro medium term note.

Medium-Term Financial Strategy A financial strategy with a term longer than the short term but shorter than the long term. The exact length varies according to the usage; it could be a few weeks or a few years. In general, however, a medium-term financial strategy outlines investment and other financial goals for any time between roughly six months and one year.

Medium-Term Loan A loan with a maturity generally between one year and 10 years. For example, if one borrows $10,000 to pay for college, and must repay it in seven years, then one has taken out a medium-term loan. A major example of a medium-term loan is a 10-year Treasury note.

Medium-Term Note Retail An unsecured bond issued by a multinational corporation in order to finance its operations, with a maturity of between one and 10 years. Retail notes are issued at par for $1,000 per note; they pay a fixed interest rate for the first nine months or so, after which the coupon payments may vary. Retail notes invested in an IRA may be tax-deferred.

Meeting Assassin A derogatory term for a person who asks numerous questions and makes an excessive number of comments during a business meeting, extending its time and annoying the other participants.

Meff Renta Fija A derivatives exchange in Barcelona. It is especially known for the trade of derivatives on financial instruments such as interest rates. See also: Bolsa de Barcelona, Madrid Interbank Offered Rate.

Mega Cap Describing a publicly-traded company with an extraordinarily large amount of market capitalization. Though there is no fixed measurement, a mega-cap company typically has a market capitalization over $200 billion. Some brokerages or exchanges may have slightly different definitions of mega-cap. Some indices track mega-cap companies, as do some exchange traded funds. See also: Large-cap, Mid-cap, Low-cap, Micro-cap.

Megye In Hungary, a political subdivision equivalent to a county.

Mei Moses World All Art Index An index tracking sales of fine art. Though art is an illiquid investment, it is used as a hedge against inflation as it tends to maintain its value over time.

Meile A German unit of length equivalent to 7,420.54 meters. It should be noted that this measure was for a geographic meile; traditional measures varied in different German-speaking areas. The meile became obsolete as German-speaking countries adopted the metric system in the 1870s.

Meisrin An obsolete Irish unit of volume approximately equivalent to 660 milliliters.

Melbourne Mint A former mint in Australia. In the 19th and early 20th centuries, it was used exclusively to issue gold sovereigns. Between 1927 and 1967, it issued all coins in Australia.

Mello Roo A form of financing allowing a municipality or other local government such as a county or school district to issue bonds for very expensive projects. The municipality pays for Mello Roo bonds with a special tax levied exclusively for that purpose. In order for a municipality to become eligible to issue Mello Roo bonds, its residents must approve a measure by a two-thirds margin.

Melon An informal term for zero. For example, an investment may be said to generate a melon.

Melting Slang; a situation in which a trader suffers such large losses (usually in a short period of time) that he/she can no longer continue to trade on the market.

Member A person, normally a broker, who has a seat on a stock exchange. This means that he/she is allowed to make trades on the floor of that exchange. Most exchanges do not allow a company to be a member, so the membership for a member firm formally belongs to an individual employee. Memberships are bought and sold at market price because most exchanges have a finite number.

Member Bank In the United States, a federally- or state-chartered bank that has joined the Federal Reserve System. Such banks must buy stock in the Federal Reserve. In general, member banks are subject to more regulations than nonmember banks. However, they have access to more of the Federal Reserve's services.

Member Firm A broker-dealer firm in which at least one of the principal officers is allowed to trade on the floor of an exchange. To become a member, one needs to purchase a membership or a seat on the exchange, which can be very expensive. There are usually a set number of memberships in an exchange; for example, on the New York Stock Exchange, there are 1,366 seats, which may cost up to $1 million each, and which may be bought or sold to different firms. Most exchanges do not recognize member firms, only individual members; that is, they consider members to be the brokers or dealers on the floor, rather than the firms they represent.

Member of Household Any person who may be claimed as a dependent on one's tax return. A member of the household may qualify one for the dependent exemption. Members of a household include children, spouses, parents, nieces or nephews, and anyone not related who has lived at one's house for an entire year.

Member Short Sale Ratio In technical analysis, a ratio of short sales made by members of the New York Stock Exchange to the total short sales on a given trading day. Members of the NYSE are thought to be especially knowledgeable about the direction of the market and investors often sell short when they are feeling bearish. Thus, a high member short sale ratio is considered a bearish signal, while a low ratio can be thought bullish.

Membership An individual or firm's right to trade on an exchange floor. Memberships are bought and sold according to an individual's or firm's needs and desires, and they can be very expensive. Most exchanges have a set number of memberships; for example on the New York Stock Exchange there are 1366 seats, which may cost up to $1 million each. Most exchanges do not recognize only recognize individual members; member firms are usually informal terms for broker-dealer firms that have at least one principal officer with a seat on an exchange.

Memorandum 1. Any written document recording a proposal, decision, policy or anything else. Memorandums are very common in business and are used to ensure that information is communicated. **2.** See: Private placement memorandum. **3.** See: Memorandum of understanding.

Memorandum of Understanding An agreement between two parties, usually two companies, outlining the rights and responsibilities each has for a particular venture or project. A memorandum of understanding is intentionally vague and is usually the first step toward a full contract. Negotiations usually continue after the MOU is signed. However, an MOU is more formal and legally binding than a handshake agreement and is enforceable in a court of law.

Meng In Inner Mongolia, a political subdivision below a province but above a county.

Mental Accounting A concept stating that investors and people divide up their current and future assets into different categories. These categories may be roughly thought of as "safety capital," which one uses to fulfill personal needs and make low-risk investments, and "risk capital," which one uses for high-risk transactions. Mental accounting is important to understanding certain investment decisions: rather than treating each unit of money as if it were exactly the same, people generally assign it into what they need and what they do not need. This effectively turns money, which is fungible, into something that is not fungible. See also: Behavioral economics.

Mental Health Parity Act of 1996 Legislation in the United States that required the annual caps and lifetime maximum benefits for mental health insurance to be equal to those for other forms of health insurance. Critics contended that the Act had little effect and was easily avoided by insurance companies. It was largely repealed as part of TARP.

Menu The bids and offers available to an investor, arranged according to price and quantity. This helps the investor or his/her broker make decisions according to one's investment goals and what can currently be done.

Mercato Italiano Futures The futures exchange for Borsa Italiana. Italian government bonds trade on the Mercato Italiano Futures.

Merchandise Any and all movable products that a company intends to sell, especially at the retail level.

Mercosur An international organization consisting of Argentina, Brazil, Paraguay, and Uruguay, as well as several associate members in Latin America. The organization mandates the lowering of tariffs and other trade barriers, with an eye toward eventually eliminating restrictions on the movement of capital, labor, and goods and services. It aims to increase trade by and between countries in South America; critics in the United States and elsewhere worry that it will prevent the proposed Free Trade Area of the Americas from coming to fruition. See also: Free trade, Gaucho.

Mercury Dime A silver coin minted by the United States between 1916 and 1945. It was worth 1/10 of one dollar. It featured the Roman god Mercury on the observe and was also called the Winged Liberty dime.

Mergent, Inc. A publisher of advisory letters and other financial information. It was formerly associated with Moody's.

Merger A decision by two companies to combine all operations, officers, structure, and other functions of business. Mergers are meant to be mutually beneficial for the parties involved. In the case of two publicly-traded companies, a merger usually involves one company giving shareholders in the other its stock in exchange for surrendering the stock of the first company. See also: Acquisition.

Merger Arbitrage A strategy in which a hedge fund buys shares in two companies that are in the process of merging and sells the shares after the merger is complete. Merger arbitrage can be profitable because stock prices often decline in the process of a merger because of the possibility that the merger negotiations will fail. They then go to a higher price after the merger is complete. Because this phenomenon is so consistent, the hedge fund using merger arbitrage effectively makes a riskless profit.

Merger Monday A Monday on which several mergers and acquisitions are announced. Merger Mondays happen when the details of the mergers are finalized over the weekend and announced on Monday.

Mergers and Acquisitions A term referring to any process by which two companies become one. In a merger, two companies integrate their operations, management, stock, and everything else, while, in an acquisition, one company buys another. Mergers and acquisitions may also refer to all legal, financial, and other issues involved before a merger or acquisition can take place.

Merhale A Turkish measure of length approximately equivalent to 45.48 kilometers. It became obsolete when Turkey made the metric system mandatory in 1933.

Merindad In medieval Spain, a political subdivision roughly equivalent to a county.

Meripeninkulma A Finnish unit of nautical distance approximately equivalent to 1,852 meters or one nautical mile. It became obsolete when Finland adopted the metric system in 1880.

Merit Good In economics, a good to which persons are believed to have a right. That is, a merit good is something that should be available for free or at reduced prices because it is necessary and the free market does not provide sufficient incentives to produce it. Examples of merit goods may include education and health care, though different jurisdictions define merit goods differently.

Merit-Based Scholarship A scholarship available to persons based only on academic qualifications. For example, a university may offer scholarships to undergraduate students who maintain a GPA over 3.75 (out of 4.0).

Meritocracy A system in which the best qualified persons are rewarded for their achievements. That is, talent and hard work are rewarded in a meritocracy, rather than other factors like personal relationships or tenure. Meritocracy in a corporation may cause better results, but certain positions are still commonly kept within a family or friendship network.

Meritocrat A person who believes that the best qualified persons should be rewarded for their achievements. That is, talent and hard work are rewarded in a meritocracy, rather than other factors like personal relationships or tenure. Meritocracy in a corporation may cause better results, but certain positions are still commonly kept within a family or friendship network.

Merke A Norwegian unit of weight approximately equivalent to 250 grams.

Merrill Lynch & Co. A formerly independent financial services company. Founded in 1914, it has been publicly traded since 1971 and specializes in investment management and advising, insurance, banking, and capital markets services, among others. It is perhaps best known for its global private client services, especially wealth management for individuals and businesses. Because of its over-exposure to mortgage-backed securities in the credit crunch that began in 2007, Merrill Lynch was acquired by Bank of America in January 2009.

Mervyn King A British economist. In 2003, he became Governor of the Bank of England, a role in which he has been known for favoring higher interest rates to fight inflation. He was born in 1948.

Mesorregiao In Brazil, a political subdivision roughly equivalent to a county. A mesorregiao consists of municipalities that band together to perform certain functions in common.

Mesta In Slovakia, a political subdivision equivalent to a city. It is a type of obce (municipality).

Method of Payment The way one pays for a transaction. The three most basic methods of payment are cash, credit, and payment-in-kind (or bartering). These three methods are used in basic transactions; for example, one may pay for a candy bar with cash, a credit card or, theoretically, even by trading another candy bar. However, they are also used in large transactions; mergers and acquisitions often occur with some combination of cash, bonds (which is a form of credit), and stock (often exchanging one stock for another). See also: Sale.

Metical The currency of Mozambique. It was introduced in 1980, replacing the Mozambican escudo. It suffered from hyperinflation for most of its history and was, for a time, the least valuable currency in the world. Inflation has slowed since the introduction of the second metical in 2006, but has remained over 10%.

Me-Too Product A product created by a company that is similar to a competitor's product in order to prevent that competitor from maximizing its market share. Creating me-too products is considered risky because the company may lack the knowledge or expertise necessary to create a competitive product.

Me-Too Response The act in which a company creates a similar product to a competitor in order to prevent that competitor from maximizing its market share. This is considered risky because the company may lack the knowledge or expertise necessary to create a competitive product.

Metretes An ancient Greek unit of liquid volume approximately equivalent to 39.3 liters.

Metric Ounce A unit of weight equivalent to 25 grams.

Metric Pound A unit of weight equivalent to 500 grams.

MEX GOST 7.67 Latin three-letter geocode for Mexico. The code is used for transactions to and from Mexican bank accounts and for international shipping to Mexico. As with all GOST 7.67 codes, it is used primarily in Cyrillic alphabets.

Mexican Mint An organization in Mexico that issues legal tender coins for general use. It was established in 1535 and is located in Mexico City.

Mexican Peso The currency of Mexico. For most of the 20th century, the peso was one of the more stable currencies in the world, and it had not been subject to the hyperinflation that plagued other Latin American countries. However, the 1970s oil crisis resulted in Mexico defaulting on its national debt in 1982; this slowed growth and caused hyperinflation throughout the 1980s. The "new peso," which was introduced in 1993, helped to stabilize the country. Now, the peso is one of the most traded currencies in the world.

Mexican Stock Exchange The only securities exchange in Mexico. Completely electronic since 1992, it trades in both equity and debt instruments, as well as some derivatives. The exchange was a mutual company until 2008 when it made an IPO. At present, its shares are traded on its own trading floor. Its main index is known as the Indice de Precios y Cotizaciones. It is abbreviated BVM after its Spanish name, Bolsa de Valores de Mexico.

Mezzanine 1. See: Mezzanine level. **2.** See: Mezzanine financing.

Mezzanine Bracket In bracketing, the second largest underwriting group responsible for placing a certain amount of a new issue with investors. It is a somewhat informal term and is also called the maker bracket. Brackets are listed in order of size on an advertisement detailing each new issue, known as the tombstone.

Mezzanine Financing A type of debt financing whereby a company issues debt that the holders may convert into equity if the debt is not repaid in due course. This debt carries a high interest rate, as there is little or no collateral, but it is low-risk compared to other forms of debt financing because of its convertibility. Mezzanine financing is listed on a company's balance sheet as an asset; some companies use mezzanine financing because it makes it easier for them to obtain financing from other sources. Mezzanine financing is sometimes associated with leveraged buyouts.

Mezzanine Level 1. Informal; In bracketing, the second largest underwriting group responsible for placing a certain amount of a new issue with investors. The term is sometimes used interchangeably with "major bracket." Brackets are listed in order of size on an advertisement detailing each new issue, known as the tombstone. **2.** In venture capital, a term used to describe a company with more risk and more potential return than an IPO, but less than a startup. It is also used to describe a company in which venture capital has been invested six to 12 months before going public. In general, the mezzanine level is a company that once was a startup but has succeeded and is progressing toward public trade. See also: Mezzanine financing, Mezzanine debt.

MFN Tariff A tariff applied to a country with most favored nation status. An MFN tariff is the lowest possible tariff a country can assess on another country. For example, if a country's lowest tariff is 2% of the value of a good, this is its MFN tariff, and it charges this percentage on an import from a country with most favored nation status. Members of the World Trade Organization are required to extend most favored nation status to other members, though exceptions exist. In the United States, most favored nation status is formally called permanent normal trade relations.

MG 1. ISO 3166-1 alpha-2 code for the Republic of Madagascar. This is the code used in international transactions to and from Malagasy bank accounts. **2.** ISO 3166-2 geocode for Madagascar. This is used as an international standard for shipping to Madagascar. Each Malagasy province has its own code with the prefix "MG." For example, the code for the Province of Toamasina is ISO 3166-2:MG-A.

MGA ISO 4217 code for the Malagasy (Madagascar) ariary. Issued in 1961, it existed alongside the Malagasy franc until 2005, during which time one ariary was equal to five francs. It is divided into five iraimbilanja, making it one of two currencies in the world not divided into 100 subunits.

MGF ISO 4217 currency code for the Malagasy franc, which was the currency of Madagascar from the early 1970s until 2005. From 1963 until the early 1970s, Madagascar belonged to the Financial Community of Africa, but subsequently issued the MGF pegged to the French franc. An inconvertible currency, it underwent a series of devaluations and floated in the last period of time prior to its abolition. It existed alongside the Malagasy ariary, which is the current currency in Madagascar.

MH 1. ISO 3166-1 alpha-2 code for the Republic of the Marshall Islands. This is the code used in international transactions to and from Marshallese bank accounts. **2.** ISO 3166-2 geocode for the Marshall Islands. This is used as an international standard for shipping to the Marshall Islands. Each Marshallese subdivision has its own code with the prefix "MH." For example, the code for Kili Island is ISO 3166-2:MH-KIL.

MHL GOST 7.67 Latin three-letter geocode for Marshall Islands. The code is used for transactions to and from Marshallese bank accounts and for international shipping to Marshall Islands. As with all GOST 7.67 codes, it is used primarily in Cyrillic alphabets.

MHS A debt security whose value is derived from mortgages on manufactured houses. This entitles the owner to a claim on the principal and interest payments on the particular mortgages underpinning the security. MHSs pay an interest rate that is usually related to the interest rates the homeowners are paying on their mortgages. The equivalent of the coupon on a mortgage backed security is a percentage of the interest and principal paid on the mortgages backing the security. MHSs are subject to many of the same risks as conventional mortgage-backed securities, but they carry an additional risk of depreciation. Unlike most homes, manufactured houses have a greater risk of losing value over time.

MI 1. ISO 3166-1 alpha-2 code for the Midway Islands before their re-designation as part of the U.S. Minor Outlying Islands. This was the code used in international transactions to and from bank accounts in the territory. **2.** ISO 3166-2 geocode for the Midway Islands. This was used as an international standard for shipping to the Midway Islands. In both cases, the code is obsolete.

Miar An obsolete Polish unit of area approximately equivalent to 1,918 square meters.

Michael Bloomberg An American businessman and politician. He spent his early career in investment banking and, in 1981, established what became known as Bloomberg LP, a news company that offers real time and historic prices, trends, and analysis of securities, as well as information and reporting on the economy as a whole. In 2002, he became mayor of New York City.

Michael R. Milken An American investor and philanthropist. In the 1970s and 1980s, he helped develop the junk bond market as a way to raise capital for greenmail, leveraged buyouts, and other purposes. In 1989, he pled guilty to illegal activities connected to insider trading (though he was not convicted of insider trading itself). He has also donated to research of prostate cancer.

Michael Spence An American economist born in 1943. He is most noted for the signalling model, which states that employees pay for education to attract employers. According to Spence's model, even if the education itself lacks any intrinsic value, its ability to attract an employer gives it value for the employee. Spence also has done work on information asymmetry, for which he shared the Nobel Prize for Economics in 2001.

Micharia In Brazil, a slang term for a small amount of money.

Michigan Consumer Sentiment Index An index on the level of consumer confidence in the United States. It takes the form of a survey conducted by the University of Michigan. It is published each month. A rising index indicates rising confidence while a falling index indicates the opposite.

Mickey In auto sales, a loan that a dealership arranges for a customer to make the down payment on an automobile. While the dealership does not extend the mickey directly, it works with a separate financial institution to ensure that the customer receives it.

Micro Cap Fund A mutual fund that invests predominately or exclusively in stocks with very low market capitalization. In general, a micro-cap company has a market capitalization of less than $250 million, but there is no hard-and-fast rule. Some brokerages or exchanges have slightly different definitions of micro-cap. Micro cap funds often contain new companies with strong growth potential; however, for this reason, they may be high risk.

Micro Country Risk The risk that a foreign government will significantly alter its policies or other regulations so that it significantly affects a particular industry, company, or project. Rather than the risk of hurting, say, exporters or foreign-owned businesses in general, micro country risks imply that a government will deliberately target someone or something. For example, the political climate of a country in which defense contractors operate may turn against one particular company because of its perceived excesses. The government may then revoke its contract while allowing other contractors to work in the country. See also: Reputational risk, political risk, country risk.

Micro-Cap Stock A stock with a very low amount of market capitalization. In general, a micro-cap company has a market capitalization of less than $250 million, but there is no hard-and-fast rule. Some brokerages or exchanges have slightly different definitions of micro-cap. Some indexes track micro-cap companies. See also: High-cap, Mid-cap, Low-cap.

Microcredit The practice of making loans to extremely poor persons to help them rise from poverty through entrepreneurship. That is, one may make a loan of, say, $25 which gives someone the start-up capital necessary to make something small to sell. Microcredit loans are usually either interest-free or carry interest that does not compound. Additionally they offer flexible repayment plans; generally one is asked to pay anything one can so long as one pays something. Microcredit is most common in the developing world; it started in Bangladesh in the 1970s. See also: Grameen Bank, Mohammed Yunus.

Microeconomics The study of the behavior of individuals, companies, and industries. That is, macroeconomics studies economic decisions at the individual and small unit level. It does not look at the function of larger data sets like GDP or national debt. It is useful in helping determine what motivates individual buyers and sellers to do what they do. See also: Macroeconomics, Bottom-up investing.

Micro-Hedge The practice of hedging the risk on a particular security or asset. An investor micro-hedges when he/she seeks to reduce the risk associated with a single investment. A common way to micro-hedge is to take a roughly equal but opposite position on the same or similar security. For example, one may take a long position in oil while taking a short position in natural gas. It is important to note, however, that micro-hedging usually has little or no effect on a portfolio consisting of several securities.

Microlender A person or bank that makes loans in small amounts. In the developing world, microlenders often make loans of only a few dollars to facilitate the start of small businesses. In this case, the interest can be a flat fee that does not compound. In the developed world, microlenders make loans of $5,000 to $25,000 and charge higher interest rates than they would for larger loans.

Microrregiao In Brazil, a political subdivision consisting of municipalities geographically close to each other. While in theory these may perform certain municipal functions, in practice they are used only for statistical purposes.

Mid-Atlantic Option An option contract that may only be exercised on certain days. For example, if one buys a Mid-Atlantic call giving him/her the right to buy shares in X expiring on the final Friday in March, the call may only be exercised on certain days, usually one day per month. The term "Mid-Atlantic" comes from the fact that it combines features of a European option, which may only be exercised on the expiration date, and an American option, which may be exercised at any time. A Mid-Atlantic option is also called a Bermudan option.

Mid-Cap Describing a publicly-traded company with medium amount in market capitalization. In general, a mid-cap company has a market capitalization of between $2 billion and $10 billion, but there is no hard-and-fast rule. Some brokerages or exchanges have slightly different definitions of mid-cap. Some indexes track mid-cap companies, as do some exchange traded funds. See also: High-cap, Low-cap.

Mid-Cap Fund A mutual fund that invests primarily or exclusively in mid-capitalization stocks. In general, a mid-cap fund invests in companies with market capitalizations between $2 billion and $10 billion, but there is no specific definition. Some brokerages or exchanges have slightly different definitions of mid-cap. Mid-cap stocks are sometimes attractive because they are considered to have less volatility than small cap stocks, but more growth potential than large cap or blue chip stocks.

Mid-Cap SPDR An exchange-traded fund that tracks the Standard and Poor's Midcap 400 Composite Price Index. The organization issuing the SPDR owns each of the stocks traded on the S&P Midcap Index in approximate ratio to their market capitalization. SPDR shares can be bought, sold, short-sold, traded on margin, and generally function as if they were stocks. Investors use midcap SPDRs (and indeed all exchange-traded funds) as a way to easily diversify their portfolios at relatively low cost. Investors also see the demand for midcap SPDRs as an indicator of which direction the market believes the S&P Midcap Index is going.

Midcareer Plateau A situation in which one is no longer challenged by his/her current position and/or he/she is not making a desired salary, but lacks the education or training to advance or change courses. A midcareer plateau may be overcome by further education or simply a change in job.

Middle East Development Bank A proposed bank intended to promote economic and regional development in the Middle East. It was suggested by the United States and regional partners in the mid-1990s but was never actually established.

Middle Market Manufacturing Exporter An exporting firm that is also a small business or a medium-sized business. Generally speaking, a middle market manufacturing exporter has fewer than 500 employees and averages less than $1 million in revenue each year.

Middle Office A section of a financial services company that deals with accounting and risk management. That is, the middle office calculates profits and losses and helps the front office determine what projects to conduct or clients with whom they will work. Sometimes the middle office handles information technology as well. The middle office uses resources from both the front office and back office in the accomplishment of its tasks.

Middle Rate In securities, the price halfway between the current bid and ask prices. For example, if the bid is $12.72 and the ask is $12.76, the middle rate is $12.74. It is also called the mid-price. See also: Bid-ask spread.

Midget A mortgage-backed security pool, issued by Ginnie Mae, with a maturity of 15 years. See also: Dwarf.

Midmarket 1. Describing a medium-sized company. There is no specific definition of how many employees a midmarket company has, but, in general, experts say the number is between 50 and 1000. Midmarket companies are often subject to stricter regulations than small businesses; for example, some states exempt small businesses from minimum wage laws. For this reason, companies ought to be cautious when hiring their fiftieth or hundredth employee. **2.** Describing a price that is neither too expensive nor too cheap. Midmarket prices may apply to a bid/ask spread, or to middling prices in a retail chain.

Mid-Market Price A price that is neither too expensive nor too cheap. Midmarket prices may apply to a bid/ask spread, or to middling prices in a retail chain.

Mid-Month Convention A method in which the owner of some asset is allowed one half-month of depreciation in the month that the asset is purchased or sold (or otherwise disposed of). That is, the mid-month convention treats assets purchased or sold any time during a month as having been purchased or sold on the day half-way through that month.

Mid-Quarter Convention A method in which the owner of some asset is allowed one half-quarter of depreciation in the quarter that the asset is purchased or sold (or otherwise disposed of). That is, the mid-quarter convention treats assets purchased or sold any time during a quarter as having been purchased or sold on the day half-way through that quarter. In general, one uses the mid quarter convention if the cost basis of assets purchased or placed in service during the fourth quarter of the year is greater than 40% of the total basis of all property purchased or placed in service that year.

MIFI A slang abbreviation for "most important financial issues," which are the priorities for which an organization exists and for which it must ensure adequate funding. The term is most common in the context of financial management of small Christian churches and ministries.

Mijl An obsolete Dutch unit of length roughly equivalent to five kilometers, with slight regional variations.

Mil In Norway or Sweden, a unit of length equal to 10 kilometers.

Mileage Allowance In the United States, a tax deduction for driving one's own car for certain purposes. If a taxpayer keeps track of miles driven for moving, medical issues, job-seeking, and some business purposes, the IRS allows a deduction of so many cents per mile, depending on the specific use and the tax year. It is important to note that commuting to and from one's place of business or employment is not covered under the mileage allowance, nor is the use of public transportation for any reason.

Milia A Russian unit of length equivalent to 24,500 feet, or approximately seven and a half kilometers. It was rendered obsolete when the Soviet Union began to use the metric system in 1924.

Milin An ancient Hebrew unit of length approximately equivalent to one kilometer.

Milion An ancient Greek unit of length approximately equivalent to 1,479 meters.

Military Family Tax Relief Act of 2003 Legislation in the United States that provides a number of tax benefits for military personnel and their families. For example, pay received by a service member in combat is tax free. Military families must fill out a special tax form to take advantage of these benefits.

Milk Income Loss Contracts Payments Commonly called MILC payments. In the United States, a program to pay dairy farmers when the price of milk falls below a certain level. The program is intended to keep dairy farmers in business during difficult times. This in turn keeps the supply of milk from radically declining, which can cause large price fluctuations. The U.S. Department of Agriculture administers the program.

Milk Spot In numismatics, a white spot that causes the surface of a coin to appear unclear. Milk spots are most common on silver coins. They may affect the value of a coin.

Milky In numismatics, describing a surface of a coin that appears unclear due to a white spot somewhere on it. This occurs most commonly on silver coins. This may affect the value of a coin.

Mill 1/1,000, or 10% of 1% of a measure. Mills are used in the calculation of property taxes. See also: Mill rate.

Mill Rate The way a property tax assessment is expressed. It is called the mill rate because it is expressed in mills (one tenth of one cent) per dollar. The mill rate is the number of mills per dollar of a property's value.

Mille pasuum An ancient Roman unit of length approximately equivalent to 1.48 kilometers. It was also called a milliarium.

Milled Coinage Coins that are produced by machine rather than by physically hammering them. All modern coins are milled.

Millennial A member of the generation that was born roughly between 1980 and 2000. Millennials grew up during economic and political flux, experiencing the end of the Cold War, the dotcom bubble, the 9/11 terrorist attacks and the late 2000s recession. Perhaps because of the sometimes volatile environment in which they were raised, millennials tend to marry and undergo other rites of passage later than earlier generations. They also tend to be technically savvy, which makes them a major demographic for technology marketers.

Miller and Modigliani's Irrelevance Proposition A theory stating that if financial markets are perfectly efficient, then how a company is a financed has no bearing on its performance. That is, without taxes, asymmetric information, or government and other unnecessary fees, then a company is equally likely to perform well regardless if it is financed by equity issues, debt, or something else. It also states that a company's dividend policy is irrelevant in these circumstances. This theory has been used to justify the increased use of leverage since the 1980s and critics contend that it has led to needless risk-taking.

Miller, Merton A financial academic and theoretician. Along with Franco Modigliani, he developed the Modigliani-Miller theory, which states that if financial markets are perfectly efficient, then how a company is a financed has no bearing on its performance. That is, without taxes, asymmetric information, or government and other unnecessary fees, a company is equally likely to perform well regardless of whether it is financed by equity issues, debt, or something else. It also states that a company's dividend policy is irrelevant in these circumstances. Miller's theory has been used to justify the increased use of leverage since the 1980s. He was awarded the Nobel Prize in Economics (along with Harry Markowitz and William Sharpe) in 1990 for this and other contributions. Critics contend his theory has led to needless risk-taking. He was born in Boston in 1923 and died in Chicago in 2000.

Miller-Tydings Fair Trade Act Legislation in the United States that allows manufacturers or distributors of goods to require retailers to charge a minimum price. The Act was designed to protect small retailers who were being driven out of business by large chains who could undercut prices, especially using loss leader strategies. The Act was passed in 1937 and was repealed in 1975. See also: Consumer Goods Pricing Act.

Millieme A subdivision of the Egyptian pound. One millieme is equal in value to 1/1,000 of one pound. It is not used in practice.

Millime A subdivision of the Tunisian dinar. One millime is equal in value to 1/1,000 of one dinar.

Milline Rate In newspapers, a measure of the cost effectiveness of advertising in a newspaper. It is not a widely used measure. One calculates the milline rate thusly: Milline rate = cost per agate line * 1,000,000 / circulation

Million Dollar Round Table Also called the MDRT. A trade association for financial advisors. It was established in 1927 by a group of insurance agents who had each sold $1 million or more in policies that year. The MDRT promotes best practices and ethical conduct among members.

Millionaire on Paper A person with net assets in excess of $1 million (or the equivalent in another currency) but with less than that amount available in cash or cash equivalents. For example, a millionaire on paper may own a house worth $2 million, but have significantly less in salary or savings. A millionaire on paper may be able to borrow against his/her assets but otherwise does not have access to his/her wealth unless he/she liquidates.

Milreis The former currency of Portugal and Brazil. It was subject to persistently high inflation. In 1911, it was replaced by the escudo in Portugal; in 1942, the cruzeiro was introduced in Brazil.

Mina An ancient Greek unit of weight approximately equivalent to 431 or 630 grams, depending on the region.

Minah An ancient Hebrew unit of weight approximately equivalent to 425 grams.

Mine A slang term in foreign exchange indicating a willingness to buy.

Mine and Yours In foreign exchange, informal for buying and selling. That is, a trader on a floor seeking to buy may shout "mine" or "it's mine." Likewise, a trader seeking to sell may shout "yours" or "it's yours."

Mingel An obsolete Dutch unit of volume roughly equivalent to 1.21 liters.

Mini Perm In construction and project finance, an informal term for debt financing that is payable over three to five years. Generally speaking, a developer accesses mini perm financing to complete the project to the point where it can begin to produce revenue. The developer then uses the revenue to pay off the mini perm.

Minicoupon Bond A bond in which the coupon payments are lower than the market rate at the time of the bond's issue. Minicoupon bonds are usually sold at a discount from their face value so as to attract investors. Zero-coupon bonds are a subset of minicoupon bonds.

Mini-Manipulation The act or practice of buying or selling a security underlying an option one holds in order to increase or decrease its price so that the option will be in-the-money on or before the expiration date. For example, suppose one holds a near-the-money call option on a certain number of shares of Stock A. The holder may buy Stock A in a large enough quantity to cause its price to go up. When this happens, the option becomes in-the-money, and the contract increases in value. He/she may then sell the contract at a high price and rid himself/herself of the shares previously bought. Like all forms of manipulation, mini-manipulation is illegal in most jurisdictions.

Minimum Finance Charge A fee on some credit cards that one must pay each billing period unless charges to the credit card for that billing period exceed it. For example, suppose the minimum finance charge is $1 per month. If one does not use the credit card for the month, one must still pay the credit card company $1. On the other hand, if one charges $10 to the card for the month, the minimum finance charge is waived and one must only pay the $10 (plus any applicable interest).

Minimum Investment The least amount of money one may place in a portfolio or fund. Some brokerages, such as boutiques, only accept clients who are willing to put up a large minimum investment. Likewise, most hedge funds exclude small investors by having a minimum investment, usually in the millions of dollars. Examples of investment vehicles with small minimum investments are IRAs and 401(k)s.

Minimum Price Contract A forward contract where the underlying asset is guaranteed to have a minimum price upon delivery. A minimum price contract exists in order to reduce the risk of fluctuations in the forward's price. This is useful for farmers and other producers of commodities, as well as for investors wishing to hedge the risk in their positions.

Minimum Purchases The minimum amount one may invest in a mutual fund should one decide to buy shares. For example, a mutual fund may set a minimum purchase of $1000 in order to make the purchase of shares worth the effort for the company managing the fund while still keeping shares affordable for most investors.

Minimum Required Distribution The amount that an IRA must begin to distribute to an annuitant by the age of 70.5 or the age of retirement, whichever is greater. The minimum required distribution may or may not be taxable, depending on the type of IRA. The amount of the minimum required distribution is determined by the value of the IRA, the length of time the annuitant has contributed, and the amount of contributions.

Minimum Tick The smallest possible change in price to a security. Various regulations exist regarding what the minimum tick is for different securities, and which trades may occur on a tick. For example, until 2007, a short sale could not occur at the same price as the security's previous trade, when that price was itself a downtick from the trade before that. A minimum tick is also called a trading variation. See also: Tick test.

Minimum-Variance Frontier In Markowitz portfolio theory, the frontier on a chart representing a portfolio with the least amount of volatility. That is, a minimum-variance frontier consists of data points representing stocks with a certain level of volatility and therefore risk, while the frontier represents a portfolio in which the volatilities of each individual stock offset each other. A minimum-variance frontier is also a Markowitz efficient frontier if it also represents the maximum level of return for its level of risk.

Minimum-Variance Portfolio A portfolio of individually risky assets that, when taken together, result in the lowest possible risk level for the rate of expected return. Such a portfolio hedges each investment with an offsetting investment; the individual investor's choice on how much to offset investments depends on the level of risk and expected return he/she is willing to accept. The investments in a minimum variance portfolio are individually riskier than the portfolio as a whole. The name of the term comes from how it is mathematically expressed in Markowitz Portfolio Theory, in which volatility is used as a replacement for risk, and in which less variance in volatility correlates to less risk in an investment.

Mini-Sized Dow Option A highly leveraged index option on a futures contract in which the underlying index is the Dow Jones Industrial Average. The option has a multiplier of five, meaning that the option allows one to buy (for a call) or sell (for a put) up to five times the value of the DJIA. This allows one to profit from the option for a lower price than one would otherwise be able to do. As with all index options, a mini-sized Dow option is settled in cash.

Minister for the Cabinet Office The head of the Cabinet Office, which is the department of the British government that provides ancillary and support staff to the government and has some oversight of the civil service. The minister is appointed by the monarch on the advice of the prime minister.

Minister for Women and Equalities The head of the Government Equalities Office, which is an office of the British government responsible for encouraging equality for all persons in the United Kingdom regardless of gender, race, disability, ethnicity, or sexual orientation. The minister oversees enforcement of anti-discrimination legislation for the U.K. He/she is appointed by the prime minister.

Ministry of Agriculture, Fisheries and Forestry A cabinet-level department of the Japanese government responsible for food safety and land reclamation. It is

also responsible for employee safety in the food industry and agricultural commodity trades.

Ministry of Defence A department of the British government responsible for national defense and management of the British Armed Forces. It advises the government on defense policy coordinates the actions of the Royal Navy, the British Army, and the Royal Air Force. It was created in 1964, but traces its origins to the interwar period.

Ministry of Economy, Trade and Industry A cabinet-level department of the Japanese government responsible for economic policy, international trade, and technology. It is responsible for regulating many Japanese businesses. It was established in 2001 as the result of a merger of MITI and other agencies.

Ministry of Finance A cabinet-level department of the Japanese government responsible for the national budget, the printing of currency, foreign exchange policy, and other areas. Before the 1990s, it was also responsible for banking regulation and monetary policy. It was regarded as the most powerful Japanese ministry for most of the postwar period. It traces its origins to the 6th century.

Ministry of Foreign Affairs A cabinet-level department of the Japanese government responsible for formulating and implement foreign policy. It aims to promote profits for Japanese companies abroad. It works with JETRO, the Ministry of Finance, and other agencies in accomplishing its goals.

Ministry of Foreign Economic Relations and Trade A former name of the Chinese Ministry of Commerce. It was created in 1983 with the merger of the Ministry of Foreign Trade, the Ministry of Foreign Economic Liaison, the State Import and Export Regulation Commission and the State Foreign Investment Regulation Commission. This merger was part of a broader effort to reform the Chinese economy after the radical failure of the Great Leap Forward and the Cultural Revolution.

Ministry of Health and Welfare 1. See: Japanese Ministry of Health, Labor and Welfare. **2.** See: Korean Ministry of Health, Welfare and Family Affairs.

Ministry of International Trade and Industry A former cabinet-level department of the Japanese government. It was responsible for directing private investment and setting business policy. Because garnering favor with the ministry was key to success in business, it was considered one of the most powerful Japanese ministries. It was merged into the Ministry of Economy, Trade and Industry in 2001.

Ministry of Posts and Telecommunications A former cabinet level department of the Japanese government. It oversaw the postal service and regulated telecommunication. It merged with several other ministries in 2001 to form the Ministry of Internal Affairs and Communications.

Mini-Tender Offer A tender offer for less than 5% of shares outstanding. A tender offer is an offer to buy a significant amount of stock in a publicly-traded company directly from shareholders, an act that bypasses the board of directors. A tender offer may be part of a hostile takeover and therefore any offer exceeding 5% of the company's shares must be registered with the SEC and submitted to oversight. A mini-tender offer avoids this requirement, which can be detrimental to shareholders, as the SEC does not have the ability to protect their rights.

Minneapolis Grain Exchange Also called MGEX. An exchange for agricultural commodities, notably corn, soybeans and wheat. Futures, options and actual commodities are traded on MGEX. It was established in 1881.

Minor A person who has not reached the age of majority, which varies from 15 to 25 depending on jurisdiction and situation. A minor has fewer legal rights and responsibilities than a legal adult. For example, a minor may not enter contracts or vote, and often has personal restrictions on tobacco or alcohol consumption and sexual activity.

Minor Bracket In bracketing, the third largest underwriting group, which is responsible for placing a certain amount of a new issue with investors. Brackets are listed in order of size on an advertisement detailing each new issue, known as the tombstone.

Minority Interest 1. A percentage of ownership in a company that is significant but does not give the owner the ability to control the company. In accounting, one includes only the dividends from a minority interest on a balance sheet, unless the owner has enough ownership to exert influence (but not outright control) over the company's direction. In that case, one includes both dividends and ordinary income on the balance sheet. **2.** A liability on a parent company's balance sheet indicating the amount of a subsidiary that the parent company does not own. For example, if a parent company owns 95% of a subsidiary and the remaining percentage is publicly traded, the dollar amount of that 5% is recorded as a liability on the balance sheet.

Minority Shareholder A shareholder who holds a significant amount of stock in a company but still has less than 51%. While technically even a person who owns one share is a minority shareholder, the term most frequently applies to persons and companies with large stakes. For example, a person who owns 5% of the shares outstanding in Johnson & Johnson is considered a minority shareholder in that company. See also: Minority interest.

Minority Squeeze-Out In joint stock companies, to buy the stocks of a minority group of shareholders without their necessary consent. A group of shareholders owning the large majority of the company have the ability to squeeze out remaining shareholders. The percentage of shareholders needed varies between jurisdictions. For example, the United Kingdom requires shareholders owning 90% of the company to consent to squeeze out the other shareholders, while Germany requires 95%. Minority shareholders receive compensation in return for surrendering their shares.

Mint A place where coins are manufactured. In general, the coins produced at a government-sponsored mint are legal tender, though private minted coins may have an intrinsic value due to their metal content. Before fiat money became common, many paper notes were exchangeable for a minted coin containing some specified level of gold or silver.

Mint Condition In numismatics, the state in which a coin has the exact same quality as it had when it was produced. A mint condition coin has never circulated and has been protected from touch or other human use. These coins can be valuable to collectors, but they tend to be illiquid assets.

Mint Luster In numismatics, the shininess of a coin that has never circulated. Coins with mint luster may have the most value, though they remain illiquid assets.

Mint Mark A letter inscribed on a U.S. coin identifying the mint at which it was created. A mint mark of "P" means the coin was made in Philadelphia, while a mint mark of "D" means the coin was made in Denver.

Mint of Finland An organization in Finland that issues legal tender coins for general use. In addition to Finland, the Mint produces euro coins for other nations, including Ireland and Greece. It also produces commemorative coins. It was established in 1860 and is located in Vantaa.

Mint of Norway An organization in Norway that issues legal tender coins for general use. It was established in 1686 and was controlled by Norges Bank from 1962 until 2003, after which ownership was transferred to two private companies. It is located in Kongsberg.

Mint Proofing Piece A high-quality gold ingot. Mint proofing pieces are melted in mints with less high-quality gold to make an alloy of 90% pure gold. This gold is then minted into coins. It is also called simply a proofing piece.

Mint Set In numismatics, a set of coins consisting of one coin in each denomination produced by a given mint. For example, a U.S. mint may make a mint set of a penny, a nickel, a dime, a quarter, a 50-cent piece, and a dollar coin. The coins in a mint set are usually in mint condition. These sets generally are bought by collectors and the coins do not circulate.

Mintage The number of coins made by a particular mint, or on a certain date, or with certain features. Mintage indicates the number of coins with certain, stated traits.

Minting The process of making coins. Minting generally consists of pressing pieces of metal with images. These images usually show the denomination of the coin, contain security features, and may say something about the country minting it. For example, the reigning monarch of the United Kingdom appears on all British coins. Coins generally are minted in small denominations, but this is not always the case.

Mintiqah In some Arabic-speaking countries, a political subdivision equivalent to a province.

Minus 1. Informal; a security with a closing price lower than its opening price. **2.** See: Minus tick.

Minus Tick On an exchange, a transaction in which a security was traded at the lower price than its previous trade. Some regulations and rules on exchanges forbid certain transactions following a minus tick or a zero-minus tick, though some rules, notably as the short sale rule, have become obsolete with increased digitalization of the market. A minus tick is also called a downtick.

Minutes A record of a meeting. The minutes from the previous meeting are read and approved at a meeting to ensure an accurate history of the meeting is kept. The secretary of an organization generally records the minutes.

MIP 1. Monthly income plan. An investment vehicle, especially for retired persons, that makes equal disbursements each month. This allows the receiver to budget one's retirement more carefully; that is, rather than spending all of one's retirement income at once, an MIP only allows the receiver a certain amount each month. See also: Annuity. **2.** Monthly income preferred security. A preferred stock issued by a company's subsidiary in a tax haven. The subsidiary sells these preferred stocks and then lends the money to the parent. This allows the parent to avoid or evade taxes on the money raised in that round of financing.

Mirror Fund A mutual fund in which a shareholder may invest through his/her life insurance policy with another company. For example, one may use his life insurance policy at Company A to invest in a mirror fund with Company B. Mirror funds provide flexibility, but usually have higher fees than other mutual funds.

Mirror Voting A practice in which a brokerage votes in proportion to how a vote has gone overall. A brokerage technically owns the shares under its charge even though the actual owners (called the beneficial owners) are the brokerage's clients. The brokerage votes with these shares according to how the beneficial owners direct. However, not all beneficial owners send directions. In this case, the brokerage may practice mirror voting. For example, if all other shareholders vote 85% in favor of a measure and 15% against, the brokerage may vote 85% in favor and 15% against with its shares that otherwise would not vote. This can be particularly useful when a quorum of voters is required and would not be met otherwise.

Misery Index An informal index that adds the unemployment rate and the inflation rate. For example, if inflation is 11% and unemployment is 6%, the misery index is 17. The misery index is of limited economic import, but politicians often use it to show the success of their programs (or the failure of their opponents' policies).

Miskal A Turkish measure of weight approximately equivalent to 0.312 grams. It became obsolete when Turkey made the metric system mandatory in 1933.

Mismatch A situation in which the purchase of a currency has a different value date (the foreign exchange term for delivery date) than the sale of the same currency. A mismatch may create liquidity problems in foreign exchange transactions.

Misqal A Tatar unit of weight approximately equivalent to 4.27 grams. It was rendered obsolete when the Soviet Union began to use the metric system in 1924.

Miss the Price/Market 1. To fail, through negligence, to execute an order on terms favorable to a client. A broker who misses the price/market consistently is thought to be poor at his/her job. **2.** To receive an order to buy or sell a security at a certain price immediately after that price has ceased to be available.

Mission Statement A brief statement of what a company wishes to accomplish in the course of its operations. A mission statement may be placed in a business plan, on a website or nearly anywhere else. A mission statement is often one or two sentences and is the most concise possible statement of the company's goals. For example, Ford's mission statement in the early 1900s was simply, "Democratize the automobile." See also: Vision statement.

Mississippi Bubble An 18th-century speculative bubble resulting from the Mississippi Company, which had a charter from the King of France for overseas trade with the Louisiana Territory and elsewhere. The Company's founder, John Law, promoted the trade of the stock, which was guaranteed indirectly by the King. The company issued notes (through the Banque Royale) until the government admitted it did not have sufficient coinage to cover the notes it had printed. This resulted in a bank run and the burst of the bubble in 1720. The Mississippi bubble was one of the first times a bank issued paper money.

Mista Zi Spetsial'nym Statusom In Ukraine, a political subdivision for cities not under the jurisdiction of a province. There are two such cities in Ukraine.

MIT 1. Market if touched. An order to a broker to buy or sell a security at a certain price when that price becomes available. MITs are common in futures markets, and the prices ordered are often derived from technical analysis. An MIT may be a day order or a GTC order, but not an immediate or cancel order. For example, if shares are trading at $10 and an MIT is made to buy at $11, the broker buys no securities until the price is actually $11 per share. **2.** Municipal Investment Trust. A unit investment trust that invests primarily or exclusively in municipal bonds. The MIT buys these bonds and holds them until maturity, passing the coupons and principal on to unit holders.

Mitbestimmung A concept in German law whereby employees are given a significant role in the management of a corporation. Under Mitbestimmung, almost half the representatives on most supervisory boards must be elected by employees and/or unions. The word translates as co-determination.

MIUM ISO 3166-3 code for the Midway Islands, which were re-designated as part of the U.S. Minor Outlying Islands. ISO 3166-3 codes are used to indicate names of countries and territories that are no longer used.

Mixed Account A brokerage account that includes a long position in at least one security and a short position in at least one security. That is, a mixed account has at least one security an investor owns and at least one that the investor has borrowed. A mixed account is a type of margin account.

Mixed Bag An informal term for a group of securities, some of which are trading above their opening prices, some of which are trading below them, and some that are trading roughly at their opening prices.

Mixed Credit A series of loans offered to a borrower containing loans with both prevailing interest rates and discounted interest rates.

Mixed Deposit A deposit into a bank account containing both checks and cash. For example, if one deposits $100 in cash and $300 in checks, one has made a mixed deposit.

Mixed Forecasting A situation in which one or more analysts arrive at the same conclusion on a company's future price movement, performance, or some other metric by using several different forecasting methods.

Mixed Lot An order to buy or sell a security that consists of at least one round lot and one odd lot. For example, if one makes an order to buy 153 shares of a security, this is a mixed lot because it combines a round lot (100 shares) with an odd lot (53 shares).

Mixed Perils Describing an insurance policy that covers several different types of risk. For example, a car insurance policy may cover both repair costs and medical bills for injured passengers.

Mixed Provinces Sack A sack of mail sorted to be delivered across multiple Canadian provinces. A mixed provinces sack cannot be sorted into more specific sacks because there are low volumes of mail going across a large area. In other words, mixed provinces sacks contain mail for very rural areas.

Mixed States Sack A sack of mail sorted to be delivered across multiple American states. A mixed states sack cannot be sorted into more specific sacks because there are low volumes of mail going across a large area. In other words, mixed states sacks contain mail for very rural areas.

MJSD Abbreviation for March, July, September, and December. This is used to option cycles to determine the expiration date of an option contract.

MK 1. ISO 3166-1 alpha-2 code for the Former Yugoslav Republic of Macedonia. This is the code used in international transactions to and from Macedonian bank accounts. **2.** ISO 3166-2 geocode for Macedonia. This is used as an international standard for shipping to Macedonia. Each Macedonian municipality has its own numeric code with the prefix "MK." For example, the code for the Municipality of Berovo is ISO 3166-2:MK-03.

MKD GOST 7.67 Latin three-letter geocode for Macedonia. The code is used for transactions to and from Macedonian bank accounts and for international shipping to Macedonia. As with all GOST 7.67 codes, it is used primarily in Cyrillic alphabets.

Mkhare In Georgia, a political subdivision approximately equivalent to a province.

MKN ISO 4217 code for the old Macedonian denar. It was issued in 1992, replacing the Yugoslav dinar at a one-to-one ratio. A year later, the new denar replaced it at a ratio of 100 old denars to one new denar.

Mkoa In Kenya and Tanzania, a political subdivision equivalent to a province.

ML 1. See Merrill Lynch and Co. **2.** ISO 3166-1 alpha-2 code for the Republic of Mali. This is the code used in international transactions to and from Malian bank accounts. **3.** ISO 3166-2 geocode for Mali. This is used as an international standard for shipping to Mali. Each Malian region has its own code with the prefix "ML" and a number following. For example, the code for the Region of Gao is ISO 3166-2:ML-7. The city of Bamako has its own lettered designation: ISO 3166-2:ML-BKO.

MLF ISO 4217 code for the Malian franc. It was issued in 1962, replacing the West African CFA franc at a one-to-one ratio. The Malian franc was a weak currency. In 1984, Mali adopted the CFA franc again at a ratio of two Malian francs to one West African CFA franc.

MLI GOST 7.67 Latin three-letter geocode for Mali. The code is used for transactions to and from Malian bank accounts and for international shipping to Mali. As with all GOST 7.67 codes, it is used primarily in Cyrillic alphabets.

MLT GOST 7.67 Latin three-letter geocode for Malta. The code is used for transactions to and from Maltese bank accounts and for international shipping to Malta. As with all GOST 7.67 codes, it is used primarily in Cyrillic alphabets.

MM 1. ISO 3166-1 alpha-2 code for the Union of Myanmar (Burma). This is the code used in international transactions to and from Burmese bank accounts. **2.** ISO 3166-2 geocode for Burma. This is used as an international standard for shipping to Burma. Each administrative division in Burma has its own code with the prefix "MM." For example, the code for the State of Mon is ISO 3166-2:MM-15.

MMK ISO 4217 code for the Burmese (or Myanmar) kyat. It was introduced in 1953, replacing the Burmese rupee. The Burmese government has been known to follow unusual policies with regard to printing money. For example, it introduced 45 and 90 kyat banknotes in 1987 because they both incorporated a leading general's favorite number (nine). Also in 1987, the government demonetized the 25, 35, and 75 kyat banknotes without warning. This led to a general uprising because those notes composed three-fourths of the currency in circulation.

MMR GOST 7.67 Latin three-letter geocode for Burma. The code is used for transactions to and from Burman bank accounts and for international shipping to Burma. As with all GOST 7.67 codes, it is used primarily in Cyrillic alphabets.

MN 1. ISO 3166-1 alpha-2 code for Mongolia. This is the code used in international transactions to and from Mongolian bank accounts. **2.** ISO 3166-2 geocode for Mongolia. This is used as an international standard for shipping to Mongolia. Each Mongolian province and the capital city has its own code with the prefix "MN." For example, the code for the City of Ulan Bator is ISO 3166-2:MN-1.

MNG GOST 7.67 Latin three-letter geocode for Mongolia. The code is used for transactions to and from Mongolian bank accounts and for international shipping to Mongolia. As with all GOST 7.67 codes, it is used primarily in Cyrillic alphabets.

MNP GOST 7.67 Latin three-letter geocode for Northern Mariana Islands. The code is used for transactions to and from local bank accounts and for international shipping to Northern Mariana Islands. As with all GOST 7.67 codes, it is used primarily in Cyrillic alphabets.

MNT ISO 4217 code for the Mongolian tugrik. It was introduced in 1925 and pegged to the Soviet ruble. It currently floats.

Mo 1. ISO 3166-1 alpha-2 code for the Macau Special Administrative Region of the People's Republic of China. This is the code used in international transactions to and from Macanese bank accounts. **2.** ISO 3166-2 geocode for Macau. This is used as an international standard for shipping to Macau.

MOB Spread The difference in yield between tax-exempt and taxable bonds, especially tax-free municipal bonds and taxable corporate bonds. A corporate bond yields less than its stated interest rate because of taxation, whereas a tax-exempt municipal bond does not. Thus, a municipal bond paying a lower interest rate will often net the bondholder more than a corporate bond with a slightly higher interest rate, depending upon one's tax bracket. See also: After-tax basis.

Mobile Home Certificate A mortgage-backed security guaranteed by the Government National Mortgage Association (Ginnie Mae). It is backed exclusively by mortgages on mobile homes and trailers. Because these homes are less expensive than permanent homes and consequently have shorter mortgage payback periods, the maturity of a mobile home certificate is almost always shorter than other mortgage-backed securities. They derive their interest payments from the timely payment of interest and principal on the mortgages that back them.

Mock Auction A con in which a gang sells low quality merchandise in an auction setting at a high price. Mock auctions usually involve gang members pretending to buy items and acting as if they are satisfied. This encourages real customers to spend too much for inferior products.

Mock Trading A computer simulation of trade used in training brokers and investment managers. Different companies offer mock trading programs at different price ranges, but a few companies offer mock trading programs for free over the Internet, much like a computer game. Most programs are fairly realistic, tracking markets and simulating trade at current prices. Different programs concentrate on specific markets. For example, mock trading programs have been developed for the foreign exchange and commodity markets.

Modd A Maltese unit of land area approximately equivalent to 1.8 hectares. It is largely obsolete but is still used in some circumstances.

Mode In statistics, the most frequently occurring value in a given data set.

Model Any mathematical formula or other structure that economists use to explain or predict occurrences. Economists test their models with real world facts before they gain wide acceptance, but, even then, there is no guarantee that a model will always be a correct predictor. See also: Model risk.

Modeling The process of creating a coherent picture on diverse amounts of data. Modeling often involves the use of charts and is important in technical analysis. See also: Forecasting.

Modern Portfolio Theory A theory of investing stating that every rational investor, at a given level of risk, will accept only the largest expected return. More specifically, modern portfolio theory attempts to account for risk and expected return mathematically to help the investor find a portfolio with the maximum return for the minimum about of risk. A Markowitz efficient portfolio represents just that: the most expected return at a given amount of risk (sometimes excluding zero risk). Harry Markowitz first began developing this theory in an article published in 1952 and received the Nobel prize for economics for his work in 1990. See also: Homogenous expectations assumption, Markowitz efficient set of portfolios.

Modified Accelerated Cost Recovery System An accounting technique used in the United States to tax a tangible asset based upon its estimated depreciation. The estimated depreciation bears only a rough relationship to an asset's actual life, and is designed to decrease the taxation in the early years of an asset's ownership. The Modified Accelerated Cost Recovery System replaced the Accelerated Cost Recovery System in 1986, and increased the deductions an owner is allowed to take in the early years of ownership. See also: Absolute Physical Life.

Modified Adjusted Gross Income In the United States, the amount of income used to determine how much of a taxpayer's IRA contributions are tax deductible. One calculates the modified AGI by taking the adjusted gross income and adding back various deductions, notably interest on student loans, foreign income deductions, foreign housing deductions, and higher education costs. Depending on the modified AGI, some or all of one's IRA contributions will not be deductible.

Modified Duration A formula that attempts to explain a change in the price of a bond as a function of a change in interest rates. It is based on the assumption that rises in interest rates depress bond prices and drops in rates do the opposite. It is calculated as: Modified Duration = Macauley Duration / (1 + YTM/Number of coupon payments per year)

Modified Internal Rate of Return A form of the internal rate of return that assumes all returns are reinvested at a company's cost of capital. As such, it measures the profitability, as opposed to the raw cash flow, of an investment or project. It is considered a more accurate way of measuring the net present value of future cash flows.

Modified Pass-Throughs Pass-through securities with principals and interest guaranteed by a U.S. Government agency. A pass-through security is backed by assets or debt; in a modified pass-through security, a government agency reduces the risk of default to the pass-through holder by guaranteeing payment. Ginnie Mae makes most of these guarantees, but Freddie Mac and Fannie Mae do as well.

Modified Union Shop A company that has made an agreement with a labor union stating that current employees may choose to join the union or not, but all new employees will be required to become members.

Modius An ancient Roman unit of dry volume approximately equivalent to 8.73 liters.

Mofu-tan Employees of private companies in Japan who are responsible for networking with employees at the Ministry of Finance. Mofu-tan maintain friendships with MOF employees to extract information and to lobby for their companies. The term is Japanese for "MOF handlers."

Mohar The currency of Nepal from the 18th century until 1932. It was issued in both silver and gold and was divided into 128 "dams." It was replaced by the Nepalese rupee (NPR).

Mohur A gold coin issued in British India and associated states. It was equivalent to 15 rupees. British India stopped minting mohurs in 1918, but some states kept issuing them until the independence of India in 1947.

Moldovan Cupon The currency of Moldova immediately after the fall of the Soviet Union. It was issued in 1992 as a temporary measure to remove the Soviet ruble from circulation. It replaced the ruble at par and was itself replaced by the Moldovan leu in 1993.

Moldovan Leu The currency of Moldova. It was introduced in 1993, replacing the Moldovan cupon, which was itself a temporary currency to replace the Soviet ruble.

Molotov Cocktail An explosive consisting of a flammable liquid like gasoline or alcohol contained in a glass bottle. One ignites the cocktail with a makeshift wick placed in the bottle. Molotov cocktails are used when hand grenades or other "formal" weapons are unavailable or unaffordable. For that reason, they may be used in terrorist or paramilitary activities.

Mom and Pop 1. Describing a small business, usually run by a family with few or no other employees. Prices at mom and pop businesses are usually unable to compete with large retail corporations, but they generally have a reputation for providing individualized service. **2.** Describing an investor who does not invest for his/her primary income. Mom and pop investors are usually seeking to supplement their incomes or save for retirement.

Momentum The likelihood of a price movement to sustain itself. For example, if a price for a security begins to increase, momentum is its likelihood to continue to increase. There are various ways to measure momentum, but most involve volume in some way. Generally speaking, a gain or loss on high trading volume tends to indicate that the movement has momentum and is likely to continue.

Momentum Fund A mutual fund that invests predominantly or exclusively in securities experiencing short term price increases. That is, a momentum fund buys stocks in companies that are on an uptrend and sells them when the trend reverses itself. This kind of mutual fund was relatively popular in the 1990s but has since fallen out of favor because of concerns over its sustainability. It is informally called a momo fund.

Momentum Indicators Measures of a security's or market's movements taking into account both price changes and trading volume. Momentum indicators are not exact measurements, but subjective calculations of market sentiment taking those two factors into account. Momentum indicators may be positive or negative, and they may be fast or slow. For example, if an index rises quickly on heavy trading volume, it is said to have a great deal of market momentum. However, if it rises only slowly on heavy trading volume, it has less market momentum.

Momentum Investing An investment philosophy in which the investor buys (or short sells) securities that had been performing well over the previous three to 12 months and sells those that have been performing poorly over the same period. This is a form of short-term investing based on the underlying belief that trends generally continue for a long period of time. This belief is at odds with efficient markets theory, because momentum investing assumes that even inefficiently priced securities tend to remain inefficiently priced. Economists therefore disagree on whether momentum investing is a sound investment strategy. See also: Market momentum.

Momentum Player An investor who buys securities that have performed well over the previous three to 12 months and sells those that have been performing poorly over the same period. This is a form of short-term investing based on the underlying belief that trends generally continue for a long period of time. This belief is at odds with the efficient markets theory, because momentum investing assumes that even inefficiently priced securities tend to remain inefficiently priced. Economists therefore disagree on whether momentum players pursue a sound strategy.

Momme A unit of weight in Japan equivalent to 3.75 grams.

Mommy Track A path in one's career in which one has little chance of advancement. The term implies that because one prioritizes family obligations over work obligations, one is unlikely to receive promotions or major responsibilities. See also: Career-limiting move.

Monarchist A person who favors a government headed by a hereditary figure such as a king or queen. Monarchists may believe that a monarchy is preferable to a system in which politicians promote their own interests, instead of those of the state. Others may be culturally or just sentimentally attached to the days when monarchies were more common.

Monarchy A system of government headed by a hereditary figure such as a king or queen. There are two basic types of monarchies. In an absolute monarchy, the monarch theoretically has complete control as an autocrat, though in practice other officials have varying degrees of control as well. In a constitutional monarchy, the monarch shares power with an elected chamber or other elected leaders and, in extreme cases, has little actual power.

Monday Effect The belief that securities market returns on Mondays are less than the other days of the week, and are often negative on average. This effect has been observed in both American and foreign exchanges. Studies have documented it since the 1920s, but no theory has adequately explained the reasons it exists. Studies have suggested the existence of a Monday effect for a diverse range of securities, from equities to debt to commodities. However, since the mid-1970s or mid-1980s (depending on the study and methodology), large firm securities seem to have exhibited what might be called a 'reverse Monday effect,' in which differences between Monday trading and the rest of the week are not statistically significant. Small firm securities have continued to exhibit the Monday effect. It is also known as the "weekend effect."

Monegasque Franc The former currency of Monaco. It was introduced in 1837. From 1960 until it was replaced by the euro in 1999, all coins in circulation corresponded with those of the French franc. The Monegasque franc was pegged to the French franc at a one-to-one ratio and the two currencies circulated alongside each other in Monaco.

Monetarism In economics, a theory stating that inflation results directly and exclusively from the expansion of a country's money supply. That is, if a government prints money, inflation will result. Monetarists believe that a government ought to set target interest rates to encourage or slow growth in the supply. For example, when an economy is growing rapidly, monetarists recommend raising interest rates. On the other hand, they recommend lowering interest rates in a recession. In general, however, monetarists recommend that a government maintain a relatively steady money supply, with an allowance for growth to keep up with GDP expansion. Many of its beliefs, notably the one on interest rates, are still commonly held, though many

economists believe the relationship between money supply and inflation is more complex than monetarism theorizes. Milton Friedman is considered the father of modern monetarism.

Monetarist An economist who believes that inflation results directly and exclusively from the expansion of a country's money supply. That is, if a government prints money, inflation will result. Monetarists believe that a government ought to set target interest rates to encourage or slow growth in the supply. For example, when an economy is growing rapidly, monetarists recommend raising interest rates. On the other hand, they recommend lowering interest rates in a recession. In general, however, monetarists recommend that a government maintain a relatively steady money supply, with an allowance for growth to keep up with GDP expansion. Many monetarist beliefs, notably the one regarding interest rates, are still commonly held, though many economists believe the relationship between money supply and inflation is more complex than monetarism theorizes. Milton Friedman is considered the father of modern monetarism.

Monetary Accord of 1951 An agreement between the U.S. Treasury and the Federal Reserve that restored the Reserve's independence. During World War II, the Federal Reserve agreed to keep interest rates on Treasury bills very low in order to monetize the deficits the United States experienced because of the war effort. Following the war, the Treasury expected the Fed to keep rates low to further support the deficit. However, this caused inflation and many in the Fed wanted to raise interest rates. The Accord allowed it to do so.

Monetary Asset An asset held in cash or cash equivalent. That is, monetary assets are assets that can easily be liquidated. Examples include stocks and savings accounts.

Monetary Authority of Macau The central bank of Macau. It is responsible for issuing the Macanese pataca. The pataca is pegged to the Hong Kong dollar using a currency board system. That is, the Monetary Authority of Macau is legally obligated to redeem pataca for the equivalent amount of Hong Kong dollars on demand. It was established in 1989 and re-formed in 1999 upon the transfer of Macau from Portuguese to Chinese control

Monetary Authority of Singapore The central bank of Singapore. It is responsible for issuing the Singapore dollar and setting exchange rates. It also regulates banking in Singapore. Unlike many central banks, which set key interest rates, the Monetary Authority of Singapore alters its exchange rates to control its monetary policy. It was established in 1971.

Monetary Conditions Index An index tracking various measures affecting monetary policy. Different central banks include different measures in their MCIs, but they always include major exchange rates and prevailing interest rates. The MCI can help a central bank determine whether its monetary policy is too loose or too tight. The Bank of Canada was the first, and is the most prominent user of an MCI.

Monetary Easing The policy in which a central bank lowers interest rates and deposit ratios to make credit more easily available. This makes borrowing easier for businesses, which stimulates investment and expansion of operations. The immediate result of monetary easing is generally a boost in stock prices. In the medium term, it promotes economic growth. However, if this policy remains for too long, it can lead to a situation in which there is a glut of currency or too many dollars chasing too few goods and services, leading to inflation. For this reason, most central banks alternate between policies of monetary easing and monetary tightening to encourage growth while keeping inflation under control.

Monetary Gain An increase in value that occurs through inflation. Suppose one's monetary liabilities exceed one's monetary assets; that is, the debt one owes exceeds the money one has in the bank. When inflation occurs, the value of the debt is reduced, which, if the debt exceeds assets, effectively increases one's net worth. This increase in net worth is called a monetary gain.

Monetary Gold Gold owned by a government, usually as part of its currency reserves. While no country now uses a gold standard, many states hold monetary gold as a (small) part of the many things that determine a currency's value, the bulk of which is the reserve of foreign currencies. As such, monetary gold has a small role in determining nations' monetary policies. Monetary gold is not traded, except between central banks and occasionally with international organizations such as the International Monetary Fund. See also: Foreign Exchange, Reserve asset.

Monetary Indicators Indicators that would influence a central bank to change a country's monetary policy. For example, high inflation may result in the central bank raising interest rates or devalue the currency. In this case, inflation is a monetary indicator.

Monetary Items Assets and liabilities that are fixed in dollar amounts and are thus not affected by inflation. Examples of monetary items include cash, accounts receivable, accounts payable, bonds, and short-term loans. In periods of high inflation, holding monetary liabilities increases a firm's purchasing power, while holding monetary assets decreases it.

Monetary Policy The actions and inactions a central bank takes to control a country's money supply. Generally speaking, monetary policy refers to the setting of interest rates. If the central bank sets low interest rates, it increases the supply of money by easing the availability of credit. This promotes economic growth but in the long term can cause inflation. On the other hand, the central bank may adopt a restrictive monetary policy by setting high interest rates, which constricts credit and slows or eliminates growth while reducing inflation. Monetary policy may also refer to the printing of money, especially to repay government debts; this always causes inflation and is used as a last resort. See also: Hyperinflation.

Monetary Reserve The foreign currencies and precious metals that a central bank holds. A central bank's monetary reserve allows it to regulate its own currency; that is, a central bank with a large amount of reserves in euros is likely to closely follow or even peg its currency to the euro. On the other hand, central banks that keep monetary reserves in multiple currencies are more likely to follow either a basket peg or to have a floating currency. A monetary reserve is also called a currency reserve.

Monetary Tightening The policy in which a central bank raises interest rates and deposit ratios to make credit less easily available. This usually happens when the central bank is seeking to control or is concerned about inflation. Monetary tightening can negatively impact security prices and make it hard to receive a loan for a house or business.

Monetary Union A group of independent countries that share a single currency. That is, these countries, while maintaining sovereignty on economic policy, taxes, and similar issues, have transferred responsibility for a monetary policy to a central bank shared by participating members. The most famous monetary union is the eurozone, though another example is the West African Monetary Union. A monetary union is also called a currency union.

Monetary Union Index of Consumer Prices The official measure of the euro's inflation. It is calculated by taking the weighted average of inflation in each country of the eurozone. The MUICP is published annually by Eurostat, the agency responsible for collecting statistics for the European Commission. Eurostat also determines the weighting each country receives. The individual data used in calculating the weighted average results in Harmonized Indices of Consumer Prices for each eurozone country, which are compiled by the European Central Bank. See also: Consumer price index.

Monetary/Non-Monetary Method A method of accounting in which liquid assets are calculated according to their current market value while illiquid assets are calculated according to their historical value.

Monetization 1. The determination and execution of plan to make a profit from a good, service, or company. **2.** See: Monetize the debt. **3.** The liquidation of a position in order to use the cash for some other purpose.

Monetize 1. To liquidate. **2.** To print money in order to cover a debt. A government may monetize its deficit in order to finance its operations. Monetizing in this sense causes inflation. **3.** To convert into cash. One may monetize an asset by selling it or monetize a venture by producing revenue.

Monetize the Debt In government, to print money in order to repay the national debt. For example, suppose a government is $1 trillion in debt. Theoretically, the government can simply expand the money supply by $1 trillion and reduce the national debt to zero. It is not uncommon for governments monetize their debts, but because it increases the amount of money in circulation, it is considered highly inflationary.

Money A commodity, asset, or (most commonly) currency that may be exchanged for goods and services. Usually, the domestic government issues its own money and provides penalties to persons and businesses in its jurisdiction that do not accept it. Money and the money supply are integral to determining interest rates, inflation, and especially economic growth. There is no uniform agreement as to what qualifies as money; some economists include more mediums of exchange than other economists. Every society throughout history has used some sort of money, even bartering economies traded for something perceived to be equivalent. See also: Money supply, Liquidity.

Money Center Bank A large commercial bank in a major city. Smaller banks use the interest rates and business practices of money center banks to influence their own. For that reason, money center banks are considered leaders (at least regionally). They are also called money market center banks.

Money Flow In technical analysis, a measure of the change in value to a security on a trading day. It is calculated by averaging the high price, low price, and closing price and multiplying the result by the trading volume. One compares money flow to the money flow of the previous trading day to determine if it is positive (meaning day 2 is higher than day 1) or negative (meaning the opposite). A negative money flow on a rising share price may indicate that the price increase is unsustainable.

Money Gift Cash or a cash equivalent that an individual transfers to another individual while neither receiving nor expecting anything in return. As with all gifts, a money gift is taxable in the United States, but only if its value exceeds $13,000 (in 2009) and is not specifically excluded. For example, gifts between spouses are not taxable under any circumstances. See also: Estate, Gift Tax.

Money Illusion In economics, the tendency of persons not to consider inflation or deflation when making decisions. That is, the money illusion states that people think in terms of the amount of money they have, rather than in terms of its value (which tends to decline over time). The money illusion was described by John Maynard Keynes and Irving Fisher.

Money Income The dollar amount of income, without regard for purchasing power, inflation, or other factors that may affect an income's value. See also: Real Income, New York Dollar.

Money Laundering An illegal act in which one makes illegally obtained money appear to be legally obtained. For instance, one may route money obtained in drug trafficking through a shell company to give it the veneer of legitimacy. One formerly common example is the practice of exchanging illegally obtained money for coins and placing them into a soda machine. One then deposits money from the soda machine such that it looks like the money came from the purchase of sodas rather than from its real source.

Money Management 1. The act or practice of an investment advisory firm making investment decisions on behalf of a client. Money management often opens up more potential investment vehicles up to the client. Another advantage is that, theoretically, money managers have more knowledge and experience in making appropriate investment decisions than the client. This is also called investment management. **2.** The act or practice of handling one's personal finances. Money management involves paying the bills, making investments, and paying taxes.

Money Market The trading of highly liquid, short-term assets and securities. Examples include U.S. Treasury bills and commercial paper. The money market is often, though not always, included in counts of the money supply. One may trade on the money market either on an exchange or over-the-counter.

Money Market Account An account at a bank that pays a higher than normal (relative to other bank accounts) interest rate in exchange for a high minimum balance and a restriction on how many transactions may take place on the account in a given month. For example, a bank may require a minimum balance of $1,000 and require that no more than 10 transactions occur on that account each month. In exchange, it offers an interest rate competitive with the money market funds interest rate.

Money Market Demand Account An account, such as a checking or savings account, that pays a certain (low) interest rate to the holder and from which funds may be withdrawn on demand. Money market demand accounts are included in most counts of money supply.

Money Market Fund A mutual fund that invests exclusively in short-term, low-risk securities. Examples of investments in money market funds are certificates of deposit and U.S. Treasury securities. Money market funds attempt to keep their net asset values at $1 per share, such that only the yield changes. Money market funds are usually not federally insured, but the risk is so low that they very rarely lose principal for the investor. However, yields are very low and thus money market funds are subject to inflation risk; that is, the yield on a fund may be less that the inflation rate, resulting in a loss. See also: Money market security, Money market note.

Money Market Investment A highly liquid, short-term asset or security. Examples include U.S. Treasury bills and commercial paper. Money market investments are often, though not always, included in counts of the money supply. One may trade on the money market either on an exchange or over-the-counter.

Money Market Note A publicly traded debt security collateralized by a mortgage or a mortgage-backed security. Generally speaking, a money market note is unsecured and uninsured.

Money Market Operations The borrowing and re-lending of highly liquid, short-term assets and securities. Examples include the borrowing and re-lending of U.S. Treasury bills and commercial paper. Money market operations are conducted between banks. See also: Banker's acceptance.

Money Market Security A short-term investment, especially a bond, lasting one year or less. Treasury bills are exceptionally popular money market securities because they are low-risk and backed by the full faith and credit of the United States government.

Money Mudharaba In Islamic finance, a mudharaba contract in which the provider of capital gives the entrepreneur the initial investment in cash. In a mudharaba, a provider of capital agrees to invest in an entrepreneur in exchange for a portion of the profit of the entrepreneur's venture. A money mudharaba, because it utilizes cash, is the preferred form of the mudharaba contract.

Money on the Table Informal; a deal less advantageous than desired. For example, if an acquisition is made at a price different from what one party wants, that party is said to leave money on the table.

Money Order A certificate entitling the payee (and sometimes simply the holder) to the stated amount of cash immediately upon receipt by the appropriate organization. For example, one may send a money order through the U.S. Postal Service; when the payee receives the money order he/she can present it to the Post Office and receive the requisite cash. The money order is considered secure because the issuing body must receive cash in advance of providing the money order. Some companies prefer money orders to checks because money orders do not bounce. However, their relative anonymity can be used for money laundering and other illegal purposes. As a result, banks and other organizations issuing money orders often place a limit on how much can be sent, and brokerages do not generally accept them for payment. An issuer charges a fee in exchange for writing a money order. See also: Certified check, Western Union.

Money Purchase Plan An employer-contribution retirement plan in which the employer is required to place a certain amount in the retirement account each year. Usually this is a certain percentage of the employee's wages or salary. The employer is required to contribute the agreed-upon amount regardless of how the company performs in a given year. This reduces the risk for the account holder, but increases the risk for the employer. It is also called an individual account plan.

Money Rate of Return The return on an investment over and above the inflation rate. For example, if the inflation rate is 3% and the return on an investment is 5%, the money rate of return is only 2%. Investors must consider the money rate of return in order to make gains even in times of high inflation. See also: Real return.

Money Supply A measure of the total amount and value of money in an economy. There are various ways of calculating the money supply. The most conservative includes only currency in circulation and instruments that can be converted to currency on demand (e.g. the amount in a checking account). Other calculations are much broader and include comparatively illiquid assets, such as money market funds.

Central banks control the money supply in their own countries. See also: M0, M1, M2, M3, M4.

Money Wages The dollar amount of an hourly wage, without regard for purchasing power, inflation, or other factors that may affect a wage's value. See also: Real Income, New York Dollar.

Money Zero Maturity A measure of money supply that includes only money ready to be used and spent. One calculates the MZM by taking the M2 measure of money supply, subtracting time deposits (like certificates of deposit) and adding money market funds. Some analysts use the MZM to measure money supply because it is a very liquid measure.

Moneybags Slang; a wealthy person who spends freely or ostentatiously. See also: Conspicuous consumption.

Moneychanger A person or, less commonly, an institution that exchanges one currency for another on behalf of a client. For example, if one presents a moneychanger with U.S. dollars, the moneychanger may provide one with an equivalent amount of British pounds. Modern moneychangers originated in medieval Europe and were instrumental in the development of banking.

Money-Purchase Pension Plan A defined contribution pension in which an employer must contribute an amount equal to a certain percentage of the employee's compensation, usually 25%. While the amount of employer contribution is fixed, the amount of benefit is not. There are also penalties associated with receiving payments from the pension before retirement. These contributions are tax-deductible for the employer and guarantee the employee a certain amount of principal in the pension plan.

Mongo One one-hundreth of a Mongolian tugrik. It is the Mongolian equivalent of a cent. See also: MNT.

Mongolian Dollar The currency of Mongolia between 1921 and 1925. It was issued to replace the Chinese yuan but in practice it had no value. It was replaced by the tugrik in 1925.

Monism The concept that domestic and international law form a complete whole. That is, monist courts are required to enforce international law when it contradicts municipal law. For example, when a treaty becomes the law of the land upon passage, the legislature does not have to change contradictory laws because the treaty does so already. The United States has a monist state because its Constitution states that treaties are the law of the land upon ratification. See also: Dualism.

Monist A legal scholar or a jurisdiction following the theory that domestic and international law form a complete whole. That is, monist courts are required to enforce international law when it contradicts municipal law. For example, when a treaty becomes the law of the land upon passage, the legislature does not have to change contradictory laws because the treaty does so already. The United States has a monist state because its Constitution states that treaties are the law of the land upon ratification. See also: Dualism.

Monkey In the United Kingdom, a slang term for 500 pounds.

Monoline A business that only has one competency. For example, a factory that only makes one component part of an oil pump and nothing else may be called a monoline.

Monopolistic Competition Competition between two or more companies where all companies produce similar (but not exactly the same) products, but all leave some excess production capacity so that total supply for the market does not meet demand. This results in product prices remaining artificially high and therefore larger profits for the companies involved. Monopolistic competition, when it is the result of collusion between companies, can be illegal under some circumstances. It contrasts with perfect competition.

Monopoly A situation in which one company that has total or near total control of a given market. This state allows the monopolist to dictate the price most people pay in that market. For example, if one company produces 99% of the widgets sold in a country, that company can set prices because there are few other options for consumers. While monopolies are often the result of competitions, they are, by their nature, anti-competitive. Antitrust laws are in place in many countries to prevent monopolies from forming.

Monopsony Describing a market for a good or service with several potential sellers and only one potential buyer. Low prices mark the monopsonies because the sellers must compete for the buyer, perhaps to below sustainable level. One may thing of a monopsony as the polar opposite of a monopoly. See also: Buyer's Market.

Monte Carlo Simulation A computer simulation that seeks to determine the likelihood of various scenarios by running multiple simulations using random variables. The results of the Monte Carlo simulation show the most likely outcomes.

Montenegrin Perper The currency of Montenegro between 1906 and 1918. It was replaced by the Yugoslav dinar when Montenegro became part of Yugoslavia following World War I.

Montenegrin Perun A proposed currency for Montenegro. It was planned in 1851 but never implemented. Montenegro went without its own currency until 1906.

Monthly Income Preferred Securities Preferred stock representing a portion of ownership in a limited partnership. The limited partnership is a subsidiary of another company and exists only for the purpose of issuing the MIPS. The proceeds from MIPS are lent to the partnership's parent company. These securities thus combine aspects of stocks and bonds; they mature on a monthly basis and usually have a par value of $25. Returns on MIPS come out of the partnership's pretax earnings.

Monthly Investment Plan An investment plan or vehicle in which the investor adds a small amount each month to the portfolio. Perhaps the most common type of monthly investment plan is a retirement account. For different retirement accounts, one makes a monthly contribution, which is then invested so as to provide a steady return when the account holder reaches retirement. However, any investment vehicle may be made into a monthly investment plan; for example, one may make a monthly contribution to a mutual fund.

Monthly Payment Debt service or another liability one must pay on a monthly basis. Examples of monthly payments include mortgage payments and salaries to some employees.

Monthly-Income Debt Securities Also called MIDS. Tradable debt securities representing the debt of a limited partnership. The limited partnership is a subsidiary of another company and exists only for the purpose of issuing the MIDS. The proceeds from MIDS are lent to the partnership's parent company. These securities thus combine aspects of stocks and bonds; they pay coupons on a monthly basis and usually have a par value of $25.

Moody's Bond Survey A weekly report the Moody's publishes listing all changes to bond ratings that occur in a given week. It also lists new ratings for bonds, preferred stock, and commercial paper. In addition, the Survey contains commentary on the bond market more generally. It is also called the Moody's Credit Survey.

Moody's Investment Grade 1. A ratings system used by Moody's to gauge the risk of municipal bonds and the creditworthiness of their issuers. The ratings are number one through four, with a one (MIG 1) representing the highest quality and a four (MIG 4) representing the lowest quality. **2.** In other bonds, a rating higher than Baa, indicating that the issue is sufficiently low risk as to allow banks to invest in them. See: Investment-grade.

Moody's Investors Service A financial services company that primarily offers credit ratings for different kinds of bonds. That is, it serves as a credit ratings agency and a research firm. It is one of only ten firms the SEC recognizes as a credit rating agency; though, like other CRAs, its methods have been subject to criticism. For example, it gave the nation of Iceland a near top rating until its bankruptcy in 2008. It is based in New York and was established in 1909.

Moonlighting The act or practice of taking a second or third job in order to make extra money. Moonlighting may or may not be related to one's actual career. For example, one may wait tables at a restaurant in the evenings even though one's main job is teaching. Moonlighting may be temporary; for instance, one may use the extra money to pay for a trip and then leave the second job.

Moore's Law In technology, a theory stating that the number of transistors on an integrated circuit doubles every 18 months. Moore's Law was first articulated by George Moore, who co-founded Intel, in 1965. His original statement was that the doubling occurred every 12 months, but the pace has not been that fast for some time. Nevertheless, Moore's Law is expected to apply until at least 2017, when physical limitation is predicted to force the rate of development to slow.

MOP ISO 4217 code for the Macanese pataca. It was introduced in 1894. Macau is a special administrative region of China; perhaps because of this the pataca is pegged to the Hong Kong dollar using a currency board system. That is, the Monetary Authority of Macau it legally obligated to redeem pataca for the equivalent amount of Hong Kong dollars on demand.

Moral Hazard The risk that a party to a transaction or activity is not acting in good faith, or that one party has perverse incentives to act in a manner detrimental to the counter party. Moral hazards may exist for almost anything. For example, a plan for a government to bail out delinquent mortgages has the moral hazard that it will encourage mortgage holders to refrain from making their home payment. Likewise, deregulation has the moral hazard that companies will use it as incentive for short-term, unsustainable profits, rather than proper economic growth.

Moral Obligation Debt A municipal bond or another government bond that is not secured by the full faith and credit of the issuer. Unlike general obligation bonds, which are secured in this way, moral obligation bonds carry higher risk and, therefore, a higher yield. However, because they are still government bonds, their interest is usually deductible from federal income taxes.

Moral Suasion Statements or acts by a regulatory authority to encourage, rather than coerce, compliance with accepted standards. For instance, given a non-compliant thrift, the Office of Thrift Supervision may increase the number of inspections, privately tell executives what needs to be done, and use other persuasive tactics to change the thrift's behavior, rather than simply reporting the violations and fining it accordingly. The idea behind moral suasion is that sometimes the threat of punishment changes behavior just as well and with less embarrassment than punishment itself. The term is often applied to the Federal Reserve Board's statements in which it makes vague threats of certain actions (such as raising interest rates) in an attempt to change market actors' behavior. Moral suasion is known less formally as jawboning.

Moratorium A temporary delay. An example of a moratorium is a delay in the payment of debt. That is, if too many people are unable to repay loans, the government may declare that no one is legally obligated to make debt service payments for a period of six months. Likewise, if a company is having a difficult year, it may declare a moratorium on research and development funding for two years in order to save money.

Morbidity Table In actuarial analysis, a table of the likelihood a person of a certain age, health or occupation will be injured or become sick in the next year. This is important in determining one's eligibility for many insurance plans. See also: Mortality table.

Mordida Spanish for "bite." It is used in Mexico as a slang term for bribery.

Morg An obsolete Polish unit of area approximately equivalent to 0.5755 hectares.

Morga An obsolete Polish unit of area approximately equivalent to 0.5985 hectares.

Morgan Dollar A $1 coin minted in the United States between 1878 and 1904, and again in 1921. It featured Lady Liberty on the obverse and is named for George T. Morgan, who designed it.

Morgan Stanley Capital International A financial services company based in New York. Founded in 1970, it has been publicly-traded since 1986 and specializes in market analysis and the publication of various indices. It is perhaps best known for the MSCI World Index and the MSCI EAFE Index. While it is a publicly-traded company, the majority shareholder is Morgan Stanley. For this reason, some Morgan Stanley products, notably iShares, track MSCI indices.

Morgan Stanley Capital International Emerging Markets Global Index A capitalization-weighted index of stocks traded in 29 emerging markets. It is managed and published by Morgan Stanley Capital International (MSCI). It is considered a benchmark of equity performance in developing countries. It is one of the best known indices published by MSCI.

Morgan Stanley Capital International Europe Index An index published by Morgan Stanley Capital International (MSCI) that tracks stocks in 15 European countries. Examples of countries with stocks tracked by the index are Austria, Italy, and Norway. German, French, and British stocks form the majority of the index. As with all MSCI indices, it is weighted for market capitalization.

Morgan Stanley Capital International Europe, Australia, Far East Index An index published by Morgan Stanley Capital International that tracks stocks in Europe, Australia, and East Asia. It is considered one of the most important indices for stocks outside the United States; indeed, its strong performance in the 1980s and early 1990s has been credited with spurring American interest in foreign investment. It is weighted for market capitalization.

Morgan Stanley Capital International Index Any of several indices managed and published by Morgan Stanley Capital International (MSCI). Some Morgan Stanley Capital International indices are considered benchmarks of global equity performance. Perhaps the best known indices are the MSCI World Index and the MSCI EAFE Index. Because MSCI's majority shareholder is Morgan Stanley, some Morgan Stanley products, notably iShares, track Morgan Stanley Capital International indices.

Morgan Stanley Capital International Pacific Free Index An index published by Morgan Stanley Capital International that tracks stocks in Pacific and Far Eastern countries. It is weighted for market capitalization.

Morgen An obsolete Dutch unit of area roughly equivalent to nine square meters, with slight regional variations.

Morning Drive The period of radio broadcasting on weekdays between 6 a.m. and 10 a.m. Radio stations typically charge advertisers more per commercial during the morning drive because more people than average are listening to their radios during their daily commutes to work.

Morningstar Rating System A system used to measure a mutual fund's risk compared to other similar mutual funds. For example, the Morningstar rating system may compare the volatility of a bond fund to that of other bond funds. According to the system, average risk equates to a rating of 1, with riskier funds receiving higher ratings.

Morningstar Risk Rating A measure of a mutual fund's risk compared to other, similar mutual funds. For example, it may compare the volatility of a bond fund to other bond funds. A mutual fund with average risk receives a Morningstar risk rating of 1. Riskier funds receive higher ratings.

Morningstar, Inc. A corporation that provides research and advisory services to clients. Its clients tend to be institutional investors, though a wide range of investors read its advisory newsletters. Morningstar is particularly well-known for its one page newsletters on more than 2,000 mutual funds and exchange-traded funds. Some of its information is available for free on its website, but more detailed information is provided through subscription services.

Moroccan Dirham The currency of Morocco. It was introduced in 1960, replacing the Moroccan franc. It is illegal to export locally circulating dirhams.

Moroccan Franc The former currency of Morocco. It was introduced in French Morocco in 1921, and became the currency of the independent Morocco in 1957. The Moroccan dirham was introduced in 1960, but the franc remained as a subdivision of the dirham until the santim replaced it in 1974.

Mortality and Expense Risk Charge An annual fee that some annuities and insurance policies assess on holders to compensate the provider for additional risk of death or the occurrence of some other insured event. For example, an insurance company will likely add a mortality and expense risk charge for a life insurance policy if someone purchases the policy at the age of 88 (indeed, some insurance companies do not provide policies for someone of this age). However, the company will be unlikely to add the charge if a person in good health purchases a policy at the age of 25.

Mortality Assumption A statistical estimate of the number of deaths a life insurance company expects to occur over a given period of time. The mortality assumption influences the underwriting decisions an insurer makes.

Mortality Table In actuarial analysis, a table of the likelihood a person of a certain age will die in the next year. This is important in determining one's eligibility for some insurance and annuity plans.

Mortgage A loan used to buy real estate. A mortgage is secured by the property it is used to purchase. One must make monthly payments on a mortgage, and there is a set term before full payment is due, often 15, 20, or 30 years. Some mortgages have fixed interest rates, while others have variable interest rates. If one defaults on a mortgage, the bank making it may take possession of the real estate and sell it to recover its investment. Some banks, notably savings and loans, specialize in making mortgage loans. See also: Mortgage-backed security.

Mortgage Bank A bank that primarily or exclusively offers loans to clients to purchase real estate, especially of private residences. The bank loans its own capital to clients and either collects payments (with interest) or sells its loans on the secondary market. Other revenue comes from origination fees and similar fees attached to making loans.

Mortgage Banker One who works for, or, especially, manages, a mortgage bank. Mortgage bankers are responsible for making mortgage loans and ensuring their timely payment. Because they specialize exclusively in mortgage loans, they often have greater access to Fannie Mae, Freddie Mac, or similar federal banking institutions. This gives them access to capital to make loans that they may not otherwise have because they work for non-depository institutions. Very often, mortgage bankers sell the mortgages they issue so as to have easier access to capital without having to wait for the loans' repayments. This in turn allows them to make more mortgage loans. See also: Mortgage-backed securities.

Mortgage Bond A long-term bond secured by the payments on one or more mortgages. For example, a mortgage corporation may issue a bond backed by payments it receives from clients. This provides the issuer with working capital while providing a relatively safe investment for bondholders. In the event of default, bondholders have the right to take possession of and sell the property underlying the mortgage in order to recover their investments. See also: Mortgage-backed security.

Mortgage Broker One who facilitates transactions between mortgage borrowers and lenders. Mortgage brokers are responsible for providing paper work between the parties and generally streamlining the process of making a mortgage. It is important to note that a mortgage broker neither originates nor provides funds for a loan. If the mortgage broker is unaffiliated with the lender, he/she may negotiate on behalf of the borrower for better terms. In any case, the mortgage broker receives a fee from the lender for locating the borrower and bringing him/her to the lender. See also: Mortgage banker.

Mortgage Credit Certificate A security issued by a state or local government allowing holders to claim a tax credit on a portion of the interest they pay on their mortgages. In general, one may not purchase a mortgage credit certificate if one has owned a home in the previous three years; it is intended to help first-time home buyers afford to purchase a house.

Mortgage Debt The balance still owed on a mortgage. One's level of mortgage debt compared to his/her equity or other assets may determine how much he/she can borrow. See also: Refinancing.

Mortgage Derivative A security with a value based upon principal and interest payments on a pool of mortgages. This entitles the owner to a claim on the principal and interest payments on the particular mortgages backing the security. The risk of a mortgage derivative ultimately comes from the risk of default of the underlying mortgages. A mortgage-backed security is the most common type of mortgage derivative.

Mortgage Duration The number of years until an investor receives the present value of all income from a mortgage-backed security (including interest and principal). It is used to gauge a mortgage-backed security's sensitivity to interest rate changes. The longer a mortgage duration is, the more an MBS declines in value when interest rates rise, and the more it rises when they fall.

Mortgage Insurance An insurance policy that provides coverage to a lender in the event that a borrower defaults on a mortgage. This ensures that the lender does not incur a loss if the borrower is unable to repay the loan. While the lender pays the premium, it generally passes on payment to the borrower (and may roll it into the monthly mortgage payment). A lender may require a borrower to pay for mortgage insurance in certain high risk situations. See also: Loan-to-Value Ratio.

Mortgage Insurance Policy Premium The premium paid on an insurance policy that provides coverage to a lender in the event that a borrower defaults on a mortgage. This ensures that the lender does not incur a loss if the borrower is unable to repay the loan. While the lender pays the mortgage insurance premium, it generally passes on payment to the borrower, either by requiring payment in the closing costs or by rolling it into the monthly mortgage payment. See also: Mortgage Insurance.

Mortgage Interest The interest on a loan secured by a piece of real estate. For example, the interest on a home loan is mortgage interest. In the United States, mortgage interest on one's primary residence is tax deductible.

Mortgage Interest Deduction In the United States, a tax deduction on the interest paid on one's mortgage. That is, one may reduce one's taxable income by the amount one pays in interest on all eligible mortgages. There are some limits to the mortgage interest deduction: for example, one may only deduct interest on the first $1,000,000 worth of mortgages, aggregated with other home debt. However, most homeowners can deduct all of their mortgage interest.

Mortgage Interest Relief A program in Ireland providing a tax benefit for a portion of the interest that one pays on a mortgage. One is able to reduce the amount of one's monthly mortgage payment to the bank by the amount of the benefit; the government reimburses the bank. The program is intended to promote home ownership.

Mortgage Interest Relief at Source Also called MIRAS. A former benefit in the United Kingdom in which individuals could take a tax deduction for the interest paid on mortgages up to 30,000 pounds (25,000 pounds before 1983). It was instituted to encourage home ownership. MIRAS was established in 1969 and eliminated in 2000.

Mortgage Lien The right of a lender to take possession of a designated piece of real estate if a borrower does not repay a mortgage. For example, if Joe buys a house with a mortgage loan and then defaults, the lender may take possession of the house. The lender releases the lien when the mortgage is fully repaid.

Mortgage Life Insurance An insurance policy that pays off a policyholder's mortgage in the event of his/her death. This protects a mortgage holder's heirs in the event of his/her untimely demise. There are two basic types of mortgage life insurance. Decreasing term insurance charges premiums that decrease as the mortgage holder gradually pays off the mortgage. Level term insurance has premiums that do not decrease; it is recommended for borrowers with interest-only mortgages. Both types of mortgage life insurance exist only for the life of the mortgage. If the beneficiary dies after he/she has finished paying for the house, no mortgage life insurance is paid out.

Mortgage Out To borrow more than is necessary to secure the purchase or improvement of real estate. Formerly, mortgaging out was most common in construction projects, but it has become difficult with increasingly strict underwriting standards.

Mortgage Pipeline Informal; the process by which a mortgage lender conducts all due diligence, files all necessary paperwork, and generally makes preparation for a new mortgage. This includes investigating the potential borrower's credit history and determining whether making the loan is a good risk. See also: Mortgage-pipeline risk.

Mortgage Pool A group of mortgages that may be placed into the same investment vehicle, especially a mortgage-backed security. The mortgage pool is collected and then divided up into smaller pieces, each containing the same proportion of the individual mortgages; the pieces are then sold as securities. Generally speaking, the mortgages in a mortgage pool have the same characteristics, such as similar maturities.

Mortgage Protection Insurance An insurance policy that makes mortgage payments on behalf of the policyholder in the event of financial hardship. For example, if a policyholder loses his job, mortgage protection insurance would make his house payment for up to, say, six months as he looks for work. Mortgage protection insurance allows one to face difficulty without the immediate fear of losing one's home.

Mortgage Rate The interest rate on a loan used to buy real estate. Some mortgages have fixed mortgage rates, meaning that it remains constant over the life of the mortgage, while adjustable-rate mortgages have variable mortgage rates, meaning that interest rates change according to prevailing interest rates, at least within certain limits. The mortgage rate, along with the amount of the loan and the time until it comes due, helps determine one's monthly payment. See also: Mortgage-backed security.

Mortgage REIT A real estate investment trust (REIT) that invests in mortgages, rather than buys and owns property outright. The revenue for mortgage REITs comes mainly from the principal and interest on the mortgages owned. Like all REITs, they may be traded as if they were stocks. Owning a mortgage REIT is more liquid than directly owning the real estate underlying it.

Mortgage-Backed Revenue Bond A municipal bond that is issued in order to finance low-cost mortgages for residents of the municipality. The bonds are guaranteed by the payments made on these mortgages. In many ways, they are similar to mortgage-backed securities, but they are issued by a local government instead of private entity. A mortgage-backed revenue bond is also called a housing bond.

Mortgage-Backed Security A derivative whose value is derived from unpaid mortgages. This entitles the owner to a claim on the principal and interest payments on the particular mortgages backing the security. MBSs pay an interest rate that is usually related to the interest rates the homeowners are paying on their mortgages. The equivalent of the coupon on a mortgage-backed security is a percentage of the interest and principal paid on the mortgages backing the security. An obvious risk to an MBS is the possibility that interest rates may decline, causing homeowners to refinance their mortgages. This provides capital to MBS holders, but it comes at a time when purchasing more MBSs would yield less due to the decline in interest rates. More complicated versions of MBSs include the collateralized mortgage obligation and the mortgage derivative. These attempt to reduce the risk associated with declines in interest rates. Another risk associated with mortgage-backed securities is the possibility that a substantial number of mortgages will default. A main proximate cause of the credit crunch, which began in 2006-2007, was the fact that many mortgage-backed securities backed by subprime mortgages began to default. See also: Credit risk, Liquidity risk, Credit crunch.

Mortgaged to the Hilt A slang term describing someone with so much debt that he/she is unlikely to be able to repay it. Being mortgaged to the hilt may lead to bankruptcy.

Mortgagee A mortgage lender. A mortgagee is ordinarily a bank or savings and loan corporation.

Mortgage-Pipeline Risk In mortgages, the risk that the prospective borrower will decline a mortgage within a certain period of time. Many lenders agree to set the interest rate at the prevailing rate at the time the sale of the property closes. The lender is therefore exposed to the risk that the prevailing interest rate will fall between the time the agreement is reached and the closing of the sale. If the borrower declines the mortgage between that agreement and the close, the lender will have lost the potential gain from the higher interest rate. See also: Reverse Price Risk.

Mortgagor In a mortgage, the party that borrows funds. The mortgagor must repay the amount borrowed to the mortgagee (which is usually a bank).

Mortise In printing, a hole cut into a block or plate so type can be inserted.

Moscow Interbank Currency Exchange One of the largest stock exchanges in Russia. The MICEX trades stocks, bonds, currencies, and derivatives in more than 600 publicly-traded companies with a market capitalization of tens of trillions of rubles. Tracing its roots to before the fall of the Soviet Union, MICEX quoted official exchange rates on behalf of the Bank of Russia until 1992. Among its largest companies by market capitalization is Gazprom, which has a large role in the global oil and gas industries.

Most Active List The list of stocks on an exchange with the highest trading volume, especially on a given trading day. A stock is often listed on the most active list when relevant information on the company becomes available. Being on the most active list is not necessarily positive; that is, the information could be either good or bad, and investors could buy or sell accordingly. Technical analysts may use the high trading volume to determine how strong or sustainable a bullish or bearish trend is.

Most Favored Nation A status in which a country assesses the lowest possible tariffs that it can assess on another country. For example, if a country's lowest tariff is a certain percentage of the value of a good, it charges this percentage on an import from a country with most favored nation status. Members of the World Trade Organization are required to extend Most Favored Nation status to other members, though exceptions exist. In the United States, most favored nation status is formally called permanent normal trade relations.

Most Likely Time In PERT, the statistical time in which an activity has the greatest probability of occurrence.

Most Recent Quarter The quarter that ended most previously. For example, if the first quarter of a fiscal year runs from January through March and it is currently April, the first quarter is the MRQ. The abbreviation is sometimes used in financial statements.

Mothballing A practice in which a company keeps equipment in a factory or other production facility in working order but does not use it on a constant basis. This is useful when a company has high operating costs and it would be more expensive to use the facility. Mothballing allows the company to save its expenses and still use the facility when needed.

Mother Chip A slang term for stock in Intel. The term derives from the fact that Intel is one of the largest and most prominent semiconductor chip companies.

Mothers High-growth stocks listed on the Tokyo Stock Exchange. Mothers are start-up, publicly-traded companies. There are fewer mothers on the Tokyo exchange than any other type of company. See also: First Section, Second Section.

Motor Truck Cargo Insurance An insurance policy that protects a trucking company from legal liability resulting from the loss, theft or destruction of cargo on a truck. This replaces the value of the lost cargo. As with all insurance, the policyholder must pay a premium to receive the coverage.

Motti A Finnish unit meaning one cubic meter. It is used for firewood or scrap paper.

Mottle Discoloration in processed food, which can be unappetizing and may result in the return of the food to the store for a refund.

Motto A saying inscribed on a coin, especially but not necessarily the official motto of a country. For example, all American coins are inscribed with "In God We Trust," the motto of the United States.

Motza An Australian slang term for a great deal of money, especially used with reference to gambling winnings.

Mouse House A slang term for a finance company. The term is most common in auto sales.

Moving Average The average price of a security over a certain time period, calculated continuously. For instance, one may calculate a moving average by adding prices from the most recent trading days (for example, the last 10 days) and dividing by the number of trading days considered (in this case, 10). A moving average may or may not be weighted. Moving averages help smooth out noise that may be present in a security's price on a given trading day. See also: Simple Moving Average, Exponential Moving Average.

Moving Average Convergence Divergence In technical analysis, an indicator of momentum calculated by subtracting the 26-day exponential moving average of a security's price from the 12-day exponential moving average. Technical analysts calculate a nine-day exponential moving average of the MACD to trace price movements and determine buy and sell signals.

Moving Average Ribbon In technical analysis, a method of determining the strength of a price movement in which one charts a large number of moving averages on the same graph. Each moving average measures a different period of time (trailing 10-day, trailing 12-month, and so forth). When all the moving averages move in the same direction, the security's price trend is believed to be strong and sustained.

Moving Expense Deduction A reduction in one's taxable income because of money spent in the course of moving to start a new job or to transfer in one's current job. This deduction is subject to certain restrictions. Specifically, only expenses incurred from the physical act of moving are deductible. For example, meals taken while traveling are not deductible, but the cost of gasoline may be.

Moving Expenses Money that one spends in the course of moving to start a new job or because of a transfer in one's current job. In the United States, one may deduct moving expenses from one's taxable income, after certain thresholds are met with regard to time and distance. This deduction is subject to certain restrictions. Specifically, only expenses incurred from the physical act of moving are deductible. For example, meals taken while traveling are not deductible, but the cost of gasoline may be.

Moving Insurance An insurance policy that provides a moving company with coverage for losses to furniture and other assets while it is in the possession of the company. For example, if a mirror breaks in transportation and the moving company is responsible for replacing it, moving insurance would cover the cost. As with all insurance, one must pay a premium to receive the coverage.

Moving Shot In cinematography, a shot in which the camera moves, whether against a stationary or moving object. Moving shots are often used in action scenes, which may influence the advertisements the broadcast garners.

MOZ GOST 7.67 Latin three-letter geocode for Mozambique. The code is used for transactions to and from Mozambique bank accounts and for international shipping to Mozambique. As with all GOST 7.67 codes, it is used primarily in Cyrillic alphabets.

Mozambican Escudo The currency of Mozambique between 1914 and 1980. It was pegged to the Portuguese escudo until 1977. It was replaced by the metical.

Mozambican Metica A proposed currency for Mozambique. It was produced in 1975 and 1976, but never went into circulation.

MP 1. ISO 3166-1 alpha-2 code for the Commonwealth of the Northern Mariana Islands. This is the code used in international transactions to and from Northern Mariana bank accounts. **2.** ISO 3166-2 geocode for the Northern Mariana Islands. This is used as an international standard for shipping to the Northern Mariana Islands.

MR 1. ISO 3166-1 alpha-2 code for the Republic of Mauritania. This is the code used in international transactions to and from Mauritanian bank accounts. **2.** ISO 3166-2 geocode for Mauritania. This is used as an international standard for shipping to Mauritania. Each subdivision has its own code with the prefix "MR." For example, the code for the District of Nouakchott is ISO 3166-2:MR-NKC.

MRO ISO 4217 code for the Mauritanian Ouguiya. It was introduced in 1973, when Mauritania left the CFA franc currency zone. Interestingly, it is one of only two currencies not based on factors of 10; each ouguiya is divided into five khoums.

MRT GOST 7.67 Latin three-letter geocode for Mauritania. The code is used for transactions to and from Mauritanian bank accounts and for international shipping to Mauritania. As with all GOST 7.67 codes, it is used primarily in Cyrillic alphabets.

MS 1. ISO 3166-1 alpha-2 code for Montserrat. This is the code used in international transactions to and from Montserrat's bank accounts. **2.** ISO 3166-2 geocode for Montserrat. This is used as an international standard for shipping to Montserrat.

MSCI EM EMEA Index An index published by Morgan Stanley Capital International (MSCI) that tracks stocks in eight developing countries in Europe, the Middle East and Africa. Countries with stocks tracked by the index include the Czech Republic, Egypt and South Africa. As with all MSCI indices, it is weighted for market capitalization.

MSCI Europe Index An index published by Morgan Stanley Capital International (MSCI) that tracks stocks in Europe. As with all MSCI indices, it is weighted for market capitalization.

MSCI World Index An index consisting of a wide selection of stocks traded in 23 developed countries. It is weighted for market capitalization and is considered an important benchmark of the state of global stock markets. It is managed by MSCI and has existed since 1969.

MSR GOST 7.67 Latin three-letter geocode for Montserrat. The code is used for transactions to and from Montserratian bank accounts and for international shipping to Montserrat. As with all GOST 7.67 codes, it is used primarily in Cyrillic alphabets.

MT 1. ISO 3166-1 alpha-2 code for the Republic of Malta. This is the code used in international transactions to and from Maltese bank accounts. **2.** ISO 3166-2 geocode for Malta. This is used as an international standard for shipping to Malta. Each local council has its own code with the prefix "MT." For example, the code for Isla is ISO 3166-2:MT-20.

Mtaa In Kenya, a political subdivision equivalent to a township or village within a tarafa (or municipality).

MTL ISO 4217 currency code for the Maltese lira, which was the currency of Malta from 1972 until 2007. Prior to 1972, Malta used the British pound; when the pound decimalized, Malta decided to issue its own lira, which it pegged to the pound on a 1:1 basis. It later was pegged to a currency basket and became the second highest valued currency in the world. It was replaced by the euro on January 1, 2008.

MTQ GOST 7.67 Latin three-letter geocode for Martinique. The code is used for transactions to and from local bank accounts and for international shipping to Martinique. As with all GOST 7.67 codes, it is used primarily in Cyrillic alphabets.

MU 1. ISO 3166-1 alpha-2 code for the Republic of Mauritius. This is the code used in international transactions to and from Mauritian bank accounts. **2.** ISO 3166-2 geocode for Mauritius. This is used as an international standard for shipping to

Mauritius. Each Mauritian district has its own code with the prefix "MU." For example, the code for the District of Black River is ISO 3166-2:MU-BL.

Muang In Laos, a political subdivision approximately equivalent to a county.

Mubaah'umuumii In Islamic law, anything that no one person is entitled to own. Examples include sunlight, water in a river, and pastures. Mubaah'umuumii must be shared by all at no cost to any one individual.

Muban In Thailand, a political subdivision equivalent to a village.

Muckraker A term for a journalist or other person who exposes corruption, especially in business or politics. The term has had both positive and negative connotations throughout its history. In the positive sense, muckrakers are thought to champion truth by exposing corruption. In the negative sense, the term connotes a person who is willing to compromise truth for a good story. That is, some muckrakers may exaggerate or in some cases simply make up their allegations.

Mud A Dutch unit of volume equivalent to 100 liters. It was adopted in 1817, soon after the establishment of the Kingdom of the Netherlands.

Muddakhar In Islamic law, describing any item that can be stored. According to the Maliki school of jurisprudence, riba al-fadl (interest in kind) may occur if a muddakhar item is lent in exchange for receiving more of the same item at a later date.

Muderiah In Yemen, a political subdivision approximately equivalent to a county.

Mueang In parts of Southeast Asia, an archaic political subdivision roughly equivalent to a province.

Muhafazah In some Arabic-speaking countries, a political subdivision equivalent to a province or district. In general, a muhafazah is smaller than a mitiqah.

Mukim In Brunei, a political subdivision approximately equivalent to a municipality.

Mullah A Muslim who is religiously educated. Some mullahs are experts in Islamic finance.

Multibank Holding Company A company that is the majority shareholder in at least two banks. A multibank holding company controls the operations of the banks it owns. Multibank holding companies have access to liquidity from regulators through the loans made to the banks themselves. In the United States, all bank holding companies must register with the Federal Reserve and are subject to its regulation, though they may also be responsible to other regulators as well.

Multibuyer A customer who appears on the client lists of two or more companies. Multibuyers may be more likely to buy new products than others.

Multibuyer Policy An insurance policy that protects the holder from the credit risk associated with selling goods to many different buyers. In the United States, multibuyer policies are sold to exporters by the Ex-Im Bank.

Multicoded City Any city in the United States with more than one zip code. All major American cities are multicoded cities.

Multicurrency Clause A clause in some eurocurrency loan agreements allowing the borrower to begin making payments in another currency at some point in the future, at his/her discretion.

Multi-Currency Line of Credit A line of credit on which a company may draw in one of several currencies. For example, the company may borrow from the same credit line in either U.S. dollars or euros, depending on its specific needs at the moment. A multi-currency line of credit may save a multinational corporation the time and expense incurred in foreign exchange transactions.

Multicurrency Loans Loans in which the borrower, at his/her discretion, may receive the funds from the loans in more than one currency. Some multicurrency loans only use two currencies, while others give the borrower the choice of several currencies. Multicurrency loans are particularly useful to multinational corporations that wish to reduce the foreign exchange risk in financing a project that may need to occur in several countries at once. See also: Dual currency issue.

Multi-Discipline Account A discretionary account to which several different money managers may have access. A multi-disciplined account is divided into several sub-accounts, with each money manager having access to one. Each money manager has a different expertise and invests the money in his/her sub-account accordingly. For example, an investor may wish to divide the account as half equity and half debt securities and hire two different money managers to do so. A multi-discipline account helps diversify one's portfolio with less complication. Most multi-discipline accounts require a minimum investment of $150,000.

Multifactor CAPM A form of the capital asset pricing model that includes macroeconomic risks left out in other versions of the CAPM. These macroeconomic variables are called factors, and are included as the model calculates prices of portfolios. Proponents claim that the multifactor CAPM better accounts for systemic risks and fits data better, while critics contend that the model does not calculate the relative riskiness of each factor compared to other factors.

Multifamily Loan A loan secured by the receivables on mortgages on apartment buildings, condominiums, and/or other multifamily residential complexes.

Multi-Fibre Arrangement An expired international agreement that set quotas on the textiles and clothing developing countries could export to developed countries. The purpose behind the Multi-Fibre Arrangement was to allow developed countries time to adjust to competition from developing countries, which could produce the same textile products much more cheaply. It was thought that developing countries could flood the markets in developed countries with less expensive textiles, which would have had a negative effect on the developed countries' economies. Critics of the Arrangement argued this hampered development. It was in effect from 1974 through the end of 2004. It is formally called the Agreement on Textile and Clothing. See also: World Trade Organization.

Multilateral Investment Guarantee Agency An agency of the World Bank that seeks to promote foreign direct investment in developing countries. It does this primarily by selling political risk insurance to corporations that wish to expand into the developing world. It also provides advisory services to governments in these countries on how best to attract investment. It was established in 1988 and is based in Washington, DC.

Multilateral Steel Agreement A proposed agreement to reduce or eliminate tariffs and other trade barriers on steel. Negotiations for the Multilateral Steel Agreement took place among 35 countries under the General Agreement of Tariffs and Trade, but were suspended in 1992, and the treaty never came to fruition.

Multilith A printing machine on which paper is placed on a cylinder, which presses it down to imprint text or images. Multiliths are used mainly by small businesses.

Multinational Corporation A corporation that maintains assets and/or operations in more than one country. A multinational corporation often has a long supply chain that may, for example, require the acquisition of raw materials in one country, a product's manufacture in a second country, and its retail sale in a third country. A multinational often globally manages its operations from a main office in its home country. Multinational corporations are controversial among groups such as environmentalists and worker advocates, who claim that multinationals exploit resources and employees. On the other hand, proponents argue that multinationals create wealth in every country where they operate, which ultimately benefits workers as well as shareholders.

Multinational Netting The practice of eliminating offsetting cash flows from the balance sheet of a multinational corporation. For example, if a multinational corporation owes a bank $50 million and the bank owes the corporation $30 million in a separate transaction, the corporation may use multinational netting and record that it owes the bank only $20 million.

Multinational Restructuring The act of changing the terms on the assets and/or liabilities of a multi-national corporation. That is, a multinational corporation may consolidate its debts, significantly change the size and scope of its operations, and take other measures to reduce the strain of continuing operation. Most companies, whether or not they are multinational corporations, restructure either as part of a bankruptcy or as an effort to avoid it.

Multi-Option Financing Facility A credit line with option contracts attached to it to increase the flexibility available to the borrower.

Multiperiod Immunization An immunization strategy in which one matches the duration of bonds in a portfolio to the duration of one's liabilities. Duration is the number of years until the investor receives the present value of all income from a bond (including interest and principal), and is used to gauge a bond's sensitivity to interest rate changes. A multiperiod immunization strategy is intended to reduce the portfolio's sensitivity to interest rates; that way, the return on the portfolio will enable the holder to pay for his/her liabilities regardless of fluctuations in interest rates. See also: Duration matching strategy.

Multiple Arbitrage In hedge funds, the use of more than one arbitrage strategy at the same time. Hedge funds conduct multiple arbitrages to extract the highest possible return at the fund's level of risk.

Multiple Bank A bank that provides more than one type of banking service. For example, a bank that provides retail services, investment banking services, and brokerage services is a multiple bank. In the United States, multiple banks have become more common since the repeal of the Glass-Steagall Act in 1999.

Multiple Compression A situation in which a publicly-traded company's share price does not rise, or may fall, even on strong earnings. That is, multiple compression occurs when the price-earnings multiple falls. Multiple compression is usually the result of investors' skepticism on growth prospects. Generally, investors buy stocks with high price-earnings ratios if they are confident in high, future growth; when multiple compression occurs, it may indicate that investors believe that growth rates are leveling off, and that the company is unlikely to grow much more. To an extent, this is a positive sign, as it shows confidence that the company has become well-established, but, on the other hand, it may be a sign that investors believe the company's stock is overvalued.

Multiple Discriminant Analysis A practice of analyzing a security using a variety of different factors. For example, an analyst may use many different financial ratios in deciding whether or not to buy a given stock. The goal of MDA is to create a Markowitz efficient portfolio.

Multiple Insurance 1. Two or more insurance policies covering the same thing. For example, a person may hold two life insurance policies. **2.** See: Multiple peril insurance.

Multiple Listing An agreement between real estate brokers to share the commissions on one or more houses sold by one of the brokers. This allows the brokers to collaborate rather than compete.

Multiple Management The act or practice of multiple money managers working on a single, particularly large portfolio. As with other forms of asset management, these managers make investment decisions on behalf of a client. Each manager has autonomy in the decisions he/she makes, which is intended to both foster a spirit of competition and allow individual investments to be more closely monitored. However, multiple management is not always conducive to coordination between the managers, a fact that may hinder the accomplishment of the client's investment goals.

Multiple management is usually limited to institutional investors and high net-worth individuals, as it is usually expensive.

Multiple Protection Life Insurance Policy An insurance policy in which the death benefit varies depending on when the insured dies. If the insured dies in the first 10 years of the policy, three times the face value of the policy is paid to survivors. Otherwise, they are paid only the face value. This may be beneficial if one expects one's family to have significant short term but fewer long term expenses. As with all insurance, one must pay a premium to receive the coverage.

Multiple Rates of Return A situation in which the internal rate of return for a project has more than one value. The internal rate of return is the present value of cash flows that will result in a project breaking even; multiple rates of return occur when one calculates cash inflows and cash outlows in the internal rate of return.

Multiple Regression In statistics, an equation showing the value of a dependent variable as a function of two or more independent variables. As with regression analysis, multiple regression analysis is important for determining certain economic phenomena.

Multiple Round Lots Two or more sets of 100 shares in a security that are traded in a single transaction.

Multiple Shop A company in which both professional and nonprofessional employees are represented by the same union. For example, in a multiple shop, both the professional mechanics and the untrained workers at an airline may have the same union. All affected workers must consent before they form a multiple shop.

Multiple Taxation A situation in which the same earnings are taxed more than twice. For example, multiple taxation may occur when a publicly-traded company pays corporate taxes on its earnings. It then passes on some of those earnings to shareholders as dividends, on which they must pay a capital gains tax at the federal level and then again at the state level. Various means exist to reduce multiple taxation. See also: Tax avoidance.

Multiple-Issuer Pool A pool of mortgages from multiple lenders. GNMA-II securities are formed by creating a multiple-issuer pool and dividing up the mortgages contained in it to form the individual securities.

Multiplier 1. The expression of a currency in terms of one U.S. dollar. For example, if a pound is worth $2.05 on a given day, it has a multiplier of 2.05. This is also called an American currency quotation. See also: Currency pair **2.** In Keynesian economics, the change in income (such as GDP or GNP) that results from a capital injection. For example, if a government spends a certain amount of money building a bridge, it must hire and pay workers to do so. These workers in turn spend their earnings on other goods and services, which fuels economic growth. The multiplier measures how much each dollar the government spends increases economic growth. See also: Demand-side economics.

Multiplier Effect A measure of the change in a country's money supply that occurs as the result of banks' ability to lend. The multiplier effect is dependent on banks' required reserves, or the amount of money in deposits they are legally required to keep in-house. If a bank has a low reserve requirement, it is able to lend more of its deposit money, which in turn increases the money supply. This indicates a high multiplier effect. On the other hand, a high reserve requirement leads to a low multiplier effect. See also: M1, M2.

Mummonmarkka A slang term for the Finnish markka. The term began to be used after the adoption of the euro; literally, it means "grandmother's markka."

Municipal Bond A bond issued by a local or state government. Municipal bonds are usually used to raise capital for improvements in infrastructure or other aspects of the municipality. For example, a city or school district may issue a bond to build a new school or a new playground. Municipal bonds are exempt from federal income taxes and sometimes from state and local taxes as well. Municipals usually pay lower coupons than corporate bonds, but because the yield is tax-free, the after-tax basis may be higher for a municipal bond. Risk varies with the municipality and the particular type of municipal bond. It is sometimes called a municipal improvement certificate.

Municipal Bond Fund A mutual fund that invests predominantly or exclusively in municipal bonds. A municipal bond fund is often tax-efficient, as municipal bonds are exempt from federal taxes and in some circumstances also from state and local taxes. As a result, municipal bond funds tend to be attractive to persons who fall into higher tax brackets. Municipal bond funds generally carry lower risks than mutual funds investing primarily in stocks, but the levels of risk vary according to the credit ratings of the municipalities whose bonds are represented in the fund.

Municipal Bond Insurance A guarantee that the principal and coupon on a municipal bond will be paid at the appropriate times. Municipal bond insurance is usually structured in such a way that a private organization such as a bank is the actual issuer of the municipal bond, rather than the municipality itself. The bank does this in exchange for a fee. Municipal bond insurance grants a higher credit rating to the bond.

Municipal Bond Unit Trust A unit investment trust that invests exclusively in municipal bonds. A unit investment trust is an unmanaged portfolio of securities, the rights to which are sold to investors as shares or units. In a municipal bond unit trust, coupons from the bonds are passed on to unit holders, just as in a mutual fund. Unit holders pay a certain percentage of the value of their purchases to the investment company creating the municipal bond unit trust. It can be advantageous to bond investors because it creates a diversified portfolio and is less expensive than the investor going out and buying the individual municipal bonds.

Municipal Finance Officers Association One of several organizations for auditors, accountants and other personnel who work in the finance departments for municipalities. Associations meet periodically to discuss matters of mutual interest. Several U.S. states have their own municipal finance officers association.

Municipal Inflation-Linked Securities Municipal bonds that pay coupons indexed to the Consumer Price Index. The coupon rate varies according to changes in the underlying inflation. The coupon rate is usually lower than those for other municipal bonds, as they have lower risk. Like other municipal bonds, they are exempt from most taxes. For these reasons, municipal inflation-linked securities often provide a solid return at little risk.

Municipal Investment Trust A unit investment trust that invests primarily or exclusively in municipal bonds. The MIT buys these bonds and holds them until maturity, passing the coupons and principal to unit holders.

Municipal Issuer A local, provincial or state government that issues a bond. Municipal issuers seek to raise capital for improvements in infrastructure or other aspects of the municipality. For example, a city or school district may issue a bond to build a new school or a new playground. Bonds from municipal issuers are exempt from federal income taxes and sometimes from state and local taxes as well. Risk varies with the issuer and the particular type of municipal bond.

Municipal Jurisdiction The area over which a municipality governs. For example, the municipal jurisdiction of a city extends to the city limits. Municipalities must enforce laws and may tax within their jurisdictions.

Municipal Note A short-term debt security issued by a local or state government. Generally speaking, a municipal note has a maturity from three months to three years. Municipal notes are usually used to raise capital for improvements in infrastructure or other aspects of the municipality. For example, a city or school district may issue a note to build a new park or a new playground. Municipal notes are exempt from federal income taxes and sometimes from state and local taxes as well. Municipal notes usually pay lower coupons than corporate notes with similar maturities, but because the yield is tax-free, the after-tax basis may be higher for a municipal bond. Risk varies with the municipality and the particular type of municipal note. See also: Tax Anticipation Note.

Municipal Revenue Bond A municipal bond that is not secured by the issuer's general revenue but instead by the revenue of the project it intends to finance. For example, a city may issue a revenue bond to finance improvements to the local sewer system. It expects to be able to pay back the bond with money raised from citizens' water bills. Generally speaking, a revenue bond is riskier than other municipal bonds because the project has no revenue to tax on its own. However, it is usually a fairly safe investment. See also: Authority Bond.

Municipal Securities Rulemaking Board A self-regulatory organization in the United States that provides regulations and guidelines for municipal bonds and other municipal securities. Its rulings apply both to municipalities that issue securities and to the firms that underwrite them. While it makes and publishes all guidelines, responsibility for enforcement resides with the SEC. Established in 1975, the MSRB consists of fifteen members chosen to represent bank dealers, securities firms, and the general public; these serve in staggered three year terms.

Municipal Service Tax A flat wage tax imposed on all employees in a municipality. For example, an employee who works in the jurisdiction of a township may have to pay $40 per year, regardless of how much he/she earns in that township. Most employers in these municipalities deduct municipal service taxes from employees' paychecks.

Municipal Short-Term Bond Fund A mutual fund that invests predominantly or exclusively in municipal bonds with maturities of less than a few years. The idea behind a short-term bond fund is to provide a return at little risk (compared to other investments) that is nonetheless better than the risk-free rate of return. Because it invests in municipal bonds, dividends from the fund are tax-free at the federal level (though they may be subject to state taxes unless all bonds in the fund are issued in the state where the holder resides).

Municipal Utility District In the United States, an area for which a government-owned utility company provides electricity, water, and/or other utilities. The company may be authorized to issue bonds to finance its operations. These bonds are generally exempt from federal taxes. See also: Rural Water District.

Municipiu In Romania, a political subdivision equivalent to a municipality with a population over 15,000.

Munifacts A wire service advisory letter that provides information to traders in municipal bonds.

Muniment A document proving ownership. A muniment may simply be the title to a property; on the other hand, a muniment may be another document, such as a death certificate, indicating that title has passed to another person.

Munjandie An obsolete Indian unit of dry volume approximately equivalent to 0.259 grams.

Muppet In investment banking, a derogatory slang term for a client. The term is used especially when the client takes an investment adviser at his/her word and buys or sells whatever securities the adviser recommends.

Muppet Shuffle The transfer of an unproductive or otherwise bad employee to another department. This saves the trouble of firing the employee, though the term implies that the new department is unaware of his/her lax work habits.

Muqarada In Islamic finance, a way to structure a bond for which bondholders are entitled to cash flow from the project that the bond intends to finance. Unlike

conventional bonds, however, muqarada "coupons" are not guaranteed and the bondholder takes a risk that the project will not generate cash flow. Holders are only entitled to cash flow as it becomes available. See also: Sukuk.

Muqtaat In Islamic law, a term describing foodstuffs. According to the Shafii school of jurisprudence, riba al-fadl (interest in kind) only occurs if a muqtaat item is lent in exchange for receiving more of the same item at a later date.

MUR ISO 4217 code for the Mauritian rupee. It was introduced in 1874, replacing the Mauritian dollar and the Indian rupee. It was pegged at par to the Indian rupee until 1934, when it changed its peg to the British pound (the currency to which the Indian rupee was itself pegged). Mauritius maintained the peg to the pound until 1979.

Muraahanah In Islamic law, the confiscation of real estate or other property by the state without paying the owner due compensation.

Murabaha A structure in Islamic finance in which one party buys a good for cash and then sells it to a second party for deferred payments. For example, if Joe wishes to buy a house, he asks a bank to purchase it and then sell it to him for a higher price than the bank paid. While the bank pays cash up front, Joe amortizes his payments over an agreed-upon number of years. From Joe's perspective, this is similar to a conventional mortgage because the payments are likely the same. Because there is no debt with interest, a murabaha is thought to conform to Islamic law. However, murabahas are controversial even within Islamic finance because some scholars believe the profit on the second sale imitates interest too closely.

Muriel Siebert An investor, researcher and broker on Wall Street. In 1967, despite opposition, she became the first woman to own a seat on the New York Stock Exchange. She later served as Superintendant of Banks for New York State. She was born in 1932.

Murphy's Law An adage stating, "Anything that can go wrong, will go wrong." Murphy's Law is used in business because of the inherent unpredictability of risk.

MUS GOST 7.67 Latin three-letter geocode for Mauritius. The code is used for transactions to and from Mauritian bank accounts and for international shipping to Mauritius. As with all GOST 7.67 codes, it is used primarily in Cyrillic alphabets.

Musaru An ancient Akkadian unit of area approximately equivalent to 36 square meters.

Musharika A partnership in Islamic finance in which all partners contribute capital. For example, if Joe wants to start a business, he may form a musharika into which he places $20,000. A bank may then contribute $40,000 and split profits with Joe based upon some agreed-upon formula. Musharikas are important in Islamic finance in part because they are the most straightforward. That is, a musharika does not attempt to imitate a debt product, which is controversial. Rather, it simply involves equity financing by an investor. However, musharikas are difficult to structure in some non-Muslim countries, especially the United States, because some banks are not permitted to make equity financing arrangements.

Musical Instrument Insurance An insurance policy that provides coverage for damage, theft or loss of a musical instrument. This is especially important for valuable instruments like Stradivarius violins. As with all insurance, one pays a premium for musical instrument coverage.

Mustard Gas A chemical made from sulfur that causes blisters on human skin. It has been used in chemical warfare since World War I. See also: Chemical Weapons Convention.

Mustron An ancient Greek unit of liquid volume approximately equivalent to 11.4 milliliters.

Mutamadiyah In Tunisia, a political subdivision roughly equivalent to a county.

Mutaqabbil An Arabic term for a tax farmer. A mutaqabbil is also called simply a qabil.

Mutchkin An obsolete Scottish unit of liquid volume approximately equivalent to 0.212 liters.

Mutha A Burmese unit of mass approximately equivalent to two grams.

Mutilated Security A stock or bond certificate on which the owner's or issuer's name cannot be read. This can occur because of damage, negligence, or other reasons. A mutilated security can only be transferred when the owner has received a guarantee of ownership from a third party to ensure that there is no fraud or other foul play.

Mutual 1. See: Mutual fund. 2. See: Mutual assent. 3. See: Mutual insurance. 4. See: Mutuality of obligation.

Mutual Assent In law, the requirement that each party to a contract must agree to the same thing and must know what the other party intends. Mutual assent is necessary for a contract to be legal and enforceable.

Mutual Atomic Energy Reinsurance Pool A group of mutual insurance companies that provide coverage to insurance companies against the possibility that they will lose money due to nuclear liability. That is, the insurance companies provide coverage for nuclear liability and the mutual atomic energy reinsurance pool covers those insurance companies. The federal government supplements the mutual atomic energy reinsurance pool. It is also simply called atomic energy reinsurance.

Mutual Company A company structure in which the company's owners are also its clients. That is, the mutual company's profits are distributed to its participating customers each year in proportion to their individual exposures to the company. Many insurance companies are structured as mutual companies, meaning that policyholders have the right to receive portions of the company's profits, and often may elect the company's management. Savings & loan associations are also common structured as mutual companies.

Mutual Exclusion Doctrine The principle that the U.S. federal government does not tax the interest one earns on municipal bonds and debts issued by state and local governments; likewise, the state and local governments do not tax the interest on federal debts, such as Treasury securities and others. The mutual exclusion doctrine was established very early in the history of American tax law. See also: McCulloch v. Maryland.

Mutual Fund A pool of liquidity that an investment company places in various securities and/or derivatives with the goal of producing a certain return. Mutual funds may carry greater or lesser risk, depending on their particular investment goals. Mutual funds are actively managed by the company to maintain the investment goals. The company issues shares that represent a portion of ownership in each of the securities underlying the fund. Mutual funds are designed for investors who wish to take advantage of a highly diversified portfolio without a large amount of capital. See also: Open-end, Close-end.

Mutual Fund Cash-to-Assets Ratio In a mutual fund, the assets held in cash as a proportion of the fund's total assets. The cash-to-assets ratio is an important measure of a mutual fund's liquidity; a higher ratio indicates higher liquidity. Generally speaking, mutual funds keep large amount of cash on hand when they are about to make large purchases of securities. As such, a higher ratio is considered bullish while a low ratio is sometimes considered bearish because it may mean that the fund is choosing to hold its assets in low risk investment vehicles, such as bonds.

Mutual Fund Custodian A third party, usually a bank or trust, that holds the securities underlying a mutual fund. The mutual fund custodian may or may not also maintain the records for the mutual fund. The existence of mutual fund custodians is thought to reduce the risk from dishonest brokers by not allowing them to maintain the actual securities. See also: Transfer agent.

Mutual Fund Liquidity Ratio A ratio of a mutual fund's cash and cash equivalents to the assets in which it is currently invested. That is, if a mutual fund has a large amount of cash that it has not invested in securities, the ratio is higher, while, if all or nearly all of its liquidity is invested, the ratio is lower. A high ratio is considered a bearish indicator because it means that the mutual fund is having difficulty finding investments with solid returns, and is therefore keeping larger cash reserves. Mutual funds publish liquidity ratios each month.

Mutual Fund Share Class In mutual funds, a type of share with a particular load. The load, which is the sales fee for buying into the mutual fund, is charged at different times depending on the stock class. For example, a class A stock has a load that is paid up front, while a class B stock has a load that is paid when one sells the shares in the mutual fund.

Mutual Fund Theorem A theory stating that all investors ought to place all their risk capital into a mutual fund containing the exact same securities. They then ought to place the remainder of their investments in risk-free securities. The theory recommends a single mutual fund because Markowitz portfolio theory states that there is precisely one portfolio with the maximum return for each level of risk. The mutual fund theorem purports to maximize the return for all capital that an investor puts at risk. It was first suggested by James Tobin.

Mutual Fund Timing The practice of buying and selling shares in a mutual fund in order to profit from changes to its closing price each trading day. This is legal, but it can harm long-term investors in the mutual fund. As a result, most mutual funds charge a redemption fee on shareholders who sell their shares before a certain number of days have passed. Mutual fund timing should not be confused with market timing, which is a different concept altogether.

Mutual Insurance Company An insurance company owned by its own policyholders. That is, policyholders elect the board of directors, and profits, if any, are distributed to policyholders each year in proportion to their individual exposures to the company. Many insurance companies are structured in this way.

Mutual Life-Assurance Company A life insurance company owned by its own policyholders. That is, policyholders elect the board of directors, and profits, if any, are distributed to policyholders each year in proportion to their individual exposures to the company. Many insurance companies are structured in this way.

Mutual Mortgage Insurance Fund A pool of liquidity that provides insurance on FHA mortgages. That is, the mutual mortgage insurance fund compensates the Federal Housing Administration in the event of default on a single family home purchased with an FHA loan. Home buyers must pay the premiums for the mutual mortgage fund, including 1.5% of the value of the loan at closing and 0.5% every year until the buyer has 22% equity in the home.

Mutual Offset A system that allows positions on one exchange to transfer to another.

Mutual Recognition Agreement An agreement between two or more jurisdictions to consider licenses and certifications given by one jurisdiction as being valid in the others. For example, if one is licensed to practice dentistry in Oregon and Oregon has a mutual recognition agreement with Washington, one is by extension licensed to practice dentistry in Washington. Mutual recognition agreements may take place within a country (as between U.S. states) or they may be international.

Mutual Savings Bank A savings and loan association that has no stockholders and, as a result, reinvests all profits in itself. Most mutual savings banks are owned by their depositors and borrowers. Because there are no stockholders to please, mutual savings banks are often very conservative with how they invest deposits. As a result, they tend to survive periods of financial distress relatively well. This was especially true during the Great Depression. In the United States, most mutual savings banks are in the Northeast.

Mutual Will A will executed by a married or partnered couple. Under a mutual will, the surviving spouse is bound by the will's terms after the first spouse dies. In general, mutual wills exist to ensure that property is passed to children of the couple after both spouses die; for that reason, they are most useful if the surviving spouse remarries.

Mutual-Fund Advisory Program An investment vehicle in which an investor works with an investment adviser to take a long position in several mutual funds. The program utilizes an asset allocation method that matches the investor's goals. The investor does not pay fees for each mutual fund, but rather pays the average fee to the investment adviser. A mutual fund advisory program allows the investor greater autonomy over his/her portfolio. It is also called a mutual fund wrap. See also: Fund of funds.

Mutuality of Obligation The state in which both parties to a contract are required to perform some service. For example, one party may make a widget and the other may pay for it. Mutuality of obligation is one of the conditions that must exist for a contract to be legal and enforceable.

Mutualization A change of a company's structure to one in which the company's owners are also its clients. That is, once mutualization occurs, the company's profits are distributed to its participating customers each year in proportion to their individual exposures to the company. Many insurance companies are structured as mutual companies, meaning that policyholders have the right to receive portions of the company's profits, and often may elect the company's management. Savings & loan associations are also commonly structured as mutual companies. See also: Demutualization.

Mutualization of Risk The spread of risk among several parties. For example, if five investors each put in $200,000, and the total amount of the investment equals $1 million, risk is mutualized because no one investor can possibly lose the whole million.

Mutually Exclusive 1. See: Mutually exclusive investment. **2.** See: Mutually exclusive project.

Mutually Exclusive Investment An investment that prevents one from making a different investment. Some investments are mutually exclusive by nature; for example, taking a long position in a stock precludes taking a short position in the same stock at the same time. Others are mutually exclusive circumstantially; for example, if one only has so much money to invest and buys stocks A, B, and C, there may not be enough left over to buy stock D. See also: Opportunity cost.

Mutually Exclusive Investment Decision The decision to make an investment that prevents making a different investment. Some investment decisions are mutually exclusive by nature; for example taking a long position in a stock precludes taking a short position the same stock at the same time. Others are mutually exclusive circumstantially; for example, if one only has so much money to invest and buys stocks A, B, and C, there may not be enough left over to buy stock D. See also: Opportunity cost.

Mutually Owned Stock Exchange A stock exchange owned jointly by members, which are usually the companies whose stocks are traded on the exchange. That is, when a company is listed on a mutually owned stock exchange, it becomes a joint owner of that exchange. These exchanges are nonprofit organizations. Some exchanges, such as the Chicago Mercantile Exchange, formerly were mutually owned but became for-profit, publicly-traded companies. See also: Demutualization.

Muzuna A division of the budju, which was the currency of Algeria prior to 1848. One budju was divided into 24 muzuna, which was itself divided into 29 asper or two kharub.

MV 1. ISO 3166-1 alpha-2 code for the Republic of Maldives. This is the code used in international transactions to and from Maldivian bank accounts. **2.** ISO 3166-2 geocode for the Maldives. This is used as an international standard for shipping to the Maldives. Each administrative atoll has its own code with the prefix "MV." For example, the code for Raa is ISO 3166-2:MV-13.

MVQ ISO 4217 code for the old Maldivian rufiyaa. It was issued in 1947 and was replaced by the current rufiyaa (code MVR) in 1981.

MVR ISO 4217 code for the Maldivian rufiyaa. It was issued in 1947 and was pegged to the Ceylonese rupee. It is currently pegged to the U.S. dollar.

MW 1. ISO 3166-1 alpha-2 code for the Republic of Malawi. This is the code used in international transactions to and from Malawian bank accounts. **2.** ISO 3166-2 geocode for Malawi. This is used as an international standard for shipping to Malawi. Each district has its own code with the prefix "MW." For example, the code for Dowa District is ISO 3166-2:MW-DO. Additionally, three regions in Malawi have codes; for example the code for the Central Region (wherein lies Dowa District) is ISO 3166-2:MW-C.

MWI GOST 7.67 Latin three-letter geocode for Malawi. The code is used for transactions to and from Malawian bank accounts and for international shipping to Malawi. As with all GOST 7.67 codes, it is used primarily in Cyrillic alphabets.

MWK ISO 4217 code for the Malawian kwacha. It replaced the Malawian pound in 1971 at a ratio of two kwachas to one pound. It is a floating currency.

MX 1. ISO 3166-1 alpha-2 code for the United Mexican States. This is the code used in international transactions to and from Mexican bank accounts. **2.** ISO 3166-2 geocode for Mexico. This is used as an international standard for shipping to Mexico.

Each Mexican state has its own code with the prefix "MX." For example, the code for the State of Hidalgo is ISO 3166-2:MX-HID.

MXN ISO 4217 code for the Mexican peso. The symbol was adopted following the revaluation of the peso that took place in 1993. For most of the 20th century, the peso was one of the more stable currencies in the world, and it had not been subject to the hyperinflation that plagued other Latin American countries. However, the 1970s oil crisis in Mexico defaulting on its national debt in 1982; this slowed growth and caused hyperinflation throughout the 1980s. The "new peso," which was introduced in 1993, helped to stabilize the country. Now, the peso is one of the most traded currencies in the world.

MXP ISO 4217 code for the first Mexican peso. For most of the 20th century, the peso was one of the more stable currencies in the world, and it had not been subject to the hyperinflation that plagued other Latin American countries. However, the 1970s oil crisis resulted in Mexico defaulting on its national debt in 1982; this slowed growth and caused hyperinflation throughout the 1980s. The "new peso," (MXN) which was introduced in 1993, helped to stabilize the country, and now the peso is one of the most widely traded currencies in the world. See also: Managed float, Mexican economic crisis.

MXV ISO 4217 code for the Mexican unidad de inversion. It is a unit of account in Mexico that does not circulate. It is adjusted for inflation relative to the Mexican peso so that its value remains stable. Because of this stability, major purchases (notably mortgages) in Mexico are often quoted in MXV terms.

MY 1. ISO 3166-1 alpha-2 code for Malaysia. This is the code used in international transactions to and from Malaysian bank accounts. **2.** ISO 3166-2 geocode for Malaysia. This is used as an international standard for shipping to Malaysia. Each state (along with each federal territory) has its own code with the prefix "MY." For example, the code for the State of Johor is ISO 3166-2:MY-01.

Myeon In South Korea, a political subdivision equivalent to a town with at least 6,000 residents.

Myo In Myanmar (Burma), a political subdivision approximately equivalent to a town, which is contained inside a myo ne (township).

Myo Ne In Myanmar (Burma), a political subdivision approximately equivalent to a township.

Myong-Dong A district in Seoul, South Korea, noted for financial services offices and upscale shopping. A number of insurance companies, banks and investment houses are based in Myong-Dong.

MYR ISO 4217 code for the Malaysian ringgit. It was issued in 1967 as the Malaysian dollar, though it was called the ringgit in Malay. The name ringgit was used in both languages starting in 1975. It was pegged to the U.S. dollar between 1998 and 2005 as a result of the East Asian financial crisis. In 2005, it became a currency with a managed float.

MYS GOST 7.67 Latin three-letter geocode for Malaysia. The code is used for transactions to and from Malaysian bank accounts and for international shipping to Malaysia. As with all GOST 7.67 codes, it is used primarily in Cyrillic alphabets.

Mysterious Disappearance Exclusion In insurance, a clause exempting the insurer from paying for a loss if an insured event occurs without explanation. This applies most commonly to property insurance. For example, an insurance policy on a diamond necklace may not provide the benefit if the necklace is lost or otherwise disappears for no apparent reason. The exclusion exists to prevent insurance fraud.

MYT GOST 7.67 Latin three-letter geocode for Mayotte. The code is used for transactions to and from Mahoran bank accounts and for international shipping to Mayotte. As with all GOST 7.67 codes, it is used primarily in Cyrillic alphabets.

MZ 1. ISO 3166-1 alpha-2 code for the Republic of Mozambique. This is the code used in international transactions to and from Mozambican bank accounts. **2.** ISO 3166-2 geocode for Mozambique. This is used as an international standard for shipping to Mozambique. Each subdivision has its own code with the prefix "MZ." For example, the code for the Province of Gaza is ISO 3166-2:MZ-G.

MZM ISO 4217 code for the first Mozambican metical. It was introduced in 1980, replacing the Mozambican escudo. It suffered from hyperinflation for most of its history and was, for a time, the least valuable currency in the world. It was replaced by the second metical (code MZN) in 2006.

MZN ISO 4217 code for the Mozambican metical. It was introduced in 1980, replacing the Mozambican escudo. It suffered from hyperinflation for most of its history and was, for a time, the least valuable currency in the world. Inflation has slowed since the introduction of the second metical in 2006, but has remained over 10%.

N.L. On a mutual fund transaction table, an abbreviation indicating that a share belongs to a no-load fund.

N.O.H.P. Not Otherwise Herein Provided. Describing a circumstance that applies unless stated otherwise elsewhere in a document. This is used most commonly in legal documents.

N.O.I.B.N. Not Otherwise Identified by Name (or Number). Describing a circumstance that applies to cargo unless cargo is specifically provided for by name or number elsewhere in a document.

Naamloze Vennootschap The Dutch term for a publicly-traded company, often abbreviated as "NV." It is the legal term for this type of corporation in several Dutch speaking countries.

Naazir al-awqaf In Islamic law, the administrator of a waqf; a trustee.

Naazir al-sikkah In late medieval Spain, an official who determined the authenticity of coins in circulation.

NAB Code A voluntary code for decency in advertising used by the National Association of Broadcasters until the 1980s. It promoted and discouraged content; for example, adherents agreed not to air advertisements for liquor.

NACIMFP National Advisory Council on International Monetary and Financial Policies. A council that reviews loans and other transactions made by banks of which the United States is a shareholder and advises accordingly. The Council consists of the U.S. Secretary of the Treasury, the Secretary of State, the U.S. Trade Representative, the Federal Reserve Chairman, the Director of the IDCA and the President of the Import-Export Bank. It was established in 1966.

Nacional Financiera Also called Nafinsa. A bank in Mexico responsible for industrial and financial development. It provides funds to banks and other financial institutions to accomplish its goals. It maintains branches in London and Grand Cayman, as well as representative offices in Tokyo and Washington, D.C. It was established in 1934.

NAD ISO 4217 code for the Namibian dollar. It was introduced in 1993, replacing the South African rand. It is pegged to the rand at par; because of this, both the dollar and the rand are accepted as legal tender in Namibia.

Nafa In Israel, a political subdivision equivalent to a county. A nafa is smaller than a mahoz.

Nagoya Stock Exchange A stock exchange in Japan. It was originally established in 1886 and re-established in 1949 following the Second World War. The Nagoya Stock Exchange is itself a stock corporation and is the third largest exchange in Japan by market capitalization. See also: Demutualization.

Nahia In Jordan, a political subdivision equivalent to a county.

Nahiyah In several Arabic-speaking countries, a political subdivision approximately equivalent of a municipality, or at least an association of several villages.

NAICS North American Industrial Classification System. A system of six digit codes used in business to classify the industry to which a company belongs. The NAICS was created by the U.S. Office of Management and Budget in 1997 to facilitate communication within and between businesses and industries. For example, an iron ore mining company might file under the code 212210.

Nail A unit of length equivalent to 2.25 inches.

Naive Diversification Diversification of a portfolio without regard, or with incorrect regard, for the mathematical formulas in the capital asset pricing model. Naive diversification rests on the assumption that simply investing in enough unrelated assets will reduce risk sufficiently to make a profit. Alternately, one may diversify naively by applying the capital asset pricing model incorrectly and finding the wrong efficient portfolio frontier. Such diversification does not necessarily decrease risk at a given expected return, and may in fact increase risk. See also: Markowitz Portfolio Theory.

Naive Model A very complicated economic or political science model that is likely to be highly inaccurate. Naive models are sometimes created intentionally in academia to demonstrate the idea that complex models are not necessarily predictive. Sometimes, however, they are used to clarify thinking, even if their results are inaccurate.

Nakasone Bond A Japanese government bond issued in a currency other than the yen. It derives its name from Prime Minister Yasuhiro Nakasone, who was premier when the bond was introduced in 1982.

Naked Call An investment strategy in which one sells a call without owning the underlying asset to hedge the risk. Unlike more complex spreads and straddles, which involve the purchase or sale of multiple options in order to profit in different ways, naked calls are straightforward calls. An investor using a naked call strategy makes a profit or loss depending on the movement of the underlying asset. The risk to a naked call is that the option will be exercised, requiring the seller to buy the underlying asset at the market price and then immediately sell it (usually at a loss) to fulfill the terms of the call. Naked calls are also called uncovered calls. See also: Covered Options. Naked Put.

Naked Debenture A certificate of debt that is not secured by an asset or lien, but rather by all the issuer's assets not otherwise secured. This means that the debt represented by a naked debenture carries no collateral; in case of bankruptcy, the debt holder is considered a general creditor.

Naked Intervention A situation in which a central bank makes a major purchase or sale of a currency in order to affect the exchange rate for its own currency. While every central bank does this to some extent, naked interventions may negatively impact other currencies' exchange rates, potentially leading to retaliatory measures. See also: Currency war.

Naked Option An option contract without another, opposite option hedging the risk. Unlike more complex spreads and straddles, which involve the purchase or sale of multiple options in order to profit in different ways, naked options are straightforward calls or puts. An investor with a naked option makes a profit or loss depending on the movement of the underlying asset. Naked options are also called uncovered options. See also: Covered options.

Naked Option Strategy An investment strategy in which one enters a position on option contracts without other, opposite options to hedge the risk. Unlike more complex spreads and straddles, which involve the purchase or sale of multiple options in order to profit in different ways, naked options are straightforward calls or puts. An investor using naked option strategies makes a profit or loss depending on the movement of the underlying asset. A naked option is also called an uncovered option strategy. See also: Covered options.

Naked Position A position that is not hedged. That is, the holder of a naked position has taken no step to reduce the risk inherent to the position. For example, if one buys 100 shares of AT&T, one is exposed to the risk that AT&T will decline in price. If one takes no action to prevent this (by buying put options or short selling AT&T, for instance), one holds a naked position in AT&T. Avoiding naked positions and hedging as much risk as possible is a substantial concern for many institutional investors.

Naked Put A short position on a put option without having enough cash or cash equivalent to buy the underlying asset should the holder exercise the option. An investor with a naked put makes a gain or loss depending on the movement of the underlying asset. This position is quite risky and can result in large losses should the underlying asset not move in the investor's preferred direction. Naked puts are also called uncovered puts. See also: Covered Options.

Naked Short Seller An investor who sells shares that he/she has neither borrowed nor made arrangements to borrow. Under Regulation SHO, naked short sellers must abide by a "locate" requirement and a "close-out" requirement. The locate requirement forces brokers to have reasonable grounds to believe that the short-sold security can be borrowed; the broker must document this prior to the security's sale. With some exceptions, the close-out requirement means that brokers who have failed to deliver a short-sold security for 13 days must purchase similar securities and present those instead. Naked shorting is very high risk.

Naked Short Selling The sale of shares one has neither borrowed nor made arrangements to borrow. Under Regulation SHO, investors engaging in naked shorting much abide by a "locate" requirement and a "close-out" requirement. The locate requirement forces brokers to have reasonable grounds to believe that the short-sold security can be borrowed; the broker must document this prior to the security's sale. With some exceptions, the close-out requirement means that brokers who have failed to deliver a short-sold security for 13 days must purchase similar securities and present those instead. Naked shorting is very high risk.

Naked Swap A credit default swap in which the buyer does not have an exposure to the underlying security. In a credit default swap, the buyer makes a series of payments and, in exchange, receives a guarantee against default from the seller on a designated debt security. That is, the buyer transfers the risk of a debt security to the seller, who receives a series of fees for assuming this risk. In a naked swap, because the buyer does not hold the underlying security, the buyer is essentially betting the underlying security will default and then the buyer will receive payment. Because of the obvious moral hazard associated with this, some regulators took steps to limit or even abolish naked swaps in the wake of the late 2000s recession.

Naked Trust A trust in which the grantor leaves assets to the care of a trustee, whose only duty is to transfer those assets to a stated beneficiary. This contrasts with most other trusts, in which the trustee invests or otherwise safeguards the assets and gives the income they generate to the beneficiary.

Naked Writer The seller of an option contract who does not own the underlying asset (for a call) or have enough cash to purchase the underlying asset (for a put). This is very high risk.

NAM GOST 7.67 Latin three-letter geocode for Namibia. The code is used for transactions to and from Namibian bank accounts and for international shipping to Namibia. As with all GOST 7.67 codes, it is used primarily in Cyrillic alphabets.

Name A wealthy individual who provides a great deal of capital that underwrites the activities of Lloyd's of London. Names spread risk of insurance among themselves along with corporations. For most of Lloyd's centuries-long history, names had unlimited liability for any losses associated with being a name. Lloyd's introduced names with limited liability in 1994, and they have become increasingly important.

Name Position Bond A bond or insurance policy covering a company in the event that it loses money as the result of theft or fraud on the part of employees in certain, stated positions. For example, a name position bond may cover theft by the chief financial officer, regardless of who holds that position at a given time. It is important to note that blanket fidelity bonds generally only cover situations in which an employee commits fraud for personal gain; it does not cover situations in which the employee, without support or knowledge of management, falsifies trading so that it makes the company appear healthier than it is. See also: Bonding, Operational Risk.

Name Schedule Bond A fidelity bond covering two or more employees named on the bond. A fidelity bond compensates a company in the event it loses money as the result of employee theft or fraud. A name schedule bond limits this coverage to the employees named in it. See also: Position bond.

Named Insured The person or company covered by an insurance policy. The named insured may or may not be the policyholder, or may include the policyholder along with other named insured. For example, one may buy a health insurance policy in which the named insured are the policyholder and his/her spouse.

Named Nonowner Coverage An addition to a car insurance policy providing coverage in the event that a named person other than the owner of the car is driving when an accident occurs. Without this coverage, only the owner or the primary operator of a car may be insured. Named nonowner coverage may cover family members or others who might commonly operate the insured vehicle.

Named Perils Insurance A homeowner's insurance policy that only provides coverage for events named in the policy. For example, a named perils policy may cover tornadoes and fires, but not hurricanes and burglaries. These policies are less expensive than comprehensive policies; named perils insurance is designed to cover only the most likely events. However, comprehensive policies themselves do not cover all likelihoods, and a named perils policy may also serve as supplemental insurance to fill holes in one's broader policy.

Namespace In computer languages, the context in which a term can have only a single meaning. For example, two files may not have the same name within a directory. In this case, the directory forms the namespace for the files.

Namibian Dollar The currency of Namibia. It was introduced in 1993, replacing the South African rand. It is pegged to the rand at par; because of this, both the dollar and the rand are accepted as legal tender in Namibia.

Nano Cap Describing a publicly-traded company with an extremely low amount of market capitalization. In general, a nano-cap company has a market capitalization of less than $50 million, but there is no specific definition. Some brokerages or exchanges have slightly different definitions of nano-cap. Nano-cap describes the smallest possible amount of market capitalization, and, for this reason, nano-cap stocks are quite risky. See also: High-cap, Mid-cap, Low-cap, Micro-cap.

Nanometer A measure of length equal to one one-billionth of a meter. In other words, a nanometer is .000000001 meters. Nanometers are important in the semiconductor industry.

Nanotechnology The technology that controls products at the atomic or molecular state. Nanotechnology has uses in information technology, heavy industry and energy.

Naples Terms A form of debt relief for heavily indebted poor countries in which the present value of payments is reduced by up to two-thirds. The Naples terms were introduced by the Paris Club in 1995. This form of debt relief is a type of concessional restructuring.

NAPM Index A monthly survey of 250 companies in 21 sectors measuring growth or decline in deliveries, inventories, jobs, order and production. The information is aggregated and disseminated as a numerical value between one and 100. A value above 50 indicates growth in manufacturing, while a value below 50 indicates the opposite.

Narcoterrorism Violent activities targeted at anti-narcotic police and similar forces. The term is also used for terrorism funded by drug trafficking. Narcoterrorism poses significant political risk in various areas of the world, notably in part of South America.

Narcoterrorist A person or group that conducts violent activities targeted at anti-narcotic police and similar forces. The term is also used for terrorism funded by drug trafficking. Narcoterrorism poses significant political risk in various areas of the world, notably in part of South America.

Narrow Basis A situation in which there is only a small difference between the spot price and the futures price for a commodity. This occurs when investors expect there to be little shift in supply or demand between the present time and when the commodity is delivered under the futures contract. A wide basis often becomes a narrow basis the closer a futures contract comes to maturity because there is less uncertainty; when this does not occur, arbitrage opportunities arise.

Narrow Money A measure of the money supply used by the various central banks that includes only currency in circulation and very near money instruments. In the Federal Reserve System, narrow money includes all physical currency and deposits in checking accounts as well as Negotiable Orders Withdrawal accounts. It does not include savings accounts, certificates of deposit, or money market accounts. This is called narrow money because it applies the most restrictive definition of money. It is also called the money base. See also: M1, M0.

Narrow the Spread To reduce the bid-ask spread. That is, narrowing the spread occurs when a potential buyer is willing to pay more for a security, when a potential seller is willing to accept less, or both. Narrowing the spread often occurs during a period of high trading volume. See also: Tight market.

Narrow-Based Describing an index that consists of only a few stocks. Generally speaking, a narrow-based index only includes stocks from one industry. These indices are often useful in gauging the performance of the industries they track, but rarely give an indication on movements in the broader economy. See also: Broad-based.

Narrow-Based Weighted Average Describing an index that consists of only a few stocks and is weighted for price or market capitalization. Generally speaking, a narrow-based weighted average only includes stocks from one industry. These indices are often useful in gauging the performance of the industries they track but rarely give an indication on movements in the broader economy. See also: Broad-Based.

Narrow-Range Securities Fixed-return securities in a trust as a proportion of all securities in that trust. That is, if 60% of a trust consists of bonds and 40% consists of stocks, it is said to have 60% narrow-range securities. The term is most common in the United Kingdom.

NASDAQ The largest electronic exchange in the world and the second largest exchange in the United States. It was established in 1971 and was originally organized as a successor to over-the-counter "curb trading" that was previously popular in New York. As a result it was considered in some circles an over-the-counter trading system as late as the mid-1980s. NASDAQ has the highest trading volume of any exchange in the world, and is a popular exchange for technology companies. It was originally owned by the NASD (now FINRA) and was spun off in 2000 and 2001. See also: NASDAQ Composite Index, Dot-Com Bubble.

NASDAQ 100 Index A stock index of the 100 largest companies by market capitalization traded on NASDAQ. The NASDAQ 100 Index includes publicly-traded companies from most sectors in the global economy, the major exception being financial services. Various exchange-traded funds follow the NASDAQ 100 Index. Its symbol on the NASDAQ ticker is QQQ. It is informally called the Cubes.

NASDAQ Bank Index An index tracking several hundred banks and bank holding companies whose shares trade on NASDAQ.

NASDAQ Biotechnology Index An index tracking pharmaceutical, biological research and similar companies whose shares trade on NASDAQ. It is weighted under a modified market capitalization scheme; the securities that compose it are updated semi-annually.

NASDAQ Composite Index An index of all common stock that trade on NASDAQ. Approximately 4000 stocks are included in the NASDAQ Composite Index. This index was established in 1971.

NASDAQ Computer Index An index tracking several hundred software, semiconductor and other companies whose shares trade on NASDAQ.

NASDAQ Industrial Index An index tracking all stocks on NASDAQ that do not already belong to the NASDAQ Bank Index, NASDAQ Biotech Index or the NASDAQ Computer Index. The industrial index includes agricultural and retail companies, as well as companies in several other industries.

NASDAQ International A publicly-traded company listed on NASDAQ but based outside the United States. Many, though not all, NASDAQ international companies are listed as American Depository Receipts.

NASDAQ LIFFE Markets An electronic futures exchange. Formed in 2001 as a joint venture between NASDAQ and LIFFE, it trades in futures contracts on the most actively traded stocks that are listed on NASDAQ and the New York Stock Exchange.

NASDAQ National Market Securities Large (by market capitalization) securities that trade on the NASDAQ National Market. NASDAQ National Market securities must register with the SEC and meet certain requirements in order to trade on the NASDAQ National Market. Specifically, publicly-traded companies wishing to list on the NASDAQ National Market must have a certain amount in net tangible assets or operating income, at least 500,000 shares and 400 stockholders, and a minimum bid price of $5 per share. NASDAQ stocks that do not meet these requirements trade on the NASDAQ Small Cap Market. Most of the time, when one refers to "NASDAQ," one is referring to the National Market.

NASDAQ Small-Capitalization Companies Small (by market capitalization) companies with stocks that trade on the NASDAQ Small Cap Market. NASDAQ small capitalization companies are those that do not meet the requirements to be listed on the NASDAQ National Market. Specifically, these companies: do not meet the minimum requirements for net tangible assets or operating income, have fewer than 500,000 shares and 400 stockholders, or do not meet the minimum bid price of $5 per share. See also: SOES.

Nasdead A derogatory nickname for NASDAQ. The name is used sarcastically when the NASDAQ is bearish.

Nasiib al-mithl An Arabic term meaning "similar share." In Islamic law, a contract of partnership may indicate that the parties will receive nasiib al-mithl if for some reason a portion of the contract is declared invalid. This means that the parties will split profits according to the generally accepted custom of society.

Nass In Islamic law, a legal text written by a sharia scholar.

Nation A group of persons with a common identity completely separate from other groups. There is no consensus as to what separates a nation from, say, an ethnic group beyond wide acceptance of a group's identity as a nation. Many nations also have their own states or countries, though most countries are multinational.

Nation Building The practice in which a foreign military force occupies a country to build infrastructure (such as roads and schools) and/or to protect the local government until it becomes stable. Nation building is highly controversial. Proponents argue that it stabilizes nascent democracies and protects local citizens, while critics contend that it is an unnecessary use of resources and can protect unpopular governments.

National Accord for Raising Productivity and Quality Also called ANEPC. A policy in Mexico whereby companies and unions voluntarily agreed to work toward higher productivity by employees. Companies agreed to provide more and better training for employees and to raise wages in exchange for higher productivity. Unions, on the other hand, agreed to make concessions on work rules to make increased productivity possible. ANEPC was introduced by President Carlos Salinas in 1992.

National Agricultural Library A federal library in the United States that provides resources on livestock, food, history, rural development, water quality, marketing, and other topics. The National Agricultural Library coordinates regional libraries and facilitates agricultural research in the U.S. It was established in 1862 and is based in Maryland.

National Association of Broadcasters A trade association for American radio and television broadcasters. It schedules educational events and programs for members to meet and share ideas and advocates for favorable legislation. It is based in Washington, D.C.

National Association of Export Companies An organization for banks, chambers of commerce, private companies and others with interest in international trade. It serves as a lobbying group for U.S. exports and conducts educational programs. It was founded in 1963 and maintains its headquarters in New York City.

National Association of Federal Credit Unions An organization for federally-chartered credit unions in the United States. It serves as a lobbying group for credit unions before the U.S. government and conducts public relations to promote credit unions to the public. It was founded in 1967 and maintains its headquarters in Arlington, Virginia.

National Association of Home Builders An organization for builders in the United States. It serves as a lobbying group for housing and other builders before the U.S. government and it conducts educational seminars for members. It was founded in 1942 and maintains its headquarters in Washington, D.C.

National Association of Insurance Brokers Also called the NAIB. A trade association for insurance brokers in the United States. The NAIB sets ethical standards for members, lobbies for favorable legislation and provides educational materials for members. It is headquartered in Washington, D.C.

National Association of Insurance Commissioners Also called the NAIC. A non-profit organization in the United States consisting of the heads of the insurance departments of each state and U.S. territory. The NAIC drafts model legislation and conducts other activities geared toward bringing together the insurance regulation laws in each state. The NAIC exists because each state may regulate insurance autonomously but it is advantageous for the states to have similar laws for the sake of consistency and to reduce jurisdictional arbitrage. The NAIC was established in 1871.

National Association of Investors Corporation An umbrella organization of thousands of local clubs across the United States that encourages successful investment practices among members. In particular, the NAIC encourages members to make long-term investments in companies with high growth potential. It runs educational and support programs for members. It was established in 1951 and is based in Michigan. It is also called BetterInvesting.

National Association of Manufacturers An organization for large and small manufacturers in the United States, regardless of industry. It serves as a lobbying group for manufacturers before the U.S. government. It also has an affiliated think tank that conducts research on the manufacturing industry. It was founded in 1895 and maintains its headquarters in Washington, D.C.

National Association of Realtors An organization for real estate brokers and real estate agents in the United States. It serves as a lobbying group for realtors before the U.S. government. It is also a self-regulatory organization for the sale of real estate. It has an affiliated think tank that conducts research on the manufacturing industry. It was founded in 1908 and maintains its headquarters in Washington, D.C.

National Association of Securities Dealers and Investment Managers Also called NASDIM. A former self-regulatory organization in the United Kingdom for security dealers, insurance brokers and investment advisers. In 1986, it was replaced by the Security and Futures Authority. See also: FINRA.

National Association of State Boards of Accountancy Also called NASBA. A non-profit organization in the United States consisting of representatives of boards governing accounting in each state and U.S. territory. NASBA provides mutual recognition for CPA certification in each state and lobbies other organizations and the federal government in matters of common interest.

National Association of State Departments of Agriculture Also called NADSA. An organization in the United States consisting of the agricultural departments or the equivalent in each state. NASDA exists to discuss issues of common interest and to promote agricultural policy to the federal government. It was established in 1915.

National Bank In the United States, a bank that has received its charter from the Office of the Comptroller of the Currency (OCC). National banks are regulated by the OCC and are required to be member banks of the Federal Reserve System. Deposits in national banks are insured by the FDIC.

National Bank of Poland The central bank of Poland. It controls issue of the Polish zloty. It was established under its current name in 1945, but traces its origins to the Bank of Poland in the 19th century. Its president is appointed by the Sejm (Polish parliament) upon the request of the President of Poland.

National Bank of Romania The central bank of Romania. It controls issue of the Romanian leu, sets the monetary policy, holds currency reserves, manages the exchange rate, and has other similar responsibilities. It was established in 1880.

National Best Bid and Offer An SEC regulation stating that brokers are required to seek the best possible price for their customers. This means that brokers may not find less favorable prices in order to extract a higher commission. See also: Fiduciary Responsibility.

National Brand A brand name sold all over a country rather than in a certain area. A national brand may be lower in price than a local brand because it is able to utilize economies of scale. A national brand may give the impression (whether accurate or not) of higher quality.

National Bulk Mail System The system of 21 centers in the United States where extremely large volumes of mail are processed and distributed to the appropriate destinations. Bulk mail centers are highly automated.

National Bureau of Economic Research A private organization that conducts research into how the American economy works. Its goal is to provide non-partisan analysis to policymakers, businesspersons, academics, and the wider public. NBER divides its research into four main components: the development of new ways to make statistical measurements, estimating quantitative data on economic behavior, researching possible effects of policy proposals, and researching the effects of policy alternatives. It is particularly well-known for chronicling the beginning and end dates of American recessions.

National Credit Union Administration An agency of the United States government that charters and regulates credit unions and insures their deposits up to a certain level so as to reduce pressure for bank panics. Created in 1970 to succeed the Bureau of Federal Credit Unions, which had become inefficient because of the rapid expansion of credit unions in the middle of the 20th century, the NCUA insures deposits up to $100,000 or $250,000, depending on the type of account. This amount may be changed by statute. It does this through the National Credit Union Share Insurance Fund, which is capitalized by the credit unions themselves. The NCUA is also responsible for handling bankruptcies in credit unions. The agency is overseen by a three-member board appointed by the President and confirmed by the Senate for a six-year term. See also: FDIC, Office of Thrift Supervision.

National Debt The total of all bonds and other debt owed by a government. Most of the time, the national debt comes from bonds and other debt securities, but some countries in the developing world borrow directly from international institutions such as the World Bank. The national debt may be internal, that is, owed to bondholders and banks within the country, or external, that is, owed to foreign governments, institutions, and/or individuals. In the United States, paying the interest on the national debt is a major part of the federal budget. See also: Deficit.

National Economic Development Council A former forum that brought together members of the British government, unions, and business interests to make recommendations for the government to promote economic growth. It was based on the corporatist idea that discussion between classes encouraged the best result for all. It was created in 1962 and was abolished in 1992.

National Environmental Policy Act Legislation in the United States, passed in 1969, requiring all entities other than the president, the Congress and the court system to prepare and present reports on the impact a proposed federal action would have on the environment. The Act established different levels of impact and created a Council of Environmental Quality to advise the president.

National Ethics Law for Central Government Public Servants Legislation in Japan, enacted in 2000, prohibiting civil servants from excessive socialization with the companies they regulate. It explicitly prohibits private companies from taking civil servants out to dinner. Previously, using personal friendships in regulation was assumed to be part of the way the system worked. The law established the National Public Service Ethics Board for interpretation and enforcement.

National Federation of Independent Businesses A trade organization for small businesses in the United States. It lobbies the government for favorable legislation. It is especially known for seeking tort reform and allowing small businesses to pool insurance in order to create more affordable health care for employees. It also seeks the repeal of the federal estate tax. Members of the NFIB vote to decide what issues to lobby. It was established in California in 1943 and is based in Nashville, Tennessee.

National Foundation for Consumer Credit In the United States, a non-profit organization with branches nationwide that aims to help consumers with too much debt to resolve their problems without resorting to bankruptcy. The NFCC provides individualized services to clients by helping them structure (or restructure) payment plans and providing advice on how to improve their situations.

National Futures Association A self-regulatory organization that works with the Commodity Futures Trading Commission to regulate the futures and commodities markets. Among its most important duties is the provision of arbitration and mediation services for traders and other interested parties. It was established in 1982 and is based in Chicago.

National Health Service Most commonly called the NHS. The collective name for the publicly-funded health care systems in the United Kingdom. The governments of Northern Ireland, Scotland and Wales operate their NHS systems independently, while the UK government controls the NHS in England. Each NHS system is funded entirely by the government and provides most services free of charge for patients. Critics contend that the NHS is too expensive for taxpayers and that inefficiency has led to long wait times for medical care. However, it has remained popular among many people in the UK.

National Housing Act Legislation in the United States, passed in 1934, that established the Federal Housing Administration and the Federal Savings and Loan Insurance Corporation. The FHA provides mortgages to those who otherwise may not be able to afford them. The FSLIC gave insurance to savings and loan corporations, which reduced the likelihood that savings and loans would go bankrupt and therefore made it less risky for them to make mortgage loans. Both aspects of the Act were intended to increase American homeownership. It was part of the New Deal.

National Income The total income of the persons in a nation. Gross domestic product is calculated by adding together total consumer spending, total government spending, total business spending, the value of net exports and payments received from other countries. One then subtracts all payments made to other countries and indirect business taxes. While it is not as common a measure as GDP, it may be used as a measure of the health of a country's economy. See also: GNP.

National Institute of Standards and Technology A federal research laboratory in the United States. Established in 1901, it conducts research in various scientific fields and has contributed to developments in x-rays, smoke detectors, and pollution control, among other things. It is an agency under the U.S. Department of Commerce.

National Insurance Contributions Deductions from paychecks or other payments made to National Insurance in the United Kingdom. National Insurance pays for the state pension, unemployment benefits and also funds the National Health Service. Both employees and employers must make National Insurance contributions, and employers must make further contributions on certain employee benefits. They do not fund other government functions, but the government may borrow against them.

National Intelligence Council An organization within the U.S. intelligence community that prepares and presents information on world events to the U.S. president and other, relevant leaders. It leads the preparation of National Intelligence Estimates and prepares a Global Briefing every four years for each incoming President. It also serves as a hub for answering government leaders' questions. It was established in 1979.

National Investor Relations Institute Also called NIRI. A trade association in the United States for corporate managers and others who facilitate communication between companies, shareholders, governments and the broader financial community. It was founded in 1969 and is based in Virginia.

National Labor Relations Act Legislation in the United States, passed in 1935, that protects workers from employer retaliation if they form a labor union. It prohibits employers from coercing employees into refraining from organizing. It also prohibits employers from discriminating against employees who argue publicly in favor or against organizing and requires companies to negotiate with employee representatives. It requires each unit of employees to be represented only by one organization. The Act created the National Labor Relations Board, which investigates and enforces potential violations. It is also called the Wagner Act.

National Labor Relations Board Also called the NLRB. An agency of the U.S. federal government that monitors union elections and guards against unfair labor practices such as featherbedding or employer discrimination against union members. It also serves as an administrative court for labor disputes. The NLRB consists of five members, appointed by the president and confirmed by the Senate to a five-year term. It was established by executive order in 1934.

National List Securities that trade on an exchange that links itself to other exchanges as part of the national market system.

National Market The domestic and foreign market in a given country. That is, the national market describes the supply and demand for all securities that are traded in a country. Each national market is governed by the regulations of its own country.

National Market Advisory Board A board that advised the Securities and Exchange Commission in the United States on the proposed creation of a national market, which would allow continuous trading of securities across all exchanges while still allowing the individual exchanges to function independently.

National Market System A trading system listing securities that trade in both New York and on regional exchanges. This allows investors to find the best price available for securities. The NMS also facilitates trading of certain over-the-counter stocks. It is sponsored and managed by NASDAQ and FINRA. See also: 19c-3 stock.

National Monetary Council An organization that sets monetary policy for the Central Bank of Brazil. It consists of the Finance Minister, the Planning Minister and the Governor of the Central Bank. It was created in 1964 by the same legislation that created the Bank itself.

National Newspaper Association An organization that promotes small community newspapers in the United States. It provides resources to members, markets their newspapers to advertisers, and lobbies for favorable legislation. It was founded in 1885 and is based in Columbia, Missouri.

National Opinion Research Center An organization that conducts data collection and survey activities. Research areas include economics and personal finance, social development, education, mental health, and criminal justice. It was established in 1941 and is based at the University of Chicago.

National Personnel Authority An agency of the Japanese government responsible for publishing the names of civil servants who take high positions in private companies and vice versa. The National Personnel Authority exists to promote transparency in Japanese government-business relations.

National Pharmaceutical Stockpile Large quantities of medicine maintained by the Centers for Disease Control and Prevention for use in national emergencies. The CDC may tap into the National Pharmaceutical Stockpile in the event of a natural disaster, epidemic, terrorist attack or any other event in which local medicinal stockpiles prove insufficient. Medicines are delivered within 12 hours of request by both federal and local authorities. They are available for free.

National Plan 1. See: IRA. **2.** See: 401(k). **3.** See: Insurance policy.

National Printing Bureau An agency of the Japanese government that prints paper money. That is, the National Printing Bureau is responsible for the production of cash yen that circulate in Japan and worldwide. It also produces postage stamps. It was established in 1871.

National Public Accountant A periodical of accounting news and commentary published by the National Society of Accountants in the United States.

National Public Service Ethics Board An agency in Japan established to interpret and enforce the National Ethics Law for Central Government Public Servants, which prohibits excessive socialization between civil servants and the companies they regulate. It rules on the meaning of the law and whether new situations that arise are permitted or prohibited. Its members are not allowed to come from the civil service.

National Quotation Bureau A company that provides quotes for over-the-counter stocks and corporate bonds. The National Quotation Bureau provides information such as the bids, asks, and the market makers giving them. Because stocks and bonds listed by the National Quotation Bureau are over-the-counter, they do not have to meet any listing requirements and may, therefore, come from quite small issuers. The Bureau provides all quotes in real time and publishes a review each week. Its quotes are divided into Yellow Sheets (for bonds) and Pink Sheets (for stocks).

National Registration Database A system in Canada allowing brokers, dealers, and investment advisers to file registration paperwork with regulators online. Formerly, everyone had to file physical copies of paperwork with the appropriate agency. It was established in 2003.

National Research and Education Network Commonly called NREN. An Internet service provider for educational and research institutions. New protocols are often introduced on NRENs before they are used on other ISPs.

National Reserve Bank of Tonga The central bank of Tonga. It controls issue of the Tongan pa'anga. Among other responsibilities, it sets the monetary policy, regulates financial institutions and advises the government on fiscal policy. It is the main fiscal agent for the Tongan government. It was created in 1988 and began operations in 1989.

National Salary The average amount that a person makes in a year. A national salary may be considered as a whole or it may be broken down by occupation. For example, one may discuss the national salary for teachers in the United States. See also: National wage.

National Savings The proportion of public and private savings as a percentage of national income. In simple economic models, the national savings is assumed to be the same as national investment, which is the total amount spent on securities and similar investment vehicles. That is, anything not spent by consumers or the government is assumed to be saved. A high national savings rate indicates lower levels of debt, which is positive. However, in an economy driven by consumer spending, a high savings rate may indicate uncertainty or lack of consumption, which can lead to a slowdown or a recession. That is, low or negative national savings usually indicates excessive borrowing, spending, or both. On the other hand, high national savings may result in slower economic growth, as persons, companies and the government are saving instead of purchasing goods and services.

National Savings Bank A state-owned bank in Sri Lanka specializes in taking deposits for checking and savings accounts and other retail banking services. It also conducts postal banking in conjunction with the Sri Lankan Post. It was established in 1971.

National Savings Certificate An investment vehicle in India whereby one is able to gather savings tax-free. The interest on a national savings certificate is taxable but is considered to have been reinvested and is therefore not actually taxed. Additionally, one receives an income tax rebate for the amount one invests in a national savings certificate. Interest on national savings certificates compounds twice a year. Middle class families in India commonly use national savings certificates as a way to save and invest. They are available for purchase at every post office. See also: Certificate of deposit.

National Savings Stock Register An investment vehicle in the United Kingdom whereby one is able to gather savings. The amount one uses to purchase a national savings stock register is invested in government gilts (which are British debt securities). The interest on a national savings stock register is taxable. They are available for purchase at every post office. See also: Certificate of deposit, National savings certificate.

National School Lunch Program A program in the United States giving subsidies to schools in order to provide free or low-price lunches to eligible children. The NSLP was created in 1946 both to feed underprivileged children and to stabilize food prices for farmers. Counting the number of children eligible for the NSLP is one way of measuring poverty in an area.

National Securities Clearing Corporation A subsidiary of the Depository Trust and Clearing Corporation. The NSCC is a clearing house that provides settlement services for securities traded on the American Stock Exchange and the New York Stock Exchange. It also provides services for FINRA. It operates settlement according to continuous net settlement practices.

National Securities Markets Improvement Act of 1996 Legislation in the United States that exempted many securities, notably those nationally registered, from state registration and regulation. The Act was intended to streamline the process of registering and offering new issues of securities, which was thought to spur investment. See also: Deregulation.

National Securities Trading System An automated quotation system connecting brokers on the National Stock Exchange (Cincinnati Stock Exchange) to other brokers around the country, allowing them to make orders for certain securities without regard for the specific exchange on which they are traded. The system is exclusive to the National Stock Exchange, but contains a blueprint for what some envision as a future nation-wide exchange. See also: Intermarket Trading System.

National Security Controls Restrictions on the export or re-export of goods from the United States. In general, the U.S. (like most countries) promotes its own exports, but national security controls may be implemented on certain goods whose export is deemed not to be in the interests of the U.S. Nuclear materials, for example, have some national security controls placed on them. The president has the authority to issue or rescind national security controls.

National Security Council A general term for a statutory or ad hoc committee in a country that forms policy and/or advises the chief executive on matters related to national security and foreign relations. National security councils vary by country, but ordinarily they consist of high ranking officials. In the United States, for example, the National Security Council includes the president, the vice president, the secretaries of State and Defense, and the national security advisor.

National Security Directive #53 A memorandum issued in 1990 by President George H.W. Bush stating that there is a presumption of approval on any application for an export license. That is, if there may be a national security reason to deny an application, the directive places the burden of proof on an objecting department or agency. This contrasts with the alternative, in which a company would be required to prove its application does not pose security risks.

National Security Directives Memoranda issued by the president of the United States indicating how he/she intends to interpret and implement the law as it relates to national security. National security directives are approved by the National Security Council before they take effect. While they are not legislative, they have the force of law.

National Security Override A restriction on the export of a good from the United States even after a federal agency has authorized it. A national security override may occur, for example, if one department approves the export but another department does not.

National Stock Exchange The oldest fully electronic stock exchange in the United States. Founded as the Cincinnati Stock Exchange in 1885, it closed its trading floor in 1980 and became America's first fully computerized exchange, largely due to the efforts of Bernard Madoff. Six years later, it became the first exchange to adopt the Intermarket Trading System, which allowed its members to interface with all other exchanges.

National Stock Exchange of India The largest stock exchange in India. It was incorporated in 1992 by a number of Indian financial institutions at the request of the government. In the 2000s, it became one of the fastest-growing exchanges in the world. Stocks, bonds, mutual funds and derivatives all trade on the National Stock Exchange.

National Tax-Exempt Money Market Fund A mutual fund that invests predominantly or exclusively in municipal bonds with maturities of less than one year. Tax-exempt money market funds are intended to provide a return at little risk (compared to other investments) that is nonetheless better than the risk-free rate of return. Because it invests in municipal bonds, dividends from the fund are tax-free at the federal level (though they may be subject to state tax unless all bonds in the fund are issued in the state where the holder resides).

National Tourism Policy Act Legislation in the Philippines, enacted in 2009, that increased funding to the Tourism Ministry in order to encourage tourism. The purpose of the Act was to create jobs and spur economic growth by developing the tourist industry.

National Trade Data Bank A database maintained by the United States federal government containing a great deal of information, such as the trade balance, the balance of payments, foreign investment in the U.S., American investment in other countries, agricultural information, and exchange rates, among other things.

National Trade Estimates Report An annual report by the United States Trade Representative discussing the best export markets for the U.S. It includes information like market size and trade barriers that exporters may face.

National Transportation Safety Board An agency in the United States responsible for investigating airline, waterway and rail accidents, and some highway car accidents. It also investigates oil and gas pipeline incidents. The board consists of five members appointed by the president with Senate confirmation. It was created in 1967.

National Treatment A feature of numerous international agreements in which the parties treat each other's persons and goods the same as their own persons and goods. That is, they have equal access to markets, courts and so forth. National treatment is used in a number of World Trade Organization treaties in order to promote international trade by reducing uncertainty.

National Wage The average amount that a person makes per hour. A national wage may be considered as a whole or it may be broken down by occupation. For example, one may discuss the national wage for construction workers in the United States. See also: National salary.

National Wealth The value of all assets less all liabilities held within a country. Assets included in natural wealth calculations include technologies, natural resources, infrastructure and so forth. It is a way to measure a country's economy (and is especially useful in measuring a nation's ability to control debt), but it is not as commonly used as the gross domestic product.

National ZIP Code Area The first digit of a zip code in the United States. The number may be between zero and nine and indicates the state (or district) to which mail is directed or from which it comes. This helps in sorting mail.

Nationalism The philosophy in which one promotes the interests of one's own country or ethnic group over others. For example, nationalism may advocate secession of a region to form a new country in which one's own ethnic group predominates. What qualifies as a "nation" in nationalist terms is a matter of some disagreement.

Nationalist One who promotes the interests of one's own country or ethnic group over others. For example, nationalism may advocate secession of a region to form a new country in which one's own ethnic group predominates. What qualifies as a "nation" in nationalist terms is a matter of some disagreement.

Nationalization The taking of a private business or industry by a government. Compensation to shareholders, bondholders, and/or other stakeholders may be made in a nationalization, but the word connotes forcible seizure. Developing countries and socialist governments nationalize companies and assets more often than developed countries, but even the United States took majority ownership of several major private companies in 2008 and 2009. Nationalization is very controversial. See also: Too-big-to-fail.

Nationally Recognized Statistical Ratings Organization A credit rating agency that the Securities and Exchange Commission in the United States uses for regulatory purposes. Credit rating agencies provide assessments of an investment's risk. The issuers of investments, especially debt securities, pay credit rating agencies to provide them with ratings. Investments must receive a high rating from two or more nationally recognized statistical ratings organizations before banks in the United States may purchase them. There are 10 nationally recognized statistical ratings organization; Fitch, S&P, and Moody's are the three most prominent.

NATO The North Atlantic Treaty Organization. A military alliance originally designed to deter against potential Soviet invasion. Members pledge mutual defense; that is, an attack on one is considered an attack on all. Since the end of the Cold War, NATO has been involved in other military engagement, notably in the Balkans and Afghanistan. Members include the United States and a number of European countries. It was founded in 1949 and is based in Brussels.

Natural Describing a security or trade in which a prospective buyer or seller actually intends to buy or sell, as opposed to an indication of interest where the inquirer has other intentions.

Natural Advantage The ability for an economic actor to produce a good or service because the resources to do so are physically available. For example, the economy of Nebraska has a natural advantage relative to the economy of Bahrain because it is easier to grow corn in Nebraska. On the other hand, Bahrain has a natural advantage over Nebraska because there are more fish located around Bahrain. See also: Absolute advantage.

Natural Business Year A fiscal year that runs according to something other than the calendar year. A natural business year often is chosen according to when most sales in a year are completed. For example, a swimsuit manufacturer may end its natural business year in September, after most swimsuits for the year are sold.

Natural Capitalism Any economic system that incentivizes profit based on proper care of the environment. In other words, natural capitalism assigns an economic value to stewardship of the planet. Income from natural capital includes yield from trees and plants. Natural capitalism assumes that goods and services have a value apart from their potential sale price on the market. Natural capitalism remains largely theoretical.

Natural Capitalist A scholar who favors an economic system that incentivizes profit based on proper care of the environment. In other words, natural capitalists assign an economic value to stewardship of the planet. Income from natural capital includes yield from trees and plants. Natural capitalists assume that goods and services have a value apart from their potential sale price on the market. Natural capitalism remains largely theoretical.

Natural Corner A situation in which an investor achieves significant control over a company or its share price without intending to do so. This may occur, for example, when a single investor is accumulating a stock at the same time a large number of investors are short selling it. When the short sellers need to buy back the stock, the single investor suddenly has a great deal of control over the price.

Natural Death Death resulting from sickness or old age, as opposed to an accident or homicide. Life insurance provides coverage for natural death, as well as most other types of death (sometimes with the exception of suicide).

Natural Environment The living and nonliving things in an area of the Earth. The natural environment both enables human life and is affected by human activity. That is, whether a human builds a house, grows a crop or mines a mineral, the natural environment is changed. The natural environment is necessary for commerce to take place. See also: Sustainability.

Natural Expenses Expenses categorized by type. Employee salaries, rent and bills for the office, and supplies for programs are all examples of natural expenses.

Natural Gas A fossil fuel consisting primarily of methane and hydrocarbons. It is used as a fuel and to produce fertilizer. Although it produces carbon, natural gas is considered the cleanest fossil fuel. It is a major commodity.

Natural Gas Storage Report A weekly report on the natural gas produced and stored in the 48 contiguous U.S. states. It considers both the natural gas previously stored and the additions and subtractions occurring each week. It is published by the Energy Information Administration, a government agency.

Natural Growth Rate The national income growth rate necessary to neither increase nor decrease unemployment. The natural growth rate assumes there are no advances in technology and the labor force enlarges at a constant rate.

Natural Guardian A parent of a minor or incapacitated person. The natural guardian has the right to make financial, legal and medical decisions on behalf of the child. A natural guardian contrasts with an appointed guardian, who is assigned by a court.

Natural Law In philosophy, the idea that that right and wrong are fixed, immutable things that human reason can discern. Some natural law theorists base natural law on

their ideas about God, but one does not need to believe in God in order to believe in natural law. It forms the philosophical basis for what are now called human rights and for that reason is an important contributor to modern liberalism.

Natural Log In mathematics, the exponent to which one must raise the number e (a mathematical constant approximately equal to 2.718) to produce a given number. The natural log has a number of applications across mathematics, including in compound interest.

Natural Loss A loss occurring from an act of God. Examples of events that may cause natural losses include tornados, earthquakes and floods. Insurance may mitigate natural losses.

Natural Monopoly A situation in which the barriers to entry for an industry or product are so high that it is not profitable for a second company to make an attempt. For example, an area may have only one utility company because it is prohibitively expensive to start another one. Governments generally regulate profits for natural monopolies to protect consumers.

Natural Person An individual belonging to the human race. In law, natural persons have rights, such as the right to own property, the right to enter into a contract, the right to vote, and the right to engage in commerce. Natural persons may be held liable for criminal and civil penalties. A natural person is distinguished from a juridical person, which is an artificial entity with some of the rights of a natural person.

Naula A Finnish unit of weight approximately equivalent to 425.6 grams. It became obsolete when Finland adopted the metric system in 1880.

Naya Paisa A subdivision of the Bhutanese rupee, the former currency of Bhutan. One naya paisa was equal in value to 1/100 of one rupee.

NBC The common abbreviation for the National Broadcasting Company, which was the first major broadcasting network in the United States. NBC launched as a radio network in 1926 and began television broadcasts in 1938 (it ended its radio component in 2003). With a market share of more than 40% of the viewing audience, it is very popular among advertisers who wish to disseminate their messages to as wide a group as possible.

NC 1. ISO 3166-1 alpha-2 code for New Caledonia. This is the code used in international transactions to and from New Caledonian bank accounts. **2.** ISO 3166-2 geocode for New Caledonia. This is used as an international standard for shipping to New Caledonia. **3.** A slang term for non-callable bond.

NCL GOST 7.67 Latin three-letter geocode for New Caledonia. The code is used for transactions to and from New Caledonian bank accounts and for international shipping to New Caledonia. As with all GOST 7.67 codes, it is used primarily in Cyrillic alphabets.

Near Money A highly liquid asset that may easily be converted to cash. Examples include savings accounts, bonds (especially near their maturities), and money markets. Central banks and statisticians sometimes, but not always, use near money when computing the money supply. See also: M2.

Nearby Month Among several different futures contracts or options, describing the one with the shortest maturity. For example, given three futures contracts, one expiring in March, one in June, and one in September, the nearby month contract is the one expiring in March. It is also called the spot month. See also: Most distant futures contract.

Necessities of Life Things one requires to avoid death. Examples include food, sleep, shelter and clothing. Most necessities of life require money to purchase them. Jobs, investments and even insurance can be utilized to pay for the necessities of life. See also: Maslow's hierarchy of needs, Activities of daily living.

Neckline In technical analysis, a line, sometimes with zero-slope and sometimes with slight slope, representing a buy point on a head and shoulders pattern. In a chart showing a head and shoulders pattern, the "head" and "shoulders" fall toward a certain near-horizontal line before rising again; this is the neckline. When technical analysts see a security falling toward the neckline, they view this as a buy signal because historical patterns have shown that the security's price will rise soon thereafter. However, if the security falls significantly below the neckline, technical analysts see this as a reversal of a previous trend.

Need-Based Aid Loans, grants, and scholarships available to post-secondary students who have an expected family contribution above zero, but who may not be able to pay that amount. Examples of need-based aid include Stafford loans and PLUS loans. To become eligible for federal need-based aid, one must file a FAFSA.

Need-Based Scholarship A scholarship available to persons with incomes below a certain level. For example, a university may offer scholarships to academically qualified students who make less than $30,000 per year.

Negative Acknowledgment Also called NAK. In telecommunications, acknowledgement of the receipt of a file, with a note that the information is incomplete or corrupted.

Negative Amortization A situation in which the principal amount of a loan increases if a payment does not cover the full interest due. For example, if the interest due for a given month is $300, and the borrower pays $200, then $100 will be added to the principal. Negative amortization is used in some mortgages. This allows more people to be eligible to borrow with lower monthly payments, but negative amortization will inevitably increase the payments when it comes time to repay the principal. See also: Payment option ARM.

Negative Amortizing Mortgage A mortgage loan in which the principal amount increases if a payment does not cover the full interest due. For example, if the interest due for a given month is $300 and the borrower pays $200, then $100 will be added to the principal. A negative amortizing mortgage allows more people to be eligible to borrow with lower monthly payments, but negative amortization will inevitably increase the payments when it comes time to repay the principal. See also: Payment option ARM.

Negative Authorization A system that compares a credit card number to a list of lost or stolen numbers. When a credit card is used, the transaction will not be approved if the number matches a number on the list.

Negative Balance An account balance in which debits exceed credits. A negative balance indicates that the account holder owes money. A negative balance on a loan indicates that the loan has not been repaid in full, while a negative bank balance indicates that the account holder has overspent.

Negative Carry A situation in which an investment has a lower yield than the cost of funding for it. For example, an investor may borrow money at 6% interest to invest in a restaurant with only a 4% yield. In this case, the investor has a negative carry of 2% and is actually spending money to invest in the restaurant. One may think of a negative carry as a bad investment, but it sometimes results in a net profit if the interest on the cost of funding is tax deductible and the investment itself is a tax free security, such as a municipal bond.

Negative Cash Flow A situation in which a company is spending more money than it is receiving. While this is common in many companies, especially in the first year or two of operation, it is obviously unsustainable in the long-term. A company with a negative cash flow often has to resort to loans or equity financing in order to keep its doors open.

Negative Convexity In callable bonds, a situation in which the principal is returned, either before maturity when interest rates are declining or after maturity when interest rates are rising. This exposes bondholders to the risk of realizing a lower return.

Negative Duration **1.** A situation in which the price of a bond or other debt security moves in the same direction of interest rates. That is, negative duration occurs when the bond prices go up along with interest rates and vice versa. **2.** In banking, a situation in which the duration of a bank's liabilities exceeds that of its assets. Negative duration means that the bank's equity is negative.

Negative Equity A situation in which one owes more on a loan used to pay for an asset than that asset's current market value. For example, if one borrows $100,000 to buy a house and, for whatever reason, the value immediately drops to $60,000, the homeowner is said to have negative equity. Negative equity is most common after the burst of an asset bubble. One with negative equity is said to be upside down in the loan.

Negative Goodwill Income, perhaps even a profit, that comes from the sale of an asset at less than its fair market value. Negative goodwill is most common during a distressed sale, in which one must raise cash immediately to pay some liability. The buyer records the difference between the negative goodwill and the fair market value as a gain on the balance sheet.

Negative Income Tax A tax system or bracket in which persons with an adjusted gross income below a certain amount receive money from the government. This system intends to bring people out of poverty, or at least to make their situations less difficult.

Negative Interest Rate An interest rate paid by a lender to a borrower rather than the other way around. Negative interest rates may occur when the interest rate is below the inflation rate, or when the lender actually pays the borrower more. Negative interest rates occur during periods of high volatility.

Negative Obligation New York Stock Exchange requirements on its specialists. The negative obligation forbids specialists from trading on their own accounts when enough matching orders exist to ensure a two-sided market. That is, when investors do not need a specialist to provide liquidity to the market, the negative obligation prohibits the specialist from trading on its own account. See also: Positive obligation.

Negative Pledge A negative covenant in a bond indenture in which the issuer agrees not to use any of its assets as security for another debt obligation or other liability if doing so would adversely impact the riskiness of the bond. This protects bondholders and also allows the issuer to pay a lower coupon rate.

Negative Saving A situation in which the persons in an economy save, in the aggregate, less than they spend. For example, suppose a small economy exists in which the people spend in total $1 million, but only manage to save $800,000. This economy has negative savings. By its nature, negative saving requires an economy (though not necessarily the government) to take on debt.

Negative Volume Index In technical analysis, a measure of change in various market indicators on days when trading volume is low. The idea behind the NVI is that intelligent investors quietly buy or sell securities ahead of the trend, and that the crowd buys or sells only on days when trading volume is high. Tracking whether a market or security is bullish or bearish when trading volume is low is thought to be a lead indicator of a market's general direction. See also: Positive Volume Index.

Negeri In Malaysia, a political subdivision equivalent to a state or province.

Neglected-Firm Effect A theory stating that publicly-traded companies that analysts do not track or follow closely tend to outperform those receiving a great deal of attention. Analysts sometimes pay less attention to companies because there is limited information available on them. Part of the neglected-firm effect may be explained by the fact that these firms are riskier and therefore have higher returns.

Negligent Trustee A trustee who violates his/her fiduciary responsibility through lack of attention rather than malice. For example, a trustee may be negligent if he/she does not perform due diligence on the investments the trust makes.

Negotiable A security that may be bought or sold. Generally, a negotiable security is traded on the secondary market, but the initial sale takes place on the primary market. Negotiable securities may be low-risk, such a Treasury bonds, or high-risk, such as stocks. They are also known as marketable securities. See also: Nonmarketable security.

Negotiable Certificate of Deposit A certificate of deposit of large value that can be bought and sold but not redeemed before maturity. See also: Jumbo CD, Callable CD.

Negotiable Order of Withdrawal Account A checking account at a bank or thrift that earns interest. The account holder is allowed to write checks or drafts against the money in the account and may withdraw any amount of money from it on demand. See also: M1.

Negotiated Commission A fee that a client negotiates with a broker to conduct trades on the client's behalf. Some brokerages charge set commissions, but some allow clients, especially large ones, to apply negotiated commissions. They became more common after commissions were deregulated in 1975. See also: May Day.

Negotiated Market A secondary market in which potential buyers and sellers negotiate the price of each transaction. Most stock exchanges are negotiated markets: buyers express interest by posting bid prices and sellers do the same with ask prices. A negotiated market operates according to the law of supply and demand. See also: Market price, Fair market value.

Negotiated Offering A way of making a new issue of securities in which the issuer hires an underwriting firm or syndicate and negotiates all terms of the issue with them. In general, a negotiated offering involves the underwriters guaranteeing that the issue will be placed with investors at a certain price in exchange for a fee to the underwriters. It contrasts with multiple competitive bidding. Most offerings, however, are negotiated.

Negotiated Sale An agreement made directly between an issuer of a security and an underwriter whereby the underwriter will place the new issue with investors in exchange for a commission or fee. The commission or fee is negotiated directly between the issuer and the underwriter; this contrasts with competitive bidding, where an issuer attempts to extract the best price from many different underwriters.

Negotiated Underwriting A process in which an issuer of securities approaches an underwriting firm to facilitate a new issue. The issuer and the underwriter negotiate a purchase price, which is the price for which the underwriter buys the new issue, and an offering price, the price at which the underwriter sells the issue to investors. The difference between these forms the underwriter's profit. In negotiated underwriting, these discussions occur on an individual basis between the issuer and the underwriting firm. It contrasts with competitive bidding, whereby a number of underwriters make offers to the issuer, who picks the most favorable offer.

Neighborhood Council In Guyana, a political subdivision equivalent to a municipality.

Nelikko A Finnish unit of dry volume approximately equivalent to 44 liters. It became obsolete when Finland adopted the metric system in 1880.

Nemawashi The informal process of gathering support for a major change before any formal actions are taken. Nemawashi may involve formulation of ideas, identification of potential problems, and/or discussions with colleagues. The term originated and is used most frequently in Japan, but the concept is universal.

Nemo A television or radio broadcast that originates some place other than the studio. A prominent example is a sports broadcast, which originates at the field or court of play.

Neo-Conservatism A political philosophy that advocates an expansive foreign policy, as well as a role (though limited) for government in poverty reduction and welfare programs. Neo-conservatism is associated with nation building, in which a country uses its military force to occupy a country to protect a nascent government until it becomes stable. Neo-conservatives favor an activist foreign policy intended to prevent potential rivals from becoming a threat. Neo-conservatives believe this philosophy makes their own countries safer, while critics contend that their philosophy leads to instability.

Neo-Conservative One who advocates an expansive foreign policy, as well as a role (though limited) for government in poverty reduction and welfare programs. Neo-conservatism is associated with nation building, in which a country uses its military force to occupy a country to protect a nascent government until it becomes stable. Neo-conservatives favor an activist foreign policy intended to prevent potential rivals from becoming a threat. Neo-conservatives believe this philosophy makes their own countries safer, while critics contend that their philosophy leads to instability.

Neo-Liberal One who favors free trade, globalization, and openness to the free market. The term is used frequently in an international context, but it may also refer to the politics of a single country. Neo-liberals advocate floating exchange rates, the reduction or elimination of tariffs, privatization of nationalized companies, and similar practices. International organizations well-known for advocating neo-liberal policies include the International Monetary Fund and the World Trade Organization.

Neo-Liberalism A political philosophy that favors free trade, globalization, and openness to the free market. The term is used frequently in an international context, but it may also refer to the politics of a single country. Neo-liberalism advocates floating exchange rates, the reduction or elimination of tariffs, privatization of nationalized companies, and similar practices. International organizations well-known for advocating neo-liberal policies include the International Monetary Fund and the World Trade Organization.

Nepalese Rupee The currency of Nepal. It was introduced in 1932, replacing the mohar. Since 1993, it has been pegged to the Indian rupee at a rate of 1.6 Nepalese rupees to 1 Indian rupee.

NER GOST 7.67 Latin three-letter geocode for Niger. The code is used for transactions to and from Nigerien bank accounts and for international shipping to Niger. As with all GOST 7.67 codes, it is used primarily in Cyrillic alphabets.

Nervous Nellie An unduly risk-averse investor. Nervous Nellies tend to invest in fixed-income securities. If they invest in stocks at all, they tend to sell at the first negative sign, resulting in a loss.

Neselje In Croatia, an administrative subdivision approximately equivalent to a rural village.

Nest Egg A reserve of money set aside, especially for a specific purpose. Generally speaking, a nest egg refers to savings for a major expense, such as retirement. However, it may also refer to smaller expenses that nonetheless require savings. Examples of the latter include nest eggs for vacations or down payments for a house.

Net Profit or loss on a transaction. For example, in the sale of an asset, one calculates the net by taking the sale price and subtracting the outlay for buying or producing the asset. If the net is positive, one has made a profit; if it is negative, one has suffered a loss.

Net Adjusted Present Value The net present value of any project financed exclusively by equity and the present value of debt, less the cost of the project. Using the net adjusted present value can carry some tax benefits.

Net Advantage of Refunding The net present value of a refund. The net present value is the value in current dollars of some future cash flow and a refund is the practice of redeeming a bond before maturity by issuing another bond with a lower cost (such as a lower interest rate). If the net present value of a refund is above a certain amount, then it may be worth the cost of issuing a new bond.

Net Advantage to Leasing The difference between the cost of leasing an asset and the cost of borrowing funds to buy it, where the cost of leasing is less. When calculating whether there is a net advantage to leasing, one takes into account the present value of the funds, the cost of capital, the useful life and depreciation, and so forth.

Net Advantage to Merging A measure of whether a merger will be profitable for a company. It is calculated by subtracting the market value before the merger and its costs from the expected market value after the merger. If the number is positive, the merger will be profitable. This is an important aspect of risk analysis for both friendly takeovers and hostile takeovers.

Net Advertising Circulation 1. The actual or projected number of contacts an advertisement has. For example, if a stretch of highway has 1 million cars driving through it every day, a billboard on that highway has a net advertising circulation of 1 million per day. **2.** See: Circulation.

Net After-Tax Gain Capital gains after one has paid capital gains taxes. The net after-tax gain is usually higher than other after-tax income because capital gains taxes are lower than other taxes.

Net Asset Value In stocks and businesses, an expression of the underlying value of the company. That is, it is a statement of the value of the company's assets minus the value of its liabilities. One way of thinking about the net asset value is that it is the underlying value of a company, not the value dictated by the supply and demand of shares or its market capitalization. It is also called the book value.

Net Asset Value Arbitrage An investment strategy in which one takes advantage of a discrepancy in the net asset value between a mutual fund trading on two different exchanges. The net asset value of a mutual fund is calculated at the end of a trading day. However, because of differences in time zones, different exchanges close at different times. Thus, one example of NAV arbitrage involves buying a mutual fund in after-hours trading on one exchange on which the NAV has been set for the day at a certain price, and then selling it on an exchange that is still open and on which the same fund's NAV has not been set and is trading at a higher price. It is also called stale price arbitrage.

Net Asset Value Per Share The expression of the value of a company or fund per share. In the case of a mutual fund, this is the per share prorated value of the securities underlying the fund. It is calculated once per day at the end of the trading day and functions as the share price of the mutual fund for the next trading day. In the case of an exchange-traded fund, closed-end fund, or stock, this is the expression of the underlying value of the company or fund per share. That is, it is a statement of the value of the company's assets themselves minus the company's liabilities and the difference divided by the number of outstanding shares. One way of thinking about the net asset value per share is that it is the underlying value of the share, not the value dictated by the supply and demand of shares. Because cost accounting tends to undervalue the value of certain assets, the net asset value per share is usually lower than the market price of shares. It is also called the book value per share.

Net Assets In accounting, the value of a company's total assets less its total liabilities and intangible assets. Put another way, the book value is the shareholders' equity, or how much the company would be worth if it paid of all of its debts and liquidated immediately.

Net Book Value In accounting, an asset's original price minus depreciation and amortization. For example, if a company bought piece of technological equipment for $100,000 with an absolute physical life of ten years and a patent lasting 20 years, one would account the net book value as the original price and subtract $10,000 per year (for depreciation due to reduced physical life) and $5,000 per year (for amortization). In accounting a company, the net book value is the value of the company's assets minus the value of its liabilities and intangible assets. Put another way, the book value is the shareholders' equity, or how much the company would be worth if it paid of all of its debts and liquidated immediately. It is also known as the written-down value.

Net Borrowing The money that a company has borrowed less its cash on hand. Net borrowing may affect a company's long-term sustainability.

Net Capital Formation The transfer of capital from individuals, organizations, or governments for business use after deductions for depreciation. For example, a widget company experiences capital formation when people buy widgets. It calculates its net capital formation by deducting the depreciation on its widget-manufacturing equipment.

Net Cash Balance The amount of money in an account. It is calculated by adding the initial deposit to all subsequent deposits and then subtracting all disbursements. A positive net cash balance indicates that money is present and available in the account, while a negative one indicates that the account is overdrawn.

Net Cash Inflow A situation in which more money is coming into an organization than is going out of it. This results in a profit.

Net Cash Outflow A situation in which more money is going out of an organization than is coming into it. This results in debt.

Net Debt A measure of a company's ability to repay all debt if it were called immediately. It is calculated by adding short-term and long-term debt and subtracting all cash and cash equivalents. Many investors use net debt in making investment decisions, as it gives them an idea of a company's financial health and its level of leverage compared to liquid assets. Some industries may have more net debt than others; therefore, investors often compare a company's net debt to others in the same business.

Net Debt Per Capital The debt a government holds divided by the number of citizens under that government's jurisdiction. The government involved may be a municipality, a national government, or anything in between. It is calculated by taking the total debt, subtracting the government's cash and cash equivalents, and dividing the quantity by the number of citizens. Net debt per capita is important in determining a government's creditworthiness and may help a potential lender or bondholder calculate the likelihood of default. See also: National debt.

Net Debt to Assessed Valuation In a municipal bond, a ratio of the level of the issuing municipality's debt to the value of the property or other asset that the bond intends to finance. A lower net debt to assessed valuation ratio indicates that the municipal bond carries less risk of default on the part of the issuer; it therefore is likely to result in a higher bond rating.

Net Debt to Estimated Valuation A ratio of the par value of a municipal bond to the market value of the property on which the bond is secured. A lower net debt to estimated valuation is considered preferable because it indicates that the issuer has sufficient assets to repay the bond when it matures. See also: Net Debt to Assessed Valuation

Net Domestic Product A country or other geographical unit's gross domestic product less the collective depreciation on its capital assets. For example, the net domestic product may calculate the depreciation on all the factories in a country. In order for an economy to grow, the gross domestic product must exceed the net domestic product; otherwise, this indicates that depreciation on capital assets is outpacing other economic growth.

Net Effects Slang; in a non-profit, an expense that is only partly passed on to users or participants. The term is most common in the context of small Christian churches and ministries. An example of a net effects expense is a mission trip in which the church partly subsidizes the cost.

Net Errors and Omissions When accounting a country's balance of payments, the calculation of statistical inaccuracies that were made in the collection of data.

Net Financing Cost 1. In interest rate futures, the difference between the cost of purchasing an instrument and its yield. See also: Profit, Loss. **2.** Fees a firm charges for making a loan. The largest single net financing cost is the interest, but it also includes charges such as an origination fee or an application fee. See also: All-in cost.

Net Float The total amount of float in a bank account. It is calculated by subtracting the disbursement float money spent but not yet taken out of the account from the collection float money deposited but not yet cleared. The net float, when added to or subtracted from the previous balance, shows how much money is in the bank account. The net float is important when an account holder deal primarily in checks, and, thus, transactions take longer to process; it is less important when an account deals primarily in direct deposits and debit cards. See also: Check hold.

Net Income per Share In a given fiscal year, a publicly-traded company's profit divided by the number of shares outstanding. This is considered the single most important aspect in determining a share's price and value, because the calculation of earnings per share shows the amount of money to which a shareholder would be entitled in the event of the company's liquidation. In general, earnings per share apply only to common shares. It is calculated thusly: Earnings per share = (net income - preferred dividends) / average shares outstanding.

Net Interest Cost The cost of capital for a bond issuer; that is, a calculation of how much an issuer will spend in interest on one of its bonds. The way the net interest cost is calculated involves the average interest rate weighted for the time to maturity. One increases or decreases the net interest cost according to various discounts or premiums that the issuer allows or is paid. Critics contend that calculating the net interest cost is less accurate than the total interest cost.

Net Interest Margin A measure of the return on a company's investments relative to its interest expenses. The net interest margin helps a company determine whether or not it has made wise investment decisions. A negative net interest margin indicates that interest expenses exceed investment returns and that the company therefore has a net negative return. A positive net interest margin indicates the opposite. It is calculated thusly: Net interest margin = (Investment returns - interest expenses) / Average earning assets.

Net Interest Margin Security A security based on the value of excess cash flows received by a mortgage-backed security. That is, if an MBS receives more cash flows than are needed to make coupon and principal payments to holders, it may place these cash flows into a different account and issue NIMS entitling the holders to these cash flows.

Net Investment The amount a person or company has invested in a certain venture less the depreciation on the venture's assets.

Net Investment Income The income one derives from capital gains, dividends and other activities related to the purchase and sale of securities. It is calculated by subtracting losses on securities transactions from gains. Investment income differs from wages and salary primarily in that one does not need to work for investment income. One can manage one's investments oneself or one can hire a money manager to do it. Both individuals and companies can have net investment income; indeed a publicly-traded company must list its net investment income on its balance sheet. Investment income is often taxed differently than other income. See also: Capital gains tax.

Net Investment Income per Share A way to measure dividends. One calculates the net investment income per share by taking the total dividend a company declares, subtracting administrative expenses and other fees, and dividing the quantity by the number of shares outstanding.

Net Lease A lease in which the lessee pays the lessor (the property owner) a flat fee at agreed-upon intervals (usually once per month), and, in addition, some or all of the taxes, utilities, and maintenance due on the leased property. That is, the lessee becomes responsible for at least some of the duties of ownership of the leased property. See also: Triple Net Lease, Gross Lease.

Net Liq A slang term for liquidation value. The term is most common in futures and options trading.

Net Liquid Assets A measure of a company's total liquid assets less current liabilities. Liquid assets include all cash and other assets that could easily be converted into cash, and current liabilities include debts and other obligations due in the next year. Determining net liquid assets helps show how easily a company can make new investments without financing.

Net Long A situation in which an investor, fund, or portfolio has more long positions than short positions. That is, an investor has a net long position if he/she has bought more securities than he/she has sold or short-sold. This means that the investor would benefit if prices increased so that he/she could then close out his/her long positions and make a profit. If the positions decline in value, the investor will lose money. See also: Net short.

Net Loss In a business, a situation or a time period during which expenses exceed revenue. A company with a net loss does not necessarily go bankrupt as it may have recourse to retained earnings or loans. Obviously, however, net losses are not sustainable in the long term.

Net Operating Profit After Tax A company's operating profit after subtracting its tax liability. It is calculated as follows: NOPAT = Operating Profit * (1 - tax rate) Because operating profit does not deduct interest expenses, NOPAT shows what a company's net profit would have been if it were debt free. As such, it may provide a more accurate description of a company's efficiency of operations for highly leveraged companies.

Net Operating Profit Less Adjusted Taxes In accounting, a calculation of a business' operating income after all taxes are paid. The NOPLAT is not a recognized practice in the Generally Accepted Accounting Practices and so it is vital to note how each accountant and each firm arrive at the calculation. It is closely related to the after-tax operating income calculation, which is also unrecognized in GAAP.

Net Period On a bill that carries a discount, the period of time between the last date the customer may apply the discount and the date by which payment must be made.

Net Position The value of one's investment position, calculated as the position's market value less the initial cost of entering that position. For example, if one spends $10,000 buying a stock and the value of that investment goes to $11,000, the net position is $1,000. See also: Net present value.

Net Present Value A measure of discounted cash inflow to present cash outflow to determine whether a prospective investment will be profitable. For example, if a dentist wishes to purchase a new dental practice, he may calculate the net present value over a number of years to see if he will recover his investment in a reasonable period of time. If the ask price for the dental practice is $500,000, this is the present cash outflow used in the calculation. If the discounted cash inflow over, say, two

years, is greater than or equal to $500,000, then the investment will likely be profitable. See also: Present value.

Net Present Value Rule In investing, a rule stating that one should only make an investment if the net present value of its return is positive. That is, an investment only results in a profit for the investor if the discounted value of future cash flows is more than the amount one invests.

Net Proceeds The money one receives from a transaction after all commissions, fees, and related expenses. For example, if one sells his/her house, the net proceeds are the funds one receives from the buyer after all realtor's fees and other closing costs. Net proceeds differ from profit because they do not account for what one originally paid for (in this instance, the house).

Net Quick Assets A measure of a company's liquidity. It is calculated as taking all current assets and subtracting inventories and current liabilities. Higher net quick assets are considered desirable.

Net Realizable Value The net asset value of an asset or investment if it were sold, less the estimated cost of the sale and the amount the seller would have to spend to bring the asset or investment to a state where it can be sold. The NRV is used in GAAP accounting rules to ensure that the value of an asset or investment is not overstated.

Net Realized Capital Gains Per Share The long-term capital gains of an investment company less its long-term capital losses, divided by the number of shares outstanding. For example, in a mutual fund, the net realized capital gain per share is what the holder of a single share will receive from dividends and capital appreciation on all the securities held by the mutual fund after the fund has accounted for all losses. See also: Net investment income per share.

Net Receivables A measure of accounts receivable that a company expects to actually be paid. Accounts receivable is money that a customer owes a company for a good or service purchased on credit. One calculates net receivables by taking the accounts receivable and subtracting bad debt and expressing the result as a percentage of the total accounts receivable. For example, if a company's accounts receivable is $100,000 and it has $10,000 in bad debt, the net receivables is 90%.

Net Revenue Pledge A provision in some municipal bonds requiring the issuer to use the revenue the bond raises after expenses to pay for the debt service. For example, if a bond issue raises $10 million, but the project it intends to finance only costs $8 million, a net revenue pledge would require the issuer to use the remaining $2 million to service the debt from the bond. A net revenue pledge exists in order to make the municipal bond less risky for investors; a bond indenture that contains a net revenue pledge is more likely receive a higher credit rating than one that does not have one.

Net Sales The amount a company receives from the sale of its products, after deducting discounts, returns of products by customers, and damaged, missing, or stolen products. Net sales provide the most accurate calculation of what a company has received or expects to receive in revenue from sales. Any financial statement indicating "sales" refers to net sales.

Net Salvage Value In accounting, an estimate of the after-tax value of an asset at the end of its depreciation. For example, a firm's computer depreciates each year. When it breaks down or becomes obsolete, it has a net salvage value; it is calculated by the best guess of the net cash inflow when it is sold at the end of its life after taxes. In price regulated industries, the salvage value may be a negative value because it includes the net cash outflow in removing the asset from where it was used. For example, nuclear energy plants must store the nuclear waste at the end of their useful life. This cost is a contributing factor in the salvage value. In such a case, the net salvage value is zero. See also: Absolute physical life, Obsolescence.

Net Short Describing a situation where one has more short positions than long positions on a security or derivative. To give a very simple example, if one buys nine futures contracts on corn, and then sells short 10 identical futures contracts on corn, one has a net short position on corn. When one has a net short position, one profits when the price for the underlying position declines.

Net Tangible Assets In stocks and businesses, an expression of the underlying value of the company. That is, it is a statement of the value of the company's total assets minus the value of its total liabilities and the value of its intangible assets such as patents and goodwill. One way of thinking about the net tangible asset is that it is the underlying value of a company, not the value dictated by the supply and demand of shares or its market capitalization. See also: Net asset value.

Net Tangible Assets Per Share One expression of the underlying value of a stock. That is, it is a statement of the value of the company's total assets minus the value of its total liabilities and the value of its intangible assets, such as patents and goodwill. This quantity is divided by the number of shares outstanding. One way of thinking about the net tangible assets per share is that it is the underlying value of a stock, not the value dictated by the supply and demand of share or its market capitalization. Corporate raiders use this measure looking for undervalued stocks. See also: Net asset value.

Net Transaction A transaction of a security in which there are no fees or in which the fees are included in the price. That is, the price quoted for such a transaction is the price the buyer will pay, regardless of anything else. A common net transaction is an initial public offering. See also: All-in cost.

Net Unrealized Appreciation The tax difference between a stock placed into a tax-deferred account such as a 401(k) or IRA and the same stock in a brokerage account. Most withdrawals from a retirement account are taxed as ordinary income, whereas most withdrawals from a brokerage account are taxes as capital gains. In the

United States, capital gains tax is often less than the income tax rate; this means that even though the fair market value of two shares of a stock may be the same, the net yield of the share withdrawn from the retirement account will be less than the share withdrawn from the brokerage account. For this reason, many money managers advise rolling-over the stock an employer places into one's tax-deferred retirement account into a regular brokerage account.

Net Volume In technical analysis, the trading volume of a security on an uptick minus the trading volume of the same security on a downtick. Analysts use this to indicate buy signals and sell signals. See also: Money flow index.

Net Weight In maritime commerce, the weight of goods being shipped. The net weight does not include the weight of packaging such as containers or wrapping.

Net Working Capital Cash and short-term assets expected to be converted to cash within a year less short-term liabilities. Businesses use net working capital to measure cash flow and the ability to service debts. A positive net working capital indicates that the firm has money in order to maintain or expand its operations. Net working capital tends not to add much to the business' assets, but helps keep it running on a day-to-day basis.

Net Worth An individual or company's assets minus liabilities, in which assets exceed liabilities. For example, if a company has $3 million in assets and $1 million in debt and other liabilities, it has a net worth of $2 million. The term may apply to companies or individuals, but is often used colloquially to refer to wealthy individuals.

Net Yield The return on a security after all expenses. That is, the net yield is the profit one makes from a security. For example, the net yield may be calculated as the return less commissions, fees, and the cost of purchasing the security.

Netherlands Antillean Guilder The currency of Netherlands Antilles. The currency traces its origins to the 18th century, but took its current name in 1952. Throughout most of its history, it was pegged to the Dutch guilder. However, after the occupation of the Netherlands during World War II, it switched the peg to the U.S. dollar. It has maintained this peg at different values ever since. It is known colloquially as the florin.

Net-Net 1. A way to value a company that considers only its net current assets, which are current assets less current liabilities. It is a value investing technique originally introduced by Benjamin Graham. **2.** A slang term for a brief, verbal summary of a report, conversation, or event.

Netting Out Informal; listing as profit.

Network A A service some brokerage firms and cable news channels carry; it reports price and trading volume on the New York Stock Exchange and regional exchanges. It also reports on over-the-counter trades for stocks listed on the NYSE. While it is a private reporting service, its overall regulation is governed by NYSE Alternext. It is less commonly called A-Network. See also: Network B.

Network B A service some brokerage firms and cable news channels carry; it reports price and trading volume on the American Stock Exchange and regional exchanges. It also reports on over-the-counter trades for stocks listed on AMEX. It is less commonly called B-network. See also: Network A.

Network Distribution Center One of several processing centers where the U.S. Postal Service sorts enormous amounts of mail. Letters and other mail are sent to network distribution centers, where they are routed to their proper destinations. This process is highly automated; machines are capable of reading even handwritten addresses. They were formerly called bulk mail centers.

Neuer Markt A segment of the Deutsche Borse for information technology, biotechnology and similar companies. Neuer Markt companies are generally younger than other German companies. The Neuer Markt was established in 1997.

Neural Net A computerized system designed to imitate human thought. Specifically, neural nets are designed to make or recommend investment decisions in light of changing circumstances in a market. Using neural nets has become more common as computers have become more accessible.

Neutral Of or relating to an opinion that a market will neither trend up or down in the near term. That is, a neutral analyst is neither bearish nor bullish; he/she believes that the market in question will remain roughly in its current value. Neutral analysts design neutral investment strategies, which are designed to perform the best if the market(s) in which one is investing do not move significantly. One example is a portfolio that is exactly half long and half short. See also: Market neutral.

Neutral Hedge A series of positions and offsetting positions on a security the results in a risk-free return. See also: Compound option.

Neutral Hedge Ratio The change in the price of a call for every one unit of change in the price of the underlying asset. The neutral hedge ratio varies according to length of time until the expiration date and whether or not the call is in-the-money.

Neutral Stock A stock with volatility exactly the same as the wider market. This means that the stock's riskiness is quantified at the exact same rate as the wider market. This is expressed by stating that the stock as a beta of exactly 1. See also: Gamma neutral.

Neutral Taxes A tax structure that does not change the incentives in the market. Neutral taxes are rare; for example, a sales tax may encourage people to shop on the black market (to avoid paying the tax). Likewise, an income tax may encourage persons not to work, so as to reduce their income. An example of a neutral tax is a poll tax.

New Account Report A fact sheet containing information about a new client to a brokerage. The new account report includes information on the client's income, debt,

net worth, and so forth. The report helps the brokerage determine the client's investment goals and therefore what strategies may be most appropriate for him/her.

New Arrangements to Borrow Also called the NAB. A collective agreement among 26 nations and financial institutions and the International Monetary Fund whereby the nations and institutions lend a certain amount of capital to the IMF. The IMF utilizes the funds of the NAB in case its normal funds fall short of its borrowers' needs. It was established following the Mexican economic crisis. See also: General Arrangements to Borrow.

New Brunswick Dollar The currency of New Brunswick between 1860 and 1867. The dollar was equal in value to the Canadian dollar (at that time, Canada and New Brunswick were separate jurisdictions). The Canadian dollar replaced the New Brunswick dollar at par when New Brunswick joined the newly-formed Canadian Confederation.

New Brunswick Pound The currency of New Brunswick between 1852 and 1860. The pound was based on the Canadian pound (at that time Canada and New Brunswick were separate jurisdictions). It was replaced by the New Brunswick dollar following Canada's adoption of the Canadian dollar.

New Cedi The former currency of Ghana. It was introduced in 1967, replacing the first cedi, which had replaced the Ghanaian pound. It was initially pegged to the British pound at various values. It became a floating currency briefly in 1978, but too-rapid depreciation led Ghana to re-peg the cedi to the U.S. dollar very quickly. It floated again in 1990; consistently high inflation led to its replacement by the third cedi (code GHS) in 2007.

New Economy An informal term for the changes that came to developed economies during the late 1990s. The new economy came about largely as a result of the popularization of the Internet. For example, because of the new economy, online companies can provide information for free and derive their revenue from advertising. Likewise, many jobs can now be done anywhere. That is, many jobs no longer require one to be present in the office; for example, one can do work in Oklahoma for a company based in Pennsylvania. See also: Dot-com bubble.

New France Livre The currency of New France, which roughly corresponds to Quebec in modern Canada. The livre was introduced in the 1600s, and was for some time valued at a premium to the French livre. It was taken out of circulation after New France was ceded by the French to the British.

New Guy Gene The polite and somewhat shy demeanor that new employees exhibit at work until they adapt to the corporate culture and generally adjust to their new positions.

New Home Sales A measure of how many newly constructed homes are sold in the United States over a given period of time. They are reported monthly and seasonally-adjusted annually. The measure of new home sales month-on-month and year-on-year is an important indicator of demand for houses. As a result, it greatly impacts the construction industry and related sectors.

New Issue Any offering of stock by a publicly-traded company. If it is the first such offering, it is called an initial public offering (IPO); otherwise, it is called a follow-on offering. A company makes a new issue through underwriters, who have the responsibility to place the offering with individual and institutional investors. Companies make new issues in order to raise financing for expanded operations, or because they have become cash poor and need to finance their current operations. The offerings themselves give investors a portion of ownership in the company issuing them.

New Jurisprudence A derogatory term used from the late 19th through the mid-20th century to describe the use of social contract theory in law. That is, new jurisprudence represented the idea that law should reflect popular will, as opposed to natural law.

New Listing A stock that begins to be traded on an organized exchange. New listings occur when a company makes an IPO that meets an exchange's listing requirements or if an OTC stock begins to meet the listing requirements.

New Money 1. Funds that the U.S. Treasury receives when the face value from a new issue of Treasury securities exceeds the face value of maturing securities. It is calculated as the difference between the new issue and the maturing issue. **2.** Informal for nouveau riche.

New Money Bond A mortgage revenue bond that is issued because the issuer has additional leeway to sell private activity bonds. That is, a new money bond is a mortgage revenue bond that would not be issued if the issuer lacked the statutory authority to do so. A new money bond is never a refunding bond.

New Money Preferred Any preferred stock issued after October 1, 1942. A feature of new money preferred stocks is that corporations owning them may exclude 80% of dividends from taxation.

New Old Stock Goods a store seeks to sell that were made some time ago but have not been used. New old stock may be offered at a discount because the store already purchased the items and wishes to recoup the cost. However, this is not always the case: new old stock may be offered at full price if it not has been previously offered in retail or if it is no longer manufactured.

New Orleans Cotton Exchange A former exchange for cotton and cotton derivatives. It opened in 1871 to counterbalance the New York Cotton Exchange. It closed in 1964, in part due to the decline of cotton in the American South.

New Paradigm A new and innovative way to do business. The term "new paradigm" was common during the dotcom bubble and referred to any business practice that utilized the Internet. During this period, investors tended to buy stocks thought to be using a new paradigm.

New Party Sakigake A former political party in Japan. Holding centrist and environmentalist views, it was established in 1993 by former Liberal Democratic Party of Japan members. It is notable primarily for participating in a coalition government with the LDP in the mid-1990s, with one of its members becoming Minister of Finance. The party dissolved itself in 2004.

New Taiwan Dollar The currency of Taiwan. It was introduced in 1949, replacing the old dollar at a ratio of 40,000 old dollars to one new dollar. Technically, it existed alongside the silver yuan, which was the official currency of the Republic of China (not to be confused with the People's Republic of China); however, the silver yuan was never actually used, and, in 2000, the Taiwanese dollar became the sole currency. It is a floating currency.

New Ugandan Shilling The currency of Uganda. The new shilling replaced the first Ugandan shilling in 1987 following a period of hyperinflation. The new shilling was issued at an exchange rate of 1 new shilling for 100 old shillings. Currently, it is used in Uganda alongside the U.S. dollar, the British pound, and the euro.

New York Board of Trade A commodity futures exchange based in New York. Founded as the New York Cotton Exchange in 1870, it was a privately owned company until it became a wholly owned subsidiary of Intercontinental Exchange in 2007. It trades a variety of commodities, notably cotton, cocoa, coffee, and sugar.

New York Cotton Exchange A commodity exchange in New York City. Established in 1870, it trades cotton and cotton derivatives almost exclusively, though it has established subsidiaries over the years to trade commodities like citrus and wool. It was a very important exchange in the United States for much of the late 19th and early 20th centuries because of the centrality of cotton to the American economy. In 1998, it became a subsidiary of the New York Board of Trade.

New York Dollar The purchasing power of a U.S. dollar in New York City relative to the remainder of the United States. The New York dollar is important to consider because New York is an extremely expensive city in which to live. One calculates the New York dollar by subtracting the additional cost of living of the city and the higher wages and salaries one normally makes there.

New York Mercantile Exchange The largest physical futures commodity exchange in the world. Established in 1882, it came into its current form as the result of a 1994 merger between the New York Mercantile Exchange and the Commodity Exchange. NYMEX trades almost exclusively in energy products and metals, among other commodities. It is regulated by the Commodity Futures Trading Board. Unlike some exchanges, it requires firms trading on its floor to send their own employees as brokers. Thus, employees of NYMEX itself only record transactions, and do not involve themselves with actual trade.

New York Stock Exchange The oldest securities exchange in the United States and the largest in the world by dollar value. Founded in 1792, it merged with Euronext in 2007 to form NYSE Euronext, which operates the exchange. Equities in 3,000 companies and 2,000 bonds are traded on the NYSE floor, with a market capitalization of $10.1 trillion in October 2008. The exchange operates as an auction, in which potential buyers and sellers gather around an appropriate floor specialist, who is employed by an NYSE member firm (not the NYSE itself) and who acts as an auctioneer to the buyers and sellers, who attempt to buy at the lowest possible price or sell at the highest. The right to trade on the floor belongs to any one of the owners of the 1366 seats on the exchange floor.

New York Stock Exchange Composite Index An index, weighted for market capitalization, of all stocks and other securities traded on the New York Stock Exchange relative to their value on December 31, 1965. It contains four sub-indices for transportation, utility, finance, and industrial companies.

New Zaire The former currency of Zaire. The new zaire was the currency of Zaire between 1993 and 1997. It replaced the first zaire because of the older currency's persistently high inflation. It was replaced by the Congolese franc in 1997 when Zaire became the Democratic Republic of the Congo.

New Zealand Dollar The currency of New Zealand. It was introduced in 1967, replacing the New Zealand pound. It was initially pegged to gold through the U.S. dollar. After the end of the Bretton Woods system, it remained pegged to gold, then later to a currency basket. It has been a floating currency since 1985.

New Zealand Pound The former currency of New Zealand. It was pegged to the British pound and was replaced by the New Zealand dollar in 1967.

New Zealand Stock Exchange The only stock exchange in New Zealand. It traces its roots to a number of smaller exchanges in the 1870s that originally traded mainly gold. These exchanges combined in 1974 to form the New Zealand Stock Exchange. It became fully computerized in 1991 and changed its name to the New Zealand Exchange Ltd in 2003.

Newfoundland Dollar The currency of Newfoundland between 1865 and 1949. The dollar was on a gold standard and was worth slightly more than the Canadian dollar. In 1895, however, it was pegged to the Canadian dollar following a banking crisis in Newfoundland. When Newfoundland joined Canada, its dollar was replaced by the Canadian dollar.

Newfoundland Pound The currency of Newfoundland prior to 1865. It was equal in value to the British pound, which circulated alongside it. It was replaced by the Newfoundland dollar.

Newly Industrialized Countries Countries with a lower GDP relative to the developed world but with a higher level of GDP growth. Newly industrialized

countries are characterized by a great deal industry and/or international trade. Newly industrialized countries have relatively (though not entirely) stable governments. Some newly industrialized countries have a great deal of government intervention while others have a lesser amount. Examples of newly industrialized countries include Mexico and China. See also: International development.

Newly Industrializing Economies Economies with a lower GDP relative to the developed world but still with healthy levels of GDP growth. Newly industrializing economies are characterized by a great deal of industry and/or international trade. Newly industrializing economies have relatively (though perhaps not entirely) stable governments. Some newly industrializing economies have a great deal of government intervention while others have virtually none. Examples of newly industrializing economies include India and Brazil. See also: International development.

News Sandwich A slang term for spending one's lunch hour reading the newspaper or, more commonly, online news sites instead of eating. This is relatively common practice in white collar office jobs.

News-Driven Market The supply and demand for a commodity, stock, or anything else that is highly volatile depending on the information available in the media. Suppose, for example, there is a revolution in a major oil exporting country. This may drive the price of oil higher without any change to the fundamentals of the market. In this sense, oil may be said to be traded in a news-driven market.

Newsstand Draw Copies of a magazine or other periodical distributed to a retailer (traditionally a newsstand) a few days in advance of the official publication date. The newsstand draw is sold to the general public at the appropriate time. It is abbreviated as N/S draw.

Newsstand Return Copies of a magazine or other periodical remaining at the end of a publication cycle. The newsstand return is the unsold portion of the newsstand draw. The newsstand return is given back to the publisher. Because publishers cannot earn income from unsold periodicals, they try to keep the newsstand return as low as possible. It is abbreviated as N/S return.

Next Best Price Stop-Loss Order A stop-loss order that one instructs a broker to execute immediately when the most favorable price is reached.

Next Day Referring to a transaction on which the settlement date is the trading day immediately following the trade date. Some transactions are required to be next day; for example, options contracts are next day transactions.

Nexus of Contracts Any contract or other thing that is related to anything else, especially something that causes something else.

NF 1. ISO 3166-1 alpha-2 code for Norfolk Island. This is the code used in international transactions to and from Norfuk bank accounts. **2.** ISO 3166-2 geocode for Norfolk Island. This is used as an international standard for shipping to Norfolk Island.

NFD ISO 4217 code for the Newfoundland dollar, which was the currency of Newfoundland between 1865 and 1949. Initially, the dollar was on a gold standard and was worth slightly more than the Canadian dollar. In 1895, however, it was pegged to the Canadian dollar following a banking crisis in Newfoundland. When Newfoundland joined Canada, its dollar was replaced by the Canadian dollar.

NFK GOST 7.67 Latin three-letter geocode for Norfolk Island. The code is used for transactions to and from Norfolk Islander bank accounts and for international shipping to Norfolk Island. As with all GOST 7.67 codes, it is used primarily in Cyrillic alphabets.

NG 1. ISO 3166-1 alpha-2 code for the Federal Republic of Nigeria. This is the code used in international transactions to and from Nigerian bank accounts. **2.** ISO 3166-2 geocode for Nigeria. This is used as an international standard for shipping to Nigeria. Each Nigerian state has its own code with the prefix "NG." For example, the code for Abia State is ISO 3166-2:NG-AB

NGA GOST 7.67 Latin three-letter geocode for Nigeria. The code is used for transactions to and from Nigerian bank accounts and for international shipping to Nigeria. As with all GOST 7.67 codes, it is used primarily in Cyrillic alphabets.

Nga Mutha A Burmese unit of mass approximately equivalent to 8.16 grams.

Ngase Tha A Burmese unit of mass approximately equivalent to 816.47 grams.

NGN ISO 4217 code for the Nigerian naira. It was introduced in 1973, replacing the Nigerian pound. It has been marked by relatively high (though not excessive) inflation. The Central Bank of Nigeria restricts the convertibility of the naira.

Ngultrum The currency of Bhutan. It was introduced in 1974, replacing the Bhutanese rupee. Like the rupee before it, the ngultrum is pegged to the Indian rupee at par.

Ngwee A currency subdivision in Zambia. It is equal in value to 1/100 of a Zambian kwacha. See also: Cent.

NH 1. ISO 3166-1 alpha-2 code for New Hebrides before it changed its name to Vanuatu. This was the code used in international transactions to and from bank accounts in Vanuatu. **2.** ISO 3166-2 geocode for New Hebrides. This was used as an international standard for shipping to New Hebrides. In both cases, the code is obsolete.

NHVU ISO 3166-3 code for New Hebrides, which changed its name to Vanuatu in 1980. ISO 3166-3 codes are used to indicate names of countries that are no longer used.

NI 1. ISO 3166-1 alpha-2 code for Nicaragua. This is the code used in international transactions to and from Nicaraguan bank accounts. **2.** ISO 3166-2 geocode for Nicaragua. This is used as an international standard for shipping to Nicaragua. Each

Nicaraguan department and autonomous region has its own code with the prefix "NI." For example, the code for the Department of Rio San Juan is ISO 3166-2:NI:SJ.

NIC GOST 7.67 Latin three-letter geocode for Nicaragua. The code is used for transactions to and from Nicaraguan bank accounts and for international shipping to Nicaragua. As with all GOST 7.67 codes, it is used primarily in Cyrillic alphabets.

Nicaraguan Cordoba Oro The currency of Nicaragua. It was introduced in 1991, replacing the second cordoba after a period of hyperinflation. It is a floating currency.

Niche 1. See: Niche market. 2. See: Niche marketing.

Nick Leeson A derivatives broker employed in the Singapore office of Barings Bank, which, before Leeson was sent, had not actively traded on SIMEX before. Leeson was permitted to conduct arbitrage by buying futures on Nikkei and at the same time selling them on SIMEX. Instead, he made unhedged futures transactions on Nikkei and reported his losses as gains. His trading was exposed following large losses on Nikkei after an earthquake. His losses totaled more than $1 billion, twice Barings' available capital. He spent about three years in jail and was released in 1999. He was born in 1967.

Nickel In the United States, a very common term for the five-cent coin. Interestingly, a nickel contains no nickel.

Nickel Note In the United States, a rarely used nickname for a $5 bill.

Nifty 50 50 blue-chip stocks that were regarded as profitable long-term investments during the 1960s and 1970s. The practice of buying and holding the nifty 50 is considered to be largely responsible for the bull market of the early 1970s; indeed the prices for the nifty 50 were driven up to very high, unsustainable levels. Most of the nifty 50 had strong growth rates and low P/E ratios. Examples included Anheuser-Busch and American Express. They were also called the Favorite 50.

Nigerian Naira The currency of Nigeria. It was introduced in 1973, replacing the Nigerian pound. It has been marked by relatively high (though not excessive) inflation. The Central Bank of Nigeria restricts the convertibility of the naira.

Nigerian Security Printing and Minting An organization in Nigeria that issues legal tender banknotes for general use. It is controlled by the Central Bank of Nigeria.

Nikkei A price-weighted index consisting of 225 prominent stocks on the Tokyo Stock Exchange. The Nikkei has been calculated since 1950 and its direction is considered an indicator of the state of the Japanese economy. Most analysts consider it the Japanese equivalent of the Dow Jones Industrial Average.

Nil-Paid A tradeable security that did not incur any costs on its original owner. A common example is renounceable cum rights on a stock, which are attached to a stock and are issued to the original owner free of charge. However, the owner may separate the cum right from the stock and sell it. Thus, while a nil-paid has value, at least insofar as there are potential buyers, it does not cost the original owner anything in order to acquire it. Therefore, it results in pure profit when it is sold.

Nindan An ancient Sumerian unit of length approximately equivalent to six meters.

Nindanu An ancient Akkadian unit of length approximately equivalent to six meters.

Nine-Bond Rule On the New York Stock Exchange, a rule requiring that members place their customers' orders for nine or fewer bonds on the trading floor for one hour. This may or may not expedite execution, but it exposes small orders to the trading floor, which may extract a better price for the customer. It is also called Rule 396.

NIO ISO 4217 code for the Nicaraguan cordoba oro. It was introduced in 1991, replacing the second cordoba after a period of hyperinflation. It is a floating currency.

Nippon Credit Bank A former bank in Japan. Established in 1957, it was implicated in the cozy relationship many banks shared with the Ministry of Finance. In 1998, it was nationalized because of the excessive bad debt it acquired as a result of Japan's bubble economy. It was privatized in 2000 and changed its name to Aozora Bank in 2001.

NIU GOST 7.67 Latin three-letter geocode for Niue. The code is used for transactions to and from Niuean bank accounts and for international shipping to Niue. As with all GOST 7.67 codes, it is used primarily in Cyrillic alphabets.

Nixie Slang; mail that is returned to the sender because its address is illegible, nonexistent or otherwise nondeliverable.

Nizaam al-misahah In Islamic law, a system of taxation for agricultural land. Under the system, taxes are assessed based on the amount of land under cultivation, regardless of how much produce actually grows.

Nizaam al-muqaasamah In Islamic law, a system of taxation for agricultural land. Under the system, taxes are assessed based on the amount of produce grown, regardless of the amount of land under cultivation.

NL 1. ISO 3166-1 alpha-2 code for the Netherlands. This is the code used in international transactions to and from Dutch bank accounts. 2. ISO 3166-2 geocode for the Netherlands. This is used as an international standard for shipping to the Netherlands. Each province has its own code with the prefix "NL." For example, the code for the Province of Utrecht is ISO 3166-2:NL-UT.

NLD GOST 7.67 Latin three-letter geocode for the Netherlands. The code is used for transactions to and from Dutch bank accounts and for international shipping to the Netherlands. As with all GOST 7.67 codes, it is used primarily in Cyrillic alphabets.

NLG ISO 4217 code for the Dutch guilder. It was introduced in 1680 as a silver coin. It was one of the most important currencies in early stock exchanges because of Holland's importance in world markets. The guilder was decimalized in 1817 and pegged to gold for a number of years in the late 19th and early 20th centuries. The peg to gold (by way of the U.S. dollar) was re-adopted during the Bretton Woods System. The guilder ceased circulation in 2002 with the introduction of the euro.

NO 1. ISO 3166-1 alpha-2 code for the Kingdom of Norway. This is the code used in international transactions to and from Norwegian bank accounts. 2. ISO 3166-2 geocode for Norway. This is used as an international standard for shipping to Norway. Each county has its own code with the prefix "NO." For example, the code for the County of Finnmark is ISO 3166-2:NO-20.

No Book Describing a situation in which a security has such a low trading volume that few or no shares are being bid on or offered at a given time. This results from a general lack of interest in that security. The term comes from a reference to a market maker's or specialist's book in which he/she must list all securities being bid on or offered.

No Documentation Mortgage A mortgage in which the income and assets of the borrower are not verified. While the borrower generally still passes a credit check, this is still extremely high risk for the lender. However, it can be useful for the borrower, for example, if he/she is moving to a new country and has no income history there.

No Par A stock that is not assigned a face value at issue. This was once important but no longer is because the prices of stocks vary constantly.

No Protest An instruction to a collection agency not to attempt to collect a certain portion of a default or other unpaid sale.

No Quote A situation in which no market makers on an exchange are making an inside market. That is, no quote indicates that market makers are not giving bid or ask prices for their own securities. This usually means that it is impossible to trade on the securities affected. See also: Bid-ask spread.

No Scraps Hit the Floor An axiom meaning that inefficient companies eventually will go bankrupt or be acquired by competitors. It is said to promote efficiency and good use of resources.

No Substitution A situation in which a shareholder gives his/her proxy to a proxy committee but states that he/she will withdraw proxy if there is a change in the makeup of the proxy committee. Most of the time, when a shareholder gives proxy to a committee, he/she automatically agrees to let the committee vote for him/her regardless of who actually sits on it. If the shareholder wishes to withdraw this permission, he/she must expressly state so; this is called a no substitution situation.

No-Action Letter A letter from the SEC stating that it will seek no civil or criminal penalties for a given activity. The SEC sends no-action letters in response to inquiries from organizations regulated by it. For example, if a company wishes to take a certain action but is uncertain as to its legality, it requests clarification from the SEC. Receiving a no-action letter equates to permission to take the action in question.

No-Brainer Informal; a market that is obviously making a certain movement. Generally speaking, this refers to a strong bull market or a strong bear market in which every investor is either making or losing a great deal of money. A no-brainer means that little analysis is required to know whether to buy or sell.

Nofs 1. A Maltese unit of volume approximately equivalent to 568.3 milliliters. It was originally used to measure alcohol. It is largely obsolete but is still used in some circumstances. 2. A Maltese unit of volume approximately equivalent to 639.3 milliliters. It was originally used to measure milk and oil. It is largely obsolete but is still used in some circumstances.

Nohijahoi Tobei Cumhuri In Tajikistan, a political subdivision for 13 districts under direct control of the central government.

Nohiya In Tajikistan, a political subdivision approximately equivalent to a county.

Noise A slight uptick or downtick in a security's or market's price and/or volume representing little or no actual change in its fundamentals. Noise occurs in the short-term; if noise continues in a certain direction, it becomes a trend, and, therefore, an indication of the general direction of the security or market. Noise, on the other hand, means little or nothing.

Noise Trader A trader that makes investment decisions based on perceived market movements rather than a security's fundamentals. Put simply, a noise trader buys when everyone else seems to be buying and sells when everyone else seems to be selling. Behavioral economists classify most traders as noise traders, though few investors admit to it. Interestingly, behavioral economists classify all technical information as noise, though not all investors do so.

Noise Trader Risk The risk of a loss on an investment that comes from a noise trader. A noise trader is an investor who makes decisions based on feelings such as fear or greed, rather than fundamental or technical changes to a security. If enough noise traders panic, they can drive down the price of the security unnecessarily. Suppose an investor owns 1,000 shares of a stock and they are currently at $50 per share. If noise traders overreact to bad news, the price could drop to $40 per share without any fundamental justification. This costs the investor $10,000. The possibility that this could happen is noise trader risk. See also: Behavioral economics.

NOK ISO 4217 code for the Norwegian krone. Originally issued in 1875 when Norway joined the (now defunct) Scandinavian Monetary Union, it was a gold standard currency, off and on, until it became pegged to the British pound in 1931. After World War II, it maintained its peg to the pound, which was itself pegged to the

U.S. dollar; it was later pegged to the dollar directly. In 1992, it became a floating currency.

Nokta A Turkish measure of length approximately equivalent to 0.219 millimeters. It became obsolete when Turkey made the metric system mandatory in 1933.

No-Load DRIP A reinvestment plan in which a publicly-traded company allows shareholders to buy more shares with the proceeds from their dividends at no commission or other transaction charge. This encourages shareholders to leave their capital with the company and, in return, allows them the possibility of a higher return.

No-Load Mutual Fund A mutual fund that does not charge shareholders a sales charge or commission. Some no-load funds charge a distribution fee, which is a small percentage of the amount one invests used to cover the fund's costs. Other no-load funds, however, do not have distribution fees. Some investors prefer no-load funds because the total amount of their investment is used to purchase shares with little or no deduction. Studies have shown that no-load funds perform neither better nor worse than load funds. See also: 12B-1 fee.

No-Load Stock Stock in a publicly-traded company one purchases without using a broker as an intermediary. Some companies also offer plans called direct purchase plans which allow the investor to bypass his/her broker and buy no-load stocks. This saves the investor the expense of commissions and fees ordinarily paid to the broker. However, no-load stocks are rather illiquid (it is difficult to sell one's shares without a broker), and are therefore bought for long-term investing.

Nominal Describing a variable that does not take inflation into account. For example, when considering GDP growth, if GDP has grown 10% in nominal terms and the inflation rate is 3%, real GDP growth is only 7%.

Nominal Account A business account in which the balance is closed out after the end of the fiscal year. See also: Real account.

Nominal Anchor A government policy that provides stability to an economy at the expense of some of that government's autonomy. For example, if a government pegs its currency to another, it reduces the uncertainty in exchange rates but also gives the government less ability to combat inflation or otherwise change the money supply.

Nominal Cash Flow Cash flow in absolute terms without adjusting for inflation. In the short term, nominal cash flow equates to real cash flow, but if a cash flow remains that same in a period of high inflation, this results in a real loss for the person or company receiving a cash flow and a real gain for the one giving it.

Nominal Exchange Rate The official quote of an exchange rate. For example, when one changes dollars for pounds, the bank lists an exchange rate of, say, two dollars for one pound. This is the nominal exchange rate. While this indicates the number of pounds one receives for a dollar (or vice versa), it does not show the purchasing power of the pound versus that of the dollar. See also: Real Exchange Rate.

Nominal Exercise Price The price one pays for a Ginnie Mae pass-through. It differs from the adjusted exercise price because, before one buys the pass-through, mortgage borrowers are paying down the principals on the underlying mortgages. One calculates the nominal exercise price as follows: Nominal exercise price = Adjusted exercise price * Total amount of the remaining principal

Nominal GDP Gross domestic product without or before accounting for inflation. Comparing nominal GDPs from year to year shows the amount an economy has grown or shrunk in dollar amounts, but does not show how the buying power of those dollars has been affected. Real GDP accounts for inflation. For example, if the nominal GDP has grown 10% and the inflation rate is 3%, the real GDP growth is 7%.

Nominal Interest Rate The interest rate on an investment or loan without adjusting for inflation. The nominal interest rate is simply the interest rate stated on the loan or investment agreement. If one makes a loan at a high nominal interest rate, this does not guarantee a real profit. For example, if the nominal interest rate on a loan is 7% and the inflation rate is 4%, the real interest rate is only 3%.

Nominal Price An estimated price that may or may not resemble an asset's market price. A nominal price may be established as part of a negotiation, or as an arbitrary, initial price when a product has just been introduced.

Nominal Quote A quote for the price of a security in which the price is subject to change. Market makers occasionally make nominal quotes for valuation purposes only. It may also refer to a quote that is not an offer, but simply supplied for informational purposes.

Nominal Return The rate of return on an investment without adjusting for inflation. It is calculated simply by taking the dollar amount of the return and comparing it to the amount invested. A high nominal return does not guarantee a real profit. For example, if the nominal return on an investment is 7% and the inflation rate is 4%, the real rate of return is only 3%.

Nominal Value 1. See: Book value. **2.** See: Par value.

Nominalism The legal principle that the dollar amount of a debt remains the same regardless of the inflation rate. Inflation and deflation, which both change the real value of repayment, do not affect the amount of a debt recorded on a balance sheet. In theory, this places risks on both the lender and the borrower, but, in practice, the lender has most of the risk, as inflation, which reduces the real value of repayment, is more likely than deflation.

Nominee A company, usually a brokerage, which holds legal ownership of a security while beneficial ownership is held by someone else, usually a client. Allowing the nominee to hold title to the security facilitates trade; that is, the brokerage can sell the security directly rather than needing to seek the client's

permission for each transaction. The client receives all dividends and other benefits of ownership.

Nominee Dividend A dividend that one receives on behalf of another person or company. The nominee is responsible for paying the appropriate tax on the dividend.

Nominee Holding The act or practice in which a company, usually a brokerage, holds legal ownership of a security while beneficial ownership is held by someone else, usually a client. Nominee holding facilitates trade; that is, the brokerage can sell the security directly rather than needing to seek the client's permission for each transaction. The client receives all dividends and other benefits of ownership. This has become more common as securities have become increasingly digitized.

Nominee Interest Interest that a person receives on behalf of another person. One is not taxed for nominee interest because the interest ultimately goes to someone else. One must file a form 1099-INT in order to have nominee interest remitted from one's taxable income.

Nominee Name The brokerage or other company that is the legal owner of a security held on behalf of a client. Even though the client is the actual owner, the nominee holds title to the security because this makes the legalities of transferring the security easier if and when it is sold. The nominee must turn the security over to the client if requested. The nominee name is also called the street name. See also: Beneficial Ownership, Safekeeping.

Nomos In Greece, a political subdivision, roughly equivalent to a province, that existed before 2010.

Non Performing Loan A loan in or near default. According to the International Monetary Fund, a non-performing loan is any loan in which: interest and principal payments are more than 90 days overdue; or more than 90 days' worth of interest has been refinanced, capitalized, or delayed by agreement; or payments are less than 90 days overdue but are no longer anticipated. Another definition of a non-performing loan is one in which the maturity date has passed but at least part of the loan is still outstanding. The specific definition is dependent upon the loan's particular terms.

Non Resident Alien In the United States, a foreigner who does not possess a green card and who has not been present in the United States for more than a certain number of days over a period of time. A non-resident alien is subject to a 30% tax on dividends that are taxable in the United States; however, he/she is not liable for capital gains taxes and is only taxed on income earned in the United States instead of worldwide income to which resident aliens and U.S. citizens are subject. See also: W-8.

Non Vessel Operating Common Carrier A company that ships goods on behalf of a client, especially internationally, but that does not own its own ships or airplanes. It operates much like any other carrier, issuing its own bills of lading or air waybills. The only difference is that an NVOCC does not own the means of transport. An NVOCC is also called a non vessel owning carrier.

Non-Accelerating Inflation Rate of Unemployment Also called NAIRU. The unemployment rate in an economy below which inflation will begin to rise. The idea behind NAIRU states that a certain unemployment rate is built in to an economy. If unemployment falls too far, the economy will begin to overheat and inflation will rise. This analysis is highly controversial; some economists hold full employment is possible without these negative side effects. Milton Friedman was a major proponent of the NAIRU idea. See also: Phillips curve.

Non-Accredited Investor An investor with a net worth of less than $1 million who has had an annual income of less than $200,000 ($300,000 with a spouse) in each of the past two years. Under Regulation D, no more than 35 non-accredited investors are allowed to participate in the private placement of a security, company, or hedge fund. As a result, many investment vehicles target high net-worth individuals.

Nonaccrual Loan A loan on which the lender is not generating the expected interest rate due to non-payment. A loan is classified as nonaccrual if no principal or interest has been paid in 90 days. A nonaccrual loan is rather likely to default

Nonacquiescence A statement of disagreement that the Commissioner of Internal Revenue makes after an unfavorable decision by the Tax Court. A statement of nonacquiescence essentially means the Internal Revenue Service will ignore the Tax Court. While this practice is controversial, there are no penalties associated with it.

Nonactionable Subsidy A subsidy on which the World Trade Organization does not permit a member state to impose countervailing duties. Most of the time, a country may impose a countervailing duty (which is a type of tariff) on an import if the exporting country has subsidized it so as to make it significantly less expensive than domestically produced products. Nonactionable subsidies, however, are not subject to these tariffs. For example, environmental and scientific subsidies are nonactionable.

Nonaligned Movement An international organization for countries not allied with the United States or any other major bloc. It was founded in 1961 by nations not wishing to take sides in the Cold War; since the fall of the Soviet Union, it has concentrated on facilitating cooperation between countries in the Global South.

Nonassessable Capital Stock Stock in a publicly-traded company that limits the holder's liability to the amount invested. That is, if the company issuing nonassessable capital stock is liquidated, the holder of the stock cannot lose more than he/she invested in the first place. Nonassessability contrasts with unlimited liability. Most stock issued in the United States is nonassessable capital stock.

Nonbank Bank An institution that provides most banking services without belonging to the Federal Reserve System or receiving a state charter. Nonbank banks do not offer checking accounts per se, but offer credit cards, loans and savings accounts. They developed to circumvent regulations preventing banks from operating in multiple states. They became unnecessary after the passage of the Riegle-Neal Act, which deregulated banks.

Nonboard Company 1. An insurance company that does not belong to a rating bureau, which is a cooperative organization that prepares documents for insurance companies according to local and state law. Every state has slightly different laws, and a rating bureau may save an insurance company some of the costs associated with changing its policy details every time it opens up in a new state. Nonboard companies, then, may have higher costs, especially when moving into a new market. 2. A company that does not have a board of directors.

Nonborrowed Reserves The portion of a bank's reserves that has not been borrowed from a discount window at the Federal Reserve. One calculates the nonborrowed reserves by adding all deposits the bank has at the Federal Reserve to its cash on hand and subtracting its borrowed funds. Nonborrowed reserved are calculated each week.

Nonbusiness Expense Deduction An expense that a company may remove from its taxable income even though it is not directly related to its operations. For example, while employee salaries are a business expense, sales taxes are non-business. The latter may be taken as a nonbusiness expense deduction. There are limits on nonbusiness expense deductions. For example, one may not deduct expenses from a trip unless it relates to one's business.

Nonbusiness Income Income a business derives from its investments not directly related to its operations. For example, if a dental office has excess cash and invests it in stocks, its dividends will be treated as nonbusiness income. It is used to calculate the net operating loss deduction.

Noncallable A security that the issuer cannot redeem before maturity.

Non-Callable Bond A bond whose holder is not permitted to exchange it with the issuer in return for its face value. Non-callable bonds may be either traded or held to maturity. A non-callable bond should not be confused with a nonnegotiable security.

Noncancellable Health Insurance A health insurance policy that the insurer is not allowed to cancel. That is, the insurer must renew the policy and may not change the terms or raise the premium at renewal. Because of the upward trend of medical costs, noncancellable health insurance is rare.

Noncancellable Insurance Policy An insurance policy that the insurer is not allowed to cancel. That is, the insurer must renew the policy and may not change the terms or raise the premium at renewal.

Non-Cash Charge Any charge to a company that does not result in a cash outlay. Examples of non-cash charges include depreciation and amortization. For example, depreciation reduces the value of an asset but does not require a reduction in the cash on hand. A non-cash charge reduces a company's earnings.

Noncash Item A negotiable instrument that may be used to pay for goods and services but is not credited to the seller until it is cleared through a bank. Examples of noncash items include checks and debit cards.

Non-Circulating Legal Tender A coin that, due to its rarity or some other reason, does not circulate. As a result, while a vendor would be required to accept it as payment (because it is legal tender), it can actually be worth (and sold for) much more than its face value.

Noncity Delivery Mail that is delivered along a rural route in an area with light population. The U.S. Postal Service is not permitted to charge more for noncity delivery.

Nonclearing Member A member firm on an exchange that does not provide clearing services for other members and does not clear its own transactions. Nonclearing members must use a clearing house on the exchange to clear and settle trades. It pays a clearing fee for these services.

Non-Client Order An order to a broker to buy or sell a security made by a member firm on an exchange, rather than a client. Non-client orders are permissible, but brokers must give priority to client orders. A non-client order is also called a professional order.

Noncommercial Trader A trader on a futures exchange who conducts transactions on commodities for speculative reasons. That is, if a noncommercial trader buys a futures contract for corn, he/she will not need the corn for his/her business purposes when the contract matures. Rather, the trader enters that contract to profit from the movement of price in the meantime. A noncommercial trader may be an individual, but is often an institutional investor such as a hedge fund. The term "noncommercial trader" is used by the CFTC.

Noncompete Describing a clause in many employment contracts forbidding an employee from working for another firm that competes with the employer for a certain number of years after the termination of the contract. A noncompete clause may have a geographic limit. For example, a dentist who goes to work for corporate dental practice may sign a noncompete clause forbidding him from working for a competing dental practice within 25 miles for five years after the completion of the contract.

Noncompetitive Bid One of two bidding processes for buying Treasury securities and some other debt securities, in which the investor agrees to purchase a certain number of securities at the average price of all competitive bids over a given time. The noncompetitive bid process allows smaller investors to buy Treasury securities in a market that would otherwise be dominated by wealthy institutional investors. The minimum price in a noncompetitive bid is $10,000.

Non-Compliance The state of performing incomplete or poor quality work for pay. For example, suppose a video editor is hired to produce five 10-minute videos. If the client receives four two-minute videos, the video editor may be non-compliant with regard to the contract. Non-compliance may be actionable.

Non-Complying Purchase A purchase in excess of some amount above which the purchaser lacks discretionary authority. For example, the executive director of a small non-profit may have the ability to spend up to $1,000 of the organization's money at will, but must go to the board of directors for larger purchases. If the executive director buys a $2,300 computer network, he/she has made a non-complying purchase.

Nonconcurrency A situation in which two insurance policies covering the same thing have different start and end dates. This can be problematic for umbrella insurance because some losses from one's regular insurance may not count toward the limit at which the umbrella policy begins to pay because they operate on different calendars.

Non-Contestability Clause 1. A clause in an insurance contract giving the insurance company a certain, limited period of time during which it may contest a claim on the grounds of fraud or something similar. A non-contestability clause protects a policyholder from the risk of non-payment of a claim. 2. In a will, a clause forbidding beneficiaries from contesting the will. A non-contestability clause states that any contest of the will results in the contester's inheritance to other beneficiaries.

Noncontributory Pension Plan A pension where the pensioner (or employee) makes no contributions. Instead, the employer makes all contributions on the pensioner's behalf. This contrasts with most pension plans, where both employee and employer make contributions. See also: Matching Contribution, Contributory Pension Plan.

Nonconvertible Currency A currency that may not be converted into another currency on the foreign exchange market, or that may be converted only in limited amounts. Some countries limit convertibility to prevent citizens from making bad investment decisions in, say, a country experiencing hyperinflation, while a few communist countries issue nonconvertible currencies to protect their citizens from capitalist influences. A nonconvertible currency is generally traded only on the black market. It is also called a blocked currency or an inconvertible currency.

Noncumulative Preferred Stock Preferred stock for which the publicly-traded company does not need to pay all dividends. If a company misses a dividend payment for any reason, it no longer owes the dividend to noncumulative preferred stockholders. That is, all dividends that were "skipped" are treated as if they never existed. Noncumulative preferred stocks are rare because they are unattractive to preferred stock investors.

Noncurrent Liability Any liability with a term of greater than a year. In both investing and personal finance, an example of a noncurrent liability often is a loan with a payback period of longer than one year. Examples include a 30-year mortgage or a 10-year Treasury note. See also: Long-term financing.

Nondeductible Contribution A contribution to a retirement plan where the amount is taxable. For example, if one makes $2,000 in nondeductible contributions, one must still pay taxes on that $2,000 even though it was placed in a retirement plan. Nonqualifying plans usually have nondeductible contributions. Likewise, a Roth IRA takes nondeductible contributions, but this is because withdrawals following retirement are tax free.

Nondeductible Tax A tax that is not allowed as a deduction on one's federal tax return. Income taxes paid to state and local authorities are deductible, but sales taxes (under most circumstances) are nondeductible.

Non-Deliverable Forward A forward contract on a low-volume or inconvertible currency that cannot be settled by delivery of the underlying. In a non-deliverable forward, the parties net the difference between the exchange rate listed in the contract and the spot rate, and one party pays the other that difference. They are usually settled in U.S. dollars. Multinational corporations sometimes use non-deliverable forwards to hedge against risk associated with comparatively illiquid currencies.

Non-Deliverable Swap A swap in which the two legs are a major currency and an inconvertible currency. In a non-deliverable swap, the parties net the difference between the exchange rate listed in the swap contract and the spot rate, and one party pays the other that difference. They are usually settled in U.S. dollars. Multinational corporations and countries with minor currencies sometimes use non-deliverable swaps to hedge risk associated with comparatively illiquid currencies.

Non-Directed Order An order to a broker to buy or sell a security on the exchange of the broker's choice. A client has the ability to tell the broker his/her preferred exchange for the execution of orders. A non-directed order, however, leaves this to the broker's discretion, with the assumption that the broker will offer or bid the exchange at the best price.

Non-Discretionary Proposal A proxy vote whereby the proxy may vote on behalf of a shareholder, but only in a way that the shareholder directs. That is, in a non-discretionary proposal, a shareholder gives proxy to another party to vote at the general meeting and provides instructions as to how the proxy may vote.

Nondiscretionary Trust A trust in which the trustee has no ability to make investment decisions with regard to the assets in the trust and/or has no control over when and how the assets are distributed to the beneficiary. In a nondiscretionary trust, the trustee simply sees to it that the grantor's wishes are carried out.

Nondiscrimination Rule A provision of ERISA that requires employer-sponsored retirement plans to offer the same benefits in the same plans to all employees regardless of position in the company. That is, the nondiscrimination rule forbids employees of different rank from buying into the same plan and receiving different benefits. This protects both low income and high income employees. Plans violating the nondiscrimination rule are not tax deductible.

Nondiversifiability of Human Capital A term describing the fact that it is difficult or impossible to reduce the risk associated with one's employees. That is, given a set of employees, some will be good workers and some will not. While the employer can fire those employees who do not perform up to task, the fact that they are on staff at all exposes the employer to the risk that he/she will lose money from these employees' performance.

Nondiversified Management Company A private company often a venture capital firm that does not wish to accept the restrictions on investment that come from diversification. Nondiversified management companies invest in whatever companies or industries they like; they do not concern themselves with the percentage of ownership they have in a single company. A nondiversified management company carries relatively high risk, but has the possibility of a high return if it invests in the correct growth industries. Because of the risk, however, most mutual funds and similar investment vehicles are not run by nondiversified management companies.

Non-Durable Good A good that is intended to be used completely within three years. Examples of non-durable goods include office supplies, food, and newspapers. While they tend to be less expensive than durable goods, non-durable goods are a major subset of consumer goods.

Nondurable Goods Consumer products designed and intended to last less than three years. Some examples of nondurable merchandise, such as designer clothes, are expensive, while others, such as microwaveable pizza or cat food, are not. Companies that produce nondurable merchandise may be less volatile than those that produce durable goods, as consumers must return to buy more on a fairly regular basis.

Non-Equity Option An option contract on anything other than stock. Common examples of NEOs include commodities, currencies, indices, bonds, and even other options.

Non-Equity Security Any security other than a stock. Examples include bonds and options. Non-equity securities may fluctuate in value in relation to stocks. For example, futures contracts may increase in price as stocks increase, while bond prices tend to move inversely to stock prices.

No-Net-Sales Policy A practice in which a brokerage discourages clients from selling their securities. A no-net-sales policy is designed to keep a security's price higher than it otherwise would be. The policy is considered unethical.

Non-Farm Payroll In the United States, a figure compiled by the Bureau of Labor Statistics representing the total number of working-age persons working in all professions, except the following: government employees, household employees, many nonprofit employees, and farm employees. At any given time, this number represents approximately 80% of the American workforce currently employed. Economists use the non-farm payroll to help gauge the state of the overall economy.

Non-Filer A person or corporation who does not file a tax return by the required date. In general, a person who has filed taxes once must continue to do so for the rest of his/her life (or existence, if a corporation). A non-filer may be subject to interest, late fees, and other penalties.

Nonfinancial Asset In accounting, any asset that can be seen and touched. Non-financial assets include things that can be reproduced, such as widgets in a widget factory, and things than cannot be reproduced, such as the land upon which the widget factory is built. Non-financial assets are comparatively easy to price and, therefore, are often used to express the value of a company. However, because they do not include intangible (but still valuable) things like stocks and bonds, they may not truly express a company's value.

Nonfinancial Services Services provided by a company that do not include brokering, banking, or anything related to investment.

Non-Fluctuating Describing a feature, such as a price, that does not change. For example, a non-fluctuating return is fixed and does not change for any reason short of default. A non-fluctuating feature is the opposite of a volatile feature.

Nonforfeiture Clause A clause in some insurance policies entitling a policyholder to receive the benefit, or a portion of it, for a short period of time after allowing the policy to lapse. That is, if the policyholder does not pay the premium as agreed, he/she is still entitled under a nonforfeiture clause to the benefit should the insured event occur within a certain, brief period of time. Alternatively, a nonforfeiture clause may entitle a policyholder to a partial refund of the premiums paid.

Non-GAAP Describing a calculation of income or earnings not made according to Generally Accepted Accounting Principles. It is often difficult to compare non-GAAP earnings to each other because there are no standardized methods for computing them. Examples of non-GAAP earnings include free cash flow and core earnings.

Noninsurance Risk The risk of loss from not having an insurance policy. For example, if one does not purchase health insurance, one carries the noninsurance risk that an injury will leave one unable to pay one's medical bills.

Noninsured Plan A defined-benefit pension plan on which payments are not guaranteed by a third party, such as an insurance company or a government.

Non-Interest-Bearing Current Liability Liabilities that a person or company must pay within a year that do not accrue interest. Examples of NIBCL include taxes that are due but do not have interest or penalties (that is, taxes due in the current year) and accounts payable where the creditor is not charging interest. Less commonly, an NIBCL may be an interest-free loan. Non-interest-bearing current liabilities are recorded on a balance sheet under current liabilities.

Nonintermediated Debt Market A situation in which no financial institutions stand between counterparties in a transaction involving debt. For example, in the sale of a house, the seller could provide financing directly to the buyer without resorting to a bank. Alternatively, a company may issue a bond directly to investors without hiring an underwriter. That is, the issuer sells the bond on the market and no party acts as a "middle man." This can reduce transaction costs, but can deprive the parties of the expertise the intermediating party can provide. See also: Intermediated market.

Nonlegal Investment An investment that is not on a state's legal list, meaning that an insurance company may not be permitted to make it because it carries too much risk. If an insurer wishes to make a nonlegal investment, it must show how it will be able to pay on its policies and still be able to carry the investment. However, some states do not permit nonlegal investments at all.

Nonmailable Matter Any material that the U.S. Postal Service must refuse to carry. Examples of nonmailable matter include advertisements disguised as invoices, hazardous materials and perishables that may not be delivered before they go bad.

Non-Marketable Debt A right to repayment of some debt that the holder may not trade. Generally, non-marketable debt may be redeemed by the issuer, but this is often subject to some limitations. Low-risk instruments such as savings bonds are examples of non-marketable debt.

Nonmarketable Security A security that may not be bought or sold. Generally, a nonnegotiable security may be redeemed by the issuer, but this is often subject to some limitations. Low-risk instruments such as savings bonds and certificates of deposit are examples of nonnegotiable securities. They are also called nonnegotiable securities and nontradeable securities.

Nonmarketed Claims Claims and liabilities that are difficult or impossible to sell. Nonmarketed claims are important because they can be impossible to hedge. A prominent example is damages from a lawsuit.

Nonmember Bank In the United States, a state-chartered bank that has opted not to join the Federal Reserve System. Such banks are required to place a certain number of their accounts at a Federal Reserve Bank so as to meet reserve requirements. However, nonmember banks allowed access to the Federal Reserve's discount window are not required to purchase stock in the Federal Reserve. In general, nonmember banks are less regulated than member banks. For example, they are allowed to keep at least a portion of their reserves in interest-bearing securities. They are subject only to the laws of the states in which they are chartered.

Nonmember Firm A firm that does not have any employees who are allowed to trade on the floor of an exchange. To become a member, one needs to purchase a membership or a seat on the exchange, which can be very expensive. Furthermore, there are usually a set number of memberships to an exchange; for example, on the New York Stock Exchange, there are 1,366 seats. As a result, nonmember firms must work with and through member firms in order to gain access to the floor and execute trades.

Non-Monetary Job Characteristics The value of a job beyond monetary remuneration. Non-monetary job characteristics include job security, the friendliness of co-workers, the level of respect given by one's boss and so forth. While non-monetary job characteristics have worth, they may be difficult or impossible to quantify.

Non-Negotiable 1. Referring to a price for an asset where the seller has no intention to change the price at the buyer's instigation. Generally, the larger a business, the more likely its prices are to be non-negotiable. For example, a street vendor may negotiate prices, while Wal-Mart will not. **2.** Referring to a security or other asset that is difficult to sell or transfer. Describing an illiquid asset.

Non-Objecting Beneficial Owner A beneficial owner who has given his/her brokerage or bank permission to release his/her name and address to the publicly-traded companies in which the beneficial owner has stock. A beneficial owner is the effective owner of a security or asset, even though the security is actually held by the brokerage or bank. Registering oneself as a NOBO enables the company to contact the beneficial owner about the general meeting and give him/her other information.

Non-Obligatory Expenditure A government outlay that the European Parliament is not required to make in order to fulfill its responsibilities as a body of the European Union. For example, payroll for EU employees is non-obligatory because it is not mentioned in any of the treaties. However, agricultural subsidies are considered an obligatory expenditure. Changes to non-obligatory expenditures require a majority vote of the members of Parliament in attendance. However, the difference between obligatory and non-obligatory expenditures is sometimes difficult to determine.

Non-Operating Cash Flow The cash flow a company gives or receives from sources other than its operations. Non-operating cash flows are usually non-recurring. Examples of non-operating cash flows include borrowing, a new issue of stock, and a self-tender offer. While non-operating cash flow is not a good indicator of profitability, it can help an analyst find a company's cost of capital and its success in investing its revenue or earnings. Non-operating cash flows are reported on a company's balance sheet.

Nonoperating Income Income that a company derives from any source other than its operations. For example, if a company sells one of its factories or receives income from interest payments, these constitute nonoperating income. Most (though not all) nonoperating income is non-repetitive, and, as such, is excluded from many measures of profit. See also: Operating income.

Nonoperating Unit A company or department that does not manage any assets or directly conduct any business whatsoever. Rather, a nonoperating unit collects money and distributes it to the appropriate parties. For example, a nonoperating unit may own an asset but lease it to another company. If this is its only activity, the nonoperating unit does nothing except receive lease payments and distribute profits to stockholders or partners.

Nonpar Item A negotiable instrument (such as a check) drawn on one bank and cashed at another bank for a discount from the amount written on the instrument. For example, one may present a check for $100 written on Bank A at Bank B and receive $95. The deduction is to compensate the bank for cashing a check other than its own (and thus transferring the risk that the check will bounce). Nonpar items have become uncommon in the United States since the early part of the 20th century.

Nonparallel Shift in the Yield Curve A change in the yield curve for bonds with different maturities in which the changes in yields do not occur evenly. For example, given a yield curve for bonds with one-year, five-year, and 10-year maturities, the yield for the one-year bond may increase 10 basis points, the five-year may stay the same, and the 10-year may decrease 20 basis points. See also: Parallel shift in the yield curve.

Nonparticipating Describing a stock that entitles the holder to a flat dividend and nothing else. That is, the dividend will not be higher if the company performs particularly well, but instead remains the same at all times. However, nonparticipating stockholders are usually entitled to a minimum dividend, unlike common stock holders, who do not have a similar right. Most preferred stock is nonparticipating. See also: Participating preferred stock.

Nonparticipating Life Insurance Policy A life insurance policy in which the policyholder does not have the right to receive a portion of the investments that the insurance company makes with the policyholder's premiums. That is, in a nonparticipating life insurance policy, the policyholder makes his/her premiums and, in exchange, the beneficiary receives a lump sum upon the policyholder's death. This sum will not increase or decrease depending on the performance of the insurance company's portfolio.

Nonparticipating Preferred Stock A preferred stock that entitles the holder to a flat dividend and nothing else. That is, the dividend will not be higher if the company performs particularly well, but instead remains the same at all times. However, nonparticipating stockholders are usually entitled to a minimum dividend, unlike common stock holders, who do not have a similar right. Most preferred stock is nonparticipating. See also: Participating Preferred Stock.

Non-Payment The non-reception of compensation for a good or service. For example, non-payment occurs if one sells a hairdryer for $10 and never receives the $10. Non-payment may result simply from theft, but most of the time the term refers to delinquency or default from a credit sale.

Non-Performance The state of not doing the work one was hired to do. For example, suppose a video editor is hired to produce five 10-minute videos. If the client does not receive the videos in the allotted time and there is no evidence that the editor has done any work, he may be liable for non-performance on the contract. Non-performance may be actionable.

Non-Positive Describing any number or measure less than or equal to zero. For example, if one business loses $1 million in a year and a second one breaks even, both are said to have non-positive gains.

Nonprice Competition Competition between companies that involves something other than lower prices. That is, rather than advertising the lowest price for a product, a company may advertise that is has the best quality, the most convenience, or even the best branding. Nonprice competition is especially important where competition is stiff and companies cannot afford to charge much less than they already do. See also: Marketing.

Nonprobate Property An asset or other property that does not have to pass through the probate process in order to be transferred following the death of the owner. Most of the time, nonprobate property is jointly owned and ownership simply remains with the surviving owner.

Nonproductive Loan A loan that does not increase an economy's total output, but may increase the economy's total spending power. One of the most common examples of a nonproductive loan is leveraged buyout. Nonproductive loans are made by commercial banks.

Nonprofit Organization An organization that operates as if it were a business but does not seek a profit. Common examples of nonprofits include charities, private schools, and think tanks. Nonprofits do not pay taxes; donations to many are tax-deductible, at least up to certain limits. In order to qualify for this status, however, a nonprofit must register with the IRS, under section 501(c) of the tax code. See also: 403(b).

Nonpublic Information Major knowledge about a publicly-traded company that is not available to the public. Information may apply to its operations, such as its quarterly earnings, or to intangibles, such as an executive's imminent indictment. Nonpublic information almost always impacts a company's stock price, either positively or negatively, when it is made public. Prior to 2001, the use of nonpublic information in investment decisions qualified as illegal insider trading. Since then, even the possession of relevant nonpublic information may cause one to run afoul of SEC rules, even if an investor would have made a particular trade anyway. See also: Rule 10b5-1.

Nonpublic Record A record that a government holds but has not released to the public. Examples include findings from investigations or consumer complaints. In the United States, a Freedom of Information Act request is required to access nonpublic records. Most of the time, FOIA requests must be honored.

Nonpurpose Loan A loan secured by securities that is used to buy something other than more securities. An investment bank is allowed to lend up to 90% of the value of the securities used as collateral, provided the borrower submits an affidavit stating the reason for the loan. A nonpurpose loan is not subject to the same margin requirements as a purpose loan, which is used to buy securities. See also: Regulation T.

Non-Qualified Distribution A distribution from an IRA, 401(k), education savings plan, or similar vehicle that is subject to income tax when it otherwise would not be. Generally speaking, a distribution is non-qualified when one makes it before a certain age (for a retirement plan) or in excess of a certain amount (for an education plan). Non-qualified distributions may also be subject to excise taxes.

Nonqualified Plan An annuity or pension plan that one buys individually rather than through an employer. Nonqualified plans are not subject to the same restrictions as qualified plans. As a result, withdrawal penalties are smaller or non-existent, and one may continue to make contributions to a more advanced age (sometime until the annuitant is over 80). In the United States, specific restrictions on nonqualified plans are set at the state level. The IRS does not regulate them; as a result, contributions are not tax-deductible, but earnings still are.

Nonqualified Stock Option Any employee stock option that does not meet with IRS requirements for preferential tax treatment.

Nonrated Bonds Bonds with issuers that have not received a credit rating from one or more of the major credit rating agencies. A bond may be nonrated for a number of reasons, including simply not wishing to pay the fee to the credit rating agency. A nonrated bond is not necessarily risky, but they cannot be investment-grade.

Non-Recourse Finance A loan secured by the revenue of the project the loan intends to fund, and nothing else. That is, non-recourse finance does not allow the bank or other lending institution access to the borrower's other assets in the event of default. This is a relatively high-risk form of financing; projects that utilize non-recourse finance generally have uncertain revenue streams and long loan periods.

Nonrecurring Charge A charge, usually triggered by an extraordinary event, that appears on a company's financial statement only once. A nonrecurring charge is listed as an expense for the company and reduces its earnings for the time period covered in the financial statement. Most statements make it clear that a nonrecurring charge is a one-time event and does not reflect the company's broader financial health.

Nonredeemable Describing a bond or other security whose holder is not permitted to exchange it with the issuer in return for its face value. Nonredeemable securities may be either traded or held to maturity.

Nonrefundable Describing a bond that may not be retired for a certain number of years or until maturity. Nonrefundable bonds protect bondholders from the risk that the issuer may effectively refinance a bond at a lower interest rate, which would deprive bondholders of coupon payments to which they would otherwise be entitled. Most bonds are nonrefundable for at least five or 10 years after issue. See also: Refundable.

Non-Renewable Resource Any natural resource that does not replenish itself. Any use of a non-renewable resource reduces the amount available to be used in the future. The finite amount of non-renewable resources may influence their prices on the open market. Major examples of non-renewable resources are coal and oil.

Non-Renounceable Right A right that a corporation may sell to shareholders (but that shareholders may not sell) giving them the ability to buy more shares in that corporation at a discount to market value. Companies usually issue rights in conjunction with new issues of stock, which would dilute current shareholders' holdings if not accompanied by rights or something similar. Non-renounceable rights put shareholders in the position of either taking advantage of the rights or allowing one's shares to be diluted. It specifically precludes the possibility of the shareholder making a profit from the sale of the rights.

Nonreproducible Asset An asset that cannot be copied or remade. Land and antique baseball cards are both nonreproducible assets, while widgets and cars, on the other hand, are not. See also: Reproducible Assets.

Nonsmoker A person who does not use tobacco products. A nonsmoker is entitled to a lower premium on health and life insurance because of the medical risks associated with tobacco.

Nonsterilized Intervention A central bank's attempt to influence exchange rates by refusing to buy or sell assets or currencies. This allows the money supply to change without interference of the central bank. See also: Sterilized Intervention, Floating Currency.

Nonsystematic Risk Risk that is unique to a certain asset or company. An example of nonsystematic risk is the possibility of poor earnings or a strike amongst a company's employees. One may mitigate nonsystematic risk by buying different of securities in the same industry and/or by buying in different industries. For example, a particular oil company has the diversifiable risk that it may drill little or no oil in a given year. An investor may mitigate this risk by investing in several different oil companies as well as in companies having nothing to do with oil. Nonsystematic risk is also called diversifiable risk. See also: Undiversifiable risk.

Non-Tariff Barriers Trade barriers other than tariffs. A common example is a countervailing duty, which enacts a tariff under certain defined circumstances. Non-tariff barriers have the same restrictive effect on trade as tariffs. They have become more common as the World Trade Organization has gradually reduced the circumstances under which a tariff may be imposed.

Non-Tax Revenue Money that a government takes in by means other than taxation. Examples of non-tax revenue include bond issues and profits from state-owned companies. Some government agencies earn non-tax revenue through user fees. For example, a bank regulator may charge the banks that it regulates some percentage of their assets for the privilege of being regulated. Some of these revenues are mandated, while others are offered as an incentive. For example, these banks may be incentivized to pay the fees in exchange for eligibility for deposit insurance.

Nontaxable Dividends Dividends from a mutual fund or other investment company that are not subject to federal taxation. In order to issue nontaxable dividends, more than 50% of the fund's liquidity must be placed in municipal bonds or some other security that is tax-exempt.

Nontaxable Income All income that is exempt from taxation at the federal level. Coupons from municipal bonds are a common example of nontaxable income, thought they still may be taxed at the state level.

Non-Transferable 1. Describing a right that one may not sell or give away, either because of legal limitations or a standing agreement. For example, riparian rights to water are non-transferable by common law except to the owner of a neighboring property. **2.** See: Nonnegotiable.

Nontrepreneur A slang term for a demanding manager who expects employees to grow the company, but who is unwilling to take the risks necessary in order to do so.

Nonviolation Nullification of Benefits The reinterpretation of a provision of a WTO agreement or a bilateral trade agreement such that it contradicts the way it was previously interpreted. It does not accuse one party of violating the agreement. However, it can change the way it is enforced. Nonviolation nullification is very controversial because it increases uncertainty in international trade. It results in arbitration before the WTO or other appropriate body.

Nonvoting Stock Stock in a publicly-traded company that does not give the holder the right to vote at the company's annual meeting. Nonvoting stock usually has other rights associated with it to compensate for the lack of ability to vote. For example, most preferred stock is nonvoting, but preferred stock has a guaranteed dividend, while most voting stock does not.

NOR GOST 7.67 Latin three-letter geocode for Norway. The code is used for transactions to and from Norwegian bank accounts and for international shipping to Norway. As with all GOST 7.67 codes, it is used primarily in Cyrillic alphabets.

Nordic Council An international organization consisting of Scandinavian and Nordic countries: Denmark, Finland, Iceland, Norway and Sweden, as well as their autonomous territories. It maintains a common labor market and freedom of movement for all Nordic citizens. It was established in 1952.

Nordic Investment Bank A financial institution established by the governments of Denmark, Finland, Iceland, Norway and Sweden in 1975. It provides loans and similar funding to projects promoting sustainable development in member countries and in emerging markets, including the Middle East and Africa. In addition to its founding governments, members include Estonia, Latvia and Lithuania.

NOREX A joint endeavor of the Copenhagen Stock Exchange and the Stockholm Stock Exchange with the goal of establishing an exchange for all Scandinavian securities. It was established in 1997.

Norges Bank The central bank of Norway. It controls issue of the Norwegian krone. It is responsible for controlling inflation and for maintaining financial stability. It also operates Norges Bank Investment Management, which is the Norwegian sovereign wealth fund. It was established in 1816.

Norio Ohga A Japanese businessman who lived from 1930 to 2011. A musician and engineer by training, he served as president of Sony from 1982 to 1995, and as chairman of the board until 2000. He was instrumental in the development of the compact disc.

Normal Backwardation Theory In Keynesian economics, a theory stating that the future spot price for a commodity will be higher than the forward price. This is because the producers of commodities expect to sell no matter what, and are willing to sell at a loss, if necessary. In normal backwardation, no rational investor will buy on the future spot market if he/she can buy more cheaply on the forward market. The extent to which normal backwardation occurs in the market is debated.

Normal Deviate In statistics, the distance of a data point from the average value of the data set divided by standard deviation.

Normal Growth Firm A company that experiences growth at a constant, sustainable rate.

Normal Investment Practice The strategies, securities, and other investment routines that a person or company usually conducts. For example, buying investment-grade bonds might be a normal investment practice for a risk-averse investor. Because normal investment practices are observable and often predictable, underwriters and investment advisers may use them to recommend securities to investors. However, FINRA prohibits underwriters from using normal investment practices when placing hot issues.

Normal Market Size The number of shares in a publicly-traded company that can be traded at a given price. The normal market size is a set number determined by the stock's market capitalization. Market makers must trade within the parameters of the normal market size. If a market maker wants to buy or sell more shares than the normal market size, he/she must negotiate a new price. The normal market size exists

to keep particularly large orders from affecting the share price, thus reducing volatility.

Normal Portfolio The portfolio of investments a money manager ordinarily makes. If a money manager deviates from his/her investment strategy at any given time for any reason, a normal portfolio is useful to help the money manager (or his/her client) determine how the investments would have performed had he/she simply used his/her usual strategy. See also: Benchmark.

Normal Random Variable A random variable on a chart that is distributed at some point along a bell curve. See also: Normal probability distribution.

Normal Retirement A situation in which a worker stops working and is eligible to receive benefits from a pension or other retirement plan without having to pay back taxes and/or a penalty. Normal retirement may occur at a certain age, such as 65, and/or after a certain number of years working for the company.

Normal Wear and Tear Deterioration to property one would expect from reasonable, light use. For example, small scratches or chips in the paint of a wall that occur over the course of a year or two may be considered normal wear and tear. A large hole in the wall resulting from a wild party generally would not. A tenant ordinarily does not compensate a landlord when the landlord repairs normal wear and tear.

Normal Yield Curve A yield curve that trends upward, indicating that the interest rates for long-term debt securities are higher than short-term debt securities. This is the regular way a yield curve trends because investors demand a higher return for the higher risk of tying up their capital in securities with longer maturities. It is less commonly called a positive yield curve. See also: Negative Yield Curve, Flat Yield Curve.

Normal-Course Issuer Bid The act of a publicly-traded company buying its own shares in order to cancel them. By definition, this reduces the number of shares outstanding and therefore increases the earnings per share. This usually results in an increased market value per share. Therefore, a company making an NCIB usually does so in order to increase its market value. Regulations govern the number of shares a company is allowed to buy back in an NCIB. See also: Share buyback.

Normalized Earnings 1. Earnings for a company not including nonrecurring charges and gains. A one-time charge or gain that deeply affects a company's profits or losses for a given period of time might make it appear more or less healthy than it really is; normalized earnings are an indication of a company's true financial health. **2.** Earnings that account for seasonal or economic cycles. See also: Seasonally-adjusted.

North America Free Trade Agreement A controversial free trade agreement between Canada, Mexico, and the United States. Signed in 1993, it was the first free trade agreement between a developing nation (Mexico) and two developed nations. The agreement reduced or eliminated most trade restrictions between the participants. In particular, NAFTA allowed for the more or less free importation and exportation of agricultural products and textiles. Proponents of NAFTA argue that the agreement allowed for cheaper access to goods, especially food, which in turn increased the real incomes in all three countries. Critics contend that the agreement has not substantially reduced poverty in any of the participating countries. Mexican critics complain that NAFTA reduced profits for farmers and agricultural workers unable to compete with American agribusiness. American organized labor have argued that the agreement has accelerated deindustrialization and caused job losses because it has become cheaper for American companies to move factories to Mexico and hire Mexican workers. NAFTA proponents note that employment in the United States increased between 1993 and 2007, and that factories in the U.S. were closing even before NAFTA was signed. Canadian opposition to NAFTA has been largely related to environmental concerns, particularly the lack of oversight for the enforcement of its environmental provisions. Because NAFTA allows Canadian water to be bought and sold as a commodity, some environmental groups have been concerned that this would cause the degradation of Canadian wild lands. See also: Maquiladora.

North American Commission on the Environment Also called NACE. A proposal in conjunction with NAFTA for the chief environment officers of the United States, Canada and Mexico to meet to discuss matters of mutual interest. It came to fruition as the North American Agreement on Environmental Cooperation.

North American Development Bank Also called the NADB. A binational organization between the United States and Mexico that provides financing for projects intended to improve the environment along the border between the two countries. Specifically, it finances projects certified by the Border Environment Cooperation Commission as being environmentally sustainable. The NADB was established in 1994 as a side agreement along with NAFTA. Its headquarters are in San Antonio, Texas.

North American Securities Administrators Association An organization dedicated to investor protection. It provides guidance and advice for persons who buy securities or receive investment advice from any jurisdiction that is a member. It also provides seminars and other educational information. It has more than 60 members, who are governments of Mexican states, Canadian provinces & territories, and American states, territories, & districts. NASAA was established in Kansas in 1919. See also: Blue Sky Laws, Uniform Securities Act.

North Korean Won The currency of North Korea. It was introduced in 1947, replacing the Korean yen. For some period of time before 2001, it was pegged to the U.S. dollar at a rate of 2.16 won to one dollar, but this has been re-adjusted because the won's black market value was nowhere near the peg. The won is an inconvertible currency. Visitors must use foreign exchange certificates in North Korea officially, but many vendors simply accept foreign currencies.

Northern Ireland Office A department of the British government responsible for the administration of devolution of power from the central government to the Northern Irish regional government. It handles national security, elections, and similar matters in Northern Ireland. The department was created in 1972.

Northwest Atlantic Fisheries Organization An international organization dedicated to managing and conserving fish resources. It also conducts scientific research to accomplish its mission. It is responsible for most fish in the Northwest Atlantic with the exception of marlins, salmon, shellfish, tuna and whales. Twelve countries are members; it was established in 1979.

Norwegian Krone The currency of Norway. Originally issued in 1875 when Norway joined the (now defunct) Scandinavian Monetary Union, it was a gold standard currency, off and on, until it became pegged to the British pound in 1931. After World War II, it maintained its peg to the pound, which was itself pegged to the U.S. dollar. It was later pegged to the dollar directly. In 1992, it became a floating currency.

Nostro Account An account at a foreign bank where a domestic bank keeps reserves of a foreign currency. A bank keeps a nostro account so that it does not have to make a currency conversion (which brings with it foreign exchange risk) should an account holder make a deposit or a withdrawal in that foreign currency. See also: Vostro Account.

Not a Name with Us In over-the-counter trading, describing a person or company that is not a registered market maker for the OTC market.

Not Held Order An order to a broker to buy or sell a security where the broker is not held responsible for not obtaining the best available price. That is, the broker is given discretion as to when to execute the order, but if he makes a mistake and obtains an unfavorable price, he is not responsible. This is sometimes used in place of a limit order.

Not Reoffered The issue or a portion of an issue that already has a buyer or buyers and, for that reason, is not reoffered to the public by underwriters. For example, an investor may purchase a large number of bonds with the stated intent to hold them until maturity. This investor would have no interest in offering them on the secondary market. The underwriter selling the bonds then may indicate that this purchase is "not reoffered," which may or may not affect prices for the remainder of the issue. The MSRB's Rule G-32 requires underwriters to disclose price spreads, including on portions of an issue that are not reoffered. See also: Private placement.

Not Spoken For Informal; describing money to be used to pay for expenses that are not regular and recurring. For example, money for company lunches or optional travel is said to be not spoken for. Some companies (and individuals) keep spoken for and not spoken for money in separate accounts to ensure financial responsibility.

Not To Be Noted An addendum to a bill of exchange indicating that the collecting bank should not be required to pay additional expenses if the bill is dishonored. It is abbreviated as N/N.

Not to Exceed An estimate of the cost of a project that a potential contractor gives to the firm negotiating a contract. An NTE includes additional funds that might be needed in case something goes wrong. It is important to note than an NTE assumes that the scope of the project does not change; it may be revised if this occurs.

Notaphilist A person who studies or collects antique or rare banknotes and other types of paper money. These notes can be valuable to the study of economic history and often have value as collectibles.

Notaphily The hobby or practice of studying or collecting antique or rare banknotes and other types of paper money. These notes can be valuable to the study of economic history and often have value as collectibles.

Notch Slang; in bond trading, a small increase or decrease in a bond rating. For example, if a rating goes from AAA to AA+, it is said to decline by a notch.

Note A debt security with a maturity longer than one year but less than 10 years. Because of many investors' aversion to long-term investments, notes are becoming more prominent benchmarks of the bond market. A prominent example is the 10-year Treasury note.

Note Agreement An agreement between a lender and a borrower on the terms of a loan or other debt.

Note Issuance Facility An agreement by a syndicate of banks to buy short- and/or medium-term notes from an issuer in the event that it is unable to sell the notes on eurocurrency markets. This effectively provides credit for the issuer because, even if the issuer cannot place an issue, it will still be able to raise the funds it seeks. A note issuance facility thereby reduces the risk to an issuer of short- and medium-term debt securities.

Note Payable A document stating that a borrower has promised to repay some debt on or by some future date. It is listed as a liability on the borrower's balance sheet and may be either current or non-current.

Note Printing Australia An organization in Australia that manufactures cash money for general use. It was established in 1998 but traces its origins to 1913. It is owned by the Reserve Bank of Australia and is located in Melbourne.

Note Receivable A debt that a borrower had not yet repaid. Notes receivable are listed as assets on the lender's balance sheet.

Notes to the Financial Statements All passages following a financial statement giving additional information and/or explaining unusual entries.

Notgeld A type of German mark issued during and immediately after World War I in order to cope with persistently high inflation. These marks were not issued by the central bank; they were issued by private banks, local governments, or other organizations that were unable to keep up with the rising demand for money. However, the central bank generally redeemed notgeld until around 1923. It did not improve the inflationary situation.

Notice 1155 (ENG/SP) A flier published by the IRS encouraging victims of qualified disasters to call or go online for information on filing extensions and quicker tax refunds that may be available if the victims are unable to pay their taxes.

Notice 1215 A flier published by the IRS stating how one may appeal a penalty imposed for late payment of taxes. The notice states which forms must be filed, which offices must be contacted, and how long the taxpayer has to do so.

Notice 1219-A A flier sent to a taxpayer informing him/her that the IRS will try to contact neighbors, banks, or other persons who may have information about the taxpayer. Notice 1219-A is sent if the IRS is attempting to collect delinquent tax returns and has been unable to do so.

Notice 1219-B A flier sent to a taxpayer informing him/her that the IRS will try to contact neighbors, banks, or other persons who may have information about the taxpayer. Notice 1219-B is sent if the IRS is attempting to collect delinquent taxes and has been unable to do so.

Notice 1311 A form the IRS published in 2002 announcing the suspension of the requirement to file Form 5500 (Schedule F).

Notice 1315 A form the IRS sends to a taxpayer informing him/her that he/she is a potentially eligible beneficiary of the Pension Benefit Guaranty Corporation.

Notice 1316 A form the IRS sends to a taxpayer informing him/her that he/she is a potentially eligible beneficiary of the trade adjustment assistance.

Notice 1325 A form the IRS published in 2005 advising taxpayers to submit Form 1042-S along with Form 1042-T.

Notice 1339 A form the IRS published in 2005 advising taxpayers in U.S. possessions that certain tax forms had been delayed and providing a portion of what was necessary for these persons to file their taxes.

Notice 1360 A form the IRS published in 2007 outlining a rule change stating that one cannot claim a tax deduction for a cash donation to charity unless one maintains a written record, such as a canceled check or a receipt from the organization.

Notice 1367 A form the IRS published in 2007 announcing an increase on fees levied on installment agreements to pay back taxes.

Notice 1373 A form published by the IRS stating the instructions for filing FinCEN Form 103, which some casinos use to report currency transactions.

Notice 1374 A form published by the IRS informing importers of motor vehicles that the vehicles may be subject to a federal excise tax.

Notice 1376 A form the IRS published in 2008 correcting a major error in Publication 15 (Circular E) that grossly overstated tax benefits available for dependent care assistance programs.

Notice 1377 A form the IRS published in 2008 informing taxpayers of their eligibility for payment under the Economic Stimulus Act of 2008. It includes a worksheet to determine the amount for which each person is eligible.

Notice 1382 A form the IRS published in 2011 outlining changes to Form 1023, which non-profits use to file for 501(c)3 status.

Notice 1392 A form published by the IRS stating instructions that non-resident aliens of the United States must follow in preparing Form W-4.

Notice 1396 A form the IRS published announcing the deductibility on 2009 tax returns of donations for relief in Haiti following the January 2010 earthquake.

Notice 1397 A form the IRS published in 2010 announcing to small businesses that they may be eligible for the health care tax credit.

Notice 1399 A form the IRS published in 2010 informing taxpayers of two minor typos on Form 1099-INT for that year.

Notice 1400 A form the IRS published in 2010 informing individual taxpayers that it will no longer mail tax packages because so many people had begun to file their taxes electronically. The notice contains information on how to find IRS forms if one still wishes to file by mail.

Notice 1400 (PR) A form the IRS published in 2010 informing individual taxpayers in Puerto Rico (and other Spanish speakers) that it will no longer mail tax packages because so many people had begun to file their taxes electronically. The notice contains information on how to find IRS forms if one still wishes to file by mail.

Notice 1400-A A form the IRS published in 2010 informing partnerships and corporations that it will no longer mail tax packages because so many taxpayers had begun to file their taxes electronically. The notice contains information on how to find IRS forms if one still wishes to file by mail.

Notice 1400-E A form the IRS published in 2010 informing split-interest trusts that it will no longer mail tax packages because so many taxpayers had begun to file their taxes electronically. The notice contains information on how to find IRS forms if one still wishes to file by mail.

Notice 1400-J A form the IRS published in 2010 informing employers that they must file W-2 forms electronically if they have more than 250 employees.

Notice 1412 A form the IRS published in 2011 explaining how one is to report income replacement payments given as a result of the 2010 BP oil spill on one's tax return.

Notice 1418 A form the IRS published in 2011 advising certain hospitals not to file Form 990 (Schedule H) before July 1, 2011, due to an administrative delay.

Notice 433 A form providing information on the penalties and interest the IRS assesses on late and non-payment of taxes.

Notice 609 A form published by the IRS explaining rights taxpayers have under the Privacy Act of 1974. Among other things, the notice states that the IRS must explain (on forms) its legal right to ask for private information whenever it asks for it. It must also explain why it asks for the information.

Notice 703 A brief worksheet the IRS uses to help taxpayers determine whether their Social Security benefits are taxable in a given year.

Notice 746 A form published by the IRS explaining the interest rates it charges for the underpayment and overpayment of taxes.

Notice 797 A form published by the IRS explaining how to apply for a tax refund of the earned income tax credit.

Notice 844 A form published by the IRS explaining the forms that a non-profit organization must file each year to maintain its tax exempt status and to ensure that it complies with all applicable laws.

Notice 931 A form published by the IRS explaining money employers are required to deposit with the IRS to pay withholding taxes for employees. Some companies file monthly, while others file semiweekly.

Notice 989 A form published by the IRS clarifying what an individual taxpayer should do if he/she attempted to file as a self-employed person but the IRS determined that he/she is an employee. Among other things, the IRS requires such persons to report income received on Form 1099-MISC as wages (rather than profit/loss) on Form 1040.

Notice Day The day on which a clearing house informs an investor that it intends to make delivery of a commodity that the investor previously bought in a futures contract. The date is governed by the rules of different exchanges and clearing houses, but may also be stated in the futures contract itself. It occurs in the delivery month in which the contract expires. See also: First notice day.

Notice of Meeting A brief statement that the management of a publicly-traded company must issue to shareholders indicating the place, date, and time of a stockholder meeting. The notice of meeting usually is attached to the proxy statement.

Notice of Seizure In U.S. tax, a letter informing the recipient that the IRS has permission to seize the recipient's assets for nonpayment of taxes. If a taxpayer is grossly delinquent in payment of taxes, the IRS has the right and ability to seize and sell the taxpayer's assets to make up for what is owed. In order to do this, the IRS must send a Notice of Seizure, which gives the taxpayer the right to appeal the decision. If no appeal is made, or if it is found against the taxpayer, the IRS may seize any and all assets to pay back taxes and accrued interest.

Notice Period 1. In futures trading, the period of time before the expiration of the future contract during which the buyer may be called upon to accept receipt of the underlying. The specific length of the notice period varies and is set in the contract, but is generally three to six weeks prior to the contract's expiration. See also: Settlement date. **2.** A period of time before which an employee, by contract or by courtesy, must inform his/her employer of his/her intention to leave the current job. If no specific notice period is set in a contract, then it is usually assumed to be two weeks. However, notice periods may be set to as long as six months or one year.

Notification Date 1. The date by which one party to a contract must inform the other of the former's intent to either renew or withdraw from the contract. This especially applies to housing leases, marketing contracts, and long-term business arrangements. Some contracts renew automatically if neither party cancels by the notification date, while others require notification either way. For example, a rental agreement ending on August 1 may contain a requirement that the renter inform the landlord by May 1 whether or not he/she intends to renew the lease. **2.** In options, see expiration date.

Notifying Bank A bank in a foreign country to which another bank in the domestic country sends a letter of credit on behalf of a client. The notifying bank honors the letter of credit and transfers requested funds to the client. A notifying bank is also called an advising bank.

Notional Income Income one may not have received but on which one may still be taxed. The term is often associated with income from rental property. In India, for example, one must pay taxes on the amount of rent one might reasonably expect to earn in a year, whether or not one actually earns it. This fictional money is notional income because one must still pay income tax on it.

Notional Principal Amount In an interest rate swap, the arbitrary amount over which interest is calculated. Suppose the two legs of the swap are a fixed interest rate, say 3.5%, and a floating interest rate, say LIBOR + 0.5%, and the notional principal amount is $1 million. In such a swap, the only things traded are the two interest rates, which are calculated over the notional principal amount. That is, the $1 million is never exchanged, but the interest is calculated with reference to it. For example, the fixed interest is 3.5% of $1 million (or $35,000). It is also called the notional value.

Notional Value 1. In an interest rate swap, see notional principal amount. **2.** The total value of the spot price of the underlying asset in a derivative contract.

Notopfer A German term for emergency levy. During the hyperinflation of the early Weimar Republic, the German state imposed notopfer, a series of emergency taxes implemented because other forms of taxation lost their value even before they were remitted to the government, making it impossible for the government to meet its expenditures via taxation.

Not-Sufficient-Funds Check A check that a bank refuses to honor because there is not enough money in the payer's checking account to cover the amount of the check. For example, if Bob writes Joe a check for $200, but there is only $175 in Bob's account, then Bob has written a not-sufficient-funds check and the bank will refuse to transfer the funds to Joe's account. It is also called an NSF check, a bad check or a returned check.

Nouveau Marche An index on Euronext Paris that includes start-ups and other high-risk, high-growth companies. Companies on the Nouveau Marche seek capital to finance their future growth.

Nouveau Riche A person or class of person who acquired wealth themselves, or at least in recent family history. The term can have a slightly negative connotation because, stereotypically, nouveau riche do not abide by social norms usually associated with the upper class. However, in the late 20th century, the term became respectable because it became indicative of personal success.

Nova Scotia Dollar The currency of Nova Scotia between 1860 and 1871. It was worth slightly less than the Canadian dollar, though the two currencies continued to circulate after Nova Scotia joined the Canadian Confederation at its formation in 1867. It was replaced by the Canadian dollar.

Nova Scotia Pound The currency of Nova Scotia prior to 1860. It was equal in value to the British pound. It was replaced by the Nova Scotia dollar.

Novada Pilseta In Latvia, a political subdivision equivalent to a township.

Novads In Latvia, a political subdivision roughly equivalent to an unincorporated urban neighborhood.

Novation 1. The transfer of a contract from one party to another by mutual consent of the original counterparties and the concurrence of the new party. **2.** See: Rollover.

Novo Kwanza The currency of Angola between 1990 and 1995. It was issued to reduce inflation; thus, while it replaced the first kwanza at par value, holders of the currency were only permitted to change five percent of the old currency for the new currency. The rest were exchanges for government securities. This did not resolve inflationary pressures and the novo kwanza was replaced by the kwanza reajustado.

NP 1. ISO 3166-1 alpha-2 code for the Federal Democratic Republic of Nepal. This is the code used in international transactions to and from Nepalese bank accounts. **2.** ISO 3166-2 geocode for Nepal. This is used as an international standard for shipping to Nepal. Each zone has its own code with the prefix "NP." For example, the code for Seti Zone is ISO 3166-2:NP-ME.

NPL GOST 7.67 Latin three-letter geocode for Nepal. The code is used for transactions to and from Nepalese bank accounts and for international shipping to Nepal. As with all GOST 7.67 codes, it is used primarily in Cyrillic alphabets.

NPR ISO 4217 code for the Nepalese rupee. It was introduced in 1932, replacing the mohar. Since 1993, it has been pegged to the Indian rupee at a rate of 1.6 NPR to 1 Indian rupee.

NQ 1. ISO 3166-1 alpha-2 code for Queen Maud Land in Antarctica. **2.** ISO 3166-2 geocode for Queen Maud Land. This was used as an international standard for shipping to the territory. In both cases, the code is obsolete.

NQAQ ISO 3166-3 code for Queen Maud Land, which was re-designated as Antarctica in 1983. ISO 3166-3 codes are used to indicate names of countries that are no longer used.

NR 1. ISO 3166-1 alpha-2 code for the Republic of Nauru. This is the code used in international transactions to and from Nauruan bank accounts. **2.** ISO 3166-2 geocode for Nauru. This is used as an international standard for shipping to Nauru. Each Nauruan district has its own code with the prefix "NR." For example, the code for the District of Aiwo is ISO 3166-2:NR-01. **3.** See: Non-Refundable. **4.** See: Non-Rated.

NRU GOST 7.67 Latin three-letter geocode for Nauru. The code is used for transactions to and from Nauruan bank accounts and for international shipping to Nauru. As with all GOST 7.67 codes, it is used primarily in Cyrillic alphabets.

NSF Fee A fee one must pay in the event that one bounces a check. For example, if Joe writes a check to Bob for $500, but there is only $400 in Joe's checking account, Joe may have to pay an NSF fee to his bank to discourage him from writing bad checks.

NT 1. ISO 3166-1 alpha-2 code for the Iraqi-Saudi Neutral Zone, which ceased to exist in 1991. **2.** ISO 3166-2 geocode for the Iraqi-Saudi Neutral Zone. This was used as an international standard for shipping to the territory. In both cases, the code is obsolete.

NTHH ISO 3166-3 code for Iraqi-Saudi Neutral Zone, which ceased to exist in 1991. ISO 3166-3 codes are used to indicate names of countries and territories that are no longer used.

NU 1. ISO 3166-1 alpha-2 code for Niue. This is the code used in international transactions to and from Niuean bank accounts. **2.** ISO 3166-2 geocode for Niue. This is used as an international standard for shipping to Niue.

Nuclear Energy Agency An organization under the OECD that promotes the peaceful, scientific use of nuclear energy. It acts as a forum for research and sharing of information between members. It has 29 member states all over the world.

Nuclear Energy Liability Insurance An insurance policy providing coverage to an individual or, more frequently, a company in the event of a lawsuit resulting from personal or property damage due to nuclear energy. The nuclear energy need not be radioactive in order to be covered by a policy. In order to receive a license as a nuclear weapons plant in the United States, one must first procure nuclear energy liability insurance.

Nuclear Nonproliferation Act Legislation in the United States, passed in 1978, that revised previous law governing export of nuclear materials. It established safeguards so nuclear material would not be able to be used as part of a weapons program. It also increased financial aid and technical assistance to the International Atomic Energy Agency.

Nuclear Nonproliferation Treaty An international treaty by which signatories agree not to pursue nuclear weapons technology. Signatories already possessing weapons agree not to distribute them to other countries and to take steps toward disarmament. However, signatories may pursue nuclear power for energy or other peaceful uses. Most of the world's countries are signatories. It entered into force in 1970 and is renewed every five years.

Nuclear Suppliers Group A group of nations that control the transfer of nuclear energy. It encourages non-proliferation of nuclear weapons by improving safety and other standards. It was established in 1974.

Nudum Pactum In law, a contract entered without any consideration, which is something each party gives to the other to induce each other to perform the contract. A nudum pactum is unenforceable in court. The term is Latin for "naked pact."

Nuevo Peso 1. See: Mexican nuevo peso. **2.** See: Uruguayan nuevo peso.

Nugget Mortgage-backed security pools, issued by Freddie Mac, with maturities of 15 years. See also: Dwarf.

Nuisance The use of property in such a way that it violates another property owner's expectation of an orderly living environment. For example, a person may refrain from mowing his lawn for so long that field mice infest his yard. This may be a nuisance if the field mice wander over to the neighbors' yards.

Nuisance Call An unsolicited, unwanted phone call. Nuisance calls include cold calls from telemarketers, prank calls and even threatening calls. The latter two may be illegal depending on the jurisdiction. One may opt out of nuisance calls from telemarketers and others by placing his/her number on a do-not-call list.

Nuke Informal; to delete the contents of a database or other set of information on a computer. Nuking is common when information is no longer relevant or may be used when information is sensitive or restricted.

Null and Void Describing anything that cannot be enforced legally. For example, a contract may be declared null and void if one party enters it under duress or if its terms violate local law.

Number Cruncher A slang term for an accountant or other financial worker.

Numbered Account A bank account in which the owner is identified by a number instead of a name. Numbered accounts are used for discretion, and have a reputation of protecting money launderers and other criminals. Until recently, numbered accounts were almost exclusively used in the Swiss banking system.

Numeraire The unit of measure, especially of price. Historically and in the present, money, gold and other commodities have been common numeraires.

Numeric Keypad A keyboard containing the numbers zero through nine exclusively or almost exclusively. Telephones and ATMs both require numeric keypads.

Numerical Rating System In insurance underwriting, a system that assigns numbered weights to various risk factors. For example, in health insurance, a smoker will be assigned a different numerical rating than a non-smoker to compensate for the smoker's higher risk. A numerical rating system compiles numbers for all risk factors to arrive at an aggregate score. Underwriters may use this to see if one is insurable and, if so, what premium one must pay.

Numismatic Coin A historically significant or otherwise very old coin, especially one worth more than its face value. Examples of numismatic coins include buffalo nickels in the United States and Roman denarii. Numismatic coins can be important to the history of money and can be valuable to the study of economic history in general.

Numismatics The study of coins or the hobby of coin collecting. Numismatics often involves the study of the history of money and can be valuable to the study of economic history in general.

Numismatist A scholar or serious hobbyist engaged in coin collecting. Numismatists often study the history of money and can be valuable to the study of economic history in general.

Nuncupative Will A will made verbally to at least two witnesses. That is, there is no written record of a noncupative will, and one must simply trust the two witnesses. Because of the possibility for fraud, noncupative wills are considered invalid if they contradict a written will. They are often made by soldiers, sailors, or others who die unexpectedly.

Nursing Home A residential center for persons who are unable to accomplish some or all activities for daily living. Most residents of nursing homes are elderly or disabled. Many residents in the United States receive government health care aid such as Medicare or Medicaid. Nursing homes are heavily regulated because of their sensitive nature, especially if they accept government money.

Nut The total amount an advertiser spends on a television, radio or Internet marketing campaign. For example, if an advertiser sponsors a radio program and broadcasts $1 million worth of commercials, that $1 million is that advertiser's nut.

Nutrition Labeling The mandatory or voluntary declaration of the nutritional value of a foodstuff. For instance, sellers of microwave dinners may be required to display how much fat, sodium, carbohydrates and so forth are contained in the meal. Critics may contend that nutrition labeling may add to costs for some food sellers but proponents argue that the right to know what one is eating outweighs this fact.

NYMEX ACCESS A computerized, after-hours trading program on the New York Mercantile Exchange. One may use ACCESS between NYMEX's close and its open, Monday through Thursday. One may use NYMEX ACCESS anywhere in the world.

Nymil A Swedish unit of length equivalent to 10 kilometers. It is often referred to simply as a mil.

NYSE Alternext A trading platform for small- and medium-sized publicly-traded companies in Belgium, France and the Netherlands. It was established in 2005 with less stringent listing requirements so that smaller companies can have access to capital. It is owned by NYSE Euronext.

NYSE Arca An electronic stock and options exchange formed by a merger between the New York Stock Exchange and the Archipelago Exchange in 2006.

NYSE Euronext A corporation that owns and operates numerous stock exchanges in the United States and Europe. It controls 10 exchanges directly and has a minority stake in the Doha Securities Market. It was formed in 2007 with a merger of Euronext and the NYSE Group. It was the first corporation to own exchanges on multiple continents. See also: NYSE Alternext.

NYSE Group A corporation that owned the New York Stock Exchange and a few other exchanges in the United States. It was formed in 2006 as the result of a merger between the NYSE and the Archipelago Exchange. The following year, the NYSE Group merged with Euronext to form NYSE Euronext. See also: Demutualization.

NYSE International 100 Index An index, weighted for float-adjusted market capitalization, of the stocks of the 100 largest publicly-traded companies traded on the New York Stock Exchange. Because foreign companies generally trade on the NYSE as American Depository Receipts, the Index effectively measure the performance of large ADRs.

NZ 1. ISO 3166-1 alpha-2 code for New Zealand. This is the code used in international transactions to and from New Zealander bank accounts. **2.** ISO 3166-2 geocode for New Zealand. This is used as an international standard for shipping to New Zealand. Each region has its own code with the prefix "NZ." For example, the code for the Region of Canterbury is ISO 3166-2:NZ-CAN.

NZD ISO 4217 code for the New Zealand dollar. It was introduced in 1967, replacing the New Zealand pound. It was initially pegged to gold through the U.S. dollar. After the end of the Bretton Woods system, it remained pegged to gold, then later to a currency basket. It has been a floating currency since 1985.

NZL GOST 7.67 Latin three-letter geocode for New Zealand. The code is used for transactions to and from New Zealander bank accounts and for international shipping to New Zealand. As with all GOST 7.67 codes, it is used primarily in Cyrillic alphabets.

Oath of Inspectors A notarized statement made by inspectors of election before a shareholders' meeting stating that they will be impartial and fair when counting ballots from shareholder votes.

Obamacare An informal term for the Patient Protection and Affordable Care Act and the Health Care and Education Reconciliation Act of 2010. The two bills changed how health insurance functions in the United States. Among other provisions, Obamacare expanded eligibility of Medicaid and required most Americans to purchase health insurance. It also set up exchanges in the several states so insurers could compete with each other to provide the most cost effectiveness for consumers. It provided subsidies for health insurance premiums. Proponents argue Obamacare makes health insurance more affordable, while critics contend it is too expensive and constitutes excessive government interference in the U.S. economy. The legislation is named for U.S. President Barack Obama, who promoted it.

Obce In Slovakia, a political subdivision equivalent to a municipality.

Objective Probability The likelihood of the outcome of any event based upon recorded measurements rather than subjective analysis. Objective probability is considered more accurate than subjective estimates, thought it should be noted that analysts often rely on subjectivity just as much. Objective probability is important to both technical analysis and fundamental analysis.

Oblast In Russia and several other Slavic countries, a political subdivision equivalent to a province.

Obligation Any requirement, especially a legal one. For example, one may have a legal obligation to disclose one's investments to the SEC. Likewise, one has an obligation to repay debts by the agreed-upon time. On the other hand, one has an ethical obligation to deal fairly with one's clients, even if the obligation is not legally enforceable.

Obligation Bond In the United States, a municipal bond in which the face value is greater than the value of the property or project securing it. An obligation bond requires the issuing municipality to pledge its revenue to finish paying the bond. These bonds are intentionally designed this way and are used to compensate bondholders for any costs they incur that exceed the value of the project or purchase the bond is intended to finance.

Obligatory Expenditure A government outlay that the European Parliament is required to make in order to fulfill its responsibilities as a body of the European Union. For example, agricultural subsidies are considered obligatory because they are mentioned in the treaties, while payroll for EU employees is not because it is not mentioned specifically. Changes to obligatory expenditures require a majority vote of the total membership of Parliament. However, the difference between obligatory and non-obligatory expenditures is sometimes difficult to determine.

Obligee The party to an agreement to whom an obligation is owed. An obligation is a requirement, especially a legal one. For example, an investor may have a legal obligation to disclose his/her investments to the SEC. In this circumstance, the obligee is the SEC. See also: Obligor.

Obligor The party to an agreement who owes an obligation to another party. An obligation is a requirement, especially a legal one. For example, an investor may have a legal obligation to disclose his/her investments to the SEC. In this circumstance, the obligor is the investor. See also: Obligee.

Oblong Describing a book or publication that is bound by the short side. Most books are not oblong (that is, they are bound by the long side). However, coupon books are sometimes oblong to make coupon clipping easier.

Oblus A coin in ancient Greece. One drachma was subdivided into six obloi. One oblus was subdivided into eight chalkoi.

Oblysy In Kazakhstan, a political subdivision equivalent to a province.

Obol An ancient Greek unit of weight approximately equivalent to 0.72 or 1.05 grams, depending on the region.

Obolus An ancient Roman unit of weight approximately equivalent to 0.57 grams.

Obscene Mail Any mail the recipient deems to be inappropriate or abusive. Recipients of obscene mail may request that the post office not deliver mail similar to that which they believe to be obscene.

Observational Noise An error resulting from an inaccurate measurement. Many analysts use multiple indicators and multiple measurements of the same indicator to reduce observational noise as much as possible. It is also called measurement noise.

Obshtina In Bulgaria, a political subdivision equivalent to a municipal government.

Obsolescence The circumstance in which a good or service is no longer desired, especially when a new, better good or service becomes available. For example, relatively few people use VHS tapes because DVDs are both more convenient and are higher quality. VHS tapes, then, have undergone obsolescence. Some companies deliberately render their products obsolete because it makes customers more likely to come back and buy new products. See also: Planned obsolescence.

Obsolete 1. In numismatics, describing a coin that is no longer minted or no longer circulates. Obsolete coins may be valuable as collector's items, but they are illiquid assets. **2.** See: Obsolescence.

Obsolete Inventory Inventory that has not been sold to customers at the end of its useful life. A company writes off its obsolete inventory; because the company has not sold this inventory, it does not produce any revenue. Obsolete inventory can result in significant losses. Some investors look out for obsolete inventory because it can indicate either lack of demand for the company's product or poor inventory management.

Obverse In numismatics, the front of a coin; that is to say, the "heads" side. The obverse usually features a face of the head of state or some real or mythological national figure. The back of a coin is called the reverse.

Occupancy The state of living or maintaining an office in a designated building or portion thereof. For example, one who rents a house may take up occupancy on the first day of the lease.

Occupancy Rate The number of units in a building with renters, expressed as a percentage of all units. For example, an apartment building with 100 units and 40 resident families has a 40% occupancy rate. It is the opposite of the vacancy rate.

Occupant A person or company that lives or maintains an office in a designated building or portion thereof. For example, one who rents a house may become the occupant on the first day of the lease.

Occupant Mailing Direct mail sent to the person residing at an address. Occupant mailing has a low response rate.

Occupational Taxes Taxes and fees levied on particular jobs and businesses. A liquor license for a bar and a health permit for a restaurant are both examples of occupational taxes. In the United States, occupational taxes are assessed at the state and local levels and generally are flat fees.

Ocean Marine Exposure The risk that a good being transported over water will be lost or destroyed. For example, the buyer of such a good carries the risk that the ship will sink with the good on board or that damage from weather will render the good unusable. Most of the time either the buyer or the seller is required to purchase marine cargo insurance to protect against ocean marine exposure.

Ocean Marine Insurance, War Risks A rider to a marine insurancepolicy that protects the buyer of a good being transported over water from the loss of that good due to war. This form of marine insurance is important if there is a high likelihood of attack on the ship due to war. Standard marine insurance excludes war risks. See also: Incoterm.

Oceanian Pound A currency issued in British and Australian possessions occupied by Japan between 1942 and 1945. It was withdrawn from circulation after the end of World War II.

OCONUS Outside the Continental United States. OCONUS is used by the General Services Administration to determine the pay rates for U.S. government employees who are stationed outside the "lower 48."

Octet In computing, eight bits. An octet may be one byte; the terms are sometimes used interchangeably.

October Dinar A currency used in the former Yugoslavia. It was introduced in October 1993 to combat the reformed dinar's hyperinflation. This attempt failed and the January dinar replaced the October dinar at a ratio of 1 billion to one only a few months later.

October Effect A calendar effect in which the stock market declines in October. There is little evidence that the October effect is real, but some investors still fear it because the 1929 crash and the 1987 crash both occurred in October.

Octroi A local tax imposed upon a good when it is brought into a municipality for sale or consumption. Octroi taxes were common in medieval Europe and elsewhere, but by the early 21st century were used only in Ethiopia and parts of South Asia. Octrois are strongly associated with tax farming.

Odd Date In foreign exchange contracts, any date other than the expiration date. For example, if the expiration date is the 19th, an odd date is any date between the establishment of the contract and the 19th.

Odd Days Interest The interest that accrues on a loan during a period either longer or shorter than the normal period during which interest accrues. For example, if interest is usually compounded once a month, odd days interest may occur if the loan is made in middle of the month and two weeks of interest accrues at the beginning of the loan. Odd days interest is usually added to the first (or the next) payment.

Odd Lot A set of less than 100 shares. Most securities are traded in sets of 100, which are called round lots. An odd lot order may be difficult to fill because, for example, a broker trying to buy 36 shares may have a hard time finding another broker selling 36 shares or one selling 100 shares who is willing to partially fill the order with those 36. See also: Odd-Lotter.

Odd Lot Theory In technical analysis, the theory that odd-lotters (defined as small investors who deal in fewer than 100 shares at a time) are both badly informed and have low risk tolerance. Therefore, an investor may profit by doing the opposite of whatever odd-lotters are doing. For example, if a technical analyst sees that a substantial numbers of odd-lotters are selling a particular security, he/she may take this as an indicator to buy that security. The theory had some prominence in the 1960s and 1970s, but came under criticism later for lack of evidence that odd-lotters' investments underperformed the market as a whole. By the 1990s, the odd-lot theory had largely fallen into disuse, in part because of the growing popularity of mutual funds for small investors.

Oddity In numismatics, anything unusual about a coin. An oddity may have occurred during the minting process or at some point after, and may affect the value of a coin.

Odd-Lot Buy Back An offer by a publicly-traded company to buy shares in itself from odd-lotters, or those who buy and sell in portions of less than 100 shares.

Odd-Lot Dealer A dealer who buys and sells securities on his/her own account in portions smaller than 100 shares apiece. An odd-lot dealer may be a market maker for a given security on an exchange.

Odd-Lot Differential An extra commission or fee that a brokerage may assess for executing an odd-lot order. An odd-lot order is an order to buy or sell a security in a quantity other than some multiple of 100. It especially refers to orders for fewer than 100 shares. Odd-lot orders are difficult to match, and a brokerage may charge an extra fee for doing so. The differential may be waived at the brokerage's discretion or under certain circumstances.

Odd-Lot Order An order to buy or sell fewer than 100 shares of a security. Most securities are traded in sets of 100, which are called round lots. An odd lot order may be difficult to fill because, for example, a broker trying to buy 36 shares may have a hard time finding another broker selling 36 shares or one selling 100 shares who is willing to partially fill the order with those 36. See also: Odd-lotter.

Odd-Lot Resale A situation in which a publicly-traded company buys back its own shares from odd lot shareholders, repackages them as round lots, and resells them. Institutional investors are the most common buyers in odd-lot resales. Odd-lot resales save a company from the expense of a pure stock buyback, and also help make its shareholder records tidier.

Odd-Lot Sales Sales of securities in quantities of fewer than 100 shares. In general, most investors who make odd-lot sales are small investors. Because some investors consider small investors poorly informed and therefore wrong most of the time, they believe a large number of odd-lot sales may be a sign that stock prices will soon fall.

Odd-Lot Short Sales Short sales in quantities of fewer than 100 shares each. Generally speaking, one engages in short sales because one expects the price of a stock to fall. Likewise, most odd lotters are small investors. Because many investors consider small investors poorly informed and therefore wrong most of the time, they believe a large number of odd lot short sales may be a sign that stock prices will in fact rise.

Odd-Lot Short-Sale Ratio The number of odd-lot short sales as a percentage of total short sales over a given period. Odd-lot short sales are short sales in quantities of fewer than 100 shares each. Generally speaking, one engages in short sales because one expects the price of a stock to fall. Likewise most odd-lotters are small investors.

Because many investors consider small investors poorly informed and therefore wrong most of the time, they believe a high odd-lot short sale ratio may be a sign that stock prices will, in fact, rise.

Odd-Lotter An investor who deals in securities only occasionally, especially when he/she deals only in small quantities. Odd-lotters are also called (more formally) small investors. Odd-lot theory holds that odd-lotters are both poorly informed and risk averse; this theory encourages larger investors to do the opposite of whatever odd-lotters tend to be doing at a given time. This theory has little evidence to support it, and few have held it since the 1990s.

OEX Ticker symbol for the S&P 100. The S&P 100 is an index, weighted for market capitalization, of 100 blue chip stocks from a variety of industries. The stocks listed on the S&P 100 are the top 100 stocks on the S&P 500 by market capitalization. The S&P 100 was originally operated by the Chicago Board Options Exchange.

Off Center In numismatics, describing a coin on which a mistake was made in the striking such that the inscriptions are not centered properly. Because off center coins are somewhat unusual, they may be valuable, though they are illiquid assets.

Off the Books A payment for which no record is kept. Off the books payments may simply result from poor record keeping. However, the term connotes illegal or unethical payments. For example, a bribe may be kept off the books.

Off the Shelf 1. Describing goods in a store that are mass produced and are available for customers to purchase, usually at the retail level. Off the shelf items are not custom made. **2.** See: Shelf Registration.

Off Time The time during which a person is not required to work. Off time may include vacation time, sick days, or simply the time of day before and after work.

Off-Balance-Sheet Financing A type of company financing that does not appear as a liability on the company's balance sheet. A company may engage in off-balance-sheet financing if it wishes to keep its debt-equity ratio low and thereby appear as if it is carrying little debt. This, in turn, makes the company look more creditworthy than it would otherwise. A common form of off-balance-sheet financing is an operating lease, in which a company rents, rather than buys, a capital asset. In an operating lease, the company must record only the rental payments, and not the whole cost of the asset. While off-balance-sheet financing is permissible, it can become unsustainable and can hide a company's true financial state. The term came into common parlance when Enron collapsed in the wake of excessive off-balance-sheet financing. See also: Enron scandal.

Off-Board Trades on listed companies of the New York Stock Exchange that do not occur on the New York Stock Exchange. An off-board trade may occur on the NASDAQ, a regional exchange, an over-the-counter or anywhere else.

Off-Board Trade 1. The trade of a listed security on the over-the-counter market. An off-board trade avoids the commissions that must be paid to floor brokers. Most of the time, off-board trades are large block trades involving institutional investors. Dealers must attempt to fill orders on an exchange before offering them over-the-counter. See also: Rule 19c3. **2.** More generally, any over-the-counter trade.

Off-Budget Federal Entities Organizations under the jurisdiction of the United States federal government with budgets that are not included in the federal budget. That is, the revenue and outlays of off-budget federal entities are not considered when calculating the federal budget and whether it is in deficit or surplus. Currently, the United States Post Office and the Social Security trust fund are both off-budget federal entities.

Offensive Warfare A marketing strategy in which a company or product with the second or lower market share directly attempts to eclipse the market share of the largest company or product. For example, a company may lower its prices or expand into a previously untapped market. Offensive warfare differs from defensive warfare, in which the largest company or product tries to protect itself from smaller competitors.

Offer in Compromise A program whereby a person or company owing delinquent taxes asks the IRS to settle the debt for less than the full amount owed. In order to be eligible for an offer in compromise, the taxpayer must demonstrate some doubt that the assessed amount owed is correct, show some evidence that he/she will never be able to pay in full, and/or show that there are other circumstances, such as age or disability, that will hinder payment. See also: Form 433-A.

Offer Wanted An indication or announcement that an investor or broker-dealer wishes to buy a certain security at a certain price, especially when there are no current sellers. An OW is analogous to an offer, which is essentially the same thing from the seller's perspective. The price on an OW is called the bid.

Offered Market A market in which the number of sellers exceeds the number of buyers. That is, the supply of securities exceeds the demand to buy them. This generally is temporary as the price tends to decline until sellers and buyers equalize. See also: Bear market.

Offeree The person or company that receives an offer.

Offerer The person or company that makes an offer.

Offering 1. An issue of stock by a publicly-traded company. A company makes an offering through underwriters, who have the responsibility to place the offering with individual and institutional investors. Companies make offerings in order to raise financing for expanded operations, though occasionally they make offerings because they have become cash poor and need assistance to maintain current operations. The offerings themselves give investors a portion of ownership in the company issuing them. The first public offering a company issues is called an initial public offering, and marks the point when a company ceases to be privately held and becomes publicly traded. **2.** An issue of bonds. A company or government makes an offering through underwriters, who have the responsibility to place the offering with individual and institutional investors. Companies and governments make offerings in order to raise financing for expanded operations, though occasionally they make offerings because they have become cash poor and need assistance to maintain current operations. The bonds themselves represent debt that the company or government owes the investor.

Offering Circular An abbreviated prospectus detailing the structure and goals of an investment company such as a mutual fund. The SEC requires that investment companies file prospecti before issuing shares. These often contain a great deal of information that many investors do not need in order to make an investment decision. Generally speaking, offering circulars contain relevant information, such as the terms of purchase, the amount of the load (if any), the fund's investment strategy, and perhaps historical financial statements. See also: Greensheet.

Offering Price The price at which an investment, asset or other transaction is quoted to a potential buyer. That is, the offering price is what a potential seller is willing to take. It may or may not be negotiable.

Offering Statement A document filed with the SEC explaining a new issue of securities for public trade with a maturity of less than nine months. An offering statement is shorter than other registration statements and allows for an expedited process. This makes registration of new issues easier for the issuer. See also: Short-form registration.

Off-Floor Order An order to a broker to buy or sell a security in which the investor placing the order is not on the floor of the exchange. Specifically, the investor placing the order is not a market maker placing an order on his/her own account. Exchange rules require that off-floor orders be filled before identical on-floor orders.

Office Audit An IRS audit conducted at its own office. Office audits are not conducted in conjunction with the taxpayer because the matter at hand is thought to be relatively simple.

Office Burglary and Robbery Insurance An insurance policy providing coverage to a company or office building in case of robbery or other malfeasance. For example, if an office is vandalized or robbed, the insurance policy will pay for its losses. As with every policy, the policyholder pays a premium for office burglary and robbery insurance.

Office of Compliance Inspections and Examinations A division of the SEC that investigates and regulates broker-dealers, exchanges, mutual funds and other investment companies. Additionally, the Office is responsible for investment advisers and credit rating agencies.

Office of Defense Trade Controls A former office within the U.S. Department of State. It was responsible for ensuring the safety of weapons and similar materials as they were exported or temporarily imported. It was replaced by the Directorate of Defense Trade Controls in 2003.

Office of Foreign Asset Control An agency of the U.S. Treasury Department that enforces economic sanctions. It may freeze the assets of criminal and terrorist groups that are under American jurisdiction. Likewise, it ensures that countries with whom American companies may not trade do not receive U.S. products. It helps guarantee U.S. compliance with United Nations sanctions. OFAC was established during the Korean War. See also: Embargo.

Office of HM Paymaster General A department of the British government holding accounts at the Bank of England that appropriates funds for the various functions of government. That is, it is responsible for paying British departments and public servants. The office was created in 1836.

Office of Management and Budget A U.S. federal government office charged with preparing the budget and measuring the effectiveness of government programs. It was established in 1970.

Office of Thrift Supervision A bureau of the U.S. Department of the Treasury that regulates federal savings associations, savings and loan associations (thrifts), and some holding companies. Created in 1989 in the wake of the savings and loan crisis, the OTS both provides charters and creates regulations for thrifts and other institutions that fall under its supervision. Additionally, it audits the practices of financial institutions that specialize in personal savings and mortgage loans to ensure that they comply with applicable regulations. Based in Washington, D.C., the OTS also maintains offices in Jersey City, Atlanta, Dallas, Chicago, and San Francisco. See also: FIRREA.

Official Creditor A government or international organization that lends, especially to another government or international organization. A major example is the International Monetary Fund. The term is most common in international development.

Official Debt Debt owed to a government or international organization, especially debt owed by another government or international organization. A major example of a lender of official debt is the International Monetary Fund. The term is most common in international development.

Official Exchange Rate The pegged exchange rate as set by a government. An official exchange rate may be expressed with relation to a commodity such as gold, but currencies are usually pegged to other currencies. Depending on how well a government manages its currency, the official exchange rate may or may not reflect the currency's true value.

Official Notice of Sale 1. The announcement of a new issue of a municipal bond. An issuer gives official notice of sale when it seeks to attract underwriters to help it place the issue with investors. **2.** More broadly, any announcement of sale.

Official Rate 1. In foreign exchange, the exchange rate set by the local government. This especially applies to pegged currencies, but countries with floating currencies may also set an official exchange rate for a given day. **2.** The rate of inflation as set by the local government. Official rates of inflation may be accurate or not, depending on how they are calculated and whether political consideration influences the calculations.

Official Statement A statement that the issuer of a municipal bond makes before the issue takes place. The official statement describes the issuer and the bond. It is the equivalent of registration of a corporate bond.

Official Unrequited Transfer A voluntary transfer of money by a government in which little or nothing is expected in return. Examples of official unrequited transfers include foreign aid, debt forgiveness, and membership dues to an international organization.

Offlake In project finance, the act of purchasing the output of a project. This form of financing may be used in lieu of or in conjunction with a loan that must be repaid. It may be compared with accounts receivable financing.

Offset To change from a long position to a short position or from a short position to a long position. A long position is ownership of a security, while a short position is debt. Thus, to offset a long position is to sell a security, and to close a short position is to buy out the debt.

Offsetting Entry In accounting, an entry on a balance sheet that sets another entry to zero. The offsetting liability may be either an asset or a liability. For example, if a bank has an outstanding loan for $10,000 and receives a $10,000 payment, the payment is recorded as an offsetting entry on the bank's balancing sheet. See also: Offset.

Offshore Describing an institution, especially a bank, that exists in a foreign country. Colloquially, the term refers to institutions that exist in known tax havens. Individuals and companies use offshore accounts to avoid or evade taxes in their home countries. As a result, some emerging financial centers have objected to being called "offshore," asking for parity with the developed financial world.

Offshore Finance Subsidiary A wholly-owned subsidiary that exists in a foreign country, especially a tax haven. An offshore finance subsidiary issues stocks and bonds on behalf of the parent company outside the jurisdiction of the home country. The issues will therefore be subject to fewer regulations and perhaps also less scrutiny.

Offshore Financial Center 1. An institution, especially a bank that exists in a foreign country. Colloquially, the term refers to institutions that exist in known tax havens. Individuals and companies use offshore accounts to avoid or evade taxes. **2.** A country known for having a tax and legal system well-suited for offshore financial centers. A prominent example is the Bahamas.

Offshore Mutual Fund A mutual fund based outside the United States. Offshore mutual funds must comply with regulations in the countries in which they are registered, but need not comply with American regulations. Offshore mutual funds cannot be sold in the United States unless they comply with these regulations, but they may invest in U.S. securities.

Off-the-Run Issue A security for which a dealer does not provide bids and asks. See also: Run.

Off-the-Run Treasuries Any set of U.S. Treasury securities of a certain maturity except for the one most recently issued. For example, if the Treasury issues one year notes in May, June, and July, and it is now August, the off-the-run Treasuries are those issued in May and June. Off-the-run Treasuries are less actively traded than on-the-run Treasuries and as a result have a slightly higher yield.

OHLC Chart In charting, a chart showing the open, high, low, and close prices of a publicly traded security on a given day, with the time of day as the x-axis and the price as the y-axis. Tick marks on the chart then show the OHLC prices. Analyst use OHLC charts to attempt to track trends in securities, especially in the short term.

Ohm A Swedish unit of volume approximately equivalent to 150 liters.

Oil and Gas Drilling Limited Partnership A limited partnership between limited partners with limited liability and one or more general partners with unlimited liability, the purpose of which is to find and drill oil or gas from the ground. The general partner uses the investment money from the limited partners to drill in for oil or gas; the typical partnership unit for a limited partner costs $5,000, and the limited partner risks no more than this investment. There are two types of oil and gas drilling limited partnerships. A development oil and gas drilling limited partnership provides for drilling only in places with proven reserves, providing the limited partners with low risk and a steady return. An exploratory oil and gas drilling limited partnership provides for drilling in places without proven reserves, searching for previously undiscovered reserves. This latter carries higher risk, but also the possibility of an extraordinarily high return if a large reserve is discovered.

Oil and Gas Income Limited Partnership A limited partnership between limited partners with limited liability and one or more general partners with unlimited liability, the purpose of which is to purchase oil or gas-producing properties or royalties generated from such a properties. The general partner uses the investment money from the limited partners to buy the properties or royalties; the typical partnership unit for a limited partner costs $5,000, and the limited partner risks no more than this investment. See also: Oil and gas drilling limited partnership.

Oitava A Portuguese measure of weight approximately equivalent to 3.59 grams. It became obsolete after Lusophone countries adopted the metric system in the 19th century.

Okka A Turkish measure of weight approximately equivalent to 1.28 kilograms. It became obsolete when Turkey made the metric system mandatory in 1933.

Okres In the Czech Republic and Slovakia, a political subdivision roughly equivalent to a county.

Okrug In Russia and several other Slavic countries, a political subdivision roughly equivalent to a district or county.

Okruzi In Serbia, a political subdivision approximately equivalent to a county.

Okshoofd An obsolete Dutch unit of volume roughly equivalent to 232 liters.

Okun's Law A theory stating that for every 1% increase in the unemployment rate, a country or region loses 2.5% potential GDP growth. See also: GDP.

Ol A Danish unit of 80.

Old Economy The universe of companies and industries that experienced a tremendous amount of growth in the first part of the 20th century, but have since slowed down with the advent of technology companies. Examples of members of the old economy include the steel, automobile, and energy industries. It is important to note that the old economy is still relevant, with most old economy industries representing thousands of jobs and a significant proportion of GDP.

Old Krona The former currency of Iceland. It was introduced in 1874 and was identical to the Danish krone until around 1918. It was revalued in 1981 at a ratio of 100 old kronur to one new krona.

Old Lady of Threadneedle Street A nickname for the Bank of England. The term is derived from a woman named Sarah Whitehead, who, after her brother's execution for forgery, went to the Bank of England every day to ask to see him. After her death in the mid-1800s, she was buried in a field that later became the Bank's garden. She is said to haunt the Bank.

Old Macedonian Denar The former currency of Macedonia. It was issued in 1992, replacing the Yugoslav dinar at a one-to-one ratio. A year later, the new denar replaced it at a ratio of 100 old denars to one new denar.

Old Sheqel The currency of Israel between 1980 and 1985. It suffered from high inflation throughout its history and was replaced by the new sheqel as a result.

Oles A Tatar unit of weight approximately equivalent to 44.43 milligrams. It was rendered obsolete when the Soviet Union began to use the metric system in 1924.

Oligopoly A situation in which a small number of companies split all or nearly all the market share of a good or service. There are two major models for oligopoly: the Cournot model and the Bertrand model. In the Cournot model, each company assumes the output of the others, resulting in greater output than in a monopoly but less than in a state of perfect competition. This pushes prices lower but not as low as they would be in perfect competition. In the Bertrand model, the companies compete for the lowest possible price, resulting in perfect competition. Both models are applicable in different situations and times and neither expresses oligopoly perfectly. Less commonly, a third option is possible: if the companies in the oligopoly openly collude with each other, they can form a cartel.

Oligopsony A market in which there are only a few, very large buyers. Sellers in an oligopsony may have difficulty remaining in business as the buyers have a great deal of power to dictate prices. This may affect both the profit margin and other factors, such as labor conditions or wages. It is the opposite of an oligopoly.

OM 1. ISO 3166-1 alpha-2 code for the Sultanate of Oman. This is the code used in international transactions to and from Omani bank accounts. **2.** ISO 3166-2 geocode for Oman. This is used as an international standard for shipping to Oman. Each Omani governate has its own code with the prefix "OM." For example, the code for the Governate of Muscat is ISO 3166-2:OM-MA.

OM Stockholm AB A derivatives exchange in Sweden. Founded in the 1980s, it was the first exchange where standardized option contracts were traded. It acquired the Stockholm Stock Exchange in 1998. See also: OMX.

Omani Rial The currency of Oman. It was introduced in 1973, replacing the rial Saidi, which had replaced the Gulf rupee. It is pegged to the U.S. dollar.

Omavalitsus In Estonia, a political subdivision equivalent to a municipality.

Omega A measure of the change in price of an option relative to a percentage change in the price of the underlying asset. For example, if an option contract has an omega of 3.5, its price increases 3.5% for every 1% of change in the price of the underlying. Omega is also known as speed. It is calculated as a derivative of the option's gamma. See also: Delta, Volatility.

Omitted Dividend A dividend that a company would have ordinarily declared and paid but decided against doing so. For example, if a company ordinarily pays a dividend each March but decides not to do so in March 2010, that dividend is said to be omitted. A company usually omits a dividend when it is experiencing financial difficulties and wishes to keep the cash that would have gone to pay the dividend to maintain its operations. An omitted dividend is also called a passed dividend.

OMN GOST 7.67 Latin three-letter geocode for Oman. The code is used for transactions to and from Omani bank accounts and for international shipping to Oman. As with all GOST 7.67 codes, it is used primarily in Cyrillic alphabets.

Omnibus Account In futures and options, an account that one broker holds with another in which all of the first broker's sub-accounts are combined under one heading and traded in that broker's name.

Omnibus Budget Reconciliation Act of 1993 Legislation in the United States that raised taxes and cut some government spending in order to reduce the federal deficit. It cut spending on entitlement programs by $42 billion while creating higher tax brackets for some wealthy individuals and corporations. The Act came out of a theory that large deficits lead to inflation; this theory was rejected by both New Deal liberals and supply-side economics conservatives, both of whom believed that deficits are relatively unimportant. While the theory behind the Act remains controversial, it led to a projected budget surplus toward the end of the 1990s.

Omnibus Foreign Trade and Competitiveness Act of 1988 Legislation in the United States requiring the president to investigate countries with more than a 10% trade surplus with respect to the U.S. It further calls for the president to take steps to reduce that trade surplus by 10%. The Act was intended to promote American exports.

OMR ISO 4217 code for the Omani rial. It was introduced in 1973, replacing the rial Saidi, which had replaced the Gulf rupee. It is pegged to the U.S. dollar.

On a Clean Up Describing a trade where one buys or seeks to buy all of the remaining securities in a block or, more generally, any securities that remain following an earlier trade. That is, one is on a clean up if one seeks to buy the leftovers from a previous trade that the seller was unable to sell to other investors.

On Balance 1. In equities, the state of trade in which there are a roughly equal number of buy orders and sell orders on a given trading day. This indicates stability in the market. See also: Imbalance of orders. **2.** Leftover buy and sell orders that are dealt with either before or after the trading day. In this situation, brokers attempt to find a buyer or seller for the on balance equity.

On Board 1. Informal for a long position. **2.** Informal; describing a situation where goods have been loaded onto the vessel used to carry them to the destination. The term is used on a bill of lading.

On Carriage In international commerce, costs coming from the delivery of a good after it has arrived in the buyer's country. For example, an exporter in Ireland may sell Waterford crystal to a buyer in Oklahoma. The crystal may be shipped to a port in New Jersey and then carried by train to Oklahoma. The on carriage costs are those resulting from the train ride to Oklahoma. Whether the buyer or seller is responsible for on carriage costs depends on the agreement between them. See also: Incoterm.

On Jacket In publishing, describing text or an image on the outside of a book, especially on the dust jacket of a hardcover.

On the Dole A term describing one who relies on welfare or other forms of support from the state. Being on the dole may mean one receives food stamps, direct cash payments or, in rare cases, it may refer to government-sponsored medical care. The term is more common in British and Commonwealth countries than in the United States, and its use may be derogatory, depending on the context.

On the Money In equities, a term describing an ask price equal to the price of the previous sale of a security. For example, if one buys a security at $35 per share, and re-sells it at the same price, such a sale is considered to be "on the money." Obviously, no profit or loss results from on the money sales.

On the Run The most recently issued bond in a series of government bonds that have a given maturity. On the run securities are usually the most liquid of the securities in the same range.

On the Sidelines Describing investors who believe that the markets are excessively volatile to risk their money. They therefore keep their money in short-term, low-risk investments until the markets are perceived to have calmed down. Investors on the sidelines usually have lower risk tolerance than investors to keep their money in the markets during these times.

On the Take 1. Describing a situation in which a stock price moves upward because more potential buyers are taking offers. The offers are then replaced by higher offers. **2.** Describing a person who accepts bribes or other forms of illegal or unethical monetary transfers.

On the Tape Describing a trade recorded on a ticker tape.

On Track 1. Describing the delivery of a futures contract on a commodity in which the seller must deliver to a location specified by the buyer. In an on track delivery, the buyer must pay all delivery costs. **2.** Describing a commodity that is loaded onto a means of delivery, especially a train or a truck, in the process of being transferred from the seller to the buyer.

On-Balance Volume In technical analysis, a measure of the amount of money going into or out of a given security. It is calculated by comparing a security's volume to its price over a given time. Technical analysts use on-balance volume to determine a security's momentum. A change in the on-balance volume indicates a coming change in the security's overall trend.

Onca A Portuguese measure of weight approximately equivalent to 28.69 grams. It became obsolete after Lusophone countries adopted the metric system in the 19th century.

One Night Stand Investment The purchase of a security with the intent of holding it, but changing one's mind and selling the next day. In other words, a one night stand investor is a failed value investor. The sale is usually made after the security's price unexpectedly drops in the wake of bad news.

One-Cancel-All Order An order to a broker that consists of several limit orders. When one of the limit orders is filled, the others are all canceled. This gives an investor (and indeed the broker) a great deal of flexibility to buy or sell one of several securities at the best available price.

One-Cancels-the-Other Order An order to conduct two transactions such that, if one transaction is done, then the other is cancelled. For example, an investor may wish to buy both stocks and bonds at a certain price. If the price becomes available for bonds first, that part of the order is filled while the order to buy stocks is cancelled. OCO orders may apply to different types of securities or even to different types or orders; for example, one may contain both stop-loss orders and limit orders. OCO orders are useful to investors who have limited funds and perhaps are unsure about the market's direction at a given time. It is also called an either-or order.

OneChicago LLC An electronic exchange specializing in futures contracts, narrow based indices, and exchange-traded funds. A unique feature of OneChicago is the presence of lead market makers, who are assigned to individual contracts and ensure that a two-sided market exists continuously for the contracts assigned to them. It is a joint venture of the IB Exchange Board, Chicago Board Options Exchange and the CME Group; the memberships for each of these exchanges are reciprocal for OneChicago.

One-Decision Stock A stock that an investor buys and holds. That is, once an investor makes the one decision to buy the stock, he does not need to make a second decision to sell. One-decision stocks usually have strong fundamentals and/or growth potential. They can be illiquid, but they are nonetheless often solid investments. See also: Value investing.

One-Man Picture A situation in which a single broker provides both the bid and the offer for a security.

Oner In the United Kingdom, a slang term for 100 or 1,000 pounds.

One-Share-One-Vote Rule A rule in which each common share in a publicly-traded company represents one vote at meetings of shareholders. That is, two persons each holding one share have one vote each. However, one person who holds two shares has two votes. Nearly all publicly-traded companies follow the one-share-one-vote rule.

One-Stop Shop A company that offers a wide variety of goods and/or services to a customer or client. For example, a retail store may sell everything from clothes to groceries to home appliances to electronics. Likewise, a bank may offer a client a checking account, investment advisory services, and insurance. One-stop shops aim to attract customers and clients by allowing them to save the time and energy they would otherwise spend going to different companies for different activities.

One-Way Market A market in which there are only potential buyers or potential sellers, but not both. That is, quotes for a one-way market only have a bid or an ask price. One-way markets are, by their nature, illiquid, and, on most exchanges, dealers and/or market makers exist to prevent them from forming. However, regulations sometimes require a one-way market to form, at least temporarily. For example, some countries forbid the resale of an IPO for a certain period of time.

On-Floor Order An order to buy or sell a security made by a member firm on the trading floor. On-floor orders may be made when an exchange has an open outcry system. Off-floor orders have priority over on-floor orders.

Onion Futures Act Legislation in the United States, passed in 1958, that prohibited the trade of futures contracts on onions. The Act resulted from protests from onion farmers that price manipulation on the futures markets was causing unsustainably low prices, hurting their earnings. The Act represented the first time the United States banned a commodity from trading entirely. Scholars disagree as to whether the Act increased or decreased volatility in the onion market.

Online Banking Banking services offered over the Internet. Online banking often includes access to one's checking and savings accounts, the ability to view balances, and so forth. Many banks (though not all) offer online banking without any additional fees.

Online Brokerage Firm A company or division of a company that offers brokerage services over the Internet. One manages one's online brokerage account by giving orders online, which the brokerage then fills. One may also settle transactions electronically, though clients usually have an option to mail a check to the firm. Online brokerage firms usually charge lower commissions than other brokerages, but do not provide individual investment advisory services.

Online Trading The act or practice of buying and selling securities over the Internet. Generally speaking, online trading occurs when an investor makes an order to a broker online; the broker then executes the order through the ordinary means. Online trading became more common in the 1990s as more brokerages offered their services online, often for a small fee rather than a commission on the trade. Online trading should be distinguished from electronic trading, which occurs on an exchange. See also: Discount brokerage.

Ons An obsolete Dutch unit of weight roughly equivalent to 30 grams, with slight regional variations.

On-the-Run Treasuries The most recently issued set of U.S. Treasury securities with a certain maturity. For example, if the Treasury issues one year notes in May, June, and July, and it is now August, the on-the-run Treasuries are those issued in July. On-the-run Treasuries are the most actively traded Treasury securities and as a result have a slightly lower yield than off-the-run Treasuries.

Onus of Good Faith In insurance, the requirement that the insured party take necessary precautions to prevent further losses after a loss has taken place. For example, if an insured vase is chipped, the policyholder has the onus of good faith not to shatter it deliberately. The onus of good faith may reduce the amount the insurer must pay.

Opcina 1. In Bosnia and Herzegovina, a political subdivision equivalent to a municipality. **2.** In Croatia, a political subdivision equivalent to a rural township.

OPD On a ticker tape, a symbol indicating that the trade being reported is the opening trade. It is especially used when the trade is being reported late or when there has been a significant price movement from the closing price of the previous trading day.

Open 1. The time trading begins on an exchange. This is important to matters like a security's opening price or opening bid. See also: Close. **2.** An order to buy or sell a security that has not yet been filled. Some orders are only open for a certain amount of time, while some remain open until they are filled. See also: IOC, GTC.

Open Account 1. See: Credit sale. **2.** Any account where money is held or is owed. That is, a bank account with a $1,000 credit and another account with a $1,000 overdraft are both open accounts because they have non-zero balances.

Open Bid A bid in which the bidder may change the amount offered. For example, suppose a construction company makes an open bid to complete a project for $150,000. If a competing company makes a bid for $130,000, the first company reserves the right to revise its bid downward in hope of being awarded the contract.

Open Book A situation in which a bank's liabilities have a shorter term (on average) than its assets. This indicates that it may not be able to meet its obligations when the time comes. It is also called an unmatched book or a short book.

Open Box 1. The physical location where a brokerage keeps securities being held as collateral on loans. Open boxes are used for collateral on margin accounts and other transactions. See also: Free box. **2.** Collateral used to secure funds borrowed on a margin account. A margin account allows an investor to buy securities with money borrowed from a broker; the funds are payable on demand of the broker. They also must be secured by an open box, which usually consists of securities owned by the borrower. The "box" refers to a safe where the stock and bond certificates are kept until the margin account is paid off. An open box in this sense is also called an active box.

Open Cheque A check that must be paid upon presentation at the drawee bank. It contrasts with a crossed check.

Open Contracts Futures, forwards, and other contracts that have not expired. This means that the underlying asset has not changed hands, and the holder of the contract may sell it on the open market.

Open Distribution The sale or other distribution of a good by multiple dealers in the same geographic area.

Open Economy An economy in which participants are permitted to buy and sell goods and services with other countries. The GDP of open economies includes exports (which add to GDP) and imports (which subtract). Some very open economies have few or no trade restrictions such as tariffs, but this is rare in practice. Nearly every economy in the world is an open economy to a greater or lesser extent.

Open Inflation A situation in which the prices of consumer goods rise consistently. Open inflation may not indicate a drop in the value of currency; instead, it may indicate a real rise in the value of consumer goods. An example of open inflation is a situation in which food and gas prices rise, but home prices, car prices, and art prices remain flat or drop.

Open Interest 1. The options or futures contracts that an investor has not closed and that have not matured or expired. For example, if an investor buys 10 futures contracts on Monday, and sells six on Wednesday, the investor has an open interest of four at the end of the trading day on Wednesday. It should not be confused with the trading volume for an option or futures contract. **2.** The number of orders to buy a security made before the beginning of a trading day.

Open Listing In real estate, a situation in which multiple agents list the same house or property. The agent able to sell the property collects the commission. An open listing often occurs when the homeowner needs to sell the property quickly or when the property is otherwise difficult to sell.

Open on the Print A situation where a block trader has bought or sold short a large block of securities and had this trade printed on the ticker tape. When a trade is open on the print, the block trader officially has taken a long or short position, which opens him/her up to orders from other investors to close the position.

Open Outcry A system of trading on an exchange in which members stand on the trading floor and make orders to each other by crying aloud. Some open outcry systems have developed special sign languages so they can make and fill orders without needing to be heard over the noise on the trading floor. All exchanges were originally open outcry, but many have gradually shifted toward electronic trading.

Open Policy In maritime commerce, an insurance policy stating that the insurer is responsible for partial losses on the value of the covered products without stating what is specifically covered. Sometimes open policies include a deductible and sometimes they do not. Depending on the amount of the deductible, the insurer of an open policy will be liable for losses if some of the products break in transit, regardless of the reason. See also: WPA.

Open Position Any position that has not been closed. For example, an open long position is the state in which an investor owns a security and has not sold it.

Open Price The first price of a security at the beginning of a trading day.

Open Repo A practice in which a bank or other financial institution buys securities with the proviso that the seller repurchases the same securities for an agreed-upon price on an unspecified day. Because the date is unspecified, either party could end the arrangement at any time. Investors and financial institutions do this in order to raise short-term capital. Interest rates are higher on open repos than on overnight repos to compensate for the uncertainty on how long the arrangement will last.

Open Unemployment Unemployment compensation without limit. That is, open unemployment continues to be paid to unemployed persons until they find a new job or qualify for the state pension (that is, until they reach retirement age). Open unemployment is available in several European countries. Proponents call open unemployment a necessary part of human dignity, while critics contend that it encourages wastefulness and is ultimately unsustainable.

Open Up To provide full disclosure. That is, opening up involves stating a specific price or terms upon request from another party.

Open-End Indenture A provision in an indenture stating that the collateral securing the bond may also secure other bond issues. An open-end indenture means that the issuer may use the same collateral on multiple issues, which increases the number of claims on the collateral in the event of default. As a result, a secured bond with an open-end indenture carries more risk than a secured bond with a closed-end indenture, which allows only one collateral per issue.

Open-End Investment Company Primarily in the United Kingdom, a mutual fund in which the number of shares may be increased or decreased depending on the amount of money invested in the company. This means that the fund's capitalization is not fixed, and changes upon the demand of shareholders. In other words, an open-end investment company issues new stock when people invest in it, and buys back old shares when investors want to be rid of them. The latter is referred to as redeeming one's share of the mutual fund. The value of each share is the net portfolio value divided by the number of shares. In the United States, this investment vehicle is usually called an open-end mutual fund.

Open-End Mortgage In real estate, a mortgage in which the principal amount may be increased. That is, further borrowing is permitted using the same property as collateral. See also: Closed-End Mortgage.

Open-End Mutual Fund A mutual fund in which the number of shares may be increased or decreased depending on the amount of money invested in the company. This means that the fund's capitalization is not fixed and changes upon the demand of shareholders. In other words, an open-end mutual fund issues new stock when people invest in it and buys back old shares when investors want to be rid of them. The latter is referred to as redeeming one's share of the mutual fund. The value of each share is the net portfolio value divided by the number of shares. In the United Kingdom, this investment vehicle is usually called an open-end investment company.

Opening 1. The beginning of a trading session on an exchange. **2.** The first price of a security at the beginning of a trading day. In this sense, the opening is also called the opening price.

Opening Automated Reporting Service A computerized system on an exchange that allows specialists to detect order imbalances before the opening of the exchange. That is, OARS lets specialists know how many extra buy or sell orders exist for a given security. This helps in determining the opening price.

Opening Balance The amount of funds in an account at the beginning of a period, especially a month or year. For example, if one has a bank account with a balance of $1236 at the end of August, this becomes the opening balance for the beginning of September.

Opening Bell A traditional bell that is rung to signify the beginning of a trading day. The opening bell on the New York Stock Exchange is one of the more famous examples. As an increasing number of securities exchanges do most or all their trading online, a bell has become a symbol or informal term for the beginning of a trading day rather than a description of a real bell. See also: Closing Bell.

Opening Range The highest bid and the lowest offer made on an exchange traded security during the period immediately after the opening. The opening range is closely related to the opening price.

Opening Sale When creating a position of several option contracts, the first transaction that creates a short position for the investor. See also: Opening purchase, Write.

Opening Transaction 1. In options contracts, the transaction which starts either a long position or a short position. For example, if an investor writes a put option and then later exercises the option, the initial writing of the option contract is referred to as the opening transaction and its exercise is the closing transaction, because it closes a position. The opening transaction is thus an investor's first trade in a series of at least two related trades. **2.** The first trade on a given security on a given trading day. This especially refers to the price at which the security is traded. Investors like to know the price of the opening transaction because it gives them a comparison to the prices of the previous trading day, which helps them attempt to predict short-term trends. It is also important to investors who placed orders for a security after the close of the previous trading day: the price of the opening transaction is the price the investors will pay or be paid.

Open-Market Operations The buying and selling of U.S. Treasury securities. The Federal Reserve conducts open market operations as a primary way of influencing inflation and economic growth. These securities are sold at certain interest rates as a way of controlling the money supply. See also: FOMC.

Open-Market Purchase The act of buying a security at or close to the market price because of an order the buyer has placed for the security. The term especially refers to a situation where investors with inside information buy a security in accordance with the rules set forth by the SEC. See also: Open-market transaction.

Open-Market Purchase Operation 1. The practice of a central bank buying government-issued securities in order to control the money supply. When a central bank begins buying back previously issued debt, it indicates that the central bank believes that there is too much money in circulation, causing inflationary pressure. It buys these securities in order to reduce the amount of money circulating. While this eases inflation, it can reduce the economic growth rate. An open-market purchase operation is usually accompanied by an increase in target interest rates. **2.** The act or practice of buying securities or other assets in fair competition with other potential buyers.

Open-Market Rates Interest rates determined by the prevailing supply and demand for money rather than according to some benchmark, such as LIBOR, or by some government organization, such as the Federal Reserve.

Open-Market Transaction A transaction in which a person with inside information on a company buys or sells that company's stocks after filing all pertinent forms with the SEC. An open-market transaction is the only legal way for an insider to trade on a company without committing the crime of insider trading. In an open-market transaction, the insider makes the transaction as close to the market price as possible.

Operating Cash Flow A ratio of a company's cash flow to either its net income or operating income. The latter ratio provides a more accurate description of a company's profit, while the former takes into account the effects of non-operation transactions on income. Operating cash flow shows the difference, if any, between a company's reported income and actual cash on hand.

Operating Cash Flow Ratio A ratio of a company's operating cash flow to current liabilities. Operating cash flow is a measure of how much cash a company has on hand, while current liabilities show expenses it must pay in the near future. The operating cash flow ratio thus shows a company's ability to meet these liabilities without having to sell assets or take any similar actions.

Operating Company A company that makes a good or provides a service that it then sells to customers or clients. An operating company contrasts with a holding company whose main function is to own other companies.

Operating Cycle The time between the purchase of an asset and its sale, or the sale of a product made from the asset. Most companies desire short operating cycles because it creates cash flow to cover the company's liabilities. A long operating cycle often necessitates borrowing and thereby reduces profitability.

Operating Expenses A company's expenses related to the production of its goods and services. Examples of operating expenses include wages for employees, research and development, and costs of raw materials. Operating expenses do not include taxes, debt service, or other expenses inherent to the operation of a business but unrelated to production. See also: Operating income.

Operating Exposure The extent to which a company is exposed to exchange risk and inflation risk. That is, operating exposure is the exposure to the risk that a change in an exchange rate or the inflation rate will negatively impact a company's revenue.

Operating in the Red Describing a business that continues operations while losing money. A business may continue to operate in the red due to the extension of a loan or credit line, or because of cash flows that exist despite losses. Obviously, a company can only operate in the red for a certain period of time before making a profit or declaring bankruptcy.

Operating Income A company's income from the goods and services it provides, less its operating expenses and depreciation. The operating income does not include losses from interest payments or income tax. For example, a widget manufacturer earns $1,000,000 in gross revenue from the sale of widgets. The widgets cost $200,000 to make and his administrative and payroll expenses total $250,000. He also must subtract $50,000 in depreciation on his widget manufacturing equipment. His operating income is stated as: $1,000,000 - $200,000 - $250,000 - $50,000 = $500,000. Operating income is closely related to earnings before interest and taxes (EBIT), but EBIT includes nonoperating income, which is usually (but not always) significantly less than operating income. See also: Net income.

Operating Lease A lease in which the lessee maintains residence or usufruct of the leased property or asset while the lessor may claim a tax deduction on depreciation. For example, if one rents an apartment for a certain period of time and the lessor repossesses the apartment at the end of the lease, is a common example of an operating lease. See also: Off-balance-sheet financing.

Operating Leverage The level to which a company is dependent on sales of individual products. That is, a company with only a few sales has a high operating leverage because it must use these few sales to pay its operating expenses. On the other hand, a company with many sales has a low operating leverage and may therefore sell more or fewer products without it affecting its profitability as much.

Operating Loss The state in which a company's operating expenses exceed its income for a given period of time, usually a quarter or a year. A company can carry back or carry forward operating losses for a certain number of years, reducing the company's tax liability. This is positive, but an operating loss still means that the company is losing money, which cannot be sustained over the long term.

Operating Rate The percentage of capacity being utilized. For example, if a factory has a 60% operating rate, it is making 60% of the goods it is capable of making with its present equipment. Companies, government and economies all have operating rates.

Operating Ratio A ratio of a company's operating expenses to its sales or revenue. A lower operating ratio is considered ideal because it indicates that, in the event of a decline in sales or revenue, a company will maintain profitability. Most firms desire an operating ratio below 0.80.

Operating Reserves Money that an organization appropriates in case budgeted operating expenses are insufficient to cover actual expenses. Operating reserves are used for fiscal conservatism.

Operating Revenue The revenue a company receives in the course of its normal operations. Examples include sales and commissions, as well as other things that may vary according to the time of business. Importantly, operating revenue on a balance sheet reflects only ordinary revenue rather than unexpected, one-time income. One subtracts the operating expense from operating revenue to determine the operating profit.

Operating Risk Risk from sources other than inadequate funding (credit risk) or a change in market factors (market risk). Basel II defines operating risk as the "risk of loss resulting from inadequate or failed internal processes, people and systems or from external events." Thus, operating risk may come from mundane sources such as incompetent personnel or miscommunication between a buyer and a seller, or it may stem from events beyond a firm's control, such as terrorism, damage to goods in transport, or even a sudden drop in demand. Because it is not (primarily) financial, it is the most difficult type of risk to quantify. Sometimes, operating risks are predictable; for example, a farmer can prepare for a drought that would harm his/her harvest and therefore profits. On the other hand, risk from an employee's fraud is often impossible to anticipate. Consultancies often offer operating risk management, identifying and attempting to eliminate it as much as possible. See also: Political risk, Reputational risk.

Operating Unit A subsidiary that engages in business with other parties. That is, an operating unit has its own assets and liabilities and functions as if it were an independent company; the only difference is that it is owned by another company. An operating unit is useful for the profit it can produce. It contrasts with a nonoperating unit.

Operation Iraqi Freedom The official United States military name for the war between the U.S. and its allies and Saddam Hussein's Iraq and later various insurgent groups. Operation Iraqi Freedom removed Saddam Hussein, Iraq's dictator, from power. However, it created a significant power vacuum, which led to high levels of violence. Economically, it disrupted Iraq's oil production during a period of time in which oil prices quadrupled. Operation Iraqi Freedom lasted from 2003 to 2011; it was controversial both in the United States and abroad.

Opinion Shopping The act or practice of a company looking for an auditor who is likely to give an undeservedly good report on that company's financial health. The company may opinion shop for an auditor with unscrupulous ethics or perhaps who is simply not very good. Opinion shopping is illegal and as a result some analysts raise questions when a company suddenly changes its auditor.

Opportunities and Risks The potential gain and loss of all the investments a person or company is able to make at a given point in time. One investigates potential opportunities and risks and the likelihood of each to occur when making investment decisions. See also: Investment opportunity set.

Opportunity Cost of Capital The difference in return between an investment one makes and another that one chose not to make. This may occur in securities trading or in other decisions. For example, if a person has $10,000 to invest and must choose between Stock A and Stock B, the opportunity cost is the difference in their returns. If that person invested $10,000 in Stock A and received a 5% return while Stock B makes a 7% return, the opportunity cost is 2%. One way of conceptualizing opportunity cost is as the amount of money one could have made by making a different investment decision. Importantly, opportunity cost is not a type of risk because there is not a chance of actual loss.

Opportunity Set The set of all possible portfolios that one may construct from a given set of assets. One may construct both high- and low-risk portfolios from an opportunity set. Presenting an investor with an opportunity set may help him/her in making investment decisions. According to Markowitz Portfolio Theory, all things being equal, an investor will choose a portfolio with the highest possible return at the level of risk he/she is able to accept.

Opstina In Russia and several other Slavic countries, a political subdivision equivalent to a municipal government.

Optimal Contract A contract that minimizes cost to the lowest possible level for all parties.

Optimal Portfolio A Markowitz efficient portfolio that best fits one's personal risk preference. A Markowitz efficient portfolio is the portfolio that has the highest possible potential return at a given level of risk. Thus, an optimal portfolio is the portfolio that considers the investor's own greed and/or how risk averse he/she is. A key difference between a Markowitz efficient portfolio and an optimal portfolio is the fact that, while a Markowitz efficient portfolio can be determined mathematically, an optimal portfolio is subjective.

Optimized Portfolio as Listed Securities An exchange traded index created by Morgan Stanley that closely tracks a single index without purchasing all the securities listed on that index. The value of OPALS is the aggregate value of the underlying securities. In this sense, they operate like a portfolio of securities, rather than a fund. They are marketed primarily to institutional investors.

Optimum Capacity The number of units a company can manufacture at the lowest possible cost. Generally speaking, a company is said to have reached optimum capacity when the cost of the production of one additional unit is equal to the average cost for every unit.

Optimum Leverage Ratio The debt-asset ratio that allows a company to achieve the highest possible return without taking on excessive risk. The optimum leverage ratio minimizes the cost of capital without acquiring a high possibility of default.

Option A contract in which the writer (seller) promises that the contract buyer has the right, but not the obligation, to buy or sell a certain security at a certain price (the strike price) on or before a certain expiration date, or exercise date. The asset in the contract is referred to as the underlying asset, or simply the underlying. An option giving the buyer the right to buy at a certain price is called a call, while one that gives him/her the right to sell is called a put. Options contracts are used both in speculative investments, in which the option holder believes he/she can secure a price much higher (or lower) than the fair market value of the underlying on the expiration date. For example, one may purchase a call option to buy corn at a low price, expecting the price of corn to rise significantly by the time the option is exercised. The investors may then buy the corn at the agreed-upon low price and instantly resell it for a tidy profit. Cases in which the option holder is correct are called in the money options, while cases in which the market moves in the opposite direction of the speculation are called out of the money. Like all speculative investing, this is a risky venture. Other investors use option contracts for a completely different purpose: to hedge against market movements that would cause their other investments to lose money. For example, the same corn investor may buy the commodity at fair market value with the hope of the price rising. He/she may then buy a put contract at a high price in case the price of corn declines. This will limit his/her risk: if the price of corn falls, the investor has the option to sell at a high price, and, if the price of corn rises (especially higher than the strike price of the option), then he/she will choose not to exercise the option. See also: Futures, Forward Sales.

Option Account A brokerage account where the brokerages permit the account holder to hold options. The extra risks of option trading entail more regulation. As a result, the holder of a brokerage account must be provided material detailing these risks and sign an option disclosure document before his/her account may become an option account.

Option Adjusted Spread In fixed-income securities with embedded options, the yield spread between two securities calculated as if the embedded options do not exist. Different models calculate the OAS slightly differently, but the basic equation is rendered as: OAS = yield spread - spread due to the options This is important in complex derivatives such as mortgage-backed securities. See also: Black-Scholes Model.

Option Agreement An agreement that many investors must make with a brokerage in order to trade in options with that brokerage. The option agreement ensures that the investor has enough financial resources and is sufficiently familiar with the parameters of option trading in order to make sound and legal investment decisions.

Option Chain A listing of quotes for an option organized according by security. For example, given stock X, an option chain lists all prices, strike prices, calls, and puts for that stock.

Option Cycle A series of option contracts with the same terms that expire successively. Generally speaking, an option cycle includes one and only one contract in each quarter. Common option cycles are JAJO (January, April, July, and October), FMAN (February, May, August, and November), and MJSD (March, June, September, and December).

Option Disclosure Document A document that an investor must read and sign before his/her brokerage account can become an option account, or one that is allowed to hold options. The option disclosure document is issued by the Options Clearing Corporation and describes different kinds of options, along with the risks associated with them and tax implications.

Option Elasticity The change in a price of an option given a 1% change in the price of the underlying asset. This price is likely to change more if the option is near-the-money than if it is deep-in-the-money or deep-out-of-the-money. See also: Volatility.

Option Exchange A securities exchange that primarily or exclusively trades option contracts. Often, options are traded on an exchange along with futures and other derivatives. However, some exchanges, like the CBOE, specialize in option transactions.

Option Fee In Texas, a fee the potential buyer of real estate may pay the seller in exchange for the agreement not to sell to anyone other than the potential buyer for a (usually short) period of time. An option fee should not be confused with earnest money, which is related but different.

Option Holder One who owns an option contract. In a call, the option holder has the right, but not the obligation, to buy the underlying asset, while, in a put, the option holder has the right to sell the underlying asset. An option holder may sell the option contract itself, at which point the buyer becomes the option holder.

Option Margin The initial margin or maintenance margin that an investor must deposit with a brokerage as collateral in order to purchase options with borrowed money. The option margin is set by Regulation T, but some brokerages have higher requirements.

Option Mutual Fund A mutual fund that invests primarily or exclusively in option contracts and/or engages in option strategies. Option mutual funds can carry greater or lesser risk. For example, an option fund where the primary strategy is to write covered calls is likely to carry much less risk than a fund that uses other, more complex option positions.

Option Period In Texas, a short period of time during which a seller of real estate may not to sell to anyone other than the person or entity who placed a bid. This gives the potential buyer time to perform inspections without placing his/her earnest money at risk. The potential buyer pays a non-refundable option fee, which is distinct from earnest money, in order to take advantage of an option period.

Option Premium The price one pays to buy an option contract, whether it is a call or a put, when one is the first buyer. That is, when the option is written, its first buyer pays the option premium. It should not be confused it with the strike price, which is the price one would pay for the underlying asset, should the option be exercised.

Option Pricing Curve A graph showing the price of an option as a function of time. The price at a given point is calculated according to the Black-Scholes Option Pricing Model, and accounts for the market value of the underlying, the strike price, and the expiration date, among other factors. Mathematically, at each price of the option, the slope is equivalent to the delta; that is, the option pricing curve shows the changes in the price of the option over a period of time.

Option Pricing Model Any formula or theory for mathematically determining the correct price for an option contract. An option pricing model may take into account the strike price, the time until the expiration date, the price of the underlying asset, and the standard deviation of the underlying asset's return. The time until the expiration and the price of the underlying asset are particularly important. Option pricing models have a large margin of error because the price of the underlying asset or other factors may change over the life of the contract. Most option pricing models also operate under certain assumptions that may affect their accuracy. The most common option pricing models are the Black-Scholes option-pricing model and the binomial model.

Option Series All the option contracts of the same class on the same underlying security with the same strike price and expiration date that are traded on an exchange. For example, all call options on Stock X with strike price Y expiring on the last Friday in March make up one option series in the exchange on which they are traded. An option series is also simply called a series.

Option Spread An investment strategy in which one has a long position on an option contract while having a short position on another option on the same underlying asset, with a different strike price and/or expiration date. One uses an option spread to profit from price movements in the underlying asset. There are a number of different kinds of option spreads. See also: Call Spread, Put spread.

Option Writer One who originally sells an option contract. In exchange for the premium, the option writer takes on an obligation to buy or sell (depending on the type of option) the underlying asset at the discretion of the option holder. For example, in a call, the option writer must sell the underlying asset to the option holder if the holder decides to exercise the option. If the option writer does not already have a long position in the underlying asset, he/she must obtain one so as to sell the position and fulfill the contract.

Optional Call The ability of a bond issuer to redeem (or call) the bond before maturity. The optional call usually gives bondholders a premium to par to compensate them for lost coupon payments. Most callable bonds have a certain amount of time that must elapse before the issuer may exercise the optional call. See also: Doomsday call.

Optional Cash Purchase A feature of some dividend reinvestment plans allowing participants to use their own cash to buy more shares that the dividends will buy when the dividends are being used themselves to buy more shares. For example, if a dividend will pay for 1,000 more shares, and optional cash purchase will allow the investor to buy, say, another 400 on top of the 1000. Most dividend reinvestment plans limit the number of shares or the amount of cash that may be used.

Optional Dividend A dividend where the shareholder may choose how to receive it. Generally speaking, the shareholder may choose between receiving the dividend in cash or in stock. See also: PIK.

Optional Payment Bond A bond for which principal and/or interest payments may be made in one of two or more currencies. The bondholder has the discretion to choose the currency in which he/she wishes to receive payments.

Options Chain A listing of all quotes for an option, organized according by security. For example, given stock X, an option chain lists all prices, strike prices on all calls, and puts available for that stock.

Options Class The whole universe of option contracts of the same type and style on the same underlying security. For example, all of the American-style calls on Google are considered option class. This class includes all expiration dates and strike prices but does not include contracts of different types, such as puts or European-style options.

Options Clearing Corporation A clearing house that matches and settles option contracts, futures, and other derivatives on commodities and stocks. It is co-owned by and operates on American Stock Exchange, the Boston Stock Exchange, the CBOE, International Securities Exchange, NYSE Arca, and the Philadelphia Stock Exchange.

Options Price Reporting Authority An organization that provides the most recent real-time sale quotes on option contracts on participating exchanges. It provides separate quoting services for foreign exchange options and all other options. Exchanges that participate in OPRA are the American Stock Exchange, the Boston Options Exchange, the Chicago Board Options Exchange, the International Securities Exchange, the Pacific Exchange, and the Philadelphia Stock Exchange.

Options Series All option contracts on the same security of the same variety and with the same terms. For example, all puts on stock in General Electric with a strike price of $15 expiring next January belong to the same option series. See also: Triple witching.

Options-Income Fund A mutual fund where the money managers write covered calls on the securities in the fund. This allows the fund to profit from the collection of the premiums while eliminating the risk that it will lose on the option transaction. In the worst case scenario, it must sell a security in its portfolio when an option is exercised. Most of the time, the options are not exercised and the fund simply increases its income with the premiums.

Or Better The limit price in a limit order. That is, when making an OB order, the investor states that he/she wants to buy or sell at a given price or a better one if it is available.

Oral Contract A contract concluded by mutual agreement between the parties but is not written. In general, an oral contract is equally valid as a written one, though some contracts, such as those dealing with transfers of real estate, must be written. However, oral contracts can be more difficult to enforce in a court of law if there are no witnesses or other evidence attesting to the existence of the oral contract.

Orase In Romania, a political subdivision for a rural municipality.

Order An instruction, especially to a broker, to buy, sell, or conduct some other transaction involving a security or commodity. For example, if a client wishes to buy 100 shares in AT&T, he/she makes an order to a broker to that effect. Orders may take a number of forms. A market order is an order to conduct a transaction at the current market price. A limit order is an order to conduct a transaction at a stated price or better. A stop order is an order to conduct a transaction at the best available price after a certain stated price is reached. Finally, a stop-limit order is a stop order that becomes a limit order when the stated price (known as the stop price) is reached.

Order Book Official On an exchange, an employee responsible for managing the order book, which is the list of orders that have not yet been executed. Order book officials only exist on exchanges that have market makers, as opposed to specialists.

Order Driven Describing an exchange where the bid-ask spread is determined by orders made by clients to brokers. An order driven market contrasts with a quote driven market, where the bid-ask spread is determined by quotes given by market makers.

Order Flow Orders too small for a broker to fill easily that are, therefore, sent to a dealer to fill. Dealers pay brokerages a small fee per share in exchange for the right to fill these orders (and receive the commission). See also: Payment for Order Flow.

Order Period The period of time during which underwriters take orders for a new issue of a security. Before a new issue, underwriters canvass potential investors, who may or may not book an order to buy a portion the new issue. The level of interest during the order period may be an indicator of demand once the security is actually issued.

Order Protection Rule A rule requiring investors to receive a price for a security that is at least equivalent to the price for the same security on another exchange. That is, the order protection rule forbids an order from being executed at a price below the price on another exchange. There are various exceptions; notably limit orders and IOC orders do not necessarily abide by the order protection rule. The rule is a provision of Regulation NMS and is designed to help integrate American exchanges and to protect investors from bad deals. It is also called Rule 611.

Order Room A department in a brokerage in which all orders are received and processed. For instance, if an investor makes an order by telephone to sell a certain security, it is likely that the person who answers the phone works in the order room. This person then refers the order to the appropriate person or department who fills the order.

Order Splitting A practice in which an investor makes several orders to buy or sell the same security, instead of making one large order. Order splitting occurs when the investor wishes to have his/her orders processed by the Small Order Execution System, which is faster than other systems, but is only supposed to be used for small orders. FINRA prohibits order splitting.

Ordering Costs Transaction costs associated with placing an order to buy or sell a security. Perhaps the most common ordering cost is the fee for the broker.

Ordering Rules The precedence under which assets of a Roth IRA are distributed. First, the account holder's contributions are given out, followed by taxable conversions, tax-exempt conversions, and finally earnings that the contributions have made over the life of the account.

Orderly Market 1. A market in which supply and demand for a product or security are roughly equal. Because of this, orderly markets tend not to be volatile and prices tend to reflect the true value of the product or security. It is possible for orderly markets to exist for some products and securities while volatile markets prevail in others. However, major orderliness or volatility tend to spread into the markets as a whole. See also: Buyer's market, Seller's market, Panic selling. **2.** An exchange in which bid prices and ask prices are provided consistently, and in which there are few price fluctuations and no large ones. The presence of an orderly market on an exchange is often due to both diligence on the part of market specialists and the existence of an orderly market in the above sense.

Ordinary and Necessary Expenses that a company incurs in the course of its operations. O&NE expenses include the office electric bill, materials needed to make a product, and employee wages. O&NE expenses differ from startup expenses; while O&NE are deductible from the company's taxes in the year they are incurred, startup expenses generally must be amortized over several years. The IRS provides guidelines as to what expenses are both "ordinary" and "necessary" in Section 162(a) of the tax code.

Ordinary Annuity An annuity with payments that are made at the end, rather than at the beginning, of a period. For example, an ordinary annuity may require payments at the end of the month instead of at the beginning. Many credit cards have ordinary annuity payments, while most lease agreements, for example, do not.

Ordinary Dividend 1. In the United States, any dividend that is subject to income tax rather than (lower) capital gains tax. An ordinary dividend occurs if the security from which the dividend derives has not been held for at least 61 days during a certain 121-day period (for common stock) or for at least 90 days during a corresponding 181-day period. See also: Qualified dividend. **2.** Any dividend that a company pays on a regular basis most of the time. See also: Special dividend

Ordinary Income In taxation, income from wages or salaries, interest, or commissions. Ordinary income is received in the short-term; for example, one usually receives a paycheck every two weeks or interest on a bond a few times per year. Ordinary income differs from capital gain, which is income from investment and is usually realized over a longer period of time. Most ordinary income is taxed at a higher rate than capital gain, so as to encourage long-term investment. In the United States, dividends were taxed as ordinary income, but this changed in 2003. One may think of ordinary income as income from one's job and/or standard business transactions.

Ordinary Interest Interest that is calculated and therefore repaid on the basis of a 360-day year as opposed to a full 365-day year. While this is only a small difference in calculation, the difference in amount can be large, especially with large debt transactions. See also: Exact interest.

Ordlach An obsolete Irish unit of length approximately equivalent to 2.1 centimeters.

Ore A division of the Danish krone, Norwegian krone, or Swedish krona. The ore is worth 1/100 of one unit of each currency.

Organic Act of the Department of Labor Legislation in the United States, enacted in 1913, that separated the Department of Commerce & Labor into the Department of Commerce and the Department of Labor. The Act was controversial at the time because critics contended that the two departments would have similar goals, and argued that having two departments would create unnecessary barriers in bureaucracy. This criticism has been repeated since 1913, most notably during the administration of President Lyndon Johnson, but the Act remains in effect today.

Organic Growth The growth rate of a company coming from its operations. Organic growth comes about when a company has solid sales, a large client base, and/or low overhead. Organic growth can lead to an expansion of operation without resorting to issuing securities or borrowing from a bank. Specifically excluded from organic growth is growth resulting from a merger or acquisition. Organic growth is considered a leading indicator of a company's underlying performance.

Organization Chart A graph stating the hierarchy of position in an organization and how they relate to one another. For example, an organization chart would state that all departments in a company ultimately answer to the board of directors which, in turn, answers to shareholders.

Organization for Economic Cooperation and Development An international organization studying proper economic policies and promoting cooperation in those policies between members. The OECD consists of member accepting the principles of the free market and the democratic process, or, informally, it consists of the so-called developed world. The OECD produces working papers and other documents detailing economic statistics and data and often offering recommendations for policy courses. The organization also provides an open forum for members to discuss these policies, with an aim of members taking roughly the same stand on economic policy. This has not always been successful. However, the OECD also offers a forum for pursuing policies of common interest, for example, setting up an office to discourage tax havens. It was established in 1961 as a successor organization to the Organization for European Economic Cooperation, which was originally established to help implement the Marshall Plan.

Organization of African Trade Union Unity Also called the OATUU. A federation of unions and other organized labor groups in Africa. It was established in 1973 and has several dozen affiliated unions. It is based in Ghana.

Organization of African Unity A defunct international organization that promoted economic and political cooperation among African states. Its goals included eliminating colonialism and achieving greater independence from former imperial powers. It was established in 1963 and disbanded in 2002. Its successor organization is the African Union.

Organization of American States Commonly called the OAS. An international organization consisting of all independent states in North and South America (though not all members are active). It was established in 1948 to oppose the spread of communism. The OAS promotes democracy, economic cooperation and free trade. It also provides a forum for addressing grievances among members. It is based in Washington, D.C.

Organization of Arab Petroleum Exporting Countries An international organization founded in 1968 to coordinate oil policy among Arab countries. Originally intended for conservative countries like Kuwait and Saudi Arabia, it initially excluded left-wing Arab governments from membership. It is not a cartel like OPEC (which has global membership), but it aims for economic cooperation and regional integration.

Organization of Petroleum Exporting Countries An international organization founded in 1960 whose members collaborate on the production and exportation of oil. Members meet several times a year to discuss oil prices and ways to bring them to an optimal level for members. OPEC has a great influence over the world's oil supply as the organization sets production quotas for member nations. Cutting production tends to result in higher oil prices while raising production tends to lower them. Many of OPEC's member nations are heavily reliant on oil to fund their economies and, as a result, tend to prefer high prices. On the other hand, other members (though the groups overlap) suffer high inflation rates when oil prices are too high. As a result, there is often tension between so-called "price hawks" and other members. See also: Brent blend.

Organization of the Islamic Conference An international organization of several dozen Muslim-majority nations. It exists to promote Islamic economic values, international peace and similar goals. It was established in 1969 and is based in Jeddah, Saudi Arabia. See also: Islamic finance.

Organizational Awareness The extent to which a company's employees are familiar with policies, procedures, executives, and similar matters. For example, if a majority of employees in a large corporation can name the CFO, it is said to have good organizational awareness.

Organized Exchange Any securities exchange in which traders and brokers meet to buy and sell securities according to the rules set by the governing body of the exchange. See also: Self-regulatory organization.

Organized Labor A group of employees in a certain company or with a certain skill who unite in a single body for purposes of negotiating wages, benefits, working conditions, and other issues with management. Members of an organized labor group must ratify decisions made by their representatives with management. Proponents of organized labor argue that it creates better working environments and played a significant role in creating the middle class in many countries. Critics contend that it creates economic inefficiency and can drive companies out of business with employees' high demands. In the United States, organized labor is regulated by the National Labor Relations Board. An organized labor group is called a union. See also: Strike.

Orgye An obsolete Arabic unit of length approximately equivalent to 1.92 meters.

Orgyia An ancient Greek unit of length approximately equivalent to 1.85 meters.

Original Cost The total cost of a transaction after commissions, interest rates, and other expenses. For example, a student loan has a principal and interest rate, but the original cost may include an origination fee, a federal default fee, and other expenses. Physical assets also have original costs: one must buy the asset, transport it to where it needs to be, and perhaps pay start-up fees to begin to use it.

Original Equipment Manufacturer 1. A company that makes a product that its customers then use in creating their own products. For example, the manufacturer of an automobile part may sell the part to a car maker, which then builds its own products. In this case, the original equipment manufacturer is the automobile part maker. OEMs often work closely with their customers to integrate their products; for example, an OEM may design a certain product exclusively for one customer. OEMs are especially common in computer and other technology sectors. **2.** A company that buys a product from another company and uses it to make its own product. This definition contradicts the above one, and is used predominantly informally. An OEM in this sense is more properly called a value-added reseller.

Original Face Value The amount one borrows in a loan, especially in a mortgage. The original face value is what the mortgagor repays, plus interest. See also: Par Value.

Original Issue Discount The difference between a bond's face value and the amount for which it is sold by the issuer. Many bonds, especially those with low interest rates, are issued at a price less than par in order to entice buyers. Generally, the lower the interest rate, the greater the original issue discount, with zero-coupon bonds having the largest. Short of default, the original issue discount is a guaranteed profit for a bondholder, as bonds must be redeemed at face value. It is considered a form of interest and may be taxed as such.

Original Issue Discount Security A bond or other debt instrument that is issued at a price below its face value. For example, a bond with par of $10,000 might be issued to an investor for $7,000. All zero-coupon bonds are original issue discount debt.

Original Maturity The time between the issue and the maturity date for a particular bond. For example, if a company issued a 20 years bond five years ago, its original maturity is 20 years, while its current maturity (or time between the present date and maturity) is 15 years. See also: Yield to maturity, Duration.

Origination The act of making a mortgage loan. Origination is usually a rather lengthy process, as it requires the lender to investigate the borrower's risk, negotiate the terms of the loan and agree upon a loan amount. It is also called loan origination. See also: Origination fee.

Origination Fee A percentage of the total amount of a loan that one pays for the privilege to take out that loan. A bank or brokerage assesses this fee in theory to help defray costs. Banks and brokerages must disclose the amount of the origination fee to the borrower within three hours of applying for the loan. See also: Activation fee.

Originator 1. A bank that makes a loan, especially a mortgage loan, to a client. The originator has the ability to sell that loan to another party, usually to create a derivative product of some kind. As a result, one often hears about originators in discussions of mortgage-backed securities. **2.** An investment bank that works with a

company in planning a new issue from the earliest stage. The originator usually becomes the syndicate manager when the issue actually is made.

Orphan Stock A stock that is not often tracked by analysts. This may be because it is not very well known or because it belongs to an industry that is generally performing poorly. As a result these stocks have low demand and often a low price. Some value investors recommend buying orphan stocks because they could be undervalued. However, because demand is low, orphan stocks have low trading volume and a small change in demand may result in volatility in price. An orphan stock is also called a wallflower.

Ort A Norwegian unit of weight approximately equivalent to a kilogram.

Orthodoron An ancient Greek unit of length approximately equivalent to 211.9 millimeters.

OS&D A report a buyer files with a shipping company stating which items in a shipment were over-shipped, which were under-shipped and which were damaged upon receipt. The buyer may request compensation with the OS&D report. The abbreviation stands for over, short and damaged.

Osaka Securities Exchange The second largest exchange in Japan. Established in 1878 with origins in the early 17th century, the Osaka Securities Exchange trades stocks, bonds, and derivatives.

Oscillator In technical analysis, a model for finding prices at which a security is overbought and oversold. An oscillator finds two extreme prices using various methods and finds buy signals and sell signals when the price of the security approaches each. One of the most common oscillators is the Stochastic oscillator. See also: Price ceiling, Price floor.

Osiedla In Poland, a political subdivision roughly equivalent to an urban neighborhood.

Osiedle In Poland, a political subdivision equivalent to a district within a city or township. Occasionally, an osiedle may encompass a whole town.

Oslo Stock Exchange The main stock market in Norway. Tracing its origins to the early 19th century, it was first organized in 1881. It is particularly known for stock in oil and international shipping companies.

Osmina A Russian unit of dry volume approximately equivalent to 105 liters. It was rendered obsolete when the Soviet Union began to use the metric system in 1924.

Ostan In Iran, a political subdivision equivalent to a province.

Ostruble A currency that circulated in German-occupied areas in Eastern Europe during World War I. It was issued in 1916 and was equal in value to the Russian ruble. It was replaced by the Polish marka 1917, though it continued to circulate in some areas along with the ostmark for some time.

OT Mail An e-mail sent to one's supervisor late at night, not because a matter is particularly pressing, but because one simply wants to remind the supervisor that one is working late.

OTB Overseas Trust Bank. A bank in Hong Kong that was, at one time, one of the largest in the country. In 1985, it suddenly collapsed due to bad debt, much of which was caused by criminal misdealing among its senior management. The day following the announcement, the Hong Kong government nationalized OTB. It has since been sold a number of times.

OTC Bulletin Board An electronic listing of over-the-counter securities on NASDAQ. The OTCBB lists several thousand securities, including stocks, bonds, ADRs, and others. Since 1999, the SEC has required all companies listed on the OTCBB to report their financial information.

OTC Options Option contracts that are not traded on an exchange. Because they are over-the-counter, OTC options are not standardized contracts and, as a result, can have any number of unusual features. This allows investors more flexibility, but creates additional risk. See also: Exotic option.

Other Assets On a balance sheet, assets of low value. Examples include scrap and prepaid expenses; other assets are listed in a single place on the balance sheet to save space and time.

Other Capital In a balance of payments, all capital that does not fit into the direct investment, portfolio investment, or reserves categories. It is classified as short-term or long-term based on whether or not it is likely to be liquidated in the coming year.

Other Current Assets On a balance sheet, the value of all non-cash assets for the next year. Examples include accounts receivable and prepaid expenses. Other current assets are included in a company's financial statements.

Other Current Liabilities On a balance sheet, all current liabilities that do not fall under a specific category. Categories for liabilities on a balance sheet include accounts payable and debt obligations. A company usually specifies what individual liabilities are included in other current liabilities when preparing its balance sheet.

Other Income Income for a company that comes from anything other than its ordinary operations. Other income includes items such as interest from the company's bank accounts, profit from the sale of a fixed asset, and so forth. Other income is not recurring and, as a result, is not included in some calculations of profit or loss.

Other Liabilities Liabilities that a company must pay but that are too small to record separately on a balance sheet. That is, other liabilities are all miscellaneous obligations that a company lumps together on financial statements.

Other Long-Term Liabilities On a balance sheet, items that do not currently require interest payments, but will require payments in the future for a period of longer than one year. Common examples of other long-term liabilities include deferred taxes, future employee benefits, such as pensions for employees currently working, and lease payments. Failing to account for other long-term liabilities may make a company look like it has a stronger financial position than it actually does. That is, while its profits may be strong for a given year, it may have to meet its other long-term liabilities in future years, and profits may not be as strong, even if revenue remains the same.

Other People's Money Informal term for the use or investment of borrowed funds. For example, a bank uses OPM to lend to its borrowers as the money it uses for loans (theoretically) comes from its deposits.

Other Revenue Revenue that a company derives from any source other than its operations. For example, if a company sells one of its factories or receives income from interest payments, it is considered other revenue. Most (though not all) other revenue is non-repetitive and, as such, is excluded from many calculations of profit. See also: Operating income.

Ottav A Maltese unit of weight approximately equivalent to 3.3 grams. It is largely obsolete but is still used in some circumstances.

Ottoman Lira The currency of the Ottoman Empire between 1862 and its demise after World War I. The lira's issue marked the first time the Ottoman Empire printed paper money. It was pegged to gold. It was replaced by the Turkish lira and a number of other national currencies.

Ounceland An obsolete Scottish unit of area. An ounceland was the amount of land on which rent of one ounce of silver could be charged. This system was used in western Scotland.

Out Describing a canceled order.

Out of Line Describing a stock with a price-earnings ratio significantly above or below that of other stocks in the same industry or other group. This may lead to larger than usual differences in price.

Out of the Name Informal; a situation in which a stock is no longer actively traded, either by an individual or by the market generally. See also: Out of favor stock.

Out of Town Check A check written in a municipality different than that of the bank on which the check is drawn. For example, if Bob holds an account in a different state and pays his landlord with a check from that account, Bob has written an out of town check. These checks may not be accepted, especially in small towns.

Out There Informal; a subjective assessment stating that sellers or (occasionally) buyers are in the market because they are looking for a transaction on a security. For example, if AT&T is described as "out there," it usually means that investors are looking to sell shares in AT&T.

Out Trade A trade that cannot be settled by a clearing house because the counterparties have contradictory or otherwise inconsistent information on the trade. The clearing house may become aware of the discrepancy by reviewing the comps the brokers give one another, or by some other method. Out trades are returned to the counterparties for resolution; if they are unable to agree on the transaction, the trade is referred to the appropriate body on the exchange for arbitration. See also: Don't Know.

Out With In equities, an inquiry to a broker by a client regarding a security.

Outbid To make a higher bid than another party. This means the second party will not buy the good or service being bid on unless it in turn makes a higher bid. For example, if Joe bids $10 for an antique desk and Frank bids $12, Frank has outbid Joe. The term is important in the securities trade. See also: Counteroffer.

Outlays Payments made in cash or cash equivalents. Common examples of outlays include employee salaries and coupon payments on bonds. Revenue outlays are those made currently or those that will be made within a year, while capital outlays are those made for periods longer than one year. Outlays are recorded as liabilities on a balance sheet and are also called expenditures.

Outlier A data point significantly different from others in the same set. An outlier is generally due to statistical noise and not to any fundamental difficulty with the data set. Taking the mean and median values of a data set can help reduce the influence of outliers. They are also called outlying observations.

Out-of-Favor Industry or Stock An industry or stock to which many analysts and investors do not pay attentions. Out-of-favor industries or stocks tend to have a low price-earnings ratio and may therefore be undervalued. That is, the low price does not necessarily come from a fundamental problem with the company, but may result simply from apathy on the part of investors. Value investors sometimes seek out-of-favor industries and stocks for long-term investments.

Out-of-Pocket Expenses Expenses that one must pay from one's personal, instead of business, income. Out-of-pocket expenses include mundane, recurring expenses such as paying the home electric bill or buying groceries. Often, however, the term refers to expenses incurred by an employee in the service of the employer. For instance, an employee may buy a more efficient computer program to accomplish his/her office work. These out-of-pocket expenses are usually reimbursed by the employer. Some out-of-pocket expenses, especially those related to education or health care, are tax deductible.

Out-of-the-Money Option 1. A call option with a strike price more than the value of the underlying asset. **2.** A put option with a strike price less than the value of the underlying asset. In both these situations, the option contract has no intrinsic value. If an option is deep out of the money, it is unlikely that the option will be in-the-money by the expiration date. If possible, out-of-the-money options are sold; if not, they expire worthless and the option holder loses the premium.

Output Gap The difference between an economy's GDP and its potential GDP. That is, the output gap measures GDP against what the GDP ought to be if the economy were using its resources efficiently. A positive output gap occurs when the GDP exceeds the efficient GDP, usually through the over-utilization of resources, while a negative output gap occurs when the GDP undershoots the potential GDP. Most analysts believe that a positive output gap leads to inflation.

Output Tax In the United Kingdom, the value added tax that a business charges customers on the products it sells. This contrasts with the input tax, which is the VAT that the business pays on its inventory and other goods. If the output tax exceeds the input tax, the business must pay the difference to the government. On the other hand, if the input tax exceeds the output, the government refunds the difference to the business.

Outright Deal A forward contract that is not part of a larger swap. That is, an outright deal is simply a forward contract on its own.

Outright Futures Position An unhedged position on a futures contract. That is, an outright futures position is a long or short position on a futures contract that is not offset by another contract that reduces the risk. One gains on an outright futures position when the price of the contract or the underlying asset increases (for a long position) or decreases (for a short).

Outright Quote A quote for the price of a security using decimals rather than fractions to represent divisions of a dollar.

Outright Rate The exchange rate on an outright forward. An outright forward is a forward contract in which a party agrees to buy a currency from another party at some definite point in the future at a given exchange rate. This exchange rate is an outright rate.

Outside Director A member of a publicly-traded company's board of directors that is not otherwise employed by or engaged with the company. That is, he/she does not represent shareholders or major executives in the company. Outside directors are thought to be advantageous because they offer objectivity and have little or no chance of conflict of interest. However, there is the possibility that an outside director might be unengaged with the issues involved in the company's governance. The Sarbanes-Oxley Act of 2002 mandates that a certain percentage of boards of directors be outside directors. It is illegal for outside directors to sit on multiple boards in the same industry as this may result in conflicts of interest.

Outside Earnings In the United States, any money received by a beneficiary of Social Security who is under the age of 70. Generally speaking, outside earnings are earnings from continuing to work. Outside earnings over a certain level result in a reduction and eventual elimination of monthly Social Security benefits. Beneficiaries under the age of 65 have a low outside earnings limit, while those between 65 and 70 have a higher limit before they begin to lose benefits. Outside earnings have historically been politically unpopular, especially among seniors, but remain in place.

Outside Market On the over-the-counter market, any bid lower than the highest bid and any ask above the lowest ask. See also: Inside market.

Outside Reversal In technical analysis, a situation in which a security's high is higher than the high of the previous trading day, and, likewise, the low is lower than the previous low. If an outside reversal occurs at a security's support level, this is a bullish indicator; if it happens at the security's resistance level, this is a bearish indicator.

Outsourcing The practice of a company hiring a different company to supplement its services at a lower cost. For example, a company may outsource its accounting to another firm, which would then prepare and provide appropriate statements for the company. Likewise, an automobile manufacturer may buy auto parts from another company and use them to make its own cars. Companies outsource in order to reduce their costs and thereby reduce the prices they charge for their goods and services. The practice is somewhat controversial, especially as some companies in the developed world outsource to firms in other, often developing nations. Critics contend that this drives jobs out of the home country, while proponents argue that this benefits consumers.

Outstanding Debt Debt that has not yet been repaid in full. For example, if one borrows $10,000 and has paid back $2,000, the outstanding debt is $8,000. In general, interest is calculated over the outstanding debt rather than the original amount borrowed.

Outstanding Dividends Dividends that have been sent by check to shareholders but have not yet been deposited into shareholders' accounts. Companies treat outstanding dividends as if they have already been paid; however, the funds remain with the company until either the checks clear or the funds revert to the state as abandoned property. See also: Declared dividend, Ex-dividend, Check hold.

Out-Thaba A Burmese unit of length equivalent to 64.008 meters.

Overadvance A short-term loan that a company takes out in order to buy more material for its inventory immediately before a period of increased sales. A company uses an overadvance to finance its expected increase in sales.

Overall Market Price Coverage The amount of the market value of a security issue that would be reimbursed in the case of the company's liquidation. It is calculated as: Overall market price coverage = $(A - I)/(S + L)$ where A is the value of the company's total assets, I represents its intangibles, S is the market value of the security issue being compared, and L is the value of the company's liabilities and issues with a prior claim.

Overapplied Overhead In accounting, a record of the overhead for a work-in-process product that is greater than the overhead actually is. This may happen for any number of reasons. Because overapplied overhead means profits are higher than the records say they should be, it is added to a company's profit at the end of the accounting period. It is also called overabsorbed overhead. See also: Underapplied overhead.

Overbase Compensation Salary and fringe benefits paid to an expatriate worker over and above what he/she would have been paid had he/she stayed in the home country. Overbase compensation may be just straight salary, but it may also include free housing, added vacation time and so forth. For example, if one's base salary is $100,000 and one is posted to perform the same work in a developing country at $130,000, the extra $30,000 is considered overbase compensation.

Overborrowed 1. Describing a company with borrowed funds that come due after funds it has lent to others. This means the company carries liabilities with longer terms than its assets. As a result, the company may not have the cash flow to repay its borrowed funds. See also: Unfunded liability. **2.** More generally, describing a person or organization that has borrowed more than is sustainable. **3.** See: Overmargined.

Overbought In technical analysis, describing a security with too high a price. This means that the technical indicators on the security do not justify its current price. Technical analysts may recommend selling overbought securities, as they are due for a price correction. See also: Oversold.

Overbought-Oversold Indicator In technical analysis, any indicator showing that a price movement is unsustainable and is likely to reverse itself. For example, a sharp drop or rise may indicate that the price of a security may soon revert to the mean.

Overcapitalization A situation in which a company has too much capital. An overcapitalized company has an excessive amount of cash or liquid assets; it may find itself in a position, for example, of paying high dividends that it would have difficulty reducing in the future. Its earnings may or may not adequately reflect the capital invested in the company. An overcapitalized company may repay its debt or make a tender offer for shares in order to reduce its capital.

Overcharge To assess a buyer too much for a product. For example, one may sell a cheap television worth $200 for $500. Because pricing is somewhat subjective, it can be difficult to determine when someone has been overcharged.

Overcollateralization The practice or process of placing an asset as collateral on a loan where the value of the asset exceeds the value of the loan. For example, a person could pledge a farm (worth $10 million) on a loan for $5 million. Usually, however, the value of the asset only exceeds the value of the loan by 10-20%. Overcollateralization reduces the risk for the lender and improves the borrower's creditworthiness. It is used most commonly when a bond issuer wishes to improve its credit rating.

Overdepreciation The act of depreciating an asset on a firm's balance sheet such that the asset is recorded as being worth less than it would be if it were sold. This results in the firm understating its earnings and/or the value of its assets.

Overdraft A situation in which a bank customer withdraws more from his/her account than he/she had previously deposited. For example, if an account holder has $1,000 in the account and withdraws $1,200, this is an overdraft of $200. The bank may or may not honor the overdraft, depending on its policies and the importance of the customer. Usually, however, an overdraft incurs a relatively steep penalty fee.

Overdraft Cap The maximum amount of money that a bank will request from another bank on a business day. This limits the first bank's exposure to the risk that too many transactions will result in overdrafts (which means the second bank may refuse to pay the first bank). Each bank has a different overdraft cap, determined by its risk adjusted capital.

Overdraft Checking Account A checking account with a negative net cash balance. That is, the owner of an overdraft checking account owes money to the bank rather than the bank holding his/her money. Overdraft checking accounts occur when a customer spends more money from the account than he/she deposited into it. This may occur when he/she has written too many checks or used a debit card to buy things with too much value. Most banks charge a fee on overdraft accounts; the amount of the fee varies from bank to bank, but is often between $15 and $30 in the United States. Some banks charge a smaller amount for the first transaction where an overdraft takes place and a larger amount every transaction thereafter to discourage irresponsible spending.

Overdraft Credit A situation in which a bank allows an account holder to spend more than is currently in the account. Overdraft credit may be attached to accounts automatically, though usually it requires payment of an NSF fee.

Overdraft Facility A short term loan that a bank makes to a business automatically if that business otherwise would face an overdraft. For example, if a business has $10,000 in the bank and withdraws $12,000 for its payroll, an overdraft facility is an automatic loan for the extra $2,000. The overdraft facility is payable on demand and, as with most loans, the business must pay interest on the amount borrowed.

Overdraft Protection The payment by a bank of a purchase by a client when that client's transaction results in an overdraft (which occurs when the account balance goes below zero). This allows the client to purchase whatever good or service led to the overdraft. The bank may assess a hefty fee for overdraft protection.

Overdue Describing any liability that should have been paid but that for some reason has not. For example, if the electric bill is due on the 15th and one still has not paid it on the 18th, the electric bill is overdue. Persistently allowing liabilities to become overdue may result in late fees and reduced creditworthiness.

Overemployment 1. A situation in which a person consistently works more hours than they can sustainably work. That is, overemployment occurs when one is overworked. Some companies, such as brokerages and other major corporations, may encourage overemployment by promoting a culture in which those who work the most hours tend to receive promotions. **2.** See: Overstaffing.

Overexposure The state of taking on too much risk. One may be overexposed to an industry, a company or even an investment vehicle. For example, a mutual fund may be overexposed to the financial sector by buying too many stocks in banks relative to its stocks in other industries.

Overfull Employment A situation in which the demand for labor exceeds supply. This results in wage and salary increases as employers try to attract employees. This, in turn, leads to employees spending more of their higher wages, which results in higher prices. According to some economists, overfull employment leads to inflation.

Overfunded Pension Plan A pension that has more assets than liabilities. That is, pensioners' contributions and the investment of those contributions amount to more than what the pension owes to retirees. This is considered a sign of financial health for the pension.

Overfunding 1. Describing any investment, annuity or other financial instrument containing more assets than liabilities. That is, contributions and the investment of those contributions amount to more than what the instrument owes to holders. This is considered a sign of financial health for the instrument. **2.** In the United Kingdom, the practice of lending more government securities than the government is expected to need to fund its activities. The excess is used to fight inflation.

Overgrowth A situation in which a mutual fund sells shares in itself so quickly and successfully that it has difficulty finding appropriate investments in which to place all of its capital. An overgrown mutual fund may have difficulty maintaining a diversified portfolio of securities and may be forced to take larger positions in the securities it already has. As a result, the fund may acquire greater risk and become a victim of its own success.

Overhanging Bond A convertible bond whose bondholders do not exercise the convertible option to turn it into common stock because it is currently trading at too low a price. Overhanging bonds therefore act like normal debt securities. This is considered a low risk investment with the possibility of high return, because an overhanging bond usually has a fixed return, and there is a small chance that the stock will recover, allowing the investor to exercise the convertible option. See also: Busted convertible.

Overhead Costs that result from having and maintaining a business. Rent is a primary (and expensive) example of direct overhead, as are office supplies.

Overheating Describing an economy that is growing too fast or otherwise unsustainably. Overheating economies tend to crash, experience high inflation, or both. The inflation occurs when the economy's producers are unable to meet demand by expanding production because it is rising too fast. To temper demand, the producers raise prices. Central banks tend to increase interest rates to temper or prevent overheating in domestic economies.

Over-Hedging The practice of taking an offsetting position on an investment to reduce its risk where the offsetting position is greater than the original position. For example, one may buy 100 shares of AT&T and then buy a put option, giving one the right, but not the obligation, to sell 125 shares of AT&T. While this completely eliminates the risk associated with the first 100 shares declining in price, over-hedging creates a new risk for the extra 25 shares in the put contract.

Overinvestment A situation in which the management of a publicly-traded company invests in too many projects, especially when the projects do not benefit shareholders. Overinvestment may be a violation of the management's fiduciary responsibility to shareholders, especially when the managers benefit from the arrangement and investors do not.

Overinvoicing 1. An invoice with a price listed that is higher than a company actually intends to charge a client. **2.** The act or practice of billing more hours than one actually works. For example, a lawyer may meet with a client for 10 minutes and bill for half an hour. Overinvoicing is difficult to track, but common in many white collar professions.

Overissue A situation in which a company issues more shares than it has authorized shares.

Overlap the Market To create a crossed market. One overlaps the market when offers to buy a security at a price higher than the lowest offer or to sell at a price lower than the highest bid.

Overlapping Debt A situation in which two governments with overlapping jurisdiction each have debt. For example, if the City and the State of New York have both issued bonds to pay for their operations, both the city and the state have overlapping debt. Having overlapping debt may affect one or both governments' ability to repay.

Overlay Strategy The practice in which a money manager keeps track of all of an investor's accounts and the securities contained in them in order to prevent duplication, overexposure, or other unnecessary risks. An overlay strategy is believed to be more efficient when one has multiple brokerage accounts and helps one accomplish his/her overall investment goals, not just the ones of a particular account.

Overmargined Describing a margin account in which the value of the securities used as collateral has dropped below the margin requirement. An overmargined account is susceptible to a margin call.

Overnight Deal An offering of previously issued stock that is not usually traded. For example, a publicly-traded company may make an overnight deal to sell some of its stock that it previously issued but still owns (because many publicly-traded companies own a portion of their own stock). Overnight deals are often less expensive than new issues because there are no underwriting costs. There is also less downward pressure on the share price because the number of shares outstanding does not increase.

Overnight Delivery Risk The risk that a difference in time zone will delay a payment from being made. Because different time zones have business days that do not overlap (for example, offices Seattle and Dubai are almost never open for business at the same time), one party may not know that a delivery or payment has not been made during the time when he/she would be able to do the most about it. As a result, one party may not know whether the other has fulfilled his/her obligations until the next business day.

Overnight Index Swap A short-term, plain vanilla swap in which the legs are a fixed interest rate and the current rate for an overnight loan. As with all interest rate swaps, an overnight index swap is calculated over some notional amount.

Overnight Position The position that a broker-dealer has at the end of a trading day. A large overnight position, either long or short, exposes the broker-dealer to the risk that events or after hours trading between the close and open of an exchange will negatively impact the price at the open. However, this risk is primarily relevant only when the overnight position is intended for the short-term.

Overnight Repo A practice in which a bank or other financial institution buys securities with the proviso that the seller repurchase the same securities the following day. Financial institutions do this in order to raise short-term capital. See also: Overnight loan.

Overnight Trading Trading on currencies that occurs between 9 pm and 8 am. Because there are so many exchanges (and indeed so many non-exchange trading platforms), currency trading is always happening, even when the local exchange is closed. Overnight trading affects exchange rates and can cause prices to rise or fall when the local exchange opens the next morning. See also: After-hours trading.

Overperform To perform better than the market as a whole for a stated period of time. To overperform does not necessarily mean to perform well. For example, if the market is expected to go down significantly, a stock may be said to overperform even if it dips slightly, provided it does not dip as far as the market as a whole.

Overreaching 1. The process by which ownership of one asset is changed into ownership of another asset. For example, one may own a car and then sell it. Afterward, one owns the cash from the sale. The process by which this occurs is called overreaching. **2.** The act of buying and/or selling a security repeatedly such that the trading volume goes to an artificially high level. If one overreaches as part of a price manipulation scheme, it is illegal.

Overreaction Hypothesis A theory stating that the crowd overreacts to both good news and bad news. For example, when a company announces unexpectedly high earnings, this can create a buying panic that unjustifiably drives up the company's stock price. Likewise, when the earnings are unexpectedly bad, there can be a selling panic that drives down the price. One can use the overreaction hypothesis to make short-term profits in either direction.

Overriding Royalty Interest The right of a person or company to royalties derived from an oil or gas producing property.

Overrun The amount by which the actual cost of a project exceeds its budget. While this does not necessarily guarantee that the project will fail, it does make it more difficult to succeed. This is also called cost overrun or budget overrun.

Overseas Economic Cooperation Fund A former fund that was responsible for providing financing to encourage Japanese international trade. It ceased to exist in 1999 when it merged with the Export-Import Bank of Japan to form the Japanese Bank for International Cooperation.

Oversight and Government Reform Committee A committee in the U.S. House of Representatives responsible for investigations into the function of the federal government. That is, the committee has jurisdiction over how efficiently the government spends its revenue. The committee was established in 1816 but took its current name in 2007.

Oversold In technical analysis, describing a security with too low a price. This means that the technical indicators on the security do not justify its current price. Technical analysts may recommend buying oversold securities, as they are due for a price correction. See also: Overbought.

Overstaffing A situation in which a company hires more employees than it can afford to keep. Overstaffing may occur, for example, if a small business makes a point of employing all of the owner's children. It may also occur if a company hires staff in anticipation of increased business. Overstaffing may be unsustainable if the increased business does not materialize.

Overstay In technical analysis, to hold an investment for too long such that it reduces one's gain or causes a loss. For example, a technical investor may see the end of an uptrend in a security's price, but believe the coming downtrend is only temporary. However, the downtrend may continue and the investor may refuse to sell, overstaying the investment until he/she loses.

Overstrike A situation in which a coin is struck over another coin, rather than over a blank disk. Usually, the overstrike is the same denomination, but sometimes two different denominations are struck on the same coin. In any case, it is so rare that it can affect the value of a coin.

Oversubscription A situation in which investors show so much interest in a new issue of a security that demand exceeds supply. Before a new issue, underwriters canvass potential investors, who may or may not book an order to buy a portion the new issue. If investors order more shares than there are shares being issued, the security is said to be oversubscribed. This may affect the price when the security is actually issued.

Oversubscription Privilege In a new issue of a stock, the right of current shareholders to receive or purchase the rights or warrants to the new issue at a discount. This allows existing shareholders to maintain their current percentage of ownership in the company. The rights or warrants that are distributed are the rights some shareholders did not want to receive. Thus, these remaining rights or warrants are distributed among existing shareholders on a prorated basis. See also: Anti-dilution provision.

Over-the-Counter Market Describing a security or trade that does not occur on an exchange. Very often, the OTC market includes securities that are very small and do not trade on an exchange because they do not meet market capitalization requirements. OTC securities may theoretically be traded informally (one may stand on a street corner and sell his/her stocks), but the term usually refers to securities traded through a dealer network.

Overtime Work by a wage earner in excess of a statutory number or hours. For example, any time that a waged employee works over 40 hours in a week is usually considered overtime. Working overtime may entitle an employee to extra compensation, such as one and a half times his/her ordinary wage, which is often called time-and-a-half.

Overtime Ban A situation in which employees refuse to work longer than is required of them. For example, if office hours are from 8 a.m. to 5 p.m., employees following an overtime ban will not work outside that time. Overtime bans may be used as labor action or another form of employee protest. It is considered less disruptive than a strike.

Overtrade 1. To make both buy and sell orders through different brokers to create the impression of increased interest in a security and thereby raise the price. This is a form of price manipulation and is forbidden by the Securities Exchange Act of 1934. It is less formally known as churning. **2.** In brokering, to make more trades on a client's holdings than are necessary in order to maximize commissions. Overtrading is illegal.

Overvaluation In technical analysis, a situation in which a security has too high a price. This means that the technical indicators on the security do not justify its current price. Technical analysts may recommend selling overbought securities as they are due for a price correction. It can be difficult to determine whether or not a company is overvalued, but a high price-earnings ratio is one way. A price-earnings ratio over 1 indicates that the stock price is more than the company's earnings per share, which may mean that the company is overvalued. See also: Undervaluation.

Overweight 1. See: Market outperform. **2.** See: Overperform. **3.** Describing a portfolio where one security or industry has too much representation. For example, an overweight portfolio may be overexposed to the financial industry, which means if the financial industry suffers a downturn the portfolio will decline in value more than other similar portfolios. See also: Diversification.

Overwithholding A situation in which an employer withholds too much money from an employee's paycheck and gives the funds to the tax agency. This occurs when the employee does not make enough to qualify for the tax bracket used on the paycheck, or when the employee takes enough itemized deductions for which the withholding does not account to reduce his/her tax liability. Overwithholding usually results in a tax refund or in the application of the amount to next year's taxation.

Overwrite An option strategy that involves writing more option contracts than the writer expects to have exercised. A writer overwrites contracts in order to collect the premiums. He/she chooses the securities underlying the contracts based on whether they are overvalued or undervalued. One overwrites calls if one believes that the underlying securities are overvalued because one expects a price correction that will result in the calls going out-of-the-money. For the same reason, one overwrites puts if one believes that the underlying securities are undervalued.

Ovoboby Slang; a situation in which stocks are overbought and therefore bonds are oversold (that is, bond prices are declining). This causes interest rates (which move inversely to bond prices) to rise to an unsustainably high level.

Owe To be required to repay money or another asset to an individual, company, or other organization. One owes a debt after one has borrowed money or another asset. In business and government, debt is often owed in the form of bonds, which are securities entitling the bearer to repayment at the appropriate time(s). Occasionally, especially for personal loans, debt is owed without interest or other compensation; one simply owes what was lent. This is exceedingly rare in business and a debtor almost always owes a creditor a certain amount of interest, representing the time value of money.

Own To have the exclusive right to use and abuse property within the limits of the law. For example, if one owns land, the owner may use it to build a house, start a farm or dump toxic waste, subject to zoning, environmental and other applicable laws. The ability of an individual to own something is the foundation of the free market system.

Own Foreign Offices In U.S. tax, a category for any company related to an American company that is based outside the United States. That is, if a company reporting American taxes has a parent company, subsidiary, or branch overseas, it must report the income of these companies under "own foreign offices."

Owner One who has the exclusive right to use and abuse property within the limits of the law. For example, if one owns land, the owner may use it to build a house, start a farm or dump toxic waste, subject to zoning, environmental and other applicable laws. The ability of an individual to own something is the foundation of the free market system.

Owner Control Investigation In Germany, an investigation conducted when a bank attempts to purchase more than a 10% stake in a German financial institution. The investigation ensures that the buyer is sufficiently transparent and well-capitalized to make the sale viable. BaFin (Germany's primary financial regulator) conducts the owner control investigation.

Owner's Equity An individual or company's net worth. This is calculated by taking the value of all assets and subtracting the value of all liabilities. Owner's equity is used in determining an individual's or company's creditworthiness, and can be used in determining the value of a business when its owner or shareholders want to sell. It is important to note than owner's equity includes the value of intangible assets and liabilities.

Ownership-Specific Advantages Intangible assets in a company, such as intellectual property, property rights, brand recognition, and other areas. Owning the copyright to a superior product is an example of an ownership-specific advantage, as is an exceptionally good organizational system. Ownership-specific advantages are less quantitative ways a company is able to remain competitive against companies in the same industry. That is, the idea behind ownership-specific advantages states that there is more to competition than simply providing the best price. Intangibles also play a significant role.

Own-Occupation Policy An insurance policy that pays benefits to the policyholder if he/she becomes unable to perform work for which he/she is qualified. For example, if a dictionary writer's hands fall off, he likely would be eligible for the benefits of an own-occupation policy because he would be unable to write definitions for the dictionary. Some own-occupation policies pay benefits if the policyholder becomes unable to perform his/her current job, while others only do so if he/she is unable to do any job that he/she would otherwise be able to do.

Oxgang An obsolete Scottish unit of area approximately equivalent to 20 acres.

Oxybathon An ancient Greek unit of volume approximately equivalent to 68.2 milliliters.

Oyaumes coutumiers In Wallis and Futuna, a political subdivision approximately equivalent to a province. Each one corresponds to a traditional kingdom.

Oyra A subdivision of the Faroese krona. One oyra is equal in value to 1/100 of one krona.

Ozalid 1. A process using ammonia to print a reproduction from a translucent, original drawing or image. **2.** A machine that uses the ozalid process.

P 1. A symbol indicating an initial dividend on a stock. It is used most often on transaction tables in a newspaper. **2.** A symbol indicating that a mutual fund charges a distribution fee. It is used most often on transaction tables in a newspaper.

P&I The principal and interest on a loan. The borrower must pay the principal and interest according to the agreed-upon schedule. See also: PITI, Amortization.

P&S 1. Purchase and sales. A statement that a brokerage gives to a client showing changes made to the client's portfolio. That is, the P&S sets forth the securities the client has bought and sold over a given period of time and the effect that has on the client's net positions. **2.** The department in a brokerage that monitors transactions and prepares P&S statements.

P/E Effect A situation in which a portfolio with a lower average P/E ratio has a higher return (when adjusted for risk) than a portfolio with a higher ratio.

P2P 1. Path to profitability. A loan to a start-up or other new company from a source other than a financial institution. A lender often charges high interest in a P2P loan. This provides the borrower with financing needed to maintain operations until it becomes profitable. See also: Angel investor. **2.** Informal for a business plan, especially for a new company or a dot-com.

PA 1. ISO 3166-1 alpha-2 code for the Republic of Panama. This is the code used in international transactions to and from Panamanian bank accounts. **2.** ISO 3166-2 geocode for Panama. This is used as an international standard for shipping to Panama. Each province has its own code with the prefix "PA." For example, the code for the Province of Bocas del Toro is ISO 3166-2:PA-1.

PAB ISO 4217 code for the Panamanian balboa. It was first issued in 1904 when Panama became independent from Colombia. It is pegged to the U.S. dollar at par and circulates alongside it.

PAC Bond A collateralized mortgage obligation that seeks to protect investors from prepayment risk. PACs do this by setting a schedule of payments; if prepayments of the underlying mortgages exceed a certain rate, the life of the PAC is shortened. If they fall below a certain rate, the life of the tranche is extended. This helps protect investors in case the holders of the underlying mortgages do not pay off their mortgages as expected.

Pac Man Defense An antitakeover measure in which a target company attempts a hostile takeover of the acquiring company. That is, an acquiring company attempts a hostile takeover, and, rather than submitting to the takeover, the target company attempts the same thing on the acquiring company.

Pacesetter The best product or company in a market. Other companies attempt to imitate or improve upon the pacesetter.

Pacific Basin Economic Council Also called the PBEC. A business association that promotes the interests of businesses in countries that border the Pacific Ocean. Among its activities, the PBEC lobbies for favorable legislation and advocates for social responsibility among private companies. It was established in 1967.

Pacific Economic Cooperation Council Also called the PECC. An informal group that seeks to promote economic and other cooperation between countries that border the Pacific Ocean. There are member countries on both sides of the Pacific, in North and South America as well as Asia and Oceania. The PECC holds a conference every two years in which business and government leaders discuss matters of mutual interest. It was founded in 1980.

Pacific Exchange A stock exchange based in San Francisco, California. It formerly had a branch office in Los Angeles, which closed in 2001. With origins tracing back to 1882, the Pacific Exchange trades primarily in stocks and options. Since the early 2000s, all stock trading has occurred electronically. However, its options market still maintains a trading floor and an open outcry system.

Pacific Rim The countries that border the Pacific Ocean, especially with reference to the cities closest to the coast. For example, while the United States is part of the Pacific Rim, the term most often refers to cities along the West Coast, such as Seattle and Portland. A great deal of trade occurs among Pacific Rim countries, and various organizations exist to promote economic cooperation.

Package Deal In futures and options, a large number of transactions that must be conducted at the same time.

Package Mortgage A mortgage in which the loan is used to buy a house as well as all furniture and other property in the house.

Pagafes Federal debt securities in Mexico that were denominated in U.S. dollars. Pagafes were considered lower risk than cetes, which were denominated in pesos, because of the uncertainty regarding the peso's stability. As a result, in the early 1990s, pagafes carried lower interest rates than cetes.

Pagasts In Latvia, a political subdivision equivalent to a rural municipality. It is also used to refer to religious parishes.

Paid Business A classification an insurance company gives a new policyholder who has been approved for life or health insurance and has paid the first premium.

Paid Cancel A classification given to a subscriber or policyholder who cancels after paying his/her monthly fee. For example, if a policyholder pays his premium on October 1 and cancels the policy on October 15, he may be considered a paid cancel. This is also called a completed cancel.

Paid In Capital Capital that a company raises in a financing round. That is, the paid in capital is the money a publicly-traded company receives when it issues new stock, either as an IPO or an additional issue. It is important to note that companies only raise paid in capital on the primary market; they do not receive any additional money from trades on the secondary market. The paid in capital goes toward expanding or improving upon a company's operations. It is also called paid-in surplus or the contributed capital.

Paid Status A classification in a database stating whether or not a customer has paid and, if so, whether or not he/she has paid in full. This is useful in determining a company's cash flow.

Paid Up Somewhat informal; referring to a situation in which a debtor has serviced debt appropriately. For example, when a debtor makes a required monthly debt payment, that portion of debt is said to be paid up.

Paid-Up Insurance Somewhat informal; insurance in which a policyholder has paid the premium appropriately. For example, when a policyholder makes a required monthly premium payment, that policy is said to be paid up.

Pain and Suffering The physical or mental distress associated with a claim in a lawsuit. A plaintiff may seek compensation for pain and suffering. For example, a person injured in an automobile accident may sue for the cost of medical bills, lost income and an additional amount (determined by the plaintiff) for pain and suffering. See also: Pain and suffering damages.

Pain and Suffering Damages Money awarded to a plaintiff in a lawsuit to compensate for physical or mental distress associated with a claim. For example, a person injured in an automobile accident may sue for the cost of medical bills, lost income and an additional amount (determined by the plaintiff) for pain and suffering. While the plaintiff may request these damages, juries have a great deal of leeway in determining how much to award. Additionally, some jurisdictions place limits on the amount of pain and suffering damages.

Painted Display Any place (usually in a high traffic area) on which a person or company can place an advertisement in exchange for a fee. A painted display is a common form of advertising for products likely to appeal to drivers or pedestrians, or to increase the visibility of companies in the display's immediate vicinity. There are two types of painted displays: a billboard (which is a freestanding structure) and a painted wall (which is an exterior wall of a building).

Painted Wall The exterior wall of a building (usually in a high traffic area) on which a person or company can place an advertisement in exchange for a fee. A painted wall is a common form of advertising for products likely to appeal to drivers or pedestrians, or to increase the visibility of companies in the immediate vicinity of the wall.

Painting the Tape A practice in which brokers make numerous buy and sell orders for a security in order to create the appearance of high trading volume. This will cause the price of the security to move in the brokers' desired direction. Because this is a form of price manipulation, painting the tape is illegal. The "tape" refers to ticker tape. See also: Pump and dump.

Paipu A bulky font that deliberately looks like computer text from the 1980s. It is used in headlines, on advertisements and in similar contexts. The word is Japanese for "pipe."

Paired Off Describing two brokerage firms that buy/sell securities to each other without delivering the physical securities. Regulations require that the delivery occur within three days of the trade date. Pairing off indicates that the two brokerages are trading non-existent securities in order to create the impression of increased or decreased demand and thereby manipulate the price. Pairing off is illegal.

Pairs Trade An investment strategy in which one owns two stocks in the same industry. In general, these stocks follow the same pattern; that is, both go up or both go down. When the pattern diverges (that is, when one increases in price and the other decreases), the investor sells the stock that has increased and buys the stock that has decreased. The idea behind a pairs trade is that the stocks will generally meet back in the middle, allowing the investor to profit from the purchase of the stock that had decreased and the sale of the one that had increased.

Paisa A generic term for a subdivision of several currencies. The Indian rupee, the Pakistani rupee and the Nepalese rupee are all divided into 100 paisa.

Paivamatka A Finnish unit of length approximately equivalent to 20 kilometers. It became obsolete when Finland adopted the metric system in 1880.

PAK GOST 7.67 Latin three-letter geocode for Pakistan. The code is used for transactions to and from Pakistani bank accounts and for international shipping to Pakistan. As with all GOST 7.67 codes, it is used primarily in Cyrillic alphabets.

Pakistan Mint An organization in Pakistan that issues legal tender coins for general use. It was established in 1942 and is controlled by the State Bank of Pakistan. It is located in Lahore.

Pakistani Rupee The currency of Pakistan. It was issued when Pakistan became independent in 1947. Originally, the rupee was divided into 16 annas, which each containing four pice. However, in 1961, it was decimalized and divided simply into 100 pice. Because of inflation, pice have not been issued since 1994. It is a floating currency.

Palaiste An ancient Greek unit of length approximately equivalent to 77.1 millimeters. It was also called a doron.

Palestinian Pound The former currency of British Mandate Palestine and Transjordan. It was replaced by the Israeli sheqel in 1948 and the Jordanian dinar in 1950, though Palestinian pounds continued to circulate in some areas.

Palladium A precious metal that may be used in jewelry, electronics, or other products. It may be traded as a commodity or on the futures and option markets.

Palme An obsolete Danish unit for circumference approximately equivalent to 8.86 centimeters.

Palmipes An ancient Roman unit of length approximately equivalent to 370 millimeters.

Palmo A Spanish measure of length approximately equivalent to 8.2 inches. It is largely obsolete.

Palmo de craveira A Portuguese measure of length approximately equivalent to 0.22 meters. It became obsolete after Lusophone countries adopted the metric system in the 19th century.

Palmus An ancient Roman unit of length approximately equivalent to 74 millimeters.

Palmus Major An ancient Roman unit of length approximately equivalent to 222 millimeters.

PAN GOST 7.67 Latin three-letter geocode for Panama. The code is used for transactions to and from Panamanian bank accounts and for international shipping to Panama. As with all GOST 7.67 codes, it is used primarily in Cyrillic alphabets.

Panamanian Balboa The currency of Panama. It was first issued in 1904 when Panama became independent from Colombia. It is pegged to the U.S. dollar at par and circulates alongside it.

Panda Informal for any trade with China, especially involving foreign exchange.

Panel Bank One of several banks that provide quotes for EURIBOR. The quote each panel bank offers is based on the interest rate the bank believes other banks are offering each other for overnight loans. Each panel bank must provide this quote each day; the quotes are aggregated to arrive at the official EURIBOR reference rate.

Panic 1. See: Bank panic. **2.** See: Panic buying. **3.** See: Panic selling.

Panic Buying A situation in which many investors buy a security on high volume, leading to a rapid rise in price. Panic buying usually occurs when investors believe that a security or market is already rising and they wish to buy it before the price rises even more. Panic buying may or may not be the result of an overreaction. Rules on many stock markets limit the amount by which a security can rise in a single session to reduce the pressure for panic buying. See also: Panic selling.

Panji In India, a slang term for a five-paisa coin, which is worth 1/20 of one Indian rupee.

Pank'a An ancient Persian unit of length approximately equivalent to 1.5 meters.

Pank'a Dva An ancient Persian unit of length approximately equivalent to 500 millimeters.

Panni A Finnish unit of dry volume approximately equivalent to 88 liters. It became obsolete when Finland adopted the metric system in 1880.

Panninala A Finnish unit of area approximately equivalent to 2,464 square meters. It became obsolete when Finland adopted the metric system in 1880.

Pantry Audit A survey of consumer goods that homes have at a given time. A pantry audit may be conducted over the telephone or using a questionnaire and is intended to inform producers and retailers of what they should make or stock.

Paper Bid A request to buy a publicly-traded company in which the offering company offers to purchase shares in the target company with shares or bonds in itself. Many offers to buy a company include both paper and cash, but a paper bid is exclusively non-cash. How profitable a paper bid is for target company shareholders depends on the market value of the stocks and bonds.

Paper Company A company with no operations that exists exclusively for a financial reason. For example, a paper company may issue a bond to fund its parent company so the parent company does not have the liability directly. A paper company has few or no assets other than those of a financial nature. See also: Back door listing.

Paper Dealer A person or company that trades commercial paper on its own behalf. That is, a dealer is a principal in a transaction; it neither does business on behalf of a client nor facilitates transactions between parties. Thus, it may purchase commercial paper from issuers and sell it to investors (including other dealers). In the United States, dealers are regulated by the SEC, and must be trading securities as a business. See also: Dealer paper.

Paper Gain A gain on an investment that has not yet been realized. That is, a paper gain occurs when the current price of a security is higher than the price the holder paid for it, but the holder still owns the security. As a result, there is the possibility that the paper gain might be erased if the price goes back down. A paper gain represents an increase in one's net worth, but it may or may not affect one's lifestyle. See also: Paper loss.

Paper Gold 1. An option contract or other derivative in which the underlying asset is gold. **2.** An informal term for Special Drawing Rights.

Paper Local A local labor union with no legitimate members that only exists to influence regional and national union elections. Paper locals are associated with organized crime.

Paper Loss A loss on an investment that has not yet been realized. That is, a paper loss occurs when the current price of a security which is still owned by the holder is lower than the price the holder paid for it. As a result, it is possible that the paper loss might be erased if the price increases again. A paper loss represents a decrease in one's net worth, but it may or may not affect one's lifestyle. See also: Paper profit.

Paper Money 1. See: Cash. **2.** See: Fiat money.

Paper Stock Weight The weight of a type of paper relative to other types of paper. In general, greater paper stock weight indicates more durable paper. For instance, card stock (used for business cards) has greater paper stock weight than notebook paper.

Paper Trade In brief, a pretend trade. Investors make paper trades to experiment investment strategies, and to generally become comfortable with the idea of trading without actually taking on risk. Paper trades are available with computer programs that link to the actual market.

Papiermark The currency of Germany between 1914 and 1923. Technically, the papiermark was the same currency as the goldmark. However, the German government broke the mark's peg to gold in 1914, making it a fiat currency in order to finance its activities in World War I. The peg to gold was not resumed after the war ended and the papiermark suffered from intense hyperinflation due to the post-war government's decision to print banknotes to pay Germany's war debts. It was replaced by the rentenmark at a ratio of 1 trillion to one.

Papua New Guinean Kina The currency of Papua New Guinea. It was introduced in 1975, replacing the Australian dollar. While the kina replaced the dollar at par, it is a floating currency.

Par 1. Of equal value. The word is often used in relation to pegged currencies; that is, if one currency pegs itself to another at par, it means that the central bank has declared that the currencies are of equal value. **2.** The full price of a bond. This is usually, but not always, $1,000 per bond. Coupon payments are calculated as a percentage of par. Likewise, bonds are often traded as a percentage of par. For example, one may buy a bond at 95% of par, meaning that the investor pays $950. It is also called face value.

Par Bond A bond with a sale price equal to its face value. Normally, this is $1000.

Par Value of Currency The dollar amount of the exchange rate between two currencies. For example, if one British pound is worth two U.S. dollars, and a person has 100 pounds, the par value in dollars is $200. The par values of currency change with exchange rates.

Para A division of the Serbian dinar equal in value to 1/100 of one dinar.

Para Tariff An extra fee or tax imposed on a good in addition to the tariff stated on the country's tariff schedule.

Parabolic Indicator In technical analysis, a method of using the stop and reverse method to determine when to buy or sell a security. When the security trades at a price below the stop and reverse point, technical analysts recommend selling while if it trades above that point they recommend buying. It is called a parabolic indicator because the prices between the buy and sell points look roughly like a parabola.

Paradox of Voting The idea that because the physical process of voting is inconvenient and each vote usually matters very little, the rational person should not vote. Yet large proportions of populations vote. The paradox occurs if one studies voters and other political actors in the same way as one would study rational economic actors.

Paraguayan Guarini The currency of Paraguay. It was introduced in 1944, replacing the Paraguayan peso. It was pegged to the U.S. dollar between 1960 and 1985; it is now the least valuable currency in North and South America.

Paraguayan Peso The currency of Paraguay between 1856 and 1944. Until 1870, it was divided into eight reales. Afterward, it was decimalized. It was replaced by the guarani.

Parallel Shift in the Yield Curve A change in the yield curve for bonds with different maturities in which the changes in yields occur evenly. For example, given a yield curve for bonds with one-year, five-year, and 10-year maturities, a parallel shift in the yield curve occurs when the yields for all three bonds increase 10 basis points each. See also: Nonparallel Shift in the Yield Curve.

Parasa An ancient Hebrew unit of length approximately equivalent to four or four and a half kilometers.

Parasang 1. An obsolete Arabic unit of length approximately equivalent to 5.76 kilometers. **2.** An ancient Persian unit of length approximately equivalent to six kilometers.

Parasanges An ancient Greek unit of length approximately equivalent to 5,548 meters.

Parastatal A slang term for state-owned enterprise, especially in Africa.

Parent Company A company that owns enough stock in another country to strongly influence or control outright the latter's operations, especially the election of its board of directors. Parent companies sometimes have operations of their own, and sometimes have no other business except to own and manage subsidiaries. These are known as holding companies. Some parent companies own subsidiaries in a single industry, while others are diversified. Parent companies become parent companies either by buying smaller companies, or by spinning off some of its operations into a separate company. See also: Mergers & Acquisitions.

Pari An ancient Indian unit of area approximately equivalent to one hectare.

Pari Passu Describing securities or debts with equal claim on some right. A new issue of a security may be issued pari passu, which indicates that it carries the same rights as shares already issued. For example, common shares are all pari passu with respect to each other; this means that no one share has a prior claim to a dividend over any other. However, all common shares are junior to any preferred share, which is likewise pari passu with respect to other preferred shares.

Paridesha An ancient Indian unit of length variously equivalent to values between 30 and 40 meters.

Paris A former slang term for the spot exchange rate for the U.S. dollar and the French franc.

Paris Club An informal group consisting of 19 wealthy countries in the developed world. Financial government official meet every six weeks to discuss debt relief in the developing world. The IMF typically recommends a country to the Paris Club when other forms of restructuring have not worked. Potential solutions proposed by the Paris Club range from payment rescheduling to debt cancellation. See also: Highly-indebted poor country.

Paris Commune A municipal government that briefly held power in Paris, France, from March to May 1871. Coming to power during a time of national upheaval, the Commune required pawn shops to return tools pawned by workers, instituted pensions for veterans' widows, abolished interest on debt, and implemented other similar measures. It was forced out of power by the French army, but was considered a model for Marxist leaders from the late-19th through the mid-20th century.

Paris Interbank Offer Rate The average interest rate participating French banks offer each other for unsecured loans. While not as prominent as LIBOR or EURIBOR, it serves as a benchmark for some euro-denominated forward rate agreements and interest rate swaps. Interest rate futures and options based on PIBOR are traded on Euronext Paris. See also: Frankfurt Interbank Offer Rate.

Parity 1. The state of being equal. Parity is used in a variety of contexts. For example, parity is achieved when the value of a convertible security equals the value of the underlying common stock. **2.** A situation in which the total of the premium and the strike price of an option are equal to the market value of the underlying asset. For example, if the premium is $5 per share and the strike is $10, then parity is achieved when the market value of the underlying is $15 per share. See also: At-the-money. **3.** See: Par.

Parity Bond A bond with an equal claim on some right as another bond. A new issue of a bond may be issued as a parity bond, which indicates that it carries the same rights as bonds already issued. For example, unsecured bonds are all parity bonds with respect to each other; this means that no one bond has a prior claim to a coupon over any other. However, all unsecured bonds are junior to any secured bonds, which are likewise parity bonds, with respect to other secured bonds. See also: Pari passu.

Parity Grid In the European Monetary System, the highest, lowest, and middle exchange rates for national currencies relative to the European currency unit. The parity grid determines the exchange rates at which naked interventions are necessary to maintain the peg to the European currency unit.

Parker v. Davis A U.S. Supreme Court case holding that fiat currency issued during the U.S. Civil War was legal tender and had to be accepted as payment. The court held that one could not demand payment in gold or another commodity instead of legal tender currency. The case was decided in 1871, confirming the earlier decision in Knox v. Lee.

Parking 1. The act or practice of investing in low risk and/or highly liquid securities while one decides where to invest in the medium and long term. For example, one may park one's money in a Treasury bond, or even a savings account, while one makes these decisions. **2.** The act of illegally holding or financing stock on behalf of another party with the intent to conceal that party's ownership. Parking occurs when an investor would otherwise own more that 5% of shares outstanding, which would require him/her to register certain information with the SEC. Parking is a method a corporate raider uses when he/she wishes to conceal his/her intent to acquire a company. The raider therefore enlists another's help in doing so by asking him/her to hold or finance a certain amount of stock. See also: Williams Act.

Parking Violation The act of illegally holding or financing stock on behalf of another party with the intent to conceal that party's ownership. Parking violations occur when an investor would otherwise own more that 5% of shares outstanding, which would require him/her to register certain information with the SEC. Parking violations usually occur when a corporate raider wishes to conceal his/her intent to acquire a company and enlists another's help in doing so by asking him/her to hold or finance a certain amount of stock. See also: Williams Act.

Parkinson's Law A somewhat tongue-in-cheek adage stating: "Work expands so as to fill the time available for its completion." This is used in project management and in other situations to describe why projects are often completed so close to deadline.

Parliamentary Secretary to the Treasury An official in the British government. Despite the name, the parliamentary secretary has no duties at HM Treasury and in general the position is given to the chief whip of the governing party of the House of Commons.

Parmak A Turkish measure of length approximately equivalent to 3.157 centimeters. It became obsolete when Turkey made the metric system mandatory in 1933.

Paroquia In several Spanish and Portuguese-speaking countries, a political or cultural subdivision. In some countries, such as Ecuador, it refers to a municipality, while in others it is simply a local neighborhood or village.

Parroquia In Andorra, a political subdivision equivalent to a county or municipality.

Parsiktu An ancient Akkadian unit of volume approximately equivalent to 60 liters.

Parsonage Allowance The housing allowance for a priest, minister or other clergy member (or the equivalent). The parsonage allowance is tax deductible for purposes of calculating the income tax owed, but not for calculating the self-employment tax. See also: Form 4361.

Part B Prospectus A supplement to a mutual fund's prospectus. It contains additional information on the fund, usually on its risks and operations. Mutual funds do not provide the part B prospectus to investors automatically, as many investors do not believe they need it to make an appropriate decision on whether to buy shares in the fund. However, regulations require that a mutual fund provide a copy of its part B prospectus free of charge upon request. It is also called a statement of additional information.

Partial Informal; a trade in which a broker only executes part of a client's order. The broker makes a partial execution based on the counter-orders currently available. Some client orders, such as all-or-none orders, preclude partial execution.

Partial Compensation A situation in which a buyer makes incomplete payment for the delivery of goods, some of which are therefore bought back by the seller, effectively withholding them from delivery.

Partial Delivery A delivery in which the seller (or his/her broker) gives to the buyer only part of the agreed-upon quantity. For example, if an investor buys 1,000 shares and the selling broker delivers 700, this is a partial delivery. In such a situation, the buyer is not obligated to make payment until full delivery has been made. See also: Fail.

Partial Execution A situation in which a broker fills part of a client's order, but is unable to fill the whole order because of the lack of a corresponding order. For example, if an investor makes an order to a broker to sell 1,000 shares at a certain price, but there are only buyers for 600 shares, the broker partially executes the order and looks for buyers for the remaining 400. The leftovers from a partial execution are called leaves.

Partial Redemption 1. A situation in which an issuer calls part of a bond issue but not the whole thing. That is, if a company issues a callable bond and decides later to redeem a portion before maturity, this is called a partial redemption. **2.** In investment companies, the decision of a shareholder to redeem some but not all of his/her shares.

Partial Release A provision in some mortgages allowing part of the collateral (which, in this case, is the property underlying the mortgage) to be released under certain stated circumstances. For example, once the property owner has repaid a given percentage of the principal, part of the property may be released from the collateral under a partial release provision.

Partial Tender Offer An offer to buy some of the stock in a publicly-traded company for a price well above fair market value. The company making the tender offer specifies the maximum number of shares it will buy. As with other tender offers, it is not intended to stop trade on its stock. It may be part of a hostile takeover or, if a company is buying back its own stock, an attempt to keep a hostile takeover from happening. See also: Self-Tender Offer.

Partial Vote A situation in which a shareholder does not vote with all available shares, or when all of a broker's clients with shares in a company do not inform the broker of their intended votes. For example, if a shareholder or broker holds 100 shares in AT&T, but only votes with 90 shares at the shareholders' meeting, that shareholder or broker has engaged in a partial vote.

Participant A person or company with a stake in a venture. Examples of participants include a shareholder, an employee in a company, or a policyholder in an insurance policy.

Participate But Do Not Initiate An instruction to a broker indicating that the investor does not want to trade in such a way that he/she affects the prices of any securities. A participate but do not initiate order occurs when the investor has made a large order to buy or sell a security.

Participating Buyer/Seller A buyer or seller who agrees to the terms of sale offered by a counterparty. This term is most often used for transactions on an exchange.

Participating Dividend A dividend from participating preferred stock. Shareholders of participating preferred stock are entitled to a minimum dividend, but the participating dividend may sometimes be higher than the minimum depending upon the company's performance.

Participating GIC A guaranteed investment contract (GIC) that receives a return based on some portfolio of assets held by the insurance company issuing the GIC. This differs from most GICs, in that most pay a fixed return.

Participating Policy In insurance, a policy (usually a whole life policy) that pays dividends. The dividends are a portion of the insurance company's profits and are paid to the policyholder as if he/she were a stockholder. However, the policyholder has a variety of options on what to do with the dividends. He/she may take the payment in cash, just like a stock. Alternately, he/she may apply the dividends to the policy premium, reducing his/her cost. Finally he/she may place the money with the insurance company, which treats the dividends like a savings account, accruing interest for the policyholder. Most participating policies pay a final dividend at the policy's maturity, and some have a guaranteed dividend, which is determined in the insurance contract. More recent participating policies have more complicated structures, such as including market value reductions on dividend withdrawals. This has led critics to complain that participating policies are overly complicated without providing the policyholder much he/she cannot have in other investment vehicles. In the United Kingdom, participating policies are called with-profits policies, and their dividends are called bonuses.

Participating Preferred Stock A stock, entitling the bearer to part ownership in the issuing company, and also to a certain minimum dividend. The dividend paid may be higher than the minimum depending upon company performance. In any case, these dividends must be paid before any dividends are paid on common stock, and if a company is unable to pay dividends on participating preferred stock, stockholders have the right to force the liquidation of the company. Private equity and venture capital firms often use participating preferred stock as a means of financing their investments. Unlike most other preferred stock owners, participating preferred stockholders sometimes have voting rights in the company. See also: Cumulative preferred stock, Non-cumulative stock, Convertible stock.

Participation A very large loan made by more than one lender to a single borrower. A participation loan exists when the lenders have a legal limit on the maximum amount they may lend.

Participation Certificate **1.** An alternative to a government or municipal bond in which an investor buys a share in the improvements or infrastructure the government entity intends to fund. This contrasts with a bond, in which the investor loans the government or municipality money in order to make these improvements. This is used primarily when the government or municipality has a charter-mandated debt ceiling. In the United States the only entities issuing or guaranteeing participation certificates are Freddie Mac, Fannie Mae, Ginnie Mae, and Sallie Mae. **2.** See: International Depository Receipt (IDR).

Participation Rate The number of persons in an economy who are willing to work, and are either working or looking for work as a percentage of the total labor force. The participation rate is one way to measure an economy's employment rate. See also: Discouraged worker.

Partisan Describing any measure or policy that draws support from only one political party. For example, in the United States, a bill drawing support only from Democrats or only from Republicans may be said to be partisan. The term can also be used to describe to the act of rigidly supporting only the interests of one's own party.

Partner In a company, one who shares with at least one other person, jointly and severally, the right to share revenue, as well as at least some of the financial risk for the company's debts. In a general partnership, all partners share this right as well as management authority over the business. In a limited partnership, one or more general partners maintain management authority while limited partners only share in profit. In a limited liability partnership, partners may or may not have management authority and share revenue according to some predetermined arrangement. The allocation of risk differs between each of these types of partnership as well.

Partnership A business structure in which two or more persons share in the ownership and profits and losses of the business. There are three main types of partnerships. In general partnerships, two or more partners, jointly and severally, share all profits and losses, management authority, and risk for the business. In a limited liability partnership, partners share profits and losses and divide management authority according to the company's specific structure. In case of liquidation, every partner is only liable for the amount he/she has invested in the company, much like a stockholder in a corporation. Limited partnerships have elements of both the previous structures, having both general partners and limited partners. General partners in a limited partnership must share a certain amount of profit and financial liability with limited partners according to an arrangement between them. In this situation, general partners have all management authority and unlimited liability, while a limited partner is only liable for his/her investment. In most jurisdictions, partnerships are preferable to corporations because partnerships' profits are not taxed prior to distribution to the partners. In other words, there is no equivalent to a corporate tax on partnerships. On the other hand, partners have more legal and financial liability in case of liquidation than would shareholders and most management in a corporation.

Partnership Account An account at a brokerage held by two or more people in which each person is equally liable. The account holders may or may not have a written agreement on the rights and obligations each one has in the partnership account. This is similar to a joint account, but is used mainly for business partnerships, rather than for married couples who are investing.

Partnership Agreement An agreement between two or more parties stating the terms of a partnership. Among the provisions of a partnership agreement are whether it is a general partnership, a limited partnership, or a limited liability partnership. The agreement also specifies the specific terms of the partnership, such as the division of profit and risk.

Party in Interest Anyone prohibited under ERISA from using a retirement plan for one's own interests. For example, the investment manager of a 401(k) may not use that 401(k) as collateral on a personal loan. See also: Fiduciary Responsibility.

Paso A Spanish measure of length approximately equivalent to 1.39 meters. It is largely obsolete.

Pass On To charge a customer for an expense that one was required to pay. For example, suppose a company spends $10 for a product, which it then re-sells to customers for $14. If the company's supplier raises the price to $12 per product, the company may pass on the expenses to customers by raising its own price to $16 per product, thereby preserving its $4 profit.

Pass the Book In a brokerage, to transfer orders from one office to another office. Passing the book enables a brokerage to continue trading when one exchange closes by simply going to an office that operates on an exchange that is still open. Ideally, this will enable trading 24 hours per day.

Passbook **1.** A ledger or book on which a depositor at a bank records all transactions in one's account, such as deposits, withdrawals, and interest payments. It is also called a bankbook. **2.** A ledger or book on which a company records the credit sales it makes to customers.

Passeree An obsolete Bengali unit of weight approximately equivalent to 4.677 kilograms.

Passive Income (or loss) from an investment in which an individual does not directly participate. The most common types of passive income are rents from property one owns and income from a limited partnership. Some analysts consider income from dividends and coupons to be passive income while others do not. Passive income is taxable, but it is often treated differently from active income.

Passive Activity An investment in which an individual does not directly participate. The most common types of passive activities are rents from a property one owns and income from a limited partnership. In both those situations, the investor puts in money but has no management authority. Some analysts consider income from dividends and coupons to be passive income, while others do not. Income from a passive activity is taxable, but it is often treated differently than active income.

Passive Activity Loss A loss resulting from a passive investment. For example, rental income is considered passive; if a tenant does not pay his/her rent, this may be considered a passive income loss. Passive income losses may only offset passive income gains; they may not offset earned income. Furthermore, passive income loss may not be carried back; it may only be carried forward.

Passive Bond A bond with no yield.

Passive Debt A debt that a creditor is not actively trying to collect, and on which the debtor is making no payments. Passive debts eventually may be written off.

Passive Foreign Investment Company A company based in a foreign country where either at least 75% of its income comes from passive sources, such as rent or dividend, or at least 50% of its assets carry dividends or interest. PFICs are subject to strict tax guidelines in the United States that intend to discourage investment by Americans. See also: Income test, Asset test.

Passive Income Income from a venture in which an individual does not directly participate. The most common types of passive income are rents and income from a limited partnership. Some analysts consider income derived from securities such as dividends and coupons to be passive income, while others put it into a separate category as portfolio income. Passive income is taxable, but it is often treated differently than active income.

Passive Income Generator Any investment that produces income from a venture in which an individual does not directly participate. The most common types of passive income are rents and income from a limited partnership. Thus, if an investor buys an apartment complex or a piece of an oil and gas limited partnership, this is considered a PIG. Passive income is taxable, but it is often treated differently than active income.

Passive Management The practice of a money manager or a team of money managers making investment decisions on what securities to include in a fund or portfolio, and then leaving those securities largely unchanged for a significant period of time. To give a very simple example, an investment manager may buy every stock on the Dow Jones Industrial Average and hold them for a period of five or 10 years. Passive investment managers seek a well diversified set of securities. See also: Indexing, Active investing, Value investing.

Passive Market Making A situation in which an underwriter makes a bid in the secondary market to buy shares in a new issue for which the underwriter is responsible before it is fully distributed. In passive market making, the underwriter is now allowed to enter a higher bid than any competing investors. See also: Stabilization period.

Passo geometrico A Portuguese measure of length approximately equivalent to 1.65 meters. It became obsolete after Lusophone countries adopted the metric system in the 19th century.

Pass-Through Coupon Rate The interest rate a holder receives on a pass-through security. A pass-through security is a negotiable security backed by the receivables on a pool of liabilities like loans or mortgages. The pass-through coupon rate is the same as the weighted average interest rate on the liabilities underlying the security, less any applicable fees.

Pass-Through Rate The interest rate that an investor in a mortgage-backed security receives. It is calculated as the weighted average interest rate on the mortgages underlying the security less management fees and other related expenses. Because of this, the pass-through rate is lower than the interest rate on the individual mortgages.

Pass-Through Security A derivative security representing the receivables on some debt. That is, a shareholder of a pass-through security is entitled to a portion of the income from the debt. Generally, a pass-through security has a large number of debts underlying it; for example, a pass-through may represent a portion of several hundred car loans. The most common type of pass-through is a mortgage-backed security.

Passus An ancient Roman unit of length approximately equivalent to 1.48 meters.

Past Due Balance Method A method for determining charges for a loan or credit sale payment that has not been received by its due date. Generally, the method is charging a certain percentage of interest on the outstanding payment. For example, if one has a $100 balance on his/her credit card and does not pay it off by the due date, interest begins to accrue on the $100 and the card holder owes for that as well.

Pataca The currency of Macau. It was introduced in 1894. Macau is a special administrative region of China; perhaps because of this, the pataca is pegged to the Hong Kong dollar using a currency board system. That is, the Monetary Authority of Macau is legally obligated to redeem pataca for the equivalent amount of Hong Kong dollars on demand.

Patent A right, granted or guaranteed by a government, giving an inventor the exclusive right to make, produce, and sell his/her invention for a certain period of time. While the time limit varies from country to country, most governments recognize each other's patent laws. In the United States, the length of a patent is 20 years. Patents exist to protect inventors from having their ideas stolen, a concept intended to encourage innovation and entrepreneurship.

Path Dependent Option An option contract whose price is determined according to some formula involving the price of the underlying asset over time. Most options have prices that are dependent upon the value of the underlying asset at the time the option is exercised. A path dependent option, on the other hand, uses a more complex formula. For example, in some Asian options, the strike price is the average of the prices of the underlying asset over the life of the contract.

Pathet Lao Kip The former currency of Laos. It was issued in 1976, though it was in circulation in some parts of the country before then. It replaced the royal kip after the Laotian Civil War. It was re-valued and replaced by the new kip in 1979.

Patriot Bond A Series EE bond issued after September 11, 2001. Patriot bonds were inspired by the war bonds issued during World War II, but they never gained the latter's popularity.

Pattern The graphical representation on a chart of a trend in security prices. Technical analysts identify patterns for a security and predict future price movements in part by matching current patterns with previous patterns.

Pattern Day Trader A designation by the SEC of an investor who conducts more than four day trades in any five, consecutive trading days and for whom these trades make up at least 6% of his/her total trading activity. Because of the risk inherent to day trading, the SEC requires all pattern day traders to maintain at least $25,000 in equity in a margin account.

Patterson v. Shumate A 1992 court case in the United States holding that assets one holds in a pension or other investment vehicle on which transfer is restricted may not be surrendered in bankruptcy. That is, these assets may not be liquidated and distributed to creditors.

Pau An obsolete unit of volume in Brunei, Malaysia, and elsewhere in the region equivalent to 0.28413 liters.

Paul v. Virginia An 1869 court case in the United States concerning insurance regulation. The Supreme Court held that a corporation is not a citizen of the U.S. under the privilege and immunities clause of the Constitution; that is, a state may treat corporations organized in another state differently from its own corporations. Additionally, the Court decided that the sale of an insurance policy did not constitute an Act of commerce and therefore the federal government could not regulate insurance at all. This decision was largely overturned in 1944. See also: United States v. South-Eastern Underwriters Association.

Paul Volcker An American economist and Chairman of the Federal Reserve from 1979 to 1987. He was credited with ending the high inflation seen in the 1970s. He raised the fed funds rate as high as 20%. This is considered to have contributed to a recession in the early 1980s. However, inflation dropped from 13.5% in 1981 to 3.2% in 1983. He was born in 1927. See also: Stagflation.

Pauper A very poor person, especially one reliant on government benefits or charity. A pauper may be able to file a lawsuit without paying filing fees.

Pavo In Spain, a slang term for the euro.

Pawn 1. To give at item to a pawnbroker in exchange for a loan. When one pawns an item, one receives the loan and gives the pawnbroker possession of the item. One may receive the item back within a certain period of time if one repays the loan with interest. If the loan is not repaid, the pawnbroker may sell the item in his/her shop. Because the pawnbroker already has possession of the item, he/she does not report non-payment of a loan and it does not affect the borrower's creditworthiness. **2.** A fairly uncommon term for collateral.

Pawn Shop A shop where one may pawn an item or buy items other persons have pawned. When one pawns an item, one receives a loan and gives the pawnbroker (the pawn shop's owner) possession of the item. One may retrieve the item within a certain period of time if one repays the loan with interest. If the loan is not repaid, the pawnbroker may sell the item in his/her shop. Because the pawnbroker already has possession of the item, he/she does not report non-payment of the loan and it does not affect the borrower's creditworthiness.

Pawnbroker The owner of a pawn shop, which is a place where one may pawn an item or buy items other persons have pawned. When one pawns an item, one receives a loan and gives the pawnbroker (the pawn shop's owner) possession of the item. One may retrieve the item within a certain period of time if one repays the loan with interest. If the loan is not repaid, the pawnbroker may sell the item in his/her shop. Because the pawnbroker already has possession of the item, he/she does not report non-payment of the loan and it does not affect the borrower's creditworthiness.

Pay Day The day on which an employer provides paychecks to employees. In the United States, pay days generally occur twice a month or every two weeks. Some jobs, however, pay weekly or monthly.

Pay Out To pay dividends to shareholders, as opposed to reinvesting profits in the company. The more of a company's profits it pays out, the less it reinvests (or plows back). Whether or not this is desirable depends on the rate of growth. Investors tend to prefer a higher pay-out in a slow-growing company and a lower one in a fast-growing company.

Pay the Piper 1. To repay a debt. **2.** To face a coming punishment, especially if one has made a serious mistake. One pays the piper by facing the wronged supervisor or client.

Pay/Collect The exchange of money that occurs between futures traders after all transactions have been marked to market and netted by a clearing house. After the end of a trading day, the clearing house offsets trades against each other so the least possible amount of money actually needs to be transferred. This exchange is called pay/collect, or more properly, payment and collection.

Payable 1. An outstanding debt. A debt that one must pay to a creditor. **2.** A current liability. Any debt that a company must pay within a year. **3.** Accounts payable. Money owed for a good or service purchased on credit. Accounts payable are a current liability for a company and are expected to be paid within a short amount of time, often 10, 30, or 90 days.

Payable Date The date on which dividends are given to shareholders, who may either receive a check from the company or elect to receive more shares.

Payable on Demand Describing a debt that must be repaid upon the request of the lender. For example, if Joe lends Bob $100 payable on demand, there is no set payment date, but Bob must pay whenever Joe asks. Some loans become payable on demand if the borrower violates the terms of the lending agreement. See also: Call the loan.

Payable to Bearer Describing a check or security containing no ownership information, for which the physical holder is therefore presumed to be the owner. One may cash a payable to bearer check at the bank on which the check is drawn, and may receive dividends or coupons on a bearer security by presenting it to the issuer.

Payable-on-Death A bank account into which a person may deposit funds that will automatically transfer to a named beneficiary upon the person's death. This can be beneficial because the payable-on-death account transfers outside the probate process and the beneficiary may begin using the money immediately. See also: Transferable-on-death.

Pay-As-You-Go The practice of a government agency funding new projects with money it has on hand from previous appropriations. That is, pay-as-you-go financing requires a government to save to pay for a project for which it does not receive a specific appropriation. The intent behind pay-as-you-go is to encourage responsible spending by a government. This is related to, but distinct from, paygo rules in the United States.

Payback The length of time until an investment makes an amount of money equal to the original amount invested. It does not account for the time value of money. That is, the payback period differs from the break-even time, which accounts for inflation, interest, and so forth.

Payback Period The time between the first payment on a loan and its maturity. For example, if one takes out a student loan with a payback period of 10 years, the full amount of the loan is due 10 years after the first payment, which occurs on an agreed-upon date. Over the course of the payback period, a borrower must either pay back the loan with his/her own funds or take out a different loan to pay off the first. It is also called the premium recovery period. See also: Refinancing.

Payday Loan A short-term loan expected to be repaid before the borrower's next pay day. Frequently, the borrower collateralizes a payday loan by presenting a postdated check for the amount of the loan (plus interest). The lender simply deposits the check on the agreed-upon date. Interest rates on payday loans are notoriously high.

Paydown 1. A payment on the interest and/or principal on a loan; debt service. **2.** When a bond is called or matures and a new one is issued, the amount by which the face value of the old issue exceeds the face value of the new one. This represents a reduction in the issuer's debt. If a company pays out $10,000,000 in bond maturities and then issues $7,000,000 in new bonds, this is an example of paydown, because the company now has $3,000,000 less in debt.

Paydown Factor In mortgage-backed securities, the amount of the principal in the underlying mortgage pool that is repaid each month, expressed as a percentage of the original total principal. Ginnie Mae requires all issuers of mortgage-backed securities to publish their paydown factors.

Payee The person or institution that receives a payment. For example, if Joe writes Bob a check for $10, Bob is the payee. He receives the check and may deposit the $10 at his bank or he may elect to take cash from either his bank or Joe's. One may be a payee on a check, wire transfer, or in any other method of sending money from one party to another.

Payer A person or institution that makes a payment. In ordinary transactions, the buyer is the payer, though a third party may be the payer in some circumstances. In bonds and loans, the issuer or borrower is the payer to the bondholder or lender. In equities, a publicly-traded company is the payer of dividends. See also: Payee.

Pay-For A tax increase or spending cut that makes proposed legislation revenue neutral. For example, if a bill proposes $150 million in spending, the pay-for may be $150 million in cuts to other programs. A pay-for is required under PAYGO budget rules.

Paygo In the United States, the practice of the federal government not to authorize increased spending or tax cuts without offsetting it by decreasing spending or raising taxes in some other place. That is, under paygo, all legislation and spending must be revenue neutral. The intent behind paygo is to encourage responsible spending by the federal government. It was in place between 1990 and 2002, and in 2007 and 2008 and was again implemented in 2010. See also: Statutory Pay-As-You-Go Act of 2010.

Paying Agent An institution, usually an investment bank, that accepts funds from the issuer of a security and distributes them to that security's holders. In stocks, a paying agent receive dividends, which it then disburses to stockholders. In bonds, it receives coupon payments, which it then gives to bondholders. A paying agent acts as an intermediary in these transactions, and receives a fee for these services. See also: Outsourcing.

Paymaster General The head of the Office of HM Paymaster General, which is the department of the British government holding accounts at the Bank of England that appropriates funds for the various functions of government. That is, he/she is responsible for paying British departments and public servants. The paymaster general is appointed by the monarch on the advice of the prime minister.

Payment The reception of compensation for a good or service. For example, if one sells a hairdryer for $10, the payment is $10. In a cash sale, payment is made immediately or almost immediately, while in a credit sale, payment may be delayed for a certain period of time.

Payment Cap The maximum periodic payment a borrower may be charged on a contract or agreement. For example, an adjustable-rate mortgage may have a payment cap stating that a payment will not rise over a certain level, even if the formula used to calculate the payment would have it do so. A payment cap reduces the risk of the party making the payments.

Payment Date The dates on which stockholders are sent dividend payments. That is, the payment dates are the dates where stockholders receive dividends that they are either guaranteed (for preferred stock) or that was previously declared by the company (for common stock). Payment dates are fixed for preferred stock because the dividends are contractually guaranteed; however, they may change for common stock, particularly when the company changes its plowback rate. See also: Interest Dates.

Payment Float A deposit into a bank account that has not yet cleared. For example, one may deposit a check for $1000 from an out-of-state bank. The funds may be posted to the account immediately, but they will not become available to the account holder until the issuing bank honors the check and transfers the funds to the receiving bank. This process can take as long as five business days. See also: Check Hold.

Payment for Order Flow A payment that a dealer makes to a brokerage in exchange for the brokerage sending business the dealer's way. For example, if a brokerage's client offers to sell 2,000 shares of a stock, the brokerage may receive a payment for order flow of three cents per share if it sells the stock to a certain dealer.

Brokerages and dealers make payment for order flow arrangements ahead of time; they are advantageous to brokerages because of the revenue, while they enable dealers to make transactions they might not have made otherwise. Critics contend that this system encourages brokerages to act in the best interest of themselves (or the dealers), rather than their clients.

Payment In-Kind 1. Describing a bond or preferred stock in which coupon payments or dividends come in the form of more bonds or shares, rather than cash. At times, the investor has the option of choosing whether to accept cash or payment-in-kind, but, more often, this option resides with the issuer. A problem with PIK securities for the issuer is the fact that it becomes tempting to pay bond coupons with more debt rather than cash when the company has a liquidity problem. Of course, doing this often adds to the issuer's liquidity problems. Likewise, payment-in-kind securities can hurt investors as they must pay taxes on the market value of these securities and may lack the cash to do so. Payment-in-kind bonds were not unusual during the private equity boom in the mid-2000s, but became rare during the credit crunch at the end of the decade. **2.** The act of compensating the seller of a good or service with another good or service rather than money. See also: Barter.

Payment Protection Insurance An insurance policy that makes loan payments on behalf of the policyholder in the event of financial hardship. For example, if a policyholder loses his job, payment protection insurance would make his credit card payments for up to, say, six months as he looks for work. Payment protection insurance allows one to face difficulty without the immediate fear of default.

Payment System Any system enabling the transfer of funds between parties. For example, when a bank processes a check, it uses a payment system to collect funds from the bank on which the check was drawn and then transfers the funds to the payee's account. Likewise, a clearing house uses a payment system for the settlement of security transactions. Most payment systems are electronic, and many involve the Federal Reserve in some way.

Payment-In-Kind Bond A bond in which coupon payments come in the form of more bonds, rather than cash. At times, the investor has the option of choosing whether to accept cash or payment-in-kind, but more often this option resides with the issuer. A problem with PIK bonds for the issuer is the fact that it becomes tempting to pay coupons with more debt rather than cash when the company has a liquidity problem. Of course, doing this often only adds to the issuer's liquidity problems. This type of bond was not unusual during the private equity boom in the mid-2000s, but became rare during the credit crunch at the end of the decade.

Payments Netting A way of settling transactions that minimizes the need for funds and securities to actually change hands. To give a very simple example, suppose a brokerage buys shares in a company for $100,000 and later sells them back to the original owner for $120,000. A payments netting method would have the securities stay with the original owner and mandate that this owner transfer $20,000 to the brokerage. Payments netting can be complex because of the number of actors involved, but maximizes the likelihood that, at the end of the trading day, every party has received exactly what it should have, and no more. Clearing houses provide most payment netting services.

Payments Pattern The likelihood of a company to receive its accounts receivable by a certain point in time. That is, if most accounts are paid in 10 days and a certain account is unpaid after 25 days, the payments pattern would state that the account is unlikely to be paid in 26 days.

Payoff Profile In options, a chart showing the profits and losses on a contract over time. It is calculated by plotting the value of the underlying asset on the x-axis and the risk on the y-axis.

Payout Period 1. The period of time during which benefits on an annuity or retirement account are paid. **2.** In entrepreneurship, a period of time in which cash flow is negative. This especially applies to an early part of a company's history before it has recovered start up costs and operating expenses. **3.** In stocks, dividends per share divided by earnings per share, expressed as a percentage. Stock analysts use this ratio to compute how much of a company's profits it pays in dividends, and perhaps how that compares to other, similar companies. Stockholders prefer companies that pay more in dividends.

Payout Phase 1. The period of time during which benefits on an annuity or retirement account are paid. **2.** In entrepreneurship, a period of time in which cash flow is negative. This especially applies to the early part of a company's history before it has recovered start up costs and operating expenses.

Payout Ratio In fundamental analysis, the opposite of the plowback ratio. That is, the payout ratio is a company's dividends paid to shareholders expressed as a percentage of total earnings. A higher ratio indicates that a company pays more in dividends and thus reinvests less of its earnings into the company. Whether or not this is desirable depends on the rate of growth: investors tend to prefer a higher plowback ratio in a slow-growing company and a lower one in a fast-growing company.

Payroll Orphan A slang term for a person who has been fired or laid off. The term derives from the fact that the person will not receive a paycheck anymore.

Payroll Tax A tax in which an employer retains a certain percentage of an employee's wages or salary and gives it to the IRS or tax agency instead of the employee. This reduces or eliminates the possibility that the employee will spend his/her tax liability, and give the government cash flow to fund certain operations. See also: Withholding.

Pay-to-Play A practice in which a politician encourages monetary contributions in exchange for benefits for an individual or company. Paying to play may involve outright bribery, but it usually refers to more subtle payments. For example, an insurance company may make large contributions to a politician re-election war chest and the politician may then be inclined to vote in the insurance company's interest. Paying to play is often in a legal gray area. See also: Campaign Finance, Campaign Finance Reform.

Payup 1. A swap for a security with a higher yield. For example, an investor may swap a bond with a certain face value and coupon for another bond with an equal face value but a higher coupon. One refers to the extra funds the investor yields from the higher coupon as a payup. **2.** The additional money an investor needs in order to buy a security with a higher market value. For example, an investor may need payup money if he/she owns a bond, but wishes to buy another bond with a higher coupon rate.

PBC In auditing, a slang term meaning "prepared by client," which indicates anything the auditor has not reviewed and corrected. "he other way around). In other words, to tie out indicates the nuts and bolts of auditing the accuracy o

PBR 1. See: Price to book ratio. **2.** See: Pre-Budget Report.

PC 1. ISO 3166-1 alpha-2 code for the Trust Territory of the Pacific Islands, which separated into several territories and independent countries. This was the code used in international transactions to and from bank accounts in the trust territory. **2.** ISO 3166-2 geocode for the Trust Territory of the Pacific Islands. This was used as an international standard for shipping to the trust territory. In both cases, the code is obsolete.

PCHH ISO 3166-3 code for the Trust Territory of the Pacific Islands, which was re-designated as the Marshall Islands, Micronesia, the Northern Mariana Islands, and Palau in 1986. ISO 3166-3 codes are used to indicate names of countries that are no longer used.

PCN GOST 7.67 Latin three-letter geocode for the Pitcairn Islands. The code is used for transactions to and from Pitcairn Islander bank accounts and for international shipping to the Pitcairn Islands. As with all GOST 7.67 codes, it is used primarily in Cyrillic alphabets.

P-Coast Informal; the Pacific Exchange or a security traded on it.

Pe 1. ISO 3166-1 alpha-2 code for the Republic of Peru. This is the code used in international transactions to and from Peruvian bank accounts. **2.** ISO 3166-2 geocode for Peru. This is used as an international standard for shipping to Peru. Each department and the constitutional province has its own code with the prefix "PE." For example, the code for the Province of Cuzco is ISO 3166-2:PE-CUS.

Peace Dividend A byword for the benefits for a government's budget (and presumably for the economy as a whole) resulting from a reduction in military spending following the end of a war or conflict. The peace dividend frees up money to spend on other things, which may have a significantly positive effect in the long term. However, it may cause job losses in some areas that are economically dependent on the military. The term was used frequently in the United States and Britain after the Cold War to justify military budget cuts.

Peace Dollar A $1 coin minted in the United States between 1921 and 1935, and again in 1964. Originally minted to make up for a shortage of silver coins after the end of World War I, it is currently illegal to own privately.

Peak 1. The point of a security's or market's highest price for a given period of time. The term comes from charting, in which the x-axis represents time and the y-axis represents price. On a chart, the high point of a business cycle looks like the peak of a mountain. See also: Bottom. **2.** In a period of economic expansion, the point of the highest GDP growth that immediately precedes the beginning of a contraction. In other words, it is the highest point in a business cycle. The term comes from charting, in which the x-axis represents time and the y-axis represents GDP growth. In this situation, the high point of a business cycle looks like the peak of a mountain. See also: Trough.

Peal Grain A measure of weight equivalent to 50 milligrams. It is used to weigh pearls and diamonds. It is also called the metric grain.

Pechys An ancient Greek unit of length approximately equivalent to 462.3 millimeters.

Peck An obsolete Scottish unit of dry volume. For beans, grass seed, peas, rye, salt, and wheat, one peck was approximately equivalent to 9.072 liters. For barley, malt, and oats, however, it was approximately equivalent to 13.229 liters.

Pecking-Order View A theory stating that, all other things being equal, companies seeking to finance a new project or product have a hierarchy of preferred financing options that progresses from the most preferred to the least preferred. The hierarchy is said to follow this order: internal funding (or simply financing a project or product out-of-pocket), debt issuance, debt-equity hybrid issuance, and equity issuance. The pecking-order view states that the hierarchy is structured this way because of the transaction costs involved in each form of financing. That is, internal funding has a lower transaction cost that debt issuance, and so forth.

Pecuniary Bequest A gift of money in a will, as opposed to some other asset. For example, if a man's will gives his son $100,000 cash, rather than ownership of his home, the man has made a pecuniary bequest.

Pedania In Span, a political subdivision roughly equivalent to a county.

Peer-to-Peer A loan to a start-up or other new company from a source other than a financial institution. A lender often charges high interest in a P to P loan. This provides the borrower with financing needed to maintain operations until it becomes profitable. See also: Angel investor.

Pegging 1. The practice of fixing the exchange rate of a currency to the value of another currency. Most countries that peg their currencies do so to the U.S. dollar, though some peg to currency baskets. See also: Fixed exchange rate. **2.** The act of buying a security in a large quantity to drive up the price. Writers of put options (and holders of short positions) practice pegging when the expiration date is approaching and it appears that the option will be exercised such that it puts the writer at a disadvantage. The idea behind pegging is to cause the price to rise so the option is not exercised and the writer can profit from the premium.

PEH ISO 4217 code for the Peruvian sol, the former currency of Peru. It was introduced in 1863, replacing the Peruvian real and the Bolivian peso, which previously had circulated in different parts of the country. It was first pegged to the French franc, then to gold, and finally to the U.S. dollar. It was plagued by hyperinflation at the end of its use, and was replaced by the Peruvian inti in 1985. See also: New sol.

PEI ISO 4217 code for the Peruvian inti, the former currency of Peru. It was introduced in 1985, replacing the Peruvian sol at a ratio of 1,000 sol to one inti. Although it was intended to reduce the sol's high inflation rate, the inti suffered from hyperinflation as well. The new sol replaced the inti in 1991.

Peittha A Burmese unit of mass approximately equivalent to 1.63 kilograms.

Pell Grant A grant that the federal government offers to students based on financial need. A Pell grant may be used to pay for education expenses (up to $5,500 in 2010-2011) for a first bachelor's degree. One must file a FAFSA to become eligible for a Pell grant.

PEN ISO 4217 code for the Peruvian new sol. It was introduced in 1991, replacing the inti, which had replaced the first sol in 1985. It was issued to stem hyperinflation, which had plagued Peru in the late 1980s. Its inflation rate has historically been very low and it developed a reputation as a reliable South American currency.

Penalty Bid An offer to buy the security offered in an IPO with the guarantee that the buyer will retain the security for a certain period of time. If the buyer sells the security before the time is over, the underwriter offering the security assesses a penalty on the buyer's broker, who may or may not pass the penalty on to the buyer. Usually the penalty is equal to the broker's commission on the trade. Underwriters accept penalty bids during an IPO to prevent the price of the security from declining through a sell-off.

Penalty Clause In a contract, especially a loan agreement, a clause stating that the payer must pay extra in the event of a late payment and/or default. The penalty clause states the amount of the penalty and the circumstances under which it must be paid.

Penalty Fee 1. See: Withdrawal penalty. **2.** See: Late fee. **3.** See: Underpayment penalty. **4.** See: Prepayment penalty.

Penalty Plan In a mutual fund, a plan in which all sales fees are paid in the first few years of ownership in the fund. This means that if the shareholder redeems his/her shares in the first few years of ownership, sales fees are deducted, and the shareholder only receives a small portion of his/her original investment. These deductions gradually lessen with time and eventually go to zero in order to encourage long-term investment in the fund. The rules governing penalty plans were established in the Investment Company Amendments Act of 1970.

Penalty Tax An excise tax imposed upon an unauthorized withdrawal from a retirement account, such as a 401(k) or an IRA. Most commonly, a penalty tax is assessed when one makes a withdrawal before the age of 59 1/2. See also: Hardship withdrawal.

Pence A subdivision of the British pound. A pound is divided into 100 pence. Its singular is penny. See also: Cent.

Pen-Down Strike A labor action in which employees come to work but do not do any work. The term connotes that this takes place in an office setting as opposed to an industrial setting. A pen-down strike is analogous to a slow down. See also: Strike.

Penetration 1. See: Market penetration. **2.** In technical analysis, a situation where a security's price falls below its support level or rises above its resistance level. A security penetrating the support (or resistance) is likely to continue to fall (or rise) until another support (or resistance) is found. Penetrating the support is considered highly bearish while penetrating the resistance is highly bullish.

Penetration Pricing The practice of undercutting competitors' prices in order to establish and gain market share. Penetration pricing is most common when a company is introducing a new product in an already saturated market. It may result in losses early on, but is intended to build brand loyalty for when it raises prices later.

Pengar In Sweden, a slang term for money. It derives its name from the penning, which was a currency used in various forms in Sweden until the 18th century.

Peninkulma A Finnish unit of length approximately equivalent to 10.7 kilometers. It became obsolete when Finland adopted the metric system in 1880.

Penni A subdivision of the Finnish markka. One penni was worth 1/100 of one markka. The penni became obsolete in 2002 with the introduction of the euro in Finland. See also: Cent.

Penning A coin minted in Sweden between the 10th and 16th centuries. It remained an accounting currency until 1777. The plural is penningar.

Penny The formal or informal name for the smallest unit of many currencies. One penny is usually equal in value to one cent or the equivalent.

Penny Stock Stock in a very small company with low market capitalization and low prices. Penny stocks are considered highly speculative and rarely are traded on an exchange because so few meet listing requirements. While there is no hard-and-fast definition of what stocks are considered penny stocks, they usually have a share price under $5 and come from a new, unestablished company. While most companies issuing penny stocks fail, investing in these stocks can lead to extraordinarily large returns.

Penny Stock Reform Act Legislation in the United States giving the SEC greater authority to regulate penny stocks. Specifically, the Act gave the SEC the ability to oversee broker-dealers who primarily transact in penny stocks. Because penny stocks trade over-the-counter, the Act also mandated the creation of automated quotes for penny stocks.

Pennyland An obsolete Scottish unit of area. A pennyland was the amount of land on which rent of 1/20 of one ounce of silver could be charged. This system was used in western Scotland.

Pension A retirement plan in which an employer makes a contribution into an account each month. The contributions are invested on behalf of an employee, who may begin to make withdrawals after retirement. Typically, pensions are tax-deferred, meaning that the employee does not pay taxes on the funds in the pension until he/she begins making withdrawals. Pensions may have defined contributions, defined benefits, or both. See also: 401(k), IRA.

Pension Benefit Guaranty Corporation A non-profit corporation under the United States Department of Labor guaranteeing the pensions of some private companies. Established in 1974, it is designed to take over the pensions of participating companies should they become insolvent. It does not derive its revenues from taxation; rather, it collects premiums from participating companies as if it were an insurance policy. It was not designed to protect bankrupt companies; rather, it exists as part of a social safety net for former employees of these companies. It is headed by a Director, who is appointed by the U.S. President upon confirmation of the Senate.

Pension Cost The expense that a company incurs each year by providing a pension plan for its employees. Major expenses in the pension cost include employer matching contributions, management fees, and so forth.

Pension Liabilities Future payouts that a pension is obligated to make. A pension run by a company that has a large number of workers nearing retirement has more liabilities than one run by a company with a smaller eligible workforce. Accounting for pension liabilities varies from country to country.

Pension Maximization A strategy in which a married couple purchases a single life annuity for the older spouse and a joint life annuity for both spouses. If the younger spouse dies first, the older spouse can continue to benefit from both annuities. If the older spouse dies first, the young spouse uses the death benefit from the single life annuity to purchase another single life annuity for himself/herself. The younger spouse will presumably be older at that point and will thus be able to receive a higher monthly payment.

Pension Parachute An antitakeover measure where a company forbids the use of funds in its pension plan to finance a hostile takeover. Many pension plans contain cash over and above what is necessary to pay retired employees. Without a pension parachute, an acquiring company could use debt (or another mechanism) to finance a hostile takeover, and then use the excess cash in the target company's pension to pay itself back. The pension parachute requires the excess cash to go to pensioners only.

Pension Protection Act of 2006 Legislation in the United States requiring companies to pay higher premiums to the Pension Benefit Guaranty Corporation (which insures pensions) if those companies' pensions are underfunded. It also provides greater tax benefits for companies that invest in their own pensions.

Pension Reversion The act of a company canceling an over-funded pension plan in order to recover the amount by which it is over-funded. In addition, pension reversion usually also involves replacing the canceled plan with a less expensive, fixed annuity plan using funds recovered from the former plan. The amount by which funds from the former plan exceed the cost of the new plan is paid to the company or employer.

Pension Rollover The transfer of funds from a retirement account to an IRA. This usually occurs when an account holder takes a new job or otherwise wishes to take advantage of the tax benefits an IRA offers over a pension plan. Most IRA programs only allow one rollover per year; with a Roth IRA, there is an income limit beyond which a rollover is not allowed. An IRA rollover may be accomplished through a direct transfer or by check; however, a check transfer brings a 20% withholding charge, so account holders are advised to make direct transfers. See also: Automatic Rollover.

Pension Shortfall A situation in which there are insufficient funds in a defined benefit plan to cover the plan's obligations. A pension shortfall may occur when the investments into which the employer placed the funds do not perform as well as hoped, or perhaps when a disproportionate number of retirees live longer than expected. The company providing the pension is liable for the pension shortfall, meaning that it must find a way to make payments, even if it reduces the company's income.

Pension Sponsor A company that establishes and/or manages a pension for participating employees. It may be, but is usually not, the same as the company that employs the participants.

Pensioner A person who is collecting a pension. That is, a pensioner has retired and is collecting on an annuity or other state-sponsored or private retirement plan. For this reason, the word is also sometimes used as a euphemism for an older person.

Penthouse A luxury apartment on the top floor of a high-rise building. Penthouses often take up multiple floors and are as large as or larger than some houses. Penthouses are very expensive and are marketed to the wealthy.

Pent-Up Demand A situation in which demand for a product rises precipitously. For example, if demand for cell phones has been low, then suddenly jumps and remains high, it may be due to pent-up demand. This may occur following a recession due to increased spending as an economy recovers.

Penultimate Profit Prospect Of the 10 stocks on the DJIA with the highest yields, the stock with the second lowest yield. According to the book, Beating the Dow, the penultimate profit prospect is the most likely of the 10 to beat the Dow over a given period of time. See also: Dogs of the Dow.

Peon An unskilled worker. The term has a highly negative connotation.

People Pill An antitakeover measure in which the entire management of the target company agrees and publicly states that it will resign collectively if the company is taken over. A people pill, if enacted, would make the takeover more difficult and costly for the acquiring company, and therefore intends to scare away potential hostile bidders. It is a form of a poison pill.

People's Bank of China The central bank of China. It is responsible for setting the country's monetary policy. Until the late 1970s, it was the only legal bank in China and made commercial loans in addition to its duties as the central bank. Since the 1980s, however, this has not been the case, and it no longer makes these loans. It holds more assets than any other central bank. It was established in 1948.

PEPFAR President's Emergency Plan for AIDS Relief. A foreign aid program instituted in the 2000s by the U.S. government to help counteract HIV/AIDS. The goal was to provide 2 million persons with HIV treatment, stop 7 million infections and support treatment for 10 million other people. PEPFAR provided $15 billion between 2003 and 2008 toward these goals.

PEPS A participating preferred stock that may be converted to common stock by a certain date. Like all participating preferred stock, a PEPS entitles the shareholder to a certain minimum dividend. The dividend paid may be higher than the minimum, depending upon company performance. In any case, these dividends must be paid before any dividends are paid on common stock; if a company is unable to pay dividends on participating preferred stock, stockholders have the right to force the liquidation of the company. The conversion feature of a PEPS gives it a great deal of flexibility for the shareholder.

PER GOST 7.67 Latin three-letter geocode for Peru. The code is used for transactions to and from Peruvian bank accounts and for international shipping to Peru. As with all GOST 7.67 codes, it is used primarily in Cyrillic alphabets.

Per Annum On a yearly basis. Taxes are (usually) calculated per annum, as is income.

Per Capita Debt The amount of municipal debt divided by the number of persons in that municipality. Because most municipal bonds are guaranteed in some way by the municipality tax revenue, the number of taxpayers in that municipality is important in determining its ability to repay the bonds. As a result, credit ratings agencies use per capita debt in rating municipal bonds.

Per Capita Income The amount of incomein an area divided by the number of persons in that area. This is, in essence, the average income in the area. It may not adequately describe wealth, as it does not consider debt and it does not consider persons with very high or very low incomes that may skew the average in one direction or another. However, it may still be used as a measure of economic health in an area.

Per Diem Money given to an employee to pay for daily expenses, for example on a business trip. For example, if the employee goes to a convention in Reno, his employer may give him $75 per day for food. If an employee (or self-employed person) pays these expenses himself/herself, they may be tax deductible. Some per diem rates are set; for instance, the IRS allows a certain write-off per diem for business trip expenses without presentation of receipts.

Per Mille Occurrences of an event per 1,000 of a population. For example, property taxes may be assessed as dollars per $1,000 of property value. See also: Millage Rate.

Per Se Latin for "in itself." Describing an act with inherent qualities. For example, in criminal law, an act may be illegal per se; in torts, an act may be negligent per se.

Per Share Basis The expression of a quantitative value regarding a stock or mutual fund divided by the total number of shares outstanding. That is, a per share basis expresses certain facts on a security as it pertains to a single share. For example, the net asset value per share takes a publicly-traded company's total net asset value and divides it by the number of shares outstanding. This shows how much of the company's net asset value is represented in one share.

Per Stirpes In wills and some retirement accounts, a provision stating that, should a beneficiary die before the testator or account holder, the assets designated for that beneficiary shall pass to his/her heirs. Most often, this provision is not used for a single asset, but rather as a means of dividing a whole estate. For example, if a testator dies leaving an estate to children Frank, Bob, and Joan, and Joan is already dead, an estate per stirpes would divide evenly among Frank and Bob, who each receive one-third, and any of Joan's living children, who collectively receive one-third.

Percent to Double In options, the percentage that the price of an underlying asset must change in order to double the price of an option contract on that asset.

Percentage Depletion A tax deduction that a miner, driller, or other producer of a non-renewable natural resource may take. It is calculated as a set percentage, which differs depending on the material, by which one may reduce one's gross income for tax purposes. For example, an oil driller in the United States may take a 15% tax deduction from his/her gross income on all income derived from the drilling of oil.

Percentage depletion exists in order to encourage the exploration for and use of natural resources within the United States.

Percentage Financial Statement A financial statement in which items are represented as percentages of the whole rather than as dollar amounts. A percentage financial statement can be useful because it allows a current or potential investor to investigate the underlying structure of a company rather than raw numbers. That is, if a company has $30 million in debt, this does not necessarily tell the investor too much. However, if that $30 million is 70% of the company's book value, the investor knows that the company is likely high risk.

Percentage Order A buy or sell order to a broker, with the added instruction to withhold executing the order until a certain number of shares in the security have been traded.

Percentage Premium The amount the price of a convertible bond exceeds its parity, expressed as a percentage. Convertible bonds may be traded like most bonds, and fluctuate in price like all securities. When its market value equals the value of the underlying common stock, the bond is said to have parity. When a convertible bond trades at a premium, this means that it is more expensive than the current value of the underlying. A convertible bond may trade at a premium if the issuer has a good credit rating and/or if investors believe that the price of the common stock will rise again.

Percentage Price Oscillator In technical analysis, an indicator of short-term momentum as percentage of long-term momentum. A positive measure indicates that the short-term momentum is higher than the long-term by the stated percentage while a negative measure indicates the opposite. It is calculated thusly: Principal Percentage Oscillator = (9 day exponential moving average (EMA) of a security's price - 26 day EMA) / 26 day EMA

Percentage-of-Completion Method In construction and project finance, a method for calculating profits and losses in which revenue is recognized as it is received, provided that it is prorated according to the percentage of the project that is complete. This differs from the completed-contract method, which only recognizes revenues after the physical completion of the contract. Each method may have its own tax advantages.

Perestroika A series of political and economic reforms in the Soviet Union in the late 1980s. Perestroika saw the introduction of multi-candidate elections for some offices and the separation of some government functions from the Communist Party. It also allowed state-owned companies to determine outputs based on consumer demand, at least within certain limits, and, for the first time in decades, permitted privately owned businesses in some sectors. Perestroika is thought to have contributed to the fall of the Soviet Union and its transition to a capitalist economy.

Perfect Capital Market Any market in which assets are priced with total efficiency. In a perfect capital market, there are no possibilities for arbitrage. See also: Efficient markets hypothesis, Perfect competition.

Perfect Forecast Line In foreign exchange, a graphic representation of a forecast exchange rate that meets the actual exchange rate over a given set of periods. It is calculated as the slope of a forecasted exchange rate against the actual exchange rate. The forecasted exchange rates at given periods are usually also put on the graph; the closer the forecasted exchange rates are to the perfect forecast line, the better the predictions. The perfect forecast line is a prime tool used to evaluate the performance of future exchange rates forecasts.

Perfect Hedge A hedge on an investment that eliminates the risk on another investment entirely. Perfect hedges are fairly rare as most investments carry at least a little unique risk that cannot be hedged. However, an example of a perfect hedge is a position on option that completely offsets a position in the underlying asset. While perfect hedges eliminate risk, they also greatly reduce or sometimes eliminate the potential for a return.

Perfect Market Assumptions The assumptions under which a market or an economy is entirely efficient. Perfect market assumptions include equal access to information by all market participants, completely rational economic actors, and no transaction costs (such as taxes). Perfect market assumptions rarely, if ever, hold true in the real world.

Perfectly Competitive Financial Markets Markets with perfect competition. That is, no single trade can affect prices and all trades are costless. This makes the market accessible to the widest possible number of participants. Perfectly competitive financial markets can only occur when all information is accessible to all market participants. See also: Efficient markets theory.

Performance 1. The total return on an investment over a period of time. **2.** A subjective measure of how an investment or the market generally is doing over a period of time. **3.** In contracts, substantial completion of an agreed-upon task. That is, a party to a contract performs the contract when he has more-or-less completed what he has agreed to do, with no or only minor work left to do.

Performance Accelerated Restricted Stock Award Plan A plan in which a company grants an employee restricted stock, which vests after a certain period of time or when a certain performance benchmark is reached, whichever comes first.

Performance Attribution Analysis An analysis of the success or failure of the performance of a money manager's investments. That is, performance attribution analysis investigates the investment decisions a money manager makes with a portfolio or fund, determines what and why investment strategies worked and what did not, and attempts to replicate success and avoid failure in the future. Performance attribution analysis may have an effect on whether the money manager receives a bonus or loses his/her job. See also: Manager Universe (benchmark).

Performance Audit A measurement and report of the effectiveness and results of certain business procedures. Performance audits are usually performed internally, and check to see that procedures have their intended effect. Unlike a compliance audit, which simply ensures that procedures are being followed, performance audits challenge the assumptions and goals of procedures, with an eye toward improving efficiency. A performance audit may recommend changes in procedures resulting from observed inefficiencies in existing procedures. See also: Audit, Assurance.

Performance Bond A bond that a company issues to another guaranteeing repayment in case some project fails. For example, suppose a company hires a construction firm to build an apartment building. The construction firm may issue a performance bond to the company. If the apartment building is not constructed according to specifications, the company will not incur any losses because the construction company must repay the bond. This reduces the risk to the bondholder that another party to a contract will not fulfill its obligations.

Performance Drag A situation in which an index fund does not perform exactly the same as the index it is supposed to follow. Performance drag occurs when the fund does not precisely track the underlying index; that is, it occurs when the fund includes other investments. Commonly, performance drag can occur when the money manager allocates part of the fund to cash and cash equivalent to improve its liquidity. However, high performance drag may indicate that the index fund is not much of an index fund at all. See also: Closet index fund.

Performance Evaluation A comparison of one money manager's performance to a group of comparable money managers. This is done periodically to maintain competitiveness and to judge a particular manager's performance. Performance evaluation judges managers based on the return he/she made for clients relative to his/her peers and on how the manager did so. Managers who do well during performance evaluations are rewarded with raises, promotions, and bonuses. Managers who do not do as well are passed over for these things and may be eventually fired. See also: Evaluation period, Manager universe (benchmark).

Performance Index Any measure of the performance of a portfolio or fund, with adjustments made for how risky it is.

Performance Index Paper A short-term debt security in which the interest rate is denominated and paid in one currency, but varies according to that currency's exchange rate with another. This is used to hedge against or speculate on foreign exchange risk.

Performance Indexed Reward A government policy in which a private company is given a strong incentive to reach a stated goal. For example, a government may offer a reward of $1 billion to the company that develops affordable space travel. Performance indexed rewards are sometimes used in economic development, for instance to promote infrastructure or trade.

Performance Measurement Any of many different mathematical measures to evaluate how well a company is using its resources to make a profit. Common examples of performance measurement include operating income, earnings before interest and taxes, and net asset value. It is important to note that no one measure of performance should be taken on its own. Rather, to arrive at a true sense of how a company is doing, one must use as many different measures as possible together.

Performance Stock A stock that is undergoing, or is likely to undergo, significant price appreciation. Performance stocks generally do not pay dividends because their companies reinvest all earnings toward further growth. Some investors seek out performance stocks because of the potential for high profit in a short period of time. They tend to have high price-earnings ratios. However, the term has a connotation referring to a stock that is fundamentally strong, as opposed to a hot stock, which does not have this connotation.

Performing Loan A loan that is not in or near default. According to the International Monetary Fund, a performing loan is any loan in which: interest and principal payments are less than 90 days overdue; less than 90 days' worth of interest has been refinanced, capitalized, or delayed by agreement; and continued payment is anticipated. All conditions must be present for a loan to be performing. However, the specific definition is dependent upon the loan's particular terms.

Perifereia In Greece, a political subdivision equivalent to a region or province.

Period of Call Protection In callable bonds, a period of time during which a bond may not be prematurely redeemed. Interest payments are guaranteed during the call protection period but not afterward. The bond may be redeemed at any point after the call date, which means that the issuer could return the principal to bondholders and interest payments would cease. The period of call protection exists to protect bondholders from the risk that interest rates will fall before the call date. The period of time is often called the cushion.

Period of Digestion The time during which the price of a new issue's early trading on the secondary market fluctuates significantly. The period of digestion occurs as the market attempts to determine the new issue's appropriate market price.

Period-Certain Annuity An annuity in which the annuitant selects a certain number of years during which he/she will receive payments. For example, an annuitant may elect to receive annuity payment each month for 20 years. This allows the annuitant higher payments each month, but it is nevertheless less common than life annuities, which provide payments for the remainder of the annuitant's life. Using period-certain annuities as retirement packages may appeal to persons who do not expect to live the full term of the annuity and/or persons who have another source of income (such as another annuity) in retirement.

Periodic Call Auction The act or practice of closing a position by selling a security slowly over the course of the trading day.

Periodic Payment Plan An agreement between a debtor and a creditor whereby the debtor makes payments on a portion of the principal and/or interest on a loan or other liability on a monthly or quarterly basis. Nearly all loans are repaid on a periodic payment plan.

Periodic Payments Payments that an account holder makes to a retirement plan each month or year over a period of time. Periodic payments are normally made over the course of one's working life in preparation for withdrawals after retirement. Periodic payments are common for many annuities as well as a variety of retirement options, including IRA, 401(k), and 403(b) plans.

Periodic Purchase Deferred Contract An annuity purchased with periodic payments by the annuitant, who does not begin to receive payments until some future date. Like all deferred annuities, a periodic purchase deferred contract has two phases, a savings phase and an income phase. The savings phase involves the annuitant making the periodic payments and having them invested on his/her behalf. In the income phase, the annuitant receives payments. It is important to note that a periodic payment deferred contract, like most deferred annuities, is not taxed until the income phase begins. It also may pay a death benefit to the survivor(s) of the annuitant. See also: IRA, 401(k).

Periodic Rate The cost of funds or interest rate for a single month instead of an entire year. For example, if the APR on a credit card is 36%, the periodic rate is 3% because the card holder pays 3% in interest each month.

Perjurer One who lies under oath. For example, one commits perjury when one knowingly gives false testimony in a court of law. As a result, perjury is illegal in practically every jurisdiction.

Perjury The crime of lying under oath or making a false statement on an affidavit. In order to be considered an act of perjury, the false statement must relate to the matter at hand; it would not be perjury, for example, to falsely state a person's eye color unless it involves the identification of a defendant. Prosecutions for perjury, however, are fairly unusual.

Perkins Loan A loan offered by the U.S. federal government to students seeking a post-secondary degree or certification. The loan is offered to students who demonstrate financial need. It is offered at a 5% interest rate and has a 10-year repayment period.

Permanent Current Assets The current assets a firm needs in order to continue operations. Examples include inventory and perhaps rapidly depreciating assets such as computers. These assets are current because they do not remain assets for longer than a year, but they are permanent because they must be replaced with similar assets. Despite the seeming contradiction in the name, they are called permanent current assets because every company must permanently maintain a certain amount in current assets in order to exist.

Permanent Financing Debt-financing or equity financing with a term of longer than several years. Permanent financing is used to build or maintain fixed assets such as factories or machinery.

Permanent Normal Trading Relations The term in the United States for most favored nation status. Permanent normal trade relations entitle a country to the lowest possible tariffs that it can assess on another country. For example, if the lowest tariff of the U.S. is 2% of the value of a good, it charges this percentage on an import from a country with which it has permanent normal trading relations.

Permanent Spontaneous Current Liabilities The minimum amount of liabilities that a firm acquires when buying the goods or services that it needs to maintain operations on credit. Specifically, permanent spontaneous current liabilities are the obligations to pay for the goods or services at some point in the future, generally on an ongoing basis.

Permanently Restricted Funds In a non-profit's year-end financial statement, money that may not be spent at any time except for specified purposes. Permanently restricted funds are expected to last over the long term. See also: Temporarily restricted funds.

Permanently Restricted Net Assets Cash or other assets that are not needed to pay liabilities but that still must never be spent freely. Permanently restricted net assets may be earmarked for a specific purpose; alternately, law or regulation may require the permanent restriction of some net assets. See also: Temporarily Restricted Net Assets.

Permissible Nonbank Activities Activities in which a bank holding company may engage that are not retail banking activities, but are close enough that the Federal Reserve permits it anyway. Examples include insurance, the secondary market for mortgages, and investment banking. In order for an activity to be classified as a permissible nonbank activity, the Federal Reserve must declare that engaging in such an activity is in the public interest. Proponents argue that this allows banks to diversify, while critics maintain that this unnecessarily increases risk to bank account holders. See also: Glass-Steagal Act, Gramm-Bliley-Leach Act.

Permit Bond A bond guaranteeing that a person with a permit from the government to perform a task will perform that task to the proper regulations. The bond provides compensation to an injured party in the event that the permit holder does not fulfill his/her obligations.

Perp Walk Informal; the practice of the police allowing the media to photograph or tape a recently arrested suspect. Some disagree with this practice as it may allow the suspect to be convicted in public opinion before the trial. On the other hand, police do it in order to assure the public that they are doing their job. Perp walks may affect

business; for example, if the police parade a recently arrested CEO of a company, it may negatively impact a company's stock price.

Perpendicular Spread An option strategy in which one buys options of the same class on the same underlying asset with the same expiration date, but with different strike prices. On or before the expiration date, the option holder exercises the option at the strike price that is most advantageous at the time. This protects the option holder from the risk of having an out-of-the-money option: the more options one has, the more likely it is that at least one will be in-the-money.

Perpetual Bond A bond in which the issuer does not repay the principal. Rather, a perpetual bond pays the bondholder a fixed coupon as long as he/she holds it. Prices for perpetual bonds vary widely according to long-term interest rates. When interest rates rise, perpetual bonds fall and vice versa. Perpetual bonds are most common in the United Kingdom, where they were used originally to pay for the military.

Perpetual Inventory A standard of accounting inventory on a daily basis, as opposed to a weekly or monthly basis. At the end of a day, a company using perpetual inventory changes the inventory that appears on its records to reflect the most current amount. This can be inconvenient to count, but allows the company to constantly maintain accurate data.

Perpetual Warrant A certificate without an expiration date, usually issued with a bond or preferred stock, giving the holder the option of buying an underlying asset (in this case, usually more securities) at a certain strike price, which is usually higher than the market value of the underlying asset at the time of issue. Some warrants expire a few years after issuance but perpetual warrants can theoretically last forever. Unlike options, warrants are issued by companies during a round of financing, rather than by an individual investor or brokerage. Companies issue warrants to attract investors who might not otherwise be interested. See also: Sweetener.

Perpetuity Cash flows paid to a person or company on an ongoing basis that are expected to go on indefinitely. The cash flows ordinarily do not increase, and as a result become less valuable over time because of inflation.

PERQS Debt securities, issued by Morgan Stanley, with a maturity value linked to the value of the underlying stock to which the security is linked. PERQS are convertible into the underlying stock, and pay fixed quarterly interest rates (the dollar value of which depends on the value of the underlying). Unlike some other debt securities, they are not redeemable early.

Persona Grata A diplomat accepted as a representative by the country to which the diplomat is sent. The term is Latin for "acceptable person."

Persona Non Grata A diplomat rejected as a representative by the country to which the diplomat is sent. The term is Latin for "unacceptable person."

Personal Account A bank account one uses for purposes other than business. One uses a personal account for one's daily and regular expenses, such as rent, utilities, debt service and groceries. One also uses a personal account for one's savings that have not been invested. Most personal accounts are thus divided into checking and savings accounts.

Personal Allowance 1. In the United Kingdom, income that is not taxed because it falls below the level at which income is taxed. For example, if one has an income of 6,000 pounds and a personal allowance of 5,000 pounds, one only pays taxes on the final 1,000 pounds. See also: Personal exemption. **2.** See: Alimony.

Personal Article Floater An insurance policy attached to another policy that insures certain, named articles. These may be very expensive articles, such as jewelry and family heirlooms. Each article covered in the floater has an assessed value listed with it, which helps determine the benefit the policyholder receives if an article is lost or stolen.

Personal Consumption Expenditures A measure of inflation in the United States that considers how much people spend on household goods and services, while also weighting for the relative demand for those particular goods and services. In addition to calculating raw changes in prices, PCE measures rises and declines in demand based on those price changes, which, in turn, may enhance or dampen the effects of inflation. The PCE is compiled by the U.S. Department of Commerce and has little effect on the market because its results are usually predictable. It is not as widely used as the Consumer Price Index, which does not consider changes in demand as they occur. See also: PCEPI.

Personal Day A day on which one does not work for some reason other than holiday or illness. A company may grant an employee a certain number of personal days, especially if he/she is not yet eligible for other employee benefits. Personal days may or may not be paid.

Personal Equity Plan An investment vehicle formerly used in the United Kingdom to encourage investment by small investors. PEPs could invest in unit trusts, investment trusts, and some other collective investment vehicles on an individual basis. Gains from PEPs were largely tax-free, though these privileges gradually eroded until individual savings accounts replaced PEPs entirely in 1999.

Personal Exemption In U.S. tax, the amount of personal income that is not taxed. That is, the personal exemption is money that is not included in one's adjusted gross income when calculating one's tax liability. One receives additional exemptions for a spouse, children, and if one is over 65 or blind. Congress sets the amount of the personal exemption each year.

Personal Finance The process of determining a person's financial needs or goals for the future and how to achieve them. Personal finance involves deciding what investments would be most appropriate under both personal and broader economic circumstances. All things being equal, short-term personal financial planning involves less uncertainty than long-term because, generally speaking, it is easier to predict one's future income. Personal finance considers future income like pensions and expenditures such as education or child support.

Personal Holding Company A corporation in which five or fewer persons control at least half of the company's stock and in which at least 60% of the company's income is passive income from companies it owns. Because personal holding companies may be used by the persons who control them to avoid personal taxes, the U.S. tax system imposes a 15% tax on personal holding company profits in addition to corporate taxes.

Personal Holding Company Tax A 15% tax added to corporate taxes in the United States on corporations in which five or fewer persons control at least half of the company's stock and at least 60% of the company's income is passive income from companies it owns. This tax is levied to discourage the existence of personal holding companies.

Personal Identification Number Commonly called a PIN. A password that a person uses to access an ATM with one's debit card, though they are increasingly being used for all debit card transactions. A PIN protects the person who owns the card from identity theft as well as the risk that a thief can steal the card and then use it without limit. Assuming the PIN is randomly generated when the card is issued and the potential thief has no other information, the thief has approximately a 0.06% chance of guessing the PIN when using the card. It was invented by James Goodfellow, who was also instrumental in developing the ATM itself.

Personal Income A regular compensation that an individual receives in the form of salary, wages, tips, rents, and/or other sources. An individual earns personal income in order to pay for personal expenses, such as one's mortgage, debt service, groceries, and so forth. Personal income is necessary for an economy to function. Most governments tax personal income differently from both corporate income and investment income.

Personal Property Any property other than real estate. Personal property includes vehicles, computers, furniture, televisions, and so forth. Personal property may be used as collateral on a loan, but it is considered less reliable collateral than real estate because the borrower could default on the loan and then steal or hide the personal property. Obviously, this is impossible with real estate.

Personal Responsibility and Work Opportunity Reconciliation Act Legislation in the United States that significantly changed the American social safety net. Among other provisions, it requires recipients of welfare to find a job within two years of receiving benefits and places a five-year lifetime maximum on benefits. It essentially transformed welfare in the United States into workfare. Proponents argue that this reduces welfare roles and promotes responsibility, while critics contend that it hurts families who need help. It was passed in 1996.

Personal Savings Money that an individual has put away for non-immediate use. For example, one may utilize personal savings to save funds for an expensive purchase, such as a house or a car. In general, it is recommended for one to maintain personal savings to cover three to six months of living expenses.

Personal Service Corporation A corporation in which employee-owners perform services helpful to individuals, such as accounting, health care, or performing arts. In order to qualify as a personal service corporation for tax purposes, the employees must own at least 10% of the fair market value of the company's stock and the company must have been engaged in the principal business of a personal service on the last day of the previous tax year or the last day of the calendar year of the company's tax year.

Personal Tax View of Capital Structure A theory stating that, all other things being equal, double taxation does not reduce a person's income from investments. This is because there is a difference in the tax rate between corporate tax and income tax (or capital gains tax). So long as one tax rate is lower than the other, the effects of double taxation are mitigated or eliminated.

Personal Use Property Property one does not use for a business or investment purpose. Examples of personal-use property include furniture, cars, family heirlooms, and so forth. Losses on personal use property are not generally tax deductible, though a loss on personal use real estate is generally an exception to this rule.

Perth Mint A mint in Australia. Opened in 1899, it minted coins for the United Kingdom until 1970, after which jurisdiction was transferred to Australia. It also provides gold refining services.

Peruvian Inti The former currency of Peru. It was introduced in 1985, replacing the Peruvian sol at a ratio of 1,000 sol to one inti. Although it was intended to reduce the sol's high inflation rate, the inti suffered from hyperinflation as well. The new sol replaced the inti in 1991.

Peruvian New Sol The currency of Peru. It was introduced in 1991, replacing the inti, which had replaced the first sol in 1985. It was issued to stem hyperinflation, which had plagued Peru in the late 1980s. Its inflation rate has historically been very low and it developed a reputation as a reliable South American currency.

Peruvian Sol The former currency of Peru. It was introduced in 1863, replacing the Peruvian real and the Bolivian peso, which previously had circulated in different parts of the country. At first it was pegged to the French franc, then to gold, and finally to the U.S. dollar. It was plagued by hyperinflation at the end of its use, and was replaced by the inti in 1985. See also: New sol.

Pes An ancient Roman unit of length approximately equivalent to 296 millimeters.

Pes quadratus An ancient Roman unit of area approximately equivalent to 0.0876 square meters.

Peseta The former currency of Spain. It was introduced in 1869 when Spain joined the Latin Monetary Union and continued to be the currency even after the union was abolished in 1927. In 1959, Spain joined the Bretton Woods System and pegged the peseta to the U.S. dollar. The peseta was replaced by the euro in 2002.

Pesewa A subdivision of the Ghanaian cedi. One pesewa is equal in value to 1/100 of a cedi.

Pesiah A Talmudic unit of length equivalent to one amah, which was itself an ancient Hebrew unit for about 50 centimeters.

Peso The name of several currencies. The word originated as the Spanish term for a large, silver coin common in international trade in the 16th century. It is currently the name of currencies in several former colonies of Spain, particularly in Latin America. See also: Mexican peso.

Peso Argentino The former currency of Argentina. It was introduced in 1983, replacing the peso ley. It suffered from high inflation and was replaced by the austral at a ratio of 1,000 to one in 1985.

Peso Boliviano The former currency of Bolivia. It was introduced in 1963 as a way to stave off inflation. It was pegged to the U.S. dollar until 1979, when it began to operate under a managed float. It suffered from high inflation throughout its history, especially in the mid-1980s. It was replaced by the boliviano in 1986.

Peso Ley The former currency of Argentina. It was introduced in 1970, replacing the peso moneda nacional. It suffered from high inflation and was replaced by the peso argentino at a ratio of 10,000 to one in 1983.

Peso Problem The phenomenon in which the market prices in (or takes into account when determining the price) the small possibility of a large change. The term especially refers to exchange rates of pegged currencies, which may be slightly different from the official rates to account for the probability that currencies will drop or change their pegs.

PEST Analysis In risk assessment, a hermeneutic used for investigating the impact of a venture or investment. The term is an acronym for political, economic, social, and technological, which are the types of issues that must be addressed before one decides whether or not to make an investment.

Petha A Burmese unit of mass approximately equivalent to one gram.

Peti A slang term for 100,000 Indian rupees. See also: Lakh.

Petrodollars Revenue that state-owned and state-influenced oil companies derive from the sale of oil. In several Middle Eastern countries, petrodollars are the predominant source of government revenue. They are available for investment and are often traded on the eurocurrency market and/or are used for development purposes. For example, Bahrain used petrodollars in the 1970s and 1980s to finance improvements in its industrial capacity. See also: OPEC, Sovereign Wealth Fund.

Petty Cash Cash that a company keeps available for small transactions with customers. For example, a mom and pop hardware store may keep petty cash to make change if a customer pays $20 in cash for a drill that costs $18.06. Most retail companies keep petty cash.

Petty Cash Fund A budgeted amount of money a company periodically replenishes to pay for minor purchases. A company may withdraw the petty cash fund from the bank every two to four weeks and keeps it in cash. This cash may be used, for example, to pay for lunch for employees once a week. Because the petty cash fund is a budgeted item, it helps reduce the likelihood that the company will overspend.

Pezata A Maltese unit of weight approximately equivalent to 238 kilograms. It is largely obsolete but is still used in some circumstances.

PF 1. ISO 3166-1 alpha-2 code for French Polynesia. This is the code used in international transactions to and from French Polynesian bank accounts. 2. ISO 3166-2 geocode for French Polynesia. This is used as an international standard for shipping to French Polynesia.

Pfandbriefe The German equivalent of a mortgage-backed security. They are issued by mortgage banks and are considered the safest non-government bond in Germany.

Pfennig A division of the deutschemark. One mark was divided into 100 pfennigs. While the mark no longer circulates, pfennig remains the slang term for euro cents in Germany.

PG 1. ISO 3166-1 alpha-2 code for the Independent State of Papua New Guinea. This is the code used in international transactions to and from Papua New Guinean bank accounts. 2. ISO 3166-2 geocode for Papua New Guinea. This is used as an international standard for shipping to Papua New Guinea. Each province has its own code with the prefix "PG." For example, the code for the Province of Chimbu is ISO 3166-2:PG-CPK.

PGK ISO 4217 code for the Papua New Guinean kina. It was introduced in 1975, replacing the Australian dollar. While the kina replaced the dollar at par, it is a floating currency.

Phantom Gain A capital gain on which one owes taxes even if one takes a capital loss in the aggregate. The most common type of phantom gain occurs when a mutual fund sells some of its securities at a gain but its own shares decline in value. Because the fund's shareholders technically owned the securities that were sold for a gain, they must pay taxes on those gains even though they have actually lost money on their investment. A phantom gain should not be confused with a paper gain. See also: Phantom Income.

Phantom Income Taxable income that does not result from cash flow. Examples include zero-coupon bonds, which are taxed as if they had a coupon, and house value increases that result in higher property taxes. See also: Phantom Gain.

Phantom Stock Award A plan to compensate senior management of a publicly-traded company in which the company grants an employee a "hypothetical" stock. That is, the company gives the employee the benefits of owning stock in the company without actually giving him/her stock. The phantom stock increases or decreases in price and pays dividends as if it were real. Eventually, the phantom stock is settled and cash is distributed to the employee. See also: Stock option.

Phantom Withdrawal A situation in which money is taken from a person's account via an ATM but the bank does not admit bank error and the account holder claims he/she never made the withdrawal. It is a type of identity theft but it may be difficult to determine whether the account holder or the bank is responsible for the loss. Phantom withdrawals are relatively rare.

Phase Out To gradually end something, especially a project. For example, a company seeking to wind down its research and development department my phase it out by cutting its budget successively over several years.

Philadelphia Federal Index An index composed of surveys of the perception of business owners on the expansion of their businesses. The Philadelphia Federal Index surveys business owners in Delaware, New Jersey, and Pennsylvania; its results are published monthly. A measure over zero indicates business expansion and a measure below zero indicates contraction.

Philadelphia Semiconductor Index An index, weighted for price, of 19 American publicly-traded companies involved at some level in the manufacture, distribution, and/or sale of semiconductors. It began in 1993 and it is considered a benchmark of stocks in the semiconductor industry.

Philadelphia Stock Exchange Founded in 1790, the oldest stock exchange in the United States. Equities in 2,000 companies and 1,700 options are traded on the PHLX floor. The exchange operates on an open outcry system, and is noted for its index options and currency options. It is currently owned by NASDAQ.

Philanthropist A wealthy individual who gives money to charity or other programs designed to help others. The term is most applicable when the individual starts his/her own organization to promote pet programs. For example, Bill Gates established the Gates Foundation to perform a variety of philanthropic activities such as agricultural development and the establishment of libraries.

Philanthropy The practice of a wealthy individual or corporation giving money to charity or other programs designed to help others. The term is most applicable when the individual or corporation starts his/her/its own programs. For example, Bill Gates established the Gates Foundation to perform a variety of philanthropic activities such as agricultural development and the establishment of libraries.

Philippine Peso The currency of the Philippines. While its origins date to 1852, the modern peso came into being following the independence of the Philippines in the 1940s. It was originally pegged to silver and gold, but overprinting and hoarding of currency caused it to become a floating currency in 1964. Since independence, the government of the Philippines has consistently devalued the peso in order to reduce the nation's debt in domestic terms. This has made it a weak currency.

Philippine Stock Exchange One of two stock exchanges in the Philippines. Established in 1927, it is one of the oldest exchanges in Southeast Asia, and it remains one of the most prominent. It contains nearly 250 listed companies with a market capitalization over $100 billion. It maintains offices in both Manila and Makati City. See also: Philippine Dealing Exchange.

Phillips Curve A curve postulating an inverse relationship between inflation and unemployment. That is, the Phillips curve theorizes that when inflation is low, unemployment is high and vice versa. This was a predominant theory for much of the mid-20th century until stagflation (high unemployment and high inflation) began to occur in the 1970s. Few economists use the Phillips curve today though it is a component in Gordon's triangle model.

Phishing The illegal practice of attempting to steal an identity by setting up a website and encouraging people to input credit card or other personal information. Phishing often purports to present a legitimate web business and asks the "customer" to give personal information in order to receive ficticious products. Alternatively, phishing may involve a criminal sending out e-mail purporting to be from a bank or credit card company asking for information as part of an "urgent" request. Phishers then steal the identity directly or sell to another party for illegal purposes.

PHL GOST 7.67 Latin three-letter geocode for the Philippines. The code is used for transactions to and from Philippine bank accounts and for international shipping to the Philippines. As with all GOST 7.67 codes, it is used primarily in Cyrillic alphabets.

Phone Switching The act of transferring one's investment from one fund to another in the same fund family over the telephone. While one can usually switch between these funds without penalty or fee, there may be a charge associated with using the telephone to do so.

Photo Financial Statement A slang term for a balance sheet or financial statement. The term is most common in the context of business consulting for small Christian churches and ministries.

PHP ISO 4217 code for the Philippine peso. While its origins date to 1852, the modern peso came into being following the independence of the Philippines in the 1940s. It was originally pegged to silver and gold, but overprinting and hoarding of currency caused it to become a floating currency in 1964. Since independence, the Philippines government has consistently devalued the peso in order to reduce the nation's debt in domestic terms. This has made it a weak currency.

Phum In Cambodia, a political subdivision equivalent to a village.

Physical Completion The time at which a project has been finished and functions, but is not yet generating revenue. Physical completion applies especially to construction and other infrastructure projects. For example, an oil company may build a series of oil pumps. The time of physical completion occurs when the oil pumps are completed and are working, but have not yet pumped any oil. Another example is a new apartment building that is ready for tenants, but in which no apartments have yet been rented.

Physical Delivery In options and futures, the act of a seller giving the actual underlying asset to a buyer. Physical delivery does not occur for most option and futures transactions; most traders offset their positions by entering an equal but opposite position. However, in order to hedge certain risks, physical delivery does occur on some contracts, notably those involving commodities. See also: Actuals.

Physical Hazard A danger to the integrity of a person or property. For example, a driver carries the physical hazard that he may crash his car. Likewise, a retail business has the physical hazard that it may be robbed. Insurance protects against many types of physical hazards.

Physical Location Exchange A securities exchange with an office where traders meet to buy and sell securities. Traditionally, physical location exchanges have operated on an open outcry system, but, increasingly, trading takes place over computers on the exchange. Physical location exchanges differ from electronic exchanges, which do not have a central location to meet.

Physical Option An option contract on an asset that is an actual thing, as opposed to a stock or futures contract. Examples of underlying assets for physical options include commodities, currencies, and U.S. Treasury securities. Other than this feature, physical options are identical to other option contracts and can be used in a variety of option strategies.

Physical Verification A practice in which an auditor ensures that the inventory recorded on a company's statements is correct by actually inspecting and counting the inventory.

Piad A Russian unit of length equivalent to seven inches. It was rendered obsolete when the Soviet Union began to use the metric system in 1924. An equivalent term was chetvert.

Pian Cha A Chinese term for bias in the statistical sense. The term refers to deviations from the statistical norm rather than any preconceived notions.

Piastre 1. The name of the subdivision equal to 1/100 of several currencies. Examples include the Egyptian pound and the Lebanese pound. **2.** See: Ottoman piastre.

Piastre de Commerce The currency of French Indochina. It was issued in 1885 and was pegged to silver until 1920. It was then pegged to the French franc, effectively pegging it to gold. It was gradually replaced in the early 1950s by national currencies, including the Lao kip and the Cambodian riel.

Pick Slang; a stock or other security that an analyst recommends his or her clients buy. For example, an analyst who is bullish on tech stocks may choose Google and Facebook as his picks.

Picking Winners The policy in which a government encourages certain sectors of an economy, or even particular companies. A government may pick winners by offering tax incentives, favorable regulation or even direct subsidies. Picking winners was a feature of post-World War II development in a number of countries. See also: Import substitution.

Pickup The increase in yield that an investor gains when he/she swaps a bond with a lower yield and shorter maturity for one with a higher yield and longer maturity. The pick up entails risk for the holder of the lower yield bond (that is, the one who receives the high yield bond). This is because the high yield bond is almost always of lower credit quality and the longer maturity exposes the bondholder to interest rate risk and perhaps inflation risk. However, the pick up represents a higher return than the bondholder would have received with the lower yield bond.

Pickup Bond A callable bond with a high coupon that is nearing the end of its call protection period. That is, the pickup bond is about to end the grace period during which it cannot be called. If prevailing interest rates fall during the remaining grace period, the pickup bond will be redeemed at a premium to its par, resulting in a profit for the bondholder, even though it will deprive her of future coupon payments.

Picture In equities, the price at which a dealer or broker is willing to buy or sell a security. See also: Bid-ask spread.

Picul A unit of weight in Taiwan approximately equivalent to 60 kilograms. It is used primarily in the sale of bulk foodstuffs.

Pie A Spanish measure of length approximately equivalent to 23.86 centimeters, or just under 11 inches. It is largely obsolete.

Pie Model of Capital Structure A graphical depiction of a company's capital structure on a pie chart. Capital structure consists of, in brief, the vehicles by which a company raises capital in order to maintain or expand operations. Thus, a pie model of capital structure would show how much capital comes from stock, how much comes from bonds, and how much comes from other vehicles, such as convertible stock or warrants. A pie model provides an easy reference for management and investors.

Piece Part of a block or exceptionally large amount or value of securities. While there is no specific definition of how many shares constitute a block, most people using the term refer to holding or trading more than 10,000 shares and/or shares worth more than $200,000. A piece is any section of this bought or sold separately from the rest of the block.

Piggies A slang term for the banking sector.

Piggy Back Registration The registration of a security in which an underwriter allows a new issue to be offered along with previously issued shares. A piggyback registration must occur with the permission of the relevant underwriter and be noted in the new issue's prospectus. Piggyback registration should not be confused with piggybacking, which is a different concept altogether.

Piggyback Freight Describing the transportation of a truck or other vehicle on a train or other land-going vehicle. See also: Fishyback.

Piggyback Loan A loan for a portion of the value of a home over and above the traditional mortgage. In general, one must have a 20% down payment to purchase a home and one finances the remaining 80%. A piggyback loan allows one to borrow at least a portion of the remaining 20% (though at a higher interest rate than the remainder of the mortgage). A piggyback loan is an alternative to private mortgage insurance. It may allow more people to purchase their own homes.

Piggyback Warrants Warrants that are attached to a security and come into effect when other warrants are exercised. Piggyback warrants, like general warrants, are usually attached as sweeteners to make the security more attractive to investors.

Piggybacking The practice in which a broker conducts a transaction on his/her own account after filling a similar order on behalf of a client. For example, if a client sells 10,000 shares and the broker owns some shares in the same company, he may piggyback by selling his own shares. A broker piggybacks when he/she believes that the client has insider information, or at least a better understanding than the broker on the market's future movements. Piggybacking should not be confused with piggy back registration, which is a different concept altogether.

Pilseta In Latvia, a political subdivision equivalent to a municipal government.

Pin Risk In options, the risk that the underlying asset of an option will close near the exercise price close to the expiration date. In this situation, the writer of the option does not know and cannot predict whether or not the option holder will exercise the option. The writer must then decide whether or not to cover the position by taking an equal but opposite position in the underlying asset. If the writer covers the position and the option is not exercised, he/she may be forced to hold securities that will result in a loss. Likewise, if the writer does not cover the position and the option is exercised, he/she must rush to fulfill the contract, which may also result in a loss.

Pineapple A slang term for a $50 note in Australia. The term is derived from the fact that $50 notes are mostly yellow.

Pingin 1. A coin that circulated in the Republic of Ireland between 1928 and 1972. It was equal in value to 1/240 of one Irish pound. See also: Penny. **2.** A coin that circulated in the Republic of Ireland between 1971 and 2002. It was equal in value to 1/100 of one Irish pound.

Pinginn An obsolete Irish unit of weight approximately equivalent to 0.4 grams.

Pink Book An annual publication of the British government detailing the country's balance of payments, which is the difference between the value of transactions in which money leaves Britain and the value of transactions in which money enters it.

Pink Sheets 1. A daily quotation system for OTC stocks. Pink sheets include information such as the bids, asks, and the market makers giving them. Because companies listed on pink sheets are over-the-counter, they do not have to meet any listing requirements, and may therefore be quite small. They are published by the National Quotation Bureau and were originally printed on pink sheets. **2.** Informal; the over-the-counter market.

Pink Slip Party A fundraiser or other gathering for recently laid-off professionals and recruiters for companies in these professionals' fields. In addition to raising money for charities, pink slip parties help professionals network with each other with the goal of finding new work.

Pink 'Un An informal name for the Financial Times, a major daily newspaper. The term refers to the salmon color of the paper on which it is printed.

Pinta A Maltese unit of volume approximately equivalent to 142.1 milliliters. It was originally used to measure alcohol. It is largely obsolete but is still used in some circumstances.

Pip A subunit of a currency. For example, a cent is a pip for the U.S. dollar and a fill is a pip for the Bahraini dinar. The term is most common in quotes for equity securities.

Pipa A Portuguese measure of liquid volume approximately equivalent to 420 liters. It became obsolete after Lusophone countries adopted the metric system in the 19th century.

Pipe An obsolete unit of volume equivalent to 126 gallons.

Pipe Smoker In auto sales, a slang term for a customer who spends a great deal of time with a salesperson, manages to negotiate the best possible deal for himself/herself, and in the end does not purchase the automobile at all.

Pipeline 1. Informal; the process by which a company or underwriter conducts all due diligence, files all necessary paperwork, and generally makes preparation for a new issue. The pipeline especially refers to abiding by regulations issued by the SEC. **2.** More broadly, any activity or project that is in the preparatory stages.

Piracy 1. Robbery committed at sea. Piracy is one of the world's oldest crimes and is a risk in international trade. Captured pirates generally are tried in military courts. A company may insure against injury or loss of goods due to piracy. **2.** The act or practice of making illegal copies of copyrighted material. For example, printing copies of a book without the author's or publisher's permission may be piracy because neither receives any compensation for sales. Piracy is a major issue in online commerce. It is common, for instance, for a private user to upload a video to a website and even profit from views of that video without permission from or compensation to the copyright owners. The best way to prevent or prosecute this form of piracy remains a controversial issue.

Pirate 1. A person who commits robbery at sea. Piracy is one of the world's oldest crimes and is a risk in international trade. Captured pirates generally are tried in military courts. A company may insure against injury or loss of goods due to piracy. **2.** A person who engages in the act or practice of making illegal copies of copyrighted material. For example, printing copies of a book without the author's or publisher's permission may be piracy because neither receives any compensation for sales. Piracy is a major issue in online commerce. It is common, for instance, for a private user to upload a video to a website and even profit from views of that video without permission from or compensation to the copyright owners. The best way to prevent or prosecute this form of piracy remains a controversial issue.

Pit Committee A committee on an exchange that deals with futures contracts. Specifically, it determines the settlement price each trading day.

Pivot A price that a security fails to either break above or fall below, or a price that a security reaches when its trading volume increases. If a security breaks above (or falls below) a pivot, it is expected to continue to rise (or fall). See also: Support level, Resistance level.

Pject to Actual A slang term for actual to budget for a non-profit, especially a small Christian church or ministry.

PK 1. ISO 3166-1 alpha-2 code for the Islamic Republic of Pakistan. This is the code used in international transactions to and from Pakistani bank accounts. **2.** ISO 3166-2 geocode for Pakistan. This is used as an international standard for shipping to Pakistan. Eight subdivisions of Pakistan have their own code with the prefix "PK." For example, the code for the Province of Sindh is ISO 3166-2:PK-SD. **3.** See: Pink sheet.

PKR ISO 4217 code for the Pakistani rupee. It was issued when Pakistan became independent in 1947. Originally, the rupee was divided into 16 annas, which each contained four pice. However, in 1961, it was decimalized and divided simply into 100 pice. Because of inflation, pice have not been issued since 1994. It is a floating currency.

PL 1. ISO 3166-1 alpha-2 code for the Republic of Poland. This is the code used in international transactions to and from Polish bank accounts. **2.** ISO 3166-2 geocode for Poland. This is used as an international standard for shipping to Poland. Each province has its own code with the prefix "PL." For example, the code for the Province of Slaskie is ISO 3166-2:PL-SL.

Placement The act or process of selling a new issue of a security to investors. Most of the time, a placement must be registered with the SEC before it can actually take place. See also: Private placement.

Placement Ratio The dollar amount of new issues of bonds that underwriters have placed with investors, expressed as a percentage of all new issues. The placement ratio is published in Bond Buyer. Only new issues worth more than $1 million are included in the calculation. This can be used as an indicator of the state of the bond market.

Plain Edge In numismatics, describing a coin with no inscription or ridges struck into it.

Plain Vanilla 1. See: Plain vanilla option. **2.** See: Plain vanilla swap.

Plaintiff In a lawsuit, the party making a complaint. A plaintiff seeks some compensation, whether monetary or otherwise, for some perceived wrong for which the other party (the defendant) is claimed to be responsible. For example, if Frank crashes his car into John's house and John sues for the damages, John is the plaintiff in the case.

Plan Administrator The person or company that manages a pension. That is, the plan administrator makes investment decisions with the contributions the employer and/or employees have made. The plan administrator is responsible for keeping the pension on sound financial footing.

Plan Agreement The final agreement between the holder of an IRA or other retirement account and the financial institution providing it. The plan agreement states the terms of the IRA(such as the contribution limit), age at which withdrawals may begin, and so forth. One must sign the plan agreement before the retirement account can go into effect.

Plan Company A company that invests in mutual funds on behalf of shareholders. Customers purchase shares, and the company uses the revenue to buy shares in one or more mutual funds. Plan companies work with shareholders to determine a specific expected return over a certain number of years and invest in mutual funds accordingly. This allows shareholders the flexibility of a changing portfolio without needing to manage its day-to-day maintenance. These mutual funds are sometimes called contractual plan companies. See also: Periodic payment plan.

Plan Completion Insurance An insurance policy for persons who have agreed to buy mutual fund shares in a periodic payment plan. If the policyholder dies before he/she has finished buying shares on the periodic payment plan, the insurance policy will purchase the remainder of the shares the policyholder agreed to purchase. This allows the policyholder's heirs to benefit from the mutual fund.

Plan Participant One who contributes to and/or is eligible to receive benefits from an employer-sponsored retirement plan or pension. This includes person(s) contributing to a 401(k), as well as retired persons who are making withdrawals from their accounts. Plan participants' rights with regard to their plans are regulated by the Employee Retirement Income Security Act (ERISA). Covered employees have the right to see the plan's annual tax forms on demand, and the right to sue the plan. Generally, planned participants need to participate in the plan for a certain number of years before becoming eligible for the maximum allowable benefits.

Plan Provider In IRAs and other retirement accounts, the investment company that manages the plan. That is, a brokerage that invests an IRA on behalf of its contributor is the plan provider for that account. A plan provider may be a brokerage, insurance company, mutual fund, or any other investment company.

Plan Sponsor An employer or company that offers a pension plan to employees. Plan sponsors may directly manage the pensions, but most allow third-party money managers to handle them. However, plan sponsors must determine which employees are eligible for the plan, and most contribute matching funds to each employee's pension, up to a certain point. A wide variety of pension plan types exist, and plan sponsors determine and may change the terms of what they offer. See also: 401(k), IRA.

Planjecting A slang term for budgeting for a non-profit, especially a small Christian church or ministry.

Planning Horizon The future time for which a person or organization plans. For example, if a company wishes to make contingency plans for the next 10 years, it is said to have a 10-year planning horizon. Many companies maintain a five-year planning horizon, though some plan for longer or shorter periods. The longer a planning horizon is, the more uncertainty it has.

Plant and Equipment The fixed assets used to produce goods for a company. A factory and the machinery therein are common examples of plant and equipment. On a balance sheet, plant and equipment are recorded according to their historical cost. It is important to note that the historical cost of net plant and equipment usually bears little or no relationship to the market value after they have been held for several years. They are also called net plant and equipment.

Plastax A tax imposed on the use of plastic bags, for example at a grocery store. A plastax is introduced to discourage use of plastic bags, which are thought to be harmful to the environment.

Plastic A slang term for a credit card, especially when being used to make frivolous or luxurious purchases.

Platform Automation A system giving the front office of a bank access to the back office's information. That is, platform automation allows a teller or other representative to see a customer's account history and other information in order to provide better service, such as telling the customer whether he/she is likely to be eligible for a loan. It is also called branch automation.

Platinum A rare and valuable metal. Platinum is used in jewelry and electronics. Platinum is traded as a commodity on various security exchanges. Platinum is volatile like other commodities, but generally maintains a relatively high price.

Play Informal for an investment or investment decision, especially one that becomes profitable.

Player Informal; an investor, especially one who trades actively.

Playing the Market The practice of making investments with little, or improper, regard for their risks. Playing the market often refers to the transactions of amateur investors. See also: Naive diversification.

Plaza Accord An agreement between the United States, the United Kingdom, West Germany, the United Kingdom, and Japan in 1985 to gradually devalue the U.S. dollar with respect to other currencies. The countries did this by selling dollars from their foreign currency reserves. In the years leading up to 1985 the dollar had become quite strong and was causing significant current account deficits and was making American exports less competitive globally. As a result of the Plaza Accord, the dollar depreciated more than 50% in an orderly fashion over the following two years. Interestingly, the Plaza Accord was the first major currency agreement involving Japan.

Plaza de soberania In Spain, a political subdivision for a territory bordering Morocco in the North African coast. There are three such territories.

Pledged Asset An asset that a borrower transfers to the possession of a lender as collateral for a loan. The borrower maintains ownership and all associated rights of the pledged asset. When the loan is repaid, the lender transfers possession back to the borrower. The pledged asset reduces the risk to the lender that the borrower will default, therefore possibly qualifying the borrower for some benefit, such as a lower interest rate. When buying a house, some mortgage borrowers will pledge an asset, such as stock, to the lender to qualify for a lower down payment. See also: Secured loan.

Plethron An ancient Greek unit of area approximately equivalent to 950 square meters.

PLN ISO 4217 code for the Polish fourth zloty. It was introduced in 1995, replacing the third zloty (PLZ) after a period of hyperinflation. It replaced the old currency at a ratio of 10,000 old zloty to one new zloty.

Ploughgate An obsolete Scottish unit of area approximately equivalent to 160 acres.

Plovman A nickname for the 500 Danish krone banknote. The name means "plowman" in Danish and derives from the fact that the note used to feature a farmer with a plow.

Plow Back To reinvest a company's earnings into its operations. A high growth company often plows back the majority of its earnings rather than pays out dividends in order to maintain its high growth rate. On the other hand, established companies tend to plow back very little, unless they are attempting to corner or create a new market. The plowback ratio tells investors the rate at which companies do this.

Plowback Rate In fundamental analysis, the opposite of the payout ratio. That is, the plowback rate is a company's earnings after dividends have been paid out, expressed as a percentage. It is expressed mathematically as: 100 - payout ratio percentage. A higher rate indicates that a company pays less in dividends and thus reinvests more of its earnings into the company. Whether or not this is desirable depends on the rate of growth: investors tend to prefer a lower plowback ratio in a slow-growing company and a higher one in a fast-growing company.

Pls Do In investment banking, a slang term for work assigned by a senior employee. The term is derived from the image of a senior banker forwarding an e-mail to a subordinate, only adding "Pls do" at the top. It is then up to the subordinate to determine what has been requested.

Plug In marketing, to mention a product or business favorably for pay. For example, the host of a game show may mention that a certain company makes good or cheap products if that company has sponsored the show. This marketing tool is thought to be effective because it provides the added feeling of a "personal" endorsement difficult or impossible to achieve on regular commercials. Plugs are common on radio shows, and are becoming increasingly common on reality television shows.

Plum In the United Kingdom, a rarely used slang term for 100,000 pounds.

Pluna The first airline company in Uruguay. It was established in 1946 and was nationalized in 1951. In the 1990s, it was partially privatized and a 49% stake was sold to a Brazilian airline. However, the government re-purchased most of Pluna in 2006, taking 98% ownership.

Plunge Team A working group of U.S. government officials constituted to maintain efficiency and stability in the financial markets. It was established by President Ronald Reagan in 1988 and consists of the Secretary of the Treasury, the Chairman of the Federal Reserve, the Chairman of the SEC, and the Chairman of the Commodity Futures Trading Commissions. The Plunge Team exists to coordinate actions of the U.S. government to deal with challenges to the American economy. It is also called the Working Group.

Plurality In an election with three or more choices, the choice that receives the most votes without attaining 50%. For example, in an election in which Candidate A receives 35% of the vote, Candidate B receives 20%, and Candidate C receives 45%, Candidate C wins with a plurality of the vote.

Plurilateral Agreement A treaty between more than two, but not very many, countries. There is no set number that differentiates a plurilateral agreement from a multilateral agreement, though a plurilateral agreement has fewer parties. For instance, the World Trade Organization considers agreements between more than two members to be plurilateral, while agreements between all WTO members are multilateral.

Plus 1. In mutual funds, the amount by which the market price exceeds the net asset value. **2.** Describing an increase in a security's price, especially a marginal one. For example, one may hear, "Stock A had a small plus tick earlier today." See also: Uptick.

PLUS Loan A loan that a parent may borrow to pay for a child's post-secondary education expenses. PLUS loans are guaranteed by the U.S. government, and have a 7.9% interest rate. Unlike some other education loans, PLUS loans are awarded on the basis of the creditworthiness of the borrower.

Plus Tick Seller A security that is sold short. The term refers to an obsolete rule whereby securities could be sold short, only after a plus tick.

Plus-Cash Convertible A convertible security in which the holder must pay a certain amount of money in addition to the exchange of the convertible in order to receive common stock in the underlying company. Because of this provision, plus-cash convertibles are susceptible to large price fluctuations.

Plutocracy A system of governance in which the wealthy rule simply by being wealthy. The term is derogatory and generally is not used officially. An example of a plutocracy is the City of London, in which companies based in the city are allowed to vote in addition to actual residents. The term may also refer to a situation in which money is perceived to have too great a role in the political process.

Plutocrat A person with real or perceived political authority due to his/her vast wealth. For example, a person who donates vast sums to candidates of all major parties in order to have influence no matter who wins may be called a plutocrat. The term is highly derogatory.

PLW GOST 7.67 Latin three-letter geocode for Palau. The code is used for transactions to and from Palauan bank accounts and for international shipping to Palau. As with all GOST 7.67 codes, it is used primarily in Cyrillic alphabets.

PLZ ISO 4217 code for the third Polish zloty. It was issued in 1950. For most of its history, it was an inconvertible currency because Poland was under Communist rule, and its exchange rate was set by the government. In 1990, it became a convertible currency. It was redenominated and replaced by the fourth zloty in 1995.

PM 1. ISO 3166-1 alpha-2 code for the Territorial Collectivity of Saint Pierre and Miquelon, an overseas department of France. This is the code used in international transactions to and from local bank accounts. **2.** ISO 3166-2 geocode for Saint Pierre and Miquelon. This is used as an international standard for shipping to Saint Pierre and Miquelon.

PN 1. ISO 3166-1 alpha-2 code for the Pitcairn Islands. This is the code used in international transactions to and from Pitcairn bank accounts. **2.** ISO 3166-2 geocode for the Pitcairn Islands. This is used as an international standard for shipping to the Pitcairn Islands.

PNG GOST 7.67 Latin three-letter geocode for Papua New Guinea. The code is used for transactions to and from Papua New Guinean bank accounts and for international shipping to Papua New Guinea. As with all GOST 7.67 codes, it is used primarily in Cyrillic alphabets.

Pociq A Tatar unit of volume approximately equivalent to the volume contained in 32 kilograms of water. It was rendered obsolete when the Soviet Union began to use the metric system in 1924.

Pod stolom A Slovak term meaning under the table. It is a slang term for bribery.

Podawqa A Tatar unit of volume approximately equivalent to the volume occupied by 16 kilograms of water. It was rendered obsolete when the Soviet Union began to use the metric system in 1924.

Pogon A largely obsolete Romanian measure of area approximately equivalent to five square meters.

Point A way of conceptualizing price changes in the trading of securities. For stocks, a point corresponds to $1, while for bonds it indicates a 1% change relative to the face value. For example, if one states that GE rose two points on Thursday, this means that it rose $2. See also: Tick.

Point and Figure Chart In technical analysis, a chart that records only changes in price to a security or derivative. A point-and-figure chart does not account for time. Price is charted along the y-axis, but nothing is measured on the x-axis. The chart is designed as a series of columns of X and O, with X representing a rising price and O representing a fall. A change in price must exceed a certain amount before it is charted, which is designed to filter out noise. As a result, a point-and-figure chart may change several times in a trading day, or not at all.

Point Balance A statement indicating the gains and/or losses on the futures contracts in a portfolio. A futures commission merchant issues point balance statements to clients at the end of each month.

Poisha A subdivision of the Bangladeshi taka. One poisha is equal in value to 1/100 of a taka. Poisha coins are rarely used. See also: Cent.

Poison Pill An antitakeover measure stipulating that shareholders on the receiving end of a hostile takeover may buy shares in their own company at a price below fair market value. Once the acquisition is complete, the provision allows these same shareholders to buy more shares in the new company for below market value. This forces shareholders in the acquiring company to suffer a devaluation and dilution of their own shares. This is done to discourage hostile takeovers among the shareholders of the acquiring companies. It is important to note that a poison pill need not use both of these tactics; sometimes it utilizes only one or the other.

Poison-Put Bond A bond that allows bondholders to redeem before maturity at a high price should certain, named events take place. These events commonly include restructuring, a leveraged buyout, an attempted hostile takeover, or paying dividends in excess of a certain amount or percentage. Poison-put bonds can act as an anti-takeover measure; they help management discourage takeovers by raising their expense. On the other hand, when the company is going through a difficult time, poison-put bonds can limit management's restructuring options for the same reason.

Poisson Distribution In statistics, a distribution representing the probability of a random event that occurs at regular intervals on average. Each event occurs independently of every other one.

POL GOST 7.67 Latin three-letter geocode for Poland. The code is used for transactions to and from Polish bank accounts and for international shipping to Poland. As with all GOST 7.67 codes, it is used primarily in Cyrillic alphabets.

Polarized Fractal Efficiency In technical analysis, a measure of price efficiency. It is measured on a scale of -100 to +100. A PFE reading greater than zero indicates a price uptrend while one below zero indicates a downtrend. The farther a reading is from zero in either direction, the more efficient the price trend is thought to be.

Pole A unit of area equivalent to 1/320th of one square mile.

Polegada A Portuguese measure of length approximately equivalent to 27.5 millimeters. It became obsolete after Lusophone countries adopted the metric system in the 19th century.

Policy Duration The length of time during which an insurance policy remains in force. Health insurance, for example, may have a policy duration of several months or several years. Many other policies last only one year before renewal. Whole life insurance remains in effect for the remainder of one's life.

Policy Limit The maximum benefit an insurance company will pay a policyholder if/when an insured event occurs. For example, a health insurance policy may have a policy limit of $2 million. This means that the most the insurance company will pay in the case of catastrophic illness is $2 million. Many policy limits are rather high and most policyholders do not need to worry about medical bills of, say, $2 million. However, some long-term illnesses may result in medical bills that approach the limit. See also: Pre-existing condition.

Policy Loan A loan that an insurance company extends to a policyholder with the cash surrender value of the policy as collateral. That is, if the policyholder does not

repay the loan, the insurance company may take an equivalent amount out of the policyholder's death benefit. The nature of collateral has historically meant that policy loans carry low interest rates, but this is not always true. It is also called a life insurance loan.

Policyholder A person or (less commonly) an organization that has an insurance policy. The policyholder receives the specific types of coverage (life, health, etc.) stated in the policy, subject to the payment of premiums, usually on a monthly basis. It is important to note that a policyholder does not make any legally enforceable promises when he/she takes out a policy. Specifically, the insurance company cannot legally compel the policyholder to pay his/her premiums; its only recourse is to stop coverage. On the other hand, the policyholder can force the insurance company to provide coverage if it refuses to do so, provided he/she has in fact paid premiums.

Policyholder Loan Bond A bond that the issuer secures with the receivables on loans made to life insurance policyholders where those loans are, themselves, secured by the cash surrender value of those policies.

Policywriting Agent An insurance agent to whom the insurance company has given the authority and responsibility to write policies. The policywriting agent sets the terms of policies.

Polish Mint An organization in Poland that issues legal tender coins and banknotes for general use. It was established in 1994 and is the only publicly-traded mint in the world. It is located in Warsaw.

Political Equity The influence that a company derives from its donations to political candidates. If a company makes large donations to a party or candidate, it is more likely to have a voice when ideas are discussed and to have politicians listen when it lobbies for its favored regulatory or other issues. Building political equity is a primary reason companies in the United States sometimes donate to both political parties.

Political Risk The risk that a foreign government will significantly alter its policies or other regulations so that it significantly affects one's investment. More broadly, it can apply to the risk that a nation will refuse to comply with an agreement to which it is a party, or that political violence will hurt an investment or business. For example, if one exports goods to a foreign nation, and that nation elects a new government that enacts protectionist tariffs, this will negatively impact the export business.

Political Risk Insurance An insurance policy protecting the policyholder from the risk that a foreign government will significantly alter its policies or other regulations so that it results in a loss for one's investment. It may also cover the risk that a nation will refuse to comply with an agreement to which it is a party, or that political violence will hurt an investment or business. For example, if one exports goods to a foreign nation, and that nation elects a new government that enacts protectionist tariffs, this will negatively impact the export business. Political risk insurance may be tailored to the policyholder's specific needs.

Political Terrorist A person or group that commits violent acts to make a statement or achieve some end. Acts of political terrorism may make it difficult to conduct business in the area in which they occur. See also: Political risk.

Political Union The transfer of most or all sovereignty from two or more states to form a single state. A political union may be a unitary state; that is, all constituent states cease to have legal existence (except maybe as administrative divisions) and they are subject to the same law. Alternatively, a political union may be federal, in which the new state is given certain responsibilities and remaining powers stay with the previously independent states. Political unions generally have one currency and have no trade barriers between constituent states.

Political Violence A violent act intended to make a statement or achieve some end. Political violence encompasses terrorism (which is carried out by a non-government group), war (which usually is carried out by a government) and other forms of civil strife. Political violence may render it difficult to conduct business in the area in which it occurs. See also: Political risk.

Poll Tax A tax one must pay in order to vote. That is, a poll tax is a fee. Poll taxes are illegal in the United States as they discourage the poor (and, in some cases, racial minorities) from voting.

Pollution Control Bond A municipal bond issued by a local government that finances some equipment intended to control pollution for use by a private company. The coupons on pollution control bonds were formerly tax exempt to encourage green investment, but this exemption ended in 1986. Payment on the coupons and principal is guaranteed by the revenue generated by the pollution control equipment. See also: Private activity bond.

Pollution Haven A jurisdiction with few environmental restrictions relative to other jurisdictions. It has been suggested that companies in "dirty" industries such as mining or milling have an incentive to relocate to pollution havens, but there is evidence of this actually happening.

Pollution Haven Hypothesis The idea that pollution-producing industries are attracted to areas with few environmental regulations. The hypothesis suggests that companies in "dirty" industries such as mining or milling have an incentive to relocate to areas where they will be comparatively free to do as do as they please and/or do not have to pay clean-up costs. However, there has been little evidence of this actually happening.

Poly Vinyl Chloride A chemical sometimes used in plastics. It has been shown to damage coins and reduce their value to collectors and investors.

Pond An obsolete Dutch unit of weight roughly equivalent to 480 grams, with slight regional variations.

Ponto A Portuguese measure of length approximately equivalent to 0.19 meters. It became obsolete after Lusophone countries adopted the metric system in the 19th century.

Pony In the United Kingdom, a slang term for 25 pounds.

Pood A Russian unit of weight approximately equivalent to 16.4 kilograms. It was rendered obsolete when the Soviet Union began to use the metric system in 1924.

Pool 1. A group of financial instruments that may be placed into the same investment vehicle. A major example is a mortgage pool, which consists of mortgages that are divided up and placed into large groups to be sold as securities. **2.** Funds that a group of investors put together to invest for mutual benefit. A major example of a pooled fund is a mutual fund.

Pooled Income Fund A mutual fund comprising of donated securities and/or cash, the proceeds of which go to charity and donors. One donates securities and cash to create a pooled income fund, which is then invested as if it were a regular mutual fund, which pays dividends to donors each quarter in proportion to the amount donated as a percentage of the whole fund. When a donor dies, what remains of his/her donation as a percentage of the total fund is given to a charity. Usually charities administer pooled income funds, and the remaining donation goes to their own charitable operations. All cash and securities donated to pooled income funds qualify as charitable gifts for tax purposes; importantly, securities so donated are exempt from capital gains tax.

Pooling of Interests A way to record a merger or acquisition where the assets and liabilities are added together and netted. The pooling of interests method does not create good will and therefore results in higher earnings for newly merged or acquired entity. The pooling of interest method contrasts with the purchase acquisition method.

Pool-Vest To manage funding for a non-profit responsibly, such that all money is deposited in the savings account or similar instrument that earns the most in interest income.

Poop (Very) informal; a person with inside information. Poops generally are not allowed to make any trades based on this information.

Poop and Scoop To spread false rumors about a security maliciously such that its price drops and then to buy the same security at the new, deflated price. A small group of investors may poop and scoop to make a quick profit when the security rises back to its former level. Pooping and scooping is a form of price manipulation and, as such, is illegal. This concept should not be confused with a poop, who is a person with inside information. See also: Pump and Dump.

Poor Mouth A slang term meaning to deny that one is rich. For example, a wealthy lawyer who visits a bar frequented primarily by blue collar workers may poor mouth herself by downplaying the success of her practice to other patrons.

Pork Bellies Futures contracts involving pork-related commodities. Pork bellies are a staple in many diversified portfolios, especially before summer, when pork products are in the highest demand. The term comes from the fact that American-style bacon is made from the underside of a pig. Due to religious prohibitions, Islamic finance forbids pork bellies and other pork-based trades.

Pork Chop An arrangement in which an employee of the New York Stock Exchange takes orders at a trading booth on behalf the broker who owns it in exchange for a fee. The pork chop enables the broker to take and solicit orders somewhere off the trading floor while still fulfilling his/her duties on the trading floor.

Poronkusema A Finnish unit of length approximately equivalent to 7.5 kilometers. It became obsolete when Finland adopted the metric system in 1880, but is still used to indicate a vaguely nearby distance.

Poronkusemaa kuukaudessa A Finnish unit of speed approximately equivalent to 2.9 millimeters per second. It became obsolete when Finland adopted the metric system in 1880.

Portability The ability to take one's benefits, particularly health insurance, from one job to another. Some U.S. states require health insurance companies to offer portability. It exists to protect people from the possibility that they will lose their health insurance and be unable to acquire a new policy because of a pre-existing condition that develops between acquiring the first policy and looking for a second.

Portability Agreement An agreement between a brokerage and a client allowing the client to take his/her accounts and transfer them to another brokerage. A portability agreement may even exist if the financial product being transferred is proprietary to the first brokerage.

Portable Alpha An investment strategy that involves making investments that have little to do with the overall trend in the portfolio. In other words, a portable alpha strategy seeks out investments that exceed the performance of the index or market upon which most of one's portfolio is based. In technical terms, a portable alpha strategy seeks to separate a portfolio's alpha from its beta.

Portable Benefits Benefits that one has accumulated on an employer-sponsored plan, usually but not always a retirement plan, that one may take with him/her to a new employer. For example, if an employee has a 401(k) with portable benefits and quits his job, he may roll over the benefits into his new employer's 401(k) plan. Most 401(k)s, 403(b)s, IRAs, and health savings accounts have portable benefits.

PORTAL A trading platform operated by NASDAQ of closely-held companies and other companies for investment by extremely high net-worth individuals. This market is largely exempt from the requirements of the Sarbanes-Oxley Act. In 2007, the Portal Market required an individual to have a minimum net worth of $100 million to qualify to trade on it.

Portfolio The set of open positions held by an investor. For example, if an investor owns shares in AT&T, GM, and bonds in Disney, one collectively refers to these as the investor's portfolio. Rational economic actors are expected to seek the highest possible return at the lowest possible risk. They do this by creating diversified portfolios, which spread risk out among several investments. See also: Portfolio Management.

Portfolio Allocation By Region Investment of one's portfolio in securities that are traded in various countries. This is done to reduce risk, often political risk. For example, if one country's government announces a larger than normal budget deficit, or the central bank raises interest rates, this may affect security prices in one country but not necessarily in other countries that did not take equivalent steps. Likewise, if a whole industry fails in one country but thrives in another, investing in the same industry in both countries hedges one's risk. Some analysts argue that country diversification is less effective in an era of globalization, but other analysts dispute that.

Portfolio Asset Allocation An active management strategy for a portfolio with a basic set of securities. The investor changes the securities represented in the portfolio as his/her investment goals change. It is important to note, however, that asset allocation implies diversification to the portfolio. The investor or money manager may use fundamental, technical and/or macroeconomic analysis in determining when and how to change the securities in the portfolio.

Portfolio Beta A measure of a portfolio's volatility. A beta of 1 means that the portfolio is neither more nor less volatile or risky than the wider market. A beta of more than 1 indicates greater volatility while a beta of less than 1 indicates less. Beta is an important component of the Capital Asset Pricing Model, which attempts to use volatility and risk to estimate expected returns.

Portfolio Diversification In risk management, the act or strategy of adding more investments to one's portfolio to hedge against the investments already in it. Ideally, this reduces the risk inherent in any one investment, and increases the possibility of making a profit, or at least avoiding a loss. This may also reduce the expected return on a portfolio, but it depends on level and type of diversification. There are two main types of diversification. Horizontal diversification involves investing in similar type investments. Examples include investing in several technology companies or in different types of bonds. Vertical diversification involves investing in very different securities; for example, one may choose to invest in securities traded in different countries, or in both winter clothing and swimsuit companies. Both types of diversification may be as broad or narrow as the investor chooses. In general, the broader the diversification, the less risk and less return. See also: Markowitz Portfolio Theory.

Portfolio Effect The reduction in the value of a portfolio relative to the reduction in value of the individual assets represented in that portfolio. The portfolio effect is weighted for the percentage of the portfolio each asset represents. For example, suppose a portfolio consists of 50% of stock A and 25% each of stocks B and C. If stock A declines 10% and B and C each decline 20%, then the portfolio effect is calculated as: portfolio effect = $(.5(.1) + .25(.2) + .25(.2)) * 100 = 15\%$ decline

Portfolio Expected Return The aggregated expected return on the securities and other assets in a portfolio, where the return on each security or asset is weighted for the proportion of its representation in the portfolio.

Portfolio Insurance A strategy used to protect against potential losses to a portfolio. For example, one may short sell futures contracts on securities in a portfolio where one makes a profit if the securities decrease in price. Alternatively, one may buy put options allowing one to sell the securities at a predetermined price regardless of market movements. See also: Hedge.

Portfolio Management The act or practice of making investment decisions in order to make the largest possible return. Portfolio management takes two basic forms: active and passive. Active management involves using technical, fundamental, or some other analysis to make trades on a fairly regular basis. For example, one may sell stock A in order to buy stock B. Then, a few days or weeks later, one may sell stock B to buy bond C. Passive management, on the other hand, involves buying an index, an exchange-traded fund, or some other investment vehicle with securities the investor does not directly choose. For example, one may buy an exchange-traded fund that holds all the stocks on the S&P 500. See also: Asset management, Investment adviser.

Portfolio Opportunity Set Given a set of assets, the total number of portfolios that can be constructed at different levels of risk and expected returns. The portfolio opportunity set helps an investor construct a portfolio with the assets he/she has at his/her risk tolerance.

Portfolio Pumping The practice of a mutual fund attempting to appear to improve its performance before it must report results to shareholders. For example, it may short sell losing stocks and buy gaining ones. It may also buy thinly-traded stocks with the intent of driving up the price. Portfolio pumping makes a portfolio look healthier (and, therefore, a better investment) than it really is.

Portfolio Restructuring An active management strategy for a portfolio or fund in which the investor or money manager changes the securities represented in the portfolio or fund as changes to one's investment goals change. Portfolio restructuring involves the sale of assets no longer needed or wanted and the purchase of different ones. The term implies that this occurs at a fundamental level; that is, rather than selling a few securities here and there, the investor or money manager is changing the basic structure of the portfolio or fund. The investor or money manager may use fundamental, technical, and/or macroeconomic analysis in determining when and how to change the securities in the portfolio or fund. See also: Asset allocation.

Portfolio Runoff A reduction in the mortgages represented in a mortgage-backed security as a result of prepayment of some of the mortgages in it. This can reduce the yield on an MBS and, at times, force the security holder to reinvest proceeds at a lower coupon rate than the MBS paid. Most mortgage-backed securities provide safeguards against portfolio runoff unduly affecting yields. See also: Prepayment risk.

Portfolio Separation Theorem An economic theory stating that the investment decisions of a firm are independent from the firm's owner's wishes. The Portfolio Separation Theorem states that the productive value of a firm's management neither affects nor is affected by the owner's business decisions. As a result, the performance of a firm's investments has no relation to how they are financed, whether by stock, debt, or cash. The theorem was devised by economist Irving Fisher. See also: Irrelevance result.

Portfolio Theory 1. See: Markowitz portfolio theory. 2. See: Post-modern portfolio theory.

Portfolio Transaction Costs Miscellaneous fees associated with the trade of securities. These fees include commissions, exchange fees, early redemption fees, and anything else not directly related to the price of the security. Under SEC rules, mutual funds and closed-end funds must disclose their commissions both as a dollar amount and as an expression of cents per share, but this disclosure is separate from any other transaction costs.

Portfolio Turnover Rate The ratio at which a portfolio trades the securities in it. A higher turnover rate indicates active management; if it becomes very high, this may indicate that the broker or manager is trading securities for the sake of collecting more fees. It is calculated as the trading volume of the portfolio as a percentage of the entire portfolio. See also: Prudent person rule.

Portfolio Variance A measure of volatility in a portfolio. It is calculated by taking the variance and co-variance of each security in the portfolio and weighting them in proportion to that security's representation in the portfolio. It differs from a weighted average of the variances of the securities because it includes the co-variances.

Portuguese Escudo The former currency of Portugal. It was introduced in 1911 following the republican revolution, and was marked by high inflation throughout its history. It was removed from circulation and replaced by the euro in 2002.

POSIT An electronic system that matches buy and sell orders made on an exchange by institutional investors. It was established jointly by BARRA and Investment Technology Group in 1987.

Position The state of owning or owing a security or other asset. One has a long position when one owns something, while one has a short position when something is sold, especially sold short. See also: Close a position.

Position Bond A fidelity bond covering the jobs named on the bond. A fidelity bond compensates a company in the event it loses money as the result of employee theft or fraud. A position bond limits this coverage to the positions named in it. For example, a position bond may cover theft by the vice president of marketing, regardless of who fills that position at a given time. See also: Name schedule bond.

Position Building The practice of buying and short selling securities to create one or more open positions. Position building may occur constantly for traders while other investors may build a position then maintain it for a long period of time.

Position Clerk An employee at a dealer firm who records transactions made on an exchange floor and relays them to the back office for recordkeeping.

Position Day The day on which the seller of a commodity must inform the buyer of the delivery date of the commodity. This especially applies if the delivery date is different from the first permissible day. On the Chicago Board of Trade, the seller's clearing corporation also must notify the Board of intent to deliver.

Position Diagram A chart or other diagram showing the profits and losses on a derivative over time. It may be calculated in a number of different ways.

Position Limit In futures on foreign exchange, the largest position (either long or short) that an investor is permitted by his/her employer to take.

Position Self To buy or sell a security in the belief that its price will soon rise or fall. Positioning oneself is perhaps the most basic and easily understood investment one can make in a security. See also: Long position, Short position.

Position Sheet A list of the positions represented in a portfolio or fund.

Position Sizing The dollar amount of an investment. When determining a position sizing, an investor usually accounts for his/her own risk tolerance and the total amount he/she has to invest. One may think of position sizing as the dollar amount of the part of a portfolio in a single security. See also: Risk capital.

Position Trader An investor who practices buying and holding. That is, position trading occurs when a trader buys a security and does not sell it until it is at or near maturity. If the security is a stock or otherwise does not have a maturity date, the position trader holds it indefinitely. The term "position trading" is most common in commodities, where it refers to a trader that does not sell a commodity contract until the delivery date is close (usually for several months). See also: Value investor.

Position Trading The act or practice of buying and holding. That is, position trading occurs when a trader buys a security and does not sell it until it is at or near maturity. If the security is a stock or otherwise does not have a maturity date, the trader holds it indefinitely. The term "position trading" is most common in

commodities, where it refers to a trader who does not sell a commodity contract until the delivery date is close (usually for several months).

Positive Carry A situation in which an investor has two opposite positions and in which the cash inflow from one position exceeds the cash outflow of the other. For example, if one borrows money, owes 10% interest, and then promptly lends the same amount of money at 12% interest, then the borrower/lender has a positive carry.

Positive Convexity The phenomenon that bond prices increase more in absolute terms more when interest rates go up than bond prices decrease when interest rates go down.

Positive Covenant A bond covenant that requires the issuer to take certain actions. For example, a positive covenant may require an issuer to maintain enough liquid assets to cover the principal of the bond. More commonly, a positive covenant requires the issuer to have a certain amount of insurance or submit to periodic audits. It contrasts with a negative covenant, which prevents the issuer from taking the enumerated actions. It is also called an affirmative covenant.

Positive Volume Index An index that tracks trading days with high trading volume. Some technical analysts recommend against trading on days with high volume because they advise against conducting the same transactions that most investors (including the bad ones) are conducting. As a result, these analysts recommend conducting trades on days when the PVI is low. See also: Negative volume index.

Possessions Corporation A U.S. corporation that does a significant amount of business in an American overseas possession, usually in Puerto Rico. The IRS allows these corporations to take a tax credit for the business they conduct in the possessions. See also: Form 5735.

Post 1. The physical place on an exchange where transactions occur. Posts are most important to exchanges that use the open outcry or a similar system. They are becoming increasingly irrelevant as more exchanges conduct trading electronically. Posts are also called trading posts. 2. To recognize a transaction on an account. For example, if one writes a check for $100 and $100 is deducted from that account three days later, the transaction is set to post on the third day.

Post 30 Stock On the New York Stock Exchange, a stock that trades in lots of 10, instead of the usual 100. That is, if one orders a lot of a Post 30 stock, one will buy or sell 10 shares. These stocks are traded on an area of the NYSE known as Post 30, which has given its name to the stock type.

Post Execute Reporting System A computerized order-entry system that sends buy or sell orders to the appropriate specialist on the floor of an American Stock Exchange, bypassing the floor broker.

Post Mortem A slang term for a meeting or series of meetings in which participants attempt to discover what went wrong with a failed project. For example, if a marketing campaign does not increase sales of a product, the company may conduct a post mortem to determine why it did not.

Postal Code A series of letters and/or numbers identifying the area of a country to which to deliver mail. Most of the world's countries use postal codes of one kind or another because they enable more efficient sorting of mail. The first postal codes were introduced in the Soviet Union in 1932.

Post-Audit Perceptions, feelings, and impressions of a company after an internal audit or external audit. This is especially important when the company needs to make budget decisions in light of the new information the audit brings to light.

Post-Dated Check A check dated for one or more days after it is written. For example, if one dates a check for January 31st, and it is currently January 25th, it is a postdated check. Theoretically, banks do not honor postdated checks, though many do anyway.

Post-Money Valuation The value of a company's stock after adding external financing, such as a new issue of bonds or an IPO. Venture capitalists can compare the estimated post-money valuation to the pre-money valuation to determine a company's potential profitability when they are making investment decisions. This comparison helps the venture capitalists find how much capital the company needs to maintain or expand its operations.

Posto In Mozambique, a political subdivision approximately equivalent to a county.

Postponement Option The ability or decision to delay a planned project without canceling it. This decision is undertaken if a party, often a financial backer, wants to undertake a project but unexpectedly lacks the capital to do so. In the case of a new issue of a stock or bond, the the postponement option may be exercised if the issuer believes that demand for the issue will be low. In some cases, it may simply be an indication that a financial backer is no longer interested in a project.

Postponing Income The act or practice of not receiving otherwise expected income in a given tax year in order to reduce one's tax liability. For example, a company may postpone income if it has had a net operating loss in the year to date and wishes to apply it to future tax liability. Realizing income in the current tax year may eliminate that possibility. See also: Future Income Tax.

Post-Trade Benchmarks The price of a security or other investment after an investor has decided to buy or sell it.

Pot The portion of a new issue that the lead underwriter places with institutional investors. Sometimes the underwriters in a syndicate give the pot back to the lead underwriter from their remainder and sometimes it is specifically set aside at issue.

Pot Is Clean Informal for fully subscribed.

Potable Water Water that a human is able to drink safely. Lack of potable water in some areas is a major impediment to economic development.

Pot-de-Vin A French term for a glass of wine. It is a slang term for a small bribe.

Pote A Portuguese measure of liquid volume approximately equivalent to 8.4 liters. It became obsolete after Lusophone countries adopted the metric system in the 19th century.

Potential Default A situation that may cause a default on a loan. Alternatively, potential default may refer to a person, especially a loan applicant, who is in such a situation. An obvious example of potential default is a situation in which a borrower loses his/her job. Lenders attempt to identify potential defaults before they make a loan.

Potential Dilution The reduction in value of stock that occurs if more stock is issued. That is, if more stock is issued, there will be more stock outstanding. Among other things, this reduces the dividend per share because each diluted stock represents a smaller ownership interest in the company than it did before. Generally speaking, potential dilution applies to the situation if convertible bonds or warrants are exercised, though it may apply to a completely new issue. Many stock issues have antidilution provisions to reduce the risk incumbent to potential dilution to shareholders. See also: Diluted earnings per share.

Potte An obsolete Danish unit of volume approximately equivalent to 966 milliliters.

Pottle A unit of liquid volume equivalent to half of one gallon.

Pourboire The French word for tip or gratuity. It may also be used as a term for bribery.

Pous 1. An ancient Greek unit of length approximately equivalent to 308.2 millimeters. **2.** An ancient Greek unit of area approximately equivalent to 0.095 square meters.

Poverty Line The minimum yearly income that a person or family needs in order to provide for basic needs. Frequently, a government agency sets the poverty line for a jurisdiction; this line may bear only a rough relationship to one's actual poverty. However, a poverty line is often used to determine eligibility for welfare and other benefit programs.

Poverty Trap An obstacle or disincentive for a person to work to raise himself/herself out of poverty. For example, an increase in income from a job may reduce the welfare benefits for which one is eligible. Likewise, a lack of affordable educational opportunities may prevent one from acquiring skills necessary to earn more money.

Pow Wow Informal; a meeting, especially an urgent meeting. For example, a manager may have a pow wow with an employee who is underperforming to warn him about his situation.

Power Luser In an office setting, a slang term for an employee who consistently (and always accidentally) causes his/her computer to malfunction. Such an employee, for example, may have a hard time differentiating between legitimate attachments to e-mails and attachments with viruses.

Power of Attorney The legal transfer of the authority to act on behalf of another person. That is, power of attorney gives the designee (called an agent) the authority to sign legal documents and manage the finances of the principal in the event of the principal incapacitation. For example, one may designate power of attorney to a relative in case one develops Alzheimer's disease and is unable to manage one's own affairs. The power of attorney may be limited or unlimited; that is, the principal may only allow the person with power of attorney to manage affairs within certain parameters.

Power of Attorney of Property A legal document giving an assignee the ability to make decisions on behalf of the assignor with regard to the assignor's property in the event of the assignor's mental or physical incapacity. The assignor grants power of attorney of property while he/she is still competent, and it comes into effect at incapacity. A person with power of attorney of property may make any and all decisions regarding the assignor's assets, including securities, within the parameters of the document. For example, the document may prohibit the person with power of attorney of property from selling certain assets intended for the assignor's heirs in his/her estate. See also: Power of attorney, Proxy directive.

Powers of Appointment A grant of the ability to dispose of property, especially of an estate. The person who receives the powers of appointment may be the executor of an estate or the trustee of a trust. The person with the powers of appointment must dispose of the property according to the wishes of the grantor, unless the grantor gives unlimited powers of appointment, which transfers discretion to the executor or trustee.

Powiat In Poland, a political subdivision equivalent to a county.

Powiaty grodzkie In Poland, a political subdivision for an urban county.

Powiaty ziemskie In Poland, a political subdivision for a rural county.

PR In numismatics, an abbreviation for proof. An equivalent abbreviation is PF.

Pradesh In India, a political subdivision equivalent to a state or province.

Prajina A largely obsolete Romanian measure of area approximately equivalent to 195 square meters.

PRB A currency code for the Transnistrian ruble. It was issued in 1994, replacing the Soviet ruble. It suffered from extremely high inflation at first, but this has eased somewhat since 2000. Because Transnistria has limited recognition, this code is not recognized by the ISO. An equivalent code is RUP.

Preapproval A commitment by a mortgage lender to provide a loan with a certain monthly payment to a borrower. A lender offers pre-approvals in hopes that the borrower to whom it is offered will use that lender in securing a mortgage. It should be noted that, while the monthly payment is fixed, the interest rate and therefore the total amount available to be borrowed are not. This can limit the potential borrower's options as he/she seeks to buy real estate.

Prearranged Trading The practice of two commodity dealers trading with each other at prices upon which they have agreed in advance. Pre-arranged trading is designed to exclude other dealers from the market, to gain a tax advantage, or both. As a result, pre-arranged trading is illegal.

Preauthorized Electronic Debit A situation in which an account holder at a bank allows deductions from his/her account without explicit authorization. That is, an account holder may give a creditor authorization to take payment out of his/her bank account on a certain date or series of dates. Preauthorized electronic debits are most common and perhaps most useful for standing payments that do not fluctuate, such as loan or mortgage payments. They are known informally as electronic checks.

Preauthorized Payment Any agreement between a bank and an account holder whereby the account holder gives the bank permission to automatically debit the account by a certain amount every month. The amount may go to the bank to pay a standing fee, but most often goes to a third party. For example, a customer may set up a pre-authorized payment plan to pay his internet bill each month. See also: Direct Debit, Standing Order.

Pre-Carriage Describing a fee assessed by a port or airport on a good to be shipped internationally. See also: International Trade.

Precautionary Demand for Money In Keynesian economics, a need for money resulting from an unforeseen situation. Medical bills following an accident are an example of precautionary demand. According to John Maynard Keynes, people keep savings accounts, as well as some stocks and commodities, in order to cover precautionary demand if and when it occurs.

Precautionary Motive The desire to keep extra money in case an unforeseen situation requires a capital outlay. For example, one may wish to save extra money to pay for medical bills in case of an accident. According to John Maynard Keynes, people keep savings accounts, as well as some stocks and commodities, with a precautionary motive in order to cover unexpected events. See also: Precautionary demand (for money).

Precedence On an exchange, the succession in which floor traders must execute orders. Invariably, the orders with the highest bid or the lowest ask are executed first. If two orders have an identical price, the one entered first has precedence. The specific rules of precedence are set by each exchange individually.

Preceding-Year Basis In budgeting and other estimates, the practice of using the previous year's numbers as guidance. For example, if a company's expenses from salaries were $2 million in 2009, it may estimate that they will be in the range of $2 million in 2010. However, one may make adjustments to account for changes from the previous year.

Precious Metals Rare or otherwise valuable metals. Metals are considered precious based upon their rarity, usefulness in industry, or history as an investment commodity. Examples of precious metals include iridium, gold, and silver. Precious metals are traded as commodities on various security exchanges. Many precious metals are volatile, like other commodities, but generally maintain relatively high prices.

Precious Metals/Gold Fund A mutual fund or other investment company that invests predominantly or exclusively in securities related to gold or other precious metals. For example, it may invest in futures contracts or options in silver and platinum.

Precompute To calculate the annual interest owed on a loan by either deducting the annual interest from the face amount of the loan, or adding the compound interest together and dividing it out equally over 12 monthly periods. This means that the effective interest paid will be higher than the stated amount on the loan. Because of this, most jurisdictions require lending institutions using precomputation to express the interest rate in simple interest terms.

Predatory Lender A lender who makes a loan in the hope or expectation that the borrower will default. A lender may have an incentive to commit predatory lending if he/she receives a commission for each loan made (regardless of creditworthiness), or if the lender easily can bundle and sell the mortgage to a third party, passing on the risk while still profiting. A predatory lender may be an individual or institution. Predatory lending is illegal in many jurisdictions, though the exact definition may vary from place to place.

Predatory Lending The practice in which a loan is made to a borrower in the hope or expectation that the borrower will default. A lender may have an incentive to commit predatory lending if he/she receives a commission for each loan made (regardless of creditworthiness), or if the lender easily can bundle and sell the mortgage to a third party, passing on the risk while still profiting. Predatory lending is illegal in many jurisdictions, though the exact definition may vary from place to place.

Preemptive Right In stock, the ability of a shareholder to maintain the same percentage of ownership in a company should the company issue more stock by subscribing to a proportional number of shares at or below the market price. This protects the investor from devaluation of his/her shares if the company decides to hold a round of financing. The purchase of this proportional number of shares usually takes place before the new issue is offered to the secondary market, and must be exercised before a certain date (known as the expiration date) if the shareholder is to maintain the same percentage of ownership. It is also called a subscription right. See also: Anti-dilution provision.

Preexisting Condition In insurance, a medical condition that existed before one applied for and/or received a health insurance policy. Most private health insurance companies refuse to cover preexisting conditions, at least for a certain period of time. Depending on the severity of the preexisting condition, a provider may refuse to provide health insurance at all. However, employer-provided health insurance must cover preexisting conditions if an employee switches insurance plans as the result of a job change.

Preference The practice of executing trades and other transactions by means other than the open market. For example, if one needs roofing repairs on one's house, one may select one's brother's roofing business even if it is more expensive. In securities, preference often occurs in over-the-counter trades, especially within a brokerage. Preference can, but does not always, lead to economic inefficiency.

Preferred Dividend Coverage Ratio A measure of a publicly-traded company's ability to pay dividends to preferred stockholders. It is calculated by taking the company's net income and dividing it by the total preferred dividends it must pay. A ratio over 1 indicates that the company is able to make dividend payments, while a ratio below 1 indicates that it cannot. The preferred dividend coverage ratio is particularly important because dividends to preferred stockholders are set and guaranteed. Failure to pay them can be highly detrimental to the company because preferred stockholders, under some circumstances, can force its liquidation to receive back dividends.

Preferred Equity Redemption Stock A convertible preferred stock that automatically converts to common stock or cash on a certain date. PERCs have higher, guaranteed returns than common stock; however, the issuer reserves the right to exchange them for common stock at any time.

Preferred Provider Organization A health insurance plan in which the policyholder receives a discount from the full price if he/she receives medical services from a participating doctor, hospital, or other medical organization. In many ways, a PPO operates like other insurance policies: the policyholder pays a premium each month and, in exchange, the insurance company pays for the cost of medical care, after a deductible and co-insurance. What distinguishes a PPO from other policies is the fact that a group of doctors or hospitals may negotiate a discounted rate with the insurance company. This provides the policyholder with an incentive to receive care from this group. However, medicals services provided by organizations outside the group are also covered. See also: Health maintenance organization.

Preferred Redeemable Increased Dividend Equity Security A forward contract to buy a certain security and an interest-bearing deposit at a certain time for a certain price. PRIDES operate much like mandatory convertible bonds, but have different structures. PRIDES allow an investor to receive the interest on the deposit at regular intervals and also take advantage of the underlying security when the forward contract matures. Whoever holds the PRIDES at maturity must purchase the underlying security. They were introduced by Merrill Lynch.

Preferred Stock Stock in a publicly-traded company without voting rights, but otherwise with more rights than common shares. Preferred stocks receive dividends before common shares and sometimes have guaranteed dividends, while common shares only receive the leftovers. Preferred stocks also have a prior claim on capital in the event of liquidation; if the company is liquidated, all preferred shareholders must be paid off before a single common shareholder. Some preferred stocks are convertible, which means they can be changed into common shares at a certain ratio so that even preferred shareholders without voting rights have the possibility of gaining them. Preferred stocks tend not to appreciate as fast as common stocks.

Preferred Stock Agreement A contract stating the terms for a preferred stock.

Preferred Stock Ratio A ratio of a publicly-traded company's preferred stock to its total capitalization. In the ratio, the preferred stock is valued at par. The preferred stock ratio measures how much of a company's capitalization consists of preferred stock.

Pregnancy Discrimination Act Legislation in the United States, passed in 1978, requiring companies with 15 or more employees to treat pregnant women the same as all other employees. That is, employers cannot fire or refuse to give hours to a woman on account of pregnancy, childbirth or a similar condition.

Pre-IPO An offering of shares in a company before its initial public offering (IPO). Pre-IPO offerings are available only to a limited number of individuals, and are done in advance of an expected IPO. Pre-IPO prices are generally much lower than they would be at the IPO, but are risky for the investor, as their value is contingent upon the company eventually making an IPO. This is because pre-IPO shares attract little demand in situations in which there is insufficient demand for an IPO soon after; they usually become illiquid securities.

Preliminary Estimate 1. In calculating quarterly GDP, a second estimate published approximately two months after the end of a quarter. It includes information not available at the time of the advance estimate, as well as any necessary data revisions. However, it is still subject to scrutiny and potential alteration. See also: Final estimate. **2.** An early calculation of the cost of a project. This calculation is made and presented to a buyer before a project has begun, and is subject to change due to both exogenous factors and endogenous factors. See also: Revised estimate.

Preliminary Prospectus The first prospectus distributed prior to a new issue of a security. The first prospectus contains information such as the terms of issue, the size

of issue, and other, relevant data about the security. Importantly, however, it does not contain the new issue's price. Because the preliminary prospectus is subject to change and because the SEC requires part of it to be printed to red ink, it is informally called a red herring.

Preliminary Scale The yield and price of a bond quoted by the issuer before it is issued and before any bids have been submitted. The preliminary scale may change as this process unfolds.

Pre-Market Describing trading that occurs on a security before an exchange opens for the day. Pre-market trading is often less liquid than regular trading because participation by market makers is voluntary, whereas market makers are required to serve as a counterparty for a security during trading hours. However, pre-market trading can give some indication on the likely direction of the security's price movement over the course of the trading day. See also: After-hours trading.

Premature Exercise A situation in which an option holder exercises the option before the expiration date. For example, suppose one has a call to purchase shares at $10 each that does not expire for some time. If the current price of the shares is $35, the holder may find it advantageous to exercise prematurely because there is no guarantee that the shares will remain that high closer to expiration. Premature exercise can be disadvantageous to the writer of the option, depending on his/her option strategy.

Premium 1. The price by which a security, especially but not necessarily a bond, exceeds its face value. **2.** The price of an option contract. **3.** A payment that a policyholder makes, usually monthly, in order to be covered by an insurance policy. **4.** The extra return that an investor expects to make from a position in exchange for accepting extra risk.

Premium Bond A bond with a price higher than its face value. A premium bond occurs when a particular bond's coupon rates exceed the interest rates prevailing at the time. For example, if a bond was issued with a 5% coupon and most other bonds are paying 2%, this bond has more value on both the primary and secondary markets. As a result, it is more expensive and is sold at a premium.

Premium Income The money one makes from selling (or writing) an option contract. The term derives its name from the fact that the original sale price of an option is called the premium. One easy way to make money investing at little risk is to write covered options one does not expect to be exercised, and profiting from the premium income.

Premium Put Convertible A bond with two unusual features. First, it has a convertible option and may be exchanged for common stock in the underlying company. Secondly, it has a feature whereby the bondholder may redeem the bond from the issuer for a certain price at any time before maturity. In addition to these, it contains regular features of a bond such as regular coupon payments. The premium put option gives the bondholder a great deal of flexibility when the value of the bond changes.

Premium Raid A tactic in hostile takeovers in which the acquiring company offers to buy shares of the target company at a substantial premium to their market value. A premium raid is intended to force control of the company away from its board of directors, either by making the acquiring company the majority shareholder or by giving it effective veto power over board elections. That said, a premium raid can be very expensive.

Pre-Money Valuation In venture capital, an estimate of the value of a privately held company before its IPO. Venture capitalists use the pre-money valuation to help determine how much money an IPO is likely to raise. However, the pre-money valuation is, at best, an educated guess, and there is no guarantee that the IPO will actually raise that much. It is also called simply pre-money.

Prenuptial Agreement A legal and binding agreement that a couple enters prior to their marriage. Prenuptial agreements are commonly associated with the division of assets in the event of a divorce later in life, but they may also include other details such as how assets are distributed in the event of the death of a spouse. Prenuptial agreements are somewhat controversial as some see them as providing an expectation of divorce; they are designed, however, to reduce financial uncertainty in a marriage.

Prepackaged Bankruptcy A situation whereby a company and its creditors agree on the terms of bankruptcy before it is filed with bankruptcy court. That is, the company and its creditors agree how and how much each creditor will be repaid and the terms of repayment. All parties, including shareholders if applicable, must agree to the prepackaged bankruptcy before it takes effect. A prepackaged bankruptcy makes it easier and less expensive for all parties when a company files Chapter 11 and reorganizes.

Prepaid Interest Interest on a loan that is paid before it is billed to the borrower. Generally speaking, the IRS does not allow the deduction of prepaid interest even when the interest would be deductible otherwise.

Prepayment 1. The payment of a debt in full before it is due. Prepayment is good for the borrower because it relieves him/her of the debt, but it deprives the lender of interest he/she would have received otherwise. As a result, some lenders attach prepayment penalties to loans to disincentivize prepayments. Prepayment can me a major risk to collateralized mortgage obligations as coupon payments are based on interest received from the underlying mortgages. Less commonly, this is called anticipation. See also: Prepayment risk. **2.** Payment in advance for a good or service not yet received.

Prepayment of Premiums The payment of premiums on an insurance policy before they are due. For example, one may pay six months' worth of premiums in January instead of paying each month from January to June.

Prepayment Penalty A fee that a lender may assess if a borrower repays a loan before the scheduled maturity. The prepayment penalty is used to discourage early payment of loans because it deprives the lender of future interest payments. The prepayment penalty is often 2% of the total amount borrowed. Some jurisdictions and organizations prohibit or limit prepayment penalties; if a jurisdiction does not, it may be assess on all loans that do not exclude the possibility in the loan agreement. See also: Prepayment risk.

Prepayment Privilege The right of a borrower to repay a debt in full before it is due. The prepayment privilege is favorable to the borrower because it relieves him/her of the debt, but it deprives the lender of interest that he/she would have received otherwise. However, some lenders offer the prepayment privilege to encourage potential borrowers to borrow from them instead of their competitors.

Prepayment Risk The risk that a borrower will repay a loan before its maturity, depriving the lender of future interest payments. Prepayment risk is most important for callable bonds, in which the issuer may repay the principal and cease paying coupons after a certain date, and mortgage-backed securities, in which the mortgage holder may refinance his/her mortgage, which will result in the security holder losing future interest. Some callable bonds and mortgage-backed securities have structures embedded within them to reduce prepayment risk. See also: Collateralized mortgage obligation, Yield-to-worst, Yield-to-maturity.

Prepayment Speed In mortgage-backed securities, the estimated rate at which mortgage borrowers will pay off the mortgages that underlie an MBS. The equivalent of the coupon on a mortgage-backed security is a percentage of the interest and principal paid on the mortgages backing the security. A riskassociated with mortgage-backed securities is that too many homeowners will pay off their mortgages with too much prepayment speed, depriving the holders of the MBS from future coupon payments.

Prepetition Liability A liability that a company incurs before filing for bankruptcy protection. Most prepetition liabilities are reduced or discharged in bankruptcy proceedings; the person or company to whom a prepetition liability is due should not expect to receive the full value of the liability unless it is secured by some asset. A prepetition liability contrasts with a postpetition liability, which usually must be paid in full.

Prequalification The act or process of determining the approximate amount a borrower will be able to borrow before he/she actually applies for a loan. Prequalification looks at the borrower's current income and debt to make this determination. Prequalification is most common with mortgages. Because the borrower has not applied for the loan, it is not a guarantee of approval, but is rather an estimation. See also: Pre-approval.

Prerefunding The act or practice of a company issuing a second bond with a lower coupon rate in order to pay off a previously issued callable bond. In this circumstance, the callable bond is referred to as a prerefunded bond. Companies engage in prerefunding when more favorable interest rates become available, reducing the company's overall borrowing costs.

Presale Order An order by an investor to buy a municipal bond before it is issued and even before all terms, such as the coupon or the maturity, have been set. The SEC disallows presale orders for other securities and, as a result, they are only available for municipal bonds because they are not subject to SEC registration requirements.

Present Value The worth of a future amount of money at specific point in time. If one expects an investment to result in a cash flow at a certain time in the future, calculating the cash flow's present value will help the investor decide whether the investment results in a real profit. Calculating the present value assumes that the investor knows both the future amount and the applicable interest rate or rate of return. One discounts the interest rate or rate of return from the future amount in order to arrive at the present value. Mathematically, this is expressed as: $Ct = C(1 + i)$-t where C is money, t is a number of years, and i is the interest rate or rate of return. Present value of money is important in calculating bond yields, the value of annuities, and many other transactions. It is also used in comparing the value of two amounts of money existing in different times. See also: Adjusted for inflation.

Present Value Factor An estimate of the present value of future cash flow for a project.

Present Value Index The ratio of the net present value of an investment to its total expense. A ratio of more than 1 indicates a profitable investment, while a ratio of less than 1 indicates one that will likely result in a loss. A present value index is used most often when one is making an investment decision and only has a finite amount of risk capital.

Presentation Department In investment banking, a slang term for employees who specialize in creating graphics or other polishing touches that make a presentation stand out. These employees may or may not be involved in the creation of the presentation's content, but they are expected to make it look creative and attractive.

Presenteeism A slang term for the practice of working an incredibly high number of hours. For example, an employee who never works less than 80 and frequently as many as 100 hours per week practices presenteeism. The term is a play on the word "absenteeism."

Presenteeist A slang term for an employee who works an incredibly high number of hours. For example, an employee who never works less than 80 and frequently as many as 100 hours per week is a presenteeist.

Presenting Bank A bank that gives a demand for payment to another bank. For example, the presenting bank may submit a check to another bank and receive payment. The presenting bank does this if the financial instrument is drawn on another bank.

Presentment 1. See: Deposit. **2.** See: Bill presentment. **3.** The act in which a bank submits a financial instrument to another bank and demands payment on the instrument.

Preservation of Capital A conservative investment strategy that attempts merely to avoid the loss of value. Retirees often prefer this strategy for their savings because the rate of return is designed only to keep up with inflation, ensuring that the value of their savings does not decrease over time. This often works in the short-term for pensioners, but using capital preservation as a long-term strategy often adds exposure to inflation risk rather than reduces it. Capital preservation strategists usually invest in fixed-income securities and other low-risk investments.

Pre-Settlement Risk The risk that a trade will not settle. For example, a buyer may not receive delivery of the securities he/she bought by the settlement date. A failure to deliver can occur because of the negligence or deliberate withholding on the part of the seller. If a buyer does not receive the securities, he/she is not obligated to make payment until delivery is made, but it renders him/her unable to resell or conduct other activities that would advance his/her investment goals.

Pre-Shipment Finance A short-term loan or other financing arrangement that an institution extends to a company to pay for inventory or other costs while it prepares its products for export.

President In a publicly-traded company, the second-highest ranking officer in the company. In smaller companies, the office of president may be combined with the chief executive officer (the highest officer). The president may or may not also be a member of the board of directors.

Presidential Election Cycle A theory of market performance stating that markets are weakest in the year following a presidential election, regardless of whether a new president or party take power. This theory held up well until the late 20th century, when the presidents' first years saw strong performance. For example, the first year of George H.W. Bush's presidency had strong market performance, but his administration ended with a recession.

Pre-Sold Issue An issue of a security, especially a bond, that is completely placed with investors before it is actually issued and before all relevant details, notably the price, are announced. Before a new issue, underwriters canvass potential investors, who may or may not book an order to buy a portion the new issue. Pre-sold issues occur almost exclusively with municipal and other government bonds, mainly because most other issues must register all their details with the SEC before they are allowed to place them. See also: Subscribed.

Press Release A statement given to the press regarding news in a company or other organization. A company may announce a merger, an expansion, a bankruptcy, or any other major event. Press releases are designed to put the announcement in the best possible light for the company or organization; therefore, it is important to check the accuracy of any information contained therein.

Pre-Syndicate Bid An order by a managing underwriter to buy or sell a security immediately before a secondary offering of the same security. The managing underwriter makes a pre-syndicate bid in order to stabilize the price of the security, which will make the secondary offering easier to place with investors. Pre-syndicate bids are only permissible under certain, defined circumstances set forth in SEC Rule 10b-7.

Pret An obsolete Polish unit of area approximately equivalent to 0.01995 hectares.

Pre-Tax Contribution A contribution made to a retirement plan with taxable withdrawals. That is, when one makes pre-tax contributions to a retirement plan, one does not pay taxes on the contributions in the year they are made, but defers taxation until one begins to make withdrawals from the plan. One makes pre-tax contributions to traditional IRAs and most 401(k)s. See also: After-Tax Contributions.

Pretax Earnings or Profits A company's total revenue less its operating expenses, interest paid, and depreciation, but not taxes. For example, a widget manufacturer earns $1,000,000 in total revenue. The widgets cost $200,000 to make and his administrative and payroll expenses total $250,000. He also must subtract $50,000 in depreciation on his widget manufacturing equipment. His net income is stated as: $1,000,000 - $200,000 - $250,000 - $50,000 = $500,000. It is important to note, however, that this number does not include any taxes that the widget manufacturer must pay that year; this fact is what differentiates pretax earnings or profits from net income.

Pretax Income An individual's total income before he/she pays any income tax or other tax, but after he/she takes deductions. For example, suppose one's salary is $50,000. If the person takes $10,000 in tax deductions, his/her pretax income is only $40,000.

Pretax Rate of Return The rate of return on an investment before capital gains or other taxes. Most of the time, when one sees a calculation of the rate of return it is the pretax rate of return. For a tax-free investment, the pretax and post-tax rates of return are identical.

Pretax Writedown In accounting, the reduction in value of an asset before one accounts of taxes owed. Pretax writedowns may reduce one's tax liability. See also: Depreciation.

Pretax Yield A return rate on an investment before accounting for either income taxes or capital gains taxes. The pretax yield is not as useful for determining yield as the after tax yield, particularly given the fact that some investments are tax-exempt.

Pretendgineer A slang term for a person who works in a technical or professional field, such as engineering or accounting, but who has aspirations for working in the arts. For example, a person who is working as a tax preparer until she finishes her novel may be called a pretendgineer. The term is slightly derogatory, implying that the pretendgineer will never reach his/her goals.

Pre-Trade Benchmark The price for a security before a trade occurs. A large trade or a large trading volume may raise or lower this price.

Prevention of Unfair Competition Act Legislation in Japan intended to protect intellectual property as defined by the Paris Convention. It was originally passed in 1934, but has been amended several times since then.

Previous Balance Method An accounting method in which interest owed on a good or service is calculated based on what is owed at the end of the month. Most credit cards calculate cost and interest on top of the balance at the end of the previous month. Payments on instruments that use the previous balance method are due at the beginning of the month.

PRI GOST 7.67 Latin three-letter geocode for Puerto Rico. The code is used for transactions to and from Puerto Rican bank accounts and for international shipping to Puerto Rico. As with all GOST 7.67 codes, it is used primarily in Cyrillic alphabets.

Price The value of a thing with real or perceived worth. Price represents the amount of value the market has assigned, fairly or unfairly, to a good or service. Normally, prices are expressed in terms of money, but practices such as countertrade and PIK securities indicate that prices may be expressed in goods: "four chickens for two sheep." Price is a necessary component of trade. Prices tend to be regulated by the law of supply and demand; that is, a price of a good or service increases with smaller supply and/or greater demand. A corollary to this is the idea that commoditization drives prices down because it increases supply (sometimes vastly) while leaving demand the same. Prices likewise rise when the value of money declines. Governments can and have controlled the prices of certain goods and services by subsidy or decree. This is usually an anti-inflationary measure and tends to distort, rather than eliminate, the law of supply and demand. It is thus not generally sustainable as a mechanism for controlling price.

Price Basing The practice of using futures contracts on a commodity to influence the price of a similar product intended for sale to consumers. For example, gasoline retailers may use the price of futures contracts on crude oil to help determine the appropriate price of their gasoline.

Price Ceiling The highest price for a good or service permitted by a government. A government may impose a price ceiling to protect consumers or to combat inflation. Many economists believe setting price ceilings is economically inefficient and a better response is to find a way to increase the supply of a good or service in order to bring down prices.

Price Change The difference between the closing price on a trading day and the closing price on the previous trading day. The price change may be positive or negative. For example, if a stock closes at $11 on Tuesday and $12 on Wednesday, it has a price change of +$1. On the other hand, if the stock falls to $10 on Thursday, it has a price change of -$2 with respect to Wednesday. Price change is also called net change. See also: Technical Analysis.

Price Compression The downward pressure on a callable bond's price appreciation during a period of declining interest rates. Declining interest rates normally raise a bond's price because interest rates are usually fixed at issue; buying such a bond will entitle the buyer to a higher interest rate than he/she would otherwise be able to receive when rates are declining. Callable bonds also rise in price, but price compression means that they do not rise as much because of the risk that the issuer will call the bond and simply repay the principal, depriving the bondholder of future interest.

Price Control A government regulation limiting the percentage (or, rarely, dollar amount) by which a price for a good or service can change over a given period of time. Price controls have been used to combat inflation, though they are rarely successful. Price controls may also be utilized to protect a favored industry, and are used most commonly to provide a minimum price for agricultural products. See also: Wage control, Price ceiling, Price floor.

Price Control Act of 1953 Legislation in Norway giving the government power to preempt mergers and acquisitions that are determined to give a company too much control over an industry or sector. It is a type of anti-trust legislation.

Price Discovery The process by which buyers and sellers interact to determine the fair market price of an asset. See also: Law of supply and demand.

Price Effect The results of a change in prevailing interest rates on bond prices. Generally speaking, when interest rates increase, bond prices go down. When they decrease, bond prices go up.

Price Fixing A practice whereby all competitors in an industry agree to charge the same price for their competing products. Price fixing deprives consumers of the fair market price for the products because the fixers can simply raise and lower prices at will. Most economists (with objectivists being a major exception) believe price fixing to be anti-competitive, thus they oppose it. In the United States, price fixing is illegal under the Sherman Anti-Trust Act. See also: Monopoly, Duopoly.

Price Floor The lowest price for a good or service permitted by a government. A government may impose a price floor to protect a favored industry and/or to keep employees working at a reasonable wage. Price floors are particularly common in agriculture. Many economists believe setting price floors is economically inefficient

and limits demand in the market, causing an oversupply of the controlled good or service.

Price Gap In technical analysis, a break on a chart representing a sudden and large price movement accompanied by high trading volume. Generally speaking, charts do not show price gaps because price movements, even when large, occur smoothly enough to not require a break in the chart. Price gaps may occur, for example, when the price of a security suddenly doubles or halves. As with many charting terms, it may be bullish or bearish; a sudden movement upward is a bullish price gap, while a sudden movement downward is bearish. It is also called a breakaway gap.

Price Give The willingness of a potential buyer or seller to negotiate a price for a security. A price give requires a nominal quote, which can be negotiated, instead of a firm quote, which cannot.

Price Immunization A strategy of matching assets to future liabilities. That is, price immunization involves investing in certain securities with a certain expected return so that the investor will be able to pay for future liabilities. Pension funds and annuities use price immunization more than many investors because they have future liabilities that are both large and relatively easy to estimate. Portfolios that practice price immunization usually invest in low-risk, investment-grade securities. See also: Portfolio dedication.

Price Improvement A situation in which a buyer pays less than the previous ask price for a security or in which a seller is paid more than the previous bid price. Price improvement usually occurs when a good broker is able to find a better price than the market price currently quoted.

Price Leader A company that sets a price for a product and whose market share and/or brand loyalty is so strong that other companies are compelled to match or beat the price. The company that first changes the price is said to show price leadership.

Price Leadership A situation in which a company sets a price for a product and this company's market share and/or brand loyalty is so strong that other companies are compelled to match or beat the price. The company that first changes the price is said to show price leadership.

Price Limit 1. See: Daily trading limit. **2.** See: Limit price.

Price Maker A monopoly or a similar company that is able to heavily influence the prices charged for its products because no other companies have the same product or a similar product of the same quality. A price maker is essentially able to charge whatever it wants so long as it does not run afoul of antitrust laws.

Price Momentum The performance of a stock relative to its industry or the performance of an industry relative to the market as a whole. A stock (or industry) that outperforms its industry (or market) for a given period of time is seen as a bullish sign for that stock (or industry). The concept is also called relative strength.

Price Movement A change in the price of a security or other asset, especially in the short term. For example, whether a stock rises or falls on Monday, it undergoes price movements throughout the trading day.

Price of Admission In equities, the cost to a trader of becoming involved in an unusually aggressive market. When a market becomes very aggressive, the prices of stocks go up, which in turn makes it more expensive for a trader to become involved in the market by buying stocks. As the market becomes more aggressive, some traders are unwilling to pay the price of admission. On the other hand, others do pay it and become aggressive traders themselves.

Price per Share What a willing buyer will pay a willing seller for one share of a security. Most stocks are quoted per share even though most shares are purchased and sold in multiples of 100 shares.

Price Range The high and low prices between which a security trades over a given period of time. The size of the price range is an indicator of volatility, with a large price range showing a great deal of volatility and a low range showing the opposite. A price range is also called simply a range.

Price Risk The risk of loss that occurs if the value of a security or portfolio falls below the price one paid to buy it.

Price Sensitive The state in which a security's or product's price changes dramatically in the face of increased or decreased demand. Price sensitivity generally refers to securities with comparatively few shares outstanding; a large order to buy or sell is likely to affect the price more strongly than a similar order for a company with more shares outstanding. In other products, price sensitivity largely comes from whether a given product is considered a necessity or a luxury. A "luxury" product is likely to be more sensitive.

Price Sensitive Market A market in which a security's or product's price changes dramatically in the face of increased or decreased demand. Price sensitive markets generally contain securities with comparatively few shares outstanding; a large order to buy or sell is likely to affect the price more strongly than a similar order for a company with more shares outstanding. In other products, price sensitivity is largely based on whether a given product is considered a necessity or a luxury. A "luxury" product is likely to be more sensitive.

Price Skimming The practice of a company offering a new product and charging a high price at first, but gradually reducing it before competitors begin to sell similar products. For example, a company may offer a new product at $40 per unit, then in six months reduce the price to $35, to $30 in another six months, and so forth. Price skimming allows the company to recover its sunk costs (such as research and development) while still remaining competitive when other companies begin to offer substantially the same product. It is also called a high price strategy.

Price Stability The state in which a security or product's price changes fairly little in the face of increased or decreased demand. Price stability generally refers to securities with comparatively large number of shares outstanding; a large order to buy or sell is likely to affect the price less strongly than a similar order for a company with fewer shares outstanding. In other products, price stability is largely based on whether a given product is considered a necessity or a luxury. A "necessary" product is likely to be more stable.

Price Stabilization The ultimate goal of the steps a central bank takes to reduce inflation. That is, when prices are rising rapidly, the central bank may reduce the amount of money in circulation and/or raise interest rates to bring down the rate at which prices are rising. Price stabilization does not bring prices down to their former levels, but it does reduce the rate at which they rise to a more sustainable level. While this is popular in theory, it is important to note that Federal Reserve chairman Paul Volcker caused a recession in the early 1980s when he raised interest rates to 18% to achieve price stabilization.

Price Support A government subsidy that keeps the price for a good or service higher than it otherwise would be. For example, the government may set a price support for milk by mandating that suppliers may not accept anything less than the stated price. Price supports exist to protect the livelihoods of suppliers who cannot afford a price war or anything approaching one;many economists oppose price supports because they claim they interfere with competition and the free market.

Price Taker An investor who makes orders that are not large enough to affect the price. That is, when price takers make orders, they must accept the price offered by another investor. A price taker may be an individual or a (small) company. A price taker contrasts with a price maker, which makes orders of sufficient quantity to affect the market price.

Price Talk The range of prices rumored or estimated for a new issue. For example, the price talk may indicate that a new issue will trade at $10-11 per share when it is placed with investors.

Price Target 1. An estimate for the future price of a security. For example, an investment adviser may inform a brokerage or a client that, after careful analysis, he/she believes that a given security's price will rise or fall to a certain level in a certain period of time. This speculative price is called the price target. A price target far in the future has more uncertainty that one in the short-term. **2.** A security's price that will result in the desired return for an investor. For example, if an investor buys a stock at $10 per share and wishes to double her money, her price target is $20 per share.

Price Transparency The ability to retrieve and access all information regarding a stock or other security's price. This includes the security's historic price and all current bids and asks. Exchanges have different levels of price transparency; for example, the NYSE only provides information on the highest bid and the lowest ask. In general, more transparency is seen as positive and more efficient.

Price Trend The direction and momentum of the price of a security or other asset. For example, if the price of a security is going mainly downward with only a few inconsistent gains, it is said to be on a downward price trend. Identifying and predicting trends is important to finding the right moment to buy and sell securities. Trends are especially important in technical analysis, which recommends buying at the bottom of a downward trend and selling at the top of an upward trend.

Price Uncertainty The chance or speculation that the price of an asset will change. This affects prices for stocks, commodities, and even bonds, whether directly or indirectly. Most of the time, price uncertainty refers to the possibility that a specific commodity is unstable. For example, a rice famine might produce uncertainty in the price of rice. However, it can also refer to uncertainty as to the real value of securities and their derivatives. According to Alan Greenspan, long-term, widespread price uncertainty is inimical to stable economic growth. See also: Price stability.

Price Value of a Basis Point The amount the price of a bond changes when the required yield changes by one basis point. Various factors influence the amount of the price value of a basis point, including the time until maturity and the coupon rate. However, in general, there is an inverse relationship between the price and the required yield.

Price/Earnings to Growth and Dividend Yield A ratio of a stock's valuation, that is, how expensive a stock is relative to its earnings and expected growth and the dividend yield. It is calculated as: PEGY = Price/Earnings/(Projected Annual Earnings Growth per Share + Dividend Yield) A lower ratio indicates a less expensive stock with higher earnings growth and dividends, while a higher ratio indicates the opposite. A PEGY may not be entirely accurate, as it is based on expected rather than actual growth. See also: PEG ratio.

Price/Earnings-to-Growth Ratio A ratio of a stock's valuation, that is, how expensive a stock is relative to its earnings and expected growth. It is calculated as: PEG = Price/Earnings/Annual Earnings Growth per Share A lower ratio indicates a less expensive stock with higher earnings and growth, while a higher ratio indicates the opposite. According to Peter Lynch, who popularized the ratio, a fairly priced stock has a ratio of 1.

Price/Growth Flow A measure of a company's earnings and the amount it spends on research and development. A high ratio indicates that the company has high earnings and/or spends significantly on its R&D, while a low ratio indicates the opposite. It is important to note that while the ratio measure the amount spend on R&D, it does not measure how successful or efficient the R&D spending is. The price/growth flow is calculated as follows: Price-growth flow = (earnings per share + R&D per share) / price per share.

Price-Anderson Act Legislation in the United States seeking to incentivize nuclear power by limiting the liability of nuclear plants in the event of an accident. Under the Act, the nuclear power industry is responsible for the first $10 billion of damages resulting from a spill or other accident, while the federal government is responsible for any losses exceeding that amount. It was passed in 1957 and has been renewed several times since.

Price-Based Option An option contract giving the holder the right but not the obligation to buy (for a call) or sell (for a put) a debt security at a certain strike price. One chooses whether to exercise a price-based option based on the direction of the yield curve relative to the yield of the underlying debt security. Price-based options are relatively uncommon investments, having been largely supplanted by yield-based options, which are structured in a similar way.

Priced Out In securities, describing a situation in which the market has already incorporated expected information into the price of a stock. That is, if a company's earnings are large for a particular quarter, it may leak the information so that the stock is priced out. That way, when the information is actually announced, it will not cause a sudden jump in price, which might suggest volatility. For this reason, the Federal Reserve issues statements indicating what policy changes it might make before it makes them, allowing the markets to price out the information. See also: Efficient markets theory.

Price-Earnings Growth Ratio A ratio of a stock's price to its increase in earnings over a given period of time. This is used in place of the price-earnings ratio in situations where the company has poor earnings that are gradually increasing. That is, PREG is most useful when the raw data on earnings may not show the company's fundamental strength or potential profitability. It is used often for dot-coms and other companies that may have poor earnings in their first few years of operation.

Price-Earnings Ratio The price of a security per share at a given time divided by its annual earnings per share. Often, the earnings used are trailing 12 month earnings, but some analysts use other forms. The P/E ratio is a way to help determine a security's stock valuation, that is, the fair value of a stock in a perfect market. It is also a measure of expected, but not realized, growth. Companies expected to announce higher earnings usually have a higher P/E ratio, while companies expected to announce lower earnings usually have a lower P/E ratio. See also: PEG

Price-Earnings Relative A comparison of an individual stock's price-earnings ratio compared to the price-earnings ratio of an index. One calculates the price-earnings relative by dividing the stock's P/E ratio by that of the index. The price-earnings relative is a tool used to estimate a stock's value compared to the value of the market as a whole; in general, a high price-earnings relative is better for the stock and its shareholders.

Price-Fixing Contract A contract between competitors in an industry in which the parties agree to charge the same price for their competing products. Price fixing contracts deprive consumers of the fair market price for the products because the fixers can simply raise and lower prices at will. Most economists (with objectivists being a major exception) believe price fixing to be anti-competitive, and thus oppose it. Price fixing is very often illegal.

Prices of Equity The amount of money for which one may buy or sell a share of common stock. The price of equity changes throughout a trading day, especially in times of high trading volume.

Price-Specie Flow Mechanism An argument David Hume made against those who argued that a favorable balance of trade is always good public policy. The price-specie flow mechanism states that under a gold standard, countries with positive trade balances are effectively importing gold (money) in exchange for their exports while those with negative trade balances are exporting gold in exchange for imports. The increase in gold in countries with positive trade balances causes inflation, which makes prices rise and in turn makes imports more competitive. Conversely, the decrease in gold in countries with negative trade balances causes deflation, which makes price fall and exports more competitive internationally. This cause the balance of trade to shift in both countries. Thus, Hume argued that a trade balance is relatively unimportant because it tends to balance itself out in the long term.

Price-to-Book A ratio of the share price of a publicly-traded company to its book value per share, which is the company's total asset value less the value of its liabilities. The P/B is a ratio of investor sentiment on the value of a stock to its actual value according to the Generally Accepted Accounting Principles. A high P/B means either that investors have overvalued the company, or that its accountants have undervalued it.

Price-to-Cash Flow Ratio The ratio of a company's stock price to the quantity of its cash inflows, minus its cash outflows over a given time, usually a year. The price-to-cash flow is similar to a company's price-earnings ratio, but it does not take into account earnings that have not actually been received. Some analysts prefer the price-to-cash flow ratio because it allows them to assess risk relative to the company's cash on-hand, instead of the cash it ought to have.

Price-to-Research Ratio The ratio of a company's share price to the amount it spends on research and development. A low ratio is considered desirable because it indicates that the company is spending a great deal on R&D. This can (but does not always) mean that the products developed in R&D will be profitable.

Price-to-Sales Ratio A ratio of a company's share price to its revenue from sales over a given period of time, especially a quarter or a year. Fundamentalists and value investors see a low ratio as more positive because it indicates that the company has a great deal of revenue and a fair price, while technicians see a high ratio as more positive because it indicates that share price has increased and will likely continue to increase. In both cases, however, analysts believe the ratio reveals less than other ratios, such as the price-earnings, because price-to-sales does not account for operating expenses in any way.

Price-Volume Relationship In technical analysis, a theory stating that changes in a security's trading volume affect the security's price. For example, in a time of low volume, a large order to buy or sell the security can cause a drastic change in price.

Price-Weighted Index An index that tracks a number of securities in which price changes in stocks that already have higher prices affect the index's price changes more than other securities. For example, suppose an index tracks three stocks: A, B, and C. If A has a higher price than B and C, an uptick in A will be more likely to result in an uptick in the index as a whole (depending on how much more weighted it is). Price weighted indices are less common than capitalization-weighted indices, but the Dow Jones Industrial Average is a prominent example.

Pricing The process of an issuer determining the appropriate price of a new issue. That is, the issuer prices when it figures out what coupon rate to promise for a bond or price at which to issue a stock. This can be complex because pricing too far in one direction means the issue will not sell while too far in the other direction raises the cost of funds too high.

Priestly v. Fowler An 1837 court case in the United Kingdom holding that an employer is not responsible for on-the-job injuries to its employees if the employer has taken due care to ensure safety. The case came about after a wagon owned by Fowler collapsed and severely injured his servant, Priestly, while they were transporting Fowler's mutton to sell. The initial jury verdict held Fowler was responsible for injury and awarded Priestly 100 pounds. The case was overturned on appeal; it was held that an employer is not responsible to ensure higher safety standards for an employee than he ensures for himself. This precedent remained until 1948.

Prima Facie In law, describing facts that, unless successfully refuted, would be sufficient to prove a fact. In both criminal and civil trials, the side with the burden of proof must establish at least a prima facie case. If this side fails to do so, the case is dismissed and the other side does not need to present its evidence. See also: Res ipsa loquitur.

Primary Dealer A firm to and from which the New York Federal Reserve directly sells and buys Treasury securities. That is, primary dealers help the Federal Reserve control the money supply by underwriting Treasury securities and placing them with investors. Primary dealers tend to be well-respected and well-known financial institutions. Merrill Lynch and Citigroup are examples of primary dealers.

Primary Distribution The sale of a new issue on the primary market. That is, the seller in a primary distribution is the issuer. Most primary distributions are placed through underwriting. The primary distribution can at times be more volatile than trading the secondary market because it is difficult to determine the underlying value of new issues. In any case, the primary distribution accounts for only a portion of trade on a given trading day. See also: Rights Issue, Preferential Issue, Initial Public Offering.

Primary Election An election in which candidates compete against members of their own party to receive the nomination for a political office. The nominee then goes on to face candidates from other parties. The rules in primary elections vary by both party and jurisdiction. In some U.S. states, for example, one needs a plurality to win the primary; in others, a plurality win leads to a run-off election between the two top contenders.

Primary Market The first group of investors to whom a new issue of a security is sold. The primary market consists of the issuer and the first buyers of the issue. All subsequent trading takes place on the secondary market. Underwriting is the process by which the primary market functions, that is, how issues are sold to the primary buyers. The primary market can at times be more volatile than the secondary market because it is difficult to determine the underlying value of new issues. In any case, the primary market accounts for only a portion of trade on a given trading day. See also: Rights issue, Preferential issue, Initial public offering.

Primary Shares Shares traded in the primary market. That is, a primary share is a share traded when the seller is the issuer. Thus, the money the buyer pays for a primary share goes directly to the company the share represents.

Primary Trend An overarching, long-term trend for a security. Generally, a primary trend refers to a trend over a period of four years or so. A primary trend may be bullish or bearish, and, in market analysis, it takes precedence over opposite, short-term trends that occur periodically. For example, a security may climb 15% in annualized terms from 2000 through 2003; if the security dropped 3% in 2002, this does not change the primary, upward trend.

Prime 1. In commercial banking, the best available interest rate under most circumstances. Generally speaking, only the most creditworthy customers receive the prime, but this is not always true. In any case, a prime serves as a benchmark against which other interest rates are compared. In this sense, it is also called the prime rate. **2.** Describing the highest possible credit rating on a bond, either Aaa (for Moody's) or AAA (for S&P and Fitch).

Prime Bank One of the approximately 50 largest banks in the world. Prime banks are well known and trade in extremely large investments. However, the term has a negative connotation because of its association with a prime bank scheme, in which a con man attempts to persuade a person to invest in supposed investment vehicles through a prime bank that does not really exist.

Prime Bank Scam A scheme in which a con man attempts to persuade a person to invest in supposed investment vehicles through a prime bank (or one of the 50 largest banks in the world). These investment vehicles do not really exist; the con man promises lavish returns on these investments, but instead pockets the money. See also: Pyramid scheme.

Prime Broker A broker-dealer on an exchange who maintains records and provides brokering services, including leveraged transactions, for other broker-dealers, money managers, hedge funds, and other major investors that trade on the same exchange.

Prime Brokerage A brokerage that provides services exclusively to institutional investors, especially hedge funds. Prime brokerage services include clearance, lending of securities, lending of money for leveraged transactions, and technical and support services. Prime brokerage services allow institutional investors to effectively outsource these aspects of investment to another party, freeing it up to concentrate on its investment strategy.

Prime Paper Commercial paper with a very high credit rating. Commercial paper is unsecured, short-term corporate debt. Because prime paper has a high credit rating, banks are allowed to invest in it and it carries very little risk.

Prime Rate The best available interest rate under most circumstances. In general, only the most creditworthy customers receive the prime rate, but this is not always true. In any case, a prime rate serves as a benchmark against which other interest rates are compared.

Prime Rate Fund A mutual fund that invests predominantly or exclusively in corporate loans. That is, the prime rate fund buys corporate loans (which are distinct from bonds) from the banks making them and passes the interest to shareholders. The risk of a prime rate fund depends on the weighted average risk of the loans represented in it.

Primitive Security An investment vehicle for which dividends, coupons, or other payments depend on the financial health of the issuer. For example, an unsecured bond may be an example of a primitive security as coupons may only be paid if the issuer has the cash flow to pay them. Primitive securities have the potential to have higher risk than other securities, especially those coming from new or relatively unknown issuers.

Prince Edward Island Dollar The currency of Prince Edward Island between 1871 and 1873. It was equal in value to the Canadian dollar, which replaced it when Prince Edward Island joined the Canadian Confederation.

Prince Edward Island Pound The currency of Prince Edward Island prior to 1871. It was equal in value to the British pound, which circulated alongside it. It was replaced by the Prince Edward Island dollar.

Principal 1. A person or organization party to a transaction or event. **2.** The amount that one borrows. For example, if one borrows $100,000, the principal amount is $100,000. Interest is calculated over the principal (and often over unpaid interest that accumulates).

Principal Amount The amount of money one borrows. Unless the loan is interest-free, one always pays more than the principal amount to the lender. The interest is calculated over the principal amount still outstanding. As a result, many loans are amortized so that a greater amount of principal amount remains outstanding for a longer period of time so the lender can make the most profit from the loan. It is also simply called the principal.

Principal Exchange Rate Linked Security A debt security denominated in U.S. dollars. The principal to be repaid on the security is determined by a particular exchange rate that exists between the dollar and a given currency at a certain time. For example, a company wishing to expand its overseas operations may buy this security in order to finance the expansion in the foreign currency while still linking it to the U.S. dollar. Companies use principal exchange-rate-linked securities to hedge against foreign exchange risk.

Principal Market The primary exchange on which a security is traded. For example, most blue chip companies list their principal market as the New York Stock Exchange because it is a large exchange with a high trading volume. Nevertheless, these stocks can and do trade on other exchanges, as well as in the over-the-counter market.

Principal Only Describing a derivative in which the underlying assets are the future principal payments on a pool of mortgages or other debt obligations. Principal-only derivatives are issued at a deep discount to their par value; that is, one buys such derivatives for an amount less than the principal payments to which the holder is entitled. The gain on a principal-only derivative comes from the amount by which principal payments exceed the amount that the holder pays for the security. For that reason, holders of these derivatives can benefit from prepayment risk because when property owners repay their mortgages more quickly, principal-only derivative holders receive their returns more quickly.

Principal Order An order made by a brokerage on its own account, as opposed to a client's. Principal orders must be registered as such on the exchange where they are made to protect investors from abuse or possible insider trading. In a principal order, the broker acts as a dealer because it seeks to trade on its own account. See also: Principal Trade.

Principal Risk The risk that an investment will decline in value below the amount one invested. For example, if one buys a security for $10 per share, there is a principal risk that it will decline to $8 per share and never recover. Principal risk is virtually non-existent for bank accounts, which are guaranteed by the FDIC up to a certain amount. However, it is significant for investments like stocks and, to a lesser extent, bonds.

Principal Stockholder A person or company that owns more than 10% of the voting stock in a publicly-traded company. All principal stockholders must announce themselves to the SEC and abide by all rules governing the prevention of insider trading.

Principal, Interest, Taxes, and Insurance The components of a real estate owner's mortgage payment. When considering whether to loan money for a mortgage, a bank often considers what the PITI will be as a percentage of the potential borrower's gross monthly income. Generally speaking, mortgage banks prefer PITI to be 28% or less of the borrower's income.

Principal-Protected Note A security in which the original investment is put at no or very little risk. An example is a bond, in which the bondholder is guaranteed (short of default) to receive at least the amount he/she originally invested. The main risk to the bondholder is that the bond issuer will not pay coupons (or interest) on time. Principle-protected notes tend to have small, fixed returns. See also: Fixed-income security, principal.

Principal-Protection Fund A mutual fund that invests predominately or exclusively in securities with principal protection, meaning holders are guaranteed to receive back at least what they originally invested. This results in a low risk mutual fund. However, principal-protection funds often have relatively low returns and, if the fund invests in a disproportionate number of short-term securities, can lead to higher capital gains taxes.

Principle of Diversification A principle of investing stating that a portfolio containing many different assets and kinds of assets carries lower risk than a portfolio with only a few. The principle of diversification states that unsystemic risk may be alleviated through diversification, but systemic risk is more difficult to reduce. That is, the risk associated with a single investment or type of investment may be offset by the risk of another investment or type of investment. See also: Diversification.

Print 1. Informal; to execute an order by making a trade. **2.** Informal; a trade. In both cases, the term is most applicable when the trade appears on a ticker tape or is otherwise publicly recorded.

Print Advertising Weight 1. The number of pages in a periodical consisting of advertising divided by the number of total pages. This is also called simply advertising weight. **2.** The actual or projected number of contacts a print advertisement has. For example, if a newspaper has a circulation of 1 million per day, an ad in that paper has a print advertising weight of 1 million per day.

Printing Block A wooden block used to print ink onto paper. This was used in printing before the invention of the movable type.

Printing on the O 1. Slang; a situation in which demand to buy a security is so intense that the bid price rises above the ask price. This is a highly bullish signal. **2.** Slang; a situation in which demand to sell a security is so intense that the ask price drops below the bid price. This is a highly bearish signal.

Prior Income The average income a person earns each month over the course of a tax year. An insurer uses prior income to determine how much to pay a policyholder each month for a claim on loss of income insurance.

Prior Insurance The insurance that a policyholder had before switching policies. For example, if Joe switched health insurance companies in October, the prior insurance is the policy that was in effect before October.

Prior Lien A lien on an asset that has a stronger claim than other liens on the same asset. For example, the first mortgage on a house has a prior lien on the house, which takes precedent over the second and third mortgages. See also: Rule of Absolute Priority.

Prior Preferred Stock A preferred stock that has priority over other preferred stock. This occurs when a publicly-traded company has more than one class of preferred stock. Thus, while all preferred stock receives dividends before common stock, prior preferred stock receives dividends before other preferred stock. It is also called a preference stock.

Prior-Charge Debt A secured debt, especially in the form of a bond.

Priority In an auction market, a rule stating that the orders for a new issue must be executed in the order in which they are received. That is, as long as an offer or bid is made at the requested price, it must be executed before an offer or bid that is made after it, even if the second one is larger.

Priority Foreign Country A designation by the United States trade representative of a country that does not adequately protect intellectual property rights. A priority foreign country is the lowest designation that the trade representative can make.

Priority List A list of projects for which a department has not received funding, categorized according to which project is to receive funding next.

Priority of Lien 1. See: Absolute priority. **2.** See: Priority of tax lien.

Priority of Tax Lien The legal requirement that, in the event of liquidation of a person's or company's assets, all unpaid taxes must be paid before any other creditors receive any payment at all. See also: Absolute Priority Rule.

Prior-Lien Bond A bond with precedence over other secured and unsecured bonds from the same issuer. Coupon payments are owed on these bonds before other bonds; in other words, prior-lien bonds will default after other bonds from the same issuer. These bonds are usually the result of a company reorganization,

Prisoner's Dilemma A classic problem in game theory. In the problem, two suspects are arrested and questioned separately by police. If one accuses the other while the other remains silent, the accuser will go free and the silent party will go to jail for 10 years. If each accuses the other, both go to prison for five years. If both remain silent, they only go to jail for one year. According to the dilemma, the rational response for each of the prisoners is to accuse the other (maximizing the possibility each will go free), even though this produces an irrational result (that both go to jail for five years). The prisoner's dilemma is used to explain a variety of economic and political phenomena when all parties involved are self-interested, rational and have imperfect information. For example, two companies may compete for a promising employee. They offer increasingly attractive salaries. If one company gives up, the other company will take the employee. So both quite rationally increase the offers. This however could produce the irrational result that a new employee is paid too highly. The prisoner's dilemma seeks to explain why rational actions sometimes lead to irrational conclusions.

Private Accountant An accountant employed by a company and charged with managing the company's own finances. That is, a private accountant does not handle the finances of a client or any other company. A private accountant is the accounting equivalent of an internal auditor. See also: Comptroller.

Private Activity Bond A tax-exempt municipal bond in which a local government entity is seeking to raise money for a private company. A municipality issues a private activity bond when it wishes to attract a business and the jobs it brings to the area, especially when the business may be otherwise unable to obtain financing for the project. The municipality issuing the bond must be able to prove that a public benefit derives from the private activity bond in order to qualify for tax-exempt status. Private activity bonds generally are not guaranteed by the revenue of the municipality.

Private Bank 1. A bank structured as a sole proprietorship or a partnership. That is, a private bank is any bank that is not a corporation. The proprietor or general partner of a private bank is personally liable for the bank's losses. Private banks are rare. **2.** See: Private Banking.

Private Banker 1. A person who works for a private bank, which is any bank structured as a sole proprietorship or a partnership. If a private banker is also the sole proprietor or general partner, he/she is personally liable for the bank's losses. **2.** An investment banker who offers services to high net worth individuals. See also: Private Banking.

Private Banking Banking services offered to high net-worth individuals. Private banking services are largely related to asset management; that is, a private banking institution assists the high net-worth individual in investing his/her money in exchange for commissions and fees. Private banking combines some of the services of a brokerage with normal banking services. Importantly, high net-worth individuals have some investment vehicles open to them that are prohibitively expensive for other investors, notably hedge funds. Some private banks allow clients who invest $50,000 or more, but others require a minimum investment of $500,000.

Private Branding The practice in which a manufacturer sells large quantities of its inventory to a retailer, who then puts its own brand name on the inventory for resale. Private branding guarantees the manufacturer a certain level of sales. It also increases the retailer's profit margins because it generally may purchase from the manufacturer at a lower price.

Private Equity 1. Ownership in a corporation that is not publicly-traded. That is, private equity involves investing in privately held companies. Most of the time, private equity investors are institutional investors and high net-worth individuals who have a large amount of capital to commit to these investments. Private equity is usually held for a long period of time, and trading in it is useful when a company is in danger of bankruptcy, because it provides access to a great deal of capital very quickly. **2.** A company that trades in private equity. Often, private equity firms band together and buy out publicly-traded companies, making them privately held.

Private Export Funding Corporation An American company that seeks to facilitate American exports by purchasing the debt obligations of importers of American goods. PEFCO concentrates on supporting the export of expensive goods.

Private Investment Fund An investment company with fewer than 100 investors, no intention of making a public offering, and members who have a significant amount of funds invested elsewhere. Under section 3C1 of the Investment Company Act of 1940, private investment funds are not required to register with the SEC. These companies usually have very wealthy individual investors who are thought to be sufficiently knowledgeable about the market so as not to require the same oversight other investors and companies need. A hedge fund is a common example of a private investment fund. It is also called a private investment company.

Private Investment in Public Equity The form of equity financing in which a private investment company purchases a certain amount of stock in a publicly-traded company at a discount from its market value. Publicly-traded companies commit to PIPE in order to raise equity without going through expense and regulatory issues involved in making a secondary offering. This form of financing is popular especially with small and medium-sized publicly-traded companies, as they often lack the resources to raise capital using other methods. There are two types of PIPE. A traditional PIPE allows the private investment company to simply buy stock in the publicly-traded company. This is a direct form of equity financing. A structured PIPE, however, involves the publicly-traded company issuing a certain amount of convertible debt. This carries less risk for the private investment company and does not dilute the publicly-traded company's shares outstanding, at least not immediately. See also: Venture capital.

Private Law Legislation having to do with relations between individuals without government intervention. Examples of private law include statutes and customs governing torts and contracts. Private law contrasts with public law, which has to do with relationships between individuals and their government.

Private Limited Partnership A limited partnership with no more than 35 general partners and limited partners. Investments in a private limited partnership is considered to be sufficiently illiquid that the venture is not required to register with the SEC. See also: Publicly-Traded Partnership.

Private Mortgage Insurance An insurance policy that a mortgage holder buys on behalf of a lender, protecting the lender in the event of default on the mortgage. Most lenders require their mortgage borrowers to purchase PMIs if the mortgage's loan-to-value ratio is more than 80%. Generally speaking, annual premium payments on PMIs are equal to 0.5% of the value of the mortgage at the time it is borrowed. When the loan-to-value ratio falls below 78%, most lenders are required to inform homeowners that they may cancel their PMI policies. Some borrowers avoid PMI by taking out a piggyback mortgage, that is, a second mortgage allowing one to borrow up to 100% of the home's value in which the loan-to-value ratio is approximately 80% in the first mortgage and 20% in the piggyback.

Private Placement The sale of a new issue to a few large institutional investors without registering with the SEC. A private placement is exempt from SEC registration, subject to certain restrictions, because it is not offered to the general public. In order to make a private placement, the issuer must file a private placement memorandum (PPM), which explains exactly why the issue complies with SEC Regulation D exempting certain companies from registration; this is done to protect both the issuer and the investors. According to Regulation D, a PPM must contain a complete description of the security and the terms of the sale. It must also include applicable information about the issuer's financial situation and applicable risk factors. Private placement is also called direct placement.

Private Placement Memorandum A document explaining a new offering of securities for private placement. Private placement involves selling securities without registering with the SEC. A private placement memorandum must then explain exactly why the offering complies with SEC Regulation D exempting certain companies from registration; this is done to protect both the issuer and the investors. According to Regulation D, a PPM must contain a complete description of the security and the terms of the sales. It must also include applicable information about the issuer's financial situation and applicable risk factors. Because securities for general issue must be registered under Regulation D, a PPM is not allowed to contain a general offer for investment.

Private Unrequited Transfer A remittance that an immigrant makes to his family or friends in the home country. For example, if a Jordanian immigrates to the United States, he may choose to make private unrequited transfer to his mother back home to help her financially. In some countries, private unrequited transfers from abroad form a significant part of the economy.

Private Voluntary Organization Also called a PVO. A charity or other organization that provides international assistance and is eligible for financial support from USAID. Organizations must register as PVOs to apply for this support, and ordinarily must provide audited financial statements and the like.

Private-Label Pass-Through A mortgage-backed or other pass-through security that is not guaranteed by a U.S. Government agency such as Freddie Mac or Ginnie Mae. Until the early 2000s, such securities needed a third-party guarantee or other credit enhancement in order to receive a triple-AAA credit rating. At the beginning of the 2000s, more private-label pass-throughs, especially subprime mortgage-backed securities, began to be issued. Many of these defaulted starting in early 2007, causing a global liquidity crisis. It is also called a conventional pass-through. See also: Credit crunch.

Privately Held Company A company in which a small group of shareholders control all of the shares. These shareholders tend to hold onto the company's stock and, in any case, no shares are publicly traded. Privately held companies are, by their nature, impervious to hostile takeovers and proxy wars. They tend to be more stable than other companies because their share prices are not determined by (sometimes irrational) investment decisions, but by the value of the company itself. However, privately held companies do not have access to as much working capital as corporations with more shareholders have. See also: Closely Held.

Privileged Subscription A new issue of stock in which current shareholders are permitted to buy an amount equal to their percentage of ownership in the company at a price below the new issue's value. For example, a shareholder who owns 1% of the company is eligible to buy 1% of the new issue at a special price available only to current shareholders. Privileged subscriptions exist so current shareholders do not find their holdings suddenly diluted without their consent. See also: Anti-dilution provision.

PRK GOST 7.67 Latin three-letter geocode for North Korea. The code is used for transactions to and from North Korean bank accounts and for international shipping to North Korea. As with all GOST 7.67 codes, it is used primarily in Cyrillic alphabets.

Pro Bono Describing work done for no pay. Pro bono work is done as a favor for a friend, but the term especially applies to work done for a client who lacks the ability to pay. Lawyers in the United States, for example, are required to do a certain amount of pro bono work to guarantee that everyone has access to the court system.

Pro Forma Capital Structure Analysis An analysis of the current or potential effects a company's capital structure may have on its credit rating, tax benefits, and profitability.

Pro Forma Earnings A company's earnings that are not calculated according to the Generally Accepted Accounting Principles. For example, a company may exclude non-cash expenses that the GAAP would ordinarily include. Companies often publish pro forma earnings to highlight positive aspects of their earnings. While this may indeed show positive earnings for a company that the GAAP can miss, pro forma earnings can also be manipulated more easily to make a company appear healthier than it is.

Pro Forma Financial Statement A financial statement that a company prepares to consider the effects of a potential activity. For example, if a company is considering acquiring another, it may prepare a pro forma financial statement to estimate what effect the acquisition would have on its own financial circumstances. A pro forma financial statement can be part of the risk analysis of a situation. See also: Due diligence.

Pro Rata Describing a distribution according to some proportion. For example, a salary may be stated as $120,000 per year pro rata. This means that if an employee only works for six months, his/her salary will be $60,000. Likewise, dividends are distributed pro rata, meaning that shareholders receive them according to the proportion of shares that they own.

Probability Distribution All the possible values a random variable can take under a given set of circumstances, as well as the probability that it will take each value. A normal probability is a bell curve.

Probability Function In statistics, a measure of the probable distribution of some random variable. When plotted on a chart, the area under the graph represents the probable values of the random variable. It is used in foreign exchange and equities as a means of assessing probable future market trends.

Probate The process by which a will is authenticated and carried out. That is, probate ensures that the will is in fact the decedent's final wishes and that everyone is receiving what they ought to receive. The executor of the estate usually handles probate, but his/her actions can be challenged in probate court. Some property, notably property co-owned with a spouse, is exempt from probate.

Probate Estate The total value of a decedent's assets. Probate estate includes the decedent's own property, but not the assets placed in trust, payable-on-death accounts, or other assets over which the decedent had control, but did not directly belong to him/her. The probate estate is discharged through the decedent's will. It should not be confused with gross estate, which is used in determining the estate tax one owes.

Probation 1. An initial period of employment during which an employee is evaluated. Typically, it is easier to dismiss a new employee during probation. At the conclusion of the probation, the employer decides whether or not to keep the employee on staff. A new employee may not be eligible for some benefits during probation. **2.** A period during which an employee has been warned that his/her performance may result in termination if it does not improve.

Probinsya In the Philippines, a political subdivision equivalent to a province.

Problem Child In growth share matrices, the quadrant representing companies, especially subsidies, that require large cash injections but have low market shares, and therefore usually operate at a loss or with little profit. These companies are normally growing rapidly (hence the need for cash) but represent new markets, products, or brands. Problem children represent an initial stage in growth share matrices; they have the potential to become stars or cash cows, but also to become dogs, depending on how the relevant markets grow. Analysts carefully evaluate problem children to determine whether or not they should be divested. A problem child is also called a question mark. See also: Marketing, Portfolio analysis.

Proceeds The money one receives from a transaction, usually before all commissions, fees, and related expenses. For example, if one sells his/her house, the proceeds are the funds one receives from the buyer. In many ways, proceeds are identical to revenue, but they often refer to a single sale or transaction rather than all of the money one receives over a period of time.

Proceeds Sale The sale of a security where the revenue from the sale is used immediately to buy another security. FINRA considers both the sale and the purchase to be a single transaction and one may not charge more than a 5% markup in a proceeds sale.

Processing Delay The time between the receipt of an order or payment and the appropriate response. Processing delay may involve the time between receiving a payment and depositing it in the bank or between a customer requesting a product and that product being shipped. The increase in electronic communication has greatly reduced processing delay for many transactions.

Procurement The act of buying, especially for business purposes. This term is often used in the energy industries; for example, one may procure oil in order to refine it.

Producer Price Index An index tracking the price of goods bought and sold in bulk before they reach the retail level. The producer price index usually tracks changes in these prices on a monthly basis. A large change in producer prices can lead to a change in retail prices, which affects consumers most directly. As a result, a few countries use the producer price index as a measure of inflation, but most do not. A dramatic increase in producer prices, however, may be seen as an early indicator of inflation. It is also called the wholesale price index.

Product Cycle The period of time from the introduction of a product to its decline and stagnation. Different analyses posit different numbers of stages in a product cycle (usually four to five), but all emphasize that a product has a beginning, with technological innovation; a period of rapid growth; maturity and consolidation; and, finally, decline and possibly death. For example, in the video cassette recording (VCR) industry, the mid-1970s were a period of decentralized technological innovation, with VHS and Betamax formats vying for dominance. Later, video cassettes very quickly became a common household item. In the maturity phase, different companies selling VCRs attempted to corner a greater market share for their own (identical) versions of the product. Finally, the industry declined and was eventually supplanted by DVD players. Factors that may prolong a product cycle include the opening of new markets for the product, finding new uses for the same product, or even attaining government subsidies. The concept of product cycles applies most readily to the sale of goods and it is difficult to gauge how it works in a service economy.

Product Differentiation Any marketing strategy that seeks to highlight differences between products. That is, in addition to advertising the lowest price for a product, a company may differentiate its products by advertising that is has the best quality, the most convenience, or even the best packaging. Product differentiation is especially important where competition is stiff and companies cannot afford to charge much less than they do. See also: Brand Loyalty.

Product Life Cycle The period of time from the introduction of a product to its decline and stagnation. Different analyses posit different numbers of stages in a product life cycle (usually four to five), but all emphasize that a product has a beginning, with technological innovation; a period of rapid growth; maturity and consolidation; and, finally, decline and possibly death. For example, in the video cassette recording (VCR) industry, the mid-1970s were a period of decentralized technological innovation, with VHS and Betamax formats vying for dominance. Later, video cassettes very quickly became a common household item. In the maturity phase, different companies selling VCRs attempted to corner a greater market share for their own (identical) versions of the product. Finally, VCRs declined and were eventually supplanted by DVD players. A product life cycle can be prolonged by several factors, including opening new markets to the product, finding new uses for the same product, or even attaining government subsidies. The concept of a product life cycle applies most readily to the sale of goods, and it is difficult to gauge how it works in a service economy.

Product Mix The set of goods and services a company provides. Generally speaking, a company offering a wider product mix carries less risk but also usually has a lower profit margin. That is, the profit margin for a company like Wal-Mart may not be high, but so long as most of its products have strong sales, it is in no danger of bankruptcy. On the other hand, a company may only offer a few products; this is high risk because there may be low demand for the products, but specializing in a niche market can result in exceptionally large profits.

Product Recall A request by a company for customers to return their products, often for a replacement or some other compensation. A product recall may be voluntary or mandated by a government. Recalls may occur if a product is found to be defective or dangerous.

Product Risk The risk that a mortgage bank will arrange a complex or otherwise unusual mortgage with no guarantee that the borrower will actually accept the terms of the agreement.

Production **1.** The process of turning raw material into a product that is sold. For example, a company's production may involve turning silver, zinc, and mercury into a dental filling. **2.** Less commonly, the revenue one derives from production.

Production Cost Advantage The ability for an economic actor to produce a good or service at a lower cost. For example, if a company produces 100 widgets for $50 and a second company produces 100 widgets for $25, the second company has a production cost advantage in the production of widgets. See also: comparative advantage, absolute advantage.

Production Opportunity The ability to turn a cost into a benefit. For example, an investor who buys a stock has the production opportunity to make capital gains. Likewise, an employee who pays money to receive certification expects a higher salary.

Production Payment Financing An unsecured debt or line of credit for a business project in which a certain percentage of proceeds from the project's sales are devoted to debt service. For example, if a business borrows $100,000 to expand its widget production, a percentage of the revenue from the sales of the extra widgets is given to the bank until the debt is settled. Because there is no asset securing the debt when it is borrowed, the lender has no recourse in case of default.

Production Possibility Frontier A graphical representation of the possible outputs using two or more inputs assuming that all inputs are used efficiently. For example, if one wishes to determine the most efficient use of raw material and labor to make as much of a product as it efficient, one may design a PPF that would show all possible production outputs, which is shown as a curve. One would then find the most efficient point on a curve and use resources accordingly.

Production Rate The highest interest rate payable on mortgage-backed securities guaranteed by the Government National Mortgage Association (Ginnie Mae). The current production rate is usually half a point less than what the homeowners are paying in interest on their mortgage. For example, if homeowners whose mortgages back the securities are paying 6% on their mortgages, the maximum interest payable is almost always 5.5%. See also: Ginnie Mae Pass-Through.

Production Subsidy A subsidy a government provides to an industry in order to enable it to make more of a product. For example, a government may provide production subsidies to a munitions factory so that it can double the armaments it produces. Production subsidies generally are used in import-substitution industrialization.

Productive Mudharaba In Islamic finance, a contract under which the owner of raw material gives the material to another person, who turns it into a finished product. When the product is sold, the parties share the profit according to an agreed-upon ratio. Some sharia scholars disapprove of a productive mudharaba, arguing that the person who fashions the finished product is an employee and should receive a wage.

Productivity A measure of the units of benefit for each unit of work. Benefits include results of work such as GDP or revenue, while units of work include capital and labor. Productivity in the United States is measured by the U.S. Department of Labor on a quarterly basis. It is beneficial for both individual companies and economies to have the maximum amount of productivity possible.

Productize To turn a good, experience, or anything else into something that can be sold. For example, a retired civil servant may productize his experience in bureaucracy by founding a consulting company.

Profane Mina An ancient Persian unit of volume approximately equivalent to 500 milliliters.

Professional Coin Grading Service A company in the United States that will, for a fee, certify whether or not a coin is authentic or counterfeit. It also appraises the value of coins. The PCGS is used most commonly by numismatists.

Professional Judgment The discretion of an individual with the educational, work-related or other experience to make a decision. For example, given 10 fairly equal candidates for a job, the hiring manager may use his/her professional judgment to advance three candidates to the next round of interviews, even if there are few quantitative reasons for doing so.

Profit A company's total revenue less its operating expenses, interest paid, depreciation, and taxes. For example, suppose a widget manufacturer earns $1,000,000 in total revenue. The widgets cost $200,000 to make and his administrative and payroll expenses total $250,000. He also must subtract $50,000 in depreciation on his widget manufacturing equipment and pay $200,000 in taxes. His net income is stated as: $1,000,000 - $200,000 - $250,000 - $50,000 - $200,000 = $300,000.

Profit and Loss Statement An annual report, and other quarterly reports, a publicly-traded company publishes giving information over a given period of time. The report contains information on the company's financial state, most notably statements on revenue, expenses, and earnings (which is the difference between the two). It is in general less detailed that a stockholder's report but contains much of the same information. A profit and loss statement goes by a number of other names, including income statement, earnings statement, earnings report, and operating statement. See also: Balance Sheet.

Profit Forecast The prediction of the future profit of a company. Profit forecasts are usually made by analysts thought to be experts in the company or industry. Various methods exist for forecasting; experts differ on which ones, if any, work. See also: Technical analysis, Fundamental analysis, Random walk theory.

Profit Graph A chart plotting the potential profits or losses from an option strategy. On a profit graph, the x-axis represents different prices for the underlying asset and the y-axis represents the profit or loss that will result from the option being exercised at a given price.

Profit Margin A measure of how well a company controls its costs. It is calculated by dividing a company's profit by its revenues and expressing the result as a percentage. The higher the profit margin is, the better the company is thought to control costs. Investors use the profit margin to compare companies in the same industry and well as between industries to determine which are the most profitable.

Profit Range The total universe of possible profits. With many investments, potential profit (and/or loss) is unlimited; that is, an investment theoretically could gain (and/or lose) an unlimited amount. With some option strategies, however, profit is limited to a certain, finite set. In such a case, calculating the profit range is useful.

Profit Sharing A plan by which an employer distributes a set percentage of the company's profits to its employees. Employers may distribute the portion of its profits immediately (that is, employees may receive what amounts to a bonus) or it may set up a series of accounts for employees and defer the profit sharing until employees retire. The idea behind profit sharing is to give employees an incentive to work for the company's profitability. See also: DPSO, ESOP.

Profit Squeeze A decrease in revenue from one time period to the next, usually quarterly or annually. A profit squeeze may happen for any number of reasons. Examples include rising costs, changes in regulations, or more competition.

Profit Table A table of the potential profits and losses that may result from following a particular business strategy. This may be used in risk analysis. See also: Profit graph.

Profit Taking The act of selling a large quantity of security immediately after it has spiked in price, such that the seller will realize a great deal of capital appreciation. For example, suppose one buys a security at $5 and it suddenly rises to $15, and an investor sells the security. If enough investors do this, it can cause a significant, but temporary, drop in price. However, technical analysts see it as a signal of an uptrend. It is also called taking profits.

Profit Warning An informal announcement by a publicly-traded company that its earnings for a given quarter or year will be less than expected. This is done to price out the company's share price and avoid a sell-off or other volatility when the earnings are actually announced.

Profitability Ratio Any ratio that measures a company's ability to generate cash flow relative to some metric, often the amount invested in the company. Profitability ratios are useful in fundamental analysis which investigates the financial health of companies. An example of a profitability ratio is the return on investment which is the amount of revenue an investment generates as a percentage of the amount of capital invested over a given period of time. Other examples include return on sales, return on equity, and return on common stock equity.

Profits Tax A term for the corporate tax in Hong Kong.

Proforma Invoice A price quote that a potential seller gives to a potential buyer that details the sale price and any applicable commissions and fees. It is given in the form of an invoice. A proforma invoice exists in order to give a potential buyer a precise figure of the final cost of a transaction. This helps the buyer in making his/her investment decisions. The proforma invoice also helps the seller avoid ill feelings that may result from unexpected fees charged to the buyer, which could drive away future business.

Program Trade A large trade executed automatically by a computer on behalf of institutional investors. Program trades are usually open orders in which the computer is programmed to wait until a certain price prevails before buying or selling a large quantity of securities. Because of the large number involved, program trading may lead to increased market volatility; because of this, program trading has been blamed for the 1987 Stock Market Crash, selling automatically as prices were reached, making the problem worse. Exchanges now limit the times when program trades may occur to prevent a recurrence. Program trading is also called basket trading. See also: Algorithmic trading.

Progress Payments The act or practice of paying a contractor in installments as different stages of work are completed, rather than providing a single lump sum at the completion of the project. Progress payments reduce the client's working capital needs for the project.

Progressive Tax System A system of taxation in which persons or corporations are assessed at a greater percentage of their income according to the theoretical ability to pay. That is, taxpayers pay more in taxes if they earn more in income. For example, taxpayers may pay 25% of their income in taxes up to a certain amount, and 35% of everything earned over that amount. A theory behind progressive taxation states that persons or corporations who earn the same or a similar amount of money should be taxed in the same or a similar way. For example, the theory states that two individuals making $50,000 per year should be taxed the same amount, regardless of how they earned their income. This is known as horizontal equity. While most countries have some form of progressive taxation, it is usually coupled with other taxes, such as a sales tax, and few countries treat all income as exactly the same. See also: Regressive tax system.

Prohibited Transaction A transaction that would cause a tax deferred structure under ERISA to lose its deferred status. A prohibited transaction is any transaction involving a retirement account and a disqualified person.

Prohibitionism The legal philosophy that the best way to reduce unwanted actions is to ban them. For example, a prohibitionist may believe that the best way to end smoking is to forbid the possession or sale of tobacco. The effectiveness of prohibitionism is highly controversial.

Prohibitionist A person who subscribes to the idea that the best way to reduce unwanted actions is to ban them. For example, a prohibitionist may believe that the best way to end smoking is to forbid the possession or sale of tobacco. The effectiveness of prohibitionism is highly controversial.

Prohibitive Tariff A tariff so high that it makes an import prohibitively expensive. A prohibitive tariff discourages importers from bringing goods into the country in the first place because they will be difficult to sell. For example, a country may levy a 900% tariff on a good that it wishes to keep out.

Project Any series of tasks or activities intended to accomplish a goal, which is ultimately to make a profit. For example, a construction company may have a project to build a house. This project involves laying in the foundation, setting up the frame, installing insulation, and so forth. A company may receive a lump sum payment at the completion of the project, or it may receive progress payments as different benchmarks on the way to completion are met. See also: Project finance.

Project Completion Restriction A clause in a bond agreement requiring the issuer to issue more debt securities if necessary to finance the completion of whatever project that bond was intended to finance. That is, if the bond's financing is insufficient for the project for any reason, a project completion restriction requires the issuer to finish financing the project even if it requires acquiring more debt. Without the project completion restriction, the issuer may cancel the project if it becomes apparent that the bond's level of financing will not cover its costs. This clause exists to protect bondholders from the risk that the project will be abandoned, and, therefore, that the issuer will not secure the revenue from the project to cover the original bond issue. The project completion restriction is most common in municipal bonds.

Project Contract An agreement between two or more parties to accomplish a certain goal in a certain way. For example, a project contract may take the form of an agreement between a builder and a property owner in which the builder agrees to build a house on the property by a certain time in a certain way, and, in exchange, the property owner makes certain remuneration. Project contracts are important to have in the event of a dispute.

Project Creep A slang term for the gradual extension of a deadline, especially if the parameters of a project are moved repeatedly. See also: Scope creep.

Project Finance Loan Program Any program that a private or government-owned bank uses to extend credit for project finance.

Project Financing A way to finance an activity using debt where the debt is repaid from the funds generated by the activity. For example, project financing may involve issuing a bond to pay for the construction of a museum and repaying it from ticket sales for that museum. Project financing is often very complex and is most common in the telecommunications, utilities, transportation, and mining industries. Very often, a company conducting project finance will set up a different corporation or other entity for the project to shield the remainder of the company from liability if the debt goes into default.

Project Link A system used to estimate the impact that the economy in one country has on the economies in other countries. For example, project link would seek to establish the relationship that significant GDP growth in China has on GDP growth (or lack thereof) elsewhere. See also: Globalization.

Project Loan A mortgage loan guaranteed by the Federal Housing Administration or another branch of the Department of Housing and Urban Development. Project loans are usually used to finance a large-scale building that provides some public benefit. Examples of uses for project loans include nursing homes, hospitals, and public housing.

Project Loan Security A mortgage-backed security issued by Ginnie Mae on mortgages for larger properties. As with all mortgage-backed securities, the coupons on guaranteed mortgage securities are paid out of the principal and interest on a pool of mortgages underlying the securities. Project loan securities are issued on mortgages on multi-family homes or large construction projects.

Project Note A short-term debt security issued by a municipality, usually in order to finance a federally-sponsored real estate or urban renewal project. When project notes are issued for this purpose, they are guaranteed by the U.S. Department of Housing and Urban Development. These are considered very low-risk bonds, and help the issuer cover the costs of a project while also avoiding taking on long-term debt.

Projected Benefit Obligation An estimate of the present value of the future liability of an employee's pension. The projected benefit obligation assumes that the employee will continue to work and make contributions to the pension plan. It also assumes that contributions will increase as the employee's salary also increases. See also: Accumulated benefit obligation.

Projected Maturity Date The date on which a collateralized mortgage obligation (CMO) is expected to mature and coupons are expected to cease. The maturity date is projected because of the uncertainty of whether or not the mortgages underlying the CMO will be paid on time, paid early, or will go into default. See also: Prepayment Risk.

Projection The use of certain data to predict future market movements, economic trends, and other things. Various methods exist for making projections; experts differ on which ones, if any, work. See also: Technical Analysis, Fundamental Analysis, Random Walk Theory.

Promissory Note A written promise made by one party to make a stated payment in full by a certain date. A promissory note is a binding, legal contract.

Proof A coin made with a polished die or using some other special method. It may be struck twice to make the images clearer. Proofs generally do not circulate, but are made for collectors or for sale as illiquid assets.

Proof Gold Any amount of pure gold used to test the purity of gold coins. In the United States, proof gold is disseminated by the Philadelphia Mint. See also: Assay, numismatics.

Proof Silver Any amount of pure silver used to test the purity of silver coins. In the United States, proof silver is disseminated by the Philadelphia Mint. See also: Assay, numismatics.

Prop Desk Slang; traders who buy and sell securities on behalf of the company they work for, rather than for that company's clients. Their incentive is to profit for the company rather than for themselves or their clients.

Property Casualty Insurers Association of America Also called the PCI. A trade association for property insurance companies in the United States. The PCI lobbies for favorable legislation and provides educational materials and networking opportunities for members. It is headquartered in Des Plaines, Illinois, and Washington, D.C., with satellite offices elsewhere in the U.S.

Property Dividend A dividend paid to shareholders in anything other than cash. Common property dividends include shipping the company's product to shareholders and giving out certificates in stocks in other companies held by the company. They are taxed like cash dividends at the fair market value of whatever property is paid out. See also: Payment-in-Kind.

Property Inventory A list of personal property for insurance or tax purposes. One lists the properties along with the price one paid and their current values.

Property Line A set line denoting the extremities of a property. Property lines are set by a government or the original owner. An owner of property sometimes may subdivide and sell pieces, thereby creating new lines within his/her old property.

Property Rights The legal protection by a government of the ability for an individual or a corporation to own real estate and personal property. Nearly every theory of economics (with the exception of some more extreme versions of socialism) state that property rights are a necessary condition for successful, economic development. However, property rights are rarely absolute. For example, a government may exercise eminent domain over real estate to build something for public use.

Property Tax A tax on the value of land or improvements (i.e. buildings). Occasionally, property taxes are levied on personal property, such as automobiles or securities, as well. All property taxes are calculated as a percentage of the value of the property. In the United States, most property taxes are levied at the city or county levels, and are used for municipal improvements, such as roads or snow removal. Municipalities can issue bonds that are secured by the proceeds on property taxes.

Proportional Representation In a publicly-traded company, a method of voting for members of the board of directors in which a shareholder can give multiple votes to the same candidate rather than voting individually for each available seat. Proportional representation allows individual and small groups of shareholders a greater likelihood of having a representative on the board. See also: Statutory voting.

Proportionate Redemption A way of conducting a management buyback in which a stockholder maintains the same percentage of ownership in the company that he/she had before the buyback. A management buyback is the act of a company buying its own shares to reduce the number of shares outstanding; a proportionate redemption exists in order to protect stockholders from the risk of loss in the buyback. For example, if a stockholder owned 4% of the company before the buyback, the company will structure the buyback such that he/she continues to own 4% after the buyback.

Proprietary Describing knowledge or another asset that properly belongs to one person or company. Proprietary knowledge and assets are protected and their owner is not required to reveal them. For example, a restaurant that makes the best fried chicken in town cannot be compelled to reveal its recipe as this knowledge gives it a competitive advantage over other restaurants. See also: Trade secret.

Proprietary Debit Card A debit card issued by or in conjunction with a certain company. For example, a retail shop may issue a proprietary debit card along with a bank. The use of a proprietary debit card may entitle one to discounts or other incentives to buy from the issuer (or co-issuer).

Proprietary Desk A group of traders that invest an investment bank's own capital, rather than the capital of the bank's clients. Proprietary desks may engage in high-risk transactions that can lead to large gains for the bank.

Proprietary Fund A mutual fund sponsored and managed by a certain financial institution. For example, all funds managed by Bank XYZ are considered Bank XYZ's proprietary funds. While some financial institutions offer other institutions funds along with their own, many only sell their own proprietary funds to investors.

Proprietary Information The information, concepts, designs or anything else that sets a business apart from its competitors and that is therefore kept secret. Other examples of proprietary information may include a company's computer systems, employee salaries, and so forth. Proprietary information may always be kept secret and is never subject to public disclosure. For instance, a fried chicken restaurant is never required to reveal the spices used in its recipe. Proprietary information is also called a trade secret.

Proprietary Trading The act or practice of an investment bank conducting trades on its own account, rather than on behalf of a client. Proprietary trading has three primary benefits. First, it allows the investment bank to profit on its own instead of simply collecting commissions and fees from clients. Secondly, it lets the bank build an inventory of securities. This can be useful if a client places an order for the securities in an illiquid market. In such a situation, the investment bank can fill the order from its own inventory. Finally, proprietary trading allows the bank to make a market when it is assigned to ensure the liquidity for a given security.

Proratable Factor The percentage of shares that may be exchanged for other stock or cash. This may happen in a bankruptcy or in a takeover. For example, if so many shareholders seek to trade in their stocks at one time that the company lacks to cash to cover it, the company may use a proratable factor to cover at least a proportion of the exchanges. To give another example, if a company is taken over for cash and equity, the proratable factor is used to determine how much of each a shareholder receives for each share of the company that has been taken over. See also: Proration, Exchange ratio.

Prospect 1. A potential seller or buyer. **2.** To network in order to find potential, new clients, especially for a brokerage.

Prospect List A list of potential clients or customers. Often, a broker compiles a prospect list of persons known personally to him/her or persons who are likely to have sufficient net worth to invest with the brokerage. See also: Cold calling, Networking.

Prospect Theory A theory stating that investors are more likely to make an investment if it is advertised in terms of growth rather than loss. That is, an advertiser is more likely to be successful if he argues that an investment will probably return 10% than if he argues that it might lose 100%. Prospect theory is a fairly obvious concept, but it important to remember when making recommendations. See also: Behavioral Economics.

Prospectus A legal document detailing the structure and goals of an investment company such as a mutual fund. The SEC requires investment companies to file a prospectus before issuing shares and to provide one to a potential investor on demand. Each prospectus must contain relevant information, such as the terms of purchase, the amount of the load (if any), the fund's investment strategy, and historical financial statements. A prospectus is also called a circular.

Prospero A blog on the website of The Economist that covers art, literature, and the market for both.

Pro-Tanto Describing partial fulfillment of an agreement, contract, or payment. The term is usually used in a legal sense; that is, a judge may order a pro-tanto payment.

Protected Fund A mutual fund backed by an insurance policy that guarantees a shareholder's initial investment assuming he/she does not sell his shares for a certain period of time. A protected fund allows the shareholder to make a return from investing in the stock market while also guaranteeing that he/she will not lose any money. Because this increases the possible return while reducing the risk, a protected fund is relatively expensive compared to other mutual funds.

Protected Risk A risk against which an investor has hedged. For example, if one buys a stock, one carries the risk that the stock will fall in price. If one then short sells the same stock (while maintaining the long position), that risk becomes a protected risk.

Protection 1. See: Call protection. **2.** A slang term for a credit default swap.

Protection Money Money paid to a powerful person or organization for protection from rivals or enemies. For example, a small business may pay protection money to a criminal organization to keep it from being sabotaged by rival criminal organizations. Protection money is a common form of extortion practiced by organized crime.

Protection Racket The practice in which businesses and/or individuals in an area periodically pay money to an organized crime syndicate in return for freedom from harassment. In other words, when the money is paid, the syndicate will protect businesses from acts of violence from other groups (or from the syndicate itself).

Protectionism Any government policy or regulation that restricts international trade. Examples include import quotas, which set a maximum number of imports for a certain good over a given period of time, and import substitution, in which the state subsidizes businesses and industries to make domestic goods less expensive. By far the most common example, however, is the tariff, which is a tax on imports. Proponents of protectionism argue that it encourages domestic production of goods and helps working class people, while critics contend that it hurts the people it aims to help by discouraging competition, which may drive down prices. The balance of protectionism and free trade is a controversial topic regarding the government's role in international trade. See also: General Agreement on Tariffs and Trade.

Protectionist A scholar or other person who favors government policy or regulation restricting international trade. Examples of policies supported by protectionists include import quotas, which set a maximum number of imports for a certain good over a given period of time, and import substitution, in which the state subsidizes businesses and industries to make domestic goods less expensive. By far the most common example of protectionism, however, is the tariff, which is a tax on imports. Protectionists argue that protectionism encourages domestic production of goods and helps working class people, while critics contend that it hurts the people it aims to help by discouraging competition, which may drive down prices. The balance of protectionism and free trade is a controversial topic regarding the government's role in international trade. See also: General Agreement on Tariffs and Trade.

Protective Stop An investment strategy designed to limit losses on a security by means of setting up a stop-loss order or stop-limit order. For example, a protective stop may involve an investor giving an order to his/her broker to sell a stock if its price drops more than 5% below what the investor paid. So, if the investor paid $30 per share, the protective stop would mean selling automatically if the price reached $28.50. Protective stops are risk averse and assume that if the price reaches (in this case) $28.50, it will continue its downward trend.

Protest An instruction to a collection agency to attempt to collect a certain portion of a default or other, unpaid sale.

Proved Reserves The estimated amount of a natural resource, especially an energy resource, that has been measured with reasonable certainty and is obtainable with existing equipment and under current operating conditions. Proved reserves are important to energy companies that wish to extract as much of a resource as possible at the least amount of risk. See also: Developmental oil and gas partnership.

Provinsi In Indonesia, a political subdivision equivalent to a province.

Provision for Income Taxes In a financial statement or personal budget, an estimate for one's total income tax liability for a given year. This is especially important when the government or an employer does not automatically deduct estimated tax payments from paychecks or other revenue. Generally speaking, one must set the provision for income taxes aside and pay it quarterly or annually.

Provisional Call Feature In convertible bonds, a feature that allows the issuer to call and redeem the bonds during the non-call period under certain circumstances. Specifically, if the price of the underlying stock exceeds the conversion price by a certain amount for a certain period of time, the issuer may exercise the provisional call feature. The provisional call feature exists to protect the issuer from needing to honor conversions of bonds into common stock at a vastly unfavorable price.

Provisional Call Trigger Price In convertible callable bonds, the price at which the underlying stock must trade in order to invalidate the call protection. For example, a convertible bond indenture may specify that if the share price of the underlying stock trades at 200% of the conversion price for a certain number of days, the issuer may call the bond before maturity during the period when it otherwise would be unable to do so.

Provisional Rating A bond rating that is subject to change based upon certain conditions. For example, if the project a bond was intended to finance is completed and begins generating revenue, a provisional rating is likely to increase. On the other hand, if an issuer's debt reaches too high a level, a provisional rating is likely to decrease. It is also called a conditional rating. See also: investment-grade, junk.

Prowincja In Poland, a political subdivision equivalent to a province.

Proxy 1. In publicly-traded companies, the transfer of a right to vote to another individual or group of individuals. At the annual meeting, shareholders who are unable to attend may give proxy to other shareholders, the board of directors, or some other representative. The persons with proxy are usually expected to vote as the shareholder would wish. Most companies encourage shareholders to vote by proxy if they are unable to come to the annual meeting, as this gives decisions the greatest possible legitimacy. **2.** A person who has proxy. See also: Proxy committee.

Proxy Committee A committee appointed by the board of directors to vote on behalf of shareholders who have given proxy to the board. It is important to note that the proxy committee does not necessarily have the discretion to vote as it wishes; it must vote as the shareholders who have given it proxy intend.

Proxy Committee Ballot The ballot that the proxy committee of a publicly-traded company completes at the annual meeting. The proxy committee is appointed by the board of directors to vote on behalf of shareholders who have given proxy to the board. The proxy committee does not necessarily have the discretion to vote as it wishes; it must vote as the shareholders who have given it proxy intend.

Proxy Directive A legal document giving an assignee the ability to make medical decisions on behalf of the assignor in the event of the assignor's mental or physical incapacity. A proxy directive is made while the assignor is still competent, and comes into effect at incapacity. A proxy directive gives far-reaching powers; for example, the form for a proxy directive in the state of New Jersey states allows the assignee the ability to "provide, withhold or withdraw life-sustaining measures" from the assignor. It is important to note that a proxy directive does not allow the assignee access to the assignor's finances, nor obliges the assignee to pay for any treatment. See also: Power of attorney.

Proxy Fight A situation in which two investors (usually two companies) compete with one another in the attempt to gain the proxy votes of shareholders in a third company. The two investors engage in the proxy fight because both wish to have enough proxy to elect a new board of directors that will effectively do whatever the investor wants. The winner of a proxy fight, if any, is able to control the third company through the board of directors and does not need to directly acquire it, though many often do anyway.

Proxy Materials Documents a publicly-traded company must provide its shareholders at least annually. SEC Regulation 14A requires that proxy materials describe procedures on how the company functions, the number of outstanding shares, the composition and compensation of the board of directors, and other relevant information. As of January 2009, the SEC requires registered companies to make their proxy materials available to shareholders online.

Proxy Solicitor A company that seeks to buy or otherwise acquire the proxy of shareholders. That is, a proxy solicitor seeks to influence a company by buying the right to vote at the annual meeting from common shareholders.

Proxy Statement In publicly-traded companies, a statement indicating the transfer of a right to vote to another individual or group of individuals. At the annual meeting, shareholders who are unable to attend may give proxy to other shareholders, the board of directors, or some other representative. The persons with proxy are usually expected to vote as the shareholder would wish. Most companies encourage shareholders to vote by proxy if they are unable to come to the annual meeting as this gives decisions the greatest possible legitimacy.

Proxy Tax In the United States, a tax levied on the political or lobbying activity of certain tax-exempt organizations. Subject to certain restrictions, the proxy tax applies to organizations under section 501(c)4, 501(c)5, and 501(c)6. Generally speaking, this includes labor unions, civic groups, chambers of commerce, and similar groups. Unless the organization meets exemption requirements (usually meaning the organization is a veterans' group or volunteer fire department), it must pay the proxy tax on its lobbying efforts. The proxy tax rate is 35%. An organization may avoid the proxy tax if it establishes to the IRS that members do not deduct membership dues, contributions, or other similar amounts on their personal or business taxes.

Proxy Vote At the annual meeting of a publicly-traded company, a vote that a shareholder allows to be cast by another on his/her/its behalf. Proxy votes are relatively common, especially when a shareholder cannot personally attend the annual meeting. Generally, but far from always, a shareholder allows the company's management to have his/her/its proxy vote. This gives the management greater control of the company. See also: Beneficial ownership.

PRT GOST 7.67 Latin three-letter geocode for Portugal. The code is used for transactions to and from Portuguese bank accounts and for international shipping to Portugal. As with all GOST 7.67 codes, it is used primarily in Cyrillic alphabets.

Prudent Man Rule A legal rule requiring investment advisers to only make investments for their clients' discretionary accounts that a "prudent person" would make. This means that investment advisers operating discretionary accounts are not allowed to make investments they believe will lose money for the client. It does not require that the investment adviser always make correct decisions; it merely requires him/her to make decisions that will be generally accepted as sound for someone of

average intelligence. The rule has its origins in an 1830 court decision in Massachusetts, stating that trustees must manage the affairs of others as if they were managing "their own affairs." See also: Suitability rules, Twisting.

Pruta An ancient Hebrew unit of weight approximately equivalent to 0.022 grams.

PRY GOST 7.67 Latin three-letter geocode for Paraguay. The code is used for transactions to and from Paraguayan bank accounts and for international shipping to Paraguay. As with all GOST 7.67 codes, it is used primarily in Cyrillic alphabets.

PS 1. ISO 3166-1 alpha-2 code for the Palestinian Territories. This is the code used in international transactions to and from Palestinian bank accounts. **2.** ISO 3166-2 geocode for the Palestinian Territories. This is used as an international standard for shipping to the Territories.

PSSG A financial ratio measuring how a company's share price relates to its sales. It is often used for dot-com stocks and may be useful when earnings are low or non-existent. It is calculated as follows: PSSG = Share price / sales / sales growth

Psychic Income The value of an item over and above its cost. For example, one may spend $100,000 on one's first house, but this is offset psychologically by the pride of owning a home. Psychic income is intangible, but can add value.

PT 1. ISO 3166-1 alpha-2 code for the Portuguese Republic. This is the code used in international transactions to and from Portuguese bank accounts. **2.** ISO 3166-2 geocode for Portugal. This is used as an international standard for shipping to Portugal. Each subdivision has its own code with the prefix "PT." For example, the code for the District of Porto is ISO 3166-2:PT-13.

PTA Bank A major bank in Africa. It is owned by the African Development Bank and 18 African governments. It provides financing to further the goals of the Common Market for Eastern and Southern Africa. It was established in 1985 as the Eastern and Southern African Trade and Development Bank.

PTE ISO 4217 code for the Portuguese escudo. It was introduced in 1911 following the republican revolution, and was marked by high inflation throughout its history. It was removed from circulation and replaced by the euro in 2002.

PU 1. ISO 3166-1 alpha-2 code for the U.S. Miscellaneous Pacific Islands prior to re-designation as part of the U.S. Minor Outlying Islands. This was the code used in international transactions to and from bank accounts in the territory. **2.** ISO 3166-2 geocode for the U.S. Miscellaneous Pacific Islands. This was used as an international standard for shipping to the U.S. Miscellaneous Pacific Islands. In both cases, the code is obsolete.

Publ 1321 A form published by the IRS providing instructions for Puerto Rico residents who must file Form 1040 or Form 1040-A in addition to Form 1040 (PR) or Form 1040-A (PR). Persons who file in Puerto Rico may be eligible to exclude their Puerto Rican income from taxation in the continental U.S., provided certain income adjustments are made.

Publ 1345 A handbook published by the IRS outlining instructions for professionals who e-file individual tax returns.

Publ 1346 A handbook published by the IRS outlining detailed instructions on how to prepare and file individual tax returns electronically.

Publ 1431 A flier published by the IRS stating the names of various tax publications that may be useful, along with telephone numbers that taxpayers may call to ask for help.

Publ 1436 A guidebook that the IRS published in 2011 stating software guidelines for individual taxpayers filing electronically.

Publ 1437 A guidebook published by the IRS giving detailed instructions for filing taxes for an estate electronically. It outlines, for example, how to prepare and e-file Form 1041.

Publ 1438 A package published by the IRS stating software guidelines for taxpayers filing returns for estates electronically.

Publ 1450 A form published by the IRS outlining how one may request a document certifying the release from a tax lien. It also provides a list of phone numbers in every state that a taxpayer may call for more information.

Publ 1457 A form published by the IRS providing examples of how to use actuarial tables for the value of various types of annuities. It also provides the website where the tables themselves are located.

Publ 1458 A form published by the IRS providing actuarial tables for the return of various types of annuities.

Publ 1459 A form published by the IRS providing actuarial tables for depreciation adjustment factors for the purpose of computing one's income tax.

Publ 1460 A form the IRS published in 2006 outlining the various types of tax relief available to residents of Alabama, Florida, Louisiana, Mississippi, and Texas who were victims of Hurricanes Katrina, Rita, or Wilma.

Publ 1461 A form published by the IRS outlining how the Attributed Tip Income Program works and what benefits it offers to employers and employees in the food services industry.

Publ 1468 A form published by the IRS stating how federal tax liens are processed, imposed, and removed.

Publ 1474 A form published by the IRS providing detailed instructions for preparing and filing Form 8655, which e-filers use to authorize a reporting agent.

Publ 1476 A flier published by the IRS advertising Retirement News for Employers, which is a quarterly newsletter intended to help business owners manage their retirement plans.

Publ 1494 A form published by the IRS providing tables stating how much income per pay period is exempt from withholding to pay for back taxes.

Publ 1516 A form published by the IRS stating the instructions for preparing and filing Form 8596, which federal contractors use to provide information on their contracts.

Publ 1518 A calendar published by the IRS stating relevant tax information for self-employed persons and small businesses. For example, it states the days that self-employed persons should pay their quarterly estimated taxes.

Publ 1524 A guidebook published by the IRS stating instructions filing returns for partnerships electronically.

Publ 1525 A form published by the IRS stating software guidelines for taxpayers filing returns for partnerships electronically.

Publ 1542 A form published by the IRS containing a table describing the per diem rates of permissible write-offs for business travel in the United States.

Publ 1544 A form published by the IRS stating the instructions for filing Form 8300, which is used to report cash payments above $10,000.

Publ 1546 A booklet published by the IRS giving detailed information about the Taxpayer Advocate Service, including contact and confidentiality information.

Publ 1546-EZ A flier published by the IRS giving basic information, including contact information, for the Taxpayer Advocate Service.

Publ 3066 A flyer published by the IRS advertising information on the tax treatment of retirement plans. It also recommends receiving an outside opinion from an expert on one's own or retirement plan or the retirement plan of one's business.

Publ 3067 A flyer published by the IRS announcing the availability of a tax deduction for the total or partial loss of a home, household goods, or personal effects due to a natural disaster. It outlines several forms that may be relevant in such a situation. The flyer is available in several languages.

Publ 3079 A guidebook published by the IRS detailing information related to the tax treatment of gambling sponsored by a tax exempt organization. For example, income earned from bingo in a church hall may, under some circumstances, be taxed as unrelated business income.

Publ 3106 A brochure published by the IRS outlining information for gas station owners on the tax treatment of payments made for improving the image of a gas station.

Publ 3112 A document published by the IRS detailing how an organization may participate in the e-file program. It also contains an application to join the program.

Publ 3114 The flyer published by the IRS briefly summarizing the definitions of an audit and a compliance review.

Publ 3125 A flyer published by the IRS advising against potentially fraudulent IRA schemes. Specifically, it indicates that the IRS does not formally approve of any IRA investment, despite what some advertisements may say.

Publ 3144 A reference guide published by the IRS for employers outlining the major tax issues regarding tips. It summarizes different programs employers may employ to report their employees' tip income.

Publ 3148 A reference guide published by the IRS for employees outlining the major tax issues regarding tips. For example, it states that employees must report all tips and summarizes what kind of records of tips must be kept.

Publ 3151 A reference guide published by the IRS outlining the major issues surrounding federal tax deposits for businesses. For example, it provides a chart stating the frequency with which taxes should be deposited, which is based on the amount of a business's payroll.

Publ 3151-A A guidebook published by the IRS detailing the issues surrounding federal tax deposits for businesses. For example, it states what taxes must be deposited and how often.

Publ 3187 A report that the IRS published in 2005 outlining the strategy for promoting continued growth in the practice of filing taxes electronically.

Publ 3189 A document published by the IRS stating the guidelines and standards of conduct for volunteers who assist taxpayers in filing their taxes electronically.

Publ 3202 A brochure that the IRS published in 2001 advertising a training seminar on search and seizure of financial information from a computer. The seminar was available to investigators and auditors in multiple countries.

Publ 3204 A form published by the IRS outlining tax information for automobile salespersons who receive incentive payments from manufacturers to sell their cars. This income is taxable and the publication states how it is taxed.

Publ 3211 (EN/SP) A flyer published by the IRS outlining the eligibility for and calculation of the earned income tax credit. It also summarizes what qualifies as earned income for purposes of claiming the credit and how to claim it for a child. It is available in both English and Spanish.

Publ 3218 A report that the IRS published in 1999 outlining the loss of tax revenue due to transfer pricing, which is the practice of reallocating U.S.-sourced income and deductions to a non-U.S. corporation, which does not pay U.S. taxes. The report estimated that the U.S. lost $2.8 billion in revenue each year due to transfer pricing.

Publ 3319 A grant application published by the IRS for the Low Income Taxpayer Clinic program. Non-profit organizations and others submit the application to receive funding to offer the clinic to qualified persons.

Publ 3326 A brochure published by the IRS advertising a 2006 continuing education seminar for tax professionals.

Publ 3328 A flyer published by the IRS outlining information for parents in Alaska to file tax returns for their children for the purposes of Alaska Permanent Fund dividends.

Publ 3366-A A poster published by the IRS stating where photocopies of IRS forms are available.

Publ 3373 A report published by the IRS providing its required disclosures to federal, state, and local government agencies for fiscal year 2001.

Publ 3385 A report published by the IRS providing its financial statements and auditor's statement for fiscal year 2001.

Publ 3386 A booklet published by the IRS providing detailed information on tax issues related to tax exempt veterans' organizations. For example, it outlines how these organizations may apply and maintain tax exempt status for various parts of Section 501(c) of the tax code.

Publ 3415 A form published by the IRS containing the Electronic Tax Administration Advisory Committee's annual report to Congress for 2011. It includes information such as the progress of the IRS toward meeting its stated goal of processing 80% of its forms electronically. The publication also includes legislative recommendations to Congress.

Publ 3416 A publication that the IRS published allowing one to file Form 1065 (a tax return for a partnership) and all supplemental forms electronically for tax year 2005. In other words, Publ 3416 is an editable PDF of Form 1065 and supplemental forms.

Publ 3441 A brochure that the IRS published in 2007 advertising a financial fraud training seminar available to tax professionals, prosecutors, and investigators in multiple countries.

Publ 3442 A brochure that the IRS published in 2002 advertising a 10-week computer audit training seminar available to auditors in multiple countries.

Publ 3498 A form published by the IRS outlining the steps of a tax audit process conducted in person or by mail. It states what the IRS does when it conducts an audit, how one replies to the audit decision, and how one may appeal an adverse decision.

Publ 3498-A A form published by the IRS outlining the steps of a tax audit process conducted by mail. It states what the IRS does when it conducts an audit, how one replies to the audit letter, and how one may appeal an adverse decision.

Publ 3512 A pamphlet published by the IRS outlining relief available to an innocent spouse. That is, if a spouse filed a joint return and the IRS demands more taxes be paid due to actions of the other spouse without the knowledge of the former, Publ 3512 states the options that the wronged spouse may have. See also: Form 8857.

Publ 3524 A poster published by the IRS outlining the eligibility requirements of the earned income tax credit in a checklist format.

Publ 3524-A A handout published by the IRS outlining the eligibility requirements of the earned income tax credit in a checklist format.

Publ 3535 A poster published by the IRS advertising the earned income tax credit. It is available in both English and Spanish.

Publ 3536 A document published by the IRS providing detailed information on excise taxes on motor vehicles. For example, it outlines monthly reporting requirements.

Publ 3560 A document the IRS published in 2005 outlining proposed changes to its strategic and operational goals and the methods by which the goals are measured. Publ 3560 was disseminated in order to invite comments on the proposed changes. See also: Publ 3561.

Publ 3561 A pamphlet published by the IRS outlining its strategic and operational goals, the methods by which they are measured, and the steps the IRS takes to achieve them. For example, it discusses increasing overall payment of taxes, employee satisfaction, and taxpayer satisfaction.

Publ 3598 A form published by the IRS outlining the audit reconsideration process. The audit reconsideration process is used if the taxpayer submits information that the IRS previously has not seen; if the taxpayer believes the IRS made a mathematical error in calculating taxation; or if the taxpayer filed a tax return after the IRS created a theoretical return for that taxpayer and levied taxes on that basis. Unlike an audit appeal, audit reconsideration is an informal process.

Publ 3605 A flyer published by the IRS outlining fast track mediation, explaining how it works, and advertising it as a quick way to resolve disputes with the IRS.

Publ 3608 A brochure published by the IRS outlining information on its tax-exempt and government entities division. Specifically, it states the duties of the division, and provides contact information for key personnel.

Publ 3609 A booklet published by the IRS outlining how businesses can use the e-file system, which allows them to electronically file their corporate, employment, and other taxes.

Publ 3611 A brochure published by the IRS advertising the e-file system, which allows taxpayers to file their taxes electronically.

Publ 3614 An agreement the IRS prepared in 2005 allowing one to participate in a pilot program for the electronic filing of debt indicator forms, on which one lists income and debt to determine whether one is eligible for an offer in compromise or a similar arrangement.

Publ 3618 A report the IRS published in 2000 outlining the strategic goals for the National Taxpayer Advocate for fiscal year 2001. It listed six major goals: to help taxpayers having a problem with the IRS; to identify systemic procedural problems within the IRS; to identify and resolve operational problems; to represent taxpayers effectively in the formulation of policy; to develop legislation favorable to taxpayers; and to reach out to more taxpayers.

Publ 3636 A pamphlet published by the IRS outlining various tax issues related to retirement plans for employees of non-profit organizations.

Publ 3637 A booklet published by the IRS detailing filing requirement for non-profit organizations. These organizations generally do not pay taxes (except on unrelated business income), but are still required to file various information returns and pay FICA taxes for their employees.

Publ 3669 A flyer published by the IRS to recruit applicants to become special agents in its Criminal Investigation division and Internal Revenue division. It features a quote and the picture of a special agent named Kathy. See also: Marketing.

Publ 3676-A A flyer published by the IRS advertising e-filing with the VITA program, in which volunteers prepare and file taxes online for qualifying persons.

Publ 3684 A flyer published by the IRS to recruit applicants to become special agents in its Criminal Investigation division. It features a quote and the picture of a special agent named Chris. See also: Marketing.

Publ 3688 A flyer published by the IRS to recruit applicants to become special agents in its Criminal Investigation division. It features a quote and the picture of a special agent named Annette. See also: Marketing.

Publ 3706 A brochure published by the IRS to recruit applicants to become special agents in its Criminal Investigation division.

Publ 3722 A flyer published by the IRS advertising the Electronic Federal Tax Payment System, which is a way to make tax deposits and similar payments online or over the phone.

Publ 3747 A brochure published by the IRS outlining information on its office of Indian Tribal Governments. Specifically, it states the duties of the office, and provides contact information for key personnel.

Publ 3748 A flyer published by the IRS outlining information on its office of Indian Tribal Governments. Specifically, it states the duties of the office, and provides contact information for key personnel.

Publ 3749 A newsletter published periodically by the IRS providing information on employee retirement plans.

Publ 3755 A booklet published by the IRS detailing filing requirement for tax-exempt bond issuers. These issuers, while they do not pay taxes on their bonds, are still required to file various information returns and submit records of coupons (which may be taxable) to bondholders.

Publ 3780 A pamphlet published by the IRS outlining tax issues relevant to small construction companies. For example, it provides guidance on which accounting method may be most beneficial.

Publ 3809 A flyer published by the IRS outlining the functions of the Office of Federal, State and Local Governments, which is a division of the IRS dealing with government agencies. Because these agencies do not pay taxes themselves, the office works primarily with information returns and employment taxes.

Publ 3823 An instruction book published by the IRS detailing how the e-file system works for employers who file 940, 941, and similar forms.

Publ 3830 A report the IRS published in 2004 documenting the results of a study of the customer satisfaction of employers who filed their 940 or 941 forms electronically. The report noted wide levels of satisfaction among these employers.

Publ 3833 A booklet published by the IRS detailing the natural disaster aid that it offers through charitable organizations. It outlines the help that it offers to these organizations and the tax relief available to victims.

Publ 3834 A flyer published by the IRS outlining information on its tax-exempt bond division. Specifically, it states the duties of the tax-exempt bond division, and provides contact information for key personnel.

Publ 3835 A brochure published by the IRS outlining various forms and publications that may be relevant to tax exempt and government organizations, especially but not exclusively those related to pensions and retirement plans for their employees.

Publ 3847 A document published by the IRS containing the 2003 business report of its criminal investigation division. Among other things, it provides statistics and reports on its progress toward fulfilling the division's strategic goals.

Publ 3857 A flyer published by the IRS providing examples of warning signs that may indicate fraudulent returns and advising tax professionals whom they should contact if they suspect a return to be fraudulent.

Publ 3861 A pamphlet outlining the responsibilities of the criminal investigation division of the IRS. For example, it states that its priorities are cases involving underpayment of taxes on legal income, followed by money laundering and cases involving illegal income.

Publ 3864 A flyer published by the IRS outlining tax issues for seniors, specifically those related to a change in marital status. For example, it states that gifts given to one's spouse generally are not subject to the gift tax.

Publ 3865 A flyer published by the IRS outlining favorable tax treatment available to persons who have been domestically abused. Specifically, it highlights other forms and publications that may be useful to such persons

Publ 3891 A directory of offices that is published the IRS. The directory is intended for tax professionals, and states where taxpayers may file forms based on their location and the type of form.

Publ 3908 A booklet published by the IRS explaining tax issues related to gambling conducted by a Native American tribal government. That is, it explains the government's tax obligations related to its employees and its customers who win money through gaming.

Publ 3909 A booklet published by the IRS explaining the e-file system to businesses. The booklet explains the benefits of filing taxes electronically, and outlines how businesses might go about doing so.

Publ 3932 A flyer published by the IRS summarizing the forms that must be filed to receive the maximum possible tax benefits from casualty losses.

Publ 3935 A report the IRS published in 2006 documenting the results of a study of the customer satisfaction of those non-profit organizations that filed their 990 or 990-EZ forms electronically. The report noted wide levels of satisfaction among these organizations.

Publ 3948 An envelope stuffer published by the IRS advertising favorable tax treatment available to taxpayers who pay education expenses. The stuffer states how taxpayers can learn more information.

Publ 3949 A poster published by the IRS advertising favorable tax treatment available to taxpayers who pay education expenses. The poster states how taxpayers can learn more information.

Publ 3953 A form published by the IRS answering frequently asked questions about tax court proceedings that are used to determine whether or not one is considered an employee for tax purposes. For example, it explains how to file a petition to determine employment status.

Publ 3954 A flyer published by the IRS outlining the eligibility requirements for the earned income tax credit. The form is available in English, Spanish, and Chinese.

Publ 3961 An envelope stuffer published by the IRS advertising the child tax credit. It states what the credit is, how one may claim it, and where more information can be found.

Publ 3966 A flyer published by the IRS outlining tax credits and other favorable tax treatment available to persons with disabilities. Specifically, it highlights other forms and publications that may be useful to disabled persons.

Publ 3995 A flyer published by the IRS highlighting common practices of fraudulent tax avoidance schemes. For example, it states that if an advertisement or salesperson recommends omitting income from one's tax return, it usually means the tax avoidance structure being advertised conducts fraudulent or other illegal activity.

Publ 3998 A brochure published by the IRS outlining various retirement plans available to employees and employers in small businesses. For example, it summarizes the tax benefits of IRAs, SEP IRAs, SIMPLE plans, and other retirement structures.

Publ 4003 A flyer published by the IRS advertising the QuickAlerts message system, which is available to providers of the IRS e-file system.

Publ 4011 A booklet published by the IRS for persons preparing taxes for foreign students and scholars as part of the Volunteer Income Tax Assistance or Tax Counseling for the Elderly programs. It states the income limits of students and scholars from various countries before they cease to be exempt from filing taxes.

Publ 4012 A volunteer guide published by the IRS for persons working for Volunteer Income Tax Assistance or Tax Counseling for the Elderly. It provides guidance on how to prepare tax returns for clients and gives standards of conduct for volunteers.

Publ 4019 A chart published by the IRS outlining how one can give different types of third party authorization and who can exercise it. For example, the chart states that one files Form 2848 to give someone power of attorney for tax purposes.

Publ 4025 A flyer published by the IRS providing the IRS mission statement and its non-discrimination policy for employees, contractors, subcontractors, and grantees.

Publ 4034 A flyer published by the IRS outlining information on its tax-exempt bond division. Specifically, it states the duties of each branch of the tax-exempt bond division, and provides the contact information for key personnel.

Publ 4038 A flyer published by the IRS with a graphic showing where individual and business tax returns from different states are processed.

Publ 4048 A pamphlet published by the IRS outlining how to apply for and receive refunds for late payment penalties through the Electronic Federal Tax Payment System.

Publ 4053 A flyer published by the IRS stating a strict non-discrimination policy applying to its employees, contractors, subcontractors, and grantees.

Publ 4072 A list published by the IRS providing the names and contact information of companies that provide e-filing services for businesses. It is available in English and Spanish.

Publ 4077 A booklet published by the IRS detailing filing requirements and compliance rules for 501(c)3 issuers of tax-exempt bonds. For example, it lists the forms that issuers are required to file each year.

Publ 4078 A booklet published by the IRS detailing filing requirements and compliance rules for issuers of tax-exempt private activity bonds. For example, it lists the forms that issuers are required to file each year.

Publ 4079 A booklet published by the IRS detailing filing requirements and compliance rules for issuers of government bonds. For example, it lists the forms that issuers are required to file each year.

Publ 4109 A flyer published by the IRS outlining information on the Office of Taxpayer Burden Reduction. Specifically, it states the duties of the tax-exempt bond division and provides contact information.

Publ 4117 A flyer published by the IRS outlining the additional child tax credit. It states eligibility requirements and explains how the credit can be claimed.

Publ 4118 A brochure published by the IRS encouraging small business owners to set up retirement plans for their employees. It outlines the benefits of doing so both for the business and for the employees.

Publ 4119-A A pamphlet the IRS published in 2006 advertising a one-day workshop in New York City discussing tax issues applicable to small and medium-sized non-profit organizations.

Publ 4119-B A pamphlet the IRS published in 2006 advertising a one-day workshop in Oklahoma City discussing tax issues applicable to small and medium-sized non-profit organizations.

Publ 4119-C A pamphlet the IRS published in 2006 advertising a one-day workshop in Miami discussing tax issues applicable to small and medium-sized non-profit organizations.

Publ 4126 A flyer published by the IRS advertising the Electronic Federal Tax Payment System aimed at persons and companies who pay taxes on their coupons several times a year.

Publ 4128 A pamphlet published by the IRS outlining some of the tax issues surrounding the loss of one's job. For example, it states that unemployment compensation and severance pay are taxable.

Publ 4131 A flyer published by the IRS advertising the ability to pay taxes online, along with a chart showing various options for doing so.

Publ 4132 A flyer published by the IRS advertising the Electronic Federal Tax Payment System, along with information on how to enroll in and pay taxes in the EFTPS.

Publ 4134 A list published by the IRS of organizations that offer low income taxpayer clinics. It also provides income limits of persons and families who are permitted to use low income taxpayer clinics.

Publ 4141 A flyer published by the IRS highlighting required minimum distribution rules and advising senior citizens to begin to take distributions from their IRAs before reaching the age of 70 1/2 to avoid penalty excise taxes.

Publ 4146 A recruitment brochure outlining how to qualify for jobs at the IRS. Specifically, it states the basic qualification for the GS-5, GS-7, and GS-9 U.S. government pay grades.

Publ 4149 A recruitment brochure advertising career opportunities with the IRS. It highlights training, advancement opportunities, and employee benefits.

Publ 4152 A volunteer guide published by the IRS for persons working for Volunteer Income Tax Assistance or Tax Counseling for the Elderly. It provides guidance on how to prepare tax returns and gives detailed information on tax issues specifically concerning non-resident aliens.

Publ 4156 A flyer published by the IRS outlining tax credits and other favorable tax treatment available to parents and caretakers of children. Specifically, it highlights other forms and publications that may be useful to parents and caretakers.

Publ 4162 A package published by the IRS containing Form 1120, Form 1120-S, Form 1120-F, and Form 7004, along with detailed information on how to file them (and accompanying forms) electronically.

Publ 4163 A guidebook published by the IRS providing detailed information on how e-file providers may more efficiently process tax returns for businesses.

Publ 4164 A guidebook published by the IRS providing detailed information for software developers and other information technology workers on how e-filing works.

Publ 4165 A pamphlet published by the IRS providing general information on how the IRS conducts due process hearings for the collection of back taxes. If a taxpayer appeals a negative finding, Publication 4165 explains the agency's expectations of the appellant and its obligations to him/her.

Publ 4167 A pamphlet published by the IRS providing general information on alternative dispute resolution for disputes of tax payments. Publication 4167 explains how the process works when a taxpayer appeals a negative finding and elects arbitration.

Publ 4169 A document published by the IRS providing general information on how tax professionals (such as accountants) may use the Electronic Federal Tax Payment System. It describes, for example, the different types of the EFTPS and which type is best suited for each type of tax professional.

Publ 4170 A flyer published by the IRS advertising the Electronic Federal Tax Payment System. It states the benefits that the EFTPS offers and how one may find more information.

Publ 4175 A recruitment pamphlet advertising career opportunities with the IRS in the Tax Exempt and Government Entities Division. It highlights training, advancement opportunities, and employee benefits.

Publ 4184 A flyer published by the IRS advertising the Electronic Federal Tax Payment System. It is used at IRS booths where one may sign up for the EFTPS.

Publ 4190 A flyer published by the IRS outlining tax issues for seniors, specifically those who have recently retired or plan to retire soon. For example, it states what kinds of income are taxable in retirement.

Publ 4194 A poster published by the IRS stating the general eligibility requirements for claiming the earned income tax credit, along with the most common errors that lead to denial of that credit. It is available in both English and Spanish.

Publ 4196B A poster published by the IRS stating the most common errors that lead to a denial of the earned income tax credit when it is claimed. The poster is available in both English and Spanish.

Publ 4205 A package published by the IRS containing numerous forms relevant for government entities and non-profit organizations. These forms are provided as a test package for the modernized e-file system. Examples of the forms included are Form 990 and Form 1120-POL.

Publ 4206 A guidebook published by the IRS providing instructions and other information for e-file providers who file tax returns on behalf of government entities and non-profit organizations. Publ 4206 contains information relevant to the e-filing of Form 990, Form 990-EZ, Form 990-PF, Form 1120-POL, and Form 8868.

Publ 4207 A report published by the IRS in 2007 documenting the results of a study of the customer satisfaction of those who filed Form 1065 electronically. The report noted wide levels of satisfaction among respondents.

Publ 4208 A report published by the IRS in 2003 documenting the results of a study of the awareness and usage of the e-filing system. The report noted near universal knowledge of the e-file system and stated that about half of taxpayers had used it.

Publ 4209 A report published by the IRS in 2003 documenting the results of a study of taxpayer attitudes toward the e-file system. The report noted near universal knowledge of the e-file system and stated that most taxpayers (and about 40% of what it called "tech laggards") would consider e-filing, at least with the help of a professional.

Publ 4210 A presentation published by the IRS in 2009 documenting the use of e-filing over the past several years and suggesting ways to encourage 80% of taxpayers to file electronically, a 2007 goal that was not realized.

Publ 4215 A book published by the IRS to help persons use the IRS website for political organization filing and disclosure. It contains a step-by-step guide on how to use each page of the website.

Publ 4216 A guidebook published by the IRS stating the filing requirements for tax exempt political organizations. Specifically, it provides detailed information on how to prepare and file Forms 8871 and 8872.

Publ 4220 A guidebook published by the IRS outlining how to apply for 501(c)3 status. It explains what types of organizations are eligible for the status, what it entails (beyond simple exemption from taxation), and what forms must be filed.

Publ 4221-NC A guidebook published by the IRS giving tax compliance guidance for organizations with 501(c)3 status that are not private foundations or public charities. It states what forms a nonprofit organization must file with the IRS, and how it might lose its tax exempt status.

Publ 4221-PC A guidebook published by the IRS giving tax compliance guidance for public charities with 501(c)3 status. Iit states what forms a public charity must file with the IRS, and how it might lose its tax exempt status.

Publ 4221-PF A guidebook published by the IRS giving tax compliance guidance for private foundations with 501(c)3 status. It states what a private foundation is (a nonprofit organization with most of its funding from a single source and whose primary purpose is to make grants), what forms it must file with the IRS, and how it might lose its tax exempt status.

Publ 4222 A brochure published by the IRS outlining 401(k) plans for smalls businesses. It states the tax benefits of 401(k)s and explains how to set up and manage them.

Publ 4224 A pamphlet published by the IRS outlining the programs available to businesses that accidentally underpay taxes on retirement plans offered to employees. It also summarizes how businesses can correct their own mistakes. These programs are offered by both the IRS and the U.S. Department of Labor.

Publ 4225 A pamphlet published by the IRS outlining the education services that it offers to help underserved communities to file and pay their taxes. It also directs readers where to retrieve further information.

Publ 4227 A pamphlet published by the IRS outlining the appeals process for adverse tax findings. It states that the appeals process is designed to solve tax problems without litigation. It lists the responsibilities of the IRS and of taxpayers.

Publ 4234 A pamphlet published by the IRS advertising the Business Marketing Service for the Small Business and Self-Employed Taxpayer Education and Communication office. It states the duties of the Business Marketing Service (which include assisting small businesses in meeting their tax responsibilities), and provides contact information for key staff members.

Publ 4235 A list published by the IRS of addresses that persons in each state should use for correspondence related to a notice of a federal tax lien.

Publ 4240 A flyer published by the IRS in 2004 advertising new products for the e-filing system. For example, it stated that Form 1120 (Schedule M-3) was available for e-filing for the first time.

Publ 4241 A report published by the IRS in 2005 documenting the results of a study of customer satisfaction with the e-filing system. The report noted widespread satisfaction with the e-filing system.

Publ 4242 A report published by the IRS in 2003 documenting the results of a study of the advertising of the e-filing system. The report noted increased awareness of the advertising, but was inconclusive on whether or not respondents had a positive view of the advertising.

Publ 4245 A pamphlet published by the IRS containing hints for and common mistakes committed in filing Form 2848, which is used to declare power of attorney before the IRS.

Publ 4248 A pamphlet published by the IRS explaining how to use the Electronic Federal Tax Payment System to make federal tax deposits. The pamphlet is sent to companies that the IRS has enrolled in the EFTPS.

Publ 4261 A flyer published by the IRS advising that persons who hold foreign bank accounts may be required to report these accounts to the IRS. According to the law, one must declare foreign bank accounts if one has more than $10,000 in all the accounts.

Publ 4262 A flyer published by the IRS encouraging businesses not to make any changes to a Form W-2 if they discover discrepancies between employees' names and Social Security numbers. In such a case, businesses are supposed to encourage employees to correct discrepancies themselves. Except for size, it is identical to Publication 4262-A.

Publ 4262-A A poster published by the IRS encouraging businesses not to make any changes to a Form W-2 if they discover discrepancies between employees' names and Social Security numbers. In such a case, businesses are supposed to encourage employees to correct discrepancies themselves. Except for size, it is identical to Publication 4262.

Publ 4263-C A flyer published by the IRS advertising publications related to the Electronic Federal Tax Payment System.

Publ 4263-D A flyer published by the IRS advertising publications intended to help small businesses report tips correctly for tax purposes.

Publ 4263-E A flyer published by the IRS advertising workshops available online and in the classroom to help small businesses file and pay their taxes correctly.

Publ 4263-F A flyer published by the IRS advertising tax products and publications intended to help small businesses choose retirement plans.

Publ 4263-G A flyer published by the IRS advertising Spanish-language tax products and publications intended to help small businesses in the Spanish-speaking community. It also contains phone numbers of bilingual tax services offered by the IRS.

Publ 4267 A periodic newsletter published by the IRS containing tax and other government information relevant to Indian nations.

Publ 4267-A A periodic newsletter published by the IRS containing tax and other government information relevant to Indian nations. This newsletter is specifically targeted at Native Americans living in Alaska.

Publ 4267-B A periodic newsletter published by the IRS containing tax and other government information relevant to Indian nations. This newsletter is specifically targeted at Native Americans living in Oklahoma.

Publ 4267-C A periodic newsletter published by the IRS containing tax and other government information relevant to Indian nations. This newsletter is specifically targeted at Native Americans living in the Great Lakes.

Publ 4267-D A periodic newsletter published by the IRS containing tax and other government information relevant to Indian nations. This newsletter is specifically targeted at Native Americans living in Great Plains states.

Publ 4267-E A periodic newsletter published by the IRS containing tax and other government information relevant to Indian nations. This newsletter is specifically targeted at Native Americans living in the Pacific Northwest.

Publ 4267-F A periodic newsletter published by the IRS containing tax and other government information relevant to Indian nations. This newsletter is specifically targeted at Native Americans living in Southwestern states.

Publ 4267-G A periodic newsletter published by the IRS containing tax and other government information relevant to Indian nations. This newsletter is specifically targeted at Native Americans living in Western states.

Publ 4267-H A periodic newsletter published by the IRS containing tax and other government information relevant to Indian nations. This newsletter is specifically targeted at the Navajo Nation.

Publ 4268 A guidebook published by the IRS providing detailed information on FICA taxes and other employment taxes relevant to Indian tribal governments. For example, it states that wages paid for fishing activity may be exempt from FICA taxes if both the employer and the employee belong to the same Indian tribe.

Publ 4269 A list of languages published by the IRS on which one marks the language one speaks or reads. The list contains about 40 language options. It is intended to help the IRS understand how it may help persons who speak various languages.

Publ 4275 A list published by the IRS containing frequently asked questions about how businesses can activate their enrollments in the Electronic Federal Tax Payment System. Among other things, it explains how the EFTPS works and provides key contact information.

Publ 4278 A periodic newsletter published by the IRS containing tax and other information relevant to employers and other sponsors of retirement plans. It is published by the Office of Tax Exempt and Government Entities.

Publ 4278-B A document published by the IRS containing retirement tips for employers and other plan sponsors. For example, it explains rules and limits concerning employer contributions.

Publ 4281 (PR) A pamphlet published by the IRS explaining how residents of Puerto Rico can claim the additional child tax credit. It explains, for example, how children of Puerto Rico residents qualify for the credit.

Publ 4283 A document published by the IRS containing information on how partnerships can file Form 1065 electronically. It lists, for example, which businesses are eligible to e-file and states the benefits of e-filing. It points out that partnerships with more than 100 partners are required to file electronically.

Publ 4284 A checklist published by the IRS regarding the eligibility to operate a SIMPLE IRA plan. For example, it asks whether a company has 100 or fewer employees who earned at least $5,000. If a company has more than this number of qualifying employees, it cannot open a SIMPLE IRA.

Publ 4285 A checklist published by the IRS regarding the eligibility to operate an SEP IRA plan. For example, it asks whether a company's employees have contributed less than the mandated annual maximum to their IRAs. Contributions over this amount qualify as an error in the operation of the SEP IRA plans.

Publ 4286 A checklist published by the IRS regarding the eligibility to operate a SARSEP plan. For example, it asks whether the SARSEP was created before January 1, 1997. SARSEPs cannot be opened legally on or after that date, and opening one qualifies as an error in the operation of the SEP IRA plans.

Publ 4297 A pamphlet published by the IRS advertising the Industry Issue Resolution Program. It states that the program exists for industry associations and some other businesses to submit frequently encountered tax issues for resolution before they actually file their taxes. The pamphlet also states how the IIR Program may be contacted.

Publ 4298 A poster published by the IRS advertising the earned income tax credit. It lists eligibility requirements and benefits in both English and Spanish.

Publ 4299 A guidebook published by the IRS listing the responsibilities of tax preparers who work in the Volunteer Income Tax Assistance and Tax Counseling for the Elderly programs. Such responsibilities include the duty of tax preparers to maintain confidentiality and not to use the information they learn for illegal or unethical purposes. The guidebook states that tax preparers must keep the information that they learn about clients confidential unless required by law not to do so. The document highlights penalties for non-compliance.

Publ 4300 A flyer published by the IRS advertising the e-filing system for Form 1065 and related forms. It also stated that Form T, Form 970, and Form 8886 would be available on the e-filing system for the first time in 2005.

Publ 4301 A flyer published by the IRS containing an article advertising the e-filing system for Form 1065 and related forms. It highlighted the system's convenience, and stated that Form T, Form 970, and Form 8886 would be available on the e-filing system for the first time in 2005.

Publ 4302 A guidebook published by the IRS outlining the rules surrounding a charity's acceptance of a donated vehicle. It states that a charity may accept a donated vehicle if it later sells and uses the earnings to finance its charitable programs.

Publ 4303 A guidebook published by the IRS outlining a donor's rules for the donation of a vehicle to a charity. For example, it states what documentation the donor must have to prove the donation in order to claim a tax deduction.

Publ 4320 A document published by the IRS stating the how one can order or download various publications related to the Electronic Federal Tax Payment System.

Publ 4324 A flowchart published by the IRS outlining the process for the audit of an employee retirement plan. The publication highlights the on-site visit of the company sponsoring the plan in order to review documentation. It also states that the process may require a second visit or further information from the employer.

Publ 4327 A pamphlet published by the IRS outlining how to obtain an individual taxpayer identification number, which a person ineligible for a Social Security number uses to prepare a U.S. tax return. For example, it states that one must file Form W-7 and estimates how long the form takes to be processed.

Publ 4333 A brochure published by the IRS providing an overview of SEP retirement plans for small businesses. Among other things, it outlines the tax advantages of SEP plans, states eligibility requirements, and provides contact information for further help.

Publ 4334 A brochure published by the IRS providing an overview of SIMPLE IRA retirement plans for small businesses. Among other things, it outlines the tax advantages of SIMPLE plans, states how to establish and manage them, and provides contact information for further help.

Publ 4336 A brochure published by the IRS providing an overview of SARSEP retirement plans for small businesses. Among other things, it outlines the tax advantages of SARSEP plans, states how to establish and manage them, and provides contact information for further help.

Publ 4341 A guidebook published by the IRS answering frequently asked questions about classifying workers as employees for purposes of filing Form 941 or Form 944. It includes information on amending previous returns and how to reduce an employer's taxes if workers are misclassified as employees.

Publ 4345 A flyer published by the IRS explaining the taxability of judicial settlements. For example, it states that settlements for medical bills are taxable unless one did not previously deduct medical expenses.

Publ 4346-A A flyer published by the IRS answering frequently asked questions on tax processing. It explains, for example, how long it takes to process paper returns versus how long it takes to process returns filed electronically. The publication is available in English and in several other (primarily Asian) languages.

Publ 4346-B A flyer published by the IRS answering frequently asked questions such as why one must pay taxes, what sort of penalties exist for non-payment, and so forth. The publication is available in English and in several other (primarily Asian) languages.

Publ 4346-C A flyer published by the IRS advertising an automated system that Spanish-speaking persons may call with tax questions, as well as a Spanish help line for those who wish to speak with a person. The publication is available in English and Spanish.

Publ 4346-D A flyer published by the IRS advertising the earned income tax credit and explaining how it may be claimed. The publication is available in English and in several other (primarily Asian) languages.

Publ 4346-E A flyer published by the IRS explaining various types of IRS notices. For example, it states that the IRS may send a notice due to a mathematical error in tax calculation, for underpayment of taxes, or simply to ask for information. The publication is available in English and in several other (primarily Asian) languages.

Publ 4346-F A flyer published by the IRS advertising the Taxpayer Advocate Service. It states what the TAS does and how it may be contacted. The publication is available in English and in several other (primarily Asian) languages.

Publ 4347 A report published by the IRS in 2003 documenting the results of a study on customer satisfaction among taxpayers who filed Form 941 over the telephone. The report noted wide satisfaction with the system.

Publ 4350 A report published by the IRS in 2003 documenting why some taxpayers do not use the e-file system, why some do not use it more frequently, and how those who use it frequently differ in attitude from the others. The report found that many tax preparers at that time simply did not like the e-file system, and those taxpayers who did use it suggested that it be made simpler and less expensive.

Publ 4351 A report published by the IRS in 2003 documenting the results of a study on the demographics of those who use the e-file system. The report noted that, on average, users were in their 50s and tended to be male.

Publ 4386 A flyer published by the IRS describing the difference between a compliance check and an audit. For example, it states that a compliance check ensures that a non-profit organization maintains appropriate records and does not conduct activities that would endanger its tax exempt status, while an audit is a review of the records themselves.

Publ 5500 A postcard published by the IRS that reminds pension funds and other retirement plans to file Form 5500, Form 5500-SF, or Form 5500-EZ on time.

Publ 6149 A report published by the IRS stating the number of tax returns of any type that it expects to be filed between the years 2011 and 2019, divided by state (and including the District of Columbia).

Publ 6186 A report published by the IRS stating the number of tax returns of any type it expects to be filed between the years 2011 and 2018, divided by IRS campus.

Publ 6187 A report published by the IRS stating the number of tax returns of any type it expects to be processed at major tax processing centers between the years 2011 and 2014.

Publ 6292 A report published by the IRS stating the number of tax returns of any type that it expects to be filed between the years 2011 and 2018.

Publ 6388 A pamphlet published by the IRS stating minimum participation standards for employee benefit plans to receive favorable tax treatment. It contains copies of relevant worksheets.

Publ 6389 A pamphlet published by the IRS stating minimum vesting requirements related to defined contribution retirement plans for employees. It contains copies of relevant worksheets.

Publ 6391 A pamphlet published by the IRS stating various requirements related to joint and survivor annuities for employees to receive favorable tax treatment. It contains copies of relevant worksheets.

Publ 6392 A pamphlet published by the IRS stating various requirements for employee benefit plans to receive favorable tax treatment. It contains copies of relevant worksheets.

Publ 6393 A pamphlet published by the IRS stating minimum coverage requirements and non-discrimination laws related to defined contribution retirement plans for employees. It contains copies of relevant worksheets.

Publ 6961 A report published by the IRS stating the number of withholding documents (such as Form W-2) and other information returns that it expects to be filed between the years 2011 and 2019, divided by IRS campus.

Publ 7001 A worksheet published by the IRS intended to help retirement plan trustees determine whether or not a plan meets requirements limiting contributions and benefits paid, which may affect a plan's qualification for preferential tax treatment.

Publ 7002 A worksheet published by the IRS intended to help retirement plan trustees determine whether or not a plan is top-heavy (meaning 60% of beneficiaries are highly-compensated employees) and whether a top-heavy plan interferes with qualification for preferential tax treatment.

Publ 7003 A worksheet published by the IRS intended to help retirement plan trustees determine whether or not issues related to employee leasing interfere with plans' qualification for preferential tax treatment.

Publ 7004 A worksheet published by the IRS intended to help retirement plan trustees and others determine whether or not their retirement plans fulfill rules governing required distributions. Most retirement plans require distributions after a beneficiary reaches a certain age. Otherwise, the retiree must pay penalties.

Publ 7005 A worksheet published by the IRS to help affiliated service groups (which are groups of two or more related employers sharing a retirement plan for employees) determine whether or not their retirement plans qualify for preferential tax treatment.

Publ 7334 A worksheet published by the IRS intended to help determine whether employee and matching contributions to a retirement plan qualify for preferential tax treatment.

Publ 7335 A worksheet published by the IRS intended to help determine whether a 401(k) qualifies for preferential tax treatment.

Publ 8160-E A pamphlet published by the IRS promoting the e-file system. It states the advantages of e-filing (such as faster tax refunds) and informs readers how to find more information about how to e-file.

Publc 3685 A flyer published by the IRS to recruit applicants to become special agents in its Criminal Investigation division and Internal Revenue division. It features a quote and the picture of a special agent named Deborah. See also: Marketing.

Public 1. Describing anything available to the population at large. For example, a publicly-traded company may be owned and traded by anyone with the money to buy shares. **2.** Describing anything owned or administered by a government. For example, a municipality owns and maintains a public park.

Public Automated Routing System A computerized system that increases the speed at which orders are executed and reported to the exchange. It is used on the CBOE.

Public Book of Order A list of all buy and sell orders for a certain security that were placed by members of the public. The public book contains orders that have not yet been filled. The orders, however, are not public; only the book keeper has access to the details of most orders. Market makers and specialists have access only to the highest and lowest orders in order to facilitate trade.

Public Company Accounting Oversight Board A regulatory body in the United States that oversees auditors and auditing firms. The PCAOB has the authority to register and regulate public accounting firms and to investigate them to ensure that they comply with applicable laws. The PCAOB consists of five members appointed by the SEC, which oversees its activities. Only two members of the PCAOB may be current or former CPAs. It is a private organization created by the U.S. government in the Sarbanes-Oxley Act.

Public Debt The total of all bonds and other debt owed by a government. Most of the time, the national debt comes from bonds and other debt securities, but some countries in the developing world borrow directly from international institutions (such as the World Bank). The national debt may be internal, that is, owed to bondholders and banks within the country, or external, that is, owed to foreign governments, institutions, and/or individuals. In the United States, paying the interest on the national debt is a major part of the federal budget. See also: Deficit.

Public Distribution Any offering of stock by a publicly-traded company to individual investors. If it is the first such offering, it is called an initial public offering (IPO); otherwise, it is a follow-on offering. Companies make public distributions in order to raise financing for expanded operations, or because they have become cash poor and need to finance their current operations. There is a sales fee attached to public distributions that the issuer includes in the offering price.

Public Domain The arena of any work that may not be owned by any individual. Any person may distribute or profit from a work in the public domain. For example, because William Shakespeare has been dead for several centuries, anyone may publish and sell copies of his plays without permission from anyone. How long it takes for a work to enter the public domain depends on the laws in force in the jurisdiction where the work originated.

Public Elevator A grain elevator in which grain producers may store excess grain. Since one producer's grain is not differentiated from another producer's, grain may (and probably will) be mixed together. Some public elevators are recognized as an appropriate storage facility for the underlying assets on futures contracts, but they must be certified as such by an exchange.

Public Housing Authority Bond A municipal bond issued by a local agency that is used to finance the construction or repair of low-income housing projects. Because the U.S. government wishes to reduce homelessness, these bonds are guaranteed by the federal government and their interest is exempt from federal taxation.

Public Interest Accounting Accounting services provided free of charge to charities and other nonprofit organizations that cannot afford them. Accountants for the Public Interest are a prominent group providing these services.

Public Law Legislation having to do with the relationship individuals have with their government. Examples of public laws are criminal codes, laws creating social safety net programs, and statutes governing lawsuits. Public law contrasts with private law, which has to do with relations between individuals without government intervention.

Public Limited Company A primarily British term for a publicly-traded company. The term derives from the facts that the company issues shares that may be bought and sold by the general public and all shareholders have limited liability.

Public Limited Partnership A limited partnership with no limit on the number of partners allowed. A public limited partnership is registered with the SEC and is available to be traded through brokers and/or dealers. A public limited partnership combines some of the characteristics of a limited partnership and a publicly-traded company.

Public Offering An issue of stock by a publicly-traded company. A company makes a public offering through underwriters, who have the responsibility to place the offering with individual and institutional investors. Companies make public offerings in order to raise financing for expanded operations; the offerings themselves give investors a portion of ownership in the company issuing them. The first public offering of a company is called an initial public offering, and marks the point when a company ceases to be privately held and becomes publicly traded.

Public Offering Price The first price for which a company offers to sell stock in itself when it makes a new issue, whether or not that is its first new issue. For example, if a publicly-traded company is issuing new stock, it may set the public offering price at $10 per share for primary trading. Investing at the public offering price can be a risky investment, because one does not know how much demand will exist for the stock after its initial offering; the risk comes from the uncertainty of the stock's resale value. However, it is usually less risky if the company has made public offerings before. See also: Initial public offering.

Public Official Bond A bond or insurance policy covering losses resulting from the negligence or mistakes made by a bureaucrat or other public official. For example, if a bureaucrat mismanages a government-owned bank account such that there are significant losses, the public official bond will compensate the government. See also: Public employees blanket bond.

Public Ownership 1. The ownership of a company represented by a stock that is traded on the open market, either on a stock exchange or on the over-the-counter market. Individual and institutional shareholders each have a portion of this public ownership, in proportion to the amount of stock they own as a percentage of all outstanding stock. Thus, shareholders have final say in all decisions made by the company and its managers, especially through its annual shareholders' meeting. Public ownership allows a company to have greater access to financing than other companies, as they have the ability to issue more stock. However, these companies are subject to greater regulation: for example, they must file 10-K reports with the SEC on their earnings, and they are more likely to be subject to corporate taxes. **2.** Ownership of a company by the government. Command economies have a large number of companies under public ownership, but even free market economies have some degree of government involvement in this form. Many countries have public ownership of one or more companies that produce their main exports. For example, many oil-rich states have oil companies under partial or total public ownership.

Public Power Bond A bond issued by a publicly-owned utility company. Because utility companies have very large capital expenditures (they must build expensive infrastructure to provide their services), they use public power bonds to finance many of their projects. Because they are publicly-owned, interest is usually tax exempt at the federal level.

Public Sector Borrowing Requirement The former name for the deficit in the United Kingdom budget. It is financed with government debt, usually through gilts. Its name has been changed to the public sector net cash requirement.

Public Sector Deficit A situation in which government spending of money exceeds taxes collected. That is, a public sector deficit occurs when a government spends more than it receives in a given period of time, usually a year. The deficit adds to the government's debt, and, therefore, many analysts believe that public sector deficits are unsustainable over the long-term. See also: Surplus.

Public Securities Association Standard Prepayment Model One of several ways to calculate changes to the prepayment rate on a mortgage-backed security. The PSA model assumes that the prepayment rate will increase 0.2% per month for the first 30 months of the life of the MBS. Obviously, this will change the expected yield of the security. If prepayment rate changes at a different pace, the PSA model expresses this as a percentage of the 0.2%. For example, a change of 0.2% is 100%, while a change of 0.4% is 200%.

Public Securities Offering 1. An issue of stock by a publicly-traded company. A company makes an offering through underwriters, who have the responsibility to place the offering with individual and institutional investors. Companies make offerings in order to raise financing for expanded operations, though occasionally they make offerings because they have become cash poor and need assistance to maintain current operations. The offerings themselves give investors a portion of ownership in the company issuing them. The first public offering a company is called an initial public offering, and marks the point when a company ceases to be privately held and becomes publicly traded. **2.** An issue of bonds. A company or government makes an offering through underwriters, who have the responsibility to place the offering with individual and institutional investors. Companies and governments make offerings in order to raise financing for expanded operations, though occasionally they make offerings because they have become cash poor and need

assistance to maintain current operations. The bonds themselves represent debt that the company or government owes the investor.

Public Unit Account An account, especially at a bank, containing funds provided by a government. The government could be national or local. The government places funds into the public unit account when it receives revenue from taxation, borrowing, or another source and it withdraws when it spends public money. In other words, a public unit account is the government's bank account.

Public Utility Holding Company Act of 1935 Legislation in the United States limiting the activities of utility companies such as electric companies. Specifically, the Public Utility Holding Company Act requires utility companies to restrict their businesses to either a single state or to a small, manageable geographic area in order to be subject to state regulations. It also requires them to obtain approval from the SEC in order to engage in business unrelated to the utility industry. The Act was passed in response to near monopolistic activities on the part of utility companies. Most of its provisions were repealed in the Public Utility Holding Company Act of 2005.

Public Utility Holding Company Act of 2005 Legislation in the United States that largely deregulated multi-state utility companies in the United States. It provides subsidies to electric companies to enable them to operate in more than one state. The Act largely repealed the Wheeler-Rayburn Act.

Public Warehouse A place used for storing inventory for sale in the future, where the warehouse is managed by the same company that owns it.

Publication 1 A form published by the IRS stating the rights U.S. taxpayers have. For example, Publication 1 explains the tax refund and appeals processes, how to contact the Taxpayer Advocate Service, the circumstances under which tax penalties can be waived, and so forth.

Publication 1075 A set of guidelines published by the IRS outlining how federal, state, and local agencies should protect the security and confidentiality of tax information with which they are entrusted.

Publication 1084 A handbook published by the IRS outlining the policies and procedures for the Volunteer Income Tax Assistance and Tax Counseling for the Elderly programs. In both of these programs, volunteers provide advice and tax preparation for vulnerable and distressed populations.

Publication 1101 A handbook published by the IRS stating the eligibility criteria and application procedures of grants that non-profit organizations use to finance the Tax Counseling for the Elderly program.

Publication 1113-A A flier published by the IRS that one may post to publicize the Voluntary Income Tax Assistance and Tax Counseling for the Elderly programs.

Publication 1114 A brochure published by the IRS providing information on the Tax Counseling for the Elderly program.

Publication 1141 An instruction book published by the IRS providing detailed instructions for preparing and filing (both electronically and by mail) substitute Forms W-2 and W-3.

Publication 1153 A brief form published by the IRS stating how a taxpayer may apply for the subordination of a tax lien.

Publication 1167 An instruction book published by the IRS providing detailed instructions for preparing and filing (both electronically and by mail) substitute various substitute forms.

Publication 1179 An instruction book published by the IRS providing detailed instructions for preparing and filing (both electronically and by mail) substitute Form 1096, Form 1098, Form 1099, Form 5498, and Form W-2G.

Publication 1187 An instruction book published by the IRS providing detailed instructions for preparing and filing (both electronically and by mail) Form 1042-S.

Publication 1212 A form published by the IRS explaining tax matters related to original issue discount bonds. The publication contains information relevant to both bondholders and to brokers and dealers.

Publication 1220 An instruction book published by the IRS providing detailed instructions for preparing and electronically filing Form 1096, Form 1098, Form 1099, Form 3921, Form 5498, Form 8935, and Form W-2G.

Publication 1223 An instruction book published by the IRS providing detailed instructions for preparing and filing (both electronically and by mail) substitute Form W-2c and Form W-3c.

Publication 1235 A flier published by the IRS outlining eligibility for receiving an advance tax refund for the earned income credit. The publication is attached to Form W-5, which is used to apply for the refund.

Publication 1239 An instruction book published by the IRS providing detailed instructions for preparing and electronically filing Form 8027, which employers file to report their employees' income from tips.

Publication 1244 A form published by the IRS stating the instructions that an employee must follow in keeping records of his/her tips and reporting those tips to his/her employer. It also contains Form 4070 and Form 4070-A, which are used for these record-keeping and reporting purposes.

Publication 1244 (PR) A form published by the IRS stating the instructions that an employee in Puerto Rico must follow in keeping records of his/her tips and reporting those tips to his/her employer. It also contains Form 4070 (PR) and Form 4070-A (PR), which are used for these record-keeping and reporting purposes.

Publication 1245 An instruction book published by the IRS providing detailed instructions for preparing and filing (both electronically and magnetically) Form W-4.

Publication 1278 A flier published by the IRS advertising online classes and resources for persons who wish to become certified tax volunteers.

Publication 1281 An instruction book published by the IRS providing detailed instructions for paying backup withholding due to missing or incorrect names or tax identification numbers.

Publication 1299 A study the IRS published consisting of a number of papers summarizing and analyzing tax statistics for 2006.

Publication 15 A form published by the IRS explaining to employers the taxes they must withhold from employees as well as which forms must be filed on which dates. The form also explains who does and who does not qualify as an employee under U.S. law. Publication 15 is also called Circular E.

Publication 1542 A form published by the IRS containing information on acceptable per diem rates for business travel in the continental United States. A self-employed person is permitted to write off the per diem rate for each day he/she travels on business. The rate varies based on the cost of living of an area.

Publication 1544 A form published by the IRS explaining how a business should report cash payments in excess of $10,000. These payments are documented on Form 8300 in order to discourage potential money laundering.

Publication 1546 A detailed pamphlet published by the IRS outlining the services offered by the Taxpayer Advocate Service. For example, it states that the TAS will assign an individual advocate to help each client as he/she attempts to deal with an audit. The publication is directed toward the general public.

Publication 1546-EZ A brief pamphlet published by the IRS outlining the services offered by the Taxpayer Advocate Service. For example, it states that the TAS will assign an individual advocate to help each client as he/she attempts to deal with an audit. The publication is directed toward the general public.

Publication 1546-P A pamphlet published by the IRS outlining the services offered by the Taxpayer Advocate Service. For example, it states that the TAS will assign an individual advocate to help each client as he/she attempts to deal with an audit. The publication is directed toward tax practitioners such as accountants.

Publication 1577 A flyer published by the IRS explaining the information and forms that an individual needs to file for federal financial aid for education. See also: FAFSA.

Publication 1582 A list published by the IRS of companies allowing one to electronically file Form 1097-BTC, Form 1098, Form 1099 (or any form related to 1099), Form 3921, Form 3922, Form 5498, Form W-2G, and/or Form 1042-S.

Publication 1586 A form published by the IRS outlining how one can avoid penalties for incorrectly entering a taxpayer's name, Social Security number, or taxpayer identification number, or for leaving these spaces blank altogether. It also states the penalties that normally apply.

Publication 1588 A flyer published by the IRS advertising Publication 4460, which is used to help taxpayers find the retirement plan that best meets their needs.

Publication 15-A A form published by the IRS clarifying the responsibilities employers have for withholding taxes from employees. It helps delineate the difference between an employee and an independent contractor, and contains various rules on withholding for wages and certain benefits.

Publication 15-B A form published by the IRS clarifying the responsibilities employers have for withholding taxes from employees. Specifically, Publication 15-B deals with tax treatment of fringe benefits.

Publication 15-T A form published by the IRS stating certain rules of withholding for non-resident aliens, as well as rules for advance payment of the earned income tax credit.

Publication 1600 A form published by the IRS outlining how a taxpayer can receive copies of tax returns and other financial statements from the IRS if the originals were lost in a natural disaster. It also provides a list of IRS forms that may be useful to a person in such a situation.

Publication 1620 A flyer published by the IRS advertising the earned income tax credit.

Publication 1635 A booklet published by the IRS stating how employer identification numbers are used. It states the circumstances under which various types of businesses (including sole proprietorships, C corporations, and partnerships) are required to receive EINs.

Publication 1660 A pamphlet published by the IRS outlining the rights that taxpayers have to appeal adverse decisions the IRS makes regarding tax collection.

Publication 1693 A newsletter published by the IRS for employers. It provides information related to Social Security taxes and retirement plans.

Publication 17 A form published by the IRS explaining how individuals can file their taxes. Among other things, it explains how to report income, take deductions and apply credits.

Publication 1771 A booklet published by the IRS outlining tax law related to recordkeeping of charitable contributions and disclosure of contributions made. In general, contributors are required to maintain records of contributions for which they claim a tax deduction, and tax exempt charitable organizations must disclose goods and services they provide to donors who contribute more than $75.

Publication 1779 A form published by the IRS outlining the differences between an employee and an independent contractor. For example, it states that the opportunity for profit or loss is indicative of an independent contractor, while the offering of health insurance is indicative of an employee. See also: Form SS-8.

Publication 1819 A flyer published by the IRS outlining tax issues related to divorced persons, non-custodial parents, separated persons, and parents who never married. For example, the publication states that if a divorced couple files a joint return, the IRS will not divide the tax refund into two checks. Rather, it mails one check to the address on file.

Publication 1828 A booklet published by the IRS outlining the tax laws applied to churches, other religious organizations, and some clergy. While religious organizations ordinarily are not subject to taxation, they still must fulfill certain requirements to acquire and retain tax exempt status. These organizations may be subject to taxation on unrelated business income.

Publication 1854 A form published by the IRS stating the instructions for filing Form 433-A, which is used to collect information on the income and assets of self-employed persons and waged (though not salaried) employees who owe back taxes and/or penalties.

Publication 1915 A booklet published by the IRS stating how individual taxpayer identification numbers are used. Individual taxpayer identification numbers are issued to individual taxpayers such as non-resident aliens who are not eligible to receive Social Security numbers.

Publication 1932 A flyer published by the IRS stating the instructions for filing federal tax deposits correctly. See also: Publication 15 (Circular E).

Publication 1971 A flyer published by the IRS advertising the Free File software system, which allows taxpayers to file their taxes online at no cost. It is available in both English and Spanish.

Publication 1976 A form published by the IRS stating the requirements for a business's eligibility for relief from employment taxes. It is sent to businesses that the IRS believes may have treated certain employees as independent contractors.

Publication 1-TEB A form published by the IRS stating the rights U.S. taxpayers have with regard to tax exempt bonds. The IRS periodically may examine returns to ensure that the interest paid really is tax exempt. Publication 1-TEB explains how this process works and what recourse a taxpayer has.

Publication 2043 (EN/SP) A flyer published by the IRS stating the estimated dates on which tax refunds will be sent based on the dates tax returns are filed. The publication is available in English and Spanish.

Publication 2053-A A form published by the IRS stating several ways that a taxpayer can receive assistance with filing taxes and order tax products. The publication states where information is available online, over the telephone, and at libraries, grocery stores, and other places.

Publication 2071 A flyer published by the IRS advertising seasonal work opportunities for processing tax returns.

Publication 2101 A bookmark published by the IRS advertising the benefits of filing taxes electronically. Publication 2101 is available in both English and Spanish.

Publication 2104 A form published by the IRS containing the first volume of the National Taxpayer Advocate's annual report to Congress for 2010. The full report is contained in Publication 2104-C. See also: Publication 2104-B.

Publication 2104-B A form published by the IRS containing the second volume of the National Taxpayer Advocate's annual report to Congress for 2010. The full report is contained in Publication 2104-C. See also: Publication 2104.

Publication 2104-C A form published by the IRS containing the National Taxpayer Advocate's annual report to Congress for 2010. It includes information such as the timeliness of IRS response to requests and how well it administrates its programs. The publication also includes legislative recommendations to Congress.

Publication 2105 A flyer published by the IRS stating some constitutional and legal provisions requiring the payment of taxes. It states the sources of U.S. government income and what it spends on outlays. It summarizes and responds to common myths used to perpetuate the notion that taxation is unconstitutional or voluntary.

Publication 2108 A form published by the IRS stating the instructions for the Taxpayer Identification Number matching program available to payers of 1099 income.

Publication 2108-A A form published by the IRS stating the instructions for the Taxpayer Identification Number matching program available online to payers of 1099 income.

Publication 213 A form published by the IRS reminding individuals that they may have too much or too little withheld from their paychecks if they have married or divorced or have had a significant change in income or some other major change since they last filed a W-4.

Publication 2181 A flyer published by the IRS advertising the resources that it makes available to classroom teachers to help their students understand how taxes work.

Publication 2188 A form published by the IRS allowing a retiree or a survivor or an employee of a retiree to request that the IRS determine how much of an annuity is taxable. The response of the IRS to such a request is an official ruling. Therefore, the filer is charged a fee.

Publication 2193 A flyer published by the IRS containing information about what it regards as "too good to be true" trusts. Specifically, it points to warning signs that a trust may be fraudulent. For example, if a trust's office lacks a physical address, the IRS cautions against using it in an attempt to avoid taxes.

Publication 2194 A package published by the IRS containing forms, instructions, and other resources for individuals describing relief available to them followings losses from floods or other natural disasters.

Publication 2194-B A package published by the IRS containing forms, instructions, and other resources for businesses describing relief available to them followings losses from floods or other natural disasters.

Publication 225 A form published by the IRS explaining special tax rules applying to farmers. For example, Publication 225 states the rules for the depreciation of livestock.

Publication 3 A form published by the IRS explaining special tax rules applying to members of the U.S. Armed Forces. Certain income earned by military personnel (such as combat pay) is subject to reduced (or eliminated) taxation. Publication 3 states how these rules work.

Publication 334 A form published by the IRS explaining the special tax rules applying to owners of small businesses and some other self-employed persons. For example, Publication 334 states the rules for calculating gross profit. It is intended for persons who file Schedule C or Schedule C-EZ.

Publication 3402 A form published by the IRS explaining taxation rules for limited liability companies. Because the federal government does not recognize LLCs (which are organized at the state level only), some LLCs may be taxed as partnerships, some as corporations, and others may be ignored entirely.

Publication 3920 A form published by the IRS explaining how one can apply for and receive tax forgiveness if one is the victim of a terrorist attack.

Publication 393 A form published by the IRS providing instructions on how to file and utilize the W-2 and W-3 forms.

Publication 3991 A form published by the IRS explaining tax changes that occurred under the Job Creation and Worker Assistance Act of 2002. Among other things, the publication explains more favorable tax treatment of loss carrybacks and new deductions for education expenses.

Publication 4387 A document published by the IRS in 2004 reporting the results of a customer satisfaction survey of estates and trusts that filed Form 1041 electronically. The report found extremely high levels of satisfaction among users. The vast majority of respondents stated that they would recommend e-filing Form 1041 to others.

Publication 4389 A flyer published by the IRS advertising various services available online. For example, the publication highlights the fact that one can obtain an employer identification number or check the status of one's tax refund online.

Publication 4391 An envelope stuffer published by the IRS containing a request for information from volunteers or potential volunteers in the Tax Counseling for the Elderly and similar programs. The stuffer states that information obtained may be used for contact, organizational, or other purposes. It also briefly cites the law under which the IRS has a legal right to ask for such information.

Publication 4393 A flyer published by the IRS advertising the ITIN acceptance agent program. An acceptance agent is a person or company that can assist non-U.S. citizens and residents in obtaining an individual tax identification number, which is necessary to file U.S. taxes if one does not have a Social Security number or employer identification number. The publication contains a return envelope with which one may apply to become an acceptance agent. It is published in both English and Spanish.

Publication 4396-A A guidebook published by the IRS providing detailed information about its tax preparation programs, notably Voluntary Income Tax Assistance and Tax Counseling for the Elderly. It outlines policies and procedures and states how volunteers and organizations should conduct themselves. The guidebook is aimed at private organizations partnering with the IRS to administer these programs.

Publication 4403 A flyer published by the IRS advising of updates in 2010 for the Link and Learn program, which is an online course that the IRS uses to train volunteers in the Voluntary Income Tax Assistance and Tax Counseling for the Elderly programs.

Publication 4407 A pamphlet published by the IRS advertising the SARSEP retirement plan. It outlines eligibility requirements, gives the names of more detailed publications, and provides contact information for further help.

Publication 4416 A document published by the IRS in 2004 reporting the results of a customer satisfaction survey of S-corporations that filed Form 1120-S electronically. The report found extremely high levels of satisfaction among users. The vast majority of respondents stated that they would recommend e-filing Form 1120-S to others.

Publication 4417 A document published by the IRS in 2009 reporting the results of a customer satisfaction survey of corporations that filed Form 1120 and Form 1120-S electronically. The report found extremely high levels of satisfaction among users. The vast majority of respondents stated that they would recommend e-filing to others.

Publication 4418 A pamphlet published by the IRS outlining how the IRS may levy one's Social Security benefits to pay back taxes. For example, the publication

explains that the IRS may manually levy benefits up to any amount, while it may only automatically levy 15% of benefits.

Publication 4419 A flyer published by the IRS providing a brief explanation of how to request a transcript of a previously filed tax return on Form 4506-T, which is used to verify income for purposes of obtaining a mortgage.

Publication 4425 A presentation published by the IRS in 2011 reporting on those who filed Form 940 in processing year 2010. It noted that more than a million of these returns were filed, almost a quarter of them electronically.

Publication 4431 A document published by the IRS in 2004 reporting the results of a survey of customers who file their tax returns electronically regularly and those who use v-code regularly. The study found that both groups agree e-filing is easier than v-coding.

Publication 4436 A guidebook published by the IRS stating the instructions for preparing substitutes for Form 941, Form 941 (Schedule B), and Form 941 (Schedule R). It also provides information for preparing substitutes for the equivalents of these forms in Puerto Rico and other U.S. territories.

Publication 4437 A newsletter published by the IRS providing information for tax preparers. It answers frequently asked questions, explains new regulations, and gives hints for filing returns for preparers' clients.

Publication 4445-B A flyer published by the IRS outlining which types of income taxpayers should report. The publication states that, in general, all payment of services rendered in a year should be reported on one's tax return.

Publication 4445-D A list of all IRS forms that are available in Spanish. The list is published by the IRS in both English and Spanish.

Publication 4445-E A flyer published by the IRS outlining the differences between an employee, a self-employed person, and an independent contractor. It highlights differing tax responsibilities between the three groups.

Publication 4445-F A flyer published by the IRS outlining why people should pay taxes. It highlights that the law requires payment of taxes and that non-payment can result in serious penalties. It is published in both English and Spanish.

Publication 4445-G A pamphlet published by the IRS providing tips on how to find and select a tax preparer. For example, it recommends that taxpayers check with the Better Business Bureau for a potential preparer's history. It is published in both English and Spanish.

Publication 4446 A flyer published by the IRS in 2005 providing information that politicians can relate to constituents about tax law. For example, it announced new criteria for claiming the earned income tax credit and provided contact information for the Taxpayer Advocate Service.

Publication 4449 A flyer published by the IRS announcing tax information relevant to non-custodial parents. For example, it states the circumstances under which the non-custodial parent is eligible for the child tax credit and is eligible to claim children as dependents.

Publication 4451 A document published by the IRS reporting the results of a study on awareness of communications about the e-filing system before an advertising campaign was launched. The report was used as a baseline to track the success of the campaign.

Publication 4452 A pamphlet published by the IRS advertising the e-filing system for filers of Form 1120 and 1120-S. It highlights, for example, the benefits of e-filing and explains which organizations can utilize the system.

Publication 4453 A pamphlet published by the IRS advertising the e-filing system for filers of the Form 990 series. It highlights, for example, the benefits of e-filing and explains which organizations can utilize the system.

Publication 4454 A pamphlet published by the IRS outlining the rights that Americans have when paying their taxes. Specifically, it states that discrimination on the basis of race, gender, or national origin is prohibited.

Publication 4456 A document published by the IRS reporting the results of a study on awareness of communications about the e-filing system. The report noted about 70% knowledge among various groups.

Publication 4460 A document published by the IRS outlining major retirement plans. It provides the name of other publications that might be helpful in creating, maintaining, and correcting the management of a retirement plan.

Publication 4463 A flyer published by the IRS advertising the Electronic Federal Tax Payment System. It particularly highlights the convenience of the EFTPS so users can file on time to avoid tax penalties.

Publication 4465-A A pamphlet published by the IRS containing tips on how IRS contractors should protect sensitive information. For example, it encourages contractors not to leave clients' income information on their desk where unauthorized persons might see it.

Publication 4471 A pamphlet published by the IRS advising tax preparers to practice due diligence when claiming the earned income tax credit for their clients. The pamphlet also advertises training modules for due diligence responsibilities.

Publication 4476 A pamphlet published by the IRS advertising the discontinuation of the telefile system and advising taxpayers to use the e-file system instead.

Publication 4481 A pamphlet published by the IRS outlining the rights that Americans have when paying their taxes through the Volunteer Income Tax Assistance or Tax Counseling for the Elderly programs. Specifically, it states that discrimination on the basis of race, gender, or national origin is prohibited.

Publication 4482 A pamphlet published by the IRS outlining common mistakes participants make on their 403(b) plans. For example, the pamphlet highlights the circumstances under which rollovers and distributions are permissible.

Publication 4483 A pamphlet published by the IRS outlining common mistakes that employers make when creating or managing a 403(b) plan. Some mistakes, such as failing to report withholdings on Form 941, may endanger the status of the plan.

Publication 4484 A pamphlet published by the IRS outlining retirement plans available to employees of tax-exempt entities such as churches or charities. It provides a list of the retirement plans available, along with basic information about their benefits. It also provides a list of other IRS publications that may be helpful.

Publication 4485 A guidebook published by the IRS providing information on state FUTA credits, which are used in a system by which states and the IRS jointly check employers for discrepancies in the filing and paying of unemployment benefits.

Publication 4486 A report published by the IRS in 2005 documenting the results of a study of the awareness of the e-file system. The report noted extremely wide knowledge of the system.

Publication 4488 A report published by the IRS in 2005 documenting the results of a study of the difficulty that committed users experienced with the V-coder system. The report noted that most users could use the system easily.

Publication 4489 A report published by the IRS in 2005 documenting the results of a study of the awareness of a communication campaign for the e-filing system among persons who use the system heavily. The report noted wide knowledge of the campaign.

Publication 4491 An instruction book published by the IRS showing volunteers in the VITA and TCE programs how to prepare and file taxes. It includes basic information such as how to calculate adjusted gross income and how to claim the standard deduction, as well as more complex matters such as important tax law changes each year.

Publication 4491-W A workbook published by the IRS containing problems that volunteers in the VITA and TCE programs must solve as part of their training. It supplements Publication 4491, which is the primary instruction book for these programs.

Publication 4491-X An instruction book published by the IRS correcting errors or outdated information in Publication 4491, which is the primarily instruction book for volunteers in the VITA and TCE programs.

Publication 4492 A form published by the IRS outlining tax benefits available to victims of Hurricanes Katrina, Rita, and Wilma in 2005. For example, the publication announces extended deadlines for filing taxes for victims, and provides an overview of casualty and other losses that are deductible.

Publication 4492-A A form published by the IRS outlining tax benefits available to victims of severe storms in Kansas on May 4, 2007. For example, the publication provides an overview of casualty and other losses that are tax deductible.

Publication 4492-B A form published by the IRS outlining tax benefits available to victims of severe storms in various American Midwestern states during the summer of 2008. For example, the publication provides an overview of casualty and other losses that are tax deductible.

Publication 4505 A package published by the IRS containing e-filing tests for Form 1065 and Form 1065-B. E-file software designers and others must pass these tests before being permitted to e-file for clients.

Publication 4512 A flyer published by the IRS advertising the Volunteer Income Tax Assistance program and highlighting its usefulness in completing one's taxes. It includes a phone number one can contact for more information on sites where VITA is offered.

Publication 4512-A A flyer published by the IRS stating how one can obtain copies of tax returns filed in previous years. It also states how one can obtain the Social Security numbers of oneself and one's dependents.

Publication 4512-B A flyer published by the IRS stating how one can obtain a copy of one's Form W-2. It is intended to ensure that taxpayers can file their tax returns on time.

Publication 4512-C A flyer published by the IRS providing guidance on whether or not one can claim a tax deduction for a casualty loss. It states the steps one must take to determine whether the loss is deductible and, if so, how much the tax deduction will be.

Publication 4513 A flyer published by the IRS outlining withholding rules for military pensions. For example, it states that retired pay is taxable.

Publication 4515 A pamphlet published by the IRS advertising Form 944, which some small employers may use to report and pay FICA taxes and similar taxes once per year instead of quarterly.

Publication 4521 A brochure published by the IRS advertising the e-filing system. It lists some forms that may be filed electronically, and indicates some differences between the electronic and paper versions of these forms.

Publication 4523 A flyer published by the IRS warning about phishing, which is a scam in which a person solicits personal information online under false pretenses. The flyer particularly warns about phishing scams in which the scammer poses as the IRS. It suggests what to do and who to contact if one believes one is a victim of phishing.

Publication 4524 A flyer published by the IRS outlining various steps one can take to avoid identity theft. For example, it recommends checking credit card statements.

Publication 4525 A report published by the IRS in 2006 outlining all of the taxpayer assistance services the IRS offers and providing a preliminary account of taxpayer perceptions on services offered and needed. It was issued as part of a broader effort to improve taxpayer assistance services.

Publication 4527 A brochure published by the IRS advertising the Pre-Filing Agreement program, under which taxpayers can request rulings by the IRS on tax issues before they file their tax returns. It notes that audits go more quickly under the program and that the program intends to develop more cooperative relations between the IRS and taxpayers.

Publication 4528 A document published by the IRS explaining administrative wrongful levy claims, which are requests for the return of property seized in a levy if the taxpayer did not in fact own the property. In other words, one makes an administrative wrongful levy claim if the IRS seized one's property believing that it belonged to a delinquent taxpayer.

Publication 4530 A brochure published by the IRS explaining the differences between a Roth 401(k), a Roth IRA, and a traditional IRA. It notes, for example, differing income limits, maximum contributions, and required distributions.

Publication 4531 A checklist published by the IRS providing a non-comprehensive list of management tips for 401(k)s. For example, it recommends updating a plan every few years to keep abreast of law changes, and states that all employees eligible for a 401(k) should be identified.

Publication 4535 A pamphlet published by the IRS explaining what identity theft is, as well as what to do and who to contact if one is a victim. It is published in both English and Spanish.

Publication 4537 A pamphlet published by the IRS advising tax preparers to perform due diligence in checking whether their clients are eligible for the earned income tax credit. It also provides resources to learn how to perform this due diligence.

Publication 4539 A pamphlet published by the IRS advertising the fast track settlement system, which is how some large- and medium-sized businesses can resolve tax issues quickly. It states what businesses can use the system, how one can start the process, and what appeal rights one has.

Publication 4541 A pamphlet published by the IRS informing financial institutions about the options that taxpayers have for using direct deposit for tax refunds. It states that taxpayers may deposit refunds in multiple accounts, or may use them to buy up to $5,000 in series I savings bonds.

Publication 4542 A pamphlet published by the IRS informing IRS partners about the options that taxpayers have for their tax refunds. It states, for example, how long it takes for direct deposits or paper checks to be received.

Publication 4543 A pamphlet published by the IRS in 2007 advertising online seminars for self-employed persons and small businesses. It provides the dates and times of the seminars and states how one can find more information.

Publication 4546 A checklist published by the IRS providing a non-comprehensive list of management tips for 403(b)s. For example, it states that only 501(c)3 organizations may offer 403(b) plans, and outlines the rules for contributions and distributions required of these plans.

Publication 4547 A pamphlet published by the IRS outlining how to create and manage a 403(b) plan. It also includes information on how to rectify mistakes that, if left alone, could endanger the tax benefits of the plan.

Publication 4554 A flyer published by the IRS advertising the fact that the federal government is required to refund excise taxes paid on long-distance services between March 2003 and July 2006. It states that one may claim the refund by filing Form 8913. It is published in both English and Spanish.

Publication 4555 An instruction book published by the IRS to help instructors train volunteers for the VITA and TCE programs how to prepare and file taxes. It provides detailed information on how to fill out tax forms. For example, it shows how to calculate adjusted gross income and how to claim the standard deduction.

Publication 4555-E An instruction book published by the IRS providing tips to instructors to help train volunteers for the VITA and TCE programs. It provides advice on useful instruction. It supplements Publication 4555.

Publication 4556 A report published by the IRS in 2008 showing the results of the survey on customer satisfaction with the free file system, which is one way to file taxes electronically. The report found wide satisfaction with the system: more than 90% of users said that they would use it the following year and would recommend free file to others.

Publication 4557 A pamphlet published by the IRS outlining various steps a business can take to protect its taxpayer information. It also summarizes various laws and regulations governing the privacy rights that taxpayers have.

Publication 4573 A form published by the IRS explaining a group exemption, which is tax exempt status given to several organizations connected to a single, parent non-profit organization.

Publication 4579 A report published by the IRS in 2007 outlining potential improvements to taxpayer assistance services that the IRS offers. It was issued as part of a broader effort to improve taxpayer assistance services.

Publication 4581 A form published by the IRS explaining tax issues related to foreclosures, repossessions or abandonment of property, and canceled debts.

Publication 4587 A pamphlet published by the IRS explaining payroll deduction IRAs, which are IRAs in which employees choose a certain amount to be deposited automatically with each paycheck. The publication is aimed at small business owners considering retirement plans for their employees.

Publication 4588 A brochure published by the IRS outlining the tax responsibilities of permanent residents of the United States. For example, it states that green card holders owe taxes on worldwide income, even if they are absent from the United States for a long period of time.

Publication 4589 A flyer published by the IRS advising that tax exempt charities and places of worship can receive a tax refund for excise taxes paid on long distance phone calls between March 2003 and July 2006. It explains how the organizations can claim the tax refund.

Publication 4591 A brochure published by the IRS outlining the tax responsibilities of small businesses. It points to further resources that small business owners can use to help determine their tax obligations, and it lists a number of forms that small businesses may have to file.

Publication 4594 A package published by the IRS containing e-filing tests for Form 720, Form 2290, and Form 8849. E-file software designers and others must pass these tests before being permitted to e-file for clients.

Publication 4596 A template poster published by the IRS containing blank spaces on which one can write locations where taxpayers can find tax forms.

Publication 4600 A pamphlet published by the IRS outlining tips for protecting one's personal tax information. For example, it recommends maintaining a list of all the places where one keeps tax information.

Publication 4604 A poster published by the IRS stating various ways in which taxpayers can access or receive IRS forms and publications. It is printed in both English and Spanish.

Publication 463 A form published by the IRS explaining the allowed write-offs for expenses related to gifts, travel and entertainment for business purposes.

Publication 4630 A brochure published by the IRS outlining the various services offered to tax exempt organizations (such as churches). It also describes the forms and publications relevant to these organizations, and provides useful contact information.

Publication 4639 A document published by the IRS providing information on privacy law relevant to taxation. For example, it outlines the circumstances under which the IRS may reveal taxpayer information to a third party.

Publication 4640 A report published by the IRS in 2010 providing detailed demographic information on U.S. taxpayers with disabilities. The report was commissioned as part of a broader effort to reach out to disabled taxpayers.

Publication 4643 A flyer published by the IRS outlining common tax mistakes made by persons older than 65. For example, it states that senior citizens frequently do not take the largest standard deduction for which they qualify.

Publication 4644 A pamphlet published by the IRSoutlining common tax mistakes made by persons older than 65. For example, it states that senior citizens frequently do not take the largest standard deduction for which they qualify. It also advertises the e-filing system.

Publication 4650 A flyer publication by the IRS advertising free file, a simple way for persons making less than $54,000 per year (in 2011) to file their taxes electronically. It emphasizes that the system may expedite tax refunds.

Publication 4651 A report published by the IRS in 2007 detailing the results of a study on customer satisfaction among taxpayers who filed Form 1120 or Form 1120-S electronically. The report noted widespread satisfaction with the e-file system, but stated that those required to e-file were somewhat less satisfied.

Publication 4652 A report published by the IRS in 2008 detailing the results of a study on awareness and usage of online IRS services. The report noted vast awareness and usage of e-services.

Publication 4653 A report published by the IRS in 2007 detailing the results of a study on customer satisfaction among non-profit organizations that filed Form 990 or Form 990-EZ electronically. The report noted widespread satisfaction with the e-file system.

Publication 4656 A report published by the IRS in 2007 detailing the results of a study on customer satisfaction among taxpayers who used the free file system, which is a way for low and middle-income persons to file taxes electronically. The report noted that the vast majority of respondents said they intended to use the system again the following year.

Publication 4665 A document published by the IRS outlining tax benefits available to Social Security, Railroad Retirement, and veterans' benefits recipients under to the Economic Stimulus Act of 2008. The publication advises that one must file a 2007 tax return in order to receive any benefits.

Publication 4671 A package published by the IRS containing an application for a grant to manage a local Volunteer Income Tax Assistance program. While the IRS provides financing for the VITA program, it is executed by local non-profit partners.

Publication 4674 A document published by the IRS for small businesses outlining automatic enrollment 401(k) plans, which are employer-sponsored 401(k) plans that employees must opt out of rather than opt into. The document describes the tax advantages of these plans and explains how a small business can start one.

Publication 4680 A pamphlet published by the IRS outlining the grant programs sponsored by the IRS to provide financing for the Volunteer Income Tax Assistance and Tax Counseling for the Elderly programs. The IRS provides financing for these programs, but they are executed by local non-profit partners.

Publication 4681 A document published by the IRS detailing the tax treatment of property abandonment, canceled debts, foreclosures, and repossessions. In general, any debt forgiveness is treated as income for tax purposes; this document outlines exceptions to this rule.

Publication 4684 A report published by the IRS in 2009 detailing the results of a study on taxpayers who used the Free File (an electronic filing system available to taxpayers making less than about $50,000 per year) in one year but did not use it the following year. The report noted widespread confusion about the system: about one-fifth of respondents stated that they thought they had used Free File in both years.

Publication 4685 A report published by the IRS in 2008 detailing the results of a study into the awareness of the requirement to file Form 990-N among non-profit organizations not previously required to file information returns. The report noted that only 59% of respondents were aware of the new requirement.

Publication 4687 A brochure published by the IRS setting due diligence requirements by which tax preparers must abide in claiming the earned income tax credit for their clients.

Publication 4694 A flyer published by the IRS outlining tax issues relevant to persons who are raising their grandchildren. For example, it states that such persons may be eligible to claim the child tax credit.

Publication 4695 (PR) A test published by the IRS that volunteers for the VITA and TCE programs must pass before they can prepare tax returns in Puerto Rico. The test is published side-by-side in English and Spanish, and is open book.

Publication 4696 (PR) A guidebook published by the IRS providing information on how to file tax returns in Puerto Rico. It states, for example, who must file taxes, how to calculate adjustments to income, and how to claim deductions.

Publication 470 A form one files to apply to become a representative before the IRS under limited circumstances.

Publication 4701 A report published by the IRS highlighting strategic changes made to the Taxpayer Advocate Service between April 2009 and September 2010 in order to make it more responsive to taxpayer needs. For example, it states that the IRS uses comprehension tests of tax products to improve how it communicates with taxpayers. The report was originally prepared for Congress.

Publication 4703 A brochure published by the IRS stating how one can claim the saver's credit, which is a tax credit applied to qualifying contributions to employer-sponsored retirement plans.

Publication 4704-FS A test published by the IRS that volunteers for the VITA and TCE programs must pass before they can prepare tax returns for non-American students and scholars.

Publication 4705 A brochure published by the IRS outlining tax benefits and help available to homeowners in difficult situations. For example, it states that tax relief is available to some homeowners whose mortgages were partly or totally forgiven. The brochure lists IRS forms that may need to be filed.

Publication 4705-SP A brochure published by the IRS outlining tax benefits and help available to homeowners in difficult situations. For example, it states that tax relief is available to some homeowners whose mortgages were partly or totally forgiven. The brochure lists IRS forms that may need to be filed. Except for the fact that it is published in Spanish, it is identical to Publication 4705.

Publication 4706 A brochure published by the IRS outlining tax responsibilities of those who have gambling winnings. It lists forms that may need to be filed and publications that may be useful to persons in this situation.

Publication 4710 A flyer published by the IRS advertising the Voluntary Income Tax Assistance and Tax Counseling for the Elderly programs. It emphasizes that volunteers in these programs prepare and file taxes for free for qualifying clients. It includes a space on which local VITA and TCE programs can provide their locations and hours of operation.

Publication 4714 A flyer published by the IRS outlining various ways that one can pay current year taxes and back taxes. Among other things, it states that one can adjust withholding rates or one can pay taxes electronically using the Electronic Federal Tax Payment System.

Publication 4716 A pamphlet published by the IRS describing the documents that one must have in order to prove income and other eligibility requirements to claim the earned income tax credit. It is published in both English and Spanish.

Publication 4717 A pamphlet published by the IRS encouraging taxpayers to provide appropriate documents to tax preparers and to answer all questions asked in order to ensure that the earned income tax credit is properly claimed. It is published in both English and Spanish.

Publication 4718 A poster published by the IRS outlining general eligibility requirements for the earned income tax credit. For example, it states that persons who earn less than $49,078 (in 2011) and have a relative living with them may be eligible for the EITC.

Publication 4731 A checklist published by the IRS for volunteers with the VITA and TCE programs outlining the conditions under which discharges of debt reported on Form 1099-C may be excluded from a taxpayer's gross income. It also states the types of discharge that fall outside the mandate of the VITA and TCE programs; volunteers are required to refer taxpayers with these discharges to other resources.

Publication 4732 A brochure published by the IRS outlining tax information for U.S. citizens and nationals living outside the United States. It states, for example, that they must report all income in U.S. dollar figures and that they may have additional time to file their tax returns. It lists other publications that may be helpful to these taxpayers.

Publication 4740 A flyer published by the IRS in 2009 highlighting changes to Form 990, an information return that many non-profit organizations are required to file. It was released after the first overhaul of Form 990 in about 30 years.

Publication 4742 A brochure published by the IRS encouraging persons who have not filed tax returns in several years to do so in order to claim refundable tax credits for which they are eligible. It provides pointers on how to file their returns accurately. It is published in both English and Spanish.

Publication 4743 A poster published by the IRS advertising ways in which one can prepare and file tax returns without cost. It particularly highlights the e-file system.

Publication 4747 A poster published by the IRS advertising "Super Saturday," March 21, 2009, on which VITA and TCE programs across the country were available to prepare tax returns for clients. Except for size, it was identical to Publication 4748.

Publication 4748 A flyer published by the IRS advertising "Super Saturday," March 21, 2009, on which VITA and TCE programs across the country were available to prepare tax returns for clients. Except for size, it was identical to Publication 4747.

Publication 4750 A poster published by the IRS encouraging persons who have not filed tax returns in several years to do so in order to claim refundable tax credits for which they are eligible. It states what information taxpayers should have before they file their taxes. It is published in both English and Spanish.

Publication 4751 A flyer published by the IRS advertising a $250 payment made to U.S. citizens and nationals in 2009 to aid in economic recovery from the late 2000s recession. It states that persons do not have to file tax returns to receive the payment, and also explains how the payments are made.

Publication 4761 A brochure published by the IRS advising government employees about the responsibilities they have to protect taxpayers' personal and tax information. In general, this information is required to be kept private unless otherwise authorized.

Publication 4763 A form published by the IRS providing answers to frequently asked questions related to loss of job or reduction in income. For example, it states that severance pay and unemployment benefits are taxable, but that a reduction in income may qualify one for certain deductions and credits.

Publication 4766 A flyer published by the IRS advising that some taxpayers may want to increase their withholding rates due to changes in tax law (specifically to the Making Work Pay tax credit) that may increase the taxes that certain groups of taxpayers owe.

Publication 4767 A flyer published by the IRS advertising the Making Work Pay tax credit available to taxpayers in 2009.

Publication 4768 A flyer published by the IRS advertising tax benefits available to students under the American Recovery and Reinvestment Act. It states that up to a $2,500 tax credit is available on 2009 and 2010 tax returns to students for tuition and other education expenses.

Publication 4771 A flyer published by the IRS advertising a tax credit of up to $8,000 for persons who purchased homes for the first time before June 30, 2010. This credit was created by the American Recovery and Reinvestment Act. Except for size, it is identical to Publication 4775.

Publication 4772 A flyer published by the IRS advertising a tax credit of up to $2,500 for money spent on tuition and other tax benefits related to education expenses. These benefits applied in 2009 and 2010 and were created by the American Recovery and Reinvestment Act.

Publication 4773 A flyer published by the IRS advertising a tax credit of up to $1,500 and other tax benefits for various environmentally friendly home improvements. These benefits were created by the American Recovery and Reinvestment Act. Except for size, it is identical to Publication 4777.

Publication 4775 A poster published by the IRS advertising a tax credit of up to $8,000 for persons who purchased homes for the first time before June 30, 2010. This credit was created by the American Recovery and Reinvestment Act. Except for size, it is identical to Publication 4771.

Publication 4776 A poster published by the IRS advertising the Making Work Pay tax credit available in 2009 and 2010. This credit was created by the American Recovery and Reinvestment Act.

Publication 4777 A poster published by the IRS advertising a tax credit of up to $1,500 and other tax benefits for various environmentally friendly home improvements. These benefits were created by the American Recovery and Reinvestment Act. Except for size, it is identical to Publication 4773.

Publication 4778 A report published by the IRS in 2010 providing the results of a study into awareness and satisfaction with IRS e-services. The report noted universal knowledge and widespread satisfaction with these e-services.

Publication 4779 A pamphlet published by the IRS outlining issues related to the termination of a non-profit organization. For example, it states that an organization must file a final Form 990 (or an equivalent form) to inform the IRS of the dissolution of the organization.

Publication 4780 A brochure published by the IRS explaining the Making Work Pay tax credit. It outlines eligibility requirements and advises taxpayers to adjust their withholdings to claim the credit.

Publication 4787 A pamphlet published by the IRS outlining the tax benefits created by the American Recovery and Reinvestment Act. It mentions, for example, the Making Work Pay tax credit, the credit available to first-time homebuyers, and special benefits for retirees.

Publication 4789 A brochure published by the IRS providing an overview of the enrolled retirement plan agent program, in which persons may register to represent retirees before the IRS on their tax issues. The brochure outlines what an agent does and how one can become an agent.

Publication 4798 A report published by the IRS in 2009 providing the results of a study on customer satisfaction among taxpayers who file Form 2290 electronically. The report noted widespread satisfaction, thought it was noticeably lower than the average satisfaction rate among users of other e-file products.

Publication 4799 A document published by the IRS answering frequently asked questions of probation officers when they work with the IRS on tax cases. For example, it states whom the probation officer should contact to ensure that the person on probation pays back taxes or other restitution.

Publication 4800 A flyer published by the IRS advertising certain tax benefits of the American Recovery and Reinvestment Act. It asks people to go to the IRS website for more information.

Publication 4806 A pamphlet published by the IRS detailing tax issues surrounding profit-sharing plans for small business. It outlines what profit-sharing plans are, why they may be beneficial and how to establish and operate them.

Publication 4807 A form published by the IRS explaining how to fill out an intake form that tax preparers may use to prepare an accurate tax return. It highlights, for example, the necessity of stating whether or not one received income reported on a W-2 or 1099-MISC.

Publication 4808 A brochure published by the IRS outlining requirements for the earned income tax credit related to persons with disabilities. It provides eligibility information for disabled persons and persons whose dependent children (both minors and adults) are disabled.

Publication 4810 A guidebook published by the IRS outlining the steps used to file Form 8955-SSA electronically.

Publication 4814 A pamphlet published by the IRS describing restrictions placed on IRS employees after they leave for other places of employment. For example, it states that former employees may not represent another party before the government for two years on matters that were pending under that employee's responsibility while he/she worked for the IRS. These requirements are intended to avoid potential conflicts of interest.

Publication 4819 A flyer published by the IRS outlining changes made to the tax credit available to first-time homebuyers in 2010. It noted that legislation extended eligibility for the credit on home sales that were to close before September 30, 2010, but reminded taxpayers of income and home price limits on eligibility.

Publication 4821 A brochure published by the IRS advertising the free file system to file taxes electronically. It lists the benefits of the system, emphasizing that it works well for taxpayers who cannot wait until a volunteer is available to prepare their tax returns. See also: VITA, TCE.

Publication 4821-A A brochure published by the IRS advertising the universal eligibility to file taxes using the free file system. It states the differences between the traditional free file system and free file fillable forms, as well as which taxpayers should use each system. It is published in both English and Spanish.

Publication 4822 A chart published by the IRS outlining information on tax returns filed in 2008, 2009, and 2010. It states, for example, the total number of returns filed, the total number of returns claiming the earned income tax credit, and the total number of returns prepared by the taxpayer and filed online.

Publication 4829 A report published by the IRS in 2011 providing the results of a study on the demographic information of those who used the free file system in tax year 2009. The report noted that about half of users had an adjusted gross income under $17,000, that most had no dependents, and that the majority did not claim the earned income tax credit.

Publication 4830 A flyer published by the IRS recommending that taxpayers use their tax refunds to buy Series I savings bonds, which are government-backed savings bonds, the principals of which are protected from inflation. The flyer describes what Series I bonds are and states how they can be purchased with tax refunds.

Publication 4830-A A flyer published by the IRS recommending that taxpayers use their tax refunds to buy Series I savings bonds, which are government-backed savings bonds, the principals of which are protected from inflation. The flyer states both how one can request to purchase the bonds and how the IRS processes the requests.

Publication 4832 A report published by the IRS providing an overview of the tax preparer business, noting both the common practice of paying another party to prepare one's tax return and the relative lack of oversight over the preparers themselves. The report recommends strengthening relationships with tax preparers in order to discourage faulty or fraudulent tax returns.

Publication 4833 A report published by the IRS stating the results of a focus group study on free file system users and potential users. The focus groups found numerous benefits to the free file system, but some participants found its dialogue unrealistic or awkward.

Publication 4836 A flyer published by the IRS advertising the Volunteer Income Tax Assistance and Tax Counseling for the Elderly programs. It states that potential volunteers should file Form 13615.

Publication 4839 A flyer published by the IRS outlining the requirements for whether a tax-exempt organization needs to file Form 990, Form 990-PF, or Form 990-N. It also states that tax-exempt organizations that fail to file the necessary forms for three years in a row automatically lose tax exempt status.

Publication 4839-B A flyer published by the IRS detailing how organizations that have lost tax exempt status due to non-filing of Form 990 or an equivalent form can apply for a one-time waiver to regain tax exempt status.

Publication 4840 A flyer published by the IRS advising taxpayers to buy Series I savings bonds with their tax refunds.

Publication 4845 A flyer published by the IRS outlining the tax benefits available under the American Recovery and Reinvestment Act to persons and companies that invest in energy efficient or environmentally friendly products.

Publication 4849 A flyer published by the IRS outlining what taxpayers should do if they cannot pay the taxes they owe. It states that taxpayers should file on time to avoid interest and penalties, and advises that persons in this situation should contact the IRS immediately.

Publication 4852 A pamphlet published by the IRS containing information relevant to federal employee tax compliance. While the pamphlet is published for managers, it encourages managers to share this information with employees under their supervision.

Publication 4853 A pamphlet published by the IRS advising taxpayers on what to do if they owe taxes. It states how one can pay in full without penalty or set up a payment plan. It also encourages these taxpayers to file their tax returns on time.

Publication 4854 A pamphlet published by the IRS containing month-by-month information relevant to employee tax compliance. While the pamphlet is published for employers, it encourages readers to share this information with employees as it becomes timely.

Publication 4855 A report published by the IRS presenting the results of a survey into customer satisfaction with IRS e-services. The report noted universal knowledge and near-universal satisfaction with these services.

Publication 4867 A brochure published by the IRS outlining various ways one can spend a tax refund to improve one's financial situation. It recommends, for example, financial management classes (which normally are free or inexpensive). It also advises one to read other relevant publications.

Publication 4868 A flyer published by the IRS encouraging taxpayers to use their tax refunds to purchase Series I savings bonds.

Publication 487 A form published by the IRS explaining how to make an application to release a property from a tax lien imposed by the federal government.

Publication 4870 A brochure published by the IRS outlining various ways one can spend a tax refund to improve one's financial situation. It recommends, for example, starting a retirement plan. It also advises one to read other relevant publications.

Publication 4873 A flyer published by the IRS outlining tax issues created by the Gulf oil spill in 2010. Specifically, it states that income replacement payments made to workers are taxable.

Publication 4873-A A flyer published by the IRS outlining tax issues created by the Gulf oil spill in 2010. Specifically, it states that income replacement payments made to workers are taxable, but payments made for personal injury or property damage are not.

Publication 4874 (VN) A flyer published by the IRS advertising a clean-up day for the Gulf of Mexico due to the Gulf oil spill in 2010. It was published in Vietnamese.

Publication 4883 A guidebook published by the IRS detailing the grant-making process for the Volunteer Income Tax Assistance and Tax Counseling for the Elderly programs, both of which are financed by the IRS but are independently operated.

Publication 4884 A flyer published by the IRS describing some changes to health savings accounts due to the Affordable Care Act of 2010. For example, it states that a prescription is necessary before an HAS will reimburse for the cost of an over-the-counter medicine.

Publication 4885 A checklist published by the IRS providing eligibility requirements to receive the tax benefits of a health savings account.

Publication 4893 A brochure published by the IRS outlining forms that taxpayers may need to file. For example, a business owner may need to file Form 1040 (Schedule C) along with his/her own Form 1040. The publication is aimed at persons who used to receive tax packages but no longer receive them.

Publication 4894 A brochure published by the IRS outlining tax issues surrounding the 2010 health care reform laws known colloquially as Obamacare. For example, it explains tax credits available to small businesses that provide health insurance to employees.

Publication 4895 A form published by the IRS explaining tax issues related to the inheritance of property from a person who died in 2010, a year during which there was no estate tax in the United States.

Publication 4899 A flyer published by the IRS providing a decision tree detailing tax issues related to the 2010 Gulf of Mexico oil spill. The decision tree states whether or not various payments made to victims are taxable.

Publication 4900 A brochure published by the IRS outlining the ways in which one can electronically pay heavy highway vehicle use taxes.

Publication 4902 A pamphlet published by the IRS detailing tax issues relevant to barbers and hair stylists. It distinguishes between shop owners and booth renters, who are considered self-employed and must pay self-employment tax, and employees, who are not considered self-employed.

Publication 4903 A flyer published by the IRS advertising an expansion of the adoption tax credit in 2010 and 2011 due to the passage of the Affordable Care Act of 2010.

Publication 4906 A document published by the IRS providing an overview of the tax issues caused by the 2010 Gulf of Mexico oil spill. The document is aimed at volunteers in the VITA and TCE programs who prepare tax returns for victims.

Publication 4907 A brochure published by the IRS advertising the benefits of the self-service free file system, under which taxpayers can prepare their own tax returns and file electronically with only minimal help from VITA or TCE volunteers.

Publication 4913 A form that IRS employees file to inform supervisors of the number of taxpayers with whom they communicate for EITC, e-services, compliance, or other purposes. This way, the IRS keeps track of its outreach.

Publication 4914 A flyer published by the IRS informing taxpayers of delayed processing of certain tax returns until February 2011 to ensure that returns comply with tax changes passed in the Tax Relief, Unemployment Insurance Reauthorization and Job Creation Act of 2010, which was not passed until December 2010.

Publication 4915 A flyer published by the IRS informing taxpayers of delayed processing of certain tax returns until February 2011 due to system reprogramming.

Publication 4916 A flyer published by the IRS advising taxpayers that certain tax returns cannot be filed until February 2011 because they do not comply with tax changes passed in the Tax Relief, Unemployment Insurance Reauthorization and Job Creation Act of 2010, which was not passed until December 2010.

Publication 4917 A flyer published by the IRS informing taxpayers that certain tax returns cannot be filed until February 2011 due to system reprogramming.

Publication 4921 A pamphlet published by the IRS outlining various services offered by the Taxpayer Advocate Service to taxpayers who cannot resolve IRS problems directly. It also states that taxpayers should deal with the IRS directly before the TAS can become involved.

Publication 4922 A report published by the IRS stating the results of a study on the e-filing and other electronic needs of Form 1040, Form 1040 (Schedule C), Form 1040 (Schedule E), and Form 1040 (Schedule F). The study was part of a broader effort to strategize to meet the electronic needs of taxpayers.

Publication 4924 A pamphlet published by the IRS outlining a program to help outgoing prisoners meet their tax obligations. The publication is aimed at facilitators who meet with outgoing prisoners either one on one or in a seminar setting.

Publication 4925 A brochure published by the IRS outlining tax information applicable to a wide variety of taxpayers. It outlines, for example, the earned income tax credit and cautions against illegal schemes to evade taxes. It also advertises a program to help outgoing prisoners meet their tax obligations.

Publication 4928 A report published by the IRS in 2011 stating the results of a survey on knowledge of and attitudes toward the free file system among non-users. The report found that only a little more than half of respondents were aware of the free file system and a little under half said they probably would use the system in the future.

Publication 4929 A flyer published by the IRS advising taxpayers to adjust their withholding if it does not approximate the taxes they actually owe in a year. It also states how taxpayers can make these adjustments.

Publication 4931-A A Spanish-language script published by the IRS for a DVD to help Spanish-speaking taxpayers understand their tax obligations. The camera directions are in English while the script itself is in Spanish.

Publication 4940 A flyer published by the IRS outlining the tax credits and other benefits available to active duty and reserve personnel in the U.S. military. For example, it states the circumstances under which a military member's tax liability can be forgiven.

Publication 4941 A brochure published by the IRS stating that the federal government requires dyeing of diesel fuels on which no excised taxes were paid, and advising truck drivers that there is a penalty for the use of dyed diesel fuels in the performance of any taxable act.

Publication 4942 A guidebook published by the IRS providing detailed information on the tax implications of the cancellation of debts and health savings accounts. The publication is aimed at volunteers in the Tax Counseling for the Elderly and Volunteer Income Tax Assistance programs.

Publication 4944 A flyer published by the IRS stating the various ways in which taxpayers can file their tax returns and receive their tax refunds. It also provides detailed contact information for persons who have any questions.

Publication 4945 A presentation published by the IRS explaining its Understanding Taxes website, which is used to teach volunteers and others how to prepare tax returns.

Publication 4961 A guidebook published by the IRS explaining standards that must be followed to prove that an employer is abiding by non-discrimination and coverage requirements on employee benefit plans.

Publication 4962 A guidebook published by the IRS explaining vesting standards for defined benefit employee plans.

Publication 4963 A guidebook published by the IRS explaining non-discrimination and coverage requirements on employee benefit plans.

Publication 4964 A pamphlet published by the IRS explaining qualification requirements for favorable tax treatment on employee benefit plans.

Publication 4965 A guidebook published by the IRS providing detailed information on non-discrimination and coverage requirements for defined benefit retirement plans.

Publication 4967 A flyer published by the IRS advertising several Twitter feeds run by the IRS.

Publication 5 A form published by the IRS explaining how to appeal an adverse decision. For example, if the IRS audits a return and claims that a taxpayer owes $4,000 more than he/she paid in taxes, Publication 5 outlines the rights the taxpayer has and how the decision might be overturned. It also explains how the taxpayer may recover litigation and other costs from the IRS if he/she ultimately prevails.

Publication 501 A form published by the IRS explaining the standard deduction, various tax exemptions and other information on filing taxes.

Publication 502 A form published by the IRS explaining the tax treatment of dental and medical expenses.

Publication 503 A form published by the IRS explaining the tax treatment of child care and similar expenses.

Publication 504 A form published by the IRS explaining the tax treatment of alimony, child support and other information pertinent to divorced and separated persons.

Publication 505 A form published by the IRS explaining rules regarding withholding and estimated tax payments.

Publication 509 A form published by the IRS stating due dates for numerous forms that individuals and business may be required to file with the IRS.

Publication 51 A form published by the IRS explaining to agricultural employers the taxes they must withhold from employees. It also explains which forms must be filed on which dates. Publication 51 is also called Circular A.

Publication 510 A form published by the IRS explaining the excise taxes, including those levied on fuel.

Publication 514 A form published by the IRS explaining how and under what circumstances one can claim a foreign tax credit on taxes paid to another government.

Publication 515 A form published by the IRS explaining withholding for non-resident aliens of the United States. Non-resident aliens may be subject to special withholding rules.

Publication 516 A form published by the IRS explaining special tax rules applying to civilian employees of the U.S. government living outside the United States.

Publication 517 A form published by the IRS explaining special FICA tax rules applying to clergy members. Some clerics may be exempt from the self-employment tax, for example. Publication 517 shows how these exemptions work.

Publication 519 A form published by the IRS explaining tax rules applying to non-U.S. citizens who are subject to U.S. taxation. Aliens may be subject to special tax treatment, depending on, for example, whether or not they are legal residents of the United States. Publication 519 shows how this treatment works.

Publication 521 A form published by the IRS explaining tax rules applying to moving expenses. Some moving expenses are tax deductible while others are not. Publication 521 shows how these deductions work.

Publication 523 A form published by the IRS explaining tax treatment of the sale of one's home. The publication shows, for example, how to calculate profit (or loss) from the sale, which can affect one's tax liability.

Publication 524 A form published by the IRS explaining the tax credit available for disabled or elderly persons whose incomes do not exceed certain limits. Publication 524 shows who qualifies for the credit and how qualified persons may claim it.

Publication 525 A form published by the IRS explaining the various types of income one may earn or receive in a year, and whether or not each type is taxable.

Publication 526 A form published by the IRS explaining the rules and limits governing the tax deductions one may claim for contributions to charities.

Publication 527 A form published by the IRS explaining the tax treatment of income and expenses related to the rental of residential real estate. For example, expenses such as maintenance on residential real estate may be tax deductible as business expenses. Publication 527 shows how this tax treatment works.

Publication 529 A form published by the IRS explaining various deductions not covered in other publications. It also lists a number of expenses that are never tax deductible.

Publication 530 A form published by the IRS explaining tax deductions and tax credits available to homeowners. Interest on one's mortgage loan, for example, may be deductible. Publication 530 explains how these deductions and credits work.

Publication 534 A form published by the IRS explaining the rules governing the depreciation of property purchased and used in a business before 1987.

Publication 535 A form published by the IRS explaining the rules governing tax deductions for business expenses, such as rent, employee wages and so forth.

Publication 536 A form published by the IRS explaining how to calculate net operating losses, as well as the rules governing carryforwards and carrybacks and similar issues.

Publication 537 A form published by the IRS explaining the tax rules governing installment sales.

Publication 538 A form published by the IRS explaining how accounting methods (such as cash accounting and accrual accounting) and calendars (such as the fiscal year and calendar year) affect the tax treatment of companies.

Publication 54 A form published by the IRS explaining special tax rules applying to U.S. citizens and resident aliens living outside the United States. Certain income earned abroad is subject to reduced (or eliminated) taxation. Publication 54 states how these rules work.

Publication 541 A form published by the IRS explaining the tax treatment of partnerships.

Publication 542 A form published by the IRS explaining the tax treatment of corporations.

Publication 544 A form published by the IRS explaining the tax treatment of asset sales and other dispositions. For example, it states how to calculate gains and losses and how this affects the former owner's tax liability.

Publication 547 A form published by the IRS explaining the tax treatment of theft, loss or destruction of assets. Some of these losses may be tax deductible. Publication 547 shows how these losses work. See also: Publication 584.

Publication 551 A form published by the IRS explaining how cost basis and adjusted basis work, as well as how else costs are calculated for the purpose of taxing gains and losses.

Publication 552 A form published by the IRS explaining how individuals should keep records of income and expenses for tax purposes, as well as how long these records should be kept.

Publication 553 A form published by the IRS explaining changes in tax laws taking effect in 2008, 2009 and 2010. Some of these changes were temporary.

Publication 554 A form published by the IRS explaining tax issues most relevant to persons 65 and older. For example, it explains tax treatment of Social Security income and reverse mortgages.

Publication 555 A form published by the IRS explaining the tax treatment of community property.

Publication 556 A form published by the IRS explaining the audit process. It discusses interest, penalties, offers in compromise and similar matters. It also explains the appeals process in the event of an adverse decision.

Publication 557 A form published by the IRS explaining issues related to tax exempt organizations under Section 501(c) of the tax code. Among other things, it shows how an organization can receive and maintain its tax exempt status.

Publication 559 A form published by the IRS explaining tax issues relevant to the survivors of a recently deceased person. It shows how to file the last Form 1040 for the decedent, how to file a tax return for the estate, and similar matters.

Publication 560 A form published by the IRS explaining tax issues related to small business retirement plans. For example, it discusses SEP IRAs and SIMPLE 401(k)s.

Publication 561 A form published by the IRS explaining how to determine the value of a property that has been given for free for tax purposes.

Publication 570 A form published by the IRS explaining how to treat income from certain U.S. possessions for tax purposes. The possessions included in Publication 570 are American Samoa, Guam, Northern Mariana Islands, Puerto Rico, and the U.S. Virgin Islands.

Publication 571 A form published by the IRS explaining the tax treatment of 403(b) plans.

Publication 575 A form published by the IRS explaining how the tax exempt portion of an annuity payment is calculated under the Simplified Rule, which is one of the two methods for making such calculations.

Publication 583 A form published by the IRS explaining tax matters related to starting a business. It also discusses record-keeping.

Publication 584 A workbook the IRS publishes to help calculate the allowable tax deductions for theft, loss or destruction of assets. See also: Publication 547.

Publication 584-B A workbook the IRS publishes to help calculate a business's allowable tax deductions for theft, loss or destruction of assets. See also: Publication 547.

Publication 587 A form published by the IRS explaining allowable expenses and deductions for the business use of one's own home.

Publication 590 A form published by the IRS explaining the tax treatment of various types of IRA.

Publication 593 A form published by the IRS explaining tax issues applicable to U.S. citizens and nationals who leave the United States to work and therefore draw foreign income, even though they still may live in the U.S.

Publication 595 A form published by the IRS explaining tax issues related to the Capital Construction Fund, which is an investment vehicle fishermen may use to defer taxation on income invested in it, provided it is used later to build, purchase or repair fishing vessels.

Publication 596 A form published by the IRS explaining eligibility for and application of the earned income tax credit.

Publication 597 A form published by the IRS explaining tax issues related to the U.S.-Canadian Tax Treaty of 1980. It discusses rights and obligations U.S. and Canadian citizens have when they may owe taxes to the other country.

Publication 598 A form published by the IRS explaining taxation on unrelated business income of tax exempt organizations such as churches and political action committees. While there are a number of exemptions, the IRS taxes unrelated business income at ordinary corporate tax rates.

Publication 600 A form published by the IRS explaining the tax deductibility of sales taxes paid to state and local governments. While sales taxes are deductible, one cannot deduct both sales taxes and state income taxes.

Publication 721 A form published by the IRS explaining tax issues related to the retirement plans of employees of the U.S. federal government.

Publication 730 A form published by the IRS stating the major forms taxpayers should keep on record for at least three years. For example, it suggests that taxpayers keep W-2 and 1099 forms for this period of time. The publication is available in both English and Spanish.

Publication 783 A form published by the IRS explaining how to apply for the removal of a tax lien.

Publication 784 A form published by the IRS explaining how to apply for the subordination of a tax lien to another obligation.

Publication 785 A form published by the IRS explaining how to apply for a purchase money mortgage or a purchase money security interest, which are used to enable a bank to make a loan to a person against whom a federal tax lien has been filed.

Publication 786 A form published by the IRS explaining how one can apply to purchase a property against which the federal government has filed a tax lien. Publication 786 is relevant only if the sale of the property was not ordered by a judge.

Publication 794 A form published by the IRS explaining how to apply for a favorable determination letter, which is a certification that a retirement plan or employee benefit package complies with applicable tax law.

Publication 80 A form published by the IRS explaining the taxes employers must withhold from employees as well as which forms must be filed on which dates to employers in American Samoa, Guam, Northern Mariana Islands and the U.S. Virgin Islands. Publication 80 is also called Circular SS.

Publication 850 A form published by the IRS containing translations of various tax terms in both English and Spanish.

Publication 892 A form published by the IRS explaining how an organization can appeal an adverse decision regarding tax exempt status. For example, if the IRS does not accept an initial application for 501(c)3 status, Publication 892 discusses how the organization can attempt to receive the designation anyway.

Publication 901 A form published by the IRS explaining tax issues related to tax treaties between the U.S. and various countries. It discusses rights and obligations U.S. citizens have when they may owe taxes to other countries.

Publication 907 A form published by the IRS explaining tax issues affecting persons with disabilities.

Publication 908 A form published by the IRS explaining tax issues affecting personal or corporate bankruptcy.

Publication 910 A form published by the IRS outlining services the IRS offers to taxpayers free of charge. For example, it discusses a free movie the IRS can send to explain tax filing.

Publication 915 A form published by the IRS explaining tax issues related to Social Security and Railroad Retirement Board benefits.

Publication 919 A form published by the IRS explaining withholding policies and how to change them periodically.

Publication 925 A form published by the IRS explaining tax issues related to the at-risk rule and passive activities.

Publication 926 A form published by the IRS explaining tax issues related to employers of household employees.

Publication 929 A form published by the IRS explaining tax issues related to income earned by one's minor child or other dependent.

Publication 936 A form published by the IRS explaining tax issues related to tax deduction for the interest paid on one's home mortgage.

Publication 938 A form published by the IRS explaining reporting requirements for real estate mortgage investment conduits and other collateralized debt obligations. Specifically, it outlines who has the right to a REMIC or CDO's tax information and how such persons may request it.

Publication 939 A form published by the IRS explaining how the tax exempt portion of an annuity payment is calculated under the General Rule, which is one of the two methods for making such calculations.

Publication 946 A form published by the IRS explaining various ways one may depreciate the property one owns.

Publication 947 A form published by the IRS explaining how one can become a representative before the IRS. It also explains power of attorney procedures.

Publication 950 A form published by the IRS explaining gift taxes and estate taxes. The form discusses exemptions and limits to these taxes, as well as how to file a return if they are payable.

Publication 957 A form published by the IRS explaining how to report back pay, bonuses, accumulated vacation pay and similar income for tax purposes.

Publication 962 A flyer published by the IRS explaining, in bullet points, eligibility for the earned income tax credit.

Publication 963 A comprehensive guide published by the IRS explaining the FICA taxes state and local government agencies must pay, as well as the Social Security and Medicare eligibility for state and local employees.

Publication 966 A form published by the IRS explaining how to pay federal taxes electronically, whether online or over the phone.

Publication 967 A form published by the IRS explaining how it calculates tax liabilities using Form 1040, Form 1040A or Form 1040EZ. It also explains the circumstances under which the IRS cannot calculate the tax liability.

Publication 969 A form published by the IRS explaining tax issues related to health savings accounts and certain other health care structures with preferential tax treatment.

Publication 970 A form published by the IRS explaining tax deductions, tax credits and other preferential tax treatment available for persons who pursue higher education.

Publication 971 A form published by the IRS explaining how a spouse or former spouse can apply for relief from taxation incurred by the other spouse. In general, spouses who file jointly are both responsible for the tax liability. Publication 971 discusses how a spouse can have this liability lifted if, for example, he/she was a victim of desertion.

Publication 972 A form published by the IRS explaining how to claim the child tax credit.

Publicly Traded Asset Any asset that is traded on an exchange. Publicly traded assets are almost always stocks.

Publicly-Traded Company A company issuing stocks, which are traded on the open market, either on a stock exchange or on the over-the-counter market. Individual and institutional shareholders constitute the owners of a publicly-traded company, in proportion to the amount of stock they own as a percentage of all outstanding stock. Thus, shareholders have final say in all decisions taken by a publicly-traded company and its managers, especially through its annual shareholders' meeting. Publicly-traded companies have greater access to financing than other companies, as they have the ability to issue more stock. However, they are subject to greater regulation: for example, they must file 10-K reports with the SEC on their earnings and they are more likely to be subject to corporate taxes. A publicly-traded company is also called a public company.

Public-Purpose Bond A municipal bond that is issued in order to finance public works. For example, a city may issue a public purpose bond to build a road or school, which improves the city but does not directly attract private investment. The federal government does not tax the interest on a public-purpose bond. This exemption occurs automatically, unlike a private purpose bond, which must prove that it benefits the public in some way to qualify for the tax exemption.

Puddee An obsolete Indian unit of dry volume approximately equivalent to 1.59 liters.

Puke Informal; the sale of a losing position. This is done to avoid further losses and to free up money that may be used in a more profitable investment. While rebounds are possible, puking a security indicates the investor's acknowledgement that further losses are unacceptable and a price recovery is unlikely. Reaching this attitude is known as reaching the "puke point." Knowing whether one is correct in reaching the puke point at a certain time is the subject of much speculation and depends greatly on one's investment strategy. See also: Close a position.

Pul A subdivision of the Afghan afghani. One pul is equal in value to 1/100 of one aghani. The pul does not circulate in practice.

Pula The currency of Botswana. It was introduced in 1976, replacing the South African rand. It has historically been one of the strongest currencies in Africa, and is used in Zimbabwe (along with other currencies) because the Zimbabwean dollar is effectively worthless.

Pulgada A Spanish measure of length approximately equivalent to 23.22 milliliters, or just under one inch. It is largely obsolete.

Pullback In a price uptrend, a security's retreat from its previous high. A pullback may be a signal that the uptrend is ending and may be taken as a sign to sell. On the other hand, the pullback may be temporary and the uptrend could continue. In that case, it may be taken as a sign to buy. The meaning of a pullback depends on other technical indicators.

Pulling in Their Horns Informal; the practice in which investors close positions or set up offsetting, hedge positions when a security has recently seen a sudden increase in price. When investors pull in their horns, they lock in the gain they made from their positions. This happens in order to protect the investor from sharp turnarounds in price.

Pulzier A Maltese unit of length approximately equivalent to 2.2 centimeters. It is largely obsolete but is still used in some circumstances.

Pulzier Kubu A Maltese unit of cubic volume approximately equivalent to 10.4 milliliters. It is largely obsolete but is still used in some circumstances.

Pulzier Kwadru A Maltese unit of area approximately equivalent to 4.77 square centimeters. It is largely obsolete but is still used in some circumstances.

Pump and Dump An illegal practice in which investors attempt to artificially inflate the price of a stock by disseminating inaccurate or misleading information. These investors have a long position on the stock in question and seek to inflate the price in order to sell their shares for a higher profit. Pumping and dumping violates securities laws and can lead to hefty fines. Victims often stand to lose a good deal on pumping and dumping as the price of the stock usually falls to its previous level in a relatively short period of time.

Pump Priming Any government action taken to spur economic growth, especially when growth is sluggish or negative. Pump priming is nonpartisan; that is, pump priming policies may be conservative (e.g. tax cuts), liberal (e.g. increased spending) or some combination of the two. The term originated during the Great Depression and fell out of use after World War II. However, it came back to some extent during the late 2000s recession.

Pumping 1. See: Portfolio pumping. **2.** See: Pump and dump.

Pund A Norwegian unit of weight approximately equivalent to 500 grams.

Pundion An ancient Hebrew unit of weight approximately equivalent to 0.35 grams.

Punitive Tax 1. A tax imposed to discourage a behavior. For example, retirement plans usually have excise taxes placed upon them if one makes a withdrawal prior to a certain age. **2.** An extraordinarily high tax. For example, a government theoretically could impose a tax of 99% on all income over $20,000. There is no consensus as to what qualifies as a punitive tax.

Punt Informal for a speculative investment. A punt is an attempt to make fast profits from an investment regardless of its underlying fundamentals. This means that a punt carries higher risks than most investments, but may see very high returns very quickly. Punts almost always are leveraged highly and are especially common in futures and options markets. They may utilize any of a number of techniques to make investment decisions. See also: Arbitrage.

Punter Informal for speculator. A punter attempts to make fast profits from his/her investments regardless of the underlying fundamentals of a company. This means that a punter takes more risks than most investors, but may see very high returns very quickly. Punters almost always leverage highly in order to make their investments, and are especially common in futures and options markets. They may use any of a number of techniques to make investment decisions. See also: Arbitrage.

Puntti A Finnish unit meaning 20 matchboxes.

Pup Company Informal; a small company owned by a large company. See also: Wholly-owned subsidiary.

Pur Autre Vie Describing a right to a property that lasts as long as the life of a second party. For example, a man may have pur autre vie right to property if he is legally able to live there as long as his wife lives. The term is French, meaning "for another's life."

Purchase Accounting In mergers and acquisitions, a method of accounting that treats the acquiring company as if it bought the assets and assumed the liabilities of the target company; all the assets and liabilities are placed on the acquiring company's balance sheet according to their current market value. Because the purchase price of the target company often exceeds this, pooling-of-assets accounting is more common. See also: Goodwill.

Purchase Acquisition In accounting, a way of recording a merger or acquisition in which the acquiring company treats the target company like an asset such as equipment or stock. That is, in a purchase acquisition, the acquiring company simply adds the fair market value of the target company's assets to its balance sheet. If the acquisition cost more than the fair market value, the excess is recorded as goodwill. Purchase acquisition is less common than pooling-of-interests, because goodwill is recorded against future earnings, reducing the company's profit.

Purchase Agreement 1. An agreement between a buyer and a seller in which the buyer agrees to buy a good at a certain price at regular intervals for a given period of time. **2.** See: Sale.

Purchase and Resale Agreement An agreement between the Bank of Canada and a dealer on an exchange in which the Bank buys Canadian Treasury securities from the dealer and the dealer agrees to buy the same securities back the following day. A PRA provides liquidity to a dealer, which in turn provides liquidity to market trading. See also: Murabaha, Double Sale.

Purchase and Sale A method of underwriting in which an underwriter buys an issue for his/her own account and then attempts to sell the issue to other investors. If the underwriter is unsuccessful in placing the issue, he/she keeps what remains. It contrasts with various other forms of underwriting, notably best-efforts sale, in which the underwriter returns the remaining issue to the issuer. The Bank of Canada uses a form of the purchase and sale method, known as a Purchase and Resale Agreement, when selling its treasury securities. It is also called an underwritten offering.

Purchase Fee Any fee that a third party assesses on an investor in exchange for helping the investor buy a security. One of the most common kids of purchase fees is the broker's commission.

Purchase Frequency The number of times a person or company buys a good or service or buys goods and services from a single seller. For example, milk has a high purchase frequency because it is consumed quickly. The purchase frequency of cars is lower than that of milk but higher than houses. Because items with high purchase frequency present more opportunities for customers to buy from different sellers, these sellers advertise themselves and their products on a nearly constant basis. This is not as necessary for products with lower purchase frequency because brand loyalty tends to be higher.

Purchase from Foreign Seller To buy a good or service from a person or company in a foreign country. Purchasing from a foreign seller can be more expensive due to added shipping costs as well as potential tariffs and other trade barriers. However, the fixed costs of making a product may be lower in a foreign country, which may reduce the overall price.

Purchase Fund A sinking fund where a company sets money aside to repurchase its own securities if their prices fall below par. If the prices fall below par value, the purchase fund enables the company effectively to redeem its securities at a discount. The purchase fund reduces the risk that the company will be unable to redeem its bonds when they mature.

Purchase Loan A loan made to a borrower to finance the buying of some asset. For example, one may take out a purchase loan to buy a house, car, or some other expensive asset one could not otherwise afford. The terms of a purchase loan vary according to the lender's rules and the borrower's creditworthiness. A purchase loan differentiates from loans used to finance intangible things, such as an education or a business. See also: Credit card, Consumer good.

Purchase Order An authorization that a company sends to a supplier to buy specified goods at a certain price. When the supplier accepts a purchase order, it becomes a legal contract that both parties are required to fill.

Purchase Tax A proposed tax on a purchase, rather than on a sale. That is, the purchaser of a good, rather than the seller, is obligated to pay the tax. In practice, there is little difference between a purchase tax and a sales tax because sellers usually pass on the tax to purchasers in the form of a higher price. A purchase tax has been suggested as an alternative to the income tax in the United States.

Purchase-Money Mortgage A mortgage in which the home buyer borrows from the seller instead of, or in addition to, a bank or thrift. Purchase-money mortgages usually are made when the buyer cannot qualify for an ordinary home loan due to lack of credit or income. Alternately, a seller may offer a purchase-money mortgage in a mortgage-takeover agreement, that is, when the sale price of the home is equal to what remains on the seller's own mortgage.

Purchasing Manager An employee of a company who purchases the goods that the company needs, especially to make its own products. A purchasing manager may supervise the purchase of office supplies, or the raw materials needed to make a company's finished goods. A purchasing manager is also called a procurement manager.

Purchasing Managers' Index An index gauging sentiment in manufacturing. It measures increases and decreases in manufacturing employment, inventories, orders for goods, production, and deliveries. Each component is weighted for importance and seasonality. A PMI above 50 indicates that the manufacturing industry is expanding, while a measure below 50 indicates contraction.

Purchasing Power 1. The value of a currency expressed as the amount of goods or services one unit of the currency can buy. Purchasing power is important to inflation, as the higher an inflation rate is, the fewer goods and services one unit of a currency can buy. To measure purchasing power, one must compare it with an objective standard; that is, one might compare how much one dollar can buy now versus how much it could buy 10 year ago. See also: CPI, Purchasing power parity. **2.** The dollar amount of securities one can buy on a margin account. Different jurisdictions have different rules on how to measure purchasing power.

Purchasing Power of the Dollar The goods and services that $1 can buy when compared to other currencies or to the dollar in a different time period. One can use the purchasing power of the dollar to gauge both the dollar's value in the currency market and to measure inflation. See also: Exchange rate.

Purchasing Power Parity The theory stating that, in an efficient market, the exchange rate of two currencies results in equal purchasing power. That is, if one pound is worth two dollars, one pound in England should buy the same amount in goods and services that two dollars can buy in the United States. Fixed exchange rates, taxes, and other inefficiencies are thought to disrupt purchasing power parity. Some theorists believe the idea holds most true when comparing countries or regions with similar standards of living.

Pure Expectations Theory In foreign exchange, a theory that forward exchange rates for delivery at some future date are equal to the spot rates for that date. The theory only functions in the absence of a risk premium. Critics contend that the evidence shows that pure expectations do not occur in actual trading.

Pure Food and Drug Act Legislation in the United States, passed in 1906, that required inspection of American meat by the federal government. It also required labeling of some addictive substances and prohibited poisonous medicines. It was superseded by the Food, Drug, and Cosmetic Act of 1938.

Pure Index Fund A portfolio or fund that is actively managed such that its return exactly matches the return of the broader market. For example, if the market portfolio (a hypothetical portfolio of all assets available to investors) returns 3% in a given year, a pure index fund also returns 3%.

Pure Monopoly A company that has total control of a given market. Most of the time, a pure monopoly exists in a situation in which a company has a patent or uses some technology that is popular with consumers, but is protected from use by another company, at least for limited period of time. See also: Duopoly, Antitrust.

Pure Play A company that works exclusively in a single industry. A pure play company can carry higher risks than diversified companies, but some, especially start-ups, can only afford to be pure plays for the first few years of operation. On the other hand, if a pure play's products are successful in its industry over a long period of time, it may be a stable investment.

Pure Risk Any risk in which there is no possibility of gain, only the avoidance of loss. For example, if a company car is stolen, the company endures a loss, but if it is not stolen, the company does not make a gain. Individuals and companies purchase insurance to mitigate the potential damage from a loss from pure risk. It is also called absolute risk.

Pure Yield Pickup Swap A swap in which two investors exchange two bonds, one with a lower yield and shorter maturity and one with a higher yield and longer maturity. This is a high risk transaction for the holder of the lower yield bond (that is, the one who receives the high yield bond). This is because the high yield bond is almost always of lower credit quality and the longer maturity exposes the bondholder to interest rate risk. However, it does guarantee a higher return that the bondholder would have received with the lower yield bond.

Purpose Credit Money that an investor may borrow from a broker in order to buy securities. Purpose credit is secured by cash and/or securities in a margin account. An investor who buys with purpose credit can realize huge gains if the price of the security moves in a favorable direction; however, he/she also takes on a great deal of risk because it may not move in such a direction. Purpose credit is also called a margin loan. See also: minimum maintenance, margin call, nonpurpose loan.

Purpose Loan A loan with securities pledged as collateral in which the proceeds from the loan are used to buy other securities. See also: Margin loan.

Purpose Statement A form banks require borrowers to fill out when borrowing funds secured by margin stock in excess of a certain amount. The purpose statement indicates the reason the borrower is taking out the loan and guarantees that he/she will not use the funds to buy securities in violation of SEC or other regulations.

Push Money Money a manufacturer or wholesaler pays a retailer in exchange for displaying its goods prominently. Push money may increase sales of the goods, which could improve the likelihood that the retailer will order that manufacturer or wholesaler's products again.

Put an Option To exercise a put. This means that the holder forces the writer to sell the underlying asset at the agreed-upon strike price.

Put Guarantee Letter A letter issued by a bank stating that the writer of a put option has enough money in a bank account to pay the exercise price should the holder of the put exercise the option. A put option allows the holder to sell a security at a given strike price at his/her discretion. A put guarantee letter reduces the risk to the holder by guaranteeing that the option will be covered if necessary.

Put On Informal; to trade.

Put Option An option contract in which the holder has the right but not the obligation to sell some underlying asset at an agreed-upon price on or before the expiration date of the contract, regardless of the prevailing market price of the underlying asset. One buys a put option if one believes the price for the underlying asset will fall by the end of the contract. If the price does fall, the holder may buy and resell the underlying asset for a profit. If the price does not fall, the option expires and the holder's loss is limited to the price of buying the contract. Put options may be used on their own or in conjunction with call options to create an option spread in order to hedge risk.

Put Price The strike price for a put option. When one buys a put option, one buys the right, but not the obligation, to sell a security to the writer of the option at a certain price. This price is called the put price.

Put Provision A provision in some floating-rate bonds allowing a bondholder to redeem the bond at par on the date coupons are paid. This allows the bondholder to reinvest at a more favorable interest rate when the coupon rate changes on the floating-rate bond.

Put Ratio Backspread A bearish investment strategy in which an investor sells a put option at a high strike price and then uses the proceeds from that sale to buy two or more put options at a lower strike price. The puts have the same underlying security or asset, and, ideally, have the same premiums; most importantly, they must have the same expiration date. If the underlying moves modestly in the direction the trader wants, he/she can realize exceptional profits; however, even if the underlying moves away from the trader, he/she can make a small profit or at least break even. This is a hedging strategy in which the investor is likely to attain neither significant profit nor loss, but may return a modest profit. Risk is limited to the premiums of the puts bought, and profits are theoretically (though rarely actually) unlimited. This is a favored investment strategy of many risk-averse option traders. See also: Call Ratio Backspread.

Put Spread An option spread in which one has a long position in a put while having a short position on another put on the same underlying asset with a different strike price and/or expiration date. One uses a put spread to profit from price movements in the underlying asset. See also: call spread.

Put Swaption An option on an interest rate swap in which the buyer of the option has the right to enter into an interest rate swap as the payer of the floating rate and the receiver of the fixed rate. This means that the seller (writer) is the receiver of the floating rate and payer of the fixed rate. This is an attractive option when interest rates are expected to rise as the buyer of the option would generally receive more in interest than he/she/it pays out. See also: Call swaption, Plan vanilla swap.

Put To Seller Informal; to exercise a put option. The "seller" in this case is the option seller (writer), not the seller of the underlying (option holder). To put to seller especially applies when the put is in the money and the writer must purchase the underlying at a higher price than the current fair market value. For example, the strike price in a put may be double the market value when the option is exercised. The writer must then pay the holder the strike price rather than fair market value.

Put Together In auto sales, to squeeze the highest possible profit out of a customer. In other words, to put together a deal means to convince the customer to pay the maximum price for an automobile.

Put Warrant A warrant attached to a share giving the shareholder the right to sell the share at a certain strike price on or before a stated expiration date. A put warrant operates much like a put option. The main difference is that a put option is a separate contract between two parties, while a put warrant is attached to a share directly, especially as a sweetener.

Put-Call Ratio The ratio of the trading volume of puts to the trading volume of calls in a given market. Investors sell puts when they believe that prices on the underlying assets will fall by the expiration date. Analysts thus use the put-call ratio to determine market sentiment, with a high ratio indicating a bearish sentiment and a low ratio indicating a bullish sentiment.

Puttable Common Stock Common stock in a publicly-traded company that an investor may sell back to the issuing company at a certain price. This price is determined when the stock is issued. Generally, the price is relatively low in order to discourage abuse of the option, but it protects the investor from the risk that the share price will collapse.

PUUM ISO 3166-3 code for the U.S. Miscellaneous Pacific Islands, which were re-designated as the U.S. Minor Outlying Islands in 1986. ISO 3166-3 codes are used to indicate names of countries that are no longer used.

PW 1. ISO 3166-1 alpha-2 code for the Republic of Palau. This is the code used in international transactions to and from Palauan bank accounts. **2.** ISO 3166-2 geocode for Palau. This is used as an international standard for shipping to Palau. Each Palauan division has its own code with the prefix "PW." For example, the code for Koror is ISO 3166-2:PW-150.

PY 1. ISO 3166-1 alpha-2 code for the Republic of Paraguay. This is the code used in international transactions to and from Paraguayan bank accounts. **2.** ISO 3166-2 geocode for Paraguay. This is used as an international standard for shipping to Paraguay. Each Paraguayan department has its own code with the prefix "PY." For example, the code for the Department of San Pedro is ISO 3166-2:PY-2.

Pya A subdivision of the Burmese (or Myanmar) kyat. A pya is equal in value to 1/100 of a kyat. See also: Cent.

PYF GOST 7.67 Latin three-letter geocode for French Polynesia. The code is used for transactions to and from French Polynesian bank accounts and for international shipping to French Polynesia. As with all GOST 7.67 codes, it is used primarily in Cyrillic alphabets.

PYG ISO 4217 code for the Paraguayan guarani. It was introduced in 1944, replacing the Paraguayan peso. It was pegged to the U.S. dollar between 1960 and 1985; it is now the least valuable currency in North and South America.

Pygme An ancient Greek unit of length approximately equivalent to 346.8 millimeters.

Pygon An ancient Greek unit of length approximately equivalent to 385.3 millimeters.

Pyi A Burmese unit of volume approximately equivalent to 255.71 milliliters.

Pyi Ne In Myanmar (Burma), a political subdivision approximately equivalent to a state. They are dominated by ethnic minorities. See also: Taing detha gyi.

Pylon A large tower containing power lines. Pylons are used in the operations of some utility companies.

Pyramid 1. To use unrealized profits from margin transactions to increase one's margin. That is, one uses unrealized profits as collateral on a margin account in order to borrow more money from a brokerage to buy more securities. **2.** To borrow to expand a company's operations. **3.** See: Ponzi Scheme.

Pyramiding 1. The practice of using unrealized profits from margin transactions to increase one's margin. That is, one uses unrealized profits as collateral on a margin account in order to borrow more money from a brokerage to buy more securities. **2.** The practice of borrowing to expand a company's operations.

Pyrrhic Victory A successful endeavor that came with such high costs, that it was almost not worth the effort. For example, a company may succeed in a hostile takeover, but only after overcoming so many anti-takeover measures and spending so much money that it overpaid and may have nearly bankrupted itself.

PZ 1. ISO 3166-1 alpha-2 code for Panama Canal Zone. This was the code used in international transactions to and from bank accounts in the Panama Canal Zone. **2.**

ISO 3166-2 geocode for the Panama Canal Zone. This was used as an international standard for shipping to the Panama Canal Zone. In both cases, the code is obsolete.

PZPA ISO 3166-3 code for the Panama Canal Zone, which acceded to Panama in 1979. ISO 3166-3 codes are used to indicate names of countries that are no longer used.

Q A symbol appearing next to a stock listed on NASDAQ indicating that the stock represents a company currently in bankruptcy proceedings. All NASDAQ listings use a four letter abbreviation; if a Q follows the abbreviation this indicates that the security being traded is in bankruptcy.

Q & A Format A way to conduct a meeting in which a speaker stands in front of participants and answers questions they may have. The speaker may make a presentation prior to answering questions. The Q & A format is very common in all kinds of business meetings.

Q Schedule A list of expenses a life insurance company in New York must file with state regulators. The Q schedule ensures that life insurers abide by laws limiting their expenses. It should not be confused with Schedule Q.

QA 1. ISO 3166-1 alpha-2 code for the State of Qatar. This is the code used in international transactions to and from Qatari bank accounts. **2.** ISO 3166-2 geocode for Qatar. This is used as an international standard for shipping to Qatar. Each state has its own code with the prefix "QA." For example, the code for the Municipality of Doha is ISO 3166-2:QA-DA.

Qadaa In Islamic law, the act of performing a duty on a later day if one was unable to perform it at the appointed time.

Qadaq A Tatar unit of weight approximately equivalent to 409.5 grams. It was rendered obsolete when the Soviet Union began to use the metric system in 1924. An equivalent term is goranka.

Qafiz A Maltese unit of volume approximately equivalent to 20.46 liters. It was originally used to measure milk and oil. It is largely obsolete but is still used in some circumstances.

Qai-Qabaalah In Islamic law, a form of tax farming in which the tax farmer pays a lump sum to the state. In exchange, he receives the right to collect all actual taxes from a given area. The tax farmer earns his living by retaining all taxes collected from subjects over the amount he pays to the state.

Qalalar In Kazakhstan, a political subdivision equivalent to a city outside the jurisdiction of any province.

Qantar A Maltese unit of weight approximately equivalent to 79 kilograms. It is largely obsolete but is still used in some circumstances.

Qanu An ancient Akkadian unit of length approximately equivalent to three meters.

QAR ISO 4217 representation for the Qatari riyal. Since 1980, the riyal has been pegged to the U.S. dollar at a rate of 1 USD = 3.64 QAR. This exchange rate is important especially to energy deals as Qatar is rich in natural gas and, to a slightly lesser extent, oil. See also: Currency pair.

Qardhul Hasan In Islamic finance, an interest-free loan. In qardhul hasam, the borrower only repays the principal amount. Because the Quran forbids paying or receiving interest, qardhul hasam is the only permissible loan in Islamic finance. However, this does not preclude a number of other investment vehicles that imitate the payment of interest. See also: Sukuk, Murabaha, Mudharaba.

Qaris A Tatar unit of length equivalent to 44.45 millimeters. It was rendered obsolete when the Soviet Union began to use the metric system in 1924.

Qark In Albania, a political subdivision approximately equivalent to a province.

Qaryah In Iraq, a political subdivision equivalent to a village.

Qasab An obsolete Arabic unit of length approximately equivalent to 3.84 meters.

Qasba A Maltese unit of length approximately equivalent to 2.1 meters. It is largely obsolete but is still used in some circumstances.

Qasba Kubu A Maltese unit of cubic volume approximately equivalent to 9.2 kiloliters. It is largely obsolete but is still used in some circumstances.

Qasba Kwadru A Maltese unit of area approximately equivalent to 4.4 square meters. It is largely obsolete but is still used in some circumstances.

QAT GOST 7.67 Latin three-letter geocode for Qatar. The code is used for transactions to and from Qatari bank accounts and for international shipping to Qatar. As with all GOST 7.67 codes, it is used primarily in Cyrillic alphabets.

Qatari Riyal The currency of Qatar. Since 1980, the riyal has been pegged to the U.S. dollar at a rate of 1 USD to 3.64 QAR. This exchange rate is important especially to energy deals as Qatar is rich in natural gas and, to a slightly lesser extent, oil. See also: Currency pair.

Qi In Inner Mongolia, a political subdivision approximately equivalent to a county.

Qian A unit of mass in China approximately equivalent to five grams.

Qindar The Albanian word for cent. A qindar is 1/100 of one Albanian lek. Qindar coins do not circulate.

Qindarke A non-circulating division of the Albanian lek equal in value to 1/100 of one lek. Its plural is qindarka.

Qiran The currency of Iran between 1825 and 1932. Its value was based on silver and gold, though it was pegged to the British pound toward the end of its circulation.

Qirsh A subdivision of a currency in several Arabic-speaking countries. A qirsh is equal to 1/100 of a Jordanian dinar or an Egyptian pound. It is also equal to 1/20 of a Saudi riyal. The term comes from a currency subdivision used during the Ottoman Empire. It is also spelled qursh or ghirsh.

Qismatul ghuramaa' In Islamic bankruptcy law, the distribution of liquidated assets to all creditors according to the proportion of debt each held. For example, if one creditor holds 25% of a person's debt, he receives 25% of the liquidated assets. This contrasts with the absolute priority principle in conventional finance, whereby all secured creditors must be paid in full before any unsecured creditors are paid.

Qiyas An Arabic term for analogy. Qiyas is used in Islamic law to deal with new situations as they arise. For example, the Quran forbids the use of alcohol but does not mention narcotics. Because alcohol and narcotics are both intoxicating, one may use qiyas to determine that Islamic law forbids narcotics as well. This has implications in Islamic finance.

Q-Rating A measure of the popularity of a celebrity. Opinion polls determine q-ratings; they are used to help guide decisions about casting for television shows. See also: Advertising.

Qsima A Maltese unit of weight approximately equivalent to 992 grams. It is largely obsolete but is still used in some circumstances.

Qstick Indicator In technical analysis, an indicator of whether pressure to buy a stock is increasing or decreasing. It is calculated by taking a moving average of the difference between the opening price and the closing price of a stock over a given period of time. A positive indicator shows that buying pressure is increasing, while a negative number indicates the opposite. The Qstick indicator is used most often with candlestick charts.

Qu An ancient Akkadian unit of volume approximately equivalent to one liter.

Quad In printing, a type with no letter attached to it. The quad exists to put spaces between words.

Quadrans 1. An ancient Roman unit of area approximately equivalent to 631 square meters. **2.** See: Teruncius.

Quadrant In Cartesian coordinates, one fourth of the area divided by the x- and y-axes. Quadrants are numbered starting in the upper right and continuing clockwise. That is, the quadrant above the x-axis and to the right of the y-axis is the first quadrant, the one below the first is the second and so forth. Quadrants are used in technical analysis, economic analysis, and other fields involving mathematics.

Quadrat Caqrim A Tatar unit of area approximately equivalent to 1.14 square kilometers. It was rendered obsolete when the Soviet Union began to use the metric system in 1924.

Quadrat Sajin A Tatar unit of area approximately equivalent to 4.5 square meters. It was rendered obsolete when the Soviet Union began to use the metric system in 1924.

Quadruple Heqat An ancient Egyptian unit of volume approximately equivalent to 19.2 liters.

Quadruple Indemnity A type of accidental death insurance that pays four times the face value of the policy should the insured die as the result of an accident. In general, to be eligible for the additional death benefit, one must die within a certain number of days of the accident and must be under a stated age. Otherwise, the ordinary death benefit is paid.

Quadruple Witching Day The expiration date for four types of standardized contracts: stock options, stock index options, stock index futures, and single stock futures. Quadruple witching day occurs four times a year, on the third Friday in the last month of each quarter. Investors often unwind their positions on these contracts on or immediately before quadruple witching days, which leads to increased trading volume on those days. See also: Triple witching hour.

Quadruple Witching Week The week in which four types of standardized contracts expire: stock options, stock index options, stock index futures and single stock futures. Quadruple witching week occurs four times a year, in the week containing the third Friday in the last month of each quarter. Investors often unwind their positions on these contracts during or immediately before quadruple witching weeks, which leads to increased trading volume on those days. See also: Triple witching hour.

Qualification Period In insurance, a period of time during which a policyholder is making premium payments but during which the insurer is under no obligation to provide coverage. That is, during the qualification period, the policyholder and insurer have entered into a binding contract in which the insurer does not have to fulfill its end if an insured event occurs. The qualification period exists to give the insurer time to determine whether there is any fraud on the part of the policyholder, and to ensure that the policyholder will not abuse the policy. The qualification period usually lasts a few weeks or months.

Qualified Describing any investment vehicle eligible for favorable tax treatment. In general, the personal income placed in a qualified vehicle is exempt from taxation until withdrawal. This increases the return on investment of that income. Common qualified vehicles include retirement plans and education trusts.

Qualified Acceptance 1. The agreement by a bank to pay only a portion of a bill of exchange, or to pay only after it changes the terms under which payment is made. This differs from a general acceptance, in which the bank honors the bill without condition. **2.** The agreement to a contract, contingent upon some change being made.

Qualified Acquisition Cost An early withdrawal from an IRA that is used to buy or build a home and/or to pay appropriate closing costs. While early withdrawals are usually subject to penalties and/or excise taxes, qualified acquisition costs are exempt from both of these.

Qualified Adoption Expenses In U.S. tax law, the expenses eligible for the adoption credit, which is a direct dollar-for-dollar reduction in one's tax liability for each child under the age of 18 that a taxpayer adopts. Qualified adoption expenses include attorney's fees, court costs, and traveling expenses. It is important to note, however, that expenses incurred while adopting one's spouse's child are not qualified adoption expenses.

Qualified Charity A non-profit organization in the United States devoted exclusively to religious, charitable, scientific, educational, or other similar purposes. Qualified charities are not allowed to lobby for political candidates. Qualified charities are exempt from federal taxation and, in most cases, contributions and donations made to them are also tax exempt. For this reason, many philanthropic foundations do not provide grants to organizations that are not qualified charities.

Qualified Circulation The number of readers a periodical, such as a newspaper or magazine, has. That is, if a magazine has 100,000 subscribers, it is said to have a qualified circulation of 100,000. Periodicals with higher qualified circulations generally command higher advertising rates. It is also simply called circulation.

Qualified Default Investment Alternative An investment vehicle a fund manager may use for retirement plan contributions in the absence of direction from the plan participant. A qualified default investment alternative must be diversified, may not directly consist of securities in the company for which the plan participant works, and may not penalize the participant for early withdrawal. Qualified default investment alternatives were defined in the Pension Protection Act of 2006 as part of a broader effort to ease automatic enrollment in retirement plans.

Qualified Discount Rate The lowest possible rate a credit card company may assess on a merchant per transaction. It is calculated as a percentage of the value of the transaction. For example, if there is a 1% qualified discount rate and one charges $100 on a transaction, the credit card company assesses $1 on the merchant. The qualified discount rate is assessed on those merchants that follow the credit card company's guidelines. See also: Merchant Account.

Qualified Distribution A tax-exempt payment made to an annuitant from a Roth IRA. In order to be qualified, a distribution must occur at least five years after the Roth IRA was established and the annuitant must be at least 59.5 years old (unless there are extenuating circumstances such as a disability). A distribution is qualified because the contributions to the IRA are not deducted from the annuitant's taxable income.

Qualified Dividend In the United States, a dividend eligible for capital gains tax rather than income tax. This is advantageous to the investor as capital gains are usually taxed at a lower rate than ordinary income. To become a "qualified" dividend, the security from which the dividend derives must be held for at least 61 days during a certain 121-day period (for common stock) or for at least 90 days during a corresponding 181-day period. Also, the corporation paying the dividend must either be American or at least have stock readily tradable in American securities markets. See also: Ordinary dividend.

Qualified Domestic Relations Order In divorces, a court order giving one party a certain percentage of his/her ex-spouse's retirement plan. Usually, the courts split retirement plans in half through qualified domestic relations orders. The spouse receiving benefits from a retirement plan through a qualified domestic relations order becomes responsible for any taxes that would be due on his/her portion of the plan.

Qualified Domestic Trust A trust into which the trustor deposits funds and other assets to provide for a surviving, non-U.S. citizen spouse while also maintaining control of what happens to those assets after the surviving spouse dies. In a Q-DOT, the trustor names his/her surviving spouse as beneficiary and provides that income and/or principal from the trust shall pass to that spouse upon the trustor's death. This enables the surviving spouse to avoid estate taxes to which the non-American spouse would otherwise be subject. See also: Q-TIP.

Qualified Endorsement An endorsement on a financial instrument, such as a check, that limits the endorser's liability. That is, the endorser may write "without recourse" as a qualified endorsement. It indicates that the endorser is not responsible in the event that an institution such as a bank refuses to make payment on the instrument.

Qualified Funeral Trust A trust constituted exclusively to pay for the funeral expenses of beneficiaries. In order to qualify for favorable tax treatment by the IRS, contributions made to the trust may not exceed certain limits per beneficiary and the trust must be the result of a contract with a funeral director or the equivalent.

Qualified Gracing The copies of a periodical that are delivered reasonably close to, but still after, the expected delivery date. For example, Monday's newspaper may not be delivered until Tuesday due to weather or an inefficient delivery person. The Audit Bureau of Circulations counts qualified gracing as part of a periodical's qualified circulation.

Qualified Higher Education Expense Tuition and related expenses that one pays to a university, college, technical school, or other post-secondary institution. Most of the time, qualified higher education expenses are tax deductible, and one may also be able to deduct the interest on savings bonds if the proceeds are used to pay for these expenses. See also: 529.

Qualified Impairment Insurance A rider attached to a health insurance policy providing coverage for an illness or injury for which the policyholder ordinarily would not qualify. This is especially useful for a preexisting condition or some other impediment to insurance. For example, if one has Crohn's disease, one's regular health insurance policy may not pay for treatment related to that illness. However, one may purchase qualified impairment insurance that would pay for these treatments.

Qualified Institutional Investor An institutional investor allowed to privately place securities with other institutional investors without registering the trade with the SEC. This requires that the private placement be for investment purposes and not for resale to the general public; it also requires that the institutional investors have at least $100 million dollars under management. It is also known as a Qualified Institutional Buyer (QIB). See also: Private placement memorandum, Rule 144A.

Qualified Lead A potential customer. A qualified lead has expressed interest in purchasing a good or service, but has not given a time frame or a solid commitment to buy. A salesperson may follow up with a qualified lead at a later date.

Qualified Long-Term Care Non-taxable benefits one receives from a long-term care insurance policy covering a long-term, non-life-threatening condition. In order for the benefits to be non-taxable, one must require care for at least 90 days and must be unable to perform at least two of the activities of daily living. Qualified long-term care was instituted in the United States in 1997.

Qualified Mail Mail that is eligible for a discount on postage before it is sorted. In general, mail must have a certain level of volume to be qualified. It is beneficial for businesses that use the mail frequently.

Qualified Opinion An auditor's statement that he/she is unable to render a full opinion about a company's finances, or a portion thereof, because the company's accounting does not meet the Generally Accepted Accounting Principles or because the information was for some reason incomplete. In other words, a qualified opinion states that the company's accounting is so sloppy that the auditor cannot render an opinion. This is placed on the front page of an audit. See also: Except for opinion.

Qualified Personal Residence Trust Also called a QPRT. In the United States, a trust to which the grantor transfers his/her personal residence. A QPRT is irrevocable. Therefore, the value of the residence is removed from the grantor's estate, which reduces his/her estate tax liability. The grantor may continue to live in the home for no charge for a certain number of years. The grantor, however, usually must pay a gift tax proportionate to the value of the home he/she owns free and clear.

Qualified Plan An annuity that one buys along with one's employer. That is, the annuitant and his/her employer both make tax-deferred contributions to the plan for a certain period, with withdrawals coming upon retirement. If the annuitant begins withdrawals before a certain age, withdrawal penalties apply. One may continue to make contributions until a certain age, usually around 65.

Qualified Prospect A company or other organization that has expressed interest in purchasing a seller's product. Sales persons identify qualified prospects on whom to spend most of their time. Each sales person has a slightly different definition of what makes a qualified prospect.

Qualified Replacement Property A property of the same type that is not necessarily the same as another property. Under U.S. tax law, a qualified replacement property is not subject to capital gains taxes. For example, if a person trades a rusty 1993 Chevrolet Cavalier for a mint-condition 1968 Chevrolet Corvette, the Corvette is a qualified replacement property. The person will not be liable for capital gains taxes on the extra value of the Corvette because both properties are automobiles. See also: Like-Kind Exchange.

Qualified Residence The place where a person primarily lives. If one owns his/her qualified residence, he/she may write off the interest on the mortgage from his/her income.

Qualified Residence Interest The interest one pays on the mortgage for one's qualified residence, which is one's primary residence. In the United States, one may take a tax deduction on qualified residence interest. That is, one may reduce one's taxable income by the amount one pays in interest on all eligible mortgages. There are some limits to the deduction: for example, one may only deduct interest on the first $1,000,000 worth of mortgages, aggregated with other home debt. However, most homeowners can deduct all of their mortgage interest.

Qualified Savings Bond A savings bond issued after December 1989 to a person 24 years old or older. This bond may be used to pay for education expenses; when the bondholder does so, the interest is tax-free.

Qualified Settlement Fund A fund into which a defendant in a lawsuit may deposit assets to pay multiple plaintiffs. Under a qualified settlement fund, the plaintiffs may not have agreed how to distribute the assets among themselves, but they have agreed that the defendant has no further liability to pay beyond what is in the qualified settlement fund. This means that the defendant cannot be forced to pay any more to settle the claim with the plaintiffs. The amount the defendant puts into a qualified settlement fund is tax deductible. Qualified settlement funds are also called 468B settlement funds or 468b settlement trusts.

Qualified Special Representative Agreement An agreement between brokers and/or dealers to settle a transaction without using the NASDAQ ACT system. Under a QSR, the brokers and/or dealers agree to settle the trade directly through the National Securities Clearing Corporation. This may be an inconvenience to the brokers and/or dealers, but processing tends to be simpler and there are fewer costs to the transaction.

Qualified Terminable Interest Property Trust A trust into which the trustor deposits funds and other assets to provide for a surviving spouse while also maintaining control of what happens to those assets after the surviving spouse dies. In a Q-TIP, the trustor names his/her surviving spouse as beneficiary and provides that income and/or principal from the trust shall pass to that spouse upon the trustor's death. However, when the surviving spouse also dies, what remains in the trust is distributed to heirs as if it had been a part of the trustor's estate. A Q-TIP is a common trust when a person has children from a previous marriage; that Q-TIP provides for the surviving spouse but later is transferred to children from one's first marriage to ensure that the estate takes care of them as well.

Qualified Thrift Lender A bank that may borrow from a Federal Home Loan Bank. In order for a bank's portfolio to be eligible as a qualified thrift lender, at least 65% of it must contain mortgages on private residences. See also: Savings & loan.

Qualified Total Distribution The total amount to which a person is entitled from his/her qualified retirement plan. Depending on the nature of the retirement plan, this amount can be fixed, or it could vary according to how long the person lives. See also: Qualified distribution.

Qualified Trust An annuity that one buys with personal contributions and contributions from one's employer. That is, the annuitant and the employer both make tax-deferred contributions to the plan for a certain period, with withdrawals coming upon retirement. If the annuitant begins withdrawals before a certain age, withdrawal penalties apply. One may continue to make contributions until a certain age, usually around 65.

Qualifying Annuity An annuity that one buys along with one's employer. That is, the annuitant and his/her employer both make tax-deferred contributions to the plan for a certain period, with withdrawals coming upon retirement. If the annuitant begins withdrawals before a certain age, withdrawal penalties apply. One may continue to make contributions until a certain age, usually around 65.

Qualifying Loss In insurance, the value of an insured event for which the insurance company must pay. For example, if the deductible for a policy is $1,000 and the insurer must pay all losses above that amount, the qualifying loss for a policyholder who endures a loss of $1,500 is $500.

Qualifying Person A person whom the head of household may claim as a dependent when filing his/her taxes. Examples of qualified persons may include spouses, children and elderly relatives for whom one financially provides.

Qualifying Ratio The maximum debt-to-income ratio for a mortgage. If one's debt-to-income is not too high, one has a qualifying ratio and is eligible for a mortgage. The qualifying ratio varies by lender.

Qualifying Share A common share one must own in order to become eligible for the company's board of directors. It is important to note that qualifying shares are not, in themselves, different from other common shares.

Qualifying Utility Dividends and other income from stock in a utility company. Between 1981 and 1985, one could defer paying taxes on qualifying utilities if one reinvested this income in the same utility company. This was useful because some governments limited the profits these companies were allowed to make.

Qualitative Describing economic, market and other research not directly related to mathematical data. Qualitative factors are based on the assumption that economic actors, being human beings, are susceptible to acting on factors that may not directly correlate with facts. Qualitative factors may include management practices or brand recognition when recommending investment decisions to clients or brokers. See also: Assurance, Panic selling, Quantitative research.

Qualitative Research Economic and/or market research into areas not directly related to mathematical data. Qualitative research is based on the assumption that economic actors, being human beings, are susceptible to acting on factors that may not directly correlate with facts. Qualitative research may look into management practices or brand recognition when recommending investment decisions to clients or brokers. See also: Assurance, Panic selling, Quantitative research.

Quality The state of being superior to something else. For example, a good is high quality if it is more durable, tastes better, looks more appealing or is otherwise generally better than similar goods. High quality is an important aspect for many goods because it may increase sales. Most companies seek to have or make high quality products because doing so promotes repeat business. On the other hand, some companies sell low quality goods for very low prices and rely on high volume. See also: Quality control.

Quality Assurance The processes a company or organization uses to make sure its products do what they are supposed to do. There are two primary aspects of quality assurance. The first ensures that a product functions. That is, if a product is supposed to cut watermelons, quality assurance operatives see to it that it is designed in such a way that it actually cuts watermelons. The second works to eliminates mistakes so the products are created as they are designed. Quality assurance may be conducted in almost any industry. See also: Quality, Quality control.

Quality at the Source A concept in which each employee, department and/or other party must ensure the quality of every product.

Quality Circle A voluntary group of employees who discuss goings-on at work and present potential solutions to management. Members of the group may elect a chairman, or managers may appoint one. A quality circle exists to improve efficiency and productivity in the workplace, and consists of employee input so managers can receive feedback from the persons actually making the products. Quality circles originated in Japan and have met with some success there and in India. They have not worked as well in the United States.

Quality Control The processes a company or organization uses to test products to ensure that they are not defective. Quality control operatives may investigate the procedures used to make a product, the knowledge of employees or even intangibles like company morale. Quality control is distinguished from quality assurance in that

quality control tests for errors while quality assurance seeks to put in place systems to ensure that the errors do not happen in the first place. See also: Quality.

Quality Cost The expenses a company incurs to improve the quality of its products. Quality is the state of being superior to something else. For example, if a company uses a more durable raw material to make its products, the material is usually more expensive, which causes the company to incur a quality cost. However, poor quality can also result in costs. For example, customers may complain about defective products that may be replaced for free, which costs the company lost revenue.

Quality Ladder The practice in which a company gradually improves the quality of its products over time. For example, a company may make cheap, threadbare socks that are unlikely to last more than a few weeks. As it sells more socks, however, it may improve the quality such that it eventually makes warm, wool socks that keep feet warm no matter what the weather. It may be able to charge a higher price for the new socks. Quality ladders are associated with companies in developing nations.

Quality of Work Life Employees' level of happiness at work. Quality of work life may come from salaries, flexibility in allowing employees to attend family events or other things. Different persons have different definitions of quality of work life. For example, one person may derive satisfaction from traveling while another may consider it the worst part of his/her job.

Quality Review The formal inspection of a product in development. Quality review seeks to find flaws in design or implementation as early as possible to minimize costs (and delays) that later discovery would bring. Quality review is a type of quality control.

Quality Spread The difference in the yield of two debt securities whose features are identical other than the differing creditworthiness of the issuers. Issuers with lower credit ratings must issue debt at a higher interest rate to compensate holders for the added risk of default. The quality spread can help potential bond investors make decisions as to whether the higher yield is worth the extra risk. See also: Quality Spread Differential.

Quality Training Any program that teaches one how to test products to ensure that they are not defective. Quality training shows one how to investigate the procedures used to make a product, the knowledge of employees or even intangibles like company morale. Certifications, concentrations and even degrees are offered in quality training. See also: Quality control.

Quan In Vietnam, a political subdivision of an urban district.

Quango Quasi-Autonomous Non-Governmental Organization. An organization, which itself is not part of the government, to which the government has given a large degree of power, as a regulator or in another capacity. A prominent example is the Water Services Regulation Authority, which regulates sewage in the UK, among other things. However, it is not part of the government. The term is most common in the British Isles.

Quant Informal for a quantitative analyst. It is more generally applied to any securities analyst who uses quantitative analysis to determine buy or sell signals. Investment advisory firms employ quants to help them make investment decisions on behalf of clients. A quant is also called a rocket scientist. See also: Technical analysis.

Quant Fund A mutual fund managed by a computer program. Theoretically, a computer program can make investment decisions without emotion or bias; it simply buys and sells the securities according to a pre-determined formula. However, there is no guarantee as to how well designed a quant fund's program is, and it may not be able to adapt its program to changing market conditions. See also: Behavioral finance.

Quantify To express economic, market or other research directly in terms of mathematical data. Quantitative factors include facts such as P/E ratios, GDP growth, and other data that are objectively measurable. See also: Qualitative research.

Quantitative Research Economic and/or market research in areas directly related to mathematical data. Quantitative research is based exclusively on facts such a P/E ratios, GDP growth, and other data that are objectively measurable when recommending investment decisions to clients or brokers. See also: Qualitative research.

Quantity Demanded The number of goods demanded at a particular price. Demand-side economics states that, unless non-price factors (like brand loyalty) are involved, demand will drop in proportion to each rise in price. See also: Keynesianism.

Quantity Discount A lower price per unit a company charges in exchange for the purchase of a large number of units. For example, if the usual price for a product is $5 per unit and a buyer asks to purchase 10,000 units, the company may offer a quantity discount and only charge $3 per unit. Quantity discounts exist to encourage large orders, which, while they may reduce profit margin, increase revenue and therefore raw profit.

Quantity Prints A set of videotapes, photographs or other forms of media that are manufactured at the same time by the same person or company.

Quantity Risk The risk that an insufficient amount of an investment will be hedged and will result in a loss of the unhedged portion.

Quantity Supplied The number of goods or services available at a given price. In general, prices decline with greater supply, but this is not always the case.

Quantity Theory of Money The idea that the amount of money in an economy directly correlates to the price of goods and services. According to this theory, more

435

money in an economy results in higher prices. Nearly all economists agree with the quantity theory of money in the long run, but there is significant disagreement over how true it is in the short term. There is also disagreement over what kinds of money (cash, notes or others) affect prices. The quantity theory of money is a major component of monetarism. See also: Real bills doctrine.

Quantity Variance The difference between sales actually made and the estimated sales, multiplied by the sales price, over a period of time. For example, suppose a company expects to sell 1,000 units at $5 per unit each week. If it sells 1,200 units in week one, its quantity variance is $1,000 ([1,200 - 1,000] * $5). Likewise, if it only sells 700 in week two, the variance is -$1,500 ([700 - 1,000] * $5).

Quantize To express or convert an asset or liability as a quantity of a currency other than the one in which it usually trades. For example, Americans trading stocks on the IPE in London must report their assets in dollars for United States tax purposes. See also: Foreign exchange.

Quanto Option A cash-settled futures contract or other derivative in which the underlying asset is denominated in a currency other than the one in which it is settled. For example, two investors may enter into an agreement to buy/sell a futures contract on an index in which the index is in British pounds but the contract is settled in euros. The exchange rate at which the contract is settled is determined at the beginning of contract, protecting the investors from the foreign exchange risk that the currencies will adversely change in value.

Quanto Swap A swap of any kind in which the assets swapped are denominated in two different currencies, but are settled in the same currency. For example, two investors may swap interest rates, one calculated in British pounds and one calculated in U.S. dollars, and settle in dollars. The exchange rate at which the contract is settled is specified at the beginning of the contract to protect the counterparties from foreign exchange risk.

Quarta A Portuguese measure of weight approximately equivalent to 0.115 kilograms. It became obsolete after Lusophone countries adopted the metric system in the 19th century.

Quartarius An ancient Roman unit of volume approximately equivalent to 136 milliliters.

Quarter Three months of a year, often abbreviated as "Q." Q1 is January, February, and March; Q2 is April, May, and June; and so forth. Publicly traded companiesmust report on their earnings and other business performance measures every three months. Analysts also use quarters to measure performance internally. For example, one might compare sales in Q1 of 2009 to those in Q1 of 2008 to measure the company's health without having to account for seasonal variance. Often, quarters are abbreviated along with the calendar year; for example, the second quarter of 2006 is expressed as Q2 2006 or Q2/06.

Quarter Day In Britain and Ireland, one of four traditional dates each year when rent on land was due and when new servants were hired. While they are not generally observed anymore, rents on English leaseholds often are due on quarter days. In England and Ireland, the quarter days are March 25, June 24, September 29 and December 25. In Scotland, they are February 2, May 15, August 1 and November 11. The dates correspond to traditional pagan and Christian holidays.

Quarter Eagle A gold coin minted in the United States between 1792 and 1929. It was worth $2.50.

Quarter of Coverage The personal income one must earn in a year to be eligible for one quarter of the Social Security benefits to which one may be entitled. That is, one who earns a quarter of coverage has that year counted as part of his/her working life for calculating benefits after retirement. One cannot earn more than four quarters of coverage per year, regardless of one's income.

Quarter on Quarter The measure of performance in one quarter compared to the same quarter of a different year. This is done so that growth or decline might be measured without having to account for seasonal variance. For example, one might compare sales in Q1 of 2009 to those in Q1 of 2008. If a company sold 1,000,000 widgets in Q1/08 and 1,250,000 in Q1/09, this indicates 25% growth in sales, and is a positive sign for investors. See also: Quarter.

Quarter Showing When advertising on a train, taxi cab or other mode of transportation, the placement of an ad in 25% of all cars. This gives the ad a great deal of exposure. See also: Full showing.

Quarter Stock A stock with a face value of $25 per share. Quarter stocks are rare because few stocks have face values anymore.

Quarterland An obsolete Scottish unit of area. A quarterland was the amount of land on which rent of two ounces of silver could be charged. In some areas, however, it indicated an area on which 1/4 ounce of silver was assessed. This system was used in western and northern Scotland.

Quarterly Earnings A company's total revenue for a quarter less its quarterly operating expenses, interest paid, depreciation, and taxes. For example, a widget manufacturer may earn $1,000,000 in total revenue in Q1 2010. The widgets cost $200,000 to make, and the manufacturer's administrative and payroll expenses total $250,000. He/she also must subtract $50,000 in depreciation on widget manufacturing equipment and pay $200,000 in taxes. The manufacturer's quarterly earnings are stated as: $1,000,000 - $200,000 - $250,000 - $50,000 - $200,000 = $300,000. See also: EBIT.

Quarterly Earnings Growth The amount by which the earnings in a quarter exceed the earnings in a corresponding quarter from a previous year, expressed as a percentage. For example, if earnings in Q1 2009 were $1.5 million and were only $1

million in Q1 2008, quarterly earnings growth is 50%. Obviously, higher earnings are considered beneficial for a company, though there is no guarantee that they are sustainable.

Quarterly Earnings Report A report that a publicly-traded company publishes giving information for its performance each quarter. The report contains information on the company's financial state, most notably statements on revenue, expenses, and earnings. In general, it is less detailed than a stockholder's report but contains much of the same information. It is also called a quarterly profit-and-loss statement and a quarterly income statement. See also: Annual earnings report, Balance sheet.

Quarterly Financing A debt security in which portions of the same issue are offered four times per year, on the 15th of February, May, August, and November. That is, rather than making a new issue, an issuer may use quarterly financing instead; this usually saves on the expense of making a whole new issue. Examples of quarterly financing include three-year and 10-year notes, as well as 30-year bonds.

Quarterly Income Debt Securities Also called QUIDS. Tradable debt securities representing the debt of a limited partnership. The limited partnership is a subsidiary of another company and exists only for the purpose of issuing the QUIDS. The proceeds from QUIDS are lent to the partnership's parent company. These securities thus combine aspects of stocks and bonds; they pay coupons on a quarterly basis and usually have a par value of $25. They are similar to QUIPS, but, in the event of liquidation, QUIDS have higher priority.

Quarterly Income Preferred Securities Preferred stock representing a portion of ownership in a limited partnership. The limited partnership is a subsidiary of another company and exists only for the purpose of issuing the QUIPS. The proceeds from QUIPS are lent to the partnership's parent company. These securities thus combine aspects of stocks and bonds; they mature on a quarterly basis and usually have a par value of $25. Returns on MIPS come out of the partnership's pretax earnings, and, therefore, can result in tax advantages.

Quarterly Returns In securities, the amount of revenue an investment generates in a quarter as a percentage of the amount of capital invested. The quarterly returns may show the number of quarters it will take to recover one's investment. For example, if one invests $1,000 in a bond and receives $125 in the first quarter of the investment, the quarterly return rate is 12.5%, and the investor will recover his/her initial $1,000 in eight quarters.

Quarterly Revenue Growth The amount by which the revenue in a quarter exceeds the earnings in a corresponding quarter from a previous year, expressed as a percentage. For example, if revenue in Q1 2009 was $1.5 million and was only $1 million in Q1 2008, quarterly revenue growth is 50%. Obviously, higher revenues are considered beneficial for a company, though there is no guarantee they are sustainable.

Quarter-to-Date A term used to describe any information for the current quarter up to the current date. For example, if the quarter goes from January 1 to March 31 and today's date is February 5, any QTD statement includes information from January 1 to February 5.

Quartier In Mali and Monaco, a political subdivision equivalent to a neighborhood in a city or a portion of a village.

Quartieren In Luxembourg, a political subdivision equivalent to a quarter or neighborhood within Luxembourg City.

Quartile In statistics, the set of values encompassing one-quarter of points in a data set.

Quartilho A Portuguese measure of liquid volume approximately equivalent to 350 milliliters. It became obsolete after Lusophone countries adopted the metric system in the 19th century.

Quasi-Contract In law, an agreement imposed upon the parties by a court to establish legal equity. A quasi-contract is imposed when the parties should have signed a real contract, but did not, and therefore may find themselves in an inequitable situation.

Quasi-Loan An agreement between two parties whereby one pays the debts of the other. In exchange, the debtor party agrees to repay the debts to the other party at some point in the future. This point may or may not be specified.

Quasi-Public Corporation A publicly traded company partially owned or at least guaranteed by a government for some purpose thought to benefit the community. For example, a government may create a quasi-public corporation that sells mortgages to encourage homeownership. Quasi-public corporations are considered low-risk investments because of the express or implied guarantee that the government would not allow the company to go bankrupt. However, quasi-public corporations are required to place their mission above providing a profit to stockholders. See also: GSE.

Quasi-Rent Income one earns on a sunk cost. A quasi-rent occurs when one makes an investment and pays for it, and then earns income from it without needing to make further investment. In order to be considered quasi-rent, the income must exceed the opportunity cost of the investment.

Quasi-Reorganization In American accounting, the act of changing a company's records to eliminate a deficit in retained earnings by restating its balance sheet as if it were in bankruptcy. No bankruptcy is actually filed, however, and shareholders must agree to the changes. Quasi-reorganizations are controversial because they do not improve a company's actual state; rather, they simply make its books appear healthier. It is rarely done in practice.

Quattro Pro A spreadsheet program. Introduced in 1990, it was one of the first programs (but not the first) to use tabs (allowing a single file to contain multiple spreadsheets). It also contained more columns and rows than any version of Microsoft Excel prior to 2007. However, it has historically occupied a relatively small market share.

Quay A place where ships may dock in order to load and unload cargo. It is also called a wharf.

Queen of the Pigs A derogatory slang term for the best person or thing among a group of defective, poor, or simply bad things. For example, the most productive employee among a group of unproductive employees, or the lease expensive good among a group of overpriced, similar goods may be referred to as the queen of the pigs.

Query 1. The words an Internet search engine attempts to find on the web. A query may be for any of the words searched, all of the words, or even an exact phrase. **2.** More broadly, a question.

Questionable Payment A payment that may be illegal or unethical. In brief, a questionable payment is a suspected bribe.

Questionnaire A sheet with a series of (usually multiple choice) questions on it. Participants are asked to answer the questions in order to provide information to the person or organization issuing the questionnaire. Questionnaires are frequently used in marketing to gauge interest in a product, campaign, price, or almost anything else.

Queue An ordered collection of persons or things in which one is serviced after another. For example, persons may form a queue to buy tickets to the cinema. Likewise, an employee may form a list of tasks to be done each day and perform them each in turn. The word queue is most common in Britain and the Commonwealth; the equivalent in American English is waiting line or simply line.

Queue Discipline The rules a company or other organization follows to process orders, inventory, or other things that it receives. For example, a queue discipline may handle things as they are received or may categorize them by importance. See also: LIFO, FIFO.

Queuing Theory The use of quantitative measures to balance supply and demand for services in order to minimize wait times. Queuing theory is most beneficial in retail establishments; for example, one may use it to determine how many cashiers to have at the grocery store. It is also called waiting line theory.

Quick Assets Highly liquid assets that a company holds. Quick assets are either cash and cash equivalents or anything that can quickly be changed into them. Examples include stocks and bonds. See also: Current assets.

Quick Win An investment highly likely to profit in the short term. For example, oil prices may temporarily jump on news of unrest in the Middle East. While the trend is unlikely to be sustainable and probably will reverse itself, it presents an opportunity for an investor to make an easy gain.

Quickbooks A major line of accounting software primarily for small businesses. Quickbooks allows one to complete taxes, payroll and end-of-year forms, among other services. Quickbooks historically has had by far the largest market share of any similar software system.

Quicken A major line of accounting software primarily for individuals and microbusinesses. Quicken allows one to complete taxes and track expenses. Quicken is marketed toward businesses that are too small to justify the extensive services offered by Quickbooks.

Quid A slang term for the British pound. See also: Buck.

Quid Pro Quo An agreement between any firm and a brokerage firm in which the first firm makes use of the other's financial research free of charge. In exchange, the firm agrees to conduct any trades it may decide to conduct as a result of the research with the second firm as broker. More generally, quid pro quo may describe any financial agreement thought to be mutually beneficial. This may apply to positive things such a trade agreement or to illegal activities such as pay-to-play schemes in municipal contracts.

Quiet Enjoyment The right to be present on and to use a piece of property in a legal way. Quiet enjoyment is usually guaranteed in a lease for a residence or office. It also may be guaranteed in title to property ownership, in which case the previous owner must defend the new owner against competing claims to the title.

Quiet Filing The registration of a new issue with the SEC where some of the details are intentionally omitted. The issuer "fills in the blanks" by making amendments to the original filing. This process takes longer than a filing where all information is complete; a company uses it when it wishes to start the process of a new issue but has not yet set all of the issue's terms.

Quiet Period 1. A time during which the issuer is not allowed to promote a new issue. The quiet period begins on the filing date when the issuer registers the security with the SEC and ends 25 days after the security is actually issued. **2.** A time during which a company's employees may not change the portfolios of their retirement plans. This usually occurs when the company sponsoring the plans is making some administrative changes. It is more commonly called a lockdown.

Quiet Title Action A court hearing to determine the true owner of a piece of real estate. Quiet title action occurs when two or more persons or companies claim a parcel of land. In general, one may not take title in a quiet title action unless one proves the superiority of one's own claim; weakness in another claim is not relevant. Quiet title action is also called action to remove a cloud.

Quincunx 1. An ancient Roman unit of area approximately equivalent to 1,051 square meters. **2.** An ancient Roman unit of weight approximately equivalent to 137 grams.

Quindark Ari A subdivision of the Albanian franga. One quindark ari was equal in value to 1/100 of franga. Quindark ari did not circulate in practice, however.

Quintal 1. In South Asia and some European countries, a measure of weight equivalent to 100 kilograms. It is commonly used in India in the trade of agricultural goods. **2.** In Germany, a measure of weight equivalent to 50 kilgrams.

Quire A unit equivalent to 24 sheets of paper.

Quitclaim Deed A deed releasing the interest or ownership, if any, that the writer, known as a grantor, has in a property. It is important to note that a quitclaim deed does not attest that the grantor actually has an ownership interest in the property; it merely states that the grantor no longer claims to have one. One who buys a property in exchange for a quitclaim deed therefore accepts the possibility that another person or persons have an ownership interest in it. For this reason, some property insurance companies do not provide coverage for a property with only a quitclaim deed.

Quite Virtual Envelopes A way of budgeting for an individual or small organization in which money for different purposes is placed in different accounts. For example, a person may keep two checking accounts, one for monthly bills and one for discretionary spending. While the monies are not physically placed in separate envelopes, they are still segregated so as to encourage financial responsibility. See also: Spoken for, Not spoken for.

Quits Termination of employment. Quits may occur due to retirement, firing for incompetence or some other reason, elimination of the positions or simply because the employee wishes to leave.

Quittance 1. In law, special exemption from the requirement to pay a certain tax, debt, or other obligation. For example, one receives quittance when a lender forgives a debt. **2.** Official acknowledgement that repayment of a debt has been made.

Quo Warranto A concept requiring a person to show proof of his/her legal authority to undertake an action. It is largely obsolete and has been abolished in some jurisdictions. When it is used, it is generally part of a claim that a government official either was not validly elected or a government or corporation lacked capacity to commit an act.

Quod Apostolici Muneris An encyclical letter written by Pope Leo XIII in 1878 in which he condemns revolution against civil governments and declares that Christians owe the duty of obedience to the state, provided the state does not direct one to violate his/her conscience. It also upholds marriage and family life and the right to private property. The letter is one of the foundational documents of Catholic social justice theory.

Quorum The minimum number of shareholders or board members that must be present at a meeting in order to make binding decisions for a company. Especially in the case of shareholders, the quorum may not be a number of persons, but a percentage of equity in the company represented by the owners who are present. The quorum is defined in the corporate charter. See also: Annual shareholders meeting.

Quota 1. The amount a country contributes to finance the International Monetary Fund. The IMF determines quota based upon how much each country contributes to the global GDP. Each country's quota also influences its voting power in matters of IMF governance. Larger countries both contribute and vote more. The quota system has proven to be controversial, as it gives smaller and less prosperous countries a lesser voice. **2.** The most barrels of oil an OPEC member state may produce per day. OPEC sets quotas in order to influence the price of oil. It raises quotas when it wishes to lower the price and lowers them when wishes to increase the price. **3.** Any minimum or maximum limit, especially one imposed by an authority. For example, a journalist may be required to write a minimum quota of articles per week, or an employee may not be allowed to work more than the maximum quota of hours to avoid charging his company overtime. **4.** See Import quota.

Quota 90 The 1927 peg of the Italian lira to the British pound instituted by Benito Mussolini. Quota 90 came out of a desire on the part of Italian economists to revalue the lira, but the rate (92.46 lira to one pound) was considered too low, overvaluing the lira. This led to increased unemployment and a decline in real wages.

Quota Sample In focus groups, the predetermination to include only a certain number of persons from stated demographic groups. The quota sample system allows focus groups to be representative while keeping them manageable. For example, a quota sample may limit itself to three persons under 25, three between 25 and 50, and three over 50.

Quota Share Reinsurance An agreement between an insurer and a reinsurer whereby the reinsurer pays an agreed-upon percentage of all losses the insurer sustains, regardless of type. The insurer compensates the reinsurer for this agreement.

Quotation Board On an exchange, a display of all current security prices, volume, and other relevant information. The quotation board is posted in a prominent place on the exchange, especially when it has a physical (instead of electronic) trading floor. See also: Big Board.

Quote 1. The highest price that a buyer is willing to pay for a security and the lowest price that a seller is willing to receive. The quote is displayed on a ticker and provides investors with the current price for each security. **2.** On an exchange, the last price at which a security, commodity, or derivative traded. This changes throughout a trading day and is recorded on the ticker.

Quote Currency In foreign exchange, the second currency listed in a currency pair. Normally, it is a foreign currency, as one usually calculates the quote currency in terms of the domestic currency. The quote currency is expressed in terms of the base currency when calculating exchange rates. For example, if one is calculating the exchange rate of the U.S. dollar to the British pound and the pound is the base currency, it is expressed as GBPUSD and read as "dollars per one pound."

Quote Driven Describing an exchange where the bid-ask spread is determined by quotes given by dealers or market makers with the duty to maintain a liquid market. A quote driven market contrasts with an order driven market, where the bid-ask spread is determined by orders directly by investors. A quote driven market is also called a price driven market and is usually on an electronic exchange.

Quote Rule An SEC rule requiring market makers and specialists on different exchanges to provide public quotes on the securities for which they are making markets (that is, serving as a counterparty for transactions when no one else is available). The quote rule is intended to increase transparency in the market.

Quote-Only Period A period of time during which relevant parties give quotes for an IPO, but during which shares are not traded. That is, interested parties state for how much they would be willing to buy or sell shares, but they do not actually do so. The quote-only period lasts for a few minutes and is intended to reduce some of the volatility inherent to an IPO.

Quotron A computer service that gives quotes for securities. It was originally the name of a single computer system, but the term has become generic.

R A symbol appearing next to a stock listed on NASDAQ indicating that the share being traded comes with a right. All NASDAQ listings use a four letter abbreviation; if an R follows the abbreviation this indicates that the share has rights attached to it.

R Square In statistics, the percentage of a portfolio's performance explainable by the performance of a benchmark index. The R square is measured on a scale of 0 to 100, with a measurement of 100 indicating that the portfolio's performance is entirely determined by the benchmark index, perhaps by containing securities only from that index. A low R square indicates that there is no significant relationship between the portfolio and the index. An R Square is also called the coefficient of determination. See also: Beta.

Rabb al-salam In a bai al salam (an Islamic finance credit sale), the buyer.

Rabbi Trust A trust in which one may deposit employee compensation such that taxation is deferred to a future date. This is done most commonly when the compensation would be deposited otherwise into a retirement plan that is not tax deductible. It derives its name from the fact that the first one was intended to benefit a rabbi.

Rachmanism In Britain, a slang term for a greedy landlord. The term derives its name from Peter Rachman, who became notorious in the mid-20th century for evicting tenants protected by rent control laws and replacing them with new immigrants without such protection.

Racial Discrimination Deliberate or unintentional preferential or detrimental treatment toward persons of a given race. For example, a person may prefer to hire persons of race A or may be more likely to dismiss persons of race B. In many jurisdictions, racial discrimination is illegal in business settings, though the specific measures taken to prevent it have proven controversial. See also: Affirmative action.

Racist A person who deliberately or unintentionally gives preferential or detrimental treatment to persons of a given race. For example, a racist may prefer to hire persons of race A or may be more likely to dismiss persons of race B. In many jurisdictions, racial discrimination is illegal in business settings, though the specific measures taken to prevent it have proven controversial. See also: Affirmative action.

Rack Folder In marketing, a small flier folded such that it fits into a display case designed for fliers folded in such a way.

Rack Jobber A wholesale company that allows a retailer to display its products on racks in a store. The rack jobber maintains ownership of the products until they are sold to customers. The retailer and the rack jobber then share the profits from these sales. A rack jobber reduces the risk to retailers that they will purchase merchandise no one will buy.

Rack Rent 1. The total amount the owner of property should be able to make from the rental of his/her property. The rack rent is especially important if the property has already been rented and the owner is bound to collect potentially lower rent. The rack rent is the same as the market rent. **2.** Excessive rent.

Racket 1. A fraudulent or otherwise illegal business practice. For example, a Ponzi scheme is a racket because no service is offered: new investors simply pay old investors. **2.** A company that engages in illegal or fraudulent activities.

Racketeer Influenced and Corrupt Organizations Act United States legislation passed in 1970 that increased criminal and civil penalties for participating in organized crime and also strengthened law enforcement tools in the investigation of illegal enterprises. Its provisions included the ability to indict individuals for witness intimidation or extortion, prosecution for acts of terrorism or murder for hire, and so forth. One can be prosecuted under RICO for offenses such as counterfeiting money, securities fraud, and bankruptcy fraud.

Racketeering The crime of engaging in an illegal business. Originally, racketeering referred to forms of extortion, in which one extracted "protection money" from local persons and businesses. The definition has extended to include offenses such as counterfeiting money, securities fraud, and bankruptcy fraud. See also: RICO.

Radar Alert A practice that a publicly-traded company uses to identify a possible hostile takeover. For example, a company may monitor for large purchases of shares

by a single person or group of persons. Radar alert may give a company time to prepare or implement an anti-takeover strategy.

Radd bi al-ayb In Islamic law, the act of returning a good to its seller or maker due to some defect.

Radio and Television Transmitting Equipment Insurance Radio and Television Transmitting Equipment, Transmission Lines, Pipelines, Traffic Lights Insurance. An insurance policy providing coverage for the loss of any of the mentioned assets a company may own. An additional rider may also compensate for lost revenue due to the loss of one of these assets. This is especially important for hospitals, brokerages and similar organizations. As with all insurance, one must pay a premium to receive the coverage.

Radio Button In programming, a prompt following a series of options that only allows the user to choose one. For example, a user may be asked if he/she wishes to save his/her work. The user may choose either yes or no but not both.

Radioactive Contamination Insurance An insurance policy providing coverage for goods being transported within a country for damage or loss resulting from radioactivity. For example, if a truck transporting goods contains both radioactive and non-radioactive material, this type of insurance would cover the losses if the non-radioactive material become radioactive due to contamination. As with all insurance, one must pay a premium to receive the coverage.

Radiogram A message sent between two or more amateur radio operators, with other radio operators acting as intermediaries. Radiograms are spoken with various headers so that each intermediary can transmit them to the next destination.

Radium Floater A supplement to an insurance policy protecting a business from damage to its property caused by radiation or other damage due to nuclear material. A radium floater is important because most insurance policies do not cover nuclear damages.

Radix In mathematics, the base number when an exponent is considered. For example, in the number 25, the radix is 2 and the exponent is 5.

Rag Content Cotton fiber in paper. If one holds the paper up to light, one is able to see the rag content (which may be arranged in a small design).

Ragged Left In printing, an uneven margin on the left side of a page.

Ragged Right In printing, an uneven margin on the right side of a page.

Raghabah In Islamic law, commonly owned property that neither the state nor an individual may own or regulate.

Rahn bil darak In Islamic law, a situation in which a buyer withholds a portion of the purchase price of goods in case a third party lays claim to them and proves the seller had no right to sell.

Raiding The act or practice of an investor or a group of investors buying a majority stake or a significant minority stake in a publicly-traded company such that it can dismiss current managers and replace them with handpicked successors. Raiding often occurs when the company's share price has recently fallen significantly. It is less commonly called venture arbitrage. See also: Hostile takeover, Greenmail.

Rail Waybill A receipt issued that indicates to the customer that his/her goods have been received and have been passed on for freight by railway. Rail waybills often include tracking numbers so that the customer can check the status of the shipment.

Railroad Retirement Act of 1934 Legislation in the United States that established the first federally administered pension system intended to benefit non-government employees. The Act was found to be unconstitutional, but it laid the foundations for the Social Security Act of 1935. See also: Railroad Retirement Act of 1974.

Railroad Retirement System A federal system in the United States providing pensions to railroad workers. Persons are eligible to draw funds from the system if they worked 10 years for a railroad (or five years if performed after 1995). It is financed through payroll taxes levied on railroads and their employees. It is distinct from the Social Security Administration, but the two perform largely the same function in their respective spheres.

Railroad Rolling Stock Insurance An insurance policy providing coverage for a railroad against damages that it causes to another railroad's equipment, as well as to any goods belonging to a third party that the second railroad carries. The policy provides all risks coverage, meaning it pays for any damage not specifically excluded. For example, if a train crashes into a train belonging to another railroad company, rolling stock insurance will pay for damages. As with all insurance, the railroad must pay a premium to receive the coverage.

Railroad Sidetrack Agreement An agreement between a railroad company and the owner of a property on which a rail sidetrack is built. The owner agrees not to sue the railroad for covered accidents that might occur on the owner's property. It is also simply called a sidetrack agreement.

Railroad Travel Policy An insurance policy providing coverage if one is injured or if one's belongings are damaged while in transit on a train. One may purchase railroad travel policies at rail stations. As with all insurance, one must pay a premium to receive the coverage.

Rain Check A receipt or verbal promise by a seller that if a product is out of stock potential buyers will be able to buy the same product at the current price when the seller receives the next shipment. This is important if the seller wishes to attract or retain the buyer's business; that is, the seller issues rain checks to discourage buyers from going to a competitor.

Rain Forest A forest that receives at least 68 inches of rain per year. Rain forests are responsible for a large proportion of Earth's oxygen turnover, and are home to numerous plant and animal species. Environmental degradation has threatened the future of rain forests, and various governments have taken steps to protect them.

Rain Insurance A type of business interruption insurance that pays for business expenses and lost income due to rain. For example, if a baseball game is rained out, rain insurance may provide a benefit to a t-shirt vendor outside the stadium. It is not property insurance and does not cover damage to facilities. As with all insurance, one must pay a premium to receive the benefit.

Rainmaker Informal; a facilitator of a deal. The term especially applies to an employee whose sole duty is to bring in new business from wealthy clients. That is, the rainmaker meets with potential clients and convinces them to come to business with the rainmaker's company. See also: Finder's Fee.

Rainy Day Fund 1. In the United States, savings put aside by individual states to pay for services when revenues fall below expenditures. That is, when the state is required to spend money in excess of its tax and other revenue, it may use the rainy day fund to make up the difference. States put a certain percentage of their budget surpluses into their rainy day funds. Rainy day funds are especially important for states that have balanced budget amendments in place. **2.** More broadly, any savings especially set aside for a specific purpose.

Raioane In Moldova, a political subdivision equivalent to a county or province.

Raion In several Slavic countries, a political subdivision referring to either a portion of a province or a portion of a large city.

Raise An increase in one's wages or salary. A company may offer a raise for seniority, exceptional work performance or some other reason. Some raises are automatic, especially to account for the cost of living, while others must be requested or earned. In the UK, a raise is sometimes called a rise.

Raised Check A check in which the face amount has been increased. For example, one may write a check for $10, then cross out that number and write $15. Unless the other party agrees, one is not obliged to honor a raised check for the higher amount and may simply pay the lower one.

Rajju An ancient Indian unit of length variously equivalent to values between 15 and 20 meters.

Rajon In Kosovo, a political subdivision equivalent to a province.

Rajons In Latvia, a political subdivision equivalent to a district or county.

Rally A rapid increase in stock prices. A rally occurs when investors begin buying one or more stocks in large amounts, which represents an increase in demand and therefore raises the price. A rally may happen following a prolonged decrease in price, indicating that a security has been oversold and the rally is likely to be sustained. Alternately, it may be a bear market rally, which is a brief respite between two downturns.

Ralph Nader An American lawyer and major consumer advocate. He rose to prominence in the 1960s exposing unsafe American automobiles, leading to numerous lawsuits against General Motors. In the 1970s, he became an environmentalist and ecologist. He also ran unsuccessfully for president of the United States several times. He was born in 1934.

Ramadan The ninth month of the Islamic lunar calendar. Most Muslims are required to fast from sunrise to sunset during Ramadan. Economically, the use of electricity and the purchase of food and medicine may increase during Ramadan in Muslim-majority areas, due to the physical hardships of adjusting one's schedule from eating during the day to eating at night.

Ramp A slang term for a market rally that occurs quickly and decisively. For example, a stock that has generally been flat or in decline but suddenly jumps 9% in a few hours may be said to experience a ramp.

Ramp Down Informal; to reduce operations in anticipation of declining demand. For example, a toy store may ramp down its operations by buying fewer toys from its wholesaler immediately after the Christmas season, when people are less likely to buy toys in large quantities. See also: Seasonality.

Ramp Up Informal; to increase operations in anticipation of increased demand. For example, a toy store may ramp up its operations by buying more toys from its wholesaler immediately before the Christmas season.

Ramping 1. See: Ramp down. **2.** See: Ramp up.

Random Access In computer systems, the ability to access any point of a sequence in an equal amount of time. Random access contrasts with sequential access, in which different points in a sequence take varying amounts of time to access. Random access is also called direct access.

Random Access File A computer file in which the user has the ability to access any point of a sequence in an equal amount of time. Random access files contrast with sequential access files in which different points in a sequence take varying amounts of time to access.

Random Digit Dialing The practice in which a computer generates random telephone numbers to dial. This is done in some phone surveys to ensure a random sample. Random digit dialing can include unlisted phone numbers. It is cost effective in some marketing campaigns, provided the area being dialed has a relatively high phone ownership rate. See also: Do not call list.

Random Variable In statistics, a variable expressing all possible outcomes of a set of circumstances. It is important in probability density function and probability distribution.

Random Variance A change in a statistical sample due to chance and not to a change in the underlying data. For example, 47% of one sample may prefer product A to product B, while only 42% do in a second sample. If the change is due to random variance, it does not indicate a decline in support for product A. Various models exist to account for random variance, notably large sample sizes and multiple surveys. See also: Outlier.

Random Walk Theory An investment philosophy holding that security prices are completely unpredictable, especially in the short term. Random walk theory states that both fundamental analysis and technical analysis are wastes of time, as securities behave randomly. Thus, the theory holds that it is impossible to outperform the market by choosing the "correct" securities; it is only possible to outperform the market by taking on additional risk. Critics of random walk theory contend that empirical evidence shows that security prices do indeed follow particular trends that can be predicted with a fair degree of accuracy. The theory originated in 1973 with the book, A Random Walk Down Wall Street. See also: Efficient markets theory.

Randomization 1. The selection of a representative, random section of the population. Randomization is important in generating accurate statistics, which is vital in marketing. **2.** See: Random Number Generation.

Random-Number Generation The production of a series of numbers with no pattern. Random number generation may be simple, such as rolling dice or flipping a coin. Other mechanisms involve complex computers. Random number generation is used in gambling, particularly in slots and lotteries.

Random-Number Generator Any machine or activity that produces a series of numbers with no pattern. A random number generator may be simple, such as rolling dice or flipping a coin. Many others are complex computers. Random number generators are used in gambling, particularly in slots and lotteries.

Range Forward A forward contract on a currency with a collared payout. It is used to hedge a short position on the underlying currency. See also: Cylinder.

Rangebound Describing a security that trades between two relatively close prices. That is, a rangebound security is not trending in either direction. For example, a stock that trades between $45 and $46 over the course of a trading day may be described as rangebound.

Rank Correlation In statistics, the extent to which two rankings match each other. There are various systems to calculate rank correlation. However, rank correlation is expressed on a scale from -1 to +1. A measure of -1 indicates the rankings disagree perfectly (meaning they are opposite one another), while a measure of +1 means they agree perfectly (meaning they are the same). A measure of 0 means the rankings are independent of one another.

Rank in Person In a foreign service, the rank an officer holds regardless of the specific position he/she holds. That is, the rank in person is the officer's rank even when he/she performs the duties of an officer with higher or lower rank.

Rank-and-File The members of an organization as opposed to its leaders. The term is especially common when some individual members disagree with leadership. For example, the rank-and-file members of a union may oppose some policies proposed by organizers and representatives.

Ranking Any way of arranging investments in a hierarchy according to return, risk, or any number of other metrics. For example, one may compare investments to each other to determine which are most likely to outperform, underperform, and perform the same as the market as a whole. Ranking systems may assign categories using letters (say A-E), numbers (1-5), or even with individual names.

Rappen A division of the Swiss franc equal in value to 1/100 of one franc. A rappen is also called a centime or a centesimo in the French and Italian-speaking sections of Switzerland.

Rapport The state of affinity between two people who are communicating. Rapport is vital in person-to-person marketing because one is more likely to buy from someone with whom one has an established relationship. Salespersons work to build rapport with their customers because it helps to increase their success. They use a variety of tactics to do this, including eye contact, smiling and even gift-giving.

Rare Describing a coin that is extremely difficult to find. Depending on its quality, a rare coin may be quite valuable, depending on demand from collectors and investors. However, a rare coin may be a highly illiquid asset. See also: Numismatics.

Rasgez Akababiwach In Ethiopia, a political subdivision for an autonomous region.

Rast An archaic Norwegian unit of length approximately equivalent to nine kilometers.

Ratable 1. Describing a property of which an appraisal is possible. For example, a farm is a ratable property because its value is able to be assessed. **2.** See: Taxable.

Ratable Value The value of real estate as estimated by the rent the owner could charge a tenant on a year's lease. The ratable value assumes the property is vacant when the real estate is sold.

Ratal A Maltese unit of weight approximately equivalent to 794 grams. It is largely obsolete but is still used in some circumstances.

Rate Anticipation Swap The exchange of bonds in one's portfolio for different bonds that will better mature at the portfolio's desired duration, given the investor's expectation about the future direction of interest rates. For example, an investor may buy bonds that will mature at a time when the investor believes that interest rates will rise, theoretically allowing him/her to receive a higher yield.

Rate Base The value of the assets of a utility company. The rate base helps the local government determine the price the utility company is allowed to charge its customers. The rate base determines prices because it helps to ensure a reasonable profit for the utility company while keeping utilities (which are perceived as necessary) affordable for customers.

Rate Book A document describing a company's prices. Rate books are especially used in marketing to show how much an advertisement costs.

Rate Capping A former policy of the British government that restricted the taxes that local councils were able to levy. Rate capping began with about 18 councils deemed to be overspending, and was later extended to other councils. Rate capping led to the rate capping rebellion over the 1985-1986 local budgets, in which some local governments refused to abide by the restrictions (though most eventually backed down). Rate capping was formally abandoned in the late 1990s.

Rate Card A short document containing maximum advertising rates for magazines and other publications. Most advertisers actually pay less than the prices listed on the rate cards as publications prefer to sell as much space as possible.

Rate Covenant A provision in an indenture for a revenue bond stating guidelines for the prices that the facility the bond intends to finance is allowed to charge its customers. For example, if a revenue bond finances an electric facility, a rate covenant may state that the electric company must charge enough to cover its ongoing expenses, but not so much that it is unfair to consumers.

Rate Holder 1. The smallest possible advertisement in a publication. An advertiser may purchase a rate holder as part of an agreement to purchase a minimum number of advertisements over a certain number of issues. **2.** The shortest possible advertisement in a broadcast. Advertisers purchase these rate holders for the same reason as above. They are approximately 10 seconds long.

Rate Lock An agreement between a mortgage bank and a potential borrower promising that that the bank will not change the proposed interest rate on a loan that has not been concluded for a certain period of time. The rate lock usually lasts for 60 days.

Rate Making In insurance, the process of determining premiums for large groups of policyholders. In rate making, the insurer must make certain that the premium is practical (that is, it covers actual risk of loss), fair to the policyholders, and non-discriminatory. Rate making is done for groups of policyholders because it is not cost effective to individually determine premiums for every policyholder.

Rate of Change In technical analysis, a measure of how fast the price of a security changes over time, expressed as a fraction or decimal. It is calculated as follows: Rate of change = (closing price today - closing price X days ago) / closing price X days ago

Rate of Effective Protection The added value to a domestically produced good or service resulting from a tariff that keeps out (or makes more expensive) foreign goods and services. That is, because the tariff make foreign goods and services more expensive than they otherwise would be, domestic goods and services are not forced to cut their own prices, which adds value and results in higher profits.

Rate of Mudharaba In a mudharaba contract, the agreed-upon ratio by which the parties share the profit. In a mudharaba, a provider of capital agrees to invest in an entrepreneur in exchange for a portion of the profit of the entrepreneur's venture. The rate of mudharaba states exactly what portion.

Rate of Return In securities, the amount of revenue an investment generates over a given period of time as a percentage of the amount of capital invested. The rate of return shows the amount of time it will take to recover one's investment. For example, if one invests $1,000 and receives $150 in the first year of the investment, the rate of return is 15%, and the investor will recover his/her initial $1,000 in six years and eight months. Different investors have different required rates of return at different levels of risk.

Rate Protection In an adjustable-rate loan, a period of time during which one's interest rate may not rise if prevailing interest rates rise. However, rates may drop in that time period if prevailing interest rates drop. Rate protection is usually extended for 90 or 120 days. See also: Call protection.

Rate Relief The ability of a price controlled company to increase the prices that it charges customers. Companies in some industries thought to be necessary for consumers, notably utilities, may be allowed to charge only certain prices, which may or may not give them a profit. If the prices are resulting in a loss, a company may apply to the government for rate relief. If rate relief is granted, it can cause a significant increase in it stock price.

Rate Setting The process of determining how much to charge for a product. Rate setting can be difficult. In rate setting, one usually considers expected expenses such as direct and indirect overhead and one's target profit. One may also consider other factors, such as competitors' prices. See also: Pricing strategy.

Rate Sheet A schedule that a bank distributes to auto dealerships stating amounts of money that the bank will pay the dealership for each incremental interest rate the dealership manages to convince the customer to pay. That is, a dealership may have an arrangement with a bank whereby the bank provides financing for the dealership's sales. If the dealership is able to convince a customer to accept a higher interest rate, the bank earns a higher profit. As a result, it offers a monetary incentive to the dealership to encourage this. The rate sheet states how much money the bank pays for each interest rate.

Rate Support Grant Direct grants made by the British government to local councils. Rate support grants were made between 1967 and 1990 because local

taxation was not considered sufficient to pay for governance. During the Thatcher premiership, these grants were cut for councils thought to be overspending. See also: Rate-capping.

Rated Down Describing an insurance policy in which one pays a lower premium because of lower risk. For example, women pay lower premiums on life insurance than men of the same age because women generally live longer than men; this fact reduces the risk of the policy.

Rated Policy An insurance policy with a higher than normal premium because of a particularly dangerous aspect of the policyholder's life. For example, if a policyholder is known to go skydiving every week, his life insurance may be a rated policy.

Rated Up Describing an insurance policy with a higher premium because of an unusual or at least higher risk. For example, a health insurance policy will likely rate up a policy for an obese person.

Rate-Reduction Mortgage A mortgage in which the interest rate may not rise, but may decline. Rate-reduction mortgages are most advantageous when interest rates are generally moving lower, increasing the likelihood the loan's rate will also decline.

Rates and Classifications A department within the United States Postal Service that enforces postage rates and works within the organization to promote efficiency.

Ratification by Agency The act in which an insurance company confirms the act of an insurance agent, thereby making it valid, legal and enforceable. This should not be confused with agency by ratification, which is a different concept altogether.

Rating 1. See: Bond rating. **2.** See: Credit score.

Rating Class In insurance, the relative risk of a policyholder. For example, in life insurance, rating classes indicate how likely a group of policyholders is to die before the insurer recoups the amount of the death benefit in premiums. Different rating classes are assessed higher or lower premiums.

Rating Service A company that evaluates preferred stocks and debt securities based on the likelihood of default. The ratings service provides an objective rating to the security; the rating is higher when the likelihood of default is lower. There are three main ratings services: Moody's, Fitch, and Standard & Poor's. Companies issuing new preferred stocks or debt securities pay one or more of the ratings services to have their securities rated. Banks are not allowed to invest in securities with ratings below a certain level. See also: Investment-grade, Junk.

Rating Trigger A provision in a loan agreement or bond indenture allowing one party or the other to take a certain action if the borrower's credit rating changes for any reason. For example, if a bond issuer's credit rating falls, a rating trigger may release bondholders from certain obligations specified in the indenture.

Ratio The division of one piece of financial information by another. Financial ratios are very common in fundamental analysis, which investigates the financial health of companies. An example of a financial ratio is the price-earnings ratio, which divides a publicly-traded company's share price by its earnings per share. This and other ratios help analysts determine whether a company's share price properly reflects its performance.

Ratio Analysis The study of the significance of financial ratios for a company. Ratio analysis is very important in fundamental analysis, which investigates the financial health of companies. An example of ratio analysis is the comparison of price-earnings ratios of different companies. This helps analysts determine which companies' share prices properly reflect their performances and therefore what investments are most likely to be the most profitable.

Ratio Calendar Combination An option strategy in which one conducts two calendar spreads, one with calls and one with puts. A calendar spread is the simultaneous purchase and sale of calls or puts with the same strike price but with different expiration dates. A ratio calendar combination (like a calendar spread itself) seeks to profit from price movements in underlying asset.

Ratio Calendar Spread An option spread in which an investor buys options with a long maturity while buying more options with a shorter maturity. All options have the same strike price and may be either calls or puts, but not a combination of the two. A ratio calendar spread is used to reduce risk on price movements to the underlying security.

Ratio Covenant Any covenant in a loan agreement that uses a financial ratio. For example, a ratio covenant may prohibit more than a certain amount of leverage and may use a gearing ratio to determine this.

Ratio Spread An option strategy that involves buying a certain number of option contracts and selling a different number (according to a stated ratio) of options on the same underlying asset with the same expiration date but with a different strike price. One hopes to profit from the change in price of the underlying asset over the life of the options, but a ratio spread is most useful when one does not expect the price to be volatile.

Ratio Writer A writer (seller) of a call option contract who does not own a sufficient number of shares of the underlying asset. That is, while some of the calls are covered, the ratio writer sells a certain number of naked options. Ratio writers carry less risk than naked writers but more than sellers who write only covered calls.

Ratio Writing An options investment strategy in which the owner of an underlying security writes a number of calls at different strike prices on that security. Generally, only one of those options is exercised (if any are at all), leaving the owner with only the profit of the option premiums. Ratio writing thus has limited profit potential, but carries the possibility that an option will be exercised at a price favorable to the writer. The "ratio" in the term comes from the fact that the writer may write a theoretically unlimited number of options per 100 shares of the underlying security actually owned. Often, the owner writes two options per 100 shares, resulting in a 2:1 ratio.

Rational Expectations Theory In economics, a theory stating that economic actors make decisions based on their expectations for the future, which are based on their observations and past experiences. A basic example of rational expectations theory is a situation in which a consumer delays buying a certain good because, based on his/her observations and experiences, he/she believes that the price will be less expensive in a month. If enough consumers believe that, demand eases and the good is likely to actually be less expensive next month. Thus, the consumer waits a month before buying the good. Rational expectations theory states that current expectations strongly influence future performance. Economists disagree about how well the rational expectations theory works in the real world.

Rational Number Any number that can be expressed as a quotient of two integers. For example, one-tenth is a rational number because it can be expressed as 1/10.

Rationalization The process of reorganizing and overhauling a company's operations, policies, and anything else needed to make the company more efficient. Rationalization is thought to be more widespread than a reorganization; it may involve closing some operations while expanding others. It usually involves a shift in investment or other policy. Rationalization is intended to improve a company's profitability.

Ratl al-fiddah In Islamic law, a measure of weight roughly equivalent to 1428 grams.

Ratl bil 'ashyaa' In Islamic law, a measure of weight roughly equivalent to 408 grams.

Ratti A customary Indian unit of weight approximately equivalent to 0.12125 grams.

Raw Describing a coin that has not been officially appraised or put in some protective casing by an appraisal company.

Raw Material Supply Agreement An agreement between a producer and a supplier in which the supplier provides the producer with a stated amount of raw material for the producer to make its product. The raw material comes on a regular basis (e.g. once a week), and, in exchange, the producer gives the supplier a fixed amount each time the raw material is delivered.

Raymond Kroc A 20th-century American businessman. He started as a milkshake mixer salesman. In 1961, he purchased a small chain of fast food restaurants from the McDonald brothers. Kroc standardized an assembly line for food preparation and turned McDonald's into one of the largest corporations in the world. He lived from 1902 to 1984.

Razoo In Australia, a slang term for a hypothetical worthless coin. The term indicates a situation of poverty.

Razor-Razorblade Model A way to price two goods dependent on the other in which one good is priced at a loss while the other has a large mark-up. The idea is to encourage consumers to buy one product for the lesser price, necessitating them to buy the other at a higher price in order to use the first product. The model takes its name from the fact that razors are very cheap, while the replacement blades are often quite expensive. The model is commonly used with video game consoles and the games themselves.

RE 1. ISO 3166-1 alpha-2 code for the French Overseas Department of Reunion. This is the code used in international transactions to and from Reunion's bank accounts. **2.** ISO 3166-2 geocode for Reunion. This is used as an international standard for shipping to Reunion.

Reachback The ability for a tax shelter or limited partnership to wait until the end of a calendar year to apply deductions or credits it incurred over the entire previous year.

Reaction A decrease in price following an increase in price. A reaction connotes a slow decline; it is the opposite of a recovery.

Read the Lines A slang term meaning to look at and analyze technical information. For example, reading the lines may involve analyzing a company's price-earnings ratio over a period of time. The general direction of the ratio may influence whether one buys or sells the company's stock.

Read the Tape Informal; to observe transactions on the market without participating. Investors generally read the tape in order to identify buy and sell points. Regulators may also read the tape to look for evidence of illegal or unethical trades.

Reader Response In print media, a measure of reader interest in an advertisement based on the number of letters and other communications the magazine or periodical receives in relation to the ad.

Readies In the United Kingdom, a slang term for cash, especially cash kept in a wallet for immediate use.

Ready, Fire, Aim A slang term for the practice of putting a product on the market before it is ready. This is done either to impress investors or to meet an unrealistic deadline set by management. Sometimes, it is accompanied by a promise to fix the product later.

Ready, Willing, and Able Describing a person prepared to undertake an action. The term is especially used in reference to one ready to enter a contract.

Reaffirmation An agreement in which a borrower agrees to continue to be obliged to repay a debt, even if it otherwise would be discharged in bankruptcy. The reaffirmation must be signed before the debt is discharged. It is often used if a debtor wishes to maintain ownership of an asset, such as a car, that secures the reaffirmed debt.

Reaganomics An informal term for supply-side economics, which is a macroeconomic theory stating that a government can best promote growth by providing incentives for persons to produce goods and services. The primary way a supply-side oriented government does this is by maintaining low tax rates so that investors and entrepreneurs may use their money toward production. Maintaining low tax rates on the wealthy is one of the most important and controversial aspects of supply-side economics; the theory states that well off persons have the capital available to produce goods and services and thereby create jobs and grow the economy. Critics contend that this does not happen in reality, and that the wealthy are more likely to keep, rather than invest, their money. Reaganomics acquired the name because it was crucial to the economic policies of the administration of U.S. President Ronald Reagan. See also: Keynesian economics, Monetarism, Trickle-down economics.

Real 1. Describing a variable that takes inflation into account. For example, when considering GDP growth, if GDP has grown 10% in dollar terms, and the inflation rate is 3%, real GDP growth is only 7%. See also: Nominal. **2.** See: Tangible.

Real Account A business account in which the balance is carried forward after the end of the fiscal year. See also: Nominal account.

Real Asset Any asset with intrinsic value. Examples include real estate, a factory, or a patent. Real assets explicitly exclude financial instruments like a debt or a currency.

Real Body In candlestick charting, a representation of the range between the opening price and the closing price. It looks like the body of a candle, and excludes the "wicks" or shadows at either end.

Real Buying The level at which institutional investors are buying a security. Because institutional investors buy at much larger volumes than other investors, and because they are sometimes thought to be more sophisticated, real buying may indicate the future direction of a security's price. It may also (but does not necessarily) indicate technical or fundamental strength.

Real Capital 1. Assets used to produce goods. Farm land is a major example of real capital: the farmer uses this asset to produce commodities, which he then sells to make a profit. See also: Financial capital. **2.** Wealth that can be expressed in monetary terms. Major examples include the funds in savings accounts, as well as the value of real estate. Real capital is part of the calculation of an individual's or company's net worth.

Real Cash Flow A company's cash flow for a certain period of time adjusted for inflation. For example, if a company wishes to compare its annual cash flows between 1995 and 2005, it may adjust all figures and reflect them in 2005 dollars. The real cash flow gives a company an idea of how it is really performing from one period of time to the next.

Real Cost 1. The total cost of a product after considering all ancillary costs, including opportunity costs. **2.** The cost after considering inflation. See also: Real.

Real Currency A currency expressed in terms adjusted for inflation. See also: Real, Nominal.

Real Earnings 1. A company's profit after considering the impact of inflation. **2.** An individual's income after considering the impact of inflation. See also: Real.

Real Economic Growth Rate The change in a nation's GDP after accounting for inflation. The economic growth rate (or GDP growth) shows how much GDP has grown or shrunk in raw dollar amounts and may not be an accurate accounting of how well or poorly an economy is performing. The real economic growth rate adjusts for how much buying power has been affected and therefore provides a more accurate view. For example, if the economic growth rate is 10% and the inflation rate is 3%, the real economic growth rate is 7%. See also: Real GDP, Nominal GDP.

Real Estate Land and the improvements on it. Real estate is one of the primary (and indeed one of the only) assets whose value does not depreciate over time. Depending on the particular title, ownership of real estate may include mineral rights to any geophysical aspects occurring thereon. Ownership of real estate does not automatically include the right to develop it, depending on local regulations. However, development of real estate (for example by building a house on it) usually increases the value. While supply of real estate does not vary, demand may change greatly depending on its particular features, number of people in the area, and cultural differences regarding land ownership. It is an attractive form of collateral because it cannot be stolen or destroyed. See also: Plot, zoning law.

Real Estate Agent A person who facilitates the sale of real estate. Real estate agents network with potential buyers, show properties to them, and generally act in a way that will help sell the property in the shortest possible period of time. A real estate agent receives a commission for his/her services, usually a percentage of the value of the property sold. In the United States, a real estate agent must receive a license from the state in which he/she works. A real estate agent is an employee of a real estate broker.

Real Estate Alert A weekly newsletter that publishes information on the commercial real estate market in the United States. It disseminates news on relevant investment vehicles and strategies. The publication is based in New Jersey.

Real Estate Appraisal The act of estimating the value of real estate by a person licensed to do so. A person performing an appraisal must receive authorization from the appropriate body of the state in which he/she resides. A real estate appraisal may take into account the quality of the property, values of surrounding properties, and market conditions in the area. It is important for determining the property taxes for which the owner is liable, as well as a potential sale price, if the owner wishes to sell his/her property.

Real Estate Certificate of Deposit A certificate of deposit in which the provider uses the proceeds to purchase a piece of real estate. The CD holder is then entitled to receive rental payments and/or capital appreciation on the value of the property in addition to the interest rate to which he/she otherwise receives. A real estate CD therefore carries a lower interest rate than other CDs, but provides the possibility of a higher return.

Real Estate Investment Trust An investment company that invests exclusively in real estate and mortgages. The REIT issues a fixed number of shares at its establishment, and afterward neither increases nor decreases the number of shares. An REIT is actively managed, meaning that the real estate underlying the trust change from time to time in accordance with the fund's investment goals. A shareholder may trade shares in the REIT as if they were stocks. The value of shares in a real estate investment trust is determined by supply, demand, and the trust's net asset value. Importantly, the REIT itself is not taxed; rather taxes are passed on to shareholders.

Real Estate Limited Partnership A limited partnership in which the limited partners provide capital and the general partner in turn manages the development of real estate, for example, to build an apartment complex or housing subdivision. The general partner uses the investment money from the limited partners to construct and sell or rent the property. This gives the limited partners a good chance at a steady return, and the potential of high growth. A real estate limited partnership may also provide tax benefits for the partners.

Real Estate Mortgage Investment Conduit The most common type of mortgage-backed security. A REMIC entitles the owner to a claim on the principal and interest payments on the particular mortgages underpinning the security. REMICs pay an interest rate that is usually related to the interest rates the homeowners are paying on their mortgages. The equivalent of the coupon on a mortgage-backed security is a percentage of the interest and principal paid on the mortgages backing the security. REMICs can take different legal forms: trusts, partnerships, and assets without a legal status. They qualify for special tax treatment. REMICs were established by the Tax Reform Act of 1986.

Real Estate Owned Describing property owned by a lender after a foreclosure and the lender's subsequent failure to sell at a foreclosure auction. That is, if a bank forecloses on a property, it attempts to sell the property at an auction for an amount at least equal to the outstanding loan and associated fees. If it fails to do this (usually because the market value of the property is less than the outstanding loan), the property becomes real estate owned. The bank then attempts to sell the property at whatever price it can find. Real estate speculators often seek out real estate owned property because they can sometimes buy it for less than the market value.

Real Exchange Rates The purchasing power of two currencies relative to one another. While two currencies may have a certain exchange rate on the foreign exchange market, this does not mean that goods and services purchased with one currency cost the equivalent amounts in another currency. This is due to different inflation rates with different currencies. Real exchange rates are thus calculated as a nominal exchange rate adjusted for the different rates of inflation between the two currencies. See also: Purchasing power parity.

Real Gain An increase in price or value after adjusting for inflation. For example, if a stock gains 10% over a year and the annualized inflation rate is 3%, its real gain is said to be 7%. See also: Capital gains, Paper gain, Realized gain.

Real GDP Gross domestic product after accounting for inflation. Comparing real GDP from year to year shows the amount an economy has grown or shrunk and how this actually affects the economy because they show how the buying power of money has been affected. Nominal GDP, on the other hand, does not account for inflation. For example, if the nominal GDP has grown 10% and the inflation rate is 3%, the real GDP growth is 7%.

Real GNP Gross national product after accounting for inflation. Comparing real GNP from year to year shows the amount an economy has grown or shrunk and how this actually affects the economy by determining how the buying power of money has been affected. Nominal GNP, on the other hand, does not account for inflation. For example, if the nominal GNP has grown 10% and the inflation rate is 3%, the real GNP growth is 7%. The real GNP measure is rarely used since the gross domestic product has become widely accepted.

Real Income Personal, corporate, or national income after accounting for inflation. Comparing one's real income from year to year shows how much income has grown or shrunk after adjusting for how much the buying power of the money has been affected. Nominal income compares only raw dollar amounts and does not account for inflation. For example, if one's nominal income has grown 10% and the inflation rate is 3%, the real income growth is 7%. Real income is also known as real wages. See also: Real GDP.

Real Interest Rate An interest rate after accounting for inflation. A nominal interest rate shows by how much an investment or account has grown in raw dollar amounts and may not be an accurate accounting of how well or poorly an investment is performing. The real interest rate adjusts for how much buying power has been affected and, therefore, provides a more accurate view. For example, if one has bond with a 5% coupon, and the inflation rate is 3%, the real interest rate is only 2%. The real interest rate does not take compounding into account.

Real Loss A company or investment's losses after considering the impact of inflation. See also: Real.

Real Market The bid and ask quotes at which a security is traded. The real market does not account for a security's fundamental value, only the price at which it may actually be traded. A dealer engaging in the real market gives quotes that are likely to be taken. A dealer who does not wish to engage the real market may give quotes, but the quotes are purposely too high (if an ask) or too low (if a bid).

Real Money 1. An informal term for a large amount of money. **2.** A highly polemical term for sound money. **3.** In the bond market, a slang term for price movements caused by fundamentals without regard for speculation. For example, if speculators buy bonds because risk has declined, and afterward prices rise (and yields fall), the price movement is said to have been caused by real money.

Real Option A situation in which an investor is able to choose between two different investments where both choices involve tangible assets. That is, in a real option, the investor may choose between assets like land or inventory; financial instruments like stocks and bonds are not involved in a real option. It should be noted that a real option has nothing to do with an option contract.

Real Profit The profit of a company or investment after adjusting for inflation. It is calculated simply by subtracting the inflation rate from the gross profit margin. For example, if a company's profit margin is 7% and the inflation rate is 4%, the real profit is 3%.

Real Property Tax A property tax on local real estate that is calculated according to the fair market value of the real estate. That is, a real property tax is assessed as a percentage of the amount for which the owner would be able to sell the property in the current market. As a result, real property taxes increase when the local property market is bullish and decline when it is bearish.

Real Rate of Return The rate of return on an investment after adjusting for inflation. It is calculated simply by taking the gross return and subtracting the inflation rate. For example, if the return on an investment is 7% and the inflation rate is 4%, the real rate of return is 3%.

Real Return Bond A bond issued by the Bank of Canada that protects the bondholder from inflation. Most fixed dollar obligations pay a fixed coupon rate periodically and mature at par. While this carries low risk, it exposes investors to the possibility that the inflation rate will outpace the interest rate represented on the coupon. In order to protect against this, a Real Return Bond automatically changes its coupon rate according to the inflation rate as tracked by the Canada All-Items Consumer Price Index. Because Real Return Bonds are so safe, they offer very low rates of return.

Real Right In Louisiana law, any right attached to a property rather than a person. For example, the owner of a property with real rights has usufruct as well as the ability to borrow against the property. Real rights may attach to both real estate and movable property.

Real Risk-Free Rate of Return The risk-free rate of return after taking inflation into account. For example, if the risk-free rate of return is 3% and the inflation rate is 2%, the real risk-free rate of return is 1%. Because the risk-free rate is low in the first place, the real return can sometimes be negative, particularly in times of high inflation.

Real Selling The level at which institutional investors are selling a security. Because institutional investors sell at much larger volumes than other investors, and because they are sometimes thought to be more sophisticated, real selling may indicate the future direction of a security's price. It may also (but does not necessarily) indicate technical or fundamental weakness.

Real Time Describing the immediate reporting of an occurrence. Many quotes offered by brokers to clients are in real time, which means changes to the quotes occur as soon as the brokerage itself receives the information.

Real Time Gross Settlement An online system allowing the instantaneous transfer of funds and securities between banks. Real time gross settlement exists to settle large transactions between banks so that they can continue to extend credit to each other and to customers. Examples include the fed wire in the United States and CHAPS in the United Kingdom.

Real Wages The wages that a person earns or that a company pays after adjusting for inflation. For example, if an employee makes $25,000 per year in both Year 1 and Year 2, but the inflation rate is 10%, that $25,000 is only worth 90% of its previous value ($22,500) in Year 2. This is good for the employer, but bad for the employee.

Real Yield Security A debt security that protects the bondholder from inflation. Most debt securities pay a fixed coupon rate periodically and mature at par. While this carries low risk, it exposes investors to the possibility that the inflation rate will outpace the interest rate represented on the coupon. In order to protect against this, a real yield security automatically increases its principal and/or coupon rate according to the inflation rate as tracked by the Consumer Price Index or some other inflation-tracking index. Thus, the return on a real yield security keeps pace with inflation. Because real yield securities are so safe, they usually offer a very low rate of return. See also: TIPS.

Realignment A situation in which the governments or central banks of several countries coordinate to revalue one or more currencies. This may occur when currencies become so strong or weak that they negatively impact international trade or a country's balance of payments. Central banks may effect a realignment, for example, by buying or selling the relevant currencies in large volume.

Realistic on Price Describing a situation where one or both counterparties to a transaction must negotiate the price to a certain extent before the buyer and the seller will agree.

Realization Principle In accounting, a principle stating that a company can realize revenue only when it earns revenue.

Realize To close a position such that one finally sees the profit or loss from an investment. For example, if an investor buys a stock at $5 per share and the price goes to $10, the investor has a paper profit of $5 per share. However, if the investor waits to sell the stock until the price drops to $8, he/she only realizes $3 per share in profit. Investors often wait before realizing substantial profits or losses, as locking in a profit may result in higher taxation, while realizing a loss removes the possibility that the investment can be recovered. See also: Cut losses.

Realized Compound Yield The yield on a bond calculated by assuming that the bondholder reinvests all coupons at the current interest rate and holds those positions until the bond matures.

Realized Gain The amount by which the sale price of an asset exceeds its purchase price. Unless the realized gain came from a tax-exempt or tax-deferred asset, it is taxable. However, the type of taxation to which it is subject varies according to how long the asset has been owned. A realized gain from an asset owned longer than one year is usually taxed at the capital gains rate, while an asset owned for a period shorter than a year is often subject to the higher income tax rate. It is also called the recognized gain. See also: Unrealized gain.

Realized Yield The return on a bond during the time one holds the bond, usually expressed in annualized terms. The realized yield is calculated by taking the income and other gains on the bond and dividing by the historical cost. It is a useful way to compare the expected return to the actual return, though with bonds there is rarely a difference unless the bond defaults.

Reallowance A fee that an underwriting syndicate pays to a company that helps place a new issue with investors, but is not part of the syndicate.

Real-Time Trade Reporting A requirement that market makers on NASDAQ report each transaction publicly within 90 seconds of its taking place. Real-time trade reporting exists to improve efficiency and transparency in the market.

Realtist Informal; a member of the National Association of Real Estate Brokers.

Realtor A person who facilitates the sale of real estate. A realtor networks with potential buyers, shows the property to them, and generally acts in such a way that will help sell the property in the shortest possible period of time. A realtor receives a commission for his/her services, usually a percentage of the value of the property sold. The title of "realtor" is a designation reserved for members of the National Association of Realtors, and encompasses both real-estate agents and real-estate brokers.

Reappraisal An estimation of the value of a property, conducted by a person licensed to do so after an appraisal was previously conducted. Reappraisals are conducted periodically, for example, for property tax purposes.

Reassessment The value of a property as determined by an appraisal after an appraisal was previously made. A reassessment usually occurs every year when a municipality orders appraisals to determine the liability for property taxes. Additionally, if a property owner wishes to dispute the value of an appraisal, he/she may request a reassessment. The reassessed value may take into account the quality of the property, values of surrounding properties, and market conditions in the area.

Rebalancing The act of changing the percentages of different types of securities in a portfolio, especially according to changes in one's investment goals. Most portfolios are diversified to a greater or lesser degree; that is, they contain different types of securities in different proportions. If one's investment goals change (or if the portfolio is not meeting them satisfactorily), one rebalances the portfolio in order to achieve them. For example, if a portfolio is half bonds and half stocks and an investor wishes to have lower risk, he/she might rebalance the portfolio to be three quarters bonds and one quarter stocks.

Rebate 1. In an option, the amount that the holder is paid by the writer if the contract expires unexercised. It is usually a portion of the premium the holder originally paid. **2.** In a short sale, the interest or dividends to which the lender of a security otherwise would be entitled but instead passes on to the borrower (who is the short seller).

Rebate Barrier Option A knock-out option that refunds the holder a certain amount of money should the knock-out occur. A knock-out option is an option contract that automatically expires, even before the expiration date, if the underlying asset reaches a certain price that would be disadvantageous to the option writer. If this price is reached for a rebate barrier option, the holder receives a portion of the premium back. Because this reduces the writer's profit, a rebate barrier option is relatively uncommon. See also: Barrier option.

Recalculation Method A way to calculate the distributions from retirement accounts, where the amount in each distribution is recalculated every so often based on the current life expectancy of a retiree.

Recall Election An election to decide whether or not to retain a political office holder. In general, a recall election occurs when a sufficient number of voters petition for it. If a majority in the recall election vote to retain the incumbent, the status quo continues. If a majority vote not to retain, the incumbent is said to be recalled.

Recapitalization The act of changing a company's capital structure. For example, a highly leveraged company (one that is largely financed with debt) may repay most of its debt and issue stock so that it is financed with equity. On the other hand, a company may make a self-tender offer and buy back most of its stock while issuing bonds so that it becomes debt-financed. Some companies may believe that recapitalization can be advantageous, but the capital structure irrelevance principle states that a company's capital structure has no bearing on its profitability. Recapitalization is also called an e-type reorganization.

Recapitalization Proposal A plan for a company to change its capital structure. For example, a company may propose buying back its own shares and issuing debt to change from an equity-based capital structure to a debt-based capital structure. Very often, a company makes a recapitalization proposal when it is a target and wishes to ward off a hostile takeover.

Recapture 1. An agreement between a buyer and a seller whereby the seller is allowed to repurchase the good or other asset within a certain period of time. **2.** See: Depreciation Recapture.

Receipt Zeros Formerly-issued Treasury securities whose coupons had been stripped by an intermediary. Receipt zeros therefore paid no interest. They were sold at a significant discount from par and matured at par. Receipt zeros fluctuated in price because changes in interest rates made them more or less desirable. Common receipt zeros in the 1980s were CATS, which were issued by Salomon Brothers. Receipt zeros became largely obsolete after 1986, when the U.S. Treasury began issuing its own stripped bonds.

Receivables Balance Fraction The percentage of a company's total sales that consist of accounts receivable at the end of a period, especially a month. In other words, the receivables balance fraction represents the sales on which the company has not collected. The figure can be valuable in determining a company's cash flow and credit risk.

Received for Shipment Bill of Lading A bill of lading that is issued when goods are delivered at a ship or dock and not when they are loaded onto the ship. It serves as a receipt that the goods arrived at the port but not that they were actually loaded. When the goods are loaded, the received for shipment bill of lading is replaced by an on-board bill of lading.

Receiver In corporate bankruptcy, a person or entity whom a court or regulator appoints as custodian to administer all assets and debts. The receiver's main duty is to pay off as many debts as possible as cheaply as possible. One obvious way to do this is to liquidate the company, but this is not always done. The receiver may restructure the company to put it on a path toward solvency. Some jurisdictions have a very short period during which a receiver may operate, sometimes as brief as two weeks. When a receiver has only this long, he/she usually liquidates the company. When a receiver is appointed, the company is said to be in receivership. In the United States, different financial regulators have the authority to decide whether receiverships are necessary. The Office of Thrift Supervision may do this for savings and loans; the Office of the Comptroller of the Currency may do it for national banks. In any federally-chartered savings and loan or bank, the FDIC must be appointed receiver.

Receiver's Certificate A short-term debt security issued by a receiver (or party appointed by secured creditors in a bankruptcy) to finance his activities during bankruptcy proceedings. Despite the fact that they involve bankruptcy, receiver's certificates are low risk because they are secured by the same assets to which the secured creditors hold liens.

Receivership In corporate bankruptcy, a situation in which a court or regulator appoints a custodian to administer all assets and debts. This custodian is known as a receiver; his/her duty is to pay off as many debts as possible as cheaply as possible. One obvious way to do this is to liquidate the company, but this is not always done. The receiver may restructure the company to put it on a path toward solvency. In the United States, different financial regulators have the authority to decide whether receiverships are necessary. The Office of Thrift Supervision may do this for savings and loans; the Office of the Comptroller of the Currency for national banks. In any federally-chartered savings and loan or bank, the FDIC must be appointed receiver.

Receiving Bank A bank that collects an electronic transfer from another bank. It is also called a receiving depository financial institution.

Recession A prolonged economic retraction. While there is no technical definition of a recession, they are conventionally defined by two or more consecutive quarters of negative GDP growth. Recessions are marked by declines in productivity and investment and high unemployment. See also: Depression.

Recharacterization In IRAs, the act of making a contribution to a certain account, then deciding to apply the contribution to a different type of IRA. For example, if one has both a traditional IRA and a Roth IRA, one may make a contribution to the traditional account, then decide that it would be more beneficial to apply the contribution to the Roth account. Recharacterization is subject to certain rules. Primarily, one may not recharacterize tax-free rollovers or employer contributions.

Reciprocal Currency In foreign exchange, a currency whose exchange rate is quoted in U.S. dollars per unit of the foreign currency. One quotes a reciprocal currency by stating the dollars needed to buy one unit of that currency. That is, a reciprocal currency is a currency quoted in European terms.

Reciprocal Marketing Agreement An agreement in which two companies agree to market each other's products. For example, a peanut butter manufacturer might agree to market a certain jelly product when attempting to sell to consumers and retailers. In exchange, the jelly manufacturer does the same for the peanut butter. This is a relatively common marketing tactic for companies offering complementary, but not competing, products.

Reciprocal Quote In foreign exchange, a quote in European terms when it is normally made in American terms or vice versa.

Reckoning 1. See: Bill. **2.** See: Account. **3.** Informal; an estimation.

Reclamation **1.** The right of a seller to repossess property from a buyer when the buyer does not pay. For example, if someone buys 100 widgets on credit and does not make payments according to the agreed-upon arrangement, the seller has the right to reclaim the widgets and assume ownership once again. A major example of reclamation is foreclosure. **2.** The right of a buyer to collect the money paid on a purchase that was not delivered or not delivered according to expectations. For example, if a buyer pays in advance for the purchase of 100 widgets and the seller instead delivers 100 whatsits, the buyer generally has a right to be reimbursed.

Reclassification In mutual funds, the act or process of changing one type of fund into another type. For example, one may reclassify a front-load fund to a back-load fund or vice versa. One of the most common types of reclassification occurs when a load fund, after a certain number of years, becomes a no-load fund. This happens because the load generally only exists for a certain number of years. The IRS does not consider reclassification to be a taxable event, even if it results in more income or capital gains.

Recognized Loss In accounting, the sale of an investment or asset for less than the purchase price. Individuals and companies may use recognized losses to offset taxable income from other gains. For example, if a company has $5,000 in capital gains in a given year and $2,500 in recognized losses, its taxable income on the capital gains is only $2,500. Recognized losses can also be applied to future years. For example, if a company has no taxable income in a given year, recognized losses may offset taxes on profits for up to a certain number of years. See also: Future income taxes.

Record Date The last date on which any dividend on a stock that has been declared but not distributed belongs legally to the buyer, rather than the seller. That is, when one sells a stock on or before the record date, the dividend will go to the buyer when the next dividend comes. On the other hand, if it is sold after the record date, the dividend will go to the seller. In practical terms, the record date is the trading day immediately before the ex-dividend date. It is also called the date of record.

Record Holder The person or company who holds a security, as recorded on the security issuer's official lists. This is important around the record date, which determines who receives dividends or coupons.

Recording Fee In real estate, a fee the local government assesses for placing the sale of a property in the public record.

Recourse Describing a loan for which there is a co-signer. That is, if the borrower defaults on the loan, the co-signer becomes legally liable for repayment of a recourse loan. Thus, in addition to any collateral that may or may not secure the loan, the lender is further protected from default by the existence of the co-signer. See also: Non-Recourse Loan.

Recourse Loan A loan for which there is a co-signer. That is, if the borrower defaults on the loan, the co-signer becomes legally liable for repayment. Thus, in addition to any collateral that may or may not secure the loan, the lender is further protected from default by the existence of the co-signer. See also: Non-recourse loan.

Recovery **1.** Rising stock prices or GDP growth following a recession or period of declining growth. See also: Business cycle. **2.** The use of depreciation or other deductions or tax credits to receive a refund for what one pays in taxes in a given year. Recovery must sometimes (though not always) be reported as taxable income for the next year.

Recovery Period The period during which a company depreciates an asset. That is, the recovery period is that during which a company is able to write off a portion of an asset's value each year until the end of that asset's useful life. The length of the recovery period varies from asset to asset, and is often set by the IRS. It often bears only a rough relationship to the time during which the asset can actually be used. See also: MACRS.

Rectangle In technical analysis, a situation in which the price of a security stays within a fairly narrow band. It is called a rectangle because the resistance price and the support price, when drawn as lines, look vaguely like a rectangle.

Red **1.** See: In the red. **2.** See: Refunding escrow deposits.

Red Chip A stock in a company operating in the People's Republic of China that trades on the Hong Kong Stock Exchange. Generally speaking, only Chinese citizens are allowed to invest on Chinese stock exchanges. Red chips are therefore separately incorporated in Hong Kong in order to allow foreign investment in Chinese companies. The term refers to the color red, which is the official color of the Communist party.

Red Ink Informal; a loss or deficit. A company or organization may continue to operate in red ink for a time, but it is not sustainable. See also: In the red, In the black.

Redeemable Bond A bond that the issuer may buy back from investors before maturity. The bond may be called at the discretion of the issuer, within certain limits. When the bond is called, the bondholder receives the par value (or sometimes slightly more) and does not receive any more coupons. Redeemable bonds are issued to allow the issuers to hedge against interest rate risk. That is, if interest rates fall significantly, they can call the bond and issue a new bond at a lower interest rate, reducing their liabilities. However, to protect the bondholder, most redeemable bonds also include call protection, which prevents the bonds from being called for a certain period of time and thereby guarantees the current interest rate for that time. A redeemable bond is also called a callable bond.

Redemption **1.** In bonds, the act of an issuer repurchasing a bond at or before maturity. Redemption is made at the face value of the bond unless it occurs before maturity, in which case the bond is bought back at a premium to compensate for lost interest. The issuer has the right to redeem the bond at any time, although the earlier the redemption take place, the higher the premium usually is. This provides an incentive for companies to do this as rarely as possible. **2.** The act of the issuing company repurchasing stocks or mutual funds. In the case of mutual funds, the repurchase is made at net asset value per share. Stocks may be redeemed in cash or by proration. See also: Proratable factor.

Redemption Date The date on which a bond's face value is repaid to bondholders. Generally speaking, this is the maturity date, but in cases of a callable bond it may be the call date.

Redemption Fee A fee that some mutual funds assess when a shareholder redeems shares from the fund during a certain, usually brief period of time after purchase. It may be a flat fee or a percentage of the value of the shares redeemed. Mutual funds charge redemption fees to discourage new investors from withdrawing from the mutual fund if the fund's net asset value drops unexpectedly.

Redemption Premium Money over and above the face value of a callable bond that the issuer pays to bondholders if the bond is called. A callable bond is a bond that the issuer is permitted to redeem or repay before the maturity date, depriving the bondholder of future coupon payments. Usually the issuer does this if it can reissue the same amount of debt at a lower interest rate. The redemption premium exists to compensate bondholders for some of their lost interest payments. It is especially useful if they can only reinvest in securities with a lower return rate. The redemption premium is also called the call premium.

Redemption Price The price at which a bond may be repurchased by the issuer before maturity. The price is set at the time of the issue. Redemption prices are set to reduce the issuer's risk of default; that is, the issuer may have a concern that it will not be able to make all coupon payments and redemptions at maturity and may cut its losses by redeeming at the redemption price. One may refer to the redemption price as the call price.

Redenomination A reduction in the face value of a currency that a government or central bank makes because of hyperinflation or chronic weakness as a currency. For example, a country may declare that a "new" dollar is worth 1,000 "old" dollars and print new denominations reflecting this change. This may or may not stem the tide of inflation, depending on how the redenomination is approached and what other steps are taken.

Rediscount To declare a discount for the second time. For example, an issuer may offer a bond at a discount from its par value to entice investors. If this does not work, the issuer may discount the bonds further in order to encourage people to buy the bond.

Red-Lining A practice in which a company refuses to market its products in a certain area because it is disproportionately poor, has a high rate of default, and/or has a large minority population. Examples of products where a company may practice red-lining are health insurance and mortgages. Red-lining is illegal because these products should be offered based on individual creditworthiness. Those who support the illegality of red-lining argue that it promotes equality between races and classes, while critics contend that it leads to needless distortions in the market. See also: Fair Housing Act of 1968, Community Reinvestment Act.

Reduction-Option Loan A mortgage loan that combines aspects of fixed-rate and adjustable-rate mortgages. A reduction-option loan is a fixed-rate mortgage, but the rate may drop if prevailing interest rates drop more than a certain amount in a year. Usually, this reduction must be 2% or more. If that happens, the new, lower interest rate becomes the interest rate for the remainder of the mortgage.

Redundant Tariff A tariff that is imposed or changed but does not affect trade because some non-tariff barrier such as an import quota is already in place. Alternatively, a minutely changed tariff may be considered a redundant tariff because the change is not large enough to entice or discourage trade.

Reeded Edge In numismatics, describing a coin with grooves or ridges struck into it. It is intended to make the coin harder to counterfeit.

Ref A Swedish unit of length approximately equivalent to 27.7 meters. It is used in land measurement.

Reference Rate A floating interest rate or other benchmark used in some investment vehicles. For example, in an interest rate swap, the reference rate is the floating interest rate that one of the counterparties is paid. Likewise, in an adjustable-rate mortgage, the reference rate is the floating interest rate that helps determine the interest rate the property owner pays. Usually, the reference rate is LIBOR or some other interest rate that is adjusted on a daily basis.

Refinance To repay a loan by taking out another loan. Refinancing can allow one to secure a lower interest rate; for example, one can replace a loan at an 8.5% rate with one at 5.5%. In the case of a balloon loan, refinancing can repay the principal if one does not have sufficient funds to do it; that is, if one has made only interest payments over the life of the loan and has not saved the principal amount when the loan comes due, refinancing can prevent bankruptcy. There are two main drawbacks to refinancing. First, there is no certainty that one will be approved for it. One thus takes a risk every time one decides to make only interest payments on a loan or mortgage. Secondly, refinancing generally resets the repayment period; that is, if one refinances six years into a 10 year loan, the one generally repays the new loan over 10 years instead of the remaining four.

Refinanced Mortgage A mortgage one repays by taking out another mortgage. Refinancing a mortgage can allow one to secure a lower interest rate; for example, one can replace a mortgage at an 8.5% rate with one at 5.5%. In the case of a balloon loan, refinancing can repay the principal if one does not have sufficient funds to do so; that is, if one has made only interest payments over the life of the loan and has not saved the principal amount when the loan comes due, refinancing can prevent bankruptcy. There are two main drawbacks to refinancing. First, there is no certainty that one will be approved for it. One thus takes a risk every time one decides to make only interest payments on a mortgage. Secondly, refinancing generally resets the repayment period; that is, if one refinances six years into a 10 year mortgage, then one generally repays the new mortgage over 10 years instead of the remaining four.

Reflation The act of a government printing money or taking similar actions to combat deflation. Deflation occurs when a recession is so severe that prices are reduced to inspire demand. This often leads to further economic decline. Reflation marks an attempt to increase money supply to increase spending in an attempt to spur growth. See also: Inflation.

Reformed Dinar A currency used in the former Yugoslavia. It was introduced in 1992, quickly succumbing to hyperinflation. It was replaced by the October dinar in 1993 at a ratio of 1 million to one.

Refund 1. See: Tax refund. **2.** The sale price of an asset that the seller may give back to the buyer if the buyer returns the asset. **3.** See: Redeem. **4.** See: Refunding.

Refund Annuity An annuity that makes fixed payments to the annuitant throughout his/her life, but, more importantly, guarantees the return of the original amount paid into the annuity. Thus, if the annuitant dies before the original amount is paid out, his/her survivors receive the remaining amount. Premiums for refund annuities are usually higher than for other annuities.

Refundable A bond that may be retired before maturity. Nonrefundable bonds does not protect bondholders from the risk that the issuer may effectively refinance a bond at a lower interest rate, which exposes bondholders to the risk that they could be deprived of coupon payments to which they would otherwise be entitled. Most bonds are nonrefundable for at least five or 10 years after issue but may become refundable afterward. See also: Refundable tax credit.

Refundable Credit A direct, dollar-for-dollar reduction of one's tax liability in which one still receives a tax refund even if one's liability drops below zero. That is, if a taxpayer otherwise owes $2,000 to the government, but takes $3,000 in refundable credits, then the government owes $1,000 to the taxpayer. Relatively few tax credits are refundable; most are limited to the amount of one's tax liability. However, the earned income tax credit is a common example of a refundable credit.

Refunded Bond A bond whose principal is held in an escrow account, generally invested in Treasury securities or something else risk-free, until such time as the bond matures. That means that there is no possibility of default on the principal; as a result, refunded bonds usually have the highest possible credit ratings. They are also called prerefunded bonds.

Refunding The act or practice in which a company repays a bond by making a new issue of another bond. That is, a company refunds a bond when it borrows more money to repay the money it already owes to bondholders. One may think of refunding as the company refinancing a bond.

Refunding Bond A bond that retires another bond before the first bond matures. A company may issue a refunding bond for a number of reasons, but mainly because of a decline in interest rates, which reduces the cost of funding. Refunding bonds deprive bondholders of the first bond from future coupon payments to which they would otherwise of have been entitled. Most bonds are nonrefundable for at least five or 10 years after issue, but a refunding bond may be issued afterward.

Refunding Escrow Deposits A forward contract in which the holder is obligated to purchase a certain bond (usually a municipal bond) with a given yield at some point in the future. Until that purchase is made, the money used to purchase the RED is held in an escrow account and used to buy Treasury securities. This allows the holder of an RED to work around rules against pre-refunding of certain municipal bonds; REDs therefore have a tax advantage.

Regiao In Guinea-Bissau, a political subdivision roughly equivalent to a province.

Regiao autonoma In Portugal, a political subdivision for Madeira and the Azores, which are the parts of Portugal outside continental Europe.

Regierungsbezirk In Germany, a political subdivision of a state or province. It is larger than a county or rural district.

Regional Bank A bank that only operates in one state or province, or in only a few neighboring states or provinces. A regional bank differs from a money center bank, which has a national and/or global presence. Regional banks usually specialize in retail banking, making loans and taking deposits. See also: Thrift, Regional exchange.

Regional Check Processing Center A center run by a Federal Reserve Bank that expedites the settlement of checks. A regional check processing center processes and delivers checks to the appropriate bank on the same day it receives them, which helps money move through the economy more smoothly. A regional check processing center handles corporate checks, personal checks, food stamps, money orders, and checks drawn on the U.S. Treasury.

Regional Fund A mutual fund that invests predominantly or exclusively in the securities of a single region of the globe. While a regional fund may be diversified in other ways (e.g. it may hold both stocks and bonds), it selects securities based upon the countries in which they trade or are issued. Regional funds usually carry less political risk than single-country funds. Some analysts argue that, in an age of globalization, there is little difference between regional, single-country, and global funds, but others dispute that.

Regional Stock Exchange 1. In the United States, all stock exchanges operating outside New York City. Examples include the National Stock Exchange and the Chicago Stock Exchange. **2.** More broadly, all stock exchanges located outside a nation's main financial center.

Regionalism In political science, the ideology that seeks to decentralize government, or at least promote the interests of a given set of groups. Regionalism may advance geographic areas and/or ethnic groups. Despite growing international trade, regionalism is fairly popular in many countries. See also: Federalism.

Regionalist In political science, a scholar who believes in decentralized government, or at least promotes the interests of a given set of groups over the central group. Regionalism may advance geographic areas and/or ethnic groups. Despite growing international trade, regionalism is fairly popular in many countries. See also: Federalism.

Regioni In Macedonia, a political subdivision approximately equivalent to a province.

Registered Competitive Market Maker 1. A market maker registered with the National Association of Securities Dealers. As market makers, they seek to maintain stable prices by offering consistent buy and sell prices on over-the-counter trades. They list their bid and ask quotes on NASDAQ, which requires at least two registered competitive market makers per listed stock. Their bid and ask quotes are compared to ensure a representative spread. **2.** See: Registered competitive trader. An independent member of the New York Stock Exchange, who does not represent a firm and who acts as his/her own broker. Registered competitive traders are expected to correct imbalances of orders. Because they do not pay commissions, they deal actively in stocks, but because they represent only themselves they account for less than 1% of trade volume. Orders from specialists take precedence over registered competitive traders. See also: Registered equity market maker.

Registered Education Savings Plan In Canada, an account into which a person makes contributions up to a certain limit in order to save for a university education and from which he/she begins to take distributions to pay for tuition and other expenses. A Registered Education Savings Plan allows for tax deductible contributions and taxable distributions; that is, contributions are tax-deferred until withdrawals are made. Registered Educations Savings Plans may be invested in securities and usually own common stock and certificates of deposit. See also: Registered Retirement Savings Plan.

Registered Equity Market Maker A trader firm registered on the American Stock Exchange. They are expected to make purchases and sales that encourage stability in the market and for its own account. It is also charged with helping to correct imbalances. See also: Registered competitive market maker, Registered options trader.

Registered Exchange A securities exchange with sufficient trading volume and other activity to require registration with the SEC. Most exchanges about which one hears in the news are registered exchanges. A prominent example is the New York Stock Exchange.

Registered Investment Advisor A person or business regulated by the SEC that provides investing advice or counsel to an investor. All investment advisers managing over $25 million must register with the SEC; the actions of all registered investment advisers are governed by the Investment Advisors Act of 1940. Importantly, it is a criminal offense for investment advisers to provide false or misleading information, and to buy or sell his/her own securities to or from a client. Registration helps the SEC enforce these provisions.

Registered Investment Company A mutual fund or other investment company that is registered with the SEC. Registered investment companies are required to report their policies and financial conditions, much like a publicly-traded company. Most investment companies in the United States must register with the SEC; they are regulated by the Investment Company Act of 1940.

Registered Name The name of a business on record with the appropriate government authority. In general, a registered name must be unique within the jurisdiction. A company need not use its registered name in its advertising and daily operations, but if it does not, it may have to file a doing business as application.

Registered Office The address of a business on record with the appropriate government authority. The registered office may be important for determining the business' status for tax purposes.

Registered Options Trader A floor trader or specialist on the American Stock Exchange concentrating on options. These traders are expected to ensure that options are being traded fairly and, if necessary, to help correct imbalances in the market. See also: Registered competitive market maker, Registered equity market maker.

Registered Owner The person or company whose name is listed on a security certificate or some other title. The registered owner is recognized as the legal owner of the property or asset represented by the certificate, and has full rights of ownership subject to the restrictions of law.

Registered Representative Rapid Response Service An automated system on the NYSE filling buy and sell orders for certain securities at the best available price. The system allows registered representatives to fill certain orders without resorting to a specialist.

Registered Retirement Income Fund In Canada, a tax-deferred retirement plan that invests the funds the holder has placed in a Registered Retirement Savings Plan (RRSP) and pays the beneficiary out of the income from those investments. Generally speaking, one does not buy an RRIF directly, but rather rolls over funds from an RRSP, which one may do anytime by the age of 71. The advantage to an RRIF is that it allows one to invest tax-free until one actually receives the income from those investments.

Registered Retirement Savings Plan In Canada, an account into which a worker makes contributions up to a certain limit throughout his/her working life, and from which he/she begins to take distributions following retirement. A registered retirement savings plan allows for tax deductible contributions and taxable distributions; that is, contributions are tax-deferred until retirement. Registered retirement savings plans may be invested in securities and usually own common stock and certificates of deposit. It is the Canadian equivalent of an IRA.

Registered Retirement Savings Plan Contribution An amount of money that a worker places into a Registered Retirement Savings Plan at regular intervals. In Canada, an RRSP is an account into which a worker may make these contributions up to a certain limit throughout his/her working life, and from which he/she begins to take distributions following retirement. The contributions are tax deductible, and they are invested in securities, usually common stock and certificates of deposit.

Registered Retirement Savings Plan Deduction A tax deduction one takes from contribution to a Registered Retirement Savings Plan. An RRSP is an account into which a worker makes contributions up to a certain limit throughout his/her working life, and from which he/she begins to take distributions following retirement. The contributions one makes are taken out of one's taxable income. The trade-off for an RRSP deduction is the fact that distributions are taxable. The RRSP deduction can reduce one's tax liability in the years contributions are made, but it is especially important because the taxation on distributions almost certainly results in lower tax liabilities after retirement.

Registered Secondary Offering An offering of a large block of previously issued stock that is not usually traded after registering the offering with the SEC. For example, a mutual fund that owns a large portion of an issue of stock may decide to sell it. Most of the time, the seller of a registered secondary offering is an institutional investor who acquired the stock through private placement. It is also called a registered secondary distribution. See also: Overnight deal.

Registered Security A security with the owner's name printed on the certificate or, in the case of an electronic registration, where the owner's name is listed in a database. Registered securities contrast with bearer forms, which the person physically holding them is presumed to hold. Virtually all securities currently traded are registered securities; this has become truer as registration has become computerized.

Registrar A company or other organization that handles records for stocks and bonds. That is, a registrar maintains records of who owns individual shares or bonds in exchange for a fee paid by the issuer. Registrars help ensure that shares and bonds are authentic and that bonds represent a legitimate legal obligation on the part of the issuer.

Registration The process of submitting appropriate documents to a government regulator before an activity may be conducted. For example, a company must register with the SEC or the equivalent state agency before it may issue stock. In other words, registration is the process of publicly announcing that one intends to conduct an activity and taking all steps to ensure that the activity is done legally and correctly.

Registration Fee A fee that a company pays to the SEC when registering a new issue. The fee changes from year to year; its amount is governed by the Investor and Capital Markets Fee Relief Act.

Registration Right The right of a holder of a restricted security to have his/her security registered with the SEC on demand. A restricted security is a stock or right one acquires through some means other than the open market. One may receive a restricted security through a merger or acquisition, private placement prior to an IPO, or sometimes through a stock option. Perhaps most importantly, it is not registered with the SEC and thus may not be sold publicly until registration has been made. The registration right protects holders from the risk that they will be forced to retain a security that they do not want and that may become detrimental to their investment goals.

Registration Statement A document filed with the SEC explaining a new offering of securities for public trade. A registration statement must contain a complete description of the security and the terms of the sales. It must also include applicable information about the issuer's financial situation and applicable risk factors. This is done to protect investors from fraud.

Regression Analysis In statistics, the analysis of variables that are dependent on other variables. Regression analysis often uses regression equations, which show the value of a dependent variable as a function of an independent variable. For example, a regression could take the form: $y = a + bx$ where y is the dependent variable and x is the independent variable. In this case, the slope is equal to b and a is the intercept. When plotted on a graph, y is determined by the value of x. Regression equations are charted as a line and are important in calculating economic data and stock prices.

Regression Coefficient A mathematical measure of the effect that an independent variable has on a dependent variable. It may be used on any number of financial measures. For example, one may calculate the effect that earnings have on the share price.

Regression Equation In statistics, an equation showing the value of a dependent variable as a function of an independent variable. For example, a regression could take the form: $y = a + bx$ where "y" is the dependent variable and "x" is the independent variable. The slope is equal to "b," and "a" is the intercept. When plotted on a graph, "y" is determined by the value of "x." Regression equations are charted as a line and are important in calculating economic data.

Regressive Tax A tax that is applied to all persons equally and therefore adversely affects persons with lower income. For example, if a city institutes a 5% sale tax on groceries, everyone who buys groceries (that is, everyone) must pay 5% extra. Because the poor and the lower middle class make less money than other classes, the extra 5% is more difficult for them to afford. As a result, regressive taxes are less popular among left-wing political groups. However, proponents argue that regressive taxes are fair, at least to a certain extent, because they do not punish success.

Regret Theory A theory stating that many investors consider the possibility that they will regret their investment decisions. The spectre of regret may have different effects on different persons. For example, it may motivate one investor to take more risks because he/she would regret not doing so if the price of securities increases a great deal. Likewise, it may motivate another investor to be more risk averse because he/she would regret buying some stocks if the price drops significantly. The study of regret is one example of behavioral finance.

Regular Settlement A situation in which a buyer or, more commonly, his/her broker, receives delivery of the securities he/she bought and makes payment for them on the normal settlement date. Regular settlement occurs on the date set by the exchange, which is usually three to five days after the trade date, depending on the type of transaction and the country in which it occurs. See also: Early settlement, Delayed settlement.

Regular-Way Trade Any trade that does not take any longer to settle than is legally required. The settlement date occurs anywhere from one to five days following the trade date, depending on the type of trade. Regulators set the settlement date, allowing the buyer a certain number of days to make payment. Regular-way trades occur when the buyer follows the regulations. The large majority of trades are regular-way trades.

Regulated Commodities All options and futures where the underlying assets are commodities that are traded on an exchange in the United States. They are regulated by the Commodity Futures Trading Commission.

Regulated Investment Company An investment company that does not pay taxes on its earnings. Mutual funds and closed-end investment companies are both regulated investment companies. RICs are able to escape corporate taxes because they profit from investments by shareholders and do not have any real operations. They are therefore able to pass profits to shareholders and avoid double taxation. In order to qualify as an RIC, a company must derive at least 90^ of its profits from investment activities.

Regulation The set of rules and legislation governing certain actions. For example, the U.S. Tax Code and the rules the IRS publishes regulate federal taxation in the United States. In securities, regulations often require companies to disclose their actions to see to it that as much information as possible is publicly available. Other regulations govern business practices; for example they may set minimum or maximum wages and salaries, prohibit discrimination on certain grounds, and/or ban certain policies or practices deemed unfair for consumers or competitors. While nearly everyone agrees that some regulations are necessary, there is significant disagreement as to how many and what kind. Proponents of more regulation state that it ensures a fair market place and sustainable growth, while critics argue that many regulations do more harm than good.

Regulation A An SEC regulation governing an issue of securities worth $5 million or less. Regulation A exempts these issues from many SEC regulations. While companies making these issues must still make filing statements, the issue's prospectus may be shorter and directors and officers have less liability for false or misleading statements. Many companies making regulation A issues are small businesses.

Regulation A Issue An issue of securities worth $5 million or less. Regulation A issues are exempt from many SEC regulations. While companies making these issues must still make filing statements, the issue's prospectus may be shorter and directors and officers have less liability for false or misleading statements. Many companies making regulation A issues are small businesses.

Regulation D An SEC regulation governing an issue of securities for private placement. Private placement involves selling securities without registering with the SEC. Regulation D requires that those offering must file a private placement memorandum (PPM) explaining exactly why the offering complies with SEC Regulation D exempting certain companies from registration; this is done to protect both the issuer and the investors. According to Regulation D, a PPM must contain a complete description of the security and the terms of the sales. It must also include applicable information about the issuer's financial situation and applicable risk factors. Regulation D securities are not subject to the same oversight that other issues must follow.

Regulation Fair Disclosure An SEC regulation requiring that all publicly-traded companies in the United States disclose relevant, or "material," information to all shareholders at the same time. Adopted in 2000, this was a response to a common practice in the 1990s in which large companies disclosed financial information on conference calls to certain analysts and neither the public at large nor even all shareholders were invited. The regulation mandates that intentional disclosures be made publicly and unintentional disclosures be made public within 24 hours. Controversial when introduced, it has increased access to information on larger firms, but some analysts suggest that it has decreased the information available, and therefore increased stock volatility for smaller firms.

Regulation G A former regulation of the Federal Reserve defining the terms under which investors other than broker-dealers and banks may purchase U.S. Treasury Securities. It was rescinded in 1998.

Regulation M 1. A Federal Reserve regulation requiring member banks to maintain a certain amount in reserves against the borrowings by their foreign branches. Member banks may use the average of the reserves over a 28-day period in order to comply with the regulation. **2.** An IRS regulation allowing mutual funds and other investment companies to forego capital gains taxes and other taxes on dividends and coupons if they pass down the liability to shareholders. This regulation exists to prevent double taxation.

Regulation Q A former regulation of the U.S. federal government forbidding banks from paying interest on certain demand deposits, and imposing a low interest rate on savings account deposits. The result of the regulation was the proliferation of money market funds (which did pay interest). Regulation Q was almost entirely revoked by the Depository Institutions Deregulation and Monetary Control Act of 1980.

Regulation S An SEC regulation allowing publicly-traded companies not to register stocks sold outside the United States to foreign investors. Created in 1990, this regulation was intended to encourage foreign investors to purchase American stocks in order to increase the liquidity of American markets.

Regulation SHO An SEC regulation, adopted in 2005, restricting naked short selling. Naked short selling involves selling shares one has neither borrowed nor made arrangements to borrow. The regulation requires these brokers and short sale buyers to abide by a "locate" requirement and a "close-out" requirement. The locate requirement forces brokers to have reasonable grounds to believe that an equity security can be borrowed; the broker must document this prior to the security's sale. With some exceptions, the close-out requirement means that brokers who have failed to deliver a short-sold security for 13 days must purchase similar securities and present those instead. Brokers failing to do this may not engage in naked short selling until the position is closed. The rule also requires stock exchanges to publish daily a list of companies whose stock has failed to deliver over a certain threshold. See also: Short selling, Open fail, Threshold security.

Regulation T A Federal Reserve Board rule governing the opening and maintaining of margin accounts. Specifically, Regulation T governs the initial margin and the maintenance margin, which are, respectively, the collateral necessary to open and to maintain a margin account. While the percentages have changed over time, the initial margin is currently 50% of the amount borrowed, and the maintenance margin is 25%.

Regulation T Call On an initial transaction on a margin account, an order by a brokerage for an account holder to deposit more cash or securities into the account because the value of the cash and securities currently in it is below 50% of the value of the securities purchased on margin. The name comes from Regulation T, a Federal Reserve regulation requiring the initial margin requirement to be at least 50% of the amount borrowed for the account. If the account holder is not able to make the necessary deposit, he/she must close out enough positions in order to make the deposit or risk the account becoming blocked.

Regulation U A regulation of the Federal Reserve Board governing the total amount a bank may lend a customer for purposes of buying securities. This contrasts with Regulation T, which governs the same thing for brokers and dealers.

Regulation Z A Federal Reserve regulation requiring lenders to disclose all terms of loans to potential borrowers, including, but not limited to, the interest rates, applicable fees, and the length of loans. The regulation also allows consumers to cancel some credit transactions that require a lien to be placed on the consumer's primary residence. For the most part, the regulation does not place limits on the fees lenders may charge but instead requires transparency. Regulation Z is more or less the regulatory implementation of the Truth in Lending Act of 1968.

Regulator An agency enforcing legislation and setting rules governing certain actions. For example, the Internal Revenue Service in the United States is a regulator because it collects taxes, enforcing the U.S. Tax Code. In securities, regulators often require companies to disclose their actions to see to it that as much information as possible is publicly available. Other regulators govern business practices. For example, they may enforce minimum or maximum wages and salaries, prohibit discrimination on certain grounds, and/or ban certain policies or practices deemed unfair for consumers or competitors. While nearly everyone agrees that some regulations are necessary, there is significant disagreement as to how many and what kind are needed. Proponents of more regulation assert that it ensures a fair market and sustainable growth, while critics argue that many regulations do more harm than good.

Regulatory Arbitrage The practice of making small changes to one's company so as to come under the jurisdiction of a different regulator agency with more lenient rules. For example, a corporation unwilling to pay corporate taxes to the state of California may move its head office to Arizona, outside the jurisdiction (in most circumstances) of the California tax authorities. See also: Jurisdictional Arbitrage, Federal Deposit Insurance Act of 2005.

Regulatory Climate A legal situation describing the extent to which government regulations enhance or impede earnings growth. The term is used most often in the utilities industry, which must receive government approval for increases in the prices of its products. Generally speaking, the business world favors a regulatory climate with as little government oversight as possible, as this usually enables higher profits. Critics allege, however, that this sort of regulatory climate encourages unsustainable growth and/or harms the poorer segments of society. See also: Deregulation.

Regulatory Pricing Risk In insurance, the risk that regulators will directly set or exert influence on the premiums that insurance companies may charge. If premiums are required to be too low on a certain class of policyholders, this means the insurance company has to raise them on other policyholders, which may cost the companys clients. On the other hand, if all premiums are regulated, the insurance companies may have to sacrifice profitability.

Rehiyon In the Philippines, a political subdivision equivalent to a super-provincial region.

Rehypothecate To pledge securities as collateral for a loan when the same securities have already been pledged for another loan. Generally speaking, a brokerage rehypothecates when it needs to secure a loan for a client. That is, the client pledges securities for a loan on a margin account and the brokerage uses those same securities to procure a loan from a bank to finance the loan for the client.

Reichsmark The currency of Germany between 1924 and 1948. It was issued following the hyperinflation that crippled Germany in the early 1920s. It was pegged to gold. During World War II, the government set exchange rates between the Reichsmark and other Axis powers, as well as the occupied territories. In 1948, it was replaced by the Deutschemark in West Germany and the Ostmark in East Germany.

Reimbursement The act or concept of repaying a person or organization for expenses it incurred that rightly belonged to another party. Reimbursement is common between employees and employers. For example, if an employee pays for his/her own hotel room while on a business trip, the employer will likely reimburse him.

Reimport To bring a finished product into a country after the raw materials to make that product were exported from that same country. For example, a company may export crude oil to another country for refining, and then reimport the finished gasoline.

Reinstatement The act of an insurer putting an insurance policy back into effect after it has lapsed because of missed premium payments. Generally speaking, a policyholder is under no legal obligation to make premium payments, but if he/she fails to do so, the insurer has the right to rescind the policy. Reinstatement may require proof of continued eligibility for the policy and may also require the policyholder to pay back all missed premium payments.

Reinsurance An insurance policy for insurers. In reinsurance, one insurer cedes a portion of its portfolio of policyholders to another insurer in exchange for paying a fee. There exists the possibility that too many policyholders will make a claim and a single insurer will be unable to pay the benefit without ruining itself. This is especially true for disaster insurance and other similar policies. Reinsurance reduces this risk. It is also called stop-loss insurance.

Reinvestment The act or practice of taking profits or other proceeds from investments and making other investments with them. It nearly always means that one is investing in more of the same security. For example, one may take dividends from a stock and buy more shares with it or may take coupon payments to buy more of the same bond issue. Reinvestment often increases the value of a security.

Reinvestment Effect The phenomenon that rising interest rates on bonds mean that the investor will earn more interest over the same amount of time, and is therefore more likely to reinvest in bonds to earn even more. Likewise, falling interest rates mean that the investor will earn less in coupons and he/she will be less inclined to reinvest in bonds.

Reinvestment Plan A practice or agreement in which dividends on a security are used to buy more of the same security, rather than disbursed to the investor in cash. A reinvestment plan is relatively common in mutual funds; investors agree to use dividends and other capital gains to reinvest in more shares of the mutual fund. While this involves assuming more risk in the mutual fund, it carries the possibility of higher returns.

Reinvestment Privilege The right of shareholders to use dividends to buy more shares of a publicly-traded company or mutual fund. Many publicly-traded companies and most mutual funds carry a reinvestment privilege as a perk for investors. Shareholders who avail themselves of the reinvestment privilege do not pay any additional fees on the extra shares they buy.

Reinvestment Rate The coupons that a bondholder uses to buy more of the same bond as a percentage of total coupons received. The reinvestment rate tends to increase when interest rates rise because the bondholder will earn more interest with less risk. See also: Reinvestment Effect, Plowback Rate.

Reinvestment Risk A risk that an investment, usually a bond, will be paid off early and that the money earned may not be able to be reinvested in a security with a comparable return. Suppose one invested in a bond with coupon payment of 4%. However, the issuer calls the bond and pays the par value. The investor has made a profit, but interest rates have fallen and now he/she may only purchase a bond with coupons of 2.5%. Theoretically, one might purchase a mortgage-backed security or other investment in which all the mortgage holders backing the MBS may pay back their mortgages early, exposing one to reinvestment risk. However, in reality, this risk exists primarily in callable bonds and certificates of deposit.

Reinvestment Stock Stock that an investor purchases with dividends on that same stock. For example, if one receives $500 in dividends from his stock in Johnson & Johnson, one may purchase $500 worth of reinvestment stock in Johnson & Johnson. While this involves assuming more risk in the stock, it carries the possibility of higher returns. See also: Automatic reinvestment plan.

Rejection 1. A bank's refusal to grant a line of credit. This often applies to the refusal to grant a mortgage loan to an uncreditworthy person or a business loan to someone without a proper business plan. **2.** An investor's refusal to accept a security presented to him/her/it. Reasons for this include suspicion of fraud or improperly filled-out forms. **3.** Refusal to provide insurance coverage because the insurance company believes that the claim describes a service or situation that the policy does not cover.

Related-Party Transaction A transaction between two businesses that have a personal or other relationship. For example, a publicly-traded company may be inclined to hire a large, minority shareholder as a supplier. In small businesses, a company may hire the owner's brother-in-law to repair the driveway. Related-party transactions are legal, but create the potential for conflicts of interest. Thus, publicly-traded companies are required to report them on their 10-K forms.

Relational Banking A form of banking in which the length of time the client has known the bank is considered, sometimes strongly, in risk assessment. For example, in relationship banking, a borrower with mediocre creditworthiness but who has been with the bank for 30 years may be likely to receive a loan regardless of his credit history. Relational banking has played a role in the economic development of some countries. For example, banks tend to finance favored firms, which contributes to their long-term success.

Relative PE The price-earnings ratio of a company compared to other companies in the same industry or other companies of the same size. The relative PE is useful in helping people make investment decisions. One may desire a higher relative PE or a lower PE, depending on one's investment strategy.

Relative Purchasing Power Parity A theory that the purchasing power of two currencies differs by the same proportional rate. This differs from the absolute form of purchasing power parity, which states that the purchasing power between two currencies is the same. However, the concepts are similar because RPPP holds that the absolute form would be true if there were no interference of taxes, quality of products, and other circumstances that change the market. One must take into account all these circumstances to calculate the proportional rate by which the purchasing power changes.

Relative Return In investing, the return on an asset or other investment compared to some benchmark. For example, the return on a stock may be 8% over a given period of time. This may sound rather high, but if the return on the designated benchmark index is 20% over the same period of time, then the relative return on that stock is in fact -12%. The relative return is important for determining how the return of a given stock or fund compares to that of other potential investments. This can be useful in making investment decisions.

Relative Strength Index A measure of the performance of a stock relative to its industry or the performance of an industry relative to the market as a whole. A stock (or industry) outperforming its industry (or market) for a given period of time has a relative strength index value above 1; this is seen as a bullish sign for that stock (or industry). On the other hand, a stock (or industry) underperforming its industry (or market) for a given period of time has a relative strength index value under 1; this is seen as a bearish sign.

Relative Value The value or desirability of one investment with reference to another. One may compare the relative values of many things, with start-up costs, return, risk, maturity, and liquidity being among the most popular. Comparing relative values helps investors make investment decisions that will maximize returns at the lowest possible level of risk.

Relative Yield Spread In bonds, it is the ratio of the yield spread of more than one bond to the yield of a single bond. The relative yield spread is important to determining how the yield of a given bond compares to that of other bonds, especially those in different classes. This can be useful in making investment decisions.

Release Written statement by a creditor to the effect that a debtor has either paid off the debt or the debt is otherwise discharged. A creditor may release a lien if the loan has been paid or if other collateral has been offered. Most mortgages contain release clauses indicating under what circumstances the borrower obtains release from the mortgage lien.

Release Clause In some mortgages, a clause allowing part of the property that has been pledged to have its lien removed once the borrower has made a defined number of payments on the mortgage.

Release on Recognizance In law, the release of a prisoner without assessing bail because the prisoner publicly recognized that he/she is obliged to appear in court on a later date. A prisoner may be released on recognizance if he/she is not considered to be a flight risk and/or if the person's accused crime is not too grave.

Relevant Costs In managerial accounting, costs relating to decisions executives are able to make. For example, employee salaries may be a relevant cost because executives (usually) decide how much to pay their employees and can raise or lower them according to need and efficiency. Some costs may be irrelevant under some circumstances but relevant under others.

Relief In numismatics, an image on a coin that rises above the background and is not pressed into it.

Relief Printing A way to print paper in which the image is raised from the printing plate. This contrasts with gravure printing, in which the image is carved into the plate's surface.

Relief Rally A general increase in stock or other security prices because an expected negative situation did not materialize or began to reverse itself. For example, if stocks were falling all week because oil prices were rising, but oil prices suddenly dip on Friday, stock prices may recover some of their lost ground in a relief rally. See also: Behavioral Economics.

Reload Option Employee stock options that can be traded for more employee stock options. When this option is exercised, the option holder pays the strike price in stock already in his/her possession, rather than in cash. A reload option must be exercised prior to the expiry date because the new stock options retain the former expiry date. When the reload option is exercised a new strike is set; it is equal to the market value of the underlying stocks at the time the first option is exercised. This is useful to an employee if he/she wishes to set a new, lower strike for the option. See also: Early Exercise.

Reloading The act or practice of borrowing money in order to pay off some other debt. Depending on the type of reload loan, this may be advantageous to the borrower as he/she may pay a lower interest rate and the interest may be tax-deductible. For example, credit card debt has a high interest rate and is not tax-deductible. Someone with a large amount of credit card debt may take out a home equity loan in order to pay off the credit card. In the long run, the borrower will pay less because home equity loans come with a lower interest rate and he/she may write off the interest. While they may be advantageous, it is possible to reload too much or too often, resulting in a greater amount of debt.

Remainder Man The person or organization that receives what remains of a trust at its dissolution. That is, once all obligations to the beneficiary have been satisfied and all expenses have been paid, the remainder man receives the rest of the assets in the trust. The remainder man only receives these assets at the end of the trust's life; it may or may not be the same person as the trustor.

Remaining Maturity The time between the present date and the time at which a bond matures. This is important in the pricing of a bond; the price approaches the bond's face value as the remaining maturity shortens. This is in part because the bondholder will receive fewer coupons (and eventually no coupons) as the remaining maturity approaches zero. See also: Duration.

Remaining Principal Balance The amount of the principal of a loan that a borrower has not repaid. For example, suppose a person borrows $1,000 for a year and repays an equal amount of principal every month in addition to the interest payment. After six months, the remaining principal balance is $500. It should be noted, however, that not all loans have the same amount of principal repayment every month. The remaining principal balance is particularly important in mortgages. See also: Amortization.

Remargin To place more cash or securities into a margin account as collateral following a margin call. In a margin call, a brokerage requires a client to remargin because the market value of the collateral currently in the account has fallen below the margin requirement, which is a least 25% (and sometimes 50%) of the value of the securities the client has purchased with borrowed money. Remargining occurs to force the client to comply with federal regulations and/or the brokerage's own rules.

Remarketed Preferred Stock A preferred stock with an adjustable dividend that changes every so often on the decision of a designated agent. Every preferred stock has a guaranteed dividend; what distinguishes remarketed preferred stock is that the amount of its dividends changes from time to time. A dividend changes so that the preferred stock may always be resold at its original offer price. See also: Auction rate preferred stock.

Rembrandt Bond A foreign bond denominated in euros and traded in the Netherlands. In order to raise capital from Dutch investors, a non-Dutch company may choose to sell a bond in the Netherlands. See also: Yankee bond, Samurai bond.

Rembrandt Market Informal; a stock market in The Netherlands. The term is most often used by foreigners outside of The Netherlands.

Remen An ancient Persian unit of length approximately equivalent to 400 millimeters.

Remit To send money to remove an obligation or liability, especially electronically or through a wire service. For example, if one receives a speeding ticket and wires the city government the fine, one is said to have remitted the speeding ticket. As a noun, "remittance" also refers to the amount of money that is sent.

Remittance 1. See: Remit. **2.** See: Migrants' remittance.

Renegotiable Rate An adjustable interest rate in a balloon loan. The renegotiable rate is constant throughout the life of the balloon loan, but, when the loan comes due, the lender has the right to refinance the loan at a higher interest rate. This is advantageous for both the borrower and the lender, as the borrower does not have to pay the entire principal when the loan comes due, and the lender may take advantage of the higher payments.

Renewable Term Life Insurance A life insurance policy that provides coverage only for a certain period of time, but which may be renewed at the end of that period. A term life insurance policy provides a benefit upon the death of the policyholder, but ceases to provide this benefit if he/she is still alive when the policy expires. Upon expiration, the policyholder may decide to renew the policy or let it lapse. If the policy lapses, the policyholder is not reimbursed for the premiums paid over the life of the policy. Like other term life policies, renewable term life insurance does not include some of the other benefits of a whole life policy, such as a savings component.

Renewal A day order with the exact same terms as a day order made the previous trading day that expired unfilled.

Renewal FAFSA A FAFSA form filed in each subsequent year of attendance at a post-secondary educational institution after the first year. A FAFSA is a form that a post-secondary student files with the federal government to determine eligibility for federal financial aid.

Renko Chart In technical analysis, a chart that does not account for volume or time. That is, a renko chart is a series of small bricks, each representing a change in price. When a price goes above or below a previous price, a new brick is added to the chart. A white brick represents an increase in price while a black brick represents a decline. A renko chart is useful because it can help technical analysts find support and resistance levels accurately.

Renounceable Right A right attached to a security that one may buy or sell separately from that security. The right is usually the ability to buy more shares in a publicly-traded company at a discount, especially after a new issue of stock that would otherwise dilute the stockholder's holding. If one sells a renounceable right, its buyer receives this ability. It differentiates from a nonrenounceable right, which always must remain attached to the security with which it was originally issued.

Rent A regular, usually monthly, payment that a person makes in exchange for the use of an asset he/she does not own. That is, rent is the payment on a lease. The term is most often used to refer to payments on a leased dwelling or other piece of real estate.

Rent Control A local law setting maximums on the amount landlords can charge tenants on certain properties. This is done primarily to protect tenants from certain actions, such as increases in rent at the end of a lease on tenants who ask for repairs. Proponents argue that rent control gives tenants a degree of stability that would not otherwise exist. Opponents contend that rent control discourages investment in housing, reducing the quantity (and perhaps the quality) of rental housing available.

Rent-a-Cow The practice in which a person places livestock on his/her residential or commercial property in order to have access to favorable tax treatment available to agricultural real estate. The term implies abuse of the tax system because the livestock are not used for legitimate agricultural purposes.

Rental Lease A lease whereby the lessee pays a certain amount of rent in exchange for use of a property; in exchange, the lessor agrees to provide maintenance and insurance for the property. It is also called a full-service lease.

Rentenmark A temporary currency in Germany in the 1920s. It was introduced in 1923 as part of a successful effort to end the hyperinflation suffered by the papiermark. While it was not pegged to gold as the goldmark was, it was backed by mortgages on real estate and industrial infrastructure. For this reason, the rentenmark effectively served as a bond that was used as currency. The last rentenmarks matured in 1948 but in 1924 the Reichmark became legal tender and was used for most purposes.

Rentier 1. A person who makes most or all of his/her income from the rental or property. 2. A state or government that has access to a great deal of liquidity and uses it to maintain hegemony over its population. For example, it may provide free or inexpensive health care using its excess money. Rentier states rarely assess taxes, and often acquire their liquidity through the sale of their natural resources, such as oil. Citizens of rentier states often (though not always) have little loyalty to these countries, which may go through difficult transition periods when the natural resources run out. See also: Rents.

Rentier Class A class of people who rely largely on rent, pensions, or similar means for their income. For example, a landlord who agrees to rent out a house for a set amount each month for a year is a member of the rentier class. So is a pensioner living on a fixed income. The rentier class may be particularly susceptible to bouts of high inflation.

Rent-Seeking The practice of an individual, company, or government attempting to make a profit without making a product, producing wealth, or otherwise contributing to society. For example, a company may seek subsidies from the government, which would count as income for that company. Likewise, a government may seek rent by seizing control of natural resources and charging citizens for use. Some rent seeking is legal, while others, such as some forms of blackmail, are not. Rent-seeking behavior is most common when the rent seeker is also a monopoly or has sufficient economic or political power to act as one. The concept was originated by Adam Smith.

Reoffering Yield The yield of a municipal bond if one buys it from an underwriter and holds it until maturity.

Reopening After a period of suspended trade, an indication by an exchange or regulator that trade may resume. Reopening often occurs half an hour after trading is suspended, but this is not a hard-and-fast rule.

Reorganization The act or process of changing the terms on the assets and/or liabilities of a company. That is, a company may consolidate its debts, significantly change the size and scope of its operations, and take other measures to reduce the strain of continuing operations. Most companies reorganize either as part of a bankruptcy or as an effort to avoid it. If the company is reorganizing as part of a corporate bankruptcy, it is said to be in receivership.

Reorganization Bond A bond issued by a debtor in possession, which is a company that maintains its operations during a Chapter 11 bankruptcy. A debtor in possession is generally attempting to fulfill its reorganization plan, discharging certain debts and changing any structural weaknesses to put it on a path to profitability. A company often requires financing in order to restructure, and a reorganization bond enables it to do so. Because of the risk inherent to buying a bond issued by a debtor in possession, reorganization bonds carry a high interest rate.

Reorganization Plan In chapter 11 bankruptcy, a plan filed with bankruptcy court describing the process of how an insolvent company will change structurally to help it pay its debts and stay in business. This plan is subject to court oversight to ensure enforcement. Depending upon the specific plan, a company's original owner or managers may maintain control. Other times, the company's creditors become the new owners of the business; this especially happens when one or more creditors have had their debt completely discharged. Changes also must occur structurally, perhaps in risk management or marketing or perhaps in something more fundamental, to ensure that the bankruptcy does not repeat itself.

Repaired In numismatics, describing a damaged coin that has been fixed. A repaired coin generally is worth more than a damaged coin, but is not as valuable as a coin in mint condition or even a used coin that has never been damaged.

Repatriated Profit Profit earned in a foreign country that one wishes to bring into the borders of one's own country. For example, a corporation in the United States may repatriate the profits earned by a French subsidiary. Repatriated profit may be subject to special tax rules.

Repatriation The act of an individual or company bringing foreign capital into a home country and converting it to the domestic currency. Generally speaking, an individual who repatriates capital is usually converting foreign earnings into his/her home country's currency, perhaps in the process of moving back to the home country after having a job abroad. A company that repatriates capital is usually bringing over the returns on foreign investment. Repatriation can expose the individual or company to foreign exchange risk.

Repayment The act of paying off debts. If one borrows a certain amount, one must eventually repay it to the lender.

Repayment Date The date by which a borrower must repay the principal and interest on a loan in total. For example, a mortgage with a period of 10 years has a repayment date 10 years after it is issued. The repayment date also indicates the period of time during which the lender will receive interest (and often principal) payments. Despite the existence of a maturity date, many debts may be repaid early, though they may be subject to penalties in such cases.

Repeat Prices Omitted On a ticker tape, a notice that only the initial transaction will be reported for each price. Other trades that occur at the same price are not reported on the ticker tape. This is most common in period of heavy volume.

Replacement Cost Accounting An accounting practice in which liabilities and assets are recorded on a balance sheet according to the cost of replacing them, rather than the original amount spent on the liabilities or assets. This practice is intended to take into account current prices when calculating a company's value. It is the opposite of historic cost accounting.

Replacement Cost Insurance An insurance policy in which the insurer will pay the entire cost of replacing the insured asset in the case it is damaged or destroyed. That is, there is not maximum benefit on the policy; the insurer simply pays the replacement cost regardless of what it is. Importantly, a replacement cost plan does not take depreciation into account.

Replacement Cycle A period of time between the purchase of an asset and its replacement with an equivalent asset. The replacement may be the result of the end of the asset's absolute physical life or its obsolescence or some other reason. It is especially important in the information technology industry in which improvements occur with (sometimes variable) frequency. See also: Depreciation.

Replacement Reserve In real estate accounting, money set aside to purchase new materials that are expected to be bought as older materials wear out and need to be replaced. The replacement reserve may be listed on a financial statement as a phantom expense, and may be credited back if it is not actually spent.

Replacement Value The cost of replacing an asset in the case that it is damaged or destroyed. That is, the replacement value changes according to the market value of the asset. An individual or company may buy a replacement cost insurance policy to cover the replacement value. It is also called the replacement cost.

Replacement-Chain Problem When deciding among several projects that a company could pursue, the consideration of the costs associated with replacing the individual assets that one project, but not any of the others projects, requires.

Replica A coin struck using the same or similar equipment, but not with official sanction or at a later date. For example, a collector may make a replica of a Mercury dime. Replicas are illegal to sell in the United States unless "replica," "facsimile," or "copy" are printed on them.

Replicating Portfolio A portfolio that attempts to match, as closely as possible, some benchmark or index. See also: Index fund, Exchange-traded fund.

Replication Ministry A non-profit, especially a small Christian ministry, with the primary purpose of investing donations and then re-donating to another non-profit. Examples include credit unions and church investment companies.

Repo A practice in which a bank or other financial institution buys securities with the proviso that the seller must repurchase the same securities for an agreed-upon price on a certain day. Investors and financial institutions do this in order to raise short-term capital. A repo is also called a repurchase agreement or an overnight repo.

Repo Rate The interest rate at which the central bank in a country repurchases government securities (such as Treasury securities) from commercial banks. The central bank raises the repo rate when it wishes to reduce the money supply in the short term, while it lowers the rate when it wishes to increase the money supply and stimulate growth.

Report 1. See: Stockholder's report. **2.** Confirmation that a broker makes to a client that an order has been executed. The report includes all relevant information, such as price and order size. It may be made orally or in writing. See also: Fresh picture.

Report of Condition and Income A quarterly report that every bank, bank holding company, and Edge Act corporation must file giving information over a given period of time. The report contains information on the bank's financial state, most notably including statements on income, assets, liabilities, and write-offs for bad debt. It is informally called a call report. The report of condition and income must be filed within 30 days following the end of each quarter. It is the equivalent of a thrift financial report, which must be filed by savings and loan associations. See also: earnings report.

Reporting Currency The currency a publicly-traded company, investment company, or other organization uses in its financial statements and other reports. Generally speaking, the reporting currency is the domestic currency, but this is not always the case. It is important for an investor or auditor to note the reporting currency, especially when a company has international investments or interests.

Reporting Dealer A firm that must report its transactions and positions in Treasury securities to the Federal Reserve. A reporting dealer must make these reports because it helps the Federal Reserve make decisions with regard to the money supply. That is, reporting dealers help the Fed decide whether to sell or buy Treasury securities to affect interest rates and, therefore, the money in circulation. See also: Primary dealer.

Reporting Level The level of a position one must have in a futures contract at which one must file daily reports with the Commodity Futures Trading Commission. An investor with an exceptionally large long position in a futures contract has the ability to disproportionately affect the price of both the contract and the underlying commodity, especially if the market is unaware of the position's size. Thus, an investor with a position above the reporting level must file reports with the CFTC in order to increase transparency in the market and help ensure smooth trades. It is also called the reporting limit.

Representative 1. See: Agent. **2.** See: Broker. **3.** See: Attorney.

Repricing The act of a manager or other high level employee exchanging an out-of-the-money stock option in the company for an at-the-money stock option. Companies issue new at-the-money options and make the exchanges in order to reward the employee and/or to provide an incentive for the employee to continue to perform well even when the company's stock price has declined.

Reproducible Asset An asset that can be copied and remade. Buildings and widgets are both reproducible assets while an antique baseball card, on the other hand, is not.

Republic A polity governed by elected officials. In a republic, the citizens elect representatives who vote on issues of governance. Often, republics are called democracies, in which citizens themselves vote on issues of governance, but the two terms are not identical.

Republican A person who believes or participates in a polity governed by elected officials. In a republic, the citizens elect representatives who vote on issues of governance. Often, republics are called democracies, in which citizens themselves vote on issues of governance, but the two terms are not identical.

Republika Pilseta In Latvia, a political subdivision equivalent to a city.

Repurchase 1. See: Repurchase agreement. **2.** See: Buyback.

Repurchase Price The price at which a seller (dealer) agrees to buy a security back from a purchaser (customer) on a designated future date. The repurchase price represents repayment of a collateralized short-term loan. See also: Repurchase agreement.

Repurpose 1. To use a product, a concept, or research for something other than for what it was intended originally. Repurposing products is common when they fail in their original market but their makers do not wish to lose the money they spent preparing the products. **2.** To make slight changes to a product and sell it on a different market. For example, a book may be recorded as an audiobook and sold in both formats.

Required Beginning Date The date by which an IRA must begin distributing payments to the annuitant. Under most circumstances, the date is April 1 of the year following the time that the annuitant turns 70.5. Occasionally, the required beginning date is postponed until the date of retirement, but this is not allowed in situations in which the annuitant owns 5% or more of the company sponsoring the IRA. The amount distributed on the required beginning date may or may not be taxable, depending on the type of IRA. See also: Minimum required distribution.

Required Insurance An insurance policy an individual or organization is legally mandated to carry. For example, employers are often required to have workers compensation insurance, and drivers usually must have some form of car insurance.

Required Minimum Distribution The amount that an IRA must begin to distribute to an annuitant by the age of 70.5 or the date of retirement, whichever comes later. The required minimum distribution may or may not be taxable, depending on the type of IRA. The amount of the minimum required distribution is determined by the value of the IRA, the length of time the annuitant has contributed, and the amount of contributions.

Required Rate of Return In securities, the minimum acceptable rate of return at a given level of risk. Different investors have different reasons for choosing their required returns. Normally, it is determined by a person's or institution's cost of capital. For example, an investor may also carry a debt with a high interest rate; if an investment does not meet a required rate of return, it would make more sense for the investor to pay down his/her debt. The required return is also related to the amount of risk an investor is willing to accept. One with a portfolio consisting largely of bonds will generally have a lower required return than one whose portfolio contains mainly stocks. See also: Markowitz Portfolio Theory.

Required Yield In securities, the minimum acceptable yield at a given level of risk. Different investors have different reasons for choosing their required yields. Normally, a person's or institution's cost of capital determines it. For example, an investor may also carry a debt with a high interest rate; if an investment does not meet a required yield, it would make more sense for the investor to pay down his/her debt. The required yield is also related to the amount of risk an investor is willing to accept. One with a portfolio consisting largely of bonds will generally have a lower required yield than one whose portfolio contains mainly stocks. See also: Markowitz Portfolio Theory.

Rerun A television or other program that has already been broadcast and is being broadcast again. Reruns are an inexpensive way for a television station to make money from advertising, especially if it already owns the rights to the program.

Res 1. A property owned by a trust. **2.** In law, a matter about which litigation takes place. In both cases, the word derives from the Latin word meaning "thing."

Res Ipsa Loquitur The legal concept that some acts are so obviously negligent that no further explanation is necessary to prove legal liability. A res ipsa loquitur case ordinarily requires one to show that an act usually would not occur without negligence, that the act probably was the result of negligence, that the defendant caused the negligence, and that the plaintiff did not contribute to it. A res ipsa loquiture case contrasts with a prima facie case, which requires more evidence to prove liability. The phrase "res ipsa loquitur" is Latin for "the thing speaks for itself."

Res Judicata In law, a case that has already been decided and is no longer subject to appeal. A res judicata case prohibits litigants from bringing up the same matter repeatedly. For example, res judicata disallows creditors from trying to collect a debt after it has been discharged in bankruptcy. The term is Latin for "a thing judged."

Rescaled Range Analysis A method of analysis of financial information over time to see what patterns, if any, arise. Theoretically, R/S analysis can be useful to determine potential future price movements for a stock or future performance for a company, but critics contend that its accuracy is limited.

Rescheduled Loan A loan made to a borrower where the lender has extended the repayment period. Rescheduled loans are most common when the borrower informs the lender that he/she will be unable to repay the loan in time, or when the borrower cannot afford payments. Because a default would hurt both the borrower and the lender, the lender often works with the borrower through options, such as rescheduling the repayment.

Rescheduling of Debt The extension of the repayment period of a loan. Rescheduled loans are most common when the borrower informs the lender that he/she will be unable to repay the loan in time, or when the borrower cannot afford payments. Because a default would hurt both the borrower and the lender, the lender often works with the borrower through options, such as rescheduling the repayment.

Rescind To cancel a contract and declare it invalid from its beginning. When a contract is rescinded, both parties are restored to the status quo before the contract was entered (as much as possible). Rescission may occur by mutual agreement, or when one of the parties misrepresented himself/herself before the contract was signed.

Rescission The act of abolishing a contract and restoring, as far as possible, the status quo ante. While legal systems differ on the precise reasons for which a contract may be rescinded, it may occur due to an act of God or by mutual consent, provided that no substantial progress has been made toward completion of the contract. In the context of finance and economics, some contracts may be rescinded up to a certain point after they come into effect. For example, some mortgage refinance contracts allow the homeowner a period of three business days after signing the contract in which he/she may unilaterally rescind it. Likewise, the sale of land may be rescinded by either party up to the point the sale is recorded. Sometimes an option contract, especially a stock option, can be rescinded for a certain time after its exercise; in this situation, the person who exercised the option surrenders the underlying in exchange for the cash he/she paid for it.

Research and Development 1. The process of discovering what goods and services best suit the company's needs and developing those products in order to sell them. For example, a vacuum cleaner company may conduct research into improvements to the vacuum cleaner most likely to be profitable, and then develop new vacuum cleaners in response to the research. It is important to note that not all research and development leads directly to a new product; that is, the developers may find it impossible to develop Product A, but the research generated from the project may lead to the development of Product B. **2.** A department in a company that deals with research and development.

Research and Development Costs The costs a company incurs in process of developing new goods and services to best suit the company's and consumer needs. For example, a vacuum cleaner company may spend a significant amount of money researching and developing profitable vacuum cleaner improvements. The costs decrease the company's profit in the short term but create the potential for higher profits in the medium and long term. As a result, many analysts consider it a positive sign when companies devote a large amount to their research and development costs.

Research and Development Limited Partnership A limited partnership where limited partners (who have no management authority) provide capital for the general partner (who manages the venture) to conduct research and development activities for a new product, or perhaps new uses for an old product. In return, the limited partners are entitled to a share of the profit on any new inventions, uses, or products developed in the process of R&D.

Research Department A department in a brokerage or institutional investor with the task of evaluating securities and other investment vehicles to determine which to recommend to brokers, clients, and other interested parties. The research department develops investment strategies depending on the current and projected future conditions of markets. It may use technical analysis, fundamental analysis, or any other technique in performing its duties. See also: Investment adviser, Advisory letter.

Research Portable Research from a brokerage or investment bank that may be made available to a client electronically. For example, a brokerage may e-mail a client its information and recommendations on a security in exchange for a fee. See also: Research department.

Reseaux Associes pour la Recherche Europeenne Commonly called RARE. A former organization that attempted to promote open protocols in computer networking. It was established in 1985 and in 1994 merged with EARN to form TERENA.

Reservation Price The price for an asset above which a buyer is not willing to pay and/or below which a seller is not will to take. This tension between the buyer wanting a low price and the seller wanting a high price helps create the market price for the asset. The reservation price is important in microeconomics, where it is used to help determine an asset's equilibrium price. See also: Reservation wage.

Reserve Currency A foreign currency held by a central bank or occasionally a major financial institution that may be used to settle international debts or transactions. A reserve may also be used to affect the exchange rate of the domestic currency. The most common reserve currency worldwide is the U.S. dollar, though the British pound, Japanese yen, and euro are also very common. See also: SDR.

Reserve Deficiency A situation in which a company must meet some unexpected expenses, perhaps resulting in a shortage of cash. For example, a company may set aside a certain amount of funds to cover bad debt. If bad debt exceeds expectations, and the company must write off more funds than it intended, it is said to have a reserve deficiency. Reserve deficiencies reduce profits and may cause a problem with liquidity.

Reserve for Contingencies A company's retained earnings that are not reinvested but set aside to protect against future losses. A company may set up a reserve for contingencies when it is performing well to guard against the risk that it may eventually perform poorly. A reserve for contingencies allows a company to maintain its operations smoothly even when it has suffered an operating loss.

Reserve Fund An account used to save for unexpected expenses. In most cases, a reserve fund is a savings account from which one can withdraw at will. In other cases, a reserve fund may be a money market fund or may be invested in something like U.S. Treasury securities. In any case, a reserve fund is highly liquid and easy to access.

Reserve Price At an auction, the price below which the owner of the item may refuse to sell. For example, if the reserve price is $1,000, and bidding does not rise above $900, the owner may withdraw the item from the auction. The reserve price is also called the upset price.

Reserve Ratios The liquid assets that a central bank or other body mandates that a bank keep at all times. The reserve ratio is expressed as a percentage of the bank's total deposits. The reserve ratio exists to ensure that the bank is able to pay an unusually high number of withdrawals on demand accounts should that event occur. It also helps ensure that the bank does not over-leverage itself. In some countries, increasing or decreasing reserve ratios may be used to help control the money supply. See also: Basel II, Monetary Policy.

Reserve Tranche Twenty-five percent of an IMF member state's membership fees. Any IMF member has access to its reserve tranche without preconditions, and is not obligated to repay what it withdraws.

Reserves 1. See: Foreign exchange reserves. **2.** See: Reserve for bad debt.

Reset Bond A bond that, on designated days, increases its coupon rate to bring its market value back to its original value. For example, suppose a bond is issued with a price of $1,000 at a coupon of 5%. If the bond's price declines for any reason to $900 by the first designated day, the coupon rate is increased to 7% or whatever percentage will bring the price back up to $1,000. Reset bonds are structured this way to protect bondholders' investment, but they can create hardship for the issuer. The extra coupon rate has been known to cause an issuer to go into bankruptcy.

Reset Frequency In adjustable-rate loans, the rate at which changes to a loan's interest rate occur. Sometimes, the interest rate changes once a year, but some loans change interest rates as often as once a month or as seldom as every five years. The higher the reset frequency, the higher the financial risk for the homeowner. For example, if the reset frequency is once a month, a homeowner could find his/her mortgage payment increasing every month for five months before it goes down again. This ties up more of the homeowner's income and increases the likelihood of default.

Reset Margin In an adjustable-rate loan or other security, the reference rate against which the adjustable rate is calculated.

Residence The place where a person lives most of the time. A residence may be eligible for certain tax breaks. For example, one may be able to write off the interest on a mortgage on a primary residence. Various rules exist to determine what constitutes one's residence for tax purposes.

Residency Visa A general term for a visa allowing a person to live in a country, either on a temporary or permanent basis. A residency visa permits one to work while living in the country issuing the visa. A residency visa may be a step on the way to gaining citizenship in a country. See also: Green Card.

Resident Agent A person who is licensed to sell insurance in the state in which he/she lives. Because most insurance is regulated at the state level, state agents are registered on a state-by-state basis.

Resident Alien A non-citizen who has permission to live and work in a country on a permanent basis. In the United States, a resident alien is subject to the same taxation as an American citizen, but may take foreign tax credits on taxes that are paid to the alien's home country.

Residential Mortgage A loan that one or more persons receive in order to buy a house or other residential property in which they will live. The loan is secured by a lien on the property; the borrowers repay it over a specified period of time. The interest on a residential mortgage is tax deductible under most circumstances.

Residential Mortgage-Backed Security A derivative whose value is derived from home equity loans and mortgages on properties where people live. As with all mortgage-backed securities, this entitles the owner to a claim on the principal and interest payments on the particular mortgages underpinning the security. MBS's pay an interest rate that is usually related to the interest rates the homeowners are paying on their mortgages. The equivalent of the coupon on a mortgage backed security is a percentage of the interest and principal paid on the mortgages backing the security. An obvious risk to a residential MBS is the possibility that interest rates on home loans may decline, causing homeowners to refinance their mortgages and deprive the holder of the security from future interest payments.

Residential Property Any property that a municipality has designated for single family homes, apartments, co-operatives, townhouses, and any other place where people live. Mortgages on and income from residential property are often (though not always) entitled to preferential tax treatment.

Residual Assets A person's or company's assets after all secured obligations have been paid. That is, the residual assets are those left over after all senior creditors have had their claims satisfied. For example, in a bankruptcy or other liquidation, the residual assets are those used to pay unsecured creditors or common shareholders, if any. See also: Precedence.

Residual Cover Remaining cash flow on a project after debt service, expressed a percentage of the loan amount.

Residual Dividend Approach A dividend policy for a publicly-traded company stating that the company will not pay dividends to shareholders unless there are no acceptable investment opportunities for the money that would be paid as dividends. Companies following a residual dividend approach therefore have a high plowback rate. This approach is most common among start-ups that are seeking to establish themselves.

Residual Return A return on an investment that is independent of the investment's benchmark. It is calculated as follows: Residual return = Excess return - (Benchmark's excess return * beta).

Residual Risk Any risk remaining to an investment after all other risks have been eliminated, hedged, or otherwise accounted. For example, a residual risk to an international shipment may be the part that is not insured by the export credit agency. Some residual risks may not be known during risk analysis, and indeed may not be knowable.

Residual Security A security that has the potential to dilute its issuer's earnings per share. For example, a convertible bond can be exchange for so many shares of common stock. If it is exchanged, then the earnings per common share are diluted because there are now more common shares by which to divide earnings. For that reason, a convertible bond is a residual security.

Residual Value In accounting, an estimate of the value of an asset at the end of its depreciation. For example, a firm's computer depreciates each year. When it breaks down or becomes obsolete, it has a residual value; it is calculated by the best guess of the net cash inflow when it is sold at the end of its life. It will never be above the blue book value. In price regulated industries, the residual value may be a negative value because it includes the net cash outflow in removing the asset from where it was used. For example, nuclear energy plants must store the nuclear waste at the end of their useful life. This cost is a contributing factor in the residual value. It is also called the salvage value or scrap value. See also: Absolute Physical Life, Obsolescence.

Resiliency The ability of equipment to continue to function at the same level even after its components stop working. This can be an important concept for complex machinery.

Resistance Level In technical analysis, a price that a security does not, or only rarely, rise above. Technical analysts identify a resistance level by looking at past performance. When the security approaches the resistance level, it is seen as an indication to sell the security, which will increase the supply, causing the security's price to fall back below the resistance level. If there are too many buyers, however, the security rises above the resistance level. When this occurs, the price of the security will likely continue to rise until it finds another resistance level. It is also called the overhead resistance level. See also: Price ceiling, Support (Support level).

Resolution An official statement by a board of directors. A resolution is binding on a company unless overruled by shareholders.

Resolution Funding Corporation An agency established by the Financial Institutions Reform, Recovery and Enforcement Act of 1989 to fund the Resolution Trust Corporation, which in turn was charged with bailing out insolvent savings & loan associations. REFCORP funded its own activities by issuing zero-coupon bonds through the US Treasury.

Resolution Trust Corporation An agency of the United States government that was charged with closing thrifts declared to be insolvent. It also issued bailout bonds and paid for the reorganization and the financing of thrifts that were bankrupt but could still function. It was established by the Financial Institutions Reform, Recovery and Enforcement Act of 1989 and was closed in 1996.

Resource Recovery Revenue Bond A municipal bond used to construct a waste processing or recycling center. The coupons and principal on a resource recovery revenue bond are secured by the fees paid by users of the center and/or by the sale of the recycled products.

Resourcing The act or practice of providing an employee or other person with the necessary tools to complete a task. For example, if a constructions company hires a worker, it may provide him/her with a hammer and nails. One the other hand, if a company hires a technical writer, resourcing involves giving him/her the information required to do the work.

Respite Care Occasional or temporary care that a nurse or nurse's aide gives to an elderly or disabled person. Some health insurance policies may provide coverage for respite care, and it has been known to reduce the risk of abuse or neglect that comes from putting a loved one in a nursing home.

Respondent A person or organization required to answer a legal proceeding. For example, if a company is sued, the company is called the respondent because it must respond to the charges or risk a summary judgment. See also: Petitioner.

Respublika In Uzbekistan, an autonomous region, which is roughly a province with less oversight from the central government.

Ressorten In Suriname, a political subdivision equivalent to neighborhood or municipality.

Rest and Recreation Leave Paid time off from work given to persons who work in a foreign country under difficult circumstances. For example, aid workers in least developed countries may receive rest and recreation leave. Rest and recreation leave may give employees time to go home and see their families. It is given over and above regular vacation time.

Restatement The release of a previously issued financial statement amended with new information. For example, if a company issues a profit-loss statement and then discovers new information that affects the statement, it may amend the profit-loss statement to reflect the new information. When it releases this to the public, the company is said to make a restatement.

Restricted 1. See: Gray list. **2.** See: Restricted account.

Restricted Account A margin account in which the amount of equity is below SEC or brokerage requirements. Such an account is not allowed to buy any more stocks until the level of equity is raised; a portion each sale of stock must be used to pay down the account's debt. Regulation T sets the minimum equity standards, but individual brokerages may set higher standards. In general, however, an account becomes restricted when the market value of the stocks purchased on margin falls below the amount owed on the stocks. A restricted account is sometimes referred to as a blocked account.

Restricted Asset Money or another asset that may be used only for a certain purpose. For example, a donor may give to a nonprofit, provided the donation is used exclusively to fund a scholarship for underprivileged children. Restricted assets must be accounted separately from an organization's other funds.

Restricted Donation A donation in which the donor requires a specific use. For example, a donor may make a restricted donation to a non-profit organization requiring the money to be used for after-school tutoring. In such cases, the non-profit may not use the donation to subsidize student lunches. See also: Unrestricted donation.

Restricted Fund Money that may be used only for a certain purpose. For example, a donor may give to a nonprofit, provided the donation is used exclusively to fund a scholarship for underprivileged children. Restricted funds must be accounted separately from an organization's other funds. It is a common type of restricted asset.

Restricted Letter of Credit A letter of credit issued by a bank to a customer that the customer may redeem only at a certain, stated bank. See also: Unrestricted Letter of Credit.

Restricted Market The market for a currency whose value is not determined by the free market. A restricted market may involve a pegged currency or even a nonconvertible currency. In extreme cases, the official value of a restricted currency bears only a rough relationship to its actual value.

Restricted Net Assets Cash or other assets that are not needed to pay liabilities but still may not be spent freely. Restricted net assets may be earmarked for a specific purpose; alternately, law or regulation may require the restriction of some net assets. See also: Temporarily Restricted Net Assets, Permanently Restricted Net Assets.

Restricted Option An option contract that the rules of an exchange do not permit to be used in a naked option strategy. That is, one must own the underlying asset (for a call) or sufficient cash to buy the underlying asset (for a put), or have some way to acquire it easily, in order to use a restricted option. An option may become restricted if it is worth less than $50 and is out-of-the-money. Restricted options exist in order to prevent volatility in the market. See also: Covered Option, Straddle.

Restricted Retained Earnings The earnings of a publicly-traded company that it is legally or contractually obligated not to pay as dividends. The most common reason for earnings to become restricted is the existence of dividends in arrears. That is, if a company has not made legally promised dividend payments to preferred stockholders, it must make these payments before it can pay any other dividends. Thus, the earnings become known as restricted retained earnings. Restricted retained earnings are also called the restricted surplus.

Restricted Security A stock or right that one acquires through some means other than the open market. One may receive a restricted security through a merger or acquisition, private placement prior to an IPO, or sometimes through a stock option. A restricted security is not registered with the SEC and thus may not be sold publicly until registration has been made. It is less commonly called a letter security.

Restricted Stock Award An award of stock through some means other than the open market. One may receive a restricted stock through a merger or acquisition, private placement prior to an IPO, or sometimes through a stock option. A restricted stock is not registered with the SEC and thus may not be sold publicly until registration has been made.

Restricted Stock Grant A stock option given to an employee, especially a senior manager, allowing that employee to buy the company's shares, which are not registered with the SEC. The stocks in a restricted stock grant must be registered before the employee may sell them.

Restricted Stock Unit A restricted stock, usually acquired through the exercise of a stock option, that does not vest until some date in the future. Restricted stock units do not pay dividends until they vest. Likewise, one is not responsible for taxes on these units until they vest, unless one chooses a section 83(b) election.

Restriction 1. See: Credit control. **2.** See: Exchange control. **3.** See: Import control.

Restrictive Covenant A bond covenant that forbids the issuer from taking certain actions. For example, a restrictive covenant may prevent an issuer from issuing more debt until the bond matures. More commonly, a restrictive covenant limits the dividends an issuer may pay to shareholders so as to reduce the risk to the bond. It contrasts with a positive covenant, which requires the issuer to take certain enumerated actions. It is also called a negative covenant.

Restrictive Endorsement An endorsement on a check with restrictions. An endorsement is a signature on the back of a check stating that the payee has consented to receive the funds from the payer. A restrictive endorsement states the circumstances under which the payee will accept the funds under the signature.

Restructured Loan A loan for which the parties have agreed to alter the terms, usually to make them more favorable to the borrower. For example, the borrower may restructure a loan to receive a lower interest rate or monthly payment. Restructured loans are most common if the borrower states that he/she can no longer afford payments under the old terms. For example, a borrower may have to accept a new job with less income, forcing a tighter budget.

Restructuring The act or process of changing the terms on the assets and/or liabilities of a company. That is, a company may consolidate its debts, significantly change the size and scope of its operations, and take other measures to reduce the strain of continuing operation. Most companies restructure either as part of a bankruptcy or as an effort to avoid it. If the company is restructuring as part of a corporate bankruptcy, it is said to be in receivership.

Restructuring Charge A cost that a company incurs when it reorganizes its operations. Restructuring charges include costs with opening or closing a factory, hiring new employees or paying the severances for lay-offs, and so forth. Restructuring charges are included in the calculation of a company's net income, but because they are unusual, a high restructuring charge is less likely to result in a steep decline in the company's share price.

Resume Stain A job at a company with a bad reputation, or any low-prestige job. Resume stains may be removed from one's resume in order to preserve one's marketability. See also: Career-limiting move.

Retail 1. Relating to the sale of goods or services to consumers, rather than producers or intermediaries. For example, a retail clothing store sells to people who will (most likely) wear the clothes. It does not include the sale of the clothes to other stores that will resell them. Retail contrasts with wholesale. **2.** Relating to the sale of securities to individual investors rather than institutional investors or broker-dealers. See also: Retail banking.

Retail Banking Banking services that are offered to individual customers through local branches of the bank. Examples of retail banking services include checking and savings accounts, credit cards, personal lines of credit, mortgages, and so forth. Some retail banks offer basic brokerage services, though this is not always the case. Retail banking contrasts with commercial banking, which primarily offers services to businesses. See also: Private banking.

Retail House A brokerage in which most clients are individuals, rather than institutional investors. While there are small retail houses for elite clients, most of these brokerages are large organizations with high overheads because they usually need larger client bases than other brokerages. Brokers at a retail house often earn high commissions, and their research departments produce investment recommendations for individual, as opposed to institutional, investors.

Retail Investor An investor who invests small amounts of money for himself/herself rather than on behalf of anyone else. Retail investors are the polar opposite of institutional investors, which are large firms who invest on behalf of clients. Some investment vehicles require minimum investments so as to discourage retail investors from them. Retail investors are thought to be risk-averse and poorly informed compared to other investors, though there is disagreement as to how true that is. See also: Odd-Lot Theory.

Retail Market 1. The market for the sale of goods or services to consumers rather than producers or intermediaries. For example, a retail clothing store sells to people who will (most likely) wear the clothes. It does not include the sale of the clothes to other stores who will resell them. The retail market contrasts with the wholesale market. **2.** The market for the sale of securities to individual investors rather than institutional investors or broker-dealers. See also: Retail banking.

Retail Price The price the end user of a product pays. That is, if one buys a vacuum in order to use it instead of to sell it to another store, one likely pays the retail price. The retail price includes all expenses the retailer incurs, plus a mark-up.

Retail Price Index A measure of inflation that considers what people spend on staple goods and services. It is calculated by taking the average of changes in price to a basket of goods and services compiled by the appropriate government agency. The goods and services in the basket are weighted according to their perceived importance. The RPI was considered a primary tool in determining how people are experiencing inflation, but it has largely been superseded by the Consumer Price Index. It is primarily used today in the British news media.

Retailer A company that sells goods or services to consumers, rather than to producers or intermediaries. For example, a clothing retailer sells to people who will (most likely) wear the clothes. Retailers generally do not sell their products to other stores that will resell them. A retailer contrasts with a wholesaler.

Retainage The amount that a construction company is owed but is not paid until a project is completed and passes muster with the client. Retainage is a form of quality control.

Retained Earnings Statement A financial statement that a publicly-traded company files each year stating its net income that has not been paid out as dividends. See also: Plowback rate.

Retender To sell the delivery notice on a futures contract. When a futures contract matures, the seller of the underlying asset gives his/her intent to deliver to the clearing house, which then gives delivery notice to the buyer. The buyer then may retender, or sell the delivery notice, to a third party to ensure that the buyer does not actually receive the underlying asset. Retendering occurs because most futures investors do not wish to actually receive what they buy; sometimes, it may be avoided by settling in cash. It is important to note that some futures contracts do not permit retendering.

Retention Prior to a new issue, the percentage of securities given to an underwriting syndicate to place with investors after making allowances for any underwriters that are not part of the syndicate as well as placement with institutional investors.

Retired in Place A slang term for an employee who works just hard enough not to be fired and who waits until he/she is eligible to take retirement benefits. The term implies that one is not a reliable or responsible employee, at least not beyond the bare minimum required.

Retired Securities 1. A situation in which a firm buys back its own stock. A publicly-traded company may retire its stock in order to reduce the number of shares available, with the hope of driving up the price. Alternatively, it may retire securities in order to prevent one or more shareholders from acquiring too large a stake in the company. See also: Self-tender offer. **2.** The removal of debt securities from trade due to their maturity. For example, when a bond issue matures, it is obviously no longer traded. The issue is then said to be retired.

Retiree A person who has stopped working in his/her old age, or at least when he/she has saved enough money to last the remainder of his/her life. Generally, retirement occurs after the age of 65, but not always. Both governments and companies offer pensions, annuities, and other plans to provide for one's financial needs in retirement. Luxury products such as cruises often are targeted at retirees because they tend to have expendable income and relatively few expenses.

Retirement 1. The act or process of causing a security to cease to exist. It especially applies to debt securities; when a bond for example matures is said to be retired. However, a stock or other security may also be retired if its issuer buys it back. **2.** A situation in which one stops working in one's old age, or at least when one has saved enough money to last the remainder of one's life. Generally, retirement occurs after the age of 65, but this is not a hard-and-fast rule. Both governments and companies offer pensions, annuities, and other plans to provide for one's financial needs in retirement.

Retirement Age The age at which a person is expected to retire. The retirement age varies from country to country (and even company to company), but tends to be between 55 and 70.

Retirement Annuity An annuity one purchases to provide for oneself in retirement. In general, one purchases a retirement annuity well before retirement and makes contributions to it throughout one's working life. The contributions are invested on behalf of the annuitant, who begins to receive payments from the annuity after retirement. Many retirement annuities (especially those sponsored by an employer) are tax-deferred, meaning that the annuitant does not pay taxes on the funds in the pension until he/she begins making withdrawals. Annuities may have defined contributions, defined benefits, or both. See also: 401(k), IRA.

Retirement News for Employers A newsletter published by the IRS relating news items of interest to employers who manage retirement plans for themselves or employees. The newsletter contains relevant tax information on the subject.

Retirement Protection Act of 1994 Legislation in the United States designed to protect pensions for retirees and strengthen a government-administered program insuring them. Among its provisions, the Act required pension plans deemed to be underfunded to obtain enough cash and securities to cover benefits they were required to make. It increased the premiums for pensions insured by the Pension Benefit Guaranty Corporation that were in danger of default.

Retirement Relief A capital gains tax cut formerly given in the United Kingdom to persons over 50 who sold their assets related to business.

Retiring a Bill The removal of debt securities from trade due to their maturity. For example, when a bond issue matures, it is obviously no longer traded. The issue is then said to be retired.

Retracement A situation in which a price begins to move back toward its former price after it has changed significantly in a brief period of time. An example of retracement occurs when a stock falls 10% but then recovers 8%.

Return If Exercised The return that the writer, or seller, of a covered call would make if the buyer decides to exercise the option (or buy the underlying asset at the stated strike price). This return will likely be less than if the writer sold the underlying asset at the current market price. Otherwise, the option probably would not have been exercised.

Return on Capital Employed A measurement of return on the investment needed for a business to function, otherwise known as capital employed, expressed as a dollar amount or a percentage. It is used to show a business' health, specifically by showing how efficiently its investments are used to create a profit. A good ROCE is one that is greater than the rate at which the company borrows. Because capital employed has no set definition, there are different ways to calculate ROCE. Two common ways are: ROCE = (Operating Profit Before Tax) / (Total Assets - Current Liabilities) and ROCE = ((Profit before Tax) / (Capital Employed)) * 100. One limitation to ROCE is the fact that it does not account for depreciation of the capital employed. Because capital employed is in the denominator, a company with depreciated assets may find its ROCE increases without an actual increase in profit. It also neglects inflation, which might depress ROCE unnecessarily. See also: Return on Average Capital Employed (ROACE), Required return.

Return on Capital Gains The yield on an investment that comes from an increase in the purchase price, expressed as a percentage. For example, suppose one buys a share for $30. If one sells that share for $40, one has a capital gain of $10. The return on capital gains is calculated as follows: Return on capital gains = $10 / $30 * 100 = 33.3%

Return on Common Equity A publicly-traded company's earnings (less dividends on preferred shares) divided by the amount of money invested in common stock, expressed as a percentage. This is a measure of how well the company is investing the money invested in it. A high return on common equity indicates that the company is spending wisely and is likely profitable; a low return on common equity indicates the opposite. As a result, high returns on common equity lead to higher stock prices. Some analysts believe that return on common equity is an extremely important indicator in publicly-traded companies' health. See also: Growth stock.

Return on Equity A publicly-traded company's earnings divided by the amount of money invested in stock, expressed as a percentage. This is a measure of how well the company is investing the money invested in it. A high return on equity indicates that the company is spending wisely and is likely profitable; a low return on equity indicates the opposite. As a result, high returns on equity lead to higher stock prices. Some analysts believe that return on equity is the single most important indicator of publicly-traded companies' health. See also: Growth stock.

Return on Gross Invested Capital A measure of a company's return on its total capital, expressed as a percentage. ROGIC is calculated by taking the company's returns and dividing by the total amount of capital it has invested (that is, the value of common stock, preferred stock, and bonds) and multiplying the quotient by 100. ROGIC is an important measure because it does not take into account depreciation and amortization, which means that the company's return cannot be artificially inflated through non-cash earnings.

Return on Investment The money that a person or company earns as a percentage of the total value of his/her/its assets that are invested. It is calculated thusly: Return on investment = (Income - Cost) / Cost Because it is easy to calculate the return on investment, it is a relatively popular measure of the profitability on an investment and can help in making investment decisions.

Return on Investment Capital A measure of how efficiently a company generates cash flow compared to how much capital is invested in the company. It is calculated by taking its net operating profit after taxes and dividends and dividing by the total amount of capital invested and expressing the result as a percentage. Companies seek to have a return on investment capital greater than its cost of capital. It is also called return on invested capital and simply return on capital.

Return on Net Assets A ratio of a company's financial performance. It is calculated by taking its net income and dividing it by the quantity of its fixed assets and net working income. The return on net assets measures how efficiently a company is using its net assets (its fixed assets and net working income) in order to make a profit. The higher the ratio is, the better the company's performance is thought to be.

Return On Revenue The ratio of a company's net income (or profit) to its revenue. The return on revenue helps determine the company's profitability and is particularly useful if compared year to year. An increase in the return on revenue indicates that a company is reducing its expenses relative to its revenue because net income, simply put, is revenue minus expenses.

Return on Sales A company's earnings divided by the amount of sales, expressed as a percentage. This is a measure of how much the company is profiting from its sales. A high return on sales indicates that the company is selling its products well and its profits are likely sustainable; a low return on sales indicates the opposite. Management often uses the ROS to determine how efficient the company is.

Return on Total Assets A publicly-traded company's earnings before interest and taxes, divided by its total assets, expressed as a percentage. This is a measure of how well the company is using its assets to generate earnings. A high return on total assets indicates that the company is investing wisely and is likely profitable; a low return on equity indicates the opposite.

Returned Without Action A situation in which an application for an export license is not granted, generally because it is incomplete or the applicant is eligible for a general license.

REU GOST 7.67 Latin three-letter geocode for Reunion. The code is used for transactions to and from Reunionese bank accounts and for international shipping to Reunion. As with all GOST 7.67 codes, it is used primarily in Cyrillic alphabets.

Reul A coin that circulated in the Republic of Ireland between 1928 and 1972. It was equal in value to 1/40 of one Irish pound. See also: Sixpence.

Reunion Franc The former currency of Reunion, an overseas department of France. After 1973, the franc was equivalent to the French franc. It was replaced by the euro in 1999.

Re-Use Fee A fee paid to the creator or owner of a product by its user for permission to continue to use the product. An example of a re-use fee is a SAG fee, which is paid to an actor or other performer every time his/her program is rerun.

Revaluation A change to the exchange rate of a pegged currency. For example, if the central bank has declared a currency to be worth 10 U.S. dollars and later changes the exchange rate to $8, one refers to this as a revaluation. A revaluation generally, but does not always, refer to an increase in value.

Revenue The amount of money a company earns through the sale of goods or services, rents, and other sources. Revenue is the amount the company makes; it should not be confused with profit, which is revenue less expenses. Likewise, it should not be confused with cash flow, as revenue can be money owed but not yet paid.

Revenue Agent An employee at the IRS who is responsible for helping the agency collect all federal taxes derived from sources other than tariffs and associated fees. Generally speaking, revenue agents perform audits on random tax returns to ensure appropriate payment of taxes.

Revenue Agent's Report An IRS agent's report following an audit. The RAR contains information such as adjustments to the taxpayer's income, but it states the bottom line as to whether the taxpayer overpaid, underpaid, or paid the correct amount. If the taxpayer overpaid, he/she receives a refund. If one underpaid, one must pay additional taxes, often with interest and penalties. See also: Form 4549.

Revenue Anticipation Note A municipal bond, with a maturity of one year or less, that is repaid to bondholders with expected revenues from the project the RAN intends to finance. For example, a city may issue an RAN to finance improvements to the local museum. It expects to be able to pay back the bond with money raised on increased ticket sales at the museum after improvements are completed.

Revenue Bond A municipal bond that is not secured by the issuer's general revenue but instead by the revenue of the project it intends to finance. For example, a city may issue a revenue bond to finance improvements to the local sewer system. It expects to be able to pay back the bond with money raised from citizens' water bills. Generally speaking, a revenue bond is riskier than other municipal bonds because the project has no power to tax on its own. However, it is usually a fairly safe investment. See also: Authority Bond.

Revenue Enhancement A politically correct term for raising taxes. When a government or politician refers to revenue enhancement, it usually refers to raising taxes indirectly, especially by eliminating deductions or credits.

Revenue Officer 1. A person who works for the IRS, especially for its collections department. **2.** Any person at a company whose position involves the collection of revenue. Examples include sales persons, marketers, and persons working for accounts receivable.

Revenue Passenger Miles A measure of consumer demand for an airline, bus, train, or other form of mass transportation. One calculates revenue seat miles by taking the number of passengers who pay for their seats and multiplying by the number of miles in the trip. Some overnight trips, especially on trains with sleeper cars, use a more complex measure. One excludes employees and others who receive free tickets from the calculation, but usually includes those who pay through a frequent flyer or a similar program. Revenue passenger miles are also called revenue seat miles.

Revenue per Available Room In the hotel industry, a measure of the average daily rate for a room multiplied by the number of rooms used. It is calculated by taking the total revenue for a particular period of time and dividing by the number of rooms rented over the same period. It is important to note that RevPAR only accounts for revenue from room rental and does not include other sources of revenue, such as that from room service or alcohol.

Revenue per Employee The revenue that a company generates over a given period of time divided by the number of employees. Companies seek to have the highest possible revenue per employee. Analysts often compare revenue per employee of different companies in the same industry to measure productivity.

Revenue Per User A measure of revenue of a company or a product divided by the total number of customers or the customers using that product. Companies use RPU to determine the average amount they make from each customer, especially on certain products. It is especially important in the telecommunications industry, which uses the measure to identify the demand (and therefore the profitability) of its various products.

Revenue Reconciliation Act of 1993 Legislation in the United States that raised certain taxes on certain income, including on some entitlements like Social Security. It was part of the broader Omnibus Budget Reconciliation Act of 1993, which raised taxes and cut some government spending in order to reduce the federal deficit. The Act came out of a theory that large deficits lead to inflation; this theory was rejected by both New Deal liberals and supply-side economics conservatives, both of whom believed that deficits are relatively unimportant. While the theory behind the Act remains controversial, it led to a projected budget surplus toward the end of the 1990s.

Revenue Sharing 1. The practice of splitting a company's profits and losses between parties. For example, a partnership shares revenue between partners in accordance with each one's share in the company. Alternatively, revenue sharing may indicate any arrangement where a company gives a portion of its profits to its employees or other companies in an alliance. **2.** The practice of a government giving a portion of tax revenue to subdivisions of government. For example, a province may apportion a certain percentage of the taxes it collects to municipalities and a national government may do the same for its provinces. In the United States, the federal government practiced revenue sharing with the states until the 1980s, when the Reagan administration stopped the practice to reduce the national deficit.

Reversal A change in a security's price trend.

Reversal Amount In charts that account only for a security's price without regard for time, the amount of change in price needed to move the chart. Most charts that do not account for time are a series of columns (variously conceptualized), each representing a price. Thus, a reversal amount may be thought of as the amount of price movement needed to create a new column on the chart.

Reversal Arbitrage A series of transactions in which an investor short sells a security, buys a call, and sells a put. The call and the put both have the short sold security as the underlying asset. Reversal arbitrage is riskless because, if the value of the underlying increases, the call is exercised and negates the short sale. On the other hand, if the value decreases, the put will be exercised and also negates the short sale.

Reversal Pattern In technical analysis, any pattern on a chart that indicates a previous trend is changing to a new trend. Generally speaking, any trend in which the highs are lower than the previous highs is a bearish reversal pattern, while any trend in which the lows are higher than the previous lows is bullish. However, some reversal patterns are more complex. Examples include a head-and-shoulders pattern and an outside reversal.

Reverse In numismatics, the back of a coin; that is to say, the "tails" side. The reverse often usually features some national monument or commemorates some event. The front of a coin is called the obverse.

Reverse a Swap To engage in a swap in which the legs are the same as a previous swap, but are held by different parties. For example, suppose two counterparties swap bond A and bond B. The party that receives bond A (who is the same party that gave away bond B) may reverse the swap by giving away bond A and receiving bond B back. One usually reverses a swap if there are tax advantages associated with it, or if the new position is not as profitable as previously thought.

Reverse Acquisition An act where a private company purchases a publicly traded company and shifts its management into the latter. It also normally involves renaming the publicly traded company. This allows private companies to become publicly traded while avoiding the regulatory and financial requirements associated with an IPO. In order for a reverse acquisition to happen smoothly, the publicly traded company is usually a shell corporation, that is, one with only an organizational structure and little or no activity. The two businesses can then merge the private company's product(s) with the public company's structure. It also makes initial trading less dependent on market conditions, a key risk in IPOs. However, it is important to note that a reverse acquisition only provides the private company with more liquidity if there is a real market interest in it.

Reverse Convertible Note A security that combines aspects of a stock and a bond. An RCN operates like a debt security that pays a fixed coupon, which is usually higher than the coupons for regular bonds. At maturity, the holder may choose to receive a certain amount of stock or cash equal to the value of that stock. RCNs allow the investor to diversify his/her portfolio while only incurring the expense of a single investment vehicle.

Reverse Crush A commodity trade in which one sells soybean futures at the same time one buys futures in soybean mean and soybean oil. Reverse crushes are useful because they can take advantage of price spread between the underlying soybeans and products that can be derived from soybeans. See also: Crush.

Reverse Dandruff In technical analysis, an indicator in which the price of a security falls to a low, rises, falls to a lower point, then rises again, and, finally, drops to a low roughly equal to the first and then rises again. While, in general, a reverse dandruff pattern is considered a bullish indicator, it contains various bearish points, namely immediately before the price drops. On the other hand, the third price low is considered a buy signal. Reverse dandruff is the opposite of a head and shoulders pattern.

Reverse Leverage 1. A situation in which a company is spending more money than it is receiving. While this is common in many companies, especially in the first year or two of operation, it is obviously unsustainable in the long-term. A company with reverse leverage often has to resort to loans or equity financing in order to keep its doors open. It is also called negative cash flow. **2.** A situation in which the interest a company pays on a loan exceeds the return on any investments acquired with that loan. This usually results in a loss to the company, but some companies may do this deliberately to reduce their tax liabilities. It is also called reverse carry.

Reverse Leveraged Buyout The issue of stock by a company that had previously gone private through a leveraged buyout (or an acquisition financed mainly with debt). A reversed leveraged buyout often occurs when the company is having difficulty repaying the debt used for the leveraged buyout and wishes to raise capital to do so.

Reverse Merger An act where a private company purchases a publicly traded company and shifts its management into the latter. It also normally involves renaming the publicly traded company. This allows private companies to become publicly traded while avoiding the regulatory and financial requirements associated with an IPO. In order for a reverse merger to happen smoothly, the publicly traded company is usually a shell corporation, that is, one with only an organizational structure and little or no activity. The two businesses can then merge the private company's product(s) with the public company's structure. It also makes initial trading less dependent on market conditions, a key risk in IPOs. However, it is important to note that a reverse merger only provides the private company with more liquidity if there is a real market interest in it.

Reverse Mortgage A loan borrowed against the value of one's home. In this situation, the lender gives the borrower the amount of the loan and the borrower makes no payments and retains title to his/her home. When the borrower moves from the house or dies, the lender takes possession of the home, which it then sells to repay the loan. Any extra profit is remitted to the borrower or his/her estate. A lifetime reverse mortgage allows a homeowner to access his/her home's equity without the inconvenience of moving. It is a financial instrument designed to help homeowners who are cash poor, and is limited to senior citizens. In the United States, one must be 62 years old in order to be eligible for a lifetime reverse mortgage, while the U.K. requires potential borrowers to be at least 55. It is also known as a lifetime reverse mortgage.

Reverse Price Risk In mortgages, a situation in which a lender agrees to set the interest rate at the prevailing rate at the time the sale of the property closes. The lender is therefore exposed to the risk that the prevailing interest rate will fall between the time the agreement is reached at the closing of the sale. See also: Mortgage pipeline risk.

Reverse Repurchase Agreement A practice in which a bank or other financial institution buys securities or another asset with the proviso that it will resell these same securities or asset to the same seller for an agreed-upon price on a certain day (often the next day). Investors and financial institutions do this in order to raise short-term capital. Indeed, it is the equivalent of a short-term loan with the securities or asset serving as collateral. A reverse repurchase agreement is the same as a repurchase agreement, but from the perspective of the buyer rather than the seller. It is also called a matched sale transaction or simply a reverse.

Reverse Stock Split The act of a publicly-traded company reducing the number of outstanding shares while maintaining the same market capitalization. In other words, a company engages in a reverse stock split in order to increase its share price. For example, a company with a share price of $1.50 may cut its number of shares in half so that the price goes to $3. Companies only conduct a reverse stock split if it desires to boost its share price when it is unable to do so by other means. Some companies consider reverse stock splits a last resort to avoid delisting from the exchange as the result of a share price that is too low.

Reverse Swap A swap that restores an earlier position. For example, one may swap U.S. dollars for British pounds when doing so is advantageous to one's investment strategy, then reverse swap the pounds back to dollars when that becomes advantageous.

Reverse Triangular Merger In mergers and acquisitions, a situation in which a company is acquiring a publicly-traded target company and, in the process, a subsidiary of the acquiring company merges with the target company. When this occurs, the equity of the subsidiary is reflected in the target company's stock. The result makes the target company a wholly owned subsidiary, and shareholders in the target company instead receive shares in the acquiring company. Reverse triangular mergers occur when regulations or contracts require that certain assets not change hands.

Reversing Trade A term for closing a position. It is usually used with respect to futures positions.

Revised Estimate 1. In calculating quarterly GDP, a third estimate published approximately three months after the end of a quarter. It includes information not available at the time of the advance estimate or preliminary estimate, as well as any necessary data revisions. However, it is still subject to scrutiny and potential alteration. See also: Final estimate. **2.** A change in the calculation of the cost of a project. This calculation is made and presented to a buyer, usually while a project is in progress, and may be subject to further changes due to both exogenous factors and endogenous factors. See also: Preliminary estimate.

Revisionary Trust An irrevocable trust that becomes a revocable trust after a certain number of years. An irrevocable trust is one where the grantor forfeits his/her ability to dissolve the trust and to reclaim the assets placed in it, while a revocable trust is one where the grantor retains these rights. If the grantor dies while the trust is irrevocable, the trust is not considered part of his/her estate for estate tax and inheritance tax purposes. On the other hand, if the grantor is still living when the trust become revocable, the assets can be considered part of the estate, but at the same time the grantor may revoke the trust and use the assets if he/she runs into financial difficulty or for any other reason.

Revocable 1. See: Revocable trust. **2.** See: Revocable beneficiary. **3.** See: Revocable letter of credit.

Revocable Beneficiary The beneficiary of a life insurance policy that the policyholder may remove from the policy at his/her discretion. For example, suppose a policyholder names her husband as a revocable beneficiary. Should the policyholder be divorced, she may remove her (now ex-) husband from the policy and replace him with someone else, say a child or other relative. Most life insurance policies have revocable beneficiaries to give the policyholder a great deal of flexibility. A revocable beneficiary should not be confused with a revocable trust. See also: Irrevocable Beneficiary.

Revocable Letter of Credit A letter of credit that the grantingbank or the letter holder (who is the buyer of some good) may cancel under some or any circumstances. This does not provide the seller with any extra assurance that he/she will be paid on time and in the correct amount. As a result they carry higher risk than irrevocable letters of credit.

Revocable Trust A trust that the trustor may terminate at any point prior to his/her death. A trust relationship in which one party, known as the trustor, gives to a person or organization, known as the trustee, the right to hold and invest assets or property on behalf of a third party, known as the beneficiary. Most trusts exist to provide for the financial future of a minor child or mentally incompetent person, or may benefit charitable organizations. Many trusts are exempt from taxation on money given to the beneficiary, but because revocable trusts may be terminated, they are considered part of the trustor's estate and are thus subject to estate taxes.

Revoked IRA An IRA that the holder decides to cancel within seven days of forming it. All funds contributed to the revoked IRA are returned to the holder, and the sponsoring institution may not charge any cancellation or other penalty fees.

Revolving Acceptance Facility by Tender Commonly called a RAFT. A way to provide financing for international trade in which a bank places a banker's acceptance through a network of acceptable banks on behalf of a creditworthy buyer of the underlying good.

Revolving-Loan Fund A pool of liquidity that may be loaned to a business. When it is repaid, the capital becomes available to be loaned to another business. A revolving loan fund is intended to assist in business development but, because money is limited, it may only be loaned out to one company at a time. A revolving loan fund begins with a donation; that is, the initial capital that forms the fund need not be repaid.

Reward-to-Volatility Ratio The excess return on an investment divided by the standard deviation from its average price. This can be used to determine the risk of an investment.

RH 1. ISO 3166-1 alpha-2 code for Southern Rhodesia before it changed its name to Zimbabwe. This was the code used in international transactions to and from bank accounts in Southern Rhodesia. **2.** ISO 3166-2 geocode for Southern Rhodesia. This was used as an international standard for shipping to Southern Rhodesia. In both cases, the code is obsolete.

Rho The dollar amount that the price of an option or other derivative changes for each 100 basis points the risk-free interest rate changes. This is a measure of the option's or derivative's responsiveness to interest rates. See also: Volatility.

Rhodesian Dollar The currency of Rhodesia. It was issued in 1970, soon after Rhodesia became a republic. It was a strong currency throughout its history, being roughly equal in value to the British pound. There were limits on its convertibility. It was replaced by the Zimbabwean dollar.

RHZW ISO 3166-3 code for Southern Rhodesia, which changed its name to Zimbabwe in 1980. ISO 3166-3 codes are used to indicate names of countries that are no longer used.

Ri A unit of length in Japan equivalent to approximately 4,295 yards, or a bit less than two and a half miles.

Rial 1. The currency of Iran. Issued to replace the qiran in 1932, it was pegged to the British pound at various rates until 1945. After this, it was pegged to the U.S. dollar until 1975. Since the Islamic Revolution in 1979, the rial has been marked by high inflation and low value. **2.** The currency of Yemen. It was the currency of South Yemen before unification in 1990. Following unification, the rial remained in circulation along with the North Yemeni dinar until 1996. After the dinar was withdrawn from circulation, the rial became a floating currency. **3.** The currency of Oman. It was introduced in 1973, replacing the rial Saidi, which had replaced the Gulf rupee. It is pegged to the U.S. dollar.

Rial Saidi The currency of Oman between 1970 and 1973. It was pegged to the British pound at par. It was replaced by the Omani rial.

Riba The Arabic word for "excess," which is used as a byword for interest. The Quran explicitly prohibits Muslims to receive or take riba; many Muslims believe this forbids them from taking advantage of financial products based on interest. Because this removes most conventional products, Islamic finance was developed to offer an alternative, though critics contend these products still accumulate riba because they imitate "regular" finance.

Riba al-jadl In Islamic law, interest that accrues immediately upon the completion of a transaction. As with all forms of interest, riba al-jadl is prohibited. It is also called riba al-ajlaan.

Riba al-Quran In Islamic law, interest charged on money lent. It is called riba al-Quran (as opposed to simply riba, which has much the same meaning in everyday use) because it is explicitly forbidden in the Quran. This contrasts with riba al-sunnah, which refers to subtler forms of interest prohibited in traditions surrounding the Quran, but not in the Quran itself.

Riba al-sunnah In Islamic law, an alternate term for riba al-fadl, which is the exchange of different amounts of the same good in which the delivery of one occurs at a later date. For example, two parties may exchange 10 bushels of corn now for 12 bushels next month. It is called riba al-sunnah because this type of riba is not specifically prohibited in the Quran, but is disallowed by the traditions surrounding the Quran, which are called the Sunnah.

Richard Roll An economist who researches portfolio theory and asset pricing. He was among the first to analyze how stock prices react to the announcements of particular events, such as a merger or an earnings report. See also: Price out.

Ricin A protein found in castor beans. Ricin is poisonous and has been used in biological warfare.

Riddler In coin minting, a machine that finds and discards coins with errors or that are the wrong size.

Ride-Along In marketing, a small sample of a product that is sent in the mail along with a periodical. Ride-alongs are intended to entice recipients to want more of the product and therefore to buy it.

Rider An amendment to a document, especially an insurance policy. More formally, it is called an endorsement. The insurance company may issue the rider to change the terms of coverage, or the policyholder may do so, especially to add a family member to the policy. Generally, riders increase coverage in exchange for higher premiums.

Riding the Yield Curve An investment strategy in which one buys a long-term bond and sells it before maturity. Riding the yield curve allows the bondholder to profit from the declining yield that occurs over the life of the bond.

Riegle-Neal Interstate Banking and Branching Efficiency Act of 1994 Legislation in the United States repealing previous restrictions on banks from operating in more than one state. The Riegle-Neal Act allowed banks, under certain circumstances, to acquire banks or set up branches in other states without creating a separate subsidiary. The Act streamlined banking regulation in the United States, and, for the first time, allowed out-of-state residents to set up bank accounts. It also gave federal regulators the authority to ensure that out-of-state deposits do not dominate American banking.

Riel The currency of Cambodia. It was issued in 1980, ending a five-year period during which Cambodia had no monetary system. The U.S. dollar also circulates in Cambodia, particularly in urban areas. Additionally, merchants along the border often accept the Thai baht.

Rifle Approach A marketing strategy that focuses on only one target. That is, a rifle approach attempts to market a product to a small, narrowly defined demographic. See also: Shotgun Approach.

Rigged Market An illegal act or practice in which a person or company causes a price to be more favorable to an investor than market forces really justify. Rigged markets exist in order to attract investors to a company or project, but it is often not sustainable and in any case dupes the investor. There are a variety of ways to create a rigged market. See also: Price Manipulation.

Right Here In equities, describing an order that is almost ready to be executed. An order is called "right here" especially when the client making the order asks when it will be filled. Right here means that the requested price has almost been reached. See also: In-line.

Right of Establishment The right of a citizen of any country in the European Union to start a company, set up a subsidiary or generally to conduct business in any other EU country. The right of establishment is part of the common market of the EU. It is guaranteed by the Treaty of Lisbon.

Right of First Refusal The right of a person or organization to take advantage of a transaction before it is open to other parties. For example, a seller and potential buyer of a house may agree that the buyer has right of first refusal. Then, if the seller receives a better offer from another potential buyer, she must take the offer to the first buyer and, if that buyer accepts, sell to him rather than the second buyer. One party may pay for the right of first refusal, and it may be built into a contract. See also: Earnest money.

Right of Foreclosure The legal right of a mortgage lender to take ownership of a property securing a mortgage if the borrower does not meet the terms of the lending agreement. Most obviously, the right of foreclosure is exercised if the borrower does not pay the mortgage.

Right of Redemption In foreclosure or repossession, the right of a borrower to receive back the stated property before it is re-sold (and sometimes after it is re-sold) in exchange for repaying the debt guaranteed by the property that was foreclosed or repossessed. The length of time one has the right of redemption varies, but it can be for up to one year.

Right of Return The legal right that an individual has to go back to his/her country. The right of return is guaranteed by the Universal Declaration of Human Rights, but there is debate about what is meant by "country," whether it refers to one's physical place of birth or the state with which one's ethnicity is associated. The right of return remains controversial in many places, notably Israel and the Palestinian territories.

Right to Privacy The right not to be violated without one's consent. For example, the right to privacy includes the right to be secure in one's own person or home. The right to privacy in guaranteed in many jurisdictions. Other jurisdictions that do not explicitly provide a right to privacy may provide some protections. For example, a government may prohibit searches in a private area without a warrant.

Right-Angle Fold In printing, a way to fold paper in which each new fold occurs at a right angle to the previous fold. Right-angle folds may be used in all kinds of pamphlets and flyers.

Right-Hand Side In foreign exchange, a slang term for buying a currency.

Rights of Accumulation In loaded mutual funds, the right of a shareholder to a reduced load or sales fee when he/she purchases more than a certain a dollar amount of the mutual fund. The dollar amount is known as the breakpoint. For example, if the breakpoint for a certain mutual fund is $50,000, an investor has the right to reduce the load by, say, half when he/she invests more than $50,000 in the fund. It thus becomes advantageous for the investor to invest $50,000 instead of, say, $45,000, because this will entitle him/her to half the load for the entire investment, and not just for the amount invested past $50,000. Mutual funds that allow investors to buy at just below the breakpoint may run afoul of Financial Industry Regulatory Authority regulations. The right of accumulation is not limited to a single investment; an investor putting two tranches of $25,000 into the above mutual fund will usually find his excess load refunded.

Rights of Set-Off A portion of a loan agreement stating the rights of each party should one party or the other default on his/her obligations. Rights of set-off are most often stated explicitly when two parties are lending money to each other. See also: Parallel loan.

Rights of Survivorship In a situation where two or more persons jointly own property, the right of the other owner(s) to continue to own the property when one owner dies. In other words, a jointly-owned property with right of survivorship does not become part of a decedent's estate; rather, his/her co-owner(s) continue to own the property. Couples may have rights of survivorship on a jointly-owned house, for example. It may also be used in a joint business venture: if two persons own an apartment complex and one of them dies, the whole of the complex belongs to the co-owner and not the decedent's heirs. It is important to note, however, that the decedent's liabilities may remain attached to this property and may be used to pay off creditors, even if the creditor had nothing to do with the property in question. See also: Tenants in common.

Rights Off Describing the sale of a share without any rights attached to it. That is, any rights that may be attached to the share remain with the seller. It is also called ex-rights and contrasts with rights on. See also: Rights offering, Ex-dividend.

Rights Offering In stock, the ability of a shareholder to maintain the same percentage of ownership in a company should the company issue more stock by buying a proportional number of shares at or below the market price. This protects the investor from devaluation of his/her shares if the company decides to hold a round of financing. The purchase of this proportional number of shares usually takes place before the new issue is offered to the secondary market, and must be exercised before a certain date (known as the expiration date) if the shareholder is to maintain the same percentage of ownership. Rights offerings or issues are also called subscription rights or simply rights. See also: Anti-dilution provision.

Rights On Describing the sale of a share with rights attached to it. That is, any rights that are attached to the share but have not been distributed go to the buyer, rather than remaining with the seller. It is also called cum rights and contrasts with rights off. See also: Rights offering.

Right-Shoring The practice of moving jobs to the place where the company can maximize profits at the lowest cost. Often, right-shoring is identical to offshoring, but the term implies a more comprehensive search for the correct location.

Rightsizing The act or process of reducing the workforce at a company to the perceived correct number. The term is identical in meaning to layoffs or downsizing, but the word was invented to have a positive connotation. Instead, it is often used in a tongue-in-cheek fashion.

Right-to-Work Legislation at the state level in the United States prohibiting union shops, which are companies in which the employer agrees to require union membership from employees after a probationary period. In effect, right-to-work laws allow employees to benefit from union agreements without paying union dues. Right-to-work laws are controversial; both proponents and opponents claim that they reduce union power. The argument is over whether or not this is a good thing.

Riisi A Finnish unit meaning 500 sheets of paper.

Rijnlandse voet An obsolete Dutch unit of area roughly equivalent to 10 square centimeters.

Riksbanken The central bank of Sweden. It issues the Swedish krona and sets basic interest rates for commercial banks dealing in it. Established in 1668, it is the oldest central bank still in existence.

Rin A unit of length in Japan equivalent to 0.03030 millimeters.

Ring A place on an exchange assigned for the trading of certain commodities, futures, or options. It is also called a pit or a trading pit.

Ring Fencing The practice of a company creating a legal entity separate from itself in order to protect certain assets. For example, ring fencing may protect assets from taxation, regulation, or allow the company to hide it from creditors. Ring fencing often makes use of offshore accounting. It is usually legal, but there are limitations, such as maximum amounts that may be protected.

Ring Trading A term for floor trading on the London Metals Exchange. It derives its name from the fact that traders sit in a circle to buy and sell securities to each other.

Ringgit The currency of Malaysia. It was issued in 1967 as the Malaysian dollar, though it was called the ringgit in Malay. The name ringgit was used in both languages starting in 1975. It was pegged to the U.S. dollar between 1998 and 2005 as a result of the East Asian financial crisis. In 2005 it became a currency with a managed float.

Ringi System A management technique in Japanese companies in which low-level managers discuss a new idea among themselves and come to a consensus before presenting it to higher managers. The higher ranking managers then discuss the new idea themselves and arrive at their own consensus. This process continues until the idea comes to the highest management level and the idea is (or is not) implemented. Proponents claim that this system allows whole sections of a company to take credit for a new idea, while critics contend that it is time-consuming and hampers innovation.

Rio Trade Informal; a high-risk trade that an investor or company makes in order to recover previous losses. An investor makes a Rio trade when he/she needs to recover losses in the shortest possible amount of time so he/she can avoid bankruptcy. The slang term comes from the image of a ruined investor buying a plane ticket to Rio de Janeiro to avoid creditors.

Riparian Rights The right to use running water as it comes on to one's property. Riparian rights include, for example, the right to fish and the right to use the water to power machinery on one's land. Riparian rights come with various duties and responsibilities, such as not to pollute water such that it would affect the rights of property owners downstream and not to prevent the free passage of fish. With certain, limited exceptions, riparian rights are non-transferable. The rights have their origins in English common law.

Rippage A slang term for a market rally. See also: Ramp.

Ripping Out Eyeballs In investment banking, the act or practice of working against a client's interest in order to advance the interest of the investment bank. For example, a bank may encourage a client to go long on a security when it believes the price will drop because doing so raises the price in the short term and enables the bank to profit from a short sale. In some circumstances, ripping out eyeballs may be illegal.

Ripple In technical analysis, an informal term for a security's performance over a certain period of time, usually a few hours to a few days. Analysts look for cyclical behavior in a security to account for a ripple; that is, if a long-term bull market is observed with a bad trading day in a certain week, an analyst might view the ripple as moderately bearish without detracting from the long-term bullish trend.

Ris 1. An ancient Hebrew unit of length approximately equivalent to 135 meters. **2.** A Talmudic unit of length approximately equivalent to 32 or 35 meters.

Rise To increase in price, especially for a security. If a stock's price is $10 per share at the start of the trading day and $15 at the end, the stock is said to have risen.

Rising Bottom In technical analysis, a situation in which the low price for a security increases each day over a number of days. This is usually seen as a bullish signal. They are also called ascending bottoms.

Rising Market An exchange or sector that is generally increasing in price. For example, if an index starts at 10,000 in January and ends at 13,000 in December, it may be said to be a rising market over the course of that year.

Risk The uncertainty associated with any investment. That is, risk is the possibility that the actual return on an investment will be different from its expected return. A vitally important concept in finance is the idea that an investment that carries a higher risk has the potential of a higher return. For example, a zero-risk investment, such as a U.S. Treasury security, has a low rate of return, while a stock in a start-up has the potential to make an investor very wealthy, but also the potential to lose one's entire investment. Certain types of risk are easier to quantify than others. To the extent that risk is quantifiable, it is generally calculated as the standard deviation on an investment's average return.

Risk Adjusted Return on Capital A measure of the profitability of an investment or business after accounting for its risk. This can help inform one's investment decisions. It is calculated as follows: RAROC = (revenue - expenses - expected loss + income from capital invested) / capital It should be noted that an investment's RAROC has become a less common measure than the risk adjusted return on risk adjusted capital (RARORAC).

Risk Arbitrage In hedge funds, an investment strategy related to mergers and acquisitions involving the purchase and/or shorting of an acquired company's stock. In a cash merger, the stock of the acquired company often trades below the offer price until the deal is completed. A hedge fund may buy at the lower price and wait for the deal to be completed, at which point it makes a profit. In a stock-for-stock merger, the acquiring company (with more valuable stock) offers to exchange the acquired company's stock for its own at a certain ratio. A hedge fund may then short sell the

acquiring company's stock while simultaneously buying stock in the acquired company. When the deal goes through, the acquired company's stock is converted and the new stock returned to the owner from which the hedge fund borrowed. In both these situations, the primary risk is the possibility that the deal may fail in the middle of the hedge fund's transactions. See also: Exchange ratio.

Risk Aversion The subjective tendency of investors to avoid unnecessary risk. It is subjective because different investors have different definitions of unnecessary. An investor seeking a large return is likely to see more risk as necessary, while one who only wants a small return would find such an investment strategy reckless. However, most rational economic actors are sufficiently risk averse such that, given two investments with the same return and different levels of risk, they would choose the less risky investment.

Risk Capital Extra money that one has in order to invest in high-risk investment vehicles. That is, it is money that one can afford to lose in case the investments turn sour. Most investment advisers recommend using only risk capital for highly speculative investments.

Risk Classes Securities that are divided into different groups, each with a different level of risk. That is, Treasury securities are in one risk class because they are risk-free while speculative stocks are in a different risk class because they are extraordinarily risky.

Risk Factor In arbitrage pricing theory, any risk, especially a macroeconomic situation, that may affect an asset or investment. Examples of risk factors include inflation and interest rates.

Risk Graph A chart describing the potential profit or loss of an option if it is exercised when the underlying asset is at different prices. A risk graph provides a quick reference as to whether an option is in-the-money or out-of-the money. It can be helpful in determining whether an option is worth buying, depending on how close it is to expiration and the expected movement of the underlying asset.

Risk Hedge The practice of taking opposite positions in two different but similar assets in order to profit from the price movements between them. See also: Hedge.

Risk Indexes Categories of risk used in risk analysis. Examples include financial risk, political risk, and credit risk.

Risk Lover An investor who is willing to take big risks to increase the potential return on investments. For example, a risk loverwould be more likely to invest in the IPO of a company with a new and exciting product about which little is known, than to invest in the secured bond issued by a company everyone knows and trusts. Critics maintain that risk lovers accept lower returns for their risk and, as such, are not investing efficiently. See also: Markowitz efficient portfolio.

Risk Management The process of identifying risks to an investment and, if possible, mitigating them. The first stage of risk management is determining the types and magnitudes of risk. For example, a risk manager might look at a bond and identify the possibility of default as a risk and evaluate the likelihood of that scenario. The second stage is taking steps to remedy risk, insofar as it is possible. In the above example, the risk manager might recommend buying other bonds to offset the risk of default on any single bond. Sometimes risk cannot be mitigated; in that case, risk managers evaluate how central the investment is to one's investment goals and risk tolerance. Generally speaking, investors seek the highest possible return at the lowest possible risk. Risk management helps them achieve this goal by showing how their investments may be affected and finding ways to alleviate the situation.

Risk Manager A professional who identifies risks to an investment and, if possible, attempts to mitigate them. The first stage of risk management is determining the types and magnitudes of risk. For example, a risk manager might look at a bond and identify the possibility of default as a risk and evaluate the likelihood of that scenario. The second stage is taking steps to remedy risk, insofar as it is possible. In the above example, the risk manager might recommend buying other bonds to offset the risk of default on any single bond. Sometimes risk cannot be mitigated; in that case, risk managers evaluate how central the investment is to one's investment goals and risk tolerance. In general, investors seek the highest possible return at the lowest possible risk. Risk managers help them achieve this goal by showing how their investments may be affected and finding ways to alleviate the situation.

Risk Neutral A situation in which an investor effectively ignores risk in making investment decisions. Given two investments with different levels of riskiness, a risk neutral investor considers only the expected return from each investment. As such, being risk neutral differs significantly from both risk aversion and risk seeking.

Risk Premium The return over and above the risk free rate of return that an investor expects in exchange for each additional unit of risk. According to Markowitz portfolio theory, rational investors only accept additional risk if they expect a greater return. One refers to this greater return as the risk premium. See also: Risk capital, Eat well, Sleep well.

Risk Premium Approach In active portfolio management, a way to classify different assets according to their risk. In a risk premium approach, one seeks to find investments with higher returns for higher risks. See also: Risk Premium.

Risk Profile 1. A measure of how risk averse an investor is. One may conduct a risk profile to determine what securities will likely fit an investor's investment goals. **2.** In options, a chart showing the profits and losses on a contract over time. It is created by plotting the value of the underlying asset on the x-axis and the risk on the y-axis. It is also called a payoff profile.

Risk Ratio An analysts' estimate of the likelihood that a security will increase or decrease in price by a certain amount. For example, if a security currently trades at

$50, but an analyst believes it could increase $30 but could also decrease $10, the security is said to have a risk ratio of 3:1.

Risk Reversal 1. The sale of a call and the purchase of a put with the exact same terms. One conducts a role reversal when the price for the underlying asset is falling and one wishes to hedge one's risk. A risk reversal reduces profit potential and eliminates it if the underlying asset rises back above the strike price. **2.** In currency options, the difference between the delta of a call and the delta of a put. Because delta is a measure of volatility, risk reversal helps one determine the potential return of investing in one as opposed to the other.

Risk Taker 1. See: Risk lover. **2.** See: Speculator.

Risk Tolerance The extent to wish an investor is willing to accept more risk in exchange for the possibility of a higher return. An investor with a high risk tolerance is likely to invest in securities, such as stocks in startup companies, and is willing to accept the possibility that the value of his/her portfolio will decline, at least in the short-term. An investor with a low risk tolerance, on the other hand, tends to invest predominantly in stable stocks and/or highly-graded bonds. One's risk tolerance is subjective and may vary according to age, needs, goals, and even personal dispositions. See also: Eat well, sleep well.

Risk Transfer The reduction of risk to a position by buying an insurance policy or taking an offsetting position. For example, a person may reduce the risk of loss due to medical expenses by buying health insurance. Likewise, a person may reduce the risk of loss to a long position by entering an equal but opposite short position. See also: Hedge.

Risk-Adjusted Discount Rate The discount rate calculated by adding a risk premium to the risk-free rate of return. This is used to calculate the rate of return on a risky investment.

Risk-Adjusted Performance The performance of a security or investment relative to its risk. One may calculate the risk-adjusted performance in a number of ways. One may consider the investment's volatility. Alternatively, one may compare its performance to the performance of the market as a whole or relative to securities or investments with similar levels of risk.

Risk-Adjusted Return The return on an asset or investment relative to the return on assets and investments with similar risk. The risk-adjusted return can help an investor determine whether he/she is extracting the highest possible return for the least possible risk. One way to calculate the risk-adjusted return is to take the Sharpe ratio.

Risk-Free Describing a transaction or investment in which the return is known with certainty. The certainty generally comes from a supreme amount of confidence in the issuer of the investment; for example, Treasury securities are considered risk-free investments because the United States government is considered the best possible issuer. Critics contend that there is no such thing as a risk-free investment because, in theory, even the US government could default. However, risk-free investments have such a low level of risk that it may be ignored. Risk-free investments usually have a low rate of return and, as a result, are exposed to inflation risk.

Risk-Free Asset An asset in which the return is known with certainty. The certainty generally comes from a supreme amount of confidence in the issuer of the asset; for example, Treasury securities are considered risk-free because the United States government is considered the best possible issuer. Critics contend that there is no such thing as a risk-free asset because, in theory, even the US government could default. However, risk-free assets have such a low level of risk that it may be ignored. Nonetheless, risk-free assets usually have a low rate of return, and, as a result, even these are exposed to inflation risk.

Risk-Free Return The return on any investment with such low risk that the risk is considered to not exist. A common example of a risk-free return is the return on a U.S. Treasury security. The risk-free return exists in order to compensate the investor for the temporary tying up of his/her capital, even though it is not put at risk. See also: Capital Allocation Line, riskless investment.

Riskless Arbitrage The act of buying an asset and immediately selling the same asset for a higher price. For example, one may execute two orders at once, one to buy a security at $10 and one to sell the same security at $12. The short time frame involved means that riskless arbitrage occurs without investment; there is no rate of return or anything like it because the asset is immediately sold. One simply makes a profit on the deal.

Riskless Investment An investment where the return is known with certainty. The certainty generally comes from a supreme amount of confidence in the issuer of the investment; for example, Treasury securities are considered riskless investments because the United States government is considered the best possible issuer. Critics contend that there is no such thing as a riskless investment because, in theory, even the US government could default. However, riskless investments have such a low level of risk that it may be ignored. Riskless investments usually have a low rate of return and, as a result, are exposed to inflation risk.

Riskless Transaction A transaction where a gain is guaranteed by the structure of the transaction. To give a very simple example, one may find a client who wishes to purchase a security at $10 per share when one knows that the current price is $9.50 per share. One then buys the security at the current price and instantly re-sells to the client for a 50 cent per share guaranteed profit. This is also called a simultaneous transaction. See also: Arbitrage, Risk-free return.

Risk-Loving Describing an investor who is willing to take big risks to increase the potential return on investments. For example, a risk loving investor would be more likely to invest in the IPO of a company with a new and exciting product about which

little is known, than to invest in a secured bond issued by a well known and widely trusted company. Critics maintain that risk loving investors accept lower returns for their risk and, as such, are not investing efficiently. See also: Markowitz efficient portfolio.

Risk-Return Trade-Off The concept that every rational investor, at a given level of risk, will accept only the largest expected return. That is, given two investments at the exact same level of risk, all other things being equal, every rational investor will invest in the one that offers the higher return. The risk-return tradeoff is pervasive throughout economics and finance. It is the reason that riskier bonds pay higher coupons than other bonds. It is also the reason that bonds pay lower returns than most stocks because they are a less risky investment. The Markowitz Portfolio Theory attempts to mathematically identify the portfolio with the highest return at each level of risk. See also: Markowitz Efficient Portfolio.

Risk-Reward Ratio The ratio of the standard deviation of an investment to its expected return. The higher the ratio is, the lower the return for the amount of risk one is taking. This can inform one's investment decisions. See also: Risk adjusted return on capital.

Risks and Opportunities An identification of what could go wrong and what might go right with a company or organization. For example, a company may determine that it carries the risk that its primary product may become obsolete, but also determines that it has the opportunity to spread the product into a new market. Companies use these identifications to minimize their risks and to maximize long-term profitability.

Risk-Weighted Assets The reserve requirements for a bank, weighted according to risk. Risk-weighted assets are the capital a bank must keep to cover its liabilities. They are calculated as follows: Government bonds have a risk weight of 0% while all other assets have a risk weight of 100%. One calculates the units of each type of asset a bank carries to find how risky its assets are.

Risky Asset An investment with a return that is not guaranteed. Assets carry varying levels of risk. For example, holding a corporate bond is generally less risky than holding a stock. Government bonds are generally not considered risky assets. A risky asset should not be confused with a risk asset.

Risky Operation A business venture with a return that is not guaranteed. Ventures carry varying levels of risk. For example, founding a company in a new industry that is not yet established is generally riskier than starting a dental office in a town that has no dentist.

River Measure An ancient Egyptian unit of length approximately equivalent to 10.5 kilometers.

Riyal 1. The currency of Qatar. Since 1980, the riyal has been pegged to the U.S. dollar at a rate of 1 USD to 3.64 QAR. This exchange rate is important especially to energy deals as Qatar is rich in natural gas and, to a slightly lesser extent, oil. **2.** The currency of Saudi Arabia. It became the official currency of the Kingdom at its establishment in 1932; it is the successor currency of the Hejaz riyal. Between 1986 and 2003, the riyal was pegged to Special Drawing Rights, but, in practice, this was effectively a peg to the U.S. dollar. The peg was officially changed to the dollar in 2003 and has been in effect since (with the exception of a brief period in 2007). It is issued by the Saudi Arabian Monetary Agency.

Ro 1. ISO 3166-1 alpha-2 code for Romania. This is the code used in international transactions to and from Romanian bank accounts. **2.** ISO 3166-2 geocode for Romania. This is used as an international standard for shipping to Romania. Each Romanian county has its own code with the prefix "RO." For example, the code for Alba is ISO 3166-2:RO-AB.

ROA 1. Right of accumulation. In loaded mutual funds, the right of a shareholder to pay a reduced load (or sales fee) when he/she purchases more than a certain a dollar amount of the mutual fund. The dollar amount is known as the breakpoint. For example, if the breakpoint for a certain mutual fund is $50,000; an investor has the right to reduce the load by, say, half when he/she invests more than $50,000 in the fund. It thus becomes advantageous for the investor to invest $50,000 instead of, say, $45,000, because this will entitle him/her to half the load for the entire investment, and not just for the amount invested past $50,000. Mutual funds that allow investors to buy at just below the breakpoint may run afoul of Financial Industry Regulatory Authority regulations. The right of accumulation is not limited to a single investment; an investor putting two tranches of $25,000 into the above mutual fund will usually find his excess load refunded. **2.** Return on assets. A measure of how efficiently a company is using its assets in order to produce a profit. It is calculated by taking the aftertax profit over a given period of time and dividing by the value of the net assets. A higher return on assets is seen as a sign of stronger financial health. See also: Earning power.

Road Show A presentation that an underwriter and/or issuer makes to potential investors. The term has a connotation of travel; that is, the issuer may go to the potential investors' offices (which may or may not be in the same country) in order to make the presentation. The road show consists of information on a new issue or IPO, set up in a way to make investors want to buy it. The road show has an important, often instrumental role to play in the successful placing of a new issue.

Robber Barons A pejorative term for wealthy industrialists in the late 19th century United States. Robber barons are credited with leading American industrialization and creating a great deal of wealth; however, they often did so through unethical means, many of which later became illegal. Price manipulation, union busting, and anti-competitive practices were common among robber barons. Well known robber barons include Andrew Carnegie, John W. Rockefeller and Cornelius Vanderbilt.

Robbery A crime in which one takes the property of another by force or threat of force. Robbery generally requires the victim to be put in a state of fear when the crime occurs. The element of force distinguishes robbery from theft. Robbery is considered a serious crime; under Islamic law, for example, highway robbery historically has been punishable by death or amputation of limbs.

Robert Ng An investor who in the 1980s was responsible for the crash of the Hong Kong Futures Exchange due to a number of trades in which he was accused of illegally avoiding margin calls. These trades resulted in the collapse of the exchange, though Ng avoided criminal charges because it was thought that prosecution would further disrupt the market. He later became chairman of the Sino Group, a property development company, and one of the wealthiest people in the world.

Robert Rhea An investor who was a major proponent of Dow theory, which states that when the Dow Jones Industrial Average and the Dow Jones Transportation Average both hit a new high or a new low for a period of time, it can confirm a previous, bullish or bearish signal. Rhea was a student of William Peter Hamilton. He died in 1939.

Robert Rubin An American businessman who served as Secretary of the Treasury from 1995 to 1999. He assisted President Bill Clinton in setting up the Exchange Stabilization Fund, which helped Mexico through its financial crisis of the early 1990s. His lobbying contributed to the Gramm-Leach-Bliley Act, which is thought to have contributed to the late 2000s recession.

Robert Zoellick An American lawyer who spent most of his career in government service. He served in the U.S. Department of State and later was the U.S. Trade Representative. In 2007, he became president of the World Bank.

Rock the Boat Informal; to change the way things are done, especially in a sudden or abrupt way. For example, a new manager may rock the boat by dramatically changing a company's production process. Rocking the boat is sometimes successful, though it is often difficult.

Rod A rarely used unit of length in the U.S. system equal to five and a half feet.

Roede An obsolete Dutch unit of length roughly equivalent to five meters, with slight regional variations.

Rogue Trader A trader who makes frequent, large, and usually reckless investments without regard for his/her client or institution. The rogue trader does not work in concert or consultation with anyone else, but typically handles other people's money. Obviously, the investments the rogue trader makes are very high risk, and he/she usually ultimately fails. See also: Nick Leason, John Rusnack, Chen Jiulin.

Rogue Trading The practice of trading securities using another person or institution's money without input or oversight from others. For example, an employee of an investment bank may trade with the bank's money without receiving authorization from or reporting it to his supervisor. Rogue trading generally is risky and usually is discovered when it leads to a large loss.

ROL ISO 4217 code for the third Romanian leu. It began circulating in 1952 when Romania was under Communist rule. It began suffering from high inflation after the fall of communism in the 1990s and was replaced by the new leu (RON) in 2005.

Roll 1. To buy or sell an option and then later buy or sell the same option with a different strike price because one believes the price trend will continue. For example, suppose one buys a call option giving one the right but not the obligation to buy a stock at $10. One does this if one believes the underlying price will be above $10 when the option expires. However, if it appears near expiration that the option is well above $10 and likely will continue to, say, $20, one may buy another call option with a longer expiration and a strike price of $14 in order to capture higher gains. Rolling options may provide an investor with time to take full advantage of a prolonged price trend. It may be done with both call options and put options. **2.** See: Roll over.

Roll Back To sell an option position and buy another with the same underlying asset and strike price, but with an earlier expiration date. One may also call this rolling backward.

Roll Down To liquidate one option in order to buy a similar one with a better strike price. Most often, rolling down refers to an investor who wishes to maintain a position when he/she is bearish on the price of the underlying. See also: Roll Up.

Roll Order 1. See: Dividend Trade Roll/Play. **2.** The replacement of one investment that is maturing with an identical investment with a longer maturity. For example, one may take the proceeds of a bond as it matures and buy an identical bond that does not mature for another 10 years. **3.** An order to buy or sell a security such that it realizes a gain or loss.

Roll Over 1. The act or practice of taking profits or other proceeds from investments and making other investments with them. It nearly always means that one is investing in more of the same security. For example, one may take dividends from a stock and buy more shares with it or may take coupon payments to buy more of the same bond issue. It is also called reinvesting. Colloquially, rolling over refers to reinvesting proceeds from one retirement account in another retirement account without causing a taxable event. **2.** A loan that a borrower may renew upon maturity. This may happen when the borrower has only been making interest payments over the life of the loan. See also: Refinancing.

Roll Up 1. In venture capital and hedge funds, the purchase and merging of two or (often) more small firms in the same sector. This is done to hedge risk; given the choice between two firms in which to invest, one more risky than the other, a fund or venture capital firm may simply buy out both of them and force a merger, hoping to split the difference in risk and return. Roll ups become more common in times of economic downturn as part of a market consolidation process. **2.** To liquidate one

option in order to buy similar one with a better strike price. Most often, an investor does this in order to maintain a position when he/she is bullish on the price of the underlying.

Roller Stripping A situation in which an ink roller begins to repel ink. This causes problems in printing.

Rollercoaster Swap Any swap in which payments to the counterparties vary at different times. Rollercoaster swaps are most common among companies with highly seasonal sales. Receiving higher payments and giving higher payments at different times helps the counterparties meet their financing needs on a year-round basis, when they likely could not do so on sales alone. For example, an ice cream company and a winter coat company may enter a rollercoaster swap in which the ice cream company pays more to the winter coat company in the summer and the opposite occurs in the winter.

Rolling a Stop Down To reduce a stop price to keep profiting from a short position. For example, suppose one sells short a stock at $20 with a stop price of $18 (meaning the stock will be sold automatically if the price hits $18 in order to lock in profit). If the price appears to be trending downward, the holder may roll the stop down to $16 to try for higher gains.

Rolling a Stop Up To increase a stop price to keep profiting from a long position. For example, suppose one buys a stock at $20 with a stop price of $22 (meaning the stock will be sold automatically if the price hits $22 in order to lock in profit). If the price appears to be trending upward, the holder may roll the stop up to $24 to try for higher gains.

Rolling Billboard A billboard on which the advertisement changes every few seconds. A rolling billboard attracts attention to multiple advertisements at roughly the same time, which enables the company owning the billboard to derive more revenue.

Rolling Earnings per Share A publicly-traded company's profit over the previous two quarters added to its projected profit for the next two quarters, with the quantity divided by the number of shares outstanding. This is considered an important aspect in determining a share's price and value, because it takes into account both historical and expected factors. In general, the rolling EPS (like earnings per share more broadly) applies only to common shares. It is calculated thusly: Rolling earnings per share = ((Net income from previous two quarters - Preferred dividends) + (Projected net income from two forthcoming quarters - projected preferred dividends) / Average shares outstanding.

Rolling Forward The act or practice of selling an option and buying another of the same type and with the same terms, but with a longer period until the expiration date. For example, one may sell a call with a strike price of $25 expiring in June and buy another call with a strike price of $25 that expires in September.

Rolling of Futures The sale of one futures position before its maturity and the purchase of another with identical terms but a longer maturity. Rolling of futures may occur if one does not wish to accept delivery of the underlying asset and/or if maintaining the futures position remains important to one's investment strategy.

Rolling Position A constant position in which the underlying securities or assets change over time. For example, one has a rolling position if one always has a call and a put on crude oil, even if the specific calls and puts maintaining that position are bought and sold (or expire).

Rolling Returns Annualized returns for a given number of years. For example, if one holds a stock for 15 years, one refers to its returns in annualized terms as rolling returns.

Rolling Settlement Settlement of multiple transactions in successive days. For example, if an investor sells a stock, buys another stock, and sells a bond such that all transactions settle on Wednesday, Thursday and Friday, the investor is said to have a rolling settlement.

Rolling Stock Automobiles, railroad cars, trucks, and similar assets. Rolling stock is used as collateral on some loans because it is easy for the lender to take possession of them in the event of default.

Rolling the Tortoise In business, the practice of giving a slow-moving project more resources than it actually needs in order to increase momentum. For example, if a project has two people working on it and could use two more, the supervisor may roll the tortoise by adding five more.

Rollover IRA An IRA to which one has transferred funds from an employer-sponsored qualified retirement account. This usually occurs when an account holder takes a new job or otherwise wishes to take advantage of the tax benefits an IRA offers over, say, a 401(k). Most IRA programs only allow one rollover per year; with a Roth IRA, there is an income limit beyond which a rollover is not allowed. An IRA rollover may be accomplished through a direct transfer or by check; however, a check transfer brings a 20% withholding charge, so account holders are advised to make direct transfers. It is less commonly called a conduit IRA.

Rollover Mortgage A mortgage that automatically refinances at a new interest rate every few years. The new interest rate causes payments to go either up or down. This entails risk for both the borrower and the lender as neither can predict future directions of interest rates. A rollover mortgages behaves much like an adjustable-rate mortgage (ARM). The primary difference is that a rollover mortgage requires a new loan, while an ARM simply changes the rate.

Roll's Critique A theory stating it is impossible to create a fully diversified portfolio and, therefore, the capital asset pricing model (of which a diversified portfolio is an important part) cannot be completely accurate. According to Roll's critique, a diversified portfolio would include all assets in the world. Thus, the CAPM uses a large index, such as the S&P 500 or the Wilshire 5000, as a proxy for the fully diversified portfolio.

ROM GOST 7.67 Latin three-letter geocode for Romania. The code is used for transactions to and from Romanian bank accounts and for international shipping to Romania. As with all GOST 7.67 codes, it is used primarily in Cyrillic alphabets.

Romanian Leu The currency of Romania. It was issued in 1867 and was pegged to silver and gold until 1878, when the peg shifted exclusively to gold. The peg was dropped in 1914. Revaluations occurred twice during the Communist era in Romania to enhance collectivist goals. In 2005, a third revaluation occurred following a period of high inflation.

Rome Convention An agreement harmonizing at least some of the contract law among members of what became the European Union. Under the Rome Convention, parties to a contract generally may choose which EU member's law shall govern the contract. The Convention was established in 1980.

RON ISO 4217 code for the new Romanian leu. It began circulating in 2005 following a period of high inflation. It was issued at a ratio of 1 new leu to 10,000 old lei.

Rood A unit of area equivalent to one-quarter of one acre.

Roosevelt Dime A coin minted by the United States starting in 1946. It is worth 1/10 of one dollar. It features a portrait of Franklin D. Roosevelt on the obverse.

Rotating Shift A work schedule that changes on a regular, predictable basis. For example, an employee may work the day shift for three weeks followed by the evening shift for three weeks, and so on.

Rotation of Directors A requirement in a company's bylaws or articles of incorporation stating that one third of the members of the board of directors shall resign at each annual general meeting. However, they may be re-elected. Rotation of directors allows a company to bring in new leadership as needed while still keeping institutional memory in the form of the other two thirds of directors. Most British companies have rotation of directors. See also: Staggered terms.

Roth 401(k) A 401(k) in which a contributor makes post-tax contributions in exchange for tax-free withdrawals after retirement. Instituted in 2006, this investment vehicle involves a worker placing a portion of his/her post-tax income into a 401(k) account and allowing it to be invested. When the investor begins withdrawals, all contributions and income resulting from its investment are free from taxation. Withdrawals prior to the age of 59.5 are subject to excise taxes, but the investor must begin disbursements before the age of 70.5, unless he/she is still employed with the company offering the 401(k). Most employees are allowed to place up to $16,500 (as of 2009) into a 401(k), and some employers have matching contributions. As with traditional 401(k)s, a Roth 401(k) is an employee benefit, and a worker must have a sponsoring employer to take advantage of one. However, a self-employed person may also set up a 401(k) for himself/herself.

Roth IRA An investment retirement account in which a worker makes non-tax deductible contributions up to a certain limit throughout his/her working life. Unlike traditional IRAs, withdrawals are tax-free but contributions are not deductible. The limit to annual contributions varies by year according to inflation ($5,000 in 2008 and 2009). Roth IRAs are allowed to invest in securities and, in practice, normally own common stock and certificates of deposit. See also: 401(k).

Roth IRA Conversion The rollover of assets from a SIMPLE plan, traditional IRA, or other retirement savings plan into a Roth IRA. A Roth IRA receives post-tax contributions and gives out tax-free distributions. This is a different structure from most retirement plans; because they are taxed differently, a Roth IRA conversion may be taxable.

Rough Cut In film, a stage in the production process in which a movie or television show is nearly complete but requires further editing.

Round Lot 1. 100 shares of a stock or other security. **2.** $1,000 or $5,000 in bonds. Most trading takes place in multiples of round lots.

Round Trip In futures and equities, to take a position and then later to close it. For example, an investor who buys a futures contract and then sells it and an investor who short sells a contract and then covers it are both round tripping. The practice is also called a round turn.

Round Trip Transaction Costs All commissions and other expenses related to trading a security. When an investor buys or sells a security, he/she must usually pay a fee to his/her investment adviser, who may or may not also be the broker, who is also entitled to a fee. Research and other indirect costs informing investment decisions are not usually considered transaction costs unless they directly relate to or result from a specific transaction. The investor accounts for these expenses when calculating whether an investment made a profit or loss. See also: All in Cost.

Round-Trip Trading The act or practice of two or more companies trading assets or securities back and forth at approximately the same price. For example, Company A may sell securities to Company B and agree to buy them back at the same price at a later time. Round-trip trading creates the impression of a high trading volume, suggesting interest in assets or securities that may not actually be there. It also increases a firm's earnings and expenses without increasing or decreasing its net income. It is a form of market manipulation. See also: Churning.

Route Type The classification of an area in which the U.S. Postal Service must deliver mail. Examples of route types include rural routes and city delivery.

Royal Australian Mint A mint in Australia. It mints coins for Australia and several other nations in the South Pacific. It was opened in 1965 and is located in Canberra.

Royal Bank of Scotland A major retail bank in the United Kingdom. Established in 1727, it gradually expanded its operations throughout the rest of the British Isles. It is one of three banks permitted to issue banknotes in Scotland. It was the world's first bank to offer customers an overdraft facility, which it has done since the year after it opened.

Royal Canadian Mint An organization in Canada that issues legal tender coins for general use. It was established in 1908 and is owned by the government of Canada as a Crown corporation. It is located in Ottawa, Ontario.

Royal Canadian Mounted Police The national police force of Canada. It is responsible for enforcing federal laws, including but not limited to laws against counterfeiting, organized crime and drug trafficking. It also enforces provincial and territorial laws everywhere except Ontario and Quebec, and to a lesser extent in Newfoundland & Labrador. It was formed in 1920.

Royal Cubit An ancient Egyptian unit of length approximately equivalent to 52.5 centimeters.

Royal Dutch Mint An organization in the Netherlands that issues legal tender coins for general use. It was established in 1567 and is owned by the government of the Netherlands. It is located in Utrecht.

Royal Mint A body that issues coins (but not notes) for the United Kingdom. It also mints the coins for more than 100 countries. It traces its origins to 886 and is based in Wales.

Royalty A fee that one receives in exchange for allowing another party to use and profit from one's property. For example, a publisher who prints and sells a book must compensate the author for use of his/her intellectual property. Usually a royalty is a percentage of the revenue or profit that the other party (in this example, the publisher) makes.

Royalty Income Trust A unit investment trust in which the trustee buys the rights to income from a natural resource, such as oil or real estate, and distributes the profit to beneficiaries. A company, such as an oil company, may sell the right to income from an oil well to a royalty income trust because it usually pays more than other ways of raising capital. Likewise, an investor may be interested in buying into such a trust because yields are often higher than stocks or bonds. For example, an oil company may sell oil wells to a royalty income trust instead of issuing stock or a bond in order to raise capital to increase its capacity for pumping oil out of the ground.

Royalty Trust A corporate structure for companies involved in oil, gas, mining, or similar industries. In a royalty trust, profits are not subject to corporate taxation, provided that at least 90% are distributed as dividends to shareholders. Royalty trusts prevent double taxation of dividends. Royalty trusts are generally publicly traded and their shares behave just like ordinary stocks. They exist in both Canada and the United States. T. Boone Pickens created the first royalty trust in 1979.

RPIX A measure of inflation. It measures price changes to what the average family buys, but excludes changes to the interest paid on mortgages. The RPIX was the primary gauge of inflation in the United Kingdom between 1992 and 2003.

Rrethe In Albania, a political subdivision approximately equivalent to a county.

RSD ISO 4217 code for the Serbian dinar. It was introduced in 2003 when Yugoslavia formally separated into Serbia and Montenegro. It replaced the Yugoslav dinar at par. Montenegro had already abandoned the Yugoslav dinar in 2000.

Rt On a ticker or in a newspaper listing of stocks, a symbol indicating a transaction involving a right rather than a specific security. See also: Warrant.

RTS An electronic stock market in Russia. It was established in 1995 and was modeled on NASDAQ. Its securities experienced an extraordinary amount of growth in the early 2000s. See also: RTS Index.

RTS Index An index tracking stocks that trade on the RTS, an electronic stock market in Russia. It was established in 1995 and is calculated in real time.

RU 1. ISO 3166-1 alpha-2 code for the Russian Federation. This is the code used in international transactions to and from Russian bank accounts. **2.** ISO 3166-2 geocode for Russia. This is used as an international standard for shipping to Russia. Many Russian federal subjects have their own codes with the prefix "RU." For example, the code for the City of Moscow is ISO 3166-2:RU:MOW.

RUB ISO 4217 code for the Russian ruble. It was issued in 1998, replacing the Soviet ruble (which was also called the Russian ruble after the fall of the Soviet Union). Despite the issue of a new currency, it lost 70% of its value against the U.S. dollar in six weeks as a result of the Russian financial crisis. It is a floating currency.

Rubber Band Effect A situation in which a security or market drops precipitously and rises just as much just as fast. On a graph, the rubber band effect looks like a capital "V" because of the price declines and increases. The rubber band effect usually occurs due to the execution of limit orders by computer programs.

Rubber Cheque A predominately British term for an NSF check.

Rubber Stamp Informal; a term for a person or institution that theoretically could take an action independently but in practice follows the advice or counsel of another party. For example, shareholders may ratify the decision of the board of directors with little scrutiny. In this case, the shareholders act as a rubber stamp to the board.

Rube Goldberg A slang term for an unnecessarily complicated solution to a problem, or a problem with a solution that is itself problematic. The term refers to a

20th-century American cartoonist who drew large machines performing simple actions for which a machine is not necessary.

Rubu A Turkish measure of length approximately equivalent to 8.5 centimeters. It became obsolete when Turkey made the metric system mandatory in 1933. An equivalent term is urup.

Rug Ranking A situation in which the career of an administrative assistant is inexorably connected to the career of the person he/she works for. That is, the assistant receives higher salaries when his/her boss is promoted, moves to a different company when the boss moves, and so forth. Rug ranking displays loyalty and trust between the boss and the administrative assistant.

Rule 104 On the New York Stock Exchange, a rule requiring designated market makers to trade on their own accounts to help ensure a fair and orderly market. The rule also outlines other rights and responsibilities for designated market makers; for example, they must help the NYSE remain sufficiently liquid to provide for fair quotes. Previously, Rule 104 mandated that designated market makers (then known as specialists) not trade on their own accounts, but this was amended in 2008 as part of a wider streamlining of NYSE rules.

Rule 105 On the New York Stock Exchange, a rule allowing specialists to enter positions on options contracts to hedge their positions on equity.

Rule 105b-1 A plan in which an investor holding a long position on a security sets forth conditions under which the security will be sold automatically. The selling plan is particularly important if the investor has inside information because Rule 105b-1 of the SEC permits what would otherwise be insider trading as long as the process is set in motion automatically with a selling plan. This construction is controversial, with critics maintaining that selling plans are open to manipulation that allows what amounts to insider trading by stealth.

Rule 10a-1 An SEC rule that formerly prohibited a short sale except on a plus tick or a zero plus tick. That is, Rule 10a-1 disallowed short sales at a price below the price at which the security traded most recently. This rule was intended to prevent short sellers from artificially deflating a security's price so that it harmed other investors. It was also called the uptick rule. It was replaced by Regulation SHO in 2007. Some have argued for its reintroduction.

Rule 10b-10 An SEC rule requiring broker-dealers to disclose certain information to clients before or at the completion of a transaction. Information includes the date and time of the transaction, whether the broker-dealer is acting as an agent for any other party, especially the other party to the transaction, and any information particular to the security being traded. The rule is not considered exhaustive and the broker-dealer is also required to disclose any potential fraud to the client, even though that is not specifically included.

Rule 10b-13 An SEC rule prohibiting a company that has made a tender offer or an exchange offer for another company's stock or bonds from acquiring the stock or bonds by any other means until the offer expires. This rule exists to help ensure fair play in the market.

Rule 10b-16 An SEC rule requiring brokerages to reveal to clients the terms and conditions under which margin accounts are set up before the customer may open a margin account. The rule also requires that the client receive quarterly updates on the status of his/her margin account.

Rule 10b-2 A rule of the SEC prohibiting the placement of a new issue in any way except as indicated in the new issue's filing statement.

Rule 10b-4 An SEC rule prohibiting the short sale of securities, the sale of borrowed securities, to an investor making a tender offer. A tender offer is usually made at a premium to the market price of the security; the sale of borrowed securities for such an offer creates the possibility of unsustainable price fluctuations.

Rule 10b5-1 An SEC rule that allows an employee of a publicly-traded company to create a plan of when and how to sell shares in that company. The employee writes and files this plan while he/she has no nonpublic knowledge about the company. Following this plan and selling shares according to it allows the employee to sell shares without fear of being accused of insider trading, regardless of what nonpublic knowledge he/she may later come to possess.

Rule 10b-6 An SEC rule forbidding broker-dealers, insurers, and underwriters (except those involved in the syndicate placing an issue) from buying shares in a new issue before it is offered to the general public.

Rule 10b-7 An SEC rule that limits the use of pre-syndicate bids. A pre-syndicate bid is an order by a managing underwriter to buy or sell a security immediately before a secondary offering of the same security in order to stabilize the price of the security. Theoretically, this will make the secondary offering easier to place with investors. However, the rule only allows this under certain circumstances.

Rule 13e An SEC rule governing "going private" or situations in which publicly-traded companies buy enough of their own stock to become its own majority shareholder. Among other things, Rule 13e requires the company going private to disclose all relevant information on the transaction to the SEC.

Rule 144 An SEC rule that allows the executive of a publicly-traded company who owns restricted stock to sell some shares without registering them with the SEC. An executive may do this once every six months if he/she has held the shares for at least two years.

Rule 144A An administrative rule under the SEC allowing, under certain circumstances, for qualified institutional investors to trade certain securities with other institutional investors without registering the trade with the SEC. The rule requires that the private placement be for investment purposes and not for resale to the general public. These securities are traded on the NASDAQ Portal Market; only NASDAQ members who are qualified institutional investors have access to it. Some firms may trade under Rule 144A as a prelude to an IPO.

Rule 145 An SEC rule allowing the sale of certain securities without first registering the securities with the SEC. Specifically, stocks an investor has acquired as the result of a merger, acquisition, or reclassification do not need to be registered prior to sale. Rule 145 allows investors more flexibility following the uncertainty of, say, a merger.

Rule 14a An SEC rule governing the distribution of proxy materials to shareholders. Among other provisions, the rule requires companies to state clearly (and in bold face) the issues on which shareholders shall be voting in the general meeting.

Rule 14-d An SEC rule restricting tender offers and regulating how disclosures of tender offers are made. This is an important rule in risk arbitrage.

Rule 14e-3b A rule requiring a party making a tender offer for a company to file a statement with the SEC if the terms of the offer change before it is completed. It also requires the party to file the results of the tender offer.

Rule 156 An SEC rule prohibiting investment companies from giving investors or potential investors false or misleading information in their literature. For example, Rule 156 prohibits a mutual fund from making false statements in any of its prospectuses.

Rule 15c2-1 An SEC rule that governs how broker-dealers must treat securities they hold in safekeeping. For example, the rule forbids them from using securities from one customer's account for another customer.

Rule 15c3-1 An SEC rule setting capital requirements for brokers and dealers. Under Rule 15c3-1, a broker or dealer must have sufficient liquidity in order to cover the most pressing obligations. This is defined as having a certain amount of liquidity as a percentage of the broker/dealer's total obligations. If the percentage falls below a certain point, the broker or dealer may not be allowed to take on new clients and may have restrictions placed on dealings with current clients.

Rule 15c3-2 An SEC rule that requires broker-dealers to inform a client if the client's free credit balance is about to be withdrawn.

Rule 15c3-3 An SEC rule requiring broker-dealers to keep securities for which a client has paid in full separate from securities the client has purchased on margin as well as from securities used as collateral on a margin account.

Rule 17f-1 A rule of the SEC requiring brokerages and other financial institutions to inform the authorities immediately if securities under its charge are lost or stolen. See also: Safekeeping.

Rule 19b-3 An SEC rule that requires commissions for brokers to compete with each other. That is, under Rule 19b-3, brokerages are not allowed to collude to fix commissions. This rule is intended to protect the clients of brokers from anti-competitive practices.

Rule 19c-3 An SEC rule stating that stock listed on a given exchange after April 26, 1979 may be traded off the physical confines of the exchange. These stocks are eligible for over-the-counter trading. The rule was adopted as part of a move toward an experimental National Market System. See also: 19c-3 stock.

Rule 209 A rule on the New York Stock Exchange requiring signatures on a registration statement to be guaranteed by a bank, trust company, or member of the Exchange.

Rule 2310 A FINRA rule stating that a broker or investment adviser must reasonably believe that a certain investment decision will benefit a client before making a recommendation to him/her. That is, the broker or investment adviser must act in good faith, and must not knowingly recommend bad investments. Rule 2310 requires investment advisers to know their clients' needs. See also: Due diligence, Prudent-person rule, Twisting.

Rule 254 A section of the Securities Act of 1933 governing solicitations of interest in a new issue. Among other provisions, the rule allows companies to advertise a potential new issue via written communications or over radio or television, provided it is made clear that the advertisement is only a solicitation of interest and not an offering. As such, the company is not allowed to ask for or accept money when it is in this stage of a new issue.

Rule 27-11 A FINRA rule requiring analysts to state whether they or their family members own a security that they discuss. It also requires recommendations to be divided into three categories: buy, neutral and sell. Rule 27-11 is intended to make recommendations as clear as possible while reducing potential conflicts of interest.

Rule 390 A rule on the New York Stock Exchange stating that members must receive permission from the exchange's management before conducting trades on listed securities anywhere other than the trading floor. Rule 390 was rescinded in 2000.

Rule 3b-3 An SEC rule defining a short sale. It is no longer in effect.

Rule 405 A New York Stock Exchange rule requiring investment advisers to only make or recommend investments for their clients' accounts that a "prudent person" would make. This means that investment advisers are not allowed to make investments they believe will lose money for the client. It does not require that the investment adviser always make correct decisions; it merely requires him/her to make decisions that will be generally accepted as sound for someone of average intelligence who seeks to do what is in the client's best interests as the client defines them. It is an example of a suitability rule. See also: Prudent-Person Rule.

Rule 415 An SEC regulation allowing a publicly-traded company to register a new issue of stock and actually offer it at any time over a two-year period, subject to compliance with other appropriate regulations. This offering is covered by a single prospectus but may be offered to the public in different tranches. This practice is called shelf registration.

Rule 419 An SEC rule stating that funds received from a penny stock offering by a blank check company must be placed in an escrow account until certain conditions have been met. A blank check company issues penny stock for business operations that have not yet begun; it effectively asks investors to trust it. Rule 419 exists in order to protect these investors from the possibility that the company is a fraud.

Rule 434 A former SEC rule allowing a prospectus on some new issues to be delivered incrementally, that is, in several documents given out over a period of time. The rule was rescinded in December 2005.

Rule 500 On the New York Stock Exchange, a rule regarding the voluntary delisting of a publicly-traded company. If the management of a company wishes to delist from the NYSE, it must have the consent of at least two thirds of shareholders, with no more than 10% of shareholders opposing.

Rule 72(t) An IRS rule allowing IRA account holders to make withdrawals before the age of 59.5 without any penalty, provided they make at least five substantially equal periodic payments. This exempts the account holder from the 10% penalty that would otherwise be assessed. On the other hand, it reduces the amount of principal in the IRA, which may result in an account that is unable to cover the entirety of one's retirement.

Rule 80A On the New York Stock Exchange, a rule restricting the trade of S&P 500 Index stocks when the Dow Jones Industrial Average index has gained or lost more than 2% from the previous trading day. This is done to prevent wild swings in index prices that might result from speculative investing. Rule 80A exists to attempt to maintain stability in share prices. It is also informally called the Uptick/Downtick Rule and the Collar Rule.

Rule 80B A rule on the New York Stock Exchange mandating that trades stop for a certain amount of time if the Dow Jones Industrial Average falls 10%, 20%, or 30% in a single trading day. This measure is designed to prevent panic selling by stopping trading after a security or an index has fallen by a certain amount. For example, if the Dow Jones Industrial Average falls 10% in a trading day, the New York Stock Exchange suspends trade for at least one hour. Rule 80B is intended to allow investors to determine whether a situation is really as bad as it looks. See also: Suspended trading, collar.

Rule Against Accumulations In trusts, the legal concept forbidding interest or coupons from being added back into a trust's principal after a given number of years. The rule effectively sets a limit on the number of years a trust can exist, or at least prevents trusts from accumulating income and not distributing it. See also: Rule against perpetuities.

Rule Against Perpetuities The legal concept forbidding a testator from leaving portions of his/her estate unvested in a beneficiary after a certain number of years. The rule against perpetuities disallows an estate from holding back certain assets for descendents who will not be born for several generations. While it is part of the common law, not all jurisdictions have a rule against perpetuities. Among those that do have it, the rule begins to apply between 20 and 90 years after a person's death. See also: Rule against accumulations.

Rule G-32 A rule of the Municipal Securities Rulemaking Board requiring brokers and dealers to provide buyers of a new issue of a municipal bond with information regarding that bond. Delivery of the information must be made prior to delivery of the bond. The rule also provides for an Internet-based portal on which buyers can look up the information themselves.

Rule Line A line that surrounds a print advertisement in a periodical. The rule line emphasizes the advertisement and visually separates it from the rest of the page.

Rule NMS An SEC rule that requires exchanges to adopt policies to prevent trading through, which is the practice of trading a security on a given exchange when a better price is available on a different exchange. It mandates most electronic orders to buy or sell a security to be sent to the exchange with the best price for that security. It became effective in 2004.

Rule of 18 A general investing rule stating that the sum of the inflation rate and the price-earnings ratio of the Dow Jones Industrial Average determines the general trend of stock prices. If the sum is below 18, stocks are supposed to increase, while if it is above 18, they are thought to be ready to decrease. For example, if the inflation rate is 5% and the DJIA's price-earnings ratio is 19, the sum is 24, and, according to the Rule of 18, stocks will soon decrease.

Rule of 300 In marketing, a general rule stating that one should send out enough direct mail to receive at least 300 responses. The rule of 300 involves establishing an expected response rate. For example, if the expected response rate is 10%, the marketer should send 3,000 pieces of mail. The rule of 300 ensures a fairly representative response. In this sense, the rule of 300 is rather like polling.

Rule of 69 A general rule estimating how long it will take for an investment to double, assuming continuously compounding interest. One calculates this by dividing 69 by the rate of return. The rule of 69 is not exact, but it provides a quick look at the effects of compounding on an investment. It is similar to the rule of 72, which is more useful for non-continuously compounding interest.

Rule of 72 A rule of thumb estimating how long it will take for an investment to double. One calculates this by dividing 72 by the rate of return. The rule of 72 is not exact, but it provides a quick look at the effects of compounding on an investment.

Rule of 78 A practice in which lenders amortize repayment of short-term loans in a way that the borrower pays most of the interest earlier. For example, in a 12-month loan, the borrower will pay nearly all of the interest over the first, say, six or seven months before his/her payments cover any principal at all. The Rule of 78 guarantees that the lender will still make a profit if the borrower repays the loan early. However, it does not do anything to protect the borrower and is illegal to use for loans with a term longer than 61 months.

Rule Off In bookkeeping, to underline a total figure or other amount derived from adding or subtracting other numbers. Ruling off indicates that this number should not be changed.

Rule-Based Monetary Policy A monetary policy in which a jurisdiction rarely or never deviates from established norms. A rule-based monetary policy does not make exceptions based upon extenuating circumstances.

Rule-Based Policy Any government policy in which a jurisdiction rarely or never deviates from established norms. A rule-based policy does not make exceptions based upon extenuating circumstances.

Rule-Based Trade Policy A trade policy in which a jurisdiction rarely or never deviates from established norms. A rule-based trade policy does not make exceptions based upon extenuating circumstances.

Rules of Fair Practice A set of rules FINRA uses to govern the broker-dealers that belong to it. In general, the Rules of Fair Practice govern reporting and disclosure, and they require broker-dealers to exercise loyalty and deal equitably with clients.

Rules of Navigation Statutory or regulatory standards that govern how to operate a water-going vessel within a certain jurisdiction. Rules of navigation may enforce speed limits, rights of way and so forth. Rules of navigation facilitate safe travel, which may affect trade.

Rules of Origin Regulations determining where a product was created for the purpose of determining what tariff, if any, applies. In general, rules of origin consider a product to come from the country where the last substantial change occurred. For example, suppose raw material comes from Britain, is sent to Russia for refining and then is finished in Japan. If the final product is sent to the United States, rules of origin generally consider it as having come from Japan.

Rules of the Game Informal for regulation. Rules of the game should not be confused with the Rules of Fair Practice.

Ruling An official opinion by the IRS on how it interprets U.S. tax law. The IRS may make a ruling, for example, after seeing taxpayers apply a deduction or credit to an unusual, but still relevant situation. The IRS determines whether or not it will accept the situation, and, afterward, applies the ruling to all comparable situations. It is also called a revenue ruling, a letter ruling, or a private letter ruling.

Rump In a merger or acquisition, the shareholders who refuse to sell their stock. If the merger or acquisition is successful, the rump becomes powerless; however, refusal to sell can deprive the acquiring company from some of the company's cash flow. This can discourage the acquiring company from completing the merger or acquisition in the first place.

Run An event in which many account holders at a bank withdraw all of their funds at the same time because they do not believe the bank is solvent. In the United States, runs were fairly common before the creation of the FDIC, which insures bank deposits up to a certain amount. See also: Panic.

Run Charge In computer services, a charge offered per-file or per-item. For example, a computer programmer may offer a certain amount per file to process 80 files. Likewise, a marketer or political campaign may rent a list of potential contacts for a per name run charge.

Run of Paper In newspaper advertising, the publisher's ability to place an ad anywhere space allows. While the paper may attempt to put the ad in the advertiser's preferred space, run of the paper gives the publisher significant leeway, depending on the availability of column space. It is also called run of press. See also: Run of schedule.

Run of Schedule In broadcast advertising, the broadcaster's ability to place an ad anywhere space or time allows. While the broadcaster may attempt to run the ad during the advertiser's preferred time, run of the schedule gives the publisher schedule leeway, depending on the availability of time. However, less favorable times often provide better rates. It is also called run of station. See also: Run of paper.

Run Rate The estimation of future financial data that assumes present trends continue. For example, if a company earns $1 million in a month, it may announce $12 million estimated annual earnings according to the run rate. This can be very inaccurate, particularly if a company's performance is seasonal.

Run to Settlement The state of holding a futures contract until its expiration date. After a run to settlement, the holder receives the underlying asset. For example, if one holds a contract for 100 barrels of oil and runs it to settlement, one must buy the oil. Running to settlement is relatively uncommon as most contracts are settled in cash.

Run with the Land Informal; describing rights that are conveyed with the transfer of real estate. For example, the owner of real estate is permitted to build a house on the property. Rights that run with the land are relatively all encompassing, though they generally exclude mineral rights.

Runaround Slang; deceptive tactics. For example, a dishonest salesman may be said to give a victim "the runaround" by not disclosing hidden fees associated with the price.

Runaway 1. A slang term for high inflation that proves difficult to control. **2.** See: Runaway gap.

Runaway Gap In technical analysis, a gap on a chart representing a sudden and large price movement accompanied by high trading volume. A runaway gap usually occurs in the middle of an upward or downward trend and is used to confirm the intensity of the trend. Runaway gaps may occur, for example, when the price of a security suddenly doubles when it has been increasing, or halves when it has been decreasing. As with many charting terms, it may be bullish or bearish; a sudden movement upward is a bullish breakaway gap, while a sudden movement downward is bearish. See also: Breakaway Gap.

Rundlet A unit of volume equivalent to 15 gallons.

Rundown In municipal bonds, a list of bonds in a serial issue still available for purchase. The rundown includes the sizes and prices of the relevant bonds.

Runner 1. See: Book runner. **2.** See: Running broker. **3.** See: Front runner.

Running a Position The act or practice of keeping a risky position open with the goal of earning eventual gains through speculation.

Running Ahead An illegal act in which a broker or other representative, just before filling a large order on behalf of a client, conducts a transaction in the same security on his/her own account. A large order to buy or sell usually affects the price of a security; the broker conducts the transaction hoping to profit on the movement in price after he/she fills the client's order. This is a form of insider trading, as the broker filling the order knows something about the market's probable movement that other market participants do not know. It is also known as tape racing.

Running Broker A broker who facilitates transactions in bills of exchange between investors and discount houses (banks that buy securities at a discount and re-sell them). The running broker receives a commission for these services.

Running Down Clause A clause in an ocean marine insurance contract that eliminates the policyholder's legal liability in the event of a collision. It is distinct from hull insurance in that it covers damage to (and a lawsuit by) another party, not damage to the ship itself.

Running Head A title that appears at the top of each page of a publication. The running head may be the name of a chapter, article or even the book or magazine.

Running Text The main body of text on a page in a periodical. The most common example is an article.

Running Time The period of time during which a computer program is performing.

Runoff A situation on the NYSE in which a trade is not reported on a ticker tape until after the end of the trading day because trading volume is so heavy for a security that the ticker quotes are delayed by a significant amount of time. This was fairly common before electronic tickers were used, but has become largely a non-issue because electronic tickers announce prices in real time. See also: Tape is Late.

Runup 1. A sudden increase in price, especially of a stock. Runups are usually temporary. **2.** A sudden increase in some economic measure. For example, the Federal Reserve may run up interest rates, or a recession may lead to a runup in unemployment.

Runway A slang term for the amount of time before a project, report, or anything else must be completed. That is, a runway is the length of time until a deadline. See also: Drop-dead date.

Rupee 1. The currency of India. Prior to the independence of India, there were various Indian rupees and other currencies in circulation, many issued by different colonial powers. The modern rupee is descended from the rupee issued by the British. It was pegged to gold for much of its history, finally floating after the end of the Bretton Woods System in 1971. **2.** The name of several now defunct currencies in South Asia and the Middle East. Examples include the Bhutanese rupee and the Gulf rupee.

Ruq'ah al-sairif A term for a promissory note used in some Muslim-majority areas during the 12th century.

Ruqbaa In Islamic law, a gift given with the stipulation that the giver will receive the gift back if the recipient dies before him. If the giver predeceases the recipient, on the other hand, the recipient keeps it.

RUR ISO 4217 code for the Russian ruble prior to 1998. The code was adopted in 1992 after the fall of the Soviet Union. Legally, the currency was identical to the old Soviet ruble, though for the most part it only circulated in Russia. The ruble was redenominated at a ratio of 1,000 to one in 1998, at which point it received the new code "RUB."

Rural Describing a town or vicinity outside a major, metropolitan area. Rural areas have low population density. Most people in rural areas work in urban or suburban areas, but some still work in agricultural or energy producing industries. In the United States, living in a rural area can qualify one for some forms of government assistance, such as a USDA mortgage.

Rural Carrier An employee of the United States Postal Service who delivers mail in areas with low population density. Rural carriers were introduced in the 1890s; previously, people who lived in rural areas had to go to the nearest post office to pick up their mail. Unlike other letter deliverers, rural carriers do not wear uniforms. They also have their own labor union.

Rural commune In Mali, a political subdivision equivalent to a rural municipality.

Rural Delivery Service The delivery of mail by the United States Postal Service to areas with low population density. The Rural Delivery Service was introduced in

the 1890s; previously, people who lived in rural areas had to go to the nearest post office to pick up their mail.

Rural Direct A service in Scotland that helps local voluntary organizations to prepare applications for financing. Rural Direct is available to organizations seeking to repair civic buildings, pay for new services or generally improve their communities. While Rural Direct does not provide funding directly, it helps organizations apply to other funding sources.

Rural Housing A program to construct and/or maintain residences outside a major, metropolitan area. Government loans may be available to encourage rural housing.

Rural Route In the United States, a mail route outside the city or township limits in a rural area. The U.S. Postal Service must deliver mail regardless of where one lives.

Rural Water District In the United States, a local government institution that supplies water to farms and homes in a rural area. Because the provision of water in low-population areas can be expensive, the federal government offers various assistance programs to help pay for rural water district services.

Rurban An area close to the country with many of the amenities of a city. A rurban area may be more scenic than an urban area. See also: Suburban.

RUS GOST 7.67 Latin three-letter geocode for Russia. The code is used for transactions to and from Russian bank accounts and for international shipping to Russia. As with all GOST 7.67 codes, it is used primarily in Cyrillic alphabets.

Rush Sudden, increased interest in a commodity. For example, a gold rush occurs when a large number of people flock to a certain area to mine for gold.

Russell 1000 An index, weighted for market capitalization, of 1,000 large cap, publicly-traded companies. Companies tracked on the Russell 1000 account for upwards of 90% of the market capitalization of companies traded in the United States. While not as famous as the Dow Jones Industrial Average or the S&P 500, some analysts believe that the Russell 1000 accomplishes much the same thing: providing a snapshot of how well the U.S. economy is doing by gauging demand for shares in its largest publicly-traded companies. It is managed by the Russell Investment Group. See also: Benchmark, Russell 2000 Index, Russell 3000 Index.

Russell 2000 Index An index, weighted for market capitalization, of 2,000 small cap, publicly-traded companies. It is considered the premier benchmark for small cap mutual funds. It is managed by the Russell Investment Group. See also: Russell 3000 Index, Russell 1000 Index.

Russell 3000 Index An index, weighted for market capitalization, of the 3,000 largest publicly-traded companies in the United States. While not as famous as the Dow Jones Industrial Average or the S&P 500, some analysts believe that the Russell 3000 Index accomplishes much the same thing: providing a snapshot of how well the U.S. economy is performing by gauging demand for shares in its largest publicly-traded companies. It is managed by the Russell Investment Group. See also: Benchmark, Russell 2000 Index, Russell 1000 Index.

Russell Indexes Three indices that track the 3,000 largest (by market capitalization) publicly-traded companies in the United States. The Russell 1000 tracks the 1,000 largest, the Russell 2000 tracks the 2,000 next-to-largest companies, and the Russell 3000 tracks them all together. All the indices are weighted for market capitalization.

Russell Investment Group A company that provides consulting services to money managers, retirement funds and others. It is especially well known for publishing the Russell indices. It was established in 1936 and is based in Seattle.

Russell Sage An American businessman, investor and politician (1816-1906). He started his career as a grocer and in local politics, eventually being elected to U.S. Congress. In later life, he purchased a seat on the New York Stock Exchange and financed the expansion of American railroads westward.

Russian Country Fund A mutual fund that invests predominantly or exclusively in the securities issued in Russia. While a Russian country fund may be diversified in other ways (for instance, it may hold both stocks and bonds), it is usually exposed to political risk, which, in Russia, has historically been considerable. It is a type of single-country fund.

Russian Option An option giving the holder the right but not the obligation to buy (for a call) or to sell (for a put) the underlying asset at the best price that occurs between the start of the option and the time it is exercised. What distinguishes a Russian option is the fact that there is no expiration date. The holder can wait indefinitely for an advantageous price and exercise the option. It is a type of lookback option.

Russian Project Finance Bank A bank intended to improve development in Russia by providing consulting services and medium-to-long-term loans to businesses. It is a subsidiary of the European Bank for Reconstruction and Development.

Russian Ruble The currency of Russia. It was issued in 1998, replacing the Soviet ruble (which was also called the Russian ruble after the fall of the Soviet Union). Despite the issue of a new currency, it lost 70% of its value against the U.S. dollar in six weeks as a result of the Russian financial crisis. It is a floating currency.

Russian Trading System A stock exchange in Russia. The Russian Trading System was established in 1995 by combining regional exchanges in the country into a large, electronic exchange. It is considered one of the more important exchanges in Russia; it publishes the RTS Index, which is considered an important benchmark on the direction of Russian stocks.

Russian Union of Industrialists and Entrepreneurs An organization that lobbies the Russian government on behalf of business interests. Members include private and state companies, as well as domestic and foreign companies. It especially works with investment and industrial companies.

Rust Belt An area of the United States known for manufacturing and heavy industry. The area is broadly contiguous with the upper Midwest and parts of the mid-Atlantic. States generally considered part of the Rest Belt include Michigan, Pennsylvania, Ohio and Indiana. In the early and mid 20th century, companies in the Rust Belt made cars, steel and other products. It has declined since the 1970s, though information technology and other sectors have started to take root.

Rust Bowl Any area that was once the home of many manufacturing plants and related companies, but has seen decline as companies have either gone bankrupt or moved to areas with a lower cost of doing business. Rust bowls are most common in the developed world. Pennsylvania, for example, forms part of the Rust Bowl in the United States.

Rust Spot In numismatics, a red or brown area on a gold coin caused by rust. They may affect the value of a coin.

Rute A German unit of length. Its measure varied in different German-speaking areas, but generally was between two and a half and five meters. It became obsolete with the adoption of the metric system in the 1870s.

RW 1. ISO 3166-1 alpha-2 code for the Republic of Rwanda. This is the code used in international transactions to and from Rwandan bank accounts. 2. ISO 3166-2 geocode for Rwanda. This is used as an international standard for shipping to Rwanda. Each Rwandan province and town council has its own code with the prefix "RW." For example, the code for Nord Province is ISO 3166-2:RW-03.

RWA GOST 7.67 Latin three-letter geocode for Rwanda. The code is used for transactions to and from Rwandan bank accounts and for international shipping to Rwanda. As with all GOST 7.67 codes, it is used primarily in Cyrillic alphabets.

Rwanda and Burundi Franc The currency of Rwanda and Burundi between 1960 and 1964 while the two were territories under Belgian Mandate. Circulation ended when the two became independent countries.

Rwandan Franc The currency of Rwanda. It was introduced in 1964, replacing the Rwanda and Burundi franc. The proposed East African shilling may replace the franc.

RWF ISO 4217 code for the Rwandan franc. It was introduced in 1964, replacing the Rwanda and Burundi franc. Rwanda is planning to replace the franc with the proposed East African shilling sometime in 2009 or 2010.

Rybczynski Theorem The concept that, assuming constant prices, an increase in an endowment will result in increased output of a product using that endowment and reduced output for another product. The theorem was developed by Tadeusz Rybczynski in 1955.

S A symbol appearing next to a stock listed on NASDAQ indicating that the stock has beneficial ownership. All NASDAQ listings use a four-letter abbreviation; if an S follows the abbreviation, it indicates that the security is trading beneficial ownership rather than actual ownership.

S Corporation A business with few shareholders that is exempt from some taxes levied on other corporations. Specifically, an S corporation is not responsible for taxes on its profits (corporate taxes) and is taxed as if it were a partnership. However, it may have no more than 100 shareholders. An S corporate structure allows a company to take advantage of some of the benefits of incorporation without all of the responsibilities attached to it.

S&P 100 An index, weighted for market capitalization, of 100 blue chip stocks from a variety of industries. The stocks listed on the S&P 100 are the top 100 stocks on the S&P 500 by market capitalization. Its ticker symbol is OEX, and it was originally operated by the Chicago Board Options Exchange. See also: Dow Jones Industrial Average.

S&P 700 A stock market index tracking 700 companies outside the United States in various industries with a large amount of market capitalization. It is a capitalization-weighted index, meaning that stocks with higher market caps affect the average more. The decision to include companies on the S&P 700 is made by committee and is updated periodically. The index also scales its averages to account for stock splits and other changes in the companies tracked. See also: S&P 700.

S&P Commodity Index An index in the United States tracking a large number of commodities in various industries. Sectors in the S&P Commodity Index include energy, fibers, grains, livestock and metals. Different sectors receive different weights, which are updated periodically.

S&P Core Earnings A standard used to determine a company's core earnings, which are the profits a company derives from its main business. Because there is no hard-and-fast rule of what constitutes a "main business" or the activities associated with it, S&P core earnings are useful for providing a basic standard to the measurement of core earnings. S&P core earnings are more conservative than some other measurements; among other things, it excludes revenue from pensions while including expenses related to them.

S&P Effect The increase or decrease in the price of a stock when it is added to or deleted from the S&P 500. When a stock is added to or deleted from the index, all index funds tracking the S&P 500 must buy or sell that stock in order to continue being index funds. This increases pressure to buy or sell that stock, resulting in an increase or decrease in price.

S&P Global 100 Index A stock index of 100 large cap, international companies. All stocks on the index come from the S&P Global 1200 Index. It is useful to

investors wishing to monitor the performance of multinational companies. It is weighted for market capitalization.

S&P Global 1200 Index A stock index of 1,200 international companies. Stocks on the index represent about 70% of the world's market capitalization. It is useful to investors wishing to monitor the performance of multinational companies. It is weighted for market capitalization.

S&P Phenomenon A common situation in which a stock newly added to the S&P 500 undergoes a sharp but temporary increase in price. This occurs because portfolios, ETFs, and other investment vehicles tracking the S&P 500 add this stock, usually in large quantities. This results in a sudden increase in interest in the stock, causing it to jump up in price. Normally, it returns to equilibrium once everyone's portfolio has adjusted to the change.

S&P Rating A credit rating by Standard & Poor. As with other credit ratings, an S&P rating measures the level of risk associated with a particular issuer of debt securities. S&P is one of only 10 firms the SEC recognizes as a credit rating agency, and, along with Fitch and Moody's, it is one of the three most prominent. However, the methods of S&P ratings have been subject to criticism. For example, it gave the nation of Iceland a top rating until its bankruptcy in 2008.

S&P/ASX 200 An index in Australia tracking 200 stocks listed on the Australian Securities Exchange. It is weighted for market capitalization and adjusted for float. It is published by Standard and Poor's.

S/D Abbreviation for shutdown, as of a government or a factory.

S-3 Filing The simplest document one may file with the SEC explaining a new offering of securities for public trade. An S-3 filing requires less information from the issuer, and is only available to companies that have met filing requirements in the past and have been required to file for at least 12 months.

Sa 1. ISO 3166-1 alpha-2 code for the Kingdom of Saudi Arabia. This is the code used in international transactions to and from Saudi bank accounts. 2. ISO 3166-2 geocode for Saudi Arabia. This is used as an international standard for shipping to Saudi Arabia. Each Saudi province has its own code with the prefix "SA." For example, the code for the Province of Riyadh is ISO 3166-2:SA-01. 3. An abbreviation for a number of corporate structures, including Sociedad Anonima (Spanish) and Societe Anonyme (French).

Sa Le A Burmese unit of volume approximately equivalent to 63.93 milliliters.

Saahib al-'iinah In Islamic law, the borrower in a bai al-inah. In this contract, the borrower buys an item on credit and immediately sells it back to the original owner at a lower price for cash. This effectively creates a loan at interest, which is prohibited in Islam.

Saahib al-maal In Islamic law, a person who possesses sufficient wealth to be required to pay zakah, which are the charitable donations Muslims are required to pay. Different schools of jurisprudence have different views on how much one must have to be a sahib al-maal. The requirement also varies by the type of wealth one has.

Saahib al-maks In Islamic law, a term for a corrupt tax collector who collects more than is due to him. The practice of taking more than is owed in taxes is prohibited in Islam.

Sacagawea Dollar A $1 coin that began to be minted in the United States in 2000. Unlike the Susan B. Anthony dollar, it is gold colored, to reduce the likelihood of confusion with other coins.

Sachwerte A German term for something of real value. The pursuit of Sachwerte was constant in Germany and Austria in the early 1920s, when cash lost its value almost as soon as it was printed. Examples of Sachwerte include real estate, businesses, and even furniture.

Sack Predominately British; to terminate a person, especially with cause. For example, an employee caught stealing may be sacked, meaning he will no longer be employed at the company. The term is equivalent to firing.

Sacred Mina An ancient Persian unit of volume approximately equivalent to 600 milliliters.

Sacrifice Ratio The cost to an economy when growth slows or stops in order to combat inflation. The ratio shows the cost for each percentage of decrease in inflation. It is calculated thusly: Sacrifice ratio = (Dollar cost of lost production) / (Percentage of change to the inflation rate)

Safe Harbor 1. An anti-takeover measure in which a potential target company buys a subsidiary in an industry that is so strictly regulated that it makes acquiring the target company difficult and/or expensive. 2. Legal protection from a lawsuit. Regulators often apply safe harbor to some corporate actions as long as those actions are taken in good faith.

Safe Harbor Rule An IRS rule protecting taxpayers from losing favorable tax treatment as long as their actions are taken in good faith.

Safe Haven Currency A currency that investors trust more than others and which they therefore buy in times of uncertainty. Safe haven currencies are considered low risk because their issuing governments are stable and their economies tend to be strong, among other reasons. Examples of safe haven currencies include the U.S. dollar and the British pound.

Safe Rate The rate of return on a low-risk investment. Examples of investments with safe rates include U.S. Treasury securities and investment grade bonds. See also: Safety-net return.

Safekeeping The act of a brokerage holding a client's securities or other assets on his/her behalf. This reduces the risk of the client losing his/her assets or having them stolen. They are also available to the brokerage to sell at the client's demand. Like a bank, safekeeping provides an investor a place to store assets with little risk. Unlike a bank, brokerages are not allowed to use the items in safekeeping for their own ends. Assets in safekeeping are not fungible for the brokerage because they remain in the client's name; for this reason, brokerages normally require a fee for safekeeping services. See also: Street name safekeeping.

Safekeeping Certificate A certificate identifying the ownership of an asset. The term is most commonly used with respect to ownership of an international depositary receipt or a certificate of deposit. See also: Stock certificate.

Safety Cushion In a contingent immunization strategy, the difference between a portfolio's value and the agreed-upon safety net return. A contingent immunization strategy prescribes an actively managed portfolio that is risk tolerant until a series of bad investments brings the return on the portfolio down to a certain level, known as the safety net. At that point, the portfolio becomes risk averse. Thus, the safety cushion is the amount in investment that the money manager may lose before he/she is required to change the goal of the portfolio from capital gain to capital protection.

Safety Net 1. See: Safety net return. **2.** See: Social safety net.

Safety Responsibility Law Laws in U.S. states protecting persons injured, killed or required to pay money due to a traffic accident involving an uninsured motorist. Penalties differ, but the uninsured motorist generally has his/her driver's license suspended.

Safety Stock Inventory a company keeps in order to avoid running out. For example, a grocery store may buy more apples than it expects to sell in case there is a sudden uptick in demand or if the next delivery is delayed. Safety stock is considered a drain on a company's finances because it very likely will not sell. However, it may be necessary for the smooth function of a business. See also: Supply chain management.

Safety-Net Return In an actively-managed portfolio, the minimum return the portfolio must make in order to remain actively managed. If the return falls below this minimum, the portfolio automatically initiates an immunization strategy to reduce the portfolio's risk. The safety-net return is part of a contingent immunization strategy.

SAG Fee A fee paid to an actor or other performer for a rerun of a program in which he/she was part of the cast. An advertiser or a broadcaster may pay the fee, which is set in a union contract. It is also called a residual fee.

Saher In Turkmenistan, a political subdivision for the capital city, Ashgabat, which is not under the jurisdiction of any province.

Sahib al-suuq An Arabic phrase meaning "guardian of the marketplace." A sahib al suuq was a local official responsible for regulation of trade and similar matters in the early days of Islam.

Sahrawi Peseta The currency of the Sahrawi Arab Democratic Republic, a country in the Western Sahara with limited recognition. The peseta does not circulate, though in theory it is pegged to the euro.

Sahu In Nepal, a term for a small-time lender or businessperson.

Saint Helena Pound The currency of Saint Helena. It has existed side by side with the British pound since the early 19th century. It is pegged to the British pound at a one-to-one ratio. Saint Helena does not have a central bank, and pounds are issued through a private, commercial bank.

Saint Petersburg Mint An organization in Russia that issues legal tender coins for general use. It was established in 1724 and is owned by Goznak, a state-owned minting and banknote printing organization.

Saitori A member on the Tokyo Stock Exchange that matches buy and sell orders with each other in order to facilitate trading and promote liquidity on the exchange. Unlike specialists on the NYSE, however, they are not allowed to trade on their own accounts. See also: Market maker.

Sajin A Tatar unit of length approximately equivalent to 2.13 meters. It was rendered obsolete when the Soviet Union began to use the metric system in 1924.

Salad Oil Scandal A famous fraud perpetrated by Allied Crude Vegetable Oil in 1963. In this year, Allied Crude began using its inventory of vegetable oil to obtain millions of dollars in loans from banks and other financial institutions. In order to inflate its capital, it began shipping tanks of water into the United States with only a small amount of oil on top of the tanks. Because oil floats on water, inspectors were fooled into believing that the tanks were full of oil, and would then approve additional loans against the non-existent vegetable oil. The scheme became so large that, when it was finally exposed, it created one of the largest corporate scandals of the century. The ensuing panic caused American Express to lose more than half its stock price; Bank of America and Bank Leumi also suffered considerably. Allied Crude's leader ultimately served seven years in prison.

Salariat Persons who earn salaries (or set amounts of money each month or year) as a class. The salariat contrasts with wage earners, who are paid by the hour and are not paid for hours not worked. See also: Proletariat.

Salaried Partner A partner who owns a portion of a company and thus is entitled to part of its profit, but who also receives a regular salary in exchange for his/her services for the company. A salaried partner usually works for the company exclusively, while an unsalaried partner may have another job or other investments. A salaried partner may be a part of the company's management team (or even its only manager) while an unsalaried partner has little or no management role. See also: Silent partner.

Salary A regular compensation that an employee receives for working at a company. A salary is set by agreement between the employee and the employer and is not dependent on the number of hours worked. That is, the employee does not make more for working more than 40 hours per week and does not make less for working less than that.

Salary Freeze A temporary policy in which a company refrains from giving any workers, or a certain subset of workers, any increases in salary or wages. Salary freezes are most common in companies that ordinarily give raises at regular intervals. The policy is adopted when a company is experiencing financial difficulties and wishes to avoid layoffs, if possible. See also: Cutting Hours.

Salary Reduction Plan An employer-sponsored plan whereby the employee does not receive a check for his/her entire salary. Rather, the employer puts a portion of the salary into the plan directly; the contribution is automatically invested for the employee's retirement. This sort of plan may make this reduction either before or after the employee's taxes. This determines whether or not the withdrawals after retirement are taxable. See also: IRA, 401(k).

Salary Reduction Simplified Employee Pension Plan A former 401(k) for small businesses, defined as those with fewer than 25 employees. This plan minimized costs for the employer, and employees could make contributions through paycheck deductions. It was replaced by the SIMPLE plan in 1996.

Salary-Reduction Contribution A contribution to an employer-sponsored plan whereby the employee does not receive a check for his/her entire salary. Rather, the employer puts a portion of the salary into the plan directly; the contribution is automatically invested for the employee's retirement. A salary reduction contribution may come before or after the employee's taxes. This determines whether or not the withdrawals after retirement are taxable. See also: IRA, 401(k).

Sale The act of relinquishing ownership of some asset in exchange for some monetary compensation. Sales may take any of several forms. In a cash sale, the seller receives cash or a cash equivalent immediately in exchange for the asset. In a credit sale, the seller surrenders ownership immediately in exchange for future payment, often with interest. An example of a sale is a simple transaction involving widgets. If the seller is willing to accept $2 per widget, and the buyer wishes to purchase 100 widgets, then the seller gives the buyer 100 widgets in exchange for $200. See also: Buy.

Saleh Abdul Aziz Al-Rajhi A 20th-century Saudi investment banker. At the beginning of his career, he co-founded a foreign exchange service for Muslim pilgrims traveling to Mecca and Medina. This service grew into Al Rajhi Bank, one of the largest banks in Saudi Arabia. Rajhi himself became one of the wealthiest persons in the country not connected to the royal family. He lived from 1921 to 2011.

Sale-Leaseback The sale of a property in which the seller immediately begins to rent the property from the buyer. That is, the seller no longer has ownership of the property, but maintains residence and/or use for the duration of the rental agreement. A sale-leaseback gives the seller profit from the sale while the buyer is guaranteed income from the rental agreement in the medium or long-term. Sometimes, a sale-leaseback occurs in order to grant the seller access to capital to make improvement on the property; for example, the seller may use the proceeds from the sale to build a factory. A form of sale-leaseback, known as sukuk al-ijara, is a common structure for sukuk, or the equivalent of a bond, in Islamic finance. Sale-leaseback is also called simply leaseback.

Sale-Manageback A transaction in which a company is sold but the previous owners remain in place as managers. For example, Joe may sell his company to Bob but remain as the chief executive officer. The seller may receive a share of the company's profits, but no longer has any liability for losses.

Sales The revenue that a company derives from the sale of its products. This is distinguished from sources of revenue like interest income, investments, and others. A company records its sales on a balance sheet. Obviously, high sales are usually thought desirable, particularly when expenses are high.

Sales Completion In project finance, the time at which a project has been finished, functions, and has generated the expected revenue. Sales completion applies especially to construction and other infrastructure projects. For example, an oil company may build a series of oil pumps. The time of sales completion occurs not when the oil pumps are completed and are working, but when they have pumped enough oil to meet revenue expectations. Another example is a new apartment building that has collected enough rent to meet expectations for the owner(s). See also: Physical completion.

Sales Contract A contract between two parties in which one relinquishes ownership of some asset in exchange for some monetary compensation. Sales contracts specify the terms of sale, which may take any of several forms. In a cash sale, the seller receives cash or a cash equivalent immediately in exchange for the asset. In a credit sale, the seller surrenders ownership immediately in exchange for future payment, often with interest.

Sales Forecast An estimate of a company's future sales based historical patterns, macroeconomic factors, and expected future trends. The sales forecast is important when a company is making financial plans; sales that fall short of the forecast may cause the company to be unable to meet the obligations it has assumed based on those financial plans.

Sales Growth The amount a company derives from sales compared to a previous, corresponding period of time in which the latter sales exceed the former. For example, a company has experienced sales growth when its sales were $1 million in Q1 2009 and are $1.2 million in Q1 2010. Sales growth is considered positive for a company's survival and profitability. It may result in increased dividends for shareholders and/or higher stock prices.

Sales Letter Direct mail intended to convince the recipient to purchase a certain product. Sales letters are primarily textual, though they may include graphics. Some web pages expounding the benefits of a product are considered sales letters.

Sales Literature Brochures, pamphlets, and other documents that a company writes to encourage investment in its securities. The sales literature contains information designed to present the securities in the best, possible light. However, regulators often require sales literature to include disclaimers stating that investing is always a risky venture.

Sales Per Share A ratio of a company's annual revenue to its average number of shares outstanding for a given year. This is a measure of how well a company uses its resources to produce sales. A higher ratio is seen as a positive sign.

Sales Return A product given back to the seller for a refund, usually due to a defect or malfunction. Sales returns reduce a seller's revenue and may also reduce a salesperson's commission.

Sales Tax A tax imposed on the sale of retail goods and services. That is, the government collects a certain percentage of the sale price on transactions where goods and services are traded at the retail level. While the retailers are responsible for paying the sales tax, most of the time they simply pass on the cost to customers. For example, if an item costs $10 and there is a 5% sales tax, the retailer will charge the customer $10.50. Proponents of sales taxes argue that they reward those who spend less and, therefore, do not punish those who earn more. Critics argue that sales taxes harm the poor disproportionately and can drive business to other jurisdictions. See also: VAT, Regressive tax.

Sales Territory A designated area in which a salesperson works. For example, a sales territory may include a neighborhood, a town or even a whole state. Sales territories are assigned to reduce competition between commission-based salespersons working for the same company. Most of the time, only one (or a few) salespersons are placed in a territory.

Sales to Cash Flow Ratio A company's sales per share divided by its cash flow per share. A higher ratio is considered desirable for a company, while a lower ratio could mean that the company is in danger of bankruptcy or other hardship.

Sales, General, and Administrative Expenses Overhead costs to a company. Sales, general, and administrative expenses are usually recurring; they include things like rent, salaries, and money spent on office supplies. They do not generally include one-time costs. They form one of the single largest expenses a company can incur in its operations. These expenses are included in one category on financial statements and are subtracted from revenue when calculating operating income.

Sales-Type Lease A lease whereby a company rents its own assets that it needs to run its business. For example, an automobile factory may lease its machinery to another factory.

Sallie Mae The Student Loan Marketing Association (SLMA). A publicly-traded company chartered by the U.S. Congress to guarantee student loans and to provide a secondary market for student loans made by other lenders. In order to do this, it buys student loans and repackages them, selling them as short-term and medium-term debt obligations. Sallie Mae also provides other services, such as debt management, to students, universities, and businesses. It was established as a government-sponsored enterprise in 1972, but ended its federal charter in 2004. See also: Farmer Mac, Fannie Mae, Freddie Mac.

Salmonella A genus of bacteria known to cause illness in humans and animals, especially after they have eaten infected food. Salmonella infections have been associated with chicken eggs, a fact that in the past has caused marketing and other business problems in the poultry industry in the United States. However, fatal poisonings are extremely rare.

Salomon Brothers Non-U.S. Dollar World Government Bond Index An index of all fixed-rate bonds traded between institutional investors and not issued in U.S. dollars. It is considered an important benchmark of the bond market.

Salomon Brothers World Equity Index An index that tracks both debt securities and stocks in publicly-traded companies worldwide where the total number of shares available for trade in each company is worth at least $100 million. Each company in the index is weighted according to the total value of its shares available for trade. The Salomon Brothers World Equity Index tracks more than 6,000 companies in 22 countries.

Salong A subdivision of the Cambodian tical, the currency of Cambodia before 1875. One salong was worth one-fourth of a tical.

Salt Name A false name and address placed on a list for quality assurance. A salt name may be placed on a list to monitor improper use of the list (for example, if one sends correspondence to the list without permission). A salt name is also called a dummy name or a decoy name.

Saltus An ancient Roman unit of area approximately equivalent to 201.9.

Salvadoran Colon The currency of El Salvador between 1919 and 2004. It was initially pegged to the U.S. dollar, but began to float in 1931. As part of El Salvador's liberalization policy, it began to accept the dollar as legal tender in 2001 and stopped circulating the colon in 2004. See also: Dollarization.

Sam Walton An American businessman who is best known for founding the Wal-Mart chain. He began in the retail store business in 1945 when he purchased a Ben Franklin franchise. Throughout the 1950s, he opened more franchises until he established the first Wal-Mart in 1962. He was one of the first retailers to always buy from the lowest priced wholesaler; this drove sales higher, which allowed him to negotiate still lower prices from wholesalers. This practice, while controversial, became a staple of Wal-Mart. He also was among the first to offer managers the ability to become limited partners in his stores. Walton lived from 1918 until 1992.

Same Day Funds 1. Funds in a financial institution that may be withdrawn or otherwise used on the same day they are deposited. **2.** Fed funds transferred through the Fedwire. **2.** See: Same-day funds settlement.

Same Store Sales When a retail company owns several stores, the amount in sales made by stores that have been open for more than one year. It is calculated by subtracting the amount in sales made by new stores from the total sales in a given period. Same store sales are useful because they allow a company to have an indication how much demand for its products is growing in stores that currently exist. Increases in same store sales may be as useful to expansion as opening new stores as they do not carry the overhead associated with it. Same store sales are released on a monthly basis and are also known as comps.

Same-Day Funds Settlement Describing a transaction on which the settlement date occurs on the same day as the trade date. Most of the time, same-day funds settlement occurs for funds transferred over the Fed Wire service; in other words, this type of settlement occurs only for the least risky securities and funds.

Same-Day Substitution In a margin account, a situation where the value of some securities rise and some others decline on the same day, such that there is no net change to the account's aggregate value at the end of the trading day.

Sammarinese Lira The former currency of San Marino. It was introduced in the 1860s and was pegged to the Italian lira at a one-to-one ratio. Sammarinese and Italian coins circulated alongside each other in both San Marino and Italy. The euro replaced both currencies in 1999.

Samsarah In Islamic law, a term for a brokerage.

Samuel Waksal Founder of ImClone, a pharmaceutical company in the United States. While serving as CEO in 2002, he was arrested for insider trading, eventually pleading guilty to securities fraud and similar charges. This scandal was noted for also leading to the arrest of noted television personality Martha Stewart. Waksal was born in 1947.

Samurai Bond A foreign bond denominated in Japanese yen and traded in the Japan. In order to raise capital from Japanese investors, a non-Japanese company may choose to sell a bond in Japan. See also: Bulldog Bond, Yankee Bond.

Samurai Market Informal; a stock market in Japan. The term is most often used by those outside of Japan.

San Francisco Stock and Bond Exchange A former exchange in the United States. Established in 1882, it merged with the Los Angeles Oil Exchange to form what became known as the Pacific Exchange.

Sanar A currency subdivision in Afghanistan between 1891 and 1925. A sanar was worth one-sixth of an Afghan rupee.

Sanchi A Burmese unit of length equivalent to 0.079375 millimeters.

Sandbag 1. Informal; an anti-takeover measure. **2.** When a company desires a takeover and it has a potential buyer, a stalling tactic the company uses to find a better buyer without scaring off the buyer it already has. **3.** In sales, the practice of a salesperson to delay the completion of a deal until such time as he/she will be able to maximize his/her commission.

Sandwich Coin A slang term for a clad coin, which is a coin made of two different metals, one at the center of the coin and one that is plating. The term originated in the United States when it began producing clad coins in 1965.

Sandwich Generation The collection of middle-aged individuals who must provide financial support to both their parents and their children. Additionally, many attempt to save for their own retirements. Because these responsibilities are financially draining, members of the sandwich generation are often under a great deal of personal stress.

Sandwich Lease A lease in which a party who previously rented a property re-rents to another party. In a sandwich lease, the lessee becomes a lessor.

Sangam An ancient Indian unit of area approximately equivalent to one-quarter hectare.

Sangkat In Cambodia, a political subdivision equivalent to a quarter of a district, which is a subdivision of a city.

Sanmekai One of 13 banks in Japan that together set short-term interest rates for other Japanese banks.

Santeem A subdivision of the Algerian dinar. One santeem is equal in value to 1/100 of one dinar. While santeem do not circulate in practice, prices frequently are quoted in terms of santeem.

Santim A subunit of several currencies. A santim is 1/100 of a Moroccan dirham, a Latvian lat or an Ethiopian birr. See also: Cent.

Santims A subdivision of the Latvian lats. One santims is equal in value to 1/100 of one lats. Its plural is santimu.

Sao Tome and Principe Dobra The currency of Sao Tome and Principe. It was introduced in 1977, replacing the Sao Tome and Principe escudo. In the mid-2000s, the dobra's inflation rate accelerated significantly. In 2009, it was pegged to the euro.

Sao Tome and Principe Escudo The currency of Sao Tome and Principe between 1914 and 1977. It was equivalent to the Portuguese escudo. Soon after Sao Tome and Principe became independent, the dobra replaced the escudo.

Sar ISO 4217 code for the Saudi Arabian riyal. It became the official currency of the Kingdom at its establishment in 1932; it is the successor currency to the Hejaz riyal. Between 1986 and 2003, the riyal was pegged to Special Drawing Rights, but in practice, this was effectively a peg to the U.S. dollar. The peg was officially changed to the dollar in 2003 and has been in effect since (with the exception of a brief period toward the end of 2007). It is issued by the Saudi Arabian Monetary Agency.

Sarbanes Oxley Act of 2002 Legislation in the United States, passed in 2002, intended to increase transparency in accounting practices. It was adopted in the wake of a series of scandals involving aggressive accounting on the part of a number of major accounting firms, notably Arthur Andersen. Among other provisions, it created the Public Accounting Oversight Board to regulate accounting firms that provide auditing services. It established and enhanced provisions for auditor independence and financial disclosures to limit potential conflicts of interest. It introduced a requirement that the chief executive officer must sign a corporation's tax return and enhanced punishments for white collar crime. Proponents argue that the Act has increased transparency in public accounting, while critics contend that it has driven business outside the United States.

Sarin A liquid that may be used as a chemical weapon. Stockpiling sarin is illegal under the Chemical Weapons Convention.

Satang A division of the Thai baht worth 1/100 of the baht. See also: Cent.

Satisficing The act or practice of doing the absolute minimum necessary to complete a project. That is, when one satisfices a contract, one did no more than was required. This may reduce costs, but may not be the best way to conduct business because there may be fewer repeat customers.

Saturday Night Special Informal; an unexpected attempt at a hostile takeover. The term comes from the fact that such takeover attempts are often announced over the weekend when the fewest investors are paying attention.

SATURNS An equity derivative linked to some stated collateral. The credit rating of SATURNS depends on the risk of the underlying collateral.

SAU GOST 7.67 Latin three-letter geocode for Saudi Arabia. The code is used for transactions to and from Saudi bank accounts and for international shipping to Saudi Arabia. As with all GOST 7.67 codes, it is used primarily in Cyrillic alphabets.

Saucer In technical analysis, an indicator that a downtrend is reversing itself. It is marked by a gradual decline in a security's price, followed by a bottom, and finally by a gradual increase. It is important to note that the bottom has low trading volume. The term comes from the fact that, when charted, a saucer trend looks like a small bowl. It is also called a rounded bottom.

Saudi Arabian Monetary Agency The central bank of Saudi Arabia. It controls issue of the Saudi riyal, sets the monetary policy, holds currency reserves, manages the exchange rate and regulates banks and financial markets. It was established in 1952.

Saudi Arabian Riyal The currency of Saudi Arabia. It became the official currency of the Kingdom at its establishment in 1932; it is the successor currency to the Hejaz riyal. Between 1986 and 2003, the riyal was pegged to Special Drawing Rights, but in practice, this was effectively a peg to the U.S. dollar. The peg was officially changed to the dollar in 2003 and has been in effect since (with the exception of a brief period in 2007). It is issued by the Saudi Arabian Monetary Agency.

Saudi Arabian Standards Organization An organization that oversees development of standards of quality for products, utilities and facilities in Saudi Arabia. It has the authority to enforce the standards it sets. It was founded in 1972. See also: ISO.

Saundaung An obsolete Burmese unit of length approximately equivalent to 558.86 meters.

Savings Account An account at a bank in which the customer deposits money for any non-immediate use. For example, one may utilize a savings account to save funds for an expensive purchase, such as a house or a car. Because most customers keep money in a savings account for a longer period than a checking account, a savings account pays a slightly higher interest rate. However, the interest rate is not as high as a bond or another low-risk investment. Generally speaking, one may not write a check on a savings account without paying a penalty. This is to disincentivize withdrawals on savings.

Savings Are Vital to Everyone Retirement Act of 1997 Legislation in the United States requiring the Department of Labor to better inform the American public about the necessity of saving for retirement. Among other provisions, it mandated that the president of the United States conduct three programs on retirement: one in 1998, one in 2001 and the last in 2005.

Savings Association Insurance Fund A pool of money created in 1989 by the FDIC to insure deposits made in savings and loan associations (or thrifts). The SAIF was created to separate thrift insurance money from regular bank insurance money (which came from the Bank Insurance Fund). While this was likely beneficial for a time because of the savings and loan crisis, it created a perverse incentive for banks and thrifts to reclassify themselves as the other (i.e., a bank to a thrift or a thrift to a bank), depending on which fund had lower fees. This led to the passage of the Federal Deposit Insurance Act of 2005, which abolished the Savings Association Insurance Fund and the Bank Insurance Fund and created a single Deposit Insurance Fund.

Savings Bond In the United States, a non-tradable bond issued by the federal government for savings purposes. A savings bond allows citizens to receive a guaranteed return for their investments and helps raise revenue for the government. There are two types of savings bond in the United States: Series EE and Series I, with the main difference being that Series I bonds have interest rates indexed to inflation. Savings bonds pay coupons semi-annually; they are sold at face value and pay par upon maturity, which is 30 years after purchase. Bonds not held for at least five years are subject to a redemption penalty. Federal taxes on interest are deferred until redemption or maturity. Savings bonds are non-transferable and must be either held or redeemed.

Savings Element The portion of a whole life insurance policy that is set aside and invested by the insurance company. Part of the policyholder's premium each month becomes part of the savings element, as do any gains from investment. The savings element becomes available to the policyholder upon the cancellation of the policy. Furthermore, the savings element is an asset belonging to the policyholder; it can be borrowed against or used as collateral. The amount of money in the savings element is called the cash-surrender value. Any investment gains in the savings element are tax-deferred until the policy is canceled.

Savings Incentive Match Plan for Employees of Small Employers An IRA or 401(k) plan for employees of small businesses, usually with fewer than 100 employees. The employee may make tax deductible contributions, and the employer may contribute in one of two ways. The employer may either match employee contributions up to 3% of the employee's annual salary, or provide a contribution of 2% of the salary regardless of how much the employee contributes. The employee controls the investment of the contributions.

Savings Rate The amount a person or organization places in a savings account or similar vehicle as a percentage of total disposable income. Savings are important for long term financial stability as it gives a person or organization a cushion for bad times. The savings rate may be calculated at microeconomic level for personal finances or may be aggregated at the national level to gauge financial health. A low or negative savings rate usually indicates excessive borrowing, spending, or both. On the other hand, a high savings rate may result in slower economic growth as persons and companies are saving instead of purchasing goods and services. See also: Rainy day fund.

Savivaldybe In Lithuania, a political subdivision equivalent to a municipality.

Savivaldybes In Lithuania, a political subdivision equivalent to a municipality.

Sawbuck In the United States, a slang term for $10. It is rarely used.

Say's Law The concept that, because that which is consumed must be produced, supply creates its own demand. That is, supply of products will eventually be consumed by demand. This is an important concept for supply-side economics; Keynesianism, however, holds the opposite view.

Sazen Wiedenski An obsolete Polish unit of area approximately equivalent to 3.6 square meters.

Sazhen A Russian unit of length equivalent to seven feet. It was rendered obsolete when the Soviet Union began to use the metric system in 1924.

SB 1. ISO 3166-1 alpha-2 code for the Solomon Islands. This is the code used in international transactions to and from Solomon Islander bank accounts. 2. ISO 3166-2 geocode for the Solomon Islands. This is used as an international standard for shipping to the Solomon Islands. Each province and the capital territory has its own code with the prefix "SB." For example, the code for the Province of Isabel is ISO 3166-2:SB-IS.

SBA Administrator The head of the Small Business Administration, an agency of the U.S. government that guarantees loans made to entrepreneurs and small businesses. It also provides special assistance to businesses run by women and minorities. The SBA Administrator is appointed by the president of the United States and confirmed by the Senate.

SBD ISO 4217 code for the Solomon Islands dollar. It was introduced in 1977, replacing the Australian dollar, to which it was pegged until 1979. Since becoming a floating currency, the Solomon Islands dollar has been marked by high inflation. Indeed, in some parts of the Solomon Islands, citizens have reverted to traditional currencies such as dolphin teeth.

Sberkassa A savings bank in Russia. During the Soviet era, sberkassas were extremely important because personal loans were virtually impossible to obtain. As a result, one used a sberkassa to save up for large purchases. In the post-Soviet era, a sberkassa is analogous to a postal savings bank.

SC 1. ISO 3166-1 alpha-2 code for the Republic of the Seychelles. This is the code used in international transactions to and from Seychellois bank accounts. 2. ISO 3166-2 geocode for the Seychelles. This is used as an international standard for shipping to the Seychelles. Each district has its own code with the prefix "SC." For example, the code for the District of Bel Air is ISO 3166-2:SC-09.

Scab In organized labor, an employee who breaks a strike. That is, a scab does not go on strike with other employees but instead keeps working. A scab may do this out of concern for his/her livelihood, because he/she does not agree with the reasons for striking, or for some other reason. Because scabs are thought to reduce the effectiveness of a strike, the term is highly derogatory.

Scalage In shipping, a deduction of the price of a set of goods considered likely to be lost during transport due to normal depletion.

Scale The range of prices at which an underwriter offers to place with investors a serial bond, where the individual bonds have different maturities.

Scale In To deliberately buy a stock when its price is falling. When one scales in, one sets a maximum price for that stock. When it falls below that price, one begins buying in small increments until the price stops falling or one reaches one's desired holding. The idea behind scaling in is to lower the average price at which one buys the stock, which can result in a higher return. Scaling in is risky, however, because there is no guarantee that the stock will rise back to its previous level. See also: Average Down.

Scale Order 1. An order to buy a security where the client requests the order be executed at several, different times at successively lower prices. For example, a scale order may be an order to buy on three different occasions when the prices are $11, $10 and $9. **2.** An order to sell a security where the client requests the order be executed at several, different times at successively higher prices. For example, a scale order may be an order to sell on three different occasions when the prices are $9, $10 and $11.

Scale-Enhancing Describing a new project that carries the same amount and type of risk as other projects a company is currently running. A scale-enhancing project does not diversify the company's risk in any way. However, it may be beneficial, as the project is likely within the company's core competence.

Scaling The change in size of a measurable object accomplished when one of its dimensions is enlarged or shrunk. For example, given a rectangle, if one changes the length and/or width, this will by definition change the measure of its area.

Scalp To hold a position for a very short period of time and receive a small gain. For example, a trader who buys and instantly sells a security hoping to profit from the bid-ask spread is said to scalp that security. A scalper hopes that the series of small gains over the course of the trading day will result in a much larger gain.

Scalper 1. A trader who holds a position for a very short time and sells it for a small gain. A scalper buys and instantly sells a security hoping to profit from the bid-ask spread. Scalpers hope the series of small gains over the course of the trading day will result in much larger gains. See also: Day Trader. **2.** An investment adviser who makes a trade on his/her own account immediately before recommending a client to take a position on the same security. A scalper takes advantage of his/her insider knowledge and the client's trust to make a gain. Scalping, in this sense, is illegal.

Scalping The investment practice of holding a position for a very short period of time and selling it for a small gain. That is, a trader who buys and instantly sells a security hoping to profit from the bid-ask spread is said to scalp that security. A scalper hopes that the series of small gains over the course of the trading day will result in a much larger gain. See also: Day trader.

Scandinavian Monetary Union A currency union between Sweden and Denmark established in 1873. Norway, which was politically united to Sweden but set its own currency policy, joined two years later. Each country continued to issue its own currency, but each was pegged to gold at the same value. This led to each currency being accepted in the other jurisdictions. The Union was dissolved in 1914 with the onset of World War I.

Scarcity In classical economics, the fact that resources are limited while desires are unlimited. The existence of scarcity requires the efficient allocation of resources and drives innovation to work around limitations. That is, scarcity often refers to trading one good or service for another, but it may cause an economic actor to invent something that will satisfy as many desires as possible. See also: Land, labor, and capital.

Scenario Analysis In risk analysis, the process of considering different, possible outcomes of a decision. Scenario analysis may take a number of forms; for example, a company may consider the various potential returns on an investment and how each will affect the company's other business. Scenario analysis can also be used in policy making: the president can weight potential effects of a tax increase when deciding whether or not it would be beneficial to do so.

Schar A slang abbreviation for school accounts receivable, which is the tuition and similar monies that a private school has billed to students (or their families) but has not yet collected. The term is used most commonly in the context of business consulting for small Christian schools.

Schedule 13D A form that an individual or organization must file with the SEC declaring the purchase of 5% or more of a publicly-traded company's voting stock. The Schedule 13D form must be filed within 10 days of such a transaction. When an investor buys a large amount of voting stock, it gives him/her a degree of control over the company's operations and may be a harbinger of a takeover attempt. Schedule 13D exists to promote transparency in the market and to comply with Rule 13D.

Schedule 13E-3 A form that a company must file with the SEC during a management buyout. That is, the schedule 13E-3 is filed when the senior management of a publicly-traded company buys all of the company's shares outstanding. A schedule 13E-3 is necessary because it stops trade on the company's stock and allows the company to operate without recourse to shareholders.

Schedule 13E-4 A form that a publicly-traded company formerly filed with the SEC when making a self-tender offer, a situation in which it offers to buy back its own stock directly from shareholders. It was replaced in 2000 with Schedule TO-I.

Schedule 14D-1 A form one must file with the SEC when making a tender offer for a publicly-traded company if the success of the tender offer will result in one holding more than 5% of that company. Schedule 14D-1 is intended to increase transparency in the market and makes a stealth hostile takeover much more difficult.

Schedule A A form in the United States on which a taxpayer reports itemized deductions. These expenses over the course of the year reduce one's income for purposes of reducing one's tax liability. Examples of expenses that may be reported on Schedule A include medical bills, business costs for a sole proprietorship, and so forth.

Schedule B An IRS form on which one lists all dividends and interest income over $400 per year. Schedule B helps one calculate the taxes one owes on these sources of income.

Schedule C A section of the bylaws for the NASD used to determine eligibility of an organization for membership. It became less relevant when the NASD merged with the NYSE to form FINRA.

Schedule D A form that a taxpayer sends to the IRS claiming all gains and losses from securities and other assets that may be subject to the capital gains tax. Part I of Schedule D includes all income listed on the investor's 1099-OID.

Schedule E A form one files with the IRS to report the revenues and expenses from leasing of real estate, activities from S-corporations, REMICs, trusts, or estates, partnerships, or royalties. For example, one may report rental payments from tenants as revenues, and report repairs and advertising as expenses.

Schedule F A form one files with the IRS to report the revenues and expenses from farming activities. For example, one may report payments for the sale of corn as revenues, and report repairs and wages paid to farmhands as expenses.

Schedule J A form one files with the IRS to calculate taxes due on farming or fishing businesses. One calculates this by averaging one's taxable income (or part of it) for each of the past three years.

Scheduled Cash Flows The debt service on a mortgage that is scheduled each month. That is, the scheduled cash flows are what the mortgage borrower must pay to the bank (or perhaps the holders of mortgage-backed securities) every month. The scheduled cash flows do not account for late payments or prepayments. See also: Amortization.

Scheduled Coverage Insurance coverage for the assets of the policyholder's choice. Scheduled coverage is tailored to the individual needs of the policyholder. As with all insurance, one must pay a premium to receive scheduled coverage.

Scheduled Floater An addendum to an insurance policy providing coverage for the assets of the policyholder's choice. A scheduled floater is tailored to the individual needs of the policyholder. As with all insurance, one must pay a premium to receive the coverage.

Scheduled Injury An injury specified in workers compensation law as having a certain period of time during which one receives disability payments. For example, a thumb injury may be a scheduled injury if the workers comp law specifies 15 weeks of disability payments.

Scheduled Policy An insurance policy providing coverage for the assets of the policyholder's choice. A scheduled policy is tailored to the individual needs of the policyholder. As with all insurance, one must pay a premium to receive the coverage.

Scheepslast An obsolete Dutch unit of weight roughly equivalent to 2,000 kilograms.

Schmir Yiddish for grease or smear. It is used as a slang term for bribery.

Schnitzeling Slang; the act or practice of making small trades. Schnitzeling may be associated with individual investors.

Schoinos An ancient Greek unit of length approximately equivalent to 7,397 meters.

Scholarship A reduction in tuition for an educational institution or program. Scholarships may be awarded for any number of reasons, including financial hardship, academic or professional achievement, or athletic ability. Students must often fulfill certain criteria both to be awarded a scholarship and to maintain it. For example, a student awarded an academic scholarship may be required to keep a high GPA.

Scholarship Search Services Any company, organization or system that searches for scholarships, grants, or other forms of financial aid for which a post-secondary student may be eligible. Students provide information such as GPA, academic achievements, ethnic background, and athletic achievements to the scholarship search service, and in turn are provided with a list of potential scholarships. More detailed consulting services may also be available.

School Code An identifying number that the U.S. Department of Education assigns to post-secondary education institutions for purposes of determining financial aid.

Scienter In law, knowledge of wrongness of an act or the danger of a situation. A person with scienter may be held legally liable in criminal or civil cases.

Scilling A coin that circulated in the Republic of Ireland between 1928 and 1993. It was equal in value to 1/20 of one Irish pound. See also: Shilling.

Scooby Snack A derogatory slang term for a small bonus or other token reward. For example, if an employee receives a $25 bottle of wine in lieu of the usual Christmas bonus, he may be said to have been given a Scooby snack. The term comes from the name of the treats given to Scooby-Doo, the cartoon dog.

Scoop 1. To buy, especially at a discount. See also: Poop and Scoop. **2.** Information, especially that which is not publicly known. A person who invests on a scoop may be guilty of insider trading.

Scope In business, the objectives and parameters of a project or department. Good management prevents a project from going beyond its scope, which may require more resources, take up more time, and lead to a less focused conclusion.

Scope Creep A slang term for the gradual extension of the goal or parameters of a project, especially if they are changed by a manager attempting to make himself/herself look good to his/her own managers.

Scorched Earth Policy An antitakeover measure in which a company sells many or all of its "good" or desirable assets and/or issues an extraordinary amount of debt.

A scorched earth policy is designed to make the company less attractive to potential acquirers. The obvious disadvantage to a scorched earth policy is the possibility that, even if the company remains independent, it may have acquired so many liabilities that it may not be able to maintain its operations easily. See also: Poison pill, Suicide pill.

Score In the United Kingdom, a slang term for 20 pounds.

Scotland Office A department of the British government responsible for the administration of devolution of power from the central government to the Scottish regional government. The department was created in 2003 but traces its origins to 1885.

Scots Drop An obsolete Scottish unit of weight approximately equivalent to 1.921 grams.

Scots Gallon An obsolete Scottish unit of liquid volume approximately equivalent to 13.638 liters.

Scots Mile An obsolete Scottish unit of length equivalent to 1,760 yards, with some minor regional variations.

Scots Ounce An obsolete Scottish unit of weight approximately equivalent to 31 grams.

Scots Pint An obsolete Scottish unit of liquid volume approximately equivalent to 1.696 liters. It was also called a joug.

Scots Pound An obsolete Scottish unit of weight approximately equivalent to 496 grams.

Scots Stone An obsolete Scottish unit of weight approximately equivalent to 7.936 kilograms.

Scott Sullivan An American accountant who, as CFO of WorldCom, managed one of the largest accounting frauds in U.S. history. Investors lost billions of dollars because of his actions. Sullivan received a five-year jail sentence and was released in 2009.

Scottish Ministers' Widows' Fund An insurance fund constituted in 1748 to take care of the widows of ministers in the Church of Scotland. Annual premiums were invested, and benefits were paid out of the gains on these investments. It was the first insurance fund to pay benefits out of investments rather than directly out of premiums.

SCR ISO 4217 code for the Seychelles rupee. Introduced in 1914, it initially circulated alongside the Mauritian rupee, the previous currency. For a long time, it was pegged to a currency basket consisting of euros, British pounds, and U.S. dollars. It began to float in November 2008 and devalued considerably.

Screen Actors Guild A labor union for American film and television actors. It lobbies and negotiates contracts for better pay and working conditions; it also advocates for members in the event of a labor dispute. It was established in 1933 and is based in and Los Angeles. It is affiliated with the AFL-CIO.

Screen Stocks To investigate stocks for potential investment according to a predetermined set of criteria. For example, an investor may screen stocks according to the lowest price, the most market capitalization, the most favorable price-earnings ratio, or any number of other variables. One may also combine criteria while screening stocks. The process is designed to help one make the best investment decisions, and is often accomplished with the help of a computer.

Screpall An obsolete Irish unit of weight approximately equivalent to 1.2 grams.

Scrip 1. A private sector substitute for currency. Historically, scrip was used in logging and mining communities dominated by a single company, and employees had to buy goods from the company store. Presently, it is more closely associated with gift certificates, gift cards, and re-loadable debit cards. Militaries also occasionally pay soldiers in scrip when they are on deployment. In Australia, buyout offers including stock in place of or in addition to cash are known as scrip bids. See also: Money. **2.** An IOU from a publicly-traded company that is short on cash. Such a company pays dividends in scrip until it resolves its liquidity problems.

Scrip Bid In Australia, a term for a buyout offer of a company made in stock instead of or in addition to cash. Scrip bids may be advantageous, as stock is taxed at a capital gains rate, which is lower, and losses on the stock may be used to offset other gains, reducing one's tax liability.

Scrip Dividend An IOU from a publicly-traded company that is short on cash. Such a company pays dividends in scrip until it resolves its liquidity problems.

Scripophilist A person who collects expired or antique bond and stock certificates. These certificates can be valuable to the study of economic history and often have value themselves as collectibles.

Scripophily The hobby or practice of collecting expired or antique bond and stock certificates. These certificates can be valuable to the study of economic history and often have value themselves as collectibles.

Scrub A slightly disrespectful term for a new or inexperienced employee.

Scruple A unit of weight equivalent to 1/24th of one ounce.

Scrupulum 1. An ancient Roman unit of area approximately equivalent to 8.76 square meters. It was also called decempeda quadrata. **2.** An ancient Roman unit of weight approximately equivalent to 1.14 grams.

Scumming A situation in which a part of a printing plate not intended for ink takes on ink anyway. The ink is transferred to paper by accident. Printers seek to avoid scumming.

SD 1. ISO 3166-1 alpha-2 code for the Republic of Sudan. This is the code used in international transactions to and from Sudanese bank accounts. **2.** ISO 3166-2 geocode for Sudan. This is used as an international standard for shipping to Sudan. Each state has its own code with the prefix "SD." For example, the code for the State of An-Nil is ISO 3166-2:SD-04.

SDD ISO 4217 code for the Sudanese dinar. It was introduced in 1992, replacing the first Sudanese pound. It was a highly volatile currency throughout its history and was replaced by the second Sudanese pound in 2007.

SDG ISO 4217 code for the second Sudanese pound. It was issued in 2007 as part of a peace agreement between northern and southern Sudan. It replaced the Sudanese dinar (in the north) and the first Sudanese pound (in the south).

SDN GOST 7.67 Latin three-letter geocode for Sudan. The code is used for transactions to and from Sudanese bank accounts and for international shipping to Sudan. As with all GOST 7.67 codes, it is used primarily in Cyrillic alphabets.

SDP ISO 4217 code for the first Sudanese pound. It was introduced in 1956, replacing the Egyptian pound. The pound was itself replaced by the Sudanese dinar in 1992, but it continued to circulate in Southern Sudan and the dinar was used only in the North. Both currencies were replaced by the second Sudanese pound in 2007.

Se 1. An ancient Sumerian unit of length approximately equivalent to 0.0025 meters. **2.** An ancient Sumerian unit of weight approximately equivalent to 50 milligrams.

Searah An ancient Hebrew unit of area approximately equivalent to nine square millimeters.

Seasonal Unemployment Unemployment due to lack of demand during certain times of the year. For example, an agricultural worker may not be needed between the harvest and the next planting. Likewise, a restaurant in a resort town may reduce the number of wait staff after the busy season is over. Seasonal unemployment may lead some to pursue another career in the off-season or may lead others to a different place to look for jobs. See also: Migrant worker.

Seasonal Variation A situation in which a company has better sales in certain times of the year than in other times. For example, a swimwear company likely has better sales in the summer, and toy companies likely perform better in the period preceding Christmas. Sales forecasts and reports often adjust to account for seasonal variation, and the companies often change the amount of inventory they carry to ensure that they are able to meet demand at the lowest cost.

Seasonally Adjusted Annual Rate A rate used to reduce seasonal noise on a company's sales or revenue information. For example, many retail companies tend to have higher sales figures at the end of the calendar year because of the holiday season. Comparing the raw data may make the company's sales look better than they are. The SAAR is designed to even out that trend. It is calculated by taking the raw annual rate for a given month and dividing by a seasonality factor.

Seasoned 1. Of or relating to a security that has been traded long enough to establish a positive reputation for liquidity and trade volume. Seasoned securities tend to have stable prices and meet with success of the secondary market. **2.** Any euromarket security that has been traded for 40 days or longer. SEC regulations do not allow certain American investors to trade in euromarket securities before they have been traded for at least 40 days.

Seasoned Issue An issue of a security that has been traded long enough to establish a positive reputation for liquidity and trade volume. Seasoned issues tend to have relatively stable prices and meet with success on the secondary market.

Seasoned Loan A loan that has been out for at least a year in which the borrower has a good payment history. This is considered a sign that the loan is unlikely to default. They may therefore command higher prices on the secondary market.

Seasoned New Issue 1. See: Seasoned issue. **2.** See: Secondary issue.

Seasoned Securities A security that has been traded long enough to establish a positive reputation for liquidity and trade volume. Seasoned securities tend to have stable prices and meet with success on the secondary market.

Seat An individual or firm's right to trade on an exchange floor. Seats are bought and sold according to an individual's or firm's needs and desires, and they can be very expensive. Most exchanges have a set number of seats; for example, on the New York Stock Exchange there are 1366 seats, which may cost up to $1 million each. Most exchanges only recognize individual members; member firms are usually informal terms for broker-dealer firms that have at least one principal officer with a seat on an exchange. A seat is also called a membership.

Seated Liberty Dime A silver coin minted by the United States between 1836 and 1891. It was worth 1/10 of one dollar. It featured a portrait of Lady Liberty seated on a throne.

Seated Liberty Dollar A $1 silver coin minted by the United States between 1836 and 1873. It featured a portrait of Lady Liberty seated on a throne.

Seated Liberty Half Dime A silver coin minted by the United States between 1836 and 1891. It was worth 1/20 of one dollar. It featured a portrait of Lady Liberty seated on a throne.

Seated Liberty Half Dollar A silver coin minted by the United States between 1836 and 1891. It was worth 1/2 of one dollar. It featured a portrait of Lady Liberty seated on a throne.

Seated Liberty Quarter A silver coin minted by the United States between 1836 and 1891. It was worth 1/4 of one dollar. It featured a portrait of Lady Liberty seated on a throne.

Seattle Ministerial A meeting of the World Trade Organization that occurred over several days in November and early December 1999. It exposed disagreements between the developed world and developing countries on trade policy. It is also noted for the sometimes violent conflicts between anti-globalization activists and law enforcement.

SEC Fee A nominal fee the SEC levies on equity transactions on an exchange. Created by the Securities Exchange Act of 1934, the fee was 1% of 1/300 of the dollar amount of the transaction until 2007. Since then, the fee is 1% of 1/800 of the dollar amount. The fee is collected by the brokerages involved in a transaction; these brokerages forward the fees to the SEC. The fees help pay for the SEC's operating expenses. It is important to note that debt instruments are not assessed this fee.

SEC Release IA-1092 A protocol by the SEC providing a uniform set of interpretations on how state and federal authorities will deal with similar issues in their respective jurisdictions. This was published to reduce uncertainty and increase regularity in financial regulation. SEC Release IA-1092 was released in 1987.

SEC Yield The yield on a bond fund calculated by a formula issued by the SEC. The SEC yield is calculated by taking the interest each share in the fund earns for a 30 day period and subtracting all expenses and sales charges the fund's managers assess. Each bond fund in the United States must publish its SEC yield. The SEC yield is used to compare the yields on different bond funds. It is also called the standardized yield.

Second 1. See: Second mortgage. **2.** See: Second round.

Second Cruzeiro The currency of Brazil between 1967 and 1986. It replaced the first cruzeiro at a rate of one new cruzeiro to 1,000 old cruzeiro. It was subject to high inflation and it was replaced by the cruzado.

Second Fundamental Welfare Theorem The theory that one can achieve any desired Pareto efficient outcome by a one-time redistribution of wealth, followed by a reversion to the invisible hand of the market. Pareto efficiency is the allocation of resources such that one cannot improve the lot of one economic actor without hurting the lot of another economic actor.

Second Mortgage A mortgage secured by a property lien that is subordinate to another mortgage on the same property. One may take out a second mortgage to pay for home repairs or for any number of other reasons. A second mortgage carries a higher interest rate than a primary mortgage because the lien is less secure.

Second Round Any type of financing that occurs after a company has sufficient revenue or profits to no longer be considered a start-up but is not yet fully established. A second round may be an IPO or debt issue, but it usually refers to a venture capital arrangement.

Second Section Stocks in medium-sized companies listed on the Tokyo Stock Exchange. There are far fewer second section stocks on the Tokyo exchange than first section stocks. See also: Mothers.

Second State Pension A voluntary state pension scheme available to citizens of the United Kingdom. It grants higher payments to pensioners following retirement in exchange for higher National Insurance contributions. Payments are based on average earnings over a pensioner's career. It was created in 2002 to replace the State Earnings-Related Pension Scheme, which offered lower benefits to lower and middle income pensioners.

Second Sudanese Pound The currency of Sudan. It was issued in 2007, replacing both the first pound and the Sudanese dinar, which each circulated in different parts of the country.

Second Zimbabwean Dollar The former currency of Zimbabwe. It was issued in 2006, replacing the first Zimbabwean dollar at a ratio of 1,000 to one. Its introduction was intended to slow inflation in Zimbabwe, but this attempt failed and the third Zimbabwean dollar was introduced in 2008.

Secondary Bank 1. A bank that provides financing for purchases that require repayment on an installment plan. **2.** A bank that provides financing to other banks, rather than to businesses or individuals.

Secondary Distribution The sale of a security that has already been issued. Generally speaking, it refers to the sale of a security by a private investor (usually a corporation) to a member of the general public. It is also called a secondary offering. See also: Secondary market.

Secondary Issue 1. The sale of a security that has already been issued. Generally speaking, it refers to any sale of a security other than transactions at the initial public offering, in the case of a stock, or the issuance, in the case of a bond. **2.** The procedure followed when a firm attempts to sell more than 10,000 stocks or $200,000 worth of bonds that have previously been issued. See also: Seasoned stocks, Block.

Secondary Market The market for all investors in a security, except for the first ones to whom a new issue of a security is sold. The secondary market consists of all sellers and buyers, except for the issuer and the first group of investors who bought the issue. The secondary market is often less volatile than the primary market because it is easier to determine the underlying value of a security after it has already begun trading. Nearly all trading of a security occurs on the secondary market.

Secondary Mortgage Market The market for buying and selling mortgages. After a bank makes a mortgage loan to a client, it may choose to sell the loan to another party, which reduces its risk of non-payment; this transaction is based on the same concept as accounts receivable financing. Often, these mortgages are re-packaged together as mortgage-backed securities.

Secondary Public Offering Any issue of stock after the initial public offering. That is, in a secondary public offering, a company sells shares that it has not previously issued. This increases the number of shares outstanding, which can (though does not always) lead to dilution of share value. A secondary public offering occurs on the primary market and therefore should not be confused with secondary market transactions.

Secondary Stock Any stock issued by a publicly-traded company other than a blue chip company. Secondary stocks are issued by less well-established and less well-known companies; as a result, they carry higher risk than blue chip stocks. However, they can have higher growth potential. Secondary stocks tend to have a smaller market capitalization, often under $1 billion.

Secondary Trade Any trade of a security other than the first trade. Prices for secondary trades are often less volatile than those that occur on the primary market because it is easier to determine the underlying value of a security after it has already begun trading. Nearly all trades are secondary trades.

Secondary Trend A situation in which a security, or the broader market, temporarily moves in the opposite direction from where it usually moves. For example, if a market is trending downward but moves upward for a brief period of time, this upward movement is said to be a secondary trend. Secondary trends are inevitable, but when trends are forming it is difficult or impossible to determine whether one is primary or secondary.

Second-Class Mail In the United States, the mail rate given to newspapers and magazines. To qualify for a second-class mail rate, the periodical must be at least quarterly and must not have advertising as its primary goal. On time delivery of second-class mail is given lower priority than first-class mail, which includes all mail and correspondence weighing less than 13 ounces.

Second-Preferred Stock A preferred stock with a guaranteed dividend that, in the event of liquidation, ranks below another issue of preferred stock. That is, if the company issuing the second preferred stock liquidates itself, a designated issued of preferred stock must have all back dividends paid before the holders of second preferred stock receive anything. However, second preferred stock ranks above all common stock. See also: Absolute priority rule.

Second-Tier Stock A stock investors favor less than others. This results in the price of a second-tier stock being lower, sometimes significantly so. This may occur for a number of reasons: for example, the stock may have lower market capitalization. Alternatively, it may simply trade on a less prestigious exchange. The specific stocks in a second-tier change as investors' expectations change. See also: Tiered market, Two-tier market.

Second-to-Die Insurance An insurance policy that covers a married couple and pays the death benefit on the death of the second spouse. Generally speaking, the death benefit is intended to cover the estate tax. Because the second spouse does not owe the estate tax upon the death of the first spouse, second to die insurance helps the heirs of the married couple rather than either the husband or the wife. It is also called survivorship life insurance or dual-life insurance.

Secret Reserve The amount by which shareholder equity in a company exceeds the amount claimed on its financial statements. Secret reserves arise when a company overstates its liabilities or understates its assets, usually because its accounting practices depart from GAAP. In such cases, the company must declare that its accounting is different from that of most other companies. The secret reserve may eventually be converted to cash and distributed to shareholders. It is also called the hidden reserve.

Secretariat The administrative headquarters of an organization. The secretariat maintains all paperwork and other documents for the organization's operations. It may also be where the organization conducts its meetings. The word is most commonly applied to political, especially international, organizations.

Secretary of Agriculture The head of the U.S. Department of Agriculture, which is charged with assisting farmers and ranchers. The secretary is responsible for food inspections, rural development (for example, by providing mortgages outside cities), and some agricultural research. He or she is appointed by the president of the United States and confirmed by the Senate.

Secretary of Commerce The head of the U.S. federal government department charged with encouraging economic growth. The secretary is responsible for issuing patents, setting standards for companies and sectors, and gathering data on the state of the American economy. He or she is appointed by the president of the United States and confirmed by the Senate.

Secretary of Defense The head of the U.S. Department of Defense, which is charged with supervising the military and conducting war. The secretary oversees military training and education and advises the president on military policy. He or she is appointed by the president of the United States and confirmed by the Senate.

Secretary of Energy The head of the department of the U.S. federal government charged with implementing American energy policy. The secretary promotes domestic energy production, conducts research, and sets standards for safe handling of nuclear materials. He or she is appointed by the president of the United States and confirmed by the Senate.

Secretary of Housing and Urban Development The head of the U.S. federal government department charged with promoting homeownership. He or she oversees the Federal Housing Administration and has a relationship with Fannie Mae and Freddie Mac. The secretary also provides vouchers to make rent more affordable and provides grants for community development. He or she is appointed by the president of the United States and confirmed by the Senate.

Secretary of Labor The head of the U.S. federal government department charged with enforcement of laws regulating workplace conditions, minimum wages, and other federal labor laws. The secretary is also responsible for the administration of unemployment insurance and collection of some economic statistics, particularly regarding unemployment. He or she is appointed by the president of the United States and confirmed by the Senate.

Secretary of State The head of the U.S. federal government department charged with conducting foreign relations. The secretary is responsible for advising the president on foreign policy, assisting American businesses abroad, and overseeing U.S. embassies. He or she is appointed by the president of the United States and confirmed by the Senate.

Secretary of State for Business, Enterprise and Regulatory Reform A former official of the British government responsible for business regulation, enforcement of employment law, promotion of business growth and entrepreneurship, and economic growth in sub-national regions. The position ceased to exist when the Department for Business, Enterprise and Regulatory Reform became part of the Department of Business, Innovation and Skills.

Secretary of State for Business, Innovation and Skills The head of the Department of Business, Innovation and Skills, which is the cabinet department of the British government responsible for advising the government and implementing law related to corporate governance, business regulation, intellectual property, international trade, and other business issues. For example, he/she oversees the issue of export licenses. The secretary is appointed by the monarch on the advice of the prime minister.

Secretary of State for Communities and Local Government The head of the Department of Communities and Local Government, which is a department of the British government responsible for administration of municipalities in England (but not elsewhere in the United Kingdom). He/she is responsible for a wide variety of matters, including issues such as fire services, building regulations, and urban planning. The secretary is appointed by the monarch on the advice of the prime minister.

Secretary of State for Culture, Media and Sport The head of the Department of Culture, Media and Sport, which is the department of the British government responsible for Internet and media regulation in the United Kingdom and for the promotion of the arts, sports, and creative economic sectors in England alone. The secretary is appointed by the monarch on the advice of the prime minister.

Secretary of State for Defence The head of the Ministry of Defence, which is a department of the British government responsible for national defense and management of the British Armed Forces. He/she advises the government on defense policy and coordinates the actions of the Royal Navy, the British Army, and the Royal Air Force. The secretary is appointed by the monarch on the advice of the prime minister.

Secretary of State for Education The head of HM Department of Education, which is the department of the British government responsible for schools and other services for children up to the age of 19. He/she advises the government on education policy. The secretary is appointed by the monarch on the advice of the prime minister.

Secretary of State for Energy and Climate Change The head of the Department of Energy and Climate Change, who is responsible for advising and managing government energy policy. For example, he/she oversees efforts to gradually decrease the United Kingdom's reliance on fossil fuels. The secretary is appointed by the monarch on the advice of the prime minister.

Secretary of State for Environment, Food and Rural Affairs The head of the Department for Environment, Food and Rural Affairs, which is the department of the British government responsible for regulation of agriculture and fishing, enforcement of safety standards in food, and protection of the environment. He/she advises and enforces government policy on these and similar issues. The secretary is appointed by the monarch on the advice of the prime minister.

Secretary of State for Foreign and Commonwealth Affairs The head of the British Foreign and Commonwealth Office. He/she advises the government on foreign policy and matters related to the Commonwealth of Nations (which primarily consists of former territories of the British Empire). He/she is also responsible for British overseas territories. The foreign secretary is appointed by the monarch on the advice of the prime minister.

Secretary of State for Health The head of HM Department of Health, a department of the British government responsible for managing and advising government health policy. Most importantly, he/she administrates the National Health Service, the comprehensive government medical program, in England (though not elsewhere in the United Kingdom). The secretary is appointed by the monarch on the advice of the prime minister.

Secretary of State for Innovation, Universities and Skills A former official of the British government responsible for the administration of universities, adult learning programs, and other public bodies (such as the Medical Research Council) intended to promote education. The position ceased to exist when the Department for Innovation, Universities and Skills became part of the Department of Business, Innovation and Skills.

Secretary of State for International Development The head of the Department for International Development, which is the department of the British government responsible for the administration of foreign aid. He/she oversees donations of money and the sponsorship of programs all over the world to assist in international development. The secretary is appointed by the monarch on the advice of the prime minister.

Secretary of State for Justice The head of HM Ministry of Justice. He/she is responsible for administering the British (and in some cases only the English and Welsh) justice system. He/she oversees the prosecution of criminal cases, appeals of immigration decisions, civil liberty issues, sentencing and penalty laws, and other similar issues. He/she also advises the government on matters relating to the British constitution. The secretary is appointed by the monarch on the advice of the prime minister. In practice, he/she is also lord chancellor of the United Kingdom.

Secretary of State for Northern Ireland The head of the Northern Ireland Office, which is the department of the British government responsible for the administration of devolution of power from the central government to the Northern Irish regional government. He/she oversees national security, elections, and similar matters in Northern Ireland. The secretary is appointed by the monarch on the advice of the prime minister.

Secretary of State for Scotland The head of the Scotland Office, which is the department of the British government responsible for the administration of devolution of power from the central government to the Scottish regional government. He/she represents Scottish interests in the government. The secretary is appointed by the monarch on the advice of the prime minister.

Secretary of State for Transport The head of the Department for Transport, which is the department of the British government responsible for highway maintenance, motor vehicle registration, the coastguard, and other similar issues. He/she advises the government on transportation issues. The secretary is appointed by the monarch on the advice of the prime minister.

Secretary of State for Wales The head of the Wales Office, which is the department of the British government responsible for the administration of devolution of power from the central government to the Welsh regional government. He/she represents Welsh interests in the government. The secretary is appointed by the monarch on the advice of the prime minister.

Secretary of State for Work and Pensions The head of the Department for Work and Pensions, a department of the British government responsible for administration of welfare policy, British Social Security, state pensions, and similar matters. Because the secretary oversees most government payments to citizens, he/she administers the largest budget of any department in the U.K. He/she is appointed by the monarch on the advice of the prime minister.

Secretary of State of the Home Department The head of the Home Office. He/she advises the government on immigration, police, and other matters related to law enforcement. The secretary is appointed by the monarch on the advice of the prime minister.

Secretary of the Interior The head of the U.S. federal government department charged with overseeing national parks and most other land owned by the federal government. The secretary is also responsible for conserving wildlife and managing U.S. relations with Native Americans. He or she is appointed by the president of the United States and confirmed by the Senate.

Secretary of the Treasury In the United States, the head of the Department of the Treasury, which is responsible for the printing of money, the collection of taxes, the regulation of banks and the management of public debt. He/she is appointed by the president with the consent of the Senate.

Secretary of Transportation The head of the U.S. federal government department that oversees aviation, federal highways, shipping, and railroads. He or she is appointed by the president of the United States and confirmed by the Senate.

Secretary of Veterans Affairs The head of the U.S. federal government department charged with serving the interests of American military veterans. Among other things, the secretary is responsible for guaranteeing mortgages borrowed by veterans to increase veteran homeownership. He or she is appointed by the president of the United States and confirmed by the Senate.

Section 1031 A section of the Internal Revenue Code that allows for the deferral of capital gains taxes on the exchange of two assets, of like kind even if of different quality, provided that the assets are used for a business purpose. Under Section 1031, the goods exchanged are not assessed capital gains taxes, or more properly, capital gains taxes are deferred until an asset is resold with no intention of reinvestment. Section 1031 also allows one to sell an asset with the intention to use the proceeds to buy a similar asset. For example, if a farmer sells his farm and uses the money to buy another farm, capital gains taxes are likely deferred on the money he made on the sale of the first farm. The same would be true if the he traded a farm for a farm. Stocks and bonds are expressly excluded from this preferential treatment.

Section 1035 Exchange The tax-exempt exchange of two annuities or life insurance policies. The annuities exchanged are not assessed capital gains or any other taxes. Section 1035 exchanges allow a policyholder to avoid taxes that would have been levied on the first annuity or policy as long as the second is of equal or greater cost. The IRS only recognizes a Section 1035 exchange as such if the annuities or policies are directly exchanged. Selling one and buying another, for example, does not count.

Section 1245 A section of the IRS tax code indicating that any depreciable property that is sold for more than the depreciated value qualifies for capital gains taxation rather than income taxation. Equally importantly, Section 1245 qualifies this type of property for favorable capital gains treatment: sellers pay less in capital gain tax than they otherwise would on this property. Section 1245 applies to real, personal, and intangible property so long as it can be depreciated and amortized. See also: Accounting.

Section 1250 A section of the Internal Revenue Code that the IRS uses to maximize tax revenue from depreciating assets by requiring the profit on the sale of a depreciating asset to be reported as ordinary income rather than capital gain. Because capital gains are taxed at a lower rate than most ordinary income, the IRS uses Section 1250 to make up for some of the tax revenue lost in the depreciating asset. This is called recapture of depreciation; it is assessed if the assets are sold for a price higher than their depreciated value. For example, suppose one buys a computer for $700 and, after a year, it depreciates to $600. If one then sells the computer for $650, one has recaptured $50 worth of depreciation. This $50 is taxed as ordinary income.

Section 1256 Contracts Investments that fall under Section 1256 of the U.S. Tax Code, namely, any regulated futures contract, any foreign currency contract, any non-equity option, any dealer equity option, and any dealer securities futures contract. Section 1256 contracts are treated differently from other securities for tax purposes. Specifically, rather than waiting to tax them until they are sold, Section 1256 contracts are treated as if they were sold at market value on the last day of the tax year. This means that one may be liable for capital gains taxes on a Section 1256 contracts even though the positions are still open. See also: Form 6781.

Section 179 An alternative to depreciation, which is a way of deducting expenses gradually over an asset's useful life. Under Section 179, one may deduct the entire cost of the certain assets in the year they were purchased (or put into service). One may not use Section 179 for certain assets, notably real estate.

Section 179 Property Real estate or personal property purchased specifically for investment or business purposes in the United States. Expenses on Section 179 property are tax deductible up to a certain level, which changes each year. However, one must declare that such property should be given Section 179 tax treatment by filing Form 4562.

Section 31 Fee A fee the SEC charges to register and trade securities. Each transaction of a registered security incurs a small Section 31 fee, which is a tiny portion of 1% of the value of the transaction. While the fee is technically levied on FINRA and other self-regulatory organizations, they pass it on to individual investors.

Section 423 A section of the Internal Revenue Code governing the taxation of an employee stock purchase plan (ESPP). Under an ESPP, a company allows certain employees to buy its stock at a discount from fair market value. According to Section 423, an employee who holds stock purchased under an ESPP for at least two years does not have to treat the discount as income and therefore does not have to pay taxes on it. Stocks held for this long are called "qualified" because they qualify for favorable tax treatment under Section 423.

Section 482 A section of the U.S. Tax Code allowing the IRS to allocate assets, income, deductions, and so forth between different branches of the same company or between different companies controlled by the same interests. That is, the IRS may treat these branches or companies as one branch or one company for tax purposes. This section exists to reduce tax evasion by preventing a company from hiding its taxable income in a subsidiary or a separate company.

Section 521 A section of the Internal Revenue Code in the United States exempting cooperatives of farmers, fruit growers, and similar person from taxation. These cooperatives must file Form 1028 to apply for this exemption.

Section 83(b) Election When one receives restricted stock, a decision to pay taxes on the value of the stock in the year and value at which it is received, rather than when it vests. Many executives receive restricted stock as part of their compensation. It may vest years later when the stock is trading much higher. If one does not make a Section 83(b) election, one must pay taxes on the stock when it vests, which can result in a much higher tax rate. A Section 83(b) election, on the other hand, means that the stock is treated as if it vests immediately, which results in higher taxes in the short-term but possibly much lower taxes in the long-term. A Section 83(b) election must take place within 30 days of receiving the stock.

Sectoare In Romania, a political subdivision for a quarter or sector within Bucharest, the capital.

Sector A set of securities or individual companies that are similar to each other. For example, all automotive companies in the United States are said to belong to the American automotive sector. See also: Industry.

Sector Allocation The act or practice of including securities in different industries in one's portfolio. This is done to reduce systemic risk. For example, if one includes both Industry A and Industry B stocks in one's portfolio, and most Industry A companies go bankrupt, this will not necessarily affect Industry B stocks. Industry allocation thus increases the possibility of making a profit, or at least avoiding a loss. This may also reduce the expected return on a portfolio, but it depends on the level and type of diversification. In general, the broader the industry allocation, the less risk and the less return. See also: Horizontal diversification, Vertical diversification.

Sector Analyst A person who examines information related to a single sector of the economy to determine what the information indicates about a company, situation, or anything else in that sector. For example, a sector analyst may be an expert in oil but know comparatively little about trading in other areas. Sector analysts are sought for their expertise in their fields.

Sector autonomo In Guinea-Bissau, a political subdivision for the capital city of Bissau.

Sector Equity Fund A mutual fund or other fund that invests predominantly or exclusively in stocks in a single industry or sector. For example, a sector equity fund may invest only in energy companies, or, even more narrowly, only in natural gas

companies. Sector equity funds perform well when their industries perform well, but they are risky because there is little attempt at diversification.

Sector Fund A mutual fund or other fund that invests predominantly or exclusively in a single industry or sector. For example, a sector fund may invest only in energy companies, or, even more narrowly, only in natural gas companies. Sector funds perform well when their industries perform well, but they are risky because there is no attempt at diversification. A sector fund is also called a specialized market fund.

Sector Neutral Index Fund A mutual fund that tracks an index of multiple sectors where the fund maintains the same ratio of sectors with respect to the index, but actively manages the individual securities within each sector. For example, suppose an index consists of stocks where 25% of the companies are in manufacturing, 25% in retail, and 50% in financial services. The money managers of a sector neutral index fund will see to it that the fund consists 25% of manufacturing stocks, 25% of retail, and 50% of financial services. However, the individual stocks within each of those sectors in the fund will change from time to time. A sector neutral index fund seeks to have a higher return than the benchmark index. See also: Enhanced indexing.

Sector Rotation An investment strategy in which a portfolio overweights or underweights certain sectors in accordance with expected performance. Sector rotation is a form of active investment management; the portfolio manager observes market trends and alters the composition of the portfolio in order to earn the highest possible return. Sector rotation is fairly high risk, as a portfolio's systematic overweighting and underweighting means that is not efficiently diversified. See also: Markowitz portfolio theory.

Secular Market A market as defined by its overarching, long-term trends. Generally, a secular market refers to trends over a period of five or more years. A secular market may be bullish or bearish, and, in market analysis, takes precedence over opposite, short-term trends that happen within the secular market. For example, the Great Depression in the United States lasted from 1929 until World War II (certainly a bearish secular market). Even though some years saw significant GDP growth (including 14.2% growth in 1936), this did not prevent the secular market from being bearish. Thus, a secular market describes general trends in the market without regard for anomalous trends in the interim. See also: Cyclical market.

Secured Bond A bond with collateral. That is, the issuer pledges a property or other asset to the bondholders and states that they may take ownership if the issuer defaults. For example, a municipality may secure a bond with future receipts on property taxes. Likewise, a company may secure its bonds with a factory. Secured bonds carry less risk than unsecured bonds and therefore have lower coupon rates, which reduces the issuer's borrowing costs. All secured bonds must be repaid before any unsecured bonds are repaid.

Secured Credit Card A credit card with a credit limit that is at least partially collateralized by funds in a special savings account. That is, a cardholder places a certain amount of money into an account with the credit card company, and this is used to protect the company from the cardholder's default. Depending on the cardholder's credit history, he/she may be required to place anywhere from 50% to 100% of the credit limit into the savings account. These funds still belong to the cardholder, and he/she may retrieve it if he/she pays off or cancels the secured card. Because these reduce the risk to the credit card company, it may charge a lower interest rate. Secured cards are particularly useful for persons with bad credit or little credit history.

Secured Creditor One who is owed a collateralized debt. A secured creditor has a lien or collateral on the debt, depending on the nature of the goods. In the event of bankruptcy in the United States, a general creditor has a right to repossess the property if the debt is not paid, especially in case of bankruptcy. In Chapter 7 bankruptcy, secured creditors are usually allowed to repossess the property even if the debt is discharged. The creditor may waive this right if the debtor reaffirms the debt, that is, signs a statement indicating that the debt still exists. See also: General creditor.

Secured Debt A debt on which payment is guaranteed by an asset or lien. This means that a secured debt has collateral; if the debtordoes not repay the debt in due course, the creditor has the legal right to take possession of the collateral and resell it to recover losses. In case of bankruptcy, the creditor is considered a secured creditor, which means the creditor receives proceeds from the sale of the collateral to satisfy the debt. If the collateral is insufficient, all secured creditors must have their debts satisfied before any unsecured creditors receive any funds.

Secured Lease Obligation Bond A debt security that is secured by a lease on an asset. That is, the revenue the issuer obtains from the lease guarantees payment on the bond. It is important to note that only the lease (or a lease coupled with a lien on the asset) secures the bond. This is a common financing tool for electric companies building power stations.

Secured Loan A loan with collateral. That is, the borrower pledges a property or other asset to the creditor and states that the creditor may take ownership if the borrower defaults on the loan. Sometimes the creditor even takes possession of the collateral, though this is not always the case. A common example of a secured loan is a mortgage, in which the lender has the right to take ownership of the real estate purchased with the mortgage if the property owner does not make payments in a timely manner. In corporate finance, all secured loans must be repaid before any unsecured loans are repaid.

Secured Note A boilerplate lending agreement. The secured note states the amount to be borrowed, the interest rate, and the time until the loan is due.

Securities & Exchange Commission An agency of the U.S. Government that serves at the primary regulator of the securities trade. It attempts to ensure that all trades are fair, and that no price manipulation or insider trading occurs. Additionally, the SEC promotes full disclosure and monitors mergers and acquisitions to ensure continued competitiveness. It works with several self-regulatory organizations, notably FINRA, to enforce its regulations. Most securities offered through interstate commerce must be registered with the SEC. The SEC was created in 1934 as part of the New Deal to prevent excessive speculation. It is overseen by five commissioners, who are appointed by the President of the United States upon confirmation by the Senate. No more than three commissioners may belong to the same political party.

Securities Act of 1933 Legislation in the United States that formed the first major federal regulation of the securities trade. Among other provisions, it requires companies traded under interstate commerce to register with the federal government and disclose their financial statements and other activities. Before 1934, registration and disclosure were made with the Federal Trade Commission but, following the creation of the Securities & Exchange Commission, this changed. See also: New Deal.

Securities Acts Amendments of 1975 Legislation in the United States that attempted to integrate American markets by encouraging the creation of nationwide settlement and clearing system, as well as a national market.

Securities and Exchange Board of India An agency of the Indian Government that serves at the primary regulator of the securities trade. It drafts regulations under the parameters of its jurisdiction, creates rules to enforce these regulations, and investigates potential abuses. SEBI was created in 1988 and became a permanent body in 1992 under the SEBI Act 1992. It is overseen by eight members.

Securities and Exchange Commission of Brazil Also called the Comissao de Valores Mobiliarios or the CVM. An agency of the Brazilian government that serves as the primary regulator of the securities trade. It attempts to ensure that all trades are fair, and that no price manipulation or insider trading occurs. Additionally, the CVM promotes full disclosure and transparency to ensure competitiveness. It was established in 1976.

Securities and Investment Board The original name for the Financial Services Authority in the United Kingdom. It was established as the SIB in 1985. After a series of financial scandals in the early 1990s, pressure came to increase the scope of the SIB's authority. It changed its name to the FSA in 1997 and its powers were expanded by the Financial Services Act 2000.

Securities Exchange Act of 1934 Legislation in the United States that regulated broker-dealers and secondary trades on American stock exchanges. This Act also created the Securities and Exchange Commission to help it accomplish its goals. The act prohibited certain trades that would unfairly or dangerously manipulate prices. For example, the Act forbids churning, in which an investor makes both buy and sell orders through different brokers to create the impression of increased interest in the security and to raise the price. It was one of the most important regulatory laws that came out of the New Deal.

Securities Industry Association A defunct trade association for broker-dealers of taxable securities. The SIA set common practices for the industry, compiled statistics and other information, and lobbied governments. In 2006, the SIA formed the Securities Industry and Financial Markets Association in a merger with the Bond Market Association.

Securities Industry Automation Corporation Also called SIAC. On the New York Stock Exchange, AMEX, and affiliated exchanges, an organization that provides computer services. Consequently, SIAC runs DOT, which is a computerized order-entry system that sends smaller buy or sell orders to the appropriate specialist on the floor of a stock exchange, bypassing the floor broker. It also provides the Consolidated Quotation System and the Options Price Reporting Authority. The NYSE owns two-thirds of the SIAC, while AMEX owns the remainder.

Securities Industry Conference on Arbitration An organization set up in 1977 to arbitrate disputes between and within self-regulatory organizations. SICA was designed to avoid the need for courts because the process of lawsuit can often take very long. SICA sets its own procedures, known as a Uniform Arbitration Code, which it periodically revises. Various SROs are members of SICA and sponsor its activities.

Securities Information Center A branch of the SEC responsible for lost, stolen, and counterfeit securities. An investor who has lost securities or has had them stolen is required to report the incident to the Securities Information Center. The same applies to an investor who discovers counterfeit securities. It was established in 1977.

Securities Investor Protection Act of 1970 Legislation in the United States that established the Securities Investor Protection Corporation (SIPC). The SIPC insures investors in case their broker-dealer firms fail. In the event of failure of a broker-dealer firm, its clients are protected up to $500,000 of their total equity investments and up to $100,000 in cash. It also protects investors from fraud or misappropriation on the part of their broker-dealers. It is important to note that the SIPC does not protect against bad investments, nor does it cover any futures or commodity contracts. It is not a government entity; it is a non-profit organization to which most brokers and dealers registered with the SEC are required to belong.

Securities Investor Protection Corporation A not-for-profit organization mandated under American law to insure investors against the potential bankruptcy of a broker-dealer. If a broker or dealer goes bankrupt after a client has entrusted it with cash or securities, the SIPC will compensate the client up to $500,000 (or $100,000 if the client is owed only cash). All brokers, dealers, and exchanges registered with the

SEC are required to be members of the SIPC and fund its activities. It is important to note that the SIPC does not insure against losses by investors, only against the possibility of a broker-dealer being unable to conduct a transaction because of bankruptcy.

Securities Law Enforcement Remedies Act Legislation in the United States, enacted in 1990, that established additional civil penalties for officers and board members in publicly-traded companies deemed to be "unfit." The SEC was granted increased enforcement powers in order to carry out the provisions of the Act.

Securities Lending The act of loaning a stock, derivative, or other security to an investor or firm. Securities lending requires the borrower to put up collateral, whether cash, security, or a letter of credit. The completion of this transaction requires a securities lending agreement, which states, among other things, how long the loan lasts, what fee the lender receives, and the amount and type of collateral. Securities lending is important to short selling, in which an investor borrows securities in order to immediately sell them. The advantage of securities lending to the borrower is the fact that he/she may profit from shorting the securities; the advantage to the lender is the fee (and, if the borrower fails to repay, the collateral).

Securities Lending Agreement An agreement governing the loan of a stock, derivative, or other security to an investor. A securities lending agreement requires the borrower to put up collateral, such as cash, security, or a letter of credit. It also states how long the loan lasts, what fee the lender receives, and the amount and type of collateral. Securities lending agreements are important to short selling, in which an investor borrows securities in order to immediately sell them.

Securities Subsidiary A brokerage or other financial services company owned by a bank. A securities subsidiary deals in commercial paper, mortgage-backed securities and often stocks and bonds as well. Securities subsidiaries have become more popular in the United States since banks were deregulated in the 1980s and 1990s.

Securities Trade The sale of a security from one investor to another. The seller receives compensation in exchange for giving up ownership of a security. Securities trades may take place on an exchange or over-the-counter. The securities trade is regulated by special agencies in the appropriate jurisdiction; trade in the United States is regulated by the SEC, among other organizations.

Securities Transfer Association A professional organization of transfer agents in the United States and Canada. Transfer agents are responsible for smooth transfers in securities (e.g. issuing certificates reflecting changes in ownership); the STA is thus charged with providing a forum for the exchange of information that may prove useful to this business. For example, it publishes books and holds educational events for transfer agents. It also sponsors the Medallion Stamp Program, which seeks to protect investors from securities fraud. It is based in Hazlet, New Jersey.

Securitization The process by which a company packages its illiquid assets as a security. For example, when a company makes an initial public offering, it effectively packages the company's ownership into a certain number of stock certificates. Securities are backed by an asset, such as equity, or debt, such as a portion of a mortgage. Securitization allows a company access to greater funding to expand its operations or investments, or some other reason.

Securitized Mortgage A mortgage that is packaged into a mortgage-backed security (MBS). One mortgage may be securitized over several MBSs, and each MBS contains many securitized mortgages. A securitized mortgage gives the holder of the security, rather than the bank originating the loan, the right a claim on the principal and interest payments on that mortgage. Mortgages are securitized to remove them from a bank's balance sheet (which reduces risk) and to improve its cash flow.

Security A document; historically, a physical certificate but increasingly electronic, showing that one owns a portion of a publicly-traded company or is owed a portion of a debt issue. Securities are tradable. At their most basic, securities refer to stocks and bonds, but the term sometimes also refers to derivatives such as futures and options.

Security Analyst A person who researches and reports on the state of securities. That is, a securities analyst uses technical or fundamental signals to determine which securities are likely to be profitable and which are not. Analysts help persons and organizations in making investment decisions. See also: CFA.

Security Characteristic Line A line on a graph where one axis is the excess return on a security over the risk-free return and the other axis is the excess return of the market in general. The slope of the security characteristic line is its beta. See also: Markowitz portfolio theory.

Security Deposit 1. See: Maintenance Margin. **2.** An amount that a lessor, lender, seller or provider of a service requires up front to compensate for the risk that he will not receive payment or the agreement will be violated. For example, a landlord may require one month's rent as a security deposit just in case a tenant knocks a hole in the wall and leaves the landlord to pay for it. Generally speaking, if the agreement is followed, the one who pays the security deposit receives the money back. See also: Earnest Money.

Security Depository An organization where security certificates are stored until they are ready to be transferred at a later date to the holder or to another party.

Security Industry and Financial Markets Association Formerly known as the Public Securities Association, a professional organization for banks, broker-dealers, and other organizations that underwrite securities. It serves as a lobbying group and provides education and training to members and non-members. It maintains offices in New York, Washington DC, and London, with affiliated offices in Hong Kong and other locations.

Security Interest A creditor's legal right to take possession of certain property offered as security or collateral. For example, in a margin account, the brokerage making the margin loan may require its client to deposit some or all of the borrowed securities with the brokerage. The right of the brokerage to demand that is its security interest.

Security Market Line In Markowitz Portfolio Theory, a line on a chart representing the capital asset pricing model. The security market line plots risk versus expected return of the market. The security market line is a useful tool in determining whether a given security is undervalued and/or a market outperform. If a security plots the security market line, it indicates a higher expected return for a given level of risk than the market as a whole.

Security Market Plane A chart showing the relationship between the expected return on an investment and its beta, which is its risk relative to the market as a whole.

Security Plant Complex An organization in the Philippines that issues legal tender coins for general use. It was established in 1978 and is controlled by the Central Bank of the Philippines. It is based in Manila.

Security Selection The process by which one chooses the securities, derivatives, and other assets to include in a portfolio. In making securities selections, one considers the risk, the return, the ethical implications, and other factors affecting both of the individual securities and the portfolio as a whole. See also: Diversification.

Security Traders Association A trade association for individuals who trade in securities. Established in Chicago in 1934, the STA provides educational, informational, and social opportunities for members.

Security Valuation The process of determining how much a security is worth. Security valuation is highly subjective, but it is easiest when one is considering the value of tangible assets, level of debt, and other quantifiable data of the company issuing a security. For example, determining a company's earnings for the current year is easier than determining what the value of the company's brand recognition might be in 10 years. Valuation is important in fundamental analysis, the practitioners of which usually consider a company's earnings to be indicative of its value.

Security Valuation Model Any model used to estimate the appropriate price of a security. This helps investors make investment decisions on which securities are undervalued and are therefore good to buy and likewise, which are overvalued and good to sell. All security valuation models use a series of mathematical relationships to make their determinations. As with all things, some models are more accurate than others.

Seed Capital Money used for the initial market research and/or operations for a company. Seed money is vitally important because, without it, a company can hardly come into being, let alone become successful. It may come from a loan, and initial public offering, or from another source. For example, it is famously said that Ross Perot established Electronic Data Systems with $1,000 in personal savings; in this case, Perot's savings account contained his seed money. See also: Seed round.

Seehandlung The central bank of Prussia. During the hyperinflation under the Weimar Republic, it became notable for its corruption, including bribery and fraud. It was liquidated in 1983.

Seek a Market To look for a counterparty for a transaction. For example, a potential buyer seeks a market when he/she searches for a potential seller of the security he/she wishes to have.

Seer 1. An obsolete Sri Lankan unit of volume approximately equivalent to 1.024 liters. **2.** An obsolete unit of mass in India and elsewhere approximately equivalent to one kilogram. **3.** An obsolete unit of mass in Afghanistan approximately equivalent to seven kilograms.

Segmented Market A market that is isolated from other markets. Markets usually become segmented through government intervention; for example, a government can erect tariff barriers. However, a segmented market can occur because of distance, lack of available information, or other inefficiencies. A segmented market prevents the free flow of labor and capital. Economists dispute the extent if any to which segmented markets are harmful, though most agree that excessive segmentation is not desirable.

Segregated Fund An investment company in Canada that has features of a life insurance policy and a mutual fund. The investment company sells life insurance to policyholders, who have rights to all benefits, just like any other life insurance policy. It then uses the proceeds to buy securities, which it packages and sells as shares in a mutual fund. The two aspects of a segregated fund must be kept separate from each other, except in the manner described above.

Segregation The practice of broker-dealers keeping securities for which a client has paid in full separate from securities the client has purchased on margin as well as from securities used as collateral on a margin account. Rule 15c3-3 requires segregation of these securities.

Seigniorage The money a government generates when it prints more money. This usually is calculated as the difference between the face value of the money and the value of the bullion backing it.

Seir An obsolete Arabic unit of length approximately equivalent to 192 meters.

Seirei Shitei Toshi In Japan, a political subdivision for a city with a population of more than 500,000 people. Many of the functions of its associated prefecture are delegated to it.

Seisrech An obsolete Irish unit of area equivalent to 120 acres.

Seit A Burmese unit of volume approximately equivalent to 1.02 liters.

SEK ISO 4217 code for the Swedish krona. It was introduced in 1873 when it replaced the former currency at the beginning of the Scandinavian Monetary Union. After World War I, the Monetary Union ended, but the Swedish government kept the krona as its own currency. In 1995, Sweden committed to joining the eurozone at an indeterminate date. However, a 2003 referendum rejected this course of action.

Sela An ancient Hebrew unit of weight approximately equivalent to 17 grams.

Select Ten Portfolio A unit investment trust that seeks dividend income for unit holders. It accomplishes this by buying and holding the 10 stocks on the Dow Jones Industrial Average with the highest dividend yields for a period of one year. At the end of the year, the portfolio's managers reassess which stocks have the highest yields and adjust the portfolio accordingly.

Selected Dealer Agreement An agreement between the underwriters in a syndicate stating what rules the underwriters will follow as they place a new issue with investors. The selected dealer agreement is temporary because every syndicate is itself a temporary arrangement.

Selective Hedging The practice of making investments that reduce the risk to part of one's portfolio, but not the whole portfolio. Alternatively, selective hedging may involve making offsetting investments on the whole portfolio, but only at certain times. Selective hedging carries higher risk than other hedging strategies simply because it leaves some of one's investments un-hedged.

Selective Service Certification Verification that a male post-secondary student in the United States has signed up for Selective Service, a U.S. military program. Selective Service certification is required before a male student can become eligible for any federal financial aid

Self Exam An assessment that a non-profit conducts on itself to identify potential profit areas. Questions are generally qualitative, which is the primary difference between self exams and internal audits. See also: Management audit.

Self Service A business model in which a company sells a product that the buyer selects and/or uses without direct supervision by the seller. One of the most common examples is a gas station, where customers normally put gas in their automobiles themselves. Another example is a grocery store, where customers select items and put them in a shopping basket before check out. Self service may reduce costs and, in any case, it frees employees to perform other tasks.

Self-Amortizing Loan A loan where the borrower pays for part of the principal and the interest each month. A self-amortizing loan differs from an interest-only mortgage, where the borrower does not make principal payments over the life of the mortgage. An advantage of a self-amortizing loan is the fact that the borrower does not have to make a lump sum payment of the principal at maturity (or refinance at a potentially higher interest rate). However, self-amortizing loans have higher monthly payments than other types of loans. See also: Self-amortizing mortgage.

Self-Amortizing Mortgage A mortgage in which the holder pays for part of the principal and the interest each month. A self-amortizing mortgage differs from an interest-only mortgage, in which the holder does not make principal payments over the life of the mortgage. An advantage of a self-amortizing mortgage is the fact that the holder does not have to make a lump sum payment of the principal at maturity (or refinance at a potentially higher interest rate). However, self-amortizing mortgages have higher monthly payments than other mortgage types.

Self-Assessment In taxation, any system that allows the individual taxpayer to determine how much he/she owes in taxes. In a self-assessment, the taxpayer declares his/her income, makes deductions and credits, and arrives at the amount owed. A self-assessment is subject to review (and perhaps an audit) by the tax authorities.

Self-Correcting Describing a situation where a trend is likely to reverse itself and restore the status quo. For example, if a security drops in price by $5, a self-correcting trend would provide some indication that it will soon rise (roughly) $5 to its previous price. See also: Reversion to the Mean.

Self-Directed IRA An IRA in which the account holder has a great deal of control over the investments made on the account. That is, either the account holder or a designated representative has the ability to make investments with the contributions made to the account. Generally speaking, a self-directed IRA exists through a brokerage, which makes investments on behalf of the account holder. The brokerage may charge an annual fee for managing a self-directed IRA in addition to the commissions it charges on the individual trades.

Self-Directed Portfolio An investment portfolio in which the account holder has a great deal of control over the investments made on the account. That is, the holder has the ability to make investments with the capital in the account because he/she has not delegated the power to an investment adviser.

Self-Directed Retirement Plan A retirement plan in which the account holder has a great deal of control over the investments made on the account. That is, either the account holder or a designated representative has the ability to make investments with the contributions made to the account. Generally speaking, a self-directed retirement plan exists through a brokerage, which makes investments on behalf of the account holder. The brokerage may charge an annual fee for managing a self-directed retirement plan in addition to the commissions it charges on the individual trades.

Self-Directed RRSP In Canada, registered retirement savings plan (RRSP) in which the account holder has a great deal of control over the investments made on the account. That is, either the account holder or a designated representative has the ability to make investments off of the contributions made to the account. However, investments not ordinarily permitted on an RRSP are still not permitted on a self-directed RRSP. The individual account holder must ensure that investment conforms to this rule, or risk losing the tax deductible nature of contributions.

Self-Employed Contributions Act Legislation in the United States, passed in 1954, requiring self-employed persons to pay the full 15.3% of their net earnings in FICA taxes.

Self-Employed Income Net profit derived as the result of owning a business or for work as an independent contractor. In the United States, self-employed persons pay double the social security tax of employed persons, but are entitled to more tax deductions. One calculates self-employed income by taking one's gross income and deducting all business expenses. For example, a self-employed person working from home may deduct a certain percentage of his/her rent or mortgage and not pay taxes on that portion of his/her income. Self-employed income is reported to the IRS on Schedule C of the 1040 Form.

Self-Employed Taxpayer A taxpayer who derives his/her income from his/her own business or from work as an independent contractor. In the United States, self-employed taxpayers pay double the social security tax of employed persons, but are entitled to more tax deductions. One calculates self-employed income by taking one's gross income and deducting all business expenses. For example, a self-employed taxpayer working from home may deduct a certain percentage of his/her rent or mortgage and not pay taxes on that portion of his/her income. Self-employed income is reported to the IRS on Schedule C of the 1040 Form.

Self-Employment The state of owning a business or working as an independent contractor. In the United States, self-employed persons pay double the social security tax of employed persons, but are entitled to more tax deductions. One calculates self-employed income by taking one's gross income and deducting all business expenses. For example, a self-employed person working from home may deduct a certain percentage of his/her rent or mortgage and not pay taxes on that portion of his/her income. Self-employed income is reported to the IRS on Schedule C of the 1040 Form.

Self-Financing The act or practice of using one's own capital to provide funding for a project or company. Self-financing allows the creator of the project or company to maintain control apart from outside influence. It also allows the project or company to grow without debt. It is famously said that Ross Perot established Electronic Data Systems with $1,000 in personal savings. This is an example of self-financing.

Self-Help Aid Loans, grants, or scholarships that a post-secondary educational institution (as opposed to the federal government or some other party) awards a student as part of a financial aid package. See also: FAFSA.

Self-Inflicted Injury The deliberate injury of oneself. Self-inflicted injuries may be the result of depression or may be a form of insurance fraud. In any case, many insurers exclude self-inflicted injuries from coverage.

Self-Liquidating Bond A bond used to finance the purchase of assets intended to be sold within a short period of time. For example, a company may issue a self-liquidating bond to pay for its inventory, which it intends to quickly sell. It is called a self-liquidating bond because the proceeds from the sale of the assets provide the capital with which the issuer may repay the bond.

Self-Liquidating Loan A loan used to finance the purchase of assets intended to be sold within a short period of time. For example, a company may use a self-liquidating loan to pay for its inventory, which it intends to quickly sell. It is called a self-liquidating loan because the proceeds from the sale of the assets provide the capital with which the debtor may repay the loan.

Self-Regulatory Organization A professional organization, unaffiliated with a government, having certain, limited regulatory authority over members. An example is the American Dental Association, which has the ability to set standards and enforce discipline over dentists in the United States. In trading, most exchanges are self-regulatory organizations, as are trading-related professional organizations. SROs assist the SEC and government regulators in the maintenance of operating standards and the arbitration of disputes. See also: SICA.

Self-Selection A situation in which only one person or group can take advantage of a contract.

Self-Similar In mathematics, describing a condition in which the parts of an object are substantially the same as its whole. See also: Fractals.

Self-Supporting Debt A bond, especially a municipal bond, where the coupons and principal are paid with funding from the project the debt seeks to finance. It may be used, for example, to build a hospital or a toll bridge, and bondholders are repaid with the revenue the hospital or toll bridge derives. Self-supporting debt is usually slightly higher risk than a general obligation bond because if the project fails to generate revenue, the bond will default. However, self-supporting debt is generally low risk and highly liquid.

Self-Tender Offer A firm's offer to buy back its own stock for a price well above fair market value. A self-tender offer usually excludes a targeted number of shareholders; it is not intended to stop trade on its stock. Rather it is an attempt to prevent a real or suspected hostile takeover. If a firm becomes its own majority or plurality shareholder, it either makes a hostile takeover impossible or much more expensive for the company attempting to buy it out. See also: Antitakeover measure.

Sell To relinquish ownership of some asset in exchange for some monetary compensation. Selling may take any of several forms. In a cash sale, the seller receives cash or a cash equivalent immediately in exchange for the asset. In a credit sale, the seller surrenders ownership immediately in exchange for future payment, often with interest. An example of a sale is a simple transaction involving widgets. If the seller is willing to accept $2 per widget and the buyer wishes to purchase 100 widgets, then the seller gives to the buyer 100 widgets and in their place receives $200. See also: Buy.

Sell a Spread In options, to write a contract for a higher premium than a contract with the same underlying asset that one buys. For example, one my write a put option with a certain underlying after buying a similar put option with the same underlying, though often with a shorter expiration date. One sells a spread to hedge investments: in this case, if either option is exercised, the investor has still made a profit by selling the contract at a higher premium that the one he/she paid for buying the other contract.

Sell Hedge The sale of a futures contract or option on a security or commodity one owns in order to hedge against the risk of a decline in its price. In a sell hedge, the price of the futures contract or option should move inversely in relation to the price of the underlying asset.

Sell in May and Go Away An expression describing the supposed seasonal trend of the stock market in which it rises toward the end of each year and begins to decline the following summer. The existence of this phenomenon is disputed.

Sell Off The rapid sale of a security by a large number of holders. This increases the supply of the security available for sale and therefore drives down the price. Sell-offs occur for a number of reasons. A stock may drop suddenly in price if its company issues a negative earnings report, or if there are reports of a new technology rendering the company's product obsolete, or if the company's costs rise. Sell-offs also happen for other, perhaps less rational reasons. For example, a natural disaster, which may or may not affect supplies, can cause a sell-off. See also: Panic Sale.

Sell Order An order to a broker to sell a security. A sell order may take any of a number of forms. Depending on the nature of the order, the broker may execute it at the best available price when the order is made, at a set price designated by the client, or according to a more complicated formula. Additionally, the sell order may or may not have an expiration date (though most do). See also: Buy order.

Sell Out 1. To liquidate. 2. In a brokerage, to sell a security bought on behalf of a client when the client has not paid for the security by the agreed-upon time. 3. In a brokerage, to sell the securities in a margin account when a client has failed to pay for a margin call. 4. To sell the entire stock of a security or product.

Sell Plus Order 1. An order to a broker to sell a security above its current price. 2. An order to a broker to sell a security at its current price only if the current price is higher than the previous plus tick or zero plus tick. A sell plus order also requires that the current price be higher or the same as the previous trade if the last trade was a zero minimum tick or a minimum tick.

Sell Short To sell borrowed securities. In selling short, one borrows securities, usually from a brokerage, and sells them. One then buys the same securities in order to repay the brokerage. Selling short is practiced if one believes that the price of a security will soon fall. That is, one expects to sell the borrowed securities at a higher price than the price at which one buys in order to return the securities. Selling short is one of the most common practices of hedge funds. See also: Margin account.

Sell Side The retail brokers and small investors who sell securities on Wall Street. See also: Buy side.

Sell Stop Order An order to a broker to sell a security if its price falls below a certain level. A sell stop order exists to stop the losses, should a security's price fall. That is, it protects against further losses. See also: Buy stop order, stop-loss order.

Sell the Book An order to a broker to sell as much of a position as possible at the current, market price. That is, one sells the book when one wishes to close the position on the stated security. The term refers to the specialist's book on an exchange.

Sell the Spread In an option spread, to sell an option contract at a higher price than one pays to buy another option in the same spread.

Sell to Close Informal; to sell an option contract in order to close the position. That is, when one sells to close, one is liquidating the position and ending whatever option strategy one was using. This may occur because the investor has already extracted whatever profit is going to result, or because the position was not profitable in the first place.

Sell to Open Informal; to sell an option contract in order to open a position. That is, when one sells to open, one is beginning to implement an option strategy that requires a net short position in order to be profitable. For example, one may write a call expecting it not to be exercised, allowing one to keep the premium (or sale price). Alternatively, selling to open may be the first of several steps in a complex strategy. See also: Sell to close.

Sell to Rent To sell one's house and to rent it back from the buyer such that one continues to live there. Selling to rent may be useful if one is in arrears on one's mortgage or has some other debt and needs access to cash. It is advantageous to the buyer because it provides some instant cash flow in exchange for one's investment.

Seller A person or organization that relinquishes ownership of some asset in exchange for some monetary compensation. In a cash sale, the seller receives cash or a cash equivalent immediately in exchange for the asset. In a credit sale, the seller surrenders ownership immediately in exchange for future payment, often with interest. A seller is distinguished by the fact that he/she receives payment, as opposed to a buyer, who gives payment, or a donor, who relinquishes an asset for free. See also: Buyer.

Seller Financing An agreement between a buyer and a seller of an asset, usually real estate, where the seller directly holds the debt. That is, rather than going through a financial intermediary such as a bank, the seller and the buyer conclude the transaction and the buyer makes payments on the asset at the agreed-upon rate of interest directly to the seller. This is useful for the buyer when he/she could not otherwise obtain financing. It can also be useful because the interest rate is often lower. Likewise, the seller can often receive a higher return on the sale of the house because he does not have to pay commissions or other costs to the financial intermediary.

Seller's Call A commodity contract in which the parties agree that the seller will determine the price at some point in the future. The contract specifies by when the seller will set the price. The seller informs the buyer that the buyer either will pay a certain price or will purchase equivalent commodity futures on behalf of the seller. See also: Buyer's Call.

Seller's Fee In an auction, a fee paid to the person or organization holding the auction on top of the highest bid. For example, if one bids $1,000 for an antique bed, the seller may have to pay a 10% buyer's fee (or $100) if that is the winning bid. A seller's fee is one way an auctioneer makes money from the auction.

Seller's Option Contract A contract between a buyer and a seller where the seller has the ability to delay settlement of the contract beyond the normal time. A seller may exercise this option if he/she has difficulty in making delivery on the contract for any reason at all. The farthest possible settlement date is stated in the seller's option contract. This contrasts with a cash contract, where settlement is made before the regular settlement date.

Seller's Points A lump sum that the seller of real estate pays to the lender that finances the transaction for the buyer. Seller's points are part of the seller's closing costs and are used to make the loan less expensive for the lender. Seller's points are usually made when the seller needs to rid himself/herself of the property in short order and wants to encourage the lender to qualify the buyer. Most of the time, one point equals 1% of the amount of the loan.

Selling Away 1. The act of a broker seeking to sell a client a security not offered by the brokerage. This is usually part of a private placement. Except in limited circumstances, selling away is illegal. **2.** The act of a broker selling a client's security without the client's authorization.

Selling Climax The point at which a security becomes so oversold at high trading volume that it precipitates an upward market correction. It is an example of a market bottom that precedes a rally. See also: Buying Climax.

Selling Concession The compensation that an underwriter receives for placing a new issue with investors. It is calculated as a discount from the price of the new issue. For example, an issuer may sell the underwriter a bond at $990 per bond. The underwriter will then place the issue at $1,000, allowing it to make a $10 profit. This profit is the selling concession. It is also simply called a concession.

Selling Dividends An act or practice in which an underwriter, investment adviser, or anyone else attempts to sell a security to an investor by arguing that the investor can collect future dividends. That is, rather than discussing the company's technical or fundamental information, the dividend seller instead talks about scheduled dividends that the investor can collect.

Selling Group In an initial public offering or bond issue, a group of institutions who help the issuer place a new issue without necessarily participating in the underwriting group. This means they are not responsible for any unsold securities. The selling group therefore receives lower fees than the underwriters and is listed last on the tombstone. The specific agreement governing a selling group's duties in a new issue is called a selected dealer agreement. More generally, a selling group may refer to all underwriters in a new issue, that is, every person and institution on the tombstone.

Selling Into Strength The act or practice of selling a security while the price is rising but when the seller expects the trend to reverse. This could result in a smaller profit but allows the seller to lock in profits before the reversal begins, which reduces the potential for loss. Selling into strength carries no risk for the seller, but it does come with the opportunity cost that the reversal will not take place and the seller will miss more profit. However, selling into strength may prevent a serious loss that comes from waiting until the reversal materializes.

Selling on the Good News Informal; an investment strategy that involves selling a stock when its company announces good news. Selling on the good news assumes that the price of the stock rises, sometimes dramatically, on the good news. This is a minor variation on the buy low, sell high investment strategy, in that it assumes that the good news always causes the price to rise, and that the price will fall again soon thereafter. To some extent, selling on the good news also assumes that the market has not priced the news prior to the announcement.

Selling Out A derogatory term for compromising one's personal beliefs or demographic group for more money or some other gain. For example, a person who believes that corporations are harmful to society but goes to work as a corporate lawyer may be said to sell out. Selling out is a charge often leveled by critics of modern capitalism.

Selling Panic The rapid selling of a security by a large number of investors. This increases the supply of the security available for sale while leaving constant or decreasing the demand to buy; this drives down the price. Selling panics occur for a number of reasons. For example, a stock may drop suddenly in price if its company issues an unexpectedly negative earnings report. The panic comes from investors' desire to sell the stock immediately before the price falls even more. See also: Buying panic, Sell-off.

Selling Plan A plan in which an investor holding a long position on a security sets forth conditions under which the security will be sold automatically. The selling plan is particularly important if the investor has inside information because Rule 105b-1 of the SEC permits what would otherwise be insider trading as long as the process is set in motion automatically with a selling plan. This construction is controversial, with critics maintaining that selling plans are open to manipulation that allows what amounts to insider trading by stealth.

Selling Rate The foreign exchange rate of a foreign exchange transaction in which a dealer is the seller. For example, if a dealer is selling British pounds, the selling rate is the exchange rate that he accepts for them.

Selling, General & Administrative Expense Overhead costs to a company. SGAs are usually recurring; they include things like rent, salaries, and money spent on office supplies. They do not generally include one-time costs. They form one of the single largest expenses a company can incur in its operations. These expenses are included in one category on financial statements and are subtracted from revenue when calculating operating income.

Sellout A broker's sale of securities on behalf of a client when the client has failed to settle transactions as promised. A common cause of a sellout is a client's failure to meet a margin call.

Sell-Side Analyst A securities analyst who works for a brokerage. The observations and recommendations of sell-side analysts are given to brokers, who in turn pass them along to the firm's clients. They are also called Wall Street analysts.

Sell-to-Cover To sell stock in a company for which one works in order to raise the necessary funds to exercise an employee stock option. Because employee stock options allow one to buy shares at a discount, selling to cover usually allows one come out of the activity with more shares than when he/she started. If this is not the case, the employee usually does not exercise the stop option. The SEC may restrict to the extent to which one may sell to cover through its rules against insider trading, among other restrictions.

Selsoviet In Russia, a political subdivision equivalent to a rural municipality.

Semi A slang term for a stock in a company in the semiconductor industry.

Semiannual Describing a situation, event, statement, or anything else that occurs or is filed twice per year. For example, most bonds pay coupons on a semiannual basis. See also: Annual, Quarterly.

Semiconductor Any substance that conducts electricity more slowly than a conductor. Semiconductors are common in products like computer chips and, as such, may be traded as commodities. Silicon and germanium are both semiconductors.

Semimodius An ancient Roman unit of dry volume approximately equivalent to 4.36 liters.

Semimonthly Describing a situation, event, statement, or anything else that occurs or is filed twice per month. For example, interest on a loan may be compounded semimonthly. See also: Annual, Quarterly.

Semisextula An ancient Roman unit of weight approximately equivalent to 2.28 grams.

Semistrong Form of the Efficient Markets Theory A controversial model on how markets work. It states that the market efficiently deals with nearly all information on a given security and reflects it in the price immediately. The model holds that technical analysis, fundamental analysis, and any speculative investing based upon them, are useless because any facts that might cause technical or fundamental changes are already reflected in the security price. Investors and academics disagree on how well the model works. See also: Weak form of the EMT, Strong form of the EMT.

Semiuncia 1. An ancient Roman unit of area approximately equivalent to 105 square meters. **2.** An ancient Roman unit of weight approximately equivalent to 13.7 grams.

Semi-Variable Cost A cost for an individual or company that consists of a fixed base cost and another cost that changes from time period to time period. For example, suppose one's landlord rolls utility costs together with the rent. One's rent thus becomes a semi-variable cost because one pays the rent (a fixed cost) and the electric, gas, and water bills (variable costs) together with the same check.

Sen GOST 7.67 Latin three-letter geocode for Senegal. The code is used for transactions to and from Senegalese bank accounts and for international shipping to Senegal. As with all GOST 7.67 codes, it is used primarily in Cyrillic alphabets.

Senate Appropriations Committee A committee of the U.S. Senate responsible for drafting legislation to spend federal money. According to the U.S. Constitution, any federal spending must be authorized by legislation. The Appropriations Committee spearheads that effort in the Senate. It consists of approximately 30 members, most of whom belong to the Senate majority party. It was established in 1867. See also: Senate Finance Committee.

Sene A subdivision of the Western Samoan tala. One sene is equal in value to 1/100 of a tala. See also: Cent.

Sengi A subdivision of the old Zairean zaire. One sengi was equal in value to 1/10,000 of one zaire.

Senior Bond A bond that has higher priority compared to another in the event of liquidation. That is, if a company goes bankrupt and is liquidated, holders of a senior bond must be paid before holders of junior debt. It is a type of senior security. See also: Absolute priority rule.

Senior Citizen A person over a certain age, usually 55 or 65. Senior citizens are often entitled to discounts for certain entertainment services like restaurants and cinemas. Very often, a senior citizen collects a retirement annuity from the government and/or a private plan. See also: Pensioner, Medicare, Social Security.

Senior Citizen's Freedom to Work Act of 2000 Legislation in the United States that made it easier for persons to continue to work between 65 and 69. Prior to its passage, persons in this age group had their Social Security benefits reduced significantly (and, in some circumstances, almost eliminated) if they continued to work after beginning to collect from the program and earned more than $17,000 per year. This was considered to be detrimental to middle class persons who continued to work. The Act eliminated this penalty.

Senior Debt A debt that has higher priority compared to another in the event of liquidation. That is, if a company goes bankrupt and is liquidated, holders of secured debt must be paid before holders of unsecured debt. In this case, the secured debt is senior debt with respect to the unsecured debt. It is a type of senior security. See also: Absolute priority rule.

Senior Mortgage A mortgage that is secured by a lien on a property and that has preference to another mortgage on the same property. In general, the senior mortgage is the original mortgage; one takes out a junior mortgage to pay for home repairs or for other reasons. In the event of default or bankruptcy, the senior mortgage must be paid entirely before the junior mortgage is paid at all. As a result, a senior mortgage carries a lower interest rate than a junior mortgage. See also: Piggyback mortgage.

Senior Mortgage Bond A bond secured by a mortgage on one or more properties that, in the event of bankruptcy and/or liquidation, has priority over other liabilities secured by the same mortgages. See also: Absolute Priority Rule, Second Mortgage.

Senior Refunding The act of an issuer redeeming a bond by replacing it with a bond with a longer maturity. For example, a company may conduct a senior refund by redeeming its 10-year bonds and granting bondholders 30-year bonds. This is a useful tactic when a company wishes to delay payment or consolidate its debt.

Senior Security A security that has higher priority compared to another in the event of liquidation. That is, if a company goes bankrupt and is liquidated, holders of secured debt must be paid before holders of unsecured debt. Holders of unsecured debt must be paid before preferred shareholders and finally, preferred shareholders must be satisfied before common shareholders. In the forgoing, each security is a senior security compared to the following one. See also: Absolute Priority Rule.

Seniti A division of the Tongan pa'anga worth 1/100 of the pa'anga. See also: Cent.

Seniunija In Lithuania, a political subdivision consisting of a small town, a small group of villages, or a neighborhood in a city.

Sensex An index of the 30 most actively traded stocks on the Bombay Stock Exchange (BSE). The Sensex is considered the most important benchmark index on the BSE, and it is the oldest stock index in India. Unlike many indices, it is not weighted for price or market capitalization, but rather for "free-float capitalization." This is similar to market capitalization, but uses shares available for trade rather than the total shares outstanding. Thus, it excludes shares that have not been vested, among others. Sensex is formally known as the Bombay Exchange Sensitive Index.

Sensitive Market A market that can become highly volatile at good news or bad news. Sensitive markets are susceptible to wild fluctuations in price. Many companies attempt to avoid sensitive market by pricing out the news or gradually leaking good and bad news so its stock price rises or falls smoothly and consistently. See also: Price sensitive market.

Sensitivity Analysis The analysis of an investment's profitability according to various changes. That is, sensitivity analysis considers potential changes to interest rates, costs, and/or other variables and measures how this will affect the return on the investment. Sensitivity analysis is a form of quantitative research. It can be useful in making investment decisions. It is sometimes called a what-if analysis. See also: Volatility.

Sent A division of the Estonian kroon equal in value to 1/100 of one kroon. Its plural is senti.

Sente A subdivision of the Lesotho loti. One sente is equal in value to 1/100 of one loti. Its plural is lisente.

Sentiment Index A mathematical calculation on average or median forecast made by well-respected analysts on the future direction of the market. That is, the sentiment index uses certain data to show what analysts believe future market movements will be. See also: Earnings Expectations, Forecasting.

Sentneri A Finnish unit of weight approximately equivalent to 42.6 kilograms. It became obsolete when Finland adopted the metric system in 1880.

SEOG Supplemental Educational Opportunity Grant. A grant that the federal government offers to students based on financial need. The SEOG may be used to pay for education expenses (up to $4,000) for a first bachelor's degree.

Separate Account An account at an insurance company where funds are invested for a variable annuity. Because the annuitant in a variable annuity assumes the risk of the investment of his/her contributions, his/her funds are held in a separate account away from the general pool of funds that are invested for fixed annuities.

Separate Account Fund 1. An investment account, bought through a brokerage, in which the investor buys a pool of securities and directly owns them. A separate account fund operates much like a mutual fund, the main difference being that in a separate account fund, one owns the securities directly. In a mutual fund, one owns shares in a pool of securities. In both cases, however, ones closes the position by trading his/her shares for the net asset value per share. Most separate account funds require a minimum investment of $100,000. **2.** In variable annuities, an account in which one places money to invest in securities. A single variable annuity may contain several separate account funds, depending on the investor's specific portfolio needs. Money in these funds must be kept separate from each other, and from the annuity's general funds.

Separate Customer The way that the Securities Investor Protection Corporation treats each account. The Securities Investor Protection Corporation is a not-for-profit organization mandated under American law to insure investors against the potential bankruptcy of a broker-dealer. According to the SIPC's rules, each account is treated as a separate customer, even if multiple accounts have the same owner. This insures each account and not just the owners personally.

Separate Property In marriage and divorce law, real or personal property owned by only one spouse. Separate property exists even in community property jurisdictions. It includes property owned by each spouse before the marriage, and any property given to one spouse as a gift or inheritance. It may also include property that the spouses agree to keep separate. If separate property is liquidated during the marriage (e.g. if a spouse sells a house he/she owns separately) the cash resulting from the sale may also qualify as separate property.

Separate Trading of Registered Interest and Principal of Securities Also called STRIPS, a Treasury security whose coupons have been separated from the principal. STRIPS therefore pay no interest. They are sold at a significant discount from par and mature at par. STRIPS fluctuate in price, sometimes dramatically, because changes in interest rates made them more or less desirable. STRIPS could be invested IRAs and other pension accounts; however, unlike other Treasury securities, they are subject to federal taxes. STRIPS are quoted according to their yields rather than their prices. They began to be issued in 1985, rendering obsolete similar securities, such as CATS, which behaved similarly. See also: zero-coupon bond.

Separation Property In Markowitz portfolio theory, the ability of a portfolio manager to identify a client's needs by separating them into two separate duties. The first duty is to pick the risky securities that will have the highest return. This is a mathematical equation and can be accomplished easily. The second duty is to decide which securities meet individual clients' own desires for risk. Portfolio managers must discuss investment goals and risk averseness with clients in order to perform the second duty.

Separation Theorem An economic theory stating that the investment decisions of a firm are independent from the firm's owner's wishes. The Separation Theorem states that the productive value of a firm's management neither affects nor is affected by the owner's business decisions. As a result, the performance of a firm's investments has no relation to how they are financed, whether by stock, debt, or cash. The theorem was devised by economist Irving Fisher. See also: Irrelevance result.

Septunx 1. An ancient Roman unit of area approximately equivalent to 1,472 square meters. **2.** An ancient Roman unit of weight approximately equivalent to 191.9 grams.

Sepu An ancient Akkadian unit of length approximately equivalent to one meter.

Sequential Access In computer systems, the state in which it takes varying amounts of time to access different points in a sequence. This contrasts with random access, in which any point of a sequence can be accessed in an equal amount of time.

Ser An obsolete Indian unit of dry volume equivalent to one liter.

Serbian Dinar The currency of Serbia. It was introduced in 2003 when Yugoslavia formally separated into Serbia and Montenegro. It replaced the Yugoslav dinar at par. Montenegro had already abandoned the Yugoslav dinar in 2000.

Serial Bond with Balloon A bond issue that combines features of a serial bond and a term bond. A serial bond matures gradually over the course of the life of the issue, while a term bond matures all at once. A serial bond with balloon has certain parts that mature gradually, but the majority of the issue matures at the end of the issue. This majority of the issue is called the balloon. See also: Balloon maturity.

Serial Bonds An issue of bonds that gradually matures at regular intervals until the whole issue matures. Corporate bonds are sometimes serial bonds. In these situations, a corporation issues bonds and it sells them to any investor who will buy, and the bonds mature at different times. Serial bonds are most useful to finance a project with regular income streams with which to pay off the serials. Some municipal bonds and corporate bonds combine aspects of both term and serial issues in which some parts of the issue mature at various times but in which the bulk matures all at once. See also: Term Bonds.

Serial Correlation In technical analysis, a measure of how well past occurrences predict future occurrences. Most importantly, serial correlation checks whether and how often a particular price movement will result in a different price movement. Serial correlation lies at the heart of technical analysis. It is also called autocorrelation.

Serial Entrepreneur A person who starts several different businesses with little intention of operating any of them for very long. That is, a serial entrepreneur may start one business and work at it until it becomes profitable, then sell it and start another business. A serial entrepreneur is not interested in a career with the individual companies he/she runs, but rather enjoys the process of starting a business. Serial entrepreneurship is risky, as is entrepreneurship in general.

Serial Redemption The gradual maturity of a serial bond. A serial bond is an issue of bonds that gradually matures at regular intervals until the whole issue matures. The serial redemption feature of these bonds is most useful in the financing of a project with regular income streams with which to pay off the serials. Serial bonds (and therefore serial redemption) are more common among corporate bonds than municipal bonds.

Serienscheine Elaborate notgeld printed in 1920 and 1921 in Germany under the Weimar Republic. Serienscheine featured flashy colors and pictures of famous buildings and German legends. It did not actually go into circulation.

Series 24 A license issued by FINRA enabling the holder to manage and administer a branch of a brokerage. In order to qualify for a Series 24, one must already possess a Series 7 and pass an exam covering a variety of subjects, notably regulation, trading, securities, and real estate investment trusts.

Series 26 1. A license allowing one to manage sales staff at an investment company or annuity. One must complete a Series 26 exam in order to obtain the license. **2.** The exam required to obtain a Series 26 license. It consists of 110 multiple choice questions; topics covered in the exam include hiring, training, supervision, sales and business practices, and book keeping. To take the Series 26 exam, one must already possess a Series 6 or Series 7 license.

Series 27 A license allowing one to become the chief financial officer at a FINRA member firm. One must complete a Series 27 exam in order to obtain the license. **2.** The exam required to obtain a Series 27 license. It consists of 145 multiple choice questions; topics covered in the exam include balance sheets, net capital rules, regulations of the SEC and FINRA, and book keeping.

Series 3 A license, granted by FINRA, entitling a holder to trade in commodities and futures. In order to be eligible for a series 3, one must complete an exam covering a number of topics, including: futures trading theory; margins, limits, and settlements; orders, accounts, and analysis; hedging; spreads; speculation; options; and regulation. There is no prerequisite for a series 3, but it is a prerequisite for a series 30.

Series 30 In futures trade, a license allowing one to manage a futures branch office. To acquire a Series 30 license, one must complete a 50 question test. While there are no prerequisite licenses, the test covers various rules and regulations, notably disclosure requirements. The Financial Industry Regulatory Authority administers the test.

Series 31 In futures trade, a license allowing one to sell managed futures funds. It also authorizes the holder to manage a commodities pool account and raise funds for it, and to engage in certain types of futures trading. To acquire a Series 31 license, one must complete a forty-five question test and already possess a Series 7 license, in addition to already being registered with the Financial Industry Regulatory Authority, which administers the test.

Series 4 An exam one must pass to become a registered options principle, which authorizes one to regulate and supervise the options trading of the firm for which one works. The exam tests one's knowledge of options and options trading; specifically, it deals with equity options, debt options, index options, currencies, and strategy, among other things. One must already have a Series 7 license in order to be eligible for this exam. It is administered by the Financial Industry Regulatory Authority.

Series 55 A license giving the holder the right to trade in stocks. To obtain a Series 55, one must complete a multiple-choice exam measuring one's knowledge of practices on the New York Stock Exchange and over-the-counter markets, as well as knowledge of customer accounts, electronic trading, and trading regulations. The exam is administered by FINRA.

Series 6 A license entitling the holder to buy and sell mutual funds, variable annuities, and some insurance products on behalf of clients. In order to receive a Series 6 license, one must pass a multiple choice examination covering each of these investment vehicles, as well as the securities and tax regulations involved with them. The license and examination are administered by FINRA.

Series 65 A license, granted by FINRA, entitling a holder to act as an investment adviser representative, who assists a registered investment adviser. In order to be eligible for a series 65, one must complete an exam covering a number of topics, including law & regulation, various investment vehicles, and ethics. There is no prerequisite for a series 65. See also: Series 7.

Series 7 An exam one must pass to become a registered representative with FINRA, a designation that authorizes one to trade for the brokerage or other firm for which one works. It authorizes one to sell any security except commodity futures contracts. The Series 7 license is a prerequisite for most other FINRA exams.

Series A-Preferred Stock A preferred stock with rights or privileges distinguishing it from other preferred stock in the same company. That is, a company issues series A preferred stock when it wishes to have several different types of preferred stock. For example, series A preferred stock may have a different guaranteed dividend from series B and series C preferred stock.

Series Bond A single issue of a bond made in two or more tranches. For example, a company may announce that it intends to issue $10,000,000 in bonds in two tranches of $5,000,000. Series bonds are common to collateralized mortgage obligations, which are backed by pools of mortgages. These mortgages are arranged in tranches that mature at different times, for instance, in 10 years, 15 years, and 30 years. See also: Serial bond.

Series E Bond In the United States, a formerly-issued savings bond, exempt from state and local taxes, with a fixed interest rate. These bonds were sold at three-fourths of face value and pay par upon maturity, which was originally 10 years, but later became 30 or 40 years. They began to be issued to help finance American involvement in World War II; they were known colloquially as war bonds. They were non-transferable and must either have been held or redeemed. In 1980, the government stopped issuing Series E bonds and replaced them with Series EE bonds.

For a time, Series E bonds were exchangeable for Series H or Series HH bonds, but this is no longer the case.

Series EE Savings Bond In the United States, a savings bond, exempt from state and local taxes, with a fixed interest rate. The interest is adjusted every six months and is equal to 90% of the average 5-year Treasury security yield over the six months preceding the calculation. These bonds are sold at half of face value and pay par upon maturity, which is 30 years after purchase. They must be held for at least one year, and United States Treasury guarantees that it will double in value after 20 years. They are non-transferable and must either be held or redeemed. When used to pay for college education, they are exempt from federal taxes. Series EE bonds are the successors to Series E bonds, better known as war bonds.

Series Fund A mutual fund with multiple portfolios. Series funds are designed to spread their investments out among multiple sectors so as to diversify and reduce risk.

Series HH Savings Bond In the United States, a formerly-issued savings bond, exempt from state and local taxes, with an interest rate fixed for 10 years. These bonds paid par upon maturity, which was 20 years after issue. They were non-transferable and must either have been held or redeemed. Very often, the interest rate dropped to 1.5% after 10 years, which rarely kept pace with inflation. Series HH bonds were discontinued in 2004. See also: Series H bond.

Series I Savings Bond In the United States, a savings bond with either a fixed interest rate or an inflation-indexed interest rate. The inflation-indexed version pays a fixed amount plus an amount adjusted every six months according to the Consumer Price Index. For both types of Series I bonds, the interest rate is announced twice annually. These bonds are sold at face value and pay par upon maturity, which is 30 years after purchase. Series I bonds not held for at least five years are subject to a redemption penalty. Federal taxes on interest are deferred until redemption or maturity. Savings bonds are non-transferable and must either be held or redeemed.

Series of Catastrophes Coverage under a reinsurance plan that protects an insurance company from losses over and above its retention limit. It is a type of excess of loss reinsurance.

Serif In typography, a small mark attached to a letter. Serifs do not alter the meanings of letters. They are decorative and are not present in some fonts.

Serigraphy The act or practice of printing on woven surface, especially silk. Serigraphy is used in art. It was popularized by Andy Warhol.

Serious Fraud Office An agency of the British government that investigates and prosecutes complex cases of fraud, especially in business and the financial sector. It is independent from other departments, though it frequently coordinates with them. The SFO was established in 1988.

Serious Injury Frequency Rate In business, the number of employee injuries per 1 million man-hours worked. For example, 100 injuries in 1 million man-hours equates to a serious injury frequency rate of 0.0001.

Service Charge A fee a company or bank assesses for providing an unusual service. For example, a bank may assess a service charge if a person who does not have an account withdraws money from that bank's ATM. It is also called a service fee.

Servicemembers Group Life Insurance Also called SGLI. Life insurance offered by the Veterans Administration to members of the United States uniformed services. Premiums on SGLI are very low and the death benefit is very high. Benefits are also paid for traumatic injuries.

Servizi Assicurativi del Commercio Estero An export credit agency (ECA) in Italy. It provides a wide range of export credit and advisory services, and especially extends credit for trade with Africa and the Balkans. Like other export credit agencies, SACE is controversial; critics allege that ECAs negatively impact international development, as developing countries cannot compete with insured exports. Proponents of ECAs argue that they enable developing countries to import products they otherwise would not be able to afford.

Sescuncia An ancient Roman unit of weight approximately equivalent to 41.1 grams.

SESDAQ Stock Exchange of Singapore Dealing and Automated Quotation System. A system that facilitates trading of securities on the Stock Exchange of Singapore. Unlike some other systems, IPO prices on SESDAQ are fixed; an investor may either buy at the offered price or choose not to do so, but it will not change

Sestaky A Slovak slang term for eurocent coins. Literally, the term refers to coins with little value.

Set of Contracts Perspective The belief that different stakeholders in the corporation have different interests that often, or always, conflict. For example, managers may be concerned about the company's ability to make a long-term profit while shareholders (especially traders) may consider primarily short term gains. Likewise, management may be interested in reducing expenses, while the union representing employees are most concerned with increasing members' wages and benefits.

Set Up In arbitrage, the practice of taking a long position on a convertible security and taking a short position on the underlying asset of that convertible security. The investor makes a set-up hedge in hopes that the price of the underlying asset will rise, allowing him/her to profit from the increase in the price of the convertible security. On the other hand, if the underlying asset falls in price, the investor profits from the short sale of the underlying asset. A set-up hedge is the opposite of a Chinese hedge. See also: Convertible arbitrage.

Set-Aside The portion of a contract that is guaranteed to go to a minority owned company. For example, suppose a city wishes to contract out its trash collection services to a number of privately-owned companies. It may declare that 20% of the total value of the contract must go to one or more companies owned by a member of a minority group. While this is intended to reduce corruption in (especially local) governments, critics allege that this practice is, itself, subject to abuse. See also: Affirmative action.

Setat An ancient Egyptian unit of area approximately equivalent to 2,756.5 square meters.

Setoff 1. The ability of a debtor to reduce the amount of one's debt by an amount the creditor owes to the debtor. Thus, if a debtor owes a creditor $20,000 but the creditor owes the debtor $5,000 in an unrelated matter, setoff allows the debtor effectively to owe only $15,000. **2.** In banking, the right of a bank to seize a debtor's account balance held at that bank if a debt is in or near default. Some jurisdictions limit the right of setoff; for example, the United States does not allow it to apply for commercial loans or credit card debt.

Settle Price 1. The last price for an option or futures transaction on a derivatives exchange in a given trading day. It is calculated by averaging the last bid and offer, the final sale price, and a weighted average of the transaction prices over the last few minutes of trading. Clearing houses use the settle price to determine whether or not margin accounts and other accounts are current. It is also called a settlement price. **2.** See: Closing price.

Settlement The process in which a buyer makes payment and receives the agreed-upon good or service. This term is used on exchanges to indicate when a security actually changes hands, which often occurs several days after a trade is made. See also: Clearance.

Settlement Agent A person responsible for ensuring that all laws and regulations are followed in transferring real estate from one owner to the next. For example, when one sells his/her house, the settlement agent performs the title search and conducts other activities necessary for the real estate to close smoothly. Generally speaking, a settlement agent does not represent either party in a real estate transaction. Some U.S. states require a settlement agent to work on real estate transactions.

Settlement Date 1. The date upon which the buyer of a security must pay the seller. The settlement date depends upon the type of security traded; for example, stocks usually have a settlement date three days after the trade date. On the other hand, government bonds must be settled on the next trading day. It is important to note that when calculating the capital gains or losses, one uses the trade date and not the settlement date. **2.** In life insurance, the day the benefit is paid. This usually follows the death of the beneficiary, unless he/she cashes in the policy.

Settlement Month The month during which the underlying asset of a futures contract or forward contract is delivered to the contract holder. A contract holder may offset the contract by taking an opposite position before it matures, but any investor holding such a contract on the expiration date must take delivery during the settlement month. See also: Delivery date, Notice day.

Settlement Options Any of a number of possibilities for the beneficiary of a life insurance policy to receive payment. Among the options are the reception of a lump sum, monthly payments for a certain number of years, smaller monthly payments for the remainder of the beneficiary's life, and leaving the benefit with the insurance company and collecting interest with the option of withdrawing the principal at any time.

Settlement Period The number of days between the trade date and the settlement date. The trade date is the day on which investors agree on the security transaction, while the settlement date is the day securities change hands and payment is made. Different types of transactions have different settlement periods. For example, stock trades usually settle on T+3 (three trading days since the trade date) while bonds settle on T+1 (one trading day since the trade date).

Settlement Price In futures, the average price at which a futures contract trades on a given day. It is calculated by taking the average of the opening price and the closing price on that day. The settlement price helps a broker determine whether a client's margin account needs to be called, if the price changes too much, and the client holds the contract in question.

Settlement Rate The suggested way to calculate the net present value of a pension plan. The settlement rate is devised by the Financial Accounting Standards Board and is used by companies who wish to discontinue their pension plans. That is, a company may use the settlement rate to calculate lump sum payments to plan participants to relieve itself of the future liability of making payments on the pension over time.

Settlement Risk The risk that a trade will not settle. For example, a buyer may not receive delivery of the securities he/she bought by the settlement date, or the seller may not receive payment. This may occur because of the negligence or deliberate withholding by one party or the other. If a party does not receive the securities or payment, he/she is not obligated fulfill his/her end of the bargain until delivery or payment is made, but this can render him/her unable to conduct other activities that would advance his/her investment goals.

Seutukunta In Finland, a political subdivision equivalent to a sub-region or county.

Seutukuntaa In Finland, a political subdivision approximately equivalent to a county.

Severability A clause in a contract stating that if one clause in the contract is ruled illegal or unenforceable, the remainder of the contract remains in effect. Severability exists to protect the counterparties to the contract from the possibility that the whole contract will be ruled invalid. This is especially important if one or both parties must spend money in the execution of the contract. A contract without a severability clause could be declared entirely invalid if a single section is declared invalid. It is also called a savings clause.

Severally But Not Jointly Describing an underwriting agreement in which several underwriting firms agree to buy a new issue together, but state specifically that they are not responsible for any other firm's unsold portion of the issue. That is, while the underwriting syndicate works together in coordinating the placement of the new issue with investors, each firm is ultimately only responsible for its own portion. See also: Jointly and severally.

Severance A payment often (but not always) made in a lump sum that occurs when an employee is laid off or fired. Severance is sometime voluntary; that is, an employee may choose to quit and take a severance that is offered instead of staying and risking a layoff with no severance. The amount of severance is determined by the employee's length of time at the company, previous pay rate, and other factors. Accepting a severance makes one ineligible to collect unemployment insurance or to initiate a wrongful termination lawsuit. A severance exists in order to reduce the risk of the company when layoffs become necessary and to improve employee morale.

Sextans 1. An ancient Roman unit of area approximately equivalent to 421 square meters. **2.** An ancient Roman unit of weight approximately equivalent to 54.8 grams.

Sextarius An ancient Roman unit of volume approximately equivalent to 546 milliliters.

Sextula 1. An ancient Roman unit of area approximately equivalent to 35 square meters. **2.** An ancient Roman unit of weight approximately equivalent to 4.57 grams.

Seychelles Rupee The currency of the Seychelles. Introduced in 1914, it initially circulated alongside the Mauritian rupee, the previous currency. For a long time, it was pegged to a currency basket consisting of euros, British pounds and U.S. dollars. It began to float in November 2008 and devalued considerably.

Seymour In the United Kingdom, a slang term for a 100,000-pound salary. The term is most common in the media industry, and is derived from Geoff Seymour, a 20th-century advertisement writer who was apparently the first person in media to earn 100,000 pounds per year.

SG 1. ISO 3166-1 alpha-2 code for the Republic of Singapore. This is the code used in international transactions to and from Singaporean bank accounts. **2.** ISO 3166-2 geocode for Singapore. This is used as an international standard for shipping to Singapore. Each district has its own code with the prefix "SG." For example, the code for Central Singapore is ISO 3166-2:SG-01.

SGD ISO 4217 code for the Singapore dollar. It was issued in 1965 after the end of the currency union between Singapore, Brunei, and Malaysia. It was at different times pegged to the British pound, the U.S. dollar, and a currency basket. Since 1995, it has been a managed float currency. It is interchangeable with the Brunei dollar.

SGL-1 A rating of the risk, published by Moody's, that a company will not be able to meet its short-term liabilities due to illiquidity. An SGL-1 rating is the most liquid rating. This indicates a company very likely has cash on hand to pay immediate obligations. See also: SGL.

SGL-2 A rating of the risk, published by Moody's, that a company will not be able to meet its short-term liabilities due to illiquidity. An SGL-2 rating is the second most liquid rating. This indicates a company likely has cash on hand to pay immediate obligations. See also: SGL.

SGL-3 A rating of the risk, published by Moody's, that a company will not be able to meet its short-term liabilities due to illiquidity. An SGL-3 rating is the second least liquid rating. This indicates a company may or may not have cash on hand to pay immediate obligations. See also: SGL.

SGL-4 A rating of the risk, published by Moody's, that a company will not be able to meet its short-term liabilities due to illiquidity. An SGL-4 rating is the least liquid rating. This indicates a company may not have cash on hand to pay immediate obligations. See also: SGL.

SGP GOST 7.67 Latin three-letter geocode for Singapore. The code is used for transactions to and from Singaporean bank accounts and for international shipping to Singapore. As with all GOST 7.67 codes, it is used primarily in Cyrillic alphabets.

SGS GOST 7.67 Latin three-letter geocode for the South Georgia and South Sandwich Islands. The code is used for transactions to and from local bank accounts and for international shipping to South Georgia and South Sandwich Islands. As with all GOST 7.67 codes, it is used primarily in Cyrillic alphabets.

SH 1. ISO 3166-1 alpha-2 code for Saint Helena. This is the code used in international transactions to and from Saint Helenian bank accounts. **2.** ISO 3166-2 geocode for Saint Helena. This is used as an international standard for shipping to Saint Helena. Each administrative divisionshas its own code with the prefix "SH." For example, the code for the Dependency of Ascension is ISO 3166-2:SH-AC.

Shaar In Kyrgyzstan, a political subdivision equivalent to a city outside the jurisdiction of any province.

Shabiyah In Libya, a political subdivision equivalent to a province.

Shadow In candlestick charting, the "wicks" above and below each candle. Each candle represents a single trading day; the shadow above a candle represents the highest price on that day while the shadow below represents the lowest price. See also: Real body.

Shadow Calendar A list of potential new issues that have been filed with the SEC but have not yet been processed. As such, the shadow calendar is the list of new issues that are waiting for permission to be made.

Shadow Open Market Committee An organization that meets bi-annually to evaluate and critique the policies of the Federal Reserve, as well as to discuss macroeconomics generally. The SOMC consists of various monetarist economists from academia and the private sector. It is frequently critical of the Federal Reserve, blaming it for both recessions and inflation throughout the 1970s and 1980s. It is not widely thought to have much influence on the policies the Fed actually adopts. See also: Federal Open Market Committee.

Shadow Pricing In a cost-benefit analysis, the assignment of a dollar value to an intangible asset or liability that cannot be sold. Shadow pricing is arbitrary; that is, because these assets and liabilities cannot be sold, and analysts must make an educated guess on their value. An example of shadow pricing occurs in the cost-benefit analysis of building a factory. The analysis must calculate the cost of blight on the neighborhood in which the factory is built. Because there is no way to put a real value on the cost of blight, shadow pricing assigns an arbitrary value to it.

Shadow Rating A credit rating given to a bond issue by a credit agency that is not reported to the general public. Credit ratings of bonds generally must be made public eventually, but the credit rating agency gives the shadow rating to the issuer before the issue is made. This gives the issuer an idea of the likely demand for the bonds.

Shadow Stock A term used to describe the stock of a publicly-traded company that has already been listed on an exchange after the listing of a new company in the same or a similar industry. For example, stock in an already established oil company is a shadow stock to that of a newly listed oil company. When a new company is listed on an exchange, its share price tends to increase rapidly. This often causes shadow stocks to increase as well. However, the increase in the shadow stock's price is not sustainable, as it is unrelated to its actual performance, and it tends to drop soon after.

Shahar In Uzbekistan, a city that is not a constituent within a province or other political subdivision. The only shahar in Uzbekistan is Tashkent, the capital.

Shaharlar In Uzbekistan, a political subdivision for a city.

Shahi A currency subdivision in Afghanistan between 1891 and 1925. A shahi was worth 1/12th of an Afghan rupee.

Shahrestan In Iran, a political subdivision equivalent to a county.

Shakeout A consolidation of the number of companies in an industry. Shakeouts occur because of stiff competition and the ability of some companies to offer a better product at a lower price than other companies. Shakeouts are generally considered a normal part of an industry life cycle.

Shake-Out Formation In technical analysis, a situation in which a price rises to its resistance level, then falls below its support level, but then rises again. This is considered a bullish signal.

Shaku A unit of length in Japan equivalent to approximately one foot.

Share A certificate giving the person or company listed a portion of ownership in a stock, mutual fund, or some other investment vehicle. A share is the smallest unit of ownership. They may be bought or sold on or off an exchange.

Share Account An account at a credit union. A share account gives the account holder a percentage of ownership in the credit union. Because of this, share accounts earn dividends rather than interest.

Share Broker A broker or brokerage that charges a flat fee per each share that one trades, rather than a percentage of the whole value of the trade. This can result in lower transaction costs for an investor and, for that reason, appeals to those seeking a discount broker.

Share Draft A withdrawal from a share account, which is an account at credit union. While share accounts are structured differently from accounts at ordinary banks, share drafts behave the same as any other withdrawal.

Share Issued at Discount A stock issued at a price below its face value. For example, a share with par of $100 might be issued to an investor for $70. Shares issued at discount are rare because stocks almost never have face values anymore.

Share Premium Account Capital raised in an issue of shares that exceeds the nominal value of the shares. The share premium account is recorded on the company's balance sheet and cannot be returned to shareholders as dividends.

Share Purchase Right A right attached to some shares giving the shareholder the ability to buy more shares of the same stock at a given price. It is similar to a stock option, but is distributed to existing shareholders rather than bought and sold. However, share purchase rights may be traded like any other option.

Share Turnover A measure of the liquidity of a security calculated by taking the average trading volume for a given period and dividing by the average shares outstanding for the same period. The higher the share turnover ratio is, the more liquid the security is because it indicates that the security can be bought and sold easily.

Shared Appreciation Mortgage A mortgage where the lender allows the borrower to pay a lower interest rate in exchange for giving the lender a portion of the property's appreciated value when it is sold. For example, if the borrower buys a house for $100,000 under a SAM and sells it five years later for $130,000, the lender would be entitled to an agreed-upon portion of the extra $30,000. Most of the time, there is a limit on how long the borrower can hold the house under a SAM. That is, if the SAM is not repaid within, say, 10 years, and the borrower has not sold the house, he must generally refinance at the prevailing interest rate.

Shareholder Communications Improvement Act Legislation in the United States, passed in 1989, requiring investment companies holding proxy powers on behalf of beneficial owners to provide proxy statements and other information to the appropriate parties.

Shareholder Meeting Any meeting in which the shareholders of a publicly-traded company discuss and vote on matters pertaining to the company. At a shareholder meeting, the company may present its financial reports. Shareholders also may ask questions of the board of directors. Publicly-traded companies are required to have at least one such meeting each year; management may also call an extraordinary general meeting at its discretion.

Shareholder Proposal A proposal for a publicly-traded company to take a certain course of action, submitted by a shareholder. Any shareholder who owns more than $2,000 in stock or 1% of the company is permitted to initiate a shareholder proposal. It must be placed on the agenda and put to a vote at the next available annual shareholders meeting, unless the SEC gives the company special permission to exempt it. Generally speaking, a shareholder makes a shareholder proposal to force the company to do something that the management does not want it to do. As a result, management tends to urge shareholders to vote against shareholder proposals, though they may seek a compromise with the shareholders if the proposal is popular.

Shareholder Value Added The value of a company to its stockholders. That is, the SVA measures whether or not it is worth the expense for an investor to buy stock in a company. It is calculated by taking the net operating profit after taxes and subtracting the cost of capital. See also: Market Value Added, Economic Value Added.

Shareholder Value Transfer A measure of the amount of equity going out of a publicly-traded company when the company's executives exercise stock options. It is measured as the difference between the strike price of the stock options and the fair market value of the company's stock. When an executive receives a stock option, he/she has the right to buy shares in the company at a certain price, regardless of the company's market value. When these options are exercised, the company is deprived of the equity it otherwise would have received had those shares been sold to someone else.

Shareholder Vote An election in a corporation in which all shareholders may participate. Shareholder votes are most often associated with electing directors and setting company policies at the annual meeting of shareholders. In order to be able to vote, one must hold voting stock. The right to vote gives the holder of voting stock a great deal of control over the company.

Shareholders' Letter A section of an annual report providing general information to shareholders. Every publicly-traded company is required to distribute an annual report to shareholders each year. The shareholders' letter contains information on the company's financial state, such as operational income and net profit. Sometimes it also contains an accountant's opinion on the general health of the company. Generally, the shareholders' letter states the "bottom line," and shareholders may read the rest of the annual report to learn more detailed financial information. For example, the shareholders' letter may contain a brief essay stating, "Our company is healthy for reasons A, B, and C."

Shares Outstanding The number of shares an issuing entity, such as a publicly-traded company, has not repurchased and that are available for trade by the general public. This is sometimes known as collection float or float.

Shark A company that is offering or executing a hostile takeover. If a firm makes an offer to shareholders to acquire a publicly-traded company after the board of directors refused, or if it bypasses the board completely, one refers to the acquiring firm as a shark. This is a derogatory term, and so one might expect the board, management, or even employees, to use it more than shareholders. See also: Shark repellent.

Shark Watcher A specialist or firm that specializes in early detection of hostile takeovers. Client corporations hire shark watchers to monitor trade patterns and see what companies might be accumulating shares. Common clients include firms concerned about a possible takeover and third-party firms interested in engaging in risk arbitrage. A shark watcher's primary business is often the solicitation of proxies from shareholders. See also: Antitakeover measure.

Sharpe Benchmark In financial econometrics, a model for a portfolio's performance that attempts to account for a money manager's index-like tendencies. In other words, the Sharpe benchmark attempts to statistically calculate whether a portfolio's success was due to good management or the taking of excessive risk. The model measures a company's or portfolio's performance against a series of securities indices.

Shaykhat In Tunisia, a political subdivision roughly equivalent to a municipality.

Sheetwise Describing a paper on which only one side has print.

Shelf Registration A method the SEC uses to allow a publicly-traded company to register several new issues of stock and actually offer them at any time over a two-year period, subject to compliance with other appropriate regulations. These offerings are covered by a single prospectus, but may be offered to the public in different tranches. See also: Rule 415.

Shelf Talker A sign or other display intended to attract a shopper's attention to a shelf or product at a retail store. A shelf talker is intended to persuade a shopper to buy the stated product. A shelf talker is also called a shelf screamer.

Shell Branch A branch of an American bank outside the United States with few operations other than to handle the bank's overseas transactions. They often are located in an offshore banking center. Records at shell branches may be kept at a different branch altogether.

Shell Corporation A company that exists as a vehicle for transactions without any independent activities or assets. Shell corporations are formed sometimes to obtain financing before they begin operations, or after a bankruptcy and business has ceased. They are also used in tax avoidance and tax evasion schemes: for example, companies may set up shell subsidiaries in tax havens and hide profits in them. See also: Reverse acquisition.

Sheltered Monopoly A monopoly that a government or, rarely, another body protects from competition. For example, a company may receive a charter to be the only company in its industry to operate in a certain area. Sheltered monopolies such as the British East India Trading Company were common in the early development of capitalism. In the United States, the insurance industry and Major League Baseball are exempt from most antitrust law, which may make them a type of sheltered monopoly.

Shematy An ancient Egyptian unit of weight approximately equivalent to 1.13 grams during the Old and Middle Kingdoms or 7.58 grams during the New Kingdom.

Sheng In China, a political subdivision approximately equivalent to a province.

Shengxiashi In Taiwan, a political subdivision equivalent to a municipality under the direct control of its province.

Shenzhen Stock Exchange One of the major stock exchanges in the People's Republic of China. Shares in more than 500 companies with a market capitalization of over $225 billion trade on its floor. It is one of the largest stock exchanges in Asia.

Shequ In China, a political subdivision equivalent to a residential area within a city or town.

Sheriff's Sale An auction to sell private property that an authority has seized in order to pay a judgment. For example, suppose a man is found guilty of managing a Ponzi scheme. If he lacks the cash to repay the persons he defrauded, his house may be seized and later sold at a sheriff's sale.

Sherman Antitrust Act The first legislation passed in the United States limiting trusts and monopolies. The Act prohibits agreements and collusion restricting trade, without providing many specifics. The Act was largely unenforced against the organizations it was intended to curtail. Indeed, the Act was invoked early on to restrict organized labor more than any other group. As a result, Congress passed the Clayton Act in 1914 to clarify American antitrust law. The Sherman Act has been criticized by many, notably Ayn Rand and her followers, for unfairly and inefficiently restricting the Invisible Hand of the market.

Sherwan In Nepal, a political subdivision approximately equivalent to a rural municipality.

Shibosai Bond A bond issued in yen to private investors outside Japan. That is, a shibosai bond, unlike other samurai bonds, is not offered to financial institutions. See also: Private placement.

Shield Nickel A copper coin minted by the United States between 1866 and 1883. It was worth 1/20 of one dollar.

Shikuchoson In Japan, a political subdivision equivalent to a municipality.

Shilling 1. In the United Kingdom, an informal term for a five pence coin. The term dates back to before decimalization, when a shilling was worth 1/20 of a pound. The term also persists with the same meaning for 1/20 of an Australian dollar. **2.** The name of the currency in several Commonwealth countries.

Shimming The act or practice of a broker or dealer stealing a few cents (or the equivalent) from a client while conducting a trade. Shimming results in a small gain for the broker or dealer, but, with volume, may add up to a significant amount. Shimming is illegal in most jurisdictions.

Shingle Theory Informal for a fiduciary duty. The term refers to a broker who "hangs a shingle" or a sign advertising his/her services and therefore has a legal and ethical responsibility to act in the client's best interests.

Shipper's Export Declaration A form that an exporter or a shipping company must file with the U.S. Department of Commerce if the value of the commodity one is exporting exceeds a certain value. In 2000, this value was $2,500. The form is administered by the U.S. Census Bureau. See also: International trade.

Shipping Certificate A document stating that an approved facility must make delivery of the underlying asset to the buyer of a futures contract. Shipping certificates are used on futures exchanges.

Shipping Documents All appropriate papers and forms needed for international shipping. Necessary shipping documents vary with different goods, but common examples include permission to take the goods out of the country, a statement of inventory, and insurance documentation.

Shirkah In Islamic finance, an agreement between two or more parties forming a business or other venture. There are two basic types of shirkah: mudharaba and musharika. In a mudharaba, one party contributes capital and another manages the business. In a musharika, multiple parties contribute capital. In both cases, the shirkah must comply with Islamic law.

Shirking The act of working less when there is no chance of earning a higher return. For example, a company may have punitive taxes levied on it if its profits are considered excessive. The owners of the company therefore have an incentive to shirk their responsibilities and to not work as hard as they otherwise would. Likewise, employees who are paid poorly may shirk their responsibilities since there is no incentive rewarding hard work.

Shixiaqu In China, a political subdivision consisting of a section within a city.

Shkalik A Russian unit of liquid volume approximately equivalent to 61.5 milliliters. It was rendered obsolete when the Soviet Union began to use the metric system in 1924. An equivalent term is kosuskha.

SHN GOST 7.67 Latin three-letter geocode for Saint Helena. The code is used for transactions to and from local bank accounts and for international shipping to Saint Helena. As with all GOST 7.67 codes, it is used primarily in Cyrillic alphabets.

Shoehorning The practice of picking and choosing data to fit a previous prediction. For example, if one predicts a recession but the recession does not materialize, one may identify negative economic information to "prove" that the recession (or at least a slowdown) really happened. Shoehorning connotes ignoring contradictory data.

Shogun Bond A bond issued in Japan by a non-Japanese organization in any currency other than the yen. The shogun bond market is relatively small, but the World Bank has issued them in the past. Less commonly, it is called a geisha bond.

Shoko Chukin Bank A bank in Japan that provides loans and other forms of financing to small and medium-sized business cooperatives. It originally was owned by the Japanese government, but its privatization began in 2008. It is also called by its English name, the Central Bank for Commercial and Industrial Cooperatives.

Shooting Star In candlestick charting, a situation in which a security, which was trading above its opening price for most of the trading day, suddenly reverses and closes down for the day. This is represented on the candlestick chart by a (usually short) black candle with a long upward shadow, which looks like a wick. Shooting stars occur during a bullish trend and may indicate reversal.

Shootout Informal; a bidding war between two venture capital firms over financing for a startup. This usually gives the startup the best possible terms.

Shop 1. Among workers on Wall Street, informal for a company, especially a publicly-traded company. **2.** To seek out the best bid price or ask price possible for a security by contacting a large number of broker-dealers.

Shopped Stock An inquiry or offer to sell a stock that the seller makes to several dealers before receiving any indication of interest.

Shopping The practice of an investor or broker investigating bids and/or offers from a number of sources, possibly on multiple exchanges, in order to find the best price for a trade.

Short Bias An investment strategy in hedge funds in which much or all of a fund's investments consist of short sales.

Short Bond A bond with a short current maturity. That is, a short bond is a bond with a comparatively short amount of time before it matures. While there is no hard and fast rule as to how "short" the time is that would make a short bond qualify as such, it usually means that the bond will mature in less than one or two years.

Short Coupon 1. A bond with a short maturity, often defined as two years or less. **2.** The first coupon payment on a bond that includes less than six months' worth of interest. For example, if a company issues a bond on May 1, with coupon payments due on June 15 and December 15, the first payment will only include a few weeks' worth of interest.

Short Cover The act of buying a security one has previously sold short in order to close a position. In order to make a profit on a short cover, one must buy the security at a price less than the price at which one sold it. It is also simply called a cover.

Short Exempt A short sale exempt from the short sale rule, which was a rule requiring that short sales occur only after upticks or zero plus-ticks. Convertible securities were sometimes short exempt. This is no longer important as the short sale rule is not in effect anymore.

Short Form Prospectus Distribution System A standard system Canadian regulators use to distribute a changes to the prospectus for each issue of a security. Firms may use the SFPDS if they continuously distribute information to their investors and therefore do not want to go through the trouble of issuing a completely new prospectus for every new issue and every change to old issues. The SFPDS requires less information than the full prospectus otherwise would. It is governed by the Securities Act and applicable provincial laws.

Short Forward Date A date less than two months in the future on which a forward contract expires. That is, a short forward date is the expiration date for a short-term forward contract.

Short Hedge The sale of a futures contract or option on a security or commodity one owns in order to hedge against the risk of decline in its price. In a short hedge, the price of the futures contract or option should move inversely to the price of the underlying asset. It is also called a selling hedge.

Short Interest The number of shares of a security that have been short sold, expressed as a percentage of the shares outstanding. Short selling is the sale of borrowed securities; those who engage in it must buy the same security soon thereafter in order to repay them. Some analysts thus believe that a high percentage of short interest is an indication that demand to buy a security will rise in the short-term.

Short Interest Ratio In technical analysis and fundamental analysis, a ratio of the short-sold shares of a publicly traded company to the trading volume over a given period of time. This is an indication of the market's sentiment regarding a particular stock. A higher ratio indicates a feeling that the stock will decline in value, while a lower ratio indicates general belief that it will rise. It is not an exact indication, as it fails to take into account matters such as the potential exercise of convertible shares. Fundamental analysts interpret a high ratio as bearish because it shows an expectation for lower prices; on the other hand, technical analysts see a middling ratio as bullish as it may indicate a demand for a stock among hedge funds unable to cover a short sale. The short interest ratio is also called days to cover. See also: Hedge fund.

Short Interest Theory In technical analysis, a theory stating that when an exceptionally large number of investors have a short position on a security, the price of that security will soon rise because those same investors will need to buy to close their positions. For example, if many investors have short sold a stock, they must soon buy that stock to repay it to the brokerage. This results in an increase in demand for the stock, which increases the price.

Short Leg In an option spread, any option contract on which one has a short position. For example, if one has bought a call and sold a put as part of one's option strategy, the put is said to be the short leg of the spread.

Short Market Value The market value of all of an investor's short positions at the end of a trading day. The short market value is calculated each day to determine whether or not the investor has maintained his/her maintenance margin and therefore whether he/she is subject to a margin call.

Short Position The sale of a security or derivative, or the state of having sold one or the other. It is important to note that a short position is not closed, and is applied only to sales where further action may be required. For example, one who has borrowed securities and has then sold them is said to be have a short position with respect to that security, because he/she must eventually return an equivalent amount of the borrowed securities. Likewise, one who has sold (or written) an option is in a short position, because the option may be exercised at a later date. See also: Long position, Close a position.

Short Ratio In technical analysis, a ratio of short sales made by investors to the total trading volume on a given trading day. Investors often sell short when they expect security prices to fall. Thus, a high short ratio is considered a bearish signal, while a low ratio is thought to be bullish.

Short Run Informal for short term.

Short Sale The sale of borrowed securities. In a short sale, one borrows securities, usually from a brokerage, and sells them. One then buys the same securities in order to repay the brokerage. Selling short is practiced if one believes that the price of a security will soon fall. That is, one expects to sell the borrowed securities at a higher price than the price at which one will buy in order to return the securities. Selling short is one of the most common practices of hedge funds. This is also called establishing a bear position. See also: Margin account.

Short Sale Rule An SEC regulation in effect from 1938 until 2007 forbidding short sales on a stock after a downward tick in its transaction price. In other words, if the price of a stock decreased in the trade immediately prior to a transaction, that transaction is not allowed to be a short sale. Short sales were only permitted after an uptick or a zero-plus tick. This rule was instituted to prevent panic selling in an era when lack of computerization made markets more easily to manipulate. With the increased digitalization of stock markets, this rule was no longer necessary.

Short Sell Against the Box Describing the action of short selling a security one owns. When one sells against the box, gains and losses are equalized by the long position on a security combined with the short position created by the short sale. One formerly sold against the box generally in order to be able to claim profits on the sale in the following tax year, but the Taxpayer Relief Act of 1997 largely removed this loophole.

Short Settlement A trade that is settled before it otherwise would have been, because one party or the other requests it.

Short Squeeze A situation in which a rapid increase in demand coupled with a small supply causes a stock price to rise significantly. This occurs most commonly in small companies with relatively few shares outstanding.

Short Tender The use of borrowed shares to receive proceeds from a tender offer. That is, if one borrows shares during a tender offer, and then sells them to the party making the offer, one has engaged in a short tender. The SEC prohibits short tenders under Rule 10b-4. See also: Short sale.

Short the Basis In futures, to take a short position on a commodity and a long position on a futures contract on the same commodity. This allows the investor to lock in the price of the commodity for when he/she must make delivery on the commodity. Shorting the basis is important especially when the investor believes that the price of the commodity will soon rise. See also: Long the basis.

Shortfall The amount by which an obligation or liability that is due exceeds one's ability to pay. For example, if a company has a $5,000 payroll for a given two week period, but only has $4,200 in its checking account, the company has a shortfall of $800. Obviously, shortfalls are causes of significant concern and can force an individual or company to borrow money to pay the obligation or liability. See also: Budget.

Shortfall Risk The risk that an investment's actual return will be less than the expected return, or, more properly, the return needed to meet one's investment goals.

Short-Form Registration A document filed with the SEC explaining a new issue of securities for public trade. A short-form registration allows the registering company to reference its previous registration statement to avoid repeating information. This especially applies to information on the issuer's financial situation. Short-form registration makes registration of new issues easier for the issuer.

Shorting Salomon During the 1980s, the practice in which a Salomon Brothers employee would line up an alternative job in case an investment caused a loss for the company and the employee was fired. Shorting Salomon was a way for employees to hedge their career choices. The practice was exposed in the book Liar's Poker, which describes the author's experience as a bond trader on Wall Street in the 1980s.

Shorts and Puts 500 A derogatory nickname for the S&P 500 index. The name is used sarcastically when the S&P 500 is bearish. Other nicknames with the same connotation are the Stupid and Poor 500 and the S and Flee 500 Miles.

Short-Short Test A former IRS restriction that limited returns on investments of less than three months to 30% of gross income. The penalty for accruing more than this was the loss of certain other tax breaks. This test negatively impacted mutual funds, the managers of which needed to ensure that they were not too successful. The short-term test was repealed with the Taxpayer Relief Act of 1997.

Short-Term Referring to any investment, financial plan, or anything else lasting for one year or less. Short term investments and financial plans usually involve less uncertainty than long-term investments and financial plans because, generally speaking, market trends are more easily predictable for one year than for any longer period. Likewise, short-term financial plans are more easily amendable as a result of the short time frame. Short-term financial plans usually involve investing in short-term securities, such as T bills or commercial paper See also: Long Term.

Short-Term Bond Fund A mutual fund that invests predominantly or exclusively in bonds with maturities of less than a few years. The idea behind a short-term bond fund is to provide a return at little risk (compared to other investments) that is nonetheless better than the risk-free rate of return.

Short-Term Capital Gain The gain one realizes by closing a position one has held for less than one year. For example, if one buys a stock or bond and sells it five months later for more than what one paid, the gain is considered a short-term capital gain. The government wishes to encourage long-term investment and, as such, short-term capital gains are usually not entitled to preferential treatment for tax purposes; that is, they are taxed at a higher rate than gains from long-term investments. See also: Short-term capital loss.

Short-Term Capital Loss The loss one realizes by closing a position one has held for less than one year. For example, if one buys a stock or bond and sells it five months later for less than what one paid, the loss is considered a short-term capital loss. One may write off short-term capital losses against any capital gains.

Short-Term Debt Any bond or other debt that must be repaid or refinanced within one year. Short-term debts are recorded on a balance sheet as current liabilities.

Short-Term Discount Note A debt security with a maturity of one year or less issued at a discount to its face value. For example, if a short-term discount note has a face value of $1000, it may be issued to the holder at $900. When it matures, the holder receives the full $1000. A short-term discount note does not pay a coupon; rather the difference between the discount and the face value takes the place of the coupon. They are often issued by governments and low risk corporate borrowers. See also: Coupon-Equivalent Yield, Zero-Coupon Bond.

Short-Term Financial Plan A financial plan outlining investment and other financial goals for the coming fiscal year. Short-term financial plans involve less uncertainty than long-term financial plans because, generally speaking, market trends are more easily predictable in the short term. Likewise, short-term financial plans are more easily amendable as a result of the short time frame. Short-term financial plans usually invest in short-lived securities, such as T bills. A short-term financial plan aims to achieve goals that would be beneficial for one's long-term financial plan.

Short-Term Greed In investment banking, a term describing the placing of a bank's interests above those of one's client. That is, short-term greed encourages the bank to make money from trades or other investments, even if it causes some clients to lose out. Short-term greed may be detrimental to an investment bank in the long run as clients eventually may steer their assets elsewhere.

Short-Term Interest Rate The interest rate on a loan or other obligation with a maturity of less than one year. A commonly followed short-term interest rate is the rate on a Treasury bill. Short-term interest rates are also called money market rates.

Short-Term Investment Fund A mutual fund or other fund that invests exclusively in short-term, low-risk securities such as Treasury bills, money markets, and so forth. A STIF aims to protect the funds invested in it while also providing a (low) return. STIFs have exceptionally low management fees.

Short-Term Loan Any loan that must be repaid or refinanced within one year. Short-term loans are recorded on a balance sheet as current liabilities.

Short-Term Moving Average The average price of a security over several days, calculated continuously. For instance, one may calculate a short-term moving average by adding the closing prices from each day for the past week and dividing by the number of trading days considered. As with all moving averages, short-term moving averages may or may not be weighted. Moving averages help smooth out noise that may be present in a security's price on a given trading day. See also: Simple Moving Average, Exponential Moving Average.

Short-Term Municipal Bond Fund A mutual fund that invests predominantly or exclusively in short-term municipal bonds. The returns on a short-term municipal bond fund derive from coupons on the municipal bonds and are therefore tax exempt. The short-time frame of the bonds makes the fund quite liquid. As a result, these funds are beneficial for short term investors who wish to minimize their tax liability.

Short-Term Reserves Savings and investments that are expected to be liquidated in less than one calendar year. Examples of short-term reserves include deposits in banks, U.S. Treasury bills, and short-term certificates of deposit. See also: Money Market.

Short-Term Tax Exempts A short-term debt security issued by a municipality, agency, or other government or quasi-government body. Most short-term tax exempts are issued by housing agencies for development or urban renewal projects.

Short-Term Trading Index In technical analysis, a ratio indicating whether to buy or sell securities in the short term. It is calculated thusly: Short-term trading index = (Volume of advancing securities - Volume of declining securities) / (Number of advancing securities - Number of declining securities) A ratio above 1.3 is considered a buy signal, while a ratio below 0.7 is seen as a sell signal.

Short-Term Trend Any price movement that occurs over a few hours or days. Short-term trends can be predicted with some accuracy with technical analysis. Traders make large profits (and sometimes large losses) from predicting short-term trends. Value investors, on the other hand, tend to discount the importance of short-term trends.

Shotgun Approach A marketing strategy that focuses on a wide range of targets. That is, a shotgun approach attempts to market a product to as many demographics as possible. See also: Rifle Approach.

Shotgun Clause A provision in some shareholder or partnership agreement stating that if one shareholder offers to buy out the company at a certain price, the other shareholder(s) either must accept the offer or buy out the first shareholder at the same price. This is most common when two shareholders each own 50% of a business.

Shout Option An option contract that allows the holder the opportunity at certain points in the life of the contract to lock in a certain profit while continuing the holder the contract. For example, if a contract is in the money by $10 per share at a given time, the option holder may "shout" or lock in the profit. This means that he/she will make at least $10 per share regardless of the future price movements of the underlying asset. If the option is only $5 in the money at expiration, the holder still makes $10 per share. On the other hand, if it is in the money by $15 per share at expiration, the holder can collect the higher profit. A shout option gives a great deal of flexibility to the option holder. It is a type of exotic option.

Show Stopper 1. Any law or regulation that makes a hostile takeover impossible or prohibitively expensive. A show stopper may take the form of a court order or an act of legislation. The term implies that the target company takes some action in order to make the takeover difficult or impossible, but this is not always the case. See also: Antitakeover measure. **2.** More generally, anything that prevents an activity or transaction from taking place as planned.

Show-Through Describing print on paper that shows on the other side of the paper. Show-through print occurs when the paper is too thin.

Show-Up Time Money paid to union members who are required to arrive at a job site but not to work. Show-up time is associated with organized crime.

SHP ISO 4217 code for the Saint Helena pound. It has existed side by side with the British pound since the early 19th century. It is pegged to the British pound at a one-to-one ratio. Interestingly, Saint Helena does not have a central bank, and pounds are issued through a private, commercial bank.

Shrapnel In the United Kingdom, a slang term for loose coins in one's pocket.

Shrink A slang term for the losses a retail company suffers from shoplifting. Some companies, such as grocery stores, may build shrink into their earnings estimates.

Shrinkage A reduction in inventory due to a loss, theft, deterioration, or accounting error. Deterioration is a normal part of trading perishable goods. For example, a grocery store selling milk will likely experience shrinkage due to some of the milk spoiling. Shrinkage can be a tax write-off for the company experiencing it.

Shrinking Asset 1. An asset that depreciates. For example, an automobile is a shrinking asset because it loses value over time due to its limited useful life. Shrinking assets are important in taxation: one pays less in taxes on an asset the more it depreciates. See also: Absolute physical life. **2.** An asset that is consumed. These shrinking assets are usually commodities; for example, a trucking company may buy a large amount of gasoline, which could theoretically be resold or liquidated, but is in fact used in the operation of the trucking company.

Shruggy A slang term for a stock that rises in price (or at least does not fall) in the wake of bad news, such as a negative earnings report.

Shunto In Japan, annual negotiations between trade unions and corporations on wage increases. Traditionally, shunto began in March each year. Over time, wage increases during shunto became almost automatic. Shunto has become less common since the 1990s with the weakening of unions in the wake of the Asian financial crisis.

Shutdown 1. See: Government shutdown. **2.** See: Liquidation. **3.** See: Lockout.

Shut-Down Price The price of a product below which it is cheaper for a company not to make the product than to continue to sell it. That is, the shut-down price is the price at which the company will begin to lose money for making the product.

Shuttle Trade A small retailer's purchase of goods in a different country in order to re-sell them. For example, a retailer in the United States may buy a limited amount of Belgian chocolate to sell in his gift shop. Shuttle trades often are snuck through customs without declaration in order to save on tariffs.

Shyster 1. A crook or a con man who tries to sell inferior goods or to cheat customers. **2.** A corrupt lawyer or politician.

Si 1. ISO 3166-1 alpha-2 code for the Republic of Slovenia. This is the code used in international transactions to and from Slovenian bank accounts. **2.** ISO 3166-2 geocode for Slovenia. This is used as an international standard for shipping to

Slovenia. Each municipality has its own code with the prefix "SI." For example, the code for the Municipality of Bled is ISO 3166-2:SI-003.

Sicilicus 1. An ancient Roman unit of area approximately equivalent to 52.6 square meters. **2.** An ancient Roman unit of weight approximately equivalent to 6.85 grams.

Side Collateral Collateral that only covers a portion of the value of a loan. For example, one may pledge a $10,000 certificate of deposit to cover a $50,000 loan. Side collateral lessens the risk of a loan, but not as much as full collateral.

Side Effects The effect a company's activity has on other activities in the company. For example, if an investment performs poorly, it may have the side effect of depriving other departments of funds needed for their own operations.

Side-by-Side Trading The practice of buying or selling a security while also buying or selling an option on that security at the same time. The SEC watches side-by-side trading closely because it opens the possibility for price manipulation.

Sidelined Describing a currency that is no longer traded at high volume because foreign exchange traders have begun to favor another currency.

Sidelines 1. Describing investors who believe that the markets are too volatile to risk their money. They therefore keep their money in short-term, low-risk investments until the markets are perceived to have calmed down. Investors on the sidelines usually have lower risk tolerance than investors who keep their money in the markets during these times. **2.** Describing investors who are watching a security instead of taking a position on it.

Siege Economy An economy under such heavy government regulation that it cannot function properly. Examples of circumstances that may result in a siege economy include excessive taxes or laws that prevent growth. The appropriate amount of government intervention in an economy remains highly controversial.

Siegh A Maltese unit of land area approximately equivalent to 187.4 square meters. It is largely obsolete but is still used in some circumstances.

Sight Draft A check or other draft that is payable to the payee when the payee presents the draft to the appropriate party. It contrasts with a time draft, which is not payable until a stated date in the future.

Sight Unseen Describing a bid to buy a good or other asset without seeing it first. For example, one may purchase a house through an agent without ever going to the house oneself. Another example would be an offer to buy a rare coin after reading a description without actually seeing it.

Signal An indication of a company's health and/or actions. Signaling a certain state or action may cause a company's stock to rise or fall in price. Generally speaking, the more money a signal costs a company to make, the stronger the signal is thought to be. For example, a company may make a statement indicating financial distress, but reducing its dividends is thought to be a stronger signal.

Signaling Approach on Dividend Policy The belief that the amount per share a company pays in dividends is a strong indication of what the management believes about future earnings. For example, if the company pays $5 per share when it had paid $8 per share the previous time dividends were disbursed, shareholders may take this as a signal that the management believes that earnings will soon decline. Some investors may use the signaling approach on dividend policy as a means to determine whether to buy or sell a stock.

Signature Guarantee A statement by a financial institution that a signature on a document is genuine. A signature guarantee is needed in some transfers of securities and other transactions. The signature guarantee is usually made by a commercial bank or a member firm. See also: Medallion Stamp Program.

Signature Loan A loan with no collateral that one borrows from a bank upon request. Signature loans may have high interest rates (because of the risk of no collateral), and they may be fairly small. For example, one may borrow a signature loan of $4,000 to consolidate and pay old medical bills.

Signatures on Proxies The name of the owner of a stock printed and signed on a proxy ballot to show that the proxy is legitimate.

Significant Influence The state of holding a substantial minority stake in a publicly-traded company such that one does not have outright control but is still a major player in the company's decisions. Usually, an investor is considered to have significant influence if he/she has at least a 20% holding in the company. One has significant influence because the number of voting shares gives one virtual veto power over company decisions, particularly when other stockholders are closely divided. These investors must be listed on the company's financial statements.

Significant Order An order to buy or sell a security that, because of its size, will likely cause a considerable price fluctuation. The exact size of a significant order varies according to security. For example, a stock with relatively few shares outstanding will likely have a smaller threshold for a significant order than others. Most of the time, significant orders are made by institutional investors. Generally speaking, they try to avoid price fluctuations by splitting significant orders into several parts and filling them over a certain period of time.

Significant Order Imbalance The excess of buy orders or sell orders for a given security. That is, a significant order imbalance occurs when brokers or investors have made many more orders of one type such that they cannot be matched to orders of the opposite type. Significant order imbalance in either direction reduces the liquidity of a security and thus specialists and market makers attempt to keep order imbalance at the lowest possible level. If the order imbalance becomes too extreme, the exchange may suspend trade.

Sila An ancient Sumerian unit of volume approximately equivalent to one liter.

Silent Partner In a partnership, a partner who owns a share in the company's equity, but does not take part in management. A partner provides capital in order to fund the company's operations and is liable for loss up to the amount of an investment. A silent partner is also responsible for at least a portion of the company's tax liability. Less commonly, a silent partner is called a sleeping partner.

Silicon Valley An area in California, centering on San Francisco and San Jose, known for the large number of computer and internet companies. Silicon Valley became important during the dot-com bubble in the 1990s. It remains important both in investing and for the technical expertise of its companies and employees. Prominent companies such as Google and Intel are headquartered in Silicon Valley.

Siliconaires Informal; young entrepreneurs, especially during the 1990s, who founded or were deeply involved with dot-com companies. When these companies went public at vastly inflated prices, these entrepreneurs suddenly found themselves to be millionaires. Some of them sold their remaining stock and retired very young, while others lost much of their fortunes when the dot-com bubble burst.

Silo Funds, assets, or anything else kept separate from other funds or assets of a similar type. For example, an investment company that manages both Islamic funds and conventional mutual funds must keep the Islamic funds siloed in order to prevent violations of the sharia.

Sil'rady In Ukraine, a political subdivision approximately equivalent to a municipality.

Silver A precious metal with the highest electrical conduction properties of any metal. It is used mainly in jewelry, photography, and for scientific and industrial purposes. It has been used as the basis for currencies in the past. Silver is traded as a commodity on various security exchanges. Like many precious metals, silver is volatile but generally maintains relatively high prices.

Silver Ceiling An unspoken barrier to promotion that is experienced by some older employees. A silver ceiling may exist because management believes older employees are not sufficiently innovative, or simply because they are too close to retirement to implement a long-term vision.

Silver Certificate A document entitling one to ownership of a certain, stated amount of silver. Most of the time, silver investors hold silver certificates rather than the physical silver itself in order to avoid the expense, security issues, and other difficulties associated with owning a precious metal. However, the holder of the silver certificate can take possession of the silver he/she owns upon demand.

Silver Clad Describing U.S. 50-cent pieces consisting of 80%/20% silver-copper core plated with a 21%/79% silver-copper alloy. These coins were minted from 1965 to 1970.

Silver Krugerrand An object purporting to be a South African coin containing silver. In South Africa, a krugerrand is minted only in gold. Silver krugerrands have no legal status and are sold only on certain disreputable websites.

Silver Parachute A clause in a hiring contract describing a relatively lucrative severance package once an employee leaves a company, especially after a merger or acquisition. Such a package often includes cash and stock options, as well equity in the company. A silver parachute is not normally as large as a golden parachute, but a greater number of employees are eligible for one.

SIMEX A former futures exchange in Singapore. It was established in 1984. It became defunct in 1999, following a merger with the Stock Exchange of Singapore; the two formed the Singapore Exchange.

Simple Interest Interest that does not compound. That is, simple interest is a percentage of the principal amount and is not added to the principal itself. For example, if one buys a $1000 bond that pays a 2% coupon in simple interest, one receives $20 each coupon date. The $20 is never added to the $1000. See also: Compound interest.

Simple Linear Regression In statistics, the analysis of variables that are dependent on only one other variable. Regression analysis uses regression equations, which shows the value of a dependent variable as a function of an independent variable. For example, a simple regression equation could take the form: $y = a + bx$ where y is the dependent variable and x is the independent variable. In this case, the slope is equal to b and a is the intercept. When plotted on a graph, y is determined by the value of x. Regression equations are charted as a line and are important in calculating economic data and stock prices. See also: Multiple regression.

Simple Linear Trend Model A way to predict a trend by taking a previous statistic and plotting out its future movement on the assumption that its growth rate remains the same. For example, if one is estimating a country's GDP according to a simple linear trend model, one takes the previous GDP growth rate (say 3% or -1%) and extrapolates the GDP indefinitely. The problem with simple linear trend models is the fact that many statistics simply do not grow or shrink at the same rate at all times.

Simple Moving Average The average price of a security calculated by adding closing prices from the most recent trading days (for example, the last 10 days) and dividing by the number of trading days considered (in this case, 10). A simple moving average is easy to calculate and provides a quick look at a security's short-term trend. See also: Exponential moving average.

Simple Prospect An investment in which only one of two outcomes is possible. For example, buying a stock is usually a simple prospect. The investment will either make money or lose money. This contrasts with other investments, such as an option, which has at least four possible outcomes.

Simple Rate of Return An estimate of the return on an investment. It is calculated simply by finding the investment's profit before taxes and interest expenses. The simple rate of return is easy to calculate but is not always accurate because it considers the investment's profit rather than cash flow. It also does not take into account the effects of compounding. It is also called the accounting rate of return or the book value method.

Simple Trust A trust in which the beneficiary may take ownership of the assets in the trust at any time. He/she may also take any and all income the trust produced whenever he/she wishes. The trustees of a simple trust must act in accord with the beneficiary's wishes. A simple trust contrasts with other types of trusts, in which the trustees are not answerable to the beneficiary. A simple trust is also called a bare trust.

Simplified Employee Pension Plan Also called a SEP IRA. A retirement plan designed for persons with self-employed income and their employees. It operates like an IRA: it has contribution limits and may be invested in securities. When an employer sets up an SEP, he/she creates a different account for each employee and puts a certain percentage of each person's income into these accounts. The percentage must be the same for the employer and all employees (although the dollar amounts will differ because of different levels of compensation). The employer makes all contributions, which are tax deductible for him/her; when the employee makes withdrawals upon retirement, the withdrawals are tax-free. SEPs may exist side-by-side with 401(k)s.

Simsar In Islamic law, a term for a broker or agent.

Simulation The use of a mathematical model with different values as variables in order to determine the likelihood of a particular outcome. A simulation is run many times (often thousands) in order to find the most likely outcome. Running simulations is important for analysts who, for example, wish to predict a security's future price movements.

Sin deudas A Spanish term describing a company with little or no debt. The phrase literally means "without debts," but it may be translated as "clean."

Sin Tax A tax on a good or service considered socially or ethically undesirable. For example, a government may levy a tax on the sale of alcohol. A sin tax finances programs to discourage the undesirable practice (in this example, it may fund anti-teen drinking programs). However, a sin tax may simply be a way for a government to generate revenue from something people are expected to do anyway.

Sine Die The adjournment of a committee or assembly without scheduling a date for the next meeting. Legislatures adjourn sine die at the end of a session, while a board of directors may do so if its company is closing down, being sold, or otherwise ceasing operations.

Sine Wave Any curve plotted along an axis where the y-value moves above and below zero at a rate of $y = \sin(x)$. The Composite Index of Lagging Indicators is thought to be roughly a sine wave because interest rates and inflation, which make up the index, move in relation to each other in a way resembling the sine.

Sinful Stock Stock in a publicly-traded company that engages in a business many people consider to be immoral. Common example of these "sinful" industries include alcohol, tobacco, pornography, payday loans, and weapons. While investors have different definitions of sinful stocks, many refuse to invest in these industries. See also: Ethical investing, Islamic finance.

Singapore Exchange Also called SGX. An exchange formed in 1999 through the merger of the Stock Exchange of Singapore and the Singapore International Monetary Exchange. Stocks, bonds, derivatives and other securities all trade on SGX. At its formation, it was the first demutualized exchange in Asia-Pacific on which both securities and derivatives traded.

Singapore Ministerial Declaration A statement made after a 1996 World Trade Organization meeting in Singapore that summarized the views of the participants. The document discussed customs, transparency in government procurements, investment, and competition.

Singaporean Dollar The currency of Singapore. It was issued in 1965 after the end of the currency union between Singapore, Brunei and Malaysia. It was, at different times, pegged to the British pound, the U.S. dollar and a currency basket. Since 1995, it has been a managed float currency. It is interchangeable with the Brunei dollar.

Single In American taxation, the filing status for a legally unmarried person who does not qualify for any other filing status. In other words, single is the default filing status. This may affects one's tax liability; for example, single filers have lower income limits for most exemptions.

Single Annuitant The annuitant for a single life annuity, which only provides payments to one person. That is, payments cease when the single annuitant dies. This contrasts with other annuities that make a lump sum payment to the annuitant's survivors, or continue payments to them for a certain number of years.

Single Currency Peg An exchange rate for a currency whose value the government has decided to link to another currency, as opposed to a currency basket or a commodity like gold. For example, under the Bretton Woods System, most world currencies fixed themselves to the U.S. dollar, forming a single currency peg across most of the world. Under a single currency peg, a government must hold enough reserves of the peg in the central bank. For example, if a country fixes its currency to the British pound, it must hold enough pounds in reserve to account for all of its currency in circulation.

Single European Act An agreement among European Community members to gradually reduce tariffs and trade barriers with a goal of creating a Common Market in Europe. The Act aimed to unify trade and other laws among participating nations. It came into effect in 1987 and was replaced by the institutions of the European Union in 1993.

Single Life Annuity An annuity that only provides payments to one person. That is, payments cease when the annuitant dies. This contrasts with other annuities that make a lump sum payment to the annuitant's survivors, or continue payments to them for a certain number of years.

Single Option An option contract. Unlike more complex spreads and straddles, which involve the purchase or sale of multiple options in order to profit in different ways, a single option is a straightforward call or put. An investor in a single option makes a profit or loss depending on the movement of the underlying asset.

Single Premium A lump sum used to purchase an annuity, insurance policy, or similar instrument. A single premium is expensive, but it causes less strain on one's monthly budget as it does not require one to make recurring payments. See also: Single Premium Immediate Annuity, Single Premium Deferred Annuity.

Single Premium Deferred Annuity An annuity purchased with a lump sum payment by the annuitant, who does not begin to receive payments until some future date. Like all deferred annuities, an SPDA has two phases, a savings phase and an income phase. The savings phase involves the annuity taking the lump sum payment and investing it on behalf of the annuitant. In the income phase, the annuitant receives payments. It is important to note that an SPDA, like all deferred annuities, is not taxed until the income phase begins. It also pays a death benefit to the survivor(s) of the annuitant. See also: IRA, 401(k).

Single State Municipal Bond Fund In the United States, a mutual fund that invests exclusively in municipal bonds issued in a single state. The returns from such a fund are exempt from all federal taxes and all state taxes if the bondholder is a resident of that state. A single state municipal bond fund is attractive to locals and encourages them to invest in the fund. It is particularly important in states such as New York, with large populations, and states with high capital gains taxes, such as Oregon.

Single Stock Future A derivative in which the buyer and seller agree to exchange one stock at a certain price at a certain time. Single stock futures are bought on margin and, because they are futures and not actual stock, one may short sell single stock futures without being subject to the downtick rule. Single stock futures are usually traded in lots of 100 at a time. South Africa contains the largest market for single stock futures, though they are traded worldwide. In the United States, they are usually traded on OneChicago LLC. See also: Commodity Futures Modernization Act of 2000.

Single-Buyer Policy A practice in which the Ex-Im Bank allows exporters to buy separate insurance policies for separate transactions.

Single-Country Fund A mutual fund that invests predominantly or exclusively in the securities of a single country. While a single-country fund may be diversified in other ways (for instance, it may hold both stocks and bonds), it is usually exposed to political risk. Some analysts argue that in an age of globalization, there is little difference in single-country and multi-country funds, but others dispute that. See also: Country diversification, WEBS.

Single-Factor Model A mathematical calculation of the extent to which one macroeconomic factor affect the securities in a portfolio. Single-factor models attempt to account for contingencies like changes in interest rate or inflation. Usually, however, a single-factor model considers how the market return affects the return on the portfolio. See also: Risk analysis, Factor model.

Single-Index Model The relationship between a security's performance and the performance of a portfolio containing it. The market model states that the security's performance is related to its portfolio's performance, according to its beta. It is calculated as follows: Return on security = alpha + beta * return on portfolio + residual return

Single-Payment Bond A bond that does not make coupon payments but rather allows interest to accrue and pays the entire liability in full at maturity.

Single-Premium Life Insurance A life insurance policy purchased with a large, lump sum payment. Single-premium life insurance may take any number of forms: it may be structured as whole life or term life, or nearly any other kind of life insurance. What distinguishes it is the one-time payment at the purchase of the policy.

Sinik A Turkish measure of volume approximately equivalent to 0.009 cubic meters, or slightly less than two and a half gallons. It became obsolete when Turkey made the metric system mandatory in 1933.

Sinking Fund A fund or account into which a person or company deposits money on a regular basis in order to repay some debt or other liability that will come due in the future. For example, if one has a loan with a balloon maturity of seven years, one may put money into a sinking fund for seven years in order to be ready to pay off the principal when it comes due. Some bonds have sinking fund provisions, requiring the issuer to put money aside to repay bondholders at maturity.

Sinking Fund Bond A bond with a fund or account into which an issuer deposits money on a regular basis to repay the bond when it matures. For example, if a company issues a bond with a balloon maturity of seven years, one may put money into a bond sinking fund for seven years in order to be ready to pay off the principal when it comes due. Some bonds have sinking fund provisions, requiring the issuer to put money aside to repay bondholders at maturity. See also: Sinking Fund Call.

Sinking Fund Call A provision in some bond indentures allowing the issuer to redeem a bond before maturity using money it had previously set aside in a sinking fund. A sinking fund is an account into which the issuer deposits money on a regular basis in order to repay the bond at some point in the future. A sinking fund call gives the company the ability to reduce its debt at its discretion. As with other callable bonds, a sinking fund call provision may only be exercised after a stated call date.

Sinking Fund Provision A provision in some bond indentures requiring the issuer to put money aside to repay bondholders at maturity. In bonds with such a provision, a fund or account is set up into which a issuer deposits money on a regular basis to repay the bond when it matures. See also: Sinking Fund Bond.

Siqlu 1. An ancient Akkadian unit of length approximately equivalent to one square meter. 2. An ancient Akkadian unit of weight approximately equivalent to nine grams.

SIT ISO 4217 code for the Slovenian tolar. It was introduced in 1991, replacing the Yugoslav dinar. In 2004, the tolar was pegged to the euro, which eventually replaced it in 2006.

Sit Tight A message to a client from a trader or broker advising patience and stating that an order will be executed as soon as possible.

SITC Standard International Trade Classification. A system used to classify goods traded internationally by type. Each type of good is given a numerical code, which is used to calculate statistics related to international trade. For example, the SITC code for organic chemicals is 51. The United Nations manages the SITC system.

Sit-Down Strike A strike in which union members or, rarely, other employees, come to work but sit at their workstations and do not perform their duties. The purpose behind a sit-down strike is to make it difficult or impossible for the employer to hire replacement workers to replace the strikers. This is supposed to make the strike more effective. See also: Lock-out.

SIX Swiss Exchange The primary exchange in Switzerland. Stocks, government and corporate bonds, derivatives and other securities all trade on the SIX Swiss Exchange. It was one of the first exchanges in the world to become fully automated. It was created in 1995 as the Basel, Geneva and Zurich exchanges moved their trading to a central, computerized floor. See also: Swiss Electronic Bourse.

Sixpence A former coin in the United Kingdom equal in value to 1/40 of one British pound. Sixpence ceased to circulate with the decimalization of the pound in 1971.

Sixteenth 1. In bonds, 0.0625% of one point. This is used when quoting bond prices. For example, a bond may have the price of 95 3/16 points, meaning that the bond is selling for 95.1875% of its par value. 2. In stocks, 0.0625% of one dollar. This format was used when stocks were quoted in fractions instead of decimals. It is less common today.

Size Informal; Referring to a large trading volume or number of securities. It often refers to 100,000 shares to buy or sell, but is a non-specific term relative to the market.

Size Effect The relative advantage the size of a company has on returns. Some analysts suggest that investing in a small company can lead to a higher return than investing in a large company, even after accounting for unsystematic risk.

Sizing The process of determining how many shares or bonds to place in a new issue. Sizing depends on the issuer's financing needs and other factors, such as its desired earnings per share.

Sizu An ancient Akkadian unit of length approximately equivalent to 333 centimeters.

SJ 1. ISO 3166-1 alpha-2 code for Svalbard and Jan Mayen. This is the code used in international transactions to and from local bank accounts. It is important to note that Svalbard and Jan Mayen are both part of Norway, but are unlike other ISO 3166 definitions in that they are not otherwise related. 2. ISO 3166-2 geocode for Svalbard and Jan Mayen. This is used as an international standard for shipping to Svalbard and Jan Mayen.

SJM GOST 7.67 Latin three-letter geocode for Svalbard and Jan Mayen. The code is used for transactions to and from local bank accounts and for international shipping to Svalbard and Jan Mayen. As with all GOST 7.67 codes, it is used primarily in Cyrillic alphabets.

Sjomil A Swedish unit of nautical distance equivalent to 7,408 meters.

SK 1. ISO 3166-1 alpha-2 code for Sikkim before it merged into India. This was the code used in international transactions to and from bank accounts in Sikkim. 2. ISO 3166-2 geocode for Sikkim. This was used as an international standard for shipping to Sikkim. In both cases, the code is obsolete.

Skalpund A Swedish unit of weight approximately equivalent to 425 grams or about one pound.

Skeppspund A Swedish unit of weight approximately equivalent to 170 kilograms.

Skewed Distribution A probability distribution where more data points lie on one side of the mean than the other. This means that the distribution will not form a bell curve.

Skid On a ship, a plank of timber set parallel to other planks in order to support weight.

Skill The ability to perform a task well. For example, a locksmith has the skill to make new keys for customers' homes and cars. Skills are required to perform many jobs and employers will only hire persons who fit the required skill set. As a result, skilled workers are often more highly paid than unskilled workers.

Skilled Labor The ability to perform a specific task or occupation. For example, a locksmith has the skill to make new keys for customers' homes and cars. Other examples of skilled laborers include carpenters, mechanics, graphic designers, and so forth. Skilled workers are often more highly paid than unskilled workers.

Skilled Worker A worker who is able to perform a specific task well. For example, a locksmith is a skilled worker because he/she can make new keys for customers' homes and cars. Skilled workers need some training and many acquire a certification from an institute stating that they have passed coursework in a skill. Because of this additional training and ability, skilled workers are often more highly paid than unskilled workers.

Skilling A subdivision of the speciedaler, the former currency of Norway. A skilling was worth 1/120 of one speciedaler.

Skimming 1. The act of stealing a person's credit card information on an electronic device and transferring the information to a different card. It may occur during a normal business transaction. For example, if one uses a credit card to make a purchase, the person handling the card may surreptitiously swipe the card through another electronic device that copies the information contained on it. The skimmer then transfers the information to another card. **2.** The act or practice of stealing a small amount of money from a company, especially over a long period of time, so that it adds up to a large amount. One example is a worker neglecting to ring up a sale and simply keeping the money. A more sophisticated example involves a banker stealing a few fractions of a cent each time a transaction occurs. Over time, this can add up to a great deal of money.

Skin ISO 3166-3 code for Sikkim, which acceded to India in 1975. ISO 3166-3 codes are used to indicate names of countries that are no longer used.

Skin in the Game Informal; a situation in which an executive in a publicly-traded company uses his/her own money to buy stock in that company. It is fairly common for an executive to receive stock as compensation or to exercise stock options to buy stock at a discount. It is less common for an executive to risk his/her own money in the company for which he/she works as if he/she were an outside investor. Putting skin in the game is seen as a sign of good faith or a show of confidence in the future of the company. The term was coined by Warren Buffett.

Skip Person The transfer of a property to a person two or more generations younger than the person making the transfer. This may trigger a taxable event.

Skip-Day Settlement On an exchange, the practice of settling a transaction one day after the normal time period in which it is settled. For example, if a trade is usually settled five business days after the transaction, skip-day settlement requires the trade to settle six days after the original transaction. See also: delayed settlement.

Skip-Payment Privilege A clause in some mortgage contracts allowing the borrower to skip payments if he/she is ahead of schedule on repayment or has given advance notice to the lender that the payment will be skipped. If the borrower skips a payment under the skip-payment privilege, it does not change or affect the repayment schedule, interest accumulation, or anything else. This gives the borrower some degree of flexibility if he/she has unexpectedly high expenses in a given month. The borrower can miss a payment without risking default, which is detrimental to both the lender and the borrower. It is also called a skip payment clause.

Skippund A Norwegian unit of weight approximately equivalent to 159.5 kilograms.

Skirt Length Theory A theory of investing stating that market trends follow the length of women's skirts. That is, when women wear short skirts, there is or will be a bull market because of high consumer confidence. On the other hand, when they wear long skirts, there is or will be a bear market because consumer confidence is low. There is little evidence that the skirt length theory is true.

SKK ISO 4217 code for the Slovak koruna. It was first issued in 1993 with the separation of Slovakia and the Czech Republic, replacing the Czechoslovakian koruna at par. It was the sole currency of Slovakia until the end of 2008, when the nation adopted the euro.

Skogsmil A Swedish unit of length approximately equivalent to five kilometers.

Skojec A unit of account used in medieval central and eastern Europe. Also used as a unit of weight, it is believed to have derived its name from cattle, which were used in bartering.

Skrupel A Norwegian unit of length approximately equivalent to 0.18 millimeters.

Skunkworks 1. A division of Lockheed Martin responsible for developing military aircraft for several countries. **2.** More generally, a division of a company responsible for research and development with little or no regard for bureaucracy or protocol. That is, creativity is highly valued in a skunkworks.

Skyscraper Indicator A sign that a company or economy may soon begin to experience hardship based on recent construction of lavish buildings. For example, Northern Rock Bank in the United Kingdom began building a new, 10-story headquarters in 2006. In 2007, Northern Rock nearly collapsed and for a time was nationalized. The building was not completed until 2008.

Skywriting The selective release of smoke from an airplane so that it forms letters and words in the sky. The obvious visibility of skywriting may make it attractive in marketing, especially when a large crowd is gathered.

SL 1. ISO 3166-1 alpha-2 code for the Republic of Sierra Leone. This is the code used in international transactions to and from Sierra Leonean bank accounts. **2.** ISO 3166-2 geocode for Sierra Leone. This is used as an international standard for shipping to Sierra Leone. Each subdivision has its own code with the prefix "SL." For example, the code for the Eastern Province is ISO 3166-2:SL-E.

Slab A casing for a coin made and applied by a coin grading service. A coin grading service may put a slab on a coin that it has appraised and authenticated to preserve its condition and value.

Slave One whose person, or at least whose labor, is owned by another person. In either case, the owner does not compensate the slave for his/her work. Slavery is one of the world's oldest institutions. In the modern world, it is considered one of the most egregious human rights violations. It is illegal in nearly every country, but still exists. Today it is strongly associated with sexual trafficking and forced domestic servants.

Slavery The practice in which one person owns another person, or at least that person's labor. In either case, the owner does not compensate the slave for his/her work. Slavery is one of the world's oldest institutions. In the modern world, it is considered one of the most egregious human rights violations. It is illegal in nearly every country, but still exists. In the present, it is strongly associated with sexual trafficking and forced domestic servants.

SLB GOST 7.67 Latin three-letter geocode for the Solomon Islands. The code is used for transactions to and from Solomon Islander bank accounts and for international shipping to the Solomon Islands. As with all GOST 7.67 codes, it is used primarily in Cyrillic alphabets.

SLD Last Sale On a ticker tape, an indication that security significantly increased or decreased in price in a single transaction.

SLE GOST 7.67 Latin three-letter geocode for Sierra Leone. The code is used for transactions to and from Sierra Leonean bank accounts and for international shipping to Sierra Leone. As with all GOST 7.67 codes, it is used primarily in Cyrillic alphabets.

Sled In auto sales, a trade-in automobile with little or no value.

Sleeper Cell A group that lives in society and conducts no activities until it receives an order or otherwise decides to take action. A sleeper cell is associated with clandestine operations, such as espionage and terrorism.

Sleeping Beauty A company, especially a start-up, that might make a profitable takeover, but has not been approached by a potential acquirer. Qualifications for a sleeping beauty include high potential with bad management or perhaps an undervalued share price.

Slide Ruler In auto sales, a buyer who insists on justification for each price offered. A slide ruler picks apart each new price the salesperson quotes, and may calculate taxes and other fees on his/her own. In other words, a slide ruler does not trust the numbers the dealership offers until he/she proves their accuracy himself/herself.

Slider In numismatics, a slang term for a coin that has been cleaned in order to make it appear to be in mint condition. This may actually reduce the value of the coin. That is, a slightly used coin in good condition may be worth more than a slider.

Slippage In futures, the difference between the estimated and actual transaction costs. These costs may increase because of a broker's mistake, or because of reduced liquidity, increased transportation costs for the underlying commodity, or any number of other reasons. Some brokerages use algorithmic trading to avoid slippage. See also: All-In Cost.

SLL ISO 4217 code for the Sierra Leonean leone. It was introduced in 1964, replacing the British West African pound. It has been marked by high inflation for much of its history.

Sloe Gin Fizz A slang term for a market with low trading volume and no major price movements. This should not be confused with an inactive market or an illiquid market. Sloe Gin Fizz simply indicates that a market that is unusually quiet.

Slovak Koruna The former currency of Slovakia. It was first issued in 1993 with the separation of Slovakia and the Czech Republic, replacing the Czechoslovakian koruna at par. It was the sole currency of Slovakia until the end of 2008, when the nation adopted the euro.

Slovenian Tolar The former currency of Slovenia. It was introduced in 1991, replacing the Yugoslav dinar. In 2004, the tolar was pegged to the euro, which eventually replaced it in 2007.

Slow Loan A loan that a regulator or bank considers to be at risk of default. Payments on a slow loan are generally 60 to 90 days late, depending on a regulator's definition and the maturity of the loan. A slow loan may be referred to a collection agency, which attempts to enforce repayment.

Slow Market A market with low volume and typically little change in prices. Slow markets tend to be illiquid and many analysts advise against selling in these markets because it is often difficult to achieve the price one desires.

SLS A currency code for the Somaliland shilling. It was issued in 1994, replacing the Somali shilling. Because of Somaliland's lack of international recognition, the shilling must be exchanged either through the Somaliland Central Bank or informally through a hawalah dealer. Because Somaliland has limited recognition, this code is not recognized by the ISO. An equivalent code is SLSH.

Slump Informal for a downturn in an industry or economy. It specifically refers to a recession, which is defined as negative GDP growth for two consecutive quarters. However, there is no set definition for what constitutes a slump.

Slush Fund An account in which a business, government, or individual in either of those hides money for later use. Businesses sometimes hide profits for a given quarter in a slush fund to make later profits look more robust, or even to hide later losses. In government, politicians sometimes use slush funds to hide illegal contributions or bribes to finance re-election campaigns or an extravagant lifestyle. It is important to note that not all monies set aside for entertainment or other future use constitute a slush fund; the term implies that the money is hidden or used for illegal or unethical purposes.

Slusher A slang term for an individual (or, rarely, an institution) who makes informal loans at an exorbitantly high interest rate. The term is most common in the U.S. Navy. See also: Loan shark.

Slushing A slang term for the practice of making informal loans at an exorbitantly high interest rate, especially if the lender is an individual rather than an institution. The term is most common in the U.S. Navy.

SLV GOST 7.67 Latin three-letter geocode for El Salvador. The code is used for transactions to and from Salvadorian bank accounts and for international shipping to El Salvador. As with all GOST 7.67 codes, it is used primarily in Cyrillic alphabets.

SM 1. ISO 3166-1 alpha-2 code for the Republic of San Marino. This is the code used in international transactions to and from Sammarinese bank accounts. **2.** ISO 3166-2 geocode for San Marino. This is used as an international standard for shipping to San Marino. Each municipality has its own code with the prefix "SM." For example, the Faetano municipality is assigned the code ISO 3166-2:SM-04.

Small Bundle A superdivision of a tin ingot, which was a currency used in Malacca in the 15th century. Ten tin ingots were equivalent to one small bundle.

Small Business Administration An agency of the U.S. federal government that guarantees loans made to entrepreneurs and small businesses. It also provides special assistance to businesses run by women and minorities. It was established in 1953.

Small Business Issuer A company that issues stock when its revenue and/or shares outstanding are worth less than $25 million. Small business issuers are subject to slightly less stringent requirements when making a new issue. See also: SB-2.

Small Business Policy An insurance policy that a start-up or other small business may purchase to protect it against losses, at least for a certain period of time.

Small Firm Effect A theory stating that publicly-traded companies with low market capitalization tend to outperform larger ones. Part of the small firm effect may be explained by the fact that these firms are riskier and, therefore, have higher returns. Additionally, small firms have lower stock prices and, thus, what would be a small price appreciation for a large firm can, in fact, be huge for a small firm. See also: Neglected-firm effect.

Small Order Execution System A computerized order-entry system on NASDAQ that bypasses brokers and automatically executes orders at the best available price. The SOES is available for buy and sell orders for 200, 500, and 1,000 shares. NASDAQ market makers are required to use SOES where appropriate. It was established in 1987 following the stock market crash of that year.

Small Span An ancient Egyptian unit of length approximately equivalent to 22.5 centimeters.

Small Trader A trader, especially on an options or futures exchange with positions having a value below the value at which the Commodity Futures Trading Commission requires registration and reporting. That is, small traders are exempt from many requirements imposed upon larger traders. See also: Small Investor.

Small-Capitalization Fund A mutual fund that invests primarily or exclusively in small-capitalization (small-cap) stocks. In general, a small-cap fund invests in companies with market capitalizations of less than $1 billion or $2 billion, but there is no specific definition. Some brokerages or exchanges have slightly different definitions of small-cap. See also: High-cap, Mid-cap.

Small-Capitalization Stock A stock in a publicly-traded company with low amount of market capitalization. In general, a small-cap company has a market capitalization of less than $1 billion or $2 billion, but there is no specific definition. Some brokerages or exchanges have slightly different definitions of small-cap. Some indexes track small-cap companies, as do some exchange traded funds. See also: High-cap, Mid-cap.

Small-Issue Bond Part of a small municipal bond that is used for private purposes. As a municipal bond, the interest is tax-deductible; however, there is a limit on the amount of debt and number of issues a municipality is allowed to use for private purposes and still qualify for the deduction.

Smallmin Slang; a Christian church or ministry that manages less than $500,000 per year. The term is most common in business consulting for these organizations.

Smart Money Money controlled and invested by institutional investors and market insiders. Supposedly, smart money investments perform better than others, and, because of this, some investors follow the smart money by buying and selling the same securities as institutional investors. Many analysts, however, dispute the idea that smart money is any "smarter" than that of the average investor.

Smidge A very small change in a security's price, usually only a few cents.

Smithsonian Agreement A December 1971 agreement between 10 nations that effectively ended the Bretton Woods System. Because of high government spending due to the Vietnam War and the Great Society program, the U.S. dollar became overvalued and was under significant inflationary pressure. In August 1971, President Richard Nixon unilaterally devalued the dollar and ended the ability to exchange it for gold. The Smithsonian Agreement formalized this act as the participating nations agreed to allow their currencies to appreciate relative to the dollar. While this Agreement kept the Bretton Woods System in place, the precedent led to its final abandonment in 1973.

SML ISO 4217 code for the Sammarinese lira. It was introduced in the 1860s and was pegged to the Italian lira at a one-to-one ratio. Sammarinese and Italian coins

circulated alongside each other in both San Marino and Italy. The euro replaced both currencies in 1999.

Smoking Gun Very strong evidence that proves a crime. Perpetrators of financial crimes have a reputation of destroying paperwork because doing so reduces the possibility that authorities will find a smoking gun.

Smoot-Hawley Act Legislation in the United States, passed in 1930, that raised tariffs on thousands of imports. The idea behind the Act was to protect American jobs, especially those of farmers, from cheap imports. However, the Act is considered to have been a failure because it led to retaliatory measures in foreign countries, which reduced U.S. exports. Some economists consider the Act to have been a contributing cause to the depth of the Great Depression. See also: NAFTA, Trade war.

Smortonde An obsolete Danish unit of volume approximately equivalent to 1,314 liters. It was used to measure barrels of butter.

SMR GOST 7.67 Latin three-letter geocode for San Marino. The code is used for transactions to and from Sammarinese bank accounts and for international shipping to San Marino. As with all GOST 7.67 codes, it is used primarily in Cyrillic alphabets.

Smuggler A person who secretly transports goods in violation of law or regulation. For example, a smuggler may transport drugs or other illegal goods. Alternately, one may smuggle legal goods by taking them to a prohibited area (such as a prison) or by not following applicable rules (such as not paying a tariff).

Smuggling The secretive transportation of goods in violation of law or regulation. For example, one may smuggle drugs or other illegal goods. Alternately, one may smuggle legal goods by taking them to a prohibited area (such as a prison) or by not following applicable rules (such as not paying a tariff).

Smurf An informal term for one who commits money laundering.

Smurfing The act of breaking down a transaction into smaller transactions to avoid regulatory requirements or an investigation by the authorities. For example, suppose a jurisdiction requires shareholders to register with regulators if they purchase more than 5% of a company's stock. A shareholder may smurf by having dummy shareholders purchase smaller quantities of stock so that he controls more than the statutory percentage but does not have to register. Smurfing is a crime in many jurisdictions.

SN 1. ISO 3166-1 alpha-2 code for the Republic of Senegal. This is the code used in international transactions to and from Senegalese bank accounts. **2.** ISO 3166-2 geocode for Senegal. This is used as an international standard for shipping to Senegal. Each Senegalese region has its own code with the prefix "SN." For example, the code for the Region of Dakar is ISO 3166-2:SN-DK.

Snail Mail A popular slang term for correspondence sent through the post, rather than by e-mail. Snail mail is much slower than e-mail (hence its name) and has become less common for correspondence in which a physical signature or package is not required.

Snes A Danish unit of 20.

Snowballing A situation in which a price rises or falls, which triggers stop orders, resulting in increased pressure to buy or sell the security. The increased or decreased demand for the security drives the price up or down even further, and the cycle continues until a price correction occurs. Snowballing should not be confused with a snowball, which is a different concept altogether.

SO 1. ISO 3166-1 alpha-2 code for the Republic of Somalia. This is the code used in international transactions to and from Somali bank accounts. **2.** ISO 3166-2 geocode for Somalia. This is used as an international standard for shipping to Somalia.

Soccer Mom Indicator An indicator that a current trend is ending. The theory behind the soccer mom indicator states that listening to parents at their children's soccer games shows how the economy, a security, or a sector has been performing. However, because soccer moms and dads (stereotypically) do not know much about future trends, their comments show that the opposite is about to occur. For example, if parents are expressing concern about high oil prices, this may indicate that oil prices are about to decline. See also: Lagging indicator, Behavioral economics.

Social Accounting A way to calculate economic growth in which one aggregates the growth or decline of each sector of an economy. For example, suppose a simple economy has three equally-sized industries: agriculture, manufacturing, and construction. If agriculture has grown 5%, manufacturing has grown 2%, and construction has declined 1%, then the total growth is 6% (5% + 2% - 1%). A major example of social accounting is the calculation of a country's GDP.

Social Capital Valuable personal and business connections between people and organizations. Social capital can enhance or even create success for a person or company. For example, a person may use his social capital by contacting friends and former colleagues to procure a job. Likewise, a company may use the collective social capital of its management to attract clients. See also: Networking.

Social Contract Theorist A person who believes that morality is a manifestation of the mutual consent of all persons involved in a society. For example, murder is wrong according to social contract theory because society has generally agreed that it would not be conducive to prosperous relations, and not because it is wrong in and of itself. Social contract theory is used in government as one of the foundations of the modern state. "Government by consent of the governed," one of the most fundamental ideas of democracy, has its origins in social contract theory.

Social Contract Theory The theory that morality is a manifestation of the mutual consent of all persons involved in a society. For example, murder is wrong according to social contract theory because society has generally agreed that it would not be conducive to prosperous relations, and not because it is wrong in and of itself. Social contract theory is used in government as one of the foundations of the modern state. "Government by consent of the governed," one of the most fundamental ideas of democracy, has its origins in social contract theory.

Social Democratic Party A political party in Germany. It was established in 1875, making it the oldest party in Germany currently in existence. Throughout its history its ideology has shifted between socialism and seeking social justice within a capitalist state.

Social Justice Any theory or practice that encourages members of a society to behave more justly to each other. For example, a social justice policy may seek to alleviate the consequences of racism or improve relations between classes. In economics, social justice is associated with policies seeking to help the poor, especially but not necessarily at the expense of the wealthy. While generally critical of capitalism, social justice is not necessarily a socialist ideology, and is often opposed to socialism due to human rights concerns or similar grounds. See also: Justice.

Social Responsibility The practice of appropriate behavior in a public setting, regardless of the behavior's legality. In investing, social responsibility helps inform the investment decisions of some individuals and companies. For example, an individual may have a moral objection to smoking and therefore may refrain from investing in tobacco companies. Social responsibility in investing may be either positive or negative; that is, it may inform where an individual makes investments (e.g. in environmentally friendly companies) and where he/she does not (e.g. in arms manufacturers). Some mutual funds and even whole subdivisions are dedicated to promoting socially responsible investing. See also: Green fund, Islamic finance.

Social Security A program of the United States federal government that provides income to disabled and (especially) elderly people. That is, persons who have paid into the Social Security system for a certain period of time are eligible to receive what amounts to a government pension in retirement or in the event of disability. It is paid out of the Social Security trust fund and is financed through FICA taxes. Because Social Security is the single largest expense of the federal budget, periodic attempts are made to wholly or partly privatize Social Security, though opponents claim that doing so would make the American social safety net less secure. See also: SSI, TANF, SCHIP.

Social Security Benefits In the United States, a social program providing, among other things, disability insurance, the national pension, unemployment insurance, Temporary Assistance for Needy Families, and Supplemental Security Income. In common parlance, however, Social Security benefits refer to the monthly check received by pensioners starting generally after retirement. All U.S. citizens who have paid the Social Security tax for a certain number of years are eligible for Social Security benefits at age 65 (or 62 for reduced benefits). Widows (or widowers) are also eligible for benefits even if they were never employed, so long as their deceased spouses paid into the system.

Social Security Disability Income Insurance A program, run by the Social Security Administration, that provides for the lost income of individuals who become disabled for an extended period of time. Persons who have paid enough of the FICA tax for a long enough period of time are eligible for Social Security Disability Income Insurance. Payment begins at the start of the sixth month of a person's disability. The amount of the benefit varies according to a number of factors.

Social Security Number A number given to every American citizen and national. The number is unique to each person and is necessary to work. Government organizations use Social Security numbers for a variety of purposes, notably to ensure that each citizen is billed for his/her own taxes, and not those of someone else with the same name. It is also used to determine eligibility for certain government services, especially Social Security benefits.

Social Security Reform Act of 1983 Legislation in the United States that improved the short- and medium-term solvency of the Social Security Administration. The act raised taxes in order to pay for benefits. It also separated Social Security from the general federal budget.

Socialism An economic system in which the state or the people generally own most or all of the means of production. That is, under socialism, industries, agriculture and corporations are nationalized. The government may also manage the nationalized companies, or they may delegate this to a private company. Most socialist systems, however, allow some degree of private enterprise. Because it favors a strong role for the state, socialism should not be confused with Marxism, which holds that the state will eventually disappear.

Socialist A scholar or partisan who believes in an economic system in which the state or the people generally own most or all of the means of production. That is, under socialism, industries, agriculture, and corporations are nationalized. The government may manage the nationalized companies, or they may delegate this to a private company. Most socialist systems, however, allow some degree of private enterprise. Because socialists favor a strong role for the state, socialism should not be confused with Marxism, which holds that the state will eventually disappear.

Societa a Responsabilita Limitata Also called an Srl or an S.r.l. A company in which the owners' risk is limited to the capital that they contribute. That is, they cannot lose and they cannot be held responsible in court for losses above their individual contributions. An Srl must abide by strict requirements (compared to other corporate structures) in issuing bonds. Owners make corporate decisions by vote. An Srl is a corporate form in Italy. See also: Public Limited Company.

Societe a Responsabilite Limitee A company in which owners' risk is limited to the capital they contribute. That is, they cannot lose and they cannot be held responsible in court for losses above their individual contributions. Owners make corporate decisions by vote, but they may not transfer their portions of ownership without unanimous consent of the other owners. A SARL is a corporate form in Francophone countries, notably France, Switzerland, Lebanon and a few countries in North Africa. See also: Public limited company.

Societe d'investissement a capital variable An actively-managed investment company in Europe in which the amount of capital is dependent on the number of shareholders in the SICAV. It is structured much like a mutual fund in the United States and is a very common investment vehicle in Luxembourg, France, and Italy.

Societe par Actions Simplifiee Also called an SAS. A French company based upon a limited liability company in the United States. Unlike some other French corporations, SAS companies do not have a board of directors. Rather, the organization is responsible to a President, who may hire a General Manager at his/her discretion. The company's balance sheet is published and its annual statements are controlled by an outside party.

Society A group of persons who, by accident or design, are related to each other in some way and therefore have to deal with each other. Examples of societies include everyone who attends the same church, lives in the same country, or belongs to the same club. According to most political and economic theories, persons in a society have the responsibility to care for other members of that society, though exactly how to do so remains a matter of contention. While some theories emphasize the role of society, more individualistic theories tend to minimize its role.

Society for Worldwide Interbank Financial Telecommunications A cooperative society that provides highly secure message communications between banks. It does not transfer money or any other financial materials, but simply provides information. It also standardizes forms between members so as to reduce costs and operational risk. Founded in 1973 and headquartered in Belgium, SWIFT has thousands of members in more than 200 countries worldwide.

Sode-No-Shita A Japanese term for "under the sleeves." It is used as a euphemism for bribery.

SOES Bandit A trader who uses the Small Order Execution System (SOES) on NASDAQ to manipulate prices. The SOES bandit conducts a small transaction on a security in order to affect the price, and then executes a larger transaction to take advantage of the price inefficiency. This is a form of insider trading, as the broker executing the order knows something about the market's probable movement that other market participants do not know. An SOES bandit is also simply called a bandit.

Soft Call Provision In some callable bonds and other fixed income securities, a provision in the indenture stating that the issuer will pay a premium to the face value or market value of the security if it calls it before maturity. Soft call provisions exist to encourage investment in the securities carrying them because they provide a disincentive for early redemption.

Soft Commodity A commodity that is grown. Soft commodities include most agricultural products; examples include sugar, corn, and wheat. See also: Hard commodity.

Soft Currency A currency that fluctuates in value frequently. Soft currencies are generally issued by governments that are less stable and/or have weaker economies than stronger currencies. As such, most soft currencies come from countries in the developing world. Central banks rarely hold reserves of foreign soft currencies as they do little or nothing to stabilize the local currency. A soft currency is also called a weak currency. See also: Strong currency.

Soft Dot A portion of a halftone image with a blurred edge. A halftone image is used to print an illustration, and a soft dot produces a lower quality print. Often, new halftones have hard dots, which have sharp edges, and they degenerate over time to soft dots.

Soft Insurance Market A period of time during which insurance companies assess low premiums and therefore achieve relatively low profits. A soft insurance market occurs after companies begin to meet their profit goals and are able to loosen their underwriting standards, writing more policies on more clients. It can be easy to obtain insurance during a soft insurance market. However, the possibility exists that insurers may write too many policies, taking losses or at least reducing profits. A soft insurance market is considered a normal part of the business cycle of insurance. See also: Hard insurance market.

Soft Landing A situation in which a central bank raises interest rates gradually, but steadily, to curb inflation, while still attempting to keep the economy out of a recession. A hard landing is more effective at reducing inflation, but it slows down growth. However, soft landings are considered more desirable than allowing inflation to run amok, which could necessitate a hard landing.

Soft Loan A loan made at no interest or at a below market interest rate. Soft loans usually refer to loans made to developing countries and others in need of financing, but without the ability to borrow at the market rate. Soft loans may also have a longer grace period or a different amortization schedule that makes repayment easier. This is also called soft financing.

Soft Metrics Informal; intangible information that may predict the success or failure of a start-up. Examples of soft metrics include the previous track record of its management and consumer excitement about the area or sector in which it is operating.

Soft Money 1. An indirect contribution to a political campaign. Soft money is money raised for political activities in favor of or opposed to a certain candidate or issue that stops short of actually endorsing anything. In other words, any ad stopping short of asking for a vote for or against someone or something is funded by soft money. Colloquially, soft money connotes large amounts donated by special interest groups for these purposes. The McCain-Feingold Act forbade political parties and some other organizations from raising soft money, but most organizations can still do so. **2.** See: Fiat money.

Soft Offer In marketing, an offer to receive a product and to make payment later. For example, a soft offer may send a customer a magazine subscription and send an invoice for it later. A soft offer contrasts with a hard offer, in which payment is demanded in advance. Companies making soft offers have higher response rates than those making hard offers, but they generally carry more bad debt.

Soft Patch A period of weak economic performance amid a longer strong performance. That is, a soft patch is mild slowdown between two periods of high economic growth. Central banks usually cut target interest rates during a soft patch to encourage a return to growth. The term is somewhat informal and usually used in the media and by the Federal Reserve.

Soft Price 1. The price of a security or other asset that is either remaining the same or gradually falling. **2.** A price for anything that is open for negotiation.

Soft Sell An advertisement that subtly encourages the target to purchase the product. For example, a soft sell commercial may state the advantages to a product with or without specifically asking a customer to buy it. A soft sell contrasts with a hard sell, which is more demanding.

Soft Side An informal term for customer care and relationship management issues that a company faces in trying to remain in business. It contrasts with the hard side, which refers to financial and operational issues.

Soft Spot A stock that does not trend upward when the majority of the market does. There are a number of explanations for a soft spot's existence. A soft spot may be a countercyclical stock or it may belong to an industry that is in decline. Alternatively, it may simply be a poorly managed company. See also: Bear Market, Bull Market.

Sogo Shosha A type of general company in Japan. A sogo shosha buys material from large companies and distributes it to medium and small companies. It also markets Japanese products from small and medium companies internationally. Sogo sosha companies handle substantial portions of Japan's imports and exports.

Soju A Korean term for whiskey. In South Korea, it is a slang term for a small bribe.

SOL Project A proposed electronic currency system designed to help the disadvantaged in society. The SOL project uses electronic cards rather than paper money. It is intended to complement, rather than replace, the euro. Pilot tests were conducted in three regions in France.

Sole Proprietor The one and only owner of an unincorporated business. That is, the business of a sole proprietor is not a corporation, a limited liability company, or anything else. The sole proprietor must list all profits and losses on his/her personal tax return and does not file a separate return for the business. Additionally, the sole proprietor is personally responsible for all losses and debts the business incurs. Some small businesses begin as sole proprietorships and then become something else. Other sole proprietorships are part-time businesses that the owners operate on the side.

Sole Proprietorship A business owned by a single person that is not a corporation, a limited liability company, or anything else. The sole proprietor who owns the proprietorship must list all profits and losses on his/her personal tax return and does not file a separate return for the business. Additionally, the proprietor is personally responsible for all losses and debts the business incurs. Some small businesses begin as sole proprietorships and then become something else. Other sole proprietorships are part-time businesses that their owners operate on the side.

Solectwa In Poland, a political subdivision roughly equivalent to a rural village.

Solectwo In Poland, a political subdivision equivalent to a village or township.

Solidarity In Catholic social justice theory, the idea that all persons have a right and obligation to work with each other in order to achieve the common good. That is, solidarity states that humans are not atomistic and therefore economies should not be structured in such as a way that prioritizes profits or anything else over human good. This concept has been used to criticize unregulated capitalism and the free market more generally. See also: Subsidiarity.

Solomon Island Dollar The currency of the Solomon Islands. It was introduced in 1977, replacing the Australian dollar, to which it was pegged until 1979. Since becoming a floating currency, the Solomon Islands dollar has been marked by high inflation. In some parts of the Solomon Islands, citizens have reverted to traditional currencies such as dolphin teeth.

Solvency The state of a company being able to service its debt and meet its other obligations, especially in the long-term. Solvency is a necessary condition for a business to operate. If a company is unable to meet its obligation, it is said to be insolvent and must undergo bankruptcy in order to either liquidate or restructure. See also: Insolvency risk, Accounting insolvency.

Solvency II Proposed regulation for insurers in the European Union. Solvency II would harmonize the insurance regulation in EU member states, permitting any insurer registered in one member state to operate in any other member state. Solvency II would put in place capital requirements for insurers to reduce the risk that they would be unable to meet obligations when an unusually high number of claims has been made. Solvency II is expected to take effect in January 2013.

Solvency Ratio A measure of a company's ability to service debts, expressed as a percentage. It is calculating by adding the company's post-tax net profit and depreciation, and dividing the sum by the quantity of long-term and short-term liabilities; the resulting amount is expressed as a percentage. A high solvency ratio indicates a healthy company, while a low ratio indicates the opposite. A low solvency ratio further indicates likelihood of default. Different industries have different standards as to what qualifies as an acceptable solvency ratio, but, in general, a ratio of 20% or higher is considered healthy. Potential lenders may take the solvency ratio into account when considering making further loans.

SOM GOST 7.67 Latin three-letter geocode for Somalia. The code is used for transactions to and from Somali bank accounts and for international shipping to Somalia. As with all GOST 7.67 codes, it is used primarily in Cyrillic alphabets.

Somali Shilling The currency of Somalia. While the East African shilling was in use in parts of present-day Somalia since 1921, the present shilling was introduced in 1962. It suffered from hyperinflation in the 1980s and again in the early 2000s. Currently, the shilling is used mainly for small transactions, with U.S. dollars or (less frequently) euros being used for large ones. The breakaway region of Somaliland issues its own shilling, which is accepted there and is not related to the Somali shilling.

Somaliland Shilling The currency of Somaliland, a country with limited recognition. It was issued in 1994, replacing the Somali shilling. Because of Somaliland's lack of international recognition, the shilling must be exchanged either through the Somaliland Central Bank or informally through a hawalah dealer.

SONIA Sterling Overnight Index Average. A major reference rate used in calculating the exchange rate for the British pound. It is calculated as the average interest rate on unsecured overnight transactions on the pound conducted between midnight and 3:15 p.m. by members of the London WMBA.

Sortino Ratio A variation on the Sharpe ratio that measures the risk-adjusted return on an investment. The Sortino ratio considers the possibility that an investment will fall below the required rate of return, rather than volatility in general. It is calculated as follows: Sortino Ratio = (Realized return - Required return) / Downside risk.

SOS ISO 4217 code for the Somali shilling. While the East African shilling was in use in parts of present-day Somalia since 1921, the present shilling was introduced in 1962. It suffered from hyperinflation in the 1980s and again in the early 2000s. Currently, the shilling is used mainly for small transactions, with U.S. dollars or (less frequently) euros being used for large ones. The breakaway region of Somaliland issues its own shilling, which is accepted there and is not related to the Somali shilling.

Sound Money A somewhat polemical term for a currency backed by a tangible commodity such as gold, silver or platinum. Sound money has an intrinsic value, but is more susceptible to deflation than fiat money. Many countries used sound money throughout most of their histories; however, most countries today use fiat money and have since the United States left the Bretton Woods System in the 1970s. The term "sound money" is often used by those who favor its reintroduction. The more common term is hard money.

Sour Bond A bond that has missed a scheduled coupon payment or has not paid the full principal at maturity. Because the sour bond is in default, it trades at a significant discount from its par value. There is a high risk that the buyer of a sour bond will not recover his/her investment, but if the bond is eventually repaid, he/she can receive a high return.

Source of Funds Seller A person selling a security to raise money for another purpose, usually not related to investment. For example, a source of funds seller may sell some shares of stock to acquire the funds for an engagement ring. A source of funds seller is not aggressive and usually waits for an advantageous price before selling.

Sourcing In private equity, a slang term for cold calling potential clients.

Sous-prefecture In Guinea, a political subdivision equivalent to a municipality.

South African Futures Exchange A branch of the Johannesburg Stock Exchange specializing in derivatives. Originally established in 1988 and owned by the JSE since 2001, the South African Futures Exchange consists of two main subdivisions, one for equity derivatives and one for agricultural derivatives. Both subdivisions offer a variety of investment vehicles, but the latter is well known for its futures contracts based on maize.

South African Pound The former currency of South Africa. It was introduced in 1921 when the South African Reserve Bank was established. It was equal in value to the British pound for its entire history except between 1931 and 1933, when the British government briefly left the gold standard. It was replaced by the South African rand in 1961.

South African Rand The currency of South Africa. It was introduced in 1961, replacing the South African pound when South Africa became fully independent from the United Kingdom. It was a very valuable currency for most of its early history, but mounting international pressure over apartheid and the uncertainty during reforms since then have greatly weakened it. It has been marked by fairly steady depreciation since the mid-1980s. However, it is a regionally important currency, being used in Namibia and Zimbabwe as well as South Africa.

South Asian Association for Regional Cooperation Also called SAARC. An international organization dedicated to mutual assistance and economic cooperation among nations in South Asia. Heads of state of member nations meet once a year and foreign secretaries twice a year. It was established in 1985 and maintains its headquarters in Kathmandu.

South Korean Won The currency of South Korea. It became the currency of South Korea in 1962, replacing the hwan. It was pegged to the U.S. dollar at various rates until 1997, when it became a floating currency. See also: Asian financial crisis.

South Yemeni Dinar The currency of South Yemen. It was introduced in 1965, replacing the East African shilling two years before South Yemen became independent. After South and North Yemen united in 1990, the South Yemeni dinar remained in circulation until 1996. It was replaced by the Yemeni rial.

Southern African Customs Union An international organization that establishes the free movement of goods and services across member nations. It also maintains a common tariff policy with respect to countries that are members; that is, members negotiate as a bloc for trade agreements. Established in 1910, it is the oldest extant customs union in the world. Its members are Botswana, Lesotho, Namibia, South Africa and Swaziland.

Southern African Development Community An international organization that promotes economic development and integration for 15 countries in southern Africa. It encourages regional trade, common security measures and coordination on health policy, among other things. It was established in 1980 as the Southern African Development Coordination Conference and took its current name in 1992.

Sov In the United Kingdom, a slang term for 1 pound. The term derives from the sovereign coin.

Sovereign 1. A gold coin in the United Kingdom. It has a face value of one British pound, but because it is made of gold, its actual value far exceeds one pound. Investors use sovereigns as bullion coins. **2.** See: Sovereignty.

Sovereign Risk In foreign exchange, the risk that a foreign central bank will significantly alter its monetary policy or other foreign exchange regulations so that it significantly affects one's currency trades. More broadly, it can apply to any political risk that a nation will refuse to comply with an agreement to which it is a party. For example, if one conducts a currency trade involving a pegged currency and the country in question decides to let its currency float, it can significantly impact the profitability of the currency trade. See also: Liquidity risk, Credit risk.

Sovereign Wealth Fund A government-owned company that invests that government's excess reserves. That is, if a country has a current account surplus or a positive balance of trade the government may deposit the excess funds into a sovereign wealth fund. The funds are invested in securities, companies, or projects in order to increase the government's net worth. Often a sovereign wealth fund pays for a government's social programs such as welfare or a state pension. The funds in a sovereign wealth fund are kept separate from the country's regular currency reserves. Sovereign wealth funds are common in oil-rich countries where the government owns a significant portion of the oil production facilities.

Sovereignty The legal right of a state to govern its own affairs in its own territory without outside interference. Sovereignty may reside with an individual (such as a monarch, sometimes known as a sovereign), a body (such as a parliament) or with the populace as a whole. The notion of sovereignty is less clear in federal governments like the U.S. and Canada, as sovereignty is split between the national government and the regional governments. This is a matter of considerable controversy in some countries.

Soviet Ruble The currency of the former Soviet Union. It was first issued in 1917 and underwent five redenominations over the course of its history. It was replaced by various currencies, starting in 1991 with the fall of the Soviet Union. See also: Russian ruble.

Span A unit of length equivalent to nine inches.

SPAN Margin Standardized Portfolio Analysis of Risk Margin. A system of determining the appropriate amount of margin on an option or futures trader's account in order to cover potential losses from his/her trades. Options and futures traders are required to maintain a certain margin on their positions to reduce the risk of failing to settle. The SPAN margin uses a complex system of algorithms to calculate the margin for each position that a trader holds and transfer excess margin from some positions to cover the margin that is lacking for others. Most options and futures exchanges require their traders to use the SPAN margin.

Spanish Ounce An obsolete unit of weight equivalent to 28.75 grams.

Spann A Norwegian unit of weight approximately equivalent to 18 kilograms. It is used most commonly to measure the weight of grains and similar commodities.

Spannland A Swedish unit of area approximately equivalent to two and a half square kilometers.

Spark Spread In energy financing, the theoretical gross income produced by the sale of a unit of electricity, less the cost of the fuel to produce the electricity. All of the plant's other expenses must come out of the spark spread. It is the benchmark used to gauge the financial health of gas-powered electricity plants. Occasionally, if the spark spread is too low, plants will refrain from producing electricity until it becomes more profitable. Since the Kyoto Protocols, the formula for determining the spark spread must include the financial effects of carbon emissions. This is called the clean spread. See also: Dark spread.

Spave To spend money in the mistaken belief that one is saving money. For example, a lower price for a good psychologically may encourage a buyer to buy several when ordinarily he/she would have bought only one. In this way, buyers may believe they are saving money when in reality they have spent more than they intended.

Spear In auto sales, a tactic in which a salesperson speaks with a person away from the dealership site and offers an impossibly high price for a trade-in, provided the person comes to the dealership that same day to finalize the deal. The intent of a spear is to encourage the customer to come back to that dealership, at which time the salesperson will quote the real price for the trade-in.

Special Administrative Region In China, a province with a great deal political and economic autonomy. Special administrative regions largely govern their own affairs and even conduct (extremely limited) foreign policy. The special administrative regions, currently Hong Kong and Macau, are major players in international trade and as a result play a large role in bringing foreign currencies into China.

Special Agent An agent authorized to perform a single transaction on behalf of a client. The special agent's authority and responsibilities are terminated at the conclusion of this transaction. For example, a real estate agent is usually a special agent. Once the client buys or sells a property, the special agent ceases to have a legal relationship with that client.

Special Assessment Bond A municipal bond whose proceeds sponsor a certain, defined project. Property taxes paying for the bond are levied only on those directly benefiting from the project. For example, if a special assessment bond is issued to pay for road repairs on a certain street, only the houses and other buildings on that street will pay higher property taxes. Generally speaking, special assessment bonds are not backed by the full faith and credit of the municipality and as such carry more risk than most general obligation bonds. Special assessment bonds that do have full faith and credit are called "general obligation special assessment bonds."

Special Bid A situation in which a member of the NYSE seeks to fill an order to buy a large number of shares by finding a series of smaller orders to sell the same shares. See also: Block trade.

Special Bond Account A margin account that exclusively uses borrowed funds to buy bonds. That is, one is not permitted to buy stocks or derivatives on a special bond account. Because bonds both carry fewer risks and have less volatile prices than other securities, special bond accounts have lower minimum maintenance requirements than other margin accounts.

Special Cash Account A brokerage account in which the customer must pay the full amount for securities purchased by an agreed upon date, often within two days of the purchase. Customers are not allowed to borrow in order to pay off the account. Special cash accounts in the United States are governed by Regulation T and are the most basic kind of investment account. Examples of special cash accounts include Individual Retirement Accounts(IRAs) and trusts for minor children.

Special Claim on Residual Equity A unit investment trust entitling the holder to the capital appreciation on the securities in the trust but not to dividends, coupons, or other claims. In other words, a SCORE behaves much like a warrant on the capital appreciation of stock. A SCORE has a strike price (known as a termination price) and an expiration date (known as a termination date). It contrasts with a PRIME. See also: Americus Trusts.

Special Dividend A non-recurring dividend that a company may choose to distribute to shareholders after a particularly profitable period. A company may also choose to distribute special dividends if it wishes to restructure its financing from equity-based to debt-based. In general, however, one may think of a special dividend as a "bonus" for shareholders in good times. It is also called an extra dividend or a bonus dividend.

Special Drawing Rights A reserve currency created by the International Monetary Fund to reduce the pressure on gold and the U.S. dollar in international transactions. It was established in the late 1960s and is mainly used in the IMF's internal accounting. A few currencies are pegged to the SDR; they derive their value from a currency basket consisting of the U.S. dollar, the Japanese yen, the British pound, and the euro.

Special Memorandum Account The amount of extra money an investor is allowed to borrow on a margin account. Suppose an investor buys $20,000 worth of securities on margin and places securities worth 50% of the value of the amount as collateral (in this case, $10,000) as required by Regulation T. If that collateral increases in value to $13,000, the investor has an extra $3,000 in the margin account he/she did not previously have. This $3,000 is placed in the special memorandum account. The investor may use it for a loan of up to $3,000 or may use it to buy up to $6,000 more on margin. A special memorandum account is also called a special miscellaneous account.

Special Needs Child A child with physical or mental disabilities or who otherwise requires attention above and beyond what other children require. When adopting a special needs child, parents often receive a larger tax deduction than they would have if they had adopted another child without special needs. See also: Adoption expenses.

Special Purchase and Resale Agreement A practice in which the Bank of Canada buys securities from a bank with the proviso that the bank repurchases the same securities for an agreed-upon price the following day. The Bank of Canada does this to increase the amount of money in circulation (the purchase price for the securities), which reduces overnight interest rates and increases the availability of credit. See also: Open-market operation.

Special Purpose Acquisition Company A company that is set up specifically to buy an existing company. The SPAC issues an IPO and collects investments in exchange for common shares in itself. It then uses the capital it raises to identify and then purchase a target company. Sometimes at the outset it may have identified the industry in which it wishes to buy a company, but never the company itself. If, after two years, the SPAC has not found and purchased a company successfully, the initial investments are returned to shareholders. A SPAC is also called a targeted acquisition company.

Special Purpose Enterprise A subsidiary created for a specific purpose. A common example of a special purpose enterprise occurs often when a company wishes to use certain assets as collateral on a loan but does not wish to directly acquire more debt. It may spin off a special purpose enterprise and sell it those assets, which are then used as collateral on a loan. The debt then belongs to the SPE rather than the company. Some regulations govern special purpose enterprises so that they do not become havens for bad debt or unprofitable assets designed to make the parent company's financial situation look better than it really is. See also: Aggressive accounting.

Special Purpose Fund Money set aside for a particular purpose. For example, a non-profit organization specializing in childhood development may designate a special purpose fund for subsidizing school lunches and another for after-school tutoring. It is rarely abbreviated "spfund."

Special Purpose Vehicle A subsidiary of a company that attempts to isolate risk from the parent company by maintaining its assets and liabilities on a completely separate balance sheet. It can be used as a counterparty in swap transactions, or the parent company can finance a project through an SPV that would put the parent company in danger of bankruptcy if the project does not perform well. During the Enron scandal, SPVs developed notoriety because Enron hid much of its debt in SPVs.

Special Sauce A slang term for proprietary information. The term may derive from the sauce McDonald's puts on its Big Mac sandwiches, the recipe for which is a trade secret.

Special Situation An occurrence that may lead an investor to trade a particular security, usually to make a short-term gain. For example, if a company announces an earnings surprise, an investor may buy its stock in the hope of selling it later in the trading day for a higher price. Other examples of special situations include mergers and acquisitions and bankruptcy.

Special Subscription Account A brokerage account into which one deposits cash exclusively for buying securities to which one has a subscription privilege. A subscription privilege is a right to buy more shares in a company one already holds before the shares become available to the general public. One may open a special subscription account to take advantage of these opportunities if and when they arise.

Special Tax Bond A government bond where repayment is guaranteed by a tax that the issuer levies specifically for that purpose. For example, suppose a city issues a special tax bond to build a new campus for the community college. It may levy an excise tax on alcohol sold in the city in order to pay coupons and eventually the principal on this bond. While excise taxes commonly pay for special tax bonds, increases in property taxes, sales taxes, or any other duty may be used.

Specialist A member firm on a securities exchange that the exchange's management charges with keeping a fair and orderly market on one or more securities. That is, a specialist serves as a market maker on its assigned securities by buying and selling them to ensure liquidity in the market. Brokers approach specialists to conduct to conduct transactions on their assigned securities. Each security on the exchange has exactly one specialist. A specialist is less commonly called an assigned dealer. See also: Book.

Specialist Block Purchase and Sale The purchase of a large block of securities by a specialist, especially with the intent to re-sell them nearly immediately to another investor.

Specialist Market The market for a security that only exists because a specialist stands ready to make a market if need be. That is, there are few or no orders on the security and a potential buyer or seller would have a difficult time conducting a transaction if the specialist were not ready to serve as a counterparty. A specialist market would otherwise be highly illiquid.

Specialist Short Sale Ratio The ratio of short sales made by specialists on an exchange to total short sales over a given period. Specialists are thought to be especially knowledgeable about the direction of the market, and most investors generally sell short when they are feeling bearish. Thus, a high specialist short sale ratio is considered to be bearish signal, while a low ratio is thought to be bullish. See also: Member short-sale ratio.

Specialist's Book A list of all long and short positions that a specialist holds. The book also contains all orders by other member firms on an exchange that the specialist may be able to fill. It is also called simply a book. See also: New York Stock Exchange Display Book.

Specialists' Sentiment An assessment of how bearish or bullish specialists are on a security, measured by a ratio of short sales made by specialists on a security to the total short sales on a given trading day. Specialists are thought to be especially knowledgeable about the direction of the market, and most investors generally sell short when they are feeling bearish. Thus, a high short sale ratio is considered to be a bearish signal, while a low ratio is thought to be bullish.

Specialty Fund A mutual fund or other fund that invests predominantly or exclusively in a single industry, sector, or region of the world. For example, a specialty fund may invest only in energy companies, or, even more narrowly, only in natural gas companies. Specialty funds perform well when their industries perform well, but they are risky because there is no attempt at diversification. See also: Country fund.

Specie Payment Resumption Act Legislation in the United States, passed in 1875, that made greenbacks (fiat currency issued during the U.S. Civil War) exchangeable for silver. This increased the value of the U.S. dollar and reduced inflation. However, agricultural and other interest groups found the higher inflation desirable as it made their debts more affordable. As a result, the act was controversial both before and after its passage.

Speciedaler The currency of Norway from 1816 to 1875. It circulated until Norway joined the Scandinavian Monetary Union, when it was replaced by the krone.

Specific Return The return on an asset or investment over and above the expected return that cannot be explained by common factors. That is, the specific return is the return coming from the asset or investment's own merits, rather than the merits common to other, similar assets or investments. It is also called the idiosyncratic return.

Spectail A dealer on an exchange who conducts transactions for clients but primarily makes transactions on his/her own account. The term is a portmanteau of "speculative" and "retail." That is, the dealer is involved in retail transactions for his/her clients, but is most interested in his/her own speculative investments.

Speculation An investment with an exceptionally high risk. Speculators may invest in a start-up company or in a volatile commodity. These risks carry the possibility of very high returns. Speculators often trade actively and many have hedging strategies to reduce their risks. See also: Hedge fund.

Speculative Bubble A situation in which prices for securities, especially stocks, rise far above their actual value. This trend continues until investors realize just how far prices have risen, usually, but not always, resulting in a sharp decline. Speculative bubbles usually occur when investors, for any number of reasons, believe that demand for the stocks will continue to rise or that the stocks will become profitable in a short time. Both of these scenarios result in increased prices. A famous example of a bubble is the dot-com bubble of the 1990s. Dot-com companies were hugely popular investments at the time, with IPOs of hundreds of dollars per share, even if a company had never produced a profit and in some cases, had never earned any revenue. This came from the theory that Internet companies needed to expand their customer bases as much as possible and thus corner the largest possible market share, even if this meant massive losses. NASDAQ, on which many dot-coms traded, rose to record highs. This continued until 2000, when the bubble burst and NASDAQ quickly lost more than half of its value. Other famous examples include the tulip mania of the 1630s and the housing bubble in the early 2000s.

Speculative Company A new, small, or otherwise obscure company with a high likelihood of failure but a small possibility of experiencing an extraordinarily high return. Many IPOs, especially in small companies, are considered investments in speculative companies. By definition, investing in a speculative company carries a great deal of risk. See also: Penny Stock.

Speculative Demand for Money In Keynesian economics, a need for money for investment purposes. That is, speculative demand for money is the desire to have money for transactions other than those necessary for living. Speculative demand includes risk capital for securities. According to John Maynard Keynes, speculative demand is one of the three desires governing demand for money, the others being precautionary demand and transactions demand.

Speculative Grade Liquidity Rating Also called SGL. A rating of the risk that a company will not be able to meet is short-term liabilities. SGL ratings are compiled and published by Moody's and are an assessment of a company's liquidity. SGL ratings are: SGL-1 (most liquid), SGL-2, SGL-3, SGL-4 (least liquid).

Speculative Motive A strategy in which one holds cash apart from any other investments just in case an attractive investment opportunity arises. This allows the investor to take advantage of the opportunity without closing any other positions.

Speculative Stock A stock in a new, small, or otherwise obscure company with a high likelihood of failure but a small possibility of experiencing an extraordinary return. Many IPOs, especially in small companies, are considered speculative stocks. By definition, speculative stocks carry a great deal of risk. See also: Penny Stock.

Speculator An investor who takes large risks in the hope of making large short-term gains. Speculators often use technical analysis and other tools to make investment decisions on what securities to buy. They tend to buy stocks they believe will soon see a large growth in price and then sell them at the top of the market. Speculators are controversial because some believe that they contribute to the creation of bubbles; however, others believe that they provide liquidity necessary for the market to function.

Speed 1. In mortgage-backed securities, the estimated rate at which homeowners will pay off the mortgages that underly an MBS. The equivalent of the coupon on a mortgage-backed security is a percentage of the interest and principal paid on the mortgages backing the security. A risk associated with mortgage-backed securities is that too many homeowners will pay off their mortgages with too much speed, depriving the holder of the MBS from future interest payments.

Spending Control Any tactic or strategy designed to reduce or otherwise discipline the spending of an organization. Spending controls may be adopted in a corporation, a non-profit, or even a government.

Spending Phase The time of one's life during retirement. The spending phase is the period during which one accepts payments from an annuity, pension, or a similar fund. Income almost always declines during the spending phase (unless one has a particularly fantastic pension), but expenses are usually less as well. For this reason, some companies market luxury products, such as cruises or vacations, to persons in the spending phase; they have few other items on which to spend their money.

Spider Also called a Standard & Poor's Depositary Receipt or a SPDR. An exchange-traded fund that tracks the Standard and Poor's 500. The organization issuing the SPDR owns each of the stocks traded on the S&P 500 in approximate ratio to their market capitalization. SPDR shares can be bought, sold, short-sold, traded on margin; they generally function as if they were stocks. Dividends are paid quarterly and are based on the accumulated dividends of all the stocks represented in the SPDR, less any expenses. Investors use SPDRs (and indeed all exchange-traded funds) as a way to easily diversify their portfolios at relatively low cost. Investors also see the demand for SPDRs as an indicator of which direction the market believes the S&P 500 is going. See also: Mid-Cap SPDR.

Spielkarten Notgeld issued in Germany during and immediately after World War I that was printed on playing cards. Since removed from circulation, spielkarten has become a collector's item.

Spin To attempt to present a situation in the best possible light. For example, a political operative may attempt to spin a situation in which a candidate who took a bribe by saying it was a gift or donation. The term is somewhat derogatory, but is common in business as well as politics. See also: Jawboning.

Spinning The act or practice of an underwriting or brokerage firm giving shares of an IPO, especially a popular issue, to major executives in some company unrelated to the company issuing the IPO. These executives return the favor by recommending that their clients do business to the underwriter or broker. The relationship is mutually beneficial because the executives profit from the shares in the IPO and the underwriter or broker profits from the new business. However, it is controversial and some believe spinning to be unethical. Spinning should not be confused with spinning off, which is a different concept altogether.

Spin-Off A situation in which a company offers stock in one of its wholly-owned subsidiaries or dependent divisions such that subsidiary or division becomes an independent company. The parent company may or may not maintain a portion of ownership in the newly spun-off company. A company may conduct a spin-off for any number of reasons. For example, it may wish to divest itself of one industry so it can expand into another. It may also simply wish to profit from the sale of the subsidiary. A spin off should not be confused with a split off.

Spintarella An Italian term for "little push." It is a slang term for a small bribe.

Spithame An ancient Greek unit of length approximately equivalent to 231.2 millimeters.

Split The act of a publicly-traded company increasing the number of outstanding shares, while maintaining the same market capitalization. In other words, a company engages in a stock split in order to decrease its share price by increasing the number of shares available. Current holders of the stock are given more shares so that they maintain the same percentage of ownership in the company. For example, a company with a share price of $400 may double the number of shares so that the share price drops to $200. Companies conduct stock splits for a number of reasons; one possible reason is to keep its shares affordable. See also: Last Split, Split Ratio, Split Adjusted.

Split Adjusted Describing what the price of a stock would be had a stock split not taken place. Stock splits often occur when publicly-traded companies wish to reduce their share prices to keep their stocks affordable. One can calculate a stock's split adjusted value by multiplying the current share price by the split ratio. For example, suppose a stock trading at $75 per share has a 3:1 stock split. This would send the share price to $25. If the share price then rises to $45, the split adjusted value is $45 * 3, or $135.

Split Close A situation in which futures contracts with the same underlying asset but different maturing dates close at different prices. This is relatively common in the final minute of trading on an exchange.

Split Commission A commission that two or more people share. For example, a broker may split a commission with a friend who introduced a client to the broker as a finder's fee. Alternatively, real estate agents may split the commission on a house if one represents the buyer and the other represents the seller.

Split Coupon Bond 1. A bond that pays no coupons at issue and, at some point prior to maturity, begins to pay coupons. **2.** See: Zero-Coupon Bond.

Split Funding The act or practice of using a single amount of money to buy two or more investment vehicles. Split funding is most common in insurance; for example, the premium for an insurance policy may be used to both maintain the policy and to buy shares in a mutual fund. Whole life policies operate on split funding: part of the premium pays for the benefit on death, while another part is placed in a special savings account one may redeem.

Split Gift The act of a married couple giving gifts to a single beneficiary separately in order to avoid the gift tax. Givers of gifts in excess of $10,000 are required to pay the gift tax. In order to avoid this through gift splitting, a husband and a wife may separately give up to $10,000, meaning that the beneficiary receives up to $20,000 without subjecting the giver to the tax.

Split Grade A situation in which the obverse and reverse of a coin have different conditions. This is common in numismatics. In general, a split grade coin is worth what a coin with only the lower grade would be worth. See also: Split rating.

Split Offering A new issue of a bond that consists of both serial bonds, which mature at regular intervals over a given period of time, and term bonds, which mature all at once. That is, some parts of the split offering mature at various times, but the bulk matures all at once. Both corporate and municipal issuers sometimes make split offerings.

Split Order An order to buy or sell a security that, because of its size, is executed as two or more smaller orders. The order is split in order to reduce the pressure for a large price fluctuation that can occur when such orders occur. The exact size of a split order varies according to security. For example, a stock with relatively few shares outstanding will likely have a smaller threshold for a split order than others. Most of the time, split orders are made by institutional investors. Split orders are common among significant orders.

Split Print A large trade (of over 10,000 shares or with a value over $200,000) that is reported as separate trades at different prices on an exchange's ticker.

Split Rating A situation in which two ratings agencies give a bond two different ratings. Experts disagree as to why ratings agencies may give different ratings, but many point to differences in methodology. They also disagree as to whether the higher or the lower rating affects market prices more. It is important to note, however, that most regulators do not allow banks and some other institutional investors to buy bonds that have not received an investment-grade rating from at least two agencies. Thus, a split rating in which one agency calls a bond investment-grade and another calls it junk can have major implications for issuers and some investors.

Split Ratio Following a stock split, a ratio of the new number of shares outstanding to the old one. This shows an investor by how much a publicly-traded company has split its stock. The higher a split ratio is, the more the company's share price drops.

Split Stock 1. A stock one owns with at least one other person. See also: Joint property. **2.** See: Stock split.

Split-Funded Annuity An annuity in which part of the premium is paid out to the annuitant immediately in monthly installments, while the remainder is set aside and paid to the annuitant in monthly installments in the future. A split-funded annuity allows the annuitant the flexibility of receiving monthly payments at once while still investing a significant amount of money. The deferred payments are usually higher when the annuitant begins to receive them.

Split-Off A relatively rare situation in which a parent company offers to its shareholders stock in a subsidiary in exchange for a comparable amount of stock in the parent company. This allows the parent company to divest itself of the subsidiary. See also: Splitoff IPO.

Splitoff IPO The initial public offering for an individual unit of a corporation. Because the corporation may itself be publicly traded, this may be a form of spinning off. However, the parent company rarely offers a controlling interest in the unit so as to maintain it as a subsidiary. A corporation may make a splitoff IPO for a number of reasons, including expansion of operations of the subsidiary or the need to repay its debt.

Split-Rate Tax System A tax system that taxes retained earnings (profits a company keeps) at a higher rate than the profits it pays out as dividends. This can encourage companies to have a lower plowback ratio and, instead, pay higher dividends.

Split-Up An action in which a publicly-traded company splits into two different publicly-traded companies. Stock in the company is exchanged for stock in both of the new companies according to some predetermined formula. A split-up may happen at government instigation, for example, to end a monopoly. A company may also voluntarily split up if it believes it will improve profitability.

Split-Up Value The value of the individual parts of a company if they were separate companies. Companies may consider a takeover if the split-up values of a target company's parts are higher than its purchase price. Likewise, a company may evaluate the split-up value of a department if it is considering a spin-off.

SPM GOST 7.67 Latin three-letter geocode for Saint Pierre and Miquelon. The code is used for transactions to and from local bank accounts and for international shipping to Saint Pierre and Miquelon. As with all GOST 7.67 codes, it is used primarily in Cyrillic alphabets.

SPOC Single point of contact. In management, the only person on a committee or project who is permitted to speak publicly (or in some cases, privately) about the committee's or project's actions. Assigning a SPOC is a way to streamline management of a project so supervisors (or the public) do not receive multiple stories multiple times.

Spoken For Describing a security upon which an order has been placed, but not necessarily executed. The trader of a spoken for security is no longer looking for buyers or sellers, and may tell potential trading partners that he/she or the security are "spoken for." It is the opposite of open.

Spolka Z Organiczona Odpowiedzialnoscia A Polish term for a limited liability company. It is abbreviated SP.Z O.O.

Sponsor 1. An underwriting firm. **2.** An institutional investor or high net-worth individual who takes a large position in a security, which encourages other investors to the same. Sponsors exist because other investors trust them to make the correct investment decisions most of the time. See also: Crowd.

Sponsored ADR An American Depositary Receipt issued with the knowledge and cooperation of the company whose stock backs it. Unlike other ADRs, which simply give themonetary benefits of ownership, sponsored ADRs are treated just like common stock, complete with voting rights, only denominated in the U.S. dollar. In order for an ADR to trade on the New York Stock Exchange, it must be sponsored. See also: International depositary receipt.

Spontaneous Current Liabilities Liabilities that a company must pay within a year that arise automatically as a result of its daily operations. Examples of spontaneous current liabilities include accounts payable and the cost of goods sold.

They often change as a result the company's sales. See also: Spontaneous liabilities, spontaneous assets.

Spontaneous Liabilities Liabilities that a person or firm acquires when buying goods or services on credit. Specifically, spontaneous liabilities are the obligations to pay for the goods or services at some point in the future.

Spoo Slang; an index contract traded on the Chicago Mercantile Exchange in which the underlying index is the S&P 500.

Spoofing 1. An illegal practice in which an investor with a long position on a security makes a buy order for that security and immediately cancels it without filling the order. Spoofing tends to increase the price of that security as other investors may then issue their own buy orders, which increases the appearance of demand. The first investor then closes his/her long position by selling the security at the new, higher price. Spoofing is a form of market manipulation. See also: Pump and dump. **2.** The act of impersonating a person, usually over the Internet, with the intention of gaining access to another's personal or financial information. It is a means of identity theft.

Spooz A slang term for index futures contracts on the S&P 500. Because the S&P 500 is considered representative of the broader U.S. market, spooz essentially are bets on the direction of American stocks.

Spot Commodity A commodity traded on the current market. Spot commodities involve straightforward transactions; there is a buyer and a seller and the seller makes delivery of the commodity promptly when the transaction is settled. A spot commodity differs from a futures transaction, in which the buyer and seller agree to exchange the commodity at some point in the future.

Spot Currency Market A market in which a currency bought or sold is delivered in two business days (except for the Canadian dollar, which is delivered in one business day). It differs from currency derivatives markets like futures contracts.

Spot Exchange Rate The exchange rate for which two parties agree to trade two currencies at the present moment. The spot exchange rate is usually at or close to the current market rate because the transaction occurs in real time and not at some point in the future. Some analysts believe that forward rates are an accurate predictor of future spot rates, though many others dispute this. See also: Forward exchange.

Spot Interest Rate The interest rate for loans and debt securities issued at a given time. The advantage of borrowing at the spot interest rate is the fact that it is a known quantity and one can amortize the loan accordingly. The risk of the spot interest rate is that interest rates may rise or fall in the future to the disadvantage of one of the parties to a contract. Some investors speculate on the difference between a spot interest rate and a forward interest rate.

Spot Market A market in which an asset bought or sold is delivered immediately. To give a basic example, if one buys a stock and it is delivered immediately, one utilizes the spot market. It differs from derivatives markets like futures. Perhaps less commonly, it is called the cash market.

Spot Next A swap that matures the day after the transaction.

Spot Rate The interest rate or exchange rate on a contract on the current market. Some analysts believe that forward rates accurately predict future spot rates, though others dispute this. See also: Spot price.

Spot Secondary A secondary offering that is not registered with the SEC. A spot secondary must meet certain requirements in order to avoid registration. Specifically, they are usually offered to institutional investors rather than the general public. Generally speaking, a spot secondary is faster than other secondary offerings; issuers usually offer a discount for underwriting services on a spot secondary.

Spot Trade A trade on any commodity or contract for immediate delivery. The most common spot trade is a trade on a foreign exchange contract. If one is trading a physical commodity, the buyer receives delivery of the underlying goods and compensates the seller immediately. If a spot trade is not settled immediately, the counterparty responsible is expected to compensate the other. Spot trades contrast with futures trades.

Spot Transaction Any transaction that does not occur in the futures or forward market. That is, the participants in a spot transaction agree to buy and sell, respectively, at the present market value and to settle the transaction a few days (usually one, two, or three) later. The term is most common in the foreign exchange market.

Spot Week The length of time for a currency swap at a certain exchange rate that expires one week after it is entered. It may be used to hedge other foreign exchange positions.

Spousal IRA An IRA where the beneficiary the spouse of the person making the contributions. This provides a steady stream of income for the spouse after the contributor's retirement or death, especially when he/she has little or no other income. This is especially useful should the spouse who earns the income die prematurely. A spousal IRA has the same terms as any other IRA and may be either a traditional IRA or a Roth IRA.

Spousal Remainder Trust A term trust into which the grantor deposits assets that produce income. The income passes to the beneficiary for a certain number of years, after which the assets go to the grantor's spouse. The income from the assets are taxed at the beneficiary's marginal tax rate unless the beneficiary is under 14 years old, in which case it is taxed at the grantor's rate. See also: Q-TIP.

Spread The difference between two prices. For example, if one sells an asset for a higher price than one bought it, this profit is called a spread. It may also refer to the difference between the highest bid and the lowest offer for a security. See also: Bid-ask spread, Arbitrage, Spread option.

Spread Option In options, the writing of a contract and the purchase of another with the same underlying asset, but with different strikes and expiration dates. A spread option is intended to reduce the risk of having a particular position on the underlying asset. The profit on a spread option comes from the difference in the strike prices of the two contracts. Spread options are usually traded over-the-counter. See also: Crack, Crush, Spark.

Spread Order An order to a broker to buy and sell different options on the same underlying asset but for different premiums and/or strike prices. The client who makes the spread order hopes to profit from the difference between the prices in the options sold and the options bought. See also: Spread strategy.

Spread Strategy Any of several investment strategies that involve maintaining different positions on options or futures with the same underlying asset, often with different expiration dates. Spreading may take many different forms, and is designed to hedge against loss regardless of price movements on the underlying asset.

Spread to Treasury The difference in yield between a U.S. Treasury security and any other debt security with a similar maturity. Because U.S. Treasury securities are considered zero-risk investments, the yield on the other security is almost always higher to compensate the investor for the added risk.

Spreading An options strategy in which one buys one option contract while selling another on the same underlying asset, but with either a different strike price, a different expiration, or both. Spreading allows the investor to profit from price movements between the two option contracts. It can be a form of speculation. See also: Strike spread.

Spread-Load Contractual Plan An agreement in which the load of a mutual fund is spread out evenly over a period of time. That is, the buyer of shares in the mutual fund does not pay the load the first time he/she buys shares. Rather, he/she pays a portion of the load each time he/she buys more shares until the load is paid in full. This assumes the buyer consistently buys shares over an extended time. It is also called a load spread option.

Spreadsheet A sheet or computer program organized into rows and columns for easy comparison of information. For example, there may be two columns representing two different fiscal years and several rows representing different financial variables (such as revenue, profit, and so forth). A balance sheet is a very common example of a spreadsheet.

Springing Convertible A convertible security that may be exchanged for common stock in the issuing company and, in addition, contains warrants allowing the holder to purchase more shares if he/she desires. Under certain defined circumstances, the exercise price for these warrants drops dramatically. Springing convertibles are issued in an antitakeover measure. Common circumstances under which the exercise price drops include hostile tender offers and other hostile takeover attempts.

Sprinkler Leakage Legal Liability Insurance An insurance policy that provides coverage in the event that a sprinkler system discharges at the wrong time. That is, if the sprinkler discharges for some reason other than a fire, the automatic sprinkler clause would protect the policyholder from paying for the resultant damage. It is usually an endorsement (or an addendum) to a Standard Fire Policy.

Sprinkling Trust A trust with several beneficiaries in which the trustee has the discretion to distribute funds between them. That is, the trustor gives the trustee a great deal of leeway to use the trust according to the needs of individual beneficiaries. A sprinkling trust may be a living trust or may be part of a will.

Square A unit of area equivalent to 100 square feet. It has historically been used to measure real estate in Australia.

Squawk Box An intercom or telephone on the desk of individual brokers allowing them to communicate with analysts at their brokerages to received updated information on different securities. The brokers can then pass this information along to clients.

Squeeze-Out In joint stock companies, to buy the stocks of a minority group of shareholders without their necessary consent. A group of shareholders owning the large majority of the company have the ability to squeeze out remaining shareholders. The percentage of shareholders needed varies between jurisdictions. For example, the United Kingdom requires shareholders owning 90% of the company to consent to squeeze out the other shareholders, while Germany requires 95%. Minority shareholders receive compensation in return for surrendering their shares.

Squeezing the Shorts A situation in which a rapid increase in demand coupled with a small supply causes a stock price to rise significantly. This occurs most commonly in small companies with relatively few shares outstanding.

Squiggly Lines A slang term for technical information. The term has a somewhat negative connotation.

SR 1. ISO 3166-1 alpha-2 code for the Republic of Suriname. This is the code used in international transactions to and from Surinamese bank accounts. **2.** ISO 3166-2 geocode for Suriname. This is used as an international standard for shipping to Suriname. Each Surinamese district has its own code with the prefix "SR." For example, the code for the District of Wanica is ISO 3166-2:SR:WA.

SRD ISO 4217 code for the Surinamese dollar. It was issued in 2004, replacing the Surinamese guilder following a period of high inflation. It is pegged to a currency basket denominated in U.S. dollars.

SRG ISO 4217 code for the Surinamese guilder. Originally pegged to the Dutch guilder, it changed its peg to the United States dollar during World War II. It began to suffer from high inflation at the beginning of the 1990s and, because of this, the currency was discontinued and replaced with the Surinamese dollar in 2004.

Sri Lankan Rupee The currency of Sri Lanka. The rupee was instituted as the sole currency in 1869; it separated from the Indian rupee following Sri Lanka's independence from the United Kingdom.

Srok In Cambodia, a political subdivision equivalent to a district, which is a subdivision of a city.

S's over N's A slang term indicating that the S&P 500 outperformed the NASDAQ 100 index over a certain period of time.

ST 1. ISO 3166-1 alpha-2 code for the Democratic Republic of Sao Tome and Principe. This is the code used in international transactions to and from Santomean bank accounts. **2.** ISO 3166-2 geocode for Sao Tome and Principe. This is used as an international standard for shipping to the country. Sao Tome and Principe each have their own codes with the prefix "ST." The code for the Sao Tome is ISO 3166-2:ST-ST, while for Principe it is ISO 3166-2:ST-PR.

STA 1. Securities Transfer Association. A trade association for banks and independent transfer agents. The STA performs a number of services for the industry and, significantly, operates the STAMP program. **2.** Security Trader Association. A trade association for individuals who trade in securities. Established in Chicago in 1934, the STA provides educational, informational, and social opportunities for members.

Stability The state of a security maintaining a constant or near constant price. Short-term securities tend to be more stable than long-term securities, but this is not always the case.

Stabilization Period The period between the offering of a new issue and the time at which it is fully distributed. During the stabilization period, underwriters serve as counterparties on the secondary market to help keep the price of the new issue at or above the offering price on the primary market. If the market price falls below the offering price, the underwriters will be unable to place the issue with investors because interested parties will buy at the lower price available on the secondary market. After the issue is fully distributed, there are no more shares or bonds to sell on the primary market and the stabilization period ends. See also: Price stabilization.

Stable Market A market with low trading volume that can nevertheless absorb a large sale without a major change in price. In most low volume markets, a single large sale causes a big jump or drop in price because there are relatively few other sales against which to compare the large sale. The term is most common in foreign exchange.

Stack A unit of volume equivalent to 108 cubic feet. It is used in the sale of firewood.

Stadion An ancient Greek unit of length approximately equivalent to 184.9 meters.

Staffer In investment banking, an employee responsible for parceling out work among other, usually subordinate employees. A staffer generally attempts to divide work as evenly as possible. The staffer usually has another job description and simply takes on staffer duties as extra work.

Stag Informal; an investor who buys a new issue of a security and sells it very quickly in order to make a profit. A stag makes the bet that the price of a new issue will rapidly rise, at least for the first few hours or days. His/her investment philosophy is the exact opposite of a buy and hold strategy.

Stagflation High inflation in a period of low GDP growth. Many economists thought that this was impossible, but the oil embargo of the 1970s contributed to a staggering increase in oil and food prices, which fueled inflation and hindered economic growth. Stagflation is difficult to control, as focusing on controlling inflation could hurt growth even further, while trying to ease credit to encourage growth could intensify inflation. The term is a portmanteau of stagnation and inflation.

Staggered Entry Strategy In development economics, the approach in which a government allows only a few companies in an industry, but periodically allows a new company to enter the market. The staggered entry strategy allows companies time to develop their products, which may be quite expensive, but also gives them the incentive to perform well, as the government may provide added competition at any time.

Staggered Terms An arrangement whereby only a certain number of members of a board of directors are elected in a given year. For example, a board of directors may have 10 members serving five year, staggered terms where two new members are elected each year. In addition to giving the board consistency in its membership, staggered terms makes hostile takeovers more difficult because the potential acquirer can replace only so many directors at a time.

Stagnation A period where an economy grows at an extremely low rate without actually entering a recession. During stagnation, it is unlikely that jobs will be created, wages will increase, or that the stock market will boom. While there is no exact definition of economic stagnation, most analysts agree that positive growth under 2%-3% qualifies. It may occur because a business cycle is winding down, because a catastrophic event has caused economic uncertainty, or for any number of other reasons. Classical Keynesian economics states that stagnation will result in a period of low inflation because there is no growth in demand for money, but American stagnation in the 1970s also saw a period of high inflation. See also: Brezhnev Stagnation, Stagflation.

STAIRS A convertible municipal bond. STAIRS are zero-coupon bonds that may be converted into interest-bearing bonds. Zero-coupon bonds are sold at a discount,

and, because they do not pay interest, they are more volatile in the secondary market. A bondholder may thus wish to convert STAIRS to interest-bearing bonds in order to lock in a certain return. On the other hand, more risk tolerant bondholders may wish to hold the bond in the belief that a fluctuation in interest rates will make the bond more valuable. Like all municipal bonds, STAIRS are exempt from federal taxes. They are also called municipal convertibles.

Stakeholder Management A form of management in which multiple constituencies are invited to contribute. For example, labor union representatives, shareholders, non-union employees, customers, and the general public may all be asked to provide input on a project. Stakeholder management is used to stop problems before they become significant, and, in case a project fails, to make it more difficult to assign blame to any one person or group.

Stakeholdering A way that an employee can gather support for a pet project by talking about it with clients. It is hoped that the clients will bring up the project casually with management in a way that will socially force management to approve of it.

Stakeholders All persons and institutions that have an interest in seeing a venture or company succeed. Stakeholders include shareholders, management, employees, the larger community, and even the government. While stakeholders may not have a direct financial holding in the company, they would still stand to benefit if the venture or company succeeds. For example, the local government may wish to see a company succeed because it provides tax revenue, even though the local government does not directly own any part of the company.

Stake-Out Investment An initial investment in a company that provides a certain amount of equity, with the intent to buy more of the company at a later date, especially when a certain regulatory hurdle has been met. In the early 1980s, it became relatively common for bank holding companies to make stake-out investments in out-of-state banks before interstate banking was allowed to any significant extent. This brought stake-out investments under the regulation of the Federal Reserve, which limited stake-outs to 5% equity. The bank holding companies made these stake-out investments under the assumption that interstate banking would eventually be allowed, which it finally was with the passage of the Riegle-Neal Interstate Banking and Branching Efficiency Act of 1994.

Stale Price The current price of an asset that does not reflect recently revealed or other available information. The stale price is unlikely to remain stale as the market absorbs the information and reflects it in the price. Analysts disagree on how long this takes, as different versions of the efficient markets hypothesis state that the stale price either evaporates quickly, or does not exist at all.

Stalking Horse Bid 1. In a corporate bankruptcy in which the corporation wishes or is required to sell its assets, an initial bid on those assets by a third party chosen by the corporation. This is done to ensure that the bankrupt corporation does not have to settle for unacceptably low prices for its assets. **2.** More generally, a "trial balloon" in which a third party approaches a person or company inquiring about the possibility of a (usually hostile) takeover. The party actually asking about the takeover remains anonymous so as to protect its reputational risk in case the idea does not meet with favor.

Stalwart Informal for a publicly-traded company that earns a steady but not staggering return. That is, a stalwart provides a solid return for little risk; one may think of a stalwart as the opposite of a growth stock. Peter Lynch coined the term stalwart to describe these companies. See also: Blue chip.

Stamp Duty A tax placed on legal documents upon transfer. For example, a stamp duty may be assessed on the deed to a house when it is sold before the deed can pass from the seller to the buyer. The term comes from the fact that governments used to place physical stamps on the legal documents as proof that the duty had been paid, but this practice is fairly uncommon now. Stamp duties are most common in some Commonwealth of Nations countries, such as Singapore and Australia, as well as in some U.S. states.

Stand-Alone Company A company that is not a subsidiary of another company. A subsidiary is sometimes spun off and becomes a stand-alone company because it may have higher profit potential as an independent entity.

Stand-Alone Principle The principle that a company should decide whether or not to do a project based on the profitability of similar projects with the same risk. See also: standalone profit, standalone risk.

Standard & Poor's A financial services company that offers many different types of products. It is perhaps best known for the S&P 500 American stock index and other indices in four different countries. It also serves as a credit ratings agency and a research firm. It is one of only 10 firms the SEC recognizes as a credit rating agency, though, like other CRAs, its methods have been subject to criticism. However, its research branch, Capital IQ, is one of the most active in the world, publishing information on firms and markets globally. Since 1966, it has been owned by McGraw-Hill Companies.

Standard & Poor's 500 Index A stock market index tracking 500 companies in various industries with a large amount of market capitalization. It is a capitalization-weighted index, meaning that stocks with higher market caps affect the average more. The companies included on the S&P 500 are decided by committee and are updated periodically. It also scales its averages to account for stock splits and other changes in the companies tracked. Next to the Dow Jones Industrial Average, it is considered one of the premier securities indices in the United States. Some exchange-traded funds, notably SPDRs, track the S&P 500.

Standard & Poor's Confidence Indicator A measure of investor willingness to attempt higher returns by assuming more risk. It is calculated by compiling an index of stocks categorized according to risk; a higher measure indicates higher confidence. It differs from other confidence indicators in that it is not based on subjective surveys of industry insiders.

Standard & Poor's MidCap 400 Index A stock index that tracks 400 publicly-traded companies with a medium amount of market capitalization. While not as well-known as the S&P 500 index, the S&P Midcap 400 is considered a leading index on mid-cap companies. Mid-cap SPDRs are depository receipts that track the S&P Midcap 400.

Standard & Poor's SmallCap 600 Index A stock index that tracks 600 publicly-traded companies with a small amount of market capitalization. While not as well-known as the S&P 500 index, the S&P Smallcap 600 is considered a leading index on small-cap companies.

Standard & Poor's Underlying Rating The bond rating system used by Standard & Poor's to rate municipal bonds. It attaches a rating to municipalities' creditworthiness, regardless of the creditworthiness of any guarantor or insurer. S&P provides SPURs to municipalities that request them; it may also provide an amended statement of creditworthiness if a bond is insured. However, it is important to note that a SPUR only rates the underlying bond.

Standard Cubit An ancient Egyptian unit of length approximately equivalent to 45 centimeters.

Standard Deduction In American tax law, the portion of an individual's or couple's income that is not taxed. The standard deduction is taken after computing the adjusted gross income. Taxpayers have the option of choosing between the standard deduction and making itemized deductions, based on medical expenses or local taxes paid. Itemized deductions may or may not result in a larger percentage of income that is tax free, and taxpayers usually take the larger deduction. The amount in the standard deduction varies from year to year, depending on inflation and a person's filing status. However, it is higher for persons over age 65 and blind persons.

Standard Error An estimate of the standard deviation of a data set. See also: Confidence interval.

Standard Industrial Classification A system of four digit codes used in business to classify the industry to which a company belongs. The SIC was created by the U.S. government in 1937 to facilitate communication within and between businesses and industries. For the most part, the SIC was replaced by the six digit NAICS in 1997, but the SEC still uses the SIC. For example, an oil and gas exploration company might file with the SEC under the code 1382.

Standard Industrial Classification Code A four digit code used in business to classify the industry to which a company belongs. The SIC code was created by the U.S. government in 1937 to facilitate communication within and between businesses and industries. For the most part, the SIC was replaced by the six digit NAICS in 1997, but the SEC still uses the SIC. For example, an oil & gas exploration company might file with the SEC under the SIC code 1382.

Standard Mileage Rate A small amount (less than $1) that one is allowed to deduct from one's income for business use of a vehicle. The standard mileage rate is multiplied by the number of miles that the vehicle is driven for business use. This is used in lieu of deducting actual expenses (such as gas and maintenance) on the vehicle.

Standardized Normal Distribution A bell curve with an average value of zero and a standard deviation of one.

Standardized Value The distance of a data point from the average value of the data set divided by the standard deviation. The standardized value helps minimize some of the statistical noise in individual data points.

Standby Agreement An agreement between the issuer of a security and its underwriters stating that the underwriters are responsible for any unsold portion of the issue. That is, the underwriters agree to buy the remainder of a new issue if they are unable to place its entirety with investors. This transfers the risk of the unsold portion of the issue from the issuer to the underwriters. This guarantees that the issuer will raise the capital it intends to raise, but leaves the underwriters with the possibility that they must purchase an issue with low value. As a result, underwriters charge a standby fee for a standby agreement. It is also called firm commitment underwriting or a backstopped deal.

Standby Credit Funds that the IMF sets aside to lend to needy countries as the need arises with little notice. It should not be confused with a standby letter of credit.

Standby Fee A fee paid to an underwriter in exchange for an agreement that the underwriter will purchase the remainder of a new issue that it does not place with investors. See also: Jointly and Severally.

Standby Letter of Credit A statement issued by a bank to the buyer of a good stating that the seller will receive payment on time and in the correct amount. If the buyer fails to make payment, the bank will do so on his/her behalf. The buyer presents a letter of credit to the seller, which virtually eliminates the risk that the seller will not be paid. Letters of credit have become very common in international commerce, as distance and other factors make it difficult for sellers to establish the creditworthiness of every buyer.

Standby Underwriter An underwriter who agrees with the issuer of a security and its underwriters to be responsible for any unsold portion of the issue. That is, the underwriter agrees to buy the remainder of a new issue if it is unable to place its entirety with investors. This transfers the risk of the unsold portion of the issue from the issuer to the underwriter. This guarantees that the issuer will raise the capital it intends to raise, but leaves the underwriter with the possibility that it must purchase an issue with low value. As a result, standby underwriters charge a standby fee.

Standing Liberty Quarter A silver coin minted by the United States between 1916 and 1930. It was worth 1/4 of one dollar.

Standstill Agreement An agreement between a target company and a potential hostile acquirer whereby the acquirer agrees not to buy any more of the target company in exchange for some compensation. The compensation may be monetary; that is, the company can simply buy off the acquirer. More commonly, it involves some other incentive such as a seat on the board of directors or an agreement for the company to repurchase its own stock, which would increase the value of the shares the acquirer already owns. A standstill agreement has an expiration date after which the acquirer can continue buying the company if it wishes, but the time in between gives the target company time to form a more effective antitakeover strategy.

Stang A Swedish unit of length approximately equivalent to 4.75 meters. It is used in land measurement.

Stapled Stock Shares of two publicly-traded companies operating under the same management that are traded as if they were one stock. Most of the time, certificates for each stapled stock are printed on the same stock certificate. Stapled stocks are put together usually if one share pays higher dividends while the other has the higher potential for appreciation. Variations on stapled stocks include HOLDRS, which issue stocks in more than two companies as one certificate. Stapled stocks are also called paired shares.

Start-Up Company A company in its earliest stage of development, usually before its IPO. Start-up companies concentrate on product development and build-up of capitalization. Nearly all start-up companies operate at a loss, at least at first. Some start-ups go through a period where they have no revenue at all. Start-ups spend their time perfecting their business plans and developing products that will eventually be sold on the open market. Most start-ups rely on venture capital or loans to continue operations during this phase. See also: Payout period, Dot-com bubble.

State Administrator The regulator charged with governing securities at the state level. That is, the state administrator is the unit of a state government that ensures security issues under that state's jurisdiction comply with the law. It also investigates potential wrong-doing and takes administrative action against persons and companies that violate rules and regulations. The name of state administrator comes from a provision in the Uniform Securities Act.

State Agent A person who is licensed to sell insurance in a single state. Because most insurance is regulated at the state level, state agents are registered on a state-by-state basis.

State and Local Government Series Non-negotiable securities the Federal government sells to state and local governments. SLGS are an investment vehicle for issuers of state and local debt securities in which they may invest the proceeds from such issues. SLGS may have time deposits or demand deposits. Time deposit SLGS have maturities of anywhere from 15 days to 40 years and have interest rates one basis point below Treasury securities with similar maturities. Demand deposit SLGS have one-day maturities that are automatically rolled over until the security holder withdraws the deposit; their interest rates are based on the most recent auction of 13-week Treasury securities.

State Bank In the United States, a bank that has received its charter from a state government rather than the federal government. A state bank has the option of whether or not to become a member bank in the Federal Reserve System. If it elects to become a member, there is no real difference between a state bank and a federal bank, except that the state bank generally does business only within a state. If it does not become a member, it is regulated only by the state in which it is based. See also: Nonmember Bank.

State Council of the People's Republic of China The highest administrative body in mainland China. The State Council directly oversees provincial governments and several government agencies. It indirectly supervises most other agencies through government departments. The State Council consists of the premier and the head of every department. In practice, the members of the State Council are also the senior leadership of the Communist Party of China.

State Earnings-Related Pension Scheme Also called SERPS. A voluntary state pension scheme formerly available to citizens of the United Kingdom. It granted higher payments to pensioners following retirement in exchange for higher National Insurance contributions. Payments were based on average earnings over a pensioner's career. It was replaced in 2002 by the Second State Pension, which offers higher benefits to lower and middle income pensioners.

State Guaranty Fund A fund administered by the government of a U.S. state protecting policyholders and pensioners from the default of an insurance company. That is, if an insurance company is licensed to operate in a given state, policyholders within that state are protected because, if the company defaults on its payments, the state guaranty fund will pay the policyholder instead. Insurance companies pay a small percentage of their revenues to different states to finance state guaranty funds.

State High Risk Pools for the Medically Uninsurable In the United States, a pool of liquidity sponsored by the state government for persons who, because of a severe illness or pre-existing condition, cannot purchase health insurance. One pays a premium (which is comparatively high due to the level of risk); the pool pays for medical expenses for policyholders up to a certain point and, in most respects, operates as a regular insurer. The main difference is the lack of need for profit, which enables the government to provide the insurance in the first place.

State Mint An organization in Romania that issues legal tender coins for general use. It was established in 1870 and is owned by the government of Romania. It is located in Bucharest.

State Tax-Exempt Income Fund A mutual fund with earnings that are exempt from both federal taxes and state taxes. Generally speaking, state tax-exempt income funds are limited to investing in bonds issued in the state where the mutual fund is based. Most of the time, shareholders of these funds must also live in the same state to take advantage of the tax exemption.

State Unemployment Compensation Unemployment insurance paid by an American state, as opposed to the federal government. Under the Federal Unemployment Tax Act, states pay for half of their unemployment benefits. The federal government pays the other half.

Stated Annual Interest Rate An interest rate in a given year that does not account for more frequent compounding. For example, if a loan of $100 has a stated annual interest rate of 5%, the amount owed at the end of the year is $105. However, if the interest compounds monthly, the actual amount is $105.12. See also: Effective annual interest rate.

Stated Value An arbitrary value a publicly-traded company assigns to its common stock on its financial statements. The stated value bears no relationship whatsoever to a stock's market value; however, in the event of liquidation it provides shareholders with some level of protection as the stated value shows that their stock does have some worth.

Statement A written report of an individual or company's financial or other relevant data. A prime example is the annual report that a publicly-traded company is required to distribute to shareholders. The report contains information on the company's financial state, such as operational income and net profit. Sometimes it also contains an accountant's opinion on the general health of the company. Occasionally, statements are distributed at irregular intervals to explain a major event in the company. See also: Balance sheet.

Statement Billing A bill for goods or services that collects several invoices from a given time, usually a month, into one document. The statement bill is presented to the customer, who is then responsible to pay for all goods or services listed on it. This is useful for repeat customers, who may purchase several goods and services from a business over a given period of time.

Statement of Auditing Standards A decision by the Auditing Standards Board providing information on how to conduct an audit. The Board's decisions are authoritative; auditors generally must abide by them. The Auditing Standards Board provides a uniform set of standards for conducting audits in the United States.

Stathmos An ancient Persian unit of length variously equivalent to values between 24 and 30 kilometers.

Stationary Time Series In statistics, a time series in which the data in the series do not depend on time. That is, the mean, variance, and covariance of all data in the time series are adjusted to reflect true values not dependent on time or seasonality.

Statism 1. In political science, the theory that the state exercises (or should exercise) control over a society and for that reason is a major engine of social change. **2.** See: State capitalism.

Statist A person who believes that the state exercises (or should exercise) control over a society and that it is a major engine of social change.

Statistical Massage A slang term for the manipulation of data in order to promote one's favored view. For example, one may statistically massage the results of a focus group to indicate that participants favor a new product more strongly than they actually do. If statistical massages are applied to earnings reports or similar documents, it may constitute aggressive accounting.

Statistical Office of the European Community Commonly called Eurostat. A directorate under the European Commission responsible for collecting statistical information within the European Union. Eurostat collects and analyzes demographic, economic and trade data. It also works to harmonize statistical methods used by members of the EU. It traces its origins to 1953 but was established under its present name in 1959.

Statistical Tracking Error One standard deviation from the difference between the return on a portfolio and the return on a benchmark, such as the S&P 500. If the difference varies within that standard deviation, it is not considered cause for concern. For example, it may be attributed to a rounding error in the calculations. See also: Margin of error.

Statisticne regije In Slovenia, a subdivision used only for statistical purposes.

Statutami mesto In the Czech Republic, a city that is not a constituent within a province or other political subdivision.

Statutarstadt In Austria, a city that is not a constituent within a province or other political subdivision.

Statutory Accounting Principles A system of accounting used by insurance companies. They are considered more conservative than the Generally Accepted Accounting Principles; this is because insurance companies will, at one point or another, have to pay benefits to most policyholders. Therefore, they must take all possible steps to remain solvent. SAP have minor variation by state, but are generally used by all insurance companies in the United States.

Statutory Employee In the United States, a person declared an employee by law. Persons declared to be statutory employees include: full-time life insurance agents, drivers who distribute laundry, meat, produce, or beverages (excluding milk) to customers, individuals who work from home on material provided by an employer, or full-time salespersons who seek orders for resale on behalf of an employer. While statutory employees file their expenses on a Schedule C, they are not considered independent contractors and thus do not pay the self-employment tax.

Statutory Investment Investments allowed for institutional investors under the legal and regulatory rules of the country in which they are made. Institutional investors, notably banks, handle funds on behalf of clients, who may or may not be interested in investing themselves. As a result, many institutional investors are restricted from making certain high-risk investments. In the case of bonds, statutory investments are called investment-grade. One may also refer to statutory investments as legal investments.

Statutory Merger A merger between two or more companies in which one company continues to legally exist, while all others cease to exist. That is, if Company A and Company B merge, Company A will continue to exist under its own name, while Company B will begin to operate under the name, "Company A." A statutory merger is essentially the same as an acquisition, though an acquisition carries a slight connotation of a hostile takeover, while a statutory merger does not. See also: Statutory consolidation.

Statutory Surplus The budget surplus that an insurance company has after it calculates its assets and liabilities according to all applicable state and federal laws.

Statutory Voting In common stock, a method of voting at the annual meeting and/or in elections for the board of directors in which there is one vote per share. Thus, if a shareholder has 10 shares, he/she receives 10 votes at meetings. This gives persons and companies with more equity in a company a greater voice in its decisions.

Staying Power Informal; the ability of an investor to refuse to give into fear after a loss and to remain in the market. Because every investor loses on some positions, it is necessary to have staying power in order to become (and to be considered) a "serious" investor.

STC Said to Contain. In shipping, a term in which a carrier (shipper) accepts packages for transport but does not verify their contents. Depending on the international convention used, a carrier accepting goods on an STC basis may only be legally liable for the number of packages, rather than the value of the contents. This is especially important in the event of a lawsuit or insurance claim. STC is also called shipper's load and carry (SL&C) or said to weigh (STW).

STD ISO 4217 code for the Sao Tome and Principe dobra. It was introduced in 1977, replacing the Sao Tome and Principe escudo. In the mid-2000s, the dobra's inflation rate accelerated significantly. In 2009, it was pegged to the euro.

Steady State 1. Describing an economy that is neither growing nor shrinking. While this is not technically a recession, a steady state economy is not generally considered desirable. **2.** See: equilibrium.

Stealth Parenting In business, the act or practice of lying to one's supervisor by saying that one has a company-related appointment, when in fact one is leaving to do something for one's children.

Steenth Informal; one-sixteenth (1/16, 0.0625). Steenth is a term often used in options trading, as well as other price negotiations. It is also called a teenvo.

STEER Analysis In risk assessment, a hermeneutic used for investigating the impact of a venture or investment. The term is an acronym for socio-political, technological, economic, ecological, and regulatory, which are the types of issues that must be addressed before one decides whether or not to make an investment. The term came to prominence in the early 21st century.

Steinkast A Norwegian unit of length used to refer to an undetermined short distance.

Stella A gold coin minted in the United States in 1879 and 1880. It was worth $4. Because only a few hundred were made, it never circulated.

Stem the Tide Informal; to slow down a trend or change its direction. Stemming the tide especially applies to negative situations that are beginning to turn positive. For example, gradual and slow economic growth may be said to stem the tide of a recession. To stem the tide is also called to stop the bleeding.

Stenkast A Swedish unit of length approximately equivalent to 50 meters, though it is also used to mean, roughly, "nearby."

Step Aside To allow a block trade to occur because one does not wish to make a better bid or offer.

Step Up 1. Informal; to increase. For example, one's income may increase until one "steps up" into a higher marginal tax rate. **2.** In convertible securities, a scheduled increase in the conversion price. Step-ups also apply to warrants and options. For example, if a shareholder owns convertible preferred stock at a conversion price of $10 per share, a step-up may involve an increase in the conversion price to $12 per share. The terms under which the security is sold outline the amount of the step-up and when it takes place. Because step-ups are contrary to the interest of buyers, there is little demand for securities with step-ups, and, as a result, they are a relatively rare feature of convertible securities.

Step-Down Note A debt security issued with a high coupon rate that gradually decreases over the life of the security. The decreases occur at regular intervals stated in the bond indenture. See also: Step-up bond.

Stepford Worker An employee who enthusiastically supports management policy, regardless of its actual merits. The term implies that the employee is a sycophant, and that he/she automatically agrees with management without thinking.

The term is a reference to The Stepford Wives, a novel (and films by the same name) about suspiciously submissive housewives.

Stephen Ross A neoclassical economist who developed the arbitrage pricing model in the mid 1970s. The arbitrage pricing model seeks to calculate the appropriate price of an asset while taking into account systemic risks common across an asset class. Any security with a price different from the one predicted by the model is considered "mispriced" and is an arbitrage opportunity. Ross also had a hand in developing the binomial option pricing model, which seeks to price options accurately in situations where other models do not easily apply. He is a professor at the Massachusetts Institute of Technology.

Stephen Wozniak An American engineer and co-founder of Apple. He was one of the earlier pioneers of the personal computer. He was born in 1950. See also: Steve Jobs.

Step-Out Trading The practice of one brokerage executing an order on behalf of a client but giving credit (and part of the commission) to another brokerage. This is often a gesture when the second brokerage has assisted the first in some way, especially by helping with research and analysis.

Stepped Coupon Bond A callable bond issued with a low coupon rate that gradually increases over the life of the bond. The increases occur at regular intervals stated in the bond indenture. It is also called a step-up coupon security or a dual coupon bond

Step-Up In Basis The increased cost basis of securities or other assets one has inherited. A step-up in basis is the fair market value of the securities at the time they are inherited, rather than when they were bought. For example, suppose a benefactor buys 10 shares at $10 per share in 1990 and dies in 2009, when they are $20 per share. The step-up in basis of those shares for the person to whom that benefactor wills those 10 shares is $20. This means that the person will be treated as if he/she bought the shares at $20 for tax purposes. A step-up in basis exists to limit the capital gains tax liability for persons who inherit stocks and other assets.

Step-Up Swap An interest rate swap with scheduled increases in the notional value. That is, the counterparties to the swap may agree to exchange different interest rates with a notional value of $1 million, with an increase to $1.1 million the following month, and $1.2 the month after that. Step-up swaps increases the dollar amounts of the swap, but the interest rate remains the same for the fixed rate payer and changes only according to the benchmark rate for the floating rate payer.

Stere A unit of volume used to measure quantities of firewood. The stere is equivalent to one cubic meter.

Sterile Investment An investment that does not provide dividends or interest. All gains from a sterile investment come from price appreciation. Examples of sterile investments include commodities, collectibles, and growth stocks. Sterile investments are often, but not always, high risk.

Sterilization A method by which a central bank may affect the value of the domestic currency relative to a foreign currency. To weaken the domestic currency, sterilization involves selling the domestic currency on the forex market and buying the foreign currency. This increases the supply of the domestic currency, while reducing the supply of the foreign. To strengthen the domestic currency, sterilization involves the opposite. A central bank usually conducts sterilization to counteract adverse changes to the domestic currency in foreign exchange markets.

Sterling A term for the British pound. While the official name of the currency is pound sterling, "sterling" tends to be used in accounting and foreign exchange contexts while "pound," and, less formally, "quid," are used in day-to-day transactions.

Sterling Index An index that compares the exchange rate of the British pound to other important currencies.

Sterling Note A bank note issued by the Bank of England. Sterling notes are denominated in British pounds.

Sterling Ratio A ratio of the potential return on a hedge fund to a measure of risk. A higher ratio is considered more desirable because it indicates that the hedge fund has a greater return compared to its riskiness. It is calculated thusly: Sterling ratio = Compounded annual return / (maximum possible loss - 10%) See also: Calmar ratio, Sharpe ratio, Sortino ratio.

Stet In editing, the cancellation of a correction. Stet is written over a correction indicating that the editor wishes the correction to be disregarded. The word is Latin for "let it stand."

Steve Jobs An American inventor and businessman. In 1976, he co-founded Apple, which was one of the first companies to market the personal computer successfully. In the 1980s, he also founded NeXT, whose products facilitated business communication between computers. He became CEO of Apple again in 1997. Jobs lived from 1955 to 2011.

Steward A person who believes that one has a responsibility to manage wealth and other assets equitably and sustainably. That is, a steward holds that owners do not have an absolute right to use their property however they see fit, but have the obligation to use it to help others and ensure that no harm is done to the poor, one's employees, the environment, or anything else.

Stewardship The idea that one has a responsibility to manage wealth and other assets equitably and sustainably. That is, stewardship holds that owners do not have an absolute right to use their property however they see fit, but have the obligation to use it to help others and it ensure that no harm is done to the poor, one's employees, the environment, or anything else.

Stick A slang term for a point on a security market. For example, if a share price drops five points over the trading day, it may be said to decline five stick.

Stick and Move A strategy in which one primarily or exclusively makes small trades on one's account and takes few if any large positions. See also: Diversification, Naive diversification.

Sticks In auto sales, furniture put up as collateral on a loan for an automobile.

Sticky Deal An informal term for a new issue of securities that an underwriter has a difficult time placing with investors. This may occur because of problems with the market generally; for example, in a prolonged bear market investors are unlikely to be interested in a risky IPO. Alternatively, the sticky deal may result from well known or persistent problems with the issuer.

STIR Futures & Options Short-term interest rate futures and options. A futures or option contract in which the underlying asset is the three-month interest rate on LIBOR, EURIBOR, or TIBOR. Some companies use STIR futures and options in order to hedge against the risk of borrowing and/or lending.

Stiver 1. The currency of Ceylon (modern Sri Lanka) from 1801 to 1821. **2.** A currency used in Demerara-Essequibo (modern Guyana) before 1831.

STIX An oscillator on an exchange that compares the trading volume of advancing stocks to the trading volume of declining stocks. It is used in technical analysis. See also: Advance/decline line.

Stochastic In technical analysis, a way to calculate momentum in which one only considers price movements and not trading volume. Most calculations of momentum consider both factors. See also: Stochastic oscillator.

Stochastic Modeling Any of several methods for measuring the probability of distribution of a random variable. That is, a stochastic model measures the likelihood that a variable will equal any of a universe of amounts. It is used in technical analysis to predict market movements. Insurance companies also use stochastic modeling to estimate their assets and liabilities because, due to the nature of the insurance business, these are not known quantities.

Stochastic Oscillator In technical analysis, an indicator of market momentum. A stochastic oscillator measures whether the closing price of a security is closer to the high or the low. It is based on the assumption that when a market is trending upward, the closing price will be closer to the highest price, and, when it is trending downward, the closing price will be closer to the lowest price. It is calculated as: Stochastic Oscillator = 100 * (closing price for a given day - lowest price for the previous 14 trading days) / (highest price for the previous 14 trading days - lowest price for the previous 14 trading days).

Stock A portion of ownership in a corporation. The holder of a stock is entitled to the company's earnings and is responsible for its risk for the portion of the company that each stock represents. There are two main classes of stock: common stock and preferred stock. Common stock holders have the right to vote on major company decisions, such as whether or not to merge with another corporation, and receive dividends determined by management. Preferred stock holders do not usually have voting rights, but receive a minimum dividend. Stock may be bought or sold, usually, though not always, in the context of a securities exchange. It is important to note that a single share of a stock usually represents only a tiny amount of ownership, and, therefore, most stocks are traded in batches of 100.

Stock Ahead Informal; a situation where an order is not executed because another order takes precedence over it. For example, when two orders are placed, and the first order is made at a better price, the second order is not executed because there was "stock ahead."

Stock Appreciation An increase in the value of a stock. Stocks may appreciate or depreciate depending on market conditions, such as dividend schedules, supply, demand, underlying value of the company, and so forth. Stock appreciation is used to calculate capital gains taxes. See also: Appreciation.

Stock Appreciation Right A bonus that an employer pays an employee equal to the price appreciation on the company's stock over a given period of time. This is much like an employee stock option. The primary difference is that the employee does not have to actually buy stock; that is, he/she does not have to pay anything. Rather, the employee simply receives the cash or stock bonus in the specified amount.

Stock Bonus Plan A system whereby an employer shares its profits with employees, particularly (but not necessarily) middle and upper management, by awarding stock in the company. The stock bonuses are given instead of, or in addition to, cash.

Stock Certificate A physical document that gives the person or company listed a portion of ownership in a publicly-traded company. Stock certificates often contain a great deal of information, such as the owner's name, a right attached to the ownership (such as a warrant), or something else entirely. Stock certificates are vitally important as one may use them in court to prove a fact alleged.

Stock Company 1. See: Joint stock company. **2.** See: Publicly-traded company.

Stock Compensation An agreement in which an employee, usually a high-placed executive, receives stock in the company in addition to or instead of cash as salary. If the share price for the company increases, stock compensation can be very profitable for the employee. The idea behind stock compensation is to give the employee a significant stake in the success of the company, which will, in turn, encourage him/her to act in the best interest of shareholders. See also: Qualifying stock option.

Stock Dividend A dividend that is paid in stock or bonds rather than cash. A stock dividend may be declared when the company is cash poor and cannot afford a dividend otherwise. They are generally not considered desirable because one must pay capital gainstax on stock dividends, even though there is no cash gain for the shareholder. It is also called a scrip dividend. See also: Payment-in-kind bond.

Stock Exchange A place, whether physical or electronic, where stocks, bonds, and/or derivatives in listed companies are bought and sold. A stock exchange may be a private company, a non-profit, or a publicly-traded company (some exchanges have shares that trade on their own floors). A stock exchange provides a regulated place where brokers and companies may meet in order to make investments on neutral ground. The concept traces its roots back to medieval France and the Low Countries, where agricultural goods were traded for cash or debt. Most countries have a main exchange and many also have smaller, regional exchanges. A stock exchange is also called a bourse or simply an exchange.

Stock Exchange Automated Quotation System An electronic system for trading mid-cap securities over-the-counter. Only securities traded on the London Stock Exchange but not included in the FTSE 100 can be traded on SEAQ. Its rules are considered rather stringent, and critics contend that this contributes to illiquidity on SEAQ. Because of its basic structure as an electronic, over-the-counter exchange, it is sometimes called London's NASDAQ.

Stock Exchange Automatic Execution Facility Also called the SAEF. An electronic system for trading securities on the London Stock Exchange. A broker enters an order in a terminal and it is executed immediately by the relevant market maker. See also: SEAQ.

Stock Exchange Daily Official List An identification code for each security that trades in the United Kingdom, both on the London Stock Exchange and on regional exchanges. The SEDOL consists of seven alphanumeric characters. See also: CUSIP.

Stock Exchange of Hong Kong The only stock exchange in Hong Kong. Established in 1891, it lists more than 1,200 companies with a market capitalization of more than $2 trillion. The Stock Exchange of Hong Kong is relatively unusual in that many stocks, even for well-established companies, often trade for a low dollar amount. As a result, the exchange has a rather low definition of penny stock. It is one of the premier exchanges in East Asia. It is also known as the Hong Kong Stock Exchange.

Stock Exchange of Singapore A former stock exchange in Singapore. It was established in 1973 following the separation of currencies between Singapore and Malaysia. It became defunct in 1999, following a merger with the Singapore International Monetary Exchange; the two formed the Singapore Exchange.

Stock Exchange of Thailand The main securities exchange in Thailand. It was established in 1975 out of a desire by the Thai government to maintain a securities exchange in the country following the failure of the Bangkok Stock Exchange. Securities traded on the Stock Exchange of Thailand are divided into eight industries, which are subdivided into 25 sectors. It was known as the Securities Exchange of Thailand until 1991, which is the same year it set up electronic trading.

Stock Idea A slang term for news about a stock that merits further study for analysis. That is, a stock idea may help an investor decide whether to buy or sell a stock.

Stock Index A group of stocks put together in a standardized way to provide a useful window into a sector or market's performance at a glance. That is, a stock index groups together a certain list of stocks and usually takes an average of their prices so as to provide an idea of how the industry or market represented in the stock index is doing. Very often, stock indices are weighted to prevent a few data points from overwhelming it. For example, the S&P 500 is weighted according to market capitalization, while the DJIA is weighted for price.

Stock Index Future A futures contract on a stock index. In a stock index future, the counterparties agree to trade the underlying index at a certain time for a certain price. Because it is impossible to physically deliver the index, stock index futures are settled in cash, especially if the underlying assets are indices. Financial futures may be traded like other futures.

Stock Index Option A call or put option contract in which the underlying asset is a stock index. For example, in a call, an investor may buy the right to an index on or before the expiration date at a certain strike price. Obviously, one cannot buy or sell a physical index; so, the underlying asset is said to be the dollar value of an index at a certain date and time multiplied by $100. Because physical delivery is not possible, when a stock index option is exercised, the delivery is the cash value of the strike price. See also: Exchange-traded fund, Index fund.

Stock Index Swap A swap in which one of the legs is a stock index. At the swap, one swaps the cash flow of an index for some other asset. The other leg can be almost any other index, from another stock index to an interest rate.

Stock Insurance Company A publicly-traded insurance company. Shareholders in a stock insurance company may be, but are not necessarily, policyholders.

Stock Jobber An investor who buys stocks only to resell them at a profit very quickly. Stock jobbing is a short-term investment strategy that operates on the assumption or existence of liquid markets. The practice, when done over and over by a large number of stock jobbers, can lead to a speculative bubble. See also: Flipping.

Stock Jobbing The act or practice of buying stocks only to resell them at a profit very quickly. Stock jobbing is a short-term investment strategy that operates on the assumption or existence of liquid markets. Stock jobbing, when done over and over by a large number of investors, can lead to a speculative bubble. See also: Flipping.

Stock Jockey A broker who trades very actively. That is, the stock jockey buys and sells securities for his/her clients on a nearly constant basis. Stock jockeys who trade too frequently, however, may be accused (rightly or wrongly) of churning.

Stock Option A non-tradeable call option giving an employee at a publicly-traded company the right to buy shares in that company for a certain price. Stock options in this sense are often a part of compensation for major and mid-level executives in large publicly-traded companies. If the share price for the company increases, stock options can be very profitable for the employee. These stock options have certain rules governing when and how the option can be exercised.

Stock Participating Accreting Redemption Quarterly-Pay Securities A callable bond that pays coupons in cash, but, upon maturity, is redeemed for a certain number of shares in the company issuing the bond. If it is called, the issuer must pay all interest that would have been paid had the SPARQS been held until maturity; companies call these bonds after their stock has risen quickly since they do not wish to distribute them for free. SPARQS exist to provide the low risk of a bond while also exposing the investor to the stock market. Morgan Stanley underwrites SPARQS.

Stock Power The ability to transfer stock, granted to someone other than the owner. For example, a stockholder may grant stock power to his/her broker. This allows the broker to make decisions regarding the stock without owning it. Stock power is most common when stock is pledged as collateral on a loan. It is a type of power of attorney. See also: Beneficial ownership, bond power.

Stock Quote The highest price a potential buyer is willing to pay for a stock and the lowest price a potential seller is willing to receive. This is similar to the bid-ask spread, but the stock quote refers to the prices themselves, rather than the difference between them.

Stock Record A computer system allowing brokerages to keep accurate records of the securities in which they hold ownership. This is particularly important given the complexities of many transactions and the fact that brokerages hold legal ownership on behalf of clients most of the time. See also: Street name.

Stock Register A list maintained by a publicly-traded company of all stock issues, buybacks, transfers and other major actions related to its stock.

Stock Replacement A strategy in which one closes a position on a stock but also buys an option to take the same position that was closed. This allows one to reduce risk while still taking advantage of any upside potential.

Stock Replacement Strategy An investment strategy where on buys derivatives to mimic the return on a stock. For example, one may buy deep-in-the-money options because increases in the share price on the underlying stock will likely result in equal increases in the price of the option. A stock replacement strategy seeks to make the same return for a lower cost and/or risk. See also: Synthetic Asset.

Stock Repurchase Plan 1. See: Buyback. **2.** See: Self-tender offer.

Stock Right 1. See: Right. **2.** Less commonly, a term for a stock option.

Stock Savings Plan A tax credit available in some Canadian provinces to investors who buy shares in companies based in their own province. The credit is available only on one's provincial taxes, not on federal taxes.

Stock Screener A computer program that filters stocks according to criteria listed by an investor. For example, if an investor is only interested in buying clean energy stocks with a certain PEG ratio listed in European markets, he/she may enter these requirements into a stock screener and save himself/herself the time of looking up the stocks individually.

Stock Selection An investment strategy that involves buying stocks and placing them in a portfolio according to the perceived strengths of the individual stocks. That is, one does not hedge by buying similar stocks, diversify by buying different industries, or anything else. A stock selection strategy runs the risk of not being sufficiently diversified. However, if the individual stocks perform well, the strategy can result in large gains.

Stock Split The act of a publicly-traded company increasing the number of outstanding shares while maintaining the same market capitalization. In other words, a company engages in a stock split in order to decrease its share price by increasing the number of shares available. Current holders of the stock are given more shares so that they maintain the same percentage of ownership in the company. For example, a company with a share price of $400 may double the number of shares so that the share price drops to $200. Companies conduct stock splits for a number of reasons; one possible reason is to keep its shares affordable for investors. See also: Last Split, Split Ratio, Split Adjusted.

Stock Warrant A certificate, usually issued with a preferred stock, giving the holder the option of buying an underlying asset at a certain strike price. The strike price is usually higher than the market value of the underlying asset at the time of issue. Some warrants expire a few years after issuance, but perpetual warrants can theoretically last forever. Unlike options, stock warrants are issued by companies during a round of financing, rather than by an individual investor or brokerage. Companies issue stock warrants to attract investors who might not otherwise be interested.

Stock Watch An electronic system that the management of the New York Stock Exchange uses to monitor trading. Stock Watch observes trading for potential illegal activities and other unusual trading patterns. In other words, it helps maintain honest trading on the NYSE. It is also called the Stock Watcher.

Stockholder The person or company that owns a share in a publicly-traded company or a mutual fund. The share represents a certain (usually very small) percentage of ownership in the company or the securities underlying the fund. Thus, a stockholder has the right to receive a portion of the company's profits in the form of dividends, and, depending on the type of share, may have a right to vote on matters pertaining to corporate governance. A person or company becomes a stockholder on the record date, that is, on the date that the share was bought. A stockholder is also known as a shareholder.

Stockholder Books Records that a publicly-traded company keeps of its revenue, expenditures, and other activities. They must conform to the standards set forth by the FASB, and are used to compile the company's annual report and other reports.

Stockholder Derivative Suit A lawsuit filed by one or more shareholders of a publicly-traded company in the name of the company. Often, this lawsuit is filed against a member of the company's management who committed an illegal, unethical, or negligent act. Directors' and officers' liability insurance can protect the management from losses as the result of one of these lawsuits. They are also called derivative suits and derivative action.

Stockholder of Record The person or company whose name is listed on a stock certificate. The stockholder of record is the legally recognized owner of the share in the publicly-traded company represented on the stock certificate. He/she/it is recognized as the stockholder of record as of the record date, that is, the date the share was bought.

Stockholder's Report The annual report, and other quarterly reports, a publicly-traded company is required to distribute to shareholders. The report contains information on the company's financial state, such as operational income and net profit. Sometimes it also contains an accountant's opinion on the general health of the company. Occasionally, stockholder's reports are distributed at irregular intervals to explain a major event in the company. Generally the front part of the stockholder's report states the "bottom line" while the last part contains more detailed financial information. For example, the front part of the report may contain a brief essay stating, "Our company is healthy for reasons A, B, and C." At the conclusion of that essay, the stockholder may view its financial statement. See also: Balance sheet.

Stockholm Stock Market A stock exchange in Sweden that serves as the primary stock market in Scandinavia. It was founded in 1863 and trading became completely electronic in 1990. It merged with the Helsinki Stock Exchange in 2003.

Stockout Informal; a situation in which a company sells its entire inventory. A stockout may occur, for example, when there is a delay in a scheduled delivery of new inventory, but the term usually refers to situations where demand exceeds supply, causing the company to run out of inventory earlier than expected.

Stocky In foreign exchange, a slang term for the Swedish krona.

Stone A unit of weight equivalent to 14 pounds.

Stoop An obsolete Dutch unit of volume roughly equivalent to 2.4 liters.

Stoozer A holder of multiple credit cards who profits from taking advantage of differing interest rates and moving balances between cards.

Stoozing The practice in which the holder of multiple credit cards profits from taking advantage of differing interest rates and moving balances between cards.

Stop 1. An order to a broker to buy or sell a security at the best available price once a certain, stated price is reached. Suppose that price is $50. A stop order remains inactive until that security begins trading at $50, at which point the broker may fill the order at best price he/she is able to find. See also: Stop-limit order, Stop-loss order. **2.** An order by the SEC to stop a new issue from taking place because of an omission or inaccuracy on its filing statement. See also: Deficiency letter.

Stop Hunting The act or practice in which an investor buys or sells a stock to drive the price to a level that triggers many investors' stop-loss orders, forcing many investors to close their positions. This raises the volatility of the stock, which is good for some investment strategies.

Stop Order An order to a broker to buy or sell a security at the best available price once a certain, stated price is reached. Suppose that price is $50. A stop order remains inactive until that security begins trading at $50, at which point the broker may fill the order at best price he/she is able to find. See also: Stop-limit order, Stop-loss order.

Stop Payment An order to a bank or other financial institution not to make payment on a check drawn on that account. For example, suppose Bob writes a check to Joe. Bob may go to his bank and stop payment, which means that Joe will not be able to collect the funds written to him. Generally speaking, one stops payment on a check when its has been lost or stolen.

Stop Price The price at which a stop order becomes a market order. A stop order is an order to buy or sell a security at the best available price after a certain, stated price is reached. The stated price is called the stop price. See also: Limit price.

Stop Transfer An order made to prevent the transfer of ownership of a security. One generally makes a stop transfer if the security certificate has been lost or stolen, or if another claim has been made on ownership and must be resolved.

Stop-and-Go Tactic A tactic in which a taxpayer waits to recognize revenues until the next tax year or attempts to recognize a deduction in the current tax year. Stop-and-go tactics are used in order to reduce one's tax liability in a given year. An example of a stop-and-go tactic is the purchase of a house in the current tax year in order to realize the first-time homeowner's tax credit. Another example is waiting to sell securities until the next tax year so that one can delay paying taxes on the profits.

Stop-Limit Order A stop order that becomes a limit order when the stop price is reached.

Stop-Loss Order An order to a broker to buy or sell a security at the best available price once a certain, stated price is reached. Suppose that price is $50. A stop order remains inactive until that security begins trading at $50, at which point the broker may fill the order at best price he/she is able to find. A stop-loss order is technically the same as a stop order, but carries the connotation of avoiding further losses rather than seeking to cash in on future gains. See also: Protective stop.

Stop-Out Price The highest yield or the lowest price that the U.S. Treasury will accept when conducting an auction of Treasury securities.

Stopped Order On the New York Stock Exchange, an order by a specialist on the trading floor that stops the execution of a trade because the specialist believes that a better price will become available. When this occurs, the specialist must guarantee the market price at the time of the stopping of the order in case the better price does not materialize. Stopped orders are given by specialists actively involved in the market who are associated with an NYSE member firm. It should not be confused with a stop order.

Stopped Out An executed stop order. A stop order is an order to a broker to sell a security once a certain price is reached. Once the price is reached and the security is sold, the position is said to be stopped out. Usually this refers to the protection of the investor from further losses in a time of declining prices.

Store of Value Anything with value that may be stored and retrieved at a later date with the expectation that it will still have value. The most common store of value is money, which generally will still be money after being buried underground for some number of years. Other stores of value include real estate, securities and precious metals.

Storfavn A Swedish unit of volume approximately equivalent to 3,770 liters.

Story Stock/Bond 1. A stock or bond with highly unusual characteristics that are often difficult to understand. Investors are usually hesitant to invest in stocks or bonds (or other securities) that they do not understand; thus, representatives of the issuer or the underwriters must explain the stock's or bond's features in such a way as to convince the investor to buy it. The term comes from the fact that having the stock or bond explained can feel like having a story told to the investor. **2.** Especially for stocks, a security with a price or value that is highly dependent on positive press coverage.

Stotin A subdivision of the Slovenian tolar. A stotin was equal in value to 1/100 of a tolar. Both the stotin and the tolar became obsolete in 2007 when Slovenia introduced the euro.

Stotinka A subdivision of the Bulgarian lev. A stotinka is equal in value to 1/100 of a lev. Its plural is stotinki.

STOXX A series of indices that track global markets. STOXX indices track a wide number of markets, including blue chip companies and various sectors and industries. It is important to note that while STOXX indices track markets worldwide, there is a heavy bias toward European markets. These indices trade on options and futures exchanges. They were established as a joint venture between Dow Jones, SWX, and Deutsche Borse AG.

Stoxx 600 An index tracking 600 publicly-traded companies based in one of 18 EU countries. The index includes small cap, medium cap, and large cap companies. The countries represented in the index are Austria, Belgium, Denmark, Finland, France, Germany, Greece, Holland, Iceland, Ireland, Italy, Luxembourg, Norway, Portugal, Spain, Sweden, Switzerland, and the UK.

STP GOST 7.67 Latin three-letter geocode for Sao Tome and Principe. The code is used for transactions to and from local bank accounts and for international shipping to Sao Tome and Principe. As with all GOST 7.67 codes, it is used primarily in Cyrillic alphabets.

STR 1. See: Suspicious transaction report. **2.** See: Sell to rent.

Straddle The strategy in which one has the same position in both a put option and a call option with the same underlying asset, strike price, and expiration date. An investor may have a straddle when he/she believes that the market for the underlying asset will be volatile and will undergo dramatic price changes, but is unsure of which direction the changes will go. A straddle allows the investor to profit regardless of which direction the underlying moves, provided there is a significant movement. A small price change in either direction will result in a loss. See also: Long Straddle, Short Straddle.

Straight Describing a phone that connects directly to one and only one other phone. One need not dial any number between straight phones.

Straight Bill of Lading A document in which a seller agrees to use a certain transportation to ship a good to a certain location, where the bill is assigned to a specific party. The straight bill of lading details the type, quality, and quantity of the good. It also serves as the receipt upon arrival at the destination. Because it is assigned to a specific party, it is not negotiable and may not be re-assigned to another party.

Straight Bond A bond with no special features. A straight bond has a coupon that is paid to bondholders periodically. The issuer repays the principal at maturity. It does not include a conversion feature, a floating coupon, an extendible maturity date or other characteristics.

Straight Debt Any debt that cannot be changed into something else. For example, a regular bond is straight debt because it contains no special features beyond repayment with interest. Straight debt contrasts with convertible debt which may be exchanged for something else, usually common stock.

Straight Discount A percentage used to calculate the present value of a future cash flow from a debt security without taking compounding into account.

Straight Life An annuity or other insurance plan that provides the policyholder with monthly payments for the remainder of his/her life. After death, however, the payments cease, and the policyholder does not name a beneficiary. Like all annuities, one may buy the plan with a lump sum or with a series of payments over a number of years, usually ending around retirement. Straight life policies are usually less expensive than other annuities because they end in one's death, which is presumably before the death of one's spouse, children, and other beneficiaries. However, they provide fewer services, notably a widow's benefit.

Straight Life Annuity A fixed or variable annuity that pays a certain monthly or (rarely) annual sum for life of the annuitant and carries no death benefit. Generally speaking, an annuitant buys a straight life annuity and makes installment payments for it throughout his/her working life. Following retirement, the annuitant begins to receive the benefit, the amount of which may or may not be fixed in the annuity contract. A straight life annuity is designed to provide a stable income for the annuitant in retirement. Most straight life annuities make larger payments than other annuities because there is no death benefit. See also: Income annuity, Pension, IRA, 401(k).

Straight Term Insurance Policy A life insurance policy that provides coverage only for a certain period of time. A straight term insurance policy provides a benefit upon the death of the policyholder, but ceases to provide this benefit if he/she is still alive when the policy expires. Upon expiration, the policyholder may decide to renew the policy or allow it to lapse. If the policy lapses, the policyholder is not reimbursed for the premiums paid over the life of the policy. A term life insurance policy does not include some of the other benefits of a whole life policy, such as a savings component.

Straight Through Processing An as-yet unimplemented process that would allow transactions and payments to occur without re-entering information manually. That is, STP would permit all information on a transaction to transfer electronically to the appropriate broker, dealer, or other party.

Straight Value In convertible security, the value of the security itself (usually a bond or preferred stock) without considering the fact that it may be converted to common stock. That is, the straight value is the value of a convertible bond less the value of the conversion option. It is also called the bond value or the investment value.

Straight Voting The act of using all of one's shares to vote for the same way. Most of the time, a shareholder in a publicly-traded company has one vote per share. The shareholder can divide these votes at his/her/its discretion. For example, a shareholder may wish to vote for candidate A for the board of directors with 60% of shares and for candidate B with the remaining 40%. In straight voting, however, the shareholder may vote for candidate A with 100% of shares.

Straight-Line Depreciation A system of depreciation in which one deducts the same amount every year. For example, suppose an asset costs $1,200 with a usable life of three years and a salvage value of $300. If one uses straight-line depreciation, one deducts $300 each year.

Strangle Strategy An option strategy in which one buys two out-of-the-money options (usually one call and one put) on the same asset at different strike prices. One profits from a strangle position when there is a large price movement on the underlying asset, regardless of the direction. This is because one of the options will become in the money, so long as the price moves in one direction or the other. Loss only occurs if the price of the underlying asset remains largely the same.

Strap A bullish investment strategy in which an investor holds two calls and one put on the same underlying asset with the same expiration date and strike price. An investor uses a strap when he/she believes that the price of the underlying will increase substantially. If it does, the investor stands to make a substantial profit by exercising the calls. On the other hand, if the underlying decreases in price, the investor will not suffer a substantial loss because the strike price of the put protects him/her. See also: Call backspread ratio.

Strategic Alliance Any agreement where two or more companies agree to cooperate with each other to achieve a certain, mutually beneficial goal. However, a strategic alliance is not a merger, and the involved companies remain separate. A common strategic alliance is a joint venture, where the involved companies partner together to conduct a certain project. Other strategic alliances include management contracts and licensing agreements.

Strategic Buyout The purchase of one company by another where the buyer believes that the acquisition will create synergy, which is a financial benefit that the buyer may derive from the acquisition. For example, the buyer may determine that the two companies together may be able to produce more revenue than either one could produce independently by combining the most efficient processes each brings to the merger. Alternatively he may decide that the strategic buyout will reduce expenses by eliminating or streamlining redundant processes. The main point of a strategic buyout is to ensure the acquirer benefits, though the purchased company often benefits as well.

Strategy The principles guiding investment practices. A strategy may be simple, such as buy low, sell high, or complex, like many option strategies. The basic aim of any strategy is to make money, but each takes a different (sometimes very different) approach to achieve this goal.

Stratified Sampling Bond Indexing A method of creating bond indices in which one assesses the different characteristics of each bond and assigns each to one of a group of sub-indices according to those characteristics.

Straw Boss A member of a work crew who supervises the crew in addition to performing normal duties alongside them.

Straw Purchase In auto sales, the purchase of a vehicle for another person. In a straw purchase, the official owner assumes all liability and pays all expenses, but does not ordinarily use the car. A straw purchase may occur if the driver has little money or insufficient credit history to buy the car on his/her own. For example, a mother may buy a car in her name with the intention of letting her 16-year-old son drive it.

Stray A random data point or event that has no significant meaning.

Streep A Dutch unit of length equivalent to one millimeter. It was adopted in 1817, soon after the establishment of the Kingdom of the Netherlands.

Street Book A list of futures transactions on an exchange. The street book is maintained in order to calculate what investor owes what to whom for margin accounts and for clearance purposes.

Street Broker A broker who facilitates trades in the over-the-counter market. That is, a street broker is not a member on an exchange and therefore does not have a right to trade on an exchange.

Street Expectation The average or median forecast made by well-respected analysts on the future performance of a security or derivative. Forecasting is the process of using certain data to predict future market movements. Various methods exist for arriving at the Street expectation; experts differ on which ones, if any, are accurate. See also: Technical Analysis, Fundamental Analysis, Random Walk Theory.

Street Sweep An offer of a stock allowing institutional investors and (occasionally) high net-worth individuals to buy a large percentage of a company's equity, usually at a price higher than the previous offer of stock. Street sweeps are fairly common in takeovers; they may also be used as antitakeover measures. A street sweep is also known as a market sweep.

Streetable Describing the management of a company that is believed to be ready for an IPO. That is, if a company is streetable, it is said to be ready for Wall Street.

Street-Side Trade A trade between two brokers. See also: Street broker.

Stress Test A simulation measuring the capital adequacy of a bank. A government conducts a stress test to attempt to ensure that a bank can remain solvent in a crisis. The term came to prominence in 2009 and 2010 when the U.S. Treasury conducted stress tests of bailed out banks before it allowed them to repay Treasury loans.

Stress Testing A process, usually computerized, that evaluates an institution's reaction to different situations. Specifically, stress testing measures whether the institution has adequate capital and/or assets to respond effectively to various, adverse scenarios presented by the computer program. Stress testing became particularly important in the United States in the spring of 2009 when Treasury Secretary Timothy Geithner conducted a series on troubled American financial institutions to determine which were able to raise private capital and could therefore begin repaying TARP funds extended the previous year.

Stretch IRA An IRA designed to keep making payments to the heirs of the annuitant even after the annuitant dies. A stretch IRA is advantageous because it allows the annuitant to provide for his/her relatives without incurring the estate tax. See also: Stretch annuity.

Striation In numismatics, small lines on the surface of a coin, sometimes only visible with magnification. Striation may be caused by polishing the die that struck the coin.

Strike The collective action in which employees do not come to work as a form of protest. That is, in a strike, workers deprive employers of their services. Often, though not always, strikers also stand outside their workplace to stage protests. A strike occurs when employees wish to force the employer to pay them better wages or benefits or to improve working conditions. Strikes are usually orchestrated by a union.

Strike Ballot A referendum by members of a union to decide whether or not to declare a strike, which is a refusal to work in an attempt to force their employer to adopt better working conditions. Under labor laws in the United States, a union must inform the employer seven days before a strike ballot takes place, and the results must have independent verification if there are more than 50 employees affected.

Strike Benefits Health insurance and other employee benefits provided by a union to members while they are on strike. In a strike, union members do not come to work as a form of protest. However, this deprives them of the wages and benefits they otherwise would have received, which increases the likelihood that people will go back to work prematurely and the strike will fail. Strike benefits help reduce this risk. See also: Strike pay.

Strike Clause A clause in a contract allowing a seller or shipper to delay delivery of a good if a strike or other collective action makes on-time delivery impossible. This reduces the risk that the seller or shipper may breach the contract due to circumstances beyond its control.

Strike Index The strike price on an index option. An index option is a call or put option contract in which the underlying asset is an index of any sort. For example, in a call, an investor may buy the right to an index on or before the expiration date at a certain strike index. Obviously, one cannot buy or sell a physical index; so the underlying asset is said to be the dollar value of an index at a certain date and time multiplied by $100. Because physical delivery is not possible, when a stock index option is exercised, the delivery is the cash value of the strike index.

Strike Insurance An insurance policy that protects the policyholder from losses due to strikes, lock-outs or other actions involving employees. Most insurance policies do not cover strikes, so strike insurance must be purchased separately. As with all insurance, one must pay a premium to receive coverage.

Strike Notice Paperwork filed with the relevant agency stating that a union intends to go on strike. These notices must be filed in many jurisdictions to ensure that a strike is in accordance with the law and does not unnecessarily disrupt the economy or orderly function of society.

Strike Pay Wages provided by a union to members while they are on strike. In a strike, union members do not come to work as a form of protest. However, this deprives them of the wages and benefits that they otherwise would have received, which increases the likelihood that people will go back to work prematurely and the strike will fail. Strike pay helps reduce this risk. See also: Strike benefits.

Strike Price In options, an agreed-upon price for which the underlying is bought (in case of a call) or sold (in case of a put) if the option is exercised. For a call option to be profitable, the strike price must be lower than the market value of the underlying at the time the option is exercised. The opposite is true for a put: the strike price must be higher than the market value. In most cases, the amount of the strike is stated in the option contract; however, in Asian options, the strike is a formula, rather than a set price. For example, the strike may be the average price of the underlying over a set period of time. The strike price is also known as the exercise price or the striking price.

Strike Spread In options, an investment strategy involving the sale of one option and the purchase of another option identical to the first in every way except the strike price. For example, an investor may write a call giving the buyer the right to buy 1,000 barrels of oil with a strike price of $50 per barrel, and, at the same time, buy a call giving himself/herself the right to buy the same amount of oil at $40 per barrel. In the event that both options are exercised, the investor profits on the difference in the strikes. A strike spread is also called a money spread, a vertical spread, or a price spread.

Strike Vote A referendum by union members deciding whether or not to go on strike, which is a form of protest in which employees do not come to work. An affirmative strike vote authorizes union leadership to give strike notice and to take other steps necessary for the strike to occur. A strike vote is always on a secret ballot.

Strikes, Riots, and Civil Commotions An insurance policy that protects the policyholder from losses due to strikes and other disruptions to civil order. Most insurance policies do not cover strikes, so SR&CC riders must be purchased separately. As with all insurance, one must pay a premium to receive coverage.

String of Ponies A British slang term for 250 pounds. It is an example of Cockney rhyming slang.

Strip A bearish investment strategy in which an investor holds two puts and one call on the same underlying asset with the same expiration date and strike price. An investor uses a strip when he/she believes that the price of the underlying will decrease substantially. If it does, the investor stands to make a substantial profit by exercising the puts. On the other hand, if the underlying increases in price, the investor will not suffer a substantial loss because the strike price of the call protects him/her. See also: Call backspread ratio, Strap.

Strip Bond A bond, especially a U.S. Treasury security, that is traded separately from its coupons such that it pays no interest. Strip bonds are sold at a significant discount from par and mature at par. They fluctuate in price, sometimes dramatically, because changes in interest rates make them more or less desirable. They can be placed in IRAs and other pension accounts; however, unlike other Treasury securities, they are subject to federal taxes. Generally speaking, strip securities are quoted according to their yields rather than their prices. In 1985, the U.S. Treasury began issuing its own strip bonds, called STRIPS, which replaced other vehicles, such as CATS and TIGRS, that had been issued by the Treasury and stripped by another party.

Stripped Mortgage-Backed Security A mortgage-backed security with a cash flow that derives exclusively from interest payments or principal payments on the underlying mortgages. That is, the underlying asset of a stripped MBS is interest or principal paid on debt securities, rather than both together. Stripped mortgage-backed securities are extremely sensitive to changes in interest rates, allowing investors to choose either an interest strip or a principal strip depending on the expected direction of interest rates.

Stripper Informal for a homeowner who re-finances his/her property in order to access the equity and spend it on consumer goods rather than investment. A stripper, rather than investing wisely with the equity, squanders his/her wealth while increasing debt. There are two main risks associated with being a stripper. The first is the possibility that the value of the home will begin to decrease, which will prevent any more re-financing. The second is the possibility that interest rates will rise, preventing re-financing at an affordable rate. Since many strippers live above their means, the realization of either of these risks could be devastating.

Stripping The act or practice of removing the coupons from a bond, especially a U.S. Treasury security, and trading the bond separately such that it pays no interest. Stripped bonds are sold at a significant discount from par and mature at par. They fluctuate in price, sometimes dramatically, because changes in interest rates make them more or less desirable. They can be invested in IRAs and other pension

accounts; however, unlike other Treasury securities, they are subject to federal taxes. Generally speaking, stripped securities are quoted according to their yields, rather than their prices. In 1985, the U.S. Treasury began issuing its own stripped securities, called STRIPS, which replaced other vehicles, such as CATS and TIGRS, that had been issued by the Treasury and stripped by another party.

Strong Currency A currency when it is worth more relative to other currencies. Because most currencies are floating, their values vary according to market trends. When one unit of a currency trades for more units of another currency, it is known as a strong currency. When a currency is strong, travelers are able to go abroad while spending less of their money, but it makes exports more expensive in other countries. A strong currency can be disinflationary for currencies pegged to it. See also: Weak currency, Exchange rate.

Strong Dollar The U.S. dollar when it is worth more relative to other currencies. Because the dollar is a floating currency, its value varies according to market trends. When one dollar trades for more units of one or more other currencies, it is known as a strong dollar. When the dollar is strong, American travelers are able to go abroad while spending less of their money, but it makes American exports more expensive in other countries. A strong dollar can be disinflationary for currencies pegged to the dollar. See also: Weak dollar, Exchange rate.

Strong Dollar Policy Any policy making the U.S. dollar worth more relative to other currencies. When one dollar trades for more units of one or more other currencies, it is known as a strong dollar. When the dollar is strong, American travelers are able to go abroad while spending less of their money, but it makes American exports more expensive in other countries. A strong dollar can be disinflationary for currencies pegged to the dollar. See also: Weak Dollar, Exchange Rate.

Strong Form of the EMT The most controversial form of the efficient markets theory on how markets work. It holds that the market efficiently deals with all information on a given security and reflects it in the price immediately. Even insider information is immediately reflected in security prices. Therefore, the model holds that technical analysis, fundamental analysis, and any speculative investing based on them are useless. Investors and academics disagree on how well the model works. See also: Weak form of the EMT, Semi-strong form of the EMT.

Strong Hands 1. In futures, an informal term for a person or firm that is a well-financed speculator. This enables the person or firm to engage in perhaps riskier, or at least larger, trades on the futures market than most other investors. **2.** In delivery of commodities and futures, the intent of the investor to receive the underlying asset of the contract. Most commodity and futures traders are speculative investors and have no desire to receive the bushels of corn or pounds of coffee or whatever underlies the contract. Those who do wish to receive the underlying are referred to as trading with strong hands; they make up only about 2% of the futures and commodity markets.

Strong Sell A recommendation by a broker or analyst to sell a security because technical and/or fundamental indicators show that the security is likely to underperform the market by a significant amount.

Strong v. Repide A U.S. Supreme Court case holding that a member of the board of directors of a publicly-traded company may not buy or sell shares while keeping the counterparty ignorant of the fact that he/she has nonpublic information on which the company's share price depends. The case was decided in 1909.

Structural Adjustment A government program in a developing country making changes to economic or monetary policies in order to better facilitate growth. For example, a structural adjustment loan may include a stipulation that the borrowing country relax any protectionist subsidies or impose higher taxes to balance the budget. Structural adjustments are necessary in some cases before the IMF or the World Bank will make loans to finance further development. See also: Structural Adjustment Facility.

Structural Adjustment Loan Facility Loans made by the World Bank and/or IMF to developing countries to finance projects, such as infrastructure, that will promote economic growth in the long term. They are often accompanied by requirements that the borrower make changes to its economic or monetary policies in order to better facilitate growth. For example, a structural adjustment loan may include a stipulation that the borrowing country relax any protectionist subsidies or tariffs.

Structural Funds Several sources of money available to member states of the European Union to encourage economic development and to bring all EU members to roughly the same stage of advancement. See also: European Regional Development Fund, European Social Fund, Cohesion Fund, Common Agricultural Policy.

Structural Inflation Inflation that occurs because a government pursues an excessively loose monetary policy. That is, if a central bank prints too much money or keeps interest rates too low for too long, the value of each unit of currency drops more than it would simply from increased demand.

Structural Unemployment Unemployment that results from a change in the way the local or national economy functions. For example, suppose the economy in a region is heavily dependent on exploiting a single, natural resource. If that resource is entirely consumed, the trained and untrained workers working on exploiting it will find themselves subject to structural unemployment, since there are no other companies exploiting that natural resource because there is no more natural resource. On the plus side, these gaps in the economy can open up new opportunities. See also: Retraining.

Structure 1. See: Capital structure. **2.** A building or other improvement to real estate.

Structured Debt Debt that the lender has tailored specifically for the borrower. Structured debt often includes incentives and options for the borrower to do business with the lender.

Structured Finance The provision of a complex financing arrangement. This service is offered to a client with financing needs are more difficult to structure than an ordinary loan or bond. Examples of structured financing arrangements include mortgage-backed securities, syndicated loans, collateralized debt obligations.

Structured Note A debt security attached to a derivative of any sort. The derivative may be an option on stock in the company issuing the note or a security that tracks some index. A structured note aims to gives both the holder and the issuer a great deal of flexibility; for this reason they are usually very complex. As a result they are marketed to investors thought to be "sophisticated."

Structured Product Any investment vehicle where the return is linked to the performance of an underlying index. For example, an exchange traded fund is a structured product that a company puts together using all the stocks that trade on a particular exchange. It compiles all the stocks and issues its own shares representing those stocks. These shares can be traded as if they were stocks. Many structured products are known by acronyms; for example, SPDRs are common structured product shares. See also: Rule 434.

Structured Settlement The judgment or final agreement in a lawsuit where one party (usually the defendant) pays the other party (usually the plaintiff) a certain amount of money over a long period of time. A structured settlement allows the "winning" party to receive a large amount while still making payment affordable for the other party. Some companies purchase insurance policies where the insurance company pays any structured settlements that may arise.

Stub **1.** See: Stub stock. **2.** See: Check stub.

Stub Stock A common stock in a publicly-traded company that the company has converted from a bond. A company converts its bonds to stub stocks when it has a negative net worth, either because of a takeover or a bankruptcy. The name "stub stock" probably derives from the fact that the common stock is typically worth much less than the bonds from which it has been converted. Because of the price uncertainty surrounding companies that issue stub stocks, they are risky investments. However, if the company recovers, they have the possibility of a high rate of return.

Student A person working toward an educational qualification, especially but not necessarily a degree. For example, one may be studying for a bachelor's degree in engineering or a professional certification as an electrician. Students often finance their studies with loans and grants. These loans may be treated favorably for tax purposes.

Student Aid Report A document that the federal government sends to a post-secondary student notifying him/her of all federal financial aid for which he/she is eligible. Among other things, the student aid report states the expected family contribution for the student's education. It is sent after the student's FAFSA is processed by the CPS.

Student Loan A loan one uses to pay for postsecondary education. A parent, guardian or the student may take out a student loan. In the United States, the federal government subsidizes or guarantees some student loans to enable more people to attend college. Interest on student loans is also tax deductible in the United States. However, because universities in the United States are often so expensive, many students spend a significant portion of their income on student debt service.

Student Loan Interest Deduction A reduction in one's taxable income by the amount one spends in interest payments in the process of repaying student loans. For example, if one's student loan payments included $800 in interest for the tax year, one is does not pay taxes on that $800. The student loan interest deduction is subject to certain restrictions, such as a modified adjusted gross income under a certain amount. Additionally, one may only take the deduction if one was legally obligated to pay interest on the loan. The maximum deduction one could take was $2500 in 2008.

Student-Specific Scholarship A scholarship available to persons of a certain gender, race, ethnicity, religion, or those with a certain cultural or other background. For example, a religious denomination may make scholarships available to academically qualified members of that denomination.

Stuffed Describing a situation in which a market rally begins to occur but is short-lived since the supply outstrips demand.

Stuffing **1.** See: Channel stuffing. **2.** See: Vanning.

Stuiver A coin that circulated in the Netherlands prior to the Dutch guilder's decimalization in the 19th century. It was worth 1/20th of one guilder.

Style Box A way to describe the features of a mutual fund graphically. There are two types of style box. An equity style box is a box divided into nine smaller boxes. The vertical boxes represent the market capitalization (low, medium, and high) and the horizontal boxes represent the type of fund (value fund, mixed, or growth fund). A bond style box is much the same. The vertical boxes represent credit quality (low, medium, and high) and the horizontal ones represent maturity (short, medium, and long term). One may place a check mark or fill in the box that best describes a particular fund. Style boxes are used by Morningstar.

Style Drift A situation in which a mutual fund's investment strategies or goals change from what they were originally. Style drift can be explicit or implicit. For example, style drift may occur implicitly when a fund manager seeks ever larger returns for shareholders and tries out any number of investment strategies to achieve them. This is usually thought to be naive or even dangerous. Style drift can arise explicitly when a fund's situation has changed a significant amount; for example, a stock in the fund may grow to the point where it is advantageous for the fund to change its capitalization requirements. Style drift, if handled responsibly, can show flexibility on the part of the fund managers.

Style Investing A strategy for managing a portfolio or fund that involves shifting between different types of investment as conditions change. Style investing is based on the assumption that not all types of investment do well at the same time. As a result, a money manager utilizing style investing may shift from growth to income stocks or from small-cap to large-cap stocks depending on various indicators. It is important to note that style investing does not mean shifting from, say, one industry to another, but rather from one type of investment to a completely different type. This form of active management became popular in the 1980s and 1990s.

Stylized Facts Facts that have been widely observed in many different contexts. Stylized facts are sometimes assumed to be always true, but this is not always the case. The term is most common in macroeconomics.

SU **1.** ISO 3166-1 alpha-2 code for the Soviet Union prior to its dissolution. This was the code used in international transactions to and from Soviet bank accounts. **2.** ISO 3166-2 geocode for the Soviet Union. This was used as an international standard for shipping to the Soviet Union. In both cases, the code is obsolete.

Subaccount An account within an account. For example, funds in a subaccount may be available only to a certain person, or may be used only for a certain purpose.

Subchapter M In American tax, an IRS regulation dealing with ways by which a publicly-traded company and its shareholders can avoid double taxation. Generally speaking, a publicly-traded company must pay corporate tax on its profits. If it paid taxes on its profits before passing along those profits to shareholders, the company's income is effectively taxed twice. Subchapter M allows these companies to deduct dividends and certain interest and capital gains paid to shareholders from its taxable income. See also: Conduit theory.

Subclass All of the varieties within a given type of security. For example, subclasses of a stock include mid-cap, small cap, high cap, growth and value stocks, among others. While all securities are most similar to others of the same type, discussing subclasses is useful to describe the differences in expense, risk, expected rate of return, and other factors within a certain type.

Subdistritu In East Timor, a political subdivision equivalent to a sub-municipality.

Subindex A set of securities in an index whose performance is also tracked independent of the other securities in the index. An index may divide itself into subindicies for the different sectors it tracks. For example, the S&P 500 contains 10 subindices representing various sectors of the economy, such as energy or health care companies. A subindex may also be created for subsets of a specific sector. Given an index of the energy sector, for example, one may create subindices of oil companies and alternative energy companies.

Subject Describing a bid or offer for a security that is still negotiable. That is, a subject bid/offer is not firm and requires confirmation before a transaction involving it can be executed.

Subject Market An exchange or financial market in which quotes given are tentative and subject to confirmation. An example of a subject market is a fast market, in which there is so much volatility and trades occur so rapidly that market orders may be executed at a different price from the price at the time the order was placed. Subject markets can be risky.

Subject Offer An offer to sell an asset to which the seller is not committed. That is, the seller may withdraw the subject offer at any time. In general, subject offers are made in order to elicit a counteroffer or at least to gauge general interest in the market.

Subject Quote A quote for the price of a security in which the price is subject to change. Market makers occasionally make subject quotes for valuation purposes only. It may also refer to a quote that is not an offer, but simply supplied for informational purposes. A subject quote is also called a nominal quote.

Subject to a Can Informal; indicating that an offer or a bid might be canceled by a trader. A broker may make on offer to sell a stock "subject to a can," meaning that the offer might be canceled if certain conditions are not met. For example, an all-or-none offering is subject to a can.

Subject to Collection A deposit of a check into a bank account to which the depositor has immediate access. That is, the deposit is treated as if it has already cleared even though it has not. Subject to collection deposits are available to longstanding or well-respected customers; however, if the check bounces, the deposit will be removed from the account. See also: Subject to verification.

Subject to Mortgage An agreement in which the owner of real estate transfers to another party the right to use the property, in exchange for which the other party makes mortgage payments to the lender. Neither the property nor the legal obligation to make the payments transfers. This is a high risk endeavor for the owner: if the other party stops paying, the lender must collect from the current owner. However, the owner maintains title to the property.

Subject to Verification A deposit of a check into a bank account to which the depositor has immediate access, but which a bank may alter if it discovers an error. For example, if the deposit slip says $100 but the total deposit only amounts to $90, the bank will remove the remaining $10 from the account. See also: Subject to collection.

Subjective Probabilities One's personal judgment about the outcome of a particular investment. At its most extreme, relying on subjective probabilities represents the exact opposite of a formula plan, which seeks to eliminate all personal judgments and biases from investing. By definition, one cannot calculate subjective probabilities because they are based ultimately on one's feeling. Most investors rely on a combination of subjective probabilities and more objective calculations when making investment decisions.

Subordinate Bond A class of bond that, in the event of liquidation, is prioritized lower than other classes of bonds. For example, a subordinate bond may be an unsecured bond, which has no collateral. Should the issuer be liquidated, all secured bonds and similar debts must be repaid before the subordinated bond is repaid. A subordinate bond carries higher risk, but also pays higher returns than other classes. See also: junior debt.

Subordinated Describing a class of security that, in the event of liquidation, is prioritized lower than other classes of security. For example, a subordinated security may be an unsecured loan, which has no collateral. Should the issuer be liquidated, all secured bonds and debts must be repaid before the subordinated security is repaid. A subordinated security carries higher risk but also pays higher returns than other classes. See also: Junior Debt.

Subordinated Debenture Bond A class of unsecured bond that, in the event of liquidation, is prioritized lower than other classes of debt. In essence, a subordinated debenture bond is an unsecured loan, which has no collateral. Should the issuer be liquidated, all other bonds and debts must be repaid before the subordinated debenture bond is repaid. This class of debt carries higher risk, but also pays higher interest than other classes. It is a type of junior debt.

Subordination Clause A clause in some contracts for debt stating that in the event of bankruptcy or liquidation, the debt in the contract will take priority over all other debts. This protects the creditor in the event that the debtor defaults. It is most common in mortgages and bonds. See also: Absolute Priority Rule.

Suborn To encourage perjury through bribery, coercion, or any other means. Like perjury itself, subornation is illegal in practically every jurisdiction.

Subpart F In U.S. taxation, income from foreign subsidiaries of American companies. Income under subpart F is subject to taxation even if it is not repatriated into the United States. Interestingly, subpart F income also includes the amount of money the subsidiary paid in bribes to foreign officials.

Sub-Penny Quoting The practice of offering a fraction of a cent (or the equivalent) higher than the bid price for a security. Sub-penny quoting is thought to complicate computerized execution programs. This may be detrimental to investors.

Subperiod Return The return on an investment or portfolio over a period of time shorter than the money manager's designated evaluation period. The evaluation period is a time during which a return is measured to evaluate the money manager's performance. A subperiod return can be useful because some money managers make excessively risky or losing investments until the end of the evaluation period, at which time he/she makes a series of "sure deal" investments to increase the return. Looking at subperiod returns helps to discount this possibility when evaluating the money manager.

Subprefecture In Japan, a political subdivision equivalent to a county.

Sub-Prime Lender A bank or other financial institution that makes loans at interest rates higher than most other loans. Subprime loans are made to borrowers who do not qualify for ordinary loans because of bad credit history or some other reason. There is a higher risk of default on subprime loans. Their prevalence was a significant factor in the 2008 credit crunch. See also: Subprime mortgage.

Subprime Loan A loan that is made at a higher interest rate than most other loans. Subprime loans are made to borrowers who do not qualify for ordinary loans because of bad credit history or some other reason. There is a higher risk of default on subprime loans. Their prevalence was a significant factor in the 2008 credit crunch. See also: Subprime Mortgage.

Subprime Mortgage A mortgage with an interest rate higher than most other mortgages. Subprime mortgages are provided to borrowers who do not qualify for ordinary loans because of bad credit history or some other reason. There is a higher risk of default on subprime loans. Their prevalence was a significant factor in the 2008 credit crunch.

Subrogation The transfer of a claim or legal right from one party to another. Subrogation is often associated with the transfer of the right to a debt from one person to another. That is, a creditor can give or sell his/her right to a debt to some third party. See also: Forfaiting.

Subrogee A party to which a claim or legal right of another party is transferred. This is often associated with the transfer of the right to be repaid for a debt from one person to another. That is, a creditor can give or sell his/her right to a debt to some third party. In this case, the third party is the subrogee. See also: Forfaiting, Subrogor.

Subrogor A party that transfers a claim or legal right to another party. This is often associated with the transfer of the right to be repaid for a debt from one person to another. That is, a creditor can give or sell his/her right to a debt to some third party. In this case, the creditor is the subrogor. See also: Forfaiting, Subrogee.

Subscription An agreement to buy a new issue of a security before it is actually issued. Before a new issue, underwriters canvass potential investors, who may or may not make an order to buy a portion of the new issue. The extent to which the issue is subscribed may affect the price when the security is actually issued. It is important to note that a subscription is not binding, as it is illegal to sell a security that has not actually been issued. To subscribe is also called to book. See also: Overbooked, Underbooked.

Subscription Agreement An application to join a limited partnership. The general partner in a limited partnership devises the subscription agreement and requires potential limited partners to complete it. The subscription agreement requires the applicant to disclose financial information relevant to his/her suitability to join the partnership. The agreement also states the terms of the partnership, should the application be approved.

Subscription Period The time during which underwriters attempt to place a new issue with investors. During the subscription period, underwriters canvass potential investors, who may or may not book an order to buy a portion the new issue. No deals are final until the new issue is actually made at the end of the subscription period.

Subscription Price The price at which an underwriter offers a new issue of a security or, more commonly, a rights offering to the public. The subscription price is fixed and subscribers may only subscribe at that price.

Subscription Ratio In a rights offering, the number of rights required to buy a share in a publicly-traded company. A rights offering allows current shareholders to buy more shares, especially of a new issue, at a discount from their market value. The subscription ratio describes the number of shares one must currently hold in order to effectively receive a free share.

Subscription Warrant In derivatives, a security, usually attached to another security, that gives the right to buy a certain amount in common stock in the company issuing the subscription warrant at or below the market price. Subscription warrants are usually issued with a bond to encourage investors to purchase the debt. They operate much like call options, but are issued by corporations, instead of individual investors; they are particularly susceptible to volatility. See also: Subscription right.

Subsidiarity In Catholic social justice theory, the idea that decisions should be made at the lowest feasible level of governance. That is, subsidiarity states that humans, while basically the same, sometimes have different needs and if possible should be able to solve their own problems without having solutions imposed upon them. This concept has been used to criticize socialism and state regulation more generally. See also: Solidarity.

Subsidiary A company that is publicly-traded but has more than half its stock owned by another company, known as the parent company. As long as the parent company owns more than half the stock, it maintains control of the subsidiary, though its other stock is still traded. Some subsidiaries belong to the same industry as the parent company, while others do not, and are part of a diversification effort on the part of the parent company. See also: Wholly owned subsidiary.

Subsidized Financing A loan or other form of financing that a government provides directly or guarantees. Subsidized financing is available at a lower interest rate because the government does not need to make a profit and can better afford the risk of loss. Subsidized financing often is offered to lower income people, for example, to encourage home ownership. See also: Co-signer.

Subsidy Financial assistance provided by a government to another entity, usually a business or industry. Subsidies are given to keep otherwise unprofitable ventures in business; for example, a family farm unable to compete with agribusiness may receive a subsidy from the government to maintain operations. Subsidies may also exist as a protectionist measure to make domestic goods less expensive than imports. Proponents of subsidies argue that they maintain employment in the domestic economy while critics state that they distort the market and make it less efficient. See also: Bailout.

Substandard Health Annuity An annuity one may buy if he/she has a health problem likely to significantly shorten his/her life. A substandard health annuity pays a higher amount to the annuitant each month because the annuitant is likely to die sooner. It may or may not cost more than other annuities that pay lower amounts each month. It is a straight life annuity and therefore does not pay a death benefit.

Substantially Equal Periodic Payments Annual distributions that one may take from an IRA without penalty, under certain conditions. Specifically, in order to avoid the penalty, one must agree to receive the payments in roughly the same amount for five years or until one turns 59 1/2 (whichever is longer). The SEPP structure allows one to access money in one's IRA before retirement without penalty, while still discouraging the abuse of the practice.

Substitute A good or service that satisfies a consumer's needs or desires just as well or almost as well as a similar good or service. A common type of substitute is an off-brand product; for example, a grocery store may sell its own peanut butter to compete with the on-brand peanut butter it also sells. Often, though not always, the price of a substitute is lower than that of the original product, but they follow generally the same trends. For example, if demand for the on-brand peanut butter rises, its price increases, but so does the price of the off-brand peanut butter, because consumers are willing to pay more for peanut butter generally, but are still looking for a bargain.

Substitute Check A digital image of the front and back of a check with the words "this is a legal copy of your check" appearing next to the image. A substitute check can be transferred electronically, while a regular check cannot. This can expedite the payment process of a check; that is, it reduces the amount of time it takes for the check to clear. Like regular checks, substitute checks can be used as proof that payment was made. Substitute checks are normally kept on file at the bank where they were deposited, but an account holder can usually receive a copy for a fee. A substitute check is also called an image replacement document.

Substitute Sale A sale of an interest rate futures contract or the short sale of a security. Substitute sales exist to hedge the risk that one's portfolio will decline in price.

Substitution Swap A swap in which one sells a bond and buys another with the same maturity, risk, and other terms; the only difference between the two bonds is the fact that the bond the investor buys has a higher yield. Alternatively, one may directly swap the bonds without selling or buying them. A substitution swap allows one to increase one's return without changing the risk, or any of the other terms, of one's portfolio. See also: Markowitz efficient portfolio.

Success Tax A tax formerly imposed on distributions from a retirement account in excess of a certain amount. If a retirement account's investments were particularly successful, the account holder has the ability to receive larger payments, depending on the nature of the account. The success tax discouraged this by levying a 15% surtax on payments deemed to be too large. It was repealed by the Taxpayer Relief Act of 1997.

Succession The rules of or process by which a person goes about filling a role previously held by another person. In estates, succession determines who owns the property of the decedent, with everything going to the next of kin in the absence of a will. In business, succession is the process by which one employee, especially a major executive like the CEO, is replaced by another person. In determining succession, a board of directors ought to exercise caution to ensure that an executive is not only competent, but also does not bring any conflicts of interest to the company.

Sudanese Dinar A former currency of Sudan. It was introduced in 1992, replacing the first Sudanese pound. It was a highly volatile currency throughout its history and was replaced by the second Sudanese pound in 2007.

Sudanese Pound The currency of Sudan. It was introduced in 1956, replacing the Egyptian pound. The pound was itself replaced by the Sudanese dinar in 1992, but it continued to circulate in Southern Sudan while the dinar was used only in the North. Both currencies were replaced by a second Sudanese pound in 2007. Both Arabic and English appear on notes, but coins are minted only in Arabic.

Sudden Wealth Syndrome Feelings of depression, guilt, or alienation thought to be caused by earning a great deal of wealth in a short period of time. For example, if one purchases a stock that inexplicably skyrockets and makes one a millionaire overnight, one may begin to feel isolated from family or friends. Sudden wealth syndrome is not generally recognized as an actual disease.

Su-Du-A An ancient Sumerian unit of length approximately equivalent to 333 centimeters.

SUHH ISO 3166-3 code for the Soviet Union, which dissolved in 1991. ISO 3166-3 codes are used to indicate names of countries that are no longer used.

Suicide Bombing An act of war or terrorism in which one explodes a bomb such that it kills oneself and the people in the vicinity. Suicide bombings are usually acts of desperation. The possibility of a suicide bombing is a type of political risk, especially in areas where they are already known to occur.

Suicide Pill An antitakeover measure stipulating that shareholders on the receiving end of a hostile takeover may buy shares in their own company at a price below fair market value. Once the acquisition is complete, the provision allows these same shareholders to buy more shares in the new company for below market value. This forces shareholders in the acquiring company to suffer a devaluation and dilution of their own shares. This is done to discourage hostile takeovers among the shareholders of the acquiring companies. In essence, a suicide pill is identical to a poison pill except for degree; the term suicide pill indicates that the target company may intentionally go bankrupt, rather than simply weaken itself.

Suitability The legal requirement than an investment adviser, broker, or other party act in a way most likely to fit a client's investment goals. See also: Fiduciary responsibility.

Suitability Rule A stated or implied requirement by a regulatory body that a broker or investment adviser must reasonably believe that a certain investment decision will benefit a client before making a recommendation to him/her. That is, the broker or investment adviser must act in good faith, and may not knowingly recommend bad investments. Different regulators and self-regulating organizations incorporate suitable rules in different places in their bylaws. Two commonly referenced suitability rules are Rule 2310 for the Financial Industry Regulatory Authority and Rule 405 for the NYSE. See also: Due diligence, Prudent-person rule, Twisting.

Suitor A company that makes an offer to buy another company. The term has a positive connotation and may therefore refer especially to a friendly takeover attempt. See also: White Knight, Acquiring firm.

Sukaa A subdivision of the Nepalese rupee. One sukaa is worth half a rupee.

Suku In East Timor, a political subdivision equivalent to a neighborhood within a sub-municipality.

Sum In Mongolia, a political subdivision equivalent to a county.

Sum Certain In law, a specific amount of money stated in a contract. For example, a company may agree to buy another for $10 million. The $10 million price is sum certain, as opposed to an agreement to buy the other company for whatever its market value happens to be when the deal is finalized.

Sum of Years Digits Also called SYD. A depreciation method. The SYD method writes off more of an asset's value each year than the straight line method, but less than the declining balance method. Under the SYD method, more value is written off at first, such that very little value above the salvage value is available to be written off at the end of the asset's useful life.

Summary Plan Description A statement of the terms and conditions of a pension or other retirement account. It states all benefits, restrictions, and other relevant information. An employer must give a summary plan description to an employee before that employee enrolls in an employer-sponsored retirement plan.

Summer Doldrums A supposed seasonal trend in which a stock market declines or remains flat during the summertime. Some analysts and traders believe markets rise toward the end of each year and begin to decline the following summer. The existence of this phenomenon is disputed.

Summi Pontificatus An encyclical letter written by Pope Pius XII in 1939. In it, he criticizes the notion that law should not necessarily conform to God's will. He blames this for class war and racism, as well as for the idea that the state is supreme over individual notions of right and wrong. Written in the context of the outbreak of World War II, it was a call for all people to cooperate for the common good.

Sun A unit of length in Japan equivalent to approximately 30 millimeters.

Sundry Income A company's income that comes from sources other than its operations or investments. Common examples of sundry income include royalties and income from foreign exchange. Sundry income is outside the control of the company. It is also called miscellaneous income.

Sunk Costs Money that has already been spent. Sunk costs are important because a company may use, for example, an old piece of equipment to make a new product. In this case, sunk costs are positive because no further investment is required. On the other hand, a sunk cost may be negative; for example, that old piece of equipment may break down after its warranty has expired. This means that the owner will not recover the costs no matter what happens.

Sunrise Industries Industries in an economy that are growing rapidly and may become market leaders in the future. One example is the Internet industry in the 1990s. While many such companies were just part of the dot-com bubble, companies like Google and Amazon grew very quickly throughout the decade and are now considered fairly prominent stocks. Identifying sunrise industries can be risky, as one may be wrong about a market's direction. However, a correct investment can provide rapid capital appreciation in the near term and a steady return in the long term. See also: Industry life cycle, Sunset industry.

Sunset To discontinue a product slowly. For example, a company may cut 25% of original production every quarter for a year.

Sunset Clause A clause in a law or regulation automatically abolishing that law or regulation after a stated period of time. In order for the law or regulation to continue to have effect, specific action must be taken. A law or regulation without a sunset clause continues indefinitely. The U.S. state of Texas has sunset clauses abolishing nearly every state agency every 12 years unless they are specifically renewed.

Sunshine Enema Any actions that a company takes to increase morale or productivity among the employees after a round of layoffs.

Sunshine Laws Laws at both federal and state levels requiring regulators to make meetings and decisions public. Some sunshine laws allow ordinary citizens to attend the meetings, but all aim to increase transparency in economic regulation. The SEC, for example, makes many of its decisions available for public view on its website.

Sunshine Trade A trade involving a large number or volume of securities that is publicized to the market before the order for the trade is formally made. Sunshine trades exist to reduce volatility in the market; that is, if the trade is likely to drive the price for the security up or down, the sunshine trade can help the market price in relevant information and thereby avoid wild price swings. See also: Transparency.

Supachai Panitchpakdi A Thai economist and politician. He served as Deputy Minister of Finance in the late 1980s and Deputy Prime Minister from 1992 to 1995. In 1999, he became Director General of the World Trade Organization. In 2003, he became the head of the UN Conference on Trade and Development. He was born in 1946.

Super Bowl Rule An indicator that few follow seriously stating that a Super Bowl win by an NFC team will result in a market uptrend for the coming year, while a win by an AFC team portends a downtrend. The Super Bowl indicator has been correct more than four years out of every five, but most believe this to be simply coincidence.

Super NOW Account A checking account at a bank or thrift that earns higher interest than other NOW accounts and carries a higher minimum balance. The account holder is allowed to write checks or drafts against the money in the account and may withdraw any amount of money from it on demand. Super NOW accounts are not very common. See also: M1.

Super Sinker Bond A short-term bond with a coupon equivalent to that of a long-term bond. That is, the bondholder receives a long-term yield in a short period of time. Most super sinker bonds are collateralized by mortgages and are used to reduce prepayment risk.

Superfund A U.S. federal program dedicated to cleaning and/or removing environmentally hazardous sites in the United States. Superfund works with state, local and tribal governments to clean brownfields and to eliminate hazardous waste, whether it was dumped purposely, accidentally or even legally.

Supermajority A percentage of shareholders, usually 67% to 90%. A supermajority is often required for a company to take certain actions, such as amending the charter. Some companies require supermajorities as anti-takeover measures. For example, a company may require two-thirds of shareholders to approve of a merger or acquisition. Supermajority provisions exist primarily to ensure the company's independent survival, but they may limit the board of directors' authority in even a friendly takeover.

Supermajority Provision In a publicly-traded company's bylaws, a provision mandating that the consent of more than a simple majority of shareholders is needed for certain actions. These actions, and the specific percentage needed for consent, are outlined in the bylaws and are often used as an anti-takeover measure. For example, a company may require that two-thirds of shareholders must approve of a merger or acquisition. Supermajority provisions exist primarily to ensure the company's independent survival, but they may limit the board of directors' authority in even a friendly takeover. See also: Board-out clause.

SuperMontage The electronic system that operates the NASDAQ trading system. It was introduced in 2002.

Supernormal Growth Stock A stock that increases in price at an unusually fast rate for an extended period of time. Usually, this period of time lasts longer than one year, but eventually the stock starts growing at a "normal" rate. Supernormal growth is considered a normal part of an industry life cycle, particularly when there is high demand for a new product.

Superregional Bank 1. A bank holding company with banks operating in at least two U.S. states. **2.** A bank operating in all regions of the United States.

Superseded Suretyship Rider An addendum to the conditions of some surety bonds covering losses that are discovered after the expiration of the original bond. Many surety bonds only cover losses that occur while a bond is in force and that are discovered no later than one year following expiration. Superseded suretyship riders extend this period to permit additional time to discover losses. See also: Discovery period.

Superstation A television satellite that broadcasts locally and also uses satellite technology to broadcast nationally. While superstations have become rather uncommon, they were the forerunners to cable television. The technology behind superstations was pioneered by Ted Turner.

Supervisory Analyst An analyst for a member firm on the New York Stock Exchange who is qualified to approve of research and other reports in order to make them available to the public quickly. To become a supervisor analyst, one must pass a Series 16 exam, which measures one's knowledge of research standards for the NYSE.

Supervisory Capital Assessment Program A program in the United States that conducted assessments of the capital adequacy of bank holding companies under two different scenarios. Bank holding companies in the United States with assets worth more than $100 billion were tested in 2009. The first scenario assumed generally accepted macroeconomic conditions for 2009 and 2010, while the second made pessimistic assumptions. The program was intended to determine banks' likelihood of failure in the event of a financial crisis.

Supervoting Stock Common stock designated by the publicly-traded company issuing it as having more voting rights than other common stock. This gives a shareholder of supervoting stock a greater amount of control over the company. For example, a company can designate its supervoting stock as having three votes and its regular common stock as having one vote. It is also called control stock. See also: Limited-voting stock, Golden share.

Supplemental Security Income Income that one receives from the government if one is blind, disabled, or over 65 and has no other sources of income. In order to qualify for Supplemental Security Income, one must be able to prove one has one of those conditions and have applied for all other government benefits for which one is eligible. Supplemental Security Income is administered by the Social Security Administration, but is paid through the U.S. Treasury instead of the Social Security trust fund.

Supplier A company that provides goods or services to another company. These goods or services may be used to make a different good or service (which is then sold to customers). Alternately, the supplier may provide retail goods or services that a company simply re-sells.

Supplier Credit An agreement between a supplier and a buyer whereby the supplier defers payment. That is, supplier credit occurs when the supplier accepts installment payments for the supplies he/she sells.

Supply In economics, the amount of a good available to be sold. Generally speaking, the greater the supply of a good is, the lower its price is. Likewise, a scarce supply usually results in a high price. However, this price fluctuation also depends on the demand for the good. See also: Law of supply and demand.

Supply and Demand The availability of goods and services in the market and the desire of consumers to buy them. Supply and demand is a major factor (some economists believe the only factor) in determining the price of a good or service. See also: Law of Supply and Demand.

Supply Chain Management The act or process of ensuring that one's business has the proper supplies in order to continue operations. Supply management involves ensuring that supplies are procured as cheaply as possible. For example, a construction company must procure cement, wood, and nails efficiently and inexpensively; equally, a consulting firm must make sure that research materials are easily available. Large companies often devote whole divisions to supply chain management, giving them budgets of millions of dollars to help the company save money. There are two basic types of supply chain management: just in time and just in case. A just in time supply chain management strategy involves keeping only enough inventory to meet immediate business needs. This requires constant monitoring but can save a significant amount money. A just in case strategy, on the other hand, keeps a larger inventory to meet unexpected increases in demand. This saves less money (depending on the nature of the business and matters like carrying costs) but can be easier to manage.

Supply Price The price per unit for a good or service that justifies the production of a given amount of that good or service. If the market price falls below the supply price, production of the good or service will fall accordingly.

Supply Risk The risk that a company will suffer a loss because it becomes unable to buy the raw materials necessary to make its products. For example, a corn mill has the supply risk that not enough corn will grow or farmers will be unable to transport it to the mill or something else will happen that will render the mill unable to provide its services.

Supply Shock Any sudden event that dramatically but (usually) temporarily increases or decreases supply for one or more goods or services. The event may result from government intervention, such as a change in money supply, or may be a random occurrence in the market. For example, a sudden discovery of oil in a field previously thought mainly dry will increase the supply of oil, which will lower the price, assuming demand remains constant. See also: Demand shock.

Supply-Side Economics A macroeconomic theory that a government can best promote growth by providing incentives for persons to produce goods and services. The primary way a supply-side oriented government does this is by maintaining low tax rates so that investors and entrepreneurs may use their money toward production. Maintaining low tax rates on the wealthy is one of the most important and controversial aspects of supply-side economics; the theory states that well off persons have the capital available to produce goods and services and thereby create jobs and grow the economy. Critics contend that this does not happen in reality, and that the wealthy are more likely to keep, rather than invest, their money. In the United States, supply-side economics was crucial to the economic policy in the Ronald Reagan administration. See also: Keynesian economics, Monetarism, Trickle-down economics.

Support In technical analysis, a price that a security does not or only rarely falls below. Technical analysts identify a support level by looking at past performance. It is seen as an indication to buy the security, which will increase the demand, causing the security's price to move above the support level. The demand comes from investors who fail to buy the security at the support price, and resolve to do so if it reaches that price again. If buyers are not forthcoming, however, the security falls below the support level. When this occurs, the price of the security will likely continue to drop until it finds another support level. See also: Price floor, Resistance (Resistance level).

Supranational Describing an organization that exists in multiple countries. While, theoretically, supranational could refer to multinational corporations, the term most often describes an international government or quasi-government organization. Examples include the United Nations and the International Monetary Fund. Supranational organizations often have a direct role in regulation. For example, an international treaty may set up certain standards for international trade. It is important to note, however, that enforcement of these provisions is left to individual, sovereign governments.

Supranational Organization An organization that exists in multiple countries. While, theoretically, supranational could refer to multinational corporations, the term most often describes an international government or quasi-government organization. Examples include the United Nations and the International Monetary Fund. Supranational organizations often have a direct role in regulation. For example, an international treaty may set up certain standards for international trade. However, enforcement of these provisions is left to individual, sovereign governments.

SUR ISO 4217 code for the Soviet ruble. It was first issued in 1917 and underwent five re-denominations over the course of its history. It was replaced by various currencies, starting in 1991 with the fall of the Soviet Union. See also: Russian ruble.

Surcharge An additional fee one must pay over and above some other fee. For example, one may be required to pay a surcharge for a late payment, or for using a service under unusual circumstances.

Surety A sum of money or the guarantee by a third party that a loan or credit extension will be paid. This reduces the risk the lender will lose the money he/she has distributed in the loan. For example, a third party may sign an agreement with the lender with the condition that if the borrower fails to repay the loan, the third party will assume legal liability for it. Often, persons with poor credit cannot receive a loan without surety. See also: Guarantee, Lien.

Surety Bond 1. A fee that a security holder must pay to the security's issuer, should the holder lose the physical certificate. The holder receives a replacement certificate in exchange for the surety bond. A surety bond helps reduce fraud. **2.** See: Blanket fidelity bond.

Suriname Guilder The former currency of Suriname. Originally pegged to the Dutch guilder, it changed its peg to the U.S. dollar during World War II. It began to suffer from high inflation at the beginning of the 1990s and, because of this, the currency was discontinued and replaced with the Surinamese dollar in 2004.

Surinamese Dollar The currency of Suriname. It was introduced in 2004, replacing the Surinamese guilder. Its exchange rate closely follows the U.S. dollar.

Surplus The amount by which the revenue of a government from taxes, tariffs and other sources exceeds its expenditures. A surplus means that the budget is likely healthy, at least in the short-term, and in any case the government does not have to resort to borrowing. Some economists believe that a budget surplus or deficit has only minor importance, while others believe that it is very important to maintain a surplus if at all possible. Most U.S. states are required to maintain either a surplus or a balanced budget, while the federal government is not. See also: Federal deficit.

Surplus Funds Money remaining after all liabilities, including taxes, insurance, and operating expenses, are paid. Having surplus funds means that a company has made a profit or perhaps that it has completed a project under budget. Surplus funds indicate prudent management of funds over the course of the company's operations or project.

Surrender Charge 1. A fee one must pay when canceling a life insurance policy. A surrender charge is levied to encourage a policyholder to remain with the same insurer. **2.** A fee one must pay to a mutual fund for selling one's shares within a certain period of time. For example, one may be required to pay a surrender charge if one sells shares in the first year or two of ownership. The surrender charge exists to encourage stability in ownership of the mutual fund; that is, it discourages traders from speculating on the fund. **3.** A penalty charge one owes if one makes a premature withdrawal from an annuity, insurance contract, or some other investment vehicles.

Surtax An additional tax placed on a person or corporation on a tax liability. For example, a government may calculate one's tax liability and simply add, say, 5% to it. Surtaxes are often politically unpopular. A surtax is also called a supertax.

Surveillance Department A department on an exchange charged with enforcing the rules of the exchange as well as applicable regulations and ethics. It monitors trading on a daily basis in order to accomplish this.

Survivorship Annuity An annuity that is paid to a beneficiary upon the death of the purchaser. That is, one purchases a survivorship annuity and designates a beneficiary. When the purchaser dies, the beneficiary receives a monthly payment for the remainder of his/her life. If the beneficiary dies before the purchaser, then the annuity contract is canceled. The purchaser may not change beneficiaries after the annuity is purchased. It is also called a reversionary annuity.

Survivorship Bias In finance, the tendency to exclude failed companies or managers from performance evaluations or studies simply because they do not exist. Survivorship bias can result in skewed findings in a study and lead a casual reader to believe that a study shows a rosier picture than it really does. Mutual funds, especially smaller ones, are especially susceptible to survivorship bias. At any given time, 90% of mutual funds will claim to be in the top 25% of performers. Technically, they are correct, but only because the other 75% have closed or merged. Manager universe comparisons have also been criticized for exhibiting signs of survivorship bias. It is also known as survivor bias.

Susan B. Anthony Dollar A $1 coin minted in the United States between 1979 and 1981, and again in 1999. It did not circulate widely because its size and shape led to confusion with the 25 cent coin.

Sushi Bond A bond issued by a Japanese company outside of Japan and denominated in a currency other than the yen. A sushi bond is outside the jurisdiction of the Bank of Japan. If another Japanese company buys a sushi bond, it does not count against its legal limits on ownership of foreign securities.

Sushi Roll In candlestick charting, a pattern of 10 candlesticks, each representing a trading day, in which the first five are all smaller than the second five. This means that the daily highs on the first five trading days are all below the second five highs; likewise, the first five lows are all above the second five lows. A sushi roll may indicate the coming reversal of a trend, and may be either bullish or bearish.

Su-Si An ancient Sumerian unit of length approximately equivalent to 15 centimeters.

Suspended Trading A situation in which trading on a security is halted, usually for about half an hour, but sometimes longer, by the exchange's management or by regulators. Trading on a security is suspended usually in order to discourage volatility. For example, suspended trading may occur for the period immediately around a major announcement by the company's management that may cause the price to unsustainably rise or fall. Likewise, the SEC may suspend trading on a security if it is thought to be engaged in illegal activities.

Suspense Account 1. A brokerage or some other account in which an investor deposits securities or cash while he/she decides how to invest it. A suspense account is, by definition, low-risk, as the investor has no intention of losing the deposit while making appropriate investment decisions. **2.** An account in which a company deposits and withdraws funds for transactions that have not yet been completed. A suspense account exists in order to keep ongoing transactions off of a balance sheet.

Suspicious Transaction Report A report a drug store or other company may file with the authorities if one believes a person is purchasing goods to produce methamphetamine. In general, a suspicious activity report is filed if a person is buying legal goods (such as cough medicine, which contains ingredients used to make methamphetamine) in such large quantities that the seller reasonably believes that there may be an ulterior motive in the purchase.

Sustainable Growth Rate The amount that a company or economy can grow without having to increase borrowing. A sustainable growth rate is desirable because it satisfies the needs of the company or economy without increasing its fixed costs (in this case, borrowing costs), which can create significant problems if the growth slows or begins to decline.

Sutu An ancient Akkadian unit of volume approximately equivalent to 10 liters.

SV 1. ISO 3166-1 alpha-2 code for the Republic of El Salvador. This is the code used in international transactions to and from Salvadoran bank accounts. **2.** ISO 3166-2 geocode for El Salvador. This is used as an international standard for shipping to El Salvador. Each Salvadoran department has its own code with the prefix "SV." For example, the code for the Department of La Paz is ISO 3166-2:SV-PA.

SVC ISO 4217 code for the Salvadoran colon. The colon was the currency of El Salvador between 1919 and 2004. It was initially pegged to the U.S. dollar, but began to float in 1931. As part of El Salvador's liberalization policy, it began to accept the dollar as legal tender in 2001 and stopped circulating the colon in 2004. See also: Dollarization.

Sveitafelog In Iceland, a political subdivision equivalent to a municipality.

SVK GOST 7.67 Latin three-letter geocode for Slovakia. The code is used for transactions to and from Slovakian bank accounts and for international shipping to Slovakia. As with all GOST 7.67 codes, it is used primarily in Cyrillic alphabets.

SVN GOST 7.67 Latin three-letter geocode for Slovenia. The code is used for transactions to and from Slovenian bank accounts and for international shipping to Slovenia. As with all GOST 7.67 codes, it is used primarily in Cyrillic alphabets.

Swap The exchange of two securities, interest rates, or currencies for the mutual benefit of the exchangers. For example, in an interest rate swap, the exchangers gain access to interest rates available only to the other exchanger by swapping them. In this case, the two legs of the swap are a fixed interest rate, say 3.5%, and a floating interest rate, say LIBOR + 0.5%. In such a swap, the only things traded are the two interest rates, which are calculated over a notional value. Each party pays the other at set intervals over the life of the swap. For example, one party may agree to pay the other a 3.5% interest rate calculated over a notional value of $1 million, while the second party may agree to pay LIBOR + 0.5% over the same notional value. It is important to note that the notional amount is arbitrary and is not actually traded.

Swap Arrangements Agreements between 15 central banks and the Bank for International Settlements whereby any of the participating institutions can borrow a foreign currency from one of the other ones in order to buy its own domestic currency on the open market. Swap arrangements allow participating institutions to effect changes on their exchange rates, while still allowing their currencies to trade according to market factors.

Swap as Percentage The return on a swap, expressed as an annual percentage rate.

Swap Assignment A swap in which one party pays a leg to the counterparty, then assigns the other leg to a third party. Thus, the first party steps out of the deal, receiving or paying the net amount of the deal. It is also called a swap sale or swap novation.

Swap Book A list of potential swaps kept by a swap bank or a broker. A swap bank acts as an intermediary; it looks for potential counterparties for investors who want to engage in a swap. A swap book assists in this task; it is usually arranged by currency and maturity.

Swap Buy Back A situation in which a counterparty to a swap sells the right to receive payments to the other counterparty. This ends the swap agreement.

Swap Curve A yield curve for a swap. The swap curve states the possible return for a swap on different maturity dates. See also: Bond yield curve.

Swap Order An order to a broker to buy a security and sell the same security, but only if the broker can achieve a certain price differential. For example, an investor may make a swap order to buy a certain number of shares of Stock X and sell the same number of shares, but only if the broker can sell them at $1 more per share. If the broker is unable to do this, then no part of the order is executed. A swap order is also called a switch order.

Swap Price The return on a swap expressed as the difference in price on the day the swap was issued and the day it matures.

Swap Reversal An interest rate swap with the exact opposite terms as another interest rate swap. An investor makes a swap reversal in order to close the position in the interest rate swap she already has.

Swap Spread The difference between the expected return on a swap and the expected return on a government bond. A swap spread is used to measure the riskiness of a swap. Calculating the swap spread is determined by the current LIBOR rate, the credit of the counterparties to the swap, and other macroeconomic factors that might affect interest rates.

Swaption An option in which the buyer of the option has the right to enter into to an interest rate swap. The terms of the swaption specify whether the buyer will be the payer of the floating rate or the payer of the fixed rate. It is called a swaption because it is an option on a swap. A swaption is useful if an interest rate swap may be useful for the buyer's investment strategy, but there is still some uncertainty as to whether that will be the case. See also: Call swaption, Put swaption, Plain vanilla swap.

Swazi Lilangeni The currency of Swaziland. It was first issued in 1974 and pegged to the South African rand at a 1:1 ratio. Interestingly, the rand is also accepted in Swaziland alongside the lilangeni, and it is also issued by the Central Bank of Swaziland. The plural of lilangeni is emalengeni.

SWE GOST 7.67 Latin three-letter geocode for Sweden. The code is used for transactions to and from Swedish bank accounts and for international shipping to Sweden. As with all GOST 7.67 codes, it is used primarily in Cyrillic alphabets.

Sweat Equity The physical work that one puts into an asset, company, or venture that increases its value. For example, one may work constantly on one's writing business so as to increase the revenue one receives from various contracts. This, in turn, increases the value of the business when the writer decides to sell the contracts to someone else. Likewise, one may build a new front porch onto one's house to increase its resale value. In both cases, the physical work is called sweat equity.

Sweat the Asset Slang; to extract the most possible work out of the most productive employee. Sweating the asset may not be sustainable as it can sometimes lead to overwork and exhaustion.

Sweated Labor Work done in a sweatshop. Sweated labor is work done in poor conditions for low level, often below subsistence, wages. See also: Minimum wage, Living wage.

Sweating The act or practice of removing gold or some other precious metal from a coin. This has occurred since Roman times. When coins derive their value from the intrinsic value of the metals, sweating has been known to cause significant inflation.

Sweatshop A factory or other workplace where persons work for unusually low pay. The word connotes places where labor laws are consistently violated. For example, sweatshops may pay below minimum wage and hire underage persons. Alternatively, sweatshops may be legally set up in countries that have very few labor laws, but many still consider them unethical or immoral.

Swedish International Development Cooperation Agency An agency of the Swedish government that administers most of the country's foreign aid. Developing countries seeking assistance from Sweden likely receive aid from the Agency.

Swedish Krona The currency of Sweden. It was introduced in 1873 when it replaced the former currency at the beginning of the Scandinavian Monetary Union. After World War I, the Monetary Union ended, but the Swedish government kept the krona as its own currency. In 1995, Sweden committed to joining the eurozone at an indeterminate date. However, a 2003 referendum rejected this course of action.

Sweep 1. To use all cash flow currently available to service debt. This can lead to liquidity problems. **2.** To transfer funds into an interest-bearing account automatically. Some brokerages sweep extra cash into such accounts on behalf of their clients.

Sweep-to-Fill Order An order to a broker to buy or sell a certain number of shares in a security as quickly as possible. A sweep-to-fill order accomplishes this by splitting an order into several pieces and fills each piece with a different investor. For example, if an investor wishes to sell 500 shares very quickly, he may sell 250 shares to buyer A, 100 to buyer B, and 150 to buyer C, all at different prices. A sweep-to-fill order is most useful when an investor wishes to take a position because he/she thinks there will soon be a large change in price. Therefore, the specific prices at which the investor buys or sells matter little.

Sweet Crude Crude oil with a low percentage of hydrogen and sulfur mixed in it. Compared to sour crude, sweet crude is easier to refine. As a result, sweet crude is the most popular futures contract in the oil market.

Sweetener An extra incentive to encourage investors to buy a bond or preferred stock. For example, a bond may include a right to buy common stock in the issuer for 10% below its market value. A sweetener is designed to help sell securities. It is also called a kicker, a wrinkle, or bells and whistles.

Sweetheart Deal A sale with exceptionally attractive terms, especially offered between persons with an ongoing business or personal relationship. A sweetheart deal may be offered, for example, to a long-time client. The term may, under some circumstances, connote corruption. See also: Fiduciary Responsibility.

Swindler A person who commits fraud, especially as his/her primary career.

Swing High On a chart, a peak in an indicator or price. Swinging high may indicate that a trend is nearing reversal; on the other hand, swinging high at successively higher levels may be a bullish indicator. See also: Swing Low

Swingline Facility A line of credit or other loan that a bank extends to a company to help pay down its debt. A swingline facility is most useful when a company is having difficulty with its debt service. See also: Loan consolidation.

Swingline Loan A large loan that a company may take out in order to repay other debts. A swingline loan is much like a line of credit or a demand loan, but differs in that it must be used to repay outstanding debt. See also: Refinancing, Debt consolidation.

Swiss Bank A bank based in Switzerland. Swiss banks are famous worldwide for their secrecy, which is mandated by Swiss law. This secrecy has resulted in a great deal of laundered and other illegal money to be deposited in Swiss accounts. Historically, this has formed a significant portion of the Swiss banking sector. However, the secrecy is not absolute and may be lifted by following appropriate procedures. See also: CHF, Gnomes of Zurich.

Swiss Dinar An Iraqi dinar issued prior to the First Gulf War. They are possibly called Swiss dinars because the printing plates used to print them were made in Switzerland. After the war, the Iraqi government no longer used these plates and instead printed money using inferior plates. Companies in Kurdistan, in northern Iraq, continued to use Swiss dinars and refused to accept new dinars. This resulted in Swiss dinars being worth more than the new dinars. Both were replaced following the U.S.-led invasion in 2003.

Swiss Electronic Bourse A computerized system linking the trading floors of the Basel, Zurich, and Geneva stock exchanges. This allows a bid or an order made on one exchange to be executed on any of the three.

Swiss Exchange The main exchange in Switzerland. Stocks, derivatives and government bonds all trade on the Swiss Exchange. It was established in 1995 as an automated system to replace regional exchanges in Basel, Geneva and Zurich.

Swiss Franc The currency of Switzerland. Although the first Swiss franc was used briefly at the end of the 18th century, the modern franc was introduced in 1850, replacing almost two dozen local currencies. Switzerland was a member of the Latin Monetary Union until its demise in 1927 and later belonged to the Bretton Woods System. Until 2000, at least 40% of the franc was required to be backed by gold. The Swiss franc is known for having almost no inflation and, for that reason, is considered a very safe currency for investment.

Swiss Market Index An index of 20 blue chip companies in Switzerland. It is considered a benchmark index for Swiss stocks. It consists of large cap companies and is weighted for market capitalization, meaning price changes for companies with higher market caps affect the price of the index more. It was established in 1988.

Swiss Options and Financial Futures Exchange The first fully electronic exchange in the world. It became defunct in 1998 when it merged with Deutsche Terminborse to form Eurex.

Swissie A slang term for the Swiss franc, often used in foreign exchange.

Switch 1. See: Swap. **2.** See: Roll forward.

Switching 1. The act of closing a position and opening another with better prospects. This term often applies to securities and mutual funds. See also: Load. **2.** In futures, the act of liquidating a contract and using the proceeds to buy another on the same type with a longer maturity. This is often done to avoid receiving delivery of the underlying.

Switching Costs In microeconomics, what one must spend in order to upgrade to a higher technology. For example, switching costs may involve purchasing a new, higher quality mobile phone. The higher the switching costs are for a consumer, the less likely that consumer is to adopt the higher technology.

Switching Option An option, the exercise of which creates one or more options. The most basic example of this is a compound option, which is an option on an option. A reload stock option may also be a switching option. Switching options may be useful if an investor believes he/she can secure a lower (in the case of a call) or higher (in the case of a put) strike price.

SWOT Analysis A way to identify and analyze a company's goals by assessing its strength, weaknesses, opportunities, and threats. An advantage to SWOT analysis is that it separates internal factors (strengths and weaknesses) from external ones (opportunities and threats). This allows the company to match what it could do in theory with what is possible in reality. Another advantage is the fact that conducting SWOT analysis is straightforward if the company conducting it is honest with itself. See also: Qualitative Analysis.

SWX Group A holding company for exchanges and financial companies. It is primarily known for owning the Swiss Exchange; it also holds partial ownership in a number of other exchanges, including EUREX and STOXX. It was founded in 2001.

SWZ GOST 7.67 Latin three-letter geocode for Swaziland. The code is used for transactions to and from Swazi bank accounts and for international shipping to Swaziland. As with all GOST 7.67 codes, it is used primarily in Cyrillic alphabets.

SY 1. ISO 3166-1 alpha-2 code for the Syrian Arab Republic. This is the code used in international transactions to and from Syrian bank accounts. **2.** ISO 3166-2 geocode for Syria. This is used as an international standard for shipping to Syria. Each province has its own code with the prefix "SY." For example, the code for the Province of Idlib is ISO 3166-2:SY-ID.

SYC GOST 7.67 Latin three-letter geocode for Seychelles. The code is used for transactions to and from Seychellois bank accounts and for international shipping to Seychelles. As with all GOST 7.67 codes, it is used primarily in Cyrillic alphabets.

Sydney Futures Exchange The former primary derivatives exchange in Australia. In 2006, it merged with the Australian Stock Exchange to form the Australian Securities Exchange.

Sydney Mint A former mint in Australia. Established in 1855, it was the first branch of the Royal Mint located outside the United Kingdom. It closed in 1926, though the building retains the name.

Syli The currency of Guinea between 1971 and 1985. It replaced the first Guinean franc and itself was replaced by the second franc. The second franc's initial value matched the syli's at a 1:1 ratio. See also: GNF.

Symmetric Cash Matching The process of borrowing in the short-term to pay a liability before it is due such that it reduces the cost of funds. For example, symmetric cash matching may reduce the interest rate a company owes. Symmetric cash matching is a form of cash flow matching and allows a company to maintain balance in a portfolio and the lowest possible cost.

Sympvertizing The use of an advertisement or other marketing tactic in which the seller attempts to commiserate or identify with the potential buyer. For example, a television commercial may start with, "Don't you hate it when you can't have things your way?"

Synchronous Data Information collected or available at the same time. Investment decisions must be made according to data synchronous to the general public in order to avoid committing insider trading. Likewise, in options, one must use synchronous data in order to evaluate the validity of the various option pricing models.

Syndicate 1. In banking, a group of banks that each lend an amount of money to a borrower, all at the same time and for the same purpose. The banks in a syndicate cooperate with each other for the duration of the project, even if they are otherwise competitors. Bank syndicates usually only lend large amounts of money. Every syndicate is a temporary arrangement. **2.** In investment banking, a group of underwriters responsible for placing a new issue of a security with investors. As with banking syndicates, the members of an underwriting syndicate work together for the duration of the project. Every syndicate is a temporary arrangement. It is also called a purchase group or a selling syndicate.

Syndicate Bid An order by a managing underwriter to buy or sell a security immediately before a secondary offering of the same security. The managing underwriter makes a syndicate bid in order to stabilize the price of the security, which will make the secondary offering easier to place with investors. This is only permissible under certain defined circumstances set forth in SEC Rule 10b-7.

Syndicated Eurocredit Loans Loans made on the eurocredit market by a group of banks.

Syndicated Loan A loan made by many lenders to a single borrower. Syndicated loans are made in large amounts that would be too big for one lender to handle. In many ways, a syndicated loan operates like an ordinary loan; there is an interest rate (fixed or floating) and a time until repayment is due. It may be a direct loan or a revolving line of credit or a combination of the two. However, syndicated loans are usually made on a best effort basis, meaning that if the lenders are unable to find enough capital or additional lenders to cover the amount requested, the amount borrowed will be less than anticipated. They are common in leveraged buyouts.

Syndication The process of finding underwriters to place a new issue. See also: Syndicate.

Synergistic Effect The financial benefit (or, more rarely, detriment) that two companies may derive from a merger or acquisition. For example, two companies that merge may be able to produce more revenue than either one could produce independently by combining the most efficient processes each brings to the merger. The synergistic effect may also refer to the cost reduction a merger brings about by eliminating or streamlining redundant processes. The synergistic effect usually has a positive connotation, but one also occasionally hears of a negative synergistic effect, such as when the management teams of newly merged corporations do not work well with each other. Generally speaking, however, a synergistic effect makes the merged company worth more than its individual components were before the merger.

Synergy The financial benefit (or, more rarely, detriment) two companies may derive from a merger or acquisition. For example, two companies that merge may be able to produce more revenue than either one could produce independently by combining the most efficient processes each brings to the merger. Synergy may also refer to the cost reduction a merger brings about by eliminating or streamlining redundant processes. Synergy usually has a positive connotation, but one also occasionally hears of negative synergy, such as when the management teams of newly merged corporations do not work well with each other.

Synthetic Asset A position in which one takes various positions to create the same effect as holding a certain asset or other investment vehicle. For example, one may borrow funds in one currency and lend the same amount in another currency in order to create the same effect as having a forward contract on one of the currencies.

Synthetic Call The purchase of an asset combined with the sale of a bond and the purchase of a put option on that asset. The strike price of the put is equal to the face value of the bond. Combined, these investments produce the same effect as buying a call option.

Synthetic Collateralized Debt Obligation A collateralized debt obligation that invests in credit default swaps. This investment can lead to large returns for holders of the CDO; however, the nature of credit default swaps may leave the holders liable for more than their initial investments, should there be significant changes in the credit default swaps.

Synthetic Convertible A bond and a warrant or right that are issued separately, but are combined together to create the same effect as a convertible bond.

Synthetic Forward Position A position in which one borrows funds in one currency and lends the same amount in another currency. One then offsets these positions by making trades on the currencies.

Synthetic Futures Contract 1. The purchase of calls and the sale of puts with the same expiration date and strike price. **2.** The purchase of puts and the sale of calls with the same expiration date and strike price. In both cases, the position creates the effect of holding a long position (for the first definition) or a short position (for the second) on a futures contract.

Synthetic Index The purchase of futures contracts and/or options such that one's exposure and potential payout resemble that of an index. One creates a synthetic index if one believes doing so will result in a higher return than a security tracking a real index.

Synthetic Investment A combination of investment vehicles that, when used together, can create a profit. An example is an option spread, where one takes two or more positions in option contracts in order to profit from the difference in their prices. Likewise, one may create a synthetic index in order to outperform a real index. Institutional investors are the main creators of synthetic investments.

Synthetic Lease The creation by a parent company of a special purpose entity to which is given a certain property and which leases the same property back to the parent company. A synthetic lease allows the parent company to use the property for any purpose it wants while not recording it as an asset on its balance sheet. Instead, it is recorded as an expense. This way, rather than paying taxes on the property, it may write off the rent from its taxable income.

Synthetic Short Sale An option strategy in which one buys a put while selling a call on the same underlying asset. This is called a synthetic short sale because the investor makes a profit if the price of the underlying asset falls and a theoretically unlimited loss if the price rises.

Synthetic Stock A position in which one owns a call option and has sold a put option on the same underlying asset, which is a stock. A synthetic stock acts like a stock because both open the investor to theoretically unlimited gains and losses depending on the price movements of the stock. Because of this, a synthetic stock is taxed like a regular stock.

Synthetic System The use of two or more steps to create a product. This may refer to the assembly line at an auto plant, the writing and editing processes in journalism, or almost anything else.

SYP ISO 4217 code for the Syrian pound. It was introduced after the First World War under the French Mandate. It was first pegged to the French franc, then the British pound and finally the U.S. dollar. Now, the Central Bank of Syria sets official exchange rates, but these can vary widely from the black market exchange rates. There are restrictions in place on how many pounds can leave the country at a given time. Interestingly, it is known as the pound in English, the livre in French, and the lira in Arabic.

SYR GOST 7.67 Latin three-letter geocode for Syria. The code is used for transactions to and from Syrian bank accounts and for international shipping to Syria. As with all GOST 7.67 codes, it is used primarily in Cyrillic alphabets.

Syrian Pound The currency of Syria. It was introduced after World War I under the French Mandate. It was first pegged to the French franc, then the British pound and finally the U.S. dollar. Now, the Central Bank of Syria sets official exchange rates, but these can vary widely from the black market exchange rates. There are restrictions in place on how many pounds can leave the country at a given time. It is known as the pound in English, the livre in French, and the lira in Arabic.

Sysla In Iceland and the Faroe Islands, a political subdivision equivalent to a police precinct.

System for Electronic Document Analysis and Retrieval An electronic system that Canadian regulators use to allow publicly-traded companies to make necessary filings more quickly and efficiently. Most publicly-traded companies in Canada use SEDAR to file their quarterly and annual reports and other information they must submit. SEDAR provides a website where investors can review this information, which is useful in conducting fundamental analysis.

Systematic Risk Principle A theory stating that unsystemic risks are irrelevant in properly diversified portfolios. According to this principle, only systemic risks affect the expected return on such a portfolio, because the process of diversification eliminates the risk attached to any particular company, and only the systemic risks endemic to the wider economy may affect the portfolio.

Systematic Withdrawal Plan A way to receive regular payments from an annuity, mutual fund, or other investment vehicle. One way of conducting a systematic withdrawal by selling one's interest in an investment vehicle slowly over time and keeping the cash from the sales. This reduces the risk that the investor will sell all of one's interest at once and receive a lump sum payment when the market is in a downturn. Systematic withdrawals may occur automatically, such as in Social Security or in some retirement plans.

Systemic Risk A risk that is carried by an entire class of assets and/or liabilities. Systemic risk may apply to a certain country or industry, or to the entire global economy. It is impossible to reduce systemic risk for the global economy (complete global shutdown is always theoretically possible), but one may mitigate other forms of systemic risk by buying different kinds of securities and/or by buying in different industries. For example, oil companies have the systemic risk that they will drill up all the oil in the world; an investor may mitigate this risk by investing in both oil companies and companies having nothing to do with oil. Systemic risk is also called systematic risk or undiversifiable risk.

Systems Safety Engineering The use of engineering to find, resolve and eliminate hazardous aspects of a system. Systems safety engineering helps reduce a company's risk.

SZ 1. ISO 3166-1 alpha-2 code for the Kingdom of Swaziland. This is the code used in international transactions to and from Swazi bank accounts. **2.** ISO 3166-2 geocode for Swaziland. This is used as an international standard for shipping to Swaziland. Each Swazi district has its own code with the prefix "SZ." For example, the code for the District of Manzini is ISO 3166-2:SZ-MA.

SZL ISO 4317 code for the Swazi lilangeni. It was first issued in 1974 and pegged to the South African rand at a 1:1 ratio. Interestingly, the rand is also accepted in Swaziland alongside the lilangeni, and is also issued by the Central Bank of Swaziland.

Sznur An obsolete Polish unit of area approximately equivalent to 0.1995 hectares.

SZSE Component Index An index tracking 40 securities traded on the Shenzhen Stock Exchange. It was introduced in 1995.

T A symbol appearing next to a stock listed on NASDAQ indicating that the stock is not common issue, but has a warrant attached to it. All NASDAQ listings use a four letter abbreviation; if a T follows the abbreviation, this indicates that the security being traded has a warrant attached.

T. Boone Pickens An American oilman and business man. He founded an oil company, Mesa Petroleum, in 1956, and built it into one of the largest independent oil companies in the world. In the 1980s, Mesa was deeply involved in mergers and acquisitions, buying and attempting to buy companies much larger than it was. Pickens developed a reputation as a greenmailer, one who buys stock in a company and forces the company to buy it back at a large premium to avoid a hostile takeover. In 1997, he established BP Capital Management, which manages hedge funds. He is also a noted patron of his alma mater, Oklahoma State University. He was born in 1928.

T+1 Informal for a settlement date that occurs one trading day after the trade date. T+1 trades are fairly unusual.

T+1 (T+2,T+3) Informal; the number of trading days since the trade date on which a trade is settled. Different types of transactions settle on different days. For example, stock trades usually settle on T+3 (three trading days following the trade date), while bonds settle on T+1 (one trading day following the trade date).

T+2 Informal for a settlement date that occurs two trading days after the trade date.

T+3 Informal for a settlement date that occurs three trading days after the trade date. Different types of transactions settle on different days, but stock trades usually settle on T+3.

Ta A Burmese unit of length equivalent to 3.2004 meters.

TA-100 Index An index of the 100 largest companies (by market capitalization) that trade on the Tel Aviv Stock Exchange. The index is weighted for market capitalization; that is, price changes in stocks with higher market caps will affect the index more than stocks with lower market caps. The index is published every 30 seconds during a trading day by the Tel Aviv Stock Exchange. The TA-100 was first calculated in 1992.

Table of Denial Orders A list of companies or individuals who are prohibited from seeing receiving American goods via ship. One may be placed on the table if one violates U.S. trade policies or other policies.

Tabular Cost of Insurance The total amount life insurance policyholders must pay in premiums in order to compensate an insurance company for the death benefits it must pay in a year. The tabular cost of insurance is calculated using a mortality table.

Tabular Plans A way to calculate a premium for an insurance policy using a table to set a minimum and maximum premium for various types of plans. An insurance underwriter uses the table as a guide and applies various discounts and additions based on the policyholder's risk and the underwriter's judgment.

Tabulation Report A report at any stockholder meeting indicating the results of each vote and whether or not a quorum is met.

Tackoscope An instrument that measures the stickiness of ink. Tackoscopes are used in printing to ensure that ink is able to be easily transferred without causing damage to the page. A tackoscope is also called an inkometer.

Tactical Asset Allocation An active management strategy for a portfolio or fund with a basic set of securities. The money manager changes the securities represented in the portfolio or fund as needed in order to take advantage of short-term profits. However, once the portfolio or fund attains those profits, the money manager returns to the basic set of securities it originally contained. The money manager may use fundamental, technical, and/or macroeconomic analysis in determining when and how to change the securities in the portfolio or fund.

Tael A unit of weight in Taiwan approximately equivalent to 37.5 grams. It is used primarily in the sale of bulk foodstuffs. An equivalent term is niu.

Taft-Hartley Act Legislation in the United States, enacted in 1947, that amended and rolled back some of the provisions of the National Labor Relations Act. Specifically, the Act provided a list of "unfair labor practices" in which unions and other forms of organized labor could not engage. It prohibited jurisdictional strikes, wherein workers protest transfers to another division or role within the same company, and wildcat strikes, or strikes unauthorized by a union. It also forbade solidarity or other political strikes, and disallowed unions from donating to federal political campaigns. Importantly, the Taft-Hartley Act allowed individual states to pass right-to-work laws. See also: Featherbedding, National Labor Relations Board.

Taft-Hartley Pension Plan A pension plan in which an employer makes fixed contributions to a fund on behalf of employees, who receive a fixed benefit upon retirement. The employer negotiates the amount of the contribution with an employee union, and a third party (consisting of an equal number of representatives of the employer and the union) is responsible for investing contributions. The employer is therefore not responsible for the pension's investment losses, if any. This structure was created in 1947 by the Taft-Hartley Act.

Tafwid 1. In Islamic law, authorization to perform an action. For example, a party to a contract may give tafwid by delegating the ability to negotiate to his/her lawyer. **2.** In Islamic law, an arrest warrant.

Tag Ends The shares of a new issue that have not been placed with investors after most of the issue has been sold. Failing to place the tag ends may or may not result in the whole issue being canceled.

Tag Line In marketing, a brief phrase used in advertising a product. It is intended to embed itself in the memories of members of the target audience in order to entice them to buy the product. For example, the tag line for a mousetrap company may be "No rodent escapes."

Tag Sale A garage sale in which the seller affixes price tags to the items. These prices may or may not be negotiable. A tag sale contrasts with a garage sale, in which no prices are set.

Tag-Along Right The contractually guaranteed right of a minority shareholder to sell his/her stake in a company if the majority shareholder does so. The tag-along rights further guarantee the exact same terms to the minority shareholder. This protects the minority shareholder from the possibility that a new majority owner will come along and ruin the company or take it in a direction disadvantageous to the

minority shareholder. Tag-along rights are also called co-sale rights and are common in venture capital agreements.

Tail 1. In a bond auction, the difference between the lowest bid and the average bid in the auction. **2.** In a quote, the cents rather than the whole dollar amount. For example, in the quote $32.59, tail is 59 cents. This term is most common in new issues of a security. **3.** See: Residual Value.

Tail Coverage A form of insurance in which the insurer will pay claims on events occurring during the policy period even if they are filed after the insurance has lapsed. For example, if an employee falls off a ladder in June and the employer allows the employee's workers compensation insurance to expire in July, tail coverage would pay the claim even if the employee does not file until August.

Tailgating The act of entering a restricted area without authorization by following a person with authorization. For example, one may enter a door immediately behind a person who has the key. The term implies that the tailgater does not have the consent of the person who has access, but this is not always the case. Tailgating is a violation of security protocol and may be a form of trespassing.

Tailored Life Insurance Life insurance with provisions specific to the policyholder's individual needs or desires. For example, an ill policyholder may tailor his policy so that a portion of the death benefit can be used in advance to pay medical bills. One may pay a higher premium for tailored life insurance.

Taing Detha Gyi In Myanmar (Burma), a political subdivision approximately equivalent to a province. They are dominated by ethnic Burmese. See also: Pyi ne.

Tai-Pan A colloquial, Cantonese term for a business executive. It literally means "top class." The term originated as an expression for Western executives who did business in Hong Kong during the late 19th and early 20th centuries.

Taiwan Capitalization Weighted Stock Index An index tracking all stocks that trade on the Taiwan Stock Exchange, including preferred stock and stock in companies listed for less than a month. As the name implies, the index is weighted for market capitalization; that is, price changes in stocks with higher market caps will affect the index more than stocks with lower market caps. The index was first published in 1967. See also: Taiwan weighted index.

Taiwan Stock Exchange The only stock exchange in Taiwan. Trading began on it in 1962. It operates the Taiwan Capitalization Weighted Stock Index.

Taiwan Weighted Index An index tracking all common stocks that trade on the Taiwan Stock Exchange. The index is weighted for market capitalization; that is, price changes in stocks with higher market caps will affect the index more than stocks with lower market caps. The index's base year is 1966. See also: Taiwan Capitalization Weighted Index.

Tajikistani Ruble The former currency of Tajikistan. It was introduced in 1995, replacing the Russian ruble, which had itself only recently replaced the Soviet ruble. It suffered from high inflation for five years, and, in 2000, was replaced by the Tajikistani somoni.

Tajikistani Somoni The currency of Tajikistan. It was issued in 2000, replacing the Tajikistani ruble after a period of high inflation. The somoni is one of the highest-valued currencies in Central Asia.

Takaful An insurance structure compatible with Islamic law. According to most Muslim jurists, conventional insurance is disallowed, in part because it requires the insurer to gamble on the likelihood of an insured event's occurrence. This uncertainty is not permitted under the sharia. Under a takaful, subscribers pay a certain amount, which is deposited into a pool of liquidity with other subscribers' contributions. Insured losses are paid out of that pool. In effect, a takaful is a mutual aid society in which the aim is not profit. However, a company may invest the pool of liquidity in sharia-compliant instruments and may keep a management fee. Takafuls have existed in one form or another for most of the history of Islam.

Take a Bath Informal; to lose a significant amount on an investment very quickly. For example, if one buys a stock for $95 per share and a year later it is trading for $40 per share, one has taken a bath in that stock.

Take a Beating Informal; to lose a significant amount on an investment very quickly. For example, if one buys a stock for $95 per share and a year later it is trading for $40 per share, one has taken a beating in that stock.

Take a Flier Informal; to take a significant risk by investing in a highly speculative venture or security. To take a flier is to make such an investment knowing full well that it might result in the loss of the investor's capital. See also: Take a bath.

Take a Position The state of owning or owing a security or other asset. One has a long position when one owns something, while one has a short position when something is sold, especially sold short. See also: Close a position.

Take a Powder To temporarily cancel an order to buy or sell a security when the investor still wishes to buy or sell it. One takes a powder when one believes that one can pay or receive a better price. See also: Sidelines.

Take a Swing Informal; to make a trade at a price that the investor or broker ordinarily would consider to be disadvantageous. One takes a swing at a trade on the chance that the investment may become profitable.

Take Delivery To receive the underlying asset from a derivative, especially a futures contract. For example, if one holds a futures contract on 1000 barrels of oil at the time it matures, one receives the oil, taking delivery. In many futures contracts and other derivatives that are settled in cash, the holder does not take delivery.

Take Home Pay The paycheck actually issued to an employee after all withholding taxes are taken out. Examples of taxes withheld from an employee's pay are income taxes and FICA taxes. An employee must base his/her personal budget on take home pay and not on gross pay.

Take Off Informal; to increase significantly in price in a short period of time. A security may take off, for example, if analysts raise its profile unexpectedly or if it belongs to an industry that is in favor at a certain period of time. Taking off is often unsustainable unless a security's fundamental information justifies it.

Take or Pay An agreement between two parties where one agrees to either buy certain goods or services from the other on a certain date or to pay for them even if that party does not need them on that date. A take-or-pay agreement provides guaranteed revenue for the seller even if the buyer decides against actually purchasing the goods or services. It is common in transactions involving electric utilities.

Take the Knock A slang term meaning to sell for less money than one paid. To take the knock means to lose money. See also: Loss.

Take the Offer Informal; to agree to buy a security at a price offered by a dealer at an agreed-upon volume.

Take-and-Pay Contract A contract of sale in which the buyer becomes legally obligated to pay for the goods or services purchased in the contract upon delivery or upon the buyer's agreement to take delivery. The buyer incurs a penalty if he/she does not pay for the goods or services at the time. It contrasts with a take-or-pay contract.

Take-Away Acquisition The acquisition of a company when the target firm already has another offer from a second potential acquirer. For example, when Company A buys Company B for $200 million when Company C had previously made an offer on Company B for $150 million, the purchase is called a take-away acquisition. A take-away acquisition carries the risk that the acquiring company rushes too quickly to finalize the transaction and will not do sufficient due diligence.

Takedown The price that members of an underwriting syndicate pay for a new issue. The syndicate has the responsibility to place the new issue with investors. The amount by which the underwriters' selling price exceeds the takedown represents their profit on the placement of the new issue.

Take-One A flyer that advertises something, usually an event or service, and is passed out to individuals.

Takeout 1. Informal; to borrow. **2.** Extra cash that an investor derives when he/she sells a position and then buys a similar position for a lower price. **3.** To make a bid for the entirety of a security that a seller owns. **4.** Informal for a merger or acquisition. The term comes from another informal term, "in play," which refers to a company either soliciting offers for a buy-out or vulnerable to a hostile takeover. A takeout means that the company involved as been "taken out of play."

Take-Out Commitment An agreement by a financial institution or another investor to make a long-term loan at a certain, stated date in the future. A take-out commitment may be made in construction or other projects when short-term financing is initially beneficial but the borrower anticipates long-term financing to become more advantageous at a later time.

Take-Out Lender A financial institution or, less commonly, another investor, that makes a long-term loan at a certain, stated date in the future. A take-out commitment may be made in construction or another project when short-term financing is initially beneficial but the borrower anticipates long-term financing to become more advantageous at a later time.

Takeover Attempt An effort by a corporation or, less commonly, an individual, to purchase a majority of the stock in a publicly-traded company. A takeover attempt may be friendly or hostile but, in order to be successful, must be approved by a majority of shareholders (or, more specifically, the holders of a majority of shares).

Takeover Bid An offer in which an investor or company attempts to buy a publicly-traded company, or, more commonly, most of the shares in that company. For example, if Corporation A offers to buy 51% or more of Corporation B, then Corporation A is making a takeover bid. Takeover bids are made for cash, stock, or both. Likewise, they may be friendly or hostile; a friendly takeover bid occurs when the board of directors supports the acquisition and a hostile takeover bid occurs when it does not. See also: Antitakeover measure, Greenmail.

Takeover Panel An organization in the United Kingdom that arbitrates both acquisitions and mergers While it has no ability to enforce its decisions, it carries a great deal of moral authority and attempts to treat individual and corporate shareholders with equity. It is more formally called the Panel on Takeovers and Mergers.

Takeover Stock Stock in a company that is considered a primary target for a hostile takeover. Takeover stock is likely to rise significantly in price as rumors of a takeover are thought to increase demand.

Takeover Target A publicly-traded company that is the object of a takeover, especially, but not necessarily, a hostile takeover. That is, another company is interested in buying the takeover target, often by buying its shares with the intent of obtaining a majority stake without the authorization of its board of directors. An acquiring company identifies takeover targets based on a variety of factors, including share price and growth potential; it may buy up to 5% of the takeover target without publicly disclosing its intentions. A takeover target is also called a target company.

Takeover Tax Treatment The way the tax authority of a jurisdiction treats a merger or acquisition of a company. Takeover tax treatment varies by accounting method used. The amount a company spends defending against a hostile takeover attempt may be deductible.

Taker Slang; a buyer or potential buyer. For example, one may offer a product at a certain price and ask, "Any takers?"

Takes a Call Describing a transaction that a broker cannot complete until he/she has placed a phone call to the client to receive the client's approval. See also: Show me.

Takes Price A price that one party must raise (for a buyer) or lower (for a seller) for a counterparty to be willing to accept the offer. See also: Market price.

Takeunder An offer for the takeover of a publicly traded company in which the offer price is significantly lower than the market value. These offers are made (and accepted) when a company's stock is under downward pressure. The offering company makes the offer to purchase a company cheaply, and shareholders accept the offer because they believe that the price, while below the market value, will soon be more than the company is worth if the trend continues.

Take-Up Rate The percentage of persons who are eligible for some benefit or compensation who take advantage of it. The take-up rate may refer, for example, to persons eligible for a portion of a class action judgment or persons who qualify for some government assistance. Due to lack of information and other reasons, it is virtually impossible for a take-up rate to approach 100% in most situations.

Take-Up Reel A film reel containing no film. It is placed in a projector in front of a reel with film and collects the film gradually as a movie plays.

Takhayyur In Islamic law, the practice of choosing which rules to follow from various schools of thought. For example, if one school of jurisprudence permits one action while a different school prohibits the same action, takhayyur allows an individual scholar to choose which school to follow. Choosing the most lenient rules from different schools of jurisprudence is a controversial practice.

Taking a View Informal; the act or process of forming an opinion on the direction of the market and taking appropriate action. The expression is most common in the UK.

Taking off a Leg The act or practice of selling one option contract in a combination option while maintaining one or more different ones. This will likely destroy the option strategy of the combination option. Therefore, one only does it when the premium makes the entire combination profitable. See also: Cliquet, Straddle, Strangle.

Taking the Street The practice in which a hedge fund buys the entire inventory of a stock from several banks and brokerages with the intention to sell it in a short period of time. The hedge fund takes the street knowing that the banks and brokerages will need to buy the inventory soon for their clients. This increase in demand raises the stock's price. The hedge fund is then able to sell the stock to the same banks and brokerages (and others) at a profit.

Talent An ancient Greek unit of weight approximately equivalent to 25.86 or 37.8 kilograms, depending on the region.

Talent Charge Payment given to an actor who appears in or voices a commercial. A talent charge is a one-time fee, though it may be accompanied by a residual.

Taliban A political movement that ruled most of Afghanistan from 1996 to 2001. When it was in power, the Taliban was noted for brutal treatment of women and for almost entirely wiping out the cultivation of opium, which was until then one of Afghanistan's primary cash crops. It based its teachings and rule on an austere interpretation of Islam combined with Pashto tribal law. In 2001, it was overthrown by the United States and coalition forces. Since 2004, the Taliban has become a major insurgent group in Afghanistan, funded through opium trade.

Talk Down To encourage a stock price to decline. Talking down can be a form of price manipulation (in which case it is illegal) or it simply may be a self-fulfilling prophesy. For example, an analyst may believe a stock is overvalued and publish an article saying so. This may spook investors into selling, which itself would cause the price to decline.

Talk Turkey Informal; to speak candidly, especially about a problem or a situation one wishes to resolve. Talking turkey is often necessary in order to conclude any business deal.

Talking One's Book 1. The act of promoting a stock one owns in order to entice others to buy it. This would in turn benefit one's own investment portfolio. Talking one's book is not a well-regarded strategy. **2.** More generally, the act of promoting one's company, product or other good or service.

Tallyman 1. A salesman who sells products and accepts installment payments. **2.** A person who keeps track of shipped, received or produced inventory. A tallyman may account for products by unit or by weight.

Taluka In Sindh (a province of Pakistan), a political subdivision equivalent to a county.

Talukdar In Nepal, a term for a tax collector.

Tambala A subdivision of the Malawian kwacha. One tambala is equal in value to 1/100 of a kwacha. See also: Cent.

Tambon In Thailand, a political subdivision roughly equivalent to a township.

Tandem Describing two or more related trades one makes at the same time. Tandem trades are most common when an investor wishes to profit from a spread, or the difference in price between two securities. See also: Exotic option.

Tandem Programs A program, begun in 1974, in which Ginnie Mae would provide a mortgage to a low-income family at a below market interest rate and then sell the loan to a private investor. The program has been discontinued. See also: Ginnie Mae pass-through.

Tanga A division of the Tajikistani ruble worth 1/100 of the ruble. Because the ruble was such a weak currency, no coins or notes for the tanga were ever printed. It was discontinued and replaced by the diram when the somoni replaced the ruble in 2000.

Tangentery A slang term for a distraction at work. The proliferation of the Internet has increased tangentery in office settings.

Tangibility In law, the ability to be apprehended by the human senses. Many assets have tangibility, including but not limited to, cash, commodities, real estate, and personal property. Some more abstract things also have tangibility, at least in certain circumstances. For example, accounts receivable is a tangible asset for accounting purposes. Tangibility explicitly does not include patents, brands, or intellectual property. An asset must have tangibility in order to be used as collateral on a loan. For example, one may not use a patent as collateral, but may use his/her house. See also: Intangibility; Tangible net worth.

Tangible Asset In accounting, any asset that can be seen and touched. Tangible assets include things that can be reproduced, such as widgets or a widget factory, and things that cannot be reproduced, such as the land upon which the widget factory is built. Tangible assets are comparatively easy to price, and therefore they are often used to express the value of a company. However, because they do not include intangible but still valuable things like patents and brand recognition, they may not truly express a company's value. Less commonly, tangible assets are called hard assets. See also: Intangible Assets.

Tangible Net Worth A calculation of a company's value that does not include the value of intangible assets. It is calculated by taking the value of the company's total assets and subtracting the value of intangible assets and total liabilities. Tangible net worth is easier to measure than net worth because physical things are easier to value. On the other hand, tangible net worth may not be accurate, as it excludes the value of things such as patents, copyrights, and brand recognition.

Tank Slang; to drop precipitously in price.

Tankan A survey of Japanese executives measuring their perceptions on the state of the national economy. The tankan is published quarterly; its publication can cause significant changes to stock and yen prices because a high level of business confidence is considered bullish, while a low level is considered bearish.

Tanshi Company A type of brokerage firm in Japan that deals primarily or exclusively in short term, money market investments. For example, a tanshi company may assist a client in buying and selling commercial paper, but may not do so for 10-year corporate bonds.

Tanzanian Shilling The currency of Tanzania. It was introduced in 1966, replacing the East African shilling. It is one of the least valuable currencies in the world.

Tap Issue An issue of a bond that is not placed immediately with investors. That is, the issuer authorizes the bond and makes it available, but holds it back until it needs or desires the cash flow that the sale of the issue would bring. The French and British governments are the most common tap issuers. A tap issue is also called tap stock.

Tape Is Late A situation in which trading volume for a security is so heavy that the ticker publicly announcing quotes is delayed by a significant amount of time, usually one or two minutes. This was fairly common before electronic tickers were used, but has become largely a non-issue since electronic tickers announce prices in real time.

Tarafa In Kenya, a political subdivision equivalent to a municipality.

Tare Weight The weight of an empty container and packing materials. One subtracts the tare weight from the total weight of a good being shipped in order to arrive at the weight of the good itself. This helps companies price their services.

Target Date Fund A fund of funds that invests predominantly or exclusively in mutual funds with a certain maturity. For example, a target date fund may hold funds with securities that all mature in 2015. A target date fund is useful when one wishes to have all of one's investments mature on the date of one's retirement.

Target Fund A mutual fund that invests exclusively in bonds with maturities around a certain date. Once that date is reached, all proceeds are distributed to shareholders; the fund liquidates and ceases to exist. A target fund operates much like a unit investment trust (UIT) because both have final maturity dates; however, a target fund is actively managed, while a UIT is not.

Target Leverage Ratio The level of debt that a company wishes to maintain expressed as a percentage of its market value. Some companies are more comfortable with debt than others. Increased leverage increases the risk to a company, but can increase returns.

Target Payout Ratio The dividend that a publicly-traded company attempts to pay to shareholders each year as a percentage of its total earnings in a given year. There is no guarantee that the company will be able to pay the target payout ratio; if its earnings are particularly low in a year, it may pay a smaller percentage or even no dividend at all. It is important to note that even if the target payout ratio remains the same, the actual dividend may differ as earnings change each year and the payout ratio is a percentage rather than a dollar amount. See also: Omitted Dividend.

Target Price 1. In mergers and acquisitions, the purchase price of the target company. **2.** The price at which an investor hopes to buy or sell a security. That is, when an investor takes a position on a security he/she hopes that the investment will become profitable. The target price is the price at which the investment becomes worth the effort and money put into it. **3.** In options, the price at which a contract becomes in-the-money.

Target Risk 1. A term for prospective policyholders of an insurance company, organized by demographic information such as age and gender. **2.** The amount of risk an investor is willing to take. Target risk varies according to the investor's risk tolerance.

Target Risk Fund A fund of funds that invests predominantly or exclusively in mutual funds with a certain level of risk. That is, a target risk fund may be conservative, investing largely in bond funds and the like, or aggressive, investing in funds with initial public offerings. The target risk fund may also be somewhere between the two. A target risk fund is useful when an investor has a certain level of risk tolerance.

Target Zone Under a managed float, the ideal range of exchange rates of a currency that a government seeks to maintain. The target zone may encourage a weak currency regime in order to encourage exports or a strong currency to reduce inflationary pressures. The central bank or other relevant body intervenes in the forex market with some frequency in order to keep the exchange rate within the target zone.

Target Zone Arrangement An agreement between two countries and/or central banks to keep the exchange rates of their currencies within a certain range of a fixed rate. A target zone arrangement combines factors of a pegged currency and a floating currency in that it allows market factors to have an effect on the exchange rate while also giving one country or the other a competitive advantage in their imports or exports.

Target-Benefit Plan A pension plan with a defined contribution but no guaranteed payout. That is, when the annuitant purchases the plan, he/she makes a contribution each month according to a formula that is most likely to result in a certain payout when he/she begins receiving payments. The formula assumes a certain interest rate and/or market movements will take place. If these do not occur according to the formula's projections, the plan's operators are under no obligation to provide the projected payout. Instead, they provide what the contributions have actually earned over the life of the pension.

Targeted Amortization Class Bond A collateralized mortgage obligation that seeks to protect investors from prepayment risk. Like PACs, a targeted amortization class bond does this by setting a schedule of payments; if prepayments of the underlying mortgages exceed a certain rate, the life of the bond is shortened. Unlike PACs, however, if prepayments fall below a certain rate, the life of the tranche is not extended. Targeted amortization class bonds help protect investors in case the holders of the underlying mortgages do not pay their mortgages back as expected.

Targeted Employment Area In the United States, a rural area or a place with an unemployment rate more than 150% of the national rate. Immigrants who wish to start businesses in a targeted unemployment area are given preferential treatment for the issue of visas. It is abbreviated as TEA.

Targeted Registered Offerings New issues of a security in the United States that are sold to foreign companies and investors in accordance with SEC guidelines. These foreign companies and investors provide a secondary market for the targeted registered offerings in their own countries.

Tariff Anomaly A situation in which the tariff on raw material imports is higher than the tariff on finished products made from those raw materials. Tariff anomalies are unusual and may encourage import of finished products, which may hurt manufacturing in the importing country.

Tariff Barrier A tariff designed to make imports more expensive than domestically produced products. That is, a tariff barrier is a tax imposed upon imports to protect local industries and companies. Critics, notably the WTO, have criticized tariff barriers because they believe they discourage international trade and because they may have net negative effects on the economy in the long run. However, proponents of tariff barriers argue that they can force countries to develop their own domestic industries. See also: Import substitution industrialization, Free trade.

Tariff Equivalent A non-tariff barrier that has the same effect as a tariff. That is, a tariff equivalent discourages imports and promotes domestic industries and companies. Examples of tariff equivalents include import quotas or licensing restrictions. The GATT and the WTO have both tried to reduce tariff equivalents to promote more international trade.

Tariff Escalation A situation in which the tariff on raw material imports is lower than the tariff on semi-finished goods, which is lower still than the tariff on finished products. Tariff escalation is the most common tariff regime.

Tariff Quota A reduced tariff applied to a certain quantity of an import. For example, a country may apply a tariff quota of 5% for the first 100,000 units of a good received each year, at which time the tariff increases to 10%.

Tariff Redundancy A policy in which a tariff is imposed or changed but it does not affect trade because some non-tariff barrier such as an import quota is already in place. Alternatively, a minute change in a tariff may be considered tariff redundancy because the change is not large enough to entice or discourage trade.

Tariff Suspension The European Union policy of temporarily or permanently waiving tariff duties on raw material and semi-finished products in order to encourage trade within the EU. Tariff suspension only applies to certain industries (notably pharmaceuticals and information technology) and is not granted for finished products.

Tassel Loafers In the construction sector, a slang term for a corporate manager when he/she visits a worksite in person. The term derives from the fact that executives on construction sites can be identified by their fancy shoes.

Tatemae A Japanese term for the feelings a person projects in public, which may or may not conform to his/her true feelings. Tatemae usually corresponds to social necessities and expectations for what one's feelings ought to be. Tatemae contrasts with honne, which is how one really feels.

Tax Abatement A reduction of taxes for a certain period or in exchange for conducting a certain task. For example, if one receives a tax credit for purchasing a house, one receives tax abatement because one pays less in taxes than he/she otherwise would. A sales tax holiday is another instance of tax abatement. Tax abatement represents a reduction of government revenue and therefore may add to a deficit.

Tax Advantage Any act or structure that reduces the amount of tax one pays. For example, one may derive a tax advantage by investing in a tax-exempt bond as opposed to a corporate bond (on which one pays taxes). Numerous tax advantages are built into tax codes in order to encourage certain behavior. For example, in the United States, one derives a tax advantage from writing off the interest on one's mortgage. This structure exists to encourage homeownership.

Tax Allowance Income that is not taxed. For example, a government may not subject the first $10,000 of earnings to an income tax or the first $20,000 in investment income to a capital gains tax.

Tax and Loan Account An account that a Federal Reserve bank maintains at a private bank containing funds from taxes and government debt. The tax and loan account finances the operations of the U.S. Treasury.

Tax and Spend A pejorative term for a political liberal in the United States. The term connotes the idea that a liberal wants to increase both taxes and government spending.

Tax Anticipation Bill A U.S. Treasury bill that an investor purchases at a discount from par and, upon maturity, uses the proceeds to pay a tax liability. Corporations and individuals with large tax liabilities are the main investors in tax anticipation bills. It should not be confused with a tax anticipation note.

Tax Anticipation Note A municipal bond, usually with a maturity of less than one year, issued on the assumption that the debt will be paid back on future tax revenue. Municipalities issue tax anticipation notes to provide cash for immediate or time sensitive needs. For example, a city may issue a bond to pay for school construction rather than wait for tax revenues to pay for it because either the school is desperately needed or construction can only occur in certain times of the year when the city is cash poor. At maturity, tax anticipation notes are paid with tax revenues in the months following the issue.

Tax Arbitrage A form of arbitrage in which one attempts to profit on price differences on the same security resulting from different tax systems in the countries or jurisdictions in which the security is traded.

Tax Assessment The determination of how much a person or company owes in taxes. One usually determines one's own tax assessment by declaring one's income and capital gains from the previous year and applying the methodology the government requires to arrive at the tax liability. The government has the right to audit any tax assessment.

Tax Audit In taxation, the process in which the tax collection agency reviews the reports of an individual or company to see if all income, deductions, and/or credits reported accurately reflect reality. This is done to ensure that each individual or company pays his/her/its full tax liability. Audits are conducted on a random basis, or when something appears remiss on a tax return. See also: Tax Avoidance, Tax Evasion.

Tax Avoidance The act or practice of taking steps to legally reduce one's tax liability. One may do this directly by taking advantage of an applicable tax credit or tax deduction. More often, however, the term refers to a person or company making trades or conducting other activities specifically to avoid taxes. For example, one may sell a stock at a loss to offset a gain on the sale of another stock. It is important to note that tax avoidance is different from tax evasion, which is the minimization of one's tax liability through illegal means, though it is generally acknowledged that the line between the two can be murky.

Tax Base The value of all assets that a government may tax. The tax base may increase for a number of reasons, particularly with the creation of wealth or when persons with high income move to an area. The tax base is particularly important to local governments because persons with large amounts of assets can move in and out with relative ease. The tax base is also the reason that government revenues tend to increase during economic growth and shrink during recessions.

Tax Basis 1. The cost of an asset less depreciation. This is used when calculating one's tax liability related to that asset. **2.** The all-in cost of a security when it is bought. That is, it is the price of the security plus any applicable fees. This is the price against which any capital gains or losses are calculated for tax purposes. For example, if the tax basis for a stock is $5 per share and the investor sells it for $7, then the capital gain for which one is liable is $2 per share. It is also called the cost basis or simply the basis.

Tax Books Records that a company must keep in order to comply with IRS regulations. Tax books must conform to the Generally Accepted Accounting Principles.

Tax Break 1. See: Write off. **2.** See: Tax cut.

Tax Clientele The universe of investors who have a preference for one type of security or another because that type of security minimizes their tax liabilities.

Tax Counseling for the Elderly A program the IRS sponsors to provide free tax advice and preparation to persons 60 years of age and older. The IRS provides grants to non-profit organizations to train volunteers to provide these services. While the volunteers are not paid, they are reimbursed through grants for meals, transportation, and similar expenses. The program was created in 1978.

Tax Court of Canada A court in Canada charged with settling disputes regarding taxation between the Canada Revenue Agency (and/or the Department of Justice) and individuals or companies. That is, the Tax Court of Canada resolves disagreements as to whether an individual or company paid the correct amount in federal taxes. In its proceedings, a taxpayer has the obligation to show he/she paid correctly, but the government has the obligation to prove that civil penalties should be levied. The Tax Court of Canada was established in 1983.

Tax Credit A direct, dollar-for-dollar reduction of one's tax liability. That is, if a taxpayer otherwise owes $2,000 to the government in income tax, but has $1,000 in tax credits, then the taxpayer only owes $1,000. Tax credits may be either refundable or non-refundable. A refundable tax credit means that if one's tax liability goes below zero, the government owes the taxpayer the remainder of the credit. Non-refundable credits mean that the tax liability cannot go below zero. Relatively few tax credits are refundable; most are limited to the amount of one's tax liability. However, the earned income tax credit is a common example of a refundable credit.

Tax Deductible Interest The interest one must pay on a loan that one may also remove from one's income for the purpose of calculating taxes. For example, if one pays $2,500 in interest on a student loan, one may be able to remove $2,500 from his/her taxable income. Mortgage interest is often tax deductible.

Tax Deed An instrument proving ownership of a piece of real estate purchased in a government tax sale. That is, if a government confiscates property due to lack of payment of taxes and then sells it to another party, the tax deed proves the other party's ownership.

Tax Deferral A situation in which one is not required to pay taxes one would otherwise owe until some date in the future. Most of the time, tax deferral refers to contributions to an IRA or a 401(k) or other retirement instrument. Under many structures, one is able to make contributions from one's pre-tax income; this means that taxation is deferred until withdrawals are made, generally after retirement.

Tax Deferral Option The right of a taxpayer to refrain from paying capital gains tax on the price appreciation of an asset until he/she has locked in that appreciation by selling the asset. Suppose one bought a stock at $5 and its price is currently $15. Theoretically, the person owes capital gains tax on the extra $10, but the tax deferral option means that he/she will not have to pay until he/she sells the stock.

Tax Deposit In the United States, payment of taxes through a Federal Reserve bank or other designated institution rather than directly to the IRS. Tax deposits are used for corporate taxes, withholding taxes and excise taxes.

Tax Deposit Certificate In the United Kingdom, an account into which one may deposit a future tax liability for later payment to Inland Revenue. In the meantime, the deposit earns interest, which the taxpayer may keep. See also: Certificate of Deposit.

Tax Differential View of Dividend Policy A theory stating that investors prefer capital gains to dividends because capital gains are usually taxed at a lower rate. A company whose management subscribes to this theory may concentrate on increasing its share price and is likely to have a low target payout ratio.

Tax Equity And Fiscal Responsibility Act of 1982 Legislation in the United States, passed in 1982, that rolled back some of the tax cuts the federal government enacted the previous year. It repealed accelerated depreciation deductions and created a 10% withholding tax on all dividends sent to accounts without tax identification numbers. It also increased the unemployment tax. While TEFRA raised taxes, they remained well below what they were prior to Ronald Reagan's accession to the presidency. See also: Reaganomics.

Tax Evasion An illegal act or practice of not paying one's true tax liability. One may do this directly simply by not paying taxes in a given year. More often, however, the term refers to a person or company hiding assets or income in certain vehicles deemed to be improper by the IRS. It is important to note that tax evasion is different from tax avoidance, which is the minimization of one's tax liability through legal means, though it is generally acknowledged that there is a fine line between the two. See also: Shell corporation, Tax haven.

Tax Exempt Describing income or organization that is not subject to taxation. Examples of tax exempt organizations include religious groups and charities. Additionally, certain income an individual or corporation derives may be tax exempt. For example, coupons from a municipal bond are tax exempt at the federal level. See also: Tax credit, tax deduction.

Tax Exile A person who resides outside his/her country of citizenship in order to avoid paying taxes in that country. For example, one may earn most of one's income from a business in France but actually live in Monaco, where there are no taxes. Tax exiles often may not go to their home country more than a certain number of days per year in order to avoid taxes legally. American citizens may not be tax exiles legally unless they leave the United State, earn no money in the United States, and renounce their citizenship.

Tax Expenditure The way in which a government uses a tax code to spend money. For example, suppose a government offers a tax credit for adopting a child. In such a case, an adoptive parent would pay less in taxes than he/she otherwise would, effectively receiving a subsidy from the government for adopting a child. Tax expenditures are popular ways for governments to encourage behaviors such as purchasing a home or having children.

Tax Free Acquisition A merger where the value of the assets a stockholder receives at the end of the transaction is substantially the same as the value of assets before the transaction began. For tax purposes, stockholders are treated as having kept their old shares, and are therefore not subject to capital gains taxes.

Tax Haven A country that has a low tax liability compared to other countries or no taxes at all. Some countries deliberately set themselves up as tax havens in order to encourage international corporations to register themselves there. Some countries that are not tax havens have loopholes in their tax codes in order to allow certain persons and companies to place some of their assets in an account in a tax haven.

Tax Haven Affiliate A wholly owned subsidiary of an American corporation in a foreign tax haven. Prior to the Tax Reform Act of 1986, a corporation could avoid taxes by placing a certain amount of its income in its tax haven affiliate, but this benefit is generally no longer permissible.

Tax Holiday A temporary suspension of a tax, especially a sales tax. Jurisdictions declare tax holidays at certain times of the year on the theory that doing so will stimulate consumer spending and thereby induce economic growth. Some U.S. states routinely declare tax holidays before school begins each year, for example. Critics of tax holidays maintain that they deprive the jurisdictions of revenue and that their effect on growth is overstated.

Tax Identification Number A number the IRS assigns to businesses and other entities, such as trusts, for tax purposes. While the TIN exists for a variety of reasons, its main function is to ensure that each organization is billed for its own taxes, and not those of another entity with the same name. Social Security numbers serve as TINs for individuals.

Tax Liability The money one owes to the government in a given year. At its most basic, a tax liability is usually a certain percentage of one's income, and varies according to income. That is, one who makes $100,000 per year usually has a higher tax liability than one who makes $25,000. Different taxable events command different tax liabilities. For example, income taxes are usually higher than capital gains taxes. Certain taxable events do not occur for everyone in every year; for example, inheritance taxes only apply when someone dies. See also: Tax bracket.

Tax Lien A claim on private property by a government that allows that government to take over and sell the property until it recovers what its owner owes in taxes. That is, if a taxpayer does not pay the appropriate amount in taxes and steadfastly refuses to do so, the government has the right to confiscate and sell his/her property until it takes in what the taxpayer owes. An investor may buy a tax lien from the government.

Tax Lien Certificate A security one may purchase giving the owner the right to collect unpaid property taxes from a property on which there is a tax lien. The tax lien certificate does not guarantee that the property owner will actually pay, and, for that reason, it is a risky investment. A tax lien certificate exists to preserve the cash flow of the municipality assessing the tax.

Tax Loophole A deliberate or accidental provision in tax law that allows an individual or corporation to be exempt from some provision. Most loopholes are deliberate and are created to ensure that the law is not draconian, to please a lobbyist, or for some other reason. For example, a country may pass a law requiring most companies to pay taxes on their net assets each year. However, it may contain a loophole allowing the exemption of companies that would find this tax too difficult or expensive. Occasionally, the government may close a loophole, which means that it takes away the exemption.

Tax Loss A loss of value that results in a tax deduction. A tax loss may be a business loss or it may be the loss of a personal asset such as a house. For example, the amount one spends repairing a car after a wreck may be a tax loss. In order to qualify as deductible, the loss must not be covered by insurance and (for the loss of an asset) must be the result of a real disaster such as theft. Gradual damage generally does not qualify.

Tax Loss Harvesting The sale of securities at a loss toward the end of a calendar year. One conducts tax loss harvesting to offset the losses against gains made earlier in the year. This reduces one's tax liability. In order for tax loss harvesting to work properly, one must offset short-term losses against short-term gains, and long-term losses against long-term gains. This is because of the difference between income taxes (paid on short-term gains) and capital gains taxes (paid on long-term gains).

Tax Lot Accounting A method of accounting for a portfolio in which one keeps a record of the purchase price and sale price of each security in the portfolio, along with each one's cost basis and transaction size. One maintains the same record for each security even if one performs more than one transaction with it. The goal of tax lot accounting is to minimize one's taxes by reducing the net present value for accounting purposes.

Tax Map An electronic or written document detailing the size and value of a piece of taxable real estate, among other information. A tax map may be useful to a potential buyer. Written tax maps are kept in the local tax office.

Tax Opinion An official opinion by an attorney stating how an investment (especially a bond) should be treated for tax purposes. For example, in the case of a municipal bond, the issuer may hire an attorney to write a tax opinion detailing how it complies with requirements exempting the interest from taxation.

Tax Planning The practice of making adjustments so as to reduce one's tax liability to the least possible amount. For example, one may wait to sell a security until the next tax year so as not to realize capital gains.

Tax Preference Item Income or other event that is excluded when calculating one's ordinary tax liability but is included when calculating one's liability for the alternative minimum tax. That is, a tax preference item is an item that would be tax deductible under normal circumstances but is not for purposes of the alternative minimum tax. Examples include depreciation and some interest on municipal bonds.

Tax Preparation Services The act of writing and sometimes filing a tax return for an individual or corporation in exchange for a fee. The individual or corporation must turn over relevant information to the provider of tax preparation services in order to ensure the return is accurate. Both individual accountants and large firms may offer tax preparation services.

Tax Rate A percentage of one's income that one must pay in taxes. Tax rates vary according to incomes. That is, one who makes $100,000 per year usually has a higher tax rate than one who makes $25,000. See also: Marginal tax rate, Average tax rate.

Tax Reform Act of 1976 Legislation in the United States that expanded various tax credits and deductions. Among other provisions, it increased the standard deduction to 16% and created a $175,000 exemption from the estate tax.

Tax Reform Act of 1986 Legislation in the United States dictating the reduced marginal tax rates, the number of tax brackets, and the deductions and tax shelters that individuals can have. It also increased corporate tax rates and equalized capital gains tax and income tax rates. It was designed to be revenue neutral; this was accomplished by reducing deductions to offset the lower tax rates. It also changed incentives; for example, it increased the home mortgage interest deduction to encourage home ownership. While proponents hail this Act as a major tax cut, critics maintain that it did little to accomplish its main goal of simplifying the tax code. See also: Economic Recovery Tax Act of 1981.

Tax Refund Money given back to a taxpayer if he/she/it has paid too much in taxes for a given year. Tax refunds are most common for employees from whose paychecks too much has been withheld because of deductions and credits for which the withholding does not account. One may only collect a tax refund for a certain number of years after it was originally due.

Tax Return A document that individuals and some corporations must file with the tax collection agency each year. The tax return calculates income, deductions, and credits, and ultimately determines how much tax the filer owes for the year. In the United States, Form 1040 is the basic tax return form. See also: 1040EZ.

Tax Sale The sale of real estate in order to pay back taxes. In a tax sale, the taxing authority seizes the property for non-payment and then conducts the sale, generally selling to the highest bidder. For example, the IRS may hold a tax sale of a person's house for chronic non-payment of income taxes.

Tax Schedule The amount of tax one owes depending on one's filing status. That is, in addition to income, the amount one is assessed in tax depends on whether one files as a single person, married filing jointly, married filing separately, or head of household.

Tax Selling 1. The act or practice of selling stock or other securities at a loss in order to offset gains from other investment or income. In the United States, one is able to reduce one's taxable income by the amount one has lost in investing. Therefore, it is common to sell securities that have declined anyway at the end of the year and thereby reduce one's tax liability. **2.** The act or practice of selling stock or other securities at a gain in order to reduce an expected higher tax liability. Tax selling at a gain is common in December when an investor expects his/her income to be higher the following year. Thus, one pays the higher income tax on the gains this year rather than pay the higher still gains next year.

Tax Shelter An investment vehicle that reduces one's tax liability. For example, a 401(k) defers taxation until withdrawal from the account and may therefore be considered a tax shelter. Tax shelters are legal unless their sole purpose is to avoid taxes. See also: Tax evasion.

Tax Shield The reduction of one's taxable income as the result of a properly qualified deduction. Examples of tax shields include mortgage interest deductions, charitable donations, and others. The mortgage interest deduction is a particularly important tax shield to middle-class households because the value of their properties constitutes the greatest part of their net worths. Creating tax shields is also important to wealthy individuals to help them avoid as many taxes as possible.

Tax Software Any of a number of computer programs purporting to help the user complete his/her own tax forms without the expense of hiring an accountant or the potentially expensive possibility of overlooking certain deductions and credits. Most of these programs explain basic tax information to the user, and some use a series of questions and answers to determine what deductions and credits most likely apply to the user. While tax software was originally bought and installed on one's personal computer, programs are increasingly available online.

Tax Status Election The decision by a person or company about one's filing status. For example, a married person may file jointly with, or separately from, his/her spouse. Likewise, a company often may file as an S corporation or a C corporation. One makes a tax status election depending on one's circumstances and the filing status that is most advantageous.

Tax Stop A clause in a lease stating that the lessee is responsible for payment of property taxes should they rise above a certain level. The tax stop limits the lessor's liability for property taxes.

Tax Straddle A practice in which two futures or options contracts, one expected to gain and one expected to lose, are sold in two different tax years. The contract expected to lose is sold at the end of one tax year while the one showing a gain is sold at the beginning of the following year. This is done in order to avoid taxation on a futures or option until the following year. This was formerly a common practice until the IRS began to require that all open positions be treated as if they were closed on the last day of the tax year for tax purposes. See also: Form 6781.

Tax Swap A situation in which an investor sells a long position to claim a capital loss for tax purposes and immediately buys an equivalent position in a similar (but not the same) company or industry. A tax swap allows the investor to reduce his/her tax liability while not running afoul of the wash sale rule, which states that one cannot claim a capital loss for tax purposes if one repurchases the same position within 30 days. See also: Wash sale.

Tax Table In American taxation, a table showing the tax due at a certain level of income and/or capital gain. A tax table may state a dollar amount, a percentage, or a combination in order to determine the tax liability of a taxpayer. For example, taxpayers may pay 25% of their income in taxes up to a certain amount, and 35% of everything earned over that amount. A tax table takes these and averages them so a taxpayer may have a convenient way to know how much he/she will pay in taxes for a given year. The IRS publishes a tax table every year to assist persons earning less than $100,000 per year to determine their tax liability. See also: Progressive taxation.

Tax Treaty A treaty between two countries governing double taxation and other matters when a company or individual owes taxes to both countries. Tax treaties are written because double taxation with no exceptions could result in a decrease in trade between the two countries. Most countries (except tax havens) have entered into tax treaties with their trading partners and others. A tax treaty is also called a bilateral tax agreement.

Tax Umbrella A tax loss carryforward from a previous year. A tax loss carryforward is a business loss in one year that may be used for up to five years to offset profits in future years. For example, if a business loses $800,000 in year one but makes a $1 million profit in year three, it may only be taxed for $200,000 in income for year three. The remaining $800,000 is a tax umbrella.

Tax Value The amount that a real estate owner pays in property taxes each year. The municipal government assesses and updates the tax value periodically, basing each assessment on the appraised value of the real estate.

Tax Year The year during which one's taxable income is considered. That is, the tax year is any 12-month period during which a government calculates one's tax liability. Normally, this is simply the calendar year, but it may also be a fiscal year.

Taxable Acquisition A merger where the value of the assets a stockholder receives at the end of the transaction is substantially different from the value of assets before the transaction began. For tax purposes, stockholders are treated as having sold their shares, and are therefore subject to capital gains taxes.

Taxable Bond A bond on which the yield is taxable. All corporate bonds and some municipal bonds are taxable. On a taxable bond, one is usually assessed capital gains tax on the coupon payments. One is also liable for taxation if the bond was issued at a discount and redeemed at face value. See also: Tax-exempt bond.

Taxable Equivalent Yield The yield of a taxable investment that equals the yield of a tax-free investment with a lower stated yield. A corporate bond yields less than its stated interest rate because of taxation, whereas a tax-exempt municipal bond does not. Thus, a municipal bond paying a lower interest rate will often net the bondholder more than a corporate bond with a slightly higher interest rate, depending upon one's tax bracket. The taxable equivalent yield is the extra yield required on a corporate bond to equal the yield of a municipal bond. See also: Municipals-over-bonds spread, After-tax basis.

Taxable Estate The value of an individual's estate that is subject to taxation. The taxable estate includes the actual value of the estate and most gifts and transfers made for a certain period of time before death. It is important to note that any assets left to a surviving spouse and all assets under a certain dollar amount (under $1 million, depending on the year) are usually excluded from the taxable estate. See also: Estate tax.

Taxable Event A transaction or other action that results in one receiving income that may be taxed. Common taxable events are the reception of a paycheck or the sale of stock for a profit. Often, investors wait to sell securities until a certain time (such as a new calendar year) in order to minimize the taxable events that occur in a given period of time.

Taxable Gain Any income or other money that is subject to taxation.

Taxable Income In U.S. tax, an individual's income after all deductions. Individuals and corporations may eliminate certain expenses from their incomes for tax purposes. For example, if someone makes $30,000 per year and spends $4,000 on tuition for college, that person's taxable income is reduced to only $26,000, and the person pays a portion of that to the government. Everyone may take a standard deduction or may itemize deductions to arrive at one's taxable income. In corporations, profits may be offset by business losses to arrive at the taxable income. See also: Adjusted gross income, Modified adjusted gross income.

Taxable Municipal Bond A municipal bond in which a local government entity seeks to raise money for a private company with no obvious public benefit. The municipality issues a taxable municipal bond when it wishes to attract a business and the jobs it would bring to the area, especially when the business may be otherwise unable to obtain financing for the project. While this may benefit the area in the long term, the bond remains taxable unless then municipality can prove that a public benefit derives directly from the bond. Taxable municipal bonds generally are not guaranteed by the revenue of the municipality. See also: Private activity bonds.

Taxable Person The person or company from whom a government collects a value-added tax. A value-added tax is a tax on the new value of a good or service at each stage of the production process. The taxable person is thus assessed a tax on the value added to the product, rather than the total value of the sale. The taxable person is always the seller, though the tax is almost always passed on to the customer in the form of a higher price.

Taxable Security A security with interest or dividends subject to taxation. All securities other than some government bonds are taxable securities. See also: Tax Exempt Security.

Taxable Transaction A transaction that results in one receiving income that may be taxed. Common taxable transactions are the reception of a paycheck or the sale of stock for a profit. Often, investors wait to sell securities until a certain time (such as a new calendar year) in order to minimize the taxable transactions that occur in a given period of time.

Tax-Appraised Value The value of a property as estimated by a person licensed to do so for tax purposes. The tax-appraised value may take into account the quality of the property, values of surrounding properties, and market conditions in the area. It is important for determining the property taxes for which the owner is liable. See also: Mill Rate.

Tax-Deductible Interest Interest paid on certain loans that one may take off of one's taxable income. For example, in the United States, interest on mortgage loans and student loans are deductible, at least up to a certain limit. For example, if a person spends $1,200 in student loan interest in a year, he may reduce his taxable income by $1,200.

Tax-Deferred Account 1. See: 401(k). 2. See: Traditional IRA.

Tax-Deferred Annuity A retirement plan in which an employee makes tax-deferred contributions from his/her pre-tax income. The employee is not taxed on the contribution until he/she begins to make withdrawals after retirement. Strictly speaking, a 401(k) is a tax-deferred annuity, but the term especially applies to a 403(b) plan, which is directed at teachers and employees of tax-exempt organizations, such as charities or churches.

Tax-Deferred Contribution A contribution to a retirement plan on which the contributor does not pay taxes until a later date. One reduces one's taxable income by the amount of the tax-deferred contributions, shielding those contributions from taxation. However, one eventually pays taxes on these contributions when one begins to make withdrawals from the retirement plan. Those contributions (and their investment income) are taxed as ordinary income upon withdrawal. One makes tax-deferred contributions to reduce one's tax liability in the near term in hopes that one's income (and therefore one's tax liability) will be lower after retirement.

Tax-Deferred Income Any income that one earns but does not receive until a later date, resulting in a situation in which taxes on the income are not paid until later. Common examples of tax-deferred income fall into two broad categories. The first is income in certain retirement accounts; the account holder is not liable for taxes until funds are disbursed. The second is the capital gain on some bonds such as U.S. Treasury securities; taxes on these gains are deferred until maturity. It is important to note that tax-deferred income is not the same as tax-free income, which has no tax liability at all.

Tax-Deferred Retirement Plan A retirement investment plan in which a contributor does not pay taxes on contributions until after withdrawal at retirement. That is, one places a portion of his/her pre-tax income into a retirement account that allows it to be invested. Taxation is deferred until withdrawal from the account following retirement. Presumably, one's tax rate will be lower after retirement because one's income is usually lower after retirement. Common examples of tax-deferred retirement plans include IRAs and traditional 401(k)s. Some employers make matching contributions to these plans.

Tax-Efficient Fund A mutual fund that invests in securities thought to give fund shareholders the least possible tax liability. Common securities in which a tax-efficient fund invests are municipal bonds, which are usually tax-free, and non-dividend paying stocks, which reduce a shareholder's capital gains tax liability. Tax-efficient funds often retain stocks in which they invest, as stocks held for more than a year are taxed at a lower capital gains rate. They are often thought of as an alternative to tax-deferred investment vehicles, such as 401(k)s and IRAs.

Tax-Equivalent Income The income one derives from a taxable investment that equals the yield of a tax-free investment with less income. A corporate bond yields less than its stated interest rate because of taxation, whereas a tax-exempt municipal bond does not. Thus, a municipal bond that pays a lower interest rate will often net the bondholder more than a corporate bond with a slightly higher interest rate, depending upon one's tax bracket. The tax equivalent income is the extra income required from a corporate bond to equal the post-tax income of a municipal bond. See also: Municipals-over-bonds spread, After-tax basis.

Tax-Equivalent Yield The yield of a taxable investment that equals the yield of a tax-free investment with a lower stated yield. A corporate bond yields less than its stated interest rate because of taxation whereas a tax-exempt municipal bond does not. Thus, a municipal bond that pays a lower interest rate will often net the bondholder more than a corporate bond with a slightly higher interest rate, depending upon one's tax bracket. The tax equivalent yield is the extra yield required on a corporate bond to equal the post-tax yield of a municipal bond. See also: Municipals-over-bonds spread, After-tax basis.

Tax-Exempt Bond A bond issued by a local or state government. Municipal bonds are usually used to raise capital for improvements in infrastructure or other aspects of the municipality. For example, a city or school district may issue a tax-exempt bond to build a new school or a new playground. They are called tax-exempt bonds because they are exempt from federal income taxes and sometimes from state and local taxes as well. Tax-exempt bonds usually pay lower coupons than corporate bonds, but because the yield is tax-free, the after-tax basis may be higher for the tax-exempt bond. Risk varies according to the municipality and the particular type of bond.

Tax-Exempt Commercial Paper A short-term, unsecured loan issued by an organization that provides exemption from at least some taxes on its yield. Universities are the most common issuers of tax-exempt commercial papers; they do so with the permission of the government, which wants to help the universities fund their operations without directly injecting cash. Like other commercial papers, tax-exempt commercial papers are rarely for a term longer than a few months and they are usually issued at a discount. They are usually issued to cover short-term liabilities.

Tax-Exempt Income Income that is not subject to taxation. Additionally, certain income an individual or corporation derives may be tax exempt, even though the individual or corporation would owe taxes otherwise. For example, coupons from a municipal bond are tax exempt at the federal level. See also: Tax credit, tax deduction.

Tax-Exempt Income Fund An income fund that invests predominantly or exclusively in securities exempt from taxes, at least at the federal level. The easiest investment for such a fund is in U.S. Treasury securities.

Tax-Exempt Interest In the United States, interest on a bond not subject to federal taxes. Generally speaking, tax-exempt interest comes from a municipal bond. It is also important to tax-efficient funds because dividends on these funds coming from tax-exempt interest are also tax free. However, tax-exempt interest is required to be reported to the IRS and may affect one in other ways, notably on eligibility for Social Security benefits.

Tax-Exempt Money Market Fund A mutual fund that invests predominantly or exclusively in short-term municipal bonds. The returns on a short-term municipal bond fund derive from coupons on the municipal bonds, and are therefore tax exempt. The short-time frame of the bonds makes the fund quite liquid. As a result, these funds are beneficial for short term investors who wish to minimize their tax liability.

Tax-Exempt Property Real estate that is not subject to property tax. A tax-exempt property may be owned by a government or by a charity, especially a house of worship. See also: Waqf.

Tax-Exempt Sector The market for investments exempt from federal taxes. All, or nearly all, investments in the tax-exempt sector are municipal bonds. This is because U.S. law forbids the federal government from taxing debt issues made by state and local government bodies.

Tax-Free Exchange Under Section 1031 of the Internal Revenue Code, the exchange of two assets of like kind, even if of different quality, that are used for a business or for investment purposes. The goods exchanged are not assessed capital gains taxes. More precisely, capital gains taxes are deferred until an asset is resold with no intention of reinvestment. Tax-free exchanges also apply if one sells an asset with the intention to use the proceeds to buy a similar asset. For example, if a farmer sells his farm and uses the money to buy another farm, capital gains taxes are likely deferred on the money he made on the sale of the first farm. The same would be true if the he traded farm for farm.

Tax-Free Investment An investment, the income from which is not subject to taxation. Certain income an individual or corporation derives may be tax free, even though the individual or corporation would owe taxes otherwise. For example, coupons from a municipal bond are tax-free investments at the federal level. See also: Tax credit, tax deduction.

Tax-Loss Selling The act or practice of selling stock or other securities at a loss in order to offset gains from other investment or income. In the United States, one is able to reduce one's taxable income by the amount one has lost in investing. Therefore, it is common to sell securities that have declined anyway at the end of the year and thereby reduce one's tax liability.

Tax-Managed Mutual Fund A mutual fund that invests in securities thought to have given fund shareholders the least possible tax liability. Common securities in which a tax-managed fund invests are municipal bonds, which are usually tax-free, and non-dividend paying stocks, which reduce a shareholder's capital gains tax liability. Tax-managed funds often hold on to stocks in which they invest, as stocks held for more than a year are taxed at a lower capital gains rate. They are often thought of as an alternative to tax-deferred investment vehicles, such as 401(k)s and IRAs.

Taxpayer A person who pays taxes. In the United States, nearly everyone is a taxpayer at some level because almost everyone pays FICA taxes, sales taxes and other taxes. Colloquially, however, the word refers to persons who pay income and capital gains taxes. The word is sometimes used in a political context to make both conservative and liberal arguments.

Taxpayer Advocate Service An office within the IRS that provides free assistance to individual and corporate taxpayers who are experiencing trouble with the IRS. If one is facing immediate IRS action and has experienced a delay of at least 30 days (or the IRS has not resolved the problem by a promised date), Taxpayer Advocate Service may be able to stop asset seizures and similar measures while one's case is being processed. It was established in 1996.

Taxpayer Relief Act of 1997 Legislation in the United States devoted exclusively to lowering taxes. Among other things, it reduced the top capital gains rate to 20% from 28%, and nearly doubled the exemption from the estate tax. The Act also introduced a credit for each child under the age of 17 living at home; that is, a taxpayer could take a direct dollar-for-dollar reduction in his/her tax liability for each child subject to certain income limits. See also: Short-short test.

Tax-Sheltered Income Income that would normally be taxable but because of a non-cash deduction, notably depreciation, is not taxed. For example, income from the lease of a car where the lessor maintains title to the car can be tax-sheltered income because of the depreciation on the value of the car.

Tax-Timing Option An option every investor has to either sell an asset for a loss and thereby reduce one's tax liability or continue to hold it and maintain the possibility that one may eventually sell it for a gain.

Taylors Rule A general rule for central banks when deciding interest rates. The rule states that interest rates should be increased in times of high inflation and when employment is higher than full employment, and should be decreased in periods of low inflations and higher unemployment. The rule states that following these principles will encourage growth while discouraging inflation. The Federal Reserve follows this rule implicitly, even though it does not explicitly endorse it.

TC 1. ISO 3166-1 alpha-2 code for the Turks and Caicos Islands. This is the code used in international transactions to and from local bank accounts. 2. ISO 3166-2 geocode for the Turks and Caicos Islands. This is used as an international standard for shipping to the Turks and Caicos Islands.

TCA GOST 7.67 Latin three-letter geocode for the Turks and Caicos Islands. The code is used for transactions to and from local bank accounts and for international shipping to the Turks and Caicos Islands. As with all GOST 7.67 codes, it is used primarily in Cyrillic alphabets.

TCD GOST 7.67 Latin three-letter geocode for Chad. The code is used for transactions to and from Chadian bank accounts and for international shipping to Chad. As with all GOST 7.67 codes, it is used primarily in Cyrillic alphabets.

TD 1. ISO 3166-1 alpha-2 code for the Republic of Chad. This is the code used in international transactions to and from bank accounts in Chad. 2. ISO 3166-2 geocode for Chad. This is used as an international standard for shipping to Chad. Each region in Chad has its own code with the prefix "TD." For example, the code for the Region of Batha is ISO 3166-2:TD-BA.

TD Ameritrade A company that offers brokerage services over the Internet. It allows clients to buy, sell, and short sell stocks, bonds, mutual funds, and other investment vehicles. A client manages his/her online brokerage account by giving orders online, which TD Ameritrade then fills. TD Ameritrade sometimes charges a flat fee per trade (as opposed to a commission) for conducting transactions, but it does not provide individual investment advisory services. It was established in 1983 as a clearing broker and launched the first online brokerage service for individuals in 1996. It is based in Omaha, Nebraska.

Tea Money Informal; a bribe made for business purposes in China.

Tear Sheet Informal; a brief statement of information Standard & Poor's compiles and disseminates on various publicly-traded companies. Investment advisers and brokers often share tear sheets with clients to encourage them to invest in certain companies. Originally, these were actual one-page summaries that one could tear out of a book, but most tear sheets are now available online.

Teaser Rate In an adjustable-rate mortgage, an initial interest rate that one pays for a certain period of time, at which point the interest rate rises. A teaser rate exists in order to encourage people who would otherwise be unable to qualify for a mortgage to be able to buy a house. While a lender is required to disclose the higher interest rate and payment, their existence has been accused of creating a perverse incentive for unqualified borrowers to buy houses. Many believe this contributed to the housing bubble and the subsequent credit crunch.

Tech Street Informal; the technology sector. Stocks such as Intel and Apple are said to be on Tech Street. The term is a reference to Wall Street.

Technical Analysis The practice of using statistics to determine trends in security prices and make or recommend investment decisions based on those trends. Technical analysis does not attempt to determine the intrinsic value of securities, but instead focuses on matters such as trade volume, demand, and volatility. Technical analysts evaluate short-term trends almost exclusively, which is both a strength and a weakness in their analysis. They are sometimes called chartists because of the importance charts have in technical analysis. See also: Fundamental analysis.

Technical Analyst A person who engages in technical analysis, especially professionally. Technical analysts use statistics to determine trends in security prices, and make or recommend investment decisions based on those trends. They do not attempt to determine the intrinsic value of securities, but instead focus on matters such as trade volume, demand, and volatility. Technical analysts often evaluate short-term trends almost exclusively, which is both a strength and a weakness in their analysis. They are sometimes called chartists because of the importance charts have in technical analysis. See also: Fundamental analysis.

Technical Bankruptcy The state of a person or company that has defaulted on a liability and lacks the ability to pay it, but has not yet filed for bankruptcy or been declared bankrupt by a court.

Technical Condition of a Market In a given market, activities that affect the supply or demand for a security. For example, if there are equal numbers of buyers and sellers of a security, a number of factors could drive the price down (creating more buyers) or drive it up (creating more sellers). An increase in buyers results in a greater demand for the security; equally, an increase in sellers results in a greater supply. Examples of activities that may change the technical condition of a market include stop loss orders, floating supply, and short interests.

Technical Correction A temporary decline in a stock's price after a series of extremely high gains. If a stock is overbought, its price often become unsustainably high and a technical correction brings it back to a level that ideally reflects its true value.

Technical Descriptors Statistics used to determine trends in security prices, and make or recommend investment decisions based on those trends. In general, technical descriptors are available in chart patterns. Technical descriptors do not show the intrinsic value of securities, but instead focus on matters such as trade volume, demand, and volatility. Technical descriptors are useful for short-term trends almost exclusively, which is both a strength and a weakness in their analysis. See also: Technical Analysis.

Technical Forecasting The practice of using statistics to determine future trends in security prices and make or recommend investment decisions based on those expected trends. Technical forecasting does not attempt to determine the intrinsic value of securities, but instead focuses on matters such as trade volume, demand, and volatility. Technical forecasters evaluate short-term trends almost exclusively, which is both a strength and a weakness in their analysis. See also: Fundamental Analysis.

Technical Indicator Statistical information that is used to determine future trends in security prices and to make or recommend investment decisions based on those trends. Technical indicators have nothing to do with the intrinsic value of securities, but instead focus on matters such as trade volume, the number of odd-lot sales or short sales, and volatility. Technical indicators show short-term trends almost exclusively; this is both a strength and a weakness in their analysis. See also: Economic indicator.

Technical Inflection Point In technical analysis, a support level or resistance level. The support level is the price below which a security rarely falls. Reaching the support level is an indication to buy, as the price generally rises. The resistance level is the price above which a security rarely rises, and is therefore an indication to sell. A technical inflection point may be a sign to buy or sell a security. That is, a technical inflection points requires some action from the security holders.

Technical Rally An increase in a security's price following a downward trend. It is important to note that a technical rally is caused by technical factors, rather than by any fundamental changes to the security. For example, an increase in price resulting from investors' needs to buy the security to return shares sold on margin is a technical rally. An actual change to the security's value, such as the announcement of stronger-than-usual sales, may result in an increase in the share price, but this is not considered a technical rally.

Technical Trader A person who uses technical analysis to make investment decisions. Technical traders use statistics to determine trends in security prices, and decide to buy or sell based on those trends. These traders do not attempt to determine the intrinsic value of securities, but instead focus on matters such as trade volume, demand, and volatility. Technical traders often evaluate short-term trends almost exclusively, which has both positive and negative consequences for their analysis.

Technically Strong Market In technical analysis, a market that is rising on high volume or falling on low volume. Technical strength is important to determining a security's or market's momentum. Rising on high volume or falling on low volume means that it is likely that the security or market is on a bullish trend. See also: Technically weak market.

Technically Weak Market In technical analysis, a market that is falling on high volume or rising on low volume. Technical weakness or strength is important to determining a security's or market's momentum. Falling on high volume or rising on low volume means that it is likely that the security or market is on a bearish trend.

Technological Unemployment Unemployment that occurs because advances in machinery renders workers redundant. For example, a machine that mass produces shoes may cause a cobbler to lose his business. Technological unemployment is the result of a disparity between the collective skills of the workforce of an economy and the skills necessary to perform the available jobs. As such, it is a type of structural unemployment.

Technology Company A company that sells products involving sophisticated technology. Commonly, high-technology companies deal in electronics, computers and scientific research. Investing in high-technology companies is high risk because the market is stiffly competitive, but it may yield a high return, particularly if a technology suddenly becomes very popular. This was the case in the 1990s when the Internet became a part of daily life. Many high-technology stocks trade on NASDAQ. See also: Dot-com bubble.

Ted Spread A measure of credit risk, calculated by subtracting the price of three-month U.S. Treasury securities and three-month eurodollar contracts. These contracts must have the same expiration month. Because Treasury securities are risk-free and eurodollar contracts are not, an increased Ted spread indicates a greater likelihood of default.

Ted Turner An American media businessman. Born in 1938, he took over his father's advertising company when he was only 24. He used developing satellite technology to pioneer advances in cable television; he was the first person to broadcast a local station nationally. In 1980, he founded CNN, the first 24-hour news channel. He also became the largest landowner in the United States.

Teenage Scribblers A derogatory term for currency analysts and traders on the London markets. Teenage scribblers were blamed, rightly or wrongly, for some of the United Kingdom's financial woes in the 1980s and 1990s.

Teenie 1. Prior to decimalization, one-sixteenth of one point. That is, if a stock price falls a teenie, it falls 1/16 of a dollar. **2.** After decimalization, one cent.

Tefach An ancient Hebrew unit of length approximately equivalent to eight or nine centimeters.

Tehsil In India and most of Pakistan, a political subdivision equivalent to a county.

Tel Aviv Stock Exchange The only stock exchange in Israel. Its roots can be traced back to 1935. Its trading became fully electronic in 1999. See also: TA-100 Index.

Telecommunications Act of 1996 Legislation in the United States that deregulated telecommunications. It changed regulations for telephones, television broadcasts and cable in order to reduce barriers to entry and increase competition. It also regulated explicit material broadcast on television. See also: Communications Decency Act.

Telecommunications Consumer Protection Act of 1991 Legislation in the United States curtailing the use of unsolicited phone calls to make sales. The Act limits the hours during which a telemarketer may call, and requires that all telemarketers provide the households they call with their names and phone numbers. It further stipulates that telemarketing companies must comply with any request not to call the household back if requested. The TCPA was a precursor to the federal do-not-call list, which the Federal Communications Commission and the Federal Trade Commission created in 2003.

Telephone Banking Banking services offered over the telephone. Telephone banking often includes access to one's checking and savings accounts and the ability to view balances, make transfers and so forth. Generally, one must state one's social security number, answer a security question or provide some other information in order to verify that one is really the account holder. Many banks (though not all) offer telephone banking without any additional fees. See also: Online banking.

Telephone Booth Informal; a cubicle containing a telephone on the New York Stock Exchange. Member firms use these telephones to take orders for trade, which are then executed on the trading floor. Members then use the telephone booth to communicate the trade back to a client. With the advent of Blackberries and other personal digital devices, some members have begun using these instead of the telephone booths.

Telephone Consumer Protection Act Legislation in the United States, enacted in 1991, restricting the activities of telemarketers. It prohibits, for example, unsolicited faxes and phone calls after 9 p.m. It also requires telemarketers to maintain do not call lists for persons who opt out of unsolicited phone calls. The Act was intended to protect consumers.

Telephone Switching An order given over a telephone, especially to transfer assets from one mutual fund or annuity to another. A client has the right to call his/her investment adviser and direct that money be invested only in certain ways. See also: Telephone booth.

Teletubbie A derogatory slang term for financial analysts who make regular news appearances and give financial advice on television.

Temporal Method In accounting, a convention where assets and liabilities listed according to their market cost and denominated in a foreign currency are translated to the domestic currency at the current exchange rate while all assets and liabilities listed at their historical cost are translated at the exchange rate in effect when each asset or liability was acquired. See also: Current/Noncurrent Method.

Temporarily Restricted Funds In a non-profit's year-end financial statement, money that may not be spent for a certain period of time except for specified purposes. Temporarily restricted funds, which may come from restricted donations, are expected to be spent in fairly short order.

Temporarily Restricted Net Assets Cash or other assets that are not needed to pay liabilities but still may not be spent freely for a period of time. Temporarily restricted net assets may be earmarked for a specific purpose; alternately, law or regulation may require the restriction of some net assets until certain benchmarks are met.

Temporary Account An account whose balance is quickly reduced to zero after its creation by a company. For example, a company may create a temporary account for dividends after they are announced but before they are distributed. After distribution, the temporary account goes to zero. A temporary account is also called a nominal account.

Temporary Assets A subset of a company's current assets that changes according to seasonal fluctuations. For example, a retail store's current inventory may include holiday decorations around Christmas. These decorations would be temporary assets with respect to the remainder of the store's inventory.

Temporary Investment An investment in short-term, low-risk securities such as Treasury bills, money markets and so forth. A temporary investment aims to protect the funds invested in it while also providing a (low) return.

Temporary Liquidity Guarantee Program A rule adopted by the FDIC guaranteeing certain transaction accounts and unsecured loans that banks make to one another. The rule was implemented in 2008 to promote liquidity in interbank lending in the wake of the global financial crisis that started that year. It began to expire in 2010, though the Dodd-Frank Act made certain portions permanent.

Ten Largest Holdings The percentages of a portfolio's total holdings that come from its 10 largest investments. That is, a portfolio's 10 largest holdings are simply the 10 investments that have the highest degree of representation. The smaller the 10 largest holding are, the more diversified the portfolio is.

Ten Windows Ten companies in China permitted to borrow money from financial institutions outside China.

Tenancy at Will A lease binding the parties to each other on a month-to-month basis. A tenancy at will occurs because of some defect in the original lease that renders its term invalid.

Tenancy by the Entirety The joint ownership of a property with rights of survivorship. In other words, a property with tenancy by the entirety does not become part of a decedent's estate; rather, the other tenants continue to own the property. Couples may be tenants by entirety on a jointly-owned house, for example. Likewise, two business partners may be tenants by entirety on a business property: if two persons own an apartment complex and one of them dies, the whole of the complex belongs to the co-owner and not the decedent's heirs. It is important to note, however, that the decedent's liabilities may remain attached to this property and may be used to pay off creditors, even if the creditor had nothing to do with the property in question.

Tenancy in Common A way for two or more persons to own property together. Tenants in common may own equal or unequal shares of the property, and there are no rights of survivorship. That is, when one of the co-owners dies, his/her share of the property becomes part of his/her estate and passes on to heirs. This is an arrangement common in joint business ventures: if two persons own an apartment complex and one of them dies, his/her share of the complex passes to his/her beneficiaries and does not pass to the other co-owner.

Tenant One who has obtained the right to use land, a house, and/or other property owned by someone else. Sometimes, this includes the right to develop land belonging to another, but normally it is the right to live on an already developed property. The contract governing a lessee's rights is a lease; it generally includes the lessee's right to use the property under certain conditions without undue interference from the lessor for the period of time described in the lease. In exchange, the lessee pays rent.

Tenant at Will A person who pays rent to use a property, but is only bound to the property on a month-to-month basis. A tenancy at will occurs because of some defect in the original lease that renders its term invalid.

Tenants by Entirety Two or more persons who jointly own a property with rights of survivorship. In other words, a property with tenancy by entirety does not become part of a decedent's estate; rather, the other tenant(s) continue to own the property. Couples may be tenants by entirety on a jointly-owned house, for example. Likewise, two business partners may be tenants by entirety on a business property: if two persons own an apartment complex and one of them dies, the whole of the complex belongs to the co-owner and not the decedent's heirs. However, the decedent's liabilities may remain attached to this property and may be used to pay off creditors, even if a creditor had nothing to do with the property in question.

Tenants in Common Two or more persons who own property together with no rights of survivorship. That is, when one of the co-owners dies, his/her share of the property becomes part of his/her estate and passes on to heirs. Tenants in common may own equal or unequal shares of the property. This is an arrangement common in joint business ventures: if two persons own an apartment complex and one of them dies, the decedent's share of the complex passes to his/her beneficiaries and does not pass to the other co-owner.

Tenbagger A stock with a price that eventually rises to 10 times what a shareholder paid for it. Tenbaggers are obviously very profitable for an investor and one is considered lucky if one finds a tenbagger. While there is no method for finding a tenbagger, they tend to be small-cap companies with large growth potential. They eventually become blue chip stocks. Examples of stocks that have become tenbaggers are Wal-Mart and General Electric. The term was coined by Peter Lynch.

Tend to Infinity Describing a variable that, for any reason, becomes extremely large.

Ten-Day Rule In shareholder meetings, a rule on the New York Stock Exchange allowing member firms to vote with the management of a company that trades on the NYSE if there are 10 or fewer days until a meeting. The 10-day rule only applies if the member firm has attempted to contact the beneficial owners of shares in a timely manner, have received no response, and the meeting would otherwise not be able to make a quorum unless the member firm votes.

Ten-Day Window The period of time an investor who buys more than 5% of a publicly-traded company has before it must file with the SEC. That is, the investor has 10 days to announce that it has purchased more than 5% of the company. This requirement is intended to give the investor an appropriate amount of time to organize his/her records while also encouraging transparency in the market.

Tender 1. To agree to take an offer. 2. To bid for U.S. Treasury securities. 3. To settle.

Tender Offer An offer to buy some or most of the stock in a publicly-traded company directly from shareholders for a price well above fair market value. A tender offer may be made by the company's management in a bid to prevent a hostile takeover. Alternatively, it may be a made by an outside company as part of a hostile takeover. See also: Self-Tender Offer.

Tender Offer Premium A tender offer made above the fair market value of the offering.

Tenement An apartment building, especially a shoddy or poorly maintained one. A tenement may only meet the minimum standards for the owner to rent its units legally.

Tennesi A subdivision of the Turkmenistani manat. One tennesi is equal in value to 1/100 of a manat. See also: Cent.

Tennessee Public Service Commission A former agency in the state of Tennessee responsible for regulating utility companies and the railroad and trucking industries. It consisted of three members, one elected from each of Tennessee's regions. It existed from 1897 to 1996.

Tenor The length of time before a loan is due. For example, if a homeowner is 10 years into a 30-year mortgage, the tenor is 20 years.

Tent Card A card with printing on either side that may be mounted on a stand or placed on a flat surface. Tent cards are used to advertise, especially by restaurants to showcase their specials.

Tentative Order An order that an investor makes to an underwriter before a new issue. Before a new issue, underwriters canvass potential investors, who may or may not book a tentative order to buy a portion. Tentative orders are not final until the new issue actually takes place, because it is illegal to sell a security that has not been issued. Tentative orders help underwriters gauge the level of interest in the new issue. See also: Overbooked, Underbooked, Fully Subscribed.

Term 1. The period of time during which a fixed-income security, investment, or agreement is in force. For example, term life insurance lasts only for a certain number of years. The exact number of years is called the term. 2. The period of time during which an individual serves in an office. For example, a member of a board of directors may serve a term of two years.

Term Bond An issue of bonds that mature at the same time. Corporate bonds are sometimes term bonds. In these situations, a corporation issues bonds and sells them to whatever person or institution will buy them; all the bonds mature at the same time. Both municipal bonds and corporate bonds combine aspects of both term and serial issuances in which some parts of the issue mature at various times, but in which the bulk matures all at once. See also: Serial bonds.

Term Certain Annuity An annuity that makes payments (either monthly or in a lump sum) to the annuitant only for a certain period of time. A term certain annuity guarantees these payments for the term but ceases payments if the annuitant is still alive when the policy expires. While these may be a useful part of a larger retirement plan, term certain annuities could leave the annuitant with no income at all if they form the entirety of one's retirement. See also: Life Annuity.

Term Certificate A certificate of deposit with a maturity of greater than one year. Term certificates pay more in interest to compensate for the time value of money.

Term Deposit A deposit at a bank or other financial institution that has a fixed return (usually via an interest rate) and a set maturity. That is, the depositor does not have access to the funds until maturity; in exchange, he/she is usually entitled to a higher interest rate. One of the most common examples of a term deposit is a certificate of deposit. It is also called a time deposit. See also: Demand deposit.

Term Fed Funds Federal funds that a bank borrows for a period of more than one day. Generally speaking, term fed funds have a maximum maturity of 90 days. Banks borrow term fed funds when they need to borrow funds for an extended (but still short-term) period of time and wish to lock in a low interest rate.

Term Life Insurance A life insurance policy that provides coverage only for a certain period of time. A term life insurance policy provides a benefit upon the death of the policyholder, but ceases to provide this benefit if he/she is still alive when the policy expires. Upon expiration, the policyholder may decide to renew the policy or let it lapse. If the policy lapses, the policyholder is not reimbursed for the premiums paid over the life of the policy. A term life insurance policy does not include some of the other benefits of a whole life policy, such as a savings component.

Term Loan A loan from a bank with a floating interest rate, the total amount of which must be paid off in a certain period of time. An example of a term loan is a loan to a small business to buy fixed assets, such as a factory, in order to operate. The length of a term loan varies between one and 10 years, depending on the loan agreement.

Term Premium The amount by which the yield-to-maturity of a long-term bond exceeds that of a short-term bond. Because one collects coupons on a long-term bond for a longer period of time, its yield-to-maturity will be more. The amount of a term premium depends on the interest rates of the individual bonds.

Term Repo A practice in which a bank or other financial institution buys securities with the proviso that the seller repurchases the same securities for an agreed-upon price on a certain day more than one day after the establishment of the agreement. Investors and financial institutions do this in order to raise short-term capital. A term repo differs from other types of repo because the term is more than one day.

Term Sheet A document indicating a corporation's intent to undertake a merger or acquisition. A term sheet outlines the details of the merger or acquisition, including the purchase price, and whether it will be paid in cash, stock, and/ordebt. It is important to note that a term sheet it not legally binding and may not be enforced. It is similar to a letter of intent, but it is usually less formal. It may also indicate a company's unilateral intentions, rather than what two companies have agreed to say.

Term to Maturity The amount of time that must elapse before a contract expires. The term to maturity can greatly affect the price of an option or futures contract. It is also called time to expiration. See also: Time value premium.

Term Trust A unit investment trust with a maturity date. That is, a term trust is an unmanaged portfolio of securities that an investor may buy. At the maturity date, all shares in the term trust are redeemed, and shareholders are entitled to the profits (or must suffer the losses) that the portfolio has achieved over its life. It is a type of closed-end investment company.

Terminable Marital Trust A trust giving the beneficiary, the spouse of the trustor, access to the trust's income, but not assets, upon the death of the trustor. That is, the spouse is able to access the capital gains or other income deriving from the trust, but not the assets of the trust itself. The assets usually pass to other survivors upon the death of the second spouse.

Terminal Elevator A large storage facility for agricultural products, especially grain. A terminal elevator allows investors to store their purchases prior to or after delivery. A terminal elevator does not differentiate which investor owns what grain; therefore, it is possible that products will mix together. An exchange must recognize a facility as a terminal elevator before it may be used as one.

Terminal Value 1. In accounting, the salvage value. **2.** In finance, the present value of future cash flows. **3.** In investing, the value of an investment after a given period of time at a given interest rate. The terminal value is calculated in the same way as compound interest.

Terminal Year The year in which a person dies. Special tax rules apply during a person's terminal year.

Terminally Ill Describing a person who is expected to die soon, usually within a year. Gifts of terminally ill persons are considered distributions of the estate; they may be subject to the estate tax. Obviously, terminally ill persons are unlikely to be sold health insurance or life insurance.

Termination Date The date on which a contract is canceled. This may apply to any contract, whether for employment, construction or anything else. Sometimes notice must be given prior to the termination date, depending on the terms of the contract.

Termination Fee A one-time fee charged to an account holder if he/she transfers or cancels an IRA. The termination fee is levied by the brokerage or bank that manages the IRA and must be spelled out in the agreement that created the account. Some brokerages and banks do not charge a termination fee. See also: Prepayment penalty.

Terms of Delivery In international commerce, an agreement between the seller and the buyer as to who is responsible for the cost and risk of delivering the goods. Cost and risk may rest exclusively with either party, or may be split at a certain point. The International Chamber of Commerce has set approximately a dozen different terms of delivery. See also: Incoterm.

Terms of Sale The conditions the parties agree to follow in the trade of a good or service. Necessary terms of sale include price, quantity, and, if necessary, quality. The terms of sale may also include special conditions. See also: Terms of trade.

Terms of Trade 1. The conditions the parties agree to follow in the trade of a security. Necessary terms of trade include the price and the number of shares or bonds traded. The terms of trade may also include special conditions. **2.** In international trade, the difference between price indices on imports and exports. **3.** See: Balance of trade.

Terotechnology The study of the cost of an asset over its absolute physical life. Terotechnology looks at not only the initial cost of buying an asset, but also maintenance costs and how they may affect the asset's ability to produce profits for the company that owns it. The internal rate of return, net present value, and discounted cash flow are all tools used in terotechnology. It is important to note that a terotechnological analysis of an asset before buying it is only an estimate, and not an exact science.

Territorial Tax System Any tax system that only taxes income earned in that country. For example, if one lives in Belgium, one only owes taxes on income earned in Belgium. If one conducts a great deal of business in Great Britain, income from that business is not taxed in Belgium (though it may be taxed by the UK). Only a few countries have territorial tax systems; prominent examples include Hong Kong and France.

Territory Bond A bond issued by a non-state territory of the United States, such as Puerto Rico or Guam. Territory bonds are exempt from all federal, state, and local taxes. This gives a territory bond preferential treatment to a state or municipal bond, which is generally only exempt from state and local taxes in the state and locality in which it is issued.

Terrorist A non-state individual who perpetrates or attempts to perpetrate violent acts directed at civilians to achieve a political or ideological end. A terrorist differs from an insurrectionist, who attempts to overthrow a government. While terrorists may try to influence government policy, they generally have no interest in actually running a government. Terrorism is a type of political risk, especially in unstable areas.

Terrorist Group A non-state group that perpetrates or attempts to perpetrate violent acts directed at civilians to achieve a political or ideological end. A terrorist group differs from an insurrectionist group, which attempts to overthrow a government. While terrorists may try to influence government policy, they generally have no interest in actually running a government. Terrorism is a type of political risk, especially in unstable areas.

Teruncius An ancient Roman unit of weight approximately equivalent to 82.2 grams. It was also called a quadrans.

Terz 1. A Maltese unit of volume approximately equivalent to 284.1 milliliters. It was originally used to measure alcohol. It is largely obsolete but is still used in some circumstances. **2.** A Maltese unit of volume approximately equivalent to 319.6 milliliters. It was originally used to measure milk and oil. It is largely obsolete but is still used in some circumstances.

Testacy The state of having a will. Assuming that the will is legal and enforceable, the assets of testate person are distributed, upon his/her death, according to the will's terms.

Testamentary Trust A trust created in a will. A testamentary trust is considered part of an estate and is therefore subject to estate taxes, if any. However, a testamentary trust is useful if the deceased has minor children whose assets need to be managed before they reach maturity. The trustee of the testamentary trust does this on behalf of the estate.

Testate Describing a person with a will. Assuming that the will is legal and enforceable, the assets of such a person are distributed according to the will's terms.

Testator A person who writes and, if necessary, registers a will. The will states how and to whom the testator wants his/her property transferred after death. In addition to transferring property, the testator may specify how certain responsibilities are to be performed. For example, he/she may indicate who shall take care of the decedent's minor children, how they are to be educated, and so forth. Many advisers recommend writing a will to ensure that the testator's wishes are carried out. Rarely, a female testator is called a testatrix.

Testcheck To check a representative sample to verify accuracy. For example, a tax agent may substantiate every fourth tax deduction to see if they were properly applied. If testchecking uncovers any irregularities, a more thorough investigation is conducted.

Testdeck To check a computer calculation of accounting or other information against a manual calculation. Testdecking ensures that calculations are performed accurately and/or the computer program functions properly.

Tetarton An ancient Greek unit of liquid volume approximately equivalent to 136.4 milliliters. It was also called a hemikotyle.

Tetra A fish food manufacturing company. It was established in the 1950s to market recently invented fish food flakes. Tetra's product made fish keeping much easier, resulting in a dramatic increase in participants in the hobby.

Tetri A subdivision of the Georgian lari. One tetra is equal in value to 1/100 of one lari.

TEU An inexact unit of capacity equal to the size of a cargo container 20 feet in length. See also: FEU.

Teuro In Germany, a slang term for euros when describing something that costs a great deal. The term combines "euro" and the German word "teuer," which means expensive.

Texas Hedge A hedged position that increases rather than reduces risk. A Texas hedge is made without regard, or with incorrect regard, for the mathematical formulas necessary to lessen exposure. A Texas hedge may involve applying models incorrectly and finding the wrong efficient portfolio frontier and therefore investing in the "wrong" securities.

TF 1. ISO 3166-1 alpha-2 code for the French Southern and Antarctic Territories. **2.** ISO 3166-2 geocode for the French Southern and Antarctic Territories. This is used as an international standard for shipping to the Territories.

TG 1. ISO 3166-1 alpha-2 code for the Togolese Republic. This is the code used in international transactions to and from Togolese bank accounts. **2.** ISO 3166-2 geocode for Togo. This is used as an international standard for shipping to Togo. Each Togolese region has its own code with the prefix "TG." For example, the code for the Centre Region is ISO 3166-2:TG-C.

TGO GOST 7.67 Latin three-letter geocode for Togo. The code is used for transactions to and from Togolese bank accounts and for international shipping to Togo. As with all GOST 7.67 codes, it is used primarily in Cyrillic alphabets.

TH 1. ISO 3166-1 alpha-2 code for the Kingdom of Thailand. This is the code used in international transactions to and from Thai bank accounts. **2.** ISO 3166-2 geocode for Thailand. This is used as an international standard for shipping to Thailand. Each Thai province has its own numeric code with the prefix "TH." For example, the code for the Province of Bangkok is ISO 3166-2:TH-10. The exception to this is the Province of Pattaya, which has a geocode of ISO 3166-2:TH-S.

THA GOST 7.67 Latin three-letter geocode for Thailand. The code is used for transactions to and from Thai bank accounts and for international shipping to Thailand. As with all GOST 7.67 codes, it is used primarily in Cyrillic alphabets.

Thai Baht The currency of Thailand. In use since the late 1800s, the baht at different times has been pegged to silver, gold, and various other currencies. After World War II, it was pegged to the U.S. dollar. It began to float during the Asian Financial Crisis in 1997, decreasing in value significantly in a short period of time. It has since stabilized.

Thanh Pho Truc Thuoc Tinh In Vietnam, a political subdivision for a provincial city.

Thatcherism A term for deregulation, privatization and other conservative policies associated with Margaret Thatcher, who was prime minister of the United Kingdom between 1979 and 1990. Thatcherism promoted monetarism and free markets and is intellectually closely related to Reaganomics.

Thatcherist A politician or other person who favors the deregulation, privatization, and other conservative policies associated with Margaret Thatcher, who was prime minister of the United Kingdom between 1979 and 1990. The beliefs of Thatcherists, which include monetarism and free markets, are intellectually closely related to Reaganomics.

THB ISO 4217 code for the Thai baht. In use since the late 1800s, the baht at different times has been pegged to silver, gold, and various other currencies. After World War II, it was pegged to the U.S. dollar. It began to float during the Asian Financial Crisis in 1997, decreasing in value significantly in a short period of time. It has since stabilized.

The Accounting Review A journal for accounting professionals. Articles in The Accounting Review cover a variety of topics related to accountancy. It is published every other month by the American Accounting Association. Both members and non-members of the Association may submit articles for publication.

The Arabs During the 1980s, a slang term describing the cause for any unpredictable or unexplainable upswing or downswing in the markets. That is, when traders could not explain why the market moved in a certain way, they would jokingly blame (or credit) "the Arabs." The term was popularized by the book Liar's Poker, which describes the author's experience as a bond trader on Wall Street in the 1980s.explain why the market moved in a certain way, they would jokingly blame (or credit) "he ich trader could disply the

The Bond Market Association Also called the BMA. A defunct trade association for investors in debt securities. Members of the Bond Market Association consisted of brokers, dealers, banks, and underwriters. The BMA set common practices for the industry, compiled statistics and other information, and lobbied governments. In 2006, the BMA formed the Securities Industry and Financial Markets Association in a merger with the Securities Industry Association.

The City An area in London that forms the center of its financial district. The City is legally called "the City of London" and once formed the entirety of London. The Bank of England, the London Stock Exchange and Lloyd's, among others, are headquartered in the City. In the 1800s, the City was the world's primary financial center and it remains very important. Because of its influence on the wider financial world, the City is often used as a byword for the financial industry in the United Kingdom and its lobbyists. The sheer amount of money traded in the City renders it vitally important to the global economy as well. Interestingly, both businesses and individuals may vote in City elections.

The Clearing Corporation Also called CCorp. The oldest company in the United States to provide clearing and settlement services for futures and derivatives. It operated both on exchanges and over-the-counter. It was established in 1925 as the Board of Trade Clearing Corporation. The Intercontinental Exchange purchased it in 2009. It should not be confused with a clearing corporation, which is a generic term.

The Conference Board A networking and informational organization for corporate management. Based in the New York, over 1,000 corporations are members and more than 10,000 executives attend its events annually. In addition to its numerous events, it publishes information on market trends, economic trends, and provides other research services related to corporate management to its members. It is a registered not-for-profit organization in the United States. See also: 501(c)(3)

The Curb Informal for the American Stock Exchange, which, prior to its 2008 acquisition by NYSE Euronext, was a mutually owned stock exchange located in Manhattan. Of the three main U.S. stock exchanges, it has the most liberal policies on company listing, having more small companies than either the NYSE or NASDAQ. As a result, it is smaller than either of those stock exchanges by trading volume, handling only about 10% of American securities.

The Desk The Securities Department at the New York Federal Reserve, which carries out all of the Federal Reserve's orders to increase or decrease the dollar supply when interest rates are changed.

The Intelligent Investor A 1949 book by Benjamin Graham promoting value investing, which is an investment strategy in which one seeks securities thought to be undervalued. That is, one tries to buy securities at prices lower than their true value. In The Intelligent Investor, Graham uses the character "Mr. Market," who offers securities at different prices every day. According to Graham, the smart investor waits to buy a security until Mr. Market offers a good price. See also: Buy and hold.

The Outlook A weekly advisory letter published by S&P. It provides research on stocks and discusses investment strategies. It is available in .pdf format by subscription.

The Public Informal for non-professional investors. See also: Crowd.

The Securities Association Ltd. In the United Kingdom, the name of the Securities and Futures Association Ltd. from March 1986 to January 1987. The organization was disbanded in 2003 and replaced by the Financial Services Authority.

The Touch Informal; the inside market, which is the bid-ask spread in the over-the-counter market. The term is used mainly in the United Kingdom.

The Value Line Investment Survey A research survey on hundreds of stocks conducted by Value Line Inc. The Value Line Investment Survey uses financial data and other information to attempt to predict future performance for stocks representing the vast majority of American market capitalization. The Survey is available by subscription and is updated regularly.

The Wall Street Journal A major newspaper in the United States. While it covers all news, it is particularly well known for its coverage of financial markets, stocks, business and similar issues. Its editorial page is commonly considered to have

a conservative viewpoint. It was founded in 1889 and was purchased by News Corp (which bought its parent company, Dow Jones) in 2007.

Thebe A subdivision of the Botswana pula. One pula is equal in value to 100 thebe. See also: Cent.

Theft Insurance An insurance policy that provides coverage losses resulting from the theft of personal property. An individual item, such as a diamond ring, may have an individual theft policy, or a policy may cover all property in a given area, like a house. In the latter case it may be part of a larger policy such as homeowner's insurance.

Thekka Patta In Nepal, a term for contract work.

Theme Fund A mutual fund that invests predominately or exclusively in securities representing a single thing. For example, a theme fund may invest only in energy stocks, securities related to real estate, or in investment vehicles that conform to a set of ethical standards. While some theme funds can be relatively diversified, many are exposed to the risk that a downturn in the "themed" industry will impact the fund disproportionately. See also: Green fund, Islamic fund, Ethical fund.

Theoretical Dow Jones Index A way to calculate the daily high and low of the Dow Jones indices, assuming that all stocks on an index hit their highs and lows at the same time. That is, one takes the high and low for each stock on each trading day and averages them according to Dow Jones' methodology. This does not present an entirely accurate picture for the index because the daily highs and lows do not actually occur at the same time. The Dow Jones indices stopped using this method in 1992 when it began calculating the average every 10 seconds on a rolling basis.

Theoretical Value In options and futures contracts, a mathematically derived estimate of the value of the contract. The most frequently used method to calculate the theoretical value is the Black-Scholes Pricing Model. Depending upon the efficiency of the market and/or the presence of inside information, an option may trade at, above, or below its theoretical value. The concept has come under criticism for not accurately describing true market value: because theoretical value is based on past performance, it does not take into account potential future events such as changes in demand.

Theory of Elasticities A theory attempting to explain how markets move foreign exchange rates. The theory of elasticities states that the foreign exchange rate for a currency is the rate that puts the balance of payments of the country issuing the currency at equilibrium.

Thesaban In Thailand, a municipal government roughly equivalent to a township or city.

Theta The decline in value of an option contract over the passage of time. Assuming all other factors (such as the price of the underlying security) remain constant, the price of the option will decline as the expiration date nears because it becomes less likely that the option will be in-the-money or out-of-the-money at expiration. Theta is an attempt to quantify this fact. It is important to note that because other factors do not always remain constant, the price of the option does not always decline according to the theta.

Thi Xa In Vietnam, a political subdivision equivalent to a township.

Thin Market A market for a security with few transactions. Because of the low trading volume, a single, large order to buy or sell the security can affect the price significantly. It is also called a narrow market. See also: Inactive Security, Broad Market.

Thinly Traded Security An inactive or infrequently traded bond or stock. Thinly traded securities are usually traded in small batches, approximately five shares at a time. Thinly traded securities are fairly illiquid and may be difficult to sell in a downturn. Their prices are also volatile because a small change in demand can greatly affect the price. Thinly traded securities are sometimes called cabinet securities because they are kept in cabinets on the trading floor until they are needed. See also: Cabinet crowd, Inactive post.

Third Baseman In auto sales, a slang term for an outside party who accompanies a customer to a dealership. The third baseman comes along because he/she is more knowledgeable about automobiles than the customer. This makes it less likely that the customer will buy a bad car (or spend too much for a good one).

Third Cruzeiro The currency of Brazil between 1990 and 1993. It replaced the cruzado novo at par. It was issued as part of an attempt to control Brazilian inflation; this attempt failed and the cruzeiro was replaced by the cruzeiro real in 1993.

Third Market The trading of listed securities on the over-the-counter market. The third market avoids the commissions that must be paid to floor brokers. Most of the time, trades on the third market are large block trades involving institutional investors. Dealers must fill orders on the exchange before offering them over-the-counter.

Third Market Maker A third party on an exchange that is willing to buy or sell for a given price. Brokers often execute orders through third market makers either because the broker does not belong to a member firm on the exchange or because the third market maker pays the broker a small commission to direct trades to him/her.

Third World A term for developing countries. Originally used for countries that did not side explicitly with either the United States (the First World) or the Soviet Union (the Second World) during the Cold War, it has become a byword for countries with less wealth relative to others. The term is sometimes considered politically incorrect.

Third Zimbabwean Dollar The former currency of Zimbabwe. It was introduced in August 2008, replacing the second Zimbabwean dollar at a ratio of 10 billion to one. It failed to temper the dollar's hyperinflation and the fourth Zimbabwean dollar was introduced in February 2009. Both currencies were demonetized in June 2009.

Third Zloty The former currency of Poland. It was issued in 1950. For most of its history, it was an inconvertible currency because Poland was under Communist rule, and its exchange rate was set by the government. In 1990, it became a convertible currency. It was redenominated and replaced by the fourth zloty in 1995.

Third-Country Dumping The act of exporting a good to a country where the exported good is much less expensive than an exported good from a different country. For example, suppose Countries A and B both export products to Country C. If A's exports are less expensive than B's exports of the same type (as well as C's domestically produced goods), people in C are more likely to buy from A. This can result in a handsome profit for the first exporter, but can be detrimental both to domestic producers and other exporters to the same country. Importing countries attempt to counteract dumping by setting up tariff barriers. Some countries peg their currencies artificially low so as to enable dumping. See also: Outsourcing.

Third-Party Distributor A company that sells mutual funds on behalf of the investment company managing the funds. A third-party distributor receives a portion of the loads (or sales fees) that the mutual funds charge shareholders. This system can be beneficial if an investment company lacks the knowledge or resources to market funds directly.

Thirteenth Month An accounting method that recognizes write-offs and unusual income in an artificially created 13th month. This allows an organization to consider the strength of its finances from ordinary operations in the other 12 months.

Thirty-Day Visible Supply A new issue of a municipal bond that is not currently being sold, but will be sold in the next 30 days.

Thirty-Day Wash Rule An IRS regulation stating that one may not claim a capital loss for tax purposes if one repurchases the same position within 30 days. Suppose one sells a stock at a substantial loss but immediately buys back the same stock at the same price. Effectively, the locked in loss is "unlocked" and one can still make a profit on the investment in the long term. The 30 day wash rule exists to prevent investors from taking tax deductions on losses they do not actually incur. Some investors find a way around this by exercising a tax swap. The 30 day wash rule should not be confused with wash trading, which is a different concept altogether.

Thirty-Year Treasury A debt security backed by the full faith and credit of the United States government with a maturity of 30 years. They may be purchased directly from the government or from a bank; they have coupon payments payable every six months. Thirty-year Treasury bonds may be bought competitively or non-competitively. In a non-competitive transaction, one takes the interest rate he/she is given on a T-bond. In competitive investing, one bids on a desired yield, but this does not mean it will be accepted. Treasury bonds are low-risk, low-return investments. The minimum purchase is $1,000, and the maximum is $5 million in non-competitive bidding or 35% of the offering in competitive bidding. They are known informally as T-bonds. See also: Treasury bill, Treasury note.

Thomas Edison An American businessman and inventor. He is especially known for inventing the light bulb, but he also created the phonograph, which laid the foundation for much of modern telecommunications. He founded General Electric. Edison lived from 1847 to 1931.

Thomas J. Watson, Sr. A salesman who served as president of IBM from 1914 to 1956. He began by selling organs and pianos to farmers in New York in the 1890s. He became interested in selling for technology companies when he purchased a cash register for his butcher shop. As head of IBM, he cornered 90% of the market for tabulating machines in the United States. During his tenure, IBM also began research into what became analog computers. He lived from 1874 to 1956.

Thomas Sowell An American economist born in 1930. He is known for his criticism of Marxism and for his advocacy of free market economics. He is also a critic of affirmative action and has sparked controversy for suggesting that some ethnic groups may be more intelligent, on average, than others.

Thomson Financial A former company that provided financial information to clients and the public at large. It was particularly well known for its FirstCall system, which was later consolidated with the I/B/E/S when Thomson acquired Primark. In 2008, Thomson Financial merged with Reuters to form Thomson Reuters. The new company's major competitor is Bloomberg.

Three Steps and a Stumble Rule A rule of thumb stating that the prices of stocks fall significantly after the Federal Reserve raises interest rates three times in a row. In a booming economy, minor adjustments in key interest rates, both up and down, are fairly normal. However, if the Fed raises interest rates three times in a row, this is taken as an indicator that it intends for interest rates to remain at a comparatively high level for the foreseeable future. This leads investors to sell stock, because the businesses underlying the stock now have the added cost of high interest rates, which reduces profits. The selling of stock causes stock prices to drop.

Three-Cent Piece A coin minted in the United States between 1851 and 1873 worth 3% of one dollar.

Three-Digit Zip Code A prefix in a zip code representing a general geographic area. An area denoted by a three-digit zip code is serviced by a single postal facility (though a post office may have more than one three-digit code assigned to it).

Three-Dollar Piece A gold coin minted in the United States between 1854 and 1889. It was worth $3.

Three-Martini Lunch A byword for an expensive lunch claimed as a tax deduction for business purposes. For example, a company may take a client out to lunch but spend more than it otherwise would because of the deduction. The presumed prevalence of three-martini lunches led to an alteration of the U.S. tax code making only half of business meals deductible.

Three-Month Euroyen Futures Contract A futures foreign exchange contract on yen deposits outside the jurisdiction of the Bank of Japan. As the name implies, a three-month euroyen futures contract matures three months after issue. These contracts have been traded on the Tokyo Financial Exchange since 1989.

Three-Months Copper A futures or option contract on copper with an expiration date three months following the trade date. Three months copper contracts allow traders to speculate on the future price of copper. Three months copper contracts are traded on exchanges such as the London Metals Exchange.

Three-Phase DDM A form of the dividend discount model that divides a company into three phases. A dividend discount model is a calculation of the value of a publicly-traded company's common stock based on the present value of its future dividends. The three-phase DDM assumes that a company's dividend policy is determined by one of three phases: a growth phase, a transition phase, and a maturity phase. The company's goals differ in each phase and its dividend policy changes accordingly. The three-phase DDM attempts to account for this in its calculation.

Three-Sheet Paper A term noting the number of pages that the U.S. Postal Service states can be sent in an envelope with one stamp. In practice, this is not enforced, as paper rarely weighs enough to qualify for a higher postage rate.

Threshold 1. See: Threshold list. **2.** See: Threshold price. **3.** See: Threshold security.

Threshold for Refinancing The interest rate on a mortgage or a mortgage-backed security that is high enough to encourage property owners to refinance their mortgages at lower rates. If enough property owners refinance, this may affect the yield on a mortgage-backed security, depending upon its particular type. Generally speaking, the threshold for refinancing is two percentage points above prevailing interest rates.

Threshold List A list of securities for which a significant number of shares fails to deliver after five days. A security is placed on the list if 10,000 shares fail to deliver, if more than 0.5% of shares outstanding fail, or if a self-regulatory organization declares it a threshold security. The list is maintained by the National Securities Clearing Corporation. See also: Regulation SHO.

Threshold of Divergence In the European Monetary System, a series of steps by which a currency can exit the EMS. Under the threshold of divergence, steps other than a naked intervention by the central bank must be taken to attempt to stabilize a currency under pressure. It should be noted that no similar system exists for countries already in the eurozone.

Threshold Price The price that psychologically encourages a potential buyer to purchase a product. For example, a company may price a product at $19.99 because it finds that it begins to lose buyers at $20. This maximizes the company's revenue because it makes slightly less money from significantly more buyers.

Threshold Security A security in which a significant number of shares fails to deliver after five days. A security crosses the threshold if 10,000 shares fail to deliver, if more than 0.5% of shares outstanding fail, or if a self-regulatory organization declares it to be a threshold security. See also: Regulation SHO.

Thrift Institutions Advisory Council An organization that advises the Federal Reserve on issues affecting savings & loan associations, credit unions, and mutual savings banks, which operate much like banks, but over which the Federal Reserve does not have direct regulatory authority. The Council consists of representatives from S&Ls, credit unions, and mutual savings banks; it meets three times per year in Washington, DC.

Thrift Plan A retirement account in which a worker and an employer each make contributions up to a certain limit throughout the working life of the employee, usually on a before-tax basis. Under a thrift plan, a worker places a portion of his/her pre-tax income into an account and allows it to be invested. Taxation is deferred until withdrawal from the account, generally after retirement. It is important to note, however, that unlike some retirement plans, the employer makes a defined contribution to the account as well. Thrift plans are employee benefits, and workers must have a sponsoring employer to take advantage of one. See also: 401(k).

Thromde In Bhutan, an administrative subdivision of a municipality. See also: Gewog.

Throughput Agreement An agreement within a company, or between a company and a transporter, to route some or all units of a product through a certain mode of transportation. This is used by energy companies; for example, an oil company may agree to use a certain pipeline or ship to transport some of its oil.

Thruppenny Bit A British coin worth three pence. It has not been minted since the decimalization of the British pound in 1971. As a result, a thruppenny bit was worth 1/80 of one pound. It was also called threepence or a thrip.

Thundering Herd Informal for Merrill Lynch. This company is sometimes called the Thundering Herd because of the bull in its symbol.

Thursday/Friday Dollars A foreign exchange transaction in which a bank buys U.S. dollars on Thursday and sells them on Friday using a clearing house check. Because the check is issued on Friday, the exchange will not clear until the following Monday. As a result, one is entitled to higher interest on Thursday/Friday dollars.

Tick On an exchange, a trade in which a security was traded after another trade. There are three basic types of tick. A plus tick occurs when the price is higher than the previous trade. A minus tick occurs when the price is lower, and finally a zero tick happens when the price is the same. Ticks are recorded and published in real time throughout a trading day. Certain regulations govern the types of trade that can occur after certain kinds of ticks. See also: Zero-plus Tick, Zero-minus Tick.

Tick Index The number of securities on an uptick minus the number of securities on a downtick. A positive tick index is a bullish indicator, while a negative index is bearish. Because a tick index reflects only the directions of the most recent trades, its usefulness beyond the very short term is limited.

Tick Indicator In technical analysis, a signal of whether to buy or sell shares in a company based on whether its last price movement was an uptick or a downtick. A tick indicator can be a signal of market sentiment, which could indicate whether the crowd is going to buy or sell. A tick indicator is subject to confirmation, especially by other tools of technical analysis.

Tick Mark In accounting, a mark on a document indicating that a specific task has been done. Accountants generally provide information on what each tick mark means.

Tick Test A temporary suspension on trading on a security in which trading is allowed to continue but only in certain directions. For example, if the security is falling dramatically, an exchange may put in place a tick test only allowing trades for a higher or the same price. Likewise, if the security is rising unsustainably, the tick test may only allow lower or the same prices on trades. Tick tests are designed to reduce volatility in the market. See also: Trading curb.

Ticker A record of the transactions occurring on an exchange on a given trading day, updated in real time or with only a slight delay. Before electronic tickers became common, most records of trading were printed out on strips of paper known as tape. It is more common now to refer to an exchange's live record as a ticker. When tape was common, trading volume sometimes became so heavy for a security that the tape publicly announcing quotes was delayed by a significant amount of time, usually a minute or two. This was called a tape is late situation.

Ticker Symbol A series of letters, often an abbreviation, that represents a stock, option, mutual fund, or other security that trades on an exchange. A ticker symbol allows securities to be listed on an exchange's overhead board conveniently and provides a useful reference for traders and investors. NASDAQ ticker symbols have four letters, while those on the NYSE have no more than three. Mutual fund ticker symbols sometimes include numbers. Examples of ticker symbols include F, for Ford, and MSFT, for Microsoft.

Ticker Tape A record of the transactions occurring on an exchange on a given trading day, updated in real time or with only a slight delay. Before electronic tickers became common, most records of trading were printed out on strips of paper known as tape. It is more common now to refer to an exchange's live record as a ticker. When tape was common, trading volume sometimes became so heavy for a security that the tape publicly announcing quotes was delayed by a significant amount of time, usually a minute or two. This was called a tape is late situation.

Ticket Informal for the form on which an investor makes an order to a broker. It is not always necessary to fill out a ticket, as some orders can be made over the phone or via the Internet. It is also called an order ticket.

Tide In technical analysis, an informal term for a security's performance over a long period of time, usually over a year or more. Analysts look for cyclical behavior in a security to interpret the tide properly; that is, if a long-term bull market is observed with a bad trading day in a certain week, an analyst might view the short-term trend as moderately bearish without detracting from the long-term bullish tide. The term was coined by Robert Rhea. See also: Ripple, Wave.

Tie Out Slang; in auditing, to check source documents to ensure that the statements on the balance sheet are correct (or to check the balance sheet against the source documents). In other words, to tie out means to implement the means of auditing the accuracy of documents.

Tiebreaker A random character assigned to a matchcode to prevent duplicate codes This is important when matchcodes are derived from personal information such as addresses or zip codes in which repetitions are probable. A tiebreaker is also called a unique character.

Tied Loan A loan that a government makes to a foreign borrower in exchange for the promise that the borrower will use the loan to purchase goods from the lender's country. A tied loan may be mutually beneficial; for example, it may spur business in the lending country while aiding the borrower's economic development.

Tied Selling An illegal practice in which a company agrees to sell a customer some good or service only if the customer also buys some other good or service. Tied selling is most often associated with banks. For example, tied selling may occur when a bank informs its customer that it will only approve a mortgage for him/her if the customer transfers all his/her bank accounts to that bank.

Tie-In Agreement An agreement between an investor and an underwriter requiring the investor to buy more shares of a new issue in the secondary market as a condition of buying shares from the underwriter in an initial public offering. This maintains a higher share price for the new issue as demand is inflated artificially. Tie-in agreements are illegal.

Tier A group of securities according to company size or quality. For example, blue chip stocks may belong in one tier, while startup stocks belong in another. See also: Secondary stock, Credit rating.

Tier 1 Capital Capital in a bank that is easy to calculate or liquidate, especially compared to Tier 2 capital. Under the Basel I Accord, Tier 1 capital includes retained earnings and common stock, and occasionally also some preferred stock. Tier 1 capital is considered the bank's core capital and is less risky than Tier 2 capital. It is included in the calculation of a bank's reserve requirements.

Tier 2 Capital Capital in a bank that is difficult to calculate or liquidate, especially as compared to Tier 1 capital. Under the Basel I Accord, tier 2 capital includes revaluation reserves (or the increase in the value in an asset after it is reappraised), general provisions (or money that the bank has lost but has been unable to calculate), and subordinated debt (or debt that, in the event of default, receives payment only after some debt). Tier 2 capital is included in calculations of a bank's reserve requirements but is not considered as reliable as Tier 1 capital.

Tiered Market The situation in which investors favor a group of securities over other, similar groups of securities. This results in the price of the first group being higher than all other groups, sometimes significantly so. This may occur for a number of reasons: for examples investors may expect future earnings on the first group to be higher. Alternatively, the first group may simply employ better marketing tactics. The specific securities in different tiers change as investors expectations change. The term should not be confused with "two-tier market."

TIFFE Tokyo International Financial Futures Exchange. A former name for the Tokyo Financial Exchange, which is an exchange in Japan on which futures are traded on Euroyen, Eurodollar, and the U.S. dollar-yen exchange rates. Options are traded on Euroyen as well.

Tifundza In Swaziland, a political subdivision roughly equivalent to a province.

Tiger Economy A collective name given to the economies of East and Southeast Asia, which experienced nearly unprecedented growth, especially in the 1980s and early 1990s. The Asian financial crisis in the late 1990s ended the idea that the tiger economies were unstoppable, though most have recovered well and remain important players in the global economy. See also: Keiretsu, chaebol, ASEAN.

Tight Credit A situation in which it is difficult to find a loan. That is, tight credit occurs when banks are unwilling to part with their money, even on an interim basis. Tight credit may occur during periods of uncertainty or simply during times of high interest rates. See also: Credit Crunch.

Tight Market A market or security with high trading volume and a small bid-ask spread. However, an investor can profit in a tight market, especially if he/she trades large numbers of securities. When the bid-ask spread is narrow, an investor may have difficulty making more than a small return for each trade, but sheer numbers can make returns add to a substantial amount.

Tight Money A situation in which it is difficult to receive credit because of the monetary policy of the central bank. Tight money occurs when the central bank has enacted relatively high target interest rates. While this usually happens when the central bank is seeking to control or is concerned about inflation, tight money can negatively impact security prices and make it hard to receive a loan for a house or business.

Tight Stop The act or practice of raising a stop price to minimize losses from a long position. For example, suppose one buys a stock at $20 with a stop price of $18 (meaning the stock will be sold automatically if the price hits $18 in order to prevent further losses). If the price appears to be trending downward, the holder may put in a tight stop at $18.60 to try to keep from losing more money.

Tighter Slang; in bond trading, a decline in yield spread, indicating lower risk.

Tiin A subdivision of the Kazakhstani tenge. One tiin is equal in value to 1/100 of one tenge. It does not circulate in practice.

Tiki The number of upticking stocks less the number of downticking stocks traded on the Dow Jones Industrial Average on a given trading day. A tiki tells how well the DJIA performed on a certain day. Specifically, if a tiki is positive, it indicates that more DJIA stocks upticked, while, if it is negative, it shows that more stocks downticked. One can chart tikis over a number of days to help determine market trends. Tikis are thus relevant to technical analysis of the DJIA. See also: Tick, Trin.

Till 1. A term for government funds. **2.** A British term for a cash register.

Till Money Money kept in a register at a bank that a bank teller may distribute to customers making withdrawals. Till money is distinguished from cash in a vault.

Tilla A former currency super-division in Afghanistan. One tilla was worth 10 Afghan rupees.

Till-Forbid An order that is left standing until it is canceled. For example, a restaurant may order 100 steaks daily on a till-forbid basis. This means that a distributor will sell 100 steaks to the restaurant each day until the restaurant requests otherwise. See also: GTC.

Tilted Portfolio A portfolio that combines aspects of active management and passive management. In general, a tilted portfolio tracks a particular index. However, a money manager may weight parts of the index more than others depending on interest rates, company performance, what industries are in favor, and other factors. See also: Closet Index Fund.

Time and a Half Payment of one and a half times one's ordinary hourly wage. For example, a company may be required to pay its waged employees time and a half for any time they work over 40 hours in a week. See also: Double time.

Time Card A card an employee inserts into a machine in order to record when he/she arrives and leaves the work space. The employee is paid for the period of time indicated on the card. Time cards are used for wage earners, especially but not necessarily in manufacturing.

Time Decay The decline in value of an option contract as it approaches the expiration date. In an out-of-the-money option, the closer the contract is to expiry, the less likely it is that the option will become in-the-money, reducing its value. Time decay is also called time-value decay.

Time Draft A check or other draft that is not payable to the payee until a stated date in the future. It contrasts with a sight draft, in which the payee may demand payment upon presentation of the draft to the appropriate party.

Time Horizon The length of time an investment is intended to last, usually expressed in years. Having a time horizon helps an investor set his/her short-term and long-term investment plans. See also: Horizon analysis, Horizon return.

Time is of the Essence A clause in a contract indicating that an unnecessary delay in the execution of a contract constitutes breach of contract. The delay is only a breach if it causes material harm to the contract.

Time Letter of Credit Letter of credit requiring payment a certain number of days after the appropriate documents are presented. It is also called a usance letter of credit.

Time Loan A loan that must be repaid by a certain, stated date. For example, a time loan's terms may state that all interest and principal must be repaid within six months.

Time Order An order that changes its form after a certain period of time. For example, a limit order may become a market order if it is not filled within a few days. Likewise, a time order may be automatically canceled if it is not filled after the specified period of time.

Time Preference for Consumption In economics, the preference that consumers have to spend immediately rather than to save for future needs. Time preference for consumption is important in economies driven by consumer spending. It can result in unsustainable growth if it leads to excessive debt.

Time Series A comparison of a variable to itself over time. One of the most common time series, especially in technical analysis, is a comparison of prices over time. For example, one may compile a time series of a security over the course of a week or a month or a year, and then use it in the determination of future price movements.

Time Slot A period of time during which something takes place. For example, a meeting may be scheduled from 3 pm to 4 pm, or a work order may be processed between 5 pm and 6 pm. In both cases, the scheduled occurrence is the time slot.

Time Spread An options strategy in which an investor takes the same position in two different option contracts that are identical in every way except the expiration date. For example, an investor utilizing a time spread strategy may buy or write two puts on the same underlying asset at the same strike price; the only difference is that one of the puts has a longer expiration. A time spread allows the investor to profit from the difference in price on the underlying asset between the two expiration dates. It is also called a horizontal spread and a calendar spread.

Time Stamping The practice of marking an order with the time it is made and the time it is executed. Time stamping is mandatory on many option exchanges, among others.

Time Standard A legal or customary measure of the rate at which time passes. Most time standards are based upon the earth's rotation, that is, upon the passage of days. Nearly all modern time standards divide time into seconds, minutes and hours.

Time Value 1. See: Option time value. **2.** See: Time value of money. **3.** See: Extrinsic value.

Time Value of an Option The portion of the value of an option determined by the amount of time until it expires and the likelihood that it will be in the money at that time. The time value of an option is generally calculated as the difference between the premium and its intrinsic value. See also: Time value of money.

Time Value of Money A fundamental idea in finance that money that one has now is worth more than money one will receive in the future. Because money can earn interest or be invested, it is worth more to an economic actor if it is available immediately. This concept applies to many contracts; for example, a trade in which payment is delayed will often require compensation for the time value of money. This concept may be thought of as a financial application of the saying, "A bird in the hand is worth two in the bush."

Time Value Premium The amount by which the premium on an option contract exceeds its intrinsic value. The time value premium becomes smaller as the expiration date approaches. Volatility to the underlying asset also affects the time value premium; a lower premium comes from a security with lower volatility.

Time-and-a Half Informal; the period of time during which a wage earner makes 150% of his/her normal, hourly rate. For example, a worker who ordinarily earns $10 per hour makes time and a half when he earns $15 per hour. Time and a half usually is paid when an employee is required to work more than a certain number of hours, or is required to work on a holiday.

Timeliness A system for rating stocks according to earnings and price performance. A stock being rated for timeliness is assigned a letter between A and E, with A indicating the highest earnings and price performance. A stock with a high timeliness rating usually has a higher return in the short term, but also tends to be more volatile than a stock with a lower rating.

Time-Poor A slang term describing a person who has little or no free time due to his/her workload. It may refer to a person who is unable to take on additional projects, or to one who has no life outside work because he/she works almost constantly.

Times Interest Earned A measure of a company's ability to service its debts. It is calculated by dividing the company's earnings before interest and taxes by the total interest payable on its debts, expressed as a ratio. Investors prefer publicly-traded companies to have a middling times-interest-earned ratio. A low ratio indicates an inability to service debts, while too high a ratio indicates a lack of debt that investors may find undesirable.

Time-Series Analysis An analysis of the relationship between variables over a period of time. Time-series analysis is useful in assessing how an economic or other variable changes over time. For example, one may conduct a time-series analysis on a stock to help determine its volatility.

Timesheet A document indicating the hours in a pay period during which an employee worked. This may be used to determine how much to pay an employee or it may serve as proof of work when billing a client.

Time-Zone Arbitrage A form of arbitrage in which an investor takes advantage of price discrepancies that occur when some stock markets are open while others are closed. For example, one may buy a stock on an American exchange when it has experienced a rally, guaranteeing that the same stock will surge when Asian exchanges open the next day. This is used for international stocks.

Timing Difference In accounting, the amount of time between the point at which an asset or transaction affects a company's finances for reporting purposes and the point at which it affects it for tax purposes. This is especially important in depreciation: tax depreciation and reporting depreciation are sometimes calculated differently.

Timing Option The ability of the seller of a Treasury security or futures contract to decide at what point in the delivery month actual delivery shall be made.

Timothy Geithner An American economist and civil servant. He worked in the U.S. Treasury Department for most of his early career. In 2003, he became president of the New York Federal Reserve. In 2009, he became the United States Secretary of the Treasury. In these capacities, he helped arrange the bailouts of the American financial and automotive industries. Geithner was born in 1961.

Tin A Burmese unit of volume approximately equivalent to 40.9 liters.

Tin Ingot A currency used in Malacca in the 15th century. A tin ingot was made of tin and shaped like a hexahedron block, weighing around half a kilogram.

Tinh In Vietnam, a political subdivision equivalent to a province.

Tinkhundla In Swaziland, a political subdivision roughly equivalent to a county.

Tip 1. Information on a security, company, or anything else provided by one investor or trader to another that is not available to the general public, that can produce significant profits if it proves to be accurate. See also: Inside information. **2.** See: Gratuity.

Tip from a Dip Information given to an investor by a person purporting to have inside information on a stock or company who in fact does not have that information. It is important to note that even if the "dip" had inside information, it would be illegal for him/her or anyone to whom he/she divulges the information to use it for investment purposes.

Tip Income For those employed in service jobs, regular income that does not come from either salaries or wages, but from extra money left by a patron or customer in exchange for adequate or exceptional service. Some employees, especially those in hospitality, receive most of their income through tips. Tip income is taxable in the United States, and an employee receiving more than $20 in tips for a single job in a given month must report all tips to his/her employer.

Tippee A person who receives inside information. Unless reported to the authorities, tippees can be held legally liable for illegal inside information, even if the tippee does not use it in trading. This exists to encourage tippees to come forward to eliminate insider trading and increase transparency. See also: Insider trading.

Tipster A person who provides insider information. In doing so, the tipster commits a crime, regardless of whether or not the information is used in investing.

Tir-cumaile An obsolete Irish unit of area approximately equivalent to 9.3 hectares.

Tire Kicker In auto sales, a slang term for a potential customer who is unlikely to buy a vehicle. A tire kicker arrives at a dealership, does not approach any salespersons (and dismisses those who approach), generally looks around for a few minutes and then leaves.

Tissue Overlay Strong, transparent paper that an artist can use to trace a previous drawing. Tissue overlays are used in advertising as an artist develops marketing graphics. Tissue overlay allows the artist to trace the parts of the previous drawing that have been accepted and to make requested changes. Tissue overlay is also called layout paper.

Tithe Ten percent of one's income or production donated to a religious institution. Historically, one could pay a tithe in cash or in kind. In a few jurisdictions, tithes are enforced by law. More broadly, a tithe may refer to a religious donation, even if it is less than 10% of one's income.

Title 1. The right of ownership over a piece of tangible or intangible property. In countries and economic systems recognizing private ownership, title represents a recognition by government and society that a person or organization owns something. **2.** A certificate acknowledging title. See also: Stockholder of record.

Title Company A company that conducts a title search, which is research done to trace a title back to its original owner or back to some date dictated by statute. A title search is done before the sale of property to ensure that there are no competing claims for the same property. Paying a title company is part of a real estate sale's closing costs.

Title Defect Something that prevents a title to a property from being a clear title. That is, a title defect is a situation in which there may be a legitimate, contrary claim to the true ownership of the property. A title defect can prevent the sale of a property. See also: Title search, Title insurance, Quitclaim deed.

Title Insurance An insurance policy protecting a property owner from the risk that another claim to the property will arise in the future and prove successful in court. This occurs in cases in which property records are inaccurate or incomplete. If there is a reasonable risk of this, a mortgage lender will require a borrower to obtain title insurance with a term equal to the term of the mortgage. Most of the time, one pays the total premium of title insurance as part of the closing costs on the property.

Title IV Funds All monies that the federal government administers as financial aid under the Higher Education Act of 1965.

Title Search In real estate, research done to trace a title back to its original owner or back to some date dictated by statute. A title search is done before the sale of property to ensure that there are no competing claims for the same property. A title search protects the mortgage lender from the possibility that that a competing claim will be honored in court, resulting in a loss. See also: Clean Deed, Quitclaim Deed, Title Insurance.

Title Sponsor A company that purchases naming rights to a building or venue. This is usually part of a marketing strategy to increase a company's visibility or improve its reputation. For example, a natural gas company may become the title sponsor for the baseball stadium in the town where it maintains its headquarters.

Tiu A Finnish term for 20 eggs.

Tiyin A subdivision of the Uzbekistani som. One tiyin is equal in value to 1/100 of one som.

Tiyn A subdivision of the Kazakhstani tenge. One tiyn is equal in value to 1/100 of a tenge. The tiyn is not used in practice. See also: Cent.

TJ 1. ISO 3166-1 alpha-2 code for the Republic of Tajikstan. This is the code used in international transactions to and from Tajik bank accounts. **2.** ISO 3166-2 geocode for Tajikistan. This is used as an international standard for shipping to Tajikistan. Each Tajik region has its own code with the prefix "TJ." For example, the code for the Region of Republican Subordination is ISO 3166-2:TJ-RR.

TJK GOST 7.67 Latin three-letter geocode for Tajikistan. The code is used for transactions to and from Tajikistani bank accounts and for international shipping to Tajikistan. As with all GOST 7.67 codes, it is used primarily in Cyrillic alphabets.

TJR ISO 4217 code for the Tajikistani ruble. It was introduced in 1995, replacing the Russian ruble, which had itself only recently replaced the Soviet ruble. It suffered from high inflation for five years, and, in 2000, was replaced by the Tajikistani somoni.

TJS ISO 4217 code for the Tajikistani somoni. It was issued in 2000, replacing the Tajikistani ruble after a period of high inflation. The somoni is one of the highest-valued currencies in Central Asia.

TK 1. ISO 3166-1 alpha-2 code for Tokelau. This is the code used in international transactions to and from Tokelauan bank accounts. **2.** ISO 3166-2 geocode for Tokelau. This is used as an international standard for shipping to Tokelau.

TKL GOST 7.67 Latin three-letter geocode for Tokelau. The code is used for transactions to and from Tokelauan bank accounts and for international shipping to Tokelau. As with all GOST 7.67 codes, it is used primarily in Cyrillic alphabets.

TKM GOST 7.67 Latin three-letter geocode for Turkmenistan. The code is used for transactions to and from Turkmen bank accounts and for international shipping to Turkmenistan. As with all GOST 7.67 codes, it is used primarily in Cyrillic alphabets.

TL 1. The ISO 3166-1 alpha-2 code for the Democratic Republic of Timor-Leste (East Timor). This is the code used in international transactions to and from East Timor's bank accounts. **2.** A former ISO 3166-2 geocode for East Timor. This is used as an international standard for shipping to East Timor.

TM 1. ISO 3166-1 alpha-2 code for Turkmenistan. This is the code used in international transactions to and from Turkmen bank accounts. **2.** ISO 3166-2 geocode for Turkmenistan. This is used as an international standard for shipping to Turkmenistan. Each Turkmen province has its own code with the prefix "TM." For example, the code for the Province of Ahal is ISO 3166-2:TM-A.

TMM ISO 4217 code for the Turkmenistani manat. It was introduced in 1993, replacing the Soviet ruble. It suffered from high inflation in the 1990s and 2000s, and was replaced by the new manat (code TMT) in January 2009 at a ratio of 5000 old manat to one new manat.

TMP GOST 7.67 Latin three-letter geocode for East Timor. The code is used for transactions to and from East Timorese bank accounts and for international shipping to East Timor. As with all GOST 7.67 codes, it is used primarily in Cyrillic alphabets.

TMT ISO 4217 code for the new Turkmenistani manat. It was introduced in January 2009, replacing the old manat after it suffered from high inflation in the 1990s and 2000s.

TND ISO 4217 code for the Tunisian dinar. It came into circulation in 1960, replacing the Tunisian franc. It was pegged to the French franc until 1964 and then the U.S. dollar until 1971. There are significant restrictions on the convertibility of the dinar.

TO 1. ISO 3166-1 alpha-2 code for the Kingdom of Tonga. This is the code used in international transactions to and from Tongan bank accounts. **2.** ISO 3166-2 geocode for Tonga. This is used as an international standard for shipping to Tonga. Each division has its own code with the prefix "TO." For example, the code for 'Eua is ISO 3166-2:TO-01.

To Be Announced A forward contract on a mortgage-backed security. The seller agrees to deliver the MBS for an agreed upon price on an agreed upon date (usually 48 hours after the contract is made), but makes no guarantee as to which or how many securities are to be delivered. In other words, the seller delivers the amount of mortgage-backed securities that equal the market value of the selling price at the time of delivery.

To Order Describing a purchase or other transaction that is specialized to one's direction. For example, if one orders a burger cooked medium-well, the burger is said to be "made to order."

Tobin Tax A proposed tax on foreign exchange transactions. The tax is intended to reduce excessive speculation on currencies by making it more expensive. First proposed after the collapse of the Bretton Woods system, the Tobin tax is often re-proposed after major currency crises because speculation can cause unsustainable rises and crashes in foreign exchange rates.

Tobin's Q Ratio A ratio of a company's market value to its total asset value. Tobin's Q ratio is based on the work of James Tobin, who suggested that a fairly priced company ought to have a price equal to its total asset value. Thus, when Tobin's Q ratio is less than one, it means that the market value of the company is less than the total asset value, indicating that it is undervalued. Likewise, when it is more than one, it indicates that the market value is higher than the total asset value and that the company might be overvalued. Tobin's Q ratio is also called simply a Q ratio.

Tochka A Russian unit of length equivalent to 1/100 of one inch. It was rendered obsolete when the Soviet Union began to use the metric system in 1924.

Tod A unit of weight equivalent to 28 pounds. It is used in the sale of wool.

Toea A subdivision of the Papua New Guinean kina. One toea is equal in value to 1/100 of a kina. See also: Cent.

Toehold Purchase A purchase of less than 5% of the stock of a publicly-traded company. This is called a toehold purchase because one is not required to register and explain one's purchase to the SEC until one meets the 5% threshold. This allows one to begin the process of a potential hostile takeover by accumulating stock quietly, though one eventually would have to disclose one's intent.

Toesa A Portuguese measure of length approximately equivalent to 1.98 meters. It became obsolete after Lusophone countries adopted the metric system in the 19th century.

Token Money A currency with cash and coin that circulate in an economy. This contrasts with account money, which is used for accounting purposes but is not the money people actually use. For example, in 1999, the euro became the account money in many countries in the EU; that is, company books began to be kept in euros. However, it became token money in 2002, when euro notes and coins were first issued.

Tokenism The practice of including only a certain number or percentage of a minority group in a business or other organization. Tokenism may or may not be deliberate. For example, a company, intentionally or not, may hire one and only one member of a minority race to its executive team. It could be an attempt to avoid a discrimination lawsuit, but some believe it is itself a form of discrimination.

Tokkin A fund or investment company owned by a Japanese corporation (other than a financial services company). A tokkin invests in speculative, often high risk securities in Japanese companies.

Tokugawa Currency A gold, silver and bronze coin system that served as Japan's currency between 1601 and 1867. Originally used for international trade, export of Tokugawa coins was eventually restricted because of the scarcity of precious metals in Japan. See also: Japanese yen.

Tokyo Commodity Exchange An exchange in Japan on which commodities are traded. It was established in 1984 with the merger of the Tokyo Gold Exchange, Tokyo Rubber Exchange, and the Tokyo Textile Exchange. Futures contracts on a number of commodities, notably gold, oil, and rubber, trade on TOCOM, as do option contracts on gold.

Tokyo Financial Exchange An exchange in Japan on which futures contracts and other derivatives are traded. It was established in 1989.

Tokyo Grain Exchange An exchange in Japan on which futures contracts and options on beans, silks, coffee, and corn are traded. It is organized as a nonprofit organization and was established in 1952.

Tokyo Round A global discussion on the role of tariffs that took place over several years and resulted, in 1980, in the Tokyo Declaration, which called for a significant reduction in tariffs over the next eight years. It also led to the adoption of an agreement on the appropriate times to use countervailing duties. See also: General Agreement on Tariffs and Trade.

Tokyo Stock Exchange The second largest stock exchange in the world by market capitalization. The TSE was established in 1878. After World War II, it experienced growth unprecedented in history. By the early 1990s, it accounted for approximately 60% of the world's market capitalization. It has since fallen because of the Asian Financial Crisis, but it remains one of the world's most important exchanges.

Tokyo Stock Price Index Commonly called TOPIX. A major index on the Tokyo Stock Exchange that tracks the First Section, which consists of the largest companies by market capitalization. Along with the NIKKEI average, TOPIX is considered a major indicator of the state of Japanese investment, and of the economy at large.

Tola A customary Indian unit of weight approximately equivalent to 11.66 grams.

Toll Revenue Bond A municipal bond with a coupon and principal guaranteed by the revenue on a toll road. Generally speaking, a toll revenue bond builds some improvement, such as a bridge or road, and the toll is placed on that road to repay the bond. A toll revenue bond helps some municipalities avoid its debt ceilings.

Toll-Free A telephone number that never results in charges to the caller. That is, one is not assessed long distance or other charges when one calls a toll-free number. It is often used for charities and technical support services in which the owner of the number solicits phone calls. In the United States, toll-free numbers usually begin with 800 or 888.

Tolling Agreement An agreement between two companies in which one agrees to supply a certain amount of a raw material every so often. For example, an oil refinery and a drilling company may agree that the drilling company will sell the refinery a certain number of barrels of crude oil every month so that the refinery has something to refine. Tolling agreements are relevant to supply chains; because of the tolling agreement, the refinery in the above example may be more confident that it can sell refined oil to other companies along the supply chain. Tolling agreements can therefore be mutually advantageous.

Toltti A Finnish term for 12 pieces of lumber.

Tom Next Short for "tomorrow next;" referring to a eurocurrency or foreign exchange transaction in which delivery of the underlying currency occurs the following trading day. Tom next transactions occur on the interbank market.

Toman In Iran, an informal expression for 10 rials. See also: IRR.

Tombstone An advertisement detailing a new issue of a security. Most importantly, the tombstone lists the underwriting syndicate responsible for placing the new issue with investors. Tombstones list the syndicate according to bracket, which is a place on a hierarchy indicating how much of an issue each individual underwriter is placing with respect to the others. The brackets are called, from largest to smallest: bulge bracket, major bracket, minor bracket, underwriter, and selling group. A tombstone derives its name because, in print, it looks vaguely like a stereotypical tombstone from the Old West.

Tomme A Norwegian unit of length approximately equivalent to 26.1 millimeters. Before the 1970s, it was used to measure Norwegian timber. Since then, the word has been used to denote an inch.

Tomna A Maltese unit of land area approximately equivalent to 1,124 square meters. It is largely obsolete but is still used in some circumstances.

TON 1. GOST 7.67 Latin three-letter geocode for Tonga. The code is used for transactions to and from Tongan bank accounts and for international shipping to Tonga. As with all GOST 7.67 codes, it is used primarily in Cyrillic alphabets. **2.** Informal; in bond trading, $100 million.

Tonel A Portuguese measure of liquid volume approximately equivalent to 840 liters. It became obsolete after Lusophone countries adopted the metric system in the 19th century.

Tonelada A Portuguese measure of weight approximately equivalent to 793 kilograms. It became obsolete after Lusophone countries adopted the metric system in the 19th century.

Tong An ancient Indian unit of area approximately equivalent to 1/32 hectare.

Toning In numismatics, the color of a coin. The color of coins changes over time due to use and corrosion. How much or how little the toning corresponds to the toning of the coin when it was first minted is one aspect of determining its condition, which in turn determines its value.

Tonni An informal Finnish unit meaning 1,000 kilograms. It is sometimes used to indicate other bunches of 1,000.

Tontine Describing any investment jointly held by two or more persons in which, when one investor dies, his/her share is reapportioned among the surviving investors. For example, if there are three persons who own a tontine company equally, and one of them dies, the surviving partners then divide the company 50-50. See also: Last survivor annuity.

Too-Big-To-Fail Describing a concept or policy that certain companies are so systematically important to an economy that the government must intervene if they are in danger of bankruptcy or other failure. The idea behind a too-big-to-fail policy is that these companies do business with too many other companies, and their failure will cause a cascade effect adversely impacting the economy on a grand scale. Supporters of too-big-to-fail policies argue that they maintain economic stability, while critics allege that they encourage unnecessary risk taking.

Toonie An informal term for the Canadian two-dollar coin. It was introduced in 1996. See also: Canadian dollar.

Tooth Describing paper with rough texture, which makes the paper able to receive ink more easily.

TOP ISO 4217 representation for the Tongan pa'anga. It is officially pegged to a currency basket that includes the Australian dollar and the New Zealand dollar, as well as the yen and United States dollar. However, the National Reserve Bank (Tonga) sets the exchange rate to the Australian dollar each day. Critics contend that this official exchange rate bears little reflection to the currency basket. The pa'anga is divided into 100 seniti. See also: Currency pair.

Top a Bid To make a bid for a security or other asset higher than the previous one. See also: Auction.

Top Line Informal; revenue or sales. The term is used most frequently in connection to earnings reports, where revenue is listed at the top and profit at the bottom.

Top of Mind The state in which a significant proportion of potential customers think of a certain brand first to serve their needs. This may occur, for example, when a brand name for a product becomes synonymous with its generic name. A product may come to the top of the mind as the result of a successful marketing campaign or simply from a vastly superior product.

Top Up 1. Informal, to refill, especially when the thing being refilled is not completely empty. The term is chiefly British. **2.** See: Top Up Investing.

Top-Down Investing An investment philosophy that considers macroeconomic factors. When making investment decisions a top-down investor first considers the broad condition of the economy, then factors affecting specific industries expected to outperform the economy, and, finally, individual companies expected to do the best in those industries. Proponents of top-down investing argue that it identifies good companies more efficiently, while critics contend that it does not let the investor know the details of each specific stock. See also: Bottom-up investing.

Top-Heavy Informal; describing a security trading at a price at which there are more sellers than buyers. Because there is a lack of demand at the top-heavy price, the security is likely to undergo a price correction. See also: Resistance level.

Topline Growth An increase in a company's revenue over a given period of time. Topline growth does not necessarily indicate an increase in profit; if expenses at the same or a greater rate, topline growth could mean that profits remain flat or even decrease. See also: Bottomline growth, Top Line.

Topping Out A situation in which a price or stock has reached its highest point and is unlikely to continue to increase. It may even begin to decrease. See also: Mature phase (of an industry).

Toronto Stock Exchange The largest stock exchange in Canada. Tracing its roots to the 1850s, the Toronto Stock Exchange in 1997 became one of the largest exchanges in North America to close its trading floor and begin operations electronically. It is a leader in the oil, gas, and mining industries, with more such companies trading on it than on any other exchange in the world.

Toronto Terms A form of debt relief for heavily indebted poor countries in which the present value of payments is reduced by up to one-third. The Toronto terms were introduced by the Paris Club in 1988. This form of debt relief is a type of concessional restructuring.

Torpedo Stock A stock that is declining in price very quickly with no foreseeable reversal. A torpedo stock may occur when a company's fundamentals suddenly change or when it becomes gradually apparent over time that the company is unprofitable and is not taking appropriate steps to change course. This causes many or most shareholders to sell their stock for whatever they can receive.

Toshihiko Fukui A Japanese businessman who served as Governor of the Bank of Japan from 2003 to 2008. As governor, he refused to establish an inflation target or take other steps that were thought to help combat deflation. In the 1980s (during the Japanese bubble), he was the head of the Bank's business department.

Total Describing completion, especially of an amount. The total cost of a transaction includes not only the sale price but also commissions, interest rates, and other expenses. For example, a student loan has a principal and interest rate, but the total cost may include an origination fee, a federal default fee, and other expenses.

Total Cost of Ownership The all-in cost for purchasing and maintaining an asset. For example, the total cost of ownership of a house is not simply the purchase price, but also includes the cost of taxes, utility bills, perhaps the cost of replacing or repairing parts of the structure, and any other relevant costs incurred during the time one owns the house.

Total Debt to Total Assets A measure of a company's risk. It is taken by adding its short-term debt to its long-term debt and dividing the quantity by its total value of its assets. A ratio over 1 indicates that the value of the company's debt exceeds that of its assets while a ratio below 1 indicates the opposite. Generally speaking, a low total debt to total assets ratio is thought to be desirable.

Total Dollar Return The total return on an investment made in a foreign currency expressed in U.S. dollars. This is especially important for companies that make foreign investments but whose profits and losses are denominated in dollars.

Total Enterprise Value The market value of a company if it were (hypothetically) to be taken over. It is calculated by adding its market capitalization to its debt, minority interest, and preferred equity at market value, then subtracting its cash and cash equivalents. This is an important aspect of business valuation and accounting.

Total Expense Ratio A measure of an investment fund's costs of operation as a percentage of its total assets. It is calculated by dividing the fund's total costs by its total assets. As the total costs include things like management fees and commissions, the total expense ratio is important to determining the actual return on a fund. For example, a mutual fund may have a 10% return per year, which is quite high; however, if the total expense ratio is 8%, this means that shareholders only receive

2% of the return. It is also called the management expense ratio or simply the expense ratio.

Total Liabilities A line on a balance sheet representing the sum of a company's long-term debt, current liabilities and irregular or miscellaneous expenses. In other words, total liabilities include the full amount that a company is required to pay.

Total Loss Only Insurance Also called TLO insurance. A marine insurance policy that only provides coverage if an insured item is completely destroyed, damaged beyond use or disappears without explanation. TLO insurance is typically a form of reinsurance.

Total Reserves The cash and coin a bank keeps in its vault and all of its deposits with a Federal Reserve bank. Total reserves are the assets that a bank has immediately available to cover its liabilities. Total reserves count against the bank's reserve requirements.

Total Return The complete amount one receives on an investment, expressed either as the rate of return or as a dollar figure. One calculates the total return simply by adding coupons or dividends to capital gains.

Total Return for Calendar Year The complete amount one receives on an investment in a year, expressed either as the rate of return or as a dollar figure. One calculates the total return simply by adding coupons or dividends to capital gains for the period between January and December.

Total Return Index An index of stocks that assumes that all dividends are reinvested in the stocks issuing them. Thus, a total return index is effectively weighted according to how often dividends are distributed and how much they are worth. It is important to note that a total return index is only a statistical calculation and that not all dividends of stocks represented in the index are actually reinvested.

Total Return Swap A swap in which the two legs are an interest rate, whether fixed or floating, and the return on a set asset. The second party owns the asset, which is usually a set of loans, bonds, or an equity index. The advantage to a total return swap for the payer of the interest rate is that it allows him/her to benefit from the ownership of the asset without owning it. However, if the asset falls in price over the life of the swap, the payer of the interest rate is required to compensate the owner of the asset for the amount the asset has lost.

Total Revenue The total amount of a company's sales and other sources of income. It is important to note that revenue is distinct from earnings or profits, which takes expenses into account. Obviously, however, high total revenue is desirable for any company.

Total Risk Systemic risk plus unsystemic risk on an investment. Every investment has sytemic risk (any risk carried by an entire class of assets and/or liabilities) and unsystemic risk (any risks unique to the investment). When making investment decisions, investors must account for the total risk to the investment.

Total Utility In economics, the level of satisfaction a person derives from a good or service. Utility is inherently subjective and thus difficult to measure, but it is important to determining how much supply of a product the market can handle without diminishing demand. Historically, it has been thought that one can quantify the utility of each unit, but some economists disagree with this. See also: Austrian school, Law of Diminishing Marginal Utility.

Total Volume The aggregate number of trades that take place for a security or on an exchange on a given trading day. A high total volume is an indicator of a high level of interest in a security at its current price. It is an especially important tool in technical analysis, in which volume is used to determine the strength of a market indicator. For example, a price rise on heavy trading volume indicates that that price rise is a true indicator, while a technical analyst likely would be more skeptical of the same rise on lighter trading volume. The method for determining total volume is called volume counting. In the United States, the SEC determines the methodology of volume counting. It is often called volume or trading volume.

Tote a Note Slang; to finance a loan. The term is most common in the automotive industry.

Totten Trust A trust into which the grantor places banking assets such as savings accounts and certificates of deposit while maintaining control of them. That is, the grantor maintains the ability to invest, profit from, or otherwise use the assets in the Totten trust. The assets in the Totten trust pass on to the beneficiary following the death of the grantor. However, because the grantor maintains the rights of ownership (though not ownership itself), the trust is subject to the estate tax.

Touchline The highest price a buyer of a security is willing to pay and the lowest price a seller is willing to sell at a given time. The touch line, like the bid-ask spread, represents the best price available for a security. Generally speaking, the more liquid an asset is, the lower the bid-ask spread is. As a result, currency, which is considered the most liquid asset, has an extremely low bid-ask spread.

Tour of Duty In the military, a period of deployment, especially overseas. In business, the term may be used informally to describe a brief stint in a company or department, especially if the stint is undesirable but necessary.

Tourist Baggage Insurance An insurance policy providing coverage for a policyholder's clothes, jewelry, photographs, electronics and other personal effects while he/she is traveling. The policy covers the insured items if they are lost, stolen, damaged or destroyed during travel. As with all insurance, one must pay a premium to receive the coverage.

Tout To strongly encourage investors to buy a particular security. Touting usually comes from someone with a strong interest in seeing the security's price rise, such as a large shareholder, a public relations firm, or even the issuing company itself. To tout is illegal in some circumstances, notably around the date of registration with the SEC.

Towing Insurance An insurance policy providing coverage for tow trucks. Towing insurance covers damage to a tow truck in the event of an accident, as well as its owner's legal liability. As with all insurance, one must pay a premium to receive the coverage.

Town Check A check written within the same municipality as the bank on which the check is drawn. For example, if Bob holds an account at a local bank and pays his landlord with a check from that account, Bob has written a town check. These checks are almost always accepted.

Town Clearing A computerized system allowing transfers of large payments by companies between banks in the same town or vicinity. Town clearing may be processed after regular clearance systems are done for the day. The system is used in the United Kingdom.

Town Hall A meeting in which management makes a presentation to all staff, followed by a question and answer session. Town halls are sometimes accused of being scripted in order to give the appearance of transparency without actually providing any useful information.

Town Marker In the U.S. Postal Service, a designation indicating that a sack of mail is going to a stated municipality. Zip codes have replaced the use of town markers.

Toxic Waste Informal for an illiquid or otherwise unattractive security. The term most often applies to a few collateralized mortgage obligations in which only the most risky mortgages are the underlying assets. Toxic waste is illiquid, but its existence makes other CMOs more liquid because it enables them to represent less risky mortgages.

Toxin Any poisonous substance a living thing produces as part of its metabolic or other natural process. That is, toxins themselves are not living things, but are produced by living things. Toxins are defined by the Biological Weapons Convention.

Toyoo Guyohten A Japanese official who served as vice minister of finance for international affairs until 1989. He was well known for his collaboration and good working relationship with Federal Reserve Chairman Paul Volcker.

TP 1. A former ISO-3166-1 alpha-2 code for the Democratic Republic of Timor-Leste. This was the code used in international transactions to and from Timor's bank accounts. The current code is TL. **2.** A former ISO 3166-2 geocode for Timor-Leste. This was used as an international standard for shipping to Timor-Leste. The current code is TL.

TPSC 1. Trade Policy Staff Committee. A standing committee of 19 federal agencies in the United States that coordinates policy on matters of international trade. It is chaired by the United States trade representative. **2.** Tennessee Public Service Commission. A former agency in the state of Tennessee responsible for regulating utility companies and the railroad and trucking industries. It consisted of three members, one elected from each of Tennessee's regions. It existed from 1897 to 1996.

TPTL ISO 3166-3 code for East Timor, which changed its name to Timor-Leste in 2002. ISO 3166-3 codes are used to indicate names of countries that are no longer used.

TR 1. ISO 3166-1 alpha-2 code for the Republic of Turkey. This is the code used in international transactions to and from Turkish bank accounts. **2.** ISO 3166-2 geocode for Turkey. This is used as an international standard for shipping to Turkey. Each province has its own code with the prefix "TR." For example, the code for Ankara Province is ISO 3166-2:TR-06.

Tracking Error An excessive deviation between an investment or portfolio and some benchmark. It is commonly used with respect to mutual funds, hedges, or other investment vehicles designed to track some index or other benchmark. If the portfolio's performance falls short of the benchmark, especially by a large amount, there is said to be a tracking error; an investor or investment company may wish to re-evaluate how it puts together the portfolio.

Tracking Stock A stock in a department (but not an independent corporation) of a publicly-traded company. For example, a company may issue tracking stock representing its new green energy division. A tracking stock allows the company to gauge the performance of a new or untested product or department while still maintaining control over it. They were common during the dot-com bubble, as established companies formed internet divisions and wished to observe their performance.

Trade The voluntary exchange of goods and/or services for money or an equivalent good or service. In ancient times and frequently even now, trade was conducted through the bartering of goods. In developed economies, trades are usually made with an intermediary, especially money or credit. Trade is regulated by laws of the particular jurisdiction in which a trade is made. Common restrictions include prohibitions on selling stolen property or non-existent goods. Most states, however, have much more complex regulations for trade, depending on the complexity of goods and services traded in their jurisdiction. States also regulate trade between parties in different jurisdictions. For example, two countries may encourage trade between each other, or, more famously, discourage trade through quotas and/or tariffs. In modern finance, trade especially refers to trade on securities exchanges. For example, the sale of a stock from one investor to another is known as a trade. This type of trade is regulated by special agencies in the appropriate jurisdiction; trade in the United States is regulated by the SEC, among other organizations. See also: Countertrade, Free trade, Protectionism.

Trade Acceptance A bill of exchange that has not been countersigned by the drawee's bank. A trade acceptance is presented as payment for a good or service. It is only as valuable as the drawee's creditworthiness. It is also called an accepted bill of exchange, an accepted draft, or a trade bill.

Trade Act of 1974 Legislation in the United States that gave the president the authority to negotiate trade agreements with other countries with relatively little interference from Congress. Specifically, Congress could disapprove of a trade agreement but could not amend it. It also allowed the president to impose trade barriers unilaterally against countries found to engage in unfair trade practices. The act expired in 1994. See also: Trade Act of 2002.

Trade Adjustment Assistance 1. A program of the U.S. Department of Labor providing financial assistance and employment retraining for persons who have lost jobs or suffered wage or hour reductions due to imports or outsourcing outside the United States. **2.** A program of the U.S. Department of Commerce providing financial assistance for companies that have suffered hardship due to competition from cheaper imports. The assistance is intended to make these companies more competitive through diversifying products and other means. **3.** A program of the U.S. Department of Agriculture providing payments to farmers who suffer reduced prices for their crops resulting from increased supply due to imports.

Trade Adjustment Assistance Center One of several offices throughout the United States charged with implementing the Trade Adjustment Assistance program, which provides financial assistance for companies that have suffered hardship due to competition from cheaper imports. The assistance is intended to make these companies more competitive through diversifying products and other means. Each TAAC is responsible for companies in a certain region of the U.S.

Trade Advertising Advertising aimed at a business and designed to entice it to purchase a product to sell to its customers, or at least to recommends it to its customers. Trade advertising is directed at stockbrokers, wholesalers and others who are not intended to be the end user of a product. It is also called business-to-business advertising.

Trade and Tariff Act of 1984 Legislation in the United States that requires the president of the United States to inform the House Ways and Means Committee and the Senate Finance Committee before opening free trade negotiations. Each committee then has 60 legislative days to permit or deny the negotiations. The Act increased congressional influence over American trade agreements.

Trade Away To execute a trade through another broker or dealer.

Trade Bust The cancellation of an offer to buy or sell a security because an error on an electronic exchange causes the price to leave its usual range.

Trade Credit A loan or line of credit that a company extends to another in order for the second company to buy goods and services, especially those necessary to conduct its operations.

Trade Creditor A seller who delivers goods to a buyer and does not require payment for a certain period of time. This means that the buyer owes money to the seller for the trade, making the buyer a debtor and the seller a trade creditor.

Trade Date The date on which a transaction occurs, especially the trade of a security or derivative. It is important to note that the trade date differs from the settlement date, which can range from one to five days following the trade date. On the trade date, ownership of the securities being traded transfers from the seller to the buyer, but the seller does not receive payment until the settlement date.

Trade Discount The amount by which a company reduces its price per unit when selling units (usually in large quantities) to a reseller. Trade discounts exist to encourage large orders, which, while they may reduce profit margin, increase revenue and therefore raw profit. They also tend to increase the reseller's profit margin, which may encourage repeat business with the supplier.

Trade Dollar A $1 coin minted in the United States between 1873 and 1885. It was produced in order to open up U.S. trade with East Asia. It contained 90% pure silver.

Trade Expansion Act of 1962 Legislation in the United States giving the president the authority to reduce tariffs on imports up to 50% in order to encourage international trade. While the act expired in 1967, the Johnson administration used its authority to reduce tariffs in the Kennedy Round of the General Agreement on Tariffs and Trade.

Trade Finance The institutions or transactions involved in the financing of international trade. Trade finance looks at banks, credit agencies, insurers, forfaiters, and any other person or institution who enables importers and exporters to trade across borders.

Trade Flat 1. In stocks, to trade without a change in price. That is, one trades flat when one sells a stock for the same price at which one bought it. **2.** In bonds, to trade without accrued interest. That is, the buyer is not responsible for paying the seller for any interest that has accumulated since the last coupon payment.

Trade House A company that trades commodities.

Trade Minister A general term for a government official responsible for international trade. The trade minister may negotiate trade agreements, advise the administration on trade policy, and promote the country's products on the world stage. The trade minister may be a cabinet level official, but this is not always the case.

Trade Month The month during which the trade of a security takes place. Unlike the trade date, the trade month rarely matters for settlement purposes, but it may have tax implications if the trade month is just before or just after the end of a fiscal year.

Trade Name 1. The name used by a business, even if that is not its legal name. For example, the trade name for Investment Corporation may be InvestCorp. The trade name sometimes has no relation to the company's actual name. **2.** See: Brand Name.

Trade Not Aid A slogan in support of fair trade. The slogan indicates a desire to buy products from developing countries instead of giving them foreign aid. Proponents of "trade not aid" believe that it represents a more sustainable, and less dependent, form of development. The slogan became popular in the late 1960s.

Trade on the Wire To make a bid or give an offer without checking surrounding conditions. That is, an investor may trade on the wire when he/she gives his/her broker an order to buy a security at a given price without first checking whether a better price is available.

Trade Policy Review Group A standing committee of 19 federal agencies in the United States that reviews policy on matters of international trade. It is chaired by the United States trade representative.

Trade Policy Staff Committee A standing committee of 19 federal agencies in the United States that coordinates policy on matters of international trade. It is chaired by the United States trade representative.

Trade Rate 1. A special, lower price that members of a trade group offer each other for work. For example, a plumber may charge an electrician the trade rate for work because they are both skilled tradesmen. The term is chiefly British. **2.** More broadly, a lower rate given to regular customers.

Trade Reporting The practice of announcing the trade or issue of a security to the appropriate regulator. Trade reporting is mandatory and serves to increase transparency in the market. It also helps keep the regulator abreast to what is happening, which may help it find wrongdoing.

Trade Sanction One or more trade barriers that a country places upon another country as a punitive action. A country may institute a trade sanction because it disagrees with its trade policies; for example, if country A subsidizes domestic corn so that it reduces demand for country B's imports, country B may restrict the import of country A's wheat as punishment. Alternatively, a trade sanction may occur when two countries disagree on a more fundamental level. A trade sanction should not be confused with an economic sanction.

Trade Surplus The difference between the value of a country's exports and the value of its imports, where the value of exports is greater. Analysts disagree on the impact, if any, of a trade surplus on the economy. Some economists believe that a trade surplus creates employment and increases GDP growth. Others believe that the balance of trade has little impact. A trade surplus is also called a favorable balance of trade. See also: Trade deficit.

Trade Through To trade a security on a given exchange when a better price is available on a different exchange. Computerized links between exchanges have made trading through inadvertently less common and more difficult for unscrupulous brokers. Rule NMS attempts to prevent trading through by requiring most orders to be sent to the exchange with the best possible price.

Trade Working Capital The amount of money a company has on hand, or will have for a given year. Trade working capital is calculated by subtracting current liabilities from current assets. That is, one takes the value of all debts and obligations for the current year and subtracts that total from the value of all cash and assets that might reasonably be converted into cash in the current year. This is a good measure of the short- and medium-term financial health of a company, and may indicate by how much it can expand its operations without resorting to borrowing or another capital raising tactic.

Trade-for-Trade Settlement A securities transaction that the buyer and seller settledirectly, without recourse to a clearing house.

Trademark A logo, insignia, or other distinctive sign identifying a company, product, or anything else. A trademark may be registered with a country's patent office and is protected from duplication. An example of a trademark is the unique check mark seen on Nike products. Trademarks are intangible assets because they can help build brand recognition and as such have value.

Trader An investor who makes many trades throughout a trading day, buying and selling securities in order to profit from short-term changes in prices. For example, a trader may buy Stock A at $15 per share because he/she believes it will be $18 a few minutes, or hours, later. Traders engage in high risk activities because there is no guarantee that the price will move in the desired direction. However, traders provide a great deal of liquidity to the market. See also: Registered Competitive Trader.

Trades by Appointment Describing an illiquid stock. A stock that trades by appointment may be difficult to sell for any number of reasons.

Trade-Weighted Dollar The average value of the U.S. dollar with respect to a basket of 10 foreign currencies. The Federal Reserve calculates the value of the trade-weighted dollar. When the value increases, American exports become more expensive in foreign countries; when it decreases, they become more affordable. See also: Strong Dollar, Weak Dollar.

Trade-Weighted Exchange Rate The exchange rate for a currency as adjusted against a currency basket consisting of the currencies of a country's main trading partners. This allows a currency to be judged against the currencies that it is most likely to be converted into, rather than against the market as a whole.

Trading Ahead A trade in which a specialist, one who trades only to maintain liquidity in the market, makes a trade when there is an offsetting trade from someone else. For example, suppose a specialist receives an order to buy 100 shares of a stock. Ordinarily, the specialist would look for an offsetting order from the public and only sell the shares from its own account if no such order exists. The specialist trades ahead when it sells 100 shares to the buyer when another order is on record. The specialist does this in order to make a profit for itself. Trading ahead is a violation of NYSE and other rules. See also: Front running.

Trading Authorization A document giving another party the ability to make trades of securities and/or derivatives on one's behalf. Generally speaking, one gives trading authorization to a broker, but theoretically, one may give it to someone else. See also: Discretionary Account.

Trading Below Cash Describing a stock with less market capitalization than cash on hand. That is, the share price times the number of shares outstanding in a company trading below cash is less than its total cash minus its debt. A company may be trading below cash if its financial prospects are poor.

Trading Channel In technical analysis, the range of prices between a security's resistance level and support level. A resistance level is the price below which a given security does not normally fall, and a support level is the price above which it does not usually rise. A trading channel is particularly useful to technical analysts as it enables them to recommend buying the security when it is toward the bottom and selling when it is near the top. A trading channel may be steady, or it may be gradually rising or falling.

Trading Costs All commissions and other expenses related to the trade of a security. When an investor buys or sells a security, he/she must usually pay a fee to his/her investment adviser and/or broker. Research and other indirect costs informing investment decisions are not usually considered trading costs unless they directly relate to or result from a specific transaction. The investor accounts for these expenses when calculating whether an investment earned a profit or loss. See also: All in cost.

Trading Curb On an exchange, a measure designed to prevent panic selling by stopping trading after a security or an index has fallen by a certain amount. For example, if the Dow Jones Industrial Average falls 10% in a trading day, the New York Stock Exchange institutes a trading curb that suspends trade for at least one hour. A trading curb is intended to allow investors to determine whether a situation is really as bad as it looks. It is sometimes called a collar or a circuit breaker. See also: Suspended trading.

Trading Currency The currency used to settle an international transaction, especially when it is the currency of neither country involved in the transaction. For example, if a buyer in Romania uses U.S. dollars to purchase goods from a seller in Brazil, the dollar is the trading currency.

Trading Day A day on which an exchange is open for the buying and selling of securities. The trading days for most exchanges are Monday through Friday. However, some exchanges, notably in Muslim-majority countries, have different trading days.

Trading Desk A physical desk at an investment bank where one may buy or sell securities or derivatives. Generally speaking, each trading desk at an organization specializes in one type of security. For example, one may buy and sell stocks, other bonds, and so forth. Trading desks allow users to trade securities instantaneously, which can be important in arbitrage. A trading desk is also called a dealing desk.

Trading Dividends The act or practice of buying shares in a company before the ex-dividend date so as to maximize one's income from dividends. Trading dividends is normally practiced by corporate investors because the large majority of their income from dividends is tax free.

Trading Dollars Informal; a term for a company breaking even on an investment. For example, an oil company may spend $1 million placing an oil pump' on an unproven reserve and drill only $1 million worth of oil. In this situation, the company trades $1 million in investment for an equal number of dollars from the oil, hence the term.

Trading Floor The physical place where trading occurs on an exchange with an open outcry system. For example, the New York Stock Exchange has a place where traders and members gather to buy and sell securities. Many exchanges are moving away from trading floors and toward conducting more trades electronically. It is also called a floor.

Trading Gap In technical analysis, a break on a chart representing a sudden and large price movement accompanied by high trading volume. Generally speaking, charts do not show trading gaps because price movements, even when large, occur smoothly enough to not require a break in the chart. Trading gaps may occur, for example, when the price of a security suddenly doubles or halves. As with many charting terms, it may be bullish or bearish; a sudden movement upward is a bullish trading gap, while a sudden movement downward is bearish. It may occur when there is a significant break between the bid and the ask, or when trading temporarily stops in anticipation of a major news announcement by the company.

Trading Hours The hours during which an exchange is open for the buying and selling of securities. For example, an exchange may be open from 9 am to 12 pm, and again from 1:30 to 4 pm. Market makers generally are required to trade during trading hours. See also: After-Hours Trading.

Trading on the Equity The practice of borrowing capital in order to increase the cash one has available to invest. For example, if one has $50,000 to invest and an investment vehicle has a minimum investment of $100,000, one may borrow an additional $50,000. In order for trading on the equity to be worth the effort, the return on the investment must exceed the interest on the loan.

Trading on the Perimeter The act of trading near a trading post when trading is particularly active. A trading post is a place on an exchange assigned to a specialist for the trading of certain securities. When the trading is very active, trading on the perimeter occurs because the crowd around the trading post renders investors unable to speak with the specialist directly. Instead, investors speak and trade between themselves.

Trading Paper The act or practice of buying or selling a certificate of deposit. Trading paper especially refers to situations in which the buyer is likely to re-sell the CD. The term is most common on the Euromarket.

Trading Pattern The graphical representation on a chart of a trend in security prices. Technical analysts identify trading patterns for a security and predict future price movements, in part, by matching current patterns with previous patterns.

Trading Pool Two or more investors who manipulate a stock's price by making buy or sell orders so as to create the impression of high volume and general interest in the stock. This could raise or lower the price, according to the needs of the trading pool. See also: Price manipulation.

Trading Posts The physical places on exchanges where transactions occur. Trading posts are most important to exchanges that use the open outcry or a similar system. They are becoming increasingly irrelevant as more exchanges conduct trading electronically.

Trading Price In the context of a trading day, the price at which a security is being bought or sold at any given time. The trading price is advertised on an exchange's overhead board, and is often also posted on the Internet with updates up to every minute.

Trading Profit The profit that an investor derives from buying and selling short-term securities, or those that the investor holds for less than one year. Trading profits can be substantial if the investor knows what he/she is doing, but there is a good deal of risk involved. Governments often seek to encourage long-term investment at the expense of short-term, and because of this, trading profit is usually taxed at the (higher) income tax rate instead of the capital gains rate.

Trading Ring 1. An area of the NYSE trading floor on which bonds are traded. **2.** A group or syndicate of traders and/or trading firms, especially one engaged in illegal activities. This sense of the term is most often used in journalism. See also: Insider trading.

Trading Session The period of time during which a securities exchange is open. That is, orders may be placed and filled during the trading session, but generally not outside it. An exchange may have several trading sessions during a day. For example, the exchange may be open from 9 a.m. until 10:30 a.m., from 11:30 a.m. until 1 p.m., and from 2 p.m. to 3:30 p.m. Holding several trading sessions gives the market more time to digest information rationally without having to respond immediately.

Trading Volume The measure how many trades take place for a security or on an exchange on a given trading day. A high trading volume is an indicator of a high level of interest in a security at its current price. It is an especially important tool in technical analysis, in which trading volume is used to determine the strength of a market indicator. For example, a price rise on heavy trading volume indicates that that price rise is a true indicator, while a technical analyst likely would be more skeptical of the same rise on lighter trading volume. The method for determining trading volume is called volume counting. In the United States, the SEC determines the methodology of volume counting. Trading volume is often simply called volume.

Traditional 401(k) A retirement investment plan in which a contributor defers taxation on contributions until after withdrawal. Under a traditional 401(k), a worker places a portion of his/her pre-tax income into a 401(k) account and allows it to be invested. Taxation is deferred until withdrawal from the account, generally after retirement. Withdrawals prior to the age of 59 1/2 are subject to excise taxes, but the investor must begin disbursements before the age of 70 1/2, unless he/she is still employed with the company offering the 401(k). Most employees are allowed to place up to $16,500 (in 2009) per year into a 401(k), and some employers have matching contributions.

Traditional IRA An investment retirement account in which a worker makes tax deductible contributions up to a certain limit throughout his/her working life. Unlike Roth IRAs, contributions are tax deductible but withdrawals are taxed, effectively deferring tax on the account until the worker begins making withdrawals in retirement. Importantly, however, tax deductibility of contributions depends on one's tax bracket. The limit to annual contributions varies by year and is indexed to inflation. Traditional IRAs are allowed to invest in securities and, in practice, normally own common stock and certificates of deposit. See also: 401(k).

Traditional Whole Life Policy A life insurance policy with no expiration date. That is, a traditional whole life policy provides coverage for the entire life of the policyholder (provided he/she continues to make premium payments). When the policyholder dies, his/her beneficiaries receive the death benefit. Traditional whole life policies also include a cash surrender value, allowing the policyholder to recover part of the premium he/she has invested in the policy should he/she ever decide to cancel the policy.

Trailing Referring to a recently completed time period. For example, trailing 12-month earnings refers to a company's earnings over the 12 months ending on the last day of the most recent month. Showing developments on a trailing basis is common way of tracking a company's finances.

Trailing Commission A commission that the salesperson of a mutual fund receives each year an investor remains a shareholder. That is, the salesperson receives the first trailing commission when the investor first buys shares in the fund, and a new trailing fee each year thereafter. Critics of this practice point out that it can create a moral hazard that the salesperson will aggressively sell a fund because of his own financial incentive, rather than because he believes it to be a good investment for the potential shareholder. Not all mutual funds pay their sales staff trailing commissions. A trailing commission is also calling a trailer fee. See also: Load.

Trailing Earnings A company's earnings over a previous period of time. Commonly, one examines a company's earnings over the most recently completed fiscal year; these may be considered trailing earnings. However, the term "trailing" often implies a value calculated on a rolling basis. That is, trailing earnings may describe the most recent 12 month period. These earnings will change each month as the nearest month is added to the calculation and the most distant month is dropped. See also: Trailing 12 Month.

Trailing EPS A company's earnings per share over a previous period of time. Commonly, one examines a company's earnings per share over the most recently completed fiscal year; these may be considered trailing EPS. However, the term "trailing" often implies a value calculated on a rolling basis. That is, trailing EPS may describe the most recent 12 month period. These earnings per share will change each month as the nearest month is added to the calculation and the most distant month is dropped. See also: Trailing 12 month.

Trailing P/E The price of a security per share at the present time divided by the trailing earnings per share over the previous year. It is the most commonly used form of the P/E ratio because it is based on actual, rather than projected, earnings. A trailing P/E ratio is thus the most accurate way to measure a security's valuation, that is, the fair value of a stock in a perfect market.

Trailing Sales A company's revenue from sales over a period of time in the past. Often, a company will use trailing sales over the past 12 months to help forecast its expected sales over the coming 12 months. Trailing sales are useful because they can be known with certainty; however, their predictive value is often limited because of forces outside the company's control.

Trailing Stop An order to sell a security when the price drops below a certain percentage of a given price. If the price rises, the trailing stop remains the same percentage below the new price. However, if the price drops, the trailing stop remains the same. For example, suppose an investor buys a security at $10 per share and sets a trailing stop at 20% below the price. If the price drops to $8, the security is automatically sold. If the price rises to $20, the trailing stop moves to $16. However, if the security is bought at $10 and the price drops to $9.50, the trailing stop remains at $8. Likewise, if the price rises to $20 and then drops to $18, the new trailing stop remains $16. See also: Advisory account.

Trailing Twelve Months Referring to the most recently completed 12 month period. For example, trailing 12 month earnings refers to a company's earnings over the 12 months ending on the last day of the most recent month. Showing developments on a trailing 12 month basis is common way of tracking a company's finances. It is less commonly called last 12 months.

Trambiyo A subdivision of the kori, the currency of Kutch while it was part of British India. A trambiyo was worth 1/48 of one kori.

Tranche A part of an issue. A tranche sometimes refers to a single issue of a security released at different times. For example, a company may announce that is intends to issue $10,000,000 in bonds in two tranches of $5,000,000. Tranches are important to collateralized mortgage obligations, which are backed by pools of mortgages. These mortgages are arranged in tranches that mature at different times, for instance in 10 years, 15 years, and 30 years.

Tranchette A small issue of bonds issued by the Bank of England and sold to the British government. The government then sells the tranchettes to the public.

Transaction Account A bank account from which payments can be made to a third party. Perhaps the most common type of transaction account is a checking account where one can write a check or use a debit card to deduct an amount from the account and give it to a third party without having to go personally to the bank to make a withdrawal. See also: NOW Account, Demand Account.

Transaction Cost The total cost of a security transaction after commissions, taxes, and other expenses. For example, a security has a price, but transaction costs include the fee one must pay the broker, capital gains taxes, among other things.

Transaction Date The date on which the trade of a security or derivative occurs. It is important to note that the transaction date differs from the settlement date, which can range from one to five days following the trade date. On the transaction date, ownership of the securities being traded transfers from the seller to the buyer, but the seller does not receive payment until the settlement date.

Transaction Demand The amount of money needed to cover the needs of an individual, firm, or nation. That is, transaction demand for money is a measure of how much of a certain currency people need in order to buy the goods and services they use. Generally speaking, if an economy is healthy, there is a high transaction demand for money because people are buying more goods and services. Conversely, if an economy is in trouble, people buy fewer goods and services. Unless there is a significant, sudden change in the transaction demand, central banks have little trouble adjusting the money supply to accommodate the changes that do occur.

Transaction Exposure In international trade, the risk that exchange rates will change after a company has agreed to a transaction but before it is accomplished, such that it adversely affects the transaction. For example, suppose an American company agrees to buy goods from a British company and settle the transaction in pounds. The American company has the transaction exposure that the pound will appreciate with respect to the U.S. dollar, causing the company to spend more dollars to buy the same number of pounds to be able to settle the transaction.

Transaction Fee A fee that a broker-dealer assesses on a client for the service of filling an order. Usually, the transaction fee is a percentage of the value of the transaction, but sometimes it is a flat rate, such as two cents per share or seven dollars per trade.

Transaction Insured Trade Acceptance Locator In international trade, a certificate issued by an insurance company guaranteeing payment to an exporter, depending upon the exporter's performance.

Transaction Loan A loan for a specific purpose. For example, a mortgage is a transaction loan because it is used to buy a piece of property, a fact both the lender and the borrower know when they begin the process. A transaction loan contrasts with a line of credit, which may be used for any number of purposes within a broad range.

Transaction Price The price of a good or service expressed relative to the same quantity of another good or service. Transaction prices help distinguish price changes due to inflation from real price changes.

Transaction Tax A tax on a sale of property, especially the sale of a security. This is rarely used in the United States. In 1968, the City of Philadelphia levied a small transaction tax on all shares traded on the Philadelphia Stock Exchange, which caused the Exchange to move to Bala Cynwyd, immediately outside Philadelphia, until the tax was rescinded. More rarely, the term transaction tax may refer to a tax on the transfer of title on any property such as real estate. In this sense, capital gains taxes and estate taxes are transaction taxes. It is also called a transfer tax. See also: Stamp duty.

Transactions Motive The desire of an economic actor to maintain sufficient funds in a bank account in order to write checks on that account for daily needs and wants. A person with higher income has a greater transactions motive than a person with lower income; that is, that person wants to have more money in order to spend more. In Keynesian economics, the transactions motive is one of three reasons persons demand liquidity. See also: Liquidity preference, precautionary motive, speculative motive.

Transcribe To take dictation of speech and put it into an electronic or written format. Transcription businesses are common in the legal and medical fields; for example, one may hire a company to transcribe court records.

Transcript of Account A list of information all current and past holders of a security.

Transfer 1. To sell. 2. To deliver. 3. To change ownership between parties for any reason.

Transfer Agent A financial institution that acts, for a fee, as a record keeper for a publicly-traded company, investment company, or similar company. A transfer agent is responsible for issuing stock certificates, dealing with lost or stolen certificates, and generally maintaining accurate records for the client company. A transfer agent is particularly important because many investment companies have a large number of investors with a small amount of equity.

Transfer Deed In England and Wales, a document affixed to the title of a piece of real estate indicating its transfer (whether by sale, gift or other means) to another party. A transfer deed must be filed with HM Land Registry. See also: Stamp duty, Transfer stamp.

Transfer on Death A brokerage account into which the account holder places assets while maintaining control of them, with the proviso that the assets pass on to beneficiaries after the account holder's death. That is, the account holder maintains the ability to invest, profit from, or otherwise use the securities and other assets in the transfer-on-death account. The assets in the account pass on to the beneficiary following the death of the account holder. This helps the beneficiary avoid the sometimes lengthy probate process. However, because the account holder maintains the rights of ownership (though not ownership itself) the account is subject to the estate tax. See also: Totten trust.

Transfer Payment Money that a government gives to individuals, usually through a social welfare program. For example, elderly people in the United States who have paid FICA taxes for a certain number of years receive a Social Security check from the government every month. This is a transfer payment. Another type of transfer payment is money given to a state or province with the proviso that it will fund the state or province's social welfare programs. For example, under the Personal Responsibility and Work Opportunity Reconciliation Act in the United States, each state receives a certain amount of money from the federal government to fund welfare and similar programs for the poor.

Transfer Price The price a division of a company charges a different division of the same company for a good or service. Transfer prices are important especially for large, decentralized corporations where each division reports its own profits and losses separately. The transfer price is usually roughly the same as the market price for the good or service. See also: Section 482.

Transfer Procedures The procedures by which the SEC governs the exchange of money for securities. That is, transfer procedures are the regulations concerning the sale of securities. Transfer procedures include strict requirements of documentation and guarantees that all signatures of parties agreeing to transfers are valid. See also: Stamp Medallion Program.

Transfer Risk In international trade, the risk that a transaction cannot take place because a government or central bank will not allow currency to leave a country. For example, a government may theoretically declare that its currency is inconvertible, disallowing a transaction. Alternatively, a government may restructure its national debt service in such a way that it affects transfers of currency out of the country. See also: Political risk.

Transfer Stamp Documentation (often a physical stamp) affixed to a transfer deed to indicate that a stamp duty (which is a tax on a property transfer) has been paid.

Transferable Letter of Credit An irrevocable letter of credit with three parties. The first party is the bank issuing the letter of credit. The second party is an intermediary who accepts the letter of credit from the bank, and is called the first beneficiary. The third party is called the second beneficiary and is often an importer or exporter. Generally speaking, the first beneficiary is the second beneficiary's representative in the country in which the letter of credit is issued. In order for the letter of credit be transferable, the bank must be aware of the situation and agree to the transfer. This agreement allows the first beneficiary to transfer the letter of credit to the second beneficiary. A transferable letter of credit is relatively common for international transactions in the Far East.

Transferable Put Right An option contract that a publicly-traded company issues to a shareholder giving the shareholder the right but not the obligation to sell his/her shares back to the company at a certain strike price on or before the contract's expiration date. A transferable put right protects the shareholder from the possibility that the share price will drop precipitously, resulting in a massive loss. However, the right increases the company's risk that it may have to honor the exercise of a number of options at a high price, resulting in financial difficulty.

Transferable Stock Option An employee stock option that allows the employee to give to another party. Usually, transfers are limited to members of the employee's family, an investment vehicle designed to benefit family members, and/or a charity.

Transferable-on-Death A brokerage account into which the account holder places assets while maintaining control of them, with the proviso that the assets pass on to beneficiaries after the account holder's death. That is, the account holder maintains the ability to invest, profit from, or otherwise use the securities and other assets in the transferable-on-death account. The assets in the account pass on to the beneficiary following the death of the account holder. This helps the beneficiary avoid the sometimes lengthy probate process. However, because the account holder maintained the rights of ownership (though not ownership itself), the account is subject to the estate tax. See also: Totten trust.

Transferee The person or organization to whom a transfer of funds or assets is made. For example, if Joe writes a check to Bob, Bob is the transferee because he receives the stated amount of money from Joe's bank account. See also: Payee.

Transferor In law, a party that makes a tranfer of property or another asset to a second party. The transferor may or may not receive compensation for the transfer.

Transition Industry An industry at a state in its life cycle in which growth slows to the growth rate of the economy at large. This is marked by a slowdown in earnings growth and often results in a change to the company's dividend policy. See also: Growth phase, Maturity phase, Three-phase DDM.

Transition Phase A stage in a company's life cycle where growth slows to the growth rate of the economy at large. This is marked by a slowdown in earnings growth and often results in a change to the company's dividend policy. See also: Growth phase, Maturity phase, Three-phase DDM.

Translation When a parent-subsidiary relationship exists between two companies in different countries using different currencies, the act or practice of changing the financial statements of the subsidiary to conform to the accounting standards of the parent's country, as well as re-denominating the subsidiary's currency into the parent's currency. According to the Generally Accepted Accounting Principles in the United States, the translation of a foreign currency to U.S. dollars must be accurate as of the date on the financial statement. If there have been substantial changes to the exchange rate since that date, the consolidated financial statement must note this.

Translation Gain The gain that occurs when one exchanges one floating currency for another, then back into the first currency after it has become weaker. For example, suppose one has 1,000,000 U.S. dollars and exchanges them for 500,000 British pounds; this means the exchange rate was two dollars per pound. Later, if one still has those 500,000 pounds when the exchange rate is three dollar per pound and exchanges them back to dollars, suddenly one has $1,500,000. In this case, the translation gain is $500,000.

Translation Loss The loss that occurs when one exchanges one floating currency for another and then trades back into the first currency after it has become stronger. For example, suppose a person has 1,000,000 U.S. dollars and exchanges them for 500,000 British pounds; this means the exchange rate is two dollars per pound. Later, if that person still has those 500,000 pounds when the dollar has risen (quite dramatically) to one dollar per pound and exchanges them back to dollars, he/she has $500,000 instead of $1 million. In this case, the translation loss is $500,000.

Transmittal Letter A letter describing a transaction of a security. That is, a transmittal letter states the nature of a trade and the number of shares contained therein. A transmittal letter is sent with security certificates when they change ownership.

Transnistrian Ruble The currency of Transnistria, a country with limited recognition. It was issued in 1994, replacing the Soviet ruble. It suffered from extremely high inflation at first, but this has eased somewhat since 2000.

Transparency The state in which all relevant information is fully and freely available to the public. Nearly every analyst agrees that transparent markets are desirable because they lead to greater efficiency. Laws and regulations exist in most jurisdictions encouraging or mandating transparency. For example, the SEC requires disclosure forms declaring a great many different actions when or immediately after they occur. Likewise, the Sarbanes-Oxley Act is designed to increase transparency in accounting. A minority view holds that these laws and regulations intended to create transparent markets in fact reduce efficiency. Others contend that markets are efficient with or without transparency. See also: Efficient market hypothesis.

Transparent Market Any market where all relevant information is fully and freely available to the public. Nearly every analyst agrees that transparent markets are desirable and lead to greater efficiency. Laws and regulations exist in most jurisdictions encouraging or mandating transparency. For example, the SEC requires disclosure forms declaring a great many different actions when or immediately after they occur. Likewise, the Sarbanes-Oxley Act is designed to increase transparency in accounting. A minority view holds that these laws and regulations intended to create transparent markets in fact reduce efficiency. Others contend that markets are efficient with or without transparency. See also: Efficient Market Hypothesis.

Transportation Costs The expenses a company incurs when it transfers its inventory or other assets to another location. For example, a company must pay a trucking or shipping company. If a company is delivering a product, it may pass on the costs to the customer. Alternatively, it may spread its transportation across all products, or it may simply absorb the costs. See also: Incoterm, Shipping and handling, Transportation risk.

Transshipment The transfer of goods from one ship or other vessel to another, especially while in transit. One may think of transshipment as a layover in the importing and exporting of goods. Because it exposes the buyer to the risk that the goods will be damaged in transit, some letters of credit prohibit transshipment. The term is also spelled as transhipment.

Travel and Entertainment Expense Deduction A reduction in one's taxable income based on money one spends on traveling and entertainment for business purposes. Examples include expenses for hotels and meals while traveling on business. Travel and entertainment expenses can significantly reduce one's tax liability, but they are not unlimited. For example, one cannot deduct entertainment considered "lavish." Some entertainment is only deductible at 50% of its value.

Travel Dazzle A slang term for an attempt to become indispensible for one's supervisor while on a business trip with him/her. One does this in hopes that the indispensability will continue after the business trip ends.

Travel Expenses Expenses incurred when a person conducts business away from home. For example, if one must travel to another location to conduct a meeting with an important client, any lodging, meals, or transportation costs usually count as travel expenses. One may deduct travel expenses from one's taxable income, provided they are in fact directly related to business. For this reason, travel expenses are somewhat controversial; some companies, for example, book a business meeting at a major resort and deduct the entire cost. Whether this is an actual travel expense is a matter for debate.

Traveling Salesperson A person who makes a living by going from place to place to sell products. For example, a traveling salesman may visit dental offices in various towns to sell dental supplies. A traveling salesperson generally earns a commission on sales.

Trayas An ancient Persian unit of length approximately equivalent to 300 millimeters.

Treasure Trove Informal; great wealth or a large amount of money.

Treasurer An officer in a corporation responsible for filing financial statements, tax returns, and similar documents with the appropriate authorities and agencies. The treasurer may be, but is not always, the chief financial officer.

Treasury **1.** The department of the federal government responsible for the printing of money, the collection of taxes, the regulation of banks, and the management of public debt. Created in 1789, the Treasury issues Treasury securities, which is debt that the American government uses to pay for some of its functions. It also administers the Internal Revenue Service, which collects taxes and decides how tax laws and regulations are enforced, and the U.S. Mint, which prints and disburses currency. The Treasury Department is responsible for investigating and prosecuting certain financial crimes, such as tax evasion and counterfeiting. It is headed by the Secretary of the Treasury, who is appointed by the President with the consent of the Senate. **2.** See: U.S. Treasury Security.

Treasury Bill A debt security backed by the full faith and credit of the United States government with a maturity of one year or less. Very commonly, T bills have a maturity of a few weeks to a few months. They are purchased at a discount and then redeemed for par; T bills do not pay interest. For example, an investor may purchase a $5,000 bill for $4,500. While he/she will not earn any coupon payments, he/she will receive $5,000 in no more than a year. They are low-risk, low-return investments. Private investors may purchase T bills in small quantities, but the bulk of the T bill market comes from institutional investors, especially banks. See also: Treasury note, Treasury bond.

Treasury Bill Auction A weekly Dutch auction held for the sale of 13-week and 26-week U.S. Treasury bills, or a monthly auction for 52-week bills. In a Treasury bill auction, the bills are offered at a relatively high price, which is gradually lowered until a potential buyer indicates it wishes to buy at that price. The interest rates on these Treasury bills are used as benchmarks for short-term interest rates. It should be noted that the Treasury also sets aside securities for those who do not enter a , but have indicated they are willing to pay whatever the winning bid happens to be.

Treasury Bond Receipt A receipt one receives proving that one has been paid the coupon and/or principal on a U.S. Treasury bond.

Treasury Certificate A debt security issued by the U.S. Treasury with a short maturity, usually only a few months, and a rather unusual interest rate, such as 4.586%. They are no longer issued to the public and are only issued at all when the Treasury seeks to borrow from the Federal Reserve. In that situation, the Treasury issues Treasury certificates to the New York Federal Reserve Bank; this can only occur with the approval of the Fed's Board of Governors.

Treasury Credit Certificate In Italy, a government-issued debt security with a variable rate coupon linked to the rates of Italian Treasury bills. The variable coupon rate is intended to protect the holder from inflationary pressures. Treasury credit certificates first were issued in 1977.

Treasury Direct The act or practice of buying U.S. Treasury securities without using a broker as an intermediary. The federal government sells its securities to the public using both competitive and non-competitive bidding; both of these are examples of Treasury direct. This eliminates fees the counterparties would have to pay otherwise.

Treasury Futures Contract A futures contract in which one agrees to buy a U.S. Treasury security at a certain price at some stated date in the future, regardless of what the spot price is on that date. One buys a Treasury future if one expects Treasury securities to rise in price (because one wants to lock in the lower price). For the same reason, one sells a Treasury future if one expects the price to fall. Treasure futures are traded on the CBOT.

Treasury Index An index based on recent auctions of United States Treasury securities. Treasury indices are used as a benchmark for interest rates of some bank accounts and floating-rate mortgages. Each Treasury index is calculated differently, but it usually is based on the yield of some combination of five-year and 10-year Treasury notes and Treasury futures contracts.

Treasury Inflation-Protected Security A U.S. Treasury security that protects the bondholder from inflation. Most Treasury securities, like most fixed dollar obligations, pay a fixed coupon rate periodically and mature at par. While this carries low risk, it exposes investors to the possibility that the inflation rate will outpace the interest rate represented on the coupon. In order to protect against this, a Treasury Inflation-Protected Security automatically increases its principal according to the inflation rate as tracked by the Consumer Price Index. Thus, while the coupon rate does not increase, the dollar amount paid does. Because TIPS are so safe, they offer a very low rate of return. See also: Real Return Bond.

Treasury Investment Growth Receipt A Treasury security whose coupons have been stripped by Merrill Lynch. TIGRs therefore pay no interest. They are sold at a significant discount from par and mature at par. TIGRs fluctuate in price, sometimes dramatically, because changes in interest rates have made them more or less desirable. TIGRs can be invested IRAs and other pension accounts; they are also exempt from state and local taxes. They were originally issued between 1982 and 1986, becoming more-or-less obsolete when the U.S. Treasury began issuing its own stripped bonds. They still exist, but are fairly uncommon investments. See also: zero-coupon bonds, STRIPS. .

Treasury Lock A derivative whereby one guarantees oneself a particular yield on a Treasury security. That is, one purchases a Treasury lock for a certain price; if the actual price of the designated Treasury security is higher than the price of the lock, the buyer must pay the difference. On the other hand, if price is lower than the price of the lock, the buyer receives the difference. One buys a Treasury lock when a certain yield is important to his/her investment strategy but there is uncertainty on the future direction of Treasury yields. Treasury locks are settled in cash.

Treasury Offering The sale of a company's treasury shares to investors. Treasury shares are stock that a publicly-traded company issues but does not place with investors, or which it has bought back from shareholders. Selling treasury shares to the public can be a less expensive way for the company to raise capital because the amount it spent issuing them previously is a sunk cost. However, it should be noted that a treasury offering is not necessarily beneficial to shareholders as it can cause dilution of holdings.

Treasury Shares Stock that a publicly-traded company issues but does not place with investors, or which it has bought back from shareholders. That is, the company holds its treasury shares back until such time as selling them becomes beneficial. Treasury shares have been issued, but they are not considered shares outstanding. Selling treasury shares to the public can be a less expensive way for the company to raise capital because the amount it spent issuing them previously is a sunk cost. Treasury shares are not included in "per share" calculations.

Treasury Tax and Loan Account An account at a bank where a Federal Reserve bank deposits taxes that it receives from individual and corporate taxpayers. This increases the liquidity of the banks with the TT&L accounts; this in turn keeps the banking system stable.

Treasury Yield The income one receives from an investment in a U.S. Treasury security. The yield is calculated as the coupons that the investor receives in a year expressed as a percentage of the cost of the investment. Trends in Treasury yields indicate what the market expends in future interest rates or inflation. See also: Treasury yield curve.

Treasury Yield Curve A representation on a chart of the yields on U.S. Treasury securities with different maturities. On the yield curve, the maturities are represented on the x-axis, and the yield is represented on the y-axis. If the yield curve trends upward, it indicates that interest rates for long-term Treasurys are higher than short-term Treasurys; this is called a normal yield curve. A negative yield curve indicates that interest rates for short-term Treasurys are higher, and a flat yield curve indicates

that they are roughly the same. The Treasury yield curve is used to predict future trends in interest rates and inflation.

Treaty of Rome A 1957 agreement establishing the European Economic Community. Under the Treaty, the EEC shared a parliament and Court of Justice with the European Coal and Steel Community. These organizations eventually merged and formed the basis for what became the European Union.

Tree Killer In an office setting, an employee who uses the printer excessively.

Trend The direction and momentum of a market, price, economy, or other measure. For example, if the price of a security is going mainly downward with only a few gains here and there, it is said to be on a downward trend. Identifying and predicting trends is important to finding the right moment to buy and sell securities. Trends are especially important in technical analysis, which recommends buying at the bottom of a downward trend and selling at the top of an upward trend.

Trend Ratio Analysis The analysis of a financial ratio by comparing it to the same ratio in previous years. For example, a person may compare earnings in November 2009 to earnings in November 2008, November 2007 and November 2006. This helps analyze whether a company's financial state is becoming more or less healthy over time.

Trend Trading An investment strategy in which one makes investment decisions based on the perceived momentum of the securities in which one invests. That is, an investor buys when he/she believes a security is trending upward, and sells when he/she believes it is trending downward. Trend trading may be used for short-term and long-term investing, though the indicators for a trend reversal may change for each.

Trendline In technical analysis, a line on a chart representing the price movements of a security. The direction of the line shows whether the security is advancing or declining. Technical analysts use trendlines and patterns within them to determine whether a security or the broader market is bullish or bearish.

Trente Sous In French-speaking Canada, a slang term for a 25-cent coin. Ironically, the term literally means 30 cents.

Treuhandanstalt An agency of the German government charged with privatizing numerous state-owned companies in East Germany. Created a few months before the reunification of Germany in 1990, Treuhandanstalt was responsible for 8,500 publicly-owned companies. It privatized many; this was controversial as it necessitated the laying off of two and a half million state employees. The agency was dissolved in 1994 and its remaining assets were transferred to successor agencies. The term "Treuhandanstalt" is German for "trust agency."

T-Rex Fund A venture capital firm with more than $1 billion. T-Rex funds invest in start-ups and guide them typically to the initial public offering. Because they have so much capital to invest, they are generally able to acquire a great deal of control over the start-ups and are known for enforcing a good deal of fiscal discipline on them.

Treynor Performance Measure A measurement of return on a portfolio in excess of what a riskless investment would have earned per unit of risk. It is calculated by taking the portfolio's rate of return, subtracting the return on the riskless investment (usually a Treasury bond), and dividing by the portfolio's beta. It is important to note that the Treynor performance measure does not account for the effect, if any, of active portfolio management. It is simply a measurement of actual returns. It is also called the return to volatility ratio.

Triangle In technical analysis, a series of high and low prices for a security that, when plotted on a chart, looks vaguely like a triangle. A triangle indicates that investors do not know whether a bull market or a bear market will prevail. If the triangle breaks upward, it is a bullish sign, but if it breaks downward, it is a bearish sign. A triangle is also called a wedge. See also: Ascending sign, Descending sign.

Triangular Arbitrage A series of three currency trades in which the exchange rates do not exactly match up. In triangular arbitrage, an arbitrageur may profit from the inefficiency in pricing of the exchange rates. The process of triangular arbitrage involves converting one currency to another, then to a third, then back to the first. Opportunities for this are rare because the currency markets are so liquid as to provide almost perfect efficiency. It ordinarily requires advanced computer software to accomplish it successfully.

Tribal Agency In Pakistan, a political subdivision inhabited largely by nomadic tribes and administered by the central government.

Trickle Down Theory An informal term for a macroeconomic theory that a government can best promote growth by providing incentives for persons to produce goods and services. The primary way a government does this is by maintaining low tax rates so that investors and entrepreneurs may invest their money in production. Maintaining low tax rates on the wealthy is one of the most important and controversial aspects of trickle down theory; the theory states that if well off persons have the capital available to produce goods and services, they create jobs and thereby grow the economy. In other words, the growth "trickles down" from the wealthy to the remainder of the economy. Critics contend that this does not happen in reality and that the wealthy are more likely to keep, rather than invest, their money. In the United States, trickle down theory was crucial to the economic policy of the Ronald Reagan administration. See also: Keynesian economics, Monetarism, Thatcherism.

Triens 1. An ancient Roman unit of area approximately equivalent to 841 square meters. 2. An ancient Roman unit of weight approximately equivalent to 109.6 grams.

Trigger List A list of materials that could be used in the manufacture of nuclear weapons. Trigger List materials cannot be exported to non-nuclear states except under the guidance and supervision of the International Atomic Energy Agency.

Trigger Point An event that causes another event. For example, an exchange may stop trade on a stock if its price drops by 10% in a single trading session. In that case, the trigger point is the 10% drop.

Trigger Price A price at which an import causes the importing country automatically to impose a tariff or quota. For example, a country may have a law stating that if an import falls below $10 per unit, a tariff is imposed that results in the import becoming $13 per unit. Trigger prices are used when the importing country generally wishes to promote free trade but does not want importers to undercut domestic industry.

Triggering Event 1. A milestone that a person must attain to become eligible for a benefit or annuity. Usually the triggering event is retirement, but it could be reaching a chronological age, such as 65. **2.** A movement in a security's price that causes an investor to become interested in trading that security. For example, if a stock were trading at $70, and the price moves to $75, a shareholder may become interested in selling his/her shares. **3.** An event that changes the terms of an agreement or contract. For example, a student loan may include a provision forgiving the debt if the student to whom it is loaned dies. In this case, the triggering event is the student's death. See also: Act of God.

Trilateral Commission An informal group of 300 to 400 people from North America, Europe, and East Asia who meet several times a year to discuss public policy with an eye toward promoting globalization and integration. Membership is by invitation and current government officials are excluded from membership. However, many members go on to become high political executives. The Trilateral Commission has been controversial throughout its history, with some accusing it of promoting a one-world government. It was established in 1973 by David Rockefeller. See also: Council on Foreign Relations.

Trillion 1. In the short form, one million million. In business and economics, the GDP of highly developed countries is often given in trillions of dollars. **2.** In the long form, one million million million. This is increasingly called one quintillion.

Trime A nickname of three cent-coin in the United States. Trimes have not been minted since the 1800s.

TRIN In technical analysis, a measure of the strength of short-term market movements. It is calculated thusly: TRIN = (Advancing securities / Declining securities) / (Volume of advancing securities / Volume of declining securities) A TRIN measure below 1 indicates that there are more advancing securities on higher volume and is therefore a bullish indicator. A TRIN above 1 indicates the opposite and is thought to be bearish.

Trinidad and Tobago Dollar The currency of Trinidad and Tobago. It was introduced in 1964, replacing the East Caribbean dollar at par. While it was originally pegged to the British pound, it is now pegged to the U.S. dollar.

Trip Slang; in bond insurance, an AAA rating from Standard and Poor's or Fitch. See also: Trip trip.

Trip Trip In bond insurance, a slang term used to describe the situation in which one has received both an Aaa rating from Moody's and an AAA from Standard and Poor's or Fitch. See also: Trip.

Triple Tax-Exempt Describing a municipal bond that is exempt from federal, state, and local taxes. The United States Constitution forbids the federal government from taxing any state and local bonds. Most states and municipalities offer tax exemptions for residents who invest in their bonds; thus, to be eligible for triple-tax-free status, a bondholder must be resident in the municipality and/or state issuing the bond. Triple-tax exempt bonds almost always offer low returns, exposing bondholders to inflation risk. See also: After-Tax Basis.

Triple Top In technical analysis, a situation in which a security peaks at roughly the same price three times in a relatively short period. That is, the price peaks and then drops back down, which is then repeated twice. Technical analysts consider a triple top a bullish signal if the price continues to rise following the third peak. However, if the price drops significantly after the third peak, it is seen as a bearish indicator.

Triple Witching The last hour of trade on an exchange on the third Friday of March, June, September, and December. It is the time of expiration for three types of standardized contracts: stock options, stock index options, and stock index futures. Investors often unwind their positions on these contracts during or immediately before triple witching hour, which leads to increased trading volume on those hours. See also: Quadruple witching day.

Triple Witching Day The third Friday of March, June, September and December. It is the expiration day for three types of standardized contracts: stock options, stock index options and stock index futures. Investors often unwind their positions on these contracts during or immediately before triple witching days, leading to increased trading volume. See also: Quadruple witching day.

Triple Witching Week The week of trade on an exchange containing the third Friday of March, June, September and December. It is the week of expiration for three types of standardized contracts: stock options, stock index options and stock index futures. Investors often unwind their positions on these contracts during or before triple witching weeks, leading to increased trading volume. See also: Quadruple witching day.

Triple-Net A lease in which the tenant is responsible for costs in addition to rent. The tenant is responsible for net property taxes, net insurance, and net maintenance for the duration of the lease, which is the origin of the name. Because the tenant is responsible for costs that the lessor would otherwise pay, rent on a triple-net lease is usually lower than on other leases.

TRL ISO 4217 code for the Turkish lira. It traces its history back to the Ottoman Empire. Until 2005, the lira was subject to high (though not crippling) inflation. The "new lira," which revalued the currency, was introduced in 2005. It 2009, the moniker, "new," was removed from coins, and it became the lira again.

Troighid An obsolete Irish unit of length approximately equivalent to 25 centimeters.

Trojan Horse A computer virus that poses as an innocuous program. A Trojan horse appears to be harmless so that the user will install it, but then performs damaging activities like data theft or file deletion. The virus derives its name from the legendary wooden horse used by the Greeks to clandestinely gain access to Troy.

Trough In a recession, the point of the most negative GDP growth that immediately precedes the beginning of recovery. In other words, it is the lowest point in a business cycle. The term comes from charting, in which the x-axis represents time and the y-axis represents GDP growth. In this situation, the low point of a business cycle looks like a trough or pit. A trough is also called a valley. See also: Peak.

Troy Candareen A measure of weight in East Asia roughly equivalent to 374 milligrams. See also: Candareen.

Troy Grain A measure of weight equivalent to 64.79891 milligrams.

Troy Ounce A unit used to measure the mass of precious metals. It is equal in weight to 31.1034768 grams.

Troy Pound An obsolete unit of weight approximately equivalent to 373.24 grams. See also: Troy ounce.

Troy Weight A system to measure mass. It originated in the Middle Ages in France and is arranged into (from lightest to heaviest) grains, pennyweights, ounces and pounds. Of these, only troy ounces are still used, and only to weigh precious metals. A troy ounce is heavier than an imperial ounce but lighter than an imperial pound.

True and Fair View In British accounting standards, the requirement for companies not to obfuscate their financial statements so as to mislead shareholders or the wider market.

True Lease A multi-year lease in which the lessee maintains residence or usufruct of the leased property or asset while the lessor may claim a tax deduction on depreciation. Likewise, the lessee may claim a capital expense deduction. An operating lease in which the lessor repossesses the property or asset at the end of the lease is a primary example of a true lease.

True North A slang term for success, especially if one is not headed in the direction of success. For example, one may discuss ways that a company can change course and begin to head true north.

Trust 1. A relationship in which one party, known as the trustor, gives to a person or organization, known as the trustee, the right to hold and invest assets or property on behalf of a third party, known as the beneficiary. Most trusts exist to provide for the financial future of a minor child or mentally incompetent person. Trusts may also be set up to benefit charitable organizations. The trust agreement indicates at what time, if any, the beneficiary takes direct control of the assets. The beneficiary often receives disbursements to meet basic expenses until the time comes when the beneficiary takes control. Trusts are taxed on all money not given to the beneficiary. See also: Escrow, Charitable trust. **2.** See: Monopoly.

Trust Company A company, usually a division of a bank or brokerage, that acts as a trustee. In this relationship, one party, known as the trustor, gives to the trustee the right to hold and invest assets or property on behalf of a third party, known as the beneficiary. Most trusts exist to provide for the financial future of a minor child or mentally incompetent person, or may benefit charitable organizations. Many trusts are exempt from taxation on money given to the beneficiary, but trust companies may charge a fee in order to administer the assets. See also: Trust.

Trust Deed 1. In real estate, an agreement in which the title to the property is held in a trust until the mortgage is paid. A trust deed is not given to the homeowner in order to provide an extra amount of security for the lender; the trustee for a trust deed does nothing except in the event of default, in which case the trustee sells the real estate. **2.** An agreement stating the terms of a trust. A trust deed is most common when mutual funds are held in trust, and outlines the responsibilities and restrictions on the fund.

Trust Fund Transaction Any transaction involving two trust funds managed by the same trustee or given by the same grantor.

Trust Indenture Act of 1939 Legislation in the United States requiring the appointment of an independent trustee to act on behalf of bondholders in each issue of debt securities. The Act also mandates that bond indentures must conform to certain standards set forth by the SEC and the Act itself, and that issuers must report their financial information periodically. The Trust Indenture Act was designed to increase transparency in the bond market and to protect the rights of bondholders.

Trust Letter A monthly periodical detailing regulatory and legislative news related to trusts. It has been published since the mid-1970s by the American Bankers Association.

Trust Preferred Security A security that has every feature of a debt security except for the fact that it is not actually debt. That is, TruPS have fixed coupons, a maturity date when the holder receives the face value, and an early redemption option. However, the holder does not lend the issuer money when he/she purchases a TruPS. Some companies favor TruPS to bonds and preferred stock because they are taxed like bonds but may be included as assets (and not liabilities) on a balance sheet.

Trust Receipt An acknowledgment that goods intended to be held in a trust have been duly received.

Trust Share A share in a closed-end fund entitling the holder to a share of the fund's profits.

Trustbuster A person or, less commonly, an organization that seeks to break monopolies into several companies or to shut them down entirely in order to encourage competition in the free market. The word is strongly associated with Theodore Roosevelt, the early 20th-century U.S. president who opposed the early industrial monopolies.

Trustee 1. The individual or company who manages assets in a trust on behalf of the beneficiary. **2.** More generally, any individual or company who manages assets on behalf of another. For example, a bank may hire a trustee to distribute funds from a loan to the borrower. In both cases, the trustee has a fiduciary responsibility to act on behalf of the beneficiary or client, rather than in his/her own interests.

Trustee In Bankruptcy A court- or government-appointed person who manages assets in bankruptcy. In the United States, trustees in bankruptcy have different duties depending on the type of bankruptcy filed. In Chapter 7 bankruptcy, the trustee liquidates all non-exempt assets and distributes the proceeds to creditors according to bankruptcy law and the court's directions. In Chapter 13 bankruptcy, the trustee reviews the debtor's plans and collects and distributes payments to creditors. In Canada, trustees in bankruptcy hold assets in trust and distribute them to creditors according to the dictates of the Bankruptcy and Insolvency Act.

Trustor One who gives money and/or other assets to a trust. A trustor usually sets up a trust in order to provide for the financial future of a minor child or mentally incompetent person. A trustor may also set up a trust to benefit a charitable organization. It is important to note that the trustor does not hold or invest the assets once they are given to the trust, as that is the duty of the trustee. See also: Escrow, Charitable trust.

Truth-in-Advertising Any law or regulation mandating fairness in marketing. Most of the time, truth-in-advertising requires a company not to lie about its products and to be able to support its claims with facts. Truth-in-advertising may only apply to certain services or products, such as pharmaceuticals, but laws vary by jurisdiction.

Truth-in-Savings Act Legislation in the United States, passed in 1991, that requires banks to disclose interest (in APY terms), fees and other information when one seeks to open a savings account. It is enforced through Regulation DD.

TRY ISO 4217 code for the Turkish lira. It traces its history back to the Ottoman Empire. Until 2005, the lira was subject to high (though not crippling) inflation. The "new lira," which revalued the currency, was introduced in 2005. It 2009, the word "new" was removed from coins, and it became the lira again.

TSX Venture Exchange A Canadian stock exchange based in Calgary with offices in Winnipeg, Vancouver, Toronto, and Montreal. It was established in 1999 as the Canadian Venture Exchange, and listed securities that were generally too small to be listed on the Toronto Stock Exchange. It specializes in companies with small capitalization and often high risk. It was purchased by the TSX Group, which owns the Toronto Stock Exchange, in December 2007.

TT 1. ISO 3166-1 alpha-2 code for the Republic of Trinidad and Tobago. This is the code used in international transactions to and from Trinidadian and Tobagonian bank accounts. **2.** ISO 3166-2 geocode for Trinidad and Tobago. This is used as an international standard for shipping to Trinidad and Tobago. Each of the country's subdivisions has its own code with the prefix "TT." For example, the code for the Borough of Arima is ISO 3166-2:TT-ARI.

TTD ISO 4217 code for the Trinidad and Tobago dollar. It was introduced in 1964, replacing the East Caribbean dollar at par. While originally pegged to the British pound, it is now pegged to the U.S. dollar.

TTO GOST 7.67 Latin three-letter geocode for Trinidad and Tobago. The code is used for transactions to and from local bank accounts and for international shipping to Trinidad and Tobago. As with all GOST 7.67 codes, it is used primarily in Cyrillic alphabets.

Ttokkap In South Korea, the practice in which businesspersons give colleagues envelopes containing small amounts of cash. Ttokkap is given on holidays and is a major part of networking in South Korea. Some businesspersons, however, use ttokkap to give a great deal of money, using the practice to cover up bribery.

Tuath An obsolete Irish unit of area equivalent to 4,320 acres.

Tuck-In Acquisition The acquisition of a company where the acquiring company intends to merge the target company into one of its departments. For example, a broad-based financial services company may conduct a tuck-in acquisition where it buys a research company and then transfers all of its resources into its own research department. A tuck-in acquisition is also called a bolt-on acquisition.

Tudse A nickname for the 1,000 Danish krone banknote. The name means "toad" in Danish, but is a play on the Danish word for thousand, which is tusinde. An alternate nickname is egern, which means "squirrel."

Tugrik The currency of Mongolia. It was introduced in 1925 and was pegged to the Soviet ruble. It currently floats.

Tuition The money one must pay for an educational program. While the word may apply to any program, it is especially used in reference to private primary and secondary schools and post-secondary education. For example, a university may charge a student $30,000 to attend for a year. Various scholarships, grants, loans and other forms of financial aid exist to reduce the burden of tuition.

Tuition Fees Insurance An insurance policy covering a school for tuition that it must refund. For example, if a natural disaster forces a college to cancel a semester and it returns tuition to students, tuition fees insurance will reimburse the college for this expense. As with all insurance, the school must pay a premium to receive the coverage.

Tuition Form An insurance policy covering a school for tuition that it must refund due to the destruction of a building. For example, if a class building burns down, forcing a college to return tuition to students, a tuition form will reimburse the college for this expense. As with all insurance, the school must pay a premium to receive the coverage.

Tuition Reduction Any plan by which one may pay lower than normal tuition for an educational program. One may be eligible for tuition reduction based on need, merit or any number of other criteria. For example, a veteran may have his/her tuition reduced when he/she returns from service.

Tuition Tax Credit Any direct, dollar-for-dollar reduction in one's tax liability based on tuition paid for higher education. Common examples include the Hope Tax Credit and the lifetime learning credit.

Tularemia An infectious bacterium that can cause lesions, fever, anorexia and death in humans. It has been used in American, Japanese and Soviet bioweapons programs. See also: Biowarfare.

Tulip Mania History's first major asset bubble. Tulips were introduced to Europe from the Ottoman Empire in the mid-1500s and became very popular in the Netherlands. As they grew in popularity, prices for tulips rose steadily, then unsustainably, in the 1630s. Prices suddenly collapsed in February 1637. Interestingly, tulip mania resulted in the creation of a formal futures market and marked one of the first times when contracts were traded without exchanging the underlying asset.

Tum A Swedish unit of length approximately equivalent to 2.96 centimeters.

Tuman In Uzbekistan, a political subdivision approximately equivalent to a county.

Tun GOST 7.67 Latin three-letter geocode for Tunisia. The code is used for transactions to and from Tunisian bank accounts and for international shipping to Tunisia. As with all GOST 7.67 codes, it is used primarily in Cyrillic alphabets.

Tuna-Dolphin Case The discovery that tuna fishers were ensnaring dolphins in their netting, injuring or killing many. Tuna swim near dolphins in the wild for protection from sharks. As a result, tuna fishing boats tracked dolphins to find tuna. Because dolphins are considered among the most highly intelligent species on Earth, many found this practice to be unethical. As a result, various companies and governments began taking steps to ensure tuna fishing practices were "dolphin safe" and did not injure dolphins. The U.S. Department of Commerce began issuing dolphin safe labels in 1990.

Tunisian Dinar The currency of Tunisia. It came into circulation in 1960, replacing the Tunisian franc. It was pegged to the French franc until 1964 and then the U.S. dollar until 1971. There are significant restrictions on the convertibility of the dinar.

Tunisian Franc The former currency of Tunisia. It was issued in 1891 during the French protectorate of Tunisia. It was pegged to the French franc at par. The Tunisian franc ceased circulation in 1960 with the introduction of the Tunisian dinar.

Tunnel Insurance An insurance policy providing coverage for damage to an underground tunnel. It covers all damages except for defects, normal wear and tear and war.

Tunnland A Swedish unit of area approximately equivalent to five square kilometers or one acre.

Tuoppi A Finnish unit of volume approximately equivalent to 1.33 liters. It became obsolete when Finland adopted the metric system in 1880.

TUR GOST 7.67 Latin three-letter geocode for Turkey. The code is used for transactions to and from Turkish bank accounts and for international shipping to Turkey. As with all GOST 7.67 codes, it is used primarily in Cyrillic alphabets.

Turban Head Eagle A gold coin minted in the United States between 1795 and 1804. It was worth $10. It derived its name from the turban worn by Lady Liberty in the picture on the obverse.

Turkey Informal; a bad investment.

Turkey Farm A slang term for a department staffed by unfireable employees. Examples of people who work in a turkey farm include the owner's relatives and people married to litigious lawyers.

Turkish Lira The currency of Turkey. It traces its history back to the Ottoman Empire. Until 2005, the lira was subject to high (though not crippling) inflation. The "new lira," which revalued the currency, was introduced in 2005. It 2009, the word "new" was removed from coins, and it became the lira again.

Turkmenistani Manat The currency of Turkmenistan. It was introduced 1993 and was revalued in January 2009 at a rate of 5,000 to one after the old manat suffered from high inflation in the 1990s and 2000s.

Turn the Corner Informal; to begin to recover. For example, an economy may be said to have turned the corner after a recession when GDP starts to grow again.

Turnaround 1. A change in a security's price trend, especially from a downtrend to an uptrend. See also: Reversal. **2.** A change in a company's situation from one of losses or low profitability to one with higher profits. **3.** To buy a security, then to sell in the same trading day. See also: Day trader.

Turnaround Document A document resulting from a computer output to which information is added. The information is then fed back into the computer. A common example is a utility meter reading.

Turnaround Time 1. The time it takes for share prices that had been declining to begin to improve. For example, if a publicly-traded company has been in a prolonged bear market, but its share price eventually stabilizes and begins to move back up, the turnaround time describes the entire duration of this process. **2.** The time it takes for an unprofitable company to begin to become profitable. For example, if a company has been posting losses, but it restructures and becomes profitable, the turnaround time describes the entire duration of this process. **3.** In supply chain management, the amount of time between a supplier receiving an order and its delivery to the distributor or customer. This is important for both custom-made products and mass production, and suppliers are expected to know the lead times for their different products. It is particularly important for just-in-time supply chains, in which each step in the supply chain is expected to know precise turnaround time. It is also known as lead time.

Turnbull Report A 1999 report to listed companies on the London Stock Exchange reminding them of their obligations to maintain good corporate governance, specifically through internal controls and audits. It derives its name from Nigel Turnbull, the head of the group that authored the report.

Turnkey Business A new company with a business model that has already been set. Most franchises operate in this way. For example, if one wishes to open a McDonald's franchise, everything from the products to the uniforms has already been determined. One merely needs to put up the appropriate capital and start the business.

Turnkey Construction Contract A construction contract in which the price is fixed at the time the contract is signed. As a result, the construction company is held responsible for exceeding the budget. Turnkey construction contracts reduce the risk to the buyer of the construction services and provide an incentive for the company to stay within budget.

Turnkey Insurance An insurance policy providing coverage for a contractor or architect in the event that he/she does not perform his/her duties well and it results in harm to a client. That is, turnkey insurance covers negligence on the part of a contractor or architect. It is a type of errors and omissions insurance.

Turn-of-the-Month Effect A temporary increase in stock prices during the last few days and the first few days of each month. Some analysts credit the turn of the month effect to distributions from pension funds and other retirement accounts that the pensioners immediately reinvest in the stock market. See also: Calendar effect.

Turnover 1. In accounting, the number of times or the speed at which a company replaces an asset in a given period of time. This usually refers to the amount of time it takes for the company to collect its accounts receivable or the number of times it has to procure new inventory to replace that which it has already sold. Companies desire a fast or high turnover, as this indicates financial health. **2.** The number of shares traded in a portfolio over a given period of time, expressed as a percentage of the number of shares in the portfolio. A low turnover means that the portfolio is not being very actively managed; it also means that one's broker is making less in commissions, as he/she is paid per trade. See also: Churning.

Turnover Rate The ratio at which a fund or portfolio trades the securities in it. A higher turnover rate indicates active management; if it becomes very high, this may indicate that the broker or manager is trading securities for the sake of collecting more in fees. It is calculated as the trading volume of the fund or portfolio as a percentage of the entire portfolio. See also: Prudent person rule.

Turnover Tax A tax paid on a good during or after its manufacture, rather than when it is sold. It is usually calculated as a percentage of the value of a good.

Tuuma A Finnish unit of length approximately equivalent to 24.74 millimeters. It became obsolete when Finland adopted the metric system in 1880.

TUV GOST 7.67 Latin three-letter geocode for Tuvalu. The code is used for transactions to and from Tuvaluan bank accounts and for international shipping to Tuvalu. As with all GOST 7.67 codes, it is used primarily in Cyrillic alphabets.

Tuvaluan Dollar The currency of Tuvalu. Tuvaluan dollars only circulate as coins because Tuvalu uses Australian dollar banknotes; Australian coins are used as well. The two dollars are pegged at a one-to-one ratio. The Tuvaluan dollar was issued in 1976.

Tuvan Aksa The currency of Tannu Tuva, a satellite state of the Soviet Union prior to its takeover in 1944. Most aksa notes were overstamped Soviet rubles. It was replaced by the Soviet ruble at a one-to-one ratio.

TV 1. ISO 3166-1 alpha-2 code for Tuvalu. This is the code used in international transactions to and from Tuvaluan bank accounts. **2.** ISO 3166-2 geocode for Tuvalu. This is used as an international standard for shipping to Tuvalu. Each island of the nation has its own code with the prefix "TV." For example, the code for the island of Nui is ISO 3166-2:TV-NIU.

Tvarhand A Swedish unit of length approximately equivalent to four inches.

TVD A currency code for the Tuvaluan dollar. Tuvaluan dollars only circulate as coins because Tuvalu uses Australian dollar banknotes; Australian coins are used as well. The two dollars are pegged at a one-to-one ratio. The Tuvaluan dollar was issued in 1976. This code is not recognized by the ISO.

TW 1. ISO 3166-1 alpha-2 code for Taiwan (Province of China). This is the code used in international transactions to and from Taiwanese bank accounts. **2.** ISO 3166-2 geocode for Taiwan. This is used as an international standard for shipping to Taiwan. Each Taiwanese subdivision has its own code with the prefix "TW." For example, the code for the Municipality of Taipei is ISO 3166-2:TW-TPE. It is important to note that because the People's Republic of China regards Taiwan as a province, Taiwan also has a separate ISO 3166-2 designation as a Chinese province.

TWD ISO 4217 code for the new Taiwanese dollar. It was introduced in 1949, replacing the old dollar at a (somewhat staggering) ratio of 40,000 old dollars to one new dollar. Technically, it existed alongside the silver yuan, which was the official currency of the Republic of China (not to be confused with the People's Republic of China); however, the silver yuan was never actually used, and, in 2000, the Taiwanese dollar became the sole currency. It is a floating currency.

Twenty Bond Index An index tracking the yields of 20 municipal bonds with 20-year maturities and a high average credit rating. It is considered a benchmark for municipal bond yields.

Twenty-Cent Piece A coin minted in the United States between 1875 and 1878 worth 1/5 of one dollar.

Twenty-Five Percent Rule 1. A cautionary guideline for municipal bond investors stating that a municipality carries excessive debt if its long-term debt exceeds 25% of its annual budget. Investors are generally advised to be cautious about buying bonds from municipalities in violation of the 25% rule. **2.** A rule stating that a person or company selling a product based on the intellectual property of another must pay a 25% royalty to the owner of the intellectual property. The 25% rule is applied to copyrights, trademarks, trade secrets, and other forms of intellectual property.

Twenty-Pay Life Insurance Policy A life insurance policy in which the policyholder must pay premiums for 20 years. After 20 years have elapsed, the policyholder owes no more premiums even though the policy remains in effect. This reduces the policyholder's costs, especially as he/she ages.

Twin Pack Two units of a retail item in the same wrapping such that the buyer must purchase at least two. For example, two bottles of shaving cream may be offered in a twin pack. A twin pack usually has a higher price than a single unit of the item, but a lower price than two individually wrapped units.

TWN GOST 7.67 Latin three-letter geocode for Taiwan. The code is used for transactions to and from Taiwanese bank accounts and for international shipping to Taiwan. As with all GOST 7.67 codes, it is used primarily in Cyrillic alphabets.

Two Bob In the United Kingdom, a slang term for a 10-pence coin, which is worth 1/10 of one British pound.

Two Comma A slang term describing any contract worth between $1 million and $10 million. For example, an investment in $4 million in stock in a two comma deal.

Two Pillar Strategy The approach the European Central Bank uses to analyze price stability. The first pillar is economic analysis, which examines movements in business, unemployment and so forth. The second pillar is monetary analysis, which considers the supply and demand for money. The ECB checks these pillars against each other for confirmation of trends; this in turn influences its decisions.

Twobicle In an office setting, a large cubicle that two people share.

Two-Cent Piece A coin minted in the United States between 1864 and 1873 worth 1/50 of one dollar.

Two-Dollar Broker A broker who conducts trades for another broker's client because the second broker is too busy to do so. The commission the client pays goes to his/her own broker, but the two dollar broker receives a portion from the other broker. Originally, this commission was $2, but now it is negotiated between the two brokers.

Two-Factor Model 1. An economic model that states that production is derived from two factors. These factors are the availability of cost of labor and the availability and cost of capital. **2.** A form of the capital asset pricing model that does not account for beta. This form of the CAPM was developed by Fischer Black. **3.** Any economic model that discusses two factors as predominate or exclusive causes of some event.

Two-Fund Separation Theorem A theory stating that under conditions in which all investors borrow and lend at the riskless rate, all investors will either choose to possess a risk-free portfolio or the market portfolio. See also: Markowitz portfolio theory.

Two-Part Tariff A set fee assessed with a purchase along with a per-unit charge. For example, a credit card carries a two-part tariff if it has an annual fee and a minimum fee with each purchase. A two-part tariff is not necessarily an import tariff.

Twopence A coin in the United Kingdom equal in value to 1/50 of one British pound.

Two-Pillar Strategy The approach the European Central Bank uses to analyze price stability. The first pillar is economic analysis, which examines movements in business, unemployment and so forth. The second pillar is monetary analysis, which considers the supply and demand for money. The ECB checks these pillars against each other for confirmation of trends; this in turn influences its decisions.

Two-Step Earnings A term describing a situation in which two companies have earnings that tend to mirror each other. Companies with two-step earnings usually grow slowly in tandem then quickly in tandem. The process then repeats itself. The term derives from the two-step country dance, where the partners dance together slowly then quickly.

Two-Tier Board A corporate structure with two boards of directors. A management board oversees the company and provides general direction, while a supervisory board must approve of major business decisions. Half the supervisory board is elected by shareholders while the other half represents employee interests. It appoints the management board. A two-tier board is seen in German companies with the Aktiengesellschaft corporate structure.

Two-Tier Market A system whereby a country maintains one exchange rate for some transactions and another for different transactions. For example, one exchange rate may apply to investments and another may apply to international trade. It is a type of managed float. A two-tier market should not be confused with a tiered market.

Two-Tier Tender Offer A tender offer in which a buyer offers to buy enough shares to gain control of the company at a certain price, then offers to buy the remaining shares at a lower price. For example, a buyer may purchase 50% + 1 of a company at $20 per share and then offer to buy the rest of the company at $12 per share. See also: Blended price.

Two-Way Market A market for a security where both an open bid and an open ask are quoted. This indicates that there are both willing buyers and sellers for the security, though their prices may not be the same. While a two-way market is not necessarily liquid, it is by definition more liquid than a one-way market, where there is either no willing buyer or no willing seller currently available. It is also called a two-sided market.

Two-Way Trading The legal ability to convert Global Depository Receipts into ordinary shares and vice versa. A Global Depository Receipt is a certificate issued by a bank representing shares of a stock the bank holds in trust but that are traded on a foreign stock exchange. It is denominated in the local currency, and entitles the bearer to any dividends and other benefits associated with the shares. Different governments have different regulations as to how shares may be converted into Global Depository Receipts; those that allow two-way trading have the fewest regulations.

Tyco International A Swiss and American manufacturing conglomerate. Established in 1960, it initially operated primarily in semiconductor products and in research. It acquired more than 1,000 companies between the 1970s and 1990s, building itself into a health care, electronics and security company. These components separated into three companies in 2006. Tyco International took the security portion of its former operations. The company primarily sells security systems, CCTV equipment and related products for individuals, businesses and governments.

Tycoon A very wealthy businessperson, especially one who made his/her fortune in a single industry. For example, one may be called an oil tycoon or a steel tycoon.

Tyiyn 1/100 of a Kyrgyz som. It is the Kyrgyz equivalent of a cent.

Tynnyri 1. A Finnish unit of dry volume approximately equivalent to 175 liters. 2. A Finnish unit of liquid volume approximately equivalent to 125.6 liters. Both versions of the term became obsolete when Finland adopted the metric system in 1880.

Tynnyrinala A Finnish unit of area approximately equivalent to 4,936.5 square meters. It became obsolete when Finland adopted the metric system in 1880.

Type One of two kinds of option contract. In other words, a type is either a call or a put.

Type I and II Errors 1. See: Type 1 error. 2. See: Type 2 error.

Typo An unintentional mistake in typing, short for "typographical error." In 1962, a typo in the code of the computer instructions for an unmanned satellite traveling to Venus allegedly caused the failure of the mission.

Tyyn A subdivision of the Kyrgyzstani som. One tyyn is worth 1/100 of one som.

TZ 1. ISO 3166-1 alpha-2 code for the United Republic of Tanzania. This is the code used in international transactions to and from Tanzanian bank accounts. 2. ISO 3166-2 geocode for Tanzania. This is used as an international standard for shipping to Tanzania. Each Tanzanian region has its own code with the prefix "TZ." For example, the code for the Region of Arusha is ISO 3166-2:TZ-01.

TZA GOST 7.67 Latin three-letter geocode for Tanzania. The code is used for transactions to and from Tanzanian bank accounts and for international shipping to Tanzania. As with all GOST 7.67 codes, it is used primarily in Cyrillic alphabets.

TZS ISO 4217 code for the Tanzanian shilling. It was introduced in 1966, replacing the East African shilling. It is one of the least valuable currencies in the world.

U A symbol appearing next to a security listed on NASDAQ indicating that the security trades in units rather than shares. All NASDAQ listings use a four-letter abbreviation; if a "U" follows the abbreviation, this indicates that the security being traded is a unit security.

U.S Department of Commerce A department of the United States federal government charged with encouraging economic growth. It issues patents, sets standards for companies and sectors and gathers data on the state of the American economy. It also supervises the U.S. Census. It was established in 1903 as the Department of Commerce and Labor; Commerce split from what became the Labor Department in 1913.

U.S. Agency for International Development An agency of the U.S. federal government that provides foreign aid and financial assistance to other countries. It helps after natural disasters and conducts anti-poverty programs in various parts of the world. It was established in 1961.

U.S. Agricultural Adjustment Act of 1933 Legislation in the United States intended to provide relief for farmers and other agricultural workers during the Great Depression. Because of high production in the years leading up to the passage of the Act, prices for agricultural commodities were extremely low. The Act paid farmers not to grow more than a certain amount of crops in order to raise prices. It also paid them to reduce populations of pigs and cows for the same reason. The pork and beef resulting from the slaughter of excess animals were distributed through the Federal Emergency Relief Administration. The Act was part of the New Deal.

U.S. Agricultural Export Development Council A trade association in the United States that was established to promote the export of American agricultural products. It provides a forum for members to discuss matters of mutual interest and lobbies the U.S. government for favorable legislation. It was established in 1983 but traces its origins to the mid-1950s. It is based in Virginia.

U.S. Attorney General The head of the Department of Justice. The attorney general is responsible for the prosecution of federal crimes and also serves as counsel for the government. He/she also supervises law enforcement agencies such as the FBI and the Bureau of Alcohol, Tobacco, Firearms and Explosives. The attorney general is appointed by the president of the United States and confirmed by the Senate.

U.S. Chamber of Commerce An organization in the United States representing the interests of private businesses. It lobbies for legislation perceived to be favorable to business. For instance, it supports free trade and deregulation. It was established in 1912 and is based in Washington, D.C.

U.S. Code The codification of all U.S. federal law into 50 titles. The U.S. Code exists to organize American law by topic rather than by chronology (as would be done if acts or bills were listed as they were enacted). Parts of the U.S. Code, notably the Internal Revenue Code, are sometimes called codes in their own right, but they are in fact titles under the U.S. Code. It is updated and published every six years. The first U.S. Code was published in 1926.

U.S. Commercial Service An agency of the U.S. Department of Commerce that promotes U.S. exports. It conducts market research, introduces companies to buyers and conducts other services for American exporters. It charges a fee for many of these services. The Commercial Service also promotes American goods in foreign markets. It has offices in American embassies around the world to accomplish these activities.

U.S. Council for International Business Also called the USCIB. An organization that promotes American businesses. It lobbies the U.S. government, the World Trade Organization, the OECD and other organizations for favorable legislation and regulation. It also provides dispute resolution services for members. The USCIB is an affiliate of the International Chamber of Commerce. It is based in New York and maintains an office in Washington, D.C.

U.S. Department of Agriculture A department in the United States charged with assisting farmers and ranchers. The USDA inspects foods for safety, promotes rural development (for example, by providing mortgages outside cities) and conducts research. It was established in 1862.

U.S. Department of Defense A department in the United States charged with supervising the military and conducting war. It oversees military training and education and advises the president on military policy. It was established in 1947, but traces its origins to the Department of War and the Department of the Navy, both created in the late 1700s.

U.S. Department of Education A cabinet-level body of the U.S. federal government responsible for establishing and implementing policies related to federal funding and other assistance for education. It also is charged with enforcing civil rights as they relate to education. The department was established in 1980.

U.S. Department of Energy A department in the United States charged with implementing American energy policy. It promotes domestic energy production, conducts research and sets standards for safe handling of nuclear materials. It was created in 1977.

U.S. Department of Health and Human Services Also called HHS. A cabinet-level body of the U.S. federal government responsible for protecting the public health. It conducts drug inspections, assists in the implementation of Medicare and Medicaid, runs the health service for Native Americans, and performs many similar operations. Until 1995, it also administered the Social Security Administration. It was created in 1953 and took its current form in 1980.

U.S. Department of Housing and Urban Development A department in the United States charged with promoting homeownership. It oversees the Federal Housing Administration and has a relationship with Fannie Mae and Freddie Mac. It also provides vouchers to make rent more affordable and provides grants for community development. It was established in 1965.

U.S. Department of the Interior A department in the United States charged with overseeing national parks and most other land owned by the federal government. It is also responsible for conserving wildlife and managing U.S. relations with Native Americans. It was established in 1849.

U.S. Department of Transportation A department in the United States that oversees aviation, federal highways, shipping and railroads. It began operations in 1967.

U.S. Depository An organization in the United States, which may be either for-profit or non-profit, that takes money from clients and places it in any of a variety of investment vehicles for the benefit of both the client and the organization. Common examples of depository institutions are retail banks and savings and loan associations, both of which take deposits into safekeeping and use them to make loans to other customers. U.S. depositories are regulated by federal and state law.

U.S. Direct Investment Abroad A major investment by an American corporation outside the United States. For example, an American company may buy a factory in Indonesia because labor costs are lower. Many economists believe that U.S. direct investment abroad is good for an economy, as it provides jobs and increases domestic capital. Critics point out that profits usually leave the invested country and go to the American company. U.S. direct investment abroad is a type of foreign direct investment.

U.S. Dollar The currency of the United States. First issued in 1792, it is the currency used most often in international transactions. After World War II, most world currencies were pegged to the dollar, which was pegged to gold. In 1971, the dollar became a fiat currency. Nevertheless, many currencies are still pegged to the dollar, and it is one of the most important reserve currencies in the world.

U.S. Dollar Area The area in which the U.S. dollar circulates as a primary currency, either officially or unofficially. The U.S. dollar area includes the United States and its territories, as well as the nations of the British Virgin Islands, Cambodia, East Timor, Ecuador, El Salvador, Liberia, Marshall Islands, Micronesia, Palau, Panama, Turks and Caicos Islands and Zimbabwe. Some of these countries have their own currencies but the dollar may be just as accepted or even more widely accepted.

U.S. Environmental Protection Agency A regulatory body of the U.S. federal government responsible for environmental health and well-being. Its writes and enforces regulations within the parameters set up by law. It is charged with protecting water, air, land, and endangered species, as well as with the handling of hazardous waste. For example, the EPA administers legislation requiring registration of all pesticides sold in the U.S. The EPA was established in 1970.

U.S. Information Agency A former organization of the U.S. State Department that distributed information to foreign countries. It advocated American policy abroad. During the Cold War, its content was largely pro-American propaganda. It existed from 1953 to 1999.

U.S. International Trade Commission An agency of the U.S. federal government that maintains American tariff schedules, arbitrates disputes and advises the president and Congress on matters of international trade. It was established in 1916.

U.S. League of Savings Institutions A former professional association for savings banks in the United States. Its goals were to establish and enforce best practices among members, to lobby policymakers on behalf of the industry and to educate the public about banking issues. It was established in 1892 and merged with the National Council of Community Bankers in 1992.

U.S. Mint An agency of the United States that strikes coins for circulation and for collectors. It was established in 1792; its first office (in Philadelphia) was the first building commissioned by Congress under the Constitution. It is part of the U.S Treasury Department.

U.S. Mission to the European Union The equivalent of an embassy from the United States to the European Union. It promotes U.S. interests before the European Union and seeks mutual cooperation. The United States has had diplomatic representation at the EU's predecessor organizations since 1953.

U.S. Mission to the United Nations The equivalent of an embassy from the United States to the United Nations. It promotes U.S. interests before the UN and, like the missions of four other countries, has veto power over Security Council resolutions. Because the U.S. is a founding member of the UN, the mission has existed since 1947.

U.S. Munitions List In American law, the list of weapons and similar items that are subject to licensing because of the danger they pose. The U.S. Munitions List is related to the International Traffic in Arms Regulations.

U.S. Person A U.S. citizen, permanent resident, American corporation or an association of persons in which a large percentage are U.S. citizens. A U.S. person is entitled to protection by the U.S. government and to anonymity in foreign intelligence reports unless one's information is relevant to a report.

U.S. Postal Service A government organization in the United States that delivers mail to individuals and businesses. It is required to offer the same prices for the entire U.S., regardless of geography. It is also the only organization allowed access to mail boxes with "U.S. Mail" stamped on them. It traces its origins to 1775.

U.S. Price The price of a good or service in the United States, especially compared to its price in another country. That is, the U.S. price measures the purchasing power of a dollar. See also: Purchasing power parity.

U.S. Secretary of Education The head of the U.S. Department of Education. The secretary is responsible for establishing and implementing policies related to federal funding and other assistance for education. He/she is also charged with enforcing civil rights as they relate to education. The secretary is appointed by the president of the United States and confirmed by the Senate.

U.S. Secretary of Health and Human Services The head of the Department of Health and Human Services. The secretary is responsible for protecting the public health. He/she has jurisdiction over drug inspections, implementation of Medicare and Medicaid, health service for Native Americans, and many similar operations. Until 1995, the secretary was also charged with the administration of the Social Security Administration. He/she is appointed by the president of the United States and confirmed by the Senate.

U.S. Source Income Personal income earned inside the United States. As with most other countries, U.S. source income is taxable in the United States.

U.S. State Department A department in the United States charged with conducting foreign relations. It advises the president on foreign policy, assists American businesses abroad and oversees U.S. embassies. It was established in 1789 and was the first department created by Congress.

U.S. Stock Exchanges Stock exchanges in the United States. U.S. stock exchanges contain greater market capitalization than the stock exchanges of any other country in the world.

U.S. Tax Code The set of laws governing U.S. federal taxation. It covers the credits and deductions for which one is eligible, as well as the tax rates for different types of income or wealth. The U.S. Tax Code is rarely replaced, but it is amended with some frequency.

U.S. Taxation The system under which American persons are taxed. There are many types of taxation in the United States. At the federal level, personal income, corporate income and capital gains are all taxed on a progressive scale: corporations and persons making more are taxed at a higher rate. Most states also have income taxes and some have corporate taxes as well. Most states and localities also have sales taxes and some local governments have wage taxes on top of everything else. Numerous deductions and credits exist so U.S. taxation does not become crippling. Compared to the rest of the world, U.S. corporate taxes are rather high and income taxes are rather low.

U.S. Trade and Development Agency An agency of the United States government charged with economic development in foreign countries and the promotion of American exports with those countries. It helps other countries develop their infrastructure, which helps improve their sustainability as trading partners. It works with other agencies, notably USAID, in executing its tasks.

U.S. Trade Representative An official in the United States with ambassadorial rank who is responsible for conducting trade negotiations and recommending policy to the president. The trade representative reports annually on countries that do not protect intellectual property or that pursue other policies that make trades difficult. The office of the trade representative is based in Washington, D.C., with satellite offices in Geneva and Brussels.

U.S. Travel and Tourism Administration Also called the USTTA. A former U.S. government agency that had offices in numerous foreign countries and promoted tourism to the United States. Because its purpose was largely being filled by the Visit USA Committee, the USTTA shut down in 1996.

U.S. Treasury Bond A debt security backed by the full faith and credit of the United States government with a maturity of more than 10 years. They may be purchased directly from the government or from a bank; they have coupon payments payable every six months. Treasury bonds may be bought competitively or non-competitively. In a non-competitive transaction, one takes the interest rate he/she is given on a T-bond. In competitive investing, one bids on a desired yield, but this does not mean it will be accepted. Treasury bonds are low-risk, low-return investments. The minimum purchase is $1,000 and the maximum is $5 million in non-competitive bidding or 35% of the offering in competitive, They are known informally as T-bonds. See also: Treasury bill, Treasury note.

U.S. Treasury Note A debt security backed by the full faith and credit of the United States government with a maturity between one and 10 years. They may be purchased directly from the government or from a bank; they have coupon payments payable every six months. Treasury notes may be bought competitively or non-competitively. In a non-competitive transaction, one takes the interest rate he/she is given on a Treasury note. In competitive investing, one bids on a desired yield; however, this does not mean it will be accepted. Treasury notes are low-risk, low-return investments. The minimum purchase is $1,000 and the maximum is $1 million in competitive bidding, or $5 million in non-competitive. They are known informally as T notes. See also: Treasury Bill, Treasury Bond.

U.S. Treasury Security A tradable debt security owed by the United States government for a certain stated period. Each note has a stated interest rate which is paid semi-annually. Because the United States is seen as a very low-risk borrower, many investors see Treasury security interest rates (especially 10-year Treasury notes) as indicative of the wider bond market. Normally, the interest rate decreases with greater demand for the securities and rises with lower demand. For example, in December 2008, 10-year interest rates were the lowest in history due to deteriorating economic conditions and the consequent desire of investors for low-risk investments. U.S. Treasury securities are sold in auctions, usually once every few weeks. They are secured by the full faith and credit of the United States government. They should not be confused with U.S. savings bonds, which are not tradable, or indirect government obligations, which are not issued by the U.S. government itself. See also: Yield, Bond, Treasury Bond, Treasury Bill, Treasury Note.

U.S. vs. O'Hagan A U.S. Supreme Court case holding that a person who profits from nonpublic information may be held liable even if he/she does not owe a fiduciary duty to a company in question. O'Hagan was a lawyer representing a company considering buying Pillsbury. He discovered this information and bought call options on Pillsbury, to which he had no responsibility as he only represented the buyer. In the decision, the Supreme Court upheld O'Hagan's conviction. It was decided in 1997.

U.S.-Canada Free Trade Agreement A treaty between the United States and Canada that went into effect in 1988 and in which each country pledged to reduce their tariffs over a period of 10 years. It also eased the conditions under which cross-border investment could occur. The agreement greatly increased international trade between Canada and the U.S. NAFTA superseded it in 1994.

U.S.-Israeli Free Trade Agreement A treaty between the United States and Israel that came into effect in 1985 and reduced tariffs between the two countries. It was the United States' first free trade agreement.

U.S.-Japan Semiconductor Trade Arrangement A treaty between the United States and Japan opening up the Japanese market for semiconductors to American businesses. It also contains provisions disallowing Japan from dumping semiconductors into the United States. It went into effect in 1991.

U/lc An abbreviation for upper and lower case. In business correspondence (and in writing generally), using U/lc is considered a mark of both good grammar and professionalism.

UA 1. ISO 3166-1 alpha-2 code for Ukraine. This is the code used in international transactions to and from Ukrainian bank accounts. **2.** ISO 3166-2 geocode for Ukraine. This is used as an international standard for shipping to Ukraine . Each Ukrainian oblast and several other subdivisions have their own codes with the prefix "UA." For example, the code for the City of Kiev is ISO 3166-2:UA-30.

UAH ISO 4217 code for the Ukrainian hryvnia. It was introduced in 1996, replacing the karbovanets following a period of hyperinflation in the latter. Since its introduction, it has been pegged to the U.S. dollar at various values.

UAK ISO 4217 code for the karbovanets, which was the currency of Ukraine from 1992 to 1996. It replaced the Soviet ruble and suffered from hyperinflation. It was replaced by the Ukrainian hryvnia.

Ubanu An ancient Akkadian unit of length approximately equivalent to 15 centimeters.

Uberrima Fides A legal principle in which all parties to a contract must make full disclosure of material facts in order for the contract to be effective. It is used in insurance contracts, in which the potential policyholder must declare all illnesses, injuries or other facts that would change the policy's level of risk. The phrase "uberrima fides" is Latin for "utmost good faith." It is also the motto of Lloyd's.

Uberrimae Fidei Contract A contract in which all parties must make full disclosure of material facts in order for the contract to be effective. It is most relevant in insurance, in which the potential policyholder must declare all illnesses, injuries or other facts would change the policy's level of risk.

Ubi Arcano Dei An encyclical letter written by Pope Pius XI in 1922. Written only a few years after the end of World War I, it laments a large gap between the richest and the poorest, greed, and general moral decay after the war. It represents an early use of the figure of Christ the King in the Roman Catholic teaching of social justice.

Ubu An ancient Akkadian unit of area approximately equivalent to 1,800 square meters.

UCC-1 Statement A statement filed for personal property used as collateral on a loan. The statement derives its name from the Uniform Commercial Code (UCC), which requires its filing.

UDDI Universal Description, Discovery and Integration. A registry for businesses to list themselves online. UDDI also allows users to access web services. Businesses listed on UDDI are organized by name and contact information, industry or sector, and the specific services offered. UDDI was written in 2000 but was not widely adopted. It was largely abandoned by 2010.

U-Formation In technical analysis, a situation in which a security or economy declines in price, and only gradually recovers. A U-formation may be bullish in the long run, but one may not realize gains or profits immediately. In the case of an economy, a U-shaped recovery may indicate that job growth and investment gains are slow in coming. See also: W-type bottom, V-shaped recovery, W-shaped recovery.

UG 1. ISO 3166-1 alpha-2 code for the Republic of Uganda. This is the code used in international transactions to and from Ugandan bank accounts. **2.** ISO 3166-2 geocode for Uganda. This is used as an international standard for shipping to Uganda. Each Uganadan district has its own code with the prefix "UG." For example, the code for the District of Arua is ISO 3166-2:UG-ARU.

UGA GOST 7.67 Latin three-letter geocode for Uganda. The code is used for transactions to and from Ugandan bank accounts and for international shipping to Uganda. As with all GOST 7.67 codes, it is used primarily in Cyrillic alphabets.

Ugandan Shilling The currency of Uganda. It was introduced in 1966, replacing the East African shilling. It was marked by high inflation and was revalued in 1987. See also: UGS, UGX.

UGS ISO 4217 code for the first Ugandan shilling. It was introduced in 1966, replacing the East African shilling. It was marked by high inflation and in 1987 was replaced by the second shilling (UGX).

UGX ISO 4217 code for the second Ugandan shilling. The new shilling replaced the old Ugandan shilling (UGS) in 1987 following a period of hyperinflation. The new shilling was issued at an exchange rate of 1 second shilling for 100 first shillings. The second shilling is stable, though there are plans to replace it with a common currency for the East African Community at the end of 2009. Currently, it is used in Uganda alongside the U.S. dollar, the British pound, and the euro.

UIC Unit Identification Code. A unique, six-digit code utilizing both letters and numbers for each unit of the Unite States Armed Forces.

Ujrah In Islamic finance, a generic term for a fee, especially one charged for a service.

UK Payments Administration A trade organization in the United Kingdom that provides banks, credit card companies, and other financial institutions with a forum under which they can process payments and work together in areas in which they do not compete. It sets national standards for debits, standing orders, and other types of payments. It organized and oversaw the UK's transition to the chip and PIN system. It was known as the Association for Payment Clearing Services (APACS) until 2009.

UKR GOST 7.67 Latin three-letter geocode for Ukraine. The code is used for transactions to and from Ukrainian bank accounts and for international shipping to Ukraine. As with all GOST 7.67 codes, it is used primarily in Cyrillic alphabets.

Ukrainian Hryvnia The currency of the Ukraine. It was introduced in 1996, replacing the karbovanets following a period of hyperinflation in the latter. Since its introduction, it has been pegged to the U.S. dollar at various values.

Ukrainian Karbovanets The currency of Ukraine from 1992 to 1996. It replaced the Soviet ruble and suffered from hyperinflation. It was replaced by the Ukrainian hryvnia (UAH).

Ulcer Index In technical analysis, a measure of a security's volatility in a downward direction. That is, the Ulcer Index is a measure of the depth and duration of a security's downward trend. The UI is thus a measure of a security's risk. The higher a security's rating on the UI, the more risk it carries. It was designed as a corrective to measurements of standard deviation, which, according to proponents of the UI, does not adequately calculate risk.

Ultimate Beneficial Owner The person or company that owns a U.S. affiliate of a foreign company. The ultimate beneficial owner may not own the affiliate directly; for example, he/she may own 51% of a company that owns 51% of the U.S. affiliate.

Ultimate Consignee In international commerce, the buyer of a good being shipped, as opposed to the freight forwarder or other intermediary.

Ultimate Consignor In international commerce, the seller of a good being shipped, as opposed to the freight forwarder or other intermediary.

Ultimate Mortality Table In actuarial analysis, a table of the likelihood that a policyholder of a certain sex and age will die in the next year, excluding recently issued policies. These policies are excluded because new policyholders are generally healthier than the rest of the sample due to selection bias. An ultimate mortality table provides more accurate information than a regular mortality table of a life insurer's risk.

Ultimate Net Loss The amount an insurance company pays on a claim after recouping some of its cost from reinsurance and other sources (but not premiums).

Ultimo Day The previous day. For example, if today is the 23rd, the ultimo day is the 22nd. It is used primarily in letter writing.

Ultra Vires Activities Activities in which a publicly-traded company engages that are outside the powers delegated to it in its charter and/or bylaws. Every publicly-traded company has a charter and bylaws, which both outline the powers of executives and the board of directors and actions they are allowed to take. While both the charter and the bylaws can be amended by shareholders, companies sometimes take actions outside the scope of their charters without first receiving permission to do so. If shareholders deem ultra vires activities to be harmful to them or to have the potential of harm, they may sue the company for damages.

Ultradot Software that allows a company to send orders on derivative products to the appropriate exchange for execution.

Ultra-Short-Term Bond Fund A mutual fund that invests exclusively in bonds with a maturity of one year or less. Like all bond funds, it carries fewer risks than other mutual funds, but it may still be risky if it invests in short-term junk bonds.

Ulus In the Sakha Republic (a subdivision of the Russian Federation), the equivalent of a raion.

UM 1. ISO 3166-1 alpha-2 code for the United States Minor Outlying Islands. This is the code used in international transactions to and from local bank accounts. **2.** ISO 3166-2 geocode for the US Minor Outlying Islands. This is used as an international standard for shipping to the Islands. Each island has its own code with the prefix "UM." For example, the code for Baker Island is ISO 3166-2:UM-81.

Umbrella Personal Liability Policy An insurance policy that guards the policyholder from unusual legal expenses from a lawsuit that other liability policies do not cover. This includes both attorneys' fees and damages that the policyholder must pay. Umbrella personal liability policies cover extraordinarily large jury awards or other highly unusual expenses. Premiums on liability insurance are sometimes considered prohibitively expensive, depending on the policyholder's profession.

Umbrella Policy An insurance policy that covers the policyholder for all claims that his/her other insurance policies do not cover. For example, if a health insurance policy only covers an individual up to $1 million, an umbrella policy would pay for all claims above that. Likewise, if an export insurance policy covers loss but not damage to the exports, an umbrella policy would cover damage. Umbrella policies exist to cover all possible contingencies for the policyholder that are not covered under other policies.

Umbrella Reinsurance A reinsurance policy that covers the policyholder for all claims that his/her other reinsurance policies do not cover. For example, if an insurer has an individual reinsurance policy for its health and life policies, an umbrella reinsurance policy would cover its property, liability and other policies. Umbrella policies exist to cover all possible contingencies for the insurance companies that are not covered under other policies.

UMI GOST 7.67 Latin three-letter geocode for the U.S. Minor Outlying Islands. The code is used for transactions to and from local bank accounts and for international shipping to the U.S. Minor Outlying Islands. As with all GOST 7.67 codes, it is used primarily in Cyrillic alphabets.

Umlage During the Weimar Republic in Germany, the policy in which farmers were required to deliver a certain number of tons of wheat to the market earlier than they otherwise would have done. Umlage was instituted to keep bread as affordable as possible during Germany's bout of hyperinflation during the early 1920s.

Umurenge In Rwanda, a political subdivision equivalent to a municipality.

Unadjusted Basis In the accelerated cost recovery system and the modified accelerated cost recovery system, the price of an asset used to calculate depreciation. Generally speaking, the unadjusted basis is based on the original purchase price.

Unadjusted Trial Balance In accounting, a record of the assets and liabilities of a company made during an accounting period before any mistakes are corrected or any other adjustments (such as unearned revenue or prepaid expenses) are calculated. The unadjusted trial balance contrasts with the adjusting journal entry, which includes these considerations.

Unaffiliated Investments Total investments in anything other than a subsidiary, a company owned by the same parent company or other affiliate corporation. The term is most commonly used in insurance.

Unaffiliated Union A union in the United States that is not a part of the AFL-CIO, which is America's biggest labor group. The Teamsters and the SEIU are two of the largest unaffiliated unions, both having split from the AFL-CIO in 2005.

Unaided Recall In marketing, a technique to determine how well viewers or listeners remember an advertisement. In unaided recall, a test audience is shown an advertisement and is asked questions about it. The testers do not give verbal cues to help the test audience remember; the better the audience members recall the ad the more effective it is thought to be. This technique contrasts with aided recall, in which some help is given.

Unallocated Benefit A way to structure a pension in which money deposited into an account is not used immediately to buy an instrument to fund retirement. Interest and principal are not guaranteed in an unallocated benefit plan. Upon retirement, the pensioner is either given the funds that have accumulated or those funds are used to purchase an immediate annuity. An unallocated benefit structure is also called an unallocated funding instrument.

Unamortized Bond Discount The difference between the face value of a bond and the price below face value at which it is issued, less any interest that has already been amortized. Issuers of original discount bonds are required to keep a record of the unamortized bond discount.

Unamortized Bond Premium The difference between the face value of a bond and the price above face value at which it is issued, less any interest that has already been amortized. Issuers of original discount bonds are required to keep a record of the unamortized bond premium.

Unamortized Cost The historical cost of an asset (which is what the owner originally paid for it) less its total depreciation (which is the portion of value removed each year for accounting purposes) up to that point. That is, the unamortized cost of an asset is the value of the asset that has not yet been subtracted for depreciation. This affects the owner's net asset value, but the unamortized cost often has only a rough relationship with the asset's actual fair market value.

Unamortized Premiums on Investments The difference between the face value of an investment and its purchase price that has not yet been amortized.

Unaudited Statement A financial statement that an auditor has prepared, but not according to the Generally Accepted Auditing Standards (GAAS). Auditors preparing unaudited statements are required to issue a disclaimer stating that they are not rendering opinions and that the statement does not abide by the GAAS. Unaudited statements are subject to less rigorous standards than audited statements and, as such, are more prone to errors.

Unauthorized Insurance An insurance policy sold by a company that has not received permission to do business in one's state. For example, if Tom lives in Oklahoma and an insurance company only authorized to operate in Texas sells Tom a policy, it has sold unauthorized insurance. Selling unauthorized insurance is illegal.

Unauthorized Insurer An insurance company that has not received permission to do business in one's state. For example, an insurance company only authorized to operate in Texas is an unauthorized insurer in Oklahoma. It is illegal for an unauthorized insurer to do business.

Unauthorized Investment An investment that does not meet the investment goals of a bank or trust. An unauthorized investment may be legal; that is, a bank or trust may be allowed to purchase an unauthorized investment. However, it does not suit the particular needs of the bank or trust. It contrasts with a nonlegal investment, which is not permitted by law.

Unauthorized Practice of Law 1. The crime in which one poses as one qualified to give legal advice. **2.** The act in which one acts as a lawyer (before a court, for example) without permission. Unauthorized practice of law in this sense may not be a crime, but does violate regulations or court rules.

Unauthorized Reinsurance The sale of an insurance policy to a reinsurer that is not allowed to do business in a state. For example, an insurance company in Oklahoma may cede some of its policies to a reinsurer only authorized to operate in Texas. Selling unauthorized reinsurance is illegal.

Unauthorized Transfer The illegal transfer of funds without permission from the person or company who owns the funds. Unauthorized transfers can be fairly basic; for example, one may steal and use a debit card. Often, however, unauthorized transfers involve using computer programs to find a person's financial information and conduct large transactions with that person's money. The person who owns the funds is responsible for the loss of the first $50 if he/she informs the bank within 60 days. Otherwise, he/she is responsible for the first $500. See also: Identity theft.

Unauthorized Use The illegal use of a credit card without permission from the card holder. Unauthorized use can be fairly basic; for example, one may steal and use a credit card. Often, however, unauthorized use involves using computer programs to find a person's financial information and conduct large transactions with that person's credit. The card holder may be responsible for the loss of the first $50 if he/she informs the bank within 60 days, but many card issuers waive this responsibility. See also: Identity theft.

Unavoidable Costs Costs a company incurs regardless of the operational decisions it makes. Examples of unavoidable costs include rent, office supplies and some taxes.

Unbalanced Growth A situation in which economic growth is significantly higher in some sectors than others. For example, banking may be growing rapidly while manufacturing may be growing more slowly or even declining. Unbalanced growth portends an eventual economic slowdown or recession, though economists disagree on how a country should address it.

Unbanked Describing a person or group of people who do not have an account at any bank. Unbanked persons are either paid in cash or cash their paychecks rather than deposit them. Unbanked persons are often poor; lack of a bank account often renders one ineligible to buy a house or take advantage of some social services.

Unbiased Estimator A mathematical estimation of the value of some unknown that does not differ from the unknown's true value.

Unbiased Expectations Hypothesis In foreign exchange, a theory that forward exchange rates for delivery at some future date are equal to the spot rates for that date. The hypothesis only functions in the absence of a risk premium. Critics contend that the unbiased expectations evidence shows that unbiased expectations do not occur in actual trading. It is also called an unbiased predictor.

Unbranding Describing the act of removing the advertisements from a billboard, television or radio station or some other medium.

Unbundled Life Insurance Policy A whole life insurance policy in which the savings element, standard element and cost are analyzed and invested independently of each other. This may result in a return for the policyholder that is higher than that of other whole life policies.

Unbundling The practice of separating previously joined products and selling them. Unbundling tends to become more common under deregulatory policies.

Uncalled Capital Capital that a company has raised by issuing shares or bonds but that the company has not collected because it has not requested payment. See also: Authorized Shares.

Uncap To remove a cap previously instituted. For example, a government may uncap its debt ceiling by allowing itself to borrow more money.

Uncashed Describing a check, bond or other financial instrument that has not been redeemed. That is, an uncashed instrument is something that may be exchanged for cash or some other liquidity but has not been.

Uncertain Tax Position In accounting, a situation in which a taxpayer believes its interpretation of earnings recognition is less strong than what the interpretation of the IRS is likely to be. While the FASB does not allow companies to report uncertain tax positions on financial reports, they may take these positions on their tax returns in hope that the IRS will not conduct audits.

Uncertified Unit A building constructed according to industry standards but which, for any reason, may not be eligible for a permit. An uncertified unit also may be ineligible for a warranty.

Uncharged An amount for which a client or customer has not been billed, but for which he/she will be billed in a short time.

Uncharged Arrearage A past due amount for which a customer or client was billed previously, but which will not be due until the next bill is sent. For example, if a client did not pay February's bill, February becomes uncharged arrearage for March's bill and the two months are due at once.

Uncia 1. An ancient Roman unit of length approximately equivalent to 24.6 millimeters. It was also called a pollex. **2.** An ancient Roman unit of weight approximately equivalent to 27.4 grams. **3.** An ancient Roman unit of area approximately equivalent to 210 square meters. **4.** An obsolete unit of weight in the early metric system approximately equivalent to 32 grams.

Uncirculated Describing a coin that has never been touched or put into general use. An uncirculated coin usually is in mint condition, which means it has no evidence of wear and tear. Depending on demand for the coin among collectors and investors, an uncirculated coin may be quite valuable, though it is an illiquid asset.

Unclaimed Balance Money in a bank account that has not been accessed or use for an exceptionally long period of time. After a certain number of years (usually about five), unclaimed balances become abandoned property and the state may claim ownership.

Uncollectible Account Accounts receivable that a company cannot collect because the client is unable or unwilling to pay. If the client is simply unwilling to pay, the company can sue to collect what is owed; however, this incurs its own expenses and may not be worth the effort. If the client is unable to pay, for instance because of bankruptcy, the company writes off the amount lost as bad debt. This reduces the company's revenue, but also reduces its taxable income.

Uncommercial Describing anything that harms commerce. For example, a law that requires businesses to pay confiscatory taxes may be described as uncommercial.

Uncommitted Facility An agreement between a bank and a company or, rarely, an individual to provide an unspecified amount in loans on demand from the borrower. The borrower is under no obligation to actually take out a loan at any particular time. Funds borrowed are not repaid on any particular schedule, but they must be repaid on demand from the bank. This agreement is fairly common in situations where a business must make payroll but does not always have the operating income to do so. See also: Committed facility, Line of credit, Overdraft facility.

Unconditional Bid In a takeover of a publicly-traded company, an offer to pay a stated price per share, regardless of how many shares the acquirer purchases. An unconditional bid is most common after the acquirer already has a majority stake in the target company.

Unconditional Vesting The process by which an employee with a qualified retirement plan and/or stock option becomes entitled to the benefits of ownership, even if he/she no longer works at the company providing the retirement plan or stock option. Once unconditional vesting occurs, the plan or option belongs to the employee even if the employer no longer makes contributions. As with all vesting, the benefits of the plan or stock option cannot be revoked.

Unconfirmed Letter of Credit A letter of credit where only the bank issuing it has agreed to guarantee payment. This differs from a confirmed letter of credit, where at least two banks guarantee payment. This increases the risk for the bank that honors the letter of credit, as it only has one, rather than two, ways to seek recourse.

Unconscionable In law, describing anything that violates or ought to violate one's conscience. An unconscionable act is unenforceable by a court. For example, a court may rule a contract invalid because its provisions so obviously favor one party that it becomes unconscionable.

Unconscionable Bargain In law, a contract with provisions that so obviously favor one party that no honest person would agree to it. An unconscionable bargain is unenforceable by a court and may result in the declaration of an invalid contract.

Unconsolidated Subsidiary A subsidiary whose financial statements are accounted differently from its parent company. That is, an unconsolidated subsidiary publishes its balance sheets, 10-K statements and other information separately. On the parent company's financials, an unconsolidated subsidiary is listed as an investment.

Uncovered Interest Arbitrage The transfer of funds into another currency in order to achieve a higher interest rate at the same level of risk. For example, one may transfer a money market fund denominated in U.S. dollars to one denominated in euros because euro interest rates may be slightly higher. The interest arbitrage is uncovered because it does not hedge against foreign exchange risk.

Uncreditworthy Describing a person or company unable to borrow money. An uncreditworthy person or company may have defaulted on a previous loan, overspent in the past and/or may not have sufficient history to establish credit. Individual creditworthiness is measured by the FICO score, while a company's or other organization's creditworthiness usually is measured by its credit rating.

Undated Security A debt security with no maturity date. That is, an undated security pays interest in perpetuity. Undated securities are rare outside of a few government securities in the United Kingdom.

Undeliverable Billing Document An invoice that cannot be delivered and is returned to the sender. Usually this occurs because of a faulty address. The sender will not collect on an undeliverable billing document until the address is corrected. See also: Accounts uncollectable.

Undeliverable-As-Addressed Any piece of mail that cannot be delivered because the address is incomplete or illegible. Such mail can be costly to marketers and others who rely on high mail volume.

Under In bond insurance, a slang term for underlying. It is used to describe what a bond rating would be if there were no insurance covering it.

Under Reporting The act of deliberately understating personal income or corporate earnings. One usually underreports in order to pay less in taxes. For example, if one makes $50,000 in a year and reports $35,000, one does not pay taxes on the extra $15,000. Underreporting is illegal because it deprives the government of tax revenue. Occasionally, underreporting refers to an illegal practice in which a company refrains from reporting earnings in one quarter in order to report them the following quarter. Companies usually do this to drive up the stock price.

Under the Counter Describing an illegal payment for a good or service. An under the counter payment often involves paying more than a good's value as a form of bribery.

Under the Table Describing a payment in which no involved party reports the payment to tax authorities. An under the table payment usually occurs when one party or both wishes to hide income and thereby evade paying taxes on it. Under the table payments are illegal.

Under-Allowance In auto sales, the act or practice in which a dealership pays less than the actual value for a trade-in. Suppose a customer has a car worth $5,000 and wishes to buy another worth $10,000. In an under-allowance, the dealership may accept $3,000 for the trade-in, leaving the customer to pay $7,000 for the new car.

Underapplied Overhead In accounting, an estimate of overhead for a work-in-process product that is less than the overhead actually is. This may happen for any number of reasons. Because underapplied overhead means profits are lower than the records say they should be, it is subtracted from the cost of goods sold at the end of the accounting period. See also: Overapplied overhead.

Underbanked Describing a situation when an issuer or syndicate manager has difficulty finding enough underwriters to place a new issue with investors.

Underbooked Describing a situation in which investors show a lack of interest in a new issue of a security. Before a new issue, underwriters canvass potential investors, who may or may not book an order to buy a portion of the new issue. If investors do not show interest, the security is said to be underbooked. This may affect the price when the security is actually issued. See also: Fully circled.

Undercapitalized Describing a company that has insufficient capital to maintain operations without outside assistance. Undercapitalized companies often rely on short-term loans for funding, though they may issue stock or bonds at some point to raise capital.

Undercharge To assess a buyer too little for a product. For example, one may sell an antique car worth $50,000 for $10,000. Because pricing is somewhat subjective, it can be difficult to determine when someone has been undercharged.

Underclass The lowest level of the socioeconomic spectrum. The underclass may be intermittently employed but generally are thought to include long-term welfare recipients, drug and alcohol addicts, and petty criminals. They are distinguished from the working poor and the lower middle class.

Undercolor Removal In printing, the use of black ink instead of grey to reduce the amount of colored ink used.

Underconsumption The reduction of demand by consumers. That is, underconsumption is the desire of consumers to buy fewer goods. Some early Keynesian thinkers believed that underconsumption causes recessions or stagnation, but most now argue that aggregate demand consists of more than consumption. Classical and Austrian School economists reject the notion that underconsumption is harmful.

Underemployed The group of persons with part time jobs who are willing and able to work full time. Underemployment is most common during difficult economic times, when job growth is stagnant or declining. Underemployed persons are bringing in an income, but it may not be sufficient to pay their bills and usually is not enough to support the lifestyle they were living when they were employed full time. For this reason, the underemployment rate is sometimes called the "real" unemployment rate. See also: U6.

Underemployment A term used to describe persons who are working part time but would like to work full time, or persons whose skills exceed those needed for the job they are performing. For example, an economist working as a retail clerk may be described as underemployed. Underemployment increases during recessions and periods of slow economic growth.

Underfunded Describing a program, account or anything else with insufficient assets to meet liabilities, especially but not necessarily in the short term. The term is often used with respect to pension schemes.

Underfunded Pension Plan A pension plan that has more liabilities than assets. That is, the retirees covered under the pension plan have been promised more than the plan contains. This may happen for a variety of reasons, such as the pension's investments not going as expected, or perhaps retirees are living longer than expected. It can lead to bankruptcy, though some pension plans have government guarantees.

Undergrading In numismatics, the act or practice of appraising a coin for less than it is actually worth. This is an unethical practice, often conducted by persons who are trying to buy a valuable coin without paying full price.

Underground Storage Insurance An insurance policy providing coverage to a company that stores oil tanks and other hazardous materials underground. For example, underground storage insurance may pay for losses if a policyholder's tank explodes underground, causing damage. As with all insurance, a company must pay a premium to receive underground storage insurance.

Underhand Describing a secret or sneaky action. For example, one may underhandedly plot to remove the CEO of a corporation. Some underhand actions are illegal or unethical, but very often they are simply part of doing business.

Underinsurance The state in which one's health insurance or other insurance policy does not provide sufficient benefits. In an extreme example, one may be underinsured if one's policy does not cover cancer. Underinsurance may be deliberate: young persons often underinsure themselves because they are healthy and wish to pay lower premiums. However, some insurers have at times underinsured even those paying higher premiums to save on their own costs.

Underinsured A person or company with insufficient insurance to pay for a negative event. For example, if one's health insurance has a maximum benefit of $1 million and one contracts a chronic disease whose treatment costs $2 million over several years, one may be said to be underinsured.

Underinsured Motorist Coverage Limits Trigger The point at which an underinsured motorist endorsement becomes effective. That is, one may make a claim if the trigger is reached. The trigger occurs when an underinsured motorist's insurance stops paying for a tort determined to be to that motorist's responsibility.

Underinsured Motorist Coverage Modified Limits Trigger The point at which an underinsured motorist endorsement becomes effective in situations when there are multiple claimants. That is, one may make a claim if the trigger is reached. The trigger occurs when an underinsured motorist's insurance must pay multiple persons and, because of this, it is unable to pay the full amount to any one claimant.

Underinsured Motorist Endorsement An insurance policy or supplemental providing coverage to a motorist and/or his family in the event of a car accident with another driver who does not have sufficient car insurance to cover the motorist's repairs and/or medical bills. Underinsured motorist insurance only provides coverage if the policyholder is not at fault in the accident.

Underinvestment Problem A situation in which a company refuses to make low-risk investments to the detriment of bondholders. The company does this in order to placate its shareholders, who seek a higher return, but this exposes bondholders to more risk without the promise of a higher return. That is, the high-risk investments or projects may not perform as expected, resulting in bankruptcy, but the nature of bonds does not allow them to participate in any extra rewards from these investments or projects. The underinvestment problem may encourage bondholders to sell their bonds. See also: Asset substitution problem.

Underinvoicing The act or practice of stating the price of a good on an invoice as being less than the price actually paid. Underinvoicing occurs if the importer and/or exporter wish to reduce a tariff or if a buyer and/or seller wish to reduce their apparent profits so as to pay less in taxes. See also: Fraud.

Underleveraged Describing a company with too little debt. While it sounds strange, a company may be underleveraged because interest on bonds are usually tax deductible for the issuing company; thus, a bond issue can create higher earnings per share for stockholders. There is no metric for determining when a company is underleveraged and investors decide on it based on their personal perceptions.

Underlying Asset In a derivative or warrant, the security, property, or other asset that gives value to the derivative or warrant. For example, in an option giving one the right to buy stock in Johnson and Johnson, the underlying asset is the stock in Johnson and Johnson. An underlying asset may many things, such as a physical commodity, a security, a piece of land, or part of a business.

Underlying Debt A bond or other debt issued by a municipality and guaranteed by another government entity. For example, if a state guarantees payment, at least in part, for municipal bonds issued by cities in that state, those bonds are called the state's underlying debt. This debt is usually lower risk than other debts.

Underlying Futures Contract In an option on a futures contract, the futures contract. The underlying futures contract supports the option; that is, if the option is exercised, the futures contract is executed. For example, an investor may buy a call giving him/her the right to buy a pork belly if the option is exercised. In this case, the pork belly is the underlying futures contract.

Underlying Index An index tracked by an investment vehicle. For example, an exchange-traded fund may track every stock traded on the New York Stock Exchange. In this case, the underlying index is the NYSE Composite.

Underlying Inflation Inflation caused by a reduction in the value of money rather than price changes in volatile products. For example, rising gasoline prices may reduce the spending power of one's income, but this may be due to factors external to money such as excessive speculation. Underlying inflation measures changes to the supply and demand for money itself. See also: Core Inflation.

Underlying Instrument A security, commodity, or other asset described in a derivative contact. For example, in an option contract giving the holder the right to buy so many shares of AT&T, the underlying instrument is stock in AT&T. Likewise, in a futures contract on so many barrels of refined oil, the underlying instrument is refined oil.

Underlying Investment The sum of the investments represented in a mutual fund or annuity. When one buys a share in either of these investment vehicles, the share represents a right to the dividends, coupons, and capital gains or losses in each of the securities represented in the fund or annuity in proportion to their representation in it. For example, suppose a mutual fund consists of 50% of Stock A, 25% of Stock B, and 25% of Bond C. All other things being equal, ownership of a share in that mutual fund effectively means that one owns half a share of Stock A and one quarter of a share in Stock B and Bond C. One refers to these investments collectively as the underlying investment. See also: Underlying asset.

Underlying Mortgage In a mortgage-backed security, a mortgage or a piece of a mortgage that gives value to the security. For example, if a bank sells the mortgage on Joe's house to another bank and that bank repackages it into an MBS, Joe's mortgage is one of the underlying mortgages for the security. See also: Underlying asset.

Underlying Price The spot price of the underlying asset of a derivative. For example, suppose one owns a call option to buy so many shares of Marinelli Enterprises. If Marinelli Enterprises is currently trading at $15 per share, the underlying price is $15. The difference between the underlying price and the strike price greatly influences the value of a derivative.

Underlying Retention A limit on an insurance policy's coverage past which an umbrella policy begins to pay claims. For example, if one holds an umbrella policy paying all expenses over the $200,000 limit on one's homeowners insurance, the underlying retention is $200,000.

Underlying Security In a derivative or warrant, a security that gives value to the derivative or warrant. For example, in an option giving one the right to buy stock in Johnson and Johnson, the underlying security is the stock in Johnson and Johnson. An underlying security may be a stock or a bond.

Underlying Service The issues of a periodical scheduled to be sent to a subscriber after his/her current subscription expires. That is, the underlying service includes renewals and gift subscriptions that have been paid for but that have not been sent because the current subscription has not run out. For example, if one renews a newspaper subscription for a year starting June 1, the underlying service includes all issues scheduled to be sent to that subscriber after June 1. A high underlying service rate indicates that a periodical is in strong financial shape and has engaged in effective marketing (and/or simply has a superior product).

Underlying Value The fundamental value of a company, and not its speculated or estimated future value. The underlying value may reflect both tangible and intangible value and, for that reason, may be difficult to calculate. However, it comes from present, fundamental information and not conjecture.

Undermargined Account A margin account in which the value of the assets purchased on margin falls below the maintenance requirement on the account. A margin account holder is required to maintain money or securities worth a certain amount in order to continue trading on margin; this rule exists to protect the broker from financing excessive and irresponsible trading. An undermargined account may result in a margin call or in the account becoming restricted.

Underpayment The act of paying an amount under the full amount. For example, if one's mortgage payment is $600 per month but one only pays $400 for July, one has underpaid the mortgage. Underpayment is not sustainable and may lead to serious financial difficulties. However, paying what one can afford when one cannot pay the full amount may be easier for both the obligor and the obligee.

Underpayment Penalty A penalty that a taxpayer must pay if he/she fails to pay enough in estimated taxes and withholding. In order to reduce the incentive for persons and companies to pay taxes late, the IRS has instituted an underpayment penalty. In order to avoid the underpayment penalty, one must either pay 100% of his/her tax liability for the previous year or 90% of the liability for the current year.

Underperform A broker's or brokerage firm's rating of a security. Such a security is expected to do marginally worse than the market as a whole for the period of time it holds the "underperform" rating. Some firms call the rating "market underperform" "moderate sell" or "weak hold." Different firms have different rating systems, but "underperform" is usually one rating above "sell" and one rating below "market perform" or "neutral." For example, if the market is expected to rise slightly, but a certain company's fundamentals are thought to be slightly weaker than the rest of the market, a brokerage firm might change that company's rating from market perform to underperform.

Underperforming Asset An asset that is not generating an expected or necessary return. While the asset may produce income for the company or person possessing it, the income may not be sufficient and is certainly less than expected. Examples of underperforming assets include loans in which payments are irregular or products that have been inefficiently marketed. Companies with underperforming assets are often candidates for both hostile and friendly takeovers. See also: Nonperforming asset.

Underpricing Describing a situation in which a company prices an IPO lower than its market value. This results in the company raising less capital in the IPO than it could have raised. There is no definite way to determine if a stock issue is underpriced until it is too late and the price of the first secondary trade is much higher than the IPO.

Underresourced Describing a project or other activity with too few people or too little money to accomplish the objectives.

Undersell To deliberately charge a lower price for a good or service than a competitor. For example, if a grocery store sells apples for $2 per pound, a competitor may undersell by charging only $1.50 per pound. Underselling may result in losses in the short term (depending on how much of a discount one offers), but it may build market share.

Underspend To spend less than one was allotted in a budget. Underspending in personal finance is almost always a good thing as it allows one to save more or to pay down debts. In corporations, however, underspending can be negative; for example, if a department does not spend its entire budget, the executives may conclude that it does not need such a high budget and cut that department's allotment. This creates a perverse incentive for departments and other subdivisions to spend their entire budget whether or not they need to.

Understandability The articulation of financial terms in words whose meanings can be understood by a layperson.

Undertakings for Collective Investment in Transferable Securities Also called UCITS. A system intended to allow mutual funds and other investment vehicles to operate throughout the European Union. That is, UCITS aims to unify investment regulation throughout Europe so that a company registered in one country can conduct operations in other countries as well. UCITS has been marginally successful, though differing regulations intended to protect local investment companies have remained in place. UCITS was first adopted in 1985.

Undertone An implied meaning. Undertones may have detrimental effects on a business. For example, a newspaper may imply, but never directly state, that a company is cheating on its taxes. This may cause shareholders to sell their stock even if the undertones are not true.

Undervaluation The state in which a security's price is lower than it ought to be. A stock may be undervalued, for example, when its earnings and financial outlook are both strong, but its share price is still comparatively low. A number of factors may cause undervaluation, including lack of investor knowledge about the company, which, in turn, leads to low demand for its securities. Value investors seek out undervalued companies because they tend to provide solid returns for lower prices.

Undervalued Company A company with a stock price lower than its asset value and/or earnings potential. It can be difficult to determine whether or not a company is undervalued, but a low price-earnings ratio is one way. A price-earnings ratio below 1 indicates that the stock price is less than the company's earnings per share, which may mean that the company is undervalued. Undervalued companies are often target companies in hostile takeovers. See also: Undervalued, Overvalued.

Undervalued Currency A currency with an exchange rate lower than it ought to be. A currency may be undervalued, for example, when its purchasing power, supply and demand are all strong, but its price is still comparatively low. Some governments keep their currencies undervalued deliberately because it makes their exports less expensive, but this is usually an unsustainable policy. See also: Weakening of a currency.

Undervalued Security A security with a share price lower than its asset value and/or earnings potential. It can be difficult to determine whether or not a security is undervalued, but a low price-earnings ratio is one way to estimate it. A price-earnings ratio below 1 indicates that the security's price is less than the company's earnings per share, which may mean that the company is undervalued. Undervalued companies are often target companies in hostile takeovers. See also: Undervalued, Overvalued.

Underwater 1. Describing an out-of-the-money stock option. That is, it describes an option in which the underlying asset is a stock that is currently trading for less than the strike price of the option. For example, an executive at a publicly-traded company may have stock options in which he may buy the stock of his/her own company for $80 per share. If the stock is currently trading at $60 per share, the options are worthless. **2.** Insolvent; unable to meet a financial obligation. The term especially applies to being unable to meet a margin call.

Underwater Loan A loan in which one owes more than the value of the asset the loan was intended to buy. For example, if one borrows $15,000 to buy a car, but the car depreciates rapidly to a value of only $12,000, the borrower has an underwater loan. See also: Underwater.

Underwater Option An out-of-the-money stock option. That is, it describes an option in which the underlying asset is a stock that is currently trading for less than the strike price of the option. For example, an executive at a publicly-traded company may have stock options in which he/she may buy the stock of his/her own company for $80 per share. If the stock is currently trading at $60 per share, the options are worthless.

Underweight 1. Describing a portfolio or fund with too little exposure to an industry, sector, or something else. See also: Overweight. **2.** See: Underperform.

Underwithholding A situation in which an employer withholds too little from an employee's paycheck; that is, the employer gives too little of the employee's wages or salary to the tax agency. This occurs when the employee makes enough to qualify for a higher tax bracket that the one used for the paycheck. Underwithholding results in the employee owing taxes at the end of the year.

Underwriter A company, usually an investment bank, that an issuer hires to place a new issue with investors. The issuer normally hires several underwriters for a single issue, where each is responsible for placing a certain amount of the new issue. The underwriters contact potential investors to gauge interest and sell the issue. Underwriters guarantee the price for a certain number of shares of the new issue. Because of their expertise on placing securities with investors, using underwriters often increases the chance that the placement will be successful. An underwriting firm is also called a house of issue. See also: Bracketing, Oversubscribed, Undersubscribed, Underwriting agreement.

Underwriters Laboratories, Inc. Also called UL. A nonprofit organization in the United States that develops and tests standards for product safety. It also evaluates products to ensure that they are not dangerous. UL is especially known for testing the safety of drinking water. It was founded in 1894 and is based in Illinois.

Underwriting 1. The process of placing a new issue with investors. Underwriting involves the issuing company using one or (usually) more companies who are each responsible for placing a certain amount of the new issue. The underwriting firms contact potential investors to gauge interest and sell the issue. Underwriters guarantee the price for a certain number of shares of the new issue. See also: Bracketing, Oversubscribed, Undersubscribed. **2.** Due diligence a lender conducts to ensure that a potential borrower is able to repay the loan.

Underwriting Agreement A contract between the issuer of a security and a managing underwriter stating the responsibilities and rights of each party as the security is placed with investors. The underwriting agreement may state the size of the new issue, the percentage of the sale that the underwriters are allowed to keep, and whether or not it is sold on a best efforts basis, among other things. The contract helps define and avoid problems before they start.

Underwriting Cycle The business cycle in the insurance sector. In the underwriting cycle, insurers compete with each other for clients, resulting in falling premiums and low underwriting standards. Insurers therefore write more policies than they can reasonably risk, which results in higher underwriting standards and premiums. Eventually, insurers write too few premiums to sustain and the cycle begins again.

Underwriting Expenses The expenses associated with running an insurance agency. Underwriting expenses include salaries and commissions for agents, travel,

training sessions, rent on offices and so forth. Underwriting expenses do not include taxes.

Underwriting Factors 1. See: Underwriting Factors: Health Insurance. **2.** See: Underwriting Factors: Life Insurance.

Underwriting Factors: Health Insurance The factors that a provider of health insurance considers before issuing a policy and determining how much the premium should be. Underwriting factors in health insurance are used to estimate how likely a potential policyholder is to become ill and how much treatment is likely to cost the insurer. Factors include age, height, weight, preexisting conditions and so forth. See also: Underwriting Factors: Life Insurance.

Underwriting Factors: Life Insurance The factors that a provider of life insurance considers before issuing a policy and determining how much the premium should be. Underwriting factors in life insurance are used to estimate how likely a potential policyholder is to die before issuing the policy becomes profitable for the insurer. Factors include age, gender, whether or not the potential policyholder smokes, and so forth. See also: Underwriting Factors: Health Insurance.

Underwriting Fee The compensation that an underwriter receives for placing a new issue with investors. It is calculated as a discount from the price of the new issue. For example, an issuer may sell the underwriter a bond at $990 per bond. The underwriter will then place the issue at $1,000, allowing it to make a $10 profit. This profit is the underwriting fee. It is also called a concession.

Underwriting Gain The profit an insurance company generates after paying all claims. That is, the underwriting gain is what is left over after the premiums the company collects are added to its investment income and the amount the company pays for claims on its policies is subtracted. An underwriting gain is also called an underwriting profit.

Underwriting Income In insurance, the profits generated from premiums in relation to the cost of settling claims. Underwriting income is the revenue generated by premiums on the insurance policies the company offers, less the cost of settling claims. For example, if a company generates $10,000,000 in revenue from premiums and spends $6,000,000 settling claims, its underwriting income is $4,000,000. See also: Loss ratio.

Underwriting Risk The risk that what an insurance company collects in premiums and investments will not be enough to cover its expenses from paying claims on its policies. This differs from its risk of loss, which is the risk that its income will be insufficient to cover all expenses, not just those related to policies.

Undetachable Stock Warrant A warrant attached to a bond that one may redeem for stock but may not sell separately from the bond. That is, a bond with an undetachable stock warrant is simply a convertible bond; it may not be separated into a normal bond and a warrant.

Undifferentiated Marketing A type of marketing in which a whole population receives the same message, whether or not individual persons belong to the target audience. A billboard in Times Square in New York is an example of undifferentiated marketing because the millions of people who go to Times Square every year will all see it. Undifferentiated marketing has a lower response rate and must therefore rely on large volume, but may be less expensive in the long run because the advertiser does not need to spend to determine how best to appeal to a certain target audience. See also: Market research.

Undigested Securities The shares or bonds in a new issue that are not placed with investors because investors do not want them. Depending on the agreement with the issuer, the underwriting syndicate may be required to buy undigested securities itself. See also: Underbooked.

Undischarged Bankrupt A person or organization who has filed for bankruptcy but has not received permission from the court to stop making payments on debts. Many debts are ultimately discharged (meaning forgiven), but some debts must be repaid even after the bankruptcy is finalized.

Undisclosed Principal In law, a person or company on whose behalf an agent acts, but who is not revealed. That is, the agent does not tell any other party who the undisclosed principal is. This secrecy may sometimes be necessary for a variety of reasons, such as the avoidance of some controversy. However, due to the secrecy, in the event of a dispute, the agent for the undisclosed principal may be held personally liable for the principal's actions.

Undiscounted Describing anything for which one pays full price. See also: Discount.

Undistributed Profits The amount of a publicly-traded company's post-tax earnings that are not paid in dividends. Most earnings retained are re-invested into the company's operations. Year-on-year tracking of the ratio of undistributed profits to dividends is important to fundamental analysis to investigate whether a company is increasing or decreasing its rate of re-investment. Undistributed profits form part of a company's equity, and are owned by shareholders. They are also called retained earnings, accumulated profits, undivided profits, and earned surplus.

Undiversified In risk management, the state of one's portfolio when it contains only a few securities or classes of securities. For example, if one invests exclusively in automotive companies or only in bonds, one has an undiversified portfolio. An undiversified portfolio carries a great deal of risk; for instance, if automotive companies or bonds perform poorly, it does not matter how well the rest of the market performs. On the other hand, the potential for gains is higher. In general, broader diversification equates to less risk and less return. See also: Markowitz Portfolio Theory.

Undivided Account In underwriting, a portion of a new issue that a member of a syndicate is responsible for placing with investors, where each member is responsible for placing the whole issue. Each underwriting firm in a syndicate is responsible for its own undivided account, but if a member of the syndicate fails to place its portion with investors, the other underwriters are under an obligation to "help out" that member until the entire issue is placed. This contrasts with a divided account, where underwriters are each assigned a portion of a new issue, and no underwriter is responsible for placing any part of the issue that it is not explicitly assigned.

Undivided Interest A form of communal ownership in which all owners share possession jointly and severally. That is, owners with undivided interest collectively own a single piece of property rather than each owning a portion of it. Decisions regarding the property must be made as a group.

Undocumented 1. Describing a circumstance for which there is no proof in the form of paperwork. For example, if one takes an undocumented deduction on his/her tax return, the IRS may not allow the deduction. **2.** A term for a non-citizen working in a country without proper paperwork (that is, illegally).

Undue Debt A debt that one is not yet required to pay. An example is a bond that has not yet matured.

Undue Influence In law, a situation in which one person uses his/her position or authority to extract an agreement from another person that is regarded as unfairly favorable to the first person. For example, if a physician executes an unreasonably favorable contract with a patient, the physician must be able to prove he/she did not exercise undue influence. A contract found to have undue influence is voidable.

Unearned Discount A finance charge a lender assesses at the beginning of a loan, but only recognizes as income gradually over the loan's life. In accounting, the unearned discount is listed at first as a liability on the lender's balance sheet, but is slowly recognized as income.

Unearned Increment Appreciation in the value of real estate without any improvement undertaken by the owner. For example, a parcel of land may become more valuable if a university is built nearby and the parcel becomes desirable for developers. The term originated in the 18th century as part of a proposal to tax the added value. See also: Unearned Income, Property Tax.

Unearned Interest Interest on a loan that the lender has received, but that may not be recorded as earnings because the principal has not been outstanding for a long enough time.

Unearned Premium A premium paid on an insurance policy before it is due. For example, one may pay six months' worth of premiums in January instead of paying each month from January to June. If the policyholder cancels before February, the insurer should refund the premiums for March, April, May and June. For that reason, they are listed as liabilities on the insurer's balance sheet.

Unearned Premium Insurance An insurance policy compensating a policyholder for the loss of premiums that it must refund due to the occurrence of an insured event. For example, suppose one prepays premiums on car insurance for January, February and March. If the car is destroyed in February, unearned premium insurance reimburses the policyholder for at least a portion of March's premium. As with all insurance, one must pay a premium to receive the coverage.

Unearned Premium Reserve An account into which an insurer deposits unearned premiums, which are paid on insurance policies before they are due. For example, one may pay six months' worth of premiums in January instead of paying each month from January to June. Unearned premiums are listed as liabilities on an insurer's balance sheet and regulators thus require insurance companies to maintain reserves to refund these amounts if necessary.

Unearned Reinsurance Premium A premium paid on a reinsurance policy before it is due. For example, one may pay six months' worth of premiums in January instead of paying each month from January to June. If the policyholder cancels before February, the reinsurer should refund the premiums March, April, May and June. For that reason, they are listed as liabilities on the reinsurer's balance sheet.

Unearned Revenue Revenue for a company from a project that has not been completed or a product that has not been delivered. A common example of unearned revenue is prepayment for a lease or asset. Unearned revenue is a liability for the company until the project has been completed or the product delivered; at that point, it becomes earned revenue.

Uneconomic Growth Economic growth that reduces quality of life. It is sometimes difficult to determine what qualifies as uneconomic growth (some may argue that it is subjective). For example, one person may believe the advent of the Internet was positive because of the improved technology, business opportunities and other benefits it brought. However, another person may argue that the Internet has reduced people's connection to their own land and communities. One often considers environmental and social impacts when discussing uneconomic growth. See also: Degrowth.

Unemployable Describing a person who is unable to find a job, especially one that suits his/her skill set. A person may be unemployable due to personal reasons (for example, he may interview poorly or he may be subject to racial or age discrimination). However, the term may also refer to a person whose skill set has become obsolete. Unemployable persons often must retrain to be able to find jobs in the future, though doing so is often very difficult.

Unemployed Labor Force The portion of the population able and willing to work that is not working. Members of the unemployed labor force may have been terminated for cause or they may have been laid off because of circumstances beyond their control. The unemployed labor force may collect some benefits from the government while they look for jobs. Because unemployed persons have less money to spend than they otherwise would, a large unemployed labor force is detrimental to economic growth.

Unemployment The state of not having a job, especially if one is available for work. For example, a person who is laid off and still wishes to work may be considered unemployed. The unemployment rate of a region is an important indicator of economic health.

Unemployment Benefit A payment made, especially by a government, to an unemployed person. Unemployed benefits are available to persons who have been laid off or terminated against their will. These benefits help them pay their bills until they can find more work.

Unemployment Compensation Amendment of 1992 Legislation in the United States that requires employers terminating an employee to allow the employee to take all employer-sponsored retirement savings and place them in the qualified retirement plan of the employee's choice. This allows the employee to keep the money he/she has saved and invested while at the company. The employee may also receive the savings directly, but the employer must then pay a 20% penalty tax on of the savings.

Unemployment Compensation Tax A tax levied on an employer that pays the unemployment insurance for the unemployed labor force. The tax is assessed as a proportion of the employer's payroll; the employer generally passes on payment of the tax to his/her employees.

Unemployment Rate The percentage of a population's workforce not working but willing to work and actively seeking a job. A high unemployment rate is considered a negative sign both economically and socially. However, the unemployment rate is a lagging indicator: it rises and falls in response to a macroeconomic change rather than in anticipation of one. This may be because employers do not hire employees unless they are confident that they will be able to afford to retain them.

Unencumbered Describing the title of a property where there are no competing claims, liens, or anything else that would hinder its transfer. That is, if a property has undisputed ownership, its owner is said to be unencumbered. An owner with unencumbered property may sell the property without any legal difficulties. Generally speaking, a real estate broker researches a property to ensure that there are no competing claims. See also: Quitclaim Deed, Clear Title, Title Search.

Unencumbered Balance In government accounting, an amount appropriated for a project or department that has not been spent and has not been earmarked for a specific task.

UNE-P Unbundled Network Element-Platform. A phone service by which Baby Bells were required to allows competitors to use their networks. The UNE-P was intended to increase competition between Baby Bells and telecommunications start ups. It was authorized by the Telecommunications Act of 1996.

Unethical Describing inappropriate behavior, even if the behavior is legal. Unethical behavior may violate a code of conduct for a particular industry or sector. Professional organizations may censure or revoke the licenses of those professionals who are found to have committed unethical acts. In investing, ethics helps inform the investment decisions of some individuals and companies. For example, an individual may have a moral objection to smoking, and therefore may refrain from investing in tobacco companies. Ethics may be both positive and negative in investing; that is, it may inform where an individual makes investments (e.g. in environmentally friendly companies) and where he/she does not (e.g. in arms manufacturers).

Unexercised Option An option in which the holder does not buy (in a call) or sell (in a put) the underlying asset by or on the expiration date. An option holder may let a contract expire unexercised because the price of the underlying has moved in an unfavorable direction or if exercising would harm his/her overall investment strategy. In an unexercised option, the contract becomes worthless and the holder loses the premium he/she paid to purchase it.

Unexpected Inflation A situation in which the inflation rate is higher than economists, regulators or others anticipated. Unexpected inflation may occur when the currently held macroeconomic model does not adequately account for new circumstances. For example, in the 1970s, the United States experienced unexpected inflation when classical Keynesianism held that inflation was virtually impossible when GDP growth was sluggish; this turned out to be untrue. As with all inflation, unexpected inflation is good for borrowers, but detrimental to both lenders and persons who save. See also: Stagflation.

Unexpired Cost The difference between the price one paid for an asset and the revenue it has generated, when the latter is less. That is, an asset has an unexpired cost when it has not yet paid for itself. An asset that has an expired cost for too long or never recovers its initial cost represents a bad investment.

Unfair Claims Practice The practice by an insurer to refuse to pay claims it is contractually obliged to pay. An insurer may engage in unfair claims practices to reduce its costs; however, it is illegal in many jurisdictions.

Unfair Dismissal 1. In British law, the termination of an employee without proper procedure. In general, an employer must give warnings, discipline an employee in other ways, offer alternative duties, and/or allow the employee to have counsel present at any disciplinary hearing. Specific requirements are complex, but an employer must usually give the employee a chance to defend himself/herself. If the employer unfairly dismisses an employee, a tribunal may order reinstatement, compensation or assistance in finding a new job. **2.** More broadly, any termination in violation of the law or an employee's employment contract.

Unfair Labor Practice Any practice that violates labor law in the United States. Both employers and employees can commit unfair labor practices. For example, an employer is not permitted to refuse to negotiate with a properly recognized labor union. Likewise, a union or group of employees may not require an employer to hire workers the company does not need. Unfair labor practices are defined primarily in the Taft-Hartley Act and the National Labor Relations Act.

Unfair Trade Practice Any trade practice that provides or is thought to provide an inequitable advantage to one party. For example, a country may keep its currency artificially weak so as to make its exports cheaper than the situation warrants.

Unfair Trader A country or corporation that conducts practices providing an inequitable advantage to one party. For example, a country may keep its currency artificially weak so as to make its exports cheaper than the situation warrants.

Unfavorable Balance of Trade The difference between the value of a country's exports and the value of its imports such that imports exceed exports. Analysts disagree on the impact, if any, of an unfavorable balance of trade on the economy. Some economists believe that an unfavorable balance of trade, especially if sustained, causes unemployment and lowers GDP growth. Others believe that the balance of trade has little impact, because the more international trade occurs, the more likely it is that foreign companies will invest in the home country, negating any negative effects. An unfavorable balance of trade is also called a trade deficit.

Unfavorable Variance The actual costs of a project over and above the normal costs of a similar project. Companies try to avoid unfavorable variances by budgeting carefully.

Unfilled Orders Any obligation to provide a good or service that has not been filled. For example, a salmon distribution company that has not shipped salmon to one of its clients is said to have an unfilled order. The length of time orders go unfilled is one measure of the efficiency of a company's supply chain.

Unfranked Income In the United Kingdom, any income that does not come from a dividend with a tax credit attached to it. Franked income exists in order to avoid double taxation of dividends. Unfranked income may be a dividend that is double taxed, or it may be any other income at all. See also: Franked Dividend.

Unfreeze To remove a restriction on an account, asset, or anything else. For example, a government may unfreeze salaries that it previously controlled, or a bank may unfreeze an account after a debt has been repaid.

Unfunded Describing any liability or other expense that does not have savings or investments set aside to pay it. That is, the party responsible for paying an unfunded liability pays for it out of current income or by borrowing. The risk of an unfunded liability is that a payee may not receive that which he/she is entitled to if the payer goes through a difficult financial period. It also increases the payer's current liabilities.

Unfunded Pension Plan A pension plan where a former employer pays pensioners out of current income. That is, the employer does not place money aside or invest funds on a regular basis to finance the pension. Obviously, an unfunded pension carries higher risk for both the pensioner and the employer; if the company goes through a difficult period, the pensioner may not have a pension for all his/her retirement while the employer has higher current liabilities.

Unga An obsolete Irish unit of weight approximately equivalent to 28 grams or exactly one ounce.

Unglie An obsolete Indian unit of length approximately equivalent to 1.905 centimeters.

Unidad de Fomento A non-circulating currency in Chile. It is adjusted for inflation relative to the Chilean peso (it was formerly adjusted relative to the Chilean escudo) so that its value remains constant. It was created in 1967 and was originally used to help the Chilean government pay its loans for international development.

Unidad de Valor Constante An accounting currency introduced in 1993 to control inflation of the Ecuadorean sucre. Its initial value was set at 10,000 sucres to one UVC. This value was readjusted to account for inflation of the sucre. The UVC was abandoned in 2000 when Ecuador adopted the U.S. dollar.

Unidade Real de Valor An accounting currency used in Brazil in 1994. It was pegged to the U.S. dollar at par, as well as to three price indices. Prices were expressed in URV even though the cruzeiro real, which suffered from hyperinflation, continued to circulate. It was used to adjust people in Brazil to a stable currency in anticipation of the introduction of the Brazilian real later the same year.

Unidentified Transaction Payment sent to a company without an invoice, computer matchcode, or other clearly identifying information. Unidentified transactions may result in a mistake: that is, the company may think that payment was not made when it in fact was.

Unified Budget In government accounting, a general term for on-budget and off-budget items. Off-budget items include dedicated spending paid with specially levied taxes. For example, Social Security is an off-budget item because FICA taxes exclusively pay for it. On-budget items include all other mandatory and discretionary spending. Most discussion of the federal budget in the United States refers to the unified budget, unless otherwise stated.

Unified Credit In the United States, a tax credit on estates and large gifts. The unified credit is exceptionally large so that most people will not need to pay federal taxes on their estates and large gifts. For example, the unified credit on an estate is usually around $1 million, meaning that the estate has to be worth more than that in order to be subject to the estate tax.

Unified Managed Account An actively managed portfolio that contains many different investment vehicles, such as stocks, bonds, mutual funds, ETFs, and so forth. Some portfolios are structured such that they may only contain one investment vehicle or another, requiring an investor to open multiple accounts in order to diversify. A UMA prevents this.

Uniform Bank Performance Report In the United States, a system that federal regulators use to examine banks' capital adequacy, liquidity and general solvency. It was created by the Federal Financial Institutions Examination Council.

Uniform Business Rate Also called the UBR. The local tax rate for commercial property in England and Wales. The rate changes every year due to inflation. Even though it is paid to local governments, it is determined by the central government.

Uniform Commercial Code A template for a law governing the transfer of personal property, commercial goods, and other property (though generally excluding real estate). The Uniform Commercial Code governs sales, leases, bank deposits, letters of credit, auctions, securities, and other transactions when they are subject to state, rather than federal, law. The Uniform Commercial Code was developed in the 1950s by the American Law Institute and the National Conference of Commissioners on Uniform State Laws in order to unify legal codes in all American states. All 50 states (as well as the District of Columbia and several commonwealths) have adopted a version of the Uniform Commercial Code, though some states, notably Louisiana, have made various changes to it.

Uniform Fiduciaries Act Legislation enacted in several U.S. states outlining the responsibilities and liabilities that principals have toward fiduciaries acting on their behalf. It was written by the National Conference of Commissioners of Uniform States Laws in 1922.

Uniform Gifts to Minors Act Legislation in several U.S. states allowing cash or securities to be transferred from a donor to a minor child without needing to set up a trust. Specifically, this act was intended to allow transfers to persons under 18 or 21 (depending on the jurisdiction). The act allows for the giving of gifts to children up to a certain amount in value without any tax consequences. These gifts are held in a custodianship until the child reaches the age of majority. The custodian is appointed by the donor (and is often the donor himself/herself). The UGMA was set up to allow these transfers to occur without a lawyer needing to set up a trust, a process that can be quite complicated and sometimes expensive. See also: Uniform Transfers to Minors Act.

Uniform Individual Accident and Sickness Policy Provisions Act Legislation enacted in all U.S. states outlining some of the responsibilities that health insurers have toward policyholders. The Act deals with the methods and circumstances under which an insurer or a policyholder can make changes to a policy. It was written by the National Association of Insurance Commissioners.

Uniform Order Bill of Lading A form sheet for a bill of lading used in rail and air shipping.

Uniform Partnership Act Model legislation proposed by the National Conference of Commissioners on Uniform State Laws governing business partnerships. The Act determines how assets are distributed, governs the fiduciary duties of partners, and so forth. The NCCUSL has promulgated several versions of the Act since 1914. Versions of the Act have been adopted in every state except Louisiana.

Uniform Practice Code A code issued by FINRA governing over-the-counter transactions. The Uniform Practice Code mandates certain things, such as the number of days after the trade date that settlement must take place. It is intended to increase certainty in the over-the-counter market and thereby reduce risk.

Uniform Price Auction A way to issue a security or commodity using the following steps. Potential buyers submit the quantity desired and a price per unit in sealed bids. When all bids are collected, the seller gives the desired quantity to the bidder who offered the highest price, then the second highest, and so forth, until all available units are sold. All buyers pay the price per unit of the lowest bid that was awarded units. For example, suppose there are 100 available units and three bidders. Bidder A offers $45 per unit and wants 60 units; Bidder B wants 40 units at $60 per unit. Finally, Bidder C wants 30 units at $35 per unit. Under this scenario, Bidders A and B both receive their desired units and they both pay $45 per unit.

Uniform Rules for Collections Guidelines issued by the International Chamber of Commerce to govern collections. See also: Accounts receivable.

Uniform Securities Act Model legislation for regulating securities at the state level. The National Conference of Commissioners on Uniform State Laws originally drafted the Uniform Securities Act in 1930; it has periodically updated the Act and recommends that state legislature enact it. The Act deals with security issues not subject to SEC regulation. As of 2009, 12 states and the U.S. Virgin Islands have enacted a form of the most recent update of the Act, which was passed in 2002.

Uniform Securities Agent State Law Examination In many states, an exam one must pass to become a registered representative with FINRA, a designation that authorizes one to trade for the brokerage or other firm for which one works. It authorizes one to sell any security except commodity futures contracts. It is important to note that some states require the Uniform Securities Agent State Law Examination in addition to the Series 7. It is not an alternative to the Series 7.

Uniform Simultaneous Death Act Model legislation enacted in various forms in most U.S. states that provides for the estates of two or more intestate relatives who die at the same time. Under the Act, when two or more relatives die within 120 hours of each other, each is treated as having predeceased the other. For example, if a husband and wife die in the same car crash and either has a will (or its terms are not explicit), the husband and wife's relatives are equally entitled to their assets.

Uniform Transfers to Minors Act An extension of the Uniform Gifts to Minors Act allowing assets other than cash or securities to be considered gifts. Specifically, this extension was intended to allow gifts of property to persons under 18 or 21 (depending on the jurisdiction). Both acts allow for the giving of gifts to children up to so much in value without any tax consequences. These gifts are held in a custodianship until the child reaches the age of majority. The custodian is appointed by the donor (and is often the donor himself/herself). The UTMA was set up to allow these transfers to occur without a lawyer needing to set up a trust, a process that can be complicated and sometimes expensive. The National Conference of Commissioners on Uniform State Laws drafted the UTMA in 1986, and a version of it has been passed in most U.S. states.

Unilateral Transfers Gifts that foreigners make to citizens of a country or vice versa. Unilateral transfers are recorded in the country's balance of payments.

Unincorporated Joint Venture A joint venture where the parties do not form a corporation. That is, an unincorporated joint venture is either an ad hoc project or legally structured as a partnership.

Uninsurable Describing a person or event for which no insurance company will provide coverage. Someone or something may be uninsurable because the cost of protection is too high or because there is too great a risk of an insured event occurring. An example of the former is a nuclear blast while an example of the latter is the impending death of a person who is 110 years old. Thus, a life insurance policy is unlikely to cover death from a nuclear event and probably will not be sold to a super-centenarian in the first place.

Uninsurable Property In the United States, a piece of real estate not eligible for insurance through the FHA because it is in need of serious repairs. A property is considered uninsurable if it is a bad risk for the FHA, whose mortgages are guaranteed by the federal government. An uninsurable property is usually not eligible for an FHA mortgage, though, in some circumstances, it may qualify for an FHA refinancing loan.

Uninsurable Risk A risk against which one cannot purchase insurance, either because it is very likely to occur or because it would be too expensive to cover if it did. For example, a 118-year-old person may be an uninsurable risk for life insurance because the person is very likely to die before the insurer collects a sufficient amount in premiums. Likewise, one generally cannot insure against nuclear war because, even though nuclear war is unlikely, repairs and medical bills would be prohibitively expensive.

Uninsurable Title Real estate that a title insurance company would refuse to insure because of significant doubt about whom the legitimate owner is. That is, insurance is refused because it is considered likely that a court will award ownership to another party. Many banks will not provide mortgages on properties with uninsurable titles.

Uninsured Describing any person, property, business or anything else without an insurance policy. Some uninsured persons and things may be self-insured, in cases in which insurance is a poor financial decision because the responsible party has sufficient income or wealth to pay for whatever might happen. Most of the time, however, uninsured persons and items are very risky. In some circumstances, it is illegal to be without certain kinds of insurance.

Uninsured Bond A bond on which payment is not guaranteed by a bond insurance company. An uninsured bond is not protected from default; that is, if the issuer states that it is unable to pay the bond, there is no recourse for bondholders to recoup their investment. Because of this added risk, uninsured bonds often carry a higher coupon rate than insured bonds.

Uninsured Depositor A municipal bond for which a bond insurance company does not guarantee payment. An uninsured bond is only protected by the revenues of the issuing municipality, and does not have an outside guarantor. For that reason, an uninsured bond carries more risk, and therefore usually carries a higher coupon rate than an insured bond.

Uninsured Motorist Insurance An insurance policy or supplemental providing coverage to a motorist and/or his family in the event of a car accident with another driver who either has no car insurance or does not provide it on request. Uninsured motorist insurance only provides coverage if the policyholder is not at fault in the accident.

Unintentional Tort An injury caused without intent because one does not abide by the legally required standard of care. Unintentional torts are a form of negligence.

Uninvested Money that a person or company could invest but does not. Uninvested funds may be savings, money placed aside for dividends, another optional expense, or even spending money.

Union Busting A derogatory term for the attempt to reduce the power of a labor union, or an organization designed to protect worker interests. Union busting generally is intended to allow employers to force employees to accept less favorable terms or working conditions. Union busting may involve espionage, hiring of scabs (or workers who agree not to abide by a union agreement), lockouts, or even violence. See also: Anti-unionism.

Union Contract A contract governing the relations between an employer (or industry) and its employees represented by a union. The union contract may govern wages, benefits, retirement packages, working conditions, and other matters. Union contracts are renegotiated periodically and can be a source of considerable tension.

Union de Paises Exportadores de Banano An organization established to attempt to create a cartel for countries exporting bananas to North America, especially the United States. Most members were located in Central and South America. The organization proposed that member states enact a tax on banana exports to improve government revenues from banana trade. The organization was formed in 1974; the following year, it was revealed that the chairman of United Brands had bribed the president of Honduras to lower the tax. Since then, the Union has been less active. See also: Bananagate.

Union Label A label on a product indicating that the employees who made the product are represented by a labor union. Union labels are affixed to encourage interested parties (such as other union members or persons who support unions) to buy such a product rather than a similar product made by a non-union company.

Union Recognition In the United States, certification by the National Labor Relations Board indicating that a majority of the employees at a company have requested to form a union to represent them. This union is then given the right to negotiate with the employer on the employees' behalf.

Union Salter A member of a labor union who applies and receives a job with a non-union company with the intent of organizing the company's other employees into a labor union. The union member may or may not announce that he/she is a member when applying for the job. Sometimes, the union member will file a complaint with the NLRB after being fired, quitting, or not receiving a job from a non-union company. This forces the company either to defend the charge or to organize its employees.

Union Salting The practice in which a member of a labor union applies and receives a job with a non-union company with the intent of organizing the company's other employees into a labor union. The union member may or may not announce that he/she is a member when applying for the job. Sometimes, the union member will file a complaint with the NLRB after being fired, quitting, or not receiving a job from a non-union company. This forces the company either to defend the charge or to organize its employees.

Union Scale A minimum wage guaranteed by a union contract. The union scale may vary by the type of job performed, but all union members working a covered job must be paid the scale.

Union/Non-Union Wage Differential The amount a union member is paid compared to the amount a non-union member is paid for approximately the same service. Almost always, a union member is paid more. The differential helps measure the effectiveness of unions. A highly effective union is good for employees but increases the costs of doing business, which some believe to be detrimental to economic growth.

Unique Character Random digits added to a computer matchcode to prevent a duplicate where one otherwise would exist.

Unique Coin A coin that is the only one of its kind still in existence. Depending on demand for it among investors and collectors, it may be very valuable. However, a unique coin is an illiquid investment.

Unique Diversification Benefit The reduction in the likelihood of financial difficulties that occurs when a person or company diversifies his/her/its investments. The downside to the unique diversification benefit, however, is the fact that it generally reduces the expected return.

Unique Impairment An unusual circumstance that makes a life insurer unable to offer coverage. For example, a potential policyholder may have an untreatable disease.

Unique Records Records with no duplicates. Database coordinators seek to keep unique records in order to promote efficiency.

Unique Three-Digit City A city in the United States large enough to be assigned the same three digits in all its zip codes.

Unisex Legislation Any legislation restricting the ability of an insurance company to charge higher premiums to one gender or the other simply because one belongs to that gender. Unisex legislation does not apply to all forms of insurance; for example, young men tend to pay higher rates for car insurance than young women.

Unissued Capital Stock Stock that a publicly-traded company is authorized to issue but has not. Generally, the company's charter specifies the maximum number shares it is allowed to issue, but shareholders can increase or decrease it according to procedures listed in the charter. There is normally a larger amount of unissued capital stock than is required in order to give a company the greatest amount of flexibility. See also: Authorized shares.

Unit 1. A combination of securities or types of securities packaged together and bought and sold as one. For example, a preferred share may have warrants and/or common shares attached to it when it is sold. See also: Paired shares, Cum warrant. **2.** One thing that may be exchanged. For example, one dollar is a unit of money.

Unit Banking A system of banking in which the government restricts or does not permit a bank to open branch offices. Unit banking systems encourage either small, independent banks or banks that are theoretically independent but are in fact owned by a bank holding company. In the United States, unit banking is largely confined to the Midwest and Southwest.

Unit Benefit Formula In a defined-benefit plan, a method used to determine how much money the beneficiary receives each month. A defined-benefit plan is a retirement plan or other annuity in which the annuitant knows in advance how much he/she will be entitled to when he/she begins receiving payments. The unit benefit formula is thus stated in the annuity contract and is usually some function of the amount the annuitant contributed combined with the number of years he/she contributed.

Unit Convertible A convertible security that differs from most other convertible securities because it may be changed into a portfolio or other package of investments rather than a certain number of shares in common stock.

Unit Cost The amount that a company spends to produce or purchase one unit of a good or service. For example, if a company buys 100 widgets for $100, the unit cost is $1.

Unit Growth The extra number of units of a product sold over a given period of time, compared to the number of units sold in a comparable past period of time. For example, if a company sold 8,000 units in January 2008 and later sold 10,000 units in January 2009, it experienced year-on-year unit growth of 2,000. Unit growth is measured in units, instead of dollar amounts, to eliminate the effects of inflation.

Unit Holder 1. The owner of a combination of securities or types of securities that have been packaged together and bought and sold as one. For example, a unit holder may own a preferred share with warrants and/or common shares attached to it. See also: Paired shares, Cum warrant. **2.** The owner of a portion of a company other than a corporation. For example, a unit holder may own part of a limited liability company.

Unit Investment Trust An investment company that offers an unmanaged portfolio of stocks and/or bonds, packaging the portfolio as shares that are redeemable from the trust after a certain period of time. Unit investment trusts are designed to give shareholders income from dividends and/or coupons. See also: Mutual fund.

Unit Load Items packaged together into a compact container that may be easily transported. For example, three weeks' worth of diet meals may be placed together in the same box for shipment.

Unit of Account A measure of an amount of money. Units of account, for example, divide one dollar into 100 cents or one pound into 100 pence. Units of account are somewhat arbitrary, but are necessary to measure value and price fairly.

Unit of Trading 1. One thing that may be exchanged. For example, one dollar is a unit of money. **2.** See: Lot.

Unit Sales A measure of the total amount of revenue a product generates divided by the total number of units of that product that were sold in a given time period. Companies use unit sales to determine how profitable a certain product is and, if necessary, to make improvements, expand, or cancel the product. Analysts may also use it as a way of determining changes in demand.

Unit Share A combination of securities or types of securities packaged together and bought and sold as one. For example, a preferred share may have warrants and/or common shares attached to it when it is sold. It is also called simply a unit. See also: Paired shares, Cum warrant.

Unit Trust A British term for an open-ended mutual fund. See also: OEIC.

Unitary Falloff A situation in which sales of a product decline by a percentage equal to an increase in price. For example, a unitary falloff occurs when there is a 10% drop in sales following a 10% price raise.

Unitary Tax A corporate tax on a corporation's global income. Some countries levy unitary taxes on corporations operating in their borders in order to prevent them from avoiding taxes by transferring income to another country with a low or no corporate tax. See also: Transfer pricing mechanisms, Aggressive accounting.

Unitary Thrift A company that owns one thrift, which is a bank specializing in residential mortgages and checking/savings accounts. A unitary thrift has more freedom than a bank holding company: for example, up to 20% of its holdings may be commercial loans. New unitary thrifts were banned after the Gramm-Leach-Bliley Act.

United Arab Republic A brief political union between Egypt and Syria, formed in 1958. It was formed as part of a plan eventually to unite all Arab countries. Gamal Abdel Nasser, the President of Egypt, was the UAR president. He nationalized industry and sought to give aid to farmers; these policies were already being followed in Egypt but were thought to hurt the Syrian economy. Additionally, Nasser was accused of treating Syria more like an Egyptian province rather than as a state in a federal union. The UAR was dissolved in 1961, but Egypt continued to use the name for another 10 years.

United Auto Workers A U.S. labor union based in Detroit that was established in 1935 to represent workers in the American automotive industry.

United Nations An international organization consisting of a large majority of the nations in the world. Its mission is to promote peace, international development, human rights and global health. It formerly helped prepare colonies for independence. It was established in 1945 following the end of World War II.

United Nations Children's Fund Commonly called UNICEF (formerly United Nations International Children's Emergency Fund). An organization within the United Nations that provides humanitarian and other aid to women and children, especially in the developing world. It provides food, shelter, medicine and other necessary supplies. It is financed by governments and individuals globally. It was established in 1946.

United Nations Commission on International Trade Law Also called UNCITRAL. An organization under the United Nations that was established to promote international trade by standardizing regulations to promote predictability in trade. Among other activities, UNCITRAL prepares model laws for member states to implement and coordinates with other bodies that work in the same field. It was established in 1966.

United Nations Conference on Environment and Development A major United Nations conference held in Rio de Janeiro in 1992. Participants discussed environmental issues, notably continued production of toxic materials in industry and elsewhere. The conference was considered a success: it led directly to the Kyoto Protocol in 1997. The conference is also called the Rio Summit and the Earth Summit.

United Nations Conference on Trade and Development Also called UNCTAD. An organization created by the United Nations in 1964 and charged with increasing international trade and investment, especially in developing countries. It was responsible for implementing the Generalized System of Preferences, which exempted some developing countries from WTO trade requirements.

United Nations Development Programme Also called the UNDP. An organization within the United Nations that provides grants, training and other forms of assistance in developing countries. The UNDP promotes democratization, anti-poverty initiatives, and environmental protection, among other things. Its head is the third highest ranking official at the UN.

United Nations Economic Commission for Africa A commission established by the United Nations to foster economic and other cooperation among African states. It promotes trade, food security and other development goals. It was founded in 1958.

United Nations Economic Commission for Latin America and the Caribbean A commission established by the United Nations to foster economic and other cooperation among Central, South American and Caribbean states. Interestingly, members include North American and Western European countries as well. It was founded in 1948.

United Nations Educational, Scientific, and Cultural Organization Also called UNESCO. An organization within the United Nations that promotes greater respect for the rule of law, freedom of the press, freedom of speech and other areas. UNESCO fosters scientific development through education and the administration of several institutes of learning. It was created in 1945 and is based in Paris.

United Nations Environment Programme An organization created by the United Nations and charged with providing assistance to developing countries and others in developing guidelines for sustainable environmental policies. It also publishes reports on the state of the environment and has had a significant role in the discussion of climate change. See also: Kyoto Protocol.

United Nations High Commissioner for Refugees Also called UNHCR. An organization created by the United Nations in 1950 and charged with providing assistance to and protection of persons displaced by a government as the result of a war, persecution or another reason. It helps them return to their homes or to settle in another country.

United Nations Industrial Development Organization Also called UNIDO or ONUDI. An organization created by the United Nations in 1966 and charged with helping developing countries accelerate the pace of their industrialization. It also performs the same services for countries transitioning from communism to the free market.

United Nations Institute for Training and Research Also called UNITAR. An organization created by the United Nations in 1965 and charged with training local and national government officials, particularly from developing countries. UNITAR seeks to educate personnel in peace making, human rights, international law, finance and trade and other matters.

United Nations Population Fund An organization created by the United Nations and charged with promoting reproductive health. It provides funding for programs to discourage the spread of sexually transmitted diseases, to promote the use of contraceptives and to support healthy pregnancies and childbirths. The alleged role of the United Nations Population Fund in funding abortions and forced sterilizations has been a source of controversy.

United Nations Regional Economic Commissions One of five organizations under the United Nations charged with encouraging economic development in a different part of the world. There are regional economic commissions for Africa, Asia and the Pacific, Europe, Latin America and the Caribbean and Western Asia (Arab countries in the Middle East plus Egypt and Sudan).

United Nations Relief and Works Agency Also called UNRWA. An organization created by the United Nations in 1948 and charged with providing assistance and humanitarian relief to Palestinians living in Jordan, Lebanon and Syria, as well as those living in Palestinian territories. Most of those whom the agency helps were displaced following the Israeli War for Independence in 1948, or are their descendants. UNRWA is the only UN relief agency concentrating in a specific area.

United Nations Special Commission An organization created by the United Nations in 1999 to ensure that Iraq complied with Security Council resolutions not to produce biological, chemical or nuclear weapons after the Gulf War. UNSCOM was created in 1991 and dissolved in 1999 amid allegations that the U.S. Central Intelligence Agency was using it to spy on the Iraqi military.

United Nations University A think tank that conducts research into international development, human rights and other areas. It provides opportunities for PhD students and others to perform research at its facilities. It is based in Tokyo with satellite campuses all over the world. It is not funded out of the United Nations budget.

United Nations Volunteers A program of the United Nations that encourages volunteerism. It recruits volunteers throughout the world who are placed in various development programs depending on their skills and the UN's needs. It also assists NGOs in finding volunteers for their programs. United Nations Volunteers began in 1971.

United Parcel Service An American delivery company. It delivers packages all over the world, in addition to supply chain delivery and less than truckload services. It was established in 1907 by two teenagers who delivered packages on foot, bicycle and motorcycle.

United States Citizen A person entitled to all rights and responsibilities offered under the Constitution of the United States. A U.S. citizen is protected by the United States government when abroad. Unless one loses one's rights (for example, by committing a felony), a U.S. citizen may vote, run for political office and conduct business without special permission. However, a U.S. citizen must also pay taxes on worldwide income and may be called to serve in the armed forces.

United States Customs Service A former agency of the U.S. Government responsible for keeping illegal substances out of the United States as well as collecting tariffs and other import duties. The Customs Service was responsible for, among other things, enforcing the trade embargo on Cuba and trade agreements between the U.S. and other countries. In 2003, the Customs Service combined with Immigration and Naturalization Services to form Immigration and Customs Enforcement.

United States Department of the Treasury The department of the federal government responsible for the printing of money, the collection of taxes, the regulation of banks, and the management of public debt. Created in 1789, the U.S. Treasury issues Treasury securities, which is debt that the American government uses to pay for some of its functions. It also administers the Internal Revenue Service, which collects taxes and decides how tax laws and regulations are enforced, and the U.S. Mint, which prints and disburses currency. The Treasury Department is responsible for investigating and prosecuting certain financial crimes, such as tax evasion and counterfeiting. It is headed by the Secretary of the Treasury, who is appointed by the President with the consent of the Senate.

United States Government Life Insurance A former program in which the United States government offered renewable term life insurance with $10,000 coverage for military men and women as well as other members of the federal uniformed services. The program has been replaced by the SGLI and the VGLI.

United States Government Securities A debt instrument issued directly by the government of the United States. United States government securities are backed by the full faith and credit of the United States and are considered zero-risk. The most common examples of United States government securities include Treasury securities and savings bonds. It is important to note that United States government securities are distinct from debt issues from government-sponsored agencies.

United States Junior Chamber An organization in the United States that promotes business leadership in persons between the ages of 18 and 41, who are informally called Jaycees, after the pronunciation of the initials of "Junior Chamber." The Junior Chamber helps members develop management skills and training and encourages community service. Jaycees also advocate before the U.S. government. The organization was established in 1920 and is based in Tulsa, Oklahoma.

United States Merchant Marine The fleet of private and government-owned, non-military ships operating in the United States. The Merchant Marine delivers cargo and passengers in peacetime. During times of war, it may be ordered to assist the U.S. Navy. Since 1988, mariners who served in wars have had access to veterans' benefits.

United States Treasury Money Mutual Fund A mutual fund that invests primarily or exclusively in U.S. Treasury securities and repurchase agreements guaranteed by Treasury securities. Because U.S. Treasury securities are considered some of the lowest-risk investments in the world, a U.S. Treasury money mutual fund is likewise low-risk.

United States v. South-Eastern Underwriters Association A Supreme Court case in the United States in which it was held that the insurance sector was responsible to the Sherman Act (and could therefore be found in violation of anti-trust laws) and that the government had the ability to regulate insurance pursuant to the Commerce Clause of the Constitution. The decision was made in 1944; the following year, Congress passed the McCarran-Ferguson Act, which exempts insurance from most anti-trust law.

Unity of Command In an organization, the concept that each employee is responsible to only one supervisor, who himself reports to one supervisor and so forth. This prevents the possibility that an employee may not know whose orders to follow. This applies even when an organization is governed by a committee. For example, in the United States, a superintendent of public schools is responsible to the president of the school board, not the school board as a whole, in daily activities.

Universal Banking Banking services including savings, loans and investments. That is, universal banking combines both commercial banking and investment banking. The term universal banking is more common in Europe than the U.S. because of stricter regulation of American banks.

Universal Life Insurance A life insurance policy that combines features of term life and whole life insurance. That is, a person pays a premium and, in exchange, receives at least a guaranteed death benefit (as with term life insurance). Additionally,

one has a cash value account that may be invested and may offer a higher return for the policyholder. A person may use the funds in the cash value account to pay premiums, increase the death benefit, or even serve as collateral for a loan. Premiums are higher for universal life policies than for other forms of life insurance.

Universal Market Integrity Rules A set of rules governing trading on exchanges in Canada. All Canadian exchanges are required to adhere to UMIR, which, among other provisions, prohibit price manipulation and other practices deemed to be unfair. UMIR were written in part to create uniform practices throughout Canada so that a trader on one exchange would know and be able to abide by the rules on all other exchanges.

Universal Product Code Commonly called a UPC. A bar code system used in the United States, Canada and elsewhere. Groceries and other products commonly have UPCs on them so a machine can display how much they cost. This ensures that consistent, accurate prices are paid on retail goods.

Universe A group of securities, assets or anything else with similar characteristics. One may consider, for example, a universe of stocks in the same industry. Universes are useful when comparing one data point to others in order to maintain control over systematic factors.

Universe of Securities In technical analysis, a group of similar securities compared to each other. Securities may be in the same industry, or have similar market capitalizations, or may be listed on the same index. There is no rule stating what criteria can be used for creating a universe of securities; all that matters is that an analyst believes they are alike enough to be compared so that he/she may determine and analyze market trends. Testing a theory on a specific universe of securities helps technical analysts create methodologies for analyzing markets.

Unjust Enrichment In law, a situation in which one person profits from a venture but does not provide adequate compensation to another person who helped in the venture. Unjust enrichment may result from underpayment, failure to honor a contract, or slavery. One found liable for unjust enrichment may have to pay the person who was mistreated.

Unlawful Loans Any loan made in a way contrary to the legal framework of the jurisdiction in which it is made. In general, an unlawful loan refers to a loan with an interest rate that is too high or with insufficient disclosure by one of the parties. See also: Truth in Lending Act.

Unleveraged Beta A measure of an asset or company's volatility with respect to a market index when the asset or company has been financed entirely with equity. That is, the unleveraged beta helps determine the asset company's risk when it has no debt.

Unleveraged Program A policy or project in which a company borrows less than 50% of the amount used to purchase an asset. An unleveraged program carries fewer risks than a leveraged program, but may prevent the company from purchasing as many assets as it needs or wants for its operations.

Unleveraged Required Return The required return on an investment that one makes using only cash or equity and no debt.

Unlimited Company A company in which all members or shareholders have total and joint responsibility to cover all debts and other liabilities the company generates, regardless of how much capital each contributes. An unlimited company presents higher risk than a limited company (such as a publicly-traded company or a limited liability company). However, the finances of an unlimited company are able to remain private and, for that reason, it may be a preferable business structure in some circumstances. One may register an unlimited company in the United Kingdom, Germany, Ireland and many Commonwealth countries.

Unlimited Liability The responsibility of one or more owners of a business for the total amount of debt and other liabilities that the business accrues, regardless of how much the owner(s) has personally invested. That is, suppose two persons form a general partnership and each invests $10,000. If the business later accrues $100,000 in liabilities, both partners are equally responsible for the $80,000 over and above what they have invested. If the business defaults, the personal assets of the partners may be seized to repay debts. Unlimited liability contrasts with limited liability, which limits the amount one can lose on an investment to the total amount invested. Unlimited liability is most common in general partnerships, sole proprietorships, and for general partners in limited partnerships.

Unlimited Marital Deduction An exemption that allows spouses to transfer an unlimited amount of property between themselves without incurring the gift tax. Most gifts over a certain (large) amount are subject to the gift tax. In order to prevent this from negatively impacting spouses who have not joined all their property, the unlimited marital deduction exempts married couples from the tax entirely.

Unlimited Risk The risk that one's loss on an investment will be larger than the amount one originally invested. For example, in short selling one will lose money if the short sold security rises in price. Because the potential rise in price is theoretically infinite, one may lose much more than one invests. Likewise, a general partner of a company has unlimited liability, meaning that in the event of bankruptcy he/she must pay all debts the company incurs regardless of how much he/she invested in it. See also: Limited liability.

Unlisted Company A company with stock that is not traded on an exchange. Very often, unlisted companies are very small and do not trade on an exchange because they do not meet market capitalization requirements. Unlisted companies may be traded informally (theoretically, one may stand on a street corner and sell his/her stocks), but the term usually refers to companies traded through a dealer network. See also: Over-the-counter.

Unlisted Security A stock that is not traded on an exchange. Very often, unlisted securities are very small and do not trade on an exchange because they do not meet market capitalization requirements. Unlisted securities may be traded informally (theoretically, one may stand on a street corner and sell his/her stocks), but the term usually refers to securities traded through a dealer network. They are also called over-the-counter securities.

Unlisted Trading Privileges Special permission an exchange gives to its member firms to trade an unlisted security. In order to be able to give unlisted trading privileges, the exchange itself must receive permission from the SEC.

Unload To sell securities, especially all the shares one owns. Unloading has a connotation of selling at a loss, especially in a bear market or following a bad investment decision. See also: Bull trap.

Unmanaged Portfolio A portfolio into which a money manager or investor places securities and then does not change those securities for a significant period of time. For example, an investment manager may buy all of the stocks on the Dow Jones Industrial Average and hold them for a period of five or 10 years. Money managers of unmanaged portfolios seek to have a well diversified set of securities. See also: Indexing, Passive investing, Value investing.

Unmerchantable Describing goods or services of such poor quality that they cannot be sold. Unmerchantable merchandise may be damaged or simply poorly made.

Unofficial Service Charge An informal, somewhat tongue-in-cheek term for a bribe.

Unpaid Balance An amount that has been borrowed but not repaid. This term applies to loans, lines of credit, cash advances and other forms of debt.

Unparted Bullion Gold or silver bars that have other metals mixed together with the gold or silver. Unparted bullion has lower value than pure gold or silver; how much lower depends on the value of the particular metals and the level to which they are mixed. See also: Bullion.

Unpeg To remove a peg to which a country's currency previously subscribed. For example, Kuwait unpegged the Kuwaiti dinar from the U.S. dollar and shifted to a currency basket in 2007 because the dollar was weak at the time, resulting in high inflation. When a country unpegs a currency, it may choose to peg the currency to something else or to let it float.

Unperfected Lien An invalid lien on the property of a borrower, usually resulting from a previous lien on the same property or simply poor record keeping. In a dispute or bankruptcy, a court normally treats unperfected liens as valid, provided there are no disputes from other parties.

Unpriced Describing a good or service to which a price has not been assigned. The word is used especially when it is expected that a price will be given. For example, inventory for a new product may be temporarily unpriced while a retailer decides how much to charge.

Unprofitable Describing a company or investment that consistently loses money. Very often, one cuts one's losses with respect to an unprofitable instrument; failure to do so may lead to bankruptcy.

Unqualified Mail Mass mailing not sent in sufficient volume to qualify for a postage discount. Unqualified mail is also called unqualified sort.

Unquoted Company A publicly-traded company that previously traded on an exchange but no longer does. A company may become unquoted if its market capitalization falls to the point that it no longer meets an exchange's listing requirements. This is an extremely negative sign for a company; an unquoted company may be in danger of ceasing operations. However, its stock price is likely to be low and, if it comes back, an unquoted company can provide a substantial return.

Unquoted Security A security that previously traded on an exchange but no longer does. A security may become unquoted if the market capitalization of its issuing company falls to the point that it no longer meets an exchange's listing requirements. An unquoted security, then, is very high risk. However, its price is likely to be low and, if it comes back, an unquoted security can provide a substantial return.

Unrealized Appreciation An increase in the value of a property or other asset that the owner does not receive because the asset has not been sold. Unrealized appreciation occurs most commonly in real estate and securities because most other assets depreciate. Unrealized appreciation is not taxed until the asset is sold. However, unrealized appreciation may be used to calculate property taxes. See also: Net unrealized appreciation.

Unrecorded Deed Title to property, especially real estate, that is not registered with the appropriate body. An unrecorded deed is valid, but there is no guarantee that it is authentic. As a result, some insurance companies refuse to provide coverage for properties with unrecorded deeds. See also Quitclaim deed.

Unregistered Exchange An exchange that is not required to register with the SEC or submit to most of its requirements. Unregistered exchanges are very small and trade predominantly or exclusively in local issues. An unregistered exchange should not be confused with unregistered stock.

Unrelated Business Income Income a nonprofit organization produces on a regular basis from a trade or business that is not connected to its ordinary operations. For example, a charity may sell t-shirts at a profit to the general public. While there are a number of exemptions, the IRS taxes unrelated business income at ordinary corporate tax rates.

Unrelated Person A person to whom one is not related by blood or marriage. In most business transactions, one is generally not required to disclose the nature of one's relationship with an unrelated person because it is less likely that an unrelated person will create a conflict of interest.

Unrestricted Donation A donation in which the donor does not require a specific use. For example, when a donor makes an unrestricted donation to a non-profit organization, the non-profit, at its discretion, may use the donation for whatever purpose it chooses. See also: Restricted donation.

Unrestricted Letter of Credit A letter of credit issued by a bank to a customer that the customer may redeem at any bank he/she wishes. See also: Restricted Letter of Credit.

Unrestricted Net Assets Cash or other assets that are not needed to pay liabilities and are not earmarked for a specific purpose. The governing body of a company or organization may use unrestricted net assets for any purpose it wishes.

Unsatisfied Judgment Fund A fund established by a state government to compensate persons who are involved in automobile accidents that are not sufficiently covered by the other motorists' insurance. In general, drivers are required to carry insurance on their automobiles in case they are at fault in an accident. Unsatisfied judgment funds exist so as not to punish the wrong person in case the other party does not carry the mandatory insurance.

Unscheduled Property Floater An insurance policy providing coverage up to a certain amount for all property of the type listed in the policy. To give a very simple example, an unscheduled property floater may cover all the lamps that a person owns without describing any particular lamp. This contrasts with a scheduled property floater, in which each piece of covered property is listed individually. As with all insurance, one must pay a premium to receive the coverage.

Unseasoned Issue A new issue that only recently started trading. It is called unseasoned because investors do not know with certainty how the market will treat the issue, and whether or not it will be successful.

Unsecured Bond A debt security, issued by a government or large company, that is not secured by an asset or lien, but rather by the all issuer's assets not otherwise secured. That is, an unsecured bond carries no collateral; in case of bankruptcy, the bondholder is considered a general creditor. Thus, the bondholder is paid out of funds that do not have a prior claim on them with a secured debt. Like most bonds, an unsecured bond can be traded. Some unsecured bonds, such Treasury securities, are considered risk-free. See also: Debenture.

Unsecured Creditor One who is owed an uncollateralized debt. That is, an unsecured creditor has no lien or collateral on the debt. An unsecured creditor has no right to repossess any property in the event of default or bankruptcy. In the event of liquidation of the debtor's property, the unsecured creditor receives nothing until all secured creditors are repaid in full. Because of the extra risk associated with unsecured credit, it usually commands a higher interest rate. See also: Secured creditor.

Unsecured Debt A debt that is not secured by an asset or lien, but rather by the all issuer's assets not otherwise secured. This means that an unsecured debt carries no collateral; in case of bankruptcy, the debt holder is considered a general creditor. Thus, the debt holder is paid out of funds that do not have a prior claim on them with a secured debt. Some unsecured debts, such as Treasury securities, are considered risk-free.

Unsecured Liability A debt or other liability that is not secured by an asset or lien, but rather by the all issuer's assets not otherwise secured. This means that an unsecured liability carries no collateral; in case of bankruptcy, the bondholder is considered a general creditor. Thus, the bondholder is paid out of funds that do not have a prior claim on them with a secured debt. Like most bonds, an unsecured bond is tradeable. Some unsecured bonds, such Treasury securities, are considered risk-free.

Unsecured Loan A loan that is not secured by an asset or lien, but rather by the all issuer's assets not otherwise secured. This means that an unsecured liability carries no collateral; in case of bankruptcy, the bondholder is considered a general creditor. Thus, the bondholder is paid out of funds that do not have a prior claim on them with a secured debt. Like most bonds, an unsecured bond is tradeable. Some unsecured bonds, such as Treasury securities, are considered risk-free.

Unsecured Loan Stock A loan made to a company with no collateral. In many respects, unsecured loan stock behaves like a bond (both offer fixed returns, have maturity dates, and so forth). However, unlike a bond, in the event of default or liquidation, the holder of unsecured loan stock does not have a claim on the company's assets. For that reason, unsecured loan stock carries higher risk than a bond. Despite the name, it has nothing to do with shares of stock.

Unsettled Transaction A sale on which payment has not been made. See also: Clearing House.

Unskilled Work Work that requires no special training or education. Unskilled work includes washing dishes or mopping floors. Many companies require unskilled work to operate; however, it generally is low-paid work.

Unskilled Worker Persons in the work force with no special job training or education. For example, unskilled workers may wash dishes or mop floors. Many companies require unskilled workers to operate; however, they generally are low-paid employees.

Unsold The portion of a company's inventory that customers or clients have not purchased, especially by the end of an accounting period. Unsold inventory may be sold at a discount, given away or even discarded. Too much unsold inventory results in losses.

Unsponsored American Depository Receipt An American Depository Receipt issued without the knowledge or cooperation of the company whose stock backs it. Unlike other sponsored ADRs, which are treated just like common shares denominated in the U.S. dollar, an unsponsored ADR simply gives the monetary benefits of ownership. That is, the bank issuing the ADR pays out dividends as if it were common stock, but the ADR does not carry voting rights. Unsponsored ADRs may not be traded on the New York Stock Exchange, and are usually traded over-the-counter. See also: International depositary receipt.

Unssi A Finnish unit of weight approximately equivalent to 28 grams. It became obsolete when Finland adopted the metric system in 1880.

Unstable Transition A difficult, unsustainable change from one form of government to another. For example, a state may undergo an unstable transition from a dictatorship to a democracy, or from communism to capitalism. An unstable transition is marked by war, civil unrest, hyperinflation, and other social ills.

Unstated Interest Paid The percentage of interest the IRS assumes was paid on a loan, even if that interest was not actually paid. Taxes are assessed on unstated interest. For example, if one makes an interest-free loan to a family member, the IRS assumes that the loan is repaid with interest. The same applies to zero-coupon bonds (unless the bond is otherwise tax exempt, like a T bill).

Unsterilized Intervention A central bank's attempt to influence exchange rates by refusing to buy or sell assets or currencies. This allows the money supply to change without interference of the central bank. See also: Sterilized intervention, floating currency.

Unsubscribed A new issue in which investors show a lack of interest. Before a new issue, underwriters canvass potential investors, who may or may not book an order to buy a portion of the new issue. The portion that is not booked is called the unsubscribed portion. The existence of an unsubscribed portion may affect the price when the security is actually issued. Sometimes an issuer requires underwriters to buy the unsubscribed portion in order to raise its target capital. See also: Underbooked, Fully subscribed.

Unused License A license giving one the legal ability to do something even though one works in a different field. For example, a person may have a Series 7 license but work in construction. In such a case, the Series 7 is an unused license.

Unweighted Index An index where all securities represented in it affect the index equally. That is, an unweighted index does not give any preference to aspects like market capitalization or price when one calculates its value. For example, given an unweighted index of three stocks, one priced at $10, one at $15, and one at $20, the value of the index will be $15, which is simply the average of the three prices. The Value Line averages are prominent examples of unweighted indices.

Unwelcome Assignment A situation in which an option writer (that is, the one who sells the option and has no control over its exercise) is required to fulfill the terms of the contract when doing so results in a loss or is otherwise detrimental to his/her investment strategy. For example, one may write a call with an exercise price of $30. If the price of the underlying asset is $40, the exercise of the contract is an unwelcome assignment because the writer must sell the underlying asset for $10 below its market price. One can avoid an unwelcome assignment by taking an offsetting position.

Unwind 1. See: Close a position. **2.** To correct a mistake. For example, if an investor instructs his/her broker to sell a security and the broker instead buys it, the broker must re-sell the security, and pay the client what he/she may have lost in the mistake. This process is known as unwinding.

Up In North Korea, a political subdivision equivalent to an urban municipality.

Up Volume The trading volume of a security on a trading day on which it closed up for the day. That is, when the closing price is higher than the opening price, all volume on that security for the day is considered up volume. Technical analysts use up volume and down volume to determine buy and sell signals.

Up/Down Volume Ratio In technical analysis, the trading volume on a security on days when its price increases, divided by the trading volume on days when the price decreases. This indicates whether more investors are buying the security or selling it. A high ratio is a bullish signal, while a low ratio is considered bearish.

Up-and-In Option An option contract that may be exercised only if the price of the underlying asset falls below or rises above a certain, stated barrier. An up-and-in option is often less expensive to buy than another option because of this limitation on exercise. See also: Knock-In Option, Barrier Option.

Up-and-Out Option An option contract that expires worthless automatically, even before the expiration date, if the price of the underlying asset exceeds a certain stated amount. For example, one may purchase an up-and-out option with a "knock-out price" of $45 and a strike price of $35. If the price of the underlying asset reaches $45 at any point over the course of the option's life, the option is treated as if it never existed in the first place. If it does not exceed this price, it remains a plain vanilla option (that is, a regular option) with a strike price of $35. It is a type of knock-out option. See also: Up-and-in option, Down-and-in option, Down-and-out option, Knock-in option.

Upazila In Bangladesh, a political subdivision equivalent to a sub-district or county.

Upfront Fee A fee paid before a good is produced or a service is performed. The upfront fee is generally a portion of the total fee that the buyer must pay. For example, one may commission an artist to paint a portrait and pay a 20% upfront fee, paying the remainder when the portrait is finished. It is also called an advance fee.

Upgrade 1. An improvement to an existing product. Some companies, especially technology companies, offer upgrades to customers for free or at a discount. **2.** An improvement to the quality of securities in a portfolio. For example, one may sell a stock with a given risk and return and buy another stock with a higher return at the same level of risk. Alternatively, a security may upgrade by itself; for example, its issuer may announce higher than expected earnings, and, therefore, a higher dividend. **3.** An increase in a bond rating. For example, if a bond goes from a junk rating to an investment-grade rating, the bond is said to be upgraded. This usually occurs when the issuer reduces its exposure to one or more risks.

Upkeep 1. The activities one must conduct in order to maintain a good or property. For example, upkeep on a house may include cleaning, exterminating termites and periodically replacing the roof. Upkeep is sometimes expensive, but generally costs less than the major repairs that result if a good or property is not maintained. **2.** The costs of upkeep.

Upmarket Describing products intended to appeal to upper class customers. For example, a designer handbag may be described as upmarket. Upmarket products are generally high quality.

Upscale Describing a high quality good, product, service or property. For example, an upscale neighborhood is assumed to contain nice, desirable homes, and an upscale clothing store may sell designer fashions. Upscale products are usually expensive.

Upside Down Mortgage A mortgage in which the amount that a property owner owes on the loan is more than that property's current market value. For example, if one borrows $100,000 to buy a house and, for whatever reason, the value immediately drops to $60,000, the homeowner is said to have an upside down mortgage. Upside down mortgages are most common after the burst of an asset bubble.

Upside Potential The opinion of an analyst on how far a security may rise in price. It is usually expressed in terms of the price to which it might possibly rise. For example, if an analyst believes that a stock trading at $10 will rise to $12, it has an upside potential of $12. Obviously, there is no guarantee that the security will actually rise to the predicted level. See also: Downside Risk.

Upside/Downside Ratio On the New York Stock Exchange, the ratio of the volume of publicly-traded companies closing up for the day to the volume of those closing down. A high upside/downside ratio indicates a bullish trend on the NYSE, and is used as an indicator of trends in the wider equity market.

Upstairs Market The trading of listed securities that occurs off the floor of the exchange. That is, the upstairs market is essentially over-the-counter trading for a listed security. Much of the time, upstairs trades occur within a broker-dealer firm with the broker-dealer acting as the agent for both counterparties. Some exchanges prohibit these trades.

Upstairs Order An order to a brokerage to buy or sell a security in which the counterparty is the brokerage itself. That is, the brokerage fills the order from its own inventory of the security. Some exchanges prohibit these trades.

Upstairs Trade A trade of a listed security that occurs off of the floor of the exchange. An upstairs trade is essentially an over-the-counter trade for a listed security. Sometimes upstairs trades occur within a broker-dealer firm, with the broker-dealer acting as the agent for both parties. Some exchanges prohibit these trades.

Upstream In energy companies, relating to exploration and production operations. For example, an oil company's operations related to discovering new oil reserves and the pumping of new oil from the ground are considered upstream. Upstream operations may also include initial operations like political risk analysis. Some companies provide upstream operations exclusively, but most are integrated, providing both upstream and downstream operations.

Upswing A situation in which a security or stock market increases in price after a period of falling or flat prices. An upswing often refers to a short-term gain, but this is not always the case. See also: Bull market.

Uptick On an exchange, a transaction in which a security was traded at the higher price than its previous trade. Some regulations and rules on exchanges only permit certain transactions following an uptick or a zero-plus tick, though some, such as the short sale rule, have become obsolete with increased digitalization of the market. An uptick is also called a plus tick.

Uptick Volume In technical analysis, the trading volume of a security that is trading higher than its previous price. This is used to calculate the net volume, which is the uptick volume minus the downtick volume. Some analysts use this to find buy signals and sell signals.

Uptick/Downtick Ratio In technical analysis, a ratio of block trades on a security conducted on an uptick (that is, at a higher price than the previous trade) to those conducted on a downtick (that is, at a lower price). Generally speaking, buyers initiate uptick transactions. A high ratio is therefore an indication that there are too many buyers and that the security may soon undergo a price correction. As such, a high ratio is a bearish indicator.

Uptitling The act or practice of changing an employee's title to something that sounds more impressive without any actual increase of responsibility or jurisdiction. It is a way to preserve the employee's morale without taking on additional risk or further expenditures.

Uptrend A situation in which a security price is moving mostly upward. Though there may be, and usually are, a few downward price movements in-between, this does not stop the overall bullish trend. For example, a security may be priced at $100 per share on January 1, $105 on January 10, and $109 on January 31. This indicates an uptrend, even if the security closed lower on certain days in January.

Uptrend Line In technical analysis, a line on a chart indicating a consistent upward movement in price or some other variable. For example, if inflation is increasing over time, this may be expressed as an uptrend line on a chart.

Upu An ancient Sumerian unit of area approximately equivalent to 1,800 square meters.

Uqija A Maltese unit of weight approximately equivalent to 26.5 grams. It is largely obsolete but is still used in some circumstances.

Uqud al-isytirak In Islamic law, a contract of partnership between two or more parties. Major examples of uqud al-isytirak include mudharaba and musharika.

Uqud al-mu'awadhat In Islamic law, a contract in which parties make an exchange. For example, the parties may agree to exchange a good or service for money.

Uqud al-tabarruat In Islamic finance, a contract in which one party voluntarily gives money or something valuable to another. A major example is a hibah contract, in which a borrower freely gives money to a lender as a gratuity for making the loan.

Urban commune In Mali, a political subdivision equivalent to an urban municipality.

Urban Development Act of 1970 Legislation in the United States that provided federally guaranteed (but privately managed) insurance to business owners and residents in high-crime areas. The Act was intended to improve the business climate in urban areas that could not previously acquire insurance because of the excessive risk.

Urbun In Islamic finance, a term for earnest money.

Urna An ancient Roman unit of liquid volume approximately equivalent to 13.1 liters.

Urstromtaler A non-legal tender currency used in Brandenburg and Saxony-Anhalt in Germany. It is accepted by some local retail businesses, but generally not by large chains. It was issued in order to promote small business in Brandenburg and Saxony-Anhalt. It circulates alongside the euro, which is legal tender.

Uruguay Round A series of meetings between more than 120 countries between 1986 and 1994. The round created the World Trade Organization and required signatories to reduce trade barriers on agricultural products, which before then had been subject to significant subsidization.

Uruguayan Nuevo Peso The currency of Uruguay between 1973 and 1993. It replaced the first peso at a rate of 1,000 old pesos to one new peso. It was subject to high inflation toward the end of its circulation, also at a rate of 1,000 nuevo pesos to one Uruguayan peso.

Uruguayan Peso The currency of Uruguay. It was introduced in 1993, replacing the Uruguyan nuevo peso after a period of hyperinflation. The peso uruguayo historically has been subject to high inflation. Until 1982, the peso was on a crawling peg to the U.S. dollar. The end of this peg drove many businesses into bankruptcy because most large debt in Uruguay was denominated in dollars. After a banking crisis in 2002, the peso appreciated against the dollar for the first time in the mid-2000s.

URY GOST 7.67 Latin three-letter geocode for Uruguay. The code is used for transactions to and from Uruguayan bank accounts and for international shipping to Uruguay. As with all GOST 7.67 codes, it is used primarily in Cyrillic alphabets.

US 1. ISO 3166-1 alpha-2 code for the United States of America. This is the code used in international transactions to and from American bank accounts. **2.** ISO 3166-2 geocode for the United States. This is used as an international standard for shipping to the United States. Each American state, the federal district, and six outlying areas have their own codes with the prefix "US." For example, the code for the State of Oklahoma is ISO 3166-2:US-OK.

USA GOST 7.67 Latin three-letter geocode for the United States. The code is used for transactions to and from American bank accounts and for international shipping to the United States. As with all GOST 7.67 codes, it is used primarily in Cyrillic alphabets.

USA PATRIOT Act Legislation in the United States, enacted in 2001 shortly after the September 11 terrorist attacks, that increased the federal government's surveillance and enforcement powers with the intent of combating terrorism. Among other provisions, it expanded the powers of the Secretary of the Treasury to monitor financial transactions, especially internationally, and cracked down on money laundering.

USAEDC U.S. Agricultural Export Development Council. A trade association for companies that export American agricultural products. It provides a forum for members to discuss issues of common interest and lobbies the government for favorable legislation. USAEDC was established in 1983 but traces its origins to the 1950s. It is based in Virginia.

Usage Variance The difference between estimated inputs in a production process and actual inputs, multiplied by their cost, over a period of time. For example, suppose a company expects to use 1,000 hours of work at $5 per hour each week. If it needs to pay for 1,200 hours in week one, its usage variance is $1,000 ([1,200 - 1,000] * $5). Likewise, if it only needs to pay for 700 hours in week two, its variance

is -$1,500 ([700 - 1,000] * $5). Obviously, negative usage variance reduces costs while positive variance increases them.

Usance 1. The use of goods and services to fulfill needs. For instance, one who buys food and then eats it is getting usance out of the food. Likewise, a company that buys crude oil in order to produce refined oil is getting usance from the crude. **2.** The customary period between the time a bill is sent and the time payment is due. Depending on the good or service being provided, usance can be anywhere from a few days to a few months. Usance in this sense is also called usage or tenor.

USD ISO 4217 code for the United States dollar. First issued in 1792, it is the currency used most often in international transactions. After World War II, most world currencies were pegged to the dollar, which was in turn pegged to gold. In 1971, the dollar became a fiat currency. Nevertheless, many currencies are still pegged to the dollar, and it is one of the most important reserve currencies in the world.

USD LIBOR The London Interbank Offer Rate computed with respect to the U.S. dollar. This is used to determine the interest rate on some American mortgages.

Use and Occupancy A payment one makes periodically for the right to live in and occupy a piece of real estate while a court case related to the property is pending. Use and occupancy is identical to rent, but the landlord and tenant do not have rights and obligations toward each other, often because a lawsuit is in progress.

Use and Occupancy Insurance A former term for boiler and machinery business interruption insurance. The term is no longer used.

Use Value The satisfaction derived from a commodity. That is, use value is the ability of a commodity to extinguish a want. The concept dates at least to Aristotle, but is used most commonly in Marxist economics. It is analogous to utility in neoclassical economics. It differs from exchange value in that use value measures quality while exchange value measures quantity.

Useful Life The amount of time, as determined by the IRS, that an asset is expected to be used. The useful life is important in determining taxes assessed on the depreciated value of the asset each year. Theoretically, an asset's useful life is equal to its absolute physical life, but, because the useful life is an estimation, this is not always the case.

User Fee Money one must pay in exchange for the ability to use a service. User fees generally are collected by municipal governments. For example, one may pay a fixed fee every month for sewer services.

U-Shaped Average Cost Curve A model of how the average cost for producing a unit changes over time. The average cost per unit begins high and drops as production increases. Eventually, the cost begins to rise again as marginal costs increase. It is so called because, when plotted on a chart, the cost curve looks like the letter U.

USN ISO 4217 code for U.S. dollar exchange rate transactions settling on the next business day.

USS ISO 4217 code for U.S. dollar exchange rate transactions settling on the same business day.

Usual Marketing Requirements Regulations intended to ensure that American agricultural exports do not cause unnecessary volatility in global commodity prices.

Usufruct The temporary right to use and profit from a property that belongs to another, provided one does not damage the property. For example, a farmer may have usufruct of another person's land. If he grows crops on that land, they belong to the farmer and not the property owner. Only a few jurisdictions in North America recognize usufruct, but it is an important concept in some investment vehicles in Islamic finance.

Usury An excessively high interest rate. Different jurisdictions have different regulations as to what constitutes usury, but most places have laws protecting consumers from the practice of borrowing at such an interest rate. In some cases, as in Islamic finance, any interest at all is considered to be usury, and, therefore, providers of funding must find different ways to provide financing at a profit.

Usury Law Any law restricting banks, credit cards, and financial services companies from charging an excessive amount in interest. In 1978, the U.S. Supreme Court held that a company may charge the legal interest rate in the state in which it is registered, regardless of where the borrower lives. As a result, many American credit card companies are registered in South Dakota, which has quite loose restrictions.

Usury Rate The highest, legal interest rate on a financial instrument in a jurisdiction. In 1978, the U.S. Supreme Court held that a company may charge up to the usury rate in the state in which it is registered, regardless of where the borrower lives. As a result, many American credit card companies are registered in South Dakota, which has loose restrictions.

ut In newspapers and other media reports, an abbreviation indicating that a stock was traded as a unit share.

Utilitarian A person who believes moral actions must provide the greatest good to the greatest number of persons. Utilitarians emphasize the consequences of actions when evaluating their morality. For example, a utilitarian may regard a lie to a regulator as moral if it saves 2,000 jobs. Critics of utilitarianism contend that consequences are unknowable and argue that it could be used to defend atrocities. Utilitarians, on the other hand, argue that their philosophy is the best way to improve happiness in the aggregate.

Utilitarianism The philosophy holding that moral actions must provide the greatest good to the greatest number of persons. Utilitarianism emphasizes the consequences of actions when evaluating their morality. For example, a utilitarian may regard a lie to a regulator as moral if it saves 2,000 jobs. Critics of utilitarianism contend that consequences are unknowable and argue that it could be used to defend atrocities. Utilitarians, on the other hand, argue that their philosophy is the best way to improve happiness in the aggregate.

Utility 1. In economics, the level satisfaction the person derives from a good or service. Utility is inherently subjective and thus difficult to measure, but it is important in determining how much supply of a product the market can handle without diminishing demand. Historically, it has been thought that one can quantify the utility of each unit, but some economists disagree with this. See also: Austrian school, Law of Diminishing Marginal Utility. **2.** A company that provides electricity, water, or gas to customers. These companies are subject to a number of regulations at the local and national levels. They borrow more than most other companies; thus, a decline in utility stocks is often seen as an indicator of a coming rise in interest rates. See also: Dow Jones Utility Average - DJUA.

Utility Bill The amount a household or office is expected to pay for electricity, water and/or gas each month. Utility bills vary according to one's usage. However, many local and national governments regulate the profits of utility companies, limiting the amount they can charge customers. Utility bills are almost always a significant business expense. See also: Dow Jones Utility Average.

Utility Bond A long-term bond issued by a utility company. Because utility companies have very large capital expenditures (they must build expensive infrastructure to provide their services), they use utility bonds to finance many of their projects. See also: Utilities sector.

Utility Company A company that provides electricity, water or gas to customers. These companies are subject to a number of regulations at the local and national levels. They borrow more than most other companies; thus, a decline in utility stocks is often seen as an indicator of a coming rise in interest rates. See also: Dow Jones Utility Average.

Utility Function The expression of desire in mathematical terms. Utility function is important in investing; it may show the usefulness of investing in some securities as opposed to different ones. For instance, a stock with low risk and a high return has a higher utility function than a stock with high risk and a low return. See also: Marginal Utility.

Utility Revenue Bond A municipal bond issued in order to finance the construction of a public utility, such as a power plant or a water treatment plant. A utility revenue bond is guaranteed by and is paid out of the revenues derived from the sale of those utilities.

Utility Value A subjective assessment of the expected return on an investment at a given risk. The utility value an investor assigns to a particular investment depends largely on the investor's risk tolerance. For instance, one investor may find that expected return X is appropriate for risk level Y, but a second investor may believe that X is too low for the riskiness.

Uttatu 1. An ancient Akkadian unit of length approximately equivalent to 0.0025 meters. **2.** An ancient Akkadian unit of weight approximately equivalent to 50 milligrams.

Utugari In Rwanda, a political subdivision roughly equivalent to a village.

UY 1. ISO 3166-1 alpha-2 code for the Oriental Republic of Uruguay. This is the code used in international transactions to and from Uruguayan bank accounts. **2.** ISO 3166-2 geocode for Uruguay. This is used as an international standard for shipping to Uruguay. Each Uruguayan department has its own code with the prefix "UY." For example, the code for the Department of San Jose is ISO 3166-2:UY:SJ.

UYN ISO 4217 code for the Uruguayan nuevo peso. It replaced the first peso at a rate of 1,000 old pesos to one nuevo peso. It was subject to high inflation toward the end of its circulation. It was replaced by the peso uruguayo at a rate of 1,000 nuevo pesos to one peso uruguayo.

UYU ISO 4217 code for the Uruguayan peso uruguayo. It was introduced in 1993, replacing the Uruguyan nuevo peso after a period of hyperinflation. The peso uruguayo historically has been subject to high inflation. Until 1982, the peso was on a crawling peg to the U.S. dollar. The end of this peg drove many businesses into bankruptcy because most large debt in Uruguay was denominated in dollars. After a banking crisis in 2002, the peso appreciated against the dollar for the first time in the mid-2000s.

UZ 1. ISO 3166-1 alpha-2 code for the Republic of Uzbekistan. This is the code used in international transactions to and from Uzbekistani bank accounts. **2.** ISO 3166-2 geocode for Uzbekistan. This is used as an international standard for shipping to Uzbekistan. Each Uzbekistani province has its own code with the prefix "UZ." For example, the code for the Province of Andijon is ISO 3166-2:UZ-AN.

UZB GOST 7.67 Latin three-letter geocode for Uzbekistan. The code is used for transactions to and from Uzbekistani bank accounts and for international shipping to Uzbekistan. As with all GOST 7.67 codes, it is used primarily in Cyrillic alphabets.

Uzbek Sum The currency of Uzbekistan. It was introduced in 1993, replacing the Soviet ruble. In 1994, a new sum was issued, replacing the old sum at an exchange rate of 1 new sum to 1,000 old sum. The sum is a floating currency.

UZS ISO 4217 code for the Uzbek sum. It was introduced in 1993, replacing the Soviet ruble. In 1994, a new sum was issued, replacing the old sum at an exchange rate of 1 new sum to 1,000 old sum. The sum is a floating currency.

VA 1. ISO 3166-1 alpha-2 code for the Vatican City State. This is the code used in international transactions to and from Vatican bank accounts. **2.** ISO 3166-2 geocode for Vatican City. This is used as an international standard for shipping to the Vatican.

Vaaksa A Finnish unit of length approximately equivalent to 148.44 millimeters. It became obsolete when Finland adopted the metric system in 1880.

Vacancy A job that has not been filled. A job vacancy may occur when an employee quits or is terminated or when a company creates a new position. A large number of job vacancies in an area may indicate that unemployment is about to decline or that workers have sufficient job security to hold out for higher wages or other benefits. Alternatively, vacancies may indicate that the workforce is poorly trained for what needs to be done. See also: Help-Wanted Index.

Vacancy Rate The number of units in a building without renters, expressed as a percentage of all units. For example, an apartment building with 100 units and 40 resident families has a 60% vacancy rate. It is the opposite of the occupancy rate.

Vacant Land Land with no houses, offices or other permanent structures. Vacant land may be available for development, or it may be set aside by a government or a private owner to remain vacant.

Vacation A period of time during which one ordinarily would work but does not, normally to engage in some pleasure. One may spend a vacation traveling, relaxing or simply organizing one's personal life. Many companies offer paid vacation time to employees after a certain period of employment. Some jurisdictions require paid vacations.

Vacation Home A residence other than the owner's primary residence that is used for vacations or other recreational purposes. A vacation home is often rented to tenants during times when the owner is not using it. For example, if a person in Connecticut owns a winter home in Florida, this is a vacation home and may be rented to other persons during the summer. Different tax rules apply for how much interest can be deducted and how much rental income can be declared, depending on how often the owner uses the vacation home, how often it is rented, and how often it is unoccupied.

Vacation Pay Time for which an employee is paid even though he/she is on vacation. Many companies offer paid vacation time to employees after a certain period of employment. Some jurisdictions require paid vacations. If one has accumulated vacation time (based on length of employment) and quits or retires without using it, the employer often must pay for the time in cash.

Vadra In some parts of Romania, a term used to indicate 10 liters.

Vag A Norwegian unit of weight approximately equivalent to 18 kilograms.

Vakomitta A Finnish unit of length approximately equivalent to 213.6 meters. It became obsolete when Finland adopted the metric system in 1880.

VAL ISO 4217 code for the Vatican lira. It was introduced in 1929 upon the Vatican's independence from Italy. It was pegged to the Italian lira at a one-to-one ratio. Vatican and Italian coins circulated alongside each other in both the Vatican and Italy. The euro replaced both currencies in 1999.

Vald In Estonia, a political subdivision for a rural municipal government.

Valid Contract A contract that conforms to the law of the jurisdiction in which it is entered. In the event of a dispute, a court will enforce a valid contract.

Validated Export License A license issued by the Bureau of Industry and Security of the U.S Department of Commerce allowing the holder to export specified goods (usually commodities) during the time the license is valid.

Valuables Items worth a significant amount of money. Valuables include things like jewelry, high quality furniture, and electronics. Some insurance policies limit coverage on valuables without additional premiums as they can be expensive to replace. Valuables are also called high-ticket items.

Valuation The process of determining how much an asset, company, or anything else is worth. Valuation is highly subjective, but it is easiest when one is considering the current value of tangible assets. For example, determining how much a willing buyer will pay a willing seller for a house right now is easier than determining the value of what a company's brand recognition might be in 10 years. Valuation is important in fundamental analysis, the practitioners of which usually consider a company's earnings to be indicative of its value.

Valuation Clause A provision in some insurance policies stating the amount of money the insurer will pay the policyholder if the insured event occurs. That is, the valuation clause states that the insurance company will pay a fixed amount, neither more nor less, under the circumstances described in the policy.

Valuation Reserve A charge against a company's earnings set aside to account for changes in the value of a company's assets. These changes are normally due to depreciation, but also may come from bad debt.

Value A measure of worth. Value is generally expressed in monetary terms. For example, the value of a house may be $100,000. Generally, the value of a product depreciates over time, though it sometimes appreciates instead (notably in real estate). How easily one can sell a product for its value helps determine how liquid the product is.

Value Added The increase to the value of a product at each stage in a production cycle or supply chain. For example, a timber company cuts down trees, which adds value to the wood because it can then be used. It may then sell the timber to a miller, who adds value by refining the timber into planks of wood. A carpenter who buys the planks adds value by making them into a table, which can then be sold to a customer. The concept of value added is most important in countries and other jurisdictions that have a value-added tax.

Value Additivity Principal 1. A situation in which the market value of a portfolio or other group of assets exactly equals the market value of the individual assets or securities represented therein. **2.** A situation in which the net present value of a portfolio or other group of assets exactly equals the net present value of the individual assets or securities represented therein.

Value at Risk In risk analysis, a method to measure the probability of loss on an investment. One calculates the value at risk by measuring the historical trends and volatility of the investment. The method is used most often by investors in highly volatile commodities, such as energy products.

Value Chain The set of activities whereby a company take raw materials and turns them into finished products by adding value at each step. For example, take a conglomerate that controls every step of a supply chain. It may have a timber division that cuts down trees, which adds value to the wood because it can then be used. It then sends the timber to the milling division, which adds value by refining the timber into planks of wood. The carpentry department refining the planks adds value by making them into a table, which can then be sold to a customer. The value chain analyzes how much value each activity adds to the final product against how much each step costs. The two may not be equivalent; making a table may add a great deal to the wood's value without costing very much. Analyzing the value chain is one strategy a company can use to identify and cut costs in a way that maximizes profit.

Value Date In eurocurrency and foreign exchange, the delivery date. That is, if a buyer and seller agree to trade a currency, the value date is the day that the currencies are actually traded, not the date on which the traders agree to the exchange rate.

Value Fund A mutual fund that invests predominantly or exclusively in stocks that have a great deal of growth potential. These stocks may be undervalued and have an exceptionally low P/E ratio. Likewise, these stocks may pay dividends on a regular basis.

Value Impaired A loan to a foreign country on which the borrower has not made payments for more than six months. There is a high likelihood that a value impaired debt will not be repaid. Value impaired loans do not comply with IMF credit adjustment requirements.

Value Index An index tracking value stocks, which are stocks with prices lower than their intrinsic values. One may identify stocks for a value index in a variety of ways, but two of the most popular are finding companies with low P/E ratios or low price-to-book ratios. In both cases, the share price for a company is lower than its earnings per share or its asset value per share. Value indices may have high profit potential because it is thought that the share prices will eventually rise to match the stocks' real value.

Value Investing An investment strategy in which one seeks securities thought to be undervalued. One may do this in a variety of ways, but two of the most popular are finding companies with low P/E ratios or low price-to-book ratios. In both cases, the stock price for a company is lower than its earnings per share or its asset value per share. These companies are thought to have high profit potential. Analysts disagree on the tools for value investing, but most use some form of fundamental analysis and look for companies with an underlying value of more than its price. See also: Buy and hold.

Value Investment An investment in securities thought to be undervalued. One may make a value investment in a variety of ways, but two of the most popular are finding companies with low P/E ratios or low price-to-book ratios. In both cases, the stock price for a company is lower than its earnings per share or its asset value per share. These companies are thought to have high profit potential. Analysts disagree on the tools for value investing, but most use some form of fundamental analysis and look for companies with an underlying value that is higher than their price. See also: Buy and hold.

Value Investor An investor who seeks securities thought to be undervalued. One may do this in a variety of ways, but two of the most popular are finding companies with low P/E ratios or low price-to-book ratios. In both cases, the stock price for a company is lower than its earnings per share or its asset value per share. These companies are thought to have high profit potential. Analysts disagree on the tools for value investing, but most use some form of fundamental analysis and look for companies with an underlying value that is higher than their price. See also: Buy and hold.

Value Judgment A decision based on what one believes is the right thing to do. The value involved may come from any number of sources. For example, one may make an investment decision based on one's moral values, one's view of the macroeconomic situation, and/or one's willingness to take risks. Often, value judgments occur when the correct decision is not immediately clear.

Value Line Composite Index An index of more than 1,500 companies traded on the American Stock Exchange, NASDAQ, NYSE, and Toronto Stock Exchange. It ranks the stocks listed on it according to their performance over trailing six to 12 month periods, and publishes each one's volatility compared to the market average. The Value Line Survey also has both arithmetic and geometric indices.

Value Line Ranking The performance for a stock as measured in the The Value Line Investment Survey. The ranking is on a scale from 1 to 5, with 1 being the best possible score.

Value Line, Inc. A corporation that provides research and advisory services to clients. Its wholly-owned subsidiary, Value Line Publishing, sells both print and online editions of more than a dozen advisory letters. Some are broad and discuss macroeconomic trends, while others offer specific advice, providing in-depth coverage of one or two stocks. Value Line also operates the Value Line Index, an equal-weighted index of more than 1,700 stocks traded in the United States. It provides services as a registered investment advisor.

Value Manager A money manager who uses value investing, which is a strategy that seeks securities thought to be undervalued. A value manager may do this in a variety of ways, but two of the most popular are finding companies with low P/E ratios or low price-to-book ratios. In both cases, the stock price for a company is lower than its earnings per share or its asset value per share. These companies are thought to have high profit potential. Value managers disagree on the tools for value investing, but most use some form of fundamental analysis and look for companies with an underlying value of more than its price. See also: Buy and Hold.

Value Maximization The act or process of adding to an individual's net worth by increasing the share price of the common stock in which that individual has invested. See also: Expected value maximization principle.

Value Proposition In marketing, an advertisement or other tactic in which one is encouraged to buy a product because it will save time or money or otherwise add value to one's business or personal life.

Value Quota A price for a good including both the quantity and the price per unit. For example, given five apples priced at 20 cents each, the value quota is $1.

Value Stocks Stocks with prices lower than their intrinsic value. One may identify value stocks in a variety of ways, but two of the most popular are finding companies with low P/E ratios or low price-to-book ratios. In both cases, the stock price for a company is lower than its earnings per share or its asset value per share. These companies are thought to have high profit potential because it is thought that the share price will eventually rise to match the company's real value. See also: Buy and hold, Warren Buffett, Benjamin Graham.

Value Stream All changes made during the production of a product between its conception and sale. The term implies that each change adds value, but this is not necessarily the case.

Value Trap A stock with a lower-than-usual price that appears to be a value stock but is not. A value trap appears to be undervalued at first glance but its fundamentals are unhealthy and the stock is unlikely to recover in price. One may fall into a value trap by looking only at the stock's price but not at any other financial information.

Value-Added Activity An activity that increases the value of a product at a given stage in a production cycle or supply chain. For example, a timber company cuts down trees, which adds value to the wood because it can then be used. It may then sell the timber to a miller, who adds value by refining the timber into planks of wood. A carpenter who buys the planks adds value by making them into a table, which can then be sold to a customer. The concept of value added is most important in countries and other jurisdictions that have a value-added tax.

Value-Added Monthly Index A method of tracking the return on an investment over a given period of time in relation to a theoretical $1,000 investment. For example, suppose the yearly return on an investment is 10%; the VAMI would then be 1100. It is calculated thusly: VAMI = Previous VAMI for equal period of time * (1 + return rate)

Value-Added Tax A tax levied at each stage in the production of a good or service that results in value being added to the product. For example, a timber company pays a percentage on the timber it sells to a miller. The miller then pays the same percentage (less what the timber company paid) on the timber it has refined into planks of wood, which it then sells to a carpenter. The carpenter likewise pays the same percentage (less what the timber company and miller paid) on the planks of wood he/she makes into a table, which he/she then sells to a customer. Proponents of a VAT state that each person or company along the supply chain has an incentive to ensure that every other person or company pays the VAT, reducing the likelihood of tax evasion. They also argue that it is more straightforward than other taxes because there are no exemptions or loopholes. Opponents of a VAT counter that the tax is regressive and unduly harms poor people, who, as a rule, spend more of their discretionary income on necessary items.

Value-Adding Cost A cost that increases the value of a product. For example, a company may spend $1 to increase the value of a widget from $10 to $12. In this case, the $1 is a value-adding cost.

Value-Based Pricing A method of pricing a product in which one estimates the value of the product to the customer. That is, rather than considering the cost to the company and marking up according to some formula, value-based pricing looks at factors such as how many customers want the product, how badly and how often they want it, and determine the price from these data.

Valued Basis A benefit in disability income insurance replacing an insured's total lost income. For example, suppose a machinist makes $40,000 per year and is injured on the job so he cannot work. The valued basis of his disability insurance would enable him to continue to make $40,000 per year.

Valued Clause A clause in an insurance policy stating how much the insurer will pay per insured property. For example, the valued clause may state that the insurer will pay $1,000 per computer, $500 per piece of furniture, and so forth. The insurer pays this regardless of the actual value of the property at the time of the loss. See also: Value Policy.

Valued Marine Policy A marine insurance policy that pays a specified amount in the event of a loss, regardless of the value of the loss. For example, a policy may pay $1,000 per lost box of cargo, whether the value of the cargo is $100 or $2,000 per box.

Valued Policy An insurance policy that pays a specified amount in the event of a loss, regardless of the value of the loss. For example, a life insurance policy may pay $100,000 upon the death of the insured, regardless of when or how the death occurs.

Valued Policy Law Any law requiring an insurer to pay the full amount of an insurance policy in the event of a claim of loss. This requirement exists even if the value of the claim is less than the full value of the policy.

Values-Based Corporation A company that prioritizes its corporate values over short-term profits. The idea behind values-based corporations is that behaving morally will increase the sustainability in the long term.

Vampire Squid A derogatory slang term for Goldman Sachs. The term denotes the outsized influence that current and former Goldman executives had on (especially American) finance and government before and during the late 2000s recession.

Vandalism Endorsement An addition to a Standard Fire Policy providing coverage for vandalism or other acts of deliberate harm. For example, the endorsement may cover graffiti on the side of a building. Schools and places of worship commonly purchase vandalism endorsements because they are unoccupied for long periods of time (such as summers or during the week) when vandals are unlikely to be discovered.

Vanilla Issue An issue of a stock or bond with no unusual provisions. There are no warrants or other rights attached to the issue as sweeteners, nor are there any relevant tax provisions. A vanilla issue is simply a straightforward issue of a security.

Vanilla Option An option contract with no special characteristics. It is either a call or a put, and has a standard expiry date and strike price. The contract contains no unusual provisions. It is also called a plain vanilla option. See also: Exotic option.

Vaporware An upgrade to a product that is not yet available that a salesperson sells in order to avoid a customer's complaints about the current version.

Vara 1. A Portuguese measure of length approximately equivalent to 1.1 meters. It became obsolete after Lusophone countries adopted the metric system in the 19th century. **2.** A Spanish measure of length approximately equivalent to 0.84 meters. It is largely obsolete, but is still used in the sale of lumber in Costa Rica.

Variable Anything that does not have a set value. In basic algebra, a variable is often expressed as "x." Variables in economics and finance may be measures such as GDP, prices, or interest rates. Analysts use complicated equations to determine the value of some variables at the present time and even more complicated equations to predict their possible future values. See also: Regression.

Variable Annuity An annuity that provides the annuitant a small guaranteed return for the life of the annuity along with another return that depends on the performance of a portfolio. Like any annuity, the annuitant buys into a policy, either with a lump sum or premiums over a period of time. When the annuitant reaches a certain age or retirement (whichever is greater), he/she begins to receive payments. Generally speaking, the insurance company issuing a variable annuity invests the premiums in investment vehicles such as stocks or mutual funds. This exposes the annuitant to the risk that he/she will be stuck with a smaller return, but it also carries the possibility of a much larger return. See also: Fixed annuity.

Variable Cost A cost to a person or business that varies over time according to a number of factors. For example, a dental office must buy dental supplies, which usually cost about the same. This is a fixed cost. On the other hand, the dental office must also pay the electric and gas and water bills, which may fluctuate considerably. This is a variable cost.

Variable Coupon Renewable Note A debt security that matures every week with the principal automatically reinvested at a new interest rate. This process continues until the holder of the note asks the principal not to be reinvested. The interest rate is generally linked to the rate on a Treasury bill. It is also called a VCR note.

Variable Death Benefit A benefit in some life insurance policies where the designated beneficiary is guaranteed a minimum death benefit and an additional benefit, depending on the performance of some investment portfolio. This allows the beneficiary the possibility of a much larger death benefit that she/he would otherwise receive. However, the minimum benefit can be smaller than normal death benefits paid in other life insurance policies. See also: Variable life insurance.

Variable Levy A tariff that changes in such a way that the domestic price of an imported good always remains the same (or almost the same). A variable levy increases when the raw price of the import drops and decreases when the raw price rises.

Variable Life Insurance A whole life insurance policy in which some, or all, of the premium is allocated to a separate account, which is invested in common stock. If the common stock portfolio does well, the death benefit increases accordingly; if it performs poorly it decreases, though all variable life insurance policies have a benefit floor. A significant advantage to a variable life insurance policy is the fact that the policyholder does not have to pay taxes on earnings from the portfolio until it is cashed in, usually through death. In the United States, variable life insurance policies are considered securities contracts and, as such, they are regulated by federal law.

Variable Plan A new issue in which the number of shares and/or their price is not known for a certain, relatively long period of time.

Variable Price Limit In commodities, price variations above or below the general limits imposed by the exchange at which a commodity may trade. Because commodities can be quite volatile, exchanges impose limits above or below which a commodity's price cannot move in a given period. In times of heavy volume, however, an exchange may institute a temporary, variable price limit to allow commodities greater leeway.

Variable Ratio Option Writing An options investment strategy in which the owner of an underlying security writes a number of calls at different strike prices on

that security. Generally, only one of those options is exercised (if any are at all), leaving the owner with only the profit of the option premiums. Variable ratio writes thus have limited profit potential, but carry the possibility that an option will be exercised at a price favorable to the writer. The "variable ratio" in the term comes from the fact that the writer may write a theoretically unlimited number of options per 100 shares of the underlying security actually owned. Often, the owner writes two options per 100 shares, giving a 2:1 ratio.

Variable Ratio Write An options investment strategy in which the owner of an underlying security writes a number of calls at different strike prices on that security. Generally, only one of those options is exercised (if any are at all), leaving the owner with only the profit of the option premiums. Variable ratio writes thus have limited profit potential, but carry the possibility that an option will be exercised at a price favorable to the writer. The phrase "variable ratio" in the term comes from the fact that the writer may write a theoretically unlimited number of options per 100 shares of the underlying security actually owned. Often, the owner writes two options per 100 shares, giving a 2:1 ratio.

Variable-Price Security A security with a price that changes periodically or constantly according to market forces. Most marketable securities, notably stocks, bonds, and derivatives, are variable price securities. The foundational principle behind stock exchanges and over-the-counter trading states that securities have variable prices. These securities contrast with those whose prices do not change, such as certificates of deposit.

Variable-Rate Certificate of Deposit A certificate of deposit for which the interest rate changes according to some formula at set intervals. Investors use variable-rate certificates of deposit when they want a low-risk investment but expect prevailing interest rates to rise during the life of the CD. See also: Variable-rate bond.

Variable-Rate Demand Note A debt security that a holder may require the issuer to redeem before maturity. When this occurs, the issuer must pay par to the holder, and the holder loses any future coupon payments that he/she might otherwise have been due. An advantage to a variable-rate demand note from the holder's standpoint is the fact that the holder may reinvest the par value in a new bond in a time of rising interest rates. This protects the holder from certain types of interest rate risk. Variable-rate demand notes come in two main forms. The first allows the holder to demand redemption on any of several days throughout the life of the bond, while the second only allows this on one particular day. Variable rate demand notes are also known as variable rate demand obligations, option tender bonds, or put bonds. In Canada, the most common term is a retractable bond.

Variable-Rate Loan A loan with an interest rate that changes periodically. Generally speaking, a variable rate loan is linked to some major benchmark rate; for example, the interest rate may be stated as "LIBOR + 1%." The loan may or may not have a cap on how much the interest rate can rise or fall, or on how often the interest rate may change. Very often, the initial interest rate for a variable-rate loan is lower than that for a fixed-rate loan. This allows more people to qualify for a loan; however, this kind of loan can be risky because the interest rate (and therefore the monthly payment) can rise unexpectedly. See also: Adjustable-rate mortgage.

Variable-Rate Note A bond with an interest rate that changes periodically. These bonds typically have coupons renewable every three months and pay according to a set calculation. For example, a note may have an interest rate of "EURIBOR + 1%" and pay whatever the EURIBOR rate happens to be at the time plus 1%. Some variable-rate notes have maximum and minimum interest rates, known as capped notes and floored notes, respectively. A variable-rate note with both a maximum and a minimum interest rate is called a collared note. In the United States, government sponsored enterprises issue most variable-rate notes, while banks do the same in Europe. See also: Adjustable-rate mortgage.

Variable-Rate Preferred Stock A preferred stock paying a dividend that varies from time to time. Usually, the dividend rate is based on an index or on the interest rate on a Treasury security. They may also be backed by mortgages or mortgage-backed securities.

Variance 1. In accounting, the difference between the estimated and actual cost of a project or other operation. **2.** In risk, the average deviation of a set of data points from their mean.

Variance Rule The upper and lower limits of how many mortgage-backed securities are delivered in a TBA transaction. A TBA transaction is a forward contract on a mortgage-backed security. The seller agrees to deliver the MBSs for an agreed upon price and agreed upon date (usually 48 hours after the contract is made) but makes no guarantee as to which or how many securities are to be delivered. Generally speaking, the seller delivers the amount of mortgage-backed securities that equal the market value of the selling price at the time of delivery. However, the variance rule places a limit on how much this can vary from the market value of the securities at the time the TBA occurs. This reduces the risk for both the buyer and the seller.

Variance Swap A forward contract on the variance of a security. The variance is the square of the standard deviation. As a result, the payout on a variance swap is higher when the volatility increases. A variance swap allows the investor to speculate on volatility, just as a trader might speculate on the price of a stock; it is most advantageous when the volatility is or is expected to be high.

Variation Margin Extra money that a member of a clearing house must pay to the clearing house to meet its minimum maintenance requirements. Members pay the variation margin each day or more often to protect the clearing house from the risks inherent to its members buying on margin.

Variety One of two or more types of the same line of coin. For example, all the pennies made in one year may include a line of 100 with a double die. A variety may affect the value of the coin.

VAT 1. GOST 7.67 Latin three-letter geocode for the Vatican. The code is used for transactions to and from Vatican bank accounts and for international shipping to the Vatican. As with all GOST 7.67 codes, it is used primarily in Cyrillic alphabets. **2.** See: Value-added tax.

Vatican Lira The former currency of Vatican City. It was introduced in 1929 upon the Vatican's independence from Italy. It was pegged to the Italian lira at a one-to-one ratio. Vatican and Italian coins circulated alongside each other in both the Vatican and Italy. The euro replaced both currencies in 1999.

Vatu The currency of Vanuatu. It was introduced when Vanuatu became independent in 1982, replacing the New Hebrides franc and the Australian dollar. It has no subdivisions; as a result, large transactions are sometimes quoted in "dollars," though the currency has no current relationship to the Australian dollar.

Vault Cash Capital kept at a bank or other financial institution to cover day-to-day expenses such as cash withdrawals. It is called vault cash because the bulk of it is traditionally kept in a heavily-guarded vault.

Vault Receipt A guarantee that a seller will deliver commodities to a certain warehouse for storage. A vault receipt is a way to settle a futures contract, especially one on precious metals, in lieu of actual delivery. A vault receipt is also called a warehouse receipt.

VC 1. See: Venture capital. **2.** ISO 3166-1 alpha-2 code for Saint Vincent and the Grenadines. This is the code used in international transactions to and from Vincentian bank accounts. **3.** ISO 3166-2 geocode for Saint Vincent and the Grenadines. This is used as an international standard for shipping to the nation. Each Vincentian parish has its own code with the prefix "VC." For example, the code for the Parish of Charlotte is ISO 3166-2:VC-01.

VCT GOST 7.67 Latin three-letter geocode for Saint Vincent and the Grenadines. The code is used for transactions to and from local bank accounts and for international shipping to Saint Vincent and the Grenadines. As with all GOST 7.67 codes, it is used primarily in Cyrillic alphabets.

VD 1. ISO 3166-1 alpha-2 code for North Vietnam prior to its reunification with South Vietnam. This was the code used in international transactions to and from North Vietnamese bank accounts. **2.** ISO 3166-2 geocode for North Vietnam. This was used as an international standard for shipping to North Vietnam. In both cases, the code is obsolete.

VDVN ISO 3166-3 code for North Vietnam, which merged with South Vietnam in 1976. ISO 3166-3 codes are used to indicate names of countries that are no longer used.

VE 1. ISO 3166-1 alpha-2 code for the Bolivarian Republic of Venezuela. This is the code used in international transactions to and from Venezuelan bank accounts. **2.** ISO 3166-2 geocode for Venezuela. This is used as an international standard for shipping to Venezuela. Each subdivision has its own code with the prefix "VE." For example, the code for the Capital District is ISO 3166-2:VE-A.

VEB ISO 4217 code for the Venezuelan bolivar. It was introduced in 2008 following a revaluation of the previous currency. It has suffered from high inflation throughout its history.

Vedro 1. A Russian unit of dry volume approximately equivalent to 13.12 liters. **2.** A Russian unit of liquid volume approximately equivalent to 12.3 liters. Both versions of the term were rendered obsolete when the Soviet Union began to use the metric system in 1924.

VEF ISO 4217 code for the Venezuelan bolivar fuerte. It was issued in 2008, replacing the old bolivar at a ratio of 1,000 old to one new. Though it is pegged to the U.S. dollar, it has been subject to high inflation, and its black market exchange rate differs widely from the official rate.

Vega In the Black-Scholes Model, the amount of change to the price of an option contract as a result of a 1% change to the implied volatility of the underlying. The vega is calculated mathematically, and can be large in a new options contract. The vega tends to decline closer to the expiry date of the contract. It is not necessary for the price of the underlying to change in order for the vega to change; only the expected volatility of the underlying needs to change. The concept of vega is one of the three Greeks often used in the Black-Scholes Model. See also: Delta, Theta.

Veinat In Andorra, a political subdivision equivalent to a neighborhood.

Velaya'at In Afghanistan, a political subdivision equivalent to a province.

Vellum Finish Slightly rough, uncoated paper with an antique finish. Vellum finish is useful in high speed printing.

Velocity of Money The rate at which money changes hands. For example, assume an economy with $100 and two people in it. In a given year, if Person A charges Person B $50 for a widget, and Person B charges Person A $100 for a whatsit, then $150 worth of transaction has occurred even though there are only $100 in the economy. This means that, on average, one dollar is spent one and a half times in a year, expressed as a velocity of 1.5/year. Velocity of money is useful as a measure of how strong and/or liquid an economy is, and it is usually compared with some figure such as GDP or money supply.

VEN GOST 7.67 Latin three-letter geocode for Venezuela. The code is used for transactions to and from Venezuelan bank accounts and for international shipping to Venezuela. As with all GOST 7.67 codes, it is used primarily in Cyrillic alphabets.

Vendee A buyer, especially but not necessarily of real estate.

Vendor Financing The act or practice of a company lending money to a customer so the customer can buy the company's products. Vendor financing allows the company to increase its sales because the customer likely would not have bought from the company otherwise. However, it carries a great deal of credit risk, especially since the customer may or may not have a good credit history and may not pay back the debt. In a situation in which the company is not repaid, it essentially has bought its own products and given them to the customer. In such cases, it writes off the loss as bad debt. See also: Credit sale.

Venture Capital The provision of funding for a start-up. For example, suppose a company with little access to capital is attempting to open a new market or access an old one with a better product. It may not be able to receive loans, either because of an unproven track record or because it is already significantly in debt, and it may have exhausted financing from family and friends. Venture capital allows this company to begin and build upon its operations by providing necessary funding. Usually, the provider of venture capital takes equity in the company in exchange for the money. Venture capital firms may also provide needed expertise in how to run a business than can help the start-up become successful.

Venture Capital Fund A pool of funds from investors that exists to provide funding for a start-up. For example, suppose a company with little access to capital is attempting to open a new market or access an old one with a better product. It may not be able to receive loans, either because of an unproven track record or because it is already significantly in debt, and it may have exhausted financing from family and friends. Venture capital funds allow this company to begin and build upon its operations by providing necessary funding. Usually, the provider of venture capital funds takes equity in the company in exchange for the money. Venture capital firms may also provide needed expertise in how to run a business than can help the start-up become successful. Venture capital funds are considered high risk investments, but have the potential for a high return.

Venture Capital Limited Partnership An agreement between a venture capital firm and a start-up company in which the venture capital firm provides funding and, in exchange, receives a certain percentage of ownership in the company. In other words, the venture capital firm is the limited partner and the start-up is the general partner, which manages the company. This structure gives the venture capital firm limited liability; that is, if the company goes bankrupt, the venture capital company can lose no more than the amount it invested. It also provides the start-up with capital necessary to continue operations and perhaps become profitable.

Venture Capitalist An individual or company that provides funding for a start-up. For example, suppose a company with little access to capital is attempting to open a new market or access an old one with a better product. It may not be able to receive loans, either because of an unproven track record or because it is already significantly in debt, and it may have exhausted financing from family and friends. A venture capitalist allows this company to begin and build upon its operations by providing necessary funding. Usually, the venture capitalist takes equity in the company in exchange for the money. Venture capital firms may also provide needed expertise in how to run a business than can help the start-up become successful.

Verbatim Using the same words. For example, a market researcher may transcribe the responses of a focus group verbatim in order to ensure accurate findings.

Verbiage Business jargon added to a proposal or report to make it sound more impressive.

Vereinsthaler A silver coin used in German-speaking countries prior to the unification of Germany in 1873. It served as the basis for several German countries in the 19th century. It was replaced in the united Germany by the goldmark.

Vereniging zonder winstoogmerk A Dutch term for non-profit organization. It is a name for the legal corporate form of non-profits in Belgium. It is abbreviated VZW. See also: Association sans but lucratif.

Vermin Exclusion In transportation insurance, the denial of coverage for damage to goods due to rats or other pests.

Vermogenszuwachssteuer The term for the capital gains tax in Austria. The imposition of Vermogenszuwachssteuer in Austria remains controversial. Proponents argue that it promotes income equality while critics cite it as an example of Marxism.

Versailles Treaty A 1919 treaty that solemnized the end of World War I. It required Germany, Austria, and Hungary to accept responsibility for causing the war and Germany to pay heavy reparations to the victorious powers. While some scholars disagree, others believe these reparations contributed to Germany's hyperinflation in the early 1920s. In any case, the reparations were humiliating and financially damaging for Germany, which did not make the final payment until 2010.

Vershok A Russian unit of length equivalent to 1.75 inches. It was rendered obsolete when the Soviet Union began to use the metric system in 1924.

Verst A unit of length approximately equivalent to two-thirds of one mile.

Versta A Russian unit of length equivalent to 3,500 feet, or approximately one kilometer. It was rendered obsolete when the Soviet Union began to use the metric system in 1924.

Vertical 1. See: Vertical integration. **2.** See: Vertical diversification. **3.** See: Vertical keiretsu.

Vertical Acquisition An acquisition where one company buys another company in the same industry, but at a different stage of the production cycle. A vertical acquisition can reduce the costs of the two companies by eliminating redundant processes. It also reduces reliance of one company on another. For example, an upstream oil company can merge with a downstream oil company to streamline operations.

Vertical Agreement An agreement between two companies at different levels of the supply chain to work together. At its worst, a vertical agreement can indicate collusion. However, this is ordinarily not the case; a franchise contract, for example, is a vertical agreement.

Vertical Analysis On a balance sheet, a means of calculating assets, liabilities, and equities in which each intake or outlay is represented as a percentage of each group. For example, suppose a company has three liabilities: a debt to the bank, a bond issue, and salaries to employees. Vertical analysis would record each of these on a balance sheet as a percentage of the total amount the company carries in liabilities.

Vertical Audit An audit that investigates all aspects of an activity or department. For example, a vertical audit may measure the effectiveness of training, cost controls and operations in the accounting department. This contrasts with a horizontal audit, which investigates one activity across all departments.

Vertical Conflict Competition between two or more companies at different levels on the channel of distribution. For example, a manufacturer may stop selling to a retailer because another company offers a better deal. See also: Horizontal Conflict.

Vertical Contiguity The purchase of several advertisements on television or radio for broadcast several times over the course of a day. Buying vertical contiguity may lead to a vertical discount.

Vertical Contract In social contract theory, a contract between the people and their rulers. That is, a vertical contract is the actual or implied agreement giving a state the right to govern. An example of a vertical contract is a constitution. See also: Horizontal Contract.

Vertical Discount A reduced price to broadcast an advertisement on television or radio several times over the course of a day. See also: Horizontal Discount.

Vertical Disintegration The separation of one company into several, with each performing activities leading to a single, finished product. Vertical disintegration occurs generally because diseconomies of scale, which are the result of inefficiency due to large size, make it more advantageous than remaining one corporation.

Vertical Diversification In risk management, the act or strategy of adding very different investments to one's portfolio to hedge against the investments already in it. Ideally, this reduces the risk inherent in any one investment, and increases the possibility of making a profit, or at least avoiding a loss. Vertical diversification involves investing in very different securities; for example, one may choose to invest in securities traded in different countries, or in both winter clothing and swimsuit companies. Vertical diversification may be as broad or as narrow as the investor chooses. In general, broader diversification equates to less risk and lower return. See also: Markowitz Portfolio Theory, Horizontal diversification.

Vertical Equity The concept that persons with more income and/or wealth should pay higher tax rates than those with less. This should, in theory, lead to a more equal society. While vertical equity is controversial, most countries have adopted some form of a progressive income tax, which is based on the idea.

Vertical Export Trading Company An export company that handles multiple parts of the exportation process. For example, a vertical export trading company both buys from the domestic producer and sells to the customer in the foreign country.

Vertical Half Page An advertisement in a periodical that is printed on half of a page, divided from the top to the bottom.

Vertical Integration A business strategy in which a company expands its operations to offer similar goods and services at a different point on the supply chain. For example, a widget wholesaler may expand into retailing widgets directly with consumers. More concretely, an oil exploration company may also begin refining oil in addition to its exploration operations. Vertical integration always occurs at different points on the supply chain: a retailer does not expand into retailing other products. Rather, it may move into wholesaling. See also: Horizontal integration.

Vertical Keiretsu In Japan, a number of independent but related companies financed by a single bank and/or a joint stock company that controls every stage of the supply chain. For example, a mining company may sell a metal to a refinery in the same keiretsu, who then sells it to an auto company, who then sells cars to consumers. These consumers are often employees of the very same keiretsu because they have such strong company loyalty. Critics of this system contend that it is inefficient; proponents, however, argue that it is sustainable and has helped Japan recover from the post-war period.

Vertical Line Chart A chart that consists of vertical bars, each representing a trading day. The top of each bar represents the highest price of the day, while the bottom represents the lowest price. The closing price is shown by a short, horizontal line to the right of the bar, while the opening price is shown by the same thing to the left of the bar. The vertical axis of the chart shows prices, while the horizontal axis shows trading days. It is also called a bar chart.

Vertical Market The market for a product that only appeals to a single industry. For example, an airplane manufacturer is likely to sell airplanes predominantly or exclusively to airlines. A vertical market can be very profitable when there are only a few sellers in it; however, even a small amount of competition can drive down profit margins significantly. See also: Horizontal market.

Vertical Merger A merger between two companies in the same industry but at different stages of the production cycle. A vertical merger can reduce the costs of the two companies by eliminating redundant processes. It also reduces reliance on one company on another. For example, an upstream oil company can merge with a downstream oil company to streamline operations.

Vertical Organization An organization in which one manager has authority over others. For example, one manager may be assigned to human resources, a second to operations, and a third to accounting, but all three must answer to the company president.

Vertical Promotion A promotion to a position of greater managerial authority (and therefore more compensation). For example, the vice president for operations may receive a vertical promotion to company president. See also: Horizontal Promotion.

Vertical Publication A periodical intended for a single company, industry or trade. For example, the American Dental Association publishes the ADA Guide to Dental Therapeutics, which is designed to appeal only to those interested in dentistry.

Vertical Security Exchange The trade of one type of security for another. For example, two investors may agree to trade a stock one holds for a bond the other holds. This is often tax-free.

Vertical Specialization A management style in which one manager has authority over another. For example, one manager may be assigned to human resources, a second to operations, and a third to accounting, but all three must answer to the company president. See also: Horizontal Specialization.

Vertical Third Page An advertisement in a periodical that is printed on one third of a page, divided from the top to the bottom.

Vertical Union A labor union representing all workers in a given industry in a geographic area, regardless of the company for which they work. For example, a horizontal union may represent all auto workers in Michigan. It is also called an industrial union.

Very High Frequency Also called VHF. Radio frequency between 30 and 300 megahertz. Very high frequency is used for FM radio and television broadcasts, among other things.

VES An abbreviation for "vessel," as in a ship. The term is used in international trade.

Vessel A ship or other vehicle of transportation over water. Vessels are important in international commerce. See also: Incoterm.

Vessel Ton In shipping, a measure of volume equal to 100 cubic feet.

Vest Pocket Dealer A slang term for a coin dealer who buys and sells coins primarily as a hobby rather than for investment or for a living. The term connotes someone who carries coins in his/her pocket.

Vested Benefits Benefits from a pension or other retirement account that belong to the employee and that he/she keeps regardless of his/her future employment with the company offering the pension. While different companies have different rules as to the number of years at which benefits vest, the time period is usually five years. If an employee quits before five years (or before the set time period), he/she loses the benefits that he/she has accrued up to that point. If the employee quits after the benefits vest, he/she may keep them.

Vested Interest 1. A stake that a person or company has in a certain outcome. For example, a shareholder and an employee both have a vested interest in a company performing well. 2. See: Right.

Vesting The process by which an employee with a qualified retirement plan and/or stock option becomes entitled to the benefits of ownership, even if he/she no longer works at the company providing the retirement plan or stock option. Vesting occurs after an employee has worked at the company for a certain number of years; once vesting occurs, the benefits of the plan or stock option cannot be revoked.

Vesting Schedule The time according to which an option or restricted stock is able to be exercised (in the case of restricted stock, without forfeiture). The vesting schedule is dependent up on the details of the option or restricted stock agreement. See also: Vesting.

Veterans Administration Mortgage A mortgage made by a private bank to a qualifying veteran that is guaranteed by the U.S. Department of Veterans Affairs. In order to be eligible for a VA mortgage, the veteran cannot have been dishonorably discharged and must have served a certain number of years in one of the branches of the American military (the number varies by branch). During the credit crunch, obtaining a VA mortgage became the only way one could obtain a mortgage with no down payment.

Veterans Group Life Insurance Also called VGLI. Term life insurance offered by the Veterans Administration in the United States to former service members who purchased Servicemembers Group Life Insurance while they were in the military. Veterans who sign up for VGLI within 120 days of discharge are not required to submit evidence of good health to be eligible. Premiums are the same for both male and female veterans and are not higher for smokers. Likewise, veterans may not be excluded for mental problems such as post-traumatic stress disorder.

Vette A Norwegian unit of weight approximately equivalent to 6.3 kilograms.

V-Formation In technical analysis, a situation in which a security steeply declines in price, and then steeply recovers. A V-formation may be bullish, but many analysts believe that a V-formation is risky because of the possibility that another steep decline could occur. See also: W-type bottom, V-shaped recovery, W-shaped recovery.

VG 1. ISO 3166-1 alpha-2 code for the British Virgin Islands. This is the code used in international transactions to and from bank accounts in the British Virgin Islands.

2. ISO 3166-2 geocode for the British Virgin Islands. This is used as an international standard for shipping to the British Virgin Islands.

VGB GOST 7.67 Latin three-letter geocode for the British Virgin Islands. The code is used for transactions to and from local bank accounts and for international shipping to the British Virgin Islands. As with all GOST 7.67 codes, it is used primarily in Cyrillic alphabets.

VI 1. ISO 3166-1 alpha-2 code for the U.S. Virgin Islands. This is the code used in international transactions to and from U.S. Virgin Island bank accounts. **2.** ISO 3166-2 geocode for the U.S. Virgin Islands. This is used as an international standard for shipping to the U.S. Virgin Islands.

Viager Predominantly in France, the sale of a house, usually by an elderly person, in which the seller retains usufruct of the house. The buyer makes a down payment and continual monthly payments until the seller decides to move or dies. At that point, the payments cease and the buyer takes possession of the property. This gives the seller the right to remain in his/her home while also allowing him/her to tap into the house's equity. The buyer has the possibility of purchasing a house for a small amount of money, especially if the seller dies soon after the sale. See also: Lifetime reverse mortgage.

Viatical Settlement A transaction in which a life insurance policy holder sells his/her policy to a third party. The situation occurs when the policy's fair market value exceeds the cash surrender value that the insurance company offers. The third party is known as a life settlement provider, who, in the United States, must abide by applicable state regulations. The life settlement provider becomes the policy's new beneficiary, is responsible for maintaining premiums, and upon the death of the insured person, receives the benefit. The secondary market for life insurance began growing in the last part of the 20th century. In a viatical settlement, the life settlement provider is speculating on how long the insured person will live; indeed, it is in the life settlement provider's financial interest for the insured person to die as soon as possible. A viatical settlement is also known as a life settlement.

Viatical Settlement Company A company to which a life insurance policy holder sells his/her policy in exchange for a lump sum. The situation occurs when the policy's fair market value exceeds the cash surrender value that the insurer offers. The viatical settlement company must abide by applicable regulations, which, in the U.S., are set by individual states. The viatical settlement company becomes the policy's new beneficiary, is responsible for maintaining premiums, and, upon the death of the insured person, receives the benefit. The secondary market for life insurance began growing in the last part of the 20th century. The viatical settlement company is speculating on how long the insured person will live; indeed, it is in the company's financial interest for the insured person to die as soon as possible. A viatical settlement company is also called a life settlement provider.

Viator A dying person who sells his/her life insurance policy. The viator sells the policy at a deep discount (often as little as half) to its cash value. This is beneficial to the buyer because he/she receives a much larger amount when the buyer dies. This helps the viator pay for his/her medical expenses.

Vice President A senior manager in a corporation. While the duties of a vice president vary from company to company, the title often refers to the head of a department. For example, a company might have a vice president of operations, a vice president of human resources, and so forth. A vice president reports directly to the president or CEO of a company.

Victory Bond A bond issued by the British and Canadian governments in the early 20th century, used to finance their involvement in World War I.

Video Conference A meeting in which one or more participants participate by projecting their images on an audio-visual device. This allows one to attend a meeting from a great distance. Proponents of video conferencing argue that it saves on the cost of travel, especially in a multinational corporation. Critics contend that video conferences restrict the camaraderie and informal exchanges that facilitate the conduct of business.

Video Financial Statement A financial statement prepared as a visual presentation instead of as text. For example, a video financial statement may involve a video of the CEO explaining the company's fiscal situation. Video financial statements do not conform to the Generally Accepted Accounting Principles.

Vienna Convention Formally known as the United Nations Convention on Contracts for the International Sale of Goods; an international treaty governing international commerce, defining the rights and duties of an exporter/seller and an importer/buyer. For example, it states that the seller must deliver the goods and the buyer must pay for them. Importantly, the treaty sets forth a variety of agreements into which exporters and importers may enter. This list of agreements lays out when the risk associated with delivery of the goods transfers from the seller to the buyer, and who is responsible for what costs. For example, a CPT agreement states that the seller must pay for shipment, but the buyer assumes all risk once the goods are transferred to the first transporter. More than 70 nations subscribe to the Vienna Convention. See also: Incoterm.

Vienna Stock Exchange The only stock exchange in Austria and one of the largest in eastern Europe. Established in 1771 as a forum for selling state bonds, it is now responsible for approximately 60% of Austria's stock trade, with the remaining 40% being over-the-counter. Stocks, bonds, options, and futures trade on the Vienna Stock Exchange; all trading occurs electronically. It serves as the primary sponsor for other exchanges in eastern Europe, notably the Zagreb Stock Exchange and the Budapest Stock Exchange.

Vierkante roede A Dutch unit of area equivalent to 100 square meters. It was adopted in 1817, soon after the establishment of the Kingdom of the Netherlands.

Vietnam-Era Veteran A person who served in the United States Armed Forces in Vietnam between 1964 and 1975. Because of the controversy surrounding the Vietnam War, these veterans were sometimes mistreated upon their return home. However, the Vietnam-Era Veteran Readjustment Assistance Act gives these veterans preference in the award of federal contracts.

Vietnamese Dong The currency of Vietnam. It was introduced in 1978, replacing the previous dong of North and South Vietnam. It was subject to high inflation from the mid-1980s through the early 1990s.

Vig Interest paid on a loan to a loan shark. Vig is usually very high, or at least higher than the legal limit for interest. It is also called shy.

Vignette A picture or symbol on a stock certificate or unit of cash that is difficult to copy, making counterfeiting less likely. For example, the dollar bill has a picture of George Washington on the front and a number of other symbols. These are all vignettes.

Vigorish 1. A commission charged by a betting parlor in exchange for placing a bet. **2.** An excessive amount of interest on a loan, especially one made by a loan shark. See also: Usury.

Vikas Kshetra In Nepal, a political subdivision equivalent to a region. It is used for international development purposes.

Village Hall A small meeting between the middle management of a company and representatives of upper management. A village hall is designed to invite discussion and debate of the topic at hand, though this is sometimes viewed cynically, as if upper management really intends to control the meeting regardless of other people's thoughts. The term derives its name from the fact that it is a miniature version of a town hall meeting.

Viloyat In Uzbekistan and Tajikistan, a political subdivision equivalent to a province.

Viloyati Mukhtor In Tajikistan, a political subdivision equivalent to an autonomous province. There is one such province, which has a great deal of internal independence.

Vingerhoede A Dutch unit of volume equivalent to 10 milliliters. It was adopted in 1817, soon after the establishment of the Kingdom of the Netherlands.

VIR GOST 7.67 Latin three-letter geocode for the U.S. Virgin Islands. The code is used for transactions to and from local bank accounts and for international shipping to the U.S. Virgin Islands. As with all GOST 7.67 codes, it is used primarily in Cyrillic alphabets.

Virgate An obsolete unit of area equivalent to 30 acres.

Virsta A Finnish unit of length approximately equivalent to 1,069 meters. It became obsolete when Finland adopted the metric system in 1880.

Virtual Bank A bank that offers services predominately or exclusively over the Internet. A virtual bank offers normal banking services, including access to one's checking and savings accounts and personal and business loans. Even non-virtual banks almost always offer virtual banking services.

Virtual Cooperation The act in which an association of independent companies use the same computer network to accomplish mutually beneficial goals. Virtual cooperation is temporary and may be used for only a single project.

Virtual Corporation The act in which independent companies work together as an association to accomplish mutually beneficial goals. Virtual cooperation is temporary and may be used for only a single project. However, for the duration of the project, the companies act as if they were a single corporation.

Virtual Currency Option An option contract that trades in a foreign currency on the Philadelphia Stock Exchange, but is settled in U.S. dollars. This protects the option holder from foreign exchange risk, while allowing him/her to participate in foreign markets.

Virtual Debt Servicing The act or practice of servicing debt by borrowing more money. Virtual debt servicing can be useful but revenue eventually must increase to pay down all debt.

Virtual Mall A website from which one may buy a wide variety of goods. For example, one may purchase books, clothes, electronics, and many other items from a virtual mall. One pays for goods from a virtual mall with a credit card or debit card and they are shipped from a centralized location. A virtual mall is an example of e-commerce. See also: Virtual storefront.

Virtual Private Network Also called a VPN. A computer network connecting the main office of a company to its regional offices, and sometimes to individuals using the network remotely. Until the 1990s, a VPN was a dial-up connection or a network set up especially for the company. Since then, most VPNs simply use the Internet.

Virtual Reality A computer simulation that takes data inputs and uses a stated methodology to create outputs. Virtual reality is used in gaming. Likewise, it is important in science and business to predict future trends.

Virtual Storefront A website that allows a person to research, order and pay for a good online. For example, one may visit a website to find a book, read reviews and then purchase it. See also: Virtual mall.

Visa 1. A document allowing a person to enter, study and/or work in a country in which the person is not a citizen. There are many types of visas; most have time limits and restrictions. Visa holders ordinarily are not permitted recourse to welfare or other public funds. **2.** A financial services company that issues a large share of credit cards and debit cards in the United States and worldwide. It began as a credit card issued by Bank of America that was accepted by multiple merchants, and not simply by a single company. In 1970, Visa became its own company and revolutionized the way for which goods and services are paid, especially at the retail level. Because of Visa, customers may pay with a card almost everywhere and are not required to use cash or check.

Visa Waiver Program Reciprocal agreements between the United States and a number of countries whereby one may travel to other countries for up to 90 days without needing to purchase a tourist visa or other documentation. The Visa Waiver Program does not allow one to take a job in the United States (or another country), but one may conduct business for one's job in one's home country. Most European countries, along with Australia, Japan, New Zealand and South Korea, are part of the Visa Waiver Program.

Visegrad Group An informal grouping consisting of the Czech Republic, Hungary, Poland and Slovakia. Leaders meet to discuss common issues. The group administers a scholarship fund and a working group on energy policy. It was established in 1991 following the end of the Cold War.

Visibility Somewhat informal; the extent to which a future situation is predictable. Low visibility means that analysts have little confidence in their predictions, while high visibility means the opposite. Low visibility may occur because of an unexpected fluctuation in the market or uncertainty in the macroeconomic situation. Visibility is often used with regard to upcoming sales or earnings figures for a given quarter. See also: Volatility.

Visible Balance The aggregate value of a country's exports and imports of goods but not services. The visible balance is a subset of the balance of trade, which is the same thing, but includes services.

Visible Supply 1. A new issue of bonds that is not currently being sold, but will be sold in the next month. **2.** Commodities that are in a warehouse and are able to be delivered for a spot or futures contract.

Visible Trade The sale of a good as opposed to a service or an intangible asset (such as a copyright). See also: Invisible trade.

Vision 1. See: Vision care insurance. **2.** See: Vision statement.

Vision Care Insurance An insurance policy that pays all or a portion of one's eye care. For example, vision care insurance may pay for check-ups, contact lenses or eye surgery. Most health insurance policies do not cover vision and thus vision care insurance must be purchased separately. As with all insurance, one pays a regular premium to receive vision care insurance.

Vision Statement A fairly detailed statement of what a company wishes to accomplish in the course of its operations. A vision statement may be placed in a business plan, on a website or nearly anywhere else. While brief, it explains the company's goals and how it intends to accomplish them to potential investors and other interested parties. It is more detailed than a mission statement.

Visioning Meeting A meeting in which the future direction of a company or organization is decided. A visioning meeting usually involves the board of directors and/or senior management. It occurs especially as a company or organization is in its beginning stages or after a major readjustment such as a leadership change or bankruptcy. However, an organization may elect to have visioning meetings periodically to ensure its mission and vision statements remain relevant over time.

Visit USA Committee An organization with a presence in numerous countries that promotes tourism to the United States. Members of Visit USA Committees are usually private companies who would benefit from travel to the United States. See also: USTTA.

VITA Volunteer Income Tax Assistance. A program the IRS administers each year to help low income persons prepare their tax returns. VITA certifies volunteers to work at centers all over the United States. In general, persons under certain income limits are allowed to have their taxes prepared for free by a VITA volunteer.

Vitasti An ancient Indian unit of length variously equivalent to values between 188 and 250 millimeters.

Vj On a ticker tape or stock table, a symbol describing a company in bankruptcy. The symbol vj precedes the name of the company on the tape or table.

VN 1. ISO 3166-1 alpha-2 code for the Socialist Republic of Vietnam. This is the code used in international transactions to and from Vietnamese bank accounts. **2.** ISO 3166-2 geocode for Vietnam. This is used as an international standard for shipping to Vietnam. Each province has its own code with the prefix "VN." For example, the code for Hanoi is ISO 3166-2:VN-64.

VND ISO 4217 code for the Vietnamese dong. It was introduced in 1978, replacing the previous dong of North and South Vietnam. It was subject to high inflation from the mid-1980s through the early 1990s.

VNM GOST 7.67 Latin three-letter geocode for Vietnam. The code is used for transactions to and from Vietnamese bank accounts and for international shipping to Vietnam. As with all GOST 7.67 codes, it is used primarily in Cyrillic alphabets.

Voblast In Ukraine, a political subdivision equivalent to a province.

Vocational Rehabilitation A joint program between the U.S. federal government and all state and territorial governments that trains and provides other services to persons with disabilities in order to help them find jobs. Vocational rehabilitation programs work with both disabled persons and employers to find the best solution for all involved. The programs began as federal state partnerships in 1973, but some states had similar programs before then.

Voet An obsolete Dutch unit of length roughly equivalent to 30 centimeters, with slight regional variations.

Voice of America The internationally broadcast radio and television service of the United States federal government. It is broadcast in 44 languages and attempts to portray the U.S. positively. It began in 1942 following the United States' entry into World War II. It was later used during the Cold War to promote America behind the Iron Curtain.

Voicemail A program that stores messages for missed telephone calls. Voicemail differs from earlier answering machines in that voicemail messages are stored on a computer network, while answering machine messages were recorded on an audio tape. Voicemail messages can thus be retrieved from anywhere.

Voidable Describing a contract that comes into force, but which a court may or is likely to nullify it before its completion. A voidable contract may (but does not necessarily) violate the law. See also: Rescission.

Voidable Preference The transfer of assets to a secured creditor less than 90 days before a bankruptcy filing. The voidable preference means one secured creditor is favored over others. After bankruptcy is filed, the trustee in bankruptcy may prevent this creditor from receiving the assets and instead transfer them to another creditor.

Voivodeship In Poland, a political subdivision equivalent to a province.

Volatile Market A market with a great deal of price instability. Volatile markets are highly risky; for example, a security with a volatility of 50% is considered very high risk because it has the potential to increase or decrease by up to half its value.

Volatility A measure of a security's stability. It is calculated as the standard deviation from a certain continuously compounded return over a given period of time. It is an important measure in quantifying risk; for example, a security with a volatility of 50% is considered very high risk because it has the potential to increase or decrease up to half its value. Volatility may influence the type of investments one makes: one may directly invest in non-volatile securities, such as a certificate of deposit, but highly volatile securities lend themselves more to short selling and other forms of hedging.

Volatility Quote Trading A way to quote an option contract according to its volatility rather than its price. Option investors use volatility quote trading when they are more interested in the likelihood of contract increasing or decreasing in price rather than the price itself.

Volatility Swap A forward contract on the volatility of a security. The underlying of a volatility swap is usually the volatility of a currency. A volatility swap allows the investor to speculate on volatility, just as a trader might speculate on the price of a stock.

Volost In Imperial Russia, a political subdivision roughly equivalent to a county that was abolished in the 1920s after the rise of the Soviet Union.

Volume Counting On an exchange, the process of computing trade volume, that is, determining how many trades take place on a given trading day. In the United States, the SEC determines the methodology of volume counting. For example, if a broker orders 1,000 shares of a stock, it counts as 1,000 trades for purposes of volume counting. On the other hand, if a broker orders 1,000 shares from another firm, but the firm does not have 1,000 shares to sell, the firm buys them from another firm and immediately re-sells them to the broker. In this case, the SEC counts these transactions as 2,000 trades.

Volume Deleted On a ticker tape, an announcement that trading volume is so heavy that small trades (defined as those transactions under 5,000 or 10,000 shares) are not recorded. Tape with volume deleted also further abbreviates the abbreviations used to represent securities, volume, and price.

Volume Discount A decrease in the price for a product that occurs when the buyer acquires a particularly large quantity. A seller may offer a volume discount to entice buyers to conduct business with the seller. A volume discount reduces the profit that the seller makes on each, individual product, but it allows him/her to make a large sale quickly and receive the proceeds from it in short order.

Volume Index An index that measures the aggregate production of a given set of goods and services over a period of time. For example, a volume index may measure changes in the amount of refined oil, corn and automobiles. A volume index may be an indicator of an economy's direction. That is, if production is falling, it may portend an economic downturn.

Volume Merchandise Allowance A discount that a wholesale company offers to a retailer in exchange for a bulk sale. This benefits the retailer because of the lower price per unit, which can increase the retailer's profit. However, it also benefits the wholesaler because it encourages higher revenue through the sale of more units.

Volume Price Trend Indicator In technical analysis, an indicator that is calculated by taking the cumulative volume line and adding (or subtracting) a multiple of the percentages of the price change and volume change. The VPT is used to help determine the supply and demand for a security.

Volume Rate of Change The percentage change in trading volume of a security over a period of time. For example, if 10 million shares trade on Wednesday and only five million trade on Thursday, the volume rate of change is -50%. The volume rate of change may determine how likely a price trend is to be sustained; that is, the higher the volume is, the more likely it is that a price change will become a trend.

Volume Weighted Average Price The price of a security in which a higher trading volume affects the price more than a lower trading volume. It is calculated by dividing the dollar value of transactions by the average volume. It is sometimes used to determine the relative strength of a trend.

Voluntary Accidental Death and Dismemberment Insurance An insurance policy that provides coverage if the policyholder (or his/her dependent) dies as the result of a non-work related accident. It differs from regular accidental death insurance in that it is effectively a rider one purchases through an employer providing a death benefit in addition to the one one would have received from a policy the employer offers to all employees. One may pay premiums through paycheck deductions.

Voluntary Accumulation Plan An investment strategy in which shareholders of a mutual fund to buy more and more shares in the fund on a regular basis. It especially refers to situations in which a shareholder puts in a fixed amount of money on a regular basis, regardless of how many shares that amount buys. Generally speaking, this lowers the average price one pays per share. Thus, if one buys using a voluntary accumulation plan and later sells all shares at once, this could result in a higher profit. It is also called a contractual plan.

Voluntary Arrangement An agreement between a debtor and one or more creditors whereby the debtor repays according to a certain schedule arranged between all parties. A voluntary arrangement benefits creditors because it ensures that they are repaid. However, it also benefits the debtor because it keeps him/her out of bankruptcy.

Voluntary Bankruptcy A situation in which a debtor files for bankruptcy with a court. That is, no creditor forces the debtor into voluntary bankruptcy. A debtor may file for bankruptcy if it finds repaying its debts difficult or impossible. There are different kinds of voluntary bankruptcy. A company may file for liquidation, where a company ceases operations and sells its assets to repay creditors as far as possible. Likewise, a company may file a reorganization plan where some or all debts are forgiven and the company puts itself on a path toward solvency. See also: Chapter 7, Chapter 11, Chapter 13.

Voluntary Compensation Endorsement An addition to workers compensation insurance that provides the same coverage for partners, executives and other employees who ordinarily are not eligible for workers compensation. The policyholder pays an additional premium for this endorsement.

Voluntary Compliance 1. The principle that all taxpayer pay their taxes according to the law. That is, the IRS or other tax agency assumes that one has paid the appropriate amount of taxes unless something looks wrong on the tax return of the person or company. **2.** A situation in which a person or company complies with a government request before it becomes an order. Voluntary compliance gives the person or company more leeway in how strictly the request is enforced; it can also be a good public relations move. Perhaps most importantly, voluntary compliance does not create the precedent that a government can simply order the release of documents, records, or anything else.

Voluntary Conveyance 1. The sale of real estate without regard for its value. For example, one may voluntarily convey a house if one sells it for $1. Voluntary conveyance may be a form of fraud under some circumstances. **2.** A situation in which one gives real estate to the bank holding the mortgage on that real estate. Voluntary conveyance is done if the owner of the real estate can no longer make payments and wishes to avoid foreclosure.

Voluntary Deductible Employee Contribution Plan An optional, individual plan in which employees join a pension and pay the premiums by having their employer deduct a portion of their paycheck every month or pay period. The employer does not make any contributions to the plan and, as a result, employees may take the plan with them if they change jobs.

Voluntary Deferral Plan An employee retirement plan in which an employee may elect to place a portion of his/her wages or salary into an account. The money in this account is invested and distributed following retirement and the employee does not have to pay tax on this income until retirement. What distinguishes a voluntary deferral plan is the fact that it is not governed by the Employment Retirement Income Security Act. For that reason, the employer may choose which employees can participate in the voluntary deferral plan.

Voluntary Employees Beneficiary Association Also called a VEBA. A non-profit organization in the United States that administers employee benefits. Under the subsection, profits from a VEBA are tax free, provided employees are not required to join, members control the organization, earnings do not benefit any one member or group of members and the VEBA does not substantially engage in any activities other than administration of benefits.

Voluntary Exchange An agreement between two free individuals and/or organizations to buy, sell or trade a good or service. A voluntary exchange contrasts with an exchange that is mandated, for example, by a government. Voluntary exchanges are the basis of a free market economy.

Voluntary Export Restraint A situation in which one country agrees to restrict the export of one or more goods to another country. The voluntary export restraint allows a country to protect its internal market for the designated goods without erecting tariff or other trade barriers. A voluntary export restraint may be informal or it may be codified in a voluntary restraint agreement. It may or may not be reciprocal.

Voluntary Government Insurance A government social program with an option not to participate. For example, one may or may not elect to sign up for food stamps, even if one is eligible. In general, one must still pay for voluntary government insurance through one's taxes, whether or not one takes advantage of it.

Voluntary Import Expansion A change in a country's policies to allow more imports. Examples include lowering tariffs or dropping import quotas. Voluntary import expansion may occur as part of a trade agreement with another country, in which both partners move to expand imports, or it may be a result of international pressure. See also: Economic imperialism.

Voluntary Insurance Any insurance policy that an employee may elect to purchase if an employer does not pay for insurance or if the employee feels the employer-sponsored insurance does not provide sufficient coverage. The employee pays all premiums on his/her own (that is, without help from the employer). However, the employer may assist in payment by deducting contributions from the employee's paycheck every month or pay period. Voluntary insurance is particularly useful for small companies or for firms with many part-time employees, for whom employer-paid insurance may not be cost effective.

Voluntary Lien A consensual claim to the property of another as collateral to ensure the repayment of a debt. The lien is voluntary because the debtor agreed to it; the placement of a voluntary lien is often necessary in order to secure a loan. An example is the lien placed on real estate to guarantee a mortgage. A voluntary lien contrasts with an involuntary lien, which may be imposed by a court or other body for non-payment of a debt.

Voluntary Life Insurance A life insurance policy that an employee may elect to purchase if he/she feels the employer-sponsored insurance does not provide sufficient coverage. The employee pays all premiums on his/her own (that is, without help from the employer). The death benefit of a voluntary life insurance plan is usually expressed as a multiple of the employee's annual income. For example, the plan may pay three times the employee's final salary when he/she passes away.

Voluntary Liquidation The decision by shareholders in a publicly-traded company to cease operations, sell all assets, and use the proceeds to repay its creditors as far as possible. A voluntary liquidation differs from a bankruptcy, where the company files with a court without taking a vote of shareholders.

Voluntary Payroll Deduction Plan An optional, individual plan in which employees purchase life insurance and/or disability income insurance and pay the premiums by having their employer deduct a portion of their paycheck every month or pay period. The employer does not make any contributions to the plan and, as a result, employees may take the plan with them if they change jobs.

Voluntary Plan Termination The act in which an employer ceases to sponsor a pension plan for his/her employees. In the United States, a voluntary plan termination may occur at any time, but the employer is required to distribute employee contributions and any applicable gains according to the terms of the Employee Retirement Security Act.

Voluntary Redundancy Early retirement from a position when one's employer has offered sufficiently attractive retirement benefits. Employers typically offer voluntary redundancy when they are considering layoffs. A voluntary redundancy package is less expensive than keeping an employee on staff. It is also less traumatic to the employee because he/she comes to an agreement with the employer for the terms of the redundancy. The term is more common in Britain than in the United States.

Voluntary Reserve Money or other liquid assets a bank or insurance company puts aside over and above what regulators require. The voluntary reserve may exist to pay unforeseen liabilities or to make the bank or insurance company more fiscally sound. However, a company may keep a voluntary reserve to pay for expected, future liabilities such as dividends. The voluntary reserve is listed as a liability on the company's balance sheet.

Voluntary Restraint Agreement An agreement between two or more countries in which each limits exports to the other. While this reduces trade between the counties involved, it can help domestic industries and, in any event, can reduce tensions because fewer workers in the involved countries may be worried about outsourcing.

Voluntary Termination A situation in which a person quits his/her job. One may undergo voluntary termination for any number of reasons, including finding a better job, dissatisfaction with one's current position, or retirement.

Voluntary Trust A trust in which property is transferred to a beneficiary by a grantor who keeps legal title to the property. Despite this arrangement, the beneficiary has actual title and use of the property. See also: Revocable trust.

Voluntary Unemployment The number of persons in an economy without jobs because they choose to be unemployed. An example of a voluntarily unemployed person is one who rejects a position while looking for one with better pay or benefits. Most frictional unemployment (unemployment when one is between jobs) is considered voluntary because one is looking for work rather than taking any job one finds. See also: Involuntary unemployment.

Volunteer Income Tax Assistance An IRS program providing free tax advice and preparation to persons who make less than $49,000 per year or who are eligible for the earned income tax credit. The IRS recruits and trains volunteers each year to implement this program. Volunteer Income Tax Assistance was created in 1971.

Volunteer Protection Act of 1997 Legislation in the United States that protects volunteers at a nonprofit from legal liability for actions they take in good faith that unintentionally cause harm to another. For example, if a person volunteering at a homeless shelter unknowingly assigns a homeless person to a bunk that cannot hold his/her weight, the Act will protect the volunteer from liability in a resultant lawsuit if the bunk collapses. The Act was intended to promote volunteerism.

Voluntold A slang term for a situation in which an employer or manager requires an employee or subordinate to perform a task that is, in theory, voluntary.

Voodoo Accounting Any accounting system that uses unscrupulous methods, especially to please investors. For example, voodoo accounting may inflate profits by transferring funds to an off-the-books account set aside just for that purpose. It may also hide losses in subsidiaries or do other things to misrepresent a company's financial state. In the early 2000s, voodoo accounting came into focus in the United States when it was revealed that Enron and several other companies were using the practice. See also: Sarbanes-Oxley Act of 2002.

Voodoo Economics A derogatory term for supply-side economics, which is a macroeconomic theory stating that a government can best promote growth by providing incentives for persons to produce goods and services. The primary way a supply-side oriented government does this is by maintaining low tax rates so that investors and entrepreneurs may use their money for production. Maintaining low tax rates on the wealthy is one of the most important and controversial aspects of supply-side economics; the theory states that well off persons have the capital available to produce goods and services and thereby create jobs and grow the economy. Critics contend that this does not happen in reality, and that the wealthy are more likely to keep, rather than invest, their money. It is also known as Reaganomics, and acquired the name because it was crucial to the economic policies of the administration of U.S. President Ronald Reagan. See also: Keynesian economics, Monetarism, Trickle-down economics.

Vostro Account An account that a bank holds on behalf of another bank in another country. The term is most common in the United States and the United Kingdom.

Vote To make a choice along with other parties asked to make the same choice. In business and finance, voting is most often associated with electing directors and setting company policies at the annual meeting of shareholders. In order to be able to vote under these circumstances, one must hold voting stock. The right to vote gives the holder of voting stock a great deal of control over the company. In democratic forms of government, voters elect politicians, who may promote certain business or financial policies as part of their platform. In turn, bodies of elected politicians often vote on proposed policies or programs.

Voting Instruction Card A certificate issued by a voting trust to common shareholders. The voting instruction card is given in exchange for common stock and gives the shareholder every right associated with the common share except voting rights. Specifically and perhaps most importantly, the shareholder continues to receive dividends. A voting trust receives the voting rights (and legal title) to the common stock for a set period of time in order to combine the voting power of common shareholders who set up the voting trust.

Voting Right The right of some shareholders to participate in the company's decision making process, especially at the annual meeting or at other special meetings. Some decisions, such as friendly takeovers or whether to make a new issue, must be put to shareholder votes, though the list of what decisions are included varies by company. Because voting rights give these shareholders the most control over the company, other shareholders are compensated with benefits, such as guaranteed dividends. See also: Voting stock.

Voting Stock Stock in a publicly-traded company that gives the holder the right to vote at the company's annual meeting. Votes are usually allocated on the basis of one vote per share. The right to vote gives the holder of voting stock a great deal of control over the company; in exchange, voting stock usually has few or no other rights associated with it. For example, most preferred stock is nonvoting, but preferred stock has a guaranteed dividend while most voting stock does not.

Voting Trust A trust that common shareholders create in order to combine their votes at the annual meeting. Each shareholder transfers his/her voting rights to the trust, while retaining title to the dividends and other rights associated with the stock. The voting trust receives legal title to the common stock and issues voting trust certificates, representing the other rights of common stock, to shareholders. The voting trust uses these shares to vote as a block. This gives participating shareholders a degree of control over the company that they would not otherwise have. Typically, a voting trust can only exist for a certain period of time, depending on the laws of the state in which the company is incorporated.

Voting Trust Agreement A contract creating a trust through common shareholders in order to combine their votes at the annual meeting. Each shareholder transfers his/her voting rights to the trust while keeping title to the dividends and other rights associated with the stock. The voting trust receives legal title to the common stock and issues voting trust certificates, representing the other rights of common stock, to shareholders. The voting trust uses these shares to vote as a block. This gives participating shareholders a degree of control over the company they would not otherwise have. Generally speaking, a voting trust can only exist for a certain period of time, depending on the laws of the state in which the company is incorporated.

Voting Trust Certificate A certificate issued by a voting trust to common shareholders. The voting trust certificate is given in exchange for common stock and gives the shareholder every right associated with the common share except voting rights. Specifically, and perhaps most importantly, the shareholder continues to receive dividends. A voting trust receives the voting rights (and legal title) to the common stock for a set period of time in order to combine the voting power of the common shareholders who set up the voting trust.

Voucher A document entitling the holder to some payment. For example, one may be provided with a voucher for a discount on some product a company sells. Likewise, one may have a voucher for a rebate on a product already purchased.

Vouchers have entered political discussions as well, with some advocating the provision of vouchers to local taxpayers, which may be used to finance education at a private school.

Voucher Check A check with a perforated or other attachment indicating the reason for and the amount of the check. The voucher allows one to keep records of one's checks after they are deposited. This is important for balancing one's checkbook.

Voucher Register Any organized list of vouchers.

Voucher System A system in which a receipt representing monetary value is issued, but can only be spent on certain items. For example, a charity may use a voucher system to provide assistance in paying recipients' utility bills. The vouchers may be redeemed for credit at the utility company but they may not be used for other purposes like groceries or rent. Likewise, in an educational voucher system, parents could use a receipt representing a portion of tax money to pay tuition at a private school.

Vouching In accounting, the act or process of testing the accuracy of a statement by checking supporting documentation.

Voyage Policy In shipping, an insurance policy that provides coverage for the entirety of the voyage (rather than a stated period of time). A voyage policy usually covers damage or loss to the cargo, but not to the ship.

V-Shaped Recovery A situation in which an economy enters a steep recession but quickly and strongly recovers. A V-shaped recovery may be bullish and lead to GDP growth and job creation, but it may be risky because of the possibility that another steep decline could occur. See also: W-type bottom, V-Bottom, W-shaped recovery.

VT100 An early computer video terminal. Its technical aspects became standard for later models. It was introduced in 1978 and replaced by the VT200 in 1983.

Vubicle In an office setting, a slang term for a cubicle with a window. In a drab and undifferentiated office, a vubicle may be highly desirable.

Vulture Capitalist 1. An investor who buys companies in or near bankruptcy in order to save them. 2. An investor who buys the rights to a new product or invention in order to profit from its sale. The term is somewhat derogatory as vulture capitalists deprive inventors of the money they would make otherwise. However, vulture capitalists may be in a better position to market these new products than the inventors themselves. See also: Vulture fund, Venture capital.

Vulture Fund A mutual fund that invests predominately or exclusively in high risk stock and high-yield debt. That is, a vulture fund invests in companies that are in or near bankruptcy. The idea behind a vulture fund is to buy securities at low prices and to earn an extraordinarily high return, even if it forces a company to do things against its best interest. For example, some vulture funds may force a company to repay debt when the company would be better served by declaring bankruptcy and not paying. As a result, the term is somewhat derogatory. See also: Vulture Capitalist.

Vulture Investor 1. In venture capital, an investor who buys a company with an excessive amount of debt in the hopes that streamlining and reorganization will make the company profitable. Vultures engage in a high risk, high reward type of investment. 2. An investor who buys an invention from the inventor. The term in this sense is slightly derogatory, as the vulture investor usually profits from the invention while the investor does not.

VUT GOST 7.67 Latin three-letter geocode for Vanuatu. The code is used for transactions to and from Vanuatuan bank accounts and for international shipping to Vanuatu. As with all GOST 7.67 codes, it is used primarily in Cyrillic alphabets.

VUV ISO 4217 code for the Vanuatu vatu. It was introduced when Vanuatu became independent in 1982, replacing the New Hebrides franc and the Australian dollar. Interestingly, it has no subdivisions; as a result, large transactions are sometimes quoted in "dollars," though the currency has no current relationship to the Australian dollar.

VXN The volatility of an index option in which the underlying index is the NASDAQ 100, also called an NPX option. It is calculated by taking into account near-the-money NPX calls and puts.

W A symbol appearing next to a security listed on NASDAQ indicating that the security is a warrant. All NASDAQ listings use a four-letter abbreviation; if a "W" follows the abbreviation, this indicates that the security being traded is a warrant.

W Formation In technical analysis, a price trend characterized by a sharp fall, then a sharp rise, then a second sharp fall, and finally a second sharp rise. It is called a W formation because the series of rises and falls vaguely looks like the letter W. Technical analysts may consider a W formation a buy signal if the second sharp rises outpaces the two previous price highs.

W-2 Form A form that an employer provides an employee each year indicating the employee's wages, salary, and/or tips and the amount of tax withheld over the course of the year. This helps the employee calculate his/her income tax liability. The W-2 form is the most common tax form in the United States, and every employer is required to provide it to every employee. See also: W-4 Form.

W-4 A form that employees fill out when starting a job in the United States. The form calculates the tax withholding from an employee's paychecks, depending on the number of persons in his/her household and the employee's expected filing status for that year. The W-4 form does not determine one's tax liability; one may receive a refund (or be required to pay extra) depending on his/her specific deductions, credits and income.

W-8 A form that must be filed with the IRS guaranteeing that a person is a nonresident alien, and, as such, is not subject to U.S. taxation. One must file a W-8 whether the person involved is an employee or an investor.

W-9 A form filed with the IRS stating a person or company's Social Security number or Tax Identification Number, and listing all the income that the filer has paid to the person or company he/she regard. This income may be ordinary income, dividends, or something else. The W-9 form states that the person or company is not subject to withholding. That is, it states that the party making payments is not responsible for withholding income for taxes, and places the onus on the person or company the form regards. W-9 forms are frequently used for independent contractors.

Wafer Seal A small adhesive, shaped like a wafer, that holds the pages of a magazine or other periodical together when it is sent in the mail. A wafer seal may also be placed on an envelope. Its purpose is to ensure that one does not read the enclosed material without leaving evidence of doing so. It is also called a mailing tab.

Waffle A mechanized process that destroys old or defaced coins. A waffle scratches a coin so that it can no longer be recognized. The former coin is demonetized and may then be sold as scrap metal.

Wage An amount of money paid each hour to compensate an employee for the amount of time he/she spends working. Wages are paid for both skilled and unskilled labor. For example, one may pay an employee $8 per hour for working at a fast food restaurant or $45 per hour for highly trained work at a car factory. What distinguishes wages from salaries is the fact that wages are only paid for the hours worked; an employee is paid more if he works for more hours. Salaries, on the other hand, are the same whether one works five hours or 50. See also: Overtime, Minimum Wage.

Wage and Salary Administration A department or subset of a department in a company that sets wages and salaries for employees. The wage and salary administration may use a variety of factors, including the company budget and the amount that competitors pay, in making its decisions.

Wage and Salary Survey A survey of employers in the same industry and the same area showing the wages and salaries they pay to their employees. Wage and salary surveys are useful because they show the prevailing compensation in a given city or other place, which may result in employers making upward or downward adjustments.

Wage Assignment A voluntary deduction from a person's paycheck. One may contribute to a retirement account, repay a debt, or make any number of other payments through wage assignment. It contrasts with wage garnishment (which is done for taxes or child support, for example) because it is voluntary.

Wage Bracket The range of potential wages a company offers to a person with a given job description. One's individual wage depends on education, experience, and even one's negotiating skills.

Wage Ceiling The highest possible wage within a wage bracket, which is the range of potential wages offered to a person with a given job description. For example, if a wage bracket is $12 to $15 per hour, the wage ceiling is $15.

Wage Control A government regulation limiting the percentage (or, rarely, the dollar amount) by which a wage or salary can increase in a given year. Wage control generally is practiced only during national emergencies, or when inflation is particularly high. Wage controls were attempted during the 1970s in the United States and the United Kingdom, but were unsuccessful in curbing inflation.

Wage Differential The difference in wage or salary between two employees of different classes who perform the same work. Examples of classes include age, gender, race, religion or even union and non-union membership. Wage differentials may be legal in some circumstances, but are generally illegal when based on gender, ethnicity, sexual orientation and similar classes.

Wage Drift The amount by which the wage or salary of a worker or group of workers exceeds a previously negotiated agreement. Wage drift may occur, for example, if an employee is asked to work unexpected overtime or if persons in a region are offered wages higher than the national rate during a labor shortage.

Wage Flexibility The extent to which wages and salaries can rise or fall due to rising or falling profits. That is, a company or economy has wage flexibility if, when times are good, it provides employees raises but has the ability to impose cuts when times are difficult. Proponents of wage flexibility contend that it leads to lower unemployment because employers can cut wages instead of jobs. Critics, however, contend that it leads to lower financial security among workers.

Wage Floor The lowest possible wage within a wage bracket, which is the range of potential wages offered to a person with a given job description. For example, if a wage bracket is $12 to $15 per hour, the wage floor is $12.

Wage Freeze 1. A policy in which a company refuses to raise wages and salaries for a period of time. A wage freeze is usually instituted when a company is having a difficult time financially and wishes to avoid layoffs or other cutbacks. **2.** A policy in which a government forbids or severely restricts rises in wages and salaries for a period of time. A wage freeze is usually instituted to combat inflation, but the policy often does not have its intended effect.

Wage Incentive A policy in which a company pays a higher wage in exchange for greater productivity. For example, a company may pay $10 per hour most of the time, but if a worker's output exceeds a certain level, he/she may receive a temporary raise to $12 for as long as that level of productivity lasts. See also: Bonus.

Wage Index In the United States, a table one uses to calculate how much to pay a retired person in Social Security benefits. Factors affecting a wage index include the number of years a person worked and his/her average wage or salary during his/her working life.

Wage Protection Laws Laws at the state or federal level protecting an employee's right to be paid. Examples of wage protection laws include minimum wage statutes, laws protecting vacation pay and laws that put employee wages ahead of other creditors if the company goes bankrupt. Wage protection laws are often controversial.

Wage Resistance Opposition to reductions in wages or salaries. Employees apply wage resistance out of self-interest. Employers often try to avoid cuts, whether for personal or practical reasons. Wage resistance comes to the forefront in union negotiations or when a company is facing losses or lower profits.

Wage Restraint An agreement between an employee and an employer not to demand wage or salary increases. Wage restraint may occur when a company is facing losses or lower profits and needs to live within its means. The employee may receive concessions (such as better health insurance) in exchange for wage restraint.

Wage Rigidity The general difficulty a company experiences in trying to reduce wages. Whether because of a labor agreement, fears for lost productivity or other reasons, companies often find it hard to reduce employee wages or salaries. For this reason, many (though far from all) companies elect to conduct layoffs rather than wage reductions when facing losses or lower profits. See also: Wage resistance.

Wage Round A periodic negotiation for pay rates between a company and its employees, especially if those employees are unionized. Wage rounds set how employee pay is to be determined until the next round.

Wage Scale The range of wages paid to employees in a certain company, organization, or locality. The relevant authority often publishes a wage scale so current and potential employees know how much they may be paid for performing certain jobs.

Wage Stabilization During a period of high inflation, the system of policies a government uses to prevent wages from increasing. A government may adopt a wage freeze, in which it simply forbids wage and salary increases. Because this does not attack underlying inflation, the most effective method of wage stabilization is to reduce currency in circulation, specifically by raising key interest rates.

Wage Tax 1. Any tax deducted from one's paycheck automatically. Most income taxes for employees come from wage taxes. See also: FICA. **2.** A local tax on one's wage or salary directly. For example, a township may elect to take $50 from every $1,500 one makes in wages or salary in that township.

Wage-Price Spiral The phenomenon in which prices for goods and services rise, which causes employees to demand higher wages. This added expense on business causes higher prices, which leads to still higher wages, and so forth. The wage-price spiral is alternately described as a cause or a symptom of inflation, depending on one's economic philosophy.

Wage-Push Inflation Inflation caused by increased costs as a result of higher wages. To give an extreme example, suppose a state raises its minimum wage from $5 per hour to $30 per hour. In order to be able to pay workers, an employer is forced to significantly increase the prices on his/her products. This in turn makes goods and services more expensive, and the $30 per hour suddenly lacks the purchasing power it had when the minimum wage was $5 per hour. Soon, it is no longer sufficient to purchase necessary goods and services and the minimum wage must be raised again. The cycle starts over, creating an inflation spiral.

Wagering v. Insurance The difference between gambling and insurance lies in the nature of the risk involved. In gambling, no risk exists before a wager occurs. Thus, gain or loss depends on one's decision. In insurance, risk pre-exists the contract. The possibility of loss therefore is not a choice; insurance simply attempts to mitigate it.

Wages Council One of a number of boards in the United Kingdom that formerly set minimum wages. One wages council existed for each low-pay industry and each had the authority to raise or lower the minimum wage for that industry. Most wage councils were abolished in the early 1990s. In the late 1990s, the National Minimum Wage was passed, eliminating the need for the councils.

Wait Order A request by an advertiser to a periodical to refrain from running an ad it has already produced and paid for until it receives some further confirmation. For example, a winter coat company may issue a wait order during an unseasonably warm period because it would be more beneficial to advertise coats when the weather is cold.

Waiting for the Other Shoe to Drop The act or process of waiting for an impending decision or announcement. For example, an investor may wait for the other shoe to drop if he waits for an earnings announcement before deciding to buy.

Waiver A statement of the voluntary surrender of a right. For example, suppose a company provides customers a service that might be dangerous, such as bungee jumping. The company may require customers to sign a waiver relinquishing the right to sue the company for negligence if a problem occurs. This reduces the company's risk in the conduct of its business.

Waiver of Coinsurance Clause A clause in a property insurance contract relinquishing the normal requirement that the policyholder pay some coinsurance, which is a type of payment the policyholder must make along with the insurer if an insured event occurs. The policyholder may be required to pay a higher premium for this waiver.

Waiver of Demand An agreement by a check depositor to be responsible without any notice if the check defaults or bounces.

Waiver of Exemption A clause in a credit card or other lending agreement stating that the creditor may seize certain assets of the debtor in the event of default, even if local law ordinarily exempts such assets from seizure. Waivers of exemption reduced the risk to the creditor, but were considered unfair to the debtor. As a result, the Federal Trade Commission does not permit them to be used.

Waiver of Notice 1. A bank's relinquishment of the right to be notified formally when it presents a bill to the Federal Reserve. Endorsing the bill is considered, on its own, waiver of notice. **2.** See: Waiver of demand.

Waiver of Premium An agreement between an insurance company and a policyholder allowing the policyholder not to pay premiums if he/she is seriously injured, ill or disabled. In general, the policyholder must pay a one-time fee for the insurer to include a waiver of premium clause in a policy.

Waiver of Premium Disability Claim A claim a policyholder makes to an insurer to activate a waiver of premium rider, which is an agreement with the insurer allowing the policyholder not to pay premiums if he/she is seriously injured, ill or disabled. In general, the policyholder must pay a one-time fee for the insurer to include a waiver of premium clause in a policy.

Waiver of Premium for Payer Benefit An agreement between an insurance company and the payer on a policy allowing the policyholder not to pay premiums if he/she becomes disabled or dies. This is used if the policyholder is a child but an adult (such as a parent) actually pays the premiums. In general, one must pay a one-time fee for the insurer to include a waiver of premium clause in a policy.

Waiver of Restoration Premium An agreement between an insurer and a policyholder for a liability policy exempting the policyholder from a restoration premium. A restoration premium is an amount of money the policyholder must pay to re-activate a policy after a claim is paid. The waiver ensures that the restoration premium does not need to be paid.

Wales Office A department of the British government responsible for the administration of devolution of power from the central government to the Welsh regional government. The office represents Welsh interests in the government. It was established in 2003.

Walid Chammah A Lebanese banker. He joined Morgan Stanley in 1993, becoming head of investment banking in 2005 and co-president of the company in 2007. In late 2009, he became chairman of Morgan Stanley.

Walk Away Describing a lease where the lessee must return the asset at the end of the lease's term. A walk away lease gives a great deal of flexibility to the lessee because the costs are all known in advance; likewise, the lessee does not need to predict the fair market value of the asset because he/she will not possess it. The lessor carries all risk. A walk away lease is most common with car loans. It is also called a closed-end lease.

Walk-In A client who arrives at a brokerage without appointment or a personal relationship with one of the brokers. A walk-in is usually assigned a broker at random unless he/she requests someone specific.

Walking Figures In auto sales, a situation in which a potential customer tells a salesperson that he/she wishes to look at some other dealerships. The salesperson will respond by quoting an impossibly low sales price for a vehicle. The intent of walking figures is to encourage the customer to come back to that dealership, at which time the salesperson will quote the real price.

Walking Liberty Half Dollar A silver coin minted by the United States between 1916 and 1947. It was worth 1/2 of one dollar.

Walkout The act in which all the employees of a company leave the workplace and refuse to work any longer that day. A walkout is a type of protest for better wages, benefits or other demands. It may be sustained (and therefore part of a strike) or it may be a one-off event.

Walk-Through Test In an audit, a procedure in which the auditor looks at each step taken when accounting for an item from the beginning until the end. The walk-through test looks at the adequacy of the accounting system used.

Wall Banner In advertising, a poster affixed to a wall. A wall banner is most useful for small-scale events or businesses because it likely will be seen by relatively few people. See also: Billboard.

Wall of Worry Informal; a market uptrend that occurs when there is significant uncertainty about its sustainability. For example, if the market is concerned about potential, new regulations or the possibility of recession but stocks increase anyway, this is called climbing a wall of worry. Price correction often follows a wall of worry.

Wall Street A street in New York City that forms the center of its financial district. The NYSE, NASDAQ, and American Stock Exchange, among others, are headquartered on Wall Street. Additionally, several investment companies maintain their primary offices on or near Wall Street. Because of its influence on the wider financial world, Wall Street is often used as a byword for the financial industry in the United States and its lobbyists. In this sense, Wall Street is important to political discourse in the United States. The sheer amount of money traded on Wall Street render it vitally important to the global economy as well.

Wall Street Week A television show that aired on PBS between 1970 and 2005. The show summarized stock market performance for the week and featured a panel that made recommendations for the coming week. Panelists routinely made predictions for future market movements. It was the first major show of its type and, at its peak, was one of the most followed programs for investment advice. See also: Elves, Wall Street Week Index, Elves Index.

Wall Street Week Index An index featured on the television program Wall Street Week, which aired between 1970 and 2005. The index consisted of 10 technical indicators, each of which was assigned a value of +1, 0 or -1, depending on whether the indicator was bullish, neutral or bearish. The index was relatively accurate over time and was well regarded for its usefulness. The index was used from the show's inception in 1970 until 1989.

Wallet Share The amount that a customer spends at a company, especially when compared to the amount spent by the same customer at other times. For example, if a customer spent $12,000 in 2010 and $15,000 in 2011, a company may be said to have increased its wallet share for that customer by $3,000.

Wallpaper A security that has become worthless due to a bankruptcy or for some other reason. For example, when General Motors went into bankruptcy in 2009, its stock continued to be traded over-the-counter. However, because there was very little value to the company, it was treated as wallpaper. That is, the owners of GM stock might as well use the certificates as wallpaper in their houses because the stock was worth nothing.

Wallpaper a Meeting Slang; to populate a business meeting with persons likely to agree with one's position. One may wallpaper a meeting, for example, to bully a minority of members of the board of directors into accepting a certain point of view.

Wal-Mart A very large discount retail store chain. Wal-Mart is one of the largest corporations in the world. The first Wal-Mart was established in 1962. It was one of the first companies to practice the just-in-time supply chain management system in order to reduce costs to a minimum. Wal-Mart's founder, Sam Walton, was one of the first retailers to always buy from the lowest priced wholesaler; this drove sales higher, which allowed Wal-Mart to negotiate still lower prices from wholesalers. This practice, while controversial, became a staple of Wal-Mart. It is based in Bentonville, Arkansas.

Walras' Law The principle that, if all markets for all goods and services in an economy are balanced, then the market for a specific good or service must also be balanced. Walras' law is based on the idea that excess demand and supply in an economy must add to zero. Thus, if there is no excess demand or supply elsewhere in an economy, then there can be no excess in a given market. Walras' law contradicts the Keynesian notion that involuntary unemployment can exist when an economy is otherwise in equilibrium because, according to the law, the labor market must itself be balanced. Critics of the law maintain that it does not consider financial markets and their effect on the markets for goods and services.

Walt Disney An American entertainer and businessman. In 1923, he co-founded an animation studio with his brother, Roy. The company expanded to other media, including film, television and theme parks. Disney created Mickey Mouse, Donald Duck and other iconic fictional characters. The Walt Disney Company (as the studio was renamed) became a hugely successful corporation. Disney lived from 1901 to 1966.

Wanted for Cash A notice or statement on a ticker stating that an investor wishes to buy a security for same-day settlement. That is, a wanted for cash indication means that the investor wishes to pay for and receive delivery of the security on the same day.

War Babies Informal; a term for securities in the defense industry. Examples of war babies include stocks in arms manufacturers or ship-building companies. In or immediately before wartime, war babies tend to be market outperforms.

War Bond In the United States, a formerly-issued savings bond, exempt from state and local taxes, with a fixed interest rate. These bonds were sold at three-fourths of face value and paid par upon maturity, which was originally 10 years, but later became 30 or 40 years. They began to be issued to help finance American involvement in World War II but they continued to be issued thereafter. They were non-transferable and must either have been held or redeemed. They were known formally as series E bonds. In 1980, the government stopped issuing war bonds and replaced them with Series EE bonds. For a time, war bonds were exchangeable for Series H or Series HH bonds, but this is no longer the case.

War Chest Informal; money a corporation sets aside to pay for or defend against a hostile takeover. A war chest is highly liquid, and while it can cut into short-term profits, it may open up investment opportunities for the long-term. The term is commonly used in journalism.

War Damage Corporation A state-sponsored corporation in the United States that provided coverage for damage to property in the mainland United States due to attacks by the enemy during World War II. The War Damage Corporation was extremely profitable for the U.S. government because the mainland United States did not experience major attacks during the war.

War Exclusion Clause 1. A clause in some life insurance policies stating that the insurer does not have to pay the death benefit if the insured dies from a war-related injury. War exclusion clauses are most common in wartime; they generally cannot be added if a war starts after a policy is issued. **2.** A clause in some bills of lading and other transport documents exempting the insurer from paying losses if a ship is damaged or destroyed as the result of an act of war. For example, if a torpedo fires on a ship as part of a declaration of war or other hostile act, the war exclusion clause protects the insurer from covering the value.

War Nickel A five-cent coin manufactured in the United States during World War II. The war nickel eliminated the use of real nickel in the coin, replacing it with silver, manganese, and copper. This was done because nickel was considered an important commodity for the war effort. It no longer circulates, but is more valuable than its face value due to the silver content.

War Profits Tax A tax on industries that do especially well during wartime. For example, a war profits tax may be imposed on armaments manufacturers. In general, war profits taxes are implemented only during war, and are used to finance the war.

War Rate The higher premium that an insurer charges a policyholder who is exposed to a warzone or other high-risk area. The war rate pays for the increased likelihood that the insurer will have to pay a claim. See also: War Risk.

War Risk The likelihood that a person or property will be injured, killed or destroyed in an act of war. For example, if an employee is transporting goods in a truck to a customer, war risk is the possibility he/she may drive over a landmine, killing himself/herself and destroying the goods. War risk is a type of political risk and is often excluded from insurance policies.

War Risk Insurance An insurance policy covering risk from war, terrorism, coups or other armed conflict in the country in which the covered party does business. War risk insurance takes two forms: war risk liability, covering employees, customers, and other persons and their effects, and war risk utility, covering property. For example, a company may take out war risk insurance protecting a luxury passenger ship from an act of terrorism while at sea. The war risk liability covers the persons on a cruise and their luggage while war liability utility protects the ship itself. See also: Political risk.

War/Strike Clause A clause in an insurance contract providing coverage for a loss that occurs due to an act of war, a strike (when employees refuse to show up to work) and some other forms of civil strife. Many insurance contracts do not provide coverage for these events, but a war/strike clause reduces the risk of a loss due to war by increasing the number of covered events. See also: Force majeure risk.

Ward A subdivision used in local governments in a number of countries. Wards are sometimes the constituencies for local, elected officials. They are often equivalent to a neighborhood or a portion of county.

Warehouse A building in which goods are stored, especially in large quantities and for commercial purposes. Warehouses may be used to store imports before they are distributed, commodities whose contracts are being traded, goods intended for retail sale, and many other purposes. Goods stored in warehouses may be owned by a company and sold to another for resale. Warehousing is an important part of many supply chains. See also: Wholesale.

Warehouse Club A retail store where one may buy goods at or close to wholesale prices. Warehouse clubs are often actual warehouses (or are at least made to look like them); they have little decoration and goods are stored and sold in large quantities. Many warehouse clubs require annual membership fees, which help to keep prices low. They began in their modern form in the 1970s but have their origins in other discount stores.

Warehouse Entry The entry of bonded goods into a country. Bonded goods are stored in a location where they may be kept without payment of tariffs or other duties for a certain period of time. Warehouse entry allows goods to be kept in a place where they may be cleaned, repackaged or even completed. Upon being granted warehouse entry, importers have a given period of time (such as five years) to pay the tariffs and remove the bonded goods. See also: Bonded warehouse.

Warehouse Financing A loan or line of credit available to a business secured by raw materials held in a warehouse. The materials may be held in a place designated by the lender or in the borrower's own warehouse (provided it is managed by a third party). The business places these materials as collateral in exchange for an operating loan. Repayment may be flexible in warehouse financing as it may be tied to the rate at which the borrower uses the raw material to make a finished product. See also: Inventory financing.

Warehouse to Warehouse An insurance policy providing coverage during the transport of a good from one warehouse to another. That is, the policy becomes effective the moment the good leaves the premises of the first warehouse and ends when it enters the second. As with all insurance, the policyholder must pay a premium to receive the coverage.

Warehousers Liability Form An insurance policy that provides coverage to owners and operators of warehouses for legal liability for goods that may break or be destroyed while in their care. That is, if a good breaks while in a warehouse and the warehouser is deemed to be at fault, a warehousers liability form protects him/her from paying to replace the good. As with all insurance, one must pay a premium to receive the coverage.

Warehousing 1. The act or process of storing inventory for sale in the future. **2.** The act or practice of a company gradually buying the stock of another company it later intends to acquire. It need not register its warehousing with the SEC until it has bought a certain percentage of shares outstanding. See also: Accumulation, Significant order.

Wares An informal word for goods for sale.

Warm Card A bank card that may only be used for certain transactions. For example, a warm card may permit one to make a withdrawal from an ATM but may not be used for purchases. Likewise, some warm cards allow a company to make deposits but not withdrawal at an ATM, so any employee may deposit daily revenue without the risk of theft.

Warm Color Colors related to red and yellow. Examples include pink and orange. Warm colors may be used in advertising and marketing to provoke feelings of vitality, sexuality and/or excitement.

Warm-Up An act or skit before the recording of a television or radio show to make the audience comfortable and to make it more likely to respond well to the television or radio show as it is being recorded. A warm-up usually involves one or more persons from the show telling jokes, answering questions and explaining how the production works. Warm-ups are intended to make the live audience more responsive, which in turn makes the television or radio audience more responsive. This helps marketing because it helps increase the number of viewers or listeners, which allows the show to charge more for advertising.

Warrant A certificate, usually issued with a preferred stock, giving the holder the option of buying an underlying asset, in this case usually more stock, at a certain strike price. The strike price is usually higher than the market value of the underlying asset at the time of issue but lower than the expected market value at some point in the future. Some warrants expire a few years after issuance, but perpetual warrants can theoretically last forever. Unlike options, stock warrants are issued by companies during a round of financing, rather than by an individual investor or brokerage. Companies issue stock warrants to attract investors who might not otherwise be interested.

Warrant Agreement A statement governing a warrant issue. A warrant is a document attached to a security giving the holder the right to buy more shares of the same security at a certain price on a certain date. Because each warrant is different, the terms in a warrant agreement are vitally important for determining the warrant's value.

Warrant Coverage A situation in which a company attaches to its stock a percentage of the dollar amount of one's investment in the form of more shares. For example, a person who buys 100 shares at $X per share may receive warrant coverage for a 10%of X, which allows the investor, if he/she desires, to buy 10 more shares at $X. A company may issue warrant coverage as a form of preemptive dilution protection: if it intends to issue more shares, it may issue warrant coverage to existing investors to protect their percentages of ownership up to a certain amount. It does not protect investors from downtrends in the stock, but does protect them from missing out on uptrends. See also: Cum warrant.

Warrant Leverage Ratio A measure of the sensitivity of the price of a warrant to a change in the price of the underlying security. A high warrant leverage ratio indicates that the price changes significantly when the price of the underlying security changes. Therefore, investing in the warrant carries high risk and the possibility of a high return.

Warrant Premium The amount by which the price of a warrant exceeds the value of its underlying stock. A warrant is a document attached to a security giving the holder the right to buy more shares of the same security at a certain price on a certain date. If, for example, a warrant allows one to buy 10 shares at $5 each (for a total of $50) but the warrant is trading at $60, the warrant premium is $10. The warrant premium usually declines as the warrant approaches its expiration date.

Warranted Growth Rate In the Harrod-Domar model, the growth rate at which an economy will neither expand unsustainably nor go into recession. The warranted growth rate is equal to the savings rate of the economy divided by its capital output ratio. In order to be true, the savings rate is assumed to be a constant proportion of national income and the capital output ratio is derived in part from the investment rate, which is also assumed to be a proportion of the national income.

Warranty A guarantee that the manufacturer of a product will repair damage or defects for free for a certain period of time. For example, a computer often comes with a warranty for a year. If the computer breaks in the first year of ownership, the manufacturer will repair or replace it without cost to the computer owner. Most warranties are limited warranties, meaning that there is a maximum amount the manufacturer will pay for repairs and/or that certain damage is not covered by the warranty. For example, a warranty on a computer generally does not cover water damage. Some warranties come with a product while others are purchased separately. Often, one may purchase an unlimited warranty, which has no constraints, or an extended warranty, which has a longer expiry, in addition to the ordinary warranty.

Warranty Deed In real estate, a deed providing a number of guarantees from a seller to a buyer. A warranty deed contains the promise that the seller's title is legitimate and no non-disclosed encumbrances exist. It may be passed to the buyer (and the buyer may in turn pass it to someone else). Generally, it also contains the promises that the seller will resolve any remaining problems and he/she will come to the buyer's aid if a competing claim is made. See also: Title search, Clear title, Quitclaim deed.

Warranty of Habitability The guarantee by a landlord that one may safely live in a residence. For example, a warranty of habitability implies that the landlord must provide a structurally sound residence with suitable drinking water, locks on the doors, and so forth. A warranty of habitability is implied in a lease; depending on the jurisdiction, if a landlord does not live up to the warrant, a tenant may withhold rent, refuse to pay rent, or even break the lease and move out.

Warranty of Merchantability A guarantee by a seller that a good or service reasonably meets the buyer's expectations. For example, if one buys a telephone, the warranty of merchantability requires the seller to ensure that the phone is able to make and receive calls. The warranty of merchantability is implied unless the seller specifically states otherwise. See also: Caveat emptor.

Warren Buffett An American investor and businessman. In 1962, Buffett began buying shares in Berkshire Hathaway, eventually taking a controlling stake in the company. He expanded Berkshire Hathaway's business into insurance and used the proceeds to finance other investments. These investments turned Buffett into a billionaire in 1990. In 2008, he was the richest man in the world, but dropped to second place in 2009. Nicknamed the "Oracle of Omaha," Buffett is a major proponent of value investing, which holds that it is better to invest in companies based on their intrinsic values rather than their technical information. This philosophy generally has been highly profitable for Buffett. Between 2000 and 2010, under Buffett's guidance, Berkshire Hathaway returned 76% to shareholders.

Warsaw Convention An international agreement regulating legal liability for passengers, luggage and cargo traveling by air. The Warsaw Convention denotes liability limits in French francs (which are obsolete) and Special Drawing Rights (which are not). It set a two-year limit for a passenger to make a claim against an airline and requires airlines to issue tickets for passengers and checked luggage. The Convention was signed in 1929 and has been amended a few times since.

Warsaw Pact A military pact between the Soviet Union and a number of Eastern European countries that existed between 1955 and 1991. Members of the Warsaw Pact pledged mutual defense. It was established in response to the formation of NATO and was a key alliance during the Cold War.

Warsaw Stock Exchange A major stock exchange in Poland. It was established in 1991 after the fall of Communism. Upon its establishment, only five stocks were listed. It grew by leaps and bounds in the 1990s and, in 2008, it was designated as an "advanced market" by FTSE.

Wash A situation in which the profit on one activity or investment equals the loss on another. When an investment is a wash, it is said to break even.

Wash Sale 1. An illegal act in which an investor buys and sells the same security at the exact same time, especially through two different brokerages. This results in neither profit nor loss for the investor, but creates the impression that the security is undergoing heavy trading, which could drive up the price or generate unwarranted interest. **2.** An illegal act in which an investor takes essentially the same position as one he/she closed at a loss less than 30 days earlier. Wash sales are intended to provide the investor with a write-off (through the loss) without fundamentally changing the position he/she holds.

Washington Quarter A coin minted by the United States starting in 1931. It is worth 1/4 of one dollar. It features of portrait of George Washington on the obverse.

Washington, D.C. v. Greater Washington Board of Trade A United States Supreme Court decision holding that states cannot require private employers to provide health insurance to disabled employees who are eligible for workers compensation insurance.

Wash-Sale Rule An IRS regulation stating that one may not claim a capital loss for tax purposes if one repurchases the same position within 30 days. Suppose one sells a stock at a substantial loss but immediately buys back the same stock at the same price. Effectively, the locked in loss is "unlocked" and one can still make a profit on the investment in the long term. The 30 day wash-sale rule exists to prevent investors from taking tax deductions on losses they do not actually incur. Some investors find a way around this by exercising a tax swap. The 30 day wash-sale rule should not be confused with wash trading, which is a different concept altogether.

Washup In printing, to clean one ink color from a printer in preparation of loading another.

Waste In real estate, a change in a property's value caused by a lessee or another person who has possession but no ownership rights. Waste usually results in a reduction in the property value, for which the owner ordinarily is entitled compensation. Waste may be positive or negative; positive waste results from the possessor's act, while negative waste results from his/her omission. An example of the former is destroying the floor with a sledge hammer, while an example of the latter is neglecting a termite infestation for so long that the floor collapses.

Waste Circulation The portion of readers of a periodical (such as a newspaper or magazine) unlikely to purchase a good or service being advertised and/or who live in an area where it cannot be obtained. By advertising in the appropriate periodicals (according to interest or location), an advertiser attempts to minimize the waste circulation.

Wasting Asset An asset, especially a derivative, that loses value over time. A primary example is an out of the money option, which declines in value close to the expiry date because it becomes less likely that the option will become in the money. It can also apply to assets that are consumed, such as oil or food products. In this situation, the asset reaches its highest value at its sale, and then rapidly depreciates. In accounting, a wasting asset is anything subject to depreciation. See also: Absolute physical life.

Wasting Trust 1. A trust in which the principal does not generate sufficient income to meet desired payouts and therefore the beneficiary receives a portion of the principal each month. Obviously, this reduces the future income potential of the remaining principal. A wasting trust only occurs if further contributions .(which increase the principal) are not made. **2.** A trust that holds assets that dissipate over time, such as contracts on corn and gas.

Watch List A list of securities that the SEC or other body is observing closely because their companies are suspected of regulatory or legal violations, or because it has simply attracted an unusual amount of attention recently. For example, a company about to make a new issue of stock may be placed on the watch list to ensure that it abides by all regulations, even if it has never been suspected of violating any.

Watchdog Group An organization, often nonprofit, that researches and publishes information on alleged abuses in a certain area or sector. For example, a watchdog group may investigate the truth of stories reported in the media or poor environmental practices in private companies. At their best, watchdog groups may expose real corruption, but they may be susceptible to bias themselves.

Water In auto sales, a slang term for false equity. For example, water occurs when a car owner claims $3,000 in equity on a vehicle when she only has $1,500 in equity.

Water and Sewer Bond A municipal bond used to construct or expand a water and sewer lines for the municipality. The bond is secured by the revenue the utilities derive in the course of its operations; that is, the issuing municipality does not back the bond itself and the principal and interest are repaid from water bill collections. Generally speaking, a water and sewer bond (like all revenue bonds) is riskier than other municipal bonds because the water and sewer department has no power to tax. However, it is a fairly safe investment because most people will pay their water bills most of the time.

Water Backup and Sump Overflow An addition to a property insurance policy that protects the owner from expenses related to the overflow or backup of water through a sewer system and/or a sump pump. Coverage is provided whether the damage is caused by a malfunction or an act of God. It may be especially useful in areas where flooding is likely. As with all insurance, one must pay a premium to receive the coverage.

Water Bill The amount one must pay to use water and sewage services each month. Normally, water and sewage is provided by a municipality, but this is not always the case. Water bills usually are based upon one's usage, such that those who use more water are charged more. See also: Utilities.

Water Damage Insurance An insurance policy that provides coverage for damage due to flooding or water. Some insurers exclude water damage from their property insurance contracts because of the substantial damage water can cause; property owners with this exclusion may purchase water damage insurance to account for this risk. As with all insurance, one must pay a premium to receive the coverage.

Water Exclusion Clause A clause in some property insurance contracts stating that flood or other water damage does not receive coverage. Water exclusion clauses exist because the substantial amount of damage water can cause poses a significant risk for insurers. Some private insurers refuse to insure against flood damage at all; as a result, some governments institute their own insurance programs.

Water in the Tariff A tariff so high that it makes an international trade almost completely impossible. That is, water in the tariff has the same effect as forbidding the import of a good.

Water Pollution Liability The obligation of a ship's owner or other relevant party to pay to clean up pollution his/her ship causes. At the U.S. federal level, water pollution liability was instituted by the Water Quality Improvement Act of 1970.

Water Quality Improvement Act of 1970 Legislation in the United States requiring ship owners to pay to clean up their ships' pollution. Ships may be refused the right to travel in certain waters if their owners cannot show that they have the ability to pay for any potential clean-ups.

Water Quality Insurance Syndicate A group of insurers that provide insurance for water pollution liability, which is the obligation of a ship's owner to pay to clean up his/her ship's pollution. The Syndicate formed in 1971 in response to the Water Quality Improvement Act of 1970.

Watercraft Endorsement A rider to a liability policy or homeowners insurance that provides coverage for boats one owns or uses. For example, if one owns a boat not covered under one's other insurance and it sinks, a watercraft endorsement would pay for the replacement boat. As with all insurance, one must pay a premium to receive the coverage.

Watercraft Nonowned Insurance A rider to a liability policy that provides coverage for boats a business uses but does not own. For example, if a company leases a boat for business purposes and it sinks, watercraft nonowned insurance would pay for the replacement boat. As with all insurance, one must pay a premium to receive the coverage.

Watered Stock An overvalued stock. A stock may be overvalued for any number of reasons; speculation and over-issue are only two of the most common. Watered stocks are often subject to a price correction.

Watermark An image in a piece of paper that may be seen more clearly when it is held up to light. This is used in printing some money and passports to prevent counterfeiting. For example, if one holds a $20 American bill up to light, one would see a watermark of Andrew Jackson's face.

Watermelon Note A nickname for the Federal Reserve Note issued for the $500 bill. The name was not used for the $500 gold certificate. It featured William McKinley.

Waterschap In the Netherlands, a municipal subdivision responsible for sewage treatment and the provision of fresh water.

Wave A short-term movement that goes against the general trend. For example, if the DJIA rallies on a given trading day but overall is in the midst of a prolonged bear market, the rally is called a wave against the bearish tide.

Waybill A document describing goods to be transported, usually internationally. A carrier, such as a shipping line or airline, issues a waybill to prove that the goods have been received and are ready for transport.

Ways and Means Advances A system whereby the Reserve Bank of India (the country's central bank) extends loans to the central and state governments to offset temporary cash flow problems they may have. Ways and means advances may be issued without collateral (normal WMAs) or they may be guaranteed by Indian government bonds (special WMAs). Ways and means advances come due three months after issue.

Ways and Means Committee 1. A committee in the U.S. House of Representatives that recommends measures to raise funds for budgets. As such, taxation and tariff bills are referred to the Committee. It is considered one of the most powerful committees in the House. **2.** A former Committee of the British House of Commons that performed much the same function. It was abolished in 1967.

W-Cubed In sales, a slang term meaning that one's company can deliver whatever the client needs, whenever the client needs it, wherever the client needs it. This claim is sometimes criticized as unrealistic.

Weak 1. See: Weak form of the EMT. **2.** See: Weak currency.

Weak Dollar The U.S. dollar when it is worth less relative to other currencies. Because the dollar is a floating currency, its value varies according to market trends. When one dollar trades for fewer units of one or more other currencies, it is known as a weak dollar. See also: Strong dollar, Exchange rate.

Weak Dollar Policy The policy under which the U.S. government seeks to maintain a U.S. dollar that is worth less than other currencies. This makes U.S. products less expensive in other countries, which encourages exports. The U.S. pursues a weak dollar policy primarily by buying foreign debt. It carries the risk of leading to unsustainable debt and/or inflation.

Weak Form Efficiency A version of the efficient markets theory on how markets work. It holds that the market efficiently deals with most information on a given security and reflects it in the price immediately. Specifically, weak form efficiency states that technical analysis is ineffective and that prices are on a random walk. Investors and academics disagree on how well the model works, but it is less controversial than the semi-strong form of the EMT and the strong form of the EMT.

Weak Hands 1. A holder of a futures contract who does not intend to take delivery of the underlying asset. While this strategy is a fairly common speculative investment, an investor with weak hands connotes a small investor who lacks the capital to actually buy the underlying asset and simply trades in contracts. **2.** In foreign exchange, an investor who sells at the first negative news or price change. This has a slightly negative connotation and other investors seek to profit from the sales of investors with weak hands.

Weak Market A market for one or more securities in which there are few buyers and many sellers. A weak market comes about due to declining prices, and it is sometimes associated with high trading volume. See also: Bear market, Panic sell.

Weak Sister Informal for the security in a portfolio or fund that performs worse than all other securities in the portfolio or fund. One may consider dropping the weak sister unless there is significant growth potential in the future.

Weakest Link Theory A concept holding that each action in a sequence is dependent upon the performance of the action that came before it. According to the theory, the quality of the series of actions is limited to the quality of the weakest performance in the sequence.

Wealth The state of having strong financial resources. There is no strict definition of how much one needs to have in order to be "wealthy," but, in general, it refers to one with significantly more assets than liabilities. However, socially, a person with too much debt may be considered to be wealthy because others are not aware of his/her true financial state. Excess wealth (and wealthy persons) drives economic growth. Some believe this ought to be encouraged, as it eventually makes the remainder of society wealthier. Others, however, believe growth is strongest when the needs of multiple classes, and not just the wealthy, are balanced. A few others believe most wealth ought to be confiscated and redistributed, but this is a minority opinion.

Wealth Added Index A measure of the wealth created for the shareholders of a publicly-traded company. Unlike most such measures, it does not account for profits or dividends; rather, the WAI assumes that wealth is created only if the return for the shareholders is greater than the cost of equity. Cost of equity is the return investors demand in exchange for taking on risk; the WAI holds that if the return does not exceed this, then shareholders are not receiving what they demand and are effectively destroying their own wealth by maintaining a position in the company.

Wealth Creation 1. Accumulation of assets (especially those that generate income) over a long period of time. A major example of wealth creation is a retirement plan. **2.** A byword for economic growth, especially when used at the macroeconomic level.

Wealth Tax A tax levied on a person's or company's net assets, as opposed to income. For example, if a person has a net worth of $1 million, the government may assess a wealth tax on this amount over and above the tax on that person's income. Proponents believe this tax promotes equality while critics maintain it discourages accumulation of wealth, which is thought to drive economic growth.

Wealthy Describing a person or entity with strong financial resources. There is no strict definition of how much one needs to have in order to be "wealthy," but, in general, it refers to one with more money or assets relative to others in a society. The wealthy drive economic growth. Some believe this ought to be encouraged, as it eventually makes the remainder of society wealthier; others, however, believe growth is strongest when the needs of multiple classes are balanced. A few others believe wealthy persons ought to have most of their resources confiscated and redistributed, but this is a minority opinion.

Weapon of Mass Destruction Any weapon designed to kill human beings in exceptionally large numbers. Examples include biological, chemical and nuclear weapons. International agreements limit the spread of these weapons and they are rarely used in practice. However, they remain a significant political risk in some parts of the world.

Wear and Tear Exclusion In insurance, a category prohibiting payment on claims for normal wear and tear, which is the degrading of the quality of an item that is expected over time. Because this decline in value is inevitable, insurers will not pay for these losses.

Wearout Factor In marketing, the point at which an advertisement no longer affects its target audience. It can be very difficult to measure when the wearout factor occurs; it depends on the catchiness of the advertisement, how long it has been public, and other factors.

Weather Derivative A derivative security in which an investor hedges against the future state of the weather. For example, two investors may enter a weather derivative, where one investor pays the other if rainfall in a given place over a given period of time is above a certain amount. Likewise, the other investor pays if the rainfall is below the agreed-upon amount. One of the most common weather derivatives is a weather future, in which the buyer is required to pay the seller $20 for each day in a given month that the daily temperature is below 65 degrees (a heating degree day) or above 65 degrees (a cooling degree day), depending on the nature of the contract. A weather future allows a business to hedge against potential losses resulting from an unexpected change in weather. Energy companies are some of the most common sellers of weather derivatives.

Weather Future A weather derivative in which the buyer is required to pay the seller $20 for each day in a given month that the daily temperature is below 65 degrees (a heating degree day) or above 65 degrees (a cooling degree day), depending on the nature of the contract. A weather future allows a business to hedge against potential losses resulting from an unexpected change in weather. Energy companies are the most common sellers of weather futures; they have become relatively popular investments.

Weather Insurance An insurance policy protecting one from loss of income due to adverse weather conditions. For example, a recreational horseback riding facility is unlikely to have many customers during heavy rain, which could cause significant drops in profit. Weather insurance can replace at least some of what the profits would have been. It is a type of business interruption insurance.

Web 2.0 Informal; the development of the Internet in such as way as to facilitate interactive and user-generated content. This contrasts with older uses for the Internet, in which websites provided information and the user could read it or not. Examples of Web 2.0 services include blogs (on which users may comment) and social media (in which users create and share content on a massive scale). Web 2.0 does not refer to technical advances in the Internet. Web 2.0 has opened new avenues for monetization of the Internet, particularly regarding customized advertising. User generated content means advertisers are better able to identify the interests of a single user of the Internet and to cater to him/her. The term dates to 1999 and was popularized in the early 2000s.

Web Browser A program that allows one to search, find and disseminate information over the Internet. Web browsers have become almost indispensable in business because of the sheer volume of information currently available.

Web Page A virtual document that displays information on the Internet. The ability to access Web pages has become almost indispensable in business because of the sheer volume of information currently available.

Web Press A printer using a roll to churn out paper.

Web Server Any hardware or software allowing a computer to connect to the Internet. A web server allows one to visit websites, post or share content, and view advertisements.

Web Tension The force used to pull paper through a web press, which is a printer using a roll to churn out paper. Too much or too little web tension affects the quality of the print job.

Web-Based Application Software used online rather that downloaded onto one's hard drive. Some financial assistance programs for individuals and organizations are web-based applications.

Webb-Pomerene Act of 1918 Legislation in the United States that exempts associations of exporters from the provisions of the Sherman Antitrust Act. That is, it allows exporters to engage in acts that otherwise might be considered collusion in order to promote American trade abroad. However, they may not engage in importation or sales within the United States. These exporters may not combine services; that is, they may only collude to export similar products.

Webb-Pomerene Association An association of exporters exempt from some of the provisions of the Sherman Antitrust Act. That is, a Webb-Pomerene Association may engage in acts that otherwise might be considered collusion in order to promote American trade abroad. However, they may not engage in importation or sales within the United States. They may not combine services; that is, they may only collude to export similar products. They derive their name from the Webb-Pomerene Act of 1918, which authorized their creation.

Weber's Law In psychology, a concept stating that change in a stimulus is noticeable in proportion to the strength of the original stimulus. Weber's law is used in marketing to increase prices for products. That is, marketers have found a company may change its prices by a certain percentage before customers notice they are higher or lower.

Webinar A seminar conducted online. For example, one may conduct a business meeting, a college class or any number of other discussions via webinar using various video chat technologies. Webinars have become more common due to increasingly reliable technology and the expense of traveling to in-person meetings. The term is formed from the combination of "Web" and "seminar."

Webmaster An employee or independent contractor who manages the website of a company or organization. This may involve managing content, such as editing and updating information, or it may involve more technical aspects, such as coding.

WEBS An exchange-traded fund that tracks various Morgan Stanley Capital International country indices. An organization issuing WEBS owns each of the securitiestraded on an MSCI country index in approximate ratio to their market capitalization. WEBS are available for 17 MSCI indices and can be bought, sold, short-sold, traded on margin, and generally function as if they were stocks. Investors use WEBS (and indeed all exchange-traded funds) as a way to easily diversify their portfolios at relatively low cost. WEBS trade on the American Stock Exchange.

Website Development Costs What a company or organization spends in creating or updating its website. These costs can vary widely. One may put together a basic website for the cost of a small program and of writing the content. On the other hand, one may spend a great deal of money on a website with custom designed graphics and interactive features. How much an organization spends in website development costs depends on how much business it can expect from the Internet and the extent to which a well-presented website will affect its reputation.

Wedding Presents Floater An insurance policy providing coverage for all gifts a couple receives for their wedding until they are moved to the couple's permanent place of residence. The floater covers all wedding gifts no matter where they are. This is particularly useful because the gifts would not be covered by homeowner's insurance until they are present in the home.

Wednesday Scramble The sudden increase in the buying and selling of excess reserves by banks so they meet their required reserves each Wednesday, as mandated by the Federal Reserve. The Wednesday scramble can have significant, short-term effects on the federal funds rate.

Weekly Coal Production Report A report published by the U.S. Department of Energy detailing how much coal each state produces each week. This is watched by energy investors and may affect commodity prices.

Weekly Premium Insurance An insurance policy in which one pays the premium weekly, instead of monthly, like most insurance. Weekly premium insurance is usually inexpensive and has a benefit under $1,000.

Wegstunde A German unit of length equivalent to 3.71 kilometers in Germany and 4.8 kilometers in Switzerland. It became obsolete with the adoption of the metric system in the 1870s.

Weigh Count In direct mail marketing, the practice of weighing responses to a promotion each day and comparing the total to the weight of the total mail sent out. The weigh count provides a rough estimate of the response rate to a promotion each day and is quicker than actually counting responses.

Weighing a Pig Slang; the practice of spending so much time trying to measure results that one is distracted from producing results. For example, a manager may spend so much energy finding innovative ways to measure market share that she does not do enough to actually improve it.

Weight Break The weight of cargo to be transported that is sufficient for the owner to become eligible for some sort of bulk rate. The weight break is the quantity necessary for a per unit reduction in price for the cargo's transportation. It is also called the weight threshold.

Weight of Ice, Snow, or Sleet Insurance An insurance policy providing coverage due to damage from the weight of winter weather. For example, if accumulated snow on one's roof becomes too heavy and the roof collapses, this insurance would pay for repairs. Normally, it does not cover damage to sidewalks, swimming pools and the like. As with all insurance, one must pay a premium for this coverage.

Weighted Describing an average in which some values count for more than others. For example, if an index consisting of 10 stocks is weighted for price, this means that the average price of the stocks will move more when the stocks with higher price move. Most indices use weighted averages so "smaller" values do not affect the index inordinately. This helps correct for the fact that averages tend to be affected by extreme values. One of the most common ways of weighting an average is to weight for market capitalization.

Weighted Alpha In technical analysis, a measure of the amount by which a stock has gained or lost over a period of time, often a year, with weight being given to more recent price movement. A positive weighted alpha indicates a stock that has risen over the year, sometimes significantly, while a negative weighted alpha indicates the opposite. A weighted alpha helps analyst identify stocks with upward or downward momentum, which helps determine buy and sell signals.

Weighted Average An average in which some values count for more than others. For example, if an index consisting of 10 stocks is weighted for price, this means that the average price of the stocks will move more when the stocks with higher price move. Most indices use weighted averages so that "smaller" values do not affect the index inordinately. This helps correct for the fact that averages tend to be affected by extreme values. One of the most common ways of weighting an average is to weight for market capitalization.

Weighted Average Contribution Margin The average amount that each unit of product contributes to a company over the cost of producing it, after accounting for the different price of different products. For example, suppose half a company's sales come from Product A and half come from Product B. If the sale of each unit of

Product A results in a $5 profit, and the sale of each unit of Product B results in $15, the weighted average contribution margin is $10.

Weighted Average Cost of Capital A calculation of a company's cost of capital in which every source of capital is weighted in proportion to how much capital it contributes to the company. For example, if 75% of a company's capital comes from stock and 25% comes from debt, measuring the cost of capital weights these accordingly. A high WACC indicates that a company is spending a comparatively large amount of money in order to raise capital, which means that the company may be risky. On the other hand, a low WACC indicates that the company acquires capital cheaply.

Weighted Average Credit Rating The average credit rating of the bonds in a bond fund or a portfolio consisting entirely of bonds. This credit rating is weighted for the percentage each bond represents in the fund or portfolio. As with individual bonds, the higher a bond fund's weighted average credit rating, the less risk and the lower return it carries.

Weighted Average Inventory Method A way to calculate the weighted average cost of goods that a company sells. The weighted average cost is what a company spends per unit of inventory after accounting for the different cost of different products. Under the weighted average inventory method, one adds all the sale prices for each unit of each good and divides by the number of goods available for sale.

Weighted Average Life The amount of time for the principal on a loan or a mortgage to be paid off. The length of the weighted average life depends on the amount of principal paydowns and how often they are made. Once the WAL is calculated, one can determine how long it will take to pay off half of the remaining principal.

Weighted Average Market Capitalization Describing an index in which the average price is weighted for market capitalization. For example, if an index consisting of 10 stocks is weighted for market capitalization, this means that the average price of the stocks will move more when the stocks with higher market capitalization move. Most indices use weighted averages so that "smaller" values do not affect the index inordinately. This helps correct for the fact that averages tend to be affected by extreme values. Most indices weight for market capitalization. A prominent example is the S&P 500. See also: Weighted average price.

Weighted Average Maturity The average amount of time remaining before maturity in the mortgages underlying a mortgage-backed security, weighted by the percentage of the MBS that each mortgage constitutes. For example, suppose a mortgage-backed security contains two mortgages, one worth $10,000 and one worth $20,000, for a total of $30,000. The $10,000 mortgage matures in five years, and the $20,000 mortgage in 10 years. The weighted average remaining maturity is calculated as: WAM = ($10,000 / $30,000) * 5 years + ($20,000 / $30,000) * 10 years = 8 1/3 years The weighted average maturity is also known as the weighted average remaining maturity.

Weighted Average Maturity Date The average amount of time remaining before the securities in a portfolio reach maturity, weighted by the percentage of the portfolio that each security constitutes. For example, suppose a portfolio contains two bonds, one worth $10,000 and one worth $20,000, for a total of $30,000. The $10,000 bond matures in five years, and the $20,000 bond in 10 years. The weighted average remaining maturity date is calculated as: WAMD = ($10,000 / $30,000) * 5 years + ($20,000 / $30,000) * 10 years = 8 1/3 years

Weighted Average Portfolio Yield The total yield on a bond portfolio divided by the number of bonds contained in it, weighted for the size of each bond so that the yield of large holdings does not drown out the calculation of yields on small holdings.

Weighted Ballot After an oversubscription for a new issue, a ballot used to allot new shares in such a way that either those who have subscribed to larger or smaller portions of the issue receive a disproportionate amount. That is, the weighted ballot is used to allocate available shares in the new issue either to small investors or large investors.

Weighted Cost Driver In accounting, the process of treating some cost drivers (that is, factors that directly contribute to overhead such as labor and machines used) as affecting overhead more or less than they actually do.

Weighted Moving Average An average in which some values count for more than others, and in which less recent values are dropped off the average. For example, if an index is weighted for prices over the previous 20 days, this means that the average price of the stocks will move more when the values with higher price move and values are removed from the average after 20 days have elapsed. This helps correct for both outdated information and the fact that averages tend to be affected by extreme values.

Weighted Stock Index An index that tracks a number of stocks in which price changes in some stocks affect the index's price changes more than others. For example, suppose an index tracks three stocks: A, B, and C. If A is weighted more highly than B and C, an uptick in A will be more likely to result in an uptick in the index as a whole (depending on how much more weighted it is). It is common for weighted stock indices to be weighted for market capitalization, meaning the stocks with more capitalization affect the index more. The S&P 500 is a well-known weighted stock index. See also: Unweighted stock index.

Weighted-Average Coupon Rate The interest rate the holder of a mortgage-backed security is paid. It is calculated by taking the gross of the interest rates owed on the mortgages underlying the security and weighting them according to the percentage of the security that each mortgage represents. For example, if a very simple MBS is backed by three mortgages, one representing the gross interest rate and the other two representing one-quarter each, one gives twice the weight to the first mortgage when calculating the weighted average coupon. It is important to note that the weighted average coupon rate may change over the life of the MBS because different mortgage holders pay down their mortgages at different rates, changing the weights. See also: Prepayment risk.

Weighting When calculating an average from a given data set, the process of allowing some data points to affect the average more than others. For example, if one is calculating the average value of a stock index, one may weight the stocks with higher market capitalization greater than other stocks. Likewise, if one is determining a moving average over a given number of trading days, one may weight more recent trading days than those more distant. Weighting can lessen some of the disadvantages of taking the average of a data set instead of taking the median.

Wejba A Maltese unit of land area approximately equivalent to 4,497 square meters, or slightly more than one acre. It is largely obsolete but is still used in some circumstances.

Welayat In Turkmenistan, a political subdivision equivalent to a province.

Welcome Tax An informal term for a land transfer tax in Quebec. The welcome tax is assessed on the buyer of real estate. It derives its name from Bienvenu, which is the French word for welcome and also the name of the minister who originally proposed it.

Welfare A generic term for many government assistance programs. In general, it refers to programs in which the government pays money to indigent and unemployed persons. However, it may include non-cash payments such as food stamps. It may or may not include a requirement that able-bodied persons on welfare attempt to find work. Welfare is very controversial. Proponents argue that it helps the persons least able to help themselves, while critics contend it encourages people not to work. See also: TANF, Dole.

Welfare and Pension Plans Disclosure Act Legislation in the United States regulating employee pension plans. It requires pensions with more than 25 employees participating to register with the Labor Department and to file information regarding the plan. Larger plans with more than 100 participants must also file a financial report annually. The Act requires all paperwork to be made available to plan participants on request. The intent of the Act is to increase transparency in employee pension plans.

Welfare Criterion The basis by which one measures the benefits of a change against its drawbacks. For example, one may elect to make a change if everyone gains and no one loses, or if the number or the quality of the gains outpaces the number or quality of the losses. There is no single welfare criterion; the criterion used varies according to the ethics or preferences of the one(s) considering the change.

Welfare Economics The study of how to distribute income in order to achieve social good. In other words, welfare economics takes the preferences of individuals at the microeconomic level and tries to apply them in macroeconomics. It attempts to discourage inequality to improve utility. Welfare economics is rather controversial, in part because there is no one way to measure social good; therefore, its study can be subjective.

Welfare State The concept in which a government is or views itself as responsible for providing some minimum economic security for citizens. For example, the government may guarantee housing, work and a minimum income for all citizens. Less comprehensively, a government may provide income during periods of unemployment or poverty. Most governments have a welfare state to some degree. Proponents view welfare states as a form of economic justice. Critics contend that they are detrimental to GDP growth and promote needless dependency.

Well-Diversified Portfolio A portfolio that has invested in many different types of security in order to hedge against the securities already in the portfolio. Ideally, this reduces the risk inherent in any one investment, and increases the possibility of making a profit, or at least avoiding a loss. This may also reduce the expected return on the fund, but it depends on level and type of diversification. There are two main types of diversification that a well-diversified portfolio may utilize. Horizontal diversification involves investing in similar types of investments. Examples include investing in several technology companies or in different types of bonds. Vertical diversification involves investing in very different securities; for example, one may choose to invest in securities traded in different countries or in both winter clothing and swimsuit companies. Both types of diversification may be as broad or narrow as the fund's manager chooses. In general, the broader the diversification, the less risk and less return.

Well-Heeled Informal for rich or wealthy.

Wellness Program Any program that promotes health, especially for employees of a company. A wellness program may offer seminars on quitting smoking, free access to a gym, and any number of other benefits. Wellness program are aimed to improve employee health, which in turn can improve morale and increase productivity.

Wells Notice Written documentation of a coming enforcement action from the Securities and Exchange Commission to the respondent. While a Wells notice is not legally required, it has been standard practice since the 1970s.

Wertbestaendige Notgeld printed in Germany during and immediately after World War I that purported to be pegged to some asset. For example, some Wertbestaendige was based on rye, while some was based on coal. The intention behind this was to help the notgeld to keep its value as a medium of exchange. It was largely unsuccessful.

West Africa Rice Development Association Also called WARDA. An international organization that conducts academic and scientific research to promote the development of rice cultivation. WARDA primarily benefits small farmers in West Africa. It works with governments, universities and other organizations in conducting its activities. It was established in 1971.

West African CFA Franc The currency of several former French colonies in West Africa, namely Benin, Burkina Faso, Cote d'Ivoire, Guinea-Bissau, Mali, Niger, Senegal, and Togo. It was introduced in 1945 to spare French colonies from the severe devaluation necessary to the French franc following World War II. Between 1949 and 1999, it was pegged to the French franc. Since then, it has been pegged to the euro. While it is of equal value to the Central African CFA franc, the two currencies are not interchangeable.

West African Monetary Union An organization of several countries in West Africa whose members are politically separate but have free movement of goods and services and labor across borders and, most importantly, use a single currency: the West African CFA franc. Members include Benin, Burkina Faso, Cote d'Ivoire, Guinea Bissau, Mali, Niger and Togo. It was established in 1994.

West Texas Intermediate Crude Oil A blend of light, sweet crude oil drilled in the Midwestern United States and the Gulf of Mexico. It is the underlying commodity for oil futures and other derivatives traded on the New York Mercantile Exchange. West Texas Intermediate is stored and shipped from Cushing, Oklahoma. It is considered a major benchmark for the global price of oil.

Western Account An offering of a new issue in which underwriters are liable for placing only a certain percentage of the total offering. An underwriting firm is not liable for placing unsold portions of the issue from other underwriters. For instance, suppose an underwriting firm is responsible for placing 15% of an issue and does so. If the entire issue is not placed, the firm is not responsible for placing any of the unsold portion of the issue. This contrasts with an Eastern account, in which the whole syndicate of underwriters is jointly and severally responsible.

Western European Union Also called the WEU. An international organization dedicated to mutual defense of member states. It was established in 1948 at the outset of the Cold War and was intended to counteract the Soviet bloc. The WEU's operations were gradually taken over by the European Union beginning the 1990s. The WEU treaty was abolished in 2010.

Western Hemisphere Trade Corporation An American company that derives 95% or more of its income from countries in the Western hemisphere except for the United States. Under the 1939 Internal Revenue Code, western hemisphere trade corporations qualified for lower than normal corporate tax rates.

Western Samoan Tala The currency of Western Samoa. It was introduced in 1967, replacing the Western Samoan pound. It was pegged to the New Zealand dollar until 1975.

Western Union An American financial services company. It provides wire transfers, money orders and similar services. It is especially popular among persons without bank accounts who need to transfer money. It began as a telegraph company in 1851. It is based in Englewood, Colorado.

Westlaw An online research service for legal professionals in the United States. It provides users with thousands of documents, including statutes, court decisions, articles and so forth. Westlaw began in 1970.

Wet Printing A practice in printing in which one places ink on a previously printed surface that has not dried. Wet printing is used if a press prints too rapidly to allow print to dry.

Wetlands An area in which water is permanently trapped in the soil. Examples of wetlands include swamps and bogs. Wetlands improve the quality of water in the area, provide fish (thereby creating jobs), and present other economic benefits.

Wey A unit of dry volume equivalent to 30 bushels.

WF In publishing, a mark by a proofreader indicating a work or part of a work has accidentally been printed with an incorrect font. The WF tells the designer or printer to correct the mistake before the work goes to final press.

WG The former alpha-2 code for Grenada. See also: GD.

Whacked Slang; describing an investor who has experienced a quick loss on a trade. For example, an investor who experiences a sudden turnaround in a security's price may be said to have been whacked.

Wharfage A fee that a ship's owner or operator must pay in order to have the right to use a wharf, which is a place where ships dock to load or unload cargo.

Whatsit A generic term for any product, especially a manufactured product. It is used in text books and academic papers to provide an example without using specifics. A whatsit is a less common term than a widget, and usually is used if the example includes two products: widgets and whatsits.

Wheat A cereal used in a large number of products, especially food. Wheat is contained in bread, cake, beer, pasta and even some fuels. Wheat is a major commodity and its contracts are traded on exchanges.

Wheat Back Cent A penny manufactured in the United States featuring grains of wheat on the reverse. These were made between 1909 and 1958.

Wheel of Retailing A long-term strategy in which a discount retailer gradually begins to sell higher quality goods. The wheel of retailing allows the retailer to increase its prices over time, leading to higher revenues and perhaps higher profits. The ultimate goal of a wheel of retailing is to develop a discount company into a department store or the equivalent.

Wheelbarrow Inflation A slang term for hyperinflation. The term is a reference to the inflation seen in Germany under the Weimar Republic in the early 1920s, when cash was worth so little that people had to carry it in wheelbarrows to buy basic necessities.

Wheeler-Lea Act Legislation in the United States, passed in 1938, that prohibited practices deemed unfair to competitors. It gave the Federal Trade Commission power to enforce this prohibition.

When Issued Referring to a conditional offer for a new security, subject to the security actually being issued. Before a new issue, underwriters canvass potential investors, who may or may not book an order to buy a portion the new issue. Orders made are said to be effective "when issued" because they may not be completed, especially if the offering is cancelled. Less formally, orders when issued are referred to as orders "with ice" or orders "when distributed."

Whipsaw 1. A change in a security's price quickly followed by another change in the opposite direction. For example, a security could rise $1 then quickly lose $2, or it could fall 50 cents then rise 75 cents. Whipsaws are significant risks for day traders and speculators who may lose large amounts of money in short-term trading. **2.** To buy securities at a market top or to sell at a market bottom. That is, one whipsaws when one buys or sells securities at exactly the worst possible time. One whipsaws out of fear or out of misreading market signals. To whipsaw is also called to chatter.

Whisper Number or Forecast An informal forecast of a publicly-traded company's earnings per share. One arrives at the whisper number by a combination of past performance, perceived optimism by company officials, and just plain rumor. The whisper number can be useful, as it is occasionally more accurate than official forecasts. However, the Sarbanes-Oxley Act restricts the availability of some information that previously contributed to the whisper number, making it more difficult for some investors to determine. See also: Price out.

Whisper Stock Stock in a company rumored to be the target of a hostile takeover. Investments in whisper stocks can be highly speculative because the rumor may turn out to be false. Furthermore, if one knows the rumor to be true for a fact and buys or sells the whisper stock accordingly, one may be guilty of insider trading.

Whistle Blower An employee of a company who has knowledge of illegal activities and reports them to the authorities. Generally speaking, a whistle blower reports the activities out of a sense of conscience or out of a desire to avoid criminal charges himself/herself. Under federal law, whistle blowers may not be fired, but some companies find ways around this.

Whistle Blowing The practice in which an employee or other person publicly exposes the wrongdoings of a private company. For example, if a company is illegally dumping chemicals in a protected environment, a whistle blower may inform the proper authorities or, failing that, the media. Certain laws may protect whistleblowers from being fired or other negative consequences within the company.

Whistleblower An employee or other person who publicly exposes the wrongdoings of a private company. For example, if a company is illegally dumping chemicals in a protected environment, a whistleblower may tell the proper authorities or, failing that, the media. Certain laws may protect whistleblowers from being fired or other negative consequences within the company.

White Collar Crime A crime committed by an office worker within the context of his/her job, especially when the worker is educated or respected. For instance, a bank employee may divert pennies from customers' to his/her own account. White-collar criminals take advantage of their positions in the commission of their illegal acts. Ordinarily, white-collar crimes involve money; major examples include embezzlement, money laundering and some computer crimes. While white-collar crimes may appear victimless in their commission, they may have broader ramifications than street crimes such as burglary or theft. For example, a robber can only steal from one person or home at a time, while a white-collar criminal can embezzle funds from thousands or millions of investors.

White Collar Crime Penalty Enhancement Act of 2002 The portion of the Sarbanes-Oxley Act (which strengthened accounting disclosure requirements) that increased the criminal penalties for white collar crimes such embezzlement, money laundering and some computer crimes.

White Collar Worker An office worker, especially an educated or respected one. White collar works include (but are not limited to) clerical employees, salespersons, retail managers, bankers and so forth. White collar workers are usually salaried (though many others work primarily on commission). White collar workers contrast with blue collar workers, who generally perform manual labor of some kind and/or have less education. Stereotypically, white collar workers earn more than blue collar workers, but this varies by job, industry and experience.

White Elephant An investment, especially in real estate, that is expensive, unprofitable, and difficult to sell. An example is a house that is overbuilt for its neighborhood. A white elephant is perhaps one of least desirable investments possible.

White Goods Durable goods, generally purchased for household or office use. Examples include refrigerators, microwaves and air conditioners. They are called white goods because, historically, they have been available only in white.

White Knight Informal; an acquiring company in a friendly takeover. One usually refers to a white knight when the target company would be otherwise subject to a hostile takeover. That is, the white knight rescues the target company from the prospect of the hostile takeover. While the target company does not remain independent, it is able to negotiate terms with the white knight. Management usually

remains in place and shareholders are often paid a higher price. See also: Black Knight, Gray Knight.

White List State A U.S. state maintaining a list of insurance companies that are allowed to provide surplus line insurance in that state. Surplus line insurance is provided in special circumstances by a company not otherwise authorized to provide insurance in a certain state. A white list state restricts these activities only to those companies on the list.

White Paper An official document issued by a company describing and promoting a new product it intends to begin offering to customers. A white paper can both encourage customers to buy the product and encourage investors to buy shares in the company. The information provided in the white paper is generally quite detailed. See also: Marketing.

White Sale A period of time during which a company discounts some of its inventory in order to increase sales when they might otherwise be sluggish. One of the most common times to have a white sale is immediately following Christmas. The idea behind a white sale is to make up in volume of sales what the seller loses in profit margin. White sales are thought to trace their origins to John Wanamaker's department store in Philadelphia in the 1870s.

White Sheets Quotes for over-the-counter securities traded in Chicago, Los Angeles, and San Francisco. The National Quotation Bureau provides white sheets to American market makers.

White Space Any empty space in a print advertisement. White space generally looks sleek and, for that reason, is frequently used to promote luxury or other expensive products.

White Squire A friendly investor who buys a large minority interest in a struggling company. This provides the company with more capital to improve its financial situation, while still allowing the current owners to maintain control of the company. See also: White knight.

White-Coat Rule A rule of the Federal Trade Commission officially disapproving of the use of persons wearing white coats to advertise a product unless they are actually doctors or other medical professionals. The white-coat rule regards the use of actors as doctors in a broadcast marketing campaign as misleading.

Whitehouse Decision A slang term for a policy or other decision that only the CEO and/or other members of upper management are permitted to make. Whitehouse decisions may have far-reaching consequences.

Whitemail An anti-greenmail provision whereby a publicly-traded company sells a significant portion of its stock to a friendly company, usually at a discount to its market value. Greenmail is a practice in which a corporate raider buys stock directly from shareholders with no intention to actually take over the company, but instead wishes to force the company to buy back its own shares at a significant premium. When the target company engages in whitemail, it sells its shares to the friendly company in the belief or assurance that the friendly company will sell to the corporate raider only at a significant premium. Whitemail makes the greenmail more expensive for the corporate raider, who may then be forced to abandon the attempt.

White's Ratings A ratings servicethat investigates tax exempt bonds. It rates a bond on a scale of one to 100 according to its liquidity, that is, the ease with which it can be bought and sold. Importantly, unlike other rating services, White's Ratings does not account for the issuer's creditworthiness.

White-Shoe Firm Informal; a broker-dealer that does not engage in hostile takeovers on principle. That is, white-shoe firms believe hostile takeovers to be an unfair business practice.

Whitespace A slang term for an unexploited opportunity. That is, whitespace is a potential source of profit, almost always associated with some level of risk.

Whizzing The act or practice of scrubbing a coin with a special brush in order to make it appear as if it is in mint condition. This causes wear and tear to the surface of the coin and may therefore reduce the coin's value. It is also called buffing.

WHOIS A query into a computer system seeking the identity of a domain name, IP address or other unknown information. The WHOIS query promotes security on computer systems.

Whole Dollar Any amount of a currency expressed without using subdivisions of that currency. For example, if one rounds $3.76 to the nearest whole dollar, one arrives at $4.

Whole Life Annuity Due A payment on a life annuity that must be made at the beginning, rather than at the end, of a period. That is, a whole life annuity due requires payments at the beginning of the month instead of at the end.

Whole Life Insurance A life insurance policy with no expiration date. That is, a whole life insurance policy provides coverage for the entire life of the policyholder (provided he/she continues to make premium payments). When the policyholder dies, regardless of when that is, his/her beneficiaries receive the death benefit. Whole life insurance policies also include a cash surrender value, allowing the policyholder to recover part of the premium he/she has invested in the policy should he/she ever decide to cancel the policy.

Whole Loan Describing a collateralized mortgage obligation that is too large to be issued or guaranteed by Ginnie Mae, Freddie Mac, or Fannie Mae. That is, a whole loan CMO represents jumbo mortgages, which can be riskier than other mortgages. As a result, whole loan CMOs pay a higher yield than those issued by a government agency; because of the lack of a government guarantee on coupon payments, they have a higher exposure to prepayment risk.

Whole Pool The underlying instrument in a mortgage-backed security representing ownership interest in entire mortgages as opposed to pieces of mortgages. Whole pools are fairly unusual among mortgage-backed securities as they are thought to carry higher risk: if a mortgage goes into default, the holder of the whole pool has little or nothing with which to hedge the investment. However, because they are not divided and re-divided as with other MBSs, whole pools are easier for investors to understand.

Whole-Life Cost The total amount a company spends on an asset over its entire usable life. Examples of whole-life costs include planning, research, purchase price, and maintenance. Companies estimate the whole-life cost prior to purchasing a new asset to determine whether or not it will be cost effective. It is also called the life cycle cost.

Wholesale 1. Relating to the sale of goods to a retailer. That is, a wholesaler receives large quantities of goods from a manufacturer and distributes them to stores, where they are sold to consumers. A wholesaler generally is able to extract a better price from the manufacturer because it buys so many good relative to an individual retailer. In theory, this enables the retailer to sell the good at a better price for the consumer. See also: Economies of scale. **2.** Relating to the sale of securities to institutional investors rather than individuals.

Wholesale Bank A bank that offers services to institutional investors, businesses (especially large businesses), other banks, and investment vehicles such as mutual funds or pensions. Wholesale banks usually conduct transactions worth large amounts of money, and wholesale clients can be prioritized above individual customers. This contrasts with retail banking, which specializes in individual clients.

Wholesale Banking Banking services offered to institutional investors, businesses (especially large businesses), other banks, and investment vehicles such as mutual funds or pensions. Wholesale banking usually conducts transactions worth large amounts of money, and wholesale clients can be prioritized more highly than individual customers. It compares with retail banking, which specializes in individual clients.

Wholesale Deposit A deposit at a bank made by an institutional investor, a large business, another bank or an investment vehicle such as a mutual fund or pension. Wholesale deposits are usually large amounts of money, and wholesale clients are sometimes prioritized more highly than individual customers.

Wholesale Insurance An insurance policy for a small group of persons, usually sponsored by an employer. Wholesale insurance is offered if a group is not large enough to qualify for group insurance; such groups generally range from five to 50 members. In wholesale insurance, the individual policyholder owns the policy, but the employer or another party subsidizes the premium.

Wholesale Inventory The inventory of a good a wholesaler that is unable to sell to a retailer. Retailers generally reduce their orders in response to lower demand at the consumer level. Wholesale inventories may therefore be an indicator of consumer good sales.

Wholesale Life Insurance A life insurance policy for a small group of persons, usually sponsored by an employer. Wholesale life insurance is offered if a group is not large enough to qualify for group insurance; such groups generally ranges from five to 50 members. In wholesale life insurance, the individual policyholder owns the policy, but the employer or another party subsidizes the premium.

Wholesale Market 1. The market for the sale of goods to a retailer. That is, a wholesaler receives large quantities of goods from a manufacturer and distributes them to stores, where they are sold to consumers. A wholesaler is generally able to extract a better price from the manufacturer because it buys so many good relative to an individual retailer. In theory, this enables the retailer to sell the good at a better price for the consumer. See also: Economies of scale. **2.** The market for the sale of securities to institutional investors rather than individuals.

Wholesale Price The per unit price of a good that a wholesaler (or distributor of large quantity of goods) charges a retailer (which resells the goods to the general public). A wholesaler is generally able to extract a better price from the manufacturer because it buys so many good relative to an individual retailer. Wholesale prices are thus able to be lower than what the retailer would pay if it went directly to the manufacturer. In theory, this enables the retailer to sell the good at a better price for the consumer. See also: Economies of scale.

Wholesaler A company that purchases large quantities of goods from a manufacturer and sells them to stores, where they are resold to consumers. A wholesaler generally is able to extract a better price from the manufacturer because it buys so many good relative to an individual retailer. In theory, this enables the retailer to sell the good at a better price for the consumer. See also: Economies of scale, Warehouse.

Wholly Owned Subsidiary A company that, while theoretically publicly-traded, has all of its common stock owned by a single company. Some wholly owned subsidiaries belong to the same industry as the parent company, while others do not, and are part of a diversification effort on the part of the parent company. A wholly owned subsidiary's board of directors is directly appointed by the parent company, and is ultimately responsible to the shareholders of the parent company. Some wholly owned subsidiaries were once part of the parent company but were spun off, while others were smaller companies bought outright by their parent companies. See also: Holding company.

Whoops An informal and derogatory term for the Washington Public Power Supply System. This company issued more than $2 billion in bonds in the 1970s to build nuclear power plants and defaulted on these obligations in 1983. It is now known as Energy Northwest.

Whore's Market A slang term for a market with almost no barriers to entry that already has a large number of participants. That is, in a whore's market, several companies are already competing with each other and there is little to stop more companies from entering the market. This can result in great prices for customers, but tends to dramatically reduce profitability.

Wiardunek A unit of account used in medieval central and eastern Europe, primarily Germany and Poland. It was considered to be equal in value to 12 groschen, the rough equivalent of the penny.

Wicker Basket A British slang term for 15 pounds.

Wide Area Network Also called WAN. A network that allows computers to connect to the Internet over an exceptionally large area, such as a metropolitan area, a region or even a country.

Wide Area Telephone Service Also called WATS. A long distance service in the United States allowing a single telephone line to call one of several lines at a central location (such as a call center) or vice versa. This service may be used for outbound or inbound calls, though using it for outbound calls became obsolete by the 1990s. The service is used by 800 numbers, enabling customers to call a center to place an order or conduct some other activities. It was developed in the 1960s by AT&T.

Wide Basis A situation in which there is a large difference in the spot price and the futures price for a commodity. This occurs when investors expect there to be a large shift in supply or demand between the present time and when the commodity is delivered under the futures contract. A wide basis should narrow as a futures contract comes closer to maturity; when this does not occur, arbitrage opportunities arise.

Wide Opening An unusually large bid-ask spread on a security at the open of an exchange. A wide opening is most common when specialists and/or market makers have not yet submitted their first bids and asks, which are usually the most competitive offers.

Wide-Angle Lens A camera lens allowing one to take an image with a broader spectrum. That is, one may see more on either side of the focal point of the image. However, a wide angle lens may compress depth, potentially resulting in a blurred image. It is used in both photography and film.

Wider Slang; in bond trading, an increase in yield spread, indicating greater risk.

Wider-Range Securities The proportion of a trust's pool of liquidity that is invested in higher risk securities such as stocks or junk bonds. A trust generally invests in both wider-range securities and narrow-range securities, which carry less risk. It adjusts the proportion according to how risk averse the trust's managers are.

Widget A generic term for any product, especially a manufactured product. It is used in text books and academic papers to provide an example without using specifics.

Widow A woman whose husband has died. In many countries, widows are eligible for certain state benefits. Widows generally receive at least a portion of their husband's pension or other retirement plan. Likewise, a man whose wife has died is called a widower.

Widow-and-Orphan Stock A stock that pays high dividends because it has a strong financial position and is in a non-cyclical industry. Widow-and-orphan stocks are generally issued by well-established companies and are considered low-risk investments. See also: Blue chip.

Widow's Allowance In probate, a portion of a decedent's estate that a court allows the surviving spouse to use to provide for his/her needs until the case is settled and property is distributed.

Widow's Benefit In the U.S., a state-level deduction from taxable income of the amount a widow or widower receives from the estate of his/her deceased spouse. The benefit means the widow or widower pays little or nothing in state inheritance taxes.

Widow's Exemption 1. The reduction of a taxable inheritance one receives because one is the widow or widower of the deceased. For example, if a woman passes away and leaves her husband all her assets, the widow's exemption is the amount to which the husband is entitled before he becomes liable to pay inheritance taxes. **2.** More generally, any tax deduction given to a widow or widower.

Wiggle Room The amount by which a sale can be reduced before it significantly cuts into profit. Wiggle room can determine how much of a discount a company can give a customer for things like volume, new client promotions, or other promotions.

Wigtje A Dutch unit of weight equivalent to one gram. It was adopted in 1817, soon after the establishment of the Kingdom of the Netherlands.

Wiki An online project allowing any participant to comment, add, delete or change the product. A wiki is generally an online dictionary or encyclopedia. Wiki software has been developed to ease the editing process. It is an example of Web 2.0. The first wiki came online in 1994.

Wilayah In parts of North Africa and Central Asia, a political subdivision equivalent to a province.

Wild Card Option The ability for the seller of a futures contract on a Treasury note or Treasury bond to give notice of delivery for a certain period of time after the exchange on which the contract was trading has already closed for the days. This gives the seller the ability to deliver the cheapest to deliver issue. See also: Wild Card Play.

Wild Card Play The ability for the seller of a futures contract to give notice of delivery for a certain period of time after the exchange on which the contract was trading has already closed for the days. This gives the seller the ability to deliver the cheapest to deliver issue. See also: Wild Card Option.

Wildcat Banking A period in the United States between 1816 and 1863 in which there was no federal regulation of banks. Currency was issued by private banks, which were only regulated by the individual states. These currencies were often backed by the debt the banks held and were often unstable, which frequently caused the currencies to become worthless. See also: National Bank Act of 1863.

Wildcat Drilling The practice of drilling for oil in an area with no proven reserves. That is, the wildcatter has no idea if the venture will yield a significant amount of oil. This is extremely high risk but has the potential for large profits if the wildcatter strikes "black gold." See also: Exploratory Oil and Gas Partnership.

Wildcat Strike A strike that employees take in small or large groups without the authorization of union representatives. This may happen when the employees believe both the union and the employer are treating them unfairly. Wildcat strikes are illegal in the United States. See also: Winter of Discontent.

Will A document stating how and to whom a person wants his/her property transferred after death. In addition to transferring property, a will may specify how certain responsibilities are to be performed. For example, a will may state who shall take care of the decedent's minor children, how they are to be educated, and so forth. A court must enforce the provisions of a will unless there is some overriding legal reason for it not to do so. Many advisers recommend writing a will to ensure that the writer's wishes are carried out.

Will Variation A law allowing the widow(er) or children of a decedent to contest a will if they believe the will does not adequately provide for them. Wills are intended to carry out the wishes of the deceased; thus, will variation does not guarantee that the decedent's relatives will actually receive anything from the estate.

William Hewlett An engineer and businessman (1913-2001) who co-founded the Hewlett-Packard Company in 1939. He served as president from 1964 to 1977 and CEO from 1968 to 1978. He remained involved well into the 1980s. He was also a noted philanthropist.

William Levitt An American real estate investor whose mass production of affordable, private homes to middle class persons led to the development of modern suburbs. He founded a number of towns in the mid-20th century and marketed the homes to middle class (and largely white) persons and families. He lived from 1907 to 1994.

William M. Allen A 20th century businessman who served as President of Boeing from 1945 to 1970. He became well-regarded during his tenure, overseeing the launch of the Boeing 727, 737, and 747 aircrafts.

William McDonough An American economist. He served as president of the New York Federal Reserve from 1993 to 2003, and chairman of the Public Company Accounting Oversight Board from 2003 to 2005. He was born in 1934.

William Peter Hamilton An investor who was a major proponent of Dow theory, which states that when the Dow Jones Industrial Average and the Dow Jones Transportation Average both hit a new high or a new low for a period of time, it can confirm a previous, bullish or bearish signal. He was a student of Charles Dow and an editor of the Wall Street Journal. He died in 1930.

William S. Paley An American businessman who brought CBS to prominence. He started in his family's cigar business, which purchased a number of radio stations in Philadelphia, primarily to advertise the cigars. Paley pioneered quality programming to draw advertisers. He served as owner and executive of CBS for most of his career. He lived from 1901 to 1990.

William Sharpe An American economist and professor. His major contributions include both the capital asset pricing model and the Sharpe ratio, which attempts to account for a money manager's index-like tendencies in portfolio management. Sharpe won the Nobel Prize for economics in 1990. He was born in 1934.

Williams %R In technical analysis, an indicator showing a security's closing price compared to its price over the last N days. Somewhat unusually, it rates on a scale of -100 to 0, with -100 representing a closing price equal to the low of the past N days and 0 representing a closing price equal to the high. Mathematically, it is represented as: %R = ((closetoday - highN days) / (highN days - lowN days)) * 100 The Williams %R was created by Larry Williams, who concluded that a %R below -80 indicates a security is oversold; on the other hand, a %R above -20 indicates an overbought security. Most analyst use N = 10 or N = 14.

Williams Act Legislation in the United States, enacted in 1968, requiring persons or companies who own or make a tender offer for more than 5% of the common stock of a publicly-traded company to register with the SEC. The information contained in the registration includes the person or company's intentions, the terms of a tender offer, and how the person or company is paying for it. The Williams Act is designed to increase transparency in the market, especially in the event of a hostile takeover. The SEC enforced the Williams Act through Rule 13d and Rule 14d.

Willie Sutton Rule A rule in management accounting stating that activity-based costing (in which activities are prioritized by necessity and budgeted accordingly) should be applied where the highest costs occur because that is where the biggest savings can be found. That is, one attempts to find savings in the most expensive activities. The rule derives its name from bank robber Willie Sutton, who reportedly said he stole from banks "because that's where the money is."

Wilshire 5000 Total Market Index A capitalization-weighted index that tracks as many stocks being traded in the United States as possible. It tracks all stocks traded on the NYSE, American Stock Exchange, NASDAQ, and any other stock for which data is easily available. Thus, despite its name, it is usually tracking more than 5,000 stocks. It is the broadest index in the United States. The Wilshire 5000 is subdivided into four indices: one for large-cap, one for mid-cap, one for small-cap, and one for micro-cap stocks.

Wilshire Indexes A series of capitalization-weighted indexes that tracks as many stocks being traded in the United States as possible. They track all stocks traded on the NYSE, American Stock Exchange, NASDAQ, and any other stock for which data is easily available. It is the broadest index in the United States. The Wilshire indexes are subdivided into four indexes: one for large-cap, one for mid-cap, one for small-cap, and one for micro-cap stocks.

Wilson-Gorman Act Legislation in the United States, enacted in 1894, that imposed the first income tax in peacetime. Primarily, the act significantly lowered tariffs, but levied an income tax of 2% on incomes over $4,000 to make up the lost federal revenue. The act is formally called the Revenue Act of 1894.

Windfall A sudden, unexpected profit or gain. A windfall may occur, for example, after a company announces an earnings surprise and its stock consequently jumps significantly. Companies may also experience windfall when demand for their products skyrockets; for example, an umbrella manufacturer may see windfall during an especially rainy year. See also: Windfall shares, Windfall tax.

Windfall Profits Tax A tax on profits seen as excessive. For example, a windfall profits tax may be imposed on oil companies when their profits rise above a certain amount. The idea behind a windfall profits tax is to encourage the taxed persons or companies to lower their prices, which is thought to be good for consumers. However, it may have the effect of reducing investment because the aftertax profit may not be worth the effort. See also: Windfall shares, Windfall tax.

Windfall Shares Shares given without charge to the owners of a mutually-owned company when that company is in the process of demutualizing. Because the owners will no longer be the owners when the company demutualizes, windfall shares are designed to compensate them for their previous ownership. This is intended to encourage goodwill. It also gives the former owners a continued stake in the company.

Winding Up The process of a company liquidating the assets, paying off creditors, and generally ceasing operations. The company may continue its normal business during winding up, but will gradually bring it to an end.

Winding-Up Order An order by a court for a company or organization to liquidate, especially to pay its debts. A winding-up order forces the company to cease operations and sell its assets.

Windmill A software framework one may use from almost any browser or across any platform to test web applications.

Window 1. A physical place at a bank or brokerage where a customer goes to receive services. For example, a client may approach a window at a bank to deposit a check or make a withdrawal. Likewise, a client goes to a window at a brokerage to settle an account or deliver and receive securities. **2.** A time during which it would be advantageous to conduct a certain transaction. For example, an investor has a window in which to make a profit on a security by buying while the price tends to rise and selling when it tends to fall.

Window Dressing The act or practice of buying and selling securities on a portfolio immediately before a report is due in order to make the portfolio look more profitable or otherwise healthier than it has been. For example, the portfolio manager may sell stocks that have performed poorly and buy those that have performed well. Portfolios receive window dressing in order to make them look more attractive to prospective investors, which in turn makes the portfolio manager look more successful. The practice is also called dressing up a portfolio or portfolio dressing. See also: Manager Universe (benchmark).

Window Envelope An envelope with one or more transparent portions where the addresses are ordinarily written. Pre-printed addresses are placed so they can be seen through the windows. Window envelopes are often used to mail paychecks, which usually contain both the payer's and the payee's addresses.

Window Guaranteed Investment Contract A pension plan purchased through a bank or an insurance company in which one puts a series of payments in an account such that the principal is guaranteed. After retirement, one may receive payments from the investment. Window GICs contrast with most guaranteed investment contracts in that they are are purchased over time with a series or payments rather than with a lump sum.

Window Licker Slang; an employee who unsuccessfully vies for his/her supervisor's approval in order to achieve a promotion.

Window Period The period of time during which the SEC allows executives and certain employees to trade in stock of their own company. Window periods exist in order to prevent insider trading while also allowing executives to keep skin in the game.

Window Settlement A way to settle a transaction where two dealers physically meet and exchange the underlying asset for the payment. Window settlement occurs when one or both dealers do not belong to a clearing house. Window settlement has become less common with increased computerization of the securities trade.

Window Streamer In advertising, a large banner hung from the window of a store to attract attention.

Window Tax A tax on the number of windows on a house. Window taxes existed in Britain and France during the 18th and 19th centuries. They were intended primarily to affect the wealthy, who tended to live in houses with more windows. In England, the tax was structured as a flat rate per window, with a variable rate applying after 10 windows. Because of the window tax, some homes had bricked up spaces for windows so owners easily could install windows if the tax were reduced or repealed.

Windshield Survey When doing field work or visiting a work site, the act or practice of only giving a cursory examination. The term implies that one does not even bother to leave one's car while on the visit.

Windstorm Hazard The risk that a windstorm will cause damage to a property. Most standard homeowner insurance policies do not provide coverage for this hazard, and one must purchase windstorm insurance to protect oneself.

Windstorm Insurance An insurance policy providing coverage for the risk that a windstorm will cause damage to a property. Most standard homeowner insurance policies do not cover this hazard, and one must purchase windstorm insurance to protect oneself.

Winkelbankier A currency speculator in German in the early 1920s. A Winkelbankier bought and sold currencies to profit from the arbitrage from the official and free market exchange rates of the German mark, which was constantly depreciating due to hyperinflation.

Winner's Curse In auctions, the tendency for the winning bid to exceed the intrinsic value of what is being offered. This trend was first noted among energy companies during auctions for bidding rights to drill in the Gulf of Mexico. It is thought that insufficient information and, perhaps more so, the emotional desire to win in the heat of an auction contribute to the winner's curse. See also: Behavioral economics.

Winnipeg Commodity Exchange An exchange in Canada on which futures and options contracts on barley, canola and wheat are traded. It is Canada's only futures exchange for commodities. It was established in 1887. In 2007, it became a subsidiary of the Intercontinental Exchange.

Winter Range Form An insurance policy providing coverage to owners of livestock inhabiting states in the Western US between October 1 and May 1. The winter range form protects the owner from loss due to theft, natural disasters and, most importantly, inclement weather. For example, if a portion of a herd of cattle freezes to death during the winter, a winter range form covers the owner for the loss. As with all insurance, one must pay a premium to receive the coverage.

Wipe In film, a transition between two shots or scenes in which a second shot gradually replaces a first. Wipes are done in editing.

Wipeout A significant loss on an investment. For example, a wipeout occurs if one buys a stock at $100 per share and the price later drops to $4. An investment is unlikely to recover from a wipeout.

WIR Bank A non-profit bank in Switzerland that finances transactions between members. It encourages members (which consist of medium-sized and small businesses) to trade with each other and provides the financing for them to do so. For its bookkeeping, it uses the WIR euro, a non-circulating accounting currency. It was established in 1934 and is credited with contributing to the stability of the Swiss economy.

WIR Euro An accounting currency used by medium-sized and small businesses in Switzerland. The WIR euro is used by members of the WIR Bank, which encourages member businesses to trade with each other and facilitates transactions between them. Although the WIR euro does not circulate, it helps maintain the stability of the Swiss economy.

Wire Fate Item Notification by one bank to another in a different jurisdiction of payment or non-payment of a check. The term derives from the fact that these notifications were originally sent by telegraph. See also: Fedwire.

Wire Fraud The use of any electronic communications device to defraud anyone. Using false promises to gain something over the phone or internet is wire fraud, regardless of whether or not any money is actually stolen. In the United States, wire fraud is a federal offense.

Wire House A company or other institution with multiple offices that are connected via an independent computer system. This allows for the easy and secure sharing of financial and other information. The term is usually used for banks and brokerages.

Wire Room A department (or a physical room in the office) of a brokerage that receives orders from clients and transmits them to the appropriate broker on an exchange for execution. Likewise, when the order is executed, the wire room is responsible for informing the client. The wire room helps keep the process of placing orders and making transactions as organized as possible. See also: Front office.

Wire Side In printing, a cloth made from brass, bronze or nylon. It is used to form paper.

Wire Transfer The direct, electronic transfer of funds from one bank account to another. Wire transfer is instantaneous and is a fairly common way to send funds to another party very quickly. However, wire transfers sometimes have higher fees than, say, writing checks. Outside North America, wire transfers are sometimes known as telegraph transfers.

Wireless Technology The ability to connect to the Internet or another computer without attaching an Ethernet cord or telephone wire to one's computer. It was invented in 1994 and became popular in the 2000s. Wireless technology has facilitated mobility in both study and many occupations. Many wireless devices use technology certified as Wi-Fi, a brand name. See also: Work from home.

Wireline The use of an Ethernet or other cable to connect a computer to the Internet or another computer. The advent of wireless technology has made it less common for home computers.

Wire-O Binding A type of bookbinding in which O-shaped rings attached to the binding are placed within holes punched in the paper. This is used most commonly with notebooks and instruction manuals.

Wirtschaftswunder The rapid development in West Germany and Austria following the devastation of World War II. The Wirtschaftswunder saw low inflation and quick growth in industrial production starting around 1950. The impetus for the Wirtschaftswunder came from replacement of the Reichsmark with the deutschemark (in West Germany) and the schilling (in Austria), as well as the development package offered by the United States in the Marshall Plan.

Wisconsin State Life Fund A program in the State of Wisconsin in which life insurance is offered to any resident who applies. As with all insurance, the policyholder must pay a premium to receive the coverage.

Wisse A Dutch unit of volume equivalent to one cubic meter. It was adopted in 1817, soon after the establishment of the Kingdom of the Netherlands. It is also called a teerling el.

With Approved Credit Describing a situation in which a potential borrower must have a sufficient credit rating and/or credit history in order to qualify for a loan. This term is most commonly used when a company provides financing for the sale of its products. For example, a car dealer may finance automobiles to buyer "with approved credit."

With Average A provision in maritime transport insurance stating that the insurer is responsible for partial losses on the value of the covered products. Sometimes with-average plans include deductibles, and sometimes they do not. Depending on the amount of the deductible, the insurer of a with-average plan will be liable for losses if some of the products break in transit. For example, if one is transporting $10,000 worth of goods over sea and $2,000 in goods are washed overboard, the with-average policy covers the owner of the goods for $2,000 (assuming no deductible). This contrasts with a free of particular average plan, in which the insurer is generally only responsible for catastrophic losses.

With Interest Describing a bond being traded for which the buyer is entitled to all interest that has accumulated since the last coupon was paid. That is, the seller sells the right to the accumulated interest along with the actual bond.

With or Without Describing an order to buy or sell an odd-lot of a security immediately at the best available price. An odd-lot is any quantity of shares other than 100. Odd-lot orders are more difficult to execute because there are fewer of them; many sellers charge more for odd-lot orders and many buyers will not pay as much. As a result, many odd-lot orders look for a counter-order without this premium attached. A with or without order does not wait for this and is simply executed immediately.

With the Grain The practice of folding paper or feeding it into a printer in the same direction as the fibers of the paper run. Going with the grain leads to less bulky material that presents better. For that reason, it is usually preferred, especially in marketing.

Withdrawal A transaction in which a customer receives back money he/she had previously deposited at a bank, pension, or trust. When one makes a withdrawal on a pension or similar plan, it may carry a penalty depending on the pension's rules. For example, one must usually be of a certain age in order to make a withdrawal. There is rarely such a penalty when making a withdrawal from a bank. For instance, when one closes an account, the client makes a withdrawal on all the money he/she owns at that bank.

Withdrawal Benefits The right of an employee to contributions made to his/her employer-sponsored retirement plan when he/she leaves an employer. The employee has withdrawal benefits to all his/her own contributions and all interest earned. He/she may have a right to employer contributions, but only if they are vested. See also: Rollover.

Withdrawal Notice A written statement informing a bank that a depositor wishes to make a withdrawal from an account. Depending on the type of account, some withdrawal notices must be made a certain number of days in advance. Most of the time, however, a withdrawal may be made on demand.

Withdrawal Plan 1. A strategy in which an investor sells a certain number or type of securities each year. One may use the proceeds to fund any number of things, such as a child's college education or one's own retirement. The risk of a withdrawal plan is the possibility that one may not have sufficient cash to buy replacement securities or, more simply, that one may run out of securities to sell. **2.** See: Systematic withdrawal plan.

Withdrawals from the Circular Flow of Incomes Any structure that takes money out of the circular flow of incomes, which is a simple model for the flow of money. Under the model, consumers buy goods and services from producers, who make a profit. The producers then use that money to pay consumers to make their products (say, in factories). The consumers use that money to buy more goods and services and the cycle continues. Withdrawals from the circular flow include imports (in which money is sent outside the economy), savings (in which money is not spent at all) and taxes.

Withholding The act or practice of not giving a certain percentage of money that otherwise belongs to a person. Withholding must occur in accordance with appropriate laws and may not be arbitrary. Withholding is most common in taxes, in which an employer retains a certain percentage of an employee's wages or salary and gives it to the IRS instead of the employee. Likewise, a manual rollover to an IRA is subject to a 20% withholding. Courts may order withholding for reasons such as child support or alimony. See also: Overwithholding.

Withholding Allowance A declaration on a W-4 form stating that an employee should have less money withheld from his/her paycheck. That is, the more withholding allowances an individual declares, the less money is withheld because it is likely that the individual will owe less in income tax. One may declare one withholding allowance each for oneself, one's spouse, and each of one's children and other dependents.

Without Describing a quote in a one-way market. That is, when one says "$25 ask without", that means a willing seller wants to sell a security for $25, but there is no corresponding bid.

Without Evidence of Insurability A situation in which an applicant for life or health insurance does not present documentation indicating that he/she is sufficiently healthy to be sold a policy. Many policies do not require evidence of insurability, but others mandate a health exam prior to the policy's issue.

Without Penalty Describing the early withdrawal of funds from a retirement plan without a penalty tax. A withdrawal without penalty is rare, and generally occurs only in the event of a major catastrophe, such as an unexpected illness.

Without Prejudice A legal term indicating that an act should not be taken as a precedent. For example, if a criminal charge is dismissed without prejudice, the prosecutor may refile the same charge at a later date. Statements made without prejudice may be altered later and ordinarily may not be used as evidence in a court.

Without Reserve The grant of unlimited authority to an agent, at least within certain limits. For example, an agent with the authority without reserve to buy a house for the principal does not need to seek the principal's final approval and may simply buy a house. See also: Agency problem.

Without-Profits Life Insurance A chiefly British and Commonwealth term for a nonparticipating life insurance policy.

With-Profits Bond A fixed income investment based on non-fixed income instruments. For example, one may purchase a with-profits bond with a 5% annual return, but the money one invests is placed in stocks, mutual funds and other instruments. The profits made in the "good years" are not disbursed to the investor; rather, they are used to make up for losses in the "bad years." These instruments are designed to allow one to take advantage of market movements without assuming too much risk. With-profits bonds are sponsored by insurance companies.

With-Profits Policy A chiefly British and Commonwealth term for a participating policy.

Wizna A Maltese unit of weight approximately equivalent to four kilograms. It is largely obsolete but is still used in some circumstances.

WK 1. ISO 3166-1 alpha-2 code for Wake Island before it was re-designated as part of the U.S. Minor Outlying Islands. This was the code used in international transactions to and from bank accounts on Wake Island. **2.** ISO 3166-2 geocode for Wake Island. This was used as an international standard for shipping to Wake Island. In both cases, the code is obsolete.

WKUM ISO 3166-3 code for Wake Island, which became part of the United States Minor Outlying Islands. ISO 3166-3 codes are used to indicate names of countries that are no longer used.

WLF GOST 7.67 Latin three-letter geocode for the Wallis and Futuna Islands. The code is used for transactions to and from local bank accounts and for international shipping to the Wallis and Futuna Islands. As with all GOST 7.67 codes, it is used primarily in Cyrillic alphabets.

Wloka An obsolete Polish unit of area approximately equivalent to 18 hectares.

Wolfe Wave In technical analysis, a series of price movements with waves roughly analogous to waves found in nature. The Wolfe wave holds that stock prices move up a total of five times and down a total three times in a bull market and vice versa in a bear market. Tracking Wolfe waves over time helps technical analysts estimate future price movements. A Wolfe Wave may occur in a very short or over a very long period of time.

Women Leaders Round Table A group within the National Association of Life Underwriters that discusses issues in insurance particularly relevant to female agents. All women insurance agents who underwrite more than a certain number of policies are eligible for membership.

Women's Service Magazine A magazine most likely to appeal to homemakers, especially but not necessarily female homemakers. These magazines may include articles about children, cleaning, cooking and so forth. The demographics to which women's service magazines appeal affect the type of advertisements that appear in them.

Won 1. See: North Korean won. **2.** See: South Korean won.

Wonger A chiefly British slang term for money. It is primarily used in London.

Woodcut A block of wood with a letter or image cut into it. Woodcuts were used as an early way to print materials in large quantities. They developed in Asia.

Woody Informal; describing a sudden, large uptick in market prices. This may refer to a single security, but usually refers to a stock market at large. For example, one may say, "The market has a woody," to describe this situation.

Wool Growers Floater An insurance policy that provides coverage for the loss of sheep or their wool while in transit within a country. For example, if a truck containing sheep crashes and kills the sheep, a wool growers floater would protect their owner from the loss. As with all insurance, one must pay a premium to receive the coverage.

Word Informal; an advertisement or a set of advertisements in succession. The term is most common in broadcasting. For example, a radio announcer may say, "And now a word from our sponsors."

Word Association Test A game or psychological test in which a participant is given a word and is asked to state the word he/she first thinks of upon hearing that word. A word association test is thought (though this is disputed) to reveal the contents of the participant's subconscious mind. It is used in marketing to help determine the precise words to use in an advertisement by attempting to ensure that viewers or listeners will associate the ad with the "proper" words.

Word Processing The use of a computer program to write, edit and format content. One writes the content and may either print it or save it in an electronic format. Word processing developed in the 1960s and was popularized in the 1970s and 1980s. Word processing was one of the first business uses for the personal computer.

Word Processing Center A company or a department within a company that provides secretarial or other writing and editing services, such as court reporting.

Word Processor A computer program allowing one to write, edit and format content. One writes the content and may either print it or save it in an electronic format. Word processors developed in the 1960s and were popularized in the 1970s and 1980s. Word processing was one of the first business uses for the personal computer.

Word Wrap In word processing, the feature that allows text that goes past the margin to be automatically transported to the next line without any break or hyphenation in the word. This occurs unless the word itself is longer than a line.

Words per Minute The number of words of dictation a person can type in one minute. Maintaining a high WPM rate is an important clerical skill for persons who are expected to type or retype documents.

Woreda In Ethiopia, a political subdivision approximately equivalent to a county.

Work 1. To perform a task, especially in exchange for compensation or the potential for profit. Working is necessary for any economy to function. **2.** See: Job.

Work and Materials Clause A provision in a property insurance contract enabling the property owner to safely store materials used for his/her business on the property secured by the policy. For example, a work and materials clause may enable a homeowner to keep non-perishable inventory for his store in the basement. Without such a clause, the policy may be invalidated because the presence of the material may increase the risk of theft or another insured event.

Work Experience The length of time one has been working in a particular field (or working generally). For example, one may have three years of work experience in computer programming. Greater work experience usually (but does not always) translates to greater skill in one's craft and therefore to a higher salary.

Work from Home To conduct business from one's residence as opposed to an office. Some employees may work from home on a temporary or project basis; for example, one may work from home on a weekend when the office is closed. However, others, notably the self-employed, work from home regularly because they do not have offices. The advent of home computers and the Internet have made working from home easier.

Work in Process Products of a company that are in inventory but are incomplete. They are held in inventory while they are completed and made ready for sale. In the accounting of inventory, work in process is recorded under assets and is valued at its cost or realizable value, whichever is less. Just as commonly, works in process are called goods in process.

Work Opportunity Credit A tax credit a business owner was able to receive in 2009 and 2010 for hiring an unemployed or semi-employed veteran or young person. To be eligible for the credit, the veteran must have been discharged sometime in the five years previous to hiring and must have been on unemployment insurance for at least four weeks in the year prior to hiring. Likewise, a youth must have been between 16 and 24, a high school dropout without a GED and either unemployed or employed at a job in which he/she earned less than he/she would have working for minimum wage for 30 hours a week.

Work Order A formal, written request by a client for some product to be made and delivered to him/her. For example, a car company may submit a work order to an engine manufacturer for 10,000 engines to be made according to certain specifications. The term historically has been most common in manufacturing, but other sectors use it as well. It is also called a job order or, outside the United States, a works order.

Work Papers Documents an auditor uses in performing his/her duties. Examples of work papers include balance sheets and memos. Work papers give the auditor some basis on which to base his/her work. Work papers may be subpoenaed and required to be presented in court.

Work Permit 1. Legal permission in certain U.S. states for a minor child to take a job. Work permits are required to ensure that neither the employer nor the child is in violation of child labor laws. Work permits come with certain restrictions; for example, the employee ordinarily may not work during school hours. **2.** See: Work visa.

Work Sandwich In an office setting, a slang term for the practice of hiding personal material between two batches of work material in order to hide the fact that one is working on personal matters at the office.

Work Sharing An arrangement whereby a company cuts employee hours so that two or more employees work the same amount that one employee previously did. Companies implement work sharing in difficult times in order to reduce expenses without conducting layoffs. Work sharing is also called job sharing.

Work Spasm A slang term for a brief period of productivity between long periods of non-productivity at work. Work spasms may happen, for example, right before one leaves for vacation, when one has to clear one's desk of all outstanding projects.

Work Study 1. A program whereby a college or university allows a student to work on campus in exchange for a reduction in tuition or other fees. **2.** A program whereby an educational institution combines theoretical study with practical experience. Traditionally, work study alternates semesters between classroom study and full-time, paid employment in a position related to one's field. This is more commonly called cooperative education.

Work Visa A visa giving one the ability to take a job in a country other than the one in which one is a citizen. There are different types of work visas. One kind may require the holder to have a local employer as a sponsor, and to return home if he/she loses the job. Another visa may be more general and may allow the holder to work at any job for a certain period of time. Work visas are generally temporary, though most may be renewed.

Worked Mail Mail that has been presorted and is ready to be sent to its destination.

Worker An employee or one engaged in an activity that makes money. In left-wing circles, the word especially refers to employees who earn wages (as opposed to salaries) and/or those in blue collar professions.

Worker Adjustment and Retraining Notification Act Informally called the WARN Act. Legislation in the United States, passed in 1988, that requires employers with more than 100 employees to provide at least 60 days notice before a mass layoff. The employer must also provide notice to local authorities, an employment transition organization and the labor union, if applicable. The WARN Act is intended to protect employees and allow them to look for other work during the 60 days.

Worker Buyout A situation in which an employer pays a (usually large) fee to an employee in exchange for that employee's resignation or retirement. Despite the upfront payout, a worker buyout usually is less expensive over the long term than keeping the employee on staff. As such, worker buyouts are sometimes used in lieu of layoffs.

Worker Capitalism A theory that employees should have a partial or total ownership interest in the company for which they work. The idea behind worker capitalism states that employees will work harder and better if they have an actual, tangible incentive for the company to make a profit. See also: Employee stock ownership plan.

Worker Capitalist A scholar or other person who believes that employees should have a partial or total ownership interest in the company for which they work. Worker capitalists contend that employees will work harder and more efficiently if they have an actual, tangible incentive for the company to make a profit. See also: Employee stock ownership plan.

Worker Participation The policy in which a company allows subordinate employees, usually but not always collectively, to have a say in the management of the company. For example, employees may be represented on a company's board of directors. Likewise, the company's union may negotiate a contract in which union representatives have certain management authority.

Worker-Controlled Firm A for-profit company owned by its own employees. Employees assume the risk of the company's failure (though they may have limited liability) and benefit from its success. A worker-controlled firm gives employees a vested interest in and a tangible share of the company's profitability; however, the risk exists that employees do not have the skills to be effective business owners.

Workers' Compensation Insurance that pays for an employee's medical care in the event that he/she is injured at work. Workers' comp may also provide for lost wages and compensate for disability or reduced earning potential. In exchange for receiving workers' comp, the employee surrenders the right to sue the employer for negligence. Workers' comp is mandatory in many jurisdictions and employee paychecks are reduced by the amount of the premium.

Workers' Compensation Acts American legislation at individual state levels regulating workers' compensation insurance, which covers medical care in the event that an employee is injured at work. Workers' compensation acts generally require employers to purchase this insurance for their employees.

Workers' Compensation Benefits Payment for an employee's medical care in the event that he/she is injured at work. Workers' comp benefits may also provide for lost wages and compensate for disability or reduced earning potential. In exchange for receiving workers' comp benefits, the employee surrenders the right to sue the employer for negligence.

Workers' Compensation Catastrophe Cover An insurance policy providing coverage for a self-insured employer in the event workers compensation claims rise above a certain amount. Employers who are not required to purchase workers comp insurance may elect simply to set money aside to pay for claims rather than buy a

policy. Workers compensation catastrophe cover pays for claims if this money is insufficient to pay for a claim. An employer may pay a lower premium for catastrophe cover as it is fairly unlikely he will have to file a claim.

Workers' Compensation Income, Disability Benefit Payment to replace a portion of an employee's wages or salary in the event that he/she is injured on the job and is unable to work. That is, if the employee is no longer able to perform his/her required tasks due to a work-related injury, he/she receives workers' compensation income, which, for example, may be equal to two thirds of one's ordinary wage or salary. See also: Workers compensation benefits.

Workers' Compensation, Coverage A A workers' compensation policy covering an employee for all situations required in the jurisdiction in which the employee works. Workers' comp is mandatory in many jurisdictions and employee paychecks are reduced by the amount of the premium.

Workers' Compensation, Coverage B A workers' compensation policy covering an employee for situations not required in the jurisdiction in which the employee works. That is, coverage B covers injuries for which the employee otherwise would be allowed legally to sue the employer.

Workfare A somewhat informal term for government benefits or other aid given in exchange for state-sponsored work. Workfare labor may or may not be compensated, but, if it is, the government is responsible for payment. Workfare contrasts with welfare, in which recipients have few requirements beyond low income.

Working 1. In investing, a term describing the process of a broker attempting to find a counterparty for a trade. **2.** See: Working capital. **3.** See: Work.

Working Asset A highly liquid, current asset. Working assets are taken in and distributed over relatively brief periods of time. Examples of working assets include cash, works in process and inventory. A working asset is also called a floating asset or a circulating asset.

Working Away The act of conducting a transaction between broker-dealers.

Working Capital The amount of money a company has on hand, or will have, in a given year. Working capital is calculated by subtracting current liabilities from current assets. That is, one takes the value of all debts and obligations for the current year and subtracts that from the value of all cash and assets that might reasonably be converted into cash in the current year. This is a good measure of the short and medium-term financial health of a company, and may indicate by how much it can expand its operations without resorting to borrowing or another capital raising tactic. Working capital is also called operating assets or net current assets.

Working Capital Loan A short-term loan to finance day-to-day operations of a business. It is normally a loan for a comparably small amount, and is not used for long-term investment purposes. Rather, it funds immediate needs, such as payroll and accounts payable.

Working Capital Management An accounting strategy in which a company seeks to maximize its cash flows so as to pay for its current liabilities and operating expenses. Examples of working capital management include active monitoring of accounts receivable and maintaining little short-term debt. Working capital management, if done properly, can help a company improve its earnings and maintain a healthy financial state.

Working Capital Ratio Cash and short-term assets expected to be converted to cash within a year as a percentage of the amount of annual sales. Because expansion requires capital on hand, the working capital ratio is considered a prime indicator of a company's ability to expand its operations without taking on additional debt. Perhaps more straightforwardly, it is often known as the working capital to sales ratio.

Working Class The class of persons who perform physical labor, skilled labor, domestic duties or similar tasks. Persons in the working class often earn an hourly wage and many (though far from all) have low job security. Examples of those with working class occupations include food servers, miners and construction workers. Some, though not all, are poorly paid. The working class is closely related to, but distinct from, the working poor. See also: Blue collar.

Working Control The state of holding a substantial minority stake in a publicly-traded company such that one does not have outright control, but is still a major player in the company's decisions. Often, an investor is considered to have working control if he/she has at least a 20% holding in the company. One has working control because the number of voting shares gives one virtual veto power over company decisions, particularly when other stockholders are closely divided. These investors must be listed on the company's financial statements.

Working Families Tax Relief Act of 2004 Legislation in the United States that extended tax cuts to middle class families and restored business tax cuts that were scheduled to expire. Among other provisions, it extended the $1,000 child tax credit, which was set to change to $700 per child.

Working Group Persons gathered together to solve a common problem or to set a particular goal. For example, a working group may be gathered to set standards for a nascent industry. A working group is expected to complete its task within a certain amount of time, usually with the publication of a paper or report. While working groups are founded as temporary, ad hoc committees, many go on to become semi-permanent bodies.

Working Life The time during which an adult is expected to be working or pursuing work. One's working life begins after the completion of education and ends at retirement. In general, most of one's savings and investments occurs during the working life because this is when one has the highest cash flow and, sometimes, the willingness to take risks.

Working Mother A woman who has a full-time job in addition a family. Some working mothers are professionals such as lawyers and doctors who work for personal and financial advancement. Others are working poor who have jobs out of utter necessity. Working mothers must balance time between their families and their careers. Working mothers are fairly new in the Western world because of the feminist movement in the 20th century. Some working mothers seek out companies with benefits such as maternity leave or flexibility when a child is sick.

Working Papers Special certification that some jurisdictions require before a person under age 18 may work. The working papers attest that the minor will abide by applicable laws, such as not working during school hours. See also: Child labor.

Working Ratio A measure of a company's ability to recover its operating expenses from its gross income in a given year. It is calculated by taking the company's total expenses, except for depreciation and debt service, and dividing them by its gross income. A ratio under 1 indicates that the company is recovering its expenses and therefore has a certain amount of financial health, while a ratio over 1 indicates the opposite.

Working Stiff Informal; an employee in a non-management position, especially one who is treated poorly. The term often is used in reference to tensions between corporate authorities and those under them.

Workout An informal process by which a debtor and creditors agree to debt forgiveness and/or a different repayment plan when the debtor states that he/she/it is unable to repay debts. A workout may be part of a Chapter 11 bankruptcy process, or the debtor and the creditors may work out their differences to avoid the painful,and often expensive, process of bankruptcy.

Workout Market A prediction made by a market maker on a security's trading range. That is, the market maker predicts a workout market when he/she makes an estimate as to the trading range over a short period of time, such as over the course of a trading day. Workout markets are easier to predict when there are fewer potential buyers and sellers for the security. See also: Narrow market.

Works Council A chapter of a labor union representing the workers of a single company. The works council coordinates its activities with the larger union. In some countries, notably Germany, works councils have the authority to alter national labor agreements to fit the circumstances of their own company. In some countries, representatives of a works council sit on the board of directors of the corporation.

Workstream A slang term for a project with such vague parameters that it is extremely difficult to define deliverables, let alone actually make any progress.

Work-Study A program in which a post-secondary student works a (usually menial) job on campus in exchange for tuition reduction or some other form of payment. Work-study programs may be part of a school's financial aid package, and may make post-secondary education more affordable.

World Administrative Radio Conference Also called WARC. A former periodic conference of the International Telecommunications Union at which member-delegates met to discuss changes to international regulations concerning radio broadcast. Conferences were held in Geneva. In 1993, the WARC became known as the World Radiocommunication Conference.

World Agricultural Outlook Board A division of the U.S. Department of Agriculture that gathers and disseminates information on the current and expected future state of the global agricultural markets. To this end, it publishes a periodical, World Agricultural Supply and Demand Estimates, on a monthly basis and hosts an annual forum for persons with interests in the business of agriculture.

World Bank A bank that provides loans and grants to developing countries. Formed by the Bretton Woods negotiations in 1944 and founded in 1945, it was established to rebuild Europe and Asia after World War II. It loans money for infrastructural, business, and environmental development worldwide. It charges developing countries low interest rates, raising its funds from bonds issued to governments and institutions. Because its largest shareholder is the United States, the president of the World Bank is traditionally American. See also: International Monetary Fund.

World Confederation of Labor A former European labor union. Founded in 1920, it originally catered to Catholic workers. It worked to improve working conditions for members, to assist women, to fight against child labor and to train members and build capacity. It merged into the International Trade Union Confederation and ceased to exist in 2006.

World Economic Forum 1. An annual meeting of global business, political and academic leaders in Davos, Switzerland. Participants in the World Economic Forum discuss the economic, political, environmental and other relevant issues of the day. The World Economic Forum lasts for five days and includes of 220 conferences and other events. Meetings tend to promote globalization. As a result, the forum has been the subject of controversy. **2.** A nonprofit foundation that sponsors the World Economic Forum as well as regional and specialized meetings. It was founded in 1971.

World Federation of Development Financing Institutions Also called the WFDFI. An organization for financial institutions specializing in development finance. The WFDFI advocates for its members and provides information on the industry. It was established in Zurich in 1979.

World Federation of Exchanges An organization that sets standards for international capital flows between securities exchanges. Based in Paris, it seeks to encourage international commerce in the securities and derivatives markets. More than 50 of the largest exchanges in the world belong to the World Federation of Exchanges. It was founded as the International Federation of Exchanges.

World Food Council An organization established by the United Nations in 1974 to reduce global hunger. It was suspended in 1993.

World Food Program A branch of the United Nations that provides food in needy areas worldwide. It was established in 1960 and has distributed food in areas where food security is lowest. It is based in Rome.

World Gold Council A professional organization of mining companies that produces gold. It exists to promote the use of, and investment in, gold through research, lobbying, and other means. Importantly, it has worked for reducing regulation on the gold trade. It also provides educational opportunities for members and the general public through its Goldipedia service, among other things. It was established in 1987 and is headquartered in Geneva. See also: Gold bug, Gold fund.

World Health Organization Also called the WHO. An organization under the United Nations that promotes and coordinates programs related to public health. It conducts activities aimed to reduce the effect of infectious diseases, notably polio, tuberculosis and HIV/AIDS, among others. It worked to successfully eradicate smallpox in the 1970s. It was founded in 1948 and is based in Geneva.

World Insurance An optional addition to a commercial liability policy that provides coverage in the event that the policyholder is sued anywhere in the world. This contrasts with most commercial liability policies, which have a geographic limit for coverage. One pays an additional premium in order to receive world insurance.

World Intellectual Property Organization Also called WIPO. An agency of the United Nations that seeks to protect intellectual property globally. It administers a number of international treaties and provides information about and for patent offices (or the equivalent) in most countries. It was established in 1967 and is based in Geneva.

World Investible Wealth The percentage of the global GDP that is available for investment. The world investible wealth includes all things of value that may be bought and sold for investment purposes. Examples include securities, commodities, real estate, and others.

World Meteorological Organization Also called the WMO. An international organization that sets standards and shares information on meteorology between members. Virtually every member of the United Nations (which sponsors the WMO) belongs to the organization. Among other activities, it assists in preparedness for natural disasters and attempts to improve the ability to predict dangerous weather. It was established in 1950 but traces its origins to the 1870s.

World Price A price for a good or service in all countries other than one's own. The world price influences international trade. Barring any trade barriers, a country exports goods and services with local prices lower than the world price. On the other hand, it imports goods and services with higher local prices than the world price.

World Radiocommunication Conference Also called WRC. A periodic conference of the International Telecommunications Union at which member-delegates meet to discuss changes to international regulations concerning radio broadcast. Conferences occur every three to five years and are usually held in Geneva. WRCs have been held since 1993, when they replaced the World Administrative Radio Conference.

World Tourism Organization An organization within the United Nations that promotes tourism worldwide. It conducts activities to encourage sustainable, business friendly tourism. It was established in 1974 and is based in Madrid.

World Trade Organization An international organization with the goal of liberalizing international trade. It was established in 1995, succeeding the General Agreement on Tariffs and Trade. The WTO aims to reduce tariff barriers and promote global economic integration. It sponsors periodic gatherings of representatives of member states to discuss trade issues and further integration, though talks have been marked by disagreement and little resolution. Particularly notorious were the protests and riots at the WTO meeting in Seattle in 1999. See also: Doha Round, Globalization.

WorldCom A telecommunications company that was at one time the second largest long distance provider in the United States. It had a large role in the expansion of Internet use in the 1990s. It is known for its notorious bankruptcy in 2002 following massive accounting fraud that resulted in several executives receiving jail sentences and investors losing billions of dollars. WorldCom is often associated with the Enron scandal because they occurred at about the same time and because both WorldCom and Enron used the accounting firm Arthur Andersen. It is now called MCI and is a subsidiary of Verizon.

Worn Currency Cash and coin that has been used so much it is no longer recognizable. Worn currency ceases to be legal tender and is no longer useable. In the United States, the Federal Reserve burns worn currency.

Worry 1. See: Risk. **2.** See: Going concern.

Worthless Describing anything with no substantial value. For example, a stock certificate in a company that has gone bankrupt is almost always worthless.

Worthless Security A security with no value. Examples include bonds past maturity or stocks in a bankrupt company. Obviously, holding worthless securities represents a loss to the owner.

Would Ya, Could Ya Slang; in auto sales, an attempt to extract a commitment from a customer to buy a vehicle, provided the seller offers the right price. The idea behind the attempt is to keep the customer on the lot for as long as possible in order to persuade him/her to buy the vehicle in order to fulfill this supposed promise.

Wow Factor A buzzword for an intangible quality that causes a product to be perceived as perfect. Because a wow factor cannot be articulated, it can be frustrating when a client demands a wow factor on a project.

Wrap Account A brokerage account where the brokerage agrees to conduct transactions for the client for a flat fee, usually assessed on a quarterly or yearly basis. This differs from most brokerage accounts where transactions occur in exchange for a commission on the size of the transaction. A wrap account exists to protect the client from overtrading, which is the (illegal but sometimes hard to detect) practice of a broker making transactions to extract commissions rather than to benefit the client. Because this can result in less profit for the brokerage, a wrap account often requires a minimum investment of anywhere from $50,000 to $100,000.

Wrap Fee A fee a money manager charges a client for all services the money manager offers. The wrap fee covers investment advice, portfolio management brokerage services and anything else to which the manager and client agree. The wrap fee is usually calculated as a percentage of the assets under management. Paying a set fee for all services rather than individual fees repeatedly can help streamline the management process for all involved.

Wraparound A loan whereby the borrower re-finances a previous loan at an interest rate between the current market rate and the interest rate at which the first loan was made, which is presumably lower. This allows the borrower to re-finance the first loan without being forced to accept a significantly higher interest rate.

Wraparound Annuity An annuity contract allowing an investor some control over the underlying securities and assets. The funds in a wraparound annuity are tax-deferred until withdrawal. The IRS does not allow the purchase of a wraparound annuity if it is possible to purchase the same investments without a tax deferral. Therefore, a wraparound annuity is not a permitted tax avoidance vehicle.

Wraparound Mortgage A second mortgage that a borrower takes out to guarantee payment on the original mortgage. In this situation, the borrower makes payments on both mortgages to the wraparound lender, which then makes payments on the original mortgage to the original lender.

Wrapped Slang; describing a bond that is insured. For example, if one says a bond is wrapped by MBIA, it means that MBIA has insured the issue.

Wreath Cent A one-cent piece minted by the United States in 1793. It was worth 1/100 of one dollar.

Wright Brothers Two brothers who are credited with inventing the airplane. The Wright brothers developed a way for a pilot to control a motor-powered flying machine. This invention revolutionized transportation, trade, warfare and myriad other businesses. Wilbur Wright lived from 1867 to 1912. Orville Wright lived from 1871 to 1948.

Wrinkled Describing a publication printed on improperly folded or otherwise bungled paper. Wrinkled paper can be expensive to replace and can be detrimental to a marketing campaign.

Writ A court order commanding that a party perform an action. For example, a writ may demand that a party make an appearance before the court, and may require that the party stop conducting an action that affects the matter at hand in the meantime. See also: Subpoena, Cease and desist.

Writ of Attachment An order by a court to seize an asset. A writ of attachment may be issued if one has been convicted of fraud or some other crime that requires the relinquishment of property. It may also be used while a case is pending in order to freeze the assets of the accused.

Writ of Error An order by a court to another court to review a previously made decision. A writ of error is issued if a mistake in law or in fact may have been made.

Writ of Seizure and Sale An order by a court that permits a creditor to take ownership of a property belonging to a borrower and to use law enforcement if necessary to take possession of it. This same order allows the creditor to sell the property once it is seized. Obviously, a writ of seizure and sale is a drastic step, and creditors do not request it unless all other steps have yielded no response. See also: Foreclosure.

Write To originate and sell an option contract. The writer of an option contract must sell (in a call) or buy (in a put) the underlying asset of the contract if the holder exercises the option.

Write Out A situation in which a specialist on the floor of an exchange fills an order using his/her own store of inventory with the expectation that the customer will pay him/her back. For example, if a specialist receives an order to sell 1,000 shares of Security A, he/she may sell 1,000 of his/her own shares in Security A, with the expectation that the customer will then sell the specialist the 1,000 shares he/she wished to sell at the agreed-upon price.

Write-Back An increase in the value of an asset after a previously made write down, which is a record of a decrease in value. A write-back may have capital gains tax implications, as higher value generally translates to higher taxes.

Write-Off A reduction in an individual's or a company's income as the result of an expense. For example, an unpayable credit sale may be a write-off for the creditor, especially if the debtor declares bankruptcy. The bankruptcy means that the debtor is unable to pay the debt, which results in a loss of income for the creditor. A write-off may usually be deducted from one's taxable income.

Writeup In accounting, an increase in the value of an asset without an expenditure. For example, if a company spends money to renovate its office and that causes the value of the office to increase, this is not a writeup. A writeup, however, may occur if the value of the office increases for some other reason, such as gentrification.

Writeups are most common during a period of price inflation in situations in which the company conducts accounting according to the fair market value of its assets.

Writing Cash-Secured Puts The act of writing a put option with the intention to avoid a margin account. Because a put writer is obligated to buy the underlying should the option buyer exercise the option, the writer must have easily available cash in order to cover the exercise. Rather than borrowing this money from a broker, the writer deposits with the broker a cash amount equal to the exercise price of the option. This way, the option is immune to margin calls.

Writing Naked An investment strategy that involves selling naked options. A naked option is an option contract without another, opposite option hedging the risk. Unlike more complex spreads and straddles, which involve the purchase or sale of multiple options in order to profit in different ways, naked options are straightforward calls or puts. An investor with a naked option makes a profit or loss depending on the movement of the underlying asset.

Writing-Down Allowance A reduction in the taxable income of a corporation due to assets acquired in a year. To calculate the writing-down allowance, one adds a percentage of the value of the assets purchased in the current year to the depreciation on assets purchased in previous years. The writing-down allowance reduces a company's corporate tax liability.

Wrongful Act An accidental or deliberate violation of fiduciary responsibility by a member of a board of directors. Examples include relatively minor mistakes like misstatements to reporters that affect stock prices, as well as felonies such as theft or fraud. Wrongful acts can result in lawsuits. Directors and officers insurance protects companies from liability due to wrongful acts.

Wrongful Death A claim that a person or organization is directly responsible for the death of a person. A wrongful death claim is brought in a lawsuit in a few common law jurisdictions, notably the United States, the United Kingdom and Australia. Wrongful death lawsuits are brought by relatives of the deceased. Some analysts believe these lawsuits are an easier way to punish suspected murderers because only a "preponderance of evidence" or a "balance of probabilities" (as opposed to "proof beyond a reasonable doubt") is required for a judgment. One prominent example of this occurred in the 1990s when former football player O.J. Simpson was found not guilty of murder but judged liable for wrongful death.

Wrongful Dishonor The failure or refusal by a bank to pay a check that is properly printed and endorsed. If the bank wrongfully dishonors a check and the check writer suffers financial hardship, the writer may sue for damages.

Wrongful Dismissal The termination of an employee in violation of relevant law, the contract of employment or the employer's own dismissal procedures. What constitutes wrongful dismissal varies by jurisdiction. Generally, however, termination because of race, sex or other protected class is illegal. Likewise, dismissal outside the parameters the employer himself has set in place may be considered wrongful. Wrongful dismissal may result in a lawsuit.

Wrongful Termination Clause A clause in a contract defining the circumstances under which wrongful dismissal takes place. In a wrongful dismissal, an employer terminates an employee in violation of relevant law, the contract of employment or the employer's own dismissal procedures.

Wrongful Termination Lawsuit A lawsuit resulting from a situation in which an employer terminates an employee in violation of relevant law, the contract of employment or the employer's own dismissal procedures. What constitutes wrongful termination varies by jurisdiction. Generally, however, termination because of race, sex or other protected class is illegal. Likewise, dismissal outside the parameters the employer himself has set in place may be considered wrongful. A wrongful termination lawsuit may result in damages being awarded to the former employee, and possibly in mandatory reinstatement.

WS 1. See: Warrant. **2.** ISO 3166-1 alpha-2 code for the Independent State of Samoa. This is the code used in international transactions to and from Samoan bank accounts. **3.** ISO 3166-2 geocode for Samoa. This is used as an international standard for shipping to Samoa. Each Samoan district has its own code with the prefix "WS." For example, the code for the District of Atua is ISO 3166-2:WS-AT

WSM GOST 7.67 Latin three-letter geocode for Western Samoa. The code is used for transactions to and from Western Samoan bank accounts and for international shipping to Western Samoa. As with all GOST 7.67 codes, it is used primarily in Cyrillic alphabets.

WST ISO 4217 code for the Western Samoan tala. It was introduced in 1967, replacing the Western Samoan pound. It was pegged to the New Zealand dollar until 1975.

Wt On a stock transaction table, an abbreviation indicating that a stock has a warrant attached to it.

Wuleswali In Afghanistan, a political subdivision roughly equivalent to a county.

WW On a ticker tape, an indication that a security has a warrant attached to it. That is, the buyer of the security is eligible for a warrant that was declared prior to the purchase of the security, but had not been distributed. See also: Cum warrant.

WYSIWYG An abbreviation for "what you see is what you get." This is an informal way to say that conditions are final and a sale cannot be refunded.

WYSIWYP An abbreviation for "what you see is what you pay." This is an informal way to say that a price is not negotiable.

X 1. A symbol appearing next to a stock listed on NASDAQ indicating that the share being traded is a mutual fund. All NASDAQ listings use a four-letter abbreviation; if an X or XD follows the abbreviation, this indicates that the share was a mutual fund.

2. A symbol appearing next to a stock indicating that the stock is being traded without its next dividend. This occurs when the company the stock represents declares that the next dividend is coming to the seller before he/she decides to sell it. A buyer purchasing such a stock begins to receive dividends the next time they are declared.

XAF ISO 4217 code for the Central African CFA franc. Introduced in 1945, it was used in five former French colonies and one former Spanish colony in Africa: Cameroon, Central African Republic, Chad, Congo (Republic of), Equitorial Guinea, and Gabon. For most of its history, it was pegged to the French franc, but, in 1999, the peg switched to the euro. See also: XOF.

XAG ISO 4217 code for silver, a precious metal with the highest electrical conduction properties of any metal. It is used mainly in jewelry, photography, and for scientific and industrial purposes. It has been used as the basis for currencies in the past. Silver is traded as a commodity on various security exchanges. Like many precious metals, silver is volatile but generally maintains relatively high prices.

XAU ISO 4217 code for gold, a particularly valuable precious metal. Gold is an element with the atomic number 79. It is used for jewelry, electronics and for other purposes. Historically, gold was used in many cultures as the basis for currency, but this is no longer the case. Investments in gold are often used as a hedge against inflation because it tends to maintain its value over time.

XBA The ISO 4217 currency code for a European Composite Unit, which was a bond market unit.

XBB The ISO 4217 currency code for a European Monetary Unit, which was a bond market unit.

XBC The ISO 4217 currency code for a European Unit of Account 9, which was a bond market unit.

XBD The ISO 4217 currency code for a European Unit of Account 17, which was a bond market unit.

XBWD ISO 4217 code for the British West Indies dollar, which was the currency of British Guiana and various British possessions in the Caribbean between 1935 and 1955. Starting in 1949, it was pegged to the British pound at a ratio of $4.80 to one pound. It was replaced by different currencies, but mainly the East Caribbean dollar.

XCD ISO 4217 code for the East Caribbean dollar. It is the legal currency for all members and associate members of the Organisation of Eastern Caribbean States except for the British Virgin Islands. It traces its origins to the Spanish dollar, the world's leading currency in the 18th century, but it was first issued in 1965, replacing the British West Indian dollar at par.

XDIS On a ticker tape, an abbreviation indicating that a stock is trading ex-distribution, or that it is trading after the distribution of a dividend and, therefore, its price is lower by the amount of the dividend.

XDR ISO 4217 code for Special Drawing Rights (SDR), a reserve currency created by the International Monetary Fund to reduce the pressure on gold and the U.S. dollar in international transactions. It was established in the late 1960s and is mainly used in the IMF's internal accounting. A few currencies are pegged to the SDR; they derive their value from a currency basket consisting of the U.S. dollar, the Japanese yen, the British pound, and the euro.

Xeme An ancient Greek unit of liquid volume approximately equivalent to 9.1 milliliters.

Xenophobe A person who hates or distrusts foreigners. Xenophobes can cause trouble in business; one may, for example, refuse to hire a foreigner who may be better qualified for a position than a native candidate. In many jurisdictions, xenophobic business practices may violate anti-discrimination law. Xenophobia in business should be distinguished from refusing to hire foreigners who are not legally authorized to work.

Xenophobia Hatred of foreigners. Xenophobia can cause trouble in business; one may, for example, refuse to hire a foreigner who may be better qualified for a position than a native candidate. In many jurisdictions, xenophobic business practices may violate anti-discrimination law. Xenophobia in business should be distinguished from refusing to hire foreigners who are not legally authorized to work.

Xerox Subsidy A slang term for the (usually frowned-upon) practice of using a copy machine, printer, or scanner for personal use at work. A Xerox subsidy can be expensive for a company if employees abuse the privilege.

Xestes An ancient Greek unit of volume approximately equivalent to 545.5 milliliters.

Xetra The world's first electronic trading system. It offers users an up-to-the-minute look at trading on many exchanges throughout Europe. Prices reported on Xetra are used to calculate various indices, including Deutscher Aktienindex. It was created in 1997 for use on the Frankfurt Stock Exchange and today accounts for more than 90% of the trade on that exchange.

XEU ISO 4217 currency code for the European currency unit. Prior to the adoption of the euro, the XEU was set up as currency basket to provide a methodology for reconciling differing exchange rates between currencies who wished to participate in the single European currency. Established in the 1979, it was known as a "semi-pegged" system in which currencies were variable with respect to each other only within a certain range. After the introduction of the euro in 1999, the exchange rate mechanism was replaced by ERM II, which reconciles exchange rates for countries wishing to join the eurozone. See also: Exchange rate mechanism.

XFO ISO 4217 code for the gold franc, which was an accounting currency used by the Bank for International Settlements between 1930 and 2003. The gold franc was equal in value to 0.290 grams of fine gold, which was also the peg used by the Swiss franc for a time. The BIS replaced the gold franc with Special Drawing Rights.

XFU ISO 4217 code for the UIC franc. This is a non-circulating currency used for accounting purposes to settle transactions involving the International Union of Railways.

Xian In China, a political subdivision approximately equivalent to a county.

Xiang In Taiwan, a political subdivision approximately equivalent to a rural township.

Xianjishi In China, a political subdivision of a county centered on at least one city but usually also including rural areas.

Xianxiashi In Taiwan, a political subdivision equivalent to a municipality under the direct control of its county. A city must have at least 150,000 residents to qualify to become a xianxiashi.

Xiber A Maltese unit of length approximately equivalent to 26.2 centimeters. It is largely obsolete but is still used in some circumstances.

Xiber Kubu A Maltese unit of cubic volume approximately equivalent to 18 liters. It is largely obsolete but is still used in some circumstances.

Xiber Kwadru A Maltese unit of area approximately equivalent to 686.1 square centimeters. It is largely obsolete but is still used in some circumstances.

XMI Ticker symbol for the Major Market Index, which is managed by the American Stock Exchange.

XOF ISO 4217 currency code for the West African CFA franc. The West African CFA franc is used in former French colonies in West Africa, namely Benin, Burkina Faso, Cote d'Ivoire, Guinea-Bissau, Mali, Niger, Senegal, and Togo. It was introduced in 1945 to spare French colonies from the severe devaluation necessary to the French franc following the Second World War. Between 1949 and 1999 it was pegged to the French franc; since then it has been pegged to the euro. It is of equal value to the Central Africa CFA franc, but the two currencies are not interchangeable. See also: CPF franc, XAF.

XPD ISO 4217 code for palladium, a metal used in jewelry, electronics, and other products. It may be traded as a commodity or on the futures and option markets.

XPF ISO 4217 currency code for the CPF franc. The CPF franc is used in former French colonies in the South Pacific, namely French Polynesia, New Caledonia, and Wallis and Futuna. It was introduced in 1945 to spare French colonies from the severe devaluation necessary to the French franc following World War II. Between 1949 and 1999, it was pegged to the French franc; since then, it has been pegged to the euro. See also: CFA franc.

XPT ISO 4217 code for platinum, a rare and valuable metal used primarily in jewelry and electronics. It is traded as a commodity on various security exchanges. It is volatile like other commodities, but generally maintains a relatively high price.

XR On a ticker, a symbol indicating that a security is trading with no rights attached. The symbol is an abbreviation of the term, ex-rights.

XRT An abbreviation on a ticker tape indicating the sale of a share without any rights attached to it. That is, any rights that may be attached to the share remain with the seller. XRT is an abbreviation of ex-rights. See also: Rights Offering, Ex-Dividend.

XTS ISO 4217 code used for testing.

Xu A subdivision of the Vietnamese dong. One xu is equal in value to 1/100 of a dong. In practice, the xu is not used. See also: Hao, Cent.

XW Ex-Warrant. Describing the sale of a security after a warrant has been announced but before it has been distributed such that the warrant remains with the seller. Selling an ex-warrant almost invariably reduces the price for which the security is sold. See also: Cum Warrant.

XXX ISO 4217 code used to indicate that no currency is meant.

Y A symbol appearing next to a security listed on NASDAQ indicating that the security is an American Depository Receipt. All NASDAQ listings use a four-letter abbreviation; if a "Y" follows the abbreviation, this indicates that the security being traded is an ADR.

Yacht Insurance An all risks insurance policy protecting against a loss of one's yacht. For example, if one's yacht is stolen or sinks, yacht insurance replaces it. Likewise, if a crash causes injury to another and the yacht owner is sued, the insurance may cover his/her legal liability. As with all insurance, one must pay a premium to receive the coverage.

Yankee Bank A bank with significant operations in the United States but registered in another country. See also: Yankee bond, Yankee certificate of deposit.

Yankee Bond A foreign bond denominated in U.S. dollars and traded in the United States. In order to raise capital from American investors, a non-American company may choose to sell a bond in the United States. Most of the time, the issuers must register Yankee bonds with the SEC. See also: Bulldog bond, Samurai bond.

Yankee CD A foreign certificate of deposit denominated in U.S. dollars and issued in the United States. In order to raise capital from American investors, a non-American company may choose to issue a CD in the United States. See also: Yankee bond.

Yankee Market Informal; a stock market in the United States. The term is most often used by foreigners outside of the United States. See also: Bulldog Market, Samurai Market.

Yaounde Convention A treaty between the European Community and several newly independent states in Africa. The relationship the Yaounde Convention established was relatively similar to the one that existed between the European countries and their former colonies. It expired in 1975 and was replaced by the Lome Convention.

Yard 1. In foreign exchange, informal for one billion. On an open outcry exchange, a trader may bid or offer one yard of a currency instead of one billion in order to avoid confusion of billion with million or trillion. **2.** A slang term in Hong Kong for $1 billion. See also: Hong Kong dollar.

Yardland A unit of land area equivalent to 30 acres.

Yat Kwet In Myanmar (Burma), a political subdivision approximately equivalent to a ward within a township (myo ne).

YAWN Young and Wealthy but Normal. Self-made wealthy young persons (usually under 35) who live fairly simply. That is, YAWNs tend not to buy fancy cars and houses, but rather work hard and spend time with their families. YAWNs contrast with yuppies, who embrace their wealth rather more ostentatiously. It can be difficult to market products to YAWNs, though some are noted for their philanthropy.

YD 1. ISO 3166-1 alpha-2 code for South Yemen before it merged with North Yemen in 1990. This was the code used in international transactions to and from South Yemeni bank accounts. **2.** ISO 3166-2 geocode for South Yemen. This was used as an international standard for shipping to South Yemen. In both cases, the code is obsolete.

YDD ISO 4217 code for the South Yemeni dinar. It was introduced in 1965, replacing the East African shilling two years before South Yemen became independent. After South and North Yemen united in 1990, the South Yemeni dinar remained in circulation until 1996. It was replaced by the Yemeni rial.

YDYE ISO 3166-3 code for South Yemen, which merged with North Yemen in 1990. ISO 3166-3 codes are used to indicate names of countries that are no longer used.

Year A 12-month period. The tax year, the period of time during which annual taxes are calculated, runs from January 1 to December 31. A company's fiscal year, the period of time for which it makes its annual budget, may run for a different 12-month period.

Year Bill A U.S. Treasury security with a maturity of one year. The Treasury Department sets auctions for year bills each month.

Year End Describing anything that occurs toward the end of a fiscal year or calendar year.

Year over Year The measure of performance in one year compared to a different year, especially the most recent one. This is done so that growth or decline might be measured without having to account for seasonal variance. For example, one might compare sales in 2009 to those in 2008. If a company sold 1 million widgets in 2008 and 1.25 million in 2009, this indicates 25% growth in sales, and is a positive sign for investors.

Year-End Bonus A bonus paid to employees at the end of a calendar year. Year-end bonuses are popular with employees, but bad feelings can result if they received a bonus one year but not the next. However, they are good for morale, especially since they come close to Christmas and other end-of-year holidays. Year-end bonuses may be calculated based on sales, collections, performance or in some other way.

Year-End Dividend A final dividend declared toward the end a given fiscal year. A company announces a year-end dividend especially if revised estimates show a greater than expected profit; it waits until the end of the year to revise and attempt to verify these estimates before declaring the dividend. More broadly, it may refer to the last dividend declared in a year.

Year-End Rally A rise in stock prices that sometimes occurs on the trading days between Christmas and New Year's Day, occasionally extending into the first few trading days of January. Year-end rallies are thought to occur in anticipation of the January effect, which is a rise in demand for stocks resulting from the increased liquidity among investors who closed positions prior to the end of the year for tax purposes. A year-end rally is also called a Santa Claus rally.

Year-Over-Year The measure of performance in one year compared to the previous year. This is done so that growth or decline might be measured. For example, one might compare sales in 2009 to those in 2008. If a company sold 1,000,000 widgets in 2008 and 1,250,000 in 2009, this indicates 25% growth in sales, and is a positive sign for investors. See also: Quarter.

Year-to-Date The period between the beginning of the calendar year and the present date. It is often used to calculate a company's income up to the present date and may be compared to the same period of the previous year to evaluate a company's financial health.

Yellow Knight A company that offered a hostile takeover but has since changed its mind and decided to discuss a merger. A yellow knight's management may decide that a hostile takeover would be too expensive or otherwise difficult but still believes that the target company would be advantageous. The term is derogatory and implies that the acquiring company (who would have been a black knight) has cold feet or has gone "yellow." One would expect the term to be used by the board, management, or even employees, rather than shareholders.

Yellow Sheets A daily quotation system for taxable bonds (that is, most non-government bonds). Yellow sheets include information such as the bids, asks, and the market makers giving them. They are published by the National Quotation Bureau and were originally printed on actual yellow sheets. See also: Pink sheets.

YEM GOST 7.67 Latin three-letter geocode for Yemen. The code is used for transactions to and from Yemeni bank accounts and for international shipping to Yemen. As with all GOST 7.67 codes, it is used primarily in Cyrillic alphabets.

Yemeni Rial The currency of Yemen. It was the currency of South Yemen before unification in 1990. Following unification, the rial remained in circulation along with the North Yemeni dinar until 1996. After the dinar was withdrawn from circulation, the rial became a floating currency.

Yen Bond A bond denominated in Japanese yen. A yen bond is usually issued by a Japanese entity and is traded in Japan, but this is not always the case. For example, a yen bond may be issued in Japan by a foreign company or even issued outside Japan. See also: Euroyen bond.

YER ISO 4217 code for the Yemeni rial. It had been the currency of South Yemen before unification in 1990. Following unification, the rial remained in circulation along with the North Yemeni dinar until 1996. After the dinar was withdrawn from circulation, the rial became a floating currency.

Yield The income one receives from an investment, rather than its capital appreciation. The yield is calculated as the coupons or dividends the investor receives in a year expressed as a percentage of the cost of the investment.

Yield Advantage The yield of a publicly-traded company's convertible securities minus the yield on the dividends of its common stock. The yield advantage is important in determining whether it would be better to buy convertible securities or common stock, and whether it would be profitable to exercise the convertible option on the convertible securities.

Yield Basis A method of quoting a bond price in which one quotes the yield instead of the dollar amount. The yield basis is usually more useful to investors because a bond's yield determines its value.

Yield Burning The practice of an investor deliberately attempting to raise the price of a bond in order to reduce its yield. Because the reduction of yield reduces the tax owed on the bond, yield burning is illegal.

Yield Curb In convertible bonds, the difference between the price of the convertible and the underlying common stock.

Yield Curve A representation on a chart of the yields on bonds with identical credit ratings but different maturities. On the yield curve, the maturities are represented on the x-axis, and the yield is represented on the y-axis. That is, if the yield curve trends upward, it indicates that interest rates for long-term debt securities are higher than short-term debt securities; this is called a normal yield curve. A negative yield curve indicates that interest rates for short-term debt securities are higher, and a flat yield curve indicates that they are roughly the same. Yield curves are most commonly plotted with U.S. Treasuries with different maturities; this is used to predict future trends in interest rates.

Yield Curve Note A debt security structured so that its yield increases when prevailing interest rates decrease and declines when these interest rates increase. Because yield curve notes are the opposite of most other debt securities, investors use them to hedge against possible changes in interest rates that might be unfavorable to their other investments.

Yield Curve Option-Pricing Models Any formula or theory for mathematically determining the correct price for an option contract that considers the yield curve of a bond at different levels of volatility. An example is the Black-Derman-Toy Model.

Yield Curve Strategy Any investment strategy that seeks to profit from changes in the yield curve of U.S. Treasury securities. For example, one may buy a bond at a certain interest rate expecting prevailing interest rates to decline. If and when they do, the price of the bond one holds will increase, allowing one to sell the bond for a profit.

Yield Elbow The highest point on a yield curve. That is, the yield elbow shows the period of time when an economy has the highest interest rate on bonds. The yield elbow occurs most often when there are concerns for current or future inflation. It also corresponds roughly to low prices for bonds.

Yield Maintenance The extra money a prepaying borrower would have to pay to make the yield the same for the lender if the borrower made all, regularly scheduled payments until maturity. When a borrower prepays a loan or other debt investment, the lender loses the interest the borrower otherwise would have paid. The lender may charge the yield maintenance as a prepayment penalty to ensure that it makes the yield regardless of whether or not the borrower prepays. This has the effect of making prepayment or refinancing unattractive to the borrower.

Yield Pickup The extra yield an investor receives when he/she exchanges a bond with a lower yield (and usually a shorter maturity) for one with a higher yield (and usually a longer maturity). While this exchange sounds advantageous, it is risky because the yield pickup often comes from a bond with lower credit quality, and the longer maturity likewise exposes the investor to interest rate risk. However, the yield pickup is still a guaranteed higher return, and many investors take advantage of them. See also: Pure yield pickup swap.

Yield Ratio A comparison of the expected yield of one bond to the expected yield of another. A yield ratio is important when deciding whether to invest in one bond or another; generally, the one with the higher yield wins out. However, it is important to take into account the after tax basis when taking the yield ratio of a corporate bond and a tax-exempt municipal bond. A corporate bond yields less than its stated interest rate because of taxation, whereas a tax-exempt municipal bond does not. Thus, a municipal bond paying a lower interest rate will often net the bondholder more than a corporate bond with a slightly higher interest rate, depending upon one's tax bracket.

Yield Spread The difference in yield between two bonds or other debt securities with different credit quality. For example, an investment grade bond and a junk bond have different yields to compensate the bondholder for the risk (or lack of risk). The difference between these is called the yield spread.

Yield Spread Strategy In bonds, an investment strategy in which one attempts take advantage of the yield spread of a particular bond. For example, one may take a short position on a bond with a low yield while taking a long position on a bond with a higher yield. See also: Relative yield spread.

Yield to Average Life A calculation of the yield of a bond assuming the bond's average life. The yield to average life is useful if a bond is likely to be retired before maturity because of sinking fund requirements. This method helps the investor determine how much he/she is likely to make from a given bond investment, regardless of its actual maturity. See also: Yield to worst.

Yield to Current Call The lowest possible yield on a callable bond. If a callable bond is called before maturity, the bondholder only earns interest on the time that has elapsed between purchasing the bond and its early redemption. This yield can be significantly less than what would have been earned had the bond been held until maturity. The yield to current call assumes that the bond is called on the first date permitted in the bond agreement. Determining the yield to current call is an important part of risk analysis in evaluating a callable bond. It is also called yield to worst. See also: Yield to call, yield to maturity.

Yield to Maturity The rate of return on a bond if it is held until maturity. This is expressed as an annual rate; the calculation of the YTM includes the coupon rate (if any), length of the bond, market value, and face value. Bond quotes are made in terms of the YTM, but an individual investor's yield may be different if he/she does not hold the bond, or if the bond is called before maturity.

Yield to Warrant Expiration In convertible securities, the yield of a bond between the present date and the date any warrants attached to the bond expire.

Yield-Based Option An option where the underlying asset is a debt security. The strike price of a yield-based option is expressed as a yield. The payoff on such an option is the difference between the "strike yield" and the actual yield on the underlying debt security on or before (depending on the type of option) the expiration date. Yield-based options are settled in cash. See also: Cash settlement.

Yin A unit of length in China approximately equivalent to 33.33 meters.

Yojana An ancient Indian unit of length variously equivalent to values between 13 and 16 kilometers.

Yoroshiku Onegai Shimasu A Japanese phrase meaning "I ask you for a favor." The phrase is fairly formal, and is used in business settings. See also: Yoroshiku Tanomu.

Yoroshiku Tanomu A Japanese phrase meaning "I ask you for a favor." The phrase is informal. That is, it may be used between friends and is not appropriate for business settings. See also: Yoroshiku Onegai Shimasu.

Yours A slang term in foreign exchange indicating a willingness to sell.

Yo-Yo Stock Informal; a stock that moves upwards and downward in price frequently and with little pattern. Yo-yo stocks are highly volatile and, as such, can be very risky.

YT 1. ISO 3166-1 alpha-2 code for Mayotte. This is the code used in international transactions to and from Mahoran bank accounts. **2.** ISO 3166-2 geocode for Mayotte. This is used as an international standard for shipping to Mayotte.

YU 1. ISO 3166-1 alpha-2 code for Yugoslavia before it changed its name to Serbia and Montenegro. This was the code used in international transactions to and from Yugoslavian bank accounts. **2.** ISO 3166-2 geocode for Yugoslavia. This was used as an international standard for shipping to Yugoslavia. In both cases, the code is obsolete.

YUCS ISO 3166-3 code for Yugoslavia, which became Serbia and Montenegro. ISO 3166-3 codes are used to indicate names of countries that are no longer used.

YUD ISO 4217 code for the hard dinar, a currency used in the former Yugoslavia. It was introduced in 1966 and suffered from high inflation throughout its history, especially toward the end of its circulation. The convertible dinar replaced the hard dinar in 1990.

YUG ISO 4217 code for the January dinar, a currency used in the former Yugoslavia. It was introduced in January 1994 but suffered from hyperinflation so extreme that it was withdrawn only a month later. It was replaced by the new Yugoslav dinar, which was pegged to the deutschemark.

Yugen-Kaisha A Japanese term for a limited company. Yugen-kaisha could have up to 50 investors, called members, who collectively were required to contribute 3 million yen in capital. Yugen-kaisha were required to have one director, but not a full board of directors. After 2006, no new yugen-kaisha could be formed; the structure was replaced by godo gaisha.

Yugoslav Dinar The currency of Yugoslavia. It was introduced in 1994 following a period of hyperinflation and pegged to the Deutsche mark at par. It was used in Montenegro until 2000. It was replaced by the mark, which was later replaced by the euro. Serbia continued to use the new dinar until 2003, when Yugoslavia officially split into Serbia and Montenegro. At that time, it was replaced by the Serbian dinar at a 1:1 ratio.

Yugoslav New Dinar The currency of the former Yugoslavia. It was introduced in 1994 following a period of hyperinflation and was pegged to the deutschemark at par. It was used in Montenegro until 2000, when it was replaced by the deutschemark, which was later replaced by the euro. Serbia continued to use the new dinar until 2003, when Yugoslavia officially split into Serbia and Montenegro. At that time, it was replaced by the Serbian dinar at a 1:1 ratio.

Yukichi A slang term for 10,000 yen. The term derives from the Japanese translator and political scientist Fukuzawa Yukichi, whose picture appears on the 10,000 yen banknote.

YUM ISO 4217 code for the Yugoslav new dinar. It was introduced in 1994 following a period of hyperinflation and pegged to the Deutsche mark at par. It was used in Montenegro until 2000; it was replaced by the mark, which was later replaced by the euro; Serbia continued to use the new dinar until 2003, when Yugoslavia officially split into Serbia and Montenegro. At that time, it was replaced by the Serbian dinar at a 1:1 ratio.

YUN ISO 4217 code for the convertible dinar, a currency used in the former Yugoslavia. It was introduced in 1990, replacing the hard dinar. As most of the constituent countries of Yugoslavia became independent, it was replaced by the reformed dinar in 1992.

YUO ISO 4217 code for the October dinar, a currency used in the former Yugoslavia. It was introduced in October 1993 to combat the reformed dinar's hyperinflation. This attempt failed and the January dinar replaced the October dinar at a ratio of 1 billion to one only a few months later.

Yuppie Informal; an abbreviation for "young urban professional." A person in his/her twenties or thirties who makes significantly more money than most of his/her peers. Stereotypically, yuppies are extremely conscious of their social status, and some luxury products may be marketed especially to them. They tend to live in very large cities like New York or Chicago. The term was most common during the banking boom of the 1980s. It has a somewhat derogatory connotation.

YUR ISO 4217 code for the reformed dinar, a currency used in the former Yugoslavia. It was introduced in 1992, quickly succumbing to hyperinflation. It was replaced by the October dinar in 1993 at a ratio of 1 million to one.

Yuzana A Burmese unit of length approximately equivalent to 20.48 kilometers.

Yway Gyi A Burmese unit of mass approximately equivalent to 0.2722 grams.

Yway Lay A Burmese unit of mass approximately equivalent to 0.1361 grams.

Z 1. A symbol appearing next to a stock listed on NASDAQ indicating that the share being traded has a miscellaneous right, warrant, or receipt attached to it. All NASDAQ listings use a four-letter abbreviation; if a Z follows the abbreviation, it indicates that the share's category does not easily fit into other categories. **2.** In over-the-counter trading, a symbol meaning that no quote is available for a security. **3.** On a table, a symbol indicating an exact number, instead of an estimate, of securities traded.

Z Bond A bond on which interest accrues but is not paid to the bondholder until maturity. That is, the interest is added back into the principal and further interest is calculated over the new, larger principal. A Z bond is also called an accrual bond. See also: Accretion, Balloon Mortgage.

Z Score In statistics, the number of standard deviations a data point is from the mean value. Measuring the Z-score of a company is used to help determine a company's likelihood of bankruptcy.

ZA 1. ISO 3166-1 alpha-2 code for the Republic of South Africa. This is the code used in international transactions to and from South African bank accounts. **2.** ISO 3166-2 geocode for South Africa. This is used as an international standard for shipping to South Africa. Each province has its own code with the prefix "ZA." For example, the code for Free State is ISO 3166-2:ZA-FS.

Zabara A system of equity trading in which an order with a better price has priority over other orders; if two orders have the same price, the order made first is executed first.

Zacks Estimate System A system that compiles information on analyst recommendations for more than 5,000 publicly-traded companies. These recommendations are collected and disseminated from several thousand analysts. The system is known for its interpretations of "consensus" recommendations. Zacks Estimate System services are available on a subscription basis.

Zacks Investment Research A company that compiles information on analyst recommendations for more than 5,000 publicly-traded companies. Zacks collects and disseminates recommendations from several thousand analysts, and is known for its interpretations of "consensus" recommendations. Its services are available on a subscription basis.

ZAF GOST 7.67 Latin three-letter geocode for South Africa. The code is used for transactions to and from South African bank accounts and for international shipping to South Africa. As with all GOST 7.67 codes, it is used primarily in Cyrillic alphabets.

Zagreb Stock Exchange An exchange in Croatia. Both stocks and bonds are traded on the Zagreb Stock Exchange. It was established in 1991.

Zaibatsu A group of companies owned by the same family that more or less controlled the Japanese economy in the late 19th and early 20th centuries, especially between the two World Wars. Each zaibatsu consisted of a holding company, which entirely owned a bank that financed the zaibatsu's operations. These operations were carried out by subsidiary companies in different industries. For example, a zaibatsu might own a chemical company, a mining company, and a military supply company, which may, in turn, have owned their own subsidiaries for more specialized work. One zaibatsu still in existence (albeit in a much different form) is the Mitsubishi corporation. See also: Keiretsu.

Zaichik A slang term for the Belarusian ruble. Literally, the term means "little hare," a reference to the picture of a hare that appeared on banknotes in the 1990s.

Zaikai A term for the business, investment and finance community in Japan. The term connotes executives and other elites.

Zaire The currency of Zaire between 1967 and 1997. The first zaire, used until 1993, suffered from hyperinflation. The second zaire was replaced by the Congolese franc in 1997 when Zaire became the Democratic Republic of the Congo.

Zairean First Zaire A former currency of Zaire. It was introduced in 1967 and suffered from persistently high inflation. It was replaced by the new zaire in 1993 at a ratio of 3 million old zaires to one new zaire.

ZAL ISO 4217 code for the financial rand, an accounting currency used in South Africa between 1985 and 1995. Under this system, the South African rand continued to circulate but investments made by non-South Africans could be sold only for the financial rand, which had strict conditions placed on its convertibility. The financial rand was introduced in order to prevent massive outflows of capital that began in response to South Africa's apartheid policy. It was abolished after apartheid was ended.

Zambian Kwacha The currency of Zambia. It was introduced in 1968, replacing the Zambian pound. It has suffered from high inflation throughout its history.

Zambian Pound The former currency of Zambia. It was introduced upon Zambia's independence in 1964. It was pegged to the British pound. It was replaced by the Zambian kwacha (ZMK) in 1968.

ZAR GOST 7.67 Latin three-letter geocode for the Democratic Republic of the Congo. The code is used for transactions to and from DRC bank accounts and for international shipping to the DRC. As with all GOST 7.67 codes, it is used primarily in Cyrillic alphabets.

Zentner A German term for quintal. It should be noted that a quintal is equivalent to 50 kilograms in Germany, but 100 kilograms in other German-speaking countries.

ZEP Zone d'Exchanges Preferentiels pour les Etats de l'Afrique de l'Est et de l'Afrique Australe. An international organization that promotes cooperation between member states in agriculture, the use of industrial and natural resources, trade, monetary issues and customs. Members include Burundi, Comoros, Djibouti, Ethiopia, Kenya, Lesotho, Malawi, Mauritius, Rwanda, Somalia, Swaziland, Tanzania, Uganda, Zambia and Zimbabwe. It was established in 1981 and is based in Zambia.

Zeret An ancient Hebrew unit of length approximately equivalent to 25 centimeters.

Zero Balance Account An account that maintains no funds in it because the account holder transfers only enough funds into it to cover checks written on it. A zero balance account exists so companies can prevent excessive balances on accounts and more effectively control how they distribute funds.

Zero Based Budgeting A system of budgeting where each department or division of a company must justify all expenditures and allocations rather than simply increases over the previous fiscal year. That is, the budget is made with every department starting at zero dollars to spend, and each department must demonstrate need for what it wants to receive. Zero-based budgeting is advantageous because it is more detail-oriented than other forms of budgeting; among other things, it makes it easier to detect and eliminate over-inflated budgets. On the other hand, zero-based budgeting is more difficult and time consuming to put together and often has a bias toward departments that directly produce revenue instead of departments like R&D.

Zero Basis Risk Swap An interest rate swap between a municipality and a financial institution. The municipality is the fixed rate payer and the financial institution is the floating rate payer. The floating rate the financial institution pays (and that the municipality receives) is identical to the adjustable interest rate on a floating rate note that the municipality previously issued. A ZEBRA makes a municipality's borrowing costs more predictable and therefore reduces its risk.

Zero Bracket Amount In the United States, the amount of income not taxed before the Tax Reform Act of 1986. Taxpayers who chose not to itemize deductions subtracted the zero-bracket amount from their adjusted gross income. The amount was indexed to inflation and therefore had the potential to change every tax year. It has since been replaced by the standard deduction.

Zero Cost Collar An investment strategy in which one buys or sells one position while taking an opposite position for the same price that will limit both the return and the risk of one's investment. An investor sells a position that caps return while buying one that limits loss, while a borrower does the opposite. A zero-cost collar may be used for options, stocks, interest rates, or commodities. See also: Collar.

Zero Dividend Preference Share A preferred share that does not pay a dividend. Rather, the shareholder receives an agreed-upon, fixed amount when he/she redeems the share with the issuer. As with all preferred shares, in the event of liquidation, holders are entitled to receive proceeds from liquidation before any common shareholders.

Zero Growth A situation in which the GDP of an economy is neither increasing nor declining. While zero growth is not technically a recession, it may be marked by high unemployment or at least no job growth.

Zero Inventory A system in which a company keeps no or very little inventory in storage, simply ordering exactly what it needs to sell and receiving it in a timely manner. Zero inventory is the goal of just-in-time inventory management and the two terms are sometimes used to mean the same thing.

Zero Minus Tick A trade on a security that occurs at the same price as the security's previous trade, which was itself less than the price on the trade before that. For example, a security that trades for $5 at 10:00, $4.90 at 10:01, and $4.90 at 10:02 has experienced as zero-minus tick. Until 2007, a short sale was not permitted on a zero minus tick. See also: Tick test.

Zero Plus Tick On an exchange, a transaction in which a security was traded at the same price as its previous trade, which was in turn higher than the trade before that. Some regulations and rules on exchanges only permit certain transactions following a zero-plus tick or an uptick, though some, such as the short sale rule have become obsolete with increased digitilization of the market.

Zero Population Growth A situation in which the number of persons born in a population equals the number of persons who die. The fertility rate necessary for zero population growth varies, but is generally between 2 and 3. Some countries concerned about overpopulation aim for zero-population growth, while others dealing with an aging population may wish to increase the growth rate.

Zero Risk Describing an investment or security in which the return is known with certainty. The certainty generally comes from a supreme amount of confidence in the issuer of the investment; for example, Treasury securities are considered zero risk investments because the United States government is considered the best possible issuer. Critics contend that there is no such thing as a zero risk investment because, in theory, even the US government could default. However, zero risk investments have such a low level of risk that it may be ignored. Zero risk investments usually have a low rate of return and, as a result, are exposed to inflation risk.

Zero Tick On an exchange, a transaction of a security in which the price is the same as the previous transaction. Whether the price before zero tick was higher or lower may affect what kind of transaction may take place next. See also: zero-minus tick, zero-plus tick.

Zero Time Describing a small task that managers consider to take no time. The term is especially used when managers assign several zero time tasks, which in fact can be time consuming.

Zero-Beta Portfolio A portfolio with no systematic risk. A zero-beta portfolio is most useful for a risk averse investor; however, its expected return is the risk-free rate of return, which is very low.

Zero-Coupon Bond A bond that pays no interest. It is sold at a discount from par and matures at par. These are fairly illiquid investments because they do not benefit from changes in interest rates. However, they tend to be low-risk. Zero-coupon bonds fluctuate in price, sometimes dramatically, with changes in interest rates. Sometimes zero-coupon bonds are issued as such; other times they are bonds stripped of their coupons by a financial institution and resold as zero-coupon bonds. A zero-coupon bond is less formally known as a zero.

Zero-Coupon Certificate of Deposit A certificate of deposit that pays no interest. One may purchase a zero-coupon CD for less than its face value; it matures at its face value. See also: Coupon equivalent yield, zero-coupon bond.

Zero-Coupon Convertible Bond 1. A bond that may be converted into common stock in the company issuing it. A zero-coupon convertible bond is sold at a discount from par and matures at par. They tend to be volatile in the secondary market because the convertible option may or may not become worthwhile, depending on how the company is performing. Additionally, like all zeros, they can fluctuate in price, sometimes dramatically, with changes in interest rates. **2.** A municipal bond that may be converted into a corporate bond in the company issuing it. A zero-coupon convertible bond is sold at a discount from par and matures at par. They tend to be volatile in the secondary market because the convertible options may or may not become worthwhile, depending on how the companies they represent are performing. These zero-coupon convertibles are tax-exempt, but are convertible to other bonds that may yield more.

Zero-Coupon Mortgage A mortgage in which all principal and interest are deferred until maturity. All interest that accrues is rolled into the principal, which is payable in a lump sum. A zero-coupon mortgage may be beneficial for a business property in which cash flow is expected to be low for the foreseeable future, but in which the value of the real estate is expected to increase. The owner in this case could refinance the mortgage at maturity with more valuable real estate securing the loan. See also: Accrual note.

Zero-Floor Limit In retail transactions, a system in which a bank card will not be authorized to make a purchase if it would result in an overdraft. A zero-floor limit system also checks for past due accounts.

Zero-Interest Loan A loan on which interest does not accumulate. Rather, the borrower must only repay the principal. For example, one may borrow $5,000 and pay the lender $5,000 over a period of two years, at which point the debt is considered repaid. Zero-interest loans are the only loans permitted in Islamic finance. They are also extended to persons, companies and countries in desperate need of aid. See also: Zero-coupon bond.

Zero-Investment Portfolio A portfolio consisting of long positions and short positions with no combined net worth. To give a very simple example, suppose one buys 100 shares in AT&T while simultaneously selling 100 shares; this creates a zero-investment portfolio. A zero-investment portfolio has the advantages of carrying little or no risk and reducing taxes. Obviously, however, there is little or no return on a zero-investment portfolio.

Zero-One Programming In integer programming, a way to make decisions in which there are only two mutually exclusive solutions. These possible decisions are assigned the values zero and one.

Zero-Rated Goods and services that are not subject to a VAT. Examples of potentially zero-rated goods and services include financial services and items donated to a charity that the charity later sells.

Zero-Sum Game A situation where the gain of one person equates to the loss of another person. That is, for every dollar one person makes in a zero sum transaction, another person loses a dollar. Not every transaction is a zero sum game; stock trading is not because some trades are mutually beneficial to the buyer and the seller. Options and commodity markets, however, are zero sum games because wealth cannot be created from these transactions, only shifted. See also: Wealth creation.

Zero-Zero Split A dishonest practice in which an employee is responsible for two projects but avoids giving his/her supervisors updates on either because he/she claims to be busy with the other. A zero-zero split may catch up to the employee as the projects come due.

Zeta Model A model used to predict the likelihood that a publicly-traded company will file bankruptcy in the coming two years. The zeta model derives a company's z-score, in which a high z-score indicates low likelihood of bankruptcy. The z-score is calculated as follows: Z-Score = $1.2a + 1.4b + 3.3c + 0.6d + e$ The variables are as follows: a: the ratio of working capital to total assets; b: the ratio of retained earnings to total assets; c: the ratio of EBIT to total assets; d: the ratio of the market value of the equity to total liabilities; and e: the ratio of sales to total assets.

Zhang A unit of length in China approximately equivalent to 3.33 meters.

Zhen In Taiwan, a political subdivision approximately equivalent to an urban township.

Zhixiashi 1. In Taiwan, a political subdivision for a large city such as Tapei. **2.** In the People's Republic of China, a political subdivision for a city under the direct control of its province.

Zig Zag In technical analysis, an indicator of the momentum of a security when its price trend changes. Because the indicator does not begin to function until the price trend changes, many technical analysts use it to confirm a trend rather than to predict one. In any case, the zig zag indicator helps technicians profit from trend changes.

Zila In Bangladesh, a political subdivision equivalent to a district or province.

Zilla In India, a political subdivision equivalent to a district, which is smaller than a state but larger than a county.

Zimbabwe Mining Index An index tracking five mining companies in Zimbabwe. The companies represented mine a number of materials, including gold, nickel, copper, and coal.

Zimbabwean Dollar The former currency of Zimbabwe. It replaced the Rhodesian dollar following (official) independence from Britain in 1980 and was used until extreme hyperinflation forced a change to a new currency code in early 2009 and was abandoned in April of that year. Its inflation rate in December 2008 was $6.5 \times 10^{108}\%$.

Zionism The political view that Jews have a right to national homeland in Palestine roughly corresponding to the borders of Biblical Israel. Zionism emerged as a nationalist movement in 19th-century Europe as secular and assimilated Jews did not find wide acceptance in European society. Many, though not all, early Zionists were socialists; this led to the establishment of communal farms in Palestine. Religious Zionism was initially a minor part of the movement, but has grown in importance since the 1960s. After the establishment of the States of Israel in 1948, the Zionist movement has concentrated on maintaining or expanding Israel's borders and/or influence. Proponents of Zionism believe a Jewish homeland is the only place Jews can be perfectly safe from persecution, while critics contend that Palestinian Arabs have been displaced and discriminated against since the early 20th century.

Zionist A person who believes that Jews have a right to a national homeland in Palestine roughly corresponding to the borders of Biblical Israel. Zionism emerged as a nationalist movement in 19th-century Europe as secular and assimilated Jews did not find wide acceptance in European society. Many, though not all, early Zionists were socialists; this led to the establishment of communal farms in Palestine. Religious Zionists initially were a minor part of the movement, but have grown in importance since the 1960s. After the establishment of the state of Israel in 1948, Zionists have concentrated on maintaining or expanding Israel's borders and/or influence. Zionists believe a Jewish homeland is the only place Jews can be perfectly safe from persecution, while critics contend that Palestinian Arabs have been displaced and discriminated against since the early 20th century.

ZIP Code Zoning Improvement Plan Code. A series of five numbers identifying the area of the United States in which to deliver mail. While some ZIP codes are reserved for post office boxes and single addresses receiving large volumes of mail, most identify the general area, such as the town or neighborhood, to which correspondence is addressed. They were introduced in 1963.

ZIP Code Analysis A way to target a marketing campaign. It is based on the assumption that like-minded people tend to live near each other. Thus, a marketer may concentrate equal resources to small populations in multiple ZIP codes as a test. If one ZIP code has a higher response rate than the others, the marketer concentrates on that ZIP code for future campaigns. It is also called a ZIP code count.

ZIP Code Correction A manual task or automated program that adds missing ZIP codes to lists of addresses. This is used in marketing and for other business purposes to ensure that all correspondence is delivered to the correct recipient. To accomplish ZIP code correction, one compares the ZIP codes in one's list to a database of valid ZIP codes.

ZIP Code Omission In ZIP code analysis, the process of deleting a ZIP code from a database of marketing targets. In ZIP code analysis, a marketer may concentrate equal resources to small populations in multiple ZIP codes as a test. If one ZIP code has a higher response rate than the others, the marketer concentrates on that ZIP code for future campaigns and conducts ZIP code omission for the others.

Zip Pan In filmmaking, a pan of a camera from one subject to another. The zip pan occurs very quickly and is used to emphasize the second subject. It may be used in television or other film advertising.

ZIP Sort A computer system that separates large volumes of mail according to its ZIP code. The zip sort eases the efficient transport of mail.

ZIP+4 A more specific type of ZIP code used to identify a smaller area, such as an apartment building, a city block or even an individual post office box. The ZIP+4 was introduced in 1983.

Zirai A Turkish measure of length approximately equivalent to 75.77 centimeters. It became obsolete when Turkey made the metric system mandatory in 1933.

Zizhiqi In Inner Mongolia, a political subdivision approximately equivalent to a county in which the majority population is an ethnic minority.

Zizhiqu In China, an autonomous region. A zizhiqu is like a sheng (or province), but theoretically is subject to less control from the central government.

Zizhizhou In China, a political subdivision of an autonomous prefecture. That is, a zizhizhou is a province in which more than half the population belongs to an ethnic minority, or which is historically associated with a minority.

Zloty The currency of Poland. It was introduced in 1995, replacing the third zloty (PLZ) after a period of hyperinflation. It replaced the old currency at a ratio of 10,000 old zloty to one new zloty.

ZM 1. ISO 3166-1 alpha-2 code for the Republic of Zambia. This is the code used in international transactions to and from Zambian bank accounts. **2.** ISO 3166-2 geocode for Zambia. This is used as an international standard for shipping to Zambia. Each Zambian province has its own code with the prefix "ZM." For example, the code for the Western Province is ISO 3166-2:ZM-01.

ZMB GOST 7.67 Latin three-letter geocode for Zambia. The code is used for transactions to and from Zambian bank accounts and for international shipping to Zambia. As with all GOST 7.67 codes, it is used primarily in Cyrillic alphabets.

ZMK ISO 4217 code for the Zambian kwacha. It was introduced in 1968, replacing the Zambian pound. It has suffered from high inflation throughout its history.

Zoba In Eritrea, a political subdivision approximately equivalent to a province.

Zolotnik A Russian unit of weight approximately equivalent to 4.27 grams. It was rendered obsolete when the Soviet Union began to use the metric system in 1924.

Zombie A publicly-traded company that continues operations despite a merger or bankruptcy. Stocks in zombies are usually low in price because the companies are likely to cease operations (and the stocks will consequently become worthless). However, a few bottom feeders may be interested in a zombie if they believe that it can restructure and become profitable.

Zone 1. See: Free trade zone. **2.** In marketing, an area that a single sales representative or team of sales representatives are assigned to cover. A sales representative whose zone is, for example, Oklahoma, is not allowed to try to sell products in Texas and vice versa. This helps prevents sales reps from competing with each other for commissions.

Zone Charges Charges the U.S. Postal Service assesses for delivering heavy mail a long distance from the point of origin. Zone charges depend on the weight of the mail and how far it is going.

Zone-Restricted Merchandise Goods that are imported into a country but are not permitted to be used for domestic consumption. Zone-restricted merchandise may be stored or improved upon in the importing country. It is then re-exported.

Zoning Laws at the municipal level regulating the uses of real property in certain areas. For example, land in a certain area may be zoned only for commercial use or residential use. Zoning laws exist to improve the quality of life in a local area; for instance, they guard against an oil refinery being placed in an area where families with children live. Depending on the laws of the municipality, zoning laws may be suspended at certain times for certain developments, especially those likely to result in an economic boon for the community.

Zoning Map A map showing the allowed uses of real property in certain areas. For example, land in a certain area may be zoned only for commercial use or residential use. Zoning maps exist to assist developers, businesspersons and residents in finding out what they can build in certain areas. See also: Zoning law.

Zoom To focus the lens of a camera such that it appears that a photographer is closer to or farther away from a picture he/she takes. If the photographer focuses so that the subject appears closer, he/she is said to zoom in; if the photographer focuses so that the subject appears farther away, he/she is said to zoom out. Zooming became possible with the invention of the Zoomar lens in 1959.

Zoom Lens A lens that allows a photographer to focus so that it appears that a picture is closer to or farther away from the viewer. The first zoom lens was developed by Frank Back and was introduced in 1959.

Zoomar Lens The first camera lens that allowed a photographer to focus so that it appeared that a picture was closer to or farther away from the viewer. The Zoomar lens was developed by Frank Back and was introduced in 1959.

Zou Hou Mien A Chinese term for bribery. Literally, the term means "going through the back door."

ZR 1. ISO 3166-1 alpha-2 code for Zaire before it changed its name to the Democratic Republic of the Congo. This was the code used in international transactions to and from Zairean bank accounts. **2.** ISO 3166-2 geocode for Zaire. This was used as an international standard for shipping to Zaire. In both cases, the code is obsolete.

ZRCD ISO 3166-3 code for Zaire, which is the former name of the Democratic Republic of the Congo. ISO 3166-3 codes are used to indicate names of countries that are no longer used.

ZRN ISO 4217 code for the Zairean new zaire. The new zaire was the currency of Zaire between 1993 and 1997. It replaced the first zaire because of the older currency's persistently high inflation. It was replaced by the Congolese franc in 1997 when Zaire became the Democratic Republic of the Congo.

ZRZ ISO 4217 code for the first Zairean zaire. It was introduced in 1967 and suffered from persistently high inflation. It was replaced by the new zaire in 1993 at a ratio of 3 million old zaires to one new zaire.

Z-Score In statistics, a quantification of the distance of a datapoint from the average of a set of datapoints. A z-score of zero indicates that that the data point is equal to the mean or average. It is often used to measure a person's or company's likelihood of bankruptcy.

Zupanija In Croatian-speaking areas, a political subdivision roughly equivalent to a county.

ZW 1. ISO 3166-1 alpha-2 code for the Republic of Zimbabwe. This is the code used in international transactions to and from Zimbabwean bank accounts. **2.** ISO 3166-2 geocode for Zimbabwe. This is used as an international standard for shipping to Zimbabwe. Each Zimbabwean province has its own code with the prefix "ZW." For example, the code for the Province of Midlands is ISO 3166-2:ZW-MI.

ZWC ISO 4217 code for the Rhodesian dollar. It was issued in 1970, soon after Rhodesia became a republic. It was a strong currency throughout its history, being roughly equal in value to the British pound. There were limits on its convertibility. It was replaced by the Zimbabwean dollar.

ZWD Former ISO 4217 code for the Zimbabwean dollar. It replaced the Rhodesian dollar following (official) independence from Britain in 1980 and was used until hyperinflation forced a change to a new currency code in 2009. It was used for the first, second, and third Zimbabwe dollars. See also: ZWL.

ZWE GOST 7.67 Latin three-letter geocode for Zimbabwe. The code is used for transactions to and from Zimbabwean bank accounts and for international shipping to Zimbabwe. As with all GOST 7.67 codes, it is used primarily in Cyrillic alphabets.

ZWL ISO 4217 code for the Zimbabwean dollar. The new code replaced the old code (ZWD) in February 2009, when the government of Zimbabwe dropped 12 zeros from the dollar in response to hyperinflation. However, inflation continued, and, in April, the government permitted Zimbabweans to use any currency for transactions (which most people were doing anyway). This effectively ended the Zimbabwean dollar.

ZWN ISO 4217 code for the second Zimbabwean dollar. It was issued in 2006, replacing the first Zimbabwean dollar at a ratio of 1,000 to one. Its introduction was intended to slow inflation in Zimbabwe, but this attempt failed and the third Zimbabwean dollar was introduced in 2008.

ZWR ISO 4217 code for the third Zimbabwean dollar. It was introduced in August 2008, replacing the second Zimbabwean dollar at a ratio of 10 billion to one. It failed to temper the dollar's hyperinflation and was demonetized in June 2009.

Zyklon B A deadly chemical based on cyanide noted for use in gas chambers during the Holocaust. It is used occasionally as a pesticide.

ZZZZ Best A company established in the 1980s that engaged in massive fraud. Originally a carpet cleaning company, it later began insurance restoration services. It went public in 1996 and eventually acquired a market capitalization of more than $100 million. Unfortunately, much of that was stolen or simply fabricated. In addition to engaging in aggressive accounting, ZZZZ Best's CEO, Barry Minkow, borrowed from organized crime groups and lied to shareholders about insurance contracts that did not exist. Minkow was eventually convicted and sent to federal prison.

Dear Reader,

We hope you have found *The Farlex Financial Dictionary* to be an indispensable guide to understanding the complex world of finance.

If this book has helped you, we would like to ask you to consider supporting Farlex as an independent publisher by telling others about it in an Amazon review.

Your feedback helps us make all our books better! Thank you for choosing Farlex as your guide to the English language.

Sincerely,

The Farlex Team

Explore more books by Farlex at
farlex.com/books

Complete English Grammar Rules

All the rules of English grammar, all in one book, explained in simple terms.

- 500+ pages of proper grammar instruction—2X more information than the leading grammar book!

- Hundreds of quizzes, thousands of example sentences, and more.

Complete English Punctuation Rules

The only punctuation guide with simple, easy-to-remember rules for how to use— and not use—every punctuation mark.

- Side-by-side examples of both correct and incorrect punctuation.

- Quizzes after every topic to help you retain what you learn.

Complete English Spelling & Pronunciation Rules

Learn the rules and patterns that tell you exactly how any word should be spelled and pronounced.

- Go beyond "I before E except after C" and get all the rules and exceptions, all in one place, all explained in plain English.

- Simple tips and tricks to avoid the most common mistakes.

The Farlex Idioms & Slang Dictionary

The most complete collection of idioms and slang in the English language.

- 17,000+ entries covering idioms, slang, phrasal verbs, and more.

- Example sentences for every definition showing how the term is used in real life by native speakers.

Made in the USA
Coppell, TX
23 August 2020